D1345677

How To Use The Edge Index

Bend the pages of the book nearly double and hold them that way with your right hand.

Locate the letter you want in the Edge Index.

Match up the 1- or 2-line symbol next to the letter you have selected with the corresponding 1- or 2-line symbol on the page edge, and open there.

License No. 308. Machol Edge Index. U.S. Patent No. 2680630. Ten Foreign Patents Issued.

А	
Б	
В	
Г	
Д	
Е	
Ж	
З	
И	
К	
Л	
М	
Н	
О	
П	
Р	
С	
Т	
У	
Ф	
Х	
Ц	
Ч	
Ш	
Щ	
Э	
Ю	
Я	

CALLAHAM'S
RUSSIAN–ENGLISH
Dictionary of
SCIENCE AND TECHNOLOGY

CALLAHAM'S
RUSSIAN–ENGLISH
Dictionary of
SCIENCE AND TECHNOLOGY

Fourth Edition

LUDMILLA IGNATIEV CALLAHAM
Chemist, Translator, Pioneering Lexicographer (1912–1990)

PATRICIA E. NEWMAN

JOHN R. CALLAHAM

A Wiley-Interscience Publication
JOHN WILEY & SONS, INC.

New York | Chichester | Brisbane | Toronto | Singapore

Library of Congress Cataloging-in-Publication Data
Callaham, Ludmilla Ignatiev.
    [Russian–English dictionary of science and technology]
    Callaham's Russian–English dictionary of science and technology /
edited by Ludmilla I. Callaham, Patricia E. Newman, and John R.
Callaham. — 4th ed.
        p. cm.
    "A Wiley-Interscience publication."
    Rev. ed. of: Russian–English chemical and polytechnical
dictionary. 3rd. 1975.
    ISBN 0-471-61139-5 (cloth)
    1. Chemistry—Dictionaries—Russian. 2. Technology—Dictionaries—
Russian. 3. Russian language—Dictionaries—English. I. Newman,
Patricia E. II. Callaham, John R. III. Callaham, Ludmilla
Ignatiev. Russian–English chemical and polytechnical dictionary.
IV. Title.
QD5.C33 1995
603—dc20   94-37599
                                                         CIP

Printed in the United States of America

10 9 8 7 6 5 4 3 2 1

To my supportive family,
all four generations of them

L. I. Callaham
February 1990

Ludmilla Ignatiev Callaham about the time
she began her 50-year career in technical
Russian–English lexicography.

PREFACES TO THE FOURTH EDITION

Ludmilla Ignatiev Callaham

Those who are familiar with the three earlier editions of my dictionary already know in what high esteem I hold Patterson's German–English and French–English dictionaries for chemists. They served as my model and I can still say that of all the foreign–English dictionaries I have ever used in my work, none can compare with his in organization, dependability, and consistency. I have tried to emulate him to the best of my ability.

Since chemistry reaches out into so many fields and so many sciences, this dictionary is as much polytechnical as it is chemical. Naturally, the most complete coverage is given to inorganic and organic chemistry; physical and nuclear chemistry; analytical chemistry; chemical engineering and broad chemical technology.

It is only logical—and therefore necessary—to include terms used in the major chemical process industries: plastics; synthetic elastomers; man-made fibers; ceramics; petroleum refining; pulp and paper; pharmaceuticals; food processing; fertilizers; insecticides, fungicides, and herbicides; paints and varnishes; light metals.

Emphasis on chemical process technology inevitably led to comprehensive coverage of related technical fields: mineralogy; mining, and geology; metallurgy; general engineering; mechanical engineering and machinery; metalworking; electrical engineering; automatic control systems; computer technology; nucleonics; agriculture; botany ...; and finally, in addition, the more frequently used terms in medicine; anatomy; zoology; aeronautics; space technology; electronics; meteorology; physics, mathematics and other pure sciences.

The life sciences are becoming increasingly important, and this is where my husband was especially helpful. He spent several years researching zoological and botanical terms to find their English equivalents when possible. Environment has become of worldwide interest now, so we included many plants and animals that are not yet known to be useful, but are certainly part of the environment.

In this edition I have added something new, something I have not seen in any other Russian–English technical dictionary. Since Russian geographic adjectives are not capitalized, they can pose a real problem to the translator. For example, **калужский** is the adjective of **Калуга**; **онежский** the adjective of **Онега**; **окинский** the adjective of **Ока**. To find them, I literally read several Russian geographic encyclopedias.

As has always been my custom, I made every effort to check each term in several reliable sources, both Russian and English. A limited number of terms could be found in only one good source, but these were also included if they appeared particularly useful or interesting.

Some people climb mountains simply because they are there; other people compile dictionaries because they are not there. Back in 1940 no Russian–English chemical or technical dictionary was generally available. Since I was a technical translator and needed one badly in my work, I started collecting such terms. This is a common custom with translators, but I became so engrossed in collecting that it became my life work. There are obvious advantages to being first in any field. My 1947 edition received quite a bit of attention, for one thing, and reviewers tended to use it as a base of comparison for books that came out later. I also had the opportunity to make observations in my first preface that have since become clichés and do not need to be repeated here. Most users of such a dictionary seem to realize how much tedious work is involved in the compilation of a reliable dictionary. And all knowledgeable people recognize the fact that the word "complete" can no longer be honestly applied to any existing dictionary. Today's technical vocabulary has grown so extensively that no one work could include it all. A lexicographer can only try, so I gave preference to the most frequently used terms and to the rare, hard-to-find definitions.

This work is intended chiefly for English-speaking scientists and engineers with a fair knowledge of Russian and a very good knowledge of their own specialities. It therefore includes a general vocabulary consisting of all types of words that are likely to appear in the technical literature. Many of these nontechnical terms acquire either special, or entirely different, meanings when used in a technical context. It is also much handier to use one volume instead of two, as Patterson proved long ago. Besides, how can a non-Russian distinguish a technical from a nontechnical word when he has never seen it before? How does he know what type of reference to seek next?

I am glad to see so many specialized Russian–English dictionaries being published, but it is convenient to start with a wide-coverage dictionary like mine and then go on to specialized dictionaries for more detail. My dictionary serves as a kind of directory and, judging from the letters I have received, many translators approve of this approach. The time never comes when a lexicographer can stop work and say with satisfaction that she has reached her goal. There will always be terms not encountered, equivalents overlooked, and endless improvements in presentation.

A remarkable number of people have written to me, sending from two words to several hundred. These contributions and suggestions for improvement not only added to my dictionary and/or confirmed entries already in my files, but they also showed me the type of words serious users want to find. Many of them regard my dictionary as the "technical man's basic dictionary." It is very encouraging to get letters like that from busy, professional people. Their feedback has given me the moral strength to keep at this work for so many decades.

My most valuable ally in my work is my husband, John R. Callaham. He has not only given me every kind of support—material, moral and mental—but he has put all his experience at my disposal. For more than 32 years he was with McGraw-Hill Publishing Co., starting as an editor on *Chemical Engineering* and finishing as Senior Vice President-Editorial in charge of their many technical publications. He has made it possible for me to devote my entire time to the dictionary, with only the interruption of raising four children. What is even more important, he has always been ready with technical advice. With his broad technical background, he has usually been able to supply me with the right English word for almost any definition I offer him. I translate the meaning of a new Russian word, he suggests the English equivalent or where to go to find it. He presents me with new words with the same kind of flourish that other men bring home roses, but he does not limit his gift-giving to anniversaries and birthdays. He provides me with a perfect study, hundreds of prized reference books, and all the time in the world to do the work I love. Best of all, he has always been deeply interested in my work and encouraged me when lesser men would have found the situation intolerable. It takes a lot of man to live with an obsessed lexicographer.

I can list the names of only a few of the generous people who have taken the time and trouble to write me—giving me constructive suggestions, moral encouragement, and new entries. Some years ago, I received a New Year's greeting from several professors at the University of Warsaw, just thanking me for compiling my dictionary. I do cherish that card!

Several contributors have sent me so many words over the years that I could almost call them collaborators:

Dr. Kurt Gingold of Cos Cob, Connecticut

Ben Teague of Athens, Georgia

Paul Hopper of Washington, D.C., who sent me 243 terms from his father's files.

Sidney Glazer of Bethesda, Maryland

Lucile S. Davison of Woodbury, Connecticut

Robert K. Johnston of Las Vegas, New Mexico

Roger Marcinic of Palm Beach, Florida

Dorothy B. Vitaliano of Bloomington, Indiana

My uncle, Nikolai Ilyich, who gleaned words from a Soviet reference and prepared cards in his meticulous engineer's hand.

Michael Zimmerman, well-known technical lexicographer in the USSR, who helped with advice and supplied me with hard-to-get Soviet books for more than 25 years.

These professional people specialize in a variety of subjects, so their contributions are very valuable. Even those who sent two or three words were a big help. And I would like to pay homage once again to the late Michael Kay, the bilingual White Russian engineer, who contributed so much of himself to my third edition.

Perhaps my most valuable contributor is Lee Nolan, of Nolan and Rogers, Scranton, Pennsylvania. This talented and ingenious young man volunteered to make me a bilingual daisy wheel for my typewriter. Before this, I had to use two typewriters, one Russian, one English, to prepare the manuscripts for the three preceding editions. You can imagine the time I wasted transferring my manuscript back and forth between the two typewriters. I discussed the possibility of using a computer or word processor before I tackled this edition, but experts told me it would take more time to learn the program than I could spare. Dr. Gingold coined the word "computer-unfriendly," but I am not so much unfriendly as practical.

My publisher, John Wiley & Sons, Inc., merits a very special thank you.

Their people have been my loyal friends throughout the forty-five years we have worked together. They backed me up in every aspect of my dictionary, and gave me understanding and encouragement whenever I needed it.

American users of my dictionary who need a source of current Soviet technical reference books can get such books from Victor Kamkin Bookstore, Inc., Rockville, Maryland. This firm imports USSR technical books regularly and has been a valuable source for my own reference library. Another excellent source of Soviet references is Associated Technical Services, of Glen Ridge, New Jersey. They sell a wide assortment of dictionaries, and their catalog is well worth getting.

Having been born in this country, I am not as much of a fatalist as Russians tend to be, but I must admit that fate, or luck, played a big part in the course of my career. First of all, I was born into a word- and work-oriented family, all of whom spoke a flawless Russian. My grandmother, Elizaveta Andreyevna, had been a teacher in Russia; my grandfather, Ilya Grigorevich, was editor of a newspaper. They saw to it that I spoke only Russian the first five years of my life. And it had to be pure Russian, with no English words thrown in for convenience, or from laziness. I found out how wise they had been when I visited the USSR in 1979, for I was often taken for a Soviet citizen, and that gave me a chance to get to really know the people.

My career is going to be somewhat shorter than I had expected for I was diagnosed as having myelogenous leukemia three years ago. Three intensive chemotherapy treatments have kept me alive so far. None of our children have followed in my lexicographer footsteps—they all carved out deep footsteps in their own professions, which is as it should be. But once again fate has intervened and provided me with an ideal successor to take up where I will have to leave off. Patricia Newman is an accomplished linguist-engineer and, most important of all, she has the same values as I do. Patricia is much like us Callahams—we all tend to bite off more than we can chew, and then persist in chewing it. It takes that kind of stubbornness to be a lexicographer. As former president of the American Translators Association, she has proven her organizational talents. That position has also given her many valuable contacts. And she will do what I cannot—bring the dictionary into the computer age—for she has had a great deal of successful experience with computers and word processors. Incomputerate that I am, I can only be humbly impressed.

The Introduction on the following pages explains the organization of this book in detail and offers suggestions for determining the meaning of words not included herein. We shall be grateful for any further suggestions regarding improvements, omissions, and errors. And I know that Patricia Newman will be glad to hear from our users, whether or not they have any words or definitions to add to our files.

Newfoundland, Pennsylvania
February 1990

PATRICIA E. NEWMAN

When I first discovered Ludmilla Callaham's dictionary, which I call simply "*Callaham,*" many years ago when I was first trying to translate Russian technical articles into English, I felt as though I had come into sunlight out of a fog. It was such a *useful* book, and I was astonished that my Russian professors seemed to be unaware of it. Here in one book were most of the technical terms I needed, plus many of the common words that bind one technical term to another, and, at no extra cost, many of the common abbreviations and acronyms that are one of the most difficult aspects of translation. When the precise term I needed was not included, I found that I could frequently infer its meaning from the related words that were listed, and I could then go searching English technical literature for the accepted way of expressing the concept in English. I know of no other scientific and technical dictionary in the other languages I translated that could match those qualities.

At that time I had no inkling that I would ever meet Ludmilla Callaham, much less work with her and help finish her fourth edition. I was an electrical engineer with experience in missile systems and weapon components, and I was entering a second career as a technical translator. I took *Callaham* with me when I went back to work at Sandia National Laboratories as a technical information specialist and translator, translating scientific and technical papers from Russian, German, French, and Spanish into English. When I became president-elect of the American Translators Association, I invited Ludmilla Callaham to speak at the group's twenty-fifth annual conference in 1984. She refused the invitation (she never liked to attend such functions or speak in public) and invited me to visit her instead. I accepted with alacrity and came to consider her a great personal friend.

When leukemia struck Ludmilla, she fought back tenaciously. It was only after several cycles of chemotherapy and remission, followed by a renewed attack, that she realized she would not complete the fourth edition of her beloved dictionary. She asked my help in finding someone to help her finish it. Fortunately for me, her first choice declined for reasons of health, and she asked me to do it instead. Once again, I accepted with alacrity.

This edition represents a considerable change in content over earlier editions. Many terms from Ludmilla's planned life sciences dictionary were incorporated into this book, since it was obvious that plans for the biological dictionary must be abandoned. The scope of biological coverage extends to medicine, physiology, botany, entomology, ornithology, ecology, and many other areas. Computer terminology is finally approaching a generally accepted form in Russian, and many terms have been added from that field. My own experience working with specialists in nuclear power, weapons, disarmament, safeguards, and security has produced a significant number of new terms. The fledgling field of Russian business warrants a more cautious approach to the terminology of trade, contracts, imports, and exports, but some terminology from those fields has been included nonetheless.

So much cannot be added without deleting something. Many of the more esoteric chemical compounds that had crept into the third edition were deleted, as were the names of specific minerals, many of which are cognates of the English names. Some outmoded Russian words and some relating to outdated technology have been deleted, even though former translators like these authors recognize the need for help in translating old documents as well as new ones. Subject specialists like Bob Johnston, a chemist in Las Vegas, New Mexico, and Lev Feigin at the Institute of Crystallography in Moscow were invaluable in pointing out obsolete or incorrect terminology in the third edition and making suggestions for the fourth edition.

This book is a collaboration in the truest sense of the word. Ludmilla Callaham did the vast majority of the research and more than half of the compilation. John Callaham helped in all the essential ways she describes so lovingly in her preface. I did a small part of the research, finished the compilation—at first under her guidance, then alone after her untimely death—, revised the entire book to include ё, and proofread all the galleys. Since mine was the last opportunity to make changes and corrections, any and all errors are my responsibility. I will be grateful to the kind readers who point them out and give me the opportunity to correct them.

Language, particularly today's Russian language, does not stand still. This dictionary, like all dictionaries, is only a snapshot of the language. As we approach publication, I look back over the years I have spent on this book with a sense of amazement. The world has changed drastically, even in the short time since Milla's death. The Soviet Union has disappeared, and independent states have blossomed from its ashes. Not just Western goods, but Western words and concepts are pouring into the vacuum left by the collapse of the Socialist world, and the Russian language is changing to reflect the changing conditions in which its speakers live. It will be fascinating to watch as Russian technology and its scientific and technological vocabulary leap over stages that Western technology plodded through. Imagine, for example, an essentially computer-less society suddenly acquiring today's most modern computers with the most up-to-date operating systems and software. As all these new concepts and devices appear, the language must accommodate them somehow. A lexicographer could have no more fun than watching this explosive evolution. I have already started collecting terms for the next edition, and I welcome contributions from readers who are as intrigued by words as I am.

My grateful thanks must go to the Callahams, Ludmilla and John, for their generosity and warm support of my work on this dictionary. I couldn't have done it without the help of my mother, Helen Tolmie, who proofread every word I wrote, and my husband, Wallace, who bore uncomplainingly the many weekends, vacations, and early mornings I spent on dictionary work instead of family fun.

Albuquerque, New Mexico
September 1995

INTRODUCTION

When a dictionary is reasonably consistent in its organization, a user soon learns what he or she can expect to find in it, and how to go about it most efficiently. It expedites matters, however, if the author provides a few instructions and suggestions.

Alphabetical Order. All Russian terms are entered in strictly alphabetical order, and hyphenated compound words are treated as one word. [Newman's note: Strict alphabetical order is sometimes sacrificed in favor of user-friendliness and space-saving. In particular, consider the letter ё. The distinction between е and ё is important in pronunciation, since the former is pronounced *ye*, and the latter is pronounced *yo* and usually carries the stress. That is why I went to considerable effort to show the occurrence of ё in this edition of the dictionary. Russian alphabetical order places ё after е, therefore **ёж** after **ею** and **жёлтый** after **жечь**, for example. However, ё is usually printed without its distinctive dots, making it look exactly like е. Those who are not native speakers of Russian generally do not know how to pronounce these words and consequently cannot find them in a strictly alphabetical dictionary. For that reason, the alphabetical distinction between ё and е is ignored in this dictionary.

In order to avoid repetition and thereby save space, verb endings are placed together even though one of them may be out of alphabetical order. For example, **полз/ать, —ти** are placed together before **ползком**, although strictly speaking **ползком** should be placed between the two verbs.

Following accepted practice, adjectives are listed under the masculine form. Phrases using the feminine or neuter endings follow the masculine form even though they should precede if put in strict alphabetical order. Adjectives used as nouns are exceptions to this rule.]

Words derived from one root are listed in a single paragraph, as Patterson has done. This type of entry is a great space saver compared with the practice of entering each term on a separate line. The latter method is much easier for the lexicographer, but much more expensive for the purchaser of a dictionary. It increases the ratio of white space to printed matter, which means fewer Russian terms per page and therefore a higher cost for each term. In fact, it often doubles the cost of each term.

The paragraph method of entry has another advantage for the user—it makes the meaning of each part of speech much clearer. I have combined space saving with more consistent sets of English equivalents by using the verb in the paragraph as the key word. The following is a good example of how this works: "**обрабатывать** *v.* process, treat, digest; work, machine, tool; turn (on lathe); size, cut; trim; finish, dress; face, surface; process, handle (data); adapt, condition; prepare, manufacture; develop, elaborate (plans); (agr.) cultivate, till, farm;" Adding "—ing" to each of these verb equivalents makes an adjective or noun out of them. A translator can do this just as well as I can, and save himself the space it takes to repeat all these forms. **Обработанный** in the same paragraph, followed by "processed, etc., *see v.*" is just as clear as listing 24 English equivalents ending with "—ed". This practice not only eliminates endless repetition, it ensures more consistent translations of each part of speech. Many lexicographers enter their terms without matching up the English equivalents, so that very good translations may be given for the verb but not for the noun.

Transliterations. The lexicographer gets little satisfaction from including transliterations, and one knowledgeable professor suggested that I omit the obvious ones. This is not possible, since most scientific terms are transliterations. And what is obvious to an expert in a given field is not at all obvious to the nonspecialist. In fact, one of the greatest dangers of lexicography is the omission of important words that the lexicographer knows too well. He has seen them in the literature so frequently that he is confident they must be in his files—and does not check. This results in many serious gaps in an otherwise good dictionary. An extensive vocabulary is the product of experience, not intelligence, and many users of a dictionary have very limited experience. A lexicographer must have the attitude of a good teacher and consider every type of dictionary user. He must take nothing for granted.

Synonyms. English equivalents are preferably of American usage and spelling, rather than British. Wherever possible, the meaning of English equivalents is made clear by means of suitable synonyms, logically grouped. The synonym appearing first is usually the one most commonly used. Many Russian words have a large number of English equivalents, and I tried to track down as many of the pertinent ones as I could. Many changes have taken place in the last few decades. Everyday words have assumed special technical meanings. Other words have wandered far from their original habitats and taken on new meanings in new environments. The most conspicuous example of this is the word "barn." Some technical terms have assumed more meanings, and others have become narrower in their scope. Some writers use their vocabulary loosely, and it takes skill on the translator's part to render it into acceptable English. **Слышный**, for example, means "audible," but should be translated as "perceptible" when referring to an odor.

Glosses. To help the nonspecialist, most technical terms (except chemical ones) are identified by field or discipline. This is not intended to restrict the user since many of the words can also be used in other fields, but it does help to identify subtle differences in meaning, as well as to guide the user to more specialized references.

Prefixes and Suffixes. A very large number of prefixes and suffixes have been included in the body of the dictionary, since these are the material for constructing words which do not appear in this dictionary. English equivalents are given in parentheses when the prefix is of Latin or Greek origin. It is often a help to be reminded of the meaning of a prefix. For my 1947 edition I had laboriously compiled a table of word endings.

[Newman's note: Most suffixes have been removed from the body of the dictionary and placed in an expanded table of technical word endings at the front.

Copious examples of usage have been added, and the suffixes have been arranged in alphabetical order to make them easier to find.]

Abbreviations. These are given in strictly alphabetical order in the text. If they consist of more than one part, they are alphabetized as one word. All the abbreviations of important units of measure and most of the frequently used abbreviations of technical idioms are included. If all pertinent abbreviations were included, they would make a large volume in themselves. **РП**, for example, stands for 27 different idioms and would lead to more confusion than usefulness. As in English, a diagonal line in an abbreviation signifies "per," e.g., **лм/м²** (lumen per square meter).

Idioms. Idioms are usually listed under the modifying adjective or the more distinctive word in the phrase. The idioms given here are those which cannot be translated literally into idiomatic English or which provide a very special example of a word's use. Except in rare cases, each idiom appears only under one key word. This avoids repetition and cross references which occupy space without serving any useful purpose. Every effort has been made to avoid including phrases which are obvious translations. **Атомная энергия** or **пустотелый кирпич**, for example, cannot be translated as anything but "atomic energy" or "hollow brick." They are pure fill, and it doesn't take much fill to double the size, and therefore the cost, of a dictionary.

Old and Modern Terms. Obsolete and little-used Russian words are frequently included, since many old articles containing such words require translation. Emphasis is made, however, on Soviet terminology. The Russian words are spelled as they were found in Soviet periodicals, reference books, and dictionaries. Some of these may not always be in the approved form, but, since their purpose is to help in the translation of Soviet technical articles, it was considered desirable to give such words as they appeared in the literature. **Камфара** and **камфора** are good examples. The first is the approved form, as given in the *Soviet Orthographic Dictionary,* but the second is the one seen most frequently in chemistry textbooks. It is also well to remember that spellings have changed in the last fifteen years. If you cannot find a word spelled with a single consonant, look for it with a double consonant.

Cross References. These have been kept to a minimum since they are generally as much of a nuisance as they are a help to the user. When they are given, they usually refer to words that are only a few pages, or less, away.

Russianized Words. When words are encountered which do not appear in this dictionary and the meaning of which is not readily determined, it is well to remember that Soviet writers frequently use foreign words written with Russian letters. For example, the German words *Träger, Abscheider,* and *Vorstoss* appear as **трегер, абшайдер,** and **ворштосс** in Russian and retain their original meanings. The French term *terre de Sienne* becomes **тердесьен,** and the English word *timer* is **таймер.** Another custom is to add verb, noun, and adjective endings to a man's name; for example, **шерардизовать,** to sherardize; **шерардизация,** sherardization; **томасовский** *a.,* Thomas. Wherever possible, names have been included in the dictionary, since Russian spelling usually makes them difficult to recognize. Walker, for example, is **Уокер** in Russian. Since many minerals are named after men, these also serve as an indication of the English spelling of such names.

Chemical Compounds. Since the number of chemical compounds is extremely large, only the most common and exemplary ones were chosen for each element. In general, those given should be sufficient to assist in the translation of almost any compound. With a few exceptions, Russian organic nomenclature is very similar to the English. The Russian alphabet, however, made it desirable to include a fairly wide range of organic compounds.

Botanical Terms. Such a common term as **капуста,** for example, is translated as "cabbage." There is very little point in adding the Latin *"Brassica oleracea"* in this case, since there is no chance of confusing this plant with any other. However, if a plant's Latin name is commonly used, like Aquilegia, that should be sufficient translation for **водосбор.** Both the English and Latin equivalents of a Russian botanical term are given when confusion may result from not doing so.

Grammatical Structure

Technical Russian is not particularly difficult, since sentence structure is very similar to the English, but it is necessary to have a firm knowledge of Russian grammar. Both nouns and adjectives are declined, and recognition of their endings, as well as those of conjugated verbs, is necessary to understand the meaning of a sentence. It is also convenient for looking up the particular word in the dictionary, since all nouns are indexed under the nominative case, all adjectives under the masculine singular form, and verbs under the infinitive. All idioms starting with a particular adjective are listed in a paragraph under the masculine form, even if the feminine form would appear elsewhere if considered alphabetically.

Nouns. Russian nouns have three genders, the recognition of which is important in the determination of modifying adjectives and clauses. The masculine nominative usually ends in a hard consonant, —**ь** or —**й**; the feminine in —**а,** —**я,** —**ь**; the neuter in —**о,** —**е,** —**мя,** —**тя**; the plural in —**ы,** —**и,** —**а,** —**я,** —**ья.**

I have introduced a practice in this dictionary that I have never seen elsewhere. I have included the genitive and/or plural of most one and two-syllable nouns, in their proper alphabetical order. These forms can be very confusing to the user of a dictionary, as I once discovered when I tried to look up an irregular Latin noun, the nominative case of which I did not know. (I never did find it.) The genitive and plural usually provide the key to other cases as well. The genitive of many such nouns has the deceptive appearance of a masculine noun in the nominative case. It is also far removed from the nominative alphabetically. A good example is **меток** which looks like a masculine noun but is actually the genitive plural of **метка** and the shortened masculine form of the adjective **меткий.** And anyone who needs to look up the word **лед** is not likely to recognize its genitive **льда. Шеек** too has very little resemblance to the nominative **Шейка.**

Adjectives. All adjectives agree with the noun they modify in gender, number, and case. The masculine nominative singular endings are —**ый,** —**ой,** —**ий**;

the feminine, —**ая,** —**яя**; the neuter, —**ое,** —**ее**; the plural, —**ые,** —**ие**. The comparative degree is usually formed by replacing —**ый** or —**ой** with —**ее,** —**ей** or —**е**; the superlative, by adding —**ейший** or —**айший** to the stem. Past and present participles have been considered as adjectives in this dictionary.

Here too I have introduced a practice which I believe to be an innovation in dictionaries. I have included the shortened forms of adjectives in their proper alphabetical order. **Полон,** for example, is the shortened form of **полный** and is more than a column removed from it alphabetically. A translator should probably know his grammar well enough to recognize this shortened form, but it saves a lot of time if he doesn't have to rack his memory for rules.

Adverbs. A large proportion of adverbs are formed by changing the adjective endings —**ый** and —**ой** to —**о**; **ский** to —**ски**; and sometimes —**ий** to —**е**. The adverb form is also used to express the impersonal verb, as **холодно,** which is translated "it is cold." **Удобно** is translated "It is convenient"; **хорошо** is translated "It is good; it is well."

Verbs. As is customary, verbs are indexed under the infinitive form, the ending of which is usually one of the following: —**ть,** —**ать,** —**еть,** —**ить,** —**оть,** —**уть,** —**ыть,** —**ять,** —**йти,** —**зть,** —**зти,** —**сть,** —**сти,** —**чь**. The reflexive form is often used to express the passive voice and is formed by adding —**ся** or —**сь** to the infinitive.

In my 1962 edition, I had followed the advice of one of my contributors and included typical conjugated forms of many of the irregular verbs. The third person singular of **пить** in the present tense is **пьет,** which also appears in the proper alphabetical order in the text. With this form given, the student will immediately recognize the first person plural or any other form in the immediate vicinity. The inclusion of such verb forms has been greatly expanded in this edition.

The present tense of a perfective verb is usually translated as the future in English and is therefore referred to as the future form. With very few exceptions, the perfective aspect of a verb is cross-referred to the imperfective aspect which is given with all its English equivalents.

In the 1962 edition, I had also introduced another table which I had prepared to assist students of Russian when case endings slip their minds. This table gives a brief resume of typical noun and adjective declensions of each gender—on one line. This makes it easier to match a modifying adjective with its noun in the text. In all the grammars I have seen, all noun declensions are handled separately from adjective declensions, which makes matching them a cumbersome task. This table is given below, followed by typical regular verb endings.

L. I. CALLAHAM

ABBREVIATIONS

a.	adjective	gen.	genetics
abbr.	abbreviation	geobot.	geobotany
acc.	accusative	geod.	geodesy
act.	active	geog.	geography
acous.	acoustics	geol.	geology
adv.	adverb	geom.	geometry
aero.	aeronautics	gram.	grammar
aerodyn.	aerodynamics	hemat.	hematology
agr.	agriculture	herp.	herpetology
AI	artificial intelligence	hist.	histology
amph.	amphibians	horol.	horology
anat.	anatomy	hort.	horticulture
apid.	Apidae; apiculture	hydr.	hydraulics,
arch.	architecture		hydrology
archeol.	archeology	ichth.	ichthyology
art.	artillery	illum.	illumination
astr.	astronomy	immun.	immunology
aut.	automation	*imp.*	imperative
av.	aviation	*imp.v.*	impersonal verb
bact.	bacteriology	instr.	instruments,
bal.	ballistics		instrumentation
biochem.	biochemistry	*instr.*	instrumental
biogeog.	biogeography	*m.*	masculine noun
biol.	biology	mach.	machinery
bot.	botany	mal.	malacology
carp.	carpentry	mam.	mammals
cer.	ceramics	mar.	maritime
chem.	chemistry	math.	mathematics
com.	commerce	mech.	mechanics
commun.	communications	med.	medicine
comp.	comparative	met.	metallurgy; metals
comp.	computers	meteor.	meteorology
conj.	conjunction	micros.	microscopy
constr.	construction	mil.	military
cosm.	cosmology	min.	mineralogy; mining
crust.	crustaceans	*n.*	neuter noun
cryst.	crystallography	naut.	nautical
cyt.	cytology	nucl.	nucleonics
dat.	dative	*num.*	numeral
dim. of	diminutive of	obs.	obsolete
ecol.	ecology	ocean.	oceanography
educ.	education	ophth.	ophthalmology
elec.	electricity, electrical	orn.	ornithology
	engineering	pal.	paleontology
elec. commun.	electrical communication	*part.*	participle
embr.	embryology	*pass.*	passive
ent.	entomology	petr.	petrology, petrography
enz.	enzymology	petrol.	petroleum
esp.	especially	pharm.	pharmacy, pharmaceuticals
expl.	explosives	phot.	photography
f.	feminine noun	phys.	physics
fut.	future	physiol.	physiology
gen.	genitive	phyt.	phytopathology

ABBREVIATIONS

pl.	plural	spec.	specifically
pr.	present	stat.	statistics
prep.	preposition	*superl.*	superlative
prepos.	prepositional	surv.	surveying
pron.	pronoun	tech.	technical
prot.	protozoa	tel.	telephone
pyro.	pyrotechnics	teleg.	telegraphy
rad.	radio	telev.	television
rr.	railroad	text.	textiles
seism.	seismology	top.	topology
sh. f.	shortened feminine form	typ.	typography, printing
sh. m.	shortened masculine form	*v.*	verb
sh. n.	shortened neuter form	vet.	veterinary medicine
silv.	silviculture	zool.	zoology
sing.	singular	*3*	3rd person

RUSSIAN ALPHABET

STANDARD		ITALICS	NAME	TRANSLITERATION
А	а	*а*	ah	a
Б	б	*б*	beh	b
В	в	*в*	veh	v
Г	г	*г*	geh	g
Д	д	*д*	deh	d
Е	е	*е*	yeh	e
Ё	ё	*ё*	yoh	e
Ж	ж	*ж*	zheh	zh
З	з	*з*	zeh	z
И	и	*и*	ee	i
Й	й	*й*	ee kratkoye	ǐ
К	к	*к*	ka	k
Л	л	*л*	el	l
М	м	*м*	em	m
Н	н	*н*	en	n
О	о	*о*	aw	o
П	п	*п*	peh	p
Р	р	*р*	ehr	r
С	с	*с*	ess	s
Т	т	*т*	teh	t
У	у	*у*	oo	u
Ф	ф	*ф*	ef	f
Х	х	*х*	hha	kh
Ц	ц	*ц*	tseh	ts
Ч	ч	*ч*	tcheh	ch
Ш	ш	*ш*	sha	sh
Щ	щ	*щ*	shcha	shch
Ъ	ъ	*ъ*	mute hard sign	—
Ы	ы	*ы*	yeri	y
Ь	ь	*ь*	mute soft sign	—
Э	э	*э*	eh oborotnoye	e
Ю	ю	*ю*	yoo	yu
Я	я	*я*	ya	ya

COMMON RUSSIAN TECHNICAL
WORD ENDINGS

The following table shows a selected list of Russian word endings and suffixes that may be useful to a translator wrestling with a word that does not appear in the dictionaries. The English equivalents given are suggestions only; they will not fit all cases, as many of the examples show.

RUSSIAN ENDING	ENGLISH EQUIVALENT	RUSSIAN EXAMPLE	ENGLISH EQUIVALENT
—авший	*see* —вший		
—аемость	—ability, —ibility, —ubility	поглащаемость	absorbability
—аемый	—able, —ible, —uble, —ed	пологощаемый	absorbable
—аза	—ase	лактаза	lactase
—акс	—ax	антракс	anthrax
—ал, —аль	—al	ацетал, ацеталь	acetal
—алевый	—al, —alic	фталевый	phthalic
—аловый	*see* —алевый		
—альдегид	—aldehyde	гептальдегид	heptaldehyde
—альный	*see* —алевый, —ильный; *see also* —гон(альный)		
—альня	—ery, —ry, —ing mill, —ing shop, —ing works	плавильня	smeltery, smelting works, foundry
—ание	—ation, —ence, —ing, —sion, —tion	1) выпаривание 2) сцепление	1) evaporation 2) coherence, cohesion
—ан	—an, —ane	1) меркаптан 2) бутан	1) mercaptan 2) butane
—анный	*see* —нный		
—ановый	—an, —ane, —anic, —anoic	1) меркаптановый 2) бутановый	1) mercaptan 2) butane
—арность	—arity	молекулярность	molecularity
—арный	—ar, —arian, —ary	1) молекулярный 2) утилитарный 3) санитарный	1) molecular 2) utilitarian 3) sanitary
—ат, —атный	—ate	сульфат, сульфатный	sulfate
—атель	—ant, —ator, —ent, —er, —ing agent	1) поглотитель 2) окислитель	1) absorbent, absorber 2) oxidizer, oxidizing agent
—ательный	—ent, —ing	поглотительный	absorbent, absorbing
—атический	*see* —тический		
—атный	*see* ат		
—атор(ный)	—ator, —er	1) генератор(ный) 2) трансформатор	1) generator 2) transformer
—атый	*see* —тый		
—ацетил	—acetyl	бромацетил	bromacetyl
—ационный	*see* —ционный		
—ация	*see* —ция		
—ающий(ся)	*see* —щий(ся)		
—бежный	—dromous	дуговиднокривобежный	campylodromous
—биоз	—biosis	метабиоз	metabiosis

COMMON RUSSIAN TECHNICAL WORD ENDINGS

RUSSIAN ENDING	ENGLISH EQUIVALENT	RUSSIAN EXAMPLE	ENGLISH EQUIVALENT
—бойный	combatting, fighting	1) маслобойный	1) oil-extracting
		2) морозбойный	2) frost damaged
—бочный	—lateral, —sided	равнобочный	equilateral
—боязнь	—phobia	водобоязнь	hydrophobia (rabies)
—брюхий	—bellied	голобрюхий	bare-bellied
—брюшинный	—peritoneal	позадибрюшинный	retroperitoneal
—ватый	—ish	влажноватый	dampish
—вед	person who does …	1) законовед	1) lawyer
		естествовед	2) naturalist
—ведение	—ology	китаеведение	sinology
—ветвистый	—branched	многоветвистый	polycladous, many-branched
—вид	—species	геновид	genospecies
—видные	—ales (order), —oidei (suborder)		
—видный	—form, —oid, —like, —(ac)eous	1) волосковидный	1) piliform
		2) волосовидный	2) hair-like
		3) газовидный	3) gaseous, gasiform
—вод	guide, conductor, conduit; farmer, grower, breeder; specialist	1) голубевод	1) pigeon breeder
		2) группповод	2) group leader
		3) зверовод	3) fur (animal) breeder
		4) лесовод	4) forester
—водство	breeding, raising; growing, culture; cultivating, farming	голубеводство	pigeon breeding
—водческий	breeding, raising	звероводческий	fur farming
—волокнистый	—fibered, —fibrous, —grained	грубоволокнистый	coarse-fibered, coarse-grained
—волосистый	—trichous, hairy, haired	грубоволосистый	rough-haired, shaggy
—вший(ся)	—ed, —en, —ened, —t	1) потонувший	1) drowned, sunken
		2) сгоревший	2) burnt
—выпухлый	—convex	вогнутовыпухлый	concavo-convex
—гамический	—gamous	моногамический	monogamous
—гамия	—gamy, union	полигамия	polygamy
—гамный	see —чамический		
—гаус	—house	пакгауц	warehouse
—генез(ис)	—genesis, —geny, —formation	1) гетерогенез(ис)	1) heterogenesis
		2) геогенезис	2) geogeny
—гения	see —генезис		
—генный	—genic, —geny	гистогенный	histogenic
—гипс	—plaster	газогипс	porous plaster
—главый	—headed, —cephalous, —capitate	1) многоглавый	1) polycephalous
		2) молотоглавый	2) hammerhead
—гнат	—gnathus, —jawed	описгогнат	opisthognathus, having retreating jaws
—глоточный	—pharyngeal	позадиглоточный	retropharyngeal
—гнозия	—gnosy		
—головый	see —главый		
—голосый	—glot(tous), —voiced	многоголосый	polyglot(tous)
—гон(альный)	—gon(al)	гептагон(альный)	hexagon(al)
—гония	—gony, —production	моногония	monogony, asexual reproduction
—гонный	—agogue, —agogic, —producing	1) медогонная машина	1) honey extractor
		2) молокогонный	2) galactalogue
—гранник	—hedron	шестигранник	hexahedron
—гранный	—hedral, —faced	шестигранный	hexahedral
—графический	—graphic, diffraction	микрографический	micrographic
—грудый	—breasted	белогрудый	white-breasted
—дел	—maker, manufacturer	винодел	wine maker
—делие	industry; manufacture	маслоделие	butter making
—дер, —дёр	remover, extractor, doer of an action	1) трубодёр	1) tube extractor
		2) детандер	2) expander
		3) лыкодёр	3) bast peeler
—дёрка	disintegrator		

COMMON RUSSIAN TECHNICAL WORD ENDINGS

RUSSIAN ENDING	ENGLISH EQUIVALENT	RUSSIAN EXAMPLE	ENGLISH EQUIVALENT
—дерма	skin, dermis	полидерма	polyderm
—десят	—ty	семьдесят	seventy
—десятый	—ieth	семьдесятый	seventieth
—дневка	—day period	семидневка	seven-day period
—дневный	—day	короткодневный	short-day
—домный	—oec(i)ous	двудомный	dioec(i)ous
—дший	*see* —вший		
—еватый	—ish	синеватый	bluish
—евший	*see* —вший		
—евые	—aceae, ata, eae	1) гераниевые	1) Geraniaceae
		2) целомные	2) Coelomata
—ед	—phage, —eater, —vore	грибоед	mycetophage, fungivore
—ёз	—osis	аргулёз	argulosis
—ез	*see* —з; —ia; *see also* —генез	анурез	anuria
—еин	—eine	эвкодеин	eucodeine
—ен	—en, —ene	1) глутен	1) gluten
		2) бутен	2) butene
—ение	*see* —ание		
—ёнок	young animal, e.g. calf	1) слонёнок	1) elephant calf
		2) лисёнок	2) fox cub
—енный	*see* —нный		
—еновые	—en, —ene, —enic, —enoic	1) блутеновый	1) gluten
		2) бутеновый	2) butene, butenoic
		3) нафтеновый	3) naphthenic
—ентность	—ence, —ency	турбулентность	turbulence
—ентный	—ent	турбулентный	turbulent
—енция	—ence, ency	тенденция	tendency
—енциозность	—ence, —ency	тенденциозность	tendency
—ер, —ёр	—er, operator	1) дистиллер	1) distiller
		2) лифтёр	2) elevator operator
—есть	—ism, —ity, —ness (*see* —ость)	аморфность	amorphism
—етический	*see* —тический		
—етый	*see* —тый		
—еций	—*ecium*	апотеций	apothecium
—еющий	*see* —щий		
—жаберные (pl.)	—branchia	нитежаберные	Filibranchia
—з	—sis	гидролиз	hydrolysis
—завр	—saur(us), lizard	динозавр	dinosaur
—защитный	—repellent, —proof	влагозащитный	water-repellent, moisture-proof
—звуковой	—sonic	гиперзвуковой	hypersonic
—зём	earth, soil	чернозём	black earth
—зёрный	—grained	белозёрный	white-grained
—зионный	—sion	телевизионный	television
—зия	—sion, —sia	1) телевизия	1) television
		2) аплазия	2) aplasia
—зубчатый *a.*	—dentate, —toothed	многозубчатый	multidentate
—ивность	—ivity	селективность	selectivity
—ивный	—ive	селективный	selective
—ивший	*see* —вший		
—ид(ный)	—ide	сульфид(ный)	sulfide
—иевый	—ic, —ium	таллиевый	thallic, thallium
—из	—sis	гидролиз	hydrolysis
—изация	—ization, —izing, —yzing	гомогенизация	homogenization, homogenizing
—изирование	*see* —изация		
—изированный	—ized, —yzed	1) кристаллизированний	1) crystallized
		2) анализированный	2) analyzed
—изировать	—ize, —yze	1) гомогенизировать	1) homogenize
		2) анализировать	2) analyze
—изм	—ism	аморфизм	amorphism
—изна	—ness		

COMMON RUSSIAN TECHNICAL WORD ENDINGS

RUSSIAN ENDING	ENGLISH EQUIVALENT	RUSSIAN EXAMPLE	ENGLISH EQUIVALENT
—изование	*see* —изация		
—изованный	*see* —изированный		
—изовать	*see* —изировать		
—ий	—ium, —um	1) кальций	1) calcium
		2) алюминий	2) aluminum
—ийский	—ian, —ic	пермский	Permian, Permic
—ик	—ant, —er, —ic,	1) механик	1) mechanic
	—ist, —yst	2) химик	2) chemist
—ика	—ics; *see also*	механика	mechanics
	—техника		
—ил	—il, —ile, —yl	1) бензил	1) benzil; benzyl
		2) нитрил	2) nitrile
—иловий	—il, ile, —ilic, —yl,	1) бензиловый	1) benzyl, benzilic;
	—ylic		benzil
		2) нитриловый	2) nitrile
—ильный	—ing; *see also*	плавильный	smelting
	—иловый		
—ильня	*see* —альбя		
—имость	*see* —аемость		
—имый	*see* —аемый		
—ин	—in, —ine, —ol	1) глутин	1) glutin
		2) анилин	2) aniline
		3) арбистерин	3) arbusterol
—иновый	—in, —ine, —inic	1) глутиновый	1) glutin, glutinic
		2) анилиновый	2) aniline
—ирование	—ating, —ation,	1) окклюдирование	1) occlusion
	—ing, —ion	2) метилирование	2) methylating, methylation
—ированный	—ated, —ed	метилированный окклюдированный	methylated occluded
—ировать	—ate, —e	метилировать окклюдировать	methylate occlude
—ист	*see* —ик	аналист	analyst, analyzer
—истый	—ous, —y,	1) пористый	1) porous
	—containing	2) тинистый	2) slimy
—ит	—ite, —itis, —yte	3) гранит	3) granite
		4) неврит	4) neuritis
		5) электролит	5) electrolyte
—итель	*see* —атель		
—итический	*see* —тический		
—итный	—ite, —itic, —ytic	1) гранитный	1) granitic
		2) электролитный	2) electrolytic
—итовый	*see* —итный		
—итый	*see* —тый		
—ификация	*see* —ция		
—ихт	—ichthys (fish)	каламоихт	reedfish, calamoichthys
—ихтовые	—ichthyidae	каллихтовые	Callichthyidae
—иционный	*see* —ционный		
—иция	*see* —ция		
—ический	—ic, —ical, —ous	1) металлический	1) metallic
		2) оптический	2) optical
—ичный	*see* —ический		
—ия	—ia, —ium; *see also*	афония	alphonia
	—ция, —ология	парамеция	paramecium
—калий	potassium	монокалий	monopotassium
—кальций	calcium	монокальций	monocalcium
—ка (with number)	—year-old	семилетка	seven-year-old
—кислота	acid	гетерополикислота	heteropoly acid
—кислый *a.*	acid; ...ate (of)	сернокислый	sulfuric acid; sulfate (of)
—клеточный	—cellular, —celled	гетероклеточный	heterocellular
—колейный	(rr.) track, —gage	узкоколейный	narrow-gage
—кор	correspondent, reporter	спецкор	special correspondent
—конечный	—finite	бесконечный	infinite
—коричный	—cinnamic	гидрокоричный	hydrocinnamic (acid)

COMMON RUSSIAN TECHNICAL WORD ENDINGS

RUSSIAN ENDING	ENGLISH EQUIVALENT	RUSSIAN EXAMPLE	ENGLISH EQUIVALENT
—корый	—barked, —skinned	белокорый	white-bark(ed)
—костный	—osseous, bone	1) бескостный	1) boneless
		2) внутрикостный	2) intraosseous
—кратный	—ple	восьмикратный	octuple
—крахмал	starch	нитрокрахмал	nitrostarch
—кровие	—(a)emia	белокровие	leukemia
—крылые	—ptera	двукрылые	Diptera
—крылый	—pterous, winged	легкокрылый	light-winged
—кс	—x	антракс	anthrax
—ксильный	—xylous, wood		
—ксия	*see* —ия		
—летие	—year period, anniversary, birthday	пятилетие	five-year period, fifth birthday or anniversary
—летка	—year plan	пятилетка	five-year plan
—летний	—year(-old), —ennial	семилетний	seven-year, septennial, seven-year-old
—лиз	—lysis, breaking down	катализ	catalysis
—лист(вен)ный	—leaved, —phyllous, —folious	1) вальковатолистный	1) teretifolious;
		2) гладколистный	2) smooth-leaved, leiophyllous
—листый	—leaf, —leaved, foliate	перистолистый	feather-leaved
—лит	—lith (stone); *see also* —ит	монолит	monolith
—лицый	—face(d)	круглолицый	round-faced
—логия	—ology	геология	geology
—ловка	catcher, trap	мухоловка	fly catcher
—лом	break	волнолом	breakwater
—ломный	—fragous, breaking	бероломный	devious
—лопастный	—lobate, —lobed	многолопастный	multilobate, multilobed
—лый	*see* —вший		
—любивый	—philous, —loving	водолюбивый	hydrophilous, water-loving
—ман	maniac, lover of…	наркоман	drug addict
—мания	—mania	опиомания	opiomania, craving for opium
—мейстер	master, specialist		
—мер	gage, meter	1) водомер	1) water meter, water (flow) gage
		2) высотомер	2) altimeter
—меритель	*see* —мер	газомеритель	gas meter
—мерный *a.*	—dimensional	трехмерный	three-dimensional
—мёт	launcher, firer, thrower	1) пулемёт	1) machine gun
		2) гранатомёт	2) grenade launcher
—метил	—methyl	гидроксиметил	hydroxymethyl
—метр	—meter	гальванометр	galvanometer
—метрия	—metry, measuring	телеметрия	telemetry
—миксис	—mixis, mingling, mixing	панмиксис	panmixis, nonselective mating
—мильный *a.*	—mile	семимильный	seven-mile, seven-league (e.g. boots)
—морфный *a.*	—morphous, —shaped	аморфный	amorphous, shapeless
—мочевой	—urinary	генитомочевой	genitourinary
—мужие *n.*	—andry	многомужие	polyandry
—навтика	—nautics	аэронавтика	aeronautics
—надсать	—teen	семнадцать	seventeen
—надцатый	—teenth	семнадцатый	seventeenth
—натриевый *a.*	sodium	мононатриевый	monosodium
—ная	*see* —альня		
—нёбный	—gnath, palatine	язычнонёбный	glossopalatine
—ник	worker	1) высотник;	1) steeplejack;
		2) голубник	2) pigeon breeder
—нит	*see* —ит		
—нный	—ed	поглощенный	absorbed

COMMON RUSSIAN TECHNICAL WORD ENDINGS

RUSSIAN ENDING	ENGLISH EQUIVALENT	RUSSIAN EXAMPLE	ENGLISH EQUIVALENT
—ногий	—legged, —footed	**голоногий**	bare-legged, bare-footed
—номия	—nomy (systematized knowledge)	**таксономия**	taxonomy
—носец	—phore, —bearer	**плодоносец**	carpophore
—носный	—bearing, —iferous; —containing	**водоносный**	water-bearing, aquiferous
—ность	*see* —**есть**, —**арность**		
—носый *a.*	—nosed	**горбоносый**	hook-nosed
—ные	*see* —**евые**		
—ный	*see* —**ический**		
—ия	*see* —**альня**		
—образный *a.*	—iform, —shaped; —like, —aceous	1) **бенцеобразный** 2) **воскообразный**	1) coroniform 2) wax-like, ceraceous
—образование *n.*	—poiesis, formation	**мочеобразование**	uropoiesis, urine formation
—оватый *a.*	—ish	**красноватый**	reddish
—овые	*see* —**евые**		
—овый	*see* —**ический**		
—оза	—ose	**целлюлоза**	cellulose
—оз	*see* —**з**		
—озный	—ose-, —ous	**фистулозный**	fistulose, fistulous
—оидальный	—oid, —oidal	**коллоидальный**	colloid(al)
—ойский	—oic	**мезозойский**	Mesozoic
—окисный	oxide	**медноокисный**	copper oxide
—оксид	—oxide	**гидроксид**	hydroxide
—оксил	—oxyl	**гидроксил**	hydroxyl
—ол	—ol, —ole, —ene	1) **нафтол** 2) **бензол**	1) naphthol 2) benzene
—олиз	*see* —**из**		
—оловый	*see* —**ольный**		
—олог	—ologist	**вирусолог**	virologist
—ология	*see* —**логия**		
—оль	*see* —**ол**		
—ольный	—ol, —ole, —olic	**алкогольный**	alcoholic
—ома	—oma, tumor	**карцинома**	carcinoma
—он	—on, —one	1) **электрон** 2) **ксантон**	1) electron 2) xanthone
—онный, —оновый	—on, —one, —onic	1) **электронный** 2) **ксантоновый**	1) electron, electronic 2) xanthone, xanthonic
—ор	—or	**активатор**	activator
—основный	—basic	**многоосновный**	polybasic
—осный	—axis, —axial, —axle	**двухосный**	biaxial, two-axled
—ость	*see* —**есть**		
—ота	*see* —**изна**		
—отвод	vent, outlet	**газоотвод**	gas vent, gas outlet
—отделение	evolution; separation	**газоотделение**	gas evolution; gas separation
—отический	*see* —**тический**		
—отый	*see* —**тые**		
—очный	*see* —**ательный**		
—пад	—ptosis, falling	**водопад**	waterfall
—палый *a.*	—dactylous, —fingered	**трёхпалый**	tridactylous
—патия	—pathy	**логопатия**	logopathy, speech disturbance
—педия	—pedics, therapy	**логопедия**	logopedics, speech therapy
—пёр	—pterus, fin	**многопёр**	Polypterus
—переменный	—variable	**гиперпеременный**	hypervariable
—перистый	—pinnate	**полуперистый**	semipinnate
—пёрые	—pterygii	**лучепёрые**	Actinopterygii
—пёрый	—finned		
—писец	—graph, —recorder	**высотописец**	altigraph, altitude recorder

COMMON RUSSIAN TECHNICAL WORD ENDINGS

RUSSIAN ENDING	ENGLISH EQUIVALENT	RUSSIAN EXAMPLE	ENGLISH EQUIVALENT
—питек	—pithecus, ape	ореопитек	oreopithecus, a genus of fossil primates
—платеат	—platinate	гексахлороплатеат	chloroplatinate
—плегия	—plegia, paralysis	крадриплегия	quadriplegia
—плечевой	—humeral	лучеплечевой	radiohumeral
—плечий	—brachial	одноплечий	monobrachial
—плодный	—carpous, —carpic	1) вершиноплод-ный	1) acrocarpous
		2) воздутоплод-ный	2) cystocarpic
—поэз	—poiesis	гемопоэз	hemopoieses
—проводный	—conducting	теплопроводный	heat-conducting
—протеид	—protein	гемопротеид	hemoprotein
—растворимый	—soluble	водорастворимый	water-soluble
—рёберный	—costal, —rib(bed)	грудо-рёберный	sternocostal
—пезущий	cutting	металлорежущий	metal cutting
—рея	—rrhea	гематорея	hematorrhea
—рогий	—ceros, —horn(ed)	винторогие	Strepsiceros
—семянный	—seeded, —spermous	волосистосемянный	hairy-seeded, trichospermous
—сердечный	—cardiac, —hearted	позадисердечный	retrocardiac
—сернистый	—sulfurous, —sulfite	гидросернистый	hydrosulfurous, hydrosulfite (of)
—серный	—sulfuric	гепоринсерный	heparin sulfuric (acid)
—силовой	—power	гидросиловой	water power
—сионный	see —зионный		
—сиз	see —зионный		
—ский	see —ийский		
—содержащий	—containing, —iferous	металло-содержащий	metal-containing, metalliferous
—соединение	—compound	гетеросоединение	heterocompound
—сома	—some, chromosome	гетеросома	heterosome, sex chromosome
—сотый	—hundredth	пятисотый	five-hundredth
—спинный	—backed	голоспинный	naked-backed
—спирт	alcohol	галоидоспирт	halogen alcohol
—стаз	—stasis	гипостаз	hypostasis
—ство	—ism, —ity, etc.	1) людоедство	1) cannibalism
		2) электричество	2) electricity
		3) мастерство	3) skill, mastery
		4) материнство	4) maternity
—ствольный	—bore	гладкоствольный	smooth-bore (gun)
—стилия	—styly	гетеростилия	heterostyly
—стебельный, –стебельчатый	—stalked, —cal(ous), —stemmed	1) высокостебельчатый;	1) tall-stalked;
		2) голостебельный	2) nudicaul(ous), bare-stemmed
—стойкий	—resistant, —stable, —proof	1) биостойкий;	1) biostable
		2) брызгостойкий;	2) splashproof;
		3) вибростойкий	3) shock-resistant
—стомный	—stomatous	гимностомный	gymnostamatous
—строительный	—building, —engineering, —construction	машино-строительный	mechanical engineering
—сфера	—sphere	тропосфера	troposphere
—тека	—theca, spore case	оотека	ootheca
—тепловой	—thermal	гипертепловой	hyperthermal
—терапия	—therapy, treatment	гидротерапия	hydrotherapy, water treatment
—термальный	see тепловой		
—термия	—thermia	гипотермия	hypothermia
—техник	—engineer, technician, —ician	1) гидротехник;	1) hydraulics engineer;
		2) электротехник	2) electrician, electrical engineer
—техника	—engineering, —ics, technology	1) биотехника;	1) bioengineering;
		2) роботехника;	2) robotics;
		3) гиалотехника	3) glass technology
—теций	—thecium	клейстотеций	cleistothecium

COMMON RUSSIAN TECHNICAL WORD ENDINGS

RUSSIAN ENDING	ENGLISH EQUIVALENT	RUSSIAN EXAMPLE	ENGLISH EQUIVALENT
—тический	*see* —пческий		
—тый	—ed, —en, —n	1) тянутый;	1) pulled, drawn;
		2) битый	2) beaten
—увший	*see* —вший		
—угольник	—agon	восьмиугольник	octagon
—уемость	*see* —аемость		
—уемый	*see* —аемый		
—уксусный	—acetic	бромоуксусный	bromoacetic
—упорный	—proof; *see also* —стойкий	бзрывоупорный	explosion-proof
—устойчивый	—resistant, —proof; *see also* —стойкий	ветроустойчивый	wind resistant windproof
—утый	*see* —тый		
—ухий	—eared	вислоухий	lop-eared
—ушной	—otic, —aural	внутриушной	entotic, intra-aural
—ущий	*see* —щий		
—ующий	*see* —щий		
—фаг	—phage	гематофар	hematophage
—фагия	—phagy, eating	онихофагия	onychophagy, nailbiting
—фермент	—enzyme	апофермент	apoenzyme
—фильный	—philous, —loving	геофильный	earth-loving, geophilous
—фит	—phyte	биофит	biophyte
—фобный	—phobic, —phobous	1) гелиофобный	1) heliophobic
		2) гемерофобный	2) hemerophobous
—хвостый	—tailed	гладкохвостый	smooth-tailed
—хинин	—quinine	апохинин	apoquinine
—хозяйство	—culture, management	водохозяйство	water management, aquiculture
—холевый	—cholic	апохолевый	apocholic
—цветный	—iferous	венчикоцветный	corolliferous
—целе	—cele	гематоцеле	hematocele
—цен(овый)	—cene	миоцен(овый)	Miocene
—цепной	—chain	гетероцепной	heterochain
—цефалия	—cephaly, —cephalus	гидроцефалия	hydrocephaly, hydrocephalus
—цеховой	—shop	внутрицеховой	intrashop
—циан	—cyan	гексоциан	hexocyan
—цид	—cide	гербицид	herbicide
—ций	—cium	апотеций	apothecium
—цикл(ический)	—cyclic, —cycle	гетероцикл	heterocyclic ring
—ционный	—ing, —tion, —tional	1) агитационный	1) agitating, agitation
		2) фрикционный	2) friction(al)
—циста	—cyst; *see also* —ит	литоциста	lithocyst
—цит	*see* —ит		
—ция	—tion	эволюция	evolution
—часовой	—hour	сорокачасовой	40-hour
—чатый	—ar, —ated	трубчатый	tubular, tubulated
—черепной	—cranial	внутричерепной	intracranial
—членный	—membered, —amerous	семичленный	seven-membered, heptamerous
—чик	*see* —ник		
—ший	*see* —вший		
—щатый	*see* —чатый		
—шей, —шейный	—necked	голошейный	bare-necked
—щий	—ent, —ing, —ive	поглощающий	absorbent, absorbing, absorptive
—шийся	—able, —ible, —ing, —ive	1) окисляющийся	1) oxidizable, oxidizing
		2) сцепляющийця	2) cohesive
—щик	worker, operator	инструментальщик	tool maker, tool worker
—щина	city and its surroundings, region	киевщина	Kiev region
—ытый	*see* —тый		
—эдр	—hedron	гексаэдр	hexahedron
—эдрический	—hedral	гексаэдрический	hexahedral
—эз	*see* —поэз		

COMMON RUSSIAN TECHNICAL WORD ENDINGS

RUSSIAN ENDING	ENGLISH EQUIVALENT	RUSSIAN EXAMPLE	ENGLISH EQUIVALENT
—ющий	*see* —щий		
—яд	—eater, —ivore	травояд	herbivore
—ядный	—ivorous, —phagous	1) травоядный	1) herbivorous
		2) листоядный	2) phyllophagous
—яемость	*see* —аемость		
—яемый	*see* —аемый		
—язычный	—glot, —lingual	многоязычный	polyglot, multilingual
—яльный	*see* —ильный		
—яльня	*see* —альня		
—янный	*see* —нный		
—янтарный	—succinic	диоксиянтарный	dihydroxysuccinic
—ярность	*see* —арность		
—ярный	*see* —арный	гетерополярный	heteropolarity
—ятор(ный)	*see* —атор(ный)		
—ятый	*see* —тый		
—яционный	*see* —ционный		
—яция	*see* —ция		
—ячеистый,	—cellular, —cell(ed)	многоячеистый	multicellular, multi-cell
—ячейковый			
—ящий	*see* —щий		
—яющий	*see* —щий		

DECLENSIONS

MASCULINE SINGULAR ADJECTIVE ENDINGS

Nom.	перв/ый	дорог/ой	син/ий
Gen.	—ого	—ого	—его
Dat.	—ому	—ому	—ему
Acc.		like nom. or gen.	
Instr.	—ым	—им	—им
Prepos.	о —ом	—ом	—ем

TYPICAL REGULAR MASCULINE SINGULAR NOUN ENDINGS

	HARD	SOFT	SOFT	SOFT
Nom.	стол	словар/ь	случ/ай	критер/ий
Gen.	—а	—я	—ая	—ия
Dat.	—у	—ю	—аю	—ию
Acc.	стол	—ь	—ай	—ий
Instr.	—ом	—ем	—аем	—ием
Prepos.	—е	—е	—ае	—ии

FEMININE SINGULAR ADJECTIVE ENDINGS

Nom.	перв/ая	дорог/ая	син/яя
Gen.	—ой	—ой	—ей
Dat.	—ой	—ой	—ей
Acc.	—ую	—ую	—юю
Instr.	—ой,	—ой,	—ей,
	—ою	—ою	—ею
Prepos.	о —ой	—ой	—ей

TYPICAL REGULAR FEMININE SINGULAR NOUN ENDINGS

	HARD	SOFT	SOFT	SOFT
Nom.	масс/а	сол/ь	реакц/ия	мил/я
Gen.	—ы	—и	—ии	—и
Dat.	—е	—и	—ии	—е
Acc.	—у	—ь	—ию	—ю
Instr.	—ой,	—ью	—ией,	—ей,
	(—ою)		(—иею)	(—ею)
Prepos.	—е	—и	—ии	—е

NEUTER SINGULAR ADJECTIVE ENDINGS

Nom.	перв/ое	дорог/ое	син/ее
Gen.	—ого	—ого	—его
Dat.	—ому	—ому	—ему
Acc.	—ое	—ое	—ее
Instr.	—ым	—им	—им
Prepos.	о —ом	—ом	—ем

TYPICAL REGULAR NEUTER SINGULAR NOUN ENDINGS

	HARD	SOFT	SOFT
Nom.	тел/о	пол/е	знан/ие
Gen.	—а	—я	—ия
Dat.	—у	—ю	—ию
Acc.	—о	—е	—ие
Instr.	—ом	—ем	—ием
Prepos.	—е	—е	—ии

PLURAL ADJECTIVE ENDINGS— ALL GENDERS

Nom.	перв/ые	дорог/ие	син/ие
Gen.	—ых	—их	—их
Dat.	—ым	—им	—им
Acc.		like nom. or gen.	
Instr.	—ыми	—ими	—ими
Prepos.	о —ых	—их	—их

MASCULINE PLURAL NOUN ENDINGS

Nom.	стол/ы	словар/и	случ/аи	критер/ии
Gen.	—ов	—ей	—аев	—иев
Dat.	—ам	—ям	—аям	—иям
Acc.	—ы	—и	—аи	—ии
Instr.	—ами	—ями	—аями	—иями
Prepos.	—ах	—ях	—аях	—иях

FEMININE PLURAL NOUN ENDINGS

Nom.	масс/ы	сол/и	реакц/ии	мил/и
Gen.	масс	—ей	—ий	—ь
Dat.	—ам	—ям	—иям	—ям
Acc.	—ы	—и	—ии	—и
Instr.	—ами	—ями	—иями	—ями
Prepos.	о —ах	—ях	—иях	—ях

NEUTER PLURAL NOUN ENDINGS

Nom.	тел/а	пол/я	знан/ия
Gen.	тел	—ей	—ий
Dat.	—ам	—ям	—иям
Acc.	—а	—я	—ия
Instr.	—ами	—ями	—иями
Prepos.	о —ах	—ях	—иях

DECLENSIONS

TYPICAL REGULAR VERB ENDINGS—PRESENT TENSE

читать		терять		греть		образовать	
я	чит/аю	я	тер/яю	я	гр/ею	я	образ/ую
ты	—аешь	ты	—яешь	ты	—еешь	ты	—уешь
он, она		он, она, оно		он, она, оно		он, она, оно	
	—ает		—яет		—еет		—ует
мы	—аем	мы	—яем	мы	—еем	мы	—уем
вы	—аете	вы	—яете	вы	—еете	вы	—уете
они	—ают	они	—яют	они	—еют	они	—уют

малевать		говорить		учить	
я	мал/юю	я	говор/ю	я	уч/у
ты	—юешь	ты	—ишь	ты	—ишь
он, она		он, она		он, она	
	—юет		—ит		—ит
мы	—юем	мы	—им	мы	—им
вы	—юете	вы	—ите	вы	—ите
они	—юют	они	—ят	они	—ат

PAST TENSE ENDINGS

m.	чита/л
f.	—ла
n.	—ло
pl.	—ли

FUTURE IMPERFECTIVE

Formed by future of **быть** followed by
the infinitive: **я буду читать**, etc.

А

а *abbr.* (**ампер**) ampere; (**ар**) are; (**атто**) atto (10^{-18}).

а *conj.* but, and; while; if; **а** (**не**) **то** or else; otherwise.

Å *abbr.* (**ангстрем**) ångstrom.

а— *prefix* a—; non-; without.

ААИ *abbr.* (**амплитудный анализатор импульсов**) pulse height analyzer.

аапа *f.* aapa (a woodless bog).

ааронова борода (bot.) arum.

АБ *abbr.* (**препарат Боргарда**) a copper sulfate-carbonate seed disinfectant.

абажур *m.* (lamp) shade, screen.

абак *m.,* **—а** *f.* abacus; abaca (hemp).

абаканский *a.* Abakan (river).

абаксиальный *a.* (biol.) abaxial.

абампер *m.* (elec.) abampere (10 amp).

абасин *m.* Abasin, acetylcarbromal.

Аббе конденсатор (micros.) Abbe condenser.

аббревиа/тура, —ция *f.* abbreviation.

аб/вольт *m.* (elec.) abvolt; **—газ** *m.* waste gas; **—генри** *m.* (elec.) abhenry.

абграт/пресс *m.,* **—штамп** *m.* trimming press, dressing or burring machine.

абдом/ен *m.* abdomen; **—инальный** *a.* abdominal; **—ино—** *prefix* abdomino—.

абдук/тор *m.* (anat.) abductor; **—ционный** *a.* abducent, abducting; **—ция** *f.* abduction.

абел/евский, —евый *a.* (math.) Abel's, Abelian; **—ит** *m.* (expl.) abelite.

абелия *f.* (bot.) Abelia.

абельмош *m.* (perfumery; flavoring) abelmosk.

Абеля прибор Abel tester (for flash point).

аберрац/ионный *a.* (astr.; opt.) aberration(al); aberrant; **—ия** *f.* aberration, deviation.

абзац *m.* paragraph, item; indentation.

абиетин *m.* abietin; **—ат** *m.* abietate; **—овая кислота** abietic acid, sylvic acid.

абинский *a.* (geog.) Aba.

абио— *prefix* abio— (without life); **—генез** *m.* abiogenesis; **—генетический, —генный** *a.* abiogenetic, abiogenous; **—тический** *a.* abiotic.

абисс/аль *f.* abyssal zone or fauna; **—альный** *a.* abyssal, deeper bathyal; **—инский** *a.* Abyssinian.

абиссо— *prefix* abysso— (deep; depths of the sea); **—лит** *m.* abyssolith; **—пелагический** *a.* abyssopelagic.

абитуриент *m.* matriculant, applicant.

абихит *m.* (min.) abichite, clinoclasite.

АБК *abbr.* (**ацидофильная бульонная культура**) acidophilus culture.

аблактиров/ание *n.,* **—ка** *f.* (hort.) inarching, side-grafting; **—ать** *v.* inarch.

абляция *f.* ablation, removal.

аб/мо *n.* (elec.) abmho; **—ом** *m.* abohm.

абон/емент *m.* subscription; (library) circulation or work; loan system; library card; **—ент** *m.* subscriber, user, borrower; **—ентский** *a.* subscriber's, customer; **—ировать** *v.* subscribe; borrow.

аборальный *a.* (zool.) aboral.

аборнген *m.* aborigine, native, indigenous species; **—ный** *a.* indigenous, local, native, aboriginal.

аборт *m.* abortion; miscarriage; **—ивный** *a.* abortive; **—ировать** *v.* abort.

абрадировать *v.* abrade, wear off.

абраз/ив *m.,* **—ивный** *a.,* **—ивный материал** abrasive; **—ивность** *f.* abrasability; **—ивостойкий** *a.* abrasion-resistant; **—ионный** *a.* abrasion, abrasive; **—ия** *f.* abrasion, attrition.

абраумзальц *m.* abraum (potash) salts.

абрауский *a.* (geog.) Abrau.

абрико/с *m.,* **—сный, —совый** *a.* apricot; **—тин** *m.* apricot liqueur.

абрин *m.* abrin, jequiritin; abrine, N-methyltryptophan.

абрис *m.* contour, outline, sketch, description; cut-out; (geod.) traverse.

абс. *abbr.* (**абсолютный**) absolute.

абсанс *m.* (med.) absence, absentia.

абс. в. *abbr.* (**абсолютный вес**) absolute weight; **абс. выс.** *abbr.* (**абсолютная высота**) absolute elevation; **абс. ед.** *abbr.* (**абсолютная единица**) absolute unit, ab-unit.

абсент *m.* absinth(e) (liqueur); **—ин** *m.* absinthin.

абсинт/ат *m.* absinthate; **—ин** *m.* absinthin; **—овый** *a.* absinth; absinthic (acid).

абсолютиров/ание *n.* dehydration (of alcohol); **—ать** *v.* dehydrate.

абсолютн/о *adv.* absolutely, perfectly; ideal (black body); **—ый** *a.* absolute; positive; **—ый нуль** absolute zero.

абсорб/ат *m.* absorbate; **—ент** *m.* absorbent; **—ер** *m.* absorber, absorbing apparatus; **—ированный** *a.* absorbed; **—ировать** *v.* absorb, take up; **—ируемый** *a.* absorbable; absorbed; **—ирующий** *a.* absorbing, absorbent; **—ирующее средство** absorbent; **—циометр** *m.* absorptiometer; **—циометрический** *a.* absorptiometric; **—ционный** *a.* absorption, absorptive; **—ционная способность** absorptivity; **—ция** *f.* absorption.

абстатампер *m.* (elec.) abstatampere.

абстиненц/ия *f.* abstinence; **симптом —ии** withdrawal symptom.

абстра/гировать *v.* abstract; **—ктный** *a.* abstract; **—кция** *f.* abstraction.

абсурд *m.,* **—ность** *f.* absurdity; **—ный** *a.* absurd, preposterous; inept.

абсце/дированный *a.* abscessed; **—сс** *m.* abscess.

абсцисса *f.* (math.) abscissa, x-coordinate.

абс. эл. магн. ед. *abbr.* (**абсолютная электромагнитная единица**) absolute electromagnetic unit, abs. emu; **абс. эл. ст. ед.** *abbr.* (**абсолютная электростатическая единица**) absolute electrostatic unit.

абулия *f.* (med.) abulia.

абутилон *m.* (bot.) Abutilon.

абх. *abbr.* (**абхазский**) *a.* Abkhasian.

аб/цуг, —штрих *m.* (met.) dross, scum.

ав, а-в *abbr.* (**ампервиток**) ampere-turn.

а.в. *abbr.* (**атомная единица веса**) atomic weight unit.

ав— *see also under* **авиа—, ау—**.

авагис *m.* (mam.) wooly lemur (*Avahi*).

аван— *prefix* ante—, preliminary; **—гардный** *a.* leading (role); **—дек** *m.* (dock) end platform; **—камера** *f.* antechamber; air lock; **—порт** *m.* outer harbor.

аванс *m.* advance (payment); **—ировать** *v.* advance; **—ом** *adv.* in advance, on account.

авантитул *m.* fly title, foretitle.

авантюрин *m.* (min.) aventurine; **—ный, —овый** *a.* aventurine, spangled.

аванцистерна *f.* preliminary tank.

аварийн/о-защитный *a.* emergency, safety; **—о-спасательный** *a.* emergency rescue (service); survival (gear); **—ость** *f.* accident rate.

авар/ийный *a. of* **авария**; stand-by; damaged (vehicle); hazardous; (comp.) postmortem (dump); **а. рабочий** trouble shooter; **а. режим** emergency conditions; malfunction; **а. случай** emergency; **а. стержень** (nucl.) scram rod, emergency safety rod; **—ийная установка** emergency service; **—ия** *f.* accident, breakdown, trouble; emergency; damage, injury; failure; defect; crash, wreck; mishap.

авачинский *a.* (geog.) Avacha.

авгит *m.* (min.) augite; **—ит** *m.* (petr.) augitite; **—овый** *a.* augitic, augite.

август *m.,* **—овский** *a.* August.

авдотк/а *f.* (bot.) globe flower (*Trollius*); (ichth.) stone loach (*Noemacheilus barbatulus*); (orn.) stonecurlew (*Burhinus oedicnemus*); **—и, —овые** *pl.* (orn.) thick-knee family (*Burhinidae*).

авезасит *m.* (petr.) avezacite.

авелизин *m.* (pharm.) Avelizin(e).

авеназеин *m.* avenacein (antibiotic).

авенин *m.* avenine (alkaloid); avenin, legumin.

авер/роа *f.* (bot.) Averrhoa; **—сивный** *a.* aversive; **—сия** *f.* aversion; **—тин** *m.* Avertin, tribromoethanol.

авиа— *prefix* aviation, airplane, aero—; air, aerial; **—база** *f.* air base; **—бензин** *m.* aviation gasoline; **—бомба** *f.* aerial bomb; **—горизонт** *m.* gyrohorizon; **—двигатель** *m.* airplane engine; **—десант** *m.* (mil.) airborne force; **—десантный** *a.* airborne; **—диспетчер** *m.* air traffic controller; **—древесина** *f.* aircraft wood; **—завод** *m.* airplane factory; **—звено** *n.* flight; **—инструктор** *m.* flight instructor; **—камера** *f.* inner tube (of tire); **—компания** *f.* airline; **—конструктор** *m.* aircraft designer; **—космический** *a.* aerospace; **—крыло** *n.* airplane wing; **—линия** *f.* airway; air route; airline.

авиал/ит *m.* Avialite (alloy); **—ь** *m.* Avial.

авиа/магистраль *f.* major airline; **—масло** *n.* aviation oil; **—матка** *f.* aircraft carrier; **—маяк** *m.* beacon; **—метео—** *prefix* aerometeorological; **—метеорологический** *a.* air weather; **—метеослужба** *f.* air weather service; **—метстанция** *f.* aeronautical weather station; **—метод борьбы с вредителями** aerial pest control; **—механик** *m.* airplane mechanic; **—модель** *f.* model airplane; **—моторостроение** *n.* airplane engine manufacture; **—носец** *m.* aircraft carrier; **—обработка** *f.* (agr.) aerial treatment (with chemicals); **—обучение** *n.* air training; **—опрыскивание** *n.* (agr.) aircraft spraying; **—опрыскиватель** *m.* sprayer plane; **—опыливание** *n.* crop dusting; **—опыливатель** *m.* crop duster; **—отряд** *m.* flight; **—подкормка** *f.* (agr.) aerial application of fertilizer; **—покрышка** *f.* airplane tire (tread); **—почта** *f.* air mail; **—предприятие** *n.* airline; **—приборы** *pl.* aircraft instruments; **—прицел** *m.* bomb sight; **—промышленность** *f.* aviation industry; **—радист** *m.* radio operator; **—разведка** *f.* aerial reconnaissance; **—ремонтный** *a.* aircraft maintenance; **—сев** *m.* aerial sowing; **—станция** *f.* landing site; **—строение** *n.* aircraft industry; **—таксация** *f.* aerial forest survey; **—техник** *m.* aircraft mechanic; **—тика** *see* **авиация; —тор** *m.* aviator.

авиатранспорт *m.,* **—ный** *a.* air transport; **—ом** by air.

авиа/трасса *f.* air route; **—фоторазведка** *f.* aerial photo reconnaissance; **—химборьба** *f.* aerochemical pest control; **—химический** *a.* aerochemical.

авиаци/онно-космический *a.* aerospace; **—онный** *a.* aviation, aircraft, aeronautical; airborne; air-launched; **—я** *f.* aviation; aeronautics; aircraft.

авиваж *m.,* **—ный** *a.* (text.) brightening, avivage, freshening; (rubber, plastics) finishing, dressing.

авидин *m.* avidin (a protein).

авиетка *f.* light plane.

авиз *m.,* **—о** *n.* aviso; letter of advice.

авикулярия *f.* (zool.) avicularium.

авирулентн/ость *f.* (biol.) avirulence; **—ый** *a.* avirulent.

авитаминоз *m.* avitaminosis, vitamin deficiency; **—ный** *a.* avitaminotic.

авифауна *f.* (orn.) avifauna.

авк— *see* **аук—**.

авлейка *see* **аулейка**.

ав/м *abb.* (ампер-виток на метр) ampere-turn per meter; **АВМ** *abbr.* (аналоговая вычислительная машина) analog computer; (автономный воздушный морской аппарат) aqualung.

а.в.н., АВН *abbr.* (аппарат высокого напряжения) high-voltage equipment.

а-во *abbr.* (агенство) agency.

Авогадро число Avogadro number.

авокадо *n.* or *m.* (bot.) avocado.

авометр *m.* avometer, ampere-volt-ohm-metter, multimeter.

авост *m.* emergency stop.

АВР *abbr.* (автоматическая выходная регулировка) automatic output control.

авр— *see also under* **аур—**.

авраамово дерево (bot.) chaste tree (*Vitex agnus-castus*).

авран *m.* (bot.) hedge hyssop (*Gratiola*).

аврикуляриевые грибы (bot.) Auricularia.

австр. *abbr.* (австрийский) Austrian.

австрал/ен *m.* australene, pinene; **—ийский** *a.* Australian; **—ит** *m.* (petr.) australite.

австралогубановые *pl.* (ichth.) Odacidae.

австралопитек *m.* (pal.) Australopithecus.

австрийский *a.* Austrian.

авт. *abbr.* [автоматический; автомобиль(ный); автономный; автор(ский)].

автентичный *a.* authentic.

авт. л. *abbr.* (авторский лист).

авто *n.* car, automobile.

авто— *prefix* auto—, self-, automatic; automobile; carborne, truck-mounted; author's; *see also under* **ауто—**; **—база** *f.* service station; garage; car or truck fleet; **—бензоцистерна** *f.* (fuel) tanker; **—бетономешалка** *f.,* **—бетоносместитель** *m.* concrete mixer (truck); **—биографический** *a.* autobiographic(al); **—блокировка** *f.* automatic block(ing); **—броневик** *m.* armored car; **—бус** *m.* bus; **—вагон** *see* **автомотриса**; **—вакцина** *f.* (med.) autovaccine; **—весы** *pl.* automatic scales; **—воз** *m.* truck; **—вокзал** *m.* service station; bus terminal; **—восстановление** *n.* auto-restoration (of arc).

автогам *m.* autogamous plant; **—ия** *f.* autogamy; **—ный** *a.* (biol.) autogamous, self-fertilizing.

авто/генез *m.* (biol.) autogenesis; **—генератор** *m.* self-excited oscillator; **—генный** *a.* autogenous; gas, oxyacetylene (cutting, welding); **—генщик** *m.* oxyacetylene welder; **—граф** *m.* autograph; recorder; (phot.) setting device; **—грейдер** *m.* (road) grader; **—грузчик** *m.* fork lift; **—гудронатор** *m.* paver; **—дегазационная машина** decontamination truck.

авто/дезоустановка *f.* (vet.) portable disinfecting unit; **—дело** *n.* automobile engineering; **—дин** *m.* (pharm.; rad.) autodyne; **—диспетчер** *m.* automation dispatcher; **—доение** *n.,* **—доильный** *a.* machine milking; **—дорога** *f.* highway, road; **—дорожный** *a.* highway, road; **—дрезина** *see* **автомотриса**; **—дром** *m.* race track; testing or proving grounds; **—дупликация** *f.* (gen.) reduplication; **—душевой** *a.* mobile shower; **—жижеразбрасыватель** *m.* liquid manure spreader; **—жир**

m. gyroplane, autogyro; —**завод** *m.* automobile factory; self-winder; —**заправочный** *a.* refueling, gas; —**заправщик** *m.* gas truck, tanker.

авто/инспекция *f.* car inspection; —**интоксикация** *f.* autointoxication, self-poisoning; —**камера** *f.* inner (tire) tube; —**кар** *m.,* —**кара** *f.* autotruck, shop truck; —**катализ** *m.* autocatalysis; —**каталитический** *a.* autocatalytic; —**качка** *f.* automatic pumping unit.

автоклав *m.* autoclave, digester; (med.) sterilizer; **красильный** *a.* pressure-dyeing machine; —**ирование** *n.* autoclaving; —**ировать** *v.* autoclave, digest; sterilize; —**ный** *a.* autoclave; steam (and pressure) cured.

автокластический *a.* (petr.) autoclastic.

автоколеб/ания *pl.* self-excited vibrations, auto-oscillation(s); hunting; —**ательный** *a.* self-oscillating, self-vibrating, self-excited; free-running (operation).

авто/коллимационный *a.,* —**коллимация** *f.* (opt.) autocollimation; —**колонна** *f.* truck convoy; —**компенсатор** *m.* (elec.) self-balancing potentiometer; —**корд** *m.* tire cord; —**кормушка** *f.* automatic feeder; —**ректор** *m.* self-correcting device; —**корреляционный** *a.* (math.) autocorrelation, self-correlated; —**кран** *m.* vehicle-mounted crane; —**л** *m.* motor oil; —**лавка** *f.* shop van; —**лаки** *pl.* automobile lacquers; —**лебёдка** *f.* winch truck; —**лесовоз** *m.* (lumber) straddle carrier; —**лиз** *m.* (cyt.) autolysis, self-digestion; —**лист** *m.* (automobile) sheet steel; —**лит** *a.* (petr.) autolith; —**литический** *a.* (cyt.) autolytic; —**магистраль** *f.* main highway; —**массажер** *m.* (med.) belt massager.

автомат *m.* robot, automat(on); automatic machine or device; (elec.) circuit breaker; submachine gun; telephone booth; **винторезный** *a.* automatic threader; **а.-водоотводчик** *m.* automatic steam trap.

автоматиз/ация *f.* automation, automatic control; **а. программирования** automatic programming; **а. производства** automation, process control; —**ированный** *a.* automated, automatically controlled; computer-aided; —**ированное проектирование** computer-aided design; CAD; —**изированное рабочее место** workstation; —**ировать** *v.* automate.

автомат/изм *m.* automatism, automatic performance, action or behavior; —**ика** *f.* automatics; automation; automatic machines or equipment; —**ический** *a.* automatic, auto—, self-acting; unattended; power (-driven or -propelled); —**ическая линия** transfer machine; **с —ическим питанием** self-feeding; —**ия** *see* **автоматизм;** automaticity; automatic activity; —**ный** *a.* of **автомат;** screwstock, free-cutting (steel); —**чик** *m.* machine operator.

авто/машина *f.* motor vehicle, car, truck; —**механик** *m.* auto mechanic; —**механический** *a.* automotive; —**миксис** *m.* (gen.) automixis.

автомобилестро/ение *n.,* —**ительный** *a.* automobile manufacture.

автомобил/изм *m.* motoring, driving; —**ист** *m.,* —**истка** *f.* motorist, driver.

автомобил/ь *m.* auto(mobile), car, vehicle; truck; **на —е** truck-mounted.

автомобиль/носанитарный транспорт ambulance; —**ный** *a.* of **автомобиль;** motorized; automotive (parts); truck-mounted (equipment); —**ный транспорт** motor vehicle.

автомобиль-/пескомёт *m.* sanding truck; —**платформа** flatbed truck; —**рефрижератор** refrigerator truck; —**самосвал** dump truck; —**тягач** *m.* tractor; —**фургон** van; —**цистерна** tank truck.

автомод/ельный *a.* self-similar, self-simulating; progressive; self-modeling (problem); —**улировать** *v.* self-modulate; —**уляция** *f.* self-modulation.

автомолит *m.* (min.) automolite, zinc spinel, zinc gahnite.

автоморф/изм *m.* automorphism; —**ный** *a.* automorphic; (petr.) idiomorphic.

автомотриса *f.* railway (motor) car.

авто/мутаген *m.* (gen.) automutagen; —**навеска** *f.* automatic hitch; —**нагрузчик** *m.* truck loader; fork lift.

автоном/ия, —**ность** *f.* autonomy, self-regulation; noninteraction; —**ный** *a.* autonomous, independent, self-contained; stand-alone; (comp.) off-line; noninteraction; self-reacting (device); (biol.) autonomic; —**ный воздушный морской аппарат** aqualung; —**ный режим,** —**ная работа** (comp.) off-line operation; —**ное испытание** stand-alone test.

авто/окисление *n.* autoxidation; —**оператор** *m.* (mach.) transfer arm; —**опрыскиватель** *m.* mobile sprayer; —**ответчик** *m.* answering machine; —**парк** *m.* car or truck fleet; —**перевозка** *f.* haulage, trucking; —**переключатель** *m.* automatic switch; —**пилот** *m.* autopilot, mechanical pilot; —**погрузчик** *m.* loader, fork lift; —**подаватель** *m.* self-feeder; —**податчик** *m.* power feed; —**подача** *f.* self-feeding, automatic feed; —**подий** *m.,* —**подия** *f.* autopodium, limb; —**подъёмник** *m.* self-lift; —**поезд** *m.* tractor and trailer (rig); —**поилка** *f.* (livestock) automatic fountain; —**покрышка** *f.* tire (tread or casing); —**полимеризация** *f.* autopolymerization; —**полиплоид** *m.,* —**полиплоидный** *a.* (gen.) autopolyploid; —**полярный** *a.* autopolar, self-polar; —**посадочный** *a.* mechanical planting; —**потенциометр** *m.* self-balanced potentiometer; —**правка** *f.* (paper) automatic guiding; —**прицеп** *m.* trailer; —**проводимость** *f.* (elec.) autoconduction; —**прокладчик** *m.* automatic position plotter; —**пром** *insert, suffix,* —**промышленность** *f.* automobile industry; —**пуск** *m.* automatic start(-up); starter.

автор *m.* author.

авторадио/грамма *f.,* —**граф** *m.* autoradiogram, autoradiograph; —**графирование** *n.,* —**графия** *f.* autoradiography; —**снимок** *m. see* **авторадиограмма.**

авторегул/ирование *n.,* —**ировка** *f.* automatic control; —**ятор** *m.* automatic regulator or controller.

авто/режим *m.* automatic performance; —**резина** *f.* car tires and tubes; —**ремонтный** *a.* auto repair.

автореферат *m.* author's abstract.

авторефрижератор *m.* refrigerated truck.

авторизованный *a.* authorized.

авторитет *m.* authority, power; —**ный** *a.* authoritative, expert.

авторс/кий *a.* author's; **а. лист** author index; author's quire; —**кое право** copyright; —**кое свидетельство** inventor's certificate; —**тво** *n.* authorship.

авторучка *f.* fountain or ball point pen.

авто/самосвал *m.* dump truck; —**сани** *pl.* motor sleigh; snowmobile; —**сборка** *f.* automatic assembly; —**свеча** *f.* spark plug; —**син** *m.* (elec.) autosyn, selsyn, synchro; —**синдез(ис)** *m.* (gen.) autosyndesis; —**синный** *a. of* **автосин;** —**смазка** *f.* automatic lubrication or lubricant; —**сома** *f.* (gen.) autosome; —**сом(аль)ный** *a.* autosomal; —**спора** *f.* (bot.) autospore; —**спуск** *m.* (phot.) tripping device, delayed action release.

автостабилиз/атор *m.* (aut.) autostabilizer; —**ация** *f.* autostabilization.

авто/стелла *f.* motel; —**стерильность** *f.* (biol.) autosterility, self-sterility; —**стоп** *m.* automatic stop or brake; —**стоянка** *f.* parking lot; —**страда** *f.* superhighway, turnpike; —**строение** *n.* automobile construction; —**сцепка** *f.*, —**сцепной** *a.* automatic coupling; (agr.) automatic hitch; —**таймер** *m.* (aut.) autotimer; —**тележка** *f.* shop truck; —**телеуправление** *n.* remote control; —**термический** *a.* autothermic; —**терморегулятор** *m.* thermostat; —**тип** *m.* (biol.; phot.) autotype; —**типный** *a.* autotypic; —**томия** *f.* (biol.) autotomy, self-division; —**топливозаправщик** *m.* (fuel) tank truck; —**тормоз** *m.* automatic brake; —**тракторный** *a.* automobile and tractor; automotive.

автотранспорт *m.* motor transport; vehicle; **грузовой а.** trucking; —**ёр** *m.* self-propelled conveyer; —**ное загрязнение, —ные выбросы** traffic pollution.

авто/трансформатор *m.* (elec.) autotransformer; —**тропизм** *m.* (biol.) autotropism; —**тропный** *a.* autotropic.

автотроф *m.* (biol.) autotroph, autotrophic organism; —**ия, —ность** *f.* autotrophy; —**ный** *a.* autotrophic, self-nourishing.

авто/тягач *m.* tractor; —**управление** *n.* automatic control; —**фазировка** *f.* phase stability; automatic phase stabilization; —**фар** *m.* headlight; —**фертильность** *f.* (biol.) autogamy, self-fertilization; —**фильтровальный** *a.* mobile water-filtering; —**фотолаборатория** *f.* darkroom van; —**фрет(т)аж** *m.*, —**фрет(т)ирование** *n.* (mech. eng.) autofrettage; self-loading; —**фургон** *m.* van; caravan; —**хозяйство** *n.* truck or car fleet.

автохтон *m.* (biol.; geol.) autochthon, —**ный** *a.* autochthonous, indigenous.

авто/цидный *a.* insecticide-impregnated (band); —**цистерна** *f.* tanker; —**шина** *f.* (automobile) tire; —**штурман** *m.* (aero.) autonavigator; —**электронный** *a.* auto-electronic, field (emission); field-emission (breakdown, microscope); —**эмиссия** *f.* field emission.

автур *m.* automatic level controller.

АВУ *abbr.* (**аналоговое вычислительное устройство**) analog computer.

ага *f.* giant toad (*Bufo marinus*).

АГА Gorodilin food processor.

агава *f.* (bot.) agave.

агальматолит *m.* (min.) agalmatolite.

агам/ета *f.* (zool.) agamete; —**ия** *f.* agamy; —**маглобулинемия** *f.* (immun.) agammaglobulinemia; —**ный** *a.* agamous, agamic, asexual.

агамо— *prefix* agamo— (agamous, asexual); —**вид** *m.* agamospecies; —**генез** *m.*, —**гония** *f.* agamogenesis, agamogony, asexual reproduction.

агар/(-агар) *m.* agar(-agar); —**изованный** *a.* agar-containing; —**ицин** *m.* agaricin; —**ициновый** *a.* agar(ic)ic (acid); —**овый** *a.* agar.

агат *m.* (min.) agate; —**ис** *m.* (bot.) Agathis; —**овый** *a.* of **агат**; agathic (acid); —**оподобный** *a.* agate-like.

агглломер— *see* **агломер**—.

агглютин/ация *f.* agglutination; —**ин** *m.* agglutinin; —**ировать** *v.* agglutinate; —**ирующий** *a.* agglutinating; —**ирующее средство** agglutinant; —**оген** *m.* agglutinogen.

агградация *f.* aggradation.

аггре— *see under* **агре**—.

аге/взия *f.* (med.) ageus(t)ia, loss of taste; —**незия** *f.* agenesia, agenesis; sterility, impotence.

агент *m.* agent, factor; —**ant, —ent; дезактивирующий а.** decontaminant; —**ский** *a.* agent, acting; —**ство** *n.*, —**ура** *f.* agency.

агератум *m.* (bot.) floss flower (*Ageratum*).

агиларит *m.* (min.) aguilarite.

агинский *a.* (geog). Aga.

агирн/о-примитивный *a.* (cryst.) monohedral; **а.-центральный** *a.* pinacoidal; —**ый** *a.* triclinic.

агит/атор *m.* agitator; —**ационнопенный процесс** (flotation) agitation-froth process; —**ационный** *a.*, —**ация** *f.* agitation, stirring; —**ировать** *v.* agitate, stir; persuade; campaign.

АГК *abbr.* (**активационный гамма каротаж**) neutron gamma logging.

агликон *m.* aglycone.

агло— *prefix* agglomerated, agglomeration; —**лента** *f.* (sintering machine) grate.

агломер/ат *m.* agglomerate, sinter (cake); —**ационный** *a.* agglomeration, sintering; sinter (roasting); —**ация** *f.*, —**ирование** *n.* agglomeration, sintering; —**ировать** *v.* agglomerate; —**ирующий** *a.* agglomerating; —**ирующее средство** agglomerant.

агло/спек *m.* agglomerated cake; —**фабрика** *f.* agglomeration plant; —**чаша** *f.* agglomeration basin; —**шихта** *f.* agglomerated charge.

аглюкон *m.* aglycone, aglucone.

агмаль *m.* Agmal (alloy).

агматин *m.* agmatine, aminobutyl guanidine; —**оплоидия** *f.* (gen.) agmatoploidy.

агна/тия *f.* (med.) agnathia, —**ты** *pl.* (zool.) Agnatha; —**ция** *f.* (gen.) agnation, kinship.

агнозия *f.* (med.) agnosia.

агностерин *m.* agnosterol.

агойский *a.* (geog.) Agoi.

агон/а *f.* agonic line; —**альный** *a.* (med.) agonal; terminal (illness); —**иадин** *m.* agoniadin, plumierin; —**(из)ировать** *v.* agonize, be in agony; —**ист** *m.* (anat.) agonist; —**ический** *a.* agonic (line); —**ия** *f.* agony; —**овые** *pl.* (ichth.) sea poachers (*Agonidae*).

агранул/о— *prefix* agranulo— (nongranular); —**оцит** *m.* agranulocyte; —**ярный** *a.* agranular, nongranular.

аграр/ий *m.* landholder; —**ный** *a.* agrarian, agricultural, landholding.

аграфия *f.* (med.) agraphia.

аграхан/ка *f.* (ichth.) agrakhanka (a shad) (*Alosa brashnikovi agrachanica*); —**ский** *a.* (geog.) Agrakhan.

агрег/ат *m.* aggregate, set, outfit; assembly, collection; unit, plant; package; —**аты** *pl.* hardware; —**ативно-неустойчивый** *a.* unstable in the state of aggregation; —**ативный** *a.* aggregative; —**(ат)ирование** *n.* aggregating, aggregation, etc. *see v.*; —**(ат)ировать** *v.* aggregate; design as a unit, unitize; hook up, couple, hitch, mount (implements); —**атная** *f.* power room; —**атность** *f.* (soil) aggregation; —**атный** *a. of* **агрегат**; (mach.) gang(ed); unit-head, standard-unit (machine tool); in units, in blocks; modular; —**атная головка** power pack; —**атное состояние** state of aggregation; —**ация** *f.* aggregation; aggregate, set, collection.

агресс/ивность *f.* aggressiveness; —**ивный** *a.* aggressive, corrosive; —**ин** *m.* aggressin, virulin; —**ия** *f.* aggression.

агресте *n.* agreste, woodland savanna.

агри/колит *m.* (min.) agricolite; —**культура** *f.* agriculture; —**культурный** *a.* agricultural; —**мония** *f.* (bot.) agrimony (*Agrimonia*).

агро— *prefix* agro—, agricultural; —**база** *f.* agricultural base; —**биология** *f.* agrobiology, agricultural biology; —**город** *m.* agricultural town; —**зоотехнический** *a.* crop and animal husbandry; —**клавин** *m.* agroclavine; —**климат** *m.* agricultural climatic conditions.

агролесомелиор/ативный *a.*, —**ация** *f.* conservational afforestation, forest and land improvement.

агромелиор/ативный *a.* soil-improving, soil-conserving; **—ация** *f.* land improvement, land reclamation, soil conservation.

агромет/еорологический *a.* agrometeorological; **—прогнозы** *pl.* (agr.) weather reports.

агроном *m.* agronomist; **а.-зерновик** *m.* grain-growing specialist; **—ический** *a.* agronomic, agricultural; **—ия** *f.* agronomy, agriculture; **а.-механизатор** *m.* agricultural engineer; **а.-полевод** *m.* field-crop agronomist; **а.-почвовед** *m.* soil scientist; **а.-семеновод** *m.* seed-growing specialist; **а.-химизатор** *m.* agricultural chemist.

агро/нормативы *pl.* agricultural standards; **—помощь** *f.* farm extension service; **—почвенный** *a.* agropedological; **—почвоведение** *n.* agropedology, soil science; **—приёмы** *pl.* agricultural methods; **—пульверизатор** *m.* sprayer; **—пункт** *m.* agricultural experiment station; **—стология** *f.* (bot.) agrostology; **—техника** *f.* agricultural technology, agronomical practices; **—технический** *a.* agrotechnical, agronomical; **—учёба** *f.* agricultural training; **—фак** *m.* agricultural division; **—фитоценоз** *m.* agrophytoceno(e)sis; **—фон** *m.* soil preparation; soil fertility.

агрохим/ик *m.* agricultural chemist; **—икат** *m.*, **—ический** *a.* agrochemical; **—ия** *f.* agricultural chemistry.

агроцибин *m.* agrocybin (antibiotic).

АГ соль *f.* nylon salt, hexamethylenediamine adipate.

агульский *a.* (geog.) Agul.

агума *f.* soybean meal.

агурин *m.* Agurin, theobromine sodium acetate.

агути(евые) *pl.* (mam.) agutis (*Dasyproctidae*).

АГ-цемент *m.* anhydride cement.

адаксиальный *a.* adaxial (towards the axis).

адалин *m.* Adalin, carbromal.

адамантан *m.* adamantane, tricyclodecane.

адамантовый *a.* adamantine; firm, steadfast.

адамеллит *m.* (petr.) adamellite.

адам/ин *m.* (min.) adamite; **—ит** *m.* (min.; abrasive) adamite.

адамово дерево (bot.) royal paulownia (*Paulownia tomentosa*); **а. яблоко** (anat.) Adam's apple.

адам/он *m.* adamon; **—сит** *m.* (min.; poison gas) adamsite; **—сия** *f.* Adamsia (a sea anemone).

адансонин *m.* adansonine.

адапт/ационный *a.* adaptation; adaptive; **—ация** *f.* adaptation; **—ер** *m.* adapter; (sound) pickup; **—ивный** *a.* adaptive, self-adjusting; **—ированный** *a.* adapted; acclimated; **—ировать(ся)** *v.* adapt; **—ометр** *m.* adaptometer.

адатом *m.* adsorbed atom, adatom.

адвек/тивный *a.* (meteor.) advective, advection; **—ция** *f.* advection.

адвент/ивный *a.* adventive, accidental; **—ициальный** *a.* (anat., biol.) adventitious; **—иция** *f.* adventitia.

адвокат *m.* lawyer, attorney; advocate; **—ура** *f.* bar; legal profession.

адгез/ионный *a.* adhesion, adhesive; **—ия** *f.* adhesion, adherence; attachment.

адда *f.*, **—кс** *m.* (mam.) antelope adaxe (*Addax nasomaculatus*).

адденд *m.* complexing agent.

аддисонова болезнь (med.) Addison's disease, bronzed skin.

адди/тивность *f.* additivity; **—тивный** *a.* additive; **—ционный** *a.* addition(al); association (complex).

аддук/т *m.* (chem.) adduct, addition product, inclusion complex; **—тор** *m.* (anat.) adductor; **—ция** *f.* (physiol.) adduction.

адекватн/о *adv.* adequately, sufficiently; equally; **—ость**

f. adequacy; **—ый** *a.* adequate, sufficient; equal (to); equivalent (to); suitable (for).

аделит *m.* (min.) adelite.

адело— *prefix* adel(o)— (not apparent, concealed); **—морфный** *a.* (biol.) adelomorphous.

адельфо— *prefix* adelpho— (brother); **—гамия** *f.* (gen.) adelphogamy.

аден— *see* **адено—**; **—аза** *f.* adenase; **—илат** *m.* adenylate; **—иловый** *a.* adenylic (acid); **—илянтарный** *a.* adenylsuccinic (acid); **—ин** *m.* adenine, 6-aminopurine; **—иннуклеотид** *m.* adenine nucleotide; **—ит** *m.* (med.) adenitis; **—ия** *f.* (bot.) Adenia.

адено— *prefix* adeno— [gland(ular)]; **—вирус** *m.* adenovirus; **—гипофиз** *m.* (anat.) adenohypophysis; **—з** *m.* (med.) adenosis; **—зилметионин** *m.* adenosylmethionine.

аденозин *m.* adenosine, adenine riboside; **—дифосфат** *m.* adenosine diphosphate, ADP; **—монофосфат** *m.* adenosine monophosphate, AMP; **—трифосфат** *m.* adenosine triphosphate, ATP.

адено/ид *m.*, **—идный** *a.* (anat.) adenoid; **—иднокистозный** *a.* adenocystic (carcinoma); **—кистома** *f.* (med.) adenocystoma; **—ма** *f.* adenoma; **—матозный** *a.* adenomatous; **—цит** *m.* adenocyte.

аденский *a.* (med.) Aden (ulcer).

адергнейс *m.* (petr.) banded gneiss.

адермин *m.* adermine, vitamin B_6.

адето— *prefix* adeto— (free).

адж. *abbr.* **(аджарский)** *a.* (geog.) Adzhar.

адж/ирик *m.* Bermuda grass (*Cynodon dactylon*); **—ур** *m.* snake melon (*Cucumis melo flexuosus*).

адзуки *m.* adzuki bean (*Phaseolus angularis*).

адиабат/а *f.* adiabatic curve; **—ический**, **—ичный**, **—ный** *a.* adiabatic.

адиактинический *a.* adiactinic.

адиант(ум) *m.* (bot.) maidenhair (*Adiantum*).

адинамич/еский *a.* (med.) adynamic, asthenic.

адинол(ь) *m.* (petr.) adinole.

адип/ил *m.* adipyl; **—иновая кислота** adipic acid, hexanedioic acid; **—иновый альдегид** adipaldehyde; **—о—** *prefix* adip(o)— (fat); **—олитический** *a.* adipolytic, lipolytic; **—рен** *m.* Adiprene (polyurethane rubber).

адиуретин *m.* adiuretin, antidiuretic hormone.

администр/ативно-управленческий *a.* administrative and managerial; **—ативный** *a.* administrative; routine; **—ация** *f.* administration; **—ировать** *v.* administer.

адмиралтейс/кий *a.* admiralty (metal); **—тво** *n.* shipyard, dockyard.

адмитанц *m.* (elec.) admittance.

адмонский двойной купорос Salzburg vitriol (cupric and ferrous sulfate).

адник *m.* (met.) Adnic (alloy).

адокса *f.* (bot.) moschatel (*Adoxa*).

адолескар/ий *m.*, **—ия** *f.* (zool.) adolescaria.

адон/идин *m.* adonidin; **—изид** *m.* Adonisid; **—ин** *m.* adonin; **—ис** *m.* (bot.) Adonis; **—ит** *m.* adonite, adonitol.

адрагант *m.*, **—гумми** tragacanth (gum).

адраспан *m.* (bot.) African rue (*Peganum harmala*).

адрен/алин *m.* adrenaline; **—ергический** *a.* (physiol.) adrenergic; **—о—** *prefix* adreno— (adrenal gland); **—окортикальный** *a.* (anat.) adrenocortical; **—окортикотропный гормон** adrenocorticotropic hormone, ACTH; **—остерон** *m.* adrenosterone; **—охром** *m.* adrenochrome; **—эргический** *a.* adrenergic.

адрес *m.* address; location; destination; **—ант** *m.* addresser; **—ат** *m.* addressee; destination; **—ация** *f.*

(comp.) addressing; **а.-календарь, —ная книга** directory; **—ность** *f.* number of addresses; **—ный** *a.* address(ing); **—овальный** *a.*, **—ование** *n.*addressing; **—овать** *v.* address, direct; refer; **—ограф** *m.* addressing machine, addressograph; **а.-операнд** *m.* immediate address; **—уемый** *a.* addressable; addressed.

адрианихтовые *pl.* (ichth.) Adrianichthyidae.

адрианопольский красный Turkey red.

адриатический *a.* (geog.) Adriatic.

адский *a.* hellish, infernal; awful, terrible; Hell's (gate); **а. камень** lunar caustic, silver nitrate.

адсорб/ат *m.* adsorbate; **—ент** *m.* adsorbent; **—ер** *m.* adsorber; **—ирование** *n.* adsorption; **—ированный** *a.* adsorbed; **—ировать** *v.* adsorb; **—ируемый** *a.* adsorbable; adsorbed; **—ирующий** *a.* adsorbing, adsorbent; **—ирующее средство** adsorbent; **—тив** *m.* adsorbate; **—ционность** *f.* adsorptivity; **—ционный** *a.* adsorption, adsorptive; **—ция** *f.* adsorption.

АДУ *abbr.* (**аппаратура дистанционного управления**) remote control equipment.

адуляр *m.* (min.) adular(ia).

адурол *m.* (phot.) adurol.

адус/ация *f.*, **—исаж** *m.* (met.) softening, malleablizing.

АДФ *abbr.* (**аденозиндифосфат**) adenosine disphosphate, ADP.

адъективные красители mordant dyes.

адъюнкт *m.*, **—а** *f.* (math.) adjunct, cofactor; (mil.) advanced student, postgraduate.

адыгейский *a.* (geog.) Adigey; Adige.

адыры *pl.* adyry (low foothills bordering the Ferghana depression).

адэкватный *a.* adequate.

АЕ *abbr.* (**антигенная единица**) antigen unit; (**антитоксическая единица**) antitoxin unit.

АЕМ, а.е.м. *abbr.* (**атомная единица массы**) atomic mass unit, amu.

ажгон *m.*, **—овый** *a.* ajowan (fruit of *Carum copticum*).

ажит/ация *f.* agitation, excitement; **—ированный** *a.* agitated.

ажрык *m.* (bot.) Aeluropus litoralis.

ажур *adv.* up to date; *m.* openwork; **—ный** *a.* openwork; skeleton; fret (saw).

аз *m.* letter A.

аз— *prefix* Azerbaijan; Azov.

азал/еин *m.* azalein, fuchsin, aniline red; **—ия** *f.* (bot.) azalea.

азар/ин *m.* azarin (dye); **—овое масло** asarum oil; **—он** *m.* asarone, asarum camphor; **—оновая кислота** asaronic acid, 2,4,5-trimethoxybenzoic acid.

азарт *m.* fervor; risk, hazard; **—ный** *a.* fervent; risky.

аза/серин *m.* azaserine, serine diazoacetate; **—соединение** *n.* aza-compound; **—фрин** *m.* azafrin.

азбест *see* **асбест.**

азбу/ка *f.* alphabet; code; **—чный** *a.* alphabetical; code(d).

азелаин *m.* azelain; **—овая кислота** azelaic acid, nonanedioic acid; **—овокислый** *a.* azelaic acid; azelate (of); **—овокислая соль** azelate.

азеотроп *m.* azeotrope; **—ический, —ный** *a.* azeotropic; **—ность** *f.* azeotropy.

азерб. *abbr.*, **азер(б)—** *prefix,* **азербайджанский** *a.* Azerbaijan.

азиатикозид *m.* asiaticoside.

азиатский *a.* Asiatic, Asian.

азиго— *prefix* azygo— (azygous, odd, not one of a pair); **—та** *f.* (gen.) azygote.

азид *m.* azide; **—о—** *prefix* azid(o)—, triazo.

азимина *f.* (bot.) papaw (*Asimina*).

азимино— *prefix* azimino—, azimido—.

азиминовое дерево *see* **азимина.**

азимут *m.* (astr.; surv.) azimuth, bearing; **—альный** *a.* azimuth(al); **а.-квадрант** *m.* azimuth dial.

азин *m.*, **—овый** *a.* azine.

Азия Asia.

Азнефть *f.* Azneft' (State Association of the Azerbaijan Petroleum Industry); **АзНИИ . . .** *abbr.* Azerbaijan Research Institute (of).

азо— *prefix* azo—; **—амин** *m.* an azo dye series; **—белок** *m.* azoprotein; **—бензол** *m.* azobenzene.

азов/о-черноморский *a.* Azov-Black Sea; **—ский** *a.* Azov.

азо/группа *f.* azo group; **—имид** *m.* azoimide, hydrazoic acid; **—иминосоединение** *n.* azoimino compound; **—йский** *a.* azoic (without life); **—кислотный** *a.* azo acid; **—красители, —краски** *pl.* azo dyes; **—кси—** *prefix* azoxy—; **—ксибензол** *m.* azoxybenzene; **—ксипроизводное** *n.* azoxy derivative; **—ксисоединение** *n.* azoxy compound; **—ксисочетание** *n.* azoxy coupling; **—л** *m.* azole; **—литмин** *m.* azolitmin (dye); **—метин** *m.* azomethin.

азональный *a.* azonal (soil).

азооспермия *f.* (zool.) azoospermia.

азо/производное *n.* azo derivative; **—реакция** *f.* (dyes) coupling reaction.

азорский *a.* (geog.) Azores.

азо/соединение *n.* azo compound; **—составляющее** *n.* azo component; **—сочетание** *n.* azo coupling.

азот *m.* nitrogen, N; **двуокись —а** nitrogen peroxide; **закись —а** nitrous oxide; **окись —а** nitric oxide; **—выделяющий** *a.* nitrogen-releasing; nitrogen-fixing (bacteria); **—емия** *f.* (med.) azotemia; **—изация** *f.*, **—ирование** *n.* nitration; (met.) nitriding; **—ировать** *v.* nitrate; nitride.

азотисто/амиловый эфир amyl nitrite; **—аммониевая соль** ammonium nitrite; **—водородная кислота** hydrazoic acid; **—калиевая соль** potassium nitrite; **—кальциевая соль** calcium nitrite; **—кислый** *a.* nitrous acid; nitrite (of); **—кислый натрий** sodium nitrite; **—кислая соль** nitrite; **—натриевая соль** sodium nitrite; **—этиловый эфир** ethyl nitrite.

азотист/ый *a.* nitrous, nitrogenous, nitride (of); **а. ангидрид** nitrous anhydride, nitrogen trioxide; **а. бор** boron nitride; **а. кальций** calcium nitride; **—ая известь** calcium cyanamide; **—ая кислота** nitrous acid; **соль —ой кислоты** nitrite; **—ое равновесие** (biol.) nitrogenous equilibrium.

азотно/амиловый эфир amyl nitrate; **—аммониевая соль** ammonium nitrate; **—бариевая соль** barium nitrate.

азотноват/ая кислота hyponitric acid (old name for nitrogen peroxide); **—истая кислота** hyponitrous acid; **соль —истой кислоты** hyponitrite; **—истоаммиачная соль** ammonium hyponitrite; **—истокислый** *a.* hyponitrous acid; hyponitrite (of); **—истокислая соль** hyponitrite; **—истосеребряная соль** silver hyponitrite; **—ый ангидрид** nitrogen peroxide.

азотно/висмутовая соль bismuth nitrate; **основная —висмутовая соль** bismuth subnitrate; **—глицериновый эфир** glycerol trinitrate, nitroglycerin; **—железистая соль** ferrous nitrate; **—железная соль** ferric nitrate; **—калиевая соль** potassium nitrate; **—кальциевая соль** calcium nitrate; **—кислотный** *a.* nitric acid; **—кислый** *a.* nitric acid; nitrate (of); **—кислый калий** potassium nitrate; **—кислый сплав** niter cake; **—кислая соль** nitrate; **—натриевая соль** sodium nitrate; **—ртутистая соль** mercurous nitrate; —**ртутная соль** mercuric nitrate; —**серебряная соль** silver nitrate; —**стибиловая соль** antimonyl nitrate; —**стронциевая соль** strontium nitrate; —**туковый** *a.* nitrogen fertilizer; —**этиловый эфир** ethyl nitrate.

азотн/ый *a.* nitric, nitrogen(ous); **а. ангидрид** nitric anhydride, nitrogen pentoxide; —**ая кислота** nitric acid; **соль —ой кислоты** nitrate.

азотобактер *m.* Azotobacter, nitrogen-fixing bacteria; —**ин** *m.* azotobacterin, bacterial fertilizer.

азотолуол *m.* azotoluene.

азото/люб *m.* nitrophyte, nitrogen-loving plant; —**метр** *m.* azotometer, nitrometer; —**накопители** *see* **азотобактер;** —**оборот** *m.* nitrogen cycle; —**отдающий** *a.* nitrogen-liberating; —**потребление** *n.* nitrogen consumption or requirement; —**р(р)ея** *f.* (med.) azotorrhea; —**свяявающий** *a.* nitrogen-fixing; —**собиратель** *m.* nitrogen-fixing bacterium; nitrogen-storing plant; —**содержащий** *a.* nitrogen-containing; —**тдающий** *a.* nitrogen-liberating; —**углеродистый титан** titanium carbonitride; —**усваивающий** *a.* nitrogen-assimilating, nitrogen fixing; —**фиксатор** *m.* nitrogen fixer.

азот/собиратель *see* **азотособиратель;** —**содержащий** *see* **азотосодержащий;** —**урия** *f.* (med.) azoturia; —**фиксирующий** *a.* nitrogen-fixing.

азо/фенол *m.* azophenol; —**фос** *m.* azophos (nitrogen-phosphorus fertilizer); —**фоска** *f.* azophoska (nitrogen-phosphorus-potassium fertilizer).

Азрыба *f.* Azerbaijan State Fish Industry Trust.

АЗС *abbr.* (**автозаправочная станция**) gas station.

азул/ен *m.* azulene; —**ин** *m.* azulin; —**ьмовая кислота** azulmic acid, azulmin.

азур *m.* (micros.) azure blue dye; —**ин** *m.* azurine; —**ит** *m.* (min.) azurite, azure stone; —**офиль** *m.* azurophil; —**офильный** *a.* azurophil(e), azurophilic.

азчер— *prefix* Azov-Black Sea.

АИ *abbr.* (**анализатор импульсов**) pulse analyzer.

АИГ *abbr.* (**алюмоиттриевый гранат**) yttrium-aluminum garnet, YAG.

аизовые *pl.* (bot.) Aizoaceae.

АИМ *abbr.* (**амплитудно-импульсная модуляция**) pulse-amplitude modulation, PAM.

аир *m.* (bot.) sweet flag (*Acorus calamus*); —**а** *f.* hairgrass (*Aira*); —**ник** *m.* Acorellus; —**ный** *a.* sweet flag, calamus.

аист *m.* stork (*Ciconia*); —**ник** *m.* (bot.) storksbill (*Erodium*); —**овые** *pl.* (orn.) Ciconiidae; **а.-разиния** *m.* openbill (*Anastomus*).

ай *m.* (mam.) ai (*Bradypus tridactylus*); **ай-ай** *m.* aye-aye (*Daubentonia madagascariensis*).

айва *f.* (bot.) quince (*Cydonia*).

айдарский *a.* (geog.) Aydar.

айкинит *m.* (min.) aikinite, needle ore.

айлант *m.* (bot.) ailanthus; —**овая кислота** ailanthic acid.

айлот *m.* a worm lizard (*Bipes biporus*).

аймалин *m.* ajmaline, rauwolfine.

айован *see* **ажгон.**

айонский *a.* (geog.) Ayon.

Айри спиралы (cryst.) Airy's spirals.

айрол *m.* Airol, bismuth iodosubgallate.

айрширский *a.* Ayrshire (cattle).

айсберг *m.* iceberg.

айский *a.* (geog.) Aye, Ai.

Айткена счётчик Aitken counter.

Айха металл Aich's metal.

айюовые *see* **аю(о)вые.**

академ/ик *m.* academician, member of the Academy (of Sciences); —**ический** *a.* academic; —**ия** *f.* academy.

акадиалит *m.* (min.) acadialite.

акажу *n.* cashew nut; acajou.

акакатехин *m.* acacatechin.

акалифа *f.* (bot.) Acalypha.

акальцикоз *m.* (med.) acalcicosis.

акан/т *m.* (arch.; bot.) acanthus; —**тит** *m.* (min.) acanthite; —**то**— *prefix* acanth(o)— (thorn, spine); —**тобделла** *f.* Acanthobdella (a leech); —**товые** *pl.* (bot.) Acanthaceae; —**товый** *a. of* **акант;** —**тоз** *m.* (med.) acanthosis; —**толитический** *a.* acantholytic; —**тома** *f.* acanthoma; —**тоцефалёз** *m.* acanthocephalid infection; —**туриды** *pl.* surgeonfishes (*Acanthuridae*); —**ф** *see* **акант.**

акар/иазис, —идоз *m.* acariasis, mite infestation; —**ид** *m.* acarid, mite; —**ицид** *m.* acaricide; —**ицидность** *f.* acaricidal action; —**ицидный** *a.* acaricidal; —**о**— *prefix* acar(o)—, mite; —**оз** *m.* mange; —**оид** *m.* acaroid resin; —**ология** *f.* acarology.

акатастатический *a.* acatastatic, irregular.

акац/иевый *a.* (bot.) acacia —**ия-робиния** *f.* locust tree (*Robinia*).

аква— *prefix* aqua— (water); —**даг** *m.* Aquadag (lubricant); —**жел** *m.* Aquagel (bentonite clay); —**ланг** *m.* aqualung; —**марин** *m.*, —**маринный, мариновый** *a.* (min.) aquamarine; —**метрия** *f.* aquametry (determination of water); —**наут** *m.* aquanaut; —**панист** *m.* skindiver, frogman; —**полисоединение** *n.* aquapolycompound; —**рель** *f.* watercolor(s); —**рельный** *a.* watercolor; water (color); —**риды** *pl.* (astr.) Aquarids.

акв/ариум *m.* aquarium; —**ариумист** *m.* aquarist; —**асоединение** *n.* aquo complex; —**атационный** *a.*, —**атация** *f.* aquat(at)ion; —**атинта** *f.* aquatint; —**атический** *a.* aquatic; —**атория** *f.* area, expanse (of water); (spawning) ground; —**едук** *m.* aqueduct, conduit; —**илегия** *f.* (bot.) columbine (*Aquilegia*).

акво— *prefix* aquo— (water); —**ион** *m.* aquoion, hydrated ion; —**кислота** *f.* aquo acid; —**комплекс** *m.* aquo complex; —**соединение** *n.* aquo compound; —**соль** *f.* aquo salt; —**тизирование** *n.* aquation, hydrolysis; —**тизировать** *v.* aquate.

а/кг *abbr.* (**ампер на килограмм**) amperes per kilogram.

акенобеит *m.* (petr.) akenobeite.

ак/еринский *a.* (geog.) Akera; —**ерит** *m.* (petr.) akerite; —**жарский** *a.* (geog.) Akzhar; —**и** *m.* akee tree (*Blighia sapida*); —**иба** *f.* (mam.) ringed seal (*Phoca hispida*); —**илей** *see* **аквилегия.**

акин/ез *m.*, —**езия** *f.* akinesis, akinesia, temporary paralysis; —**ета** *f.* (bot.) akinete.

акисовые *pl.* (ichth.) Akysidae.

акка Селлова *f.* (bot.) pineapple guava (*Acca sellowiana*).

акклиматиз/ация *f.*, —**ирование** *n.* acclimatization; —**ированный** *a.* acclimatized; —**ировать** *v.* acclimatize; naturalize.

аккольский *a.* (geog.) Akkol.

аккомод/ационный *a.* accomodative; —**ация** *f.* accommodation, adjustment; —**ировать** *v.* accommodate, adjust, adapt; —**ометр** *m.* (med.) accommodometer.

аккомпанировать *v.* accompany.

аккорд *m.* accord; (acous) chord; piece work (terms); —**еон** *m.* accordion; —**ный** *a. of* **аккорд;** contract, piece (work); by the piece.

аккредит/ив *m.* letter of credit; —**ированный** *a.* accredited; —(ир)овать *v.* accredit, give credit, open credit (with).

аккреция *f.* accretion, growth.

аккульский *a.* (geog.) Akkul.

аккумулиров/ание *n.* accumulation, storage; magnification; (geol.) sedimentation, accretion; —**анный** *a.* accumulated, stored; accumulative; —**ать** *v.* accumulate, store (up), collect; retain (heat).

аккумулятивный *a.* accumulative.

аккумулятор *m.* (elec.) accumulator, storage cell, storage battery; reservoir, tank; —**ная** *f.* battery room; —**нозарядный** *a.* battery-charging; —**ный** *a.* of аккумулятор; —**ный элемент** battery cell, storage cell; —**ная батарея** storage battery; —**ная кислота** battery acid.

аккумуляция *see* **аккумулирование.**

аккуратн/о *adv.* accurately, exactly; neatly; —**ость** *f.* accuracy, exactness, precision; neatness; —**ый** *a.* accurate, precise, punctual; neat, careful.

аклад/ий *m.* Acladium (fungus); —**иоз** *m.* (med.) acladiosis.

аклин/а(ль) *f.* aclinic line, magnetic equator; —**альный** *a.* aclinal, horizontal; —**ический** *a.* aclinic.

акм/е *n.* acme; —**еа, —ея** *f.* (mal.) marine limpet (*Acmaea*); —**ит** *m.* (min.) acmite.

акмолит *m.* (geol.) akmolith.

акн/е *n.* (med.) acne; —**ида** *f.* (bot.) Acnida; —**ит** *m.* (med.) acnitis.

акобальтозный *a.* (med.) cobalt-deficient.

акодон *m.* Akodon (a field mouse).

акоин *m.* acoin(e), guanicaine.

аколитин *m.* acolytine, lyaconine.

аком *m.* acoustic ohm.

акон/ин *m.* aconine; —**ит** *m.* (bot.) aconite; —**итаза** *f.* akonitase; —**итин** *m.* aconitine, acetylbenzoylaconine; —**итиновый** *a.* aconitic; —**итовая кислота** aconitic acid, 1,2,3-propene tricarboxylic acid; —**итовокислая соль** aconitate; —**ия** *f.* (ent.) acone; —**овый** *a.* aconic (acid); —**ция** *f.* (zool.) acontium.

акория *f.* acoria, insatiable appetite.

акр *m.* acre (4,047 sq. meters).

акр— *prefix* acr— (sharp, sour, pungent).

акральный *a.* acral.

акрибометр *m.* acribometer.

акрид/ан *m.* acridan, 5,10-dihydroacridine; —**ил** *m.* acridyl; —**ин** *m.* acridine; —**иновый** *a.* acridine (dyes); acrid(in)ic (acid); —**ол** *m.* acridol; —**он** *m.*, —**оновый** *a.* acridone, ketodihydroacridine.

акрил *m.* acryl; —**амид** *m.* acrylamide; —**ан** *m.* (text.) Acrilan; —**ат** *m.* acrylate; —**ил** *m.* acrylyl; —**овый** *a.* acryl(ic); —**овый альдегид** acrylaldehyde, acrolein, propenal; —**овая кислота** acrylic acid, propenoic acid; —**овокислая соль** acrylate; —**онитрил** *m.* acrylonitrile, propenenitrile; —**опласт** *m.* acrylic resin; —**офенон** *m.* acrylophenone.

акри/пласт *see* **акрилопласт; —т** *m.* acritol; —**флавин** *m.* acriflavin; —**хин** *m.* Acriquine, quinacrine hydrochloride; —**хиновый** *a.* quinacrine(-induced).

акро— *prefix see also under* **акр—**; acr(o)— (extremity, extreme, terminal; top, summit); —**батолитовый** *a.* (geol.) acrobatholitic; —**бласт** *m.* (gen.) acroblast; —**диния** *f.* (med.) acrodynia; —**донтный** *a.* (zool.) acrodont; —**за** *f.* acrose; —**карпический, —карпный** *a.* (bot.) acrocarpous.

акрол/еин *m.* acrolein, acrylaldehyde; —**ит** *m.* acrolite (synthetic resin).

акромегалия *f.* (med.) acromegaly.

акроми/(альн)о— *prefix* (anat.) acromio—; **а.-ключичный** *a.* acromioclavicular; —**альный** *a.* acromial; —**он** *m.* acromion, acromial process.

акро/н *m.* (ent.; zool.) acron; —**петальный** *a.* (bot.) acropetal; —**подий** *m.* (orn.) acropodium, digits; —**пома** *f.* (ichth.) Acropoma; —**помовые** *pl.* acropomids (*Acropomidae*); —**порит** *m.* (min.) acroporite; —**сома** *f.* (zool.) acrosome; —**фит** *m.* acrophyte, alpine plant; —**фобия** *f.* (med.) acrophobia.

акрофут *m.* acre-foot.

акро/хордит *m.* (min.) akrochordite; —**центрический** *a.* (gen.) acrocentric; —**цефалия** *f.* (med.) acrocephaly, oxycephaly.

акселер— *see* **акцелер—.**

аксенический *a.* axenic, not contaminated.

аксерофтол *m.* axerophthol, vitamin A_1.

аксессуары *pl.* accessories.

аксиальн/о-векторный *a.* axial-vector; —**о-симметричный** *a.* axisymmetric, axially symmetric; —**ый** *a.* axial; axial-flow (pump).

аксил/ла *f.* axilla, armpit; axil; —**ярный** *a.* (anat.) axillary.

аксин *m.* axin; —**ит** *m.* (min.) axinite.

аксиолит *m.* (petr.) axiolite.

аксиома *f.* axiom; principle; —**тизировать** *v.* axiomatize; —**тический** *a.* axiomatic.

аксис *m.* axis; axis deer (*Axis axis*).

аксо— *prefix* ax(o)— (axis); —**ид** *m.* (geom.) axoid; —**лотль** *m.* (amph.) axolotl, Ambystoma larva; —**н** *m.* (anat.) axon, neurite; —**но—** *see* **аксо—**; —**нометрический** *a.* axonometric; —**нометрия** *f.* axonometry, perspective geometry; —**плазма** *f.* (zool.) axoplasm; —**подий** *m.*, —**подия** *f.* axopodium; —**стиль** *m.* axostyle.

аксуский *a.* (geog.) Aksu.

акт *m.* act, event; statement, report; record, certificate, document; (law) deed; (insurance) policy; **а. ионизации** ionizing event; **на а. деления** per fission.

акт. *abbr.* (**активный**) active.

акташский *a.* (geog.) Aktash.

АКТГ *abbr.* (**адренокортикотропный гормон**) adrenocorticotropic hormone, ACTH.

акт/еон *m.* Actaeon (a snail); —**ея** *f.* (bot.) baneberry (*Actaea*).

актив *m.* assets, funds; active members.

актив/атор *m.* activator, promoter, stimulant; sensitizer; peptizer, catalyst, reagent; —**ационный** *a.*, —**ация** *f.* activation, etc., *see v.*; —**изатор** *see* **активатор**; —**(из)ирование** *see* **активация**; —**(из)ированный** *a.* activated, etc., *see v.*; —**(из)ировать** *v.* activate, promote, accelerate; sensitize, stimulate; stir up, excite; —**(из)ирующий** *a.* activating, etc., *see v.*; —**(из)ирующее вещество** activator.

активн/одействующий *a.* active; —**оплавающий** *a.* actively swimming; —**оплавающее население** nekton, necton; —**ореактивный** *a.* impulse-reaction (turbine); —**остный** *a.*, —**ость** *f.* activity, radioactivity; (biol.) potency; —**ый** *a.* active; (elec.) resistive, in-phase; industrious; operating; (nucl.) radioactive (sample), fissionable (material); available (oxygen); impulse (turbine); (com.) asset(s); —**ая единица** unit of activity; —**ая зона** (nucl.) core; —**ая масса** (battery) filling paste.

актидион *m.* actidione (antibiotic).

актин *m.* actin; —**ид** *m.* actinide; —**идиевые** *pl.* (bot.) Actinidiaceae; —**идия** *f.* Actinidia; —**иевый** *a.* actinic; actinium; —**изм** *m.* actinism; —**ий** *m.* actinium,

Ac; **эманация —ия** actinon, An; **—ин** *m.* actinine; **—ический, —ичный** *a.* actinic; **—ичность** *f.* actinism; **—ия** *f.* (zool.) Actinia, sea anemone.

актино— *prefix* actino— (rays, ray- or star-shaped); **—бациллёз** *m.* (vet.) actinobacillosis; **—ид** *see* **актинид;** **—идный** *a.* actinoid, raylike; **—лит** *m.* (min.) actinolite; **—логия** *f.* actinology.

актинометр *m.* actinometer; **—ический** *a.* actinometric; **—ия** *f.* actinometry.

актино/микоз *m.* (vet.) actinomycosis; **—микотический** *a.* actinomycotic; **—миксидии** *pl.* (zool.) Actinomyxidia; **—мицетин** *m.* actinomycetin; **—мицеты** *pl.* (bact.) Actinomycetes; **—мицин** *m.* actinomycin; **—морфный** *a.* actinomorphic, star-shaped; **—н** *m.* actinon, An; **—родин** *m.* actinorhodin (antibiotic); **—скоп** *m.* actinoscope, solar radiation meter; **—троха** *f.* (zool.) actinotrocha; **—уран** *m.* actinouranium, AcU; **—фаг** *m.* (med.) actinophage; **—фотометр** *m.* actinic photometer; **—химия** *f.* actinochemistry; **—электричество** *n.* actinoelectricity.

актинула *f.* (zool.) actinula.

актировать *v.* certify the presence or absence (of).

акт/ный *a.* of **акт;** **—овый** *a.* assembly (hall); stamped (paper).

актол *m.* Actol, silver lactate.

актомиозин *m.,* **—овый** *a.* actomyosin.

актор *m.* (chem.) actor.

акт-рекламация *f.* damage claim.

актуальн/ость *f.* actuality; urgency; **—ый** *a.* actual; present; urgent, pressing; of current interest, timely.

аку— *see also under* **акку—.**

акул/а *f.* shark; **колючая а.** spiny dogfish (*Squalus,* spec. *S. acanthias*); **а.-бык** *f.* bull shark (*Carcharhinus leucas*); **а.-каркародон, а.-людоед** *f.* man-eater shark (*Carcharodon carcharias*); **—ий** *a.* shark; **—овые** *pl.* sharks and skates (*Selachii*); **—ообразный** *a.* selachoid; **—ы-молоты** *pl.* hammerhead sharks (*Sphyrnidae*).

аку— *prefix* acou— (hearing); acu— (needle); **—метр** *m.* acoumeter; **—прессура** *f.* (med.) acupressure; **—пунктура** *f.* acupuncture.

акусти/к *m.* sound technician; **—ка** *f.* acoustics; **—ческий** *a.* acoustic; **—ческая антенна, —ческая база** (sonar) transducer (array).

акушер *m.* (med.) obstetrician; **—ка** *f.* obstetrician; midwife; **—ский** *a.* obstetric; **—ство** *n.* obstetrics.

акцелер/атор *m.* accelerator; **—ация** *f.* acceleration; **—ин** *m.* accelerin (a coagulation factor); **—ограф** *m.* accelerograph; **—ометр** *m.* accelerometer.

акцент *m.,* **—ный** *a.* accent(uation); **—(ир)овать** *v.* accent(uate).

акцепт *m.* (com.) acceptance; **—ант** *m.* acceptor; **—(ир)овать** *v.* accept; **—ование** *n.* acceptance; **—ор** *m.,* **—орный** *a.* (chem.) acceptor.

акцессор/ия *f.* accessory; **—ный** *a.* accessory, auxiliary.

акциден/тный *a.* accidental; job (printing); **—ция** *f.* job(bing), job printing.

акциз *m.,* **—ный** *a.* excise.

акци/онер *m.* (com.) stockholder, shareholder; **—онерный** *a.* joint-stock; **—я** *f.* share, stock; action.

акш/ийракский *a.* (geog.) Akshirak; **—инский** *a.* Aksha.

ал *sh. m. of* **алый; ал—** *see under* **аль—.**

ала/балах *m.* (ichth.) alabalakh (*Salmo ischchan*); **—бандин** *m.* (min.) alabandite, manganblende; **—бетовые** *pl.* (ichth.) Alabetidae; **—бута** *f.* (bot.) Tartarian orach (*Atriplex tatarica*); **—джа** *f.* aladzha (an ozocerite); **—занский** *a.* (geog.) Alazan(ic); **—зейский** *a.* Al-

azeya; **—ит** *m.* (min.) alaite; **—йский** *a.* (geog.) Alai; **—кольский** *a.* Alakol; **—кульский** *a.* Alakul; **—лит** *m.* (min.) alalite; **—лия** *f.* (med.) alalia; **—мозит** *m.* (min.) alamosite; **—ндский** *a.* (geog.) Aland.

алан/ил *m.* alanyl; **—ин** *m.,* **—иновый** *a.* alanine, 2-aminopropanoic acid.

алант/ин *m.* alantin, inulin; **—овый** *a.* alantic, inulic (acid); inula (oil); **—олактон** *m.* alantolactone, helenin.

алария *f.* Alaria (a seaweed).

алас *m.* (geol.) alass (depression).

ала/тауский *a.* (geog.) Alatau; **—тырский** *a.* Alatyir; **—ша** *f.* (ichth.) alasha, golden sardine (*Sardinella aurita*); **—шский** *a.* (geog.) Alash.

алб— *see also under* **альб—;** **—анит** *m.* albanite (an asphalt); **—анский** *a.* (geog.) Albanian; **—ат** *m.* Caspian salmon (*Salmo trutta caspius*).

алг— *see also under* **альг—.**

алгебра *f.* algebra; **—ический** *a.* algebraic.

алгидный *a.* (med.) algid, cold.

алгинский *a.* (geog.) Alga.

алгол *m.,* **—евый** *a.* (comp.) algol, algorithmic language; **—ь** *m.* (astr.) Algol.

алгор/итм *m.* (math.) algorithm; **—итмизация** *f.* algorithm(ic) presentation; **—итмический** *a.* algorithm(ic).

алд— *see* **альд—; —анский** *a.* (geog.) Aldan.

алебастр *m.,* **—овый** *a.* (min.) alabaster (gypsum); plaster of Paris.

алевр/(и)о— *see* **алейро—; —ит** *m.* **—итовый** *a.* aleurite, silt; (bot.) Aleurites; **—олит** *m.* aleurolite, siltstone.

алей/дрин *m.* aleudrin, dichloroisopropyl carbamate; **—кемия** *f.* (med.) aleukemia; **—коцитарный** *a.* aleukocytic.

алейр/итиновая кислота aleuritic acid; **—о—** *prefix* aleuro— (flour); **—одиды** *pl.* white flies (*Aleyrodidae*); **—ометр** *m.* aleurometer; **—он** *m.* aleurone; **—оновый** *a.* aleurone, aleuronic.

алейский *a.* (geog.) Alei.

александри/йский *a.* Alexander; royal (paper); **а. лист** (pharm.) senna leaves; **—т** *m.* (min.) alexandrite.

алекс/еевит *m.* alexejevite (a tar); **—ин** *m.* (immun.) alexin, complement; **—инский** *a.* (geog.) Alexin; **—ия** *f.* (med.) alexia, word blindness.

алект/ис *m.* threadfish (*Alectis*); **—ория** *f.* Alectoria (a lichen).

аленка *f.* (ent.) chafer.

алеп/изавр *m.* lancetfish (*Alepisaurus*); **—изавровые** *pl.* Alepisauridae; **—пский** *a.* (geog.) Aleppo.

алет *m.* (orn.) Eleonora's falcon (*Falco eleonorae*); (ichth.) squaretail (*Tetragonurus cuvieri*); **—овые** *pl.* Tetragonuridae.

алетр/ис *m.* (bot.) Aletris; **—оид** *m.* aletroid, aletrin.

алеть *v.* redden, glow; show red; (physiol.) flush.

алеу/ро— *see* **алейро—; —тит** *m.* (min.) aleutite; **—тский** *a.* (geog.) Aleutian.

алеф-нуль *m.* (math.) aleph zero.

алецитальный *a.* alecithal, without yolk.

алжирский *a.* (geog.) Algerian.

АЛЗ *abbr.* alizarin.

алзиновые *pl.* chickweed family (*Alsinaceae*).

аливал *m.* alival, iodopropyleneglycol.

алидад/а *f.,* **—ный** *a.* (surv.) alidade.

ализар/ат *m.* alizarate; **—ин** *m.* alizarin; **—иновый** *a.* alizarin (dyes); alizaric (acid); **—иновокислая соль** alizarate.

аликантная сода kelp (ashes).

аликв/антный *a.* (math.) aliquant; —**ота** *f.*, —**отный** *a.* aliquot.

алиментарный *a.* alimentary, nutritional.

алименты *pl.* (law) alimony, maintenance.

алипин *m.* Alypine, Amydricaine.

алиседикахиты *pl.* alicyclic components of organic matter in sedimentary rocks.

алит *m.* (cement) alite.

алитиров/ание *n.* (met.) calorizing, etc., *see v.*; heat treatment; —**ать** *v.* calorize, aluminize, alit(iz)e.

али/фатический *a.* aliphatic; —**цикл** *m.* alicyclic compound; —**циклический** *a.* alicyclic.

алкадиен *m.* alkadiene.

алкали *n.* alkali; —**зация** *f.* alkalization; —**зировать** *v.* alkalize; —**йность** *f.* alkalinity; —**метр** *m.* alkalimeter; —**метрический** *a.* alkalimetric; —**метрия** *f.* alkalimetry; —**целлюлоза** *f.* alkali cellulose; —**ческий** *a.* alkaline.

алкалоз *m.* (med.) alkalosis.

алкалоид *m.*, —**ный** *a.* alkaloid; —**ность** *f.* alkaloid content; —**оносный** *a.* alkaloid-bearing.

алк/амин *m.* alkamine, amino alcohol; —**ан** *m.* alkane, alkyne.

алкан/(н)а *f.* (bot.) alkanet (*Alkanna*); —**нин** *m.* alkannin, alchusin; —**ный** *a.* alkanna; alkannic (acid); —**овый** *a.* alkanoic.

алк/аптон *m.* alkapton(e); —**аптонурический** *a.* (med.) alkaptonuric; —**ен** *m.* alkene; —**ид** *m.*, —**идный** *a.* alkyd.

алкил *m.* alkyl; —**аминогруппа** *f.* alkylamino group; —**ат** *m.* alkylate; —**атор** *m.* alkylation tower; —**бензол** *m.* alkylbenzene; —**бромид** *m.* alkyl bromide; —**ен** *m.* alkylene; —**замещённый** *a.* alkyl substituted; —**иден** *m.*, —**иденовый** *a.* alkylidene; —**ирование** *n.* alkylation; —**ированный** *a.* alkylated; —**ировать** *v.* alkylate; —**мочевина** *f.* alkyl urea; —**овый** *a.* alkyl; —**серный** *a.* alkylsulfuric (acid); —**сульфокислота** *f.* alkylsulfonic acid; —**хлорид** *m.* alkyl chloride; —**ьный** *a.* alkyl; —**эфир** *m.* alkyl ether or ester.

алкин *m.* alkyne.

алклэд *see* **альклэд.**

алкогель *m.* alcogel.

алкогол/из *m.* alcoholysis; —**изация** *f.* alcoholization; —**изм** *m.* alcoholism; —**изовать** *v.* alcoholize; —**ик** *m.*, —**ичка** *f.* alcoholic; —**иметр**, —**ометр** *m.* alcoholometer; —**иметрия,** —**ометрия** *f.* alcoholometry; —**ический** *a.* alcoholic; —**ь** *m.* alcohol; —**ьдегидрогеназа** *f.* alcohol dehydrogenase; —**ьный** *a.* alcohol(ic); —**ят** *m.* alcoholate.

алкозоль *m.* alcosol.

алкокси— *prefix* alkoxy—; —**алкилировать** *v.* convert into an alkoxy compound by alkylation; —**арилровать** *v.* convert into an alkoxy compound by arylation; —**группа** *f.* alkoxy group; —**кислота** *f.* alkoxy acid; —**л** *m.*, —**льный** *a.* alkoxyl; —**лировать** *v.* alkoxylate; —**производное** *n.* alkoxy derivative; —**соединение** *n.* alkoxy compound.

алкомакс *m.* Alcomax (magnetic alloy).

алкон *m.* alkone.

алкумит *m.* Alcumite (alloy).

алл— *see* **алло—;** —**агит** *m.* (min.) allagite; —**аиховский** *a.* (geog.) Allaikha; —**актит** *m.* allactite; —**алинит** *m.* (petr.) allalinite; —**анит** *m.* (min.) allanite, orthite; —**ановый** *a.* allanic (acid).

алланто— *prefix* allanto— (sausage); —**зома** *f.* (zool.) Allantosoma; —**идный** *a.* allantoid, sausage-shaped; —**ин** *m.* allantoin, glyoxyl diureide; —**иновый** *a.* al-

lantoic (acid); —**иновокислая соль** allantoate; —**ис** *m.* (anat.) allantois; —**исный** *a.* allantoic.

алл/антуровая кислота allanturic acid, glyoxalylurea; —**ахский** *a.* (geog.) Allakh; —**ацил** *m.* (pharm.) aminometradine; —**егани(и)т** *m.* (min.) alleghanyite; —**еганский** *a.* (geog.) Allegheny, Alleghenian.

аллейный *a. of* аллея; alley, avenue.

аллел/изм *m.* (gen.) allelism, alternative inheritance; —**о—** *prefix* allel(o)— (reciprocally, one another); —**оморф** *m. see* **аллель;** —**оморфный** *a.* allelomorphic, allelic; —**отип** *m.* allelotype; —**отропический,** —**отропный** *a.* allelotropic; —**отропия** *f.* allelotropism, equilibrium isomerism; —**ь** *m.* (gen.) allele, allelomorph; —**ьный** *a.* allelic.

аллемонтит *m.* (min.) allemontite.

аллен *m.* allene, propadiene.

алленопитек *m.* Allen's monkey (*Allenopithecus*).

аллерг/ен *m.* (immun.) allergen; —**енный** *a.* allergenic; —**изированный** *a.* allergized; —**изирующий** *a.* allergenic; —**ический** *a.* allergic; —**ия** *f.* allergy; —**олог** *m.* allerg(olog)ist.

аллея *f.* alley, avenue; lane.

аллигатор *m.*, —**ный** *a.* alligator.

аллигация *f.* alloy.

аллиин *m.* alliin.

аллил *m.* allyl; —**бензол** *m.* allyl benzene; —**горчичное масло** allyl mustard oil, allyl isothiocyanate; —**ен** *m.* allylene, propyne; —**овый** *a.* allyl; —**овый альдегид** allyl aldehyde, acrolein; —**овый спирт** allyl alcohol, 2-propen-1-ol; —**тиомочевина** *f.* allyl thiourea; —**хлорид** *m.* allyl chloride; —**ьный** *a.* allyl.

алли/т *m.* allite (sugar alcohol); —**тировать** *see* **алитировать;** —**тный** *a.* allitic (soil); —**тол** *see* **алит;** —**цин** *m.* allicin.

алло— *prefix* allo— [(an)other]; —**бар** *m.* allobar; —**биоз** *m.* (ecol.) allobiosis; —**гамия** *f.* (bot.) allogamy, cross-fertilization; —**ген** *m.* (gen.) allogene, recessive allele; —**диплоид** *m.*, —**диплоидный** *a.* allodiploid; —**за** *f.* allose; —**каин** *m.* allocaine; —**клаз(ит)** *m.* (min.) alloclas(it)e; —**коричный** *a.* allocinnamic (acid); —**ксазин** *m.* alloxazine.

аллоксан *m.* alloxan, mesoxalylurea; —**овая кислота** alloxanic acid; —**овокислая соль** alloxanate; —**тин** *m.* alloxantin.

алло/мерия *f.* (cryst.) allomerism; —**мерный** *a.* allomerous, allomeric; —**метрический** *a.* (biol.) allometric, heterogonic; —**морфизм** *m.* (cryst.) allomorphism; —**морфный** *a.* allomorphic.

аллонж *m.* adapter; extractor.

алло/новый *a.* allonic (acid); —**палладий** *m.* (min.) allopalladium; —**патия** *f.* allopathy, heteropathy; —**патрический** *a.* (biogeog.) allopatric; —**плоидия** *f.* (gen.) alloploidy; —**прен** *m.* alloprene (chlorinated rubber); —**слизевой** *a.* allomucic (acid); —**сома** *f.* (gen.) allosome; —**стерический** *a.* allosteric (enzyme); —**триоморфный** *a.* (cryst.) allotriomorphic, xenomorphic; —**троп** *m.* allotrope, allotropic modification; —**тропизм** *m.*, —**тропия** *f.* allotropy, allotropism; —**тропический,** —**тропный** *a.* allotropic; —**трофный** *a.* (bot.) allotrophic.

аллофан *m.* (min.) allophane; —**овая кислота** allophanic acid, urea-carboxylic acid; —**овокислая соль** allophanate.

алло/феновый *a.* (gen.) allophenic, mosaic; —**хроит** *m.* (min.) allochroite; —**хронический,** —**хронный** *a.* allochronic, not contemporary.

аллохтон *m.* (biol.; geol.) allochthon; —**ный** *a.* allochthonous, exotic; acquired.

аллюв/иальный *a.* (geol.) alluvial, superficial; **—ий** *m.* alluvium.

аллюр *m.* gait, pace, step (of horse).

алм— *see also under* **альм—**.

алмаз *m.* diamond; diamond cutter.

алмазно/белый *a.* diamond-white; **—расточный** *a.* diamond boring.

алмаз/ный *a.* diamond (drill, etc.); adamantine (luster, spar, etc.); **—одержатель** *m.* diamond holder; **—оподобный** *a.* diamond-like, adamantine; **—содержащий** *a.* diamond-bearing; **—чик** *m.* diamond cutter.

ални *see* **альни;** **—ко** *see* **альнико.**

ало *adv. and sh. n. of* **алый;** *n.* halo; *prefix* reddish; **—ватый** *a.* reddish.

аловольт *m.* alowalt (abrasive).

алое *see* **алоэ;** **—тин** *m.* aloetin (resin); **—тиновая кислота** aloetic acid, tetranitro-anthraquinone.

ало-жёлтый *a.* reddish yellow.

ало/за *f.* (ichth.) Alosa (a shad); **—ин** *m.* aloin; **—иноза** *f.* aloinose; **—йный** *a.* aloe; aloetic; aloe-fiber; **—казия** *f.* (bot.) Alocasia; **—ксит** *m.* aloxite (alumina abrasive).

алонж, —а *see* **аллонж.**

ало/пеция *f.* alopecia, baldness; **—са** *see* **алоза.**

алость *f.* ruby color, ruby redness.

алоэ *n.* (bot.) aloe; **американское а.** agave; **смола а.** aloetin (resin).

алсифер *see* **альсифер.**

алстон/ин *m.* alstonine, chlorogenine; **—ит** *m.* (min.) alstonite, bromlite; **—ия** *f.* (bot.) Alstonia.

алтаит *m.* (min.) altaite.

алтайский *a.* (geog.) Altai(an), Altay.

алтеин *m.* altheine, asparagine.

алтей *m.,* **—ный** *a.* (bot.) Althaea.

алтер— *see* **альтер—; алтр—** *see* **альтр—.**

алтыарыкский *a.* (geog.) Altiyaryik.

алудель *m.* aludel (vessel).

алудур *m.* Aludur (alloy).

алукснеский *a.* (geog.) Aluksne.

алумнол *m.* Alumnol.

алунд, —ум *m.* alundum (abrasive).

алун/ит *m.* (min.) alunite; **—итизированный** *a.* alunitized; alunite (ore); **—оген** *m.* (min.) alunogen.

алфавит *m.* alphabet; (comp.) character set; **—но-цифровой** *a.* alphanumeric; **—ный** *a.* alphabetic; **—ный указатель** *m.* index.

алфил *m.* alphyl, alkyl-phenyl.

алхим/ик *m.* alchemist; **—ия** *f.* alchemy.

алыдша *see* **алыча.**

алый *a.* scarlet, vermilion, crimson; ruby-colored; light (brick).

алыча *f.* cherry plum (*Prunus divaricata* or *P. cerasifera*).

альб— *see* **альбо—;** **—акор** *m.* (ichth.) albacore (*Thunnus alalunga*); **—ан** *m.* alban(e); **—атрос** *m.* (orn.) albatross (*Diomedea*); **—едо** *n.* (astr.; illum.) albedo (reflection factor); **—едометр** *m.* albedometer.

альберт/ит *m.* (min.) albertite; **—ол** *m.* albertol (a phenol-formaldehyde resin); **—шлаг** *m.* twist in the same direction.

альбикация *f.* (bot.) albication, whitening.

альбин/изм *m.* (biol.) albinism; **—ос** *m.,* **—осный** *a.* albino.

альбион-металл *m.* Albion metal.

альбит *m.* (min.) albite; **—изация** *f.* albitization; **—ит** *m.* (petr.) albitite; **—овый** *a.* albite.

альби/хтол *m.* (pharm.) albichtol, leukichthol, ichthyol; **—ция** *f.* (bot.) Albizzia.

альбо— *prefix* albo— (white); **—лен** *m.* albolene; **—лит** *m.* (cement) albolite.

альбом *m.* album.

альбо/мицин *m.* albomycin (antibiotic).

альбомный *a.* (comp.) landscape (format).

альбоферрин *m.* alboferrin, iron phosphoalbuminate.

альбул/а *f.* ladyfish, bonefish (*Albula,* spec. *A. vulpes*); **—евые; —иды** *pl.* Albulidae.

альбумин *m.* albumin; (egg) albumen; **молочный а.** lactalbumin; **—ат** *m.* albuminate; **—иметр** *m.* albuminometer; **—ный, —овый** *a.* albumin(ous); albumen; **—оглобулиновый коэффициент** (med.) albumin-globulin ratio, A-G ratio; **—оза** *f.* albuminose; **—озный** *a.* albuminous; **—оид** *m.* albuminoid; **—урия** *f.* (med.) albuminuria.

альбумоза *f.* albumose.

альбуцид *m.* Albucid, Sulfacyl.

альв/ар *m.* Alvar (a polyvinylacetal resin); **—ары** *pl.* (geobot.) alvares; **—еин** *m.* alvein (antibiotic); **—еола** *f.* (anat.) alveole, alveolus; (tooth) socket; **—еолированный** *a.* alveolate; **—еоло—** *prefix* alveolo— (alveolus); **—еолярный** *a.* alveolar.

альг/а *f.* (bot.) alga; **—альный** *a.* algal; **—ароба** algaroba bean, mesquite (*Prosopis juliflora*); **—аробаль** *m.* (phytogeog.) algarrobal; **—аротов порошок** algaroth (powder), antimony oxychloride; **—езиметр** *m.* (med.) algesimeter; **—езия** *f.* algesia; **—инат** *m.* alginate; **—иновый** *a.* alginic (acid); **—ический** *a. suffix* —algic (painful); **—одонит** *m.* (min.) algodonite; **—ол** *m.,* **—олевый** *a.* algol; **—ология** *f.* algology, phycology.

альграфия *f.* (typ.) al(umino)graphy.

альдаровый *a.* aldaric (acid).

альдебаран *m.* (astr.) Aldebaran.

альдегид *m.,* **—ный** *a.* aldehyde; **а. уксусной кислоты, уксусный а.** acetaldehyde; **—аммиак** *m.* aldehyde ammonia; **а.-дегидрогеназа** *f.* aldehyde dehydrogenase; **—ин** *m.* aldehydine; **—мутаза** *f.* aldehyde mutase; **—ный** *a.* aldehyde; **—ная смола** aldehyde resin; **—о—** *prefix* aldehyde; **—окислота** *f.* aldehyde acid, aldehydic acid; **—оксидаза** *f.* aldehyde oxidase; **—оспирт** *m.* aldehyde alcohol; **—раза** *f.* xanthine oxidase.

альди/мин *m.* aldimine; **—н** *m.* aldin, aldehyde base; **—т(ол)** *m.* alditol, glycitol.

альдо— *prefix* ald(o)— (aldehyde; aldose); **—бионовый** *a.* aldobionic (acid); **—гексоза** *f.* aldohexose; **—за** *f.* aldose; **—кетен** *m.* aldoketene; **—ксим** *m.* aldoxime; **—лаза** *f.* aldolase, zymohexase; **—лизация** *f.* aldolization; aldol addition; aldol condensation; **—лиз(ир)оваться** *v.* be aldolized, be converted into an aldol; **—ль** *m.,* **—льный** *a.* aldol, 3-hydroxybutanal; **—ль-сырец** *m.* crude aldol; **—новый** *a.* aldonic (acid); **—стерон** *m.* aldosterone (hormone); **—триоза** *f.* aldotriose.

аль/дрей *m.* Aldrey (alloy); **—дрин** *m.* Aldrin (insecticide); **—дрованда** *f.* Aldrovanda (aquatic plant); **—дюраль** *m.* Aldural (Duralumin sheet); **—зен** *m.* Alzene (alloy); **—золь** *m.* alsol, aluminum acetotartrate.

альк/лед, —эд *m.* (met.) Alclad.

альков *m.,* **—ный** *a.* alcove, niche.

альмаг *m.* aluminum-magnesium alloy.

альмана/х *m.,* **—шный** *a.* almanac, calendar, anthology.

альмандин *m.* (min.) almandine.

альмасилиум *m.* Almasilium (alloy).

альмелек *m.* Almalec (alloy).

Альмена-Ниландера проба Almen-Nylander test (for sugar).

альмукантар(ат) *m.* (astr.) almucantar, equal-altitude circle.

альн/еит *m.* (petr.) alnoite; **—еон** *m.* Alneon (alloy); **—и** *m.* alni (aluminum-nickel alloy); **—ико** *n.* Alnico (alloy); **—иси** *m.* Alnisi (alloy).

альпака *f.* (mam.) alpaca (*Lama pacos*).

альпари *n., adv.* at par, par.

альп/ийский *a.* alpine, Alpine; **—инарий** *m.* rock garden, alpine garden; **—инизм** *m.* mountain climbing; **—инист** *m.,* **—инистка** *f.* mountain climber; **—инистский** *a.* mountain climbing; **—иния** *f.* (bot.) Alpinia; **Альпы** the Alps.

альсифер *m.* Alsifer (alloy).

альст— *see under* **алст—**.

альт *m.* alto (voice or instrument).

альтазимут *m.* (astr.) altazimuth.

альтаир *m.* (astr.) Altair.

альтакс *m.* Altax (rubber accelerator).

альтер/ация *f.* alteration; **—ированный** *a.* altered.

альтерн/антера *f.* (bot.) Alternanthera; **—ариоз** *m.* (phyt.) alternaria blight; **—аровый** *a.* alternaric (acid); **—атива** *f.,* **—ативный** *a.* alternative; **—ативное имя** (comp.) alias; **—атор** *m.,* **—аторный** *a.* (elec.) alternator; **—ация** *f.,* **—ирование** *n.* alternation; **—ированный** *a.* alternated; alternating; **—ирующий** *a.* alternating.

альтея *see* **алтей**.

альти— *prefix* alti— (high; altitude); **—граф** *m.* altigraph; **—метр** *m.* altimeter; **—метр-анероид** *m.* aneroid altimeter; **—туда** *f.* altitude.

альтовый *a. of* **альт**.

альтр/оза *f.* altrose; **—оновый** *a.* altronic (acid).

альтруистический *a.* altruistic, unselfish.

альфа *f.* alpha (α); (bot.) *see* **альфа-трава; а.-железо** *n.* alpha iron; **а.-излучатель** *m.* (nucl.) alpha emitter; **а.-излучение** *n.* alpha emission, alpha radiation; **а.-лучи** *pl.* alpha rays; **—метр** *m.* alphameter, electrophysical gas analyzer; **а.-превращение** *n.,* **—распад** *m.* alpha decay or disintegration; **а.-трава** *f.* esparto grass (*Stipa tenacissima*); **—фетопротеин** *m.* alphafetoprotein, AFP.

альфа-част/ица *f.,* **—ичный** *a.* alpha-particle; **счётчик —иц** alpha counter.

альфовый *a. of* **альфа**; top-ranking.

альфоль *f.* aluminum foil.

альц/геймера болезнь Alzheimer's disease, presenile dementia; **—иона** *f.* (astr.) Alcyone; **—ихт** *m.* (ichth.) Alcichthys.

альянс *m.* alliance.

алюм/ель *m.* Alumel (alloy); **—илит** *m.* alumilite; **—инат** *m.,* **—инатный** *a.* aluminate; **—инид** *m.* aluminide.

алюминиево/калиевая соль potassium aluminate; **—калиевые квасцы** potash alum; **—кислый** *a.* aluminic acid; aluminate (of); **—натриевая соль** sodium aluminate; **—кислая соль** aluminate; **—кобальтовая соль** cobalt aluminate.

алюминиев/ый *a.* aluminum, aluminiferous; aluminic (acid); **соль —ой кислоты** aluminate; **—ые квасцы** potash alum.

алюминиево/натриевая соль sodium aluminate; **—фтористый натрий** sodium aluminum fluoride, cryolite.

алюмин/ий *m.* aluminum, Al; **азотнокислый а.** aluminum nitrate; **гидрат окиси —ия** aluminum hydroxide; **окись —ия** aluminum oxide, alumina; **хлорид —ия, хлористый а.** aluminum chloride; **—ийорганический** *a.* organoaluminum.

алюмин/ировать *v.* aluminize; coat with aluminum; **—ит** *m.* (min.) aluminite.

алюмино— *prefix* alumin(o)—, aluminum; **—з** *m.* (med.) aluminosis; **—н** *m.* (colorimetry) aluminon; **—(о)ксид** *m.* (cer.) sintered alumina; **—силикат** *m.* aluminosilicate; **—термический** *a.* aluminothermic; **—термия** *f.* aluminothermy.

алюмо— *see also* **алюмино—; —боросиликатный** *a.* aluminoborosilicate; **—гель** *m.* alumogel, alumina gel; **—гидрид** *m.* aluminum hydride; **—гидрогель** *m.* alumina hydrogel; **—гранат** *m.* (min.) garnet in clay; **—железистый** *a.* pedalferic (soil); **—иттриевый гранат** yttrium-aluminum garnet, YAG; **—калиевые квасцы** potash alum; **—кальцит** *m.* (min.) alumocalcite; **—кремнекислородный** *a.* aluminum silicate; **—лит** *m.* (min.) bauxite; **—натриевые квасцы** soda alum; **—нитросиликотермия** *f.* aluminonitric silicothermic method; **—силикат** *m.* aluminosilicate; **—хромовый** *a.* (petrol.) chromoalumina (catalyst).

алярия *see* **алария**.

аляск/аит *m.* (min.) alaskaite; **—инский** *a.* Alaskan; **—ит** *m.* (petr.) alaskite.

ам. *abbr.* (**американский; аморфный**).

а/м *abbr.* (**ампер на метр**) ampere per meter.

АМ *abbr.* (**амплитудная модуляция**) amplitude modulation, AM; (**амплитудномодулированный**) amplitude-modulated; (**акриламид**) acrylamide.

амавроз *m.* (med.) amaurosis, blindness.

амаду *m.* amadou, punk (fungus).

амазон/а *f.* (orn.) Amazona; **—ит** *m.* (min.) amazonite, amazonstone; **Амазонка** Amazon River; **—ский** *a.* Amazon(ian).

амалиновая кислота amal(in)ic acid.

амальгам/а *f.* amalgam; **—атор** *m.* amalgamator; **—ационный** *a.,* **—ация** *f.,* **—ирование** *n.* amalgamation; **—ированный** *a.* amalgamated; **—ировать** *v.* amalgamate; **—ирующий** *a.* amalgamating; **—ический, —ный** *a.* amalgam.

аман/дин *m.* amandin; **—итин** *m.* amanitin(e).

амар/ант *m.* Amaranthus; **—антит** *m.* (min.) amarantite; **—антовые** *pl.* (bot.) Amaranthaceae; **—ил(лис)** *m.* (bot.) amaryllis; **—иллисовые** *pl.* Amaryllidaceae; **—ин** *m.* amarine; **—он** *m.* amaron, tetraphenyl-*p*-pyrimidine.

амасийский *a.* (geog.) Amasia.

аматол *m.* (expl.) amatol.

АМБ *abbr.* (**препарат автохтонной микрофлоры Б**) autochthonous microflora B fertilizer.

амбар *m.,* **—ный** *a.* storehouse, granary, barn; (petrol.) reservoir, pit, sump; **хлебный а.** granary.

амбатоаринит *m.* (min.) ambatoarinite.

амбач *m.* (bot.) a vetch (*Aeschynomene*).

амбер/ит *m.* (expl.; plastics) amberite; **—лит** *m.* Amberlite (ion-exchange resin).

амби— *prefix* ambi— (both); **—валентный** *a.* ambivalent; **—дентный** *a.* ambident; **—офонический** *a.* ambiophonic; **—полярный** *a.* ambipolar; **—сексуальный** *a.* bisexual; **—стома** *f.* Ambystoma (a salamander).

амбиция *f.* ambition.

амбли— *prefix* ambly— (blunt, dull, obtuse; faint); **—гонит** *m.* (min.) amblygonite; **—опия** *f.* (med.) amblyopia.

амбо/инский *a.* (geog.) Amboina; **—мицин** *m.* ambomycin (antibiotic); **—цептор** *m.* (immun.) amboceptor.

амб-препарат *see* **АМБ**.

амбра *f.* amber (fossil resin); **серая а.** ambergris.

амбразура *f.* embrasure; (window) frame; port hole.

амбр/еин *m.* ambrein; **—еиновый** *a.* ambreic (acid); **—еиновокислая соль** ambreate; **—ет** *see* **абельмош; —ин** *m.* ambrin; (pharm.) Ambrine; **—ит** *m.* ambrite (fossil resin); **—овый** *a.* amber; **—овое дерево** (bot.) sweetgum (*Liquidambar styraciflua*); **—озия** *f.* ragweed (*Ambrosia*); ambrosia (fungus).

амбулакр *m.* (zool.) ambulacrum; **—альный** *a.* ambulacral, ambulacriform, tube (foot).

амбулатор/ия *f.* dispensary, outpatient clinic; (vet.) surgery; **—ный** *a.* outpatient (care); ambulatory, out(patient); dispensary.

амбушюр *m.,* **—а** *f.* embouchure, opening; (telephone) mouthpiece.

амг/инский *a.* (geog.) Amga; **—унский** *a.* Amgun.

амёб/а *f.* (zool.) ameba; **—иаз, —иоз** *m.* (med.) amebiasis; **—ный** *a.* amebic; **—овидный, —оидный, —ообразный** *a.* ameboid, amebiform; **—осодержащий** *a.* ameba-containing; **—оцид** *m.* amebicide; **—оцит** *m.* amebocyte.

амезит *m.* (min.) amesite.

амей/ва *f.* Ameiva (a lizard); **—оз** *m.* (gen.) ameiosis.

амел/анотический *a.* amelanotic, unpigmented; **—иорационный** *a.,* **—иорация** *f.* amelioration, improvement; **—областический** *a.* (cyt.) ameloblastic.

амен/ор(р)ея *f.* (med.) amenorrhea; **—сализм** *m.* (ecol.) amensalism; **—тивный** *a.* (med.) amential; **—тула** *f.* Amentula (moss); **—ция** *f.* amentia, feeble-mindedness.

американ/ец *m.* American (male); **—ка** *f.* American; (min.) washer; (oil well drillling) sand pump; (typ.) platen press; **—ский** *a.* American; United States (patent); **—ские орехи** Brazil nuts.

америций *m.* americium, Am.

аметаболический *a.* (zool.) ametabolic.

аметист *m.,* **—овый** *a.* (min.) amethyst.

аметоптерин *m.* amethopterin, methotrexate.

аметропия *f.* (med.) ametropia.

амиант *m.,* **—овый** *a.* (min.) amianthus.

амигдал/ат *m.* amygdalate; **—ин** *m.* amygdalin; **—иновокислая соль** amygdalate; **—иновый** *a.* amygdalic (acid); **—оза** *f.* amygdalose; **—оид** *m.* (petr.) amygdaloid; **—оидный** *a.* amygdaloid(al), almond-like; **—ярный** *a.* amygdaline; tonsillar.

амид *m.* amide; **а. уксусной кислоты** acetamide; **—аза** *f.* amidase; **—ин** *m.* amidine; **—ирование** *n.* amidation; **—ировать** *v.* amidate; **—ный** *a.* amide, amido.

амидо— *prefix* amido—; amino—; **—бензол** *see* **аминобензол; —ген** *m.* amidogen, amino group; **—группа** *f.* amido group (or radical); amino group; amides; **—кислота** *f.* amino acid; **—ксим** *m.* amidoxime; **—л** *m.* (phot.) amidol; **—пирин** *m.* amidopyrine; **—соединение** *n.* amido compound; **—стом(ат)оз** *m.* (vet.) Amidostomum infection.

ам/иевые, —ии *pl.* mudfishes (*Amiidae*).

амиксис *m.* (zool.) amixis.

амикрон *m.* amicron (particle).

амил *m.* amyl, pentyl; **уксуснокислый а., —ацетат** *m.* amyl acetate; **—аза** *f.* amylase; **—амин** *m.* amylamine; **—ан** *m.* amylan (a gum); **—ен** *m.* amylene, 1-pentene; **—коричный альдегид** amyl cinnamaldehyde; **—нитрит** *m.* amyl nitrite; **—о—** *prefix* amylo— (starch; amyl); **—огенный** *a.* amylogenic, starch-producing.

амиловый *a.* amyl; **а. альдегид** amyl aldehyde, pentanal; **а. ацетат** amyl acetate; **а. спирт** amyl alcohol, pentanol; **а. эфир уксусной кислоты** amyl acetate.

амило/ген *m.* amylogen; **—декстрин** *m.* amylodextrin; **—за** *f.* amylose; **—ид** *m.,* **—идный** *a.* amyloid; **—идоз** *m.* (med.) amiloidosis; **—идоподобный** *a.* amyloid, starch-like; **—ин** *m.* amyloin, maltodextrin; **—кластический** *a.* amyloclastic; **—лиз** *m.* amylolysis; **—литический** *a.* amylolytic, starch-splitting; **—пектин** *m.* amylopectin; **—пласт** *m.* (bot.) amyloplast; **—псин** *m.* amylopsin, pancreatic amylase; **—фил(л)ьный** *a.* amylophyllous, starch-loving.

амил/пенициллин *m.* amyl penicillin; **—фенол** *m.* amyl phenol; **—формиат** *m.* amyl formate.

амимия *f.* (med.) amimia.

амин *m.* amine; **—азин** *m.* Aminazine, chlorpromazine; **—арсон** *m.* Aminarsone, Carbarsone; **—изация** *f.* (soils) aminization; **—ирование** *n.* amination; **—ировать** *v.* aminate; **—ировщик** *m.* worker in amination process; **—ный** *a.* amine, amino; amino acid (nitrogen).

амино— *prefix* amino—; **—адипиновый** *a.* aminoadipic (acid); **—азобензол** *m.* aminoazobenzene; **—азосоединение** *n.* aminoazo compound; **—акриловый** *a.* aminoacrylic (acid); **—алкилпроизводное** *n.* aminoalkyl derivative; **—антрахинон** *m.,* **—антрахиноновый** *a.* aminoanthraquinone; **—ацетон** *m.* aminoacetone; **—ацил** *m.* aminoacyl; **—ацил-тРНК** *f.* aminoacyl-tRNA.

аминобенз/альдегид *m.* aminobenzaldehyde; **—оил** *m.* aminobenzoyl; **—оилировать** *v.* aminobenzoylate; **—оильный** *a.* aminobenzoyl; **—ойный** *a.* aminobenzoic (acid); **—ол** *m.* aminobenzene, aniline.

амино/валерьяновый *a.* aminovaleric (acid); **—вый** *see* **аминный; —глутаровый** *a.* aminoglutaric, glutamic (acid); **—группа** *f.* amino group or radical; amines; **—з** *m.* (med.) aminosis; **—замещение** *n.* amino substitution; **—изомасляный** *a.* aminoisobutyric (acid); **—капроновый** *a.* aminocaproic (acid); **—кетон** *m.* aminoketone; **—кислота** *f.,* **—кислотный** *a.* amino acid; **—кислот-РНК** aminoacyl-tRNA; **—ксилол** *m.* xylidine, dimethylaniline; **—левулиновый** *a.* aminolevulinic (acid); **—лиз** *m.* aminolysis; **—масляный** *a.* aminobutyric (acid); **—нафтол** *m.* aminonaphthol; **—основание** *n.* primary amine; **—пептид-(аминоацидогидрол)аза** *f.* aminopeptidase; **—пласт** *m.* aminoplast (resin); **—производное** *n.* amino derivative; **—пурин** *m.* aminopurine, adenine; **—сахар** *m.* amino sugar; **—соединение** *n.* amino compound, amine; **—спирт** *m.* amino alcohol; **—толуол** *m.* aminotoluene, toluidine; **—(транс)фераза** *f.* aminotransferase, transaminase; **—углеводород** *m.* amino hydrocarbon; **—уксусный** *a.* aminoacetic (acid); **—фераза** *f.* transaminase; **—янтарный** *a.* aminosuccinic (acid).

амио/стенический *a.* (med.) amyosthenic; **—тония** *f.* amyotonia; **—трофический** *a.* amyotrophic; **—трофия** *f.* amyotrophy, muscular atrophy.

амирантский *a.* (geog.) Amirantes.

амир/ин *m.* amyrin; **—ол** *m.* amyrol.

амитал *m.,* **—овый** *a.* Amytal, amobarbital.

амито/з *m.* (biol.) amitosis; **—тический** *a.* amitotic.

ами/уровые *pl.* freshwater catfishes (*Ameiuridae*); **—я** *f.* (ichth.) bowfin (*Amia*).

АМК- *abbrev.* (**аминокислотный**).

амм. *abbrev.* (**аммиак; аммиачный**).

аммат *m.* ammonium sulfamate.

аммел/ид *m.* ammelide, cyanuramide; **—ин** *m.* ammeline, cyanurodiamide.

амметр *see* **амперметр.**

амми *f.* (bot.) Ammi.

аммиа/к *m.* ammonia (gas); **едкий а.** aqua ammonia,

ammonium hydroxide; **хлорид —ка, хлористый а.** ammonium chloride; **—(ка)т** *m.* ammoniate, ammine; ammonia liquor.

аммиачн/ожелезные квасцы ammonium iron alum; **—орастворимый** *a.* ammonia soluble; **—охромовые квасцы** ammonium chrome alum; **—ый** *a.* ammonium, ammonia(cal); **—ая вода** ammonia water, ammonium hydroxide; **—ая селитра** ammonium nitrate; **—ая смола** gum ammoniac; **—ая сода** ammonia soda or ash, sodium carbonate; **—ые квасцы** ammonium alum.

аммин *m.* ammine, ammoniate.

аммо— *prefix* ammo— (sand); **—дендрон** *m.* (bot.) Ammodendron; **—дил** *m.* (mam.) ammodille (*Ammodilus*); **—дитес** *m.* (ichth.) sand eel (*Ammodites*); **—крипта** *f.* Ammocrypta.

аммон/ал *m.* (expl.) ammonal; **—бактерии** *pl.* ammoniacal bacteria; **—иакум** *m.* ammoniac (gum); **—иев рог** (anat.) cornu Ammonis, hippocampus; **—иевый** *see* **аммиачный; —изация** *f.,* **—изирование** *n.* ammoniation, ammonification; **—изированный** *a.* ammoniated; **—изировать** *v.* ammoniate.

аммон/ий *m.* ammonium; **гидроокись —ия** ammonium hydroxide; **сернокислый а., сульфат —ия** ammonium sulfate; **хлористый а.** ammonium chloride; **—ийный** *see* **аммиачный; —ийное основание** ammonium hydroxide; **—иофосфат** *m.* ammonium phosphate; **—ит** *m.* (expl.; pal.) ammonite; **—итовый** *a.* ammonite; (geol.) ammonitic; **—ификатор** *m.* ammonizing agent; **—ификация** *f.* ammonification, ammonization; **—ов рог** *see* **аммониев рог; —оидеи** *pl.* (pal.) Ammonoidea; **—олиз** *m.* ammonolysis.

аммофил/а *f.* beach grass (*Ammophila*); **—ьный** *a.* ammophilous, sand-loving.

аммофос *m.* ammophos (an ammonium phosphate fertilizer); **—ка** *f.* ammophoska (a complete fertilizer).

амнезия *f.* (med.) amnesia, memory loss.

амнио— *prefix* (anat.) amnio—, amnion, amniotic; **—н** *m.* amnion; **—т** *m.* amniote; **—тический** *a.* amniotic.

АМО *abbr.* (**анодно-механическая обработка**) electromachining.

амомум *m.* (bot.) Amomum.

амортиз/атор *m.* shock absorber, bumper; buffer, cushion; (elec.) damper; surge damper; **—ационный** *a.* shock-absorbing; amortization, depreciation; buffer (inventory); obsolete, old (scrap); **—ационная пружина** shock absorber; **—ация** *f.* absorption (of shock), etc., *see v.*; cushioning; (elec.) damping; buffer action; amortization, depreciation; **моральная —ация** obsolescence; **с —ацией отказов** (comp.) fail-soft; **—ирование** *n.* absorption (of shock), etc., *see v.*; **—(ир)ованный** *a.* shockproof; spring-mounted; absorbed, etc., *see v.*; **—ировать** *v.* absorb, cushion (shock); amortize, depreciate; damp; **—ирующее устройство** shock absorber; **—уемый** *a.* depreciable.

аморф *m.* (gen.) amorph; **—a** *f.* (bot.) false indigo (*Amorpha*); **—изация** *f.* conversion to amorphous state; vitrification; **—изировать** *v.* render amorphous; **—изм** *m.,* **—ность** *f.* amorphism; **—ный** *a.* amorphous, shapeless; **—офаллус** *m.* (bot.) Amorphophallus.

амп *abbr.* (**ампер**) ampere.

АМП *abbr.* (**аминопласт**) aminoplast.

ампангабеит *m.* (min.) ampangabéite.

ам. пат. *abbr.* (**американский патент**) United States patent.

амп-вит *abbr.* (**ампер-виток**).

ампелит *m.* (petr.) ampelite.

ампело— *prefix* ampel(o)— (vine); **—графия** *f.* (agr.) ampelography; **—псис** *m.* (bot.) Ampelopsis.

ампер *m.* (elec.) ampere (unit of current); **—аж** *m.* amperage; **—весы** *pl.* ampere balance; **—виток** *m.* ampere-turn; **—вольтметр** *m.* ampere voltmeter, voltammeter; **—метр** *m.* ampere meter, ammeter; **—ный** *a.* ampere; **—ометрический** *a.* amperometric (titration); **а.-секунда** ampere-second; **а.-час** ampere-hour.

ампир *m.,* **—ный** *a.* (arch.) Empire style.

ампициллин *m.* ampicillin (antibiotic).

амплидин *m.,* **—ный** *a.* (elec.) amplidyne.

амплитуд/а *f.* amplitude, range; width; unevenness (of crop yield); crest, peak; (pulse) height; **а. качания** swing; **а. сброса** (geol.) fault amplitude, total throw; **иметь —у** *v.* be peak to peak; **коэффициент —ы** (elec.) crest factor; **—но-модулированный** *a.* amplitude-modulated, AM; **—но-частотный** *a.* amplitude-frequency, amplitude (compensator).

амплитудный *a.* amplitude; maximum, crest, peak (value); pulse-height (selector, etc.); **а. анализатор (импульсов)** (nucl.) pulse-height analyzer; **а. фазовый** *a.* gain-phase (characteristic); **а частотный** *a.* gain-frequency.

амплифика/тор *m.* amplifier; **—ция** *f.* amplification.

амп-сек *abbr.* (**ампер-секунда**).

ампул/а *f.* ampoule, ampulla, vial, tube; (duct) enlargement; **—ария** *f.* (mal.) apple shell (*Ampullaria*); **—овидный, —оподобный** *a.* ampullaceous, ampulliform, flask-shaped; **—ярный** *a.* ampullar.

ампут/ация *f.* amputation; **—ированный** *a.* amputated; **—ировать** *v.* amputate.

амп-час *abbr.* (**ампер-час**).

амрад гумми amrad gum.

амселитра *f.* ammonium nitrate.

амударьинский *a.* (geog.) Amu Darya.

амуниция *f.* (mil.) equipment, accoutrements.

амур, белый (ichth.) white amur (*Ctenopharyngdon idella*); **чёрный а.** black amur (*Mylopharyngodon piceus*); **—ский** *a.* (geog.) Amur; **—ско-зейский** *a.* Amur-Zeya (plain).

АМФ *abbr.* (**аденозинмонофосфат**) adenosine monophosphate, AMP.

амфетамин *m.* (pharm.) amphetamine.

амфи— *prefix* amphi— (about, around; both; on both sides); **—артроз** *m.* (anat.) amphiarthrosis; **—астер** *m.* (embr.) amphiaster; **—биальность** *f.* amphibious nature; **—бии** *pl.* amphibians (*Amphibia*); **—бластический** *a.* (embr.) amphiblastic.

амфибол *m.* (min.) amphibole, hornblende; **—изация** *f.* (petr.) amphibolization; **—ит** *m.* amphibolite; **—овый** *a.* amphibole, amphibolic.

амфи/гастрий *m.,* **—гастрия** *f.* (bot.) amphigastrium; **—ген** *m.* (min.) amphigene, leucite; **—генез** *m.,* **—гония** *f.* amphigenesis, amphigony, sexual reproduction; **—генит** *m.* (petr.) amphigenite; **—д** *m.* (zool.) amphid; **—диплоид** *m.* (gen.) amphidiploid; **—дный** *a.* amphoteric (salt); **—карион** *m.* (gen.) amphikaryon; **—лофис** *m.* (bot.) Amphilophis; **—миксис** *a.* (gen.) amphimixis; **—микт(ич)ный** *a.* amphimictic; **—он** *m.* amphoteric ion, zwitterion; **—под** *m.,* **—подный** *a.* (zool.) amphipod; **—прион** *m.* anemonefish (*Amphiprion*); **—сбены** *pl.* (herp.) Amphisbaenidae.

амфистом/атический, —атный *a.* (bot.) amphistomatic; **—ный** *a.* (zool.) amphistomous; **—оз** *m.* (med.) amphistomiasis.

амфи/театр *m.* amphitheater; **горный а.** (geol.) cirque; **—токия** *f.* (gen.) amphitoky; **—трита** *f.* (zool.) amphitrite (*Amphitrita*); —**тропный** *a.* (bot.) amphitropous; —**ума** *f.* (amph.) Amphiuma; —**ура** *f.* (zool.) brittle star (*Amphiura*); —**хро(мат)ический** *a.* amphichro(mat)ic; —**цельный** *a.* amphicoelous, biconcave.

амфо— *prefix* ampho— (both); —**лит** *m.* ampholyte, amphoteric electrolyte; —**литоид** *m.* (soils) ampholytoid; —**теризация** *f.* amphoterization; —**терицин** *m.* amphotericin (antibiotic); —**терность** *f.* amphoteric nature; —**терный** *a.* amphoteric; —**тропин** *m.* amphotropin, methenamine camphorate.

АН *abbr.* (**Академия наук**) Academy of Sciences.

ана— *prefix* an(a)— [up(ward), up again, throughout]; (chem.) ana— (position).

анабад/уст, —эст *m.* anabadust (anabasine sulfate-lime insecticide).

ана/базин *m.* anabasine, neonicotine; —**базис** *m.* (bot.) Anabasis; —**барский** *a.* (geog.) Anabar; —**бас** *m.* (ichth.) climbing perch (*Anabas*, spec. *A. testudineus*); —**басовые** *pl.* Anabantidae; —**батический** *a.* (meteor.) anabatic, upward-moving; —**биоз** *m.* anabiosis, resuscitation; —**болизм** *m.* anabolism, constructive metabolism; —**болит** *m.* (physiol.) anabolite; —**болитик** *m.* anabolic agent; —**болический** *a.* anabolic; —**галактический** *a.* (astr.) anagalactic; —**генез** *m.* anagenesis, tissue regeneration; —**гирин** *m.* anagyrine; —**глиф** *m.* (phot.) anaglyph; —**дромный** *a.* (ichth.) anadromous; —**дырский** *a.* (geog.) Anadyr.

анакард/иевые, —овые *pl.* (bot.) cashew family (*Anacardiaceae*); —**ия** *f.* cashew; —**овокислая соль** anacardate; —**овый** *a.* cashew; anacardic (acid).

анаконда *f.* (herp.) anaconda (*Eunectes murinus*).

анаксиальный *a.* anaxial, asymmetric.

аналгезия *see* **анальгезия.**

аналепт/ик *m.* analeptic, restorative drug; —**ический** *a.* analeptic, restorative.

анал/из *m.* analysis, assay; test, examination; (stat.) estimation; (blood) count; —**изатор** *m.* analyzer; meter; —**изаторы** *pl.* analytical equipment; —**изирование** *n.* analysis; —**изированный** *a.* analyzed; —**изировать** *v.* analyze, assay; examine; —**изируемый** *a.* test, sample; —**изируемая проба** test sample; —**ист, —итик** *m.* analyst, assayer; —**итика** *f.* (math.) analytics; —**итический** *a.* analytic(al); structural (characteristics); —**итичность** *f.* (math.) analyticity.

аналл/актический *a.* (geod.) anallactic; —**обар** *m.* anallobar, isallobaric height.

аналог *m.* analog; analogy, similarity; —**ический, —ичный** *a.* analogous, similar, like; —**ично** *adv.* in much the same way (as); —**ично этому** similarly.

аналог/ия *f.* analogy, similarity, comparison; analog method; —**овый** *a.* analog (computer); analogous; —**о-цифровой** *a.* analog-digital (computer).

анальг/езин *m.* analgesine, antipyrine; —**езирующий** *a.* (med.) analgesic, pain-relieving; —**езия** *f.* analgesia; —**етик** *m.,* —**етический** *a.* analgesic; —**ин** *m.* analgin, methampyrone; —**ический** *a.* analgic, insensible to pain.

анальн/ый *a.* (anat.) anal; —**ое отверстие** anus.

анальцим *m.* (min.) analcite, analcime; —**изация** *f.* analcimization.

анам/езит *m.* (petr.) anamesite; —**нез** *m.* (med.) anamnesis, case history; —**нии, —ниоты** *pl.* (zool.) Anamniota.

анаморф/ировать *v.* anamorphose; —**ный** *a.* anamorphous, anamorphic; —**оз** *m.,* —**оза** *f.* anamorphism; (gen.) anamorphosis; —**от** *m.* (opt.) anamorphic lens.

ананас *m.,* —**ный, —овый** *a.* pineapple (*Ananas*); —**ная трава** feijoa (*Feijoa sellowiana*); —**ные, —овые** *pl.* Bromeliaceae.

ана/ньевский *a.* (geog.) Ananyev; —**плазия** *f.* (med.) anaplasia; —**плазмоз** *m.* anaplasmosis; —**плазмы** *pl.* (biol.) Anaplasma; —**пластический** *a.* anaplastic, restorative (surgery); —**пломовые** *see* **анопломовые.**

анап/сид *m.* (herp.) anapsid; —**сиды** *pl.* Anapsida; —**ский** *a.* (geog.) Anapa; —**тих** *m.* (pal.) anaptychus.

ана/ртрия *f.* (med.) anarthria; —**стигмат** *m.,* —**стигматический** *a.* anastigmatic (lens).

анастомоз *m.* (anat.; biol.) anastomosis; *suffix* —**стомы**; —**ировать** *v.* anastomose, interjoin; —**ирующий, —ный** *a.* anastomotic; —**ит** *m.* anastomositis.

ана/стральный *a.* (gen.) anastral; —**таз** *m.* (min.) anatase, octahedrite; —**тан** *m.* (mam.) Anathana; —**тексис** *m.* (geol.) anatexis, refusion; —**токсин** *m.* anatoxin, toxoid; —**толический** *a.* (geog.) Anatolian, Anatolic.

анатом *m.* anatomist; —**ирование** *n.* dissection; —**ировать** *v.* dissect, anatomize; —**ический** *a.* anatomical; —**ия** *f.* anatomy; dissection.

ана/тропный *a.* (bot.) anatropous; —**фаза** *f.* (gen.) anaphase; —**физ** *m.,* —**физа** *f.* anaphysis, outgrowth.

анафилак/сия *f.* (med.) anaphylaxis; —**тин** *m.* anaphylactin; —**тический** *a.* anaphylactic.

ана/форез *m.* (chem.; med.) anaphoresis; —**фронт** *m.* (meteor.) anafront, upslide surface; —**циклюс** *m.* (bot.) Anacyclus.

анаэроб/(ионт) *m.* (biol.) anaerobe; —**иоз** *m.* anaerobiosis; —**ный** *a.* anaerobic.

анг. *abbr.* (**ангидрид**).

ангал/амин *m.* anhalamine; —**ин** *m.* anhaline; —**онин** *m.* anhalonine.

ангар *m.* hangar, shed.

ангармонич/еский *a.* (math.) anharmonic; —**ность** *f.* anharmonicity.

ангарный *a.* hangar, shed.

ангарский *a.* (geog.) Angara.

ангедральный *a.* (petr.) anhedral.

ангел *m.* angel; angelfish; **морской а.** angel shark (*Squatina,* spec. *S. squatina*); —**ика** *f.* (bot.) angelica; —**иковый** *a.* angela (oil); angelic (acid); **морской —ок** (mal.) sea butterfly (*Clione*); **морские —ы** Squatinidae.

ангидр/аза *f.* anhydrase; —**емия** *f.* (med.) anhydremia; —**ид** *m.* anhydride; —**идный** *a.* anhydride; anhydrous; —**изация** *f.* dehydration; —**ит** *m.,* —**итовый** *a.* (min.) anhydrite; —**о**— *prefix* anhydr(o)— (waterless; anhydride); —**оглюкоза** *f.* anhydroglucose; —**он** *m.* anhydrone, magnesium perchlorate; —**основание** *n.* anhydro base; —**осахар** *m.* anhydro sugar.

ангин/а *f.* (med.) angina, *spec.* quincy, tonsillitis; —**озный** *a.* aginose.

ангио— *prefix* (bot.; med.) angi(o)— (vessel; blood vessel); —**бласт** *m.* (embr.) angioblast; —**графия** *f.* angiography; —**литический** *a.* angiolithic (degeneration); —**логия** *f.* (anat.) angiology; —**ма** *f.* (med.) angioma; —**матоз** *m.* angiomatosis; —**невротический** *a.* angioneurotic; —**патия** *f.* angiopathy; —**саркома** *f.* angiosarcoma; —**спазм** *m.* angiospasm; —**стомия** *f.* angiostomy; —**тензин, —тонин** *m.* (horm.) angiotensin, angiotonin; —**фиброма** *f.* (med.) angiofibroma.

англ. *abbr.* (**английский**).

англезит *m.* (min.) anglesite.

английск/ий *a.* English; British (patent); **а. порошок** algaroth, antimony oxychloride; **а. цемент** marble cement, Keene's cement; **—ая болезнь** (med.) rickets; **—ая булавка** safety pin; **—ая соль** Epsom salts; **—ие белила** white lead.

Англия England.

англоязычный *a.* English-speaking.

ангоб *m.* (cer.) engobe; **—аж** *m.,* **—ирование** *n.* engobing; **—ировать** *v.* engobe.

анг/ольский *a.* (geog.) Angola; **—орский** *a.* Angora (wool, etc.); **—остуровый** *a.* angostura (bark); **—стрем** *m.* ångström (10^{-8} cm.); **—урия** *f.* bur cucumber (*Cucumis anguria*); **—усский** *a.* Angus (cattle).

анд/аксин *m.* Andaxin, meprobamate; **—алузит** *m.* (min.) andalusite; **—алузский,** **—алусский** *a.* (geog.) Andalusian; **—езин** *m.* (min.) andesine; **—езит** *m.* (petr.) andesite; **—ерсонит** *m.* (min.) andersonite; **—ижанский** *a.* (geog.) Andizhan; **—ийский** *a.* Andean; **—ира** *f.* (bot.) Andira; **—ирин** *m.* andirine, surinamine; **—овый** *a.* anda(-assu) (oil); **—орит** *m.* (min.) andorite; **—радит** *m.* andradite; **—реэя** *f.* Andreaea (Alpine moss).

андский *a.* (geog.) Andean, Andes.

андро— *prefix* andro— (male); **—гамета** *f.* (gen.) androgamete; **—ген** *m.* androgen, male hormone; **—генез** *m.* androgenesis; **—генный** *a.* androgenous, androgenic; **—генный гормон** androgen; **—гинный** *a.* androgynous; **—меда** *f.* (astr.; bot.) andromeda; **—сома** *f.* (gen.) androsome; **—спора** *f.* (bot.) androspore; **—стан** *m.* (horm.) androstane; **—стерон** *m.* androsterone; **—фор** *m.* (bot.) androphore; **—цей** *m.* androcoecium.

андский *a.* (geog.) Andean, Andes.

ане/вризм *m.,* **—а** *f.* (med.) aneurysm; **—врин,** **—йрин** *m.* aneurin, vitamin B.

анелло— *prefix* anello— (ring).

анем/изация *f.* becoming anemic; pause in circulation; **—ический,** **—ичный** *a.* anemic; **—ичность,** **—ия** *f.* anemia.

анемо— *prefix* anemo— (wind); **—гамия** *f.* anemogamy, wind pollination; **—грамма** *f.* (meteor.) anemogram; **—граф** *m.* anemograph; **—метр** *m.* anemometer, wind gage; **—метрический** *a.* anemometric, wind (measuring); **—метрия** *f.* anemometry.

анемон *m.,* **—а** *f.* (bot.) anemone; **—ин** *m.,* **—овая камфара** anemonin, pulsatilla camphor; **—иновый** *a.* anemoninic (acid); **—овый** *a.* anemonic (acid).

анемо/румбограф *m.* (meteor.) anemorumbograph; **—скоп** *m.* anemoscope; **—тахометр** *m.* anemotachometer; **—фикация** *f.* wind power utilization; **—фил** *m.* anemophile, anemophilous plant; **—филия** *f.* (bot.) anemophily; **—фильный** *a.* anemophilous, wind-pollinated; **—хор** *m.* anemochorous plant; **—хория** *f.* (bot.) anemochory; **—хорный** *a.* anemochorous, wind-dispersed.

анемузит *m.* (min.) anemousite.

анергический *a.* (med.) anergic, inactive.

анероид *m.* (meteor.) aneroid (barometer); **—ный** *a.* aneroid.

анесте/зин *m.* Anesthesin, benzocaine; **—зиолог** *m.* anesthesiologist; **—зировать** *v.* anesthetize; **—зирующее средство,** **—тик** *m.,* **—тический** *a.* anesthetic; **—зия** *f.* anesthesia.

анетол *m.* anethole, anise camphor.

анеуплоид *m.,* **—ный** *a.* (gen.) aneuploid.

анж/еро-судженский *a.* (geog.) Anzhero-Sudzhensk; **—усский** *a.* Anzhu.

анзерин *m.* anserine, N-methylcarnosine.

анивский *a.* (geog.) Aniva.

анид *m.* anid (USSR equivalent of nylon).

аниз— *see* **анизо—**; **анис—**; **—ет** *m.* (bot.) star anise (*Pimpinella anisetum*); **—идин** *m.* anisidine, anisidino—; **—ил** *m.* anisyl; **—о—** *prefix* aniso— (unequal, dissimilar); not; (chem.) aniso—, uneven; **—обарический** *a.* anisobaric; **—огамета** *f.* (embr.) anisogamete; **—огамия** *f.* anisogamy; **—одесмический** *a.* (cryst.) anisodesmic; **—оил** *m.* anisoyl; **—ол** *m.* anisole, phenylmethyl ether; **—омерный** *a.* anisomeric, not isomeric; (bot.) anisomerous; **—ометр** *m.* anisometer; **—ометрический** *a.* anisometric; **—опараклаз** *m.* (geol.) strike fault, longitudinal fault; **—отропический,** **—отропный** *a.* anisotropic; **—отропия** *f.* anisotropy, **—отропность** *f.* anistropy; **—офильный** *a.* (bot.) anisophyllous; **—охромисовые** *pl.* (ichth.) Anisochromidae.

аникшяйский *a.* (geog.) Anikshchyai.

анил *m.* anil (dye); *prefix* aniline-dye; **—ид** *m.* anilide; **—ид уксусной кислоты** acetanilide; **—ин** *m.* aniline, phenylamine; **—иновый** *a.* aniline; **—иновая соль** aniline hydrochloride; **—инокрасочный** *a.* aniline-dye; **—иносульфоновый** *a.* aniline-sulfonic (acid).

анимал/изация *f.* (stat.) animalization, animal population; **—ьный** *a.* animal; (biol.) holozoic.

аниме, смола anime (resin).

анимик/ит *m.* (min.) animikite; **—ский отдел** (geol.) Animikean system.

анингаль *m.* (geobot.) aningal.

анион *m.* anion; **—ировать** *v.* soften water by anion exchange; **—ит** *m.,* **—итный,** **—итовый** *a.* anionite, anion-exchange resin; **—ный,** **—овый** *a.* anion(ic); **—оактивный** *a.* anionic (detergent); **—оидный** *a.* anionoid, nucleophilic.

анионообмен *m.,* **—ный** *a.* anion-exchange; **—ник** *m.* anion exchanger.

анис *m.* (bot.) anise (*Pimpinella anisum*); **—идин** *m.* anisidine, methoxyaniline; **—ил** *m.* anisyl; anisil; **—ный** *a.* anise; **—овка** *f.* anise liqueur; **—овокислый** *a.* anisic acid; anisate (of); **—овокислая соль** anisate; **—овоэтиловый эфир** ethyl anisate.

анисов/ый *a.* anise, anisic; **а. альдегид** anisaldehyde; **а. спирт** anisalcohol, anisyl alcohol; **—ая кислота** anisic acid, p-methoxybenzoic acid; **—ое масло** anise oil; **—ое семя** aniseed.

анисо/ил *m.* anisoyl; **—л** *see* **анизол.**

анкер *m.* anchor; stay, tie rod; (rack) lever; (horol.) pallet; **—аж** *m.* anchorage.

анкерит *m.* (min.) ankerite.

анкер/ный *a.* anchor; tie (beam); tension (chain); lever (fork); **а. камень** bonder; **—овать** *v.* anchor, fix; brace (a boiler); **—овка** *f.* anchoring, etc., see *v.*; **—ок** *m.* (water) breaker.

анкет/а *f.,* **—ный** *a.* questionnaire, form.

анкило— *prefix* ankyl(o)— (bent, crooked); **—з** *m.* (med.) ankylosis; **—завр** *m.* (pal.) ankylosaurus; **—зированный** *a.* ankylosed, fused, obliterated (joint); **—стомоз** *m.* ankylostomiasis, hookworm disease.

анлауфрад *m.* (mach.) pallet wheel.

аннабергит *m.* (min.) annabergite.

анналин *m.* annalin, calcium sulfate.

анналы *pl.* annals, records.

аннато *n.,* **—вый** *a.* annato (tree) (*Bixa orellana*).

аннекс *m.* annex; (commun.) end panel; **—ировать** *v.* annex; **—ия** *f.* annexation.

аннелид *m.* annelid, segmented worm.

аннелиров/ание *n.* annelation; **—аться** *v.* annelate, link (with), fuse, condense.

аннигил/ировать *v.* annihilate, obliterate; **—ятор** *m.*, **—яторный** *a.* annihilator; **—яционный** *a.*, **—яция** *f.* annihilation, destruction, obliteration.

аннидалин *m.* annidalin, thymol iodide.

анн/инский *a.* (geog.) Anna; **—ит** *m.* (min.) annite.

аннот/ация *f.* annotation, note; abstract, resume; (publisher's) blurb; **—ировать** *v.* annotate, comment; summarize.

аннуитет *m.* annuity.

аннулир/ование *n.* cancelation, etc., *see v.*; **—ованный** *a.* canceled, etc., *see v.*; **—овать** *v.* cancel, strike out, annul, abrogate, revoke; annihilate, abolish; **—оваться** *v.* (math.) vanish; **—уемый** *a.* annihilated; **—ующая** *f.* annihilator; **—ующий** *a.* canceling, etc., *see v.*

аннулярии *pl.* (pal.) Annularia.

аннулятор *m.*, **—ный** *a.* annihilator.

аноа *m.* (mam.) anoa (*Anoa depressicornis*).

анод *m.* (elec.) anode; **—альный** *a.* (bot.) anodal, anodic; **—замыкательный** *a.* (physiol.) anodal closure (contraction); **—изация** *see* **анодирование; —инин** *m.* anodynine, antipyrine; **—ирование** *n.* (met.) anodizing, anodic oxidation; **—ировать** *v.* anodize; **—номеханическая обработка** electromachining; **—ный** *a.* anode, anodic; plate (capacitor, current, etc.); B-(battery); **—ный контур** plate tank; **—ная масса** anode paste; **—ная цепь** plate tank circuit; **—ное покрытие** *see* **анодирование; —одержатель** *m.* anode mount.

анодонта *f.* (mal.) Anodonta.

анодразмыкательный *a.* (physiol.) anodal opening (contraction).

анокс(ем)ия *f.* anoxia, oxygen deficiency.

анол *m.* anol, propenylphenol; **—ис** *m.* Anolis (a lizard); **—ит** *m.* anolyte.

аномал/истический *a.* anomalistic; **—ия** *f.* anomaly; abnormality; **—оскоп** *m.* anomaloscope; **—ьновязкий** *a.* quasi-viscous; **—ьносвязочные** *pl.* (mal.) Anomalodesmaceae; **—ный** *a.* anomalous, atypical, irregular, abnormal.

аном/ер *m.* anomer; **—ерный** *a.* anomeric; **—ит** *m.* (min.) anomite; **—ия** *f.* (mal.) jingle shell (*Anomia*); **—о—** *prefix* anomo— (abnormal, unusual, irregular); **—оцельные** *pl.* (amph.) Anomocoela.

анона *f.* (bot.) custard apple (*Anona*).

анонимный *a.* anonymous, unknown.

ано́новый *a.* (bot.) custard apple.

анонс *m.* announcement, notice; **—ированный** *a.* announced, advertised; **—ировать** *v.* announce, advertise.

анопло/помовые *pl.* sablefishes (*Anoplopom(at)idae*); **—фрий** *m.* (prot.) Anoplophrya; **—цефалиды** *pl.* tapeworms (*Anoplocephalidae*).

аноп/сия *f.* (med.) anopsia; **—тих** *m.* Mexican cave fish (*Anoptichthys*, spec. *A. jordani*); **—тральный** *a.* (opt.) anoptral.

анорексия *f.* (med.) anorexia.

анормальн/ость *f.* abnormality; **—ый** *a.* abnormal.

анорт/ит *m.* (min.) anorthite; **—огенез** *m.* (gen.) anorthogenesis; **—озит** *m.* (petr.) anorthosite; **—оклаз** *m.* (min.) anorthoclase.

ано/сматики *pl.* anosmatic mammals; **—сматический** *a.* anosm(at)ic; **—смия** *f.* (med.) anosmia, olfactory anesthesia; **—стомовые** *pl.* (ichth.) Anostomidae **—топтеровые** *pl.* javelinfishes (*Anotopteridae*); **—трон** *m.* (rad.) anotron; **—фелес** *m.* malarial mosquito (*Anopheles*).

анса— *prefix* ansa— (compound).

ансамбль *m.* ensemble, set, group.

анса-соединение *n.* ansa compound.

ансерин *see* **анзерин.**

анский *a.* (geog.) Ana.

ант *m.*, **—а** *f.* (arch.) anta (a pier); **—абка** *f.* swivel; **—аблемент** *m.* (arch.) entablature (a wall); entablement (platform).

антагон/изм *m.* antagonism; counteraction, reaction; (min.) antipathy; **—ист** *m.* (anat., biol., etc.) antagonist; **—истический** *a.* antagonistic.

Антаркти/да *f.* Antarctica (the continent); **—ка** *f.* Antarctic (region).

антарктический *a.* Antarctic.

антацидный *a.* (med.) antacid.

антверпенский *a.* Antwerp (blue).

антгельминтный *a.* (med.) anthelmintic.

анте— *prefix* ante— (before; prior); **—анальный** *a.* (anat.) pre-anal; **—версия** *f.* anteversion; **—гмит** *m.* Antegmit (antifriction molding material); **—датинг** *m.* antedating; **—дон** *m.* (zool.) Antedon; **—дорсальный** *a.* (anat.) predorsal.

антекл/аза *f.* (geol.) anteclase; **—иза** *f.* anteclise (broad structural uplift).

антеклимакс *m.* (geobot.) anteclimax.

анте/ла *f.* (bot.) anthela; **—лий** *m.* (meteor.) anthelion; **—мол** *m.* anthemol, camomile camphor; **—натальный** *a.* prenatal; fetal (death).

антенн/а *f.* (tech.; zool.) antenna, feeler; **—ула** *f.* (zool.) antennule; **—ый** *a.* antenna; **—ая сеть** antenna (array).

антерид/иальный *a.* (bot.) antheridial; **—ий** *m.* antherid(ium); **—иофор** *m.* antheridiophore.

антериорный *a.* anterior.

антерозоид *m.* (bot.) antherozoid, spermatozoid.

антецедент *m.*, **—ный** *a.* antecedent.

анти— *prefix* anti— (opposite, against, instead, counter); non—; **—агрессивный** *a.* antiaggressive; **—анемический** *a.* (med.) antianemic; **—апекс** *m.* (astr.) antapex; **—ароза** *f.* antiarose; **—ауксин** *m.* antiauxin; **—бактериальный** *a.* antibacterial; **—барион** *m.* (nucl.) antibaryon; **—барический** *a.* (meteor.) antibaric; **—батно** *adv.* in opposition, in disagreement; in opposite direction; **—бесский** *a.* (geog.) Antibes.

антибио/з *m.* (biol.) antibiosis; **—тик** *m.* antibiotic; **—тикоустойчивый** *a.* antibiotic-resistant; **—тический** *a.* antibiotic.

анти/блок *m.* (text.) antiblocking agent; **—вещество** *n.* (phys.) antimatter; **—вибратор** *m.* antivibrator, vibration damper; (mach.) shock absorber; **—винная кислота** mesotartaric acid; **—вирус** *m.* (med.) antivirus; **—вирусный** *a.* antiviral, antivirus; **—витамин** *m.* antivitamin; **—вспениватель** *m.* antifrothing agent; **—гелий** *m.* (meteor.) anthelion, countersun; **—гельминтный** *a.* (med.) anthelmint(h)ic; **—геморрагический** *a.* antihemorrhagic; coagulation (factor); **—ген** *m.* (immun.) antigen; **—генный** *a.* antigenic; **—гигиенический** *a.* unsanitary; **—гистамин** *m.* antihistamine; **—гнилостное средство** preservative; **—гония** *f.* boarfish (*Antigonia*); **—горит** *m.* (min.) antigorite; **—гормон** *m.* antihormone; **—гравитационный** *a.* antigravity; **—гризутный** *a.* safety (explosive); **—дерапан** *m.* nonskid (tire) tread; guide path.

антидетон/атор *m.* antiknock (compound); **—ационный, —ирующий** *a.* antiknock.

анти/диазосоединение *n.* antidiazo compound; **—дизентерийный** *a.* antidysenteric; **—динатронный** *a.* (elec.) suppressor (grid); **—диуретический** *a.* antidiuretic (hormone); **—дот** *m.* antidote; **—дотный** *a.* antidotal; **—дромный** *a.* antidromic; (bot.) antidromal; —**затухание** n. (phys.) antidamping; —**змейная сыворотка** snake bite serum; —**инфекционный** a., —**инфекционное средство** anti-infective; —**катализатор** m. anticatalyst, catalyst poison; —**катод** m. anticathode.

антиклин/аль f. (geol.) anticline, anticlinal fold; —**(аль)ный** a. anticlinal; —**орий** m. anticlinorium.

антикоагул/ин m. anticoagulin, stabilizer, preservative; —**янт, —ятор** m. anticoagulant.

анти/кодон m. (gen.) anticodon; —**коллектор** m. (flotation) defrothing agent, depressant; —**компенсатор** m. (av.) antibalance tab; —**компенсация** f. antibalance; —**комплемент** m. (immun.) anticomplement, antialexin; —**конвульсант** a. anticonvulsant; —**коррозийный, —коррозионный** a. anticorrosive, corrosion-resisting, antirust; —**ксерофтальмин** m. antixerophthalmic vitamin, vitamin A; —**логарифм** m. (math.) antilogarithm.

антилопа f. (mam.) antelope.

анти/луетический a. antiluetic, antisyphilitic; —**луна** f. (meteor.) antiselene; —**льский** a. (geog.) Antillean, Antilles; —**люизит, британский** British Anti-Lewisite, BAL (detoxicant for poison gases, etc.); —**магнитный** a. antimagnetic, nonmagnetic; —**материя** f. antimatter; —**мер** m. (anat.) antimere; —**метаболит** m. (physiol.) antimetabolite; —**микозиый** a. antimycotic, fungus-suppressing; —**микробный** a. antimicrobial; —**микрофонный** a. antimicrophonic, jarproof; —**митотический** a. (gen.) antimitotic; —**мицин** m. antimycin (antibiotic).

антимон/ат m. antimonate; —**ид** m. antimonide; —**ий** m. antimony; —**ил** m. antimonyl; **(виннокислый)** —**ил-калий** tartar emetic, antimony potassium tatrate; —**ит** m. antimonite.

анти/мора f. (ichth.) longfin cod (*Antimora rostrata*); —**морфный** a. (gen.) antimorphic; —**мутаген** m. antimutagen; —**накипин** m. boiler or antiscaling compound; —**научный** a. unscientific; —**нейтрино** n. (nucl.) antineutrino; —**нейтрон** m. antineutron; —**номия** f. antinomy; —**нуклеарный** a. antinuclear; —**нуклон** m. antinucleon; —**обледенитель** m. (av.) deicer; —**озонант** m. (plast.; rub.) antiozonant, sunproofing agent; —**окислитель** m. antioxidant, age resistor; —**окислительный** a. antioxidant; (petrol.) antisludge; —**оксиген, —оксидант** m. antioxidant.

анти/параллельный a. (math.) antiparallel; —**пассат** m. antitrade (wind); —**патарии** pl. (zool.) Antipatharia; —**патия** f. antipathy; —**пеллагрический** a. antipellagric (vitamin); —**переполнение** n. (comp.) underflow; —**пертит** m. (petr.) antiperthite; —**пирен** m. fireproofing compound; —**пиретик** m., —**пиретический** a. (med.) antipyretic; —**пирин** m. antipyrine, Analgesine.

антипка f. mahaleb cherry (*Prunus mahaleb*).

анти/под m., —**а** f. antipode; **оптический а.** enantiomer; —**под(аль)ный** a. antipodal; —**подокоттус** m. (ichth.) Antipodocottus; —**полимеризатор** m. (rub.) shortstop(ping) agent; —**производная** f. (math.) antiderivative; —**протон** m. antiproton, negative proton; —**рад** m. (plast.; rub.) antirad; —**ракета** f. antimissile missile; —**рахитический** a. antirachitic, D (vitamin); —**резонанс** m. (electron.) antiresonance, parallel resonance; —**р(р)инум** m. (bot.) Antirrhinum; —**род** m. antigenus; —**санитарный** a. unsanitary; —**сегнетоэлектрик** m., —**сегнетоэлектрический** a. antiferroelectric; —**сейсмический** a. earthquake-proof; —**селена** f. (meteor.) antiselene.

антисеп/син m. Antisepsin, bromoanilide; —**тик** m. antiseptic; —**тика** f. antisepsis; antiseptic; —**тирование** n. antiseptization; wood preservation treatment; —**тический** a. antiseptic; antifouling (paint); —**тическое средство** antiseptic.

антисимметрич/еский, —ный a. antisymetric, skew (-symmetric), alternating; —**ность** f. antisymmetry.

анти/скорбутный a. antiscorbutic; —**скорчинг** m. (rub.) antiscorching; —**совпадение** n. (electron.) anticoincidence; —**спазматический, —спастический** a. antispasmodic; —**спазмин** m. antispasmin, alverine citrate; —**спутник** m. antisatellite (missile); —**старитель** m. anti-ager, age resistor; —**статик** m. static eliminator; —**статический** a. antistatic; —**стерильный** a. antisterility, E (vitamin); —**стоксовой** a. (phys.) anti-Stokes (lines); —**сыворотка** f. (immun.) antiserum; —**твердитель** m. anti-hardening agent; —**теза** f. antithesis, direct opposite; —**телехор** m. (bot.) antitelechore; —**тело** n. (immun.) antibody; —**тетанический** a. (immun.) antitetanic; —**тетический** a. antithetic, opposite; —**тиреоидный** a. antithyroid; —**токсин** m. (immun.) antitoxin; —**токсический** a. antitoxic; antitoxin (unit); —**трипсин** m. antitrypsin; —**тромбин** m. antithrombin; —**тромбоновый** a. antithrombotic; —**узел** m. (phys.) antinode; —**упорядоченный** a. inversely ordered; —**фагин** m. (bact.) antiphagin; —**фебрин** m. antifebrin, acetanilid; —**фермент** m. antienzyme.

антиферромагн/етизм m. antiferromagnetism; —**етик** m., —**итный** a. antiferromagnetic.

анти/фидинг m. animal repellent; —**фламинг** m. (av.) flame damper, back-fire screen; —**фон** m. antiphone, ear-plug; —**формин** m. Antiformin; —**фриз** m. antifreeze; —**фрикционный** a. antifriction; —**фздинговый** a. antifading; —**хлор** m. antichlor; —**цепь** f. antichain, inverse chain.

антициклон m. (meteor.) anticyclone; —**ический, —ный** a. anticyclonic.

анти/цинготный a. antiscorbutic, C (vitamin); —**частица** f. (nucl.) antiparticle.

античный a. antique.

анти/шумовой a. antinoise; antistatic; —**электрон** m. (nucl.) antielectron; —**эмульгатор** m. demulsifier, emulsion inhibitor; —**эрмитовый** a. (math.) anti-Hermitian.

анто— prefix anth(o)— [flower, floral; (zool.) asexual]; —**дий** m. (bot.) anthodium.

антодин m. Antodyne, phenylglyceryl ether.

анто/ксантин m. anthoxanthin; —**медузы** pl. (zool.) Anthomedusae.

антоним m. antonym; —**ичный** a. antonymous, of opposite meaning.

антонов огонь (med.) gagrene; —**ка** f., —**ское яблоко** (bot.) Antonoff apple.

анто/филлит m. (min.) anthophyllite; —**фит** m. (bot.) anthophyte; —**хлор** m. anthochlor (pigment); —**церотовые** pl. Anthocerotaceae (mosses).

антоциан m. anthocyan; —**идин** m. anthocyanidin; —**ин** m. anthocyanin.

антр—, —а— prefix anthr(a)— [coal; (chem.) anthracene]; —**агаллол** m. anthragallol, alizarin brown; —**азин** m. anthrazine; —**азо** n. anthrazo; —**акноз** m. (phyt.) anthracnose.

антрако— prefix anthrac(o)— (coal; carbuncle); —**з(ис)** m. (med.) anthracosis, blackling; —**лит, —нит** m. (min.) anthracolite, anthraconite; —**нитовый** a. anthraconitic.

антракс m. (med.) anthrax.

антраксолит m. (min.) anthraxolite.

антральный *a.* (anat.) antral.

антр/амин *m.* anthramine, aminoanthracene; **—анил** *m.* anthranyl; anthranil; **—анило—** *prefix* anthranilo—; **—аниловая кислота** anthranilic acid, *o*-aminobenzoic acid; **—анол** *m.* anthranol, 9-hydroxyanthracene; **—анон** *m.* anthranone, dihydroketoanthracene.

антра/пурпурин *m.* anthrapurpurin; **—руфин** *m.* anthrarufin; **—флавиновый** *a.* anthraflavic (acid); **—хинон** *m.*, **—хиноновый** *a.* anthraquinone; **—хинонсульфокислота** *f.* anthraquinonesulfonic acid.

антрацен *m.*, **—овый** *a.* anthracene.

антрац/ил *m.* anthracyl; **—ит** *m.*, **—итный, —итовый** *a.* anthracite, hard coal; **—итизация** *f.* (geol.) anthracitization.

антресоль *f.* entresol; mezzanine.

антр/ил *m.* anthryl; **—имид** *m.* anthrimide; **—оиновый** *a.* anthroic (acid); **—оксан** *m.* anthroxan, anthronil; **—ол** *m.* anthrol, hydroxyanthracene; **—он** *m.* anthr(an)one.

антроп/ический *a.* anthrop(e)ic; **—о—** *prefix* anthropo—(man).

антроповский *a.* (geog.) Antrop(ovo).

антропоген *m.* (geol.) Anthropogen, Quaternary period; **—ез** *m.* anthropogenesis; **—ный** *a.* anthropogenic; man-made, man's (impact); man-induced (erosion).

антропо/ид *m.*, **—идный** *a.* (zool.) anthropoid; **—лог** *m.* anthropologist; **—логия** *f.* anthropology; **—метрия** *f.* anthropometry; **—морфический, —морфный** *a.* anthropomorphous, man-like; **—томия** *f.* anthropotomy, human anatomy; **—фильный** *a.* anthropophilic; **—фит** *m.* (bot.) anthropophyte; **—хор** *m.* anthropochore.

антье (от) *n.* (math.) greatest integer (in).

антэций *m.* (bot.) anthoecium.

ануйский *a.* (geog.) Anyuy, Anuy.

анур/ез *m.*, **—ия** *f.* (med.) anuria.

анучинский *a.* (geog.) Anuchino.

анфас *adv.* facing front.

анфельция *f.* ahnfeltia (a seaweed).

анфилада *f.* suite (of rooms).

анфлераж *m.* (perfumery) enfleurage.

анх/имы *pl.* (orn.) screamer family (*Anhimidae*); **—истропус** *m.* (zool.) Anchistropus; **—уза** *f.* (bot.) bugloss (*Anchusa*); **—узовокислая соль** anchusate; **—узовый** *a.* anchusic (acid).

анцестральный *a.* ancestral.

анцил/ит *m.* (min.) ancylite; **—овый** *a.* Ancylus (clay; Lake).

анчар *m.* upas tree (*Antiaris toxicaria*).

анч/инский *a.* (geog.) Ancha; **—оа** *f.* (ichth.) Anchoa; **—оус** *m.*, **—оусный, —оусовый** *a.* anchovy (*Engraulis*); **—оусовые** *pl.* anchovies (*Engraulidae*).

анш/лаг *m.*, **—лажный** *a.* try square; head (of depth gage); **—лаш** *m.* stopping device; **—лиф** *m.* (min.) polished section; **—пуг** *m.* crowbar.

анюйский *a.* (geog.) Anyuy.

анютины глазки (bot.) pansy.

аорт/а *f.* (anat.) aorta; **—(аль)ный, —овый** *a.* aortal, aortic; **—ит** *m.* (med.) aortitis.

апаранский *a.* (geog.) Aparan.

апарель *m.* approach ramp.

апастр(он) *m.* (astr.) apastron.

апатит *m.*, **—овый** *a.* (min.) apatite.

апат/ический, —ичный *a.* apathetic, indifferent; **—ия** *f.* apathy.

АПВ *abbr.* (**автоматическое повторное включение**) automatic reclosing.

апджонит *m.* (min.) apjohnite.

апекс *m.* apex.

апелл/ировать *v.*, **—яция** *f.* (law) appeal.

апельсин *m.*, **—ный, —овый** *a.* orange; **морской а.** Tethya aurantium (a sponge).

Апеннинские горы (geog.) The Apennines.

апериодич/еский, —ный *a.* aperiodic; **—ность** *f.* aperiodicity.

аперт/ометр *m.* (opt.) apertometer; **—ура** *f.*, **—урный** *a.* aperture, opening.

апи/генин *m.* apigenin, trihydroxyflavone; **—дология** *f.* apiculture, beekeeping; **—ин** (chem.) apiin; **—кальный** *a.* apical; **—ко—** *prefix* apico—(apex); **—нол** *m.* apinol, *l*-menthone; **—оза** *f.* apiose; **—ол** *m.* apiole, parsley camphor; **—оловый** *a.* apiolic (acid); **американский —ос, клубневой —ос** ground nut (*Apios americana*).

апираза *f.* apyrase, ATP-diphosphatase.

аплазия *f.* (med.) aplasia.

апланат *m.* aplanat, aplanatic lens; **—изм** *m.* aplanatism; **—ический, —ичный** *a.* aplanatic.

аплано— *prefix* aplano— (fixed, nonmotile); **—гамета** *f.* (gen.) aplanogamete.

апл/екса *f.* Aplexa (a snail); **—изия** *f.* (mal.) sea hare (*Aplysia*); **—иката** *see* **аппликата**; **—ит** *m.* (petr.) aplite.

аплод/ировать *v.* applaud; **бурно а.** acclaim; **—исменты** *pl.* applause.

апло/донтовые *pl.* (mam.) mountain beavers (*Aplodontiidae*); **—хитоновые** *pl.* (ichth.) Aplochitonidae.

апноэ *n.* (med.) apnea.

апо— *prefix* apo— (away from, separate, detached); **—астр** *m.* (astr.) apastron; **—гам(ет)ия** *f.* (embr.) apogam(et)y; **—гей** *m.* culmination, climax, peak; (astr.) apogee; **—гон** *m.* cardinalfish (*Apogon*); **—гонихт** *m.* Apogonichthys; **—гоновые** *pl.* Apogonidae; **—дальный** *a.* (zool.) apodal; **—зимаза** *f.* apozymase; **—кодеин** *m.* apocodeine; **—кринный, —криновый** *a.* apocrine (glands); **—лизин** *m.* apolysin.

аполярный *a.* apolar, nonpolar.

апо/мейоз *m.* (gen.) apomeiosis; **—миксис** *m.* (bot.) apomixis; **—миктический** *a.* apomictic; **—морфин** *m.* apomorphine; **—нал** *m.* aponal; **—невроз** *m.* (anat.) aponeurosis; **—ногетоновые** *pl.* (bot.) Aponogetonaceae.

апоплек/сический *a.*, **—тик** *m.* (med.) apoplectic; **—сия** *f.* apoplexy.

апо/репрессор *m.* aporepressor; **—рфин** *m.* aporphine; **—сафранин** *m.* aposafranine; **—сематический** *a.* (zool.) aposematic, warning (coloration); **—спория** *f.* (bot.) apospory; **—стема** *f.* (med.) apostem, abscess.

апостериорный *a.* a posteriori, empirical.

апо/стильб *m.* (illum.) apostilb (10^{-4} lambert); **—столовский** *a.* (geog.) Apostolovo; **—стоматы** *pl.* (prot.) Apostomata; **—строф** *m.*, **—строфа, —строфия** *f.* apostrophe; **—теций** *m.* (bot.) apothecium; **—фема** *f.* (math.) apothem; **—фермент** *m.* apoenzyme; **—физ** *m.* apophysis, outgrowth, offshoot; **—физарный, —физовый** *a.* apophyseal; **—филлит** *m.* (min.) apophyllite; **—фит** *m.* (bot.) apophyte; **—хинин** *m.* apoquinine; **—холевый** *a.* apocholic (acid).

апохромат *m.* apochromat, apochromatic lens; **—изм** *m.* apochromatism; **—ический** *a.* apochromatic.

апо/центр *m.* (astr.) apocenter; **—цианин** *m.* apocyanine; **—цит** *m.* (cyt.) apocyte.

аппалачский *a.* (geog.) Appalachian.

аппарат *m.* apparatus, instrument, device, contrivance, mechanism, means; equipment; staff, employees;

(phot.) camera; (space) vehicle; (reference) aid, matter, guide; subsidiary pages (of book); (petrol.) vessel; (chem.) reactor; (anat.) organs, part(s), system; **—er, —or**, e.g. **приёмный а.** receiver; **—ик** *m.* (micro-analysis) absorption tube; **—ная** *f.* instrument or control room; **—ный** *a. of* **аппарат;** **—ный** *a.* (opt.) spread (function); **—ная поддержка** (comp.) hardware; **—ная реализация** hardware implementation; **—ные средства** (comp.) hardware; **—остроение** *n.* equipment design; **а.-смеситель** *m.* mixer.

аппаратур/а *f.* apparatus, equipment, gear; instrumentation; set, outfit; **оснащать —ой** *v.* equip; **—но реализуемый** *a.* (comp.) hardware; **—ный** *a. of* **аппаратура;** hardware.

аппаратчик *m.* instrument control person.

аппарель *f.* (access) ramp.

аппенд/икс *m.* appendix; **—икула** *f.* appendicle, small appendage; **—икулярии** *pl.* (zool.) Appendicularia; **—икулярный** *a.* appendicular; **—ицит** *m.* (med.) appendicitis.

апперципироиать *v.* (ap)perceive.

аппетит *m.* appetite; **—ность** *f.* palatability; **—ный** *a.* appetizing, tasty.

аппли/ката *f.,* **ось —кат** (math.) z-coordinate, z-axis; **—катор** *m.* applicator, applier; **—кация** *f.* application; applique (work); **—ке** *n.* plated ware; **—цировать** *v.* apply.

аппозиц/ионный *a.* apposite; **—ия** *f.* apposition, juxtaposition.

аппрет *m.,* **—ирование** *n.* (text.; leather) dressing, finish, size; **—ированный** *a.* dressed; **—ировать** *v.* dress, finish, size; **—ура** *f.,* **—урный** *a.* dressing, finish(ing), size; **—урщик** *m.* dresser.

аппро— *see also under* **апро—.**

аппроксим/альность *f.* approximateness; approximation; **—альный** *a.* approximate; **—ация** *f.,* **—ирование** *n.* approximation; **—ированный** *a.* approximate(d); **—ировать** *v.* approximate; **—ируемость** *f.* approximability; **—ирующий** *a.* approximating; approximate.

апраксия *f.* (med.) apraxia.

апрель *m.,* **—ский** *a.* April.

априорный *a.* a priori, prior.

апроб/ационный *a.* approbatory; **а. акт** deed of approval, certification; **—ация** *f.* approbation; approval; certification; variety control; **—ированный** *a.* approved, officially accepted; certified; **—(ир)овать** *v.* approve; certify (seeds).

апро/тонный *a.* aprotic (acid, solvent, etc.); **—фен** *m.* (pharm.) Aprophen.

апсид/а *f.* (arch.; astr.; math.) apsis, apse; **—альный** *a.* apsidal; **—ы** *pl.* apsides.

апт *m.* (geol.) Aptian (stage).

аптека *f.* drug store, pharmacy, dispensary; **—рский** *a.* pharmaceutical; **—рь** *m.* druggist, pharmacist.

аптер/ий *m.,* **—ия** *f.* (orn.) apterium, featherless tract; **—онотовые** *pl.* (ichth.) Apteronotidae.

аптеч/ка *f.* medicine chest; first-aid kit; repair kit; **—ный** *a.* pharmaceutical; (bot.) officinalis; **—ное дело** pharmaceutics; **—ные товары** drugs, pharmaceuticals.

аптский ярус (geol.) Aptian (stage).

АПУ *abbr.* (**автоматический переключатель усиления**) automatic gain change-over switch.

апулийский *a.* (geog.) Apulia(n).

апуриновый *a.* apurinic (acid).

АПФ *abbr.* (**автоматический переключатель фильтрации**) automatic filter change-over switch; **АПЧ**

abbr. (**автоматическая подстройка частоты**) automatic frequency control, afc.

апшеронский *a.* (geog.) Apsheronsk.

а-пятно *n.* (phys.) a-spot.

ар *m.* are (100 sq.m.).

ара *f.* (orn.) Ara; **—бан** *m.* araban.

арабеск/а *f.,* **—и** *pl.* (arch.) arabesque.

араб/ин *m.* arabin; **—иновая кислота** arabic acid, *d*-tetrahydroxyvaleric acid; **—иновокислая соль** arabate; **—иноза** *f.* arabinose, gum sugar; **—ит(ол)** *m.* arabitol; **—овый** *a.* arabic (acid); **—оновый** *a.* arabonic (acid).

арабский *a.* (geog.) Arabian.

араван/овые *pl.* (ichth.) bonytongues (*Osteoglossidae*); **—ский** *a.* (geog.) Aravan.

аравийск/ий *a.* (geog.) Arab(ian), Arabic; **—ая камедь** gum arabic; **Аравия** Arabia.

арагонит *m.* (min.) aragonite.

арайан *m.* (bot.) arrayan (*Myrtus arayan*).

арак *m.* arrack (liquor).

аракановые *pl.* (ichth.) Aracanidae.

аракача *f.* (bot.) arracacha (*Arracacia*).

араксинский *a.* (geog.) Arax, Araks.

арал/иевые *pl.* (bot.) ginseng family (*Araliaceae*); **—ия** *f.* Aralia.

аралкил *m.,* **—ьный** *a.* aralkyl.

арал/окаспийский *a.* (geog.) Aral-Caspian; **—ьский** *a.* Aral (Sea).

араминировать *v.* ar(yl)aminate.

арамы *pl.* (orn.) limpkins (*Aramidae*).

аранеиды *pl.* orb-weaving spiders (*Araneidae*).

арапаймовые *pl.* (ichth.) Arapaimidae.

арапка *f.* Kafir corn (*Andropogon sorghum*).

араратский *a.* (geog.) Ararat.

арароба *f.* araroba, goa powder.

арастра *f.* (min.) drag-stone mill.

араукария *f.* (bot.) Araucaria.

арах/идный *a.* peanut; **—идоновый** *a.* arachidonic (acid); **—ин** *m.* arachin; **—иновый** *a.* arachi(di)c; **—ис** *m.,* **—исовый** *a.* peanut (*Arachis*).

арахн/иды *pl.* (zool.) arachnids; **—(о)—** *prefix* arachn(o)— (spider); arachnoid membrane); **—ология** *f.* arachnology.

арбажский *a.* (geog.) Arbazh.

арбитр *m.* arbitrator; **—аж** *m.* arbitration; **—ажный** *a.* arbitrary; official (sample); umpire (analysis).

арбо/лит *m.* wood-chip board; **—рет(ум)** *m.* arboretum; **—рицид** *m.* arboricide, sylvicide.

арбуз *m.,* **—ный** *a.* watermelon; **—инский** *a.* (geog.) Arbuzinka; **—овидный** *a.* melon-like.

арбу/скула *f.* (bot.) arbuscule; **—стерин** *m.* arbusterol; **—тин** *m.* arbutin, arbutoside.

арга/зиды *pl.* (zool.) argasids (*Argasidae*); **—зинский** *a.* (geog.) Argazi; **—ли** *m.* (mam.) argali (*Ovis ammon*); **—н** *m.* arghan (fiber); **—ндова горелка** Argand burner; **—с** *m.* (zool.) Argas; **—салинский** *a.* (geog.) Arga-Sala; **—совые** *pl.* soft ticks (*Argasidae*); **—яшский** *a.* (geog.) Argayash.

аргемон/е *m.,* **—овый** *a.* (bot.) Argemone.

аргент— *prefix* argent(i)—, silver; **—ан** *m.* argentan, German silver; **—ин** *m.* (met.; min.) argentine; **—ина** *f.* (ichth.) argentine (*Argentina*); **—иновые** *pl.* deepsea smelts (*Argentinidae*); **—инский** *a.* (geog.) Argentine, Argentinian; **—ит** *m.* (min.) argentite, silver glance.

аргенто/метр *m.* argentometer; **—метрический** *a.* argentometric; **—метрия** *f.* argentometry; **—пирит** *m.* (min.) argentopyrite.

аргилл/изация *f.* (geol.) argillization; **—ит** *m.* argillite;

mudstone; —**итовый** *a.* argillic, argillaceous; —**офит** *m.* argillophyte, clay-loving plant.

аргин/аза *f.* arginase; —**ил** *m.* arginyl; —**ин** *m.* arginine; —**инфосфат** *m.* phosphoarginine; —**инянтарный** *a.* argininosuccinic.

аргир/ея *f.* (bot.) Argyreia; —**ит** *m.* (min.) argyrite; —**ия** *f.* argyria, silver poisoning; —**о—** *prefix* argyro— (silver); *see also under* **аргенто—**; —**оз** *see* **агририя**; —**опирит** *m.* (min.) argyropyrite.

арго/л *m.* argol; —**н** *m.*, —**новый** *a.* argon, Ar; —**навт** *m.* (mal.) Argonauta; —**но-дуговой** *a.* argon-arc (welding).

аргулёз *m.* argulosis, Argulus infestation (of fish).

аргумент *m.* argument, reasoning; (math.) argument, amplitude; independent variable (of function); —**ированно** *adv.* plausibly; —**ировать** *v.* prove, argue, deduce.

аргу/нский *a.* (geog.) Argun; —**с** *m.* argus fish (*Scatophagus argus*); (orn.) argus pheasant (*Argusianus*); —**совые** *pl.* (ichth.) scats (*Scatophagidae*).

ард/атовский *a.* (geog.) Ardatov(ka); —**еннит** *m.* (min.) ardennite; —**еннский** *a.* (geog.) Ardennes; —**ометр** *m.* ardometer (pyrometer); —**онский** *a.* (geog.) Ardon.

АРЕ *abbrev.* Arab Republic of Egypt.

ареа *f.* area; *prefix* (math.) inverse hyperbolic; **а.-косинус** *m.* inverse hyperbolic cosine, cosh^{-1}.

ареакт/ивность *f.* absence of reactivity; —**ивный** *a.* non-reactive; —**огенный** *a.* not causing a reaction or side effects.

ареал *m.* (biol.) geographic range, locality, area; —**ьный** *a.* area(l).

ареа-функции *pl.* (math.) inverse hyperbolic functions.

арек/а *f.* betel palm (*Areca catechu*); —**аидин** *m.*, —**аидиновый** *a.* arecaidine; —**аин** *m.* arecaine, *n*-methylguvacine; —**овый** *a.* areca; betel (nuts); —**олин** *m.* arecoline.

арен *m.* arene, aromatic hydrocarbon.

арена *f.* arena, field, area.

аренга *f.* (bot.) Arenga.

аренд/а *f.*, **сдавать в** —**у** *v.* rent, lease.

арендалит *m.* (min.) arendalite.

аренд/атор *m.* lessee, tenant; —**ный** *a.*, —**ная плата** rent; —**ный договор** lease; —**ование** *n.* renting, leasing; —**ованный**, —**уемый** *a.* rented, leased; —**овать** *v.* rent, lease.

аренит *m.* (petr.) arenite.

Арентса сифон Arents tap (for lead).

ареол/а *f.* area; areole; (anat.) areola; —**ярный** *a.* areolar.

ареометр *m.* areometer, hydrometer; **а. для кислот** acidimeter; **нефтяной а.** densimeter, oleometer; —**ический** *a.* areometric; —**ия** *f.* areometry.

арео/пикнометр *m.* areopycnometer; —**центрический** *a.* areocentric.

арест *m.* arrest, seizure; —**ованный** *a.* arrested; —**ов(ыв)ать** *v.* arrest, seize.

арецин *m.* arecin, areca red.

аржан/ец *m.* (bot.) timothy (*Phleum*); —**ница** *f.* Heleochloa.

арзгирский *a.* (geog.) Arzgir.

арибин *m.* aribine, loturine.

арид/ность *f.* aridity; —**ный** *a.* arid; —**офильный** *a.* xerophilous, drought-resistant.

ариевые *pl.* sea catfishes (*Ariidae*).

аризема *f.* (bot.) Arisaema.

аризон/ит *m.* (min.; petr.) arizonite; —**ский** *a.* (geog.) Arizona.

арил *m.* aryl; —**амин** *m.* arylamine; —**аминировать** *v.*

ar(yl)aminate; —**аминопроизводное** *n.* arylamino derivative; —**арсоновый** *a.* aromatic arsonic (acid); —**ирование** *n.* arylation; —**ировать** *v.* arylate.

ариллус *m.* (bot.) aril(lus).

арил/сульфокислота *f.* arylsulfonic acid; —**ьный** *a.* aryl; —**эстераза** *f.* arylesterase.

ариоммовые *pl.* (ichth.) Ariommidae.

арион/иды, —**овые** *pl.* (mal.) Arionidae.

арист/а *f.* (bot.) arista, awn; (ent.) arista; —**ида** *f.* (bot.) Aristida; —**олохин** *m.* aristolochine; —**олохия** *f.* (bot.) Aristolochia; —**отелев(ский)** *a.* Aristotelian, Aristotle's; —**охин(ин)** *m.* aristochin, aristoquinine.

арит *m.* (min.) arite.

аритм/ический, —**ичный** *a.* arrhythmic; —**ичность** *f.* arrhythmic nature; —**ия** *f.* (med.) arrhythmia.

ариус *m.* a sea catfish (*Arius*).

арифмет/ика *f.* arithmetic; —**ический** *a.* arithmetical; —**ический ряд** arithmetical progression; —**ическое устройство** (comp.) arithmetic unit; **среднее** —**ическое** arithmetical mean.

арифмометр *m.* arithmometer, calculating or adding machine, adder.

арицин *m.* aricine, quinovatine.

АРК *abbrev.* (**автоматический радиокомпас**) automatic direction finder, ADF.

арк— *prefix* (math.) arc—, inverse, anti—.

арка *f.* arc(h); (mal.) ark shell (*Arca*); —**да** *f.* (arch.) arcade.

аркадакский *a.* (geog.) Arkadak.

аркал *m.* (mam.) ark(h)al (*Ovis orientalis*).

аркан *m.* lasso, loop.

арканз/ас *m.* Arkansas stone; —**асский** *a.* (geog.) Arkansas; —**ит** *m.* (min.) arkansite.

аркан/ит *m.* (min.) arcanite; —**овые** *pl.* (ichth.) Arcanidae.

арканчик *m.* (zool.) lasso cell.

аркатн/ый *a.*, —**ая связь** harness.

аркатом *m.* atomic-hydrogen welding.

аркверит *m.* (min.) arquerite.

арк/косеканс *m.* (math.) arc or inverse cosecant, cosec^{-1}; —**косинус** *m.* arc cosine, cos^{-1}; —**котангенс** *m.* arc cotangent, cot^{-1}; —**овидный** *a.* arcuate, arched; —**овые** *pl.* (mal.) ark shells (*Arcidae*); —**оген** *m.* (welding) arcogen.

аркоз *m.*, —**а** *f.* (petr.) arkose.

аркообразный *a.* arched, arcuate.

арк/секанс *m.* (math.) arc or inverse secant, sec^{-1}; —**синус** *m.* arc sine, sin^{-1}; —**тангенс** *m.* arc tangent, tan^{-1}.

Арктика Arctic regions.

арктический *a.* arctic, northern.

аркто— *prefix* arcto— (bear; north); —**гейский** *a.* (biogeog.) Arctogaean; —**цебус** *m.* (mam.) golden potto (*Arctocebus*).

арк(ус-)функция *f.* (math.) inverse trigonometric function.

арлекиновый *a.* harlequin (snake).

арм., арм— *abbr., prefix* army; Armenian.

АРМ *abbr.* (**автоматизированное рабочее место**) (comp.) workstation.

армавирский *a.* (geog.) Armavir.

армадиллы *pl.* (mam.) armadillos.

арматур/а *f.* fittings, fixtures, accessories, hardware; outfit, equipment; mounting, framework; reinforcement; (biol.; elec.) armature; **а. котла** boiler fittings; —**ный** *a.* of **арматура;** reinforcing, reinforced.

армейский *a.* army.

армерия *f.* (bot.) Armeria.

армиллярный *a.* armillary, ring-like.

арминженер *m.* army engineer.

армир/ование *n.* reinforcement; **—ованный** *a.* reinforced, etc. *see v.*; wire (glass); **—овать** *v.* reinforce, armor, sheathe, support; **—ующий** *a.* reinforcing.

армия *f.* army, troops.

армко-железо *n.* (met.) Armco iron.

армо/каменный *a.* reinforced stone; **—пенобетонный** *a.* reinforced foam-concrete; **—цемент** *m.* ferrocement, reinforced concrete.

армянский *a.* Armenian.

арнаутка *f.* hard wheat (*Triticum durum*).

арн/ебия *f.* (bot.) Arnebia; **—и** *m.* (mam.) Indian buffalo (*Bubalus b.*); **—ика** *f.* (bot.) Arnica; **—ицин** *m.* arnicin; **—оглосс** *m.* (ichth.) Arnoglossus; **—ольдовский** *a.* Arnold's.

ароидные *pl.* (bot.) arum family (*Araceae*).

арок *gen. pl. of* **арка**.

аромат *m.* aroma, scent, fragrance; (wine) flavor; **—изатор** *m.* aromatic ingredient; flavoring material; odorant; **—изация** *f.* aromatization; **—изированный** *a.* aromatized; **—изировать** *v.* aromatize, convert into aromatic hydrocarbons; flavor; **—ика** *f.,* **—ический,** **—(ич)ный** *a.* aromatic; **—ический ряд** aromatic series; **—ическое вещество** aromatic principle; **—ичность** *f.* aroma; aromatic nature; **—ообразователь** *m.* aroma-producing oraganism.

ароморфоз *m.* (gen.) aromorphosis.

арон/ия *f.* (bot.) Aronia; **—ник** *see* **арум**.

ароч/ка *dim. of* **арка**; **—ный** *a.* arch(ed).

аррен/ал *m.* arrhenal, sodium methyl arsenite; **уравнение А—иуса** Arrhenius equation; **—о—** *prefix* arrheno— (male); **—оид** *m.,* **—оидный** *a.* (gen.) arrhenoid; **—отокия** *f.* arrhenotoky.

арретир *m.* arrest(er), stop, catch, detent, checking device; locking device; **без —а** nonlocking (key).

арретиров/ание *n.* arresting, etc. *see v.*; **—анный** *a.* arrested, etc., *see v.*; **—ать** *v.* arrest, stop, catch, check; hold, lock, secure; cage; **—ка** *see* **арретир**; **—(оч)ный** *a.* arresting, stop(ping).

аррип *m.* (ichth.) Arripis; **—(ис)овые** *pl.* Arripidae; **—ус** *see* **аррип**.

арройо *n.* arroyo, dry water course.

арро(у)рут *m.* arrowroot (a starch).

арс/аниловая кислота arsanilic acid, *p*-aminophenylarsinic acid; **—ацетин** *m.* arsacetin, acetylatoxyl; **—еназо** *n.* arsenazo indicator.

арсенал *m.,* **—ьный** *a.* arsenal, store(s); armory.

арсен/ат *m.* arsenate; **—диметил** *m.* dimethylarsine; **—ид** *m.* arsenide; **—ик** *m.* arsenic, *see also* **мышьяк**; **—иосидерит** *m.* (min.) arseniosiderite; **—ировать** *v.* arsenate; **—ит** *m.* arsenite.

арсено— *prefix* arseno—; **—бензол** *m.* arsenobenzene; **—бисмит** *m.* (min.) arsenobismite; **—зосоединение** *n.* arsenoso compound; **—ксид** *m.* arsenoxide; **—лит** *m.* (min.) arsenolite, white arsenic; **—пирит** *m.* (min.) arsenopyrite, mispickel; **—соединение** *n.* arseno compound; **—феррит** *m.* (min.) arsenoferrite, iron arsenide.

арсеньевский *a.* (geog.) Arsenyev.

арс/ил *m.* arsyl; **—илен** *m.* arsylene; **—ин** *m.* arsine, arsenous hydride; **—инистый** *a.* arsinous; **—ино—** *prefix* arsino—; **—иновый** *a.* arsonic; (sometimes) arsinic.

арский *a.* (geog.) Arsk.

арсмаль *m.* a copper-arsenic insecticide.

арсон/иевый *a.,* **—ий** *m.* arsonium.

арсфенамин *m.* arsphenamine, Salvarsan.

арт. *abbr.,* **арт—** *prefix* artillery; **АРТ** *abbr.* (адсорбер распыливающего типа) spray chamber.

арта/ботрин *m.* artabotrine; **—н** *m.* artane.

артачиться *v.* be restive (of horse); be obstinate.

арташатский *a.* (geog.) Artashat.

артедиеллус *m.* (ichth.) Artediellus.

артезианский *a.* artesian (well).

артель *f.,* **—ный** *a.* artel, cooperative; crew (of workers); **сельскохозяйственная а.** collective farm.

артем/иевые *pl.* (zool.) brine shrimps (*Artemiidae*); **—изин** *m.* artemisin, oxysantonin; **—изия** *f.* (bot.) Artemisia; **—ия** *f.* (zool.) Artemia; **—овский** *a.* (geog.) Artem(ovsk).

артер/енол *m.* arterenol (hormone); **—иализация** *f.* arterialization; **—иальный** *a.* arterial; **—иит** *m.* (med.) arteritis; **—ийка** *f.* (anat.) arteriole; **—ио—** *prefix* arterio—, artery; **—иола** *f.* arteriole; **—иосклероз** *m.* (med.) arteriosclerosis; **—ия** *f.* artery.

арт/ефакт *m.* artifact; **—икль** *m.* (bot.) article (joint); **—икский** *a.* (geog.) Artik; **—икул** *m.* type of merchandise.

артикул/ировать *v.* articulate; **—яты** *pl.* (zool.) Articulata; **—ятор** *m.* (med.) articulator; **—яционный** *a.,* **—яция** *f.* articulation, intelligibility, distinctness; **расстройство —яции** (med.) dysarthria.

артиллер/ийский *a.* artillery; **—ийскотехнический** *a.* (mil.) ordnance; **—ист** *m.* artillery-man; **—ия** *f.* artillery.

артинский *a.* (geog.) Arti.

артист *m.* artist; **—ический** *a.* artistic.

артишок *m.* (bot.) artichoke (*Cynara*).

артр— *see* **артро—**; **—альгия** *f.* arthralgia, joint pain; **—ит** *m.* arthritis; **—итик** *m.,* **—итический,** **—итный** *a.* arthritic; **—о—** *prefix* arthr(o)— (joint, articulation); **—опатия** *f.* arthropathy, joint disease; **—оспора** *f.* (bot.) arthrospore.

АРУ *abbr.* (автоматическое регулирование усиления) automatic gain control, AGC.

арум *m.* (bot.) arum.

арун *m.* (mam.) arui (*Ovis tragelaphus*).

арунд/инария *f.* (bot.) Arundinaria; **тростниковый —о** giant reed (*Arundo donax*).

арфа *f.* harp; (agr.) cribble, sieve; (aeolian) tones; (mal.) harp shell (*Harpa*).

арфведсонит *m.* (min.) arfvedsonite.

арфообразный *a.* harp(-shaped).

арх— *see* **архи—**; **архивный; архитектурный; —аический, —аичный** *a.* archaic; **—аллаксис** *m.* (zool.) archallaxis; **—ангелика** *f.* (bot.) Archangelica; **—ангельский** *a.* (geog.) Archangel(sk); **—ар** *m.* argali, Marco Polo sheep (*Ovis ammon*); **—аринский** *a.* (geog.) Arkhara; **—бюро** *n.* bureau of archives.

архегон/иальный *a.* (bot.) archegonial; **—иеносец** *m.* archegoniophore; **—ий** *m.* archegonium.

арх/едиктион *m.* (ent.) archedictyon, **—ей** *m.,* **—ейский** *a.* (geol.) Archean; **—ентерон** *m.* (embr.) archenteron, archigaster.

архео— *prefix* arch(a)eo— (ancient); **—зой** *m.,* **—зойский** *a.* (geol.) archeozoic; **—лог** *m.* archeologist; **—логический** *a.* archeological; **—логия** *f.* archeology; **—птерикс** *m.* (pal.) Archaeopteryx; **—фит** *m.* (bot.) arch(a)eophyte; **—циаты** *pl.* Archaeocyathidae.

архе/спориальный *a.* (bot.) archesporial; **—спорий** *m.* archespore; **—тип** *m.* (biol.) archetype.

архи— *prefix* arch(i)— (first, original; chief; ancient; principal, extreme, great); **—аннелиды** *pl.* marine worms (*Archiannelida*); **—бентический** *a.* (biol.) archibenthic; **—бластический** *a.* (embr.) archiblastic.

архив *m.,* **—ный** *a.* archives, records, file(s); **—ариус** *m.* archives custodian.

архи/гаструла *f.* (embr.) archigastrula; **—карп(ий)** *m.* (bot.) archicarp; **—медова сила** buoyancy force; **—медов(ский)**, **—медовый** *a.* Archimedean, Archimedes'; **—мицеты** *pl.* (bot.) Archimycetes; **—пелаг** *m.,* **—пелагский,** **—пелажный** *a.* (geog.) archipelago; **—птеригий** *m.* archipterygium (primitive fin); **—тевтис** *m.* (mal.) squid (*Architeuthis*).

архитект/оника *f.* architectonics, structural design; **—онический** *a.* architectonic; **—ор** *m.* architect; **—ура** *f.* architecture; **—урный** *a.* architectural.

арцелла *f.* (prot.) Arcella.

арцизский *a.* (geog.) Artsiz.

АРЧ *abbr.* (**автоматическое регулирование частоты**) automatic frequency control, AFC; (**автоматическое регулирование чувствительности**) automatic sensitivity control, ASC.

арча *f.* (bot.) juniper (*Juniperus*).

арчак *m.* saddle tree; pommel; (tech.) bow.

арч/евник *m.* (bot.) juniper stand; **—евый, —овый** *a.* juniper.

аршин *m.,* **—ный** *a.* arshine (0.71 m).

ары/к *m.* irrigation ditch; **—чный** *a. of* **арык**; ditch (irrigation).

а-с *see* **а-сек.**

аса *f.,* **—н** *m.,* **—фетида** *f.* asafetida (a gum resin).

асб *abbr.* (**апостильб**) apostilb.

асбест *m.* (min.) asbestos; **—ин** *m.* asbestine; **—ировать** *v.* line or cover with asbestos; **—ит** *m.* asbestos insulation; **—обетон** *m.* asbestos concrete; **—овидный** *a.* asbestiform, fibrous; **—овый** *a.* asbestos; **—опластик** *m.* asbestos plastic; **—оцемент** *see* **асбоцемент;** **—шифер** *m.* asbestos roofing shingles; **а.-сырец** *m.* crude asbestos.

асбо— *prefix* asbestos; **—бумага** *f.* asbestos paper; **—картон** *m.* asbestos board; **—лан** *m.* (min.) asbolane, asbolite; **—наполненный** *a.* asbestos-filled; **—пеколит** *m.* asbopekolite (asbestos-pitch composition); **—пластик** *m.* asbestos plastic; **—труба** *f.* asbestos-cement pipe; **—фанера** *f.* asbestos-cement sheeting; **—цемент** *m.,* **—цементный** *a.* asbestos cement; **—шифер** *m.* asbestos roofing; corrugated asbestos sheets.

асейсмический *a.* (geol.) aseismic.

а-сек *abbr.* (**ампер-секунда**) ampere-second.

асек/вентный *a.* asequential; **—еевский** *a.* (geog.) Asekeyevo; **—суальный** *a.* asexual.

асепт/ика *f.* (med.) asepsis; **—ический** *a.* aseptic.

АСИ *abbr.* (**амплитудный селектор импульсов**) pulse height selector.

асидерит *m.* (min.) asiderite.

асидол *m.* acidol (naphthenic acid mixture); **—мылонафт** *m.* naphthenic soap and acid mixture.

асиминин *m.* asiminine.

асимметр *m.* asymmeter; **—ический, —ичный** *a.* asymmetric; **—ичность, —ия** *f.* asymmetry, skewness; **—ичность свойств** (phys.) anisotropy.

асимпто/мный *a.* asymptomatic, showing no symptoms; **—та** *f.* (geom.) asymptote; **—тика** *f.* asymptotics; **—тический** *a.* asymptotic; **—тичность** *f.* asymptotic property.

асин/апсис *m.* (gen.) asynapsis; **—дез** *m.* (med.) asyndesis; **—ергия** *f.* asynergy, faulty coordination; **—овский** *a.* (geog.) Asino.

асинхрон/изм *m.* asynchronism; **—(ич)ный** *a.* asynchronous, nonsynchronous; induction (motor).

асистолия *f.* (med.) asystolia, cardiac arrest.

аск *m.* (bot.) ascus, sac.

аскан/гель *m.* a bentonite clay preparation; **—ийский** *a.* Ascanian (sheep); **—ит** *m.* askanite (clay).

аскарид/а *f.* ascarid, roundworm (*Ascaris*); **—иаз, —оз** *m.* ascar(id)iasis, ascarid infestation; **—ол** *m.* ascaridole.

аскарит *m.* Ascarite (asbestos material).

аскарицид *m.* ascaricide.

аскизский *a.* (geog.) Askiz.

аскинский *a.* (geog.) Askino.

аско— *prefix* asc(o)— (bag, bladder); **—генный** *a.* (bot.) ascogenous; **—гон(ий)** *m.* ascogonium; **—лизация** *f.,* **—лирование** *n.* Ascoli test (for anthrax).

аскольдовский *a.* (geog.) Askold.

аскомицеты *pl.* (bot.) Ascomycetes.

аскорбин/ат *m.* ascorbate; **—овый** *a.* ascorbic (acid); **—оксидаза** *f.* ascorbate oxidase.

аскоспор/а *f.,* **—овый** *a.* (bot.) ascospore.

аскохитоз *m.* (phyt.) Ascochyta blight.

асманит *m.* (min.) asmanite.

аспарагин *m.* asparagine; **—аза** *f.* asparaginase; **—овый** *a.* aspartic, aminosuccinic (acid); **—овокислая соль** aspartate.

аспарт/аза *f.* aspartase; **—ил** *m.* aspartyl; **—овый** *a.* aspartic (acid).

аспект *m.* aspect, appearance; (classification) facet; **—нокарточный** *a.* card per item, feature card (system); **—ный** *a.* feature, subject, term (card).

аспергилл/ёз *m.* (med.) aspergillosis; (phyt.) Aspergillus blight; **—ин** *m.* aspergillin; **—овый** *a.* aspergillic (acid).

аспид *m.* shale, slate; (herp.) asp; *prefix see* **аспидо—**; **—ин** *m.* aspidin; **—инол** *m.* aspidinol; **—ноголубой** *a.* slate blue; **—ный** *a.* slate, slaty; **—ный сланец, —ная доска** slate; blackboard; **—о—** *prefix* aspid(o)— (shield); **—огастер** *m.* (zool.) Aspidogaster; **—офороидес** *m.* alligator fish (*Aspidophoroides,* spec. *A. monopterygius*).

аспиндзский *a.* (geog.) Aspindza.

аспирант *m.* aspirant, post-graduate (student); **—ура** *f.* post-graduate work, course or students; **—урский** *a.* post-graduate.

аспир/атор *m.* aspirator, suction apparatus, exhauster; dust separator; **—ационный** *a.,* **—ация** *f.,* **—ирование** *n.* aspiration, suction; air cleaning; winnowing (of grain).

аспирин *m.* aspirin, acetylsalicylic acid.

аспит *m.* shield volcano.

асплен/ий, —иум *m.* (bot.) spleenwort (*Asplenium*); **—ический** *a.* (med.) asplenic.

аспорогенн/ость *f.* (biol.) asporogenicity; **—ый** *a.* asporogenic.

аспредовые *pl.* banjo catfishes (*Aspredinidae*).

ассамбл/ея *f.* assembly, convention; **—яж** *m.* assemblage, collection.

ассамский *a.* (geog.) Assam.

ассафетида *see* **асафетида.**

ассектатор *m.* (ecol.) assector.

ассениз/атор *m.* sanitation worker, sewage-disposal worker; **—ационный** *a.* sanitary, sanitation; sewage (pump); **—ационное устройство** waste management system; **—ация** *f.* sanitation; sewage disposal; ;**—ировать** *v.* make sanitary.

ассигн/ование *n.,* **—овка** *f.* assigning, assignment, etc. *see v.;* grant; **—ов(ыв)ать** *v.* assign, allot, allocate, appropriate, grant.

ассимил/ирование *n.* assimilation; **—ированный** *a.* assimilated; **—ировать** *v.* assimilate; **—ируемый** *a.* assimilable; **—ятивный** *a.* assimilative; **—ятор** *m.* assimilator; —**яторный** *a.* assimilatory; —**яционный** *a.,* —**яция** *f.* assimilation.

асс/инский *a.* (geog.) Assa; —**ирийский** *a.* Assyrian.

ассист/ент *m.,* —**ентка** *f.* assistant; —**ировать** *v.* assist.

ассортимент *m.* assortment, choice, selection; set; broad range, wide variety; (frequency) distribution; (product) line; product mix.

ассоци/ативность *f.* (math.) associativity; —**ативный** *a.* associative; community (ecology); —**ации-близнецы** *pl.* twin associations; —**ационный** *a.* association; —**ация** *f.* association; —**ированный** *a.* associated, etc., *see v.*; —**ировать(ся)** *v.* associate, unite, combine (with); —**ирующий** *a.* associating; —**ула** *f.* (geobot.) associule; —**я** *f.* associes.

астабилизация *f.* astabilization.

астазиров/ание *n.* (phys.) astatizing; —**ать** *v.* astatize, render astatic.

астазирующий *a.* labilizing (force).

астазия *f.* (med.) astasia.

астар/инский *a.* (geog.) Astara; —**та** *f.* (mal.) Astarte.

астат/(ий), —**ин** *m.* astatine, At; —**ический** *a.* astatic, nonstatic, unstable; floating (action, etc.); —**ичность** *f.* astaticism.

астен— *prefix* asthen(o)— (weak); —**ический** *a.* (med.) asthenic; —**ия** *f.* asthenia; —**осфера** *f.* (geol.) asthenosphere.

астер *m.* (gen.) aster; *prefix* aster(o)— (star); —**изм** *m.* (cryst.) asterism; —**ин** *m.* asterin; —**иск** *m.* asterisk, star; —**оид** *m.,* —**оидный** *a.* (astr.) asteroid.

астианакс *m.* (ichth.) Astyanax.

астигмат *m.* astigmat, astigmatic lens; —**изм** *m.* (med.; opt.) astigmatism; —**ический** *a.* astigmatic.

астильбе *f.* (bot.) Astilbe.

астма *f.* (med.) asthma; —**тик** *m.,* —**тический** *a.* asthmatic.

астоматы *pl.* (prot.) Astomata.

Астона закон Aston rule (of isotopes).

астра *f.* (bot.) aster.

астрабадский *a.* (geog.) Astrabad.

астрагал *m.* (bot.) Astragalus; (anat.) astragalus, ankle bone.

астра/лин *m.* astral oil, kerosene; —**лит** *m.* (glass; expl.) astralite; —**льный** *a.* astral, star; —**нция** *f.* (bot.) Astrantia; —**ханит** *m.* (min.) astrak(h)anite; —**ханский** *a.* (geog.) Astrakhan.

астрингентный *a.* astringent.

астро— *prefix* astro— (star); celestial, astronomical; —**биология** *f.* astrobiology; —**блеповые** *pl.* (ichth.) Astroblepidae; —**ботаника** *f.* astrobotany; —**геология** *f.* astrogeology; —**граф** *m.* astrograph; —**графирование** *n.* astrography; —**графический** *a.* astrographic; —**датчик** *m.* star tracker; —**динамика** *f.* astrodynamics; —**ида** *f.,* —**идный** *a.* (geom.) astroid; —**камера** *f.* astrocamera, astronomical camera; —**кариум** *m.* (bot.) Astrocaryum; —**климат** *m.* astroclimate; —**компас** *m.* astrocompass; —**коррекция** *f.* stellar monitoring; —**купол** *m.* astrodome; —**люк** *m.* astrohatch; —**лябия** *f.* astrolabe (instrument); —**метрия** *f.* astrometry.

астронав/едение *n.* star tracking, celestial guidance; —**игационный** *a.,* —**игация** *f.* astronavigation, star tracking; —**т** *m.* astronaut; —**тика** *f.* astronautics; —**тический** *a.* astronautical.

астро/нестовые *pl.* (ichth.) snaggletooths (*Astronesthidae*); —**ном** *m.* astronomer; —**номический** *a.* astronomical; —**номия** *f.* astronomy.

астроориент/атор *m.* astrotracker, star tracker; —**ация** *f.,* —**ировка** *f.* celestial navigation, star tracking.

астро/спектроскопия *f.* astrospectroscopy, stellar spectroscopy; —**сфера** *f.* (gen.) astrosphere; —**труба** *f.* astronomical telescope; —**физика** *f.* astrophysics; —**филлит** *m.* (min.) astrophyllite; —**фотография** *f.* astrophotography, celestial photography; —**фотометрия** *f.* astrophotometry; —**химия** *f.* cosmochemistry; —**цит** *m.* (cyt.) astrocyte.

АСУ *abbr.* (**автоматизированная система управления**) automated control system.

АСУП *abbr.* (**автоматизированная система управления производством**) computer-aided manufacturing, CAM.

асфальт *m.* asphalt; —**ен** *m.* asphaltene; —**ирование** *n.* asphalting; —**ированный** *a.* asphalted; —**ировать** *v.* asphalt, pave (with asphalt); —**ит** *m.* (min.) asphaltite; —**ный** *see* **асфальтовый**.

асфальтобетон *m.,* —**ный** *a.* asphalt concrete; —**осмеситель** *m.* asphalt concrete mixer; —**оукладчик** *m.* asphalt concrete paver.

асфальто/вый *a.* asphalt(ic), asphalt-bearing, asphalt-base (oil); —**геновые кислоты** asphaltogenic or polynaphthenic acids; —**подобный** *a.* asphalt-like; —**распределитель** *m.* asphalt spreader; —**смеситель** *m.* asphalt mixer; —**укладчик** *m.* aphalt paver.

асферический *a.* aspherical, nonspherical.

асфиксия *f.* (med.) asphyxia.

асфод/елина *f.* (bot.) asphodeline; —**ель,** —**иль** *f.* asphodel (*Asphodelus*).

асхистовый *a.* (petr.) aschistic.

асц/елихтовые *pl.* (ichth.) Ascelichthyidae; —**ендент** *m.* (meteor.) ascendent; —**идии** *pl.* (zool.) Ascidia; —**ит** *m.* (med.) ascites, abdominal dropsy; —**итический,** —**итный** *a.* ascitic.

ат *abbr.* (**атмосфера техническая**) technical atmosphere; **ат.** *abbr.* (**атомный**) atomic; **Ат** *abbr.* (**антитело**) antibody, Ab.

ата *abbr.* (**атмосфера абсолютная**) absolute atmosphere, abs. atm.

атабрин *m.* Atabrine, quinacrine.

атав/изм *m.* (biol.) atavism, throwback; —**истический** *a.* atavistic.

атайка *f.* red duck (*Tadorna ferruginea*).

атака *f.* attack, assault; incidence; breakdown, decomposition; **мозговая а.** brainstorming.

атакамит *m.* (min.) atacamite.

атаковать *v.* attack, assault, charge; corrode, eat (away).

атак/сит *m.* ataxite (meteorite); —**сический,** —**тический** *a.* atactic, ataxic, irregular, random; —**сия** *f.* (physiol.) ataxia; —**тичность** *f.* atacticity.

атакуем/ость *f.* vulnerability, susceptibility; —**ый** *a.* vulnerable, susceptible.

атаманствовать *v.* be in command.

атба/сарка *f.* a locust (*Dociostaurus kraussi*); —**сарский** *a.* (geog.) Atbasar; —**шинский** *a.* Atbashi.

ат. в. *abbr.* (**атомный вес**) atomic weight.

Атвуда машина Atwood's machine.

атебрин *see* **атабрин**.

ат. ед. массы *see* AEM.

ател/ектаз *m.* (med.) atelectasis; —**ектатический** *a.* atelectatic, marginal; —**еоповые** *pl.* (ichth.) Ateleopidae; —**ит** *m.* (min.) atelite; —**о—** *prefix* atelo— (imperfect, incomplete).

ателье *n.* studio; workshop.

атерин/а, —**ка** *f.* (ichth.) silverside (*Atherina*); —**иды,** —**овые,** —**ы** *pl.* Atherinidae.

атеро— *prefix* athero— [groats, meal; (med.) atheroma]; **—генный** *a.* (med.) atherogenic; **—ма** *f.* atheroma; **—склероз** *m.* atherosclerosis; **—спермин** *m.* atherospermine.

атетоз *m.* (med.) athetosis, mobile spasm.

ати *abbr.* (**атмосфера избыточная**) gage atmosphere.

атизин *m.* atisine.

атипический *a.* atypical, irregular.

атирео/з *m.* (med.) athyreosis, hypothyroidism; **—идный** *a.* athyreoid.

аткарский *a.* (geog.) Atkarsk.

Аткинсона проба *Atkinson test.*

атлант *m.* (anat.) atlas.

атлант/ический *a.* Atlantic; **—о—** *prefix* atlanto— (Atlantic; atlantal; huge creature); **—озатылочный** *a.* (anat.) atloido-occipital, atlanto-occipital.

атлас *m.* (text.) satin; (anat.; geog.) atlas; (color) chart; **—истый** *a.* satin(y); **—истый шпат** (min.) satin spar; **—ит** *m.* (min.) atlasite; **—ить** *v.* make as smooth as satin; **—ный** *a. of* атлас; silklike; **—ное дерево** satinwood.

атлет *m.* athlete; **—ика** *f.* athletics.

атм *abbr.* (**атмосфера физическая**).

атм. *abbr.* (**атмосфера; атмосферный**).

атм—, —о— *prefix* atm(o)— (atmospheric; steam, vapor); **—идометр** *see* атмометр; **—огенический** *a.* (petr.) atmogenic; **—огенный** *a.* atmospheric; **—олиз** *m.* (gas separation) atmolysis; **—олит** *m.* (geol.) atmolith; **—ометр** *m.* atm(id)ometer, evaporimeter; **—остойкий** *a.* weatherproof; **—остойкость, —оустойчивость** *f.* weather stability, resistance to weather(ing).

атмосфера *f.* atmosphere; air; **а. абсолютная** absolute atmosphere; **а. избыточная** gage or excess atmosphere; **а. нормальная, а. стандартная, а. физическая** normal, standard or physical atmposhere (760 mm of Hg column); **а. техническая** technical atmosphere (735.5 mm of Hg column).

атмосфер/ик *m.* atmospheric disturbance; **—ика** *f.* atmospherics; **—ический, —ный** *a.* atmospheric (precipitation, pressure, etc.); air, vent (tube); **—остойкий, —оустойчивый** *a.* weatherproof.

атмофильный *a.* atmophile (elements).

ат. н. *abbr.* (**атомный номер**).

атоксил *m.* atoxyl, sodium arsanilate; **—овый** *a.* atoxylic, arsanilic (acid).

атоксический *a.* atoxic, nonpoisonous.

атолл *m.,* **—овый** *a.* (geog.) atoll.

атом *m.* atom; **вес —а** atomic weight; **знак —а** atomic symbol; **однородные —ы** atoms of the same element; **разнородные —ы** atoms of different elements; **порядковое число —ов** atomic number; **а.-акцептор** acceptor atom; **—арный** *a.* atomic; nascent; **а.-донор** *m.* donor atom; **а.-заместитель** *m.* substituting atom.

атомиз/атор *m.* atomizer; **—ация** *f.* atomization; **—ировать** *v.* atomize.

атом/изм *m.* atomism, atomic theory; **—изобар** *m.* (nucl.) isobar; **—истика** *f.* atom(ist)ics; atomic theory; **—истический** *a.* atom(ist)ic; **—ический** *a.* atomic; **—ник** *m.* nuclear scientist.

атомно/водородный *a.* atomic-hydrogen (welding); **—молекулярный** *a.* atomic (theory); **—сть** *f.* atomicity, valence, valency; basicity (of alcohols).

атомн/ый *a.* atomic; nuclear (physics, reactor, etc.); nuclear-powered (vessel); *suffix* **—гидрид** (alcohol); **а. вес** atomic weight; **а. номер, —ое (порядковое) число** atomic number; **а. объём** atomic volume; **—ая**

единица веса atomic weight unit, awu; **—ая единица массы** atomic mass unit, amu; **—ая техника** nucleonics; **—ая энергия** atomic energy; nuclear power; **—ое обозначение** atomic symbol; **—ое учение** atomic theory.

атомо— *prefix* atomic; nuclear-powered; **—воз** *m.* nuclear-powered locomotive; **—ход** *m.* nuclear-powered vessel.

атон/альный *a.* (acous.) atonal; **—ический** *a.* (med.) atonic; **—ия** *f.* atony.

атоп/ический *a.* atopic; **—ия** *f.* atopy, hereditary allergy; **—омиктер** *m.* (ichth.) Atopomycterus.

атофан *m.* Atophan, cinchophen.

атравматический *a.* atraumatic, non-injuring.

атразин *m.* Atrazine (herbicide).

атрактиловый *a.* atractylic (acid).

атрезия *f.* (med.) atresia.

атрепсия *f.* (med.) athrepsia, marasmus.

атриальный *a.* (anat.; zool.) atrial.

атрибут *m.* attribute, property, quality; **—ивный** *a.* attributive.

атр/ий *m.* (anat.; zool.) atrium; **—ио—** *prefix* atrio—, atrium; **—иовентрикулярный** *a.* atrioventricular; **—иум** *m.* atrium; **—их** *m.* Atrichum (moss); **—ихоз** *m.* atrichosis, body baldness.

атро— *prefix* atro— (atropine; black and); **—глицериновый** *a.* atroglyceric (acid); **—ментин** *m.* atromentin; **—молочный** *a.* atrolactic, α-phenyllactic (acid).

атроп/а *f.* (bot.) deadly nightshade (*Atropa belladonna*); **—амин** *m.* atropamine, apoatropine; **—ин** *m.,* **—иновый** *a.* atropine, *dl*-hyoscyamine; **—ный** *a.* (bot.) atropous; **—овый** *a.* atropic, α-phenylacrylic (acid); **—оизомерия** *f.* atropoisomerism.

атросцин *m.* atroscine, *i*-scopolamine.

атроф/ированный *a.* atrophied, shrunken; **—ироваться** *v.* atrophy; **—ический** *a.* atrophic; **—ия** *f.* atrophy, wasting away.

АТС *abbr.* (**автоматическая телефонная станция**) automatic telephone exchange; **приборы АТС** dialing equipment.

аттеню/атор *m.* attenuator; **—ация** *f.* attenuation; **—ированный** *a.* attenuated, thinned, weakened.

аттест/ат *m.* certificate; reference, recommendation; (mil.) allotment; **—ационный** *a.,* **—ация** *f.* certification, etc., *see v.*; **—ованный** *a.* certified, fully qualified; **—ов(ыв)ать** *v.* certify, testify; recommend.

атти/к *m.,* **—ческий** *a.* (anat.) attic.

атто— *prefix* atto— (10^{-18}).

аттрактант *m.* attractant, lure.

аттрит *m.* (geol.) attritus.

АТФ *abbr.* (**аденозинтрифосфат**) adenosine triphosphate, ATP; **АТФ-аза** adenosine triphosphatase, ATPase.

атюрьевский *a.* (geog.) Atyurevo.

атяшевский *a.* (geog.) Atyashevo.

АУ *abbr.* (**автоматическое управление**) automatic control; (**активированный уголь**) activated carbon; (**арифметическое устройство**) arithmetic unit.

аугментация *f.* augmentation, increase.

ауди/альный *a.* audio; **—о—** *prefix* audi(o)— (hearing); **—овизуальный** *a.* audiovisual; **—ограмма** *f.* (med.) audiogram; **—олог** *m.* audiologist; **—ометр** *m.* audiometer; **—ометрия** *f.* audiometry; **—он** *m.* (rad.) audion; **—тория** *f.* auditorium, lecture room; audience; **—фон** *m.* hearing aid.

Ауески болезнь (vet.) Aujeszky's disease, pseudorabies.

аукс— *prefix* aux—, auxan(o)— (increase, growth);

—аномет *m.* auxanometer; **—илиарный, —илярный** *a.* auxiliary; **—ин** *m.* auxin (plant hormone); **—отроф** *m.* (gen.) auxotroph; **—охром** *m.*, **—охромная группа** auxochrome.

аукуб/а *f.* (bot.) Aucuba; (phyt.) aucuba potato mosaic; **—ин** *m.* aucubin.

аукцион *m.*, **—ный** *a.* auction.

аул/акомний *m.* Aulocomnium (moss); **—ейка** *f.* (orn.) old squaw (*Clangula hyemalis*); **—о—** *prefix* (biol.) aulo— (tubular structure); **—оп** *m.* (ichth.) yellowfin (*Aulopus*); **—оповые** *pl.* Aulopidae; **—оринховые** *pl.* tubesnouts (*Aulorhynchidae*); **—офит** *m.* (bot.) aulophyte.

аур— *see* **аури—**; **—а** *f.* (med.) aura; **—амин** *m.*, **—аминовый** *a.* auramine; **—анция** *f.* aurantia (dye); **—ат** *m.* aurate; **—ата** *f.* (ichth.) gilthead (*Sparus aurata*); **—елия** *f.* (zool.) Aurelia; **—еомицин** *m.* aureomycin (antibiotic).

аури— *prefix* aur(i)— [gold; (anat.) ear]; **—д** *m.* auride; **—куло—** *prefix* auriculo— (ear); **—кулярия** *f.* (zool.) auricularia; **—кулярный** *a.* (anat.) auricular; **—н** *m.* aurin, p-rosolic acid; **—нтрикарбоновая кислота** aurintricarboxylic acid, ATA; **—пигмент** *m.* (min.) orpiment, yellow arsenic; **—хальцит** *m.* aurichalcite.

ауротио— *prefix* aurothio—.

АУС *abbr.* (**агрегатная унифицированная система**) modular pneumatic instrumentation system.

аускультировать *v.* (med.) auscultate.

аустенит *m.* (met.) austenite; **—ный, —овый** *a.* austenite, austenitic.

аустроглосс *m.* (ichth.) Austroglossus.

аутбридинг *m.* (gen.) outbreeding.

аутигенный *a.* (petr.) authigenic.

аут/изм *m.* (med.) autism; **—инит** *see* **аутунит**; **—истический** *a.* autistic, self-centered.

ауто— *see under* **авто—**; **—псия** *f.* autopsy; **—флора** *f.* endogenous flora.

аутунит *m.* (min.) autunite, lime uranite.

аутэкология *f.* autecology, individual ecology.

ауха *f.* Chinese perch (*Siniperca chua-tsi*).

ауэр/бахово сплетение (anat.) Auerbach's plexus; **—лит** *m.* (min.) auerlite.

афаз/ия *f.* (med.) aphasia; **—мидиевые** *pl.* (zool.) Aphasmidea (nematodes).

афалина *f.* (mam.) bottlenose dolphin (*Tursiops*).

афан/асьевский *a.* (geog.) Aphanasyevo; **—ит** *m.* (petr.) aphanite; **—итовый** *a.* aphanitic, diabasic; **—о—** *prefix* aphan(o)— (obscure, invisible).

афареевые *pl.* (ichth.) Aphareidae.

афвиллит *m.* (min.) afwillite.

афган/ец *m.*, **—ка** *f.* Afghan (native); a dry, hot wind; **—ский** *a.* (geog.) Afghan.

афел/ий *m.* (astr.) aphelion; **—ины** *pl.* (ent.) Aphelinidae.

афенил *m.* afenil, calcium chloride urea.

АФИ *abbr.* [(**метод) амплитудно-фазовых изменений**] amplitude-phase variation method (of geophysical prospecting).

афидиус *m.* (ent.) Aphidius.

афил/лин *m.* aphylline; **—(л)ия** *f.* aphylly; **—(л)ьный** *a.* aphyllous, leafless.

афио/новые *pl.* (ichth.) Aphyonidae; **—семион** *m.* Aphyosemion.

афипс(с)кий *a.* (geog.) Afips.

афицид *m.* aphicide, aphid insecticide.

афиш/а *f.*, **—ный** *a.* bill, poster, placard; **—ировать** *v.* make a display (of).

афлебии *pl.* (bot.) aphlebia.

афокальный *a.* afocal.

афония *f.* (med.) aphonia, loss of voice.

афотический *a.* aphotic, lightless.

афр. *abbr.* (**африканский**) African.

афредодер/овые, —усы *pl.* (ichth.) pirate perches (*Aphredoderidae*).

афро— *prefix* aphro— (foam); Afro—, African; **—дитиды** *pl.* (zool.) sea mice (*Aphroditidae*); **—европейский** *a.* Afro-European; **—золь** *m.* afrosol (foam stabilizer); **—метр** *m.* (wines) aphrometer; **—нитр** *m.* (min.) aphroniter; **—сидерит** *m.* aphrosiderite.

афрэгле *n.* (bot.) Afraegle.

афта *f.* (med.) aphtha (small ulcers).

афтершок *m.* (geol.) aftershock.

афт/италит *m.* (min.) aphthitalite; **—озный** *a.* aphthous; **—ы** *pl.* aphthae.

афунд *m.* (bot.) afund.

аффек/т *m.* affect; **—тивный** *a.* affective; **—тированный** *a.* affected; **—тировать** *v.* assume an appearance (of); **—ция** *f.* affection, morbid condition.

афферентный *a.* (physiol.) afferent.

аффикс *m.* (nomenclature) affix.

аффин/аж *m.*, **—ажное производство, —ирование** *n.* (met.) refining; **—ация** *f.* (sugar) affination; **—ировать** *v.* refine.

аффин/итет *m.*, **—ость** *f.* affinity; **—ный** *a.* affine, adjoining; **—ор** *m.* (math.) affinor.

ахал/азия *f.* (med.) achalasia; **—калакский** *a.* (geog.) Akhalkalaki; **—текинский** *a.* Akhaltekin; **—цихский** *a.* Akhaltsikhe.

ахатин(ид)ы *pl.* (mal.) Achatinidae.

ахил/ический *a.* (med.) achylous; **—ия** *f.* achylia; **—(л)еин** *m.* achilleine; **—лесово сухожилие** (anat.) Achilles' tendon; **—летин** *m.* achilletin; **—ло—** *prefix* (anat.) achillo— (Achilles' tendon).

ахироклина *f.* (bot.) Achyrocline.

ахматит *m.* (min.) achmatite.

ахметский *a.* (geog.) Akhmeta.

ахол/ический *a.* (med.) acholic, bile-free; **—ия** *f.* acholia.

ахондрит *m.* achondrite (a meteorite).

ахорион *m.* Achorion (parasitic fungi).

ахро— *prefix* achro— (absence of color); **—ит** *m.* (min.) achroite; **—мат** *m.* achromatic lens; **—матизированный** *a.* achromatized; **—матизм** *m.* achromatism; **—матин** *m.* (cyt.) achromatin; **—матический** *a.* achromatic, colorless; **—мицин** *m.* Achromycin, tetracycline (antibiotic); **—мия** *f.* (med.) achromia; **—одекстрин** *m.* achroödextrin.

ахсуинский *a.* (geog.) Akhsu.

ахтер/пик *m.*, **—пиковый** *a.* (naut.) afterpeak; **—штевень** *m.* sternpost.

ахт/убинский *a.* (geog.) Akhtuba; **—ынский** *a.* Akhtyi; **—ырский** *a.* Akhtyirka.

ахурянский *a.* (geog.) Akhuryan.

АЦ *abbr.* (**ацетилцеллюлоза**) cellulose acetate.

ац. *abbr.* (**ацетон**) acetone (solvent).

аце— *prefix* ace— (acetic); **—антрен** *m.* aceanthrene; **—лы** *pl.* flatworms (*Acoela*); **—льный** *a.* (anat.) acoelous; **—нафтен** *m.* acenaphthene.

ацервулевидное тело (bot.) acervulus.

ацет/абулум *m.* (anat.) acetabulum; **—алевый** *a.* acetal; **—алировать** *v.* acetalize; **—ал(ь)** *m.* acetal, 1,1-diethoxyethane; **—альдегид** *m.* acetaldehyde, ethanal; **—альдегид-аммиак** acetaldehyde ammonia; **—альдоксим** *m.* (acet)aldoxime; **—альдол(ь)** *m.* (acet)aldol; **—альный** *a.* acetal; **—амид** *m.* acetamide, ethanamide;

—амидин *m.* acetamidine; **—анилид** *m.* acetanilide; **—ат** *m.*, **—атный** *a.* acetate; **—атцеллюлоза** *f.* cellulose acetate; **—енил** *m.* acetenyl, ethynyl.

ацетил *m.* acetyl; **—аза** *f.* acetylase; **—активирующий фермент** acetate thiokinase; **—анизол** *m.* acetylanisole; **-аш-кислота** *f.* acetyl-H-acid.

ацетилен *m.* acetylene, ethyne; **—дикарбоновый** *a.* acetylenedicarboxylic (acid); **—ид** *m.* acetylide; **—истая медь** cuprous acetylide; **—истое серебро** silver acetylide; **—овый** *a.* acetylene; acetylene gas (producer); **—овая сажа** acetylene black; **—окислородный** *a.* oxyacetylene (welding).

ацетил/ид *m.* acetylide; **—ирование** *n.* acetylation; **—ированный** *a.* acetylated; **—ировать** *v.* acetylate; **—ируемый** *a.* acetylizable; **—КоА, —кофермент А** *m.* acetyl-CoA, acetyl coenzyme A; **—мочевина** *f.* acetylurea; **—овый** *a.* acetyl; **—овый альдегид** acetaldehyde; **—производное** *n.* acetyl derivative; **—салициловая кислота** acetylsalicylic acid, aspirin; **—серная кислота** acetylsulfuric acid; **—хлорид** *m.* acetyl chloride; **—холин** *m.* acetylcholine, Ach; **—целлюлоза** *f.*, **—целлюлозный** *a.* cellulose acetate; (text.) acetate; **—ьный** *a.* acetyl; **—ятор** *m.* acetylizer.

ацет/иметр *m.* acetimeter (obs. for hydrometer); **—иметрия** *f.* acetimetry; **—ин** *m.*, **—иновый** *a.* acetin.

ацето— *prefix* aceto—; **—бактерия** *f.* (microbiol.) Acetobacter; **—ин** *m.* acetoin, 3-hydroxy-2-butanone; **—клетчатка** *f.* cellulose acetate; **—ксим** *m.* acetoxime, 2-propanone oxime; **—л** *m.* acetol, 1-hydroxy-2-propanone; **—лиз** *m.* acetolysis; **—масляный** *a.* acetobutyric (acid); **—метр** *m.* acetometer; **—н** *m.* acetone; **—ндикарбоновая кислота** acetone dicarboxylic acid ADA; **—немия** *f.* (med.) acetonemia, ketonemia; **—нил** *m.* acetonyl; **—нилацетон** *m.* acetonylacetone; **—нитрил** *m.* acetonitrile, ethanenitrile.

ацетонов/окислый *a.* acetonic acid; acetonate (of); **а. эфир, —окислая соль** acetonate; **—ый** *a.* acetone; **—ый спирт** acetone alcohol, acetol; **—ая кислота** acetonic acid, *a*-hydroxyisobutyric acid.

ацето/нерастворимый *a.* acetone-soluble; **—нпроизводное** *n.* acetone derivative; **—нурия** *f.* (med.) acetonuria, ketonuria; **—тиоамид** *m.* acetothioamide; **—уксусный** *a.* acetoacetic (acid); **—уксусный эфир** acetoacetic ester, spec. ethyl acetoacetate; **—фенетидин** *m.* acetophenetidin, phenacetin; **—фенон** *m.* acetophenone, methyl phenyl ketone; **—форм** *m.* acetoform.

ацетуровая кислота aceturic acid.

ацет. ч. *abbr.* (**ацетильное число**) acetyl number, acetyl value.

ацефальный *a.* acephalous, headless.

аци/демия *f.* (med.) acidemia; **—диметрический** *a.* acidimetric; **—диметрия** *f.* acidimetry; **—дит** *m.* acid(ic) rock; **—дифицировать** *v.* acidify; **—добутирометр** *m.* acidobutyrometer; **—доз** *m.* (med.) acidosis; **—доид** *m.* acidoid; **—дол** *m.* Acidol, betaine hydrochloride; **—дометр** *m.* acidometer; **—дофил** *m.* acidophil(e), acidophilous organism; **—дофилин** *m.* acidophilin; acidophilus milk; **—дофилия** *f.* acidophilic nature; **—дофильный** *a.* acidophilic; (biol.) acidophilous; acidophilus (milk); **—дофобный** *a.* acidophobic, acidofuge.

ациклический а. acyclic; aliphatic.

ацикула *f.* (zool.) acicula, acicle.

ацил *m.* acyl; **—аза** *f.* acylase; **—аль** *m.* acylal; **—ирование** *n.* acylation; **—ировать** *v.* acylate; **а.-КоА, —кофермент А** *m.* acyl-CoA, acyl coenzyme A; **—оин** *m.*, **—оиновый** *a.* acyloin; **—производное** *n.* acyl derivative; **—трансфераза** *f.* acyltransferase; **—ьный** *a.* acyl.

ацин/озный *a.* acinous, grape-like; acinar; **—ус** *m.* (anat.; bot.) acinus.

а-ч *abbr.* (**ампер-час**) ampere-hour.

Ачесона электропечь Acheson furnace.

ач/инский *a.* (geog.) Achinsk; **—исуйский** *a.* Achi-Su; **—итский** *a.* Achit; **—хой-мартановский** *a.* Achkhoi-Martan.

ашарит *m.* (min.) ascharite.

Ашберри сплав Ashberry metal.

ашеб *m.* (bot.) asheb.

ашель *m.*, **—ский** *a.* (archeol.) Acheulean.

ашинский *a.* (geog.) Asha.

аш-кислота *f.* H acid (dye intermediate).

аш/крофтин *m.* (min.) aschcroftine; **—таракский** *a.* (geog.) Ashtarak; **—хабадский** *a.* Ashkhabad.

ащикульский *a.* (geog.) Aschikul.

аэр— *prefix* aer—, air; **—атор** *m.* aerator; **—ация** *f.* aeration; **—енхима** *f.* (bot.) aerenchyma, aeration tissue; **—ирование** *n.* aeration; **—ированность** *f.* degree of aeration; **—ировать** *v.* aerate.

аэро— *prefix* aero—, air, aerial; airplane; airborne; *see also under* **авиа—**; **—б** *m.* (biol.) aerobe; **—биоз** *m.* aerobiosis; **—бный** *a.* aerobic; **—бус** *m.* airliner; **—взвесь** *f.* aerosuspension; **—вокзал** *m.* air terminal (building); **—гаммарадиометр** *m.* airborne gamma radiometer; **—гамма-съёмка** *f.* airborne radio-activity survey; **—гель** *m.* aerogel; **—ген** *m.* aerogen, aerogenic bacterium; **—генный, —геновый** *a.* aerogenic; **—геосъёмка** *f.* aerial geological survey.

аэрограф *m.* (paint) sprayer, air brush; aerograph; **—ия** *f.* aerography.

аэродвигатель *m.* airplane engine.

аэродинам/ик *m.* aerodynamics specialist; **—ика** *f.* aerodynamics; **—ический** *a.* aerodynamic; oil-film (bearing); **—ический спектр** (av.) streamline flow pattern; **—ическая поверхность** airfoil; **—ическая труба** wind tunnel; **—ическое качество** lift-drag ratio.

аэро/дром *m.* airdrome, airport, air field; **—желоб** *m.* pneumatic tube; **—затвор** *m.* aerial camera shutter; **—золь** *m.*, **—зольный** *a.* **—золь-туман** *m.* aerosol; **—зонд** *m.* sounding weather balloon; **—зондирование** *n.* atmospheric sounding; **—изыскание** *n.* aerial survey; **—клуб** *m.* flying club; **—кулер** *m.* air cooler; **—лаг** *m.* air log; **—лак** *m.* (airplane) dope; **—лит** *m.* (geol.) aerolite, stony meteorite; **—лифт** *m.* air lift (pump); **—логический** *a.* (meteor.) aerological; **—логия** *f.* aerology; **—лодка** *f.* sea plane; **—лоток** *m.* pneumatic tube; **—лоция** *f.* flight log.

аэромагнит/ный *a.* (geol.) aeromagnetic; **—ометр** *m.* airborne magnetometer.

аэро/маяк *m.* beacon; **—метеорограф** *m.* aerometeorograph, recording densimeter; **—методы** *pl.* (geol.) aerial prospecting.

аэрометр *m.* aerometer, densimeter; **—ический** *a.* aerometric; **—ия** *f.* aerometry.

аэромеханик *m.* airplane mechanic; **—а** *f.* aeromechanics.

аэрон *m.* Aeron (alloy or antiemetic).

аэронав/игатор *m.* air navigator; **—игационный** *a.* aeronautical, air navigation; aircraft; **—игация** *f.* air navigation; **—т** *m.* aeronaut; **—тика** *f.* aeronautics; **—тический** *a.* aeronautical.

аэро/негатив *m.* aerial negative; **—номический** *a.* (meteor.) aeronomic; **—номия** *f.* aeronomy; **—обследование** *n.* aerial survey; **—опрыскивание, —опыли-**

вание *n.* (agr.) crop dusting; **—опрыскиватель, —опыливатель** *m.* crop duster; **—пауза** *f.* aeropause; **—план** *m.* airplane; **—планктон** *m.* (biol.) aeroplankton; **—планный** *a.* airplane; **—плёнка** *f.* aerial film; **—порт** *m.* airport; **—посев** *m.* aerial sowing; **—почта** *f.* airmail; **—проектор** *m.* aerial photograph projector; **—пыл** *m.* crop duster; **—пыль** *f.* dust cloud.

аэро/разбрасыватель, —распыливатель *m.* (agr.) crop duster; **—разведка** *f.* airborne prospecting; **—рекогносцировка** *f.* aerial reconnaisance; **—сани** *pl.* aerosleigh (propeller-driven sleigh); **—сев** *m.* aerial sowing; **—сидерит** *m.* (astr.) aerosiderite; **—сил** *m.* Aerosil (silica powder); **—снимок** *m.* aerial photograph; **—спорин** *m.* Aerosporin, polymyxin A.

аэростат *m.* aerostat, balloon, airship; (ent.; orn.) aerostat, air sac; **управляемый а.** dirigible, airship; **—ика** *f.* aerostatics; **—ический** *a.* aerostatic, pneumatic; **—ный** *a.* balloon(-borne).

аэро/суспензия *f.* aerosuspension, gaseous suspension; **—сфера** *f.* aerosphere; **—съёмка** *see* **аэрофото-съёмка; —таксация** *f.* aerial forest survey; **—танк, —тенк** *m.* aerotank, aeration tank, bio-aerator; **—тенк-смеситель** *m.* stirred aeration tank; **—термодинамика** *f.* aerothermodynamics; **—термоупругость** *f.* aerothermoelasticity; **—термохимия** *f.* aerothermochemistry; **—тит** *m.* (med.) aerotitis, barotitis; **—тория** *f.* aerodrome limits; **—тропизм** *m.* (biol.) aerotropism.

аэро/упругость *f.* aeroelasticity; **—фагия** *f.* (vet.) aerophagia, air swallowing; **—физика** *f.* aerophysics; **—фил** *m.* (biol.) aerophil(ic organism); **—фильм** *m.* aerial film; **—фильный** *a.* aerophilic; **—фильтр** *m.* aeration filter, biofilter; **—финишер** *m.* (av.) arrester (of carrier); **—фит(он)** *m.* aerophyte, air plant; **—флот** *m.* aerofloat (flotation agent); **Аэрофлот** Aeroflot (Russian airlines); **—фобный** *a.* aerophobic.

аэрофото/аппарат *m.* aerial camera; **—грамметрия** *f.* aerophotogrammetry; **—графия** *f.* aerial photography; **—затвор** *m.* (camera) shutter; **—камера** *f.* aerial camera; **—объектив** *m.* aerial camera lens; **—разведка** *f.* aerial photo reconnaissance; **—снимок** *m.* aerial photograph; **—съёмка** *f.* aerial photography, aerial mapping; **—установка** *f.* camera mount.

аэро/целе *n.* (med.) aerocele (air-filled tumor); **—змболия** *f.* aeroembolism.

АЭС *abbr.* (**атомная злектростанция**) nuclear power plant.

аэтобатус *m.* (ichth.) Aetobatus.

аю *m.* ayu, sweetfish (*Plecoglossus*); **—(о)вые** *pl.* Plecoglossidae.

ая/гузский *a.* (geog.) Ayaguz; **—клинский** *a.* Ayakla, Ayakli.

Аякс-Виатта печь Ajax-Wyatt furnace.

ая/нский *a.* (geog.) Ayan; **—пана** *f.* ayapana tea; **—тский** *a.* (geog.) Ayat.

аяцин *m.* ajacine.

Б

б *see* **бы;** *abbr.* (**бар**) bar; (**барн**) barn; (**бел**) bel; **б.** *abbr.* (**бывший**) former.

Б *abbr.* (**Бомэ**) Baumé, Bé.

баба *f.* ram, monkey, drop weight, block; (hammer) head; peasant woman.

бабабуданит *m.* (min.) bababudanite.

баба/дагский *a.* (geog.) Baba-dag; **—евский** *a.* Babayevo.

бабануха *f.* (ent.) horseradish leaf beetle (*Phaedon cochleariae* or *Ph. armoraciae*).

баба-рыба *f.* (ichth.) sculpin.

бабасу *n.* babassu (oil).

бабасуаль *n.* babasual (a palm forest).

бабаюртовский *a.* (geog.) Babayurt.

баббит *m.,* **—ный** *a.* babbit (alloy).

бабез/иеллёз, —иоз *m.* (vet.) Babesia infection, babesiasis; **—ия** *f.* (prot.) Babesia.

бабец *m.* (ichth.) sculpin.

бабингтонит *m.* (min.) babingtonite.

Бабинэ принцип Babinet's principle.

бабирусса *f.* (mam.) Babirussa.

бабка *f.* (lathe) head(stock), mandrel; kingpost, central post; (drill) chuck; monkey; weight, ram (of pile driver); sheaf (of grain); pastern (of horse); one of several species of fish; **задняя б., центрирующая б.** tailstock (of lathe); **передняя б.** headstock.

Бабо закон (phys.) Babo's law.

бабок *gen. pl. of* **бабка**.

бабоч/ка *f.* butterfly; (ichth.) roach (*Rutilus r.*); butterfly fish (*Pantodon buchholzi*); **—ки** *pl.* (ent.) Lepidoptera; **клапан —кой** butterfly valve; **—ницы** *pl.* moth flies (*Psychodidae*).

бабуин *m.* (mam.) baboon (*Papio*).

бабынинский *a.* (geog.) Babyinino.

бабье лето Indian summer.

бавалит *m.* (min.) bavalite.

баварская голубая Bavarian blue.

бавенский закон (cryst.) Baveno law.

бавлинский *a.* (geog.) Bavlyi.

багаж *m.,* **—ный** *a.* baggage, luggage, goods; **—ник** *m.* carrier, rack; trunk.

багамский *a.* (geog.) Bahama.

баган *m.* heap, pile.

баганский *a.* (geog.) Bagan.

багар/иевые *pl.* (ichth.) Sisoridae; **—ий** *m.* a catfish (*Bagarius*).

багас *m.,* **—са** *f.* (sugar) bagasse.

багдадский *a.* (geog.) Bag(h)dad.

багер *m.,* **—ный** *a.* dredge(r), excavator; bagger; **—зумф** *m.* dredging sump.

багет *m.,* **—ный** *a.* baguet, molding.

багийский *a.* (geog.) Bahia.

багон *m.* mshara (a mossy swamp forest).

багор *m.* (boat) hook, gaff; harpoon.

багрение *n.* spearing, harpooning (fish).

багрец *m.* (mal.) purple snail (*Purpura*); **б.-кошениль** *m.* (ent.) cochineal (*Dactylopius coccus*).

ба́грить *v.* spear, harpoon; fish out.

багр/и́ть *v.* redden, color reddish purple; **—оветь** *v.* redden, flush; **—овый** *a.* reddish purple; crimson; **—яник** *see* **багрянник; —янистый** *a.* purple; **—янить** *see* **багри́ть; —яница** *f.* (med.) purpura; **—янка** *f.* (mal.) Murex; **—янки** *pl.* (bot.) red algae (*Rhodophyceae*); **—янник** *m.* (bot.) redbud (*Cercis*); Cercidiphyllum; **—янниковые** *pl.* Cercidiphyllaceae; **—яный** *a.* (reddish) purple.

багульник *m.,* **болотный б.** (bot.) wild rosemary (*Ledum palustre*).

бадан *m.* (bot.) Bergenia.

бадделеит *m.* (min.) baddeleyite.

баде/ечный *a.,* **—йка** *f.* small bucket, tub, basin; **—йный** *a. of* **бадья.**

бадис *m.* (ichth.) Badis; **—овые** *pl.* leaffishes (*Badidae*).

бадхызский *a.* (geog.) Badkhyiz.

бадь/евой *a.,* **—я** *f.* bucket, pail, tub; scoop; trough; **б. транспортер** bucket conveyer.

бадьян *m.,* **б.-трава** *f.,* **—овый** *a.* (bot.) star anise (*Illicium anisatum*).

бадяга *see* **бодяга.**

баевский *a.* (geog.) Baevo.

баз *m.* corral, pen, yard, paddock.

база *f.* base, basis, foundation, starting point; (surv.) datum line, base line; (comp.) base address; (mach.) reference surface; supply, source (of materials); reserve(s), resources; facilities; depot.

базальн/о(плоско)клеточный *a.* (med.) basal cell; **—ый** *a.* basal.

базальт *m.* (petr.) basalt; **—овый** *a.* basalt(ic); **—ообразный** *a.* basaltiform, columnar.

базанит *m.* (min.) basanite, lydite.

базар *m.,* **—ный** *a.* market; (orn.) rookery; colony (of animals).

базардаринский *a.* (geog.) Bazar-Dara.

базедов/изм *m.* (med.) Basedow's disease, exophthalmic goiter; **—ик** *m.* basedowian.

базельский *a.* Basle.

бази— *prefix* basi— (base; basis).

базид/иальные *pl.* (bot.) Basidiomycetes; **—иальный** *a.* basidial; **—иеносец** *m.* basidiophore; **—ий** *m.* basidium; **—ио—** *prefix* basidio—, basidial; **—иомицеты** *pl.* Basidiomycetes; **—иоспора** *f.* basidiospore; **—ия** *f.* basidium.

бази/лик *m.,* **—иковый** *a.* (bot.) basil (*Ocimum*); **—лихт** *m.* (ichth.) Basilichthys; **—птеригий** *m.* (ichth.) basipterygium; **—птероидный** *a.* basipterygoid (bone).

базиров/ание *n.* basing, etc. *see v.;* **—ать** *v.* base, ground, found (on); **—аться** *v.* be based, rest (on).

базис *m.* basis, base, foundation; (geol.) base line or level; reference; (petr.) mesostasis; (cryst.) basal plane; **—ный** *a. of* **базис;** reference (point); fixed-base (index); baseline (studies).

базисфеноид *m.,* **—ная** *f.* basisphenoid (bone).

базит *m.* basic rock; **—овый** *a.* basic.

базифильный *a.* (bot.) basiphil(ic).

баз-навес *m.* livestock shed.

базо— *prefix* baso— (base); **—вый** *a. of* **база;** basic; base-stock; host (computer); reference (point); *a. of* **баз;** **—к** *m.* cattle pen; **—к-ловушка** *f.* box trap.

базофил *m.* (cyt.) basophil(e), basocyte; **—ия** *f.* (med.) basophilia; **—ьный** *a.* basophil(ic).

базоцентрированный *a.* base-centered.

байбак *m.* (mam.) steppe marmot (*Marmota bobac*).

байд/а *f.* small fishing boat; **—ак** *m.* a commercial boat; **—ар(к)а** *f.* canoe, dugout, kayak.

байевое масло bay oil, myrcia oil.

Байера способ Bayer process (for aluminum oxide); **Б. теория напряжения** Baeyer tension (or strain) theory.

байесовский *a.* (stat.) Bayes'.

байка *f.* (text.) baize; (filter) cloth.

байк/алит *m.* (min.) baikalite; **—альский** *a.* (geog.) Baikal; **—итский** *a.* Baikit; **—овый** *a. of* **байка;** **—уру** *n.* baycuru root.

баймакский *a.* (geog.) Baimak.

байонет *m.* bayonet joint; **—ный** *a.* bayonet.

байпас *m.* by-pass; **—ирование** *n.* by-pass(ing); **—ировать** *v.* by-pass; **—ный** *a.* by-pass; auxiliary.

байрак *m.* ravine, gorge, deep gully.

байрам-алийский *a.* (geog.) Bairam-Ali.

байрачный *a. of* **байрак.**

байсунский *a.* (geog.) Baisun.

байт *m.* (comp.) byte.

бай-тайгинский *a.* (geog.) Bai-Taiga.

байховый *a.* (geog.) Baikhovi.

байчунасский *a.* (geog.) Baichunas.

байю *m. or n.* bayou.

байя-грас(с) *m.* Bahia grass.

бак *m.* tank, cistern, vat, tub, reservoir, container; mess kit; (naut.) forecastle.

бак-аккумулятор *m.* storage tank.

бакалавр *m.* (educ.) Bachelor.

бакале/йный *a.,* **—я** *f.* grocery.

бакальский *a.* (geog.) Bakal.

бакан *m.* beacon; buoy; lake (pigment).

бакаут *m.,* **—овое дерево** (bot.) lignum vitae, guaiac (*Guaiacum officinale*); **—овый** *a.* guaiac.

бакборт *m.* (naut.) port side.

бак-дегазатор *m.* degassing tank.

бакел/изация *f.* (plastics) bakelization; **—изировать** *v.* bakelize; **—ит** *m.,* **—итовый** *a.* bakelite.

бакен *m.* floating beacon, buoy.

бакерит *m.* (min.) bakerite.

бакинский *a.* (geog.) Baku.

бакинститут *m.* bacteriological institute.

бак-коллектор *m.* accumulator tank.

баккорея *f.* (bot.) Baccaurea.

баклаб *m.* bacteriological laboratory.

баклага *f.* flask, canteen.

баклажан *m.,* **—ный** *a.* (bot.) eggplant (*Solanum melongena*).

баклан *m.* (orn.) cormorant (*Phalacrocorax*).

бакланец *m.* small rocky island, rock.

баклан/овые, —ы *pl.* (orn.) Phalacrocoricidae.

баклейка *f.* (ichth.) bleak (*Alburnus a.*)

баклуш/а *f.* chip; block (of wood); cast iron wheel; **—ка** *f.* gate pin.

бак-мерник *m.* measuring tank.

баковый *a. of* **бак.**

бак-отсек *m.* (rockets) integral tank.

бакрузякский *a.* (geog.) Bakruziak.

баксанский *a.* (geog.) Baksan.

бакстромит *m.* (min.) backstromite.

бактер/иальный *a.* bacterial; **—иальное разложение** bacteriolysis; **—иевидный** *a.* bacteriform; **—иеубивающий** *a.* bactericidal; **—изовать** *v.* bacterize, inoculate with bacteria; **—ии** *pl.* bacteria; **—ийный** *a.* bacterial; **—ийубивающий** *a.* bactericidal; **—иоз** *m.* (phyt.) bacteriosis, bacterial blight; **—иолиз** *m.* bacteriolysis; **—иолизин** *m.* bacteriolysin; **—иолитический** *a.* bacteriolytic.

бактерио/лог *m.* bacteriologist; **—логический** *a.* bacteriological; **—логия** *f.* bacteriology; **—носитель** *m.* bacteria carrier; **—подобный** *a.* bacteroid; **—проницаемость** *f.* bacterial permeability; **—пурпурин** *m.* bacteriopurpurin; **—скопия** *f.* bacterioscopy; **—статический** *a.* bacteriostatic, bacteria-inhibiting; **—убивающий** *a.* bactericidal; **—убивающее средство** bactericide; **—фаг** *m.* bacteriophage; **—хлорофилл** *m.* bacteriochlorophyll; **—цин** *m.* bacteriocin.

бактерицид *m.* bactericide; **—ность** *f.* bactericidal action; **—ный** *a.* bactericidal; **—ное средство** bactericide.

бактер/ия *f.* bacterium; **—оид** *m.,* **—оидный** *a.* bacteroid.

бактриан *m.* Bactrian camel.

бакуин *m.* bakuin (lubricating oil).

бакулятный *a.* baculiform, rod-shaped.

бакун *m.* a low-grade tobacco.

бак-хранилище *m.* storage tank.

бакча *see* **бахча;** **–рский** *a.* (geog.) Bakchar.

бакша *see* **бахча.**

бакштаг *m.* backstay, guy (rope).

бакштов *m.* (naut.) guess-rope, cable.

Бал. *abbr.* Balling (degrees); **БАЛ** *abbr.* (**британский антилюизит**) (chem.) British Anti-Lewisite, BAL.

балаболка *f.* (bot.) Campanula.

бала/ганский *a.* (geog.) Balagansk; **—клейский** *a.* Balakleya; **—ковский** *a.* Balakovo.

баламут *m.* (ichth.) mackerel (in spring).

баламутить *v.* stir up, muddy; disturb, agitate, confuse.

балан/ит *m.* (med.) balanitis; **—(о)–** *prefix* balan(o)— [acorn; (anat.) glans penis]; **—оглосс** *m.* (mal.) Balanoglossus; **—офорин** *m.* balanophorin.

баланс *m.* balance, equilibrium; balance sheet, account; budget; distribution (of energy); pulpwood; **—ер** *m.* balancer.

балансир *m.* balancer; equalizer; balance beam, walking beam; rocking lever, rocker, bob; (horol.) balance wheel; **—ный** *a. of* **балансир;** balance(d); balancing, rocking, equalizing; **—ование** *see* **балансировка;** **—ованный** *a.* balanced, in equilibrium; **—овать** *v.* balance, compensate; even up; (av.) trim; **—овка** *f.,* **—овочный** *a.* balancing, etc. *see v.*

баланс/ный, —овый *a. of* **баланс;** balanced; pulp (wood); economic, proven (reserves); **—омер** *m.* radiation balance gage; **—ы** *pl.* pulpwood (logs).

балантид/иаз *m.* (med.) balantidiasis; **—ий** *a.* (prot.) Balantidium.

балат/а *f.,* **—овый** *a.* balata (latex).

бала/ханский *a.* (geog.) Balakhanyi; **—хонский** *a.* Balakhonka; **—хтинский** *a.* Balakhta; **—шинский** *a.* Balashikha; **—шовский** *a.* Balashov.

балбер *m.,* **—очный** *a.* (fishing) float.

балвский *a.* (geog.) Balvyi.

балда *f.* sledge hammer; knob.

балдахин *m.* (arch.) baldachin, canopy.

балеган *m.* (ichth.) grayling (*Thymallus nigrescens*).

бал/езинский *a.* (geog.) Balezino; **—ейский** *a.* Balei; **—есан** *see* **балеган;** **—ийский** *a.* Bali.

балистовые *pl.* triggerfishes (*Balistidae*).

балка *f.* beam, girder, bar; joist; ravine, gully, gorge; (anat.) trabecula.

балканский *a.* (geog.) Balkan.

балка-распорка *f.* (arch.) purlin; **б.-спица** *f.* needle beam; **б.-стенка** *f.* wall beam.

балкашинский *a.* (geog.) Balkashino.

балкер *m.* (naut.) bulk carrier.

балкон *m.,* **—ный** *a.* balcony.

балл *m.* mark, point, number, rating; index; degree, severity; (mach., petrol.) (merit) rating, demerit rating; **ветер в 1 б.** wind force of 1.

баллас *m.* ballas (type of diamond).

балласт *m.* ballast; rubble; inert material, dead weight; **—ер** *m.* (rr.) ballasting machine; **—ина** *f.* ballast pig; **—ирование** *n.,* **—ировка** *f.* ballasting; **—ировать** *v.* ballast; gravel (road); **—ный** *a. of* **балласт;** inactive; (physiol.) indigestible; **—овыгружатель** *m.* ballast unloader; **—оочиститель** *m.* gravel washer.

баллер *m.* (naut.) stock.

баллист *m.* ballistic fruit, catapult fruit; **—ик** *m.* ballistician; **—ика** *f.* ballistics; **—ит** *m.* (expl.) ballistite; **—ический** *a.* ballistic; **—окардиограмма** *f.* (med.) ballistocardiogram, BCG.

балловый *a. of* **балл.**

баллон *m.* balloon; (gas) cylinder; (acid) carboy; bottle;

vessel, container, tank; bulb; (pneumatic) tire; **—ет** *m.* (aero.) ballonet; **—ировать** *v.* balloon; inflate, distend; **б.-комко-давитель** *m.* (agr.) clod-breaking roller; **—чик** *dim. of* **баллон.**

баллотиров/ание *n.* (med.) ballottement; **—ировать** *v.* vote (by ballot); **—аться** *v.* run (for office).

балльн/ость *f.* intensity (of an earthquake); **—ый** *a. of* **балл.**

балобан *m.* (orn.) saker (*Falco cherrug*).

баловать *v.* spoil, coddle; humor; indulge; **—ся** *v.* indulge (in); play around (with).

бал/ок *gen. pl. of* **балка; —очка** *dim. of* **балка;** arm; (anat.) trabecula; **—очный** *a. of* **балка; с —очными выводами** (microelectronics) beam-lead(ed).

балт/айский *a.* (geog.) Baltai; **—асинский** *a.* Baltasi; **—ийский** *a.* Baltic; **—ский** *a.* Balta.

балхаш/ит *m.* balkhashite (a bitumen); **—ский** *a.* (geog.) Balkhash.

балык *m.,* **—овина** *f.,* **—овый** *a.* dried fish.

балыкчинский *a.* (geog.) Balyikchi.

бальза *f.* (bot.) balsa (*Ochroma lagopus*).

бальзам *m.* balsam; **—ин** *m.* (bot.) balsam (*Impatiens*); **—иновые** *pl.* Balsaminaceae; **—ировать** *v.* embalm; **—ический** *a.* balsam(ic); **—ник** *m.* balsam (tree); **—ный, —овый** *a.* balsam; **—оносный** *a.* balsam-yielding.

бальзовый *a.* balsa (wood).

бальма *f.* overhang, rock shelter.

бальмеровский *a.* Balmer (series).

бальнео— *prefix* balneo— (bath); **—грязевой** *a.* mud-bath; **—логия** *f.* balneology.

бальный *a. of* **бал(л).**

бальтиморит *m.* (min.) baltimorite.

Бальца-Шимана реакция Balz-Schiemann reaction (for fluorobenzenes).

балюстрада *f.* balustrade, guard rail.

балянус *m.* (zool.) rock barnacle (*Balanus*).

балясина *f.* baluster; rail post; rung (of ladder).

бамбу/за *f.,* **—к** *m.,* **—ковый** *a.* (bot.) bamboo (*Bambusa*); **—кокрысиные** *pl.* (mam.) bamboo rats (*Rhizomyidae*); **—раль** *m.* bamburral (open woodland).

бамия *f.* (bot.) okra (*Hibiscus esculentus*).

бампер *m.* bumper.

банадос *m.* banados, shallow swamp.

банан *m.* banana; **райский б.** plantain; **текстильный б.** Manila hemp; **—овые** *pl.* (bot.) Musaceae; **—оеды** *pl.* (orn.) touracos (*Musophagidae*).

банаховый *a.* (math.) Banach.

бангиевые *pl.* marine red algae (*Bangiaceae*).

бандаж *m.* tire, rim, band(ing), strap(ping); belt(ing); (turbine) shroud(ing); riding ring (of dryer); (med.) truss; **—епрокатный** *a.* tire- or strip-rolling; **—ировать** *v.* band, wrap; shroud; reinforce; **—ный** *a. of* **бандаж;** strip (mill).

бандероль *f.* wrapper; printed matter.

банд/жовые *pl.* (ichth.) Banjosidae; **—икота** *f.* (mam.) bandicoot rat (*Bandicota*); **—икут** *m.* bandicoot (*Perameles*).

бани *gen., etc. of* **баня.**

баниевые *see* **банджовые.**

банистерин *m.* banisterine.

банить *v.* clean, swab, sponge, wash.

банк *m.* bank.

банк/а *f.* jar, can; beaker; (med.) cup; bank, shoal; (oyster) bed; (naut.) thwart; **ставить —и** *v.* cup.

банкаброш *m.* (text.) flyer, fly frame.

банкет *m.* (min.) banket; embankment; bench; banquet, dinner; **упорный б.** rockfill embankment.

банкия *f.* (zool.) a shipworm (*Bankia*).

банк/ноты *pl.* bank notes; **—овый** *a.* (com.) bank(ing); **—ротиться** *v.* go bankrupt.

банкуловое масло bancoul nut oil.

банн/ик *m.* (tube) brush; reamer; swab; **б.-протиральщик** *m.* rammer and sponger; **—о-пачечный** *a.* laundry (waste); rinse (water); **—ый** *a.* **баня.**

бан/ок *gen. pl.,* **—очка** *dim. of* **банка;** (glass) parison; **—очный** *a. of* **банка.**

бант *m.* knot, bow.

бантенг *m.* (mam.) banteng (*Bibos banteng*).

бань *gen. pl. of* **баня.**

баньян *m.* banyan (tree).

баня *f.* bath; bath house; **водяная б.** (hot) water bath.

баобаб *m.* (bot.) baobab (*Adansonia*).

бапти/зия *f.* (bot.) Baptisia; **—токсин** *m.* baptitoxine, cytisine.

бар *m.* bar, ledge; barrier; (mach.) cutter bar; (acous.) bar (1 dyne/cm^2); (meteor.) bar (10^6 dyne/cm^2) *prefix and suffix* bar—, **—бар** (weight, pressure).

барабан *m.,* **—но** *prefix* drum, barrel; roll(er), cylinder; reel; thimble (of micrometer); (anat.) tympanum; **—но-сосцевидный** *a.* (anat.) tympanomastoid; **—но-фрезерный** *a.* drum-milling; **—но-шлифовальный станок** drum sander; **—ный** *a.* drum (-type), barrel (-type); rotary (dryer, kiln); (anat.) tympanic; **—ный грохот** revolving screen; (min.) trommel; **—ная мельница** tumbler; **—ная перепонка** ear drum; **б.-фильтр** *m.* filter drum; **—чик** *dim. of* **барабан; —щик** *m.* (ichth.) drummer (*Pogonias cromis*).

барабинский *a.* (geog.) Barabinsk.

барабул/евые, —и *pl.* (ichth.) surmullets (*Mullidae*); **—ька** *f.* surmullet, goatfish (*Mullus,* spec. *M. barbatus*); **—ьки, —ьковые** *pl.* Mullidae; **—я** *see* **барабулька.**

барак *m.* (temporary) barracks.

барак(о)ута *f.* (ichth.) barracouta, snake mackerel (*Thyrsites atun*).

баран *m.* sheep, ram; (mech.) ram; **—ец** *m.* (bot.) lamb succory (*Arnoseris*); **—ий** *a. of* **баран;** mutton; sheepskin; **—ий горох** (bot.) chickpea (*Cicer,* spec. *C. arietinum*); **—ий лоб** roche moutonnée (glacier-worn rock); **—ина** *f.* mutton; **молодая —ина** lamb (meat); **—ка** *f.* steering wheel; (nucl.) doughnut; **б.-муфлон** *m.* (mam.) moufflon (*Ovis musimon*); **—ник** *m.* (bot.) Arnica; **—ок** *m.* (tech.) plane; **б.-толсторог** *m.* bighorn sheep (*Ovis canadensis*); **—чик** *m.* lamb; (text.) reel; (bot.) cowslip (*Primula officinalis*).

барасинга *f.* swamp deer (*Cervus duvauceli*).

барат *m.* (xanthation) churn.

барачный *a. of* **барак.**

бараш/ек *m.* lamb(skin); (mech.) wing nut; kink (in wire); (orn.) common snipe; **—ки** *pl.* fleece; fleecy clouds, cirrocumulus; whitecaps; **—ковый** *a.* lamb(skin); wing (nut); thumb (screw).

барбадосский *a.* (geog.) Barbados.

барба/лоин *m.* barbaloin; **—мил** *m.* Barbamyl, amobarbital sodium.

барбарис, —ник *m.,* **—ный, —овый** a. (bot.) barberry (*Berberis*); **—овые** *pl.* barberry family (*Berberidaceae*).

барбатиновая кислота barbatic acid.

барбет *m.* (mil.) barbette.

барбиерит *m.* (min.) barbierite.

барбит/ал *m.* barbital, diethylbarbituric acid; **—урат** *m.* barbiturate; **—уровая кислота** barbituric acid, malonylurea.

барбот/аж *m.* bubbling, sparging; splash oiling;

—ажный *a. of* **барботаж; bubble; air-lift (system); sparged; —ажный реактор, —ер** *m.* bubbler, sparger; diffuser; wash flask.

барботин *m.* (cer.) barbotine.

барботир/ование *n.,* **—ующий** *a.* bubbling, sparging; **—овать** *v.* bubble, pass through.

барб/оурисиевые *pl.* (ichth.) Barbourisiidae; **—удовые** *pl.* beardfishes (*Polymixiidae*); **—улька, —уля** *see* **барабулька; —урисиевые** *pl.* Barbourisiidae.

барвенковский *a.* (geog.) Barvenkovo.

барвинок *m.* (bot.) periwinkle (*Vinca*).

баргузин *m.* a strong NE wind; **—ский** *a.* (geog.) Barguzin.

бард/а *f.,* **—еный** *a.* malt residue, spent mash; vinasse, slop(s), spent wash, waste liquor.

бардинский *a.* (geog.) Barda.

бардосушение *n.* slop drying.

бардымский *a.* (geog.) Bardyim.

бардяной *a. of* **барда; б. уголь** vinasse cinder.

барель *see* **баррель.**

барельеф *m.,* **—ный** *a.* bas-relief.

барен *m.* barene (carborane).

баренцев/оморский *a.* Barents Sea; **—ый** *a.* Barents.

баретный *a.* cant (file).

бареттер *m.* (electron.) barretter, ballast tube or lamp.

барех *m.* kelp.

барж/а *f.* barge; **—евоз** *m.* barge carrier; **—евой, —евый** *a.* barge.

бари— *prefix* bary— (heavy).

барибал *m.* black bear (*Ursus americanus*).

барид *m.* snout beetle (*Baris*).

бариевый *a.* barium.

бар/ий *m.* barium. Ba; (acous.) barye (1 dyne/cm^2); **окись —ия** barium oxide, baryta; **сернокислый б.** barium sulfate.

барико— *prefix* barometric.

барилит *m.* (min.) barylite.

барильет *m.* gas-collecting main.

барион *m.,* **—ный** *a.* (nucl.) baryon.

барированный *a.* barium-coated.

баристый *see* **баритовый.**

барисфера *f.* (geol.) barysphere.

барит *m.* baryta, barium oxide; (min.) barytes, barite; **едкий б.** barium hydroxide; **сернокислый б.** barium sulfate; **—аж** *m.* baryta coating; **—изация** *f.* (geol.) barytization.

баритов/ый *a.* barytic, baryta, baryto—; **б. жёлтый, б. крон** barium yellow, barium chromate; **б. шпат** *see* **барит; —ая вода** baryta water; **—ая селитра** barium nitrate; **—ые белила** baryta white, blanc fixe, permanent white (barium sulfate).

баритокальцит *m.* (min.) barytocalcite.

баритон *m.,* **—ный** *a.* baritone.

баритоцинковые белила lithopone.

барицентр *m.* barycenter, center of gravity; **—ический** *a.* barycentric.

бари/ческий *a.* (meteor.) baric; barometric; pressure-field (analysis); **—я** *f.* (acous.) barye (1 dyne/cm^2).

барка *f.* barge; large boat; (dye) vat; **—с** *m.* (tanning) paddle (vat), launch; (naut.) launch.

баркаузия *f.* (bot.) Barkhausia.

баркометр *m.* (tanning) barkometer.

барлерия *f.* (bot.) Barleria.

барлова болезнь Barlow's disease, scurvy.

барминский *a.* (geog.) Barma.

барн *m.* (nucl.) barn (10^{-24}cm^2).

баро— *prefix* baro— (weight, pressure); **—грамма** *f.* barogram; **—грамма подъёма** (av.) climb curve;

—граф *m.* barograph, recording barometer; **—граф-анероид** *m.* aneroid barograph; **—граф-высотописец** *m.* barograph altitude recorder; **—диффузия** *f.* pressure diffusion.

барок *m.* whippletree, swingletree (of harness); *gen. pl. of* **барка.**

баро/камера *f.* (low-) pressure chamber, decompression chamber; **—клинность** *f.* baroclinic distribution; **—клинный** *a.* baroclinic.

барометр *m.* barometer; **б.-анероид** aneroid barometer; **б.-высотомер** barometer-altimeter; **—ический** *a.* barometric; **—ический ящик** barometric well.

баро/миль *m.* baromil (barometer unit); **—переключатель** *m.,* **—реле** *n.* baroswitch, barometric pressure switch; **—рецептор** *m.* (anat.) baro(re)ceptor; **—скоп** *m.* baroscope, open-end manometer; **—спидограф** *m.* velocity-height recorder; **—стат** *m.* barostat, pressure regulator; **—сфера** *f.* barosphere; **—термограф** *m.* barothermograph; **—травма** *f.* (med.) barotrauma; **—тропность** *f.* barotropic distribution; **—тропный** *a.* barotropic; **—фильный** *a.* barophilic, pressure-tolerant.

барочный *a. of* **барка.**

барраж *m.,* **—ировать** *v.* (av.) barrage.

барра/кудовые *pl.* (ichth.) barracudas (*Sphyraenidae*); **—мунда** *f.* barramunda (*Neoceratodus forsteri*); **—ндовский** *a.* (pal.) Barrande; **—нкос** *m.* barranca (ravine or cliff); **—с** *m.* barras, galipot.

баррель *m.* barrel (unit of measure).

барретер *see* **бареттер.**

баррикад/а *f.,* **—ный** *a.* barricade.

барс *m.* (mam.) ounce, (snow) leopard (*Uncia u.*); panther; (av.) porpoising; (bucking) ram (for drill); **—ение** *n.* porpoising.

барс/ёнок *m.* young badger; **—ук** *m.* (mam.) badger (*Meles*); **сумчатые —уки** bandicoots (*Paramelidae*); **—уковые,** **—учьи** *pl.* badger family (*Melinae*); **—уковый,** **—учий** *a. of* **барсук.**

Барта реакция Bart reaction.

бартолиновый *a.* Bartholin's (glands).

бартонеллёз *m.* (med.) bartonellosis.

барх *see* **бархатное дерево.**

бархан *m.* barkhan, sand dune; **—ный** *a.* barkhan; aeolian (sands).

бархат *m.* (text.) velvet; (bot.) corktree (*Phellodendron*); **амурский б.,** **—ное дерево** Amur cork (*P. amurense*); **бумажный б.** (text.) velveteen; **—ец** *m.,* *see* **бархатцы;** **—источёрный** *a.* velvet black; **—источелковистый,** **—истый** *a.* velutinous, velvety; **—ки** *see* **бархатцы;** **—ный** *a. of* **бархат;** barette (file); **—ный сезон** Indian summer; **—ное дерево** Amur cork; **—ные бобы** (bot.) Mucuna; Stizolobium; **—цы** *pl.* marigolds (*Tagetes*).

бархоут *m.* (naut.) rubbing strip.

барщин/а *f.,* **—ный** *a.* forced labor.

барыш *m.* profit, gain.

барышский *a.* (geog.) Baryish.

барьер *m.,* **—ный** *a.* barrier, wall, enclosure; obstacle, impediment; rail, bar; (protective) belt; **б. деления** fission barrier.

барятинский *a.* (geog.) Baryatino.

бас *m.* bass; *prefix see* **бассейновый.**

басаргечарский *a.* (geog.) Basargechar.

басистый *a.* bass, deep.

баскский *a.* Basque.

баскунчакский *a.* (geog.) Baskunchak.

басма *f.* a black dye.

басовый *a.* bass.

басон *m.* galloon, braid, trimming.

бассейн *m.* tank, reservoir, basin; drainage or catchment area, watershed; pond, pool; watering place (for livestock); (coal) field; **б.-грязевик** *m.* sump (tank); **—изация** *f.* sea salt recovery in basins; **—овый** *a. of* **бассейн;** (nucl.) swimming-pool (reactor); **б.-отстойник** *m.* settling tank.

бассетит *m.* (min.) bassetite.

бассия *f.* (bot.) Bassia.

бассогигас *m.* (ichth.) Bassogigas.

бассор/ин *m.* bassorin, tragacanthose; **—иновая кислота** bassoric acid; **—ская камедь** bassora gum.

бастард *m.* (biol.) hybrid; mongrel.

бастион *m.* bastion, bulwark.

баст/ит *m.* (min.) bastite; **—незит** *m.* (min.) bastnäsite.

бастов/ать *v.* (go on) strike; **—ка** *f.* strike.

бастр *m.* brown sugar, raw sugar.

бастующий *a.* striking, on strike.

бата *f.* (bot.) batha, phrygana.

батавские слёзки Prince Rupert's drops, glass tears.

батальон *m.* battalion.

батан *m.* batten (lumber); (text.) sley.

батар/ейка *f.* small battery; **—ейная** *f.* battery room; **—ейный** *a.* battery; multiple (cyclone); **—ея** *f.* battery; set, bank, range; (heating) radiator; **—ея котлов** bank of boilers.

батат *m.* sweet potato (*Ipomoea batatas*).

батенсы *see* **баттенсы.**

бати— *prefix* bathy—, batho— (deep; depth; height); **—аль** *f.* bathyal zone, deep-sea zone; **—альный** *a.* bathyal; **—завровые** *pl.* lizardfishes (*Bathysauridae*); **—клюпеевые** *pl.* (ichth.) Bathyclupeidae; **—лаговые** *pl.* deepsea smelts (*Bathylagidae*); **—лаковые** *pl.* bonythroats (*Bathylaconidae*).

батиловый спирт bathyl alcohol.

бати/мастеровые *pl.* (ichth.) ronquils (*Bathymasteridae*); **—метр** *m.* (ocean.) bathymeter; **—метрия** *f.* bathymetry, echo sounding; **—пелагиаль** *f.* bathypelagic zone; **—план** *m.* bathyplane, towed submersible craft; **—птеровые** *pl.* spiderfishes (*Bathypteroidae*); **—скаф** *m.* bathyscaphe, depth boat.

батист *m.* (text.) cambric, lawn.

бати/сфера *f.* bathysphere, diving sphere; **—фильный** *a.* (bot.) bathyphilous, lowland-dwelling; **—фит** *m.* bathyphyte.

баткак *m.* batkak (black saline silt).

баткенский *a.* (geog.) Batken.

батлачок *m.* (bot.) foxtail (*Alopecurus*).

батмотропический *a.* (physiol.) bathmotropic.

бато— *see* **бати—;** bato— (bramble).

батог *m.* whip, cane, staff.

батокс *m.* buttock (of ship).

бато/лит *m.* (petr.) batholite, batholith; **—литовый** *a.* batholitic; **—метр** *m.* (ocean.) bathometer; water bottle, sampler.

батон *m.* (candy) bar; bread stick; long loaf; **—лак** *m.* button lac.

бато/порт *m.* caisson gate, pontoon dock gate; **—фил** *m.* (ichth.) Bathophilus; **—хром** *m.* (chem.) bathochrome; **—хромный** *a.* bathochromic (shift).

батрак *m.* hired hand, farm laborer.

батрах/ит *m.* (min.) batrachite; **—о—** *prefix* batracho— (frog; amphibian); **—овые,** **—оидиды** *pl.* toadfishes (*Batrachoididae*); **—ология** *f.* batrachology.

батра/цкий *a. of* **батрак;** **—чество** *n.* farm work; farm hands; **—чить** *v.* be a farm hand, work as a farm hand.

баттенсы *pl.* battens (lumber).

баттер/фиш *m.* butterfish; **—фляй** *m.* (mech.) butterfly; **затвор —фляй** butterfly gate.

батумский *a.* (geog.) Batumi.

батун *m.* Welsh onion (*Allium fistulosum*).

батут *m.* trampoline.

батчелорит *m.* (min.) batchelorite.

баугиниевый *a.* (anat.) Bauhin's (valve).

бауденовский *a.* Bowden.

баул *m.* trunk, grip, case.

баулит *m.* (petr.) baulite, krablite.

баумгауерит *m.* (min.) baumhauerite.

баунтовский *a.* (geog.) Baunt(ov).

бауский *a.* (geog.) Bauska.

Бауш-Лом (opt.) Bausch and Lomb.

баф/иин *m.* baphiin; **—ия** *f.* (bot.) Baphia.

бафтинг *m.* (av.) buffet(ing).

бахада *f.* (geol.) bajada (slope).

бахмачский *a.* (geog.) Bakhmach.

бахмутский *a.* (geog.) Bakhmut.

бахонадо *n.* (ichth.) jolthead porgy (*Calamus bajonado*).

бахрейнский *a.* (geog.) Bahrein.

бахром/а *f.* fringe, border, edge; outskirt; (anat.; biol.) fimbria; **—ка** *f.* fimbrilla; **—ный** *a. of* **бахрома; —чато—** *prefix* fimbriate; crosso— (tassels, fringe); thysan(o)— (tassel); **—чатокрылые** *pl.* (ent.) thrips (*Thysanoptera*); **—чато-лопастный** *a.* (bot.) fimbriate-laciniate; **—чатость** *f.* fringing; **—чатый** *a.* fringed, fimbriate.

бахтак *m.* Sevan trout (*Salmo ischchan*).

бахтарм/а *f.,* **—яный** *a.* flesh side of hide.

бахч/а *f.* (agr.) field of cucurbits; **—еводство** *n.* cucurbit cultivation; **—евой** *a.* (bot.) cucurbitaceous.

бахчисарайский *a.* (geog.) Bakhchisarai.

бацилл/а *f.* bacillus; **—оз** *m.* bacillosis, bacillary infection; **—омицин** *m.* bacillomycin; **—оноситель** *m.* (bacilli) carrier; **—оподобный** *a.* bacilliform, bacillar; **—оубивающее средство** bacillicide; **—ярный** *a.* bacillary.

бацитрацин *m.* bacitracin (antibiotic).

баццит *m.* (min.) bazzite.

бачатский *a.* (geog.) Bachatyi.

бач/ковый *a.,* **—ок** *m. dim. of* **бак;** tank, container; canister, can.

башен *gen. pl.,* **—ка** *dim. of* **башня;** turret; cupola; **—ница** *f.* (bot.) tower cress (*Turritis*); **—ный** *a. of* **башня; —ный биофильтр** multistage tower; **—ный охладитель** cooling tower.

башк— *prefix* (**башкирский**).

башка *f.* jowl, head (of fish).

башкирский *a.* (geog.) Bashkir.

башклейка *f.* (ichth.) bleak (*Alburnus a.*)

башковка *f.* (agr.) spring harrowing.

башм/ак *m.* shoe; chock, block; (leveling) footplate; **—ачник** *m.* shoemaker; **—ачный** *a.* shoe; **—ачок** *dim. of* **башмак;** (bot.) Cypripedium.

башх/евидный *a.* tower-shaped, turriform; **—я** *f.* tower; **—я-сатуратор** *f.* saturation tower.

баштан *see* **бахча.**

бв. *abbr.* (**безводный**) anhydrous.

б.г. *abbr.* (**без года**) no date (given); **б.г., б/г** *abbr.* (**будущего года**) next year.

бдел/ий *m.* bdellium (a gum resin).; **—ла** *f.* (zool.) snout mite (*Bdella*); **—ло—** *prefix* bdello— (leech); **—лоз** *m.* leech infestation.

бдительный *a.* vigilant, watchful, alert.

б.е. *abbr.* (**белковая единица**) protein unit.

Бе *abbr.* (**градусы Бомэ**) degrees Baumé.

беб/еерин, —ирин *m.* bebeerine; **—ееру** *n.* bebeeru bark.

беватрон *m.* (nucl.) bevatron.

бег *m.* run, course; **—ание** *n.* running; **—ательный** *a.* cursorial; cannon (bone); **—ать** *v.* run (about); **—ать от** *v.* avoid, shun; **—ающий** *a.* running, cursorial; *see also* **бегущий.**

бегемот *m.* (mam.) hippopotamus; **—овые, —ы** *pl.* Hippopotamidae.

беген/ат *m.* behenate; **—овый** *a.* behenic, docosanoic (acid); behen (oil); **—олевый** *a.* behenolic (acid).

бегичевский *a.* (geog.) Begicheva.

бегл/ец *m.* fugitive; refugee; **—ость** *f.* dexterity; speed; fluency; **—ый** *a.* fluent, rapid; sketchy, superficial; cursory (inspection); fugitive, runaway; brief, passing; **—ый огонь** rapid fire.

бег/овой *a.* running, race; carpal (bones); **—овая дорожка** race track; (mach.) race; **—ом** *adv.* on the run, running; *m.* (elec.) begohm (10^9 ohms).

бегон/иевый *a.,* **—ия** *f.* (bot.) begonia.

бегство *n.* flight, escape, hasty retreat.

бегун *m.* runner; millstone, crusher roll; edge roll; leading pulley; (paper) kollergang; **зобатые —ки** *pl.* (orn.) seedsnipe family (*Thinocoridae*); **—ковый** *a. of* **бегунок; —ковая тележка** trailer; **—ок** *m.* runner, roller, traveler; (ball bearing) race; rider, slide (valve); (slide rule) cursor, indicator; (rr.) pilot truck; (orn.) courser (*Cursorius cursor*); **—ы** *pl.* edge runner mill.

бег/ут *pr. 3 pl. of* **бежать; коэффициент —учести** traveling-wave ratio; **—учий, —ущий** *a.* running; traveling (wave); scanning (beam); **с —ущей волной** traveling wave.

бегхауз *m.* bag house; filter plant.

бед/а *f.* misfortune, trouble, mishap, predicament; **на—у** unfortunately.

бедантит *m.* (min.) beudantite.

беден *sh. m. of* **бедный.**

бёдер *gen. pl. of* **бедро; —ный** *see* **бедренный.**

бедленд *m.* (geol.) badland.

беднеть *v.* grow poor; peter out.

беднодемьяновский *a.* (geog.) Bednodemyanovsk.

бедн/ость *f.* poverty; poorness (of soil); **—ота** *f.* poverty; the poor; **деревянская —ота** the rural poor; **—ый** *a.* poor, lean (gas, ore); low, deficient (in); weak (solution); **—ый энергией** low-energy; **—як** *m.* poor peasant, poor person.

бёдра *pl. of* **бедро.**

бедренец *m.* (bot.) Pimpinella.

бедр/енно— *prefix* (anat.) femoro— (femur); **—енный** *a.* femoral; **—енная кость** femur, thigh bone; **—о** *n.* femur, thigh; ham, haunch.

бедрок *m.* (geol.) bedrock.

бедроротые *pl.* (pal.) Merostomata.

бедряный *see* **бедренный.**

бедств/енный *a.* distress(ing); disastrous; **—ие** *n.* calamity, disaster; emergency; distress; (ecol.) catastrophe; **сигнал —ия** distress signal, SOS; **—овать** *v.* be in distress; live in poverty.

беегерит *m.* (min.) beegerite.

беж *m.* beige.

бежать *v.* run, course, flow; trickle, drip; boil over; flee, escape.

бежевый *a.* beige.

бежецкий *a.* (geog.) Bezhetsk.

беженец *m.* refugee.

без *prep. gen.* without; minus, less, free (from or of); with no; not involving; with the exception (of); exclusive (of); —less, e.g. **без шва** seamless; **и б. того** anyway, already.

без— *prefix* in—, ir—, un—, —less, —free, de—, non—; *see also* **бес—**.

безаварийн/ость *f.* trouble-free operation; **—ый** *a.* trouble-free, faultless; **—ый отказ** fail-safe operation, fail-safety.

безазотистый *a.* nitrogen-free.

безалаберный *a.* without system, inconsistent; negligent, careless.

баз/алкалоидный *a.* alkaloid-free; **—алкогольный** *a.* nonalcoholic, soft (drinks).

безапелляционный *a.* peremptory, categorical.

безбелковый *a.* protein-free (diet); (bot.) exalbuminous.

безболезненн/ость *f.* analg(es)ia; perfect health; **—ый** *a.* painless; healthy.

безборный *a.* free of boron or boric acid.

безбородый *a.* beardless, imberbe.

безбоязненный *a.* fearless, brave.

безбрачный *a.* celibate; (bot.) agamous.

безбрежный *a.* vast, boundless.

безбурный *a.* stormless, calm.

безв. *abbr.* (**безводный**).

безвариантный *a.* invariant.

безваттный *a.* (elec.) wattless, idle, reactive (component).

безвершинн/ик *m.* (silv.) pollard; **—ый** *a.* pollarded (tree); topless.

безвестный *a.* obscure, unknown.

безветр/енный *a.* windless, calm; **—ие** *n.* calm, still air.

безвинный *a.* innocent, guiltless.

безвихревой *a.* vortex-free, eddy-free; irrotational (flow).

безвкус/ие *n.*, **—ица** *f.*, **—ность** *f.* tastelessness; **—ный** *a.* tasteless, bland, insipid.

безвлажный *a.* dry, moisture-free.

безвластный *a.* without authority.

безвласый *a.* hairless.

безвод/ие *n.*, **—ность** *f.* anhydrous state; dryness, aridity; drought, water shortage; **—ный** *a.* anhydrous; water-free, moisture-free; nonaqueous; absolute (alcohol); dry, arid; **—ородный** *a.* hydrogen-free; **—ье** *see* **безводие.**

безвозвратн/о *adv.* irrevocably; **—ый** *a.* irrevocable, irreversible.

безвоздушн/ый *a.* airless; deaerated, vacuum; **—ое пространство** vacuum; outer space.

безвозмездный *a.* free (of charge).

безволокнистый *a.* fiber-free; snap (bean).

безволос/ица *f.* baldness; **—ый** *a.* bald, hairless; glabrous, smooth.

безвредн/о *adv.* harmlessly; **—ость** *f.* harmlessness; **—ый** *a.* harmless, noninjurious; innocuous; innocent.

безвременн/ик *m.*, **—ица** *f.* (bot.) Colchicum; **—о** *adv.* prematurely; **—ый** *a.* premature, untimely, inopportune.

безвыборочный *a.* indiscriminate.

безвыгодн/ость *f.* disadvantage; **—ый** *a.* disadvantageous.

безвыездный *a.* uninterrupted.

безвыходный *a.* hopeless, desperate.

безвязкостный *a.* nonviscous, inviscid.

безгаремный *a.* (zool.) bachelor.

без/главый *see* **безголовый; —глазый** *a.* eyeless, anophthalmous; one-eyed; **—гласие** *n.* aphonia, loss of voice; **—гласный** *a.* mute, silent.

безгнилостный *a.* aseptic.

безголов/ые *pl.* (zool.) Acephala; **—ый** *a.* headless, acephalous; scatter-brained.

безголос(н)ый *a.* voiceless, surd.

безграмотный *a.* illiterate, ignorant.

безграничн/о *adv.* infinitely, ad infinitum; **—ость** *f.* infinity; **—ый** *a.* infinite, limitless, unlimited, boundless; unbounded (function); immense.

безгранный *a.* anhedral.

безгрунтовый *a.* one-coat (enamel).

безгумусный *a.* humus-free.

бездарн/ость *f.* want of talent: **—ый** *a.* untalented, ungifted, incapable.

бездейств/енность *f.* inactivity; ineffectiveness, inefficiency; **—енный** *see* **бездействующий; —ие** *n.* inaction, inertia, inertness; inactivity; standstill, stop; **быть в —ии** *v.* (mach.) be out of service, be out of commission, not run; **—овать** *v.* be inactive or idle, not work, **—ующий** *a.* inactive, inert, passive; idle, inoperative, out of operation.

бездел/ица *f.* trifle; **—ка, —ушка** *f.* novelty, knick-knack; **—ье** *n.* idleness; **—ьник** *m.*, **—ьница** *f.* idle person; **—ьничать** *v.* be idle, loaf; **—ьный** *a.* idle.

безденеж/ный *a.* impecunious; non-cash, clearing (payment); **—ье** *n.* shortage of money.

бездетный *a.* childless.

бездефицитный *a.* self-supporting.

бездеятельн/о *adv.* passively; **—ость** *f.* inactivity, inertia; **—ый** *a.* passive, inert, inactive, inoperative.

бездиверген/тный *a.* nondivergent; **—ционный** *a.* without divergence; (math.) solenoidal.

бездна *f.* chasm, gulf, deep, abyss; a great number (of), a great deal (of).

бездожд/ие *n.*, **—ье** *n.* drought, dry weather.

бездоказательный *a.* unproved, unsubstantiated, not based on evidence.

бездольный *a.* (bot.) acotyledonous.

бездомный *a.* houseless, homeless.

бездон/ка *f.* upright bee log or box hive; **—ный** *a.* bottomless, very deep.

бездорож/ица *f.*, **—ье** *n.* lack of good roads; impassable roads; **—ный** *a.* impassable, roadless, pathless.

бездоходн/о *adv.* without profit, unprofitable; **—ый** *a.* unprofitable.

бездугные *pl.* (herp.) Anapsida, Chelonia.

бездымный *a.* smokeless; pollution-free.

бездыханный *a.* lifeless, inanimate.

без/жаберный *a.* (zool.) abranchiate, lacking gills; **—жгутиковый** *a.* eflagelliferous; **—железистый** *a.* eglandular; **—жёлтковый** *a.* alecithal; **—жёлчный** *a.* acholic, bilefree.

безжизненный *a.* lifeless, inanimate; dull.

безжилковый *a.* veinless, ribless.

безжирный *a.* fat-free.

беззаботный *a.* carefree, unconcerned.

беззаветный *a.* selfless, dedicated.

беззакон/ие *n.* unlawful action; **—ничать** *v.* break the law; **—но** *adv.* illegally; **—ный** *a.* illegal, unlawful.

баззамков/ые *pl.* (mal.) Inarticulata; **—ый** *a.* (zool.) inarticulate, hingeless.

беззародыш/евый, —ный *a.* (biol.) inembryonate, having no embryo.

беззарядный *a.* uncharged, neutral.

беззащитный *a.* unprotected, defenseless.

беззвёздный *a.* starless.

беззвучный *a.* soundless, noiseless, silent.

безземель/е *n.* lack of arable land; **—ный** *a.* landless, lacking land.

беззольный *a.* ashless, ash-free.

беззуб/ки, —ковые p*l.* (mal.) Anodontidae; **—ый** *a.* toothless, edentate.

безизлучательный *a.* nonradiating.

безин— *see under* **безын—**.

безискр/истый, —овой *a.* sparkless.

безклеточный *a.* noncellular.

безкоготный *a.* clawless, without claws.

безконечный *see* **бесконечный**.

безконтактный *a.* noncontact (control).

безкопирочная бумага carbonless paper.

безкорыстный *a.* disinterested.

безламповый *a.* (rad.) tubeless.

безлёгочный *a.* (zool.) apulmonic, lungless.

безлепестковый *a.* (bot.) apetalous.

безлес/ный *a.* woodless, treeless, bare; **—ье** *n.* lack of forests; cut-over area.

безликий *a.* faceless, vague.

безлист/венный, —(н)ый *a.* leafless, aphyllous.

безличина *f.* (leather) mat grain.

безличный *a.* impersonal, dull (personality).

безлодочный *a.* (glass) without debiteuses.

безлопастный *a.* bladeless.

безлоскутный *a.* (med.) flapless (amputation).

безлунный *a.* moonless.

безлюд/ный *a.* thinly populated, uninhabited, desolate, **—ство, —ье** *n.* low population; manpower shortage.

безмагнитный *a.* nonmagnetic.

безмала *adv.* almost, nearly.

безмасляный *a.* oil-free.

безмассовый *a.* (phys.) massless.

безмасштабный *a.* scaleless.

без/маток *m.* (apid.) queenless hive; **—маточный** *a.* queenless (hive); **—медица** *f.* bee colony without food.

безмен *m.* steelyard, beam scale.

безмерн/о *adv.* immeasurably, very; **—ость** *f.* immensity, excess; **—ый** *a.* immeasurable, immense; boundless, infinite.

безместный *a.* without a place.

безмикробный *a.* (med.) amicrobic.

безмолв/ный *a.* silent; implicit (promise); **—ствовать** *v.* be silent, say nothing.

безмолочность *f.* dry period (of cow).

безмоментный *a.* momentless.

безморозный *a.* frost-free.

безмоторный *a.* motorless, unpowered.

безмякотный *a.* (anat.) amyelinic, nonmedullated; pulpless.

безмятежный *a.* tranquil, serene.

безнагрузочный *a.* idle, standby.

безнадёжн/ость *f.* hopelessness; **—ый** *a.* hopeless, desperate; bad (debt).

безнадзорный *a.* unsupervised.

безналичный расчёт (com.) clearing.

безнамеренный *a.* unintentional.

безнапорный *a.* free, nonartesian (water); gravity (flow); nonramming.

безнатриевый *a.* sodium-free.

безнатурный *a.* hypothetical.

безног/ие p*l.* (zool.) Apoda; **—ий** *a.* without feet, legless; (zool.) apodal.

безо *see* **без**.

безоар *m.* **—овый** *a.* (vet.) bezoar, hairball; **—овая кислота** bezoardic acid, ellagic acid.

безобидный *a.* inoffensive, harmless.

безоблачный *a.* cloudless, clear.

безобраз/ие *n.* deformity; outrage, disgrace; **—ить** *v.* mutilate, disfigure; **—ный** *a.* hideous, deformed, ugly; outrageous, shocking; unseemly, disgraceful.

безоговорочный *a.* unconditional.

безоконный *a.* windowless.

базопасн/о *adv.* safely, without danger; it is safe; **—ость** *f.* safety, security; reliability; **коэффициент —ости** safety factor, margin of safety; **мера —ости** safeguard, safety measure; **техника —ости** accident prevention; **—ый** *a.* safe, secure, reliable; foolproof; safety; permissible (load).

безориентирный *a.* featureless (terrain); random, patternless, aimless.

безоружный *a.* unarmed, defenseless; (bot.) inerm.

безосколочный *a.* shatterproof (glass); (paper) shive-free.

безосновательн/о *adv.* without basis; **—ый** *a.* groundless, unfounded.

безосный *a.* (zool.) anaxial.

безостановочн/о *adv.* continuously, without stopping; **—ость** *f.* continuousness; **—ый** *a.* continuous, unceasing, ceaseless, uninterrupted; nonstop (flight).

безостаточн/ый *a.* without residue; **—ая переработка** (petrol.) run-down distillation.

безостый *a.* (bot.) awnless, exaristate.

безотборный режим (distillation) infinite reflux conditions.

безотвальный *a.* (mold) boardless (plow).

безответственн/ость *f.* irresponsibility; **—ый** *a.* irresponsible.

безотказн/ость *f.* reliability, dependability; failure-free performance; **—ый** *a.* reliable, trouble-free, smooth; **—ая работа** no failure (operation).

безоткатный *a.* recoilless, nonrecoil.

безотл/агательно *adv.* without delay, urgently, immediately; **—агательность** *f.* urgency; **—агательный, —ожный** *a.* urgent, pressing.

безотлучн/ость *f.* constant presence; **—ый** *a.* constantly present; uninterrupted, continuous.

безотменный *a.* irrevocable.

безотносительн/о *adv.* without reference (to), irrespective(ly) (of); **—ый** *a.* irrespective (of); absolute, unconditional.

безотрывный *a.* continuous, unbroken.

безотходный *a.* pollution-free (fuel).

безотчётный *a.* involuntary, instinctive, unconscious; unaccountable.

безошибочн/о *adv.* correctly, without error; **—ость** *f.* infallibity; **—ый** *a.* correct, exact, faultless, infallible, unerring.

безпористый *a.* nonporous.

безпорядочный *a.* random (sequence).

безпредельный *a.* unlimited, boundless.

безпривязный *a.* loose.

безпристрастный *a.* unbiased.

безработ/ица *f.* unemployment; **—ные** p*l.* the unemployed; **—ный** *a.* unemployed.

безрадиоактивный *a.* nonradioactive, cold.

безраздельный *a.* undivided; wholehearted.

безразлич/ие *n.* indifference, apathy; **—но** *adv.* irrespective, no matter which; it makes no difference; **ему —но** he doesn't care; **—ный** *a.* indifferent, apathetic; insensitive; neutral (point).

безразмерный *a.* dimensionless, nondimensional; stretch (fabric).

безраковинн/ые p*l.* (crust.) fairy shrimps (*Anostraca*); **—ый** *a.* aconchal.

безрамный *a.* frameless.

безрасчётный *a.* uncalculated; careless; imprudent; wasteful, extravagant.

безрёберный *a.* ribless, acostate.

безредукторный *a.* (mach.) direct-drive.

безрезультатн/о *adv.* without result, to no effect, in vain; **—ость** *f.* futility, ineffectiveness; failure; **—ый** *a.* futile, without result, ineffective; unsuccessful, barren (well); dry (run).

безрезьбовой *a.* slip (joint).

безрельсовый *a.* railless, trackless; road, highway (transportation).

безрессорный *a.* without springs, springless; unsprung.

безрогий *a.* hornless, polled; acerous.

безротый *a.* astomatous, without a mouth.

безрыб/ица *f.,* **—ье** *n.* scarcity of fish.

безтигельн/ый *a.* without crucibles; **—ое плавление** floating zone melting, zone floating.

безубыточн/о *adv.* without loss; **—ость** *f.,* **быть —ым** *v.* (comp.) breakeven; **—ый** *a.* without loss; breakeven.

безуглеродистый *a.* carbon-free.

безугольный *a.* having no angles; without coal; carbon-free.

безударный *a.* shock-free; unaccented.

безудержный *a.* unchecked, unrestrained.

безуклон/ный, —чивый *a.* undeviating, straight.

безукоризненный *a.* irreproachable.

безум/ие *n.* insanity; folly; **—ный** *a.* mad, senseless; distracting; exorbitant (price); **—ствовать** *v.* rage, rave, carry on.

безупречный *a.* faultless, blameless, irreproachable; flawless; stainless (reputation).

безусадочн/ость *f.* resistance to shrinking; **—ый** *a.* shrink-resistant, nonshrinking.

безусловн/о *adv.* absolutely, etc., *see a.;* of course, there is no doubt that, to be sure; **—ость** *f.* absoluteness, certainty; **—ый** *a.* absolute, indisputable; positive, unconditional; inborn, instinctive, unconditioned, unlearned; (stat.) unconstrained.

безуспешн/о *adv.* unsuccessfully, without success; **—ость** *f.* failure; **—ый** *a.* unsuccessful, ineffective.

безусый *a.* whiskerless; unbearded.

безуточный *a.* (text.) weftless.

безучаст/ие *n.,* **—ность** *f.* indifference; **—ный** *a.* indifferent, apathetic.

безчешуйный *a.* scaleless, bare.

безшумный *a.* noiseless, silent.

безъёмкостный *a.* noncapacitive.

безъядерный *a.* enucleate, lacking a nucleus; non-nucleated; nuclear-free (zone).

безъязыч/ковый *a.* (bot.) eligulate; **—ные** *pl.* (amph.) Aglossa; **—ный** *a.* aglossal, tongueless.

безъячейковый *a.* cell-free.

безызвестн/ость *f.* obscurity, uncertainty; **—ый** *a.* obscure, unknown.

безызлучательный *a.* nonradiating.

безым/ённый, —янный *a.* nameless, anonymous; fourth (finger); **—янная кость** innominate bone.

безындукционный *a.* noninductive.

безынерционный *a.* inertia-free, inertialess.

безынициативный *a.* lacking initiative, passive, inert.

безынтересный *a.* uninteresting.

безыскровый *a.* sparkless, spark-free.

безысходный *a.* endless; irreparable.

Безье (comp.) Bezier (curves).

безэлектродный *a.* electrodeless.

безэховый *a.* (acous.) anechoic.

бей *imp. of* **бить.**

бейделлит *m.* (min.) beidellite.

бейерит *m.* (min.) bayerite.

бейесовский *a.* (stat.) Bayes'.

бейза *f.* (mam.) beisa (*Oryx beisa*).

бейлиит *m.* (min.) bayleyite.

Бейльби слой (met.) Beilby layer.

бейнит *m.* (met.) bainite; **—изация** *f.,* **—ирование** *n.* bainiting (of steel).

бейра *f.* (mam.) beira (*Dorcatragus megalotis*).

Бейс-Балло закон (meteor.) Buys-Ballot's law.

бейский *a.* (geog.) Beya.

бейц/евание *n.,* **—овка** *f.* staining (of woods); (met.) scouring, pickling.

Бека лампа Beck arc lamp.

бекабадский *a.* (geog.) Bekabad.

бекас *m.* (orn.) snipe (*Gallinago*); woodcock (*Scolopax*); **морской б.** *see* **бекас-рыба;** **—ик** *m.* (ichth.) Kuban dace (*Leuciscus aphipsi*); **—ики** *pl.* snipe flies (*Rhagionidae*); **—овидный** *a.* snipe-billed, snipe-like; **—овые** *pl.* (orn.) Scolopacidae; (ichth.) snipefishes (*Macroramphosidae*); **б.-рыба** *m.* snipefish.

бекеровский *a.* Baker('s).

Бекке полоска (opt.) Becke line.

беккелит *m.* (min.) beckelite.

беккерел/евский *a.* Becquerel (rays); **—ит** *m.* (min.) becquerelite.

беккросс *m.* (gen.) back-cross.

бекман/ия *f.* slough grass (*Beckmannia*); **—овское превращение** (chem.) Beckmann rearrangement.

бекмес *m.* concentrated fruit juice.

бекон *m.,* **—ный** *a.* bacon.

бекфиллер *m.* back filler.

бел *sh. m. of* **белый;** *m.* (acous.) bel, B.

белая *f.* silver salmon (*Oncorhynchus kisutch*); *f. of* **белый.**

белбор *m.* (met.) Belbor.

бел/городский *a.* (geog.) Belgorod; **—ебеевский** *a.* Belebei; **—ёвский** *a.* Belyov.

белёк *m.* whitecoat (baby seal).

белемнит *m.* (pal.) belemnite.

белена *f.* (bot.) henbane (*Hyoscyamus*).

беление *n.* bleaching; blanching.

беленной *a. of* **белена.**

белён(н)ый *a.* bleached; blanched.

белес/оватость *f.* (paints) blushing; **—(оват)ый** *a.* whitish; albicant.

бел/еть *v.* turn white, whiten; fade; **—еющий** *a.* turning white, etc. *see v.;* albescent; **—и** *gen., pl., etc. of* **бель;** (med.) leucorrhea; **—изна** *f.* white(ness); **—ики** *pl.* beliki (for the Alapaevsk iron ore deposits the term means a mass of white clastic diluvial mesozoic rocks; for the Tukansk deposits, weathered and whitened clay schists; for the Berezovsk deposits, weathered beresites).

белила *pl.* white (mineral) pigment, whiting; **свинцовые б.** white lead; **цинковые б.** zinc white, zinc oxide.

белиль/ный *a.* bleaching; **б. бак** bleacher, bleach tank; **б. порошок, —ная известь** bleaching powder, calcium hypochlorite; **б. раствор, —ная ванна** bleaching liquor, bleach; **—ное средство** bleach, decolorant; **—ня** *f.* bleachery; **—щик** *m.* bleacher.

белимый *a.* bleachable.

белит *m.* (cement; min.) belite.

белит/ель *m.* bleach, bleaching agent; **—ь** *v.* whiten, bleach; whitewash, paint white; blanch (metal, etc.).

белич/ий *a. of* **белка; —ье колесо** (mach.) squirrel cage; **—ьи** *pl.* (mam.) squirrels (*Sciuridae*).

белк/а *f.* squirrel; *gen. of* **белок; —ки** *pl. of* **белок;** *gen., pl., etc. of* **белка;** belki (snow-covered, flattened mountain summits in Siberia).

белкинский *a.* (geog.) Belka.

белки-рыбы *pl.* squirrelfishes (*Holocentridae*).

белков/ина *f.* albumen, egg-white; protein; **—(ист)ость** *f.* protein content; **—истый** *a.* protein-containing; **—о-уг-ле-водный** *a.* protein-carbohydrate; **—ый** *a.* protein(-containing), albumin(ous); **—ая оболочка** (anat.) tunica albuginea; **—ое вещество, —ое тело** protein.

белладон/ин *m.* belladonnine; **—на** *f.*, **—ный** *a.* (bot.) belladonna.

белловский *a.* Bell (telephone).

бело *adv. and sh. n. of* **белый**; *prefix* albi—, alb(o)—, white; leuc(o)— (white, colorless); **—бокий** *a.* white-sided; **—бочка** *f.* (mam.) dolphin (*Delphinus delphis*); **—бровик** *m.* (orn.) whitebrow (*Turdus musicus*); **—брюхий** *a.* white-bellied; **—брюшка** *f.* (orn.) whitebelly (*Cyclorrhynchus*).

белов/ато— *prefix* whitish; **б.-жёлтый** *a.* ochroleucous, cream-colored; **—атость** *f.* whitishness; **—атый** *a.* whitish, albicant; **—ик** *m.*, **—ой экземпляр** clean copy, final draft; **—ые товары** stationery.

беловский *a.* (geog.) Belovo.

белоглазк/а *f.* calcareous concretions; (ichth.) bream (*Abramis sapa*); (orn.) white-eye (*Zosterops*); **—и, —овые** *pl.* Zosteropidae.

белоголов, —ец *m.* (bot.) Spiraea; **—ка** *f.* mountain clover (*Trifolium montanum*); **—ый** *a.* white-headed.

белогрудый *a.* (orn.) white-breasted.

белодеревец *m.* joiner, rough carpenter.

бело/душка *f.* (mam.) stone marten (*Martes foina*); **—зем** *m.* light(-colored) soil; **—зёрный** *a.* white-grained, white-kernel; **—зерский** *a.* (geog.) Lake Beloye; **—зор** *m.* (bot.) Parnassia.

белозуб/ка *f.* (mam.) shrew (*Crocidura*); **б.-малютка** *f.* dwarf shrew (*Suncus*); **—ки, —овые** *pl.* Crocidurinae; **—(чат)ый** *a.* white-toothed.

белок *m.* albumin, protein; (egg) albumen; white (of eye); *gen. pl. of* **белка.**

белокалильн/ость *f.*, **—ый жар** incandescence, white heat; **—ый** *a.* incandescent, white hot, glowing.

бело/калитвинский *a.* (geog.) Belaya Kalitva; **—канский** *a.* Belokanyi; **—катайский** *a.* Belokatai; **—копытник** *m.* (bot.) coltsfoot (*Petasites*); **—корый** *a.* white-barked; **—кровие** *n.* (med.) leukemia; **—кровки, —кровные** *pl.* (ichth.) icefishes (*Channichthyidae*); **—крылки** *pl.* white flies (*Aleyrodidae*); **—крылый** *a.* white-winged; white-finned; **—крыльник** *m.* (bot.) Calla; **—кудренник** *m.* Ballota; **—курый** *a.* fair, blond; **—лист(вен)ный** *a.* white-leaved, silver-leaved; **—ность** *f.* (phyt.) white leaf; **—лицый** *a.* fair-skinned; **—лоз** *m.* (bot.) white willow (*Salix alba*); **—морский** *a.* (geog.) White Sea; **—мошник** *m.* sphagnum moss; **—мышечная болезнь** (vet.) white muscle disease, WMD, nutritional myopathy.

белонит *m.* (petr.) belonite.

бело/ножка *f.* (orn.) pied thrush (*Microcichla or Enicurus scouleri*); **—перый** *a.* white-feathered; white-finned; **—полосый** *a.* white-striped, white-banded; **—польский** *a.* (geog.) Belopolye; **—пятнистый** *a.* white-spotted; **—пятнистая болезнь** (vet.) white spot; **—рецкий** *a.* (geog.) Belaya (River); **—русский** *a.* Belorussian; **—рыбица** *f.* white salmon (spec. *Stenodus leucichthys*).

бело/семянный *a.* white-seeded, leucospermous; **—снежный** *a.* snow-white, nival; **—стебельный** *a.* white-stalked; **—тал** *m.* (bot.) osier willow (*Salix viminalis or alba*); **—телый** *a.* fair-skinned; **—точечный** *a.* white-dotted, white-spotted; **—турка** *f.* hard wheat (*Triticum durum*); **—ус** *m.* (bot.) matgrass (*Nardus*); **—усник** *m.* matgrass community; **—холуницкий** *a.* (geog.) Belaya Kholunitsa, **—цветковый** *a.* white-flowered, albiflorous; **—цветник** *m.* (bot.) snowflake

(*Leucojum*); **—церковский** *a.* (geog.) Belaya Tserkov.

белочн/ый *a.* of **белок**; (anat.) albugineous; **—ая оболочка** tunica albuginea; sclera (of eye).

бело/шей *m.* white-necked goose; **—щетинковый** *a.* white-bristled, albisetose; **—ярский** *a.* (geog.) Belyi Yar.

белу/га *f.*, **—жий** *a.* (ichth.) beluga, white sturgeon (*Huso huso*); (mam.) *see* **белуха**; **—жина** *f.* beluga flesh; **—кар** *m.* (geobot.) belukar; **—ха** *f.* (mam.) beluga, white whale (*Delphinapterus leucas*); **—хинский** *a.* (geog.) Belukha.

бел/ый *a.* white; blank (spot); **—ь** *f.* linen yarn; (text.) dyeing) resist; gap; (phyt.) white rust.

бельг. *abbr.* (**бельгийский**) Belgian.

бельдюг/а *f.* (ichth.) eelpout (*Zoarces*, spec. *Z. viviparus*); **—овые** *pl.* Zoarcidae.

бельё *n.* linen; (cer.) plain white china; **нижнее б.** underwear.

белевой *a.* of **бельё.**

бель/ка *gen. of* **белёк**; **—мо** *n.* (med.) leukoma (white corneal spot); **—ник** *m.* birch forest; **—ский** *a.* (geog.) Belaya (River).

бельтинг *m.* (text.) belt(ing) duck.

бельэтаж *m.* second floor; mezzanine.

беляк *m.* school, shoal (of fish); foam, white-cap (of waves); (leather) staking frame; (geol.) beliak (white clay); (mam.) blue hare (*Lepus timidus*).

белянк/а *f.* (bot.) white mushroom (*Lactarius*); spring snowflake (*Leucojum vernum*); white butterfly (*Pieris*); **—овые** *pl.* (ichth.) Sillaginidae; Lactariidae.

бембро/вые *pl.* (ichth.) Bembridae; **—псовые** *pl.* Bembropsidae.

бем/ерия *f.* (bot.) Boehmeria; **—ит** *m.* (min.) boehmite; **—ский** *a.* Bohemian (glass).

бенбери *m.* (rub.) Banbury mixer.

бенгальский *a.* (geog.) Bengal(ese).

бенедикт *m.* (bot.) blessed thistle (*Cnicus*, spec. *C. benedictus*); **—ин** *m.* benedictine (liqueur).

бенз— *prefix* benz(o)—; *see also under* **бензо—**; **—азин** *m.* benzazine; **—аконин** *m.* benzaconine; **—акридин** *m.* benzacridine, phenonaphthacridine.

бензаль *m.* benzal, benzylidene; **—азин** *m.* benzalazine, benzaldehyde azine; **—ацетон** *m.* benzalacetone, cinnamyl methyl ketone; **—ацетофенон** *m.* benzalacetophenone, cinnamyl phenyl ketone.

бенз/альдегид *m.* benzaldehyde, benzenecarbonal; **—альдоксим** *m.* benzaldoxime; **—альхлорид** *m.* benzal chloride, benzylidene chloride; **—амид** *m.* benzamide, benzenecarbonamide; **—амидин** *m.* benzamidine; **—амон** *m.* Benzamon; **—анилид** *m.* benzanilide, benzoylaniline; **—антрен** *m.* benzanthrene, naphthanthracene; **—аурин** *m.* benzaurine; **—гидрил** *m.* benzhydryl; **—гидроль** *m.* benzhydrol; **—едрин** *m.* Benzedrine, amphetamine.

бензель *m.* (naut.) seizing, lashing.

бензен *see* **бензол**; **—ил** *m.* benzenyl.

бензидин *m.*, **—овый** *a.* benzidine.

бензил *m.* benzyl; benzil, dibenzoyl; **хлористый б.** benzylchloride; **—амин** *m.* benzylamine, phenylmethylamine; **—ацетат** *m.* benzyl acetate.

бензилиден *m.* benzylidene, benzal; **хлористый б.** benzylidene chloride; **—ацетон** *m.* benzylidene acetone.

бензилир/ование *n.* benzylation; **—ованный** *a.* benzylated; **—овать** *v.* benzylate.

бензилов/ый *a.* benzyl; **б. спирт** benzyl alcohol, phenyl carbinol; **б. эфир** benzyl ether, benzyl oxide; **б. эфир уксусной кислоты** benzyl acetate; **—ая кислота**

benzilic acid, diphenylglycolic acid; **соль —ой кислоты,** —**окисная соль** benzilate.

бензил/пенициллин *m.* benzylpenicillin; —**хлорид** *m.* benzyl chloride; —**целлюлоза** *f.* benzylcellulose; —**ьный** *a.* benzyl.

бензимер *see* **бензиномер.**

бензимидазол *m.* benzimidazole.

бензин *m.* gas(oline); benzine (solvent); —**e** *n.* saturated benzol(e) wash oil; **б.-калоша** *m.* rubber solvent; —**ный** *a.* of **бензин;** —**овоз** *m.* (gasoline) tanker; —**овый** *a.* of **бензин;** —**овая колонка** gas pump; —**оизмеритель,** —**омер** *m.* fuel gage; —**омотор** *m.* gasoline engine; —**оуловитель** *m.* oil or gas separator; —**охранилище** *n.* gas tank.

бензин-растворитель *m.* benzine solvent.

бензо— *prefix* benz(o)—; gasoline; —**ат** *m.* benzoate; —**бак** *m.* gas(oline) tank; —**воз** *m.* tank truck.

бензозаправ/очный *a.* (gasoline) fueling; —**щик** *m.* (av.) fueling truck.

бензозол(ь) *m.* benzosol, guaiacol benzoate.

бензоил *m.* benzoyl; **перекись** —**а** benzoyl peroxide; **хлористый б.** benzoyl chloride; —**ацетон** *m.* benzoylacetone; —**бензойный** *a.* benzoylbenzoic (acid); —**ирование** *n.* benzoylation; —**ировать** benzoylate; —**муравьиный** *a.* benzoylformic (acid); —**уксусный** *a.* benzoylacetic (acid); —**хлорид** *m.* benzoyl chloride; —**ьный** *a.* benzoyl.

бензой *see* **бензойное дерево.**

бензойно/амиловый эфир amyl benzoate; —**кальциевая соль** calcium benzoate; —**кислый** *a.* benzoic acid; benzoate (of); —**кислый натрий** sodium benzoate; —**кислая соль** benzoate; —**метиловый эфир** methyl benzoate; —**натриевая соль** sodium benzoate; —**этиловый эфир** ethyl benzoate.

бензойн/ый *a.* benzoin, benzoic; **б. альдегид** benzaldehyde; **б. ангидрид** benzoic anhydride; **б. эфир гваякола** guaiacol benzoate; —**ая кислота** benzoic acid, benzenecarboxylic acid; **соль** or **эфир —ой кислоты** benzoate; —**ая смола** (gum) benzoin; —**ое дерево** (bot.) spice bush (*Lindera, Benzoin*).

бензо/колонка *f.* gas(oline) pump; gas station; —**кран** *m.* fuel cock; —**ксазин** *m.* benzoxazine; —**кси—** *prefix* benzoxy—.

бензол *m.* benzene, phene; —**гексахлорид** *m.* hexachlorocyclohexane, Lindane (insecticide); —**дикарбоновый** *a.* benzenedicarboxylic (acid); —**ин** *m.* Benzoline, ligroin; benzolin; —**овый** *a.* of **бензол;** —**стойкий** *a.* benzene-resistant.

бензолсульф/иновый *a.* benzenesulfinic (acid); —**окислота** *f.,* —**оновая кислота** benzenesulfonic acid; —**онат** *m.* benzenesulfonate; —**оновокислый** *a.* benzenesulfonate; benzenesulfonic acid; —**оновоэтиловый эфир** ethyl benzenesulfonate.

бензо/льный *a.* of **бензол;** —**маслостойкий** *a.* gas and oil resistant; —**маслостойкость** *f.* resistance to gas(oline) and oil; —**мер** *m.* fuel gage; —**насос** *m.* fuel pump; —**нафтол** *m.* benzonaphthol, naphthol benzoate; —**нитрил** *m.* benzonitrile, benzenecarbonitrile; —**обогреватель** *m.* (av.) gasoline preheater; —**пила** *f.* gasoline-powered saw; —**пиррол** *m.* benzopyrrole, indole; —**помпа** *f.* fuel pump; —**провод** *m.* fuel line; —**пурпурин** *m.* benzopurpurin.

бензо/раздаточный *a.* gas (pump); —**растворитель** *m.* petroleum solvent; —**рез** *m.* oxy(gen)-gasoline torch; —**система** *f.* (av.) fuel system; —**склад** *m.* gasoline storage; —**станция** *f.* gas service station.

бензостойк/ий *a.* gasoline-resistant, gasoline-proof; —**ость** *f.* resistance to gasoline.

бензо/тиофен *m.* benzothiophene; —**триазол** *m.* benzotriazole; —**трихлорид** *m.* benzotrichloride, phenylchloroform; —**указатель** *m.* fuel gage; —**фильтр** *m.* fuel filter; —**фенон** *m.* benzophenone, diphenyl ketone; —**фуран** *m.* benzofuran, coumarone; —**хинолин** *m.* benzoquinoline, α-anthrapyridine; —**хранилище** *n.* gas(oline) tank.

бенз/пинакон *m.* benzpinacone; —**пирен** *m.* benzpyrene; —**тиазол** *m.* benz(o)thiazole; —**хинолин** *m.* benzquinoline.

бенинкопал *m.* benin copal; —**овый** *a.* benin copal; benincopalic (acid).

бенит *m.* barley sugar.

бенитоит *m.* (min.) benitoite.

беннер *m.* Banner (tire) machine.

беннеттитовые *pl.* (pal.) Bennettitaceae.

бенс-джонсовый *a.* Bence Jones (protein).

бент— *prefix* benth(o)— (sea-bottom); —**аль** *f.* benthic zone; (pond) bottom; —**ический** *see* **бентонический;** —**одесма** *f.* (ichth.) Benthodesmus; —**озавр** *m.* Benthosaurus.

бентонит *m.,* —**овая глина** (geol.) bentonite; —**овый** *a.* bentonite, bentonitic.

бенто/нический, —**нный** *a.* benthonic, sea-bottom; —**с** *m.* benthos, sea-bottom organisms; —**сный** *a.* benthos, benthic; —**соядный** *a.* benthos-eating, bottom-feeding, benthophagous; —**фаг** *m.* benthophage; —**фит** *m.* (bot.) benthophyte; —**ядный** *see* **бентосоядный.**

бенч *m.* (geol.) bench.

беомицес *m.* (bot.) Baeomyces (a lichen).

бер. *abbr.* [**берег(овой); берёзовый**].

Бера закон (opt.) Beer's law.

бераунит *m.* (min.) beraunite.

берберийский *a.* (geog.) Berbera.

бербер/ин *m.,* —**иновый** *a.* berberine; —**оновая кислота** berberonic acid, 2,4,5-pyridinetricarboxylic acid.

бергамот *m.,* —**ный,** —**овый** *a.* (bot.) bergamot (*Citrus bergamia*).

бергаптен *m.* bergaptene.

берггрюн *m.* (min.) mountain green, malachite.

бергин/изация *f.,* —**ирование** *n.* (fuels) berginization, Bergius process.

бергманский *a.* Bergmann (tubing).

бергузня *f.* (mam.) marbled polecat (*Vormela peregusna*).

берг/шляг *m.* collapse (of rock); —**шрунд** *m.* (geol.) bergschrund (crevasse); —**штрих** *m.* (maps) bergstrich.

Бердана амальгаматор (min.) berdan.

бердичевский *a.* (geog.) Berdichev.

бёрдо *n.,* —**овый** *a.* (text.) reed; (naut.) loom.

бердский *a.* (geog.) Berd (river).

бердянский *a.* (geog.) Berdyansk.

берег *m.* shore, coast, beach; bank; **у —а** off-shore.

бер/ёг *past m. sing.,* —**егли** *past pl.* of **беречь.**

берегов/ой *a.* shore, coastal, littoral; riparian; offshore; —**ая линия** waterfront; —**ая охрана** coast guard; —**ушка** *f.* (ent.) brine fly (*Ephydra*); (orn.) bank swallow (*Riparia r.*).

берего/любивый *a.* shore-loving, litophilous; —**укрепительные работы** shore containment; bank protection.

берегу/т *pr. 3 pl.* of **беречь;** —**щий** *a.* keeping, preserving.

бередить *v.* irritate (a sore).

бережанский *a.* (geog.) Berezhanyi.

береж/ёный *a.* kept, preserved; —**ёт** *pr. 3 sing. of*

беречь; **—ливость** *f.* economy; **—ливый** *a.* economical.

бережник *m.* (ichth.) grayling (*Thymallus articus*); silver bream (*Blicca bjoerkna*).

бережн/ость *f.* caution, prudence; **—ый** *a.* cautious, prudent, careful.

берёза *f.* (bot.) birch (*Betula*).

березинский *a.* (geog.) Berezina.

березит *m.* (petr.) beresite, aplite.

бер/ёзка *f.* small birch (tree); bindweed (*Convolvulus arvensis*); **—езник,** **—езняк** *m.* birch grove, birch forest; **—ёзовик** *m.* birch mushroom (*Boletus scaber*); (orn.) black grouse (*Lyrurus tetrix*).

березовит *m.* (min.) beresovite.

берёзов/ица *f.* birch sap.

березовский *a.* (geog.) Berezovka; Berezovaya (River).

берёзовые *pl.* (bot.) Betulaceae; **—ый** *a.* birch.

берека *f.,* **лечебная б.** (bot.) wild service tree (*Sorbus torminalis*).

берём *pr. 1 pl. of* **брать:** we take.

беремен/еть *v.* conceive; **—ная** *a.* pregnant, gravid; **—ность** *f.* pregnancy, gravidity; gestation; conception.

беренгелит *m.* (min.) berengelite.

бересклет *m.* (bot.) Euonymus; **—овые** *pl.* staff-tree family (*Celastraceae*).

берест *m.* (bot.) elm (*Ulmus*).

берёста *f.* birch bark.

берестняк *m.* elm forest, elm woods.

берёст/о *n.,* **—овый** *a.* birchbark.

берестяной *see* **берёстовый.**

берёт *pr. 3 sing. of* **брать.**

берет *m.* beret.

беречь *v.* take care (of), look (after); watch, guard; save, keep, preserve; spare, conserve; protect; **—ся** *v.* guard (against), beware (of); be careful, take care.

бери *imp. of* **брать.**

бери-бери *f.* (med.) beriberi.

берикс/овые *pl.* (ichth.) red snappers (*Berycidae*); **усатые** **—ы** beardfishes (*Polymixiidae*).

берил/(л) *m.* (min.) beryl; **—лат** *m.* beryllate; **—лид** *m.* beryllide; **—лиевый** *see* **берилловый;** **—лизация** *f.* (met.) casehardening with beryllium; **—лий** *m.* beryllium, Be; **окись** **—лия** beryllium oxide, beryllia; **сернокислый** **—лий** beryllium sulfate; **—лийорганический** *a.* organoberyllium.

бериллов/окалиевая соль potassium beryllate; **—окислый** *a.* beryllate (of); beryllic acid; **—окислая соль** beryllate; **—ый** *a.* beryllium; beryllic (acid); **—ая земля** beryllia, beryllium oxide; **соль** **—ой кислоты** beryllate.

берилло/ид *m.* (cryst.) berylloid; **—н** *m.* (photometric analysis) beryllon; **—нит** *m.* (min.) beryllonite.

бери/нгийский *a.* (geog.) Bering; **—нговоморский** *a.* Bering Sea; **—нговский** *a.* Bering; **—славский** *a.* Berislav.

берите *imp. of* **брать.**

берк/еит *m.* (min.) berkeyite, lazulite, burkeite; **—(е)лий** *m.* berkelium, Be.

беркут *m.* golden eagle (*Aquila chrysaetos*).

беркширский *a.* Berkshire (swine).

берлин/ит *m.* (min.) berlinite; **—ский** *a.* Berlin; Prussian (green); **—ская лазурь** Berlin blue, ferric ferrocyanide.

берло/га *f.,* **—жный** *a.* den, lair.

берма *f.* berm, bench; shoulder (of road).

бер/мудский *a.* (geog.) Bermuda; **—нский** *a.* Bern(ese); **—нуллиевый** *a.* Bernoulli('s); **—о** *m.* (ichth.) Bero.

беровский *a.* Baer (knoll).

беро/е, **—з** *m.* (zool.) Beroё.

берсим *m.* (bot.) Egyptian clover (*Trifolium alexandrinum*).

Бертело бомба Berthelot's calorimeter.

бертиерит *m.* (min.) berthierite.

бертин/иевый *A.* (anat.) Bertin's; **—ирование** *n.* (fuels) bertinization.

Берт/ло *see* **Бертело:** **—оле** Berthollet.

бертол/(л)етова соль Berthollet's salt, potassium chlorate; **—лид** *m.* berthollide; **—лидный** *a.* berthollide, nonstoichiometric (compounds).

бертонит *m.* (min.) berthonite, bournonite.

бертрандит *m.* (min.) bertrandite.

бертьер/ин, **—ит** *m.* (min.) berthierite.

берул/а, **—я** *f.* (bot.) Berula.

беру/т *pr. 3 pl. of* **брать;** **—щий** *a.* taking, etc. *see* **брать.**

бёрце *n.* (anat.) tibia, shin bone.

берцел/ианит *m.* (min.) berzelianite; **—иусовый** *a.* Berzelius's (test).

берцов/таранный *a.* (anat.) tibiotarsal; **—ый** *a.* tibial; leg; **большая** **—ая кость** tibia; **малая** **—ая кость** fibula.

берчогурский *a.* (geog.) Ber-Chogur.

бёрш *m.* (ichth.) one of several species, chiefly pike perch (*Lucioperca volgensis*).

бершадский *a.* (geog.) Bershad.

бершик *see* **берш.**

беря *pr. ger. of* **брать:** taking, if we take.

бес— *see also under* **без—**.

беседа *f.* conversation, talk, discussion.

беседк/а *f.* arbor, bower; **—овые птицы** bowerbird family (*Ptilonorhynchidae*).

бесед/овать *v.* talk, discuss, discourse; **—очный** *a. of* **беседа;** bowline, slip (knot).

бесить *v.* enrage, infuriate; irritate; **—ся** *v.* rage; (vet.) become rabid.

бескамерный *a.* tubeless (tire).

бескарбонатный *a.* noncalcareous.

бесква/дратный *a.* (math.) square-free; **—дратурный** *a.* quadrature-free; **—нторный** *a.* quantor-free.

бескварцевый *a.* quartz-free.

бескил/евой *a.* keelless, ecarinate, ratite; **—евые** *pl.* (orn.) Ratitae; **—ьница** *f.,* **—ьницевый** *a.* (bot.) alkali grass (*Puccinellia; Atropis*).

бес/кислородный *a.* oxygen-free; anaerobic; **—кислотный** *a.* acid-free; **—кишечные** *pl.* (zool.) flatworms (*Acoela*); **—кишечный** *a.* acoelous, ac(o)elomate; **—клапанный** *a.* valveless; **—клеточный** *a.* cell-free, acellular; **—коготный** *a.* clawless; **—коленок** *m.* moor grass (*Molinia coerulea*).

бескомпрессорный *a.* compressorless, airless-injection (engine); **б. воздушнореактивный** *a.* ramjet (engine).

бесконечно *adv.* endlessly, infinitely, ad infinitum, forever; indefinitely; extremely; **б. большой** infinite, infinitely great; **б. малый** *a.* infinitesimal, infinitely small.

бесконечно/длинный *a.* infinitely long; **—кратный** *a.* infinite-to-one; **—листный** *a.* infinite sheeted; **—мерный** *a.* infinite-dimensional, of infinite dimensions; **—связный** *a.* of infinite connectivity; **—сть** *f.* infinity; **до** **—сти** ad infinitum; **—удалённый** *a.* infinitely far, (at) infinity.

бесконечн/ый *a.* infinite, endless, everlasting, perpetual; without end, interminable; **б. винт** perpetual screw, worm; **—ая величина** (math.) infinite (value); **—ое полотно** conveyer belt.

бесконтактный *a.* contactless, noncontact.

бесконтрольн/о *adv.* without control; **—ый** *a.* uncontrolled.

бес/конфетийный *a.* (comp.) chadless (tape); **—корковый** *a.* crust-free; blended (cheese); **—корешковый** *a.* rootless; **—кормица** *f.* lack of fodder; **—корневищный** *a.* rhizomeless; **—корневой** *a.* rootless, arrhizal; **—корпусный транзистор** chip transistor; **—корый** *a.* barkless; **—костный** *a.* boneless; **—косточковый** *a.* seedless, stone-free, apyrene; **—крайний** *a.* vast, boundless; **—кризисный** *a.* acritical, crisis-free; smooth, uneventful.

бескров/ие *n.*, **—ность** *f.* (med.) exsanguinity; **—ный** *a.* exsanguine, bloodless.

бескрыл *m.* (orn.) kiwi (*Apteryx*); **—ые** *pl.* Apterygidae; **—ый** *a.* wingless, apterous; (ichth.) finless.

беспаечный *a.* solderless (joint).

беспалый *a.* adactyl(ous), lacking digits.

беспамятн/ый *a.* forgetful, absentminded; **в —ом состоянии** unconscious.

беспанцирные *pl.* (amph.) Lissamphibia; (mal.) Solenogastres; Aplacophora.

беспарье *n.* (agr.) non-fallow cropping.

беспатентный *a.* unpatented; unlicensed.

бесперебойн/о *adv.* continuously, etc., *see a.*; without fail; **—ость** *f.* continuity, etc., *see a.*; uninterrupted operation; **—ый** *a.* continuous, uninterrupted; regular; steady, smooth, trouble-free; reliable.

беспереводный *a.* nontransferable.

бесперемен/н/о *adv.* without change; **—ый** *a.* changeless, invariable.

беспересадочный *a.* nonstop, through.

бесперспективный *a.* hopeless.

бесперый *a.* featherless; apodal (fish).

беспечный *a.* unconcerned, careless.

беспилотный *a.* pilotless, unmanned, robot, drone (aircraft).

беспламенный *a.* flameless.

беспланов/ость *f.* lack of planning; **—ый** *a.* haphazard, random, unplanned.

бесплатн/о *adv.* free of charge, gratis, at no cost: **—ый** *a.* free (of charge); public-domain (software).

бесплатформенный *a.* strapdown (intertial navigation system).

бесплод/ие *n.*, **—ность** *f.* sterility, infertility, barrenness; fruitlessness, futility; **—ный** *a.* sterile, barren, fruitless, futile; depleted, unproductive (soil); (bot.) acarpous; **—ная земля** arid land; badland.

бесповоротн/ость *f.* irreversibility; **—ый** *a.* irreversible, irrevocable; rotation-free.

бесподобный *a.* incomparable, unrivaled.

бесподпорочный *a.* unsupported.

бесподстроечный *a.* preset, pretuned.

беспозвоночн/ые *pl.* (zool.) invertebrates; **—ый** *a.* invertebrate; *m.* an invertebrate.

беспоисковый *a.* preset, pretend.

беспокоить *v.* disturb, bother, trouble, harass; **—ся** *v.* worry, be anxious, be concerned (about); trouble, bother.

беспокой/ный *a.* disturbed, agitated, restless, turbulent; **—ство** *n.* disturbance, agitation; trouble, anxiety, concern.

беспокровный *a.* naked, bare.

бесполезн/о *adv.* uselessly, in vain, (it is) of no use; **—ость** *f.* uselessness; inefficiency; **—ый** *a.* useless, of no use, vain; inefficient, ineffective, futile.

бес/поло— *prefix* agamo—, asexual; **—полостной** *a.* (biol.) ac(o)elous; **—полосый** *a.* unstriped; **—полый** *a.* asexual, agamic; vegetative (generation); **—пол-**

юсный *a.* poleless; (bot.) apolar; **—помощный** *a.* helpless; **—пористость** *f.* density; **—пористый** *a.* non-porous, dense; **—породный** *a.* non-pedigree, mongrel; **—порочный** *a.* faultless; spotless; **—поршневый** *a.* pistonless.

беспоряд/ок *m.* disorder, confusion, chaos; clutter; **—очно** *adv.* in disorder, out of order, at random; irregularly; **—очность** *f.* disorderliness, lack of order; chaos; **—очный** *a.* disorderly, confused, chaotic; out of order, random, irregular; disordered (motion); unrestricted, free (grazing); (bot.) inordinate.

беспосадочный *a.* nonstop (flight).

беспоследов/ые *pl.* pouched mammals, marsupials; **—ый** *a.* aplacental, implacental.

беснотерный *a.* loss-free, zero-loss.

беспочвенн/о *adv.* without basis, without foundation; **—ость** *f.* groundlessness; **—ый** *a.* groundless, unfounded, unsubstantiated, without sound basis; soilless (culture); **—ое выращивание** hydroponics.

беспошлинн/о *adv.*, **—ый** *a.* duty-free; **—ая торговля** free trade.

беспредельн/о *adv.* infinitely, ad infinitum; **—ость** *f.* infinity, boundlessness; **—ый** *a.* infinite, boundless, limitless, unlimited; unbounded; immense.

бес/предметный *a.* aimless, pointless; academic; **—прекословный** *a.* indisputable; absolute, unquestioning.

беспрепятственн/о *adv.* free (to), without hindrance; freely, easily; **—ый** *a.* unimpeded, unobstructed, unchecked, free.

беспрерывн/о *adv.* continuously, without interruption; **—ость** *f.* continuity; **—ый** *a.* continuous, uninterrupted, perpetual, ceaseless, incessant, unremitting.

беспрестанный *a.* continuous, constant.

беспрецедентный *a.* unprecedented.

бесприбыльн/о *adv.* without profit; **—ый** *a.* unprofitable; disadvantageous.

беспримерный *a.* unparalleled.

беспримесный *a.* pure, uncontaminated.

беспристраст/ие *n.*, **—ность** *f.* impartiality; **—но** *adv.* impartially, without bias, without prejudice; **—ный** *a.* impartial, unprejudiced, unbiased.

бесприточный *a.* without tributaries.

бесприцельный *a.* aimless, random.

беспричинн/о *adv.* without reason; **—ый** *a.* without reason or cause, groundless; (med.) idiopathic, self-originated.

бес/проволочный *a.* wireless; **—проигрышный** *a.* safe, sure; **—прокладочный** *a.* gasketless (joint); **—просветный** *a.* (utterly) dark, gloomy; **—просыпный** *a.* unbroken (sleep); **—процентный** *a.* bearing no interest; **—пыльный** *a.* dust-free; **—садочный** *a.* nonstop; **—сальниковый** *a.* (mach.) packless.

бессарабский *a.* (geog.) Bessarabian.

бессахарный *a.* sugarless, sugar-free.

бессвинцовый *a.* lead-free.

бессвязн/ость *f.* inconsistency, incoherence; **—ый** *a.* inconsistent, incoherent, disconnected.

бесселевый *a.* (math.) Bessel(ian).

бессемейный *a.* unmarried, single.

бессеменн/одольный *a.* (bot.) acotyledonous; **—ой** *a.* seedless.

бессемер *m.* (met.) Bessemer (converter); **—ование** *n.* bessemerizing, Bessemer process; **—овать** *v.* bessemerize; **—овский** *a.* Bessemer.

бессемя/дольный *a.* (bot.) acotyledonous; **—нка** *f.* seedless fruit, parthenocarpic fruit; **—нность** *f.* seedlessness; **—нный** *a.* aspermous, parthenocarpic.

бес/сепараторный *a.* cageless (bearing); **—сер-**

дечниковый *a.* coreless; —**сернистый** *a.* non-sulfurous; —**серный** *a.* sulfur-free; —**сеточный** *a.* gridless; without a grating or netting.

бессил/ен *sh. m. of* **бессильный;** —**ие** *n.* debility, weakness; **половое** —**ие** impotence.

бессиликатный *a.* without silicate(s).

бессильный *a.* impotent, weak; failed.

бессимптомный *a.* asymptomatic; masked, inapparent, silent; subclinical (infection); latent (syphilis).

бессировать *v.* lower.

бессистемн/о *adv.* without system, haphazardly, at random; —**ость** *f.* lack of system; —**ый** *a.* unsystematic, haphazard; unrestricted, free (grazing).

бесскачковый *a.* without jumps, smooth.

бесскелетный *a.* without a skeleton.

бесследн/о *adv.* without any trace, leaving no trace; —**ый** *a.* without trace, not to be traced, traceless.

бесслов(ес)н/ые *pl.* (mam.) ape men (*Pithecanthropidae*); —**ый** *a.* mute, dumb.

бессменн/о *adv.* without change, continuously; —**ость** *f.* permanency; —**ый** *a.* permanent, fixed, continuous.

бессмерт/ие *n.* immortality; —**ить** *v.* immortalize; —**ник** *m.* (bot.) immortelle, everlasting (*Helichrysum*); —**ность** *f.* immortality; —**ный** *a.* immortal, everlasting, eternal; —**ная трава** (bot.) Ambrosia.

бессмольный *a.* tar-free.

бессмысл/енно *adv.* senselessly; there is no point; —**енность,** —**ица** *f.* absurdity, senselessness, etc., *see a.;* —**енный** *a.* absurd, senseless, meaningless, insignificant, foolish; irrational.

бес/снежный *a.* snowless, bare; —**снежье** *n.* absence of snow; —**совестный** *a.* unscrupulous; —**содержательный** *a.* empty.

бессознательн/о *adv.* unconsciously; —**ость** *f.* unconsciousness; —**ый** *a.* unconscious, involuntary; instinctive; —**ое состояние** unconsciousness.

бессоновский *a.* (geog.) Bessonovka.

бес/сосудистый *a.* (anat.) avascular, non-vascular; —**сочный** *a.* sapless; —**спиновый** *a.* (nucl.) spinless, zero-spin.

бесспорн/о *adv.* indisputably, undoubtedly, without question; by far; —**ость** *f.* indisputability; —**ый** *a.* indisputable, undeniable, self-evident.

бессребреник *m.* disinterested person.

бессрочный *a.* indefinite, open-ended, without a time limit; permanent.

бес/створчатый *a.* valveless; —**стебельный** *a.* stemless, acaulous; —**столбиковый** *a.* (bot.) without a style; —**столбность** *f.* astely.

бессточн/ый *a.* without drainage or outflow, enclosed; closed drainage (area); internal-drainage (basin); zero-discharge; —**ая область** closed drainage.

бес/страстие *n.* apathy; —**страстный** *a.* indifferent, apathetic; —**стружковый** *a.* non-destructive (analysis); —**структурный** *a.* structureless, without structure; amorphous, shapeless, formless, indistinct; —**струнный** *a.* stringless.

бесступенчат/о-регулируемый *a.* continuously variable; —**ый** *a.* stepless, continuous, without stages; variable-speed (drive); infinitely variable (transmission).

бес/стыдный *a.* shameless, brazen; —**сульфатный** *a.* sulfatefree; —**суставчатый** *a.* (zool.) inarticulate; —**сучковый** *a.* trimmed, lopped (tree); branchless, clear (lumber); —**счётный** *a.* innumerable, countless.

бессяжковые *pl.* (ent.) Protura.

бесталантный *a.* untalented, incapable.

бестарный *a.* unpackaged, (in) bulk, loose.

бест-бар *m.* (met.) best bar.

бес/теневой *a.* shadowless; —**тигельный** *a.* crucible-less; —**тканевый** *a.* non-textile, non-fabric; without tissue; —**товарье** *n.* shortage of goods; —**токовый** *a.* no-current, without a current.

бестол/ковщина, —**ковица,** —**очь** *f.* disorder, confusion, chaos; —**ковый** *a.* confused; unintelligible.

бес/трубный *a.* pipeless; —**тычинковый** *a.* (bot.) stamenless, non-staminate.

бесуго *m.* (ichth.) besugo (*Pagrus p.*).

бесфакельный *a.* flameless, non-flame.

бесфланцевый *a.* flangeless, rimless.

бесфоновый *a.* no-background, free of background noise, hum-free.

бесформенн/о *adv.* without form, without shape; —**ость** *f.* shapelessness, formlessness, amorphism; —**ый** *a.* shapeless, formless, amorphous.

бесфосфорный *a.* phosphorus-free.

бесхвост/ые *pl.* (amph.) Salientia, Anura; —**ый** *a.* tailless, ecaudate, anural.

бесхлеб/ица *f.* bread shortage; famine, starvation; —**ный** *a.* famine-stricken.

бесхлопотный *a.* trouble-free.

бесхлор/ный *a.* chlorine-free; —**офил(л)ьный** *a.* chlorophyll-free, non-chlorophyll, achlorophyllaceous.

бесхозный *a.* ownerless; no man's (land); (law) in abeyance.

бесхозяйственн/ость *f.* poor management, mismanagement; negligence; —**ый** *a.* wasteful, uneconomical; inefficient; —**ый человек** poor manager; —**ое ведение дел** mismanagement.

бесхордов/ые *pl.* (zool.) non-chordates; —**ый** *a.* non-chordate.

бесцвет/ковые *pl.* (bot.) cryptogams; —**ковый** *a.* ananthous, without flowers; —**ность** *f.* achromatism; —**ный** *a.* colorless, achromatic; obscure (heat).

бесцельн/о *adv.* aimlessly, at random; it is pointless; —**ость** *f.* aimlessness, random nature; —**ый** *a.* aimless, purposeless, pointless, random.

бесценн/о *adv.* beyond price; —**ость** *f.* inestimable value; —**ый** *a.* priceless, inestimable, invaluable.

бесценок: за б. at a bargain.

бесцентров/о— *prefix,* —**ый** *a.* centerless; **б.-обдирочный станок** centerless lathe.

бесциркуля/рный, —**ционный** *a.* circulation-free, without circulation; irrotational.

бесчаше/листковый *a.* (bot.) asepalous, without sepals; —**чный** *a.* acalycine.

бесчелюстн/ой *a.* (zool.) agnathous, jawless; —**ые** *pl.* (ichth.) Agnatha; jawless vertebrates (*Cyclostomata*).

бесчерепн/ой *a.* (zool.) acranial; —**ые** *pl.* Acrania.

бесчест/ить *v.* dishonor, disgrace; —**ный** *a.* dishonest.

бесчешуйный *a.* scaleless, esquamate.

бесчисленн/о— *prefix* myri(o)— (countless); —**ость** *f.* innumerability; —**ый** *a.* innumerable, countless.

бесчувств/енность *f.* insensibility; apathy; —**енный** *a.* insensible, unfeeling, numb; —**ие** *n.* loss of consciousness.

бесшаботный *a.* counterblow (hammer).

бес/шамотный *a.* (cer.) without chamotte; —**шарнирный** *a.* hingeless; —**шерст(н)ый** *a.* without wool; hairless, glabrous; —**шипые** *pl.* (ichth.) Anacanthini, Gadiformes; —**шовный** *a.* seamless, jointless; (med.) sutureless; —**штамбовый** *a.* trunkless, boleless (tree); —**штанговый** *a.* rodless; —**шумка** *f.* sound deadener; —**шумный** *a.* noiseless, silent; —**щелевой** *a.* slotless; slitless (spectrograph); —**щелочной** *a.* alkali-free; —**щитковые** *pl.* (herp.) anapsids; —**щупальцевые** *pl.* (zool.) Atentaculata.

бета *f.* beta (β); **б.-железо** *n.* beta iron.

бета-излуч/атель *m.* (nucl.) beta-emitter; **—ение** *n.* beta-emission, beta-radiation.

бетаин *m.* betaine, trimethyl glycocoll; **—оподобный** *a.* betaine-like.

бета/-луч *m.,* **б.-лучевой** *a.* (nucl.) beta-ray; **б.-нафтол** *m.* beta-naphthol; **б.-переход** *m.* beta transition; **б.-превращение** *n.* beta transformation; **б.-радиоактивный** *a.* beta-radioactive; **б.-распад** *m.* beta disintegration, beta decay; **б.-распределение** *n.* beta-distribution; **б.-спектр** *m.* beta(-ray) spectrum; **б.-спектрометр** *m.* beta-spectrometer; **—трон** *m.,* **—тронный** *a.* betatron, induction accelerator; **—уранотил** *m.* (min.) betauranotil; **—фит** *m.* betafite; **б.-функция** *f.* beta-function; **б.-частица** *f.* (nucl.) beta-particle.

бетел/евый *a.,* **—ь** *m.* (bot.) betel (*Piper betle*); **—ьгейзе** *n.* (astr.) Betelgeuse; **—ьный, —ьский** *a.* betel.

бетол *m.* betol, beta-naphthyl salicylate.

бетон *m.* concrete; **—ак** *m.* betonac (concrete with metal particles); **—ирование** *n.* concreting; **—ированный** *a.* concreted; **—ировать** *v.* (lay) concrete; **—ировка** *f.* concreting; **—ит** *m.,* **—итный камень, —итный массив** concrete (building) block; **—итный** *a.* concrete.

бетоно— *prefix* concrete; **—бойный** *a.* concrete-smashing; **—вод** *m.* concrete delivery line; **—воз** *m.* concrete delivery truck; **—литная башня** concrete pourer; **—лом** *m.* concrete breaker; **—мешалка** *f.* concrete mixer; **—насос** *m.* concrete pump; **—отделочный** *a.* concrete-finishing; **—разбиватель** *m.* concrete breaker; **—раздатчик** *m.* concrete pourer; **—распределитель** *m.* concrete spreader or layer; **—смеситель** *m.* concrete mixer; **—смесительный, —смешивающий** *a.* concrete-mixing; **—укладочный** *a.* concrete-laying; **—укладчик** *m.* concrete layer or paver.

бетон/щик *m.* concrete worker; **—ьерка** *f.* concrete mixer.

бетруксиновая кислота betruxinic acid.

бетулин *m.* betulin(ol); **—овый** *a.* betulin; betulinic (acid); **—ол** *m.* betulinol.

бехевиоризм *m.* behaviorism.

беч *m.* batch, charge.

беч/ева *f.* towline, rope; cord, (binder) twine; **—ёвка** *f.* twine, string, yarn; **—евник** *m.* foreshore, waterfront, beach; tow path; **—евой** *a.* tow(ing); **—ёвочный** *a. of* **бечёвка.**

бешен/ик *m.,* **—ица** *f.* (bot.) poison hemlock (*Cicuta*); **—ка** *f.* (ichth.) shad (*Alosa kessleri*); **—ство** *n.* fury, frenzy; (med.) rabies; **—ый** *a.* mad, furious, raging; turbulent; rabid; **—ый огурец** (bot.) squirting cucumber (*Ecballium elaterium*); **—ая вишня, —ая ягода** (bot.) belladonna.

бештаунит *m.* (petr.) beschtaunite.

б.з. *abbr.* (**без заглавия**) no title; **бз.** *abbr.* (**бензол**).

бзыбский *a.* (geog.) Bzyib.

би— *prefix* bi—, di— (two; twice).

биакс *m.* (comp.) biax(ial ferrite core); **—иальный** *a.* biaxial.

Биаля реакция Bial's test.

биаториновый *a.* (bot.) biatorine.

биахайба *f.* (ichth.) lane snapper (*Lutjanus synagris*).

биацетил *m.* biacetyl, 2,3-butanedione.

биб— *prefix see* **библиотечный.**

бибензил *m.* bibenzyl, diphenyl ethane.

биберит *m.* (min.) bieberite.

библейский *a.* biblical.

библио— *prefix* biblio—, book; **—бус** *m.* bookmobile;

—граф *m.* bibliographer; **—графировать** *v.* compile a bibliography; **—графический** *a.* bibliographic; **—графия** *f.* bibliography, references; **—тека** *f.* library; **—текарь** *m.* librarian; **—тека-читальня** *f.* reading room; **—тековедение** *n.* library science; **—течный** *a.* library.

библьдрук *m.* bible paper (for books).

бибрихский *a.* Biebrich (red).

бивак *m.* (mil.) bivouac, camp.

бивалент *m.* (gen.) bivalent; **—ный** *a.* bivalent, double-valency; dihydric (alcohol).

бивариантный *a.* bivariant.

бивачный *a.* (mil.) bivouac(king).

бивектор *m.* (math.) bivector.

бивень *m.* incisor, tusk.

бивербальный *a.* biverbal (name).

биверит *m.* (min.) beaverite.

бивни *pl. of* **бивень.**

бивольтинный *a.* (zool.) bivoltine.

бивуак *see* **бивак.**

бивший *past act. part. of* **бить.**

биг *m.* (typ.) score, crease.

бигам/ический, —ный *a.* bigamous; **—ия** *f.* bigamy.

бигарадия *f.* Seville orange.

бигармонический *a.* biharmonic.

бигидрат *m.,* **—ный** *a.* dihydrate.

бигнон/иевые *pl.* (bot.) bignoniaceae; **—иевый** *a.,* **—ия** *f.* trumpet flower (*Bignonia*).

бигов/альцы *a.,* **—ка** *f.* (typ.) scoring, creasing, bending.

биградуированный *a.* bigraded, twice-graded, double-graded.

бигумаль *m.* bigumal (hydrochloride), chlorguanide hydrochloride.

бидезил *m.* bidesyl, dibenzoyldibenzyl.

бидистилл/ат *m.* bidistillate, twice-distilled product; redistillate; double-distilled water; **—ированный** *a.* redistilled, etc., see v.; **—ировать** *v.* redistil, double-distil, distil twice; **—ят** *see* **бидистиллат; —ятор** *m.* redistiller; **—яция** *f.* redistillation.

бидон *m.* can(ister), container, vessel.

биен/ие *n.* beat, pulse, pulsation, throbbing; wobble, play (of wheel); sag(ging), slack (of belt); **частота —ий** beat frequency; **—ия** *pl.* beat(ing); running out of true.

бизань *f.* (naut.) mizzen.

бизнес *m.* business; **—мен** *m.* businessman.

бизон *m.* (mam.) bison; **американский б.** buffalo (*Bison b.*); **—ова трава, —ья т.** buffalo grass (*Buchloë dactyloides*).

бийохинол *m.* Bijochinol, quinine bismuth iodide.

бийский *a.* (geog.) Biya (River); Biisk.

би/капсулярный *a.* bicapsular; **—карбонат** *m.* bicarbonate, spec. sodium bicarbonate.

биквадрат *m.* (math.) biquadrate, fourth power; **—ный** *a.* biquadratic.

бикварц *m.* (light) biquartz.

бикинский *a.* (geog.) Bikin.

бикомпакт *m.* (math.) (bi)compact(um); **—ный** *a.* (bi)compact.

биконический *a.* biconical.

бикристаллический *a.* bicrystalline.

бикрон *m.* bicron (10⁻⁹ meter).

бикс *m.* steam sterilizer.

бикс/а *f.* (bot.) Bixa; **—иит** *m.* (min.) bixbyite; **—ин** *m.* bixin (coloring matter).

бикфордов шнур Bickford (safety) fuse.

бикхаконитин *m.* bikhaconitine.

бил *past m. sing. of* **бить.**

билатеральный *a.* bilateral.

билеин *m.* bilein.

билет *m.,* **—ный** *a.* card; ticket, pass, permit; (examination) paper.

били *past pl. of* **бить.**

били— *prefix* (physiol.) bili— (bile); **—арный** *a.* biliary, bilious; **—вердин** *m.* biliverdin; **—вердиновый** *a.* biliverdic (acid); **—ксантин** *m.* bilixanthin.

б. или м. *abbr.* (**более или менее**) more or less.

билин *m.* bilin.

билин/еарный, —ейный *a.* (math.) bilinear; **—ейность** *f.* bilinearity.

билинейрин *m.* bilineurine.

билинза *f.* (opt.) bilens, divided lens.

били/ноген *m.* bilinogen (bile pigment); **—пурпурин** *m.* bilipurpurin; **—рубин** *m.* bilirubin, hematoidin; **—рубиновый** *a.* bilirubinic (acid); **—соидановый** *a.* bilisoidanic (acid); **—траст** *m.* Bilitrast, iodoalphionic acid; **—фусцин** *m.* bilifuscin.

биллетировка *f.* (met.) roughing up.

биллион *m.,* **—ный** *a.* billion (10^9 or 10^{12}); **—ная часть** one billionth.

биллитонит *m.* (petr.) billitonite.

билль *m.* bill.

било *n.* beater (blade or bar); (agr.) swip(p)le, swingle; *past n. sing. of* **бить.**

билоидановый *a.* biloidanic (acid).

билодержатель *m.* beater arm.

бильгарциоз *m.* (med.) bilharziasis, Schistosoma infection; **—ный** *a.* bilharzial.

бильд— *prefix* photograph, picture; **—аппарат** *m.* picture transmitter; facsimile; **—передача** *f.* transmission of photographs; **—связь, —телеграфия** *f.* phototelegraphy.

бильный *a.* beating; hammer (mill).

биметалл *m.* bimetal, clad metal, duplex metal, laminated metal; bimetal(lic) plate or strip; **прокатка —ов** cladding; pressure welding; **—ический** *a.* bimetallic.

биминеральный *a.* bimineral.

бимод/альная *f.,* **—альный** *a.* (math.; stat.) bimodal; **—уль** *m.* bimodule.

бимолекулярный *a.* bimolecular.

бимомент *m.* bitorque.

бим/с *m.* (naut.) beam; **—трал** *m.* beam trawl.

бина *f.* cattle pen.

бинант *m.* binant.

бинарн/ый *a.* binary; binomial (nomenclature); **б. пересчёт** scale of two; **б. счётчик, —ая пересчётная схема** binary scaler, scale of two circuit.

бинауральн/ость *f.* (acous.) binaural effect; **—ый** *a.* binaural.

бингамовский *a.* Bingham (viscosity).

биндгеймит *m.* (min.) bindheimite.

бинейтрон *m.* (nucl.) bineutron.

биннит *m.* (min.) binnite.

бинодаль *f.,* **—ный** *a.* binodal.

бинок/левый *a.,* **—ль** *m.* binoculars, (field) glasses; **—улярный** *a.* binocular.

бином *m.* (math.) binomial; **—и(н)альный** *a.* binomi(n)al.

бинормаль *f.,* **—ный** *a.* (math.) binormal.

бинт *m.* bandage; (book) band; **—овать** *v.* bandage, dress (a wound).

бинтуронг *m.* (mam.) Arctictis binturong.

бинуклеарный *a.* binuclear, binucleate.

Био закон (opt.) Biot's law.

био— *prefix* bio— (life); biological; **—анализ** *m.* bioanalysis; **—ассимилируемый** *a.* bioresorbable; **—газ** *m.* biogas, fermentation gas.

биоген *m.* biogen; **—ез(ис)** *m.* biogenesis, origin of life; **—етический** *a.* biogenetic; **—ия** *f.* biogeny; **—ный** *a.* biogenic; (bot.) biogenous, parasitic; essential (elements).

биогео/графический *a.* biogeographic; **—графия** *f.* biogeography; **—химия** *f.* biogeochemistry; **—ценоз** *m.* biogeocenosis, ecosystem.

биогерм *m.* (geol.) bioherm.

биограф *m.* biographer; **—ический** *a.* biographic; **—ия** *f.* biography.

био/датчик *m.* biosensor; **—деградируемый, —деградирующийся** *a.* biodegradable.

биодинам/ика *f.* (biol.) biodynamics; **—ический** *a.* biodynamic.

биоза *f.* biose; disaccharide.

биокатал/из *m.* biocatalysis; **—изатор** *m.* biocatalyst; **—итический** *a.* biocatalytic.

био/климатический *a.* bioclimatic; **—климатология** *f.* bioclimatology; **—коллоид** *m.* biocolloid; **—косные тела** (min.) biogenic bodies, bioliths.

биоксалат *m.* bioxalate.

биол/из *m.* biolysis; **—ит** *m.* (min.) biolith; **—итический** *a.* biolytic, destructive to life.

биолог *m.* biologist; **—ически** *adv.* biologically; **—ический** *a.* biological; bio—; **—ический эквивалент рентгена** roentgen equivalent man, rem; **—ическое топливо** biofuel; **—ия** *f.* biology.

био/люминесценция *f.* bioluminescence, biophotogenesis; **—м** *m.* (ecol.) biome; **—масса** *f.* biomass; stock; **—метод** *m.* biological pest control; **—метрика, —метрия** *f.* (stat.) biometrics; **—метрический** *a.* biometric; **—механика** *f.* biomechanics; **—мицин** *m.* Biomycin, chlortetracycline; **—н** *m.* bion(t); **—ника** *f.* (math.) bionics; **—номический** *a.* bionomic, ecological; **—номия** *f.* bionomy; **—нт** *m.* bion(t); **—нтизация** *f.* biontization, chemical stimulation (of seeds).

био/обрастание *n.* biological (slime) growth; **—окисление** *n.* biochemical oxidation; **—плазма** *f.* bioplasm, protoplasm; **—повреждение** *n.* biodeterioration; **—полимер** *m.* biopolymer; **—потенциал** *m.* biopotential, bioelectric potential; **—препарат** *m.* (immun.) biological (preparation); **—проба** *f.* bioassay; **—продуктивность** *f.* bioproductivity; **—псия** *f.* (med.) biopsy; **—птерин** *m.* biopterin; **—разрушающийся** *a.* biodegradable.

биортогональный *a.* biorthogonal.

биос *m.* bios, life.

Био-Савара закон Biot-Savart law.

био/сестон *m.* bioseston (microplankton); **—синтез** *m.* biosynthesis; **—сома** *f.* (cyt.) biosome; **—социология** *f.* biosociology; **—спутник** *m.* biosatellite; **—стаз(ис)** *m.* (ecol.) biostasis; **—станция** *f.* biological (research) center; **—статика** *f.* biostatics; **—стерол** *m.* biosterol, vitamin A; **—стимулятор** *m.* biostimulant; **—стойкий** *a.* biostable; **—стойкость** *f.* biostability, vitality, biological resistance; **—сфера** *f.* biosphere; **—та** *f.* biota, regional fauna and flora; **—техника** *f.* bioengineering; **—тин** *m.* biotin, vitamin H; **—тип** *m.* biotype, species; **—тит** *m.* (min.) biotite; **—тический** *a.* biotic, relating to life.

биотовский *a.* Biot('s).

био/ток *m.* biocurrent; **—топ** *m.* (ecol.) biotope; **—топливо** *n.* biofuel; **—топологический** *a.* biotopological; **—трон** *m.* (rad.) biotron; **—управление** *n.* biopotential control; **—фабрика** *f.* biofactory, biologicalsmanufacturing plant.

биофиз/ик *m.* biophysicist; **—ика** *f.* biophysics; **—ический** *a.* biophysical.

био/фильтр *m.* biofilter; (sewage) trickling filter; **капельный б.** trickling or percolating filter; filter bed; —**фильтратор** *m.* (zool.) filter feeder; —**фит** *m.* biophyte, parasitic plant; —**фор** *m.*, **фора** *f.* (gen.) biophore.

биохим/ик *m.* biochemist; —**ически пазлагаемый** *a.* biodegradable; —**ический** *a.* biochemical; —**ический расрад,** —**ическое пазложение** biodegradation; **поддающийся** —**ическому разложению** biodegradable; —**ия** *f.* biochemistry.

био/хор *m.* (ecol.) biochore; —**ценоз** *m.* biocenosis, biotic community, ecosystem; —**ценологир** *f.* bioc(o)enology; —**ценотический** *a.* bioc(o)enotic; —**ценотическая группировка** biocenosis; —**цид** *m.* biocide; —**цидный** *a.* biocidal; —**цикл** *m.* biocycle; —**цитин** *m.* biocytin; —**экология** *f.* bioecology; —**электрический** *a.* bioelectric; —**электроника** *f.* bio(electro)nics; —**энергетика** *f.* bioenergetics.

бипиннарии *pl.* (zool.) bipinnaria.

бипирамида *f.* (cryst.) bipyramid; —**льный** *a.* bipyramidal.

биплан *m.* (av.) biplane; —**арный** *a.* (geom.) biplanar.

бипол/ь *m.* dipole; —**ярность** *f.* bipolarity; —**ярный** *a.* bipolar.

бипризма *f.* (opt.) biprism.

бирадикал *m.* biradical.

биржа *f.* (com.) exchange.

биржайский *a.* (geog.) Birzhai.

биржев/ик *m.* stock broker; —**ой** *a. of* **биржа.**

бирка *f.* label, tag, nameplate; tally.

биркеланг *m.*, —**а** *f.* (ichth.) blue ling (*Molva Dypterygia*).

Биркеланд-Эйде способ Birkeland-Eyde process (for nitrogen fixation).

бирков/ание *n.* labeling, etc., *see v.;* —**ать** *v.* label, tag, brand.

бирманский *a.* (geog.) Burmese, Burma(n).

бирмингемский *a.* (geog.) Birmingham.

бирок *gen. pl. of* **бирка.**

биротативный *a.* birotatory, differential (engine); duplex (turbine).

бирочный *a. of* **бирка.**

бирский *a.* (geog.) Birsk.

бируанг *m.* (mam.) Helarctos malayanus.

бирунийский *a.* (geog.) Biruni.

бирюз/а *f.*, —**овый** *a.* (min.) turquoise.

бирюсинский *a.* (geog.) Biriusa.

бирючевский *a.* (geog.) Biriuchii.

бирючина *f.* (bot.) privet (*Ligustrum*).

бирючок *m.* (ichth.) Don ruffe (*Acerina a.*).

БИС *abbr.* (**большая интегральная схема**) large-scale integrated circuit, LSI circuit.

бис— *prefix* bis— [twice; (chem.) double; (anat., med.) both]; —**азосоединение** *n.* bisazo compound; —**диазосоединение** *n.* bisdiazo compound; —**диазосоставляющая** *f.* bisdiazo component.

бисексуал/изм *m.*, —**ьность** *f.* bisexualism, bisexuality; —**ьный** *a.* bisexual.

бисектриса *see* **биссектриса.**

бисер *m.* beads.

бисериальный *a.* biserial.

бисерный *a.* bead(ed), pearl.

бисиликат *m.* disilicate.

биск *m.* (cer.) bisque.

бискайский *a.* (geog.) Biscay(an).

бискамжинский *a.* (geog.) Biskamzha.

бисквит *m.*, —**ный** *a.* (cer.) biscuit, bisque.

бислой *m.* bilayer.

бисмалит *m.* (geol.) bysmalith.

бисмаркбраун *m.* Bismarck brown.

бисмит *m.* (min.) bismite.

бисмут— *see* **висмут—;** —**о—** *prefix* bismut(h)o—; —**осферит** *m.* (min.) bismutosph(a)erite.

бисса *f.* (herp.) hawk-bill turtle (*Eretmochelys imbricata*).

биссект/ор *m.* (geom.) bisector; —**орный** *a.* bisector, bisecting; —**риса** *f.* (geom.) bisector, bisecting line; (cryst.) bisectrix.

биссолит *m.* (min.) byssolite.

биссус *m.* (zool.) byssus.

бистабильный *a.* (comp.) bistable.

бистер, бистр *m.* bister (a pigment).

бистунки *pl.* beaded wires.

бисульф/ат *m.* bisulfate; —**ид** *m.* bisulfide; —**ит** *m.*, —**итный** *a.* bisulfite.

бисфеноид *m.* (cryst.) bisphenoid.

бит *m.* (comp.) bit, binary digit; *sh. m. of* **битый.**

битартрат *m.* bitartrate.

битва *f.* battle, fight, combat, action.

бительная машина (text.) beetle.

битенг *m.* (aero.; naut.) bitt; **б.-краспица** cross bitt.

битер *m.* (agr.) beater; **б.-сороудалитель** *m.* trash beater.

битиит *m.* (min.) bityite.

битком *adv.:* **б. набитый** *a.* packed (tight).

бито *sh. n. of* **битый.**

битовнит *m.* (min.) bytownite.

биток *m.* beetle, ramming instrument; (beef) cutlet.

биттит *m.* (elec.) bittite.

битулитный *a.* bitulithic.

битум *m.* bitumen; (petrol.) asphalt; —**енит** *m.* (min.) bitumenite, torbanite; —**(ин)изация** *f.* bituminization; bituminous grouting; —**(ин)изировать** *v.* bituminize; —**инозность** *f.* bituminosity; impregnation (with bitumen); —**(иноз)ный** *a.* bituminous; tar (sand); —**овоз** *m.* asphalt distributor.

бит/ый *a.* beaten, etc., *see v.;* **б. лёд** ice cakes, blocks; —**ь** *v.* beat, whip; sound (alarm); hammer, hit; crack, break, fracture; gush, spurt (of stream); churn (butter); strike (the hour); (belt) flap, sag, whip; (wheel) wobble, play; slaughter, kill; dress (poultry); fight, struggle (against); *f.* (met.) hammered sheet; —**ь на** *v.* aim (at); **не** —**ь** *v.* (wheel) run true, be in alignment; **медная** —**ь** hammered copper; —**ьё** *n.* beating, etc., *see v.;* —**ься** *v.* beat, throb, pulsate; strive, fight (for, about, over), struggle; knock (against); get smashed, get broken; be breakable.

битюгский *a.* (geog.) Bityug (river).

биурат *m.* biurate.

биурет *m.*, —**овый** *a.* biuret, allophanamide.

бифакторный *a.* bifactor(ial).

бифенил *m.* biphenyl, phenylbenzene; —**ен** *m.* biphenylene.

бифилярный *a.* bifilar, double-wound.

бифторид *m.* bifluoride, acid fluoride.

бифункциональный *a.* bifunctional.

бифуркация *f.* bifurcation.

бифштекс *m.* beef steak.

бихе(й)виор/изм *m.* behaviorism; —**истический** *a.* behavioristic; —**ический** *a.* behavioral.

бихлорид *m.* bichloride.

бихор/ки, —**хи** *pl.* (zool.) Solpugida.

бихромат *m.* bichromate.

бицепс *m.* (anat.) biceps.

бициклический *a.* bicyclic (compounds).

бицикло— *prefix* bicyclo—.

бицилиндрический *a.* bicylindrical.

бициллин *m.* Bicillin, benzathine penicillin G.

бициркулярный *a.* bicircular.

бич *m.* whip; (biol.) flagellum; (mach.) beater; (agr.) bar; scourge, plague; —е *prefix* mastig(o)— (whip); flagelli—.

бичев/а *f.* towline, tow rope; **тянуть** —**у** *v.* tow; —**ание** *n.* towing; flagellation; —**ать** *v.* tow, flagellate, whip, lash; —**идный** *a.* flagelliform.

бичёвка *f.* twine, string, yarn.

бичевник *m.* sloping beach.

бич/еносцы *pl.* (prot.) Flagellata, Mastigophora; —**образный** *a.* flagelliform, lash-like; —**ик** *m.* flagellum.

бишировые *pl.* (ichth.) bishirs (*Polypteridae*).

бишофит *m.* (min.) bischofite.

биюргун *m.* (bot.) Anabasis salsa.

БК *abbr.* (**бацилла Коха**) Koch bacillus; (**боковой каротаж**) lateral logging; (**бутилкаучук**) butyl rubber.

б-ка *abbr.* (**банка**) bank, shoal; (**библиотека**) library.

БКВРД *abbr.* (**бескомпрессорный воздушнореактивный двигатель**) ramjet engine.

БКЗ *abbr.* (**боковое каротажное зондирование**) lateral-log sounding.

благо *n.* the good, welfare; **общее б.** common good, public welfare; —**вещенский** *a.* (geog.) Blagoveshchensk; —**видный** *a.* seemly, plausible.

благовол/ение *n.* goodwill; favor, kindness; —**ить** *v.* (regard with) favor; be well disposed (to); have the kindness (to).

благовон/ие *n.* aroma, fragrance; —**ный** *a.* aromatic, fragrant.

благодар/ить *v.* thank; —**ность** *f.* thanks, gratitude, appreciation; acknowledgment; —**ный** *a.* grateful, appreciative; rewarding; —**я** *prep. dat.* thanks (to), owing, due (to), because of, through, by.

благоденств/ие *n.* prosperity; —**овать** *v.* prosper, thrive, flourish; live comfortably; —**ующий** *a.* prospering, etc., *see v.;* vigorous.

благодетель *m.* benefactor; —**ный** *a.* beneficial; —**ствовать** *v.* benefit.

благо/желательный *a.* well-disposed (to), favorable; —**звучный** *a.* harmonious, melodious.

благонадёжный *a.* reliable, dependable.

благонамерен/ие *n.*, —**ность** *f.* good intention; —**ный** *a.* well-meant.

бдагополуч/ие *n.* welfare, well-being; —**но** *adv.* all right, safely; —**ный** *a.* safe; successful; healthy, disease-free.

благоприобретённый *a.* acquired (trait).

благоприят/но *adv.* favorably; —**ность** *f.* favorableness; —**ный** *a.* favorable, opportune; advantageous, beneficial; contributory (factor); —**ный момент**, —**ный случай** opportunity; —**ное условие** facility; **наиболее** —**ный** optimum, optimal; —**ствовать** *v.* favor, foster, be conducive (to), be favorable (to), promote, assist, contribute (to); —**ствующий** *a.* favoring, etc., *see v.;* favorable, conducive (to).

благоразум/ие *n.* sense, prudence; **в пределах** —**ия** within reason; —**но** *adv.* reasonably, etc., *see a.;* it is reasonable, it is sound practice; —**ный** *a.* reasonable, sensible, wise, cautious, prudent; of sound practice.

благородный *a.* noble, precious (metal, stone); inert, inactive, rare (gas).

благосклонный *a.* favorable.

благо/состояние *n.* welfare, prosperity, well-being; —**творный** *a.* beneficial, wholesome; —**творное воздействие** therapy.

благоустр/аивать *see* **благоустроить;** —**оенный** *a.*

well-organized, well-managed; well-equipped; comfortable, with modern conveniences; developed (area); —**оить** *v.* put in good order; —**ойство** *n.* good order; (urban) development; civic improvement(s), public services and amenities.

благоух/ание *n.* fragrance, aroma; —**анный**, —**ающий** *a.* fragrant, aromatic, sweet-smelling; —**ать** *v.* give off fragrance.

блазиевые *pl.* (bot.) Blasiaceae (mosses).

Блана реакция Blanc reaction.

бланжирование *see* **бланшировка.**

бланк *m.* form, blank; letterhead.

бланк/вил(л)овые *pl.* tilefishes (*Branchiostegidae*); —**ет** *m.* Aphya minuta.

бланкир/ование *n.*, —**ующий** *a.* blanking.

бланкит *m.* sodium hydrosulfite.

бланков/ый *a.* blank, form; —**ая надпись** endorsement.

бланкофор *m.* (dyestuffs) Blankophor.

бланманже *n.* (food) blancmange.

бланочная продукция (typ.) blanks.

бланфикс *m.* blanc fixe (barium sulfate).

бланшир *m.* (leather) slicker; —**ование** *see* **бланшировка;** —**ователь** *m.* blancher; —**овать** *v.* blanch, scald; (leather) whiten; (text.) bowk, kier; —**овка** *f.* blanching, etc., *see v.;* kier-boiling.

бласт— *see* **бласто—;** —**ема** *f.* (embr.) blastema; —**ический** *a.* blastic; —**о—** *prefix* blast(o)— (sprout, bud, germ).

бластоген *m.* (gen.) blastogene; —**ез** *m.* blastogenesis; —**ный** *a.* blastogenic.

бласто/дерма *f.* (embr.) blastoderm, germinal membrane; —**идеи** *pl.* (pal.) Blastoidea; —**ма** *f.* (med.) blastoma; —**мер** *m.* blastomere, cleavage cell; —**микоз** *m.* (med.) blastomycosis; —**мицета** *f.* Blastomyces (fungus); *pl.* Blastomycetes; —**пор** *m.*, —**пора** *f.* (embr.) blastopore, protostoma; —**хор** *m.* (bot.) blastochore; —**целе** *n.*, —**цель** *m.* (embr.) blastoc(o)el(e), cleavage cavity.

бластула *f.* (embr.) blastula.

блау/газ *m.* Blaugas (an oil gas); —**офен** *m.* (met.) flowing furnace.

бледен *sh. m. of* **бледный.**

бледит *m.* (min.) bloedite, astrakanite.

бледн/еть *v.* turn pale, lose color, fade; —**еющий** *a.* turning pale, etc., *see v.;* exalbescent; —**ить** *v.* make pale; —**о** *adv. and prefix* pale(ly); —**оватый** *a.* rather pale, palish; —**ожёлтый** *a.* pale yellow; —**кровие** *n.* anemia; —**ооокрашенный** *a.* pale-colored, dull; —**ость** *f.* paleness, pallor; —**ый** *a.* pale, light-colored; pallid, faint, weak (color).

блей/вейс *m.* white lead; —**штейн** *m.* (met.) lead matte.

блек— *see also under* **блэк—.**

блёкло— *prefix* dull, mat, dead; pale; —**коричневый** *a.* dull brown, fallow dun; —**сть** *f.* fading; flatness (of color).

блёк/лый *a.* faded, discolored; pale, mat, dull, flat (color); —**лая руда** (min.) gray copper ore, fahlerz; —**нуть** *v.* fade, wither; —**ота** *f.* (bot.) black henbane (*Hyosciamus niger*).

блекрот *m.* (phyt.) black rot.

бленда *f.* (min.) blende, spec. zinc blende; (opt.) diaphragm; (phot.) lens hood; blind, screen, shield; (mining) lantern.

блендировать *v.* blend.

бленкер *m.* (commun.) indicator.

бленно— *prefix* blenn(o)— (mucus); —**(р)рея** *f.* (med.) blennorrh(o)ea.

блепсиевые *pl.* (ichth.) sculpins (*Blepsiidae*).

блесбок *m.* (mam.) Damaliscus albifrons.

блеск *m.* luster, gloss, shine, brilliance; glare, flash, glitter; (astr.) brightness; (min.) glance; **без —а** opaque, dull; **—ообразователь** *m.* (electroplating) brightener; **—ость** *f.* glare, glaze; flicker.

блесн/а *f.* (fishing) lure; **—уть** *v.* flash.

блест/еть *v.* shine, glitter, sparkle; gleam, glisten; **—ка** *f.* spangle; **—як, —ян** *m.* (min.) galena; (sometimes) mica; **—янки** *pl.* sap-feeding beetles (*Nitidulidae*); **—яще—** *prefix* lampr(o)— (bright); **—ящелистный** *a.* (bot.) lamprophyllous; **—ящий** *a.* lustrous, brilliant, bright, shiny, shining, sparkling; (pel)lucid, clear, translucent.

блёф *m.* bluff.

блефар—, —о— *prefix* blephar(o)— (eyelid); **—ит** *m.* (med.) blepharitis; **—опласт** *m.* (prot.) blepharoplast.

блефовать *v.* bluff.

блея/ние *n.* bleat(ing); **—ть** *v.* bleat.

блигия *f.* (bot.) Blighia.

ближ/айший *a.* near(est), proximal, next, immediate; more recent; **—ающий** *a.* nearest, most similar; **—е** *comp.* of **близкий, близко** nearer, closer; **—невосточный** *a.* Near Eastern; **—ний** *a.* near, next, neighboring; inner; short-range (order); **Ближний Восток** (geog.) Near East (West Asia and NE Africa).

близ *prep. gen.* near, around, at hand, in the vicinity (of), close (to); **—иться** *v.* approach, approximate, draw near; begin (of time); dawn, break, fall; **—кие** *pl.* kin, relatives; close friends or associates; **—кий** *a.* near, close (by); like, similar; approximating; imminent; intimate; **—ко** *adv. and sh. n.* of **близкий**; near, close (by or to).

близкодейств/ие *n.* short-range (inter)action; **—ующий** *a.* short-range.

близко/кипящий *a.* with close boiling points; **—родственный** *a.* closely related; close, in-(breeding); **—лежащий** *a.* adjacent, contiguous (to), neighboring, near.

близна *f.* flash mark.

близнец *m.,* **—овый** *a.* twin; **—овая мышца** (anat.) gemellus (muscle); **—ы** *pl.* twins; (astr.) Gemini; **—ы(-пара)** (math.) twins, prime pair.

близок *sh. m.* of **близкий.**

близорук/ий *a.* near-sighted, myopic; **—ость** *f.* myopia.

близост/ь *f.* nearness, proximity, vicinity, neighborhood, closeness, imminence; **по —и** near (at hand).

близполюсный *a.* circumpolar.

блик *m.,* **—ование** *n.* flash; high-light, spot of light; (phot.) hotspot; (met.) fulguration, blick, flashing; refining (of silver); (radar) blip; glare; **—ованный** *a.* refined; **—овать** *v.* flash, lighten; refine; **—овый** *a.* of **блик;** refined.

блин *m.* pancake; (ice) cake.

блинд/аж *m.* (mil.) shelter, dugout; **—ированный** *a.* armored, iron-clad.

блинк/компаратор *m.* blink comparator; **—микроскоп** *m.* blink microscope.

блин/ный, —овый *a. of;* **—ок** *dim. of* **блин; —ообразный** *a.* pancake (ice).

блинт *m.* (typ.) blind stamping; **—овать** *v.* blind-stamp; **—овый** *a.* blind (stamping).

блинчатый *a.* pancake.

блист/ание *n.* shining, glittering; **—ательно** *adv.* brilliantly; **—ательный** *a.* brilliant; splendid; **—ать** *v.* shine, glitter; be conspicuous, distinguish oneself, stand out.

блистер *m.* (naut.; av.) blister, bulge.

Бло драже (pharm.) Blaud's pill.

блок *m.* block, unit, module; assembly, set, section; (comp.) bucket; device; block (pulley), pulley (block), hoist; (nucl.) lump, slug; mass; (polymerization) bulk; (anat.) trochlea; ginglymus; **—и квартир** housing projects; **б. управления** control unit; **в —е** bulk (polymerization); **в —ах** lumped; **сложный б.** hoisting (tackle).

блок— *prefix* block(ing); (inter)locking; **—ада** *f.* blockade; block(ing); **—атор** *m.* blocking agent; **—гауз** *m.* blockhouse; **-диаграмма** *f.* block diagram; **—инггенератор** *m.* (electron.) blocking oscillator; **—ингпроцесс** *m.* regeneration.

блокир/ование *n.* blocking, etc., see *v.;* **—ованный** *a.* blocked, etc., see *v.;* **—овать** *v.* block, stop, obstruct, bar the way, disable; blockage; (inter)lock, interconnect; **—овка** *f.* block(ing), stop(ping); (inter)locking, interlock; (comp.) lockout; (rr.) block signalling; **взаимная —овка** (comp.) deadlock; **—овочный, —ующий** *a. of* **блокировка;** by-pass (capacitor, resistance).

блок/картный *a.* looseleaf; **-каучук** *m.* block rubber; **-комната** *f.* (building) module; **-контакт** *m.* (electron.) blocking or auxiliary contact.

блокнот *m.,* **—ный** *a.* tablet, scratchpad.

блоко/видный *a.* (anat.) ginglymoid, hingelike; trochlear; **б. сустав** ginglymus; **—вый** *a. of* **блок;** (anat.) trochlear; **—укладчик** *m.* block layer.

блок-полимер *m.* bulk polymer; block copolymer; **—изация** *f.* bulk polymerization.

блок-/пост *m.* (rr.) signal box; **б.-прокладка** *m.* (constr.) filler block; **б.-резина** *f.* cut sheet (of rubber); **б.-сигнал** *m.* block signal; **б.-сополимеризация** *f.* block copolymerization; **б.-схема** *f.* (comp.) block diagram, flow chart; **б.-счётчик** *m.* pulley block counter; **б.-участок** *m.* (rr.) blocking section.

бломстрандит *m.* (min.) blomstrandite.

блондин *m.* blond; **—ка** *f.* blond (woman); (ichth.) Decapterus ronchus.

блох/а *f.* (zool.) flea; **водяные —и** (crust.) Cladocera; **—овник** *m.* (bot.) pennyroyal (*Mentha pulegium* or *Hedeoma pulegioides*).

блоховский *a.* Bloch's.

блоч/ный *a. of* **блок;** block; in blocks, in unit form, unitized; modular; bulk (polymer), block (copolymer); (chem.) bucket; **—ок** *dim. of* **блок;** (fuel, uranium) slug, lump.

блош/иный *a. of* **блоха;** puce (color); **—иная трава** (bot.) Polygonum persicaria; **—истый, —ливый** *a.* flea-infested; **—ка** *f.* flea; **—ник** *m.,* **—ница** *f.* (bot.) fleabane; (*Pulicaria*); flea; psyllium (seed); **—ная трава** Plantago psyllium.

блу/дить *see* **блуждать; —ждание** *n.* wandering, etc., see *v.;* **—ждать** *v.* wander, stray, migrate, circulate; diffuse, err; (math.) walk; **—ждающий** *a.* wandering, etc., see *v.;* stray, erratic; traveling, intrusive (wave); free-moving, migratory (cell); floating (kidney); (elec.) surface leakage, vagabond (current); **—ждающий нерв** (anat.) vagus; **—ждающие блики** (commun.) ghosts, ghost images.

блуза *f.* blouse, shirt.

блум *see* **блюм.**

блэк— *prefix* black; **—бенд** *m.* (min.) blackband ore; **—варниш** *m.* black (asphalt) varnish; **б.-рот** *m.* (phyt.) black rot; **б.-чаф** *m.* black chaff.

блювал *m.* (mam.) blue whale (*Balaenoptera musculus*).

блюдет *pr. 3 sing. of* **блюсти.**

блюд/ечко *n.* saucer; (porcelain) crucible; (biol.) patellula; (mal.) limpet (*Patella*); **—ечковидный** *a.* patelliform, saucer-shaped; **—о** *n.* dish, plate.

блюду/т *pr. 3 pl. of* **блюсти; —щий** *a.* keeping; observing.

блюд/це *n.* saucer, dish; (biol.) patella; (geol.) shallow depression; **морское б.** jellyfish (*Aurelia aurita*); **—цевидный, —цеобразный, —чатый** *a.* patelliform, pan-shaped; saucer-shaped.

блюл *past m. sing. of* **блюсти.**

блюм *m.* (met.) bloom; **—инг** *m.* blooming mill; **б.-дуо** *m.* two-high reversing blooming mill; **—сы** *pl.* blooms.

блюсти *v.* keep, guard, protect; fulfill, observe, attend (to); **—тельный** *a.* careful, watchful.

бляринелла *f.* (mam.) Blarinella.

бля/ха *f.* metal plate; **—шечный** *a.* patchy; **—шка** *f.* platelet; (zool.) shield, scute, plate; (med.) plaque, patch, spot; **—шконоска** *f.* (bot.) Peltigera (a lichen); **—шконосные** *pl.* (zool.) Aspidochirota.

БМ *abbr.* (**бинокулярный микроскоп**) binocular microscope; **б.м.** *abbr.* (**без места**) no place; **б.м., б/м** *abbr.* (**будущего месяца**) next month; **б.м. и г.** *abbr.* (**без места и года**) no place, no year.

б/н *abbr.* (**без номера**) unnumbered.

БНР *abbr.* Bulgarian People's Republic.

БНТ *abbr.* (**быстронасыщающийся трансформатор тока**) saturation transformer.

БО *abbr.* (**бактериологическое оружие**) bacteriological weapon(s).

боа *m.* (herp.) boa.

боб *m.* (bot.) bean, pod; bean plant.

бобёр *m.* beaver (fur); (mam.) *see* **бобр.**

бобик *m.* pod.

бобин/а *f.* bobbin, spool, reel; ignition coil; **—одержатель** *m.* (text.) bobbin carrier.

боб/ковый *a.* bean; bay (oil); **—овидный** *a.* pisolitic; fabiform, bean-shaped; **—овина** *f.* bean plant; (petr.) nodule; pea ore, bean ore; hardpan; **—овник** *m.* (bot.) dwarf almond (*Amygdalus nana*); **—овые** *pl.* legumes; **—овый** *a.* leguminous; bean; nodular, pisolitic (ore); **—ок** *m.* bean (seed); **—ообразный** *see* **бобовидный.**

бобр *m.* (mam.) beaver (*Castor*); **болотный б.** nutria, coypu (*Myocastor coypus*); **камчатский б., морской б.** sea otter (*Enhydra lutris*); **мускусный б.** muskrat (*Ondatra*); **—ёнок** *m.* young beaver; **—инецкий** *a.* (geog.) Bobrinets; **—ик** *m.* (text.) castor; **—овик** *m.* (bot.) Spanish broom (*Spartium junceum*); **—овицкий** *a.* (geog.) Bobrovitsa; **—овник** *see* **бобровик; —овокрысиные** *pl.* (mam.) Hydromyinae; **—овский** *a.* (geog.) Bobrov(ka); **—овые, —ы** *pl.* beavers (*Castoridae*); **—овый** *a.* beaver; **—ая струя** (pharm.) castor(eum); **—уйский** *a.* (geog.) Bobruisk; **горные —ы** (mam.) Aplodonti(i)dae.

бобслей *m.* bobsled.

бобы *pl. of* **боб; русские б.** broad bean (*Vicia faba*).

бобыр/ец *m.,* **—ь** *m.* (ichth.) Leuciscus borysthenicus; ruffe (*Acerina a.*); et al.

бобышка *f.* boss, lug; nipple.

бобьер(р)ит *m.* (min.) bobier(r)ite.

бов/енит *m.* (min.) bowenite.

бовихтовые *pl.* (ichth.) Bovichthyidae.

бовманит *m.* (min.) bowmannite.

Бог *m.* god; God.

боганидский *a.* (geog.) Boganid.

богар *m.* (ichth.) Lutjanus griseus.

богар/а *f.* boghara, unirrigated land; **—ный** *a.* unirrigated; dry (farming).

богат/ейший *a.* very rich, very abundant; **—ень** *m.* (bot.) trefoil (*Lotus*); **—еть** *v.* get rich, thrive, prosper;

—ство *n.* riches, wealth, opulence, abundance; fertility (of soil); (biol.) wide range; **—ства** *pl.* resources, wealth; **—ый** *a.* rich, wealthy; highgrade, high (in); rich (in); abundant, copious, prolific; with wide experience (in); wide (experience); magnificent, luxurious; bumper (crop); *m.* the rich; rich man; **—ый энергией** energy-rich.

богатырский *a.* athletic; giant; robust; sound (sleep); (geog.) Bogatyir.

богаче *comp. of* **богатый.**

богдановичский *a.* (geog.) Bogdanovich.

богдинский *a.* (geog.) Bogdo.

богемский *a.* Bohemian.

бого/духовский *a.* (geog.) Bogodukhov; **—родицкий** *a.* Bogoroditsk; **—мол** *m.* (ent.) praying mantis; **—родский** *a.* (geog.) Bogorodsk; **—родская трава** wild thyme (*Thymus serpyllum*); **—сский** *a.* (geog.) Bogoss; **—толский** *a.* Bogotol.

богуславский *a.* (geog.) Boguslav.

богхед *m.,* **—ский уголь** boghead coal.

бод *m.* (commun.) baud (unit).

бодайбинский *a.* (geog.) Bodaibo.

бодать *v.* butt; gore.

боденбендерит *m.* (min.) bodenbenderite.

боджак *m.* (ichth.) bodzhak (*Salmo ischchan*).

бодливый *a.* butting, inclined to butt.

бодо *n.* (teleg.) Baudot transmitter.

бодр/ить *v.* brace, stimulate, invigorate; encourage, urge on; **—иться** *v.* take courage; **—ость** *f.* courage, nerve; cheerfulness; **—ствующий** *a.* lying awake; **—ый** *a.* bold; brisk; cheerful; **—ящий** *a.* invigorating.

Бодуина реакция Baudouin test.

бодяга *f.* (zool.) Spongilla.

бодяк *m.* (bot.) thistle (*Cirsium*).

бо/е *prepos. of* **бой;** *prefix see* **бой; боевой; —ёв** *gen. pl. of* **бой; —евик** *m.* (film) hit.

боев/ой *a.* combat, fighting; war (gas, etc.); urgent (problem); sledge (hammer); **б. заряд, —ая головка, —ая часть** (rockets) warhead; **—ая тяга** acceleration thrust.

бое/головка *f.* (rockets) warhead; **—готовность** *f.* combat readiness; **—запас** *m.* ammunition.

боёк *m.* block; (hammer) head, face; (firing) pin, striker; *sh.m. of* **бойкий.**

боем *instr. of* **бой.**

боен *gen. pl. of* **бойня; —ие** *n.* (glass) fracturing; **—ский** *a.* slaughter house, slaughter (house); **—ское дело** slaughtering; **—ское исследование** meat inspection.

бое/питание *n.* munitions supply; **—припасник** *m.* nuclear warhead designer; **—припасы** *pl.* ammunition; (nuclear) warheads; **—способность** *f.* (mil.) combat efficiency; combat effectiveness; **—способный** *a.* battleworthy; efficient; **—ц** *m.* soldier, fighter, man.

бож/ественный *a.* divine (proportion); **—ий** *a.* God's; **—ье дерево** southernwood (*Artemisia abrotanum*); **—ья коровка** (ent.) ladybird.

боз/е-частица *f.,* **—он** *m.* (nucl.) boson (Bose particle); **безмассовый —он** classon.

бозух *m.* (phyt.) mosaic disease.

бои *pl. of* **бой.**

боится *pr. 3 sing. of* **бояться.**

бой *m.* combat, battle, action; ramming; breakage, breaking; broken material, crushed material, rubble; cullet; broken glass; crushed rock, grog; shattering (of grain); face (of hammer); (text.) pick(ing) **б. икры** (ichth.) spawning.

бойга *f.* (herp.) Boiga.

Бойда огнемёт Boyd flame thrower.

бойка *sh. f. of* **бойкий**; *gen. of* **боек**; *f.* (pile) driving.

бойк/ий *a.* smart, brisk, alert; animated, busy; —**ость** *f.* briskness, alertness.

бойкот *m.,* —**ировать** *v.* boycott.

бойлер *m.* boiler, hot water heater.

Бойля закон (phys.) Boyle's law.

бойница *f.* porthole, embrasure; vent.

бойня *f.* slaughter house, abattoir; (poultry); processing plant.

бойсограмма *f.* Boys' camera photograph.

бойтесь *imp. of* **бояться**.

бойц/а *gen. of;* —**овый** *a. of* **боец**; game (cock); fighting (fish).

бойче *comp. of* **бойкий**.

бок *m.* side, flank; wall; profile plan; **б.-о-б.** side by side, alongside; **в б.** to the side, sideways; **к** —**у** to the side, laterally; **на б.** on the side, sideways; **по** —**ам** on each side; **по** —**у** set aside; **под** —**ом** near (at hand); **с** —**у** at the side (of), by the side (of), at hand; **с** —**у на б.** side to side.

бокал *m.* beaker, glass; (anat.; bot.) beaker-shaped structure; poculum, cup; caliculus; —**ец** *m.* (bot.) scyphus; —**о**—, —**ьце**— *prefix* scyphi—, scypho— (cup, can); —**овидный**, —**ообразный**, —**ьчатый** *a.* (bot.) scyphiform, cup-shaped; caliciform, goblet (cell); —**ьчик** *dim. of* **бокал**; (bot.) cyathus.

боккран *m.* trestle crane.

боко— *prefix* side-, lateri—; pleur(o)— (rib, side); —**бочный** *a.* collateral, side by side; —**вик** *m.* measuring jaw; (typ.) marginal, side head; —**вина** *f.* side, (side) member, sideframe; wall; (tire) sidewall.

боков/ой *a.* side, lateral; profile; peripheral (vision); by—, secondary, accessory, supplementary; sidelong; glancing (blow); marginal; wall (rock); (anat.) collateral (ligament); **б. канал** by-pass; —**ая грань** lateral face, facet; —**ая жидкость** (electrophoresis) auxiliary liquid; —**ая качка** rolling; —**ая реакция** side reaction; —**ая цепь** side chain; —**ого действия** (phot.) focal plane (shutter); —**ое спускное течение** (distillation) side stream, slip stream.

боковский *a.* (geog.) Bokovo.

боко/вушка *f.* margin, edged; (typ.) marginal; —**жаберные** *pl.* (ichth.) sharks (*Pleurotremata*); —**м** *instr. of* **бок**; *adv.* sideways; —**нервные** *pl.* (mal.) Amphineura; (herp.) Loricata; —**нервный** *a.* laterinerved; —**плавы** *pl.* (crust.) Amphipoda; —**плодный** *a.* (bot.) pleurocarpic; —**ходовые** *pl.* crab spiders (*Thomisidae*); —**цветковый** *a.* (bot.) lateriflorous; —**цветный** *a.* pleuranthous; —**чешуйниковые** *pl.* (ichth.) Doradidae; —**шейные** *pl.* (herp.) side-necked turtles (*Pleurodira*).

бокс *m.* (elec.; nucl.) box; cell; (firing) bay; boxing (sport); (leather) box calf; (hospital) isolation ward or room; box stall; (ichth.) Box boops; —**ировать** *v.* (sports) box.

боксит *m.,* —**овый** *a.* (min.) bauxite; —**ирование** *n.* bauxitization; —**огорский** *a.* (geog.) Boksitogorsk.

болван *m.* (met.) billet, ingot; fool; —**ить** *v.* rough-cast, rough-hew; —**ка** *f.,* —**очный** *a.* pig, ingot, billet, bar; dummy; **в** —**ках** pig (iron).

болвинский *a.* (geog.) Bolva.

болг. *abbr.* (**болгарский**) Bulgarian.

болградский *a.* (geog.) Bolgrad.

болевой *a. of* **боль**; painful, algesic.

более *comp. of* **большой, много;** more; upwards (of), (and) up; **б. всего** most of all; **б. подробно** in greater detail; **б. того** and what's more; **тем б.** all the more; **тем б., что** (especially) as.

болезн/енность *f.* ill health, sickliness; painfulness, tenderness; —**енный** *a.* sickly, unhealthy, morbid, diseased; sore, painful; —**етворный** *a.* pathogenic, disease-producing; nosogenic (conditions); ill (effect); —**етворный микроорганизм** pathogen; —**еустойчивый** *a.* disease-resistant; —**ь** *f.* disease; sickness, illness, disorder, malady; (met.) embrittlement; **возбудитель** —**и** pathogen.

болеит *m.* (min.) boléite.

болен *sh. m. of* **больной**.

болетовые *pl.* (bot.) Boletaceae (fungi).

бол/еть *v.* be ill, be sick, be down (with), suffer (from); pain, ache, hurt; be anxious (about); —**еутоляющие** *pl.* analgesics, pain killers; —**еутоляющий** *a.* analgesic, pain-relieving; —**и** *gen., pl. etc. of* **боль**.

боливийский *a.* (geog.) Bolivian.

болиголов *m.* (bot.) poison hemlock (*Conium,* spec. *C. maculatum*).

болид *m.* bolide (meteor).

болит *pr. 3 sing. of* **болеть**; it hurts.

болнисский *a.* (geog.) Bolnisi.

болометр *m.* (phys.) bolometer; —**ический** *a.* bolometric.

болона *f.* excrescence, gall (on trees).

болонский *a.* (geog.) Bologna.

болот/ина *f.,* —**истая местность** marshland, moorland; —**истый** *a.* bog(gy), swampy, marshy, paludose, paludine; —**ник** *m.* swamp plant, spec. Callitriche; —**нинский** *a.* (geog.) Bolotnoe; —**ница** *f.* (bot.) spike rush (*Eleocharis*); (zool.) Paludicola; —**нокрысиные** *pl.* (mam.) Otomyinae; —**ноцветник** *m.* (bot.) Nymphoides; —**ный** *a. of* **болото**; bog (peat); paludal; —**ный газ** marsh gas, methane; —**ная лихорадка** (med.) malaria; —**ная руда** bog (iron) ore; —**ная синяя руда** peat phosphate; —**о** *n.* bog, swamp, marsh, quagmire; moor; **лес по** —**у** swamp forest; **солёное** —**о** salina; **топкое** —**о** quagmire; —**о**— *prefix* hel(e)o— (marsh); telmat(o)— (stagnant water, mud); —**оведение** *n.* telmatology; —**о-зыбун** *n.* quaking bog; —**олюбивый** *a.* bog-loving, heleophilous; telmatophilous; —**ообразование** *n.* bog formation; —**це** *gen. of* **болото**.

болт *m.,* **скреплять** —**ами** *v.* bolt, pin.

болт/алка *f.* shaker; —**ание** *n.* shaking, etc., *see v.;* —**анка** *f.* (av.) bump(iness), buffetting, rough weather, turbulence; jiggling; —**ать** *v.* shake; mix, stir, agitate; buffet; dangle; chatter, babble; —**аться** *v.* dangle, swing, hang (loose); hang about, hang out; —**ающийся** *a.* dangling; (med.) flail (joint).

болт/-барашек *m.* wing bolt; —**ик** *dim. of* **болт;** bolt; (contact) stud.

болтливый *a.* talkative, indiscreet.

болтнуть *see* **болтать**.

болтов/ой *a.* bolt; pin; **б. шарнир** pin hinge; —**ое крепление** bolting.

болторезн/ый *a.* bolt-threading; —**ая головка** threading die.

болт/ун *m.* sterile egg, rotten egg; —**ушка** *f.* mix, mash; batter; —**ушка-мешалка** *f.* mixer.

болховский *a.* (geog.) Bolkhov.

боль *f.,* **причинять б.** *v.* pain, hurt, ache.

больверк *m.* bulwark, sea wall, rampart.

бульдо *m.* (pharm.) boldo (leaves).

больн/ая *f.* patient; —**ица** *f.* hospital, infirmary; —**ичный** *a.* hospital; inpatient (care); nosocomial (disease); —**ичный служитель** *m.* orderly; —**о** *adv.* painfully; it is painful; very, exceedingly, badly; **ему** —**о** it hurts him; —**ой** *a.* sick, unwell, ill; diseased; sore; *m.* patient.

больсон *m.* (geol.) bolson.

больцмановский *a.* (nucl.) Boltzmann.

большак *m.* highway.

больше *comp. of* **большой, много** more, larger, bigger; over, in excess (of); **б. всего** the most; **б. не** no more; **вдвое б.** twice as much; **как можно б.** as much as possible; **много б.** much more; **тем б.** so much the more; **чем б., тем** the more . . . the.

больше— *prefix* macro—, large; magni— (big, great); meg(a)— great; million); (geog.) Big, Great, Grand; **—берцово—** *prefix* (anat.) tibio—; **—берцовый** *a.* tibial; **—берцовая кость** tibia; **—глазовые** *pl.* (ichth.) sweepers (*Pempheridae*); **—глазый** *a.* big-eyed; **—голов** *m.* (ichth.) bighead (*Aristichthys nobilis*); **—головка** *f.* Cottus gobio; **—головки** *pl.* (ent.) thick-headed flies (*Conopidae*); **—головник** *m.* (bot.) Rhaponticum; **—головый** *a.* macrocephalic, big-headed; **—грузный** *a.* heavy(-load); **—ноги** *pl.* (orn.) Megapodiidae; **—порожский** *a.* (geog.) Bolshoi Porog; **—ротовые** *pl.* jawfishes [*Opist(h)ognathidae*]; **—ротые** *pl.* gulpers (*Eurypharyngidae*); **—ротый** *a.* big-mouth(ed); **—травье** *n.* tall herbaceous vegetation.

больш/ий *comp. of* **большой;** bigger, etc.; superior; **—ей частью** for the most part, mostly; **самое —ое** at most; **—инство** *n.* majority, most (of).

больш/ой *a.* big, large, great, bulky; large-sized; major, significant, considerable, substantial, profound (change); heavy (machine); coarse (grain); strong (current); high (altitude, etc.); high-power (magnification); complex (system); mainframe (computer); ample, significant; (geog.) Great, Grand; **—ая земля** the Mainland; **—ая клетка** macrocyte; **—ущий** *a.* enormous, huge, mammoth.

болюс *m.* (min.) bole (clay); (vet.) bolus.

бол/ячка *f.* sore; **—ящий** *see* **больной.**

бомб/а *f.* bomb; (gas) cylinder; (depth) charge; **сбрасывать —ы** *v.* bomb.

бомбаж *m.* bulging (of cans), bloat(ing); **—ый** *a.* bulging, buckling, bloated.

бомбаксовые *pl.* (bot.) Bombacaceae.

бомбардир *m.* bomber; **—ование** *n.* bombardment, bombarding, etc., *see v.;* **—овать** *v.* bombard, impinge, strike; bomb, shell; **—овка** *f.,* **—овочный** *a. see* **бомбардирование.**

бомбардир/овщик *m.* bomber (plane); **б.-разведчик** *m.* reconnaissance bomber; **б.-ракетоносец** *m.* missile-carrying bomber; **—уемый** *a.* bombarded, struck; **—ующий** *a.* bombarding, etc., *see* **бомбардировать.**

бомбёжка *f.* bomb(ard)ing.

бомбейский *a.* (geog.) Bombay.

бомбил/евые *pl.* (ichth.) Harpadontidae; **—ь** *m.* Bombay duck (*Harpadon*).

бомбиров/ать *v.* crown; **—ка** *f.* crown(ing) (of rolls); camber (of shaft).

бомб/ить *v.* bomb(ard); **—ицина** *f.* coarse rag paper; **—овоз** *m.* bomber (plane); **—овый** *a.* bomb; **—одержатель** *m.* bomb rack; **—олюк** *m.* bomb hatch; **—омёт** *m.* bomb thrower, mortar; (naut.) depth-charge mortar; **—ометание** *n.* bombing; **—отсек** *m.* bomb bay; **—осбрасыватель** *m.* bomb release (gear); depth-charge rack; **—оубежище** *n.* air-raid shelter; **—оупорный** *a.* bomb-proof; **—очка** *dim. of* **бомба.**

Боме *see* **Бомэ.**

бомовский *a.* Bohm (value).

бомонтит *m.* (min.) beaumontite.

Бомэ Baumé, Bé.

бон *m.* boom, floating barrier.

бона *f.* check, money order.

бонанца *f.* bonanza (body of rich ore).

бонго *m.* (mam.) Taurotragus eurycerus.

бондар/ить *v.* cooper; **—ный** *a.* cooper's; **—ное предприятие, —ня** *f.* cooperage, cooper's shop; **—ь** *m.* cooper.

бондеризация *f.* (met.) bonderizing.

бонеллия *f.* a marine worm (*Bonellia*).

Бонжана масштаб (naut.) Bonjean diagram.

бонит/ёр *m.* appraiser, grader, classifier; (livestock) judge; improver, innovator; **—ет** *m.* quality index, grade; estimated productivity; **класс —ета** quality class; **—ирование** *see* **бонитировка;** **—ировать** *v.* appraise, evaluate; grade, classify (according to quality); estimate; judge; **—ировка** *f.,* **—ировочный** *a.* appraising, etc., *see v.;* appraisal; (biol.) bonitation, taxation; class-improving; **—ировщик** *m.* classifier; judge.

бонито *m.* (ichth.) bonito; **океанский б.** skipjack tuna (*Euthynnus pelamis*).

бонифик/атор *m.* ameliorant, aid, additive; conditioner; **—ация** *f.* bonification; amelioration, improvement.

бонобо *m.* (mam.) Pan paniscus.

бон/овый *a. of* **бон;** **-поглотитель** *m.* absorbing boom (for oil spills).

бонтбок *m.* (mam.) Damaliscus dorcas.

бонус *m.* bonus; premium.

боны *pl. of* **бон; бона;** paper money.

боо/пс *m.* (ichth.) Boops; **—тит** *m.* (min.) boothite; **—фил** *m.* (zool.) Boophilus.

бор *m.* boron, B; drill; pine forest; millet grass (*Milium*); **азотистый б.** boron nitride; **иодистый б.** boron iodide.

бора *f.* bora, cold northerly wind.

Бора теория Bohr's theory.

бор/аго *n. or m.* (bot.) borage (*Borago*); **—азол** *m.* borazole, triborine, triamine; **—азон** *m.* Borazon (boron nitride); **—акс** *see* **бура;** **—аль** *m.* boral, aluminum borotatrate; (nucl.) Boral; **—ан** *m.* borane, boron hydride; **—ат** *m.* borate; **—ацит** *m.* (min.) boracite.

Боргарда препарат a basic copper sulfate-carbonate seed disinfectant.

боргес *m.* (typ.) bourgeois (9 points).

борглицерин *m.* (pharm.) boroglycerin.

бордо *n.* claret (wine); Bordeaux (dye); **—вый, —сский** *a.* wine-colored; Bordeaux; **—сская жидкость** Bordeaux mixture (fungicide).

бордс/овый фут board foot (unit of measure); **—ы** *pl.* boards.

бордюр *m.,* **—ный** *a.* border, edging; curb; list; (geol.) limb; **—ный камень** curbstone.

боре/альный *a.* boreal (region); **—й** *m.* Boreas, north wind.

борелевский *a.* (math.) Borel (set).

бор/ение *n.* fighting, etc., *see* **бороться;** **—ец** *m.* fighter, wrestler; (bot.) aconite.

боржом *m.* Borzhom mineral water.

борз/ая *f.,* **—ой** *m.* borzoi, Russian wolfhound; **—инский** *a.* (geog.) Borzya.

борид *m.* boride.

бориккит *m.* (min.) borickite.

бор/ил *m.* boryl; **—ин** *m.* borine; **—ирование** *n.* borating; (met.) boronizing; **—ировать** *v.* borate; boronize.

борис/лавский *a.* (geog.) Borislav; **—овский** *a.* Borisov; **—польский** *a.* Borispol.

бор/истый *a.* boron(-containing); boride (of); **б. алюминий** aluminum boride; **—истая камера** boron (ionization) chamber; **—истая сталь** boron steel;

—**кальк** *m.* aluminum powder-lime mixture; calcium borate; —**магниевый** *a.* boron-magnesium.

бормашина *f.* (dentist's) drill.

борметил *m.* bormethyl, trimethylborine.

бормот/ать *v.* murmur, mumble, mutter; —**ушка** *f.* (orn.) babbler (*Hippolais caligata*); —**ушки** pl. jacamars (*Galbulidae*).

борн *m.* (battery) terminal.

Борна формула Born's equation.

борнасский *a.* (vet.) Borna's (disease).

борн/ейский *a.* (geog.) Borneo; —**еол** *m.* borneol, bornyl alcohol; —**ивал** *m.* bornyval, bornyl isovalerate.

борнил *m.*, —**овый** *a.* bornyl; —**амин** *m.* bornylamine, 2-aminocamphane; —**ацетат** *m.* bornyl acetate; —**ен** *m.* bornylene; —**овый спирт** *m.* borneol; —**хлорид** *m.* bornyl chloride.

борнит *m.* (min.) bornite.

борно— *prefix* boro—; —**аммониевая соль** ammonium borate; —**вольфрамовая кислота** borotungstic acid.

борновский *a.* Born (approximation).

борно/кальциевая соль calcium borate; —**кислый** *a.* boric acid; borate (of); —**кислый натрий** sodium borate; —**кислая соль** borate; —**муравьиный** *a.* boroformic (acid); —**натриевая соль** sodium borate; —**салициловый** *a.* borosalicylic (acid); —**этиловый эфир** ethyl borate.

борнхольмский *a.* Bornholm (disease).

борн/ый *a.* bor(ac)ic; boron (counter, etc.); borax (soap); boric acid (ointment); **б. ангидрид** boric anhydride, boron oxide; **б. глицерин** boroglyceride, glyceryl borate; —**ая кислота** bor(ac)ic acid; **соль —ой кислоты** borate.

боро— *prefix* boro—, boron.

боров *m.* flue, chimney intake; (zool.) hog, boar; *gen. pl.* of **бор**.

боровик *m.* (bot.) mushroom (*Boletus edulis*); —**а** *see* **брусника.**

боровина *f.* borovina, pine forest soil.

боровичский *a.* (geog.) Borovichi.

боровковый *a.* of **боровок.**

боровлянский *a.* (geog.) Borovlyanka.

бороводород *m.* boron hydride, borane.

боровой *a.* (pine) forest.

боровок *m.* baffle (plate); furnace bridge; mound, hill, ridge.

боровольфрам/ат *m.* borotungstate, tungstoborate; —**овокислый** *a.* tungstoborate (of); tungstoboric acid.

боровский *a.* (nucl.) Bohr; (geog.) Borovsk.

боровый *a.* of **боров.**

борогидрид *m.* boron hydride.

борода *f.* beard, barba; (piston rod) lug.

бородав/ка *f.* wart, verruca; (tech.) lug; **молочная б.** mammilla, nipple; —**ко**— *prefix* verruci—, wart; —**ковидный** *a.* verruciform; —**ник** *m.* (bot.) nipplewort (*Lampsana*); —**очка** *dim.* of **бородавка;** —**очник** *m.* (mam.) wart hog (*Phacochoerus*); (bot.) celandine (*Chelidonium majus*); —**очный** *a.* of **бородавка;** —**чатки, —чатковые, —чатники** pl. stonefish family [*Synancei(i)dae*]; —**чатость** *f.* wartiness; (phyt.) wart, scab, scurf; —**чатый** *a.* warty, verrucose; (phyt.) wart.

бород/атка *f.* (ichth.) Pogonophryne; (orn.) bearded titmouse (*Panurus biarmicus*); barbet (*Capito*); —**атки** pl. (orn.) barbet family (*Capitonidae*); —**атковые** pl. (ichth.) Harpagiferidae; —**атый** *a.* bearded; (bot.) barbate, barbed; —**атая трава, —ач** *m.* beard grass (*Andropogon*); —**ач** *m.* (orn.) bearded vulture (*Gypaëtus*

barbatus); —**ачка** *f.* (ichth.) black drum (*Pogonias cromis*); —**ка** *f.* barb, tuft, brush; (key) drift, bit; —**ки** pl. (orn.) wattles; —**ок** *m.* drift, punch, broach; nail set; knock-out rod; —**чатый** *a.* barbed; (bot.) barbate, bearded.

борозд/а *f.* furrow, groove, channel, trench; ridge; trail; (anat.) sulcus, fissure; (lunar) wrinkle; rill; —**ильник** *m.* (agr.) furrower; —**ильный** *a.* furrowing, etc., *see* *v.*; —**ина** *f.* (ocean.) submarine trench or canyon; —**ить** *v.* furrow, trench; groove, channel; —**ка** *dim.* of **борозда;** slot, stria; (anat.; bot.) vallecula; (anat.) sulcu(lu)s; —**ковый** *a.* of **бороздка;** —**ник** *m.* (agr.) furrower; marker; —**ной** *a.* of **борозда;** —**няк** *m.* (casting) sow scrap; —**ование** *n.* furrowing, ridging; —**овой** *a.* furrow(ed); —**одел(атель)** *m.* furrower; —**мер** *m.* furrow depth indicator; —**оплодник** *m.* (bot.) lovage (*Ligusticum*); —**рез** *m.* furrower.

бороздчат/о— *prefix* groove, furrow; soleno— (channel); aulac(o)— (furrow); glypt(o)— (carved); —**обрюхие** pl. (mal.) Solenogastres; —**оплодный** *a.* (bot.) aulacocarpous; —**ость** *f.* striation; —**ый** *a.* grooved, furrowed, channel(ed), fluted, striated; *suffix* —sulcate.

боро/кальцит *m.* (min.) borocalcite; —**л** *m.* borol; —**лл** *m.* (soil) boroll.

боролся *past m. sing.* of **бороться.**

борона *f.* (agr.) harrow; **б.-волокуша** *f.* drag harrow; **б-гвоздёвка** *f.* peg tooth harrow; **б.-смык** *f.* brush harrow.

боронатрокальцит *m.* (min.) boronatrocalcite, ulexite.

борон/а-шлейф *f.* (agr.) drag harrow; —**ённый** *a.* harrowed; —**ить, —овать** *v.* harrow; —**ование** *n.*, —**ьба** *f.* harrowing.

бор/опластик *m.* reinforced boron-fiber plastic; —**органический** *a.* organoboron; —**осиликат** *m.* borosilicate; —**осилицирование** *n.* boron-silicon cladding.

бороскоп *m.* borescope (for tubes).

боросодержащий *a.* boron-containing.

бороться *v.* fight, combat, control; strive; (sports) wrestle.

борофтор(ист)оводородн/ый *a.* fluoboric (acid); **соль —ой кислоты** fluoborate.

боррелия *f.* (bact.) Borrelia.

борский *a.* (geog.) Bor.

борсодержащий *a.* boron-containing.

борт *m.* edge, rim, border, hem; flange, (tire) bead; bort (industrial diamond); side (of ship); curbstone; bank (of ore); **загибать б.** *v.* bead; **за —ом** overboard; **на —у** on board, aboard; **у —а** alongside.

борт— *prefix see* **бортовой.**

борт/евой *a.* wild hive; —**ень** *m.* wild hive decoy.

борт/журнал *m.* (av.) log (book); —**ик** *m.* (constr.) skirting; (hort.) border; —**инженер** *m.* flight engineer; —**механик** *m.* flight mechanic; ship mechanic; maintenance technician.

бортн/ик *m.* wild-hive beekeeper; —**ичанье, —ичество** *n.* wild-hive beekeeping.

бортовальный *a.* flanging.

борт/овой *a.* of **борт;** airborne, spaceborne, vehicleborne; flight, aircraft, aboard, (on) board; side, flank; edge, rim, border; flange, bead; (mech.) final (drive); **б. камень** curbstone; **б. фрикцион** (mach.) steering clutch; —**овая качка** (naut.) rolling; —**овое содержание** (min.) bank content; **ракетный б.** rocketborne; —**овый** *see* **бортовой;** —**одержатель** *m.* edge holder; (glass) bort holder; —**озагибочный пресс** flanger; —**орасширитель** *m.* (tire) spreader; (glass) edge widener; —**орез** *m.*, —**орезка** *f.* (glass) cutter; —**проводник** *m.*, —**проводница** *f.* flight attendant; —**радист** *m.* radio operator; —**сеть** *f.* (av.) electrical system; —**техник** *m.* maintenance technician.

борть *f.* wild bee hive.

борушистость *f.* (leather) wrinkles.

борфтор/ид *m.* boron fluoride; —**истоводородный** *a.* fluoboric (acid).

борхавия *f.* (bot.) Boerhavia.

борца *gen. of* **борец.**

борштанга *f.* boring bar.

борщ *m.* bors(h)ch (soup); —**евик** *m.* (bot.) Heracleum; —**евский** *a.* (geog.) Borshchev; —**овочный** *a.* Borshchovochnyi.

борьба *f.* struggle, fight, combat(ing); campaign, drive; (disease, fire, flood, pest, weed) control; (accident) prevention; (noise) abatement; **б. с загрязнением** pollution control.

борэт/ан *m.* borethane; —**ил** *m.* borethyl.

борю/тся *pr. 3 pl. of* **бороться;** —**щийся** *a.* fighting, combating.

босиком *adv.* barefoot.

босмина *f.* (crust.) Bosmina.

бос/ой, —оногий *a.* barefoot.

босфорский *a.* (geog.) Bosporus.

бот *m.* boat; boot, overshoe.

ботало *n.* cowbell; (fishing) beater.

ботани/зирка *f.* (bot.) specimen box; —**зировать** *v.* botanize; —**к** *m.* botanist; —**ка** *f.* botany; —**ческий** *a.* botanical; —**ическая география** phytogeography.

ботать *v.* beat (water), drive (fish).

ботв/а *f.* plant top(s), haulm; —**одробитель, —оизмельчитель** *m.* haulm shredder; —**ообрезающий** *a.* tops- or haulm-cutting; —**оотделитель, —орез, —осрезатель** *m.* haulm cutter, topper; —**отеребильный аппарат, —оудалитель** *m.* haulm remover.

бот/ик *m.* overshoe, boot; (mal.) Argonauta; Nautilus; —**инок** *m.,* —**иночный** *a.* shoe, boot.

Боткина болезнь infectious hepatitis.

ботн/ий *m.,* —**ическая свита** (geol.) Bothnian series; —**ический** *a.* Bothnian; (geog.) Bothnia.

ботнуть *see* **ботать.**

ботр/идий *m.,* —**идия** *f.* (zool.) bothridium; —**ий** *m.* bothrium, sucker; —**ио—** *prefix* botry(o)— (cluster); bothri(o)— (pit, depression; bothrium); —**иоид** *m.,* —**иоидный** *a.* botryoid; —**иомикоз** *m.* (vet.) botryomycosis; —**иоцефал** *m.* (zool.) Bothriocephalus, Diphyllobothrium; —**ический** *a.* (bot.) botryose; —**ия** *see* **ботрий;** —**опс** *m.* (herp.) Bothrops.

боттом *m.* bottom; **б.-кросс** *m.* (gen.) bottom cross.

ботул/а *f.* (mal.) Botula; —**изм** *m.* botulism, food poisoning.

ботус *m.* (ichth.) Bothus.

боты *pl.* overshoes, boots.

боуманит *m.* (min.) bowmanite.

боуто *m.* (mam.) bouto, Amazonian dolphin (*Inia geoffrensis*).

Боуэна болезнь (med.) Bowen's disease.

Бофор(т)а шкала (meteor.) Beaufort scale.

бочаг *m.,* —**а** *f.* deep pool, water hole.

бочар *m.* cooper; —**ничать** *v.* cooper; —**ничество** *n.* cooperage, coopering; —**ный** *a.* cooper's; barrel, cask; —**ня** *f.* cooperage, cooper's shop.

боч/ечка *see* **болонок;** —**ечный** *a.,* —**ка** *f.,* —**ковый** *a.* barrel, drum, cask, keg; tub, vat; (av.) roll; (naut.) buoy; (zool.) pleuron; —**ковидный** *see* **бочкообразный;** —**ком** *see* **боком;** —**конаполнитель** *m.* drum filler; —**кообразность** *f.* crown (of rolls); —**кообразный** *a.* barrel (-shaped or -type); (biol.) dolioform.

бочок *m.* (zool.) pleuron; (carcass) flank.

бочон/ки, —ковые *pl.* (mal.) Doliidae; —**ковидный, —кообразный** *a.* doliiform, dolioform, barrel-shaped; orculiform, cask-shaped; —**ок** *m.* small barrel, keg, cask; (mal.) Dolium; —**очник** *m.* Doliolum; —**очники, —очниковые** *pl.* Doliolidae.

боя *gen. of* **бой.**

бояз/ливый *a.* fearful, apprehensive; —**нь** *f.* fear, dread; (med.) phobia.

боялыч *m.* Russian thistle (*Salsola arbuscula*).

боянусов орган (mal.) organ of Bojanus.

бояр/ка *f.* (bot.) hawthorn (*Crataegus pontica* or *azarolus*); —**ышник** *m.* hawthorn (*Crataegus*); —**ышница** *f.* pierid butterfly.

бояться *v.* fear, be afraid (of), dread; suffer (from); be susceptible (to); be adversely affected (by); **не б. проколов** be puncture-proof.

боях *prepos. pl. of* **бой.**

боящийся *pr. part. of* **бояться.**

БПК *abbr.* (**биохимическая потребность в кислороде**) biochemical oxygen demand, BOD; **БПК-полная** ultimate BOD.

БПФ *abbr.* (**быстрое преобразование Фурье**) fast Fourier transform, FFT.

бр *abbr.* (**бар**) bar; **бр.** *abbr.* (**бракованный**) rejected; (**брикетированный**) briquetted; (**брошюра**) pamphlet; **бр., Бр** *abbr.* (**брутто**) gross (weight).

бра *n.* sconce, (wall) bracket.

браваизит *m.* (min.) bravaisite.

бравший *past act. part. of* **брать.**

Бравэ решетка (cryst.) Bravais lattice.

брага *f.* home-brewed beer; (naut.) span.

браг/гит *m.* (min.) braggite; —**ит** *m.* (min.) bragite, fergusonite.

брагоперегонный *a.* (beer) mash.

брадзот *m.* (vet.) braxy.

бради— *prefix* brady— (slow); —**кардия** *f.* (med.) bradycardia; —**кинин** *m.* bradykinin (hormone); —**телический** *a.* bradytelic.

брадэна головка (oil wells) bradenhead.

бражка *f.* mash.

бражники *pl.* (ent.) Sphingidae.

бражный *a.* mash.

браз. *abbr.* (**бразильский**) Brazilian.

бразил/еин *m.* brazilein; —**ин** *m.* brazilin, brasilin; —**ит** *m.* (petr.) brazilite, baddeleyite; **Бразилия** Brazil; —**овый** *a.* brasilic (acid); —**ьский** *a.* Brazil(ian); —**ьское дерево** brazilwood.

брайлевский *a.* Braille.

брайтова болезнь (med.) Bright's disease.

брайтсток *m.* bright stock (oil).

брак *m.* union, marriage; (tech.) flaw, defect; waste, wastage, refuse, scrap; reject(s), defective products; (paper) broke; **доля —а** (math., stat.) fraction defective.

бракебушит *m.* (min.) brackebuschite.

бракёр *m.* grading inspector, grader, sorter.

брак/аж *m.* grading; sorting, culling; —**овочная** *f.* grading or sorting room.

бракет *m.,* —**а** *f.* bracket.

брако/ванный *a.* condemned, etc., see *v.*; off-grade, defective, faulty; non-acceptable; refuse, waste; —**ванное изделие** reject, waste; —**вать** *v.* condemn, reject, refuse, discard, scrap; inspect; grade, sort, cull, screen out; —**вка** *f.* condemning, etc., see *v.*; rejection; inspection; —**вочный** *a.* rejected, discarded; defective; objectionable; —**вщик** *m.* quality control inspector, sorter, grader; —**дел** *m.* careless worker; —**делие** *n.* production of defective goods; —**молка** *f.* (paper) cone breaker, kneader, shredder; **—моталка** *f.* scrap baller (of wire).

бракониды *pl.* (ent.) braconid wasps.

браконьер *m.* poacher; offender; **—ский** *a.* poaching; illegal (fishing); excessive, rapacious; **—ство** *n.* poaching; **—ствовать** *v.* poach; fish illegally.

бракте/ола *f.* (bot.) bracteola; **—я** *f.* bract.

бракующий *pr. act. part. of* **браковать.**

брал *past m. sing. of* **брать.**

брам/а *f.* (ichth.) Ray's bream (*Brama*); (orn.) Brahma; **—ан** *m.* Brahman (cattle); **—овые** *pl.* (ichth.) Bramidae.

бранд— *prefix* fire; **—вахта** *f.* fire watch; guard ship.

бранденбургский *a.* (geog.) Brandenburg.

брандер *m.* fire boat, fire ship.

брандизит *m.* (min.) brandisite.

бранд/мауер *m.* fire wall; **—мейстер** *m.* fire chief; **—спойт** *m.* (fire) pump; high-pressure hose.

брандтит *m.* (min.) brandtite.

брандтрубка *f.* (art.) nipple, tube.

брандушка *f.* (bot.) Bulbocodium.

брани(ва)ть *v.* scold, reprove, rebuke; censure; **—ся** *v.* quarrel.

браннерит *m.* (min.) brannerite.

бранхи— *prefix* branchi(o)— (gills); **—огенный** *a.* branchiogenic, gill-forming; **—озавр** *m.* (pal.) branchiosaur; **—омер** *m.* (embr.) branchiomere; **—омикоз** *m.* (vet.) branchiomycosis, gill rot; **—остегит** *m.* (crust.) branchiostegite; **—остома** *f.* (zool.) Branchiostoma, Amphioxus; **—ура** *f.* (crust.) fish louse (*Branchiura*).

бранш *m.* arm; branch.

брас *m.* (naut.) brace.

брасик *m.* (naut.) tiller becket.

браславский *a.* (geog.) Braslav.

браслет *m.* bracelet; (rubber) band; **—ный станок** band builder; **—чик** *m.* band-building operator.

брасопить *v.* (naut.) brace.

брасси/(ди)новый *a.* brassidic, 12-docosenoic (acid); **—ловый** *a.* brassylic (acid).

брат *m.* brother, sibling; (geol.) earth pillar; **—аться** *v.* fraternize; **—ский** *a.* fraternal; common (grave); (geog.) Bratsk; **—ственный** *a. suffix* (bot.) —adelphous; **—ство** *n.* brotherhood, fraternity; (bot.) adelphia.

брать *v.* take (possession; into service); grasp, seize, occupy; claim, demand; require, need; accept, receive, obtain; derive (from), originate; withdraw, remove, borrow (from); prevail, succeed; put (in brackets); negotiate (turns); turn (right or left); follow (an example); **б. на себя** take upon oneself, assume; **не б.** fail; **—ся (за)** *v.* undertake, tackle, approach; start; accept (a challenge).

братья *pl. of* **брат; б. и сёстры** siblings.

браузе *n.* sprinkler, spray.

браулёз *m.* bee louse infestation.

Брауна реактив Braun's reagent.

браунинг *m.* (mil.) Browning.

браунит *m.* (min.) braunite.

браунколь *f.* (bot.) kale.

браун/миллерит *m.* (min.) brownmillerite; **—овский** *a.* Brownian (movement); Braun's (reagent).

брауншвей/гская зелень, —н *m.* Brunswick green, green copper carbonate.

брауэровский *a.* (math.) Brouwer(ian).

брахи— *prefix* brachy— (short); brachi— brachial; **—альный** *a.* brachial; arm; **—мейоз** *m.* (gen.) brachymeiosis; **—о—** *prefix* (anat.) brachio— (brachial;

arm); **—олария, —олярия** *f.* (zool.) brachiolaria; **—онихтовые** *pl.* frogfishes (*Brachionichthyidae*); **—опода** *f.*, **—оподовый** *a.* (mal.) brachiopod; **—ось** *f.* (cryst.) brachyaxis; **—пирамида** *f.* brachypyramid; **—стохрона** *f.* (math.) brachistochrone; **—телес** *m.* (mam.) Brachyteles; **—цефалический** *a.* brachycephalic, short-headed.

браун/ость *f.* (zool.) nuptiality; **—ый** *a.* nuptial, mating; breeding; *suffix* (biol.) —gamous; **—ый наряд, —ая окраска** nuptial dress or color; (orn.) nuptial plumage; **—ые игры** nuptial play.

брашпиль *m.* windlass, anchor winch.

брёвен *gen. pl. of* **бревно.**

бревен/ник *m.* mature forest; **—чатый** *a. of* **бревно;** timbered.

бревий *m.* brevium, uranium X_2.

бревно *n.* log, beam; block; (constr.) timber; **—катка** *f.* log roller, log elevator; **—мер** *m.* log scale; **—подъёмник** *m.* log hoist; **—сбрасыватель** *m.* log kicker; **—спуск** *m.* log slide, chute; **—таска** *f.* log hauler; **—укладчик** *m.* log stacker.

брег(г)ерит *m.* (min.) bröggerite.

брегма/тический *a.* (anat.) bregmatic; **—церовые** *pl.* (ichth.) Bregmacerotidae.

бред *m.* (med.) delirium; delusion; **алкогольный б.** delirium tremens.

бредень *m.* drag net.

бредёт *pr. 3 sing. of* **брести.**

бредина *f.* goat willow (*Salix caprea*).

брединский *a.* (geog.) Bredyi.

бред/ить *v.* be delirious; **—ни** *pl. of* **бредень; —овой** *a.* delirious; **—овые идеи** delusions; **—ущий** *a.* wandering, etc., *see* **бродить.**

брезг/ать *v.* be squeamish or fastidious (about); have an aversion (to), disdain; **—ливость** *f.* squeamishness; disgust; **—ливый** *a.* squeamish, fastidious.

брезент *m.*, **—овой** *a.* tarp(aulin), canvas; burlap; **—овое пальто** tarpaulin, poncho.

брезжить *v.* glimmer; dawn.

брей *imp. of* **брить.**

брейнерит *m.* (min.) breunerite.

брейслакит *m.* (min.) breislakite.

Брейта-Вигнера формула (nucl.) Breit-Wigner formula.

брейтгауптит *m.* (min.) breithauptite.

брейте *imp. of* **брить.**

брейтовский *a.* (math.) Breit('s); Breitov (breed of swine).

брекватер *m.* breakwater, jetty.

брекер *m.* breaker.

брекч/иевидный, —ированный *a.* (petr.) brecciated; **—ирование** *n.* brecciation; **—ия** *f.* breccia.

брёл *past. m. sing. of* **брести.**

брелок *m.* suspender.

бременский *a.* Bremen (green, blue).

бремза *f.* (text.) swivel tension.

бремсберг *m.*, **—овый** *a.* (gravity) incline, slope, ramp.

бремя *f.* burden, load, weight.

бренди *m.* brandy.

брентстедовский *a.* Brönsted (acid).

бренц— *prefix* pyro—; **—виноградный** *a.* pyroracemic (acid); **—катехин** *m.* pyrocatechol.

бренчать *v.* jingle; chink (of coins).

бресмадрук *m.* (typ.) reflectography.

брести *see* **бродить;** plod (along).

брест-колесо *n.* breast wheel.

брестский *a.* (geog.) Brest.

бретель(ка) *f.* shoulder strap.

бретонский *a.* (geol.) Bretonian.

брефический *a.* (zool.) nepionic, postembryonal.

брех/ать, —нуть *v.* yelp, bark; lie.

брештук *m.* (naut.) breasthook; hook.

брешь *f.* breach, gap, break, notch; flaw; (bot.) lacuna.

брею/т *pr. 3 pl. of* **брить; —щий** *a.* shaving; (av.) low-altitude.

б-рея *abbr.* (**батарея**) battery, cell.

бриг *m.* brig (a boat).

бриг— — *prefix see* **бригадный; —бриг** *m., suffix,* **—ада** *f.* brigade, squad, crew, team, gang; **—адир** *m.* team leader, foreman; **—адный** *a. of* **бригада.**

бриг(гс)овый логарифм (math.) Briggs' logarithm, common logarithm.

бригелоу-скраб *m.* (geobot.) brigalow scrub.

бридель *m.* (mooring) bridle; anchor chain.

бридер *m., —ный* *a.* (nucl.) breeder.

бриевые *pl.* (bot.) Bryaceae (mosses).

бриз *m.* breeze.

бризантн/ость *f., —ое* **действие** (expl.) brisance; **—ый** *a.* brisant, disruptive, shattering, detonating, high explosive; high (explosives).

брий *m.* (bot.) Bryum (a moss).

брикет *m.* briquet, brick, cake; wafer; brick fuel; (feed) pellet; preform; **—ирование** *n.* briquetting, etc., *see v.;* **—ированный** *a.* briquet(ted), etc., *see v.;* **—ировать** *v.* briquet; pellet; preform; **—ировочный** *a.* briquet(ting), etc., *see v.;* **—ировщик** *m.* pelleter; **б.-лизунец** *m.* salt lick.

Брикнера цикл (meteor.) Brückner cycle.

брил *past m. sing. of* **брить.**

бриллиант *m.* diamond; (typ.) brilliant; **—овый** *a. of* **бриллиант;** (zool.) diamondback(ed).

бриллуэновский *a.* Brillouin (function).

бриль *m.* (ichth.) brill (*Scophthalmus rhombus*).

брильянт *see* **бриллиант.**

Брина метод Brin (oxygen) process.

Бринел/я проба (met.) Brinell test; **твёрдость по —ю** Brinell hardness.

брио— — *prefix* bryo— (moss); **—бии(ны)** *pl.* (zool.) Bryobiidae; **—зои** *pl.* Bryozoa; **—логия** *f.* (bot.) bryology; **—ния** *f.* Bryonia; **—фит** *m.* bryophyte.

бристольский *a.* Bristol (board).

бриталь-процесс *m.* (met.) Brital process.

британ/ец *m.* Britisher; **—ия** *f.* Britannia (metal); **—ка** British woman; (elec.) Brittania splice; **—ский** *a.* British; **—ская тепловая единица** British thermal unit, Btu, BTU.

бритв/а *f.* razor; blade, knife; **—енный** *a.* razor; shaving; **—енная лапа** L-blade.

бритолит *m.* (min.) britholite.

брит/ый *a.* shaved, clean-shaven; **—ьё** *n.* shave, shaving; **—ь(ся)** *v.* shave.

брова/лол *m.* brovalol, bornyl bromoisovalerate; **—рский** *a.* (geog.) Brovaryi.

бров/астый *a.* heavy-browed; **—ка** *dim. of* **бровь;** lip, brow (of hill, etc.); edge, brink, border, shoulder; **—ник** *m.* (bot.) Herminium; **—ный** *a., —ь* *f.* (anat.) supercilium, eyebrow.

брод *m.* ford.

бродил/о *n.* leaven; ferment; yeast; enzyme; **—ьность** *f.* fermentability; **—ьный** *a.* zymotic, fermenting, fermentative; **—ьный грибок** yeast plant; **—ьный запал** ferment, leavening; **—ьный процесс** fermentation; **—ьня** *f.* fermentation room.

брод/ить *v.* wander, roam, stray; touch, graze; ferment; drag (fish net); **—ник** *m.* small haul seine.

бродовский *a.* (geog.) Brodyi.

брод/яжка *f.* (biol.) zoospore; young larva; **—ячие** *pl.* (zool.) Errantia; **—ячий** *a.* stray, wandering; erratic, restless; migratory, itinerant, nomad; **—ящий** *a.* wandering, etc., *see* **бродить.**

брожение *n.* fermentation.

брозилат *m.* bromobenzene sulfonate.

бройлер *m.* broiler.

Брока центр (anat.) Broca's (speech) center.

брокат *m.* bronze powder; (text.) brocade.

брокателло *n.* broccatello (a marble).

брокатель *f.* (text.) brocatel.

брокенский *a.* (meteor.) Brocken (specter).

брокер *m.* (com.) broker.

брокcol/и, —ь *f.* (bot.) broccoli.

бром *m.* bromine, Br; (pharm.) bromide; **гидрат —а** bromine hydrate; **хлористый б.** bromine chloride; *prefix* brom(o)—; **—аль** *m.* bromal, tribromoacetaldehyde.

бромангидрид *m.* acid bromide; **б. серной кислоты** sulfuryl bromide; **б. уксусной кислоты** acetyl bromide.

броманилин *m.* bromaniline.

бромаргирит *m.* (min.) bromargyrite.

бромат *m., —ный* *a.* bromate; **—ология** *f.* bromatology, dietetics; **—ометрия** *f.* (analysis) bromate method.

бром/аурат *m.* bromaurate, auribromide; **—аурит** *m.* bromaurite, aurobromide; **—ацетил** *m.* bromacetyl; **—ацетон** *m.* bromacetone; **—ацетофенон** *m.* bromacetophenone; **—бензилцианид** *m.* bromobenzyl cyanide; **—бензойный** *a.* bromobenzoic (acid); **—бензол** *m.* bromobenzene; **—гидрат** *m.* bromine hydrate; hydrobromide; **—гидрин** *m.* bromhydrin; **—гидрирование** *n.* hydrobromination; **—дезоксиуридин** *m.* bromodeoxyuridine, BUDR; **—елиевые** *pl.* pineapple family (*Bromeliaceae*); **—елия** *f.* bromelia, 2-ethoxynaphthaline; **—замещённое** *n.* bromo compound; **—замещённый** *a.* bromo— (compound); **—ид** *m.* bromide; **—ирит** *m.* (min.) bromyrite; **—ирование** *n.* brom(in)ation; **—ированный** *a.* brom(in)ated; **—ировать** *v.* brom(in)ate.

бромистоводородн/ый *a.* hydrobromic; hydrobromide (of); **б. хинин** quinine hydrobromide; **—ая кислота** hydrobromic acid, hydrogen bromide; **соль —ой кислоты** bromide.

бромист/ый *a.* bromine; (lower or **—ous**) bromide; **б. водород** hydrogen bromide; **б. калий** potassium bromide; **б. натрий** sodium bromide; **б. этил** ethyl bromide; **—ая медь** cuprous bromide; **—ое железо** ferrous bromide.

бром /ит *m.* bromite; **—лит** *m.* (min.) bromlite, alstonite; **—масляный** *a.* bromobutyric (acid); **—метил** *m.* methyl bromide; **—молочный** *a.* bromolactic (acid).

бромноват/ая кислота bromic acid; **соль —ой кислоты** bromate; **—истая кислота** hypobromous acid; **соль —истой кислоты** hypobromite; **—исто-кальциевая соль** calcium hypobromite; **—истокислый** *a.* hypobromous acid; hypobromite (of); **—истокислая соль** hypobromite; **—обензиловый эфир** benzyl bromate; **—окалиевая соль** potassium bromate; **—окислый** *a.* bromic acid; bromate (of); **—окислый натрий** sodium bromate; **—окислая соль** bromate.

бромн/ый *a.* bromine; (higher or **—ic**) bromide; **—ая вода** bromine water; **—ая кислота** perbromic acid; **соль —ой кислоты** perbromate; **—ая медь** cupric bromide; **—ое железо** ferric bromide.

бромо— *prefix* bromo—.

бромоводород *m.* hydrogen bromide; **—ный** *see* **бромистоводородный.**

бромо/вый *a. of* **бром; —камфара** *f.* bromocamphor; **—кись** *f.* oxybromide; **—л** *m.* bromol, tribromophenol; **—метилирование** *n.* bromomethylation; **—ниевый** *a.,* **—ний** *m.* bromonium; **—прен** *m.* bromoprene, 2-bromobutadiene-1,4; **—серебряный** *a.* silver bromide (emulsion); **—форм** *m.* bromoform, tribromomethane.

бром/производное *n.* bromine derivative; **—стирол** *m.* bromostyrene; **—сульфалеин** *m.* bromsulfalein, bromosulfophthalein; **—тимолблау, —тимолсиный** *m.* bromothymol blue; **—толуол** *m.* bromotoluene; **—уксусный** *a.* brom(o)acetic (acid); **соль —уксусной кислоты** bromoacetate; **—уксусноэтиловый эфир** ethyl bromoacetate; **—урал** *m.* Bromural; **—урацил** *m.* bromuracil, BU (mutagen); **—фенол** *m.* bromphenol; **—фенолблау** *m.* bromophenol blue; **—циан** *m.* cyanogen bromide; **—этан, —этил** *m.* bromoethane, ethyl bromide; **—юр** *m.* bromide.

броне— *prefix* armor(ed); **—автомобиль** *m.* armored car; **—башня** *f.* turret; **—бойный** *a.* armor-piercing; **—вик** *m.* armored car; **—вой** *a.* armor(ing), armored, protective, sheathing; **—вой лист** armor plate.

броней *instr. of* **броня.**

броне/кабель *m.* (elec.) armored cable; **—катер** *m.* armored boat; **—колпак** *m.* armored turret; **—лента** *f.* armoring tape (of cable); **—машина** *f.* armored vehicle; **—носец** *m.* battleship; (mam.) armadillo (*Dasypus,* etc.); **—носный** *a.* armored, armor-clad; **—носцевые, —носцы** *pl.* (mam.) Dasypodidae; **—плита** *f.* armor plate; **—поезд** *m.* armored train; **—пробивающий** *a.* armor-piercing; **—стекло** *n.* bullet-resistant glass; **—танковый** *a.* armored; **—транспортер** *m.* armored (personnel) carrier.

бронза *f.* (met.) bronze.

бронзиров/альный *a.* bronze, bronzing; **—ание** *n.,* **—ка** *f.* bronzing; **—анный** *a.* bronzed; **—ать** *v.* bronze.

бронзит *m.* (met.; min.) bronzite.

бронзов/альный *a.* bronze, bronzing; **—ание** *see* **бронзирование; —атоокрашенный** *a.* bronze-colored; **—ки** *pl.* scarabaeid beetles; **—ость** *f.* (phyt.) bronzing; spotted wilt; **—ый** *a.* bronze, bronzy; **—ый штейн** concentrated metal from copper sulfide ores); **—ая болезнь** (med.) Addison's disease; **—ые краски** bronze powders.

бронзо/крылый *a.* bronze-winged; **—литейный завод** bronze foundry; **—подобный** *a.* bronze-like, bronzy.

брониров/ание *n.* armoring, etc., *see v.;* **—анный** *a.* armored, etc., *see v.;* **—анный латунью** brass-clad; **—ать** *v.* armor, armor-plate, clad with metal, jacket; (rockets) inhibit, restrict (grain); reserve; **—овка** *f.,* **—овочный** *a.* armoring, etc., *see v.*

бронто— *prefix* bronto— (thunder); **—завр** *m.* (pal.) brontosaurus; **—метр** *m.* (meteor.) brontometer.

бронх *m.* (anat.) bronchus; *pl.* **—и** bronchi; **—иальный** *a.* bronchial; **—иола, —иоль** *f.* bronchiole; **—ит** *m.* (med.) bronchitis; **—о-** *prefix* bronch(i); broncho—(windpipe); **—оаденит** *m.* (med.) bronchadenitis; **—олёгочный** *a.* (anat.) bronchopulmonary; **—орасширение** *n.* bronchodilation; **—оскопировать** *v.* examine with a bronchoscope; **—осуживатель** *m.* bronchoconstrictor; **—оэктаз** *m.,* **—оэктазия** *f.* bronchiectasis.

брон/я *f.* armor, casing, jacket; reservation; reserved quota; **покрывать —ей** *v.* armor(-plate); **—яковые** *pl.* armored catfishes (*Doradidae*).

брос/ание *n.* throwing, etc., *see v.;* projection; abandonment; (missiles) departure; **—ать, —ить** *v.* throw, cast, toss; hurl; project; give up, quit, abandon, leave, drop; launch (missile); **—аться, —иться** *v.* throw oneself, plunge; apply oneself (to work); **—овый** *a.* worthless, unproductive, waste, refuse; unusable; useless; disposable; (petrol.) retrievable; wireline (bit); (av.) retractable; jettisonable; off, lost (heat); **—овый экспорт** (com.) dumping; **—овая земля** wasteland; **—ок** *m.* throw(ing); thrusting; (in)rush, surge; (mach.) kick; (av.) bump; (zool.) lunge; (sports) sprint.

бротул/евые, —овые *pl.* (ichth.) brotulids.

броуновский *a.* Brownian (movement).

брохидо— *prefix* brochido—, loop.

брошантит *m.* (min.) brochantite.

брошенный *past pass. part. of* **бросать.**

броширов/ка *f.,* **—очный** *a.* stitching.

брош/ка, —ь *f.* brooch; (tech.) broach.

брошюр/а *f.* brochure, pamphlet, booklet; bulletin; **—овать** *v.* stitch (books); **—овка** *f.,* **—овочный** *a.* stitching; **—овщик** *m.* stitcher.

б.р.т., БРТ *abbr.* (**брутто регистровая тонна**) gross registered ton, G.R.T.; **бр.-т** *abbr.* (**брутто-тонн**) gross tons; **бр-то** *abbr.* (**брутто**) gross (weight).

БрУ *abbr.* (**бромурацил**) bromouracil, BU.

брудер *m.,* **—ный** *a.* brooder (for poultry); **—гауз** *m.* brooder house.

брукит *m.* (min.) brookite.

бруксизм *m.* (med.) bruxism, teeth grinding.

брукхейвенский *a.* (geog.) Brookhaven.

брульон *m.* sketch, outline; field map.

брун/ирование *see* **брюнирование; —кресс** *m.* water pepper (*Polygonum hydropiper*).

бруннеровский *a.* Brunner's (glands).

брунсвигит *m.* (min.) brunsvigite.

бруньятеллит *m.* (min.) brugnatellite.

брус *m.* beam, girder, joist; (tie) rod, bar; block; (lumber) cant; square.

брусит *m.* (min.) brucite.

бруслов/ый *a. of* **брусок;** squared; joist (nail); brick-shaped; bar, flat (iron); loaf (cheese).

брусни/ка *f.,* **—чный** *a.* mountain cranberry (*Vaccinium vitis idaea*); **—чные** *pl.* Vacciniaceae.

брус/овать *v.* break down, open up (a log); **—овка** *f.* arm file, coarse file; breaking down, opening up; **—овой** *a. of* **брус; —овский** *a.* (geog.) Brusovo; **—ок** *m.* bar, strip; block; slug; pig; rail, rod; stack; (timber) square; whetstone, grinding stone; **—орезка** *f.* rod bench; **—очный** *a. of* **брусок; -помост** *m.* scaffold plank.

бруссонеция *f.* (bot.) Broussonetia.

бруствер *m.* breastwork, parapet.

брусчат/ка *f.* (paving) block; **—ый** *a.* block; stacked; (geol.) mullion, rodding (structure).

брус/штанга *m.* (rolling) spreader bar; **—ья** *pl. of* **брус;** skids.

брутто *a. and adv.,* **—вый** *a.* gross; **б.-реакция** *f.* overall reaction; **б.-тонна** *f.* gross ton; **б.-формула** *f.* empirical formula; **вес б.** gross weight.

брух *m.* (wines) casse.

бруц/еллёз *m.,* **—еллёзный** *a.* (med.) brucellosis; **—ин** *m.* brucine, dimethoxystrychnine; **—ит** *m.* (min.) brucite.

брушбрекер *m.* (agr.) brush breaker.

брушеный *a.* sealed, capped (honey).

брушит *m.* (min.) brushite.

БРФ *abbr.* (**физический бериллиевый реактор**) physical beryllium reactor.

брыж/еечный *a.* (anat.) mesenteric; **—ейка** *f.* mesenterium; **—ейка желудка** mesogastrium; **—ейка толстой кишки** mesocolon; **сердечная —ейка** mesocardium; **—ейный** *a.* mesenteric.

брызг *m.* spray, splash; **—алка** *f.,* **—ало** *n.* sprinkler, sprayer, spray nozzle, atomizer; spray; **—альный** *a.* spraying, etc., *see v.;* spray; **—альце** *n.* (zool.) spiracle; **—анье** *n.* spraying, etc., *see v.; see* **ать** *v.* spray, sprinkle, spatter, splash; jet, spurt, gush out; **—аться** *v.* spatter; **—и** *pl.* spray, splash, spatter; **давать —и** *v.* spurt.

брызго/вик *m.* mudguard; **—защищённый, —непроницаемый** *a.* splashproof, spraytight; rainproof; **—отражатель** *m.* spray deflector, guard; **—стойкий** *a.* splashproof; **—уловитель** *m.* spray trap.

брызгун *m.* archerfish (*Toxotes jaculatrix*); **—овые, —ы, —ья** *pl.* Toxotidae.

брызнуть *see* **брызгать;** spout, gush.

брык/ание *n.* kicking; **—ать, —нуть** *v.* kick (out, up); **—аться** *v.* kick; be obstinate; **—ливость** *f.* tendency to kick; **—ливый** *a.* kicking; bucking.

брынза *f.* brynza (sheep's milk cheese).

брэ *abbr.* (биологический рентген-эквивалент) Roentgen equivalent man, rem.

брзгговский *a.* Bragg('s).

брэнштедовский *a.* Brönsted (theory).

брюзжать *v.* grumble, grouse.

брюкв/а *f.,* **—енный** *a.* Swedish turnip, rutabaga (*Brassica napobrassica*).

брюки *pl.* trousers, pants.

брюнет *m.,* **—ка** *f.* brunette.

брюнировать *v.* brown, burnish, polish.

брюссельская капуста Brussels sprouts.

брюстерит *m.* (min.) brewsterite.

брюстеровский *a.* (opt.) Brewster's (law).

брюх/о *n.* abdomen, belly; **мышца —а** abdominal muscle; **—овина** *f.* entrails; rumen (of ruminant); belly; **—оногие** *pl.* (mal.) gastropods, **—оресничные** *pl.* (prot.) Hypotricha; (zool.) Gastrotricha; **—оротые** *pl.* (zool.) Gasterostomata; **—ощитник** *m.* Aspidogaster.

брючн/ый *a. of* **брюки;** **—ая лента** cuff lining.

брюшин/а *f.* (anat.) peritoneum; **воспаление —ы** (med.) peritonitis; **—ный** *a.* peritoneal.

брюшистый *a.* single-bladed (knife).

брюш/ко *dim. of* **брюхо;** abdomen; belly, venter (of muscle); face (of blade); **—но—** *prefix* abdomino—; **—ной** *a.* abdominal, ventral, enteric; peritoneal (cavity); celiac (artery); splanchnic (nerve); pelvic (fin); **—ной тиф** typhoid fever; **—ная полость** abdominal cavity; **—но-маточный** *a.* (anat.) abdominouteral; (med.) c(a)esarian (section); **—нотифозный** *a.* typhoid.

бряк/ать, —нуть *v.* rattle, clatter; jingle, clank; fling, drop; blurt out; **—аться, —нуться** *v.* fall down heavily.

брянский *a.* (geog.) Bryansk; Bryanka.

бряц/ание *n.* clang, clank(ing); **—ать** *v.* clang, clatter; jingle, chink.

БСК *abbr.* (бутадиенстирольный каучук) butadiene-styrene rubber.

б.т.е., БТЕ, *abbr.* (британская тепловая единица) British thermal unit, Btu.

б-то, Б-то *abbr.* (брутто) gross.

бубал *m.* (mam.) Alcelaphus; Damaliscus.

бубен *m.* tambourine; **—ец** *m.* bell; **—чик** *m.* bell; (bot.) Adenophora.

бублик *m.* (food) bagel.

бубон *m.* (med.) bubo; **—ный** *a.* bubonic.

бубырь *m.* (ichth.) Bubyr; Pomatoschistus caucasicus; ruffe (*Acerina cernua*).

Буво-Блан(к)а реакция Bouveault-Blanc reaction.

бугай *m.* breeding bull.

Буге закон (opt.) Bouguer's law.

бугель *m.,* **—ный** *a.* bow, loop, hoop; band, ring; stirrup, strap; (elec.) bow collector; (eccentric) clip.

бугор *m.* mound, hill(ock), knoll; heap; protuberance, tubercle; (anat.) tuber, knob, swelling, eminence; **—ково—** *see* **бугорно—;** **—ковый** *a. of* **бугорок;** tubercular, grumous, clotted; **—но—** *prefix* (anat.) thalamo—; **—но-корковый** *a.* thalamocortical; **—ок** *m.* tubercle, nodule; protuberance, prominence.

бугорчат/ка *f.* (med.) tuberculosis; **—ковые** *pl.* (ichth.) Synancei(i)dae; **—о—** *prefix* tuberculato— (tuberculate); condyl(o)— (knuckle, joint, knob); **—ый** *a.* tubercular, nodular; torulose, knobby; tuberculate, warty; (orn.) strawberry (comb).

бугр/а *gen. of* **бугор;** **—истость** *f.* tuberosity; eminence; bumpiness; **—истый** *a.* tuberous; bumpy, uneven; hummocky, hilly; grumose, knotted; (pal.) pustulous; **—овидный** *a.* tubercular.

буг/ский *a.,* **—ско—** *prefix* Bug (river); **—ульминский** *a.* (geog.) Bugulma; **—унский** *a.* Bugun; **—урусланский** *a.* Buguruslan.

Бугэ *see* **Буге.**

будапештский *a.* Budapest.

будем *fut. 1 pl. of* **быть.**

будень *m.* workday, weekday.

будет *fut. 3 sing. of* **быть.**

будильник *m.* alarm clock.

будить *v.* wake, rouse, call, raise.

будка *f.* booth, stall; cabin; (sentry) box; (mach.) cab; shelter, screen; housing; nest box.

будле(й)я *f.* (bot.) Buddleia.

будн/и *pl.,* **—ий** *a.* workday(s), weekday(s); **—ичный** *a.* week (day); everyday; dull.

будок *gen. pl. of* **будка.**

будоражить *v.* excite, agitate, disturb.

БУДР *abbr.* (бромдезоксиуридин) bromodeoxyuridine, BUDR.

будра *f.* (bot.) ground ivy (*Glechoma*).

будру-пам *m.* (herp.) Lachesis gramineus.

будто *conj.* as if, as though; **б. бы** supposedly, apparently, ostensibly.

буду/т *fut. 3 pl.;* **—чи** *pr. act. ger. of* **быть;** being; if, when, while.

будущ/ее *n.* the future; **дерево —его** thriving tree; **—ий** *a.* future, coming, next, ensuing; **на —ее время** for the future; **—ность** *f.* future; career.

будылья *pl.* sunflower stalks.

будь, —те *imp. of* **быть;** be; whether; **б. что будет** come what may; **не б. вас . . .** but for you . . .

будяк *m.* (bot.) thistle (*Cirsium*).

будящий *pr. act. part. of* **будить.**

буёв *gen. pl. of* **буй.**

буёк *m.* (small) buoy.

буен *sh. m. of* **буйный.**

буер *m.* ice boat, ice breaker.

буер/ак *m.,* **—ачный** *a.* ravine, bully; **—ачистый** *a.* gullied.

буж *m.* (med.) bougie (instrument).

буж(д)ение *n.* wakening, arousing.

буженина *f.* pork.

бужиров/ание *n.* (med.) bougi(e)nage; **—ать** *v.* examine with a bougie.

буза *f.* bouza (beverage); (min.) bay salt.

бузгунча *f.* (pharm.) pistacia galls.

бузин/а *f.,* **—ный, —овый** *a.* (bot.) elder (*Sambucus*).

бузулукский *a.* (geog.) Buzuluk.

бузульник *m.* (bot.) Ligularia.

бузун *m.* bay salt, rock salt.

буинский *a.* (geog.) Buinsk.

буй *m.* buoy, float; beacon.

буйвол *m.* (mam.) buffalo (*Bubalus*); **—ёнок** *m.* buffalo calf; **—ица** *f.* buffalo cow; **—оводство** *n.* buffalo breeding; **—овый** *a.* buffalo; **б.-рыба** *f.* buffalofish (*Ictiobus cyprinellus*).

буйка *gen. of* **буёк.**

буйнакский *a.* (geog.) Buinaksk.

буйн/о *adv.* violently; vigorously; **—ость** *f.* violence, turbulence; **—ый** *a.* violent, turbulent, ungovernable; vigorous; lush, rank, luxuriant (growth); rampant, unchecked; wild.

буйреп *m.* (naut.) buoy line or rope.

буйский *a.* (geog.) Bui (river).

буйство *n.* violence; **—вать** *v.* be violent.

бук *m.* (bot.) beech (*Fagus*).

букантауский *a.* (geog.) Bukantau.

бук/арка *f.* (ent.) snout beetle (*Rhynchites pauxillus*); **—ашка** *f.* chafer, beetle, small insect; **—ашник** *m.* (bot.) Jasione.

букв/а *f.* letter, character; (comp.) alpha (character); **—ально** *adv.* literally, word for word, verbatim; **—альность** *f.* literalness; **—альный** *a.* literal; verbal; **—арный** *a.* alphabetic; **—енно-цифровый** *a.* alphanumeric; tabular (display); **—енный** *a.* (by) letter; literal; (min.) graphic.

буквица *f.* (bot.) betony (*Betonica*).

букво/отливной *a.* type-casting; monotype; **—печатающий** *a.* printing.

букет *m.* bouquet, flavor; perfume, scent, aroma; bunch, clump (of plants); union; **—ик** *dim. of* **букет;** (bot.) cyathium; **—ировать** *v.* (agr.) block, bunch; thin (out); **—(ир)овка** *f.* blocking, etc., *see v.;* **—ировщик** *m.* blocker; **—ный** *a. of* **букет; –ная цвет(оч)ка** spray.

букинистический *a.* secondhand (book).

букинский *a.* (geog.) Bukina.

буккер *m.* drill plow.

букко *n.* bucco (leaves), buchu.

букландит *m.* (min.) bucklandite.

буклет *m.* booklet, leaflet, pamphlet.

букна *f.* (ent.) grape moth (*Theresia*).

бук/няк *m.* beech forest; **—овидный** *a.* beech-like; **—овые** *pl.* (bot.) Fagaceae; **—овый** *a.* beech(en); beechwood; beechnut; **—овый жолудь** beechnut.

букре/мет *m.* (plastics) Bukremet; **—суль** *m.* Bukresul (light stabilizer).

букс *m.* (bot.) box (*Buxus sempervirens*).

букса *f.* axle or journal box; bushing, bearing; (guiding) sleeve.

буксбаумиевые *pl.* (bot.) Buxbaumiaceae.

буксир *m.* tow(line); tug(boat); **—ный** *a.* tow, tug; **—ное приспособление** towline, towbar; **—ование** *n.* towing, etc., *see v.;* haulage; **—овать** *v.* tow, tug, haul; **—овка** *f.,* **—овочный** *a.* towing, etc., *see v.;* **—овщик** *m.* towing aircraft; **б.-толкач** *m.* pusher (tug).

буксов/ание *n.* slipping, etc., *see v.;* slip(page); **—ать** *v.* slip, slide, skid, spin.

букс/овое дерево boxwood; **—ус** *m.* (bot.) box, boxwood (*Buxus*).

буку *see* **букко.**

букциниды *pl.* (mal.) Buccinidae (snails).

булава *f.* club; (biol.) clava.

булавка *f.* pin.

булавница *f.* (bot.) Clavaria.

булаво— *prefix* (biol.) clavi—, club; **—видный** *a.* clavate, club-shaped; squarehead (wheat); (med.) clubbed; **—носец** *m.* (bot.) Corynephorus; **—носный** *a.* club-bearing, clavigerous; **—усые** *pl.* (ent.) Rhopalocera.

булавочн/ый *a. of* **булав(к)а;** pin; **—ая коррозия** pitting.

булаевский *a.* (geog.) Bulaevo.

буланжерит *m.* (min.) boulangerite.

буланый *a.* dun, cream-colored.

булат *m.* damask steel.

булат-май *m.* (ichth.) Barbus capito.

булгуннях *m.* (geol.) hydrolaccolith.

булев/ский, —ый *a.* (math.) Boolean.

булимия *f.* bulimia, insatiable appetite.

булинь *m.* (naut.) bowline.

бул/ка, —очка *f.,* **—очный** *a.* roll, bun; **—очная** *f.* bakery.

бултых/аться, —нуться *v.* splash, slop; flounder (about); fall, plunge (into water).

булунский *a.* (geog.) Bulun.

булыжн/ик *m.,* **—ый** *a.* cobble(stone).

бульб *m.,* **—а** *f.* bulb; **—арный** *a.* bulbar.

буль-блок *m.* (wire drawing) bull block.

бульбо— *prefix* bulbo— (bulb; bulbar); **—вый** *a.* bulb; **—капнин** *m.* bulbocapnine; **—уретральный** *a.* (anat.) bulbourethral.

бульбул/евые *pl.* (orn.) Pycnonotidae.

бульбус *m.* (biol.) bulbus.

бульва *f.* (bot.) Jerusalem artichoke.

бульвар *m.,* **—ный** *a.* boulevard, avenue.

бульверк *m.* bulwark; breakwater.

бульдоговые *pl.* (mam.) Molossidae.

бульдозер *m.* (mach.; met.) bulldozer; **—ист** *m.* bulldozer operator; **б.-погрузчик** *m.* loader; **б.-снегоочиститель** *m.* snow plow.

булька *f.* pellet.

булькать *v.* bubble, gurgle.

бульон *m.,* **—ный** *a.* broth, bouillon.

бум— *prefix, insert, suffix see* **бумажный.**

бумага *f.* paper; document; cotton; (met.) foil; **б.-основа** *f.* base paper.

бумаго/видный *a.* papery; **—делательный** *a.* papermaking; **—держатель** *m.* paper holder, paper clip; **—прядильный** *a.* textile, cotton-spinning; **—прядильня** *f.* cotton mill; **—реза(те)льный** *a.* paper-cutting.

бумаж/истый *a.* papery, papyraceous, paper-like; chartaceous; **—ка** *f.* slip of paper; **—ник** *m.* wallet, billfold; worker in paper industry; **—но—** *prefix,* **—ный** *a.* paper; (text.) cotton. **—ная масса** paper pulp; **—ное дерево** (bot.) paper mulberry (Broussonetia papyrifera); **—ное литьё** papier-mache; **—ное тесто** paper pulp.

бумаз/ейный *a.,* **—ея** *f.* (text.) fustian.

бумеранг *m.,* **—овый** *a.* boomerang.

буммасса *f.* paper pulp.

бумпер *m.* (ichth.) Atlantic bumper (*Chloroscombrus chrysurus*).

бумсланг *m.* (herp.) Dispholidus typus.

буна *f.* Buna (rubber); dike, jetty; (stream) bar; (min.) bank head.

бунгар *m.* (herp.) krait (*Bungarus*).

бундук *m.* (bot.) Kentucky coffee tree (*Gymnocladus canadensis*).

Бунзена-Роско закон Bunsen-Roscoe law.

бунзен/ит *m.* (min.) bunsenite; **—овский** *a.* Bunsen (burner).

бункер *m.* bin, bunker, hopper; **б.-воронка** *m.* feed hopper; —**ный** *a. of* **бункер;** —**ный фидер** feed hopper; —**ная вагонетка** hopper car; —**ная сеялка** (agr.) seed drill; —**ное топливо** oil-distillation residues; —**ование** *n.,* —**овка** *f.* (naut.) bunkering, etc., *see v.;* —**овать** *v.* bunker, coal, fuel; fill bunkers; —**овщик** *m.* fueler; **б.-охладитель** *m.* cooling hopper; **б.-питатель** *m.* feed hopper; **б.-распределитель** *m.* distributing hopper; **б.-сборник** *m.* storage bin; **б.-смеситель** *m.* blending hopper.

бунт *m.* bale, pack, bundle; coil; revolt, mutiny, riot; **в** —**ах** bulk (grain).

Бунте бюретка Bunte gas buret.

бунто/вать *v.* bale, pack; coil; revolt, rebel; rouse, incite; —**овой** *a. of* **бунт;** drum (drawing of tubes); —**держатель** *m.* (rolling) coil holder.

бунхозия *f.* (bot.) Bunchosia.

буор-хайский *a.* (geog.) Buor-Khaya.

бур *see* **бурав;** cutter; *sh. m. of* **бурый;** *prefix see* **буровой; бурятский.**

бура *f.* borax, sodium tetraborate; *sh. f. of* **бурый.**

бурав *m.* auger, borer, drill, perforator; bit; —**ить** *v.* bore, drill, perforate, pierce; —**ление** *n.* boring, drilling; —**ница** *f.* (ent.) miner; —**овидный** *a.* (zool.) terebriform; —**чатый** *a.* auger-shaped; —**чик** *m.* gimlet, borer; **правило** —**чика** (elec.) corkscrew rule, Ampere's rule; —**ящий** *a.* boring, etc., *see v.;* terebrate.

бурак *m.* beet (*Beta*); can; (met.) bootleg; (fishing) lamprey pot.

буран *m.,* —**ный** *a.* snowstorm, blizzard.

бураперл *m.* borax bead.

бурат *m.* (min.) trommel, washing drum; (flour) reel, bolter, sifter.

бурач/ище *n.* beet field; —**ная** *f.* beet shed or bin; —**ник** *m.* (bot.) borage (*Borago*); —**никовые** *pl.* Boraginaceae; —**никовый** *a.* borage, boraginaceous; —**ный** *a. of* **бурак;** —**ок** *m.* (bot.) Alyssum.

бурбон *m.* a cotton plant (*Gossypium purpurascens*); —**ский** *a.* bourbon.

бургомистер *m.* (orn.) Larus hyperboreus.

бургун *m.* (bot.) wormwood (*Artemisia*).

бургундск/ий *a.* Burgundy; —**ая жидкость** a copper sulfate-sodium carbonate fungicide.

бурда *f.* slops, waste water; muddy liquid; (zool.) dewlap, skin fold.

бурдон *m.* (gen.) burdo(n).

бурдюк *m.* wineskin.

буре/бал *m.* (silv.) windfall, blowdown; —**вестнико-вые** *pl.* (orn.) storm petrel family (*Procellariidae*); —**вой** *a. of* **буря;** —**инский,** —**йский** *a.* (geog.) Bureya; —**лом** *m.* windbreak, windfall.

бурен *sh. m. of* **бурный.**

бурение *n.* boring, drilling.

бурет *m.* (text.) bourette; floret.

бур/еть *v.* turn brown; —**еющий** *a.* turning brown, browning; fuscescent.

бурзеровые *pl.* (bot.) Burseraceae.

бурзит *see* **бурсит.**

бури *gen., pl., etc. of* **буря.**

бури/лка *f.* (fruit) fly; —**льность** *f.* drillability; —**льный** *a.* drilling, boring; jack (hammer); —**льщик** *m.* driller, drill operator; (zool.) borer; —**мость** *f.* drillability; —**имый** *a.* drillable.

буритизаль *n.* (phytogeog.) buritysal.

бур/ить *v.* drill, bore, pierce; —**ка** *f.* drill hole, blast hole.

буркеит *m.* (min.) burkeite.

бурки *pl.* warm, high boots.

буркун *m.* (bot.) medic (*Medicago flacata*); knotweed

(*Polygonum aviculare*); —**чик** *m.* black medic (*Medicago lupulina*).

бурлачить *v.* work as a barge tower.

бурл/ение *n.* swirling, etc., *see* **бурлить;** —**ивость** *f.* turbulence; —**ивый** *a.* turbulent, tempestuous.

бурлинский *a.* (geog.) Burla.

бурлить *v.* swirl, churn, boil, bubble, seethe; (glass) plain; (re)fine, found, block.

бурно *adv. and sh. n. of* **бурный.**

бурнонит *m.* (min.) bournonite.

бурн/ость *f.* violence; turbulence; intensity; —**ый** *a.* violent; stormy, turbulent; intense; vigorous, rapid, explosive (growth); (med.) peracute; projectile (vomiting); —**ый рост,** —**ое развитие** (population) explosion; —**ое течение** rip tide.

буро *adv. and sh. n. of* **бурый;** *prefix* fusco— (dark-colored); phaeo— (dark, dun-colored); brown; bore, boring, drill.

Бурова жидкость (pharm.) Burow's (aluminum acetate) solution.

буроват/ость *f.* (phyt.) leaf rust; —**ый** *a.* brownish; fuscescent, dusky-colored.

буро/вая *f.* borehole; —**взрывной** *a.* drilling and blasting; —**взрывная работа** blasthole drilling; —**вик** *m.* driller.

буровить *v.* bubble, ferment.

буров/ой *a.* drilling, boring; mud (pump); **б. журнал** driller's log; **б. раствор** mud; **б. станок** drill; rig; —**ая вышка** (oil) derrick; —**ая скважина** borehole; (oil) well.

буровский *see* **Бурова.**

буровый *a.* borax, boracic.

бурого ловый *a.* brown-headed.

бурод ержатель *m.* drill holder or chuck.

бурожелезняковый *a.* brown iron ore.

бурозём *m.* brown soil.

бурозубк/а *f.* (mam.) shrew (*Sorex*); **б.-пигмей** *f.* pigmy shrew (*Microsorex*); —**и,** —**овые** *pl.* Soricidae.

бурокислый *see* **борнокислый.**

буролом *m.* storm damage.

буро/стебельчатый *a.* brown-stalked; —**угольный** *a.* (min.) lignite; —**хвостый** *a.* brown-tailed.

бур-расширитель *m.* expansion bit.

бурс/а *f.* (anat.) bursa, sac; —**альные** *pl.* (prot.) Bursariidae; —**альный** *a.* (anat.) bursal; —**ария** *f.* (prot.) Bursaria; —**еровые** *pl.* (bot.) Burseraceae; —**ит** *m.* (med.) bursitis; —**итный** *a.* bursal.

бурт *m.* bead, rib, fillet, crimp, shoulder, collar; (agr.) storage pile, (silage) pit; —**ик** *see* **бурт;** (naut.) belting, fender (pile); —**ование** *n.* pit storing, piling; —**овой** *a. of* **бурт;** above-ground (silage); —**оуклад-чик** *m.* piler, stacker.

бурун *m.* surf, breaker.

бурунд/ук *m.* (mam.) Siberian chipmunk (*Eutamias sibiricus*); (naut.) afterguy; —**учный** *a. of* **бурундук;** banded (ore).

бур-уширитель *m.* enlarging bit.

бурчать *v.* grumble, mutter; rumble, growl.

бурщик *see* **бурильщик.**

бурый *a.* (grayish) brown, fuscous; **б. уголь** (min.) brown coal, lignite.

бурынский *a.* (geog.) Buryin.

бурьян *m.* (bot.) weeds; —**истый** *a.* weed-infested, weedy; —**ник** *m.* weed localities.

буря *f.* storm, gale; hurricane; tempest; **чёрная б.** dust storm.

бур-ямокопатель *m.* posthole auger.

бурятский *a.* (geog.) Buryat.

бус *m.* bead; (min.) smalls, slack, fines; **—ин(к)а** *f.* bead; **—овидный** *a.* moniliform.

бусский *a.* (geog.) Busk.

буссоль *f.* (surveying) compass; **б. наклонения** inclinometer; **б. склонения** declinometer; **б.-угломер** aiming circle.

бустамит *m.* (min.) bustamite.

бустер *m.* booster; **—ный** *a.* booster; power-assisted; servo-controlled.

бус/ы *pl.* beads; **—ьки** *pl.* (bot.) storksbill (*Erodium cicutarium*).

бут *m.* quarrystone, rubble (stone), debris; container.

бутадиен *m.,* **—овый** *a.* butadiene; **б.-нитрилакриловый, б.-нитрильный** *a.* butadiene acrylonitrile (rubber); **б.-стирольный каучук** styrene-butadiene rubber, Buna-S.

бутадион *m.* (pharm.) phenylbutazone.

бутан *m.* butane; **—дикарбоновый** *a.* butane-dicarboxylic (acid); **—дикислота, —диовая кислота** butanedioic acid, succinic acid; **—диол** *m.* butanediol, butylene glycol; **—дион** *m.* butanedione; **—кислота** *f.* butanoic acid; **—овый** *a.* butane; butanoic (acid); **—ойл** *m.* butanoyl, butyryl; **—ол** *m.* butanol, butyl alcohol; **—он** *m.* butanone, methylethyl ketone.

бутара *f.* (min.) trommel.

бут/вар *m.* (plastics) Butvar, polyvinyl butyral; **—езин** *m.* Butesin, butyl-*p*-aminobenzoate.

бутелуа *f.* (bot.) grama (*Bouteloua*).

бутен *m.* butene; **—ал** *m.* butenal, crotonaldehyde; **—ил** *m.* butenyl; **—овый** *a.* buten(o)ic (acid); **—ол** *m.* butenol.

бутень *m.* (bot.) chervil (*Chaerophyllum*).

бутерброд *m.,* **—ный** *a.* sandwich.

бутерлак *m.* (bot.) water purslane (*Peplis*).

бутил *m.* butyl; **хлористый б.** butyl chloride; **—амин** *m.* butylamine, aminobutane; **—ацетат** *m.* butyl acetate; **—ен** *m.* but(yl)ene; **—енгликоль** *m.* butylene glycol, butanediol; **—иден** *m.* butylidene; **—каучук** *m.* butyl rubber.

Бутилье Boutillier.

бутил/меркаптан *m.* butyl mercaptan; **—метиловый эфир** butyl methyl ether.

бутиловый *a.* butyl; **б. альдегид** *see* **бутиральдегид; б. эфир уксусной кислоты** butyl acetate.

бутил/окситолуол *m.* butoxytoluene; **—пропионат** *m.* butyl propionate; **—целлозольв** *m.* butyl Cellosolve (a solvent); **—этиловый** *a.* butyl ethyl; **—ьный** *a.* butyl.

бутин *m.* butine, butyne.

бутир—, **—о—** *prefix* butyr(o)— (butter); **—альдегид** *m.* butyraldehyde, butanal; **—амид** *m.* butyramide, butanamide; **—ат** *m.* butyrate; **—ил** *m.* butyryl; **—ин** *m.* (tri)butyrin; **—иновая кислота** butyric acid, butanoic acid; **—олактон** *m.* butyrolactone; **—ометр** *m.* butyrometer; **—он** *m.* butyrone, 4-heptanone; **—онитрил** *m.* butyronitrile.

бут/ить *v.* fill or line with rubble; **—обетон** *m.* rubble concrete; **—овый** *a. of* **бут; —овый камень** *see* **бут.**

бутокси— *prefix* butoxy—.

бутон *m.* (bot.) bud; **—изация** *f.* budding.

бутурлиновский *a.* (geog.) Buturlinovka.

бутчик *m.* (min.) packer.

бутыл/еобразный *see* **бутылковидный; —ка** *f.* bottle; **—ковидный** *a.* bottle-shaped, flask-shaped, ampullaceous, lageniform; phialine; **—комоечный** *a.* bottle-washing; **—конос** *m.* (mam.) bottlenosed whale

(*Hyperoodon*); **—кообразный** *see* **бутылковидный; —очно-зелёный** *a.* bottle-green; **—очный** *a.* bottle; bottle-top (ingot mold); **—очный камень** (min.) bottle stone; **—ь** *f.,* **—ьный** *a.* large bottle, carboy, vessel; (gas) cylinder.

бу-ут *m.* (mam.) Crateromys schadenbergi.

буфа/диенолид *m.* bufadienolide (steroid); **—нин** *m.* buphanine; **—нитин** *m.* buphanitine.

буфер *m.* buffer, bumper, shock absorber, cushion(ing); **б. вырезанного изображения, б. хранения** (comp.) clipboard; **воздушный б., масляный б.** dashpot; **б. компенсатор** *m.* compensating buffer; **—изация** *f.* spooling, buffering; **—ность** *f.* buffering, buffer action, buffering capacity; **—ный** *a. of* **буфер;** protective (zone); (comp.) annex or cache (memory); **—ный показатель** buffer index; **—ный раствор** buffer (solution); **—ная ёмкость** surge tank; **—ная реакция, —ное действие** buffering.

буферовка *f.* (met.) buffing, polishing.

буфет *m.* buffett, snack bar; cupboard; **б.-автомат** *m.* dumbwaiter.

буфо— *prefix* bufo— (toad); **—генин** *m.* bufogenin; **—нин** *m.* bufonin; **—талин** *m.* bufotalin; **—тенин** *m.* bufotenin; **—токсин** *m.* bufotoxin.

буффирование *n.* (leather) grain buffing.

бух *past m. sing. of* **бухнуть.**

бухарестский *a.* (geog.) Bucharest.

бухарник *m.* velvet grass (*Holcus*).

бухарский *a.* (geog.) Bukhara.

бухать *v.* crash down; bang, slam; ring out (of shot); blurt out; **—ся** *v.* fall heavily; plop down.

бухгалтер *m.* accountant, bookkeeper; **—ия** *f.* bookkeeping; accounts department; **—ский** *a.* accountant, accounting; **б.-эксперт** *m.* certified public accountant.

Бухерера реакция Bucherer reaction.

бухло/е, —э *n.* buffalo grass (*Buchloë*).

бухнуть *v.* swell (up); *see* **бухать.**

бухта *f.* bay, inlet, cove; coil (of rope, etc.); **ротовая б.** (embr.) buccal cavity.

бухтарминский *a.* (geog.) Bukhtarma.

бухт/ование *n.* coiling; **—ованный** *a.* coiled; **—овать** *v.* coil; **—овый** *a. of* **бухта; —одержатель** *m.* (wire-)reel holder; **—очка** *dim. of* **бухта.**

буцефал *m.* (zool.) Bucephalus.

буция *f.* (bot.) Butia.

буч *m.* bow net, lobster trap.

буча *f.* row, disturbance; selvage.

бучакский *a.* (geog.; geol.) Buchak.

бучачский *a.* (geog.) Buchach.

буч/ение *n.* (text.) bucking, etc., *see* **бучить;** (med.) purging; **—енный** *a.* bucked, etc.; **—еный** *a.* filled with rubble; **—ильник** *m.* kier, vat; **—ильный** *a.* bucking, etc., *see* **бучить.**

бучина *f.* beech forest.

бучить *v.* buck, steep (in lye), scour; (boil in a) kier; (paper) digest; fill with rubble.

бушбок *m.* (mam.) bushbuck, harnessed antelope (*Tragelaphus scriptus*).

бушевать *v.* storm, rage, roar; foam.

бушель *m.* bushel (measure).

бушинг *m.* (mach.) bushing; (glass) rotating cylinder (of feeder).

буш/ленд *m.* (phytogeog.) bushland; **—мейстер** *m.* (herp.) bushmaster (*Lachesis muta*); **—менский** *a.* Bushman.

бушприт *m.* (naut.) bowsprit.

бушующий *a.* storming, raging, turbulent.

буэа *f.* (bot.) Bouea.

буюндинский *a.* (geog.) Buyunda.

буя *gen. of* **буй.**

бц. *abbr.* (**бесцветный**) colorless.

б-ца *abbr.* (**больница**) hospital.

БЦЖ палочка (bact.) BCG bacillus, bacillus Calmette-Guerin.

б.ч. *abbr.* (**большая часть**) a large part; (**большей частью**) for the most part; (**бромное число**) bromine number.

бы *particle expressing subjunctive mood;* should, would; **где бы ни** wherever; **когда бы ни** whenever; **что бы ни** whatever.

быв. *abbr.* (**бывший**).

быв/ало *past of* **бывать:** used to, would; **как ни в чём не б.** as if nothing were the matter; **—алость** *f.* experience; **—алый** *a.* experienced, skilled; past; **—ать** *v.* be, exist, occur; happen; be held, take place; visit, frequent; come (in sizes); **как это часто —ает** as is often the case.

бывш/ий *a.* former, late, ex—; **—ая новая** (astr.) ex-nova.

быдгощский *a.* (geog.) Bydgoszcz.

бык *m.* bull (*Bos*); pier, buttress; **—и** *pl.* Bovidae; **—овский** *a.* (geog.) Byk (river); Bykovo; **б.-производитель** *m.* sire.

был *past m. sing. of* **быть; не б.** not found (on lists).

былин(к)а *f.* blade (of grass).

был/о *past n. sing. of* **быть;** *particle* nearly, on the point of; **—ое** *n.* the past; **—ой** *a.* past, bygone, former.

быльё *n.* (agr.) weeds.

быр(р)ангский *a.* (geog.) Byrranga.

быстр *sh. m. of* **быстрый; —ина** *f.* rapids, riffle; swift course, race; **—ицкий** *a.* (geog.) Bystritsa.

быстро *adv.* quick(ly), rapidly, swiftly, fast, in no time; suddenly, abruptly; readily; **—вращающийся** *a.* fast-rotating, fast-running; **—высыхающий** *a.* fast-drying; **—вяжущий** *a.* quick-setting (concrete); **—горящий** *a.* quick-burning; readily combustible; **—движущийся** *a.* high-speed, fast.

быстродейств/ие *n.* fast response; fast operation; quick action; speed; **низкого —ия** low-speed; **—ующий** *a.* fast-response; fast-operating, quick-acting, fast-acting; high-speed, fast.

быстро/замороженный *a.* quick frozen, flash frozen; **—изнашивающийся** *a.* rapidly wearing (out), not durable; **—летящий** *a.* fast(moving); **—насыщающийся** *a.* saturation (transformer); **—отверждающийся** *a.* fast-hardening; **—размыкающий** *a.* quick-break; **—распадающийся** *a.* rapidly disintegrating, short-lived; **—растущий** *a.* fast-growing; **—режущий** *a.* fast-cutting; high-speed (steel).

быстро/сгорающий *a.* free-burning; **—сканирующий** *a.* rapid-scanning, high-speed (spectrometer); **—сменный** *a.* quick-change; **—сохнущий** *a.* fast-drying; **—схватывающийся** *a.* quick-setting (concrete); **—сьёмный** *a.* easily detachable.

быстрота *f.* speed, velocity, rapidity, quickness; rate, frequency.

быстро/твердеющий *a.* fast-hardening, quick-setting, quick-curing; **—текущий** *a.* rapid, swift; (med.) galloping; **—течный** *a.* transient, brief; **—ток** *m.* chute (in spillway); **—ток-регулятор** *m.* adjustable chute.

быстро/убивающий *a.* fast-killing; **—устанавли-**

вающийся *a.* quick-adjusting, readily adjustable; **—ходность** *f.* (specific) speed (of pump); **—ходный** *a.* high-speed, fast; express (train); **—чередующийся** *a.* quick(-flashing), frequent.

быстр/ый *a.* quick, fast, rapid, sudden; prompt; high-rate; high-velocity (electron); speedy (progress); high-speed; **исключительно б.** explosive (growth); **б. ход** high speed; **—янка** *f.* (ichth.) bystranka (*Alburnoides bipunctatus*); **—янский** *a.* (geog.) Bystraya.

быт *m.* (way of) life, living conditions; *prefix, suffix or insert see* **бытовой; в —у** in homes.

бытантайский *a.* (geog.) Bytantai.

быт/ие *n.* being, existence; **—ность** *f.* stay, sojourn, presence; **в —ность** when; **—овать** *v.* exist, occur, happen; be current.

бытовн/ит *m.* (min.) bytownite; **—итит** *m.* bytownitite; **—ортит** *m.* bytownorthite.

бытов/ой *a.* everyday, usual, routine; natural, nonregulated (stream flow); domestic, household, home (appliance); general (service); **—ое обслуживание** consumer services; **—ые отходы** garbage.

быть *v.* be, exist; **б. чему б.** come what may; **—ё** *see* **бытие.**

быховский *a.* (geog.) Bykhov.

быч/ар *m.* cattleman; **—атина** *f.* beef; **—(ач)ий** *a.* bull, bovine, taurine; beef; **—ий глаз** (med.) buphthalmia; **—ье копытное масло** neat's-foot oil; **—ья жёлчь** oxgall; **—ина** *f.* oxhide; **—иный** *a. of* **бык; —ки** *pl. of* **бычок; —ки, —ковые** *pl.* (ichth.) gobies (*Gobiidae*); sculpins (*Cottidae*); **—ок** *m.* young bull, small bull; goby; sculpin; (bridge) pier; **—ок-песочник** *m.* (ichth.) Neogobius fluviatilis; Cottus gobio, **—ок-подкаменщик** *m.* sculpin (Cottus); **—ьи** *pl.* (mam.) Bovidae.

бьерк *m.* dynamic meter.

Бьеркнеса модель Bjerknes (cyclone) model.

бьёт *pr. 3 sing. of* **бить.**

бьеф *m.* water race, mill race; reach; pond, pool; **верхний б.** head or upper water, upper reach; **горизонт верхнего —а** upper-water or upstream water level; **нижний б.** tail or under water, tail race, downstream (wall); **горизонт нижнего —а** downstream water level.

бьющий a. beating, etc., *see* **бить;** untrue (wheel); **—ся** *a.* beating, pulsating.

Бэв *abbr.* (**биллион электрон-вольт**) billion electron volts, Bev.

бэватрон *m.* (nucl.) bevatron.

бэдленд *m.* badland.

БЭЗ *abbr.* (**боковое электрическое зондирование**) lateral electric sounding.

бэйевое масло *see* **байевое масло.**

Бэйли печь Baily furnace.

Бэлля способ *see* **Белля способ.**

бэр *abbr.* (**биологический эквивалент рентгена**) roentgen equivalent man, rem.

бэр/довский *a.* Byrd('s); Baird's (beaked whale); **—овский** *a.* (math.) Baire; Behre (tackmeter).

БЭСМ *abbr.* (**быстродействующая электронная счётная машина**) high-speed electronic computer.

БЭТ *abbr.* Brunauer, Emmett, and Teller equation, BET.

бэтсовский *a.* Bates'.

бювар *m.* blotting pad.

бювет *m.* pump room.

бюгель *m.* clasp.

бюджет *m.,* **—ный** *a.* budget; (vitamin) balance.

бюкс *m.,* **—а** *f.* weighing bottle.

бюллетен/ить *v.* be on sick leave; **—ь** *m.* bulletin; certificate; (weather) report; ballot paper.

бюльбюл/евые, —и *pl.* (orn.) bulbul family (*Pycnonotidae*).

бюрет/ка *f.,* **—очный** *a.* buret.

бюро *n.* bureau, office, department; desk; **б. проката** rental service.

бюрократ *m.* bureaucrat; **—изм** *m.* red tape; **—ический, —ный** *a.* bureaucratic; **—ия** *f.* bureaucracy.

бюст *m.* bust; **—гальтер** *m.* brassiere.

Бюхнера воронка Büchner funnel.

бяз/евый *a.,* **—ь** *f.* (text.) coarse calico.

В

в *prep. acc.* to indicate direction; *prepos.* to indicate location; in, into; on; at, per; with (a firm); as (a function of); **в . . . и из . . .** in and out of.

в *abbr.* (**вольт**) volt; **в.** *abbr.* (**век**) century; (**восточный**) eastern; (**выпуск**) issue; **В.** *abbr.* (**восток**) East.

в— *prefix* in, into.

ва *abbr.* (**вольт-ампер**) volt-ampere; **ВА** *abbr.* (**винилацетилен**) vinylacetylene; (**вольтамперметр**) volt-ammeter.

ваб/ик *m.,* **—ило** *n.* decoy, lure; bird call; **—ить** *v.* decoy, lure.

вабуляция *f.* wobble.

вавеллит *m.* (min.) wavellite.

вавиловский *a.* (geog.) Vavilov (Glacier).

вага *f.* crowbar, lever; weighing machine, balance; hoisting machine; (harness) swingletree.

вагайский *a.* (geog.) Vagai.

вагальный *a.* (anat.) vagal.

вагильный *a.* migratory, free-ranging.

вагин/а *f.* (anat.) vagina, sheath; **—альный** *a.* vaginal; **—ит** *m.* (med.) vaginitis; **—о—** *prefix* vagino— [vagina(l)].

вагнер/ит *m.* (min.) wagnerite; **—овский реактив** Wagner's reagent.

ваго— *prefix* (anat.) vago—, vagus.

вагон *m.* (rr) car, coach; carload; truck, wagon; (livestock) van; **в.-вертушка** *m.* turn-around car; **в.-весы** *m.* scale car; **в.-деррик** *m.* derrick car, wrecking car.

вагонетка *f.* trolley, truck, car(t), wagon; skip; **в.-самосвал** *m.* dump car; **в.-транспортер** transfer car.

вагон-/кран *m.* traveling crane, crane car; **в.-лаборатория** *m.* test(ing) car; **в.-ледник** *m.* refrigerator car; **в.-мастерская** *m.* repair car.

вагонн/ый *a.* of **вагон; в. парк** rolling stock; **—ые весы** weigh bridge.

вагоно/вожатый *m.* motorman, engineer; **—оборот** *m.* car traffic or turnover; **—опрокидыватель** *m.* car dump(er); **—погрузчик** *m.* car loader; **—подъёмник** *m.* car lift; **—поток** *m.* car traffic; **—ремонтная мастерская** car repair shop; **—строение** *n.,* **—строительный** *a.* car building.

вагон-/платформа *m.* flat car; **в.-ресторан** *m.* dining car; **в.-самосвал** *m.* dump car; **в.-холодильник** *m.* refrigerator car; **в.-цистерна** *m.* tank car; **в.-электростанция** *m.* power-generating car.

ваго— *prefix* (anat.) vago— (vagus; vagal and); **—томия** *f.* (med.) vagotomy; **—тропный** *a.* vagotropic.

вагран/ка *f.,* **—очный** *a.* (met.) cupola.

вагусный *a.* (anat.) vagal.

вад *m.* (min.) wad, bog manganese.

вади *n.* wadi, dry wash, dry stream bed.

вадоз/ный, —овый *a.* (geol.) vadose.

вадский *a.* (geog.) Vad.

ваенгинский *a.* (geog.) Vaenga.

ваер *m.* wire, cable, warp.

важен *sh. m. of* **важный.**

важенка *f.* elk cow, doe.

важивать *see* **водить; возить.**

важн/ейший *a.* major, paramount; most important; **—о** *adv.* significantly; it is important or essential; **—ость** *f.* importance, significance, concern; **—ый** *a.* important, significant; vital (role); fundamental, essential; valuable, far-reaching; **исключительно —ый** *a.* critical; **особо —ый** *a.* high-priority.

важский *a.* (geog.) Vaga.

ВАЗ *abbr.* (**внутриаптечная заготовка**) drugstore-filled prescription.

ваза *f.* vase, bowl.

ваз/елин *m.,* **—елиновый** *a.* Vaseline, petrolatum; **—ицин** *m.* vasicine.

вазо— *prefix* vaso— (vessel, duct); **—дилятатор** *m.* (physiol.) vasodilator; **—констриктор** *m.* vasoconstrictor; **—мотор** *m.,* **—моторный** *a.* vasomotor.

вазон *m.* (flower) pot.

вазо/прессин *m.* vasopressin (hormone); **—прессорный** *a.* (physiol.) vasopressor; **—ренальный** *a.* renovascular.

вазэктомия *f.* (med.) vasectomy.

вайд/а *f.,* **—овый** *a.* (bot.) woad (*Isatis*).

вайербарс *m.* wire bars.

вайма *f.* (carpentry) clamp.

вайсенберговский *a.* (cryst.) Weissenberg.

вайя *f.* (bot.) frond.

вакан/сия *f.* vacancy, hole; **—тный** *a.* vacant, empty, unoccupied; vacancy; **—тный узел** (phys.) vacancy, hole.

вакат *m.* (typ.) blank page or strip.

вакка *f.* (petr.) wacke (a residual deposit); **серая в.** graywacke.

ваккенродеровский *a.* (chem.) Wackenroder's.

вакковый *a.* (petr.) wacke.

вакс/а *f.* shoe polish; **—ить** *v.* polish.

вакуол/изация *f.* (biol.) vacuol(iz)ation; **—изированный** *a.* vacuolated; **—ь, —я** *f.* vacuole; **—ьный, —ярный** *a.* vacuolar.

вакуом *m.,* **—а** *f.* (biol.) vacuome.

вакуум *m.* vacuum; void; **перегонка под —ом** vacuum distillation; **сушка в —е** vacuum drying; **в.-аппарат** *m.* vacuum pan; **в.-бак, в.-бачок** *m.* vacuum tank; **в.-бетон** *m.* de-aerated concrete, vacuum(-processed) concrete; **в.-выпарка** *f.* vacuum evaporation.

вакуум/изация *f.,* **—(из)ирование** *n.* evacuation, exhaustion, withdrawal; vacuum processing; vacuum evaporation; (met.) degassing; **—(из)ированный** *a.* evacuated, etc., *see v;* vacuum-processed; **—(из)ировать** *v.* evacuate, withdraw, exhaust, pump out; treat under vacuum.

вакуум/-испаритель *m.* vacuum evaporator; **в.-клапан** *m.* vacuum valve; **в.-котёл** *m.* vacuum pan; **в.-манометр, —метр** *m.* vacuum gage; **б.-мешалка** *f.*

vacuum mixer; **в.-насос** *m.* vacuum pump, suction pump; **—но-космический** *a.* space (chamber); **—ный** *a. of* **вакуум; в.-отсос** *m.* vacuum suction; **в.-охладитель** *m.* vacuum cooler; **в.-перегонка** *f.* vacuum distillation; **в.-питатель** *m.* (glass) suction feeder; **—плотный** *a.* vacuum-tight, airtight; **в.-провод** *m.* vacuum line; **в.-разгонка** *f.* vacuum distillation; **в.-смеситель** *m.* vacuum blender; **в.-сушилка** *f.* vacuum dryer; **—тормоз** *m.* vacuum brake; **в.-укупорка** *f.* vacuum sealing; **в.-фильтр** *m.* vacuum filter, suction filter; **—формование** *n.,* **—формовка** *f.* (plastics) vacuum forming, vacuum molding; **в.-холодильник** *m.* vacuum cooler; **в.-щит** *m.* vacuum molding machine; **в.-эксикатор** *m.* vacuum exsiccator or desiccator.

вакценовая кислота vaccenic acid.

вакцин/а *f.* (med.) vaccine; **—ация** *f.,* **—ационный** *a.* vaccination; **—ейрин** *m.* vaccineurine; **—ированный** *a.* vaccinated; **—ировать** *v.* vaccinate; **—ный** *a.* vaccine, vaccinal.

вал *m.* (mach.) shaft, arbor, spindle, axle; roll(er); bank, embankment, rampart; levee; (crater) wall; (geol.) swell, arch; (anat.) torus, protuberance; ridge (of nose); **на —у** shaft-mounted; **мощность на —у** shaft power or output; **окружать —ом** *v.* bank.

валаамка *f.* (ichth.) valaamka (*Coregonus lavaretus widegreni*).

валаит *m.* (min.) valaite.

валах *m.* wether, castrated ram.

валгаский *a.* (geog.) Valga.

валдайский *a.* (geog.) Valdai.

валежка *f.* (av.) wing heaviness.

валежн/ик *m.,* **—ый** *a.* windfall, brushwood, deadwood, slash, debris.

валёк *m.* roll(er); bar; battledore, paddle; (harness) singletree; (naut.) loom; round whitefish (*Prosopium cylindraceum*).

валенный *a.* thrown down; felled (trees).

валентинит *m.* (min.) valentinite.

валентн/ость *f.* valence, valency; **—ый** *a.* valence; stretching (vibration); *suffix* **—valent; —ые схемы** valence bond.

валенцианит *m.* (min.) valencianite.

валеный *past. pass. part. of* **валить.**

валер/альдегид *m.* valeraldehyde, pentanal; **—амид** *m.* valeramide, pentanamide; **—ен** *m.* valerene, amylene.

валериан *m.,* **—а** *f.* (bot.) valerian; **—ат** *m.* valer(ian)ate; **—елла, —(н)ица** *f.* (bot.) Valerianella.

валерианово/калиевая соль, —кислый калий potassium valerate; **—кислый** *a.* valeric acid; valerate (of); **—кислая соль** valerate; **—этиловый эфир** ethyl valerate.

валерианов/ый *a.* (bot.) valerian; (chem.) valeric; **в. альдегид** valeraldehyde; **в. ангидрид** valeric anhydride, pentanoic anhydride; **—ая кислота** valer(ian)ic acid, pentanoic acid; **соль** or **эфир —ой кислоты** valerate.

валер/ил *m.* valeryl, pentanoyl; **—илен** *m.* valerylene, 2-pentyne; **—ол** *m.* valerol; **—олактон** *m.* valerolactone; **—он** *m.* valerone, diisobutyl ketone; **—онитрил** *m.* valeronitrile, butyl cyanide; **—ьян** *see* **валериан.**

валец *m.* roller, cylinder; drum (of roller).

валивать *see* **валить.**

валидн/ость *f.* validity; **—ый** *a.* valid.

валидол *m.* validol, menthol valerate.

валик *m.* roller, cylinder, drum; spindle, shaft; bead, fillet, ridge; (anat.) tor(ul)us; vallum, mound; **—овидный, —ообразный** *a.* (circum)vallate.

вал/ил *m.* valyl, diethyl valeramide; **—ин** *m.* valine; **—инол** *m.* valinol.

валить *v.* throw or bring down, overturn, upset; fell (trees); heap up, pile up; pour out, belch forth (of smoke); fall thickly (of snow); flock, throng; put the blame (on); **в. в кучу** heap (up); **—ся** *v.* fall (over), lean (over); tumble down, collapse; flock, throng.

валичная кожа roller leather.

валка *f.* felling (of trees); (text.) fulling; blend(ing) (of flour); *gen. of* **валок;** *sh. f. of* **валкий.**

валкий *a.* shaky, unsteady; (naut.) crank.

валков/ание *n.* (hay) swathing, windrowing; ridging (with earth); **—ать** *v.* swath, windrow; ridge.

валковский *a.* (geog.) Valki.

валко/вый *a. of* **валок;** roll (mill); **—оборачиватель** *m.* (agr.) swath turner; **—способный** *a.* (text.) suitable for milling, fulling or felting; **—сть** *f.* shakiness; (naut.) crank(i)ness, unsteadiness; (text.) tendency to felt; **—укладчик** *m.* (agr.) swather.

валкский *a.* (geog.) Valka.

валла/би *m.* (mam.) wallaby (*Wallabia*); **—ру** *m.* wallaroo (*Osphranter*); **—ховский** *a.* (chem.) Wallach (rearrangement).

валлезия *f.* (bot.) Vallesia.

валлериит *m.* (min.) valleriite.

Валлеса линия (biogeog.) Wallace's line.

валлийский *a.* Welsh; **Валлис** Wales.

валлиснерия *f.* tape grass (*Vallisneria*).

валлония *f.* (mal.) Vallonia (a snail).

валлонский *a.* (met.) Wallon (process).

валмиерский *a.* (geog.) Valmiera.

валов/ой *a.* gross, total; wholesale; empirical (formula); bulk (analysis, etc.); **в. доход** gross returns.

валогенератор *m.* shaft generator.

валок *m.* roll(er); cylinder; (agr.) swath, windrow; *sh. m. of* **валкий.**

валонея *f.* (tanning) valonia.

валопровод *m.* shaft line, shafting.

валуевит *m.* (min.) valuewite, valuevite.

валу/ек, —й *m.* (bot.) a mushroom (*Agaricus emeticus*); (*Russula foetens*).

валуйский *a.* (geog.) Valuiki.

валун *m.* boulder; rubble; **—ы** *pl.* (geol.) detritus, rock waste; float; **—ник** *m.* cobble(stone), roundstone, boulder conglomerate; **—ный** *a. of* **валун;** rubbly; erratic; **—ная глина** (geol.) boulder clay, glacier till; **—чатый** *a.* nodular (ore).

валу/х *m.* castrated ram, wether; **—шение** *n.* wethering, castration.

валховит *m.* (min.) walchowite.

вальв/арный *a.* (biol.) valv(ul)ar, valval; **—ата** *f.* (mal.) Valvata (a snail).

вальденовский *a.* Walden (inversion).

вальдовский *a.* Wald.

вальдшнеп *m.* (orn.) woodcock (*Scolopax*).

валька *gen. of* **валёк.**

вальковат/о– *prefix* tereti—, terete; **—олистный** *a.* teretifolious, round-leaved; **—ость, удельная** relative bulk; **—ый** *a.* terete, cylindrical.

вальм/а *f.* (building) hip; **—овая крыша** hipped roof.

вальнуть *see* **валить.**

вальпургит *m.* (min.) walpurgite.

вальтерит *m.* (min.) waltherite.

вальц *m.* roll(er), cylinder; **—евание** *n.* rolling, etc., *see* **в.; —евать** *v.* roll, mill; (rub.) masticate; roll-squeeze; (met.) forge-roll; (tubes) expand, flare; **—евый** *see* **вальцовый; —езагибочный станок** bending roller; **—еобразный** *a.* cylindrical; **—етокарный** *a.* roll-turning; —**масса** *f.* (typ.) roller composition; —**ованный** *a.* rolled, etc., *see* v.; —**овать** *see* **вальцевать;** —**овка** *f.* rolling, etc., *see* v.; roller, rolling mill; stretching rolls, expander; —**овщик** *m.* rolling mill operator, roller; —**овый** *a.* of **вальцевание;** roller; —**овая дробилка** crushing mill; —**уемость** *f.* millability; —**ы** *pl.* roll(er)s; (roll) mill.

вальчак *m.* (ichth.) kelt (spent salmon).

вальян *m.* (text.) doffer, stripper.

валют/а *f.,* —**ный** *a.* currency; —**ный курс** rate of exchange.

валюшка *f.* (cer.) wad, clot, mass.

вал/яльный *a.* (text.) fulling, etc., *see* v.; fuller's (soap); —**яльная глин(к)а** fuller's earth; —**яльня** *f.* fulling mill; —**яльщик** *m.* fuller; —**яние** *n.* fulling, etc., *see* v.; —**ян(н)ый** *a.* fulled, etc., *see* v.; —**ять** *v.* full, mill, felt; roll; knead; —**яться** *v.* lie about, be scattered about.

вам *dat.* of **вы,** to you, for you; —**и** *instr.* by you, with you.

вампир *m.* (mam.) vampire bat (*Vampyrus*); **адский в.** (mal.) Vampyroteuthis infernalis.

ВАН *abbr.* (**Вестник Академии Наук**) Bulletin of the Academy of Sciences.

ванад *see* **ванадий;** —**ат** *m.* vanadate; —**атометрия** *f.* vanadatometry.

ванадиево/кислый *a.* vanadic acid; vanadate (of); **в. натрий, —натриевая соль** sodium vanadate; —**кислая соль** vanadate; **кислая —кислая соль** divanadate.

ванадиев/ый *a.* vanadium; vanadic (acid, salt); **в. ангидрид** vanadic anhydride, vanadium pentoxide; **соль —ой кислоты** vanadate.

ванад/ий *m.* vanadium, V; **одноокись —ия** vanadium monoxide, vanadous oxide; **пятиокись —ия** vanadium pentoxide, vanadic anhydride; **трёхокись —ия** vanadium trioxide, vanadic oxide; **хлористый в.** vanadous chloride, vanadium dichloride; **хлорный в.** vanadic chloride, vanadium trichloride.

ванад/ил *m.* vanadyl; **сернокислый в.** vanadyl sulfate, vanadium sulfate; —**инит** *m.* (min.) vanadinite.

ванад/истый *a.* vanadium; vanadous (acid, salt); **соль —истой кислоты, —ит** *m.* vanadite.

ванг/ерия *f.* (bot.) Vangueria; —**и, —овые** *pl.* (orn.) vanga-shrike family (*Vangidae*).

вангресс *m.* front hearth of shaft furnace.

ванда *f.* (fishing) net.

Ван-де-Граафа генератор Van de Graaf generator (electrostatic accelerator).

Ван-Дейка коричневый van Dyck brown.

ванделл/иевые *pl.* parasitic catfishes (*Trichomycteridae, Pygidiidae*); —**ия** *f.* candiru (*Vandellia cirrhosa*).

ван/денбрандеит *m.* (min.) vandenbrandeite, urano-lepidite; **-дер-ваальсовский** *a.* van der Walls (forces).

вандеру *m.* (mam.) Macaca silenus.

вандрут *m.* (min.) supporting beam.

ванду *m.* wandoo (eucalyptus) forest.

ванер *see* **ваннер.**

ванил/аль *see* **ваниллаль;** —**ин** *m.* vanillin; —**иновый** *a.* vanillin; vanillic (acid, alcohol); —**лаль** *m.* vanillal, ethyl vanillin; —**лил** *m.* vanillyl; —**лин** *see* **ванилин;** —**ь** *f.* vanilla (bean); —**ьный** *a.* vanilla.

Ванкеля двигатель Wankel engine.

ванкомицин *m.* Vancomycin (antibiotic).

ванкуверский *a.* (geog.) Vancouver.

ванн/а *f.* bath; (dyeing) dip, steep; tub, tank, vat, basin; cell; pan, trough; (welding) pool; (molecular configuration) boat; (met.) smelt; hearth (of puddling furnace);

(mercury) cup; **в виде —ы** bath (thermostat, etc.); **форма —ы** boat conformation (of stereoisomers); **в.-пресс** *f.* (text.) steeping press; —**ая** *f.* bathroom.

ваннер *m.* (min.) vanner, concentrator; —**ная отсадочная машина** vanning jig.

Ваннера пирометр Wanner's pyrometer.

ванн/очка *dim.* of **ванна;** (phot.) tray; puddle (of molten metal); —**ый** *a.* of **ванна;** —**ая печь** (salt) bath furnace; (glass) tank furnace.

ваноксит *m.* (min.) vanoxite.

Ван-Слайка метод Van Slyke method.

ванта *f.* guy (rope), stay; (naut.) shroud.

Вант-Гоффа закон (phys.) van't Hoff's law.

вантгоффит *m.* (min.) vanthoffite.

вант/ина *see* **ванта;** —**овый** *a.*of **ванта.**

вантуз *m.* air escape valve; air hole, vent.

ванчесы *pl.* (building) wainscot.

ванчский *a.* (geog.) Vanch.

вапа *f.* (text.) resist; (wall) paint.

вапити *m.* (mam.) wapiti (*Cervus canadensis; C. elaphus sibiricus*).

вапор *m.* steam-cylinder oil; —**изатор** *m.* vaporizer; —**изация** *f.* vaporization; —**иметр** *m.* vaporimeter.

вапплерит *m.* (min.) wapplerite.

вар *m.* pitch, pine tar; (grafting) wax; (elec.) var (volt-ampere-reactive); var (visual-aural range).

варакушка *f.* (orn.) bluethroat (*Cyanosylvia*).

варан *m.* (herp.) monitor (*Varanus*).

варбурговский *a.* Warburg's.

варвар *m.* barbarian; —**ийский** *a.* (geog.) Barbary; —**ский** *a.* barbarian; foreign, strange.

варвикит *m.* (min.) warwickite.

варвицит *m.* (min.) varvicite.

вардит *m.* (min.) wardite.

вардовать *v.* (met.) assay.

варево *n.* soup, concoction.

варек *m.* varec, kelp.

вар/ение *n.* cooking, etc., *see* **варить;** *suffix* making, manufacture; —**еник** *m.* dumpling; —**ён(н)ый** *a.* cooked, etc., *see* **варить;** —**енье** *n.* preserves, jam.

варзеа *f.* (biogeog.) varzea.

вари *m.* (mam.) Lemur varius.

вариаб/ельность, —ильность *f.* variability; —**ельный** *a.* variable.

вариак *m.* (telecomm.) Variac, autotransformer.

вариан/са *f.* (stat.) variance; —**т** *m.* variant; variation; modification, alternate, alternative (method); version; option; model; —**та** *f.* variant; (math.) sequence; —**тность** *f.* variance; —**тный** *a.* variant, varying, alternate, alternative.

вари/атор *m.* (electron.) buncher; (mach.) variable-speed drive, (speed) regulator; (elec.) variable-ratio transformer; —**ационность** *f.* variational character; —**ационный** *a.* variation(al); —**ация** *f.* variation; (gen.) mutation; (hereditary) changes; —**етет** *m.* variety; —**ировать** *see* **варьировать;** —**ируемый** *a.* variable; —**кап** *m.* (electron.) varicap, variable capacity.

варико— *prefix* (med.) varico— (varix; twisted, swollen); —**зный** *a.* varicose; —**зный узел** varix; *pl.* varices.

варбиконд *m.* (elec.) varicond, variable condenser.

варикоцеле *n.* (med.) varicocele.

вари/мю, лампа (electron.) varimu, variable mu (tube); —**ола** *f.* (med.) variola, smallpox; —**олизация** *f.* variol(iz)ation; —**олит** *m.* (petr.) variolite; —**олитовый, —олический** *a.* variolitic, spotted; —**оловидный** *a.* varioliform; —**оль** *f.* variole; —**оляция** *f.* variolation; **—ометр** *m.* (electron.) variometer, variable inductor; (av.) rate-of-climb indicator; (torsion) balance; **—стор** *m.* (electron.) varistor, variable resistor.

варис(ций)ский *a.* (geol.) Variscian.

варисцит *m.* (min.) variscite.

варитрон *m.* (cosmic rays) varitron.

вар/ить *v.* cook, boil, digest; brew (beer); (text.) scour; (glass) found; make (steel): (rub.) cure, vulcanize; weld; (physiol.) digest; **—иться** *v.* digest, cook, be boiled; **—ка** *f.* cooking, etc., *see v.*

варковый *a. of* **варок.**

варметр *m.* (elec.) varmeter.

варненский *a.* (geog.) Varna.

вар/ница *f.,* **—ничный** *a.* salt pan; saltworks; brewery; **—ный** *see* **варочный; —ня** *f.* brewery; **—ок** *gen. pl. of* **варка;** *m.* enclosure, pen, corral.

варолиев мост (anat.) pons varolii.

варочный *a.* cooking, digesting; brewing; curing; **в. котёл** digester.

варрант *m.,* **—ный** *a.* (com.) warrant.

варташенский *a.* (geog.) Vartashen.

вартит *m.* (min.) warthite, bloedite.

вартонов проток (anat.) duct of Wharton.

варшавский *a.* (geog.) Warsaw.

варь/етет *m.* variety; **—ирование** *n.* variation; (electron.) bunching, etc., *see v.;* **—ированный** *a.* varied, etc., *see v.;* **—ировать** *v.* vary, diversify, modify, change; tailor (to); bunch; **—ироваться** *v.* vary, range; **—ирующий** *a.* varying, variable.

варящий *a.* cooking, etc., *see* **варить.**

вас *acc. of* **вы,** you.

василёк *m.* (bot.) Centaurea.

василиск *m.* (herp.) basilisk.

васил/ист(н)ик *m.* (bot.) meadow rue (*Thalictrum*); **—ьевский** *a.* (geog.) Vasilyevka; **—ьки** *pl.* (bot.) larkspur (*Delphinium consolida*); **—ьковский** *a.* (geog.) Vasilkov; **—ьковый** *a.* cornflower (blue).

васкул/ит *m.* (med.) vasculitis; **—яризация** *f.* vascularization; **—ярный** *a.* vascular.

вассерглас *m.* water glass, specif. sodium silicate solution; **калиевый в.** potassium silicate.

Вассермана реакция (med.) Wasserman test.

васхегиит *m.* (min.) vashegyite.

васюганский *a.* (geog.) Vasyugan.

ват/а *f.* cotton (batting); (glass) wool; **на —е** padded, quilted.

ватер *m.* (text.) ringspinning frame.

ватер/вейс, —вельс *m.* (naut.) waterway; **—жакет** *m.* water jacket; water-jacketed furnace; **—жакетный** *a.* water-jacket(ed); jacket (cooling, etc.); **—клозет** *m.,* **—клозетный** *a.* toilet, lavatory; **—линия** *f.* water line, water mark; **—машина** *see* **ватер.**

ватерпас *m.* level (the instrument); **—ный** *a.* level, horizontal.

ватерпруф *m.* raincoat.

ватин *m.* fleecy jersey fabric.

ватман *m.* Whatman drawing paper.

ват/ник *m.* quilted jacket; **—ный** *a.* quilted; cotton; **симптом —ных ног** wadded leg symptom; **—ообразный** *a.* gossypine, cottony, cotton-like; velvety, velvet-like; **—очник** *m.* (bot.) milkweed (*Asclepias*); **—очный** *a.* cotton(y).

ватт *m.* (elec.) watt; tidal marsh; **число в.** wattage; **—метр** *m.,* **—метровый** *a.* (elec.) wattmeter; **—ность** *f.* wattage; **—ный** *a. of* **ватт; в.-секунда** watt-second; **в.-час** watt-hour; **отдача в в.-часах** watt-hour efficiency.

вау-вау *m.* (mam.) Hylobates moloch.

ваф/ельница *f.* wafer iron or tongs; **—ельный** *a.,* **—ля** *f.* wafer, waffle.

ваханский *a.* (geog.) Vakhan.

вахня *f.* (ichth.) wachna cod, Pacific navaga (*Eleginus gracilis*).

вахт/а *f.* watch, duty; work shift; **в., в.-трава** (bot.) buckbean (*Menyanthes,* spec. *M. trifoliata*); **—енный** *a. of* **вахта;** lookout; log (book); **—енный командир** officer of the watch; officer of the deck; **—ёр** *m.* watchman; janitor.

ваху *m.* (ichth.) wahoo (*Acanthocybium soland(e)ri*).

вахшский *a.* (geog.) Vakhsh.

вачский *a.* (geog.) Vacha.

ваш *m.,* **—а** *f. pron.* your.

вашгерд *m.* (min.) buddle.

вашеты *pl.* (leather) split hides.

ваши *pl. pron.* your.

вашингтон/ия *f.* Washington palm (*Washingtonia*); **—ский** *a.* Washington.

вашкинский *a.* (geog.) Vashka.

ваял/о *n.* chisel, graver; **—ьный** *a.* chisel, sculpture; modelling (clay).

вая/ние *n.,* **—тельное искусство** sculpture; **—тель** *m.* sculptor; **—ть** *v.* sculpture, model; chisel, carve; cast.

вб *abbr.* (**вебер**) weber.

ВБ *abbr.* (**верхний бьеф**) head water.

вбегать, вбежать *v.* run in(to), rush into; flow into.

вберёт *fut. 3 sing. of* **вобрать.**

вбив/ание *n.,* **—ка** *f.* driving in, etc., *see v.;* **—ать** *v.* drive, hammer (in); pack in, ram, wedge.

вбир/ание *n.* absorption; **—ать** *v.* absorb, soak up, take up; **—аться** *v.* soak (into), infiltrate.

вбит/ый *a.* driven in, etc., *see* **вбивать; —ь** *see* **вбивать.**

вблизи *adv. and prep. gen.* near (by), close (by), in the neighborhood (of), in the vicinity (of), in proximity (to); at hand, not far from.

вб/м² *abbr.* (**вебер на квадратный метр**) weber per square meter.

в.б.о. *abbr.* (**вероятное боковое отклонение**) probable deflection error.

вбок *adv.* to the side, sideways; laterally.

вбрасывать *v.* throw in.

вбро/сить *v.* throw in, include; **—шенный** *a.* thrown in, included.

вбрыз/гивание *n.* injection; **—гивать** *v.* inject; spray in, squirt in; **—нутый** *a.* injected, etc., *see v.;* **—нуть** *see* **вбрызгивать.**

вв, ВВ, В.В., в.в. *abbr.* (**взрывчатое вещество**) explosive; **вв.** *abbr.* (**века**) ages; **В.В., в.-в.** *abbr.* (**высоковольтный**) high-voltage.

ввали(ва)ть *v.* throw in, dump; heap into; **—ся** *v.* tumble in; sink in, fall in.

ввальцовывать *v.* roll in.

ввар/и(ва)ть *v.* weld in; cast in; **—ка** *f.* welding in.

введ/ём *fut. 1 pl. of* **ввести;** let us introduce; **—ение** *n.* introduction, etc., *see* **вводить;** advent; inlet, intake; preface, prelude; **с —ением** with the advent (of); **—ение в вену** intravenous injection; **—ение через рот** oral administration; **—ённый** *a.* introduced, etc., *see* **вводить; -ённая информация** input; **—я** *pr. ger.* introducing.

ввез/ённый *a.* imported, brought in; **—ти** *see* **ввозить.**

ввёл *past. m. sing. of* **ввести.**

вверг/ать, —нуть *v.* plunge (into).

ввер/енный *a.* entrusted (to); **—ить** *v.* (en)trust (with); confide (to); **—иться** *v.* confide; trust (in).

ввер/нуть, —теть v. screw in, twist in, turn in.

ввёр/тка f., **—тывание** n. screwing in, etc., *see v.;* **—тный** a. screw(-in); **—тывать** *see* **ввернуть; —тыш** m. screw cap or stopper.

вверх adv. up, upward(s); over, above; **в. дном, в. ногами** upside down, inverted; **в. по течению** upstream; **перемещение в., ход в.** ascent; upstroke (of piston); **тяга в.** upward pull, lift; updraft; **—у** adv. above, overhead, at the top (of).

вверч/енный a. screwed in, etc., *see* **ввертеть; —ивать** *see* **ввертеть.**

вверять *see* **вверить.**

ввести(сь) *see* **вводить(ся).**

ввивать v. weave in, interweave, interlace.

ввиду prep. gen. in view of, on account of, because of, owing to, due to, through, for reasons of; as, whereas; **в. того, что** as, in view of the fact that.

ввин/тить, —чивать v. screw in; **—ченный** a. screwed in; **—чивание** n. screwing in; **—чиваться** v. thread (into).

ввит/(ый) a. interwoven; **—ь** *see* **ввивать.**

в-во abbr. (**вещество**) substance.

ввод m. introduction, etc., *see v.* inlet, intake; entry, entrance; (comp.) input; insertion; (elec.) lead-in; bushing; (house) sewer; **в.-вывод** m. (comp.) input-output; **—ить** v. introduce, admit, lead in, bring in, feed (into); inject, administer (medicine); commission; incorporate (in); slip in, insert; place, put into (operation); throw into (gear); set (data); coin (a new term); input; **—ить в действие** bring into use or service, put into operation; blow in (blast furnace); **—иться** v. be introduced; come into use.

вводн/ый a. introductory; incoming, inlet, leading in; (comp.) input; parenthetic; **в. провод** lead-in; **в. элемент** input component; **—ое отверстие** inlet; **—ое предложение** parenthesis; parenthetic clause.

вводя pr. ger. introducing; if we introduce; **—щий** pr. act. part. of **вводить;** feed (line).

ввоз m., **—ка** f. import(ation); **—ить** v. import, bring in; **—ный** a. imported; import (duty); **—ные товары** imports.

ввол/акивать, —очь v. drag in.

вволю adv. in any amount, to any degree; free choice; at will.

ввосьмеро adv. eight times; **в. больше** eight times as much; **в. меньше** one eighth; **—м** adv. eight (together).

ВВР abbr. (**водо-водяной реактор**) water-moderated water-cooled reactor.

ввс, ВВС abbr. (**высоковольтная сеть**) high-voltage network; **ВВС** abbr. (**военно-воздушные силы**) air force.

ВВФ abbr. (**высоковольтный фидер**) high-voltage feeder.

ввысь adv. up, upwards.

ВВЭР abbr. (**водо-водяной энергетический реактор**) water-moderated, water-cooled power reactor.

ввяз/анный a. involved, etc., *see v.;* **—ывание** n. involvement; implication; **—(ыв)ать** v. involve, implicate; tie in, knit in; **—(ыв)аться** v. get involved (in); meddle, interfere.

вгиб m. inward bend; incurve; **—ание** n. bending inward; **—ать** v. bend in, curve inward, incurve; **—аться** v. curve inwards.

вгладь adv. flush, even; **сварить в.** v. flush weld; **сварка в.** flush welding.

вглубь adv. deep (in); **в. страны** inland.

вгляд/еться, —ываться v. observe closely, examine, peer (at); take a good look.

вгнездиться v. take root in.

вгон m., **—ка** f. driving in, etc., *see v.;* **—ять** v. drive (in), knock in, force in.

вгорячую adv. hot; **ковать в.** v. (met.) forge hot; **тянутый в.** (met.) hot-drawn.

вгребать, вгрести v. rake in.

вгружать, вгрузить v. load, freight.

вгрыз(а)ться v. bite into, catch, seize; lock its teeth into; eat, bore or gnaw into.

вгустую adv. thick, solid, hard.

ВГЭС abbr. (**ветренная гидроэлектростанция**) wind and hydroelectric power plant.

в.д. abbr. (**высокое давление**) high pressure; **в.д., В.Д.** abbr. (**восточная долгота**) east longitude.

вдаваться v. devote oneself (to), go into, dwell upon; go to (extremes); jut out, protrude; press in, wedge in.

вдав/ить *see* **вдавливать; —ление, —ливание** n. pressing in, etc., *see v.;* impression, depression; **—ленный** a. pressed in, etc., *see v.;* sunken; **—ливать** v. press in, bend in, depress, cave in; force (in); pit; embed, sink in; impress, imprint, stamp; indent.

вдавшись past ger. of **вдаться.**

вдаётся pr. 3 sing. of **вдаваться.**

вдалбливать v. ram in; (educ.) drill in.

вдал/еке, —и adv. in the distance, far (off), beyond; **—ь** adv. into the distance.

вда/ться *see* **вдаваться; —ющийся** pr. act. part. of **вдаваться;** incurrent.

вдви/гание n. moving in, etc., *see v.;* **—гать** v. move in, push in, shove in, slide in, put in; be in; **—гаться** v. move in, go in, enter; **—жной** a. movable, sliding; **—нутый** a. moved in, etc., *see v.;* **—нуть** *see* **вдвигать.**

вдво/е adv. doubly, twice; di—; (folded) in two; **в. больше** twice as much or as many; **в. быстрее** twice as fast; **в. лучше** twice as good; **в. меньше** half (as much; as big); **уменьшить в.** v. halve; **—ём** adv. together; **—йне** adv. twice, twofold, doubly.

вдевать v. put in; thread (a needle).

вдевятеро adv. ninefold, nine times; **в. больше** nine times as much; **в. меньше** one ninth; **—м** adv. nine (together).

вдел/анный a. fitted in, etc., *see v.;* built in; **—ка** f., **—ывание** n. fitting in, etc., *see v.;* **—(ыв)ать** v. fit in, build in, fix in; set in, embed, incase; inlay (with).

вденет fut. 3 sing. of **вдеть.**

вдёр/гивать, —нуть v. pull in, retract, draw in; thread (a needle).

вдесятеро adv. ten times, tenfold; **в. больше** ten times as much; **в. меньше** one tenth; **—м** adv. ten (together-er).

вдет/ый a. put in; threaded; **—ь** *see* **вдевать.**

вдобавок adv. besides, in addition, as well, over and above.

вдов/а f. widow; **—еть** *see* **вдовствовать; —ица** f. widow; (ichth.) jelly cat (*Lycichthys denticulatus*).

вдоволь adv. enough, plenty, sufficiently.

вдов/ствовать v. be widowed; be a widow or widower; **—ушка** f. (bot.) Nigella damascena; (orn.) Vidua.

вдогон(ку) adv. in pursuit (of).

вдолбить v. ram into; (educ.) drill into.

вдоль adv. lengthwise, longitudinally; prep. gen. along, by, down; **в. всего** (running) the entire length; along the length (of); **в. по** along; **разрез в.** longitudinal cut; **—береговой** a. beach.

вдох m. inhalation, breath; inspiration, breathing in; **резервный объём —а** inspiratory reserve volume, IRV.

вдохнов/ение *n.* inspiration; **—енный** *a.* inspired; **—ить, —лять** *v.* inspire; **—ляться** *v.* take inspiration (from).

вдохнуть *see* вдыхать.

вдп *abbr.* (вакуум дуговой переплав стали) vacuum arc remelting of steel, VAR.

вдребезги *adv.* to pieces, to fragments.

вдруг *adv.* suddenly, all at once, abruptly.

вдув/аемый *a.* blown in; **в. воздух** air blast; **—ание** *n.* injection, etc., *see v.;* blast; blow-in; **—атель** *m.* insufflator; blower; **—ать** *v.* inject, insufflate, blow in, force in, inflate; **—ной** *a.* intake.

вдум/аться *see* вдумываться; **действовать —чиво** *v.* exercise judgment; **—чивый** *a.* thoughtful, serious; **—ываться** *v.* consider carefully, think over, go into the matter.

вду/(ну)тый *a.* injected, etc., *see* вдувать; **—нуть** *see* вдувать.

вдух/аемый *a.* inspired; **—ание** *n.* inspiration, inhalation; **—атель** *m.* inspiratory muscle; **—ательный** *a.* inspiratory, respiratory; **—ать** *v.* inspire, breathe in, inhale.

вебер *m.* (elec.) weber (10^8 maxwells), Wb; **—метр** *m.* fluxmeter; **—ов(ский)** *a.* Weber's, Weberian.

вебнерит *m.* (min.) webnerite, andorite.

вебстерит *m.* (min.) websterite.

вевелит *m.* (min.) whewellite.

вега (soil) vega; (astr.) Vega.

вегазит *m.* (min.) vegasite.

Вегарда закон Vegard's law.

вегет/арианец *m.,* **—арианский** *a.* vegetarian; **—арианство** *n.* vegetarianism; **—ативный** *a.* vegetative; autonomic (nervous system); asexual (reproduction); **—ационный** *a.* vegetation, vegetative; growing (season); (greenhouse) culture; seasonal (irrigation); culture (flask); **—ационный домик** conservatory; **—ация** *f.* vegetation; growth; **—ировать** *v.* vegetate; grow.

ведать *v.* know; manage, be in charge.

ведём *pr. 1 pl. of* вести.

веден/ие *n.* knowledge; management; supervision; authority, jurisdiction; guidance, direction; leading, guiding, conducting; conduct; working, practice; disposal; *suffix* —ology, science, study; **в. дела** business transaction; **в. файла** file maintenance.

ведённый *a.* conducted, etc., *see* вести.

вёдер *gen. pl. of* ведро.

ведрённый *a. of* ведро.

ведёт *pr. 3 sing. of* вести.

веджвуд *m.* Wedgwood china.

вединский *a.* (geog.) Vedi.

ведом/о *n.* knowledge, consent; **—ость** *f.* report, journal, log; register, list, record; statement; (charge) sheet; (pay) roll; **сопроводительная —ость** bill of lading; **—ости** *pl.* gazette, record, house organ; **—ственность** *f.* jurisdiction; **—ственный** *a.* departmental; institutional; bureaucratic; **—ственные барьеры** red tape; **—ство** *n.* department, service.

ведомый *a.* conducted, etc., *see* вести; dependent, slave (unit); known; managed; *m.* supporting aircraft; second (pilot), wingman; **в. механизм** follower.

ведро *n.* pail, bucket; vedro (12.3 liters).

вёдро *n.* (meteor.) fair weather.

ведут *pr. 3 pl. of* вести.

ведущ/ий *a.* conducting, etc., *see* вести; guide (bearing, pulley, etc.); drive (shaft, wheel, etc.); pilot, steering; master, control; leading, chief, foremost, top-level; key (industry; word); fundamental (principle); preceding (spot); basic (role); conductor (ideal); **в.-ведомый** *a.* master-slave; **в.-ведомый триггер** (comp.) master-slave flip-flop; **—ая перфорация** (comp.) feed holes; **—ее положение** leadership; **—ийся** *a.* being conducted, in progress.

ведший *pr. act. part. of* вести.

ведь *conj.* (well) but, why, in fact.

ведьм/а *f.* (geom.) witch; **—ина метла** (phyt.) witches'-broom; **—ины кольца** (bot.) fairy rings.

ведя *pr. gerund of* вести.

веелерит *m.* wheelerite (a fossil resin).

веер *m.* fan; (art.) sheaf; **—ный** *a. of* веер; (spectroscopy) twisting (mode of vibration); wagging (vibration); **с —ным лучом** fan-beam (antenna); **—овидный, —ообразный** *a.* flabellate, flabelliform, fan-shaped; **—овые** *pl.* (ichth.) Veliferidae; **—окрылые** *pl.* (ent.) Strepsiptera; **—олистный** *a.* fan-leaved; **—ом** *adv.* fan-shaped; **—оносцы** *pl.* (ent.) Rhipiphoridae; **—охвост** *m.* (ichth.) fantail.

веет *pr. 3 sing. of* веять.

вежливый *a.* courteous, polite.

вёз *past m. sing. of* везти.

везде *adv.* everywhere; commonly (used); **в. где** wherever; **—сущий** *a.* omnipresent, ubiquitous; **—ход** *m.,* **—ходный** *a.* all-terrain or cross-country vehicle.

везен/ие *n.* transportation; **—ный** *a.* conveyed, carried, transported.

везерометр *m.* (paints) weatherometer.

везик/о— *prefix* vesico (bladder, blister); **—ула** *f.* vesicle, vesicula; **—улит** *m.* (med.) vesiculitis; **—улярный** *a.* vesicular.

вез/ти *v.* carry, convey, transport, drive; **ему —ёт** he is lucky.

везувиан *m.* (min.) vesuvianite.

Везувий Mount Vesuvius.

везувин *m.* vesuvin, triaminoazobenzene.

везущий *a.* carrying, transport(ing).

вейбуллит *m.* (min.) weibullite.

вейгелия *f.* (bot.) Weigela.

Вейерштрасса функция (math.) Weierstrass' function.

вей/левский *a.* Weil; Weyl; **—марский** *a.* Weimar; **—мутова сосна** white pine (*Pinus strobus*).

вейник *m.* reed grass (*Calamagrostis*).

вейс/ит *m.* (min.) weissite; **—манизм** *m.* (biol.) Weismannism.

век *m.* century; age, period, (life)time; (geol.) age, epoch, stage; *gen. pl. of* веко; **отжить свой в.** become obsolete; **—ами** through the ages or centuries.

веко *n.* (anat.) eyelid, palpebra; *prefix* blepharo— (eyelid, eyelash), palpebro—.

веков/ечный *a.* everlasting, eternal; **—ой** *a.* secular, age-old, permanent.

вековый *a.* (anat.) palpebral, eyelid.

вексел/едатель *m.* (com.) drawer (of bill); **—едержатель** *m.* drawee; **—ь** *m.,* **—ьный** *a.* bill (of exchange), draft, promissory note; **—ьный курс** rate of exchange.

вектолит *m.* Vectolite (a magnet).

вектор *m.* (math.) vector; **—иальность** *f.* (cryst.) anisotropy; **—(иаль)ный** *a.* vector(ial); **—но-матричный** *a.* vector-matrix; **—ное исчисление** vector calculus; **в.-столбец** *m.* column vector; **в.-строка** *m.* row vector.

векша *f.* (mam.) European red squirrel (*Sciurus vulgaris*).

вёл *past m. sing. of* вести.

велась *past f. sing. of* вестись.

велд *m.* veld(t), grassland.

веленевый *a.* vellum (paper).

веление *n.* order, command; instructions.

велень *f.* vellum (paper).

велер *m.* selector.

велерит *m.* (min.) wöhlerite.

велеть *v.* order, bid, tell, instruct.

вели *past pl. of* **вести.**

велигер *m.* (mal.) veliger.

велик/ан *m.,* **—анский** *a.* giant; **—ий** *a.* great, big, huge; (geog.) Great; Pacific (Ocean).

Великобритания Great Britain.

велико/возрастный *a.* overgrown; **—душный** *a.* generous; **—лепный** *a.* magnificent, splendid; superb, fine, showy; **—лукский** *a.* (geog.) Velikie Luki; **—устюгский** *a.* (geog.) Velikii Ustiug.

велиферовые *pl.* (ichth.) Veliferidae.

велич/айший *a.* greatest, extreme; **—ать** *v.* glorify, extol, praise; call, name; **—ественный** *a.* majestic, stately; **—ие** *n.* grandeur, greatness.

величин/а *f.* size, dimension, measure; (math.) value, magnitude, quantity, amount; volume, bulk; degree, extent (of error); scope; intensity (of force, etc.); (flow) rate; (aut.) variable; bigness, greatness; stature; range (of tide); (math.) term; **в. pH** pH value; **—ы** *pl.* data; **в натуральную —у** life-size; **на значительную —у** to a considerably extent; **определять —у** *v.* measure.

веллингтония *f.* (bot.) sequoia.

веллсит *m.* (min.) wellsite.

вело *past n. sing. of* **вести.**

вело— *prefix* (bi)cycle; **—камера** *f.* bicycle (inner) tube; **—покрышка** *f.* (bi)cycle tire; **—сипед** *m.* bicycle; **—сипедный** *a.* bicycle; walking (crane).

велось *past n. sing. of* **вестись.**

вело/трек *m.* cycle track; **—шина** *f.* bicycle tire.

вёлся *past m. sing. of* **вестись.**

велум *m.* (biol.) velum, veil.

велутина *f.* (mal.) Velutina (a snail).

вельбот *m.* whaleboat.

вельвет, **—ин** *m.,* **—овый** *a.* velveteen; **—овые** *pl.* (ichth.) Caracanthidae.

вельвичия *f.* (bot.) Welwitschia.

вельд *m.,* **—енский** *a.* (geol.) Wealdian.

Вельдона способ Weldon process.

вельды *pl.* (phytogeog.) veld.

вельминский *a.* (geog.) Velmo.

вельский *a.* (geog.) Velsk; Vel'.

вельц/евание *n.* (met.) Waelz process; **—евать** *v.* process in a rotary kiln; **—окись** *f.* oxide from Waelz process; **—печь** *f.* rotary kiln.

Вельша способ (met.) Welsh process.

велюр *m.* (text.) velour; suede leather.

велярный *a.* velate, veiled; velar (sound).

Вена (geog.) Vienna.

вена *f.* vein; **воспаление вен** (med.) phlebitis; **расширение вен** varicose veins; **в.-выпускник** *f.* (anat.) emissary vein; **в.-спутница** *f.* accompanying vein.

венг. *abbr.* (**венгерский**) Hungarian.

венгерка *f.* common plum.

Венгрия (geog.) Hungary.

вендрут *m.* (min.) support.

венёвский *a.* (geog.) Venyov.

венепункция *f.* (med.) venipuncture.

Венера *f.* (astr.) Venus.

венериды *pl.* (mal.) Veneridae.

венерин башмачок (bot.) Cypripedium; **в. волос(ок)** (bot.) maidenhair (*Adiantum capillus-veneris*); **—а мухоловка** (bot.) Venus flytrap; **—ы волосы** (min.) Venus hairstone, sagenitic quartz.

венер/ический *a.* (med.) venereal; **—ологический** *a.* vener(e)ologic, venereal; **—ология** *f.* vener(e)ology.

венерупис *m.* (mal.) Venerupis.

венесекция *f.* (med.) venesection, phlebotomy.

венесуэльский *a.* (geog.) Venezuela(n).

венец *m.* corona, crown, aureole, halo; wreath; (mach.) ring, rim; (constr.) row of logs; (min.) curb; acme, highest achievement; (hoof) coronet; (antler) knob.

венецианск/ий *a.* (geog.) Venice, Venetian; **—ая ярь** verdigris.

венечн/ик *m.* (bot.) Anthericum; **—ый** *a. of* **венец;** crown; (anat.) coronary; coronoid (fossa; process); coronal (suture); **—ый сустав** (zool.) coffin joint.

вензель *m.* monogram, initials.

веник *m.* broom, sweeper; **—овидный,** **—ообразный** *a.* scopulate, scopiform, brush-like, broom-like.

венировать *v.* veneer.

вениса *f.* (min.) andradite (garnet).

венит *m.* (petr.) venite, veined gneiss.

венич/ек *dim. of* **веник;** (bot.) panicle; Lepidium; **—ный** *a.* broom; (bot.) paniculate.

венковидный *a.* garland-shaped.

веннер *m.* (min.) vanner, concentrator.

вен/ный, **—озный** *a.* venous, vein; **в. узел** (med.) varix.

венок *m.* wreath, garland.

веносклероз *m.* (med.) venosclerosis, phlebosclerosis.

веночек *dim. of* **венок.**

венск/ий *a.* (geog.) Viennese; Vienna (paste, etc.); **—ое питьё** (pharm.) senna tea.

вентерь *m.* clip net, fish trap.

вентилир/ование *n.* ventilation, airing; aeration; **—ованный,** **—уемый** *a.* ventilated; **—овать** *v.* ventilate, air, aerate.

вентиль *m.* valve; (comp.) gate; (electron.) rectifier; **в.-задвижка** slide valve.

вентильный *a. of* **вентиль;** barrier (effect); recitfying (metal); **в. преобразователь** (electron.) converter; **в. слой** depletion or barrier layer; **в. фотоэлемент** photovoltaic or barrier-layer cell; **в. фотоэффект** photovoltaic effect.

вентиля/тор *m.* ventilator, fan, blower; **в.-измельчитель** *m.* (agr.) chopper fan; **—торный** *a. of* **вентилятор;** fan-driven; **—ционный** *a.* ventilating; vent (hole); **—ционный канал** (met.) vent; **—ционная выработка** (min.) airway; **—ция** *see* **вентилирование.**

вентр/альный *a.* ventral, abdominal; **—икуло—** *prefix* (anat.) ventriculo—, ventricle; **—икулярный** *a.* ventricular.

вентский *a.* (geog.) Venta.

вентспилсский *a.* (geog.) Ventspils.

Вентури трубка Venturi tube.

вентурия *f.* (phyt.) Venturia (a fungus).

венула *f.* (anat.) venula, venule.

венус *m.* (mal.) Venus.

вен/ца *gen. of* **венец;** **—це—** *prefix* coroni—, stephano— (crown); **—ценосный** *a.* coroniferous, crown-bearing; **—цеобразный** *a.* coroniform, crown-shaped; **—чать** *v.* crown, top; marry; **—чаться** *v.* be crowned; get married; **—чающий** *a.* crowning; **—чающая часть** crown.

венчик *m.* rim, collar, bead; crown, corona, halo; (bot.) corolla; **—овидный** *a.* corollaceous; **—овый** *a. of* **венчик;** **—оносный** *a.* corolliferous; **—ообразный** *a.* corolliform; **—оцветный** *a.* corolliferous.

вены *gen., pl., etc., of* **вена;** veins, venae.

ВЕП *abbr.* (**высота единицы передачи**) height of a transfer unit, H.T.U.

вепр/евые *pl.* boarfishes (*Pentacerotidae*); **—ь** *m.* wild boar.

вера *f.* faith, belief, trust, credit.

вератр/ат *m.* veratrate; **—ил** *m.,* **—иловый** *a.* veratryl; **—ин** *m.,* **—иновый** *a.* veratrine; **—(ин)овая кислота** veratric acid, dimethoxybenzoic acid; **соль —(ин)овой кислоты** veratrate (of); **—иновокислый** *a.* veratric acid; veratrate (of); **—иновокислая соль** veratrate; **—ол** *m.* veratrole, dimethoxybenzene; **—ум** *m.* (bot.) Veratrum.

верба *f.* osier, willow.

вербальный *a.* verbal.

вербейник *m.* (bot.) loosestrife (*Lysimachia*); mullein (*Verbascum*).

вербен/а *f.* (bot.) verbena; **—овые** *pl.* Verbenaceae; **—овый** *a.* verbena; **—ол** *m.* verbenol; **—он** *m.* verbenone.

верблю/д *m.* camel; **двугорбый в.** Bactrian camel; **одногорбый в.** dromedary; **—дка** *f.* (bot.) tickseed (*Corispermum*); **—дки** *pl.* (ent.) Rhaphidioptera; **—довые** *pl.* (mam.) Camelidae; **—жатник** *see* **верблюдка; —жий** *a.* cameline), camel's; **—жонок** *m.* young camel; **—жья колючка, —жья трава** (bot.) camel's thorn (*Alhagi*).

вербн/ый *a. of* **верба; —як** *m.* willow grove.

вербовать *v.* recruit, enlist; engage, hire; **—ся** *v.* join, enlist; sign a contract.

вербо/вый *a. of* **верба; —лоз** *m.* bay willow (*Salix pentandra*).

верва *f.* cobbler's thread.

верветка *f.* (mam.) Cercopithecus pygerythrus.

вер-гинье *n.* Guignet's green.

вердикт *m.* verdict.

вердо/гемин *m.* verdohemin; **—глобин** *m.* verdoglobin; **—пероксидаза** *f.* verdoperoxidase.

Вердэ постоянная Verdet's constant.

верёв/ка *f.* cord, rope, string; line, tackle; **—ки** *pl.* cordage; **—ковидный** *a.* funiliform, rope-like; **—очный** *a.* rope; link, funicular (polygon; curve); **—чатый** *see* **верёвковидный.**

вередить *v.* irritate, chafe (a sore).

вередник *m.* (bot.) field pennycress (*Thlaspi arvense*).

верейский *a.* (geol.) Vereian (horizon); (geog.) Vereya.

верен *sh. m. of* **верный.**

вереница *f.* row, file, line; **в. импульсов** (phys.) pulse train.

верес *m.* common juniper.

верес/к *m.,* **—ковый** *a.* (bot.) heather (*Calluna* or *Erica*); **—ковые** *pl.* Ericaceae; **—няк** *m.* moor, heath.

веретен/ица *f.* (herp.) slow worm (*Anguis*); **—ицевые** *pl.* Anguidae; **—ник** *m.* (orn.) godwit (*Limosa*); spindlefish (*Paralepis,* etc.); **—никовые** *pl.* Paralepididae; **—ный** *a.,* **—о** *n.* spindle (anchor, oar) shaft; (anat.) modiolus; **—овидность** *f.* (phyt.) spindle tuber; spindle twig or leaf; **—овидный, —ообразный** *a.* spindle (-shaped); (biol.) fusiform, taper(ed).

верещатник *m.,* **—овый** *a.* heath, moorland.

верещать *v.* squeal; crackle; chirp.

верея *f.* gate post, door post, jamb.

верже *n.* laid paper.

верзор *m.* (math.) versor.

веритайпер *m.* (typ.) Vari-typer.

верит/ельные грамоты credentials; **—ь** *v.* believe, trust, give credit.

верифи/катор *m.* verifier; **—кационный** *a.,* **—кация** *f.* verification; **—цировать** *v.* verify; **—цируемый** *a.* verifiable.

веркблей *m.* (met.) crude lead.

верлит *m.* (min.) wehrlite.

верметус *m.* (mal.) Vermetus (a snail).

верми/кулит *m.* (min.) vermiculite; **—лион, —льон** *m.* vermilion.

вермишель *f.,* **—ный** *a.* vermicelli.

вермут *m.,* **—овый** *a.* vermouth; (bot.) wormwood (*Artemisia absinthium*).

верна/дит *m.* (min.) vernadite; **—лизация** *f.* (hort.) vernalization.

вернее *comp. of* **верно, верный** (or) rather, more accurately.

Вернеля печь Verneuil furnace.

вернер/ит *m.* (min.) wernerite, common scapolite; **—овский** *a.* Werner's.

Вернета голубой Vernet's blue.

верниер *see* **верньер.**

вернин *m.* vernine.

верно *adv.* correctly, right, faithfully; probably; it is correct.

верно́ния *f.* (bot.) Vernonia.

верность *f.* correctness, accuracy, precision; (acous.) fidelity; loyalty.

вернуть *v.* return, give back; get back, regain, retrieve, recover; **—ся** *v.* return, come back, get back.

верн/ый *a.* correct, accurate; valid; reliable, sure; significant (digit); faithful, true; exclusive (species); **быть —ым** *v.* hold (true).

верньер *m.,* **—ный** *a.,* **—ная шкала** vernier (scale).

верон/ал *m.* veronal, barbital; **—ика** *f.* (bot.) veronica; **—ская зелень, —ская земля** Verona green, Verona earth.

вероятие *n.* likelihood, probability.

вероятн/ейший *a.* most probable; **—о** *adv.* probably, possibly, perhaps; apt; it is probable (or likely).

вероятност/ный *a.* probability; probabilistic (machine); stochastic, random (process); **—ь** *f.* probability, likelihood, chance; (thermodynamic, etc.) potential; **по всей —и** in all probability, most likely; **теория —и** law of probability.

вероятный *a.* probable, likely.

верп *m.* kedge anchor; **—овать** *v.* (naut.) warp.

веррук/ария *f.* (bot.) wartwort (*Verrucaria*); **—озный** *a.* verrucose, warty.

Версаль (geog.) Versailles.

версен *m.* Versene (chelating agent).

версинус *m.* (math.) versed sine.

версия *f.* version.

версор *m.* (math.) versor.

верста *f.* verst (1.067 km).

верстак *m.* (work) bench.

верст/альщик *m.* (typ.) make-up man; **—ание** *n.* (typ.) making up (pages), composing; **—атка, —ать** *f.* composing stick; **—ать** *v.* compose, make up; impose; (mil.) draft, enlist; adjust, compare; allot, give.

верстачный *a. of* **верстак.**

вёрстка *f.* (typ.) make-up; making up; proof in page(s).

верстовой *a.* verst; **в. столб** mile post.

версьера *f.* (geom.) versiera, witch (of Agnesi).

вертебральный *a.* vertebral.

вертеж *m.* giddiness, vertigo, dizziness.

вертел *m.* spit, skewer; (anat.) trochanter; **—ка** *f.* (text.) warp loom; **—овидный** *a.* spit-shaped; **—ьный** *a.* (anat.) trochanteric.

вертеть *v.* turn, twirl, spin, twist; (elec.) reverse; **—ся** *v.* turn around, whirl, spin, revolve, rotate; center (around).

верти/го *n.* vertigo; **—головка** *f.* (orn.) wryneck (*Jynx*).

вертикал *m.* (astr.) vertical; vertical flue; —**изация** *f.* (rockets) vertical adjustment; —**ь** *f.* vertical (line), upright, perpendicular; observation point; **скорость по —и** vertical speed.

вертикально *adv.* vertically; **в.-взлетающий** *a.* (av.) vertical take-off; —**сверлильный** *a.* upright-drilling; —**строгальный** *a.* vertical-planing; —**сть** *f.* verticality, vertical position; —**фрезерный** *a.* vertical-milling.

вертикальн/ый *a.* vertical, upright, erect, perpendicular; updraft (furnace); portrait (orientation of image); **в. разрез, —ая проекция** front view.

вертикант *m.* roll stabilizer.

вертициллёз *m.* (phyt.) verticillium wilt.

вертишейка *f.* (orn.) wryneck (*Jynx*).

вертл/уг, —юг *m.* swivel, pivot; (anat.; zool.) trochanter; —**южный** *a.* of **вертлюг;** trochanteric; acetabular (artery, bone); —**южная впадина** (anat.) acetabulum; —**южок** *dim.* of **вертлюг.**

вертлявый *a.* restless, mobile.

вертляниц/а *f.* (bot.) Indian pipe (*Monotropa*); —**евые** *pl.* Monotropaceae.

верто/дром *m.* (av.) heliport, helipad; —**лёт** *m.,* —**лётный** *a.* helicopter; —**лёт-амфибия** amphibious helicopter; —**лётоносец** *m.* helicopter carrier.

верт/о́лист *m.* (ent.) leaf roller; —**опрах** *m.* weather vane; —**ун** *m.* weather vane; (phyt.) rust; —**унья** *f.* (ent.) bud moth; —**уха** *f.* wild buckwheat (*Polygonum convolvulus*); —**ушечный** *a.* *of* **вертушка;** —**ушка** rotator, rotor, impeller; vane; ventilator; revolving stand; revolving door; turntable; dial; current meter; special Kremlin telephone system; —**ячий** *a.* whirling; rotatory; —**ячка** *f.* (vet.) avertin; coenurosis, gid (of sheep); —**ячки** *pl.* whirligig beetles (*Gyrinidae*); —**ящийся** *a.* revolving, rotating; —**ящийся крест** turnstile.

верфь *f.* dock(yard), shipyard.

верх *m.* top, upper part, summit; head; acme (of perfection); **брать в.** *v.* get the upper hand (of), get the better (of), overcome.

верхне— *prefix* top, upper; overhead; supra—; (geog.) Upper, e.g. —**азовский** *a.* Upper Azov; —**бойный** *a.* overshot (wheel); —**бродильный** *a.* top-fermenting; —**волжский** *a.* (geog.) Upper Volga; —**глазничный** *a.* (anat.) supraorbital; —**глоточный** *a.* suprapharyngeal; —**губной** *a.* supralabial.

Верхнее (geog.) Lake Superior.

верхне/жаберный *a.* (zool.) epibranchial; —**затылочный** *a.* (anat.) supraoccipital; —**камский** *a.* (geog.) Upper Kama; —**клапанный** *a.* overhead valve; —**наливной** *a.* overshot (wheel): —**сторонний** *a.* upper side; —**ушная** *f.* epiotic (bone); —**челюстной** *a.* (anat.) maxillary; —**челюстная кость** maxilla.

верхн/ий *a.* superior, upper, top, overhead; **в. класс** (concentration) oversize; **в. привод** overhead drive; **в. резервуар** gravity tank; **в. свет** skylight; **в. цикл** (math.) cocycle; **Верхнее озеро** Lake Superior; —**яя поверхность** upper surface, top; —**яя точка** apogee, peak; —**яя часть** top.

верхн/ик, —як *m.* upper part, top (part); (min.) roof timber, capping, beam.

верхо/венство *see* **верховность;** —**вка** *f.* verkhovka (one of several species of fish, most commonly *Leucaspius*); —**вность** supremacy, superiority; —**вный** *a.* supreme; —**водка** *f.* (geol.) perched water table; (ichth.) bleak, shad, etc.

верхо/вой, —вый *a.* top, upper; upland, high; raised (bog); upriver, upstream; tall-growing; surface (fer-

mentation); saddle (horse); *m.* rider; —**вье** *n.* upper reaches, head(water); —**гляд** *m.* (ichth.) skygazer; —**лаз** *m.* steeple jack, construction worker.

верхом *adv.* upwards, above, overflowing, heaping (full); (at or along) the top, (in the) upper part; astride, mounted; **ложка с в.** heaping spoonful.

верхо/плодный *a.* (bot.) acrocarpous; —**цветник** *m.* cyme; —**цветный** *a.* cymose; —**янский** *a.* (geog.) Verkhoyansk.

верхуш/ечноцветный *a.* (bot.) terminiflorous; —**ечный** *a.* tip, terminal, apical; crowning; —**ка** *f.* apex, tip, top; stem end; (anat.) fastigium; acme.

верчен/ие *n.* turning, etc., *see* **вертеть;** (naut.) whirl(ing); —**ный** *a.* turned, etc.

верша *f.* basket trap, creel, lobster pot, bow net; (mal.) Nassa reticulata.

верш/ать *see* **вершить;** —**ённый** *a.* topped, etc., *see v.;* —**ина** *f.* top, summit, pinnacle, crown; (geom.) vertex, apex; peak (of curve); node; apogee; crest (of hill); point (of tool); tip (of snout); acme, high point; —**инка** *dim.* of **вершина;** apicule; —**инник** *m.* top-wood; top log; —**инный** *a.* apical; vertex; —**иноплодный** *a.* (bot.) acrocarpous; —**ить** *v.* top, crown; accomplish, execute, conclude; (re)solve, decide; manage, control, direct, run; —**кование** *n.* (hort.) topping; —**ковый** *a.* of **вершок;** —**ник** *m.* head rail; —**ок** *m.* top, peak, summit; vershok (4.4 cm).

вес *m.* weight; importance, consequence; influence, authority, position; **на в.** by weight; **на —у** (freely) suspended; overhanging; **по —у** by weight; **собственный в.** gravity; **удельный в.** specific gravity; relative significance; **функция —а** weighting function.

вес. *abbr.* (весовой).

вёсел *gen. pl.* of **весло.**

весел/еть, —ить *v.* cheer up, gladden; —**иться** *v.* enjoy oneself.

веселковые *pl.* (bot.) Phallaceae.

весёлый *a.* cheerful, happy.

весельный *a.* oar, oar-like.

веселящий газ laughing gas (nitrous oxide).

вёсен *gen. pl.* of **весна.**

вес/не-посевной *a.* spring-planted; —**ний** *a.* spring, vernal; (ichth.) spring-run.

вес/ить *v.* weigh; —**кий** *a.* heavy; weighty, significant, impressive; —**кость** *f.* weight(iness), heaviness.

весло *n.* oar, paddle; (bot.) ala; —**ногие** *pl.* (crust.) Copepoda; (orn.) Pelecaniformes; —**носые** *pl.* paddle-fishes (*Polyodontidae*); —**образный** *a.* oar-like, oar-shaped, remiform.

веслянский *a.* (geog.) Veslyana.

весна *f.* spring.

весноватый *a.* freckled.

весно/вспашка *f.* spring plowing; —**й, —ю** *adv.* in the spring.

веснуш/ка *f.* freckle; —**чатый** *a.* freckled.

веснянка *f.* stone fly; (bot.) Erophila.

весов/ой *a.* of **вес** *and* **весы;** (by) weight; weighing (bottle, etc.); gravimetric (analysis); mass (velocity); weighting (function); balance (pan, barometer, etc.); ponderable (amount); **в. износ** wear measured by weight loss; **в. мерник** weigher, weighing device; **в. номер** weight ratio; **в. процент** percent by weight; —**ая платформа** platform scale(s) or balance; —**ая часть** part by weight; —**ым способом** gravimetric (determination); —**щик** *m.* weigher, weigh master.

весоизмеритель *m.* weighing device.

весо/к *sh. m of* **веский;** *m.* plumb bob, plummet; —**м** *adv.* in or by weight; —**мер** *see* **весовой мерник;**

—**мость** *f.* ponderability; weight(iness); —**мый** *a.* ponderable, weighable.

вес-сырец *m.* undressed weight (of fish).

вест *m.* (naut.) west; west wind.

ВЕСТ *abbr.* (**ведомственный стандарт**) departmental standard.

Веста *f.* (astr.) Vesta.

вести *v.* conduct, run, carry on, carry out (reaction); do, be engaged in (work); transact (business); keep (accounts); record, note; guide, steer, direct, lead; drive (a car); fly (a plane); wage (war); *gen., pl., etc.* of **весть; в. себя** behave.

вестиб/улярный *a.* vestibular; —**юль** *m.* vestibule, entrance, antechamber.

Вестингауз Westinghouse.

вест-индский *a.* West Indian.

вестись *reflexive of* **вести;** be underway, be in progress, proceed.

вестник *m.* messenger, herald; journal.

вестов/ой *a.* signal; warning (bell); overflow (pipe); —**ое очко** overflow.

Вестона элемент (elec.) Weston cell.

вестфальский *a.* (geol.) Westphalian.

весть *f.* news, tidings, report; *v. see* **вести.**

весцелиит *m.* (min.) veszelyite.

вес. ч. *abbr.* (**весовая часть**).

весы *pl.* scales, weighing machine; (analytical) balance; **в.-автомат** *pl.* automatic scales or balance; **в.-дозатор** *pl.* bagging scale(s).

весь *a. and pron.* all, (the) whole, total, entire, complete; overall, throughout; everything; **в. свет** the whole world; *imp.* of **весить.**

весьма *adv.* very, pretty, fairly, rather; highly; closely; readily (soluble); **в. ценный** *a.* of considerable value.

вет— *prefix* veterinary; —**баклаборатория** *f.* veterinary bacteriological laboratory.

ветв/е— *prefix* rami- [branch(es)]; clad(o)— (sprout, slip); —**ецветковый** *a.* (bot.) ramiflorous; —**и** *pl.* of **ветвь;** rami; —**истость** *f.* ramification; branchiness; —**истоусые** *pl.* (ent.) Cladocera; —**истый** *a.* branching, branched, ramified; dendritic; ram(ul)ose; *suffix* —ramose, —ramous; —cladous; —**иться** *v.* branch, ramify; —**ление** *n.* branching, ramification.

ветврач *m.* veterinarian, veterinary doctor.

ветв/ь *f.* branch, arm; bough, limb; run, leg; (trajectory) phase, path; (rr.) siding; dendrite; (anat.) ramus; prong (of tuning fork); **главная в.** (hort.) leader; **(со)отношение —ей** (nucl.) branching ratio; —**янка** *f.* (bot.) Brachiaria; —**ящийся** *a.* ramifying, branching.

ветер *m.* wind; **по —у** downwind; **против —а** upwind.

ветеран *m.* veteran.

ветеринар *m.* veterinarian, veterinary doctor; —**ия** *f.* veterinary medicine; —**ный** *a.* veterinary.

ветерок *m.* breeze.

ветивен *m.* vetivene; —**овая кислота** vetivenic acid; —**ол** *m.* vetivenol.

ветивер/ия *f.,* —**овый** *a.* (bot.) vetiver (*Vetiveria zizanioides*).

ветк/а *see* **ветвь;** —**орез** *m.* pruning shears.

ветла *f.* (bot.) white willow (*Salix alba*).

вет/лазарет *m.,* —**лечебница** *f.* veterinary hospital; veterinary clinic.

ветлужский *a.* (geog.) Vetluga.

ветляник *m.* white willow grove.

ветлянский *a.* (geog.) Vetlyanka.

вето *n.* veto.

веток *gen. pl.* of **ветка.**

ветосмотр *m.* veterinary inspection.

веточ/ка *dim.* of **ветка;** sprig, spur, twig; ramulus; —**ный** *a.* branch(y), ramal.

ветош/ка *f.,* —**ный** *a.,* —**ь** *f.* cleaning cloth, rags; litter, mulch.

вет/помощь *f.* veterinary service; —**правила** *pl.* veterinary regulations; —**пункт** *m.* veterinary hospital or dispensary.

ветр/а *gen.* of **ветер;** —**ен** *sh. m.* of **ветреный;** —**еница** *f.* (bot.) anemone; —**енник** *m.* weathercock; —**ено** *adv.* (it is) windy; —**еный** *a.* wind(y).

ветро— *prefix* wind, anemo—; air; —**бой,** —**вал** *m.* windfall; fruit drop; blow-down, storm damage; —**водоподъёмник** *m.* water-pumping windmill; —**вой** *a.* wind; —**вое стекло** windshield; —**гон** *m.* weathercock; —**гонный** *a.* (pharm.) carminative; —**двигатель** *m.* wind mill; wind turbine; —**задерживающая полоса,** —**защита** *f.,* —**защитный** *a.* windbreak; —**кальный** *a.* air-hardened (steel); —**лом** *m.* windbreak; —**мер** *m.* wind gage, anemometer; —**направляющий** *a.* wind-deflecting; —**опыление** *n.* wind pollination, anemophily; —**опыляемый** *a.* wind-pollinated, anemophilous; —**отбойник** *m.* wind deflector; —**рез** *m.* chimney hood; —**силовой** *a.* wind-power(ed), wind-driven.

ветро/указатель *m.* (av.) wind indicator; wind sock; —**улавливатель** *m.* scoop; —**устойчивость** *f.* resistance to wind; —**устойчивый** *a.* wind-resistant, windproof; —**чёт** *m.* (av.) wind-speed indicator, drift computer; —**электрический агрегат,** —**электростанция** *f.* wind-operated power plant; —**энергетика** *f.* wind-power technology.

ветря/к *m.,* —**нка** *f.* windmill; wind turbine; air vane; —**ной,** —**ный** *a.* wind(-driven); natural-draft (furnace); —**ной двигатель** windmill; —**ной конус** (meteor.) wind sleeve; —**ная оспа** (med.) chickenpox; —**чный** *a.* wind-driven.

вет/санитар *m.* veterinary attendant; —**участок** *m.* veterinary district; —**фельдшер** *m.* veterinary technician.

ветх/ий *a.* old, dilapidated, decrepit; —**ость** *f.* decay, decrepit state.

ветчин/а *f.,* —**ный** *a.* ham.

ветшать *v.* fall into decay, age.

вех *m.* (bot.) water hemlock (*Cicuta*).

веха *f.* landmark, (surveyor's) stake; post, pole, rod, peg; guide post, sign post; (naut.) beacon, (spar)buoy.

вечен *sh. m.* of **вечный.**

вечер *m.* evening; **под в.** at dusk; —**еть** *v.* get dark; —**ний** *a.* evening; night (school); (bot.) vespertine; —**ник** *m.,* —**ница** *f.* night school student; —**ник** *m.* (mam.) Lasionycteris; —**ница** *f.* (mam.) noctule bat (*Nyctalus*); (bot.) Hesperis; —**ом** *adv.* in the evening.

вечно *adv.* perpetually, always; —**мёрзлый грунт** permafrost; —**зелёный** *a.* evergreen; —**плавающий** *a.* (biol.) holoplanktonic; —**плавающие тела** holoplankton, aquatic life; —**сть** *f.* perpetuity.

вечн/ый *a.* perpetual, endless, everlasting, eternal; —**ая мерзлота** permafrost; —**ое движение** perpetual motion.

веш/алка *f.* hanger, rack, stand; peg; **сушка на —алках** rack curing; —**ало** *n.* (drying) rack; —**ание** *n.* hanging, etc., see v.; —**анный** *a.* hung, etc., see v.; —**ать** *v.* hang (up), suspend; weigh.

вешение *n.* staking out, etc. see **вешить.**

вешенка *f.* (bot.) Pleurotus ostreatus.

веш/ить *v.* (surv.) stake, mark or set out; —**ка** *dim. of* **веха;** marker; buoy.

вешняк *m.* floodgate, sluice (gate).

вещ. *abbr.* (**вещество**).

вещ/ание *n.*, **—ательный** *a.* (rad.) broadcast(ing); **—ать** *v.* broadcast; prophesy.

вещев/ой *a. of* **вещь; в. мешок** knapsack, kit bag; **в. склад** warehouse; **—ое довольство** personal equipment; clothing; **—ое снабжение** (mil.) clothing and equipment supply.

вещевременник *m.* (orn.) skylark (*Alauda arvensis*).

веществен/означный *a.* real-valued; **—ость** *f.* reality; matter, substance; **—ый** *a.* real (frequency, number, etc.); substantial, material; **—ый взнос** contribution in kind.

вещество *n.* substance, matter, material, stuff; agent; (med.) drug; **—ант, —ент, —ер, —атор**, e.g. **охлаждающее в.** coolant; **связывающее в.** binder; **потеря веществ** substantial loss; **в.-переносчик** *m.* carrier, transmitter; **в.-эталон** *m.* reference material.

вещ/ный *a.*, **—ь** *f.* thing, object, article; item, piece; entity; (law) estate.

вея/лка, —льница *f.* (agr.) winnowing machine; **—льный, —тельный** *a.* winnowing; **—льщик, —тель** *m.* winnower; **—ние** *n.* winnowing; blowing (of wind); trend, tendency; **—ный** *a.* winnowed; **—ть** *v.* winnow, fan; blow.

вживаться *see* **вжиться.**

вживл/ение *n.* implantation; **—ённый** *a.* implanted; **—яемый** *a.* implantable; **—ять** *v.* implant; introduce.

вж(им)ать *v.* force, press or squeeze in.

вжиться *v.* accustom oneself, get used (to).

вз— *prefix* up, off, away, again.

взад *adv.* back(wards); **в. и впепёд** back and forth, to and fro, up and down.

взаимен *sh. m. of* **взаимный.**

взаимно *adv. and prefix* mutually, reciprocally; inter—, *see also under* **взаимо—; в. заменимый** *a.* interchangeable (part); **в. замкнутый** interlocked, intermeshed; **в. корреляционный** *a.* cross-correlation (function); **в. превращаться друг в друга** *v.* be interconverted; **в. простой** *see* **взаимно-простой; в. уничтожающийся** *a.* compensating (errors).

взаимно/дополнительный *a.* mutually complementary; **—обменный** *a.* interchangeable; **—обратный** *a.* inverse, reciprocal.

взаимно/-однозначный *a.* (math.) one-to-one; **в.-полярный** *a.* polar reciprocal; **в.-причинный** *a.* mutually causal; **—проникающий** *a.* interpenetrating; **в.-простой** *a.* (math.) relatively prime, coprime; **—растворимый** *a.* mutually soluble; **—связанный** *a.* (inter)linked, coupled; **—сопряжённый** *a.* self-conjugate; **—сть** *f.* mutuality, reciprocity, duality, correlation; **в.-эквивалентный** *a.* (comp.) mutually equivalent.

взаимн/ый *a.* mutual, reciprocal, inter—; (inter)linked; relative (position); *see also under* **взаимо—; в. затвор, —ая сцепка** interlock; **—ая связь** (inter)linking, coupling; interrelation, interconnection; **—ое влияние** interaction; **—ое проникновение** interpenetration.

взаимо— *see* **взаимно; —влияние** *n.* interference; reciprocal influence; interaction; **—выгодный** *a.* mutually advantageous.

взаимодейств/ие *n.* interaction, interworking, interplay; reciprocal action; interface; coupling; cooperation; (chem.) reaction; (comp.) communication(s); **—овать** *v.* interact, act reciprocally; interface; cooperate; react; **—ующий** *a.* interacting, etc., *see v.;* reaction (mixture); cooperative.

взаимозависим/ость *f.* interdependence, interrelation(ship); interplay; **—ый** *a.* interdependent.

взаимозамен/а *f.* interchange; **—яемость** *f.* inter-

changeability; **—яемый** *a.* interchangeable, duplicate, standby, spare (part).

взаимо/заместимый *a.* interchangeable; **—замещающий** *a.* interchanging; representative (species); **—замыкающий** *a.* interlocking; **—индуктивность** *f.* (elec.) mutual inductance; **—индукция** *f.* mutual induction.

взаимоисключ/ать *v.* be incompatible; **—ающий** *a.* incompatible, mutually exclusive, alternative; **—ение** *n.* incompatibility.

взаимо/нерастворяющийся *a.* mutually insoluble; **—обмен** *m.* interchange; **—обменный** *a.* interchangeable; **—обратный** *a.* (mutually) inverse, reciprocal; **—отношение** *n.* (inter)relation, relationship, interdependence, correlation; **—подкрепляемый** *a.* (biol.) allied; **—положение** *n.* relative position; **—помощь** *f.* muutal aid; **—понимание** *n.* mutual understanding; **—превращаемый** *a.* interconvertible; **—превращение** *n.* interconversion, alternate or mutual conversion; (phys.) transmutation; **—проникающий** *a.* interpenetrating; **—проникновение** *n.* interpenetration, mutual penetration; **—растворимый** *a.* mutually soluble.

взаимосвяз/анный *a.* (inter)related, (inter)connected, interdependent; coupled (effect); **—ь** *f.* (inter)relation(ship), interdependence, interconnection, intercommunication, correlation; interplay; **устанавливать —ь между** *v.* relate to.

взаимоусиляемый *a.* alllied (reflexes).

взаймы *adv.* on credit; **брать в.** *v.* borrow; **дать в.** *v.* lend, advance.

взакрой: забивка в. clinch nailing; **сварка в.** split welding.

взамен *adv. and prep. gen.* instead, in return, in exchange (for).

взамок *adv. lock;* **соединение в.** lock joint; **соединённый в.** lock-joined.

взаперти *adv.* locked.

взбадривать *v.* reassure, cheer up.

взбалам/утить *v.* stir (up), agitate; **—ученный** *a.* stirred, agitated.

взбалтыв/ание *n.* shaking (up), agitation; **—ать** *v.* shake (up), agitate stir.

взбе/гать, —жать *v.* run up.

взбесить *v.* infuriate, madden; **—ся** *v.* become infuriated; go mad, become rabid.

взбив/алка *f.* (egg) beater; **—ание** *n.*, **—ка** *f.* beating, etc., *see v.;* **—ать** *v.* beat (up), whip; churn (butter); puff up.

взбираться *v.* get up, mount, climb (up).

взбит/ый *a.* beaten, etc., *see* **взбивать; —ь** *see* **взбивать.**

взблес/к *m.*, **—кивать, —нуть** *v.* flash, sparkle.

взбодрить *v.* reassure, cheer up.

взболт/ать, —нуть *see* **взбалтывать.**

взбороздить *v.* ridge, furrow.

взборон/ить, —овать *v.* (agr.) harrow.

взбраживание *n.* primary fermentation.

взбр/асывать, —осить *v.* throw up, thrust up; toss up; **—ос** *m.* ramp; (geol.) upthrust, upthrow fault, spec. reverse (thrust) fault; **—осо-сдвиг** strike-slip thrust fault; **—ошенный** *a.* thrown up, thrust up; upthrown, upthrust.

взбрыз/гивание *n.* spraying, splashing up, spurting; **—гивать, —нуть** *v.* spray, splash up, spurt.

взбудоражи(ва)ть *v.* disturb, trouble, excite; **—ся** *v.* be uneasy, become anxious (about).

взбунтовать *v.* revolt, riot; bale, pack.

взвал/ивать, —ить *v.* load.

взвар *m.* decoction.

взвед/ение *n.* leading up (to), etc., *see* **взводить;** **—ённый** *a.* led up (to); erected, raised; cocked.

взвезти *see* **взвозить.**

взвесить *see* **взвешивать.**

взвести *see* **взводить.**

взве/сь *f.* suspension, suspended matter; airborne dust; **—шенно-квадратический** *a.* (math.) weighted-square; **—шенно-полиномиальный** *a.* weighted polynomial; **—шенность** *f.* suspension, suspended state; **—шенный** *a.* suspended, in suspension; entrained (flow); weighed; weighted; fluidized (bed); **—шенное вещество** suspended solid; **—шенное состояние** suspension; **—шенное среднее** weighted mean; **—енной фазы** dilute-phase (transport reactor); **в —шенном состоянии** in suspension; (met.) levitation (melting); **—шивание** *n.* suspension; weighing; **—шивать** *v.* suspend; weigh (out); balance; consider; (stat.) weight; **—шивающий** *a.* suspending, etc., *see v.*

взвиваться *see* **звиться.**

взвин/тить, —чивать *v.* wind up; excite; raise (prices).

взвиться *v.* rise, fly up, whirl up.

взвихриться *see* **взвиться.**

взвод *m.* leading up; notch (of gun); (mil.) platoon; **—ить** *v.* lead up (to); raise; reset; cock (gun); impute.

взвоз *m.* conveyance; **—ить** *v.* convey, carry up.

взволновать *v.* disturb, agitate, stir up; upset; **—ся** *v.* be rough (of water); be upset.

взвыть *v.* howl, set up a howl.

взгля/д *m.* look, glance; (point of) view, opinion, outlook; aspect; **в. назад** retrospect; (geod.) back sight; **на в.** in appearance; **на первый в.** at first glance; **при —де на** on looking at; **—дывать, —нуть** *v.* look at, glance.

взгор/ок *m.* small hill; **—ье** *n.* hill.

вздв/аивать, —оить *v.* duplicate; double; halve; (agr.) replow; **—оенный** *a.* duplicated, etc., *see v.*

вздорожать *v.* rise in price.

вздохнуть *see* **вздыхать.**

вздрагивать *v.* shudder, start, wince.

вздремнуть *v.* nap, doze.

вздрогнуть *see* **вздрагивать.**

вздув/ание *n.* swelling, bulging, bulge, inflation; (geol.) heave; **—ать** *v.* inflate, blow up; **—аться** *v.* inflate, swell, puff up, bulge, heave; **—шийся** *a.* inflated, tumid, swollen.

вздумать *v.* get the idea.

вздут/ие *n.,* **—ость** *f.* swell(ing), intumescence, tumor; bulge, bulging; blister; inflation, distention; **—о—** *prefix* cyst(o)— (bladder); phymato— (tumor); **—оплодный** *a.* (bot.) cystocarpic; **—остебельник** *m.* Physocaulis; **—ый** *a.* inflated, distended, swollen, tumid, turgid, puffed up; **—ь** *see* **вздувать.**

вздым/ание *n.* rising; (geol.) upthrusting; **—аться** *v.* rise, billow, heave; **—ающийся** *a.* rising, upward; **—щик** *m.* resin collector.

вздыхать *v.* sigh, take a breath.

взим/аемый *a.* taxable; **—ать** *v.* levy, collect, raise (taxes).

взламывать *v.* break open, force open.

взлез(а)ть *v.* climb up, get up.

взлёт *m.* flight; upsurge; (av.) take-off, launching.

взлет/ание *see* **взлёт; —ать, —еть** *v.* fly up, rise, take off; soar; take wing.

взлёт/но-посадочная полоса runway; **—ный** *a. of* **взлёт.**

взлом *m.* breaking open; break; **—анный** *a.* broken; **—ать** *see* **взламывать.**

взлущть *v.* (agr.) peel off, take off; scuffle, break (stubble).

взмах *m.* stroke, sweep, flap; **—ивать, —нуть** *f.* flap, wave, swing.

взмести *v.* whirl up, throw up.

взмёт *m.* sudden rise; breaking (of soil).

взмет/ание *n.* flying up, rising (of dust); **—ать** *v.* throw up; (agr.) plow in; **—нуть** *v.* throw up, fling up, raise; flap, beat (wings).

взмётывать *see* **взметнуть.**

ВЗМО *abbr.* (**высшая занятая молекулярная орбиталь**) highest occupied molecular orbital, HOMO.

взмоет *fut. 3 sing. of* **взмыть.**

взморник *m.* eel grass (*Zostera marina*); **—овые** *pl.* Zosteraceae.

взморье *n.* shore, coastal waters; offing.

взму/тить *v.* roil, stir up, make turbid, muddy; **—ченный** roiled, etc., *see v.;* muddied, turbid; **—ченный асбест** asbestos slurry; **во —ченном состоянии** turbid; in suspension; **—чивание** *n.* roiling, etc., *see v.;* **—чивать** *see* **взмутить.**

взмыв/ание *n.* (av.) bouncing; **—ать** *v.* bounce; balloon; soar up.

взмыл/енный *a.* foamy, frothy, lathery; **—и(ва)ться** *v.* foam, froth, lather.

взмыть *see* **взмывать.**

взнос *m.* payment, fee, dues; deposit.

взнузд(ыв)ать *v.* bridle (a horse).

взо— *see* **вз—.**

взобраться *see* **взбираться.**

взобьёт *fut. 3 sing. of* **взбить.**

взовьётся *fut. 3 sing. of* **взвиться.**

взогн/анный *a.* sublimated; **—ать** *see* **возгонять.**

взойти *see* **восходить, всходить.**

взор *m.* look, glance, gaze.

взорв/анный *a.* exploded, blown up, blasted; **—ать** *see* **взрывать.**

взошёл *past m. sing of* **взойти.**

взра/стать, —сти *v.* grow (up); increase; **—стить, —щивать** *v.* grow, raise.

взрез *m.* cut, incision; dissection; **—ка** *f.,* **—(ыв)ание** *n.* dissection; **—(ыв)ать** *v.* dissect, cut open.

взроет *fut. 3 sing. of* **взрыть.**

взросл/еть *v.* grow up, become an adult; **—ость** *f.* adult stage, maturity; **—ый** *a.* adult, mature, grown up.

взрыв *m.* explosion, detonation, blast; burst(ing), rupture; blow up; outbreak, outburst; **ядерный в.** (nuclear) event, shot; **—аемость** *f.* explosiveness; **—ание** *n.* explosion, bursting, etc., *see v.;* (min.) shooting; **—атель** *m.* fuse, detonator, firing device; **удалять —атель** *v.* defuse; **—ать** *v.* explode, detonate, blast, demolish, blow up, dynamite; fire, set off; dig up; **—аться** *v.* explode, burst, blow up, go off; **—ающий-(ся)** *a.* explosive, detonating; **—ник** *m.* (min.) blaster.

взрывн/ой *a.* explosive, exploding, explosion; blast (wave); high-explosive (grenade); **—ая работа** blasting; **—ая сила** explosive force; brisance.

взрыво/безопасный *a.* explosion-proof, blast-resistant, safe; **—опасность** *f.* explosion hazard; **—опасный** *a.* dangerously explosive; **—стойкий, —упорный** *a.* explosion-proof; **—чный** *see* **взрывной.**

взрыв/пакет *m.* smoke-puff charge; **—чатка** *f.* explosive; **—чатость** *f.* explosiveness.

взрывчат/ый *a.* explosive; detonating; fulminating (silver); **в. воздух** firedamp; **в. желатин** blasting gelatin, nitrogelatin; **в. состав, —ое вещество** (high) explosive; **—ая сила** explosive force.

взрыт/ие *n.* digging up; **—ь** *v.* dig up.

взрыхл/ение *n.* loosening; **—ённый** *a.* loosened; **—ить,** **—ять** *v.* loosen, break up.

взъ— *see* **вз—** *before* **е, ю** *and* **я.**

взъерош/ение, —ивание *n.* dishevelling, etc., *see v.;* (leather) roughing; **—енный** *a.* dishevelled; bristling; **—и(ва)ть** *v.* dishevel, ruffle, rumple; **—и(ва)ться** *v.* bristle, stand on end.

взывать *v.* appeal, invoke; call (for).

взыск *m.* search; proceedings; claim; **—ание** *n.* penalty, fine; **—ательный** *a.* exacting, demanding, strict; **—(ив)ать** *v.* exact, claim; search.

взя/в(ший) *a.* having taken; **—тие** *n.* taking, withdrawal; **—тие пробы** sampling; **—тка** *f.* bribe; **—ток** *m.* (apiculture) nectar and pollen harvest; honey flow; **вылетать на —ток** *v.* forage; **—тый** *a.* taken; given (value); in question; **—тый у** taken or borrowed from; **—ть** *v.* take; turn (right or left); **—ться (за)** *v.* take hold of), grasp; undertake.

виадук *m.* viaduct.

виандот *m.* wyandotte (breed of poultry).

вибратор *m.,* **—ный** *a.* transducer, oscillator; jigger; (antenna) dipole; **двойной в.** folded dipole.

вибрационный *a.* vibration, vibrating, shaking; oscillating (switch, etc.); tuned-reed (indicator; vibratory (impulse).

вибрация *see* **вибрирование.**

вибрион *m.,* **—ный** *a.* (bact.) vibrio.

вибрир/ование *n.* vibration, shaking, etc., *see v.;* (concrete) compaction by vibration; (av.) buffeting; **—овать** *v.* vibrate, shake, jar; oscillate; **—ующий** *a.* vibrating, vibratory, vibration; oscillating; (astr.) rocking (mirror).

вибрисса *f.* (zool.) vibrissa.

вибро— *prefix* vibro—, vibrating, vibration; **—активатор** *m.* vibrating (bin) activater, vibrating hopper; **—анализатор** *m.* vibration analyzer; **—булава** *f.* needle vibrator; vibrating flask; **—бур** *m.* vibrodrill; **—бурение** *n.* vibrodrilling; **—возбудитель** *m.* vibration exciter; **—выпрямитель** *m.* vibrating rectifier; **—галтовка** *f.* vibration tumbling; **—гаситель** *m.* vibration damper; **—граф** *m.* vibrograph; **—грохот** *m.* vibrating screen; **—датчик** *m.* vibration pickup, vibration detector; **—жёлоб** *m.* vibrating chute; **—затирка** *f.* vibrating float; **—игла** *f.* needle vibrator.

вибро/каток *m.* vibrating roller; **—литьё** *n.* vibratory casting; **—лопата** *f.* vibrator spade; **—мельница** *f.* vibrating mill; **—метр** *m.* vibrometer, vibration meter; **—молот** *m.* vibrating hammer; **—нный** *a.* vibronic (interaction, excitation); **—перегрузка** *f.* vibration overload; **—площадка** *f.* vibrating surface; table vibrator; **—поглощающий** *a.* vibration-absorbing; **—погружатель** *m.* vibratory pile driver; **—помол** *m.* vibrational mill; **—преобразователь** *m.* (electron.) vibropack, chopper; vibrator power supply; **—продавливание** *n.* vibration packing; **—прокат** *m.* vibrorolling; vibration-rolled concrete; **—прокатный** *a.* vibration-rolled; **—прочность** *f.* (vibration) strength; shock resistance; **—прочный** *a.* shock-resistant.

вибро/рейка *f.* vibrating screed or float; **—сердечник** *m.* vibrating mandrel; **—сито** *n.* vibrating screen; **—скоп** *m.* vibroscope; **—старение** *n.* vibration aging; **—стенд** *m.* vibrator, vibration table, vibration tester; **—стойкий** *a.* vibration-proof, shock-resistant; **—стойкость** *f.* resistance to vibration; **—трамбовка** *f.* vibrating tamper; **—транспортер** *m.* oscillating conveyer; **—установка** *f.* vibrator; **—устойчивый** *see* **вибростойкий; —устройство** *n.* vibrator, shaker; **—щуп** *m.* vibroprobe.

виварий *m.* (zool.) vivarium.

виверр/а *f.* (mam.) civet (*Viverra*); **—овые, —ы** *pl.* Viverridae.

вивианит *m.* (min.) vivianite.

вивиант *m.* Prussian blue, Berlin blue.

виви/пария *f.* (biol.) viviparism, viviparous reproduction; **—секция** *f.* vivisection.

вивший *past act. part. of* **вить.**

вигантол *m.* Vigantol (vitamin D_3).

вигна *f.* (bot.) cowpea (*Vigna*).

Вигнера эффект (nucl.) Wigner effect.

вигольд *m.* wiegold (alloy).

вигон/евый *a.,* **—ь** *f.* vicuna wool; (mam.) vicuna (*Lama vicuna*).

Вигре колонка Vigreux column.

вид *m.* aspect, look, appearance, form, shape; view, prospect, outlook; type, class, kind, sort; (biol.) species; mode (of oscillations); condition, state; **в. сбоку** side view, profile; **в. сзади** back view, rear view; **в. спереди** front view; **в —е** in the form (of); as; in (terms of); **—oid,** e.g. **в —е ризоморфа** rhizomorphoid; **в том —е, в каком** as; **в том —е, как** as; **в любом —е** in any form; **в —у** in view (of); as, whereas; **в —у того, что** in view of the fact that, considering that; **в холодном —е** cold; **в чистом —е** in the pure state, when pure; **внешний в.** appearance; habit; **делать в.** *v.* pretend, feign; **для —a** pro forma; *v.* be in the form (of); **иметь —ы** *v.* aim (at;) **иметь в —у** *v.* bear (or keep) in mind, remember; intend, contemplate, aim (at); **на в.** in appearance; **на —у** in sight; **ни под каким —ом** by no means, under no circumstances; **никаких —об на** there is no prospect (of); **общий в.** general view; **при —е** at the sight (of); **придавать в.** *v.* fashion, shape, mold; **с —у** in appearance; **упускать из —у** *v.* lose sight (of), overlook.

Видаля проба (med.) Widal test; **В. чёрный** Vidal black (dyestuff).

вид/анный *a.* seen; **—ать** *v.* see often; **—аться** *v.* see (each other), meet.

вид-двойник *m.* (biol.) geminous species.

Видемана-франца закон Wiedemann-Franz law.

виден *sh. m. of* **видный; —ие** *n.* vision, sight; viewing; (med.) hallucination; **—ный** *a.* seen.

видео— *prefix* video, television; **—детектор** *m.* video detector; **—запись** *f.* video recording; **—импульс** *m.* video pulse; **—канал** *m.* video channel; **—лампа** *f.* video tube; **—магнитофон** *m.* video tape recorder; **—передатчик** *m.* video transmitter; **—помехи** *pl.* video cross talk; **—сигнал** *m.* video (signal); **—телефон** *m.* video-telephone, phonovision system; **—ток** *m.* video current; **—усилитель** *m.* video amplifier; **—частота** *f.* video or picture frequency.

вндер *m.* (agr.) weeder, cultivator.

видеть *v.* see; **—ся** *v.* it is seen; meet.

видиа режущий металл, в.-сплав (met.) widia (cemented tungsten carbide).

видикон *m.* vidicon, photoconductive camera tube.

видим/о *adv.* evidently, apparently; **—ость** *f.* visibility, visual range; semblance, appearance; **зона —ости** field of vision; **—ый** *a.* visible, visual; apparent, obvious; in sight; **—ый горизонт** skyline; **делать —ым** *v.* visualize.

вид-индикатор *m.* (biol.) indicator species.

видм/анштеттова структура (met.) Widmanstätten pattern; **—ерова колонка** (fractionation) Widmer column.

видн/еться *v.* be seen, show, appear; **—о** *adv.* apparently, evidently; it is evident, clear, or obvious; it is seen, one can see; **—ость** *f.* visibility (factor), luminosity factor, luminous efficiency; **—ые** *suffix pl.* (biol.) —ales (order); —oidei (suborder); **—ый** *a.* visible, noticeable, prominent; show; *suffix* —form, —oid, —like, resembling, —aceous.

видов/ой *a.* species, specific; **—ое богатство, —ое обилие** range of species; **—ое понятие** specific concept; **—ое развитие** phylogenesis, race history; **—о-неспецифический** *a.* heterologous (serum).

видоизмен/ение *n.* modification, etc., *see v.;* change; variation; version; **—ённый** *a.* modified, etc., *see v.;* **—ить** *v.* modify, change, alter, transform, convert; (gen.) mutate; **—иться** *v.* be transformed; vary, change; undergo mutation; **—яемость** *f.* modifiability; mutability; **—яемый** *a.* modifiable, changeable; variable; mutable; **—ять** *see* **видоизменить.**

видоискатель *m.* (phot.) viewfinder.

видо/образование *n.* speciation, species formation; **—образовательный, —образующий** *a.* species-forming; **—специфический** *a.* species-specific.

виеторисовский *a.* Vietoris.

виза *f.* visa, permit.

визави *adv.* opposite (each other).

византийский *a.* Byzantine.

виз/г *m.* squeal, scream, shriek; screech; yelp; whining (of saw); **—гливый** *a.* squealing, screeching, shrill; whining; **—гнуть** *see* **визжать; —жание** *n.* squeal(ing); **—жать** *v.* squeal, shriek, screech; whine; yelp; splutter (of arc).

визига *f.* (anat.) chorda; dried spinal cord of sturgeon.

визио— *see* **видео—; —нер** *m.* visionary.

визир *m.* sight, finder; (phot.) viewfinder; hairline (pointer); tracker; (sonar) cursor; (av.) drift indicator; **—ка** *f.* (surv.) range pole; gage glass; specimen jar; **—ный** *a.* sighting, line of sight; guide (line); peep (hole); **—ный крест** (surv.) reticle; **—ная трубка** telescopic finder; **—ная щель** aperture sight; **—ное приспособление** finder.

визиров/ание *n.* sight(ing), bearing; **обратное в.** (surv.) backsight(ing); **прямое в.** direct sighting; foresight; **—ать** *v.* sight, level, take bearings; track; visa.

визит *m.,* **—ный** *a.* visit, call; **—ация** *f.* visit; inspection; **—ёр** *m.* visitor.

визуал/изация *f.* visualization; **—изировать** *v.* visualize; **—ьный** *a.* visual; direct (reading); preliminary (observation).

вииκит *m.* wiikite (uranium mineral).

вика *f.* (bot.) vetch (*Vicia*).

Вика игла (cement) Vicat needle.

викаллой *m.* Vicalloy (alloy).

викар/иант *m.* vicariant, vicarious species; **—и(и)ровать** *v.* vicariate, typify; **—и(и)рующий, —ный** *a.* vicarious, substitute(d); representative (species).

викасол *m.* vicasol (vitamin K).

викел/евать *v.* wrap, roll, wind (up); **—ёвка** *f.* wrapping, etc., *see v.;* **—ь** *m.* roll; (rub.) rolled-up stock, uncured stock; **—ь-аппарат** rolling-up device; batching apparatus.

виккерсовый *a.* (met.) Vickers.

вико— *prefix,* **—вый** *a.* (bot.) vetch.

виксит *m.* (min.) weeksite.

виктория *f.* (bot.) Victoria.

викунья *see* **вигонь.**

вил *past m. sing. of* **вить;** *gen. of* **вилы; —а** *f.* fork; *past f. sing. of* **вить; —ась** *past f. sing. of* **виться.**

виледьский *a.* (geog.) Viled.

вилийский *a.* (geog.) Viliya.

вилк/а *f.* fork, yoke; prong; (art.) bracket; (elec.) plug; (hinge) jaw; *gen. of* **вилок; мерная в.** caliper; **соединение —ой** Y-connection.

вилкеит *m.* (min.) wilkeite.

вилко/вый *a. of* **вилка, вилок; —образный** *a.* fork(ed), bifurcate, Y-shaped; yoke (lever); Y- (tube).

виллебруния *f.* (bot.) Villebrunia.

виллемит *m.* (min.) willemite.

виллиамс/ит *m.* (min.) williamsite; **—онова синь** Williamson's blue, Prussian blue.

виллизиево кольцо (anat.) Willis' circle.

вило *past n. sing. of* **вить.**

вило/к *m.* cabbage head; *gen. pl. of* **вилка; -мотыга** *f.* (two-)prong hoe; **—образный** *a.* forked, (bi)furcate; double-pointed; **—образная лопата** digging fork; **—рог** *m.* (mam.) pronghorn (*Antilocapra americana*); **—роги (е)** *pl.* Antilocapridae.

вилось *past n. sing. of* **виться.**

вилоч/ка *dim. of* **вилка;** (orn.) wishbone; (embr.) furcula; **—ковый** *a. of* **вилочка;** thymus (gland); **—ный** *a.* fork(ed), pronged; fork (wrench); **—ный контакт** (elec.) plug; **—ный погрузчик** forklift.

вился *past m. sing. of* **виться.**

вилт *see* **вильт.**

вилуит *m.* (min.) wiluite.

вилы *pl.* (agr.) pitchfork; fork, crotch; **в.-лопата** *pl.* digging fork.

Вильгеродта реакция Willgerodt reaction (for amides).

Вильда защита (meteor.) Wild fence.

вильнуть *see* **вилять;** swerve.

вильнюсский *a.* (geog.) Vilnius.

вильо диаграмма (mech.) Williot diagram.

вильомит *m.* (min.) villiaumite.

Вильсона камера (phys.) Wilson chamber, cloud chamber.

вильт *m.* (phyt.) wilt.

Вильфлея обогатитель (min.) Wilfley concentrator; **В. стол** Wilfley table.

вильчат/о *adv.* furcately; **в. раздвоенный** *a.* bifurcate; **—ый** *see* **вилкообразный;** *a. suffix* —furcate; **с —ым захватом** fork (lift).

вильямс— *see* **виллиамс—.**

вилюйский *a.* (geog.) Vilyui.

вил/яние *n.* wagging, etc., *see v.;* (mach.) hunt, oscillating movement, rocking motion; wobble; **—ять** *v.* wag; wobble (of wheel); shift; weave, zigzag; (elec.; mach.) hunt; equivocate, hedge; **—яющий** *a.* wagging, etc., *see v.*

ВИМ *abbr.* (**временная импульсная модуляция**) pulse-time modulation, PTM.

вимба *f.* (ichth.) Vimba.

вина *f.* fault, guilt, blame; cause; *gen. and pl. of* **вино.**

Вина закон (phys.) Wien's (displacement) law; **В. мостик** (elec.) Wien bridge.

винаконовый *a.* vinaconic (acid).

винд/роза *f.* tail vane (of windmill); **—ротор** *m.* wind rotor.

виндроуэр *m.* (agr.) windrower.

винегрет *m.* mixed salad; mixture.

винеровский *a.* Wiener.

винил *m.* vinyl, ethenyl; **хлористый в.** vinyl chloride; **—ацетат** *m.* vinyl acetate; **—ацетилен** *m.* vinylacetylene; **—бензол** *m.* vinylbenzene, styrene; **—ен** *m.* vinylene; **—иден** *m.* vinylidene; **—иденхлорид** *m.* vinylidene chloride; **—ирование** *n.* vinylation; **—ит** *m.* vinylite (plastic); **—карбазол** *m.* vinylcarbazole; **—овый** *a.* vinyl; **—овый спирт** vinyl alcohol, ethenol; **—ог** *m.* vinyl analog; **—огия** *f.* vinylogy; **—уксусный** *a.* vinylacetic (acid); **—хлорид** *m.* vinyl chloride; **—циклогексен** *m.* vinylcyclohexene; **—ьный** *a.* vinyl.

вини/пласт *m.* rigid vinyl plastic, Viniplast; **—пол** *m.* a polyvinyl *n*-butyl ether oil additive; **—пор** *m.* Vinipor (sound-absorbent material).

винить *v.* accuse, blame; **—ся** *v.* confess; take the blame.

винифлекс *m.* Viniflex (plastic).

винка *f.* (bot.) Vinca.

винкель *m.*, **—ный** *a.* (try) square; (math.) vinculum.

винницкий *a.* (geog.) Vinnitsa.

винно— *prefix* wine; (chem.) tartrate.

винно/аммониекалиевая соль potassium ammonium tartrate; **—железистый** *a.* ferrotartaric; **—железистая соль** ferrous tartrate; **—железная соль** ferric tartrate; **—жёлтый** *a.* wine-yellow; **—калиевая соль** potassium tartrate; **кислая —калиевая соль** potassium bitartrate.

виннокаменн/окислый *see* **виннокислый**; **—ый** *a.* tartaric, *see also* **винный**; **—ая кислота** tartaric acid, spec. *d*-tartaric acid; **соль —ой кислоты** tartrate.

виннокисл/ый *a.* tartaric acid; tartrate (of); **в. калинатр, в. натрий-калий** sodium potassium tartrate; **—ая известь** tartrate of lime; **—ая соль** tartrate; **кислая —ая соль** bitartrate.

винно/-красный *a.* wine-red; **—натриевая соль** sodium tartrate; **—стибилокалиевая соль** potassium antimonyl tartrate, tartar emetic; **—этиловый эфир** ethyl tartrate.

винн/ый *a.* wine, vinous; tartaric; **в. камень** tartar (on teeth); cream of tartar, potassium bitartrate; **в. спирт** ethyl alcohol; **в. уксус** wine vinegar; **—ая кислота** tartaric acid; **соль —ой кислоты** tartrate; **кислая соль —ой кислоты** bitartrate; **—ая пальма** (bot.) wine palm; **—ая ягода** fig (*Ficus carica*).

вино *n.* wine; **горячее в., хлебное в.** vodka.

винов/атый *a.* guilty, to blame; **—ник** *m.* culprit, offender; **—ность** *f.* guilt; **—ный** *a.* guilty, at fault.

виновский *a.* Wien('s).

виногонный *a.* distillatory, distilling.

виноград *m.* grape(s); **—арский** *a.* vineyard, grape-growing; **—арство** *n.* (agr.) viticulture; viniculture; **—арь** *m.* grape grower; **—ина** *f.* (a) grape; **—ник** *m.* vineyard.

виноградно/аммониевая соль ammonium racemate; **—кислый** *a.* racemic acid; racemate (of); **—кислая соль** racemate; **—этиловый эфир** ethyl racemate.

виноградные *pl.* (bot.) Vitaceae.

виноградн/ый *a.* grape; racemic; **в. сахар** grape sugar, glucose; **—ая болезнь** (phyt.) grape mildew; **—ая кислота** racemic acid, paratartaric acid; **соль —ой кмслоты** racemate; **—ая чернь** vine black (a pigment); **—ое масло** grape seed oil.

виноградовит *m.* (min.) vinogradovite.

виноградов/ник *m.* (bot.) Ampelopsis; **—овые** *see* **виноградные**.

винодел *m.* wine maker; **—ие** *n.*, **—ьный** *a.* wine making; **—ьня** *f.* winery, wine cellar; **—ьческий** *a.* wine making.

вино/курение *n.* distillation; **—куренный** *a.* distilling; **—куренный завод, —курня** *f.* distillery; **—мер** *m.* wine-level gage; **—тека** *f.* collection of wine samples.

винслово отверстие (anat.) Winslow's foramen.

винт *m.* screw; propeller; rotor (of helicopter); **барашковый в.** *see* **в.-барашек; бесконечный в.** screw or worm conveyer; **воздушный в.** (av.) propeller; **в.-барашек** *m.* thumbscrew, butterfly screw.

винтергреновое масло wintergreen oil.

винтерова кора Winter's bark.

винт/ик *dim. of* **винт**; **—ить** *v.* screw; **—о—** *prefix* screw; helico— (helix, spiral); **—овальный** *a.*

screw(-threading); **—овальная доска, —овальня** *f.* screw plate; **—оверт** *m.* screwdriver.

винтовка *f.* rifle.

винтов/ой *a.* screw, spiral, helical; worm (gear); propeller; helicoidal (flow); screw (pump); ratchet-action (tool); whorled (leaf); **в. движитель** propeller; **в. домкрат** (screw) jack; **в. ключ** nut wrench; **в. конвейер, в. транспортер** screw conveyer, worm conveyer; **—ая (зубчатая) передача** helical gear; worm gear; **—ая крышка** screw cap (closure); **—ая линия** (math.) helical line, helix; spiral; **—ая муфта** sleeve nut; **—ая пара** screw gage, micrometer; bolt and nut; **—ая пружина** helical spring; **—ое движение** screw or helical motion; **—ое дерево** screw pine (*Pandanus*); **—ое колесо** helical wheel.

винтовочный *a.* rifle.

винт/-ограничитель *m.* stop screw; **—окрыл** *m.* rotorcraft; **—окрылый** *a.* rotary-wing; **—ом** *adv.* spirally; **—омоторный** *a.* (av.) propeller; **—ообразный** *a.* screw-shaped, spiral, helical, coiled; **—ообразная линия** helical line, helix; **—орез** *m.* thread-cutting die.

винторезн/ый *a.* screw-cutting; **в. патрон, —ая головка** screw die, (threading) die; **в. станок** screw-cutting lathe, threader; **—ая гребёнка, —ая плашка** (thread) chaser; **—ая доска** screw plate, die plate.

винторогие *pl.* (mam.) Strepsiceros.

винтотурбинный *a.* (av.) turboprop(eller).

винчестер *m.*, **—ский** *a.* (comp.) Winchester (disk drive); hard disk.

виньет/ировать *v.*, **—ка** *f.* (phot.) vignette.

виола *f.* (bot.) Viola; **—ит** *m.* (min.) violaite; **—кверцитрин** *m.* violaquercitrin, rutin; **—ксантин** *m.* violaxanthin; **—н** *m.* (min.) violane; **—нин** *m.* violanine; **—новый** *a.* violanic (acid); **—цеин** *m.* violacein (antibiotic).

виолевый *a.* violet.

Виолля эталон Violle's standard, Violle's platinum unit.

вио/лоуровая кислота violuric acid; **—мицин** *m.* viomycin (antibiotic); **—стерол** *m.* viosterol (vitamin D): **—форм** *m.* vioform, iodochlorohydroxyquinoline.

виперы *pl.* (herp.) vipers (*Viperidae*).

виппер *m.* (min.) whipper, dumper.

вираж *m.*, **—ный** *a.* (av.) turn(ing), etc., *see v.*; banked turn; curve, bend; (phot.) toner; **—ировать** *v.* turn, veer, bank; **в.-фиксаж** *m.* toning-fixing bath.

виргац/ионный *a.* virgate, rod-like; **—ия** *f.* (geol.) virgation.

виргин/альный, —ильный *a.* virginal; **—ский** *a.* Virgin (Islands).

виреон/овые, —ы *pl.* (orn.) Vireonidae.

вириал *m.*, **—ьный** *a.* (math.) virial.

виридин *m.* (chem.; min.) viridine.

вирилизм *m.* (med.) virilism.

вирион *m.* (med.) virion, viral particle.

вириров/ание *n.* (phot.) toning; **—ать** *v.* tone.

вирицид *m.* (med.) viricide, virucide.

вирогенетический *a.* (med.) virogenetic.

вироз *m.* (phyt.) virus disease.

вирология *f.* (med.) virology.

виртуальный *a.* virtual; (meteor.) eddy (viscosity).

виру/лентность *f.* (med.) virulence; **—лентный** *a.* virulent; **—лицид** *see* **вирицид**; **—с** *m.* virus; **—сный** *a.* virus, viral; **—солог** *m.* virologist; **—сология** *f.* virology; **—соноситель** *m.* virus carrier; **—соподобный** *a.* virus-type.

вис *past m. sing. of* **виснуть**; **—ение** *n.* hanging, etc., *see v.*; **на режиме —ения** hovering (flight); **—еть** *v.* hang, be suspended, overhang; (av.) hover.

висимский *a.* (geog.) Visim.

виска/ча *f.* (mam.) viscacha (*Lagostomus*); **—ша** *f.* mountain chinchilla (*Lagidium*).

вискеризация *f.* (cryst.) whiskering.

виски *f. and n.* whiskey; *pl. of* **висок.**

вискоз/а *f.* viscose; **—иметр** *m.* viscometer; **—иметрия** *f.* viscometry; **—ин** *m.* viscosin (a cylinder oil); viskosin (antibiotic polypeptide); **—ный** *a.* viscose.

вислинский *a.* (geog.) Vistula.

висло *past n. sing. of* **виснуть;** *prefix* hanging, sagging, droop(ing); loose; (bot.) cremo—; **—крылка** *f.* sialid (fly); **—крылки, —крылые** *pl.* (ent.) Megaloptera; **—листный** *a.* (bot.) cremophyllous; **—плодник** *m.* cremocarp; **—ухий** *a.* lop-eared.

вислый *a.* hanging, pendent, drooping.

висмит *m.* (min.) bismite.

висмут *m.* bismuth, Bi; **азотнокислый в.** bismuth nitrate; **основной азотнокислый в.** bismuth subnitrate; **карбонат —а, углекислый в.** bismuth carbonate; **основной углекислый в.** bismuth subcarbonate; **окись —а** bismuth oxide, specif. bismuth trioxide; **хлористый в.** bismuth (tri)chloride.

висмут/ат *m.* bismuthate; **—ид** *m.* bismuthide; **—ил** *m.* bismuthyl; **—ин** *m.* bismuthine, bismuth hydride; (min.) bismuthinite, bismuth glance; **—истый** *a.* bismuth(ous); **—ит** *m.* (min.) bismutite; **—ный** *a.* bismuth; **—оводород** *m.* bismuth hydride.

висмутовокисл/ый *a.* bismuthic acid; bismuthate (of); **—ая соль** bismuthate.

висмутов/ый *a.* bismuth(ic); **в. ангидрид** bismuthic anhydride, bismuth pentoxide; **в. блеск** (min.) bismuth glance, bismuthinite; **—ая белая, —ые белила** bismuth white; **—ая кислота** bismuthic acid; **соль —ой кислоты** bismuthate; **—ая обманка** (min.) bismuth blende, eulytite; **—ая охра** (min.) bismuth ocher, bismite; **—ая синь** bismuth blue; **—ая соль** bismuthic salt; **—ое золото** (min.) bismuth gold, maldonite; **—ое серебро** (min.) bismuth silver, chilenite.

висмуторганический *a.* organobismuth.

виснуть *v.* hang, droop, sag.

висок *m.* (anat.) temple.

високос *m.,* **—ный год** leap year.

височн/о— *prefix* (anat.) temporo—; **в.-нижнечелюстной** *a.* temporomandibular; **—ый** *a.* temple, temporal.

вистан *m.* Vistan (gasoline-resistant plastic).

вистария *f.* (bot.) Wisteria.

вистра *f.* (text.) a viscose wool.

висцер/альный *a.* (anat.) visceral; **—ит** *m.* (med.) visceral lesion; **—о—** *prefix* viscero— (viscera, organs); **—оплевральный** *a.* visceropleural.

висцин *m.* viscin.

висюлька *f.* pendant; icicle.

вися/челистный *a.* flaccid-leaved; **—чий, —щий** *a.* hanging, pendent, suspended, aerial; dependent (drop); suspension (bridge); drop (valve); **—чий бок** (min.) hanging wall; **—чий замок** padlock; **—чая строка** widow or orphan line; **—чие ходы** (photogrammetry) cantilever extensions.

вит *sh. m. of* **витый;** *abbr.* (виток) turn.

вита/-гляс *m.* Vita glass; **—лизм** *m.* (biol.) vitalism; **—листический** *a.* vitalistic; **—ллий** *m.* Vitallium (alloy); **—льный** *a.* (biol.) vital.

витамин *m.,* **—ный** *a.* vitamin; **—изация** *f.* vitaminization, vitamin enrichment; **—изированный** *a.* vitamin-enriched, vitamin-rich (diet); **—изировать(ся)** *v.* enrich or supplement with vitamins; **—(оз)ность** *f.* vitamin content; **—озный** *a.* vitamin-rich; **—оноситель**

m. vitamin-rich food; **—оносный, —осодержащий** *a.* vitamin-containing or yielding.

вит/ание *n.* climbing, etc., *see v.;* **скорость —ания** terminal or free-fall velocity; climb rate; **—ать** *v.* climb, soar, hover, fly, float, become airborne; stay, linger; **—ающий** *a.* climbing, etc., *see v.;* airborne (dust).

Витворта резьба Whitworth thread.

витгамит *m.* (min.) withamite.

витебский *a.* (geog.) Vitebsk.

вителин *m.* vitellin.

витерит *m.* (min.) witherite.

витиатин *m.* vitiatine.

витие *see* **витьё.**

витиеватый *a.* ornate, flowery.

витилиго *n.* (med.) vitiligo.

витимский *a.* (geog.) Vitim.

витковый *a. of* **виток;** turn; loop.

витнеит *m.* (min.) whitneyite.

вит/ой *a.* twisted, spiral, winding, coiled, curled, curly; twined; turned; **—ок** *m.* coil, loop; whorl, convolution; curl; (elec.) turn; orbit.

витраж *m.* stained glass (panel or work).

витрен *m.* vitrain (a bituminous coal); **—изированный** *a.* vitrainized.

витрина *f.* showcase, store window.

витриолизация *f.* vitriolization.

витр/ит *see* **витрен;** *m.* vitrite (a glass); **—ификация** *f.* vitrification; **—офир** *m.* (petr.) vitrophyre; **—офировый** *a.* vitrophyric.

Витстона мостик (elec.) Wheatstone bridge.

Витта теория цветности Witt color theory.

виттихенит *m.* (min.) wittichenite.

виттова пляска (med.) St. Vitus' dance.

вит/ый *a.* twisted, etc., *see v.;* **—ая экранированная пара** twisted shielded pair (of wires); **—ь** *v.* twist, spin, wind, twine; weave, build (a nest); **—ьё** *n.* twisting, etc., *see v.;* torsion; **—ься** *v.* eddy, spin, whirl; (bot.) climb, twine, creep; (orn.) hover, circle; meander (of road); curl (of hair).

витютень *see* **вяхирь.**

вихляй *m.* (orn.) Houbara bustard (*Chlamydotis undulata*).

вихл/яние *n.* wobbling, etc., *see v.;* wobble (of wheel); **—ять** *v.* reel, sway; **—яться** *v.* wobble, swing, dangle; reel, be unsteady.

вихор *m.* tuft.

вихрев/ой *a.* vortex, vortical, rotational; turbulent; eddy (mill, etc.); whirl (wind), whirling; peripheral, turbine (pump); drag (turbine); **в. размол** pulverization in eddy mill; **—ая камера** swirl chamber; **—ая нить** vortex line; **—ое движение** eddy; swirl; **—ое расположение** (anat.) vortex; **в. ток** (elec.) eddy or Foucault current; **—ость** *f.* vorticity.

вихр/екамерный *a.* swirl-chamber; **—ение** *n.* vorticity; **—еобразование** *n.* vortex formation; **—еограничивающий** confined vortex (scrubber); **—ить** *v.* whirl, swirl, spin; **—ь** *m.* vortex, whirl, eddy, rotation; (math.) curl; whirlwind; whirlpool; **—ь в потоке** vortex flow; **—ь (скорости)** vorticity.

вице— *prefix* vice-.

вицианоза *f.* vicianose.

вициналь *f.* (cryst.) vicinal form; **—ный** *a.* vicinal, adjacent, neighboring.

вишарник *m.* boxthorn thicket.

вишен *gen. pl. of* **вишня;** **—ник** *m.* cherry orchard; bush cherry; Agaricus prunulus (mushroom); **—ный** *a.* cherry.

вишерский *a.* (geog.) Vishera.

вишневит *m.* (min.) wischnewite.

виши *f.* Vichy (water).

вишнёв/ка *f.* cherry liqueur; **—окалильный** *a.* cherry-red (heat); **—окрасный** *a.* cherry-red; **—олистный** *a.* cherry-leaved.

вишн/ёвый *a.* cherry(-colored); **—еобразный** *a.* cherry-like; **—еслива** *f.* cherry plum (*Prunus cerasifera*); **—я** *f.* cherry (*Cerasus*); **—як** *m.* cherry orchard.

ВК *abbr.* [**высококипящий (компонент)**] high-boiling (component).

вкалывать *v.* stick in, spear.

вкап/ать, **—нуть** *v.* instill, drop in; **—ывание** *n.* instillation; digging in; **—ывать** *v.* instill; dig in, drive (post).

вкат/ить(ся), **—ывать(ся)** *v.* roll in.

вкач/анный *a.* pumped in; **—ать** *v.* pump in.

вкаченный *a.* rolled in.

вкачивать *see* **вкачать.**

ВКГ *abbr.* (**векторкардиограмма**) (med.) vectorcardiogram.

ВКИ *abbr.* (**виннокислая известь**).

вки/данный *a.* thrown in, added; **—д(ыв)ать,** **—нуть** *v.* throw in, add.

ВКК *abbr.* (**виннокаменная кислота**); (**высотно-компенсирующий костюм**) pressure suit.

вкл. *abbr.* (**включительно**) inclusively.

вклад *m.* contribution; deposit; investment; **внести в.** *v.* contribute; **—ка** *f.* enclosing, etc., *see v.;* enclosure; insert, inset; (typ.) supplementary sheet; **—ной** *a.* of **вклад;** (typ.) supplementary; loose (leaf); (bot.) equitant, overlapping; **—чик** *m.* depositor; **—ывание** *n.* enclosing, etc., *see v.;* **—ывать** *v.* enclose, put in, insert, embed; contribute; deposit; invest; expend, devote, apply.

вкладыш *m.* (mach.) bush(ing), lining, shell, brass; insert, insertion piece.

вкле/енный *a.* glued in, pasted in; **—и(ва)ть** *v.* glue in, paste in; **—йка** *f.* gluing in, pasting in; inset, glued-in piece.

вклёп/анный *a.* riveted in.

вклепать *v.* rivet in.

вклёп/ка *f.,* **—ывание** *n.* riveting in; **—ывать** *v.* rivet in.

вклин/ение, **—ивание** *n.* wedging in, etc., *see v;* **—и(ва)ть** *v.* wedge in; insert, intercalate.

включ/аемый *a.* included, etc., *see v.;* triggered; **—атель** *m.* (elec.) switch, circuit breaker; **—атель-выключатель** *m.* make-and-break (device); **—ать** *v.* include, enclose, insert, embed; integrate, incorporate, contain, cover, comprise; entrap, occlude (gas); (elec.) turn on, switch on or in, cut in, plug in, connect, hook up or into; engage, put (in gear; into service); apply (brake); actuate, energize; set off (alarm); **—аться** *v.* engage; **—ающий** *a.* including, etc., *see v.;* cut-in; **—ая** *pr. ger.* including, inclusive (of); **не —ая** exclusive (of), minus, less.

включен/ие *n.* inclusion, including, etc., *see* **включать;** circuit, network; engagement; entrapment; (petr.) xenolith; **—ия** *pl.* impurities; **газовые —ия** occluded gas, entrapped gas; **коробка —ия** (elec.) junction box; **положение —ия** (elec.) on positon; **схема —ия** (elec.) wiring diagram.

включ/ённый *a.* included, etc., see **включать;** in gear; on (position); **—ено-выключено** on-off; **—ительно** *adv.* inclusive(ly); **—ить** *see* **включать.**

вков(ыв)ать *v.* forge in, weld in.

вкожный *a.* (med.) intracutaneous.

вкол/ачивание *n.* driving in, etc., *see v.;* (anat.) gomphosis; (dental) impaction; **—ачивать, —отить** *v.* drive in, knock in, ram in, pack in.

вколоть *v.* stick in(to), prick in.

вколоченный *a.* driven in, etc., see **вколачивать;** impacted (tooth).

вконец *adv.* entirely, totally, wholly.

вкоп/анный *a.* dug in; embedded; buried; **—ать** *v.* dig in; embed, bury; **—ка** *f.* digging in; burying.

вкорен/ение *n.* inculcation; **—ить,** **—ять** *v.* inculcate, enroot; **—иться,** **—яться** *v.* take root.

вкось *adv. and prep. gen.* on a slant, on a bias, obliquely, awry, crookedly.

ВКР *abbr.* (**вынужденное комбинационное рассеяние**) stimulated Raman scattering, SRS.

вкрадываться *v.* creep in, slip in.

вкрап/ина *f.* embedded particle; **—ить** *see* **вкрапливать;** **—ление** *n.* dissemination, etc., *see v.;* embedment; **—ленник** *m.* (petr.) phenocryst, inset; **—ленность** *f.* (state of) dissemination; **—лённый** *a.* disseminated, etc., *see v.;* **—ливание** *see* **вкрапление;** **—ливать,** **—лять** *v.* disseminate, impregnate; intersperse (with), sprinkle (with); embed; disperse (land).

вкрасться *see* **вкрадываться.**

вкратце *adv.* briefly, in short.

вкреп/ить, **—лять** *v.* fasten in.

вкрест *adv.* transverse(ly) (to).

вкривь *see* **вкось;**

вкруг *see* **вокруг;** **—овую** *adv.* circular (plowing).

вкрутить *v.* screw in, twist in.

вкрутую *adv.* hard-boiled (egg).

вкруч/енный *a.* screwed in; **—ивать** *a.* screw in.

вкуёт *pr. 3 sing. of* **вковать.**

вку/с *m.* taste, flavor; appetite, liking; manner, style; **придавать в.** *v.* flavor; **пробовать на в.** *v.* taste; **—сить** *v.* taste, partake (of); **—сный** *a.* tasty, appetizing; **—совой** *a.* taste; flavor(ing); gustatory (sense); **—совые качества** *or* **свойства** palatability; **—шать** *see* **вкусить.**

вл. *abbr.* (**влажность**) humidity.

влаг/а *f.* moisture, humidity, dampness; (med.) humor; **количество —и** moisture content, humidity.

влагалищ/е *n.* sheath, case; (anat.) vagina; *prefix* colp(o)— (vagina); **—евидный, —еобразный** *a.* vaginiform, sheath-like; **—но—** *prefix* vagino—, vaginal; coleo— (sheath); **—ный** *a.* vaginal; (bot.) vaginant, sheathing, sheath(ed).

влагальце *dim. of* **влагалище.**

влагать *see* **вкладывать.**

влаго— *prefix* moisture, hygro—; water; **—боязливый** *a.* (zool.) hydrophobe; **—выделение** *n.* evaporation; **—ёмкий** *a.* moisture-retentive; **—ёмкость** *f.* moisture or water capacity; specific retention (of moisture by soil); **—задержание** *n.* moisture or water retention; **—зарядка** *f.,* **—зарядковый** *a.* water supply; **—зарядковый полив** reserve or winter irrigation; **—защитный** *a.* water-repellent, hydrophobe; **—изоляция** *f.* waterproofing; moisture seal; vapor barrier.

влаголюб *m.* moisture-loving organism; **—ивый** *a.* hygrophilous, moisture-loving; **—ивое растение** hygrophyte.

влаго/мер *m.* moisture gage, hygrometer; **—накопление** *n.* moisture accumulation; **—насыщенность** *f.* saturation (with moisture) **—непроницаемость** *f.* resistance to moisture, moisture impermeability; **—непроницаемый** *a.* moisture-proof, damp-proof; **—оборот** *m.* (meteor.) hydrologic cycle; water cycle; **—отдача** *f.* water-yielding capacity, release of moisture; **—отделитель** *m.* moisture separator; dehumidifier; water trap; **—отталкивающий** *a.* moisture-repellent.

влагопогло/титель *m.* dehumidifier, desiccator, desiccant; **—щаемость** *f.* moisture absorbency; **—щающий** *a.* water-absorbing, moisture-retentive; **—щение** *n.* moisture absorption, dehumidification.

влаго/потребность *f.* moisture requirement; **—проводность, —проницаемость** *f.* moisture permeability; **—прочность** *f.* wet strength **—сниматель** *m.* (foods) humectant; **—содержание** *n.* moisture content; **—стойкий** *a.* moisture-resistant, waterproof; **—стойкость** *f.* moisture resistance; wet strength; **—съём** *m.* moisture removal, dehumidification; **—удерживающий** *a.* moisture- or water-retentive; **—упорный** *a.* moisture-proof, waterproof; **—устойчивый** *see* **влагостойкий.**

влад/елец, —етель *m.* owner, possessor, proprietor; **—ение** *n.* possession, ownership; property; domain, territory; holding, tenure; estate; **—еть** *v.* possess, own, have; manage, handle, master, know; **хорошо —еть** be familiar (with); **—еющий** *a.* possessing, etc., *see v.*

владимир(ов)ский *a.* (geog.) Vladimir.

владиславия *f.* (ichth.) Ladislavia.

влаж/ить *v.* moisten; **—неть** *v.* get damp, become humid.

влажн/о *adv.* damply, wet; *prefix* moist-; **—оадиабатический** *a.* (meteor.) moist-adiabatic, saturated-adiabatic; **—оватый** *a.* subhumid, dampish; **—онеустойчивый** *a.* moist-labile; **—ость** *f.* moisture (content), damp(ness), wet(ness); humidity; **—ость завядания** wilting point; **—отропический** *a.* rain (forest); **—ый** *a.* moist, damp, humid, wet.

вламываться *v.* break into.

влапу: соединение в. lap joint.

власку: соединение в. scarf joint.

власо/глав *m.* (zool.) whipworm (*Trichuris trichiura*); **—главовые, —главы** *pl.* Trichuroidea; **—хвостый** *a.* (zool.) filicaudate.

власт/вовать *v.* rule (over), dominate; **—ный** *a.* authoritative, having the authority; **—ь** *f.* authority, power, rule.

влачить *v.* drag.

влево *adv.* to the left, counterclockwise; **—завитой** *a.* l(a)eotropic; **вращающийся в.** *a.* (opt.) levorotatory.

влез/ание *n.* getting in; intrusion; **—ать, —ть** *v.* climb in, get in; intrude.

влеи *m.* vlei, grass swamp.

влей(те) *imp. of* **влить.**

влёк *past. m. sing. of* **влечь; —омый** *a.* drawn, attracted; **—ущий** *a.* drawing, etc., *see* **влечь.**

влеп/ить, —лять *v.* paste in.

влёт *m.* (av.) arrival, entry; opening, mouth; *adv.* in flight.

влет/ание *n.* flying in, arrival; **—ать, —еть** *v.* fly in(to); come in, arrive; **—ающий** *a.* incoming, entering; oncoming (neutron).

влеч/ение *n.* inclination, bent, tendency; attraction; (math.) implication; (sexual) drive; **импульсное в.** mania; **—ённый** *a.* drawn, attracted, etc., *see v.;* **—ь** *v.* draw, attract; drag, bring; necessitate, cause, induce; imply, involve; **—ь за собой** involve, entail, imply.

вли/вание *n.* injection, etc., *see v.;* **—вать** *v.* inject, infuse; pour in, run in; blend, merge; **—ваться** *v.* run in, flow in; **—тие** *see* **вливание; —тый** *a.* injected, etc., *see v.;* **—ть** *see* **вливать.**

влия/ние *n.* influence, action, effect; impact, repercussion(s); agency; control; exposure; **взаимное в.** interference; **оказать в.** *see* **влиять; под —нием** by; under [the influence or action (of)]; in response (to); when exposed (to); **подвергаться —нию** *v.* be affected (by); **термического —ния** heat-affected

(zone); **функция —ния** influence function; weighting function; nucleus, kernel (of integral equation); **—тельный** *a.* influential; **—ть** *v.* (exert an) influence, affect, have an effect, act (on), work (on).

влож/ение *n.* enclosure; inclusion; input; investment; (comp.) nesting; (math.) embedding; **отображение —ения** (algebraic topology) inclusion map; **—енный** *a.* enclosed, etc., *see* **вкладывать; —енный один в другой** nested; **—ить** *see* **вкладывать.**

вломиться *v.* break in; burst in.

в.л.р. *abbr.* (**весьма легко растворимо**) readily soluble.

вм. *abbr.* (**вместе; вместо**); **ВМ** *abbr.* (**воздушная масса**) air mass; (**вычислительная машина**) computer; **в/м** *abbr.* (**вольт на метр**) volt per meter, V/m.

вмаз/ать, —ывать *v.* cement in, putty in; embed, fix in; **—ка** *f.,* **—ывание** *n.* cementing in, etc., *see v.*

вматывать *v.* roll up (in), wind in.

вмёл *past m. sing. of* **вмести.**

вмен/ить, —ять *v.* impute, charge (with); **—яемый** *a.* responsible, of sound mind.

вмерзать *v.* freeze in.

вмёрзнуть *see* **вмерзать.**

вмесить *v.* knead in, mix in.

вместе *adv.* together, collectedly, jointly; combined, along (with); **в. с тем** in addition to that, also, moreover; at the same time.

вмести *v.* sweep in.

вмести/лище *n.* receptacle, reservoir, tank, container, vessel, cistern; (bot.) conceptacle; **—мость** *f.* (holding) capacity; holding, storage; volume, bulk; (naut.) tonnage; **—мый** *a.* fitting, fitted; embeddable; **—ность** *f.* room(iness), spaciousness; scope; capacity; **—тельный** *a.* roomy, spacious, large, extensive, ample; bulk; high-capacity; **—ть** *see* **вмещать.**

вместо *prep. gen.* instead (of), for, in place (of), in lieu (of); as an alternative (to); **в. того, чтобы** instead of, rather than; **в. этого** instead.

вмётанный *a.* tacked in.

вмет/ать *v.* sweep in; **—ённый** *a.* swept in.

вмётывать *v.* tack in (with thread).

вмеш/анный *a.* mixed in; **—ательство** *n.* interference, intervention; **—енный** *a.* kneaded in; **—ивание** *n.* mixing in; **—(ив)ать** *v.* mix in, stir in; interfere, intervene, interpose; involve, implicate (in); **—(ив)аться** *v.* be mixed in; interfere, intervene, meddle (in); step (in).

вмещ/ать *v.* hold, contain, enclose, accommodate, house; encompass; put in, insert, embed; go (into); seat; **—аться** *v.* go in, fit in, find room; **—ающий** *a.* holding, etc., *see v.;* (country) rock; **—ение** *n.* holding, etc., *see v.;* (math.) embedding; **—ённый** *a.* held, etc., *see v.*

вмиг *adv.* in a flash, in an instant.

вминать *v.* press in, dent, crumple.

вмокрую *adv.* wet.

вмонтиров/анный *a.* built in, etc., *see v.;* stationary; **—ать** *v.* build in, mount in, install, fix, fit in; incorporate; switch into.

вмороженный *a.* frozen in.

ВМП *abbr.* [(**метод**) **вращающегося магнитного поля**] rotating magnetic field method (of geophysical exploration).

ВМС *abbr.* (**военно-морские силы**) naval forces; (**высокомолекулярные соединения**) macromolecular compounds.

ВМТ, в.м.т. *abbr.* (**верхняя мёртвая точка**) upper dead center.

вмуров/анный *a.* immured, etc., *see v.;* **—(ыв)ать** *v.* immure, embed; wall in.

вмыван/ие *n.* (soil) illuviation, inwash; **горизонт —ия** illuvial horizon.

вмят/ина, —ость *f.* hollow, dent, depression; impression; (tool) mark; nick; (rolling) pinchers; **—ый** *a.* pressed in, etc., *see v.;* **—ь** *v.* press in, (in)dent; depress; crumple in; knead in.

ВН *abbr.* (**вакуум-насос**) vacuum pump.

в.н. *abbr.* (**высокое напряжение**) high tension.

внавал(ку) *see* **внасыпную**.

внаём, внаймы *adv.* to let, to rent.

внакладку *see* **внахлёстку**.

внаклон *adv.* on a slant, at an angle.

внакрой, внапуск *see* **внахлёстку**.

внасыпную *adv.* bulk; **груз в.** bulk load, bulk freight.

внахлёстку *adv.* lap(ped), overlap(ped); **соединение в.** lap joint.

вначале *adv.* at the beginning, at first, to start (or begin) with, initially.

в н. вр. *abbr.* (**в настоящее время**) now, at present.

вне *prep. gen.* out of, outside (of), beyond, in addition (to); without; exterior (to), external (to); off; regardless of, without regard (for); *prefix* extra—, ex-; **—атмосферный** *a.* (astr.) extra-atmospheric; **—аэродромный** *a.* cross-country (flight); **—больничный** *a.* out (patient); home (care); **—брюшинный** *a.* (anat.) extraperitoneal; **—вписанный** *a.* circumscribed; **—галактический** *a.* (astr.) extragalactic; **—городской** *a.* out-of-town, suburban.

внедр/ение *n.* introduction, etc., *see v.;* (geol.) intrusion; **раствор —ения** interstitial solution; **соединение —ения** intercalation compound; **—ённый** *a.* introduced, etc., *see v.;* interstitial (atom); **—ить, —ять** *v.* introduce, inject; instill, inculcate, implant, embed; intrude, invade, penetrate; promote, adopt (system); implement; integrate; immerse; insert; **—иться, —яться** *v.* penetrate, invade; take root; strike; **—яющийся** *a.* invasive; **—яющийся вид** invader.

внежелудочковый *a.* (anat.) extraventricular.

внезапн/о *adv.* suddenly, unexpectedly; **в. возникший** *a.* accidental; **—ость** *f.* suddenness, surprise; **—ый** *a.* sudden, unexpected, abrupt; random, unpredictable; catastrophic.

вне/зародышевый *a.* (zool.) extraembryonic; **—земной** *a.* extraterrestrial, outer space; **—интегральный** *a.* (math.) integrated; **—ионосферный** *a.* beyond the ionosphere; **—капсульный** *a.* extracapsular; **—кишечный** *a.* (med.) abenteric; **—клеточный** *a.* (biol.) extracellular; **—конкурентный** *a.* noncompetitive; **—контрольный** *a.* out of control; **—корневая подкормка** (agr.) leaf feeding; **—корневое удобрение** leaf-feeding spray; **—лёгочный** *a.* (anat.) extrapulmonary; **—маточный** *a.* extrauterine; ectopic (pregnancy); **—меридианный** *a.* extrameridional; **—осевой** *a.* extra-axial, abaxial; off-axis (effect, etc.); side (blow); **—очередной** *a.* extra(ordinary), special; top-priority; out of order; **—очерёдность** *f.* top priority.

вне/пазушный *a.* (bot.) extra-axillary; **—печёночный** *a.* (anat.) extrahepatic; **—пиковый** *a.* off-peak (load); **—планетный** *a.* extraplanetary; **—плановый** *a.* unplanned, unscheduled; **—плодник** *m.* (bot.) exocarp, epicarp; **—плодный** *a.* epicarpic; **—плоскостный** *a.* out-of-plane, extraplanar; **—пойменный** *a.* unflooded; **—почечный** *a.* (anat.) extrarenal.

внесен/ие *n.* introduction, etc., *see* **вносить**; entry; payment, deposit; placement (of fertilizer); distribution (of pesticides); **в. платы** payment; **машина для —ия** feeder, injector.

внесённый introduced, etc., *see* **вносить**.

вне/сердечный *a.* (anat.) extracardial; **—системный** *a.* arbitrary (unit); **—солнечный** *a.* extrasolar; **—сосудистый** *a.* (anat.) extravascular; **—стеночный** *a.* extramural.

внести *see* **вносить**.

вне/студийный *a.* outside (the studio), outdoor, field; (TV) live; **—суставной** *a.* (anat.) abarticular, extraarticular; **—тропический** *a.* extratropical; **—уличный** *a.* underground or elevated (train); **—утробный** *a.* (anat.) extrauterine; **—фокальный** *a.* extrafocal; **—цветковый** *a.* (bot.) extrafloral; **—центренный** *a.* noncentral; eccentric; **—черепной** *a.* (anat.) extracranial.

внеш— *see* **внешний**.

вне/шкальный *a.* inferred (zero); **—школьный** *a.* extramural (education); extracurricular.

внешне *adv. and prefix* externally, outwardly, in appearance; foreign; **—образованный** *a.* externally generated; **—секреторный** *a.* exocrine (gland); **—торговый** *a.* foreign trade.

внешн/ий *a.* external, exterior, outer, outside, extrinsic; outward, out- (side); environmental; circumambient, surrounding; exogenous; ecto—; overall (size); outdoor; extraneous; surface, superficial; fringe (zone); outboard (engine); foreign (trade); male (thread); **в. вид** appearance; **в. паразит** ectoparasite; **—ее оборудование** (comp.) peripherals; **—ие контакты, —ие связи** public relations; **—ие члены** (math.) extremes; **—яя среда** environment; **—ей среды** environmental; **—ость** *f.* exterior, outside, (outward) form, appearance, aspect, look; external parts; superficiality.

внештатный *a.* not on the permanent staff; part-time, free-lance.

внешторг— *prefix* foreign trade.

вне/щёчный *a.* (anat.) extrabuccal; **—ядерный** *a.* extranuclear; (chem.) exocyclic; **—ярусный** *a.* non-layered.

ВНЗ *abbr.* (**водонефтяная зона**) oil-water zone.

вниз *adv.* down(wards), underneath; **в. по** down; **в. по склону, в под гору** downhill; **направленный в.** downward; **ход в.** descent, down stroke (of piston).

внизу *adv.* beneath, below, under(neath), at the foot (of), at the bottom (of); lower (position); downstairs.

ВНИИ . . . [**Всероссийский** (or **Всесоюзный**) **научно-исследовательский институт**] All-Russian (or All-Union) Scientific Research Institute (of).

вник/ать, —нуть *v.* investigate, examine, scrutinize, see into.

ВНИЛ . . . *abbr.* [**Всероссийская** (or **Всесоюзная**) **научно-исследовательская лаборатория**] All-Russian (or All-Union) Research Laboratory (of).

вниман/ие *n.* attention, notice, regard, care; emphasis; **достойный —ия** noteworthy; **обращать в.** *v.* pay attention, notice, give consideration (to), consider; concentrate (on); **обращать в. на себя** attract attention; **предлагать —ию** *v.* call attention (to), propose; **принимая во в.** in view (of the fact that), in consideration (of), considering (that), taking into account; **не принимая во в.** disregarding, ignoring, neglecting; **приняв всё во в.** all things considered.

внимат/ельно *adv.* attentively; **—ельность** *f.* attentiveness; **—ельный** *a.* attentive, intent, careful, close; **—ь** *v.* follow, watch.

ВНИТО . . . , **внито—** *abbr.* [**Всероссийское** (or **Всесоюзное**) **научное инженерное техническое об-**

щество . . .] All-Russian (or All-Union) Scientific Engineering and Technical Society (of).

ВНК *abbr.* (**водонефтяной контакт**) oil-water contact.

вновь *adv.* again, afresh, freshly, anew, re—, once more; newly, recently; **соединять(ся) в.** *v.* recombine.

вно/с *m.* introduction, etc., *see v.;* importation; **—симый** *a.* introduced, etc., *see v.;* **—ситель** *m.* importer; **—сить** *v.* introduce, bring in, carry in, import; run in, add; insert, enter, list; pay in, contribute; (elec.) couple (into); make (a change); place, apply (fertilizer); **—ска** *see* **внос;** entry; **—ся** *pr. ger.* introducing, if we introduce; **—сящий** *a.* introducing, etc., *see v.;* contributory; **—шение** *see* **внос.**

вну— *see* **внутренний.**

внук *m.* grandson.

внуран *see* **меркаптофос.**

внутр. *abbr.* (**внутренний**) internal.

внутренне *adv. and prefix* inwardly, intrinsically; inside, internal, endo—; **—раковинные** *pl.* (mal.) Endocochlia; **—шлифовальный станок** internal grinder.

внутренн/ий *a.* inner, inside, interior, internal, endo—; inward, in-(side); inherent, intrinsic, self—; indoor; inland (water); epeiric (sea); female (thread); domestic, home (trade); **в. паразит** endoparasite; **в. фактор** intrinsic factor; **ее горение** internal combustion; **—ей секреции** endocrine (gland); **—яя часть** interior; **—о** *see* **внутренне.**

внутренност/ный *a.* (anat.) visceral; internal; splanchnic (nerve); **—ь** *f.* interior; (angular) domain, region; **—и** *pl.* internal organs, viscera, guts, entrails.

внутреродность *f.* (math.) endomorphism.

внутри *adv. and prep. gen.* in(side), within; *prefix* intra—, endo—; **находящийся в.** *a.* internal; **—аптечная заготовка** drugstore-filled prescription; **—артериальный** *a.* (anat.) endarterial, intra-arterial; **—атомный** *a.* intra-atomic; nuclear (energy, etc.); **—блочный** *a.* intrablock; **—больничный** *a.* (intra)hospital; nosocomial (disease); **—гнездник** *m.* (bot.) endothecium; **—годовой** *a.* annual; **—городская миграция** commuting; **—горный** *a.* (geol.) intermontane; **гортанный** *a.* (anat.) intralaryngeal, endolaryngeal; **—государственный** *a.* national, domestic; **—грудной** *a.* (anat.) intrathoracic; **—долевой** *a.* intralobar; **—дольковый** *a.* intralobular; **—железный** *a.* intraglandular; **—желудочковый** *a.* intraventricular; **—желудочный** *a.* intragastric; **—жизненный** *a.* (biol.) intrabiontic; **—заводский** *a.* inplant, departmental; factory; **—зёренный** *a.* intragranular; **—капсульный** *a.* intracapsular; **—квартальный коллектор** submain sewer; **—клеточный** *a.* (cyt.) intracellular, endocellular; cell(ular); endo—(enzyme); **—книжный** *a.* in books; **—кожный** *a.* intracutaneous, intradermal; skin (test).

внутрикомплексн/о циклизованный *a.* chelated; **—ый** *a.* chelate (compound); **—ый цикл** chelate ring.

внутри/контурный *a.* internal, contour, center-to-edge (flooding); **—координированный** *a.* chelated; **—костный** *a.* (anat.) intraosseous; **—кристаллический** *a.* intracrystalline; **—лёгочный** *a.* (anat.) intrapulmonary; **—лежащий** *a.* internal, inner, interior; **—массовый** *a.* (meteor.) air-mass.

внутри/материковый *a.* inland (ice); **—маточный** *a.* (anat.) intrauterine; **—мозговой** *a.* intracerebral; **—молекулярный** *a.* intramolecular; **—мышечный** *a.* intramuscular; **—организменная селекция** (cyt.) intraselection; **—охлаждённый** *a.* internally cooled; **—пазовый** *a.* inner; **—печёночный** *a.* (anat.) intrahepatic; **—пластовый** *a.* in situ (combustion); **—пле-**

—вральный *a.* (anat.) intrapleural; **—плодник** *m.* (bot.) endocarp; **—породное разведение** inbreeding; **—порошицевые** *pl.* (zool.) Kamptozoa; **—почвенный** *a.* subsoil, internal (erosion); **—почечный** *a.* intrarenal; **—пузырный** *a.* intravesical; **—растительный** *a.* systemic (insecticide); **—реакторный** *a.* (nucl.) in-pile (test); in-core (cable); **—родовой** *a.* intrageneric; **—рядный** *a.* in row.

внутри/связочный *a.* (anat.) intraligamentous; **—секреторный** *a.* (physiol.) endocrine; **—сердечный** *a.* (anat.) endocardial; **—системный** *a.* intrasystem, internal; **—солевой** *a.* intrasalt; **—сортовой** *a.* intravarietal; **—сосудистый** *a.* (biol.) intravascular; **—союзный** *a.* domestic (in USSR); **—стенный** *a.* (anat.) intraparietal; **—сточный** *a.* intramural; **—суставной** *a.* intra-articular; **—суточный** *a.* diurnal; **—тазовый** *a.* (anat.) intrapelvic, endopelvic; **—тканевый** *a.* (hist.) interstitial; tissue.

внутри/усадебный *a.* within the farmstead; **—утробный** *a.* (anat.) intrauterine; fetal (death); prenatal (mortality); **—ушной** *a.* entotic, intra-aural; **—фермский** *a.* within or on the farm; **—формационный** *a.* (geol.) intraformational; **—хозяйственный** *a.* intradepartmental; within the enterprise; **—цеховой** *a.* intrashop, department(al); **—циклический** *a.* transannular (tautomerism); **—черепной** *a.* (anat.) intracranial; **—шейный** *a.* endocervical; **—шлифовальный станок** internal grinder; **—ядерный** *a.* intranuclear; nuclear (energy).

внутро *n.* inside(s), interior.

внутрь *adv. and prep. gen.* in, inside, inward(s), into, toward the interior; **в. страны** inland; **для приёма в.** (med.) oral.

внуш/аемость *f.* suggestibility; **—ать, —нть** *v.* suggest, prompt, inspire, instill, fill (with); impress; **—ение** *n.* suggestion; **—енный** *a.* suggested; **—нтельный** *a.* imposing, impressive.

внюх(ив)аться *v.* identify an odor.

внят/ность *f.* audibility, distinctness, intelligibility; **—ный** *a.* audible, distinct, intelligible; **—ь** *v.* pay attention (to).

во *see* **в; во—** *see* **в—** *before* й *and* о.

воб/бегонг *m.* (ichth.) wobbegong (*Orectolobus*); **—ла** *f.* (ichth.) vobla, Caspian roach (*Rutilus rutilus*).

вобрать *v.* absorb, imbibe; inhale; **—ся** *v.* soak in, be absorbed; ooze, infiltrate.

вобуляция *f.* (electron.) wobble, wobbulation.

вобьёт *fut. 3 sing. of* **вбить.**

вовек(и) *adv.* eternally, everlastingly.

вовле/кать *v.* draw in, implicate, involve; entrap, entrain; **—каться в реакцию** react; **—чение** *n.* implication, involvement; entrapment, entrainment; **—чённый** *a.* drawn in, etc., *see v.;* **—чь** *see* **вовлекать.**

во/вне *adv.* beyond, outside; **—внутрь** *see* **внутрь; —время** *adv.* in or on time; **—все** *adv.* at all; completely, entirely; **—все нет** not at all; **—всю** *adv.* to the utmost; **-вторых** *adv.* secondly, in the second place.

вовча *f.* (bot.) restharrow (*Ononis*).

вовьёт *fut. 3 sing. of* **ввить.**

вогезит *m.* (petr.) vogesite.

Вогезы the Vosges (mountains).

вогмер *m.* ribbonfish (*Trachipterus*); **—овые** *pl.* Trachipteridae.

вогнать *see* **вгонять.**

вогнут/о *prefix* concavo—, hollow; **—овыпуклый** *a.* concavo-convex; **—ость** *f.* concavity; **—ый** *a.* concave, bent in; curved; caved-in; sway (back); **—ое место** dent; **—ь** *v.* bend in, curve in; (math.) deform.

вод. *abbr.* (**водяной**) water, aqueous.

вод/а *f.* water; **в —е** waterborne (radioactivity); **выделение —ы** dehydration; **малая в.** low tide; **полная в.** high tide; **присоединение —ы** hydration; **сила —ы** water power; **содержащий —у** hydrated; **удалять —у** *v.* dehydrate.

водвор/ить, —ять *v.* install; (re)establish; send back; put back; settle.

водил/ка *f.* traverse guide; **—о** *n.* guide pole; carrier; (av.) tow bar.

вод/итель *m.* driver, operator; teamster; **—ить** *v.* lead, conduct, pass (over); drive, steer, operate, navigate; keep up (association); (agr.) raise, breed; **—иться** *v.* be (found), live, inhabit; breed; associate (with); be customary; **как —ится** as usual.

водка *f.* vodka; **крепкая в.** aqua fortis, nitric acid; **царская в.** aqua regia, nitrohydrochloric acid.

водлозерский *a.* (geog.) Vodlozero.

водн. *abbr.* (**водный**) water, aqueous.

водник *m.* water-transport worker; water reservoir.

водно— *prefix* water, aqueous; *see also under* **водо—**; **-воздушный** *a.* water-air; **—ледниковый** *a.* (geol.) fluvio-glacial; **—листниковые** *pl.* (bot.) Hydrophyllaceae; **—масляный** *a.* water-oil; **в.-минеральный обмен** (biol.) water and electrolyte balance; **—ореховые** *pl.* (bot.) Hydrocariaceae; **—растворимый** *a.* water-soluble; **—сосудистый** *a.* water-vascular; **—спиртовой** *a.* water-alcohol; **—сть** *f.* water content; **—транспортный** *a.* water-transport.

водн/ый *a.* water, aqueous, hydrous, hydrated; aquatic; water-borne; *suffix* **—hydrate; в. остаток** hydroxyl; **в. путь** waterway; **в. раствор** aqueous solution; **—ая культура** hydroponics; **—ая окись** hydroxide; **—ая соль** hydrated salt; **—ая энергия** water power; **инженер —ого хозяйства** hydraulic engineer.

водо— *prefix* water, aqua—, hydro—, hydraulic; **—аккумулирующий** *a.* water-storage; **—бой** *m.,* **—бойный** *a.* fountain, jet; (hydr.) apron; (min.) monitor; **—бойная стенка** apron; **—боязнь** *f.* (med.) hydrophobia, rabies; **—вместилище** *n.* reservoir; **—вод** *m.* water line, water conduit; waterway, channel; **—водяной** *a.* water-moderated, water-cooled (reactor); water-to-water (heat exchanger); **—воз** *m.* water carrier; **—возный** *a.* water(-carrying).

водоворот *m.* whirl(pool), swirl, eddy, vortex; **—ный** *a.* whirling, vorticose, vortical.

водовыпуск *m.* water outlet, water discharge; **—ной кран** water faucet; **—ная труба** drain.

водо/гонное средство (pharm.) hydragogue; **—грейка** *f.* water heater; **—грейный** *a.* water-heating; hot-water (boiler); **—действующий** *a.* hydraulic; water (wheel); **—делитель** *m.* water divider or separator.

водоём *m.* reservoir, cistern, (water) tank, basin, well, body of water; pond, impound; **—кий** water-retaining; **—кость** *f.* water-retaining capacity; reservoir capacity; **—ный** *a. of* **водоём.**

водозабор *m.,* **—ный** *a.* water supply, water intake; water withdrawal, water consumption; water (well); **—ник** *m.* water scoop.

водо/защитный *a.* waterproof; protective (forest); **—защищённый** *a.* watertight, waterproof; (elec.) hoseproof; **—зор** *m.* hydroscope; **—измерительный** *a.* water-metering; **—изме́щение** *n.* (naut.) displacement; **—источник** *m.* water source; **—канализация** *f.* sewer system; **—качальный** *a.* water-pumping; **—качка** *f.* water tower; water supply station, pumping station; **—кольцевой** *a.* liquid-piston (pump); **—крас**

m. (bot.) frogbit (*Hydrocharis morsus-ranae*); **—красовые** *pl.* Hydrocharitaceae.

водолаз *m.* diver; **в.-акваланги́ст** *m.* scuba diver; **—а** *f.,* **—ный шлем** diving helmet; **—ничать** *v.* be a diver; **—ный** *a.* diving, diver's.

водолей *m.* water boat, water carrier; (astr.) Aquarius.

водо/лечебный *a.* (med.) hydropahtic; **—лечение** *n.* hydropathy, hydrotherapy, water cure; **—листниковые** *pl.* (bot.) Hydrophyllaceae; **—люб** *m.* water scavenger beetle; (bot.) Hydrocotyle; **болотный —люб** bulrush (*Scirpus*); **—любивый** *a.* water-loving, hydrophilous; **—маслозаправщик** *m.* (av.) water and oil servicing truck.

водомер *m.* water (flow) gage, water meter; **—ный** *a.* water measuring, gage; **—ный пост** water-gage (station); **—ная рейка** depth stick; **—ное стекло.**

водо/мёт *m.,* **—мётный** *a.* jet, fountain; water jet (propeller); monitor; **—мойна, —мойня** *f.* gully, ravine; **—нагреватель** *m.* water heater; **—наливной** *a.* water-filling; **—напорный** *a.* water-pressure, hydrostatic pressure; water (tower); hydraulic (pump).

водонасыщен/ие *n.* saturation with water; **—ный** *a.* water-saturated; waterlogged.

водонепро/мокаемость, —ницаемость *f.* waterproofness; **—никаемый, —ницаемый** *a.* waterproof, impervious (to water), water tight.

водо/нефтяной *a.* water-oil (ratio); **—носность** *f.* rate of stream flow; **—носный** *a.* water-bearing, aquiferous; **—носный горизонт** *or* **слой** aquifer, water-bearing stratum; **—обеспеченность** *f.* (available) water supply; **—обильность** *f.* abundance of water; **—обильный** *a.* with an abundant water supply; **—обмен** *m.* replacement, turnover (of water); **коэффициент —обмена** rate of replacement; **—оборот** *m.* water cycle; **—описание** *n.* hydrography; **—опресни́тель** *m.* water-distilling unit; **—опыляемый** *a.* (bot.) hydrophilous; **—отведение** *n.* overflow drainage, water disposal.

водоотвод *m.* drainage (system), overflow; water ditch; waterway; **—ный** *a.* drain(age), overflow, waste, discharge; **—ное отверстие** drain; **—чик** *m.* steam trap.

водо/отдача *f.* water yield; water loss; **—отделитель** *m.* water separator or trap; dehydrator; **—отлив** *m.* drainage, draining, pumping out; **—отливный** *a.* water-removing, drain; pumping (shaft); bilge (pump); **—отнимающий** *a.* dehydrating; **—отстойник** *m.* water sedimentation tank; **—отталкивающий** *a.* water-repellent, hydrophobe; **—охладитель** *m.* water cooler, water-cooling system; **—охладительный** *a.* water-cooling; **—охлаждаемый** *a.* water-cooled; **—охранный** *a.* water-conservation.

водоочи/ститель *m.* water purifier; water treatment plant; **—стительный, —стной** *a.* water-purifying; **—стительная автоустановка** mobile water purifier; **—стка** *f.,* **—щение** *n.* water purification, water treatment.

водо/пад *m.,* **—падный** *a.* waterfall, falls, cascade; **линия —падов** (geol.) fall line; **—падь** *f.* decrease of water; **—перепускная труба** water circulator; **—перехватывающий** *a.* drainage, runoff control (terrace); **—плавающий** *a.* (biol.) planktonic; floating; water (fowl); **—плавающие тела** plankton; **—плавный** *a.* floated; **—плёночный** *a.* rotary jet (pump).

водопоглощ/аемость *f.* water-absorbing capacity; **—ающий** *a.* water-absorbing, hygroscopic; **—ение** *n.* water absorption.

водо/подача *f.* water supply **—подготовительный** *a.,*

—**подготовка** *f.* water treatment; —**подогреватель** *m.* water heater; —**подпорный** *a.* water-retaining.

водоподъём *m.* water lifting, water pumping; —**ник** *m.* water lift; —**ный** *a.* water-lifting, water-pumping; hydraulic (ram); ascending (pipe); —**ная способность** capillarity (of soil).

водопо/ение *n.* watering (of livestock); —**илка** *f.* drinking bowl; water trough; —**й** *m.* watering place, water hole; watering, drinking; —**йка** *see* **водопоилка;** —**йный** *a.* watering, drinking; water hole.

водо/полье *n.* flood, high water; overflow; —**пользование** *n.* water consumption; water management; water utilization; —**пользователь** *m.* water consumer; —**понижение** *n.* (geol.) drop in water table; (water) drawdown, depression; —**потребитель** *m.* water consumer; —**потребление** *n.* water consumption; water requirements; water use; —**потребность** *f.* water requirements; —**приводный канал** raceway.

водоприём *m.* water inflow; —**ник** *m.,* —**ный** *a.* water intake; catch water; —**ный колодец** drain, sump; —**ная канава** race, flume.

водоприток *m.* (petrol.) water influx.

водопробный кран gage cock (of boiler).

водопровод *m.* water pipe, water supply line, water conduit; water supply; running water; (anat.) aqueduct(us); —**ец** *m.* hydraulic engineer; —**имость** *f.* water permeability (of soil): —**но-канализационный** *a.* water-and-sewage; —**но-канализационная сеть** plumbing; —**ность** *f.* water conductivity (of soil); —**ный** *a.* water-conducting; water supply; tap (water); water (faucet); —**ная магистраль** water main; —**ная система** water supply system; —**ная станция, —ные сооружения** water works, water supply station; —**ная труба** water pipe, water supply line; —**чик** *m.* plumber; —**ящий** *a.* water-conducting; —**ящий лоток** headrace.

водопроницаем/ость *f.* water permeability; —**ый** *a.* permeable (to water).

водо/пропускливость *f.* water permeability (of soil); —**пропускной** *a.* water-permeable; —**прочность** *f.* resistance to water; —**прочный** *a.* water-resistant, water-stable; waterproof; —**проявление** *n.* water seepage; —**пуск** *m.,* —**пускной** *a.* overflow, overspill; —**пылесос** *m.* wet-dry suction cleaner.

водоразбор *m.* water distribution; —**ный** *a.* water supply; —**ный кран** hydrant.

водо/раздатчик *m.* water dispenser; —**раздел** *m.* watershed, water divide; interfluve (area); —**раздельный** *a.* divide, dividing; summit; —**распределитель** *m.* water distributor.

водораспыл/ение *n.* water spraying, water atomization; —**итель** *m.* water sprayer, water atomizer; —**ительный** *a.* water-spray; spray (nozzle).

водораствори/ость *f.* solubility in water; —**ый** *a.* water-soluble.

водо/рез *m.* cutwater (of ship or bridge); (orn.) skimmer [*R(h)ynchops*]; —**ы** *pl.* R(h)ynchopidae; —**ресурсный** *a.* water resource.

водород *m.* hydrogen, H; **перекись —а** hydrogen peroxide; **сверхтяжёлый в.** tritium; **сернистый в.** hydrogen sulfide; **хлористый в.** hydrogen chloride.

водород/истый *a.* hydrogen; hydride (of); **в. натрий** sodium hydride; —**катионирование** *n.* hydrogen zeolite softening; —**но-** *prefix* hydrogen; —**но-ионный показатель** pH value; —**но-кислородный** *a.* oxyhydrogen; —**ный** *a.* hydrogen(ous); —**ный показатель** pH value, hydrogen ion concentration.

водородо/воздушный *a.* hydrogen-air; —**кислородный** *a.* oxyhydrogen; —**подобный** *a.* hydrogen-like, hydrogenic.

водородосернисто/кислый *a.* hydrosulfurous acid; hydrosulfite (of); **в. натрий, —натриевая соль** sodium hydrosulfite; —**кислая соль** hydrosulfite.

водородосернист/ый *a.* hydrosulfurous; hydrosulfide (of); **в. натрий** sodium hydrosulfide; —**ая кислота** hydrosulfurous acid, hyposulfurous acid; **соль —ой кислоты** hydrosulfite.

водород/осодержание *n.* hydrogen content; —**отропия** *f.* hydrogenotropy; —**содержащий** *a.* hydrogenous, hydrogen-containing.

водороина *f.* gully.

водоросл/евидный *a.* (bot.) alga-like, fucoid; —**евый** *a.* algal; —**ь** *f.* alga; —**и** *pl.* algae; **бурые —и** Phaephyta; **зелёные —и** Chlorophyceae; Chlorophyta; **красные —и** Rhodophyta; **синезелёные —и, цианоые —и** Cyanophyceae; **морская —ь** seaweed.

водосбор *m.* (geol.) catchment (area), drainage basin or system; reservoir; (bot.) Aquilegia; —**ник** *m.* catchment basin; (water) header; water tank; (min.) water sump; —**ный** *a.* drainage (area, basin), catchment (basin); —**ный бассейн** *see* **водосбор;** —**ная площадь** watershed; catchment basin.

водосброс *m.,* —**ный** *a.* (hydr.) spillway; flood gates; discharge weir.

водо/свинка *f.* (mam.) capybara (*Hydrochaeris*); —**свинки, —свинковые** *pl.* Hydrochaeridae; —**связный** *a.* water-bound; —**скат** *m.* (river) rapids; —**скоп** *m.* reservoir; accumulation of water.

водослив *m.,* —**ный** *a.* overflow, runoff, spillway, weir; —**ный порог, —ная плотина** (hydr.) spillway; weir; —**ный штрек** (drift at) water level.

водо/снабжающий *a.* water-supplying; —**снабжение** *n.* water supply, water service, water works; —**содержание** *n.* water content; —**содержащий** *a.* water-bearing; water-containing, hydrated; —**спуск** *m.,* —**спускной** *a.* floodgate, drain (weir), outlet.

водостойк/ий *a.* water-resistant, waterproof; —**ость** *f.* water resistance, stability in water, water-resisting property.

водосто/к *m.* drain, runoff; (geol.) catchment area; sewage system; —**чный** *a.* drain, catch(ment); —**чный жёлоб** gutter; —**чный колодец** catch pit; —**чная канава** gully, wash; drainage ditch.

водо/струйный *a.* water-jet; **в. насос** water-jet pump; aspirator; —**тек** *m.,* —**течь** *f.* current of water; leak; —**терапия** *f.* hydrotherapy; —**ток** *m.* water course, current, stream; waterway, channel; —**точина** *f.* leak; —**точный** *a.* flowing, running; —**трубный котёл** water-tube boiler; —**тяга** *f.* drain pipe; —**удержание** *n.* water retention; —**удерживающий** *a.* water-retaining.

водоуказатель *m.,* —**ный прибор, —ное стекло** water gage.

водо/улучшающее средство water conditioner; —**умягчение** *n.* water softening; —**умягчитель** *m.* water softener.

водоупор *m.* (geol.) water-confining bed or stratum; —**ность** *f.* water resistance; —**ный** *a.* water-resistant, waterproof; impermeable, impervious.

водоустойчивый *see* **водоупорный.**

водо/хозяйственный *a.* hydroeconomic; water-management; water (district); **в. кадастр** inventory of water resources and users; —**хозяйство** *n.* water management, water distribution system; aquiculture; —**хра-**

нилище *n.* water storage; reservoir; cistern; tank; —**черпалка** *f.* pump; —**черпальный** *a.* water-drawing, pumping; —**черпание** *n.* drawing of water; —**чистилище** *n.* filtering basin.

водочный *a.* vodka; **в. завод** distillery; **в. огарок** niter cake.

водру/жать, —зить *v.* erect, set up.

вод. ст. *abbr.* (**водяной столб**).

водуотнимающий *a.* dehydrating.

воды *gen. and pl. of* **вода**; waters, stretch of water; **сточные в.** sewage.

водяник/а *f.* (bot.) crowberry (*Empetrum*); —**овые** *pl.* Empetraceae.

водянист/ость *f.* wateriness; (med.) serosity; abundance of water; —**ый** *a.* watery, aqueous, hydrated; (med.) serous; sea (blue).

водянка *f.* (med.) dropsy, hydrops; water spider (*Argyroneta aquatica*); (bot.) *see* **водяника**; **в. (головного) мозга** (med.) hydrocephalus; **в. почек** hydronephrosis; **в. яичка** hydrocele.

водян/ой *a.* water, aqueous; aquatic; hydraulic; hot-water (bath; heat); **в. газ** water gas; **в. затвор** hydraulic seal; **в. пар** steam, water vapor; **в. столб** water column; water gage; —**ая сила** water power; —**ая щель** (bot.) hydrathode; —**ое число** water equivalent, thermal capacity.

водяночный *a. of* **водянка**; (med.) dropsical, hydropic; **в. отёк** dropsy.

водящ/ий *a.* leading, guiding; —**ее приспособление** guide, carrier.

воевать *v.* fight, wage war (with).

воедино *adv.* together, jointly.

воен/изация *f.* militarization; —**изированный** *a.* militarized; —**изировать** *v.* militarize; —**инженер** *m.* military engineer; —**мор** *m.* sailor, navy man; **воен.-мор.** *abbr.* (**военноморской**); —**но-** *prefix* military; —**но-воздушный** *a.* air (force); —**но-врачебный** *a.* military-medical; —**но-инженерный** *a.* military engineering; —**но-морской** *a.* naval; —**но-обязанный** *a.* subject to military service; —**но-пленный** *a.* prisoner of war; —**но-полевой** *a.* field (surgery); —**но-продовольственный** *a.* military food supply; —**но-санитарный** *a.* military medical (service); hospital (train): —**но-служащий** *m.* serviceman; —**но-технический** *a.*, —**но-техническое имущество** materiel; —**но-учебный** *a.* military training, service; —**но-химический** *a.* chemical warfare; —**ный** *a.* military; war; shell (shock); —**ные запасы** munitions; —**порт** *m.* military harbor; —**техник** *m.* military technician.

воет *pr. 3 sing. of* **выть**.

вожа/к *m.*, —**тый** *a.* leader; driver; (zool.) dominant male; (fishing) net warp.

вожд/ение *n.* leading, etc., *see* **водить**; —**ь** *m.* leader, chief.

вожжа *f.*, —**ть** *v.* rein.

воз— *see* **вз—**; *see also under* **вос—**.

воз *m.* wagon, cart, van; cartload.

ВОЗ *abbr.* (**Всемирная организация здравоохранения**) World Health Organization, WHO.

возбуд/имость *f.* excitability; —**имый** *a.* excitable; irritable; —**итель** *m.* stimulant, irritant; incentive, inducer, agent, activator; instigator, originator; stimulus; (anat.) excitor; (elec.) exciter, energizer; (rad.) driver; (med.) pathogen; —**ительный** *a.* stimulating, exciting; exciter; —**ить** *see* **возбуждать**.

возбужд/аемость *f.* excitability, irritability; —**аемый** *a.* excitable, excitatory; —**аемая энергия** energy input; —**ать** *v.* excite, stimulate, stir, arouse, provoke,

incite, instigate; call forth, awaken, generate (interest); raise (questions); set up; activate, induce; create, give rise (to); (elec.) excite, energize; actuate, establish (magnetic field); (rad.) drive; —**аться** *v.* get excited; run up, build itself up; —**ающий** *a.* exciting, etc., *see* *v.;* —**ающее средство** stimulant, excitant.

возбужден/ие *n.* excitement, stimulation, etc., *see* **возбуждать**; (elec.) excitation; (rad.) drive (signal); **обмотка** —**ия** exciting winding; **параллельного** —**ия** shunt-wound (motor); **последовательного** —**ия** series-wound; **реостат** —**ия** (elec.) field rheostat; **смешанное в.** compound excitation; **смешанного** —**ия** compound-wound (motor); **цепь** —**ия** (comp.) energizing circuit.

возбуждённ/ость *f.* excited state; excitement; —**ый** *a.* excited, etc., *see* **возбуждать**.

возве/дение *n.* raising, etc., *see* **возводить**; (math.) raising (to a power), involution; **в. в квадрат** square, squaring; **в. в куб** cube, cubing; **в. в степень** raising to a power, involution; computing powers; —**дённый** *a.* raised, etc., *see* **возводить**; —**дённый в квадрат** squared.

возвеличи(ва)ть *v.* exalt, praise.

возве/сти *see* **возводить**; —**стительный** *a.* giving notice; —**стить, —щать** *v.* announce, give notice, notify, advertise; —**щение** *n.* announcement, notice.

возводить *v.* raise, elevate, erect, build, construct; promote; derive, deduce, trace back (to); **в. в . . . степень** raise to the . . . power.

возврат *m.* return(ing), re-entry; restitution, recovery; recovered material; regression; handling returns; (comp.) reset(ting); link(age); backspace; recycling, reinjection; reimbursement, repayment; (med.) recurrence, relapse; **коэффициент** —**а** resetting ratio; **точка** —**а** inversion point; **в. каретки** carriage return; **в. судалением** destructive backspace; —**имый** *a.* revertible; retrievable, salvageable, recoverable; —**ить** *see* **возвращать**.

возвратно-поступательн/о *adv.* back and forth, to and fro; **двигаться в.** *v.* reciprocate; —**ый** *a.* reciprocating, reciprocal; —**ое движение** reciprocation, reciprocal motion; **совершать** —**ое движение** *v.* reciprocate.

возврат/ость *f.* reflexivity; recurrence; —**ый** *a.* return(ing), recurring, recurrent; reflexive, backward, retrogressive; reflex (ligament); reusable (container); re—, e.g. —**ое рассеяние** rescattering; —**ое скрещивание** (gen.) back-cross.

возвращ/ать *v.* return, bring back, give back, restore, replace; recover; recirculate; re-enter; rest; reimburse, pay back; **в. в процесс** recycle; —**аться** *v.* return, reenter, come back, recur; revert; be back (to), regain, be restored; —**аться назад** regress; —**ающий(ся)** *a.* returning, etc., *see* *v.;* —**аясь** *pr. ger.* returning, if we return to; —**ение** *n.* return(ing), etc., *see* *v.;* reset(ting); recovery; re-entry (into atmosphere); replacement; back stroke (of piston); —**ённый** *a.* returned, etc., *see* *v.*

возвысить *see* **возвышать**.

возвыш/ать *v.* raise, elevate, exalt; increase, add; —**аться** *v.* rise, tower (over); surpass; —**ающийся** *a.* rising; —**ение** *n.* raising, elevation; rise, increase; rising; hill, mound, eminence, protuberance, prominence; —**енность** *f.* height; elevation, rising ground, high ground, upland, hill, eminence, emergence; (geom.) altitude; **плоская** —**енность** plateau, tableland; —**енный** *a.* high, elevated; raised; lofty, majestic, towering.

возглав/ить, —лять *v.* head, be at the head (of), be in charge, lead.

возгнать *see* **возгонять**.

возгон *m.* sublimate; **—ка** *f.,* **—ный, —очный** *a.* sublimation, volatilization; dry distillation; **—яемый** *a.* sublimable; sublimated; **—ять(ся)** *v.* sublimate, sublime, volatilize; **—яющий(ся)** *a.* sublimating, etc., *see v.*

возгор/аемость *f.* inflammability, combustibility; **—аемый** *a.* inflammable, combustible; **—ание** *n.* inflammation, ignition; **—аться, —еться** *v.* ignite, catch fire; **—аться самопроизвольно** be readily combustible; **—ающийся** *a.* inflammable.

возд. *abbr.* (**воздушный**).

возд(ав)ать *v.* render; show; reward, repay, recompense.

воздвиг/ание *n.* erection, raising; **—ать, —нуть** *v.* erect, raise, set up, put up.

воздейств/ие *n.* action, influence, effect; impact; modification; seeding (of clouds); attack; reaction; exposure (to); (aut.) response, input; **в. по производной** rate response; **в. сил** loading; **острое в.** impact; **подвергаться —ию** *v.* be affected (by), be subjected (to), be exposed (to); **—овать** *v.* act (on), influence, affect, attack, react; **—ующий** *a.* acting, etc., *see v.;* **—ующее устройство** actuator; agent.

воздел/анный *a.* cultivated, etc., *see v.;* **—ывание** *n.* cultivation, etc., *see v.;* **—(ыв)ать** *v.* cultivate, till, farm; grow.

воздерж/ание *n.,* **—(ан)ность** *f.* abstinence; **—анный** *a.* abstinent, temperate; restrained; **—(ив)ать** *v.* restrain, repress; **—(ив)аться** *v.* abstain, refrain (from).

воздух *m.* air; **в —е** airborne (radioactivity); **внд с —а** aerial view; **доступ —а** aeration; **кислород —а** atmospheric oxygen; **удаление —а** deaeration; **в.-в.** air-to-air (missile); **в.-земля** air-to-surface.

воздухо— *prefix* air; pneumatic; blast; **—вод** *m.* air duct, air line; **в.-водяной** *a.* air-to-water (heat exchanger); **—воз** *m.* (min.) pneumatic engine; **в.-воздушный** *a.* air-to-air (heat exchanger); **—выпускной** *a.* escape (valve).

воздуходувка *f.* (blast) blower; bellows; ventilator; pneumatic pump; **поршневая в.** air pump; **в.-сушилка** *f.* (atmospheric) dryer; desiccator.

воздуходувн/ый *a.* air-blowing, blast; **в. мех** bellows; **—ая коробка** blast box; **—ая машина** blower; **—ая труба** (met.) blast pipe, tuyere pipe.

воздухо/ёмкость *f.* air content, total pore space; **—заборник** *m.,* **—заборный** *a.* air intake; **—измещение** *n.* air displacement; **—летательные аппараты** aircraft; **—любивый** *a.* (bot.) aerophilous; **—мер** *m.* air (-flow) meter; **—нагревание** *n.* air heating; **—нагреватель** *m.* air heater; (met.) hot-blast stove; **—непроницаемость** *f.* air tightness, impermeability to air; **—непроницаемый** *a.* airtight, airproof, impermeable to air; airlocked.

воздухоносн/ый *a.* air-bearing, aeriferous; pneumatic (bones); **—ая ткань** (bot.) aerenchyma; **—ая трубка** (anat.) trachea.

воздухо/обмен *m.* air exchange; ventilation; **—осушитель** *m.* air dryer; **—отвод** *m.,* **—отводной** *a.* air draw-off, air outlet; **—отводчик** *m.* air bleeder; **—отделитель** *m.* air separator; **—отражатель** *m.* air deflector, air baffle; **—отсасывающий** *a.,* **—отсос** *m.* air ejector, exhaust; **—охладитель** *m.* air cooler; **—охладительный** *a.* air-cooling; **—охлаждаемый** *a.* air-cooled; **—очиститель** *m.* air purifier, air filter; scrubber; air cleaner; **—очистительная система** air purifier; **—очистный** *a.* air pollution control (equipment).

воздухоплав/ание *n.* aeronautics, aerial navigation; aviation; aerostatics; aerostation; **—атель** *m.* aeronaut;

—ательный *a.* aeronautical; aerostatic; **—ательные аппараты** aircraft.

воздухо/подводящий *a.* air-supply, air-feed; **—подготовка** *f.* air cleaning; **—подобный** *a.* air-like, airy; **—подогреватель** *m.* air (pre)heater; **—приводной** *a.* (met.) blast (line); **—приёмник** *m.* air inlet, air scoop, air intake; **—приёмный** *a.* intake.

воздухопровод *m.,* **—ный** *a.* air line, air duct, air pipe, air conduit; **—ящий** *a.* air-conducting.

воздухопроницаем/ость *f.* permeability (to air): **—ый** *a.* permeable, air-penetrable.

воздухоразделительный *a.* air-fractionating.

воздухораспредел/ение *n.* air distribution; **—итель** *m.* air distributor, air manifold; **—ительный** *a.* air distributing.

воздухо/сборник *m.* air collector, air receiver; compressed air tank; **—стойкий** *a.* airproof, air-resistant; **—устойчивость** *f.* stability in air; **—устойчивый** *a.* stable in air; **—эквивалентный** *a.* air-equivalent.

воздушник *m.* air vent.

воздушно— *see* **воздухо—;** **в.-водяной** *a.* air-to-water (heat exchanger); **—гашёный** *a.* air-slaked (lime); **—десантный** *a.* airborne; **—закаливающийся** *a.* (met.) air-hardening; **—камерный** *a.* air-cell (diesel engine); **в.-капельный** *a.* droplet (infection); **—космический** *a.* aerospace; **—охлаждаемый** *a.* air-cooled.

воздушно-реактивный двигатель (air-breathing) jet engine, thermojet; **бескомпрессорный в.-р.** or **прямоточный в.-р. двигатель** ramjet engine.

воздушно/сть *f.* airiness; **—сухой** *a.* air-dry, air-dried, wind-dried; air-seasoned.

воздушн/ый *a.* air; pneumatic (hammer, etc.); aerial, overhead (line, etc.); elevated (train); airborne; open-air (drying); hot-air (heat); (met.) blast; **в. винт** (av.) airscrew, propeller; **в. манометр** blast indicator; **в. мешок** (zool.) air sac; **в. насос** air pump; air compressor; **в. провод** aerial, antenna; aerial line; **в. резервуар** air chamber, air box; (met.) blast box, tuyere box; **в. сифон** air lift, monte-jus; **в. флот** (mil.) air force; **в. шар** balloon; **—ая канатная дорога** cableway; **—ая машина** pneumatic engine; **—ая прослойка** air seal; **—ая сеть** aerial; **—ая яма** air pocket; **—ое сообщение** air route; **—ое сопло** air-blast nozzle; **—ое успокоение** air cushioning; **—ые души** humidifiers.

воздым/ание *n.* rising, etc., *see v.;* rise; uplift; **—ать** *v.* rise; heave, bulge up.

возж/ечь, —игать *v.* kindle, inflame.

воззвать *v.* call, cry; invoke; appeal.

воззрение *n.* view, opinion, outlook.

возимый *a.* portable, mobile (equipment).

возить *v.* convey, transport, carry, cart.

возиться *v.* fuss (over), be busy (with).

возка *f.* carting, carriage, haulage.

возлагать *v.* place, lay, rest (on); confer, bestow; charge, entrust (with).

возле *adv. and prep. gen.* beside, by, near.

возле/жать, —чь *v.* lie, rest, recline.

возложить *see* **возлагать.**

возме/стить, —щать *v.* compensate, make good, make up (for); replace; reimburse; **—щающий** *a.* replacement, compensatory (mortality); **—щение** *n.* compensation; makeup; replacement; substitution; reimbursement.

возможн/о *adv.* possibly, perhaps; it is possible, it might be, it may; **в. скорее** as soon as possible; **(на)сколько в.** as much as possible, as far as possible; **—ость** *f.*

possibility, feasibility, opportunity, chance; —**ости** *pl.* resources, means; potential(ities), opportunities; **давать** —**ость** *v.* enable, allow, permit; **по** —**ости** as far as possible, as . . . as possible, where(ver) possible, if possible; **широкие** —**ости** wide latitude; —**ый** *a.* possible, feasible, conceivable, practicable, potential; probable; —**ое перемещение** virtual displacement.

возмуж/алость *f.* maturity; virility; —**алый** *a.* mature; virile, manly; —**ать** *v.* reach puberty, grow up; be grown-up.

возму/тительный *a.* outrageous, disgraceful, shocking; —**тить,** —**щать** *v.* disturb, perturb; make indignant, exasperate; agitate, stir up; trouble; —**щаться** *v.* be indignant; —**щающий** *a.* disturbing, etc., see *v.;* (elec.) exciting; dynamic (force); —**щающее воздействие** disturbance; —**щение** *n.* disturbance, perturbation; derangement, disorder; trouble; indignation; **по** —**щению** disturbance-stimulated (control); **теория** —**щения** (nucl.) perturbation theory; **угол** —**щений** (av.) Mach angle; —**щённый** *a.* disturbed, etc., see *v.;* turbulent (flow); indignant; —**щённое движение** perturbation.

вознагра/дить, —**ждать** *v.* reward, recompense, compensate; —**ждение** *n.* reward, compensation; fee, —**ждённый** *a.* rewarded.

вознес/ённый *a.* raised; —**ти** *see* **возносить.**

вознещение *n.* reimbursement, indemnity.

возни *gen., etc., of* **возня.**

возник/ать *v.* originate, arise (from); come up, crop up, emerge, appear; develop, result (from); occur, be brought about; —**ающий** *a.* originating, etc., see *v.;* nascent; *suffix* —genous; —**новение** *n.* origination, etc., see *v.;* rise, formation; origin, genesis; initiation, beginning, start, onset; —**нуть** *see* **возникать;** —**ший** *a.* originated, etc., see *v.;* risen.

Возничий *m.* (astr.) Auriga.

возно/сить *v.* raise (up), elevate, uplift; —**шение** *n.* raising, etc., see *v.*

возня *f.* trouble, fuss, care.

возобнов/ить *see* **возобновлять;** —**ление** *n.* regeneration, etc., see *v.;* renewal, resumption; recommencement; return; re—, *e.g.* —**ление леса** reforestation, restocking; second growth; —**ление разряда** restriking a discharge; —**лённый** *a.* regenerated, etc., see *v.;* —**ляемый** *a.* renewable; perpetual (resources); —**лять** *v.* regenerate, renew, restore; restock (forest); resume, proceed (with); reinstate (a patent); —**лять запасы** restock; —**ляющийся** *a.* regenerative.

возовой *a.* of **воз.**

возогн/анный *a.* sublimated; —**ать** *v.* sublimate.

возонавиватель *m.* (hay) loader.

возра/жать, —**зить** *v.* object, take exception (to), contradict; retort, reply, answer; —**жающий** *a.* objecting, etc., see *v.; m.* objector; —**жение** *n.* objection; retort, rejoinder.

возраст *m.* age; stage (of development); **в. по свинцу** lead age; —**ание** *n.* increase, increment, growth, augmentation, rise, gain; enhancement; (math.) slope; **сортировка по** —(comp.) ascending sort; —**ать,** —**и** *v.* increase, grow rise, ascend, augment, accelerate; —**ающий** *a.* increasing, etc., see *v.;* progressive; —**ной** *a.* age, age-group, age-class, age-related, developmental, ontogenetic; presenile (sclerosis); —**ной класс,** —**ная группа** age group; —**но-половой** *a.* age, population (pyramid).

возро/дить, —**ждать** *v.* regenerate, revive, revitalize; restore, renew, reactivate; —**ждающий** *a.* regenerating, etc., see *v.;* regenerative; —**ждающийся** *a.* reappearing; —**ждение** *n.* regeneration, etc., see *v.;* renew-

al, revival, rebirth, renaissance; —**ждённый** *a.* regenerated, etc., *see v.*

возчик *m.* driver, teamster.

возыметь *v.* conceive, form; have (effect).

возьмилка *f.* (fishing) gill net.

возьми(те) *imp. of* **взять.**

воин *m.* soldier, army man; —**ский** *a.* military, army, service; troop (train); —**ская повинность** compulsory military service; —**ственность** *f.* militancy, bellicosity; —**ственный** *a.* militant, belligerent, warlike; martial; —**ство** *n.* army, host; —**ствующий** *a.* militant.

вой *m.* howl(ing), whine, wail.

войдя *pr. ger. of* **войти.**

войло/к *m.* felt(ing); (biol.) tomentum; (root) matting; (forest) floor, litter, mulch; (glass) wool; —**корневой в.** root-hair system; **сбивать в.** *v.* felt; —**кообразный** *a.* felt-like, matted; —**чек** *dim. of* **войлок;** —**чник** *m.* felt maker; —**чноопушённый** *a.* tomentose; —**чный** *a.* felt(ed), matted; tomentose; —**чная болезнь** (phyt.) Rhizoctonia root and stem rot; —**чная ткань** aerial tissue; —**чная трава** (bot.) Cuscuta.

вой/на *f.* war(fare); —**ско** *n.* army; —**ска** *pl.* troops, forces; —**сковой** *a.* army, military.

войти *see* **входить.**

вокабуларий *m.* vocabulary.

вокальный *a.* vocal.

вокеленит *m.* (min.) vauquelenite.

вокзал *m.,* —**ьный** *a.* station, terminal.

вокодер *m.* vocoder, voice coder.

вокруг *adv. and prep. gen.* (a)round, about, on (axis); *prefix* peri—; —**желудочковый** *a.* (anat.) periventricular; —**заднепроходный** *a.* circumanal; —**сосудистый** *a.* perivascular.

вол *m.* bullock, ox.

волан *m.* (text.) fancy roller.

волглый *a.* damp.

волго— *prefix* (geog.) Volga; **в.-балтийский** *a.* Volga-Baltic; —**градский** *a.* Volgograd; **в.-донской** *a.* Volga-Don; **в.-уральский** *a.* Volga-Ural.

волдыр/еватый *a.* covered with blisters; —**ник** *m.* (bot.) campion (*Cucubalus*); —**ный** *a.,* —**ь** *m.* blister, wheal, bleb; **образование** —**ей** blistering.

вол/евой *a.* volition(al); resolute, determined, strong-willed; —**ей** *see under* **воля;** —**ен** *sh. m. of* **вольный.**

волж/анка *f.* (bot.) goat's beard (*Aruncus*); wooly milk cap (*Lactarius torminosus*); —**ский** *a.* (geog.) Volga; —**ско-камский** *a.* Volga-Kama.

воли *gen., etc. of* **воля.**

волк *m.* (mam.) wolf (*Canis lupus*); (ichth.) Black Sea shad (*Alosa kessleri pontica*); (astr.) Lupus; **морской в.** wolffish (*Anarhichas lupus*); —**и** *pl.* (mam.) Caninae; **в.-машина** *f.* (text.) willow; disintegrator, shredder, devil; —**обой** *m.* (bot.) Daphne mezereum; —**бойник** *m.* Aconitum; —**дав** *m.* wolfhound; —**зуб** *m.* (herp.) Lycodon.

волконскоит *m.* (min.) volchonskoite.

волк/орыба *see* **волк, морской;** —**осельдевые** *pl.* (ichth.) wolf herrings (*Chirocentridae*); —**оцвет** (bot.) Laburnum; -**рыба** *f.* (ichth.) spined loach (*Cobitis taenia*).

**волл
астон/ит** *m.* (min.) wollastonite; —**овский** *a.* Wollaston (prism).

волн/а *f.* wave, surge, breaker; **длина** —**ы** wavelength.

волнение *n.* agitation, disturbance; fluctuation; churning, heaving, swell (of sea); waves; sea(s), seaways.

волнист/о— *prefix* wave, wavy, undular; —**олистный** *a.* (bot.) undulifolious; —**ость** *f.* waviness, undulation, sinuosity; ridges, corrugation; ripple (marks); (wood) wavy grain; (met.) buckles; curl (of paper); —**ый** *a.* wavy, undulating, rolling, ripply; curving, sinuous; corrugated (iron); crimped (wire); buckled, warped; ropy (lava; texture).

волно— *prefix* wave, ondo—.

волновать *v.* agitate, disturb, upset, worry; —**ся** *v.* be agitated; worry; rise in waves, billow, surge; ripple, be rough (of water).

волно/видный *see* **волнообразный**; —**вод** *m.*, —**водный** *a.* (rad.) wave guide; —**вой** *a.* wave; wavelength (constant); —**вой кризис** (aerodyn.) shock stall; —**вомеханический** *a.* wave-mechanical; —**гаситель** *m.* wave suppressor; —**граф** *m.* wave recorder; —**искатель** *m.* (rad.) wave detector; —**лом** *m.* breakwater; (naut.) manger board; —**мер** *m.* wavemeter, frequency meter.

волнообраз/ный *a.* wave-like, wavy, undulating, undulatory, ripple; pulsating (current); undulant (fever); **в. изгиб** undulation; —**ная обмотка** (elec.) wave winding; —**ное движение**, —**ование** *n.* undulation; —**ователь** *m.* (rad.) oscillator.

волно/отбойный *a.* sea (wall); —**отвод** *m.* breakwater; (naut.) manger board; —**повышающий** *a.* (rad.) booster; —**поглощение** *n.* wave absorption; —**прибойный** *a.* wave-cut; ripple (marks); —**продуктор** *m.* wave generator; —**рез** *m.* breakwater; cutwater; —**стойкий** *a.* surgeproof; —**указатель**, —**уловитель** *m.* (rad.) wave detector; —**устойчивость** *f.* wave resistance.

волну/ха, —**шка** *f.* (bot.) sharp agaric (*Lactarius torminosus*).

волнующий *pr. act. part. of* **волновать.**

волны *gen. and pl. of* **волна.**

волнянка *f.* tussock moth.

волов/ий *a.* ox(en); —**ик** *m.* (bot.) bugloss (*Anchusa*); —**ина** *f.* ox hide; —**ня** *f.* ox barn; —**ья птица** cowbird; —**ья трава** (bot.) restharrow (*Ononis*).

вологодский *a.* (geog.) Vologda.

володушка *f.* (bot.) Bupleurum.

воло/жка *f.* (geol.) oxbow; —**к** *m.* portage, logway, skidding trail; (tech.) draw plate; *past m. sing. of* **волочь;** —**ка** *f.* draw plate, (wire-drawing) die; drawhole; (**бумажная**) —**кита** *f.* red tape; —**клюй** *m.* (orn.) oxpecker (*Buphagus*).

волокн/а *gen. and pl. of* **волокно;** —**ина** *f.* fibrin.

волокнисто— *prefix* fibro-, fibrous, fiber; **в.-лучистый** *a.* fibrous radiated; —**образный** *a.* fibroid; **в.-перистый** *a.* fibrovesicular; —**пористый** *a.* fibroporous; **в.-сетчатый** *a.* reticulate fibrous; —**сть** *f.* fibrous nature or structure, stringiness, fibration; —**эластичный** *a.* fibroelastic.

волокнистый *a.* fibrous, stringy, filamentous; (met.) fibriform (structure); (geol.) columnar (aggregates); (biol.) fibrillar; string (bean); **в. хрящ** (anat.) fibrocartilage.

волокнит *m.* fiber plastic.

волокно *n.* fiber, filament, thread; grain (of wood); (seism.) ribbon; —**держатель** *m.* lint retainer; —**дёрка** *f.* (text.) disintegrator; —**образный** *a.* fibriform; —**образование** *n.* fiber formation; (text.) fiber drawing; —**образующий** *a.* fiber-forming; —**отвод** *m.* lint flue.

волокноотдел/ение *n.* (text.) ginning; —**итель** *m.*, —**ительная машина** (cotton) gin; —**ительный** *a.* fiber-extracting.

волокно/очиститель *m.* post-ginning cleaner; —**очистка** *f.* post-ginning cleaning; -**сырец** *n.* raw fiber.

волоком *adv.* by traction.

волокон *gen. pl. of* **волокно:** —**це** *n.* fibril; —**чатый** *a.* filamentary.

волоку/т *pr. 3 pl. of* **волочь;** —**ша** *f.* drag harrow; rake; tuck net; drag net; sled, sledge; —**ша-выравниватель** *f.* (agr.) smoothing drag, leveller; —**ша-гвоздёвка** *f.* peg-tooth harrow; —**ша-грабли** *f.* hay rake; —**ша-подборщик** *f.* sweep rake; —**ша-шлейф** *f.* drag harrow, float; —**шка** *f.* scraper; small drag net.

Волопас *m.* (astr.) Bootes.

волос *m.* hair, crinis; capillus; bristle.

волосатик *m.* a hair; (zool.) hair worm; (bot.) maidenhair (*Adiantum*); feather grass (*Stipa capillata*); —**и**, —**овые** *pl.* hairworms (*Gordiaceae*); (min.) Venus hair.

волосат/ковые *pl.* (ichth.) sea ravens (*Hemitripteridae*); —**ость** *f.* hairiness, pilosity; (med.) hypertrichosis; —**ый** *a.* hairy, pilose; shaggy.

волос/ик *m.* a short hair; —**ина** *f.* hairline (crack), craze; —**инка** *f.* a hair.

волосисто— *prefix* trich(o)—, hairy, pilose; —**головчатый** *a.* hairy-headed, trichocephalous; —**крылые** *pl.* (ent.) Trichoptera; —**листный** *a.* (bot.) trichophyllous; —**плодный** *a.* trichocarpous; —**семянный** *a.* hairy-seeded; —**стебельный** *a.* hairy-stalked; —**сть** *f.* hairiness, pilosity.

волос/истый *a.* hairy, pilose; capillary; *suffix* —**trichous;** —**ки** *pl. of* **волосок;** (cross) hairs; whiskers; lashes, cilia; (biol.) pili.

волоско— *prefix* pili— (hair); —**видный** *a.* piliform; —**носный** *a.* piliferous.

волоснец *m.* (bot.) wild rye (*Elymus*); black-eyed Susan (*Rudbeckia hirta*).

волосн/ой, —**ый** *a.* capillary; very fine, hairline (crack); fret (saw); **в. сосуд** (anat.) capillary; —**ая трубка** capillary tube; —**ость** *f.* capillarity, capillary attraction; —**ое действие**, —**ости** capillary action.

волосо/видный *a.* hair-like; capillary, capillaceous; fibrolitic; —**вина** *f.* fine crack, seam, flaw, hair(line) crack; —**гонный** *a.* dehairing, depilatory; —**двигательный** *a.* (physiol.) pilomotor; —**зубы(е)** *pl.* sandfishes (*Trichodontidae*); —**к** *m.* hair; filament, fiber; hair spring; (biol.) pilus, crinus; —**носный** *a.* piliferous; —**образный** *a.* piliform; —**сгонный** *see* **волосогонный;** —**хвост(ов)ые** *pl.* cutlassfishes (*Trichiuridae*).

волос/ы *pl.* hair; bristles, pile; —**яник** *m.* hair mattress; —**яница** *f.* (bot.) capillitium.

волосян/ой *a.* hair(y), hirsute, crinite; capillary; **в. канал** capillary duct; —**ая соль** (min.) hair salt, silky epsomite.

волоч/ающийся *a.* dragging, trailing; paraparetic (gait); —**ение** *n.* dragging, etc., *see* **волочить;** drag, traction; **ось** —**ения** drag axis; —**ён(н)ый** *a.* dragged, etc., *see* **волочить.**

волочильн/ый *a.* (wire) drawing; **в. инструмент** wire-drawing die; **в. стан** draw bench; —**ая доска**, —**я доска** draw plate.

волоч/ильщик *m.* (wire) drawer; —**ить**, —**ь** *v.* drag, pull, haul; draw (wire); draw out; prolong; (agr.) harrow; —**иться** *v.* drag oneself, crawl along; trail; be dragged, etc.

волошский орех walnut.

волунтал *m.* voluntal, trichlorourethan.

волховский *a.* (geog.) Volkhov.

волч/анка *f.* (med.) lupus; —**ец** *m.* (bot.) thistle; (met.) tungsten (old); —**еягодник** *m.* (bot.) daphne; —**аночный** *a.* (med.) lupoid, lupiform.

волч/ий *a.* wolf, lupine; **в. боб** (bot.) lupine; —**ье лыко** (bot.) mezereon (*Daphne mezereum*); —**ье сито**

carline thistle (*Carlina vulgaris*); **—ьи ветры** (bot.) puffball (*Lycoperdon*); **—ья пасть** (med.) cleft palate; **—ья печь** (met.) blast furnace.

волч/ки *pl. of* **волчок;** (mal.) Trochidae; **—ник** *m.* (bot.) Daphne; **—никовые** *pl.* Thymelaeaceae.

волчок *m.* gyroscope; (spinning) top; hydrometer; (bot.) sucker; (text.) willow; (bur) crusher; picker roll; meat mincer; (typ.) rotary abrasive disk; (bot.) Orobanche; (orn.) little bittern (*Ixobrychus*).

волчуг *m.* (bot.) restharrow (*Ononis*).

волчь/е, –и, —я *see under* **волчий: —янский** *a.* (geog.) Volchya.

волшебный *a.* magic; **в. орех** (bot.) Hamamelis; **в. фонарь** projector.

волынка *f.* (music) bagpipes; (rad.) droning; dawdling.

волынский *a.* (geog.) Volhynia, Volyn; (med.) trench (fever).

вольвент *m.,* **—а** *f.* (zool.) volvent, desmoneme.

Вольвилля способ Wohlwill process.

вольвическая лава an acidproof lava.

вольв/окс *m.* (prot.) Volvox; **—оксовые** *pl.* Volvocaceae; **—ообразный** *a.* (bot.) volvaceous.

вольготный *a.* free.

вольер *m.,* **—а** *f.* cage; yard, corral, pen.

вольёт *fut. 3 sing. of* **влить.**

вольн/ичать *v.* take liberties, presume; **—о** *adv.* freely, voluntarily; *imp.* (mil.) at ease; **—онаёмный** *a.* civilian; **—опрактикующий** *a.* privately practicing; *m.* private practitioner; **—ослушатель** *m.* (educ.) auditor; **—ость** *f.* freedom, liberty; **—ый** *a.* free; open market, unregulated (price); unrestricted (grazing).

вольский *a.* (geog.) Volsk.

вольт *m.* (elec.) volt; **число в.** voltage.

вольта a machine oil; a light cotton fabric.

Вольта явление Volta effect.

вольта/ж *m.* (elec.) voltage; **—ит** *m.* (min.) voltaite; **—ический** *a.* (elec.) voltaic; **—метр** *m.* voltameter; **—метрический** *a.* voltametric; **—мпер** *m.* volt-ampere; **—мперметр** *m.* voltammeter; **—мперометрия** *f.* voltammetry.

вольтерровский *a.* (math.) Volterra.

вольтижировать *v.* vault.

вольт/метр *m.* (elec.) voltmeter; **—ов столб** voltaic pile; **—ова дуга** electric arc; **—одобавочный** *a.* booster.

вольтол/евый *a.,* **—ь** *m.* voltol, voltolized oil; **—изация** *f.* voltolization; **—изированный** *a.* voltolized; **—изировать** *v.* voltolize.

вольт/оммметр *m.* (elec.) volt-ohmmeter; **—оскоп** *m.* spark-plug tester; **—отрансформатор** *m.* (voltage) transformer; **-секунда** *f.* volt-second (1 weber).

вольтцин *m.* (min.) voltzine, voltzite.

Вольты элемент voltaic cell.

Вольфа процесс (flotation) Wolf process.

вольфартова муха screw-worm (*Wohlfartia magnifica*).

вольфахит *m.* (min.) wolfachite.

вольфия *f.* (bot.) Wolffia.

вольфов канал, в. проток, в. ход (embr.) Wolffian duct; **—о тело** Wolffian body, mesonephros.

вольфрам *m.* tungsten, W; **азотистый в.** tungsten nitride; **трёхокись —а** tungsten trioxide, tungstic anhydride; **—ат** *m.* tungstate; **—ировать** *v.* plate with tungsten; **—истый** *a.* tungsten; **—ит** *m.* (min.) wolframite; **—о** *prefix* tungsten.

вольфрамово/кислый *a.* tungstic acid; tungstate (of); **в. натрий, —натриевая соль** sodium tungstate; **—кислая соль** tungstate.

вольфрамов/ый *a.* tungsten, tungstic; **в. ангидрид** tungstic anhydride, tungsten trioxide; **в. камень** (min.) scheelite; **—ая кислота** tungstic acid; **соль —ой кислоты** tungstate; **—ая охра** (min.) tungstic ocher, tungstite.

вольфрамо/натриевая соль sodium tungstate; **—сернистый** *a.* sulfotungstate.

вольфсбергит *m.* (min.) wolfsbergite, chalcostibite.

волюм/(ен)ометр *m.* volumenometer, stereometer; **—етр, —(ино)метр, —ометр** *m.* volumeter; **—етрический** *a.* volumetric; **—етрия** *f.* volumetry; **—инозный** *a.* voluminous.

волюта *f.* (arch.) volute, scroll.

волютин *m.,* **—ный** *a.* (gen.) volutin; volutine.

вол/я *f.* will, volition; freedom, liberty; **—ей-неволей** *adv.* willing or not; **по доброй —е** willingly, of one's own accord; **сила —и** will power.

волярный *a.* (anat.) volar.

вомбат *m.* (mam.) wombat (*Vombatus, Phascolomis*); **—ы** *pl.* Phascolom(y)idae.

вомер *m.* moonfish (*Vomer*).

вомнёт *fut. 3 sing. of* **вмять.**

вонз/ать, —ить *v.* thrust, prod; stab, stick in; **—иться** *v.* pierce, go into; be stuck.

вонь *f.* stench, stink, bad odor, reek.

вонюч/ий *a.* malodorous, putrid, stinking; (geol.) fetid; stink (stone); **—ая смола** asafetida (gum); **—ка** *f.* (mam.) skunk; (bot.) asafetida (*Ferula asafetida*); bean trefoil (*Anagyris foetida*); **—ки** *pl.* (mam.) Mephitinae.

вонять *v.* have a bad smell, stink.

вообра/жаемый *a.* imaginary, unreal, fictitious, nonexistent, hypothetical; virtual; conceptual; proposed, visualized; **—жать** *v.* imagine, visualize, conceive; assume; **—жение** *n.* imagination; **—жённый** *a.* imagined, etc., *see v.;* imaginary; virtual; **—зимый** *a.* imaginable; **—зить** *see* **воображать.**

вообще *adv.* generally, in general, in a broad sense; at all; (all) in all, altogether; **в. говоря** generally (speaking); by and large; **в. не** at all; **если в. происходит** if ever; if any; **мало . . . если в.** little if any.

воодушев/ить, —лять *v.* inspire.

вооруж/ать *v.* arm, equip, supply, outfit (with); incite, stir up, instigate (against); **—аться** *v.* arm onself, provide oneself (with); **—ение** *n.* armament, arms, weapons, ammunition; equipment, outfitting; **поступать на —ение** *v.* go into operation; **—ённый** *a.* armed, etc., *see v.;* weapon-carrying; in possession (of); **—ить** *see* **вооружать.**

воочию *adv.* with one's own eyes; **убедиться в.** *v.* see for oneself.

во-первых *adv.* first(ly), in the first place, first and foremost; for one thing; **во-п . . . , во-вторых** for one thing . . . for another; on the one hand . . . on the other; first(ly) . . . second(ly).

воп/ить *v.* howl, wail, yell; **—иющий** *a.* howling; crying; flagrant, glaring.

вопло/тить, —щать *v.* embody, personify; translate (into); **в. в жизнв** realize, put into practice; **—щение** *n.* embodiment; personification; realization.

вопль *m.* howl, yell, cry, scream.

вопреки *prep. dat.* in spite (of), notwithstanding, despite, regardless (of), contrary (to), against.

вопрос *m.* question, problem; point, aspect; item, matter, issue, subject; query; **ещё в.** it remains to be seen; **история —а** background; **к —у о, по —у on; под —ом** open to question; **—ительный** *a.* interrogative; question(ing); **—ить** *v.* question, interrogate; **—ник** *m.,* **—ный лист** questionnaire; **—ный** *a. of* **вопрос.**

вопрошать see **вопросить.**

вопьёт(ся) fut. sing. of **впить(ся).**

вопять v. cry out, exclaim.

вор m. thief, robber; **пальмовый в.** (crust.) palm crab (Birgus latro).

ворара f. curare.

ворван/ный a., **—ь** f. blubber; oil (of fish, seals or whales).

ворваться see **врываться.**

воргашорский a. (geog.) Vorga-Shor.

ворковать v. (orn.) coo.

воркут(ин)ский a. (geog.) Vorkuta.

вормсиский a. (geog.) Vormsi.

воробей m. (orn.) sparrow; **морской в.** lumpfish (Cyclopterus lumpus); **—ник** m. (bot.) Lithospermum.

воробьевит m. (min.) vorobyevite.

воробь/ёнок m. young sparrow; **—иные** pl. (orn.) Passeriformes; **—иный** a. (orn.) passerine; sparrow; **—иные языки** (bot.) strapwort (Corrigiola littoralis).

воров/ать v. steal, rob; plagiarize; tamper (with); tap (electricity, etc.); **—ство** n. stealing, etc., see v.

ворон m. (orn.) raven (Corvus corax); (astr.) Corvus; **морской в.** (ichth.) sea raven (Hemitripterus americanus); **—а** f. crow (Corvus corone).

воронежский a. (geog.) Voronezh.

ворон/ение n. (steel) bluing.

воронёнок m. young crow; young raven.

воронён(н)ый a. blued, etc., see **воронить.**

воронец m. (bot.) baneberry (Actaea).

ворон/ий a. crow's, corvine; coracoid (bone); **в. глаз** (bot.) Paris; **—ика** f. crowberry (Empetrum); **—иковые** pl. Empetraceae.

ворон/ило n. burnisher, polisher; (typ.) planer; **—ить** v. (steel) blue, brown, subject to oxide treatment; burnish.

воронк/а f. funnel; hopper; crater, sink- (hole); cone (of depression); eddy, whirlpool; (Ford) cup; (viscosimeter) orifice; (anat.) infundibulum; (med.) speculum; (ichth.) bullhead (Cottus gobio); **—овидный, —ообразный** a. funnel-shaped, funnel(ed); (anat.) infundibuliform; **—ообразное образование** infundibulum.

ворон/овидный a. (anat.) coracoid; **—овые** pl. (orn.) crow family (Corvidae); (ichth.) Formionidae; **—ой** a. (coal-)black; **—ок** m. (orn.) city swallow (Delichon urbica); **—о-чёрный** a. raven black; **-рыба** f. black butterfish (Formio niger).

ворончатый see **воронковидный.**

воронь/и see **вороновые; —я кость** (anat.) coracoid; **—я лапка** (bot.) wartcress (Coronopus).

ворот m. windlass, winch, capstan, reel; drum, shaft; hoist, pull; collar.

ворота pl. gate(way); door, entrance; (anat.) porta; hilus, hilum; (med.) portal(s).

воротило n. mill handle.

воротить v. recall, call back, bring back; give back, return; **—ся** v. return.

воротн/ик m. collar, flange, lip; (bol.) cingulum; **—ичок** dim. of **воротник; —ичковый** a. collared; (orn.) ringnecked; **—ичковая клетка** (cyt.) choanocyte.

воротн/ый a. gate, portal; windlass, winch; **—ая вена** (anat.) portal vein.

вороток m. tap wrench, diestock; tommy bar; (leather) shoulder, front.

ворох m. grain chaff; (thrashed) heap, pile; **—овой** a. of **ворох;** grain (carrier).

ворочать v. turn, roll, move, shift; run, handle, manage; (elec.) reverse; **—ся** v. rotate, turn over.

ворош/ение n. turning, etc., see **ворошить; —илка** f., **—ило** n. agitator, stirrer; (agr.) tedder.

ворошиловградский a. (geog.) Voroshilovgrad.

ворошит/ель see **ворошило; —ь** v. turn (over), stir, disturb.

ворс m. pile, nap, fleece; (anat.) villus; (leather) suede.

Ворса элемент Vorce (chlorine) cell.

ворс/ильный a. (text.) teasing; **—инка** f. hair, fiber; down, fluff; (anat.) villus; **—инчатый** a. fluffy, wooly, tomentose, villose **—инчатая оболочка** (biol.) chorion; **—истость** f. fluffiness; **—истый** a. fluffy, fleecy, shaggy, friezed, nappy; villose, pubescent; **—ит** m. an artificial leather.

ворсить see **ворсовать.**

ворсклинский a. (geog.) Vorskla.

ворс/овальный a. (text.) teasing; teasel (bur); **—ование** n. teasing; **—овать** v. tease, raise the nap; **—овидный** a. (biol.) villiform; **—овой, —овый** a. of **ворс;** fleecy, napped; **—оносный** a. villiferous; **—янка** f. (bot.) teasel (Dipsacus); **—янковые** pl. Dipsacaceae.

вортекс m. vortex.

Вортингтона насос Worthington pump.

ворч/ание n. grumbling; growling; **—ать** v. grumble, complain; growl; **—ун** m. (ichth.) grunt (Pomadasys); **—уновые** pl. Pomadasyidae.

ВОС abbr. (станция визуально-оптических наблюдений) visual observation station.

вос— prefix up, off, away; re—, again.

восемнадцат/ый a. eighteenth; **—ь** eighteen.

восемь eight; **—десят** eighty; **—сот** eight hundred; **—ю** adv. multiplied by eight.

воск m. wax; **в.-заменитель** m. substitute wax; **—ирование** n., **—ировка** f. waxing.

воскли/кнуть v. exclaim, cry out; **—цательный** a. exclamation (mark); **—цательная совка** a cutworm (Agrotis exclamationis); **—цать** see **воскликнуть.**

воско— prefix wax(y), cer(o)—; **—беление** n., **—белильный** a. wax bleaching; **—битие** n. wax refining; **—боина** f. wax refiner; **—бой** m. wax refiner; (residual) beeswax; **—бойн(а)я f., —бойный завод** wax refinery; **—вание** n. waxing; **—видный** a. wax-like, waxy, ceraceous; **—вина, —вица** f. (orn.) ceroma, cere; **—вка** f. wax paper; tracing paper; stencil paper; **—вник** m., **—вница** f. bayberry (Myrica); **—вниковые** pl. waxmyrtle family (Myricaceae).

восков/ой a. wax(y), waxed; cer(ac)eous; ceruminous (glands); yellow (ripeness); ceric (alcohol); cer(ot)ic (acid); **соль —ой кислоты** cerotate; **—ая моль** bee moth; **—ая пальма** wax palm (Ceroxylon andicola); **—ое дерево** wax tree (Rhus succedanea); Chinese tallow tree (Croton sebiferus).

воско/выделение n. wax secretion; **—листный** a. waxy-leaved; **—носный** a. ceriferous, wax-bearing; **—образный** a. wax-like, waxy, ceraceous; **—отделительный** a. wax-producing, ceruminous (glands); **—отстойник** m. wax clarifier; **—подобный** see **воскообразный; —строительный** a. (apiculture) building (frame); **—сырьё** n. crude wax; **—топка** f. wax refinery; wax extractor; **—уловитель** m. wax trap; **—цветник** m. (bot.) honeywort (Cerinthe); **—цветный** a. waxy-flowered.

воскрес/енье n., **—ный** a. Sunday.

воск-сырец m. crude wax.

воспал/ение n. (med.) inflammation; **—itis, e.g. в. сустава** arthritis; **—ённый** a. inflamed; **—ительный** a. inflammatory, phlogistic; **—ить, —ять** v. inflame; **—иться** v. become inflamed; be sore; blaze.

воспар/ить, —ять v. soar, fly up.

воспит/ание n. education, training, etc., see v.; **—анный** a. educated, etc., see v.; well-bred; **—атель** m. educator;

trainer; —**ательный** *a.* educational; —**(ыв)ать** *v.* educate, train; raise, rear, bring up; grow, tend; breed.

воспламен/ение *n.* ignition, inflammation, combustion; kindling; **камера** —**ения** combustion chamber; **проба на в.** flash test; **температура** —**ения** fire point (of oils); ignition point; —**ённый** *a.* ignited.

воспламен/имый *see* **воспламеняемый;** —**итель** *m.* igniter, squib; (ignition) charge; blasting cap, detonator; fuse; —**ить** *see* **воспламенять;** —**яемость** *f.* ignitability, etc., *see a.;* —**яемый** *a.* ignitable, inflammable, combustible; —**ять** *v.* ignite, inflame, kindle; —**яться** *v.* ignite, catch fire; —**яющийся** *a.* (in)flammable, combustible, ignitable; ignition (mixture).

восполн/имость *f.* recruitment rate; —**имый** *a.* renewable, perpetual (resources); —**ить,** —**ять** *v.* make up, compensate (for); make good (a loss); meet, fill (a need); cancel out, counterbalance; fill up, supply; fill in, complete; fulfill.

воспользоваться *v.* profit (by), take advantage (of), avail oneself (of), make use (of), employ, resort (to).

воспомин/ание *n.* recollection; —**ания** *pl.* reminiscences, memoirs; —**ать** *v.* remember, recollect, recall.

воспрепятствовать *v.* hinder, prevent.

воспре/тительный *a.* prohibitive; —**тить,** —**щать** *v.* prohibit, forbid; —**щение** *n.* prohibition; —**щённый** *a.* prohibited.

восприимчив/ость *f.* susceptibility, etc., *see a.;* —**ый** *a.* susceptible, receptive, sensitive; absorptive, absorbent.

воспри/нимаемость *f.* perceptibility; —**нимаемый** *a.* perceptible, discernible; perceived; —**нимание** *see* **восприятие;** —**нимать** *v.* perceive, sense; interpret; take, receive, accept; take up, absorb; incorporate; ingest (food); —**ниматься** *v.* be perceived, etc.; be noticed; be noticeable; —**нимающий** *a.* perceiving, etc., *see v.;* perceptive; —**нимающий элемент** sensor; —**нятие** *n.* perception, sensing, etc., *see v.;* intake, uptake; —**нять** *see* **воспринимать;** —**ятие** *see* **восприятие.**

воспроизв/едение *n.* reproduction, breeding; (lag) representation; reconstruction; replica; playback; —**едённый** *a.* reproduced, etc., *see v.;* —**ести** *see* **воспроизводить;** —**одимость** *f.* reproducibility; —**одимый** *a.* reproducible; repeatable; —**одитель** *m.* reproducer; —**одительный** *a.* reproductive; —**одительное скрещивание** crossbreeding; —**одить** *v.* reproduce, breed; produce; repeat; regenerate; recall, call to mind; play back.

воспроизводств/о *n.* reproduction; replacement; regeneration; (nucl.) breeding; **зона** —**а** (nucl.) blanket (region); **коэффициент** —**а** breeding factor, conversion ratio.

воспроизводящий *a.* reproducing etc., *see* **воспроизводить;** fertile (medium); **в. перфоратор** (comp.) reperforator, paper tape punch.

воспротив/иться *v.* oppose, be opposed (to), object, be against, resist; —**ление** *n.* opposition, etc., *see v.*

воссоедин/ение *n.* reunion; recombination (of ions); —**ённый** *a.* reunited; reunion; —**ить,** —**ять** *v.* reunite; —**яться** *v.* reunite, rejoin; recombine.

воссозда/(ва)ть *v.* reconstruct, re-create; reconstitute, re-establish; realize; regenerate; —**ние** *n.* reconstruction, etc., *see v.*

восставать *v.* oppose; revolt, rebel.

восстав/ить, —**лять** *v.* erect, raise.

восстанавлив/аемость *f.* reducibility, etc., *see a.;* —**аемый** *a.* reproducible; restorable; recoverable; repairable; —**ать** *v.* reduce, deoxidize; restore, reestablish, recreate; reconstruct; reinstate; renew; recall, recollect; resume; regenerate, revive, recuperate; reclaim, recover; re-

condition; rehabilitate (people); retread (tires); erect, set up, raise; stir up, incite, set (against); repair; renovate; reset (a cycle); —**аться** *v.* be reduced, etc.; regenerate; —**ающий** *a.* reducing, etc., *see v.;* —**ающая способность** reducing power; recovery characteristics (of counter); —**ающийся** *a.* reducible; regenerating.

восстание *n.* rise; uprising, rebellion.

восстанов/имость *f.* reducibility, susceptibility to reduction; —**имый** *a.* reducible; —**итель** *m.* reducer, reducing agent; restorer, regenerator; renovator, etc., *see* **восстанавливать;** —**ительно-окислительный** *a.* reduction-oxidation, redox.

восстановительн/ый *a.* reducing, reduction; regenerating, restoration; full (renovation); replacement (value); progressive (succession); regenerative, restitutive; restorative (surgery); —**ая печь** reduction furnace; —**ая способность** reducing power; —**ое пламя** reducing flame; —**ое средство** reducing agent; —**ые работы** recovery.

восстановить *see* **восстанавливать.**

восстановл/ение *n.* reduction, reducing, etc., *see* **восстанавливать;** reestablishment, reinstatement; restitution, regeneration; repair; renewal; recovery; (instr.) recovery time; ре—, *e.g.,* **в. цикла** recycling; **прямого** —**ения** direct-reduction (iron); **в.-окисление** reduction-oxidation; —**енный** *a.* reduced, etc., *see* **восстанавливать;** —**яемость** *f.* reducibility; —**яемый,** —**яющийся** *a.* reducible; —**ять** *see* **восстанавливать;** —**яющий** *a.* reducing, etc., *see* **восстанавливать.**

восст/ать *v.* rise, revolt, rebel; —**ающий** *a.* rising, etc., *see v.; m.* (min.) raise, steep incline.

вост. *abbr.* (**восточный**).

восток *m.* the east, orient; —**оведение** *n.* oriental studies; —**оведный,** —**оведческий** *a.* oriental.

востор/г *m.* enthusiasm, delight, zeal; —**гаться** *v.* be enthusiastic (about); —**женный** *a.* enthusiastic.

восточн/ее *adv.* more to the east; —**о** *prefix* east; (geog.) East, Oriental; —**о-европейский** *a.* East European; —**о-китайский** *a.* East China; —**о-сибирский** *a.* East Siberian.; —**ый** *a.* east(ern), oriental.

востребов/ание *n.,* —**ать** *v.* demand.

вострец *m.* (bot.) Aneurolepidium.

востр/обрюшка *f.* (ichth.) sawbelly (*Hemiculter*); —**як** *m.* whitefish (*Coregonus pidschian*).

восхвал/ение *n.* eulogy, praises; —**ить,** —**ять** *v.* laud, praise, extol.

восхи/тительный *a.* delightful; —**тить,** —**щать** *v.* delight; —**щаться** *v.* admire, be delighted (with).

восхо/д *m.* rise, rising, ascent; —**дить** *v.* rise, ascend, climb; date back, go back; —**дящий** *a.* rising, etc., *see v.;* anabatic; upward; uptake (flue); up (flow); bottom-up (analysis); —**дящий боровок** uptake, upcast; —**дящая труба** riser; **отливать** —**дящей струёй** *v.* cast from bottom; —**ждение** *n.* ascent, ascension, climbing.

восьм/еричный *a.* octuple, octal; —**ёрка** *f.,* —**ёркообразный** *a.* figure eight; —**ерник** *m.* (cryst.) eightfold twin; —**ерной** *a.* eightfold; —**еро** *num.* eight.

восьми *gen.* of **восемь;** *prefix* oct(a)—, octo—, eight; —**атомный,** —**валентный** *a.* octavalent; —**гнездный** *a.* (biol.) octolocular; —**гранник** *m.* octahedron; —**гранный** *a.* octahedral, eight-faced; —**десятилетие** *n.* eightieth year; eightieth year; —**десятилетний** *a.* octogenarian; —**десятый** *a.* eightieth; —**значный** *a.* eight-digit, eight-unit; —**зубые** *pl.* (mam.) Octodontidae; —**кратный** *a.* octuple; —**летний** *a.* octennial; —**надрезный** *a.* (bot.) octofid; —**ног**

m. (mal.) octopus; —**образный** *a.* figure-of-eight; —**полюсник** *m.* octopole, eight-terminal network; —**сотый** *a.* eight hundredth; —**угольник** *m.* octagon; —**угольный** *a.* octagonal, octangular; —**усый** *a.* eight-whiskered (fish); —**фтористый** *a.* octafluoride (of); —**членный** *a.* octamerous.

восьмой *a.* eighth.

вот *adv.* here (is), there (is); **в. и всё** that is all; **в. как** that is how.

вотатор *m.* votator (for heat exchanger).

вотировать *v.* vote.

воткать *v.* interweave, weave in.

воткнуть *see* **втыкать.**

вотрёт *fut. 3 sing. of* **втереть.**

вотум *m.* vote.

в. оч. *abbr.* (**высшей очистки**) superpure.

вошедший *past act. part. of* **войти.**

вошерия *f.* (bot.) Vaucheria.

вошли *past pl. of* **войти.**

вошь *f.* (ent.) louse; **травяная в.** aphid.

вошьёт *fut. 3 sing. of* **вшить.**

вощ/анка *f.* wax paper; oil cloth; —**аной,** —**аный** *a.* wax(en), waxed; —**ение** *n.* waxing; wax finish(ing); —**ёный** *a.* wax(ed); —**ина** *f.* (honeycomb) foundation; unrefined beeswax; **пчелиная** —**ина** honeycomb; —**ить** *v.* wax.

воюет *pr. 3 sing. of* **воевать.**

во/ющий *pr. act. part. of* **выть;** warble (tone); —**я** *gen. of* **вой.**

вп *abbr.* (**вода питьевая**) drinking water; **ВП** *abbr.* (**высокая проницаемость**) high permeability; (**выз-ванная поляризация**) induced polarization (method); [(**метод**) **вызванного потенциала**] induced potential (IP) method.

впавший *past act. part. of* **впасть.**

впад/ать *v.* fall in; flow, run (into), discharge; sink (into), lapse; go (to extremes); —**ающий** *a.* falling into, etc., *see v.;* inflowing; —**ение** *n.* inflow; mouth, issue (of river); —**ина** *f.* hollow, cavity, depression, basin; trench; concavity, dent, indentation; recess, notch, gap, space; cut, incision; sag; trough (of wave); valley (of curve); orbit, socket (of eye); root (of screw thread); —**истый** *a.* full of cavities.

впа/ивание *n.* soldering in, sealing in; —**ивать** *v.* solder in, seal in; —**й** *m.* sealing in, seal(-in), lead; soldering in; —**йка** *see* **впаивание;** sealed-in or soldered-in piece.

впал *past m. sing. of* **впасть.**

впал/ость *f.* hollowness, concavity; —**ый** *a.* hollow, concave, sunken.

впараллель *adv.* in parallel.

впасть *see* **впадать.**

впа/ян(н)ый *a.* soldered in, sealed in; —**ять** *v.* solder in, seal in.

ВПВ *abbr.* (**высокая полная вода**) higher high water, HHW.

впервые *adv.* first, for the first time.

вперевязку: стык в. broken joint.

вперёд *adv.* on, forward, ahead, forth, onward; first; fast (of clock); in the future, henceforth; in advance, before-hand; **выступать в.** *v.* protrude; **движение в.** onward motion, advance, progress; **забегать в.** *v.* forestall; **идущий в.** advancing, progressive; **подвигаться в.** *v.* advance, progress; **ход в.** forward running; forward stroke.

впереди *adv. and prep. gen.* in front (of), before, ahead (of), in advance (of); in future; in the foreground; *prefix* pre—; —**крестцовый** *a.* (anat.) presacral.

впере/крой, —**крыш(к)у** *adv.* lap(ped), overlap(ped); —**межку** *adv.* alternately; —**мешку** *adv.* in disorder, indiscriminately; intermixed.

впечатл/ение *n.* impression, influence, effect; imprint, cast; —**ительность** *f.* susceptibility; —**ительный** *a.* impressionable, susceptible, sensitive.

впивать *v.* drink in, absorb, suck in; —**ся** *v.* dig in, hold on, fasten on, cling to, adhere to; pierce, penetrate.

впис/анность *f.* refinement; —**анный** *a.* inscribed, etc., *see v.;* —**ать,** —**ывать** *v.* inscribe, enter, insert, regis-ter; write in; (top.) refine; —**ка** *f.* inscribing; entry; —**ывание** *n.* inscribing, etc., *see v.*

впит/анный *a.* absorbed, etc., *see v.;* —**ать(ся)** *see* **впитывать(ся);** —**ываемость** *f.* absorbency; —**ыва-емый** *a.* absorbent, absorbable; absorbed; —**ывание** *n.* absorption, etc., *see v.;* seepage; —**ывать** *v.* absorb, imbibe, take up, soak up; —**ываться** *v.* be absorbed, soak in; —**ывающий** *a.* absorbing, etc., *see v.;* absor-bent; —**ывающий в себя** absorptive; saturant, satu-rable; —**ь(ся)** *see* **впитывать(ся).**

впих/анный *a.* pushed in, etc., *see v.;* —(**ив**)**ать,** —**нуть** *v.* push in, stuff in, cram in, squeeze in.

вплав/ить *v.* fuse in(to), melt in; float in; —**ление** *n.* fusion, melt; floating in; —**лять** *see* **вплавить;** —**ь** *adv.* (by) floating or swimming.

впластов/анный *a.* interbedded, etc., *see v.;* —**ываться** *v.* interbed, interstratify; be embedded.

вплёс/кивать, —**нуть** *v.* splash in, pour carelessly, dump in.

вплести *see* **вплетать.**

вплет/ание *n.* interweaving, intertwining; implication; (camouflage) garnishing; —**ать** *v.* interweave, inter-twine; splice in; plait in; implicate, involve; —**ение** *see* **вплетание;** —**ённый** *a.* interwoven, etc., *see v.*

вплот/ную *adv.* close (by or to), up to, (up) against, right up (to), immediately adjacent (to); —**ь** *adv.* up to, till; close; down (to); —**ь до** up to, up until, through, to the extent of; down to.

вплы/(ва)ть *v.* swim in, float in; sail in.

впповалку *adv.* side by side, in a row.

впол— *prefix* half; —**дерева** *adv.* half-lap; **соединение** —**дерева** half-lap joint.

вполз/ать, —**ти** *v.* crawl in, creep in.

вполнакала *adv.* (illum.) dim(ly), weak(ly).

вполне *adv.* fully, entirely, wholly, totally, completely, thoroughly, quite, perfectly; well; **не в.** incompletely, under, sub—; not quite; —**применимость** *f.* complete applicability.

впол/оборота *adv.* half-turned; —**овину** *adv.* (in or by) half; **уменьшить** —**овину** *v.* halve; —**унакрой,** —**унахлёст(ку)** *adv.* half-lap (joint); —**употай** *adv.* half-countersunk.

впопад *adv.* timely, to the point.

впопыхах *adv.* hurriedly, hastily.

впору *adv.* at the right time, in time, timely; **быть в.** *v.* fit; be fit (for).

впорхнуть *v.* fly up; flit in.

впоследствии *adv.* afterwards, later on, subsequently.

впотай *adv.* flush(-mounted), countersunk, even; **голов-ка в.** countersunk head; **углубление в.** countersinking.

впотьмах *adv.* in the dark.

ВПП *abbr.* (**взлётно-посадочная полоса**) runway.

вправду *adv.* really, seriously.

вправе *adv.* justified, in the right; on the right; **быть в.** *v.* have a right (to).

вправ/ить *see* **вправлять;** —**ка** *f.,* —**ление** *n.* setting, etc., *see v.;* —**ленный** *a.* set, etc., *see v.;* —**лять** *v.* set, reposition, reduce (a fracture); set to rights.

вправо *adv.* to the right, clockwise; **вращающийся в.** *a.* dextrorotatory; **движение в.** dextroduction (of eyes); **—завитой** *a.* (zool.) dexiotropic.

впредь *adv.* henceforth, hereinafter, from now on, in the future; **в. до** pending, until.

впрессов/анный *a.* pressed in, etc., *see v.;* press-fitted; **—(ыв)ать** *v.* press in, set in, embed, build in.

впритирку *adv.* tight(ly).

впритык *adv.* butt, abutting; butt-jointed; against, end to end; **располагать в.** *v.* butt; **сваривать в.** *v.* butt-weld; **соединение в.** butt joint.

впроголодь *adv.* half starving.

впрозелень *f.* unripe fruit.

впрок *adv.* for the future, for keeping, for preservation; **заготовлять в.** *v.* preserve, cure, lay in, store; **идти в.** *v.* be of use, be of profit.

впрочем *adv.* however, though, besides, by the way; not that; nevertheless.

впрыг/ивать, —нуть *v.* jump in.

впрыс/к *m.* injection, shot; **—кивание** *n.* injection, injecting; **—киватель** *m.* injector; **—кивательный** *see* **впрыскивающий; —кивать** *v.* inject, spray in, squirt in; **—кивающий** *a.* injecting; spray (nozzle); jet (condenser); **—нутый** *a.* injected; **—нуть** *see* **впрыскивать.**

впряг/ание *n.* harnessing; **—ать** *v.* harness; **—аться в работу** get to work.

впрядать *v.* spin in.

впряжённый *a.* harnessed (in).

впрясть *see* **впрядать.**

впрячь *see* **впрягать.**

впуск *m.* admission, etc., *see v.;* intake, inlet; induction; **—ание** *n.* admission, etc., *see v.;* **—ать** *v.* admit, inject, introduce, run in, let in, take in.

впускн/ой *a. of* **впуск;** feed, supply (line); **—ое отверстие** inlet, intake; **—ое устройство** injector.

впустить *see* **впускать.**

впустую *adv.* in vain, to no purpose.

впут/анный *a.* involved, etc., *see v.;* **—(ыв)ать** *v.* involve, implicate, entangle, enmesh; twist in; **—(ыв)аться** *v.* be mixed up (in).

впущенный *past pass. part. of* **впускать.**

впятеро *adv.* five times, fivefold; **в. больше** five times as much; **в. меньше** one fifth; **—м** *adv.* five (together).

впятить *see* **впячивать.**

в-пятых *adv.* in the fifth place.

впяч/енный *a.* (biol.) invaginate, enclosed in a sheath; introverted; **—ивание** *n.* invagination; **—ивать(ся)** *v.* invaginate, involute, draw into a sheath; retract; (mach.) back up.

вр. *abbr.* (**врач**); **в.р.** *abbr.* (**весьма растворимо**) readily soluble; **ВР** *abbr.* (**воздушная разведка**) aerial reconnaissance; (**выключающее реле**) shutdown relay.

враб/атываться, —отаться *v.* work in, run in; become familiar (with work).

вра/г *m.* enemy, foe; **—жда** *f.* enmity; **—ждебный** *a.* hostile, antagonistic.

вразбежку *adv.* alternate(ly); **расположенный в.** staggered, alternated; **стыки в.** alternate joints.

враз/бивку *adv.* out of order; haphazardly; **—брод** *adv.* separately; **—брос** *adv.* scattered, haphazard, random(ly): broadcast (sowing); **—вал: борозда —вал** open furrow; **—вилку** *adv.* forked, pronged; **—рез** *adv.* across; contrary; (elec.) in series; **идти —рез** *v.* oppose, be in conflict (with).

вразрядку *adv.* (typ.) letter-spaced.

вразум/ительный *a.* perspicuous, comprehensible; persuasive; **—ить, —лять** *v.* explain, convince; instruct.

врал *past m. sing. of* **врать.**

вранг/елевский *a.* (geog.) Wrangel(l); **—ский** *a.* V(a)rang.

вранов/ая кость (anat.) coracoid; **—ые** *pl.* (orn.) Corvidae.

врас/брос *see* **вразброс; —плох** *adv.* by surprise, unawares; **—сечку** *adv.* (elec.) in series; **—сыпную** *adv.* in all directions.

враст/ание *n.* growing in; intergrowth, interlocking; **—ать, —и** *v.* grow in; intergrow, interlock; become embedded (in); settle, subside; heal over; **—ающий** *a.* in(ter)growing, etc., *see v.*

врастяжку *adv.* at full length, prone.

врасщеп *adv.* split, fork(ed); **соединене в.** split joint.

врать *v.* lie, tell a lie; be deceiving; be wrong, make a mistake; be inaccurate.

врач *m.* doctor, physician, medical man.

врачебн/о-консультационный *a.* medical consultation; **в.-контрольный** *a.* medical control; **в.-лётная экспертиза** flight fitness determination; **в.-санитарный** *a.* medical (and sanitary); **в.-трудовой** *a.* medical labor; disability (determination); **в.-экспертный** *a.* medical expert; **—ый** *a.* medical.

врач/евание *n.* treatment, therapy; **—евать** *v.* treat, doctor; **-консультант** *m.* consulting physician.

враща/емый *a.* rotatable; **—тель** *m.* rot(at)or, spinner; swivel head.

вращательно *adv.* rotationally; **в. эллиптический** *a.* spheroidal; **в.-изомерный** *a.* rotational isomer; **в.-качающийся** *a.* rotary shaking; **в.-колебательный** *a.* rotationally oscillatory.

вращатель/ный *a.* rotary, rotating, rotation(al); revolving; trochoid (articulation); **—ая способность** (opt.) rotatory power; **—ое движение** rotary motion, rotation, gyration.

вращать *v.* rotate, revolve, turn; circulate (a liquid); circle; wind; drive; **—ся** *v.* revolve, rotate, turn, gyrate, spin; pivot, swivel; (mach.) run; mix (with), mingle (among); **—ся вокруг** revolve (around), circle.

вращающ/ий *a.* rotating; **в. момент** torque; **—ийся** *a.* rotating, rotatory, rotary (furnace, dryer, etc.); revolving; turning, turn (table); swivel, pivoted; (mach.) running; live (center); spinning (nucleus); spin-stabilized, spinner (rocket); **—ийся влево** (opt.) levorotatory; **—ийся вправо** dextrorotatory.

вращаясь *see* **вращающийся.**

вращен/ие *n.* rotation, revolution, turn(ing), spin(ning), etc., *see* **вращаться; круговое в.** revolution; **момент —ия** angular momentum; **точка —ия** pivot, fulcrum.

вращполе *n.* rotating field.

врбаит *m.* (min.) vrbaite.

ВРД, Врд *abbr.* (**воздушно-реактивный двигатель**) jet engine.

вред *m.* harm, damage, injury, hurt; impairment; **—ен** *sh. m. of* **вредный; —итель** *m.* saboteur; (agr.) pest; predator; **—ители** *pl.* pests, vermin; **—ительский** *a.* pest; harmful; **—ительство** *n.* harm, damage; sabotage.

вредить *v.* harm, damage, injure, hurt, impair, be detrimental (to).

вредн/о *adv.* harmfully; it is harmful; **—ость** *f.* harm, damage, injury; harmfulness; (health) hazard; **—ость производства** occupational hazard; **—ый** *a.* harmful, damaging, injurious, deleterious, detrimental, destructive, bad, ill (effect); unfavorable, adverse; noxious (gas); over-(dose); **—ое пространство** idle space, dead space; clearance (in cylinder); **—ые испарения** effluvium, noxious exhalation.

вредоносн/ость *f.* harmfulness; **—ый** *a.* harmful, injurious, pernicious.

врез/ание *n.* incision, gash, notch; cutting in, etc., *see v.;* **—анный** *a.* incised, etc., *see v.;* **—ать** *see* **врезывать;** **—ающийся** *a.* incisive, cutting; **—ка** *see* **врезание;** inset map; **—ной** *a.* cut in, etc., *see v.;* mortise; downcutting (stream); in-feed (grinding); **—ной замок** (rr.) deadlock **—ывание** *see* **врезание; —ывать** *v.* cut in, incise, entrench; set in, inlay, fit in, mortise; lay (into); engrave; notch, score; serrate; (geol.) downcut; **—ываться** *v.* cut (into), run (into); project (into).

времена *pl. of* **время;** **—ми** *adv.* at times, from time to time, now and then.

времениподобный *a.* time-like.

временн/ик *m.* annals; timer; **—о** *adv.* temporarily; **—о назначенный** *a.* acting officer; **—о помогающее средство** (pharm.) palliative; **—ой** *a.* time, temporal; time-division (multiplexing); **—ой механизм** timer; **—ость** *f.* temporariness; time factor; **—ый** *a.* temporary, provisional, tentative; makeshift, emergency; intermittent; interim (agreement); accidental, chance, random; time (order of reaction); **—ая мера, —ое приспособление** makeshift, expedient; **—ое согласование** timing; **—ое сопротивление** temporary resistance, breaking(-down) point, critical point.

врем/я *n.* time; period, season; duration; (oestrous) cycle; (gram.) tense; **в. года** season; **в. жизни** lifetime; time of life; **в. от —ени** occasionally, from time to time, at times, once in a while, now and again; **во в.** in the course (of), while, during; on time, in season; **во —ени** in time; **в. последнее в.** recently, in the last few years; **в своё в.** in due course **в то в. как** (where)as; **в то же (самое) в.** at the same time, simultaneously; yet, while; **в это в.** at this time, as this takes place, in this case, in the process, therewith; **к тому —ени** by then; **к тому —ени, когда** by the time; **на в.** for a while; **на всё в.** for life; **на некоторое в.** for a while, for the time being; **по —енам** from time to time, intermittently; **постоянная —ени** time constant; **регулируемый по —ени** timed; **с того —ени** since then, from then on; **с этого —ени** from now on; **со —енем** in (due) time, in due course, in the course of time; **со —ени** since; **тем —енем** meanwhile.

время/импульсный *a.* cycle-repeat (timer); time-division (multiplier); pulse-position (modulation); **—исчисление** *n.* chronology; **—нка** *f.* (elec.) temporary connection; **—образный, —подобный** *a.* time(-like); **—пролётный** *a.* time-of-flight (spectrometer).

врёт *pr. 3 sing. of* **врать.**

вровень *adv.* level, flush (with).

вроде *prep. gen. and particle* like, such as; **нечто в.** a kind of.

вроет *fut. 3 sing. of* **врыть.**

врождённ/ость *f.* innateness, inherency; congenitalness; **—ый** *a.* innate, inherent, inborn; congenital; native; original; unconditioned (reflex); **—ый семейный** *a.* heredofamilial.

врозницу *adv.* (at) retail.

врозь *adv.* apart, asunder, separately.

вронскиан *m.* (math.) Wronskian.

врос *past m. sing. of* **врасти; —ший** *a.* ingrown; grown into; incarned, healed over.

вроют *fut. 3 pl. of* **врыть.**

врс. *abbr.* (**верста**) verst.

вруб *m.* cut, notch; channel, groove; cutting, etc., *see v.;*

—ание *n.* cutting, etc., *see v.;* **—ать, —ить** *v.* cut (in), chop (in), hew; notch, groove, channel; throw in (switch); (building) frame into; **—иться** *v.* cut one's way (into); break through; **—ка** *f.* cutting, etc., *see v.;* cut, notch; joint; **соединять —кой** *v.* mortise; **—ленный** *a.* cut, etc., *see v.;* **—машина, —овка** *f.* (min.) cutter; **—о(во)-навалочный** *a.* cutting-loading; **—о(во)-отбойный** *a.* cutting-winning; **—о(во)-отбойная машина** (coal) cutter; **—о(во)-погрузочный** *a.* cutting-loading; **—овый** *a. of* **вруб;** (coal) cutting; **—овая машина** cutter; **—овая щель** kerf.

врут *pr. 3 pl. of* **врать.**

вруч/ать *see* **вручить; —ение** *n.* presentation, presenting, etc., *see v.;* **—ённый** *a.* presented, etc., *see v.;* **—ить** *v.* present, hand (in, over), deliver, give, entrust.

вручную *adv.* (by) hand, manual(ly); **отсортированный в.** handpicked; **подача в.** hand feed, manual feed; **приводимый в.** hand-operated, manual; **сделанный в.** handmade, manual.

ВРЦ *abbr.* (**водонепроницаемый расширяющийся цемент**) waterproof expanding cement.

вры/вать, —ть *v.* dig in; **—ваться** *v.* dig in; burst in.

вряд (ли) *adv.* scarcely, hardly; it is doubtful (whether), it is unlikely.

в.с. *abbr.* (**вид симметри**) class of crystal symmetry; (**водяной столб**) water column.

в/с *abbr.* (**высший сорт**) high(est) grade.

в-с *see* **в-сек.**

вс— *see* **вос—.**

вса/дить, —живать *v.* set in, embed; thrust, plunge, drive in; plant; lay out (money); **—дник** *m.* rider; **—женный** *a.* set in, etc., *see v.*

всаливание *n.* salting.

всас *m.* suction.

всасыв/аемость *f.* absorbability; **—аемый** *a.* absorbable; suction; **—ание** *n.* suction, sucking, etc., *see v.;* resorption; intake, induction; indraft; **обратное —ание** reabsorption; **—ательный** *see* **всасывающий; —ать** *v.* suck in, draw in; absorb, imbibe.

всасывающ/ий *a.* sucking, suction, pull; intake; absorption, absorbing, absorbent; exhaust (fan); **в. клапан** suction or inlet valve; **в. коллектор** intake manifold; **в. насос** suction pump; **в. ход** admission stroke, instroke; **—ая склянка** suction bottle; **—ая способность** absorbing capacity; **—ая труба** intake; **—ее действие** suction, pull; **—ее окно, —ее устройство** intake.

всачиваться *v.* seep in, be absorbed.

всвал: борозда в. plow ridge.

все *pl.* all, everybody, everyone; **в. эти . . ., вместе взятые** taken together.

всё *n. of* **весь;** *adv.* always, all the time; still; only, all; **в. более** increasingly, progressively, more and more; **в. ещё** still; **в. же, в. таки** nevertheless, however; yet; **в., что** anything that; whatever.

все— *prefix* omni—, pan—, all; All-Union; **—возможный** *a.* every kind of, all kinds of, various; all possible, of every description; **—волновный** *a.* all-wave; long (counter).

всегда *adv.* always, at all times, constantly, ever; invariably; **—жив** *m.* (bot.) Vinca; **в.-истинность** *f.* identity; **в.-истинный** *a.* identity, identically true; **—шний** *a.* usual, habitual, customary, normal.

всего *gen. of* **весь, всё;** *adv.* only, but, in all, altogether, all told; as low as; **в.-навсего** in all, only; **в.-то** only, no more than.

в-седьмых *adv.* in the seventh place.

всей *gen., etc., of* **вся;** **во в.** throughout.

всек *abbr.* (**вольтсекунда**) volt second.

всеканальный *a.* all-channel.

все.л/ение *n.* establishment, etc., *see v.;* —**ённая** *f.* universe, cosmos (outer) space; —**ённый** *a.* established, etc., *see v.;* —**ить**, —**ять** *v.* establish, install; settle; inspire, instill; give; lodge; —**иться**, —**яться** *v.* settle, move in; take root (in).

всем *instr. and prepos. of* **весь, всё**; **во в.** in all respects, throughout; **при в. том** for all that.

всемерн/о *adv.* in every possible way; —**ый** *a.* of every kind, all possible; all-out, intensified.

всемеро *adv.* seven times; sevenfold; **в. больше** seven times as much; **в. меньше** one seventh; —**м** *adv.* seven (together).

всемирн/о *adv.* universally; **в. известный** *a.* world-renowned; **в.-распространённый** *a.* with world-wide distribution; —**ый** *a.* universal, world(-wide).

все/направленный *a.* omnidirectional; —**народный** *a.* national, nation-wide; people's; —**обуч** *m.* compulsory education; —**общий** *a.* general, universal; —**общность** generality, universality; —**объемлющий** *a.* universal, all-embracing, comprehensive, total; —**погодный** *a.* all-weather, weatherproof; —**режимный** *a.* fully variable; variable (-speed); —**российский** *a.* all-Russian.

всерьёз *adv.* in earnest, seriously.

все/светный *a.* universal, common; —**союзный** *a.* All-Union.

всесторонн/е *adv.* thoroughly, in detail, comprehensively; from every point of view; —**есимметричный** *a.* (biol.) homaxonic, homaxial; —**ий** *a.* complete, thorough, detailed, comprehensive, all-round, three-dimensional (compression); close, confining; manifold.

всё-таки *adv. and conj.* nevertheless, however, all the same, for all that, still.

всеукраинский *a.* (geog.) All-Ukrainian.

всеуслышание: во в. publicly, openly.

всех *gen. pl. of* **все**.

всецел/о *adv.* wholly, completely, entirely, altogether, exclusively; —**ый** *a.* whole, complete, entire, full.

всечасн/о *adv.,* —**ый** *a.* hourly.

всеядн/ость *f.* (zool.) omnivorousness, euryphagia; —**ый** *a.* omnivorous, euryphagous; —**ое животное** omnivore.

всилу *prep. gen.* by virtue of.

вскакив/ание *n.* jumping up; —**ать** *v.* jump up, spring up, leap up; bounce up.

вскальзыв/ание *n.* slipping in; —**ать** *v.* slip in, slide in.

вскапыв/ание *n.* digging up; excavating; —**ать** *v.* dig up, trench; excavate.

вскарабк(ив)аться *v.* climb up, clamber up.

вскармлив/ание *n.* rearing, etc., see *v.;* nutrition, alimentation; —**ать** *v.* rear, raise, bring up; nurse; feed, nourish, fatten.

вски/дка *f.,* —**дывание** *n.* tossing up, etc., *see v.;* —**дывать**, —**нуть** *v.* toss up, throw up, heave (onto); jerk up, yank up, hoist.

вскип/ание *n.* boiling up, etc., *see v.;* ebullition; effervescence; (paints) blistering; —**ать**, —**еть** *v.* boil up, boil over; bubble up, froth, foam; effervesce; —**ающий** *a.* boiling up, etc., *see v.;* —**ятить** *v.* (bring to a) boil; —**ятиться** *v.* (come to a) boil.

вскло(ко)ченный *a.* matted, felted.

всколых/(ив)ать, —**нуть** *v.* stir up.

вскольз/нуть *see* **вскальзывать**; —**ь** *adv.* superficially, casually, in passing.

вскоп/анный *a.* dug up, furrowed; —**ать** *v.* dig up, furrow.

вскоре *adv.* soon, shortly after, before long.

вскорм/ить *see* **вскармливать**; —**ленный** *a.* reared, etc., *see* **вскармливать**.

вскочить *see* **вскакивать**.

вскри/кивать, —**кнуть**, —**чать** *v.* exclaim, cry out.

вскры/вание *n.* opening, etc., *see v.;* (biol.) dehiscence; —**вать** *v.* open, uncover, lay bare, reveal, discover, disclose; (min.) strip; dissect; (med.) lance, cut, open; unseal; uncap (honeycomb); (met.) break down; rip up (pavement); —**ваться** *v.* be revealed, come to light; break (of ice); burst (of abscess); —**вающийся** *a.* (biol.) dehiscent; —**тие** *see* **вскрывание**; (med.) autopsy; (met.) breakdown; break up, debacle (of river); breaking up (of ice); —**тый** *a.* opened, etc., *see v.;* —**ть** *see* **вскрывать**; —**ш(к)а** *f.,* —**шной** *a.* (min.) stripping; strip pit; overburden; soil removed from hole; —**шные работы** stripping.

вслед *adv. and prep. dat.* after; **в. за** behind, after, following, subsequent to; next to; **в. за ними** followed by; **в. за чем** following which, whereupon; **в. за этим** subsequently; **послать в.** *v.* forward.

вследствие *prep. gen.* in consequence of, owing to, on account of, due to, as a result of, because of, through; so that; **в. того, что** due to the fact that; **в. этого** as a consequence, because of this, that is why.

вслепую *adv.* (av.) blind.

в.сл.р. *abbr.* (**весьма слабо растворимо**) poorly soluble.

вслу/х *adv.* aloud; —**ш(ив)аться** *v.* listen attentively.

ВСМ *abbr.* (**высокомолекулярное соединение**) macromolecular compound.

всматриваться, всмотреться *v.* look into, examine, scrutinize, peer at; observe.

всов(ыв)ать *v.* push in, put in, shove in, slip in, insert.

всос/анный *a.* sucked in, etc., *see v.;* suction; —**ать** *v.* suck in or up, soak up, absorb, imbibe; draw in, pull in.

ВСП *abbr.* (**вертикальное сейсмическое профилирование**) vertical seismic profiling; (**временный спад проницаемости**) temporary drop in permeability.

вспаивать *v.* raise, rear (on milk).

вспархивать *v.* fly up; take wing.

вспарывать *v.* rip up.

вспа/ханный *a.* plowed; —**х(ив)ать** *v.* plow, till, cultivate; —**хивание** *n.,* —**шка** *f.* plowing, tilling; —**шка-взмёт** *f.* first tilth; —**шка-лущение** *f.* stubble breaking.

вспен/енный *a.* frothed, etc., *see v.;* —**ивание** *n.* frothing, etc., *see v.;* **бурное** —**ивание** effervescence; —**иватель** *m.* frother; frothing, foaming or blowing agent; —**и(ва)ться** *v.* froth, foam, lather; blow; —**ивающий** *a.* frothing, etc., *see v.*

всплес/к *m.* splash(ing); burst, eruption; surge, bump (of current); flash-up (of power); spike (of pulse); —**кивание** *n.* splashing; stirring; —**кивать**, —**нуть** *v.* splash; stir; —**нутый** *a.* splashed.

всплош/ную, —**ь** *adv.* without interruption, continuously, unbroken.

всплы/ваемость *f.* buoyancy; flotation; —**вание** *n.* floating (up), etc., *see v.;* (flotation) levitation; —**вать** *v.* float (up), emerge, surface, rise or come to the surface, (comp.) pop up; come up, arise, come to light; —**вающий** *a.* floating (up), etc., *see v.;* buoyant; supernatant; —**вающее меню** popup menu; —**вной** *a.* floating; flotation (process); buoyancy; —**вная сила** force of buoyancy; —**вший** *a.* emersed; surfaced; —**тие** *see* **всплывание**; pivoting; —**тый** *a.* floated, etc., *see v.;* —**ть** *see* **всплывать**.

вспоить *v.* raise, rear (on milk).
всполаскивать *v.* rinse.
всполашивать *see* **всполошить**.
всполз/ание *n.* creeping; **—ать, —ти** *v.* creep.
всполоснуть *v.* rinse.
всполохи *pl.* northern lights.
всполо/хнуть, —шить *v.* raise an alarm; rouse, startle; **—шиться** *v.* take alarm; be startled.
всполье *n.* ridge.
вспом/инать, —нить *v.* recollect, recall, remember, think (of).
вспомогатель *m.* booster.
вспомогательн/ый *a.* auxiliary, accessory, subsidiary; relief, emergency, standby, on hand, spare; booster; slave (unit); additional, added, secondary (entry); supplementary (index); intermediary (language); stabilizing (float); **в. агрегат** booster; **в. двигатель** servomotor; **—ая часть** accessory; **—ое средство** means; **—ые программы** (comp.) utilities.
вспомогать *v.* assist, aid.
вспороть *v.* rip up.
вспорхнуть *v.* fly up; take wing.
вспот/елый *a.* perspiring, perspired; **—еть** *v.* perspire, sweat.
вспрыг/ивать, —нуть *v.* jump up.
вспрыс/кивание *n.* injection; **—кивать, —нуть** *v.* inject, give a shot; sprinkle, dampen.
вспуг/ивать, —нуть *v.* frighten away.
вспузыри(ва)ться *v.* blister.
вспух/ание *n.* swelling, intumescence; **—ать, —нуть** *v.* swell; **—ающий** *a.* swelling; bulking (sludge); **—лый, —ший** *a.* swollen.
вспуч/енный *a.* swollen, bloated, etc., *see v.;* **—иваемость** *f.* bloating; expansion (of carbon anodes, etc.); **—ивание** *n.* swelling, etc., *see v.;* (geol.) heave, heaving; upwarp(ing); intumescence; **—иватель** *m.* bloater; **—ивать** *v.* swell (up), expand; puff up, bloat, blow up, inflate; **—иваться** *v.* swell up, bulk, expand; bloat, bulge, tumesce; blister; heave, upwarp; rise; **—ивающийся** *a.* swelling, etc., *see v.;* **—ина** *f.* blister; swelling; **—ить** *see* **вспучивать**.
вспушенн/ость *f.* fluffiness; looseness (of soil); **—ый** *a.* fluffy; loose.
вспыл/ить *v.* flare up; get angry; **—ьчивый** *a.* hot-tempered, irascible.
вспых/ивание *see* **вспышка**; **—ивать, —нуть** *v.* flash, flare up, flame up, blaze up, burst out; catch fire; scintillate; **—ивающий** *a.* flashing, etc., *see v.*
вспыш/ечный *a.*, **—ка** *f.* flash, flare, blaze; ignition, spark, scintillation; ignition, inflammation, firing; deflagration; explosion; outburst, spurt; outbreak (of epidemic); (astr.) burst; fulmination; **проба на —ку** flash test; **сварка —кой** flash welding; **сгорание со —кою** deflagration; **температура —ки** flash point; **температурные —ки** temperature flashes; flash temperatures.
встав/ание *n.* rising, getting up; **—ать** *v.* get up, stand up, rise.
встав/ить *see* **вставлять; —ка** *f.* insertion, etc., *see v.;* insertion piece, insert, inset; plug; (elec.) fuse; (compass) point; (comp.) embedding, (bit) stuffing; (typ.) casing-in; **метод —ки** (hort.) split grafting; **—кодержатель** *m.* fuse holder; **—ление** *n.* insertion, etc., *see v.;* **—ленный** *a.* inserted, etc., *see v.;* **—лять** *v.* insert, put in, install; set (in), fit (into), nest; fix in, encase, frame, mount; (comp.) paste; embed, inlay; secure, engage (in); introduce; intercalate, interpose; (math.) interpolate; **—ной** *a.* insert(ed), insertion; intercalary;

detachable, loose; plug-in; **—ной зуб** false tooth; (mech.) bit; **—ной-вытяжной** *a.* (elec.) push-pull; **—очный** *a.* inserted, intercalary; insertion (piece); interjected, interposed; **—чатопозвонковые** *pl.* (pal.) Embolomeri.
встанет *fut. 3 sing. of* **встать**.
встар/ину, —ь *adv.* in the past.
встать *see* **вставать**.
встопорщиться *v.* bristle (up), stand on end.
всторошенный *a.* rough (ice).
встраивать *v.* build in, install; incorporate.
встревож/енный *a.* anxious, agitated, upset; **—ить** *v.* (give the) alarm, worry; trouble, disturb, bother; **—иться** *v.* be anxious, be worried (about).
встрепать *v.* ruffle, dishevel.
встрепенуться *v.* rouse oneself; spread its wings; begin to throb (of heart).
встретить *see* **встречать**.
встреч/а *f.* meeting, encounter, contact; rendezvous (in space); convergence; collision, impact; incidence; **место —и** collision point; **—аемость** *f.* frequency, occurrence, rate of incidence; **—аемость-обилие** frequency-abundance; **—ать** *v.* meet, encounter, find, come across; strike (oil); **—аться** *v.* meet, encounter, come across, come up against, run into; rendezvous; be met, be found, occur, happen; turn up; **часто —аться** *v.* be widely met, be common, be widespread; **—ающийся** *a.* met, encountered, occurring; found; *m.* the one met; **—ающийся в природе** natural; **—ающийся при** encountered when, involved in; **—енный** *a.* met, etc., *see v.*
встреч/но-параллельный *a.* antiparallel; **в.-пересекающийся** *a.* collision (course); **—ный** *a.* counter (flow, etc.); contrary; head (wind); oncoming, head-on (collision); collision (course); **—ное излучение** (meteor.) back radiation; **первый —ный** *am.* the first comer; **—у** *prep. dat.* counter to.
встро/енный *a.* built in, fixed; embedded; **—енные программы** (comp.) firmware; **—ить** *see* **встраивать; —йка** *f.* building in.
встряска *see* **встряхивание**.
встряхив/ание *n.* shaking up, etc., *see v.;* vibration; **—атель** *m.* shaker; agitator; (rad.) scrambler; **—ать** *v.* shake (up), jar, jolt; vibrate; agitate, stir; toss out; scramble; **—ающий** *a.* shaking, etc., *see v.;* jarring (table); jigging (conveyer); vibrating (screen); **—ающий формовочный** (met.) jolt-ramming.
встряхнуть *see* **встряхивать**.
вступ/ать *v.* enter, step in; go into, come into, make (contact); join (union); act (as); **в. в действие** go into effect, become valid; **в. в реакцию** react; **—аться** *v.* intercede, stand up, stick up (for); **—ающий** *a.* entering, incoming; **—ительный** *a.* introductory; admission, ingoing, incoming; entrance (examination); **—ить** *see* **вступать; —ление** *n.* entry, entrance; introduction, opening; arrival; occurrence (of an event).
встык *adv.* butt; **приделанный в.** butted; **сваривать в.** *v.* butt-weld; **соединение в.** butt joint.
всунут/ый *a.* put in, inserted; pushed in; **—ь** *see* **всовывать**.
всухую *adv.* dry; **шлифованный в.** dry ground; **шлифовать в.** *v.* dry grind.
всучи(ва)ть *v.* interlace, intertwine; foist off.
всхо/д *m.* ascent, rise; **—ды** *pl.* young growth, sprouts, shoots; seedlings; **—дить** *v.* rise, mount, ascend, climb; (bot.) come up, sprout, germinate; **—дозащитный** *a.* (protective) mulch; **—жесть** *f.* germinating capacity, viability; germination; **—жий** *a.* germinating, germinative, viable.

всхолмлённый *a.* hilly, hillocky.

всхрап/нуть, —ывать *v.* snore; breathe heavily.

всып/ание *n.,* **—ка** *f.* filling, pouring in (dry material); **—анный** *a.* poured in; **—ать** *v.* fill (with), pour in; **—ной** *a.* pouring; bulk; random, haphazard.

всырую *adv.* wet, damp; **формовка в.** (met.) green sand molding.

всю *acc. of* **вся; во в.** fully.

всюду *adv.* everywhere; completely.

вся *f. of* **весь; —кий** *a. and pron.* any, every, each; anyone, anybody, everyone, everybody; **—кая рыба, в.-рыба** *f.* (ichth.) bream (*Abramis brama*); **—чески** *adv.* in every way; **—ческий** *a.* of every kind, every type.

вт *abbr.* (**ватт**) watt.

ВТ *abbr.* (**техническая вода**) industrial water; (**воздушная тревога**) air alert; (**вращающийся трансформатор**) rotating transformer.

втайне *adv.* secretly, confidentially.

вталкив/ание *n.* pushing in, etc., *see v.;* **—атель** *m.* pusher; **—ать** *v.* push, force, thrust or shove in; **—аться** *v.* run into, collide (with).

втаптыв/ание *n.* trampling down; **—ать** *v.* trample down, stamp in.

втаск/ивание *n.* dragging in, etc., *see v.;* **—(ив)ать** *v.* drag in, pull in, haul in.

втач/ать, —ивать *v.* stitch in.

втащить *see* **втаскивать.**

втек/ание *n.* inflow(ing), influx; **—ать** *v.* flow in, run in, discharge into; **—ающий** *a.* inflowing; influent (stream); **—ающая жидкость** inflow.

втер/еть *see* **втирать; —еться** *v.* make one's way into, insinuate oneself; soak in, rub in, penetrate.

втёртый *a.* rubbed in, smeared in.

втеч/ение *see* **втекание; —ь** *see* **втекать.**

втир/ание *n.* rubbing in; (med.) rub; **—ать** *v.* rub in, smear in.

втис/к(ив)ать, —нуть *v.* squeeze in, press in, force in, jam in; **—к(ив)аться** *v.* be forced in, etc.; force oneself in; be a tight fit.

ВТК *abbr.* (**вязкостно-температурный коэффициент**) viscosity-temperature coefficient.

вт/кг *abbr.* (**ватт на килограмм**) watts per kilogram; **вт/м²** *abbr.* (**ватт на квадратный метр**) watts per square meter.

втолк/ать, —нуть *v.* push in, shove in.

втолков(ыв)ать *v.* make understand.

втолкут *fut. 3 pl. of* **втолочь.**

втолочь *v.* grind in.

втоптать *see* **втаптывать.**

втор— *abbr.* (**вторичный**) secondary; *sec*-(compounds); **—ак** *m.* (bees) after swarm; **—ая** *f.* second part.

вторг/аться *v.* intrude, break in, encroach (upon), invade; intervene; (geol.) irrupt; **—ающийся** *a.* intruding; incoming; (geol.) intrusive, irruptive; **—нувшийся** *a.* intruding; incoming; **—нуться** *see* **вторгаться; —шийся** *a.* having entered; having invaded.

вторец: обтачивать в. *v.* face.

вторжение *n.* intrusion, etc., *see* **вторгаться;** inbreaking, ingression, injection; encroachment; (polar, etc.) outbreak.

вторить *v.* echo, repeat.

вторичн/о *adv.* a second time, again, re—; *prefix* deuter(o)— (secondary); **в. использовать** *v.* recycle; **—обутиламин** *m.* sec-butylamine; **—оводные** *pl.* (mam.) reentrants; **—опокровный** *a.* (bot.; geol.) metachlamydeous; **—ополостной** *a.* (embr.) coelomate; **—ополостные** *pl.* (zool.) Coelomata; **—опо-**

чечный *a.* (anat.) metanephric; **—оротые** *pl.* (zool.) Deuterostomata; **—оротый** *a.* deterostomatous; **—ость** *f.* (embr.) deuterogenesis; **в.-эмиттирующий** *a.* secondary-emission; **—ый** *a.* secondary; derived; re—; reiterative; deuterogenic, of secondary origin; **—ое замерзание** refreezing.

вторн/ик, —ичный *a.* Tuesday.

второ— *prefix* second(ary).

втор/ой *a.* second; **—ого порядка** secondary; **во —ых** in the second place, secondly; **—оклассный** *a.* second-class; secondary; **—окурсник** *m.* sophomore; **—олетний** *a.* second-year; **—оочередной** *a.* of secondary importance.

второпях *adv.* hastily, hurriedly.

второ/разрядный, —сортный *a.* second-rate, inferior; **—сортная руда** (min.) seconds; **—сортность** *f.* inferior quality; **—степенный** *a.* secondary, unimportant, minor, accessory, supplementary; **—тёлка** *f.* twice-calved cow; **—укосный** *a.* aftermath harvest; conducive to second crop.

вторсырьё *n.* recycled product.

в.т.р. *abbr.* (**весьма трудно растворимо**) difficultly soluble.

втрав/ить, —ливать *v.* draw into, involve.

втрамбов(ыв)ать *v.* ram in.

в-третьих *introd. word* in the third place, thirdly.

втро/е *adv.* three times (as much, as many, as large); threefold; (fold) in three; **в. больше** three times as much; **в. меньше** one third as much; **—ём** *adv.* three (together); **—йне** *adv.* threefold.

вт-с, втсек, вт-сек *abbr.* (**ватт-секунда**) watt-second.

ВТСП *abbr.* (**высокотемпературный сверхпроводник**) high-temperature superconductor, HTSC.

втуз *m.,* **—овский** *a.* technical educational institute, technical college.

втул/ка *f.* (mach.) bush(ing), sleeve, socket, collar, boss; insert, liner, housing; spigot; stopper, plug, bung; (wheel) hub; **направляющая в.** valve guide; **—ковидный** *a.* (biol.) modioliform; **—очно-роликовый** *a.* sprocket, roller (chain); **—очный** *a. of* **втулка;** socket (wrench); **—очная муфта** box coupling, sleeve coupling.

втупик *adv.* dead end; **ставить в.** *v.* perplex, baffle, puzzle.

втч, вт-ч *abbr.* (**ватт-час**) watt-hour; **в т.ч.** *abbr.* (**в том числе**) among them.

вты/кать *v.* thrust in(to), stick in(to), plug in; drive in (stake); **—чной** *a.* plug-in.

втягив/ание *n.* drawing in, etc., *see v.;* suction; retraction; **—атель** *m.* retractor; **—ать** *v.* draw in, pull in, suck in, absorb; retract (wheels); involve; engage (in); **—аться** *v.* be drawn in, take part (in), participate, become involved (in); enter; get used (to), get accustomed (to); **—ающий** *a.* drawing in, etc., *see v.;* pulling (coil); **—ающая мышца** (anat.) retractor; **—ающийся** *a.* retractable; contractile (root).

втя/жение *see* **втягивание; —жка** *f.* concavity; **—жной** *a.* retractile, retractable; suction, pull-in; plunger; **—нутость** *f.* retractility; retraction; **—нутый** *a.* drawn in (or back), etc., *see* **втягивать; —нуть** *see* **втягивать.**

ВУ *abbr.* (**вертикальный угол**) vertical angle; (**верхний уровень**) upper level; (**выпрямительное устройство**) rectifier; (**вычислительное устройство**) computer; (**вязкость условная**) conventional viscosity.

вуал/еобразный *a.* (biol.) veliform; **—еобразование** *n.* (phot.) fogging; **—ехвост** *m.* (ichth.) veiltail; **—ирование** *n.* (phot.) fogging; (paints) hazing, blooming;

—ировать v. fog; haze; veil; mask; **—ирующий** a. fogging, etc., see v.; **—ь** f. film, veil; (phot.) fog; (text.) voile.

Вуда сплав Wood's alloy.

вудвардит m. (min.) woodwardite.

Вудруф(ф)а шпонка Woodruff key.

Вудс Хол (geog.) Woods Hole.

вудсия f. (bot.) Woodsia.

вуз m., **—овский** a. higher institute of learning, college, university.

вулка— prefix Vulca— (in trade names); **—лок** m. (rubber bonding) Vulcalock.

вулкан m. volcano.

вулканиз/ат m. vulcanized rubber, vulcanizate; **ненаполненный в.** pure-gum vulcanizate; **—атор** m. vulcanizer, vulcanizing agent; **—аторщик** m. vulcanizer (operator); **—ационный** a., **—ация** f., **—(ир)о-вание** n. vulcanization; cure; (polymer) cross-linking; **замедлитель —ации** antiscorch (agent); **ускоритель —ации** rubber accelerator; **—(ир)ованный** a. vulcanized, cured; **—(ир)овать** v. vulcanize, cure; **—м** m. (geol.) volcanism, volcanicity; **—уемость** f. rate of cure; **—ующийся** a. vulcanizable, curable; cross-link-able.

вулканит m. vulcanite (hard rubber).

вулканическ/ий a. volcanic; **—ого происхождения** volcanic; igneous; **—ое стекло** (petr.) volcanic glass, obsidian.

вулканогенный a. of volcanic origin.

вулканоид m. mud volcano.

вулканолог/ический a. volcanological; **—ия** f. volcanology.

вулка/нский a. (geol.) vulcanian (eruption); **—нфибра** f. vulcanized fiber (leather substitute); **—фор** m. Vulcafor (rubber accelerator); **—цит** m. Vulkazit (rubber accelerator).

вулкмаст m. (tire) recapping shop.

вулпиновая кислота vulpic acid.

вульв/а f. (anat.) vulva; **—ит** m. (med.) vulvitis; **—ова-гинальный** a. (anat.) vulvovaginal.

вульгар/изировать v. popularize; **—ный** a. (biol.) common (vulgaris).

вультекс m. vultex (vulcanized latex).

Вульфа склянка Woulfe bottle.

вульфенит m. (min.) wulfenite.

вульфова see **Вульфа.**

вульяврский a. (geog.) Vulyavr.

вуоксинский a. (geog.) Vuoksa.

вурстер m. (Wurster) pulper, shredder.

вуртц/илит m. (min.) wurtzilite; **—ит** m. wurtzite.

вустит m. wustite (ferrous oxide-ferrous silicate).

вут m. (reinforced concrete) bracket.

ву(т)ц m. wootz steel.

вуцин m. vuzine, isooctylhydrocupreine.

ВУШ abbr. (**воспринимаемый уровень шума**) perceived noise level.

ВХ abbr. (**винилхлорид**) vinyl chloride; (**вода, химическо очищенная**) chemically purified water.

вход m. (point of) entry, entrance, door(way); entering, admission, access; (comp.) login, logon; aperture, opening, orifice; inlet, intake, input, influx; re-entry; (anat.) aditus; **на —е** inlet (temperature, etc.); input (velocity, etc.); **на три —а, с тремя —ами** three-input (adder); **в.-выход** m. (comp.) input-ouput; **—ец** m. (bot.) omphalo(i)dium; **—ить** v. enter, come or go (into), pass in penetrate; (comp.) log in, log on; re-enter (atmosphere); fit in, be contained (in); appear, be (present), occur, appear; **—ить в** fit in; become (the prac-

tice); **—ить в состав** become a component; **в число —ить** be among.

входн/ой a. of **вход**; re-entrant (angle); input, source (information); acceptance (tests); **в. триггер** (comp.) flip-flop; **в. элемент** receiver; **—ое отверстие** inlet, intake; **—ое реактивное сопротивление** (elec.) input reactance; **—ое сопротивление** input resistance; **—ое устройство** input unit.

вхо/дящая f. (com.) incoming paper; **—дящий** a. entering, etc., see **входить;** incoming; input, source (information); re-entrant (angle); male (thread); **—дящие в него** its constituent; **—ждение** n. entering, etc., see **входить;** (re-)entry; (math.) occurrence; (rad.) establishment (of contact).

вхолодную adv. cold; **окраска в.** cold dyeing.

вхолостую adv. idle, empty, no-load; **идя в., работая в., работающий в.** (mach.) idling; **работать в.** v. (run) idle.

В/Ц abbr. (**водо-цементное соотношение**) water-cement ratio.

вце/дить, —живать v. filter in; pour in; transfuse; **—женный** a. filtered in.

вцеп/иться, —ляться v. catch hold (of), seize, hook on, grasp, cling (to).

ВЧ abbr. (**высокая частота, высокочастотный**) high frequency; **в.ч.** abbr. (**весовая часть**) part by weight.

вчера adv. yesterday; **в. вечером** last night; **—шний** a. yesterday's.

вчерне adv. in the rough, unfinished; in draft form.

вчер/тить, —чивать v. draw in, sketch in, trace in, inscribe.

вчетверо adv. four times; (fold) in four; **в. больше** four times as much; **в. меньше** one fourth; **—м** adv. four (together).

в-четвёртых introd. word in the fourth place, fourthly.

вчистую adv. clean, final, in final form; **обрабатывать в.** v. finish, dress.

вчит(ыв)аться v. read up (on), become familiar (with).

вчуствоваться v. get into the spirit (of).

вш/и see **вошь; —ей** gen. pl. of **вошь.**

вшей(те) imp. of **вшить.**

вшестеро adv. six times; **в. больше** six times as much; **в. меньше** one sixth; **—м** adv. six (together).

в-шестых introd. word in the sixth place.

вши pl. of **вошь;** (ent.) lice (Anoplura); **карповые в.** (crust.) fish lice (Branchiura); **китовые в.** Cyamidae; **колючие в.** (ent.) Echinophthiri(i)dae; **пчелиные в.** bee lice (Braulidae); **растительные в., травяные в.** plant lice, aphids (Aphididae).

вшивать v. sew in, stitch in.

вшив/еть v. become louse-infested; **—ица** f. (bot.) lousewort (Pedicularis).

вшив/ка f. sewing in; **—ной** a. sewn in.

вшив/ость f. (med.) pediculosis; **—ый** a. louse(-infes-ted), lousy, pediculous.

вширь adv. in width.

вшит/ый a. sewn in; **—ь** see **вшивать.**

вшпунт adv. tongue and groove (joint).

въ— see **в—** before **е** and **я.**

въедаться v. corrode, eat into; get accustomed (to a food).

въедет fut. 3 sing. of **въехать.**

въед/ливый, —чивый a. corrosive; penetrating (smell).

въезд m., **—ной** a. drive, approach, entrance, entry; approach ramp; (text.) run-in (of carriage); **—ная виза** entry permit.

въезжать v. enter, drive in, move into.

въесться see **въедаться.**

въехать *see* **въезжать.**

вы *pron. pl.* you.

вы— *prefix* ex—, out of.

выбалансировать *v.* balance (out).

выбег *m.* running out, coasting; (mach.) running down, rundown; stopping distance (of brakes); overshoot, overswing (of pointer); (temperature) excursion; (frequency) drift; (bot.) shoot, sprout; —**гать, —жать** *v.* run out.

выбей(те) *imp. of* **выбить.**

выбели(ва)ть *v.* bleach, whiten; whitewash.

выберет *fut. 3 sing. of* **выбрать.**

выбив/алка *f.* knocker; rapper; —**альный** *a.,* —**ание** *n.* knocking out, etc., *see v.;* —**ание пастбища** overgrazing; —**ать** *v.* knock out, drive out, force out, eject, strike; shake out, dislodge; beat out, stamp (out), punch; break open, smash; deflect; emboss; —**аться** *v.* be knocked out, etc.; get out, break out, escape; extricate oneself; (av.) tumble, topple; —**ка** *see* **выбивание;** (met.) knock-out; —**ной** *see* **выбивальный;** knock-out, shake-out; bursting (charge).

выбир/аемый *a.* selective; —**ание** *n.* selection, etc., *see v.;* —**атель** *m.* selector; (elec.) selector switch; —**ать** *v.* select, choose, single out, pick (out), cull; sort out; adopt, decide (on); elect; take out, recover; take in, haul in (rope); take up (slack); weigh (anchor); —**аться** *v.* be selected, etc.; get out; go out; move.

выбит/ый *a.* knocked out, etc., *see* **выбивать; knocked-on** (atom); overgrazed (pasture); —**ь** *see* **выбивать.**

выблен/ка *f.,* —**очный** *a.* (naut.) ratline; —**очный узел** clove hitch.

выбо/ина *f.,* —**й** *m.* hollow, dent, indentation; rut, pot hole (in road).

выбой/ка *f.,* —**чатый** *a.* siftings, fines; (text.) printed linen.

выбор *m.* choice, selection, pick; sample, sampling; option; election; **в. из кучи** bulk sampling; **без —а** at random; **возможность —а** option; **остановить свой в.** *v.* fix on, decide on; **по —у** optional; **свобода —а** latitude; —**ка** *f.* selection, excerpt; sorting; (math.; stat.) sample, sampling; (comp.) access; fetch; retrieval; recovery; extract; lift, hault (of seine); **время —ки** access time; **проверять на —ку** *v.* spot check; **распределение —ки** (stat.) sample distribution; —**ный** *a.* sample; elective, electoral; *m.* delegate; —**ок** *m.* choice item; —**очность** *f.* optionality; —**очный** *a.* selective; selected (data); sample, sampling; random, spot (check); in patches; —**очный рычаг** (comp.) access arm; —**очная проба** (stat.) sample; —**очного контроля** sampling (theory); **ошибка —очного обследования** sampling error; **с —очным ответом** multiple-cohice (question).

выбражив/ание *n.* fermentation; —**ать** *v.* ferment (fully); wander over.

выбраков/ка *f.* culling, etc., *see v.;* selective harvesting; rejection; —**(ыв)ать** *v.* cull, sort; discard, reject, throw out.

выбранный *a.* selected, etc., *see* **выбирать.**

выбрасыв/аемый *a.* ejected, etc., *see v.;* vent (gases); —**ание** *n.* ejection, ejecting, etc., *see v.;* ejaculation; —**ание султанов** (bot.) tasseling; **рефлекс —ания** (orn.) rejection reflex; —**атель** *m.* ejector, knock-out (rod); extractor; shedder; lift(ing) out device; pusher; —**ать** *v.* eject, expel, vent; eliminate, discard, reject, throw out, throw away; fling out; knock out (atom); exclude, omit, leave out; waste, squander; cast (ashore); project (rays); release (for sale); reject, dismiss; (naut.) run (aground); set, shoot (a net); —**аться** *v.* be ejected, etc., jump out, bale out; —**ающий** *a.* ejecting, etc., *see*

v.; ejection; (physiol.) ejaculatory; —**ающий механизм** ejector.

выбрать *see* **выбирать.**

выбри(ва)ть *v.* shave clean.

выбро/дивший *a.* (fully) fermented; —**дить** *see* **выбраживать;** —**женный** *a.* fermented.

выброс *m.* ejection; rejection; release, emission; exhaust, waste; effluent; overshoot(ing), overswing, miss; blowout, blowing; outburst; (commun.) pip; blip (on screen); (elec.) peaked trace; (mole) hill; —**ы** *pl.* discharge, waste; (lunar) ejecta; **газовые —ы** waste gases; —**ать, —ить** *see* **выбрасывать;** —**ка** *see* **выбрасывание;** —**ный** *a.* of выброс.

выброшенный *a.* ejected, etc., *see* **выбрасывать.**

выбрыз/г(ив)ать, —нуть *v.* splash out, spatter.

выбур/енный *a.* drilled out; —**ивание** *n.* drilling out; —**и(ва)ть** *v.* drill out.

выбух/ание *n.* protrusion; **в. пупка** (med.) exomphalos; —**ать** *v.* protrude; swell out; —**ающий** *a.* protuberant.

выбы/(ва)ть *v.* leave, quit, withdraw, drop out; —**вший** *a.* leaving, quitting; —**тие** *n.* leaving, etc., *see v.;* attrition retirement.

выбьёт *fut. 3 sing. of* **выбить.**

вывал *m.* inrush; —**и(ва)ть** *v.* throw out, dump (out), tumble out; —**и(ва)ться** *v.* fall out, tumble out; rush (in or out).

вывар/енный *a.* extracted, etc., *see v.;* —**ивание** *n.* extraction, boiling out, etc., *see v.;* —**и(ва)ть** *v.* extract, boil out, decoct; boil down, boil off, evaporate (down); digest, cook; (text.) scour, degum; —**ка** *f.,* —**ной,** —**очный** *a.* extraction, etc., *see v.;* residue, remains; decoction; —**очная соль** common salt, sodium chloride.

вывев/ать *v.* (agr.) winnow, sift; —**ки** *pl.* winnowings, chaff.

выведать *see* **выведывать.**

вывед/ение *n.* deduction, etc., *see* **выводить;** withdrawal, removal; (physiol.) excretion; development (of breed); **в. на рабочую орбиту** insertion into orbit; —**ённый** *a.* deduced, etc., *see* **выводить.**

выведывать *v.* investigate, explore, find out, reveal.

вывезти *see* **вывозить.**

вывел *past m. sing. of* **вывести.**

вывер/енный *a.* adjusted, etc., *see* **выверять;** —**ить** *see* **выверять;** —**ка** *f.* adjustment, alignment, trueing, etc., *see* **выверять;** control.

вывернут/ый *a.* unscrewed, etc., *see* **вывёртывать;** —**ь** *see* **вывёртывать.**

выверочн/ый *a.* straightening, aligning, adjustment; **в. винт** fine adjustment; —**ая доска** straightedge.

выв/ертеть *v.* unscrew; —**ёртывать** *v.* unscrew, screw out, undo; turn, twist, wrench, disclocate; turn inside out; —**ёртываться** *v.* come unscrewed; slip out or away; get out, extricate oneself; be dislocated; turn up, appear suddenly.

выверчивать *v.* unscrew.

выверш/енный *a.* topped; —**ивание** *n.* topping; completion; —**ивать** *v.* top, finish off.

вывер/щик *m.* adjuster; —**ять** *v.* adjust, regulate; align, true, straighten, line up; correct; verify, test, check; gage, calibrate; set (a watch); —**яющийся** *a.* adjustable.

вывес/ить *see* **вывешивать;** —**ка** *f.* sign(board); weighing (out or up).

вывести *see* **выводить.**

выветр/елость *f.* weathered condition; —**елый,** —**енный** *a.* ventilated, aired; (geol.) weathered, eroded, windblown, wind-sculptured, eolian; efflorescent; —**еть** *v.* be dried by wind; weather; **—ивание** *n.* ventilation; weathering, disintegration, erosion, eolation; seasoning, aging; efflorescence; **кора —ивания** weathering crust; residual soil; **—и(ва)ть** *v.* ventilate, air; (geol.) weather, erode; season, age; **—и(ва)ться** *v.* be ventilated; weather, disintegrate, erode; effloresce; **—ившийся** *see* **выветренный.**

вывешивать *v.* hang out; weigh (out); test the weight (of).

вывин/тить, —чивать *v.* unscrew, screw out, undo; take out, remove (screw); loosen; **—ченный** *a.* unscrewed, etc., *see v.*

вывих *m.* (med.) luxation, dislocation, sprain, wrench; **—ивать, —нуть** *v.* dislocate, sprain; **—нутый** *a.* dislocated, sprained.

вывод *m.* deduction, conclusion, inference, corollary; finding(s), result, consequence; development; outlet, escape; withdrawal, removal; tapping (of electricity); leading out, etc., *see* **выводить;** (math.) derivation; (comp.) output, read-out; (elec.) terminal, bushing, leading-out wire, lead(out); **—ы** *pl.* summary; **делать в.** *v.* conclude, infer; **отсюда в., что** in conclusion; **при —е** in deriving; **—имость** *f.* deducibility, derivability; hatching capacity; **—имый** *a.* deducible, derivable, derived; removable.

вывод/ить *v.* deduce, conclude, infer; bring out, reveal; depict; lead out, take out, move out; destroy, remove, eliminate, eradicate; exterminate; withdraw, tap; (math.) derive; develop, evolve; erect (building); put (into orbit); disturb (equilibrium); draw (a conclusion); throw out (of gear), disengage; (chem.) separate, isolate; (physiol.) secrete, excrete; bring forth, breed; hatch; raise, grow, cultivate; show (an animal); **в. данные** *v.* (comp.) output; **—иться** *v.* be deduced, etc.; (chem., math.) derive; (physiol.) secrete; go out of use, become obsolete; die out, disappear, become extinct; hatch out; **—ка** *f.* taking out, removal; extermination; breeding, hatching; development (of variety); (animal) show; starting up; heating-up campaign (of furnace).

выводков/ые *pl.* autophagous birds; **—ый** *a. of* **выводок;** (biol.) proliferous; (orn.) precocial, nidifugous; newly hatched; **—ая камера, —ая полость** (zool.) brood pouch; **—ая почка** (bot.) bulbil, brood bulb; **—ая сумка** brood pouch.

выводн/ой *a. of* **вывод;** (physiol.) excretory, discharge, exhalant; (anat.) efferent; reserve (field); **—ая труба** outlet pipe; deliver pipe.

выводок *m.* bringing forth; brood.

выводящий *a.* deducing, etc., *see* **выводить;** outgoing, exit; (physiol.) excretory; (anat.) efferent.

вывоз *m.* export(ation); *see* **вывозка; в. на взяток** (bees) foraging; **—ить** *v.* export; remove, take out; haul, transport; **—ка** *f.* removal, taking out; delivery, transportation; **—ной** *a.* export; mobile.

вывол/акивать, —очь *v.* drag out.

вывор/ачивание *n.* reversing, etc., *see v.;* eversion; **—ачивать** *v.* reverse, turn inside out, evert, invert; tear out, pull out; distort; sprain, wrench; **—ачиваться** *v.* turn out, evert; **—от** *m.* reverse, underside; inversion; **—отить** *see* **выворачивать; —отка** *f.* (typ.) reversing; **—отный, —оченный** *a.* reversed, inverted.

вывяз(ыв)ать *v.* knit.

вывяли(ва)ть *v.* cure in open air.

выгад/ать, —ывать *v.* economize, save, spare; gain (time); **—ка** *f.,* **—ывание** *n.* economy, saving; gain.

выгар *m.,* **—ки** *pl.* slag, dross, cinder; (volcanic) scoria; burned-out forest area.

выгиб *m.* bend, curve, curvature, camber, flexure; warp-

ing; **—ание** *n.* bending, etc., *see v.;* **—атель** *m.* adjuster; **—ать** *v.* bend (out), curve, camber; **—аться** *v.* bend, be curved; arch, bulge; buckle, warp.

выгла/дить, —живать *v.* smooth (out); iron, press; burnish; **—женный** *a.* smoothed, etc., *see v.;* **—живание** *n.* smoothing, etc., *see v.*

выглублять *v.* (agr.) raise.

выгля/деть, —дывать, —нуть *v.* look, appear, seem; look out; emerge, show; find, discover.

выгнать *see* **выгонять.**

выгни(ва)ть *v.* rot out.

выгнут/ость *f.* convexity; curvature; **—ый** *a.* convex, curved (out), camber(ed), arched; **—ь** *see* **выгибать.**

выгов/аривать, —орить *v.* pronounce, enunciate, utter; stipulate, specify; reprimand, reprove, rebuke; reserve (for oneself); **—ор** *m.* pronunciation; lecture, reprimand, reproof, rebuke, admonition.

выгод/а *f.* profit, advantage, benefit, gain, interest; **—ен** *sh. m. of* **выгодный;** gained; **—нейший** *a.* most advantageous, optimal; **—но** *adv.* profitably; it is profitable, it is advantageous; **—ность** *f.* economy, advantage(ousness); utility, efficiency; **—ный** *a.* profitable, advantageous, remunerative, favorable; useful; economical, efficient.

выгодский *a.* (geog.) Vygoda.

выгозерский *a.* (geog.) Lake Vyg.

выгон *m.* distillation; pasture, pasturage; **—ка** *f.* distillation; (hort.) forcing; driving out; **—ный** *a.* grazing; **—очный** *a.* distillation; forcing; forced (plant); **—ять** *v.* drive out, expel, force out; distill; force.

выгораживать *v.* fence off, enclose, screen.

выгор/ание *n.* burning out, etc., *see v.;* burn-out, pitting; burn-off; burn-up; depletion (of fuel); **момент —ания** burn-out (of fuel); **—ать** *v.* burn out, down, up or away; be gutted; scorch, parch, wilt; die out; fade (of color); **—евший, —елый** *a.* burned out; faded; **—еть** *see* **выгорать;** come off, succeed.

выгород/ить *see* **выгораживать; —ка** *f.* compartment, enclosure.

выгравиров/анный *a.* carved out, engraved; sunken; **—ать** *v.* carve out, engrave.

выграни(ва)ть *v.* cut (facets).

выгре/б *m.* raking (out); cesspool; (agr.) bin gate; **—бание** *n.* raking out, etc., *see v.;* **—бать** *v.* rake out, clean out, scrape out, remove, empty; (naut.) row, pull (against current); **—бенный** *a.* raked out, etc., *see v.;* **—бка** *f.,* **—бной** *a.* raking (out); **—бная яма** cesspool; manure pit; **—сти** *see* **выгребать.**

выгру/жатель *m.* discharger; **—жать** *v.* discharge, unload, dump, empty, drain, evacuate; deplane, detrain, disembark; **—жаться** *v.* be discharged, etc.; deplane, detrain, disembark; **—женный** *a.* discharged, etc., *see v.;* **—зка** *f.,* **—зной, —зочный** *a.* unloading, etc., *see v.;* discharge; freight handling.

выгрыз/ать *v.* gnaw out, bite out; **—еннозубчатый** *a.* (bot.) erosodentate; **—енный** *a.* gnawed (out), bitten; (bot.) erose.

выгул *m.,* **—ьный** *a.* pasture, range; enclosure, run; **—иваться, —яться** *v.* graze, range.

выдавать *v.* distribute, give out, issue; yield, produce, turn out; grant (patent); pay out (rope); draw (a bill on); draw up; deliver; give, hand; generate (a signal); betray (a secret); (law) extradite; **в. себя** pass for, pose as; **—ся** *v.* protrude, project, jut out, stand out, be conspicuous; be remarkable, be distinguished (by); present itself, occur, happen to be.

выдав/ить *see* **выдавливать; —ка** *see* **выдавливание; —ленный** *a.* extruded, etc., *see v.;*

sunken, embossed (character); **—ливание** *n.* extrusion, squeezing out, etc., *see v.;* **—ливать** *v.* extrude, squeeze (out), force out, press (out), stamp (out); break in; squirt; emboss; spin (on lathe).

выдавшийся *a.* standing out, protruding.

выдаивать *v.* milk dry, strip (a cow).

выдай(те) *imp. of* **выдать.**

выдалбливать *v.* hollow out, chisel out, groove, slot; gouge; dig out, excavate; learn by heart.

выд/анный *a.* distributed, etc., *see* **выдавать;** **—ать** *see* **выдавать;** **—ача** *f.* distribution, etc., *see* **выдавать;** delivery, output, yield; production; presentation (of data); payment(s); **ожидается —ача патента** the patent is pending; **—ающийся** *a.* prominent, outstanding, eminent; protruding, projecting; salient (angle); **—ающийся вперёд** prominent.

выдви/г *m.* advance; **—гание** *see* **выдвижение;** **—гать** *v.* advance, promote, put forward, introduce, propose, bring forward, suggest, offer, adduce (an argument); set up, put up, pose, raise (a question); lay down (conditions); thrust out, push out; move out, slide out, open (a drawer); withdraw, draw out (of); extend; nominate; **—гаться** *v.* move forward, advance; slide out, pull out, extend; move out (of); **—женец** *m.* promoted worker; **—жение** *n.* advancing, promotion, etc., *see v.;* advance(ment).

выдвижной *a.* extensible, extension-type, pull-out, draw-out, telescopic; detachable; retractable; sliding (door); slide (gage); protractile, protrusile; **в. ящик** drawer.

выдвинут/ый *a.* advanced, etc., *see* **выдвигать; —ь** *see* **выдвигать.**

выдвор/ить, —ять *v.* turn out, evict.

выдел *m.* allotment, share; plot.

выдел/анный *a.* manufactured, etc., *see* **выделывать; —ать** *see* **выделывать.**

выделен/ие *n.* isolation, separation; selection, picking out; detection; formation (of precipitate); settling, precipitation, deposit; evolution, generation, release, liberation (of heat, gas, etc.); emanation, exhalation, emission; escape, loss; (physiol.) secretion, excretion, discharge; (met.) segregation; elimination, extraction; recovery; discrimination; (typ.) display; (comp.) (memory) allocation; **в. осадка** precipitation; **в. подсветкой** (comp.) highlight; **в. текста** display matter; **в. фосфора** dephosphorization; **момент —ия, состояние —ия** nascent state; **в состоянии —ия** nascent; **с —ием энергии** energy-yielding.

выдел/енный, —ившийся *a.* separated, etc., *see* **выделять;** preferred (axis); parting (silver); dedicated (line); **в. счётчиком** counter-defined; **—итель** *m.* separator, discriminator; extractor; (math.) eliminant; **—ительный** *a.* separating, etc., *see* **выделять;** (physiol.) secretory (gland); excretory (system); **—ить** *see* **выделять.**

выдел/ка *f.,* **—ывание** *n.* manufacture, production; make (leather) tanning, dressing; **—ывать** *v.* manufacture, make, produce, prepare; do, perform; tan, dress.

выделяем/ое *n.* excretion (product); **—ость** *f.* separability; **—ый** *a.* separated, etc., *see* **выделять;** separating; separable; precipitable.

выдел/ять *v.* separate (out), isolate; form (a precipitate); settle out, precipitate, deposit; evolve, liberate, give off (gas, heat, etc.); set free, yield, exhale; drive out, drive off, eliminate; split off; lose, detach, release; (physiol.) secrete, discharge, excrete, exude; withdraw, take away, extract; segregate; distinguish, discriminate; detect; select, choose, pick out, single out; apportion, allot, allocate, earmark, assign; **—яться** *v.* separate out; precipitate out; be given off, be liberated; escape, emanate (from); segregate; stand out; be distinguished (by, for); discharge, ooze out, exude; **—яющий** *a.* separating, etc., *see v.;* splitting off; secretory; (physiol.) apocrine; **—яющийся** *a.* separating out; precipitating; escaping (gas); prominent, outstanding, selective.

вы/дёргивание *n.* pulling out, etc., *see v.;* **—дёргать, —дёргивать** *v.* pull out, pluck out, draw (out), extract.

выдерж/анность *f.* consistency; self-control; discipline; stability, constancy; maturity (of wine); **—анный** *a.* seasoned, etc., *see v.;* consistent, uniform; self-controlled, self-restrained, disciplined, firm; ripe, mature; **—ать** *see* **выдерживать; —ивание** *n.* seasoning, etc., *see v.;* (phot.) exposure; (av.) holding off; storage; **—иватель** *m.* holder; **—ивать** *v.* season, cure, age, ripen; undergo, endure, suffer, experience, bear, (with)stand, hold out, stand up to; accept, support (a weight); allow to stand, keep, maintain, sustain, hold (at; to); store, preserve, keep; satisfy, pass (test); (phot.) expose; (met.) soak; (nucl.) cool; run (an edition); **не —ивать** *v.* fail.

выдержк/а *f. see* **выдерживание;** extract, excerpt, passage; endurance, stamina, staying power; discipline, firmness, self-control, self-restraint; constancy; maintenance; (phot.) exposure, shutter speed; **в. времени** time lag, time delay; (welding) hold time; **в. на температуре** (welding) heat time; **на —у** at random, spot (check); **с —ой времени** delayed-action; timed; **резервуар —и** (nucl.) decay tank.

выдер/ки *pl.* plucking; **—нутый** *a.* plucked, pulled; extracted; **—нуть** *see* **выдёргивать.**

выдирать *v.* rip up, rip out, tear out.

выдоить *v.* milk dry, strip (cow).

выдолб/ить *see* **выдалбливать; —ленный** *a.* hollowed out, etc., *see* **выдалбливать;** concave.

выдох *m.* expiration, exhalation, breathing out; **фаза —а** expiratory phase; **—лый** *a.* evaporated, flat; **—нуть** *v.* exhale, breathe out; **—нуться** *see* **выдыхаться; —шийся** *see* **выдохлый.**

выдра *f.* (mam.) otter (*Lutra lutra*); metal scrap.

выдразнивать *v.* (met.) tease, pole.

выдрать *see* **выдирать.**

выдрёнок *m.* young otter.

выдрессировать *v.* train (animals).

выдр/овоземлеройковые *pl.* (mam.) otter shrew family (*Potamogalidae*); **—ы** *pl.* Lutrinae.

выдубить *v.* tan (leather).

выдув/альщик *m.* (glass) blower; **—ание** *n.* blowing out, etc., *see v.;* blow off, expulsion, discharge; eolation, wind erosion; wind shifting; blowing, drifting (of soil); **—ать** *v.* blow (out, off, down); deflate; empty, discharge; **—ка** *see* **выдувание; —ной** *a.* blow(-out); blow (valve).

выдум/анный *a.* invented, etc., *see v.;* **—ка** *f.* invention; device; **—(ыв)ать** *v.* invent, devise, contrive, think up; make up, concoct; imagine.

выдут/ый *a.* blown out, etc., *see* **выдувать; —ь** *see* **выдувать.**

выдых *see* **выдох; —аемый** *a.* expired, exhaled; **—ание** *n.* evaporation; (physiol.) expiration, exhalation; **—атель** *m.* expiratory muscle; **—ательный** *a.* expiratory; **—ать** *v.* expire, exhale, breathe out; **—аться** *v.* expire; evaporate, volatilize; fade (of odor); go flat; peter out, be played out.

выед/ание *n.* eating away, etc., *see v.;* corrosion; **—ать** *v.* eat away, eat out, corrode, pit; attack; eat up, devour, consume; **—енный** *a.* eaten away., etc., *see v.*

выедет *fut. 3 sing. of* **выехать.**

выез/д *m.* departure; exit; **—дить** *v.* break in (horse); **—дка** *f.* breaking in; **—дной** *a.* of **выезд;** away (from); out-of-town (session); guest (performance); **—жать** *v.* leave, depart; break in; **—жать на** exploit; **—женный** *a.* broken in, manageable.

выел *past m. sing. of* **выесть.**

выем *see* **выемка.**

выем/ка *f.,* **—очный** *a.* hollow, recess, depression, dent, indentation; notch, gap; groove, furrow, channel(ing); (min.) cutting, excavation, digging; winning (of coal); drawing, removal, extraction (of ore); dugout, ditch, gutter; housing; sample; cavity, pit; (die) sprue) (law) seizure. **угол —ки** (surv.) angle of elevation.

выемчат/о— *prefix* sinuato—, sinuous; repando—, repand; **—озубчатый** *a.* (bot.) repando-dentate; **—окрылые** *pl.* (ent.) gelechiid moths; **—ый** *a.* emarginate, sinuate; retuse; forked (tail); dentate, toothed (leaf); notched.

выесть *see* **выедать.**

выехать *see* **выезжать.**

выжари(ва)ть *v.* roast out.

выжать *see* **выжимать, выжинать.**

выжгут *fut. 3 pl. of* **выжечь.**

выждать *see* **выжидать.**

выжелтить *v.* color yellow.

выжереб *m.,* **—ка** *f.* foaling (of horse).

выж/ечь *see* **выжигать; —женный** *a.* burned out, etc., *see* **выжигать.**

выжив/аемость *f.* survival; survival rate; viability; **—ание** *n.* survival; endurance; **—ать** *v.* survive, (out)live, pull through; stay, remain (a given time); suffer, bear, endure, stand; drive out, get rid (of); **—ший организм** survivor.

выжиг *m., see* **выжигание;** yield of calcined product; **—ание** *n.* burning out, etc., *see v.;* **—ать** *v.* burn out, burn up, burn over; roast (out), calcine; scorch; sear, cauterize; brand (cattle); (welding) penetrate.

выжид/ание *n.* waiting; expectation; **—ательный** *a.* expectant; **—ать** *v.* wait (for); expect; take one's time.

выжим/алка *f.* wringer; press, squeezer; **—ание** *n.* squeezing (out), etc., *see v.;* (hort.) heaving; **—ать** *v.* squeeze (out), press (out), force (out); centrifuge; wring (out); strip, extract; **—ка** *see* **выжимание;** spew, overflow; release, removal; fin, flash (from mold); **—ки** *pl.* residue, husks; waste; (grape) marc.

выжинать *v.* reap; mow off, mow down.

выжить *see* **выживать.**

выж/мет *fut. 3 sing. of* **выжать,** squeeze (out); **—нет** *fut. 3 sing. of* **выжать,** reap.

вызв/ан(ный) *a.* induced (by), etc., *see* **вызывать;** brought about (by), attributable (to), due to, through; **в. облучением** radiation-induced; **—ать** *see* **вызывать.**

вызвол/ить, —ять *v.* help, rescue.

выздор/авливание *n.* recovery, convalescence; **—авливать** *v.* recover, get well; recuperate, improve, get better; convalesce; **—авливающий** *a.* recovering, etc., *see v.;* convalescent; **—овевший** *a.* recovered; **—оветь** *see* **выздоравливать; —овление** *see* **выздоравливание.**

вызеленить *v.* color green.

вызимовать *v.* (agr.) winter; hibernate.

вызов *m.* summons; call(ing); ring(ing); (comp.) call, invocation; provocation, challenge; signalling; (law) summons; subpoena.

вызол/ачивать, —отить *v.* gild; **—оченный** *a.* gilt.

вызр/еваемость *f.* rate of ripening; **—евание** *n.* ripening, etc., *see v.;* **—е(ва)ть** *v.* ripen, mature, age; cure;

season; **—евший** *a.* ripe(ned), etc., *see v.;* hardwood (cutting).

вызубри(ва)ть *v.* notch; memorize.

вызыв/аемый *a.* induced (by), etc., *see v.;* (tel.) call(ed); **—ание** *n.* inducing, etc., *see v.;* **—ать** *v.* induce, evoke, cause, produce, bring about, give rise (to), lead (to), result (in), be responsible (for); elicit, call forth; provoke, attract, arouse (interest); raise (doubts); present (problems); create (complications); activate, excite, generate (current); exert (pressure); set up (vibrations); involve, send (for), summon; (tel.) call (up); invite, challenge; **—аться** *v.* be brought about (by), be due (to); arise, stem, result (from); volunteer, offer; undertake; **—ающий** *a.* inducing, etc., *see v.;* **—ной** *a.* (tel.) call(ing).

вызяб/ать, —нуть *v.* (agr.) freeze.

выи *gen., pl., etc., of* **выя.**

выигра *f.* swarming (of bees).

выигр/(ыв)ать *v.* win, gain, profit, benefit; **—ыш** *m.* gain, winnings; advantage, payoff; **коэффициент —ыша** gain factor; **функция —ыша** payoff function; **—ышный** *a.* gain(ed); advantageous.

выиск *m.,* **—ивание** *n.* search; **—(ив)ать** *v.* hunt (for) search, look for; find out, discover; **—и(ва)ться** *v.* turn up, be found.

выйдет *fut. 3 sing. of* **выйти.**

выйный *a.* (anat.) nuchal.

выйский *a.* (geog.) Vy(i)ya.

выйти *see* **выходить.**

выказ/ать, —ывать *v.* show, display, manifest; **—ной** *a.* exhibited.

выкали(ва)ть *v.* calcine (thoroughly).

выкалывать *v.* prick out, puncture; chip out.

выкапчивать *v.* smoke, cure.

выкапыв/ание *n.* digging up, etc., *see v.;* **—ать** *v.* dig up, excavate, unearth, exhume; lift, dig out (plants).

выкарабк(ив)аться *v.* scramble out; get out.

выкармливать *v.* fatten, feed; rear, raise.

выкат *m.* rolling out; **—ать, —ить, —ывать** *v.* roll out, wheel out; mangle, roll flat; **—ка** *f.,* **—ывание** *n.* rolling out, etc., *see v.;* (av.) overrun.

выкач/анный *a.* pumped out, etc., *see v.;* **—ать, —ивать** *v.* pump (out), empty, evacuate, exhaust, deflate; extract (honey); **—ивание** *n.,* **—ка** *f.* pumping (out), evacuation, etc., *see v.*

выкашивать *v.* (agr.) mow.

выкашл/ивать, —ять *v.* cough up; expectorate; **—иваться** *v.* clear one's throat.

выквасить *v.* make sour, acidify.

вык/ид *m.* discharge; **—идать** *v.* reject, eliminate, throw out, discard; discharge; omit, exclude; **—идаться** *v.* jump out; pour out (of smoke); (med.) miscarry, abort; **—идка** *f.,* **—идывание** *n.* rejection, etc., *see v.;* **—идной** *a.* discharge; delivery (line); **—идывать** *see* **выкидать; —идыш** *m.* miscarriage, abortion; fetus; **—инутый** *a.* rejected, etc., *see v.;* **—инуть** *see* **выкидать.**

выкип/ать, —еть *v.* boil away, boil out; evaporate; distill (off); **—елый** *a.* boiled away; **—ятить, —ячивать** *v.* boil (out); scald; **—яченный** *a.* boiled.

выкис/ать, —нуть *v.* turn sour.

выклад/ка *f.,* **—ывание** *n.* laying out, etc., *see v.;* (math.) calculations, computations; (mil.) pack, kit; **делать —ки** *v.* compute; **—ывать** *v.* lay out, spread out; take out, unpack; line, face, border; castrate, geld.

выкл/ев *m.,* **—ёвывание** *n.* pecking out, hatching; **—еваться, —ёвываться** *v.* peck through the shell, emerge, hatch.

выклеймить *v.* mark with a brand.

выкл/епать, —ёпывать *v.* rivet; take out rivets; dress, hammer out.

выклик/ать, —нуть *v.* call out; call the roll.

выклин/ивание *n.* thinning out, etc., *see v.;* **в. на поверхность** cropping out; **место —ивания** pinchout position; **—и(ва)ть** *v.* taper; remove wedge; **—и(ва)ться** *v.* thin out, taper (out), pinch out, peter out, wedge out, crop out, play out.

выклюнуться *see* **выклёвываться.**

выключ/аемый *a.* switch-controlled; **в. элемент** spare cell; **—атель** *m.* (elec.) switch, circuit breaker, cut-out; release, releasing device; **—атель пуска** starting switch; **—ать** *v.* disconnect, disengage, uncouple, release; turn off (current, gas), cut off, cut out, shut off; (elec.) switch off, break (contact); shut down, put out of service; throw out (of gear); exclude, leave out; (typ.) justify; **—ающий** *a.* disconnecting, etc., *see v.;* trip(ping); shutdown; shutoff, cutoff; **—ая** *pr. ger.* disconnecting, etc., *see v.*

выключен/ие *n.* disconnecting, etc., *see* **выключать;** release, disengagement; shutoff, cutoff; shutdown; **муфта —ия** release clutch; **положение —ия** off position; **—ный** *a.* disconnected, etc., *see* **выключать;** (elec.) dead; out of gear; (comp.) off-line; **—о** *adv.* off; out; open.

выключ/ить *see* **выключать;** **—ка строк** (information) justification, throw-off.

выков(ыв)ать *v.* (met.) forge, hammer (out); shape, mold.

выковыр/ивать, –ять *v.* pick out.

выколачиват/ель *m.* tapper; (typ.) planer; **—ь** *v.* knock out, beat out, drive out; tap; plane down.

выколашив/ание *n.* (bot.) earing, ear formation, heading; **—аться** ear, form ears or spikes, head.

выколка *f.* pricking out; chipping out.

выколос/ившийся *a.* (bot.) spicose, spiciferous; **—иться** *see* **выколашиваться.**

выколот/ить *see* **выколачивать;** **—ка** *f.* knocking out; knock-out (rod); drift, punch; (typ.) planer.

выколот/ый *a.* pricked out, punctured; chipped out; **—ь** *see* **выкалывать.**

выконопа/тить, —чивать *v.* caulk up.

выкоп/анный *a.* dug up, excavated, unearthed; **—ать** *see* **выкапывать;** **—ка** *f.,* **—очный** *a.* digging out, lifting.

выкоп/тить *v.* smoke, cure; **—ченный** *a.* smoked, cured.

выкорм *m.,* **—ка** *f.* fattening; **—ить** *see* **выкармливать;** **—ленный** *a.* fattened, raised (on); **—ок, —ыш** *m.* fattened animal; **—очный** *a.* reared, raised.

выкорч/евать *see* **выкорчёвывать;** **—ёвка** *f.,* **—ёвывание** *n.* uprooting, etc., *see v.;* **—ёвывать** *v.* uproot, grub up, extirpate, stub up; clear.

выко/с *m.* (agr.) mowing; **—ить** *v.* mow; **—шенный** *a.* mowed.

выкрадывать *v.* steal; tap (current, etc.).

выкраивать *v.* cut out (by pattern); make do; find, hunt up.

выкрас/ить *see* **выкрашивать;** **—ка** *f.* thorough dyeing; extraction of color.

выкрасть *see* **выкрадывать.**

выкраш/енный *a.* painted, etc., *see v.;* **—ивание** *n.* painting, etc., *see v.;* **—ивать** *v.* paint; dye; color; finish (in); **—иваться** *v.* be painted, etc.; crumble (away), break off, chip; flake, spall; (gears) pit, chip out.

выкрик *m.* shout, yell; **—ивать, —нуть** *v.* cry out, shout; call out.

выкристаллизов/анный *a.* crystallized (out); **—ать(ся), —ывать(ся)** *v.* crystallize (out); **—ывание** *n.* crystallization.

выкро/енный *a.* cut out; **—ить** *see* **выкраивать;** **—йка** *f.* pattern.

выкрош/енный *a.* crumbled; **—иться** *v.* crumble (out or away).

выкру/гливать, —глить *v.* round off; **—ж(ив)ать, —жить** *v.* round, scoop, chamfer; **—жка** *f.* rounding off; fillet, recess, chamfer; cove, concave molding; (propeller shaft) bossing.

выкру/тить *v.* unscrew, twist out; wring out; centrifuge; **—титься** *v.* unscrew; extricate oneself; **—ченный** *a.* unscrewed, etc., *see v.;* **—чивание** *n.* screwing, etc., *see v.;* removal; **—чивать** *see* **выкрутить.**

выкует *fut. 3 sing. of* **выковать.**

выкуп *m.* repurchase, redemption; buying up; payment (for).

выкупать, —ся *v.* bathe.

выкуп/ать, —ить *v.* redeem; buy out; **—ной** *a.* redeemable; purchase; **—ные платёжи** part payments, installments.

выкури(ва)ть *v.* smoke out, fumigate.

выку/с *m.* bitten or gnawed out place; **—сать, —сить** *v.* bite or gnaw out; take a bite; **—сыватель** *m.* cutting forceps; **—ывать** *v.* bite out, tear out.

выкучиваться *v.* cluster.

выкушенный *a.* bitten out, eaten out.

вылавлив/ание *n.* catching, etc., *see v.;* **в. рыбы** fishing; **—ать** *v.* catch; trap; fish out, get out; recover.

вылаз *m.* (man)hole.

вылакать *v.* lick up.

выламыв/ание *n.* breaking open, etc., *see v.;* **—ать** *v.* break open; break in or out; break off; wrench out; **—аться** *v.* break out; chip.

вылащивать *v.* polish, give a glossy finish.

вылегание *n.* lodging (of grain).

вылегчивать *v.* lighten.

вы/лежать(ся) *see* **вылёживать(ся);** **—лёживание** *n.* aging, etc., *see v.;* **—лёживать** *v.* age, mature, ripen, season; weather; store; lie (for a time); rest (in bed); be bedridden; **—лёживаться** *v.* age, mature, ripen, season; be left to ripen; (cer.) sour; **—лежка** *f.* aging, etc., *see v.;* storage; retting (of flax); secondary fermentation.

вылез/ать, —ти, —ть *v.* climb out, get out; fall out, come out, molt.

вылей(те) *imp. of* **вылить.**

выленочный узел clove hitch.

вылет *m.* flying out, departure, escape; emission, emergence; (av.) flight, takeoff; radius, sweep, reach; projection, overhang; gab, hook; arm, boom (of crane); throat, gap depth (of welder); throat clearance, sweep (of lathe); **длина —а** range; **угол —а** angle of departure; **—ать, —еть** *v.* fly out, escape; take off, depart, leave; rush out, emerge; fall out; **—ающий** *a.* flying out, etc., *see v.;* outgoing.

вылеч/енный *a.* cured; **—ивание** *n.* curing, therapy; **—и(ва)ть** *v.* cure, heal; **—и(ва)ться** *v.* recover, get well.

вылечь *v.* (agr.) be lodged.

вылив/ание *n.* pouring out, etc., *see v.;* **—ать** *v.* pour (out, off), decant; discharge, empty; discard; found, cast, mold; **—аться** *v.* run out, pour out, overflow, flood; take the form (of), develop (into); **—ка** *f.* flooding out.

вылиз(ыв)ать *v.* lick clean.

вылин/явший, —ялый *a.* faded, washed out; **—ять** *v.* fade (out), lose color; run (of dye); (zool.) molt.

вылит/ый *a.* poured out, decanted; cast; —**ь** *see* **выливать.**

вылов *m.* catch(ing); removal; **интенсивность** —**а** rate of exploitation; —**ить** *v.* catch; fish out, get out; —**ленный** *a.* caught.

вылож/енный *a.* laid out, etc. *see* **выкладывать; в. свинцом** lead-lined; —**ить** *see* **выкладывать.**

вылом *m.,* —**ка** *f.* breaking out; removal; break; quarry; —**ать** *see* **выламывать;** —**ки** *pl.* (met.) cobbings, dross; broken slag.

вылощ/енный *a.* polished, glossy, smooth; —**ить** *see* **вылащивать.**

вылу/дить, —**живать** *v.* tin, tinplate, coat with tin; —**женный** *a.* tinned.

вылуп/ившийся *a.* newly hatched; —**ить** *v.* shell (nuts); peel (fruit); husk (grain); —**иться, —ливаться, —ляться** *v.* hatch out, emerge; —**ление, —ливание** *n.* hatching, emergence.

вылущ/ение, —ивание *n.* husking, etc., *see v.;* (med.) enucleation; excision; —**и(ва)ть** *v.* husk, shell; enucleate; excise, cut out.

вырьет *fut. 3 sing. of* **вылить.**

вымаз(ыв)ать *v.* smear, daub; grease, oil; dirty, soil; —**ся** *v.* get dirty.

вымани(ва)ть *v.* coax out; lure; swindle.

вымарать *see* **вымарывать.**

вымарив/ание *n.* extirpation, etc., *see v.;* —**ать** *v.* extirpate, exterminate, eradicate, destroy; starve out.

вымарыв/ание *n.* expurgation, etc.; —**ать** *v.* soil, smear, dirty; expurgate, strike out, delete.

вымасл/ивать, —**ить** *v.* oil, grease.

выматывать *v.* wind up, wind out; deplete, drain, exhaust.

вымачив/ание *n.* steeping, etc., *see v.;* —**ать** *v.* steep, soak, drench, wet thoroughly; macerate; ret (flax).

вымащивать *v.* pave.

вымбовка *f.* (naut.) capstan bar, handspike.

вымел *past m. sing. of* **вымести.**

вымен *m.* exchange, barter; —**енный** *a.* exchanged.

вымени *gen. of* **вымя.**

вымен/ивать, —**ять** *v.* exchange, barter.

вымеобразный *a.* mammatus (cloud).

вымереть *see* **вымирать.**

вымерз/ание *n.* winterkill(ing), frost damage; —**ать, —нуть** *v.* be killed by frost; freeze (solid); —**лый** *a.* frozen, winterkilled.

вымер/ивание *n.* measuring; —**и(ва)ть** *v.* measure (out).

вымерший *a.* extinct; fossil.

вымерять *v.* measure out.

вымесить *see* **вымешивать.**

вымести *v.* sweep out.

вымет *m.* sweepings; clearing, cleaning; —**аемый** *a.* swept out; —**ание** *n.* sweeping out; —**ать** *see* **вымести; вымётывать;** (ichth.) spawn; —**енный** *a.* swept out.

выметить *v.* mark out.

вымётыв/ание *n.* throwing out, etc., *see v.;* ear formation; —**ать** *v.* throw out, cast out; spread, lay; put out (shoots); (bot.) tassel, head, ear; bind, edge, buttonhole; —**ать икру** (ichth.) spawn.

вымеченный *a.* marked out.

вымеш/анный *a.* thoroughly mixed; —**ать, —ивать** *v.* mix thoroughly; knead (thoroughly); —**енный** *a.* mixed; kneaded.

выминать *v.* soften (leather, etc.).

вымир/ание *n.* dying off, extinction; —**ать** *v.* die out, become extinct; —**ающий** *a.* dying out, becoming extinct.

вымогать *v.* extort.

вымо/ет *fut. sing of* **вымыть;** —**ина** *f.* gully, washout; gulch, ravine.

вымок/ание *n.* (bot.) wet weather loss; —**ать, —нуть** *v.* get wet; soak, be soaked, be steeped; (flax) be retted.

вымол *m.* final milling; thorough grinding; —**ачивание** *n.* thrashing; —**ачивать, —отить** *v.* thrash (out); —**от** *m.* thrashing; (total yield of) thrashed-out grain; —**отка** *f.* thrashing; —**отки** *pl.* chaff, debris.

выморажив/ание *n.* freezing (out), etc., *see v.;* winterkilling; —**ать** *v.* freeze (out), winterkill.

выморить *see* **вымаривать.**

вымор/оженный *a.* frozen, winterkilled; —**озить** *see* **вымораживать;** —**озка** *f.* freezing; —**ки** *pl.* strong alcoholic drinks (with water frozen out); —**ок** *m.* frost-killed plant.

выморочный *a.* dying out; (law) escheated.

вымостить *see* **вымащивать.**

вымот/анный *a.* depleted, exhausted; —**ать** *see* **выматывать.**

вымоч/енный *a.* wetted, steeped, soaked; —**ить** *see* **вымачивать;** —**ка** *f.* wetting, etc., *see* **вымачивать;** wet rot (of seeds); wet spot (defect).

вымощенный *a.* paved.

вымпел *m.* pennant, marker; (av.) message bag.

вымуштровать *v.* drill, discipline.

вымыв *m.* washout; —**аемый** *a.* washable; extractable; washed out; —**ание** *n.* washing (out), etc., *see v.;* removal; (geol.) erosion, washout; elution; **горизонт** —**ания** eluvial horizon; **слой** —**ания** inwash layer; —**ать** *v.* wash (out, away, off); flush, sluice; elu(a)te, rinse; displace (gas); scour, scrub (gases); lixiviate, leach out; hollow out; —**аться** *v.* wash up; —**ка** *see* **вымывание;** washout; —**ка массы** (paper) brown-stock flushing.

вымыл/ивать, —**ить** *v.* soap.

вымыс/ел *m.* invention, fiction; —**лить** *v.* invent, contrive, devise.

вымыт/ый *a.* washed (out); —**ь** *see* **вымывать.**

вымышл/енный *a.* fictitious; hypothetical; —**ять** *see* **вымыслить.**

вымьский *a.* (geog.) Vym.

вым/я *f.* udder (of cow); **воспаление** —**ени** (vet.) mastitis.

вымять *see* **выминать.**

вынашивать *v.* bear, carry; wear out.

вынес/енный *a.* taken out, etc., *see* **выносить;** remote, outlying; extension; accessible, external (instrument); —**ти** *see* **выносить.**

выним/ание *n.* removal, withdrawal; —**ать** *v.* take out, remove, withdraw, draw out, extract; back out (drill); dig out, excavate; —**аться** *v.* be removed; be removable; pull out, come out (of drawer).

вынос *m.* taking out, etc., *see v.;* export(ation); transfer (of data); removal, loss, deprivation; entrainment; evacuation; escape; drift (of river); deflection (of blade); overhanging length (of beam); outlying point; branch office; extension; (geol.) debris cone; (av.) stagger; —**итель** *m.* entrainer, entraining agent; —**ить** *v.* take out, carry out, away or off, remove; entrain; export; sustain, endure, undergo, tolerate, bear; bring forth; think out, reason out; (med.) carry to full term; train; pass (a resolution); wear out (clothes); —**ить за знак** place outside; —**иться** *v.* be taken out, etc.; dart out, fly out; —**ка** *f.* removal; marginal note, footnote.

выносляв/ость *f.* endurance, hardiness, durability, resistance, strength; tolerance; persistence; **граница** —**ости, предел** —**ости** (stat.) tolerance limit; (met.) endurance limit, fatigue limit; **—ый** *a.* durable, hardy, resistant, tolerant.

выносн/ой *a. of* **вынос;** to be carried out; for export; marginal, noted in the margin; divulged, published; external, outside, separate; **—ое слово** catchword, entry word.

выно/сящий *a.* taking out, etc., *see* **выносить;** (physiol.) efferent; (anat.) deferent; **—шенный** *a.* taken out, etc., *see* **выносить;** worn out.

выну/дить, —ждать *v.* force, compel, make; constrain; oblige; induce; stimulate (scattering); **—ждающий** *a.* forcing, etc., *see v.;* **—жденный** *a.* forced, etc., *see v.;* (geol.) coercive (texture); **быть —жденным** *v.* have to, be obliged to.

вынут/ый *a.* taken out, etc., *see* **вынимать; —ь** *see* **вынимать.**

выныр/ивать, —нуть *v.* come to the surface, emerge, appear, turn up.

вынь(те) *imp. of* **вынуть.**

вынюх(ив)ать *v.* smell out; find out.

вынянчи(ва)ть *v.* nurse, tend; bring up.

вып. *abbr.* **(выпуск)** issue.

выпа/вший *a* fallen out, precipitated; resulting; **—д** *m.,* **—дание** *n.* falling out, etc., *see v.;* extinction, dying out; mortality (of plants); **—дать** *v.* fall out, separate out, precipitate; drop out, get out (of); slip out; come out (of hair); prolapse; occur, appear; **—дающий** *a.* falling out, etc., *see v.;* (nucl.) fallout; deciduous, milk (teeth); **—дение** *see* **выпад;** precipitate, deposit; (nucl.) fallout; (med.) prolapse; shedding; loss (of function); **—дка** *see* **выпад; —дошная трава** (bot.) marsh groundsel (*Senecio paludosus*).

выпаивать *v.* water (stock); raise on milk.

выпал *m.* discharge; (min.) blasting; *past m. sing. of* **выпасть; —и(ва)ть** *v.* fire, shoot (at); discharge; singe, scorch; blurt out.

выпалывать *v.* weed (out).

выпар *m.* vaporization, evaporation; flash steam; **—ение** *see* **выпаривание; —енный** *a.* evaporated, etc., *see v.;* **—ивание** *n.* evaporation, etc., *see v.;* steaming; **отделять —иванием** *v.* boil off; **—и(ва)тель** *m.* evaporator, etc., *see v.;* **—и(ва)ть** *v.* evaporate, boil down, concentrate; vaporize; steam; **—и(ва)ться** *v.* evaporate, vaporize; **—ительный** *a.* evaporating; **—ка** *see* **выпаривание;** evaporated residue, concentrate; evaporator; **—ной, —ный** *a.* evaporating; evaporator, evaporative (cystallizer); **—ной аппарат** *see* **выпари(ва)тель; —ная колонна** (refining) stripper.

выпархивать *v.* flutter out, flit out.

выпарывать *v.* rip out; gut, disembowel.

выпас *m.,* **—ной** *a.* pasturing, grazing; pasture; **—аемый** *a.* grazing; **—ти** *v.* pasture.

выпасть *see* **выпадать.**

выпах/анность *f.* soil depletion, soil impoverishment; **—анный** *a.* plowed up, etc., *see v.;* **—(ив)ать** *v.* plow up; deplete, exhaust, impoverish (soil).

выпачкать *v.* soil, dirty; **—ся** *v.* get dirty.

выпаш/ет *fut. 3 sing. of* **выпахать; —ка** *f.* plowing.

выпей(те) *imp. of* **выпить.**

выпек *m.,* **—ание** *n.* baking; **—ать** *v.* bake (well); roast out.

выпени(ва)ть *v.* defroth; **—ся** *v.* froth out.

выпер/еть *see* **выпирать; —тый** *a.* pushed out, heaved; bulging.

выпестовать *v.* foster, nurture.

выпеч/енный *a.* baked (well); roasted out; **—ка** *f.* baking; **—ь** *see* **выпекать.**

выпи *pl., gen., etc. of* **выпь.**

выпив/ание *n.* drinking; **—ать** *v.* drink (up), drain; **—ка** *f.* (alcoholic) beverage, drink; **—ший** *a.* (having) drunk.

выпил/енный *a.* sawed out; **—ивание** *n.* sawing out; **—и(ва)ть** *v.* saw out, cut out; file out; **—ка** *f.* sawing out; sawed-out piece; **—овка** *f.* sawing out.

выпир/ание *n.* pushing out, etc., *see v.;* **—ать** *v.* push out, oust, squeeze out; (hort.) heave; protrude, bulge out.

выпис/анный *a.* copied, etc., *see v.;* **—ка** *f.* extract, copied passage; report; **—ка счётов** billing; **—ывание** *n.* copying, etc., *see v.;* **—(ыв)ать** *v.* copy, write out or down; write (for), order; extract; discharge, dismiss; strike off the list; draw carefully; subscribe, take (a periodical); **—(ыв)аться** *v.* be discharged, leave (hospital); check out.

выпить *see* **выпивать.**

выпих/ивать, —нуть *v.* push out, shove out.

выпишет *fut. 3 sing. of* **выписать.**

выплав/ить *see* **выплавлять; —ка** *see* **выплавление;** yield, output (of furnace); spalling (of refractory); **—ление** *n.* melting (out), etc., *see v.;* fusion; **—ленный** *a.* melted, etc., *see v.;* **—ляемый** *a.* meltable; dispensable; melted; **—лять** *v.* melt (out), extract; (met.) smelt, found; make, manufacture, produce; **—ной** *a. of* **выплавка; —ок** *m.* smelted ore.

выпла/та *f.* payment; **—тить, —чивать** *v.* pay off, pay out, pay in full; settle (debt).

вы/плевать, —плёвывать *v.* spit out.

вы/плеск *m.* splash, spatter; **литьё с —плеском** slush casting; **—плескать, —плёскивать** *v.* splash out, spatter, spill; **—плёскивание** *n.* splash(ing) out, spatter(ing), spill; **—плеснуть** *v.* wash ashore; *see also* **выплёскивать.**

выпле/сти, —тать *v.* plait, braid; weave; **—стись** *v.* unplait, work loose.

выплод *m.* (insect) breeding.

выплы/в *m.* (rub.) spew; **—(ва)ть** *v.* emerge, come up, turn up; float up, surface; swim out, swim ashore; **—вок** *m.* (bot.) excrescence.

выплюнуть *v.* spit out.

выпо/ить *v.* water (stock); raise on milk; **—йка** *f.* watering; raising on milk.

выполаживать *v.* flatten out, smooth out.

выполаск/(ив)ание *n.* rinsing (out), etc., *see v.;* **—ивать** *v.* rinse (out), flush out; scour; gargle.

выполз/ание *n.* creeping out or over; **—ать** *v.* creep out or over; **—ающий** *a.* creeping out; **—ок** *m.* (zool.) cast-off outer covering; **малый —ок** an earthworm (*Lumbricus rubellus*).

выполн/ение *n.* execution, fulfillment, realization, accomplishment, achievement, completion, performance; filling (of cavity); **—енность** *f.* plumpness, fullness, roundness; fulfillment; **—енный** *a.* fulfilled, etc., *see v.;* made (to order; from); be (of); (bot.) solid, plump, filled out; **—имость** *f.* feasibility, practicability; applicability; **—имый** *a.* workable; feasible, practicable; realizable, satisfiable; **—ить, —ять** *v.* fulfill, carry out, accomplish; perform, execute, achieve, realize; build (up), make; complete, do (work); implement (a program); satisfy (an equation); follow (directions); meet, comply (with conditions); take (measurements); make (to order); fill (an order); discharge (duties); **—яющий** *a.* fulfilling, etc., *see v.;* engaged (in).

выполож/енный *a.* flattened (out), smoothed out; **—ить** *v.* flatten (out), smooth out.

выполос/кать, —нуть *see* **выполаскивать.**

выполоть *see* **выпалывать.**

выпор *m.* overflow (gate, lip); (foundry) riser, vent, air gate, air hole.

выпор/аживать, —ожнить v. empty, drain.

выпор/отковый a., **—(от)ок** m. (leather) deacon, still-born calf skin.

выпороть v. rip out; gut, disembowel; flog, whip.

выпорхнуть v. flutter out, flit out.

выпот m. sweat(ing); leaking, exudation, ooze (of boiler); (met.) air gate, flow-off vent; (med.) exudate, effusion; (geol.) fumarolic sublimate; **—евание** n. sweating, etc., see v.; **—е(ва)ть** v. sweat (out); exude, ooze, bleed; **—евающий** a. sweating, etc., see v.; (med.) exudative, wet (pleurisy).

выпотрошить v. eviscerate, disembowel.

выправ/ительный a. correcting, etc., see v.; **—итель-ные работы** (hydr.) maintenance; **—ить** see **выправлять; —ка** see **выправление;** posture, bearing; **—ление** n. correcting, etc., see v.; **—ленный** a. corrected, etc., see v.; **—лять** v. correct, set right, rectify; straighten, smooth, flatten (out); direct; get, obtain (passport); **—ляться** v. straighten out; improve.

выпрастывать v. empty; work free (of), get out; **—ся** v. work free (of).

выпрашивать v. solicit, ask (for).

выпр/евание n. sweating out, etc., see v.; (bot.) asphyxiation, rotting out; blighting (of buds); (phyt.) blight; **—евать** v. sweat out; (bot.) perish; boil away; boil enough; **—елый** a. sweated.

выпрессов/ка f. pressing out, squeezing out; overflow, flash, spew; **—ывать** v. press out, squeeze out.

выпрет fut. 3 sing. of **выпереть.**

выпреть see **выпревать.**

выпров/аживать, —одить v. escort.

выпроки/дывать, —нуть v. dump out.

выпросить see **выпрашивать.**

выпростать see **выпрастывать.**

выпрыг/ивать, —нуть v. jump out or off.

выпрыс/к(ив)ать, —нуть v. spray away.

выпрягать v. unharness, unhitch.

выпряд/ать, —ывать v. spin (out).

выпрям/итель m. (elec.) rectifier; (anat.) extensor (muscle); **—ительный** a. rectifier, rectifying; righting (reflex); **—ить** v. straighten (out), unbend; flatten; (elec.) rectify; right (an airplane); **—иться** v. straighten up; **—ление** n. straightening, rectification; **—ленность** f. straightness; straightening; **—ленный** a. straightened; rectified; **—ленное напряжение** direct voltage; **—лять** see **выпрямить; —ляющий** a. straightening, rectifying; arrector (muscle); **—ляющийся** a. (bot.) assurgent.

выпрясть see **выпрядать.**

выпрячь v. unharness, unhitch.

выпуклина f. convex(ity); (biol.) umbo.

выпукл/о adv. convexly; **в.-компактный** a. convex-compact; **—овогнутый** a. convexo-concave; **в.-створчатый** a. (bot.) induplicative; **—ость** f. convexity, curvature, camber; prominence, bulge, bulging, protuberance; promontory; embossing; **—ости на поверхности** (casting) flash, bulge; **—ый** a. convex, arched, arching, domed; cambered; buckled; bulging; protuberant, prominent; raised, embossed; **—ая работа** embossing; **—ое программирование** convex programming.

выпуск m. outlet, escape, exhaust; release; discharging, discharge, tap(ping), flushing, emptying, draining, withdrawal; deflation; expulsion; output, productive capacity, delivery; issue, number (of journal); vintage; product; graduating class; (cattle) drive; **первого —а** first-generation (rocket); **—аемый** a. discharged, etc., see v.; dischargeable; output; **—ание** n. discharging,

etc., see v.; **—ать** v. discharge, drain, run off, run out, let out, empty, deflate, exhaust; flush, draw off, tap; vent, emit; eject, release, set free, liberate; publish, issue, put out, turn out; (educ.) graduate; stock (with fish); produce, manufacture; omit, leave out; **—аться** v. be discharged, etc.; be allowed to escape; come (in), be made; **—ающий** a. discharging, etc., see v.; **—ник** m., **—никовый** a. outlet; (anat.) emissary (vein); graduate, graduating student.

выпускн/ой a. exhaust, outlet, discharge; exit; drawing-off (roller); escape, release, safety (valve); imprimatur (date); **в. штуцер** exhaust (of motor); **—ая труба** outlet, exhaust pipe, waste pipe; **—ое отверстие** outlet, discharge hole, vent; tap (hole); **—ые данные** (publisher's) imprint.

выпустить see **выпускать.**

выпут(ыв)ать v. disentangle, disengage, extricate; unravel; **—ся** v. extricate onself, get out (of).

выпухлость f. curvature; vault(ing).

выпуч/енный a. bulging, protruding; **—ивание** n., **—ина** f. bulging, bulge, swelling; buckling; **—и(ва)ть** v. bulge, swell, protrude; make convex; **—и(ва)ться** v. bulge, swell (out).

выпущенный a. discharged, etc., see **выпускать.**

выпыт(ыв)ать v. question, elicit, find out.

выпых/ивать, —нуть v. puff out.

выпь f. (orn.) bittern (*Botaurus*).

выпьет fut. 3 sing. of **выпить.**

выпя/тить, —чивать v. thrust out; stick out, protrude; emphasize; **—титься, —чиваться** v. bulge out, stick out, protrude; balloon; project, overhang; **—ченный, —чивающийся** a. protruding, bulging out, protuberant.

вырабатыв/аемый a. manufactured, etc., see v.; **—ание** n. manufacturing, etc., see v.; **—ать** v. manufacture, make, produce; develop, work out, elaborate, improve; map out, draw up (a plan); (elec.) generate; (min.) work; finish, exhaust, deplete; turn out; make, earn; cultivate (a habit); **—аться** v. be manufactured, etc.; form, arise, develop.

выработ/анный a. manufactured, etc., see **вырабатывать;** spent (solution); **—анное пространство** (min.) goaf, gob; **—ать** see **вырабатывать; —ка** see **вырабатывание;** yield, output; (min.) working, opening, entry; (air) way, shaft; exhaustion, depletion; formation, production, turnout; performance; **—ка в день** daily output; **иметь —ку** v. wear out of true; **норма —ки** performance standard.

выравн/ение n. equating; **—енность** f. uniformity; **—енный** a. leveled, etc., see v.; **—ивание** n. leveling, etc., see v.; alignment; (typ.) justification; adjustment; fit; compensation; (geol.) planation; **—ивание нагрузки** load leveling; **—иватель** m. leveler, etc., see v.; (elec.) equalizer; **—ивать** v. level (off), smooth (out), even (out), flatten; straighten, align, match; fit, adjust; balance, equalize, compensate; trim; (typ.) justify; **—иваться** v. straighten out, flatten out; line up; develop; improve; **—ивающий** a. leveling, etc., see v.

выраж/ать v. express, convey; delineate; **в. через** express as or in terms of; **—аться** v. be expressed; manifest itself; **—ающийся** a. manifested (as); **—аясь** pr. ger. in terms of; **—ение** n. expression, term; **в. —ениях** in terms of, as; **в денежном —ении** in terms of money; **—енность** f. showing, appearance; prominence; **—енный** a. expressed; delineated; pronounced; marked, distinct, manifest; evolved, developed; **—енный в** or **через** expressed in terms of; **—енный чётко** clearly defined, well-defined, distinct.

выраз/ительный *a.* expressive, significant, indicative; **—ить** *see* **выражать.**

выранжировка *f.* culling; lining up.

выра/стание *n.* growing (up), etc., *see v.;* growth; **—стать, —сти** *v.* grow (up); germinate; increase; develop; emerge, appear, arise; **—стить, —щивать** raise, rear, breed; train (personnel); grow, cultivate; incubate; **—щенный** *a.* raised, etc., *see v.;* **—щивание** *n.* raising, etc., *see v.;* culture; (stock) management; **—щивание леса** sylviculture.

вырвать *v.* tear out, pull out, snatch out; tear up, pull up; vomit; **—ся** *v.* break away, escape.

вырез *m.* cut(-out), incision; notch; recess; slot; excision, cutting out; **—ание** *see* **вырезывание;** cut, excision; **—анный** *a.* cut out, etc., *see v.;* **—ать** *see* **вырезывать;** **—ка** *f.* cutting out; cut(-out); pattern; clipping; engraving, carving; (typ.) patching; excision, section; incisure, notch; tenderloin (of beef); **—ной** *a.* cut out, incised; carved.

вырезуб *m.* (ichth.) Black Sea roach (*Rutilus frisii*).

вырезыв/ание *n.* cutting out, etc., *see v.;* removal; **—ать** *v.* cut out, excise, remove; clip; carve, engrave; chisel; slaughter, butcher.

вырест *m.* (ichth.) spawning, hatching.

вырешить *v.* come to a decision.

вырисов(ыв)ать *v.* delineate, trace out; outline; inscribe; **—ся** *v.* appear, be visible, stand out.

выровн/енность *see* **выравненность;** **—енный** *a.* leveled, etc., *see* **выравнивать;** **—ять** *see* **выравнивать.**

вырод/ившийся *a.* degenerate(d), deteriorated; **—иться** *see* **вырождаться;** **—ок** *m.,* **—очный** *a.* degenerate; monstrosity, freak.

выроет *fut. 3 sing. of* **вырыть.**

вырожд/аться *v.* degenerate, deteriorate; **—ающийся** *a.* degenerating, degenerative; **—енец** *m.* degenerate; **—ение** *n.* degeneration, deterioration, degradation; degeneracy; retrogressive evolution; monstrosity; (math.) confluence; **—енность** *f.* degeneracy; **—енный** *a.* degenerate(d); (math.) confluent, singular; **—енческий** *a. of* **вырожденец.**

вырон/ить, —ять *v.* let fall, drop, lose.

вырос *past m. sing. of* **вырасти;** **—т** *m.* growth, growing; (bot.) excrescence; **—тковый** *a. of* **выросток;** **—тной** *a.* breeding; nursery; **—ток** *m.* (leather) kip, yearling calf hide; home-bred animal; **—ший** *a.* adult, grown; evolved, developed.

выруб *m.* cut, notch; **—ание** *n.* cutting (out), etc., *see v.;* **—ать, —ить** *v.* cut (out), chop out, fell, clear, cut down, strip (forest); chisel, chip off or out; stamp, punch out; **—ка** *f.* cutting (out), etc., *see v.;* notch; (met.) blank; exploitation, utilization (of forest); felling area, logging area; (typ.) die-cutting; **—ленный** *a.* cut out, etc., *see v.;* **—ной** *a.* cutting, chopping; **—ной пресс, —ной штамп** (met.) blanking die.

выругать *v.* scold, reprimand.

вырули(ва)ть *v.* (av.) taxi (out).

выруч/ать, —ить *v.* rescue, help, relieve, release; gain, profit, net, clear; recover (expenses); **—ка** *f.* rescue, assistance, aid, support; gain, profit, proceeds, receipts; income, earnings.

выры/в *m.* tear sheet, tear-out; **—вание** *n.* extraction, digging out, etc., *see v.;* (nucl.) pickup; **—вать** *v.* extract, dig (out), excavate, unearth, uncover; pull out or up, grub out; draw out; tear out; force out, eject; break away or loose (from); **—ваться** *v.* break loose, escape, get free; **—тый** *a.* dug out; **—ть** *v.* dig out, excavate.

выс. *abbr.* (**высота**) height, altitude.

высад/ить *see* **высаживать;** **—ка** *f.,* **—ной** *a.* landing, etc., *see* **высаживать;** (mach.) upset(ting); (agr.) transplant; **—ок** *m.* steckling, transplant; cutting, slip; **—очный** *see* **высадной;** **—очный пресс, —очная машина** upsetter.

высаждение *n.* precipitation.

высаж/енный *a.* landed, etc., *see v.;* (mach.) upset; **—ивание** *n.* landing, etc., *see v.;* **—ивать** *v.* land, disembark, debark, put ashore; let off, drop (passengers); push out, knock out, smash, break in; (mach.) upset, head; (chem.) precipitate; (agr.) set out, transplant; **—иваться** *v.* deboard, disembark, deplane, get off; precipitate, settle out; **—ивающий** *a.* landing, etc., *see v.;* **—ивающийся** *a.* deboarding, etc., *see v.;* precipitating.

высалив/аемый *a.* capable of being salted out; **—ание** *n.* salting out, salt precipitation; **—атель** *m.* salting out agent; **—ать** *v.* salt out; **—ающий** *a.* salting out.

высасыв/ание *n.* exhaustion, drawing off, etc., *see v.;* **—ать** *v.* exhaust, suck out, draw out, draw off, evacuate.

высачив/ание *n.* oozing, exudation, seepage, escape; **—аться** *v.* ooze (out), exude, seep, leak (out).

высверл/енный *a.* drilled, bored; bore (hole); **—ивание** *n.* drilling, boring; **—и(ва)ть** *v.* drill, bore (out).

высве/тить *v.* light up; **—тлить** *v.* brighten, polish; **—чивание** *n.* lighting up; scintillation; fluorescence, luminescence; (nucl.) de-excitation; **время —чивания** fluorescent life; de-excitation time.

высвобо/дить, —ждать *v.* (set) free; disengage, release; let out, liberate, generate; make available; **—ждаться** *v.* be freed, etc.; become available; **—ждающий** *a.* freeing, etc., *see v.;* releasing; **—ение** *n.* setting free, etc., *see v.;* release; detachment; (hormone) secretion; (chem.) formation; **—жденный** *a.* set free, released, etc., *see v.*

высев *m.* seeding, sowing; (microbiol.) inoculation; **—альный** *a.,* **—ание** *n.* seeding, sowing, planting; **—ать** *v.* seed, sow; inoculate; **—ающий** *a.* seeding, etc., *see v.;* feed (plate); **—ка** *see* **высевание;** **—ки** *pl.* siftings, screenings, chaff; bran; **—ной** *a.* seeding; sifting.

высеив/ание *n.* sifting out, etc., *see v.;* **—ать** *v.* sift out, screen; sow.

высек/аемый *a.* (being) cut; **—ание** *n.* cutting out, etc., *see v.;* **—ать** *v.* cut out, excise; hew; carve, sculpture; stamp, punch; strike (a fire).

высел/ить, —ять *v.* eject, evict; transfer, move; **—иться** *v.* move; migrate; **—ок** *m.* settlement.

высемениться *v.* shed or scatter seed.

высеребрить *v.* silver-plate.

высеч/ение *see* **высекание;** cut, excision; **—енный** *a.* cut out, excised, etc., *see* **высекать;** **—ка** *see* **высекание;** cutter; (stamping) blank; (typ.) die cutting; (min.) trench; **—ной штамп** notching die; **—ь** *see* **высекать;** flog.

высея/нный *a.* sown, sowed; sifted; **—ть** *see* **высеивать.**

выси *gen., pl., etc., of* **высь.**

выси/деть *see* **высиживать;** **—женный** *a.* hatched, etc., *see v.;* **—живание** *n.* hatching, etc., *see v.;* **—живательное пятно** (orn.) brood patch; **—живать** *v.* hatch (out), incubate, brood; breed; wait (out), sit (out), remain, stay; just manage (to).

высини(ва)ть *v.* color or dye blue.

выситься *v.* tower, rise.

выскаблив/ание *n.* scraping out; (med.) curettage; **—ать** *v.* scrape out or off; erase, rub out; scrub clean; curet(te), scoop out.

высказ/анный *a.* expressed, etc., *see v.;* explicit; **—ывание** *n.* expression, statement, proposition; opinion, view; **исчисление —ываний** propositional calculus; **—(ыв)ать** *v.* express, state, say, tell; suggest, propose, make (proposal); formulate; **—(ыв)аться** *v.* speak up (for, against); express one's opinion; advocate, favor, support.

выскак/ивание *n.* slipping out, etc., *see v.;* **—(ив)ать, —нуть** *v.* slip out, jump out, dart out, rush out; fall out; emerge; deviate (from).

выскальзыв/ание *n.* slip, slipping out; **—ать** *v.* slip (out).

выскобл/енный *a.* scraped out, etc., *see* **выскабливать; —ить** *see* **выскабливать.**

выскользнуть *see* **выскальзывать.**

выскоч/ить *see* **выскакивать; —ка** *f.* (gen.) deviation.

выскр/ёбывание *n.* scraping out, etc., *see v.;* **—ебать, —ёбывать, —ести** *v.* scrape out or off; scratch out or off; scrub clean.

высл/анный *a.* shipped, sent out; deported; **—ать** *see* **высылать.**

высле/дить, —живать *v.* trace, track down, hunt down, search out; **—живание** *n.* tracing, etc.

выслу/га *f.* service; **за —гу лет** for length of service; **—жи(ва)ть** *v.* serve, work; serve out (a given period); obtain by service; qualify (for).

выслуш/ать, —ивать *v.* listen; hear (someone) out; (med.) auscultate, sound; **—ивание** *n.* listening; auscultation.

высмаливать *v.* tar, pitch.

высматривать *v.* look out (for), be on the alert (for); notice, detect, discern; strain (eyes).

высме/ивать, —ять *v.* ridicule, deride, scoff (at), make fun (of).

высмолить *see* **высмаливать.**

высмотреть *see* **высматривать.**

высов *m.* protrusion; (tuyere) projection; **—ывать** *v.* thrust out, push out; **—ываться** *v.* protrude, show; **—ывающийся** *a.* protruding.

высокий *a.* high, tall, elevated; high-temperature (tempering, etc.); rapid (tempo); relief (printing); exacting (needs); pinpoint (accuracy).

высоко *adv. and prefix* high(ly); **—азотный** *a.* nitrogen-rich; **—активный** *a.* highly active; highly radioactive, high-activity; hot; **—вакуумный** *a.* high-vacuum; (elec.) hard; **в.-вероятный** *a.* highly probable, high-probability; **—вершинность** *f.* (stat.) excess (of curve); **—вирулентный** *a.* highly virulent; **—водный** *a.* high-water, flood (bridge); **—вольтный** *a.* high-voltage; **—вязкий** *a.* high-viscosity; **—глиноземистый** *a.* alumina-rich; **—горный** *a.* mountainous, alpine; high-altitude; **—горье** *n.* high mountains; **—градусный** *a.* of a high degree; high-grade; highly concentrated.

высоко/дисперсный *a.* highly dispersed; **—дифференциальный** *a.* highly differentiated; **—доходный** *a.* profitable; **—железистый** *a.* highly ferrous, high-iron; **—жжёный** *a.* (cer.) hard-fired; **—зольный** *a.* high-ash; **—индексный** *a.* high-viscosity (oil); **—индустриальный** *a.* highly industrial; **—интенсивный** *a.* high (flux); **—ионизированный** *a.* highly ionized; **—калорийный** *a.* high-energy (fuel); **—качественный** *a.* high-quality, high-grade, fine; high-performance, premium, (top-)quality; high-test (gasoline); rich (ore); high-fidelity; high-definition; **—квалифицированный** *a.* highly qualified, skilled or trained; **—кварцевый** *a.* quartz-rich; **—кипящий** *a.* high-boiling; **—когерентный** *a.* highly coherent; **—кон-**

диционный *a.* high-quality (seeds); **—концентрированный** *a.* highly concentrated, strong; **—кормный** *a.* (biol.) eutrophic; **—коэрцитивный** *a.* high-coercivity; **—кремнеземистый** *a.* silica-rich; **—кремнистый** *a.* high-silicon; **—кубический** *a.* cylindrical, columnar (epithelium); **—кучевые облака** (meteor.) altocumulus.

высоко/легированный *a.* high-alloy, high (alloy); **—магнитный** *a.* highly magnetic; **—марганцовистый** *a.* high-manganese; **—масличный** *a.* oil-rich; **—модульный** *a.* high-modulus; **—молекулярный** *a.* high-molecular, macromolecular; **—молочная** *a.* highly productive (cow); **—мощный** *a.* high-power, high-capacity; (mach.) heavy-duty; **—нагружаемый** *a.* high-rate (filter, pond); **—напорный** *a.* high-pressure; high-head(water); **—непредельный** *a.* highly unsaturated; **—никелевый** *a.* nickel-rich; **—номерный** *a.* high-count, high-number (yarn).

высоко/обожжённый *a.* (cer.) hard-fired; **—образованный** *a.* highly educated; **—огнеупорный** *a.* highly refractory; **—однородный** *a.* highly homogeneous; **—октановый** *a.* high-octane; **—омный** *a.* (elec.) high-resistance; **—оплачиваемый** *a.* highly paid; **—организованный** *a.* highly organized; **—основный** *a.* alkali-rich, highly basic; **—охлоренный** *a.* superchlorinated; **—очищенный** *a.* highly purified.

высоко/плавкий *a.* high-melting; **—план** *m.* high-wing monoplane; **—плодородный** *a.* highly fertile; **—плотный** *a.* very compact or dense; **—полимер** *m.,* **—полимерный** *a.* high polymer; **—пористый** *a.* highly porous; **—пробный** *a.* high-grade, high-standard; high-test (gasoline); sterling (silver); fine; **—продуктивный, —производительный** *a.* highly productive, highly efficient; high-capacity; high-duty; high-yield; high-performance; **—проходный** *a.* (elec.) high-pass (filter); **—процентный** *a.* high-percentage, high-grade, rich (ore); **—прочный** *a.* high-strength; high-impact.

высоко/радиоактивный *a.* highly radioactive, hot; **—развитый** *a.* highly developed; **—расположенный** *a.* high; **—реакционный** *a.* highly reactive; **—рентабельный** *a.* highly profitable; **—рослый** *a.* tall(-growing).

высоко/сахаристый *a.* with a high sugar content; **—сводчатый** *a.* high-domed; **—сернистый** *a.* high-sulfur; **—скоростной** *a.* high-speed; high-velocity; high-shear (viscosity); short-residence time (reaction).

высокослоист/ое облако (meteor.) altostratus; **—о-кучевое облако** high stratocumulus.

высоко/смолистый *a.* resinous, rich in resin; **—сортный** *a.* high-grade, (high-)quality; **—специфичный** *a.* highly specific.

высокоствольн/ик *m.* high forest, seedling forest; **—ый** *a.* high, full-grown, mature.

высоко/стебельный, —стебельчатый *a.* tall-stalked; **—сульфированный** *a.* with a high sulfur content; **—твёрдый** *a.* very hard; very rigid; highly consistent; **—телый** *a.* (ichth.) deep(-bodied); **—температурный** *a.* high-temperature; **—теплопроводный** *a.* highly heat-conducting; **—титанистый** *a.* high-titanium; **—товарный** *a.* market-oriented, highly marketable; highly productive, commercial (farm); **—токсический** *a.* highly toxic; **—точный** *a.* (high-)precision; sensitive; **—травный** *a.* high grass; **—травье** *n.* tall herbaceous vegetation.

высоко/углеродистый *a.* high-carbon; **—удойная** *a.* highly productive (cow); **—урожайный** *a.* (agr.) heavy-producing, high-yielding; very fertile; **—устойчивый** *a.*

very stable, highly resistant; —**фосфористый** *a.* high-phosphorous; —**хлорированный** *a.* superchlorinated; —**хромистый** *a.* high-chromium; —**частотный** *a.* high-frequency; (met.) induction (hardening) —**чувствительный** *a.* highly sensitive; —**широтный** *a.* high-latitude; —**штамбовый** *a.* high-stemmed, standard (tree); —**щелочной** *a.* alkali-rich, highly basic; (petrol.) overbased (additive).

высоко/эксцентрический *a.* highly eccentric; —**эластический** *a.* hyperelastic; —**эластичность** *f.* Mackian elasticity; —**энергетический** *a.* high-energy; —**эффективный** *a.* highly effective; —**ядовитый** *a.* highly toxic.

высолажив/ание *n.* leaching, etc., *see v.;* —**ать** *v.* leach (out), lixiviate, extract; steep, soak.

высол/енный *a.* salted (out); —**ить** *v.* salt out; —**ка** *f.* salting out; graining (of soap).

высолодить *see* **высолаживать.**

высортиров/ать *v.* sort (out), cull, —**ка** *f.* sorting, culling.

высос/анный *a.* exhausted, etc., *see* **высасывать;** —**ать** *see* **высасывать.**

высот/а *f.* height, altitude, elevation; hill; (pressure) head; depth; pitch (of tone); (geol.) throw (of fault); degree (of temperature); reading (of barometer); (floor) line; (water) level; **в. всасывания, в. подачи** lift (of pump); **в. колонны, эквивалентная одной теоретической тарелке** height equivalent to a theoretical plate, HETP; **на —ах** high-level; **набирать —у** *v.* (av.) climb, gain height.

высот/ка *f.* small height; —**ник** *m.* steeplejack, construction worker; high-altitude flyer; —**но-компенсирующий** *a.* pressure (suit); —**ность** *f.* height, altitude; altitude performance; —**ный** *a. of* **высота;** high-altitude, high-level; tall; vertical; upper-air; upper-level; elevated; high-rise (building); pressure (suit); —**ный репер** (surv.) bench mark; —**ный ход** (leveling) vertical control traverse; —**ная болезнь** altitude sickness; —**ная отметка** elevation, level, altitude, height.

высото/любивый *a.* height-loving; —**мер** *m.* (av.) altimeter, height indicator or finder; height gage; —**мер-анероид** *m.* aneroid altimeter; —**писец** *m.* altigraph, altitude recorder.

высох/нуть *see* **высыхать;** —**ший** *a.* dry, dried up; desiccated; shriveled; —**шее русло** arroyo.

высочайший *superl. of* **высокий;** highest.

высоч/иться *see* **высачиваться;** —**ка** *f.* oozing; (met.) liquation.

выспаться *v.* have enough sleep.

выспе(ва)ть *v.* ripen fully, mature.

выспр/ашивать —**осить** *v.* question.

выстав/ить *see* **выставлять;** —**ка** *f.* adjustment, setting; exhibit(ion), display, show; (agr.) fair; —**ление** *n.* setting out, etc., *see v.;* exposure; —**ленный** *a.* set out, etc., *see v.;* —**лять** *v.* set out, put out, expose; set, adjust; display, exhibit, show; present; advance, propose, bring up; take out, remove; mark (with date); —**ляться** *v.* be set out, etc.; come out, emerge; —**ляющийся** *a.* emergent; —**ной** *a.* removable (window); —**очный** *a. of* **выставка.**

выстаив/ание *n.* standing, etc., *see v.;* —**ать** *v.* stand, remain standing; withstand; lose strength, color or flavor; —**аться** *v.* mature, ripen, age.

выст/елить, —илать *v.* pave, floor, cover; line; lay; —**илающий** *a.* lining; littoral (cell); —**илающий слой** (bot.) tapetum; —**илающая ткань** epithelium; —**илка** *f.* pavement; flooring, bed; lining; corduroy (road).

выстир(ыв)ать *v.* wash (out), launder.

выстл/анный *a.* lined; —**ать** *see* **выстилать.**

выстоять *see* **выстаивать.**

выстрагивать *v.* plane (off).

выстрадать *v.* suffer, endure.

выстраив/ание *n.* alignment; building, etc., *see v.;* —**ать** *v.* build, erect, put up, set up; draw up; line up, align; —**аться** *v.* be built, etc.; line up.

выстрел *m.* shot, round, discharge, report, detonation; explosion; firing; (naut.) boom; davit; —**и(ва)ть** *v.* shoot off, fire (a gun); destroy, shoot up; launch (rocket); catapult; —**ивающий** *a.* (bot.) ballistic.

выстри/гать, —чь *v.* clip, shear, cut.

выстрогать *see* **выстрагивать.**

выстро/енный *a.* built, erected; aligned; —**ить** *see* **выстраивать;** —**йка** *f.* building, construction.

выстругать *see* **выстрагивать.**

высту/дить, —ж(ив)ать *v.* cool, chill.

выстук/ивание *n.* percussion, tapping; —**(ив)ать** *v.* percuss, tap (out).

выступ *m.* projection, protuberance, protrusion; salience; prominence; process; jut, overhang; (geol.) ledge, shelf, bench, extension; lug, cog, cam, boss, catch, horn, prong; cusp, point (of crystal); baffle, flange, shoulder, rib; embossing; jetty; **в. шероховатости** asperity (in friction); **сварка —ами** projection welding.

выступ/ать *v.* project, protrude, bulge out; jut (out), extend, overhand; crop out, emerge, come out; appear, show; step out or forward; set out, march off; speak (at meeting); deliver, give (a lecture); overflow (its banks); —**ающий** *a.* projecting, etc., *see v.;* prominent, outstanding; salient (angle); protrusive (occlusion); —**ающий отступ** hanging indent; —**ить** *see* **выступать;** —**ление** *n.* projecting, etc., *see v.;* appearance.

высты(ва)ть *v.* (become) cool.

высунут/ый *a.* thrust out, protruding; —**ь** *see* **высовывать.**

высуш/енный *a.* dried, etc., *see v.;* **вес —енного материала** dry weight; —**ивание** *n.* drying, etc., *see v.;* —**ивать** *v.* dry (out), desiccate, bake; drain (land); season (lumber); —**иваться** *v.* (get) dry; be drained; —**иваться на воздухе** airdry; —**ивающий** *a.* drying, etc., *see v.;* siccative; —**ивающее вещество** drying agent, desiccant; —**ить** *see* **высушивать.**

высчит(ыв)ать *v.* compute, calculate; count; deduct.

высш/ий *a.* higher, superior, upper(most), top(most); maximum, highest, supreme; advanced, more highly developed; sovereign; **в. спирт** higher alcohol; —**ая степень** maximum; —**ая точка** peak; —**ей огнеупорности** *a.* very fire-resistant; —**ей очистки** superpure; —**ие учебные заведения** institutions of higher learning.

высыл/ать *v.* send out, away or forward; ship; deport, exile; —**ка** *f.* sending, etc., *see v.*

высып/ание *n.* pouring out, etc., *see v.;* (med.) eruption, rash; —**анный** *a.* poured out, etc., *see v.;* —**ать** *v.* pour out, empty, spill; run out, swarm out; break out (of rash); —**аться** *v.* pour out, fall out, spill out; run out; break out; get enough sleep; —**ка** *see* **высыпание;** (geol.) rock fragments; —**ь** *f.* (med.) exanthem(a), rash, eruption.

высых/аемость *f.* drying capacity; —**ание** *n.* drying, desiccation, etc., *see v.;* dry (up, out); desiccate; run dry (of stream); fade, wither, wilt; —**ающий** *a.* drying; —**ающее масло** siccative oil, drier.

высь *f.* height; top, summit, crest.

вытаивать *v.* melt away; thaw out; appear.

выталкив/ание *n.* ejection, etc., *see v.;* (comp.) pop (out); —**атель** *m.* pusher, push rod, ejector, knock-out; lifting-out device; extruder; —**ательный** *see* **вы-**

талкивающий; —ательная сила buoyancy; —ать v. eject, expel, extrude, push out, force out, knock out; throw out, chuck out; (comp.) pop out (of stack): strip; buoy up; —ивающий a. ejecting, etc., see v.; m. (anat.) detrusor.

вытаплив/ание n. melting out, etc., see v.; —ать v. melt out; (met.) smelt out; render (fat); clarify (oil); heat (building); —аться v. be heated, get warm.

вытаптывать v. trample (down).

вытаращивать v. open (one's eyes) wide.

вытаскив/ание n. pulling out, extraction, withdrawal; —ать v. pull out, extract, draw (out), withdraw; take out, get out, haul out; tear out; take, steal.

вытачать v. sew together.

вытач(ив)ать v. turn (on lathe); sharpen; bore out, cut (grooves); (zool.) gnaw.

вытачка f. tuck, fold.

вытащить see **вытаскивать**.

вытаять see **вытаивать**.

вытвердить v. learn by heart.

вытвор/ить, —ять v. do, be up to.

вытек m. discharge, outflow, run-off; —ание n. flowing out, etc., see v.; effluence, efflux, issue, discharge; run-out, outflow; escape, leak(age); outlet; —ать v. flow out, run out, pour (out), issue, discharge, escape, drain; leak out; arise, stem (from), result, follow, be a consequence (of); rise, have its source (of river); be exhausted; —ает отсюда hence, therefore; из этого —ает it follows (that), this implies, this suggests; как —ает из термина as the term implies; —ающий a. flowing out, etc., see v.; effluent (stream); resultant; —**ающий поток**, —**ающая жидкость** effluent; —ший past act. part. of **вытекать**; effluent; resultant.

вытереб/ить v. (agr.) pull out, pluck out, tear out; harvest (flax); —ление n. pulling out, etc., see v.

вытереть see **вытирать**.

вытерпеть v. endure, bear, stand, suffer.

вытертый a. wiped (off), dried; frayed, worn out, rubbed off; threadbare.

вытесать see **вытёсывать**.

вытесн/ение n. displacement, etc., see v.; squeezing out, etc.; expulsion, ejection, expression; replacement, substitution; competition; drive; —**енный** a. displaced, etc., see v.; —**итель** m. displacer; ejector, expulsor (pump); extractant; —**ительный** a. displacing, etc., see v.; displacement; competitive (inhibitor); elution (analysis); pressurized; —ить v. displace, dislodge, supplant, supersede; replace, substitute; squeeze out, extrude; push out, eject; liberate; expel, force out, drive out, oust, exclude, crowd out; —**яемый** a. being displaced; —**ять** see **вытеснить**; —**яющий** a. displacing, etc., see v.; displacement.

вытёсывать v. cut (out), hew (out).

вытечь see **вытекать**.

вытешет fut. 3 sing. of **вытесать**.

вытир/ание n. wiping, etc., see v.; wear; —ать v. wipe (dry, off, out); dry; wear (out); abrade, scour; thrash (seeds); —аться v. dry oneself; wear out.

вытисн/ить, —уть, —ять v. impress, imprint, stamp.

вытитров(ыв)ать v. titrate.

выткать v. weave.

вытолк/анный, —**нутый** a. ejected, etc., see **выталкивать**; —ать, —**нуть** see **выталкивать**.

вытомленный a. cured (tobacco).

вытоп/ить see **вытапливать**; —ка see **вытапливание**; —ки pl. residue; (met.) scum, dross; —ленный a. melted out; smelted; rendered; heated.

вытоптать v. trample (down).

выторгов(ыв)ать v. bargain, get a discount.

выточ/енный a. turned (on lathe), etc., see **вытачивать**; в. желобок recess, groove; —ить see **вытачивать**; —ка f. turning; undercut, recess, groove, neck; journal; (gasket) seat.

вытрав/ить see **вытравливать**; —ка f., —ление, —ливание n. corrosion, pitting, etc., see v.; (dyeing) discharge; (med.) induced abortion; —**ленный** a. corroded, etc., see v.; —**ливать**, —**лять** v. corrode, erode, pit; (met.) etch, pickle; (dyeing) discharge; destroy, exterminate, poison off; damage (crops); graze, trample down (pasture); remove, take out (stain); cauterize, do away (with), remove; check (growth); ease out, slacken; —**ляющий** a. corroding, etc., see v.; corrosive; —**ляющее средство** corrosive; —**ной** a. of **вытравление**; discharge (printing).

вытрамбовать v. ram (down).

вытребовать v. send for, summon; obtain on demand.

вытрезв/итель m. treatment center for alcoholics; —ить, —лять v. sober up.

вытрепать v. (agr.) scutch, swingle.

вытр/усить, —**ясать**, —**ясти** v. shake out; —**ушенный** a. shaken out, etc., see v.; —**яхивание** n. shaking out, etc., see v.; removal; —**ях(ив)ать**, —**яхнуть** v. shake out, dump out, drop; remove.

вытыкать v. weave.

выть v. howl; —ё n. howling.

вытягив/ание n. drawing, etc., see v.; extension, etc.; —ать v. draw (wire), stretch (out), extend, pull out; elongate, lengthen, prolong; draw out, draw off, extract, remove, withdraw; exhaust (air); drain, get out; bear, endure, hold out; —аться v. be drawn, etc.; stretch out, extend, grow longer, lengthen; grow, shoot up; —**ающий** a. drawing, etc., see v.; —**ающая мышца** (anat.) protractor; —**ающийся** a. stretching out, reaching out, extending.

вытя/жение see **вытягивание**; (med.) traction; —**жка** see **вытягивание**; stretch(ing); (tires) stretch ratio; extract; (pharm.) tincture, infusion; flue; air vent; (rolling) reduction; (text.) draft; **стан повторной** —**жки** stretch reducing mill; —**жной** a. drawing; extended, extensive; exhaust (fan, hood, etc.); air (vent); vacuum (pump); suction, induced (draft); rip (cord of parachute); —**жные калибры** tension roll passes; —**нутый** a. drawn, etc., see **вытягивать**; prolate, oblong; spread, expanded (scale); —**нуть** see **вытягивать**.

выу/дить, —**живать** v. fish out; coax out.

выутюжить v. iron (out).

выучи(ва)ть v. teach, train; learn, memorize; —ся v. be trained; learn.

выхажив/ание n. raising; care; dwelling (of internal grinder); —ать v. raise, rear; tend, care for, nurse.

выхарк(ив)ать v. expectorate.

выхват m. flay mark; —ить, —ывать v. snatch out, snatch away; —**ывание** n. snatching.

выхлоп m. exhaust (fumes); discharge, expulsion.

выхлопатывать see **выхлопотать**.

выхлопн/ой a. exhaust, escape, waste; —**ые газы** exhaust; в. горшок muffler; в. коллектор exhaust manifold; в. фильтр exhaust-cleaning filter; в. штуцер exhaust (of motor); —**ое отверстие** exhaust, outlet, exit.

выхлопотать v. obtain, procure, get.

выход m. yield, output; accretion; percentage; (agr.) harvest; outlet, vent, egress, exit, (comp.) logout, logoff; (fire) escape; outflow, discharge, seepage; emergence; release; outcome, result; efficiency; (geol.) outcrop, exposure; excursion, outing; issue (of journal); publicatoin (of book); **в. 90% теории** the yield is 90% of the theoretical; **в. на** yield of; **в. по** yield (on the basis) of; **в. по току** current efficiency; **в. смешения** mixing efficiency; **в. цвета** (chromatography) color value; **в. электронов** electron yield; **в. электронов вперёд** forward electron yield; **время —а** retention time; **доза на —е** (radiation) exit dose; **зона —а** escape zone; **на —е** (at the) output, outlet, exit; **на —е из** as they leave; **работа —а** a work function (of electrons); **резервный объём —а** (med.) expiratory reserve volume, ERV; **с одним —ом** one-choice (maze); **угол —а** angle of emergence.

выходец *m.* emigrant, refugee.

выходить *v.* go out, come out, pass out; get out, escape, emanate, issue, leave; walk (in space); fall (into disuse; outside); (geol.) crop out, emerge; overflow; yield; appear, be published, be issued; front, face, open (on), overlook; go (into orbit); run out, be up (of time); come, make, be, turn out; turn up (for work); drop out, quit; put out (to sea); nurse; rear, bring up; **в. наружу** be revealed, come to light; (geol.) crop out; **выходит (что)** it seems, it appears (that).

выходн/ой *a. of* **выход;** outgoing; outside; output, target (information); front, (page); imprint, publication (date); withdrawal (roller); (chromatography) elution (curve); **в. день** day off; **в. слой** (geol.) outcrop(ping); **в. элемент** transmitter; **—ая величина** output; **—ая ёмкость** output capacitance; **—ая шина** (comp.) output line; **—ое отверстие** outlet, vent; **—ое устройство** output unit; **—ые данные** output (data); (publisher's) imprint.

выхо/дящий *a.* going out, etc., *see* **выходить;** outgoing; outcropping; output, target (information); **в. за** beyond; **—ждение** *n.* going out, etc., *see* **выходить;** outcrop, emergence; ejaculation, discharge.

выхол/аживание *n.* cooling, chilling; **фактор —аживания** (meteor.) chill factor; **—аживать, —одить** *v.* cool thoroughly, chill.

выхол/ащивать, —остить *v.* geld, castrate, emasculate; **—ощенный** *a.* castrated.

выхухол/евые, —и *pl.* (mam.) Desmanidae; **—евый, —ий** *a. of* **выхухоль; —ь** *m. or f.* Russian desman (*Desmana moschata*).

выцарап(ыв)ать *v.* scratch (out), get out.

выцве/сти, —тать *v.* fade, lose color, bleach, discolor; effloresce, bloom; (bot.) finish blooming; **—т** *m.* efflorescence, bloom; **—тание** *n.* fading, etc., *see v.;* discoloration; efflorescence; **—тший** *a.* faded, etc., *see v.;* **—ты** *pl.* efflorescence.

выце/дить, —живать *v.* filter (out); decant, pour off; tap (beer, wine); sip; **—женный** *a.* filtered, etc., *see v.*

вычегодский *a.* (geog.) Vychegda.

вычекан/енный *a.* coined, chased; **—и(ва)ть** *v.* coin, chase, emboss.

вычел *past m. sing. of* **вычесть.**

выч/еркивание *n.* deletion, etc., *see v.;* **—ёркивать, —еркнуть** *v.* delete, eliminate, obliterate, cross out, strike out, erase; cancel (out); expunge; **—еркнутый** *a.* deleted, etc., *see v.*

вычерни(ва)ть *v.* blacken, black out.

вычерп/анный *a.* dipped out, etc., *see v.;* **—ать, —нуть, —ывать** *v.* dip out, scoop out, bail out, dredge; exhaust; **—ка** *f.,* **—ывание** *n.* dipping out, etc., *see v.*

вычер/тить *see* **вычерчивать; —ченный** *a.* drawn, etc., *see v.;* **—чиваемый** *a.* plotted (function); **—чивание** *n.* drawing, etc., *see v.;* layout; map; **—чивать** *v.* draw, trace; plot, lay out, map out; design.

вычес/ать *v.* comb (out); (agr.) harrow out; **—ка** *f.* combing out; **—ки** *pl.* combings, refuse, tow.

вычесть *v.* deduct, subtract.

вычёсыв/ание *n.* combing, etc., *see* **вычесать; —ать** *see* **вычесать.**

вычет *m.* deduction; (math.) residue, remainder; **за —ом** with the deduction (of), less, minus; **теория —ов** residue theory; **—ный** *a.* deducted; residual; **—ший** *a.* deducted.

вычисл/ение *n.* computing, etc., *see v.;* estimate, rating; **—енный** *a.* computed, etc., *see v.;* **—енная стоимость** estimate; **—енное значение** (comp.) entry; **—имый** *a.* computable; **—итель** *m.* computer; calculator; **—ительный** *a.* computing, etc., *see v.;* **—ительный автомат** computer; **—ительная математика** calculus; **—ительная машина, —ительное устройство** computer; **внедрять —ительную технику** *v.* computerize; **с помощью —ительных устройств** computerized; **—ить** *see* **вычислять; —яемый** *a.* denumerable, countable; **—ять** *v.* compute, calculate; figure, reckon; estimate; evaluate.

вычистить *see* **вычищать.**

вычит/аемое *n.* (math.) subtrahend; **—аемый** *a.* deductible; **—ание** *n.* deduction; subtraction.

вычитанный *a.* (proof)read.

вычит/атель *m.* (comp.) subtractor; **—ать** *v.* subtract, deduct; (proof)read; find (in books); **—ающий** *a.* subtracting, etc., *see v.;* **—ающее устройство** subtractor; **—ка** *f.* proofreading; manuscript proof or editing; **—чик** *m.* proofreader; **—ывать** *see* **вычитать.**

вычищ/ать *v.* clean (out), scrape out; **—енный** *a.* cleaned (out).

вычлен/ение *n.* (med.) exarticulation; **—ять** *v.* exarticulate, disjoint; (math.) divide into parts.

выч/ли *past pl. of* **вычесть; —тенный** *a.* deducted, subtracted; **—тя** *pr. ger.* deducting.

вышаг(ив)ать *v.* pace out.

вышвыр/ивать, —нуть *v.* throw out.

выше *comp. of* **высокий, высоко,** higher, taller; above; upwards (of), in excess (of), over, beyond; **и в.** and up.

выше— *prefix* above-, (a)fore-; super-, over—; higher-; hyper-, supra-, epi-; **—доказанный** *a.* proved above.

вышедший *past act. part. of* **выйти.**

вышеизложенный *a.* foregoing, set forth above, above-mentioned, stated above.

вышек *gen. pl. of* **вышка.**

вышекипящий *a.* higher-boiling.

вышел *past m. sing. of* **выйти.**

вышележащий *a.* superincumbent, superposed, overlying, superjacent.

вышелуш/енный *a.* shelled, etc., *see v.;* **—и(ва)ть** *v.* shell, husk (out), peel.

выше/названный *a.* above-named, aforesaid; **—означенный** *a.* above-mentioned, aforesaid; **—описанный** *a.* described above; **—поименованный** *a.* above-named; **—приведенный** *a.* above(-mentioned), foregoing; **—сделанный** *a.* made above; **—сказанный** *a.* aforesaid; **—стоящий** *a.* higher; **—указанный** *a.* above(-mentioned), noted above; **—упомянутый** *a.* above-mentioned, referred to above.

вышиб *m.,* **—ание** *n.,* **—ка** *f.* knocking out, breaking out; **—ать, —ить** *v.* knock out, break out, drive out; chuck out, kick out; force (a door); **—ной** *a. of* **вышиб;** ejection (charge).

вышив/альный *a.* embroidery; **—ать** *v.* embroider; **—ка** *f.* embroidery.

вышин/а *f.* height; **—ой в** in height.

вышить *see* **вышивать.**

вышка *f.* tower; (oil well) derrick, rig; (mech.) pulpit.

вышколить *v.* train, discipline, school.

вышла *past f. sing. of* **выйти.**

вышлет *fut. 3 sing. of* **выслать.**

вышли *past pl. of* **выйти.**

вышлифов(ыв)ать *v.* grind, polish.

вышло *past n. sing. of* **выйти.**

вышпари(ва)ть *v.* scald.

выштампов(ыв)ать *v.* stamp out, punch.

выштукатури(ва)ть *v.* plaster, stucco.

вышу/тить, —чивать *v.* ridicule, deride.

выщел/ачиваемость *f.* leachability; **—ачиваемый** *a.* leachable; **—ачивание** *n.* leaching, lixiviation; **—ачиватель** *m.* leacher, extractor; leaching tank; **—ачивать, —очить** *v.* leach (out), lixiviate, extract; (text.) steep; **—оченный** *a.* leached, etc., *see v.*

выщепление *n.* diversion, deviation, variation.

выщерб/ить, —лять *v.* notch.

выщип *m.* notching, blazing; **—ание** *n.* picking, etc., *see v.;* **—нуть, —(вы)ать** *v.* pick, pluck (out); pull (up or out); clip (ears).

выщуп/ать, —ывать *v.* feel, probe; **—ывание** *n.* feeling, probing.

выя *f.* (anat.) nucha.

выяв/итель *m.* detector; **—ить** *see* **выявлять; —ление** *n.* exposure, revealing, etc., *see v.;* appearance; emergence; **—ленный** *a.* exposed, etc., *see v.;* **—ляемость** *f.* rate of detection; **—ляемый** *a.* detectable; **—лять** *v.* expose, reveal, uncover, show up, bring out, disclose, indicate; make manifest; find out, establish; detect, identify, recognize; prepare, isolate; trouble-shoot; **—ляться** *v.* be exposed, etc.; emerge, reveal itself.

выясн/ение *n.* clarification, etc., *see v.;* **—енный** *a.* clarified, etc., *see v.;* **—ено, что** it has been found that, it appears that; **—ить, —ять** *v.* clarify, clear (up), explain, elucidate; look into, examine, investigate; find out, learn, ascertain, determine; **остаётся (ещё) —ить** it remains to be seen; **—яться** *v.* turn out, develop.

вьёт *pr. 3 sing. of* **вить.**

вьетнамский *a.* (geog.) Vietnam.

вью/га *f.,* **—жный** *a.* snowstorm, blizzard; **—жить** *v.* storm, rage; **—жит** there is a snowstorm.

вьюк *m.* pack, load, burden; pack saddle.

вьюн *m.* (ichth.) loach (*Misgurnus fossilis*); **—ица** *f.* a single-funnel trap net.

вьюнков/ые *pl.* (bot.) Convolvulaceae; **—ый** *a. of* **вьюнок.**

вьюновые *pl.* (ichth.) loaches (*Cobitidae*).

вьюн/ок *m.* (bot.) bindweed (*Convolvulus*); *see also* **вьюн; —ообразный** *a.* curling, twisted.

вьюр/ки, —ковые *pl.* (orn.) finches (*Fringillidae*); **—ок** *m.* (orn.) brambling (*Fringilla montifringilla*); reel; (text.) scroll tube.

вьют *pr. 3 pl. of* **вить.**

вьюч/ить *v.,* **—ный** *a.* pack, load.

вьюшка *f.* damper; reel, cable drum.

вьющ/ий *pr. act. part. of* **вить; —ийся** *a.* winding, twisting, coiling; (bot.) climbing, creeping, trailing; pole (bean); **—ееся растение** vine.

ВЭЗ *abbr.* [(метод) вертикального электрического зондрования] vertical electrical sounding.

Венсана ангина (med.) Vincent's angina.

ВЕР *abbr.* (вторичные энергоресурсы) secondary power resources.

ВЭС *abbr.* (ветроэлектростанция) wind power plant.

ВЭТТ *abbr.* (высота, эквивалентная теоретической тарелке) height equivalent of a theoretical plate, HETP.

вюрм *m.,* **—ское отделение** (geol.) Würm.

вюртцит *m.* (min.) wurtzite.

Вюрца колба Würtz flask.

вюстит *m.* (min.) wüstite.

вяжет *pr. 3 sing. of* **вязать.**

вяжечка *f.* (bot.) tower cress (*Turritis*).

вяжущ/ее *n.* binder, binding agent; cement, agglutinant, adhesive; vehicle, medium; **—ий** *a.* binding, cementing; sticky, astringent, tart; **—ий материал, —ее вещество** binder, cement; astringent; matrix.

вяз *m.* (bot.) elm (*Ulmus*); *past m. sing. of* **вязнуть.**

вяз/альный *a.* binding; (text.) knitting; **—альщик** *m.* binder; knitter; **—ание, —анье** *n.* binding, etc., *see v.;* **—анка** *f.* bundle, bunch, sheaf; knit garment; **—ан(н)ый** *a.* bound, tied; knit(ted); **—ать** *v.* bound, bind, tie (up), bind together, join; make nets; knit, crochet; be astringent; **—аться** *v.* be compatible, be in keeping (with); match, fit in; tally (with).

вязель *m.* (bot.) crown vetch (*Coronilla*).

вяземский *a.* (geog.) Vyazma.

вязига *f.* dried spinal cord of sturgeon.

вязка *f.* binding, tying, joining; joint; binder; bundle; (text.) knitting, crocheting; (zool.) mating, copulation; *sh. f. of* **вязкий; в. брёвен** framework.

вязк/ий *a.* viscous, sticky; viscid; (met.) tough, tenacious, tensile, ductile, malleable; stringy, ropy; **—остно-температурная характеристика** viscosity index; **—ость** *f.* viscosity; stickiness, adhesiveness; strength, toughness, tenacity, ductility, malleability; stringiness, ropiness; thickness (of slag); **—ость по Муни** Mooney viscosity; **—отекучий** *a.* viscous-flow, plastic; viscid, semi-fluid, ropy, thick; tough, tenacious; **—оупругий** *a.* viscoelastic; **—оупругость** *f.* viscoelasticity; **—оэластичный** *a.* viscoelastic.

вязнуть *v.* stick, sink (in), get stuck.

вязовик *m.* hoptree (*Ptelea trifoliata*).

вязовник *m.* elm forest.

вяовский *a.* (geog.) Vyazovaya.

вязов/ые *pl.* (bot.) Ulmaceae; **—ый** *a.* elm.

вязок *gen. pl. of* **вязка;** *sh. m. of* **вязкий.**

вязолистный *a.* (bot.) elm-leaved.

вязочный *a.* binding, tying.

вязче *comp. of* **вязкий.**

вязьминский *a.* (geog.) Vyazma.

вял *sh. m. of* **вялый;** *past m. sing. of* **вянуть.**

вял/ение *n.* sun-curing; jerking (of meat); drying, desiccation (of fruit); **—е(н)ный** *a.* (sun-)dried, (sun-)cured; jerked; **—ить** *v.* sun-cure, dry-cure, air-dry; dry, desiccate; jerk.

вял/о *adv.* flabbily, etc., *see a.; past n. sing. of* **вянуть; —о реагирующий** *a.* sluggish; **—ость** *f.* flabbiness, etc., *see a.;* (med.) atony; inertia; **—ый** *a.* flabby, flaccid, limp, slack; sluggish, dull, relaxed; (med.) atonic; (bot.) withered, faded.

вян/уть *v.* wither, wilt, droop; fade; **—ущий** *a.* withering, etc., *see v.*

вятский *a.* (geog.) Vyatka.

вяхирь *m.* wood pigeon (*Columba palumbus*).

Г

г *abbr.* (**грамм**) gram; (**гекто—**) hecto—; (**градус**) degree; **г.** *abbr.* (**год**) year; (**гора**) mountain; (**город**) city; **Г** *abbr.* [**грамм** (**сила**)] gram (force); (**гига—**) giga—, 10⁹.

га *abbr.* (**гектар**) hectare.

гаагский *a.* Hague.

габардин *m.,* **—овый** *a.* (text.) gabardine.

габарит *m.* clearance; size, overall dimensions; (rr.) clearance diagram; (mach.) profile, bulk; **—ный** *a. of* **габарит**; overall, outside; contour, outline; **—ный контур** outline; **—ные размеры** overall dimensions; **—ометр** *m.* clearance gage; **—оустановочный чертёж** mechanical interface drawing.

габбро *n.* (petr.) gabbro; **—видный, —подобный** *a.* gabbroid; **—вый** *a.* gabbro(ic); **—ид** *m.* gabbroid (rock).

Габера процесс Haber process.

габион *m.,* **—ный** *a.* (hydr.) gabion.

габит/ет *m.* (biol.) habitat; **—ус** *m.* habitus, habit, appearance.

габонский *a.* (geog.) Gabon, Gaboon.

габронем(ат)оз *m.* (vet.) habronemiasis, Habronema infection.

гавайский *a.* (geog.) Hawaiian.

гаван/ка *f.* bunch of tobacco leaves; **—ский** *a.* (geog.) Havana.

гаван/ский *a.,* **—ь** *f.* port, harbor.

гавасайский *a.* (geog.) Gavasai.

гаверсинус *m.* (math.) haversine.

гаверсов канал (anat.) Haversian canal.

гавиалы *pl.* (herp.) Gavialidae.

гавка *see* **гага.**

гавк/ать, —нуть *v.* bark, yelp.

гавр (geog.) Le Havre.

гавра *f.* a marine trap net.

гага *f.* (orn.) eider (*Somateria*).

гагар/а *f.,* **—ий** *a.* (orn.) loon (*Gavia*).

гагаринит *m.* (min.) gagarinite.

гагарка *f.* (orn.) auk (*Alca*).

гагаровые *pl.* (orn.) loons (*Gaviidae*).

гагат *m.,* **—овый** *a.* (min.) jet; **—оподобный** *a.* jet-like.

гаг/ачий *a. of* **гага**; **г. пух** eiderdown; **—ка** *see* **гага.**

гагрский *a.* (geog.) Gagra.

гагун *see* **гага.**

гад *m.* reptile.

гадаль *m.* (ocean.) hadal zone.

гад/ание *n.* guesswork; **—ательный** *a.* hypothetical, conjectural, doubtful; **—ать** *v.* guess, conjecture, surmise.

гадикул *m.* (ichth.) Gadiculus.

гад/ить *v.* soil; spoil, damage; **—кий** *a.* dirty, foul; disgusting, bad, nasty.

Гадлея принцип (meteor.) Hadley's principle.

гадолеиновый *a.* gadoleic (acid).

гадолин/ий *m.,* **—овый** *a.* gadolinium, Gd; **—ит** *m.* (min.) gadolinite; **—овая земля** gadolinia, gadolinium oxide.

гадопсиевые *pl.* blackfish (*Gadopsidae*).

гадром *m.* (bot.) hadrome; **—икоз** *m.* (phyt.) hadromycosis, tracheomycosis.

Гадфильда процесс Hadfield process.

гад/ы *pl.* amphibians and reptiles; **—юка** *f.* (herp.) adder, viper; **морская —юка** viperfish (*Chauliodus*); **—юковидный** *a.* viperlike, viperiform; **—юковые** *pl.* Viperidae; **—ючий** *a.* viperine; **—ючий лук** (bot.) Muscari.

гаек *gen. pl. of* **гайка.**

гаечн/ый *a.* nut; female, inside (thread); **г. барашек** wing nut; **г. замок** lock nut; **г. ключ** wrench.

гажа *f.* (geol.) sea chalk (calcium carbonate mixture of sand, gypsum, etc.).

гаже *comp. of* **гадкий, гадко.**

гажение *n.* outgassing, gas removal.

газ *m.* gas; gauze (material); **сбавить г.** *v.* (mach.) throttle down; **—ация** *see* **газирование**; **г.-восстановитель** *m.* reducing gas; **—генератор** *m.* (coal) gasifier, gasification reactor; **—гольдер** *m.* gas holder.

газел/евые *pl.* (mam.) Gazellinae; **—ь** *f.* gazelle (*Gazella*).

газер *see* **газовик.**

газет/а *f.,* **—ный** *a.* newspaper, journal.

газиатор *m.* gas heater, gas stove.

газимурский *a.* (geog.) Gazimur.

газиров/ание *n.* gassing, etc., *see v.;* **—анный** *a.* gassed, etc., *see v.;* **—ать** *v.* gas(ify), aerate, bubble (up; through); carbonate (beverages).

газифи/катор *m.* gasifier, gas generator; evaporator; carburator; gasification technologist; **—кация** *f.* gasification, etc., *see v.;* **—фицированный** *a.* gasified, etc., *see v.;* gas-fired; **—цировать** *v.* gasify; produce gas, manufacture gas; carburate; install gas facilities; supply with gas.

газлинский *a.* (geog.) Gazli.

газлифт *m.* gas lift, air lift.

газ-носитель *m.* carrier gas.

газо— *prefix* gas; gas-driven; **—анализатор** *m.* gas analyzer.

газобаллон *m.* gas cylinder; **—ный** *a.* gas cylinder; bottle-gas driven (vehicle); (gas-)pressurized (rocket).

газо/безопасность *f.* prevention of gas accidents; **—безопасный** *a.* gas-safe; **—бензин** *m.,* **—бензиновый** *a.* natural gasoline; **—бетон** *m.,* **—бетонный** *a.* gas concrete, aerated concrete; **—вание** *n.* gassing; **—вать** *v.* gas; accelerate (engine); **—взвесь** *f.* suspension of matter in gas; **—видный** *a.* gaseous, gasiform; **—вик** *m.* gas producer; gas worker; **—воз** *m.* gas-driven locomotive; gas carrier (ship); **—воздуходувка** *f.* gas-engine blower; gas blast; **—воздухопровод** *m.* gas-air line; **—воздушный** *a.* gas-air; **—вщик** *m.* gas works employee; **—выделение** *n.* evolution of gas; gassing.

газов/ый *a.* gas(eous); natural (gasoline); *see also under* **газо—**; gauze; **г. завод** gas works; **г. фактор** gas-oil ratio, GOR: **—ая вода** (coal) gas liquor; **—ая колонка** (geol.) geyser; **—ая постоянная** gas constant; **—ая пробка** vapor lock; **—ая сажа** gas black, carbon black; **—ая съёмка** (petrol.) gas survey; **—ая ткань** wire gauze; **—ые сети** gas-distributing system.

газо/вырубка *f.* (oxy-acetylene) scarfing; **—вырубщик** *m.* scarfer; **—ген** *m.* gasogen.

газогенератор *m.* gas generator, (gas) producer; **—ный** *a.* gas-producing; producer-gas (engine); gas (works).

газо/гипс *m.* porous plaster; **—динамика** *f.* gas dynamics; **—дисперсный** *a.* gas-dispersion; **—диффузионный** *a.* gas-diffusion; **—добывание** *n.* gas production; **—дувка** *f.* gas blower; **—ем** *m.* gas holder; **—ёмкость** *f.* gas capacity; **—жидкостный** *a.* gas-liquid; **—золобетон** *m.* gas-ash concrete; **—испытатель** *m.* gas tester; **—йль** *m.* gas oil; **—калильный** *a.* incandescent; **—камера** *f.* (vet.) gas chamber; fumigating chamber; **—каротажный** *a.* gas-logging; **—керновый** *a.* core-gas (survey); **—кинетика** *f.* gas kinetics.

газ-окислитель *m.* oxidizing gas.

газо/кислородный *a.* gas, oxyacetylene (welding); **—конденсатный** *a.* condensed gas (deposit); gas-condensate (well); **—лин** *m.*, **—линовый** *a.* gas(oline).

газомер *m.*, **—итель** *m.* gas meter; gasometer, gas holder, gas tank.

газомёт *m.* gas ejector.

газометр *see* **газомер**; **—ический** *a.* gasometric; **—ия** *f.* gasometry.

газомото/воз *m.* gas-driven locomotive; **—р** *m.* gas engine.

газон *m.* lawn, grass (plot).

газо/наполненный *a.* gas-filled; **—насыщение** *n.*, **—насыщенность** *f.* saturation with gas; **—насыщенный** *a.* saturated with gas; **—непроницаемость** *f.* gas impermeability; **—непроницаемый** *a.* gastight, gas-proof.

газонный *a. of* **газон.**

газоносн/ость *f.* presence of gas; gas content; **—ый** *a.* gas-bearing, gas(eous).

газоноукатыватель *m.* lawn roller.

газо/обильность *f.* volume of gas; **—обмен** *m.* gas(eous) exchange, respiratory exchange, respiration.

газообразн/ость *f.* gaseousness; **—ый** *a.* gaseous, gasiform; vapor (phase); **—ое тело** gas; **—ое топливо** fuel gas.

газообраз/ование *n.* gasification, gas formation, evolution of gas; volatilization; **—ователь** *m.* gas producer, gas generator, gasifier; blowing agent, foaming agent; **—ующий** *a.* gas-forming, gas-making.

газо/окуривание *n.* gas fumigation; **—определитель** *m.* gas detector; **—освещение** *n.* gas illumination.

газоотвод *m.* gas bleeder, offtake, gas vent, gas outlet; **—ный** *a.* bleeding, offtake; vent; exhaust (pipe); gas (flue); **—ящий** *a.* (gas-)outlet, (gas-)exhaust.

газоотдел/ение *n.* evolution of gas; gas separation; gassing; **—итель** *m.* gas separator, gas trap.

газо/отравленный *a.* gassed, poisoned by gas; **—отражатель** *m.* (rockets) blast deflector; **—отсасывающий** *a.* gas-suction, exhaust; **—охладитель** *m.* gas condenser, gas cooler.

газоочист/итель *m.* gas purifier, scrubber; **—ительный,** **—ный** *a.* gas-purifying; **—ка** *f.* gas purification, scrubbing.

газо/паропроницаемость *f.* permeability to gas and vapor; **—пламенный** *a.* gas-flame; **—пламенное напыление** (met.) flame spraying; **—плотный** *a.* gastight, gas-proof.

газопогло/титель *m.* gas absorber, getter; **—щение** *n.* gettering, getter action.

газо/подводящий *a.* gas-intake, gas-feed, gas (pipe); **—подогреватель** *m.* gas heater; **—полный** *a.* gas-filled; **—предупредитель** *m.* gas detector; **—прессовый** *a.* pressure-gas, oxyacetylene-pressure (welding); **—привод** *m.* gas inlet, gas feed; **—приёмник** *m.* gas collector; **—приёмный** *a.* gas-collecting, gas-receiving.

газопровод *m.* gas (pipe)line, main or conduit; **—ный** *a.* gas-main, gas (line); **—чик** *m.* gas fitter.

газо/производитель *m.* gas producer; **—промыватель** *m.* gas scrubber; gas washer; **—промывной** *a.* scrubbing, gas-washing; **—проницаемость** *f.* gas permeability; **—проницаемый** *a.* gas-permeable; **—проточный** *a.* gas-flow (counter); **—проявление** *n.* (geol.) gas deposit, gas occurrence; (petrol.) gas show; **—пузырьковый** *a.* gas-bubble (disease of fish); **—пылевой** *a.* gaseous dust (cloud); **—разрядный** *a.* gas-discharge, glow-discharge; fluorescent (lamp).

газораспредел/ение *n.* gas distribution; valve timing; **клапанное г.** valve gear; **—итель** *m.* gas distributor; **—ительный** *a.* gas-distributing; gas (chromatography).

газорез/ательный *a.*, **—ка** *f.* cutting (with oxyacetylene torch); **—чик** *m.* cutter.

газосборн/ик *m.* gas collector; **—ый** *a.* gas-collecting.

газосвар/ка *f.*, **—очный** *a.* gas welding, oxyacetylene welding; **—щик** *m.* gas welder.

газо/светный *a.* gas-discharge; fluorescent (lamp); **—свещение** *n.* gas illumination; **—сжигательный** *a.* gas-burning; **—сигнализатор** *m.* gas detector, gas alarm; **—силикат** *m.* gas silicate; **—смеситель** *m.* gas-air mixer; (engine) carburetor; **—снабжение** *n.* gas supply; **—сос** *m.* gas exhauster; **—стекло** *n.* foam glass; **—стойкий** *a.* gasproof, gas-resistant; **—сушитель** *m.* gas drier; **—счётчик** *m.* gas meter; **—творный** *a.* gas-forming; **—техника** *f.*, **—технический** *a.* gas engineering, gas technology; **—трон** *m.* (electron.) gas-filled tube rectifier; **—трубный** *a.* gas-tube (boiler).

газотурб/ина *f.*, **—инный** *a.*, **—о**—*prefix* gas turbine; **—овоз** *m.* gas-turbine locomotive; **—огенератор** *m.* gas-turbine (driven) generator; **—онагнетатель** *m.* gas turboblower; **—оход** *m.* gas-turbine (powered) ship.

газо/убежище *n.* (mil.) gasproof shelter; **—удерживающий** *a.* gas-retaining; **—улавливание** *n.* gas trapping; **—уловитель** *m.* gas trap, gas collector; **—упорный** *a.* gasproof; **—фазный** *a.* gas-phase, vapor-phase; **—фикация** *see* **газификация**; **—ход** *m.* gas conduit; gas-powered ship; **—хранилище** *n.* gas holder, gas storage tank; **—хромирование** *n.* diffusion chromizing; **—чиститель** *m.* gas cleaner, scrubber; **—шлакобетон** *m.* gas-slag concrete; **—шлакозолобетон** *m.* gas-slag-ash concrete; **—электрический** *a.* gas-arc, gas-shielded (welding).

газский *a.* (geog.) Gaz.

газтехнологический *a.* producer gas.

газящий *a.* gassing.

гаилюссакия *f.* (bot.) Gaylussacia.

гаитян/ин *m.*, **—ка** *f.*, **—ский** *a.* (geog.) Haitian.

гаичка *f.* (orn.) tit (*Parus*).

гай *m.* small grove or thicket.

Гайда процесс (min.) Hyde process.

гайденит *m.* (min.) haydenite.

гайдингерит *m.* (min.) haidingerite.

гайдроп *m.* guide rope.

гайит *m.* (min.) gajite.

гайк/а *f.* nut, female screw; **г.-барашек, барашковая г.** wing nut; **—овёрт** *m.* impact wrench; (power) driver; **—онарезной,** **—орезный** *a.* nut-tapping.

гаймор/ит *m.* (med.) highmoritis; **—ова полость** (anat.) antrum of Highmore.

гайняча *f.* (soil) gainiacha.

гайот *m.* (ocean.) guyot.

гайпер— *see under* **гипер—**.

гак *m.* hook; **—аборт** *m.* (naut.) taffrail; **—блок** *m.* hook and tackle.

гакманит *m.* (min.) hackmanite.

гал *m.* gal [unit of linear acceleration (1 cm/sec^2)].

галаадский бальзам balm of Gilead.

галаго *m.* (mam.) bush baby (*Galago*).

галакс/иас *see* **галаксия**; **—иевые,** **—ииды** *pl.* (ichth.) Galaxiidae; **—ия** *f.* galaxid (*Galaxias*).

галакт— *see* **галакто—**.

галакт/аза *f.* galactase; **—ан** *m.* galactan, gelose; **—аровый** *a.* galactaric, mucic (acid); **—ика** *f.* (astr.)

galaxy; —**ит** *m.* (min.) galactite; (chem.) dulcitol; —**ический** *a.* (astr.) galactic.

галакто— *prefix* galacto— (milk; galactose); —**вальденаза** *f.* galactowaldenase; —**ген** *m.* galactogen; —**з** *m.* galactosis, milk formation; —**за** *f.* galactose, pentahydroxyhexanol; —**замин** *m.* galactosamine; —**зан** *m.* galactosan; —**зид** *m.* galactoside, cerebroside; —**зидаза** *f.* galactosidase; —**зофосфат** *m.* galactose phosphate; —**зурия** *f.* (med.) galactosuria; —**киназа** *f.* galactokinase; —**метр** *m.* galactometer; —**новый** *a.* galactonic (acid); —**поэз** *m.* (physiol.) galactopoiesis.

галактуроновый *a.* galacturonic (acid).

гал/алит *m.* galalith (plastic); —**ангин** *m.* galangin; —**анговый** *a.* galanga (root).

галантер/ейный *a.*, —**ея** *f.* haberdashery, notions.

галапагосский *a.* (geog.) Galapagos.

гал/бан *m.* galbanum (gum resin); —**джойновые** *pl.* (ichth.) Coracinidae; —**еа** *f.* (biol.) galea, helmet.

галево *n.* (text.) heald, harness.

гал/ега *f.* (bot.) Galega; —**егин** *m.* galegine, isoamyleneguanidine; —**еихт** *m.* sea catfish (*Galeichthys*).

галек *gen. pl. of* **галька.**

гален/ит *m.* (min.) galena, galenite, lead glance; —**итсодержащий** *a.* galenite-containing; —**обисмутит** *m.* (min.) galenobismutite; —**овы(е) препараты** galenics, organic medicines; —**овый** *a.* (min.) galena.

галер/(ей)ный *a. of* **галерея**; fringe (woodland); —**ея** *f.* gallery; tunnel; culvert.

галет/а *f.* ship biscuit; press cake; disc coil; wafer, deck; —**ный** *a. of* **галета**; disc; flat; biscuit.

галечн/ик *m.* shingle, pebble; coarse gravel; pebble bed; **крупный г.** cobble roundstone; —**иково-щебнистый** *a.* pebble-cobble; —**иковый** *a. of* **галечник**; nodular (ore); —**ый** *a.* pebbly, pebbled; pebble (mill).

галея *f.* (ichth.) shore rockling (*Gaidropsarus mediterraneus*).

гали *gen., pl., etc., of* **галь.**

галид *m.* halide.

галикт *m.* (ent.) mining bee (*Halictus*).

гал/ил *m.* galyl; —**илеев** *a.* Galilean; —**инсога** *f.* (bot.) Galinsoga.

галиотис *m.* (mal.) Haliotis.

галиофовые *pl.* (ichth.) Haliophidae.

галип/ин *m.* galipine; —**ол** *m.* galipol; —**от** *m.* galipot (resin).

галит *m.* (min.) halite, rock salt.

галицийский *a.* (geog.) Galician.

галка *f.* (orn.) jackdaw (*Coloeus*).

галл *m.* (bot.) gall (nut); —**амид** *m.* gallamide; —**аминовый** *a.* gallamic (acid); —**анилид** *m.*, —**анол** *m.* gallanilide, gallanol; —**ат** *m.* gallate; —**ацетофенон** *m.* gallacetophenone; —**еин** *m.* gallein, pyrogallolphthalein.

галлей-реал *m.* (typ.) galley rack.

галлерея *see* **галерея.**

галлерит *m.* (min.) hallerite.

галлерта *f.* jelly, gelatinous mass.

галлит *m.* (min.) hallite.

галли— *prefix* galli-, gallic.

галлиевая соль gallium salt, gallic salt.

галлизировать *v.* (wine) gallize.

галл/ий *m.* gallium, Ga; **закись** —**ия** gallous oxide, gallium monoxide; **окись** —**ия** gallic oxide, gallium trioxide.

галлит *m.* (min.) hallite.

галлиц/а *f.* (ent.) gall midge or gnat; —**ин** *m.* gallicin, methyl gallate; —**ы** *pl.* Cecidomyiidae.

галло— *prefix* gallo—, gallous; (phyt.) gall; —**бромол** *m.* gallobromol, dibromogallic acid.

галловеевский котёл Galloway boiler.

галлово/кальциевая соль calcium gallate; —**кислый** *a.* gallic acid; gallate (of); —**кислая соль** gallate; —**кислое железо** iron gallate; —**метиловый эфир** methyl gallate.

галлов/ый *a.* gall; gallic (acid); **соль** —**ой кислоты** gallate.

галло/ген *m.* gallogen, ellagic acid; —**гидрид** *m.* gallium hydride; —**дубильный** *a.* gallotannic (acid).

галлоизит *m.* (min.) halloysite.

галло/ил *m.* galloyl; —**л** *m.* gallol.

галлон *m.*, —**ный** *a.* gallon (3.79 liter).

галлообразование *n.* (phyt.) gall formation.

галлоцианин *m.* gallocyanin.

галлуазит *see* **галлоизит.**

галлюцин/ация *f.* hallucination —**ировать** *v.* hallucinate; —**оген** *m.* hallucinogen; —**огенный** *a.* hallucinogenic; —**оз** *m.* hallucinosis.

Галля цепь Gall's (sprocket) chain; **Г. явление** (elec.) Hall effect.

галм/ееподобный *a.* (min.) calamine-like; —**ей** *m.*, —**ейный** *a.* calamine, smithsonite.

гало *n.* halo; *prefix* halo— (salt).

головакс *m.* halowax.

галоген *m.* halogen; *prefix see* **галогено**—; —**алкил** *m.* alkyl halide; —**ангидрид** *m.* acid halide; —**арил** *m.* aryl halide; —**ация** *f.* halogenation; —**водород** *m.* halogen hydride; —**ез** *m.* (geol.) halogenesis, salt formation; —**замещённое** *see* **галогенозамещённое**; —**ид** *m.* halide; —**ирование** *n.* halogenation; —**ированный** *a.* halogenated; —**ировать** *v.* halogenate; —**ирующий** *a.* halogenating; —**кислота** *f.* halogen acid, hydracid.

галогенн/ый *a.* halogen(ous), halide (of); **г. водород** hydrogen halide; —**ая кислота** halogen acid.

галогено— *prefix* halo—, halogen; halide.

галогеноангидрид *m.* acid halide; **г. серной кислоты** sulfuryl halide.

галогеноводород *m.* hydrogen halide; —**ная кислота** hydrohalic acid; **соль** —**ной кислоты** halide.

галогено/замещённое *n.* halogenated compound; —**замещённый** *a.* halogen-substituted, halogenated, halo—; —**кислота** *f.* halogen acid, haloacid; —**окись** *f.* oxyhal(ogen)ide; —**производные** *pl.* halogen derivatives.

гало/геносодержащий *a.* halogenous; —**гетон** *m.* (bot.) Halogeton; —**завровые** *pl.* (ichth.) Halosauridae.

галоид *m.* halogen; haloid; halide; —**алкил** *m.* alkyl halide; —**ангидрид кислоты** acid halide; —**бензол** *m.* phenyl halide; —**замещённый** *a.* halogenated; —**ид** *m.* halide; —**ирование** *n.* halogenation; —**ированный** *a.* halogenated; —**ировать** *v.* halogenate; —**метил** *m.* methyl halide; —**ный** *a. of* **галоид**; —**ный алкил** alkyl halide; —**ный металл** metal halide; —**ная соль** halide.

галоидо— *see* **галогено**—; —**ангидрид** *m.* acid halide; —**водород** *m.* hydrogen halide; —**замещённый** *a.* halogenated; —**кислота** *f.* halogen acid; —**окись** *f.* oxyhal(ogen)ide; —**производное** *n.* halogen derivative; —**спирт** *m.* halogen alcohol; —**углеводород** *m.* halohydrocarbon; —**углерод** *m.* halocarbon.

галоидсодержащий *a.* halogen-containing.

галометр *m.* (cryst.) halometer; —**ический** *a.* halometric; —**ия** *f.* halometry.

галоп *m.*, —**ировать** *v.* gallop; —**ирование** *n.*, —**ирующий** *a.* galloping; —**ом** *adv.* at a gallop.

галос *see* **гало.**

гало/трихит *m.* (min.) halotrichite, iron alum; **—фил** *m.* halophilous organism; **—фильный** *a.* halophilous, salt-loving; **—фит** *m.* halophyte, salt marsh plant; **—фитный** *a.* halophytic; **—фитная раститель-ность** halophytes; **—фобный** *a.* halophobic; **—фоб-ное растение** (bot.) halophobe; **—фосфат** *m.* halo-phosphate; **—химический** *a.* halochemical; **—химия** *f.* halochemistry; **—хромия** *f.* halochromism.

галоч/ий *a.* of **галка**; **—ка** *dim.* of **галка**; check mark, tick.

галош/а *f.*, **—ный** *a.* overshoe, rubber; kalosha (rubber solvent).

галп *m.* (comp.) gulp (group of bits processed as a unit).

галс *m.* reach, stretch; transect; (naut.) tack.

галсту/к *m.* necktie; **—чник** *m.* (orn.) ring(ed) plover (*Charadrius hiaticula*); **—чный** *a.* necktie.

галтель *m. and f.*, **—ный** *a.* hollow chamfer, fillet, flut-ing plane; flute, channel, groove; **—ный резец** recess-ing tool.

галтов/ание *n.*, **—ка** *f.*, **—очный** *a.* tumbling; **—ать** *v.* tumble.

галтоза *f.* galtose.

галун *m.*, **—ный** *a.* galloon, lace.

галург/ический *a.* halurgic; **—ия** *f.* halurgy, mineral salt production.

галчонок *m.* (orn.) young jackdaw.

галь *f.* (text.) heald; *see also* **гал.**

гальбан *see* **галбан.**

гальваниз/атор *m.* galvanizer; **—ация** *f.*, **—ирование** *n.* galvanization, electroplating; **—ированный** *a.* gal-vanized, plated; **—ировать** *v.* galvanize, (electro)plate.

гальваническ/и *adv.* by galvanization; **—оцинко-вывать** *v.* galvanize; **г. плакировать, г. покрывать** *v.* electroplate; **—ий** *a.* galvanic, voltaic (cell); gal-vanizing, (electro)plating; **—ий покров** elec-trodeposit; **—ое золочение** electrogilding; **—ое покрытие** electroplate; electroplating.

гальвано *n.* (typ.) electrotype.

гальвано— *prefix* galvano—; electro—.

гальванограф *m.* (elec.) galvanograph; **—ия** *f.* gal-vanography.

гальвано/каустика *f.* (med.) galvanocautery; **—люми-несценция** *f.* galvanoluminescence; **—магнитный** *a.* galvanomagnetic.

гальванометр *m.* (elec.) galvanometer; **—ический** *a.* galvanometric; **—ия** *f.* galvanometry.

гальваноотложение *n.* electrotype shell.

гальванопласт *m.* galvanizer; **—ика** *f.* galvanoplastics, electroforming; (typ.) electrotyping; **—ический, —ич-ный** *a.* galvanoplastic, electroforming; electroformed.

гальванопокрытие *n.* electrodeposit(ion), (electro)plating.

гальваноскоп *m.* (elec.) galvanoscope, current detector, quadrant electrometer; **—ический** *a.* galvanoscopic.

гальваностег *m.* electroplater (operator); **—ировать** *v.* electroplate; **—ически отложенный** electrodeposited; **—ический** *a.* electrolytic (plating), electroplating; **—ическое покрытие, —ия** *f.* galvanostegy; electro-plating.

гальвано/стереотип *m.* (typ.) electrotype; **—стерео-типия** *f.* electrotype; electrotyping; **—таксис** *m.* (biol.) galvanotaxis; **—техник** *m.* electroplater; **—техника** *f.* electroplating technology; **—типия** *f.* (typ.) electro-type; electrotypy; **—тропизм** *m.* (biol.) galvanotrop-ism; **—ударный колпак** horn (of mine); **—хромия** *f.* electrocoloring.

гальк/а *f.* pebble, shingle; rubble; nodule; pebbles (fuel); boulder; beach; **—овидный** *a.* pebble-shaped.

гальмей *see* **галмей.**

гальмиролиз *m.* halmyrolysis, underwater decay.

гальтельник *m.* fillet plane, fluting plane.

Гальтона кривая (math.) Galtonian curve.

галя *pl.* pebbles, nodules.

гамада *f.* hamada (stony, flat desert).

гамадриад *m.* (herp.) king cobra (*Ophiophagus hannah*).

гамадрил *m.* (mam.) hamadryas baboon (*Papio hama-dryas*).

гамазиды *pl.* Gamasidae (mites).

гамак *m.* hammock.

гамакер *m.* Hamaker constant.

гамамел/идовые *pl.* Hamamelidaceae; **—ис** *m.* witch-hazel (*Hamamelis*); **—оза** *f.* hamamelose.

гамартит *m.* (min.) hamartite.

гамарто— *prefix* hamarto— (defect).

гаматионовый *a.* hamathionic (acid).

гамаша *f.* gaiter, legging.

гамбергит *m.* (min.) hambergite.

гамбийский *a.* (geog.) Gambia(n).

гамбин *m.* gambin (a nitroso dye).

гамбир *m.* gambier, pale catechu.

гамбуз/иевые *pl.* mosquito fishes (*Poeciliidae*); **—ия** *f.* Gambusia.

гамбургский *a.* (geog.) Hamburg.

гамет/а *f.* (gen.) gamete, sexual cell; **женская г.** gyno-gamete; **—ангий** *m.* gametangium; **—ический, —ный** *a.* gametic; **—о—** *prefix* gameto—, gamete; **—огенез** *m.* gametogenesis; **—носец** *m.* (bot.) gametophore; **—носитель** *m.* gamete carrier; **—ообразование** *n.* ga-metogenesis; **—офит** *m.* (bot.) gametophyte; **—офор** *m.* gametophore; **—оцит** *m.* gametocyte.

гамильтониан *m.* (math.) Hamiltonian.

гамлинит *m.* (min.) hamlinite.

гамма *f.* gamma (γ); gamma [magnetic unit (10^{-5} oersted)]; gamut, range, scale; **г.-активный** *a.* gamma-active, gamma-ray-emitting; **г.-аппарат** *m.* gamma (therapy) unit; **г.-глобулин** *m.* gamma globulin; **—граф** *m.* (nucl.) gammagraph; **—графирование** *n.* gamma-ray inspection; **—графия** *f.* gamma(-ray) radiography.

гаммада *f.* hammada (rocky desert).

гамма-/дефектоскопия *f.* gamma-ray flaw detection; **г.-дозиметрия** *f.* gamma-monitoring; **г.-железо** *n.* gamma iron.

гамма-излуч/атель *m.* gamma emitter; **—ающий** *a.* gamma-emitting; **—ение** *n.* gamma radiation, gamma-ray emission.

гамма-/каротаж *m.* gamma-ray logging; **г.-квант** *m.* gamma(-ray) quantum; **г.-лучи** *pl.* gamma rays; **г.-метод** *m.* gamma-ray prospecting; **г.-облучение** *n.* gamma irradiation; **г.-переход** *m.* gamma(-ray) transi-tion; **г.-резонансная спектроскопия** Mössbauer spectroscopy; **г.-спектр** *m.* gamma(-ray) spectrum; **г.-спектроскопия** *f.* gamma(-ray) spectroscopy; **г.-уран** *m.* gamma uranium; **г.установка** *f.* gamma-ray source; **г.-фаза** *f.* gamma phase; **г.-фактор** *m.* gam-ma; **г.-фон** *m.* gamma background; **г.-фотон** *m.* gamma-ray photon; **г.-функция** *f.* gamma function; **г.-цепь** *f.* gamma chain; **г.-число** *n.* gamma number.

Гаммета уравнение Hammett equation.

гамо— *prefix* gamo— (sexual union; fusion).

гамовский *a.* Gamow.

гамоген/ез *m.* gamogenesis, sexual reproduction; **—ети-ческий** *a.* gamogenetic.

гамо/н *m.* (gen.) gamone; **—нт** *m.* gamont, sprout; **—стелия** *f.* (bot.) gamostely; **—фильный** *a.* gamo-phyllous.

ганаш *m.* masseter region (of horse's jaw).

гангийский *a.* (geog.) Ganges, Gangetic.

гангл/иевидный *a.* (anat.) gangliiform; **—ий** *m.* ganglion; **—ио—** *prefix* gangli(o)—, ganglion; **—ио-блокирующий** *a.* ganglion-blocking; **—иозид** *m.* ganglioside; **—иозный** *a.* ganglionic, gangliar; **—иолитический** *a.* gangliolytic; **—иоцит** *m.* gangliocyte, nerve cell.

гангрен/а *f.* (med.) gangrene, mortification; **—озный** *a.* gangrenous.

гангский *a.* (geog.) Ganges, Gangetic.

ганшпуг *m.* (naut.) handspike; lever.

ганза *f.* yellow pigment(s).

ганзенская жёлтая Hansa yellow.

ганистер *m.* (petr.) ganister.

ганит *m.* (min.) gahnite, zinc spinel.

ганкокит *m.* (min.) hancockite.

ганксит *m.* (min.) hanksite.

ганнайит *m.* (min.) hannayite.

ганновский *a.* (electron.) Gunn.

гано— *prefix* gano— (brightness); **—идный** *a.* (ichth.) ganoid; **костные —иды** Holostei; **хрящевые —иды** Chondrostei; **—филлит** *m.* (min.) ganophyllite.

гантел/евидный, —образный *a.* dumbbell-shaped; **—и** *pl.* dumbbell(s).

Гануса раствор Hanus solution.

ганьсуйский *a.* (geog.) Kansu.

гаолян *m.* (bot.) kaoliang (*Sorghum vulgare*).

гап *m.* gap (block).

гапалемур *m.* (mam.) Hapalemur.

гапло— *prefix* haplo— (single, simple); **—бионт** *m.* (gen.) haplobiont; **—достаточный** *a.* haplosufficient; **—ид** *m.* haploid; **—идия, —идность** *f.* haploidy; **—идный** *a.* haploid; **—митоз** *m.* haplomitosis; **—недостаточный** *a.* haploinsufficient; **—нт** *m.* haplont; **—споридии** *pl.* Haplosporidia; **—фаза** *f.* haplophase, gametophyte phase.

гаптен *m.* (immun.) hapten(e).

гаптера *f.* (bot.) hapteron, holdfast.

гапто— *prefix* hapto— (grasp, hold); **—тропия** *f.* (bot.) haptotropism; **—форная группа** (biochem.) haptophore.

гараж *m.,* **—ный** *a.* garage.

гарансин *m.* garancin (dye).

гарант *m.* guarantor; **—ийный** *a.* guarantee(d), warranted; **—ийная сила тока** (expl.) minimum current (to ensure detonator firing); **—ирование** *n.* guaranteeing; **—ированный** *a.* guaranteed, etc., *see v.;* safe (from); **—ировать** *v.* guarantee, warrant, assure, ensure, secure; **—ия** *f.* guarantee, warranty, assurance.

гарвеизиров/анный *a.* (met.) harveyized, Harvey; **—ать** *v.* harveyize.

гаргоилизм *m.* (med.) gargoylism.

гаргревский *a.* Hargreaves.

гаргрот *m.* (av.) middle fuselage fairing.

гарденит *m.* (met.) hardenite (obs.), martensite.

гардения *f.* (bot.) gardenia.

гардероб *m.,* **—ная** *f.* coat closet.

гардерова железа (anat.) Harderian gland.

гардина *f.* curtain.

гардинол *m.* gardinol (a detergent).

гардистонит *m.* (min.) hardystonite.

гар/евой *a. of;* **—и** *gen. of* **гарь.**

гарига *f.* (bot.) evergreen thicket.

гарида *f.* (bot.) garide.

гаркать *v.* cry, scream, shout.

Гаркинса теория Harkins theory.

гаркнуть *see* **гаркать.**

гаркрец *m.* (met.) refinery slag.

гарлемский *a.* (geog.) Ha(a)rlem.

гармал/а *f.* (bot.) harmel, wild rue (*Peganum harmala*); **—ин** *m.* harmaline.

гарман *m.* harman, aribine.

гармахерский сок (met.) refinery slag.

Гарме способ (met.) Harmet's process.

гармин *m.* harmine, **—овая кислота** harminic acid.

гармониз/ация *f.* harmonization; **—ировать** *v.* harmonize, go (with); **—ирующий** *a.* harmonious, harmonizing.

гармон/ика *f.* harmonic(s); harmonic curve; accordion; bellows; **в виде —ики** bellow-type; **—иковая мембрана** bellows; **—ировать** *v.* harmonize, be in harmony (with); **—ическая** *f.* (phys.) harmonic; **—ический** *a.* harmonic, harmonious, rhythmic; **—ический ряд** (math.) harmonic progression; **—ичность** *f.* harmonicity; **—ичный** *a.* harmonic; **—ия** *f.* harmony, concord.

гармотом *m.* (min.) harmotome.

гармошка *f.* bellows, accordion.

гарна *f.* (mam.) blackbuck (*Antilope cervicapra*).

гарнец *m.* dry measure predating metric system in Russia, equal to 3.28 liters.

гарниерит *m.* (min.) garnierite.

гарнизон *m.,* **—ный** *a.* garrison, post.

гарнир *m.,* **—овать** *v.* garnish, trim.

гарниссаж *m.* (met.) lining slag.

гарнитур *m.,* **—а** *f.* fittings, mountings, trim(mings), furnishings; set, outfit, assembly; nest; suite; tackle; type face, font; (text.) fillet, clothing; needles (of bar).

гарное масло fuel oil.

гарнцевый *a. of* гарнец.

гарньерит *see* гарниерит.

гароннский *a.* (geog.) Garonne.

гарп/актициды *pl.* (crust.) Harpacticoida; **—идий** *m.* Harpidium (lichen).

гарпиус *m.,* **—ный** *a.* rosin, colophony.

гарпия *f.* (ent.) Dicranura; (orn.) harpy eagle (*Harpia harpyja*); (mam.) Harpionycteris whiteheadi.

гарпун *m.,* **—ировать** *v.,* **—ный** *a.* harpoon.

гарра *f.* (ichth.) Garra.

гаррига *see* гарига.

Гарриса способ (met.) Harris process.

гаррупа *f.* (ichth.) Garrupa.

гарт *m.* type metal; **—блей** *m.* hard lead, antimonial lead.

гартит *see* гарденит.

гарт/линг *m.* (met.) hardhead; **—оварка** *f.* (typ.) remelting division; **—овый** *a.* type-metal; **—оплавилка** *f.* melting furnace.

гарус *m.,* **—ный** *a.* (text.) worsted.

Гарфильда валки (met.) Garfield rolls.

гарцбургит *m.* (petr.) harzburgite.

гарцевать *v.* prance.

гарцевский *a.* Harz (jig).

гарциния *f.* (bot.) Garcinia.

Гарше система (sewage) Garchey system.

гаршнеп *m.* (orn.) jack snipe (*Lymnocryptes*).

гарь *f.* (forest) slash, burned-out clearing; ash, cinder, char(red residue); (met.) blue dust; fumes, smoke.

гас/ило *n.,* **—ильщик, —итель** *m.* extinguisher, etc., *see v.;* **—и(те)льный** *a.* extinguishing, etc., *see v.;* **—ить** *v.* extinguish, snuff out, put out (light); quench, damp, suppress; cancel; break (an arc); arrest (spark); kill (energy); clear (counter); slake (lime); **—ить пену** defoam, defroth; **—нуть** *v.* be extinguished, go out, die out; **—нущий** *a.* being extinguished, etc., *see v.*

гассар *m.* (ichth.) gassar (*Chaetostomus pictus*).

гассеров узел (anat.) gasserian ganglion.

гасталдит *m.* (min.) gastaldite.

гастеро— *see* **гастр—;** **—мицеты** *pl.* (bot.) Gasteromycetes.

гастингсит *m.* (min.) hastingsite.

гастр— *prefix* gastr(o)— (stomach); **—альгия** *f.* (med.) gastralgia, gastric colic; **—альный** *a.* gastral; **—альная полость** (embr.) gastrocoele; **—ин** *m.* gastrin (hormone); **—ит** *m.* (med.) gastritis; **—ический** *a.* gastric; **—о—** *see* **гастр—**; **—одуоденальный** *a.* (anat.) gastroduodenal.

гастролировать *v.* (be on) tour.

гастро/мизоновые *pl.* (ichth.) Gastromyzonidae; **—поды** *pl.* (mal.) Gastropoda; **—скоп** *m.* (med.) gastroscope; **—суккорея** *f.* gastrosuccorrhea; **—трихи** *pl.* (zool.) Gastrotricha; **—филёз** *m.* (vet.) gastrophilosis; **—хена** *f.* (mal.) Gastrochaena; **—хил** *m.* (bot.) Gastrochilus; **—цель** *m.* (embr.) gastrocoele; **—энтерит** *m.* (med.) gastroenteritis; **—энтеролог** *m.* gastroenterologist.

гаструл/а *f.* (embr.) gastrula; **—яция** *f.* gastrulation.

гасящий *see* **гасительный**.

г-ат *see* **г-атом**.

гатер *m.* horizontal frame saw.

гати *gen., etc., of* **гать**; **—ть** *v.* dam up; build a (swamp) road.

г-атом *abbr.* (грамм-атом) gram-atom.

гаттерия *f.* (herp.) tuatara (*Sphenodon punctatus* or *Hatteria punctata*).

гатура *f.* (map drawing) hachure.

гатчеттин *m.* (min.) hatchettite.

Гатчетта бурый Hatchett's brown (copper ferrocyanide).

гатчеттолит *m.* (min.) hatchettolite.

гать *f.* dam, dike; sea wall; corduroy road, log road, brushwood road.

гау *see* **гаур**.

Гау ферма Howe girder.

гауби/ца *f.*, **—чный** *a.* (mil.) howitzer.

гауерит *m.* (min.) hauerite.

гауйский *a.* (geog.) Gauya.

Гаукинса элемент Hawkins cell.

гаультер/ин *m.* gaultherin, monotropitoside; **—ия** *f.* (bot.) Gaultheria; **—овый** *a.* gaultheria, wintergreen.

гаунтовский *a.* Gaunt.

гаур *m.* (mam.) gaur (*Bibos gaurus*).

гаурдакский *a.* (geog.) Gaurdak.

гаус *see* **гаусс**.

гаусманнит *m.* (min.) hausmannite.

гаусс *m.* gauss (unit of magnetic induction); **—метр** *m.* gaussmeter; **—овый** *a.* Gauss(ian); **—овое распределение** (stat.) Gaussian distribution.

гауст/еллум *m.* (ent.) haustellum; **—орий** *m.*, **—ория** *f.* (bot.) haustorium; **—ра** *f.* haustrum, recess.

гауч *m.* (paper) couch; **г.-вал** *m.* couch roll; **г.-пресс** *m.* couch press.

гауянский *a.* (geog.) Gauya, Gauja.

гафель *f.*, **—ный** *a.* (naut.) gaff.

гафкия *f.* (bact.) Gaffkya.

гафний *m.* hafnium, Hf.

гафтонит *m.* (min.) haughtonite.

гач *m.* slack wax (a crude paraffin).

гаш/ение *n.* extinguishing, etc., *see* **гасить, гаснуть**; extinction; suppression; (comp.) clearance; **—енка** *f.* slaked lime; **—ёный** *a.* extinguished, etc., *see* **гасить**.

гашетка *f.* firing button, trigger (switch).

гаширование *n.* warping.

гашиш *m.* hashish.

гашпиль *m.* (leather) paddle wheel tank.

гащиватъ *v.* stay (with).

гаюин, —ит *m.* (min.) haüyn(it)e; **—овый** *a.* haüynitic.

гая *gen. of* **гай**; *f.* (herp.) hooded cobra (*Naja haje*).

гаял *m.* (mam.) gayal (*Bibos frontalis*).

гб *abbr.* (гильберт) gilbert; **гб.** *abbr.* (губа) gulf, bay.

ГБР *abbr.* (гиббереллин) gibberellin.

гвад/алказарит *m.* (min.) guadalcazarite; **—елупский** *a.* (geog.) Guadalupe.

гвай/кан *see* **гваяковое дерево**; **—ол** *m.* guaiol, tiglic aldehyde; **—эн** *m.* guaiene; **—юла** *see* **гваюла**.

гвард/ейский *a.*, **—ия** *f.* (mil.) guards.

гварея *f.* (bot.) Guarea.

гватемальский *a.* (geog.) Guatemala(n).

гваэтол *m.* guaethol, thanatol.

гваюл/а *f.*, **—овый** *a.* (bot.) guayule (*Parthenium argentatum*).

гвая/к *m.*, **—овый** *a.* guaiac (gum); **—овая кислота** guaiacic acid; **—овая смола** guaiac; **—овое дерево** lignum vitae (*Guaiacum officinale*); **—ол** *m.*, **—оловый** *a.* guaiacol, *o*-methoxyphenol.

гвая/ен *m.* guaiacene, tiglic aldehyde; **—етин** *m.* guaiacetin, sodium pyrocatechin; **—ил** *m.* guaiacyl.

гвереца *f.* (mam.) guereza (*Colobus*).

гвианский *a.* (geog.) Guiana(n).

гвизоция *f.* (bot.) Guizotia.

гвинейск/ий *a.* (geog.) Guinea(n); **—ая трава** Guinea grass (*Panicum maximum*).

гвиретка *f.* vervet monkey (*Cercopithecus*).

гвозд/арь *m.* nail manufacturer; **—е-** *prefix* nail; clavi— (club); **—евание** *n.* nailing; **—евидный** *a.* claviform, club-shaped; **—евидное укрепление** (anat.) gomphosis; **—ёвка** *f.* (agr.) spike harrow; **—евой** *a. of* **гвоздь**; **—ик** *m.* tack.

гвоздик/а *f.* clove; (bot.) Dianthus; **морская г.** (zool.) a sea anemone (*Metridium dianthus*); **—овидный** *a.* (bot.) caryophyllaceous; **—оцветковый** *a.* carnation-flowered.

гвозд/ильный *a.* nail(-making); **—ильня** *f.* nail header; nail mold; **—имый** *a.* nailable; **—ить** *v.* nail, hammer (in).

гвоздичн/ик *m.* (bot.) Statice; **—ики** *pl.* (zool.) Caryophyllaeidae (tapeworms); **—ые** *pl.* (bot.) Caryophyllaceae; **—ый** *a.* clove; (bot.) caryophyll(ac)eous; **—ый перец** allspice (*Pimenta officinalis*); **—ое дерево** clove tree (*Eugenia caryophyllata*); **—ое масло** oil of cloves; **—ые головки** cloves (spice).

гвозд/одёр *m.* nail puller, claw; **—ок** *m.* tack; **—ообразный** *a.* nail-shaped; **—очник** *m.* nail manufacturer; **—очный** *a.* nail(-making); **—ь** *m.* nail; spike; pin; (wooden) peg, dowel; (ichth.) Aspro; **—ь-холодильник** *m.* (casting) chill nail; **—яной** *a. of* **гвоздь**; **—яник** *m.* nail box.

гвт *abbr.* (гектоватт) hectowatt; **Гвт** *abbr.* (гигаватт) gigawatt.

ГВФ *abbr.* [графито-водяной физический (реактор)] graphite-water physical (reactor).

ГВЧ *abbr.* (генератор высокой частоты) high-frequency oscillator.

гг *abbr.* (гектограмм) hectogram.

гг. *abbr.* (годы) years; (города) cities.

ГГК *abbr.* (гамма-гамма каротаж), **ГГМ** *abbr.* (гамма-гамма метод), **ГГК-П** *abbr.* (гамма-гамма каротаж, плотности) gamma-gamma logging, density logging; **ГГК-С** *abbr.* (гамма-гамма каротаж, селективный) selective gamma-gamma logging.

г/г. экв. *abbr.* (грамм на грамм-эквивалент) gram(s) per gram-equivalent.

где *adv.* where; **г. бы (ни)** wherever; **г.-либо, г.-нибудь, г.-то** somewhere, anywhere.

гдовский *a.* (geog.) Gdov.

ГДФ *abbr.* (гуанозиндифосфорная кислота) guanosine diphosphoric acid.

геантиклиналь *f.* (geol.) geanticline.

геарксутит *m.* (min.) gearksutite.

гебе— *prefix* hebe (pubescent; puberty; pubes).

гебелия *f.* (bot.) Goebelia.

гебер *m.* (laboratory) siphon; (phys.) Lugin-Haber electrode.

гебефрения *f.* (med.) hebephrenia, hebephrenic schizophrenia.

гебр/идский *a.* (geog.) Hebridean, Hebrides; **—онит** *m.* (min.) hebronite, amblygonite.

гевеа *f.* (bot.) Hevea.

геветтит *m.* (min.) hewettite.

гевея *f.* (bot.) Hevea.

гегамский *a.* (geog.) Gegam.

гегаркунь *m.* (ichth.) a Sevan trout (*Salmo ischchan gegarkuni*).

Геда зона (med.) Head's zone.

геданит *m.* (min.) gedanite.

гедвигиевые *pl.* (bot.) Hedwigiaceae.

геделевский *a.* (math.) Gödel.

гед/енбергит *m.* (min.) hedenbergite; **—еомовое масло** hedeoma oil; **—ерагенин** *m.* hederagenin; **—ерин** *m.* hederine; **—ериновый** *a.* hederic (acod); **—ифан** *m.* (min.) hedyphane; **—онал** *m.* hedonal, methylpropylcarbinol urethane.

гедрит *m.* (min.) gedrite.

геевое масло ghee (a semifluid butter).

гез *see* **гэз.**

гезароль *m.* Gesarol, DDT.

гезенк *m.* (min.) blind shaft, winze.

гейбахит *m.* (min.) heubachite.

Гейгера счётчик Geiger counter; **Г.-Неттола закон** Geiger-Nuttall relation.

гейгеровская область Geiger region.

гейдельбергский *a.* Heidelberg (man).

гейзенберговский *a.* Heisenberg.

гейзер *m.* (geol.) geyser; **—ит** *m.* (min.) geyserite, siliceous sinter.

гейзинговский *a.* (electron.) Heising.

гейкиелит *m.* (min.) geikielite.

Гейланда диаграмма (elec.) Heyland diagram.

гейландит *m.* (min.) heulandite.

Гейли метод (met.) Gayley process.

Гей-люссака башня Gay-Lussac tower.

гейлюсс/ация *f.* (bot.) huckleberry (Gaylussacia); **—ит** *m.* (min.) gaylussite.

геймит *m.* (petr.) heumite.

гейнтцит *m.* (min.) heintzite, kaliborite.

Гейслера сплавы Heusler alloys; **Г. трубка** Geissler tube.

гейстер *m.* (bot.) sapling.

гейтоно— *prefix* geitono— (neighbor); **—гамия** *f.* (bot.) geitonogamy.

Гейтсхед (geog.) Gateshead.

гекбомит *m.* (min.) högbomite.

гекельный *a.* (text.) hackling.

Геккеля закон Haeckel's (biogenetic) law.

геккон *m.* (herp.) gecko (*Gekkon*); **—овые, —ы** *pl.* Gekkonidae; **—чик** *m.* Alsophylax.

гекля *f.* (text.) hackle.

гекса— *prefix* hexa— (six); *six also under* **шести—**; **—борид** *m.* hexaboride.

гексабром— *prefix* hexabrom(o)—; **—(ид)ное число** hexabromide number.

гексагидрит *m.* (min.) hexahydrite.

гексагидро— *prefix* hexahydro—; **—бензойный** *a.* hexahydrobenzoic (acid); **—бензол** *m.* hexa-hydrobenzene, cyclohexane; **—кси—** *prefix* hexahydroxy—; **—толуол** *m.* hexahydrotoluene.

гексагир *m.*, **—а** *f.* (cryst.) hexagyre (sixfold axis of symmetry); **—ноаксиальный** *a.* hexagonal trapezohedral; **—ный** *a.* hexagyric, hexagonal.

гексагон *m.* hexagon; **—альный** *a.* hexagonal, six-sided.

гекса/да *f.* (gen.) hexad; **—декан** *m.* hexadecane, dioctyl; **—децен** *m.* hexadecene, cetene; **—децил** *m.* hexadecyl; **—децилен** *m.* hexadecylene, cetene; **—диен** *m.* hexadiene; **—диин** *m.* hexadiine, bipropargyl; **—замещённый** *a.* hexasubstituted; **—йодоплатекислота** *f.* iodoplatinic (IV) acid; **—йодоплатеат** *m.* iodoplatinate.

гекса/кисоктаэдр *m.* (cryst.) hex(akiso)octahedron; **—козан** *m.* hexacosane; **—козановая кислота** hexacosanoic acid; **—контан** *m.* hexacontane **—л** *m.* hexal; **—лин** *m.* Hexalin, cyclohexanol; **—мер** *m.* hexamer (polymer); **—мерный** *a.* (biol.) hexamerous; **—метафосфат** *m.* hexametaphosphate.

гексаметил *m.*, **—овый** *a.* hexamethyl; **—ен** *m.* hexamethylene, cyclohexane; **—ентетрамин** *m.* hexamethylenetetramine; **—этан** *m.* hexamethylethane.

гекса/мидин *m.* hexamidine, Mysoline; **—мин** *m.* hexamine; **—н** *m.* hexane; **—нал** *m.* hexanal, caproaldehyde; **—нафтен** *m.* hexanaphthene, cyclohexene; **—ндиаль** *m.* hexandial, adipine aldehyde; **—ндиол** *m.* hexanediol, hexamethylene glycol; **—нит** *m.* Hexanite (a hard material); **—нитро—** *prefix* hexanitro—.

гексан/овый *a.* hexane; **—овая кислота** hexanoic acid, caproic acid; **—оил** *m.* hexanoyl; **—ол** hexanol, hexyl alcohol; **—он** *m.* hexanone, ethylpropyl ketone.

гекса/оза *f.* hexasaccharide; **—оксибензол** *m.* hexahydroxybenzene, hexaphenol; **—плоид** *m.*, **—плоидный** *a.* (gen.) hexaploid; **—рхный** *a.* (bot.) hexarch; **—симметричный** *a.* (cryst.) hexasymmetrical; **—сульфид** *m.* hexasulfide; **—фенил** *m.* hexaphenyl.

гексафтор/ид *m.* hexafluoride; **—(о)—** *prefix* hexafluoro—; **—кремнекислота** *f.* fluosilicic acid; **—кремнекислый** *a.* fluosilicate.

гексахлор— *prefix* hexachlor(o)—; **—ан** *m.* hexachloran, hexachlorocyclohexane; **—бензол** *m.* hexachlorobenzene; **—ид** *m.* hexachloride; **—оплатеат** *m.* chloroplatinate; **—оплатекислота** *f.* chloroplatinic acid; **—офен** *m.* hexachlorophene; **—оциклогексан** *m.* hexachlorocyclohexane; **—этан** *m.* hexachloroethane, carbon trichloride.

гексациан *m.* hexacyan; **—о—** *prefix* hexacyano—; **—окобальтиат** *m.* cobalticyanide; **—окобальтоат** *m.* cobaltocyanide; **—оферриат** *m.* ferricyanide; **—оферроат** *m.* ferrocyanide.

гекса/циклический *a.* hexacyclic; **—эдр** *m.* (cryst.) hexahedron, cube; **—эдрит** *m.* (min.) hexahedrite; **—эдрический** *a.* hexahedral, cubic; **—этилдиплюмбан, —этилдисвинец** *m.* hexaethyl diplumbide; hexaethyl dilead.

гексен *m.* hexene, tetrahydrobenzene; **—ал** *m.* hexenal, propylacrolein; Hexenal, hexobarbital; **—овая кислота** hexenoic acid, propylacrylic acid.

гексил *m.* hexyl; **—ен** *m.* hex(yl)ene; **—овый** *a.* hexyl; hexylic (acid).

гекс/ин *m.* hexyne; **—ит** *m.* hexitol; hexite, hexanitrodiphenylamine.

Гексли слой (anat.) Huxley's membrane.

гекс/обиоза *f.* hexobiose; **—оген** *m.* (expl.) hexogen, trimethylene trinitramine; **—оза** *f.* hexose; **—озамин** *m.* hexosamine; **—озан** *m.* hexosan; **—озодифосфат** *m.* hexose diphosphate; **—озомонофосфат** *m.* hexose monophosphate; —**озофосфат** *m.* hexose phosphate; —**озофосфорный** *a.* hexosephosphoric (acid); —**окиназа** *f.* hexokinase; —**октаэдр** *m.* hexoctahedron; —**он** *m.* hexone, methylisobutyl ketone; —**оний** *m.* hex(ameth)onium; —**оновый** *a.* hexone; hexonic (acid); —**отриоза** *f.* hexotriose; —**уроновый** *a.* hexuronic (acid).

гектар *m.* hectare (2.471 acres).

гектический *a.* hectic.

гекто— *prefix* hecto— (100); —**ватт** *m.* (elec.) hectowatt; —**ватт-час** *m.* hectowatt-hour; —**грамм** *m.* hectogram.

гектограф *m.,* —**ировать** *v.* (manifolding) hectograph; —**ирование** *n.* hectographing; —**ический** *a.* hectographic; —**ия** *f.* hectography, hectographic printing.

гекто/литр *m.* hectoliter; —**метр** *m.* hectometer; —**пьеза** *f.* hectopiezoelectric unit; —**рит** *m.* hectorite (a clay).

гелада *f.* (mam.) gelada baboon (*Theropithecus gelada*).

геластокориды *pl.* (ent.) Gelastocoridae.

гел/атин *m.,* —**атина** *f.* gelatin; —**евидный** *a.* gel-like, gelatinous.

гелен/ин *m.* helenin, inula camphor; —**ит** *m.* (min.) helenite; gehlenite; —**итодиалюминатный** *a.* gehlenite-dialuminate.

гелеобраз/ный *a.* gel-like, gelatinous, gelatinoid; —**ование** *n.* gelatin(iz)ation, gel formation; **период** —**ования** gel time; —**ующий** *a.* gel-forming, gelling.

гел/еподобный *a.* gel-like, gelatinous; —**ефицировать** *v.* jellify, make or become gelatinous; —**и** *pl.* of **гель.**

гелиакический *a.* (astr.) heliacal.

гелиант/ин *m.* helianthin(e), methyl orange; —**овый** *a.* helianthic (acid).

гелигнит *m.* (expl.) gelignite.

гелиди/евые *pl.* (bot.) red algae (*Gelidiaceae*); —**ум** *m.* Gelidium.

гел/иевый *a.,* —**ий** *m.* helium, He; —**иеносный** *a.* helium-containing.

гелико— *prefix* helico— (helix, spiral); —**ид** *m.* helicoid; —**идальный** *a.* helicoid, helical, spiral, coiled.

геликоптер *m.* (av.) helicopter.

геликотрема *f.* (anat.) helicotrema.

гелио— *prefix* helio— (sun); —**гравюра** *f.* (typ.) heliogravure, photoengraving; —**граф** *m.* (astr., etc.) heliograph; —**графический** *a.* heliographic; —**графия** *f.* heliography; —**дор** *m.* (min.) heliodor; —**з** *m.* heliosis, sunstroke; —**концентратор** *m.* solar heat collector; —**лампа** *f.* sun lamp; —**метр** *m.* (astr.) heliometer; —**н** *m.* helion, alpha-particle; —**нагреватель** *m.* solar heater; —**оранжерея** *f.* solar-heated greenhouse; —**приёмник** *m.* solar heat collector; —**скоп** *m.* helioscope; —**скопический** *a.* helioscopic; —**станция** *f.* heliostation; —**стат** *m.* heliostat; —**сушилка** *f.* sun drying; sun drying plant; —**сушка** *f.* sun drying; —**сфера** *f.* heliosphere; —**теплица** *see* **гелиооранжерея;** —**терапия** *f.* heliotherapy; —**техника** *f.* solar energy technology or engineering.

гелиотроп *m.* (bot.) heliotrope (*Heliotropium*); (min.) heliotrope; (surv.) heliotrope, heliograph; —**изм** *m.* (bot.) heliotropism; —**ин** *m.* heliotropin, piperonal; heliotropine (alkaloid); —**ист** *m.* (geod.) heliotrope operator; —**ический,** —**ный** *a.* heliotrope; heliotropic (acid).

гелио/установка *f.* solar power plant; —**физика** *f.* heliophysics, solar physics; —**филлит** *m.* (min.) heliophyllite, ecdemite; —**фильный** *a.* heliophilous, sunloving; —**фит** *m.* (bot.) heliophyte; —**фоб** *m.* helio-

phobe; —**фобный** *a.* heliophobic, shade-loving; —**химия** *f.* heliochemistry; cosmochemistry; —**центрический** *a.* (astr.) heliocentric; —**энергетика** *f.* solar power engineering.

гелихризум *m.* (bot.) Helichrysum.

гелициды *pl.* (mal.) Helicidae (snails).

гелицин *m.* helicin, salicylaldehyde glucose.

гелландит *m.* (min.) hellandite.

геллеборин *m.* helleborin.

Геллезена элемент (elec.) Hellesen cell.

Геллера процесс Heller process.

геллефлинта *f.* (petr.) hälleflinta.

Гелля-Фольгарда-Зелинского реакция Hell-Volhard-Zelinski reaction.

гело— *prefix* helo— (marsh; nail); —**бделла** *f.* (zool.) Helobdella (leech); —**дий** *m.* Helodium (moss).

гелоза *f.* gelose, galactan.

гело/фильный *a.* helophilous, marsh-loving; —**фит** *m.* helophyte, marsh plant.

гель *m.* gel.

гельбин *m.* barium yellow.

гельв/етский *a.* (geol.) Helvetian; —**еция зелёный** Helvetian green; —**ин** *m.* (min.) helvite; —**олевый** *a.* helvolic (acid).

гельдерберг/иан *m.,* —**ская формация** (geol.) Helderbergian formation.

гельзем/ий, —**иум** *m.* (bot.) Gelsemium; —**ин** *m.* gelsemine; —**иновый** *a.* gelsemine; gelseminic (acid).

гель-каучук *m.* gel rubber.

гелько— *prefix* (med.) helco— (ulcer); —**логия** *f.* helcology.

гельмгольцевый *a.* Helmholtz(ian).

гельминт *m.* (zool.) helminth (parasitic worm); —**иаз,** —**оз** *m.* (med.) helminthiasis; —**олог** *m.* helminthologist; —**ологический** *a.* helminthologic; —**ология** *f.* helminthology; —**оспориоз** *m.* (phyt.) helminthosporiosis; —**оцид** *m.* helminthocide, vermicide; —**оцидный** *a.* helminthogogue, anthelminthic.

гельмпорт *m.* (naut.) helm port.

гел/ьный *a.* gel; —**ь-полимер** *m.* gel polymer; —**ь-проникающий** *a.* gel-permeation (chromatography); —**ь-раствор** *m.* gel solution.

гельсеминин *m.* gelseminine.

гел/ь-фильтрирование *n.* gel filtration; **г.-фракция** *f.* gel fraction; —**я** *gen. of* **гель.**

гем *m.* heme; *prefix* h(a)em—, blood.

гемагглютин/ация *f.* (med.) hemagglutination; **торможение** —**ации** hemagglutination inhibition, HI; —**ин** *m.* hemagglutinin; —**ирующий** *a.* hemagglutinative.

гемальный *a.* h(a)emal, blood.

гемамель-таннин *m.* hamamelitannin.

гемангио/бласт *m.* (embr.) hemangioblast; —**ма** *f.* (med.) hemangioma.

гем/апофиз *m.* (anat.) hemapophysis; —**артроз** *m.* (med.) hemarthros(is).

гемат/еин *m.* hematein; —**ин** *m.* hematin; —**иновый** *a.* hematin; hematinic (acid).

гематит *m.* (min.) hematite, red iron ore; (met.) a high-quality foundry iron; —**овый** *a.* hematite, hematitic; —**оподобный** *a.* hematitic.

гемато— hemato—, blood; —**ген** *m.* hematogen; —**генез** *m.* hematogenesis; —**генный** *a.* hematogenous; —**глобулин** *m.* hematoglobulin, oxyhemoglobin; —**идин** *m.* hematoidin, bilirubin; —**крит** *m.* hematocrit, HCT; —**ксилин** *m.* hematoxylin; —**лиз** *m.* (physiol.) hematolysis; —**лит** *m.* (min.) hematolite; —**литический** *a.*

(physiol.) hematolytic; (min.) hematolitic; **—лог** *m.* hematologist; **—логия** *f.* hematology; **—ма** *f.* (med.) hematoma; **—миелия** *f.* hematomyelia; **—пиды** *pl.* (ent.) Haematopi(ni)dae; **—порфирин** *m.* hematoporphyrin; **—поэз** *m.* hematopoesis, blood formation; **—рея** *f.* (med.) hematorrhea; **—фаг** *m.* hematophage, blood sucker; **— фанит** *m.* (min.) hematophanite; **—физ** *m.* (anat.) hematophysis; **—хром** *m.* hematochrome; **—хроматоз** *m.* hematochromatosis; **—целе** *n.* hematocele; **—энцефалический** *a.* blood-brain (barrier).

гематур/иновая кислота hematurinic acid; **—ия** *f.* (med.) hematuria.

гемафибрит *m.* (min.) hemafibrite.

гемеллит/ен, —ол *m.* hemellitol, hemimellitene; **—овая кислота** hemellitic acid, 2,3-xylic acid.

гемер/а *f.* (geol.; pal.) hemera; **—алопия** *f.* (med.) hemeralopia; **—о—** *prefix* hemero— (day; cultivated); **—обии, —обы** *pl.* (ent.) Hemerobiidae; **—окаллис** *m.* (bot.) Hemerocallis; **—офильный** *a.* hemerophilous, easily cultivated; **—офит** *m.* hemerophyte, cultivar; **—фобный** *a.* hemerophobous, hard to cultivate.

геми— *prefix* hemi—, semi—; *see also under* **полу—**; **—анопсия** *f.* (med.) hemianopsia; **—атрофия** *f.* hemiatrophy; **—дома** *f.* (cryst.) hemidome, hemipinacoid; **—зигота** *f.* (gen.) hemizygote; **—зиготный** *a.* hemizygous; **—клейсто** *prefix* (bot.) hemicleisto—; **—криптофит** *m.* hemicryptophyte.

гемимеллит/овая кислота hemimellitic acid, 1,2,3-benzenetricarboxylic acid; **—ол** *m.* hemimellitol.

гемиметабол/ический *a.* (zool.) hemimetabolic; **—ия** *f.* hemimetaboly, incomplete metamorphosis.

гемиморф/изм *m.* (cryst.) hemimorphism; **—ит** *m.* (min.) hemimorphite, calamine; **—ия** *f.* hemimorphy; **—ный** *a.* hemimorphic.

гемин *m.* hemin, hematin chloride.

геми/паразит *m.* hemiparasite, partial parasite; **—парез** *m.* (med.) hemiparesis; **—пинакоид** *see* **гемидома; —пиновая кислота** hemip(in)ic acid, 3,4-dimethoxyphthalic acid; **—пирамида** *f.* (cryst.) hemipyramid; **—плегия** *f.* (med.) hemiplegia; **—призма** *f.* (cryst.) hemiprism; **—сфера** *f.* hemisphere; **—сферический** *a.* hemispheric(al).

гемит *m.* (elec.) Hemit (insulation).

гемитроп/ический, —ный *a.* (cryst.) hemitropic, hemitrope, twinned.

геми/хордовые *pl.* (zool.) Hemichordata; **—целлюлоза** *f.* hemicellulose; **—циклический** *a.* hemicyclic.

гемиэдр *m.* (cryst.) hemihedron; **—ический** *a.* hemihedral; **—ия** *f.* hemihedrism, hemihedry.

гем-компонент *m.* heme component.

гемлок *m.* (bot.) hemlock (*Tsuga*).

гемма *f.* gem, jewel; (biol.) gemma, bud; **—тный** *a.* gemmate.

геммула *f.* (biol.) gemmule.

гемо— *prefix* hemo— (blood).

гемоглобин *m.* hemoglobin; **—ный, —овый** *a.* hemoglobin(ous); **—ообразование** *n.* hemoglobin formation; **—опатия** *f.* (med.) hemoglobinopathy; **—офильный** *a.* (bact.) hemoglobinophilic; **—урия** *f.* (med.) hemoglobinuria.

гемо/диализатор *m.* (med.) hemodialyzer; **—динамика** *f.* hemodynamics.

гемолиз *m.* (immun.) hemolysis; **—ин** *m.* hemolysin; **—ировать** *v.* hemolyze; **—ироваться** *v.* undergo hemolysis.

гемо/лимфа *f.* (zool.) hemolymph; **—литический** *a.* (immun.) hemolytic; **—метр** *m.* hemo(globino)meter;

—нхоз *m.* (vet.) haemonchosis, Haemonchus infestation; **—пиррол** *m.* hemopyrrole; **—поэз** *m.* (cyt.) hem(at)opoiesis; **—протеид** *m.,* **—протеидный** *a.* hemoprotein.

геморр/агический *a.* (med.) hemorrhagic; **—агия** *f.* hemorrhage; **—оидальный, —ойный** *a.* hemorrhoid(al); **—оидальная шишка, —ой** *m.* hemorrhoid.

гемо/сидерин *m.* hemosiderin; **—сидероз** *m.* (med.) hemosiderosis; **—содержащий** *a.* heme-containing; **—споридии** *pl.* (prot.) Hemosporidia; **—споридиоз** *m.* (vet.) hemosporidiosis; **—стаз** *m.* (med.) hemostasis; **—статический** *a.,* **—статическое средство** hemostatic; **—терапия** *f.* hemotherapy; **—токсин** *m.* hemotoxin; **—токсический** *a.* hemotoxic; **—трансфузия** *f.* blood transfusion; **—тропный** *a.* hem(at)otropic; **—филик** *m.* (med.) hemophiliac; **—филический, —фильный** *a.* hemophilic; **—филия** *f.* hemophilia; **—хроматоз** *m.* hemochromatosis; **—целе** *n.,* **—цель** *f.* (embr.) hemocele, hemocoelom; **—цианин** *m.* hemocyanin; **—эритрин** *m.* hemoerythrin.

Гемпеля бюретка Hempel (gas) buret.

гемпил *m.* (ichth.) snake mackerel (*Gempylus*); **—евые, —овые** *pl.* Gempylidae.

гемпширский *a.* Hampshire (breed).

гем/-содержащий *a.* heme-containing; **г.-фермент** *m.* heme enzyme.

гемфриевский *a.* Humphrey.

ген *m.* (gen.) gene; *suffix* **—gene; —gen** (producing agent).

ген. *abbr.* **(генеральный)** general; **(генетика)** genetics; **(генетический)** genetic.

генвудит *m.* (min.) henwoodite.

Гендерсона процесс Henderson process.

генеалог *m.* genealogist; **—ический** *a.* genealogical; **—ия** *f.* genealogy.

генез *see* **генезис; —ерин** *m.* geneserine; **—ис** *m.* genesis, origin, source; *suffix* **—genesis, —geny** (production, formation, development).

генейкозан *m.* heneicosane; **—овая кислота** heneicosanic acid.

генекен *m.* (bot.) henequen, Mexican sisal (*Agave fourcroydes*).

генерал/изация *f.* generalization; **—изованный** *a.* generalized, etc., *see v.;* pan—; **—изировать** *v.* generalize; disseminate, disperse; **—ьный** *a.* general, basic; main, principal, leading; master, long-range (plan).

генеративный *a.* generative, reproductive.

генератор *m.* (elec.) generator, dynamo; oscillator; (gas) producer; **г. высокой частоты** radio frequency alternator; **г. звуковой частоты** audio-frequency oscillator; **г. переменного тока** alternator; **г. синхроимпульсов,** задающий **г.** timing generator, (master) clock; **оптический квантовый г.** laser; **г.-двигатель** *m.* motor-generator set; **—ная** *f.* generating plant, generator house; **—ный** *a.* generator, generating; producer (gas); power (house).

генер/атрис *m.,* **—атриса** *f.* (geom.) generatrix, generator; **—ационный** *a.* (biol.) generative, reproductive; **—ация** *f.,* **—ирование** *n.* generation, production, formation; progeny; **—ация в лазере** lasing; **—ация в мазере** masing; **—ированный** *a.* generated, etc., *see v.;* **—ировать** *v.* generate, produce, form; oscillate; **—ируемый взрывом** *a.* explosion-generated; **—ирующий** *a.* generating, etc., *see v.*

генет/ик *m.* geneticist; **—ика** *f.* genetics; **—ико-автоматические процессы** genetic drift; **—ический** *a.* genetic; **—та** *f.* (mam.) genet (*Genetta*).

гензенов(ский) проток (anat.) Hensen's duct.

ген/иальность *f.*, **—ий** *m.* genius; **—иальный** *a.* great, brilliant, genius.

генин *m.* genin.

ген/-интенсификатор *m.* (gen.) intensifier, intensifying gene; **—ипор** *m.* (zool.) pit organ; genipore; **—истеин** *m.* genistein, 4,5,7-trihydroxyisoflavone; **—италии** *pl.* genitals, sexual organs; **—альный** *a.* genital, sexual; **—ито—** *prefix* (anat.) genito—; **—итомочевой** *a.* genitourinary, urogenital.

ген/-компенсатор *m.* compensatory gene; **—контролируемый** *a.* gene-controlled.

Генле петля (anat.) Henle's loop.

ген-модификатор *m.* modifying gene; **г.-мутатор** *m.* mutator gene.

генна *f.* henna (dye).

генный *a.* gene, gen(et)ic; **—suffix —**genic, **—**genous (producing, inducing; produced by, arising in).

гено— *prefix* geno— (race, kind; sex); **—вариация** *f.* genovariation; hereditary change; **—вид** *m.* genospecies.

ген/-ограничитель *m.* restricting gene; **—оинженерия** *f.* genetic engineering; **—ом** *m.* genome; **—омер** *m.* genomere; **г.-оператор** *m.* operator gene; **—осома** *f.* genosome; **—тип** *m.* genotype, genetic complex; **—типический** *a.* genotypic; **—офонд** *m.* genetic material, genetic pool; **г.-переключатель** *m.* oligogene, key gene; **г.-подавитель** *m.* repressor gene; **г.-регулятор** *m.* regulator gene.

генри *m.* (elec.) henry (unit of induction); **закон Г.** Henry's law; **—метр** *m.* henrymeter, inductance meter.

генти/амарин *m.* gentiamarin; **—анин** *m.* gentianin; **—аноза** *f.* gentianose; **—зиновый** *a.* gentisic (acid); **—обиоза** *f.* gentiobiose; **—опикрин** *m.* gentiopicrin.

гентит *m.* (min.) genthite.

гентриаконтан *m.* hentriacontane.

генуинный *a.* genuine, real; natural; congenital (disease or deformity).

ген-усилитель *m.* intensifying gene.

генуэзский *a.* (geog.) Genoa, Genoese.

генци/ана *f.* (bot.) gentian (*Gentiana*); **—анвиолет** *m.* gentian violet; **—анин** *m.* gentianin; **—ановые** *pl.* Gentianaceae; **—обиоза** *f.* gentiobiose.

генэйкозановый *a.* heneicosanic (acid).

геня *f.* genya (treeless wasteland).

гео— *prefix* geo— (earth, land); **—активный** *a.* (astrophys.) geoactive; **—антиклиналь** *f.* (geol.) geanticline; **—биоз** *m.* geobios, terrestrial life; **—бионт** *m.* geobiont; **—биотический** *a.* geobiotic.

геоботан/ика *f.* geobotany, plant ecology; **—ический** *a.* geobotanical.

гео/генезис *m.* geogeny; **—гнозия** *f.* geognosy, structural geology.

географ *m.* geographer; **—ический** *a.* geographic; **—ия** *f.* geography.

геодез/ист *m.* geodesist, surveyor; **г.-вычислитель** *m.* geodetic computer; **г.-землеустроитель**, **г.-полевик** *m.* land surveyor; **—ическая** *f.* geodesic (line); **—ический** *a.* geodetic; (math.) geodesic; **—ическая сетка** graticule, reticule, large-scale surveying.

геод/ии *pl.* (zool.) Geodiidae (sponges); **—иметр** *m.* geodimeter; **—ин** *m.* geodin (antibiotic).

гео/ид *m.* geoid, geoidal surface; **—криология** *f.* cryopedology, permafrost study; **—кронит** *m.* (min.) geocronite.

геолог *m.* geologist; **г.-нефтяник** *m.* petroleum geolo-

gist; **—ический** *a.* geologic(al); **—ия** *f.* geology; **—опоисковый** *a.* exploration.

геологоразвед/ка *f.*, **—очный** *a.* geological exploration; **—ывательный** *a.* casing and drill (pipes).

геомагн/етизм *m.* geomagnetism; **—итный** *a.* geomagnetic; **—итофон** *m.* recording geophone.

геометр *m.* geometrician; land surveyor; **—альный**, **—ический** *a.* geometric; **—изировать** *v.* geometrize; **—ическое место** (math.) locus; **—ически** *adv.* geometrically; **—ия** *f.* geometry; configuration.

геоморф/ный *a.* geomorphic; **—оз** *m.* geomorphosis; **—ологический** *a.* geomorphological; **—ология** *f.* geomorphology.

гео/потенциал *m.* geopotential; **—разведочный** *see* **геологоразведочный.**

георгийский *a.* (geol.) Georgian.

георгин *m.*, **—а** *f.* (bot.) dahlia.

геосинклиналь *f.* (geol.) geosyncline; **—ный** *a.* geosynclinal.

гео/строфический *a.* (meteor.) geostrophic; **—сфера** *f.* (geol.) geosphere; **—таксис** *m.* (biol.) geotaxis; **—тафрогеналь** *f.* geotaphrogen (major rift zone); **—тектоника** *f.* geotectonics, structural geology; **—тектонический** *a.* geotectonic, structural.

геотерм/ика, **—ия** *f.* (geol.) geothermy; **—ический** *a.* geothermal; **—ическая ступень** (reciprocal) geothermal gradient; **—ометр** *m.* geothermometer.

геотехн/ика *f.* geotechnics; **—ический** *a.* geotechnic(al); **—ология** *f.* geotechnology.

гео/трихоз *m.* (med.) geotrichosis; **—тропизм** *m.* (biol.) geotropism; **—тропический**, **—тропный** *a.* geotropic; **—труп** *m.* (ent.) Geotrupes.

геофиз/ик *m.* geophysicist; **г.-разведчик** *m.* exploration geophysicist; **—ика** *f.* geophysics; **промысловая —ика** well logging; **—ический** *a.* geophysical; (high-altitude) sounding (rocket).

геофил *m.* geophilous organism; (zool.) Geophilus (a centipede); **—ьный** *a.* geophilous, earth-loving.

гео/фит(он) *m.* geophyte, terrestrial plant; **—фон** *m.* geophone; **—ффроин** *m.* geoffroyine, surinamine; **—химический** *a.* geochemical; **—химия** *f.* geochemistry.

геохронолог/ический *a.* geochronological; **—ия** *f.* geochronology, geological dating.

геоцентр *m.* (astr.) geocenter; **—ический** *a.* geocentric.

геоцериновая кислота geocerinic acid.

геоэлектричес/кий *a.* geoelectric; **—тво** *n.* geoelectricity.

гепард *m.* (mam.) cheetah (*Acinonyx*).

гепарин *m.* heparin; **—изировать** *v.* (med.) heparinize; **—серный** *a.* heparin sulfuric (acid).

гепат— *see* **гепато—**; **—ико—** *prefix* (anat.) hepatico— (hepatic duct); **—ит** *m.* (med.) hepatitis; (min.) hepatite; **—ический** *a.* (anat.) hepatic; **—о—** *prefix* hepat(o)— (liver); **—олит** *m.* (med.) hepatolith, gallstone; **—олог** *m.* hepatologist; **—ология** *f.* hepatology; **—ома** *f.* hepatoma; **—опатия** *f.* hepatopathy, liver disease; **—отоксичность** *f.* hepatotoxicity.

гепта— *prefix* hepta— (seven); *see also under* **семи—**; **—гон** *m.* (geom.) heptagon; **—гональный** *a.* heptagonal.

гептадекан *m.* heptadecane; **—овый** *a.* heptadecanoic (acid).

гепта/диен *m.* heptadiene; **—козан** *m.* heptacosane; **—льдегид** *m.* heptaldehyde, heptanal; **—метилен** *m.* heptamethylene, suberane.

гептан *m.* heptane; **—ал(ь)** *m.* heptanal; **—овая кислота** heptanoic acid, enanthic acid; **—ол** *m.* heptanol, heptyl alcohol; **—он** *m.* heptanone.

гептахлор *m.* heptachlor (insecticide).

гептаэдр *m.* (cryst.) heptahedron; **—ический** *a.* heptahedral.

гептен *m.* heptene, pentylethylene; **—ил** *m.* heptenyl; **—илен** *m.* heptenylene.

гептил *m.,* **—овый** *a.* heptyl; **—ен** *m.* hept(yl)ene; **—овый спирт** *see* **гептанол.**

гепт/ин *m.* Heptin, heptyne, pentylacetylene; **—ит** *m.* heptitol, a heptahydric alcohol; **—од** *m.* (electron.) heptode, pentagrid; **—оза** *f.* heptose; **—уроновая кислота** hepturonic acid.

Гепфнера процесс Höpfner process.

гераклеум *m.* (bot.) cow parsnip (*Heracleum*).

геран/иал(ь) *m.* geranial, citral; **—иевые** *pl.* (bot.) Geraniaceae; **—иевый** *a.* (bot.) geranium; geranic (acid); **—ий** *m.* geranium; **—ил** *m.,* **—иловый** *a.* geranyl; **—иол** *m.* geraniol; **—иум** *m.,* **—ь** *f.* geranium.

герапатит *m.* herapathite, quinine iodosulfate.

герб *m.* emblem, stamp; (math.) arms, heads.

гербар/изировать *v.* (bot.) herbarize, herbalize; **—ий** *m.* herbarium; **—ный** *a.* herbarial.

гербера *f.* (bot.) Gerbera.

гербертовский *a.* Herbert (process).

герби/сид, —цид *m.* herbicide, weed killer.

гербов/ый *a. of* **герб;** stamped; **г. сбор** stamp duty; **—ая марка** stamp.

герд *m.* (min.) buddle, concentrator.

гердерит *m.* (min.) herderite.

геренгрундит *m.* (min.) herrengrundite.

геренук *m.* (mam.) gerenuk (*Lithocranius walleri*).

Гересгофа печь Herreshoff furnace.

герефордский *a.* Hereford (cattle).

гериатр *m.* (med.) geriatrician; **—ический** *a.* geriatric; **—ия** *f.* geriatrics.

геркогамный *a.* (bot.) hercogamous.

геркон *m.* potted condenser.

геркулес *m.* Hercules; rolled oats; (ent.) Hercules beetle (*Dynastes hercules*); **—овый** *a.* Herculean.

геркулой *m.* Herculoy (alloy).

герм. *abbr.* (**германский**) German.

герман/ат *m.* germanate; **—ид** *m.* germanide; **—иеводород** *m.* germanium hydride, germane; **—иевокислый** *a.* germanic acid; germanate (of); **—иевокислая соль** germanate; **—иевый** *a.* germanium, germanic (acid); **соль —иевой кислоты** germanate.

германиефтороводородн/ая кислота (hydro)fluogermanic acid; **соль —ой кислоты** fluogermanate.

герман/ий *m.* germanium, Ge; **(дву)окись —ия** germanium dioxide, germanic oxide; **закись —ия** germanous oxide, germanium monoxide; **—ийорганический** *a.* organogermanic; **—ит** *m.* (min.) germanite.

Германия Germany.

германо— *see* **германие—.**

германский *a.* German.

гермафродит *m.* (biol.) hermaphrodite; **—изм** *m.,* **—ность** *f.* hermaphroditism; **—ический, —ный** *a.* hermaphroditic.

Гермес *m.* (astr.) Hermes.

герметиз/ация *f.* (hermetic) sealing, etc., *see v.;* (nucl.) containment, canning; encapsulation; potting; (av.) pressurization; **—ированный** *a.* sealed, etc., *see v.;* airtight, pressure-tight; **—ировать** *v.* seal (hermetically; in; off), make airtight; can, encapsulate; (av.) pressurize; **—ирующий** *a.* sealing, etc., *see v.;* **—ирующая паста** sealant.

герметик *m.* sealant, sealing compound.

герметич/ески *adv.* hermetically; **г. закрытый** *a.* hermetically sealed, airtight; **—еский** *a.* hermetic, (her-metically) sealed, (air)tight, leak-proof; (av.) pressurized; pneumatic (sprayer); **без —еской оболочки** naked (light); **—ность** *f.* hermetic nature, (air)tightness; impermeability (of alloy); (leak)proofness; **—ный** *see* **герметический.**

герми/нальный, —нативный *a.* germinal, germinative; **—цид** *m.* germicide.

гермо— *see* **герметический; —ввод** *m.* pressure-seal feedthrough; **—вывод** *m.* sealed lead(-out); **—кабина** *f.* pressurized cabin or cockpit; **—перегородка** *f.* pressure bulkhead; **—переходник** *m.* sealed adapter-connector; **—разъём** *m.* pressure-seal(ed) connector; **—шлем** *m.* pressure helmet.

герм. пат. *abbr.* (**германский патент**).

гернзейский *a.* Guernsey (cattle).

герни/арин *m.* herniarin, 7-methoxycoumarin; **—о— *prefix*** (med.) hernio—, hernia.

геро— *prefix* gero(nto)— (aged).

героин *m.* heroin; **—изм** *m.* heroinism, heroin addiction.

геро/ический, —йский *a.* heroic; **—й** *m.* hero.

герониевая кислота geronic acid, 2-dimethyl-6-keto-heptoic acid.

геронт/(о)— *prefix* geront(o)— (old, aged); **—олог** *m.* gerontologist; **—ологический** *a.* gerontological; **—ология** *f.* gerontology.

герп/ес *m.* (med.) herpes; **г. половых органов** genital herpes; **простой г.** herpes simplex; **—етический** *a.* herpetic; zoster; **—ето— *prefix*** herpeto— (reptile); **—етология** *f.* herpetology; **—обделла** *f.* (zool.) Herpobdella (leech).

герпол/одия, —оида *f.* (phys.) herpolhode.

герсдорфит *m.* (min.) gersdorffite.

Герти генератор Heurty generator.

Гертнера феномен (physiol.) Gärtner's phenomenon.

геру *m.* (met.) Heroult furnace.

герхардтит *m.* (min.) gerhardtite.

герц *m.* hertz, cycle per second (unit of electrical frequency).

герцин/ит *m.* (min.) hercynite, iron spinel; **—ский** *a.* (geol.) Hercynian.

герц/метр *m.* frequency meter; **—овый** *a.* Hertz(ian); **—шпрунговский** *a.* Hertzsprung (gap).

гершел/евский, —евый *a.* Herschel(ian); **—ит** *m.* (min.) herschelite.

геспер/етин *m.* hesperetin; **—етиновый** *a.* hesperetin; hesperetic (acid); **—идин** *m.* hesperidine (alkaloid); hesperidin (glucoside).

Гесса закон Hess' law.

гесс/енка *f.,* **—енская муха** Hessian fly (*Mayetiola destructor*); **—енский** *a.,* **—иан** *m.* Hessian; **—ит** *m.* (min.) hessite.

Гесслера сплав *see* **Гейслера сплавы.**

гессонит *m.* (min.) hessonite.

гестаген *m.* gestagen (hormone).

гетациллин *m.* hetacillin (antibiotic).

гётевский *a.* Goethian.

гетер/акидоз *m.* (vet.) heterakidosis; **—енхеловые** *pl.* (ichth.) Heterenchelyidae.

гетеро— *prefix* hetero— (different, mixed), *see also under* **разно—; —азеотроп** *m.,* **—азеотропная смесь** heteroazeotrope; **—аллель** *m.* (gen.) heteroallele; **—атом** *m.* hetero atom, a heterocyclic atom; **—ауксин** *m.* heteroauxin (root stimulant); **—брахиальный** *a.* heterobrachial; **—валентный** *a.* heterovalent.

гетерогам/ета *f.* (gen.) heterogamete; **—етический, —етный** *a.* heterogametic; **—етность** *f.* heterogamety; **—ия, —ность** *f.* heterogamy; **—ный** *a.* heterogamous.

гетероген/ез(ис) *m.* (gen.) heterogenesis; **—етический** *a.* heterogenetic; **—изация** *f.* heterogenization; **—ит** *m.* (min.) heterogenite; **—ия, —ность** *f.* heterogen(eit)y; **—ный** *a.* heterogen(e)ous.

гетеро/гония *f.* (gen.) heterogony; **—динный** *a.* (rad.) heterodyne; (beat) oscillator; conversion frequency source (in transmitter); **—дера** *f.* (zool.) Heterodera; **—динамический** *a.* heterodynamic; **—динировать** *v.,* **—динный** *a.* heterodyne, beat; **—донтный** *a.* (zool.) heterodont.

гетеро/зигота *f.* (gen.) heterozygote; **—зиготность** *f.* heterozygosity; **—зиготный** *a.* heterozygous; **—зис** *m.* heterosis, hybrid vigor; **—кариоз(ис)** *m.* heterocaryosis; **—клеточный** *a.* (cyt.) heterocellular; **—кольцо** *n.* hetero ring; **—конгровые** *pl.* (ichth.) Heterocongridae; **—ксенный** *a.* heteroxenous (parasite); **—лиз** *m.* heterolysis; **—лит** *m.* (min.) hetaerolite; heterolith; **—литический** *a.* heterolytic; **—логический, —логичный** *a.* (biol.) heterologous; **—мерный** *a.* (biol.) heteromeric.

гетероморф/изм *m.* heteromorphism; **—ит** *m.* (min.) heteromorphite; **—ный** *a.* heteromorphous, heteromorphic; **—оз** *m.* heteromorphosis.

гетеро/номный *a.* (biol.) heteronomous; **—переход** *m.* heterojunction; **—пикноз** *m.* (gen.) heteropyknosis; **—пический** *a.* (geol.) heteropic; **—плоид** *m.,* **—плоидный** *a.* heteroploid.

гетерополи/кислота *f.* heteropoly acid; **—конденсация** *f.* heteropolycondensation; **—соединеине** *n.* heteropoly compound.

гетерополярн/ость *f.* heteropolarity; **—ый** *a.* heteropolar.

гетеро/сома *f.* (gen.) heterosome, sex chromosome; **—спория** *f.* (biol.) heterospory; **—статический** *a.* (elec.) heterostatic; **—стилия** *f.* (gen.) heterostyly; **—сфера** *f.* heterosphere; **—сыворотка** *f.* (immun.) heterologous serum; **—таллизм** *m.,* **—талличность** *f.* (bot.) heterothallism; **—типический** *a.* (gen.) heterotypic; **—товые** *pl.* (ichth.) Heterotidae; **—топия** *f.* (biol.) heterotopy, displacement; **—тропный** *a.* heterotropic; **—трофность** *f.* heterotrophy; **—трофный** *a.* heterotrophic; **—фильный** *a.* (bot.) heterophyllous; **—хлоридные** *pl.* (prot.) Heterochloridina; **—хроматин** *m.* (gen.) heterochromatin; **—хромный, —хроматический** *a.* heterochromatic; **—хромия, —хромность** *f.* heterochromy; **—цепной** *a.* (chem.) heterochain; **—церк(аль)ный** *a.* (zool.) heterocercal; **—цикл** *m.* heterocycle, heterocyclic ring or compound; **—циклический** *a.* heterocyclic.

гетинакс *m.* Getinaks (plastic insulator).

гетит *m.* (min.) goethite.

гетол *m.* hetol, sodium cinnamate.

геттанжский *a.* (geol.) Hettangian.

геттер *m.* (electron.) getter; **—ирование** *n.* gettering.

гетчинсоновский *a.* Hutchinson('s).

Гефнера свеча Hefner unit, Hefner candle (0.9 candle-power).

Геша синтез *m.* Hoesch (ketone) synthesis.

ГЖХ *abbr.* (**газо-жидкостная хроматография**) gas-liquid chromatography, GLC.

гзимс, гзымз *m.* (arch.) stringcourse.

г.и. *abbr.* (**год издания**) year of publication.

ГИ (**генератор импульсов**) pulse generator; (**групповой искатель**) group selector.

гиады *pl.* (astr.) Hyades.

гиад— *see* **гиало—;** **—ин** *m.,* **—иновое вещество** (biochem.) hyaline; **—иновый** *a.* hyaline, glassy, clear; **—ит** *m.* (min.) hyalite; (petr.) hyalith; (med.) hyalitis.

гиало— *prefix* hyal(o)— (clear, glass); **—графия** *f.* hyalography; **—идный** *see* **гиалиновый;** **—кристаллический** *a.* hyalocrystalline; **—мелан** *m.* (petr.) hyalomelane; **—пилитовая структура** (geol.) hyalopilitic texture; **—плазма** *f.* (biol.) hyaloplasm; **—сидерит** *m.* (min.) hyalosiderite; **—текит** *m.* (min.) hyalotekite; **—техника** *f.* glass technology; **—фан** *m.* (min.) hyalophane.

гиалур/гия *f.* hyalurgy, glass manufacture; **—(он)ат** *m.* hyalur(on)ate; **—онидаза** *f.* hyaluronidase; **—оновый** *a.* hyaluronic (acid).

гиатус *m.* hiatus, gap.

гиацинт *m.,* **—овый** *a.* (bot.) hyacinth; (min.) hyacinth, zircon.

гиб *m.* bend(ing); *past m. sing. of* **гибнуть;** **г. с перегибом** backward and forward bending (test).

гиббенит *m.* (min.) hibbenite.

гиббере́лл/а *f.* gibberella (a fungus); **—ин** *m.* gibberellin; **—овая кислота** gibberellic acid, gibberellin X.

гибб/ерихтовые *pl.* gibberfishes (Gibberichthyidae); **—он** *m.* (mam.) gibbon (*Hylobates*); **—оновые** *pl.* Hylobatidae.

Гиббса правило фаз Gibbs' phase rule.

гиббсит *m.* (min.) gibbsite; **—овый** *a.* gibbsitic.

гибель *f.* destruction, annihilation, ruin(ation); catastrophe, disaster; loss; death, mortality; kill; (crop) failure; wreck; fall (of government); swarms (of insects); **г. от голода** starvation; **—ный** *a.* destructive, ruinous, pernicious; disastrous, catastrophic; fatal, suicidal.

гибернация *f.* hibernation.

гибиск(ус) *m.* (bot.) hibiscus.

гибк/а *f.* bending; **—ий** *a.* flexible, supple, pliable, pliant, bendable, ductile; springy, elastic; adaptable, versatile; variable (feedback); (comp.) floppy (disk); **—ость** *f.* flexibility, etc., see *a.;* hospitality (of classification).

гибла *past f. sing. of* **гибнуть.**

гибнуть *v.* perish; disappear.

гиб/ок *sh. m. of* **гибкий;** **—очный** *a.* bending; flexible.

гибралтарский *a.* (geog.) Gibraltar.

гибрид *m.* hybrid, cross(breed); **—изация** *f.* hybridization, crossbreeding; **—изировать** *v.* hybridize; **—ный** *a.* hybrid, crossbred.

гига— *prefix* giga— (10^9).

гигант *m.* giant; **—еновый** *see* **гигантовый;** **—изм** *m.* (med.) gigantism; **—овый** *a.* gigantic (acid); **—о—** *prefix* giganto— (huge); **—озернистый** *a.* extra coarse-grained; **—оклеточный** *a.* giant cell; **—олит** *m.* (min.) gigantolite; **—охвостые** *pl.* (ichth.) Giganturidae; **—охлоя** *f.* (bot.) Gigantochloa; **—ский** *a.* giant, huge, colossal, mammoth; **—уровые** *pl.* (ichth.) deep-sea gianturids (*Giganturidae*).

гигартиновые *pl.* (bot.) Gigartinaceae.

гигиен/а *f.* hygiene, sanitation; (public) health; preservation (of books); regimen; **—ист** *m.* hygienist; **—ический, —ичнии** *a.* hygienic, sanitary; health(ful).

гигрин *m.* hygrine; **—овый** *a.* hygric (acid).

гигро— *prefix* hygro— (wet, moist); **—граф** *m.* (meteor.) hygrograph, recording hygrometer; **—ма** *f.* (med.) hygroma; **—метр** *m.* hygrometer; **—метрический** *a.* hygrometric; **—метрия** *f.* hygrometry; **—метр-самописец** *m.* hygrograph; **—мицин** *m.* hygromycin.

гигроскоп *m.* hygroscope; **—ический, —ичный** *a.* hygroscopic, moisture-absorbing; absorbent (cotton); **—ичность** *f.* hygroscopicity.

гигро/стат *m.* hygrostat, humidity controller; humidistat, constant-humidity cabinet; **—фил** *m.* hygrophilous organism; **—фильный** *a.* hygrophilous; **—фит** *m.* (bot.) hygrophyte; **—электрометр** *m.* hygroelectrometer.

гид *m.* guide.

Гида процесс *see* **Гайда процесс.**

гид-автомат *m.* (rockets) automatic guide.

гидальго *m.* (astr.) Hidalgo.

гидантоин *m.* hydantoin, glycolylurea; **—овая кислота** hydantoic acid.

гидато— *prefix* hydat(o)— (watery); **—генезис** *m.* (geol.) hydatogenesis; **—генный** *a.* hydatogenous, hydatogenic; **—да** *f.* (bot.) hydathode.

гидденит *m.* (min.) hiddenite.

гидир/ование *n.,* **—овка** *f.,* **—ующий** *a.* guiding; **—овочный** *a.* guide, guiding.

гиднокарпов/ая кислота hydnocarpic acid; **—ое масло** hydnocarpus oil.

гидр— *see* **гидро—**; **—a** *f.* (zool.) hydra; (astr.) Hydra.

гидравлик *m.* hydraulic engineer; **—a** *f.* hydraulics; hydraulic system or drive.

гидравлическ/ий *a.* hydraulic; **г. раствор** hydraulic mortar; **г. таран, г. поршень** hydraulic ram; **—ая разработка** hydraulic mining, hydraulicking; **—ая сила** water power.

гидравличность *f.* hydraulicity.

гидраденит *m.* (med.) hydradenitis.

гидрази— *prefix* hydrazi—; **—д** *m.* hydrazide; **—дин** *m.* hydrazidine; **—л** *m.* hydrazyl; **—метилен** *m.* hydrazimethylene.

гидразин *m.,* **—иевый, —ный, —овый** *a.* hydrazine; diamine; **—ий** *m.* hydrazinium; **—окислота** *f.* hydrazino acid; **—опроизводное** *n.* hydrazino derivative; **—уксусный** *a.* hydrazi(no)acetic (acid).

гидразо— *prefix* hydrazo—; **—бензол** *m.* hydrazobenzene, 1,1-diphenylhydrazine; **—кислота** *f.* hydrazo acid; **—н** *m.* hydrazone; **—ний** *see* **гидрази-ний;** **—нопроизводное** *n.* hydrazono derivative; **—производное** *n.* hydrazo derivative; **—соединение** *n.* hydrazo compound.

гидр/акриловый *a.* hydracrylic (acid); **—акустика** *see* **гидроакустика;** **—амнион** *m.* (med.) hydramnion; **—ангея, —ангия** *f.* (bot.) hydrangea; **—анговые** *pl.* Hydrangeaceae; **—ант** *m.* (fire) hydrant; (zool.) hydranth; **—аргиллит** *m.* (min.) hydrargillite, gibbsite; **—аргирол** *m.* hydrargyrol, *p*-phenyl mercury thionate.

гидраст/ин *m.* hydrastine (alkaloid); hydrastin; **—ис** *m.* (bot.) Hydrastis.

гидрат *m.* hydrate; **г. закиси** (lower or -ous) hydroxide; **г. закиси железа** ferrous hydroxide; **г. окиси** (higher or -ic) hydroxide; **г. окиси аммония** ammonium hydroxide; **г. окиси железа** ferric hydroxide; **—аза** *f.* hydratase; **—ационный** *a.,* **—ация** *f.,* **—ирование** *n.* hydration; **—(из)ировать** *v.* hydrate; wet; **—ный** *a.* hydrate; hydrated; **—ная вода** water of hydration; **—огенный** *a.* aqueous, water; **—ор** *m.* hydrator.

гидратропов/ый альдегид hydratropaldehyde; **—ая кислота** hydratropic acid, alpha-phenylpropionic acid.

гидр/ацеллюлоза *f.* hydrated cellulose; **—афайнер** *m.* hydrafiner; **—ацетин** *m.* Hydracetin, acetylphenylhydrazine; **—ация** *see* **гидратация;** **—ид** *m.,* **—идный** *a.* hydride; **—идсилан** *m.* silane; **—ин** *m.* hydrin.

гидринд/ан *m.* hydrindane; **—ен** *m.* hydrindene, indan; **—ил** *m.* hydrindyl; **—иновая кислота** hydrindic acid, *o*-aminomandelic acid; **—он** *m.* hydrindone, indone.

гидриров/ание *n.* hydrogenation; **—анность** *f.* degree of hydrogenation; **—анный** *a.* hydrogenated; **—ать** *v.* hydrogenate, hydrogenize.

гидрир/уемый, —ующийся *a.* hydrogenable; **—ующий** *a.* hydrogenating.

гидро— *prefix* hydr(o)—, water, hydraulic; hydroelectric; hydrogen(ated); **—авиация** *f.* sea aviation;

sea planes; **—агрегат** *m.* hydraulic (turbogenerator) unit, hydroelectric generating unit.

гидроаккумул/ирование *n.,* **—ирующий** *a.* water storage; **—ятор** *m.* storage tank; hydraulic accumulator; **—яционный** *a.,* **—яция** *f.* water storage.

гидро/акустик *m.* sonar operator; **—акустика** *f.* underwater acoustics; **—акустический** *a.* hydroacoustic; **—аналогия** *f.* hydraulic analogy; **—аппарат** *m.* hydrojet, jet pump; **—ароматический** *a.* hydroaromatic; **—аэродром** *m.* sea(plane) aerodrome; **—аэромеханика** *f.* fluid mechanics.

гидро/бак *m.* hydraulic reservoir; **—биология** *f.* hydrobiology; **—бионт** *m.* hydrobiont, aquatic organism; **—бионты** *pl.* aquatic life; **—биос** *m.* hydrobios; **—борацит** *m.* (min.) hydroboracite; **—бромид** *m.* hydrobromide; **—бур** *m.* hydrodrill, water-jet borer; **—взрывание** *n.* (min.) hydraulic blasting; **—вскрыша** *f.* hydraulic stripping; **—вые** *pl.* (zool.) Hydrida; **—галоидировать** *v.* add hydrogen halide; **—гель** *m.* hydrogel; **—гематит** *m.* (min.) hydrohematite, turgite; **—ген** *see* **водород;** **—геназа** *f.,* **—геназный** *a.* hydrogenase; **—генератор** *m.* hydraulic (turbine) generator.

гидроген/изат *m.* hydrogenation product; **—изатор** *m.* hydrogenator, (fat) hardening vessel; **—изационный** *a.,* **—изация** *f.* hydrogenation; **—изованный** *a.* hydrogenated; **—из(ир)овать** *v.* hydrogenate; **—ный** *a.* hydrogen(ous); **—олиз** *m.* hydrogenolysis.

гидро/геология *f.* hydrogeology; **—геохимия** *f.* hydrogeochemistry; **—гётит** *m.* (min.) hydrogoethite, lepidocrocite; **—гранат** *m.* hydrogarnet; **—граф** *m.* hydrograph; hydrographer; **—графический** *a.* hydrographic; drainage (network); surveying (vessel); **—графия** *f.* (navigation) hydrography; **—двигатель** *m.* hydraulic engine or prime mover; **—деалкилирование** *n.* hydrodealkylation; **—дикцион** *m.* (bot.) Hydrodyctyon; **—димеризация** *f.* hydrodimerization.

гидродинам/ика *f.* hydrodynamics; **—ический** *a.* hydrodynamic; fluid flow; hydromatic (brake); **—ометр** *m.* hydrodynamometer.

гидро/добыча *f.* hydraulic mining; **—домкрат** *m.* hydraulic jack; **—дроссель** *m.* throttle valve; **—жидкость** *f.* hydraulic fluid; **—закись** *f.* (lower) oxide; **—закладка** *f.* (min.) hydraulic stowing; **—замок** *m.* pilot-controlled check valve; **—затвор** *m.* hydraulic seal; **—зои** *pl.* (zool.) Hydrozoa; **—золоудаление** *n.* hydraulic ash disposal; **—золь** *m.* hydrosol; **—ид** *m.,* **—идный** *a.* (zool.) hydroid; **—идные** *pl.* Hydrozoa; **—изогипса** *f.* (geol.) water-table contour.

гидроизол *m.* waterproofing material; **—яционный** *a.,* **—яция** *f.* waterproofing; hydraulic seal.

гидро/инженерный *a.* hydraulic engineering; **—инкубатор** *m.* hot-water incubator; **—иодид** *m.* hydroiodide; **—ионизатор** *m.* hydroionizer; **—какодил** *m.* cacodyl hydride; **—канал** *m.* flow channel, water channel; **—карбонат** *m.* hydrocarbonate, bicarbonate; **—каучук** *m.* hydrorubber, hydrogenated rubber; **—кинетика** *f.* hydrokinetics; **—кинетический** *a.* hydrokinetic; **—кись** *see* **гидроокись;** **—клапан** *m.* hydraulic valve; **—классификатор** *m.* hydraulic classifier; **—классификация** *f.* hydroclassification, hydraulic classification; **—кластический** *a.* (geol.) hydroclastic; **—копировальный** *a.* hydraulic copying (lathe).

гидро/коричный *a.* hydrocinnamic (acid); **—кортизон** *m.* hydrocortisone (hormone); **—котарнин** *m.* hydrocotarnine; **—коффеиновый** *a.* hydrocaffeic (acid); **—крекинг** *m.* hydrocracking; **—крыло** *n.* hydrofoil;

—крюк *m.* hydraulic hitch; **—кс** *m.* hydrox (coal blasting); **—ксамовый** *a.* hydroxamic (acid).

гидрокси— *prefix* hydroxy—; **—ацил** *m.* hydroxyacyl; **—бензол** *m.* hydroxybenzene; **—д** *m.* hydroxide; **—кислота** *f.* hydroxy acid; **—л** *m.* hydroxyl; **—лаза** *f.* hydroxylase; **—ламин** *m.* hydroxylamine; **—лирование** *n.* hydroxylation; **—лировать** *v.* hydroxylate; **—лсодержащий** *a.* hydroxyl-containing; **—льный** *a.* hydroxyl; **—масляный** *a.* hydroxybutyric (acid); **—метил** *m.* hydroxymethyl; **—мовый** *a.* hydroximic (acid); **—производное** *n.* hydroxy(l) derivative; **—соединение** *n.* hydroxy compound; **—цитронеллаль** *m.* hydroxycitronellal.

гидроксоний *m.* hydro(xo)nium.

гидро/л *m.* hydrol, water molecule; hydrol syrup; **—лабильность** *f.* (med.) hydrolability; **—лаг** *m.* (ichth.) Hydrolagus; **—лаза** *f.* hydrolase.

гидролакколит *m.* (geol.) hydrolaccolite.

гидролес *m.* piling.

гидролиаза *f.* hydro-lyase (enzyme).

гидролиз *m.* hydrolysis; **продукт —а, —ат** *m.* hydrolyzate; **—атор** *m.* converter; **—ация** *f.* hydrolyzation; hydrolysis; **—ер** *m.* hydrolyzer; **—(ир)овать** *v.* hydrolyze; **—ный** *a.* hydrolytic; **—уемый** *a.* hydrolyzable; hydrolyzed; **—ующий** *a.* hydrolyzing.

гидролимфа *f.* (zool.) hydrolymph.

гидролит *m.* hydrolyte; hydrolith (calcium hydride); **—ический** *a.* hydrolytic; **—ическое расщепление** hydrolytic dissociation, hydrolysis.

гидролифт *m.* water-jet pump.

гидролог *m.* (geol.) hydrologist; **—ический** *a.* hydrologic; water-supply; water (year); stream-gaging (network); **—ия** *f.* hydrology.

гидролок/атор *m.,* **—ационная станция** sonar, ultrasonic direction finder; **—ация** *f.* sonar (detection).

гидро/лоток *m.* flow channel, flume; **—лыжи** *pl.* (seaplane) skis; **—магнезит** *m.* (min.) hydromagnesite; **—масса** *f.* (peat) pulp, paste; **—машина** *f.* hydraulic machine or unit; **—медузы** *pl.* (zool.) Hydromedusae; **—мелиоративный** *a.,* **—мелиорация** *f.* water reclamation; **—металлургический** *a.* hydrometallurgic (al).

гидрометео/р *m.* (meteor.) hydrometeor; **—рологический** *a.* hydrometeorological; **—рология** *f.* hydrometeorology; **—служба** *f.* hydrometeorological service.

гидрометла *f.* (mach.) hydraulic broom.

гидрометр *m.* hydrometer, current meter; **—ический** *a.* hydrometric, gaging, stream-flow-measuring; **—ический шест** pole float; **—ическая вертушка** current meter; **—ия** *f.* hydrometry.

гидромехан/изатор *m.* hydraulic mining specialist; **—изация** *f.* hydromechanization; hydraulic mining or excavation; **—изм** *m.* hydraulic mechanism or actuator; **—ика** *f.* hydromechanics, fluid mechanics; **—ический** *a.* hydromechanical.

гидро/модуль *m.* hydromodulus, water consumption per unit of time and area; (paper) liquor ratio; **—монитор** *m.* (min.) monitor, (hydraulic) giant, excavator; **—мониторный** *a.* monitor; jet (drilling); **—морфный** *a.* (soils) hydromorphic; **—мотор** *m.* hydraulic motor; **—муфта** *f.* (mach.) hydraulic clutch or coupling; **—н** *m.* hydrone (alloy; active water molecule); **—насос** *m.* hydraulic pump; **—настуран** *m.* (min.) hydrous pitchblende; **—нефроз** *m.* (med.) hydronephrosis; **—ний** *see* **гидроксоний; —новый** *a. of* **гидрон; —обессеривание** *n.* hydrodesulfurization; **—обогащение** *n.* hydroconcentration, hydraulic ore dressing; **—окись** *f.*

hydroxide; —отвал *m.* hydraulic mine dump; **—оттаивание** *n.* hydrothawing (of frozen foundation by hydraulic method); **—очиститель** *m.* fluid cleaner; **—очистка** *f.* (petrol.) hydrorefining, hydrotreating, hydrofinishing, hydrodesulfurization.

гидро/передача *f.* (mach.) hydraulic transmission; **—перекись** *f.* hydroperoxide; **—пический** *a.* (med.) hydropic, dropsy; **—план** *m.* sea plane; **—паст** *m.* polyvinyl chloride paste; **—пневматический** *a.* hydropneumatic; **—погрузчик** *m.* hydraulic loader; **—подъём** *m.* hydraulic hoist(ing); **—подъёмник** *m.* hydraulic lift; **—полимеризация** *f.* hydropolymerization; **—помпа** *f.* hydraulic pump; **—поник** *m.* (hort.) hydroponic tank; **—поника** *f.,* **—понное выращивание** hydroponics, soilless culture; **—почты, контейнер** (nucl.) hydraulic rabbit; **—пресс** *m.* hydraulic press; **—прессование** *n.* hydraulic casting; **—привод** *m.* hydraulic drive; **с —приводом** hydraulic (tool); **—провод** *m.* hydraulic line.

гидро/пульпа *f.* (paper) pulp, slurry; **—пульпер** *m.* (hydra)pulper; **—пульт** *m.* hydraulic sprayer; spray gun; **—пята** *f.* hydraulic balancing device; **—разбиватель** *m.* (paper) (hydra)pulper, hydraulic beater; **—разгрузка** *f.* (mach.) hydraulic load relief; **—размол** *m.* (paper) beating; refining; **—разработка** *f.* hydraulic mining; **—разрыв** *m.* hydraulic fracturing; **—распределитель** *m.* hydraulic control valve; **—реактивный** *a.* hydrojet (engine); **—регулятор** *m.* hydraulic control; **—ресурсы** *pl.* water resources; **—самолёт** *m.* sea plane; **—сбив окалины** hydraulic descaling; **—сепаратор** *m.* (min.) hydroclassifier, wet collector, scrubber; coal jig; **—сепарация** *f.* wet classification.

гидросернист/ый *a.* hydrosulfurous, hydrosulfite (of); **г. натрий, —онатриевая соль** sodium hydrosulfite; sodium hyposulfite; **—ая кислота** hydrosulfurous acid, hyposulfurous acid; **соль —ой кислоты** hydrosulfite.

гидро/сеть *f.* drainage system; **—силикат** *m.* hydrosilicate; **—силовой** *a.* water power; **—силовая установка** (elec.) hydroelectric power plant; **—система** *f.* hydraulic system; piping; **—скоп** *m.* hydroscope (moisture detector); **—слюда** *f.* (min.) hydromica; **—смесь** *f.* hydraulic fluid; **—соединение** *n.* hydrocompound; **—соль** *f.* acid salt; **—сооружение** *n.* hydraulic structure; **—спуск** *m.* sea plane ramp or slipway; **—стабилизация** *f.* stabilization of liquid fuel by hydrogenation; **—станция** *f.* hydroelectric (power) plant.

гидростат *m.* hydrostat; water gage; **—ика** *f.* (phys.) hydrostatics; **—ический** *a.* hydrostatic.

гидро/стойка *f.* hydraulic prop; **—строительный** *a.* hydraulic engineering.

гидросульф/ат *m.* hydrosulfate; **—ид** *m.* hydrosulfide; **—ит** *m.* hydrosulfite.

гидро/суппорт *m.* hydraulically operated support or tool post; **—сфера** *f.* hydrosphere, earth's surface water; **—тавотница** *f.* hydraulic grease gun; **—таксис** *m.* (biol.) hydrotaxis; **—тележка** *f.* mobile hydraulic servicing unit; **—терапия** *f.* (med.) hydrotherapy (water treatment).

гидротерм *m.* (meteor.) hydrotherm; **—а** *f.* thermal spring; **—альный, —ический** *a.* hydrothermal.

гидротехн/ик *m.* hydraulic engineer; **—ика** *f.,* **—ический** *a.* hydraulic engineering; **—ическое сооружение** hydraulic structure; waterworks; water development project; **—ическое строительство** hydraulic engineering.

гидро/тионовая кислота hydrosulfuric acid, hydrogen sulfide; **—типия** *f.* (phot.) hydrotype; hydrotypy; **—торакс** *m.* (vet.) hydrothorax; **—торит** *m.* (min.) hydrothorite; —**тормоз** *m.* hydraulic brake; —**торф** *m.* hydropeat; —**транспорт** *m.* hydraulic conveying; —**транспортер** *m.* hydraulic conveyer; —**трансформатор** *m.* (mach.) torque converter; —**тропизм** *m.* (biol.) hydrotropism; —**турбина** *f.* hydraulic turbine; water wheel; —**турбогенератор** *m.* hydroelectric generator.

гидро/ударник *m.* hydraulic hammer; —**узел** *m.* hydraulic power system; water engineering system; —**управление** *n.* hydraulic control; —**упругий** *a.* hydroelastic; —**усилитель** *m.* hydraulic actuator or booster; power unit; —**установка** *f.* hydro(electric) power plant; —**файнер** *m.* hydromill; —**фан** *m.* (min.) hydrophane; —**физика** *f.* hydrophysics.

гидрофил; —**изация** *f.* (typ.) desensitization; —**из(ир)овать** *v.* make hydrophilic; —**ия,** —**ьность** *f.* hydrophily, hydrophilic nature; water-absorbing capacity, water receptivity; —**ьный** *a.* hydrophilous, hydrophilic, water-receptive.

гидро/фильтр *m.* hydrofilter; —**фит** *m.* (bot.) hydrophyte; —**фицировать** *v.* convert to hydraulic operation.

гидрофоб *m.* hydrophobe; —**изатор** *m.* water repellent; —**изация** *f.* hydrophobization, treatment for water repellency; —**из(ир)ование** *n.* hydrophobic interaction; —**из(ир)овать** *v.* hydrophobize; waterproof; —**изирующий** *a.* water-repellent; —**ия** *f.* (med.) hydrophobia, rabies; —**ность** *f.* hydrophoby, water repellency; —**ный** *a.* hydrophobic, water-repellent; (typ.) ink-receptive; (med.) rabid.

гидро/фон *m.* hydrophone, submarine detector; —**фор** *m.* hydrophore; —**формилировать** *v.* hydroformylate; —**форминг** *m.* (petrol.) hydroforming; —**форный** *a.* hydrophoric, water-carrying; —**фосфат** *m.* hydrophosphate; —**фталевый** *a.* hydrophthalic (acid); —**фталм** *m.* (med.) hydrophthalmos; —**фторид** *m.* hydrofluoride; —**химия** *f.* chemical hydrology, hydrogeochemistry; —**хинон** *m.* hydroquinone; —**хлорид** *m.* hydrochloride; —**хлорировать** *v.* hydrochlorinate; —**хорный** *a.* (bot.) hydrochoric, dispersed by water.

гидро/целе *n.,* —**цель** *f.* (med.) hydrocele; —**целлюлоза** *f.* hydrocellulose; —**централь** *m.* hydroelectric power plant; —**церуссит** *m.* (min.) hydrocerussite; —**цефалия** *f.* (med.) hydrocephaly, hydrocephalus; —**циклон** *m.* (flotation) hydrocyclone, hydraulic cyclone separator; —**цилиндр** *m.* hydraulic cylinder; —**цинкит** *m.* (min.) hydrozincite; —**шахта** *f.* hydraulically mined shaft; —**штурмовик** *m.* (av.) naval attacker; —**экстрактор** *m.* hydroextractor, whizzer (centrifuge); —**экструзия** *a.* hydrostatic extrusion, fluid-pressure extrusion; —**элеватор** *m.* hydraulic elevator; jet pump; —**электрический** *a.* hydroelectric; —**электростанция** *f.* hydroelectric power plant.

гидроэнерг/етика *f.,* —**етический** *a.* hydraulic power engineering; —**ия** *f.* hydraulic power, water power; —**остроительство** *n.* hydraulic power construction work.

гидроярокмер *m.* underwater luminance meter.

гидрюр *m.* perhydro compound; hydride; hydrogenation product.

гиен/а *f.* (mam.) hyena; —**овые** *pl.* Hyaenidae; —**овый** *a.* hyena; hyenic (acid).

гиератит *m.* (min.) hieratite.

гиетный *a.* hyetal, rain.

гиет(о)— *prefix* hyet(o)— (rain).

гижигинский *a.* (geog.) Gizhiga.

гиз *m.* State publishing house.

гизекит *m.* (min.) giesekite.

гизингерит *m.* (min.) hisingerite.

гизоция *f.* (bot.) Guizotia.

Гийо Giuyot (name).

гийот *m.* (geol.) guyot, tablemount.

гик *m.* coal-tar residue; (naut.) mainboom; —**и** *pl.* winding tackle.

гикомакс *m.* Hycomax (alloy).

гикори *m.* hickory (wood); (bot.) Carya.

гила монстр (herp.) Gila monster (*Heloderma suspectum*); —**ра** *f.* (ent.) Hilara.

гил/ейный *a.,* —**ея** *f.* hylea, tropical (rain) forest.

гиллебрандит *m.* (min.) hillebrandite.

Гиллери линейка (met.) Guillery ruler.

Гиллеспая-Лерберга уравнение Gillespie-Lerberghe equation.

Гилля способ (met.) Gill's method.

гилокомий *m.* (bot.) Hylocomium (moss).

гилпинит *see* **гильпинит.**

гилум *m.* (anat.; bot.) hilum.

гильберт *m.* (elec.) gilbert (unit of magnetomotive force); —**ит** *m.* (min.) gilbertite; —**овый** *a.* Gilbert; (math.) Hilbert.

гильз/а *f.,* —**овый** *a.* bush(ing), socket, sleeve (pipe); liner, lining; case, hull; cartridge case, shell case; tube; (paper) core; (temperature) bulb; (ichth.) Hilsa; —**овать** *v.* line down (cylinder); —**овщик** *m.* core maker; —**оотвод** *m.* case ejection chute; —**оулавливатель** *m.* shell bag.

Гильо способ Guillot method.

гильотин/а *f.,* —**ировать** *v.,* —**ный** *a.,* —**ные ножницы** guillotine.

гильош *m.,* —**ировать** *v.* guilloche.

гиль/пинит *m.* (min.) gilpinite; —**сонит** *m.* gilsonite.

гилюс *m.* (anat.) hilus.

гиляби *pl.* (petr.) bentonite.

гималайский *a.* (geog.) Himalayan.

гимантолофовые *pl.* football fishes (*Himantolophidae*).

гимен *m.* (anat.) hymen; —**альный** *a.* hymenal; —**ий** *m.* (bot.) hymenium, sporiferous layer; —**о**— *prefix* hymen(o)— (membrane); —**олепидоз** *m.* (med.) hymenolepiasis, Hymenolepis infection; —**омицеты** *pl.* (bot.) hymenomycetes; —**оносец** *see* **гименофор;** —**оптеры** *pl.* (ent.) Hymenoptera; —**офор** *m.* (bot.) hymenophore.

гиминовая кислота hyminic acid.

гимназ/ист *m.* student; —**ия** *f.* gymnasium, a preparatory school.

гимнарховые *pl.* Nile fish (*Gymnarchidae*).

гимнаст *m.* gymnast; —**ика** *f.* gymnastics; —**ический** *a.* gymnastic.

гимнел/(ис) *m.* fish doctor (*Gymnelis*); —**исы,** —**овые** *pl.* Gymnelinae; —**опс** *m.* (ichth.) Gymnelopsis.

гимнемовая кислота gymnemic acid.

гимнит *m.* (min.) gymnite, deweylite.

гимно— *prefix* gymno— (bare, uncovered); —**гобиус** *m.* (ichth.) Gymnogobius; —**карпный** *a.* (bot.) gymnocarpous, naked-fruited; —**кладус** *m.* (bot.) Gymnocladus; —**плевр** *m.* (ent.) Gymnopleurus; —**стомный** *a.* gymnostomatous; —**товые** *pl.* knifefishes (*Gymnotidae*).

гимнуровые *pl.* (mam.) Echinosoricidae; (ichth.) butterfly rays (*Gymnuridae*).

гимолальный *a.* hymolal (salts).

гимольский *a.* (geog.) Gimolskoe (lake).

ГИН *abbr.* (**генератор импульсов напряжения**) pulse voltage generator.

гин— *see* **гино**—; —**андрический** *a.* (bot.) gynandrous; —**андро**— *prefix* gynandro— (female and male); —**андроморфизм** *m.* (gen.) gynandromorphism.

гингероль *m.* gingerol.

гингив/ит *m.* (med.) gingivitis; **—о—** *prefix* gingivo— (gums).

Гиндукуш (geog.) Hindu Kush (Afghanistan).

гинезин *m.* gynesine, trigonelline.

гиней *m.* winding tackle.

гинеко— *prefix* gyneco— (female); **—лог** *m.* (med.) gynecologist; **—логический** *a.* gynecological; **—логия** *f.* gynecology.

гинецей *m.* (bot.) gynecium.

гини *pl.* of **гинь**.

гинкго *m.* (bot.) ginkgo; **—овые** *pl.* Ginkgoaceae; **—овый** *a.* ginkgo; ginkgoic (acid).

гино— *prefix* gyn(o)— (female); **—вал** *m.* gynoval, isobornyl isovalerate; **—гамета** *f.* gynogamete, egg cell; **—генез** *m.* (embr.) gynogenesis; **—кардиевый** *a.* gynocardia, chaulmoogra (oil); **—стегий** *m.* (bot.) gynostegium; **—стемий** *m.* gynostemium, column; **—фор** *m.* (biol.) gynophore.

гинсдалит *m.* (min.) hinsdalite.

гинтцеит *m.* (min.) hintzeite, kaliborite.

гинь *f.* (naut.) winding tackle; **г.-блок** gin block, whip gin, monkey wheel.

гиньетова зелень Guignet's green.

гио— *prefix* hy(o)— [(anat.) hyoid bone or arch; pig, hog]; **—одон(т)овые** *pl.* (ichth.) mooneyes (*Hiodontidae*); **—ид** *m.* (anat.) hyoid (bone); **—идный** *a.* hyoid(ean).

г-ион *abbr.* (**грамм-ион**) gram-ion.

гиоргиозит *m.* (min.) giorgiosite.

гиортдалит *m.* (min.) hiortdahlite.

гио/стилический *a.* (ichth.) hyostylic; **—сциамин** *m.* hyosciamine, daturine; **—сцин** *m.*, **—сциновый** *a.* hyoscine, scopolamine; **—холовый** *a.* hyocholic (acid).

гип— *see* **гипо—**; **—абиссальный** *a.* (petr.) hypabyssal; **—антий** *m.* (bot.) hypanthium; **—антодий** *m.* hypanthodium; **—архный** *a.* (gen.) hyparchic; **—афорин** *m.* hyphaphorine, trimethyltriptophan; **—ацидный** *a.* subacid.

гипер— *prefix* hyper—, super—, over; Hiper— (in trade names); **—активный** *a.* hyperactive; **—ареальный** *a.* hyperareal; **—ацидный** *a.* hyperacid.

гипербол/а *f.* (geom.) hyperbola; **—ический** *a.* hyperbolic; natural (logarithm); **—оид** *m.* hyperboloid.

гипер/борейский *a.* hyperborean, northern; **—вентиляция** *f.* hyperventilation; **—вещественный** *a.* hyperreal; **—генный** *a.* (geol.) supergene; **—геометрический** *a.* hypergeometric; **—гликемический** *a.* (med.) hyperglycemic; **—гликемия** *f.* hyperglycemia; **—головой** *a.* hypergolic, spontaneously inflammable; **—дин** *m.* hyperdyne; **—емия** *f.* (med.) hyperemia; **—заряд** *m.* supercharge; **—звук** *m.* (acous.) hypersound; **—звуковой** *a.* hypersonic, hyperacoustic; **—из** *m.* isopropylbenzene hydroperoxide, cumene hydroperoxide; **—ион** *m.* (astr.) Hyperion; **—ицин** *m.* hypericin; **—кальциемия** *f.* (med.) hypercalcemia; **—квадрика** *f.* (math.) hyperquadric; **—кинез** *m.* (med.) hyperkinesia; **—ко** *n.* Hiperco (alloy).

гиперком/мутация *f.* (elec.) overcommutation; **—паунд** *m.* (elec.) overcompounded generator; **—паундирование** *n.* overcompounding; **—паундированный** *a.* overcompounded; **—плекс** *m.*, **—плексный** *a.* (math.) hypercomplex.

гипер/конечный *a.* hyperfinite; **—конус** *m.* hypercone; **—коньюгация** *f.* hyperconjugation; **—куб** *m.* hypercube; **—линия** *f.* hyperline, hypercurve; **—морф** *m.* (gen.) hypermorph; **—ник** *m.* Hipernik (alloy); **—оглиф** *m.* (ichth.) Hyperoglyphe; **—ол** *m.* hyperol;

—он *m.* (nucl.) hyperon; **—осколок** *m.* hyperfragment; **—остоз** *m.* (med.) hyperostosis.

гипер/паразит *m.* hyperparasite; **—переменный** *a.* hypervariable; **—плазия** *f.* (biol.; med.) hyperplasia, abnormal growth; **—плоид** *m.* (gen.) hyperploid; **—плоскость** *f.* (math.) hyperplane; **—поверхностный** *a.*, **—поверхность** *f.* hypersurface, form; **—продукция** *f.* surplus production; **—простой** *a.* hypersimple; **—секреция** *f.* (physiol.) hypersecretion; **—сенсибилизация** *f.* (phot.) hypersensitization; **—сил** *m.* Hipersil (alloy); **—синхронный** *a.* hypersynchronous; **—сопряжение** *n.* hyperconjunction, hyperconjugation; **—сорбер** *m.* hypersorption column; **—сорбция** *f.* hypersorption; **—статический** *a.* hyperstatic.

гиперстен *m.* (min.) hypersthene; **—овый** *a.* hypersthene, hypersthenic.

гипер/сфера *f.* hypersphere; **—тензия** *f.* (med.) hypertension; **—тепловой** *a.* hyperthermal; **—термия** *f.* (med.) hyperthermia; **—тирео(ид)оз** *m.* hyperthyroidism.

гипертон/ик *m.* hypertensive (patient); **—ический** *a.* hypertonic; (med.) hypertensive; **—ическая болезнь** hypertension; **—ия** *f.* hypertonia; hypertension.

гипертрихоз *m.* (med.) hypertrichosis.

гипертроф/ированный *a.* (biol.; med.) hypertrophied, excessively developed; **—ироваться** *v.*, **—ия** *f.* hypertrophy; **—ический** *a.* hypertrophic.

гипер/флоу *m.* (petrol.) hyperflow; **—фрагмент** *m.* (nucl.) hyperfragment; **—функция** *f.* hyperfunction; **—хлорирование** *n.* superchlorination; **—холестеринемия** *f.* (med.) hypercholesterolemia; **—хроматоз** *m.* hyperchromatosis; **—хромный** *a.* hyperchromic; **—шар** *m.* hypersphere; **—ъядро** *n.* hypernucleus, hyperfragment; **—экспоненциальный** *a.* hyperexponential.

гипидиоморфный *a.* (petr.) hypidiomorphic, subhedral.

гипн *see* **гипнум**; **—ал** *m.* Hypnal, chloralantipyrine; **—о—** *prefix* hypn(o)— (sleep); **—овые** *pl.* (bot.) Hypnaceae (mosses); **—овый** *a.* Hypnum; **—овое болото** Hypnum bog, hypnetum; **—оз** *m.* (med.) hypnosis; **—озигота** *f.* (gen.) hypnozygote, dormant zygote; **—он** *m.* hypnone, acetophenone.

гипнот/изёр *m.* hypnotist, hypnotizer; **—изировать** *v.* hypnotize; **—изм** *m.* hypnotism; **—ический** *a.* hypnotic.

гипнум *m.* (bot.) Hypnum.

гипо— *prefix* hypo—, sub—, under; **—биотический** *a.* (biol.) hypobiotic; **—бласт** *m.* (embr.) hypoblast, entoderm; **—борат** *m.* hypoborate; **—бромит** *m.* hypobromite; **—витаминоз** *m.* (med.) hypovitaminosis, vitamin-deficient state; **—геальный, —гейный** *a.* hypogeal, underground; **—геевая кислота** hypogeic acid, 7-hexadecenoic acid; **—генный** *a.* (geol.) hypogene; (bot.) hypogenous; **—гликемический** *a.* (med.) hypoglycemic; **—гликемия** *f.* hypoglycemia; **—дерма** *f.* (zool.) hypoderm(is); **—дермический** *a.* hypodermic; **—идный** *a.* (mach.) hypoid(al); **—иодит** *m.* hypoiodite; **—кислота** *f.* hypoacid; **—котиль** *m.* (bot.) hypocotyl; **—креевые** *pl.* (bot.) Hypocreaceae; **—кристаллический** *a.* hypocrystalline, partly crystalline.

гипокс/антиловый *a.* hypoxanthylic (acid); **—антин** *m.* hypoxanthine, 6-oxypurine; **—емия** *f.* (med.) hypoxemia; **—ия** *f.* hypoxia, anoxia, oxygen deficiency.

гипо/морф *m.* (gen.) hypomorph; **—нейстон** *m.* (biol.) hyponeuston; **—нитрит** *m.* hyponitrite; **—нихий** *m.* (anat.) hyponychium; **—плазия** *f.* hypoplasia, incomplete development; **—плоид** *m.* (gen.) hypoploid;

—**протеиновый** *a.* low-protein (diet); —**пус** *m.* (zool.) hypopus; —**ренат** *m.* hyporhenate; —**сернистый** *a.* hyposulfurous (acid); —**синхронный** *a.* (elec.) hyposynchronous; —**спадия** *f.* (med.) hypospadia(s); —**стаз** *m.* (gen.) hypostasis; —**статический** *a.* hypostatic; recessive (gene); —**стенический** *a.* hyposthenic, weak; —**стиль** *m.* (bot.) hypostyle; —**сульфат** *m.* hyposulfate; —**сульфит** *m.* hyposulfite; —**сфера** *f.* hyposphere.

гипоталам/ический, —**ный** *a.* (anat.) hypothalamic; —**ическая область,** —**ус** *m.* hypothalamus.

гипо/теза *f.* hypothesis; conjecture, assumption; theory; —**тенуза** *f.* (geom.) hypotenuse; —**термальный** *a.* hypothermal; —**термия** *f.* (med.) hypothermia; —**тетический** *a.* hypothetical; —**тонический** *a.* hypotonic; (med.) hypotensive; —**тоническая болезнь** hypotension; —**тония** *f.* hypotonia; —**трофия** *f.* (med.) hypotrophy; —**трохоида** *f.* (geom.) hypotrochoid; —**физ** *m.* (anat.) hypophysis, pituitary body; —**физарный** *a.* hypophyseal; —**физин** *m.* hypophysin, pituitary extract; —**фосфат** *m.* hypophosphate; —**фосфит** *m.* hypophosphite; —**фтальмовые** *pl.* (ichth.) Hypophthalmidae; —**функция** *f.* hypofunction, diminished function.

гипо/хилий *m.* (bot.) hypochil(ium); —**хилия** *f.* (med.) hypochylia, chyle deficiency; —**хлорит** *m.* hypochlorite; —**хондрический** *a.* (med.) hypochondriac(al); —**хорда** *f.* (anat.) hypochord, subnotochord; —**хромный** *a.* hypochrom(at)ic; —**центр** *m.* (geol.) hypocenter, seismic center; (zool.) hypocentrum; —**циклоида** *f.* (geom.) hypocycloid.

гиппо— *prefix* hippo— (horse); —**камп** *m.* (anat.) hippocampus, Ammon's horn; —**кратовский** *a.* (med.) Hippocratic; —**потам** *m.* (mam.) hippopotamus; —**потамы** *pl.* Hippopotamidae; —**пус** *m.* (mal.) Hippopus.

гиппур/ан *m.* hippuran, sodium iodohippurate; —**ат** *m.* hippurate; —**ил** *m.* hippuryl; —**ит** *m.* (pal.) hippurite; —**итовый** *a.* hippuritic.

гиппуров/ая кислота hippuric acid, benzaminoacetic acid; **соль** —**ой кислоты,** —**окислая соль** hippurate; —**окислый** *a.* hippuric acid; hippurate (of).

гипро—, **ГИПРО . . .** *abbr.* (**государственный институт по проектированию . . .**) State Institute for the Design and Planning of . . .

гипс *m.* (min.) gypsum; (building) plaster; **жжёный г.** plaster of Paris; **землистый г.** *see* **гажа;** —**ация** *f.* (paper) gypsum precipitation; —**ировать** *see* **гипсовать;** —**о—** *prefix* (min.) gypso—, gypsum; hypso— (height); —**обетон** *m.* gypsum concrete; —**ование** *n.* (paper) gypsum precipitation; (soils) gypsum application; gypsum treatment; plastering; —**овать** *v.* apply gypsum, treat with gypsum; plaster; —**овый** *a. of* **гипс;** gypseous; —**овый слепок,** —**овая отливка** plaster cast.

гипсограф *m.* (maps) hypsograph; —**ический** *a.* hypsographic.

гипсодонт *m.* (zool.) hypsodont.

гипсолит *m.* (min.) gypsum; —**овая плита** plasterboard, sheetrock.

гипсолюб/ивый *a.* gypsophilous; —**ка** *f.* (bot.) Gypsophila.

гипсометр *m.* hypsometer (for determining altitude); —**ический** *a.* hypsometric; relief (map); —**ия** *f.* hypsometry.

гипсо/носный, —**содержащий** *a.* gypsiferous; —**подобный** *a.* gypseous; —**термометр** *m.* hypso-(thermo)meter; —**фил** *m.* gypsophilous plant; —**филл**

m. (bot.) hypsophyll; —**фит** *m.* gypsophyte; —**хром** *m.* hypsochrome, hypsochromic group; —**хромный,** —**хромовый** *a.* hypsochromic; —**шлакобетон** *m.* gypsum cinder concrete.

гипт/агин *m.* hiptagin; —**ис** *m.* (bot.) Hyptis; —**олид** *m.* hyptolide.

гипурале *n.* (ichth.) hypural (bone).

гира *f.* (cryst.) axis of symmetry.

Гира печь Geer oven.

гирардинус *m.* (ichth.) Girardinus.

гира/тор *m.* gyrator; —**ция** *f.* gyration.

гирботол *m.* (gas purification) girbotol.

гир/евой *a. of* **гира;** —**ек** *gen. pl. of* **гирька.**

гирелловые *pl.* (ichth.) nibblers (Girellidae).

гири *gen., pl., etc. of* **гиря.**

гиринохейловые *pl.* (ichth.) Gyrinocheilidae.

гирка *f.* (bot.) a variety of wheat.

гирксутит *m.* (min.) gearksutite.

гирло *n.* (river) branch; narrow strait.

гирлянд/а *f.,* —**ный** *a.* garland, chain, string; link.

гирнец *m.* gyrnets (xerophilic oak forest).

гирный *a.* weight (of balance).

гиро— *prefix* gyro— (ring; gyral; spiral); —**азимут** *m.* directional gyro(scope); —**вертикаль** *m.* gyrovertical, vertical gyroscope; —**вертикант** *m.* (missiles) pitch gyro; roll stabilizer; —**воз** *m.* (min.) inertia-type locomotive; —**горизонт** *m.* gyro horizon, artificial horizon; —**дактилёз** *m.* (vet.) gyrodactylosis, Gyrodactylus infection; —**датчик** *m.* gyro(scopic) sensor.

гироид *m.,* —**а** *f.* gyroid; (cryst.) rotation inversion axis; —**альный** *a.* gyroidal.

гиро/интегратор *m.* integrating gyro; —**компас** *m.* gyrocompass; —**котилиды** *pl.* (zool.) Gyrocotiloidea; —**лит** *m.* (min.) gyrolite; —**магнитный** *a.* gyromagnetic; —**маятник** *m.* gyropendulum; —**пилот** *m.* gyropilot; —**полукомпас** *m.* directional gyro; —**прибор** *m.* gyro instrument; —**рулевой** *m.* (naut.) gyropilot, autohelmsman; —**система** *f.* gyro(scope) system; —**скоп** *m.* gyro(scope); —**скопический** *a.* gyro(scopic).

гиростабилиз/атор *m.* gyro(scopic) stabilizer; —**ация** *f.,* —**ирование** *n.* gyrostabilization; —**ированный,** —**ируемый** *a.* gyrostabilized.

гиростат *m.* gyrostat; —**ика** *f.* gyrostatics; —**ический** *a.* gyrostatic.

гиро/тахометр *m.* rate gyro(scope); —**трон** *m.* vibrating gyro, Gyrotron; —**тропный** *a.* gyrotropic; —**успокоитель** *m.* gyro(scopic) stabilizer; —**фора** *f.* (bot.) Gyrophora (lichen); —**фор(ин)овый** *a.* gyrophoric (acid); —**частота** *f.* gyrofrequency.

гирсутизм *m.* (med.) hirsutism.

гирудин *m.* (pharm.) hirudin; —**изация** *f.* hirudinization, leeching; —**оз** *m.* hirudinosis, leech infestation.

гирциновый *a.* hircine; hircinic (acid).

гирч/а *f.* (bot.) milk parsley (Selinum); —**ёвник** *m.* Conioselinum.

гиршфельдия *f.* (bot.) Hirschfeldia.

гирька, —**я** *f.* (balance) weight; —**я-рейтер** *f.* rider, slide; —**я-противовес** *f.* tare (of weigher).

ГИС *abbr.* (**гибридная интегральная схема**) hybrid microcircuit.

гис *m.* His, histidine.

Гиса пучок (anat.) His' bundle.

гисмондин *m.* (min.) gismondite.

гисовский *a.* (anat.) His(').

гисовые *pl.* (ichth.) Pterothrissidae.

гиссарский *a.* (geog.) Gissar.

гиссоп *m.* (bot.) hyssop; —**ин** *m.* hyssopine.

гист— *see* **гисто—**.

гист/азарин *m.* hystazarin, 2,3-dihydroxyanthraquinone.

гистамин *m.,* **—овый** *a.* histamine; **—оподобный** *a.* histamine-like; **—орефрактерный, —устойчивый** *a.* histamine-resistant.

гистер— *prefix* hyster(o)— [lagging; (anat.) uterus]; **—езиметр** *m.* hysteresimeter; **—езис** *m.* hysteresis, lag(ging); **вязкий** *or* **ползучий —езис** hysteresis lag, magnetic creeping; **петля —езиса** hysteresis loop; **—езисный** *a.* hysteresis, hysteretic, lag; **—езометр** *m.* hysteresimeter; **—о—** *see* **гистер—**; **—отеций** *m.* (bot.) hysterothecium; **—эктомия** *f.* (med.) hysterectomy.

гисти/даза *f.* histid(in)ase; **—дил** *m.* histidyl; **—о—** *see* **гисто—**; **—оцит** *m.* (cyt.) hist(i)ocyte, macrophage; **—оцитоз** *m.* (med.) hist(i)ocytosis.

гисто— *prefix* hist(o)—, histio— [web; (biol.) tissue]; **—авторадиографический** *a.* autoradiographic; **—бласт** *m.* histoblast, tissue-forming cell; **—гематический** *a.* histohematic (barrier); **—генез** *m.* histogenesis, tissue development; **—генный** *a.* histogenic; **—гормон** *m.* tissue hormone; **—грамма** *f.* (stat.) histogram, bar graph or chart; **—лиз** *m.* histolysis.

гистолог *m.* histologist; **—ический** *a.* histological; **—ия** *f.* histology.

гисто/н *m.* histone; **—плазмоз** *m.* (med.) histoplasmosis; **—химический** *a.* histochemical; **—химия** *f.* histochemistry.

гису *f.* (ichth.) gissu (*Pterothrissus*).

гитагенин *m.* githagenin.

гиталин *m.* gitalin.

гитар/а *f.,* **—ный** *a.* (mech.) swinging arm or bracket, swing frame; swivel head; quadrant; gear reduction unit; (milling machine) change gear (train); (music) guitar; **морская г.** guitarfish (*Rhinobatos*); **—овидный, —ообразный** *a.* guitar-shaped, fiddle-shaped, panduriform; **—ы-рыбы** *pl.* (ichth.) Rhinobatidae.

гитов *m.* (naut.) brail, clew line.

гито/генин *m.* gitogenin; **—генический** *a.* gitogenic; **—ксигенин** *m.* gitoxigenin; **—ксин** *m.* gitoxin.

гиттия *f.* (geol.) gyttja (a mud).

Гитторфа трубка Hittorf's tube.

гиф *m.,* **—а** *f.* (bot.) hypha, filament; **—альный** *a.* hyphal; **—омицеты** *pl.* hyphomycetes; **—ообразный** *a.* hyphoid, hypha-like; **—ы** *pl.* hyphae.

гич *m.* haulm, top(s), leaves; **—ка** *see* **гич; —ь** *see* **гич**.

ГК *abbr.* (**гиббереловая кислота**) gibberellic acid; (**гамма-каротаж**) gamma-ray logging; etc.

Гкал *abbr.* (**грамм-калория**) gram-calorie.

Г-кислота *f.* G acid.

ГКН *abbr.* (**газо-нефтяной контакт**) gas-oil contact.

ГКС *abbr.* (**спектрометрический гаммакаротаж**) spectrometric gamma logging.

гл *abbr.* (**гектолитр**) hectoliter; **гл.** *abbr.* (**глава; главный; глина; глубина**).

глабелл/а, —ь *f.* (anat.) glabella.

глав— *prefix* main, chief, principal; *prefix, insert, and m. suffix* central board; **—а** *f.* head, chief, foreman; chapter (of book); **—бух** *m.* chief accountant; **—врач** *m.* chief of medical staff; **главрач; —енство** *n.* supremacy, priority; **—енствовать** *v.* take the lead, be at the head; (pre)dominate (over); have priority; **—инж** *m.* chief engineer; **—к** *m.* central board, chief directorate; **—ком** *m.* commander-in-chief.

главко *see* **глауко—**.

глав/мервес *m.* Bureau of Weights and Measures; **—нейший** *a.* chief, predominant; **—новалентный** *a.* primary or principal valency; **—командующий** *m.* commander-in-chief.

главн/ый *a.* chief, principal, main, predominant, leading, primary, prime (consideration); major (issue, etc.); (mech.) master; chief (editor, etc.); central (board); tap (root); **—ого пользования** final (felling); **—ым образом** chiefly, mainly, principally, for the most part, essentially, largely, predominantly, primarily.

главрач *m.* chief of medical staff.

глаговина *f.* (bot.) cornel (*Cornus sanguinea*).

глагол *m.* (grammar) verb.

глаголь *m.* (min.) prop, strut, pillar; **г.-гак** (naut.) pelican hook, slip hook.

гладил/ка *f.,* **—о** *n.* burnisher; planishing hammer; sleeker, smoother, flatter; trowel, float; planer; creaser, creasing tool; **—ьный** *a.* smoothing, etc., *see* **гладить; —ьщик** *m.* burnisher (operator); presser.

гладиоловая кислота gladiolic acid.

гладиолус *m.* (bot.) gladiolus.

гладить *v.* smooth, burnish, polish, planish; level (out); iron, press; stroke, pat.

гладк/ий *a.* smooth, polished; sleek; even, flat, plane; (text.) plain, unfigured; fluent (speech); **—о** *adv. and prefix* smooth(ly); lei(o)—, lio—, liss(o)—; **—оголовые** *pl.* (ichth.) slickheads (*Alepocephalidae*); **—ожгутиковые** *pl.* (prot.) Lissoflagellata; **—озёрный** *a.* smooth-grained; **—озубые** *pl.* (herp.) Aglyph(odont)a; **—окитовые** *pl.* (mam.) baleen whales (*Balaenidae*); **—олистный** *a.* smooth-leaved. leiophyllous; **—оногие** *pl.* (amph.) bell toads (*Liopelmidae, Ascaphidae*); **—оносые** *pl.* (mam.) plainnose bats (*Vespertilionidae*); **—оплодный** *a.* smooth-fruited, leiocarpous; **—опротекающий** *a.* uneventful (recovery); **—опроходной** *a.* flush (joint); **—оствольный** *a.* smooth-bore (gun); **—ость** *f.* smoothness, etc., *see a.;* fluency; **—охвостый** *a.* bare-tailed, smooth-tailed; **—ошёрст(н)ый** *a.* smooth-haired.

гладыш *m.* pebble; (bot.) Laserpitium; mushroom (*Lactarius volemus*); **—и** *pl.* (ent.) backswimmers (*Notonectidae*).

гладь *f.* smooth, mirror-like or glassy surface; (text.) satin stitch.

глаже *comp. of* **гладкий, гладко,** smoother; more smoothly; **—ние, —нье** *n.* smoothing, etc., *see* **гладить; —нный** *a.* smoothed, etc., *see* **гладить**.

глаз *m.* eye; (anat.) oculus; (ichth.) *see* **глазач; бросающийся в —а** conspicuous, outstanding; **на г.** approximately, by rule of thumb; **—ач** *m.* (ichth.) white-eyed bream (*Abramis sapa*).

Глазго Glasgow.

глазерит *m.* (min.) glaserite.

глазет *m.,* **—овый** *a.* (text.) silk brocade.

глазиров/ание *see* **глазировка; —анный** *a.* glazed, etc., *see v.;* **—ать** *v.* glaze, calender, polish; give a glossy finish; (cer.) vitrefy; frost, ice; candy; **—ка** *f.* glazing, etc., *see v.;* glaze.

глазк/и *pl. of* **глазок;** (ent.) Satyridae; **—оватый** *a.* (petr.; zool.) ocellar; birdseye (fracture).

глазн/ица *f.* orbit, socket (of eye); **область —ицы** orbital region; **—ично-височный** *a.* orbitotemporal; **—ичный** *a.* orbital; **—ой** *a.* eye, ocular, optic; ophthalmic; **—ая впадина, —ая ямка** orbit; **—ая линза** (opt.) eyepiece; **—ое пятно** (ent.) stigma, ocellus; **—ое яблоко** eyeball.

глазо— *prefix* oculo—, eye; **—видный** *a.* (zool.) ocellate; (zool.; petr.) ocellar; **—вращающий** *a.* (anat.) oculogyric; **—вский** *a.* (geog.) Glazov; **—двигательный** *a.* (anat.) oculomotor; **—едка** *f.* sulfur dioxide.

глаз/ок *m.* eye(let); (zool.) ocellus; eyepiece; inspection hole, peephole, sight; slot, aperture, hole (of die); mesh (of screen); lug, ear; (bot.) bud; (ent.) Aphantopus; (ichth.) *see* **глазач; прививать —ком** *v.* (hort.) bud, graft by budding.

глазо/мер *m.* visual estimation; **—мерный** *a.* by eye, by sight, approximate; visual (measurement); **—носовой** *a.* (anat.) oculonasal; **—образный** *a.* eye-shaped, oculiform.

глазунья *f.* eggs fried sunny-side up.

глазур/е— *prefix* glaze; **—евидный** *a.* glaze-like; **—енный, —ованный** *a.* glazed; enameled; vitrified; **—ить, —овать** *v.* glaze; enamel; **—ный** *a. of* **глазурь;** (med.) frosted (heart); **—ование** *n.,* **—овка** *f.* glaze, glazing; enamel(ing); **—ообжигательная печь** (cer.) glaze kiln; **—ь** *f.* glaze; enamel, lacquer; gloss; frosting, icing; **нанести —ь** *v.* glaze; **—ь-кракле** *f.* crackle glaze.

глаз/чатки *pl.* (ent.) Satyridae; **—чатый** *a.* spotted; ocellate (markings); **—ый** *a. suffix* -eyed.

глакрезит *m.* glakresite (a cresol resin).

гланд/а *f.* (anat.) gland, specif. tonsil; **—улярный** *a.* glandular.

глас *m.* voice; **—ить** *v.* say, state, read, run, go; **—но** *adv.* openly, publicly; **—ность** *f.* openness; publicity; **предать —ности** *v.* publish, make known; **—ный** *a.* public, open; vowel (sound); **—ящий** *a.* saying, etc., *see* v.

глаубер/ит *m.* (min.) glauberite; **—ова соль** Glauber's salt, sodium sulfate decahydrate.

глауко— *prefix* glauc(o)— (greyish blue or green); **—дот** *m.* (min.) glaucodot; **—ма** *f.* (med.) glaucoma; **—нит** *m.* (min.) glauconite; **—нитовый** *a.* glauconitic; **—пирит** *m.* (min.) glaucopyrite, lollingite; **—фан** *m.* glaucophane; **—хроит** *m.* glaucochroite.

глаукс *m.* (bot.) sea milkwort (*Glaux*).

глау/кус *m.* (mal.) Glaucus (a snail); **—цин** *m.* glaucine; **—циновый** *a.* glaucinic (acid).

глаци— *see* **гляци—**.

ГЛБ *abbr.* (**гидрофильный-липофильный баланс**) hydrophilic-lipophilic balance, HLB.

глеб/а *f.* (bot.) gleba; glebe; **—овидный** *a.* glebiform.

гледичия *f.* (bot.) Gleditschia.

глее/ватый *a.* (soils) gleyey; glutinous; **—видная почва** pseudogley; **—вый** *a.,* **—вый горизонт** gley; **—образование** *n.* gleying, gley formation.

глезер *m.* (paper) glazer, calender; **—ование** *n.* glazing.

глей *m.* gley (a soil horizon).

глейкометр *m.* (brewing) gleucometer.

глейхениевые *pl.* (bot.) Gleicheniaceae.

гления *f.* (bot.) Glehnia.

глео— *prefix* (biol.) gloeo—, gloeal, viscid; **—трихия** *f.* (bot.) Gloeotrichia.

глет *m.,* **—овый** *a.* litharge, lead monoxide.

глетчер *m.,* **—ный** *a.* (geol.) glacier.

глиадин *m.* gliadin, vegetable protein.

глиеж *m.* gliezh, naturally burnt clay.

глик— *see* **глико—; глюк(о)—; —аль** *m.* glucal; **—амин** *m.* glucamine; **—аровый** *a.* glucaric (acid); **—емия** *f.* (med.) glycemia; **—о—** *prefix* glyc(o)— (sweet, sugary); gluc(o)— (glucose).

гликоген *m.* glycogen; **—етический, —ный, —овый** *a.* glycogen(et)ic; **—овая болезнь, —оз** *m.* glycogenosis, glycogen storage disease; **—олиз** *m.* glycogenolysis; **—ообразование** *n.* glycogen formation.

глик/озамин *m.* glycosamine; **—озан** *m.* glycosan; **—озид** glycoside; **—озил** *m.,* **—озильный** *a.* gly-

cosyl; **—озурия** *f.* (med.) glycosuria; **—окол(л), —околь** *m.* glycocoll, glycine.

гликол *m.* glycol, 1,2-ethanediol; **—диацетат** glycol diacetate.

гликолево/кислый *a.* glycolic acid; glycolate (of); **—кислая соль** glycolate; **—этиловый эфир** ethyl glycolate.

гликолев/ый *a.* glycol; glycolic (acid); **г. альдегид** glycolaldehyde, hydroxyethanal; **г. эфир янтарной кислоты** glycol succinate; **—ые эфиры** glycol ethers; **соль —ой кислоты** glycolate.

гликол/ид *m.* glycolide, 2,5-*p*-dioxanedione; **—из** *m.* glycolysis; **—ил** *m.* glycolyl; **—илмочевина** *f.* glycolyl urea; **—итический** *a.* glycolytic, glycoclastic; **—липид** *m.* glycolipid; **—оил** *m.* glycoloyl; **—урил** *m.* glycoluril, acetyleneurea; **—уровая кислота** glycoluric acid, hydantoic acid; **—ь** *see* **гликол; —ьальдегид** *m.* glycolaldehyde; **—ьный** *a.* glycol; **—ят** *m.* glycolate.

глико/невый *a.* glyconic (acid); **—протеид** *m.* glycoprotein; **—стерин** *m.* glycosterin, diethylene glycol distearate; **—фит** *m.* (bot.) glycophyte; **—фосфолипин** *m.* glycophospholipin.

гликохол/ат *m.* glycocholate; **—евокислый** *a.* glycocholic acid, glycocholate (of); **—евокислая соль** glycocholate; **—евый** *a.* glycocholic (acid).

гликоциамин *m.* glycocyamine, guanidinoacetic acid.

глина *f.* clay; (met.) loam; kaolin, China clay; **белая г.,** kaolin, China clay; **формовая г.** putty; **г.-наполнитель** filler clay.

глин/ец *m.* clay sand; **—изация** *f.* argillization; clay grouting; (drilling) mudding off; **—изировать** *v.* mud (off, up); **—ий** *see* **глинозём.**

глинист/о— argillo— (argyllous, clay-containing); **—о-известковый** *a.* argillo-calcareous; **—о-песчаный** *a.* argillo-arenaceous; **—ость** *f.* clayiness; **—ый** *a.* clay(ey), argillaceous; **—ый железняк** (min.) clay ironstone; **—ый известняк** argillaceous limestone, argillocalcite; **—ый раствор** clay mortar; drilling mud; **—ый сланец** clay shale; **—ая корка** (petrol.) mud cake; **—ая порода** mud shale; **—ая суспензия** (geol.) slurry.

глин/ит-цемент *m.* brick cement; **—ице, —ище** *n.* clay pit; loam pit; **—ка** *f.* clay, kaolin.

глино— *prefix* clay, argillo—; **—бетон** *m.* gravel-clay mix; **—битный** *a.* clay, adobe; pisé (building); **—вание** *n.* addition of clay; **—железистый** *a.* argillo-ferruginous; **—завод** *m.* (drilling) mud plant.

глинозём *m.* alumina, aluminum oxide; **водный г., гидрат —а** aluminum hydroxide; **сернокислый г., сульфат —а** aluminum sulfate; **—истый** *a.* alumin(ifer)ous; **—носиликатный** *a.,* **—ный силикат** aluminum silicate; **—содержащий** *a.* aluminiferous.

глино/кислота *f.* (drilling) mud acid; **—копня** *f.* clay pit; **—мешалка** *f.* clay mixer; mud mixer; **—мялка** *f.* clay mill; pug mill; **—носный** *a.* clayey, argillaceous; **—порошок** *m.* dry mud; **—разводка** *f.* pug mill; **—резка** *f.* clay cutter; **—смеситель** *m.* clay mixer; **—содержащий** *see* **глинистый; —солома** *f.,* **—соломенный** *a.* straw adobe.

глинт *m.* clint, projecting rock or ledge.

глинтвейн *m.* mulled wine.

глинян/ый *a.* clay(ey), argillaceous; (met.) loam; **г. раствор** clay mortar; drilling mud; **—ая масса** (cer.) clay slip; **—ая посуда** earthenware, pottery.

глио— *prefix* glio— (gluey; neuroglia); **—з** *m.* (med.) gliosis; **—зный** *a.* (cyt.) glial.

глиоксал *m.* glyoxal, ethanedial; **—аза** *f.* glyoxalase;

—**ат** *m*, —**атный** *a*. glyoxalate; —**евый** *a*. glyoxalic (acid); —**ин** *m*. glyoxaline; —**ь** *see* **глиоксал.**

глиоксил *m*. glyoxyl; —**ат** *m*. glyoxylate; —**евый,** —**овый** *a*. glyoxylic (acid).

глиптали *see* **глифтали.**

глипт/ика *f.,* —**ический** *a*. glyptic, engraving; —**о**— *prefix* glypt(o)—(carved); —**огенез** *m*. (geol.) earth sculpture; —**одонты** *pl*. (pal.) glyptodonts.

глирицидия *f*. (bot.) Gliricidia.

глиссад/а *f.,* —**ный** *a*. (av.) landing beam; glide path, glide slope; —**ный огонь** angle-of-approach light(s).

глисс/ер *m*. glider; (naut.) hydroplane, hydrofoil; —**ирование** *n*. gliding, etc., *see v.;* —**ировать** *v*. glide, skim (over water), (hydro)plane.

глист *m.,* —**а** *f*. helminth, intestinal worm; **ленточный г.** tapeworm; —**ник** *m.,* —**ница** *f*. (bot.) wormwood (*Artemisia absinthium*); —**ный** *a*. helminth(ic); —**огон** *m.,* —**огонный** *a.,* —**огонное средство** vermifuge, anthelmintic.

глиф *m*. (arch.) glyph; *prefix* glyph— (carved).

глифтал/евый *a.,* —**ь** *m*. glyptal resin.

глицер– *see* **глицеро**—; —**альдегид** *m*. glyceralde-hyde; —**ат** *m*. glycerate; —**ид** *m*. glyceride; —**ил** *m*. glyceryl, propenyl.

глицерин *m*. glycerin, glycerol; *prefix* glycero—; **азот-нокислый г., нитрат** —**а** nitroglycerin; **триацетат** —**а** triacetin; —**о**— *see* **глицеро**—.

глицеринов/ый *a*. glycerin; **г. альдегид** glyceralde-hyde; —**ая кислота** glyceric acid, 2-3-dihydroxy-propanoic acid.

глицерино/серная кислота glycerosulfuric acid; **соль** —**серной кислоты,** —**сернокислая соль** glycero-sulfate; —**фосфорная кислота** glycerophosphoric acid; **соль** —**фосфорной кислоты,** —**фосфор-нокислая соль** glycerophosphate; —**фосфор-нокислый калий** potassium glycerophosphate.

глицеринтринитрат *m*. nitroglycerin.

глицеро— *prefix* glycero— (sweet, sugary); —**за** *f*. glycerose; —**фосфат** *m*. glycerophosphate; —**фос-форный** *a*. glycerophosphoric (acid).

глицид *m*. glycide, glycidol, 2,3-epoxy-1-propanol; —**ный** *a*. glycidic (acid).

глиц/ий *see* **глуциний;** —**ил** *m*. glycyl; —**илглицин** *m*. glycyl-glycine; —**ин** *m*. glycine, glycocoll, aminoacet-ic acid; (phot.) Glycin, hydroxyphenylglycine; —**иний** *see* **глуциний;** —**инин** *m*. glycinin; —**иния** *f*. (bot.) wisteria; —**иновый** *a. of* **глицин;** —**ирризин** *m*. glycyrrhizin; —**ирризиновый** *a*. glycyrrhizic (acid).

глия *f*. (anat.) (neuro)glia.

гл. о. *see* **гл. обр.**

глобальный *a*. global; total, entire.

глобар *m*. (spectrophotometry) globar.

глоб/игерина *f*. (zool.) Globigerina; —**игериновый** *a*. globigerine; —**игериновая грязь** (geol.) globigerina ooze; —**ин** *m*. globin; —**ин-цинк-инсулин** *m*. globin zinc insulin; —**оид** *m*. globoid; —**оидальный** *a*. globoid, globate, globular.

гл. обр. *abbr.* (**главным образом**) chiefly, principally, mostly, for the most part.

глобул/а *f*. globule; —**ин** *m*. globulin; —**ит** *m*. (geol.) globulite; —**ол** *m*. globulol; —**ярия** *f*. (bot.) Globularia; —**ярный** *a*. globular; **переходить в** —**ярное состояние** *v*. (chem.) coil.

глобус *m.,* —**ный** *a*. globe, sphere.

гловерный *a*. Glover (sulfuric acid).

глог *m.,* —**овина** *f*. (bot.) hawthorn (*Crataegus*); cornel (*Cornus sanguinea*).

глодать *v*. gnaw, nibble.

глокерит *m*. (min.) glockerite.

глоксиния *f*. (bot.) gloxinia.

глом/игерина *m*. (zool.) Glomeris (a millipede); —**еро**— *prefix* glomer(o)— (ball); —**ерула** *f*. (anat.) glomerulus; —**ус** *m*. glome, glomus; *pl*. glomera; —**усный** *a*. glomus, glomic.

глория *f*. (meteor.) glory.

глосс— *see* **глоссо**—; —**а** *f*. gloss; (anat.) glossa, tongue; (ichth.) a flounder (*Pleuronectes flesus*); —**арий** *m*. glossary; —**ит** *m*. (med.) glossitis; —**о**— *prefix* gloss(o)— (tongue); —**одорис** *m*. (mal.) Glos-sodoris (slug); —**отека** *f*. (ent.) glossotheca; —**офага** *f*. (mam.) Glossophaga.

Глостер (geog.) Gloucester.

глось (ichth.) *see* **глосса.**

глот/ание *n*. swallowing, gulping, deglutition; —**атель-ный** *a*. deglutitory; —**ать,** —**нуть** *v*. swallow, gulp; —**ка** *f*. throat, gullet, pharynx; —**ок** *m*. swallow, mouthful, gulp; —**очно**— *prefix* (anat.) pharyngo—, pharynx; —**очнонёбный** *a*. pharyngo-palatine; —**очно-ротовой** *a*. pharyngo-oral; —**очный** *a*. pharyngeal, throat.

глотто— *prefix* glotto— (language).

глохид/ий *m*. (biol.) glochidium; —**иоз** *m*. glochidiosis, infestation by mussel larvae; —**ион** *m*. (bot.) Glochi-dion.

глохнуть *v*. grow deaf; abate, subside, fade away, die away (of sound); go out (of fire); stall (of engine); (hort.) grow wild, choke up (with weeds).

глуб/же *comp. of* **глубокий, глубоко;** —**и** *pl., etc., of* **глубь;** —**ина** *f*. depth; profundity; intensity, degree; **на** —**ине** deep(-seated); **промерять** —**ину** *v*. fathom, sound.

глубинн/ый *a*. depth; deep-seated; subsurface, buried; submerged (culture); interior; abyssal, deep-sea; deep-well (pump); (geol.) plutonic; (petrol.) down-hole; (biol.) hypogeal; **г. калибр** depth gage; **г. разрыв,** —**ая бомба** depth charge.

глубино/измерительный прибор, —**мер** *see* **глу-бомер;** hydrometer.

глубок/ий *a*. deep(-seated), penetrating, thorough, pro-found; (in-)depth; intimate (knowledge); fundamental (understanding); high (vacuum); heavy (cracking); gra-vure, intaglio (printing); exhaustive (oxidation).

глубоко *adv. and prefix* deep(ly); low, intense (cooling, etc.); **г. находящийся** *a*. deep-seated; —**водный** *a*. deepwater; deep-sea, abyssal; —**водное растение** (bot.) benthon; —**выемчатый** *a*. (bot.) sinuate; —**из-лучатель** *m*. narrow angle lighting fixture; —**ло-пастный** *a*. (bot.) sinuate; —**мысленный** *a*. pro-found, serious; —**отпущенный** *a*. (met.) deep-drawn; —**полимеризованный** *a*. highly polymerized; —**про-каливающийся** *a*. deep-hardening; —**разрезной** *a*. laciniate, fringed; —**рыхлитель** *m*. subsoil plow; —**столбчатый** *a*. deep-columnar; —**сть** *f*. depth, pro-fundity; —**тянутый** *a*. (met.) deep-drawn; —**ува-жаемый** *a*. highly esteemed; dear (in letter); —**уко-реняющийся** *a*. deep-rooted; —**фокусный** *a*. deep-focus (earthquake).

глуб/омер *m*. depth gage, depthometer; —**очайший** *a*. deepest; —**ь** *f*. depth, bottom; —**ьевой** *a*. depths, deep-sea.

глук— *see* **глюк**—.

глуп/еть *v*. grow dull or stupid; —**ить** *v*. do something foolish; **—ость** *f.* foolishness, nonsense; stupidity; folly, foolish act; **—ый** *a.* foolish, stupid; **—ыш** *m.* dunce; (orn.) fulmar (*Fulmarus glacialis*).

глут— *prefix* glut(in)— (glue; gluten); *see also under* **глют—**; **—аконовый** *a.* glutaconic (acid); **—амат** *m.* glutamate; **—амико—** *prefix* glutamic; **—амин** *m.* glutamine; **—аминаза** *f.* glutaminase; **—а(ми)новый** *a.* glutamic (acid); **—амино-пировиноградная трансаминаза** *f.* glutamic-pyruvic transaminase, GPT.

глутар/ат *m.* glutarate; **—ил** *m.* glutaryl; **—овый** *a.* glutaric (acid).

глут/атион *m.* glutathione; **—ен** *m.,* **—еновый** *a.* gluten; **—енин** *m.* glutenin; **—ин** *m.* glutin (protein); glutine (glue).

глуто/за *f.* glutose; **—л, —ль** *m.* glutol; **—лин** *m.* glutolin, formalin gelatin.

глух *sh. m. of* **глухой.**

глухар/иный *a.,* **—ь** *m.* lag screw, coach screw; deaf person; (herp.) glass snake (*Ophisaurus apodus*); (orn.) capercaillie (*Tetra urogallus*).

глух/о *adv. and sh. n. of* **глухой; —оватый** *a.* hard of hearing; muffled (voice); muffled (sound); obscure, vague; indistinct; dead (end); dead-end, blind (passage); closed, rigid (coupling); crown (nut); anechoic (chamber); blank (test); opaque (glass); solid (bearing); slack (season); spent, indirect heating (steam); thick (forest); wild, overgrown; remote, out-of-the-way; voiceless (consonant); *m.* deaf person; **—ой переулок** cul-de-sac; **—онемой** *a.* deaf-mute, surdo-mute; **—онемота** *f.* deaf-mutism; **—ота** *f.* deafness.

глуцин/ий *m.,* **—овый** *a.* glucinum, Gl (obs.), beryllium; **—овая земля** glucina, beryllia, beryllium oxide; **—овая кислота** glucinic acid.

глуше *comp. of* **глухо(й).**

глуш/ение *n.* damping, etc., *see v.;* **—илка** *f.* blank plug; **—итель** *m.* damper; (noise) suppressor, silencer; (exhaust) muffler; baffler, buffer, attenuator; opacifier; (rad.) jammer; **—ить** *v.* damp (down), bank (fire); extinguish; muffle, suppress, deaden (sound); throttle; silence; shut off (engine); deafen; attenuate; opacify (glass); plug (pipe); choke (plants); stun (fish); **—ь** *f.* thicket.

глыб/а *f.,* **—ка** *f.* lump, clod, chunk, clump, block; heap; **каменная г.** boulder; **—истость** *f.* lumpiness; **—истый, —оватый** *a.* lumpy, cloddy; rough (plowing); **—овник** *m.* boulder (block) conglomerate; **—овый** *a. of* **глыба;** in blocks; block (mountain, etc.); **—овое строение** (geol.) block faulting; **—одроб-(итель), —окрошитель** *m.* clod breaker.

глюк— *see* **глюко—;** *see also under* **глик(о)—;** **—агон** *m.* glucagon (hormone); **—о—** *prefix* gluco— (glucose); **—огенный** *a.* glucogenic.

глюкоз/а *f.* glucose, grape sugar; **—азон** *m.* glucosazone; **—амин** *m.* glucosamine; **—ан** *m.* glucosan; **—ен** *m.* glucosene; **—ид** *m.* glucoside; **—идаза** *f.* glucosidase; **—идный** *a.* glycosidic; **—ил** *m.* glucosyl; **—он** *m.* glucosone; **—ооксидаза** *f.* glucose oxidase; **—офосфат** *m.* glucose phosphate; **—офосфорный** *a.* glucosophosphoric (acid); **—урия** *f.* (med.) glucosuria.

глюко/киназа *f.* glucokinase; **—кортикоид** *m.,* **—кортикоидный гормон** glucocorticoid (hormone); **—нат** *m.* gluconate; **—новокислый** *a.* gluconic acid; gluconate (of); **—новый** *a.* gluconic (acid); **—протеид** *m.* glucoprotein; **—фор** *m.* glucophore; **—фураноза** *f.* glucofuranose; **—холевый** *a.* glucocholic (acid).

глюкурон *m.* glucurone; **—ат** *m.* glucuronate; **—ид** *m.* glucuronide; **—овокислая соль** glucuronate.

глют— *see under* **глут—.**

глюц/ид *m.* glucide; **—иний** *see* **глуциний; —ит(ол)** *m.* glucite.

гляд/елка *f.* inspection hole, peephole, sight; **—ение** *n.* looking; **—еть** *v.* look (at); face, give (on), look out (on); show (from under or behind); point; look like; look (after), see (to), attend (to), watch.

глянец *m.* polish, luster, gloss, glaze; glare; **наводить г.** *v.* polish.

глянуть *v.* glance (at).

глянц— *prefix* gloss; brilliant; **—а** *gen. of* **глянец; —вейс** *m.* brilliant white; **—гольд** *m.* (cer.) brilliant gold; **—евание** *n.* glossing, etc., *see v.;* **—еватель** *m.* glazer; **—еватый** *see* **глянцевитый; —евать** *v.* gloss, polish, shine; glaze, enamel; (leather) scud; **—евитость** *f.* luster, gloss, glaze; **—евитый** *a.* lustrous, glossy, shiny; **—евый** *a. of* **глянец; —емер** *m.* glossmeter; **—еобразователь** *m.* (leather) finish, dressing (agent), size, sizing; **—зильбер** *m.* (cer.) brilliant silver; **—крахмал** *m.* gloss starch; **—лак** *m.* gloss varnish; **—ованный** *a.* glossed, etc., *see v.;* **—овать** *see* **глянцевать; —овка** *f.* glossing, etc., *see v.;* (leather) finish(ing), dressing, **—овый** *a.* glossy.

гляуциум *m.* (bot.) horn poppy (*Glaucium*).

гляци— *prefix* glaci— (ice); **—альный** *a.* glacial; **—ация** *f.* (geol.) glaciation; **—о—** *prefix* glacio—, glacier; **—ология** *f.* glaciology.

гм *abbr.* (**гектометр**) hectometer.

г-масса *abbr.* (**грамм-масса**) gram-mass.

гмелин/а *f.* (bot.) Gmelina; **—ит** *m.* (min.) gmelinite.

ГМК *abbr.* (**гидразид малеиновой кислоты**) maleic hydrazide; (**генератор механических колебаний**) generator of vibrations; (**гиромагнитный компас**) gyromagnetic compass; (**горно-металлургический комбинат**) integrated mining and metallurgical plant.

г-моль *abbr.* (**грамм-моль**) mole, gram molecule.

ГМСК *abbr.* (**геоакустический метод стационарных колебаний**) geoacoustical method of stationary vibrations.

ГМТ *abbr.* (**гексаметилентетрамин**) hexamethylenetetramine.

ГМФ *abbr.* (**гуанозинмонофосфат**) guanosine monophosphate, GMP.

гн *abbr.* (**генри**) henry; **ГН** *abbr.* (**гидравлический насос**) hydraulic pump.

гнато— *prefix* gnath(o)—, jaw; **—нем** *m.* (ichth.) Gnathonemus; **—цефалон** *m.* (crust.) gnathocephalon.

гнать *v.* drive, chase; hunt, pursue; race, rev up (engine); distil; **—ся** *v.* pursue, chase, run (after); seek, strive (for); be distilled.

гнафалиум *m.* (bot.) Gnaphalium.

гнев *m.* anger; **—аться** *v.* be angry; **—ить** *v.* enrage, anger; **—ный** *a.* angry.

гнедой *a.* bay (colored).

гнезд/арь *m.* nestling; **—илище** *n.* rookery; **—иться** *v.* (build a) nest, nidify.

гнёзд/ность *f.* (plastics) number of mold cavities; **—ный** *a. of* **гнездо;** nest(ing), nested; *suffix* (biol.) —locular,—loculate.

гнезд/о *m.* nest, cradle; pit, depression, hollow, recess; (peg) hole; socket, couple; seat (of valve); housing (of machine); mesh (of screen); groove, mortise, slot; nidus, breeding place; (biol.) loculus, locule; (ichth.) redd; focus (of disease); pocket (of ore); paragraph (of dictionary); (elec.) receptacle, plug-in socket; bunch, cluster; hill (of corn, etc.); seed bed; (tel.) jack; **г. и шип** mortise and tenon; **осадок —ами** (geol.) nodular deposit; **племенное г.** (zool.) litter; **расширительное г.** (comp.) expansion slot.

гнездов/ание *n.* nesting (season or habit), nidification; **—ать** *v.* nest; **—аться** *v.* build a nest; **—идный** *a.* loculiform; **—ка** *f.* (bot.) Neottia; **—ой** *a.* of **гнездо**; nestling (down); (bot.) nesting, nidulate; cluster (sowing); hill (planting); nested; hole; breeding (grounds); **—ье** *n.* breeding site or ground.

гнезд/оразрывной *a.* (bot.) loculicidal; **—остроение** *n.* nest building; **—чатый** *a.* partitioned.

гнёздышко *dim. of* **гнездо**.

гнездящийся *a.* nidificant, nest-building.

гнезиогамия *f.* (gen.) gnesiogamy.

гнейс *m.* (petr.) gneiss; **—овидность** *f.* gneiss foliation; **—овый** *a.* gneiss(ic), gneissoid; **—оподобный** *a.* gneiss-like, gneissoid.

гнести *v.* press, squeeze; oppress.

гнёт *m.* press; weight; oppression; *pr. 3 sing. of* **гнуть**.

гнетовый *a.* (bot.) gnetaceous.

гнёток *m.* plunger.

гнетум *m.* (bot.) Gnetum.

гнетущий *a.* pressing; oppressive, dismal (weather).

гнивший *past act. part. of* **гнить**.

гнид/а *f.,* **—ный** *a.* (ent.) nit.

гни/ение *n.* decay, decomposition, putrefaction, rotting; (dry) rot; **—ёт** *pr. 3 sing. of* **гнить**.

ГНИИ . . . *abbr.* (**государственный научно-исследовательский институт** . . .) State Scientific Research Institute.

гнил *sh. m. of* **гнилой**; *past m. sing. of* **гнить**; **—ец** *m.* (bees) foul brood; **—и** *gen., etc., of* **гниль**; *past pl. of* **гнить**; **—ой** *a.* decayed, decomposed, rotten, putrid; (med.) carious; **—окровие** *n.* (med.) septicemia, blood poisoning.

гнилост/(ност)ь *f.* decay, putrefaction, putrescence; **—ный** *a.* putrid; putrefactive, purulent, saprogenic, fetid; **—ойкий** *a.* rot-resistant.

гнил/ушка *f.* rotten wood, punk; **—ь** *f.* decay, putrefaction; (phyt.) rot; **—ь стеблей** stem rot; **—ьё** *n.* rotten matter; **—ьца** *f.* touch of decay.

гни/ть *v.* rot, decay, decompose, putrefy; **—ючесть** *f.* putridness; **—ючий, —ющий** *a.* putrescent, rotting.

ГНК *abbr.* (**гамма-нейтронный каротаж**) neutron gamma-gamma logging.

гное/видный *a.* (med.) puriform; **—кровие** *n.* pyemia; **—ние** *n.* rotting; suppuration; **—образовательный** *a.* pyogenic, pus-producing; **—отделительный** *a.* pus-discharging; **—подобный** *a.* pyoid; **—родный** *a.* suppurative; pyogenic; **—содержащий** *a.* pus-containing; **—содержащая моча** (med.) pyuria; **—течение** *n.* suppuration; spec. pyorrh(o)ea; **—точивый** *a.* suppurative.

гно/истый *see* **гнойный**; **—ить** *v.* rot, putrefy; suppurate, fester; manure (soil); **—иться** *v.* suppurate, fester, discharge matter; **—ище** *n.* manure pit.

гной *m.* pus, matter; **—ник** *m.* abscess; **—ничковый** *a.* pustulous; **—ничок** *m.* pustule; **—но—** *prefix* pyo— (pus); **—ный** *a.* suppurative, festering, purulent; **—ное выделение** pus.

гномон *m.* (geom., etc.) gnomon; **—ический** *a.* gnomonic.

гноскопин *m.* gnoscopine, *dl-*narcotine.

гно/ючий, —ящийся *a.* purulent, festering.

гну *m.* (mam.) gnu (*Connochaetes*).

гнус *m.* (ent.) blood-sucking flies.

гнус/авость *f.* (med.) rhinolalia; **—авый, —ливый** *a.* nasal(ized).

гну/тый *a.* bent, curved; **—ть** *v.* bend, curve, flex, de-

flect; bow; drive, aim (at); **—тьё** *n.* bending, flexure; deflection; **—ться** *v.* bend; **—щийся** *a.* flexible, elastic.

гнюс *m.* (ichth.) electric ray (*Torpedo*); **—овые** *pl.* Torpedinidae.

гоанг-нан *m.* hoangnan (bark).

гоацины *pl.* (orn.) Opisthocomidae.

гобель *m.* (bookbinding) plow.

гоби *m.* gobi, salt depression; **—йский** *a.* (geog.) Gobi; **—ус** *m.* (ichth.) Gobius.

г.-обр. *abbr.* (**газообразный**) gaseous.

говаравить *see* **говорить**.

Говарда мешалка Howard mixer.

говения *f.* (bot.) Hovenia.

говлит *m.* (min.) howlite.

говор *m.* talk, rumor; speech; speaking; **—ение** *n.* talking, speaking; **—итель** *m.* speaker; **—ить** *v.* talk, speak, say, tell; show, reveal; **—ить о том, что** indicate, suggest, point to the fact (that); **—иться** *v.* be said; **—ной раструб** (tel.) mouthpiece; **—ная воронка** (tel.) mouthpiece; **—ушка** *f.* (bot.) Clitocybe; (orn.) kittiwake (*Rissa,* spec. *R. tridactyla*); **—я** *pr. ger.* speaking; if we say; **иначе —я** in other words; **не —я (уже) о** not to mention, to say nothing of, aside from, let alone; **—ят** it is said, it is claimed.

говя/дина *f.,* **—жий** *a.,* **—жье мясо** beef.

гогманит *m.* (min.) hohmannite.

гогол/иный *a.,* **—ь** *m.* goldeneye (duck) (*Bucephala*).

гоготать *v.* cackle, cluck.

год *m.* year, annum; **—ами** for years.

годен *sh. m. of* **годный**.

годеция *f.* (bot.) Godetia.

годжкинсонит *m.* (min.) hodgkinsonite.

година *f.* time, year.

годиться *v.* suit, be suitable (for); fit, be fit (for); do; be of use; hold (good or true); be seemly; be fitted (for); serve.

годичн/ость *f.* a year's time; **—ый** *a.* yearly, annual; one year's; **—ый слой, —ое кольцо** (annual) growth ring.

годн/о *adv. and sh. n. of* **годный**; **—ость** *f.* suitability, fitness, etc., *see a.;* **—ость к полёту** airworthiness; **—ый** *a.* suitable, fit, acceptable; satisfactory; serviceable; effective; applicable, adaptable; valid; **—ый для —able**, *e.g.,* **—ый для обработки** workable.

годо— *prefix* hodo— (way, path).

годов/алый *a.* one-year-old, yearling; **—ик** *m.* yearling; **—ой** *a.* annual, yearly; per year; one year('s); seasonal; **—щина** *f.* anniversary.

годо/граф *m.* (math.) hodograph; (seism.) travel time curve; locus; **—скоп** *m.* (electron.) hodoscope.

годы *pl. of* **год**; years, age.

гой *m.* (ichth.) taimen (*Hucho periyi* or *H. taimen*).

гоймы *pl.* (min.) supporting beams.

гойяцит *m.* (min.) goyazite.

гокко *m.* (orn.) curassow (*Crax*); *pl.* Cracidae.

гокутолит *m.* (min.) hokutolite.

гол *sh. m. of* **голый**.

гол. *abbr.* [**голов(а); голландский**].

голавл/евый *a.,* **—ь** *m.* (ichth.) chub (*Leuciscus cephalus*).

гол/акант *m.* (ichth.) Holacanthus; **—андрический** *a.* (gen.) holandric; **—арренин** *m.* holarrhenine; **—арктика** *f.* Holarctic region; **—арктический** *a.* Holarctic.

голен/астобродные птицы long-legged swamp birds; **—астые** *pl.* (orn.) waders (*Ciconiiformes*); **—астый** *a.* long-legged; (orn.) wading, grallatorial; **—ища** *f.* bootleg; **—ище** *n.* boot top; single lap (of ingot);

—(н)о-подколенный *a.* (anat.) cruropopliteal; **—ный** *a.* crural, femoral; **—остопный** *a.* talocrural; **—ь** *f.* shin, crus; (orn.) tarsus; (ent.) tibia; gaskin (of horse); hock (joint); **область —и** crural region.

голец *m.* (geol.) bald peak, bald mountain; alpine tundra; (ichth.) loach (*Nemachilus*); char (*Salvelinus*).

голиаф *m.* (ent.) Goliathus.

голик *m.* besom, broom; beacon.

голландер *m.* (paper) hollander, beater; (agr.) huller, sheller.

Голландия Holland, the Netherlands.

голландский *a.* Dutch, Netherlandian.

голлевский *a.* (anat.) Goll('s).

голо *adv. of* **голый;** poorly; *prefix* (biol.) gymno—, glabro—, nudi—, psilo— (naked, bare); holo— (complete, whole, entire); **—бластический** *a.* (embr.) holoblastic, dividing completely; **—брюхие** *pl.* (ichth.) eels (Apodes); **—брюхий** *a.* bare-bellied.

голов/а *f.* head; crown; end; (ice) block; (sugar) loaf; (anat.) caput; *pl.* capita; **приходить в —у** *v.* occur; **мёртвая г.** (ent.) death's head moth (*Acherontia atropos*); **г.-рыба** *f.* headfish (*Mola mola*); **—астик** *m.* (zool.) tadpole; (mil.) specialist in nuclear warhead dismantlement; **—астый** *a.* large-headed; capitate.

головатый *a.* rather bare.

голов/ач *m.* common name for several fish, spec. bighead goby; (ent.) Lethrus; (mam.) humpback whale (*Megaptera*); (bot.) Calvatia; pistillate hemp; **—ень** *see* **голавль; —ешка** *f.* firebrand, ember, charred wood; (ichth.) goloveshka (*Percottus glehni*); **—ешковые** *pl.* Eleotridae.

головизна *f.* (food) jowl (of fish).

головк/а *dim. of* **голова;** *f.* head; cap, knob, end, tip; diehead; (drill) bit; (chisel) point; (open hearth furnace) port; (petrol.) overhead fraction; (power) pack; (garlic) clove; capitulum (of bone); (flax) boll; (anat.) glans; **боевая г.** warhead; **—овидный, —ообразный** *a.* cephaloid, capitate; capituliform; **—оотделитель** *m.* flax boll separator.

головль *see* **голавль.**

головнёв/ый *a. of* **головня; —ые грибы** smut fungi (*Ustilaginaceae*).

голов/ой *a.* head, cephalic; frontal, advanced, leading, main; primary (column); bow, forward (shock, wave); pilot (plant); head end (process); (distil.) overhead (fraction); cranial (nerve); **г. мозг** (anat.) encephalon, brain; **г. образец** pilot model, prototype; **г. погон** (chem.) head product; **г. телефон** headphone, headset; **—ая боль** headache; **—ая часть** (rockets) nose cone; **—ое сооружение** (hydr.) headwork, control works; **—омозговой** *a.* (anat.) craniocerebral.

головня *f.* ember, charred log; (phyt.) smut (*Ustilago*).

голово— *prefix* (anat.) head, cephalo—; **—грудь** *f.* cephalothorax; **—кружение** *n.* vertigo, dizziness, giddiness; **—лом** *m.* (bot.) darnel ryegrass (*Lolium temulentum*); **—ломка** *f.* puzzle, problem; **—ногие** *pl.* (mal.) Cephalopoda; **—образный** *a.* head-shaped, cephaliform; **—трубка** *f.* (ent.) proboscis; **—хордовые** *pl.* (zool.) Cephalochordata.

головчат/ка *f.* (bot.) Cephalaria; **—о—** *prefix* cephal(o)— (head); **—ый** *a.* bulbous; bulb (iron); (anat.) capitate, head-shaped; (zool.) cephalate; *suffix* —cephalous, —headed.

голо/гамия *f.* (gen.) hologamy; **—гиалиновый** *a.* (petr.) holohyaline.

голо/глаз *m.* (herp.) Ablepharus; **—головый** *a.* bare-headed; smooth (flounder).

голо/грамма *f.* hologram; **—графирование** *n.* holographing, holography.

голод *m.* hunger, famine, starvation; shortage (of land); **морить —ом, томить —ом** *v.* starve; **—ание** *n.*, **—овка** *f.* starvation; malnutrition; deficiency, lack, deprivation, hunger; fasting; **—аный** *a.* fasted (test animals); **—ать** *v.* starve, suffer from hunger; fast; **—ающий** *a.* starving, hungry, famished; *m.* starving person; **—ие** *pl.* starving population, famine-stricken people; **помощь —им** famine relief; **—ный** *a.* hungry; starvation, famine; low-calorie (diet); **—ный отёк, —ная болезнь** (med.) nutritional edema.

голо/жаберные *pl.* (mal.) Nudibranchia; **—зёрный** *a.* bare-grained, hull-free, hulled; **—зубка** *f.* hagfish (*Myxine glutinosa*).

голокаин *m.* holocaine, phenacaine.

голо/кожие *pl.* (herp.) Trionychoidea; **—корешковый, —корневой** *a.* naked-rooted.

голокринный *a.* holocrine (glands).

голол/ёд *m.*, **—едица** *f.*, **—ёдный** *a.*, **—едь** *f.* glaze (ice); ice-crusted ground.

голо/листный *a.* smooth-leaved, nudiphyllous; **—мороз** *m.* (meteor.) black frost.

голоморф *m.* (math.) holomorph; **—ность** *f.* holomorphy; **—ный** *a.* holomorphic.

голомянк/а *f.* (ichth.) Comephorus; **—овые** *pl.* Baikal fishes (*Comephoridae*).

голоногий *a.* bare-legged, bare-footed.

голо/номный *a.* (phys.) holonomic; **—планктон** *m.* (biol.) holoplankton.

голо/плодный *a.* (bot.) gymnocarpous, naked-fruited; **—пузка** *see* **гольян; —ростковый** *a.* (zool.) gymnoblastic.

голос *m.* voice; vote, ballot.

голосем/енной, —янный *a.* (bot.) gymnospermous; **—янные** *pl.* Gymnospermae.

голосистый *a.* loud-voiced, raucous.

голословн/о *adv.* without proof, without foundation; **—ость** *f.* lack of proof, unsubstantiated nature; **—ый** *a.* unsubstantiated, unfounded, unproven, assumed.

голосник *m.* (acous.) resonator.

голосов/ание *n.* vote, voting, ballot, poll; **—ать** *v.* vote; **—ой** *a.* voice; **—ой аппарат, —ая щель** (anat.) glottis; **—ой мешок** (amph.) resonator; **—ые связки** vocal chords.

голо/спин *m.* (mam.) Pteronotus; **—спинный** *a.* naked-backed; **—стебельный** *a.* nudicaul(ous), bare-stemmed.

голо/стомный *a.* (mal.) holostom(at)ous; **—тип** *m.* (biol.) holotype, type specimen; **—турии** *pl.* (zool.) Holothurioidea; **безногие —турии** Apoda; **—турия** *f.* holothurian, sea cucumber; **—фитный** *a.* (bot.) holophytic, autotrophic; **—цен** *m.*, **—ценовый** *a.* (geol.) Holocene; **—центровые** *pl.* squirrelfishes (*Holocentridae*).

голоше/ий, —йный *a.* bare-necked.

голоэдр *m.* (cryst.) holohedron; **—ический** *a.* holohedral; **—ия** *f.* holohedry.

голтель *m.* molding plane, cornice plane.

голтовка *see* **галтовка.**

голубе/видный *a.* dove-like; **—вод** *m.* pigeon breeder; **—водство** *n.* pigeon breeding.

голубель *f.* (bot.) blueberry (*Vaccinium*); spec. bog bilberry (*V. uliginosum*).

голубёнок *m.* young pigeon, squab.

голубе/образные *pl.* pigeons and doves (*Columbiformes*); **—станция** *f.* pigeon loft.

голуб/еть *v.* become azure or blue; —**еющий** *a.* turning blue.

голуби *pl.* of **голубь.**

голуб/изна *f.* blue, azure; —**ика** *see* **голубель.**

голуб/иные *see* **голубеобразные;** —**иный** *a.* pigeon; columbine, dove-like; dove-colored, palumbine; —**ица,** —**ичник** *see* **голубель;** —**ка** *f.* female pigeon; —**ки** *pl.* (bot.) columbine (*Aquilegia*).

голуб/оватый *a.* bluish; —**ой** *a.* (sky-)blue, azure, cyan; —**ое пятно** (med.) macula cerulea.

голубок, капский (orn.) Cape pigeon (*Daption capensis*); **морской г.** slender-billed gull (*Larus genei*).

голубо/лицый *a.* (zool.) blue-faced; —**серый** *a.* blue-gray, grayish blue.

голубушка *f.* (bot.) Oxytropis.

голубь *m.* pigeon, dove; (astr.) Columba.

голубянки *pl.* (ent.) Lycaenidae.

голубят/ина *f.* squab, pigeon meat; —**ник** *m.* pigeon breeder; —**ник-ястреб** *m.* (orn.) goshawk (*Accipiter gentilis*); —**ня** *f.* dovecote, pigeon loft.

голштинский *a.* Holstein.

голый *a.* bare, naked, nude; uncovered; bald, scaleless, smooth, glabrous.

голыш *m.* pebble, shingle; cobblestone; gravel; popular name for several species of fish; —**евый** *a.* pebbly, gravelly.

голь *f.* bareness, nakedness; poverty.

гольдглет *m.* a kind of litharge.

гольденит *m.* (min.) holdenite.

Гольджи аппарат (anat.) Golgi organ.

гольд/фильдит *m.* (min.) goldfieldite; —**шмидтовый** *a.* Goldschmidt('s).

голь/ё *n.,* —**евой** *a.* (depilitated) hide, pelt; viscera and feet of carcass.

гольм/иевый *a.* holmium, holmic; —**ий** *m.* holmium, Ho; **хлорный** —**ий** holmic chloride; —**квистит** *m.* (min.) holmquistite.

гольт *m.,* —**ский ярус** (geol.) Gault.

гольциевый *a.* Holtz.

гольф *m.* golf.

гольфстрим *m.* (geog.) Gulf Stream.

гольц/овый *a. of,* —**ы** *pl. of* **голец;** goltsy (alpine tundra belt).

гольшт(е)инский *a.* Holstein.

гольян *m.* (ichth.) minnow (*Phoxinus*).

голяк *m.* hide of premature lamb.

гоманнит *m.* (min.) hohmannite.

гоматропин *m.* homatropine.

гомбо *n.* (bot.) okra (*Hibiscus esculentus*).

гомельский *a.* (geog.) Gomel.

гомео— *prefix* hom(e)o— (like, similar); —**з(ис)** *m.* (biol.) homeosis.

гомеоморф *m.* (cryst.; math.) homeomorph; —**изм** *m.,* —**ность** *f.* homeomorphism; —**ный** *a.* homeomorphous.

гомеопат *m.* (med.) homeopath; —**ический** *a.* homeopathic; —**ия** *f.* homeopathy.

гомеополярн/ый *a.* hom(e)opolar; —**ая связь** homopolar bond; covalent bond.

гомео/стаз(ис) *m.* (physiol.) homeostasis; —**типический** *a.* (gen.) homeotypic.

гоми *n.* (bot.) foxtail (*Setaria italica* or *viridis*).

гомилит *m.* (min.) homilite.

гоми/ниды *pl.* man-like apes (*Hominidae*); —**цидный** *a.* homicidal.

гоммелин *m.* gommeline, dextrin.

гоммоз *m.* (phyt.) gummosis.

гомо— *prefix* homo— (same, like); —**гаметический** *a.* (gen.) homogametic; —**гамия** *f.* homogamy; —**гамный** *a.* homogamous.

гомоген/етический *a.* (gen.) homogenetic; —**изатор** *m.* homogenizer; —**изация** *f.,* —**изирование** *n.* homogenization; (met.) diffusion annealing; —**из(ир)овать** *v.* homogenize; —**изованный** *a.* homogenized; —**ность** *f.* homogeneity, homogeneousness, uniformity; —**ный** *a.* homogeneous, uniform.

гомо/гентизиновая кислота homogentisic acid, 2,5-dihydroxyphenylacetic acid; —**графический** *a.* homographic; —**графия** *f.* (geom.) homography; —**динамический** *a.* (gen.) homodynamic; —**дромный** *a.* (bot.; mech.) homodromous; —**еозис** *m.* homoeosis, metamorphosis.

гомозигот/а *f.* (gen.) homozygote; —**ность** *f.* homozygosity; homozygosis; —**ный** *a.* homozygous.

гомо/йо— *see* **гомео—;** —**йотермное** *n.* warm-blooded animal; —**йотермный** *a.* homoiothermal, warm-blooded; —**кариоз(ис)** *m.* (gen.) homokaryosis; —**клиналь** *f.* (geol.) homocline; —**лиз** *m.* (chem.) homolysis; —**литический** *a.* homolytic.

гомолог *m.* homolog; —**ический,** —**ичный** *a.* homologous; corresponding; —**ичность,** —**ия** *f.* homology; correspondence.

гомоморф *m.* (biol.; math.) homomorph; —**изм** *m.* homomorphism; —**ный** *a.* homomorphous, homomorphic; —**оз** *m.* homomorphosis.

гомо/ним *m.* (classification) homonym; —**нимический** *a.* homonymous, homonymic; —**номия,** —**номность** *f.* (biol.) homonomy; —**номный** *a.* homonomous; —**пауза** *f.* (meteor.) homopause; —**переход** *m.* homojunction; —**пластика** *f.* (med.) homoplastic transplantation; —**поликонденсация** *f.* homopolycondensation; —**полимер** *m.* homopolymer; —**полимеризация** *f.* homopolymerization; —**полярный** *a.* homopolar; —**ризный** *a.* (bot.) homorhizal; —**сексуалист** *m.,* —**сексуальный** *a.* homosexual; —**серил** *m.* homoseryl; —**стилия** *f.* (bot.) homostyly; —**сфера** *f.* (meteor.) homosphere.

гомо/таксиальный *a.* (biol.; geol.) homotaxial; —**таллизм** *m.* (bot.) homothallism; —**таллический** *a.* homothallic; —**тетичный** *a.* (math.) homothetic; —**тетия** *f.* homothety, similitude, like placement; —**тип** *m.* (anat.) homotype; —**типичность,** —**типия** *f.* homotypy; —**типный** *a.* homotypic; homologous; —**топический** *a.* (math., etc.) homotopic; —**хрония,** —**хронность** *f.* (biol.) homochronism, homochrony; —**хронный** *a.* homochronous; —**центрический** *a.* homocentric; —**церк(аль)ный** *a.* (ichth.) homocercal; —**циклический** *a.* homocyclic; —**цистеин** *m.* homocysteine.

гомункул(ус) *m.* (embr.) homunculus.

гомути *n.* gomuti (fiber).

гомфоз *m.* (anat.) gomphosis; (ichth.) a birdfish (*Gomphosus*).

гон *m.* bout, run, pass; strip; drive, driving; hunt, chase; (zool.) heat, oestrus; (geom.) grade.

гон— *see* **гоно—;** *m. suffix* —**gon** (angle).

гонад/а *f.* (anat.) gonad, sex gland; —**ный** *a.* gonadal; —**остимулятор** *m.* gonadostimulant, sex gland activator; —**отропин** *m.* gonadotropin (hormone); —**отропный** *a.* gonadotropic.

гональный *a.* (bot.) gon(idi)al; *suffix* —**gonal,** —**angle(ed).**

гонамский *a.* (geog.) Gonam.

гонг *m.* gong; —**илонем(ат)оз** *m.* (med.) gongylonemiasis, Gongylonema infection.

гонданг *m.* gondang (wax).

гондванский *a.* (geol.) Gondwanaland.

гондол/а *f.,* **—ьный** *a.* (av.) nacelle; pod; (balloon) gondola; housing; **г.-вагон** *m.* (rr.) gondola.

гондурасский *a.* (geog.) Honduras, Honduran.

гонец *m.* (ichth.) asp (*Aspius a.*); goad goby (*Mesogobius gymnotrachelus*).

гонид/иальный *a.* (bact.; bot.) gonidial; **—ий** *m.,* **—ия** *f.* gonidium; **—ио—** *prefix* gonidio—, gonidium.

гониевый *a.* (anat.) gonial.

гонио— *prefix* gonio- (corner, angle).

гониолимон *m.* (bot.) Goniolimon.

гониометр *m.* goniometer; **прикладной г.** protractor; **—ический** *a.* goniometric; **—ия** *f.* goniometry, direction finding.

гонистий *m.* (ichth.) Gonistius.

гонит *m.* (med.) gon(e)itis; *pr. 3 sing. of* **гнать.**

гонк/а *f.* race, racing, drive; haste, hurry; distillation; raft(ing), float (of wood); *suffix* separator, extractor, centrifuge; **—ий** *a.* fleet, fast; (bot.) fast-growing.

гонконгский *a.* (geog.) Hong Kong.

гонкость *f.* fast rate of growth.

гонн/ый *a.* homing, carrier (pigeon); *suffix* **—agogue, —agogic, -promoting, -stimulating, -inducing, -producing; -extracting; —ая машина** *see* **гонка,** *suffix;* **—ое средство —agogue.**

гоно— *prefix* gon(o)— (semen, seed; birth, generation, reproduction); **—бо(бе)ль** *see* **голубель; —бласт** *m.* gonoblast, reproductive cell.

гоновский очаг (med.) Ghon focus.

гоно/дукт *m.* (anat.) gonoduct, genital duct; **—зооид** *m.* (zool.) gonozooid.

гонок *m.* (text.) picker; *sh. m. of* **гонкий;** *gen. pl. of* **гонка.**

гонококк *m.* (bact.) gonococcus; **—овый** *a.* gonococcal.

гоно/мерия *f.* (gen.) gonomery; **—под** *m.,* **—подия** *f.* (zool.) gonopodium.

гонорар(ий) *m.* fee, compensation, remuneration; royalty.

гонор/ейный, —ойный *a.* (med.) gonorrheal; **—ея** *f.* gonorrhea; **—инховые** *pl.* sandfishes (*Gonorhynchidae*).

гоно/стомовые *pl.* (ichth.) bristlemouths (*Gonostomidae*); **—фор** *m.* (zool.) gonophore; **—цель** *m.* gonocoel; **—цит** *m.* (embr.) gonocyte.

гоночный *a. of* **гонка.**

гонт *m.* gravel; (roof) shingle; **—ина** *f.,* **—овой** *a.* shingle; **—овщик** *m.* shingle maker; **—орезный станок** shingle saw.

гончар *m.* (cer.) potter; **—ничать** *v.* be a potter.

гончарн/ый *a.* potter's; ceramic, earthenware; clay, argillaceous; **г. круг** potter's wheel; **—ая масса, —ое тесто** (cer.) paste, body; **—ая печь** kiln; **—ое искусство** ceramics; **—ые изделия** pottery, earthenware; **—я** *f.* pottery.

гончарство *n.* potter's trade; pottery.

гонч/ая *f.* hunting dog, hound; **—ий** *a.* hunting (dog).

гон/щик *m.* racer; driver; **—ьба** *f.* (zool.) oestrus, heat; **—ять** *see* **гнать.**

гопеит *m.* (min.) hopeite.

гопкалит *m.* hopcalite (gas mask filter).

гопкинсоновский *a.* Hopkinson.

гопл/ихтовые *pl.* (ichth.) Hoplichthyidae; **—обротула** *f.* Hoplobrotula; **—окариды** *pl.* (crust.) Hoplocarida.

гоппер-фидер *m.* feed hopper.

гор— *prefix, insert, suffix* **горный; городской; —а** *f.* mountain, hill; **в —у** uphill; **под —у** downhill.

гораздо *adv.* much, (by) far, considerably.

гораихтовые *pl.* (ichth.) Horaichthyidae.

горал *m.* (mam.) goral (*Naemorhedus*).

гора-останец *f.* residual mountain; **г.-свидетель** *f.* island mountain.

горация *f.* (mal.) Horatia (snail).

горб *m.* gibbus, hump, hunch, protuberance, bulge; (curve) peak; **—атик** *m.* (carp.) compass plane; **—атить** *v.* hump; **—атки** *pl.* (ent.) Phoridae; Mordellidae; **—атость** *f.* gibbosity; **—атый** *a.* gibbous, humped, humpbacked, hunchback(ed), protuberant.

горбахит *m.* (min.) horbachite.

горб/ач *m.* (carp.) compass plane; (mam.) humpback whale (*Megaptera nodosa; Eubalaena glacialis*); (ichth.) grayling (*Thymallus*); **—ик** *m.* little hump, gibbosity, protuberance, swelling; **—ина** *f.* bump; (zool.) umbo; **—истый** *a.* gibbous, humped; knotty (wood); **—ить** *v.* hunch (one's back); bend; **—ление** *n.* (glass) warping; **—оносный** *a.* gibbiferous, humped; **—оносый** *a.* hook-nosed; **—ун** *m.* hunchback; **—уша** *f.,* **—ушечный** *a.* (agr.) sickle; (ichth.) pink salmon (*Oncorhynchus gorbuscha*); **—ушка** *f.* (ichth.) common name for several species, spec. Erythroculter.

горбыл/ёвые *pl.* (ichth.) croakers (*Sciaenidae*); **—ёк** *m.* (window) sash bar; **—ь** *m.* slab, side piece; (ichth.) croaker (*Johnius, Otolithes, Sciaenops,* etc.)

Горвуда процесс (min.) Horwood process.

горганский *a.* (geog.) Gorganyi.

горгоны *pl.* (zool.) Gorgonocephalidae.

горд *sh. m. of* **гордый.**

горд/еин *m.* hordein; **—енин** *m.* hordenine.

гордень *m.* whip, hoisting or hauling line.

гордиев узел Gordian knot, very involved problem.

гордиться *v.* be proud (of).

гордовина *f.* (bot.) wayfaring tree (*Viburnum lantana*).

горд/ость *f.* pride; **—ый** *a.* proud.

горе *n.* grief; **—вать** *v.* grieve.

горек *sh. m. of* **горький.**

горел/ка *f.* burner, (gas) jet; (welding) torch; precombustion chamber; premix or burner cup; **—ость** *f.* hot tear (casting defect); **—очный** *a. of* **горелка; —ый** *a.* burnt, scorched; reduced to ashes; **—ые породы** coalash slag.

горельеф *m.,* **—ный** *a.* high relief.

горемик *m.* baked rock.

гор/ение *n.* combustion, burning, blazing; heating up (of hay, etc.); (apple) scald; **дистанция —ения** (rockets) firing range; **теплота —ения** heat of combustion; **—еть** *v.* burn, be on fire, blaze; glow, gleam, sparkle.

горец *m.* mountain dweller, mountaineer; (bot.) knotweed (*Polygonum*).

гореч/авка *f.* (bot.) gentian; **—авковые** *pl.* Gentianaceae; **—и** *pl.* (pharm.) bitters; **—ник** *m.* (bot.) Peucedanum; **—ь** *f.* bitterness, bitter taste; bitter principle.

горжа *f.* gorge, ravine.

горздравотдел *m.* municipal health department.

горизонт *m.* horizon, vista; level, floor; plane; (min.) gallery, adit; layer, bed; (water) line, table; height (of instrument); **вне —а** out of sight; **—аль** *f.* horizontal, level; contour (line); skyline; (mine) floor; **по —алям** contour (plowing); **установка по —али** horizontal adjustment.

горизонтальн/о *adv. and prefix* horizontal(ly); on a level; flat; **—о-ковочный** *a.* (met.) upsetting; **—о-поляризованный** *a.* horizontally polarized; **—о-расточный, —о-сверлильный** *a.* boring (machine); **—ость** *f.* horizontal position; **—офрезерный** *a.* horizontal milling (machine); **—ый** *a.* horizontal, level, flat; landscape (format); lateral (transistor); **—ая линия, —ая плоскость** level; **—ая съёмка** leveling.

горизонтировать *v.* level (off).

горилла *f.* (mam.) gorilla.

горисский *a.* (geog.) Goris.

горист/ость *f.* mountainous state; **—ый** *a.* mountainous, hilly.

гори/хвостка *f.* (orn.) redstart (*Phoenicurus*); **—цвет** *m.* (bot.) Adonis; Coronaria; **—чник** *m.* Peucedanum.

горк *past m. sing. of* **горкнуть.**

горка *f.* hill(ock), hummock, ridge, peak; (av.) steep climb; cabinet; gravity cleaner; (rr.) gravity yard, hump; (paper) descent plate, weir (of beater); (anat.) monticulus.

горкнуть *v.* turn bitter; turn rancid.

горком *m.* town or city committee.

горл/ач *m.* (ichth.) Syrman goby (*Neogobius syrman*); **—енка** *see* **горлица; —ец** *m.* (bot.) bistort (*Polygonum bistorta*); **—инка, —ица** *f.* (orn.) turtle dove (*Streptopelia*).

горло *n.* throat; neck (of vessel); vent (of volcano); (sand) bar; wave-cut niche; (math.) gorge circle; (ent.) gula; **дыхательное г.** (anat.) windpipe, trachea; **с длинным —м** long-necked; **—вина** *f.* manhole; crater, orifice, mouth, vent; throat; neck (of vessel); (steel converter) nose; hatch, scuttle (of ship); **—вой** *a. of* **горло;** (anat.) gular; (math.) striction; throttle (pipe); (med.) guttural (rale); **—овой мешок** (orn.) gular pouch; **—овой щиток** (zool.) gular; **—зубка** *f.* hagfish (*Myxine glutinosa*); **—пёрый** *a.* (ichth.) jugular; **—сечение** *n.* (med.) tracheotomy.

горл/ышко *dim. of* **горло;** mouth, spout, gullet; **—юха** *f.* (bot.) Picris; **—янка** *f.* bottle gourd (*Lagenaria vulgaris*); crookneck squash.

гормон *m.* hormone; **—(аль)ный** *a.* hormonal; **—изация** *f.* hormonization (of seeds); **—ообразующий** *a.* hormonogenic, hormonopoietic; **—оподобный** *a.* hormone-like; **—отерапия** *f.* hormone therapy.

горн *m.* (met.) hearth, forge, furnace; (cer.) kiln; crucible (of shaft furnace); (fog) horn.

горнблендит *m.* (petr.) hornblendite.

горнил/о *see* **горн; —ьный** *see* **горновой.**

горнитос *m.* (geol.) hornito, driblet cone.

горно— *prefix* mining; mountain; **г.-алтайский** *a.* (geog.) Gorno-Altaic; **г.-бадахшанский** *a.* Gorno-Badakhshan.

горно/вой *a. of* **горн;** (forge) welding; **—вой, —вщик** *m.* furnace attendant; **—вьючный** *a.* mountain pack; **—добывающий** *a.* mining (industry); **—заводский** *a.* (mining and) metallurgical.

горнокаменн/ый *a.,* **—ая порода** rock.

горно/колосник *m.* (bot.) Orostachys; **—лесной** *a.* mountain forest; **—луговой** *a.* mountain meadow; **—металлургический** *a.* mining and smelting; **—промышленность** *f.,* **—промышленный** *a.* mining industry; **—проходческий** *a.* mine-sinking; **—рабочий, —служащий** *m.* miner; **—рудный** *a.* mining; **—спасательный** *a.* (mine) rescue.

горност/аевый *a.,* **—ай** *m.,* **—айвый, —аячий** *a.* (mam.) ermine (*Mustela erminea*); **—аевые моли** (ent.) ermine moths (*Yponomeutidae*).

горно/-степной *a.* mountain steppe; **г.-таежный** *a.* mountain taiga; **—технический** *a.* mining, mine engineering; **—химический** *a.* mining and chemical; **—шахтный** *a.* mining.

горнштедтия *f.* (bot.) Hornstedtia.

горн/ый *a.* mountain(ous); mining; pit (sand, gravel); surveying (compass); air (sickness); **г. воск** (min.) miner-

al wax, ozocerite; **г. инженер** mining engineer; **г. лён** (min.) mountain flax, amianthus; **г. трут** *see* **горное молоко; г. хрусталь** (min.) rock crystal; **—ая бумага** (min.) mountain paper, mountain cork; **открытая —ая выработка** open pit mining, open cut mining; **—ая голубая** mineral blue (basic copper carbonate); **—ая губка** *see* **горное молоко; —ая зелень** mountain green, malachite; **—ая кожа** (min.) mountain leather, palygorskite; **—ая мука** mountain meal, kieselguhr; **—ая порода** rock; **—ая пробка** mountain cork; **—ая синь** *see* **горная голубая; —ая система** range (of mountains); **—ая смола** mineral tar, mineral pitch; **—ая техника** mining engineering; **—ое дело** mining (industry); **—ое дерево** mountain wood, ligneous asbestos; **—ое искусство** mining; **—ое масло** petroleum; mineral oil; **—ое молоко** rock milk, agaric mineral; **—ое мыло** mountain soap, saponite; **—ое сало** mountain tallow, hatchettite; **—ое солнце** mercury-quartz lamp; **—ые квасцы** rock alum, alunite; **—ые работы** mining.

горн/як *m.,* **—яцкий** *a.* miner; mining engineer or student.

горо— *prefix* ore(o)—, mountain.

город *m.* town, city; **изучение —ов** urban studies; **—енковский** *a.* (geog.) Gorodenka; **—ецкий** *a.* Gorodets.

городить *v.* hedge, fence, enclose.

городищенский *a.* (geog.) Gorodishche.

город/ок *dim. of* **город;** village, township; (university) campus; (mil.) post; (medical) center; (lumber) yard; **—сад** *m.* garden city; **—ской** *a.* city, municipal, urban; **—ское хозяйство** municipal services; **—спутник** *m.* satellite town.

городчат/о— *prefix* crenato—, crenate; **—ость** *f.* crenation, crenature; **—оцветковый** *a.* crenatiflorous; **—ый** *a.* cren(ul)ate, notched, indented.

городьба *f.* enclosure, fence; fencing.

горожан/е *pl.* townspeople; **—ин** *m.,* **—ка** *f.* city or town resident.

горожение *n.* enclosing, enclosure, fencing.

горо/к *gen. pl. of* **горка; —любивый** *a.* oreophilous, mountain-loving.

горообраз/ование *n.* (geol.) orogenesis, mountain formation; **—овательный, —ующий** *a.* orogenic.

горох *m.* (bot.) pea (*Pisum*); **—овидный** *a.* pea-shaped, pisiform; pisolitic; **—овик** *m.* (ent.) pea weevil (*Bruchus pisorum*); **—овище** *n.* pea field; **—овник** *m.* (bot.) gram chickpea (*Cicer arietinum*); locust tree (*Robinia*); **—овский** *a.* (geog.) Gorokhov.

горохо/вый *a.* pea; pea-green; **г. камень** (min.) aragonitic oölite; (petr.) coarse oölitic limestone; **—вая руда** pea ore; **—лущитель** *m.* pea sheller; **—мойка** *f.* pea washer; **—плодный** *a.* pea-fruited, pisiferous; **—утомление** *n.* pea soil depletion.

горочный *a. of* **горка.**

горош/ек *m. dim. of* **горох;** pea coal; (bot.) vetch (*Vicia*); **гравий —ком** pea gravel; **—ин(к)а** *f.* a pea; (mal.) pea clam (*Pisidium*); **—ковый** *a.* pea; **—чатый** *see* **гороховидный.**

горсейксит *m.* (min.) gorceixite.

горский *a.* mountain.

горст *m.* (geol.) horst, uplift.

горсть *f.* handful.

горсфордит *m.* (min.) horsfordite.

гортан/но— *prefix* (anat.) laryngo—; **—ный** *a.* laryngeal; **—ь** *f.* larynx.

гортензия *f.* (bot.) hydrangea.

гортикультура *f.* horticulture.

гортон/олит *m.* (min.) hortonolite; **—сфера** *f.* (gas) Hortonsphere.

горца *gen. of* **горец.**

горч/авка, —авка *see* **горечавка; —айший** *a.* most bitter; worst; **—ак** *m.* (bot.) smartweed (*Polygonum hydropiper*); gentian (*Gentiana*); Acroptilon; Picris; Sophora; (ichth.) bitterling (*Rhodeus*); **—е** *comp. of* **горький,** more bitter; **—инка** *f.* bitter taste; **—ить** *v.* make bitter; have a bitter taste.

горч/ца *f.,* **—чный** *a.* mustard (*Synapis*); **—чник** *m.* mustard plaster; **—чный газ** mustard gas, dichlorodiethyl sulfide.

горшечник *m.* potter; **круг —а, станок —а** potter's wheel.

горш/ечный, —ковый *a.* pot, potter's; potted (plants); **г. камень** potstone, impure talcose rock; **г. товар** pottery, earthenware; **г. шлак** (met.) first-run slag; **—ечная глина** potter's clay; **—ечная мельница** barrel mill; **—ечная печь** potter's kiln; **—кообразный** *a.* pot-shaped; **—кообразный круг** pot (grinding) wheel; **—ок** *m.* pot, vessel; (steam) trap; **—очек** *dim. of* **горшок;** (seed-starting) cube.

горы *gen., pl. of* **гора.**

горынский *a.* (geog.) Goryn.

горьк/ий *a.* bitter; **—ая настойка, —ие капли** bitters; **—ая соль** Epsom salts, magnesium sulfate heptahydrate; **—ое вещество** bitter principle; **—лый** *a.* rancid, rank; grown bitter; **—нуть** *v.* become bitter; grow rancid or rank; **—о** *adv.* bitterly; *prefix* picr(o)— [bitter; (chem.) picric; (min.) containing magnesium]; **—оватый** *a.* somewhat bitter, bitterish; **—оводный** *a.* bitter water; **—овский** *a.* (geog.) Gorki.

горько/зём *m.,* **—земистый** *a.* magnesia.

горько/миндальный *a.* bitter-almond; **—плодный** *a.* bitter-fruited; **—сладкий** *a.* bitter-sweet; **—солёный** *a.* acrid; **—сть** *f.* bitterness.

горькуша *f.* (bot.) Saussurea.

горюнский *a.* (geog.) Goryun.

горюч/ее *n.* fuel, combustible; (rocket) propellant; **газовое г.** gaseous fuel; fuel gas; **на ядерном —ем** nuclear-powered; **твёрдое г.** solid fuel; **—е-смазочный материал** fuels and lubricants; **—есть** *f.* combustibility, inflammability.

горюч/ий *a.* combustible, inflammable; **г. газ** fuel gas; flue gas; **г. материал** fuel; **—ее масло** fuel oil; **—ие ископаемые** fossil fuels.

горя *pr. ger. of* **гореть; gen. of гope.**

горяче/катаный *a.* hot-rolled; **—ломкий** *a.* (met.) hot-short; **—ломкость** *f.* hot-shortness, hot-short state; **—прессовый** *a.* shrink (fit); **—спелый** *a.* (met.) too hot; (of iron) kishy; **—тянутый** *a.* (met.) hot-drawn; **—чный** *a.* burning, feverish; **—чный бред** (med.) delirium.

горяч/ий *a.* hot; hot-air (drying); (nucl.) hot, highly radioactive; soldered (joint); **—ая камера** (nucl.) hot cell; **—а посадка** (mach.) shrink fit; **—ить** *v.* warm, heat; excite; **—ка** *f.* (med.) fever; **белая —ка** delirium tremens; **гнилая —ка** typhus; **—ность** *f.* warmth, fervor, zeal; (zool.) oestrus, heat; **—о** *adv.* warmly, hotly; eagerly.

горящий *a.* burning.

гос— *prefix* State; **—банк** *m.* State bank; **-во** *abbr.* (государство); **—издат** *m.* State publishing house.

гасларит *m.* (min.) goslarite.

гос/лесфонд *m.* State forests, national forest; **—лов** *m.* State fishery.

ГосНИИ. . . . *see* **ГНИИ. . .**

госпитал/изация *f.* hospitalization; **—изированный** *a.* hospitalized; **—изировать** *v.* hospitalize, admit to a hospital; **—ь** *m.* hospital; **походный —ь** ambulance; **—ьный** *a.* hospital; nosocomial (disease).

госплан *m.* State planning committee.

господств/о *n.,* **—ование** *n.* domination, dominance, supremacy, prevalence; **—овать** *v.* (pre)dominate, prevail; govern; **—ующий** *a.* (pre)dominant, dominating, prevailing, prevalent.

гос/предприятие *n.* State enterprise; **—распределение** *n.* State distribution; **—санинспекция** *f.* State sanitary inspection.

госсип/ин *m.* gossypin; **—иновый** *a.* gossypic (acid); **—оза** *f.* gossypose, raffinose; **—ол** *m.* gossypol.

гос/служащий *m.* State employee; **—снабжение** *n.* State supply; **—сортучасток** *m.* State strain-testing station; **—строй** *m.* State construction committee.

ГОСТ, гост *abbr.* (Государственный общесоюзный стандарт) State Standard.

госта *f.* (bot.) Hosta.

гост/евой *a. of* **гость; —еприимный** *a.* hospitable; **—иница** *f.* hotel; **—иница для автотуристов** motel; **—иный** *a.* visitor's, guest.

гостированный *a.* according to State standards.

гостить *v.* visit, stay (with).

госторг *m.* State export and import office; **—овля** *f.* State trade.

гость *m.* guest, visitor; (min.) metasome.

государств/енный *a.* state; government, public; national; federal; official (test); **—о** *n.* state; government.

гос/университет *m.* State University; **—учреждение** *n.* State institution; **—хоз** *m.* State economy; State farm.

гот/ика *f.* (phyt.) spindle tuber disease; **—ический** *a.* Gothic; **—ландий, —ландский** *a.* (geol.) Gothlandian.

готов *sh. m. of* **готовый; —альник** *m.,* **—альня** *f.* set or case of drawing instruments.

готовик *m.* honeysuckle (*Lonicera tatarica*).

готов/ить *v.* prepare, make ready; train; cook, make; lay in, provide; **—иться** *v.* prepare, get ready; be imminent; **—ность** *f.* readiness; (comp.) availability; **—о** *adv. and sh. n. of* **готовый; —ый** *a.* ready, prepared; willing; ready-made, off-the-shelf; (pre)fabricated; finished, final; cooked (food); **—ая продукция** finished output; **в —ом виде** ready for use.

гофер *m.* (mam.) gopher (*Geomys; Thomomys*).

гофереллёз *m.* (vet.) hoferellosis, Hoferellus infection.

гоферовые *pl.* (mam.) Geomyidae.

гофманский *a.* Hoffman (clamp; drops); Hofmann (reaction).

Гофмейстера ряд Hofmeister series.

гофр *m.,* **—а** *f.* corrugation, crimp; corrugated metal sheet.

гофриров/альный *a.,* **—ание** *n.* crimping, etc., *see v.;* **—анный** *a.* crimped, etc., *see v.;* **—анная мембрана,** **—анная трубка** bellows; **—ать** *v.* crimp (wire, cloth, etc.); corrugate (iron); emboss, goffer, flute (fabric, paper); **—ка** *see* **гофрирование.**

гофрить *see* **гофрировать.**

гош *a.* gauche, twisted, skew.

Гоше болезнь (med.) Gaucher's disease.

гошкорнит *m.* (min.) hauchecornite.

г-пуаз *abbr.* (гектопуаз) hectopoise.

г-р *abbr.* (грамм-рентген) gram-roentgen; **гр.** *abbr.* (градус; гражданин, гражданка, гражданский; грамм; греческий; группа); **ГР (гормон роста)** growth hormone.

граафов пузырёк (anat.) Graafian follicle.

граб *m.* (bot.) hornbeam (*Carpinus*).

грабарь *m.* excavator.

грабель/ки *pl.* (bot.) heron's bill (*Erodium*); **—ная** *f.* screen and crusher building; **—ник** *see* **грабельки;** **—ный** *a.* of **грабли;** raking.

грабен *m.* (geol.) graben.

грабин/а, **—ник** *see* **граб; —ный** *a.* of **граб.**

грабит/ельский *a.* predatory; exorbitant; **—ь** *v.* rob, plunder; rake.

грабл/ение *n.* raking; **—и** *pl.* rake, rabble; (concentration classifier) ladder; **—и-волокуша** *pl.* hay rake; **—ина** *f.* (hay) rack; (reel) bar; **—и-ползуны** *pl.* hay rake.

граб/няк, **—овник** *m.* hornbeam forest; **—овый** *a.* of **граб.**

грабшти/к, **—х(ель)** *m.* burin, graver.

гравел/истый *a.* gravelly; **—ит** *m.* gritstone; gravelite.

гравёр *m.* engraver; (ent.) Pityogenes.

грави— *prefix* gravimetric; gravitation.

гравие/ловка *f.* gravel trap; **—мойка** *f.* gravel washer; **—сортировка** *f.* gravel sorter, gravel classifier; gravel sorting.

гравий *m.* gravel, grit; **—ный** *a.* gravel(ly), gritty, tophaceous.

гравилат *m.,* **—ный** *a.* (bot.) Geum.

гравиметр *m.* gravimeter; **—ический** *a.* gravimetric; **—ия** *f.* gravimetry.

гравиразведка *f.* gravitation prospecting.

гравировальн/ый *a.* engraving; **г. станок** engraver; **—ая доска** (copper or steel) plate; **—ая игла** style, etching needle.

гравиров/альщик *m.* engraver; **—ание** *n.* engraving, etc., *see v.;* **—анный** *a.* engraved, etc., *see v.;* (min.) glyptic; sculptured; **—ать** *v.* engrave, etch, cut, carve; **—ка** *see* **гравирование;** legend.

гравистый *a.* gravelly.

гравитац/ионный *a.* gravitation(al), gravity; turbidity (current); **—ионная сортировка** (min.) gravity concentration; **—ия** *f.* gravitation; gravity concentration.

гравит/ирующий *a.* gravitating; **—он** *m.* graviton, gravitation quantum; **—оплан** *m.* (av.) gravity plane.

гравюра *f.* engraving, print, cut; (die) impression; etching.

Грагама закон *see* **Греэма закон.**

град *m.* hail; shower, volley; (centesimal) grade; *abbr.* (**градус**).

град. *abbr.* (**градус**) degree.

г-рад *abbr.* (**грамм-рад**) gram-rad.

град/ация *f.* gradation, grading, scale; shading, shade; (quantizing) level; **—ер** *m.* grader; **—иент** *m.,* **—иентный** *a.* gradient, grade, slope; grad; (temperature) lapse rate; **вертикальный —иент** lapse rate; **—иентометр** *m.* gradiometer; (surv.) gradienter.

градина *f.* hail(stone).

градинка *f.* chalaza (of bird's egg).

градир/ный *a.* graduation, evaporation; **г. аппарат** graduator; **—ня** *f.* graduating tower; (water) cooling tower; **—ование** *n.,* **—овка** *f.* graduation, evaporation; **—овать** *v.* graduate, evaporate.

град/м *abbr.* (**градус на метр**) degree(s) per meter.

градо— *prefix* hail; city; **—битие** *n.,* **—бой** *m.,* **—бойный** *a.* hail damage, hail storm; **—вой** *a.* hail; **—м** *adv.* in a shower; thick and fast; **—строительство** *n.* city designing and building.

граду/атор *m.* graduator; (elec.) induction coil; **—ирование** *n.* graduation, etc., *see v.;* **—ированный** *a.* graduated, etc., *see v.;* **—ированный диск** dial, face; **—ировать** *v.* graduate, calibrate, scale, grade; rate; divide; standardize, gage; **—ировка** *see* **градуирование;** calibrations, graduation lines; **—ировочный** *a.* calibration; calibrated.

градус *m.,* **—ный** *a.* degree; grade; **—ник** *m.* thermometer; **—ная сетка** (geod.) graticule, reticule; (maps) grade grid; **—одень** *m.* (meteor.) degree day.

граждан/ин *m.,* **—ка** *f.* citizen; **—ский** *a.* civil; civic; **—ское строительство** civil engineering; **—ство** *n.* citizenship.

грайворон *see* **грач.**

грайский *a.* (geog.) Graian (Alps).

грам— *prefix* phonograph, record(ing); **—запись** *f.* sound track; disc recording.

грам/ин *m.* gramine, donaxine; **—ология** *f.* (bot.) graminology; **—ицидин** *m.* gramicidin.

грамм *m.* gram; **г.,** **—а** *f. suffix* —gram; diffraction pattern.

граммат/ика *f.* grammar; **—ит** *m.* (min) grammatite, tremolite; **—ический** *a.* grammatical.

грамм/-атом *m.* gram-atom; **г.-ион** *m.* gram-ion; **г.-калория** *f.* gram-calorie; **г.-молекула** *f.* grammolecule, mole; **—овый** *a.* gram; **—олекулярный** *a.* grammolecular, molar; **—ометр** *m.* gram gage.

граммофон *m.,* **—ный** *a.* phonograph.

грамм—рад *m.* (nucl.) gram-rad; **г.-рентген** *m.* gram-roentgen; **г.-сантиметр** *m.* gram-centimeter; **г.-сила** *f.* gram force; **г.-эквивалент** *m.* gram-equivalent.

грамовые *pl.* (ichth.) Grammidae.

грамот/а *f.* reading and writing; charter, record; deed; certificate; **—ность** *f.* literacy; competence; **—ный** *a.* literate; competent.

грамотрицательный *a.* (bact.) Gram-negative.

грампластинка *f.* phonograph record.

грамположительный *a.* (bact.) Gram-positive.

гран *m.* grain (64.8 mg); **—а** *f.* grain, granule, particle.

гранадилла *f.* granadilla (fruit).

гранат *m.* (min.) garnet; (bot.) *see* **гранатник; благородный г.** (min.) carbuncle, red garnet; **чёрный г.** black garnet, melanite.

граната *f.* grenade, shell; heating mortar.

гранатанин *m.* granatanine, 1,5-iminocyclooctane.

гранатизированный *a.* (min.) garnetized.

гранат/ка *f.* pomegranate (fruit); granatka (sodium chloride); **—ник** *m.* pomegranate (*Punica granatum*); **—ный** *a.* (min.) garnet; (bot.) pomegranate.

гранато— *prefix* (min.) garnet; (chem.) granato—; (mil.) grenade; **—во-красный** *a.* puniceous, purplish red; garnet-red; **—вые** *pl.* (bot.) Punicaceae; **—вый** *see* **гранатный;** puniceous; **—дубильный** *a.* granatotannic (acid); **—мёт** *m.* grenade launcher or thrower; **—подобный** *a.* garnet-like; **—уловитель** *m.* grenade pit; **—эдр** *m.* rhombododecahedron.

грандидиерит *m.* (min.) grandidierite.

грандиозн/ость *f.* grandeur, magnificence; **—ый** *a.* grand, magnificent, immense, vast, far-reaching.

Гранд-Кули (geog.) Grand Coulee.

гране/ние *n.* cutting of (gems); **—(н)ный** *a.* cut, faceted; fluted, canted; **—центрированный** *a.* (cryst.) face-centered.

грани *gen., pl., etc., of* **грань.**

гранилит *m.* (petr.) granilite.

гранил/о *n.* cutter; graver, graving tool; **—ьный** *a.* cutting; lapidary; **—ьня** *f.* lapidary works; **—ьщик** *m.* lapidary, gem cutter.

гранистый *a.* faceted.

гранит *m.* (petr.) granite; **—изация** *f.* granitization; **—ит** *m.* (petr.) granitite; **—ный,** **—овый** *a.* granite, granitic.

гранито/видный *a.* (petr.) granitoid, granite-like; **—гнейс** *m.* granite gneiss; **—ид** *m.* granitoid rock; **—идный** *a.* granitoid; **—ль** *m.* a leather substitute; **—подобный** *see* **гранитовидный.**

гранить *v.* cut, grind, facet.

границ/а *f.* boundary (line); (math.) bound; line (of demarcation); dividing line; limit(ation), end, cut-off; threshold; boundary, border; (anat.) limen; margin (of error); (continental) edge; landmark; frontier; (permafrost) table; **г. газа и воды** gas-water surface; **г. раздела** interface; **в —ах** within, in the range (of); **за —ей** abroad; **имеющий общую —у** coterminous (with); **с резкими —ами** *a.* well-defined.

гранич/ащий *a.* adjacent, adjoining, next (to); limiting; frontier (area); **—ение** *n.* demarcation; **—ить** *v.* border (on), be contiguous (to), abut; adjoin, bound; **—ный** *a.* of **граница**; bounding; boundary-bound (body); interfacial; limiting, cut-off; cluster (set); edge (frequency); end (point); grenz (X-rays); fringe (zone); frontier (orbital); **—ный слой** boundary layer, interface; **—ная плоскость** boundary; **—ная частота** limit (ing) frequency; cut-off frequency; **—ное значение** (math.) limiting value; **—ные условия** (math.) boundary conditions.

гранк/а *f.* (typ.) galley proof, slip; (gem) cutting, faceting; **—ореал** *m.* (typ.) board rack.

грано— *prefix* grano— (grain); **—бластовый** *a.* (petr.) granoblastic.

грановитый *a.* faceted.

грано/диорит *m.* (petr.) granodiorite; **—зан** *m.* granosan (seed fungicide).

гранок *gen. pl. of* **гранка.**

грано/лит *m.* (cement) granolith; **—фировый** *a.* (petr.) granophyric.

Гранта топливо Grant's fuel.

гранул/а *f.* granule, small grain, shot; pellet; **—ёз** *m.* (med.) granulosis; **—ёза** *f.* (cyt.) granulosa, follicular cell; **—ёзный** *a.* granulose, granulous; **—ёма** *f.* (med.) granuloma; **—ирование** *n.* granulation; pellet(iz)ing; **—ированность** *f.* granularity; **—ированный** *a.* granulated; granular; pellet(iz)ed; **—ировать** *v.* granulate; pellet(ize); **—ит** *m.* (petr.) granulite; **—итовый** *a.* granulitic; **—оза** *f.* granulose; **—ометрический** *a.* granulometric, grain-size, particle-size; fineness (ratio); grade (analysis); **—ометрический состав** particle size distribution; **—ометрия** *f.* granulometry, granularity, screen size; **—оцит** *m.* (cyt.) granulocyte; **—оцитопения** *f.* (med.) granulocytopenia; **—ь** *m.*, **—я** *see* **гранула; —ьный, —ярный** *a.* granular; **—ярноклеточный** *a.* granular cell; **—ятор** *m.*, **—яционная машина** granulator; **—яционный** *a.* granulation; granular; **—яция** *f.* granulation; pellet(iz)ing; *pl.* granular tissue.

гран/ь *f.* (cryst.) facet, face; side, plane; edge (of tool); border, margin; (math.) bound; distinction; **—ью, —ями** facetways; **на —и** on the verge (of).

граптолит *m.* graptolite (fossil).

Грасгофа критерий Grashof number.

грассманов/ский, —ый *a.* Grassman.

грат *m.* bur, fin, edge, ridge, barb; (welding, plastics) flash.

гратиол/ин *m.* gratiolin; **—овый** *a.* gratioloic (acid).

гратосниматель *m.* flash trimmer.

грауваkk/а *f.,* **—овый** *a.* (petr.) graywacke.

граф *m.* graph; flow sheet; *prefix* graph— (drawing, writing); *m. suffix* —graph; **—графер**.

графа *f.* column (of a table); paragraph; range; (linear) complex.

графе/кон, —хон *m.* (electron.) graphecon (storage tube).

график *m.* graph, plot, curve; diagram; chart; (time) table; schedule; flow sheet; graphical representation; **в виде**

—а graphically; **представлять в виде —а** *v.* plot; **составлять г.** *v.* schedule; **укладываться в г.** *v.* be on schedule, keep schedule; **—а** *f.* graphics; graphing, plotting; **машинная —а** computer graphics.

графил/ка *f.* marking tool, scratch awl; **—ьный** *a.* marking, ruling.

графин *m.* decanter, bottle.

графит *m.* graphite, black lead; **—изация** *f.*, **—(из)ирование** *n.* graphitization; coating with graphite; **—(из)ированный** *a.* graphitized; **—(из)ировать** *v.* graphitize; **—истый** *a.* graphitic; **—ит** *m.* (petr.) graphitite; **—(н)о-водяной** *a.* graphite-water (nuclear reactor); **—ный, —овый** *a.* graphite, graphitic; lead (pencil); **—ная спель** (met.) kish, graphite segregations; **—овая кислота** graphitic acid; **—оид** *m.* graphitoid (a bitumen); **—ообразный** *a.* graphitic; **—опласт** *m.* graphite-reinforced plastics.

граф/ить *v.* rule, draw lines; (math.) graph; **—ически** *adv.* graphically; **—ический** *a.* graphic, diagrammatic, schematic; eutectic (texture); *suffix* —graphic; diffraction; **—ическая характеристика** curve; **—ическое изображение** graphic representation, diagram; **—ия** *f. suffix* —graphy; diffraction; **—ление** *n.* ruling; (math.) graphing; **—ле(н)ный** *a.* ruled; divided into columns.

графо— *prefix* grapho— (writing); **—аналитический** *a.* graphic-analytical; **—логия** *f.* graphology; **—механический** *a.* graphic mechanical; **—опостроитель** *m.* plotter; **—статика** *f.* graphostatics.

графство *n.* county; shire.

графтонит *m.* (min.) graftonite.

графт-полимер *m.* graft polymer; **—изация** *f.* graft polymerization; **г.-сополимер** *m.* graft copolymer.

грахемит *m.* (min.) grahamite.

граци/альный *a.* delicate, thin; **—альность** *f.* delicacy; **—лария** *f.* (bot.) Gracilaria; **—лярии** *pl.* (ent.) Gracilariidae.

грач *m.,* **—иный** *a.* (orn.) rook (*Corvus frugilegus*); **—онок** *m.* young rook.

ГРД *abbr.* (**гидрореактивный двигатель**) hydrojet (engine).

грёб *past m. sing. of* **грести.**

гребёнка *f.* comb; rack; rack-shaped cutter; chaser, chasing tool; manifold; (text.) hackle; (tel.) distributing block.

гребенник *m.* (bot.) Cynosurus.

гребенной *a. of* **гребень.**

гребенский *a.* (geog.) Greben.

гребенчат/ка *f.* (mal.) Cristaria plicata; **—о—** *prefix* pectinato—, pectinate; cristato—, cristate, crested; **—озубые** *pl.* (mal.) pelecypods (*Taxodonta*); **—оногие** *pl.* (crust.) Stenopoda; **—оусые** *pl.* (ent.) lamellicorn beetles; **—ый** *a.* comb(-like), comb-shaped, cristate, pectinate, pectineal; ctenoid (scale); (mech.) collar, thrust, cam (journal).

гребенщик *m.* (bot.) tamarisk (*Tamarix*); **—овые** *pl.* Tamaricaceae; **—овый** *a.* tamarisk; comb, crest.

греб/ень *m.* comb; summit, peak, crown, ridge (of hill); crest (of wave); (anat.) crista, crest, ridge; collar, flange (of wheel); ledge; hackle (for flax); (weaving) lease reed; (meteor.) wedge; **врубка —нем** cogged joint.

греб/ёт *pr. 3 sing. of* **грести; —ец** *m.* rower; (ent.) diving beetle (*Platambus*).

гребеш/ковый *a.* crested, cristate; pectineal (muscle); **—ок** *m.* comb; crest, crista; (anat.; zool.) pecten; hatch; ridge; (commutator) riser, lug; (mal.) scallop (*Chlamys; Pecten*); **морские —ки** (mal.) (*Pectinidae*); **—очек** *dim. of* **гребешок.**

греб/ковый *a.* of **гребок**; hoe-type; **—ление** *n.* (flax) hackling; **—ли** *gen.* of **гребля**; *past pl.* of **грести**; **—ло** *n.* strickle; paddle, oar; *past n. sing.* of **грести**; **—ля** *f.* raking; rowing; embankment, dike; **—ляки** *pl.* (ent.) water boatmen (*Corixidae*).

гребне— *prefix* loph(o)— (crest, tuft); **—вание** *n.* (agr.) ridging; **—видный** *a.* comb-shaped, pectinate, cristiform; ridge-like, narrow-based (terrace); **—вик** *m.* (bot.) dog's-tail grass (*Cynosurus*); **—вики** *pl.* (zool.) Ctenophora; **—вой** *a.* of **гребень**, comb; ridge; *see also* **гребневидный**; **—голов** *m.* tilefish (*Lopholatilus chamaeleonticeps*); **—держатель** *m.* comb holder; **—зуб** *m.* (ichth.) shark (*Hexanchus griseus; Heptranchias perlo*); **—мышиные** *pl.* (mam.) Ctenomyidae; **—образователь** *m.* (agr.) ridger; **—отделитель** *m.* grape stemmer; **—палые** *pl.* (mam.) gundis (*Ctenodactylidae*); **—подобный** *see* **гребневидный**; **—ротые** *pl.* (zool.) Rhabdocoela; **—укладчик** *m.* (agr.) ridge filler; **—усые** *pl.* (ent.) Lucanidae; **—хвостые** *pl.* (mam.) Dasyuridae; **—чесальный** *a.*, **—чесание** *n.* (text.) combing; **—щуковые** *pl.* (ichth.) Ctenoluciidae.

гребни *pl.* of **гребень**; cristae; spinae; **—стость** *f.* (agr.) ridge; unevenness; **—стый** *a.* ridge (plowing).

гребн/ой *a.* paddle; rowing; propelling, propeller; **г. винт** (screw) propeller; **—ая установка** propeller drive; **—уть** *see* **грести**.

гребня *gen.* of **гребень**.

гребок *m.* rake(r), rabble, hoe; paddle; strickle; stroke (of paddle).

гревиллея *f.* (bot.) Grevillea.

гревия *f.* (bot.) Grewia.

грегамит *m.* (min.) grahamite.

грегарины *pl.* (prot.) Gregarinida.

Грегема закон *see* **Греэма закон.**

греет *pr. 3 sing.* of **греть.**

греж *m.*, **—а** *f.* raw silk, greige.

Грейама *see* **Греэма.**

грейдер *m.*, **—ный** *a.* (road) grader.

грейзен *m.*, **—овый** *a.* (petr.) greisen; **—изация** *f.* greisenization.

грейнахеровский *a.* Greinacher.

грейпфрут *m.* grapefruit (*Citrus paradisi*).

Грейт-фолс (geog.) Great Falls.

грейфер *m.* grab, clamshell; gripper, grapple; grab bucket; scoop; **—ный** *a.* grab (crane, etc.); clamshell (excavator).

грел *past m. sing.* of **греть; —ка** *f.* heater; heating pad; hot-water bottle.

греметь *v.* fulminate, detonate; rattle, clank; rumble, thunder; resound.

гремуче/кислый *a.* fulminic acid; fulminate (of); **—кислая ртуть** mercury fulminate; **—кислая соль** fulminate; **—медная кислота** cuprofulminic acid; **—медная соль** cupric fulminate; **—ртутная соль** mercury fulminate.

гремуч/ий *a.* fulminating, detonating, explosive; thundering, roaring, rattling; rattle (snake); **г. воздух** (mining) firedamp; **г. газ** detonating gas, specif. oxyhydrogen gas; **г. камень** (min.) eaglestone; **г. сахар** (expl.) nitrosaccharose; **г. студень** nitrogelatin, blasting gelatin; **—ая кислота** fulminic acid; **соль —ой кислоты** fulminate; **—ая ртуть** fulminating mercury, mercury fulminate; **—ая хлопчатая бумага** pyroxylin; **—ее золото** fulminating gold, aurodiamine.

грем/учка *f.* rattle; **—учник** *m.* rattlesnake; **—учники** *pl.* (herp.) Crotalidae; **—ушка** *f.* rattle; **—ящий** *a.* rattling.

грена *pl.* silkworm eggs.

гренадерка *f.* (orn.) crested tit (*Parus cristatus*).

гренаж *m.*, **—ный** *a.* silkworm breeding.

гренай *m.* (met.) buckshot cinder.

гренария *f.* silkworm nursery.

гренвильский *a.* (geol.) Grenville.

грензавод *m.* silkworm nursery.

гренирование *n.* (typ.) backing.

гренланд/ия *f.* (bot.) Groenlandia; **Г.** (geog.) Greenland; **—ский** *a.* Greenland(ic).

гренок *m.* rusk, toast (bread).

гренпроизводство *n.* silkworm production.

грест/и, —ь *v.* rake; row, paddle, pull.

греть *v.* heat, warm.

Греффе метод (math.) Graeffe's method.

грех *m.* sin, fault.

Греца критерий Graetz number.

Греция Greece.

грецкий *a.* Greek; **г. орех** walnut.

грецовский *a.* Grätz, bridge (rectifier).

греча *see* **гречиха.**

греческий *a.* Greek.

греч/иха *f.* buckwheat (*Fagopyrum*); **красильная г.** (bot.) polygony (*Polygonum tinctorium*); **—ишка** *f.*, **—ишник** *m.* knotweed (*Polygonum*); **—ишные** *pl.* buckwheat family (*Polygonaceae*); **—ишный** *a.* buckwheat; **—ище** *n.* buckwheat field; **—ка** *see* **гречиха; —невый** *a.* buckwheat.

грешить *v.* err, make a mistake; sin.

Греэма закон Graham law.

греэмит *m.* (min.) grahamite.

греющий *pr. act. part.* of **греть.**

гриб *m.* mushroom; fungus; toadstool; *pl.* fungi; **белый г.** white mushroom (*Boletus edulis*); **морской г.** (zool.) marine sponge (*Tentorium*); **—ы-водоросли** Phycomycetes; **сумчатые —ы** Ascomycetes; **учение о —ах** mycology.

грибк/и *pl.* of **грибок**; fungi; **—овый** *a.* mushroom (-like), fungous, fungoid; fungic (acid); (med.) mycotic.

гриб/ница *f.* mushroom spawn; mycelium; **—ной** *a.* of **гриб**; fungal, fungous; **—ной сахар** mycose; **—овидный** *a.* mushroom(-shaped), fungiform; fungoid; **—овики** *pl.* (ent.) Erotylidae; **—оводство** *n.* mushroom culture; **—оед** *m.* mycetophage, fungivore; **—ожил** *m.* mushroom beetle; **—ок** *dim.* of **гриб**; fungus; mold; (valve) head; (atomizer) cone; **—окорень** *m.* (bot.) mycor(r)hiza; **—ообразный** *see* **грибовидный; —остойкий** *a.* fungus-resistant; **—остойкость** *f.* fungus resistance; **—ы-водоросли** *pl.* Phycomycetes.

грива *f.* crest, ridge; (zool.) mane; **—чевые** *pl.* manefishes (*Caristiidae*).

гривенник *m.* 10-kopeck piece.

грив/астый, —истый *a.* (long-)maned; hairy.

гривка *f.* (art.) battle sight.

гриво— *prefix* chaet(o)— (hair, mane).

Гривс-Этчеля печь Greaves-Etchell furnace (for steel).

григорианский *a.* Gregorian (calendar).

гридлик *m.* (rad.) grid leak.

гризе/ин *m.* grisein; **—офульвин** *m.* griseofulvin (antibiotic).

гриз/ли *m.* (min.) grizzly; (mam.) grizzly bear (*Ursus horribilis*); **—он** *m.* (mam.) Grison.

гризутин *m.* granulated dynamite.

грилз *m.* (ichth.) grilse.

гриллоблаттиды *pl.* (ent.) Grylloblattidae.

грильяж *m.* roasting; roasted, sugared nuts.

грим *m.* cosmetics; **—асничать** *v.* grimace; **—ировальное вещество** cosmetic; **—ировать** *v.* apply cosmetics.

грин/алит *m.* (min.) greenalite; **—вичский** *a.* Greenwich (time).

гринда *f.* (mam.) pilot whale [*Globi(o)cephala*].

гриндел/ия *f.* gum plant, tar weed (*Grindelia*); **—оид** *m.* grindeloid.

гринель *f.* broom straw.

грино/вит *m.* (min.) greenovite; **—вый** *a.* Green('s); **—кит** *m.* (min.) greenockite.

гринсбон *m.* (text.) gingham.

гринхарт *m.* greenheart (rain forest).

гриньяровский *a.* Grignard (reaction).

гриот *m.* griotte (a morello cherry).

грипп *m.,* **—озный** *a.* (med.) grippe, influenza, flu.

грисбок *m.* (mam.) grysbok (*Raphicerus melanotis*).

Грисгейма красный Griesheim red.

Грисса реактив Griess reagent.

грит *m.* grit.

гриф *m.* (rubber) stamp; (security) classification; touch, feel, handle; (music) fingerboard, neck; facsimile signature, signature stamp; (orn.) vulture.

грифа *f.* grifa, lithium acetyl salicylate.

грифел/евидный *a.* styloid, pillar-like; **—ёк** *m.* stylus; **—ь** *m.* slate; slate pencil; pencil lead; **—ька** *f.* stylus; **—ьный** *a.* of **грифель;** (anat.) splint (bones); **—ьный сланец** (geol.) grapholite, writing slate; **—ьная доска** slate.

гриф-индейка *m.* (orn.) turkey buzzard (*Cathartes aura*).

грифит *m.* (min.) griphite.

грифолин *m.* grifolin.

гриффит/ит *m.* (min.) griffithite; **—овые белила** Griffith white, lithopone.

гр-ка *abbr.* (**гражданка**); **гр-н** (**гражданин**) citizen; **гр-не** (**граждане**) citizens.

гроб *m.,* **—овой** *a.* coffin, casket; flask.

Грове элемент (elec.) Grove cell.

гродненский *a.* (geog.) Grodno.

гроза *f.* (thunder)storm.

грозд/евидный, —еобразный *a.* botryoidal, grape-like, in grape-like clusters; (biol.) racemose; **—екокк** *m.* (bact.) staphylococcus; **—ный** *a. of* **гроздь; —овник** *m.* (bot.) Botrychium; **—овый** *a.,* **—ь** *f.* cluster, bunch, raceme.

гроз/ен *sh. m. of* **грозный; —ить** *v.* threaten, menace.

грозненский *a.* (geog.) Grozny.

грозный *a.* threatening, menacing.

грозов/ой *a.* (thunder)storm, stormy; **г. воротник** roll cloud, arcus; **г. разрядник** lightning arrester; **г. шквал** thunder-squall; **—ое облако** thundercloud, cumulo-nimbus.

грозозащ/ита *f.* lightning protection; lightning protector; **—ищённый** *a.* lightning-proof.

грозо/отметчик *m.* storm indicator; **—писец** *m.* (meteor.) brontograph; **—разрядник** *m.* lightning arrester; **—регистратор** *m.* lightning recorder; **—стойкий, —упорный** *a.* lightning-proof.

грозящий *a.* threatening, imminent, impending.

гром *m.* thunder(ing); (ichth.) a roach.

громад/а *f.* mass, bulk; heap, pile; **—ина** *f.* huge thing; **—ность** *f.* hugeness, vastness, enormity; **—ный** *a.* huge, vast, enormous, large, immense.

громить *v.* destroy, smash, crush, wreck; rout, raid, loot.

громк/ий *a.* loud, noisy; **—о** *adv.* loudly; **—оговоритель** *m.* (rad.) loudspeaker; **—оговорящий** *a.* loud, loudspeaker; **—ость** *f.* loudness, volume.

громо/вой *a.* thunder(ous); **—вая стрела** thunderbolt; fulgurite, lightning tube.

громозд/ить *v.* heap up, stack, pile up; **—иться** *v.* tower, rise; **—кий** *a.* cumbersome, unwieldy, awkward,

clumsy, inconvenient; bulky, massive; **—кость** *f.* awkwardness; bulk; **—ок** *m.* bulk.

громок *sh. m. of* **громкий.**

громоотвод *m.,* **—ный** *a.* lightning rod; (text.) Gromootvod (antistatic).

громошторм *m.* thunderstorm.

громче *comp. of* **громкий, громко** louder.

громыхать *v.* rumble, rattle.

гророилит *m.* (min.) groroilite.

гросс *m.* gross (twelve dozen).

гросса *f.* (zool.) pregnant ewe.

гроссбух *m.* (com.) ledger.

гроссуляр *m.* (min.) grossularite.

грот *m.* grotto, cavern; (naut.) mainsail.

гротеск *m.,* **—ный** *a.* (typ.) grotesque; sans-serif (font).

гротит *m.* (min.) grothite.

грот-мачта *f.* (naut.) mainmast.

грото/вый *a.* grotto, cavern; **—образный** *a.* cavernous; arched (iceberg).

гроупер *m.* (ichth.) grouper.

грох/ать, —нуть *v.* drop with a crash; **—нуться** *v.* crash down; **—от** *m.* crash, rattle, roar; screen, sifter, sieve, riddle, grizzly, grid; **—отать** *v.* rattle, roar, thunder, crash; **—отить** *v.* screen, riddle, sieve, sift, bolt; **—отка** *f.* sieve; **—отнуть** *see* **грохотать; —очение** *n.* screening, etc., *see v.;* **—оченый** *a.* screened, etc., *see v.;* **—очущий** *a.* rattling, etc., *see* **грохотать.**

ГРП *abbr.* (**газораспределительный пункт**) gas-distributing center; (**гидравлический разрыв пласта**) hydraulic fracturing.

груб *sh. m. of* **грубый.**

груббер(-культиватор) *m.* (agr.) grubber.

груб/еть *v.* roughen, coarsen; **—ить, —иянить** *v.* be rude, insult; **—о** *adv.* roughly, coarsely; broadly; **—оватый** *a.* rather coarse; **—оволокнистый** *a.* coarse-fibered, coarse-grained; **—оволосистый** *a.* rough-haired, shaggy.

грубодисперс/ионный *a.* coarse-dispersion; **—ный** *a.* coarse-disperse, coarsely dispersed; **—ные примеси** suspended solids, colloidal matter.

груб/озернистый *a.* coarse(-grained); **—оизмельчённый** *a.* coarsely ground; **—омозаичный** *a.* (petr.) granoblastic; **—омолотый** *a.* coarsely milled; **—ообломочный** *a.* coarsely fragmental; **—ооднородный** *a.* roughly uniform; **—опятнистый** *a.* mottled; **—ость** *f.* roughness, coarseness; crudeness; **—ошёрстный** *a.* rough-haired, shaggy; **—ый** *a.* rough, coarse; approximate; crude, raw; gross; clumsy; hard (usage); **—ый корм** roughage.

груд *m.* grud (a kind of forest).

груда *f.* heap, pile, mass, cluster; (anat.) cumulus, mound.

груд/и *gen., etc., of* **грудь; —ина** *f.* (anat.) sternum, breast bone; **—инка** *f.,* **—инковое мясо** (meat) brisket, breast; **—ин(н)о—** *prefix* (anat.) sterno—; **—ин-(н)о-рёберный** *a.* sternocostal; **—инный** *a.* sternal; **—инная кость** sternum; **—ино-ключичный** *a.* sternoclavicular; **—ино-подъязычный** *a.* sternohyoid; **—иночный** *a.* (meat) breast; **—ка** *dim. of* **груда, грудь; —ник** *m.,* **—ника** *f.* (bot.) Abutilon; **—ница** *f.* (med.) mastitis; (text.) breast beam; (bot.) Lynosyris.

грудн/ой *a.* breast, chest, thoracic, pectoral; mammary (gland); **г. проток** (anat.) thoracic duct; **—ая жаба** (med.) angina pectoris; **—ая клетка** (anat.) chest, thorax; **—ая кость** (anat.) breastbone, sternum; **—ая упорка** breast plate; **—ая ягода** (bot.) Rhamnus; Zizyphus; **—ые ножки** (crust.) pereiopods, trunk legs.

грудо— *prefix* (anat.) thoraco— (chest); **—акромиаль-**

ный *a.* thora(ci)coacromial; —**брюшный** *a.* phrenic, diaphragm(atic); —**брюшная перегородка,** —**брюшная преграда** diaphragm, midriff; —**(над)-поясничный** *a.* thoracolumbar.

груд/ь *f.* breast, chest; (ent.) thorax; (blast furnace) front; **область** —**и** pectoral region.

груж/ение *n.* loading, etc., *see* **грузить;** —**ён(н)ый** *a.* loaded.

груз *m.* load, burden, weight; charge; goods, consignment, cargo, freight, shipment, shipload; (pendulum) bob; (mine) plummet; **без** —**а** unladen (weight); empty; **общий г.** gross weight; **с** —**ом** laden (weight); full, loaded; **транспортировка** —**ов** shipping, freight traffic, freight handling.

груз. *abbr.* (**грузинский**) Georgian.

груздь *m.* (bot.) pepper mushroom (*Agaricus* or *Lactarius piperatus*).

груз/ен *sh. m. of* **грузный;** -**заполнитель** *m.* (min.) filler cargo; —**ик** *dim. of* **груз;** weight; —**ило** *n.* plumb (bob, line); weight, lead, sinker, plummet; water gage.

грузинский *a.* Georgian.

грузить *v.* load; freight, ship; handle.

Грузия Georgia.

груз/ка *f.* loading, etc., *see* **грузить;** —**кий** *a.* heavy; —**неть** *v.* get heavy; —**но** *adv.* heavily (laden); —**нуть** *v.* sink; —**ный** *a.* heavy, massive; heavily loaded.

грузо/вик *m.* truck, van, wagon; freight car; **г.-цистерна** tank truck; —**вместимость** *f.* (load-)carrying capacity; (freight) capacity; tonnage.

грузов/ой *a.* load(ing); freight, cargo; shipping; **г. автомобиль** truck; **г. пароход,** —**ое судно** freighter, cargo ship; **г. транспорт,** —**ые перевозки,** —**ое движение** freight traffic; (naut.) shipping.

грузозахват *m.,* —**ное приспособление** load-lifting mechanism, hoisting device; sling.

грузо/напряжённость *f.* freight turnover; —**отправитель** *m.* consigner; -**пассажирский** *a.* passenger and freight.

грузоподъёмн/ик *m.* freight elevator; load lifter; —**ость** *f.,* —**ая способность** lifting capacity, lifting power; (load) capacity, carrying capacity; tonnage; —**ый** *a.* load-lifting, hoist(ing); —**ый кран** crane, derrick; —**ая машина** elevator; —**ая петля** sling; —**ая тележка** hoist trolley; —**ая цепь** chain sling; —**ое приспособление** lifting tackle.

груз/ополучатель *m.* (com.) consignee; —**опоток** *m.* freight flow, freight traffic; —**оспособность** *f.* capacity; —**охранилище** *n.* warehouse; —**ошина** *f.* truck tire.

грузчик *m.* loader; dock hand, stevedore, longshoreman.

грунд/букса *f.* (journal) box; collar bush(ing), main bush, neck bush(ing); —**роп** *m.* ground line (of trawl).

грунерит *m.* (min.) grunerite.

грунт *m.* ground, bottom; soil, earth, land; (paint) primer, ground coat, undercoat; **закрытого** —**а** hotbed, greenhouse (culture); **открытого** —**а** field (culture); —**лак** *m.* sealer, primer; —**обетон** *m.* sand-clay concrete; —**облок** *m.* earth massif, ground block.

грунтов *m.* tie rod; (naut.) gripe.

грунтов/ание *n.* grounding; (paint) priming; primer; —**ать** *v.* ground; prime, give a first coat; size; (dyeing) bottom; —**едение** *n.* soil science; —**ка** *f.* priming; primer, undercoat, ground coat.

грунто/вой *a. of* **грунт;** ground, subsoil (water); dirt (road); unpaved (airfield); prime (coat); **г. лак** sealer, filler; —**вочный** *a.* priming; —**зацеп** *m.* (wheel)

cleat; (track) grouser, lug; —**мер** *m.* soil density meter; —**нос** *m.,* —**носка** *f.* (min.) core lifter, coring tool, core barrel, sample taker; —**провод** *m.* underground pipeline; —**смеситель** *m.* soil or ground mixer; —**смесительный** *a.* ground-mixing; —**цемент** *m.* soil cement.

грунтроп *see* **грундроп.**

групер *m.* (ichth.) grouper.

групп/а *f.* group, bunch, cluster, batch; complex, set, series, assembly; battery, bank (of machines); block (of words); (chem.) radical; team (of workers); (petr.) tribe, clan; (pal.) phylum; **г. ионов** ion cluster; **метод групп** statistical classification; **разбить на** —**ы** *v.* group; **г.-заместитель** *f.* substituting group.

группиров/ание *n.* grouping, etc., *see v.;* —**анный** *a.* grouped, etc., *see v.;* —**атель** *m.* (electron.) buncher; —**ать** *v.* group (together); classify, tabulate; organize; bank; batch, bunch, concentrate; —**аться** *v.* group (together), gather, cluster; —**ка** *f.* grouping, etc., *see v.;* pooling; alignment; group; (plant) aggregation; —**очный** *a.* group(ed), grouping.

группо/вод *m.* group leader; —**вой** *a. of* **группа;** group(ed); (mach.) gang; aggregate; batch (processing); group selector (relay); (silv.) clear (cutting); institutional, group (home); (elec.) series (connection); **г. адрес** common address (in digital signal processing); —**ая команда** broadcast command; —**выбиратель** *m.* (elec. comm.) group selector.

груст/ить *v.* be sad; —**ный** *a.* melancholy, sad; lamentable; —**ь** *f.* melancholy.

груш/а *f.* (bot.) pear (*Pyrus*); (elec.; spray) bulb; (converter) vessel; **земляная г.** (bot.) Jerusalem artichoke; —**анка** *f.* (bot.) Pyrola; —**евидный,** —**еобразный** *a.* pear-shaped, pyriform; —**евый,** —**овый** *a.* pear; bulb; —**овка** *f.* pear wine.

грыж/а *f.,* —**евой,** —**евый,** —**ный** *a.* (med.) hernia, rupture; *suffix* —**cele** (tumor, swelling), *e.g.,* **г. желудка** gastrocele; —**ная трава,** —**ница** *f.,* —**(ов)ник** *m.* (bot.) Herniaria.

грыз/ение *n.* gnawing; —**ло** *n.* snaffle, bit; —**овой** *a.* edible, table, snack (food); —**ть** *v.* gnaw, nibble; eat; tease, provoke; —**ться** *v.* (zool.) fight; —**ун** *m.* (mam.) rodent; wood beetle; —**уще-сосущий** *a.* (ent.) chewing and sucking; —**ущий** *a.* gnawing, etc., *see v.;* chewing, biting.

Грэм, Грэхем *see* **Грема закон.**

грюн/ерит *m.* (min.) grunerite; —**лингит** *m.* (min.) grünlingite; —**штейн** *m.* (petr.) greenstone.

гряд/а *f.* layer, stratum, bed; ridge, range, chain (of mountains); row; bank (of clouds, etc.); **навозная г., тёплая г.** (agr.) hotbed; —**иль** *m.* (plow) beam; —**ка** *f.,* —**ковый** *a.* (seed) bed, row; ridge; (ladder) step; —**коподъёмник** *m.* ridge digger; —**ной,** —**овой,** —**овый** *a. of* **гряда;** —**оделатель** *m.* (agr.) ridger.

грязе/вик *m.* mud drum, mud box, mud trap; sludge pan, sump, bottom outlet; sediment tank; (ent.) Cercyon; —**воз** *m.* sewage barge; —**вой** *a. of* **грязь;** mud(dy); (med.) mud-bath; —**вой гейзер** (geol.) mud pot; —**лечебница** *f.* mud baths; —**лечение** *n.* pelotherapy, mud-bath treatment; —**н** *sh. m. of* **грязный;** —**отстойник** *see* **грязевик;** cesspool; —**отталкивающий** *a.* soil-repellent; —**очиститель** *see* **грязевик;** —**приёмный** *a.* mud (drum); —**уловитель** *m.* mud trap, dirt collector; sediment tank, catch basin; —**черпалка** *f.* mud dredger.

грязн/еть *v.* get dirty; —**ить** *v.* soil, dirty; pollute, contaminate; —**иться** *v.* get dirty; get contaminated; —**о** *adv. of* **грязный;** *prefix* spil(o)— (spot, stain); —**ова-**

тый *a.* rather dirty, dingy (color); **—ота** *f.* dirtiness; **—ый** *a.* dirty, muddy, soiled; sludgy, slimy, oozy; contaminated, impure.

грязовик *m.* (orn.) sandpiper (*Limicola*).

грязь *f.* dirt; mud, sludge, ooze, slurry; silt, sediment; (cer.) slip; contamination, impurity, pollutant; slime; (centrifugal) residue.

грянуть *v.* break or burst out; ring out.

гс *abbr.* (**гаусс**) gauss; *see* **г-сила**.

ГСВЧ *abbr.* (**генератор сверхвысокой частоты**) superhigh frequency generator.

ГСЗ *abbr.* (**глубинное сейсмическое зондирование**) deep seismic sounding.

г-сила *abbr.* (**грамм-сила**) gram-force.

ГСМ *abbr.* (**горюче-смазочные материалы**) fuels and lubricants.

г-см, Г-см *abbr.* (**грамм-сантиметр**) gram-centimeter.

Г-соль *f.* G acid disodium salt.

ГСП *abbr.* (**глубинное сейсмическое профилирование**) deep seismic profiling.

ГТГ *abbr.* (**гонадотропный гормон**) gonadotropic hormone.

ГТД *abbr.* (**газотурбинный двигатель**) gas turbine engine.

ГТРД *abbr.* (**газотурбинный реактивный двигатель**) gas turbine jet engine.

ГТУ *abbr.* (**газотурбинная установка**) gas turbine installation.

ГУ *abbr.* (**генератор ультразвука**) ultrasonic generator; (**газоубежище**) gasproof shelter; (**государственный университет**) State university; etc.

гуа— *see also under* **гва—**; **—ва** *f.* (bot.) guava (*Psidium guajava*); **—зета** *f.* (ichth.) guaseta, mutton hamlet (*Alphestes afer*); **—йява** *see* **гуава; —камайя** *f.* rainbow parrotfish (*Scarus guacamaia*); **—мский** *a.* (geog.) Guam.

гуаназ/а *f.* guanase; **—ил** *m.* guanazyl.

гуанако *m.* (mam.) guanaco (*Lama guanicoe*).

гуанидин *m.*, **—овый** *a.* guanidine, aminomethanamidine; **—офосфорная кислота** guanidinophosphoric acid, phosphagen; **—уксусный** *a.* guanidinoacetic (acid).

гуан/ил *m.* guanyl; **—иловый** *a.* guanyl; guanylic (acid); **—ин** *m.* guanine, imidoxanthine; **—о** *n.* guano (manure); **—озин** *m.* guanosine, guanine ribonucleiside; **—озинфосфорный** *a.* guanosine phosphoric (acid).

гуар *m.* (bot.) guar(a) (*Lupinus trifoliatus*); **—а** *f.* (mam.) Cerdocyon; **—ана** *f.* (pharm.) guarana; **—анин** *m.* guaranine; **—инит** *m.* (min.) guarinite.

гуа/са *f.* (ichth.) jewfish (*Epinephelus itajara*); **—су** *m.* guasu (tropical rain forest); **—харо** *m.* (orn.) oilbird (*Steatornis caripensis*).

гуацин *m.* guacin.

гуашь *f.* gouache (water color).

гуа/юла, —юле *see* **гваюла; —ява** *f.* (bot.) guava (*Psidium*); **—як** *m.*, **—яковый** *a.* Guaiacum.

губ— *abbr.* (**губернский**) district.

губа *f.* lip; bay, gulf, inlet; jaw (of vise, etc.); (biol.) labium; (naut.) tiller, helm.

губан *m.* (ichth.) common name for several species, e.g. wrasse, round goby, etc.; **—овые** *pl.* wrasses (*Labridae*); **—чик, г.-чистильщик** *m.* cleaner wrasse (*Labroides phthirophagus*).

губарь *m.* (ichth.) Hemibarbus labeo; silver bream (*Blicca bjoerkna*).

губаст/ик *m.* (bot.) Mimulus; **—ый** *a.* thick-lipped; labiate.

губач *m.* (ichth.) common name for several species, e.g. gubach (*Nemachilus strauchi*), thick-lipped mullet, etc.; (mam.) sloth bear (*Melursus ursinus*).

губель *m.* fillister, rabbeting plane.

губерн/ия *f.* district, province; **—ский** *a.* district, regional.

Губерта тормоз Hubert's brake.

губит/ельный *a.* destructive, injurious, lethal, fatal, suicidal; noxious, pernicious; **—ить** *v.* destroy, ruin.

губк/а *f.* sponge; (latex, plastic) foam; (tree) fungus; (phyt.) rot; (vise) jaw; *dim. of* **губа; —оватый** *see* **губчатый; —овидный, —ообразный** *a.* spongiform, sponge-like.

губ/(н)о— *prefix* labio—, lip; **—ной** *a.* lip, labial; **—нонёбный** *a.* labiopalatine; **—овидный** *a.* lip-shaped, labiate; **—овина** *f.* small bay; **—ок** *gen. pl. of* **губка; —оногие** *pl.* (zool.) centipedes (*Chilopoda*); **—оцветковый** *a.* (bot.) labiatiflorous; cheilanthous; **—оцветные** *pl.* Labiatae.

губчат/ость *f.* sponginess; **—ый** *a.* spongy, soft; sponge; blown, porous, cellular; foam (rubber); **—ое железо** sponge iron.

губы *pl., etc.,* *of* **губа; —й** *a. suffix* —labiate.

гувацин *m.* guvacine.

гуд *see* **гудение**.

гуд/айера *f.* (bot.) Goodyera; **—виновский** *a.* Goodwin('s); **—еевые** *pl.* (ichth.) Goodeidae.

гудение *n.* hum(ming), buzz(ing), drone; honk; hooting.

гудерманиан *m.* (math.) Gudermannian.

гудеть *v.* hum, drone, buzz; hoot; honk.

гуджир *m.* salt efflorescence on salt-water ice.

Гудзонов залив (geog.) Hudson Bay.

гуд/иевые *see* **гудеевые; —ировый** *a.* Goodyear.

гудок *m.* horn, siren, whistle, blast; dial tone.

гудриевый *a.* Houdry (catalyst).

гудрон *m.* tar, vacuum resid, heavy resid; asphalt; (acid) sludge; **—атор** *m.* asphalt spreader; road oiler; **—ирование** *n.* asphalting, etc., *see v.;* **поверхностное —ирование** asphalt surfacing; **—ированный** *a.* asphalted, tarred, oiled; **—ировать** *v.* asphalt, tar, oil; **—ный** *a. of* **гудрон**.

гудузия *f.* (ichth.) Gudusia.

гуж *m.* (harness) tug (strap), rope; **—евой** *a.* land (transport); wagon (road); horse-drawn, cart (traffic); **—ик** *m.* bridle (for net, etc.); **—ом** *adv.* by vehicle, by land.

гужон *m.* blunt bolt.

гуза *f.* (bot.) Gossypium; **г.-пая** *f.* guza-paya (cotton plant stalks and bolls).

гузка *f.* wider end (of egg); (stereotype) tang; tail.

гузнек *m.* gooseneck.

гузо/корчевалка *f.*, **—корчеватель, —ломатель** *m.*, **—ломка** *f.* cotton stem uprooter; boll breaker; **—уборочная машина** cotton stem picker.

гуиевский *a.* Gouy (layer).

гуитерманит *m.* (min.) guitermanite.

гуй/и *pl.* (orn.) Callaeidae; **—я** *f.* huia.

гук/ериевые *pl.* (bot.) Hookeriaceae (mosses); **—овский** *a.* Hooke('s) (joint; law).

гул *m.* boom, rumble, din; buzz, hum (of wires); roaring (of wind); **—кий** *a.* hollow, resonant, booming (sound); **—кость** *f.* hollowness, boominess.

гуллер *m.* huller, peeling machine.

Гулль (geog.) Hull.

гуло/за *f.* gulose; **—новый** *a.* gulonic (acid).

Гульдберга и Вааге закон Guldberg and Waage law, law of mass action.

гульман *m.* (mam.) entellus monkey (*Presbytis entellus*).

гульнуть *see* **гулять.**
гульсит *m.* (min.) hulsite.
гулявник *m.* (bot.) Sisymbrium.
гулярдова вода Goulard's extract (solution of basic lead acetate).
гулять *v.* stroll, take a walk; have time off; migrate, wander, drift.
гуляш *m.* (food) goulash.
гумай *m.* (bot.) Johnson grass, Guinea grass (*Sorghum halepense*).
гуман/ист *m.* humanitarian; **—истический** *a.,* **—итар-ные науки** the humanities; **—итарный** *a.* humanitarian; **—ный** *a.* humane.
гумат *m.* humate.
гумбо *n.* gumbo (clay).
гумбольдит *m.* (min.) humboldtine.
гумбрин *m.* gumbrin (bleaching clay).
гумен, гумён *gen. pl. of* **гумно.**
гумённик *m.* bean goose (*Anser fabalis*).
гумённый *a. of* **гумно;** rough (feed).
гум/идный *a.* humid; **—ин** *m.* humin.
гуминов/окислый *a.* humic acid; humate (of); **—окислая соль, соль —ой кислоты** humate; **—ый** *a.* humus, humic, mold; **—ая кислота** humic acid.
гумит *m.* (min.) humite.
гумифи/кация *f.* humification; **—цировать** *v.* humify.
гумма *f.* (med.) gumma (a tumor).
гумми *n.* gum; **—амм(он)иак** *m.* gum ammoniac; **—арабик** *m.* gum arabic; **—балата** *f.* balata; **—гут** *m.* gamboge; **—даммар** *m.* dammar; **—копал** *m.* copal; **—лак** *m.* shellac; **—лаковая кислота** laccaic acid; **—ластик** *m.* (India) rubber.
гуммиров/ание *n.* rubberizing, etc., *see v.;* **—анный** *a.* rubberized, etc., *see v.;* **—ать** *v.* rubberize; line or coat with rubber; gum, coat with adhesive; **—ка** *see* **гуммирование;** rubber coating.
гумми-смола *f.* gummed tar, gum resin.
гуммит *m.* (min.) gummite.
гуммитрагант *m.* tragacanth (gum).
гуммоз *m.* (phyt.) gummosis; **—ный** *a.* gummous, gumlike, gummy.
гуммон *m.* gummon (insulating material).
гумн/ище, —о *n.* (agr.) threshing floor.
гумо/(аммо)фос *m.* humoammophos (fertilizer); **—аммофоска** *f.* humoammophoska (humous ammonia phosphorus fertilizer); **—ген** *m.* humogen (fertilizer); **—лит** *m.* humolite, humic coal; **—ральный** *a.* (biol.) humoral; **—цериновый** *a.* humoceric (acid).
гумул/ин *m.* humulin, lupuline; **—иновый** *a.* humulinic (acid); **—инон** *m.* humulinone; **—одубильный** *a.* humulotannic (acid); **—он** *m.* humulon.
гумус *m.* humus; **—(ирован)ность** *f.* humus content; **—ированный** *a.* humus-enriched; **—ный, —овый** *a.* humus; humic (acid); **—ообразование** *n.* humus formation.
гунгаррит *m.* (min.) hoongarrite.
гунд/аринский *a.* (geog.) Gun-Dara; **—и, —у** *n.* (mam.) gundi (*Ctenodactylus gundi*); *pl.* Ctenodactylidae.
гунит *m.* gunite (cement).
гунтеровский *a.* (med.) Hunter's, hunterian.
гунтовый *a.* (geog.) Gunt.
гуньба *f.* (bot.) Trigonella coerulea.
ГУП *abbr.* (**гамма-установка, передвижная** or **промышленная**) mobile or industrial gamma unit.
гуперовский *a.* Hooper('s).
гуп(п)и *m.* (ichth.) guppy (*Lebistes*).
Гупса процесс (met.) Hoopes process.

гур *m.* (min.) guhr, kieselguhr.
гура *f.* (bot.) Hura; (geol.) butte.
гурами *m.* (ichth.) gourami (*Osphronemus goramy*); **—евые** *pl.* Osphronemidae.
гургофит *m.* (min.) gurhofite.
гуреаулит *m.* (min.) hureaulite.
Гурлера болезнь (med.) Hurler's syndrome.
Гурон Lake Huron.
гурон *m.,* **—ский** *a.* (geol.) Huronian.
гурт *m.* milled edge (of coin); (agr.) herd, flock, drove; **—ик** *m.* milling; **—ить** *v.* mill; **—овой** *a. of* **гурт;** **—овщик** *m.* herdsman; **—ом** *adv.* all together; wholesale.
гурьб/а *f.* crowd; **—ой** *adv.* in a crowd.
гурьевский *a.* (geog.) Guryev.
гурьюн/-бальзам *m.* gurjun (balsam); **—овый** *a.* gurjun (oil); gurjunic (acid).
гусак *m.* gander.
гусар *m.* rider (on a balance); (mam.) Erythrocebus; **—ик** *m.* rider.
гусеводство *n.* goose breeding.
гусевский *a.* the Gus (works).
гус/ей *gen. pl. of* **гусь;** **—ёк** *m.* gosling; (arch.) ogee, flute; bucket (of dam).
гусени/ца *f.* (ent.) caterpillar; (mach.) caterpillar (track), band, belt; **—цевидный** *a.* eruciform, caterpillar-shaped; **—цеедовые** *pl.* (orn.) Conopophagidae; **—целовка** *f.* caterpillar trap; **—цеобразный** *see* **гусеницевидный; прыгающая —чка** (ent.) diamondback moth (*Plutella maculipennis*).
гусеничн/ый *a. of* **гусеница; г. палец** track pin; **г. трактор** caterpillar, crawler; **на —ом ходу** (mounted) on caterpillar tracks.
гус/ёнок *m.* gosling; **—еобразные** *pl.* (orn.) Anseriformes; **—еферма** *f.* goose farm; **—и** *pl.* geese; **—инозерский** *a.* (geog.) Gusinoyo ozero (Goose Lake); **—иные** *pl.* Anserinae; **—иный** *a.* goose, anserine; (geog.) Gusinaya; **—иный лук** (bot.) Gagea; **—иная лапка** cinquefoil (*Potentilla anserina*).
гусматик *m.* safety tire; patching paste.
гуссакит *m.* (min.) hussakite.
густ *sh. m. of* **густой.**
густера *f.* (ichth.) silver bream (*Blicca*).
густ/еть,—иться *v.* thicken, become thick, condense; **—ить** *v.* thicken, make thick, condense, concentrate; boil down.
густо *adv.* thickly, densely; *prefix* pycn(o)— (close, compact, dense); crebri—; densi—; **—ватый** *a.* rather thick, viscous; **—ветвистый** *a.* thick-branched, densely branching; **—волосый** *a.* thick-haired; **—зубчатый** *a.* (bot.) crebridentate.
густой *a.* thick, dense, viscous; stiff (paste); heavy (oil); intimate (mixture); deep, rich (color); bushy (growth); fine (screen); soupy (fog).
густо/лесье *n.* thicket; **—лиственный, —лист(н)ый** *a.* bushy, densely leaved, densifolious; **—насаженный** *a.* thickset, close; **—населённый** *a.* densely populated, high-density (area); **—облиственный** *a.* densely leaved; **—опушённый** *a.* (bot.) hoary, canescent; (orn.) densely pubescent; **—расположенный** *a.* crowded, close together; **—растущий** *a.* bushy, dense, thick-growing; **—та** *f.* thickness, density, viscosity; consistency, body (of oil); depth, richness (of color); spacing, population (of plants); **—текучий** *a.* viscous, ropy, thick; **—тёртый** *a.* ground to a paste; **—цветковый** *a.* densely flowered, pycnanthous.
гус/ыня *f.* goose (female); **—ь** *m.* goose (*Anser*); **—ь-гуменник** *m.* bean goose (*Anser fabalis*);

—ьком *adv.* single file; tandem; **—ятина** *f.* goose meat; **—ятник** *m.* goose pen; **—ятница** *f.* (bot.) prostrate knotweed (*Polygonum aviculare*).

ГУТ *abbr.* (гамма-установка, терапевтическая) therapeutic gamma-unit.

гуталин *m.* leather cleaner; shoe polish.

гутт/а *f.* gutta; **—аперча** *f.*, **—аперчевый** *a.* gutta-percha; **—аперченос** *m.* gutta-percha(-yielding) plant; **—ация** *f.* (bot.) guttation; **—оносный** *a.* guttiferous; **—оносное растение** guttifer.

гутчинсонит *m.* (min.) hutchinsonite.

ГУЧ *abbr.* (габарито-установочный чертёж) mechanical interface drawing.

Гуча тигель Gooch crucible.

гущ/а *f.* dregs, grounds, sediment, residue; mash; thicket; **—е** *comp. of* густой, thicker; **делать —е** *v.* thicken.

гуява *see* гуава.

гф *abbr.* (гребенчатый фильтр) comb filter.

г/х *abbr.* (газоход) gas conduit.

гхариалы *pl.* (herp.) Gavialidae.

ГХЦГ *abbr.* (гексахлорциклогексан) hexachlorocyclohexane.

гц *abbr.* (герц) hertz, cycles per second.

гцк, ГЦК *abbr.* (гранецентрированная кубическая решётка) face-centered cubic lattice, Fcc.

ГЧ *abbr.* (головная часть) reentry vehicle.

гыданский *a.* (geog.) Gyda.

гырнец *m.* gyrnets (xerophilic oak forest).

гьельмит *m.* (min.) hielmite, hjelmite.

Гэв *abbr.* (гигаэлектрон-вольт) gigaelectron-volt (billion electron-volt).

гэз *m.* gaize (a sandstone).

г-экв *abbr.* (грамм-эквивалент) gram-equivalent.

ГЭП *m.* gap.

ГЭС, гэс *abbr.* (гидроэлектростанция) hydroelectric power plant; (государственная электрическая станция) State power plant.

ГЭТФ *abbr.* (гексаэтилтетрафосфат) hexaethyl tetraphosphate.

ГЭЦ *abbr.* (гидроэлектроцентраль) central hydroelectric power plant.

Гюбля раствор Hübl solution.

гюбнерит *m.* (min.) hübnerite.

гюгелит *m.* (min.) hügelite.

Гюгонио уравнение Hugoniot equation.

Гюгенса принцип Huygens principle.

гюйс *m.* (naut.) jack, signal flag.

Гюльдена теорема (math.) Guldin's theorem.

Гюльднера генератор Güldner producer.

гюнтеров *a.* hunter's.

гюнц *m.*, **—ский** *a.* (geol.) Günz.

гюргянский *a.* (geog.) Gyurgyan.

гюрза *f.* (herp.) Vipera lebetina.

Гюртля клетка (med.) Hürthle cell.

Д

д *abbr.* (деци—) deci—; **д.** *abbr.* (дюйм) inch; (день) day; (долгота) longitude; **Д** *abbr.* (диоптрия) diopter; (доминантный) dominant.

да *conj.* but, and; *particle* yes.

да *abbr.* (дека—) deca—.

дабой/а, —я *f.* (herp.) Vipera russelli.

дав/аемый *a.* given; **—ание** *n.* giving, etc., *see* давать.

даватчан *m.* (ichth.) Frolikh char (*Salvelinus alpinus erythrinus*).

дав/ать *v.* give, provide, afford, furnish, yield, deliver; produce, turn out; offer; contribute, donate; lead (to), give rise (to), result (in); let, allow, permit; incur, suffer, sustain (losses); (med.) administer, apply; **—аться** *v.* be given, etc.; let oneself; succeed in; **легко —аться** come easily; **—ая** *pr. ger.* (while) giving, etc., *see v.*

давидит *m.* (min.) davidite.

давил/ка *f.* (fruit) press, juicer, squeezer; mill; **—о** *n.* weight, press.

давиль/ник *m.* (met.) spinner, spinning tool; **—ный** *a.* press(ing); spinning; forming (pliers); **—ное производство** spinning; **—ня** *f.* (wine) press; press plant or building; **—щик** *m.* presser (operator); (met.) spinner.

давин *m.* (min.) davyne.

давить *v.* press, squeeze, squash, crush; bring pressure (on), weigh (on), bear (upon); oppress; **—ся** *v.* choke.

давка *f.* press, crowd, crush, throng.

давлен/ие *n.* pressure; compression; stress; (axial) thrust; **д. сжатия** compressive stress; **высокого —ия** *a.* high-pressure; high-density (polyethylene); **компенсатор —ия** pressurizer; **низкого —ия** *a.* low-pressure; low-density (polyethylene); **повышенное д.** (med.) hypertension; **под —ием** *a.* pressurized, (under) pressure; forced(-feed) (lubrication); pressure-die (casting); **под уменьшенным —ием** reduced-pressure, vacuum (evaporation).

давлен/ник *m.* (ichth.) European eel (*Anguilla a.*); **—ность** *f.* (paper) crush(ing), crush marks; **—(н)ый** *a.* pressed, etc., *see* давить.

давн/ий, —ишний *a.* ancient, old, long-established, of long standing; **с —их пор** for a long time.

давно *adv.* long ago, long before, long (since); **д. известно** it has long been known (that); **д. тому назад** long ago; **—сть** *f.* remoteness, antiquity; (law) prescription.

давнуть *see* давить.

давший *past act. part. of* давать.

давя *pr. ger.*; **—щий** *a.* pressing, etc., *see* давить; compression (bandage).

даг *abbr.* (декаграмм) decagram.

даганен *m.* Dagenan, sulfapyridine.

дагерротип *m.*, **—ия** *f.*, **—ный** *a.* (phot.) daguerreotype.

дагестанский *a.* (geog.) Dagestan.

дагусса *f.* African millet (*Eleusine coracana*).

да/дут *fut. 3 pl.*; **—ёт** *pr. 3 sing. of* давать; **—ётся** is given, is available.

даже *particle* even (though); **д. при этом** even so.

дази— *prefix* dasy— (hairy, shaggy, thick); **—лирион** *m.* (bot.) Dasylirion; **—метрический** *a.* dasymetric, density-measuring; **—фора** *f.* (ent.) Dasyphora.

дайка *f.* (geol.) dike.

дайкон *m.* daikon, oriental radish.

Дайнса анемограф Dines anemograph.

дайте *imp. of* давать.

дайя *f.* daya (moist wooded depression).

дакеит *m.* (min.) dakeite, schroekingerite.

дакр/ен *m.* dacrene; **—ио—** *prefix* dacryo— (tear); **—иолин** *m.* dacryolin; **—иоцистит** *m.* (med.) dacryocystitis; **—он** *m.* Dacron (synthetic fiber).

дактил/ический, —овый *a.* dactylic; **—о—** *prefix* dactyl(o)— (digit, finger); **—огироз** *m.* (vet.) dactylogyrosis, Dactylogyrus infestation; **—ограмма** *f.*

dactylogram, fingerprint; **—ология** *f.* dactylology, sign language; **—оскопия** *f.* dactyloscopy, fingerprint identification.

дал *abbr.* (декалитр) decaliter; *past m. sing. of* **дать.**

даламбер(т)иан *m.* (math.) d'Alembertian, wave operator.

далее *adv.* next, further, hereinafter; then, later; **и так д.** et cetera, and so forth.

далёкий *a.* distant, far, remote; **д. от цели** wide of the mark.

далеко *adv.* far (off); by far, much; **д. идущий** far-reaching; **д. не** far from (being), not nearly so; **д. от** far from, wide of; away from.

дали *past pl. of* **дать;** *gen., etc., of* **даль.**

далин *m.* dahlin (dye); inulin, alant starch.

далина *see* **даль.**

далия *f.* (bot.) dahlia; (ichth.) *see* **даллия.**

далл/иевые *pl.* (ichth.) Dalliidae; **—ит** *m.* (min.) dahllite; **—ия** *f.* blackfish (*Dallia pectoralis*).

далматский *a.* (geog.) Dalmatian.

дало *past n. sing. of* **дать.**

даль *f.* distance, expanse.

дальбергия *f.* (bot.) rosewood (*Dalbergia*).

дальне/видение *n.* television; **—восточный** *a.* (geog.) Far Eastern.

дальнейш/ий *a.* further, subsequent, continued; furthest; **в —ем** in what follows, from here on, hereinafter, henceforth, below; subsequently, later on.

дальне/пишущая машина teleprinter; **—привозный** *a.* imported; **—разведывательный** *a.* long-range reconnaissance.

дальн/ий *a.* distant, far (off), remote; long-range (communications; order); (tel.) long-distance, toll; **Д. Восток** (geog.) Far East; **—его действия** *a.* long-range.

дально— *prefix* distance, tele—; **—бойность** *f.* range; **—бойный** *a.* long-range.

дальновид/ение *n.,* **—ность** *f.* foresight; clear-sightedness; **—ный** *a.* far-sighted, clear-sighted; prescient.

дальнодейств/ие *n.* remote control; long-range action; **—ующий** *a.* remote-control; long-range, far-ranging.

дальноземелье *n.* remoteness of fields.

дальнозорк/ий *a.* (med.) hypermetropic, far-sighted; **—ость** *f.* hyper(metr)opia; **старческая —ость** (med.) presbyopia.

дально/измерение *n.* telemetry, telemetering; **—мер** *m.,* **—мерный** *a.* range finder, distance finder; **—мерно** *adv.* by range finder; **—мерщик** *m.* range taker; **—метрия** *f.* ranging, distance measurement; **—стный** *a.* distance, range; **—струйный** *a.* long-range (sprinkler).

дальност/ь *f.* distance, remoteness; mileage; range, compass, radius; **д. действия, д. передачи, д. полёта** range; **малой —и** short-range (missile); theater (weapon); **определение —и** (radar) ranging; **отклонение по —и** longitudinal deviation; **предельная д.** critical range, range limit.

дальноуправляемый *a.* remote-controlled.

дальтон *m.* dalton (atomic mass unit).

Дальтона закон Dalton's law.

дальтон/ид *m.* (chem.) daltonide; **—изм** *m.* (med.) daltonism, color blindness; **—ик** color-blind person.

дальше *comp. of* **далеко, далёкий,** further, farther (on), later; forward, onward, right on; beyond; **проходить д.** *v.* proceed, move on.

дам *fut. 1 sing. of* **дать.**

дама *f.* lady; (mam.) Thylogale eugenii.

даман *m.* (mam.) hyrax (*Procavia*).

дамас/к *m.* damask steel; (text.) damask; **—кет, —се,**

—т *m.* damask; **—кировать** *v.* damask, damascene; **—ковый, —ский** *a.* damask; (petr.) damascened, interwoven; **—ценин** *m.* (chem.) damascenine.

дамба *f.* dam, dike, levee, embankment.

дамбоза *f.* dambose, *i*-inositol.

даменит *m.* (expl.) dahmenite.

дамиана *f.* damiana (leaves).

даммар *m.,* **—а** *f.,* **—овый** *a.* dammar (gum); **—иловая кислота** dammarylic acid; **—лак** *m.* dammar varnish.

дамодарский *a.* (geog.) Damodar.

дамп *m.* (comp.) dump; **послесчётный д.** postmortem dump.

дампфировать *v.* damp.

дамский *a.* women's, ladies'.

дамурит *m.* (min.) damourite; **—изация** *f.* damouritization.

дан *sh. m. of* **данный.**

ДАН *abbr.* (**Доклады Академии Наук**) Proceedings of the Academy of Sciences.

данаида *f.* orifice gaging tank.

дана/иды *pl.* (ent.) Danaidae; **—ит** *m.* (min.) danaite; **—лит** *m.* danalite; **—я** *f.* (bot.) Danae.

данбурит *m.* (min.) danburite.

Данди (geog.) Dundee (port).

дани/ель *see* **даниэль; —о** *m.* (ichth.) Danio; **—о-рерио** *m.* zebra danio (*Brachydanio rerio*); **—эль(ка)** *f.* (mam.) fallow deer (*Cervus dama*).

Даниэля элемент (elec.) Daniell cell.

Дания Denmark.

даннеморит *m.* (min.) dannemorite.

данное *n.* datum, given or known quantity; ground, basis.

данн/ые *pl.* data, facts, information, evidence; findings, results; figures, estimates; records; (age) pattern; essential qualities, potential; **научные д., полученные д.** findings, evidence; **под нашим —ым** we find; **—ый** *a.* given, known; specific, particular, referred (to), under consideration, in question; present, in hand; **в —ом виде** as it stands.

дано *sh. n. of* **данный;** given.

дантикул *m.* dentil, indentation, notch.

дантист *m.* dentist.

дантония *f.* (bot.) Danthonia.

данцелловые *pl.* (ichth.) Ageneiosidae.

даны *sh. pl. of* **данный.**

дань *f.* tribute, contribution, tax.

ДАП *abbr.* (**двигатель, авиационный поршневой**) aircraft piston engine.

дар *m.* gift, donation, grant.

дарапскит *m.* (min.) darapskite.

дараф *m.* (elec.) daraf, reciprocal farad (unit of elastance).

дарвазский *a.* (geog.) Darvaz.

дарвин/изм *m.* darwinism; **—истический, —овский** *a.* Darwinian.

дар/ение *n.* donation, presentation; **—еный** *a.* donated, presented; gift; **—ивать** *see* **дарить; —итель** *m.* donor, grantor; **—ить** *v.* donate, give, grant, present.

дарминное масло wormseed oil.

дармо/вой *see* **даровой; —ед** *m.* parasite.

даров/ание *n.* gift, endowment; talent; **—анный** *a.* granted, conferred; **—ать** *v.* grant, give, confer.

даровитый *a.* gifted, clever, talented.

даровой *a.* free, gratuitous.

даром *adv.* free of charge, gratis; in vain, to no purpose, for nothing; **д. что** (al)though; **не д.** with reason; no wonder.

Дарсе металл D'Arcet metal.

дарси *m.* darcy (unit of permeability).

дарсонвализация *f.* (med.) d'Arsonval treatment, d'arsonvalization.

дарственн/ый *a.* donation; **д. акт** grant; **—ая запись** deed, settlement.

дартер *m.* (ichth.) darter.

Дарье болезнь (med.) Darier's disease.

дарьенский *a.* (geog.) Darien.

даст *fut. 3 sing. of* **давать.**

дасциллус *m.* (ichth.) Dascyllus.

дат. *abbr.* (**датский**) Danish.

дата *f.* date.

датель *m.* giver, donator, donor.

датиров/ание *n.* dating, age determination; **—анный** *a.* dated; **—ать** *v.* date; **—ка** *f.* dating; **—очный** *a.* date, dating.

датис/ка *f.* (bot.) Datisca; **—цетин** *m.* datiscetin; **—цин** *m.* datiscin.

датолит *m.* (min.) datolite.

датский *a.* Danish.

датур/а *f.* (bot.) Datura; **—ин** *m.* daturine, hyoscyamine; **—овый** *a.* daturine; daturic (acid).

датчанин *m.* Dane.

датчик *m.* pickup (unit); (elec.) transducer; monitor, controller; sender, transmitter; generator; sensor, sensing device; feeler, probe; detector; data unit; indicator, gage; (real-time) clock; (random-number) generator; **д. времени** timer; **д. детонации** knock indicator; **д. обратной связи** feedback transducer; **звёздный д.** star tracker; **д.-измеритель** *m.* gage.

дать *see* **давать.**

ДАУ *abbr.* (**дистанционно-автоматическое управление**) automatic remote control.

Дау элемент Dow (electrolytic) cell.

даугавский *a.* (geog.) Daugava.

даукостерин *m.* daucosterol.

дау-металл *m.* Dowmetal (alloy).

Дауна болезнь (med.) Down's syndrome.

Даунса метод Downs process.

даунтон *m.,* **—ский ярус** (geol.) Downtonian stage.

даурицин *m.* dauricine.

даурский *a.* (geog.) Daur.

даусон/ит *m.* (min.) dawsonite; **—овский** *a.* Dawson (producer) gas.

даутерм *m.* Dowtherm (biphenyl-diphenyl ether coolant).

дауцин *m.* daucine.

дауэкс *m.* Dowex (ion-exchange resin).

дафн/андрин *m.* daphnandrine; **—етин** *m.* daphnetin, 7,8-dihydroxycoumarin; **—ин** *m.* daphnin; **—ит** *m.* (min.) daphnite; **—ия** *f.* (crust.) water flea (*Daphnia*).

дафф *m.* duff, forest humus.

дацит *m.* (petr.) dacite; **—овый** *a.* dacitic.

дач/а *f.,* **—ный** *a.* giving, paying; (agr.) rate; plot, lot; portion, allowance; (food) ration; (med.) administration, application; intake, input, feeding; (forest) district; resort, dacha, country cottage.

даю/т *pr. 3 pl. of* **давать; —щий** *a.* giving; data.

дб *abbr.* (**децибел**) decibel.

д. б. *abbr.* (**должно быть**) probably; **дб., ДБ** *abbr.* (**доброкачественность**) good quality; **д.б.н.** *abbr.* (**доктор биологических наук**) Doctor of Biological Sciences.

ДВ *abbr.* (**длинноволновый**) long-wave; (**длинные волны**) long waves; (**Дальний восток**) Far East; (**дымоотравляющее вещество**) toxic smoke agent; etc.

дв. *abbr.* (**двоичный; двойной**).

два *m. and n. num.* two.

двадцати— *prefix* viginti—, icosi—, icosa—, twenty; **—градусный** *a.* twenty-degree; **—гранник** (cryst.) icosahedron; **—гранный** *a.* icosahedral; **—кратный** *a.* twentyfold; **—летие** *n.* twenty-year period; twentieth anniversary; **—летний** *a.* twenty-year; twentieth; **—сторонний** *a.* icosalateral; **—угольник** *m.* icosagon; **—угольный** *a.* icosagonal; **—четырёхгранник** *m.* icositetrahedron.

двадцат/ый *a.* twentieth; **—ь** *num.* twenty; **—ью** *adv.* twenty times.

дважды *adv.* twice, twofold; re—, *e.g.* **д. дистиллировать** *v.* redistil.

Двайт-Лойд *see* **Дуайт.**

ДВВ *abbr.* (**дробящее взрывчатое вещество**) high explosive.

две *f. num.* two; **—надцатеричный** *a.* duodecimal, base-twelve.

двенадцати— *prefix* d(u)odeca—, twelve-; **—гранник** *m.* (cryst.) dodecahedron; **—гранный** *a.* dodecahedral; **—перстн(окишечн)ый** *a.* (anat.) duodenal; **—перстная кишка** duodenum; **—ричный** *a.* duodecimal; **—сторонний** *a.* dodecalateral; **—угольник** *m.* dodecagon; **—угольный** *a.* dodecagonal; **—часовой** *a.* twelve-hour; twelve o'clock.

двенадцат/ый *a.* twelfth; **—ь** *num.* twelve.

двер/еэкстрактор *see* **дверцесниматель; —ка** *dim. of* **дверь; —ной** *a. of* **дверь; —ной проём** doorway; **—ца** *f.* (small) door, gate; manhole, hatch; **—цесниматель** *m.* (coke oven) door extractor; **—ь** *f.* door, gate; **д.-навес** *f.* canopy door.

двести *num.* two hundred.

двигатель *m.* engine, motor; propeller, driver; impellent, motive power; power plant, power unit; actuator; **д.-генератор** *m.* (elec.) motor-generator; **д.-маховик** *m.* motor-flywheel; **—ный** *a. of* **двигатель;** actuating, propellent, impellent, motive; (anat.) motor; **—ная сила** motive power, moving force, impetus; **источник —ной силы** prime mover; **—ное расстройство** (med.) dyskinesia; **д.-связка** *m.* coupled engines, cluster(ed) engine.

двигать *v.* move, set in motion, actuate, get started; shift; advance, promote; **—ся** *v.* move (about), stir; drive; migrate; (mach.) run, work, operate; **—ся по** move across or over, traverse; proceed along.

двигающий *see* **движущий.**

движенец *m.* transport worker.

движен/ие *n.* motion, movement; travel; traffic; flow; (rocket propulsion) flight; circulation (of blood); **без —ия** stationary, motionless, idle; **количество —ия** momentum; **момент количества —ия** angular momentum; **начало —ия** start; **приводить в д.** start, set in motion, move, activate, actuate; power; drive; **сила —ия** motive power; **энергия —ия** kinetic energy.

движет *pr. 3 sing. of* **двигать.**

движим/ость *f.* mobility; movable property; **—ый** *a.* movable, mobile, portable; moved, propelled, actuated (by); current (assets); circulating, floating, working (capital).

движ/итель *m.* propeller, propelling device; **—ковый** *a.,* **—ок** *m.* slide; cursor; arm; knob; (safety) bolt; small engine.

движущ/ий *a.* moving, motive, impellent, driving, propelling; actuating, operating (mechanism); **—ая сила** driving force, drive; propelling force; motive power; impetus; **—ийся** *a.* moving, etc., *see* **двигаться;** in motion; mobile; wandering (dunes).

двинский *a.* (geog.) Dvina; Dvinsk.

двинут/ый *a.* moved, etc., *see* **двигать; —ь** *see* **двигать.**

двое *num.* two, a pair; *prefix* bi—; **—брачный** *a.* bigamous; **—к** *gen. pl. of* **двойка; —кратный** *a.* twofold; twice (a day); **—мыслие** *n.* ambiguity; **—н** *gen. pl. of* **двойня.**

двое/ние *n.* dividing, etc., *see* **двоить;** (med.) diplopia; **—нный** *a.* divided, etc., *see* **двоить;** twice-plowed; **—связность** *f.* (chem.) double bond (character); **—тес** *m.* two-inch nail; **—точие** *n.* colon; (math.) doublet.

двои *see* **двое; —льноленточный** *a.* (leather) splitting; **—льный** *a.* dividing, etc., *see v.;* **—ть** *v.* divide (in two), split; double; (chem.) rectify; (agr.) plow a second time, replow; (TV) ghost; **—ться** *v.* bifurcate; **—ться в глазах** see double; **—х** *gen. of* **двое.**

двоично— *prefix* binary; **д.-десятичный** *a.* (comp.) binary-coded decimal; **д.-(за)кодированный** *a.* binary coded; **д.-рациональный** *a.* binary rational; dyadic; **—сть** *f.* duality, duplicity.

двоичн/ый *a.* binary, scale-of-two; (anat.) bigeminal, double; **д. знак, д. разряд, —ая единица, —ая цифра, —ое число** binary digit, bit.

двойка *f.* pair, two; (educ.) two, poor; (agr.) second plowing; rowboat.

двойник *m.* double, twin, counterpart, duplicate; sibling; return bend (of furnace, etc.); **—ование** *n.* (cryst.) twinning; **—овый** *a.* twin(ned), duplicate; twin (crystal); twinning (axis, etc.); **—овый сросток** twin; **—овое срастание** twinning.

двойнозуб *m.* (ichth.) Diplodus; gilthead (*Sparus aurata*).

двойн/ой *a.* double, twofold, duplex; dual (control, etc.); binary (compound, etc.); two-stage; compound; two-ply; di—, twin; anharmonic (ratio); parallel (publication); double-page (title); double-entry (bookkeeping); double-strength (fertilizer); cross (fertilization); double-stranded (helix); (anat.) bigeminal, paired; (bot.) geminate; folded (dipole); **—ого действия** *a.* double-acting, double-action; **д. проверка** (comp.) cross check.

двойня *f.* twins; double, duplicate.

двойственн/ое *n.* dual number; **—ость** *f.* duality, dualism, dual nature; duplicity; ambiguity; duplication; **—ый** *a.* dual, double, reciprocal; ambiguous, non-committal.

двойчат/ка *f.* double kernel; (bot.) Bifora; **—осложный** *a.* (bot.) binate; **—ый** *see* **двойной.**

двор *m.* yard, court; farm(stead); (casting) bed. **на —е** outdoors, outside; **—ец** *m.* palace; **—ик** *dim. of* **двор;** (biol.) cavity; (pleochoroic) halo; **передний —ик** vestibule; **—ник** *m.* yard man; **—ной** *a.* yard, court; **—овый** *a.* yard, outdoor; farm (buildings).

двояк/ий *a.* double, twofold, duplex; ambiguous; (chem.) binary; (bot.) dimorphous.

двояко *adv.* doubly, in two ways; *prefix* bi— (twice, two); duplic(at)o— (doubly); **—вогнутый** *a.* concavo-concave, biconcave, double concave; **—выпуклый** *a.* convexo-convex, biconvex, double convex, lenticular; **—выпуклое стекло** lens; **—гармонический** *a.* biharmonic; **—дышащие** *pl.* (ichth.) lungfishes (*Dipnoi*); **—дышащий** *a.* dipnoan; **—зазубренный** *a.* (bot.) bicrenate; **—зубчатые** *pl.* (bot.) rodents; **—зубчатый** *a.* duplicodentate; **—компактный** *a.* bicompact; **—круговой** *a.* bicircular; **—крылые** *pl.* (ent.) Diptera; **—периодический** *a.* doubly periodic; **—перистые** *pl.* (zool.) bipinnaria; **—перистый** *a.* (bot.) bipinnate; **—пильчатый** *a.* doubly serrate, biserrate; **—преломляющий** *see* **двупреломляющий; —сть** *f.* doubleness, duplicity; ambiguity; **—тройчатый** *a.* (bot.) biternate.

ДВС *abbr.* (двигатель внутреннего сгорания) internal combustion engine.

ДВТ, Двт *abbr.* (дедвейт-тонна) dead-weight ton.

дву— *prefix* bi— (twice, two); di— (twofold, double); dipl(o)—; diss(o)—; didym(o)— (twin); see also under **двух—; —аммониевый** *a.* diammonium; **—атомный** *see* **двухатомный; —бережный** *a.* (math.; topology) two-sided (cut); **—бокий** *a.* bilateral; **—борнокислая соль** diborate; **—бороздный, —бороздчатый** *a.* bisulcate, two-grooved; **—братственный** *a.* (bot.) diadelphous; **—брачный** *a.* bigamous.

двубром/замещённый *a.* dibromo (compound); **—истый** *a.* dibromide.

дву/брюшный *a.* (anat.) digastric; **—бугорковый** *a.* bicuspid(ate); **—валентность** *f.* bivalence; **—валентный** *a.* bivalent; **—вариантный** *a.* bivariant; **—вершинный** *a.* twin-cone; bicuspid(ate); **—ветвистый** *a.* bifurcate; biramose; **—видный** *a.* dimorphous; **—вильчатый** *a.* bifurcate.

двувинно/каменнокислая соль, —кислая соль bitartrate; **—кислый калий** potassium bitartrate.

дву/водный *a.* dihydrate; **—вольфрамовокислая соль** ditungstate; **—галогенный, —галоидный** *a.* dihal(ogen)ide; **—главый** *a.* two-headed; (anat.) bicipital; **—главая мышца** biceps; **—глазый** *a.* binocular; **—гнёздный** *a.* (biol.) bilocular; **—горбый** *a.* two-humped, bigibbous; double-peaked (curve); **—горлый** *a.* two-necked (bottle); **—гранный** *a.* dihedral, two-sided; **—губ** *m.* (ichth.) Bilabria; **—губый** *a.* (bot.) bilabial, bilabiate; **—дольные** *pl.* (bot.) dicotyledons; **—дольный** *a.* dicotyledonous; bipartite; **—домность** *f.* (biol.) dioecism; **—домный** *a.* dioecious; **—дужный** *a.* double-arched; (zool.) diapsid; **—дышащие** *pl.* (ichth.) Dipnoi; **—жаберные** *pl.* (mal.) Dibranchia; **—жаберный** *a.* dibranchiate; **—жгутиковый** *a.* (biol.) biflagellate; **—женный** *a.* (bot.) digynous; **—жильный** *a.* twin, twin-core (cable).

двузамещённ/ое *n.* disubstitute(d product); **—ый** *a.* disubstituted.

дву/зарядный *a.* with a double charge; **—звучный** *a.* (physiol.) dicrotic; **—зернянка** *f.* (bot.) emmer (*Triticum dicoccum*).

двузначн/ость *f.* ambiguity; two-valued property; **—ый** *a.* ambiguous; two-valued; two-digit (number).

дву/зонтичный *a.* double-umbrella (antenna); (bot.) biumbellate; **—зорка** *f.* four-eyed fish (*Anableps tetrophthalmus*).

двузуб *m.,* **—ка** *f.* (ichth.) Diodon; **—ец** *m.* (bot.) Bidens; **—ка** *f.* (bot.) cleistogene; **—(н)ый** *a.* bidentate, two-toothed; **—овые** *pl.* porcupinefishes (*Diodontidae*); **—чатый** *a.* having two rows of teeth; bidentate; bicuspidate; double-prong (forceps); **—ые** *pl.* Diodontidae.

дву/иглый *a.* two-spined, diacanthous; **—йодзамещённый** *a.* diiodo (compound); **—йодистый** *a.* diiodide; **—камерный** *a.* (biol.) bilocular; **—карбоксильный, —карбоновый** *a.* dicarboxylic; **—килевой, —кильный** *a.* bicarinate, double-keeled.

двукисл/ота *f.,* **—(отн)ый** *a.* diacid.

дву/кисточник *m.* canary grass (*Phalaris*); **—клювый** *a.* (biol.) birostrate; **—коготковые** *pl.* (mam.) ruminants; **—колка** *f.* two-wheeled cart; **—конечный** *a.* bicuspid(ate); bipartite, bifid; **—конный** *a.* team-drawn; **—конусный** *a.* biconical, double-cone; **—копытные** *pl.* (mam.) Artiodactyla; **—копытный** *a.* artiodactyl, cloven-footed; **—коренный** *a.* two-rooted (teeth); —**коробочный, —коробчатый** *a.* (bot.) bicapsular; —**косточковый** *a.* dipyrenous, two-seeded; —**костянка** *f.* didrupe; —**красочный** *a.* dichromatic.

двукратн/о *adv.* twice; *prefix see* **дву**—; duplicato— (doubly); diss(o)— (double); —**ый** *a.* twofold, double, reiterated; two-stage; push-push (circuit); through-flow (turbine); reflected-shock (compressibility).

двукремн/евый *a.* disilicic (acid); —**истый** *a.* disilicide.

двукрыл *m.* (ent.) dipteran, fly; flying fish (*Exocoetus,* spec. *E. volitans*); —**атка** *f.* double-winged seed; —**оплодник** *m.* (bot.) Dipterocarpus; —**ые** *pl.* (ent.) Diptera; —**ый** *a.* dipterous, two-winged.

дву/лёгочниковые, —лёгочные *pl.* (ichth.) Lepidosirenidae; —**лепестник** *m.* (bot.) Circaea; —**лепестный** *a.* dipetalous; —**летний** *a.* two-year; (bot.) biennial; —**летник** *m.* biennial; —**линейный** *a.* bilinear; —**листный** *a.* two-sheeted, double; (bot.) bifoliate, diphyllous; —**лопастный** *a.* bilobate; —**лоскутный** *a.* double-flap (amputation).

двулучепреломл/ение *n.* (phys.) double refraction, birefringence; —**яющий** *a.* birefringent.

двум *dat. of* **два, две.**

дву/мерный *a.* two-dimensional, dimetric, bivariate; —**местный** *a.* two-place; —**молекулярный** *a.* bimolecular; —**молочный** *a.* dilactic (acid); —**мстам** *dat. of* **двести;** —**мускульный** *a.* (zool.) dimyarian; —**мя** *instr. of* **два, две;** —**мястами** *instr. of* **двести;** —**надрезный** *a.* bifid; —**направленный** *a.* bidirectional; —**натриевый** *a.* disodium; —**нитный** *a.* bifilar.

двуног *m.* (herp.) Bipes; —**а** *f.* bipod; —**ий** *a.* two-legged, biped; —**ое животное** (zool.) biped.

двуокись *f.* dioxide; **д. серы** sulfur dioxide; **д. углерода** carbon dioxide.

дву/оксид *m.* hyperoxide (peroxide); —**орешковый** *a.* (bot.) dicoccous; —**осевой** *a.* biaxial; —**основный** *a.* dibasic; diatomic, dihydric; —**осность** *f.* biaxiality; —**осный** *a.* biaxial; —**остроконечный** *a.* bicuspid(ate); —**отражение** *n.* double reflection; —**палый** *a.* (zool.) didactylous.

двупарн/оногие *pl.* (zool.) Diplopoda; —**орезцовые** *pl.* (mam.) rodents; —**оусые** *pl.* (zool.) Teleiocerata; Branchiata; —**ый** *a.* (bot.) bijugate; bijugous; bigeminate, doubly paired.

дву/перегородчатый *a.* (bot.) biseptate; —**перисторазрезной** *a.* (bot.) bipinnatifid; —**перистые** *pl.* (zool.) bipinnaria; —**перистый** *a.* bipennate; —**пестичный** *a.* (bot.) digynian; digynous; —**печный** *a.* two-furnace; —**питаемый** *a.* double-feed; —**пламенный** *a.* double-flame; —**планный** *a.* two-plane; —**плечий** *a.* double-arm (lever); —**полосный** *a.* diplostichous; —**полостный** *a.* bilocular; two-sheeted; —**полый** *a.* bisexual, hermaphroditic; —**полье** *n.* two-field crop rotation; —**полюсный** *a.* bipolar; —**порые** *pl.* (ent.) Ditrysia; —**праворукость** *f.* ambidexterity; —**предсердные** *pl.* (mal.) Diotocardia.

двупреломл/ение *n.* (phys.) double refraction, birefringence; —**яющий** *a.* double-refracting, birefringent.

дву/пятиокись *f.* pentoxide; —**раздельный** *a.* (bot.) bifid; bipartite; dimerous, biseptate, bilobed; —**рассеченный** *a.* bisectional, bisected; —**резцовые** *pl.* (mam.) Diprotodontia; —**резцовый** *a.* diprotodont; —**рогий** *a.* two-horned, bicorn; —**родовой** *a.* bigeneric; —**ротый** *a.* (zool.) distomous; —**рукий** *a.* two-handed, bimanual; —**ручка** *f.* winter and spring crop (of wheat); —**ручий** *a.* two-hand(l)ed; crosscut (saw).

двуряд/ка *f.,* —**ник** *m.* (bot.) Diplotaxis; —**но** *adv.* biserially, bifariously; *prefix* disticho— (two-ranked); —**нооблиственный** (bot.) distichophyllous; —**ный** *a.* double(-row), two-row, two-series; (chem.) double-stranded; (bot.) di(plo)stichous, bifarious.

дву/связный *a.* doubly connected; —**селенистый** *a.* diselenide.

двусем/енник *see* **диусемянник;** —**енниковый** *a.* (anat.) diorchic; —**енодольные** *pl.* (bot.) dicotyledons; —**енодольный, —ядольный** *a.* dicotyledonous; —**янка** *f.* diachenium; —**янник** *m.* (bot.) Hutchinsia.

двусериальный *a.* biserial.

двусерн/истый *a.* disulfide (of); —**ый** *a.* disulfuric, pyrosulfuric (acid).

дву/сеточный *a.* double-grid; —**сильный** *a.* (bot.) didynamous; —**скатный** *a.* with two sloping surfaces, inverted-V; ridge(d), gable (roof); —**складчатый** *a.* biplicate, doubly folded; bilophodont (teeth); —**сложный** *a.* (bot.) binate, in pairs; —**слойный** *see* **двухслойный;** —**сменный** *a.* two-shift, double-shift; diphyodont (teeth).

двусмысленн/ость *f.* ambiguity; —**ый** *a.* ambiguous, doubtful, obscure.

дву/составный *a.* two-part, two-element; —**стадийный** *a.* two-stage.

двуствол/ка *f.* double-barreled gun; —**ьный** *a.* double-barreled; duplex well.

двуствор/ка *f.* (mal.) bivalve; —**ный** *a.* bicuspid, two-winged; —**чатые** *pl.* (mal.) Bivalvia; Lamellibranchi(at)a; —**чатый** *a.* bivalve, bivalvular; bicuspid, two-winged; double (door); —**чатая коробочка** (bot.) pod.

дву/стенный *a.* double-walled; —**степенный** *a.* two-phase.

двусторонн/ий *a.* bilateral, two-sided, bi-faced, reversible, reciprocal; two-way; duplex; double-ended; dual (control); amphoteric (oxide); —**ее весло** paddle; —**ость** *f.* two-sidedness, reversibility.

дву/ступенчатый *see* **двухступенчатый;** —**тавровая балка** I-beam, H-beam; joist; —**тактный** *a.* two-cycle (engine); push-pull; —**теллуристый** *a.* ditelluride; —**точечный** *a.* two-point, pair-wise; —**третичный** *a.* ditertiary; —**трёхокись** *f.* sesquioxide; —**тычинковый, —тычиночный** *a.* (bot.) diandrous; —**тяжевый** *a.* double-stranded.

двууглеⷞ/кислый *a.* bicarbonate (of); **д. натр, —кислая сода, —натриевая соль** sodium bicarbonate; —**кислая соль** bicarbonate; —**родный** *a.* dicarboxylic (acid).

дву/угольник *m.* (geom.) lune; —**ударность** *f.* (physiol.) dicrotism; —**узловой** *a.* binodal; —**укосный** *a.* (agr.) double-crop; —**уксусная соль** diacetate; —**урановокислая соль** diuranate; —**урановонатриевая соль** sodium diuranate; —**уст** *m.,* —**устка** *f.* (zool.) fluke; distome; —**устки** *pl.* Digenea; —**утробки, —утробные** *pl.* (mam.) Didelphidae; —**утробный** *a.* didelphic; —**ухий** *a.* double-ear (phone); (bot.) biauriculate; —**ушный** *a.* (acous.) binaural; —**фосфористый** *a.* diphosphide; —**фторзамещённый** *a.* difluoro (compound).

двух *gen. and prepos. of* **два, две;** *prefix see* **дву**—; —**адресный** *a.* two-address; —**атомный** *a.* diatomic; bivalent; dihydric (alcohol); diacid (base); —**боевой** *a.* duplex, double-faced (hammer); —**бороздчатый** *a.* double-groove, double-furrow.

двухвалентн/ость *f.* bivalence; —**ый** *a.* bivalent.

двух/валковый *a.* two-roll, two-high (rolling mill);

—**вальный** *a.* twin-shaft; —**вальцевый** *a.* double-drum (dyer); —**ванный** *a.* two-bath; —**венцовый** *a.* double (wheel); —**вершинный** *a.* double-peak; bicuspid; —**ветвевой** *a.* (mech.) bifurcate, forked; —**видовой** *a.* two-way; two-mode; —**винтовое** *n.* twin screw, twin propeller; —**винтовой** *a.* twin-screw; tandem-rotor (helicopter); —**витковый** *a.* double-coil; two-loop; —**водный** *a.* dihydrate; —**волновой** *a.* dual-frequency; (med.) diphasic.

двухвост/(и)ки, —ые *pl.* (ent.) Diplura; —**ый** *a.* bicaudate.

двух/выборочный *a.* two-sample; —**годичный, —годовой** *a.* two-year; biennial; —**годовал(ьн)ый** *a.*, —**годовик** *m.* two-year-old; —**головый** *a.* two-headed; —**гранный** *see* **двугранный**; —**групповой** *a.* two-group; —**двигательный** *a.* twin-engine(d); —**диапазонный** *a.* dual-range; —**диффузорный** *a.* dual cone (speaker); —**дневный** *a.* two-day; —**дольный** *see* **двудольный**; —**донный** *a.* double-bottom(ed); —**дорожечный** *a.* dual-track (recording); —**дорожковый** *a.* two-track; two-pronged (forceps); —**дуговые** *pl.* (herp.) Diapsida.

двухдюймов/ка *f.* two-inch (thick) board; —**ый** *a.* two-inch.

двух/желобчатый *a.* double-groove(d); —**жидкостный** *a.* double-fluid; double-solvent (extraction); —**жильный** *a.* twin (cable); —**замещённый** *a.* disubstituted; —**замещённый фосфат кальция** dicalcium phosphate; —**зарядный** *a.* two-charge, doubly charged; —**заходный** *a.* double (screw thread); —**звенник** *m.* (av.) torque link; —**звенный** *a.* two-link; —**значный** *a.* two-figure, two-place, two-valued; bivalent; —**зон(аль)ный** *a.* two-region.

двух/импульсный *a.* double-pulse; —**камерный** *a.* double-chamber, twin-chamber, two-compartment; bilocular; —**канальный** *a.* two-channel; —**каскадный** *a.* two-stage; two-circuit; —**килевой** *a.* twin-rudder, twin-tail, twin-finned.

двухкилометров/ка *f.* map with a scale of two kilometers to the centimeter; —**ый** *a.* two-kilometer.

двух/кислотный *a.* diacid; —**кисточник** *m.* (bot.) Phalaris; —**клеточный** *a.* (mach.) double squirrel-cage; —**ковшовый** *a.* twin-bucket; —**колейный** *a.* double-track; —**коленчатый** *a.* double-knee, double-throw, double-stage; —**колёсный** *a.* two-wheel(ed); —**колонный** *a.* double-housing; double-column(ed); —**кольчатый** *a.* dicyclic; binuclear; —**компонентный** *a.* two-component; binary (mixture, etc.); bi-propellant (fuel); (comp.) two-variable; —**конечный** *a.* double-end, double-pointed; —**контактный** *a.* double-contact; double-prong (plug).

двух/контурный *a.* two-circuit; double-flow; ducted-fan (turboengine); by-pass (engine); double-tuned; classifying (vacuum crystallizer); (biol.) limbate, bordered; —**координационный** *a.* twofold, two-binary; bidentate (ligand); —**корпусный** *a.* twin; double-furrow (plow); —**кратный** *see* **двукратный**; —**кулачковый** *a.* (mech.) double-jawed.

двух/ламповый *a.* (rad.) two-tube; —**лемешный** *a.* two-share, double-furrow (plow); —**ленточный** *a.* double-strand; two-band (saw).

двухлет/ие *n.* two-year period; —**ка** *f.* two-year old; two-year project; —**ний** *a.* two-year; (zool.) yearling; (bot.) biennial; —**нее животное** yearling; —**ник** *m.* biennial; —**ок** *see* **двухлетка**.

двух/линзовый *a.* two-lens; —**листный** *a.* two-sheeted; —**литровый** *a.* two-liter; —**лобный** *see* **двухбоевой**; —**лопастный** *a.* two-vane.

двухлор/замещённый *a.* dichloro (compound); —**истый** *a.* dichloride (of).

двух/лучевой *a.* two-beam, double-beam; twin-wire; —**мерный** *a.* two-dimensional; —**местный** *a.* two-place, binary; two-seat (vehicle).

двухмесячн/ик *m.* bimonthly (periodical); —**ый** *a.* two-month; bimonthly.

двух/метровый *a.* two-meter; —**минеральный** *a.* binary (rock); —**моторный** *a.* twin-engine(d); two-motor.

двухнедельн/ик *m.* biweekly, semimonthly (periodical); —**ый** *a.* two-week; biweekly; semimonthly.

двух/ниточный *a.* double (screw thread); —**ножевой** *a.* double-knife; —**оборотный** *a.* double (screw thread); —**объективный** *a.* two-lens, twin-lens.

двуход/ки, —овые *pl.* (herp.) Amphisbaenidae; —**овой** *see* **двухходовой**.

двух/олмие *n.* (anat.) bigeminal body; —**опорный** *a.* double-seat (valve); —**осевой** *a.* biaxial; —**основный** *a.* dibasic; —**основная кислота** diacid; —**осный** *a.* biaxial; two-axled; four-wheel; —**отвальный** *a.* V (blade); double-furrow (plow); —**отказный** *a.* fail-operational, fail-safe; —**палубный** *a.* double-deck; —**палый** *a.* (zool.) two-toed; —**периодичный** *a.* block key (punch); —**печной** *a.* two-furnace.

двух/позиционный *a.* two-position(ed); —**поколенный** *a.* (zool.) bivoltine; —**положенный** *a.* two-position(ed); —**полосный** *a.* double-band; —**полостный** *a.* two-sheet(ed); —**полупериодный** *a.* full-wave (rectifier); —**польный** *a.* two-field.

двухполюсн/ик *m.* (elec.) two-terminal network; bipole; dipole; —**ый** *a.* bipolar, double-pole, two-pole, two-terminal.

двух/поршневой *a.* two-piston, double-piston; —**поставный** *a.* double-blade (saw frame); —**потоковый** *a.* two-stream (instability); —**поточный** *a.* double-flow; —**предельный** *a.* double-range; —**призменный** *a.* double-prism; —**проводной** *a.* double (line), double-wire, two-wire, two-lead; —**проходной** *a.* two-way; two-pass (assembler); —**процентный** *a.* two-percent; —**пульсирующий бесклапанный реактивный двигатель** twin valveless pulse-jet engine; —**путевой, —путный** *a.* double-track; two-way, two-lane.

двух/раздельный *a.* two-part; —**размерный** *a.* two-dimensional; —**резной** *a.* split-anode (magnetron); —**резцовый** *a.* duplex (lathe); —**рельсовый** *a.* double-rail; double-track.

двухромов/окислый *a.* bichromate (of); bichromic acid; **д. натрий, —онатриевая соль** sodium bichromate; —**окислая соль** bichromate (of); —**ый** *a.* bichromic (acid).

двух/роторный *a.* two-rotor (pump); —**рычажный** *a.* double-lever (shears); —**рядный** *see* **двурядный**; —**светный** *a.* with two rows of windows; —**седельный** *a.* double-seat (valve); —**семейный** *a.* two-family; twin (hive); —**серийный** *a.* biserial; —**сигнальный** *a.* bisignal; —**скатный** *see* **двускатный**; —**скачковый** *a.* double-shock (diffuser); —**следный** *a.* tandem, double-gang (harrow); —**слойный** *a.* two-layer, two-ply; (embr.) diploblastic; —**сменный** *a.* double-shift (work); —**составный** *a.* two-part.

двухсот *gen. of* **двести**; —**летний** *a.* two-hundred-year; —**ый** *a.* two-hundredth.

двух/срезной *a.* (in) double shear; —**стадийный** *a.* two-step, two-stage; —**станинный** *a.* double-sided, double-standard; —**стах** *prep. of* **двести**; —**створный** *see* **двустворный**; —**створчатый** *see* **двуст-**

ворчатый; —стенный *a.* double-walled; —степенный *a.* two-step; dual (filtration); —стоечный *a.* (mach.) double-housing; double-pole (mast); —сторонний *see* двусторонний; —строчный *a.* double-row, two-line; —ступенный, —ступенчатый *a.* double-stage, two-stage, two-level, two-step, two-phase; —тавровый *a.* I-, H- (beam); —тактный *a.* two-stroke, two-cycle (engine); push-pull (pump).

двух/тарифный *a.* double-rate; —томный *a.* two-volume; —тональный *a.* two-tone; —точечный *a.* two-point; duplex (spot welding); point-to-point; —тысячный *a.* two-thousandth.

двух/ударный *a.* (radiobiol.) double-hit; (med.) bigeminal (pulse); —узловой *a.* binodal; —фазный *a.* two-phase, diphase; —фокусный *a.* bifocal; —ходовой *a.* two-way; two-pass; double-thread (screw); two-headed (burner).

двухцветн/ость *f.* dichro(mat)ism; —ый *a.* dichro(mat)ic, two-color, two-tone.

двух/целевой *a.* dual-purpose; —цепной *a.* double-chain; (elec.) double-circuit; —цепочный *a.* double-stranded; —цианистый *a.* dicyanide; —цилиндровый *a.* two-cylinder; double-barreled; —часовой *a.* two-hour; two o'clock; —частичный *a.* two-particle; two-body (force); —членный *see* двучленный; —шарнирный *a.* double-hinged, double-joint; —шкальный *a.* two-scale; double-dial; —шпиндельный *a.* duplex; two-spindle; —шпунтовый *a.* double-channel; —щелевой *a.* double-slotted; —ъядерный *a.* binuclear; —ъякорный *a.* double-armature; —ъярусность *f.* two-storied or double-tier arrangement; —ъярусный *a.* two-story, double-deck, double-level; double-lever (shears); —электродный *a.* two-electrode (tube); —этажный *a.* two-story, double-level; —ядерный *a.* binuclear.

двуцветный *see* двухцветный.

двучлен *m.* (math.) binomial; —ник *m.* (bot.) Diarthron; —иковый, —истый *a.* (zool.) biarticulate, double-jointed; —ный *a.* binomial; two-term; dimerous.

дву/ядерный *a.* binuclear; —язычный *a.* bilingual; —яйцевой *a.* bi(n)ovular, dizygotic, fraternal (twins); —ячеистый *a.* bilocular, two-chambered.

дг *abbr.* (дециграмм) decigram.

ДДД *abbr.* (дихлордифенилдихлорэтан) dichlorodiphenyldichloroethane.

ДДТ *abbr.* (дихлордифенилтрихлорэтан) dichlorodiphenyltrichloroethane, DDT.

де— *prefix* de(s)—, *see also under* дез—.

ДЕАЕ-целлюлоза *f.* DEAE-cellulose (diethylaminoethyl cellulose).

деазот/изация *f.*, —ирование *n.* denitration; —ированный *a.* denitrated; —ировать *v.* denitrate; denitride.

дейсер *m.* (av.) deicer.

деактивация *see* дезактивирование.

деалкилиров/ание *n.* dealkylation; —анный *a.* dealkylated; —ать *v.* dealkylate.

деароматизировать *v.* dearomatize, de-scent.

деасфальт/изация *f.* (petrol.) deasphalting; —ировать *v.* deasphalt.

деацетилирование *n.* deacetylation.

деаэр/атор *m.* deaerator; —ация *f.*, —изационный *a.* deaeration, deaerating; —ированный *a.* deaerated; —ировать *v.* deaerate.

деб/аевский *a.* Debye; —аеграмма *f.* Debye X-ray powder photograph, Debye powder pattern; —ай *m.* debye (unit of dipole moment).

дебаланс *m.* imbalance; unbalanced mass; eccentric (rotor).

дебаркадер *m.* landing stage, platform.

дебат/ировать *v.* debate, discuss, argue; —ы *pl.* debate, dispute, argument.

Дебая-Гюккеля уравнение Debye-Hückel equation.

дебет *m.*, —овать *v.*, —овый *a.* debit.

дебил *m.* mildly retarded person; —ьность *f.* mild retardation.

дебит *m.* yield, output; production (rate); capacity; discharge, flow; —ограмма *f.* (petrol.) flow diagram; —оме(т)р *m.* flow meter.

дебитор *m.* (com.) debtor.

деблокир/ование *n.* clearing, etc., *see v.*; —ованный *a.* cleared, etc., *see v.*; —овать *v.* clear, un(b)lock, release, relieve; (mil.) raise a blockade; —овка *see* деблокирование; —ующий *a.* clearing, etc., *see v.*

дебнеровский *a.* Döbner's (violet).

дебри *pl.* tropical rain forest; thicket; maze, labyrinth; —стый *a.* full of thick forests.

де-Бройля соотношение (phys.) de Broglie relation.

дебустер *m.* debooster.

дебют *m.*, —ировать *v.* debut.

девальвация *f.* devaluation.

девастация *f.* extermination of sources of infection.

девать *v.* put, dispose (of); mislay; spend, expend; quarter, put up; —ся *v.* get (to), go, disappear, vanish; take or find shelter; become.

девейлит *m.*(min.) deweylite.

Деви лампа (min.) Davy lamp, davy.

девиа/та *f.* deviation; (stat.) variance; —тор *m.* deviator; compass adjuster; —ционный *a.*, —ция *f.* deviation, error.

девиз *m.*, —ный *a.* motto, emblem.

девиндтит *m.* (min.) dewindtite.

девиометр *m.* deviometer.

Девиса печь (met.) Davis furnace.

девитрификация *f.* devitrification.

девичий *a.* virgin, maiden.

девон *m.*, —ский *a.* (geol.) Devonian.

девственн/ица *f.* virgin; —ость *f.* virginity; —ый *a.* virgin(al); primeval (community); parthen(o)—; —ая плева (anat.) hymen; —ая природа wilderness; —ое размножение parthenogenesis.

девт(ер)о— *see* дейтеро—.

девулканиз/ат *m.* reclaim(ed rubber), devulcanizate; —атор *m.* devulcanizer, digester, reclaiming tank; —ация *f.* devulcanization, etc., *see v.*; —овать *v.* devulcanize, reclaim, digest.

девушка *f.* girl, maiden, virgin.

девяност/о *num.* ninety; —ый *a.* ninetieth.

девясил *m.* (bot.) elecampane (*Inula*).

девятер/ичный *a.* nonary; nine; —ной *a.* ninefold; —о *num.* nine.

девяти *gen.* of девять; *prefix* non(a)— (ninth); novem—, ennea— (nine); —кратный *a.* ninefold; —лепестный *a.* (bot.) enneapetalous; —летие *n.* ninth anniversary; —летний *a.* nine-year(-old); —пёрка *f.* (ichth.) toothed cod (*Arctogadus borisovi*); —сот *gen. of*; девятьсот; —сотый *a.* nine-hundredth; —стам *dat. of* девятьсот; —сторонний *a.* nonagon(al); —ступенчатый *a.* nine-step(ped); —точ(еч)ный *a.* nine-point; —угольник *m.* (geom.) nonagon.

девят/ка *f.* nine; —надцатый *a.* nineteenth; —надцать *num.* nineteen; —ый *a.* ninth; —ь *num.* nine; —ьсот *num.* nine hundred; —ью *adv.* multiplied by nine.

дегаз/атор *m.* degasifier, degasser, decontaminator; stripper; deaerator; **—ационный** *a.*, **—ация** *f.* degasification, degassing, etc., *see v.*; gas decontamination; dry distillation (of wood); **—ационная жидкость** liquid decontaminant; **—ёр** *see* **дегазатор; —ированный** *a.* degasified, etc., *see v.*; **—ировать** *v.* degas(ify), outgas; strip; (coal) coke, carbonize; (plastic mold) vent, breathe; detoxify; (nucl.) decontaminate; **—ификатор** *see* **дегазатор.**

дегельминтизация *f.* (vet.) worming.

дегенер/ат *m.* degenerate; **—ативность** *f.* degeneracy; **—ативный** *a.* degenerat(iv)e; **—ация** *f.* degeneration; **—ированный** *a.* degenerate(d), vestigial; **—ировать** *v.* degenerate.

дегерминатор *m.* (agr.) degerminator.

дегидраза *f.* dehydrase.

дегидрат/ационный *a.*, **—ация** *f.*, **—ирование** *n.* dehydration; **—ировать** *v.* dehydrate; **—ирующее вещество** dehydrating agent, dehydrant; **—ор** *m.* dehydrator.

дегидрацетовая кислота dehydracetic acid, methyl acetopyronone.

дегидрация *see* **дегидратация.**

дегидрир/ование *n.* dehydrogenation; **—ованный** *a.* dehydrogenated; **—овать** *v.* dehydrogenate, dehydrogenize; **—ующий** *a.* dehydrogenating.

дегидро— *prefix* dehydro—; **—бромирование** *n.* dehydrobromination.

дегидроген/аза *f.* dehydrogenase; **—изационный** *a.*, **—изация** *f.* dehydrogenation; **—из(ир)овать** *v.* dehydrogenate.

дегидро/кортикостерон *m.* dehydrocorticosterone (hormone); **—кси—** *prefix* dehydroxy—; **—слизевая кислота** dehydromucic acid, 2,5-furandicarboxylic acid; **—соединение** *n.* dehydro compound; **—сульфирование** *n.* dehydrosulfurization; **—фторирование** *n.* dehydrofluorination; **—хлорировать** *v.* dehydrochlorinate; **—холевая кислота** dehydrocholic acid; **—циклизация** *f.* dehydrocyclization.

дегомация *f.* (text.) degumming.

дегорж/аж *m.*, **—ирование** *n.* disgorgement, disgorging (of lees from wine); **—ировать** *v.* disgorge.

дёготь *m.* tar, pitch.

дегра *f.* (leather) degras, wool fat.

деград/ация *f.* degradation, breakdown, decomposition; deterioration; (av.) longitudinal decalage; **—ированный** *a.* degraded, broken down; **—ировать** *v.* degrade, break down, deteriorate, degenerate; degress; **—ирующий** *a.* degrading, etc., *see v.*

дегресс/ивный *a.* degressive; **—ия** *see* **деградация.**

дёгте— *prefix* tar; **—бетон** *m.* bituminous concrete, tar macadam; **—видный** *a.* tarry, tar-like.

дегтевой *a.* tar.

дёгтевыделение *n.* tar separation.

дегтёвый *a.* tar.

дёгте/грунт *see* **дёгтебетон; —картон** *m.* tar paper; **—курение** *n.* tar distillation; **—образный** *see* **дёгтевидный; —образование** *n.* tar formation; **—отделение** *n.* tar separation; **—отделитель** *m.* tar separator; **—перегонный** *a.* tar distillation; **—подобный** *see* **дёгтевидный.**

дегтяр/ик *m.* tar distiller (operator); **—ица** *f.* tar container; **—ый** *a.* tar; **—я** *f.* tar works.

дегу *m.* (mam.) Octodon(tomys).

дегум(м)иров/ание *n.* degumming; **—анный** *a.* degummed; **—ать** *v.* degum.

дегуст/атор *m.* taster; **—ация** *f.* tasting; **—ировать** *v.* taste, sample; degust(ate).

дедвейт *m.* dead weight, dead load.

дедекиндово сечение (math.) Dedekind cut; **—сть** *f.* Dedekind property.

дедифференцировка *f.* (cyt.) dedifferentiation.

дедк/а *m.* (ent.) dragonfly; **—и** *pl.* Gomphidae.

дедоломитизация *f.* (geol.) dedolomitization.

деду/ктивно *adv.* deductively, by deduction; **д. равный** *a.* interducible (formula); **—ктивный** *a.* deductive; **—кция** *f.* deduction; **—цировать** *v.* deduce.

дееспособн/ость *f.* competence; **—ый** *a.* competent, capable.

деется *pr. 3 sing. of* **деяться.**

дежа *f.* pan, trough (for dough).

дежек/тивный *a.* (geol.) dejective (folding); **—ционный** *a.*, **—ция** *f.* dejection.

Дежнёва мыс (geog.) Cape Dezhney.

дежур/ить *v.* be on duty; watch, guard; **—ный** *a.* on duty; *m.* attendant; **—ный журнал** log; **—ный режим** stand-by; **—ство** *n.* tour of duty; attendance; watch; **с —ством** on duty.

дез— *prefix* de(s)—; dis—; *prefix and insert* disinfection; **—авуировать** *v.* repudiate; **—агрегация** *f.* disaggregation, disintegration; **—агрегировать** *v.* disaggregate; **—аксиальный** *a.* offset.

дезактив/ационный *a.*, **—ация** *f.*, **—ирование** *n.* deactivation; (nucl.) decontamination; **—ированный** *a.* deactivated; decontaminated; **—ировать** *v.* deactivate, inactivate; decontaminate; **—ирующее вещество** decontaminant.

дезалкилировать *v.* dealkylate.

дезами/дирование *n.* deamid(iz)ation; **—дировать** *v.* deamidate; **—наза** *f.* deaminase; **—нирование** *n.* deamin(iz)ation; **—нировать** *v.* deaminate.

дезартикуляция *f.* (med.) disarticulation.

дезассимиляция *f.* dissimilation.

дезацилоза *f.* deacylose.

дезингибитор *m.* disinhibitor.

дезинсек/тант *m.* insecticide; **—тор** *m.* insect-exterminating unit; **—ционный** *a.*, **—ция** *f.* disinfestation, disinsectization, insect control; delousing.

дезинтегр/атор *m.* disintegrator, pulverizer, shredder; (gas) scrubber, washer; **—ация** *f.* disintegration, decomposition, decay; **—ированный** *a.* disintegrated; **—ировать** *v.* disintegrate, pulverize, shred.

дезинтоксикац/ионный *a.*, **—ия** *f.* detoxicating, detoxication.

дезинфек/тант *m.*, **—ционное средство** disinfectant; **—тор** *m.* disinfector; **—ционный** *a.* disinfection, disinfecting, disinfectant; **—ция** *f.* disinfection; bacteriological decontamination.

дезинфицир/ование *see* **дезинфекция; —овать** *v.* disinfect; (bact.) decontaminate; **—ующий** *a.* disinfecting, disinfectant; antiseptic; **—ующее вещество, —ующее средство** disinfectant; decontaminant.

дезинформ/ация *f.* disinformation; dissemination of fabricated information; **—ировать** *v.* disinform.

дезкамера *f.* disinfection chamber.

дезодор/ант, —(из)атор *m.* deodorant, deodorizer, (air) freshener; **—(из)ация** *f.*, **—ирование** *n.* deodorization; **—ированный** *a.* deodorized; **—ировать** *v.* deodorize; freshen; **—ирующее средство** deodorant.

дезокамера *see* **дезкамера.**

дезоксалевая кислота desoxalic acid.

дезокси— *prefix* de(s)oxy—; **—адениловый** *a.* deoxyadenylic (acid); **—аденозин** *m.* deoxyadenosine; **—бензоин** *m.* deoxybenzoin; **—генация** *f.* (med.) deoxygenation; **—генизирующий** *a.* oxygen-consuming; **—гуаниловый** *a.* deoxyguanylic (acid); **—гуанозин** *m.* deoxyguanosine; **—дация** *f.* deoxidation; oxygen deprivation; **—кортикостерон** *m.* deoxycorticosterone, DOC.

дезоксирибо/за *f.* deoxyribose, deRib; **—нуклеаза** *f.* deoxyribonuclease; **—новая кислота** deoxyribonucleic acid, DNA.

дезокси/сахар *m.* deoxysugar; **—соединение** *n.* deoxy compound; **—тимидин** *m.* (deoxy)thymidine; **—уридин** *m.* deoxyuridine; **—холевая кислота** deoxycholic acid, DOC.

дезорб/ер *m.* desorber; **—ция** *f.* desorption.

дезорганиз/ация *f.* disorganization, confusion, disorder, chaos; **—ованный** *a.* disorganized, confused, chaotic; **—ов(ыв)ать** *v.* disorganize.

дезориент/ация *f.* disorientation, disorder; **—ированный** *a.* disoriented, randomly oriented; **—ировать** *v.* disorient, confuse; **—ироваться** *v.* get disoriented; lose one's bearings.

дезотряд *m.* disinfecting unit.

дезраствор *m.* disinfectant solution.

деион/изатор *m.* deionizer; **—ация** *f.* deionization; **—ированный** *a.* deionized; **—ировать** *v.* deionize.

дейдвуд *m.,* **—ный** *a.* (naut.) deadwood.

дейка *f.* (geol.) dyke.

дейлефиля *f.* (ent.) Deilephila.

действенн/ость *f.* efficiency, effectiveness; activity; **—ый** *a.* efficient, effective, operative; active; efficacious.

действ/ие *n.* action, work(ing), operation, performance, function(ing), running (of machine), service; agency, effect, influence; treatment, reaction; **—ием** by the action (of), by means (of); **ближнего —ия** short-range; **вводить в д.** *v.* put into operation, bring into action or force, implement, carry into effect; **вступать в д.** *v.* come into effect, become valid; **дальнего —ия** long-range; **интенсивность —ия** effective force, efficiency; **находиться под —ием** *v.* be affected (by); be exposed (to), be subjected (to); **не подвергаться —ию** *v.* be unaffected (by); **не поддающийся —ию** *a.* resistant; stable; **оказывать д.** *v.* work, operate, take effect, have an effect (on), affect; act (on); **под —ием** under (the action of), by; on exposure (to), (when) exposed (to); **подвергать —ию** *v.* expose (to), subject (to); treat; **приводить в д.** *v.* start, actuate, bring into operation, activate; (set to) work, operate; **принцип —ия** action mechanism; **прямого —ия** *a.* direct-action; direct (arc).

действительн/о *adv.* actually, in fact, indeed, in reality, real(ly); this can be proved as follows; to demonstrate; let us; **—означный** *a.* (math.) real-valued; **—ость** *f.* reality, actuality, fact; efficiency, effectiveness, practicality; validity; authenticity; **в —ости** in reality, in practice; actually, in (actual) fact; **—ый** *a.* real, true, actual, virtual; effective, efficient; valid, holding (for); authentic; current (name); net (price); **—ая производительность** effective capacity; **делать —ым** *v.* validate; **остаться —ым** *v.* remain valid, hold (for).

действ/овать *v.* act, operate, work, run, function, perform, proceed; affect; attack, react; hold (good or true), be valid; **начать д.** take effect, start; **не д.** fail, be out of order; **—ующий** *a.* active, acting, actuating, working, at work; operating, operative; in gear; efficient; effective; virtual (value); prevailing (law); efficacious; actual (resistance); *m.* operator; **—ующая среда** agent; **—ующее начало** active principle; **—ующее поле** field of action; **закон —ующих масс** law of mass action.

дейт(ер)— *see* **дейтеро—**.

дейтер/ид *m.* deuteride; **—иевый** *a.,* **—ий** *m.* deuterium, D (heavy hydrogen); **—изованный** *a.* deuterium; deuterated; **—изовать, —ировать** *v.* deuterate; **—о—** *prefix* deutero— [second(ary); deuterium]; **—огенный** *a.* (geol.) deuterogenic; **—ометка** *f.* deuterium label(ing); **—он** *see* **дейтрон**; **—оокись** *f.* deuterium oxide, heavy water; **—офлебииды** *pl.* (ent.) Deuterophlebiidae.

дейт/о— *see* **дейтеро—**; **—оплазма** *f.* (embr.) deutoplasm; **—рон** *m.,* **—ронный** *a.* (nucl.) deut(er)on.

дейция *f.* (bot.) Deutzia.

дек. *abbr.* **(декабрь)** December.

дек *m.,* **—а** *f.* deck; **—а** *f.* (agr.) hopper, concave (of combine); sounding board (of musical instrument).

дека— *prefix* deca—, ten.

декабрь, —ский *a.* December.

дека/гидрат *m.* decahydrate; **—гидронафталин** *see* **декалин**; **—гидросоединение** *n.* decahydro compound; **—гон** *m.* (geom.) decagon; **—грамм** *m.* decagram; **—да** *f.* decade; ten-day period; **—диен** *m.* decadiene; **—дный** *a.* decade, scale-of-ten; decimal.

декалесценция *f.* (met.) decalescence.

декалин *m.* decalin, decahydronaphthalene.

декалитр *m.* decaliter (10 liters).

декальк/ировать *v.* transfer (design); **—омания** *f.* transfer; decalcomania.

декальци/нация, —фикация *f.* decalcification; **—нировать(ся)** *v.* decalcify.

декаметр *m.* decameter (10 meters).

декан *m.* dean; (chem.) decane; **—ал(ь)** *m.* decanal, decyl aldehyde; **—ат** *m.* dean's office; **—овый** *a.* decane; decanoic (acid); **—ол** *m.* decanol; **—он** *m.* decanone; **—ский** *a.* dean's; (geog.) Deccan; **—ство** *n.* deanship.

декант/ат *m.* decanted liquid; **—атор** *m.* decanter; settling tank; **—атор-отстойник** *m.* settling tank, sludge separator; **—атор-сгуститель** *m.* thickener; **—ация** *f.,* **—ирование** *n.* decantation; **—ер** *see* **декантатор**; **—ированный** *a.* decanted, etc., *see v.*; **—ировать** *v.* decant, pour off, discard; **—ор** *see* **декантатор**.

декапир *m.* pickled sheet (iron); **—ование** *n.,* **—овка** *f.* pickling, etc., *see v.*; dip; **—ованный** *a.* pickled, etc., *see v.*; **—овать** *v.* (met.) pickle, dip, scour.

декапитация *f.* decapitation.

декаплоид *m.,* **—ный** *a.* (gen.) decaploid.

декапод *m.* (crust.; mal.) decapod.

декарбоксил/аза *f.* decarboxylase; **—ирование** *n.* decarboxylation; **—ировать** *v.* decarboxylate.

декарбонизировать *v.* decarbonize; (met.) decarburize.

декартовый *a.* (math.) Cartesian, Descartes.

декатил *m.* decatyl, decyl.

декатионировать *v.* (chem.) decationize.

декатир *m.* (text.) decat(iz)ing machine; **—ование** *n.* decatizing, etc., *see v.*; **—овать** *v.* decat(iz)e, steam, hot-press, sponge; flatten (curl); **—овка** *f.,* **—овочный** *a.* decat(iz)ing.

декатонна *f.* ten tons.

декатрон *m.* decatron, decade-counting tube.

декаэдр *m.* (cryst.) decahedron; **—ический** *a.* decahedral.

деквалифицировать(ся) *v.* disqualify.

декель *m.* (printing press) tympan.

декларировать *v.* declare, proclaim, state.

деклин/атор *m.* (phys.) declination compass, declinometer; **—ация** *f.* (magnetic) declination; **—ировать** *v.* decline; **—ометр** *see* **деклинатор**.

деклуазит *m.* (min.) descloizite.

декобальтизация *f.* decobaltization.

дековый *a.* of **дек(а)**.

декогер/ер *m.* (rad.) decoherer; **—ировать** *v.* decohere.

декод/ер *m.* decoder; **—ирование** *n.* decoding, etc., *see v.;* **—ированный** *a.* decoded; **—ировать** *v.* decode, decipher, interpret, translate; **—ируемый** *a.* decodable; decoded; **—ирующее устройство** decoder.

декоза *f.* decose.

декокт *m.* decoction.

деколор/ация *f.* discoloration; **—иметр** *m.* (sugar) decolorimeter.

декомпенсация *f.* (med.) decompensation.

декомпоз/ер *m.* decomposer; **—иция** *f.* decomposition.

декомпресс/ионный *a.* decompression; caisson (disease); pressure release (valve); **—ия** *f.* decompression; **—ор** *m.* decompressor, exhaust valve; relief gear.

деконъюгация *f.* (gen.) deconjugation.

декор/ативно-прикладное искусство arts and crafts; **—ативный, —ационный** *a.* decorative, ornamental; landscape (gardening); pet (animal); **—ация** *f.,* **—ирование** *n.* decoration; **—ировать** *v.* decorate.

декортик/атор *m.* decorticator; **—ация** *f.* decortication, stripping, debarking, scutching.

декрейтер *m.* uncrating machine.

декре/мент *m.* decrement, decrease; **—метр** *m.* (rad.) decremeter.

декремнезация *f.* desiliconization.

декрепитация *f.* decrepitation.

декрет *m.,* **—ировать** *v.* decree; **—ный** *a.* decree; maternity (leave); daylight saving (time).

декристаллиз/ация *f.* decrystallization; (plastics) thawing, defrosting; **—овать** *v.* thaw, defrost.

дексель *m.* (carpentry) adz(e).

дексиотропный *a.* (zool.) dexiotropic.

декстральный *a.* dextral, right-handed.

декстр/ан *m.* dextran; **—ин** *m.* dextrin, starch gum; **—инизатор** *m.* dextrin(izing) kettle; **—ин(из)ация** *f.* dextrinization, dextrin preparation; **—иниз(ир)овать** *v.* dextrinate, convert into dextrin; **—иновый** *a.* dextrin.

декстро— *prefix* dextro— (to the right, clockwise); **—за** *f.* dextrose, *d*-glucose; **—соединение** *n.* dextro(rotatory) compound.

декулятор *m.* (paper) deculator, stock deaerator.

дел *gen. pl. of* **дело;** *past m. sing. of* **деть;** *m.* (math.) del operator; **—а** *pl., etc., of* **дело;** *past f. sing. of* **деть.**

делавэрский *a.* (geog.) Delaware.

деламинация *f.* delamination.

делан/ие *n.* doing, etc., *see* **делать; —ный** *a.* done, performed, etc., *see* **делать;** simulated.

делатинит *m.* (min.) delatynite.

делать *v.* do, perform, carry out, accomplish; render, cause; turn (into); make, produce, manufacture; construct; take (photographs); **д. щелочным** alkalize; **—ся** *v.* be made, be done; become, get, grow, turn; happen.

делафоссит *m.* (min.) delafossite.

делег/ат *m.* delegate; **—ация** *f.,* **—ирование** *n.* delegation; **—ировать** *v.* (send as a) delegate; authorize; **—атка** *f.* delegate.

делёж *m.,* **—ка** *f.* share, sharing, distribution, division, partition; **—ный** *a. of* **делёж;** split (strap).

делен/ие *n.* division, dividing, etc., *see* **делить;** reading; dial; point (on scale); unit, interval; partition; splitting; (biol.; nucl.) fission; disruption; **наносить —ия** *v.* (sub)divide, graduate; index; **продукт —ия** fission product; **простое д., прямое д.** (gen.) amitosis; **размножение —ием** (biol.) fission; **с —иями** *a.* calibrated; **сложное д.** (gen.) mitosis.

делённый *a.* divided, etc., *see* **делить; д. на** divided by or into.

делесс/ерия *f.* (bot.) Delesseria (red algae); **—ит** *m.* (min.) delessite.

делеция *f.* deletion.

делигнифи/кация *f.* delignification; **—цировать** *v.* delignify, remove lignin.

деликатес *m.,* **—ный** *a.* delicacy.

деликатн/о *adv.* delicately, carefully; **—ость** *f.* delicacy, carefulness, precision; **—ый** *a.* delicate, considerate; cautious, careful, precise.

делим/ое *n.* (math.) dividend; **—ость** *f.* divisibility; (cryst.) cleavability, cleavage; (nucl.) fissionability; (petr.) fissility; **—ый** *a.* divisible, partible; cleavable; fissionable.

делинт/ер *m.* delinter, lint extractor; **—еровка** *f.,* **—еровочный** *a.* delinting; **—ировать** *v.* delint, remove lint.

делирий *m.* (med.) delirium.

делитель *m.* (math.) divisor; divider, separator; subgroup; **д. на два** (comp.) scale-of-two circuit; **общий д.** common divisor; **—ность** divisibility.

делительн/ый *a.* dividing, etc., *see* **делить;** index (head); separatory (funnel, stopcock); (nucl.) fission; **д. механизм** divider, indexer; **д. циркуль** dividers; **—ая окружность** pitch circle (of gear); **—ое приспособление** divider, indexer.

делить *v.* divide (into), part; share; index, classify; calibrate, graduate, mark off; partition; split, break down; **—ся** *v.* be divided; divide; break down, disintegrate; cleave, split; share; communicate, tell, confide; **—ся на** be divisible by, go into; come under, fall into.

делл *m.* dell, small valley.

дел/о *n.* matter, concern, thing, point; business, transaction, deal; affair; management; enterprise; occupation, work, trade; art; engineering; file, records; case; (mil.) engagement; **—ing,** i.e., **горное д.** mining; **—а** *pl.* business, affairs, doings, proceedings; **в том, что** the fact is, the point is; **д. обстоит** the situation is; **д. обстоит так** such (or this) is the case; **в самом —е** really, actually, indeed, in fact; **возбудить д.** *v.* institute proceedings (against); **иметь д.** *v.* deal, be concerned, have to do (with); **к —у** to the point; **лист —а** file or dossier sheet; **между —ом** in one's spare time; **на самом —е** as a matter of fact, actually, really; **не так обстоит д. с** not so with; **первым —ом** first of all; **по —у** on business.

делов/итость *f.* efficiency; **—итый** *a.* efficient, business-like; constructive; **—ой** *a.* business(-like), practical, workable; (zool.) surviving (litter); **—ая древесина** (construction) lumber, timber.

делокализация *f.* delocalization.

делопроизвод/итель *m.* secretary, clerk; **—ство** *n.* business correspondence, clerical work.

делоренцит *m.* (min.) delorenzite.

дельвоксит *m.* (min.) delvauxite.

дельн/о *adv.* efficiently, etc., *see a.;* **—ость** *f.* efficiency, competence; **—ый** *a.* efficient, competent, business-like, capable; sensible (suggestion).

дельт/а *f.* delta (Δ, δ); delta (of river); **д.-древесина** *f.* a laminated plywood; **д.-железо** delta iron; **д.-излучение** *n.* delta radiation; **д.-лучи** *pl.* delta rays; **—макс** *m.* Delta Max (alloy); **д.-металл** *m.* delta metal; **д.-модуляция** *f.* delta modulation; **д.-оператор** *m.* (math.) Laplacian operator; **—апланерист** *m.* hang-glider pilot; **д.-связь** *f.* delta bond; **д.-функция** *f.* (Dirac) delta function; **д.-частица** *f.* delta particle; **д.-шум** *m.* delta noise.

дельт/идий *m.* (zool.) deltidium; **—ирий** *m.* delthyrium; **—ов(идн)ый** *a.* deltoid; **—оид** *m.* deltoid, delta-shaped region; **—о(иддодека)эдр** *m.* (cryst.) deltoid dodecahedron, deltohedron; **—ообразование** *n.* (geol.) deltafication, delta formation.

дельтруксиновый *a.* deltruxinic (acid).

дельфизин *m.* delphisine.

дельфин *m.* (mam.) dolphin; (astr.) Delphinus; delphin (dye); **обыкновенный д., д.-белобочка** *m.* common dolphin (*Delphinus delphis*); **—ат** *m.* (chem.) delphinate; **—идин** *m.* delphinidin; **—ий** *m.* dolphin; **—ин** *m.* delphinine (alkaloid); delphinin (glucoside); **—ировать** *v.* (naut.) porpoise; **—ит** *m.* (min.) delphinite; **—иум** *m.* (bot.) delphinium; **—овые** *pl.* (mam.) Delphinidae; **—овый** *a.* of **дельфин;** delphinic (acid).

дельфокурарин *m.* delphocurarine.

делюв/иальный *a.* (geol.) deluvial; **—иальные отложения, —ий** *m.* deluvium, slope-wash, float, talus.

деля (на) *pr. ger.* (on) dividing (by), if we divide; **—нка** *f.* (p)lot, parcel, strip (of land); allotment.

деляпсивный *a.* (geol.) delapsing.

деляческий *a.* narrow-minded, utilitarian.

делящий *a.* dividing, etc., *see* **делить; —ся** *a.* fission (able), fissile, divisible; **—ся материал** nuclear material.

дём *m.* (ecology) deme.

демагнетиз/атор *m.* demagnetizer; **—ировать** *v.* demagnetize.

демантоид *m.* (min.) demantoid.

демаргаринизировать *v.* winterize.

демаркац/ионный *a.,* **—ия** *f.* demarcation.

демаскиров/ание *n.* disclosure; **—ать** *v.* disclose, reveal, decamouflage.

деменция *f.* (med.) dementia.

демерол *m.* demerol, meperidine.

демерсальный *a.* demersal, bottom-dwelling.

деметилиров/ание *n.* demethylation; **—ать** *v.* demethylate.

демидовит *m.* (min.) demidovite.

демиелинизация *f.* (med.) demyelin(iz)ation.

демилитаризировать *v.* demilitarize.

деминерализ/атор *m.* demineralizer; **—ация** *f.* demineralization; **—(ир)овать** *v.* demineralize.

демобилиз/ация *f.* demobilization; fixation (of nutrients, etc.); **—ировать** *v.* demobilize.

демограф/ический *a.* (stat.) demographic; vital (statistics); population (explosion); **—ические тенденции** population profile; **—ия** *f.* demography.

демодикоз *m.* (vet.) demodicosis, mange.

демодул/ировать *v.* (rad.) demodulate, detect; **—ятор** *m.* demodulator, detector; **—яция** *f.* demodulation.

демократ/ический *a.* democratic; **—ия** *f.* democracy.

демон *m.* (phys.) (Maxwell) demon.

демонстр/ативный *a.* demonstrative; **—атор** *m.* demonstrator, exponent; **—ационный** *a.* demonstration, demonstrating; **—ационный склад** showroom, exhibit; **—ация** *f.,* **—ирование** *n.* demonstration; **—ированный** *a.* demonstrated, etc., *see v.;* **—ировать** *v.* demonstrate, show, exhibit, present; **—ироваться** *v.* be demonstrated; be on display, be on exhibit.

демонт/аж *m.,* **—ирование** *n.* dismantling, etc., *see v.;* disassembly; **—ировать** *v.* dismantle, disassemble, strip, take apart, dismount, take down, knock down.

демпинг *m,* **—овый** *a.* (com.) dumping.

демпф/ер *m.* damper, shock absorber, buffer; dash-pot; (control system) anti-hunt circuit; **—ирование** *n.* damping, shock absorption, buffer action; **—ированный** *a.* damped; **—ировать** *v.* damp(en); bring to rest, prevent hunting; **—ирующий** *a.* damping.

демультиплик/атор *m.* (mach.) auxiliary transmission; (speed) reducing gear; **—ация** *f.* gearing down.

демуниципализировать *v.* return (property to private ownership).

демур/аж, —редж *m.* demurrage (of ship).

демутация *f.* reestablishment of vegetation.

дем(ь)янка *f.* eggplant (*Solanum melongena*).

демэкология *f.* population ecology.

денатур/ализовать *v.* denaturalize; **—ант, —атор** *m.* denaturant, denaturing agent; **—ат** *m.* denatured alcohol; **—ация** *f.,* **—ирование** *n.* denaturation; **—ированный** *a.* denatured; **—ировать** *v.* denature; denatur(iz)e (proteins); **—ирующее средство** *see* **денатурант.**

денге *m., лихорадка* **д.** (med.) dengue.

денгизский *a.* (geog.) Dengiz, Tengiz.

дендироль *m.* (paper) dandy roll.

дендр/арий *m.* arboretum; **—ит** *m.* (anat.; cryst.) dendrite; **—итический, —итный, —итовый** *a.* dendritic, arborescent, tree-like; **—о** *prefix* dendr(o)— (tree); **—оидный** *a.* dendroid, dendritic; **—окаламус** *m.* (bot.) Dendrocalamus; **—олог** *m.* (silv.) dendrologist; **—ологический** *a.* dendrological; **—ология** *f.* dendrology; **—ометр** *m.* dendrometer; **—ометрия** *f.* dendrometry, tree mensuration; **—онотус** *m.* (mal.) sea slug (Dendronotus); **—офильный** *a.* dendrophilous, tree-loving; **—оцел** *m.* (zool.) Dendrocoelum.

денеб *m.* (astr.) Deneb.

денег *gen. of* **деньги.**

денежн/ик *m.* (bot.) pennycress (*Thlaspi arvense*); **—ый** *a.* monetary; money (order); financial.

денет *fut. 3 sing. of* **девать.**

денитр/ация *f.,* **—(ир)ование** *n.* denitration; **—(ир)овать** *v.* denitrate; **—ирующий** *a.* denitrating; **—ификация** *f.* denitrification; **—ифицировать** *v.* denitrify; **—ифицирующий** *a.* denitrifying.

деннаж *m.* (naut.) dunnage.

денник *m.* box stall (for horse).

денонсировать *v.* denounce.

денс/иметр *m.* (phys.) densimeter; hydrometer; **—иметрия** *f.* densimetry, density measurement; **—итометр** *m.* densitometer, opacity meter; **—итометрия** *f.* (phot.) densitometry; **—ограф** *m.* recording densitometer.

дент/алиум *m.* (mal.) tooth shell (*Dentalium*); **—альный** *a.* dental; **—атность** *f.* (ligand) coordination number; **—икль** *m.* (anat.) denticle; **—ин** *m., —инный, —иновый** *a.* dentin (of teeth).

денуд/ационный *a.,* **—ация** *f.* denudation, washout; **—ированный** *a.* denuded; exposed (rock).

денут *fut. 3 pl. of* **девать.**

день *m.* day; *imp. of* **деть; изо дня в д.** (from) day to day.

деньги *pl.* money, currency; dues; **наличные д.** cash.

денье *n.,* **д.-титр** (text.) denier.

деомис *m.* (mam.) Deomys.

деонтология *f.* deontology; (med.) ethics.

депарафин/изационный *a.,* **—изация** *f.,* **—ирование** *n.* deparaffination, dewaxing; **—ировать** *v.* dewax.

департамент *m.* department, division; **—ский** *a.* departmental.

депеграмма *f.* (meteor.) depegram.

депекорация *f.* slaughtering of cattle.

депектинизатор *m.* depectinization tank.

депенсирующий *a.* depensatory (mortality).

депеша *f.* dispatch, message, telegram.

депигментация *f.* (biol.) depigmentation.

депил/ировать *v.* depilate; **—яторий** *m., —яторный, —яционный** *a.* depilatory; **—яция** *f.* depilation.

деплазмолиз *m.* (bot.) deplasmolysis.

депланация *f.* warping.

депланировать *v.* smooth, make even.

депо *n.,* —**вский** *a.* depot, station; car barn; reservoir, stock; **д. крови** (anat.) blood depot; **паровозное д.** roundhouse.

депозит *m.* deposit.

деполимер *m.* depolymerization product; —**изатор** *m.* depolymerizing agent; —**изация** *f.* depolymerization; —**из(ир)овать** *v.* depolymerize.

деполяриз/атор *m.* depolarizer; —**ация** *f.* depolarization; —**овать** *v.* depolarize.

депон/ент *m.* depositor; type gage; —**ирование** *n.* deposition; —**ировать** *v.* deposit.

депортация *f.* deportation.

депресс/ант *m.* depressor, depressing agent, depressant; —**ивный** *a.* depressive; —**иометр** *m.* depression meter; —**ионный** *a.,* —**ия** *f.* depression; dejection; lowering; draw-down; —**ор** *m.,* —**орный** *a.* (anat.) depressor.

депривация *f.* deprivation.

депротеиниз/ация *f.* deproteinization, protein removal; —**ировать** *v.* deproteinize.

депсид *m.* depside.

депула *f.* (embr.) depula.

депульпированный *a.* devitalized (tooth).

депурация *f.* (physiol.) clearance (of urea).

депут/ат *m.* representative, delegate; —**ация** *f.* deputation.

дерапаж *m.* skidding, slipping.

дератизация *f.* rat or rodent extermination.

дербенник *m.* (bot.) Lythrum; —**овые** *pl.* Lythraceae; —**овый** *a.* lythraceous.

дербилит *m.* (min.) derbylite.

дерб/ник *m.* (orn.) pigeon hawk (*Falco columbarius*); —**янка** *f.* (bot.) Blechnum.

дёрг/анец *m.* (bot.) staminate hemp; —**ание** *n.* twitching, etc., *see v.;* —**анный** *a.* twitched, etc., *see v.;* —**анье** *see* **дёргание;** —**ать** *v.* twitch, jerk, pull, tug; pluck, pull out, extract; harass.

дерг/ач, —**ун** *m.* (orn.) corncrake (*Crex crex*).

деревей *m.* (bot.) yarrow (*Achillea*).

деревен/ение *n.* lignification; —**еть** *v.* lignify, get woody; stiffen; grow numb.

дерев/енский *a.* rural, country, rustic; village; —**ня** *f.* village; country.

дерево *n.* tree; wood; lumber; (math.) tree; (anat.) arbor; —**бетон** *m.* cement wood; **д.-гигант** *n.* giant tree; **д.-камень** *n.* petrified wood; **д.-маяк** *n.* (forestry) standard.

деревообделочн/ая *f.* wood-working shop; —**ик** *m.* woodworker; —**ый** *a.* wood-working.

дерево/обрабатывающий *a.,* —**обработка** *f.* wood working; timber making; —**образный** *a.* arborescent, tree-like; dendroid; —**плита** *f.* timber slab.

дерев/це, —**цо** *n.* sapling; dwarf tree, tree-like shrub; —**цеобразный** *a.* arbusculariform, shrub-like; —**ья** *pl. of* **дерево.**

деревян/еть *see* **деревенеть;** —**исто—** *prefix* xyl(o)— [wood; (chem.) xylene; xylose; xylic]; —**истоплодный** *a.* (bot.) xylocarpous; —**истый** *a.* ligneous, woody; —**истый опал** (min.) wood opal; —**ность** *f.* woodiness; —**ный** *a.* wood(en); woody, ligneous; —**ное масло** low-grade olive oil.

деревяшка *f.* piece of wood.

дер/еза *f.* (bot.) Lycium; —**езняк** *m.* dereznyak, boxthorn thicket.

дёрен *m.* (bot.) dogwood (*Cornus*); —**енные,** —**еновые** *pl.* Cornaceae.

дерепрессированный *a.* derepressed.

дерёт *pr. 3 sing. of* **драть.**

держава *f.* state; empire, power.

держ/авка *see* **держатель;** —**ак** *m.,* —**алка** *f.* handle; —**ание** *n.* keeping, etc., *see* **держать;** (road) stability; —**анный** *a.* kept, etc., *see* **держать;** —**аный** *a.* secondhand, used.

держ/атель *m.* holder, adapter, chuck; carrier, carriage, support; bracket; mount; clip, clamp; (med.) retractor; (anat.) retinaculum; —**ать** *v.* keep, hold, retain; support; maintain, preserve; take (test); —**аться** *v.* keep (to), hold (on; out; together; up); persist; stick (to), cling, adhere; be supported, be held up (by); behave, conduct oneself; —**ащий** *a.* holding; —**и-дерево** *n.* (bot.) Christ's thorn (*Paliurus*).

дерз/ать, —**нуть** *v.* dare, risk, hazard; —**кий** *a.* daring, audacious.

дерив/ат *m.* derivative; —**атный** *a.* derived; —**ационный** *a.,* —**ация** *f.* derivation; diversion (system); (ballistics) drift.

дерихтовые *pl.* (ichth.) Derichthyidae.

дерм/а *f.* (anat.) derma; *suffix* —derm(is); —**альный** *a.* dermal, dermic, cutaneous; —**анис** *m.* (zool.) Dermanyssus (mite); —**атин** *m.,* —**атиновый** *a.* dermatin (leatherette); —**атит** *m.* (med.) dermatitis; —**ато—** *prefix* dermato— (skin, hide); —**атоген** *m.* (bot.) dermatogen; —**атоз** *m.* (med.) dermatosis; —**атозома** *f.* (bot.) dermatosome; —**атол** *m.* dermatol, bismuth subgallate; —**атолог** *m.* (med.) dermatologist; —**атология** *f.* dermatology; —**атом** *m.* (anat.; embr.) dermatome; —**атомикоз** *m.* (med.) dermatomycosis; —**атофит** *m.* dermatophyte, cutaneous fungus; —**ографизм** *m.,* —**ография** *f.* dermographism, dermatographia; —**оид** *m.,* —**оидный** *a.* dermoid.

дёрн *m.* turf, sod, lawn.

дерн/еть *v.* become covered with turf; —**ина** *f.* sod, (piece of) root mat; —**истолуговой** *a.* sod-meadow; —**истый** *a.* turfy, soddy; turf- or sod-forming; cespitose.

дернит *m.* (min.) dehrnite.

дерн/ище *n.* plowed sod; —**овать** *v.* turf, sod; —**овидный** *a.* cespitose, tufted; —**овина** *f.* turf, sod; tuft, tussock; —**овинник** *m.* click beetle; —**овинный** *a.* sod-forming; cespitous, tufty; —**овище** *n.* plowed sod; —**овка** *f.* turfing; *dim. of* **дерновина;** —**ово—** *prefix* turf, sod; soddy (soil); —**ово-подзолистый** *a.* soddy podzolic; —**овый** *a.* turf, sod(dy); (min.) meadow, bog-iron (ore).

дёрнообраз/ование *n.* sod formation; —**ующий** *a.* turf- or sod-forming.

дерн/орез *m.* sod knife, turf cutter; —**сним(атель)** *m.* skim colter, skimmer.

дёрнут/ый *a. see* **дёрганный;** —**ь** *see* **дёргать.**

деррид *m.* derrid (a resin).

деррик *m.,* **д.-вышка** derrick; **д.-кран** derrick (crane); **вагон-д.** derrick car.

деррис *m.* derris (insecticide).

дерть *f.* coarsely ground grain.

дерущий *pr. act. part. of* **драть.**

дерю/га *f.,* —**жина,** —**жка** *f.,* —**жный** *a.* sacking, sack cloth, burlap.

деряба *f.* missel bird (*Turdus viscivorus*).

дес. *abbr.* (**десятина; десятичный**).

десант *m.* (mil.) landing; landing party; —**ировать** *v.* land; —**ник** *m.* paratrooper; —**ный** *a.* landing; airborne; —**овместимость** *f.* troop capacity.

десатурация *f.* desaturation.

дёсен *gen. pl. of* **десна;** —**но—** *prefix* (anat.) gingivo—; —**ный** *a.* gingival, gum.

десенсибилиз/атор *m.* desensitizer; **—ация** *f.* desensitization; **—ировать** *v.* desensitize; **—ирующий** *a.* desensitizing.

десерт *m.,* **—ный** *a.* dessert.

десик/ант *m.* desiccant, drying agent; **—атор** *m.* drying oven; **—ация** *f.* desiccation, drying.

десили/кация *f.* (geol.) desilication; **—цировать** *v.* desiliconize.

десквам/ативный *a.* (med.; geol.) desquamative; **—(ин)ация** *f.* desquamation, scaling off, peeling.

дескрип/тивный *a.* descriptive; **—тор** *m.* descriptor; **—ция** *f.* description.

дескур/айния, —ения *f.* (bot.) Descurainia.

десм/а *f.* (zool.) desma; **—идиевые** *pl.* Desmidiaceae (algae); **—ин** *m.* (min.) desmine, stilbite; **—о—** *prefix* desm(o)— (bond, ligament); **—обактерии** *pl.* Desmobacteria; **—оген** *m.* desmogen, growing tissue; **—од** *m.* (mam.) vampire bat (*Desmodus*); **—одиум** *m.* (bot.) Desmodium; **—одовые** *pl.* (mam.) Desmodontidae; **—одонтный** *a.* (zool.) desmodont; **—оз** *m.* (med.) desmosis; **—оид** *m.,* **—оидный** *a.* desmoid; **—олаза** *f.,* **—олитический фермент** desmolase; **—олиз** *m.* desmolysis; **—ология** *f.* (anat.) desmology.

десмосома *f.* (gen.) desmosome.

десмотроп *m.* desmotrope; **—ия** *f.* desmotropism, dynamic isomerism, tautomerism; **—ный** *a.* desmotropic.

дес/на *f.* (anat.) gum, gingiva; **воспаление дёсен** (med.) gingivitis.

деснинский *a.* (geog.) Desna.

десн/ичный, —овой *a.* (anat.) gingival.

десорб/ент *m.* desorbent; **—ирование** *n.,* **—ция** *f.* desorption; **—ировать** *v.* desorb, expel, drive off; strip.

дессикация *see* **десикация.**

дестабилиз/атор *m.* destabilizer; **—ация** *f.,* **—ирование** *n.* destabilization; **—ировать** *v.* destabilize, disturb.

дест/евой *a.,* **—ей** *gen. pl. of* **десть.**

дестилл— *see under* **дистилл—.**

дестрибутор *m.* distributor.

деструирующий *a.* invasive (tumor).

деструк/тивность *f.* disruptiveness; **—тивный** *a.* destructive; disruptive; **—тированный** *a.* destroyed, etc., *see v.;* broken down; **—тировать** *v.* destroy, break down, degrade; disrupt; **—ция** *f.* destruction, etc., *see* verb; breakdown, decomposition; (biol.) catabolism.

десть *f.* quire (of paper).

десульф/атизация *f.* desulfatization; **—ирование** *n.* desulfonation; **—итация** *f.* desulfitation; **—ур(из)атор** *m.* desulfurizer; **—ур(из)ация** *f.* desulfur(iz)ation; sulfur removal; **—ировать** *v.* desulfurize.

десцендендия *f.* descent.

десятер/ичный, —ной *a.* tenfold; **—о** *num.* ten.

десяти *gen. of* **десять;** *prefix* deca—, decem—, ten; **—балльный** *a.* ten-point (scale); **—вёрстка** *f.* map with scale of 10 versts to the inch; **—водный** *a.* decahydrate; **—гнёздный** *a.* (biol.) decemolecular; **—гранник** *m.* (cryst.) decahedron; **—гранный** *a.* decahedral; **—дневка** *f.* ten-day period; **—дневный** *a.* ten-day; **—километровка** *f.* map with scale of 10 kilometers to the centimeter; **—кратный** *a.* tenfold.

десятилет/ие *n.* decade; tenth anniversary; **—ний** *a.* ten-year; decennial.

десятина *f.* tenth part; 2.7 acres.

десяти/ногие *pl.* (mal.; crust.) Decapoda; **—нормальный** *a.* decinormal; **—пёрка** *f.* (ichth.) scad (*Decapterus*); **—сторонний** *a.* decalateral.

десятиугольн/ик *m.* (geom.) decagon; **—ый** *a.* decagonal.

десятичленный *a.* ten-membered.

десятичн/о-двоичный *a.* decimal-binary; **—ый** *a.* decimal; common (logarithm); **—ый знак** decimal point.

десят/ка *f.* ten; **—ник** *m.* foreman; **—ок** *m.* (group of) ten; decade; **—ый** *a.* tenth; **—ь** *num.* ten; **—ью** *adv.* multiplied by ten.

дет— *prefix* (**детский**) children's.

детал/изация *f.,* **—изирование** *n.* detail(ing); specification; **глубина —изации, степень —изации** (comp.) granularity; **—изированный** *a.* detailed; **—из(ир)овать** *v.* (give in) detail; work out in detail; itemize; (math.) extend (an expression); **—ированность** *f.* details; **—ировка** *f.* detail(ed) drawing; **—ь** *f.* detail, part, component, member; article, piece, work(piece); element; **—и** *pl.* parts; details, particulars; hardware.

детальн/о *adv.* in detail; thoroughly; **—ость** *f.* detail(edness); **—ый** *a.* detailed, with full details, comprehensive; minute.

детандер *m.* expansion engine, expander; reducer valve.

деташёр *m.* detacher; (dyeing) spot cleaner; scroll mill.

детва *f.* (bee) larva, brood.

дет/дом *m.* children's home; **—ей** *gen. of* **дети.**

детект/ирование *n.* detection; (rad.) rectification; **—ировать** *v.* detect, find, catch; rectify; **—ирующий** *a.* detecting, etc., *see v.;* **—ор** *m.,* **—орный** *a.* detector; pickup; probe; rectifier.

детёныш *m.* youngster, offspring; cub; calf.

детергент *m.* detergent.

детермин/ант *m.* (gen.; math.) determinant; heredity factor, gene; **—ация** *f.* determination; **—изм** *m.* determinism; **—ированность** *f.* determinacy; **—ированный** *a.* determined, determinate, disciplined; definite; **—ировать** *v.* determine, fix.

дет/и *pl.* children; **—ище** *n.* offspring; creation; brain child; **—ка** *f.* (bot.) bulbil, secondary bulb, bulblet; (garlic) clove; (bee) brood; **засев на —ку** (bees) egg laying.

детойль *m.* a DDT insecticide.

детокси/кация *f.* detoxi(fi)cation; **—цировать** *v.* detoxify.

детон/атор *m.* (expl.) detonator (cap), primer, percussion cap; knock producer; **—ация** *f.,* **—ационный** *a.* detonation, explosion; knock (of motor); **ингибитор —ации** antiknock; **величина —ации, степень —ации, —ационная стойкость** knock rating (of fuel), octane number.

детонизация *f.* taking up slack.

детон/ировать *v.* detonate, explode; knock; (recording) drift, flutter, wow; **—ирующий** *a.* detonating, etc., *see v.;* **—ометр** *m.* knock indicator; flutter meter.

дето/родный *a.* genital; **—рождение** *n.* child bearing, parturition; **—убийство** *n.* infanticide.

детренированность *f.* poor physical condition.

детрит *m.* detritus, residual debris; (immun.) calf lymph; **—овый** *a.* detrital; **—ояд** *m.* detritophage, detritus eater.

детрузивный *a.* (geol.) detrusion.

дет/сад *m.,* **—ская** *f.,* **—ский сад** nursery school, preschool; **—ский** *a.* child's, children's; juvenile; infantile; childish, puerile; fetal (placenta); (med.) pediatric; **—ские годы** childhood; **—ское место** (anat.) placenta; (med.) afterbirth; **—ство** *n.* childhood, infancy.

дет/ый *a.* put; **—ь** *see* **девать.**

дет/ьми *instr.,* **—ям** *dat.,* **—ях** *prepos. of* **дети.**

дефазиров/анный *a.* out of phase; **—ка** *f.* dephasing.

дефек/ат *m.* (sugar) defecated juice; (agr.) defecation mud; **—атор** *m.* (sugar) defecator, clarifier; liming tank; **—ационный** *a.,* **—ация** *f.* defecation, etc., *see* *v.*; (voiding of) excrement; **—овать** *v.* defecate, clarify, purify.

дефект *m.* defect, flaw, fault, imperfection, blemish; deficiency, handicap; bug; **д. массы** (nucl.) mass defect; **без —а** *a.* flawless; **нахождение —ов, —ация** *f.* flaw detection, trouble shooting; **—(ив)ность** *f.* defect(iveness); **—(ив)ный** *a.* defective, deficient, imperfect, faulty; deficiency (number); handicapped, crippled; mutilated, maimed; **—овочный** *a.* defective; defective-part (list); **—ология** *f.* study of handicapped children; **—оскоп** *m.* flaw detector; **—оскопия** *f.* defectoscopy, flaw detection; non-destructive test(ing).

деферент *m.* (astr.) deferent; **—ит** *m.* (med.) deferentitis.

деферризация *f.* deferrization, iron removal.

дефибр/ер *m.* fiber separator; (paper) grinder, pulper; **—ерные камни** pulping rolls; **—иллятор** *m.* defibrillator; **—илляция** *f.* defibrillation; **—инирование** *n.* defibrination, fibrin removal; **—инированный** *a.* defibrinated; **—инировать** *v.* defibrinate; **—ирование** *n.* defibering; grinding; **—ировать** *v.* defiber; grind.

дефил/е *n.,* **—ировать** *v.* (mil.) defile.

дефин/итивный *a.* definitive; **—итный** *a.* definite; **—иция** *f.* definition.

дефис *m.* (typ.) hyphen, dash.

дефицит *m.* deficit; deficiency, scarcity, shortage, lack; (oxygen) starvation; **без —а** *a.* balanced (budget); **—ность** *f.* deficiency, shortage, short supply; unavailability; **—ный** *a.* deficient, scarce, in short supply, not readily available, critical; losing (business).

дефишенси *m.* deficiency.

дефлагра/тор *m.* deflagrator; **—ция** *f.* deflagration, burning up.

дефлегм/атор *m.* dephlegmator, reflux condenser, fractionating column; **—ация** *f.* dephlegmation, fractionation, reflux(ing); **коэффициент —ации** reflux ratio; **с —ацией** with a reflux condenser; **—ировать** *v.* dephlegmate, fractionate, reflux.

дефлект/ометр *m.* deflectometer; **—ор** *m.* deflector, baffle.

дефлированный *a.* wind-eroded.

дефлок(к)ул *n.* deflocculation; **—ированный** *a.* deflocculated; **—ировать** *v.* deflocculate; **—ирующий реагент** deflocculant; **—яция** *f.* deflocculation.

дефля/тор *m.* deflator; **—ция** *f.* (com.; geol.) deflation, wind erosion.

дефожёсткость *f.,* **жёсткость по Дефо** (rub.) Defo hardness.

дефокусиров/ание *n.* defocusing; **—анный** *a.* defocused, out of focus; **—ать** *v.* defocus, throw out of focus; **—ка** *f.* defocusing.

дефоли/ант *m.* (agr.) defoliant; **—атор-опрыскиватель** *m.* defoliating sprayer; **—ация** *f.* defoliation.

дефометр *m.* (rub.) Defo plastometer.

деформативность *f.* deformability.

деформ/ация *f.,* **—ационный** *a.,* **—ирование** *n.* deformation, distortion, warping; strain; **—ационное колебание** bending vibration, bend; **д. кручения** torsional strain; **д. при сдвиге, д. при срезе** shearing strain; **механическая д.** strain; **продольная д.** stretch; **—ированный** *a.* deformed, etc., *see v.*; wrought; **—ировать** *v.* deform, distort, warp; strain; alter; work; disorganize; **—оваться** *v.* be distorted, lose shape; warp; buckle; **—ируемость** *f.* deformability; **—ируемый** *a.* deformable; deformed; **—ирующий** *a.* deforming, etc., *see v.*

дефосфор/(из)ация *f.* dephosphorization; **—(из)иро-**

вать *v.* dephosphorize; **—илировать** *v.* dephosphorylate.

дефрост/ация *f.* defrosting, thawing; **—ер** *m.* defroster.

дефторпров/ание *n.* defluorination; **—ать** *v.* defluorinate.

дехолин *m.* Decholin, dehydrocholic acid.

децелер/ация *f.* deceleration; **—ометр** *m.* decelerometer.

децен *m.* decene.

децентрализ/ация *f.* decentralization; **—(ир)ованный** *a.* decentralized, etc., *see v.*; **—(ир)овать** *v.* decentralize, deconcentrate, scatter.

децеребр/ационный *a.* (med.) decerebrate (rigidity); **—ация** *f.,* **—ирование** *n.* decerebration.

деци— *prefix* deci— (0.1); **—бел** *m.* (acous.) decibel; **—грамм** *m.* decigram.

децидуальный *a.* (anat.) decidual.

децил *m.* decyl; **—ен** *m.* dec(yl)ene; **—еновая кислота** decylenic acid.

децилитр *m.* deciliter (0.1 liter).

децилов/ый *a.* decyl; decylic (acid); **д. альдегид** decyl aldehyde, decanal; **д. спирт** decyl alcohol, 1-decanol.

деци/ль *m.* (stat.) decile; **—мальный** *a.* decimal; **—метр** *m.* decimeter (0.1 meter); **—метровый** *a.* decimetric, decimeter (wave); **—милли—** *prefix* decimilli— (0.0001); **—молярный** *a.* decimolar.

децин *m.* decine, decyne.

децинепер *m.* (elec. comm.) decineper.

децинормальный *a.* decinormal.

дешев/еть *v.* fall in price, become cheaper; **—изна** *f.* cheapness, low price; **—ить** *v.* force the price down; undercharge; **—ле** *comp. of* **дёшево, дешёвый**; cheaper.

дёшево *adv.* cheaply, inexpensively, at a low price.

дешёвый *a.* cheap, inexpensive, low-priced, low-cost.

дешенит *m.* (min.) dechenite.

дешифр/атор *m.* decoder, code interpreter; discriminator, selector; **—ация** *f.,* **—ирование** *n.* decoding, etc., *see v.*; **—(ир)ованный** *a.* decoded, etc., *see v.*; **—(ир)овать** *v.* decode, decipher, interpret, translate; identify; (teletype) transfer; **—овка** *f.,* **—овочный** *a.* decoding, etc., *see v.*; **—овщик** *m.* decoder; interpreter.

дешламировать *v.* deslime, desludge.

Дёшм/ан, —ен Dushman (name).

деэмуль/гатор, —сатор *m.* demulsifier; **—гирование** *n.,* **—сация** *f.* demulsification; **—гировать** *v.* demulsify.

деэтилирование *n.* deëthylation.

деяние *n.* deed, act.

деятель *m.* worker, man; figure; **д. науки** scientist; **—но** *adv.* actively; **—ность** *f.* activity, work; profession, occupation; function; behavior; **—ный** *a.* active, busy, energetic; effective.

деяться *v.* happen.

дж *abbr.* (**джоуль**) joule.

джайлау *m.* jailow, high mountain pastures.

джакаранда *f.* (bot.) Jacaranda.

джакас *m.* jackass fish (*Nemadactylus*); **—овые** *pl.* Cheilodactylidae.

джаксыконский *a.* (geog.) Dzhaksyi-kon.

джалмаит *m.* djalmaite.

джалтырский *a.* (geog.) Dzhaltyir.

джамболан *m.* (bot.) jambolan plum.

джамбульский *a.* (geog.) Dzhambul.

джантак *m.* (bot.) Alhagi pseudalhagi.

джар *m.* (elec.) jar (unit of capacitance).

джасп/еризация *f.* (min.) jasperization; **—ероид** *m.* (petr.) jasperoid.

джатовое дерево teak(wood).

джебашский *a.* (geog.) Dzhebash.

Джеймс (geog.) James (River).

джейран *see* дзерен.

джейханский *a.* (geog.) Ceyhan.

джек *m.* jack; (min.) jackhammer; (orn.) Houbara bustard (*Chlamydotis undulata*); —соновский *a.* Jackson(ian).

джелада *f.* (mam.) Gelada.

джем *m.* jam.

джемпер *m.* jumper; pullover.

джемсонит *m.* (min.) jamesonite.

дженинсиевые *pl.* (ichth.) Jeninsiidae.

дженкинзит *m.* (min.) jenkinsite.

дженколовая кислота (d)jenkolic acid.

дженнеризация *f.* (immun.) jennerization.

дженни *n.* (text.) jenny.

джерзейский *see* джерсийский.

джерси *n.* (text.) jersey; —йский *a.* Jersey.

джеспилит (min.) jaspilite.

джеффер/изит *m.* (min.) jefferisite; —сонит *m.* jeffersonite.

джиг(гер) *m.* (min.; text.) jig(ger).

джигетай *m.* (mam.) kulan (*Equus hemionus*).

джида *f.* (bot.) Elaeagnus.

джидинский *a.* (geog.) Dzhida.

джизлан *m.* (ent.) cotton-boll cicada.

джилпинит *m.* (min.) gilpinite, johannite.

джин *m.* (text.) gin; gin (liquor); —ирование *n.* ginning; —ировать *v.* gin.

джин-шень *m.* (bot.) ginseng (*Panax*).

джиобертит *m.* (min.) giobertite.

джип *m.* jeep (four-wheel drive vehicle).

джиттер *m.* (opt.) jitter.

дж/кг *abbr.* (джоуль на килограмм).

джозефсоновский переход (phys.) Josephson junction.

джойнтер *m.* (building) jointer.

джойстик *m.* joystick.

джонка *f.* junk (boat).

Джонса реактив (met.) Jones' reagent.

джон/сонова трава (bot.) Johnson grass (*Sorghum halepense*); —струпит *m.* (min.) johnstrupite.

джордан *m.* (paper) Jordan (refiner).

джорджианский *a.* (geol.) Georgian.

джоул/ево тепло Joule effect, heat effect; —ометр *m.* joule meter; —ь *m.* joule (unit of work).

джу/гара *f.* (bot.) joughara (*Sorghum cernuum*); —згун *m.* Calligonum.

джугджурский *a.* (geog.) Dzhugdzhur.

джулара *f.* (ichth.) a mullet (*Mugil auratus; M. saliens*).

джулиенит *m.* (min.) julienite.

джумур-балык *m.* (ichth.) shemaia (*Chalcalburnus chalcoides*).

джунгарский *a.* (geog.) Dzungarian; Sungari.

джунгли *pl.* jungle.

джут *m.,* —овый *a.* (bot.) jute (*Corchorus*); ice coating on winter pastures; —откачество *n.* jute weaving.

джэк *see* джек.

джярра *f.* (bot.) jarra forest.

дзерен *m.* (mam.) zeren (*Gazella or Procapra gutturosa*).

дзета *f.* zeta (Z, ζ).

дзиньк/ать, —нуть *v.* tinkle, jingle.

ДЗУ *abbr.* (диодное запоминающее устройство) diode memory unit.

дзэрен *see* дзерен.

ди— *prefix* di—, bi—, two.

диа— *prefix* dia— (through, across).

диабаз *m.* (petr.) diabase; —овый *a.* diabase, diabasic.

диабантит *m.* (min.) diabantite.

диабет *m.* (med.) diabetes; —ик *m.,* —ический *a.* diabetic; —огенный *a.* diabetogenic.

диабласт/ический, —овый *a.* (petr.) diablastic, sieve texture.

диаген/ез *m.* diagenesis, recombination, rearrangement; —етический *a.* diagenetic.

диагно/з *m.* diagnosis; identification; appraisal; ставить д. *v.* diagnose; —ст *m.* diagnostician; —стика *f.* diagnostics; —стировать *v.* diagnose; —стический *a.* diagnostic; exploratory (operation); trouble-shooting; —стический признак symptom.

диагометр *m.* (elec.) diagometer.

диагонал/евый *a.* diagonal, oblique; —изуемый *a.* diagon(aliz)able, diagonalized; —ь *f.* diagonal (line); —льно *adv.* diagonally, on a bias; —льный *a.* diagonal; mixed-flow (pump).

диаграмм/а *f.* diagram, drawing, plan, figure; pattern; chart, record sheet; graph, plot; characteristic, curve; circuit, scheme; —ный *a.* diagrammatic.

диаграф *m.* (drawing) diagraph.

диада *f.* dyad, pair.

диадем/овые *pl.* (zool.) sea urchins (*Diadematidae*); —овый *a.* diadem.

диадический *a.* (math.) dyadic, binary.

диа/дохит *m.* (min.) diadochite; —дромный *a.* (ichth.) diadromous; —зин *m.,* —зиновый *a.* diazine.

диазо— *prefix* diazo—; —аминобензол *m.* diazoaminobenzene; —аминол *m.* diazoaminol (dye); —аминосоединение *n.* diazoamino compound; —бензол *m.* diazobenzene; —бумага *f.* diazo(type) paper; —гидрат *m.* diazohydrate; —графия *see* диазотипия; —кетон *m.* diazo ketone; —кислота *f.* diazo acid; —копирование *n.* diazo copying; —краситель *m.* diazo dye; —кси *prefix* diazoxy—; —л *m.* diazole; —лин *m.* diazoline; —метан *m.* diazomethane, azimethane; —ниевый *a.,* —ний *m.* diazonium; —окись *f.* diazo oxide; —плёнка *f.* diazo film; —проба *f.* diazo sample; —раствор *m.* diazo solution; —реакция *f.* diazo test (for urine); —смола *f.* diazo resin; —соединение *n.* diazo compound; —соль *f.* diazo salt; —составляющая *f.* diazo component; —тат *m.* diazotate; —типия *f.* (phot.) diazotype, diazotype process.

диазотир/ование *n.* diazotization; —ованный *a.* diazotized; —овать *v.* diazotize; —уемый, —ующийся *a.* diazotizable.

диазоуксусн/ая кислота diazoacetic acid; —окислая соль diazoacetate; —ый эфир, —оэтиловый эфир ethyl diazoacetate.

диазо/фенол *m.* diazophenol; —чёрный (пигмент) diazo black.

диак *m.* (electron.) Diac (a semiconductor).

диакарб *m.* Diacarb, acetazolamide.

диакинез *m.* (gen.) diakinesis.

диакис— *prefix* dyakis— (twice); —додекаэдр *m.* (cryst.) dyakisdodecahedron, diploid.

диа/клаз *m.* (geol.) diaclase; —клинальный *a.* diaclinal; —кризиа *f.* (ent.) Diacrisia; —критический *a.* (elec.) diacritical.

диактинический *a.* (phot.) diactinic.

диакусти/ка *f.* diacoustics; —ческий *a.* diacoustic.

диал *m.* dialdehyde; *see also* диаль.

диалектический *a.* dialectic(al), logical.

диализ *m.* dialysis, ultrafiltration; —ат *m.* dialyzate; —атор *m.* dialyzer; —ирование *n.* dialyzing; —(ир)о-анный *a.* dialyzed; —(ир)овать *v.* dialyze; —ирующий *a.* dialyzing.

диалит *m.* (elec.) dialite (insulator).

диалитический *a.* dialytic.

диалкил *m.,* —**овый** *a.* dialkyl; —**ен** *m.* dialkylene; —**ировать** *v.* dialkylate.

диалкоксисоединение *n.* dialkoxy compound.

диаллаг *m.* (min.) diallage.

диаллельный *a.* (gen.) diallelic.

диаллил *m.,* —**овый** *a.* diallyl; —**амин** *m.* diallylamine, di-2-propenylamine; —**фталат** *m.* diallyl phthalate.

диалог *m.* dialogue; —**ит** *m.* (min.) dialogite, rhodochrosite; —**ический** *a.* dialogic; —**овый** *a.* (comp.) interactive.

диалуров/ая кислота dialuric acid, 5-hydroxybarbituric acid; **соль —ой кислоты, —окислая соль** dialurate.

диаль *m.* Dial, 5,5-diallylbarbituric acid; —**дегид** *m.* dialdehyde; —**доза** *f.* dialdose; —**дрин** *m.* Dieldrin (insecticide).

диам. *abbr.* (**диаметр**) diameter.

диамагн/етизм *m.,* —**итность** *f.* diamagnetism; —**етик** *m.,* —**итный** *a.* diamagnetic (substance).

диамант *m.,* —**овый** *a.* diamond.

диаметр *m.* diameter; bore, caliber; —**ально** *adv.* diametrically, in diameter; —**альный** *a.* diameter, diametric; diametral, full-pitch (winding); —**ический** *a.* diametric(al).

диамид *m.* diamide; —**ин** *m.* diamidine; —**о**— *prefix* diamido—.

диамикрокарта *f.* microfiche.

диам/ил *m.,* —**иловый** *a.* diamyl; —**ин** *m.* diamine.

диамино— *prefix* diamino—; —**бензол** *m.* diaminobenzene; —**вый** *a.* diamine; —**дифенил** *m.* diaminodiphenyl, benzidine; —**капроновый** *a.* diaminocapronic (acid); —**карбоновый** *a.* diaminocarboxylic (acid); —**кислота** *f.* diamino acid; —**оксидаза** *f.* diamine oxidase, histaminase; —**пимелиновый** *a.* diaminopimelic (acid); —**фенол** *m.* diaminophenol; —**этан** *m.* diaminoethane, ethylene diamine.

диаммо/нийфосфат, —**фос** *m.* diammonium phosphate, diammophos (fertilizer).

диан *m.* 4,4′-isopropylidenediphenol; —**изидин** *m.* dianisidine.

дианино дерево *see* **Дианы дерево.**

диантр/ахинон *m.* dianthraquinone; —**ацил** *m.* dianthracyl; —**ил** *m.* dianthryl, bianthryl; —**он** *m.* dianthrone.

Дианы дерево arbor Dianae (silver tree).

диапазон *m.* range, compass, scope, span, interval; band, spectrum, gamut; diapason; assortment, variety; **д. использования** useful range; **д. чисел М** Mach range; **в —е** over the range, within the limits; —**ность** *f.* band characteristics, flat top response; —**ный** *a. of* **диапазон;** (wide-)band.

диа/пауза *f.* (biol.) diapause, rest period; —**педез** *m.* (med.) diapedesis; —**пенсиевые** *pl.* (bot.) Diapensiaceae; —**перис** *m.* (ent.) Diaperis; —**пиризм** *m.* (geol.) diapir fold; —**пировый** *a.* diapir(ic), piercing.

диапозитив *m.,* —**ный** *a.* (phot.) diapositive, slide, transparency.

диапроектор *m.* slide projector.

диапсид/ные, —**ы** *pl.* (herp.) Diapsida; —**ный** *a.* diapsid(ian).

диар/еальный *a.* (med.) diarrheal; —**ея** *f.* diarrhea.

ди/арил *m.,* —**арильный** *a.* diaryl; —**арилировать** *v.* diarylate; —**арсенид** *m.* diarsenide; —**арсин** *m.* diarsine, biarsine; —**артроз** *m.* (anat.) diarthrosis.

диаскоп *m.,* —**ический** *a.* slide projector; (med.) diascope; —**ия** *f.* diascopy.

диаспирин *m.* diaspirin, succinylsalicylic acid.

диаспор *m.* (min.) diaspore; —**а** *f.* (bot.) diaspore; —**овый** *a.* diaspore, diasporic.

диаст/аз *m.* (med.) diastasis; diastase (enzyme); —**аза** *f.* diastase; —**атический** *a.* diastatic; —**атический фермент** diastase; —**ема** *f.* diastem(a), interval, space; —**ер** *m.* (gen.) diaster; —**ерео(изо)мер** *m.* diastereo(iso)mer; —**ереотопия** *f.* diastereotopy; —**ола** *f.* (physiol.) diastole; —**олический** *a.* diastolic.

диастрофизм *m.* (geol.) diastrophism.

диасхистовый *a.* (gen.; geol.) diaschistic.

диатез *m.* (med.) diathesis.

диатерм/ический, —**ичный** *a.* diathermic, diathermal; —**ичность** *f.* diathermancy; —**ия** *f.* diathermy; —**окоагуляционный** *a.,* —**окоагуляция** *f.* diathermocoagulation; —**ометр** *m.* diathermometer.

диатом/а, —**ея** *f.* (bot.) diatom; —**ин,** —**ит** *m.,* —**овая земля** diatomite, diatomaceous earth; —**ный,** —**овый** *a.* diatomic; —**овые (водоросли)** diatoms.

диатрема *f.* diatreme, volcanic vent.

диауксический *a.* (bact.) diauxic.

диаф *m.* lanternfish (*Diaphus*).

диафан *m.* unglazed porcelain; —**ия** *f.* diaphanie; (phot.) transparency; —**овый** *a.* diaphanous, euphotic (zone in sea); —**ометр** *m.* diaphanometer, opacimeter; —**оскоп** *m.* diaphanoscope.

диа/физ *m.* (anat.) diaphysis; —**фильм** *m.* (phot.) slide; microfilm, film strip; —**фон** *m.* diaphone; —**фония** *f.* crosstalk; —**фораза** *f.* diaphorase (enzyme); —**форит** *m.* (min.) diaphorite.

диафрагм/а *f.* diaphragm, membrane; (phot.) stop, aperture; membrane, core wall (of dam); orifice, orifice plate; (rupture) disk; (rockets) end plate, retainer; —**ально**— *prefix* (anat.) phren(ic)o— (diaphragm); —**ально-ободочнокишечный,** —**ально-ободочный** *a.* phrenicocolic; —**ально-печёночный** *a.* phrenohepatic; —**альный** *a.* diaphragmatic; phrenic (vein, etc.); —**енный,** —**овый** *a. of* **диафрагма;** —**ировать** *v.* (phot.) stop down, select an f-stop.

диафтор/ез *m.* (geol.) diapht(h)oresis, retrograde metamorphism; —**ит** *m.* (petr.) diaphthorite.

диахильная мазь (pharm.) diachylon.

диацет/амид *m.* diacetamide; —**ат** *m.* diacetate; —**ил** *m.* diacetyl; —**илен** *m.* diacetylene, butadiene; —**илмоноксим** *m.* diacetyl monoxime; —**илморфин** *m.* diacetyl morphine, heroin; —**илуксусный** *a.* diacetyl acetic (acid); —**ин** *m.* diacetin, glyceryl diacetate; —**он** *m.,* —**оновый** *a.* diacetone, acetylacetone.

диацилировать *v.* diacylate.

диашистовый *see* **диасхистовый.**

дибазол *m.* (pharm.) Dibasol.

дибатаг *m.* (mam.) dibatag, Clarke's gazelle (*Ammodorcas clarkei*).

дибенз— *prefix* dibenz(o)—; —**амид** *m.* dibenzamide, benzoyl benzamide; —**енил** *m.* dibenzenyl; —**ил** *m.,* —**иловый** *a.* dibenzyl; —**илиден** *m.* dibenzylidene; —**оил** *m.* dibenzoyl; —**ойная кислота** dibenzoic acid; —**(о)пиррол** *m.* dibenzopyrrole, carbazole; —**(о)фуран** *m.* dibenzofuran, diphenylene oxide.

диби(-)диби *see* **диви-диви.**

дибор/ан *m.* diborane; —**ид** *m.* diboride; —**нил** *m.* dibornyl.

дибром— *prefix* dibrom(o)—; —**бензол** *m.* dibromobenzene; —**гидрат** *m.* dihydrobromide; —**ид** *m.* dibromide.

дибути/л *m.,* —**ловый** *a.* dibutyl; —**лфталат** *m.* dibutyl phthalate; —**рат** *m.* dibutyrate.

дива *f.* (geol.) diwa (a type of structural element of the continental crust).

дивал/а *f.,* —**о** *n.* (bot.) Scleranthus.

диван *m.* sofa, couch.

диванадил *m.* divanadyl.

дивариантный *a.* bivariant.

диваровый *a.* divaric (acid).

дивектор *m.* (math.) divector, screw.

дивен *sh. m. of* **дивный**.

диверг/ентный, —ирующий *a.* divergent; **—енция** *f.* divergence; **—ировать** *v.* diverge.

диверсант *m.* saboteur, wrecker.

диверсин *m.* diversine.

диверс/ионный *a.,* **—ия** *f.* sabotage, subversive activity; (mil.) diversion.

дивертер *m.* diverter.

дивертикул *m.* (med.) diverticulum.

дивиатор *m.* deviator.

дивиденд *m.* (com.) dividend.

диви-диви *n.* (bot.) American sumach, divi-divi (*Caesalpinia coriaria*).

дивиз/ия *f.* division; **—ор** *m.* divisor.

дивий *a.* (geog.) Divya.

дивинил *m.* divinyl; bivinyl, 1,3-butadiene; **—ацетилен** *m.* divinyl acetylene; **—овый** *a.* divinyl; butadiene (rubber); **д.-ректификат** *m.* purified butadiene.

дивинная кислота ditartaric acid.

дивить *v.* astonish, surprise; **—ся** *v.* wonder, marvel, be surprised (at).

дивный *a.* marvelous, wonderful, remarkable.

ди/вольфрамовый *a.* ditungstic (acid); **—галловый** *a.* digallic (acid); **—галоидный** *a.* dihal(ogen)ide; **—гаплоид** *m.* (gen.) dihaploid; **—гедральный** *a.* dihedral.

дигексагональный *a.* (cryst.) dihexagonal.

дигексил *m.* dihexyl; dodecane.

дигенетический *a.* digenetic (parasite).

дигентизиновый *a.* digentisic (acid).

дигептил *m.,* **—овый** *a.* diheptyl.

диге/рировать *v.* digest; **—стивный** *a.* digestive; **—стия** *f.* digestion.

ди/гетерозигота *f.,* **—гибрид** *m.,* **—гибридный** *a.* (gen.) diheterozygote, dihybrid.

дигидр/ат *m.* dihydrate; **—ит** *m.* (min.) dihydrite; **—(о)—** *prefix* dihydr(o)—; **—обензол** *m.* dihydrobenzene; **—оксисоединение** *n.* dihydroxy compound; **—острептомицин** *m.* dihydrostreptomycin (antibiotic); **—офосфат** *m.* dihydrophosphate.

дигир/а *f.* (cryst.) digyre, twofold axis of symmetry; **—ный** *a.* digyric, (ortho)rhombic.

дигитал/изация *f.* (med.) digitalization; **—ин** *m.* digitalin; **—ис** *m.* (bot.) Digitalis; **—оза** *f.* digitalose.

дигито/генин *m.* digitogenin; **—ксигенин** *m.* digitoxigenin; **—ксин** *m.* digitoxin; **—ксоза** *f.* digitoxose, 3,4,5-trihydroxyhexanal; **—нин** *m.* digitonin.

дигликол/евый *a.* diglycolic (acid); **—ь** *m.* diglycol; **—ят** *m.* diglycolate.

ди/глим *m.* diglyme, diethylene glycol dimethyl ether; **—глицерид** *m.* diglyceride; **—глицил** *m.* diglycyl; **—гонический** *a.* (gen.) digonic; **—граммоз** *m.* (med.) digrammosis, Digramma infestation; **—граф** *m.* (math.) digraph, directed graph; **—грессия** *f.* digression.

дидакт/ика *f.* didactics; **—ический** *a.* didactic, instructive.

дидим(ий) *m.* didymium, Di.

дидим(о)— *prefix* didym(o)—, twin.

дидодекаэдр *m.* (cryst.) didodecahedron, diploid; **—ический** *a.* didodecahedral.

диен *m.,* **—овый** *a.* diene, diolefin; **—офил** *m.* dienophile; **—эстрол** *m.* dienestrol.

диервилла *f.* (bot.) Diervilla.

диет/а *f.* diet; **—етика** *f.* dietetics; **—(ет)ический** *a.* dietetic, dietary; **—ическое лечение, —отерапия** *f.* diet therapy, dieting; **—олог** *m.* dietitian, nutritionist.

дижерминатор *m.* degerminator.

диз— *prefix* dys— (difficult, painful, bad, disordered, abnormal; unlike); *see also under* **дис—**; **—адаптация** *f.* (med.) dys(ad)aptation; maladjustment.

дизайн *m.* design; **—ер** *m.* **—ерский** *a.* designer.

дизамещённ/ое *n.* disubstituted product; **—ый** *a.* disubstituted.

дизаналит *m.* (min.) dysanalyte.

дизартрия *f.* (med.) dysarthria.

дизелевоз *m.* (min.) diesel locomotive.

дизел/из(ир)овать *v.* dieselize; **—ист** *m.* diesel operator; **—ь** *m.* diesel (engine); **—ь-генератор** *m.* diesel generator; **—ь-молот** *m.* pile hammer; **—ь-мотор** *m.,* **—ьный** *a.* diesel (engine); **—ь-электровоз** *m.* diesel (electric) locomotive; **—ь-электроход** *m.* diesel (electric) ship.

дизентер/ийный *a.* (med.) dysenteric; **—ия** *f.* dysentery.

дизодиль *m.* (min.) dysodile.

дизостоз *m.* (embr.) dysostosis.

дизурия *f.* (med.) dysuria.

дизъюнк/тивный *a.* disjunctive; **—тность** *f.* disjointness, disjunction; **—тный** *a.* disjunct, disjoint; **—ция** *f.* disjunction, separation; alteration.

диизо— *prefix* diiso—; **—бутилен** *m.* diisobutylene; **—пропил** *m.* diisopropyl.

ди/имид *m.* diimide; **—имин** *m.* diimine; **—имино—** *prefix* diimino—; **—индол** *m.* diindol.

дииод—, дийод— *prefix* diiod(o)—; **—бензол** *m.* diiodobenzene; **—ид** *m.* diiodide; **—тирозин** *m.* diiodotyrosine.

дик *sh. m. of* **дикий**.

Дика проба (med.) Dick test.

дикаин *m.* dicain, tetracaine hydrochloride.

дикакодил *m.* dicacodyl.

дикалий *m.* dipotassium.

дикальцийфосфат *m.* dicalcium phosphate.

дикамфо— *prefix* dicampho—.

дикарбо/ксильная кислота, —новая кислота dicarboxylic acid.

дикарион *m.* (bot.; gen.) dikaryon.

дикар/ский *a.,* **—ь** *m.* savage; **—ство** *n.* savage state.

дик(-)дик *m.* (mam.) dik-dik (*Madoqua*).

дикето— *prefix* diketo—; **—н** *m.* diketone; **—пиперазин** *m.* diketopiperazine; **—спирт** *m.* diketoalcohol; **—янтарный** *a.* diketosuccinic (acid).

дик/ий *a.* wild, savage; natural (growth); irresponsible; extravagant, absurd; strange; shy; **—ая местность** wilderness; **—ая природа** wilderness; wildlife; **—ие животные** wildlife; **—ое мясо** (med.) proud flesh.

дикинсонит *m.* (min.) dickinsonite.

дикислота *f.* diacid.

дик(к)ит *m.* (min.) dickite.

диклинный *a.* (bot.) diclinous.

дико *adv. of* **дикий**.

дикобраз *m.* (mam.) porcupine (*Hystrix*); **—овые** *pl.* Hystricidae.

дикод/еин *m.* dicodeine; **—ид** *m.* dicodid, dihydrocodeinone.

Дикона способ Deacon process.

дикон/овая кислота diconic acid; **—хинин** *m.* diconchinine, diquinidine.

дико/растущий *a.* (bot.) wild; spontaneous, volunteer (crop); **—сть** *f.* wildness, wild state; absurdity; shyness.

дикрановые *pl.* (bot.) Dicranaceae (mosses).

дикрезил *m.* dicresyl.

дикроти́ческий *a.* (physiol.) dicrotic.

дикроце́л/ий *m.* (zool.) dicrocoelium; **—ио́з** *m.* (med.) dicroc(o)eliosis.

диксанти́л *m.* dixanthyl.

дикси́ды *pl.* (ent.) Dixidae.

диктамни́н *m.* dictamnin.

дикти́о— *prefix* dictyo— (net); **—кауле́з** *m.* (vet.) dictyocaulosis, lungworm infection; **—кау́люс** *m.* (zool.) Dictyocaulus; **—кине́з** *m.* (gen.) dictyokinesis; **—со́ма** *f.* dictyosome; **—сте́ла, —стель** *f.* (bot.) dictyostele; **—фа́ра** *f.* (ent.) Dictyophara.

дикто́в/ание *n.*, **—ка** *f.* dictation; **—анный** *a.* dictated; **—ать** *v.* dictate.

дикт/ор *m.*, **—орский** *a.* (rad.) announcer; speaker; **—офо́н** *m.*, **—ующая машина** dictaphone, dictating machine.

дикумари́н *m.* dicoumarin.

дикуми́л *m.* dicum(en)yl.

дику́ша *f.* (orn.) a grouse (*Falcipennis*); (bot.) Tartary buckwheat (*Polygonum tataricum*).

ди́кция *f.* articulation, enunciation.

Ди́ла проце́сс (met.) Diehl process.

дилакти́л *m.* dilactyl.

дила́р *m.* (ent.) Dilar.

дилат/а́тор *m.* dilator; **—а́ция** *f.* dilation, expansion, extension; **—о́метр** *m.* dilatometer; **—оме́трия** *f.* dilatometry.

ди/лауди́д *m.* Dilaudid, hydromorphone hydrochloride; **—лейци́л** *m.* dileucyl.

диле́мма *f.* dilemma, fix, perplexity.

диле́новые *pl.* (bot.) Dilaenaceae.

диле́ны *pl.* (lumber) deal ends.

дилизи́н *m.* dilysine.

дилиту́ровая кислота́ dilituric acid, 5-nitrobarbituric acid.

диллени́евые *pl.* (bot.) Dilleniaceae.

дильдри́н *m.* Dieldrin (insecticide).

Ди́льса-А́льдера реа́кция Diels-Alder reaction.

ди́льсы *pl.* (lumber) deal(s).

дилюв/иа́льный *a.* diluvial, flood; **—ий** *m.* (geol.) diluvium, drift; glacial period.

дилю́ция *f.* dilution.

диля́татор *see* **дилата́тор.**

дим *m.* (ecol.) deme.

димагни́йфосфа́т *m.* dimagnesium phosphate.

дим/азо́н *m.* dimazon, diacetylaminoazotoluene; **—едо́н** *m.* dimedone, dimethyl cyclohexanedione; **—едро́л** *m.* Dimedrol, diphenylhydramine.

димези́тил *m.*, **—овый** *a.* dimesityl.

диме́нтил *m.*, **—овый** *a.* dimenthyl.

диме́р *m.* dimer; **—иза́ция** *f.* dimerization (a polymerization); **—ка́пто—** *prefix* dimercapto—; **—ность** *f.* dimery; **—ный** *a.* dimeric; dimerous.

димета́но— *prefix* dimethano—.

димети́л *m.* dimethyl, ethane; **—ами́н** *m.* dimethylamine; **—анили́н** *m.* dimethyl aniline; **—арси́н** *m.* dimethylarsine; **—глиокси́м** *m.* dimethyl glyoxime; **—и́ровать** *v.* dimethylate; **—кето́н** *m.* dimethyl ketone, acetone; **—овый** *a.* dimethyl; **—сульфа́т** *m.* dimethyl sulfate; **—цинк** *m.* zinc dimethyl, dimethyl-zinc.

димето́кси— *prefix* dimethoxy—.

димmetри́ческий *a.* dimetric, oblique.

ди/ми́рцен *m.* dimyrcene; **—молибда́т** *m.* dimolybdate; **—морфа́нт** *m.* (bot.) Kalopanax septemlobum.

димо́рф/изм *m.* (biol.; cryst.) dimorphism; **—ный** *a.* dimorphous, dimorphic.

димочеви́на *f.* diurea.

дин *abbr.*, **—а** *f.* dyne [unit of force (10^{-5} newton)]; (phot.) DIN-speed.

дина́м/а *f.* dyname (1000 kilogram-meters); (phys.) wrench; **—етр** *m.* (phys.) dynameter; **—и́зм** *m.* dynamism; **—ик** *m.* (rad.) dynamic loudspeaker; **—ика** *f.* dynamics; dynamic range; changes, trends; process; (car) performance; **—ика измене́ния** time history (of a phenomenon); **—и́т** *m.*, **—и́тный** *a.* (expl.) dynamite; **—и́ческий** *a.* dynamic, power; **—и́ческий винт** (phys.) wrench; **—и́ческая компенса́ция** sweep balance; **—и́ческая о́бласть** (comp.) dynamic area; heap; **—ный** *a.* dynamo; electric generator (steel).

дина́мо *n.* (elec.) dynamo, generator; *prefix* dynamo— (power, strength); **—ге́нный** *a.* dynamogenic; **—граф** *m.* dynamograph, recording dynamometer; **—дви́гатель** *see* **динамо́тор;** **—маши́на** *f.* dynamo.

динамо́метр *m.* dynamometer; **—и́рование** *n.* dynamometer test; **—и́ческий** *a.* dynamometric.

динамо́н *m.* (expl.) dynammon.

дина/мо́тор *m.* (elec.) dynamotor, rotary transformer; **—моэлектри́ческий** *a.* dynamoelectric.

дина́нтский *a.* (geol.) Dinantian.

дина́рский *a.* (geog.) Dinaric, Dinara.

дина́с *m*, **—овый** *a.* Dinas or silica brick.

динатр/и́евый *a.*, **—ий** *m.* disodium.

динатро́н *m.*, **—ный** *a.* (electron.) dynatron.

динафт/и́л *m.*, **—и́ловый** *a.* dinaphthyl; **—о—** *prefix* dinaphth(o)—; **—о́л** *m.* dinaphthol.

ди́нги *n.* dinghy (boat).

ди́нглерова зе́лень Dingler green.

ди́нго *m.* (mam.) dingo (*Canis dingo*).

ди/инди́л *m.* di(i)ndyl; **—нези́н** *m.* Dinezin, diethazine; **—нейтро́н** *m.* (nucl.) dineutron.

динери́т *m.* (min.) dienerite.

дини́т *m.* (min.) dinite.

динитр/а́ция *f.*, **—(ир)ова́ние** *n.* dinitration; **—и́л** *m.* dinitrile; **—обензо́л** *m.* dinitrobenzene; **—ова́ть** *v.* dinitrate; **—оглицери́н** *m.* dinitroglycerin; **—онафта́лин** *m.* dinitronaphthalene; **—осоедине́ние** *n.* dinitro compound; **—отолуо́л** *m.* dinitrotoluene; **—офено́л** *m.* dinitrophenol; **—охлорбензо́л** *m.* dinitrochlorobenzene.

дино— *prefix* dino— (fearful, terrible; whirling).

дино́д *m.* (electron.) dynode.

диноза́вр *m.*, **—овый** *a.* (pal.) dinosaur.

ДИНО́К *abbr.* (динитроортокрезо́л) dinitroorthocresol (herbicide).

дино/ми́ды *pl.* (mam.) Branick rats (*Dinomyidae*); **—те́рий** *m.* (pal.) dinothere; **—фил(ус)** *m.* (zool.) Dinophilus; **—флагелля́ты** *pl.* (prot.) Dinoflagellata.

дин-см *abbr.* (дина-сантиметр).

динуклеоти́д *m.* dinucleotide.

дио́д *m.* (electron.) diode (tube); **—а** *f.* (bot.) diode; **—ный** *a.* diode; **—офи́т** *m.* (bot.) diodophyte; **д.-тетро́д** *m.* diode-tetrode.

дио́за *f.* diose.

диокс/ази́н *m.* dioxazine; **—ан** *m.* dioxane, diethylene dioxide; **—диази́н** *m.* dioxdiazine.

диокси— *prefix* dioxy— (frequently used for dihydroxy—); **—азокраси́тель** *m.* dihydroxyazo dye; **—антрахино́н** *m.* dihydroxyanthraquinone; **—ацето́н** *m.* dihydroxyacetone; **—бензо́л** *m.* dihydroxybenzene; **—ви́нный** *a.* dihydroxytartaric (acid).

диокс/и́д *m.* dioxide; **—икислота́** *f.* dihydroxy acid; **—и́м** *m.* dioxime; **—има́леиновый** *a.* dihydroxymaleic (acid); **—и́н** *m.* dioxine, β-oxynaphthoquinoxime; dioxin; **—инафта́лин** *m.* dihydroxynaphthalene; **—ин-**

дол *m.* dioxindole; **—исоединение** *n.* di(hydr)oxy compound; **—итолуол** *m.* dihydroxytoluene, orcinol; **—ифениланланин** *m.* dihydroxyphenylalanine, Dopa; **—ихинон** *m.* dihydroxyquinone; **—иянтарный** *a.* dihydroxysuccinic (acid); **—ол** *m.* dioxole; **—олан** *m.* dioxolan.

диокт/аэдр *m.* (cryst.) dioctahedron, ditetragonal pyramid; **—ил** *m.,* **—иловый** *a.* dioctyl; **—илфталат** *m.* dioctyl phthalate; **—офим** *m.* (zool.) kidney worm (*Dioctophyma renale*); **—офимоз** *m.* (vet.) dioctophymosis.

дио/л *m.* diol, glycol; **—леин** *m.* diolein, glycerol dioleate; **—лен** *m.* diolen (synthetic fiber); **—лео—** *prefix* dioleo—; **—лефин** *m.* diolefin; **—нин** *m.* dionine, ethylmorphine hydrochloride.

диопсид *m.* (min.) diopside; **—овый** *a.* diopsidic.

диоптаз *m.* (min.) dioptase.

диопт/(е)р *m.,* **—ренный** *a.* (geod.) diopter; sight; **—рика** *f.* (opt.) dioptrics; **—рический** *a.* dioptric; **—рия** *f.* diopter (unit of lens power); prism diopter.

диорама *f.* diorama.

диорит *m.* (petr.) diorite; **—овый** *a.* diorite, dioritic.

диоскор/ейные *pl.* (bot.) Discoraceae; **—ея** *f.* yam (Dioscorea).

диос/пирос *m.* (bot.) persimmon (*Diospyros*); **—фенол** *m.* diosphenol, buchu camphor; **—цин** *m.* dioscin.

диотан *m.* diothane.

диотрон *m.* (comp.) diotron.

диофантовый *a.* (math.) Diophantine.

ди/пентен *m.* dipentene, terpene; **—пептид** *m.* dipeptide; **—пиколиновый** *a.* dipicolinic (acid); **—пикриламин** *m.* dipicryl amine; **—пилидий** *m.* (zool.) tapeworm (*Dipylidium*); **—пилин** *m.* dipiline.

дипир *m.* (min.) dipyre; **—амида** *f.* (cryst.) bipyramid; **—амидальный** *a.* bipyramidal.

дипирид/ил *m.* dipyridyl; **—ин** *m.* dipyridine, nicotyrine.

диплакузис *m.* (med.) diplacusis.

дипле/врула, —урула *f.* (zool.) dipleurula; **—гия** *f.* (med.) diplegia.

диплекс *m.,* **—ный** *a.* (telegraphy) diplex.

дипло— *prefix* dipl(o)— (double, twin, twofold, twice); **—бацилла** *f.* (bact.) diplobacillus; **—бионт** *m.* (biol.) diplobiont; **—гастер** *m.* (zool.) Diplogaster; **—генез** *m.* (embr.) diplogenesis; **—диноз** *m.* (phyt.) Diplodina leaf spot; **—диоз** *m.* Diplodia dry rot (of corn); **—док** *m.* (pal.) Diplodocus; **—зал** *m.* Diplosal, salicylosalicylic acid; **—з(ис)** *m.* (gen.) diplosis; **—зооноз** *m.* (vet.) diplozoonosis.

диплоид *m.,* **—ный** *a.* (cryst.; gen.) diploid; **—изация** *f.* diploidization; **—ия, —ность** *f.* diploidy.

дипло/ический *a.* diploic, double; **—кокк** *m.* (bact.) diplococcus; **—коккин** *m.* diplococcin (antibiotic).

диплом *m.* diploma; (university) degree; certificate; award; **—ант** *m.* student (working on thesis); **—ат** *m.* diplomat; **—атический** *a.* diplomatic; **—атия** *f.* diplomacy; **—ированный** *a.* graduate(d); licensed (engineer); registered (nurse).

дипло/мистовые *pl.* (ichth.) Diplomistidae; **—мицин** *m.* diplomycin.

дипломн/ик *see* дипломант; **—ый** *a. of* диплом; **—ая работа** thesis.

дипло/нема *f.* (gen.) diplonema; **—нт** *m.* diplont, diploid individual; **—пия** *f.* (med.) diplopia, double vision; **—поды** *pl.* (zool.) Diplopoda; **—сома** *f.* (gen.) diplosome; **—стихный** *a.* diplostichous, double-rowed; **—стоматоз** *m.* (vet.) diplostomatosis.

дип(-)лот *m.* (mar.) deep-sea lead.

дипло/тена *f.* (gen.) diplotene; **—фаза** *f.* diplophase; **—э** *n.* (anat.) diploe; **—эдр** *m.* (cryst.) diplohedron, diploid.

дипнон *m.* dypnone.

диполь *m.* dipole; (electric) doublet; (rad.) dipole antenna; **—ный** *a.* dipole.

диполярный *a.* dipolar, bipolar.

Диппеля масло Dippel's oil, bone oil.

дипр/ен *m.* diprene; **—ион** *m.* (ent.) Diprion; **—оксид** *m.* diproxide, diisopropylxanthogen disulfide.

дипроп/аргил *m.* dipropargyl; **—ил** *m.,* **—иловый** *a.* dipropyl; **—илкетон** *m.* dipropylketone, butyrone.

дипрофен *m.* (pharm.) diprophen.

дипсо— *prefix* dipso— (thirst); **—мания** *f.* (med.) dipsomania.

диптанк *m.* (mar.) deep tank.

диптер/икс *m.* (bot.) tonka bean (*Dipteryx*); **—о—** *prefix* diptero— (two-winged); **—ология** *f.* (ent.) dipterology.

дираковский *a.* Dirac (particle).

дирезорцин(ол) *m.* diresorcinol.

директ/ива *f.* instructions, directions; **—ивный** *a.* instruction; directive, directory; **—ор** *m.* director, manager, head; sender; **—орат** *m.* board (of directors); **—ориальный** *a.* (geom.) directrix; **—орский** *a.* director's, managerial; **—орствовать** *v.* manage, be a managing director; **—риса** *f.* directrix.

дирекц/ионный *a.* direction(al); д. угол (ballistics) grid azimuth; **—ия** *f.* direction, management, board (of directors).

диретмовые *pl.* (ichth.) Diretmidae.

дирижабль *m.* dirigible, airship.

дирижёр *m.* regulator; (music) conductor.

Дирихле признак сходимости (math.) Dirichlet's test for convergence.

дирицинолеин *m.* diricinolein.

диродан *m.* dithiocyanogen.

дирофиляр/иоз *m.* (vet.) dirofilariasis; **—ия** *f.* heartworm (*Dirofilaria*).

дис— *prefix* dis—; dys— (difficult; faulty; abnormal; unlike); *see also under* диз—.

дисазо/краситель *m.* disazo dye; **—соединение** *n.* disazo compound.

дисалициловый *a.* disalicylic (acid).

дисаналит *m.* (min.) dysanalyte.

дисахарид *m.* disaccharide.

дис/базия *f.* (med.) dysbasia; **—бактериоз** *m.* dysbacteriosis; **—баланс** *m.* unbalance, imbalance; (mech.) disbalance; (math.) disbalancement; **—болизм** *m.* (med.) dysbolism.

дисгармон/ировать *v.* clash, conflict, jar (with); **—ирующий** *a.* conflicting, incongruous (with); **—ичный** *a.* disharmonic; **—ия** *f.* disharmony, conflict.

дисгрегация *f.* (phys.) disgregation, disintegration.

диселенид *m.* diselenide.

дисил/ан *m.* disilane; **—икат** *m.* disilicate; **—ицид** *m.* disilicide.

дисимметр/ичный *a.* dissymmetric, asymmetric; **—ия** *f.* asymmetry.

диск *m.* disk, plate; wheel; dial; slice; (zool.) sucker; (anat.) discus; градуированный д., номерной д. dial.

дискант *m.,* **—овый** *a.* (acous.) treble.

дисквалифи/кация *f.* disqualification; **—цировать** *v.* disqualify, reject; **—цироваться** *v.* be struck off (professionally); be blackballed.

дискератоз *m.* (med.) dyskeratosis.

дискет *m.,* **—а** *f.* (comp.) diskette, floppy disk.

дискинезия *f.* dyskinesia.

дискобластический *a.* (embr.) discoblastic.

дисков/ание *n.* (tel.) dialing; (agr.) disking; **—ать** *v.* dial; disk; **—идный** *a.* disk-shaped, discoid; **—од** *m.* (comp.) disk drive; **—ый** *a. of* **диск;** circular; rotary (dial); **—ый фрезер** cutting disk.

диско/гнат *m.* (ichth.) Discognathichthys; **—ид(аль)-ный** *a.* discoid(al); **—котилёз** *m.* (vet.) discocotylosis, Discotyle infection; **—лит** *m.* (geol.) discolith, discoidal coccolith; **—мицеты** *pl.* (bot.) Discomycetes.

дискомфортный *a.* discomfort (glare).

дисконический *a.* discone (antenna).

дисконосный *a.* discifer, disk-bearing.

дисконт *m.*, **—ировать** *v.* (com.) discount.

дисконформный *a.* (geol.) unconformable.

дискообразный *a.* disk-like, disk-shaped, discoid(al); circular.

дискордантный *a.* discordant.

дискотека *f.* (phonograph) record library.

дискразит *m.* (min.) dyscrasite.

дискразия *f.* (med.) dyscrasia.

дискредит/ация *f.*, **—ирование** *n.* discrediting; **—ировать** *v.* discredit; **—ирующий** *a.* discrediting, discounting.

дискрет/а *f.* (stat.) sample; **—изация** *f.* quantization; digitation, analog-to-digital conversion; (time) sampling; **—ность** *f.* discreteness, discontinuity; **с —ностью** in steps, in increments (of); **—ный** *a.* discrete, distinct, separate; digital; quantified; sampled (data); **машина —ного действия** digital computer; discrete-variable device.

дискримин/ант *m.*, **—антный** *a.* (math.) discriminant; **—атор** *m.* discriminator; **—ация** *f.* discrimination; **—ировать** *v.* discriminate.

диску/ссионный *a.* controversial; disputable, debatable; **в —ссионном порядке** open to question; **—ссиро-вать**, **—тировать** *v.* discuss; debate; **—ссия** *f.* discussion; controversy, debate.

дис/лексия *f.* (med.) dyslexia; **—лизин** *m.* dyslysin.

дисло/кация *f.*, **—кационный** *a.* dislocation, disturbance; (biol.) distribution, dispersion; (mil.) stationing; deployment (of troops); **—цированный** *a.* dislocated, etc., see *v.*; **—цировать** *v.* dislocate, disturb; distribute, disperse; station; deploy.

дислуит *m.* (min.) dysluite.

дисмембратор *m.* crusher, disintegrator.

дисменор(р)ея *f.* (med.) dysmenorrhea.

дисмут/ация *f.* dismutation, disproportionation; **—ировать** *v.* disproportionate.

дисом/а *f.* (gen.) disome; **—атический** *a.* disomatic; **—овые** *pl.* (ichth.) Dys(s)om(m)idae; **—ный** *a.* (gen.) disomic.

диспансер *m.*, **—ный** *a.* dispensary; clinic, health center; **—изация** *f.* clinical observation, outpatient treatment; screening.

диспаша *f.* (com.) average statement.

диспепс/ический *a.* (med.) dyspeptic; **—ия** *f.* dyspepsia.

дисперг/атор *m.* disperser; dispergator; dispersant, dispersing agent; (powder) dispenser; **—ент** *m.* dispersion medium; **—ентный** *a.* dispergated; **—ирование** *see* **дисперсия; —ированный** *a.* dispersed; **тонко —ированный** finely divided; **—ировать** *v.* disperse, scatter, diffuse; dispergate; **—ирующий** *a.* dispersing, dispersive; **—ирующий агент**, **—ирующее вещество** dispersant, disperser; **—ующее устройство** disperser.

дисперс/ивный *a.* dispersive; **—ионный** *a.* dispersion, dispersing; (met.) precipitation, age (hardening); **—ионный анализ** (stat.) analysis of variance; **—ия** *f.* dispersion, scattering; (math., stat.) variance, deviation, vari-

ability; **коэффициент —ии** scatter coefficient; **—ность** *f.* dispersity, (degree of) dispersion; fineness; dispersibility; **—ный** *a.* disperse(d), scattered; dispersible; **—оид** *m.* dispersoid.

диспетчер *m.* dispatcher, controller; traffic supervisor; (program) monitor; **—изация** *f.* dispatching; traffic control, control (system); **—ская** *f.* control room; (av.) control tower; **—ский** *a.* dispatcher's, dispatch(ing); control.

дисплазия *f.* (med.) dysplasia.

дисплей *m.*, **—ный** *a.* display; (comp.) monitor.

диспноэ *n.* (med.) dyspnea.

диспозиц/ионный *a.*, **—ия** *f.* disposition.

диспрозий *m.* dysprosium, Dy.

диспропорц/иональность *f.* disproportionality; **—иональный** *a.* disproportional, disproportionate; **—ионирование** *n.* disproportionation; **—ия** *f.* disproportion.

диспротеинемия *f.* (med.) dysproteinemia.

диспут *m.* dispute, debate; discussion; **—ировать** *v.* discuss, dispute, debate.

диссек/тор *m.* (electron.) dissector; **—ционный** *a.*, **—ция** *f.* (med.) dissection.

диссемин/ация *f.* dissemination; **—ировать** *v.* disseminate.

диссепимент *m.* dissepiment, partition; **—арий** *m.* dissepimentarium.

диссерт/ант *m.* author of a dissertation; **—ационный** *a.*, **—ация** *f.* dissertation, thesis.

диссиметр/ичный *a.* asymmetric, unsymmetrical; **—ия** *f.* asymmetry, dissymmetry.

диссимил/ирование *see* **диссимиляция; —ирован-ный** *a.* (physiol.) dis(as)similated; **—ировать** *v.* dis(as)similate, subject to catabolism; **—ятивный**, **—яторный**, **—яционный** *a.* dis(as)similative, catabolic; **—яция** *f.* dis(as)simulation, catabolism; **биологическая —яция** biodegradation.

диссимулировать *v.* dissimulate, feign.

диссинергия *f.* (med.) dyssenergia.

диссипа/тивный *a.* dissipative; dissipation (function); **—ция** *f.* dissipation, diffusion, dispersion.

диссол/ьвер *m.* dissolving vat; **—юция** *f.* dissolution; dissolving.

диссон/анс *m.* dissonance, discord; **—ировать** *v.* be in discord, be out of tune; **—ирующий** *a.* dissonant, discordant.

диссоци/атор *m.* (petrol.) cracker; **—ация** *f.*, **—ирование** *n.* dissociation; **—ированный** *a.* dissociated, etc., *see v.*; **—ировать** *v.* dissociate, break down, split up; **—ирующий** *a.* dissociating, etc., *see v.*

диссугаз *m.* acetylene (in acetone).

дист. *abbr.* (**дистиллированный**).

дистальн/о-бороздной *a.* sulcate(d); **—ый** *a.* distal, distant, remote; **—ая борозда** sulcus.

дистанц/иометрирование *n.* ranging; **—иониру́ющий** *a.* spacer (plate, etc.); **ионно-автоматическое управление** automatic remote control; **—ион-ноуправляемый** *a.* remote-controlled; **—ионный** *a.* distant, remote, tele—; distance(-type), long-distance; range; remote-control(led); distant-reading, remote-indicating; space(r) (plate, rib, etc.); time (fuse); **—ион-ный термометр** telethermometer; **—ионная деталь** spacer; **—ионная трубка** fuse; **—ионное управление** remote control; **—ия** *f.* distance, range; interval, space.

дистеарин *m.* distearin.

дистект/ика *f.* dystectics; dystectic point; **—ический** *a.* dystectic.

дистен *m.* (min.) disthene, kyanite.

дистилл/ат *see* **дистиллят;** **—ер** *m.* distiller, still; **—ерная жидкость** (Solvay) still waste; **—ирование** *n.* distillation; **—ированный** *a.* distilled; **—ировать** *v.* distill; **—ят** *m.*, **—ятный** *a.* distillate; distilled water; **—ятор** *see* **дистиллер; —яционный** *a.*, **—яция** *f.* distillation; (urea synthesis) decomposition; **—яционный аппарат** still.

дистильбен *m.* distilbene.

дистиреоз *m.* (med.) dysthyroidism.

дистировка *f.* (glass) fine grinding.

дистирол *m.* distyrine.

дисто/матоз *m.* (med.) distomatosis, Distoma infection; **—ния** *f.* dystonia; **—пический** *a.* dystopic, misplaced; **—пия** *f.* dystopia, malposition.

дистопливо *n.* diesel fuel.

дистор/зия, —сия, —ция *f.*, **—ционный** *a.* distortion.

дистоция *f.* (med.) dystocia.

дистрибутивн/ость *f.* (math.) distributivity; **—ый** *a.* distributive.

дистроф/ия *f.* (med.) dystrophy, faulty nutrition; **—ный** *a.* dystrophic.

дисульф/ан *m.* (pharm.) Disulfan; **—ат** *m.* disulfate; **—ид** *m.*, **—идный** *a.* disulfide; **—ировать** *v.* disulfonate; **—окислота** *f.* disulfonic acid; **—онат** *m.* disulfonate; **—о(но)вый** *a.* disulfonic (acid).

дис/фагия *f.* (med.) dysphagia, **—фазия** *f.* dysphasia; **—фония** *f.* dysphonia; **—фория** *f.* dysphoria; **—фотический** *a.* (ocean.) dysphotic; **—функция** *f.* dysfunction, impaired functioning.

дисциплин/а *f.* discipline, branch of science; **—арный** *a.* disciplinary; **—ированный** *a.* disciplined, trained; **—ировать** *v.* discipline, train.

дисъюнктивный *see* **дизъюнктивный.**

дита *f.* dita bark, alstonia; **—ин** *m.* ditaine, echitamine; **—мин** *m.* ditamine.

дителлурид *m.* ditelluride.

Дитеричи уравнение Dieterici equation.

дитерпен *m.* diterpene.

дитетра/гональный *a.* ditetragonal; **—эдр** *m.* (cryst.) ditetrahedron; **—эдрический** *a.* ditetrahedral.

дити/азанин *m.* dithiazanine; **—ан** *m.* dithiane, diethylene disulfide; **—енил** *m.* dithienyl; **—зон** *m.* Dithizone, diphenyl thiocarbazone.

дитимол *m.* dithymol.

дитио/карбамат *m.* dithiocarbamate; **—карбаминовый** *a.* dithiocarbamic (acid); **—карбоновый** *a.* dithiocarboxylic (acid); **—кислота** *f.* dithio(nic) acid; **—л** *m.* dithiole, disulfole; **—н** *m.* dithion (insecticide); **—нат** *m.* dithionate; **—нистый** *a.* dithionous (acid); **—новокислый** *a.* dithionate; dithionic acid; **—новый** *a.* dithionic (acid); **—салициловая кислота** dithiosalicylic acid; **—угольная кислота** dithiocarbonic acid; **—фос** *m.* a tetraethyl dithiopyrophosphate insecticide; **—фосфат** *m.* dithiophosphate.

дитолил *m.* ditolyl, dimethyldiphenyl; **—амин** *m.* ditolylamine.

дитразин *m.* ditrazine, diethylcarbamazine citrate.

дитрем/а *f.* (ichth.) Ditrema; **—овые** *pl.* seaperches (*Embiotocidae*).

дитретичный *a.* ditertiary.

дитригон *m.* (cryst.) ditrigon, symmetrical octahedron; **—альный** *a.* ditrigonal.

дитрихит *m.* (min.) dietrichite.

дитроит *m.* (petr.) ditroite.

дитцеит *m.* (min.) dietzeite.

дитчер *m.* ditcher, ditching machine.

дитя *n.* child, infant.

диур/анат *m.* diuranate; **—ез** *m.* (med.) diuresis; **—еид** diureide; **—етик** *m.* diuretic; **—етин** *m.* diuretin, theobromine sodium salicylate; **—етический** *a.*, **—етическое средство** diuretic.

диф— *prefix* differential; diffusion.

дифацил *m.* diphacyl, adiphenine.

дифен— *prefix* diphen(o)—; **—ат** *m.* diphenate; **—ид** *m.* diphenide.

дифенил *m.* biphenyl, diphenyl; **—амин** *m.* biphenylamine, phenyl aniline; **—арсин** *m.* diphenylarsine; **—ен** *m.*, **—еновый** *a.* diphenylene; **—ил** *m.* diphenylyl; **—ин** *m.* diphenyline; **—карбазон** *m.* diphenylcarbazone; **—кетон** *m.* diphenyl ketone, benzophenone; **—метан** *m.* diphenyl methane, benzylbenzene; **—мочевина** *f.* diphenylurea; **—овый** *a.* diphenyl; **—хлорарсин** *m.* diphenylchloroarsine; **—цианарсин** *m.* diphenylcyan(o)arsine.

дифенимид *m.* diphenimide.

дифен/ин *m.* Diphenine; **—о—** *prefix* dipheno—; **—овая кислота** diphenic acid, bibenzoic acid; **соль** or **эфир —овой кислоты** diphenate; **—ол** *m.* diphenol, biphenyldiol; **—охинон** *m.* diphenoquinone.

диференциал *see* **дифференциал.**

дифилетический *a.* (gen.) diphyletic.

дифиллоботриоз *m.* (med.) diphyllobothriasis, Diphyllobothrium infestation.

дифиодонтный *a.* (zool.) diphyodont.

дифлуор— *see* **дифтор—.**

дифманометр *m.* differential manometer.

дифнасос *m.* diffusion pump.

диформил *m.* diformyl, glyoxal.

дифосген *m.* diphosgene, trichloromethyl chloroformate.

дифосф/ат *m.* diphosphate; **—ид** *m.* diphosphide; **—оглицерат** *m.* diphosphoglycerate; **—опиридиннуклеотид** *m.* diphosphopyridine nucleotide, DPN; **—орный** *a.* diphosphoric (acid); **соль —орной кислоты** diphosphate.

дифр/агированный *a.* diffracted; **—агировать** *v.* diffract; **—актограмма** *f.* X-ray pattern; **—актометр** *m.* diffractometer; **—акционный** *a.* diffraction; grating (spectroscope); **—акционная решётка** diffraction grating; **—акция** *f.* diffraction; **—акция на порошке** powder diffraction.

дифсельсин *m.* (elec.) differential selsyn.

дифсистема *f.* (commun.) hybrid set.

дифталил *m.* diphthalyl.

дифтер/ийный, —итный *a.* (med.) diphtheritic; **—ит** *m.*, **—ия** *f.* diphtheria.

дифтор— *prefix* difluor(o)—; **—гидрат** *m.* dihydrofluoride; **—ид** *m.*, **—истый** *a.* difluoride; **—этан** *m.* difluoroethane, ethylene difluoride.

дифурфурил *m.*, **—овый** *a.* difurfuryl.

диффеоморфизм *m.* (math.) diffeomorphism.

дифферент *m.* (naut.) trim; **—овка** *f.* longitudinal trimming; (submarines) ballast trim; **—овочный** *a.* trimming.

дифференциал *m.*, **—ьный** *a.* (math.; mach.) differential; **—ьная доза** (radiation) dose rate; **—ьноразностный** *a.* difference-differential.

дифференц/иатор *m.* (comp., elec.) differentiator, differentiating circuit; **—иация** *f.*, **—ирование** *n.* differentiation; **—ированно** *adv.* differentially; **—ированный** *a.* differentiated; different; **—ировать** *v.* differentiate, distinguish; **—ировать по** differentiate with respect to; **—ироваться** *v.* differ; **—ировка** *f.* differentiation; **—ируемость** *f.* differentiability; **—ируемый** *a.* differentiable; differentiated; derivable; **—ирующий** *a.* differentiating; **—ирующая схема,**

—ирующая цепь differentiator; **—ируя** *pr. ger.* if we differentiate.

диффлюгия *f.* (prot.) Difflugia.

диффлюэнция *f.* ice flow.

диффрак/тограмма *f.* diffraction pattern; **—ция** *see* **дифракция.**

диффу/зант *m.* diffusant; **—зат** *m.* diffusate; **—зивность** *f.* diffusivity; **—зивный** *a.* diffusive; **—зионный** *a.* diffusion, diffusive; **—зионный аппарат** diffuser; **—зионный перенос** mass transfer by diffusion; **—зионная способность** diffusibility; **—зия** *f.* diffusion; **коэффициент —зии** diffusion coefficient, diffusivity; **—зно** *adv., prefix* diffuse(ly); **—зность** *f.* diffuseness; **—зный** *a.* diffuse, scattered; **—зор** *m.* diffuser; (speaker) diphragm, cone; **—ндирование** *n.* diffusion; **—ндировать** *v.* diffuse, spread; **—ндируемый** *a.* diffusible; **—ндирующий** *a.* diffusing.

дихазий *m.* (bot.) dichasium.

дихинолил *m.* diquinolyl.

дихлон *m.* dichlone (fungicide).

дихлор— *prefix* dichlor(o)—; **—амин** *m.* dichloramine; **—ангидрид кислоты** acid dichloride; **—ангидрид фталевой кислоты** phthal(o)yl chloride; **—ацетон** *m.* dichloroacetone; **—бензол** *m.* dichlorobenzene; **—гидрат** *m.* dihydrochloride; **—гидрин** *m.* dichlorohydrin; **—дифенилтрихлорэтан** *m.* dichlorodiphenyl trichloroethane, DDT; **—диэтилсульфид** *m.* dichlorodiethyl sulfide, Yperite; **—ид** *m.* dichloride; **—метиловый** *a.* dichloromethyl; **—уксусный** *a.* dichloroacetic (acid); **—этан** *m.* dichloroethane; **—этил** *m.* dichloroethyl; **—этилен** *m.* dichloroethylene.

дихо— *prefix* dicho— (in two, apart); **—гамия** *f.* (bot.) dichogamy; **—стилис** *m.* (bot.) Dichostylis.

дихотом/изировать *v.* dichotomize, cut up; analyze; **—ический** *a.* dichotomous; by dichotomy, bifurcate (classification); forked (branching); **—ическое деление, —ия** *f.* dichotomy, bifurcation.

дихро/а *f.* (bot.) Dichroa; **—изм** *m.* (cryst.) dichroism; **—изный** *a.* dichroic; **—ит** *m.* (min.) dichroite, cordierite, iolite; **—ический, —ичный** *a.* dichroic; **—ичность** *f.* dichroism.

дихром/ат *m.* dichromat(ic); (chem.) dichromate; **—атизм** *m.* (opt.) dichromatism; **—атический** *a.* dichromatic; **—овокислый** *a.* dichromic acid; dichromate (of).

дихро/скоп *m.* (cryst.) dichroscope; **—соль** *f.* dichroic salt.

дицентр/ин *m.* dicentrine; **—ический** *a.* (gen.) dicentric.

дицерка *f.* (ent.) Dicerca.

дицетил *m., —овый* *a.* dicetyl.

дицефалобрахиальный *a.* (gen.) decephalobrachial.

дициан *m.* dicyan, cyanogen; **—аурат** *m.* dicyanoaurate; **—диамид** *m.* dicyandiamide; **—ид** *m.* dicyanide.

дициема *f.* (zool.) Dicyema (parasite).

дициклический *a.* dicyclic.

дицикло— *prefix* dicyclo—, bicyclo—; **—гексил** *m.* bicyclohexyl; **—пентадиен** *m.* dicyclopentadiene; **—пентил** *m.* dicyclopentyl.

ди/цимол *m.* dicymene; **—циннамил** *m.* dicinnamyl; **—цинодонт** *m.* (pal.) dicynodont; **—цистеин** *m.* dicysteine, cystine.

дич/ать *v.* go wild; run wild; **—еразведение** *n.* game breeding; **—ина** *see* **дичь;** **—иться** *v.* be shy (of); **—ок** *m.* wilding, wild (ungrafted) tree; (apid.) wild swarm; **—ь** *f.* game, wild fowl, wild life; wilderness; wildness; thicket; nonsense, absurdity.

дише-реакция *f.* Dische reaction.

диэдр *m.* (geom.) dihedron; **—альный, —ический** *a.* dihedral.

диэлдрин Dieldrin (insecticide).

диэлектр/ик *m.* (elec.) dielectric, nonconductor; insulator; **—ика** *f.* dielectric constant, permittivity; **—ит** *m.* dielectrite (insulator); **—ический** *a.* dielectric, nonconducting; **—ическая постоянная, —ическая проницаемость** *see* **диэлектрика.**

диэнантил *m.* dienanthyl.

диэрез *m.* rupture, separation.

диэструс *m.* (zool.) dioestrus.

диэта *see* **диета.**

диэтил *m.* diethyl; **—амин** *m.* diethylamine; **—анилин** *m.* diethyl aniline; **—ацетат** *m.* diethyl acetate; **—барбитуровая кислота** diethylbarbituric acid, veronal.

диэтилен *m.* diethylene; **—гликоль** *m.* diethylene glycol; **—диамин** *m.* diethylenediamine, piperazine; **—овый** *a.* diethylene.

диэтил/ировать *v.* diethylate; **—кадмий** *m.* cadmium diethyl; **—карбонат** *m.* diethyl carbonate; **—мочевина** *f.* diethyl urea; **—овый** *a.* diethyl; **—овый эфир** (di)ethyl ether; **—овый эфир винной кислоты** diethyl tartrate; **—ртуть** *f.* diethyl mercury; **—стильбестрол** *m.* diethylstilbestrol; **—сульфат** *m.* diethyl sulfate; **—фталат** *m.* diethyl phthalate; **—цинк** *m.* zinc diethyl.

ди/эфир *m.* diester; **—эичный** *a.* (biol.) dioecious.

дк *abbr.* (дека—) deca—; **дк., ДК** (доброкачественность) good quality; **дкт** *abbr.* (декаграмм) decagram; **дкл** *abbr.* (декалитр) decaliter; **дкм** *abbr.* (декаметр) decameter.

дл *abbr.* (децилитр) deciliter; **дл.** *abbr.* (длина; долгота).

длане/(видно)— *prefix* (biol.) palm(at)i—, palm; cheir(o)— (hand); **—(видно)листный** *a.* (bot.) cheirophyllous; **—(видно)надрезной** *a.* palmatifid; **—(видно)раздельный** *a.* palmipartite; **—видный** *a.* palmate(d); **—нервный** *a.* palminerve(d).

длин/а *f.* length, distance; path; stretch, run; height (of catalyst bed); **д. разбега** take-off run; **—ой, в —у** length, long; lengthwise; **во всю —у** full length; **мера —ы** linear measure; **на 3/4 —ы** 3/4 of the way through; **на единицу —ы** linear; **по —е** lengthwise.

длинн/ее *comp. of,* **—ейший** *superl. of* **длинный;** longissimus (muscle); **—еть** *v.* become longer, lengthen; **—ик** *m.* log.

длинно *adv.* long, lengthily, at length; *prefix* longi—; dolich(o)—; macr(o)—; **—волновый** *a.* long-wave; **—волокнистый** *a.* long-fibered, long-staple; **—волос(ат)ый** *a.* long-haired, hairy, crinite, pilose; **—головый** *a.* dolichocephalic; **—дневный** *a.* long-day; **—звеньевой** *a.* long-link (chain); **—земелье** *n.* narrow strip (of land); **—клювый** *a.* longirostrate, long-billed; **—корневищный** *a.* with long roots.

длиннокрыл *m.* (mam.) long-fingered bat (*Miniopterus*); **—ка** *f.* (ichth.) longfin sculpin (*Cottocomephorus inermis*); **—ые** *pl.* (orn.) Macrochires; Micropodiformes; **—ый** *a.* macropterous, longipennate, long-winged; large-finned.

длинно/лицевой *a.* dolichofacial, long-faced; **—мер** *m.* large timber; *see* **длиннорылый; —ногий** *a.* long-legged; **—носый** *a.* nasute, long- or large-nosed; **—палый** *a.* macrodactylous, long-toed; **—пёрый** *a.* long-fin(ned); **—пламенный** *a.* long-flame (coal); **—плечий** *a.* long-armed; **—плодный** *a.* dolichocarpous; **—полосица** *see* **длинноземелье; —пробежный** *a.* long-range; **—проволочный** *a.* long-wire; **—рогий** *a.* longicorn, long-horned; **—рылые** *pl.* (ichth.) Mormyridae; **—рылый** *a.* long-snout(ed);

longirostral, long-beaked; long-nose(d); —**рылая рыба** mormyrid.

длинно/сеточная машина (paper) Fourdrinier machine; —**ствольный** *a.* long-boled (tree); —**стебельчатый** *a.* long-stemmed; —**столбчатый** *a.* long-columnar; —**телый** *a.* slender, slim; —**уска** *f.* (ent.) Adela; —**усые** *pl.* Nematocera; Dolichocera; —**усый** *a.* long-whiskered; long-barbelled; —**ухий** *a.* long-eared, lop-eared; —**фокусный** *a.* long-focus; —**хвостые** *pl.* (ichth.) rattails [*Macr(o)uridae*]; —**хвостый** *a.* macrural, long-tailed; —**хоботницы** *pl.* (ent.) Nemestrinidae; —**хоботный** *a.* long-glossa (bee); —**цепной** *a.* long-chain; —**шейн** *a.* long-necked; —**шёрстный** *a.* long-wooled, wooly, lanate; long-haired; —**щупальцевый** *a.* long-tentacled; —**щупные** *pl.* (ichth.) Gigantactinidae; —**язык** *m.* (mam.) nectar-feeding bat.

длинный *a.* long, lengthy, elongated.

длино/мер *m.* length-measuring device; —**ограничитель** *m.* gage block.

длительн/о *adv.* long, a long time; **д.-импульсный** *a.* pulse-duration; —**ость** *f.* length, duration, continuance; period, time; (pulse) width; (sweep) interval; span; —**ость жизни** lifetime, life span; —**ость работы** (furnace) life, campaign; —**ый** *a.* long, lasting, prolonged, protracted; continuous, persistent, sustained; long-term; —**ая прочность** (met.) endurance limit, fatigue limit; **на —ую прочность** (stress-) rupture (test); **в течение —ого времени** long-term, for a long time.

длить *v.* protract, prolong, draw out, delay, defer; —**ся** *v.* last, continue; endure.

для *prep. gen.* for, to; for the sake of, for the purpose of; with a view to; **д. него** therefor; **д. того, чтобы** in order to, so that, for (the purpose of), for the sake of, with a view to, if one is to; **д. этого** to do this, for this purpose.

длящийся *a.* lasting, permanent.

дм *abbr.* (**дециметр**) decimeter; **дм, дм.** *abbr.* (**дюйм**) inch.

д.м.н. *abbr.* (**доктор медицинских наук**) Doctor of Medical Sciences.

ДМСО *abbr.* (**диметилсульфоксид**) dimethyl sulfoxide, DMSO.

ДМТ *abbr.* (**доза минимальной токсичности**) minimum toxic dose; (**доза максимальная толерантная**) maximum tolerated dose; (**диметилтерефталат**) dimethyl terephthalate.

дн *abbr.* (**дина**) dyne.

дна *gen. of* **дно.**

дне *prepos. of* **день** and **дно.**

днев/алить *v.* be on duty; —**альный** *m.* man on duty; —**ать** *v.* spend the day.

днёвка *f.* (day's) rest, stop.

днев/ник *m.* diary, journal, record; —**ной** *a.* day(time), diurnal; daily; —**ной свет** daylight; **лампа —ного света** fluorescent lamp; —**ный** *a. suffix* —day.

дней *gen. pl. of* **день.**

днём *adv.* in the daytime, during the day, by day; **д. и ночью** twenty-four hours a day, continuously.

днеп *abbr.* (**децинепер**) decineper.

днепровск/ий *a.* (geog.) Dnieper; —**о-азовский** *a.* Dnieper-Azov; —**о-бугский** *a.* Dnieper-Bug; —**о-донецкий** *a.* Dnieper-Donets.

днестровский *a.* (geog.) Dnestr.

дни *pl. of* **день.**

днище *n.* bottom; platform, floor; end plate; (drum; piston) head; (piston) undercrown; (zool.) tabula.

ДНК *abbr.* (**дезоксирибонуклеиновая кислота**) deoxyribonucleic acid, DNA; **ДНК-аза** *abbr.* (**дезоксирибонуклеаза**) deoxyribonuclease; **ДНК-зависимый** *a.* DNA-dependent; **ДНК-затравка** *f.* primer DNA.

дно *n.* bottom, base; ground; floor, bed (of sea, etc.); head (of bullet, drum, etc.); (electron.) face (plate); (anat.) fundus; **вверх —м** upside down.

ДНОК *abbr.* (**динитроортокрезол**) dinitro-*o*-cresol.

дноуглубитель *m.,* —**ный снаряд** dredge(r); —**ный** *a.* dredging.

дночерпатель *m.* bottom grab, dredge(r).

ДНП *abbr.* (**дезоксирибонуклеопротеид**) deoxyribonucleoprotein, DNP.

ДНФ *abbr.* (**динитрофенол**) dinitrophenol.

дн/ю *dat. of* **день;** —**юет** *pr. 3 sing. of* **дневать;** —**я** *gen. of* **день.**

до *prep. gen.* before, prior, previous to; until, pending, till; (up) to, as high as, as far as, as much as; down to, as low as, as small as; about, approximately; with; **до того как** before, previous to; **ему не до этого** he has no time for that, he is not up to it.

до— *prefix with verbs* ad—, up to; to the end, completely, until ready; to finish; till, as far as, up to, far enough, sufficiently; *with adj.* hypo—, sub—.

доб. *abbr.* (**добавление; добавочный**).

добав/ить *v.* add, append, annex; supplement; introduce, treat (with); admix, make up, fill up; replenish, top up; boost (voltage); —**ка** *f.* addition, introduction; admixture, impurity; additive, ingredient, component; complement; accessory; —**ка-замедлитель** *m.* retarder; —**ка-ускоритель** *m.* accelerator; —**ление** *n.* addition, supplement, appendix, addendum; —**ленный** *a.* added, etc., *see v.*; —**ляемое** *n.,* —**ляющийся** *a.* (math.) addend; —**лять** *see* **добавить;** —**ок** *see* **добавка;** —**очная** *f.* subscript.

добавочн/ый *a.* additional, supplementary, accessory, auxiliary, extra; more; filler; admixed; (elec.) booster; after (effect, etc.); extension (phone; rod, etc.); surplus (value); unsorted, inferior (fish); rudimentary (teat); **д. агент** addition agent; **д. налог** surtax; **д. нерв** accessory nerve; **д. полюс** (elec.) interpole; **д. усилитель** booster; —**ая плата** bonus.

добе/гание *n.* running up to; **время —гания** lag time; —**гать,** —**жать** *v.* run up to, reach.

добела *adv.* to white heat; until white; **раскалённый д.** *a.* white hot, incandescent.

добел/е(ва)ть *v.* finish bleaching; —**ение** *n.,* —**ка** *f.* (paper) final bleaching.

доберёт *fut. 3 sing. of* **добрать.**

добивать *v.* finish off, dispatch; —**ся** *v.* aim (for), try to get, strive (for), endeavor; obtain, get, attain, achieve.

добирать *v.* finish gathering; gather, collect, glean; finish typesetting; —**ся** *v.* attain, reach, come, get (to).

добит/ый *a.* finished off; obtained, etc., *see v.*; —**ь** *v.* finish off; —**ься** *v.* obtain, get, attain, gain, secure; —**ься своего** get one's way, succeed.

добор *m.* final gathering.

добр *sh. m. of* **добрый.**

дображив/ание *n.* after-fermentation, secondary fermentation; —**ать** *v.* finish fermenting.

добранный *a.* gathered up, picked.

добрасывать *v.* throw up to; throw in more, add.

добрать *see* **добирать.**

добреелит *m.* (min.) daubréelite.

добреть *v.* become kinder; be corpulent.

добри(ва)ть *v.* finish shaving.

добро *n.* good; property, goods.

доброво́л/ец *m.* volunteer; **—ьно** *adv.* voluntarily; **—ьный** *a.* voluntary, free; public-service; **—ьческий** *a.* voluntary, volunteer.

добро́дить *v.* finish fermenting.

добро́душный *a.* good-natured.

доброжела́тель/ный *a.* well-meaning, friendly; **—ство** *n.* good will; **—ствовать** *v.* wish well.

доброка́чественн/ость *f.* (high) quality, soundness; factor of merit; (med.) benignity; **—ый** *a.* high-quality, sound; benign.

доброса́ть *v.* throw in more, add.

добро́сить *v.* throw up to.

добр/осо́вестный *a.* conscientious, scrupulous; honest; diligent; **—ота** *f.* kindness; quality; **—отность** *f.* Q, Q-factor, quality (factor), figure of merit; high quality, soundness; **—отный** *a.* good (-quality); *suffix* -quality; **—ый** *a.* good, kind.

доб/ыва́ние *n.* mining, etc., *see v.*; recovery; **—ыва́ть** *v.* mine, extract, recover, quarry; obtain, get, derive, procure; capture, catch; (petrol.) produce; **—ыва́ться** *v.* come (from); **—ыва́ющий** *a.* mining, etc., *see v.*; extractive (industry, such as agriculture, mining, etc.); **—ытчик** *m.* miner, extractor; (family) provider; **—ытый** *a.* mined, etc., *see v.*; **—ыть** *see* **добыва́ть;** **—ыча** *f.* mining, extraction, recovery; output, yield; production; gain, profit; catch, take, bag, prey; getting, procurement; booty, plunder, loot, spoils; **—ычливый** *a.* productive.

добьётся *fut. 3 sing. of* **добиться.**

довар/и́(ва)ть *v.* finish cooking or boiling; digest; **—и́(ва)ться** *v.* be cooked enough; **—ива́ние** *n.*, **—ка** *f.* final cook(ing).

довегетацио́нный *a.* pre-seasonal.

довед/е́ние *n.* bringing (up to), etc., *see* **доводить;** (math.) reduction; **—ённый** *a.* brought (up to), etc., *see* **доводить.**

довез/ённый *a.* taken, etc., *see* **довозить; —ти** *see* **довозить.**

довёл *past m. sing. of* **довести.**

довер/енность *f.* trust, confidence; warrant, power of attorney; **—енный** *a.* (en)trusted; confidential; *m.* proxy, agent; **—ие** *n.* trust, confidence; credit; **коэффицие́нт —ия** (math., stat.) confidence coefficient; **—итель** *m.* **—ительница** *f.* principal; **—ительность** *f.* (stat.) confidence; **—ительный** *a.* confidential, classified; fiducial; confidence; **—ительный коэффицие́нт** or **у́ровень** confidence level; **—ить** *see* **доверя́ть.**

доверну́ть *v.* screw down, screw tight.

до́веров *a.* Dover's (powder).

доверт/е́ть, —ывать *v.* tighten.

доверху *adv.* (up) to the top, full.

доверчи́в/ость *f.* confidence, trust; **—ый** *a.* trusting; credulous.

доверш/а́ть, —и́ть *v.* complete; **—е́ние** *n.* completion, accomplishment; **—ённый** *a.* completed, accomplished.

доверя́ть *v.* trust, commit (to); entrust; confide (in); **—ся** *v.* rely, depend (on).

дове́с/ить *see* **дове́шивать; —ок** *m.* make-weight.

довести́ *see* **доводить.**

дове́шивать *v.* make up the weight; finish weighing.

дови́(ва)ть *v.* finish weaving or twisting.

дови́н/тить, —чивать *v.* screw up, tighten.

до́вод *m.* reason, argument.

довод/и́ть *v.* bring, lead, take (up to); reduce; make, work (up to); finish (up); refine; improve, shape up; size; grind, polish; lap; hone; condition; attain, reach; **д. до кипе́ния** bring to a boil; **д. до объёма** fill up; **д.**

до рН, д. на рН adust to pH; **—и́ться** *v.* have occasion (to), happen; **—ка** *f.*, **—очный** *a.* bringing (to), etc., *see v.*; development; breaking in (of engine); **—очный брусок** hone; **—очный стано́к** (met.) lapping machine.

довое́нный *a.* prewar.

дово́зить *v.* take, carry, bring (as far as), deliver.

дово́льн/о *adv.* enough, sufficiently; rather, fairly; it is sufficient; **—ый** *a.* content, satisfied, pleased (with).

дово́льств/ие *n.* ration, allowance, supply; **веще́вое д.** personal equipment; **—о** *n.* prosperity, contentment; **—овать** *v.* supply; **—оваться** *v.* draw supplies; be satisfied (with).

довооруж/а́ть, —и́ть *v.* finish arming.

дово́рот *m.* deflection; correction angle.

довраче́бная по́мощь first aid.

довсоно́вский *a.* Dowson (producer gas).

до/вспе́нивание *n.* after-foaming, final foaming; **—всхо́довый** *a.* (agr.) pre-emergence; **—вулканиза́ция** *f.* after-vulcanization, after-cure; **—вы́полнить** *v.* complete; **—вяз(ыв)а́ть** *v.* finish knitting; finish tying.

дог *m.* Great Dane; **морско́й д.** (ichth.) Port Jackson shark (*Heterodontus philippi*).

догад/а́ться, —ываться *v.* surmise, guess, conjecture, suspect; **—ка** *f.* surmise, guess, conjecture; **—ливый** *a.* ingenious, shrewd, quick.

до́ггер *m.* (geol.) Dogger, Middle Jurassic.

до́ги, морски́е (ichth.) Heterodontidae.

догла/дить, —живать *v.* finish pressing or ironing; smooth out.

догляд/е́ть, —ывать *v.* observe, watch, take care (of), look (after), see (to); stay to the end; **д. до конца́** see through.

до́гма *f.*, **—т** *m.* dogma, theory, doctrine, maxim; **—ти́ческий, —ти́чный** *a.* dogmatic, positive, authoritative.

догна́ть *see* **догоня́ть.**

догни́(ва)ть *v.* decay completely.

догов/а́ривать *v.* finish (speaking); **не д.** hold (something) back; **—а́риваться** *v.* negotiate, treat, arrange, make terms, come to an understanding; **—ор** *m.* agreement, contract; pact, treaty; **—ённость** *f.* agreement, understanding, arrangement; **—и́ть(ся)** *see* **догова́ривать(ся); —ник** *m.* contract worker; **—орный** *a.* contract, stipulated, agreed.

до́гола *adv.* naked, bare.

дого́н *m.*, **—ка** *f.*, **—я́ющий** *a.* overtaking; slewing; **—я́ть** *v.* overtake, catch up (with), reach.

догор/а́ние *n.* (av.) afterburning; **—а́ть, —е́ть** *v.* burn out, burn down; go out.

догре/ба́ть, —сти́ *v.* row (to); finish raking.

догру/жа́ть *v.* finish loading, add; recharge, replenish; **—же́ние** *n.* loading; **—жённый** *a.* (additionally) loaded; **—зи́ть** *see* **догружа́ть; —зка** *f.* additional charge, recharging.

додава́ть *v.* make up, pay up, add.

додаи́в/ание *n.* stripping, milking dry; **—ать** *v.* strip.

дода́/нный *a.* made up, added; paid up; **—ть** *see* **додава́ть; —ча** *f.* making up, addition.

дода́р/тия, —ция *f.* (bot.) Dodartia.

додека — *prefix* d(u)odeca— (twelve); **—го́н** *m.* (geom.) dodecagon.

додека́н *m.* dodecane; **—а́л(ь)** *m.* dodecanal, lauraldehyde; **—овый** *a.* dodecanoic (acid); **—о́л** *m.* dodecanol, dodecyl alcohol.

додекаэ́др *m.* (cryst.) dodecahedron; **—и́ческий** *a.* dodecahedral.

доде́л/анный *a.* finished off, completed; **—ать,**

—ывать *v.* finish off, complete; **—ка** *f.* finishing (off); finished product; **—ывание** *n.* finishing (off).

додерж(ив)ать *v.* hold, keep (until), detain.

додец/ен *m.* dodecene; **—енал(ь)** *m.* dodecenal; **—еновый** *a.* dodecenoic (acid); **—ил** *m.* dodecyl; **—иловый** *a.* dodecylic; dodecylic (acid).

дод/оек, —ой *see* **додаивание.**

до/дубливать *v.* (leather) retan; **—дувка** *f.* (glass) final blow(ing); (met.) reblow.

додум(ыв)аться *v.* conclude, come to a conclusion; think up, hit on (idea).

доедать *v.* finish (eating), eat up.

доезжать *v.* arrive, reach, get (to).

до/ение *n.* milking; **—ёнка** *f.* milk pail; **—енный** *a.* milked.

до/есть *see* **доедать; —ехать** *see* **доезжать; —жари(ва)ть** *v.* finish frying or roasting.

дожать *v.* finish reaping; finish squeezing.

дожгут *fut. 3 pl. of* **дожечь.**

дождаться *v.* wait (for, until).

дожде— *prefix* pluvio—, ombro—, rain.

дождев/альный *a.,* **—ание** *n.* sprinkling, overhead irrigation; **—альная установка, —атель** *m.* sprinkler; **—ик** *m.* raincoat; (bot.) puffball (*Lycoperdon*); **—виковые** *pl.* Lycoperdaceae; **—ка** *f.* (ent.) cleg(g), horsefly; **—ой** *a.* rain(y), pluvial, hyetal; rainfall; rainfed (pond); spray (nozzle); **—ой червь** earthworm; **—ое облако** rain cloud, nimbus; **—ые осадки** rainfall, precipitation.

дожде/любивый *a.* ombrophil(ous), rain-loving; **—мер** *m.* rain gage; **—мерное ведро** rain-gage receiver; **—носный** *a.* rainy, pluvial; **—писец** *m.* pluviograph; **—приёмник** *m.* (rain) gully; catch basin; storm water overflow.

дожд/ик *m.* drizzle, light rain; **—ить** *v.* rain; **—ливый** *a.* rainy; **—ь** *m.* rain, shower; **—ь идёт** it is raining; **золотой —ь** (bot.) Laburnum; **искусственный —ь** rainmaking.

до/жевать, —жёвывать *v.* finish chewing.

дожечь *see* **дожигать.**

дожив/ание *n.* (biol.) survival; **—ать** *v.* survive, live (until), reach, attain (the age of); stay (until; the rest of).

дожиг/ание *n.* (complete) combustion; (av.) afterburning; reheat(ing); **камера —ания, —атель** *m.* afterburner; **—ать** *v.* burn sufficiently; burn up.

дожидать(ся) *see* **дождать(ся).**

дожим/ать *v.* finish squeezing or pressing; squeeze, press (enough); **—ающий** *a.* booster (compressor); **—ный** *a.* compressor (pump).

до/жинать *v.* finish reaping; **вероятность —жития** life expectancy; **—жить** *see* **доживать.**

доз/а *f.* dose, dosage; portion, ration, quantity; batch, charge; **д. внесения** rate of application; **д. половинной выживаемости** median lethal dose, MLD; **д. облучения** radiation dose; **полной —ой** *a.* full-scale (irradiation).

дозаправ/ка *f.* refuel(ing), etc., *see v.;* **—лять** *v.* refuel, refill, replenish; fill up.

дозарив/ание *n.* artificial ripening, after-ripening; **—ать** *v.* after-ripen.

дозаря/д *m.,* **—жающий** *a.* (elec.) milking.

дозатор *m.* batcher, batchmeter; proportioner, metering device; measuring hopper; dispenser, feeder; **д. времени** timing unit; **весовой д.** weigh batcher, weigher; **д.-наполнитель** *m.* measuring and filling machine; **д.-смеситель** *m.* meter-mixer.

дозваниваться *v.* (tel.) get, reach.

дозвёздный *a.* prestellar.

дозвол/ение *n.* permission; **—енный** *a.* permitted, authorized; legal; **—ительный** *a.* permissible; **—ить, —ять** *v.* permit, allow, authorize, grant.

дозвониться *v.* (tel.) get, reach.

дозвуковой *a.* (acous.) subsonic.

дозер *see* **дозатор.**

дозидик(ус) *m.* (mal.) Dosidicus (squid).

дозиметр *m.* dosimeter, dose meter; (radiation) monitor; **—ирование** *n.* radiation monitoring; **—ист** *m.* health physicist, radiation supervisor; **—ический** *a.* dosimetric; radiation- or health-monitoring; **—ический контроль** radiation monitoring; **—ический прибор, —ическая аппаратура** dosimeter; **—ия** *f.* dosimetry, (radiation) monitoring; **д.-светофор** *m.* go-no-go radiation detector.

дозиния *f.* (mal.) Dosinia.

дозиров/ание *n.* dosing, etc., *see v.;* dosage; **—анный** *a.* dosed, etc., *see v.;* **—ать** *v.* dose; measure out, meter, dispense, proportion; apportion, ration; weigh out; (chem.) batch; monitor; determine; **—ка** *f.* dosing, etc., *see v.;* dosage, amount, weight; feed(er); **весовая —ка** proportioner, proportioning feeder; **—очный** *a. of* **дозировка;** graduated; controlled; **—очная машина** *see* **дозатор.**

дозирующий прибор *see* **дозатор.**

дозн/ан(ав)аться *v.* inquire (about), find out, ascertain; **—ание** *n.* inquiry, search, investigation.

дозор *m.,* **—ный** *a.* patrol; watch; **—щик** *m.* patrolman; (ent.) dragonfly (*Anax*).

дозре/вание *n.* ripening; **—ватель** *m.* maturing tank; **—(ва)ть** *v.* mature, ripen, finish ripening; **—лый** *a.* completely ripe.

доизбрать *v.* choose in addition.

доизвлекать *v.* extract completely.

доизмельчать *v.* (paper) regrind, fine.

доиль/ник *m.* milk pail; **—ный** *a.* milking; **—ня** *f.* dairy; **—щица** *f.* milkmaid.

доиск/аться *v.* find out, ascertain, determine, establish; **—иваться** *v.* search, try to find out, inquire.

доисторический *a.* prehistoric.

доить *v.* milk; **—ся** *v.* be milked; yield milk.

дойд/ёт *fut. 3 sing. of* **дойти; —я** *past ger.* having reached, having come that far.

дой/ка *f.* milking; **—ная** *a.* milch (cow); **—ник** *m.,* **—ница** *f.* milk pail; **—ность** *f.* milk yield, productivity.

дойти *see* **доходить.**

док *m.,* **ставить в д.** *v.* dock.

ДОК *abbr.* (**дезоксикортикостерон**) de(s)oxycorticosterone, DOC.

докадмиевый *a.* sub-cadmium.

докажем *fut. 2 pl. of* **доказать;** let us prove.

доказ/анный *a.* demonstrated, etc., *see v.;* that which has been proved; **—ательный** *a.* demonstrative, convincing, conclusive; significant; **—ательство** *n.* demonstration, argument, proof, evidence, case (for); detection, identification; **не приводя доказательства** without proof; **не требует —ательства** it goes without saying; **принимать без —ательства** *v.* take for granted; **—ать** *v.* demonstrate, argue, prove, show, substantiate, ascertain; detect, identify; **—уемость** *f.* demonstrability; **—уемый** *a.* demonstrable, provable; (being) proved; **—ывать** *see* **доказать.**

докали(ва)ть *v.* heat through.

докалывать *v.* chop up; finish chopping; stab to death.

доканчив/ание *n.* finishing, completing; **—ать** *v.* finish, complete, end up.

докапывать *v.* finish digging; —**ся** *v.* find out, uncover, reveal.

докармливать *v.* feed up; finish feeding.

докат/ать, —ывать *v.* finish rolling; —**ить, —ывать** *v.* roll (up to).

докашивать *v.* finish mowing; mow (up to).

док-бассейн *m.* (naut.) wet dock.

доквашивание *n.* after-fermentation.

докембрий *m.,* —**ский** *a.* (geol.) Precambrian.

докер *m.* docker, dock hand, longshoreman.

доки/дывать, —нуть *v.* throw (as far as, up to); finish throwing.

докип/ать, —еть *v.* boil (to a point).

док-камера *m.* testing tank; launching dock.

доклад *m.,* report, paper, talk, lecture; —**ная записка** memorandum, report; —**чик** *m.* reporter; speaker, lecturer; —**ывать** *v.* report, present (a paper); announce; add.

доклеи(ва)ть *v.* finish gluing; glue up.

доклеточный *a.* (cyt.) precellular.

доклинический *a.* preclinical.

доков/ание *n.* (naut.) (dry)docking; —**ать** *v.* dock; (met.) finish forging; —**ый** *a.* dock(ing).

докоз/ан *m.* docosane; —**ановый** *a.* docosanoic (acid).

доколоть *see* **докалывать.**

доконч/енный *a.* finished, ended, completed; —**ить** *see* **доканчивать.**

докообразный *a.* valley (iceberg).

докопать *see* **докапывать.**

докормить *see* **докармливать.**

доко/сить *see* **докашивать;** —**шенный** *a.* mowed (up to).

докрасить *see* **докрашивать.**

докрасна *adv.* to red heat; until red; **раскалённый д.** *a.* red hot.

до/кристаллизационный *a.* precrystallization; —**критический** *a.* subcritical; —**крутить, —кручивать** *v.* twist, screw (tight).

доктор *m.* doctor, physician; —**ант** *m.* doctoral candidate; —**ский** *a.* doctor('s), doctoral; —**ская диссертация** doctorate; —**ство** *n.* doctor's degree.

доктрина *f.* doctrine, teaching, tenet.

докуда *adv.* how far? until when?

документ *m.* document, papers, record; deed, instrument; —**алистика** *f.* documentation activities; —**альный** *a.* documentary; hard (copy); —**ационный** *a.,* —**ация** *f.* documentation; (file of) documents; —**ировать** *v.* document.

докуп/ать *v.* finish bathing; *see* **докупить;** —**ить** *v.* buy more, buy in addition; —**ка** *f.* additional purchase.

докури(ва)ть *v.* finish smoking.

доламывать *v.* finish breaking; break off or up.

долац *m.* (geol.) dolina, sink hole.

долбёж *m.,* —**ка** *f.,* —**ный** *a.* slotting, etc., *see* **долбить;** —**ный станок** slotter, mortising machine.

долбец *m.* (ichth.) gudgeon (*Gobio gobio*).

долб/ить *v.* slot, mortise, groove; chisel, chip, pick (at); gouge, hollow (out); shape (gears); memorize, cram (for exam); (mil.) batter, ram, bombard; —**ление** *n.* slotting, etc., *see v.;* —**лён(н)ый** *a.* slotted, etc., *see v.;* —**ня** *f.* ram; —**(н)як** *m.* ram, slide; gear-shaping cutter; —**онос** *see* **дубонос.**

долг. *abbr.* (**долгота**) longitude.

долг *m.* debt, obligation, duty; loan; liability; due; **в д.** on credit, on trust.

долгий *a.* long, protracted, prolonged.

долгинка (ichth.) a shad (*Alosa brashnikovi b.*).

долго *adv.* long, a long time; —**вато** *adv.,* —**ватый** *a.* rather long; —**вечность** *f.* longevity, lasting quality, durability, permanence; (useful) life; (plastics) rupture time; **запас —вечности** endurance limit; **средняя —вечность дуги** mean arc lifetime; —**вечный** *a.* macrobiotic, long-lived, lasting, durable, permanent.

долговой *a.* of **долг;** owing; —**ое обязательство** promissory note.

долго/временность *see* **долговечность;** —**временный** *a.* durable, lasting, permanent; of long duration; —**жданный** *a.* long-expected; —**живущий** *a.* long-lived; —**звучащий, —играющий** *a.* long-playing; —**летие** *n.* longevity, (long) life; —**летний** *see* **долговечный;** —**ноги, —ноговые** *pl.* (mam.) Pedetidae; —**ножки** *pl.* (ent.) crane flies (*Tipulidae*); —**носики** *pl.* weevils (*Curculionidae*); —**носый** *a.* long-nosed.

долго/пёр *m.* flying fish (*Exocoetus; Dactylopterus*); —**периодический** *a.* long-period; —**пёровые, —пёры** *pl.* (ichth.) Exocoetidae; Dactylopteridae; —**пёрый** *a.* long-finned; —**прочность** *f.* durability; —**прудненский** *a.* (geog.) Dolgoprudnyi; —**пят** *m.* (mam.) tarsier (*Tarsius*); —**пятовые** *pl.* Tarsiidae; —**срочный** *a.* long-term, long, lasting, long-range; —**ствольный** *a.* long-stemmed; —**та** *f.* length; (geog.) longitude; —**тный** *a.* longitudinal; —**тье** *n.* long log; —**хвостка** *f.* (herp.) Tachydromus; —**хвостовые, —хвосты(е)** *pl.* (ichth.) grenadiers (*Macrouridae*); —**хвостый** *a.* long-tailed; —**цветка** *f.* (bot.) Ageratum; —**шеий** *a.* long-necked; —**шёрстный** *a.* long-haired (sheep); —**язычный** *a.* long-tongued.

долгунец *m.* long-stemmed flax.

долевой *a.* of **доля;** per unit; longitudinal; (anat.) lobar.

доледниковый *a.* preglacial.

долее *comp.* of **долго,** longer.

до/лежать, —лёживать *v.* lie (until).

долез(а)ть *v.* climb up (to).

долей *gen. pl.* of **доля;** *imp.* of **долить.**

долек *gen. pl.* of **долька.**

долерит *m.* (petr.) dolerite; —**овый** *a.* doleritic.

долерофанит *m.* (min.) dolerophanite.

долет/ать, —еть *v.* fly (up to), reach.

долеч/ивание *n.* (med.) after-care; —**и(ва)ть** *v.* cure, heal.

долечка *dim.* of **долька; доля.**

должать *v.* borrow, owe, be in debt.

должен *imp. v.* must, should, ought, have (to); owe (to); **он д.** he must, he has (to); —**ствовать** *v.* be obliged, be forced.

должея *f.* a type of log beehive.

должн/а *f.* of **должен;** —**ик** *m.* debtor; —**о** *n.* of **должен;** —**о быть** (it) must be, should be, must have; probably, possibly; —**ое** *n.* due; required value; **воздавать —ое** *v.* do justice (to); **отдавать —ое** *v.* give credit (for).

должност/ной *a.* official, functional; —**ное лицо** official, functionary; —**ь** *f.* office, function, post, position; appointment; **в —и** as; **исполняющий —ь** acting (for).

должн/ый *a.* due, proper; **быть —ым** *v.* owe; **на —ой высоте** up to the mark; **учитывая —ым образом** with due regard (for).

доли *gen., pl., etc.,* of **доля.**

долив/ание *n.,* —**ка** *f.* adding, etc., see v.; addition; add, fill up, top up, pour full; replenish; refill; refuel.

долииды *pl.* (mal.) Doliidae.

долин/а *f.* valley, trough; —**ка** *f.* indentation, depression; (anat.) vallecula; —**ки** *pl.* (snow) coomb.

долинеевский *a.* pre-Linnaean.

долинн/о-балочный *a.* valley-ravine (relief); **—ый** *a.* valley, trough.

долиолиды *pl.* (mal.) Doliolida.

долит/ый *a.* added, etc., see **доливать; —ь** *see* **доливать.**

долиум *m.* (mal.) Dolium, Tonna.

долихо— *prefix* dolicho— (long, narrow); **—завр** *m.* (pal.) dolichosaur; **—птеровые** *pl.* (ichth.) Dolichopterygidae; **—с** *m.* (bot.) Dolichos; **—цефалический** *a.* dolichocephalic, long-headed.

доллар *m.,* **—овый** *a.* dollar.

долог *sh. m. of* **долгий.**

дологический *a.* prelogical.

долож/енный *a.* reported, etc., *see* **докладывать; —ить** *see* **докладывать.**

долой *adv.* away, off, down (with).

долок *m.* (glass) marver.

доломать *see* **доламывать.**

доломит *m.* (min.) dolomite, pearl spar; **—изация** *f.* dolomitization; **—изированный** *a.* dolomitized; **—из(ир)овать** *v.* dolomitize; **—ный, —овый** *a.* dolomite, dolomitic.

доломол *m.* dolomol (magnesium stearate).

долонский *a.* (geog.) Dolon.

долот/ить *v.* chisel; **—ной** *a.,* **—о** *n.* chisel, gouge; (drill) bit; **—овидный, —ообразный** *a.* dolabriform, hatchet-shaped; **—чатый** *a.* chisel; **—чатый бур** chisel(-shaped) bit; (min.) trepan.

доль *f.* length.

дольёт *fut. 3 sing. of* **долить.**

доль/ка *dim. of* **доля;** *f.* lobule, small lobe; section, segment, slice; (garlic) clove; (bot.) lacinule; **д. плода** (bot.) mericarp; **—ки** *pl.* lobuli; **—ковый** *a.* lobular; **—ный** *a.* lobate, lobe-like; *suffix* -lobe; -part; (bot.) **—котиледонный;** *a. and* **—** submultiple; **—чатый** *a.* lobate, lobed; laciniate, fringed; segmented.

дольше *adv.* a longer time.

дольют *fut. 3 pl. of* **долить.**

дол/я *f.* share, portion; allotment, quota; part, segment; fraction, particle; (stat.) rate; fate, lot; (bot., anat.) lobe; unit of weight (44.435 mg); **в —ях** in fractions; **весовая д.** weight proportion; **височная д. (полушария)** temporal lobe (of cerebrum); **выпадать на —ю** *v.* fall to the lot (of); **затылочная д.** occipital lobe; **лобная д.** frontal lobe; **миллионные —и** parts per million; **теменная д.** parietal lobe.

дом *m.* house, home, dwelling; lodge; domatic crystal; **—а** *adv.* at home; *pl. of* **дом; вне —а** outdoors; **на —у** *a.* (med.) home (care); house (call).

домаз(ыв)ать *v.* finish greasing or smearing.

домалывать *v.* finish grinding, grind up.

доматий *m.* domatium, shelter.

доматический *a.* (cryst.) domatic.

доматывать *v.* finish winding.

домашн/ий *a.* domestic, home, house(hold); home-made; (zool.) tame; **—ее хозяйство** domestic economy; household; housework; home; **—яя птица** poultry; **—яя хозяйка** housewife.

домбайский *a.* (geog.) Dombai.

домейкит *m.* (min.) domeykite.

домен *m.,* **—а** *f.* domain; **д.** *gen. pl. of* **домна.**

домен/ный *a.* (met.) blast furnace; metallurgical (coke); pig (iron); domain (structure); bubble (memory); **—ная печь** blast furnace; **—ное дутьё** blast-furnace air; **—щик** *m.* blast furnace operator.

домери(ва)ть *v.* finish measuring.

домесить *v.* finish kneading.

доместикация *f.* domestication.

доместицин *m.* domesticine.

домеш/ать *v.* finish mixing; **—ивать** *v.* finish mixing; finish kneading or puddling (clay).

домзак *m.* prison, house of detention.

домик *dim. of* **дом;** booth; (chicken) coop; receptacle, housing, case, shell, compartment; (bot.) perithecium; (prot.) lorica.

доминант *m.,* **—а** *f.* dominant; dominance; **—ность** *f.* dominance, preponderance; **—ный** *a.* dominant, preponderant, prevalent.

доминиканский *a.* (geog.) Dominican.

домин/ион *m.* dominion; **—ирование** *n.* domination, dominance, prevalence; **—ировать** *v.* (pre)dominate, prevail; **—ирующий** *a.* (pre)dominant; **—ьон** *m.* dominion.

домит *m.* (petr.) domite.

домкрат *m.* jack; **опускать —ом** *v.* jack down; **поднимать —ом** *v.* jack up; **—ик** *dim. of* **домкрат;** leveling jack; **—ный** *a.* jack.

домн/а *f.* (met.) blast furnace; **—ица** *f.* bloomery (furnace).

домо/владелец *m.* house owner, landlord; **—водство** *n.* domestic science; **—вый** *a.* house; domestic.

домогаться *v.* solicit, seek.

домодельный *a.* homemade.

домой *adv.* home(ward).

домол *m.* regrinding, remilling, recrushing; **—ачивать** *v.* finish threshing; **—от** *m.* end of threshing; **—отить** *v.* finish threshing; **—оть** *v.* finish grinding; regrind, remill.

доморощенный *a.* home-grown.

доморский *a.* (lunar) ante-maria.

домостить *v.* finish paving.

домостро/ение *n.,* **—ительный** *a.,* **—ительство** *n.* house building.

домотать *v.* finish winding.

дом/отканый *a.* homespun; **—оуправление, —охозяйство** *n.* house management; house manager's office; **—охозяйка** *f.* housewife; **—работница** *f.* domestic servant.

домы(ва)ть *v.* finish washing.

донакс *m.* (bot.; mal.) Donax; **—ин** *m.* donaxine, gramine.

донарит *m.* (expl.) donarite.

донасыщение *n.* final saturation.

донатор *m.,* **—ный** *a.* donor; source.

донашивать *v.* wear out, finish wearing; carry (a child) to full term.

Донбасс Donbas, Donets Coal Basin.

донга *f.* (geol.) donga, dry wash.

донейтрализовывать *v.* neutralize completely.

донельзя *adv.* completely, utterly.

донес/ение *n.* report, dispatch, account, message; **—ти** *see* **доносить.**

донец *m.* Don horse.

донецкий *a.* (geog.) Donets.

донизу *adv.* to the bottom.

донирование *n.* donation.

донка *f.* donkey (pump).

донкихотский *a.* quixotic, foolish.

доннановский *a.* Donnan (equilibrium, etc.).

донник *m.,* **—овый** *a.* (bot.) sweet clover (*Melilotus*); heading (for barrels); **—и** *pl.* benthos, bottom flora and fauna.

донн/о-моренный *a.* swell-and-swale (topography); **—ый** *a.* ground, bottom, base; (biol.) benth(on)ic; solid (phase); anchor, ground (ice); **—ый осадок** bottoms, residue, sludge; **—ая часть** base (of missile); **—ое**

население benthon, benthos; **—ые наносы** (hydr.) bed load; **площадь —ого среза** base area (of missile).

доноокругловочный станок head-rounding machine (for barrels, drums).

донор *m.* donor; **—но-акцепторный** *a.* donor-acceptor; **—ный** *a.* donor, donating; **—ский** *a.* donor's; **—ский пункт** blood bank; **—ство** *n.* blood donor system.

доно/сить *v.* carry (up to); (med.) carry to full term; report, denounce; wear out (clothes); **—ситься** *v.* be carried, reach; be heard; be worn out; **—шенность** *f.* full-term birth or pregnancy; **—шенный** *a.* carried (up to) etc., *see v.*; full-term.

донской *a.* (geog.) Don.

дон/це, **—ышко** *dim. of* **дно**; bottom, base; corm (of bulb); **—ьевырезной** *a.* head-rounding (machine); **—ья** *pl. of* **дно**.

до н.э. *abbr.* (**до нашей эры**) B.C.

до/оборудовать *v.* fit out; **—обработка** *f.* after-treatment, secondary treatment, cure; finish(ing); **—окисление** *n.* final or further oxidation; **—окорка** *f.* rossing (of bark); **—омыление** *n.* after-saponification.

доопредел/ение *n.* (pre)determination; supplement to a definition; **—ённый** *a.* (pre)determined, etc., *see v.*; **—ить**, **—ять** *v.* (pre)determine; (re)define, extend or complete a definition.

до/опыление *n.* supplementary pollination; **—отверждение** *n.* additional hardening, post-hardening, post-cure.

доохла/дитель *m.* after-cooler, recooler, additional cooler; **—ждать** *v.* recool; aftercool; **—ждение** *n.* aftercooling.

до/оценка *f.* additional evaluation, final appraisal; full appreciation; **—очистка** *f.* after-cleaning, after-purification, final purification.

доп. *abbr.* (**дополнение, дополнительный**).

допа *m.* dopa, 3,4-dihydroxyphenylalanine.

допаивать *v.* finish soldering.

допалзывать *v.* crawl or creep (up to).

допалывать *v.* finish weeding; weed (up to).

доп/амин *m.* dopamine; **—ан** *m.* Dopane.

до/пари(ва)ть *v.* finish steaming; steam (until); **—пах(ив)ать** *v.* finish plowing; plow (to); **—пашка** *f.* completion of plowing; **—паять** *v.* finish soldering; **—пекать** *v.* finish baking.

допечат/ать *v.* finish printing; make reprints; **—ка** *f.*, **—ок** *m.* reprint.

допечь *see* **допекать**.

допивать *v.* finish, drink up.

допили(ва)ть *v.* finish sawing; saw (to).

допис(ыв)ать *v.* finish (writing).

допить *see* **допивать**.

допла/та *f.* additional charge; **—тить, —чивать** *v.* pay in addition, pay up; **—ченный** *a.* paid up.

доплер *see under* **допплер**.

доплы(ва)ть *v.* swim or float (up to), reach.

доподлинн/о *adv.* for certain; **—ый** *a.* certain; authentic, genuine.

допоить *v.* finish watering (stock).

допокрытосемянный *a.* (pal.) proangiospermous.

дополаскивать *v.* finish rinsing.

дополз/ать, —ти *v.* creep or crawl (up to).

дополн/а *adv.* full; **—ение** *n.* addition, supplement, addendum; appendix; (math.) complement; (grammar) object; **—ение до** completion; **—ение нулями** zero padding; **алгебраическое —ение** (math.) cofactor; **точное —ение** radix complement.

дополн/енный *a.* supplemented, etc., *see v.*; **—ительно**

adv. in addition (to); **—ительный** *a.* supplementary, additional, added, further, more; (comp.) add-in; extra, spare; residual; subsidiary, accessory, auxiliary; ancillary (information); optional; complementary (angle; color); side (reaction); secondary (stress); after- (treatment); co- (function); **—ительный расход** overhead; **—ительная величина** (math.) complement; **—ительная клавиатура** (comp.) number pad; **—ить, —ять** *v.* supplement, add, complement, complete; augment, amplify, expand, enlarge (edition); make up, fill up, replenish; **—яемый** *a.* complemented.

дополоскать *see* **дополаскивать**.

дополоть *see* **допалывать**.

дополучить *v.* receive in addition.

допосевной *a.* pre-sowing, preplanting.

допотопный *a.* antiquated.

доппаёк *m.* supplementary ration.

доппель-машина *f.* sole-stitching machine.

доппер/ит *m.* (min.) dopperite; **—овский** *a.* Doppler (shift, etc.).

допр *m.* workhouse.

допрашивать *v.* examine, question, interrogate; **—ся** *v.* wheedle, get (by asking).

допредельный *a.* limit(ing).

допрессовывать *v.* re-press, recompact.

доприправить *v.* (typ.) correct make-ready.

доприселение *n.* settling (on existing farms).

допрос *m.* examination, questioning, interrogation; **—ить(ся)** *see* **допрашивать(ся)**; **—ный** *a. of* **допрос**.

допрясть *v.* finish spinning.

допуск *m.* tolerance, allowance, margin; limit; clearance; admission, admittance; **д. на** allowance for; **д. по частоте** frequency tolerance; **по жёстким —ам** to close tolerances; **—аемость** *f.* admissibility; **—аемый** *see* **допустимый**; **—ать** *v.* assume, suppose; admit; permit, allow, accept, tolerate, let; **не —ать** *v.* exclude, keep out; **—ающий** *a.* assuming, etc., *see v.*; accessible; **—ающий оценку** (stat.) estimable; **—ая** *pr. ger.* if we assume; allowing (for).

допустим *fut. 1 pl.* of **допустить**; **д., что** let (us assume), suppose that, let it be; **—ость** *f.* admissibility, etc., *see a.*; tolerance; allowance; **—ый** *a.* admissible, allowable, permissible, acceptable, tolerable; feasible; tolerance (dose); safe (load); **—ая точность, —ое отклонение, —ое отступление** tolerance; **предельно —ая доза** maximum permissible dose, MPD.

допустить *see* **допускать**.

допущен/ие *n.* admission, etc., *see* **допускать**; assumption, hypothesis; premise, supposition, prerequisite; **—ный** *a.* admitted, etc., *see* **допускать**.

допыт(ыв)аться *v.* (try to) find out.

допьёт *fut. 3 sing.* of **допить**.

дораб *m.* (ichth.) dorab (*Chirocentrus*).

дорабатывать *see* **доработать**.

дорабовые *pl.* (ichth.) dorabs (*Chirocentridae*).

доработ/ать *v.* finish, complete; modify, up-date, correct; **—ка** *f.* finishing, etc., *see v.*; completion; **механическая —ка** additional machining.

дорадовые *pl.* dolphinfishes (*Coryphaenidae*).

дора/стать, —сти *v.* grow (to a given size); mature; reach (the age of); **—стить, —щивать** *v.* raise, grow (until); rear (livestock); **—щивание** *n.* raising, etc., *see v.*; completion of growing.

дорвать *v.* finish tearing; tear off.

дореволюционный *a.* prerevolutionary.

дорезать *v.* finish cutting; cut (to).

дорема *f.* (bot.) Dorema.

доремонтный *a.* before repair(ing).

дорзальный *see* **дорсальный.**

дориды *pl.* (mal.) sea slugs (*Dorididae*).

дорикниум *m.* (bot.) Dorycnium.

дорилиды *pl.* (ent.) Dorylidae.

дорис *m.* (mal.) sea slug (*Doris*).

дорн *m.* mandrel, drift, core.

Дорна эффект Dorn effect.

дорнирование *n.* coring.

дорно/вать *v.* (mach.) mandrel; **—вой** *a. of* **дорн;** **—держатель** *m.* mandrel holder.

дорный *a.* split, fissured, cracked.

дорог/а *f.* road, (high)way; passage, path, course, tract; journey; **в —е** en route.

дорого *adv.* dear, expensive, high; **—визна** *f.* expensiveness; **—й** *a.* dear, expensive, costly, high-priced; *adv.* on the way; **—миловский** *a.* (geog.) Dorogomilovskaya; **—стоящий** *a.* expensive.

дородный *a.* corpulent, obese, portly.

дородовой *a.* prenatal.

дородство *n.* corpulence, obesity.

дорож/ать *v.* rise in price; **—е** *comp. of* **дорого, дорогой;** **—ить** *v.* value, prize; **—иться** *v.* overcharge.

дорож/ка *f.* path, track, trail, course; walk; furrow, groove; (anat.) flumen, stream; strip; (carpet) runner; (fishing) troll; **—ник** *m.* highway worker, road builder; (carp.) grooving plane; **—ностроительный** *a.* road-building; **—но-эксплуатационный** *a.* road-maintenance; **—ный** *a.* road, highway; laptop (computer); **—ная пробка** congestion; **—ная техника** highway engineering; **—ное дело** road management.

доросома *f.* (ichth.) gizzard shad (*Dorosoma*).

дороющий *pr. part. of* **дорыть.**

Дорра агитатор Dorr agitator.

дорс/(альн)о— *prefix* dors(o)— dorsi— (back); **—альный** *a.* dorsal; **—ивентральный** *a.* dorsiventral, bifacial; **—овентральный** *a.* dorsoventral; **—олатеральный** *a.* dorsolateral, superolateral.

дорстрой— *prefix* road building.

дортмундский чан Dortmund tank.

доруб/ать, —ить *v.* finish chopping or cutting; chop (up to).

дорш *m.* common name for various fishes.

доры/вать *v.* finish tearing; **—(ва)ть** *v.* finish digging; dig (to); **—ться** *v.* dig to, reach.

досад/а *f.* vexation, disappointment, aggravation; **—ить** *see* **досаждать, досаживать; —но** *adv.* it is a pity, it is too bad; **—ный** *a.* annoying, vexing, disappointing, unfortunate; **—ные помехи** nuisance; **—овать** *v.* be annoyed.

досажать *see* **досаживать.**

досаждать *v.* annoy, irritate, vex.

досаживать *v.* finish planting, add.

досаливать *v.* finish salting; add (more) salt; finish pickling.

досе/в *m.* (agr.) end of sowing; **—вание** *n.* completion of sowing; **—(и)вать, —ять** *v.* finish sowing; finish sifting.

доси/деть, —живать *v.* stay (until).

досинхронный *a.* hyposynchronous.

досиня *adv.* blue, to a blue color.

доск/а *f.* board, plank; (instrument) panel; slab, plate; platform; tray, pan; (tube) sheet (of boiler); **классная д.** blackboard; **обшивать —ами** *v.* plank, board up.

доскабливать *v.* finish scraping; scrape (until); finish planing.

досказ(ыв)ать *v.* finish (telling); **не д.** keep something back.

доскак/(ив)ать, —нуть *v.* jump, hop, leap, spring (up to), reach.

доскоблить *see* **доскабливать.**

доско/видный *a.* tabuliform; buttressed (root); **—вый** *a. of* **доска.**

доскональный *a.* precise, exact, thorough.

доскораспределитель *m.* pointer, tripper.

доскочить *see* **доскакивать.**

доскр/ебать, —ёбывать, —ести finish scrubbing.

досл/анный *a.* sent on; **—ать** *see* **досылать.**

доследов/ание *n.* further inquiry; **—ать** *v.* submit to further inquiry.

дословн/о *adv.* word for word, literally, verbatim; **—ый** *a.* literal, verbatim.

дослужи(ва)ть *v.* work, serve (until); **—ся** *v.* rise to the rank (of); qualify (for).

дослуш(ив)ать *v.* listen to the end.

досм/атривать, —отреть *v.* inspect, examine; watch; see to the end; look through (book); take care (of), look after; **—отр** *m.,* **—отровый** *a.* inspection, etc., *see v.*

досоветский *a.* pre-Soviet.

досок *gen. pl. of* **доска.**

досол *m.,* **—ка** *f.* final pickling; addition of salt; **—ить** *see* **досаливать.**

досохнуть *see* **досыхать.**

доспать *v.* sleep (until).

доспе/вание *n.* ripening, maturing; **—(ва)ть** *v.* ripen, mature; **—лый** *a.* ripe, mature.

досрочн/о *adv.* ahead of schedule; **—ый** *a.* premature, early.

доставать *v.* get, obtain, procure, take; reach; suffice; **не д. до** fall short of; **—ся** *v.* fall to one's lot.

достав/ить *v.* deliver, convey, transport, transmit, forward; furnish, provide, supply, give, yield, bring; **—ка** *f.,* **—ление** *n.* delivering, etc., *see v.*; delivery, conveyance; import(ation); supply; yield, recovery; **—ленный** *a.* delivered, etc., *see v.*; **—ляемый** *a.* supplied; **—лять** *see* **доставить; —очный** *a. of* **доставка; —щик** *m.* supplier; delivery man.

достаивать *v.* stand to the end.

достат/ок *m.* prosperity; sufficiency, plenty; **—ки** *pl.* income; **жить в —ке** be well off.

достаточн/о *adv.* sufficiently, adequately, enough; fairly, rather; it is sufficient or enough; **—ость** *f.* sufficiency, adequacy; competence; precision; **—ый** *a.* sufficient, enough, adequate, ample; fair, reasonable; competent; precise.

достать *see* **доставать.**

достиг/аемость *see* **достижимость; —аемый** *see* **достижимый; —ать** *v.* attain, reach, achieve, bring about, get, obtain, gain; come (up to), mount up, be as great as; amount, run (to); arrive; make (progress); take (a value); **не —ать** fail, fall short (of); **—ающий** *a.* attaining, etc., *see v.*; **—нутый** *a.* attained, etc., *see v.*; **—нуть** *see* **достигать.**

дости/жение *n.* attainment, achievement, breakthrough; **—жения** *pl.* advances, progress; **—жимость** *f.* attainability, etc., *see a.*; reachability (of points on a graph); **—жимый** *a.* attainable, accessible, achievable, practicable, within (the) reach (of); **—чь** *see* **достигать.**

достоверн/о *adv.* for certain, reliably, positively, definitely, with assurance; **—ость** *f.* certainty, reliability, trustworthiness; authenticity, truth; confidence; significance; accuracy; **граница —ости** confidence limit; **—ый** *a.* certain, reliable, sure, proved, trustworthy, sound; authentic; known; positive.

досто/инство *n.* good quality, merit, virtue, value, advantage; dignity; —**инства и недостатки** pros and cons; —**йный** *a.* worth(y), deserving.

достопримечательн/о *adv.* notably; it is notable, noteworthy or remarkable; —**ость** *f.* curiosity, rarity; (national) monument; site or area of unique interest; —**ый** *a.* notable, noteworthy, remarkable.

достояние *n.* property; ownership; contribution; **сделать** —**м** *v.* popularize.

достоять *see* **достаивать.**

достраив/ание *n.* completion; —**ать** *v.* complete, finish building; add on.

дострел *m.* shooting, perforation.

достро/ить *see* **достраивать;** —**йка** *f.* completion (of building).

доступ *m.* access, approach, entrance, admission, inlet, passage; **без** —**а** inaccessible; away (from); **прямого** —**а** *a.* direct-access; —**но** *adv.* easily, simply, accessibly; —**ность** *f.* access(ibility), availability; —**ный** *a.* accessible, within reach, available; practicable; understandable; reasonable, moderate (price); **легко** —**ный** easily available, within easy reach.

досуг *m.* leisure, spare time.

досу/ха *adv.* (until) dry; —**ши(ва)ть** *v.* finish drying; dry up or out; —**шка** *f.* completion of drying.

досчатый *see* **дощатый.**

досчит(ыв)ать *v.* count (up to); finish counting.

досыл/ание *n.,* —**ка** *f.* sending on, etc., *see v.;* —**атель** *m.* rammer, ramrod; —**ать** *v.* send on, send the rest (of); ram (home).

досып/анный *a.* filled up, added; —**ать** *v.* fill up, add; sleep enough; —**ка** *f.* filling up, addition.

досыта *adv.* to satiety, enough.

досыхать *v.* get dry, become dry.

досье *n.* dossier, file, papers.

досюда *adv.* this far, up to here.

досягаем/ость *f.* reach, range; attainability; **в пределах** —**ости** within (the) reach (of); —**ый** *a.* attainable, accessible, approachable, within reach.

досяг/ать, —**нуть** *v.* attain, reach, accomplish.

ДОТ *abbr.* (**долговременная огневая точка**) permanent emplacement, pillbox.

дотаивать *v.* melt completely.

дотаскивать *see* **дотащить.**

дотация *f.* subsidy, grant.

дотащить *v.* carry, drag (up to).

дотаять *see* **дотаивать.**

дотекать *v.* flow (up to).

дотемна *adv.* before dark.

дотерпеть *v.* tolerate, endure (until).

дотечь *v.* flow (up to).

дотитровать *v.* titrate further.

дотла *adv.* utterly, completely.

дотравка *f.* final etching or pickling.

дотрагиваться *v.* touch.

дотриаконтан *m.* dotriacontane.

дотронуться *see* **дотрагиваться.**

дотуда *adv.* up to there, to that place.

дотя/гивать, —**нуть** *v.* drag, draw (up to); last out; get by (until); drag out, delay; stretch, extend; —**гиваться,** —**нуться** *v.* reach, extend; continue; hold out, last.

доумягчать *v.* remove residual hardness.

доупорядочи(ва)ть *v.* (bring to) order.

Доусона газ Dowson (producer) gas.

доучи(ва)ть *v.* finish teaching; teach up to; finish learning; learn up to; —**ся** *v.* study until; complete one's education.

ДОФА *abbr.,* **дофа** *m.* (**диоксифенилаланин**) dihydroxyphenylalanine.

дофамин *see* **допамин.**

дох/ать *v.* choke from coughing; —**лый** *a.* dead (animal); —**лятина** *f.* carrion.

дохна *f.* (bot.) sweet sorghum.

дохнуть *v.* (zool.) die; *see* **дышать.**

доход *m.* income, return(s), revenue, profit, gain; receipt(s); —**ить** *v.* come (to), go (to), reach, attain; extend (to), go as far (as), get (to); amount, run (to), total; ripen, develop; —**ность** *f.* profitableness, productive capacity; income; —**ный** *a.* profitable, paying; lucrative, remunerative, income-bearing; —**ные статьи** revenues.

доходчив/ость *f.* clarity; —**ый** *a.* clear, understandable, intelligible.

доходящий *pr. part. of* **доходить.**

доцве/сти, —**тать** *v.* finish flowering, fade; bloom (until).

доценк *m.* (price) markup.

доцент *m.* lecturer, reader; assistant or associate professor.

дочери *gen., etc., of* **дочь.**

дочерна *adv.* (until) black.

дочерн/ий *a.* daughter, filial, subsidiary, secondary; branch (company); derived, subsequent (product); —**ее вещество** (nucl.) daughter, decay product.

дочерп(ыв)ать *v.* finish scooping out.

дочер/тить, —**чивать** *v.* finish, complete (drawing); draw up to.

дочист/а *adv.* until (perfectly) clean or pure; completely; —**ить** *see* **дочищать;** —**ка** *f.* (final) cleaning, etc., *see* **дочищать.**

дочит(ыв)ать *v.* finish reading.

дочищать *v.* finish cleaning or purifying; clean up; polish up; trim.

доч/ка, —**ь** *f.* daughter.

дошедший *past act. part. of* **дойти.**

доши(ва)ть *v.* finish sewing; sew (up to).

дошкольный *a.* preschool.

дошлёт *fut. 3 sing. of* **дослать.**

дошли *past pl. of* **дойти.**

дошник *m.* tank, vat.

дошьёт *fut. 3 sing. of* **дошить.**

дощаник *m.* flat-bottomed boat.

дощ/атый *a.* board, plank; tabular; **д. ход** boardwalk; —**ечка** *f.* small plank; tablet, slab, plate; —**ник** *m.* tan vat.

доэвтект/ический *a.* (met.) hypoeutectic; —**оидный** *a.* hypoeutectoid.

доядерн/ый *a.* (biol.) prenuclear; —**ые организмы** Procaryota.

дояр *m.* milker, dairyman; —**ка** *f.* milkmaid; —**ка-скотница** *f.* dairy woman.

дояровизировать *v.* vernalize fully.

ДПН *abbr.* (**дифосфопиридиннуклеотид**) diphosphopyridine nucleotide, DPN.

дптр *abbr.* (**диоптрия**) diopter.

др. *abbr.* (**дробь**) fraction; (**другие**) the rest; (**другой**) other; **д-р** *abbr.* (**директор**) director; (**доктор**) doctor.

дравит *m.* (min.) dravite.

драга *f.* drag, dredge; drag net.

драгант *m.* tragacanth (gum).

Драгендорфа реактив Dragendorff reagent.

драг/ер *m.* dredger; —**ирование** *n.,* —**ировка** *f.* dredging, etc., *see v.;* —**ировать** *v.* dredge, drag or scoop (out); trawl; —**лайн** *m.* dragline (excavator).

драгоценн/ость *f.* jewel, gem, precious stone; valuable; —**ый** *a.* precious.

драёк *m.* dowel, pin, fid.

драж/е *n.* (pharm.) dragee, lozenge; **—ирование** *n.*, **—ировочный** *a.* pelleting; (seed) coating; **—ированный** *a.* pelleted; coated; **—ировать** *v.* pellet; coat.

дражный *a. of* **драга.**

дразн/ение *n.* teasing, exciting; (met.) poling; **—илка** *f.* pole, stirrer; **—ить** *v.* tease, excite; pole, stir.

драить *v.* (naut.) scrub, polish.

драйвер *m.* (electron.) driver.

драйер *m.* dryer, drying machine.

драка *f.* fight.

дракон *m.* dragon; (herp.) lizard; (ichth.) weever (*Trachinus*); (astr.) Draco; **морской д.** greater weever (*Trachinus draco*); **—еттовые** *pl.* (ichth.) Draconettidae; **—ический** *a.* draconic; **—ова кровь** dragon's blood (resin); **—овые** *pl.* (ichth.) Trachinidae; Callionymidae; **—овый** *a.* dragon; draconic (acid); **д.-рыба** *f.* (ichth.) Callionymus; **—томелон** *m.* (bot.) Dracontomelon; **—чик** *m.* (ichth.) Trachinus; **морские —чики, —чиковые** *pl.* weeverfishes (*Trachinidae*).

дракункулёз *m.* (med.) dracunculosis.

драмат/изировать *v.* dramatize; **—ический** *a.* dramatic.

дран/ица, —ка *f.*, **—очный** *a.* lath(ing), slat, batten; (roof) shingle; shaving(s), slivers; **—ый** *a.* torn, tattered; superfine (meal); **—ь** *see* **дранка; —ье** *see* **дранка;** milling (of grain).

драп *m.* thick woolen cloth; **—ировать** *v.* drape; **—ировка** *f.* draping; drapery; **—ировщик** *m.* upholsterer **—овый** *a. of* **драп; —ри** *n.* drapery, curtains.

дратв/а *f.* cobbler's thread, tarred twine, waxed end; **—енный** *a. of* **дратва;** cobbler's (wax).

драть *v.* tear up, tear to shreds; pull off, strip off; scratch, lacerate; overcharge, rip off; **—ся** *v.* fight.

драфт *m.* glass rod.

драхма *f.* dram (3.73 g.).

драцена *f.* (bot.) dragon tree (*Dracaena; Cordyline*).

драч *m.* (carp.) coarse plane; hide stripper; **—евый** *a.* bastard (file).

драчливый *a.* pugnacious.

драшейоз *m.* (vet.) Drasch(e)ia megastoma infection.

ДРВ *abbr.* (Демократическая Республика Вьетнам) Democratic Republic of Vietnam.

дребезг: в —и to pieces, to fragments.

дребезж/ание *n.* rattling, etc., *see v.*; **—ать** *v.* rattle, jingle, tinkle; jar; chatter.

древен *sh. m. of* **древний.**

древес/ина *f.* wood; wood pulp; (felled) timber; lignin; (bot.) xylem; **—инник** *m.* (ent.) pinhole borer; **—инность** *f.* woodiness; **—инный** *a. of* **древесина;** woody, wooden, ligneous; **—инное вещество** lignin; **—иноведение** *n.* dendrology; xylology; wood technology; **—неющий** *a.* lignescent; **—ник** *see* **древесинник; —ница** *f.* (ent.) Zeuzera; (amph.) tree frog (*Hyla arborea*); (orn.) warbler (*Dendroica*); **—ницевые** *pl.* (orn.) Parulidae.

древесно— *prefix* xylo—, wood(y); **—волокнистый** *a.* wood-fiber; **—дикобразные** *pl.* (mam.) porcupines (*Erethizontidae*); **—кустарник** *m.* hardy shrub; **—лазающий** *a.* (orn.) scansorial; **—массный** *a.* wood-pulp; **—слоистый** *a.* laminated-wood; **—мышь** *f.* (mam.) tree mouse (*Dendromus*); **—смоляной** *a.* wood tar; **—сть** *f.* woodiness; **—угольный** *a.* (wood) charcoal; **—уксуснокислый** *a.* pyroligneous acid; pyrolignite (of); **—уксусный** *a.* pyroligneous (acid); **—ядный** *a.* xylophagous.

древесные *pl.* tree species.

древесн/ый *a.* wood(y), ligneous; fibrous; arboreal; tree; wood-pulp; (agr.) grafting (wax); tree-inhabiting; **д. картон** fiberboard; **д. порошок** sawdust; **д. сахар** wood sugar, xylose; **д. спирт** wood alcohol, methyl alcohol; **д. уголь** charcoal; **д. уксус** wood vinegar, pyroligneous acid; **—ая камедь** wood gum, xylan; **—ая масса** wood pulp; **—ая мука** sawdust; **—ая шерсть** excelsior; **—ое масло** wood oil; specif. tung oil; **—ое топливо** fire wood; **—ые опилки** sawdust.

древко *n.* staff, pole.

древмасса *f.* wood pulp.

древн/е— *prefix* paleo—, ancient; **—екрылые насекомые** (ent.) Paleoptera; **—ий** *a.* ancient, old; early; ancestral; antique; **—ик** *m.* (ent.) weevil (*Hylobius*); **—ость** *f.* antiquity, ancient times.

древо жизни *n.* (anat.) arbor vitae; (bot.) Thuja.

древо— *prefix* dendr(o)—, tree; xylo—, wood; **—вал** *m.* feller, felling machine; tree uprooter; **—валкусторез** *m.* land-clearing bulldozer; **—видность** *f.* woodiness; **—видный** *a.* woody, ligneous, xyloid; arborescent, dendritic, tree-like; **—гнёзды** *pl.* (ent.) Xylocopidae; **—грызовые, —грызы** *pl.* powder post beetles (*Lyctidae*); **—губец** *m.* (bot.) false bittersweet (*Celastrus scandens*); **—дел** *m.* woodworker, cabinet-maker; **—ед** *m.* (ent.) wood borer; **—еды** *pl.* (zool.) Xylophaga; (ent.) Eucnemidae; **—корень** *m.* mangrove (*Rhizophora mangle*); **—измерение** *n.* dendrometry.

древо/лаз *m.* (amph.) Dendrobates; (orn.) tree creeper; **—лазовые** *pl.* (orn.) Dendrocolaptidae; **—лом** *m.* (tree) windbreak; **—мер** *m.* dendrometer; **—насаждение** *n.* tree planting; forest stand; **—образный, —подобный** *see* **древовидный; —разведение** *n.* arboriculture; **—разрушающий** *a.* wood-destroying; **—руб** *m.* wood cutter; lumberjack; **—спуск** *m.* chute; **—стой** *m.* (forest) stand, crop, stock; **—сушка** *f.* timber drying or seasoning; **—тёрка** *f.* pulp grinder; **—точец** *m.* (ent.) borer; **—точина** *f.* worm hole; worm powder; **—точцевые** *pl.* (ent.) carpenter moths (*Cossidae, Zeuzeridae*); **—шёрстный** *a.* excelsior.

древпластики *pl.* wood plastics.

дреглайн *m.* dragline (excavator).

дредноут *m.* (mil.) dreadnought.

дрезденский *a.* Dresden (ware).

дрезина *f.* trolley, hand car.

дрейкантер *m.* (geol.) dreikanter, faceted pebble; (cryst.) trihedron.

дрейф *m.* drift, shift; leeway; **—ить** *v.* be hesitant, back down; **—овать** *v.* (naut.) drift; drag (at anchor); **—овый** *a. of* **дрейф; —ующий** *a.* drift(ing).

дрек *m.* grapnel, grappling anchor.

дрексель *m.* Drechsel (wash) bottle.

дрель *f.* drill, brace and bit.

дрёма *f.* (bot.) Melandrium; Silene; Lychnis; Coronaria flos cuculi.

дремать *v.* doze, slumber; **—ся** *v.* be sleepy.

дремлик *m.* (bot.) Epipactis.

дремлющий *a.* dozing, drowsy, somnolent; slumbering; latent (infection).

дремомис *m.* (mam.) Dremomys.

дремот/а *f.* drowsiness, somnolence; **—ный** *a.* drowsy, sleepy, somnolent, sluggish.

дремучий *a.* dense, thick (forest).

дрен *m.*, **—а** *f.* drain; **—аж** *m.*, **—ажный** *a.* drain(age); vent(ing); **—ажёр** *m.* drainer; **—(аж)ировать** *v.* drain, draw off; **—ажник** *m.* marsh plow; **—ажнокротовое орудие** mole (of plow); **—ажный канал** drain, gutter; **—ер** *m.* mole; **—ирование** *n.* draining, drainage; **—ированность** *f.* drainage conditions; **—ированный** *a.* drained; **—оочиститель** *m.* drain cleaner.

дренчер *m.,* **—ное оборудование** (fire prevention) drencher.

дрепано/вые *pl.* (ichth.) Drepanidae; **—цит(ар)ный** *a.* (med.) drepanocytic, sickle cell.

дресв/а *f.* grus(s), disintegrated rock, gravel; landwaste; **—яный** *a.* crumbly; gravelly.

дрессиров/ать *v.* train, school; (met.) dress (off), skin-roll; temper; **—ка** *f.,* **—очный** *a.* training, etc., *see v.*; (met.) skin (pass) rolling, temper rolling; **—очный стан** skin pass mill; **—щик** *m.* (animal) trainer, handler.

дрешер *m.* (paper) thrasher.

дриада *f.* (bot.) dryad (*Dryas*).

дрил *m.* (mam.) drill (*Mandrillus leucophaeus*).

дриллометр *m.* weight indicator.

дрильбор *m.* bur(r), bur drill.

дримис *m.* (bot.) Drimys.

дрио— *prefix* dry(o)— (oak); **—питек** *m.* (pal.) Dryopithecus.

дриттельзильбер *m.* tiers-argent (alloy).

дрифт/ер *m.* drifter (drill; boat); **—ерный** *a.* drift-net (fishing); **—овый** *a.* drift.

ДРНК *see* **ДНК.**

дроб/ей *gen. pl. of* **дробь; —емёт** *m.* (met.) shot blaster; **—емётный** *a.* shot-blasting; **—ен** *sh. m. of* **дробный; —еочистка** *f.* shot blaster; shot blasting; **—еструйный** *a.* shot-blast(ing); **—еуловитель** *m.* shot catcher; **—и** *gen. etc., of* **дробь.**

дроб/илка *f.* crusher, grinder, breaker; (hammer) mill; (knife) cutter; **д.-гребнеотделитель** *m.* crusher-stemmer; **д.-смеситель** *m.* blender-grinder; **—ильный** *a.* crushing; **—ильный прибор** crusher; **—ильщик** *m.* crusher operator; **—имый** *a.* crushable.

дробин(к)а *f.* small shot, pellet; (brewery) dregs, spent grains, mash, draff.

дроб/итель *m.* (taxonomy) splitter; **—ительный** *a.* crushing, crusher (rolls); **—ительство** *n.* (taxonomy) splitting; **—ить** *v.* crush, grind, mill, pulverize; (sub)divide, split up, break up, break down; **—ление** *n.* crushing, etc., *see v.*; breakup, breakage, fragmentation; subdivision; segmentation; cleavage; **—лёнка** *f.* crushed coal; fractured particles; **—лён(н)ый** *a.* crushed, etc., *see v.*

дробно/атомный *a.* subatomic; **—квадратный** *a.* quadratic fractional; **—линейный** *a.* linear-fractional, (bi)linear; **дискретный —линейный** *a.* discrete rational; **—рациональный** *a.* (fractional) rational; **—сть** *f.* divisibility; **—шаговый** *a.* fractional-pitch, short-pitch.

дробн/ый *a.* fractional; divided, broken; split (application; rolling; etc.); rational (function); **—ое число** fraction.

дроб/овидный *a.* buckshot; **—овик** *m.* shotgun; **—овой** *a.* shot; **—олитейный** *a.* shot-casting; **—ь** *f.* fraction; shot, pellets; **обработка —ью** shot preening; **периодическая —ь** repeating decimal; **—янка** *f.* (bot.) schizophyte; **—ящий** *a.* crushing, etc., *see* **дробить;** disruptive, shattering (action); high (explosive); molar (teeth).

дров/а *pl.* (fire)wood; **—ни** *pl.* sleigh, sled, dray; **—озаготовка** *f.* (fire)wood cutting; **—окол** *m.* woodchopper; wood splitter; **—околка** *f.* wood splitter; wood splitting; **—окольный** *a.* (wood) chopping, splitting; **—опильный** *a.* wood-sawing; **—осек** *m.* woodsman, lumberjack; (ent.) long-horned beetle;

—осека *f.* woods; **—осеки** *pl.* (ent.) Cerambycidae; **—яник** *m.* timber dealer; woodshed; **—яной** *a.,* **—яной лес** firewood.

дроги *pl.* dray cart.

дрогист *m.* druggist.

дро/гнуть *v.* shiver, shake; be chilled; tremble, quiver; jerk, twitch; waver, falter, hesitate; **—жалка** *f.* (bot.) Briza; Tremella; (ichth.) an electric ray (*Torpedo narke*); **—жание** *n.* shivering, etc., *see v.*; tremor; flicker, flutter; chatter; **—жательный** *a.* shivering, etc., *see v.*; **—жательный паралич** Parkinson's disease; **—жать** *v.* shiver, shake, vibrate; flicker; **—жащий** *see* **дрожательный.**

дрожди *see* **дрожжи.**

дрожж/евание *n.* fermentation; enrichment with yeast; **—евать** *v.* add yeast; **—евой** yeast; **—евая нуклеиновая кислота** yeast nucleic acid, RNA; **—езавод** *m.* yeast factory; **—еподобный** *a.* yeast-like, yeasty; **—и** *pl.* yeast, leaven; **прессованные —и** yeast cake; **ставить на —ах** *v.* leaven; **хлеб на —ах** yeast bread.

дрожки *pl.* droshky (an open carriage).

дрожь *f.* shiver(ing), chill, tremor.

дрозд *m.* (orn.) thrush (*Turdus*); **—овые** *pl.* Turdidae; **—овый** *a.* thrush.

дрозера *f.* (bot.) Drosera.

дрозо— *prefix* dros(o)— (dew); **—метр** *m.* (meteor.) drosometer.

дрозофила *f.* fruit fly (*Drosophila*).

дрок *m.* (bot.) Ulex; Genista; **красильный д.** dyer's broom (*G. tinctoria*).

дромадер *m.* (mam.) dromedary.

дромгед *m.* (naut.) drumhead.

дромотропный *a.* (physiol.) dromotropic.

дронго *m.* (orn.) drongos (*Dicruridae*).

дронты *pl.* (orn.) dodos (*Raphidae*).

дропмашина *f.* drop machine (for dough).

дросс *m.* (met.) dross, slag; skimmings.

дроссел/евать, —ировать *v.* throttle, choke; restrict, constrict (the flow); (av.) decelerate, throttle down; **—ирование** *n.,* **—ирующий** *a.* throttling, etc., *see v.*; throttle control; (refrigerant) expansion.

дроссель *m.,* **—ный** *a.* throttle, choke; (elec.) choke coil; restrictor, constrictor, orifice (plate) (modulation) reactor; (plate) inductor; **д.-клапан, —ный клапан** throttle (valve); **—ный орган** constrictor, restrictor; **—ный эффект** (heat) Joule-Thomson effect; **—ная заслонка** baffle plate; butterfly (throttle), throttle valve, choke; **—ная катушка** (elec.) choke (coil).

дросс/овый *a. of* **дросс; —ы** *pl.* dross.

дротик *m.* dart, javelin; **—овидный** *a.* hastate, spear-shaped.

дрот/овщик *m.* (glass) tube drawer; **—ы** *pl.* glass tubes or tubing.

дро/фа, —хва *f.* (orn.) bustard (*Otis,* spec. *O. tarda*); **—финые, —фовые** *pl.* Otididae.

друг *m.* friend; **д. —а** each other, one another; **д. за —ом** one after another, in succession; **д. с —ом** with each other, with one another; **—ие** *pl.* (the) others, the rest; **и —ие** et al.; **—ое** *n.* something else.

друг/ой *a.* (an)other, different; else; alternative; more; **в —ом месте** elsewhere; **кто-то д.** someone else; **тот и д.** both; **ни тот ни д.** neither.

друж/ба *f.* friendship; **—еский, —ественный** *a.* friendly; amicable (numbers); (comp.) user-friendly; **—ина** *f.* brigade, squad; (medical) team, unit; **—инники** *pl.* volunteer police auxiliary; **—ить** *v.* be friendly, be on friendly terms (with).

дружн/о *adv.* amicably; in unison, together; **—ый** *a.* friendly; harmonious, unanimous; (math.) amicable (numbers); sudden (spring); simultaneous (ripening); even (germination).

друза *f.* druse; nodule, node.

друзей *gen. pl. of* **друг.**

друз/овидный, —ообразный *a.* drusoid; **—овый** *a. of* **друза;** (min.) drusy, miarolitic; **—ы** *pl. of* **друза;** (med.) drusen.

друзья *pl. of* **друг.**

друк-фильтр *m.* pressure filter.

друмлин *m.* (geol.) drumlin.

друммондов свет Drummond limelight.

друшла/г, —к *see* **дуршлаг.**

дрыг/ание *n.* jerking, twitching; **—ать, —нуть** *v.* jerk, twitch.

дрызгать *v.* spatter (with); douse.

дрыхнуть *v.* sleep soundly.

др(ь)юит *m.* drewite (calcareous ooze).

дряб/лость *f.* flabbiness, etc., see *a.*; dry-rotted wood; **—лый** *a.* flabby, flaccid, limp; decayed, dry-rotted; **—нуть** *v.* wither, droop, become flabby.

дрягать *see* **дрыгать.**

дряква *f.* (bot.) cyclamen.

дрях/ление *n.* aging; **—леть, —нуть** *v.* age, grow decrepit; **—лость** *f.* senility; decrepitude; **—лый** *a.* senile; decrepit, infirm.

ДСП *abbr.* (древеснослоистый пластик) wood laminate; **ДСП, д.с.п.** (для служебного пользования) for official use.

ДСТ, дСТ *abbr.* (диэтилстильбестрол) diethyl stilbestrol.

д.с.-х.н. *abbr.* (доктор сельскохозяйственных наук) Doctor of Agricultural Sciences.

ДТА *abbr.* (дифференциальный термический анализ) differential thermal analysis.

д.т.н. *abbr.* (доктор технических наук) Doctor of Technical Sciences.

ДТРД *abbr.* (двухконтурный турбореактивный двигатель) ducted-fan turbojet.

Дуайт-Ллойда машина Dwight-Lloyd (sintering) machine.

дуализ/ация *f.* dualization; **—ировать** *v.* dualize; **—ируемый** *a.* dualizable; dualized; **—м** *m.* dualism, duality.

дуалин *m.*, **—овый** *a.* (expl.) dualin.

дуал/истический *a.* dualistic; **—ьность** *f.* duality; **—ьный** *a.* dual.

дуант *m.*, **—ный** *a.* (nucl.) duant, dee, D-electrode (of cyclotron).

дуб *m.* (bot.) oak (*Quercus*).

дуб/ас, —ень *m.* tanbark (from oak).

дубильно/железистая соль ferrous tannate; **—кислый** *a.* tannic acid; tannate (of); **—кислая соль** tannate; **—кислое железо** iron tannate.

дубильн/ый *a.* tan(ning); tannic (acid); **д. орешек** gallnut; **д. сок** tan liquor; **—ая кора** tanbark; **—ое вещество** tannin; **соль —ой кислоты** tannate; **—я** *f.* tannery.

дубильщик *m.* tanner.

дубин/а *f.* club, cudgel; **—ообразный** *a.* clavate, claviform.

дуб/итель *m.* tanning agent; (phot.) hardener; **—ить** *v.* tan; harden; **—ление** *n.* tanning; hardening; **—лёнка** *f.* leather jacket; **—лёный** *a.* tanned; **—лёный жирами** oil-tanned.

дубл/ёр *m.* doubler, doubling machine; duplicator; double, understudy, standby operator; **—ет** *m.*, **—етный** *a.* doublet; dipole; duplicate, copy; **—етов метод** (mass spectrometry) doublet method; **—етность** *f.* doubling (of lines); **—икат** *m.* duplicate, copy, replica, counterpart; **—икатный** *a.* duplicate.

дублир/ование *n.* doubling, etc., see *v.*; duplication; (card) reproduction; backup; standby system; backing (of fabric); plying (of yarn); dual (ignition); redundant; **—ованный** *a.* doubled, etc., see *v.*; dual (ignition); redundant; **—овать** *v.* double, overlap, layer, ply up; duplicate, copy, reproduce, stand by; (films) dub; **—овочный, —ующий** *a.* doubling, etc., see *v.*; redundant; backup; **—ующий агрегат** backup; **—ующий перфоратор** reproducer.

дубло *n.* tanbark.

дубл/ь *m.* (films) take; **д.-негатив** *m.* duplicate negative; **—ьтон** *m.* (typ.) duotone ink; **—яж** *m.* (films) dubbing-in.

дуб/ляк *m.* (ent.) Pentodon; **—ница** *f.* (bot.) Ajuga; **—ность** *f.* thorough tanning; **—няк** *m.* oak grove, oak forest; **—о—** *prefix* oak; **—овик** *m.* (bot.) Boletus luridus; **—овина** *f.* tanbark.

дубовский *a.* (geog.) Dubovka.

дуб/овый *a.* oak(en); **—ок** *m.* young oak; **—онос** *m.* (orn.) hawfinch (*Coccothraustes*); **—оноска** *f.* (orn.) finch.

дубоссарский *a.* (geog.) Dubossaryi.

дубр/ава *f.*, **—авник** *m.*, **—авный** *a.* dubrava, oak woods; **—овка** *f.* (bot.) Ajuga; Potentilla tormentilla; Anthoxanthum odoratum; Veronica chamaedrys; **—овник** *m.* (bot.) Teucrium; (orn.) yellow-breasted bunting (*Emberiza aureola*).

дубуазин *m.* duboisine, *l*-hyoscyamine.

дуб/ьё *n.* (silv.) clubs, sticks; **—ящий** *a.* tanning, etc., see **дубить;** *m.* tanning agent.

дувший *past act. part. of* **дуть.**

дуг/а *f.* arc, arch, bow, curve; rib; gallows (of trawler); (anat.) arcus; **сваривать в —е** *v.* arc weld; **сводить —ой** *v.* arch, curve.

дуглас/ит *m.* (min.) douglasite; **—ия** *f.* **—ова пихта** Douglas fir.

дуго— *prefix* arc, arch; curvi—; **—видный** *a.* arched, curved, arcuate.

дугов/ой *a.* arc; arch(ed), curve(d); electric arc (welding); **д. вентиль** mercury-arc rectifier; **д. переброс** arcing over; **д. угольный** carbon-arc; **—ая печь** arc furnace; **—ая плавка** arc-furnace melting.

дугога/ситель *m.* arc arrester; (magnetic) blowout; **—сительный, —сящий** *a.* arc-suppressing; blowout; **—шение** *n.* arc suppression, control or blowout.

дуго/жильный, —нервный *a.* (bot.) curvinerved.

дугообраз/но *adv.* arc-wise; in an arch; (bent) double; **—ный** *a.* arched, curved, bow-shaped, arcuate; **—ное образование** (anat.) ansa, loop; **—ование** *n.* arc formation, arcing.

дуго/отросчатый *a.* (anat.) zygapophyseal; **—позвонковые** *pl.* (herp.) Apsidospondyli; **—стойкий** *a.* arc-resistant, non-arcing; **—стойкость** *f.* arc resistance.

дуд/ак *see* **дрофа; —арь** *m.* mine worker; **—еть** *v.* pipe, whistle; **—ка** *f.* pipe, fife; whistle; tube; (bot.) fistula; (min.) open pit; **—ник** *m.* (bot.) Angelica; **—чатый** *a.* hollow, fistular.

дует *pr. 3 sing. of* **дуть.**

дужка *dim. of* **дуга;** bow, ear, shackle, U-link; parenthesis; (ent.) arculus; (orn.) furcula; **д. крыла** (av.) airfoil section; **падающая д.** chopper bar.

дуйский *a.* (geog.) Due.

дуй(те) *imp. of* **дуть.**

дук *m.* (vet.) mobile disinfecting unit.

дукер *see* **дюкер;** (mam.) duiker (*Cephalolophus*); **—ы** *pl.* Cephalophinae.

дуктил/иметр, —ометр *m.* ductilimeter; **—ьность** *f.* ductility; tack (of ink); **—ьный** *a.* ductile.

дул *past m. sing. of* **дуть.**

дулидовые *pl.* (orn.) Dulidae.

дуло *n.* bore, muzzle, mouth (of cannon); *past n. sing. of* **дуть; —ротки** *pl.* (ichth.) flutemouths (*Fistulariidae*).

дулькамарин *m.* dulcamarin.

дуль/ный *a. of* **дуло; —це** *n.* mouth.

дульц/ин *m.* dulcin; dulcine, dulcitol; **—ит(ол)** *m.* dulcite, dulcitol; **—ификация** *f.* dulcification, sweetening.

дума *f.* thought; council; **—ть** *v.* think; believe, suppose; intend, mean; **—ть над** consider; **—ться** *v.* appear, seem.

думмис *m.,* **—ный** *a.* dummy (piston).

думпкар *m.* dump car, dump truck.

дунайский *a.* (geog.) Danube.

дундазит *m.* (min.) dundasite.

дун/ит *m.* (petr.) dunite; **—нит** *m.* (expl.) dunnite, ammonium picrate.

дуновение *n.* whiff, breath, puff.

дунст *m.* dunst, finest middlings; fine shot.

дунуть *v.* blow, puff.

дуо duo, two-high (rolling mill).

дуоден/альный *a.* (anat.) duodenal; **—ит** *m.* (med.) duodenitis.

дуодецимальный *a.* duodecimal.

дуо/клеть *f.* two-high mill stand; **—плазматрон** *m.* duoplasmatron; **—стан** *m.* two-high rolling mill.

дуотал *m.* duotal, guaiacol carbonate.

дупел *gen. pl. of* **дупло.**

дупел/иный *a.,* **—ь** *m.* (orn.) snipe (*Gallinago*).

дуплекс *m.* duplex, twin; **д.-процесс** (met.) duplex process; **—ный** *a.* duplex, double, twofold; two-way.

дупл/ет *see* **дублет; —икация** *f.* (gen.) duplication; (math.) doubling.

дупл/истость *f.* hollowness; **—истый** *a.* hollow, empty; **—о** *n.* hollow, cavity, void; (anat.) alveus; **—огнёздник** *m.* (zool.) hole nester; **—яки** *pl.* (ent.) Dynastidae; **—янка** *f.* log hive.

дурайрон *m.* Duriron (alloy).

дурак *m.* fool.

дурал— *see* **дюрал—; —ьный** *a.* (anat.) dural, dura mater.

дуран-металл Durana metal.

дурангит *m.* (min.) durangite.

дуранда *f.* oil cake.

дурацкий *a.* stupid, foolish.

дурденит *m.* (min.) durdenite.

дурен *m.* durene, durol; *sh. m. of* **дурной; —ол** *m.* durenol.

дуреть *v.* become stupid.

дуриан *see* **дурио.**

дурил *m.* duryl; **—ен** *m.* durylene; **—овая кислота** durylic acid, 2,4,5-trimethylbenzoic acid.

дуримет *m.* Durimet (a ferrous alloy).

дурина *f.* (vet.) dourine, trypanosomiasis.

дур/ио *n.* (bot.) durian (*Durio zibethenius*); **—ит** *m.* (coal) durain.

дурман *m.,* **—ный** *a.* narcotic, dope, drug; (bot.) Datura; trance; **—ить** *v.* intoxicate, stupefy; **—овый** *a.* daturic (acid).

дурн/еть *v.* grow ugly; **—ика, —ица** *f.* (bot.) bog bilberry (*Vaccinium uliginosum*); **—ишник** *m.* burdock (*Xanthium*).

дурно *adv. and sh. n. of* **дурной.**

дурн/ой *a.* bad, wrong, poor; unfavorable, tough; mis—, mal—; foul (smell); venereal (disease); **—ая земля** badland; **—ое питание** malnutrition; **—ое управление** mismanagement; **—пахнущий** *a.* bad-smelling, malodorous; **—ота** *f.* giddiness, vertigo.

дуро/л *see* **дурен; —метр** *see* **дюрометр.**

дурр/а *f.,* **—о** *n.* (bot.) durra (*Sorghum vulgare durra*); **белая д.** *see* **джугара.**

дурукули *f.* (mam.) douroucouli (*Aotus*).

дуршлаг *m.* colander, strainer.

дурь *f.* foolishness, nonsense, folly.

дурьян *see* **дурио.**

дуст *m.,* **—ировать** *v.* (agr.) dust.

дутик *m.* (geol.) loess-doll, lime nodule; bulge(s); blisters (on plaster).

дут/ый *a.* blown (up), inflated; pneumatic (tire); hollow; exaggerated; **—ыш** *m.* pouter shorebird (*Calidris melanotos*); **—ь** *v.* blow (up), inflate; blast; **—ьё** *n.,* **—ьевой** *a.* blowing, blast(ing), draft; (blast furnace) air; **на полном —ьё** full blast; **подавать —ьё** *v.* blow, blast; **сушка —ья** blast drying; **—ься** *v.* sulk, pout.

дух *m.* odor, scent; breath; spirit, courage; morale; mood; specter, ghost (line; image); (spectrography) satellite line; **в —е** in the mood (for); **в этом —е** in this way; **во весь д.** (at) full speed; **присутствие —а** presence of mind.

духа *f.* (met.) air hole (of mold).

духи *pl. of* **дух;** perfume.

духовка *f.* oven, kiln.

духовн/ая *f.* will; **—ый** *a.* spiritual.

духо/вой *a.* wind, air; hot-air (heat); **д. канал** (anat.) windpipe; **—вая печь** oven, kiln; **—мер** *m.* wind gage; blast meter; **—та** *f.* close air, stuffiness; swelter.

дучка *f.* (min.) outlet ramp.

душ *m.* shower (bath); (med.) douche.

душ/а *f.* soul, mind, spirit; (stat.) person, head; **душ женского пола** (stat.) female persons; **на —у (населения)** per capita, per head.

душевая *f.* shower bath(s).

душев/ка *f.* (bot.) Acinos; **—(н)ик** *m.* Clinopodium.

душевно/больной *a.* mentally ill; *m.* mental case; **—ный** *a.* sincere, cordial; emotional; mental (illness); **—ой** *a.* per capita; shower.

душен *sh. m. of* **душный.**

душист/ость *f.* fragrance, perfume; **—ый** *a.* fragrant, scented, perfumed, aromatic; sweet (pea); **—ое вещество** perfume, aromatic principle.

душить *v.* stifle, choke, smother, throttle; suppress; scent, perfume.

душ/ица *f.* (bot.) Origanum; **—ка** *f.* Ocimum; medulla, pith (of feather).

душн/ик *m.* (air) vent, air hole, ventilator; **—о** *adv. and sh. n. of* **душный;** it is stuffy; **—ый** *a.* stuffy, close, stifling, sultry.

дующий *pr. act. part. of* **дуть;** blowing; **—ся** *a.* (geol.) heaving, swelling; growing.

ДФА *abbr.* (**дифениламин**) diphenylamine.

д.ф.-м.н. *abbr.* (**доктор физико-математических наук**) Doctor of Physics and Mathematics; **д.ф.н.** *abbr.* (**доктор фармацевтических наук**) Doctor of Pharmaceutical Sciences.

ДФПГ *abbr.* (**дифенилпикрилгидразил**) diphenylpicrylhydrazyl, DPPH.

ДФФ *abbr.* (**диизопропилфторфосфат**) diisopropyl fluorophosphate.

ДФЗ *abbr.* (**дробный факторный эксперимент**) fractional factorial experiment.

ДХМ *abbr.* (**дихлоральмочевина**) dichloralurea (herbicide).

д.х.н. *abbr.* (**доктор химических наук**) Doctor of Chemical Sciences.

ДХЭ *abbr.* (**дихлорэтан**) dichloroethane.

ДЦВ *see* **ДМВ.**

ДЦДА *abbr.* (**дициандиамид**) dicyandiamide.

дцл *abbr.* (**децилитр**) deciliter.

ДЧ *abbr.* (**делитель частоты**) frequency divider; (**допплеровская частота**) Doppler frequency.

дъенколевый *a.* djenkolic (acid).

дыба *f.* rack, beam, post.

дыбка *f.* (ent.) Saga.

дым *m.* smoke, fume(s); —**арь** *m.* (bee) smoker; smudge pot; —**завеса** *f.* smoke screen; —**илка** *f.* (bee) smoker; —**ить(ся)** *v.* smoke, fume; —**ка** *f.* haze, mist, fog; *gen. of* **дымок**; —**комер** *m.* haze meter; —**ление** *n.* smoking; fumigation; (agr.) smudging; —**но** *adv.* smokily, with smoke; —**номер** *m.* smoke meter; —**ность** *f.* (exhaust) smoke; —**ный** *a.* smoky, fuming; black (powder); —**о** — *prefix* smoke.

дымов/ой *a.* smoke; flue (gas); black (powder); **д. канал** flue; —**ая заслонка** damper; —**ая труба** chimney, smoke-stack.

дымогарный *a.* smoke-consuming; firetube (boiler); fire (box; tube).

дымо/генератор *m.* smoke generator; —**к** *dim. of* **дым**; *gen. pl. of* **дымка**; —**кур** *m.* smoky fire; —**маскировка** *f.* smoke screen; —**непроницаемый** *a.* smoke-tight.

дымообраз/ование *n.* formation of smoke; —**ователь** *m.* smoke-producing agent; mister; —**ующий** *a.* smoking, fuming; smoke or fume-forming.

дымоотвод *m.* offtake, flue; —**ный** *a.* smoke-deflecting; —**чик** *m.* smoke deflector, chimney hood.

дымо/отравляющий *a.* toxic smoke; —**ощутитель** *m.* smoke detector; —**поглощающий** *a.* smoke-consuming; —**пуск** *m.* smoke screening; —**сжигающий** *a.* smoke-consuming; —**с(о)жигание** *n.* smoke abatement; —**сос** *m.*, —**сосный** *a.* exhaust fan; —**стойкий** *a.* smoke or fume-resistant; —**улавливатель** *m.* smoke filter; —**упорный** *see* **дымостойкий**; —**ход** *m.* flue, chimney, duct, smoke stack; uptake; —**ходы** *pl.* flue system.

дымприбор *m.* smoke generator, smoker.

дымчат/о— *prefix* smoky; —**ый** *a.* smoky, smoke-colored; smoked (glass).

дымянк/а *f.* (bot.) fumitory (*Fumaria*); —**овые** *pl.* Fumariaceae.

дымящий(ся) *a.* smoking; fuming (acid); smoldering (embers).

дын/ник *m.* (agr.) melon bed; —**ный** *a.* melon; —**ное дерево** papaya; —**я** *f.* (musk)melon (*Cucumis melo*).

дыр/(к)а *f.* hole, tear, gap, perforation, puncture; aperture; (anat.) foramen; (electron.) vacancy; (met.) roak, seam; —**коватость** *f.* (phyt.) shot hole; —**ко-промежуточный** *a.* vacancy-interstitial; —**окол**, —**опробиватель** *m.* punch(er), perforator; —**омер** *m.* hole gage.

дыропробивн/ой *a.* punch(ing), piercing, perforating; **д. пресс, д. станок, д. штамп,** —**ая машина** punch(er), punch press; perforator.

дыр/опробойник *m.* punch; —**опроводный шлямбур** drift, punch; —**очка** *dim. of* **дырка**; —**очник** *m.* (prot.) foraminifer; —**очный** *a. of* **дырка**; hole (conductivity); —**чатый**, —**явый** *a.* perforated; foraminated, pitted; —**явить** *v.* pierce, perforate, make a hole.

дых/ало, —**альце** *n.* blow hole (of whale); (ent.; ichth.) spiracle; stigma, breathing hole; windpipe; —**ание** *n.* respiration, breathing; **искусственное** —**ание** resuscitation.

дыхательн/ый *a.* respiratory, breathing; pneumatic; tidal (air); **д. аппарат** respirator; **д. клапан** breather valve; **д. корень** aerating root, pneumatophore; **д. коэффициент** (med.) respiratory coefficient, R.Q.; **д. объём** tidal volume; —**ая трубка**, —**ое горло** (zool.) trachea; —**ая щель** spiracle; —**ое отверстие** *see* **дыхало**; —**ые пути** respiratory system.

ды/хнуть *v.* draw a breath; —**шать** *v.* breathe, respire; —**шаться** *v.* be able to breathe.

дышло *n.*, —**вой** *a.* shaft, pole, rod; draft bar, (trailer) tongue, tow bar.

дью *m.* (geol.) dy (a sapropel deposit).

дьюар *m.*, **сосуд Дьюара** Dewar flask.

дьявол *m.* devil; **морские** —**ы** (ichth.) devilrays, mantas (*Mobulidae*).

ДЭАЭ-целлюлоза *f.* DEAE-cellulose (diethylaminoethyl cellulose).

Дэвиса закон Davis' law.

ДЭГУ *abbr.* (**дизель-электрическая гребная установка**) diesel-electric propeller drive.

ДЭЗ *abbr.* [(**метод**) **дипольного электрического зондирования**] dipole electric sounding; **ДЭМЧЗ** *abbr.* (**дипольное электромагнитное частотное зондирование**) dipole electromagnetic frequency sounding.

д.э.н. *abbr.* (**доктор экономических наук**) Doctor of Economics.

ДЭП *abbr.* (**дизель-электрический привод**) diesel-electric drive; [(**метод**) **дипольного электрического профилирования**] dipole electric profiling (method).

ДЭС *abbr.* (**дуговая электросварка**) electric arc welding; (**дизельная электростанция**) diesel electric power plant.

ДЭТ *abbr.* [**дизель(ный)-электрический трактор**] diesel-electric tractor; (**диффузная эмиссионная туманность**) diffuse emission nebula.

ДЭЧЗ *abbr.* (**дипольное электрическое частотное зондирование**) dipole electrical frequency sounding.

дю *m.* (geol.) dy (a sapropel deposit).

дюбель *m.*, —**ный** *a.* dowel, pin, key; expansion bolt; rawlplug.

дю-Виньо синтез du Vineaud synthesis.

дюгон/говый *a.* (mam.) dugong; —**и** *pl.* Dugongidae; —**ь** *m.* dugong, sea cow.

дюжина *f.* dozen, twelve.

дюз *m.*, —**а** *f.* nozzle.

дюйм *m.* inch (2.54 cm.); —**овка** *f.* inch plank; —**овый** *a.* (one)-inch.

дюкер *m.* (hydr.) (inverted) siphon.

Дюлонга-Пти закон Dulong and Petit law.

Дюма способ Dumas method.

дюм/азин *m.* dumasin; —**онтит** *m.* (min.) dumontite; —**ортьерит** *m.* dumortierite.

дюн/а *f.*, —**ный** *a.* (sand) dune; **растение дюн** dune plant, thinophyte.

дюнштейн *m.* (met.) thin matte.

Дюпон du Pont (U.S. chemical firm).

дюпрен *m.* Duprene (synthetic rubber).

дюр— *see also under* **дур**—; —**алевый** *a.*, —**аль** *m.*, —**алюминиевый** *a.*, —**алюмин(ий)** *m.* duralumin (alloy); —**анол** *m.* duranol (dye); —**антный** *a.* lasting; —**антрен** *m.* duranthrene (dye); —**ен** *m.*, —**еновый** *a.* (min.) durain; —**ит** *m.* (min.) durite; —**ометр** *m.*

durometer, hardness tester; —**утоль** *m.* solid coconut oil.

дюфрен/ит *m.* (min.) dufrenite, kraurite; —**уазит** *m.* (min.) dufrenoysite.

дюшес(с) *m.* duchess pear.

дягиль(ник) *m.* (bot.) (Arch)angelica.

дядя *m.* uncle.

дятел *m.* (orn.) woodpecker.

дятл(ов)ина *f.* clover (*Trifolium*).

дятл/овые *pl.* (orn.) Picidae; —**овый** *a.* woodpecker; —**ы** *pl. of* **дятел.**

Е

ев— *see also under* **эв—, эй—.**

евген/ика *f.* (gen.) eugenics; —**ический** *a.* eugenic; —**ия** *f.* (bot.) Eugenia; —**овый блеск** (min.) polybasite; —**ол** *m.* eugenol.

евдиалит *m.* (min.) eudialyte.

евдо/тка *f.* (ichth.) stone loach [*Nemach(e)ilus barbatulus*]; —**шка** *f.* mud minnow (*Umbra*, spec. *U. krameri*); Don chub (*Leuciscus borysthenicus*); —**шковые** *pl.* Umbridae.

евкалипт *m.* (bot.) eucalyptus.

евклидов/(ой), —ский *a.* Euclidean.

евлиторальный *a.* eulittoral, upper littoral.

евнухоидизм *m.* (med.) eunuchoidism.

евня *f.* sheep pen, sheepfold.

евраз/иатский, —ийский *a.* (geog.) Eurasian.

Евр/азия Eurasia; —**атом** European Atomic Energy Alliance, Euratom.

еврейский *a.* Jewish, Hebrew; **е. камень** (petr.) graphic granite.

еври— *see* **эври—.**

Евро/космос Eurospace; —**па** Europe.

европ/еец *m.*, —**ейский** *a.* European; —**еизировать** *v.* europeanize; —**ий** *m.* europium, Eu.

ЕВС *abbr.* (**единая высоковольтная сеть**) unified high-voltage network.

евстахиева труба (anat.) Eustachian tube.

евфеника *f.* (sociology) euthenics.

евфратовский *a.* (geog.) Euphratean.

евший *past act. part. of* **есть.**

Егера решётка Jäger screen.

егерь *m.* hunter; gamekeeper; game warden.

Египет Egypt; **египетский** *a.* Egyptian.

его *gen. of* **он(о),** his, its; *acc.* him, it.

егорьевский *a.* (geog.) Yegoryevsk.

ед *abbr.* (**единица допуска**) tolerance unit; **ед.** *abbr.* (**единица**) unit; (**единственный**) unique; **ЕД** *abbr.* (**единица действия**) (biol.) active unit.

еда *f.* meal, food; —**ть** *see* **есть.**

едва *adv. and conj.* barely, just, hardly, scarcely, with difficulty; **е. . . . как** no sooner . . . than; **е. ли** hardly, scarcely, not likely, unlikely; it is doubtful; **е. не** nearly, almost.

еденный *a.* eaten.

едет *pr. 3 sing. of* **ехать.**

ед. изм. *abbr.* (**единица измерения**) unit of measurement.

едим *pr. 1 pl. of* **есть,** we eat.

един *sh. m. of* **единый;** —**ение** *n.* unity, accord; union; —**ить** *v.* unite.

единиц/а *f.* unit; unity, one; identity element; individual, person; (educ.) one (very poor); —**ы** *pl.* few people; (**в**) —**ах** in units (of), in terms (of); **весовой** —**ы, на** —**у веса** per unit weight; **за** —**у, на** —**у** per unit, each.

единичн/ость *f.* singleness; —**ый** *a.*, unit, single(-unit), unit(ar)y, individual; elementary (concept); solitary, separate; isolated, rare (case); job-lot (production).

едино— *prefix* uni—, mono—; —**брачие** *n.* (zool.) monogamy; —**брачный** *a.* monogamous, monogynous; (bot.) monoecious; —**временно** *adv.* once (only); —**временный** *a.* once, one-time; isochronous; —**главый** *a.* single-headed; —**гласие, —душие** *n.* unanimity, accord, unison; consensus, agreement; —**гласный, —душный** *a.* unanimous; —**душно** *adv.* unanimously; by common consent.

единокров/ие *n.,* —**ность** *f.* consanguinity, affinity; blood relationship; —**ный** *a.* consanguineous.

единоличн/ик *m.* independent farmer; —**ый** *a.* personal, individual, private.

единомысл/енный, —ящий *a.* unanimous; —**ие** *n.* agreement of opinion.

единомышленн/ик *m.* adherent, upholder; associate; —**ый** *a.* unanimous, of the same opinion.

единоначалие *n.* one-man management.

единообраз/ие *n.* uniformity, sameness; —**но-выпуклый** *a.* uniformly convex; —**ный** *a.* uniform, same.

единорог *m.* unicorn; (astr.) Monoceros; (mam.) narwhal (*Monodon monoceros*); (ichth.) filefish; unicorn fish (*Naso unicornis*); —**и** *see* **единороговые;** —**ие** *pl.* Aluteridae; —**овые** *pl.* filefishes (*Monacanthidae*).

единоутробный *a.* (zool.) monodelphic.

единственн/о *adv.* only, solely; uniquely; —**ость** *f.* oneness, singleness; (math.) uniqueness; —**ый** *a.* only, sole, unique, single, solitary.

един/ство *n.* unity, harmony; —**ый** *a.* single, only, sole; unique; unified, united, common; —**ый магистраль** (comp.) unibus; —**ое целое** unit.

ёдипода *f.* (ent.) Oedipoda.

едите *pr. 2 pl. of* **есть,** you eat.

едк/ий *a.* caustic, corrosive; biting, stinging, acrid, sharp, pungent (taste); toxic; —**ое вещество, —ое средство** caustic, corrosive; —**ие щелочи** caustic alkalis, alkali hydroxides.

едкость *f.* causticity, corrosiveness; acridness, pungency.

едо/к *m.* eater, consumer; *sh. m. of* **едкий;** —**мый** *a.* edible.

еду/т *pr. 3 pl.;* —**чи** *pr. ger.;* —**щий** *pr. act. part. of* **ехать.**

едче *comp. of* **едкий.**

едя/т *pr. 3 pl. of* **есть;** —**щий** *a.* eating.

её *gen. and acc. of* **она,** her, it(s).

ёж *m.* (mam.) hedgehog (*Erinaceus*); (mil.) portable barrier; **морской ё.** (zool.) sea urchin (*Echinus*).

ежа *f.* (bot.) orchard grass (*Dactylis*).

еже— *prefix* each, every; echin(o)— (spiny, prickly); —**видный** *a.* erinaceous; echinoid; echinulate; —**вик** *see* **ежовик.**

ежев/ика *f.* (bot.) blackberry (*Rubus*); —**ичник** *m.* blackberry patch; —**ичный** *a.* blackberry.

ежёвка *see* **ежевика.**

ежёв/ник-мордовник *m.* (bot.) globe thistle (*Echinops*); —**ые** *see* **ежовые.**

ежегодн/ик *m.* yearbook, annual (publication); —**о** *adv.*

yearly, every year, annually, per annum; —**ый** *a.* yearly, annual, anniversary.

ежеголов/ка *f.*, —**ник** *m.* (bot.) bur reed (*Sparganium*); —**(ни)ковые** *pl.* Sparganiaceae.

ежедекадно *adv.* every ten days.

ежедневн/о *adv.* daily, per diem; —**ый** *a.* daily, every day, diurnal.

ежели *conj.* if, in case.

еже/месячник *m.* monthly (publication); —**месячно** *adv.*, —**месячный** *a.* every month, monthly; —**минутно** *adv.* every minute; continually; —**минутный** *a.* occurring every minute; continual, incessant; —**мухи** *pl.* (ent.) tachina flies (*Tachinidae, Larvaevoridae*); —**недельник** *m.* weekly (publication); —**недельно** *adv.*, —**недельный** *a.* every week, weekly; —**секундный** *a.* every second; very frequent; constant; —**суточно** *adv.* every day, every twenty-four hours; —**суточный** *a.* every day, daily, diurnal; twenty-four-hour; —**часно** *adv.*, —**часный** *a.* every hour, hourly.

еж/и *see* ежовые; —**ик** *dim. of* ёж; (bot.) Acantholimon; морской —**ик** *see* ёж, морской; —**и-рыбы** *pl.* porcupine fishes (*Diodontidae*); —**ить** *v.* press together; wrinkle (nose, etc.); —**иться** *v.* shrink, shrivel; shiver; bristle.

ежов/ик *m.* (bot.) Hydnum; —**иковые** *pl.* Hydnaceae; —**ка** *f.* Echinaria, —**ник** *m.* Echinochloa; Anabasis; —**ник-мордовник** *m.* Echinops; —**ые** *pl.* (mam.) hedgehogs (*Erinaceidae*); —**ый** *a.* erinaceous; (bot.) echinate, bristly; ringed (hoof).

ез/да *f.* drive, riding; travel; —**дить** *v.* drive, ride, go; —**дка** *f.* trip; haul, run; —**довой** *a. of* езда; draft (animal), sled(ge) (dog); —**док** *m.* rider; *gen. pl. of* ездка; —**женый** *a.* ridden; well-used, frequented (road); —**ж(ив)ать** *see* ездить.

ей *dat. of* она; (to) her; (to) it.

ейский *a.* (geog.) Eya, Yeya.

ек— *see under* эк—.

ел *past m. sing. of* есть, ate; —**а** *past f. sing. of* есть, ate.

ёла *f.* fishing boat.

еланский *a.* (geog.) Yelan, Elanka.

елань *f.* glade.

елвинский *a.* (geog.) Elva, Yelva.

еле *adv.* hardly, scarcely, just.

ел/евзина, —**евзине** *f.* (bot.) Eleusine; —**евые** *pl.* Abietinae; —**евый** *a. of*, —**ей** *gen. pl. of* ель.

елец *m.* (ichth.) dace (*Leuciscus, spec. L.l.*); this name also used on other species; —**кий** *a.* (geog.) Yelets, Elets.

ели *past pl. of* есть, ate; *gen., etc., of* ель.

ёлк/а *f.* evergreen, Christmas tree; (rubber) flawed surface; кладка в —**у** herringbone brickwork.

ело *past n. sing. of* есть, ate.

еловский *a.* (geog.) Yelovka; Elovo.

елов/ые *see* елевые; —**ый** *a. of* ель.

елогуйский *a.* (geog.) Yelogui.

ёлоч/ка *dim. of* ёлка; herringbone (design); —**ный** *a. of* елка; herringbone; (cryst.) arborescent; fishbone (antenna); —**ный дефлегматор** rod-and-disk type fractionating column; —**ный кристалл** dendrite.

елшанский *a.* (geog.) Yelshanka, Elshanka.

ель *f.* (bot.) spruce (*Picea*); —**ник** *m.* spruce forest; —**ник-зеленомошник** *m.* mossy spruce forest; —**ник-лог** *m.* log, wet valley spruce forest; —**ник-черничник** *m.* bilberry spruce forest.

ельнинский *a.* (geog.) Yelnya, Elnya.

ельц/овый *a.*; —**ы** *pl. of* елец.

ем *pr. 1 sing. of* есть, eat.

ёмк. *abbr.* (ёмкость) capacity.

ёмк/ий *a.* large-capacity; capacious, roomy; voluminous; *suffix* consuming; —**остнорезистивный** *a.* (elec.) capacitance-resistance.

ёмкост/ный *a.* capacity; (elec.) capacitive; —**ное сопротивление** (elec.) capacitive reactance, capacitance; —**ь** *f.* capacity, (cubic) content, volume; (elec.) capacitance; tank, reservoir; container, vessel; (memory) size; (market) potential; *occasionally* capacitor; удельная —**ь** (elec.) permittivity.

ёмок *sh. m. of* емкий.

ему *dat. of* он(о), (to) him, (to) it.

емуранчик *m.* (mam.) emuranchik (*Stylodipus*).

енамин *m.* enamine; —**овый** *a.* enamic.

ендова *f.* (roof) valley; pouring vessel.

енисейский *a.* (geog.) Yenisei, Enisei.

еновый *a.* ene (synthesis).

енол *m.* enol; —**аза** *f.* enolase; —**изация** *f.* enolization; —**изировать** *v.* enolize; —**ьный** *a.* enol.

енот *m.* (mam.) raccoon (*Procyon*); —**овые** *pl.* Procyonidae; **е.-полоскун** *m.* Procyon lotor.

епанча *f.* mantle, cloak.

ералаш *m.* disorder, jumble, absurdity.

ервин *see* иервин.

ергенинский *a.* (geog.) Yergeni, Ergeni.

ереванский *a.* (geog.) Yerevan.

еремеевит *m.* (min.) eremeyevite.

еренениться *v.* bristle up.

ере/сь *f.* heresy; —**тик** *m.* heretic; —**тический** *a.* heretical, dissenting.

ерик *m.* erik (shallow channel).

ериоботрия *f.* (bot.) Eriobotrya.

еритр— *see under* эритр—.

ёрник *m.*, —**овый** *a.* (bot.) dwarf birch (*Betula nana*); yernik, dwarf birch thicket.

ероплан *m.* (ichth.) a goby (*Neogobius syrman*).

ерошить *v.* ruffle, rumple; —**ся** *v.* bristle, stand on end.

ерсей *m.* yersei, winding bog channel.

ерунда *f.* nonsense, absurdity.

ерунок *m.* bevel (square).

ёрш *m.* (mach.) broach; ragbolt; jagged rod; (wire) brush; go-devil, pipeline scraper; (ichth.) ruff (*Acerina*, spec. *A. cernua*); also Scorpaena; Sebastodes; Siniperca and Helicolenus; морские —**и** scorpion fishes (*Scorpaenidae*); —**ик** *dim. of* ёрш; bottle brush.

ерш/истость *f.* bristly nature; —**истый** *a.* bristly; —**иться** *v.* bristle.

ёрш-носарь *m.* (ichth.) Don ruff (*Acerina a.*).

ершов/атка *f.* (ichth.) dab (*Limanda l.*); —**ый** *a. of* ёрш.

еры/жка, —**ла**, —**шка** *f.* fishing net.

ес *abbr.* (единицы связывания) binding units.

есейский *a.* (geog.) Yesei (Lake).

если *conj.* if, in case, as long as, provided (that), should; **е. бы** if; **е. бы не** but for, if (it were) not for; **е. вообще** if at all; **е. же** but if; **е. и** even if; **е. не** unless, if not, but for; **е. только** if only, providing, provided; **е. только вообще** if at all; **е. только не** unless; **е. учесть, что** when it is considered that; **е. это возможно** when(ever) possible, if possible; **е. это так** if this is the case.

ессейский *a.* (geog.) Yessei.

ест *pr. 3 sing. of* есть.

естественн/ик *m.* naturalist; —**о** *adv.* naturally, of course; it is natural; —**оактивный** *a.* optically active; —**оисторический,** —**онаучный** *a.* natural-science; —**ость** *f.* naturalness; —**ый** *a.* natural, native, inherent, inborn, innate, intrinsic; spontaneous; internal (reaction coordinate); **в —ых условиях** field (test);

дело **—ое** it is a matter of course; **доктор —ых наук** (educ.) Ph.D.; **с —ым охлаждением** self-cooled; **угол —ого откоса** angle of repose or rest.

естество *n.* nature, substance; **—вед** *m.* naturalist; **—ведение, —знание** *n.* natural science; **—испытание** *n.* natural history; **—испытатель** *m.* naturalist.

естфак *m.* natural science division.

есть *v.* eat; corrode; *pr. 3 sing. of* **быть;** (there) is.

ефес *m.* handle, hilt.

ефремовский *a.* (geog.) Yephremov(a).

ехать *v.* go, travel, ride, drive; slip (to one side).

ехидн/а *f.* (mam.) echidna (*Tachyglossus aculeata*); (herp.) Notechis scutatus; **—ы** *pl.* Tachyglossidae; **—ый** *a.* spiteful, malicious.

ешь(те) *imp. of* **есть,** eat.

ещё *adv.* still, (as) yet, (any) more, further, else; **е. более** further; **е. в** even in, as far back as (date), back in; **е. вопрос** it remains to be seen; **е. один** one more, another.

ЕЭС *abbr.* (**единая энергетическая система**) unified electric power system.

ею *instr. of* **она,** by her, with her or it.

еюн/ит *m.* (med.) jejunitis.

Ж

ж *see* **же; ж.** *abbr.* (**жидкий, жидкость**) liquid; **Ж** *abbr.* (**журнал**) journal.

жаб/а *f.* (amph.) toad (*Bufo*); (old med.) tonsillitis; quinsy, sore throat; (ichth.) toad goby; frogfish; **грудная ж.** (med.) angina pectoris; **ж.-повитуха** *f.* obstetrical toad (*Alytes obstetricans*); **ж.-рыба** *f.,* **—ень** *f.* toad fish (*Opsanus tau*).

жаберн/одышащие *pl.* (zool.) Branchiata; **—ый** *a.* gill, branchial; **—ый луч** (ichth.) branchiostegal; **—ая дуга** gill arch, branchial arch; **—ая крышка** gill cover, operculum, opercle; **—ая тычинка** gill rake (r).

жаб/ий *a. of* **жаба; ж. глаз** (min.) toad's eye tin (a cassiterite); **—ка** *f.* (vet.) exostosis; **—ник** *m.* (bot.) cudweed (*Filago*); **—овидный** *a.* toad-like; **—овидные рыбы** toadfishes (*Batrachoididae*); **—оголовка** *f.* (herp.) Phrynocephalus.

жабр/а *f.* (zool.) gill, branchia; (naut.) sponson; *pl.* branchiae; **—ей, —ий** *m.* (bot.) Galeopsis; **—ица** *f.* Seseli.

жабро— *prefix* (zool.) branchi(o)— (gills); **—видный** *a.* branchiate; **—дышащие** *pl.* Branchiata; **—ногие** *pl.* Branchiopoda; **—образные** *pl.* (amph.) Procoela; **—образный** *a.* branchiform.

жабры *pl. of* **жабра; двоякоперистые ж., первичные ж.** (mal.) ctenidia.

жаб/ун *m.* poison toadfish (*Thalassophryne reticulata*); **—ы** *pl. of* **жаба;** (amph.) Bufonidae.

жавел/ева вода, —ь *m.* Javel water.

жаворон/ки, —ковые *pl.* (orn.) Alaudidae; **—ок** *m.* lark.

жад *m.* (min.) jade; **—еит** *m.* jadeite.

жад/ен *sh. m. of* **жадный; —неть** *v.* get greedier; **—ничать** *v.* be greedy; **—но** *adv.* greedily, avidly; **—ность** *f.* greed(iness), avidity; **—ный** *a.* greedy, avid, eager.

жажд/а *f.* thirst, craving; **—ать** *v.* thirst, long, crave (for); be thirsty; **—оутоляющий** *a.* thirst-quenching, refreshing.

жак *m.* fyke (a bag net).

жакет *m.* jacket.

жаккардова машина (text.) jacquard.

жако *m.* grey parrot (*Psittacus erithacus*).

жаксынский *a.* (geog). Zhaksyi.

жал *past m. sing. of* **жать.**

жалейка *see* **жилейка.**

жаление *n.* stinging.

жалеть *v.* regret, be sorry (for), pity, sympathize; spare, save.

жалить *v.* sting, bite; **—ся** *v.* sting (of nettles); complain.

жалк/ий *a.* sorry, pitiful, shabby, miserable; **—о** *see* **жаль.**

жало *n.* (mach.) guard pin, prong, safety finger; tip (of soldering bit); (ent.) sting(er); (biol.) aculeus.

жалоб/а *f.* complaint, grievance, claim; **—ный** *a.* sad, grievous, plaintive; complaint(s); **—щик** *m.,* **—щица** *f.* plaintiff.

жалов/анный *a.* granted, etc., *see v.;* **—анье** *n.* salary, wages, pay; **—ать** *v.* grant, bestow, confer, favor; **—аться** *v.* complain, make a complaint.

жалок *sh. m. of* **жалкий.**

жалон *m.,* **—ировать** *v.* (surv.) stake.

жало/носные *pl.* (ent.) Aculeata; **—носный** *a.* aculeate; **—образный** *a.* aculeiform.

жалост/ный *a.* regretful, sad, deplorable; **—ь** *f.* pity, compassion.

жаль *imp. v.* it is too bad, it is a pity; **ему ж.** he is sorry, he regrets.

жальный *a. of* **жало.**

жалюзи *n., pl.,* **—йный** *a.* jalousie, louver(s), shutter(s); baffle; grating; **подъёмные ж.** Venetian blinds; **—йное отверстие** louver.

жалящ/ие *pl.* (ent.) Aculeata; **—ий** *a.* stinging, biting; aculeate.

жаменовская свеча Jamin candle.

жанр *m.* genus; genre, category.

жар *m.* heat, glow; (med.) fever, temperature; **—а** *f.* heat, hot weather.

жарарака *f.* (herp.) Bothrops.

жаргон *m.* jargon; (min.) jargon.

жар/ен(н)ый *a.* fried; roasted; **—енье** *n.,* **—ильный** *a.* frying; roasting; **—ить** *v.* fry; roast, stoke up; burn, scorch (of sun); **—иться** *v.* fry; roast.

жарк/ий *a.* hot, sultry (weather); tropical; torrid (zone); ardent; **—о** *adv.* hot; it is hot; **—ое** *n.* fried or roasted meat.

жарновец *m.* (bot.) Cytisus.

жаро— *prefix* heat; **—вня** *f.* roaster, fryer; brazier; hearth; **—вой** *a.* heat, fire; **—вая труба** fire or flame tube; furnace tube.

жаровынослив/ость *f.* heat tolerance; **—ый** *a.* heat-tolerant, heat-resistant.

жарок *sh. m. of* **жаркий.**

жаропонижающ/ий *a.,* **—ее средство** (med.) antipyretic.

жаро/производительная способность heating power; **—прочность** *f.* heat resistance, high-temperature strength; **—прочный** *a.* high-temperature, heat-resistant, thermally stable; refractory; **—стойкий** *a.* heat-resistant, heat-stable; (biol.) heat-tolerant; **—стойкость** *f.* thermal stability; heat tolerance; **—трубный** *a.* fire-tube, flue (boiler, etc.).

жароупорн/ость *f.* heat resistance; **—ый** *a.* heat-resistant, heatproof, refractory; **—ый элемент** heat resistor.

жароустойчив/ость *f.* heat-resistance, thermostability;

(biol.) heat tolerance; **—ый** *a.* heat-resistant, thermostable; heat-tolerant.

жарче *comp. of* **жаркий.**

жасм/ин *m.,* **—инный, —иновый** *a.* (bot.) jasmine (*Jasminum*); mock orange (*Philadelphus coronarius*); **—он** *n.* jasmone.

жат/ва *f.,* **—венный** *a.* harvest(ing), reaping, crop, produce; **—венная машина, —ка** *f.* harvester, reaper; **—камолотилка** *f.* combine; **—ка-самосброска** *f.* side-delivery reaper; **—ка-сноповязалка** *f.* reaperbinder.

жат/ый *a.* harvested, etc.; squeezed, etc., *see v.;* **—ь** *v.* harvest, reap, mow, gather in; squeeze, press, pinch; **—ься** *v.* press (against), cling (to); hesitate; be stingy.

жауаризаль *m.* jauarizal (palm forest swamp).

жах *m.* fyke (a bag net).

жбан *m.* can, jug, tub.

жбака-галс *m.* bitter end (of cable).

жба/ло *n.* (ent.) mandible; **—чка** *f.* cud, chewing (of cud), rumination; chewing gum; **—чные** *pl.* (mam.) ruminants (*Ruminantia*); **—чный** *a.* chewing, ruminant; **—чное животное** ruminant.

Жвр *abbr.* (**временная жёсткость**) temporary hardness.

жгли *past pl. of* **жечь.**

жгун/ец *m.* (bot.) clematis; **—корень** *m.* Cnidium.

жгут *m.* braid, braided strap, band, plait; (fiber) tow, twist, packing material; bundle, bunch; (straw) wisp; (rub.) roving; (vortex) filament; (med.) tourniquet; (biol.) flagellum, cilium; *pr. 3 pl. of* **жечь.**

жгутик *dim. of* **жгут;** (biol.) flagellum, cilium; **—ование** *n.* flagellation; **—овидный** *a.* flagelliform; **—овые** *pl.* (prot.) Flagellata, Mastigophora; **—овый** *a.* flagellar, flagellum; **—оногие** *pl.* (zool.) Pedipalpi; **—оносный** *a.* flagellate; **—оносцы** *see* **жгутиковые.**

жгутник *see* **жгутик.**

жгуто/вый *a. of* **жгут;** **—ногие** *see* **жгутиконогие;** **—образный** *a.* flagelliform; **—провод** *m.* (text.) rope-feeding device; **—укладчик** *m.* (text.) piler; **—улавливатель** *m.* (paper) junk remover; **—оусые** *pl.* (zool.) Pauropoda.

жгучеволосый *a.* (biol.) stimulose.

жгуч/есть *f.* causticity, corrosiveness; smarting; **—ий** *a.* caustic, corrosive, burning, stinging, smarting; hot (spices); vital (question).

жгущий *pres. act. part. of* **жечь.**

ж.д. *abbr.* (**железная дорога**); **ж-д** *abbr.* (**железнодорожный**) railroad.

жданный *a.* awaited, expected.

ждановский *a.* (geog.) Zhdanov(sk).

жд/ать *v.* expect (a)wait; **—ущий** *a.* expecting, (a)waiting; **—ущая развёртка** (electron.) slave sweep, triggered sweep.

же *conj. and particle* but, and; as to, as for; now, then; even, still, whereas; *not translated when emphasizing preceding word;* **тот же** the (very) same.

жевание *n.* mastication, chewing.

жёван(н)ый *a.* masticated, chewed.

жев/ательный *a.* masticatory, chewing; molar (teeth); masseter (muscle); masseteric (nerve, etc.); **—ательный желудок** (zool.) gizzard; **—ать** *v.* masticate, chew; **—ок** *m.* wad of chewed food.

жёг *past m. sing. of* **жечь.**

жединский век (geol.) Gedinnian stage.

жедрит *m.* (min.) gedrite.

жезл *m.,* **—овой** *a.* rod, staff, bar.

жел/аемый *a.* wanted, desired, sought, required; **—ание**

n. wish, desire; **по—анию** as desired, at will; **—анный** *a.* desired.

желательн/о *imp. v.* it is desirable; **если ж.** if desired; **—ость** *f.* desirability; **—ый** *a.* desirable, desired, wanted.

желатин *m.,* **—а** *f.* gelatin; **—(из)ация** *f.,* **—ирование** *n.* gel(atiniz)ation, gelling; **—ированный** *a.* gel(atiniz)ed; **—ировать** *v.* gelatinize, gel(ate); form a gel; (paints) liver; **—ный, —овый** *a.* gelatin(ous); **—овидный, —озный, —ообразный, —оподобный** *a.* gelatinous, gel-like, gelatiniform.

жел/ать *v.* wish, want, desire; be willing; **—ающий** *a.* wanting, desiring.

желва/к *m.* concretion, nodule, knob; bulge; (med.) scirrhus; (resin) deposit; **—ковый** *a.* nodular; **—коносный** *a.* strumiferus, noduliferous; **—чный** *a.* nodular, knotty, lumpy; scirrhous; **—чок** *dim. of* **желвак.**

желе *n.* jelly, gel.

железа *f.* (anat.) gland; *gen. of* **железо; ж. внутренней секреции** endocrine gland.

железина *f.* iron strip, piece of iron.

железисто— *prefix* iron, ferro—, ferrous; (anat.) aden(o)— (gland); **—железистая соль** ferrous ferrite; **—кислый** *a.* ferrite (of); **—железно—** *prefix* ferrosoferric; **—кремнистый сланец** (petr.) ferruginous chert; **—листный** *a.* (bot.) adenophyllous; **—натриевая соль** sodium ferrite; **—серый** *a.* irongray.

железистосинерод/(ист)оводородный *a.* ferrocyanic (acid); **соль —истоводородной кислоты** ferrocyanide; **—истый** *a.* ferrocyanide (of); ferrocyanic (acid); **—истый калий** potassium ferrocyanide.

железисто/сть *f.* ferruginosity; glandulosity, glandulous condition; **—цианистый** *see* **железистосинеродистый.**

железист/ый *a.* iron, ferrous, ferruginous, ferriferous, chalybeate (spring, water); (anat.) glandular; **ж. препарат** (pharm.) iron tonic; **—ая глина** iron clay; **—ая кислота** ferrous acid; **соль —ой кислоты** ferrite; **—ая слюда** (min.) micaceous iron ore; **—ая соль** ferrous salt.

желез/ка *f.* small piece of iron; (anat.) gland(ule); **—ко** *n.* iron, cutter, blade (of plane); **—ковидный** *a.* glanduliform, gland-like; **—нение** *n.* (electrol.) iron plating; (concrete) floating with cement; **—нить** *v.* float with dry cement; **—ница** *f.* (bot.) Sideritis; (zool.) Demodex; (vet.) demodicidosis, Demodex infestation; (ichth.) shad (*Alosa kessleri*); spined loach (*Cobitis taenia*); **—ницевые, —ницы** *pl.* follicle mites (*Demodicidae*); **—ничный** *a. of* **железница.**

железно— *prefix* iron, ferri—, ferric; *see also under* **железо—; —аммиачные квасцы, —аммониевые квасцы** ammonium ferric alum.

железнодорожн/ик *m.* railroad man; **—ый** *a.* railroad, railway.

железно/калиевая соль potassium ferrate; **—кислый** *a.* ferric acid; ferrate (of); **—кислая соль** ferrate; **—синерод—** *see* **железосинерод—.**

железн/ый *a.* iron, ferric; **ж. блеск** (min.) iron glance; **ж. колчедан** (min.) iron pyrites, pyrite; **ж. купорос** iron vitriol (ferrous sulfate); **ж. лист** iron plate, sheet iron; **ж. лом** scrap iron; **ж. сплав** (met.) ferroalloy; **ж. сурик** iron minimum, red ocher; **ж. товар** hardware; **ж. шпат** (min.) siderite; **—ая дорога** railroad, railway; **—ая жесть** (met.) sheet iron; **—ая кислота** ferric acid; **соль —ой кислоты** ferrate; **—ая лазурь** (min.) blue iron-earth, vivianite; **—ая охра** (iron) ocher; **—ая почка** (petr.) eaglestone; **—ая роза**

(min.) hematite (formation); **—ая слюда** (min.) micaceous hematite; **—ая слюдка** (min.) specularite; **—ая сметана** (min.) micaceous hematite; **—ая соль** ferric salt; **—ая трава** (bot.) ironweed (*Vernonia*); **—ая шляпа** (petr.) iron hat, gossan; **—ое дерево** (bot.) ironwood, spec. lignum vitae (*Guaiacum officinale*); argan tree (*Argania sideroxylon*); Persian parrotia; **—ые капли** (pharm.) tincture of iron; **—ые квасцы** iron alum (ferric potassium sulfate); **—ые товары** hardware; **—ые цветы** iron flowers (ferric chloride).

железняк *m.* (min.) iron ore, ironstone; hard stock brick; (bot.) Phlomis; Parrotia; **бурый ж.** (min.) limonite, brown iron ore; **красный ж.** hematite.

желез/о *n.* iron, Fe; **ж. в болванках** (met.) pig (iron); **бористое ж., борное ж.** ferroboron, iron boride; **ванадиевое ж.** (met.) ferrovanadium; **вольфрамистое ж.** (met.) ferrotungsten; **закисное ж.** ferrous iron; **закисная соль —а, соль закиси —а** ferrous salt; **закись —а** ferrous oxide; **закисьокись —а** ferrosoferric oxide; **окисная соль —а, соль окиси —а** ferric salt; **окисное ж.** ferric iron; **окись —а** ferric oxide; **сернистое ж.** ferrous sulfide; **сернокислая закись —а** ferrous sulfate; **сернокислая окись —а** ferric sulfate; **сернокислое ж., сульфат —а** iron sulfate; **соединение закиси —а** ferrous compound; **соединение окиси —а** ferric compound; **углеродистое ж.** iron carbide; **хлористое ж.** ferrous chloride; **хлорное ж.** ferric chloride.

железо— *prefix* iron, ferro—; ferri—, ferric; sider(o)— (iron); *see also under* **железно—, ферро—**; **—аммониевые квасцы** ferric ammonium sulfate; **—бактерии** *pl.* iron (depositing) bacteria; **—бетон** *m.*, **—бетонный** *a.* ferroconcrete, reinforced concrete; **—водородное сопротивление** (elec.) barretter; **—делательный завод** iron works; **—дефицитный** *a.* iron-deficiency (anemia); **—каменный** *a.* stony-iron (meteorite); **—кирпич** *m.* reinforced brick; **—кокс** *m.* ferrous coke; **—любивый** *a.* (biol.) siderophilic; **—магнитный** *a.* ferromagnetic; **—марганцовый** *a.* iron-manganese; **—никелевый колчедан** (min.) pentlandite; **—обрабатывающий** *a.* iron-working, iron (industry); **—окисный** *a.* iron oxide; **—плавильный завод** iron foundry; **—подобный** *a.* iron-like, ferruginous; **—протопорфирин** *m.* ferroprotoporphyrin; **—прокатный стан** iron rolling mill; **—родановая кислота** ferrithiocyanic acid; **—рудный** *a.* iron-ore.

железосинеродо/(ист)оводородная кислота ferricyanic acid; **соль —истоводородной кислоты** ferricyanide; **—истый** *a.* ferricyanic (acid); ferricyanide (of); **—истый калий** potassium ferricyanide; **—истое железо** ferrous ferricyanide; **—ное железо** ferric ferricyanide.

железо/скобяные изделия hardware; **—содержащий** *a.* iron-containing, ferruginous, ferriferous; **—стекло** *n.* ferroglass; **—углеродистый** *a.* iron-carbon (alloys); **—цианистый** *see* **железосинеродистый.**

железы *gen. and pl. of* **железа.**

жел/ейный *a. of* **желе; —еобразный** *a.* jelly-like, gelatinous; **—ирование** *n.* jellification, gelatinization.

желна *f.* black woodpecker (*Dryocopus*).

жёлоб *m.* groove, gutter, trough, channel, trench, furrow, canal, conduit, chute, spout; **наклонный ж., спускной ж.** chute.

желоб/истый *a.* grooved, channeled; canaliculate; **—ить** *v.* groove, channel, slot, flute, chamfer; (leather) flex; **—коватый** *see* **желобоватый; —ковидный** *see* **желобовидный; —ление** *n.* grooving, etc., *see v.;*

—обрюхие *pl.* (mal.) Solenogastres; **—оватый** *a.* grooved, channeled, sulcate(d), furrowed; U-shaped, trough-shaped; **—овидный** *a.* sulciform, groove-shaped; **—ок** *m.* groove, flute, slot; (anat.) sulcus, furrow; (feed) trough; **—ок катания** (bearing) raceway; **—ообразный** *see* **желобоватый; желобовидный.**

желобчат/о *prefix* solen(o)— (channel, pipe); **—ый** *a.* grooved, fluted, channel(ed); corrugated, ribbed; serrated; channel (steel); trough (conveyer); rectangular-cap (tray in tower).

желон/ка *f.*, **—очный** *a.* bailer, sludge pump, sand pump; auger, spoon bit.

жёлт *sh. m. of* **жёлтый; —ая** *f.* yellow (pigment).

желт/ение *n.* yellowing; sulling, rusting (of wire); **—еть** *v.* (turn) yellow; **—еющий** *a.* yellowing; **—изна** *f.* yellow(ish)ness; **—инка** *f.* yellowish color; yellow spot; **—инник** *m.* (bot.) fustic (spec. *Rhus cotinus*); **—ить** *v.* color yellow; **—иться** *v.* turn yellow; sull; **—ковый** *a.* yolk, vitelline; **—о—** or **жёлто—** *prefix* flavo—, yellow; luteo—, yellowish; **—бровка** *f.* (orn.) wood warbler (*Phylloscopus*); **—обрюх** *m.* (herp.) Coluber jugularis.

желтоват/о *prefix*, **—ый** *a.* yellowish; **—ость** *f.* yellow(ish)ness.

желто/видение *n.* (med.) xanthopsia; **—горлый** *a.* yellow-throated; **—гривка** *see* **желтокрылка; —губка** *f.* (ichth.) a shad (*Alosa kessleri*); **—гузка** *f.* (ent.) Euproctis; **—душка** *f.* (mam.) pine marten (*Martes m.*); **жёлто-зелёный** *a.* yellowish green; **—зелье** *n.* (bot.) groundsel (*Senecio erucifolius*); **—зём** *m.* zheltozem, yellow (podzolic) soil; (min.) yellow ocher; **—зобка** *f.* (orn.) yellowcrop (*Tryngites*); **—к** *m.* yolk, vitellus; **—калильный** *a.* yellow (heat); **—клювый** *a.* (orn.) yellow-billed; **—кожий** *a.* yellow-skinned; **—корень** *m.* (bot.) Hydrastis; **жёлто-коричневый** *a.* yellowish brown; **—корневой** *a.* yellow-rooted, xanthorrhizous; **—крылка** *f.* (ichth.) a sculpin (*Cottocomephorus*); **—крылый** *a.* (ichth.) yellow-winged; **—листный** *a.* yellow-leaved; **—лоз(ник)** (bot.) purple willow (*Salix purpurea*); **—ломкость** *f.* yellow brittleness; **—мяска** *f.* (ichth.) a minnow (*Leuciscus idus*); **—носый** *a.* (orn.) yellow-billed.

желто/пёр *m.* (ichth.) Xenocypris; Plagiognathops; **—пёрый** *a.* yellow-fin(ned); **—плодный** *a.* yellow-fruited, xanthocarpous; **—полосый** *a.* yellow-striped, yellow-banded; **—пузик** *m.* (herp.) glass snake (*Ophisaurus apodus*); (ichth.) a minnow (*Phoxinus percnurus*); **—ротый** *a.* (orn.) yellow-billed; **—фиоль** *f.* (bot.) Cheiranthus; **—хвост** *m.* (ichth.) yellowtail (*Seriola*); yellowtail snapper (*Ocyurus chrysurus*); **—цвет** *m.* yellow-flowering plant; (bot.) Adonis vernalis; **—цветковый** *a.* yellow-flowering.

желточн/ик *m.* (zool.) yolk gland, vitellarium; **—о-жёлтый** *a.* egg-yolk yellow, vitelline; **—ый** *a.* yolk, vitelline; **—ый мешок, —ый пузырь** yolk sac; **—ая клетка** (embr.) vitellophag.

желтощёк *m.* (ichth.) Elopichthys.

желту/ха *f.* (med.) jaundice; (phyt.) yellows; **—шка** *f.* sulfur butterfly (*Colias*); **—шник** *m.* (bot.) Erysimum; (orn.) golden oriole (*Oriolus o.*); **—шность** *f.* (med.) jaundice, yellowness; **—шный** *a.* icteric, yellowish.

жёлт/ый *a.* yellow; **ж. корень** (bot.) golden seal (*Hydrastis canadensis*); **ж. пигмент** carotin; **—ая вода** (med.) glaucoma; **—ое дерево** fustic, yellowwood (dye); **—ое пятно** (anat.) macula lutea; **—ое тело** (anat.) corpus luteum.

желт/ь *f.* yellow (pigment); **—янка** *f.* (bot.) dyer's rocket (*Reseda luteola*).

желуд/е— *prefix* balano— (acorn); **—евый, —овый** *a.* acorn; **—еплодный** *a.* balanocarpous, acorn-bearing.

желуд/ок *m.* stomach, gaster; (orn.) crop, craw; **второй ж.** (zool.) reticulum; **железистый ж.** (orn.) proventriculе, glandular stomach; **мускульный ж.** gizzard; **относящийся к —ку** *a.* gastric; **первый ж.** (zool.) rumen; **третий ж.** omasum; **четвёртый ж.** abomasum; **—очек** *dim. of* **желудок;** (anat.) ventricle, chamber; **—очково—** *prefix* ventriculo—, ventricle; **—очковый** *a.* ventricular.

желудочн/о— *prefix* gastro— (stomach, belly; gastric); **ж.-диафрагмальный** *a.* gastrophrenic; **ж.-кишечный** *a.* gastrointestinal, gastroenteric; **ж.-ободочный** *a.* gastrocolic; **ж.-селезёночный** *a.* gastrosplenic, gastrolienal; **—ый** *a.* gastric; gastro—, *e.g.,* **—ая грыжа** gastrocele; **—ый камень** (pal.) gastrolith; **—ый сок** gastric juice.

желуд/ь *m.* acorn; (anat.) glans; **морской ж.** (crust.) barnacle (*Balanus*); **морские —и** Balanidae.

желче— *prefix* chole—, cholo— (bile, gall); **—гонный** *a.,* **—гонное средство** cholagogue; **—ние** *n.* (phyt.) yellow fermentation; **—образование** *n.* bile formation; **—отделение** *n.* bile secretion; **—провод** *m.* (anat.) bile duct; **—содержащая моча** (med.) choluria.

желчно— *see* **желче—;** **—каменный** *a.* (med.) gallstone, cholelithic; **—каменная болезнь** cholelithiasis; **—кислый** *a.* bile acid, bile (salt); **—кровие** *n.* cholemia.

жёлч/ность *f.* biliousness; jaundice; **—ный** *a.* bilious, bile; gall (stones, etc.); **ж. пузырь** (anat.) gallbladder; **ж. ход** bile duct; **жёлтый ж. пигмент** biliflavin; **—ная кислота** bile acid; **—ь** *f.* bile.

жемчу/г *m.,* **—жина** *f.* pearl; (met.) bead; **—жница** *f.* pearl oyster; (vet.) pearl disease; **морские —жницы** (mal.) Pteriidae; **пресноводные —жницы** Margaritiferidae; **—жноглазые** *pl.* (ichth.) pearleyes (*Scopelarchidae*); **—жнотелые** *pl.* Glaucosomidae; **—жночистый** *a.* as bright as a pearl; **—жный** *a.* pearl(y), margaritaceous; **—жный блеск** pearly luster; pearlstone, perlite (a volcanic glass); **—жное зерно** pearl.

жена *f.* wife; **—тый** *a.* married.

женевский *a.* (geog.) Geneva(n).

жен/ить(ся) *v.* marry; **—омужий** *a.* (bot.) gynandrous; **—ский** *a.* female, feminine, women's; (bot.) pistillate; **—ская половая клетка** ovum, egg cell; **—щина** *f.* woman.

женьшень *m.* (bot.) ginseng (*Panax ginseng*).

женья *f.* genya, pasture, plain.

жеод *m.,* **—а** *f.,* **—истый** *a.* (geol.) geode.

жерд/евой *a. of* **жердь; —ина** *see* **жердь; —инник, —няк** *m.* polewood, young forest.

жёркочка *f.* perch.

жерд/ь *f.,* **—яной** *a.* pole, rod; stake.

жерёбая *a.* (zool.) pregnant, in foal.

жеребейка *f.* (foundry) chaplet.

жереб/ёнок *m.* foal; **—ец** *m.* stallion, stud; **—иться** *v.* foal; **—ковый** *a.,* **—ок** *m.* hide of (premature) foal.

жерёбость *f.* (zool.) pregnancy.

жереб/цовый *a. of* **жеребец; —чик** *m.* colt.

жеребьёвка *f.* sorting, allotment; toss-up.

жеребя/тник *m.,* **—тня** *f.* foal stable; **—чий** *a.* foal.

жерепняк *m.* pine elfin-tree.

жере/спер, —х *m.* (ichth.) asp (*Aspius a.; Pseudaspius*); bleak (*Chalcalburnus chalcoides*).

жердица *f.* fish-catching device.

жерло *n.* mouth, orifice, crater, vent, funnel; (volcanic) pipe; **—вина** *f.* volanic neck.

жерлянка *f.* (herp.) Bombina.

жёрнов *m.* millstone; **верхний ж.** runner; **нижний ж.** bed stone.

жернов/а *f.* disk mill; **—ка** *f.* (crust.) masticatory stomach; **—ой** *a.* millstone; molar (teeth); **—ок** *m.* (ichth.) horny formation.

жертв/а *f.* sacrifice; victim, prey; **—енный** *a.* sacrificial; **—ователь** *m.* donor; **—овать** *v.* sacrifice, give (up), trade (for); do at the expense (of); donate.

жеру/ха *f.* (bot.) Nasturtium; **—шник** *m.* Roripa.

жест *m.* gesture, motion, action.

жесте/образный *a.* tinny; **—печатание** *n.* tin printing.

жёстер *m.* (bot.) Rhamnus.

жести *gen., etc., of* **жесть.**

жёсткий *a.* rigid, stiff, inflexible; exacting, stringent, tough, rigorous, severe, harsh; strong, drastic (measures); rough, coarse; close (tolerance); hard (water, disk; acid, etc.); refractory (surfactant); firm (decision); **ж. факел** inflexible flame.

жёстко *adv. of* **жёсткий;** *prefix* rigid; hard, sclero—; **—ватый** *a.* rather hard or stiff; **—волосистый** *a.* hispid, bristly-haired; **—волосый** *a.* coarse-haired; **—древесинный** *a.* hardwood(ed); **—колосница** *f.* (bot.) Sclerochloa; **—крыл** *m.* (ichth.) Trachyrhynchus; **—крылые** *pl.* (ent.) Coleoptera; **—крылый** *a.* coleopterous; **—лист(вен)ный** *a.* hard-leaved, sclerophyllous; **—мятлик** *m.* (bot.) Scleropoa; **—опушённый** *a.* hispid; **—плодный** *a.* sclerocarpous; **—подушечники** *pl.* hard cushion vegetation.

жёсткость *f.* rigidity, etc.; hardness, etc., *see* **жесткий;** tension, force (of spring); stability (of oil film); (acous.) impedance; (paper) feel, handle; (meteor.) severity; **придавать ж.** stiffen, strengthen, reinforce; **электрическая ж.** (elec. comm.) elastance.

жёстко/фокусирующий *a.* strong-focusing; **—шерстный** *a.* wire-haired (terrier); **—щетинистый** *a.* hard-bristled.

жёсток *sh. m. of* **жёсткий.**

жестокий *a.* hard, severe; **—ость** *f.* severity.

жёстче *comp. of* **жёсткий, жёстко.**

жестчение *n.* stiffening, hardening; aging.

жест/ь *f.* sheet (metal), tin (plate); **белая ж.** tin plate; **чёрная ж.** black plate, sheet iron; **—яник** *m.* tinsmith; **—яницкая** *f.* tinsmithy; **—яницкий** *a.* tinsmith's; tinware; **—янка** *f.* tin (box or can), can; **—янобаночный** *a.* tin can; **—яной** *a.* tin; **—яночный** *a. of* **жестянка; —янщик** *m.* tinsmith.

жет *m.* jet.

жетон *m.* tag, badge; counter, token.

жечь *v.* burn, roast, calcine; char; (cer.) fire, bake, kiln.

жжение *n.* burning, etc., *see* **жечь.**

жжён/ка *f.* kilned clay; roasted malt; **—(н)ый** *a.* burned, etc., *see* **жечь;** burnt (umber; alum); quick(lime).

жжёт *pr. 3 sing. of* **жечь.**

жиард/иаз *m.* (med.) giardiasis; **—ия** *f.* (prot.) Giardia.

жив *sh. of* **живой; —ать** *see* **жить.**

жив-во *abbr.* (**животноводство**).

живёт *pr. 3 sing. of* **жить.**

живетский век (geol.) Givetian stage.

живец *m.* bait fish.

живит/ельный *a.* restorative, vivifying, regenerative; **—ь** *v.* restore, vivify, regenerate, animate, revive; invigorate.

жив/ица *f.,* **—ичный** *a.* (oleo)resin, turpentine (gum), galipot; (text.) barras.

живность *f.* poultry; small game.

живо *adv.* promptly, quickly; **—глотовые, —глоты** *pl.* (ichth.) Chiasmodontidae; **—дёр** *m.* (hides) flayer; **—дный** *a.* bait.

жив/ое *n.* the quick, the living; **—ой** *a.* alive, living, animate, lively, active, brisk; bright, rich, vivid (color); keen (interest); spring (water); free, open (area); **—ая сила** kinetic energy; **закон —ых сил** principle of conservation of energy; **—ое сечение** (hydr.) (effective) cross section; discharge (section).

живокость *f.* (bot.) delphinium.

живоловка *f.* animal trap.

живопис/ный *a.* picturesque; scenic; **ж. пейзаж** scenery; **—ь** *f.* painting.

живоро/дки *pl.* (mal.) Viviparidae; **—дковые** *pl.* (ichth.) surfperches (*Embiotocidae*); **—дность** *f.* (zool.) viviparity; (bot.) vivipary; **—дящие** *pl.* viviparous animals; **—дящий** *a.* viviparous; **—ждение** *see* **живородность; —жденный** *a.* live-born.

живо/рыбный *a.* live-fish; fish (pond); **—сечение** *n.* vivisection; **—сть** *f.* animation, liveliness, briskness.

живот *m.* (anat.) venter, abdomen, belly.

животвор/ить *v.* revive; vivify, resuscitate; invigorate; **—ный, —ящий** *a.* reviving, etc., *see* v.; life-giving.

животик *dim. of* **живот.**

животина *f.* domestic animal.

животновод *m.* stock breeder; **—ство** *n.* livestock breeding, animal husbandry; **—ческий** *a.* stock-breeding.

животн/ое *n.* animal; animal life, fauna; **география —ых** zoogeography; **—оед** *m.* carnivorous animal; **ж.-переносчик** *m.* (med.) vector; **—орастение** *n.* zoophyte; **ж.-хозяин** *n.* host; **—оядный** *a.* zoophagous, carnivorous.

живот/ный *a.* animal; **ж. крахмал** glycogen; **ж. мир** animal kingdom; wildlife; **ж. танкаж** slaughterhouse waste; **ж. уголь** animal charcoal.

животрепещущий *a.* of vital importance; lively; actual, topical, timely.

живут *pr.* 3 *pl. of* **жить.**

живуч/есть *f.* viability, tenacity, persistence; life; survival, survivability; **—ий** *a.* of great vitality, tenacious of life, hardy, long-lived; fail-safe (construction); **—ка** *f.* (bot.) Ajuga; Sempervivum.

жив/ущий *a.* living; **—чик** *m.* (zool.) spermatozoon; (bot.) spermatozoid; **—шии** *past act. part. of* **жить; —ьё** *n.* living creatures; **—я** *pr. ger.* living.

жигалка *f.* stable fly (*Stomoxys calcitrans*).

Жигмонди фильтр Zsigmondy filter.

жигулёвский *a.* (geog.) Zhigulev(sk).

жигунец *m.* (bot.) Cnidium.

жиденький *a.* liquid, watery, thin.

жидк/ий *a.* liquid, fluid; watery, thin; light (oil); liquefied (air); wet (cell); (met.) molten; flexible (rod); **—ое тело** liquid, fluid; **мера —их тел** liquid measure.

жидко *adv.* in liquid form; *prefix* liquid; **—водородный** *a.* liquid hydrogen; **—кристаллический** *a.* (cryst.) mesomorphic; **—металлический** *a.* liquid-metal; **—плавкий** *a.* liquid, fluid; **—плавкость** *f.* fluidity; **—подвижность** *f.* fluidity, flowability (in liquid state); **—стно-ракетный, —стно-реактивный** *a.* liquid-propellant rocket (engine); **—стность** *f.* fluidity, liquidity; **—стно-фрикционный** *a.* fluid-friction; **—стный** *a.* liquid, fluid; fluid-flow (pump); hydraulic (brake); liquid-propellant (rocket engine); **—сть** *f.* liquid, fluid, liquor; liquidity; fluidity; **—сть-теплоноситель** *m.* heat-transfer fluid; **—текучесть** *f.* fluidity; fluid flow; (met.) flowability; **—текучий** *a.* thin, watery; **—те-**

кущий *a.* fluid, nonviscous; fluid-flow; **—фазный** *a.* liquid-phase; (petrol.) trickle-phase (desulfurization).

жидок *sh. m. of* **жидкий.**

жиж/а *f.* liquid, liquor, juice; slurry; **—е** *comp. of* **жидкий, жидко; —енный** *a. suffix* liquid, liquefied; **—еотстойник** *m.* sedimentation tank; cesspool; **—еприёмник, —есборник** *m.* liquid manure tank; cesspool; **—еразбрасыватель** *m.* liquid manure spreader; **—есборный** *a.* liquid manure collecting; **—ехранилище** *see* **жижиприёмник; —ица, —ка** *see* **жижа; —ка** *f.* pyroligneous distillate.

жизне— *prefix* life.

жизнедеятельн/ость *f.* (vital) activity, active life; life or metabolic processes; **—ый** *a.* active, vital; lively, energetic.

жизненн/о *adv.* vitally; **ж. важный, ж. необходимый** *a.* vital, essential; **—ость** *f.* vitality, vigor, life; **—ый** *a.* vital, life('s); viable; living (standard); life (cycle); biotic (energy); **—ый уровень** standard of living; **—ая ёмкость** vital capacity (of lungs); **—ое дерево** (bot.) arbor vitae (*Thuja occidentalis*).

жизне/обеспечение *n.* survival; life support (system); **—описание** *n.* biography, life; **—поддерживающий** *a.* life-support; **—радостный** *a.* cheerful, joyous, full of zest; **—сохранение** *n.* conservation of life.

жизнеспособн/ость *f.* viability, vitality; working life (of glue); germinability (of seeds); **—ый** *a.* viable, live (seeds); vital.

жизнестойк/ий *a.* vigorous, hardy, resistant; **—ость** *f.* vitality, vigor.

жизн/ь life, existence, living; **ж. доказывает** events indicate, experience shows; **время —и, продолжительность —и** lifetime, life span, existence; **дерево —и** *see* **жизненное дерево; претворить в ж., проводить в ж.** *v.* put into practice, effect or operation; realize; implement.

жиклёр *m.* jet, nozzle; metering orifice.

жил *past m. sing. of* **жить; gen. pl. of** **жила; prefix see жилищный, жилой.**

жила *f.* vein; (geol.) vein, lode, seam; filament, strand, core (of cable); (med.) catgut; *past f. sing. of* **жить; ж.-проводник** (geol.) lead vein, leader; **сухая ж.** (anat.) tendon, sinew.

жилейка *f.* pipes.

жиление *n.* (med.) strain(ing), exertion.

жилет *m.* (life) vest, jacket.

жилец *m.* dweller, tenant, resident, inhabitant.

жилист/ость *f.* (leather) venosity, veininess; **—ый** *a.* veined, fibrous, sinewy, stringy.

жилиться *v.* strain, exert oneself.

жилищ/е *n.* residence, dwelling, home(stead), house, housing, quarters; **—но-гражданское строительство** civil housing; **—но-эксплуатационный** *a.* housing operation; **—ный** *a.* housing; living (conditions); **—ный фонд** available housing; **—ное строительство, —ное хозяйство** housing.

жилк/а *dim. of* **жила;** (leaf) nerve, vein, rib; fiber; **—о—** *prefix* nervi—, nervo—, neur(o)— (nerve); phleb(o)— (vein); **—ование** *n.* (bot.) venation, nervation; veining; **—оватый** *a.* veined, ribbed; fibrous, stringy.

жиловатый *see* **жилистый.**

жилой *a.* inhabited, habitable, residential; wild, native, indigenous; (ichth.) freshwater; landlocked; **ж. дом** dwelling, residence; **ж. комплекс** community.

жилок *gen. pl. of* **жилка.**

жилотдел *m.* department of housing.

жилоч/ка *f.* small vein, fibril; **—ный** *see* **жильный.**

жил/площадь *f.* floor space; housing, accommodation; —**строительный** *a.*, —**строительство** *n.* house building; —**управление** *n.* housing management.

жильбертит *m.* (min.) gilbertite.

жиль/ё *n.* habitation, home, dwelling; **пригодный для** —**я** *a.* habitable.

жильн/ый *a.* vein(y), veined; **ж. пояс** (geol.) lode or vein system; —**ая масса** vein filling or rock; —**ая порода** vein or lode rock; matrix, vein mineral; —**ая свита** vein system; —**ое месторождение** lode, vein; —**ые минералы** gangue.

жильца *gen. of* **жилец.**

жимолост/ные *pl.* (bot.) Caprifoliaceae; —**ь** *f.* honey-suckle (*Lonicera*).

жинзенг *see* **джин-шень.**

жир *m.* fat; grease; oil; adeps, lard; suint, yolk (of wool); **дублёный** —**ами** *a.* oil-tanned.

жиральдесов орган (embr.) Giralde's organ.

жираторный *a.* gyratory, gyrating.

жираф *m.*, —**а** *f.* (mam.; min.) giraffe; —**овые,** —**ы** *pl.* Giraffidae.

жирационный *a.* gyration, gyrating.

жир/ен *sh. m. of* **жирный;** —**еть** *v.* get fat; —**компаунд** *m.* complex fat.

жирно—*prefix* fat, fatty, aliphatic; rich (in); (typ.) heavily, bold-face; —**ароматический** *a.* aliphatic-aromatic; —**вычерченный** *a.* heavily drawn, —**известковый** *a.* lime-rich; —**кислый** *a.* fatty acid; —**масляный** *a.* (bot.) oleiferous, oil-producing; —**молочность** *f.* butter-fat content (of milk); —**молочный** *a.* with high butter-fat content; —**размолотый** *a.* (paper) wet-beaten; —**сть** *f.* fat content; fatness, greasiness, oiliness; richness (of soil); fattiness; (paper) wetness; —**хвостый** *a.* fat-tail(ed) (sheep).

жирн/ый *a.* fat, greasy, oily; fatty, aliphatic (acid, etc.); fattened; rich, fertile (soil); grease (spot); lardaceous (fracture); bituminous (peat); China (pencil); wet (gas; paper stock); (typ.) bold-face; —**ая глина,** —**ая земля** (foundry) loam.

жиро *n.* (com.) indorsement.

Жиро печь (elec.) Girot furnace.

жиро— *prefix* fat, fatty, aliphatic, lipo—; adipo—; (mech.) *see under* **гиро**—.

жиров/ание *n.* greasing, etc., *see v.;* (bot.) vigorous growth; —**анный** *a.* greased, etc., *see v.;* —**ать** *v.* grease, oil, lubricate; (leather) fat-liquor, stuff; fatten; (bot.) go into foliage.

жировик *m.* (med.) lipoma, fatty tumor; (min.) steatite, soapstone; (bot.) watershoot, water sprout, sucker.

жировка *see* **жирование; жироприказ.**

жировой *a.* fatty, aliphatic; tallowy, sebaceous; (anat.) adipose; **ж. обмен** (physiol.) lipometabolism; **ж. побег** *see* **жировик** (bot.).

жиро/воск *m.* (med.) adipocere; —**заменитель** *m.* fat substitute; —**к** *dim. of* **жир.**

жироклинометр *m.* gyrolevel.

жиро/лов(уш)ка *f.* grease trap, oil trap; —**мер** *m.* butyrometer.

жирометр *m.* gyrometer.

жиромолочный *see* **жирномолочный.**

жиронепроницаем/ость. *f.* grease resistance; —**ый** *a.* greaseproof, oil-proof.

жиро/обменный *a.* (physiol.) lipometabolic; —**обрабатывающий** *a.* fat-processing; —**образный** *a.* lipoid, fatlike; —**образование** *n.* lipogenesis, fat formation; —**отделитель** *see* **жироловка;** —**отложение** *n.* adipopexis, fat deposition, getting fat; —**перерабатывающий** *a.* fat-processing.

жироплан *m.* (av.) gyroplane.

жиро/подобный *a.* fatty, oily; —**пот** *m.* (wool) suint, yolk.

жироприказ *m.* (com.) endorsement, (banking) order.

жирораствор/имый *a.* fat-soluble, liposoluble; —**итель** *m.*, —**яющий реактив** fat solvent; —**яющий** *a.* fat-dissolving.

жирорасщепл/ение *n.* lipolysis; —**яющий** *a.* fat-splitting, lipolytic.

жироскоп *m.* gyroscope, gyrostat, gyro; —**ический** *a.* gyroscopic, gyro—.

жиро/содержащий *a.* fat-containing, fatty.

жиростат/ика *f.* gyrostatics; —**ический** *a.* gyrostatic.

жиросыр/ец *m.*, —**ьё** *n.* raw or crude fat.

жиро/топление *n.*, —**топный** *a.* (fat) rendering; —**удаляющий реагент** fat extractant; —**улавливание** *n.* separation of grease, fat or oil; —**уловитель** *m.* grease trap.

жир/содержащий *see* **жиросодержащий;** —**сырец** *see* **жиросырец.**

жиря/ки *pl.* (mam.) Hyracoidea; **ж.,** —**ковые** *pl.* (orn.) oilbirds (*Steatornithidae*); —**нка** *f.* (bot.) butterwort (*Pinguicula*).

жисмондит *m.* (min.) gismondite.

жите/йский *a.* worldly; everyday; —**ль** *m.* inhabitant, resident, dweller; —**ли** *pl.* population; —**льство** *n.* abode, dwelling.

жит/ник *m.* a kind of bread; —**ница** *f.* granary; corn crib; —**ный** *a.*, —**о** *n.* corn, grain; —**няк** *m.* wheat grass (*Agropyron*).

жить *v.* live, be alive; subsist; inhabit; —**ё** *n.* life, being, existence; —**ся** *v.* fare (well or badly).

ЖК *abbr.* (**жирные кислоты**) fatty acids; **ЖК, ж.к.** (**жидкостный коэффициент**) liquor ratio.

ЖКП *abbr.* (**жидкостный кислородный прибор**) liquid-oxygen apparatus.

жмаки *see* **жмыхи.**

ЖМГ *abbr.* (**жидкометаллическое горючее**) liquid-metal fuel.

жмёт *pr. 3 sing. of* **жать,** press.

жминда *f.* (bot.) pigweed (*Chenopodium*).

жмурить(ся) *v.* screw up (one's eyes).

жмут *pr. 3 pl. of* **жать,** press.

жмых *m.*, —**и** *pl.*, —**овый** *a.* (oil) cake; —**одробилка** *f.* oil-cake grinder; —**одробление** *n.* oil cake crushing.

жн/еемолотилка *f.* (agr.) combine; —**ейка** *f.* harvester, reaper; —**ёт** *pr. 3 sing. of* **жать,** reap; —**ец** *m.* reaper; (ent.) harvester ant (*Messor*); —**ива** *f.*, —**иво,** —**ивьё** *n.* stubble (field); reaping; —**итво** *n.* reaping; standing grain; —**ущий** *a.* reaping, harvesting.

Жобера ямка (anat.) Jobert's fossa.

жолоб *see* **жёлоб.**

жолудь *see* **желудь.**

жом *m.*, —**а** *f.* press, squeezer, compressor; clamp; (beet) pulp, bagasse, chips; (anat.) sphincter; —**осушка** *f.* beet pulp drying; —**осушилка** *f.* beet pulp dryer.

жонглировать *v.* juggle.

жонкил/евый *a.*, —**ия** *f.* (bot.) jonquil.

жор *m.* (ichth.) post-spawning feeding.

жордан *m.* (paper) Jordan refiner; —**овый** *a.* Jordan; —**он** *m.* (biol.) jordanon, strain, variety.

жорение *see* **жор.**

жорнов *see* **жёрнов.**

жосефинит *m.* (min.) josephinite.

жостер *m.* (bot.) Rhamnus cathartica.

Жп. *abbr.* (**постоянная жесткость**) constant hardness.

жрать *v.* devour, eat greedily, guzzle.

ЖРД *abbr.* (**жидкостный ракетный двигатель**) liquid-propellant rocket engine.

жребий *m.* lot, fate; toss (of coin).

ЖС, жс *abbr.* (**живая сила**) kinetic energy; (**жирные спирты**) aliphatic alcohols.

жуёт *pr. 3 sing. of* **жевать.**

жужелиц/а *f.* (met.) slag, dross; (ent.) ground beetle; **—ы** *pl.* Carabidae.

жужж/ало *n.* bee fly (*Bombylius*); **—аловые** *pl.* (ent.) Bombyliidae; **—альца, —альцы** *pl.* (ent.) balancers, halteres; **—ание** *n.,* **—ащий** *a.* hum(ming), etc., *see v.;* **—ать** *v.* hum, buzz, drone, murmur.

жуинский *a.* (geog.) Zhuya.

жук *m.* beetle, bug, chafer, weevil; kink (in wire); (steel) sliver; **ж.-геркулес** *m.* (ent.) Hercules beetle (*Dynastes hercules*); **ж.-древогрыз** *m.* powder-post beetle (*Lyctus linearis*); **—и** *pl.* (ent.) Coleoptera; **—и-точильщики** *pl.* Anobiidae; **—и-щелкуны** *pl.* Elateridae; **ж.-коровка** *m.* lady beetle; **ж.-короед** *m.* bark beetle; **ж.-носорог** *m.* Oryctes nasicornis; **ж.-олень** *m.* stag beetle (*Lucanus cervus*).

жулан *m.* (orn.) red-tailed shrike (*Lanius cristatus*).

журав *m.* dolly bar; lever dolly; **—(е)ль** *m.* sweep, lever arm; (microphone) boom; (orn.) crane (*Grus*); (astr.) Grus; **—ельник** *m.* (bot.) Geranium; Erodium; **—ли(ные)** *pl.* (orn.) Gruidae; **—линый** *a. of* **журав(е)ль;** **—чик** *m.* (geol.) lime nodule, loess-doll.

журить *v.* reprove, rebuke.

журнал *m.,* **—ьный** *a.* journal, periodical, magazine; log, record; diary; register; **периодический ж.** periodical, review.

журч/ала *pl.* (ent.) Bombyliidae; **—алка** *f.* bulb fly (*Eumerus*); **—алки** *pl.* (ent.) Syrphidae; **—ание** *n.,* **—ать** *v.* murmur, gurgle, ripple.

жут/кий *a.* horrible; **—ь** *f.* terror, horror.

жух/лый *a.* faded; **—нуть** *v.* fade; (leather) become tough or hardened.

жучина *f.* wound, tapping (of trees).

жуч/ки *pl.* (zool.) scutes, bony plates; *pl. of* **жучок;** **—ок** *dim. of* **жук.**

жу/юще-сосущий *a.* (ent.) chewing-sucking; **—ющий** *a.* chewing; grinding; **—ющий зуб** molar (tooth); **—я** *pr. ger. of* **жевать.**

жюри *n.* jury.

З

з. *abbr.* (**западный**) western; **з., З.** *abbr.* west.

за *prep. acc. to indicate motion: instr. to indicate location;* after, behind, beyond, out(side) of; for, as; at; per (unit); during, in; over, across; **за и против** pro and con.

за— *prefix* beyond, trans—; behind, retro—; ad—; *with verbs to indicate the beginning of action;* **—алайский** *a.* (geog.) Trans Alai; **—алеть** *v.* redden; begin to glow; **—анкеровывать** *v.* anchor; **—арендов(ыв)ать** *v.* rent, lease; **—арретировать** *v.* cage; **—асфальтировать** *v.* asphalt; **—атлантический** *a.* transatlantic; **—атмосферный** *a.* above the atmosphere, in outer space, extraterrestrial.

забав/а *f.* amusement; **—лять** *v.* entertain, amuse; **—ный** *a.* entertaining.

забазировать *v.* store, stock.

Забайкаль/е, —ская область Transbaikal region.

забаланс/ировать *v.* start balancing; **—овый** *a.* potential (resources).

забалканский *a.* (geog.) Transbalkan.

забаллотиров(ыв)ать *v.* blackball.

забалтывать *v.* mix in, stir in.

забаррикадировать *v.* barricade; **—ся** *v.* entrench oneself.

забастов/ать *v.,* **—ка** *f.* (labor) strike.

забе/г *m.* overshoot(ing), overswing(ing) (of needle); (zool.) foray; (sports) heat, round; race; **—гание** *n.* running in, etc., *see v.;* **—гать, —жать** *v.* run in, drop in; run (ahead); forestall (events); stray; swing over; **—гающий** *a.* leading.

забей(те) *imp. of* **забить.**

забел *see* **заброд;** **—и(ва)ть, —ять** *v.* whiten; whitewash.

заберег *m.* ice-free shore; submerged off-shore ice.

забеременеть *v.* become pregnant.

заберёт *fut. 3 sing. of* **забрать.**

забеспокоиться *v.* start worrying.

забетонировать *v.* (set in) concrete.

забив/ание *n.* driving (in), etc., *see v.;* stoppage, block; **—ать** *v.* drive (in), knock in, hammer in, ram; stop up, plug up, choke, clog, block, obstruct; impound; stuff, fill in, pack; (blasting) stem; (rad.) jam; flood, glut (the market); (sports) score; overcome, subdue; (vet.) cut (hooves); slaughter, butcher, kill; **—аться** *v.* get stopped up, clog up; drive (into), get into, penetrate (of dust, etc.); hide, huddle (in a corner).

забив/ка *see* **забивание;** piling; stemming; **—ной** *a.* driving; driven; pile; **—ная крепь** (min.) prop; **—очный** *a.* driving.

забинтов(ыв)ать *v.* bandage (up).

забир/аемый *a.* input; **—ание** *n.* taking (away); **—ать** *v.* take (away); pick up; arrest; board, wall up; **—аться** *v.* get in, steal in, penetrate; climb; go away.

забир/ка *f.* (min.) prop wall, bracing, fencing; **—ное отверстие** intake.

забит/ость *f.* clogged state; **—ый** *a.* driven (in), etc., *see* **забивать;** buried, obscured (signal); (electron.) swamped; **—ь** *see* **забивать;** gush forth; begin to strike; **—ься** *v.* start beating (of heart); go (into convulsions).

заблаговременн/о *adv.* in advance, early; **—ость** *f.* term (of forecast); **—ый** *a.* done on time, early; advance (warning).

заблагорассудиться *v.* see fit, think fit, consider it necessary; like.

забл/естеть, —истать *v.* start shining.

заблу/диться *see* **заблуждаться;** **—дший** *a.* stray; **—дящий** *a.* stray(ing), accidental; **—ждаться** *v.* get lost, go astray, stray; be mistaken, err; **—ждение** *n.* fallacy, error, mistake; straying.

забодать *v.* gore.

забоечный *a. of* **забойка.**

забоина *f.* nick, dent.

забой *m.* driving in; (min.) face, stope; (drilling) bottom hole, bottom (of bore hole); (comp.) erasure; slaughter, butchering, killing; **короткий з., подготовительный з.** (min.) shortwall; **—ка** *f.* tamping (blasting) stemming; **—ник** *m.* rammer, tamper; **—ный** *a. of* **забой;** **—щик** *m.* miner, cutter, faceman; slaughterer, butcher.

заболачив/ание *n.* swamping, etc., *see v.;* bog formation; **—ать** *v.* swamp, bog up; **—аться** *v.* become boggy or marshy; get waterlogged.

заболев/аемость *f.* morbidity; sick rate, incidence of

cases; **—ание** *n.* illness, sickness, disorder, disease; falling ill; **—ать, заболеть** *v.* fall ill, get sick; start aching.

заболон/ники *pl.* bark beetles (*Scolytidae*); **—ный** *a.*, **—ь** *f.* (bot.) alburnum, sapwood.

заболо/тить *see* **заболачивать; —ченность** *f.* swampiness, bogginess; **—ченный** *a.* slack; swamped, bogged up; swampy, marshy, paludal; waterlogged (soil); stagnant (water); **—ченная местность** marshland.

заболтать *v.* mix or stir in or up.

забор *m.* fence, partition, enclosure; (air) intake; (hydr.) diversion; (sample) taking; **обнести —ом** *v.* fence in.

заборанивать *v.* harrow (in; over).

забор/ка *f.* boarding; partition; (typ.) correct linotype slug; **—ник** *m.* intake, scoop; sampler; **—ный** *a.* of забор; **—ный конус** (roll-threading) lip; **—ное отверстие** intake.

заборон/ить, —овать *v.* harrow (in, over).

забортный *a.* outboard (motor); outside, overboard.

забортовка *f.* beading.

забот/а *f.* care, trouble; attendance, attention; responsibility; **з. о потомстве** brood care; **—иться** *v.* take care (of), look after, be responsible (for); be concerned about, worry; **—ливо** *adv.* carefully; **—ливость** *f.* care(fulness); **—ливый** *a.* thoughtful, solicitous.

забраживать *v.* start fermentation.

забраков/ание *n.,* **—ка** *f.* rejection, refusal; **—анный** *a.* rejected, etc., *see v.;* faulty; **(ыв)ать** *v.* reject, refuse, condemn, scrap.

забрал/о *n.* visor (of helmet); (hydr.) boom; **—ьная стенка** boom.

забранный *a.* taken (away); picked up.

забрасыв/ание *n.* throwing, etc., *see v.;* abandonment; backing up; neglect; **з. маслом** fouling (of spark plugs); **з. ног** (vet.) capping; **—атель** *m.* spreader; **—ать** *v.* throw, (be)spatter, shower, pelt (with), bombard; spread, cover (with); abandon, give up; neglect; mislay; fill (up with), add; cast, hurl, fling; stoke, fire (furnace); launch (satellite); (vet.) cap.

забрать *see* **забирать.**

забредать *v.* wander in, stray in.

забредить *v.* become delirious.

забрезжить *v.* start to grow.

забрести *v.* go astray, stray (in).

заброд *m.* onset of fermentation; **—ить** *v.* start fermenting; start wandering; spatter.

забронировать *v.* reserve, book; armor.

забро/с *see* **забрасывание;** overshoot; **з. оборотов** overspeed(ing); **з. руля** oversteering; hardover; **—санный** *see* **заброшенный; —сать, —сить** *see* **забрасывать; —шенность** *f.* neglected state; **—шенный** *a.* thrown; abandoned, etc., *see* **забрасывать;** lonely, forlorn.

забру/с *m.* (apid.) comb cappings; (ent.) Zabrus; **—шенный** *a.* sealed, capped (honeycomb); **—шивать** *v.* seal, cap.

забрызг/анный *a.* splashed, spattered; **—ивание** *n.* splashing, spattering; **—(ив)ать** *v.* splash, spatter.

забрюшинный *a.* (anat.) retroperitoneal.

забугорная область (anat.) metathalamus.

забудь(те) *imp. of* **забыть.**

забуксировать *v.* fasten with a cable.

забуксовать *v.* start skidding.

забулькать *v.* start bubbling.

забуреть *v.* turn brown.

забур/ивание *n.* predrilling; **—и(ва)ть** *v.* (pre)drill, bore; start drilling; spud (in); collar (a hole); **—ка** *f.* starting to drill, spudding in; **—ник** *m.* drill, bore(r).

забурьяненный *a.* weedy, full of weeds.

забут *m.* packing; **—ить** *v.* fill in, pack; fill (with rubble); larry up; back(fill), bank up; **(ов)ка** *f.* filling in, etc., *see v.;* rubble(work), rubble fill(ing); packing material; **—овщик** *m.* packer.

забуференный *a.* buffer(ed).

забух/ать *v.* start swelling; **—ать, —нуть** *v.* swell (up; shut).

забучив/ание *n.* (min.) piping; **—ать** *see* **забутить.**

забы/ваемый *a.* forgotten, omitted; **—вание** *n.* forgetting, omission; **—вать** *v.* forget, omit, leave out, neglect; **—ваться** *v.* be lost in thought, drift off; doze off, drop off; be forgotten; **—вчивость** *f.* forgetfulness; **—вчивый** *a.* forgetful, absentminded, careless; **—тие** *n.* (med.) syncope; **—тый** *a.* forgotten; **—ть** *see* **забывать; —тьё** *see* **забытие.**

забьёт *fut. 3 sing. of* **забить.**

зав *m.* manager, director, chief.

завал *m.* fall, avalanche; (geol.) slide rock, scree; (min.) collapse; barrier, obstruction; reverse camber (of wheel); steep slope (of curve); droop, sag, tilt(ing); demolishing, breaking down (of a stack); (min.) debris, rubble, goaf, gob; (mil.) slashing; (med.) obstruction, constipation; (naut.) tumblehome; **—енный** *a.* heaped up, etc., *see v.;* **—ивание** *n.* heaping up, etc., *see v.;* **—ивать** *v.* heap up; load, charge, fill, prime; cover up; bury; overload (with); clog, choke, block up; **—иваться** *v.* be covered up; be mislaid; fall, slip (behind, down); collapse, fall through; fail (exam); **—ин(к)а** *f.* bank; **—ить** *see* **заваливать; —ка** *see* **заваливание;** (furnace) charge; **рабочая —ка** charge, batch; **—очный** *a.* charging.

завалуненн/ость *f.* stoniness; **—ый** *a.* stony (ground).

заваль *f.* old merchandise.

завальцовывать *v.* roll in; expand, flare out.

завальщик *m.* (furnace) charger.

завал/яться *v.* lie around, become shopworn; **—ящий** *a.* long unused; shopworn.

завар/енный *a.* welded (up), etc., *see v.;* **—ивание** *n.* welding (up), etc., *see v.;* **—и(ва)ть** *v.* weld (up), seal (up), close; scald, scour; infuse, brew; steep in boiling water; **—ка** *see* **заваривание;** seal; **—ной** *a.* scalded; **—очный** *a.* welding; (for) scalding.

завдел *m.* chief clerk, office supervisor.

завевать *v.* drift.

завед/ение *n.* establishment, institution; institute, school, college; plant, works; setting up; custom, habit, usage; **—ёт** *fut. 3 sing. of* **завести.**

заведов/ание *n.* management; **—ать** *v.* manage, superintend, direct, head.

заведом/о *adv.* known to be, knowingly, a fortiori; obviously, absolutely, certainly; it is well known; **з. зная** knowing beforehand, having previous knowledge; **—ый** *a.* well known, notorious; obvious.

завед/ующий *m.* manager, director, chief, head, superintendent; *a.* managing, directing; **—ший** *past act. part. of* **завести; —ывание** *n.* management, superintendence; **—ывать** *see* **заведовать.**

завезённый *a.* imported; ecdemic, advectitious.

завёл *past m. sing. of* **завести.**

завербов(ыв)ать *v.* recruit.

завер/ение *n.* assurance; assertion; **—ить** *see* **заверять; —ка** *f.* certification.

завёрнутый *a.* wrapped, etc., *see* **завёртывать;** involute, rolled inward; revolute; convolute.

завер/нуть *see* **завёртывать;** **—теть** *v.* start rotating.

завёрт/ка *f.* wrapping (up); wrapper; package; screw driver; catch, latch, bolt, fastener; **—очный** *a.* wrapping; turning.

завёртыв/ание *n.* wrapping (up), etc., *see v.;* involution; envelopment; **—ать** *v.* wrap (up), envelop, cover; roll in, roll up; turn (aside, up); screw up, tighten; turn off (faucet); drop in, stop (at); (naut.) belay, make fast; **—ающий** *a.* wrapping, etc., *see v.*

заверть *f.* whirlpool.

заверш/ать *v.* complete, consummate, crown (with), top off; execute, carry out, accomplish, realize; conclude, finish; **—аться** *v.* be completed, culminate (in); **—ающий** *a.* concluding, closing, final; **—ение** *n.* completion, etc., *see v.;* end; **код —ения** (comp.) completion code; **—ённость** *f.* completeness; **—ённый** *a.* completed, etc., *see v.;* complete, final; **—ить** *see* **завершать.**

заверя/ть *v.* assure; witness, certify, authenticate, confirm, attest.

завес/а *f.,* **—очный** *a.* curtain, screen; **—ить** *see* **завешивать;** **—ка** *f.* rack; (fishing) trap net.

завести *see* **заводить.**

завет *m.* will, legacy; precept, behest; **—ный** *a.* cherished, guarded; secret.

заветр/еный *a.* wind-blown, wind-dried; **—енный** *a.* protected from wind; **—еть** *v.* (foods) spoil, harden; **—ие** *n.* wind-protected area.

завешив/ание *n.* curtaining, screening; **—ать** *v.* curtain, screen, veil, cover.

завещ/ание *n.* will, testament; **—ать** *v.* will, leave, bequeath.

завеять *v.* drift.

завзятый *a.* inveterate; confirmed.

завив/ание *n.* twisting, etc., *see v.;* coiling action, convolution; **—ать** *v.* twist, curl, coil, wind; wave (hair); **—ающийся** a. twisting, etc., *see v.;* spiral; **—ка** *see* **завивание;** heading (of cabbage).

завид/еть *v.* catch sight (of); **—неться** *v.* come into sight, become visible; grow light (at dawn).

завид/ный *a.* enviable; **—овать** *v.* envy.

завизжать *v.* start squealing.

завилец *m.* peanut (*Arachis hypogaea*).

завилять *v.* start wagging; start dodging.

завин/тить, —чивать *v.* screw (in, on, up, down), tighten; put in, drive (screw); **—ченный** *a.* screwed, etc., *see v.;* **—чивание** *n.* screwing, etc., *see v.*

завиру/ха *f.* storm; **—ха, —шка** *f.* (orn.) accentor (*Prunella*); whitethroat (*Sylvia*); **—шковые** *pl.* Prunellidae.

завис/ание *n.* (av.) hovering, etc., *see v.;* **—ать** *v.* hover, hang over; get caught, stick, hang on; bridge over (of stock).

зависеть *v.* depend, be dependent (on), be governed (by); lie (with), turn (on); be related (to); be a function (of); **з. от . . . в отношении** depend on . . . for; **не з. от** be independent of.

зависимост/ь *f.* dependence, dependency, relation(ship); (math.) function; characteristic (curve); (integral) transformation; **з. масса-температура** mass-temperature relationship; **з. от температуры** temperature dependence; **з. от частоты** frequency response; **в —и от** depending on, in relation to, as a function of; according to, with; versus, against; **быть в —и от** *v.* depend on; **взаимная з.** interrelation(ship); **изменяться в —и от** *v.* vary with; **изображать з. от, наносить в —и от, откладывать в —и от, построить з.** *v.* plot

against (in graph); **кривая —и давления от температуры** temperature-pressure curve.

зависимый *a.* dependent, related, linked.

зависть *f.* envy.

зависящ/ий *a.* depending, dependent; subsidiary; **з. от времени** time-dependent; **з. от массы** mass-sensitive; **все —ие меры** all possible precautions.

завит/ки *pl. of* **завиток;** vortices; **—ковый** *a.* helicine, spiral; **—ой** *a.* spiral; (bot.) cincinnal, curled; involute; turbinal, turbinate (bone); **—ый** *a.* twisted, etc., *see* **завивать;** **—ок** *m.* curl, coil, spiral, scroll, volute; loop (of curve); (wood) knot; (anat.) helix; **—ь** *see* **завивать.**

завихр/ение *n.* turbulence, swirling, whirl(pool), eddy(ing), vortex, vorticity; convolution; (av.) backwash; (paper) spouting; **камера —ения** whirl chamber; **—ённость** *f.* vorticity; turbulence; **—енный** *a.* whirling; **—итель** *m.* swirler, swirl vane, vortex generator; **конический —итель** swirl cone; **—ить** *v.* swirl, whirl (up); **—яющий(ся)** *a.* swirling, turbulent.

зав/кант, —кон(т) *m.* office manager; **—ком** *m.* plant or factory committee.

завладе(ва)ть *v.* take over, seize; encroach (upon); engage, grip (attention).

завле/кательный *a.* enticing, attractive; **—кать, —чь** *v.* entice, lure.

завмаг *m.* store manager.

завод *m.* plant, works, factory, mill; facility, establishment; station, center; (repair) shop; (food) cannery; (ship) yard; (fish) hatchery; custom; (mech.) starter; winding mechanism; winding (up); (publishing) impression; **автоматический з.** self-starter; **своего —а** domestic; **з.-автомат** *m.* automatic plant; **з.-втуз** *m.* plant-affiliated school.

заводи *gen., pl., etc., of* **заводь;** **—(те)** *imp. of* **заводить.**

завод-изготовитель *m.* manufacturer.

завод/ить *v.* wind(up), crank, start (motor); acquire, buy; found, set up, introduce, establish; bring, take, lead (in); start (a business); put into operation; (cryst.) seed; get into the habit; **—иться** *v.* appear; be established; start up; **—ка** *f.* winding up, etc., *see v.;* (elec.) switching on; **—ка кристаллов** *see under* **завязка;** **автоматическая —ка** self-starter.

заводн/ение *n.* flooding; **—ённый** *a.* flooded; **—ить** *v.* flood.

заводн/ой *a.* winding, cranking, starting; wind-up, mechanical; **—ая ручка** crank.

заводнять *v.* flood.

завод/оуправление *n.* works or plant management; **—поставщик** *m.* supplier; **—производитель** *m.* manufacturer; producer; **—ский, —ской** *a. of* **завод;** factory-furnished; breeding, stud (farm); commercial (crop); serial (number); **—ский паспорт, —ская марка, —ская таблица** nameplate, trademark; **—ская книга** herd improvement registry; **плита —ского изготовления** (concrete) plant-precast slab.

завод/-смежник *m.* subcontractor; **—чик** *m.* manufacturer, factory owner; **—ы-смежники** *pl.* correlated plants.

заводь *f.* backwater, pool, cut-off.

завоев/ание *n.* conquest; achievement; **—атель** *m.* conqueror; **—(ыв)ать** *v.* conquer; earn, win, gain (recognition).

завоз *m.* **—ка** *f.* delivery; **—ить** *v.* bring in, deliver, drop off; take far away; **—ный** *a.* delivered, brought in.

заволакив/ание *n.* clouding up, etc., *see v.;* **—ать** *v.* cloud up, cover; (med.) heal up, close; (naut.) sludge.

заволжский *a.* (geog.) Trans-Volga.

заволноваться *v.* get excited, become agitated; get rough; start worrying.

заволочь *see* **заволакивать.**

заворачива/ние *n.* (comp.) wraparound; **—ть** *v.* turn up, roll up; wrap (up; with); (med.) entropionize, invert; manage, administer, run.

заворонить *v.* (met.) blue.

завор/от *m.* turn(ing); sharp bend; entropion, inversion (of eyelid); scraper beading tool; (met.) teeming lap; **з. кишок** (med.) ileus; volvulus; **з. корки** (casting) rippled surface; **—отить** *see* **заворачивать; —оченный** *a.* turned (up), etc., *see* **заворачивать;** reflex(ed); circumflex; inverted.

заворошить *v.* start stirring or turning.

заворчать *v.* start grumbling or growling.

завпрод *m.* food supply manager.

завтра *adv.* tomorrow.

завтрак *m.,* **—ать** *v.* breakfast.

завтрашний *a.* tomorrow's.

завуалировать *v.* veil, mist over; disguise.

зав/уч *m.* director of studies; **—хим** *m.* chemical section chief; **—хоз** *m.* (business) manager.

завшиветь *v.* become infested with lice.

завыв/ание *n.,* **—ать** *v.* howl.

завысить *see* **завышать.**

завыть *v.* start howling.

завыш/ать *v.* overstate, overestimate; set too high, raise too high; increase; (educ.) grade too high; **—ение** *n.* overstating, etc., *see v.;* **—енный** *a.* overstated, etc., *see v.;* too high, excessive.

завьёт *fut. 3 sing. of* **завить.**

завьюжить *v.* start (of blizzard).

завьючи(ва)ть *v.* pack.

завяд/ание *n.* wilting, etc., *see v.;***—ать** *v.* wilt, wither, droop, get flabby; **—ший** *a.* (e)marcid, flaccid, withered.

завяз/анный *a.* tied, bound; **—ать** *see* **завязнуть, завязывать; —ить** *v.* get stuck (in); **—ка** *f.* tie, string; bond; tying; **—ка кристаллов** crystallization; (sugar) granulation; **—ной** *a.* tying; **—нуть** *v.* stick, sink in; enter (of splinter); **—ываемость** *f.* (bot.) setting rate; **—ывание** *n.* tying, etc., *see v.;* **—ывать** *v.* tie, bind, knot; enter (into relations with); start; set (fruit); **—ываться** *v.* be tied up; begin, start; set.

завязь *f.* (bot.) ovary.

завяли(ва)ть *v.* dry(-cure).

завя/лый *a.* faded, withered, wilted; **—нуть** *v.* fade, wither, wilt, droop.

загадать *see* **загадывать.**

загадить *see* **загаживать.**

загад/ка *f.* riddle, enigma, puzzle; **—очный** *a.* enigmatic, puzzling; **—ывание** *n.* thinking (of), etc., *see v.;* **—ывать** *v.* think (of), conceive; plan, make (plans); ask (riddles); guess; conjecture; set, offer; **—ывать вперёд** try to predict events.

загаживать *v.* pollute, contaminate.

загазованн/ость *f.* gas content, gas levels; (degree of) pollution by gases; **—ый** *a.* polluted by gas.

загар *m.* sunburn, tan; tarnish; (desert) varnish.

загас/ать, —нуть *v.* go out, die out; **—ить** *v.* extinguish, put out; switch off.

зага/тить, —чивать *v.* make a corduroy road.

загашивать *see* **загасить.**

загвоздка *f.* difficulty, snag.

загиб *m.* bend, fold, crease, bead, flange, edge (of rim); (electron.) reverse breakdown; deviation (in behavior); **—ание** *n.* bending, etc., *see v.;* flexion; recurvature;

—ать *v.* bend, fold, crease; bead, flange; turn (in, back, down); **—аться** *v.* bend, fold, curl; **—ка** *see* **загибание; —ной** *a.* folding, folded; **—очный** *a.* bending, creasing; flanging; **—щик** *m.* deviator.

загипнотизировать *v.* hypnotize.

загипсов/ание *n.* plastering; **—анный** *a.* plastered; **—ать** *v.* plaster.

заглав/ие *n.* title, designation; heading; **—ный** *a.* title (page); capital (letters).

загла/дить, —живать *v.* smooth out, work smooth; iron out; make amends; **—живание** *n.* smoothing out, etc., *see v.*

заглазн/(ич)ная *f.* postorbital (bone); **—(ич)ный** *a.* (anat.) postorbital; **—о** *adv.* without seeing; in the absence (of); **—ый** *see* **заочный.**

заглатыв/ание *n.* swallowing, deglutition; **—ать** *v.* swallow, bolt down, gulp.

заглинизиров/ание *n.* mudding off, etc., *see v.;* **—анность** *f.* muddiness; **—анный** *a.* mudded off, etc., *see v.;* **—ать** *v.* mud off, mud up, silt up.

заглот *m.* swallowing; **—ать, —нуть** *see* **заглатывать; —очный** *a.* (anat.) retropharyngeal.

заглох/ание *n.* choking up, etc., *see v.;* flameout (of engine); **—нуть** *v.* choke up, be choked, smother; die out (of engine); die away, fade away, abate, subside; overgrow (with), grow wild, go to seed; **—ший** *a.* choked up, etc., *see v.;* overgrown, neglected (garden).

заглуб/ить *see* **заглублять; —ление** *n.* deepening, etc., *see v.;* depth, entry (of plow); penetration; **—лённый** *a.* deepened, etc., *see v.;* **—ляемость** *f.* cutting power (of plow); **—лять** *v.* deepen; bury, lower, place deeper, work deeper (into), cut (in).

заглухание *see* **заглохание.**

заглуш/ать *v.* suppress, smother, stifle, choke; muffle, deaden (sound); drown (noise); jam, black out; damp, bank (fire); cap, plug, blank off; soothe, alleviate (pain); opacify (glass, etc.); (hort.) overgrow; **—ающий** *a.,* **—ение** *n.* suppressing, etc., *see v.;* **—ённый** *a.* suppressed, etc., *see v.;* anechoic (chamber); **—ить** *see* **заглушать; —ка** *f.* seal, cover, closure, screw cap, end cap, plug, stopper; blank flange; (blank) panel; dead end; silencer, silencing device; (elec.) shorting plug; **—ье** *n.* thicket.

загля/дывание *n.* looking in, etc., *see v.;* **з. вперёд** (comp.) look ahead; **—дывать, —нуть** *v.* look in, peek in; glance; drop in.

загнаиваться *v.* fester.

загн/анный *a.* driven in; **—ать** *see* **загонять.**

загнёт *fut. 3 sing. of* **загнуть.**

загнив/аемость *f.* putrescibility; **—ание** *n.* rotting, etc., *see v.;* decay, putrefaction; (med.) suppuration; (phyt.) rot; **—атель** *m.* septic tank; **—ать** *v.* rot, decay, putrefy; (med.) suppurate, fester; stagnate (of water); **—ший** *a.* decayed; festered; stagnant.

загн/ить *see* **загнивать; —оённый** *a.* rotted, etc., *see* **загнивать; —оиться** *v.* fester.

загнут/ый *a.* bent, folded; recurved; **—ь** *see* **загибать.**

загов/аривать, —орить *v.* (begin to) speak, address; **—ор** *m.* plot, conspiracy; **—ориться** *v.* lose track of time while talking.

загодя *adv.* in good time, ahead of time.

заголить *v.* strip, undress, bare.

заголов/ник *m.* headrest; **—ок** *m.,* **—очный** *a.* title, head(ing), header, headline; **—очная строка** headline.

заголубеть *v.* turn blue, show blue.

заголять *see* **заголить.**

загон *m.* enclosure, pen, corral, paddock; driving in; section, strip (of land); **—ка** *f.* driving in; (plowed) strip;

(text.) scribbler; **—ный** *a. of* **загон; —ный выпас, —ная пасьтба, —ная система** rotational grazing; **—щик** *m.* drover, herdsman, beater; **—ять** *v.* drive (in); corral, pen, stable; exhaust, fatigue; dispose (of); (sports) score a goal.

загоражив/ание *n.* enclosing, etc., *see v.;* enclosure; **—ать** *v.* enclose, fence in, shut in; obstruct, block (up), bar; close, stop, shut off, cut off, screen off; **—аться** *v.* shield oneself, screen oneself.

загор/ание *n.* ignition, firing; sunburn; **—ать** *v.* get tanned; tarnish; **—аться, —еться** *v.* ignite, catch fire; fire, strike (of electric arc); break out; get tanned; **—ающийся** *a.* inflammable; ignition (mixture); **—евший, —елый** *a.* tan, sunburnt.

загорный *a.* (geol.) ultramontane.

загород/ить *see* **загораживать; —(к)а** *f.* partition, fence, enclosure.

загородный *a.* suburban; rural, country.

загороженный *a.* enclosed, fenced (in).

загорт/ать *v.* cover; **—ач** *m.* covering device.

заготавлив/ание *n.* storing, etc., *see v.;* **—ать** *v.* store, stock (up), lay up, lay in; prepare, provide; put up, preserve.

заготзерно *n.* grain procurement center.

заготов/итель *m.* purchasing agent; **—ительный** *a.* storage, storing; preparing; supply, purchasing; fixed (price); (met.) billet (mill); **—ить** *see* **заготавливать; —ка** *f.* store, stock; preparation, provision; procurement; purchase; intermediate product, half-finished article; feed; (met.) blank, billet, bar; skelp (for pipes); (wood) felling; (ice) harvesting; **плоская —ка** (met.) slab; **полосовая —ка** skelp; **трубная —ка** round billet; **—ление** *see* **заготавливание; —ленный** *a.* stored etc., *see* **заготавливать;** ready; fabricated (parts); **—лять** *see* **заготавливать; —очный** *a. of* **заготовка; —щик** *m.* supplier, provider; maker.

загот/пункт *m.* storage place, warehouse; **—скот** *m.* livestock purchasing center; **—стандарты** *pl.* quality standards (in purchase).

загра/дитель *m.* barrier; suppressor; (electron.) trap, rejector; (mine) layer; **—дительный** *a.* obstructing, etc., *see v.;* barrier; boundary; barrage (rocket); **—дить, —ждать** *v.* obstruct, block, stop, bar; dam, retain, restrain; lay mines; (electron.) reject, trap; shut in, enclose.

загражд/ающий *see* **заградительный; з. полосный** *a.* band-elimination (filter); **з. фильтр** trap, filter, blocking circuit; **—ение** *n.* obstructing, etc., *see* **заграждать;** barrier, obstacle; (road) block; barrage, rejection; enclosure; (harbor) boom; weir, counting fence; lead (of trap net); **—ённый** *a.* obstructed, etc., *see* **заграждать.**

загран/ица *f.* foreign countries; **—ицей** *adv.* abroad; **—ичный** *a.* foreign(-made).

загреб/ать *v.* rake (up), gather; bank (fire); **—ающий** *a.* raking, etc., *see v.*

загреметь *v.* crash (down); start thundering.

загрести *see* **загребать.**

загрив/ковый *a.* (anat.) nuchal; **—ок** *m.* nape (of neck); withers (of horse).

загримировать *v.* (apply) make-up.

загромо/ждать *v.* encumber, block up, obstruct, jam, clog; overload; **—ждение** *n.* encumbering, etc., *see v.;* **—ждённый** *a.* encumbered, etc., *see v.;* **—здить** *see* **загромождать.**

загрохотать *v.* start rattling or rumbling.

загруб/елость *f.* roughness; **—елый** *a.* roughened, coarsened, callous; **—ение** *n.* coarsening; (med.) cal-

losity; **—еть** *v.* coarsen, roughen; become rough, chap (of skin); **—ление** *n.* coarsening, etc., *see v.;* **—ленный** *a.* coarsened, etc., *see v.;* **—лять** *v.* coarsen; ruggedize, desensitize, make less sensitive, lower the precision (of).

загрудинный *a.* (anat.) retrosternal; substernal (goiter, etc.).

загру/жаемый *a.* (comp.) downloadable; **—жать** *v.* charge, load, fill, feed; (comp.) boot; download; stoke, fire; prime; encumber; **—жённость** *f.* capacity, load, charge; utilization; **—жённый** *a.* charged, etc., *see v.;* **—зить** *see* **загружать; —зка** *f.* charging, etc., *see v.;* charge, load; (comp.) booting; feed; batch (size); (mach.) utilization; job, work; **начальная —зка, первичная —зка** boot.

загрузнуть *v.* sink (into).

загрузо-разгрузочный *a.* handling.

загрузочн/ый *a.* charging, loading, loader, feeding; feed, charge (chute); (comp.) boot; **з. люк** hopper; **з. механизм** charger; **з. ящик, —ая воронка** hopper.

загрузчик *m.* charger; loader; stoker.

загрунтов/анный *a.* sized, primed; **—ать, —ывать** *v.* size, prime; **—ка** *f.* sizing, priming, ground coat (of paint).

загрустить *v.* grow sad, become depressed.

загрыз(а)ть *v.* worry, gnaw (to death); kill.

загрязн/ение *n.* impurity, contaminant; contamination, etc., *see* **загрязнять;** (air) pollutant; smog; **—ённость** *f.* pollution (density); **—ённый** *a.* contaminated, etc., *see* **загрязнять;** impure; **—итель** *m.,* **—яющее вещество** contaminant, pollutant; **—ить** *see* **загрязнять.**

загрязнуть *v.* get stuck, sink (in).

загрязн/яемость *f.* dirt retention, soilability; **—ять** *v.* contaminate, foul, pollute, render impure; dirty, soil; clog (up); poison (cathode); **—яться** *v.* get contaminated; get dirty; clog up; **—яющий** *a.* contaminating, etc., *see v.;* **—яющее вещество** contaminant, pollutant.

загс *m.* registry office.

загуб/ить *v.* ruin, waste, destroy; **—ленный** *a.* ruined, etc., *see v.*

загубник *m.* mouthpiece.

загудеть *v.* start buzzing, droning, humming, hooting or blowing.

загудронировать *v.* pave, tar (road).

загу/стевание *see* **загустка; —стевать** *see* **загустеть;** get sluggish; (paints) liver; **—стелый** *a.* thickened, etc., *see v.;* **—стение** *see* **загустка; —стеть** *v.* thicken, get thick, condense, become concentrated; solidify, stiffen; condense; solidify, stiffen; **—ститель** *m.* thickening agent, thickener; stiffener; **—стить** *v.* thicken, condense; stiffen; **—стка** *f.* thickening, etc., *see v.;* **—щать** *see* **загустить; —щение** *n.* thickening; getting dense; **—щённо—** *prefix* thick-, closely, densely; **—щённость** *f.* density, crowded condition; **—щённый** *a.* thickened, etc., *see v.;* close, thick(set), dense, crowded.

зад *m.* back, rear, tail; (anat.) buttock(s), rump; *pl.* clunes, nates.

задабривать *v.* cajole, coax; placate.

задав/аемый *a.* assigned, etc., *see v.;* given; **—альщик** *m.* feeder, feeding operator; **—ание** *n.* assigning, etc., *see v.;* assignment, task; target; quota; **—ать** *v.* assign, give, designate, prescribe, specify; predetermine, (pre)set, fix, define; put, pose, ask (question); allot (time); feed, (give) fodder; **—аться** *v.* be given, be described; make up one's mind; succeed, turn out well;

put on airs; **—аясь** *pr. ger.* (being) given, if we are given.

задав/ить, —ливать *v.* crush; throttle; restrain; **—ка** *f.,* **—ливание** *n.* crushing, etc., *see v.;* **—ленный** *a.* crushed.

задалбливать *v.* start hollowing out.

задалживание *n.* downtime.

задан/ие *n.* task, assignment, job; program; quota, goal, target; (math.) specification, representation; **по —ию** on the instructions (of); **техническое з. на проект** request for proposal; **—ный** *a.* assigned, etc., *see* **задавать;** given, (pre)set; desired (value); **наперёд —ный, при —ном** given.

задаром *adv.* free, gratis; in vain.

задат/ки *pl.* disposition, inclination, instincts; (inherited) properties, abilities; **—ок** *m.,* **—очный** *a.* deposit, advance (payment); **—очный корешок** radicle.

задат/чик *m.* controller, control-point adjustment, setter, set-point adjustment; reference input element; (av.) selector; **—ь** *see* **задавать.**

задач/а *f.* problem; task, job, undertaking; goal; crux, point, question; addition, feed(ing); **(сложная) з.** challenge; **—ник** *m.* problem book.

задающ/ий *a.* assigning, etc., *see* **задавать;** driving, master (frequency, oscillator, etc.); reference (axis, input); setting, set-point adjusting; **з. скорость** rate-determining; **—ее устройство** *see* **задатчик.**

задви/гание *n.* starting; **—гать** *v.* push (in), bolt, bar, shut, close; start (moving); **—гаться** *v.* start (moving), stir; shut, slide to; **—гающийся** *a.* starting; sliding; **—жка** *f.* bolt, bar, catch, fastener; gate (valve), slide (valve), shutoff; (chimney) register, damper; (anat.) obex; (hive entrance) reducer, block; **—жной** *a.* sliding; movable; **—нутый** *a.* pushed (in), etc., *see v.;* **—нуть** *see* **задвигать.**

задвоиться *v.* begin to see double.

задвор/ки *pl.,* **—ок** *m.* backyard.

задев/ание *n.* catching, etc., *see v.;* interference; **—ать** *v.* catch, graze, brush against, touch, affect; mislay; interfere; provoke, irritate; (med.) exhaust, fatigue; **не —ать** clear; **—аться** *v.* get mislaid, be missing.

задействованный *a.* equipped, fitted.

задел *m.* stock(pile), store, reserve, backlog; surplus, abundance; started project; *past m. sing. of* **задеть.**

задел/анный *a.* fixed, etc., *see v.;* built-in; **—ать** *see* **заделывать; —ка** *f.,* **—очный** *a.,* **—ывание** *n.* fixing, etc., *see v.;* (end) connection; (micros.) mount(ing); restraint, attachment; binder; fixation; termination; **—очная среда** mountant, mounting medium; **—ывать** *v.* fix, embed, build in; cover up, bury, rake in (seeds); put in, place, apply (fertilizer); stop (up), block (up), close up; fill up, plug, caulk; seal (off); fasten; (micros.) mount; (min.) frame; **—ывающий** *a.* fixing, etc., *see v.;* **—ывающая среда** mountant.

задельный *a.* task, job, piece-work.

задемпфировать *v.* damp.

заденет *fut. 3 sing. of* **задеть.**

задёрг/ать *v.* start jerking or pulling; worry; wear out; **—аться** *v.* start quivering, squirming or twitching; **—ивать** *v.* pull, draw, jerk; cover; shut; zip up.

задеревен/елый *a.* hardened stiff; numb(ed); **—еть** *v.* harden, stiffen; lignify, become woody; grow numb, grow stiff.

задерж/ание *see* **задерживание; —анный** *a.* inhibited, etc., *see v.;* arrested (development); **—анная упругость** (phys.) elastic lag; **—ать** *see* **задерживать; —ивание** *n.* inhibition, etc., *see v.;* delay; (med.) retention; **—ивать** *v.* inhibit, retard, delay, hold back,

restrain, detain, impede, moderate; stop, check, arrest; block, suppress; keep (back); sequestrate, separate; hold (one's breath); retain, hold over, entrap; **—иваться** *v.* lag; remain, be retained.

задерж/ивающий *a.* inhibiting, etc., *see* **задерживать;** inhibitory (action); delay(ing); stop; check (valve); retentive; lock (mechanism); coercive (force); depressor (nerve); **з. агент, з. препарат, з. фактор** inhibitor; **—ивающая способность** retentivity; **—ка** *f.* delay, lag, setback; check, stop, catch; impediment; entrapment, retention; inhibition, suppression; (electrochem.) arrest; *see also* **задерживание; период —ки** lag; **—ник** *m.* arrestor; **—ник затвора** tripping device.

задерн/елость *f.* turf covering; grass invasion; **—елый** *a.* planted with grass, grass-covered, soddy; matted; weedy; **—елая вырубка** glade; **—ение** *n.* turf cover(ing), turfing, sodding, sod formation; weed infestation; **—ённость** *f.* turf cover (over soil); **—ённый** *a.* turf-covered; (bot.) c(a)espitose; **—ованность** *see* **задернелость; —ованный** *see* **задернённый; —овать** *v.* cover with sod.

задернуть *see* **задёргивать.**

задет/ый *a.* caught, grazed, etc., *see* **задевать; —ь** *see* **задевать.**

задешево, задёшево *adv.* cheaply, at a low price.

задиафрагмировать *v.* (opt.) stop down.

задир *m.* fin, rib; galling; score, scoring, scratch; tear, scuffing; **—ание** *n.* lifting up, etc., *see v.;* (av.) tail heaviness; **—ать** *v.* lift up, pull up, begin to tear; scuff, break, split; scratch, score; fret, gall, chafe; tear up; (av.) pitch (nose) up; tease, provoke; **—аться** *v.* rise, turn up; abrade, graze (skin); seize (of bearings); look for trouble; **—ка** provocation; (min.) chipping; **—ковый** *a.* chip, random (sampling).

задичать *v.* grow wild.

задне— *prefix* post(ero)—, posterior; rear, tail; meta— (behind); opisth(o)— (at the back, backward); **—боковой** *a.* posterolateral; **—бороздчатые** *pl.* (herp.) Opisthoglypha; **—брюшие** *n.* (zool.) metasoma, post-abdomen; **—височная** *f.* post-temporal (bone); **—вогнутый** *a.* (zool.) opisthocoelous; **—грудь** *f.* (ent.) metathorax; **—жаберники, —жаберные** *pl.* (mal.) Opisthobranchia.

задне/ключичная *f.* (ichth.) postclavicle, postcleithrum; **—коренной** *a.* molar (teeth); **—крыловидная** *f.* metapterygoid (bone); **—латеральный** *a.* posterolateral; **—лобный** *a.* postfrontal; **—медиальный** *a.* posteromedial; **—моторный** *a.* (ent.) with rear-wing drive; **—навесной** *a.* rear-mounted; **—подъязычная** *f.* urohyal (bone).

заднепроходн/о-копчиковый *a.* (anat.) anococcygeal; **—ый** *a.* anal; **—ое отверстие** anus.

заднеспинка *f.* (ent.) metatergum.

заднестровский *a.* (geog.) Trans-Dniester.

задне/теменная *f.* postparietal (bone); **—ушная** *f.* opisthotic (bone); **—щёчная** *pl.* (pal.) Opisthoparia; **—язычный** *a.* retrolingual (gland).

задн/ий *a.* back, rear, end, tail, posterior; post(ero)—; hind (legs, etc.); trailing (edge); concealed (thought); (naut.) stern; **з. боковой** posterolateral; **з. конец** tail, back; **з. план** background; **з. проход** (anat.) anus; **з. фронт** trailing edge, tail (of pulse); **з. ход** backing (up), reversing; return stroke (of piston); **—его хода** *a.* backing, reverse; **дать з. ход** *v.* back (up), reverse; **—яя сторона** reverse, wrong side; **—ик** *m.* (elec.) heel(piece); back, counter (of shoe).

задобрить *v.* cajole, coax; placate.

задождить *v.* start raining.

задок *dim. of* **зад.**

задолбить *v.* start gouging; learn by heart; peck to death.

задолго *adv.* long in advance, long before; **з. до** well before, long before.

задолж/алый *a.* indebted, in debt; **—ать** *v.* be in debt, incur debts; **—енность** *f.* indebtedness, debt, liabilities; **—енный** *a.* in debt, indebted; **—ность** *f.* (oxygen) debt.

задом *adv.* backwards; **з. наперёд** back to front.

задор *m.* fervor, enthusiasm; splinter; **—ина** *f.* splinter; rough spot.

задох/лик *m.* addled egg, rotten egg; **—нуться** *v.* suffocate; spoil from lack of air.

задразни(ва)ть *v.* (begin to) tease, provoke; irritate, harass.

задр/и(ва)ть *v.* seal, close, batten down; **—йка** *f.* bolt bar, fastener, catch, latch.

задранный *a.* lifted up, etc., *see* **задирать.**

задрапиров(ыв)ать *v.* drape, curtain; **—ся** *v.* wrap oneself (with).

задрать *see* **задирать.**

задребезжать *v.* (begin to) rattle or jingle.

задремать, задрёмывать *v.* doze off.

задрожать *v.* (begin to) shiver, tremble.

задросселировать *v.* throttle down.

задуб/лица *m.*, **мёртвый з.** (leather) casehardening, overtanning; **—елый** *a.* coarse, roughened; **—(ен)еть** *v.* coarsen, roughen, harden; **—ливание** *n.* pretanning, etc., *see v.;* **—ливать** *v.* pretan, set the grain; (phot.) harden.

задув/ание *see* **задувка; —ать** *v.* blow in (blast furnace); start up (furnace); start blowing; blow out, extinguish; **—ка** *f.* blowing in, etc., *see v.;* blow-out; **—очный** *a.* blowing; blow-in; starting-up; **—очный кокс** (met.) bed charge.

задум/анный *a.* planned; **—(ыв)ать** *v.* plan, conceive, intend; **—(ыв)аться** *v.* ponder; become thoughtful; hesitate.

задурманить *v.* deaden (consciousness).

задут/ый *a.* blown out, extinguished; blown in (furnace); **—ь** *see* **задувать.**

задуш/ение *n.* suffocation, etc., *see v.;* **—енный** *a.* suffocated, etc., *see v.;* **—ить** *v.* suffocate, asphyxiate, strangulate, choke, stifle; suppress; **—ливый** *a.* suffocating.

задхлый *a.* musty(-smelling).

зады *pl. of* **зад;** the past.

задым/ить *v.* start smoking; smoke up, fill with smoke; **—ление** *n.* smoking up; smoke screen; **—лённость** *f.* smoke content; **—лённый** *a.* smoked up; **—лять** *v.* screen with smoke.

зады/хание *n.* asphyxiation, smothering; (vet.) broken wind; **—хаться** *v.* suffocate; pant; **—шать** *v.* begin to breathe.

заеда *f.* (med.) lip infection, perlèche.

заед/ание *n.* jamming, etc., *see v.;* **—ать** *v.* jam, stick, bind, grip, catch, hook (into); seize (of bearings); link, foul, tangle; eat (into); **—енный** *a.* jammed, etc., *see v.*

заез/д *m.* event; dropping in; pass; **—дить** *v.* exhaust, break in (a horse); **—дка** *f.* breaking in; **—док** *m.* barrier, barricade, fence; **—жать** *v.* drop in; fetch, pick up; come, approach; get (into) drive into, hit; go too far; **—женный** *a.* worn out, hard-pressed; hackneyed, trite; **—живать** *see* **заездить; —жий** *a. and m.* stranger, newcomer.

заел *past m. sing. of* **заесть.**

заём *m.* loan; (comp.) borrow; **—ный** *a.* loan; borrowed; **—ное письмо** I.O.U.

заерш/енный *a.* jagged, barbed, ragged, notched, irregular; rag (bolt); **—ивать** *v.* jag, rag.

заесть *see* **заедать.**

заехать *see* **заезжать.**

зажаберный *a.* (zool.) postbranchial.

зажари(ва)ть *v.* fry; roast; broil; grill.

зажат/ие *see* **зажимание; —ый** *a.* clamped, etc., *see* **зажимать; —ь** *see* **зажимать;** start harvesting.

зажгучивание *n.* (text.) pilling.

зажевать *v.* start chewing.

зажелт/еть *v.* turn yellow, show yellow; **—ить** *v.* (make) yellow.

зажеребляться *v.* (zool.) get with foal.

заж/ечь *see* **зажигать; —жение** *see* **зажигание; —жённый** *a.* ignited, lit.

зажив/ание *see* **заживление; —ать** *v.* (med.) close, heal; **—ить, —лять** *v.* heal; **—ление** *n.* healing, union, adhesion; **—лённый** *a.* healed.

заживо *adv.* alive; during one's life.

зажиг/алка *f.* lighter; incendiary bomb; **—ание** *n.* ignition, igniting, etc., *see v.;* **обратное —ание** backfire; **пропуск —ания** misfire (of arc); **—атель** *m.* lighter, igniter; firing electrode; **—ательный** *a.* ignition, igniting; kindling; incendiary (bomb, etc.); firing (device); fiery (speech); **—ательный шнур** fuse; **—ательная свеча** spark plug; **—ательное вещество** incendiary; **—ать** *v.* ignite, light, set fire (to), kindle; strike (match); initiate, start; switch on (lights); **—аться** *v.* ignite, catch fire, flame up; light up.

зажим *m.* clamp, clip, fastener, grip, gripping device, clutch, chuck, lock; cleat; (elec.) terminal; (tubing) pinchcock; forceps; **—ание** *n.* clamping, etc., *see v.;* **—ать** *v.* clamp, grip, grasp, hold, fasten (down), fix, clip, catch, cramp, press, pinch, clutch; squeeze, suppress, keep down; (med.) strangulate, constrict; **—ающий** *a.* clamping, etc., *see v.;* **—ка** *f.* clamp(ing); **з.-капельник** *m.* drip cock.

зажимн/ой, —ый *a.* clamp(ing), grip(ping); lock (nut); compression (condenser); chuck (jaw); terminal (board); **з. конец** (elec.) terminal; **—ое кольцо** stand ring; **—ое приспособление** clamping device, jaw, chuck; **—ые клещи** clamps.

зажим-фиксатор *m.* fixing clamp.

зажин *m.* beginning of harvest; **—ать** *v.* start harvesting.

зажир/елый *a.* fattened; **—еть** *v.* get fat; **—ивание** *n.* (typ.) filling in.

зажит/очный *a.* prosperous, well-off; **—ь** *see* **заживать;** start living; start earning.

зажмёт *fut. 3 sing. of* **зажать,** clamp.

зажмури(ва)ть *v.* screw up (eyes); blink.

зажнёт *fut. 3 sing. of* **зажать,** harvest.

зажор *m.*, **—a** *f.* accumulation of water under snow; ice jam, ice dam.

зажужжать *v.* start buzzing.

зажухнуть *v.* get dull (of colors); harden.

зазвать *see* **зазывать.**

зазв/енеть, —онить *v.* start ringing; **—учать** *v.* start sounding; (re)sound.

заз/еваться, —ёвываться *v.* be absent-minded.

зазелен/еть *v.* turn green; **—ить** *v.* color green.

заземл/ение *n.* (elec.) ground(ing); **провод —ения** ground wire; **—ённый** *a.* ground(ed); **—итель** *m.* ground(ing electrode); **—ительный, —яющий** *a.* ground(ing); **—ить, —ять** *v.* ground.

зазим/овать *v.* winter; **—ок** *m.*, **—ье** *n.* first snow, first frost.

зазнобить *v.* freeze; start shivering.

зазолотить *v.* gild.

зазор *m.* clearance, space, gap, margin; slit, slot; give, slack, (free) play, backlash; tolerance; (roll) nip; **—ный** *a. of* **зазор;** shameful, dishonorable.

зазубник *m.* mouthpiece.

зазубр/енность *f.* cren(ul)ation; **—енный** *a.* notched, etc., *see v.;* crenulate(d); castellate(d) (nut); hackly (fracture); *suffix* —crenate; **—ивать** *v.* notch, jag, (in)dent, score, serrate; **—ина** *f.* notch, jag, indentation, (in)dent; barb, burr, beard, feather; score; serration; (biol.) crena, cleft; **—инка** *dim of* **зазубрина; —ить** *see* **зазубривать;** learn by rote; cram (for exam).

зазуммерить *v.* start buzzing.

зазывать *v.* call in.

зазябнуть *v.* freeze, get chilled.

заигр(ыв)ать *v.* start playing; start sparkling; wear out.

заизвестковать *v.* (agr.) lime.

заикаться *v.* stutter, stammer.

заил/ение, —ивание *n.* silting, etc., *see v.;* sedimentation; **—енный** *a.* silted, etc., *see v.;* **—ивать** *v.* silt (up), fill in (with mud); clog (up); (firefighting) slush, inject mud.

заилийский *a.* (geog.) Trans-Ili.

заил/ование *see* **заиление; —яющий** *a.* silting, etc., *see* **заиливать.**

заимка *f.* isolated farmstead.

заим/ообразно *adv.,* **—ообразный** *a.* (taken) on credit, as a loan; **—ствование** *n.* borrowing, etc., *see v.;* **—ствованный** *a.* borrowed, etc., *see v.;* **—ствовать** *v.* borrow, take (from), copy, adopt, derive.

заинвентаризовать *v.* inventory.

заиндев/евший, —елый *a.* covered with hoar frost; **—еть** *v.* become covered with hoar frost.

заинтересов/анность *f.* interest; incentive, encouragement; involvement, role; **—анный** *a.* interested; involved, concerned (with); **—(ыв)ать** *v.* interest, attract; **—(ыв)аться** *v.* become interested.

заинтригов(ыв)ать *v.* arouse curiosity.

заиртышский *a.* (geog.) Trans-Irtysh.

заискриться *v.* (begin to) sparkle, scintillate.

зайдёт *fut. 3 sing. of* **зайти.**

займа *gen. of* **заём.**

займёт(ся) *fut. 3 sing. of* **занять(ся).**

займищ/е *n.,* **—ный** *a.* floodplain.

займ/овый *a. of* **заём; —одержатель** *m.* loan holder.

займут(ся) *fut. 3 pl. of* **занять(ся).**

займы *pl. of* **заём;** borrowing.

зайсанский *a.* (geog.) Zaisan, Zaysan.

зайти *see* **захаживать, заходить.**

зай/цегуб *m.* (bot.) Lagochilus; **—цегубые, —цероты** *pl.* (mam.) Noctilionidae; **—цехвост** *m.* (bot.) Lagurus; **—цы** *pl.* (mam.) hares and rabbits (*Leporidae*); **—чати-на** *f.* rabbit meat; **—чик** *dim. of* **заяц;** reflected light spot; **—чиха** *f.* doe; **—чонок** *m.* young hare.

закаболивать *v.* (naut.) mouse (a hook).

закавказский *a.* (geog.) Transcaucasian.

закадмиевый *a.* epicadmium.

заказ *m.* order, commission; command; **з. на** order for; **на з., по —у** to order; **выполненный по —у** custom-built, custom-made; **—ан(ный)** *a.* ordered, on order; **—ать** *see* **заказывать; з.-наряд** *m.* (work) order; **—ник** *m.* sanctuary, wildlife refuge, (p)reserve; **—ной** *a.* custom-made; registered (letter); posted (land); **—чик** *m.* client, customer, buyer, purchaser; **—ывать** *v.* order, have made; place (a call); forbid; **—ывать билет** book a seat.

закал *see* **закалка; —ённость** *f.* hardiness; **—ённый** *a.* hardened; hardenable (steel); (met.) quenched; (biol.) hardy; seasoned (soldier); **—ённый на воздухе** air-hardened; **—иваемость** *f.* hardenability; **—иваемый**

a. hardenable; **—ивание** *see* **закалка; —и(ва)ть** *v.* harden, quench; **—ивающий** *a.,* **—ка** *f.* hardening, quenching; **—ка в воде** water quenching; **поверхностная —ка** surface or case hardening; **—очная** *f.* hardening shop; **—очно-отжигательный** *a.* hardening and annealing (furnace); **—очный** *a. of* **закалка.**

закалывать *v.* stab, slaughter, butcher; pin up.

закалять *see* **закаливать.**

закамен/елый *a.* hardened, petrified; **—еть** *v.* harden, petrify.

закамуфл(аж)ировать *v.* camouflage.

заканчив/ать *v.* finish, end, complete, conclude, accomplish; **—аться** *v.* terminate (in); come to an end; **—ающийся** *a.* terminating, ending, closing.

закапать *v.* start dripping, instill drop by drop; spatter.

закапотировать *v.* cover with a hood.

закапушка *f.* (min.) gouge.

закапчивать *v.* smoke, cure; blacken.

закапыв/ание *n.* digging in, etc., *see v.;* internment; **—ать** *v.* dig in, bury; fill in, cover; *see also* **закапать.**

закармлив/ание *n.* fattening, feeding up; **—ать** *v.* fatten, feed up, overfeed.

закарпатский *a.* (geog.) Transcarpathian.

закарстован/ие *n.* (geol.) karst formation; **—ный** *a.* karst(ed) (rock).

закаспийский *a.* (geog.) Transcaspian.

закат *m.* setting; seam, crimp; (rolling) lap, backfin; **з. солнца** sunset; **—анный** *a.* rolled (up), etc., *see v.;* **—ать** *see* **закатывать;** start rolling; **—ить** *see* **закаты-вать; —ка** *f.* rolling (up), etc., *see v.;* **—ный** *a. of* **закат; —очный** *a.* rolling, etc., *see v.;* **—ывание** *n.* rolling (up), etc., *see v.;* **—ывать** *v.* roll (up), wrap; bend up, fold (over), curl, crimp; seam, bead; (text.) pill; **—ывать копий** (typ.) apply copying ink; **—ываться** *v.* roll; set of sun; burst out (laughing).

закач/анный *a.* pumped in, injected; set in rocking motion; **—ать** *see* **закачивать.**

закаченный *a.* rolled (up), etc., *see* **закатывать.**

закач/ивание *n.,* **—ка** *f.* pumping in, injection; rocking; **—ивать** *v.* pump in, inject; rock, start rocking.

закашивать *v.* (begin to) mow.

закашлять *v.* start coughing; **—ся** *v.* have a coughing fit.

заквакать *v.* (begin to) croak.

закваси/ть *see* **заквашивать; —ска** *f.* ferment(ing); leaven (for dough); (wine) starter; (bact.) culture; **—ска корма** ensilage; **—снуть** *v.* make sour; **—сочник** *m.,* **—сочный чан** starter vat; **—шение, —шивание** *n.* fermenting, etc., *see v.;* **—шивать** *v.* ferment; leaven (dough); start (wine); (make) sour.

заки/дной *a.* throwing, casting; **—душка** *f.* (angling) cast; **—д(ыв)ать, —нуть** *v.* cast, throw; bespatter; abandon, neglect; fill (in, up).

закип/ание *n.* start of boiling; **—ать** *v.* start boiling; simmer.

закированная почва (geol.) brea.

закис/ание *n.* souring; fermentation; **—ать, —нуть** *v.* (turn) sour; **—ленный** *a.* acidified.

закисн/ый *a.* (lower or **—ous**) oxide; **—ая соль** (lower or **—ous**) salt; **—ая соль железа** ferrous salt; **—ое железо** ferrous iron.

закисший *a.* sour(ed).

закис/ь *f.* (lower or **—ous**) oxide; **з. железа** ferrous oxide; **азотнокислая з. железа** ferrous nitrate; **з.-окись** mixed oxide; **гидрат —и** (lower or **—ous**) hydroxide.

заклад *m.* mortgage, pledge; investment; **—ка** *f.* laying, etc., *see v.;* location; establishment; load, batch; (hydr.) flushing; (min.) rubbish; **пустая —ка** rubbish; **—ная**

f. mortgage, investment; **—ной** *a.* mortgage; laying; insertion; **—очный** *a. of* **закладка; —чик** *m.* mortgagor, lender, investor; layer; (rivet) setter; **—ывание** *n.* laying, etc., *see v.;* **—ывать** *v.* lay (foundation), break ground (for); set, put, install, establish; build in, incorporate; block up, wall up, embed; pack, load, fill (with); mortgage, invest; plant (orchard); cut (grooves); harness (horses); sink (a well); start (an experiment).

закл/евать, —ёвывать *v.* peck to death; start pecking; start biting (of fish).

закле/енный *a.* glued, etc., *see v.;* **—ивание** *n.* gluing, etc., *see v.;* **—и(ва)ть** *v.* glue, paste (up; shut); stop up, seal; **—йка** *f.* gluing, etc., *see v.;* adhesive band.

заклейм/енный *a.* stamped, marked; **—ить** *v.* stamp, mark, brand.

заклёп *m.* rivet; **—анный** *a.* riveted; clinched.

заклепать *see* **заклёпывать.**

заклёп/ка *f.* rivet; clinch(er); pin; riveting; **—ник, —оч-ник** *m.* riveting hammer; **—ный** *see* **заклёпочный; —овидный** *a.* rivet (weld); **—очнообкатная машина** rivet spinner; **—очный** *a.* riveted (seam, joint), rivet (hole), riveting; clinch (bolt); **—щик** *m.* riveter; **—ывание** *n.* riveting; **—ывать** *v.* rivet (up); clinch.

заклин/ённый *a.* wedged, etc., *see v.;* **—ивание** *n.* wedging, etc., *see v.;* (mech.) seizure; **—и(ва)ть** *v.* wedge (up), cleat, key; block (up); pack up; jam; (mech.) seize; fasten; cotter, tighten up (cotter); **—иваться** *v.* wedge, jam, stick; **—ка** *f.* wedging, etc., *see v.;* (paper) arching, bridging (of chips).

заклокотать *v.* (begin to) bubble.

заклубить *v.* puff up, blow up; raise (dust); **—ся** *v.* mass (of smoke).

заключ/ать *v.* include, enclose, contain, house, encase (in); put (in brackets); occlude; confine, lock in, imprison; conclude, come to the conclusion, deduce, infer; close, end (with); make, enter into (a contract); strike (a bargain); **з. в себе** comprise, embody, embrace; house, hold; imply; **—аться** *v.* consist (of), be contained; reside (in), lie (in), be; end, result (in); **—аться в том** lie in the fact (that); **—ающий** *a.* including, etc., *see v.;* inclusive (of); **—ающийся** *a.* included, contained.

заключен/ие *n.* inclusion; enclosure; confinement; occlusion; conclusion, deduction, inference; closing, finishing up; summary; findings, final report; including, etc., *see* **заключать; в з.** in conclusion; **дом —ия, место —ия** prison.

заключённый *a.* included etc., *see* **заключать;** *m.* prisoner.

заключ/ительный *a.* final, closing, conclusive; terminal; **—ительная стадия** climax; **—ить** *see* **заключать; —ка** *f.* (typ.) quoin.

заков/анный *a.* fused, welded; **—ка** *f.* (met.) shortening, compression; (vet.) prick(ing); **—(ыв)ать** *v.* forge together; chain, fetter; prick.

заковылять *v.* (begin to) hobble.

закогтить *v.* lacerate, rip (with claws).

закодировать *v.* (en)code.

закожный *a.* subcutaneous.

закоксов/анность *f.* coking; **—(ыв)ание** *n.* coking, etc., *see v.;* carburization (of catalyst); **—(ыв)аться** *v.* coke, clog with coke; gum up.

закол m. slaughter(ing), butchering; fish-weir; (min.) loosened rock.

заколачивать *v.* nail (up, down), board up; drive in, hammer in.

заколашивание *n.* (agr.) earing, heading.

заколебаться *v.* start vibrating, fluctuating or oscillating; hesitate, waver.

заколоситься *v.* (agr.) come into ear, head.

заколотить *see* **заколачивать; —ся** *v.* begin to pound (of heart).

заколоть *see* **закалывать.**

заколыхаться *v.* (begin to) wave or flutter.

закольц/евать, —овывать *v.* connect (up); band (birds); girdle (tree).

закомелистый *a.* churn-butted, swell-butted.

закон *m.* law, rule, principle; relationship; **з. о том, что** law that; **—но** *adv.* legitimately, properly; **—ность** *f.* legitimacy, legality, validity; admissibility; **—ный** *a.* legal, valid, legitimate, rightful; **—овед(ец)** *m.* lawyer; jurist; **—оведение** *n.* law, jurisprudence.

законодатель *m.* legislator; **—ный** *a.* legislative; **—ство** *n.* legislation; code.

закономерн/о *adv.* regularly, uniformly, according to rule; it is in order; **—ость** *f.* regularity; trend, pattern; conformity (to principle); rule, governing laws; mechanism; characteristic; history; relationship, correlation; **—ый** *a.* natural, regular, systematic; conforming to some law, pattern or equation.

законопа/тить, —чивать *v.* calk (up), pack, plug; **—ченный** *a.* calked.

законо/положение *n.* statute; **—преступление** *n.* infringement of the law; **—проект** *m.* bill.

законсервиров/ание *n.* preservation, canning, etc., *see v.;* **—анный** *a.* preserved, etc., *see v.;* **—ать** *v.* preserve, can (food); interrupt, suspend (work); put in dead storage, mothball; (missiles) inhibit.

законспектировать *v.* summarize, sum up.

законспирировать *v.* conspire, plot.

законтрактов/анный *a.* contracted; **—(ыв)ать** *v.* make a contract, enter into contract, bind by contract.

законтривать *v.* lock, secure.

законтурный *a.* contour, boundary (zone); (petrol.) external, perimeter (flooding).

законуривать *v.* (min.) make the first cut.

законцовка *f.* tip, end.

законч/енность *f.* completeness; finish; **—енный** *a.* complete(d), finished, final; conclusive; **—ить** *see* **заканчивать.**

закоп/анный *a.* buried, dug in; **—ать** *v.* bury; (begin to) dig (in).

закопёрщик *m.* pile driver (operator).

закопошиться *v.* begin to stir or crawl.

закопт/евший, —елый *a.* smoky, soot-covered; **—еть** *v.* get smoky or soot-covered; **—ить** *see* **закапчивать.**

закопушка *f.* (min.) exploratory or test pit.

закопчённый *a.* smoky, sooty; smoked.

закорачив/ание *n.,* **—ающий** *a.* (elec.) shorting; **—а-тель** *m.* short-circuiter; **—ать** *v.* short-circuit, short out.

закорен/елый *a.* deep-rooted, inveterate, ingrained; **—ение** *n.* rooting, taking root; **—еть** *v.* (take) root; become ingrained; insist (on); **—ившийся** *a.* rooted.

закорм/ить *v.* overfeed; start feeding; **—ленность** *f.* overfeeding.

закоробить *v.* start warping or bending.

закоро/тить *see* **закорачивать; —тка** *f.* (elec.) short circuit; **—ченный** *a.* shorted, short-circuited.

закосить *v.* (begin to) mow.

закоска *f.* part of a river adjacent to a sand bar along the coast.

закос/неть *v.* become rigid, stiffen; stagnate; **—тенеть** *v.* grow stiff or numb; ossify.

закоулок *m.* secluded spot; back street.

закоченеть *v.* become numb (with cold).

закочкаренный *a.* tussock swamp (meadow).

закрадываться *v.* steal in, creep in.

закраек *see* **закраина.**

закраивать *v.* start cutting; cut out.

закра/ина *f.* edge, rim, border, flange, collar, bead, shoulder, fillet; tip; (well) curb, lining; ice rim; open water zone between ice and shore; (typ.) ridge shoulder; **—йка** *see* **закраина;** selvage.

закрапать *v.* spot; drizzle; start dripping.

закрас/ить *see* **закрашивать; —ка** *see* **закрашивание.**

закраснеть *v.* turn or show red; blush.

закрасться *see* **закрадываться.**

закрахмаливать *v.* (text.) starch.

закраш/енный *a.* painted, etc., *see v.;* **—ивание** *n.* painting, etc., *see v.;* tint; (comp.) fill pattern; **—ивать** *v.* paint (over), color, dye, tint; fill in (map).

закреп *m.,* **—а** *f.* catch, clip, fastener, holdfast, fastening, tie; tack; dowel, joint pin; (saw) buckle; **—итель** *m.* (phot.; dyes) fixer, fixative, fixing agent; (insecticides) sticker; **—ительный** *a.* fixing, etc., *see* **закреплять; —ить** *see* **закреплять; —ка** *see* **закреп(а);** fixing, etc., *see* **закреплять.**

закрепл/ение *n.* fixing, etc., *see v.;* (dyes) fixation; securing device, anchor; safety device; immobilization, stabilization; reinforcement; (gully) control; (Fermi level) pinning; **стадия —ения** (bot.) consolidation stage; **—ённый** *a.* fixed, etc., *see v.;* fast, tight; **—ённый на** fitted to; **—ять** *v.* fix, secure, fasten, affix; clamp (down), hold, grip, lock; anchor, key, bolt (down); set, install, mount, attach; tighten (screw); bind, stabilize (soil); arrest, immobilize, strengthen; consolidate; assign; confirm (reservation); stop (diarrhea); **—ять болтами** *v.* bolt; **—яющий** *a.* fixing, etc., *see v.;* lock (nut); **—яющее приспособление** fastener, clamp; **—яющее средство** *see* **закрепитель.**

закреп(оч)ный *see* **закрепляющий.**

закрещивание *n.* (min.) barrier.

закрив/ить, —лять *v.* bend, curve, distort; start bending.

закристаллизовать(ся) *v.* crystallize out; start crystallizing.

закритический *a.* (nucl.) supercritical; (av.) beyond stalling.

закричать *v.* cry out, shout.

закроет *fut. 3 sing. of* **закрыть.**

закроить *see* **закраивать.**

закрой *m.* cut, cutting out; *imp. of* **закрыть; —ка** *f.* cut, cutting out; pattern; (ichth.) summer salmon; **—ник** *m.* (carp.) molding plane; **—ный** *a.* cutting; **—щик** *m.* cutter.

закром *m.* bin, corn crib, granary; silo.

закроют *fut. 3 pl. of* **закрыть.**

закругл/ение *n.* rounding (off), chamfering; curvature, curve; **—ённость** *f.* roundness; **—ённый** *a.* rounded (off, out); round, rotund; curved; easy, slack (bilge); **—ить, —ять** *v.* round (off), chamfer.

закружить *v.* make dizzy, confuse; (begin to) whirl, turn, spin; **—ся** *v.* get dizzy; start spinning.

закру/тень *m.* (mach.) tommy bar; **—тить** *see* **закручивать; —тка** *f.* twisting, etc., *see v.;* (phys.) torsion; (aero.) vortex, swirl, whirl, spin; warp, twist; tommy bar; (med.) artery clamp; **—ченность** *f.* (av.) warping (of wing); **—ченный** *a.* twisted, etc., *see v.;* **—ченный в завиток** spirally wound; **—ченное место** kink; **—чивание** *n.* twisting, etc., *see v.;* torsion; involution; **—чивать** *v.* twist, warp, contort; spin,

swirl, whirl; curl, coil, wind, twine; bind; screw down, tighten; turn off (faucet); **—чиваться** *v.* twist, etc., (chem.) coil; kink; **—чивающий(ся)** *a.* twisting, etc., *see v.;* **—чивающий момент, —чивающая пара** (phys.) torque.

закрыв/ание *see* **закрытие; —ать** *v.* close, shut (down, off); stop, cut off, turn off (faucet); seal, plug (with), stopper; obturate; patch up; enclose, house, shelter, shield, cover; finish; **—аться** *v.* close (down), shut; end; **—ающий** *a.* closing, etc., *see v.;* occlusive; obturator.

закрылок *m.* (av.) flap.

закрыт/ие *n.* closing, etc., *see* **закрывать;** shutoff; (en)closure; cover; **—оплодные** *pl.* (bot.) flask fungi (*Pyrenomycetes*); **—опузырный** *a.* (ichth.) physoclistous; **—ый** *a.* closed, etc., *see* **закрывать;** box (groove); crossed (belt); (med.) hidden, inner; **—ый калибр** (rolling) tongue pass; **—ое помещение** enclosure; **—ого типа** enclosed; **—ь** *see* **закрывать.**

закудахтать *v.* start to cackle.

закуклив/ание *n.* (ent.; phyt.) pupation; **—аться** *v.* pupate.

закуливание *n.* (phyt.) pseudorosette virus.

закулисный *a.* secret, hidden.

закультивировать *v.* (agr.) cultivate.

закуп/ание *n.,* **—ка** *f.* purchase, purchasing, procurement; **—ать, —ить** *v.* purchase, procure, acquire, buy up.

закупор/енный *a.* stopped up, etc., *see v.;* capped (steel); **—ивание** *n.* stopping up, etc., *see v.;* **—ивать** *v.* stop up, seal, encapsulate; cork, cap; clog, plug (up); choke, obstruct; pack, make tight; **—ивающий** *a.* stopping up, etc., *see v.;* obstructive; **—ившийся** *a.* clogged up; **—ить** *see* **закупоривать; —ка** *f.* seal, plug; (med.) obstruction, occlusion; *see also* **закупоривание.**

закуп/очно-сбытовой *a.* marketing (cooperative); **—очный** *a. of* **закупка; —щик** *m.* buyer, purchaser.

закур/енный *a.* smoked, etc., *see v.;* lit (cigarette); **—жаветь** *see* **заиндеветь; —ивание** *n.* smoking, etc., *see v.;* **—и(ва)ть** *v.* (begin to) smoke; fumigate; light (cigarette, etc.); **—ка** *f.* fumigation; **—ник** *m.* fumigator.

закус/ать *v.* (begin to) bite, sting; **—ить** *v.* eat (a snack), have a bite; **—ка** *f.* snack; **—очная** *f.* snack bar.

закустар/енный *a.* overgrown with shrubs; **—ивание** *n.* shrub invasion.

закусывать *see* **закусить;** take the bit in its teeth (of horse).

закут *m.* pen, enclosure.

закутать *see* **закутывать.**

закут/ка *f.,* **—ок** *m.* pen, enclosure.

закутывать *v.* wrap up, muffle.

зал *m.,* **—а** *f.* hall, room; (milking) parlor.

залавок *m.* counter, bench; locker.

заладить *v.* make a habit (of).

залакиров(ыв)ать *v.* lacquer, varnish.

залакка *f.* (bot.) Salacca.

заламывать *v.* (begin to) break; start hurting; overcharge.

залатать *v.* patch, mend.

залащивать *v.* gloss, polish (over).

залаять *v.* (begin to) bark.

залег/ание *n.* position; (geol.) occurrence, bed(ding); preparation (for hibernating); **на месте —ания** in situ; **—ать** *v.* lie (down); occur, be deposited; be located; (mil.) take cover; prepare, get ready (for hibernation); **—ать выше, —ать на(д)** overlay; overlie; **—ать ниже, —ать под** underlay; underlie; **—ающий** *a.* lying, etc., *see v.;* deposited.

залед/еневший, —енелый *a.* ice-covered; **—енение** *n.* freezing; **—енеть** *v.* freeze over, be covered with ice; **—енить** *v.* freeze over.

залёдка *f.* (ichth.) spring salmon.

залеж/авшийся, —алый *a.* old (stock); stale; **—аться** *see* **залёживаться.**

залёж/иваться *v.* lie (too long); become stale, get old; find no market; **—ка** *f.* (mam.) rookery, breeding ground; **—ный** (*also* **залежный**) *a. of* **залежь;** long-fallow, idle, unused (land).

залежь *f.* old stock; (geol.) deposit, bed, layer, stratum; lode, vein; (oil) pool; (ore) body; fallow (land), lea, layland.

залез(а)ть *v.* get (into), penetrate; reach into; climb (up).

залей(те) *imp. of* **залить.**

залениться *v.* get lazy.

залеп/ить, —лять *v.* paste up, seal.

залес/ение *n.* reforestation; **—ённость** *f.* extent of forests; **—ённый** *a.* (re)forested, wooded; **—ённая земля** timberland; **—ить** *v.* reforest, afforest; **—ье** *n.* country beyond the woods.

залёт *m.* flight; photographic mission; flying in, arrival.

залет/ать, —еть *v.* fly (away, beyond, high, off); fly in, arrive; start flying; stop (for fuel).

залётный *a.* flown in, arriving; (orn.) accidental, casual.

залеч/ивание *n.* healing, etc., *see v.;* **—и(ва)ть** *v.* cure, heal; **—и(ва)ться** *v.* heal up, close up; weld (of cracks).

залечь *see* **залегать.**

залив *m.* gulf, bay, cove, inlet; **—ание** *n.* pouring, etc., *see v.;* **—ать** *v.* pour (over), flood, drench, soak, inundate; spill; embed; drown, extinguish; (met.) cast; lay, spread (asphalt; concrete); fill in, seal; line (bearings); fill up, prime (engine); (electron.) pot; **—ать тушью** ink in; **—аться** *v.* be poured, etc.; trickle, seep in; burst out (into laughter or tears); **—ающий** *a.* pouring, etc., *see v.;* flood (light); **—ина** *f.* (casting) flash, fin; **—ка** *see* **заливание;** inclusion; **—ка компаундом** (elec.) potting; **—ное** *n.* jelly; **—ной** *a.* flood(ed), inundated; jellied; (mach.) priming; **—ный** *a. of* **залив; —очный** *a. of* **заливка;** (met.) ladle (crane); **—чик** *m.* creek; **—щик** *m.* caster, pourer.

зализ *m.* (av.) fairing, fillet; **—(ыв)ать** *v.* lick (clean); **—(ыв)ать обводы** fair.

залиловеть *v.* turn lilac.

залип/ание *n.* sticking, etc., *see v.;* **—ать, —нуть** *v.* stick, cling; glue up, paste, seal; get sticky.

залит/ый *a.* poured, etc., *see* **заливать; з. маслом** oil-immersed; **—ь** *see* **заливать.**

залич/ка *f.,* **—ывание** *n.* (leather) pretanning, setting the grain.

залишек *m.* surplus, excess.

залобковый *a.* (anat.) retropubic.

залог *m.,* **—овый** *a.* deposit, pledge, guarantee, security, collateral; mortgage; (agr.) lea, grassland; (grammar) voice; **—одатель** *m.* depositor; **—одержатель** *m.* mortgagee.

залож/ение *n.* laying, etc., *see* **закладывать;** creation, establishment; foundation; initiation; (geod.) contour internal; **—енный** *a.* laid, etc., *see* **закладывать;** built-in, incorporated; **—ить** *see* **закладывать.**

залом *m.* break, crack, cut; stoppage, obstruction; (log) jam; (text.) crease; (ichth.) blackback shad (*Alosa kessleri k.*); **—ать** *v.* break off; **—ить** *see* **заламывать.**

залоснить *v.* rub to a shine.

залощить *v.* gloss, polish over.

залп *m.* volley, salvo, discharge; **—овый** *a. of* **залп;** immediate; **—ом** *adv.* in one volley; at one time; in one stretch; in one gulp.

залубенеть *v.* become hard or stiff.

залуж/ать, —ить *v.* sow to grass, convert to meadow; **—ение** *n.* sowing to grass; **—ённый** *a.* grass-covered, grassy.

залуп/а *f.* (med.) paraphimosis; **—ить, —лять** *v.* peel off; pare; strip; abrade, graze (skin); **—иться** *v.* peel.

залуч/ать, —ить *see* **заманивать.**

залыс/ина *f.* bald spot; **—ить** *v.* balden; blaze, mark; **—ый** *a.* with bald temples.

зальбанд *m.* (geol.) selvage, gouge.

зальёт *fut. 3 sing. of* **залить.**

зальный *a. of* **зал.**

залягут *fut. 3 pl. of* **залечь.**

заляп(ыв)ать *v.* make muddy.

зам, зам— *see* **заместитель.**

замагнезировать *v.* (typ.) dust in magnesia.

замаз/ать *see* **замазывать; —ка** *f.* puttying, etc., *see v.;* putty, plaster, paste, cement, mortar; (wallboard) compound; **—ывание** *n.* puttying, etc., *see v.;* **—ывать** *v.* putty, cement, plaster up, fill up, stop (a hole); paint over; besmear, soil; slur over; efface.

замал/евать, —ёвывать *v.* paint (over).

замалчивать *v.* hush up, conceal.

заман/и(ва)ть *v.* entice, lure, attract; decoy; **—иха** *f.* (bot.) Echinopanax elatum; **—ка** *f.* bait, lure; **—чивый** *a.* tempting, enticing; **—чик** *m.* (mam.) great gerbil (*Rhombomys opimus*).

замарать *v.* soil, smear; blot out, efface.

замаривать *v.* starve; underfeed; kill, suffocate (cocoons).

замаринов(ыв)ать *v.* marinate, pickle; shelve, put off, delay.

замаркировать *v.* mark, brand.

замаскиров/анный *a.* masked, etc., *see v.;* **—(ыв)ать** *v.* mask, disguise, conceal, hide, camouflage, screen.

замасл/енный *a.* oiled, etc., *see v.;* greasy; **—ивание** *n.* oiling, etc., *see v.;* **—иватель** *m.* lubricant; (text.) oil; **—и(ва)ть** *v.* oil, grease, lubricate; wet, soak (fiber); stain with grease or fat; **—иваться** *v.* get fouled (of spark plug).

заматерелый *a.* mature; hardened; inveterate, rooted.

заматочный *a.* (anat.) retrouterine.

заматрицировать *v.* (typ.) make matrices.

заматывать *v.* wind, twist, roll up; wear out, tire out.

замахать *v.* (begin to) wave, wag, flap.

замачив/ание *n.* wetting, etc., *see v.;* **—ать** *v.* wet, damp, moisten, humidify; soak, steep; ret (fiber).

замашка *f.* (bot.) staminate hemp.

замащивать *v.* pave, cover; fill (out).

замбар *m.* (mam.) sambar (*Cervus; Rusa*).

замб/езийский *a.* (geog.) Zambezian; **—ийский** *a.* Zambia(n); **—ониев столб** Zamboni's dry cell.

замедл/ение *n.* slowing down, deceleration, etc., *see v.;* lag(ging), delay; (nucl.) moderation; **без —ения** readily, promptly; **с —ением** delayed-action; **—енность** *f.* slowness; **—енный** *a.* slowed down, etc., *see v.;* (phot.) slow-motion; sluggish (thinking); brady—, *e.g.,* **—енная речь** (med.) bradylalia; **—енного действия** delayed action; **—итель** *m.* retarder, retardant, inhibitor; baffle; delay mechanism; (mine) delay charge; (nucl.) moderator; (speed) reducer; **—ить, —ять** *v.* slow down, decelerate, ease (up); retard, detain, delay, defer, prolong; inhibit, suppress; (nucl.) moderate; **—иться, —яться** *v.* slow down, decelerate, slacken; fall (below); **—яющий** *a.* slowing down, etc., *see v.;* timing (relay); (nucl.) moderating; **—яющий рост** growth-retarding.

замеднение *n.* copper plating.

замеж/евать, —ёвывать v. demarcate, stake off.

замёл past m. sing. of **замести**.

замели(ва)ть v. cover with chalk.

замелькать v. flash (by or past), gleam, appear; (begin to) twinkle.

замен/а f. substitution, substituting, etc., see v.; substitute, equivalent; alternative; (ex)change, replacement; renewal; **з. каучука** rubber substitute; **допускающий —у** renewable, replaceable; **—ённый** a. substituted, etc., see v.; **—имость** f. interchangeability; **—имый** a. interchangeable, replaceable, detachable; **—итель** m. **—ительный** a. substitute; replacement; alternative; **—ить** see **заменять; —яемость** f. interchangeability; **—яемый** see **заменимый; —ять** v. substitute, replace, renew, change (for, from), exchange, interchange; supersede, supplant; take the place (of); **—яющий** a. substituting, etc., see v.; interchangeable; (med.) prosthetic; vicarious.

замер m. measuring, measure(ment), gaging; gage; survey(ing); demarcation; probe, test, determination; indication, reading; past m. sing. of **замереть; —енный** a. measured; **—еть** see **замирать**.

замерз/аемость f. tendency to freeze (up); **—ание** n. freezing, etc., see v.; **температура —ания** freezing point; **—ать, замёрзнуть** v. freeze (up), congeal, solidify; **—ающий** a. freezing, etc., see v.; **—ший** a. frozen.

замер/и(ва)ть v. measure, gage; **—ная лента** measuring tape.

замертво adv. in a dead faint.

замерцать v. start scintillating or flickering.

замерший a. (apid.) addled (brood).

замерять v. gage, measure.

замес m. batch, mix; mixing; **—ить** see **замешивать**.

замести see **заметать**.

заместимость f. reciprocity.

заместитель m. substitute; assistant; deputy; (chem.) substituent; **—ный** a. substitute, substituting, acting; **—ство** n. substitution; **по —ству** by proxy.

заместить see **замещать**.

замёт m. sweeping up; casting (of net); snowdrift; bolt, bar.

замета f. mark, sign; remark, observation; memorandum, reminder.

заметать v. sweep (up), cover (up); baste, sew, tack on, affix, fasten; set (a seine); **—ся** v. (begin to) rush around.

замет/ить see **замечать; —ка** f. notice, note, memorandum; paragraph, explanation, remark; sign, mark, blaze (on tree).

заметка basting, tacking on.

замет/ливый a. observant, watchful; **—но** adv. noticeably, etc., see a.; it is noticeable; **—ный** a. noticeable, perceptible, visible; marked, appreciable, pronounced, distinct, conspicuous; material, substantial.

заметывать v. baste, sew (up), tack on, affix, fasten; cast, set, shoot (a net).

заметь(те) imp. of **заметить**.

замеч/ание n. noticing; remark, observation, comment, note; **—ательно** adv. remarkably; it is noteworthy; **—ательный** a. remarkable, notable, unusual; dramatic, striking; excellent; **—ать** v. notice, observe, remark; note, detect, mark; mention, discuss; take (a reading); **не —ать** overlook; **—аться** v. be noticed, etc.; make oneself conspicuous; **—енный** a. noticed etc., see v.

замеш/анный a. mixed (in), etc., see v.; **—ательство** n. confusion, disorder; embarrassment; **—ивание** n. mixing, etc., see v.; **—(ив)ать** v. mix (in), stir (in); knead (thoroughly); involve, implicate, connect (with).

замещ/аемый a. replaceable; replaced; **—ать** v. substitute, replace; act (for), fill (vacancy); deputize; (math.) insert; **—ающий** a. substituting, etc., see v.; replacement; vicarious (species); **—ение** n. substitution, etc., see v.; replacement; **двойное —ение, обменное —ение** (chem.) double decomposition; **раствор —ения** solution of replacement; **—ённое** n. substitution product; **—ённый** a. substituted, etc., see v.; exchanged (ions).

замзав m. acting manager.

замигать v. start blinking or twinkling.

заминать v. tread on, press down; suppress, put a stop (to); start kneading; **—ся** v. become confused, falter, stumble.

заминдаликовый a. (anat.) retrotonsillar.

заминиров/анный a. (mil.) mine-strewn, mine-studded; **—ать** v. lay mines.

заминка f. hesitation; hitch, snag, obstacle; stoppage; batch of kneaded clay.

замир/ание n. fading, etc., see v.; **—ать** v. fade, die away, sink; die off, wither; (bee brood) addle; stop, come to a standstill; falter, break off.

замка gen. of **замок**.

замкнёт fut. 3 sing. of **замкнуть**.

замкнут/ость f. reticence; (elec.) closed state (of circuit); closure; completeness; **—оячеистый** a. closed-cell (foam plastic); **—ый** a. locked, etc., see **замыкать;** closed(-type); whole, entire, intact, complete; sealed (coupling); box (groove); inland (sea); **—ый накоротко** (elec.) short-circuited; **—ь** see **замыкать**.

замков/ые pl. (mal.) Articulata; **—ый** a. of **замок;** key(stone); (zool.) cardinal; **—ая часть** lock joint; **—ое соединение** tool joint (of drill pipe).

замнач m. acting head.

замнёт fut. 3 sing. of **замять**.

замоет fut. 3 sing. of **замыть**.

замок m. lock, catch, snap; clamp, shackle; scarf (joint); joint; hinge; key(stone); (bridge) coupling; (art.) firing lock; (magnetic pole) keeper; curve (of fold); (trough) end; (hydr.) cut-off; (mal.) cardo, hinge; past m. sing. of **замокнуть**.

замокать v. get wet, get soaked.

замок-вертушка m. turnlock; **з.-задвижка** m. lock; **з.-кнопка** m. snap lock.

замокнуть v. get wet, get soaked.

замолк/ать, —нуть v. fall silent, stop (talking, etc.); stop, die away (of sound).

замолоть v. (begin to) grind.

замолчать v. stop talking; hush up.

замоноличивание n. (concrete) joinery work.

замонтировать v. build in, embed.

замор m. kill, mass destruction, asphyxiation (of aquatic animals).

заморажив/ание n. freezing, etc., see v.; **камера —ания** freezer, locker; **з.-высушивание** n. freeze-drying; **—атель** m. freezer; refrigerant; **—ать** v. freeze, congeal, refrigerate, chill; **—ающий** a. freezing, etc., see v.; **—ающее средство** refrigerant.

заморгать v. (begin to) blink, twinkle.

замор/ённый a. underfed, etc., see v.; emaciated; **—ить** v. underfeed, starve; exhaust, overwork; abuse; stain; **—иться** v. wear oneself out; **—ка** f. killing, suffocation (of cocoons).

заморо/женный a. frozen, congealed; **—зить** see **замораживать; —зок** m. (fall or spring) morning frost.

заморосить v. start drizzling.

заморочить v. bother, confuse.

заморыш m. starveling, starver; dwarf.

замостить see **замащивать.**

замот/анный a. wound, etc., see **заматывать; —ать** see **заматывать.**

замочек dim. of **замок.**

замоч/енный a. wetted, etc., see **замачивать; —ить** see **замачивать; —ка** f. wetting, etc., see **замачивать;** batching; (flax) retting; water mark; gen. of **замочек.**

замочн/ый a. of **замок; замочка; —ая скважина** keyhole.

замошка f. (bot.) staminate hemp.

замощ/ение n. paving, covering; filling (out); **—ённый** a. paved, etc., see **замащивать.**

замоют fut. 3 pl. of **замыть.**

замрёт fut. 3 sing. of **замереть.**

замуж/ество n. marriage; **—ний** a. married.

замундштучивать v. curb (a horse).

замурлыкать v. (begin to) purr.

замуров/ание n. immuring, etc., see v.; immurement; **—анный** a. immured, etc., see v.; **(ыв)ать** v. immure, wall in, brick up; build in, embed; **—ывание** see **замурование.**

замусори(ва)ть v. litter (with rubbish).

замутить v. make muddy, make turbid, disturb; **—ся** v. become turbid.

замутн/ение n. becoming turbid; **—ённый** a. turbid, cloudy, muddy; clouded, blurred; **—еть** v. become turbid, cloudy or muddy; blur; **—итель** m. turbidifying agent.

замуч/ать, —и(ва)ть v. tire out, exhaust; torment; torture; **—енный** a. exhausted; **—иться** v. wear oneself out.

замш/а f., **—евый** a. (leather) chamois; suede; **—евание** n. chamoising, suede finish(ing); **—евать** v. chamois, oil-tan; **—елый** a. mossy; **—еть** v. be coated with moss; **—иться** v. lose its nap.

замыв/ание n., **—ка** f. washing (off, away); blurring (of spectrum); **—ать** v. wash (off, away, out); efface.

замызг(ив)ать v. soil, dirty; wear out.

замык/аемый a. locked, closed; lockable; (geom.) subtended, extended under; **—ание** n. locking, etc., see v.; completion; (math.) closure; occlusion; (**короткое**) **—ание** (elec.) shorting; **—атель** m. locking mechanism; closer; (elec.) switch; (lock) catch; (anat.) sphincter; **—ательный** a. locking, closing; **—ать** v. lock, close, fasten; join, connect; complete; surround, enclose, confine; (dentistry) occlude; **—аться** v. close up, join, connect up; be completed; form (a circle); **—ающая** f. closing line; **—ающий** a. locking, etc., see v.; (anat.) obturator, closing; sphincter (muscle); **—ающий скачок** terminal shock (wave).

замыс/ел m. project, scheme, plan, intention; idea, conception; **—лить** v. plan, intend, contemplate; **—ловатость** f. intricacy; **—ловатый** a. intricate, complicated, complex, involved.

замыть see **замывать.**

замычать v. (begin to) low (of cattle).

замычка f. bolt, catch, lock, latch.

замышл/енный a. intended, planned; **—ять** v. intend, plan, contemplate.

замятие n. (paper) jam(ming).

замять see **заминать; —ся** v. become confused, falter, stop short.

занаваживать v. fertilize, manure.

занаве/с m., **—ска** f., **—сочный** a., **—сь** f. curtain, screen; **—сить, —шивать** v. curtain, screen, cover, drape (with); **—ска** f. (anat.) velum; **нёбная —ска** soft palate; **—шенный** a. curtained, etc., see v.

занаво/женный a. fertilized, manured; **—зить** see **занаваживать.**

занадобиться v. become necessary.

занаркотизировать v. narcotize, drug.

занаря/дить, —жать v. assign by order.

занашивать v. wear out.

зангинский a. (geog.) Zanga.

Зандмейера реакция Sandmeyer's reaction.

зандр m., **—овый** a. (geol.) sandr, outwash plain, (frontal) apron.

зандцемент m. sand cement.

заневоливать v. compress (spring).

занедужиться v. fall ill.

занеметь v. grow numb.

занемо/гать, —чь v. fall ill.

заненский a. (geog.) Saane.

занес/ение n. recording, etc., see **заносить; —ённый** a. recorded, etc., see **заносить;** brought in, introduced, adventitious (species); **—ти** see **заносить.**

занзибарский a. (geog.) Zanzibar.

заниж/ать v. understate; underestimate, underrate, put too low; reduce; **—ение** n. understatement; underestimation; reduction; **—енный** a. understated; too low; undersized; reduced.

занижнечелюстной a. (anat.) retromandibular.

занизить see **занижать.**

заним/аемость f. occupancy; **—ание** n. occupation, occupying, etc., see **занимать; —ательность** f. interest; **—ательный** a. interesting, entertaining, amusing, recreational.

заним/ать v. occupy, take (up), fill, hold (a place), reserve; engage, keep, secure; seize; tie up; preoccupy, interest; borrow; downgrade; **—аться** v. be occupied, be concerned (with), deal (with), be engaged (in, on), work (at), be active (in); study, examine (a question); **—ающий** a. occupying, etc., see v.; **—ающийся** a. dealing (with); oriented (toward).

занкл m. (ichth.) Moorish idol (Zanclus); **—овые** pl. Zanclidae.

занникеллия f. (bot.) Zannichellia.

заново adv. anew, re—, again.

заноет fut. 3 sing. of **заныть.**

заноз/а f. splinter; **—истый** a. splintery, hackly; **—ить** v. get a splinter in.

занорыш m. cavity.

занос m. drift, accumulation; bringing in; entry; skid(ding); (av.) side slip; (med.) mole; (apid.) honeycomb arrangement; **—ить** v. record, enter, put down, write down, register; carry, bring in, deliver; skid; choke up, block up (with); drift, accumulate; raise (arm); wear out; **—иться** v. become shabby; **—ный** a. of **занос;** brought in, imported; (biol.) adventitious, accidental; ecdemic, not native.

заносчивый a. arrogant, overbearing.

заношенный a. (badly) worn.

заноют fut. 3 pl. of **заныть.**

зануздать v. bridle, curb, bit.

зануление n. (elec.) neutral grounding.

занумеров(ыв)ать v. number, numerate, index.

заны(ва)ть v. (begin to) ache.

занят/ие n. occupation, employment, work, business; pursuit; studies; seizure, capture; **часы —ия** business hours; **—ный** a. interesting, entertaining; **—о(й)**, **—ый** a. occupied, busy, engaged; **—ость** f. employment; busyness; **коэффициент —ости** (elec.) duty factor; **сигнал —ости** busy signal; **—ь** see **занимать.**

заоблачный a. beyond the clouds.

заодно adv. at the same time, together.

заозёрный *a.* beyond the lake(s).

заокеанский *a.* transoceanic.

заокулированный *a.* (bot.) budded.

заорать *v.* (begin to) yell.

заостный *a.* (anat.) infraspinous.

заостр/ение *n.* sharpening, etc., see *v.*; taper; point, cusp, tip; emphasis; —**ённость** *f.* sharpness, keenness, taper; —**ённый** *a.* sharpened, etc., see *v.*; acuminate; sharp, acute; —**ить**, —**ять** *v.* sharpen, point, taper, grind down; —**иться** *v.* come to a point, taper; —**яющий** *a.* sharpening, etc., see *v.*; (rad.) peaking; —**яющийся** *a.* tapering.

заохренный *a.* ocherous.

заочн/ик *m.* correspondence student; —**о** *adv.* without seeing; by default; in absence (of); by correspondence; —**ый** *a.* out of sight; by default; correspondence (course).

запавший *a.* sunken, caved in, fallen in.

запад *m.* west.

запад/ание *n.* falling in; blocking; (rad.) attenuation; —**ать** *v.* start falling; fall (in, back, behind); drop in; sink (into); —**ение** *n.* retraction; —**ина** *f.* sink(-hole); (pal., etc.) patella.

западн/оевропейский *a.* (geog.) West European; —**окавказский** *a.* West Caucasian; —**окарельский** *a.* West Karelian; —**осахалинский** *a.* West Sakhalin; —**осаянский** *a.* West Sayan; —**осибирский** *a.* West Siberian; —**ый** *a.* west(ern).

западня *f.* trap, snare; trap door.

запаечный *a. of* запайка; seal(ing).

запаздыв/ание *n.* lag(ging), time lag, delay, hysteresis; retardation; tardiness, lateness; interval; **время** —**ания** (comp.) latency; **угол** —**ания** (elec.) angle of lag; **чистое з.** dead time; delay; —**ать** *v.* lag, delay, creep, retard; be late, be overdue; —**ающе-критический** *a.* (nucl.) delayed-critical; —**ающий** *a.* lagging; retarded; delayed (neutron, etc.); delay (circuit).

запа/ивание *n.* soldering, etc., see *v.*; —**ивать** *v.* solder, seal (up); overwater (stock); —**йка** *f.* soldering, seal(ing).

запаков/ать, —**ывать** *v.* pack (up); —**ка** *f.*, —**ывание** *n.* packing.

запал *m.* fuse, primer, igniter; blaster, blasting cap; ignition, firing; wind burn (of grain); (leaf) scorch; (vet.) pulmonary emphysema, heaves; —**ённый** *a.* ignited, lit, fired; scorched; exhausted (horse).

запалзывать *v.* creep in, crawl in.

запал/и(ва)ть *v.* ignite, light, kindle, (set) fire; (begin to) burn, scorch; exhaust; water (an overheated horse); —**ьник** *m.* igniter, primer, fuse; ignition chamber.

запальн/ый *a.* ignition, igniting, firing; (nucl.) seed; **з. прибор** ignition device, igniter; **з. шар** ignition chamber; hot bulb; —**ая свеча** spark plug.

запальщик *m.* blaster.

запань *f.* (logging) boom.

запараллели(ва)ть *v.* connect in parallel; operate or run in parallel.

запар/ивание *n.* scalding, etc., see *v.*; (high-pressure) steaming; —**и(ва)ть** *v.* scald; steam; start steaming; (text.) steam print; grow oppressive or sultry (of weather); stew; soak, steep; override (a horse); —**иться** *v.* be exhausted; —**ка** *f.* steaming; steamed product; steaming unit, steamer; (text.) steam-printing plant; —**ник** *m.* (feed) steamer; —**ной,** —**(оч)ный** *a.* scalding, steaming, steam(-treating).

запаршиветь *v.* (vet.) become mangy.

запарывать *v.* gore, stab; spoil (work).

запас *m.* store, stock(-pile), supply, reserve, resources, inventory; storage; (energy) content; (timber) volume; (distance) endurance; margin, allowance, provision; *past m. sing. of* запасти; —**ы** *pl.* resources; reserves; **з. истощился** (they) have run out, are out (of); **з. кожи** skin folds; **з. на** allowance for; **з. по фазе** phase margin; **з. прочности** safety factor, safety margin, assurance factor; **з. товаров** stock in trade; **з. тяги** (av.) excess thrust, thrust reserve; **коэффициент** —**а** *see* запас прочности; **с** —**ом** conservatively.

запас/ание *n.* storing, etc., see *v.*; storage, accumulation; —**ать** *v.* store (up), stock(-pile), lay in, accumulate, save up; reserve; —**аться** *v.* provide oneself (with); —**ающий** *a.* storing, etc., see *v.*; storage; —**ённый** *a.* stored (up), etc., see *v.*; —**ливый** *a.* thrifty, provident; —**ная** *f.* stockroom; —**ник** *m.* reserve soldier; —**ной,** —**ный** *a.* reserve, stored, depot (fat, etc.); storage; auxiliary, spare, standby (equipment); emergency (exit); (mil.) reservist; —**ной путь** (rr) siding; —**ная часть** spare (part).

запасовывать *v.* reeve, thread (rope).

запасти *see* запасать.

запасть *see* западать.

запасы *pl. of* запас; reserves.

запатентов/анный *a.* patented; —**(ыв)ать** *v.* patent; take out a patent.

запах *m.* odor, smell, scent; **без** —**а** odorless; **удаление** —**а** deodorization; —**и** *pl.* aroma (of wine).

запах/ать *v.* plow (in, under); —**ивание** *n.* plowing (in, under), etc., see *v.*; —**ивать** *v.* plow (in, under), turn in, bury, cover; wrap or draw tighter, close, shut; overlap; —**нуть** *see* запахивать; begin to smell.

запачкать *v.* soil, dirty; —**ся** *v.* get dirty.

запаш/ка *f.* plowing in or under; tillage; extension of arable land; —**ник** *m* shallow plow, ridger; —**ный** *a. of* запашка.

запа/янный *a.* soldered; closed, sealed (off); hardwired (logic); —**ять** *see* запаивать.

запёк *m.* (leather) sunburn.

запека *f.* (geol.) zapeka (an iron-ore cement); —**ние** *n.* baking; caking; —**нка** *f.* baked food, casserole; spiced brandy; —**ть** *v.* bake (well); —**ться** *v.* cake, sinter; clot, congeal, coagulate (of blood); crack (of lips).

запёк/шая масса (med.) clot, coagulum; —**шийся** *a.* caked, sintered; parched; clotted.

запеленать *v.* swaddle.

запеленговать *v.* take bearings; bear.

запени(ва)ть *v.* froth; cover with foam; —**ся** *v.* (begin to) foam, froth.

запер/еть *see* запирать; —**тый** *a.* closed, locked; blocked, barred, etc., see запирать; pent-up (water).

запершить *v.* have a tickle in the throat.

запесочивать *v.* oversand.

запестреть *v.* appear variegated.

запеть *v.* (begin to) sing.

запечат/анный *a.* sealed; —**ать** *v.* seal; start printing; —**ле(ва)ть** *v.* impress, imprint; show, demonstrate; —**ывание** *n.* sealing; —**ывать** *v.* seal (up).

запеч/ённый *a.* baked (well); —**ка** *f.* baking; —**ь** *v.* bake well.

запивать *v.* drink or wash down (with); take to drink.

запил *m.* notch, gash, cut, kerf, slit; *past m. sing. of* запить; —**енный** *a.* notched, etc., see *v.*; —**ивание** *n.,* —**овка** *f.* notching, etc., see *v.*; —**и(ва)ть** *v.* notch, cut; start sawing or filing; file off.

запин/аться *v.* hesitate, falter; stumble, trip; —**ка** *f.* hesitation; **без** —**ки** fluently, smoothly.

запир/ание *n.* closing, etc., *see v.; *occlusion; blackout; cut-off; **з. пучка** beam suppression; **—атель** *m.* (anat.) obturator; sphincter; **—ательный** *a.* closing, etc., *see v.;* lock(ing); obturator (muscle); **—ательство** *n.* denial, disavowal; **—ать** *v.* close (up), shut (off), seal, lock (in, up); surround, encircle; fasten, bolt; bar, block, suppress; (electron.) blank, black out, cut off; deny; **—аться** *v.* close; **—ающий** *a.* closing, etc., *see v.;* blanking (oscillator); blocking; barrier (layer); cut-off (voltage); disabling (pulse); **—ающий поток** plug flow; **—ающая мышца** (anat.) obturator.

запис/анный *a.* recorded, (on) record; **—ать** *see* **записывать;** start writing; **—ка** *f.* note, memorandum, report; (train) ticket; **—ки** *pl.* notes, records, journal; proceedings; transactions; **—ной** *a.* writing; recording; note (book); first-rate, regular.

записыв/аемый *a.* describable; recorded; **—ание** *n.* recording, etc., *see v.;* **—ать** *v.* record, put down, mark down, write (down), make a note (of); register, enroll, enter; **—аться** *f.* join, register, become a member (of); **—ающий** *a.* recording, etc., *see v.*

запис/ь *f.* record(ing), writing (down), entering, entry, notation; note; symbol; registration; (number) representation; (comp.) write-in; (geol.) log(ging), plotting; **з. на ленте** tape recording; **время —и** write time, writing time; **с прямой —ью** direct-writing (recorder); **скорость —и** recording speed.

запитка *f.* powering (of motor).

запить *see* **запивать.**

запих/(ив)ать, —нуть *v.* push in, stuff in, cram in, force in.

запишет(ся) *fut. 3 sing. of* **записать(ся).**

запищать *v.* (begin to) squeak.

заплав/ка *f.* seal(ing); **—лять** *v.* melt shut, seal, close (by fusion).

заплакать *v.* start crying.

запланиров/анный *a.* planned, etc., *see v.;* **—ать** *v.* plan, schedule, slate (to begin), project (for).

запла/та *f.* patch, piece; (comp.) patch; pay(ment); **—танный** *a.* patched; **—тать** *v.* patch, mend; **—тить** *v.* pay; **—тка** *dim. of* **заплата;** **—ченный** *a.* paid.

заплеск *m.* splash, uprush (of water); **—и** *pl.* (met.) skin, scab; **—(ив)ать** *v.* splash (up), spatter.

заплесн/евевший, —евелый *a.* moldy, mildewed; **—евелость** *f.* moldiness; **—(ев)ение** *n.* formation of mold, mildewing; **—(ев)еть** *v.* grow moldy, mildew.

заплеснуть *v.* splash, sprinkle; submerge.

запле/сти, —тать *v.* braid, plait; join, link, splice; **—тённый** *a.* braided, etc., *see v.*

заплётка *f.* braiding, etc., *see* **заплести.**

заплечик *m.* shoulder, collar, bead; (met.) bosh (of a shaft furnace); **кожух —а** bosh jacket; **—и** *pl.* bosh.

заплеч/ный *a.* shoulder (bag); knapsack (sprayer); **з. мешок** knapsack; **—ье** *n.* (anat.) shoulder blade, scapula.

заплодоносить *v.* begin to form fruit.

запломбиров/анный *a.* filled (tooth); sealed; **—(ыв)ать** *v.* fill; seal.

заплот *m.* fence.

заплутаться *v.* lose the way.

заплутонный *a.* (astr.) transplutonium.

заплы/в *m.* (sports) race; heat; (typ.) dead metal; **—вание** *n.* swimming in, etc., *see v.;* (soil) crust formation; occlusion (of wound); **—(ва)ть** *v.* swim (in; out), float in, come in; be filled (with mud, etc.); swell, bloat (with).

заплюсн/а *f.,* **—евый** *a.* (anat.) hock, tarsus, ankle.

запнуться *v.* falter, hesitate.

заповедн/ик *m.* preserve, reservation, sanctuary, reserve, refuge; park; **з. почв** soil conservation district; **—о-охотничье хозяйство** hunting reserve; **—ый** *a.* forbidden, prohibited; **—ый лес** forest reserve.

заподазривать *v.* suspect.

заподборка *f.* (typ.) wrong gathering.

заподлицо *adv.* flush(-mounted).

заподозр/енный *a.* suspected; **—и(ва)ть** *v.* suspect.

запоем *adv.* avidly, excessively.

запозд/авший —алый *a.* late, overdue; backward, retarded; delayed; **—алое развитие** backwardness; **—алость** *f.* lateness; backwardness; **—ание** *see* **запаздывание; —ать** *see* **запаздывать.**

запо/ить *v.* overwater (stock); **—й** *m.,* **—йное пьянство** (med.) dipsomania.

заполз/ать *v.* start creeping; **—ать, —ти** *v.* creep, crawl (into).

заполимеризовать(ся) *v.* polymerize.

заполн/ение *n.* filling, etc., *see v.;* coverage (of surface); occupation, population; number of counts recorded; **коэффициент —ения** (elec.) space factor; (pulse) duty factor; block coefficient (of ship); **—енность** *f.* fulness; population; **—енный** *a.* filled, etc., *see v.;* full; (nucl.) completed (shell); **—итель** *m.* filler; (concrete) aggregate; **—ить** *see* **заполнять; —яемость** *f.* fillability (of mold); **—яемый** *a.* fillable; at full capacity; **—ять** *v.* fill (in, up, out), charge, prime; pack in; stop (a hole); complete; (comp.) pad; **—яться** *v.* fill up; **—яющий** *a.* filling, etc., *see v.;* **—яющий материал** filler.

заполь/е *n.* (agr.) remote field(s), back field(s); **—ный участок** outside field.

заполяризовать *v.* polarize.

заполяр/ный *a.* (geog.) arctic; **—ье** *n.* polar region, the Arctic.

запом/инаемый *a.* (comp.) stored; **—инание** *n.,* **—инающий** *a.* memorizing, etc., *see v.;* memory, storage; mention, reminder; **—инать** *v.* memorize, remember, keep in mind; store, file; **—инаться на** *v.* be stored into; **—инающее устройство** storage, store, file, memory (bank); **—нить** *see* **запоминать.**

запонка *f.* button; stud; cuff link.

запор *m.* bolt, bar, lock, latch, fastener, catch, stop, shut-off; locking, closing, shutting off; (med.) constipation; suffocation (of fish).

запорашивать *v.* powder, dust (with).

запорн/о-выпускной *a.* shut-off, cut-off (valve); **—ый** *a. of* **запор;** cut-off (valve); **—ый кран** stopcock; **—ая жидкость** (liquid) seal.

запорожский *a.* (geog.) Zaporozhye.

запороть *see* **запаривать.**

запорошить *v.* powder, dust (with); start powdering or dusting over.

запот/евание *n.* perspiration, sweating, misting, fogging; condensation; condensate; **—евать** *v.* perspire, sweat, become misted, fog over; **—евший, —елый** *a.* sweaty, moist, misted; mowburnt (grain); **—еть** *v.* (begin to) perspire.

заправила *f.* rule; *m.* boss, chief.

заправ/ить *see* **заправлять; —ка** *f.* servicing, etc., *see v.;* charge, load, batch; delivery, supply(ing); adjustment; **—ка топливом** refueling; **—ленный** *a.* serviced, etc., *see v.;* fritted (hearth); **—лять** *v.* service, get ready; (re)fuel, fill (up); feed, load, charge; prime (engine); set (up), prepare, dress, grind, sharpen (tools); dress, fertilize (soil); fettle (furnace); guide, thread; season (food); trim (lampwick); tuck in; supervise, boss, run.

заправочн/ый *a. of* **заправка; з. валик** (paper) pinch roll; **з. пункт** (gasoline) filling station; **з. чан** (tanning) dressing vat; **—ая колонка** fuel pump; **—ое отверстие** intake.

заправщик *m.* fuel tank, fueling unit; tank truck; (av.) refueler; service man.

запрашив/ание *n.* inquiry; **—атв** *v.* inquire, ask; interrogate; request (information); ask an exorbitant price.

запревать *v.* (begin to) rot, decay; molder.

запредельный *a.* protective (inhibition).

запрессов/анный *a.* pressed (in), etc., *see v.;* **—ка** *f.* **—очный** *a.* pressing, etc., *see v.;* compression; **—ывать** *v.* press (in or on); force; embed; press-fit.

запр/ет *m.* prohibition, interdiction, ban; exclusion; veto; (comp.) inhibition; (fishing) closed season; **—ёт** *fut. 3 sing. of* **запереть; схема —ета** (electron.) inhibit(or) circuit; **—етительный** *a.* prohibitive, prohibitory; inhibiting; **—етить** *see* **запрещать; —етный** *a.* prohibited, forbidden, restricted.

запреть *see* **запревать.**

запрещ/ать *v.* forbid, prohibit, ban, bar, suppress; inhibit; **—ение** *n.* prohibition, inhibition; embargo; ban; **первого —ения** (nucl.) first-forbidden; **—ённость** *f.* (phys.) forbiddenness; **—ённый** *a.* forbidden, etc., *see v.;* unauthorized.

заприметить *v.* spot, notice.

заприходовать *v.* (com.) debit.

запрограммировать *v.* program.

запрод/(ав)ать *v.* agree to sell; **—ажа** *f.* advance contract (for future delivery).

запроектиров/анный *a.* projected, planned; **—ать** *v.* project, plan, design.

запроки/дывать, —нуть *v.* throw back, toss; overturn; **—нутый** *a.* overturned.

запропаститься *v.* get lost.

запроровые *pl.* prowfishes (*Zaproridae*).

запрос *m.* inquiry, request, question; interrogation; need, requirement; overcharging; (oxygen) demand; (comp.) query; **без —а** fixed (price); **—ить** *see* **запрашивать; —ный** *a.* request (form); **—чик** *m.* interrogator, challenger.

запротестовать *v.* protest, object.

запротоколировать *v.* enter into the records; take down minutes.

запру/да *f.* dam, dike; bar; lock, watergate; damming; artificial pond; **—дить** *see* **запруживать; —дный** *a. of* **запруда;** retaining (dam); **—жать** *see* **запруживать; —женный** (*also* **—жённый**) dammed, etc., *see v.;* back(water); **—живание** *n.* damming, etc., *see v.;* **—живать** *v.* dam (up), impound, retain; back up; block, clog.

запрут *fut. 3 pl. of* **запереть.**

запрыг/ать *v.* start jumping; **—ивать, —нуть** *v.* jump in.

запря/гать *v.* harness; yoke; **—жённый** *a.* harnessed; **—жка** *f.* harness(ing); harnessed team (and vehicle).

запрят(ыв)ать *v.* hide, conceal.

запрячь *see* **запрягать.**

запуганный *a.* frightened, intimidated.

запудри(ва)ть *v.* powder; dust.

запуск *m.* launching, etc., *see v.;* start(-up); (comp.) run; invocation (of a program); neglect; (hunting) out-of-season period; **—аемый** *a.* launched, etc., *see v.;* **—ание** *see* **запуск; —ать** *v.* launch (into space); throw, put, send (into orbit); fly (balloon); fire, shoot, start, initiate; (comp.) launch, invoke (a program); be-

gin production, go on stream; actuate, trigger; neglect; **—ающий** *a.* launching, etc., *see v.;* trigger.

запуст/ение *n.* neglect, desolation; (urban) blight; **—еть** *v.* go to waste; fall into neglect, deteriorate, get run down; **—ить** *see* **запускать.**

запут/авшийся *a.* entangled; **—анность** *f.* entanglement; complexity; confusion; **—анный** *a.* (en)tangled, etc., *see v.;* intricate; **—ать, —ывать** *v.* (en)tangle, enmesh; confuse, muddle; complicate; involve, implicate; **—аться, —ываться** *v.* become involved; get caught (in); **—ывание** *n.* entanglement; confusion; involvement.

запух/ать, —нуть *v.* swell up, puff up.

запушить *v.* coat (with snow); ice up.

запущенн/ость *f.* neglect, desolation; **—ый** *a.* launched, etc., *see* **запускать;** neglected, run down; advanced (illness): **—ый в производство** in production.

запчасти *pl.* spares, spare parts.

запылать *v.* flare up, blaze up.

запыл/ение *n.* getting or making dusty; **з. лёгких** (med.) pneumoconiosis; **—ённость** *f.* dust content, dust load, dustiness; **—ённый** *a.* dusty, dust-laden; **—ивание** *n.* dusting; **—ить** *v.* fill with dust, make dusty; begin to whirl up; **—иться** *v.* get dusty.

запыреенный *a.* infested with quack grass.

запых/аться *v.* get out of breath, pant; **—теть** *v.* begin to pant.

запьёт *fut. 3 sing. of* **запить.**

запьянеть *v.* get drunk.

запястн/о— *prefix* (anat.) carpo—, carpus; **з.-пястный сустав** carpometacarpal; **—ый** *a.* carpal; **—ье** *n.* carpus, wrist; (vet.) knee.

запят/ая *f.* comma; (decimal) point; **без —ых** comma-less (code).

запятить *v.* back up.

запятн/анный *a.* stained, etc., *see v.;* **—ать** *v.* stain, soil, spot; mark, brand.

запятовидный *a.* comma-shaped.

запячивать *v.* back up.

зараб/атывание *n.* earning; **—атывать** *v.* earn; **—атываться** *v.* overwork; **—отать** *v.* earn; start (working); **—отная плата, —оток** *m.* earnings, wages, salary, pay; paid work.

заравнив/атель *m.* (agr.) leveler; **—ать** *v.* level (off), even up, smooth, flatten.

зараж/аемый *a.* susceptible to infection; **—ать** *v.* infect; contaminate, pollute; infest (with parasites); communicate (a disease); (bact.; cryst.) inoculate; seed; **—аться** *v.* be infected, etc.; catch (a disease); **—ение** *n.* infection, etc., *see v.;* invasion (of parasites); contagion; **—ённость** *f.* infectiousness; infection; **—ённый** *a.* infected, etc., *see v.*

зараз *adv.* (all) at once, at one stroke.

зараз/а *f.* infection, contagion; (nucl.) contamination; **водяная з.** (bot.) Elodea; **—ительность** *f.* infectiousness; **—ительный** *a.* infectious, contagious, catching; contaminating; **—ить** *see* **заражать.**

заразих/а *f.* (bot.) broom rape (*Orobanche*); **—овые** *pl.* Orobanchaceae; **—оустойчивый** *a.* resistant to broom rape.

заразн/ый *a.* infectious, contagious, communicable; isolation (ward); *m.* contagious patient; **—ое начало** virus; contagious matter.

заранее *adv.* beforehand, in advance; previously; a priori; pre-; **з. отлитый** *a.* precast; **з. предвиденный** *a.* foregone (conclusion); **з. устанавливать** *v.* preset, predetermine.

зараст/ание *see* **заращивание; —ать, —и** *v.* grow

over, be overgrown (with); heal, close; **—ить —щивать** *v.* let overgrow (with).

заратит *m.* (min.) zaratite, emerald nickel.

заращив/ание *n.* obliteration, closure; encroachment (of weeds); (med.) atresia; **—ать** *v.* let overgrow (with).

зарваться *v.* go too far, go to extremes.

зард *m.* (bot.) Melo zard.

зардеть(ся) *v.* redden, grow red; flush.

зареветь *v.* (begin to) roar; start crying.

зарев/о *n.* glow, redness; **—ой** *a. of* **заря.**

зарегистриров/ание *n.* registration; **—анный** *a.* registered, recorded, on record; authorized (user); **—анная заявка** patent claim; **—ать** *v.* register, record; file (a patent application).

зарегулиров/анный *a.* regulated; with regulated flow; **—ать** *v.* regulate; discipline.

заредеть *v.* become less frequent.

зареет *fut. 3 sing. of* **зареять.**

зарез *m.* butchering; neck, throat; **до —у** desperately; **—анный** *a.* cut; butchered; cutthroat (trout); **—ать** *v.* make a deep incision; butcher, slaughter, kill.

зарезервировать *v.* reserve.

зарезинивать(ся) *v.* (paints) liver.

зарезывать *v.* butcher, slaughter; cut.

заректальный *a.* (anat.) retrorectal.

заретушировать *v.* (phot.) retouch.

зареч/ный *a.* beyond or on the other side of the river; **—ье** *n.* area beyond the river.

зареше/тить, —чивать *v.* equip with a grate; **—ченный** *a.* having a grate.

зареять *v.* start gushing.

заржав/еть *v.* rust, corrode; **—ленный** *a.* rusted, corroded, rusty.

заржать *v.* start neighing.

зари *gen., etc., of* **заря.**

зарин *m.* (mil.) sarin (nerve gas).

зарисов/анный *a.* sketched (in); **—ать, —ывать** *v.* sketch, draw; **—ка** *f.* sketch(ing); **—ывание** *v.* sketching, drawing.

зарница *f.* summer lightning.

заровн/енный *a.* leveled; **—ять** *v.* level (off).

зарод *m.* stack of hay.

зародить *see* **зарождать.**

зародыш *m.* embryo, germ; bud; (cryst.) nucleus, seed charge; **з. стебля** (bot.) plumule; **—евание** *n.* nucleation; **—евый** *a.* embryonic; fetal; germ (cell); rudimentary, primary, primordial (root); **—евый корешок** (bot.) radicle; **—евая оболочка** (embr.) amnion; **—евая полость** blastocoel; **—евое развитие** embryogenesis; **—евые растения** (bot.) Embryophyta; **—еобразование** *n.* nucleation; **—еобразующий** *a.* embryogenic; **—еотделитель** *m.* (food) germ separator.

зароет *fut. 3 sing. of* **зарыть.**

зарожд/ать *v.* conceive; produce, generate, engender; **—аться** *v.* be conceived; be born, arise, originate; **—ающийся** *a.* incipient, nascent; embryonic; originating; **—ение** *n.* conception; origin, genesis; inception; formation, generation; **—ение фронта** (meteor.) frontogenesis; **—ённый** *a.* conceived, etc., *see v.*

зарозоветь *v.* turn pink, turn rose.

зароиться *v.* (bees) start swarming.

зарой(те) *imp. of* **зарыть.**

зарокотать *v.* resound, start rumbling.

зарон/ить *v.* drop, let go; give rise (to doubt); rouse, excite; **—ять** *v.* begin to shed or lose.

зарос *past m. sing. of* **зарасти; —ль** *f.* thicket, brake; brushwood, scrub, undergrowth; bed of vegetation; **—тковый** *a.* (bot.) prothallial; **—ток** *m.* prothallium;

—ший *a.* overgrown, covered (with); **—ший растениями** plant-filled (lake).

заротовой *a.* (anat.) postoral.

зарплата *f.* wages, salary, earnings.

заруб *see* **зарубина; —ание** *n.* notching, etc., *see v.;* **—ать** *v.* notch, nick, cut, gash; cut down, fell.

зарубежн/ый *a.* frontier, beyond the border; **—ая печать** foreign press.

заруб/ина *f.* mark, incision, notch, indentation, nick, cut; **—ить** *v.* cut, notch, gash, mark, blaze; start felling (trees); **—ка** *f.* cutting, etc. *see v.;* incision, incisure, cut, notch; indentation; (safety) catch; **—ленный** *a.* cut, etc., *see v.;* **—ной бар** (min.) cutting jib.

зарубц/еваться, —овываться *v.* (med.) cicatrize, heal with a scar.

зарули(ва)ть *v.* (av.) taxi in.

зарумяни(ва)ть *v.* redden; brown (food).

зарухание *n.* devitrification.

заруч/аться, —иться *v.* secure, obtain, enlist (support, services, etc.).

зарыб/ить, —лять *v.* stock with fish; **—ленный** *a.* stocked (lake).

зары/вание *n.* burying, etc., *see v.;* **—вать** *v.* bury, inter, dig (in); **—ваться** *v.* bury oneself, dig in; go to extremes; (naut.) pitch forward.

зарыдать *v.* begin to sob.

зарыт/ый *a.* buried, interred, sunk(en); **—ь** *see* **зарывать;** start digging.

зарычать *v.* begin to roar or growl.

заря *f.* glow; dawn, daybreak, sunrise; dusk, nightfall, sunset; outset, start; (mil.) reveille; retreat; (bot.) lovage (*Ligusticum; Levisticum officinale*).

зарябить *v.* ripple; start rippling.

заряд *m.* charge, load(ing); fill(er), filling; (min.) blasting charge; cartridge; (elec.) charge, charging; supply; (solid-propellant) grain; **ядерный з.** (mil.) nuclear device; **—ить** *see* **заряжать;** persist, repeat; **—ка** *f.* charge, charging, loading; exercises, gymnastics; **—ковый** *a. of* **зарядка;** winter, reserve (irrigation); **—ник** *m.* charger; **—но-отсчётное** *or* **—носчитывающее устройство** charger-reader; **—ный** *a. of* **заряд;** warhead (compartment); **—ный дроссель** charging choke; **—ный ящик** caisson; **—овоинвариантный** *a.* charge-invariant; **—овонезависимый** *a.* charge-independent; **—овый** *a. of* **заряд;** **с —овой связью** charge-coupled (device); **—чик** *m.* (min.) charger.

заряж/аемый *a.* chargeable, charged; **—ание** *n.* charging, loading; charge; **—ать** *v.* charge, load; **—ающий** *a.* charging; *m.* loader, charger; **—ающая машина** charger; **—ённость** *f.* (battery) charge; **—ённый** *a.* charged, loaded, fed; (elec.) live, charged.

зарянка *f.* (orn.) robin (*Erithacus*).

зарящ *m.* (mil.) caisson.

заса/да *f.* ambush; **—дить** *v.* plant, set (out); sow; drive (spike); imprison, lock up, shut up; put in; compel; **—дка** *f.,* **—живание** *n.* planting, etc., *see v.;* **—женный** *a.* planted, etc., *see v.;* **—живать** *see* **засадить; —живаться** *v.* sit down (at).

засал/енный *a.* greased, etc., *see v.;* greasy; **—ивание** *n.* greasing, etc., *see v.;* **—и(ва)ть** *v.* grease, soil, smear; glaze; salt, pickle, corn; **—и(ва)ться** *v.* get greasy, glaze; clog up; **—ившийся** *a.* glazed.

засаривать *see* **засорить.**

засасыв/ание *n.,* **—ающий** *a.* suction; ingestion; **—ать** *v.* suck in, draw in; swallow up, engulf, ingest; **—ающий насос** suction pump; **—ающая банка** suction flask.

засахар/енный *a.* candied, etc., *see v.;* **—ивание** *n.* candying, etc., *see v.;* —**и(ва)ть** *v.* candy, sugar, saccharify; —**и(ва)ться** *v.* saccharify.

засвежеть *v.* renew its force (of wind).

засверкать *v.* start sparkling; flash.

засверли(ва)ть *v.* begin to drill or bore.

засве/т *m.* (flash of) light; **з. развёртки** (radar) gating, strobing; —**тить** *v.* light, kindle; (begin to) shine; (phot.) fog (film); —**титься** *v.* light up; flash; be fogged; —**тка** *f.* illumination; irradiation, exposure; (phot.) flare, light fog; (electron.) gating; (background) noise; —**тлеть** *v.* become light; begin to dawn; —**тло** *adv.* before nightfall; —**ченный** *a.* lit; fogged (film); —**чивать** *v.* illuminate; expose to light, fog; (radar) brighten, intensify (the sweep); clutter, swamp (the screen).

засвидетельствов/ание *n.* certification, etc., *see v.;* —**ать** *v.* certify, authenticate; witness, testify.

засвист/ать, —**еть** *v.* begin to whistle.

засев *m.,* —**ание** *n.,* —**ка** *f.* sowing, etc., *see v.;* seed; sown area; (bact.) inoculation; **з. (на детку)** (apid.) egg laying; (drone) brood; —**ать** *v.* sow, seed, plant; inoculate; —**ать под** sow to.

засевший *a.* stuck, caught, plugged.

засед/ание *n.* conference, meeting, session; **журнал** —**аний** minute book; —**атель** *m.* assessor; —**ать** *v.* sit in, take part (in meeting), hold meetings; meet; settle down; stick, lodge (in); hide, lie in ambush.

засеивать *see* **засевать.**

засек/а *f.* abatis, felled-tree barrier; (silv.) clearing; cut, notch, blaze; —**ание** *n.* notching, etc., *see v.; see also* **засечка;** —**ать** *v.* notch, nick, cut; intersect; locate (point); note (time); —**аться** *v.* overreach (of hooves).

засекре/тить, —**чивать** *v.* restrict, classify (information); make or keep secret; clear, give access to classified documents; —**ченный** *a.* restricted, etc., *see v.* secret, confidential; security-restricted; —**чиватель речи** *m.* scrambler.

засекшийся *a.* (vet.) hoofbound (horse).

засел *past m. sing. of* **засесть.**

засел/ение *n.* population, peopling, etc., *see v.;* settlement; —**ённость** *f.* population density; —**ённый** *a.* populated, etc., *see v.;* —**ить,** —**ять** *v.* populate, people, colonize, settle; stock (with new species); occupy, live in, inhabit.

засеребрить *v.* silver; —**ся** *v.* look silvery; start glittering.

засереть(ся) *v.* turn gray, show gray.

засесть *see* **заседать.**

засеч/ка *f.* cut, notch, mark, (in)dent; (surv.) cross bearing, intersection; (sound) ranging; (vet.) crepance (injury from hoof interference); incisure, incision; (text.) crease, break; (typ.) serif, hair stroke; **з. времени** timing, clocking; **обратная з.** (surv.) resection; **прямая з.** intersection; —**ный** *a. of* **засека;** —**ь** *see* **засекать.**

засе/янный *a.* sown, planted; seeded, inoculated; —**ять** *see* **засевать.**

заси/деть *see* **засиживать;** —**женный мухами** *a.* flyblown; —**живать** *v.* taint, spot; flyblow; —**живаться** *v.* sit or stay too long.

засилосовать *v.* (agr.) put into silage.

засилье *n.* (pre)dominance, preponderance.

засин/еть(ся) *v.* show, appear or turn blue; —**и(ва)ть** *v.* color blue; make too blue.

засичане *n.* blaze, mark, notch, incision.

засиять *v.* (begin to) shine; appear.

заскак/ать *v.* start jumping; break into a gallop; —**ивание** *n.* jumping in, etc., *see v.;* engagement; —**ивать** *v.*

jump (in, on, behind); engage, catch, drop in, snap (into place).

заскирдовать *v.* stack (hay, etc.).

заскок *see* **заскакивание;** kink, quirk, idiosyncracy, eccentricity.

заскользить *v.* start sliding; slide in.

заскоруз/лый *a.* hardened, calloused; —**нуть** *v.* harden, become calloused; become set or rigid; linger, remain; stagnate.

заскочить *see* **заскакивать.**

заскрести *v.* start scrubbing or scraping.

заскрипеть *v.* start creaking.

засластить *v.* sweeten.

заслать *see* **засылать.**

заслащивать *v.* sweeten.

засле/дить, —**живать** *v.* track up (floor).

заслезиться *v.* begin to water (of eyes).

заслеп/ить, —**лять** *v.* blind.

заслон *see* **заслонка;** (agr.) wind shelter; —**ение** *n.* screening, etc., *see v.;* —**ённый** *a.* screened, etc., *see v.;* —**ить** *v.* заслонять; —**ка** *f.,* —**очный** *a.* door, gate, flap, slide; damper, register, shutter; screen, shield; louver; baffle (plate); (throttling valve; (engine) choke; (anat.) valve; valvula; (meteor.) barrier; **поворотная** —**ка** butterfly valve; —**ять** *v.* screen, shield, cover, mask, hide; shade, overshadow; dislodge, displace, supplant.

заслу/га *f.* merit, credit; service; —**женный** *a.* merited, etc., *see v.;* honored; —**жи(ва)ть** *v.* merit, deserve, earn, be worthy (of); warrant; —**живающий** *a.* meriting, etc., *see v.;* worthy (of).

засл/уш(ив)ать *v.* hear; listen; —**уш(ив)аться** *v.* listen attentively; —**ышать** *v.* hear.

заслюн/и(ва)ть, —**явить** *v.* slobber over.

засмалив/ание *n.* pitching, etc., *see v.;* —**ать** *v.* pitch, tar; resinify; seal.

засматривать *v.* look (into).

засмеять *v.* ridicule, deride, laugh (at); —**ся** *v.* start laughing.

засмол/ение *see* **засмолка;** —**ённый** *a.* pitched, etc., *see v.;* —**ить** *v.* pitch, tar; resinify; gum; seal; —**ка** *f.* pitching, etc., *see v.;* —**ок** *m.* (timber) resinous flaw.

заснежённый *a.* snow-covered.

заснимать *v.* photograph, take, shoot.

заснуть *v.* fall asleep.

заснят/ый *a.* photographed, taken, shot; —**ь** *see* **заснимать.**

засов *m.* bolt, bar, catch; —**(ыв)ать** *v.* push, thrust, shove (in); put away; mislay.

засол *m.* pickling, salting; pickle(s); brine; —**ение** *n.* pickling, salting; salinization (of soil); —**ённость** *f.* salinity; salt content; —**ённый** *a.* salted, pickled; saline (soil); salt (marsh); —**ить** *v.* pickle, salt; —**ка** *see* **засол;** —**онение** *n.* salination (of water); —**очный,** —**ьный** *a. of* **засол;** —**яться** *v.* be salted; (soil) salinize.

засор *m.* (met.) non-metallic surface inclusion; —**ение** *n.* stoppage, obstruction, choking (up), etc., *see v.;* impurity; —**ённость** *f.* degree of contamination; dirtiness; impurity; (agr.) weediness; (grain) dockage; —**ённый,** —**ившийся** *a.* stopped, etc., *see v.;* dirty, foul; weedy; —**итель** *m.* weed; —**ить,** —**ять** *v.* stop (up), obstruct, choke (up), clog, plug up, block; foul, pollute, contaminate; soil, dirty; litter, clutter up; infest (with weeds); (med.) constipate; —**иться,** —**яться** *v.* clog up, get plugged up.

засос *m.* suction; inflow; —**анный** *a.* sucked in, drawn in, suction; **сухо —анный** dry-suction; **—ать** *v.* (begin to) suck in; swallow up, engulf.

засох/нуть *see* **засыхать; —ший** *a.* dried, withered, dead; dry, desiccated.

заспаться *v.* oversleep.

заспешить *v.* begin to hurry.

заспинка *f.* (ent.) postnotum, postscutellum.

заспиртов/анный *a.* alcoholized; **—(ыв)ать** *v.* alcoholize; preserve in alcohol.

заспорить *v.* begin to argue; dispute.

засрочный *a.* beyond the term, overdue.

заст. *abbr.* (**застывание**) solidification.

застава *f.* gate(s), barrier; (mil.) post.

заставить *v.* find (in), catch, meet.

застав/ить *see* **заставлять; —ка** *f.* (hydr.) gate, retainer; (typ.) headpiece; (elec.) fuse; **—ленный** *a.* compelled, etc., *see v.;* **—лять** *v.* compel, force, make, cause, impel; block, bar, obstruct; **—лять двинуться** *v.* impart motion, set into motion; **—ный** *a. of* **застава; —очный** *a. of* **заставка.**

застаив/ание *n.* stagnation; hanging, sticking (of charge); **—аться** *v.* stagnate, stand too long; become stale; stick.

застанет *fut. 3 sing. of* **застать.**

застар/е(ва)ть *v.* become established or chronic; **—елый** *a.* inveterate, chronic.

застать *see* **заставать.**

заст/ёгивать, —егнуть *v.* fasten, hook (up), clasp, button (up); **—ёжка** *f.* fastener, clasp, hook, buckle, hasp; (anat.) fibula; **—ёжка-молния, механическая —ёжка** zipper.

застекл/ение *n.* glazing, etc., *see v.;* **—ённый** *a.* glazed, etc., *see v.;* glass-covered; **—ить** *v.* glaze; glass in; vitrify; **—ованный** *a.* vitrified; glass-like, glassy; **—о(вы)вание** *n.* vitrification; (polymers) transition; **—ять** *see* **застеклить.**

застелить *see* **застилать.**

застенографировать *v.* take down in shorthand.

застесняться *v.* get embarrassed.

застиг/ать, —нуть *v.* catch unawares.

застил *m.* covering; **—ание** *n.,* **—ка** *f.* covering, etc., *see v.;* **—ать** *v.* cover, screen, hide from view; spread (over); sheathe; lay; **—аться** *v.* be veiled; cloud over; **—очный** *a. of* **застилка.**

застир(ыв)ать. *v.* wash off or out; wear out (by washing).

застичь *see* **застигать.**

застлать *see* **застилать.**

застоговать *v.* stack, put in stacks.

заст/ой *m.* stagnation, standstill; depression; settling; (med.) congestion, stasis; **з. крови** hemostasis; **время —оя** dull or dead season; **зона —оя** dead zone; (rolling) zone of stagnation; **—ойный** *a.* stagnant; dull, dead; static, congested, congestive.

застолбить *v.* stake, mark out (claim).

застонать *v.* begin to moan.

застопор/ивание *n.* stopping, etc., *see v.;* **—и(ва)ть** *v.* stop, check, hold back, cut off; lock (screw); clog, plug (up); (mach.) cage; **—и(ва)ться** *v.* stop, jam; come to a standstill; clog up; **—ившийся** *a.* stopped, etc., *see v.*

засто/явшийся, —ялый *a.* stagnant, stale; **—яться** *see* **застаиваться.**

застрагивать *v.* plane, shave (down.)

застраив/ание *n.* building (up); development; **—ать** *v.* build up, develop, erect buildings on.

застрахов/анный *a.* insured; **—(ыв)ание** *n.* insurance; **—(ыв)ать** *v.* insure.

застрачивать *v.* stitch up.

застрев/ание *n.* sticking, etc., *see v.;* **—ать** *v.* stick, get stuck, jam, seize.

застрежка *f.* (fishing line) snap, connector,

застрел/и(ва)ть *v.* shoot; **—ьщик** *m.* pioneer, leader; **—ять** *v.* start shooting.

застри/гать, —чь *v.* cut, shear; pare (nails); start cutting.

застрогать *v.* plane; point.

застро/енный *a.* built up, developed; **—ить** *v.* build (up); start building; develop; **—йка** *f.* building (up); development; construction (in progress); housing system; **—йщик** *m.* builder.

застропить *v.* secure slings (to cargo).

застрочить *v.* stitch (up); start stitching; start writing; start shooting.

заструг *m.,* **—а** *f.* wind-weathered ridge of snow; **—ать** *see* **застрагивать.**

заструиться *v.* start flowing or streaming.

застр/явший *a.* stuck, jammed, trapped; **—ять** *see* **застревать.**

засту/денеть *v.* freeze; gel, jell; **—дить** *v.* chill; **—диться** *v.* be chilled; (med.) catch cold; **—дневание** *n.* gela(tiniza)tion, gelling; jellying; **—дневать** *v.* gelatinize, (set to a) gel; (food) make jelly; **—женный** *a.* chilled; **—живать** *v.* chill.

застукать *v.* start knocking.

заступ *m.* spade, shovel.

заступ/ать, —ить *v.* take (someone's) place; start (work); **—аться, —иться** *v.* intercede, plead (for); defend; **—ник** *m.* defender; patron; champion; **—ничество** *n.* intercession.

заступорылый *a.* (ichth.) shovel-nosed.

застучать *v.* start knocking.

засты/вание *n.* solidification, congealing, etc., *see v.;* **проба —вания** (oils) pour test; **температура —вания** solidification point, pour point; **—вать** *v.* solidify, congeal, harden, gel, set; clot, coagulate; freeze; cool, get cold, get chilled; **—вающий** *a.* solidifying, etc., *see v.;* **—вший** *a.* solidified, etc., *see v.*

застыдить *v.* shame; **—ся** *v.* be ashamed.

засты/лый *a.* застывший; **—(ну)ть** *see* **застывать.**

засудить *v.* condemn, write off.

засуетиться *v.* (begin to) bustle, fuss.

засуживать *v.* condemn, write off.

засунуть *v.* thrust in; put away; mislay.

засупони(ва)ть *v.* fasten, tighten (straps).

засух/а *f.* drought, dry spell; dryness, aridity; dry lake; **—овынослиый —оустойчивый** *a.* drought-resistant; **—олюбивое растение** xerophilous plant, xerophyte; **—оустойкость, —оустойчивость** *f.* drought resistance.

засучи(ва)ть *v.* roll up; start twisting.

засуш/енный *a.* dried up, desiccated; **—ивание** *n.* drying (up); **—и(ва)ть** *v.* dry (up); **—ка** *f.* drying (up); **—ливость** *f.* dryness, aridity, drought; **—ливый** *a.* dry, arid; droughty, drought-stricken.

засчит(ыв)ать *v.* take into consideration, take into account, include.

засыл/ать *v.* send (away, out; to the wrong place); smuggle in, infiltrate; **—ка** *f.* sending; assignment; report; (comp.) carry, transfer (instruction).

засып/ание *n.* filling in, etc., *see v.;* **—ать** *v.* fill in, fill up (with), backfill; pour, strew; cover, bury; charge, stoke, load (with); lay in (grain); fall asleep; **—аться** *v.* be covered; get in, spill into; be caught; fail; oversleep; **—ка** *see* **засыпание;** backfill; (met.) charge, burden; —**ной** *a.* charging; feed (hopper); —**щик** *m.* charger, loader; —**ь** *f.* charge, burden.

засых/ание *n.* drying, etc., *see v.;* —**ать** *v.* dry (up), shrivel, shrink; (bot.) wither, die.

засядет *fut. 3 sing. of* **засесть.**

затавр/ённый *a.* stamped, branded, marked; —**ить** *v.* stamp, brand, mark.

затаи(ва)ть *v.* conceal, hide.

заталамическая область (anat.) metathalamus.

заталкивать *v.* push (in, about), shove, jostle; jam in, thrust in.

затаплив/ание *n.* lighting, etc., *see v.;* —**ать** *v.* light, kindle, make a fire, fire (up); heat; flood, submerge, drown.

затаптывать *v.* trample (down).

затарив/ание *n.* packaging, etc., *see v.;* —**ать** *v.* package, weigh up or out, pack, fill, bag; dispense.

затаск *m.* (text.) streak; —**и(ва)ть** *v.* wear out; make hackneyed; take, drag.

затач/(ив)ать *v.* baste, stitch loosely; —**ивать** *v.* sharpen, grind; round off; point; file (saw).

затащить *v.* bring in, drag in; take away.

затверд/евание *n.* hardening, etc., *see v.;* **температура** —**евания** solidifying point; —**е(ва)ть** *v.* harden, solidify, congeal; consolidate; (concrete) set; indurate; (plast.) become glassy; —**евший** *a.* hardened, etc., *see v.;* indurate; —**елость** *f.* hardness; hardening; induration; —**елый** *see* **затвердевший;** firm, set; indurate; caked; —**ение** *see* **затвердевание;** —**итель** *m.* hardener.

затвер/дить, —**живать** *v.* learn by rote; memorize; start repeating.

затвор *m.* bolt, bar, slide; lock, fastening, closing device, closure, shut-off, cut-off; (hydr.) gate, valve; (liquid) seal; (phot.) shutter; ram (of mixer); (art.) breechblock; (rifle) lock; (slag) tap outlet; —**ение** *n.* mixing, tempering; —**енный** *a.* closed, etc., *see v.;* —**итель** *m.* conditioner, additive; —**ить,** —**ять** *v.* close, shut (off), lock; mix (concrete); slake (lime); —**ка** *f.* closure; (anat.) valve; valvula; (mal.) Valvata; —**ки** *pl.* Valvatidae; —**ный** *a. of* **затвор;** feed (tank); solution storage (tank).

затевать *v.* undertake, start, venture.

затейливый *a.* intricate, elaborate; clever, ingenious.

затёк *m.* flow, streak; pocket.

затек/ание *n.* flowing (in), etc., *see v.;* —**ать** *v.* flow (in), fill, pour, leak (into); streak; swell; go numb.

затем *adv.* after that, then, further, next; thereupon, whereupon, subsequently; **з. что** *conj.* because, since; (inasmuch) as, seeing that; **з. чтобы** (in order) to, so that; **а з.** and then, and later.

затемн/ение *n.* darkening, etc., *see v.;* eclipse; dim-out; blackout; (cinema) fade-out; (optical) obscurity; —**ённый** *a.* darkened, etc., *see v.;* hidden, indistinct; —**еть** *v.* darken, get dark; show dark; —**итель** *m.* dimmer; —**ить,** —**ять** *v.* darken, black out; dim; obscure; screen, (over)shade, overshadow; cloud; blur; —**о** *adv.* before daybreak.

затен/ение *n.* shading, etc., *see v.;* —**ённый** *a.* shaded, etc., *see v.;* —**итель** *m.* shade; —**ить,** —**ять** *v.* shade, shadow; (aerodyn.) blanket, shield; —**яющий** *a.* shading, etc., *see v.;* —**яющий козырёк** scope hood.

затепло *adv.* before cold weather sets in.

затереть *see* **затирать.**

затеривать *v.* lose, mislay; abandon.

затерпнуть *v.* go numb.

затёртый *past part. of* **затирать;** ground (pigment); **з. льдами** icebound.

затер/янный *a.* lost, mislaid; abandoned; —**ять** *v.* lose, mislay; abandon.

затёс *m.* notch, mark, blaze; —**анный** *a.* notched, etc., *see v.*

затесать *v.* notch, mark, blaze; rough-hew; sharpen, point; —**ся** *v.* intrude on, turn up (at).

затёска *see* **затёс.**

затеснить *v.* crowd, squeeze (together).

затёсывать *see* **затесать.**

затесь *see* **затёс.**

затеч/ный *a.* congestive; —**ь** *see* **затекать.**

затея *f.* undertaking, enterprise; —**ть** *see* **затевать.**

затир/ание *n.,* —**ка** *f.* rubbing, etc., *see v.;* (concrete) float work, float finish; —**ать** *v.* rub (down, off, over, out), smooth out; wipe out, efface; (concrete) float, trowel; grind (pigments); (brewing) mash; force (in), jam; bind, trap, hold fast; get stuck; soil, dirty.

затис/к(ив)ать, —**нуть** *v.* squeeze in.

зати/хание *n.* quieting down, etc., *see v.;* —**хать,** —**хнуть** *v.* quiet down, calm down, abate, lull; stop (blowing), die away, fade (away); —**шек** *m.,* —**шь** *f.,* —**шье** *n.* calm(ness), stillness, lull; slack; leeward side; —**шный** *a.* quiet, calm.

заткать *v.* weave (in), interweave.

заткнут/ый *a.* plugged, stopped up; —**ь** *see* **затыкать.**

затл *m.* back gage (of paper cutter).

затлеть *v.* start decaying; —**ся** *v.* start glowing.

затм/евать *v.* eclipse, cover, darken; overshadow; —**евающийся** *a.* eclipsing; intermittent (light); —**евающийся огонь** (naut.) occulting light; —**ение** *n.* eclipse; —**енная,** —**енно-переменная** *f.* eclipsing variable (star); —**енно-двойная** *f.* eclipsing binary (star); —**ить** *see* **затмевать.**

зато *conj.* in return; for; but, but then, but on the other hand.

затовар/енность *f.* accumulation of stock; —**ивание** *n.* overstocking, etc., *see v.;* surplus, glut; —**и(ва)ть** *v.* overstock, hoard; glut (the market); overproduce.

затолк/ать *v.* push, jostle; start pushing; —**нуть** *v.* shove (in), push in, jam in.

затон *m.* cove, backwater, pool; creek; fish weir, dam; —**уть** *v.* sink, be submerged.

затопать *v.* begin to stamp (one's feet).

затопить *see* **затапливать, затоплять;** start heating; —**ся** *v.* warm up; be sunk.

затопл/ение *n.* flooding, etc., *see v.;* submersion; (ocean) dumping; —**енный,** —**яемый** *a.* flooded, etc., *see v.;* —**ять** *v.* flood, inundate, drown, submerge, immerse; sink, scuttle (ship); overflow; fire (furnace).

затоптать *v.* trample (down).

затор *m.* blocking, stoppage, obstruction; (traffic) jam, congestion; (ice) gorge, jam, clogging; (brewing) mash.

заторговать *v.* start trading.

заторм/аживание *n.* braking, etc., *see v.;* —**аживать** *v.* brake, check, slow down, retard; restrain, hinder; defer, delay, inhibit (reaction); —**аживаться** *v.* be inhibited; be held up; slow down; —**ожённость** *f.* inhibition; (zool.) lassitude; —**ожённый** *a.* braked, etc., *see v.;* stagnated (flow); stagnant (gas); stagnation (pressure, etc.); —**озить** *see* **затармаживать;** apply the brakes, start braking.

заторный *a. of* **затор;** ice-clogging (flood).

заторопить(ся) *v.* start hurrying.

заторфов/анный *a.* (peat-)filled (lake); —**ывание** *n.* peat formation.

заточ/ить *v.* sharpen, point, grind; file (saw); round off; start sharpening; —**ка** *f.,* —**ный** *a.* sharpening, etc., *see v.;* groove, recess, neck; **—ный станок** sharpener, grinder.

затошнить *v.* start feeling nauseated.

затравен/елый *a.* overgrown with grass; **—еть** *v.* overgrow with grass.

затрав/ить *see* **затравливать;** hunt, persecute; **—ка** *f.* primer, priming (device); detonator, blasting cap; fuse; starter; (casting) start-up piece, dummy (bar); (typ.) first bite; (cryst.) inoculation, seed(ing); (chem.) seed crystal, trigger; disinfection (of soil); chase, drive, beating; bait; **внесение —ки** seeding; **—ление, —ливание** *n.* priming, etc., *see v.;* **газовое —ливание** fumigation; smudging; **—ленный** *a.* primed, etc., *see v.;* **—ливать** *v.* prime, inoculate, seed; persecute, chase; **—очный** *a. of* **затравка; —очный кристалл** seed.

затрагив/ание *n.* touching upon, etc., *see v.;* **—ать** *v.* touch upon, broach; affect; infringe (upon).

затрамбов(ыв)ать *v.* ram; plug.

затра/та *f.* expenditure, outlay, cost, expense; investment; input, consumption; **планирование —т** budgeting; **—тить** *see* **затрачивать; —ченный, —чиваемый** *a.* expended, etc., *see v.;* input; **—чивание** *n.* expenditure, spending, etc., *see v.;* **—чивать** *v.* expend, spend, consume, use; put in, invest.

затребов/ание *n.* request; **—ать** *v.* request, ask (for); demand, require.

затрепать *v.* wear out, exhaust.

затрепетать *v.* (begin to) palpitate.

затрёпывать *v.* wear out, exhaust.

затрещать *v.* start crackling.

затро/ганный, —нутый *a.* touched upon, etc., *see* **затрагивать; —нуть** *see* **затрагивать.**

затропический *a.* extratropical.

затрубное пространство annulus (of well casing).

затруднен/ие *n.* difficulty, trouble, problem; inconvenience, embarrassment; (steric) hindrance, inhibition; **без —ия** readily, easily; **в —ии** at a loss.

затруднённ/ость *f.* difficulty; **—ый** *a.* (made) difficult, complicated (by); labored (breathing); jerky (speech); **—ые роды** (med.) dystocia, abnormal labor.

затруднительн/о *adv.* with difficulty; **—ость** *f.* difficulty; **—ый** *a.* difficult; inconvenient, embarrassing.

затрудн/ить, —ять *v.* make difficult, inconvenience, (cause) trouble; impede, hamper, block (progress); complicate (matters); embarrass; **—яться** *v.* find (it) difficult or hard, meet with obstacles; hesitate, be at a loss.

затр/усить *v.* scatter, sprinkle (over); start shaking; **—ушенный** *a.* scattered, etc., *see v.;* **—ясти** *v.* start shaking; **—ястись** *v.* start shaking or trembling.

затуман/енный *a.* clouded, etc., *see v.;* **—и(ва)ть** *v.* cloud, fog (over), blur, dim; obscure, hide; **—и(ва)ться** *v.* cloud up, grow cloudy or foggy; get dim.

затуп/ившийся, —ленный *a.* dulled, blunt; **—ить, —лять** *v.* dull, blunt; break, round off (corners); **—иться, —ляться** *v.* get dulled or blunt; **—ление, —ливание** *n.* dulling, etc., *see v.;* bluntness.

затух/ание *n.* damping, etc., *see v.;* attenuation, decrement; diminution, weakening; loss; extinguishment; (radioactive) decay; (volcano) dormancy, waning; **измеритель —ания** decrementer; **магазин —ания** (elec. comm.) attenuator; **—ать** *v.* damp, attenuate, fade, die away, die down, subside; deteriorate; be damped; become extinguished, go out; **—ающий** *a.* damping, etc., *see v.;* damped, attenuated; transient (term); **—нуть** *see* **затухать.**

затуш/евать, —ёвывать *v.* shade, overshadow; cover up, hide, conceal, obscure; suppress; tint.

затуш/енный *a.* extinguished, out; **—ить** *v.* extinguish, put out; subdue, suppress.

затхл/ость *f.* stuffiness, mustiness; stagnancy; **—ый** *a.* stuffy, stale, close, musty; moldy; stagnant (water).

затык/ание *n.* stopping up, etc., *see v.;* **—ать** *v.* stop up, plug, cork (up), close; choke up, obstruct; stuff up, pack; stick, thrust (into); start weaving.

затылов/ание *see* **затыловка; —ать** *see* **затыловывать; —ка** *f.,* **—очный** *a.,* **—ывание** *n.* (tools) relieving, backing off, back-off; **—очный станок** relieving lathe; **—ывать** *v.* relieve, back off.

затыл/ок *m.* (anat.) occiput, back of head; nucha, nape (of neck); (meat) neck; poll (of horse); (tool) back; (bit) shank; (cam) heel; **—очная** *f.* occipital (bone); **—очно—** *prefix* (anat.) occipito—; **—очно-лобный** *a.* occipito-frontal; **—очно-сосцевидный** *a.* occipitomastoid; **—очный** *a. of* **затылок;** occipital; nuchal; **—ьник** *m.* back plate (of gun).

затычка *f.* plug, bung, stopper; stop-gap; pin; (anat.) obturator.

затюков(ыв)ать *v.* bale, pack.

затя/гиваемый *a.* prolonged; **—гивание** *n.* tightening, etc., *see v.;* pulling (of frequency); (telephoto) hangover, tailing; freezing (metal seizure); **—гивать** *v.* tighten, screw down, fasten (down), tie up; (min.) lace, lag; last (shoe); cover, close; draw out, protract, prolong, delay; inhale, draw in, suck in; involve, implicate; (med.) heal over, close; **—гиваться** *v.* tighten; drag on; (mech.) work up (between); **—жка** *see* **затягивание;** tie(-beam), tie rod, tie bar, draw bar, brace; (belt) tension; bridging; delay; (stairs) string; **ванна —жки** (electrochem.) strike bath; **—жной** *a.* tightening; draw (bolt), stay (wire); slip (knot); prolonged, protracted, lingering (illness); slow, incessant (rain); delayed (drop); sluggish, dragging out; **—нувшийся** *a.* protracted; **—нутый** *a.* tightened, etc., *see v.;* **—нуть** *see* **затягивать.**

зауж/енный *a.* constricted; **—ивать** *v.* constrict, narrow.

зауза *f.* (apid.) propolis honeycomb.

заузелковый *a.* (biol.) postnodal.

заузить *see* **зауживать.**

заузленный *a.* knotted.

заузловой *a.* (anat.) postganglionic.

заумный *a.* senseless, abstruse.

заунывный *a.* (orn.) melancholy (cry).

заупрямиться *v.* be obstinate.

зауральский *a.* (geog.) trans-Ural(ian).

заурановый *a.* transuranium.

заурида *f.* (ichth.) Saurida.

заурядный *a.* ordinary, mediocre.

заусен/ец *m.,* **—ица** *f.,* **—ок** *m.* (met.) burr; (casting) seam; projection, fin, flash, spew; hangnail; **с —цами** *a.* burred; **снимать —цы** *v.* deburr.

зауч/енный *a.* memorized, etc., *see v.;* **—и(ва)ть** *v.* memorize, learn (by heart); prepare (speech).

заушн/ица *f.* (med.) mumps, parotitis; **—ый** *a.* (anat.) parotid.

зафаршировать *v.* stuff.

зафиксиров/анный *a.* fixed; recorded; **—ать** *v.* fix, settle (on); record.

зафлюгированный *a.* (av.) feathered.

заформовать *v.* mold, shape.

зафосфачивать *v.* overfertilize with phosphate.

зафрахтов(ыв)ать *v.* charter (a ship).

захаживать *v.* go in, drop in, enter.

захарк(ив)ать *v.* clear one's throat; spit.

захварывать *v.* fall ill.

захват *m.* clamp, fastener, hold; claw, grapple, grip(per), catch, clutch; grab (bucket); scoop; trap; pickup, entrainment, entrapment, capture, seizure; (comp.) lockout; (fluoride) uptake; abstraction (of atom); engagement (of gears); encroachment, inroad; intake, recharge (of well); range, span, scope, swath, sweep; (roller) bite, nip; (sonar) lock-on; involvement; (phyt.) scorch(ing), burn(ing); hot-wind burn (of grains); **з. ядром** nuclear capture; **ширина —а** (mach.) working or operating width, coverage; **—ить** *see* **захватывать.**

захват/ка *f.* dog, detent, catch, checking device; **—нический** *a.* predatory (war); **—ный** *see* **захватывающий;** intake (zone of well); **—чик** *m.* aggressor; invader; (chem.) acceptor; (geol.) pirate river, diverter.

захватыв/ание *n.* capture, seizure; entrapment; capturing, etc., *see v.;* **—атель** *m.* grip, clamp, fastener; **—ать** *v.* capture, seize, take hold (of); (en)trap, entrain; bind; grip, clamp, hold; catch, grab, engage; include, cover, deal (with); take in; engulf, enclose; occupy, take over; encroach, make inroads (upon); stop (disease); surprise; catch unawares; detect; engross; **—ающий** *a.* capturing, etc., *see v.;* catch (lock); grab (bucket); **—ающая способность** hold.

захваченный *a.* captured, etc., *see* **захватывать.**

захворать *v.* fall ill, get sick(ly).

захи/леть, —реть, grow weak, feeble or sickly; **—релый** *a.* weak, feeble.

захлам/ить, —ливать, —лять *v.* choke up, block up, clutter up.

захл/ёб *m.* choking; **—ебнуть** *v.* gulp; **—ебнуться** *see* **захлёбываться; —ёбывание** *n.* choking; flooding (of column); **—ёбываться** *v.* choke, flood; (mach.) choke, stop, die.

захл/естать *v.* start lashing; **—естнуть** *see* **захлёстывать; —ёстывание** *n.* lashing, etc., *see v.;* **—ёстыватель** *m.* wrapper; **—ёстывать** *v.* (begin to) lash, whip; knot; (mach.) collar; wrap, wind (around), throw over; splash over, overflow; sprinkle, wet; overwhelm.

захлоп/ать *v.* start clapping, flapping or clacking; **—ка** *f.* flap; clack (valve); **—нуть, —ывать** *v.* slam shut; collapse (of cavitation bubbles).

захлороформировать *v.* chloroform.

захо/д *m.* stopping in, etc., *see v.;* entry, start (of screw thread); entrance; invasion (of territory); (av.) approach; pass; (dry) run; (target) run(-in); overshoot, overswing (of pointer); throat, funnel (of net); (sun) set; **без —да** *a.* non-stop; **—дить** *v.* stop in, drop in, look in, call (on); start walking; get (in), enter; (av.) approach; make a run; go (behind); turn a corner); set, go down (of sun); **—диться** *v.* go stiff or numb; **—ка** *f.* stope, cut, web, advance; **—дность** *f.* number of starts (of screw thread); **—дящий** *pr. part. of* **заходить;** setting (sun); (mil.) marching (flank); **—ждение** *n.* (biol.) transgression; (sun)set.

захоло/дать, —деть *v.* get cold; **—дить** *v.* chill; **—женный** *a.* chilled, cold.

захолуст/ный *a.* remote, isolated; **—ье** *n.* isolated place.

захор/анивать *see* **захоронить; —онение** *n.* burial; burial place, grave; dumping (of waste); deposit; concealment; **—онение в землю** underground disposal; **—онить** *v.* bury; conceal.

захотеть *v.* want, like (to); expect.

захрапеть *v.* begin to snore.

захрипеть *v.* begin to wheeze; get hoarse.

захромать *v.* (begin to) limp.

захряснуть *v.* thicken, congeal, harden; be choked (by weeds); get stuck.

захудать *v.* get thin.

зацарапать *v.* scratch (up).

зацве/сти *v.* start blooming; **—тание** *n.* efflorescence; flowering (period); bloom (of algae); (micr.) mold cover(ing). **—тать** *v.* blossom, be in bloom; get moldy, get covered with algae; get spotted (of glass).

зацементировать *v.* cement (in); lay concrete.

зацентр/альный *a.* (anat.) postcentral; **—(ир)ованный** centered; **—(ир)овать, —овывать** *v.* (mark the) center; drill centers; **—овка** *f.* centering; **—овщик** *m.* centering machine.

зацеп *m.* hook, catch, detent, stop, checking device; cam, cog; hooking, etc., *see* **зацеплять; —а** *see* **зацепка; —ить** *see* **зацеплять; —ка** *f.* hook, catch; (biol.) holdfast; hitch, snag, obstacle; occasion, cause; hooking, etc., *see* **зацеплять.**

зацепл/ение *n.* hooking, etc., *see v.;* engagement, gear(ing); contact; entanglement; (gen.) linkage; hook, catch; **в —ении** (mach.) in gear, engaged; **входить в з.** *v.* gear, mesh, engage; **выводить из —ения** *v.* disengage; **линия —ения** (mach.) line of action or contact; **находиться в —ении** *v.* be in gear, mesh (with); **угол —ения** (mach.) generating angle; **—енный** *a.* hooked, etc., *see v.;* **—ять** *v.* hook, catch, link, couple; engage, mesh, gear; bite, lock, grapple, seize; **—яться** *v.* engage, mesh; catch (on); **—яющий** *a.* hooking, etc., *see v.*

зацикливание *n.* (re)cycling.

зацинта *f.* (bot.) Zacintha.

зачадить *v.* smoke (up).

зачали(ва)ть *v.* fasten, fix, tie (down, to).

зачаст/ить *v.* accelerate, quicken; increase; become more frequent; (begin to) frequent; **—ую** *adv.* frequently, often.

зачат/ие *n.* conception, beginning; impregnation; **—ковый** *see* **зачаточный; —ок** *m.* rudiment, vestige; embryo, source; (embr.) primordium; (root) base; (leaf) bud; **—очный** *a.* of **зачаток;** rudimentary, vestigial; initial, incipient, embryonic; stunted, dwarf; **—очный член** rudiment, vestige; **в —очном состоянии** in embryo; in its infancy; **—ь** *v.* conceive; begin, commence, start; **—ься** *v.* be conceived, germinate; begin.

зачахнуть *v.* wither, wilt, droop.

зачекан/енный *a.* calked; **—и(ва)ть** *v.* calk (in); stake (rings on rolls); **—ка** *f.* calking, etc., *see v.*

зачелюстной *a.* (anat.) retromandibular.

зачем *adv.* why, what for, wherefore; **з.-то** for some purpose (or other).

зачервиветь *v.* become worm-eaten.

зачередовать(ся) *v.* start alternating.

за/чёркивание *n.* deletion, striking out, etc., *see v.;* **—чёркивать, —черкнуть** *v.* delete, strike out, cross out, erase; cancel; **—чёркнутый** *a.* deleted, etc., *see v.*

зачерни/ение *n.* blackening; **—еть** *v.* turn black; appear or look black or dark; **—ить, —ять** *v.* blacken.

зачерп *m.* scoopful; scooping; **—ать** *v.* start scooping; **—нуть, —ывать** *v.* scoop, ladle (out), draw; **—ывание** *n.* scooping, etc., *see v.*

зачерств/елый *a.* stale; hardened; insensitive; **—еть** *v.* get stale; become hardened.

зачер/тить, —чивать *v.* (begin to) sketch, draw, trace; doodle; **—ченный** *a.* sketched, etc., *see v.*

зачесать *v.* comb; start combing; start carding; start scratching; **—ся** *v.* start scratching; start itching.

зачесть *see* **зачитывать.**

зачёсывать *v.* (begin to) comb; card.

зачёт *m.* test, examination; compensation; instalment, part payment; taking into account; **это не в з.** it does not count; **—ный** *a.* of **зачёт;** on account; record (book).

зачехлить *v.* cover, encase, enclose, house.

зачечевичный *a.* (anat.) retrolenticular.

зачинат/ель *m.* initiator, pioneer, founder; **—ь** *v.* initiate, start; **—ься** *v.* begin.

зачин/и(ва)ть *v.* fix, mend, patch, repair; sharpen (pencil); **—щик** *m.* instigator.

зачисл/ение *n.* including, etc., *see v.;* **—енный** *a.* included, etc., *see v.;* **—ить,** **—ять** *v.* include, enter, put on the list; enlist, enroll; take on (staff); **—иться,** **—яться** *v.* join; enter.

зачист/ить *see* **зачищать; —ка** *f.* clean(s)ing, etc., see **зачищать;** purification.

зачитывать *v.* take into account, take into consideration; count (toward), take in payment (of); accept; reckon in; **—ся** *v.* be taken into account; become engrossed in reading.

зачихать *v.* start sneezing.

зачищ/ать *v.* clean(se), clean off; purify; clarify, clear, defecate (liquids); (foundry) trim, fettle, deburr, deflash; scrape, skin, strip (wire); (leather) pare; (rolling) condition the surface; grind (core); (met.) refine; groom (horse); **—енный** *a.* clean(s)ed, etc., *see v.*

зачнёт *fut. 3 sing. of* **зачать.**

зачтённый *past pass. part. of* **зачесть.**

зачумлённый *a.* plague-infected.

зашагать *v.* step out; start pacing.

зашатать *v.* start shaking or rocking; **—ся** *v.* get shaky, get loose; (begin to) falter.

зашвартов(ыв)ать *v.* fasten, moor.

зашвыр/ивать, **—нуть,** **—ять** *v.* throw, cast, hurl (away, behind).

зашевелить(ся) *v.* (begin to) move, stir.

зашедший *past. act. part. of* **зайти.**

заше/ек *m.,* **—йный** *a.* nape of the neck.

зашёл *past m. sing. of* **зайти.**

зашелестеть *v.* begin to rustle.

зашелудиветь *v.* become mangy or scabby.

зашептать *v.* (begin to) whisper.

зашершаветь *v.* become rough.

зашиб/ать, **—ить** *v.* hurt, bruise, wound; gain, acquire.

зашив/ание *n.,* **—ка** *f.* sewing (up), etc., *see v.;* planking panel; **—ать** *v.* sew up; (med.) suture; (comp.) hardwire; close, seal (bag); enclose, board up; **—очный** *a. of* **зашивка;** sewing (machine).

зашипеть *v.* start hissing.

зашит/ый *a.* sewn (up), etc., *see* **зашивать;** hardwired; **—ь** *see* **зашивать.**

зашифров/ание *n.,* **—ка** *f.,* **—ывание** *n.* (en)coding; ciphering; **—(ыв)ать** *v.* (en)code, codify; cipher.

зашкал/ивание *n.* off-scale reading; **—и(ва)ть** *v.* go off scale (of pointer); read off scale.

зашлаков/ка *f.,* **—ывание** *n.* slagging, etc., *see v.;* **—(ыв)ать** *v.* slag, scorify; (coal) clinker.

зашлёт *fut. 3 sing. of* **заслать.**

зашлифов/ать, **—ывать** *v.* grind, polish; **—ка** *f.,* **—ывание** *n.* grinding, polishing.

зашло *past n. sing. of* **зайти.**

зашлют *fut. 3 pl. of* **заслать.**

зашнуров(ыв)ать *v.* lace (up).

зашпа/клёванный *a.* puttied; **—клёвка** *f.,* **—левание,** **—лёвывание** *n.* puttying; **—клевать,** **—клёвывать,** **—тлев(ыв)ать** *v.* putty (up).

зашпили(ва)ть *v.* pin up, fasten.

зашплинтов(ыв)ать *v.* (mach.) cotter, fasten with a cotter pin.

зашпонивать *v.* key (to).

зашпунтов(ыв)ать *v.* tongue-and-groove.

заштамповать *v.* stamp, punch.

заштемпел/евать, **—ёвывать** *v.* stamp.

заштиле(ва)ть *v.* (naut.) become calm.

заштифтовывать *v.* secure with dowels.

заштоп(ыв)ать *v.* darn, mend.

заштори(ва)ть *v.* curtain, screen.

заштрихов/анный *a.* hatched, shaded; **—ать,** **—ывать** *v.* (cross)hatch, shade; **—ка** *f.,* **—ывание** *n.* (cross)-hatching.

заштукатури(ва)ть *v.* plaster up.

заштуков(ыв)ать *v.* mend invisibly.

заштыбовка *f.* (min.) gumming, jamming.

зашум/еть *v.* get noisy, begin to make noise; **—енность** *f.* noise level or pollution.

зашунтиров/анный *a.* (elec.) shunted, switched; **—ать** *v.* shunt, switch.

зашуршать *v.* start rustling.

зашьёт *fut. 3 sing. of* **зашить.**

защебени(ва)ть *v.* fill with rubble.

защебетать *v.* (begin to) twitter.

защека *f.* (ent.) posterior gena.

защелачив/ание *n.* alkalization; caustic treatment; (petrol.) overbasing (of additives); **—ать** *v.* alkalize.

защёлк/а *f.* catch, latch, trigger, pawl, stop, trip, release; arrester; **—ивание** *n.* fastening, etc., *see v.;* engagement; **—ивать,** **—нуть** *v.* fasten, latch, snap, engage; **—ивающий** *a.* fastening, etc., *see v.;* lock (mechanism); snap (lock).

защем/ить *see* **защемлять; —ление** *n.* pinching, etc., *see v.;* restraint; **сила —ления** restraining force; **—лённый** *a.* pinched, etc., *see v.;* built-in; **—лять** *v.* pinch, jam, bind; fix, fasten; restrain (beam); entrap (air); **—ляться** *v.* get pinched, etc.; hook (in), bite.

защеп/ить, **—лять** *v.* pinch; intercept.

защёчн/ый *a.* (anat.) retrobuccal; **—ые мешки** (zool.) storage pouches.

защип/нуть, **—(ыв)ать** *v.* pinch, nip.

защит/а *f.* defense, protection, security, (safe-)guard, precaution, proofing; shield(ing), sheltering; (fire prevention) measures; (soil) conservation; **з. данных по записи** (comp.) write protection; **з. от вредителей** pest control; **з. от нейтронов** (nucl.) neutron shield; **—ить** *see* **защищать; —ник** *m.* defender, protector; (law) defense counsel; **—ногерметический** *a.* airtight (door).

защитн/ый *a.* protecting, protective, guard; relaying; safety (device); (nucl.) shield(ing); shielded; containment (building); defense (reaction); conservation; khaki (color); seal (coat of paint); (micros.) cover (glass); baffle (plate); **з. газ** gas envelope; **з. кожух** (nucl.) jacket, can; **з. щит** face shield; **з. экран** (nucl.) shield; **—ая зона** buffer; **—ая корка** (petr.) desert varnish; **—ое вещество,** **—ое средство** preservative; **—ые тела** immune bodies, antibodies.

защиток *m.* (ent.) postscutellum.

защищ/аемый *see* **защищённый; —ать** *v.* protect, (safe)guard, screen, shield, shelter, enclose, cover; (make) proof; defend, uphold; (law) plead (for); **—ённость** *f.* (data) security; (mil.) hardening; **повышенная —ённость** superhardening; **—ённый** *a.* protected, etc., *see v.; suffix* **—proof;** (mil.) hardened; (comp.) copy protected; **—ённый от дурака,** **—ённый от неумелого обращения** foolproof.

заэвтект/ический *a.* (met.) hypereutectic; **—оидный** *a.* hypereutectoid.

заэкранировать *v.* shield, screen.

заяв/итель *m.* applicant; **—ить** *see* **заявлять** **—ка** *f.* application; request; requisition; claim; **—ка на патент подана** patent pending; **по —ке** on request; **по-**

давать —**у на** *v.* apply for; —**ление** *n.* claiming, etc., *see v.;* application; announcement, statement; —**ленный** *a.* claimed, etc., *see v.;* —**лять** *v.* claim, state, announce, declare; present; apply (for a patent); —**очный** *a.* of **заявка**.

заядлый *a.* inveterate, confirmed.

заякори(ва)ть *v.* anchor.

заяц *m.* (mam.) hare (*Lepus*); (astr.) Lepus; stowaway; **ехать зайцем** *v.* stow away; **земляной з.** (mam.) jerboa (*Allactaga*); **морской з.** bearded seal (*Erignathus barbatus*); (mal.) sea hare (*Aplysia*); **з.-беляк** *m.* varying hare (*Lepus timidus*); **з.-песчаник** Lepus tolai; **з.-русак** European hare (*Lepus europaeus*).

заяч/ий *a.* hare, leporine; rabbit (fur); **з. глаз** (med.) lagophthalmos; —**ьи** *pl.* hares and rabbits (*Leporidae*); —**ьи лапки** (bot.) rabbit-foot clover (*Trifolium arvense*); —**ья губа** (med.) harelip.

зва/ние *n.* status, rank, title; name; —**(н)ный** *a.* called, etc., *see v.;* —**ть** *v.* call, name; invite, bid, summon.

звезд/а *f.* star; (mach.) spider; **двойная з., дочерняя з.** (gen.) diaster; **морская з.** (zool.) starfish (*Asteroidea*); **одиночная з.** (gen.) monaster.

звёздный *a.* star, stellar, astral; sidereal (time); celestial (map); meteor (shower).

звездо— *prefix* astro—, star—; —**видный** *see* **звездообразный;** —**вик** *m.* (bot.) Geaster; —**гляд** *see* **звездочёт;** —**нос** *see* **звездорыл.**

звездообраз/ный *a.* star-shaped, star-like, stellate, asteroid; radial; **з. каркас, з. остов,** —**ная опора** (mach.) spider; —**ование** *n.* star formation.

звездо/пад *m.* meteor shower; —**плавание** *a.* astronautics; —**плодник** *m.* (bot.) Domasonium; —**рыл** *m.* (mam.) starnose mole (*Condylura cristata*); —**чёт** (ichth.) stargazer; —**чётовые,** —**чёты** *pl.* Uranoscopidae.

звёздочка *dim. of* **звезда;** star wheel, sprocket; stellate cam; (bot.) Stellaria; Astrantia.

звездчат/ка *f.* (bot). Stellaria; —**ковые** *pl.* (ichth.) Ogcocephalidae; —**о—** *prefix* star, astr(o)—, aster(o)—, stellato—; —**ость** *f.* (min.) asterism; —**ый** *see* **звездообразный;** star-covered; —**ые черви** (zool.) Gephyrea.

звёзды *pl. of* **звезда.**

звенеть *v.* ring, jingle, clink, clank.

звен/о *n.* (binding) link(age), bond; member, part, unit, section, component, element; (integrating) factor; network; team, group, crew; (geol.) member, bed, stratum; —**er,** *e.g.,* **управляющее з.** controller; —**ье** *see* **звено;** —**ьевой** *a.* of **звено;** *m.* crew foreman, team leader; —**ьеулавливатель** *m.* (art.) deflection plate; —**ья** *pl. of* **звено.**

звенящий *a.* ringing; **з. камень** (petr.) phonolite, clinkstone.

звер/ёк *dim. of* **зверь;** —**ёнок,** —**ёныш** *m.* cub; —**еть** *v.* brutalize; —**и** *pl. of* **зверь; высшие** —**и** true mammals (*Eutheria*); **низшие** —**и** marsupials; —**инец** *m.* menagerie; —**иный** *a.* of **зверь;** feral, wild; savage.

зверо— *prefix* ther(o)— (wild beast); —**боецветные,** —**бойные** *pl.* (bot.) Hypericaceae, Guttiferae; —**бой** *m.* St. John's wort (*Hypericum*); —**бойный** *a.* hunting, trapping; —**вать** *v.* hunt, trap; —**вод** *m.* fur (animal) breeder; —**водство** *n.,* —**водческий** *a.* fur farming; —**вой** *a.* of **зверь;** —**головые** *pl.* (herp.) Therocephalia; —**зубые** *pl.* (pal.) Ther(i)odontia; —**к** *see* **зверёк;** —**лов** *m.* trapper; animal collector; —**ловный** *a.,* —**ловство** *n.* trapping; —**ногие** *pl.* (pal.) Theropoda; —**образные** *pl.* Therapsida; —**образный** *a.* theromorphous; —**питомник** *m.* fur farm; —**по-**

—**добные** *pl.* (pal.) Theromorpha; —**совхоз** *m.* State fur farm; —**ферма** *f.* fur farm; —**ящеры** *pl.* Theromorpha.

звер/ский *a.* brutal, savage; ravenous (appetite); —**ствовать** *v.* behave savagely; —**ь** *m.* wild animal, beast; **пушной** —**ь** fur-bearing animal; **хищный** —**ь** beast of prey; —**ьё** *n.* wild beasts.

звон *m.* ring(ing), peal; clank, clanging; chime; sound; clatter; (med.) tinnitus; —**арь** *m.* (orn.) Procnia(s); —**ец** *m.* (ent.) midge (*Chironomus*); (bot.) Rhinanthus; —**ить** *v.* ring; clang; phone, call.

звонк/ий *a.* sonorous, resounding, ringing; clear; voiced (consonant); —**овый** *a.* bell; —**ость** *f.* sonorousness, reverberation; clearness; (paper) rattle, snap.

звон/ок *m.* bell; (tel.) call; *sh. m. of* **звонкий;** (bot.) *see* **звонец;** —**цы** *pl.* (ent.) Chironomidae; —**че** *comp. of* **звонкий.**

звук *m.* sound, tone; —**о—** *prefix* phon(o)—, sono—, sound, acoustic; —**оанализатор** *m.* sound analyzer; —**овидение** *n.* ultrasonoscopy, sonic holography; —**овик** *m.* sound ranger.

звуков/ой *a.* sound, acoustic; sonic; voice; aural, audible; with sound effects; audio (frequency); **з. генератор** *see* **звукогенератор; з. удар** sonic boom; —**ая волна** sound wave.

звуковоспр/инимающий *a.* sound-perceiving; —**оизведение** *n.* sound reproduction; —**оизводящий** *a.* sound-reproducing.

звуко/генератор *m.* audio(frequency) oscillator, tone generator; —**глушитель** *m.* silencer, muffler.

звукозапис/ыватель *m.* sound recorder; —**ывающий** *a.,* —**ь** *f.* sound recording.

звуко/защитный *a.* soundproofing; —**зонд** *m.* (min.) sonoprobe; —**излучатель** *m.* sound projector.

звукоизол/ировать *v.* soundproof, insulate; deafen; —**ирующий,** —**яционный** *a.* soundproof(ing); —**ятор** *m.* sound-absorbing material; —**яция** *f.* soundproofing, sound insulation.

звуко/локатор *m.,* —**локация** *f.* sonar; —**маскировка** *f.* sound camouflage; —**мер** *m.* phonometer; —**метрический** *a.,* —**метрия** *f.* sound ranging; —**непроницаемый** *a.* soundproof.

звуко/носитель *m.* sound-recording medium; —**оператор** *m.* soundman, mixer; —**отражение** *n.* sound reflection; —**ощущение** *n.* sound sensation, tone perception; —**пеленгатор** *m.* sound direction finder; —**пеленгация** *f.* sound fixing, sound ranging; —**передатчик** *m.* sound transmitter; —**передача** *f.* sound transmission; —**писец** *m.* sound recorder; —**пись** *f.* sound recording.

звукопогло/титель *m.* sound absorber, silencer, muffler; —**щательный,** —**щающий** *a.* sound-absorbing, muffling, quieting, soundproof; —**щение** *n.* sound absorption.

звуко/подражение *n.* sound effects; (med.) onomatopoiesis; —**подражательный** *a.* onomatopoeic, imitative; —**преломление** *n.* acoustical refraction; —**приёмник** *m.* sound detector; hydrophone; —**приёмный** *a.,* —**приставка** *f.* sound pickup.

звукопровод *m.* sound duct, acoustic line; —**имость,** —**ность** *f.* sound conductivity; —**ный,** —**ящий** *a.* sound-conducting.

звукопроекция *f.* sound projection.

звукопроницаем/ость *f.* sound transmission; acoustic permeability; —**ый** *a.* sound-transmitting.

звуко/рассеивание *n.* sonic scattering; —**рассеивающий слой** (biol.) scattering layer; —**сниматель** *m.* (sound) pickup; —**сочетание** *n.* sound combination;

—стирающий *a.* sound-erasing; **—съёмник** *m.,* **—съёмочный** *a.* pickup; **—тень** *f.* sound shadow; **—техника** *f.* phonics, acoustics, acoustic engineering.

звукоул/авливание *n.* sound detection; **—авливатель, —овитель** *m.* sound detector; **—авливающий** *a.* sound-detecting.

звукоусил/ение *n.* sound amplification; **—итель** *m.* sound amplifier; **—ительный** *a.* sound-amplifying.

звукофикация *f.* public address system.

звуч/ание *n.* sound(ing), sonorousness, vibration; **—ать** *v.* (re)sound, ring, clang; be heard; **—ащий** *a.* (re)sounding, etc., *see v.;* **—ность** *f.* sonorousness, sonority; **—ный** *a.* sonorous, resounding.

звяк *m.,* **—анье** *n.* tinkling; **—ать, —нуть** *v.* tinkle, jingle, clink.

з-д *abbr.* (**завод**) plant, works; **з.д.** *abbr.* (**западная долгота**) western longitude.

здание *n.* building, structure, house.

здесь *adv.* here; in this case; **з. также, и з.** here again.

здешний *a.* local, of this place; here.

ЗДМ *abbr.* (**закон действующих масс**) law of mass action.

здороваться *v.* greet.

здоров/енный *a.* robust, big, strong; **—еть** *v.* get strong(er), improve; recover one's health; *adv.* healthily, very (much); well (done); **—ость** *f.* healthiness, etc., *see a.;* **—ый** *a.* healthy, strong, big, robust; sound; wholesome (food); **—ье** *n.* health.

здрав/ница *f.* sanatorium, health resort; **—о** *adv.* soundly, sensibly, reasonably; *prefix* health.

здравомысл/ие *n.* common sense; **—ящий** *a.* sensible, sane, sober.

здрав/оохранение *n.,* **—оохранительный** *a.* public health, health care, health service; **—ость** *f.* common sense; **—отдел** *m.* health department; **—пункт** *m.* public health center or clinic, first-aid station, dispensary; **—ствовать** *v.* be in good health, be well, thrive; **—упр** *m.* public health administration; **—ый** *a.* sound, sane, sensible; common (sense).

зеаксантин *m.* zeaxanthin.

зебр/а *f.* (mam.) zebra (*Equus zebra*); zebra fish (*Serranus scriba*); **з.-рыба** lionfish (*Pterois volitans*); **—асома** *f.* (ichth.) Zebrasoma; **—ина** *f.* (mal.) Zebrina; **—оид** *m.* (mam.) zebroid.

зебу *m.* (mam.) zebu (*Bos indicus*); **—видный** *a.* humped (cattle).

зев *m.* mouth, throat, opening, orifice; jaw opening, gap, span (of wrench); (text.) shed; **—анье** *n.* yawning, gaping.

зеваршанский *a.* (geog.) Zevarshan.

зеват/ельный *a.* yawning; **—ь** *see* **зевнуть.**

зевг/ит *m.* (bot.) zeugite; **—оподий** *m.* (anat.) zeugopodium, zygopodium.

зев/ник *m.* jaw spreader; **—нуть** *v.* yawn, gape; miss (an opportunity); **—ный** *a. of* **зев**; **—ок** *m.* yawn; **—ообразование** *n.* (text.) shedding; **—ота** *f.* yawning, gaping.

зевсовые *pl.* (ichth.) Zeidae.

зегеровский *a.* Seger (cone).

зеебековский *a.* Seebeck (effect).

зеемановский *a.* Zeeman (effect).

зеер *m.* press room; cage; (food) molder.

зеин *m.* zein.

зейбахит *m.* (min.) seebachite.

зейбертит *m.* (min.) seybertite.

зейгер/ный *a.,* **—ование** *n.* (met.) liquation, segregation; **—ованный** *a.* liquated; **—овать** *v.* liquate, segregate.

зейдлицкий *a.* Seidlitz (powder).

зеймер *m.* edger, trimmer.

зейский *a.* (geog.) Zeya.

Зейтца фильтр Seitz filter.

зелен *sh. m. of* **зелёный**; **зелёная** *f.* green (pigment); **—ей** *gen. of* **зеленя**; **—ение** *n.* turning green, etc., *see v.;* **—еть** *v.* turn green, show green; (bot.) frondesce; **—еющий** *a.* turning green; virescent, greenish; frondescent; **—ить** *v.* color green, make green.

зелёнка *f.* (bot.) Blakstonia; a mushroom (*Tricholoma flavovirens*).

зеленой *a. of* **зелень.**

зелено— *prefix* viridi—, chlor(o)—, green(ish); **—ватый** *a.* greenish; **—глазка** *f.* (ent.) green-eyed fly (*Chlorops pumilionis*); (ichth.) greeneye; **—глаз(ков)ые** *pl.* (ichth.) Chlorophthalmidae; **—глазый** *a.* green-eyed; **—жёлтый** *a.* greenish yellow; **—каменный** *a.,* **—каменная порода** (petr.) greenstone; **—лист(вен)ный** *a.* greenleaved, viridifolious; **—мошник** *m.* mossy forest; **—плодный** *a.* green-fruited, chlorocarpous; **—спинка** *f.* (ichth.) skipjack herring (*Alosa chrysochloris*).

зелёность *f.* greenness.

зеленотелка *f.* (ent.) dragonfly (*Somatochlora*); **—удобритель** *m.* green manure.

зелен/уха, —ушка *f.* (ichth.) wrasse (*Crenilabrus tinca*); damselfish (*Chromis Ch.*); (bot.) Tricholoma; (orn.) greenfinch (*Chloris*); **—ушки** *pl.* (ent.) long-legged flies (*Dolichopodidae*); **—ушковые** *pl.* (ichth.) Labridae; **—ца** *f.* greens; greenish color; **—чак** *m.* (min.) jade; (ichth.) weed goby (*Gobius ophiocephalus*); **—чук** *m.* (bot.) Galeobdolon; (ent.) Euthystira; Chrysochraon; **—щик** *m.* green grocer, produce retailer.

зелён/ый *a.* green; shade-tree (plantation); softwood (cutting); chloro—, *e.g.,* **—ый пигмент** chlorophyll.

зелен/ь *f.* greens, vegetables; verdure; green (pigment); **—я** *pl.* (agr.) young sprouts.

зелигман(н)ит *m.* (min.) seligmannite.

зельдь *f.* (ichth.) cisco (*Coregonus sardinella*).

зелье *n.* potion; greens; **вонючее з.** (bot.) coriander (*Coriandrum sativum*).

зельтерская вода Seltzer water.

зельц *m.* (food) head cheese.

зем— *prefix see* **земельный; землесосный; землечерпательный.**

земель *gen. pl. of* **земля**; **—ный** *a.* land, soil, agrarian, agricultural; land (metals).

земле— *prefix* earth, land; (foundry) sand; **—битная стена** rammed earth wall, pisé de terre wall; **—вание** *n.* earth moving; **—ведение** *v.* physical geography.

землевлад/елец *m.* landowner, landholder, landlord; **—ение** *n.* land ownership.

земледел *m.* (foundry) sand mixer; **—ец** *m.* farmer, cultivator, tiller, agriculturist; **—ие** *n.* farming, cultivation, agriculture; **—ка** *f.* (foundry) sand-mixing department; **—ьная** *f.* sand shop; **—ьческий** *a.* agricultural.

земле/использование *n.* land utilization; **—коп** *m.,* **—копный** *a.* excavator, (steam) shovel; **—коповые** *pl.* (mam.) Bathyergodae; **—люб** *m.* (zool.) centipede (*Geophilus*); **—мер** *m.* land surveyor; **—мерие** *n.* land survey(ing), geodesy; **—мерный** *a.* surveying, geodetic; **—меры** *pl.* (ent.) Geometridae; **—пашец** *m.* farmer; **—подъёмник** *m.* excavator; **—пользование** *n.* land use; **—приготовительный** *a.* (foundry) sand-mixing; **—роб** *m.* farmer.

землерой *m.* (ent.) dung beetle (*Geotrupes*); (mam.) burrowing rodent; **—ка** *f.* (mam.) shrew (*Sorex*); **—ков-**

ые *pl.* Soricidae; **—кокрот** *m.* shrew-mole; **—но-планировочный** *a.* grading; **—но-транспортные работы** earth moving; **—ный** *a.* earth-moving, excavation; digging (tool); **—ная машина** excavator.

земле/собственник *m.* land owner; **—сос** *m.,* **—сосная драга** hydraulic dredge(r), dredge pump; **—сосный** *a.* dredging; **—трясение** *n.* earthquake; **—уплотнитель** *m.* roller.

землеустро/итель *m.* land manager; **—ительный** *a.,* **—йство** *n.* land management, land use; soil improvement; **—ительное дело** land use planning.

землечерп/алка *f.,* **—ательная машина** dredge(r), excavator; **—ание** *n.,* **—ательный** *a.* dredging; **—ательные работы** dredging, excavation work.

земли *pl., etc. of* **земля; —стость** *f.* earthiness; **—стый** *a.* earthy.

земл/я *f.* earth, ground, soil; land, terrain, surface; (foundry) sand; the (planet) Earth; **з. до спутника** uplink; **белая з.** terra alba, pipe clay; **голубая з.** (min.) blue ground, kimberlite; **жёлтая з.** (min.) yellow earth or ocher; yellow soil; **редкие —и** rare earths; **у —и** surface (wind); **з.-воздух** (missiles) surface-to-air; **з.-з.** surface-to-surface; **—як** *m.* fellow countryman, compatriot; **—ян** *m.* (ichth.) nase (*Chondrostoma nasus*).

землян/ика, —ичина *f.,* **—ичный** *a.* strawberry (*Fragaria*); **—ичник** *m.* strawberry tree (*Arbutus*).

землянка *f.* mud hut, dugout.

землян/ой *a.* earth(en), earthy; (elec.) ground; (met.) sand (mold); mineral (pigments); **з. воск** ozocerite, mineral wax; **з. орех** peanut; **з. червяк** earthworm; **—ая груша** (bot.) Jerusalem artichoke (*Helianthus tuberosus*); **—ая смола** (geol.) black-stone, ampelite, carbonaceous shale; **—ая станция** (satellite) ground station; **—ые работы** excavation, earth moving.

зем/ляночный *a.* dugout; **—ляцкий** *a. of* **земляк; —ник** *m.* (min.) ground coal.

земноводн/ое *n.* amphibian; **—ые** *pl.* Amphibia; **—ый** *a.* amphibian, amphibious; terraqueous; **—ые растения** (bot.) amphiphytes.

земн/ой *a.* terrestrial, earthly; earth's; land; (elec.) ground; geo—, *e.g.,* **з. магнетизм** geomagnetism; **з. шар;** the Earth; globe; **—ая кора** earth's crust, lithosphere; **—ые работы** excavation, earth moving.

зем/орган *m.* land registry office; **—от(дел)** *m.* department of agriculture; **—снаряд** *m.* hydraulic or suction dredge(r); **—упр** *m.* land administration; **—фонд** *m.* land resources.

зензивер *m.* (bot.) Malva silvestris.

зензубель *m.* (carp.) rabbet plane.

зенит *m.* zenith; (astr.) apex; **—ка** *f.* antiaircraft gun; **—ный** *a.* zenith; antiaircraft; **з.-телескоп** *m.* (astr.) zenith telescope; **—чик** *m.* antiaircraft gunner.

зенк/ер *m.* (mach.) countersink, counterbore; spot facer; reamer, hole-enlarging multiflute drill; **—ерование** *n.,* **—еровка** *f.* reaming, hole-enlarging; **—еровать** *v.* ream; **—ование** *n.* countersinking, etc., *see v.;* **—овать** *v.* countersink, counterbore; spot-face; **—овка** *see* **зенкование; зенкер.**

зеравшанский *a.* (geog.) Zeravshan.

зёрен *gen. pl. of* **зерно.**

зеринге *m.* (herp.) sand racer (*Psammophis schokari*).

зеркал/ка *f.* reflex camera; **—о** *n.* mirror; (med.) (opt.) speculum; surface (of liquid); (water) table; (valve) face, seat; **под —о** mirror (finish); **—овые** *pl.* harvestfishes (*Pampidae*); **—о-отражатель** *m.* mirror-reflector; **—о-прожектор** *m.* mirror-searchlight.

зеркально/-линзовый *a.* catadioptic (lens); **з.-отражённый** *a.* (phys.) mirror-image; **з.-поворотная**

ось axis of mirror rotation symmetry; **—подобный** *a.* mirror-like; **з.-полированный** *a.* mirror-finished, highly polished; **—сть** *f.* reflectivity; smoothness.

зеркаль/ный *a. of* **зеркало;** smooth; specular; reflecting; reflex (camera); plate (glass); image (frequency, forces, etc.); mirror-image, optical (isomerism); **з. чугун** (met.) spiegeleisen; **—це** *dim. of* **зеркало;** (zool.) tapetum (of eye); wax plate (of bees).

зёрна *pl. of* **зерно;** grit, granulations.

зерн/а *gen. of* **зерно;** *f.* (bot.) Zerna; **—ение** *n.* granulation; pelletizing; **—ёный** *a.* granulated; **—истослан-цеватый** *a.* granular-cleavable; **—истость** *f.* granularity, grain size, mesh; (phot., etc.) graininess, grainy texture; (histol.) granulation; **—истый** *a.* granular, granulated, grainy; clotted (oil); (met.) spheroidized; **—ить** *v.* granulate; pelletize; knurl, mill; **—о** *n.* grain, granule, kernel, nodule, pellet; seed, stone, pit (of fruit); (fat) globule; (oil) droplet; cereals.

зерно— *prefix see* **зерновой; —аспиратор** *m.* pneumatic classifier, grain aspirator; **—бобовый** *a.* (bot.) leguminous, pulse; **—ведение** *n.* grain science; **—видный** *a.* granuliform, granular; **—вик** *m.* grain grower; (ent.) seed-eating beetle; **—вка** *f.* (bot.) caryopsis; (ent.) weevil (*Bruchus*); **—вки** *pl.* (ent.) Bruchidae; **—воз** *m.* grain freighter; **—возка** *f.* grain wagon.

зернов/ой *a.* grain, granular; (petr.) granulometric (composition); seed, corn, cereal; **з. спирт** grain alcohol; **—ые** *pl.,* **—ые хлеба** cereals, grain crops.

зернодробил/ка *f.* grain mill, grain grinder; **з.-плющилка** *see* **зерноплющилка; —ьный** *a.* (grain) milling, crushing.

зерно/заготовительный *a.* grain procurement; **—мёт, —метатель** *m.* grain blower, grain thrower; **—образный** *a.* granuliform, granular; **—отделитель** *m.* grain separator, classifier; **—отходы** *pl.* grain waste.

зерноочист/итель *m.* grain cleaner; (corn) sheller; **—ительный** *a.,* **—ка** *f.* grain cleaning; winnowing.

зерно/плющилка *f.* grain flattener, bruising mill; **—погрузчик** *m.* grain loader or conveyer; **—поставка** *f.* grain delivery; **—початкодробилка** *f.* corn and cob crusher; **—пульт** *m.* grain blower; **—самосев** *n.* self-seeding grain; **—склад** *m.* grain storage; granary; **—слив** *m.* grain overflow or flue; **—совхоз** *m.* State grain farm; **—сортировальный** *a.* grain-sorting; **—сортировка** *f.* grain grader; **—стой** *m.* grain crop; **—сушилка** *f.* grain dryer; **—транспортер** *m.* grain conveyer; **—уборочный** *a.* grain-harvesting; **—увлажнитель** *m.* grain humidifier; **—уловитель** *m.* grain catcher; **—фураж** *m.,* **—фуражный** *a.,* fodder grain; **—хранилище** *n.* granary, elevator; **—ядный** *a.* granivorous.

зёрнышко *dim. of* **зерно;** granule.

зеро *n.* zero.

зет *m.* (letter) Z; **—а** *f.* zeta (Z, ζ); **—образный** *a.* Z-shaped; **—овый** *a.* Z, zee— , Z-shaped; **—овая балка** (met.) Z section; **з.-хромосома** *f.* (gen.) Z-chromosome.

зефир *m.* (text.) zephyr; (food) marshmallow; (ent.) Zephyrus.

зига *f.* ridge (of corrugated metal).

зигаденус *m.* (bot.) zygadenus.

зигальгинский *a.* (geog.) Zigalga.

зигальный *a.* (anat.) zygal, H-shaped.

зиганиды *pl.* (ichth.) Siganidae.

зигапофиз *m.* (anat.) zygapophysis.

зиг/бановский *a.* Siegbahn; **—бургит** *m.* (min.) siegburgite; **—енит** *m.* siegenite.

зигзаг *m.* zigzag; **—овидный, —ообразный** *a.* zigzag, crisscross, staggered; serrated, notched, saw-like.

зигмашина *f.* creasing or beading machine.

зиго— *prefix* (biol.) zygo— (yoke, pair; joined, junction; zygosis).

зигов/ание *n.,* **—ка** *f.* (met.) bead forming.

зиго/гамия *f.* (gen.) zygogamy; **—мицеты** *pl.* (bot.) Zygomycetes; **—морфный** *a.* zygomorphic; **—спора** *f.* zygospore; **—та** *f.* (gen.) zygote; **—тический** *a.* zygotic; **—фаза** *f.* zygophase, diploid phase; **—фор** *m.* zygophore.

зиждиться *v.* be based, be founded (on).

зиз/ания *f.* (bot.) Zizania; **—ифора** *f.* Ziziphora; **—ифус** *m.* jujube (*Zizyphus jujube*).

зик— *see under* **зиг—**.

зил *m.* Zil (automobile).

зилаирский *a.* (geog.) Zilair.

зильберглет *m.* (silver met.) litharge.

зильмердакский *a.* (geog.) Zilmerdak.

зим *m.* Zim (automobile).

зима *f.* winter.

зимаза *f.* zymase (yeast enzyme).

зимнезелён/ый *a.* (bot.) wintergreen, winter-leafing; **—ые леса** hiemisylvae, monsoon forests.

зим/ний *a.* winter, hibernal, hiemal; hardwood (cutting); **—ник** *m.* winter road; **—няк** *m.* (orn.) rough-legged buzzard (*Buteo lagopus*); **—о** *prefix* winter; zymo- [ferment(ation)]; **—овал** *m.* hibernating pond; **—овалый** *a.* having wintered; **—овальник** *see* **зимовал;** **—овальный** *a.,* **—ование** *n.* wintering, hibernating; **—овать** *v.* winter, hibernate; **—овка** *f.* wintering, hibernation; winter dwelling; wintering grounds; polar station; **—овник** *m.* (bot.) Colchicum; Helleborus; winter hut; winter hive; **—овочный** *a. of* **зимовка; —овщик** *m.* (polar research) winterer; **—овье** *see* **зимовка.**

зимо/ген *m.* zymogen; **—грамм** *m.,* **—грамма** *f.* zymogram; **—зан** *m.* zymosan.

зимой *adv.* in winter.

зимол/из *m.* zymolysis; **—огия** *f.* zymology.

зимо/любка *f.* (bot.) wintergreen (*Chimaphila*); **—родки, —родковые** *pl.* (orn.) Alcedinidae; **—родок** *m.* kingfisher.

зимостерин *m.* zymosterol, mycosterol.

зимо/стойкий *a.* (winter-) hardy, cold-resistant; **—стойкость, —устойчивость** *f.* hardiness, cold tolerance.

зимофосфат *m.* zymophosphate.

зим/ою *adv.* in winter; **—ующий** *a.* wintering, hibernating.

зингиберон *m.* zingiberone, zingerone.

зинеровский *a.* Zener (breakdown).

зинтер-корунд *m.* (cer.) sintered alumina.

зис *m.* Zis (automobile).

зия/ние *n.* yawning, gaping; hiatus, chasm, gap; **—ть** *v.* yawn, gape, open; **—ющий** *a.* yawning, gaping.

зла *gen. of* **зло.**

злак *m.* grass; **—и** *pl.* cereals; **—и, —овые** *pl.* (bot.) grasses (*Gramineae*); **полевые —и** cereals; **—овидный** *a.* gramineous, grasslike; **—овник** *m.* grassland; **—овый** *a.* grass(y), gramineous, herbaceous; chloropid (flies); **—оцветный** *a.* glumiflorous.

златк/а *f.* (ent.) wood borer; **—и** *pl.* Buprestidae; **—ощелкуны** *pl.* Eucnemidae.

злато/бров *m.* (ichth.) gilthead (*Sparus auratus*); **—глазик** *m.* (ent.) deer fly (*Chrysops*); **—глаз(и)ки** *pl.* Chrysopidae; **—гузка** *f.* brown-tail moth (*Euproctis*); **—искр** *m.* (min.) aventurine; **—крот** *m.* (mam.) golden mole; **—кротовые, —кроты** *pl.* Chrysochloridae;

—лист *m.* (bot.) Chrysophyllum; **—цвет** *m.* Pyrethrum; **—чки** *pl.* (ent.) Trachyinae.

зл/ейший *a.* worse, bitterest; **—еть** *v.* become irritable; get angry; **—ить** *v.* irritate, vex, annoy, anger.

зло *n.* evil, wrong, harm; malice, anger; *adv.* maliciously; **употреблять во з.** *v.* abuse, misuse; **—ба** *f.* spite; malice; grudge; **—биться** *v.* be angry (at, with); **—бный** *a.* malicious; **—бодневный** *a.* topical, burning (question); **—бствовать** *v.* be enraged; bear malice; **—воние** *n.* bad odor, stink, stench; **—вонный** *a.* malodorous, stinking, fetid; offensive-smelling; **—вредный** *a.* harmful, noxious; pernicious.

зл/ой *a.* malicious, vicious; angry; bad (time); **—ая трава** (bot.) Thapsia.

злокачественн/ость *f.* (med.) malignancy; **—ый** *a.* malignant; destructive, detrimental; pernicious (anemia).

зло/ключение *n.* mishap; **—намеренный** *a.* ill-intentioned; **—получный** *a.* ill-fated, unlucky, unfortunate; **—словить** *v.* slander; **—стный** *a.* malicious; fraudulent; persistent (weed); **—сть** *f.* malice; fury, anger.

злоумышленн/ик *m.* evildoer, felon; adversary (of protection system); (comp.) intruder; **—ый** *a.* with criminal intent.

злоупотреб/ить, —лять *v.* abuse, misuse, exploit; **—ление** *n.* abuse; misuse.

злю/т *pr. 3 pl. of* **злить; —щий** *a.* vicious; furious.

змее— *prefix* ophi(o)—, ophid— (snake, serpent); **—видный** *a.* coil(ed), spiral; snake-like, serpentine, sinuous; **—вик** *m.,* **—виковый** *a.* coil (pipe), spiral, worm; spiral drill; (bot.) bistort (*Polygonum bistorta*); (min.) serpentine; (petr.) serpentinite; **—вик-холодильник** *m.* condenser coil, cooling coil; **—вка** *f.* (bot.) Displachne; **—глав, —голов** *m.* (ichth.) snakehead (*Ophiocephalus; Channa*); **—головка** *f.* (herp.) Ophisops; **—головник** *m.* (bot.) dragonhead (*Dracocephalum*); **—головые** *pl.* (ichth.) Ophi(o)cephalidae, Channidae; **—головый** *a.* ophiocephalous, snake-headed; **—к** *gen. pl. of* **змейка; —листный** *a.* (bot.) serpentifolious, ophiophyllous; **—носец** *m.* (astr.) Ophiuchus; **—ёныш** *m.* young snake; **—образный** *see* **змеевидный; —рыбка** *f.* a pipefish (*Nerophis ophidion*); **—собачковые** *pl.* (ichth.) Ophi(o)clinidae; **—хвостки** *pl.* (zool.) Ophiuroidea; **—шейки** *pl.* (orn.) snakebirds (*Anhingidae*); **—яд** *m.* short-toed eagle (*Circaëtus*); **—ящерица** *f.* (herp.) Ophiomorus.

змеи *pl.* (herp.) snakes (*Ophidia; Serpentes*); **морские з.** Hydrophi(i)dae; **—ногорский** *a.* (geog.) Zmeinogorsk; **—ношейный** *a.* snake-neck(ed); **—ный** *a. of* **змея;** anguine; serpentine (curve); **—ный корень** (bot.) *see* **змеевик; —стый** *a.* snake-like, sinuous, winding; **—ться** *v.* wind, coil, twist; meander; glide; glance over, skim, scan; (geol.) serpentinize.

змей *m.* kite; serpent; *gen. pl. of* **змея; воздушный з.** kite; **—ка** *dim. of* **змея;** (av.) S-turn; (agr.) spiral seed classifier; (ichth.) greater weever (*Trachinus draco*); **водяные —ки** (zool.) Naididae; **движение —кой** snaking (motion); **—ки-рыбы** *pl.* (ichth.) Trachinidae; **—ковый** *a.* kite; **—ковый аэростат** kite (balloon).

змея *f.* snake, serpent; *gen. of* **змей; з.-стрела** *f.* (herp.) Psammophis.

ЗМС *abbr.* (**зона малых скоростей**) low-velocity zone, weathered layer (in seismic surveying).

зн. *abbr.* (**знак; значение; значащий**).

знавать *v.* (used to) know.

знак *m.,* **—овый** *a.* sign, symbol, mark, indication; character, letter; (decimal) point; (weighing) place; (comp.) digit; badge; (license) number; trademark; **з. азбуки**

Морзе Morse code character; **з. pH** pH symbol, index of acidity; **з. атома** atomic symbol; **з. иона** charge; **двоичный з.** (comp.) bit, binary digit; **до . . . (десятичного) знака** to the . . . (decimal) place; **—оинвертор** *m.* (comp.) sign inverter.

знаком/ить *v.* acquaint, introduce; inform; familiarize; **—иться** *v.* get acquainted, meet; study, investigate; become familiar, familiarize oneself (with); **—ство** *n.* acquaintance (with), familiarity (with); knowledge (of); **—ый** *a.* acquainted, familiar (with); (well) known; *m.* acquaintance.

знако/определённый *a.* of fixed sign; **—переменный** *a.* alternating, of alternating sign; sign-variable; variable-polarity (excitation); reversed (stress); **—печатающий** *a.* character-writing; **—печаточная электрон-нолучевая трубка** character-writing tube; **—положительный** *a.* of positive sign; **—постоянный** *a.* of constant sign; **—чередующийся** *a.* alternating.

знамён *gen. pl.;* **—а** *pl. of* **знамя.**

знаменатель *m.* (math.) denominator; **—ный** *a.* denominative; significant, noteworthy, important.

знамени *gen. of* **знамя.**

знамение *n.* sign, phenomenon, token.

знаменит/ость *f.* celebrity, fame; **—ый** *a.* celebrated, famous, eminent.

знаменный *a. of* **знамя.**

знаменовать *v.* prove, show, indicate, express, signify, mark.

знам/ехвостый *a.* (zool.) banner-tailed; **—я** *n.* banner, standard; (mil.) colors.

знан/ие *n.* knowledge; science; skill; **сумма —ий, уровень —ий** know-how.

знатный *a.* notable, eminent, distinguished; considerable, great.

знаток *m.* connoisseur, judge, expert.

знать *v.* know, have knowledge (of), be informed (of), be aware (of), be acquainted (with); be skilled (in), have the know-how; **дать з.** inform; **дать себя з.** reveal oneself; make itself felt; **—ся** *v.* associate (with).

знахарство *n.* quackery, quack medicine.

знач/ащий *a.* meaning; meaningful; significant (digit); distinct; **—ение** *n.* value; meaning, sense; import(ance), significance; (field) data; magnitude, extent (of error); **иметь —ение** *v.* mean, be important (for); **не иметь —ение** *v.* be of no importance, be immaterial; **среднее —ение** (stat.) expectation value.

значим/ость *f.* significance, importance; meaning(fulness); index; **—ый** *a.* significant, meaningful.

значит *introd. word* so, then, hence.

значительн/о *adv.* significantly, etc., *see a.;* much; **з. больше** much more, well over; **з. выше** well above, far above; **—ость** *f.* significance; magnitude; **—ый** *a.* significant, substantial, great, considerable, appreciable, important, marked, pronounced, drastic; major (part); **в —ой степени** much (as); well into.

значить *v.* mean, signify; **—ся** *v.* be (mentioned), appear.

значкист *m.* badge wearer.

значн/ость *f.* valency; atomicity; word length (of code); significance; *suffix* **—валуедность** -valuedness; **—ый** *a.* marking; significant; (comp.) digit; *suffix* -digit, -valued.

значок *dim. of* **знак;** sign, mark, badge; index, subscript, superscript.

зна/ющий *a.* knowing; learned; expert, skilled; **—ющее лицо** expert; **—я** *pr. ger. of* **знать;** given, knowing.

зноб/ить: его —ит he has chills; **—кий** *a.* sensitive to cold; chilling.

зной *m.* heat, sultriness, swelter; hot, sultry, oppressive; torrid.

зоантарии *pl.* (zool.) Zoantharia.

зоар/ий *m.,* **—ия** *f.* (zool.) zoarium.

зоархия *f.* (ichth.) Zoarchias.

зоб *m.* (zool.) crop, craw, ingluvies; (med.) goiter, struma; **—а(с)тый** *a.* large-cropped; (med.) strum(ifer)ous; **—ик** *dim. of* **зоб; —ный** *a. of* **зоб; —ная болезнь** goiter; **—ная железа** (anat.) thymus; **—ное моло(ч)ко** (orn.) pigeon's milk; **—оватость** *f.* (phyt.) crown gall, cancer; **—овидный** *a.* strumose; **—огенный** *a.* goitrogenic.

зов *m.* call, summons, invitation; **—ущий** *a.* calling, etc., *see* **звать.**

зодиак *m.* (astr.) zodiac; **—альный** *a.* zodiacal.

зодч/ество *n.* architecture; **—ий** *m.* architect.

зо/е(а) *f.* (crust.) zoea; **—еция** *f.* (biol.) zooecium; **—ид** *m.* zo(o)id; **—идогамия** *f.* (gen.) zoidiogamy; **—идиофильный** *a.* (bot.) zoidiophilous; **—йсия** *f.* Zoysia.

зол *sh. m. of* **злой;** *gen. pl. of* **зло.**

зол/а *f.* ashes, cinders; **содержание —ы** ash content; **з.-унос** *f.* fly ash, flue dust.

золей *gen. pl of* **золь.**

золенгофенский *a.* Solenhofen (stone).

зол/ение *n.* (leather) liming; lixiviation; **—ёный** *a.* limed.

золи *gen., pl., etc., of* **золь.**

зол/ильный *a.* (leather) liming; **—истость** *f.* ash content; **—истый** *a.* ash(en); **—ить** *v.* lime; **—ка** *f.* liming.

золли *pl.* (geol.) depressions.

золо/едины *pl.* (met.) blowholes, air holes; **—обдуватель** *m.* soot blower; **—образование** *n.* ashing, incineration; **—отвал** *m.* ash dump; **—отстойник** *m.* slag settler, settling tank.

золот/арник, —ень *m.* (bot.) golden rod (*Solidago*); **—еть** *v.* turn gold (colored); shine (like gold); **—ильный** *a.* gilding; **—ина** *f.* gold grain.

золотисто— *prefix* chrys(o)—, gold(en); auro—, aurous; **—жёлтый** *a.* golden yellow; **—золотой** *a.* auroauric; **—плодные** *pl.* (ent.) Chrysididae; **—плодный** *a.* (bot.) chrysocarpous; **—родановодородный** *a.* aurothiocyanic (acid); **—синеродоводородный** *a.* aurocyanic (acid); **—сть** *f.* golden color; **—хлороводородный** *a.* chloroaurous (acid).

золот/истый *a.* golden, gold-colored; gilt; gold, aurous; **—ить** *v.* gild.

золотник *m.* slide valve, gate valve; zolotnik [old unit (4.26 g.)]; **—овый** *a. of* **золотник;** plunger (pump); **—овая пара** slide valve; spool-and-sleeve.

золот/о *n.* gold, Au; **закись —а** aurous oxide; **соль закиси —а** aurous salt; **листовое з.** gold leaf, gold foil; **окись —а** auric oxide, gold trioxide; **соль окиси —а** auric salt; **хлористое з.** aurous chloride, gold monochloride; **хлорное з.** auric chloride, gold trichloride.

золото— *prefix* gold, auri—, auric; **—бит, —боец** *m.* gold beater; **—бородник** *m.* (bot.) Chrysopogon; **—бров** *see* **златобров; —глазка** *f.* (ichth.) goldeye; **—глазки** *pl.* (ent.) Chrysopidae; **—добывающий** *a.,* **—добыча** *f.* gold mining; **—искатель** *m.* gold prospector.

золот/ой *a.* gold(en); auric; **з. дождь** (bot.) Laburnum; **з. корень, —ая печать** golden seal (*Hydrastis canadensis*); **з. песок** gold dust; **з. прииск** (min.) placer (deposit); **—ая кислота** auric acid; **соль —ой кислоты** aurate; **—ое дерево** (bot.) Aucuba; **—ое сечение** (geom.) golden section.

золото/кислый *a.* auric acid; aurate (of); **з. натрий** sodium aurate; **—кислая соль** aurate; **—мойка** *f.* gold washing.

золотонос/ость *f.* gold content; **—ый** *a.* gold-bearing, auriferous.

золото/органический *a.* organogold; **—подобный** *a.* gold-like, golden; **—промывочный** *a.* gold-washing; **—промышленник** *m.* gold miner; **—промышленность** *f.* gold mining.

золотосинерод/истый *a.* auricyanhydric (acid); auricyanide (of); **—оводородный** *a.* cyanoauric (acid).

золото/содержащий *see* **золотоносный; —тысячник** *m.* (bot.) Centaurium; **—хлор(ист)оводородный** *a.* chloroauric (acid); **—хлористый** *a.* chloroaurate (of); **—цвет** *m.* (bot.) Pyrethrum; **—цианистоводородный** *see* **золотосинеродистый; —черпательная машина** gold dredge(r).

золоту/ха *f.* (med.) scrofula; **—шник** *see* **золотарник; —шный** *a.* scrofulous.

Золотые Ворота (geog.) Golden Gate.

золо/удаление *n.* ash removal; **—удалитель** *m.* ash remover; **—улавливание** *n.* ash trapping; **—уловитель** *m* ash trap.

золоч/ение *n.* gilding, gold-plating; **—ё(н)ный** *a.* gilded, gilt, gold-plated.

золошлакоотвал *m.* ash dump.

золь *m.* sol, colloidal solution; **з.-каучук** *m.* sol rubber, latex.

зольн/ик m. ash pit, ash bin; cinder pit; (tanning) lime pit; lime (liquor); (bot.) Cineraria; Russian thistle (*Salsola ruthenica, S. kali*); **—ость** *f.* ash content; **—о-шлаковый** *a.* cinder; **—ый** *a.* ash(y), cinder; lime (water); **—ое вещество** ashes.

золь-фракция *f.* sol fraction.

зоман *m.* soman, pinacolyl methylphosphonofluoridate.

ЗОН *abbr.* (**зональная опытная станция**) zonal experimental station.

зона *f.* zone, area, field, region; belt, band, range; **—льно** *adv.* by zones; **—льность** *f.* zonality, zoning; **—льный, —рный** *a.* zonal, regional, local; **—льное распределение** zoning.

зонгорин *m.* songorine, napellonine.

зонд *m.* sound, probe; test pit, trial boring; (meteor.) sonde; sounding balloon; (surgical director; (dental) explorer; **—аж** *m.,* **—ирование** *n.* sounding, etc., *see v.;* **—ировать** *v.* sound, probe; search, explore; bore; pit test; (med.) intubate; **—ировка** *f.,* **—ировочный** *a.* sounding, etc., *see v.;* (min.) log(ging); **—ировочный бур** probe; **—ирующий** *a.* sounding, etc., *see v.;* exploratory; transmitter, transmitted (pulse); **—овый** *a. of* **зонд.**

зондские острова (geog.) the Sunda Islands.

зон/ирование *n.* zoning; **—ированный** *a.* zoned; **—ировать** *v.* zone; **—ит** *m.* (zool.) zonite, body segment; **—ный, —овый** *a. of* **зона;** zonal; (phys.) band (theory).

зонт *m.* umbrella; canopy, awning; cover; (exhaust) hood; **—ик** *see* **зонт;** (bot., zool.) umbel(la); **—иковидный** *a.* umbrella-shaped, umbelliform; **—иколистный** *a.* umbrella-leaved; **—иконосный** *a.* umbellate, umbelliferous; **—икообразный** *see* **зонтиковидный; —икоцветные** *see* **зонтичные; —икоцветный** *a.* (bot.) umbelliferous; **—ичек** *dim. of* **зонтик;** (bot.) umbellule; **—ичковый** *a.* umbellulate; **—ичнокистевой** *a.* corymbose; **—ичные** *pl.* Umbelliferae; **—ичный, —ообразный** *a.* umbrella(-shaped), umbellate; **—овидный** *a.* umbraculiform; **—овый** *a. of* **зонт; —ообразный** *see* **зонтиковидный.**

зоо— *prefix* zoo— (animal); **—бентос** *m.* zoobenthos, bottom fauna; **—ветеринарный** *a.* zootechnical-veter-

inary; **—ветпункт** *m.* veterinary station; **—ветучасток** *m.* veterinary district; **—гамета** *f.* (gen.) zoogamete; **—ген** *m.* (geol.) zoogene; **—генный** *a.* zoogenous, zoogenic; **—география** *f.* zoogeography, faunal geography; **—гигиена** *f.* animal health care; **—глейный** *a.* (bact.) zoogl(o)eal; **—глея** *f.* zoogl(o)ea; **—гонидий** *m.* (bot.) zoogonidium; **—ид** *m.* (biol.) zooid; **—ксантеллы** *pl.* (prot.) Zooxanthellae; **—кумарин** *m.* Warfarin (rat poison); **—лит** *m.* (pal.) zoolith, zoolite.

зоолог *m.* zoologist; **—ический** *a.* zoological; **—ия** *f.* zoology.

зоо/мариновый *a.* zoomaric (acid); **—мастигины** *pl.* (prot.) Zoomastigina; **—ноз** *m.* (med.) zoonosis; **—нозный** *a.* zoonotic; **—паразит** *m.* zooparasite, parasitic animal; **—парк** *m.* zoo, zoological garden; **—планктон** *m.* zooplankton; **—профилактика** *f.* zooprophylaxis, preventive veterinary care; **—сад** *m.* zoo; **—спора** *f.* zoospore; **—стерин** *m.* zoosterol; **—тамний** *m.* (prot.) Zoothamnium.

зоотехн/ик *m.* zootechnician, livestock expert; **—ика, —ия** *f.* zootechny, animal husbandry; **—ический** *a.* zootechnic, livestock.

зоо/токсин *m.* zootoxin (*e.g.* snake venom); **—том** *m.* zootomist, comparative anatomist; **—томия** *f.* zootomy; **—фаг** *m.* zoophagan, carnivorous animal; **—ферма** *f.* fur farm; **—фильный** *a.* (bot.) zoophilous; **—фит** *m.* (zool.) zoophyte; **—химический** *a.* zoochemical; **—химия** *f.* zoochemistry; **—хор** *m.* (bot.) zoochore; **—хорный** *a.* zoochoric, animal-dispersed; **—ценоз** *m.* zoocenosis, animal community; **—цид** *m.* rodenticide; **—цидный** *a.* rodenticidal; **—эций** *m.* zo(o)ecium.

зопник *m.* (bot.) Phlomis.

зораптера *f.* (ent.) Zoraptera.

зори *pl. of* **зоря; заря.**

зорилла *f.* (mam.) zorilla (*Ictonyx striatus*).

зорить *v.* ripen (produce); spoil.

зорк/ий *a.* sharp-sighted; alert, vigilant; **—ость** *f.* keen vision; vigilance.

зоркульский *a.* (geog.) Zor-Kul.

зорь *gen. pl. of* **заря; —ка** *f.* (bot.) Lychnis; (ent.) Euchloe; orange-tip (*Anthocharis cardamines*); (orn.) dawn owl (*Otus scops*).

зоря *f.* (bot.) lovage (*Levisticum*).

зостера *f.* (bot.) Zostera.

ЗПО *abbr.* (**зона противолодочной обороны**) antisubmarine defense zone, ASW zone.

зрач/ковый *a.* (anat.) pupil(lary); **—ок** *m.* pupil; **выходной —ок** (opt.) exit pupil.

ЗРБ *abbr.* (**золотник регулятора безопасности**) safety regulator valve; **ЗРД** *abbr.* (**золотник регулятора давления**) pressure regulator valve.

зрелище *n.* sight, spectacle; show.

зрел/овылупляющийся *a.* (orn.) precocial; **—ость** *f.* ripeness, maturity, readiness; puberty; **ат(т)естат —ости** secondary school completion certificate; **—ый** *a.* ripe, mature, ready; adult; **—ый возраст** maturity; **—ьник** *m.,* **—ьня** *f.* (text.) ager.

зрен/ие *n.* (eye)sight, vision; **—ия** *pl.* purpose, aim; **обман —ия** optical illusion; **поле —ия** visual field; **с точки —ия** from the viewpoint (of); in terms (of); with relation (to), as regards.

зреть *v.* ripen, mature, age; see, look (at).

зри/мый *a.* visible; **—тель** *m.* spectator, onlooker, observer; viewer; audience.

зрительн/ый *a.* visual, optic(al); signal (communication); **з. бугор** (anat.) thalamus; **з. зал** auditorium;

—**ая труб(к)а** telescope, —**ое стекло** (micros.) eyepiece.

зрительский *a.* of **зритель.**

ЗРС *abbr.* (**золотник регулятора скорости**) speed-regulator valve.

зря *adv.* in vain, to no purpose, for nothing, uselessly.

зрячий *a.* sighted; *m.* sighted person.

зряшный *a.* purposeless, absurd; groundless, unfounded, empty.

ЗС *abbr.* (**замедляющая способность**) moderating power; (**зондирование становлением**) induced electromagnetic field (method).

ЗУ *abbr.* (**запоминающее устройство**) (comp.) memory; (**звукоулавливатель**) sound detector; (**зеркальный угломер**) mirror goniometer.

зуб *m.* tooth, cog, spike, spur; tine (of fork); (cutting) blade; (hydr.) cut-off; (anat.) dens, tooth; *see also* **зубец; в з.** end on; **задний з.** molar; **морской з.** (mal.) Dentalium; —**ан** *m.* (ichth.) dogtooth (*Dentex*); —**арик** *m.* (ichth.) puntazzo; —**арь** *m.* (carp.) toothed plane; (ichth.) zander (*Stizostedion lucioperca*); damselfish (*Chromis ch.*); triggerfish (*Balistes capriscus*); (orn.) merganser (*Mergus*); —**астые** *pl.* (ichth.) Cyprinodontidae; —**астый** *a.* large-toothed; —**атка** *f.* bush hammer, crandall; tooth ax; (ichth.) wolffish (*Anarhichas*); chum salmon (*Oncorhynchus keta*); common name for several species; —**атковые** *pl.* Anarhichadidae; —**атый** *a.* toothed, dentate; **з.-выталкиватель** *m.* (agr.) knock-out pawl.

зубец *m.* tooth, cog, projection, spur, barb, claw; dent, indent(ation); notch; merlon (of wall); prong, tine (of fork); (geol.) pinnacle; (drill) bit; (med.) wave (on ECG).

зубик *dim. of* **зуб.**

зубил/о *n.,* —**ьный** *a.* chisel; calking iron, bit, punch, drift; **вырубать** —**ом** *v.* gouge, chisel out; **обрубать** —**ом** *v.* trim, chisel off; **рубить** —**ом** *v.* chisel.

зубн/ой *a.* tooth, dental; **з. камень** tartar; **з. врач** dentist; **з. протез** denture; —**ая система** dentition; —**ое вещество** dentine; —**ое средство** dentifrice.

зубо— *prefix* tooth, dent(i)—; (mach.) tooth, gear; —**видный** *a.* tooth-like, tooth-shaped, dentiform, odontoid; dent (corn); —**вик** *m.* (mal.) Dentalium; —**вой** *a.* tooth(ed.)

зубоврач *m.* dentist; —**ебный** *a.* dental; —**евание** *n.* dentistry.

зубо/долбежный *a.,* —**долбление** *n.* (mach.) gear shaping; —**закругление** *n.* gear chamfering; —**измерительный** *a.* gear-measuring.

зуб/ок *dim. of* **зуб;** bulbil; (garlic) clove; (cutting) bit; —**ки** *pl.* (min.) cutter; —**олапчатый** *a.* tenaculum (forceps).

зуболечебн/ица *f.* dental surgery; —**ый** *a.* dental, dentist's.

зубо/мер *m.* gear(-tooth) gage; —**накатывание** *n.* gear rolling; —**нарезание** *n.* gear cutting; —**ножка** *f.* (ent.) Hydrotaea dentipes; —**обкатка** *f.* gear burnishing; —**обрабатывающий станок** gear cutter; —**образный** *see* **зубовидный;** —**отделка** *f.* —**отделочный** *a.* gear finishing; —**очистка** *f.* toothpick; —**притирочный** *a.* gear-lapping; —**протезный** *a.* denture; —**рез** *m.* gear cutter; —**резный** *a.* gear-cutting; —**строгальный станок** gear planer; —**строгание** *n.* gear planing, gear shaping; —**технический** *a.* dental (laboratory, etc.); **зуб-отражатель** *m.* (agr.) cut-off pawl; —**фрезерный** *a.* gear-hobbing, gear-milling; —**шевинговальный** *a.* gear-shaving; —**шлифовальный** *a.* gear-grinding.

зубр *m.* (mam.) bison, *spec.* auroch (*Bison bonasus*).

зубр/ение *n.* serration, etc., *see v.;* —**ить** *v.* serrate, notch, (in)dent, nick; memorize, cram.

зубров/ка *f.* (bot.) sweet grass (*Hierochloë*); sweet-grass vodka; —**ник** *m.* slough grass (*Beckmannia erucaeformis*); —**ый** *a.* of **зубр.**

зуб/ца *gen. of* **зубец;** —**цевидный** *a.* dentiform; —**чатка** *f.* (mach.) gear (wheel); sprocket; (rack and) pinion; serrated pick; (bot.) Odontites; (ent.) Smerinthus.

зубчато— *prefix* denti—, odont(o)— (tooth); dentato—, dentate(ly); —**головые** *pl.* (ichth.) Denticipitidae; —**листный** *a.* (bot.) odontophyllous; —**ножка** *f.* (ent.) Denticnemis; **з.-рассечённый** *a.* (geol.) incised-dissected; —**сть** *f.* dent(icul)ation; serration, (in)dentation.

зубчат/ый *a.* toothed, gear(ed), cogged, serrate(d), (in)dented, notched, jagged, ridged; (bot.) dentate; hackly (fracture); **з. барабан, з. блок** sprocket; **з. механизм** gear train; **з. перебор** gearing; **з. рельс** rack; —**ая передача** gear (drive); **соединённый —ой передачей** geared; —**ая полоса, —ая рейка** rack; —**ое зацепление** gearing, gear system; —**ое колесо** gear (wheel), cog wheel; sprocket.

зуб/чик *dim. of* **зуб;** denticle; serration, ripple (on curve); —**чики** *pl.* (wave) ripple; —**ы** *pl.* (anat.) dentes, teeth; —**ы вне дуги** buckteeth; —**ый** *a. suffix* toothed; —**ья** (mach.) *pl. of* **зуб;** —**янка** *f.* (bot.) Dentaria.

зуд *m.* (med.) pruritus, intense itching; (mach.) buzz; —**ение** *n.* buzzing, humming; —**ень** *m.* (ent.) mite (*Acares, Sarcoptes*); —**еть, —ить** *v.* itch; yearn (for); buzz, hum; —**невые, —и** *pl.* Sarcoptidae; —**ящий** *a.* (med.) pruritic, pruriginous, itching.

зу/ек *m.* (orn.) plover (*Charadrius*); —**йки** *pl.* Charadriidae.

зулусский *a.* (geog.) Zulu.

Зуля мазер Suhl(-type) maser.

зумм/ер *m.* (elec.) buzzer, hummer; audio signal; (tel.) tone; —**ерить** *v.* buzz, hum; —**ерный** *a.* buzzer; humming; **з.-прерыватель** *m.* buzzer; —**ирование** *n.* buzzing, humming.

зум(п)ф *m.* —**овый** *a.* sump, pit; —**насос** *m.* sump pump; —**офен** *m.* pit furnace.

зунд *m.* (geog.) sound, strait.

ЗУПВ *abbr.* (**запоминающее устройство с произвольной выборки**) random-access memory, RAM.

ЗУР *abbr.* (**зенитная управляемая ракета**); **ЗУРС** *abbr.* (**зенитный управляемый реактивный снаряд**) antiaircraft guided missile.

зухтон *m.* (acous.) search tone.

зушинский *a.* (geog.) Zusha.

зыб/иться *v.* surge, swell; —**кий** *a.* unstable, unsteady, vacillating; quaking; —**кость** *f.* instability; vacillation; —**ление** *n.* vacillation, fluctuation; —**ун** *m.* quaking bog; quicksand; —**учий** *a.* shifting, unsteady; quick (sand); —**ь** *f.* ripple(s); surge, swell (of sea).

зык *m.* sharp, loud noise; cry; —**ать, —нуть** *v.* call, cry out; whizz, whistle (of bullets); cut short.

зырянский *a.* (geog.) Zyiryanka.

зычный *a.* loud, stentorian, ringing.

зюзник *m.* (bot.) Lycopus.

зюид *m.,* —**овый** *a.* (naut.) south.

зяб/кий *a.* chilly, sensitive to cold; —**кость** *f.* chilliness; —**левый** *a.* fall (plowing), fall-plowed; —**лик** *m.* —**лица, —ловка** *f.* (orn.) chaffinch (*Fringilla coelebs*); —**ликовые** *pl.* Fringillidae; —**лина** *f.* (geol.) frost cleft; —**лый** *a.* frost-damaged; —**нуть** *v.* feel chilly; freeze; —**ра** *f.* (bot.) hemp nettle (*Galeopsis speciosa*); —**ь** *f.* fall plowing; fall-plowed field; **на —ь, под —ь** fall (plowing).

И

и *conj.* and, also, too; but, although; both; even, as well as; **и . . . и** both . . . and; **и тот и другой** both.

иатрохимия *f.* (med.) iatrochemistry.

ибер/ийка *f.,* **—ис** *m.* (bot.) Iberis; **—ийский** *a.* (geog.) Iberian.

иби/жара *f.* (herp.) Amphisbaena alba; **—с** *m.* (orn.) ibis; **—совые** *pl.* Ibididae, Threskiornithidae; **—целла** *f.* (bot.) Ibicella.

ибо *conj.* for, as; in (the sense) that.

ИВ *abbr.* (индекс вязкости) viscosity index, V.I.; (идеальное вытеснение) plug flow; *and others.*

ива *f.* (bot.) willow (*Salix*).

иван-да-марья *f.* (bot.) cow wheat (*Melampyrum nemorosum*).

иванов хлеб (bot.) carob tree (*Ceratonia siliqua*); **и. червяк** (ent.) firefly; **—ский** *a.* (geog.) Ivano; late-summer (fallow).

иван-чай *m.* (bot.) willow herb [*Chamaenerion* (or *Epilobium*) *angustifolium*].

ивас/евый *a.,* **—и** *f.* (ichth.) Pacific sardine (*Sardinops sagax melanosticta; Sardinella m.*).

ивишень *m. or f.* (bot.) Clitopilus prunulus.

ив/няк *m.,* **—няковый** *a.* willow thicket, osier bed; **—овые** *pl.* (bot.) Salicaceae; **—овый** *a.* willow.

иволг/а *f.* (orn.) oriole; **—и, —овые** *pl.* Oriolidae.

иволистный *a.* willow-leaved, salicifolious.

ига/зуровый, —суровый *a.* igasuric (acid).

игап/о, —у *m.* ygapo (swamp rain forest).

игелстромит *m.* (min.) igelströmite.

игепон *m.* Igepon (detergent).

игл/а *f.* needle, stylus; (landing) spike; (zool.) spine; (bot.) thorn; spicule; pivot; (text.) card wire; (volcano) lava plug; (Pele's) tear; **и.-рыба** *f.* (ichth.) pipefish (*Syngnathus*); **и.-копьё** *f.* arrow-shaped blade; **—ецы** *pl.* (ichth.) Polyacanthidae; **—истый** *a.* needle-shaped, acicular; prickly, thorny; **—ица** *f.* (bot.) butcher's broom (*Ruscus aculeatus*); **—ицевые** *pl.* (bot.) Ruscaceae; (ichth.) Syngnathidae.

игло—*prefix* acanth(o)— [thorn(y), spine]; echin(o)— (spiny); **—бок** *m.* (mal.) Acanthopleura; **—брюх** *m.* (ichth.) puffer (*Tetraodon*); porcupine fish (*Diodon hystrix*); **—брюхие, —брюховые** *pl.* Tetraodontidae; **—видные** *see* **игловые; —видный** *a.* needle-shaped, acicular; **—вые** *pl.* pipefishes, seahorses (Syngnathidae); **—держатель** *m.* needle holder; **—кожие** *pl.* (zool.) Echinodermata; **—колюшковые** *pl.* (ichth.) Indostomidae; **—набивный** *a.* needle-felting; **—носный** *a.* acanthophorous, thorn-bearing, prickly; **—образный** *see* **игловидный; —пробивный** *a.* needle-punching; **—сдавливание** *n.,* **—терапия** *f.,* **—укалывание** *n.* (med.) acupuncture; **—фильтр** *m.* (construction) well point; **—хвост** *m.* (orn.) swift (*Chaetura*); **—шерст** *m.* (mam.) porcupine (*Erethizon*).

иглы *pl. of* **игла; морские и., и.-рыбы** *pl.* (ichth.) Syngnathidae.

игна/тьевский *a.* (geog.) Ignatiev; **—ция** *f.* St. Ignatius' bean (*Strychnos ignatii*).

игнимбрит *m.* (petr.) ignimbrite, welded tuff.

игнитрон *m.,* **—ный** *a.* (elec.) ignitron.

игнорир/ованный *a.* ignored, etc., *see v.;* **—овать** *v.* ignore, disregard, neglect; **—уемый** *a.* negligible.

игнотин *m.* ignotine, carnosine.

игол/ка *see* **игла; —очка** *dim. of* **игла; —очный, —ьный** *a. of* **игла; —ьник** *m.* needle case; (bot.) fallen needles; **—ьница** *f.* needle holder.

игольчат/ый *a.* needle(-shaped), acicular, spiny, spicular; point (contact); spiked (roller); **и. клапан** needle valve; **—ая лента** (text.) card clothing; **—ая рейка** point gage; **—ая руда** (min.) needle ore, aikinite.

игр *gen. pl. of* **игра.**

игра *f.* (free) play, freedom, slack, give, looseness, backlash; clearance; game, sport; freak (of nature); (wine) sparkling; (apid.) play flight; **и. валков** backlash; **теория игр** (math.) game theory; **—ть** *v.* play; effervesce, bubble, sparkle; glitter, scintillate.

игрек *m.* (math.) *y* (value); Y (alloy, etc.).

игр/истый *a.* sparkling, frothy, foaming; **—овой** *a. of* **игра; —унка** *f.* (mam.) marmoset; **—унковые** *pl.* Callit(h)ricidae; **—ушечный** *a.,* **—ушка** *f.* toy, plaything; **—ывать** *see* **играть.**

игуана *f.* (herp.) iguana.

ид/ант *m.* (gen.) idant, chromosome; **—ация** *f.* idiovariation, mutation.

иддингсит *m.* (min.) iddingsite.

идеал *m.* ideal; **в —е** ideally; **—изированный** *a.* ideal(ized); **—изировать** *v.* idealize; **—ьно** *adv.* ideally; perfectly, completely; **—ьнорассеянный** *a.* uniform diffuse; **—ьность** *f.* the ideal; **—ьный** *a.* ideal, optimum; theoretical; **—ьное вытеснение** plug flow; **—ьное смешение** back mixing; **в —ьном случае** ideally.

идейный *a. of* **идея;** ideological.

идемпотентный *a.* (math.) idempotent.

иденти/фикатор *m.* identifier; **—фикационный** *a.,* **—фикация** *f.* identification; **—фицированный** *a.* identified; **—фицировать** *v.* identify, determine; attach a code; **—фицируемый** *a.* identifiable, identified; **—чность** *f.* identity; **—чный** *a.* identical.

идёт *pr. 3 sing. of* **идти.**

идея *f.* idea, notion, concept(ion).

идиакантовые *pl.* (ichth.) black dragonfishes (*Idiacanthidae*).

идио—*prefix* idio— (separate, distinct; self-produced); **—бласт** *m.* idioblast; **—вариация** *f.* idiovariation, mutation; **—генит** *m.* (geol.) idiogenite; **—генный** *a.* idiogenous; **—грамма** *f.* (gen.) idiogram.

идиом *m.,* **—а** *f.* idiom; **—атический** *a.* idiomatic.

идио/морфный *a.* (min.) idiomorphic, euhedral; **—патический** *a.* (med.) idiopathic, self-originated; **—патическое заболевание** idiopathy; **—плазма** *f.* (gen.) idioplasma, germ plasm; **—синкразия** *f.* idio(syn)crasy; **—сома** *f.* (cyt.) idiosome; **—статический** *a.* (elec.) idiostatic.

идиот *m.* idiot, imbecile; **—изм** *m.* idiocy.

идиотип *m.* (gen.) idiotype.

идиот/ический, —ский *a.* idiotic, imbecile; **—ия** *f.,* **—ство** *n.* idiocy.

идио/фанизм *m.* (cryst.) idiophanism; **—фанный** *a.* idiophanous; **—хроматический** *a.* (min.) idiochromatic; **—электрический** *a.* idioelectric(al).

идит *m.* iditol (a hexahydric alcohol).

идите *imp. of* **идти.**

идитод *m.* a phenol-formaldehyde resin.

идоза *f.* idose, pentahydroxyhexanal.

идокраз *m.* (min.) idocrase, vesuvianite.

идол *m.* idol.

идоновая кислота idonic acid.

идосахарная кислота idosaccharic acid.

идофураноза *f.* idofuranose.

и др. *abbr.* (и другое) et cetera; (и другие) and others, et al.

идр/иален *m.* (min.) idrialene; **—иалит** *m.* idrialite; **—ил** *m.* idryl, fluoranthene.

ид/ти *v.* go, come (toward); operate, run, work; progress, proceed; reach; travel, traverse, cross; pass, elapse; stretch, lie, extend; leave, start, set out; walk, move (along); drive, sail, fly; be on, flow; take place; join (army); enter (school); spread (of rumor); (com.) sell; **и. за** follow; **и. во, на** or **подо** be used in, be spent on, go on, be required for.

идулия *f.* (mal.) Idulia.

идуроновый *a.* iduronic (acid).

идущий *a.* going, etc., *see* **идти**; **и. вверх** rising; **и. вниз** descending, falling; **и. назад** retrogressive.

ИДЦ *abbr.* (**радиолокационный индикатор движущихся целей**) radar moving-target indicator.

иды *pl.* ides.

идя *pr. ger. of* **идти**.

иезаконитин *m.* jesaconitine.

иезуитский *a.* Jesuit.

иекориновый *a.* jecoric (acid).

иенит *m.* (min.) yenite, ilvaite.

иенское стекло Jena glass.

иерарх/ический *a.* hierarchic, multilevel; **—ичность, —ия** *f.* hierarchy.

иервин *m.* jervine.

иероглиф *m.* hieroglyph.

иерский *a.* (geog.) Iera.

иерусалимский *a.* (geog.) Jerusalem.

иетолин *m.* jetolin (aniline black).

иецекит *m.* (min.) ježekite.

иж/евский *a.* (geog.) Izhevsk; **—емский** *a.* Izhma; **—ский** *a.* Izh (river).

из *prep. gen.* out of, of, from, with; among; **вода из рек** river-derived water; *prefix* ex-; *with verbs to mean* use up (by); *see also* **ис—**.

изадрин *m.* isoproterenol, Aludrine.

изаконитовый *a.* is(o)aconitic (acid).

изалло/бара *f.* (meteor.) isallobar; **—барический** *a.* isallobaric; **—терма** *f.* isallotherm.

изамин *m.,* **—овый** *a.* isamine.

изамовая кислота isamic acid.

изановая кислота isanic acid.

изаномал/а *f.,* **—ь** *m.* (meteor.) isanomal, isanomalous line; isabnormal line.

изарол *m.* Isarol, sulfaphenazole.

изасский *a.* (geog.) Izas.

изат/ат *m.* isatate; **—ин** *m.* isatin, indolinedione; **—иновый** *a.* isat(in)ic (acid).

иза/товая кислота isatoic acid, N-carboxyanthranilic acid; **—тогеновый** *a.* isatogenic (acid); **—токсим** *m.* isatoxime, nitrosoindoxyl; **—тофан** *m.* isatophan; **—тропил** *m.* isatropyl; **—троповый** *a.* isatropic (acid); **—фенин, —цен** *m.* isaphenine, isacen; **—феновый** *a.* isaphenic (acid).

изба *f.* hut, cottage, cabin, shack.

избав/ить *see* **избавлять**; **—ление** *n.* release; elimination; escape; **—ленный** *a.* released, etc., *see v.*; **—лять** *v.* release, relieve (from), rid (of), free (of), save (from); **—ляться** *v.* get rid (of), remove, eliminate; escape (from).

избалов(ыв)ать *v.* indulge, pamper, spoil.

изба-читальня *f.* village reading room.

избе/гать, —гнуть, —жать *v.* avoid, shun; obviate; escape, evade, dodge, avert; **—жание** *n.* avoidance, escape, averting; **во —жание** to avoid.

изби/вать *v.* beat up; damage; wear out; **—ение** *n.* beating up, etc., *see v.*; slaughter, massacre, killing; (law) assault and battery.

избир/аемый *a.* selected, chosen; preferred; **—ание** *n.* selection; **—атель** *m.* selector; (frequency) discriminator; elector, voter; *pl.* electorate; **—ательность** *f.* selectivity; discrimination; selective action; eligibility; **—ательный** *a.* selective; discriminating; electoral, election; **—ательный механизм** selector; **—ательная способность** selectivity; discrimination; selective action; eligibility; **—ать** *v.* select, choose, pick out; elect.

избит/ый *a.* beaten, etc., *see* **избивать**; **—ь** *see* **избивать**.

избоина *f.* (oil) cake.

изборо/ждать, —здить *v.* furrow, ridge, groove; striate; travel all over; **—ждение** *n.* furrowing, etc., *see v.*; (geol.) striation, striae; **—ждённый** *a.* furrowed, etc., *see v.*

избр/ание *n.* selection; election; **—анник** *m.,* **—анница** *f.* the chosen one; elect; **—анный** *a.* selected; elected; **—ать** *see* **избирать**.

избура— *prefix* brownish.

избушка *dim. of* **изба**.

избыт/ок *m.* excess, surplus, redundancy; abundance, profusion; (phase) margin; **и. нейтронов** neutron excess; **сумма —ков** (meteor.) accumulated excess; **—очно** *adv.* in excess; **—очность** *f.* excess(iveness), surplus; redundancy; **—очный** *a.* excess(ive), in excess, redundant, surplus, superfluous; overflow; over-(dose, size, etc.); gage (pressure); hyper—, e.g. **—очный метаморфоз** hypermetamorphosis.

избяной *a. of* **изба**.

изв. *abbr.* (**известия**) bulletin, news.

изва/яние *n.* sculpture; **—ять** *v.* sculpture, carve, chisel, cut; form.

изведать *see* **изведывать**.

изведённый *a.* consumed, etc., *see* **изводить**.

изведывать *v.* learn, find out; investigate, try; experience, come to know, see.

извер/гать, —гнуть *v.* erupt, eject, expel, emit, discharge; excrete; vomit; throw out, ejaculate; **—гаться** *v.* erupt; **—гнутый, —женный** *a.* erupted, etc., *see v.*; (geol.) eruptive, igneous, volcanic, plutonic, magmatic; **—жение** *n.* eruption, etc., *see v.*; discharge, outbreak.

извернуться, извёртываться *v.* evade, dodge.

известе— *prefix* lime; **—гасилка** *f.,* **—гаситель** *m.* lime slaker; **—гасильный** *a.* lime-slaking; **—любивый** *a.* lime-loving; **—мешалка** *f.* lime mixer.

известен *sh. m. of* **известный**.

известеразбрасыватель *m.* lime spreader.

извести *see* **изводить**; *gen. of* **известь**.

извест/ие *n.,* **—ия** *pl.* information, news, report; bulletin, proceedings, journal; **—итель** *m.* indicator; signaling device; **пожарный —итель** fire alarm (box); **—ительный** *a.* indicating; signaling; **—ить** *see* **извещать**.

известк/а *f.* (slaked) lime; **—ование** *n.* liming; (geol.) calcification; **—ованный** *a.* limed; **—ованность** *f.* lime content; **—овать** *v.* lime; **—овистый** *a.* calcareous, lime-like, lime-containing.

известково— *prefix* calcareo—, calcareous, lime (stone); **—обжигательная печь** lime kiln; **и.-содовый** *a.* lime-soda (treatment); **—сть** *f.* calcareousness.

известков/ый *a.* lime, calcareous, calciferous, calcium; **и. азот** calcium cyanamide; **и. зольник** (tanning) lime pit; **и. раствор** lime mortar; whitewash; **и. туф** (min.) tufa, travertine; **и. шпат** (min.) calc spar, calcite; **—ая вода** limewater; **—ая зола** lime ash; **—ая кашица** lime paste; **—ая накипь** (min.) calcareous sinter, travertine; **—ая нога** (vet.) scaly leg; **—ая селитра** calcium nitrate; **—ая синь** blue verditer, basic copper carbonate; **—ая соль** calcium salt; **—ое молоко** milk of lime; **—ое тесто** lime paste.

известконосный *a.* calciferous, lime-bearing.

известн/о *adv.* it is (well) known, it is common knowledge; **ему и.** he knows; **ещё не и.** it remains to be seen; **насколько ему и.** to the best of his knowledge; **—ость** *f.* reputation, repute, fame, publicity, notoriety; celebrity; **(по)ставить в —ость** *v.* inform, let it be known; **пользующийся —остью, —ый** *a.* well-known, familiar; famous, celebrated, notorious; some, certain; a few; **не —ый** unknown, obscure.

известняк *m.* (petr.) limestone; **—овый** *a.* limestone, calcareous, calciferous; **и.-ракушечник** *m.* shell limestone.

извест/ь *f.* lime; **азотистая и.** calcium cyanamide; **белильная и.** bleaching powder, calcium hypochlorite; **гашёная и.** slaked lime, calcium hydroxide; **едкая и., жжёная и.** quicklime, calcium oxide; **карбонат —и** calcium carbonate; **ключевая и., натёчная и.** (min.) calcareous sinter, travertine; **озёрная и.** chalk (calcium carbonate); **сернокислая и., сульфат —и** calcium sulfate; **фосфорнокислая и.** calcium phosphate; **хлорная и.** *see* **известь, белильная; и.-кипелка** *f.* quicklime; **и.-пушонка** *f.* air-slaked lime; **и.-тесто** paste.

извечный *a.* since earliest times.

извещ/атель *m.* detector; **—ать** *v.* inform, notify, let know; indicate; advertise; **—ение** *n.* information, notification, notice; **—ённый** *a.* informed, etc., *see* v.

извив *m.* winding, coil, fold; **—ание** *n.* winding, etc., *see* v.; **—ать** *v.* wind, coil; twist, twine, splice; **—аться** *v.* wind, coil, twist, meander; wriggle; **—ающийся** *a.* winding, etc., *see* v.; serpentine.

извил/ина *f.* bend, crook, curve, convolution, tortuosity, meander; detour; gyrus, convolution (of brain); **—истость** *f.* tortuosity, sinuosity; **—истый** *a.* winding, twisting, tortuous, sinuous, meandering; coiled, twisted, wound; gyrose; flexuose; anfractuose, wavy; labyrinthiform.

извин/ение *n.* apology, excuse; **—ительный** *a.* excusable; **—ить, —ять** *v.* excuse, forgive, pardon; **—иться** *v.* apologize.

извит/ость *f.* winding, twisting; crimp(iness) (of fiber); **—ый** *a.* wound, coiled; twisted, contorted; crimped; convoluted; **—ь(ся)** *see* **извивать(ся).**

извле/каемый *a.* extractable, extracted; recoverable, retrievable; **—каемая польза** benefits accruing; **—катель** *m.* extractant; **—кать** *v.* extract, derive, draw (off, out), withdraw, remove, extricate, recover, retrieve, take out; (nucl.) strip; (math.) take, extract (the root of); gain (advantage); learn (a lesson); **—кающий** *a.* extracting, etc., *see* v.; digestive; **—кающий раствор** extractant; **—чение** *n.* extraction, drawing (off, out), etc., *see* v.; withdrawal, removal, recovery; extract, abstract, excerpt, resume, summary; **—чение корня** (math.) evolution, extraction of root; **секция —чения** stripper; **степень —чения** % of all; **—чённый** *a.* extracted, drawn (off), etc., *see* v.; **—чь** *see* **извлекать.**

извне *adv.* from without, from (the) outside, external(ly).

извод *m.* consumption; waste; **—ить** *v.* consume, use up, spend; exterminate, destroy; exhaust, overwork; **—иться** *v.* be consumed, etc.; vanish, disappear.

извоз *m.* carrier's trade; delivery work; **—ничать** *v.* be a carrier; deliver; **—ный** *a.* of **извоз; —чик** *m.* carrier, delivery man; (cab) driver; cab.

изволок *m.* gently sloping hill.

извор/ачиваться, —отиться *v.* avoid, dodge, elude; **—от** *m.* turn(ing), bend; expedient; **—отливый** *a.* resourceful, clever.

извра/тить, —щать *v.* distort, misinterpret, misconstrue; corrupt, pervert; **—титься** *v.* be distorted, etc.; deteriorate, change for the worse; **—щение** *n.* distortion, etc., *see* v.; (anat., med.) inversion; **—щённый** *a.* distorted, etc., *see* v.

изга/дить, —живать *v.* mess up.

изгар/ина, —ь *f.* (forge) scale, scoria; dross.

изгиб *m.* bend(ing), deflection, inflection, curve, curvature, flexure; winding; (geol.) fold; (pipe) elbow; knee (of curve); kink (of wire); (mach.) offset; (chem.) flexion; **испытание на и.** bending test, flexing test; **линия —а** curvature; **многократный и.** flexing; **момент —а** bending moment; **продольный и.** buckling; **сопротивление —у** flexural strength; **—аемость** *f.* deflectivity; flexibility; **—ание** *n.* bending, etc., *see* v.; *also see* **изгиб; —ать** *v.* bend, deflect, curve, flex; **—аться** *v.* bend, curve, crook; buckle, sag; **—ающий(ся)** *a.* bending, etc., *see* v.; **—истый** *a.* flexuose; **—оустойчивый** *a.* resistant to flexing.

изгла/дить, —живать *v.* efface, erase, wipe out, obliterate, blot out; **—диться** *v.* become effaced, etc.; disappear.

изглодать *v.* gnaw (at, all over).

изгн/ание *n.* expulsion; **—анный** *a.* expelled, etc., *see* v.; **—ать** *v.* expel, drive out, eject; exile, banish.

изгни(ва)ть *v.* rot away.

изголодаться *v.* hunger, yearn (for); be starving, be famished.

изгонять *see* **изгнать.**

изгор/ать, —еть *v.* burn up.

изгород/ка *f.* low fence; **—ь** *f.* fence, barrier; **живая —ь** hedge.

изгот/авливать, —овить *v.* prepare, make (up), produce, manufacture, fabricate; make ready; carry out, execute; **—авливаться** *v.* get ready; **—овитель** *m.* producer, manufacturer, maker; **—овка** *f.*, **—овление** *n.* preparation, making, etc., *see* v.; manufacture; **некачественное —овление** poor workmanship; **—овленный** *a.* prepared, made, etc., *see* v.; **—овленный заранее** prefabricated; **—овлять** *see* **изготавливать.**

изгрыз(а)ть *v.* gnaw up.

изгрязн/ить, —ять *v.* soil, dirty, contaminate.

изд. *abbr.* (**издание; издательство**).

издав/аемый *a.* emitted, etc., *see* v.; **—ание** *n.* emission, etc., *see* v.; **—ать** *v.* emit, give off, exhale; publish, issue, edit; promulgate (law); utter (sound).

издавна *adv.* long since, long ago.

издалбливать *v.* chisel out (holes).

издал/ека, —ёка, —еча, —ече, —и *adv.* from afar, from a distance.

издан/ие *n.* edition, publication, issue; *pl.* transactions; **—ный** *a.* published, issued.

издатель *m.* publisher; **—ский** *a.* publisher's, publishing; **—ская деятельность** publishing; **—ское право** copyright; **—ство** *n.* publisher, publishing house.

изд/ать *see* **издавать; —ающий** *a.* emitting, exhaling, giving off; issuing.

изд-во *abbr.* (**издательство**).

издев/ательство *n.*, **—ка** *f.* ridicule, mockery; **—аться** *v.* ridicule, deride, mock, scoff, jeer.

издел/ие *n.* article, object, item, product, piece (of work); **готовое и.** finished product; purchased item; **—ия**

ware, product, goods; **каталог —ий** firm or trade catalog;

издёрг(ив)ать *v.* pull to pieces; harass, worry; **—ся** *v.* get tattered or frayed.

издерёт *fut. 3 sing. of* **изодрать.**

издерж/(ив)ать *v.* use up, spend, expend, consume; **—(ив)аться** *v.* run short (of money); **—ка** *f.* expense, cost, expenditure, outlay; **—ки** *pl.* cost(s); (shop) overhead.

издирать *see* **изодрать.**

издоль/ная аренда, —щина *f.* (agr.) share cropping, share tenancy; **—ик** *m.* share cropper.

издохнуть *v.* die (of animals).

издирать *see* **изодрать.**

издробить *v.* crumble, break up.

издыхать *v.* die (of animals).

изейкония *f.* (med.) iseiconia.

изентроп/а *f.* isentrope, adiabatic curve; **—ный** *a.* isentropic.

изень *m. or f.* (bot.) Kochia prostrata.

изерин *m.* (min.) iserine.

изжалить *v.* sting (all over).

изжарить *v.* fry, roast (thoroughly).

изжевать, изжёвывать *v.* chew up.

изжелт/а— *prefix* yellowish; **и.-бледный** *a.* pale yellow; **—ить** *v.* stain yellow.

изжечь *v.* burn up, use up (fuel); singe, burn (all over).

изживать *v.* get rid (of), eliminate, extirpate; overcome; **и. себя** be outdated, become obsolete.

изжигать *see* **изжечь.**

изжит/ый *past pass. part. of* **изживать; ещё не и.** persistent; **—ь** *see* **изживать.**

изжога *f.* (med.) pyrosis, heartburn.

из-за *prep. gen.* because of, due to, on account of, through; from (behind).

иззелен/а— *prefix* greenish; **—ить** *v.* stain green.

иззубри(ва)ть *v.* notch, serrate.

иззяб/нуть *v.* get chilled; **—ший** *a.* chilled.

изид/ий *m.,* **—ия** *f.* (bot.) isidium.

изинговский *a.* (phys.) Ising's.

излавливать *v.* catch, seize, trap, get.

излагат/ельный *a.* explanatory; **—ь** *v.* state, give an account (of), expound; present, set forth, write up, report.

изла/дить, —живать *v.* make, devise, contrive; prepare; **—диться** *v.* get ready.

изламывать *v.* smash, break (up); ruin; exhaust, wear out; deform.

излежаться, излёживаться *v.* spoil (in storage).

излени(ва)ться *v.* grow lazy.

изл/ёт *m.* last moment of flight before falling; **пуля на —ёте** spent bullet; **—етать** *v.* fly (all over); use up (fuel).

излеч/ение *n.* recovery, cure; **—и(ва)ть** *v.* cure, heal; **—и(ва)ться** *v.* heal, be cured (of), recover (from); **—имость** *f.* curability; **—имый** a. curable.

изли/(ва)ть *v.* pour (out), discharge; emit, give off; **—(ва)ться** *v.* pour (out), flow (out), issue (from); well out, gush, effuse, erupt; **—вшийся** *a.* pouring (out), etc., *see v.*; (geol.) effusive, extrusive.

излиш/ек *m.* surplus, excess; **—ество** *n.* excess; **—ества** *pl.* luxuries; **—ествовать** *v.* overindulge, be intemperate, go to excess; **—не** *adv.* in excess, superfluously; it is not necessary; **—ний** *a.* excessive, over-, superfluous, unnecessary.

излия/ние *n.* outpouring, outflow, discharge, effusion, eruption; **—ть** *see* **изливать.**

изловить *see* **излавливать.**

изловч/аться, —иться *v.* manage, contrive.

излож/ение *n.* account, statement, exposition; presentation; **—енный** *a.* stated, etc., *see* **излагать;** given.

изложина *f.* hollow.

изложить *see* **излагать.**

изложница *f.* (met.) ingot mold.

излом *m.* fracture, break, fissure, breaking (off); breakdown; deviation (from normal); angularity (of axle); cross-sectional view; **—анный, —ленный** *a.* fractured, broken; infracted, incurved; **—ать, —ить** *see* **изламывать; —остойкость** *f.* fracture toughness.

излуч/аемость *f.* emissivity, **—аемый** *a.* emitted, radiated; **—атель** *m.* emitter, radiator, radiating element; oscillator; (sonar) projector, transducer; **полный —атель** (phys.) black body; **—ательный** *a.* emitting, emissive, radiating; **—ать** *v.* emit, (e)radiate; **—аться** *v.* radiate, emanate (from); **—ающий** *a.* emitting, radiating, radiant; **—ение** *n.* emission, radiation, emanation; **биологическое действие —ения** relative biological effectiveness, RBE; **единица поглощённого —ения** radiation absorbed dose, rad; **измеритель потока —ения** fluxmeter; **энергия —ения** radiant energy; **—ённый** *a.* emitted, radiated.

излуч/ина *f.* curve, bend, winding, meander; detour; **—истый** *a.* bent, winding, meandering, tortuous.

излучить *see* **излучать.**

излюбленный *a.* favorite, preferred.

измаз(ыв)ать *v.* smear; use up; **—ся** *v.* get smeared up, get dirty; get used up.

измалывать *v.* grind, crush, break up.

измарать *v.* soil, dirty; **—ся** *v.* get dirty.

измасли(ва)ть *v.* get greasy.

изматывать *v.* deplete, exhaust, wear out.

измачивать *v.* wet, soak.

измельч/авший *a.* diminished, lessened; **—аемый** *a.* comminutable, grindable; **—ание** *n.* diminution, lessening, reduction; degeneration; getting shallow(er); *see also* **измельчение; —ать** *see* **измельчить;** become small(er), diminish, lessen; grow shallow(er); **—ающий** *a.* grinding, etc.; *see v.;* **—ение** *n.* grinding, etc., *see v.;* size reduction; breakage; **—ённый** *a.* ground, crushed, etc., *see v.;* finely divided; **—итель** *m.* crusher, pulverizer; (grain size) reducer; **—ить** *v.* grind, crush, break up, disintegrate, comminute, pulverize, mill; pound, stamp (ore); reduce; shred; cut up, mince; fragment.

измена *f.* treachery, treason.

изменен/ие *n.* change, alteration, variation, modification, conversion, transformation; fluctuation, deviation; correction; (current; sign) reversal; (biol.) mutation; **и. по глубине** depth variation; **и. фазы** phase change; **и. фазы на** phase reversal; **и. цвета** color change; discoloration; **точка —ия цвета** end point; **без —ия** unchanged, unaltered; **файл —ий** (comp.) update file.

изменённый *a.* changed, etc., *see* **изменять(ся).**

измен/имый *see* **изменяемый; —итель** *m.* changer, converter; **—ить** *see* **изменять.**

изменчив/ость *f.* variability, changeability; variation; (biol.) mutability, mutation; unsteadiness; (stat.) dispersion; **коэффициент —ости** (math.) coefficient of variation; **—ый** *a.* variable, changeable, inconstant, irregular, unsteady, floating; variegated; mutable.

измен/яемость *f.* variability, etc., *see a.;* **—яемый** *a.* variable, changeable, mutable; **—ять** *v.* vary, change, alter; reverse (direction); veer, shift (course); betray, break (promise); **—яться** *v.* change, be changed, be affected (by); fluctuate, range, vary; **—яющийся** *a.* varying, etc., *see v.;* variable; sensitive.

измер/ение *n.* measuring, measurement, gaging; survey; dimension, size; distance, length; determination; *suffix* —metry; **и. относительно** degree in; **в трёх —ениях** *a.* three-dimensional; **выполнять, делать** *or* **проводить —ения** *v.* measure, take measurements; **прибор для —ения** meter; **—енный** *a.* measured, etc., *see* **измерять**; observed, detected; **—имость** *f.* measurability; **—имый** *a.* measurable, mensurable; **—итель** *m.* meter, measurer, gage; counter; indicator; tester; —ometer, e.g., **—итель ускорения** accelerometer.

измерительн/ый *a.* measuring, gaging; gage (block); slotted (line); **и. преобразователь** transducer; **и. прибор** measuring instrument, gage; meter; **и. цилиндр** graduated cylinder, graduate; **—ая лента, —ая рулетка** tape (measure).

измер/ить, —ять *v.* measure, gage, size; meter; rate; survey; determine, take (reading); sound (depths); **—яемый** *a.* measurable; being measured; metered.

изможд/ение *n.,* **—ённость** *f.* exhaustion, prostration; **—ённый** *a.* exhausted, prostrate.

измок/ать, —нуть *v.* get wet or drenched.

измол/ачивать, —отить *v.* (agr.) thresh; **—отый** *a.* ground; **—оть** *v.* grind up.

измор *m.* starvation; **взять —ом** *v.* starve out; **—ить** *v.* wear out, exhaust.

измор/озь *f.* hoarfrost, rime; sleet; **—ось** *f.* drizzle.

измотать *v.* exhaust, wear out, deplete.

измочали(ва)ть *v.* shred; worry.

измочить *v.* wet, soak.

измуч/енный *a.* exhausted, worn out; **—(ив)ать** *v.* exhaust, fatigue, wear out.

измыли(ва)ть *v.* use up (soap).

измыслить *see* **измышлять**.

измытарить *v.* fatigue, exhaust.

измышлять *v.* contrive, devise, think up.

измять *v.* crush, (c)rumple up, trample.

изнан/ка *f.,* **—очный** *a.* back, reverse.

изнасиловать *v.* rape, violate.

изнащив/аемость *f.* wearability, endurance; depreciation; **—ание** *n.* wearing (away), etc., *see v.*; wear (and tear); erosion; consumption; deterioration, depreciation; **—ать** *v.* wear (away, down, out), fray; erode; **—аться** *v.* wear (away, down, out), be worn down; fray; erode; deteriorate, depreciate; be used up; **—ающийся** *a.* wearing, etc., *see v.*

изнеженный *a.* delicate; effeminate.

изнем/огать *v.* be exhausted; break down, collapse; **—ожение** *n.* exhaustion, breakdown; **—ожённый** *a.* exhausted, prostrate; **—очь** *see* **изнемогать**.

изнервничаться *v.* become tense and nervous.

изничтож/ать, —ить *v.* destroy, exterminate, eradicate; annihilate.

износ *m.* wear (and tear), wearing away, abrasion, erosion; (catalyst) attrition; depreciation, deterioration; depletion, impoverishment (of mine); consumption (of electrode); **—ить** *see* **изнашивать**.

износо/стойкий *a.* resistant to wear, durable; abrasion-resistant; **—стойкость** *f.* resistance to wear, durability; abrasion resistance; **—упорность, —устойчивость** *see* **износостойкость; —упорный, —устойчивый** *see* **износостойкий**.

изношенн/ость *f.* worn out state; **—ый** *a.* worn (out), etc., *see* **изнашивать(ся)**.

изнур/ение *n.* exhaustion, emaciation; **—ённый** *a.* exhausted; **—ительный** *a.* exhausting; (med.) debilitating, wasting; **—ить, —ять** *v.* fatigue, exhaust, waste, debilitate, weaken.

изнутри *adv.* from within, from inside.

изны(ва)ть *v.* burn (with thirst; from heat).

изо *see* **из**; *m.* (ichth.) Iso.

изо— *prefix* iso— (equal); insulation; *see also* **из—**; **—аг(г)лютинин** *m.* (immun.) isoagglutinin; **—аллель** *f.* (gen.) isoallele; **—аллил** *m.* isoallyl, propenyl; **—аллоксазин** *m.* isoalloxazine.

изоамил *m.,* **—овый** *a.* isoamyl; **—ацетат** *m.* isoamyl acetate; **—ен** *m.* isoamylene.

изо/андростерон *m.* isoandrosterone (hormone); **—антитело** *n.* (immun.) isoantibody.

изобар *m.* (nucl.) isobar; **—а** *f.* isobar, constant-pressure line; **—ический, —ный** *a.* isobaric; **—ический потенциал, —ноизотермический потенциал** (thermodynamics) Gibbs free energy; **—ометрический** *a.* isobarometric.

изобат/а *f.* isobath, depth contour; **—итерма** *f.* isobathytherm.

изобенз— *prefix* isobenz(o)—.

изобил/ие *n.* abundance, plenty, profusion, fertility; **—овать** *v.* abound (in), be rich (in); **—ующий** *a.* abundant, rich (in); **—ьно** *adv.* abundantly, etc., *see a.*; **—ьный** *a.* abundant, plentiful, fertile, heavy, full.

изоблич/ать, —ить *v.* show (to be), expose, unmask, reveal; convict (of).

изоборнил *m.* isobornyl.

изображ/аемый *a.* imaginary; represented, etc., *see v.*; **—ать** *v.* represent, depict, describe, portray, display, exhibit, show, picture, illustrate; express, indicate; **—ать собой** represent; **—аться** *v.* be represented, etc.; show, appear; **—ающий** *a.* representing, etc., *see v.*; (opt.) imaging (device); **—ение** *n.* representation, etc., *see v.*; picture, drawing; image; display, presentation, simulation; figure; (diffraction) pattern; **метод —ений** (electromagn.) mirror-image method; **—ение-оригинал** *m.* (phototelegraphy) subject copy; **—ённый** *a.* represented, etc., *see v.*

изобразит/ельный *a.* descriptive, imitative; graphic; figurative; **—ь** *see* **изображать**.

изобрести *see* **изобретать**.

изобретатель *m.* inventor, originator; **—ность** *f.* inventiveness, resourcefulness, ingenuity; **—ный** *a.* inventive, resourceful, ingenious; **—ский** *a.* inventor's, invention; **—ство** *n.* invention, development of inventions.

изобрет/ать *v.* invent, devise, contrive, develop; **—ение** *n.* invention, etc., *see v.*; **—ённый** *a.* invented, etc., *see v.*

изобут/ан *m.* isobutane; **—енил** *m.* 2-methyllallyl (Russian nomenclature); **—ил** *m.* isobutyl; **—илацетат** *m.* isobutyl acetate; **—илен** *m.* isobutylene; **—иловый** *a.* isobutyl; **—иральдегид** *m.* isobutyraldehyde; **—ират** *m.* isobutyrate.

изовалер/ат *m.* isovalerate; **—иановый, —ьяновый** *a.* isovaleric (acid); **—ил** *m.* isovaleryl; **—иановоэтиловый эфир** ethyl isovalerate.

изо/вела *f.* isovel, equal-speed line; **—вола, —воль** *f.* (geol.) isovol, isoanthracite line; **—вые** *pl.* (ichth.) Isonidae.

изовьётся *fut. 3 sing. of* **извиться**.

изогалина *f.* isohaline, equal-salinity line.

изогам/ета *f.* (gen.) isogamete; **—ия** *f.* isogamy; **—ма** *f.* (prospecting) isogam; **—ный** *a.* (gen.) isogamous.

изогексан *m.* isohexane.

изогелия *f.* (meteor.) isohel, isohelic line.

изоген/ез *m.* (gen.) isogenesis; **—ный** *a.* isogenic, homozygous.

изогеотерм/а *f.* (geol.) isogeotherm, isogeothermal line; **—ический** *a.* isogeothermal.

изогептан *m.* isoheptane.

изогидр/ический, —**ичный** *a.* isohydric; —**ичность,** —**ия** *f.* isohydry.

изогиет/а *f.,* —**ная линия** (meteor.) isohyet, isohyetal line.

изогипса *f.* isohypse, structure contour.

изогира *f.* (opt.) isogyre.

изогнут/о— *prefix* curvi—; —**ость** *f.* curvature, flexion, camber; bend; —**ый** *a.* curved, bent, crooked; camber (beam); —**ь** *see* **изгибать.**

изогон/а *f.,* —**аль** *m.* (magnetism) isogonic (line); —**альный** *a.* isogonal, equiangular; —**ический** *a.* isogonic.

изоград/а *f.* (petr.) isograd; —**иент** *m.* isogradient; —**ный** *a.* isograde.

изо/гель *m.* isogel; —**грамма** *f.* isogram; —**граф** *m.* isograph; —**денса** *f.* isopycnic line, equal-density line; —**десмический** *a.* (cryst.) isodesmic; —**дефа** *f.* isodef, equal-deformation line; —**диаметрический** *a.* (cryst.) isodiametric; —**диафер** *m.,* —**диафера** *f.* (nucl.) isodiaphere; —**диморфизм** *m.* isodimorphism.

изодин(ам)а *f.* (magnetism) isodynamic line.

изодинамический *a.* isodynamic.

изодовский *a.* (met.) Izod (test).

изодоза *f.* (radiobiology) isodose.

изодр/анный *a.* torn, tattered; —**ать** *v.* tear, rend; lacerate; —**аться** *v.* be all torn, be in shreds; get all scratched up.

изодром *m.,* —**ный** *a.* (aut.) proportional-integral device, PI-device; (electron.) feedback compensator.

изодульцит *m.* isodulcit, L-rhamnose.

изожжёт *fut. 3 sing. of* **изжечь.**

изо/зиготность *f.* (gen.) isozygoty; —**зим** *m.,* —**зима** *f.* iso(en)zyme; —**зома** *f.* (ent.) Harmolita; —**иммунный** *a.* isoimmune; —**индол** *m.* isoindole; —**ионный** *a.* isoionic.

изойти *v.* be drained of; go (all over), cover (ground); **и. кровью** bleed (to death).

изо/камфан *m.* isocamphane; —**капроновый** *a.* isocaproic (acid); —**карбостирил** *m.* isocarbostyril; —**клазит** *m.* (min.) isoclasite; —**климатический** *a.* isoclimatic.

изоклин/а(ль) *f.* isoclinal (line); (geol.) isocline; —**альный,** —**ический** *a.* isoclinal, isoclinic.

изо/коричный *a.* isocinnamic (acid); —**космы** *pl.* isocosmic lines; —**ксазол** *m.* isoxazol(e); —**лат** *see* **изолят;** —**лейцин** *m.* isoleucine.

изолента *f.* insulating tape, friction tape.

изо/лецитальный *a.* isolecithal (ovum); —**лизергиновый** isolysergic (acid); —**лимонный** *a.* isocitric (acid); —**линия** *f.* (meteor.) isoline.

изолир/ование *n.* insulation, etc., *see v.;* —**ованно** *adv.* separately; —**ованность** *f.* insulation; insulating property; isolation; —**ованный** *a.* insulated, etc., *see v.;* single, separate; (comp.) floating (target); closed (system); —**ать** *v.* insulate, seal (off); isolate, segregate, separate; tape (wire); (med.) quarantine; —**овка** *f.* insulation; insulation tape; —**овочный** *a.* insulating, etc., *see v.;* —**овочное вещество** insulator; —**уемый** *a.* insulated, etc., *see v.;* —**ующий** *see* **изолировочный; промежуточный** —**ующий слой** foreign layer, barrier layer.

изолог *m.* isolog; —**ический,** —**ичный** *a.* isologous; —**ический лоскут** (med.) isograft.

изольёт *fut. 3 sing. of* **излить.**

изолюкса *f.* isolux (line), equal-illumination curve.

изолят *m.* isolate, isolated population.

изолятор *m.,* —**ный** *a.* insulator; isolator; (med.) isolation ward or room.

изоляц/ионно-пропускной *a.* quarantine clearing; —**ионный** *a.* insulation, insulating; **и. материал** insulator; —**ионная лента** (elec.) insulation tape, friction tape; —**ия** *f.* insulation, insulating, etc., *see* **изолировать;** quarantine; sealing (of oil well); **полная** —**ия** (nucl.) positive confinement; **с бумажной** —**ией** paper-insulated.

изо/мальтоза *f.* isomaltose; —**масляный** *a.* isobutyric (acid).

изомер *m.* (chem.) isomer; —**а** *f.* isomer, equal-proportion line; —**аза** *f.* isomerase; —**изат** *m.* isomerizate, isomerization product; —**изация** *f.* isomerization; —**изм** *m.* isomerism; —**изование** *n.* isomerization; —**изованный** *a.* isomerized; —**изовать(ся)** *v.* isomerize; —**ия** *f.* isomerism; —**ия положения** position isomerism; **зеркальная** —**ия, пространственная** —**ия** steroisomerism; —**ный** *a.* isomerous, isomeric; —**ное превращение** isomerization; —**ное состояние** isomerism; —**ное тело** isomer.

изометамерный *a.* isometameric.

изометрический *a.* isometric(al).

изомнёт *fut. 3 sing. of* **измять.**

изомолярный *a.* isomol(ecul)ar.

изоморф/изм *m.,* —**ность** *f.* isomorphism; —**ный** *a.* isomorphous, isomorphic.

изомочевина *f.* isourea, pseudourea.

изонефа *f.* isoneph, equal-cloudiness line.

изониазид *m.* isoniazid (antibacterial).

изоникотиновый *a.* isonicotinic (acid).

изонитр/ил *m.* isonitrile, isocyanide; —**осоединение** *n.* isonitro compound.

изо/номаль *m.,* —**номальная линия** (meteor.) isonomal; —**октан** *m.* isoöctane; —**осмотический** *a.* isosmotic; —**пага** *f.* (meteor.) isopag, equiglacial line; —**пахита** *f.* (maps) isopach; —**пентан** *m.* isopentane; —**периметрический** *a.* (math.) isoperimetric; —**пикна** *f.* (meteor.) isopycn(ic), equal-density line; **пикнический** *a.* isopycnic; —**пический** *a.* (geol.) isopic(al); —**плера** *f.* (thermodyn.) isoplere, isometric line; isochore.

изо/плета *f.* isopleth, index line; —**плоидный** *a.* (gen.) isoploid; —**поверхность** *f.* isosurface; —**поды** *pl.* (crust.) Isopoda; —**поликислота** *f.* isopolyacid; —**полисоединение** *n.* isopoly compound; —**полисоль** *f.* isopoly salt; —**прал** *m.* isopral, trichloro-*i*-propanol; —**прен** *m.,* —**преновый** *a.* isoprene, 2-methyl-1,3-butadiene.

изопол/ьный, —**ярный** *a.* isopolar.

изопора *f.* isopor, isoporic line.

изопотенция *f.* isopotency, equipotency.

изопроп/анол *m.* isopropanol; —**енил** *m.,* —**ениловый** *a.* isopropenyl; —**ил** *m.,* —**иловый** *a.* isopropyl; —**илацетат** *m.* isopropyl acetate; —**иловый эфир** diisopropyl ether.

изопропункт *m.* quarantine clearing center.

изопье/за, —**ста** *f.,* —**стическая линия** (geol.) isopiestic (line); —**стический** *a.* isopiestic.

изорада *f.* isorad, equal-radioactivity line.

изорв/анный *a.* torn, tattered, ragged; —**ать** *v.* tear, rend.

изорефракт *m.* isorefract, line of equal refractive indices.

изо/родановый *a.* isothiocyanic (acid); —**родановокислая соль** isothiocyanate; —**сафрол** *m.* isosafrole.

изосейс/ма, —**та** *f.* (geol.) isoseismal line; —**мический** *a.* isoseismic, isoseismal.

изо/серин *m.* isoserine; **—споровые** *pl.* isosporous plants; **—споровый** *a.* isosporous, homosporous; **—смотический** *a.* isosmotic, isotonic; **—стазия** *f.* (geol.) isostasy.

изостат/а *f.* isostatic (curve), equal-pressure curve; **—ический** *a.* isostatic.

изостер/а *f.* (chem.; meteor.) isostere; **—ический** *a.* isosteric; **—ия** *f.* isosterism.

изо/стильбен *m.* isostilbene; **—строение** *n.* isomeric structure.

изоструктур/а *f.* (plastics) isotactic structure; **—ный** *a.* isostructural.

изотак/а *f.* (meteor.) isotac; **—тический** *a.* (polymerization) isotactic.

изотах *m.* (maps) isotach, line of equal rates of sedimentation.

изотаха *f.* isotach, equal-velocity line.

изотенископ *m.* isoteniscope, vapor pressure gage.

изотера *f.* (meteor.) isothere, isotheral line.

изотерм/а *f.* isotherm, isothermal curve, equal-temperature curve; **—ический** *a.* isothermic, isothermal; refrigerator (car).

изотеций *m.* (bot.) Isothecium (a moss).

изотима *f.* isothyme, isoatmic line, equal-evaporation line.

изотио/мочевина *f.* isothiourea; **—цианат** *m.* isothiocyanate.

изотома *f.* (bot.) Isotoma.

изотон *m.* (nucl.) isotone; **—ический, —ный** *a.* isotonic, isosmotic; **—ия** *f.* isotonicity.

изотоп *m.* isotope; **определённый и.** nuclide; **и.-индикатор** *m.* tracer isotope; **—ический, —ный** *a.* isotope, isotopic; **—ия** *f.* isotopy; **—ный анализ** tracer technique; **—ный индикатор** (isotopic) tracer; **—ное изобилие** isotopic abundance; **—ное смещение** isotope shift; **—ное число** isotopic number, neutron excess.

изотрёт *fut. 3 sing. of* **истереть.**

изотрон *m.*, **—ный разделитель** isotron (isotope separator).

изотроп/ический, —ный *a.* isotropic; **—ия, —ность** *f.* isotropy, isotropism.

изо/углеводород *m.* isohydrocarbon; **—фаза** *f.* isophase; **—фациальный** *a.* isofacial; **—фен** *m.*, **—фена** *f.* (meteor.) isophene, phenocontour; **—фенический, —фенный** *a.* isophenous; **—фермент** *m.* isoenzyme; **—фия** *f.* (ent.) Isophya; **—флавон** *m.* isoflavone; **—форон** *m.* isophorone; **—фот** *m.*, **—фота** *f.* (illumination) isophot (line); **—фталевый** *a.* isophthalic (acid); **—халина** *see* **изогалина; —химена** *f.* (meteor.) isocheim; **—хинолин** *m.* isoquinoline; **—хиона** *f.* isochion, equal-snow line.

изохор/а *f.* isochore (curve); **—ический, —ный** *a.* isochoric; **—ный потенциал, —но-изотермический потенциал** (thermodynamics) Helmholtz free energy, work function.

изохром/ата *f.* isochromatic curve; **—атический, —(атич)ный** *a.* isochromatic; **—осома** *f.* (gen.) isochromosome.

изохрон/а *f.* isochrone, isochronic curve; **—альный** *a.* isochronal; **—изм** *m.*, **—ность** *f.* isochronism; **—ический, —ный** *a.* isochronous.

изоцентр *m.* isocenter; moving point.

изоциан *m.*, **—овый** *a.* isocyanogen; **—ат** *m.* isocyanate; **—ид** *m.* isocyanide; **—иновый** *a.* isocyanin (dyes); **—овый** *a.* isocyanic (acid); **—уровый** *a.* isocyanuric (acid).

изо/ции *pl.* (biol.) isocies, habitat groups; **—циклический** *a.* isocyclic; **—цитраза** *f.* isocitrase; **—цитрат** *m.* isocitrate.

изошёл *past m. sing. of* **изойти.**

изошьёт *fut. 3 sing. of* **исшить.**

изощр/ить, —ять *v.* sharpen, refine, perfect; **—яться** *v.* become sharpened, etc., become more perceptive; outdo (oneself), excel; exercise (one's wits).

изо/эвгенол *m.* isoeugenol; **—эдрический** *a.* isohedral; **—электрический** *a.* isoelectric; **—электронный** *a.* isoelectronic; **—энергета** *f.* isenergic, constant-energy line.

изоэнтальп/а *f.* (thermodyn.) isoenthalp; **—ийный, —ический** *a.* isoenthalpic.

изоэнтроп/а *f.* isoentropic curve; **—ийный, —ический** *a.* isoentropic.

из-под *prep. gen.* from under; **и. водоземля** (missiles) underwater-to-surface; **бутылка и. вина** wine bottle.

израз/ец *m.*, **—цовый** *a.* ceramic tile.

израильский *a.* (geog.) Israeli.

изранить *v.* wound (all over).

израст/ание *n.* excrescence, outgrowth; proliferation; stooling stage, stem formation; **—ающий** *a.* excrescent; proliferous.

израсход/ование *n.* expenditure; **—ованный** *a.* spent, etc., *see v.*; **—овать** *v.* spend, consume, use; expend, lay out; run out of, exhaust.

изредить *see* **изрежать.**

изредка *adv.* rarely, seldom; from time to time, occasionally, now and then.

изреж/ённость *f.* sparsity; **—ённый** *a.* sparse, thin, intermittent (sowing); thinned out; **—ивание** *n.* thinning (out); **—ивать** *v.* thin (out).

изрез/анность *f.* irregularity, unevenness (of shore line); **—анный** *a.* irregular, uneven, rugged, dissected; angular (iceberg); **—(ыв)ать** *v.* cut (up), dissect; gash, slash (up); incise.

изре/кать *v.* utter, state, pronounce; **—чение** *n.* saying, dictum, maxim.

изреше/тить, —чивать *v.* riddle (with bullets), perforate; **—чённый** *a.* riddled, perforated, cribrate; cribrose.

изрисовать *v.* cover with drawings; decorate, adorn; use up (paper, etc.).

изроет *fut. 3 sing. of* **изрыть.**

изруб/ать, —ить *v.* cut (down, up); chop, mince; slaughter; **—ленный** cut, etc., *see v.*; hashed.

изрывать *v.* tear up; dig up.

изрыг/ание *n.* (med.) eructation; **—ать, —нуть** *v.* eructate, belch; vomit, spew.

изрыт/ый *a.* dug up; pitted; **—ь** *v.* dig up.

изрядн/о *adv.* fairly, pretty well; **—ый** *a.* fair, considerable.

изувеч/ение *n.* mutilation; **—енный** *a.* mutilated; **—и(ва)ть** *v.* mutilate, maim.

изукра/сить *see* **изукрашивать; —шенный** *a.* adorned, etc., *see v.*; variegated; **—шивать** *v.* adorn; soil, dirty; deface.

изум/ительный *a.* amazing, astounding; **—ить, —лять** *v.* surprise, amaze.

изумруд *m.*, **—ный** *a.* (min.) emerald; **—но-зелёный, —ный** *a.* emerald green.

изуродов/анный *a.* mutilated, etc., *see v.*; **—ать** *v.* mutilate, maim, disfigure.

изуч/аемый *a.* studied, etc., *see v.*; under study, under investigation, under discussion; involved; test; **—ать** *v.* study, investigate, explore, look into, examine, scrutinize; test; analyze; master, deal (with); **—аться** *v.* be under study, be under investigation; **—ающий** *a.* studying, etc., *see v.;* concerned; **—ение** *n.* investigation, research, study, examination, analysis; test; **—енность** *f.* (previous) study; **—енный** *a.* studied, etc., *see v.;* understood; **—ить** *see* **изучать.**

изъед/ать *v.* eat away, corrode; **—енный** *a.* corroded, pitted; eaten.

изъез/дить, —живать *v.* travel all over; wear out (road, vehicle); **—женный** *a.* worn out, rutted (road), beaten (track).

изъемлет *fut. 3 sing. of* **изымать.**

изъесть *see* **изъедать.**

изъяв/ить, —лять *v.* express, testify; **—ление** *n.* testimony.

изъязв/ить, —лять *v.* ulcerate, pit; **—ление** *n.* ulceration, pitting; **—лённый** *a.* ulcer(at)ed, ulcerous, pitted.

изъян *m.* defect, flaw, fault; damage.

изъясн/ить, —ять *v.* explain.

изъят/ие *n.* removal, elimination, withdrawal; exception; immobilization; confiscation, deprivation; **—ь** *v.* remove, eliminate, withdraw, take out; immobilize; confiscate; harvest (wild animals).

изымать *see* **изъять.**

изыск/ание *n.* investigation, (re)search; study; exploration, prospecting, survey(ing); **—анный** *a.* investigated, etc., *see v.;* **—атель** *m.* prospector, surveyor; investigator; explorer; scout; **—ательно-разведочный** *a.* survey-and-reconnaissance, intelligence; **—ательский** *a.* exploratory, prospecting, survey(ing); **—(ив)ать** *v.* investigate, explore, look (for), seek, search (for), (try to) find; do research (on); (geol.) prospect (for).

изэнтроп/а *f.* (thermodynamics) isentrope, isentropic line; **—ический** *a.* isentropic.

изэтионовая кислота isethionic acid, 2-hydroxyethanesulfonic acid.

изюбр/(ь) *m.,* **—евый, —овый** *a.* (mam.) wapiti, elk (*Cervus canadensis*).

изюм *m.,* **—ный** *a.* raisin.

изящный *a.* fine, graceful, elegant, neat.

ийолит *m.* (petr.) ijolite.

ийский *a.* (geog.) Iya.

ИК *abbr.* (**инфракрасный**) infrared, IR.

икар *m.* (astr.) Icarus (asteroid); (ent.) Lycaena icarus.

икать *v.* hiccup; **—ся** *v.* have the hiccups.

икациновые *pl.* (bot.) Icacinaceae.

И-кислота *f.* J acid.

ИКЛ *abbr.* (**инфракрасные лучи**) infrared rays.

ИКМ *abr.* (**импульсно-кодовая модуляция**) pulse-code modulation.

ИК-наведение *n.* infrared homing.

икнуть *see* **икать.**

иконо— *prefix* icono— (image); **—скоп** *m.* (telev.) iconoscope; **—тип** *m.* (biol.) iconotype, representation of a type.

икорный *a. of* **икра.**

икос/а—, —и— *prefix* icosa—, icosi— (twenty); **—аэдр** *m.* icosahedron; **—аэдрический** *a.* icosahedral; **—итетраэдр** *m.* icositetrahedron.

икостеевые *pl.* ragfishes (*Icosteidae*).

икота *f.* hiccup(ing).

икотин *m.* (biol.) icotype.

икотн/ик *m.* (bot.) Berteroa; **—ный** *a. of* **икота.**

ИК-приёмник *m.* infrared detector.

икр/а *f.* (ichth.) roe, spawn, ova; (anat.) calf, sura; **бить —у, метать —у** *v.* spawn; **—ин(к)а** *f.* fish egg; **—истый** *a.* full of roe; **—иться** *v.* spawn, deposit

eggs; **—омёт** *m.,* **—ометание** *n.,* **—омётный** *a.* **—омечущий** *a.* spawning; **—оножный** *a.* (anat.) sural, calf; **—оножная мышца** gastrocnemius; **—яник** *m.,* **—янка** *f.* spawner; **—яной** *a.* roe; (anat.) sural, calf; **—яной камень** (min.) roe stone, oölite.

икс *m.* (math.) *x*; any unknown; **икс(-единица)** *f.* X-unit, Siegbahn unit (10⁻³ Å).

иксинский *a.* (geog.) Ixa.

икс/лучи *pl.* X-rays; **—образный** *a.* X-shaped; **—од** *m.* (zool.) Ixodes; **—одиды, —одовые** *pl.* hard ticks (*Ixodidae*); **—олит** *m.* (min.) ixolite.

ИК-спектр *m.* infrared spectrum; **—ометрия** *f.* infrared spectrometry.

икс-хромосома *f.* (gen.) X-chromosome.

иктеро— *prefix* (med.) ictero—, jaundice.

иктидозавр *m.* (pal.) ictidosaur.

ил *m.* silt, slime, mud, sludge, ooze; (flotation) slurry; (cer.) slip; **актив(ирован)ный и.** activated sludge; **жидкий и.** ooze, liquid silt.

иланг/-иланг *m.* (bot.) ylang-ylang (*Cananga odorata*); **—ол** *m.* ylangol.

илгинский *a.* (geog.) Ilga.

илеит *m.* (med.) ileitis.

илек *gen. pl. of* **илька.**

илекс *m.* (bot.) Ilex; **—инский** *a.* (geog.) Ilexa; **—кий** *a.* Ilek.

илен *m.* ylene.

илео— *prefix* (anat.) ileo— (ileum); **—цекальный** *a.* ileocecal.

илетьский *a.* (geog.) Ilet.

илеус *m.* (med.) ileus.

илецкий *a.* (geog.) Ilek.

или *conj.* or, either; **и. вообще не** if at all; **и. же** or else; **и. . . . и.** either . . . or; **и. не** or otherwise; **и. совсем не** if at all.

илид *m.* (electrochem.) ylid(e).

ил/ийский *a.* (geog.) Ili; **—импийский** *a.* Ilimpeya; Ilimpi; **—имский** *a.* Ilim.

илио— *prefix* (anat.) ilio— (ilium, flank); **—фовые** *pl.* (ichth.) Iliophiidae.

илист/ость *f.* muddiness; **—ый** *a.* muddy, slimy, oozy, sludgy.

илициловый *a.* ilicyl (alcohol).

илиша *f.* (ichth.) Ilisha.

илли/ний *m.* illinium, Il, prometheum; **—нойский** *a.* (geog.) Illinois; **—пе** *n.,* **—повое дерево** (bot.) Illipe; **—т** *m.* (min.) illite; **—циум** *m.* (bot.) anis tree (*Illicium*).

иллудин *m.* illudin (antibiotic).

иллюв/иальный *a.* (geol.) illuvial; **—ий** *m.* illuvial deposits, illuvium.

иллюз/ия *f.* illusion, delusion; **—орный** *a.* illusory, illusive, deceptive.

иллюмин/атор *m.* illuminator; (naut.) porthole, light; (av.) window; illumination specialist; **—ация** *f.* illumination; **—ация, —овка** *f.* coloring map contours; **—ент** *m.* illuminant; **—ированный** *a.* illuminated, lit; **—(ир)овать** *v.* illuminate, light.

иллюстр/ация *f.* illustration, figure, drawing; **—ирование** *n.* illustration, etc., *see v.;* **—ированный** *a.* illustrated, etc., *see v.;* **—ировать** *v.* (serve to) illustrate, picture, portray, depict, show, display, exhibit; **—ирующий** *a.* illustrating, etc., *see v.*

илов/атый *a.* uliginous, muddy, slimy, oozy; clayey (sand); **—атая глина, —атая почва, —ка** *f.* (geol.) loam; siltstone.

иловлинский *a.* (geog.) Ilovlya.

иловый *a. of* **ил**; sludge (bed; index).

ило/ед *m.* (zool.) mud eater; **—любивый** *a.* (biol.) pelophilous; mud-loving; **—накопитель** *m.* sludge tank or lagoon; **—носковые** *pl.* (ent.) Georyssidae; **—отстойник** *m.* silt-settling tank; **—очиститель** *m.* desilter; **—сборник** *m.* sludge tank; **—скрёб** *m.* sludge collector; **—уловитель** *m.* silt pit; **—уплотнитель** *m.* sludge concentrator.

и.л.с. *abbr.* (**индикаторная лошадиная сила**) indicated horsepower, I.H.P.

илычский *a.* (geog.) Ilych.

иль *see* **или.**

ильваит *m.* (min.) ilvaite, lievrite.

ильземаннит *m.* (min.) ilsemannite.

ильинский *a.* (geog.) Ilya, Elias.

ильк/а *f.,* **—овый** *a.* (mam.) fisher (*Martes pennanti*).

ильм *m.* (bot.) elm (*Ulmus*).

ильмен/ит *m.* (min.) ilmenite, titanic iron ore; **—ный** *a.* of **ильмень**; (geog.) Ilmen; **—орутил** *m.* (min.) ilmenorutile; **—ский** *a.,* **—ь** *f.* (geol.) ilmen, bayou (Volga delta lake); (geog.) Ilmen.

ильм/овник *m.* elm grove; **—овые** *pl.* (bot.) Ulmaceae; **—овый** *a.* elm; **—олистный** *a.* elm-leaved, ulmifolious.

ильн/ик *m.* (ent.) slime beetle (*Rhantus*); (ichth.) tench (*Tinca t.*); **—ица** *f.* (ent.) Eristalis; **—ый** *a.* of **ил.**

им *instr.* of **он, оно,** by him, with it; *dat.* of **они,** to them, them.

им. *abbr.* (**имени**) named after.

имаг/инальная стадия, **—о** *n.* (ent.) imago.

имазатин *m.* imasatin.

имандровский *a.* (geog.) Imandra.

иманский *a.* (geog.) Iman.

имбецильность *f.* (med.) imbecility.

имбибиция *f.* imbibition, absorption.

имбир/ные *pl.* (bot.) Zingiberaceae; **—ный** *a.,* **—ь** *m.* ginger (*Zingiber*).

Имгофа шлам Imhoff sludge.

имезатин *m.* imesatin, 3-iminoöxindole.

имени *gen.* of **имя.**

имение *n.* property, estate.

имен/ины *pl.* name day, birthday; **—ительный** *a.* (grammar) nominative.

имен/но *particle* namely, to wit, precisely, expressly, just; it is (precisely) . . . that; **—ной** *a.* nominal, name; **—ование** *n.* naming, name, denomination; **—ованный** *a.* named, etc., *see v.*; concrete (number); **—овать** *v.* name, call, designate, identify (as), know (as), refer (to), term, denote; **—оваться** *v.* be called; **—уемый** *a.* called, known, referred (to).

имеринит *m.* (min.) imerinite.

имеритинский *a.* (geog.) Imeritian.

им/еть *v.* have, possess, be provided (with); exhibit, show, display; take (the form of); maintain, keep (staff); **не и.** be free (of); **—еться** *v.* be, exist, be available; **—еется** there is; **у него —еется** he has; **не —еться** be free (of), be lacking; be non-existent; **—еющий** *a.* having, etc., *see v.*; **не —еющий** without, **—**less, e.g., **не —еющий протоков** ductless; **—еющийся** *a.* available, at hand, provided; **—ея** *pr. ger.* having, given.

ими *instr.* of **они,** by them.

имид *m.,* **—ный** *a.* imide; **—азол** *m.* imidazole, glyoxaline; **—азолил** *m.* imidazolyl; **—азолон** *m.* imidazolone.

имидо— *prefix* imido—; **—ген** *m.* imidogen, imido group; **—кислота** *f.* imido acid; **—л** *m.* imidole, pyrrole; **—эфир** *m.* imido ester.

имин *m.* imine; **—азол** *m.* iminazole, imidazole; **—ный**

а., **—о—** *prefix* imino(—); **—огруппа** *f.* imino group, iminogen; **—окислота** *f.* imino acid; **—омочевина** *f.* iminourea, guanidine; **—опропионовый** *a.* iminopropionic (acid); **—оуксусный** *a.* iminoacetic (acid); **—оэтанол** *m.* iminoethanol; **—оэфир** *m.* imino ester.

имит/атор *m.* simulator; **—ационный** *a.,* **—ация** *f.,* **—ирование** *n.* simulation, imitation; substitute; **—ация пожара** decoy fire; **—ированный** *a.* simulated, imitated; **—ировать** *v.* simulate, imitate, copy, duplicate; **—ирующий** *a.* simulative, imitative.

ИМК *abbr.* (**индукционный метод магнитного каротажа**) magnetic induction logging.

имманентн/ость *f.* immanence; **—ый** *a.* immanent, inherent.

иммельман *m.* (av.) Immelman turn.

иммерс/ия *f.,* **—ионный** *a.* immersion; **и. в масле** oil immersion.

иммигр/ационный *a.,* **—ация** *f.* immigration; **—ировать** *v.* immigrate.

иммитанс *m.* (elec.) immittance.

иммобилиз/ация *f.* immobilization; fixation; **—ирующий** *a.* immovable, fixed; **—овать** *v.* immobilize; fix.

иммортель *f.* (bot.) Helichrysum.

иммун/изация *f.,* **—изирование** *n.* immunization; **—изин** *m.* immunisin, antibody; **—изированный** *a.* immunized; **—изировать** *v.* immunize; **—итет** *m.* immunity; **—нентный, —ный** *a.* immune; **—ность** *f.* immunity; **—ный белок** immunoprotein, immunoglobulin; **—обиологический** *a.* immunobiological; **—огенность** *f.* immunogenicity; **—огенный** *a.* immunogenic; **—оглобулин** *m.* immunoglobulin; **—одепрессант** *m.,* **—одепрессивный** *a.* immunosuppressive; **—одиагностика** *f.* immunodiagnosis; **—олог** *m.* immunologist; **—ология** *f.* immunology; **—овитительный** *a.* immunosuppressive; **—опрофилактика** *f.* immunoprophylaxis; **—ореакция** *f.* immune reaction; **—отерапия** *f.* immunotherapy; **—охимический** *a.* immunochemical; **—охимия** *f.* immunochemistry; **—оэлектрофорез** *m.* immunoelectrophoresis; **—сыворотка** *f.* immune serum, antiserum; **—ый дефицит** immunodeficiency.

имон/иевый *a.,* **—ий** *m.* imonium.

имп. *abbr.* (**импульс, импульсный**).

импала *f.* (mam.) impala (*Aepyceros melampus*).

импедан/с, **—ц** *m.,* **—сный** *a.* (elec.) impedance, apparent resistance; **измеритель —са** impedometer.

импеллер *m.* impeller, blade; (mixer) propeller, agitator.

императив *m.,* **—ный** *a.* imperative.

императорин *m.* imperatorin, peucedanin.

импер/ия *f.* empire; **—ский** *a.* imperial.

импетиго *n.* (med.) impetigo.

импидор *m.* (elec.) impeder.

имплант/ат *m.* implant; **—ационный** *a.,* **—ация** *f.* implantation.

импликант *m.* implicant (of function).

импликац/ионный *a.* implicational, graphic; **—ия** *f.* implication.

имплоз/ивный *a.* implosive; **—ия** *f.* implosion, bursting inwards.

имп/мин *abbr.* (**импульсов в минуту**) pulses per minute; counts per minute.

импозантный *a.* impressive, imposing.

импонировать *v.* impress, impose (upon).

импорт *m.* import(ation); **—ёр** *m.* importer; **—ировать** *v.* import; **—ный** *a.* import(ed).

импост *m.* (arch.) impost.

импотен/т *m.,* **—тный** *a.* (med.) impotent; **—тность, —ция** *f.* impotence.

импре/гнат, —**гнент** *m.* impregnating agent; —**гнатор** *m.* impregnator; —**гнация** *f.,* —**гнирование** *n.* impregnation; —**гнированный** *a.* impregnated; —**гнировать,** —**ньировать** *v.* impregnate; —**гнирующий** *a.* impregnating.

импринтинг *m.* (zool.) imprinting.

импровизировать *v.* improvise.

имп/сек *abbr.* (**импульсов в секунду**) pulses per second; counts per second.

импсонит *m.* (min.) impsonite.

импульс *m.* impulse, impetus, impact; momentum; (elec.) pulse; **амплитуда** —**а, высота** —**а** (electron.) pulse height; (telecomm.) pulse amplitude; **пространство** —**ов** momentum space; **усилитель** —**ов** pulse amplifier; —**атор** *m.* impulsator, pulser; **и.-врезка** *m.* (TV) serration, serrated pulse; —**ер** *m.* impulse starter; —**ивный** *a.* impulsive; —**ник** *m.* pulser; —**номо-дулированный** *a.* pulse-modulated, pulsed; —**но-приложенный** *a.* step-function (voltage); —**но-цик-лический** *a.* pulse-cycle (meter); —**ный** *a.* impulse, momentum; puls(ed), impulsive; sampled (data); flash (bulb); —**ный генератор** (im)pulse generator; —**ная модуляция** pulse modulation; —**ная мощность** pulse power, peak power; —**ная трубка** Pitot tube, impact tube; **в** —**ном режиме** pulsed; —**овидный** *a.* pulse-like; —**остойкий** *a.* surge-proof.

импфирование *n.* water softening by means of hydrochloric or sulfuric acid; (cryst.) seeding.

имуществ/енный *a.* property; —**о** *n.* property, estate; stock, goods, material(s), stores, equipment; assets; **штатное**—**о** issue or standard facilities.

имущий *a.* wealthy, well off; propertied.

им/я *n.* name; (grammar) noun; (comp.) (command) word; —**ени named for;** **институт** —**ени Ленина** Lenin Institute; **от** —**ени** on behalf (of).

ин. *abbr.* (**иностранный**) foreign; (**интенсивный**) strong; **Ин** *abbr.* (**ингибитор**).

инактив/ация *f.,* —**ирование** *n.* inactivation; —**ированный** *a.* inactivated; —**ировать** *v.* inactivate; —**ный** *a.* non-reactive.

иначе *adv.* otherwise, differently; *conj.* or (else); **и. обстоит дело** it is different (with), not so (with); **так или и.** in any case, one way or another.

инбр/едный *a.* (biol.) inbred; —**идинг** *m.* inbreeding.

инвагин/ация *f.* invagination; (med.) intussusception; —**ировать** *v.* invaginate, involute.

инваз/ивный, —**ионный** *a.* invasive; —**ия** *f.* invasion; infestation (by parasites).

инвалид *m.* invalid; disabled person; **и. войны** disabled veteran; —**ность** *f.* invalidism; disability; —**ный** *a.* invalid('s); disabled, handicapped, incapacitated; —**ное кресло** wheelchair.

инвар *m.* Invar (alloy).

инвариант *m.,* —**ный** *a.* (math.) invariant; —**ность** *f.* invariance.

инвентар/изатор *m.* inventory taker; accessioner; —**изационный** *a.,* —**изация** *f.* inventory, stock-taking; accessioning; —**изация земель** cadastral survey; —**из(ир)овать** *v.* (take) inventory, take stock; accession, record; —**ный** *a.* inventorial; accession(al); packaged-unit (substation); —**ная опись** inventory; —**ь** *m.* inventory, stock; implements, equipment; **живой** —**ь** livestock.

инверс/ионный *a.* inversion; inverted; —**ия** *see* **инвер-тирование;** —**ный** *a.* inverse; inverter (stage); —**ор** *m.* (math.) inversor; (typ.) automatic focusing device.

инверт/аза *f.,* —**ин** *m.* invertase, invertin, saccharase; —**ер** *m.* (elec.) inverter, inverted rectifier; (comp.) in-

verter, NOT gate; —**ирование** *n.* inversion, reversal; (elec.) switching from dc to ac, conversion; **температура** —**ирования** inversion point; —**ированный** *a.* inverted; invert (sugar); —**ировать** *v.* invert, reverse; convert; —**ный** *a.* invert; —**ор** *see* **инвертер.**

инвест/ирование *n.,* —**иция** *f.* investment; —**ировать** *v.* invest; —**ор** *m.* investor.

инволю/кр(ум) *m.* (biol.) involucre, involucrum; —**та** *f.* (math.) involute; —**тный** *a.* involute, coiled; —**цион-ный** *a.* involutional, involute(d); —**ция** *f.* involution; (biol.) degeneration.

инга *f.* (bot.) Inga.

ингаля/тор *m.* inhaler, inhalator; —**торий** *m.* inhalation therapy building; —**ционный** *a.,* —**ция** *f.* inhalation.

ингиб/ин *m.* inhibin (antibiotic); —**ирование** *n.* inhibition; —**ировать** *v.* inhibit; impair, hinder, retard, delay, slow down; moderate; —**итор** *m.* inhibitor, arrester; retardant; —**иторный** *a.* inhibitor, inhibiting; —**иция** *f.* inhibition.

ИНГК *abbr.* (**импульсный нейтроно-гамма каротаж**) pulsed neutron-gamma logging.

ингод(ин)ский *a.* (geog.) Ingoda.

ингот *m.* (met.) ingot; —**изм** *m.* ingot structure.

ингредиент *m.* ingredient, component, constituent; additive; **и. реакции** reactant.

ингресс/ивный *a.* ingressive, entering; —**ия** *f.* ingression, entrance.

ингу/лецкий *a.* (geog.) Ingulets; —**льский** *a.* Ingul; —**рийский** *a.* Inguri.

индазол *m.* indazole, benzopyrazole.

индаинг *m.* indaing (a tropical forest).

инд/аллой *m.* Indalloy; —**амин** *m.,* —**аминовый** *a.* indamine, phenylene blue; —**ан** *m.* indan, hydrindene; —**андион** *m.* indandione, diketohydrindene; —**анил** *m.* indanyl; —**анон** *m.* indanone, indone; —**антрен** *m.,* —**антреновый** *a.* indanthrene; —**антрон** *m.* indanthrone; —**ат** *m.* indate.

индау *m.* (bot.) roquette (*Eruca*).

индеветь *v.* be covered with hoarfrost.

индеец *m.* (American) Indian.

индейк/а *f.* turkey (hen); **горная и.** snowcock (*Tetraogallus*); —**оводство** *n.,* —**оводческий** *a.* turkey breeding.

индей/ский *a.* (American) Indian; —**цы** *pl.* Indians.

индекс *m.* index, (classification) number, identification number, notation, code, mark, symbol; (stat.) index number; **верхний и.** superscript; **нижний и.** subscript; —**ация** *f.,* —**ирование** *n.* indexing, notation, classification; —**ировать** *v.* index, classify; —**ный** *a.* index, indicial.

инден *m.* indene; —**ил** *m.* indenyl.

индентор *m.* indenter, penetrator.

индетерминатный *a.* indeterminate, indefinite; undefined; not classified.

индианит *m.* (min.) indianite, anorthite.

индивид *m.* individual; pure substance; —**уализация** *f.* individualization, individual treatment; —**уализировать** *v.* individualize, treat individually; —**уалисти-ческий** *a.* individualistic; —**уальность** *f.* individuality; (chem.) uniformity, homogeneity; —**уальный** *a.* individual; independent, separate, self-contained, single; unit (drive); personal (dosimetry); custom (work); pure, homogeneous, uniform (substance); **по** —**уаль-ному заказу** custom-built; —**уация** *f.* (biol.) individuation; —**уум** *see* **индивид.**

индигирский *a.* (geog.) Indigirka.

индиго *n.* (bot.) indigo (*Indigofera*); **белое и.** indigo white; **голубое и.** indigo blue.

индигов/ый *a.* indigo; indigotic (acid); **и. куб** indigo vat; **—ая соль** indigo salt, *o*-nitrobenzaldehyde.

индиго/золь *m.* indigosol; **—ид** *m.,* **—идный** *a.* indigoid; **—кармин** *m.* indigocarmine, sodium indigotinsulfonate; **—краситель** *m.* indigo dye; **—лит** *m.* (min.) indigolite, indicolite; **—метр** *m.* indigometer; **—метрия** *f.* indigometry; **—носка** *f.* indigo plant; **—серная кислота** indigosulfuric acid, sulfindigotic acid; **—сульфоновая кислота** indigosulfonic acid; **—тин** *m.* indigotin, indigo blue.

индигский *a.* (geog.) Indiga.

индий *m.* indium, In; **хлористый и.** indium dichloride; **хлорный и.** indium trichloride.

индийский *a.* (geog.) India(n).

индикан *m.* indican.

индикатор *m.* indicator, display; (nucl.) tracer; *suffix* **—scope; метод изотопных —ов, —ный метод** tracer technique; **химия —ов** tracer chemistry; **—ный** *a. of* **индикатор;** indicating; indicated (horsepower); rated (pressure); **—ный механизм** indicator; **—ные часы** dial indicator, dial gage; **—оподобный** *a.* indicator.

индик/атриса *f.* (math.) indicatrix, characteristic (curve); **—ационный** *a.* indicative; **—ация** *f.* indication; presentation, display; tracing; **—олит** *see* **индиголит.**

инд/ил *m.* indyl; **—илиден** *m.* indylidene; **—ирубин** *m.* indirubin, indigo red; **—итрон** *m.* (electron.) inditron.

индифферентный *a.* indifferent; inert.

индицировать *v.* indicate; index; label.

Индия (geog.) India.

индиянка *f.* (American) Indian woman.

индо— *prefix* indo—; (geog.) Indo—; **—анилин** *m.* indoaniline; **—ген** *m.* indogen; **—европейский** *a.* Indo-European; **—китайский** *a.* Indo-Chinese.

индоксил *m.* indoxyl; **—овый** *a.* indoxyl; indoxylic (acid); **—серный** *a.* indoxyl-sulfuric (acid).

индо/л *m.* indole, 1-benzazole; **—ламин** *m.* indoleamine; **—ленин** *m.,* **—лениновый** *a.* indolenine, iso-1-benzazole.

индолен/тный *a.* (med.) indolent, slow-growing; **—ция** *f.* indolence.

индо/лил *m.* indolyl; **—лилмасляный** *a.* indolylbutyric (acid); **—лилуксусный** *a.* indolylacetic, indoleacetic (acid); **—лин** *m.* indoline, 2,3-dihydroindole; **—ловый** *a.* indole; **—логенный** *a.* indologenous; **—лурия** *f.* (med.) indoluria; **—льный** *a.* indole; **—н** *m.* indone, hydrindone.

индонезийский *a.* (geog.) Indonesian.

индонил *m.* indonyl.

индоссамент *m.,* **—о** *n.* (com.) endorsement; **—ант** *m.* endorser; **—ат** *m.* endorsee; **—ирование** *n.* endorsing, endorsement; **—ировать** *v.* endorse.

индостанский *a.* (geog.) Hindustan.

индостомовые *pl.* (ichth.) Indostomidae.

индо-тихоокеанский *a.* (geog.) Indo-Pacific.

индо/фенин *m.* indophenine; **—фенол** *m.* indophenol; **—форм** *m.* indoform.

индри *m.* (mam.) Indri; **—(зиды)** *pl.* Indridae, Indri(i)sidae; **—котерий** *m.* Indricotherium.

индуз/иальный *a.* (bot.) indusial; **—ий** *m.* indusium.

индукт/анц *m.,* **—ивность** *f.* (elec.) inductance, inductivity; **катушка —ивности** inductance coil, inductor; **—ивно** *adv.* by induction; **—ивноёмкостный** *a.* inductance-capacitance; **—ивный** *a.* inductive, inductance.

индуктир/ование *see* **индукция; —ованный** *a.* induced; **—овать** *v.* induce; **—ующий** *a.* inducing, inductive.

индукто— *prefix* (elec.) inducto—, induction; **—мерный** *a.* inductometric; **—метр** *m.* inductometer; **—р** *m.* inductor, induction coil; (enzyme synthesis) inducer; **нагревательный —р** induction heater; **—рий** *m.* induction coil; **—рный** *a.* inductor, induction; **—син** *m.* inductosyn.

индукци/онный *a.* induction, inductive; **и. ролик, —онная катушка** (elec.) induction coil; **—я** *f.* induction; (magnetic) density; **вызванный —ей, обусловленный —ей** induced; **ёмкость —и** inductive capacity, dielectric constant; **коэффициент —и** (elec.) inductance.

индулин *m.,* **—овый** *a.* induline.

индурация *f.* induration, hardening.

индусск/ий *a.* (geog.) Hindu; **—ая болезнь** (med.) kala-azar.

индустри/ализация *f.* industrialization; **—ализ(ир)овать** *v.* industrialize; **—альный** *a.* industrial; **—я** *f.* industry.

индуци/бельность *f.* inducibility; **—бельный** *a.* inducible; induced (enzyme); **—рование** *see* **индукция; —рованный** *a.* induced; sympathetic (reaction); **—рованный человеком** man-induced; **—ровать** *v.* induce; stimulate.

индю/к *m.* turkey (cock); **—и** *pl.* Meleagrididae; **—шатник** *m.* turkey coop; **—шачий** *a.* turkey; **—шка** *f.* turkey hen; **—шник** *m.* turkey coop; **—шонок** *m.* turkey poult.

инее/ватый *a.* pruinose, covered with bloom; **—видный** *a.* frosted (finish).

инезит *m.* (min.) inesite.

иней *m.* hoarfrost, frost, rime.

инер *m.* Arabian-Bactrian camel hybrid.

инермиевые *pl.* (ichth.) Inermiidae.

инерт/а *f.* engineering unit of mass; **—изация** *f.* rendering inert; **—ность** *f.* inertness, inactivity, passivity; slowness (of reaction), sluggishness, lag; (phys.) inertia; **—ный** *a.* inert, inactive; sluggish.

инерци/альный *a.* inertial; **—онноплавкий** *a.* time-delay, time-lag (fuse); **—онность** *see* **инертность;** time lag; drift (of measuring instruments); (visual) persistence; **—онность действия** delay, delayed action; **—онный** *a.* inertia(l); sluggish; **—онное звено** lag network, relaxation circuit.

инерц/ия *f.* inertia, inertness; time lag; **полёт по —ии** coasting, free flight; **радиус —ии** radius of gyration; **сила —ии** (force of) inertia.

инея *gen. of* **иней.**

инж. *abbr.* (**инженер, инженерный**).

инжек/тированный *a.* injected; **—тировать** *v.* inject; **—тор** *m.* injector; **—торный** *a.* injector, injection; **—торного типа** spray-type (equipment); **—ционный** *a.,* **—ция** *f.* injection.

инженер *m.* engineer; **и.-автомобилист** *m.* automotive engineer; **и.-аквизитор** *m.* purchase engineer; **и.-атомник** *m.* nuclear engineer; **и.-вояжёр** *m.* sales engineer; **и.-геодезист** *m.* geodetic engineer; **и.-геолог** *m.* geological engineer; **и.-гидравлик, и.-гидротехник** *m.* hydraulic engineer; **и.-инструментальщик** *m.* tool engineer; **и.-испытатель** *m.* testing engineer; **—ия** *f.* engineering; **и.-конструктор** *m.* design engineer; **и.-консультант** *m.* consulting engineer; **и.-лётчик-испытатель** *m.* engineering test pilot; **и.-мелиоратор** *m.* reclamation engineer; **и.-металлург** *m.* metallurgical engineer; **и.-механик, и.-механизатор** *m.* mechanical engineer; **и.-монтажник** *m.* installation engineer; **—но-авиационный** *a.* aviation-engineering.

инженерно-/позиционный *a.* (mil.) fortification; **и.-**

разведывательный *a.* engineer-reconnaissance; **и.-ремонтный** *a.* engineer maintenance.

инженер/-нормировщик *m.* time-study engineer; **—но-сапёрный** *a.* (mil.) engineer; **—но-строительный** *a.* construction engineering; **—но-технический** *a.* engineering and technical (staff); engineer equipment (company); **—но-техническое общество** technical society of engineers; **—но-траловый** *a.* engineer mine-sweeping; **—ный** *a.* engineering; structural (seismology); **—ное дело** engineering.

инженер-плановик *m.* planning engineer; **и.-проектировщик** *m.* design and planning engineer; **и.-производственник** *m.* production engineer, works engineer; **и.-сантехник** *m.* sanitary engineer; **и.-сварщик** *m.* welding engineer; **и.-связист** *m.* communications engineer; **и.-синоптик** *m.* meterological engineer.

инженерс/кий *a.* engineer(ing); **—тво** *n.* engineering.

инженер-строитель *m.* civil engineer; **и.-термист** *m.* heat engineer; **и.-технолог** *m.* engineer-technologist, industrial engineer; **и.-физик** *m.* engineer-physicist; **и.-химик** *m.* chemical engineer; **и.-хронометражист** *m.* time-study engineer; **и.-экономист** *m.* engineer-economist; **и.-экспериментатор** *m.* testing engineer; **и.-эксплуатационник** *m.* maintenance engineer; **и.-электрик** *m.* electrical engineer.

инжир *m.*, **—ный** *a.* (bot.) fig. (*Fiscus*).

инзенский кирпич fire brick.

инзерский *a.* (geog.) Inzer.

инзухт *m.* (gen.) inbreeding.

инистый *a.* frosted, rimy.

инициал *m.* initial (letter); **—ь** *f.* (cyt.) initial, primordial cell.

иници/атив *m.* initiative; **предпринятый по —ативе** *a.* pioneered (by); **—ативность** *f.* initiative; **—ативный** *a.* (having) initiative; **—ативная творческая группа** ad-hoc think tank; **—атор** *m.* initiator, starter; trigger; pioneer; organizer; **—аторство** *n.* show of initiative, pioneering spirit; **—ирование** *n.* initiation, etc., *see v.*; **—ированный** *a.* initiated, etc., *see v.*; **—ированный светом** light-induced; **—ировать** *v.* initiate, start, trigger, induce; introduce; put into operation; **—ирующий заряд, —ирующее вещество** (expl.) initiator, priming charge.

иния *f.* (mam.) Amazon dolphin (*Inia*).

инка *f.* (mam.) rat opossum (*Lestoros inca*).

инкапсул/ирование *n.*, **—яция** *f.* incapsulation; **—ировать(ся)** *v.* incapsulate.

инкарнатный *a.* incarnate, flesh-colored.

инкарцер/ация *f.* incarceration; **—ированный** *a.* incarcerated, constricted.

инкасс/ировать *v.* (com.) collect; **—о** *n.*, **—овый** *a.* collection (of payments).

ин-кварто *adv.* (books) in quarto.

инквилин *m.* (zool.) inquiline, tenant.

инклин/атор, —ометр *m.* dipping compass, dip needle, inclinometer; **—ометрия** *f.* determination of drill hole dip and direction.

инклю/дирование *n.*, **—зия** *f.* inclusion.

инкомпетитивный *a.* non-competitive.

инконгруэнтный *a.* incongruent.

инконель *m.* Inconel (alloy).

инкорпор/ация *f.* incorporation; **—ировать** *v.* incorporate, include.

инкремент *m.* increment, growth.

инкре/т *m.* (physiol.) internal secretion, hormone; **—торный** *a.* incretory; endocrine (gland); **—тотерапия** *f.* hormone therapy; **—ция** *f.* internal secretion.

инкриминировать *v.* accuse, charge (with).

инкруст/ант *m.* incrustant, incrusting matter; **—ат** *m.* crust, scale; **—ационный** *a.*, **—ация** *f.* incrustation, scale (formation), crust; inlay, inlaid work; **—ированный** *a.* incrusted, etc., see *v.*; **—ировать** *v.* incrust, cover with a crust; inlay, line; **—ы** *pl.* incrustants.

инкуб/атор *m.*, **—аторный** *a.* incubator; **и.-автомат** *m.* automatic incubator; **—аторий** *m.* incubator house, hatchery; **—аторная станция** hatchery; **—аторно-птицеводческая станция** hatchery and poultry-breeding center; **—аторщик** *m.* incubator operator; **—ационный** *a.* incubation, incubative; **—ационная камера** (zool.) brood pouch, ovisac; **—ация** *f.*, **—ирование** *n.* incubation (period); **—ировать** *v.* incubate.

инкур/абильный *a.* incurable; **—вариевые** *pl.* (ent.) yucca moths (*Incurvariidae*).

иннерв/ация *f.* (physiol.) innervation; **—ировать** *v.* innervate.

ИННК *abbr.* (**импульсный нейтроно-нейтронный каротаж**) pulsed neutron-neutron logging.

инняха *f.* (ichth.) pond smelt (*Hypomesus olidus*).

ино— *prefix* different; other; **—видный** *a.* different (-looking).

иногда *adv.* sometimes, occasionally, in some cases, now and then.

инозем/ец *m.* foreigner; (biol.) exotic; **—ный** *a.* foreign, ecdemic, exotic.

иноз/ин *m.* inosine, hypoxanthine riboside; **—иновый, —инфосфорный** *a.* inosinic (acid); **—интрифосфат** *m.* inosine triphosphate; **—ит(ол)** *m.* inositol, hexahydroxycyclohexane; **—итофосфат** *m.* inositol phosphate; **—итурия** *f.* (med.) inos(it)uria; **—итфосфорный** *a.* phytic (acid).

ин/ой *a.* some, other; different; **в —ом случае** otherwise; **не что —ое, как** nothing but, simply.

ин-октаво *adv.* (books) in octavo.

инокул/ирование *n.*, **—яция** *f.* inoculation; **—ированный** *a.* inoculated; **—ум, —юм, —ят** *m.* inoculum.

иноломин *m.* inolomin (antibiotic).

инонациональный *a.* foreign.

инообразный *see* **иновидный.**

иноперабельный *a.* inoperable.

иноплеменн/ик *m.* foreigner, stranger, outsider; **—ый** *a.* foreign, strange.

инородный *a.* foreign, extraneous.

ино/специалист *m.* foreign specialist; **—странец** *m.*, **—странка** *f.* foreigner; **—странный** *a.* foreign; **—ходец** *m.* (horses) ambler; **—ходь** *f.* amble; **—язычный** *a.* foreign language.

ин-плано *adv.* (geom.) in plano.

инсеквентный *a.* (geol.) insequent.

инсект/арий *m.* insectarium; **—исид, —ицид** *m.* insecticide; **—ицидность** *f.* insecticidal potency; **—ицидный** *a.* insecticidal; **—ицин** *m.* insecticin (antibiotic); **—окуция** *f.* insectocution (insect electrocution); **—офунгицид** *m.* insecticide-fungicide.

инсерция *f.* insertion.

инсидентный *a.* insident; inherent.

инсинуировать *v.* insinuate.

инситный *a.* in situ, in place.

инский *a.* (geog.) Inya.

инсоляция *f.* insolation, solar radiation.

инспек/тирование *n.* inspection, examination; survey; **—тированный** *a.* inspected; **—тировать** *v.* inspect, examine; **—тор** *m.* inspector; **—торат** *m.*, **—тура** *f.* inspectorate; **—торский** *a.* inspectorial, inspection; **—торство** *n.* inspector's work; **—ционный** *a.*, **—ция** *f.* inspection; inspection center; **—ция по качеству** quality control.

инспец *m.* foreign specialist.

инспир/атор *m.* inspirator; **—ация** *f.* inspiration, inhalation; **—ированный** *a.* inspired; **—ировать** *v.* inspire.

инсталляция *f.* installation.

инстилляция *f.* instillation.

инстинкт *m.* instinct; **—ивно** *adv.* instinctively; **—ивный** *a.* instinctive.

институт *m.* institute, establishment; institution, school; **—ский** *a.* institute's, institutional.

инструк/таж *m.* instruction(s) directions; briefing; **—тивный** *a.* instructive, instruction; **—тирование** *n.* instruction; **—тировать** *v.* instruct, advise, direct; **—тировать по** brief on; **—тор** *m.,* **—торский** *a.* instructor, adviser; **—ционный** *a.,* **—ция** *f.* instruction(s), directions; order; specification; (comp.) command; handbook, manual.

инструмент *m.* instrument, tool, implement; tools, spec. machine tools; **—альная** *f.* toolroom, tool shed; **—альный** *a.* instrument(al); tool (steel, etc.); **—альная доска** dashboard; **—альное дело** tool engineering; **—альщик** *m.* tool maker, tool worker; **—арий** *m.* tool kit, set of tools; tooling; set of instruments; **—овать** *v.* (music) orchestrate; **—одержатель** *m.* tool holder; **—ораздаточный** *a.* tool- or instrument-distributing; **и.-эталон** *m.* master tool.

инсулин *m.,* **—овый** *a.* insulin (hormone); **—аза** *f.* insulinase; **—отерапия** *f.* insulin treatment.

инсульт *m.* (med.) insult(us), attack.

инсуфл/ятор *m.* (med.) insufflator; **—яция** *f.* insufflation.

инсценировать *v.* dramatize, stage; feign.

ин-т *abbr.* (институт) institute.

интактный *a.* intact, untreated; normal.

интарс(и)я *f.* intarsia (inlaid woodwork).

интегр/ал *m.* (math.) integral; **и. от квадрата** integrated square; **и. ошибок** error function; **—альный** *a.* integral, integrated, whole; mass (curve); **—альное исчисление** integral calculus; **—амма** *f.* integral curve; **—атор** *m.* integrator; **—атор импульсов** (elec.) integrating circuit; **—аф** *m.* integraph; analog integrator; **—ация** *f.,* **—ирование** *n.* integration; **—иметр** *m.* analog integrator; **—ированный** *a.* integrated; **—ировать** *v.* integrate; **—ируемость** *f.* (math.) integrability; **—ируемый** *a.* integrated; integrable; **—ируемая функция,** **—ирующийся** *a.* integrand; **—ирующий** *a.* integrating, integrant; condenser (ionization chamber); condensing (electroscope); **—ирующее звено,** **—ирующее устройство** integrator; **—одифференциальный,** **—одифференцирующий** *a.* integrodifferential; lead-lag (circuit); **—осумматор** *m.* summing integrator.

интегумент *m.* (biol.) integument, covering.

интеллект *m.* intellect, mind; (comp.) intelligence; **искусственный и.** artificial intelligence; **—уальный** *a.* intellectual, mental; intelligent; (comp.) smart; **—уальная собственность** intellectual property.

интеллигентн/ость *f.* intelligence; **—ый** *a.* intelligent, educated, cultured.

интендант *m.* (mil.) comissary, quartermaster, supply office; **—ский** *a.,* **—ство** *n.* commissariat.

интенсивн/о *adv.* intens(iv)ely, actively; **—ость** *f.* intensity, vigor; rate; severity, stength, degree; (noise) level; (traffic) density; magnitude (of earthquake); **—ость потока** (radiation) flux (level); **измеритель —ости потока** ratemeter; **—ый** *a.* intens(iv)e, high(-rate); dense, heavy (traffic); healthy (growth).

интенси/метр *m.* (nucl.) ratemeter; **—фикатор** *m.* intensifier; **—фикация** *f.* intensification; stimulation;

—фицированный *a.* intensified, etc., *see v.;* **—фицировать** *v.* intensify, enhance, step up; stimulate; **—фицирующий** *a.* intensifying, etc., *see v.;* **—фицирующая добавка** activator.

интер— *prefix* inter— (between, among); international; **—активный** *a.* (comp.) interactive; on-line; **—акция** *f.* interaction; **—амбулакральный** *a.* (zool.) interambulacral; **—бридинг** *m.* (gen.) interbreeding.

интервал *m.* interval, gap, space, spacing, interspace; pause, interruption; range; **в —е температур** in the temperature range; **—ометр** *m.* intervalometer, timer.

интервенция *f.* intervention.

интервидение *n.* international television.

интервью *n.,* **—ировать** *v.* interview.

интерградация *f.* intergradation.

интергранулярный *a.* intergranular.

интерес *m.* interest; profit; **—но** *adv.* interestingly; it is interesting; **—ный** *a.* interesting, intriguing; **—ованный** *a.* interested; **—овать** *v.* interest, attract; **—оваться** *v.* take interest; **—ующий** *a.* interesting, of interest.

интер/калярный *a.* intercalary, interposed; **—кинез** *m.* (gen.) interkinesis, interphase; **—костальный** *a.* (anat.) intercostal; **—кристаллитный,** **—кристаллический** *a.* intercrystalline; **—лейкин** *m.* (immun.) interleukin; **—локинг** *m.* interlocking.

интермед/иальный, **—иарный** *a.* intermediary, intermediate; **—иат** *m.* intermediate; **—ин** *m.* intermedin (hormone).

интерметалл/ид *m.* intermetallic compound; **—ический** *a.* intermetallic.

интер/миссия *f.* intermission, interval; **—митотический** *a.* (gen.) intermitotic; **—миттирующий** *a.* intermittent; **—молекулярный** *a.* intermolecular.

интерн *m.* (med.) intern; **—ализация** *f.* internalization; **—ат** *m.* boarding school; **—атура** *f.* internship.

интернационал/изировать *v.* internationalize; **—ьный** *a.* international.

интернировать *v.* intern.

интероперкулярный *a.* (zool.) interopercular.

интероцеп/тивный *a.* (physiol.) interoceptive; **—тор** *m.* interoceptor; **—ция** *f.* interoception.

интерплантат *m.* (embr.) interplant.

интерпозиционный *a.* interpositional.

интерпол/ирование *n.,* **—яционный** *a.,* **—яция** *f.* interpolation; **—ировать** *v.* interpolate; **—ирующий** *a.* interpolating; **—ятор** *m.* interpolator.

интерпрет/атор *m.* interpreter; interpretive program; **—ация** *f.* interpretation; **—ировать** *v.* interpret, explain; **—ирующий** *a.* interpretive.

интерсекс *m.* (biol.) intersex; intersexuality; **—уальность** *f.* intersexuality; **—уальный** *a.* intersexual.

интер/септор *see* **интерцептор;** **—сертальный** *a.* (geol.) intersertal; **—стерильный** *a.* (biol.) intersterile, non-interbreeding; **—стициальный** *a.* interstitial; **—стиций** *m.* interstice, interval, space, gap; **—фаза** *f.,* **—фазный** *a.* (gen.) interphase; **—фейс** *m.* (comp.) interface; **—фейс малых вычислительных систем** small computer system interface, SCSI.

интерфер/енциальный *a.* interference; **—енционно-поляризационный** *a.* interference-polarization; **—енционный** *a.* interference; **—енционный прибор** interferometer; **—енция** *f.* interference; **—ировать** *v.* interfere; **—ирующий** *a.* interfering; **—ограмма** *f.* interferogram, interference pattern; **—ометр** *m.* interferometer; **—ометрия** *f.* interferometry; **—он** *m.* (med.) interferon.

интер/фертильный *a.* (biol.) interfertile, able to interbreed; **—филярный** *a.* (cyt.) interfilar; **—целлюлярный** *a.* intercellular; **—цептор** *m.* (av.) interceptor; spoiler.

интерьер *m.* interior.

интим/а *f.* (anat.) intima, innermost structure; **—ничать** *v.* be on intimate terms; **—ность** *f.* intimacy, closeness; **—ный** *a.* intimate, close; subtle, innermost; (anat.) intimal.

интина *f.* (bot.) intine.

интоксикац/ионный *a.* intoxicating, toxic; **—ия** *f.* intoxication, poisoning, toxic effect.

интолерантный *a.* (med.) intolerant.

интон/ационный *a.,* **—ация** *f.,* **—ирование** *n.* intonation; **—ировать** *v.* inton(at)e.

интра— *prefix* intra— (inside, within); **—венозный** *a.* (anat.) intravenous; **—зональный** *a.* intrazonal; **—кристаллитный** *a.* intracrystalline; (met.) transcrystalline (crack).

интрамолекулярный *a.* intramolecular.

интранзитивный *a.* (math.) intransitive.

интрацеллюлярный *a.* (cyt.) intracellular.

интриговать *v.* scheme, plot, intrigue (against); arouse the curiosity (of).

интро— *prefix* intro— (into, inward; within); **—грессивный** *a.* introgressive; **—грессия** *f.* introgression; **—дукционный** *a.* introductive, introductory; **—дукция** *f.* introduction; **—дуцированный** *a.* introduced; alien (crop); **—рзный** *a.* (bot.) introrse; **—спекция** *f.* introspection, self-analysis.

интру/дировать *v.* intrude; **—зив** *m.* (geol.) intrusion, intrusive rock; **—зивный** *a.* intrusive; **—зия** *f.* intrusion.

инту/бация *f.* (med.) intubation; **—итивный** *a.* intuitive, subconscious; **—иция** *f.* intuition, instinct; **—ссуцепция** *f.* (bot.) intussusception.

инул/аза *f.* inulase; **—ин** *m.,* **—иновый** *a.* inulin, alant starch; **—инонос** *m.* inulin-yielding plant.

инфак *m.* faculty of foreign languages.

инфантил/изм *m.* (med.) infantilism; **—ьность** *f.* infantilism; infancy; **—ьный** *a.* infantile.

инфаркт *m.* (med.) infarct; infarction.

инфауна *f.* (zool.) infauna.

инфекц/иозность *f.* infectiousness; **—ионный** *a.* infectious, contagious; contagious diseases (hospital); **—ионная активность** infectivity; **—ия** *f.* infection, contagion; (gas) gangrene.

инфильтр/ат *m.* infiltrate; **—ационный** *a.* infiltrative; **—ационный** *a.,* **—ация** *f.* infiltration, seepage; **—ировать** *v.* infiltrate; **—ометр** *m.* infiltrometer, seepage gage.

инфициров/ание *n.* infection; **—анный** *a.* infected; septic (wound); **—ать** *v.* infect; contaminate.

инфлектор *m.* inflector, deflector.

инфл/уэнца, —юэнца *f.* (med.) influenza.

инфлюентная линия influence line.

инфляц/ионный *a.,* **—ия** *f.* inflation.

ин-фолио *adv.* (books) in folio.

информ/ативность *f.* information (content); **—атика** *f.* computer science; information science; **—атор** *m.* informer; information clerk; **—ационно-поисковый** *a.* (information) retrieval; index (term); **—ационно-потоковый мультиграф** information-flow network; **—ационно-справочный** *a.* information reference; **—ационный** *a.* informing, information; data-processing; indexing (language); messenger (RNA); **—ационная машина** data processor; **—ационные работы** data processing; **—ация** *f.* information; data; message; intelligence; documentation; **—ация на входе** input;

—ация на выходе output; **носители —ации** software; **—бюро** *n.* bureau of information.

информиров/ание *n.* information (distribution); **—ать** *v.* inform.

информот *m.* information department.

инфра— *prefix* infra— (below); **—звук** *m.* subsonics, infra-sound; **—звуковой** *a.* infrasonic, subsonic, sub-audio; **—красный** *a.* infrared (rays); **—низкий** *a.* subsonic; **—специфический** *a.* (biol.) subspecific; **—структура** *f.* infrastructure; **—фильтр** *m.* infrared filter.

инфуз *m.,* **—ия** *f.* infusion.

инфузор/ии *pl.* (prot.) Infusoria; **—ия** *f.* infusorian; **—ная земля** (geol.) infusorial earth, kieselguhr, diatomaceous earth.

инфундировать *v.* infuse.

инцидент *m.* incident, occurrence, case; **—ность** *f.* (math.) incidence.

инцизия *f.* incision, cut.

инцистиров/ание *n.* (biol.) encystment, cyst formation; **—аться** *v.* encyst.

инцухт *m.* (biol.) inbreeding.

инч *m.* inch.

инье/ктивный *a.* (math.) injective; **—ктировать, —кцировать** *v.* inject; **—кционный** *a.,* **—кция** *f.* injection.

иньвинский *a.* (geog.) Inva.

иньский *a.* (geog.) Inya.

иобирин *m.* yobirine.

иоганнит *m.* (min.) johannite.

иогимбин *see* **йохимбин.**

иогурт *m.* (food) yoghurt.

иод *m.* iodine, I; **бромистый и.** iodine bromide; **насыщать —ом** *v.* iodize.

иод— *prefix* iod(o)— iodide (of); **—азид** *m.* iodazide, iodine nitride; **—алкил** *m.* alkyl iodide; **—ангидрид** *m.* acid iodide; **—анилин** *m.* iodoaniline; **—ат** *m.* iodate; **—ацетамид** *m.* iodoacetamide; **—ацетат** *m.* iodoacetate; **—ацетон** *m.* iodoacetone; **—бензол** *m.* iodobenzene; **—гидрат** *m.* hydroiodide; **—гидрин** *m.* iodohydrin; **—горг(он)овый** *a.* iodogorgoic (acid); **—замещённый** *a.* iodine (compound); **—ид** *m.* iodide; **—изм** *m.* iodism, iodine poisoning; **—иный** *a.* iodine; iodide (of); **—ирит** *m.* (min.) iod(arg)yrite.

иодиров/ание *n.* iodination, iodizing; **—анный** *a.* iodinated, iodized; **—ать** *v.* iodinate, iodize, iodate.

иодистоводородн/ый *a.* hydriodide (of); hydriodic (acid); **соль —ой кислоты** iodide.

иодисто/калийный *a.* potassium iodide; **—кислый** *a.* iodous acid; iodite (of); **—кислая соль** iodite.

иодист/ый *a.* iodine; (lower or **—ous**) iodide (of); **и. водород** hydrogen iodide; **и. калий** potassium iodide; **—ая кислота** iodous acid; **соль —ой кислоты** iodite; **—ая медь** cuprous iodide; **—ое железо** ferrous iodide.

иод/ит *m.* iodite; **—крахмал** *see* **иодокрахмал; —магниймети**л *m.* methylmagnesium iodide; **—магнийэтил** *m.* ethylmagnesium iodide; **—метан** *m.* iodomethane, methyl iodide; **—метилат** *m.* methiodide; **—метилирование** *n.* iodomethylation.

иодноватист/окислый *a.* hypoiodite (of); hypoiodous (acid); **—окислая соль** hypoiodite; **—ый** *a.* hypoiodous (acid).

иодновато/бариевая соль barium iodate; **—кислый** *a.* iodic acid; iodate (of); **—кислый натрий, —натриевая соль** sodium iodate; **—кислая соль** iodate.

иодноват/ый *a.* iodic (acid, anhydride); **соль —ой кислоты** iodate.

иоднокисл/ый *a.* periodic acid; periodate (of); **—ая соль** periodate.

иодн/ый *a.* iodine; (higher or —ic) iodide (of); periodic (acid); **соль —ой кислоты** periodate; **—ая медь** cupric iodide; **—ая настойка** tincture of iodine; **—ая ртуть** mercuric iodide; **—ое число** iodine number, Wijs number.

иодо— *prefix* iodo—; **—бензол** *m.* iodobenzene; **—бромит** *m.* (min.) iodobromite; **—водород** *m.* hydrogen iodide; **—водородный** *a.* hydroiodide (of); hydriodic (acid); **—зобензол** *m.* iodosobenzene; **—зол** *m.* iodosol, thymol iodide; **—какодил** *m.* cacodyl iodide; **—кись** *f.* oxyiodide; **—крахмальный** *a.* iodized starch; **—кси—** *prefix* iodoxy—.

иодол *m.* Iodol, tetraiodopyrrole.

иодометан *m.* iodomethane, methyl iodide.

иодометр/ический *a.* iodometric; **—ия** *f.* iodometry.

иодон/ий *m.*, **—иевый** *a.* iodonium.

иодо/платинат *m.* iodoplatinate; **—пропан** *m.* iodopropane, propyl iodide; **—пропен** *m.* iodopropene, allyl iodide; **—содержащий** *a.* iodine-containing; **—соединение** *n.* iodo compound, iodine compound; **—стерин** *m.* iodosterol; **—тирин** *m.* iodothyrin, thyroidin; **—фен** *m.* Iodophene, iodophthalein; **—фор** *m.* iodophor; **—форм** *m.*, **—формный** *a.* iodoform, triiodomethane; **—формин** *m.* iodoformin; **—этан** *m.* iodoethane, ethyl iodide; **—этилен** *m.* iodoethylene, vinyl iodide; **—эфир** *m.* iodo ether.

иод/производное *n.* iodine derivative; **—пропан** *see* иодопропан; **—тиреоглобулин** *m.* iodothyr(e)oglobulin; **—тирозин** *m.* iodotyrosine; **—тиронин** *m.* iodothyronine; **—уксусный** *a.* iodoacetic (acid); **—циан** *m.* cyanogen iodide; **—этан** *see* иодоэтан; **—юр** *m.* iodide.

иолит *m.* (min.) iolite, cordierite.

ион *m.* ion; **выход пар —ов** ion-pair yield; **перенос —ов** ionic migration; **промежуточный и., средний и.** hybrid ion, amphoteric ion, zwitterion; **расщепление —ов** ionic cleavage, ionization.

ион/ен *m.* ionene; **—идин** *m.* ionidine.

иониз/атор *m.* ionizer; **—ационный** *a.*, **—ация** *f.*, **—ирование** *n.* ionization, electrolytic dissociation; **—ированный** *a.* ionized; **—(ир)овать(ся)** *v.* ionize; **—ируемый** *a.* ionizable; **—ирующий** *a.* ionizing.

ионий *m.* ionium, Io.

ионит *m.* ion exchanger, ion-exchange resin; **—овый** *a.* ion-exchange(r).

ионический *a.* (geog.) Ionian; (arch.) Ionic.

ион/-коагулятор *m.* coagulator ion; **комплексный и.-металл** metal-ion complex.

ионно— *prefix* ion—; *see also under* **ионо—**; **—дисперсный** *a.* ion-dispersed; **и.-лучевой** *a.* ion-beam; **—обменник** *see* ионообменник; **ион-носитель** *m.* ion carrier; **и.-сорбционный** *a.* getter ion (pump); **—сть** *f.* ionic character; ionization; ionic content.

ионн/ый *a.* ion(ic); gas-filled (triode); **и. обмен** ion exchange; **и. пучок** ion beam; **—ая сила** ionic strength; **—ая траектория** ionization path.

ионо— *prefix* ion(o)—, ion; ion— (violet); *see also under* **ионно—**; **—гальванизация** *f.* (med.) iontophoresis, ionotherapy; **—ген** *m.* ionogen; **—генный** *a.* ionogenic, ion-producing; **—графия** *f.* ion diffraction analysis; **—избирательный** *a.* ion-selective; **—излучающий** *a.* ion-emitting; **—колориметр** *m.* ionocolorimeter (for pH determination); **—л** *m.* ionol, butylated hy-

droxytoluene; **—мер** *m.* pH meter; **—метр** *m.* ionometer; **—н** *m.*, **—новый** *a.* ionone; **—обмен** *m.* ion exchange; **—обменитель, —обменник** *m.* ion exchanger; **—обменный** *a.* ion-exchange (resin, etc.); **—образование** *n.* ion formation, ionization; **—пауза** *f.* ionopause; **—ракета** *f.* ion rocket; **—сфера** *f.* ionosphere; **—сферный** *a.* ionospheric.

ион/отерапия *f.* (med.) ionotherapy, iontophoresis; **—отрон** *m.* ionotron; **—(т)офорез** *m.* iontophoresis.

иордан/ит *m.* (min.) jordanite; **—ский** *a.* (geog.) Jordan.

иоркширский *a.* (geog.) Yorkshire.

иорский *a.* (geog.) Iori.

иосейт *m.* (min.) josëite.

иосол *m.* iosol, thymol iodide.

иот/а *f.* iota; **ни на —у** not at all.

иотион *m.* iothion, diiodopropyl alcohol.

иотнийский *a.* (geol.) Jotnian.

иохимбин *m.* yohimbine.

Ипатиева реакция Ipatiev reaction.

ипатка *f.* (orn.) horned puffin (*Fratercula corniculata*).

ипека/куана *f.* (bot.) ipecac (*Cephaelis ipecacuanha*); **—куановый** *a.* ipecac; ipecacuanhic (acid); **—мин** *m.* ipecamine.

ипноп/(н)овые *pl.* (ichth.) Ipnopidae; **—с** *m.* Ipnops.

и под. *abbr.* (и подобное) et cetera.

ипом/еин *m.* ipom(o)ein; **—ея** *f.* (bot.) Ipomoea; **—овый** *a.* ipomic (acid).

ипоте/ка *f.* mortgage; (bot.; law) hypotheca; **—чный** *a. of* ипотека; hypothecary; **—чный долг** mortgage.

ипохондр/ик *m.*, **—ический** *a.* (med.) hypochondriac; **—ия** *f.* hypochondria.

иппо— *prefix* hippo— (horse).

и пр. *abbr.* (и прочее) and so forth.

ипрал *m.* Ipral, probarbital.

иприт *m.* (mil.) yperite, mustard gas.

ИПС *abbr.* (инкубаторно-птицеводческая станция) hatchery and poultry breeding center; (изопропиловый спирт) isopropyl alcohol; (информационно-поисковая система) information retrieval system.

ипсилон *m.* upsilon (Greek letter); (ent.) black cutworm (*Agrotis ypsilon*).

Ипсуич (geog.) Ipswich.

ипутьский *a.* (geog.) Iput.

ИПФ *abbr.* (интерференционно-поляризованный фильтр) polarizing interference filter.

ИПЯ *abbr.* (информационно-поисковый язык) information retrieval language.

ира/вадийский *a.* (geog.) Irrawaddy; **—зер** *m.* (phys.) eraser, infrared laser; **—кский** *a.* (geog.) Iraqi(an); **—нский** *a.* Iranian.

ирбис *m.* (mam.) snow leopard (*Felis uncia*).

ирбитский *a.* (geog.) Irbit.

ирвингия *f.* (bot.) Irvingia.

ирга *f.* (bot.) June berry (*Amelanchier*).

иргалон *m.* irgalon, sodium edetate.

иргизский *a.* (geog.) Irgiz.

ире/ляхский *a.* (geog.) Irelyakh; **—ндыкский** *a.* Irendyk; **—ньский** *a.* Iren.

иригенин *m.* irigenin.

иригизация *f.* (met.) ihrigizing.

ирид— *see* иридо—.

иридесценция *f.* iridescence.

иридиев/ый *a.* iridium, iridic; **—ая чернь** iridium black, iridium trioxide.

иридизация *f.* iridescence.

ирид/ий *m.* iridium, Ir; **хлористый и.** iridochloride, iridium dichloride; **хлорный и.** iridic chloride, iridium tetrachloride; **—ин** *m.* iridin.

иридирующий *a.* iridescent.

иридист/ый *a.* iridium, iridous; **и. осмий** *see* **иридосмин; —ая платина** platinum-iridium alloy.

иридо— *prefix* irid(o)— [(anat.) iris; colored circle]; **—мирмекс** *m.* (ent.) Iridomyrmex; **—мирмецин** *m.* iridomyrmecin; **—плегия** *f.* (med.) iridoplegia; **—смин** *m.* (min.) iridosmine, osmiridium; **—циклит** *m.* (med.) iridocyclitis.

иридэктомия *f.* (med.) iridectomy.

ириз/ация *f.* iridescence; irisation (of clouds); **—ин** *m.* irisin; **—ировать** *v.* iridesce, be iridescent; **—ирующий** *a.* iridescent.

ирис *m.* (anat.; bot.) iris; (ent.) Iris; toffee (candy); **—ка** *f.* a toffee.

ирит *m.* (med.) iritis.

иркинеевский *a.* (geog.) Irkineyeva.

иркутский *a.* (geog.) Irkut, Irkutsk.

Ирландия Ireland.

ирландский *a.* Irish; **и. мох** (bot.) Irish moss, carragheen (*Chondrus crispus*).

ИРН *abbr.* (**источник регулируемого напряжения**) source of regulated voltage.

и-РНК *abbr.* (**информационная рибонуклеиновая кислота**) messenger RNA.

ирный корень (bot.) Acorus calamus.

ИРО *abbr.* (**интенсивность рентгеновских отражений**) intensity of X-ray reflections.

ирокезский *a.* Iroquois (Indian).

ирон *m.* (chem.) irone.

ирон/изировать *v.* be sarcastic (about); **—ический, —ичный** *a.* ironic.

ирпеньский *a.* (geog.) Irpen.

ирради/ация *f.* irradiation; **—ировать** *v.* irradiate.

ирратен *m.* (plastics) irraten.

иррациональн/ость *f.* (math.) irrationality; irrational, surd; **освободиться от —ости, уничтожать и. в** *v.* rationalize; **—ый** *a.* surd, irrational, non-rational.

ирреальный *a.* unreal.

иррегулярн/о-особый *a.* (math) irregularly singular; **—ость** *f.* irregularity, randomness; **—ый** *a.* irregular.

ирриг/атор *m.* irrigator; **—ационный** *a.* irrigation; fountain (syringe); **—ация** *f.,* **—ирование** *n.* irrigation; **—ированный** *a.* irrigated; **—ировать** *v.* irrigate.

иррит/ативный *a.* irritative; **—ация** *f.* irritation.

ирруптивный *a.* (geol.) irruptive.

иртышский *a.* (geog.) Irtysh.

ис— *prefix* ex—, away from, out of.

исетьский *a.* (geog.) Iset, Yset.

ИСЗ *abbr.* (**искусственный спутник земли**) artificial earth satellite; spacecraft.

исима *f.* (ichth.) masu salmon (*Oncorhynchus masu*).

иск *m.* suit, action, claim; **и. о нарушении** infringement action; **встречный и.** counter-claim; **предъявить и.** *v.* sue, prosecute; **—овой** *a. of* **иск.**

иска/жать, —зить *v.* distort, deform, twist; misrepresent, falsify, alter; garble (code); **—жающий** *a.* distorting, etc., *see v.;* **—жение** *n.,* **—жениость** *f.* distortion, etc., *see v.;* **—жение по error in;* **—жённый** *a.* distorted, etc., *see v.;* abnormal.

искалечи(ва)ть *v.* cripple, maim; mutilate.

искалывать *v.* prick all over.

искан/ие *n.* search(ing), quest; hunting, seeking; selection; dialing (switch) action; **—ный** *a.* sought, looked for.

искап/ать *v.* sp(l)atter; **—ывать** *v.* sp(l)atter; dig up.

искатель *m.* selector, finder, locator; seeker; switch;

(scintillation) scanner; (phot.) view finder; **—ный** *a.* searching, seeking; **—ная трубка** (opt.) object finder; **—ство** *n.* (law) suit.

искать *v.* look (for), search, seek, hunt; look up (facts); investigate; sue; claim.

искл/евать, —ёвывать *v.* peck up; tear, maul.

исключ/ать *v.* except, exclude, rule out, preclude; omit; eliminate, delete; expel, discharge, release, eject, discard; bar; **—ающий** *a.* excepting, etc., *see v.;* **взаимно —ающий** conflicting, mutually exclusive; **—ая** *pr. ger. and prep. gen.* excepting, except (for), with the exception (of), barring, exclusive (of), less; **—ение** *n.* exception, etc., *see v.;* **за —ением** with the exception (of), except (for), exclusive (of), apart from, but for, save for, other than; **за —ением одного** with one exception; **за —ением того, что** except that; **принцип —ения** (nucl.) exclusion principle; **—ённый** *a.* excepted, etc., *see v.*

исключительн/о *adv.* exceptionally; exclusively, solely; exceedingly, extremely; **и. важный** *a.* of prime importance, critical; **—ость** *f.* exceptional nature; peculiarity, exclusiveness; **—ый** *a.* exceptional, unusual, exclusive; remarkable, outstanding, excellent; **—ое право** monopoly; patent right.

исключить *see* **исключать.**

исковерк/анный *a.* distorted, mutilated; **—ать** *v.* distort, mutilate, spoil.

исков/ой *a. of* **иск; —ое заявление** (law) statement of claim.

исков/ыривать, —ырять *v.* dig or pick out.

искол/ачивать, —отить *v.* beat up.

исколоть *v.* prick all over.

искомкать *v.* crumple, crush, wrinkle.

иском/ый *a.* sought (for), desired, required; **—ое число** unknown quantity.

исконный *a.* indigenous, native, autochthonous; primordial; age-old; **и. обитатель** autochthon.

исконопа/тить, —чивать *v.* calk.

ископаем/ое *n.* mineral; fossil; **горючие —ые** fossil fuels; **полезные —ые** mineral resources; **—ый** *a.* mineral; fossil, extinct.

ископ/анный *a.* dug up; **—ать** *v.* dig up.

искорёжи(ва)ть *v.* bend, warp.

искорен/енне *n.* eradication, etc., *see v.;* **—ённый** *a.* eradicated, etc., *see v.;* **—ить, —ять** *v.* eradicate, exterminate, extirpate, uproot, root out.

искорка *dim. of* **искра;** scintillation.

искоробить *v.* twist, bend, warp.

иско/са *adv.* askew, aslant; askance; **—сить** *v.* slant; squint; warp, distort; **—собочиться** *v.* twist to one side; **—шенный** *a.* slanted.

искр/а *f.* spark, flash; **зажигание —ой** spark ignition; **мечущий —ы** *a.* sparking; scintillating, sparkling; **не дающий —у** *a.* nonsparking; **счётчик искр** scintillation counter.

искра/сить, —шивать *v.* (use up) paint.

искрение *n.* sparking, etc., *see* **искрить(ся).**

искренн/ий *a.* sincere, frank, candid; **—ость** *f.* sincerity, candor.

искрив/ившийся *see* **искривлённый; —ить** *see* **искривлять; —ление** *n.* curve, curvature; bend(ing); twist(ing), warp(ing), buckling, distortion, deformation; deviation; curvature (of spine); **—лённость** *f.* curvature; **—лённый** *a.* curved, etc., *see v.;* **—лять** *v.* curve, bend; twist, warp, distort, contort; deflect; **—ляться** *v.* twist, warp, buckle; deviate.

искрист/ость *f.* effervescence, foaminess, frothiness; **—ый** *a.* effervescent, sparkling; scintillating, flashing.

искрить *v.* spark, flash; **—ся** *v.* (elec.) spark; sparkle, flash, scintillate; effervesce, fizz; bubble.

искров/авленный, —енённый *a.* bloodied.

искровой *a.* spark, spark-like.

искрогаситель *m.,* **—ное устройство** spark arrester, spark extinguisher; **—ный** *a.* spark-extinguishing, blow-out.

искро/гашение *n.* spark quenching, spark extinguishing; **—мер** *m.* scintillometer; **—метность** *f.* triboluminescence.

искромсать *v.* cut up, shred, tear apart.

искро/образование *n.* spark formation, sparking; **—стойкий** *a.* nonarcing, nonsparking; **—стойкость** *f.* arc resistance; **—тушение** *see* **искрогашение; —тушитель** *see* **искрогаситель; —удержатель** *m.* spark arrester; **—указатель** *m.* spark detector; **—уловитель** *see* **искрогаситель.**

искрошить(ся) *v.* crumble.

искряк *m.* (min.) aventurine.

искрящий *a.* sparking; **—ся** *a.* sparkling, scintillating; effervescent.

искуп/ать *v.* bathe, wash; *see* **искупить; —аться** *v.* take a bath; **—ить** *v.* expiate, atone (for); make up, compensate, pay (for); **—ление** *n.* expiation, atonement.

искури(ва)ть *v.* smoke (to the end).

искус *m.* test, trial.

искусать *see* **искусывать.**

искус/ить *v.* tempt; **—иться** *v.* acquire skill (in); **—ник** *m.* skilled worker; **—ный** *a.* expert, skillful.

искусственн/о *adv.* artificially; synthetically; **и. вызванный** *a.* induced (labor); **и. созданный** *a.* simulated (conditions); **—ость** *f.* artificially; **—ый** *a.* artificial; synthetic; man-made; induced (labor); therapeutic (fever); cultivated (pasture).

искусство *n.* art. craft; skill, proficiency, knack; workmanship; craftsmanship.

искусывать *v.* bite, sting (all over).

искушать *v.* tempt, seduce.

ИСЛ *abbr.* (**искусственный спутник луны**) artificial moon satellite.

исландский *a.* Iceland; **и. мох** (bot.) Iceland moss (*Cetraria islandica*); **и. шпат** (min.) Iceland spar.

ИСМ *abbr.* (**искусственные и синтетические материалы**) artificial and synthetic materials.

ИСО *abbr.* (**известково-серный отвар**) lime-sulfur spray; (**Международная организация по стандартизации**) International Organization for Standardization.

исп. *abbr.* (**испанский; испытуемый**).

Испания Spain.

испанск/ий *a.* Spanish; **и. перец** red pepper, Cayenne pepper.

испар/ение *n.* evaporaton, etc., *see* **испарить;** (petrol.) flashing, stripping; vapor, fume; (bot.) transpiration; **жидкость —ения** (meteor.) atmometry; **—ённый** *a.* evaporated, etc., *see* **испарить.**

испар/ивать *see* **испарить; —имый** *see* **испаряемый.**

испарина *f.* perspiration, sweat; condensate; (med.) diaphoresis.

испаритель *m.* evaporator, vaporizer; condenser, cooler; evaporimeter, atmometer; evaporation tank; **—ность топлива** ratio of steam generated to fuel burned; **—ный** *a.* evaporative; evaporation (tank); **—ная колонна** (petrol.) flash tower, evaporator; **—ная секция** stripper (of fractionating column); **—ная способность** evaporativity.

испар/ить, —ять *v.* evaporate, vaporize, volatilize, ex-

hale; steam; (met.) sublime; **—иться, —яться** *v.* evaporate, be evaporated; volatilize; fume; disappear, vanish; **—ометр** *m.* evaporimeter; (e)vaporability, vaporizability; volatility; **—яемый** *a.* evaporable; volatile; **—яющий** *a.* evaporating, etc., *see v.;* **—яющая способность** *see* **испаряемость.**

испах(ив)ать *v.* plow up.

испачкать *v.* dirty, soil, contaminate.

испёкший *past act. part. of* **испечь.**

испепел/ение *n.* incineration, calcination; **—ить, —ять** *v.* incinerate, calcine, reduce to ashes; **—иться** *v.* burn up.

испестр/ить, —ять *see* **испещрить.**

испеч/ённый *a.* baked, roasted; **—ь** *v.* bake, roast.

испещр/ённо — *prefix* stricto—; **—енный** *a.* speckled, etc., *see v.;* variegated; figured; irrorate; maculate; **—ить, —ять** *v.* speckle, spot, dot; mottle, streak.

испивать *see* **испить.**

испили(ва)ть *v.* saw (up).

испис(ыв)ать *v.* fill up, cover (with writing); use up (paper, etc.)

испитой *a.* worn out, emaciated; haggard.

испить *v.* take a few sips; drink up.

испод *m.* reverse side.

исподволь *adv.* unhurriedly, leisurely; gradually, by degrees, little by little.

исподн/изу *adv.* underneath, from below; **—ий** *a.* under, bottom; from below; **—ик** *m.* bottom (part), bottom tool.

испокон веков since time immemorial.

исползать *v.* creep or crawl all over.

исполин *m.* giant; **—овый, —ский** *a.* giant, gigantic, huge; **—ские щитни** (zool.) Gigantostraca.

исполком *m.* executive committee.

исполн/ение *n.* accomplishment, fulfillment, execution, observation, observance, completion; performance; implement; version, modification; design, make; construction; enclosure; **закрытого —ения** *a.* enclosed-type; **индивидуального —ения** *a.* custom-made; **приводить в и.** *v.* carry out, accomplish; **—енный** *a.* accomplished, etc., *see* **исполнить;** complete; **—имость** *f.* feasibility, practicability; **—имый** *a.* feasible, practicable.

исполнитель *m.* executor, performer; executive; (anat.) effector; **—ный** *a.* executive; control(ling); actuating; punctual, careful; **—ный механизм** actuating mechanism, actuator; servo mechanism, servo motor; power unit; slave (of a manipulator); **—ный орган, —ный элемент, —ное устройство** actuator.

исполн/ить, —ять *v.* accomplish, fulfill, carry out, perform, execute, act (for); **—яющий** *a.* accomplishing, etc., *see v.*

исполосовать *v.* cut into strips; flog.

использ/ование *n.* utilization, using, etc., *see v.;* use, employment; recovery; (sewage) treatment; **повторное и.** recycling, salvaging, reuse; **при —овании** using, with (the use of), (when) used; in (method); **процент —ования** recovery; efficiency; **—ованный** *a.* utilized, etc., *see v.;* spent, stripped (gas); **—овать** *v.* utilize, use, make use (of), employ, apply, adopt; use up, consume, spend; run, operate; treat, process (sewage); rely, depend (on); make the most (of), turn to account; follow (method); harness (power); exploit, develop, take advantage (of), profit (by); recover, salvage (waste); **—оваться** *v.* be utilized, be in use, be of use, serve (as), find application; **—уемый** *a.* usable; in use, used; **—ующий** *a.* utilizing, etc., *see v.*

исполь/ничество *n.,* **—ный** *a.,* **—щина** *f.* (agr.) metayage.

испорошковывать *v.* pulverize.

испор/тить *v.* spoil, injure, damage; deteriorate, make worse; **—титься** *v.* get spoiled, go bad (of food); get damaged; deteriorate, get worse; **—ченность** *f.* bad condition, faultiness; putrescence; **—ченный** *a.* spoiled, rotten, decomposed, putrefied; injured, damaged, faulty, unsound; in bad repair; corrupt.

исправ/дом *m.* corrective labor home; **—имый** *a.* correctable; (comp.) recoverable (error); **—ительнотрудовой** *a.* reformatory, corrective(-labor); **—ительный** *a.* corrective; **—ить, —лять** *v.* correct, (re)adjust, rectify, remedy, fix, repair, mend; improve; amend, revise; discharge (duties); reclaim; reform; **—иться, —ляться** *v.* improve, change for the better; **—ление** *n.* correction, (re)adjustment, fixing, etc., *see v.;* improvement; **вносить —ление** *v.* correct; **—ленный** *a.* corrected, etc., *see v.;* **—ляющий** *a.* correcting, etc., *see v.;* corrective.

исправн/о *adv.* duly, **—ость** *f.* punctuality, exactness, accuracy; good condition, working order; serviceability; **в —ости** in good repair, in running order, in working order; **—ый** *a.* punctual, exact, accurate, precise; efficient, fit, serviceable, in good working order, sound, healthy; **—ое состояние** working order.

испражн/ение *n.* defecation, evacuation; **—ения** *pl.* feces, excrement, stools; **—иться, —яться** *v.* defecate, evacuate, move one's bowels.

испробовать *v.* try, test; experience.

испро/сить *v.* solicit, obtain by soliciting; **—шенный** *a.* solicited.

исправм/ить, —лять *v.* straighten.

испрясть *v.* spin (all).

испуг *m.* fright, scare; terror; **—анный** *a.* frightened; **—ать** *v.* frighten, scare.

испу/скаемый *a.* emitted, etc., *see v.;* **—скание** *n.* emission, emanation; emergence; release; **—скатель** *m.* emitter; **—скательный, —скающий** *a.* emitting, emissive; **—скательная способность** emissive power, emissivity; **—скать, —стить** *v.* emit, give off, exhale; evolve, release, give up, liberate; emanate, radiate; eject; give, utter; expire; **—скаться** *v.* emerge; emanate; **—щенный** *a.* emitted, etc., *see v.*

испыл/енность *f.* pulverulence; **—енный** *a.* pulverized, pulverulent; **—ять** *v.* pulverize.

испытан/ие *n.* test(ing), experiment, trial; assay, analysis, checking, examination; research, investigation; **и. в работе, и. в эксплуатации** field test, plant test; **и. на** test for; **и. на сжатие** compression test; **и. трением** friction test; **подвергать —ию** *v.* test, try out, experiment (with); **и.-экспресс** quick test; **автономное и.** stand-alone test; **разобранное и.** interface test; **собранное и.** full(-up) systems test.

испыт/анный *a.* tested, etc., *see* испытывать; proven; **и. временем** time-tested; **—атель** *m.* tester, testing apparatus; investigator, research man; analyst, analyzer; checker; taster.

испыт/ательный *a.* test(ing), trial, experimental; examining; try (cock); laboratory (bench); probationary (period); **и. полигон** (mil.) proving ground; **и. этаж** training period; **—ательная программа** programmed checking; **—ательский** *a. of* испытатель; **—ать** *see* испытывать; **—уемый** *see* испытываемый; **—ующий** *see* испытательный; **—ываемый** *a.* tested, etc., *see v.;* experimental, test (material), under test, being tested; sample (solution); under consideration, in question; *m.* examinee; **—ывать** *v.* test, try; investigate, examine, check; sample; assay, analyze; experiment; experience, undergo, sustain, go through,

be subjected (to); encounter, run (into), meet (with), be faced (with); **—ывать на** test for; **—ывать на дорогах** road test.

испятнать *v.* spot up, spatter; patch.

иссали(ва)ть *v.* get greasy.

иссверли(ва)ть *v.* drill, bore, perforate.

иссекать *see* иссечь.

иссера— *prefix* grayish.

иссеч/ение *n.* cut(ting); carving; (med.) excision, resection; **—ь** *v.* cut, slash; hew, carve; excise, resect, exsect.

иссиза— *prefix* bluish, dove-colored.

иссиня— *prefix* bluish.

исследить *v.* track up (surface).

исследов/ание *n.* investigation, etc., *see v.;* inquiry; research, study, survey; analysis; **—ания** *pl.* investigations, research; **подвергать —анию** *v.* investigate; examine, test, analyze; **производить и.** investigate; survey; **—анный** *a.* investigated, etc., *see v.;* **—атель** *m.* investigator, researcher, research worker; (literature) searcher; explorer; **—ательский** *a.* research, exploratory, investigative; **—ать** *v.* investigate, do research (on), study, examine, inquire (into); search, explore, try, test; analyze; (met.) assay; **—аться** *v.* be investigated, be under investigation.

исследуемый *a.* under investigation, under study, being studied, under discussion, under review, covered; (under) der.

исслеживать *v.* track up (surface).

иссолить *v.* salt, pickle.

иссоп *m.* (bot.) hyssop (*Hyssopus*).

ис/сохнуть *see* иссыхать; **—стари** *adv.* from olden times; **—стир(ыв)ать** *v.* use up (in laundering); **—страдаться** *v.* suffer bitterly; **—страчивать** *v.* use up (in writing).

исстрел/ивать, —ять *v.* use up (ammunition); riddle (with bullets).

исстрочить *see* исстрачивать.

исступление *n.* frenzy; (med.) raptus.

иссуш/ать *see* иссуши(ва)ть; **—ающий** *a.* dehydrating, etc., *see v.;* **—ение** *n.* dehydration, desiccation, drying up; **—енный** *a.* dehydrated, etc., *see v.;* **—и(ва)ть** *v.* dehydrate, desiccate, dry up; scorch; waste, exhaust; wither.

иссык-кульский *a.* (geog.) Issyk Kul.

иссыхать *v.* dry up, wither, shrivel.

иссяк/ать, —нуть *v.* dry up, run dry; run low, run short; exhaust; peter out (of resources); **—нувший** *a.* dried up, etc., *see v.*

истаивать *v.* thaw, melt; waste away.

истапливать *v.* heat; melt (down).

истаптывать *v.* trample; wear out.

истаск(ив)ать(ся) *v.* wear out.

истачивать *v.* grind down; eat away, erode away; perforate, pierce.

истаять *see* истаивать.

истек/ать *v.* elapse, expire, be up (of time); become due, become void; (gas) be exhausted; drain away; emanate (from), escape, flow out, run out, issue; bleed profusely; **—ающий** *a.* elapsing, etc., *see v.;* exhaust (gas).

ист/екший *a.* past, last; **—ёкший** *a.* elapsed, etc., *see* истекать.

истереть *see* истирать.

истерзанный *a.* badly wounded, lacerated.

истер/ик *m.* hysterical man; **—ика** *f.* hysterics, hysteria; **—ический, —ичный** *a.* hysterical; imitative (tetanus); **—ичка** *f.* hysterical woman; **—ичность, —ия** *f.*

hysteria; **—о** *prefix* hyster(o)— (uterus; lagging behind).

истёрт/ость *f.* worn condition; attrition, wearing down; **—ый** *a.* worn, abraded.

истесать, истёсывать *v.* cut, hew, square.

истец *m.* plaintiff; petitioner.

истеч/ение *n.* (out)flow, discharge, efflux; emanation, emission, escape (of gas); expiration, lapse (of time); bleeding; *suffix* **—rrhea** (flow, discharge), e.g., **и. мо-лока** galactorrhea; **диаграмма —ения** effluogram; **скорость —ения** exhaust velocity, jet velocity; **—ь** *see* **истекать.**

истизин *m.* Istizin, 1,8-dihydroxyanthraquinone.

истин/а *f.* truth, fact; **—но** *prefix* true; **—нокоренной** *a.* molar (tooth); **—ность** *f.* truth; **—ный** *a.* true, actual, real, virtual; intrinsic (luminosity); (math.) proper (subgroup); **—ные солнечные сутки** apparent solar day.

истир/аемость *f.* abradability, etc., *see a.*; wear(ing properties); **—аемый** *a.* abradable, friable; (paper) erasable; abraded; **—ание** *n.* abrasion, attrition, deterioration, erosion, wear; grinding, etc., *see v.*; **—атель** *m.* abrasive; grinder, grater; **—ать** *v.* abrade, wear (away, down, off, out), erode; chafe, rub (off); use up (eraser); (met.) gall, fret; grind, grate, crush, pulverize; **—аться** *v.* abrade, wear (away, down, off, out); **—ающий** *a.,* **—ающее вещество** abrasive.

истле/вать, —ть *v.* rot, decay, decompose; be reduced to ashes, (s)moulder away; (cer.) biscuit-fire; **—вший** *a.* decomposed; **—ние** *n.* rotting, etc., *see v.*

истм/ический *a.* (anat.; geog.) isthmian, isthmic; **—ус** *m.* isthmus.

истмэновский *a.* Eastman (film).

истод *m.* (bot.) milkwort (*Polygala*); **—овые** *pl.* Polygalaceae.

исток *m.* outflow, effluent, issue, discharge, outlet; source.

истолков/ание *n.* interpretation, explanation, commentary; **—атель** *m.* interpreter, commentator; **—ательный** *a.* explanatory; **—(ыв)ать** *v.* interpret, explain, expound, comment.

истол/очь *v.* pound, crush, grind, stamp, break up; **—чённый** *a.* pounded, crushed, ground, broken up.

истом/а *f.* fatigue, lassitude; **—ить, —лять** *v.* weary, exhaust, tire (out), fatigue, wear out; **—ление** *n.* exhaustion; **—лённый** *a.* exhausted; **—ный** *a.* exhausting, tiring.

Истона циклы (meteor.) Easton cycles.

истонч/ённый *a.* thin(ned), narrow(ed); (anat.) rostral; **—иться** *v.* thin down.

истоп/ить *v.* melt (down), render (down), smelt; heat up; use, consume (fuel); **—иться** *v.* warm up; melt, dissolve; **—ник** *m.* stoker, fireman.

истоптать *v.* trample (down); track up (surface); wear out (shoes); go all over.

исторг/ать, —нуть *v.* throw out, force out, expel, banish; erupt, break out; elicit, evoke; wrest, rescue, deliver (from).

истор/ик *m.* historian; **—ический, —ичный** *a.* historic(al); historically accurate; **—ия** *f.* history; story; incident, event; unpleasant occurrence; **—ия болезни** (med.) case history; **—ия вопроса** background.

источ/ать *v.* shed, spill; give off, emit, exhale; gush forth; **—енный** *a.* ground up, etc., *see* **источить;** worn down, ground down; (worm) eaten; **—ённый** *a.* spilled, etc., *see* **источать; —ить** *v.* wear down, eat away; perforate, pierce, cover with holes; grind up; *see also* **источать.**

источник *m.* source, origin; spring, fountain, well; supply,

resource; (supply) unit; seat (of emf); **и. водорода** hydrogen donor; **и. нейтронов** neutron source; **из авторитетного —а** on good authority; **служить —ом** *v.* be a source (of), give rise (to), cause; **—овый** *a.* of **источник.**

истощ/ать *v.* exhaust, deplete, use up, drain; wear out, tire out; reduce in strength, impoverish; **—аться** *v.* be exhausted, etc.; run out, peter out; run low, dwindle; die off, come to an end; tire out, weaken, grow weak; **—ающий** *a.* exhausting, etc., *see v.*; hectic (fever); **—ение** *n.* exhaustion, etc., *see v.*; impoverishment, loss, dwindling; emaciation; (mil.) attrition; (nervous) breakdown; **предотвращение —ения** (soil) conservation; **—ённость** *f.* depleted state; **—ённый, —ившийся** *a.* exhausted, etc., *see v.*; extinct (volcano); **—ить** *see* **истощать.**

истра/тить, —чивать *v.* use (up), spend, expend; waste (time); **—титься, —чиваться** *v.* come to an end, be spent; **—ченный** *a.* used (up), etc., *see v.*

истреб/итель *m.* destroyer; fighter (plane); **и.-бомбар-дировщик** *m.* bomber; **—ительно-противотанковый** *a.* tank-destroyer; **—ительный** *a.* destroying, etc., *see v.*; fighter; **и.-перехватчик** *m.* interceptor (fighter); **и.-разведчик** *m.* reconnaissance fighter; **и.-штурмовик** *m.* pursuit plane, attack fighter; **—ить** *m.* **истреблять; —ление** *n.* destruction, etc., *see v.*; **—лённый** *a.* destroyed, etc., *see v.*; **—лять** *v.* destroy, exterminate, annihilate, obliterate.

истребовать *v.* demand (and obtain), claim, exact, require.

истренский *a.* (geog.) Istra.

истрёпанный *a.* ragged, frayed.

истр/епать, —ёпывать *v.* wear out, fray, tear; spoil; fatigue, tire out, exhaust; **—епаться, —ёпываться** get worn out; be broken (of health).

истрескаться *v.* crack (all over), craze.

истринский *a.* (geog.) Istra.

иступ/ить, —лять *v.* make (dull, blunt).

истый *a.* true, real; thorough.

истык(ив)ать *v.* stud (with nails); pierce all over.

истязать *v.* torture, torment.

исфаринский *a.* (geog.) Isfara.

исхаживать *v.* walk all over, wander through.

исхиоподит *m.* (crust.) ischiopodite.

исхлоп/атывать, —отать *v.* manage to get.

исход *m.* issue, outcome, result; outlet; way out; end, finish, close (of period).

исходатайствовать *v.* obtain by petition.

исходить *v.* issue, originate, start (from), proceed (from), come (from), emerge; emanate, radiate; be based (on); originate (in from); walk all over, wander through; grow weak; **если и. из** based on.

исходн/ый *a.* original, initial, first; starting, source, raw (materials); underlying (data); reference, base; parent; stock (culture); untreated (sewage); wild (strain); **и. пункт** starting point, point of departure, origin, base, basis; reference point; **и. район** zone of departure; **—ая линия** starting line; **—ая позиция** (comp.) home; **—ая пульпа** (concentration) feed pulp; **—ая точка** *see* **исходный пункт; —ое вещество** initial product, raw material, parent substance; **—ое угловое положение** angular reference; **—ые условия** reference conditions.

исходя *pr. ger.* issuing, etc., *see* **исходить; и. из** proceeding from, on the basis of, based (up)on; **и. из этого** hence; **—щая** *f.* outgoing paper; **—щий** *a.* issuing, etc., *see* **исходить;** outgoing; reference; **—щая информация** output.

исхуд/авший,— алый *a.* emaciated; **—алость** *f.* emaciated state; **—ание** *n.* emaciation; **—ать** *v.* become emaciated.

исцарап/анный *a.* scratched; striated, grooved; **—(ыв)-ать** *v.* scratch up.

исцел/ение *n.* healing, recovery; **—имый** *a.* curable; **—итель** *m.* healer; **—ительный** *a.* healing, curative; **—ить, —ять** *v.* heal, cure; **—иться** *v.* recover.

исчахнуть *v.* waste away.

исчез/ание *n.* disappearance, loss; **—ать** *v.* disappear, vanish, dissipate, taper out, fade away; peter out; merge (into); die out, become extinct; **—ающий** *a.* disappearing, etc., *see v.*; threatened, endangered (species); elastic (deformation); **—новение** *see* исчезание; **—нувший** *a.* extinct; **—нуть** *see* исчезать.

исч/еркать, —ёрк(ив)ать *v.* cross out; scribble all over.

исчерн/а— prefix blackish; **—ить** *v.* blacken.

исчерп/ание *n.* exhaustion, etc., *see v.*; **—анный** *a.* exhausted, etc., *see v.*; **—(ыв)ать** *v.* exhaust, deplete, work out (ore); empty, drain; use up (time); settle (dispute); **—(ыв)аться** *v.* be exhausted, etc.; be limited (to); come to an end; **—ывающе** *adv.* exhaustively, fully; **—ывающий** *a.* exhausting, etc., *see v.*; exhaustive, comprehensive, full, complete; (fractionation) stripping (section).

исчер/тить, —чивать *v.* streak, stripe, line, cover with lines, striate; use up (in drawing); **—ченность** *f.* striation; **—ченный** *a.* streaked, etc., *see v.*

исчиркать *v.* strike, use up (matches).

исчисл/ение *n.* calculation, etc., *see v.*; estimate; (math.) calculus; **—енный** *a.* calculated, etc., *see v.*; **—имый** *a.* calculable, etc., *see v.*; **—ить, —ять** *v.* calculate, compute, estimate; determine, evaluate; (e)numerate; **—иться** *v.* come (to), amount (to); **—яться тысячами** number in the thousands.

исшарить *v.* probe (all over).

исши(ва)ть *v.* sew (up); cross-link.

исштрихованный *a.* streaked, striated.

ищепать *v.* split, splinter, chip.

ищип(ыв)ать *v.* pinch all over.

ита/бирит *m.* (min.) itabirite; **—йара** *f.* (ichth.) spotted jewfish (*Promicrops itaiara*).

итак *conj.* thus, so; now, now then.

итако/лумит *m.* (petr.) itacolumite, flexible sandstone; **—новая кислота** itaconic acid, methylenebutanedioic acid.

Италия Italy; **итальянский** *a.* Italian.

ита/мэ *m.* (ent.) Itame; **—тси** *m.* (mam.) Siberian weasel (*Mustela itatsi*).

и т. д. *abbr.* (**и так далее**) and so on, etc.

итер/ативный, —ационный *a.* iterative, iterated, repetitive, repeated; **—ация** *f.*, **—ирование** *n.* iteration, repetition, replication; **—ированный** *a.* iterated, repeated; **—ировать** *v.* iterate, repeat.

ИТК *abbr.* (**истинная температура кипения**) true boiling point.

ито/г *m.* sum, total (amount), balance, summary; result; **в —ге** to sum up; as a result; **в конечном —ге** in the end, in the final analysis; **подводить и.** *v.* sum up; **—го** *adv.* altogether, in all; **—говый** *a.* of **итог**; total; (comp.) summary, gang, totalizing (punch); final (calculation); concluding; **—жить** *v.* sum up, summarize, conclude; strike a balance.

итон/иды *pl.* (ent.) gall midges (*Itonididae*); **—э** *m.* Ithone.

и т. п. *abbr.* (**и тому подобное**) and so on, and so forth, and the like, et cetera.

ИТП *abbr.* (**инженерно-технический персонал**);

ИТР (**инженерно-технические работники**) engineering staff.

итрол *m.* itrol, silver citrate.

итсегек, ит-сигек *m.* (bot.) Anabasis aphylla.

иттерб/ий *m.* ytterbium, Yb; **—ит** *m.* (min.) ytterbite, gadolinite; **—овый** *a.* ytterbium; **—овая земля** ytterbia, ytterbium oxide.

итти *see* идти.

иттр/иалит *m.* (min.) yttrialite; **—иевый, —овый** *a.* yttrium, yttriferous, yttric; **—иевый шпат** (min.) xenotime; **—иевая земля** yttria, yttrium oxide; **—ий** *m.* yttrium, Y; **окись —ия** yttrium oxide.

иттро/гуммит *m.* (min.) yttrogummite; **—колумбит, —танталит** *m.* yttrocolumbite, yttrotantalite; **—кразит** *m.* yttrocrasite; **—титанит** *m.* yttrotitanite; **—флюорит** *m.* yttrofluorite; **—церит** *m.* yttrocerite.

итурин *m.* iturin (antibiotic).

итурупский *a.* (geog.) Iturup.

ИТФ *abbr.* (**инозинтрифосфат**) inosine triphosphate, ITP.

ИТШ *abbr.* (**индекс транспортных шумов**) traffic noise index, TNI.

иуд/ейский *a.* Jewish; Jew's (pitch); **—ейское дерево, —ино дерево** (bot.) Judas tree (*Cercis siliquastrum*).

ифегена *f.* (mal.) Iphigena.

ИФК *abbr.* (**изопропилфенилкарбамат**) isopropylphenyl carbamate (weed killer).

их *gen. and acc. of* они, their; them; thereof.

ихне/вмон *m.* (ent.) Ichneumon; (mam.) ichneumon (*Herpestes ichneumon*); **—вмониды, —вмоновые, —умониды** *pl.* (ent.) ichneumon flies (*Ichneumonidae*).

ихний *a.* their.

ихно— prefix ichno— (track, trace, footprint); **—логия** *f.* ichnology, study of fossil footprints.

ихор *m.* (med.) ichor (discharge); (geol.) ichor (granitic liquid); **—озный** *a.* (med.) ichorous, serum-like.

ихт/иборовые *pl.* (ichth.) Ichthyboridae; **—инат** *see* ихтиол.

ихтио— prefix ichthy(o)— (fish); **—дин** *m.* ichthyodin; **—з** *m.* (med.) ichthyosis, xerodermia; **—завр** *m.* (pal.) ichthyosaur; **—зоподобный** *a.* ichthyosiform; **—идный** *a.* ichthyoid, fish-shaped; **—кол(ь)** *m.* ichthyocolla, fish glue, isinglass; **—л** *m.*, **—ловый** *a.* Ichthyol, ichthammol; **—лат** *m.* ichthyolate; **—лит** *m.* ichthyolite, fossil fish; **—лог** *m.* ichthyologist; **—логический** *a.* ichthyological; **—логия** *f.* ichthyology; **—масса** *f.* ichthyomass (weight of fish); **—мис** *m.* (mam.) fish-eating rat (*Ichthyomys*); **—споридоз** *m.* ichthyosporidosis, Ichthyosporidium infection; **—тический** *a.* (med.) ichthyotic; **—фаг** *m.* ichthyophage; **—фауна** *f.* ichthyofauna, fish fauna; **—фтальм(ит)** *m.* (min.) ichthyophthalmite, apophyllite; **—фтириазис, фтир(и)оз** *m.* (vet.) ichthyophthiriasis; **—фтир(иус)** *m.* (prot.) Ichthyophthirius; **—цид** *m.* ichthyocide.

ицел *m.* (ichth.) a sculpin (*Icelus*).

ицерия *f.* (ent.) cottony cushion scale (*Icerya purchasi*).

ИЧ, и.ч. *abbr.* (**иодное число**) iodine number.

ичанский *a.* (geog.) Ichang.

ичинский *a.* (geog.) Icha.

иша/к *m.*, **—чий** *a.* ass (*Equus asinus*).

иш/емический *a.* (med.) ischemic; **—емия** *f.* ischemia; **—иальгия** *f.*, **—иас** *m.* ischialgia, ischias, sciatica.

ишикаваит *m.* (min.) ishikawaite.

ишимский *a.* (geog.) Ishim.

ишио— prefix (anat.) ischio— (ischium); **—ректальный** *a.* ischiorectal.

ишнохитон *m.* (mal.) Ischnochiton.

ишнура *f.* (ent.) Ischnura.

ишурия *f.* (med.) ischuria, urine retention.
ишхан *m.* Sevan trout (*Salmo ischchan*).
ищ/ейка *f.* tracking dog, tracker; —**ет(ся)** *pr. 3 sing. of* **искать(ся)**; —**ущий** *a.* seeking.
ИЭС *abbr.* (**изменение электрического состояния**) changing the electrical state.
июддит *m.* (min.) juddite.
июль *m.,* —**ский** *a.* July.
июнь *m.,* —**ский** *a.* June.
иятрен *m.* Yatren, quiniofon.

ИАР *abbr.* (**Йеменская Арабская Республика**) Yemen Arab Republic.
йеллостонский *a.* (geog.) Yellowstone.
йеменский *a.* (geog.) Yemen.
йенский *a.* (geog.) Jena.
йерма *f.* yerma, raw desert soil.
йо— see under **ио—**.
йольд/иевый *a.* (geog.) Yoldia; —**ия** *f.* (mal.) Yoldia.
йоркширский *a.* (geog.) Yorkshire.
йосемитский *a.* (geog.) Yosemite.

К

к *abbr.* (**кило—**) kilo—, 10³; (**кулон**) coulomb; (**кюри**) curie.
к *prep. dat.* to; toward; by; for; against; **к тому же** besides, moreover, what is more; **к чему?** what for? why?
°К *abbr.* (**градус Кельвина**) degree(s) Kelvin.
ка *abbr.* (**килоампер**) kiloampere.
КА *abbr.* (**космический аппарат**) spacecraft.
каа/гапу *m.* (biogeog.) caagapu, swamp palm forest; —**гуазу** *m.* caaguazu, selva; —**поэ** *m.* caaroe; —**тинга** *f.* caatinga.
кабаит *m.* (min.) kabaite.
кабака *see* **кабачок**.
кабан *m.,* —**ный** *a.* (mam.) wild boar (*Sus scrofa*); lump, chunk, block (of ore, etc.); (av.) cabane; —**ок** *m.* block (of ice); **к.-рыба** *f.* (ichth.) boarfish; —**чик** *m.* horn.
кабарагойа *f.* (herp.) Varanus salvator.
кабарг/а *f.* (mam.) musk deer (*Moschus,* spec. *M. moschiferus*); —**овые** *pl.* Moschidae; —**овый** *a.* musk deer.
кабардин/о-балкарский *a.* (geog.) Kabardino-Balkarian; —**ский** *a.* Kabardinian.
кабар/жиный, —**ожий** *a. of* **кабарга**; —**ожьи** *see* **кабарговые**.
кабач/ковый *a.,* —**ок** *m.* squash; pumpkin.
кабел/еискатель *m.* cable locator; —**ёк** *m.* (elec.) pigtail; —**епровод** *m.* cable duct, conduit; —**епроводка** *f.* cable installation; —**еукладка** cable laying; —**еукладчик** *m.* cable layer.
кабель *m.* cable; **к.-заправочный** *a.* (rockets) umbilical (mast); **к.-кран** *m.* cableway; **к.-мачта** *f.* (cosm.) umbilical tower; —**ный** *a.* cable; dragline (excavator); **к.-план** *m.* cable layout; —**тов** *m.* (naut.) cable length (185.2 m.); —**щик** *m.* cable man.
кабестан *m.* capstan, winch.
кабин/а, —**ка** *f.* cab(in), cage, car; compartment; (av.) cockpit; (ejection) capsule; (phone) booth; (shower) stall; —**ет** *m.,* —**етный** *a.* office, room; study (center); cabinet, closet; (X-ray) unit; —**ный** *a. of* **кабина**.
кабио *m.* (ichth.) cabio, sergeantfish (*Rachycentron canadum*).
кабл/ирование *n.* cabling, cable installation; —**ировать** *v.* cable; —**ограмма** *f.* cable(gram).
каблу/к *m.,* —**чный** *a.* heel; —**чок** *dim. of* **каблук**.
Кабо кольцо Cabot's ring.
каболка *f.* (rope making) hemp yarn.
каботаж *m.,* —**ный** *a.* coast(ing); coastal trade or navigation.
кабошон *m.* cabochon, convex-cut gem.
кабрерит *m.* (min.) cabrerite.
кабрилья *f.* (ichth.) rock bass (*Paralabrax*); grouper (*Epinephelus guttatus*).
кабриолет *m.* cabriolet, convertible.

кабриров/ание *n.* (av.) pitching (up), pitch-up, tail heaviness; —**ать** *v.* pitch up.
кав/а *f.,* **к.-к., корень** —**ы** kava, kava-kava (root of *Piper methysticum*).
кавалер *m.* partner; bearer (of decoration); (ent.) Papilio; —**ы** swallowtail butterflies (*Papilionidae*).
кавалла *f.* (ichth.) Pacific mackerel (*Scomber japonicus*); king mackerel (*Scomberomorus cavalla*).
кавальер *m.* bank (of earth); dump pit.
кавальный *a.* (anat.) caval.
каверн/а *f.* cavern; vesicle, pocket; flaw, cavity; (anat.) sinus; —**овая вода** (geol.) interstitial water; —**озный** *a.* cavernous, honeycombed, porous, vesicular; —**омер** *m.* borehole caliper; —**ометрия** *f.* borehole gaging.
кавиоз *m.* (med.) khawiosis.
кавитац/ионный *a.* cavitation(al); —**ия** *f.* cavitation; cavity.
Кавказ (geog.) Caucasus; **к—ит** *m.* (petr.) kavkazite; **к—ский** *a.* Caucasian.
каволиния *f.* (mal.) Cavolin(i)a.
кавун *m.* (bot.) watermelon (*Citrullus*).
кагат *m.,* —**ный** *a.* (agr.) clamp, pit; —**ирование** *n.,* —**ировка** *f.* pit storage.
кагинский *a.* (geog.) Kaga.
кагор *m.* Cahors wine.
кагу *m.* (orn.) kagu (*Rhinochetos*); *pl.* Rhinochetidae, Rhynochetidae.
кагуан *m.* (mam.) flying lemur (*Cynocephalus volans*).
кагульский *a.* (geog.) Kagul.
кадаверин *m.* cadaverine, 1,5-pentanediamine; —**ы** *pl.* cadaverines, ptomaines.
кадастр *m.* (land evaluation) cadaster; inventory; —**альный** *a.* cadastral.
кадило *n.* (bot.) Melittis.
кадинский *a.* (geog.) Kada.
кадион *m.* cadion.
кадисский *a.* (geog.) Cadiz.
кадка *f.* tub, vat, cask.
кадмат *m.* cadmate.
кадмиев/ый *a.* cadmium; —**ая желть** cadmium yellow, cadmium sulfide; —**ая обманка** (min.) greenockite.
кадмиесодержащий *a.* cadmium-containing, cadmiferous.
кадм/ий *m.* cadmium, Cd; **бромид** —**ия, бромистый к.** cadmium bromide; **закись** —**ия** cadmous oxide; **окись** —**ия** cadmium oxide; **сернистый к., сульфид** —**ия** cadmium sulfide; —**ийорганический** *a.* organocadmium.
кадмиров/ание *n.* cadmium plating; —**анный** *a.* cadmium-plated; —**ать** *v.* plate with cadmium.
кадм/ия *f.* (met.) cadmia; —**опон** *m.* cadmopone, cadmium lithopone.
кадоксен *m.* (paper) Cadoxen.

кадр *m.* skeleton, frame(work); outline; (phot.) frame, exposure; picture, image; still; **—ы** *pl.* personnel, staff; **подготовка —ов** training of specialists; **частота —ов** picture frequency; **—овый** *a. of* кадр; **без —овых потерь** without loss of key personnel.

кадсура *f.* (bot.) Kadsura.

кадуш/ечный *a.,* **—ка** *f.* small tub, vat.

кады/к *m.,* **—чный** *a.* (anat.) Adam's apple.

кадь *see* кадка.

Кадэ жидкость Cadet's liquid.

каём *gen. pl. of* кайма; **—ка** *dim. of* кайма; **—чатый** *a.* bordered; marginate; strip (felling).

кажд/огодно *adv.* annually, every year; **—огодный** *a.* annual; **—одневно** *adv.,* **—одневный** *a.* daily, every day; **—ый** *a.* each, every; *pron.* everyone, everybody, each one.

кажется *pr. 3 sing. of* казаться.

кажущийся *a.* apparent, seeming.

казак *m.* Cossack.

казалось *past n. sing. of* казаться.

казан *m.* kettle, boiler.

казанлыкский *a.* (geog.) Kazanlyk.

казанный *a. of* казан.

казанский *a.* (geog.) Kazan.

казарка *f.* (ent.) snout beetle (*Rhynchites bacchus*) (orn.) brant (*Branta*).

казарм/а *f.,* **—енный** *a.* barracks.

казатель *m.* indicator, guide, pointer.

казать *v.* show.

казаться *v.* seem, appear; **кажется** it seems, it appears; **казалось** it seemed.

каза/хский *a.* (geog.) Kazakh; **—хстанский** *a.* Kazakhstan; **—цкий,** **—чий** *a.* Cossack; **—чок** *dim. of* казак; (ent.) cabbage bug.

казеин *m.* casein (milk protein); **—аза** *f.* caseinase, rennase; **—ат** *m.,* **—овокислая соль** case(in)ate; **—ат натрия,** **—овонатриевая соль** sodium caseinate; **—овый** *a.* casein; caseinic (acid); **соль —овой кислоты** caseinate.

каземат *m.,* **—ный** *a.* casemate.

казёнка *f.* log deck (of saw frame).

казённик *m.* (art.) breech (piece).

казённый *a.* government, state, public; fiscal; **на к. счёт** at public expense.

казеозный *a.* caseous, cheesy, cheeselike.

казимиро/един *m.* casimiroedine; **—ин** *m.* casimiroine.

казна *f.* (art.) breech; treasury; **—чей** *m.* treasurer, paymaster, cashier; **—чейство** *n.* treasury, exchequer.

казнить *v.* execute, put to death; **—ся** *v.* blame oneself.

казнь *f.* execution, capital punishment.

казолит *m.* (min.) kasolite.

казуар *m.* (orn.) cassowary (*Casuarius*); **—ина** *f.* (bot.) Casuarina; **—иновые** *pl.* beefwoods (*Casuarinaceae*); **—овые,** **—ы** *pl.* (orn.) Casuariidae.

казуистика *f.* (med.) casuistics.

казус *m.* (law) special case; **—ный** *a.* involved, intricate.

казымский *a.* (geog.) Kazym.

казырский *a.* (geog.) Kazyr.

каинит *m.* (min.) kainite.

каинк/а *f.,* **—овый корень** cahinca (root of *Chiococca racemosa*); **—овая кислота** ca(h)incic acid.

каинозит *m.* (min.) kainosite, cenosite.

каинцин *m.* caincin, cainca acid.

каир/ин *see* кайрин; **—нгорм** *m.* (min.) cairngorm; **—ский** *a.* (geog.) Cairo.

кайен(н)ский *a.* (geog.) Cayenne.

кайепутен *see* каяпутен.

Кайетэ-матиаса закон (phys.) Cailletet and Mathias law.

кайкан *m.* (ichth.) Morone labrax.

кайл/а *f.,* **—о** *n.,* **—овый** *a.* pick(ax), hack; **—ить** *v.* pick, hack.

кайлык *m.* (mam.) kylik (yak-cattle hybrid).

кайма *f.* border, margin, edge, rim, fringe; (ichth.) (fin) fold.

кайман *m.* (herp.) cayman (*Caiman*); **—овая (рыба)** (ichth.) gar (*Lepisosteus*); **—овые** *pl.* Lepisosteidae.

каймить *v.* border, edge.

кайно— *prefix* caen(o)— (new); **—генетический** *a.* c(a)enogenetic, of recent origin; **—зит** *see* каинозит; **—зой** *m.* (geol.) Cenozoic era; **—зойский** *a.* Cenozoic.

кайра *f.* (orn.) guillemot (*Uria*).

кайса *f.* dried apricots.

кайсака *f.* (herp.) Bothrops atrox.

как *adv. and conj.* how; what; suddenly; as, like; when, since; **к. будто** as if, as though; appear (to); **к. будто бы** as if there were; **к. бы** as if, as though; **к. бы не** lest; **к. бы ни** however, no matter how; **к. быть?** what is to be done? **к. вдруг** when suddenly; **к. его зовут** what is his name? **к. же** certainly, of course; **к. и** as with, as do, as is, as are; **к. и при, к. и у** as with, as in the case (of); **к. можно выше** as high as possible; **к. не** but; besides; **к. ни** however, no matter how; **к. ни в чём не бывало** as if nothing were the matter; **к. . . . , так и** both . . . and, just as . . . so (also); as well as; **к. таковой** as such; **к. только** as soon as, the moment (that); when; **к. это бывает** as sometimes happens, as is sometimes the case.

какаду *m.* (orn.) cockatoo (*Kakatoe*).

какалия *f.* (bot.) Cacalia.

какао *n.,* **—вый** *a.* cacao, cocoa; **к. боб,** **—вый боб** cocoa bean; **—велла** *f.* cacao husk; **—вое дерево, к.-шоколадное дерево** (bot.) cacao (*Theobroma cacao*); **—вое масло, к.-масло** cocoa butter.

какапо *m.* (orn.) kakapo (*Strigops*).

как-либо *adv.* somehow; **к.-нибудь** *adv.* somehow, anyhow; **к.-никак** *adv.* after all.

како— *prefix* cac(o)— (bad, ill).

каков *pron. and a.* what kind of? how? what? **к. бы ни был** whatever the material; **—о** *adv.* how.

како/гевзия *f.* cacogeusia, bad taste; **—генез** *m.* cacogenesis, defective development.

какодил *m.,* **—овый** *a.* cacodyl; **—ат** *m.,* **—овокислая соль, —овой кислоты** cacodylate; **—овая кислота** cacodylic acid, dimethylarsinic acid; **—овокислый** *a.* cacodylic acid; cacodylate (of).

какой *a.* what; how; **к. ни** whatever; **к.-либо, к.-нибудь** some (kind of), any; about; a particular; **к.-то** some; a kind (of); something like.

какоксен *m.* (min.) cacoxen(it)e.

какомицли *m.* (mam.) ringtail cat (*Bassariscus astutus*); *pl.* Bassariscidae.

какосмия *f.* cacosmia, bad smell.

какотелин *m.* cacotheline.

как-раз *adv.* exactly, just, precisely.

какри *m.* (bot.) Cucumis utilissimus.

как-то *adv.* somehow; once, one day; that is; how.

кактус *m.* (bot.) cactus; **—овидный** *a.* cactiform, cactus-like; **—овые** *pl.* Cactaceae; **—овый** *a.* cactus.

кал *m.* excrement, feces, stool(s), droppings; **кровь в —е** fecal blood.

кал *abbr.* (**калория**) calorie, cal.

кала-азар *m.* (med.) kala-azar, black fever.

калабар/ин *m.* calabarine; **—ский боб** calabar bean (*Physostigma venenosum*).

кала/брийский *a.* (geog.) Calabrese, Calabrian; **—ве-рит** *m.* (min.) calaverite; **—диум** *m.* (bot.) Caladium; **—ит** *m.* (min.) calaite; **—канский** *a.* (geog.) Kalakan; **—м** *m.* (bot.) Calamus; **—мен** *m.* calamene; **—мин** *m.* (min.) calamine, hemimorphite; **—мит** *m.* (min.; pal.) calamite; **—моихт** *m.* reedfish (*Calamoichthys*); **—мянка** *f.* (text.) calamanco.

калан *m.* (mam.) sea otter (*Ennydra*, spec. *E. lutris*).

каландр *m.*, **—овый** *a.* (text., paper) calender (roll); **—(ир)ование** *n.* calendering, calender run, glazing; **—(ир)ованный** *a.* calendered; **—(ир)овать** *v.* calender, glaze; **—овщик** *m.* calender operator.

каланус *m.* (crust.) brit (*Calanus*).

каланча *f.* fire tower, lookout.

калао *m.* (orn.) great hornbill (*Buceros bicornis*).

калаппа *f.* (crust.) Calappa.

каларский *a.* (geog.) Kalar.

калатея *f.* (bot.) Calathea.

калаусский *a.* (geog.) Kalaus.

калаха *see* **калан.**

калахарский *a.* (geog.) Kalahari.

калач *m.* kalatch (a bread); (heat) return bend; **—ик** *m.* (bot.) dieresilis; **—ики** *pl.* (bot.) Malva; **свернуться —иком** *v.* curl up.

калбасу *m.* (ichth.) Labeo calbasu.

калбинский *a.* (geog.) Kalbin.

калган *m.* (bot.) tormentil (*Potentilla erecta* or *P. tormentilla*); Alpinia; **—ный корень** galanga (root of *Alpinia officinarum*).

калгон *m.* Calgon, sodium hexametaphosphate.

калдан *m.* (grassland) litter, mulch.

Кале (geog.) Calais.

калевать *v.* channel; mold.

калёв/ка *f.*, **—очный** *a.* (channel) molding; molding plane; **—очный паз** channel.

каледон/ит *m.* (min.) caledonite; **—ский** *a.* (geol.) Caledonian; (geog.) Caledon(ian).

калейдоскоп *m.* kaleidoscope; **—ический** *a.* kaleidoscopic.

калека *m.* cripple.

календар/ь *m.*, **—ный** *a.* calendar; schedule; **—ное планирование** scheduling.

календула *f.* (bot.) Calendula.

кален/ие *n.* incandescence, heat(ing); **белое к.** white heat, incandescence; **красное к.** red heat.

каленик *m.* (ichth.) tench (*Tinca t.*); Don chub (*Leuciscus borysthenicus*).

каленица *f.* (glass) cooling arch.

калён(н)ый *a.* red-hot; hardened; roasted (nuts).

кале/пина *f.* (bot.) Calepina; **—стания** *f.* Calestania; **—сценция** *f.* calescence.

калётизанис *m.* (ent.) Calothysanis.

кали *n.* potash, potassium oxide; (ichth.) Kali; **к.-аппарат** *m.* potash bulb; **едкое к.** caustic potash, potassium hydroxide; **сернокислое к.** potassium sulfate; **углекислое к.** potassium carbonate.

калиатур *m.* caliatour (dye)wood.

калибекский *a.* (geog.) Kalibek.

калиберн/ый *a.* caliber, gage, standard; **—ая доска** wire gage (plate); **—ая дощечка** templet; **—ая плитка** gage block; **—ая скоба** snap gage.

калиборит *m.* (min.) kaliborite.

калибр *m.* caliber, gage, size, bore; gage (of wire); (rolling) pass; **выдвижной к., раздвижной к.** sliding calipers, slide gage; **косые —ы** diagonal roll pass.

калибр/атор *m.* calibrator; **—втулка** *m.* ring gage; **—(ир)ование** *n.* calibration, gaging, etc., *see v.*; groove designing (of roller); **—(ир)ованный** *a.* cali-

brated, etc., *see v.*; **—(ир)овать** *v.* calibrate, gage, graduate, standardize, adjust; grade, sort; design the roll pass; (rolling) size, groove; (mach.) finish to final dimensions; verify; **—ирующий** *a.* calibrating, etc., *see v.*; **-кольцо** *m.* ring gage; **-нутромер** *m.* internal gage, plug gage; **—овать** *see* **калибр(ир)овать**; **—овка** *see* **калибр(ир)ование**; **—овка прокатных валков** (met.) roll pass design; **—овочноинвариантный** *a.* (comp.) gage variance, gage-invariant; **—овочный** *a.* calibrating, etc., *see v.*; calibration; **—овщик** *m.* calibrator; **—овый** *a. of* **калибр**; **—омер** *m.* (thickness) gage.

калибр-плитка *m.* block gage; **к-пробка** *see* **калибр-нутромер**; **к.-скоба** *m.* snap gage; **к.-толщиномер** *m.* thickness gage.

калиг/иды *pl.* (crust.) Caligoida; **—оз** *m.* caligosis, Caligus infestation.

калиево/-известковый *a.* potash-lime; **—хромовый** *a.* potash-chrome.

калиев/ый *a.* potassium, potash, potassic; **к. белый шлам** potassium alumosilicate; **к. (полевой) шпат** (min.) potash feldspar, orthoclase; **к. щёлок** caustic potash (solution), potash lye; **—ая селитра** potassium nitrate; **—ая слюда** (min.) potash mica, muscovite; **—ое мыло** potash soap, soft soap; **—ое растворимое стекло** potash water glass, potassium silicate; **—ые квасцы** potash alum; (min.) kalinite.

кал/ий *m.* potassium, K; **гидроокись —ия** potassium hydroxide; **едкий к.** *see* **кали, едкое; иодистый к.** potassium iodide; **марганцевокислый к.** potassium permanganate; **окись —ия** potassium oxide; **—ийметил** *m.* potassium methide; **—ийный** *see* **калиевый; —ийорганический** *a.* organopotassium; **—ийэтил** *m.* potassium ethide.

каликант *m.* (bot.) Calycanthus; **—ин** *m.* calycanthine.

калико *n.* (ichth.) black crappie (*Pomoxis nigromaculatus*).

каликруг *m.* (ent.) Cryptoch(e)ilus.

каликс *m.* (bot.) calyx, cup.

калильн/ый *a.* incandescent, glowing; red (heat); (cer.; met.) annealing; hot (tube); **—ая лампа** (elec.) incandescent lamp; **—ая печь** (met.) annealing furnace; (cer.) hardening-on kiln.

калильщик *m.* annealer (operator).

калимаг *m.*, **—незия** *f.* a potassium-magnesium sulfate fertilizer.

калимантанский *a.* (geog.) Kalimantan.

калина *f.* (bot.) Viburnum; **к.-гордовина** *f.* wayfaring tree (*V. lantana*).

калинатровый полевой шпат (min.) soda-potash feldspar, anorthoclase.

калин/инградский *a.* (geog.) Kaliningrad; **—инский** *a.* Kalinin; **—ит** *m.* (min.) kalinite; **—ка** *f.* (ichth.) Leuciscus; white bream (*Blicca bjoerkna*); bleak (*Alburnus a.*).

калин/ник *m.* cranberry thicket; **—овый** *a. of* **калина**.

калип/огеевые *pl.* (bot.) Calypogeiaceae; **—со** *n.* Calypso; **—тра** *f.* (mal.) Calyptraea; (bot.) calyptra, root cap; **—троген** *m.* calyptrogen.

калистегия *f.* (bot.) Calystegia.

калитвинский *a.* (geog.) Kalitva.

калитка *f.* (wicket) gate.

калить *v.* make red hot, incandesce, heat; roast (nuts).

калифорн/ий *m.* californium, Cf; **—ийскии, —ский** *a.* (geog.) California(n); **—ийская жидкость** *see* **ИСО.**

калицин *m.* calycin (antibiotic).

кали/че, —ше *n.* (min.) caliche.

калка *f.* (leather) stuffing.

калкан *m.* (ichth.) brill (*Rhombus*); turbot (*Scophthalmus*); **—овые** *pl.* Bothidae.

калкофлуор *m.* Calcofluor (dyestuff).

каллаит *m.* (min.) kallait, turquoise.

каллефрис *m.* (ent.) Callophrys.

каллиандра кора calliandra bark.

каллидиум *m.* (ent.) Callidium.

калликреин *m.* kallikrein (hormone).

каллима *f.* (ent.) Kallima.

калли/мико *f.* (mam.) Callimico; **—морфа** *f.* (ent.) Callimorpha; **—остома** *f.* (mal.) Calliostoma.

каллиротрон *m.* (rad.) kallirotron.

каллито *f.* (orn.) Rhynocrypta.

каллитрис *m.* (bot.) Callitris.

каллифоры *pl.* (ent.) Calliphoridae.

каллихт *m.* (ichth.) Callichthys; **—овые** *pl.* callichthyid catfishes (*Callichthyidae*).

Калло элемент (elec.) Callaud cell.

каллоз/а *f.,* **—ный** *a.* (bot.) callose.

калло/ринх *m.* elephant fish (*Callorhynchus*); **—ринховые** *pl.* Callorhynchidae, Callorhinchida; **—физовые** *pl.* (ichth.) Callophysidae.

каллус *m.* (bot.; med.) callus, callosity; **—образование** *n.* callus formation.

Каллье коэффициент (phot.) Callier's *Q* factor.

каллюс *see* **каллус.**

калм/егиновый *a.* calmeghinic (acid); **—онал** *m.* Calmonal, meclizine.

калмыцкий *a.* (geog.) Kalmyk.

кало *see* **кал; —вый** *a. of* кал; fecal; **—ед** *m.* (ent.) Onthophagus.

кало/карп *m.* (bot.) Calocarpum; **—мелол** *m.* calomelol, colloidal calomel; **—мель** *f.,* **—мельный** *a.* calomel, mercurous chloride.

калонг *m.* (mam.) kalong (*Pteropus vampyrus*).

калонкоба *f.* (bot.) Caloncoba.

калоплака *f.* (bot.) Caloplaca (lichen).

калоресценция *f.* (phys.) calorescence.

калори— *prefix* calori—, heat; **—генный** *a.* high-calorie; **—затор** *m.* calorizator; (mach.) hot bulb, ignition chamber; **—заторный** *a. of* калоризатор; glow (ignition); semidiesel (engine); **—зация** *f.,* **—зирование** *n.* calorizing, coating with aluminum; **—зировать** *v.* calorize.

калорийн/ость *f.* caloricity, calorific value; caloric content, energy, fuel value (of food); **—ый** *a.* high-calorie.

калориметр *m.* calorimeter; **—ирование** *n.* calorimetric determination; **—ический** *a.* calorimetric; **—ия** *f.* calorimetry, heat measurement.

калорифер *m.* heater, heating element; radiator; (met.) hotblast stove.

калорическ/ий *a.* calori(fi)c, thermic, thermal; hot-air (engine); **—ое значение** calorific value.

калория *f.* calorie; **большая к., техническая к.** large calorie, kilogram-calorie; **британская к.** British thermal unit, BTU; **малая к.** small calorie, gram-calorie.

калот *m.* (herp.) Calotes.

калотропис *m.* (bot.) Calotropis.

калотта *f.* (arch.) calotte, cap.

калофилл *m.* (bot.) Calophyllum; **—овый** *a.* calophyllic (acid).

калош/а *f.,* **—ный** *a.* overshoe, rubber; kalosha (rubber solvent).

калу/га *f.* (ichth.) kaluga (*Huso dauricus*); **—жница** *f.* (bot.) Caltha; **—жонок** *m.* young kaluga; **—жский** *a.* (geog.) Kaluga.

калумба *f.* calumba (root).

калусцит *m.* (min.) kaluszite, syngenite.

калуфер *m.,* **—ный** *a.* (bot.) tansy (*Tanacetum*); costmary (*Leucanthemum balsamina*).

калышка *f.* kink.

Кальбаум Kahlbaum (German firm).

кальдезия *f.* (bot.) Caldesia.

кальдера *f.* (geol.) caldera, crater.

калька *f.* tracing cloth, tracing paper; tracing; copy; loan translation, calque; **бумажная к.** tracing paper; **к.-батист** *f.* tracing cloth.

калька/ммон *m.* calcammonia (lime-ammonium chloride mix); **—нео—** *prefix* (anat.) calcaneo— (calcaneus, heel bone); **—ренит** *m.* (petr.) calcarenite; **—фанит** *m.* (min.) calcaphanite.

калькгур *m.* agaric mineral.

калькиров/ание *n.* tracing, etc., *see v.;* **—анный** *a.* traced, etc., *see v.;* **—ать** *v.* trace, copy; calk; do a loan translation.

калько— *prefix* calco— (lime); chalco— (copper).

калькул/ировать *v.* calculate, estimate, figure out, work out; **—ятор** *m.* calculator; cost accountant; **—яционный** *a.* calculating; cost (sheet); **—яция** *f.* calculation estimate; accounting.

кальма *f.* (ichth.) Don ruffe (*Acerina a.*).

кальмар *m.* (mal.) squid; cuttlefish (*Sepia*); **—ы** *pl.* Teuthoidea.

кальмиусский *a.* (geog.) Kalmius.

кальмия *f.* (bot.) Kalmia.

кальсилит *m.* (min.) kalsilite.

кальцекс *m.* (pharm.) Calcex.

кальцеолярия *f.* (bot.) Calceolaria.

кальце/фил *m.* calciphil(e), lime-loving plant; **—фильный** *a.* calciphilous; **—фоб** *m.* calciphobe; **—фобный** *a.* calciphobous.

кальци— *prefix* calc(i)— [lime(stone), calcium]; **—евый** *a.* calcium; calcic, calcareous; **—евая селитра** calcium nitrate; **—ефил** *see* **кальцефил.**

кальц/ий *m.* calcium, Ca; **гидрат окиси —ия** calcium hydroxide; **кислый к.** tricalcium phosphate; **окись —ия** calcium oxide; **сернокислый к., сульфат —ия** calcium sulfate; **—ийорганический** *a.* organocalcium; **—иметр** *m.* calcimeter.

кальцин *m.* calcine, calcined phosphate.

кальцина *f.* (cer.) lime.

кальцин/ат *m.* calcination product; **—атор** *m.* calcinator, calcining furnace; **—ация** *f.,* **—ирование** *n.* calcination etc., *see v.;* **—ированный** *a.* calcined, etc., *see v.;* **—ировать** *v.* calcine, roast; calcify, treat with lime; **—оз** *m.* (med.) calcinosis.

кальци/оторит *m.* (min.) calciothorite; **—т** *m.* (min.) calcite; **—тонин** *m.* (thyro)calcitonin (hormone); **—ферол** *m.* calciferol, vitamin D_2; **—фикация** *f.* (geol.) calcification.

калэмский *a.* (geog.) Culham (England).

калютрон *m.* calutron (isotope separator).

калямус *m.* (ichth.) porgy (*Calamus*).

кам *m.* (geol.) kame.

кам. *abbr.* (**каменный**) stone.

кама/ла *f.* kamala (powder from *Mallotus philippinensis*); **—резит** *m.* (min.) kamarezite; **—цит** *m.* (min.) kamacite.

камбал *m.* (dye) camwood.

камбал/а *f.* (ichth.) plaice; flatfish; flounder; **к.-ерш** *f.* American plaice (*Hippoglossoides platessoides*); **—овидный** *a.* soleiform, slipper-shaped; soleus (muscle); **—овые** *pl.* Pleuronectidae; **—ообразный** *see* **камбаловидный; —ы** *pl.* Pleuronectidae.

камбейский *a.* (geog.) Cambay.

камберлендский *a.* (geog.) Cumberland.

камб/иальный *a.* (biol.) cambial; **к. слой, —ий** *m.* cambium.

камбоджа *f.* gamboge (gum resin).

камбоджийский *a.* (geog.) Cambodian.

камбуз *m.,* **—ный** *a.* (naut.) galley, caboose; galley stove.

камвольный *a.* (text.) worsted.

камед/евый *a.* gum; **к. клей** gum arabic; **—еносный** *a.* gummiferous; **—еобразный** *a.* gum-like, gummy; **—есмола** *f.* gum resin; **—етечение** *n.* (phyt.) gummosis, resinous exudation; **—истый** *a.* gum(my), resinous; **—истая смола** gum resin; **—ный** *a.* gum; **—ный сахар** gum sugar, arabinose; **—ная загустка** gum water; **—ное дерево** (bot.) sweet gum (*Liquidambar styraciflua*).

камед/ь *f.* gum, resin; **аравийская к.** gum arabic; **лишать —и** *v.* degum.

камелёк *m.* hearth, fireplace.

камелиевые *pl.* (bot.) Theaceae.

камелина *f.* (bot.) Camelina.

камелия *f.* (bot.) camellia.

камель *m.* camel (a type of caisson).

камен/еть *v.* (geol.) petrify, fossilize, harden, become stone; **—исто-барабанный** *a.* (anat.) petrotympanic; **—исто-затылочный** *a.* petrooccipital; **—исто-чешуйчатый** *a.* petrosquamosal; **—истость** *f.* stoniness; **—истый** *a.* stony, stone-like, petrous, rocky; gravelly; petrosal (nerve, bone); **—ка** *f.* stone stove; (ichth.) masu (*Oncorhynchus masu*); Aspro zingel; (orn.) wheatear (*Oenanthe*).

каменкский *a.* (geog.) Kamenka.

каменник *m.* bouldery area; (bot.) Alyssum.

каменноугольн/ый *a.* coal; coal-tar (dyes, oil, etc.); carboniferous (period); **к. деготь, —ая смола** coal tar.

каменн/ый *a.* stone, stony, lithoidal; jewel (bearing); masonry (work); (biol.) saxatile, lithophilous; *m.* (ichth.) local name for several species of gobies; **к. век** stone age; **к. мозг** (min.) lithomarge; **к. уголь** coal; **—ая болезнь** (med.) lithiasis; (vet.) muscadine, calcino; **—ая кладка** stonework, masonry; **—ая посуда** stoneware; **—ая соль** (min.) rock salt; **—ое дерево** (bot.) Celtis; **—ое масло** petroleum; **—ое море** boulder field; **—ые работы** masonry work.

камено— *see* **камне—;** **—боец** *m.* stone crusher; **—литейный** *a.* stone-casting; **—лом** *m.* quarrier, quarryman; **—ломка** *see* **камнеломка; —ломня** *f.* (stone) quarry; **—сек, —тёс** *m.* stone cutter; mason; **—сечный, —тёсный** *a.* stone cutter's, stone cutting; stone (chisel).

камен/ушка *f.* (orn.) stone duck (*Histrionicus*); **—щик** *m.* (stone) mason; bricklayer; (ichth.) ratan goby (*Gobius ratan*).

камень *m.* stone, rock; (concrete) block; (boiler) scale; (horol.) jewel; (med.) calculus, —lith, e.g., **к. желудка** gastrolith; (paper) grindstone, pulpstone; **к.-бегунок** runner (stone); **к.-плитняк** flagstone; **к.-поддон** bottom millstone, bedder; **к.-рыба** *f.* stonefish (*Synanceia verrucosa*); **к.-самоцвет** precious stone, gem.

камера *f.* chamber, cell, compartment; room, office; (phot.) camera; inner tube (of tire); chest, bin, case; barrel (of pump); (distribution) box; (curing) bag; (hose) lining; ramjet duct; burning system, combustor; (seed) case; **к. сгорания** combustion chamber; **к.-обскура** camera obscura.

камер/альный *a.* cameral, chamber; office (work); laboratory (work); **—а-отстойник** *f.* decantation reservoir;

—а-сборник *f.* (aero.) plenum chamber; **—а-транспортёр** *f.* (superphosphates) portable digestor; **—а-убежище** *f.* (min.) refuge room; **—ностолбовой** *a.* (min.) room-and-pillar (method); **—ность** *f.* (bot.) cameration.

камерн/ый *a.* chamber(ed), compartment; box (filter press); (min.) room-and-pillar (working); **к. способ** chamber process (for sulfuric acid); **к. печь** compartment kiln; (met.) box furnace, batch furnace; **—ые кристаллы** chamber crystals (nitrosyl sulfate).

камерон *m.* Cameron pump; **—щик** *m.* (min.) pump operator and mechanic.

камертон *m.,* **—ный** *a.* tuning fork.

камерунск/ий *a.* (geog.) Cameroon; Cameroun (in W. Africa); **—ая лихорадка** malaria.

камешек *dim. of* **камень.**

камея *f.* cameo.

камин *m.,* **—ный** *a.* fireplace; chimney, smokestack; hood; offtake.

камит *m.* (ichth.) a yearling mullet (*Mugil*).

камне— *prefix* lith(o)—, stone, calculus; rock; *see also under* **камено—;** **—бурильный станок** rock drill; **—видность** *f.* stoniness, stony appearance; (met.) coarse-grain or intergranular fracture; **—видный** *a.* stony, stone-like, lithoidal; (met.) intergranular (fracture); **—дробилка** *f.* stone or rock crusher; **—дробильный** *a.* stone- or rock-crushing; **—дробление** *n.* stone or rock crushing; (med.) lithotripsy; **—ед** *see* **камнеточец; —лом** *m.* quarrier; **—ломка** *f.* (bot.) saxifrage; **—ломковые** *pl.* Saxifragaceae; **—любивый** *a.* (bot.) lithophilous; **—мёт** *m.* (mil.) stone fougasse; **—облицовка** *f.* stone surfacing; **—обработка** *f.* stone milling.

камнеобраз/ный *see* **камневидный; —ование** *n.* (med.) lithogenesis; **—ующий** *a.* stone-forming, lapidific; (med.) lithogenous.

камне/отборник, —отделитель *m.* stone separator; **—пад** *m.* rock slide; **—печатание** *n.* lithography; **—печатный** *a.* lithographed, lithographic; **—подобный** *see* **камневидный; —растение** *n.* (bot.) lithophyte; **—рез** *m.* stone cutter; **—резка** *f.* stone saw; **—резный** *a.* stone-cutting; stone (saw); **—сверлильный станок** rock drill; **—сечение** *n.* (med.) lithotomy; **—точец** *m.* (mal.) stone borer (*Pholas*); (bot.; zool.) stone borer; **—уборочная машина, —уборщик** *m.* stone picker; **—шарка** *f.* (orn.) turnstone (*Arenaria*).

камн/и *pl. of* **камень;** **—лithiasis, e.g., к. печени** (med.) hepatolithiasis; **—я** *gen. of* **камень.**

камовый *a.* (geog.) Kamo.

камор/а *f.* (art.) chamber; lock (of sluice); **—ка** *f.* closet, small room.

кампан/ейский *a. of* **кампания;** unsystematic; **—ия** *f.* campaign, drive; season, time; operating period, run (of furnace).

кампанский *a.* (geol.) Campanian.

кампанула *f.* (bot.) Campanula.

кампеш *m.,* **—евое дерево, —евый, —ный** *a.* (bot.) logwood (*Haematoxylon campechianum*).

кампилий *m.* (bot.) Campylium.

кампилит *m.* (min.) kampylite.

кампилотропный *a.* (bot.) campylotropous.

кампина *f.* campina, woodland savanna.

кампод/еа *f.* (ent.) Campodea; **—еи(ды)** *pl.* Campodeidae; **—еовидный** *a.* campodeoid.

камполон *m.* campolon (liver extract).

кампонотус *m.* (ent.) Camponotus.

кампос *m.* campos, shrubby savanna.

кампостома *f.* (ichth.) stoneroller (*Campostoma*).

камптонит *m.* (petr.) camptonite.

камп/ус, —ы *see* **кампос(ы).**

камский *a.* (geog.) Kama.

кам.-уг. *abbr.* (**каменноугольный**).

камуфл/ет *m.* (mil.) camouflet; **—етность** *f.* containment (of underground nuclear explosion); **—етный** *a.* contained; **—етная глубина** minimum burial depth (of nuclear explosive); **—ирование** *n.* camouflaging, camouflage; **—ированный** *a.* camouflaged; **—ировать** *v.,* **—яж** *m.* camouflage.

камушек *m.* small stone, pebble.

камфан *m.* camphane; **—ил** *m.,* **—иловый** *a.* camphanyl; **—овый** *a.* camphanic (acid); **—он** *m.* camphanone.

камфар/а *f.* camphor, 2-camphanone; **—ноаммониевая соль** ammonium camphorate; **—нокислый** *a.* camphoric acid; camphorate (of); **—нокислая соль, соль—ной кислоты** camphorate; **—ный** *a.* camphor; camphoric (acid); camphor(ated) (oil); **—ный спирт** spirit of camphor; **—ное дерево** camphor tree (*Cinnamomum camphora*); **—оновый** *a.* camphoronic (acid); **—осма** *f.* (bot.) Camphorosma.

камфен *m.* camphene; **—ил** *m.,* **—иловый** *a.* camphenyl; **—иловый** *a.* camphenylic (acid); **—илон** *m.* camphenilone; **—ный, —овый** *a.* camphene; camphenic (acid).

камфил *m.,* **—овый** *a.* camphyl; **—овая кислота** camphylic acid; **—овый спирт** camphyl alcohol, borneol.

камфо— *prefix* campho—; **—ген** *m.* camphogen, cymene; **—карбоксильная кислота, —карбоновая кислота** camphocarboxylic acid, 2-keto-3-carboxycamphane; **—кислота** *f.* campho acid, carboxylapocamphoric acid.

камфол *m.* camphol, borneol; **—евый** *a.* campholic (acid); **—еновый** *a.* campholenic (acid); **—овый** *a.* campholic (acid).

камфон *m.* camphone; **—ановая кислота** camphonanic acid; **—ен** *m.* camphonene.

камфор/а *see* **камфара; —ат** *m.* camphorate; **—ный** *see* **камфарный; —оил** *m.* camphoroyl; **—оновый** *a.* camphoronic (acid); **—осма** *f.* (bot.) Camphorosma.

камфоцееновый *a.* camphoceenic (acid).

камфреновая кислота camphrenic acid.

камчат/ка *f.,* **—ный** *a.* (text.) damask.

камчатский *a.* (geog.) Kamchatka.

камчужная трава (bot.) common coltsfoot (*Tussilago farfara*).

камшафт *m.* camshaft.

камы *pl. of* **кам.**

камызякский *a.* (geog.) Kamyzyak.

камыслыбасский *a.* (geog.) Kamyslybas.

камыш *m.,* **—евый** *a.* cane, reed, rush (*Scirpus*); **—евка** *f.* (orn.) reed warbler (*Acrocephalus*).

камышек *see* **камушек.**

камыш/екосилка *f.* reed cutter; **—ина** *f.* reed stalk; **—ит** *m.,* **—итовый** *a.* reed fiberboard; **—ница** *f.* (orn.) moorhen (*Gallinula*); **—овка** *see* **камышевка; —овый** *see* **камышевый.**

канава *f.* channel, ditch, canal, trench; groove; gutter; raceway; (casting) pit; (biol.) fossa, pit; **опробование —ми** (ore concentration) trench sampling.

канавалия *f.* (bot.) Canavalia.

канаванин *m.* canavanine.

канав/ка *dim. of* **канава;** groove, flute, slot, mortise, chase, key(way); **с —ками** grooved, fluted; **—озасыпщик** *m.* trench back filler; **—окопатель** *m.* trench digger, trenching plow, ditch digger; **—окопательный** *a.* trenching, ditch-digging; **—оочиститель** *m.*

ditch cleaner, ditch dredge; **—очный** *a.* grooving, groove-cutting.

канагурта *f.* (ichth.) kembong (*Rastrelliger kanagurta*).

канад/ин *m.* canadine, tetrahydroberberine; **—иновый** *a.* canadinic (acid); **—ол** *m.* canadol; **—ский** *a.* (geog.) Canada, Canadian.

канал *m.* channel, canal, conduit, pass(age); trench; (gas) flue; (valve) port; (cable) duct; bore (of gun); (anat.) canal(is), tube; **водосбросный к.** wasteway; **—ец** *dim. of* **канал;** (anat.) canaliculus, tubule.

канализ/атор *m.* sewage disposal specialist; **—ационноочистное сооружение** sewage works.

канализационн/ый *a. of* **канализация; —ая вода** sewage, waste water; **—ая сеть** sewer system; **—ая труба** sewage pipe, sewer; water pipe, gas pipe or electric conduit.

канализ/ация *f.,* **—ирование** *n.* canalization; channeling; sewer system, sewerage, drainage, drain system; plumbing; conduit; cable-conduit system; **—ировать** *v.* canalize; channel; provide with a sewer system.

канал/овидный *see* **канальчатый; —овый, —ьный** *a.* channel, canal; (nucl.) channeling (effect); **—ьная сажа** channel black; **—овые лучи** canal rays, positive rays; **—окопатель** *m.* trenching machine, ditcher; **—ообразование** *n.* channeling; **—проходчик** *m.* mandrel (for cable conduits); **—ьцевый** *a. of* **каналец;** canalicular, tubular; **—ьчатый** channeled, grooved, furrowed, fluted; canalicular, canaliculate; tubular (tooth); **—ьчатозубые** *pl.* (herp.) Selenoglypha.

канамицин *m.* kanamycin (antibiotic).

канланговое масло cananga oil.

канап *see* **кенаф.**

канар *m.* bale of wool; harvesting sack.

канар/еечник *m.,* **—еечная трава, —ейное семя** canary grass (*Phalaris canariensis*); **—еечный** *a.* canary(-colored); **—ейка** *f.,* **—ейный** *a.* (orn.) canary; **—иум** *m.* (bot.) Canarium; **—ский** *a.* (geog.) Canary.

канат *m.* cable, rope; cord; (petrol.) wireline; **—ик** *m.* string, cord, line; stranded wire; (anat.) funiculus; **—иковидный** *a.* restiform, funicular, rope-shaped; **—(н)ик** *m.* (bot.) Abutilon.

канатно— *see also under* **канато—; —башенный, —ковшовый, —скребковый** *a.* drag-line (excavator).

канатн/ый *a.* cable, rope; funicular (railway, etc.); drag-line (excavator); **—ая дорога** cableway; **—ые изделия** cordage.

канато— *prefix* rope, cable; **—видный** *a.* restiform, rope-shaped; **—ёмкость** *f.* coiling length (of drum); **—крутильный** *a.* rope-twisting; **—нажиматель** *m.* rope tightener; **—натягивающий** *a.* rope-tightening; **—скребковый** *a.* drag-line (excavator); **—тростильная дорожка** rope-walk.

канатчик *m.* ropemaker.

канаус *m.,* **—овый** *a.* (text.) taffeta.

канва *f.* canvas; outline, groundwork.

канга *f.* (petr.) canga (iron breccia).

кандалакшский *a.* (geog.) Kandalaksha.

кандалы *pl.* shackles, fetters.

кандела *f.* (light) candela, cd.

канделильский *a.* candelilla (wax).

канделябр *m.* candelabrum; chandelier; **—овидный** *a.* candelabriform.

канделярия *f.* (bot.) Candelaria (lichen).

кандидамикоз *m.* (med.) candidiasis.

кандидат *m.,* **—ский** *a.* (educ.) candidate, applicant; candidate degree, first post-graduate degree.

канд/идоз *m.* (med.) candidiasis; **—идулин** *m.* candidulin (antibiotic); —**иру** *m.* (ichth.) candiru (*Vandellia cirrhosa*); —**олюминесценция** *f.* (phys.) candoluminescence.

кандык *m.* (bot.) dog's tooth violet (*Erythronium denscanis*).

кандым *m.* (bot.) Calligonum.

канегра *f.* (bot.) tanner's dock (*Rumex hymenosepalus*).

Канейдиан (geog.) Canadian River.

канель *f.* (bot.) Annona.

канзасский *a.* (geog.) Kansas.

каникулы *pl.* vacation, holidays.

каниловый спирт kanyl alcohol.

канинский *a.* (geog.) Kanin.

канистра *f.* (fuel) can.

канител/ить *v.* draw out; —**иться** *v.* waste time, take one's time; —**ь** *f.* long-drawn out proceedings; gold or silver thread.

канифас *m.* (text.) dimity.

канифас-блок *m.* (naut.) snatch block.

канифол/ить *v.* rub with colophony, rosin; —**ь** *f.,* —**ьный** *a.* colophony, rosin.

канкринит *m.* (min.) cancrinite.

канкроид *m.* (med.) cancroid.

канна *f.* (bot.) canna; *m.* (mam.) eland (*Taurotragus oryx*); **съедобная к.** Queensland arrowroot (*Canna edulis*).

каннаб/ин *m.* cannabine (alkaloid); cannabin (glucoside); —**инол** *m.* cannabinol; —**оид** *m.* cannaboid.

каннелюра *f.* (arch.) flute.

каннибал/изм *m.,* —**ьство** *n.* cannibalism; —**истический** *a.* cannibalistic.

Канниццаро реакция Cannizzaro reaction.

канно/вые *pl.* (bot.) Cannaceae; —**вый** *a.* canna(ceous); —**мис** *m.* (mam.) Cannomys.

канон *m.* (typ.) canon.

канон/ерка *f.* gunboat; —**ир** *m.* gunner.

канонический *a.* (math.) canonical.

канский *a.* (geog.) Kan.

кант *m.* edge, edging, border; (clothes) piping; (leather) welt.

кантабрийский *a.* (geog.) Cantabrian.

канталупа *f.* cantaloupe, muskmelon.

канталь *m.* Kanthal (alloy).

кантар *see* **кантарус**; —**ен** *m.* cantharene, dihydro-o-xylene; —**ид** *m.* Spanish fly (*Cantharis vesicatoria*); —**идин** *m.* cantharidin; —**идиновокислая соль** cantharidate; —**идиновый** *a.* cantharidic (acid); (pharm.) cantharidal; —**овый** *a.* cantharic (acid); —**офильный** *a.* (bot.) cantharophilous; —**ус** *m.* (ichth.) Black Sea bream (*Spondyliosoma cantharus*); —**ь** *see* **кантарь.**

кантегирский *a.* (geog.) Kantegir.

канто— *prefix* (anat.) canth(o)— (canthus, canthal).

кантов/ально-загибочный *a.* body-forming (machine); —**альный** *a.* cant(ing), tilting, etc., *see v.*; (rolling) turnover (table); —**альный аппарат,** —**альное устройство** tilter, turnover device; —**ание** *n.* canting, etc., *see v.*; —**атель** *m.* tilter, turner, tipper; manipulator, positioner; (met.) link-chain support; —**ать** *v.* cant, tilt; (rolling) turn over; manipulate, position; bevel, edge, square; flange; cut (stone) to size and shape; —**ка** *f.,* —**очный** *a.* canting, etc., *see v.*

кантокамптус *m.* (crust.) Canthocamptus.

кантонит *m.* (min.) cantonite.

кантонский *a.* (geog.) Canton.

кантопластика *f.* (med.) canthoplasty.

канупер *see* **калуфер.**

кануть *v.* disappear, vanish, sink, drop.

кануфер *see* **калуфер.**

канфильдит *m.* (min.) canfieldite.

канцеляр/ист *m.* clerk; bureaucrat; —**ия** *f.* office; —**ский** *a.* office, clerical; bureaucratic; —**ские принадлежности,** —**ские товары** stationery; —**щина** *f.* red tape, bureaucracy.

канцер/оген *m.* (med.) carcinogen; —**огенез** *m.* carcinogenesis; —**огенность** *f.* carcinogenic properties; —**огенный** *a.* carcinogenic, cancer-producing; —**олитический** *a.* carcinolytic, cancer-destroying.

канцлер *m.,* —**ский** *a.* chancellor.

канчаланский *a.* (geog.) Kanchalan.

канчиль *m.* (mam.) mouse deer (*Tragulus*).

каныга *f.* (zool.) stomach contents.

каньон *m.* canyon.

канюк *m.* (orn.) buzzard (*Buteo b.*); **к.-курганник** *m.* steppe buzzard (*Buteo rufinus*).

канюля *f.* (med.) cannula.

каолин *m.* kaolin, China clay, porcelain clay; —**изация** *f.* kaolinization; —**изированный** *a.* kaolinized; —**из-(ир)овать** *v.* kaolinize; —**ит** *m.* (min.) kaolin(ite); —**овый** *a.* of **каолин.**

каолисол *m.* kaolisol (kaolinite-rich soil).

каон *m.* (nucl.) K-meson.

каорский *a.* (geog.) Cahors.

кап *m.* (bot.) burl, excrescence; (wood) curly grain; wart; cap, cover; (geog.) cape.

капа *f.* sealed end.

кап/анье *n.* dropping, dripping, trickle; —**ать** *v.* drop, drip, trickle; —**ающий** *a.* dripping; —**еж** *m.* drip.

капелировать *see* **купелировать.**

капелла *f.* (astr.) Capella.

капеллировать *see* **купелировать.**

капель *f.* dripping, trickling; (met.) cupel; *gen. pl.* of **капля;** —**ка** *f.* drop(let); —**ку** *adv.* a little (bit), barely; —**ник** *m.,* —**ница** *f.* (eye) dropper, dropping tube; dropping bottle; pipet; dripcock; (geol.) dropstone, stalactite; —**но-жидкий** *a.* liquid (enough to form drops); —**но-ручьевой режим** drop-rivulet condensation.

капель/ный, —**чатый** *a.* drop(ping), trickling; condensed (moisture); dropwise (condensation); liquid-drop (model of nucleus); spot (test); **к.-ная** *a.* dropwise (condensation); **к. кран** dripcock; **к. режим** dropwise condensation; **ртутный к. электрод** dropping-mercury electrode; —**ная воронка** dropping funnel; —**ная проба,** —**ное испытание** drop test, spot test; —**ная смазка** drip lubrication.

капеляция *see* **купеляция.**

капер/аза *f.* caperase, catalase; —**с(ник)** *m.,* —**совый кустарник** (bot.) caper (*Capparis*); —**цовые** *pl.* Capparidaceae; —**сы,** —**цы** *see* **каперс(ник).**

капибара *f.* (mam.) capybara (*Hydrochoerus capybara*).

капиллиц/ий, —**иум** *m.* (bot.) capillitium.

капилляр *m.* capillary (tube); (anat.) capillary (vessel); (instruments) restrictor; —**ии** *pl.* (zool.) Capillariidae; —**иметр** *m.* capillarimeter; —**ность** *f.* capillarity, capillary attraction; —**ный** *a.* capillary; —**ная трубка** capillary (tube); —**ное притяжение** capillary attraction; —**ные волны** capillary waves, ripples.

капитал *m.* capital, assets; —**изировать** *v.* capitalize; —**ист** *m.* capitalist; —**истический** *a.* capitalist(ic); —**овложение** *n.* (capital) investment, outlay; —**оёмкий** *a.* capital-intensive; —**оёмкость** *f.* relative capital requirements; —**ьность** *f.* durability, soundness of construction.

капитальн/ый *a.* capital; chief, principal; thorough, fundamental, substantial; **к. ремонт** overhaul(ing), major repairs; —**ое вложение,** —**ые затраты** investment, outlay.

капитан *m.* captain; **к., к-рыба** (ichth.) captainfish (*Pseudotolithes*; *Otolithes*).

капитель *f.* (arch.) capital; (typ.) small capitals.

капитулировать *v.* capitulate, give up.

капкан *m.* trap.

капланкырский *a.* (geog.) Kaplankyr.

капле/видный *a.* tear-shaped, teardrop; **—защищён-ный** *a.* drip-proof; **—непроницаемый** *a.* drip-tight; **—образный** *a.* drop-shaped, drop(wise); fluid-drop (shell); **—образование** *n.* drop formation; **—отбой-ник** *m.* entrainment trap; spray separator, demister; mist collector; **—падение** *n.* drip(ping), drop(ping), trickling; **точка —падения** drop point; **—питатель** *m.* (glass) gob feeder; **—сдуватель** *m.* (film) squee-gee; **—собиратель** *m.* drip pan, gutter; **—стойкий** *a.* drip-proof; **—указатель** *m.* sight glass; **—улавли-ватель, —уловитель** *m.* (distillation) safety trap; drip pan; **—упорный** *a.* drip-proof.

каплун *m.* capon; **—ировать** *v.* capon(ize), castrate.

капл/ю *adv.* a little (bit); **—я** *f.* drop; a little, a bit; **—ями, по —ям** drop by drop, dropwise.

капно— *prefix* capno- (smoke); **—дис** *m.* (ent.) Cap-nodis; **—скоп** *m.* capnoscope, smoke gage.

капнуть *see* **капать**.

каповый *a.* of **кап**.

капок *m.*, **—овый** *a.* kapok (fibers); **к., —овое дерево** silk cotton tree (*Ceiba pentandra*).

капорка *f.* (bot.) Epilobium.

капот *m.* (mach.) hood, cowl(ing), housing; (av.) nose-over, nosing over; **—аж** *m.*, **—ирование** *n.* nose-over, nosing over; housing; **—ировать** *v.* nose over, over-turn; house, cowl; face, clad.

капоэйра *f.* (biogeog.) capoeira.

Каппа линии (elec.) Kapp lines.

каппа *f.* kappa (Greek letter); (gen.) kappa (particle); **—метрия** *f.* magnetic susceptibility measurement; **к.-тельце** *n.*, **к.-частица** *f.* kappa (particle).

капрат *m.* caprate.

капремонт *m.* overhaul(ing).

капризный *a.* capricious, freakish.

каприл *m.* capryl, octyl; **—ил** *m.* caprylyl, octanoyl; **—ин** *m.* caprylin; **—овокислая соль** caprylate; **—овый** *a.* capryl(ic); **—овая кислота** caprylic acid, octanoic acid; **соль** or **эфир —овой кислоты** ca-prylate; **—овый альдегид** caprylic aldehyde, oc-tanal.

каприн *m.* caprin; caprine, norleucine; **—ат** *m.* caprate; **—овая кислота** capric acid, *n*-decanoic acid; **соль** or **эфир —овой кислоты, —овокислая соль** caprate; **—овокислый** *a.* capric acid; caprate (of); **—овый альдегид** capric aldehyde, capraldehyde, decanal.

каприф/ига *f.* (bot.) caprifig; **—икация** *f.* caprification (of figs); **—олий** *m.*, **—оль** *f.* woodbine (*Lonicera caprifolia*).

капричо *see* **капибара**.

капро/ат *m.* caproate; **—вые** *pl.* (ichth.) Caproidae; **—ил** *m.*, **—иловый** *a.* caproyl, hexanoyl.

капрок *m.* (geol.) cap rock.

капро/лактам *m.* caprolactam; **—лан** *m.* caprolan (tire cord 528).

капрон *m.* caprone, 6-hendecanone; capron, polycapro-lactam fiber or plastic, nylon-6; **—ат** *m.* caproate; **—ил** *m.*, **—иловый** *a.* capronyl; **—итрил** *m.* capro-nitrile; **—овый** *a.* of **капрон**; **—овая кислота** caproic acid, hexanoic acid; **—овокислая соль** caproate; **—овокислый** *a.* caproic acid; caproate (of); **—овый альдегид** caproic aldehyde, caproalde-hyde, hexanal.

капрос *m.* boarfish (*Capros aper*); **—овые** *pl.* (ichth.) Caproidae.

капс/аицин *m.* capsaicin; **—антин** *m.* capsanthin; **—ан-тол** *m.* capsanthol.

капсель *m.* (cer.) sagger.

капсельный *see* **капсюльный**.

капсицин *m.* capsicine (alkaloid); capsicin (oleoresin).

капский *a.* (geog.) Cape, South African.

капсул/а *f.* capsule; **заключение в —ю, —ирование** *n.* (en)capsulation; **—ировать** *v.* (en)capsulate; **—о-видный, —ьный, —ярный** *a.* capsular.

капсюл/ь *m.* (percussion) cap, (cartridge) primer; cap-sule; cork, cap, stopper; (microphone) inset; **к.-вос-пламенитель** *m.* percussion cap, primer; **к.-детона-тор** *m.* detonator, blasting cap; **—ный** *a.* of **капсюль**; enclosed (motor); **—я** *see* **капсула**.

каптаж *m.* (hydr.) catchment; piping (of water supply); damming, harnessing (of river); capping (of well).

каптакс *m.* Captax (a mercaptobenzothiazole rubber ac-celerator).

каптал *m.* (books) headband; bead; **—орезка** *f.* head-band cutter.

каптан *m.* captan.

каптировать *v.* capture, catch, collect; pipe (water or oil).

капугиа *see* **капибара**.

капуст/а *f.* cabbage (*Brassica*); **заячья к.** orpine (*Sedum telephium*); **квашен(н)ая к., кислая к.** sauerkraut; **кудрявая к.** savoy; **лиственная к.** kale; **много-кочанчиковая к.** Brussels sprouts; **морская к.** *see* **катран; спаржевая к.** broccoli; **цветная к.** cauli-flower; (vet.) cauliflower head; **—ник** *m.* cabbage field; cabbage worm; cabbage dish; **—ник** *m.*, **—ница** *f.* (mam.) Steller's sea cow (*Hydrodamalis stelleri*); **—ники** *pl.* Hydrodamalidae; **—ница** *f.*, **—ная белянка** (ent.) cabbage butterfly (*Pieris brassicae*); **—ный** *a.* cabbage.

капутджухский *a.* (geog.) Kaputdzhukh.

капут-морту(у)м *m.* caput mortuum, polishing rouge.

капуцин *m.* (bot.) nasturtium (*Tropaeolum*); (ent.) wood borer (*Bostrychus capucinus*); (mam.) capuchin (*Cebus capucinus*); **—овые** *pl.* (bot.) Tropaeolaceae.

капцук *m.* barnacle, restraining halter.

капшак *m.* (crust.) krill (*Euphausia*).

капшинский *a.* (geog.) Kapsha.

Капштадт Cape Town.

капюшон *m.* hood, cowl; (protective) net, veil; **—ники** *see* **капюшонщики; —ная мышца** (anat.) cucullaris; **—ница** *f.* (ent.) Cucullia; **—овидный, —ообразный** *a.* cucullate, hood-shaped; hooded, cowled; **—щики** *pl.* (ent.) wood borers (*Bostrychidae*).

кар *m.* (geol.) kar, cirque, corrie.

караартский *a.* (geog.) Kara-Art.

кара-балык *m.* (ichth.) one of several species (*Schizo-thorax*, etc.).

карабахский *a.* (geog.) Karabagh.

карабильский *a.* (geog.) Karabil.

карабин *m.*, **—ный** *a.* carbine, rifle; snap hook; clamp, clasp; swivel; **—ный крючок** swivel.

карабкаться *v.* climb, clamber.

карабугазский *a.* (geog.) Kara-Bogaz-Gol.

карабутакский *a.* (geog.) Kara-Butak.

карав/аеобразный *a.* bun-shaped; **—ай** *m.* (round) loaf, bun; **—айка** *f.* (orn.) glossy ibis (*Plegadis*).

караван *m.*, **—ский** *a.* caravan; (naut.) convoy; peat storage pile.

карагайский *a.* (geog.) Karagai.

караган *m.* (mam.) fox (*Vulpes v. stepensis*).

карагана *f.* (bot.) peashrub (*Caragana*).

карагандинский *a.* (geog.) Karaganda.

караганка *f.* (mam.) fox (*Vulpes v. caragan*).

караганник *see* **карагана.**

карагач *m.,* **—евый** *a.* (bot.) elm (*Ulmus foliacea*); cork elm (*U. suberosa*).

карагенан *m.* (biochem.) carrageenan.

карагинский *a.* Karaga (River); Karagin (Island).

карадаревый *a.* (geog.) Karadarya.

карадок *m.,* **—ский ярус** (geol.) Caradocian, Lower Upper Ordovician.

карадрина *f.* (ent.) cutworm moth (*Caradrina exigua*); beet army worm (*Laphygma exigua*).

караибский *a.* (geog.) Caribbean.

караимский *a.* (geog.) Karaim.

каракал *m.* (mam.) caracal (*Felis caracal*).

каракалпакский *a.* (geog.) Kara-Kalpak.

каракара *f.* (orn.) caracara (*Polyborus*).

каракатица *f.* (mal.) cuttlefish (*Sepia*); (distillation) receiver.

каракаовый *a.* dark bay, brown.

карако/инский *a.* (geog.) Karakoin; **—йсуский** *a.* Karakoisu; **—румский** *a.* Karakorum.

карактрон *m.* (comp.) Charactron.

кара-куз(ь) *f.* (ichth.) Aral whiteeye (*Abramis sapa bergi n. aralensis*).

каракул/еводство *n.,* **—еводческий** *a.* karakul sheep breeding; **—евый** *a.,* **—ь** *m.* karakul (sheep); astrakhan (fur); **—ьский** *a.* karakul; astrakhan; (geog.) Kara-Kul; **—ьча** *f.* caraculcha, Persian lamb(skin).

каракумский *a.* (geog.) Kara-Kum.

кара(-)курт *m.* (zool.) steppe spider (*Lathrodectus tredecimguttatus*).

карамел/ан *m.* caramelan; **—изация** *f.,* **—из(ир)ование** *n.* caramelization; **—из(ир)ованный** *a.* caramelized; **—из(ир)овать** *v.* caramelize, burn, char (sugar); **—ь** *f.,* **—ьный** *a.* caramel.

каран *m.* carane (bicyclic terpene).

каранг *see* **каранкс; —иды, —овые** *pl.* (ichth.) jacks (*Carangidae*).

карандаш *m.,* **—ный** *a.* pencil, crayon; **—еобразный** *a.* pencil-shaped; **—ное дерево** (bot.) pencil cedar (*Juniperus virginiana*).

карандич *m.* (ichth.) yellow gurnard (*Trigla lucerna*).

каранкс *m.* (ichth.) jack (*Caranx*, spec. *C. hippos*).

каранская камедь (gum) carana.

карантин *m.,* **—ный** *a.* quarantine; **—ное свидетельство** bill of health; **—ные сорняки** noxious weeds.

каранчо *see* **каракара.**

карапакс *m.* (zool.) carapace.

караповые *see* **карапусовые.**

карапузик *m.* (ent.) hister beetle (*Hister*).

карапусовые *pl.* pearlfishes (*Carapidae*).

карас/евый, —ий *a. of* **карась; морские —и** (ichth.) porgies (*Sparidae*).

карасик *m.* oval file, double half-round file; (foundry) sleeker, smoother.

кара/-сингиль *m.* (ichth.) mullet (*Mugil saliens* or *M. auratus*); **—синский** *a.* (geog.) Kara Su; **—скаль, —ску** *m.* (biogeog.) carrascal, carrasco; **—сорский** *a.* (geog.) Karasor; **к.-суйский** *a.* Kara Su; **—сукский** *a.* Karasuk.

карась *m.* (ichth.) one of several species; crucian carp (*Carassius*), etc.

карат *m.* carat (0.2 g.).

карат/алыаятский *a.* (geog.) Karataly-Ayat; **—альский** *a.* Karatal; **—аауский** *a.* Kara Tau; **—егинский** *a.* Karategin.

каратный *a. of* **карат.**

каратуз *m.* karatuz (common salt from the bottom of salt lakes).

каратышский *a.* (geog.) Karatysh.

карать *v.* punish, penalize.

караугомский *a.* (geog.) Karaugom.

караул *m.,* **—ить** *v.* watch, guard.

караульский *a.* (geog.) Karaul.

карачаев/о-черкесский *a.* (geog.) Karachi-Cherkess; **—ский** *a.* Karachi, Karachai.

карб— *prefix* carb(o)—.

карбаз/ид *m.* carbazide; **—ил** *m.* carbazyl; **—ол** *m.,* **—оловый** *a.* carbazole, diphenylenimide; **—он** *m.* carbazone.

карбам/ат *m.* carbamate; **—ид** *m.,* **—идный** *a.* carbamide; **—ил** *m.,* **—иловый** *a.* carbamyl; **—инат** *m.* carbam(in)ate.

карбамино/вая кислота carbamic acid, aminoformic acid; **соль —вой кислоты, —вокислая соль** carbamate; **—воаммониевая соль, —вокислый аммоний** ammonium carbamate; **—вокислый** *a.* carbamic acid; carbamate (of); **—(во)-этиловый эфир** ethyl carbamate.

карбам/инокислота *f.* carbamic acid; **—оил** *m.,* **—оильный** *a.* carbam(o)yl.

карб/ангидраза *f.* carbonic anhydrase; **—анил** *m.* carbanil, phenyl cyanate; **—анилид** *m.* carbanilide, diphenylurea; **—аниловый** *a.* carbanilic (acid); **—анион** *m.* carbanion.

карбас *m.* fishing boat; cargo boat.

карб/атен *m.* carbatene (fungicide); **—гемоглобин** *m.* carbohemoglobin; **—ен** *m.* carbene, methylene; **—ениевый** *a.,* **—ий** *m.* carbenium, carbonium; **—еноид** *m.* carbenoid.

карбид *m.* carbide; **к. кальция** calcium carbide; **—изация** *f.* (met.) carbidizing treatment; **—изированный** *a.* carbidized; **—ка** (min.) acetylene lamp; **—ный, —овый** *a.* carbide; **—ообразующий** *a.* carbide-forming.

карб/иламин *m.* carbylamine, isocyanide; **—иловый** *a.* carbylic (acid); **—ин** *m.* carbyne; Carbyne (herbicide); **—инол** *m.,* **—инольный** *a.* carbinol, primary alcohol; methanol; **—итол** *m.* Carbitol, diethylene-glycol ethyl ether; **—катион** *m.* carbonium ion.

карбо— *prefix* carbo—; **—анализатор** *m.* carbon analyzer; **—ангидраза** *f.* carbonic anhydrase; **—бензоил** *m.* carbobenzoyl; **—бензоксигруппа** *f.* carbobenzoxy group; **—вальт, —вольт** *m.* Carbowalt (abrasive); **—воск** *m.* Carbowax; **—гемоглобин** *m.* carbohemoglobin; **—ген** *m.* carbogen; **—гидраза** *f.* carbonic hydrase; **—диимид** *m.* carbodiimide, cyanamide; **—ид** *m.,* **—идный** *a.* carboid; **—катион** *m.* carbocation; **—ксамид** *m.* carbonic acid amide.

карбокси— *prefix* carboxy—, carboxyl; **—гемоглобин** *m.* carboxyhemoglobin; **—л** *m.* carboxyl; **—лаза** *f.* carboxylase; **—латный** *a.* carboxylated, carboxyl-containing; **—лирование** *n.* carboxylation; **—лированный** *a.* carboxylated; **—лировать** *v.* carboxylate; **—лсодержащий** *a.* carboxyl-containing; **—льный** *a.* carboxyl(ic); **—льная группа** carboxyl; **—метилцеллюлоза** *f.* carboxymethyl cellulose.

карбол/ен *m.* carbolen(um) (activated carbon tablets); **—инеум** *m.* Carbolineum (wood preservative); **—инировать** *v.* carbolineate; **—ит** *m.* carbolite (abrasive); carbolite (resin); **—ка** *f.,* **—овая кислота** carbolic acid, phenol; **—овый** *a.* carbolic, phenol(ic); **—ой** *m.* (met.) Carboloy (cemented tungsten carbide); **—он** *m.* Carbolon (silicon carbide abrasive).

карбометокси— *prefix* carbomethoxy—.

карбо/метр *m.* carbometer; **—мицин** *m.* carbomycin; **—н** *m.* carbon; (geol.) Carboniferous (period); **—надо** *n.* carbonado, black diamond.

карбонат *m.* carbonate; *see* **карбонадо**; **к. натрия** sodium carbonate; **—изация** *f.* carbonate formation; **—ит** *m.* (petr.) carbonatite; **—ность** *f.* carbonate content; **—ный, —овый** *a.* carbonate; carbonaceous; calcareous (soil).

карбониевый *a.* carbonium.

карбониз/атор *m.* carbonizer; **—ационный** *a.*, **—ация** *f.*, **—(ир)ование** *n.* carbon(iz)ation; **—(ир)ованный** *a.* carbonized, etc., *see v.*; **—(ир)овать** *v.* carbonize, carbonate; carburize.

карбоний *m.* carbonium.

карбонил *m.*, **—ьный** *a.* carbonyl; **хлористый к.** carbonyl chloride, phosgene; **—ирование** *n.* carbonylation.

карбонов/ый *a.* (geol.) carbonaceous, carbon-containing, carboniferous; **—ая кислота, —окислый** *a.* carboxylic acid.

карбонолит *m.* (petr.) carbonolite.

карбон-процесс *m.* (phot.) carbon printing.

карборунд, —ум *m.*, **—овый** *a.* carborundum, silicon carbide.

карбо/сурьмировать *v.* (met.) carburize with carbon-antimony; **—тиокислота** *f.* thiocarbonic acid; **—термия** *f.* carbothermy; **—фос** *m.* a Malathion insecticide; **—холин** *m.* carbocholine, carbamylcholine chloride; **—цепной, —цепный** *a.* carbon-chain; **—цианин** *m.* (phot.) carbocyanine; **—циклический** *a.* carbocyclic.

карбро-процесс *m.* (phot.) Carbro process.

карбункул *m.* (min., med.) carbuncle.

карбур— *see* карбюр—; **—ан *m.* (min.) carburan (near thucholite).

карбэтокси— *prefix* carbethoxy—.

карбюр/атор *m.* carburetor; **—аторный** *a.* carburetor; carburetion (fuel); **—ационный** *a.*, **—ация** *f.* carburation, carburetion; (met.) carburization; **—изатор** *m.* carbonizer; carburizing agent; **—изация, —ирование** *see* **карбюрация**; **—ированный** *a.* carbureted; carburized; **—ировать** *v.* carburet; carburize.

карв/акрил *m.* carvacryl; **—акрол** *m.* carvacrol, 2-hydroxy-*p*-cymene; **—ен** *m.* carvene, *d*-limonene; **—енон** *m.* carvenone; **—естрен** *m.* carvestrene, I-*m*-terpene; **—ол, —он** *m.* carvol, carvone.

каргалинский *a.* (geog.) Kargaly, Kargala.

карган *m.* Russian thistle (*Salsola arbuscula*).

каргатский *a.* (geog.) Kargat.

карго *n.* cargo, shipload.

каргынский *a.* (geog.) Kargyn.

карда *f.* (text.) card, card clothing.

кардамон *m.*, **—ный, —овый** *a.* (bot.) cardamom (*Ellettaria cardamomum*).

кардан *m.*, **—ный шарнир** Cardan joint, universal joint; (horol.) gimbal; **—ный вал** Cardan shaft, propeller shaft; **—ный камень** trunnion block; **—ный механизм, —ная передача** *see* **кардан**; **—овский** *a.* (math.; phys.) Cardan's; Cardan's.

карди/азол *m.* Cardiazole, pentylene tetrazole; **—альный** *a.* (anat.) cardial, cardiac.

кардинал *m.* (orn.) cardinal (*Richmondena cardinalis*); **к., —ка** *f.* cardinalfish (*Apogon*); **—(к)овые** *pl.* (ichth.) Apogonidae; **—ьный** *a.* cardinal, chief, principal; basic.

кардио— *prefix* cardio— (heart); **—грамма** *f.* (med.) cardiogram; **—граф** *m.* cardiograph; **—ида** *f.* (math.) cardioid; **—идный** *a.* cardioid, heart(-shaped); **—липин** *m.* cardiolipin; **—лог** *m.* cardiologist; **—ло-**

—гический *a.* cardiological; **—логия** *f.* cardiology; **—пат** *m.* cardiopath, heart patient; **—стимулятор** *m.* pacemaker; **—тахо—** *prefix* cardiotacho— (heart rate).

кард/ит *m.* (med.) carditis; **—ита** *f.* (mal.) Cardita; **—иум** *m.* (mal.) Cardium; **—ия** *f.* (anat.) cardia.

кард/машина, —ная машина *see* **кардомашина**; **—ный** *a.* (text.) card; **—ный очёс** card waste; **—ный холст, —ная лента** card clothing.

кардо *m.* (zool.) cardo; *pl.* cardines.

кардобенедикт *m.* (bot.) blessed thistle (*Cnicus benedictus*).

кардов/ание *n.* (text.) carding; **—анный** *a.* carded; **—ать** *v.* card.

кардовый *a.* cardo, loop (polymer).

кардокс *m.* (expl.) cardox.

кардол, —ь *m.* cardol.

кардо/лента *f.* (text.) card clothing; **—машина** *f.* carder; **—наборная машина** card-setting machine; **—питатель** *m.* card filler; **—чесальный** *a.*, **—чесание** *n.* carding; **—чёсанный** *a.* carded.

Кардью вольтметр Cardew voltmeter.

карельский *a.* (geog.) Karelian.

карен *m.* carene.

карепрокт *m.* snailfish (*Careproctus*).

карет/а *f.*, **—ный** *a.* carriage, coach; **—ка** *f.* (mach.) carrier, carriage, slide; (crucible) support, stand; (drilling) rig.

каретта *f.* (herp.) turtle (*Caretta*).

каржантауский *a.* (geog.) Karzhantau.

карибский *a.* (geog.) Caribbean.

карибу *m.* (mam.) caribou (*Rangifer tarandus*).

кариес *m.* (med.) caries.

кариинит *m.* (min.) caryinite.

карий *a.* hazel, brown.

карикатура *f.* caricature; cartoon.

карико— *prefix* (bot.) caric(o)— (Carex, sedge).

карин/а *f.* (anat.; bot.) carina; **—альный** *a.* carinal; **—ария** *f.* (mal.) Carinaria.

карио— *prefix* (biol.) caryo—, karyo— (nucleus, kernel); **—гамия** *f.* (gen.) karyogamy; **—ген** *m.* karyogene, nuclear gene; (biochem.) karyogen; **—з** *m.* (med.) caries; **—зный** *a.* carious; **—ровые** *pl.* (bot.) Caryocaraceae; **—кинез** *m.* karyokinesis, mitosis, nuclear division; **—лиз(ис)** *m.* (cyt.) karyolysis; **—лимфа** *f.* (bot.) karyolymph, nuclear sap; **—литический** *a.* (cyt.) karyolyitic, karyoklastic; **—логия** *f.* karyology; **—мер** *m.* (gen.) karyomere; **—н** *m.* karyon, cell nucleus; **—плазма** *f.* karyoplasm; **—рексис** *m.* (gen.) karyorrhexis; **—сома** *f.* karyosome; **—та** *f.* (bot.) caryotype; **—тип** *m.* (bot.) karyotype; **—фаг** *m.* (med.; prot.) karyophage; **—фи(л)лёз** *m.* (vet.) caryophyllosis; **—филлен** *m.* caryophyllene; **—филлиновый** *a.* caryophyllinic (acid).

карисса *f.* (bot.) Carissa.

карист *m.* (ichth.) manefish (*Caristius*); **—иевые, —овые** *pl.* Caristiidae.

кария *f.* (bot.) hickory (*Carya*).

карканье *n.* (orn.) caw(ing), croak(ing).

каркаралинский *a.* (geog.) Karkaraly.

каркарчайский *a.* Karkarchai.

каркас *m.*, **—ный** *a.* skeleton, frame(work), chassis; body, form, shell, hull, housing, casing; cage; (tire) carcass, casing; (core) barrel, mandrel, rod; (furnace) body; structure, assembly; (bot.) hackberry (*Celtis*).

карк/ать, —нуть *v.* croak, caw.

карлик *m.* dwarf, pygmy; dwarf tree; **—овость** *f.*, **—овый рост** dwarfness, dwarfism, nanism; **—овый**

a. dwarf(ed), dwarfish, nanous; stunted; nano—, e.g., —**овый планктон** nanoplankton.

карлинг *m.* (geog.) horn (peak).

карлингс *m.* (naut.) carling.

карл/оварская соль, —сбадская соль Carlsbad salt; —**ыганский** *a.* (geog.) Karlygan; —**юдовика** *f.* (bot.) Carludovica.

кармазин *m.,* —**ный,** —**овокрасный,** —**овый** *a.* crimson (red).

карман *m.* pocket, recess, well; bag; housing, container; (anat., zool.) bursa, sac; (comp.) clipboard; **забрать в карман** (comp.) cut; **вставить из** —**а** paste; —**ный** *a. of* **карман;** pocket-sized, portable; bag (filter); —**ный фонарь** flashlight; —**овидный** *a.* sacc(ul)iform; —**чик** *dim. of* **карман.**

карматрон *m.* (electron.) karmatron, reverse-wave magnetron.

кармаш/ек *dim. of* **карман;** —**ки сливы** (phyt.) plum pockets; —**ковидный** *a.* sacculiform; —**овый** *a.* semilunar (valve).

карм/езиновый, —**инно-красный** *a.* carmine, coccineous, scarlet; —**ин** *m.* carmine, coccinellin; —**инный** *a.* carmine; —**иновокислая соль** carminate; —**иновокрасный** *a.* carmine red; —**иновый** *a.* carmine; carminic (acid).

карналлит *m.* (min.) carnallite.

карнауб/а *f.* (bot.) Brazilian wax palm (*Copernicia cerifera*); **к.-воск** carnauba wax; —**аль** *m.* Copernicia grove; —**овый,** —**ский** *a.* carnaubic (acid); carnauba (wax).

карне/гиелла *f.* (ichth.) Carnegiella; —**гиит** *m.* (min.) carnegieite; —**ол** *m.* carnelian; —**ро** *see* **кандиру.**

карниворный *a.* carnivorous.

карниз *m.* cornice; (roof) eave(s); (window) ledge; (geol.) bench; —**ник** *m.* cornice plane.

карн/ийский *a.* (geog.) Carnic; (geol.) Carnian (stage); —**ин** *m.* carnine, inosine; —**иолийский** *a.* (geog.) Carniola(n); —**итин** *m.* carnitine, vitamin B$_T$.

Карно цикл Carnot's cycle.

карно/зин *m.* carnosine, alanylhistidine; —**тин,** —**тит** *m.* (min.) carnotite.

Каро кислота Caro's acid, permonosulfuric acid.

каробовая кислота carobic acid.

каровое озеро tarn, bog, fen.

Карозерс Carothers (name).

карол *m.* carol, 5-hydroxycarane.

каролинский *a.* (geog.) Carolina, Carolinian; Caroline (Islands).

карон *m.* carone, 5-ketocarane; —**овая кислота** caronic acid.

каротаж *m.,* —**ный** *a.* (mineral exploration) logging, coring; log; —**ное зондирование** logging.

каротель *f.* carrot.

каротидный *a.* (anat.) carotid.

каротин *m.,* —**овый** *a.* carotene, primary vitamin A; —**оид** *m.* carotenoid.

карот/ировать *v.* (mineral exploration) log; —**таж** *see* **каротаж.**

карп *m.* (ichth.) carp (*Cyprinus carpio*).

карп— *see* **карпо**—; —**аин** *m.* carpaine; —**альный** *a.* (anat.) carpal.

карпатский *a.* (geog.) Carpathian.

карпел/ла, —**ль** *f.* (bot.) carpel.

карпид *a f.,* —**ий** *m.* (bot.) carpid.

карпинскиит *m.* (min.) karpinskyite.

карпи/одес *m.* (ichth.) highfin carpsucker (*Carpiodes cyprinus*); —**я** *f.* river carpsucker (*Cyprinus carpio*).

карпо— *prefix* carp(o)— [(anat.) carpus, carpal, wrist;

(bot.) fruit; (ichth.) carp]; —**видные** *pl.* (ichth.) Cyprinoidei; —**водство** *n.* carp breeding; —**вые** *pl.* Cyprinidae; —**вый** *a.* carp; —**гон(ий)** *m.* (bot.) carpogon(e); —**еды** *pl.* (crust.) fish lice (*Branchiura*); —**зубик** *m.* (ichth.) Cyprinodon; —**зубые** *pl.* killifishes (*Cyprinodontidae*); —**идеи** *pl.* (pal.) Carpoidea; —**логия** *f.* (bot.) carpology; —**спора** *f.* carpospore; —**фаг** *m.* carpophagous animal; —**фор** *m.* (bot.) carpophore.

карр *m.* (geol.) sink hole.

карра *f.* (phyt.) resin flux or blaze.

Карра долото Carr bit.

каррарский мрамор Carrara marble.

карри *n.* karri (timber).

карролит *m.* (min.) carrollite.

карсель *m.* carcel unit (9.6 candles); —**ская лампа** Carcel lamp.

карский *a.* (geog.) Kara.

карст *m.,* —**овый** *a.* (geol.) karst; —**енит** *m.* karstenite, anhydrite rock; —**овая воронка** sink hole.

карт *m.* cart.

карт/а *f.* card; map, chart; **к. в горизонталях** contour map; **чертить** —**у** *v.* map, plot, chart; **к.-бланковка** outline map.

карталинский *a.* (geog.) Kartaly.

картам/еин *m.* carthamein; —**ин** *m.,* —**овая кислота** carthamin, carthamic acid.

картезианский *a.* Cartesian; **к. водолаз** (phys.) Cartesian devil.

картел/ировать *v.* (com.) cartelize; —**ь** *m. and f.,* —**ьный** *a.* cartel.

картер *m.,* —**ный** *a.* (mach.) crankcase; casing, housing.

картеч/ь *f.,* —**ный** *a.* (mil.) canister, case shot, buckshot.

картин/а *f.* picture; figure, image; display, visualization; (diffraction, etc.) pattern; —**ка** *f.* picture, illustration; —**ный** *a.* picture, pictorial, picturesque.

картиров/ание *n.* mapping, etc., see *v.;* —**ать** *v.* map (out), chart, plot; —**очный** *a.* mapping, etc., see *v.;* core (drilling).

картлийский *a.* (geog.) Kartalin.

карто— *prefix* carto—, map, chart; card; —**ведение** *n.* cartography; —**грамма** *f.* cartogram, collation map; (recording) chart, log.

картограф *m.* cartographer, map maker; —**ирование** *n.* mapping, etc., see *v.;* —**ировать** *v.* (make or draw a) map, chart; —**ический** *a.* cartographic; —**ия** *f.* cartography, mapping.

карто/диаграмма *f.* diagrammatic map or chart; —**лентокарточный** *a.* (comp.) card-tape-card; —**метрия** *f.* cartometry.

карто/печатание *n.* map printing; —**схема** *f.* diagrammatic map, skeleton map; —**тека** *f.,* —**течный** *a.* (card) file, card catalog, card index.

картофеле— *prefix* potato; —**водство,** —**водческий** *a.* potato growing; —**запарник** *m.* potato steamer; —**копалка** *f.* —**копатель-подборщик** *m.* potato digger and picker; —**крахмальный** *a.* potato starch; —**мойка** *f.* potato washer; —**мялка** *f.* potato masher; —**посадочный** *a.* potato-planting; —**резка** *f.* potato slicer or chopper; —**сажалка** *f.,* —**сажатель** *m.* potato planter; —**собиратель** *m.* potato picker; —**сортировка** *f.* potato grader; potato grading; —**сушилка** *f.* potato-drying plant; —**тёрка** *f.* potato grater; —**уборочный** *a.* potato-harvesting; —**уборочная машина**

potato picker; **—хранилище** *n.* potato cellar; **—чистка** *f.* potato peeler.

картофели/на *f.* potato (tuber); **—ще** *n.* potato field.

картофель *m.,* **—ный** *a.* potato (*Solanum tuberosum*); **—ник** *m.* potato field; **—ный жук** Colorado potato beetle; **—ное пюре** mashed potatoes.

карточ/ка *f.,* **—ный** *a.* (index) card; postal card; (phot.) snapshot, small print; record, chart, list; (test) certificate; (ichth.) bream (*Abramis brama*); **к.-квитанция** *f.* (rad.) QSL card.

картошка *see* **картофель.**

картуз *m.* cap; (paper) bag, sac; pocket, pouch; (art.) cartridge.

картузианский *a.* Carthusian.

картузн/ик *m.* cartridge box; **—ный** *a. of* **картуз;** wrapping (paper).

картушка *f.* (compass) card, rose.

карункула *f.* (bot.) caruncle.

карусель *f.* carousel; turntable; (comp.) round-robin; **—(нотокар)ный станок** (vertical) boring and turning lathe; **—ный** *a.* rotary, revolving; turret-type; rotary-drum (dryer); rotary-hearth (furnace); spiral (seed separator); **—щик** *m.* lathe operator.

карфагенский *a.* (geog.) Carthaginian.

карфо/лит *m.* (min.) carpholite; **—сидерит** *m.* carphosiderite.

кархар/иновые *pl.* (ichth.) gray sharks (*Carcharhinidae*); **—одон** *m.* white shark (*Carcharodon carcharias*).

карцино— *prefix* carcin(o)— (cancer; crab); **—ген** *m.* carcinogen; **—генез** *m.* carcinogenesis; **—генный** *a.* carcinogenic, cancer-producing; **—литический** *a.* carcinolyitic; **—логия** *f.* carcinology, oncology; **—ма** *f.* carcinoma.

карцинотрон *m.* (electron.) carcinotron (ultra-high frequency wave generator).

карча *f.* remains of a submerged tree.

каршинский *a.* (geog.) Karshi.

карымский *a.* (geog.) Karym.

карыш *m.* (ichth.) Siberian sturgeon (*Acipenser baeri*); sterlet (*A. ruthenus*); carp (*Cyprinus carpio*).

карьер *m.* (min.) open pit, open-cut mine, quarry; career; full gallop; **во весь к.** at full speed; **разработка —ами** open-cut mining; **—а** *f.* career; **—ный** *a. of* **карьер;** run-of-bank, pit (gravel); bank-run (sand); run-of-quarry (stone).

касабе *m.* (ichth.) Atlantic bumper (*Chloroscombrus chrysurus*).

касан/ие *n.* (math.) contact, tangency; impact; **линия —ия** line of contact, tangent; **поверхность —ия** contact surface.

касарийский *a.* (geog.) Kasari.

касательн/ая *f.,* **—ая линия** (geom.) tangent; **по —ой** tangentially; **—o** *prep. gen.* about, touching (upon), concerning, relative (to); **—ость** *f.* relation, connection; **—ый** *a.* concerning, touching; tangent(ial); **—ое напряжение** tangential stress.

касательство *n.* relation(ship).

касатик *m.* (bot.) iris; **—овые** *pl.* Iridaceae.

касатка *f.* (orn.) falcated teal (*Anas falcata*); barn swallow (*Hirundo rustica*); (mam.) whale (*Orcinus orca*); (ichth.) *see* **косатка.**

кас/аться *v.* concern, touch (upon), deal (with), refer, apply (to); dwell (on), go into; hold true, be true (for); relate (to), have respect (to), affect; touch, be in contact (with); (math.) be tangent (to); **что —ается** as concerns, as regards, regarding, as to, as for; **что —ается**

меня for my part; **—ающийся** *a.* concerning, etc., *see v.*; relative (to), in respect (to); tangent.

касидоровые *pl.* (ichth.) Kasidoridae.

каска *f.* helmet.

каскад *m.* cascade; series, chain; step, stage; division circuit; **—ирование** *n.* cascading; **—ировать** *v.* cascade; **—но** *adv.* (elec.) in cascade; **—ный** *a. of* **каскад; —ный ливень** cascade shower (of cosmic rays).

каскар/а *f.* cascara; **к. амарга** cascara amarga; **к. саграда** cascara sagrada; **—илла** *f.* cascarilla; **—иллин** *m.* cascarilline; **—илловая кислота** cascarillic acid; **—ин** *m.* cascarin.

Касла фактор (physiol.) Castle's factor.

касп/ийский *a.* (geog.) Caspian; **—иосома** *f.* (ichth.) Caspian goby (*Caspiosoma* or *Neogobius caspius*).

касс *m.* (wines) casse, browning.

касса *f.* cash (box), money drawer, cash register; (typ.) case; (savings) bank; (ticket) booth; (rr.) booking office.

кассава *f.* cassava, manioc starch; (herp.) Bitis gabonica.

кассандра *f.* (bot.) Chamaedaphne.

кассансайский *a.* (geog.) Kassansai.

кассац/ионный *a.,* **—ия** *f.* (law) cassation.

кассегреновский *a.* (astr.) Cassegrain(ian).

кассельский *a.* Cassel (pigment).

кассет/а *f.* adapter, holder; cell; (phot.) film holder, plate holder, cartridge, casette, magazine; **—ка** *dim. of* **кассета; —ный** *a. of* **кассета; —ное производство** (concrete) multicell battery molding.

кассиды *pl.* (mal.) Cassididae.

кассиев пурпур Cassius' purple, gold-tin purple; **—ый** *a.* Cassia (oil).

кассики *pl.* (orn.) troupial family (*Icteridae*).

Кассиопея *f.* (astr.) Cassiopeia.

кассиопий *m.* cassiopeium (lutecium).

кассир *m.* cashier; **—овать** *v.* annul, reverse, void; collect (coins).

кассис *m.* (mal.) helmet shell (*Cassis*).

касситерит *m.* (min.) cassiterite.

кассия *f.* (bot.) cassia; **стручковая к.** purging cassia (*Cassia fistula*).

касский *a.* (geog.) Kas.

кассов/ый *a. of* **касса;** account (book); point-of-sale (terminal); **к. аппарат** cash register; **—ая наличность** cash (money).

кассореал *m.* (typ.) cabinet, case rack.

каста *f.* (ent.) caste.

кастанит *m.* (min.) castanite.

кастеламарин *m.* castelamarin.

кастильский *a.* (geog.) Castille.

кастовый *a. of* **каста.**

кастор *m.* (min.) castorite, petalite; (text.) castor; **—ка** *f.,* **—овое масло** castor oil; **—овокислая соль** castorate; **—овый** *a.* castor; castoric (acid).

кастр/ат *m.* castrate, gelding; **бычок-к.** castrated bull calf; **—ация** *f.* castration; **—ированный** *a.* castrated; **—ировать** *v.* castrate, geld, emasculate.

кастрюля *f.* pot, kettle, pan.

кат *m.* (naut.) cat.

ката *f.* (bot.) khat (*Catha edulis*).

ката— *prefix* cata—, cath—, kata—, kath— [down(ward), away; against, in accordance with; very, completely]; **—батический** *a.* (meteor.) catabatic; **—биотический** *a.* (biol.) catabiotic; **—болизм** *m.* catabolism, destructive metabolism; **—болический** *a.* catabolic.

катавлак *m.* (hort.) layer.

катавотр *m.* (geol.) swallow hole, sink hole.

ката/генез *m.* (biol.) catagenesis, retrogressive evolution; **—диоптрика** *f.* (phys.) catadioptrics; **—диоптрический** *a.* catadioptric; **—дромный** *a.* (biol.) catadromous (migration); **—клаз** *m.* (geol.) cataclasis; **—клазированный** *a.* broken down; **—кластический** *a.* cataclastic.

катакомбы *pl.* catacombs.

катaлаз/a *f.* catalase (oxidizing enzyme); **—ник** *m.* catalase tester; **—ометр** *m.* catalasometer.

каталанский *see* **каталонский.**

каталеп/сия *f.* (med.) catalepsy; **—тик** *m.,* **—тический** *a.* cataleptic.

катализ *m.* catalysis; **—ат** *m.* catalyzate, product of catalysis; **—атор** *m.* catalyzer, catalyst, catalytic agent; accelerator; **—аторный** *a.* catalytic; **—аторный яд** anticatalyst; **—ировать** *v.* catalyze, act as a catalyst (for).

каталинета *f.* porkfish (*Anisotremus virginicus*).

каталитическ/и *adv.* catalytically, by catalysis; **—ий** *a.* catalytic; **—ий яд** anticatalyst.

каталка *f.* (glass) marver (plate).

катало/г *m.* catalog; index; directory; **—гизационный** *a.,* **—гизация** *f.* cataloging, classifying; **—гизировать** *v.* catalog, classify; **—жная** *f.* catalog room; **—жный** *a. of* **каталог.**

каталонский *a.* (geog.) Catal(oni)an.

каталуф/a *f.* (ichth.) bigeye (*Priacanthus*); **—овые** *pl.* Priacanthidae; Pempheridae.

каталь *m.* wheelbarrow operator.

катальпа *f.* (bot.) catalpa.

катальщик *m.* roller; (clothes) mangler.

катамаран *m.* (naut.) catamaran.

катаморф/изм *m.* (geol.) katamorphism; **—ный** *a.* katamorphic.

катангский *a.* (geog.) Katanga.

катан/ие *n.* rolling, etc., *see* **катать; —ка** *f.* wire rod; **—ки** *pl.* felt boots; **—(н)ый** *a.* rolled, etc., *see* **катать; —ье** *see* **катание.**

ката/плазма *f.* (med.; phyt.) cataplasm; **—плеит** *m.* (min.) catapleite; **—плектический** *a.* (med.) cataplectic.

катапульт/a *f.* catapult; **—ирование** *n.* catapulting (of plane); ejection; **—ировать** *v.* catapult; eject; **—ируемый** *a.* ejection (capsule; seat); **—ный** *a.* catapult; ejection-seat.

катар *m.* (med.) catarrh; **к. влагалища** vaginitis; **к. желудка** catarrhal gastritis.

катаракт *m.,* **—ный** *a.* cataract, waterfall; cataract (hydraulic brake); shock absorber, dashpot; **—a** *f.* (med.) cataract.

катаральный *a.* (med.) catarrhal.

катарометр *m.* (phys.) katharometer; **к. с нитями** hot-wire cell.

катарр *see* **катар.**

катарский *a.* (geog.) Qatar, Katar.

катарт/ин *m.* cathartin; **—ический** *a.,* **—ическое средство** cathartic.

катаскопиевые *pl.* (bot.) Catascopiaceae.

катастроф/a *f.* catastrophe, disaster; fatal accident; (av.) crash; emergency; **—ический, —ичный** *a.* catastrophic, disastrous.

кататерм/ический *a.* (met.) catathermic; **—ометр** *m.* catathermometer.

кататон/ический *a.* (med.) catatonic; **—ия** *f.* catatonia.

катать *v.* roll; (text.) mangle; wheel, convey, drive; **—ся** *v.* roll, ride.

катафорез *m.* cataphoresis.

катафот *m.* (opt.) cat's eye.

катаянский *a.* (geog.) Cathayan.

кат-балка *f.* (naut.) cat davit.

кат/гемоглобин *m.* cathemoglobin; **—гин** *m.* cathine.

категор/ический *a.* categorical; **—ия** *f.* category, class, rank.

катекс *m.* cation-exchange resin.

кáтен/a *f.* (soils) catena, row, series, **—арный** *a.* (math.) catenary; **—оид** *m.* catenoid.

катепсин *m.* cathepsin (enzyme).

катер *m.* boat, craft, cutter, launch; **—остроение** *n.* boat building; **к.-толкач** *m.* push boat; **к.-торпедолов** *m.* torpedo recovery boat; **к.-тральщик** *m.* minesweeping boat; **к.-цель** *m.* target boat.

катет *m.* (geom.) leg (of right triangle).

катетер *m.* (med.) catheter; **—изировать** *v.* catheterize.

катеометр *m.* (phys.) cathetometer.

катех/ин *m.,* **—иновая кислота** catechin, catechuic acid; **—оламин** *m.* catecholamine; **—у** *n.* catechu.

катинга *see* **каатинга.**

катион *m.* cation, basic ion; **—активный** *a.* cation-active, cationic; **—(из)ирование** *n.* cation-exchange treatment (of water); **—(из)ировать** *v.* cationize, treat with cationite; **—ит** *m.* cation exchanger, cation-exchange resin; **—ный** *a.* cation(ic); **—оактивный** *a.* cation-active; **—ообменник** *m.* cation exchanger; **—ообменный** *a.* cation-exchange; **—отропия** *f.* cationotropy.

кат/ить *v.* roll, wheel; **—иться** *v.* roll; slide, move; flow, run, sweep along; **—ище** *n.* cold deck (of stacked logs); **—ка** *gen. of* **каток; —кование** *n.* rolling, packing (of soil).

катл/a, —я *f.* (ichth.) Catla.

катоген/ический, —ный *a.* (geol.) katogene, catogene, catogenic.

катод *m.* cathode, negative electrode; **—замыкательное сокращение** (physiol.) cathodal closure contraction, CCC; **—ический** *see* **катодный; —нолучевой** *a.* cathode-ray (tube); **—ный** *a.* cathode, cathodic; **—ное покрытие** cathodic coating; **—ные лучи** cathode rays; **—олюминесценция** *f.* cathodoluminescence; **—размыкательное сокращение** (physiol.) cathodal opening contraction, COC.

каток *m.* roll, cylinder; mangle; (road) roller; wheel, runner; truck; skating rink; **к.-глыбодроб** *m.* (agr.) clod crusher; **к.-снегоуплотнитель** *m.* snow compactor; **к.-тандем** *m.* tandem roller; **—уплотнитель** *m.* (soil) packer, compactor.

католит *m.* (electrolysis) catholyte.

катоптри/ка *f.* (opt.) catoptrics; **—т** *m.* (min.) catoptrite; **—ческий** *a.* catoptric.

катор/га *f.* penal servitude, hard labor; **—жник** *m.* convict; **—жный** *a. of* **каторга;** back-breaking (work).

катофорит *m.* (min.) katophorite.

каточек *dim. of* **каток;** roll(er); wheel.

катран *m.* (bot.) Crambe; (ichth.) spiny dogfish (*Squalus acanthias*); **—овые** *pl.* Squalidae.

катринский *a.* (geog.) Katra.

катта *f.* (mam.) ring-tailed lemur (*Lemur catta*).

кат-тали *pl.* (naut.) cat tackle.

каттиерит *m.* (min.) cattierite.

катун *m.* (bot.) Russian thistle, tumbleweed (*Salsola collina*).

катунский *a.* (geog.) Katun.

катучий *a.* rolling; traveling (crane).

катуш/ечный *a. of* **катушка;** trochlear(iform), pulley-shaped; —**ка** *f.* spool, bobbin, reel, roll; (elec.) coil; (mal.) Planorbis; —**ка-мультипликатор** *f.* geared reel; —**ки** *pl.* (mal.) Planorbidae; —**овидный** *a.* trochlear(iform); —**кодержатель** *m.* coil holder.

катыш, —ек, —ок *m.* pellet.

катэлектронический *a.* catelectronic.

катюша *f.* (mil.) katusha (rocket gun).

катящийся *a.* rolling; roller (contact).

каудальный *a.* caudal, tail.

каузальный *a.* causal.

каул— *see* **кауло—**; —**ерпа** *f.* (bot.) Caulerpa; —**ифлория** *f.* cauliflory; —**ифлорный** *a.* cauliflorous; —**о—** *prefix* caul(o)—, stem; —**офиллин** *m.* caulophyllin; caulophylline (alkaloid); —**офриновые** *pl.* (ichth.) Caulophrynidae.

Каульсья печь (met.) Cowles furnace.

каунасский *a.* (geog.) Kaunas; Kovno.

каупер *m.* (met.) Cowper hot-blast stove.

каури *n.* or *m.* kauri (gum).

каурый *a.* light chestnut (color).

каусти/затор *m.* (paper) causticizer, causticizing tank; —**зация, —фикация** *f.,* —**цирование** *n.* causticization, causticizing; —**к** *m.* caustic (soda); —**ка** *f.* caustic; *suffix* (med.) —cautery; —**фикатор** *m.* causticizer; —**цировать** *v.* causticize; —**ческий** *a.* caustic; —**чность** *f.* causticity.

каустобиол/ит *m.* (geol.) caustobiolith; —**огия** *f.* biology of combustible fossils.

каутер *m.* (med.) cautery (instrument); —**изировать** *v.* cauterize.

каучин *m.* caoutchene (dipentene).

каучук *m.* caoutchouc, rubber; —**оводство** *n.,* —**оводческий** *a.* rubber-growing; —**овый** *a.* rubber; —**овый сок, —овое молоко** rubber latex; —**овая замазка** rubber cement; —**оген** *m.* caoutchogen (monomer).

каучуконос *m.* (bot.) rubber(-yielding) plant; —**ность** *f.* rubber content; —**ный** *a.* rubber-bearing; rubber (tree).

каучуко/образный, —подобный *a.* rubbery, rubber-like, gum-like, gummy; —**образующий** *a.* rubber-forming.

каучук-сырец *m.* crude rubber.

кафедра *f.* lecture stand, rostrum; (educ.) chair; department, faculty.

кафель *m.,* —**ный** *a.* ceramic tile; —**никовые** *pl.* tile-fishes (*Branchiostegidae*).

кафетерий *m.* cafeteria.

кафрский *a.* (geog.) Kaf(f)ir.

каффеин *see* **кофеин.**

кахау *m.* (mam.) proboscis monkey (*Nasalis larvatus*).

кахек/сия *f.* cachexia, general ill health; —**тический** *a.* cachectic.

кахель *see* **кафель.**

кахетинский *a.* (geog.) Kakhetin.

кахи *m.* (ichth.) schoolmaster (*Lutjanus*).

каховский *a.* (geog.) Kakhovka.

кахрис *m.* (bot.) Cachrys.

кахский *a.* (geog.) Kakhi.

кацецица *f.* (eng.) Cacoecia.

кач. *abbr.* (**качественный**).

кач/алка *f.* rocker, rocking bar; rotating shaker; (ichth.) mackerel (in autumn); —**ание** *n.* rocking, oscillation, etc., *see v.*; (electron.) wobble; —**ательно-сочленённый** *a.* hinged; —**ательный** *see* **качающийся;** —**ать** *v.* rock, swing, sway, shake, oscillate, vibrate, agitate; pump; —**аться** *v.* rock, swing, sway; whip (of crane boom); oscillate, fluctuate; shake, wobble; vibrate; sway, reel, stagger; (naut.) lurch, roll.

качающ/ийся *a.* rocking, swinging, pendulum, oscillat-ing, oscillatory; pivot(ing), swivel(ing), free-swinging; rocking-horse (scanner); vibrating, vibratory; jigging, shaking; tipping, tilting; fluctuating; versatile; (med.) staggering (gait); —**аяся рамка** rocker.

кач-во *abbr.* (**качество**).

каче/ли *pl.,* —**ль** *f.* swing; —**ние** *n.* rolling (motion); **гайка —ния** rolling nut.

качеств/енность *f.* high quality; —**енный** *a.* (high)-quality, high-grade, high-performance, fine; qualitative (analysis); —**о** *n.* quality, grade, fineness; performance; character(istic), property, nature; **в —е** in the capacity (of), (serving) as; **высшего —а** top-quality, of highest quality.

качея *f.* sea sickness.

качим *m.* (bot.) Gypsophila.

качинский *a.* (geog.) Kachin; Kacha.

качка *see* **качание;** rolling, pitching; looseness, free play; (honey) extraction; **боковая к., бортовая к.** rolling (motion); **продольная к.** pitching (motion).

качкавал *m.* kachkaval (sheep cheese).

качкар *m.* (mam.) Marco Polo's argali (*Ovis ammon polii*).

кач/кий *a.* (naut.) unstable; —**нуть** *see* **качать;** start swinging.

качурк/а *f.* (orn.) storm petrel (*Hydrobates*); —**и, —овые** *pl.* Hydrobatidae.

каша *f.* cereal, gruel, mash; paste, pulp; (pharm.) magma; **снеговая к.** slush.

кашалот *m.* (mam.) sperm whale (*Physeter catodon*); —**овая ворвань** spermaceti oil; —**овые** *pl.* Physeteridae.

кашгарский *a.* (geog.) Kashgar.

каше *see* **кашэ.**

кашевар *m.,* —**ить** *v.* (mil.) cook.

кашель *m.* cough.

кашемир *m.,* —**овый** *a.* (text.) cashmere.

кашеобразный *a.* pasty, viscous.

каширов/альный *a.,* —**ание** *n.* vignetting, etc., *see v.*; —**ать** *v.* (phot.) vignette, mask; (books) back; paste, laminate.

каширский *a.* (geog.) Kashira.

каширующий *a.* vignetting, etc., *see* **кашировать.**

кашиц/а *f.* gruel; paste, viscous mass, slurry; (paper) pulp; (pharm.) electuary, confection, magma; **пищевая к.** (physiol.) chyme; —**еобразный** *a.* pulpy, pasty.

кашка *dim. of* **каша;** (bot.) clover.

кашкадарьинский *a.* (geog.) Kashkadarya.

кашкар/а *f.,* —**ник** *m.* (bot.) Rhododendron chrysanthemum.

кашл/евый *a.* cough, tussal, tussive; —**я** *gen. of* **кашель;** —**яние** *n.* cough(ing); —**я(ну)ть** *v.* cough.

кашмирет *m.* (text.) cashmere twill.

кашмирский *a.* (geog.) Kashmirian.

кашник *m.* (ichth.) round goby (*Neogobius melanostomus*).

каштан *m.* (bot.) chestnut (*Castanea*); (vet.) chestnut, callosity; —**ник** *m.* chestnut grove; (bot.) Castanopsis; —**овобурый** *a.* chestnut (brown) —**овый** *a.* chestnut; chestnut brown, nut brown.

кашу *see* **катеху.**

кашэ *n.* (phot.) vignette, mask; matte.

каюр *m.,* —**ка** *f.,* —**ок** *m.* dog-team driver; (orn.) pigeon guillemot (*Cepphus columba*); —**ка** *f.* (ichth.) jack (young-spawning salmon).

кают/а *f.,* —**ный** *a.* cabin, stateroom; -**компания** *f.* messroom, dining room.

каяз *m.* (ichth.) Aral barbel (*Barbus*).

каяк *m.* (naut.) kayak.

каян *m.* (bot.) Cajanus.

каяпут/ен *m.* cajeputene, limonene; **—ное масло, —овое масло** cajeput oil.

кб *abbr.* (**кабельтов**) cable length; **кб.** *abbr.* (**кубический**) cubic(al).

КБВ, к.б.в. *abbr.* (**коэффициент бегущей волны**) traveling-wave ratio.

кбт *see* **кб.**

кв *abbr.* (**киловольт**) kilovolt; (**квант**) quantum; **кв.** *abbr.* [**квадрат(ный)**] square; (**квартал**) quarter; **к.В.** *abbr.* (**камера Вильсона**) Wilson cloud chamber; **КВ** *abbr.* (**коротковолновый**) short-wave; (**короткие волны**) short waves; (**коэффициент воспроизводства**) reproduction factor, conversion ratio; **ква** *abbr.* (**киловольтампер**) kilovolt-ampere.

квагга *f.* (mam.) quagga (*Equus quagga*).

квадр *m.* cut stone.

квадрант *m.,* **—ный** *a.* (math.) quadrant; (hydr.) single-vane motor, rotary ram.

квадрат *m.* square; box, block; **возводить в к., возвышать в к.** *v.* (math.) square; **метр в —е** square meter; **обработка на к.** squaring; **—ически** *adv.* quadratically, to the second power; **—ический, —ичный** *a.* quadratic, square; square-law (capacitor); standard (deviation); **среднее —ичное** root-mean-square, RMS; **—ично-косекансный** *a.* cosecant-squared; **—но-гнездовой** *a.* square-cluster (planting); **—ичность** *f.* (electron.) square-law characteristic; **—носкуловая кость, —ночелюстная кость, —нояремная кость** (anat.) quadratomaxillary, quadratojugal; **—ность** *f.* squareness.

квадратн/ый *a.* square, quadratic; (cryst.) tetragonal; square-law; square-bar (iron); quadrate (muscle); **к. корень** (math.) square root; **к. режим** turbulent flow; **—ая кость** (anat.) quadrate; **—ое содержание** area; **—ое среднее** root mean square; **—ое уравнение** quadratic equation; **—ое число** square (number).

квадрат/ор *m.* (comp.) square-law generator, squarer; **—рикса** *f.* (math.) quadratrix; **—ура** *f.,* **—урный** *a.* quadrature, squaring; square (area); (ocean.) neap (tide); **—урный прилив** neap tide.

квадри— *prefix* quadri— four(fold) quadric; **—ка** *f.* (math.) quadric; **—ллион** *m.* quadrillion (10^{15} in USA, France and Russia; 10^{24} in Great Britain and Germany); **—плегия** *f.* (med.) quadriplegia; **—цепс** *m.* (anat.) quadriceps.

квадру/плет *m.* (nucl.) quadruplet; quartet; **—поль** *m.,* **—польный** *a.* quadrupole.

квазар *m.* (astr.) quasar.

квази— *prefix* quasi— (as if, seemingly); **—аналитический** *a.* quasi-analytic; **—звёздный** *a.* quasi-sidereal; **—импульс** *m.* quasi-momentum; **—климакс** *m.* (geobot.) quasi-climax; **—комплексный** *a.* quasi-complex; **—линейный** *a.* quasilinear; **—нейтральный** *a.* (phys.) quasineutral; **—обратный** *a.* quasi-inverse; **—однородный** *a.* quasi-homogeneous; **—периодический** *a.* (math.) quasiperiodic; **—поле** *n.* quasifield.

квази/равновесный *a.* quasi-equilibrium; **—равномерный** *a.* quasi-uniform; **—размах** *m.* (math.) semi-range; **—связанный** *a.* quasibound; **—статический** *a.* quasistatic, quasistationary; **—стационарный** *a.* quasistationary, quasistable, quasisteady; **—упругий** *a.* quasielastic; **—уровень** *m.* quasilevel; **—частица** *f.* quasiparticle; **—эргодический** *a.* (math.) quasi-ergodic; **—эруптивный** *a.* quasi-eruptive.

квак/анье *n.* croaking; **—ать** *v.* croak; **—ва** *f.* (orn.) night heron (*Nycticorax*).

квакерский *a.* Quaker.

квак/нуть *v.* croak; **—ша** *f.* tree frog (*Hyla arborea*); **—ши** *pl.* Hylidae.

квалиметр *m.* qualimeter (for X-rays).

квалифи/кационный *a.* qualification, qualifying, evaluating, classifying; **—кация** *f.* qualification(s), skill, proficiency, expertise; rating, grading; **—цированный** *a.* qualified, etc., *see v.*; skilled (labor); **—цировать** *v.* qualify; test, grade; **—цирующий** *a.* qualifying, etc., *see v.*; acceptance (number).

квант *m.,* **—а** *f.* (phys.) quantum; **к./** *abbr.* (**квантов на**) quanta per; **к. действия** Planck's constant; **к. света** photon; **теория —ов** quantum theory; **—ика** *f.* (math.) quantic; **—иль** *m.* (math.) quantile; **—ификация** *f.,* **—ифицирование** *n.* quantification; **—ировать** *v.* quantify; **—ование** *n.* quantization; **—ование времени** (comp.) time slicing; **—ованный** *a.* quantized; quantum; **—ователь** *m.* quantizer, digitizer; **—овать** *v.* quantize; **—овомеханический** *a.* quantum-mechanical; maser (amplifier); **—овохимический** *a.* quantum-chemical; **—овый** *a.* quantum; **—овый генератор света, оптический —овый генератор** laser; **—овая механика** quantum mechanics; **—ометр** *m.* (met.) quantometer; **—ор** *m.* (math.) quantifier; **навешивать —ор** *v.* quantify.

квар *abbr.* (**киловар**) kilovar.

кварта *f.* quart (unit of measure).

квартал *m.* quarter (of year); (city) block, section; district, area, region; (forestry) parcel, compartment; **—ьный** *a. of* **квартал;** quarterly.

квартер *m.* (geol.) Quaternary (era, etc.).

квартердек *m.* (naut.) quarterdeck.

квартиль *m.* (math., stat.) quartile.

квартир/а *f.,* **—ный** *a.* apartment, lodging, tenement, residence; **—анство** *n.* (biol.) commensalism, synoecy; **—ант** *m.* tenant, lodger; commensal, coenosite; **—ный вопрос** housing problem; **—овать** *v.* reside, take up residence, lodge, live; become commensalistic; **—охозяин** *m.* landlord.

кварто *n.* quarto; **стан к.** four-high rolling mill.

квартов/ание *n.* (gold and silver assay) (in)quartation; quartering (of bulk materials); **—ать** *v.* quarter.

квартплата *f.* (apartment) rent.

кварц *m.* (min.) quartz, silica; **натёчный к.** siliceous sinter, fiorite; **—евый** *a.* quartz(itic); quartzose (schist); crystal (oscillator); silica (glass).

кварц/едержатель *m.* crystal holder; **—еносный** *a.* (min.) quartziferous, quartzose; **—еподобный** *a.* quartzlike, quartz(itic); **—ин** *m.* (min.) quartzine; **—ит** *m.* quartzite, quartz rock; **—итовый** *a.* quartzitic, quartziferous, quartzose; **—ованный** *a.* (electron.) crystal-controlled; **—оидный** *a.* quartzoid, quartzose, quartzous, quartzy.

квас *m.* kvass (a fermented drink); **—ильный** *a.* fermentation; souring; leavening; **—ить** *v.* sour; leaven (dough); start fermentation; **—иться, —нуть** *v.* turn sour, ferment; **—ной** *a. of* **квас; —ный** *a.* sour; **—оварение** *n.* kvass brewing; **—ок** *dim. of* **квас;** acid taste.

квасс/иевая кислота quassic acid; **—ин** *m.* quassin; **—ия** *f.* quassia.

квасце/вание *n.* aluming, etc., *see v.*; **—вар** *m.* alum maker; **—варня** *f.* alum works; **—вать** *v.* alum, taw, tan with alum; (typ.) sensitize; **—носный** *a.* aluminous, aluminiferous; **—подобный** *a.* alum-like, aluminiform, aluminous.

квасцов/анный *a.* alumed, etc., *see* **квасцевать; —ать** *see* **квасцевать; —ик** *m.* (min.) aluminite, websterite; **—щик** *m.* alum tanner.

квасцов/ый *a.* alum, alumin(ifer)ous; **к. камень** (min.) alumstone, alunite; **к. сланец** (geol.) alum shale; **—ая земля** alumina, aluminum oxide; **—ая мука** alum powder; alum, aluminum potassium sulfate;

квасцы *pl.* alum; **жжёные к.** burnt alum, calcined aluminum potassium sulfate; **калиевые к., кубические к., нейтральные к., обыкновенные к.** potash alum; **натриевые к.** soda alum; **перистые к.** (min.) feather alum, alunogen; **римские к.** Roman alum (aluminum iron sulfate).

квасы *pl. of* квас; tanner's ooze.

кватернион *m.* (math.) quaternion.

квахтанье *n.* clucking.

квач *m.* swab.

ква-ч *abbr.* (**киловольт-ампер-час**) kilo-volt-ampere-hour.

кваш/а *f.* leaven, leavened dough; **—ение** *n.* fermentation; souring, pickling; leavening; **—ен(н)ый** *a.* fermented; leavened; sour, acid; **—еная капуста** sauerkraut; **—ня** *f.* kneading trough.

КВД *abbr.* (**котёл высокого давления**) high-pressure boiler; (**кремний в диэлектрике**) silicon-in-insulator, SII.

кв. дм *abbr.* (**квадратный дециметр**) square decimeter; **кв. дм.** *abbr.* (**квадратный дюйм**) square inch.

Квебек Quebec.

квебрах/амин *m.* quebrachamine; **—ин** *m.* quebrachine; **—ит** *m.* quebrachite, quebrachitol, methoxypinite; **—о** *n.* (bot.) quebracho (*Aspidosperma*).

квезал(ь) *m.* (orn.) quetzal (*Pharomachrus mocino*).

квенс/елит *m.* (min.) quenselite; **—тедтит** *m.* quenstedtite, copiapite.

кверия *f.* (bot.) Queria.

кверху *adv.* up(wards).

кверц/етагетин *m.* quercetagetin; **—етин** *m.* quercetin; **—итрин** *m.* quercitrin; **—ит** *m.* quercitol, acorn sugar; **—итрин** *m.* quercitrin; **—итрон** *m.* quercitron (bark).

кве́ршлаг *m.* (min.) crosscut, cross-entry.

квеста *f.* cuesta (sloping plain or ridge).

кветенит *m.* (min.) quetenite.

Квика проба (med.) Quick's test.

квил/(л)аивая кислота quillaic acid; **—лая** *f.* quillaia, soap bark.

квинкви— *prefix* quinqui—, quinque— (five); **—льон** *m.* quinquillion.

Квинке отёк (med.) Quincke's edema.

квин/оа, —оя *f.* (bot.) quinoa (*Chenopodium quinoa*).

квинс/лендский *a.* (geog.) Queensland; **—тоунит** *m.* (min.) queenstownite.

квинт— *prefix* quint(i)— (fifth; *incorrectly used for* five); **—ал** *m.* quintal (100 kg.); **—ет** *m.* (PMR spectrum) quintet; **—иллион, —ильон** *m.* quintillion (10^{18} in USA, Russia and France; 10^{30} in Great Britain and Germany); **—иль** *m.* (stat.) quintile; **—иплет** *m.* quintet; **—иплетен** *m.* (EPR spectrum) quintuplet; **—уплекс** *m.* quintuplex; **—эссенция** *f.* quintessence.

квирильский *a.* (geog.) Kvirila.

квисквеит *m.* (min.) quisqueite.

квит *m.* (bot.) quince (*Cydonia*).

квит/анция *f.* receipt, acknowledgment; **давать —анцию** *v.* (rad.) sign off; **—ирование** *n.* acknowledgment of receipt; (remote-control) signal confirmation; **—ирование установления связи** handshaking.

квиток *m.* receipt.

кв. км *abbr.* (**квадратный километр**) square kilometer; **кв. м** *abbr.* (**квадратный метр**) square meter; **кв. мм** *abbr.* (**квадратный миллиметр**) square millimeter.

к-во *abbr.* (**количество**) quantity.

квокка *f.* (mam.) quokka (*Setonix brachyurus*).

кволл *m.* (mam.) tiger cat (*Dasyurops viverrinus*).

кворум *m.* quorum.

квота *f.* quota, allotment, allowance.

квохтать *v.* cluck, cackle.

КВС *abbr.* (**кремний в сапфире**) silicon-in-sapphire, SIS.

кв. см *abbr.* (**квадратный сантиметр**) square centimeter.

квт *abbr.* (**киловатт**) kilowatt; **квт-с** *abbr.* (**киловатт-секунда**) kilowatt-second; **квт-ч** *abbr.* (**киловатт-час**) kilowatt-hour.

КВУ *abbr.* (**контрольно-выпрямительное устройство**) monitoring rectifier.

кв. фт. *abbr.* (**квадратный фут**) square foot.

квч, кв'ч, кв-ч *see* квт-ч.

Квэ *abbr.* (**квебраховый экстракт**) quebracho extract.

кг *abbr.* (**килограмм**) kilogram; **кт/** *abbr.* (**килограмм на**) kilograms per; **кГ, к-Г** *abbr.* (**килограмм-сила**) kilogram-force, shear strength, kgf; **к/г** *abbr.* (**кулон на грамм**) coulomb per gram; **кГм, кГ-м, кгм** *abbr.* (**килограмм-метр**) kilogrammeter; **кг-моль** *abbr.* (**килограмм-молекула**) kilogram-molecule.

к-гн *abbr.* (**килогенри**) kilohenry.

кгс *see* кГ; **кгс, к-гс** *abbr.* (**килогаусс**) kilogauss.

кгц *abbr.* (**килогерц**) kilohertz, kilocycles per second, kilocycle.

КД *abbr.* (**кровяное давление**) blood pressure; **кД** *abbr.* (**коэффициент дубности**) tanning index.

кдж *abbr.* (**килоджоуль**) kilojoule.

кдин *abbr.* (**килодина**) kilodyne.

КДР *abbr.* (**командно-диспетчерский пункт**) air-traffic control tower, ATC; (**кодовое реле**) code relay.

кеа *m.* (orn.) kea (*Nestor notabilis*).

кебир *m.* kebir, kevir (salt-clay desert).

кебот/а, —ов Cabot's.

кебрачо *see* квебрахо.

кевеенавит *m.* (min.) keweenawite.

кев/ир *see* кебир; **—овое дерево** turpentine tree (*Pistacia mutica*).

кегель *see* кегль; **—машина** *f.* batch roller; **—ная** *f.* (typ.) em.

кег/ельный *a. of* кегля; **—левидный, —леобразный** *a.* turbinate, top-shaped.

кегль *m.* type size, type body; point.

кегля *f.* skittle, pin; *gen. of* кегль.

к.ед. *abbr.* (**кормовая единица**) feed unit; **КЕД, кед** *abbr.* (**кошачья единица действия**) cat unit; (**крысиная единица действия**) rat unit.

кедани *m.* (med.) Japanese river fever.

кедр *m.* (bot.) cedar (*Cedrus*); **—ач** *see* кедровник; **—овка** *f.* (orn.) nutcracker (*Nucifraga, spec. N. caryocatactes*); **—овник** *m.* cedar grove; stone-pine forest; **—овый** *a.* cedar; **—овая сосна** cedar; **—овые орехи** pine kernels.

кежемский *a.* (geog.) Kezhma.

кейльгауит *m.* (min.) keilhauite.

Кейна бассейн (geog.) Kane Basin.

кейп — *prefix* (geog.) Cape.

кейпер *m.* (geol.) Keuper, Upper Triassic.

Кейптаун *m.* (geog.) Capetown.

кек *m.* (filter) cake; paste, sludge; **шламовый к.** concentrated sludge.

кеке масло cay-cay butter.

кеклик *m.* (orn.) rock partridge (*Alectoris graeca*).

кекс *m.* cake.

кекур *m.* kekur (bank of gravel pushed ashore by river ice; in Siberia, conical rocks on a sea coast).

келейный *a.* of **келья.**

келерия *f.* (bot.) Koeleria.

келесский *a.* (geog.) Keles.

келифит *m.* (min.) kelyphite, corona; **—овый** *a.* kelyphitic.

келликерова ямка (zool.) Kölliker's pit.

келлин *m.* kellin (glucoside); kelline (alkaloid); (paints) Kellin; (pharm.) khellin.

келловейский *a.* (geol.) Callovian (stage).

келоид *m.* (med.) keloid.

кельбаджарский *a.* (geog.) Kelbadzhar.

кельвин *m.* (phys.) kelvin, K.

Кельвина шкала Kelvin scale.

Кельдаля колба Kjeldahl flask.

кельма *f.* trowel.

кельнск/ий *a.* Cologne; **—ая вода** eau de Cologne; **—ая земля, —ая умбра** Cologne brown, van Dyke brown.

кельня *f.* trowel.

кельп *m.* (bot.) kelp.

кельпиния *f.* (bot.) Koelpinia.

кельтий *m. obs.* celtium (hafnium, Hf).

кельтменский *a.* (geog.) Keltma.

кельтский *a.* Celtic (race, etc.).

кельш *m.* (ichth.) Volga zander (*Stizostedion volgense*); Lucioperca volgensis.

келья *f.* cell.

кем *instr. of* **кто,** by whom.

кембриджский *a.* Cambridge.

кембрий *m., —ский период* (geol.) Cambrian period.

кембрик *m., —овый a.* (text.) cambric.

кемеровский *a.* (geog.) Kemerovo.

кемигам *m.* Chemigum (synthetic rubber).

кеммерерит *m.* (min.) Kämmererite.

кемпа берег Kemp Coast.

Кемпбелля формула (elec.) Campbell's formula.

кемпендяйский *a.* (geog.) Kempendyai.

кемпферол *m.* kaempferol.

кемпинг *m.* campsite.

кем/ский *a.* (geog.) Kem; **—чикский** *a.* Khemchik; **—чугский** *a.* Kemchug.

кенайский *a.* (geog.) Kenai.

кенаф *m.* (bot.) ambary hemp (*Hibiscus cannabinus*).

кенгур/ёнок *m.* (mam.) young kangaroo; **—овые** *pl.* Macropodidae; **—овый a., —у** *m.* kangaroo.

кендырь *m.* (bot.) dogbane (*Apocynum*); Trachomitum.

кенения *f.* (arachnology) Koenenia.

кенийский *a.* (geog.) Kenya(n).

Кенли тигельная печь Canley furnace.

кеннел/евый *a., —ь m., —ьский a.* cannel coal; **—ь-богхед** *m.* cannel-boghead.

кено/токсин *m.* kenotoxin, fatigue toxin; **—трон** *m.* (electron.) kenotron, vacuum-tube rectifier.

кенталленит *m.* (petr.) kentallenite.

кентролит *m.* (min.) kentrolite.

кентукийский *a.* (geog.) Kentucky.

кеньга *f.* kink (in rope or cable).

к.е.о., КЕО *abbr.* (**коэффициент естественной освещённости**) daylight factor.

кеплеровский *a.* Keplerian, Kepler's.

кепрок *m.* (geol.) caprock.

керазин *m.* kerasin (a cerebroside); (min.) phosgenite.

керам/ет *see* **кермет; —зит** *m.* (concrete) claydite (clay filler); **—зитобетон** *m.* claydite-concrete (lightweight aggregate concrete); **—ика** *f.* ceramics; earthenware; ceramic clay; **—иковый, —ический** *a.* ceramic, earthenware; stoneware; **—иковые изделия** pottery, earthenware; **—огалит** *m.* (min.) keramohalite.

керангас *m.* (geobot.) kerangas.

кераргирит *m.* (min.) cerargyrite, horn silver.

кератин *m.* (zool.) keratin; **—изация** *f.* keratinization, horn-formation; **—изировать(ся)** *v.* keratinize; **—овый** *a.* keratin(ous), horny.

керат/ит *m.* (med.) keratitis; **—о—** *prefix* kerat(o)—, kera— (horn; cornea); **—оз** *m.* (med.) keratosis; **—ома** *f.* keratoma; **—опластика** *f.* keratoplasty, corneal grafting; **—осульфат** *m.* keratosulfate, keratan sulfate; **—офир** *m.* (petr.) keratophyre.

керацианин *m.* keracyanin (plant dyestuff).

кербинскии *a.* (geog.) Kerbi.

кербовка *f.* girdling (of trees).

кервель *m.* (bot.) chervil (*Anthriscus*).

кер/геленский *a.* (geog.) Kerguelen; **—етьозерский** *a.* Lake Keret; **—женцевый** *a.* Kerzhenets.

керит *m.* (elec.) kerite (insulator).

кермезит *m.* kermesite, kermes mineral.

кермек *m.* (bot.) Statice; Limonium.

кермес *m.* kermes (dye); kermes insect; kermes berries; kermes mineral.

кермет *m.* cer(a)met, metal-ceramic.

керн *m.* core, core sample; center, pivot; nucleus; punch hole; base (of tube); **отливать с —ом** *v.* (foundry) hollow cast; **—ер** *m.* (center) punch.

кернит *m.* (min.) kernite, rasorite.

кернить *v.* center-punch, center-mark.

керно *n.* prick punch; indentation, mark, prick; **—вать** *v.* punch, prick.

керно/вый *a.* of **керн; —кол** *m.* (min.) core splitter; **—подъёмник, —рватель** *m.* core extractor, core lifter.

керн-пункт *m.* (topography) epipole; **к.-функция** *f.* (math.) kernel function.

керогаз *m.* pressurized-kerosene stove.

кероген *m.* (geol.) kerogen.

керонафт *m.* naphthalene-kerosene solution.

керосин *m., —ный, —овый a.* kerosene; **—ка** *f.* kerosene stove, oil burner; **—овый завод** oil refinery; **—озаправщик** *m.* kerosene fueler; **—орез** *m.* oxykerosene torch.

Керра затвор (phot.) Kerr cell.

керсантит *m.* (min.) kersantite.

керсутит *m.* (min.) kaersutite.

Кертиса диск Curtis disk.

керчак *m.* (ichth.) sculpin (*Myoxocephalus*); **—овые** *pl.* Cottidae; **—оподобные** *pl.* Myoxocephalinae.

керченит *m.* (min.) kertschenite.

керченский *a.* (geog.) Kerch.

кесар/ев разрез, —ево сечение, —ское сечение (med.) Caesarean section.

кесслеровский *a.* Kessler.

кессон *m., —ный a.* caisson; cofferdam; torsion box or cell; port (of open hearth furnace); **—ная болезнь** caisson disease, the bends; **—щик** *m.* caisson worker.

кета *f.* (ichth.) keta, chum salmon (*Oncorhynchus keta*).

кет/азин *m.* ketazin; ketazine, bisazimethylene; **—аль** *m.* ketal.

кетгут *m., —овый a.* catgut.

кетем/енский, —инский *a.* (geog.) Ketema.

кет/ен *m.* ketene; **—изация** *f.* ket(on)ization; **—имин** *m.* ket(on)imine; **—ипиновый** *a.* ketipic (acid).

кетлевать *v.* (text.) loop.

кетменский *a.* (geog.) Ketmen.

кетмень *m.* (agr.) Turkestan hoe.

кето– *prefix* ket(o)—, ketone; *see also under* **кетоно—; —альдегид** *m.* ketoaldehyde; **—амин** *m.* ketoamine.

кетовый *a.* of **кета.**

кето/гексоза *f.* ketohexose; **—генез** *m.* ketogenesis;

—**генный** *a.* ketogenic; —**глутаровый** *a.* ketoglutaric (acid); **-енольный** *see* **кето-энольный;** —**з** *m.* (med.) ketosis; —**за** *f.* ketose; —**кислота** *f.* keto(nic) acid, oxo acid; —**ксим** *m.* ketoxime, acetoxime; —**л(ь)** *m.* ketol, keto(ne) alcohol, oxo alcohol; —**масляный** *a.* ketobutyric (acid).

кетон *m.* ketone; —**изация** *f.* ketonization; —**ный,** —**овый** *a.* ketone, ketonic; —**оалкоголь** *see* **кетол(ь);** —**окислота** *see* **кетокислота;** —**оспирт** *see* **кетол(ь);** —**сахар** *m.* ketonic sugar; —**соединение** *n.* keto(nic) compound; —**урия** *f.* (med.) ketonuria.

кето/сахар *m.* ketose; —**спирт** *see* **кетол(ь);** —**форма** *f.* ketone form; **-энольный** *a.* keto-enol (tautomerism).

кетский *a.* (geog.) Ket.

кеттер/изация *f.* (books) cuttering; —**ский знак** Cutter number.

кефаелин *m.* cephaëline.

кефал— *prefix* cephal(o)— (head).

кефал/евые *pl.* (ichth.) Mugilidae; —**евый,** —**ий** *a. of* **кефаль.**

кефал/ин *m.,* —**иновый** *a.* cephalin, brain lipoid; —**ический** *a.* cephalic, head.

кефаль *f.* (ichth.) (gray) mullet (*Mugil*).

кефир *m.,* —**ный** *a.* kefir (fermented goat's milk); —**ные грибки,** —**ные зёрна** kefir yeast, kefir grains.

кеффек/елит, —**илит** *see* **кил.**

кеч *m.* (naut.) ketch (sailboat).

кечеге *m.* (ichth.) sterlet (*Acipenser ruthenus*).

кеш *see* **кэш.**

КЗ, к.з. *abbr.* (**короткое замыкание**) short circuit; **к.-з.** (**короткозамкнутый**) short-circuited; **к-з** (**колхоз**) kolkhoz.

кзади *adv.* to the rear, retro—; **смещение к.** retropulsion.

К-захват *m.* (electron.) K-capture.

КЗМ *abbr.* (**концентрированная эмульсия зелёного масла**) (agr.) 60–65% concentrate of green oil emulsion; **КЗМВ** 80% concentrate of green oil emulsion.

кзыл-кендырь, к.-курай *see* **кендырь.**

кзыл-ординский *a.* (geog.) Kzyl-Orda.

КИ *abbr.* (**кабелеискатель**) cable finder; (**кислородный ингалятор**) oxygen inhaler.

КИА *abbr.* (**контрольно испытательная аппаратура**) ground support equipment, GSE (for a spacecraft).

кианг *m.* (mam.) kiang (*Equus kiang*).

кианиз/ация *f.* (wood preservation) kyanization; —**(ир)овать** *v.* kyanize.

кианит *m.* kyanite, disthene.

киба/с, —**т** *m.* (fish net) weight, lead.

кибделофан *m.* (min.) kibdelophane, ilmenite.

кибернет/ика *f.* cybernetics; —**ический** *a.* cybernetic.

кив/ание *n.,* —**ательный** *a.* nodding.

киватин *m.* (geol.) Keewatin.

кивать *v.* nod, motion, point (to).

киви *m.* (orn.) kiwi (*Apteryx*); *pl.* Apterygidae.

кивинон *m.,* —**овый** *a.* (geol.) Keweenawan.

кив/нуть *see* **кивать;** —**ок** *m.* nod; tip (of fishing rod).

кивсяк *m.* (zool.) millipede; —**и** *pl.* Julidae.

КИВЦ *abbr.* (**Кустовой информационно-вычислительный центр**) Cluster Data Processing Center.

кигелия *f.* (bot.) Kigelia.

кигилях/и *pl.* kigilyakhi (pillared rocks of irregular shape on a slope); —**ский** *a.* (geog.) Kigilyakh.

КИД *abbr.* (**коэффициент ионной диффузии**) coefficient of ionic diffusion.

кид/ание *n.* throwing; abandoning; —**анный** *a.* thrown; abandoned, etc., *see* **кидать.**

кидас *m.* (mam.) sable-marten hybrid.

кид/ать *v.* throw, fling, cast, hurl; (naut.) toss; abandon, leave, drop, quit; —**аться** *v.* rush (at); fall on; —**ка** *f.* (text.) picking.

кидус *see* **кидас.**

киевский *a.* (geog.) Kiev.

Кижнера реакция Kishner reduction.

кижуч *m.* (ichth.) silver salmon (*Oncorhynchus kisutch*).

К-избыточное число (math.) *K*-nondeficient.

кизеловский *a.* (geog.) Kiezel.

кизельгель *m.* silica gel.

кизельгур *m.* (geol.) kieselguhr, diatomaceous earth, infusorial earth.

кизерит *m.* (min.) kieserite.

кизил *m.* (bot.) dogwood (*Cornus*); **к.-балык** *m.* (ichth.) taimen (*Hucho taimen*); Caspian salmon (*Salmo trutta caspius*); —**евый,** —**овый** *a. of* **кизил;** —**овые** *pl.* (bot.) Cornaceae; —**ь** *see* **кизил;** —**ьник** *m.* (bot.) Cotoneaster; dogwood thicket.

кизильский *a.* (geog.) Kizil.

кизирский *a.* (geog.) Kizir.

кизляк *m.* (bot.) Naumburgia.

кизляр/ка *f.* grape vodka; —**ский** *a.* (geog.) Kizlyar.

кизя/к *m.,* —**ковый,** —**чный** *a.* kizyak, dung-straw brick (for fuel or building).

киинский *a.* (geog.) Kiya.

кий *m.* cue.

кийский *see* **киинский.**

кика *f.* bow (of a ship).

кикстартер *m.* (motorcycle) kickstarter.

кил *m.* kill (a bleaching clay).

КИЛ *abbr.* (**контрольно-измерительная лаборатория**) control and measuring laboratory.

кила *f.* (phyt.) clubroot; (med.) hernia.

килев/ание *n.* careening (of boat); —**атость** *f.* dead rise; —**атый,** —**идный** *a.* (bot.) carinate, cariniform; —**ать** *v.* careen; —**ик** *m.* (ent.) Acanthosoma; —**ики** *pl.* shieldbugs (*Acanthosomidae*); —**ой** *a.* carinate, keel(ed); —**ая качка** (naut.) pitching.

киле/горлые *pl.* (ichth.) Pristigasterinae; —**грудые** *pl.* (orn.) Carinatae; —**й** *gen. pl. of* **киль.**

килек *gen. pl. of* **килька.**

киле/ногие *pl.* (mal.) sea snails (*Heteropoda*); —**образный** *see* **килевидный.**

кил/ец *m.* (ichth.) Onega cisco (*Coregonus albula kiletz*); —**ечный** *a. of* **килька.**

кили *pl. of* **киль.**

киликийский *a.* (geog.) Cilicia(n).

килиманджарский *a.* (geog.) Kilimanjaro.

килл/арнейская складчатость (geog.) Killarney folds; —**ер** *m.,* —**ерный** *a.* killer (component of T-lymphocytes); —**инит** *m.* (min.) killinite.

кило *n.* kilogram; *prefix* kilo— (10³); —**ампер** *m.* (elec.) kilo-ampere; —**амперметр** *m.* kilo-ammeter; —**бит** *m.* (comp.) kilobit, K (1024 bits); —**вар** *m.* kilovar; —**ватт** *m.* kilowatt; —**ватт-час** *m.* kilowatt-hour.

киловой *a. of* **кила.**

кило/вольт *m.* (elec.) kilovolt; **к.-ампер** kilovolt-ampere; —**гаусс** *m.* (phys.) kilogauss; —**генри** *m.* kilohenry; —**герц** *m.* kilohertz, kilocycle(s per second).

килограмм *m.* kilogram; **к.-калория** *see* **килокалория; к.-масса** *f.* kilogram-mass; **к.-метр,** —**(о)метр** *m.* kilogram-meter; **к.-молекула, к.-моль** *see* **киломоль;** —**овый** *a.* (one-) kilogram; **к.-сила** *f.* kilogram-force.

кило/джоуль *m.* (phys.) kilojoule; —**дина** *f.* kilodyne; **-Е,** —**единица** *f.* kilo unit; —**икс** *m.* kilo-X (a wavelength unit); **—калория** *f.* kilocalorie, large calorie; **—кюри** *n.* kilocurie; **—линия** *f.* kiloline (unit of magnetic flux); **—литр** *m.* kiloliter, stere; **—люмен** kilolumen; **—м** *m.* kilohm; **—максвелл** *m.* kilomaxwell; **—метр** *m.* kilometer; **—метраж** *m.* number of kilometers; mileage; **—метровый** *a.* (one-) kilometer, per kilometer; **-моль** *m.* kilomole, kilogram molecule; **—ом** *see* **килом;** **—парсек** *m.* (astr.) kiloparsec; **—понд** *see* **килограмм-сила; —резерфорд** *m.* kilorutherford; **—рентген** *m.* kiloroentgen; **—тонна** *f.* kiloton (unit of weight or force); **—уатт** *see* **киловатт; —футфунт** *m.* kilo-foot-pound; **—цикл** *m.* kilocycle; **—электронвольт** *m.* kilo-electron-volt, kev; **—эрг** *m.* kilo-erg.

килуран *m.* kilurane (unit of radioactivity).

киль *m.* (naut.) keel; (av.) (tail)fin, vertical stabilizer; (astr.) Carina; (orn.) carina; **—блок** *m.* keel block; **—ватер** *m.* (ship's) wake.

кильдинский *a.* (geog.) Kildin.

килька *f.* (ichth.) sprat (*Clupeonella; Sprattus s.*); bleak (*Alburnus a.*); minnow (*Phoxinus ph.*).

кильмезский *a.* (geog.) Kielmez.

кильский *a.* (geog.) Kiel (Bay, Canal).

кильсон *m.* (shipbuilding) ke(e)lson.

кильчевание *n.* (hort.) layering.

киля *gen. of* **киль.**

КИМ *abbr.* (**кодово-импульсная модуляция**) pulse-code modulation, PCM.

киматолит *m.* (min.) cymatolite.

ким/берлейский, —берлийский *a.* (geog.) Kimberley; **—берлит** *m.* (petr.) kimberlite, blue earth; **—еридж** *m.,* **—ериджский ярус** (geol.) Kim(m)eridgian; **—мерийский** *a.* Cimmerian.

кимограф *m.* (med.) kymograph, undulation or variation recorder.

кимолийская глина (min.) cimolite.

кимофан *m.* (min.) cymophane, chrysoberyl.

Кина испытатель (met.) Keen tester; **К. цемент** Keene's cement.

киназа *f.* kinase (enzyme activator).

кинг/(к)лип *m.* (ichth.) kingklip (*Genypterus capensis*); **—стон** *m.* Kingston valve.

киндерхук *m.* (geol.) Kinderhook beds.

кинези(о)— *prefix* kinesi(o)— (movement).

кинемат—, —о— *prefix* kinemat(o)— (motion); **—ика** *f.* (phys.) kinematics; **—ический** *a.* kinematic.

кинематограф *m.* cinema(tograph), motion picture; movie camera; **—ический** *a.* cinematographic; motion picture, movie; **—ия** *f.* cinematography.

кинескоп *m.* (telev.) kinescope, picture tube.

кинест/езия *f.* (med.) kinesthesia; **—етический** *a.* kinesthetic.

кинет—, —о— *prefix* kinet(o)— (motion); **—ика** *f.* (phys.) kinetics; **—ин** *m.* (biochem.) kinetin; **—ический** *a.* kinetic; **—огенез** *m.* (gen.) kinetogenesis; **—огенезис** *m.* (geol.) kinetogenesis; **—омер** *m.* (gen.) kinetomere; **—оскоп** *m.* kinetoscope; **—осома** *f.* (bot.; prot.) kinetosome; **—остатика** *f.* kinetostatics, dynamic force analysis; **—офон** *m.* kinetophone; **—охор** *m.* (gen.) kinetochore, centromere.

кинжал *m.* dagger; (planting) tool; **—овидный** *a.* dagger-shaped, pugioniform; **—озуб** *m.* (ichth.) daggertooth (*Anotopterus pharao*); **—озубые** *pl.* Anotopteridae.

кинза *see* **кориандр.**

киникса *f.* (herp.) Kinixys.

кинин *m.* (cyto)kinin.

кинкажу *m.* (mam.) kinkajou (*Potos flavus*).

кинкан *m.* (bot.) kumquat (*Fortunella*).

кино *n.* kino (gum); motion picture, movie; *prefix* kino— (movement).

киноа *see* **квиноа.**

киноаппарат *m.* movie camera; **—ная** *f.* projection room; **—ура** *f.* movie equipment.

киноателье *n.* movie studio.

киновар/ь *f.,* **—ный** *a.* (min.) cinnabar; vermilion (pigment); **зелёная к.** cinnabar green; **красная к.** vermilion.

кино/ведение *n.,* **—ведческий** *a.* movie making, cinematography; **—журнал** *m.* documentary film; newsreel; **—запись движений** micromotion film study.

киноин *m.* kinoin (resin).

кино/инженер *m.* motion picture engineer; **—искусство** *n.* cinematography; **—кадр** *m.* frame; **—камера** *f.* movie camera; **—картина** *f.* motion picture, movie; **копировальный** *a.* film-printing; **—лента** *f.* film; **—логия** *f.* (physiol.) kin(esi)ology; (zool.) cynology; **—механик** *m.* movie technician; projectionist; **—микросъёмка** *f.* cinemicrography; **—оборудование** *n.* movie equipment; **—оператор** *m.* camera man; **—передвижка** *f.* traveling projector; **—плазма** *f.* (cyt.) kinoplasm; **—плёнка** *f.* movie film.

кинопроек/тор *m.* movie projector; **—ционная** *f.* projection room; **—ция** *f.* movie projection.

кино/производство *n.* film production; **—прокат** *m.* film (lending) service; **—промышленность** *f.* movie industry.

киноринхи *pl.* (zool.) Kinorhyncha.

кино/сеанс *m.* performance, show; **—скоп** *m.* film viewer.

киносъём/ка *f.* motion picture photography, filming, shooting; **замедленная к.** time-lapse filming; **комбинированная к.** special effects shots; **—очный** *a. of* **киносъёмка;** movie-taking; movie (camera).

кино/театр *m.* movie theater; **—техника** *f.* movie equipment; film technique; **—токсин** *m.* kinotoxin, fatigue toxin; **—установка** *f.* movie equipment; movie projector; **—фильм** *m.* motion picture, movie, film; **—фицировать** *v.* equip for movie-showing; organize movie theaters; **—фотоклей** *m.* film cement; **—фотопулемёт** *m.* camera gun; **—фотопромышленность** *f.* motion picture industry; **—хроника** *see* **киножурнал; —экран** *m.* projection screen.

кинурен/ин *m.* kynurenine; **—овый** *a.* kynurenic, 4-hydroxyquinaldic (acid).

кинут/ый *a.* thrown; abandoned; **—ь** *see* **кидать.**

киньон-насос *m.* fluidized-solids pump.

киоск *m.* booth, kiosk, cabin; (book) stall; (news) stand; **—ёр** *m.* stall attendant.

кип *m.* (met.) boil(ing), simmering; notch, groove; (naut.) fairlead, chock; kip (unit of force, 1000 lb.).

КИП *abbr.* (**контрольно-измерительные приборы**) control and measuring instruments.

кипа *f.* bale, stack, pack; pile, heap; dump.

кипарис *m.* (bot.) cypress (*Cupressus*); **—ник** *m.* cypress grove; **—ный, —овый** *a.* cypress; **—овик** *m.* Chamaecyparis; **—овые** *pl.* Cupressaceae.

кипел/ка *f.* quicklime, unslaked lime, calcium oxide; **—ый** *a.* boiled.

кипен/ие *n.* boiling, ebullition; bubbling; (steel) rimming; **температура —ия, точка —ия** boiling point; **—ный** *a.* foam-white; **—ь** *f.* foam, froth.

кипер *m.,* **—ная ткань** (text.) twill; **—ная лента** surgical tape.

кипеть *v.* boil; bubble; (steel) rim.

КИПиА *abbr.* (**контрольно-измерительные приборы и автоматика**) control and measuring instruments and automatic equipment.

кипильник *m.* (chem.) bead.

кипня *gen. of* **кипень.**

кипов/ый *a. of* **кип(а); —ая планка** (mooring) chock, fairlead.

кипо/разбиватель, —разборщик *m.* bale opener, bale breaker.

кипп-реле *n.* (electron.) Kipp relay.

кипрегель *m.* (surv.) telescopic alidade.

кипрей *m.* (bot.) willow herb (*Epilobium; Chamaenerium*); **—ник** *m.* Epilobium; **—ные** *pl.* Onagraceae.

кипрский *a.* (geog.) Cyprus, Cyprian.

кипсейка *f.* (typ.) ink fountain.

кипсы *pl.* (leather) kips.

кип/ун *m.* bubbling or boiling spring; **—учесть** *f.* boiling state; effervescence; **—учий** *a.* boiling; bubbling; effervescent; boiling-water (nuclear reactor); rimmed, rimming (steel); **—учий слой** fluidized bed; **—ятилка** *f.* boiler room or house; **—ятильник** *m.* boiler, hot-water heater; boiling stove; **—ятильный** *a.* boiling; boiler; **—ятильный куб** beaker; **—ятить** *v.* boil, bring to a boil; **—ятиться** *v.* boil, be boiling; get excited; **—яток** *m.* boiling water; **—ячение** *n.* boiling; **—ячён(н)ый** *a.* boiled; **—ящий** *see* **кипучий.**

кир *m.* (geol.) kir (solidified petroleum).

киргизский *a.* (geog.) Kirghiz(ean).

киренгский *a.* (geog.) Kirenga.

кирз/а *f.,* **—овый** *a.* (text.) kersey; subterranean frozen layer; **к. СК** a leather substitute.

кирка *f.* pick(ax); scraper; hoe, hack.

кирказон *m.* (bot.) Aristolochia; **—овые** *pl.* Aristolochiaceae.

кир/ка-мотыга *f.* pick(ax); **—ковка** *f.* scarifying; **—ковщик** *m.* scarifier; **—ковый** *a. of* **кирка; —комотыга** *f.* pick(ax).

киров/оградский *a.* (geog.) Kirovograd; **—ский** *a.* Kirov.

кирочный *a. of* **кирка.**

кирпич *m.* brick; **пережжённый к.** clinker; **—еделательный** *a.* brick-molding (machine); **—еобжигательная печь** brick kiln; **—ина** *f.* a brick; **—ник** *m.* brick maker; **—но-красный** *a.* brick-red; **—ный** *a.* brick; masonry; brick-red, lateritious; muriform; **—ный завод** brickyard; **к.-сырец** *m.* adobe; air-dried brick.

КирССР *abbr.* Kirgiz Soviet Socialist Republic.

кирхгеймский *a.* (geog.) Kirchheim.

Кирхгофа закон Kirchhoff's law.

кирьяк *m.* large whitefish, trout or salmon.

кис *past m. sing of* **киснуть.**

кисе/евидный *a.* muslin-like; **—йный** *a.* muslin.

кисел *sh. m. of* **кислый; —евание** *n.* (tanning) drenching; **—евать** *v.* drench; **—евидный, —еобразный** *a.* viscous, paste-like, gel-like; **—ь** *m.,* **—ьный** *a.* fruit gel; any viscous mass; (tanning) bark liquor, ooze; (bran) drench.

кисет *m.* drawstring bag; **—ный** *a.* (med.) purse-string (suture).

кисея *f.* (text.) muslin, gauze.

кисл/еть *see* **киснуть; —инка** *f.* mildly acid taste; **—ить** *v.* have a mildly acid taste; make sour; **—ица** *f.,* **—ичный** *a.* any sour fruit or plant, spec. Oxalis; crab apple (*Pyrus malus*); **—ичная соль** potassium bioxalate; **—ичник** *m.* (bot.) mountain sorrel (*Oxyria*); **—ичные** *pl.* Oxalidaceae.

кисло *adv.* sourly, acid(ly); *past n. sing. of* **киснуть; —вание** *n.* acidification; **—ватость** *f.* sourness; acidulousness, (mild) acidity, subacidity; **—ватый** *a.* sourish; acidulous, subacid; **—вать** *v.* acidify, treat

with acid; **—вка** *f.* acidification, acid treatment; (text.) souring; **—молочный** *a.* sour milk.

кислород *m.* oxygen, O; **к. воздуха** atmospheric oxygen; **—но—** *see also under* **кислородо—; —нодобывающий** *a.* oxygen-producing; **—но-дыхательный** *a.* oxygen-breathing (mask); **—но-флюсовый** *a.* flux (cutting); **—ный** *a.* oxygen(ous); oxy (acid, salt); combustion (zone).

кислородо/ацетиленовая горелка oxyacetylene torch; **—водородный** *a.* oxyhydrogen (welding); **—отщепляющий** *a.* oxygen-removing, deoxidizing; **—содержащий** *a.* oxygen-containing, oxy—.

кислосладкий *a.* sourish sweet, sweet-sour.

кислот/а *f.* acid; **безводная к.** acid anhydride; **—но—** *prefix* acid; *see also under* **кислото—; —но-основный** *a.* acid-base; **—но-растворимый** *a.* acid-soluble; **—реагирующий** *a.* acid-reacting; **—ность** *f.* acid content, acidity; **показатель степени —ности** acid number; **—но-щелочной** *a.* acid-base; **—ный** *a.* acid(ic); sour.

кислото/измерение *n.* acidimetry; **—мер** *m.* acidimeter; **—нерастворимый** *a.* acid-insoluble; **—оборот** *m.* acid circulation; **—обработанный** *a.* acid-treated; **—образование** *n.* acid formation, acidification; **—образователь** *m.* acid former, acidifier; **—образующый** *a.* acid-forming; **—поглощающий** *a.* acid-absorbing; **—подобный** *a.* acid-like, of acid nature; **—понижение** *n.* deacidification, neutralization; **—растворимость** *f.* solubility in acids; **—растворимый** *a.* acid-soluble; **—содержащий** *a.* acid-containing; **—стойкий, —упорный** *a.* acidproof, acid-resisting; **—упорность** *f.* acid resistance, resistance to acid; **—упоры** *pl.* acid-resistant materials; **—устойчивый** *a.* acid-resistant.

кисл/ый *a.* acid; sour; bi— (salt); **к. характер** acid nature; acid condition, acidity; **—ая сернистокислая соль** bisulfite; **—ая углекислая соль** bicarbonate; **—ое свойство** acidity.

кислятина *f.* sour fruit or drink.

киснуть *v.* (turn) sour, become acid.

киста *f.* (med.) cyst; (tooth) abscess; **—cele,** e.g., **кровяная к.** hematocele.

кисте— *prefix* racemi—, botry(o)— (cluster); brush; **—вание** *n.* brushing; **—видный** *a.* racemose, racemiform; botryoid(al); **—вик** *m.* (bot.) Penicillium; **—вой** *a. of* **кисть;** (anat.) carpal; **—вой разряд** (elec.) brush discharge; **—й** *gen. pl. of* **кисть; —носный** *a.* (bot.) racemose; racemiferous; **—образный** *see* **кистевидный;** penicillate, penicilliform; **—пёрые** *pl.* (ichth.) Crossopterygii; **—хвост** *m.,* **—хвостка** *f.* (ent.) tussock moth (*Orgyia*); **—хвост** *m.* (mam.) marsupial rat (*Phascogale*); **—цветковый** *a.* (bot.) racemiflorous.

кисто— *prefix* cyst(o)— (bladder, sac, cyst); **—видный** *a.* cystoid, cystic; **—зный** *a.* cystose, cystic, cystous; **—ма** *f.* cystoma.

кист/очка *dim. of* **кисть;** (biol.) penicillus; **—очковидный** *a.* brush-like, bushy; penicilliform; **—очковый** *a. of* **кисточка;** penicilliform; **—очница** *f.* (ent.) Pygaera, **—очный** *see* **кистевой; —ь** *f.* brush; bunch, cluster; (bot.) raceme; (anat.) wrist.

кит *m.* (mam.) whale.

кит. *abbr.* (**китайский**).

кита/еведение *n.* sinology (Chinese culture); **—ец** *m.* Chinese (man); **—ист** *m.* sinologist; **—истика** *f.* sinology.

Китай (geog.) China.

китайка *f.* Chinese apple (*Malus prunifolia*).

китайск/ий *a.* Chinese; **к. лён, —ая крапива, —ая трава** China grass, ramie fiber; **к. орех** peanut; **—ое масло** tung oil.

китаянка *f.* Chinese woman.

кити, —ны *pl.* (bot.) runners.

кито/боец, —бой *m.* whaler; whaleboat; **—бойный** *a.* whaling; whale (industry); **—видка** *f.* (ichth.) whalefish (*Cetomimus*); **—видковые** *pl.* Cetomimidae; **—видный** *a.* cetacean, cetaceous; **—вый** *a.* whale, cetaceous; **—вый жир** whale oil; blubber; **—вый ус** whalebone, baleen; **—глав** *m.* (orn.) whale-billed stork (*Balaeniceps rex*); **—главы** *pl.* Balaenicipitidae.

китойский *a.* (geog.) Kitoi.

кито/ловный *a.,* **—ловство** *n.* whaling; **—образные** *pl.* (mam.) cetaceans; **—образный** *see* **китовидный.**

китоский *a.* (geog.) Quito.

киур *m.* mason's hammer, peen hammer.

кифо/з *m.* (med.) kyphosis, hunchback; (ichth.) sea chub (*Kyphosus*); **—зовые** *pl.* (ichth.) Kyphosidae; **—тический** *a.* (med.) kyphotic.

кихчикский *a.* (geog.) Kikhchik.

кич *m.* (stone cutting) dop(p).

кичменгский *a.* (geog.) Kichmeng.

КиШ *abbr.* (**метод кольца и шара**) ring and ball method (for melting point).

кишеть *v.* swarm, teem, be infested (with).

кишечн/ик *m.* (anat.) intestine(s); **толстый к.** large intestine— **тонкий к.** small intestine; **—о** *prefix* entero— (intestine); **—одышащие, —ожаберные** *pl.* (zool.) Enteropneusta; **—ополостные** *pl.* (zool.) Coelenterata; **—ососудистый** *a.* gastrovascular; **—ый** *a.* intestinal, enteric, gut; gastric (juice); **—ая палочка** (bact.) Escherichia coli; **—ая струна** catgut.

кишинёвский *a.* (geog.) Kishinev.

киш/ка *f.* (anat.) intestine, gut; (rubber) hose; **воспаление —ок** (med.) enteritis; **двенадцатиперстная к.** (anat.) duodenum; **ободочная к.** colon; **подвздошная к.** ileum; **прямая к.** rectum; **слепая к.** caecum; **толстая к.** large intestine; **тонкая к.** small intestine; **тощая к.** jejunum.

кишла/к *m.,* **—чный** *a.* Central Asian village.

кишмиш *m.* currant; seedless grapes; **—ность** *f.* seedlessness.

кишнец *m.,* **—овый** *a.* coriander.

кишок *gen. pl. of* **кишка.**

кияк *m.* giant rye grass (*Elymus giganteus*).

киянка *f.* wooden hammer, mallet, maul.

ккал *abbr.* (**килокалория**) kilocalorie; **ккал/** *abbr.* (**ккал на**) kilocalories per.

к/кг *abbr.* (**кулон на килограмм**) coulomb per kilogram.

ККД *abbr.* (**конусная дробилка крупного дробления**) coarse gyratory crusher.

ККМ *abbr.* (**критическая концентрация мицеллообразования**) critical micelle concentration, CMC point.

ккр, ккюри *abbr.* (**килокюри**) kilocurie.

кл *abbr.* (**килолитр**) kiloliter; **кл.** *abbr.* (**класс**) class; (**ключ**) key; spring; coulomb; **к.л.** *abbr.* (**космические лучи**) cosmic rays; **к.-л.** *abbr.* (**какой-либо**) some, any.

КЛА *abbr.* (**космический летательный аппарат**) spacecraft.

клава/риевые *pl.* (bot.) Clavariaceae; **—тин, —цин** *m.* clavatin, clavacin, patulin.

клавиатура *f.* keyboard.

клавицепс *m.* (bot.) Claviceps.

клавиш *m.,* **—а** *f.* key; **—ный** *a.* key(-actuated), keyboard (computer); multiple-section (rake); **—ный ввод на диск** (comp.) key-to-disk entry.

клад *m.* treasure.

кладбище *n.* cemetery.

кладеный *a.* castrated.

кладень *m.* beam, sleeper, ground timber.

кладестиновая кислота cladestic acid.

клад/ёт *pr. 3 sing. of* **класть; —и** *gen., etc., of* **кладь; —ка** *f.* laying, etc., *see* **класть;** masonry, walling; (furnace) lining, brickwork; stack (of lumber); clutch (of eggs); (ichth.) egg mass; castration; **—ка яиц** egg-laying, oviposition; **каменная —ка** masonry, stonework; **сухая каменная —ка** dry wall; **кирпичная —ка** brickwork.

кладо— *prefix* clado— (sprout).

кладов/ая *f.* store(room), stockroom; warehouse; larder, pantry; **—щик** *m.* warehouse attendant.

кладо/генез *m.* (gen.) cladogenesis; **—генный** *a.* cladogenous; **—дий** *m.* (bot.) cladode, cladophyll.

кладок *gen. pl. of* **кладка.**

кладо/ния *f.* (bot.) Cladonia; **—новый** *a.* cladonic (acid); **—спориоз** *m.* (phyt.) Cladosporium leaf spot, leaf mold, scab; (med.) cladosporiosis; **—фора** *f.* (bot.) cladophore.

клад/ут *pr. 3 pl. of* **класть; —ущий** *a.* laying; **—чик** *m.* layer, setter; **—ь** *f.* load, cargo, freight; bridging plank.

клажа *f.* laying, setting, piling; load, cargo.

Клайдена явление (phot.) Clayden effect.

Клайзена реакция Claisen reaction.

клайн *m.* (gen.) cline, character-gradient.

клайтония *f.* (bot.) Claytonia.

клаксон *m.* horn.

клал *past m. sing. of* **класть.**

клам/ера *f.,* **—мер** *m.* cramp iron.

клан *m.* (biol.) clan.

кланяться *v.* bow (to), greet.

клапан *m.,* **—ный** *a.* valve, vent; flap; **к.-бабочка** butterfly valve; **к.-вантуз** *m.* vent; **к.-мигалка** *m.* flap valve, clapper; **—ный** *a.* valve, valv(ul)ar.

клапейроново *a.* Clapeyron (equation).

клар-камера *f.* (phot.) folding camera.

клар/ен *m.* (coal) clarain; **—ет** *m.* claret (wine); **—иевые** *pl.* (ichth.) Clariidae; **—ий** *m.* Clarias; **—ит** *m.* (min.) clarite.

кларифик/атор *m.* clarifier; (juice) separator; **—ация** *f.* clarification.

кларк *m.* (geol.) clarke; percent(age) abundance (of element); **к. концентрации** abundance ratio; **—еит** *m.* (min.) clarkeite; **—ов столб** (anat.) Clarke's column.

кларнет *m.* (music) clarinet.

класс *m.* class, grade, rank, sort; category; (range) condition; (pal.) genus; classroom; **—ировка** *f.* grading; **—ировщик** *m.* grader.

классифи/катор *m.* classifier; **—каторщик** *m.* classifier; classification clerk; **—кационный** *a.,* **—кация** *f.* classification, sorting, etc., *see v.;* **—цирование** *n.* classifying, etc., *see v.;* **—цированный** *a.* classified, etc., *see v.;* **—цировать** *v.* class(ify), sort, grade, size; separate, assort; tabulate, group; **—цирующий** *a.* classifying, etc., *see v.*

класс/ический *a.* classic(al); **—ный** *a.* first-class; class (room); **—овый** *a.* class.

класт— *prefix* clast— (broken).

кластер *m.* cluster.

класт/ероспориоз *m.* (phyt.) Clasterosporium leaf or

fruit spot, shot hole; **—ический** *a.* (geol.) clastic, fragmental.

класть *v.* lay, deposit, put, place, set; build, erect, make; leave (mark); apply (to), spend (on); **к. начало** start, begin.

клатрат *m.,* **—ное соединение** clathrate, inclusion compound.

клаудетит *m.* (min.) claudetite.

Клаузиус-Клапейрона уравнение Clausius-Clapeyron equation.

клаузоне *n.* (cer.) cloisonné.

клаузула *f.* (law) clause, stipulation.

клаус/ия *f.* (bot.) Clausia; **—талит** *m.* (min.) clausthalite; **—трофобия** *f.* (med.) claustrophobia.

клебемасса *f.* bituminous cement, mastic.

клёв *see* **клевок.**

клева/ние *n.* pecking, etc., *see v.;* **—ать** *v.* peck; bite, nibble; (av.) pitch; **—ать носом** nod, be drowsy; **—аться** *v.* peck at each other.

Клеве кислота Cleve's acid.

клев/еит *m.* (min.) cleveite; **—еландит** *m.* cleavelandite; **—елендский** *a.* (geog.) Cleveland.

клевер *m.,* **—ный** *a.* (bot.) clover (*Trifolium*); **—ище** *n.* clover field; **—осортировка** *f.* clover grader; **—отёрка** *f.,* **—отёрочная машина** clover huller; **—оутомление** *n.* clover soil sickness.

клевет/а *f.,* **—ать** *v.* slander, libel.

клев/ец *m.* (mech.) tooth; **—ок** *m.* bite, biting; peck(ing); notcher; (art.) burst.

клее– *prefix see* **клей; —вар** *m.* glue boiler, glue maker; **—варение** *n.* glue making; **—варенный** *see* **клееварный; —варка** *f.* glue boiler, glue pot; glue making; **—вар(оч)ный** *a.* glue-making; glue (factory); size-cooking; **—видный** *a.* glue-like; **—вой** *a. of* **клей; —вое вещество** adhesive; sizing; gluten; **—к** *gen. pl. of* **клейка;** *sh. m. of* **клейкий; —мазальный** *a.* gluing; **—мешалка** *f.* glue mixer; size mixer.

кле/ёнка *f.* oilcloth; oilskin; linoleum; **—енный** *a.* glued, etc., *see v.;* **—енная фанера** plywood; **—еносный** *a.* glutenous, gummy; **—ёночный, —ёнчатый** *a. of* **клеёнка; —ёный** *see* **клеенный; —еобразный** *a.* gluey, glutinous; **—ильный** *a.* gluing, etc., *see v.;* **—ить** *v.* glue, gum, paste, cement; bond, stick together, laminate; size; (rubber) build up; **—иться** *v.* stick, be(come) sticky; get along, work.

клей *m.* glue, gum, paste, cement, adhesive; size, sizing; **извлекать к.** *v.* degum; **—дающий** *a.* collagenous; **—дающее вещество** collagen.

клейдесдальский *a.* Clydesdale (horse).

клейдит *m.* claydite (concrete filler).

клейдо— *prefix* (anat.) cleid(o)— (clavicle).

клейк/а *f.* gluing, etc., *see* **клеить; —ий** *a.* sticky, tacky, gummy, adhesive, viscous; glue; **—ий пластырь** adhesive plaster; **—ое вещество** adhesive; sizing; **—оватый** *a.* somewhat sticky; **—овина** *f.* gluten; **—овинность** *f.* gluten content; **—овинный** *a.* gluten, glutinous; **—оме(т)р** tackmeter; **—оногие** *pl.* (mam.) Natalidae.

клейкост/ь *f.* adhesiveness, stickiness, gumminess, viscosity; tack(iness); adhesion; **повыситель —и** tackifier.

клейм/ение *n.* branding, etc., *see v.;* **—ён(н)ый** *a.* branded, etc., *see v.;* **—ильный** *a.* branding, etc., *see v.;* **—ить** *v.* brand, stamp, mark, blaze; stigmatize; impress, seal; number; **—о** *n.* brand, stamp, mark, seal; notch, blaze; branding iron; **—овка** *see* **клеймение; —овщик** *m.* brander, marker.

клейн/ит *m.* (min.) kleinite, mercurammonite; **—нишиновская формула** (nucl.) Klein-Nishina formula.

клейстер *m.* paste, filling, sizing, size; dextrin glue; **—изовать** *v.* paste up; make into paste; clog; **—ная муть** (beer) amylaceous turbidity.

клейсто— *prefix* cleisto— (closed); **—гамия** *f.* (bot.) cleistogamy; **—гамный** *a.* cleistogamous; **—карпий** *m.,* **—карпия** *f.* cleistocarp; **—теций** *m.* cleistothecium.

клейтония *f.* (bot.) Claytonia.

клейтрум *m.* (pal.) cleithrum.

клекачк/а *f.* (bot.) Staphylea; **—овые** *pl.* Staphyleaceae.

клёкот *m.* (orn.) cry, scream, screech.

клек(о)тать *v.* cry, scream, screech.

клематис *m.* (bot.) Clematis.

Клемен: единица по —у Clemen unit.

клементит *m.* (min.) klementite.

клемм/а *f.* clamp, clip; (elec.) terminal; **—ник** *m.* terminal block.

клемшел *m.* clamshell (excavator).

клён *m.* maple (*Acer*).

кленовник *m.* maple grove.

клёновые *pl.* Aceraceae.

кленовый *a.* maple, aceraceous; aceric (acid).

клёнолистный *a.* maple-leaved.

клень *m.* (ichth.) chub; owsianka; dace.

клеоме *f.* (bot.) Cleome.

клеон *m.* (ent.) Chromoderus, etc.

клепало *see* **клепальный молот.**

клепальн/ый *a.* riveting; **к. зажим** screw dolly; **к. молот(ок)** riveting hammer, riveter; **к. пресс, к. станок, —ая машина** riveter.

клеп/альщик *m.* riveter; **—ание** *n.* riveting.

клёпанный *a.* riveted.

клепать *v.* rivet; dress (scythe); slander, malign.

клепец *m.* (ichth.) bream (*Abramis sapa*).

клёп/ка *f.* riveting; (barrel) stave, clapboard; **к. на прессах** press-riveting; **—очный** *a. of* **клёпка;** barrel (wood).

клепсина *f.* (zool.) Clepsine (leech).

клептомания *f.* (med.) kleptomania.

клерк *m.* clerk.

клер/ование *n.,* **—овка** *f.* clarification (of sugar); **—овать** *v.* clarify, clear, decolorize; **—с** *m.* clear liquor.

клёст *m.* (orn.) crossbill (*Loxia*); **к.-еловик** *m.* spruce crossbill (*L. curvirostra*).

клет/евой *see* **клеточный; —и** *gen., etc. of* **клеть.**

клетк/а *f.* cage; crate, box, casing, crib; (elevator) car; (biol.) cell; square; sector; cubicle; (stair) well; (screen) mesh; nip, bite (of mill rolls); **в —у** graph (paper); **отросток —и** cellular process; **физиология —и** cellular physiology; **эффект —и** (nucl.) cage effect; **к.-зерно** *f.* granular cell; **к.-киллер** *f.* killer cell; **к.-мишень** *f.* target cell; **к.-ножка** *f.* basilar cell; **к.-питомник** *f.* breeding cage; **к.-хозяин** *f.* host cell; **—ообразный** *a.* cage(-type); cellular.

клетневать *v.* lag, insulate (pipes); (naut.) parcel, serve (rope).

клеточ/ка *dim. of* **клетка;** (biol.) cell(ule); **—кообразный** *a.* cellular; **—но** *prefix* cyto— (cell); **—ный** *a. of* **клетка;** latticed; (biol.) cell(ular); **—ный сок** cell fluid; **—ная обмотка** (elec.) cage winding; **—ное тело** cytosome.

клетушка *dim. of* **клетка;** (agr.) coop.

клетчатк/а *f.* cellulose; (biol.) cellular tissue; graph paper; (diet) fiber; **жировая к.** fatty tissue; **ксантогенновый эфир —и** cellulose xanthate.

клетчатый *a.* square(d), checkered; graph (paper); meshed; cellulose; (biol.) cellular.

клеть *f.* storeroom; cage, housing; framework; stand (of rolls); crate; **к.-трио** *f.* three-high (mill) stand.

клешн/евидный, —еобразный *a.* claw-shaped; (chem.) chelate; **—евидное соединение** chelate (compound); **—еобразование** *n.* chelate formation; **—образователь** *m.* chelating agent; **—я** *f.* claw, pincer, chela; **зажимать в —ю** *v.* form a chelate.

клещ *m.* (zool.) tick, mite (*Acarus, Ixodes*, etc.); **—ак** *m.* (ent.) earwig (*Forficula auricularia*); **к.-дермацентор** *m.* wood tick (*Dermacentor*).

клещевидный *see* **клемневидный; forcipate.**

клещевин/а *f.* castor plant (*Ricinus*); (riveting) fin; **—ный** *a.* castor (oil).

клещ/евой *a. of* **клещ(и);** (med.) mite-borne, tick-borne; **—еобразный** *see* **клещевидный; —ехвостка** *f.* (ent.) Iapyx; **—ехвостки, —ехвостковые** *pl.* Iapygidae; **-железняк** *m.* (zool.) Demodex; **—и** *pl.* tongs, pliers, forceps, nippers, pincers; extractor; vise; clip; (zool.) ticks and mites (*Acarina*); **живные —и, чесотные —и** Acaridae; **—ик** *m.* mite (*Eryophyes, Tetranychus,* etc.); **—и-кусачки** *pl.* clippers; **—и-паразиты** *pl.* parasitic ticks and mites; **—накожник** *m.* scab mite (*Psoroptes*).

кле/ющий, —ящий *a.* gluing, etc., *see* **клеить;** adhesive, sticky, tacky; **—я** *pr. ger. of* **клеить;** *gen. of* **клей; —янка** *f.* glue pot.

кливаж *m.* cleavage; **расслоение по —у** cleavage foliation; **—ный** *a.* cleavage; (embr.) monozygotic.

кливлендский *a.* (geog.) Cleveland.

клидонограф *m.* klydonograph, surge voltage recorder.

клиент *m.* client; **—ура** *f.* clientele.

клизма *f.* (med.) enema, syringe.

клик *m.,* **—ать, —нуть** *v.* call, shout.

кликушество *n.* (med.) hysterics.

климаграмма *f.* (meteor.) climograph.

климакс *m.,* **—овое растительное сообщество** climax, climactic plant community; **—ный, —овый** *a.* climactic.

климактер/ий *m.* (physiol.) climacteric, menopause; **—ический** *a.* climacteric.

климат *m.* climate; **установка искусственного —а, —изёр** *m.* air conditioner; **—ип** *m.* climatype, climatic ecotype; **—ический** *a.* climatic; **—ическая станция** health resort; **—олог** *m.* climatologist; **—ологический** *a.* climatological; **—ология** *f.* climatology.

климациевые *pl.* tree mosses (*Climaciaceae*).

климениевые слои (geol.) Clymenia beds.

климограф *m.* (med.; meteor.) climograph.

клин *m.* wedge, key, cotter; cleat; chock; (agr.) strip, plot; (anat.) cuneus; (gen.) cline, character-gradient; (spectrophotometry) (attenuating) comb; **вбивать к.** *v.* wedge (in); **натяжной к., поперечный к.** cotter, split pin, forelock; **прижимной к.** (mach.) gib; **сходить на к.** *v.* taper; **—a** *f.* (gen.) cline.

клингер *m.* water gage (in boiler).

клингерит *m.* an asbestos-rubber cement.

клинидий *m.* (bot.) clinidium.

клини/ка *f.* clinic; clinical symptoms, clinical study; manifestations (of disease); **—цист** *m.* clinician; **—ческий** *a.* clinic(al); **—ческий госпиталь** clinic.

клинкер *m.,* **—ный** *a.* clinker, hard-burnt brick; Waelz slag.

клинкет *m.* (wedge) gate valve; **—ный** *a. of* **клинкет;** sliding (door).

клинковый *a. of* **клинок.**

клино— *prefix* cuneo—, spheno— (wedge); clino— (incline); **—брюхие** *pl.* (ichth.) Gasteropelecidae; **—брюшка** *f.* flying hatchetfish (*Gasteropelecus*); **—видно—** *prefix* sphen(o)— (wedge-shaped); cuneo— (wedge); **—видно-кубовидный** *a.* (anat.) cuneocuboid; **—видно-нёбный** *a.* sphenopalatine; **—видно-решетчатый** *a.* sphenoethmoid; **—видность** *f.* wedge shape; **—видный** *see* **клинообразный; —вой** *a.* wedge, key, cotter; wedge-shaped, V-shaped, V-(belt); **—вая шпонка** (taper) key; **—вые** *pl.* clipfishes (*Clinidae*).

клиногумит *m.* (min.) clinohumite.

клинозубые *pl.* (herp.) Sphenodontidae.

клинок *m.* blade, (cutting) edge.

клиноклаз(ит) *m.* (min.) clinoclas(it)e.

клино/-ладьевидный *a.* (anat.) cuneonavicular; **—листн(иков)ые** *pl.* (pal.) Sphenophyllales; **—листный** *a.* (bot.) wedge-leaved, cuneifolious.

клинометр *m.* clinometer, incline level.

клинообразный *a.* wedge(-shaped), cuneiform, sphenic, sphenoid, tapered, V-shaped; **к. интрузив** (geol.) sphenolith.

клино/ось *f.* (cryst.) clino-axis; **—пирамида** *f.* clinopyramid; **—писный** *a.* cuneiform; **—птилолит** *m.* (min.) clinoptilolite; **—ремённый** *a.* v-belt; **—ромбический** *a.* (cryst.) monoclinic; **—ромбоэдрический** *a.* clinorhomboidal, triclinic; **—хлор** *m.* (min.) clinochlore; **—цоизит** *m.* (min.) clinozoisite; **—эдрит** *m.* (min.) clinohedrite; **—энстатит** *m.* (min.) clinoenstatite.

клинский *a.* (geog.) Klin.

клинтонит *m.* (min.) clintonite.

клинтух *m.* (orn.) stock dove (*Columba onas*).

клинус *m.* (ichth.) Clinus.

клинчатый *a.* wedge-shaped, tapered.

клинчер *m.* clincher, clencher; **—ная шина** beaded-edge tire.

клин/ышек *dim. of;* **—ья** *pl. of* **клин.**

клиона *f.* (zool.) boring sponge (*Cliona*).

клионе *n.* (mal.) sea butterfly (*Clione*).

клипеальный *a.* (ent.) clypeal.

клип(п)ер *m.* clipper, fishing vessel.

клипсы *pl.* clips.

клипшпрингер *m.* (mam.) klipspringer (*Oreotragus o.*).

клир/енс *m.* clearance; **—инг** *m.* clearing.

клир(р)фактор *m.* (elec. comm.) klirr-factor, nonlinear distortion factor.

клистир *see* **клизма.**

клистрон *m.* (electron.) klystron; **—ный** *a.* klystron; reflection (oscillator).

клит *m.* (ent.) longhorn beetle (*Clytus*).

клитор *m.* (anat.) clitoris.

клитория *f.* (bot.) Clitoria.

клитоцибин *m.* clitocybine (antibiotic).

клитра *f.* (ent.) leaf beetle (*Clytra*).

клифстон *m.* chalk.

клиф/тонит *m.* (min.) cliftonite; **—ф** *m.* cliff.

клица *f.* cleat, insulating clamp.

клич *m.* call; **—ет** *pr. 3 sing. of* **кликать.**

клиш/е *n.* (typ.) cliche, stereotype, block, (engraving) plate, cut; **—ирование** *n.* plate making.

КЛК *abbr.* **(карто-ленто-карточная машина)** (comp.) card-tape-card machine.

клм *abbr.* **(килолюмен)** kilolumen; **клм-ч** *abbr.* **(килолюмен-час)** kilolumen-hour.

клоа/ка *f.* (anat.) cloaca, cesspool, sewer; **—чные** *pl.* (mam.) Monotremata; **—чный** *a.* cloacal.

клобуч/ковидный, —ковый *a.* cucullate, hooded, cowled; **—ок** *m.* cucullus, hood.

Клода способ Claude's method.

клодетит *m.* (min.) claudetite.

клозет *m.* toilet, lavatory.

клок *m.* flock, tuft; wisp, bit; **—астый** *a.* flocky, tufty, tufted.

клокичка *f.* (bot.) Staphylea.

клок/от *m.,* **—отанье** *n.* bubbling, etc.; *see v.;* **—отать** *v.* bubble, gurgle, splutter; **—тун** *m.* (orn.) bubbling teal (*Anas formosa*).

клон *m.* (gen.) clone; **—альный** *a.* clonal.

клондайкский *a.* (geog.) Klondike.

клонирование *n.* (gen.) cloning.

клонить *v.* lean, incline, bend; drive, aim, get (at); **—ся** *v.* lean, be inclined, tend (to), lead (up to); near, approach.

клоновый *a.* (gen.) clone, clonal.

клонорхоз *m.* (med.) clonorchiasis.

клонус *m.* (physiol.) clonus.

клоп *m.* (ent.) bug, spec. bed bug; **—ец** *m.* knotweed (*Polygonum linicola*); **—ик** *dim. of* **клоп**; **—иный, —овый** *a. of* **клоп**; cimicid; **—овая ромашка, —огон** *m.* (bot.) bugbane (*Cimicifuga*); **—овник** *m.* peppergrass (*Lepidium*); **—омор** *m.* bug exterminator.

клопфер *m.* (telegraphy) sounder.

клоп/-черепашка *f.* (ent.) Eurygaster; **—ы** *pl.* true bugs (*Hemiptera*); **—ы-паразиты** *pl.* Cimicidae.

клостридий *m.* (bact.) Clostridium.

клот(ик) *m.* (naut.) acorn, truck (of mast).

клоун *m.* clown; **морской к.** (ichth.) frogfish (*Antennarius*); **—изм** *m.* (med.) clownism; **—овые** *pl.* Antennariidae.

клохт/анье *n.* clucking; **—ать** *v.* cluck; cackle; **—унья** *f.* clucking hen.

клочень *m.* (ent.) bee moth (*Galleria melonella*).

клоч/кование *n.* flocculation; **—коватый** *a.* flocculent; flocky; tufty; **—ок** *m.* flake, flock; shred, scrap; flocculus, bunch, tuft; patch (of land); **—ья** *pl. of* **клок**; flakes; shreds, fragments.

клуб *m.* club, clubhouse; puff (of smoke); cloud (of dust); wreath (of mist); clump (of bees).

клубе/нёк *m.* tubercle, nodule; **—нь** *m.* tuber; nodule; **—ньковый** *a. of* **клубень**; nodular; **—ньковая бактерия** (bact.) Rhizobium; **—нькообразование** *n.* nodule formation; **—шок** *see* **клубенёк**.

клубить *v.* whirl up, raise (dust); **—ся** *v.* curl, wreathe; swirl, eddy; puff up.

клубко/видка *f.* (zool.) Glomeris; **—видковые** *pl.* Glomeridae; **—видный, —образный** *a.* glomerate, clustered.

клубне/видный *a.* tuber-like, tuberoid; **—вой** *a.* tuber(ous); **—камыш** *m.* (bot.) Bulboschoenus; **—луковица** *f.* corm, bulbous tuber; **—луковичный** *a.* corm-bearing, bulbotuber; **—мялка** *f.* potato masher; **—носный** *a.* tuberiferous; bulbiferous; **—образование** *n.* tuberization, tuber formation; **—плод** *m.* tuberous plant, root (crop); **—почка** *f.* corm, bulb; **—размножение** *n.* propagation by corms or bulbs.

клубни/ка *f.,* **—чный** *a.* strawberry.

клубный *a. of* **клуб.**

клубня *gen. of* **клубень.**

клуб/оватый *a.* ball-like, globular; **—овидный** *a.* glomerate; **—ок** *m.* ball (of thread), knot, tangle; puff (of smoke); bunch, cluster; (chem.) coil; (anat.; med.) glomus; (bot.; vet.) glome; **—очек** *dim. of* **клубок;** (anat.) glomerulus, glomerule; **—очковидный, —очковый, —очкообразный** *a.* glomerular,

glomerulate, clustered; **—очкообразующий** *a.* cluster-forming; **—очная машина** (text.) ball winder, balling frame.

Клузиуса колонна (nucl.) Clusius column.

клумба *f.* (hort.) flower bed.

клумпсы *pl.* clogs.

клуня *f.* threshing barn.

клуп/анодон *m.* (ichth.) Clupanodon; **—анодоновый** *a.* Clupanodon; clupanodonic (acid); **—еин** *m.* clupein.

клупик *see* **клупп.**

клуписудис *m.* (ichth.) Clupisudis.

клуп/ка *f.,* **—п** *m.* diestock, screwstock; tap wrench; (mach.) threading die holder; (text.) clip.

клухорский *a.* (geog.) Klukhori.

клуш/а *f.* brood hen; (orn.) lesser black-backed gull (*Larus fuscus*); **—ица** *f.* (orn.) chough (*Pyrrhocorax*); **—ка** *f.* brood hen.

клык *m.* canine tooth, cuspid; fang; tusk; detent, checking device; (art.) tow hook; **—астый** *a.* long-tusked; **—ач** *m.* (ichth.) toothfish (*Dissostichus*); **—овый** *a. of* **клык.**

клюв *m.* beak, bill, rostrum; hook; **—ач** *m.* (ichth.) Sebastes; (orn.) ibis; **—ик** *dim of* **клюв**; **—о-акромиальный** *a.* (anat.) coraco-acromial; **—о(видно)** *prefix* (anat.) coraco—, coracoid; rostri— (beak); r(h)yncho— (beaked); **—овиноключичный** *a.* coracoclavicular; **—овиднолистный** *a.* (bot.) rynchophyllous; **—о(видно)-плечевой** *a.* coracohumeral; coracobrachial; **—овидный, —ообразный** *a.* beak-shaped, rostral, rostrate; (anat.) coracoid; **—оголовые** *pl.* (herp.) Rhynchocephala; **—оносный** *a.* rhynchophorous, beaked; **—оротка** *f.* (ichth.) snipe ell (*Avocettina infans*); **—орыл** *m.* (mam.) beaked whale; **—орылы(е)** *pl.* (mam.) Ziphiidae; (ichth.) Mormyridae.

клюет *pr. 3 sing. of* **клевать.**

клюз *m.* (naut.) hawsehole, hawsepipe.

клюка *f.* rabble, poker; cane.

клюкв/а *f.,* **—енный** *a.* cranberry.

клюнийский ярус (geol.) Clunian stage.

клюнуть *see* **клевать.**

клюп— *see under* **клуп—.**

клюфт *m.* (min.) cleft, fissure.

ключ *m.* key; wrench; spring, fountain; (elec.) switch; (electron.) gate; (maps) legend; (comp.) qualifier; (music) clef; **английский к., французский к.** monkey wrench; **бить —ом** *v.* spout, jet, well up, bubble up; **кипеть —ом** boil over; **метод —ей** (ecol.) clue method; **система под к.** turnkey system; **электролитический к.** salt bridge; **—евой** *a. of* **ключ**; spring-fed; spring (water); **—евая схема** gating circuit, gate; **—евое слово** key word, catchword; **—ик** *dim. of* **ключ.**

ключи/ца *f.* (anat.) clavicle, collarbone; **—чно—** *prefix* clavi—, cleid(o)— (clavicle); **—чночерепной** *a.* cleidocranial; **—чный** *a.* clavicular.

ключки *pl.* (hort.) pricked-out seedlings.

ключ-трава *f.* (bot.) Botrychium lunaria.

клюшеногость *f.* (vet.) crooked legs.

клюшка *see* **клюка.**

клюют *pr. 3 pl. of* **клевать.**

клязьминский *a.* (geog.) Klyazma.

кляйзеновский *a.* Claisen (condensation).

клякса *f.* ink spot, blot.

клям(м)ера *f.* clinch rivet; cleat; (plumbing) roll (joint).

кляп *m.,* **—цы** *pl.* gag; (vet.) barnacle.

кляст— *see under* **класт—.**

клясть *v.* curse; **—ся** *v.* swear, vow.

клятва *f.* oath, vow.

кляча *f.* nag, old horse.

клячка *f.* chewing gum.

км *abbr.* (**километр**) kilometer; **км²** *abbr.* (**квадратный километр**) square kilometer; **км³** *abbr.* (**кубический километр**) cubic kilometer; **к/м²** *abbr.* (**кулон на квадратный метр**) coulomb per square meter; **Км** *abbr.* (**калимагнезия**) potassium magnesium sulfate; **КМ** *abbr.* (**командный модуль**) command module, CM; (**константа Михаэлиса**) Michaelis constant, K_m.

КМА *abbr.* (**Курская магнитная аномалия**) Kursk Magnetic Anomaly.

КМВ *abbr.* (**каротаж магнитной восприимчивости**) magnetic susceptibility logging.

К-мезон *m.* (nucl.) K-meson.

КМИЗ *abbr.* (**корреляционный метод изучения землетрясений**) correlational method of earthquake studies.

кмин *m.* (bot.) cumin (*Cuminum*).

кмкс *abbr.* (**киломаксвелл**) kilomaxwell.

КМОП *abbr.* (**комплементарная структура металл-оксидполупроводник**) complementary metal-oxide-semiconductor, CMOS.

КМОЭЦ *abbr.* (**карбоксиметилоксиэтил целлюлоза**) carboxymethyl hydroxyethyl cellulose, CMHEC.

КМПВ *abbr.* (**корреляционный метод преломлённых волн**) seismic refraction method.

км/сек *abbr.* (**километров в секунду**) kilometers per second; **км/ч** *abbr.* (**километров в час**) kilometers per hour.

КМЦ *abbr.* **КМ-целлюлоза** *f.* carboxymethylcellulose, CM-cellulose.

км/ч, км/час *abbr.* (**километров в час**) kilometers per hour.

Кн *abbr.* (**каинит**) (min.) kainite; **к.-н.** (**какой-нибудь**) some, any; **КН** *abbr.* (**контур нефтеносности**) outline of the oil zone; (**нефтяной кокс**) petroleum coke.

кн-во *abbr.* (**книгоиздательство**).

КНА *abbr.* (**комплекс научных аппаратов**) payload, instrument package.

КНД *abbr.* (**компрессор низкого давления**) low-pressure compressor; (**кремний на диэлектрике**) silicon-film-on-insulator, SFI; **КнД, к.н.д.** (**коэффициент направленного действия**) directivity factor.

КНДР *abbr.* (**Корейская Народно-демократическая Республика**) Korean People's Democratic Republic.

кнебелит *m.* (min.) knebelite.

кневенагелева *a.* Knoevenagel (reaction).

кнемидокопт *m.* (zool.) Cnemidocoptes.

кнериевые *pl.* (ichth.) Kneriidae.

кнефопланктон *m.* (ocean.) knephoplankton.

кнехт *m.* (naut.) bitt(s); bollard.

книг/а *f.* book, volume; register; **племенная к.** herd register; **—оставочный** *a.* (typ.) casing-in; **—одержатель** *m.* book clamp; bookend; **—оед** *m.* (ent.) book louse (*Liposcelis divinatorius*); **—оиздательский** *a.* publishing, publisher's; **—оиздательство** *n.* publishing house, publisher; **—ообмен** *m.* book exchange; **—опечатание** *n.,* **—опечатный** *a.* printing press; **—оторговля** *f.,* **—оторговый** *a.* book trade; **—охранилище** *n.* book depository; stackroom; library.

книдо— *prefix* (zool.) cnid(o)— (cnida); **—споридии** *pl.* (prot.) Cnidosporidia; **—циль** *m.* (zool.) cnidocil.

книж/ечка *f.* booklet, notebook; **к., —ка** *f.* (zool.) psalterium, third stomach; **—ка** *f.,* **—ный** *a.* book, volume; record card, register.

книзу *adv.* down(wards); **тяга к.** downward pull; downdraft.

книповичия *f.* (ichth.) Knipowitschia.

кница *f.* gusset, bracket; (naut.) knee.

кницин *m.* cnicin.

кнопер *m.* (tanning) oak gall.

кнопит *m.* (min.) knopite.

кноп/ка *f.,* **—очный,** *a.* push button, knob; (drawing) pin, tack; snap fastener; (zool.) closure; **с —кой** *a.* push-button; **к.-лампочка** *f.* illuminated push button; **—очное управление** push-button operation.

кнопперсы *pl.* (tanning) gall nuts.

Кнорра реакция Knorr (pyrrole) synthesis.

КНР *abbr.* (**Китайская Народная Республика**) People's Republic of China.

КНС *abbr.* (**кремний на сапфир**) silicon-on-sapphire (semiconductor), SOS; (**кустовая насосная станция**) cluster pump station.

кнудсеновский *a.* Knudsen (flow).

кнур *m.* (mam.) boar.

кнут *m.* whip; (ichth.) monkey goby (*Neogobius fluviatilis*); **к., —ик** *m.* toad goby (*Mesogobius batrachocephalus*); **—овина** *f.* (leather) lash mark; **—овище** *n.* whip handle.

кнутри *adv.* inwards.

кныр *m.* (mam.) boar.

кнюппель *m.* (aero.) joystick control.

княж/еника *f.* raspberry (*Rubus arcticus*); **—ик** *m.* (bot.) Clematis; Atragene.

князёк *m.* ridge of roof.

князь *m.* prince; (ichth.) roach (*Rutilus r.*); Salmo ischchan.

ко *see* **к.**

Ко *abbr.* (**компания**) Company.

КоА *abbr.* (**кофермент А**) coenzyme A.

коаг/ель *m.* coagel, coagulated gel; **—улаза** *f.* coagulase, clotting enzyme.

коагулир/ование *n.* coagulation; **—ованный** *a.* coagulated; **—овать(ся)** *v.* coagulate, clot, flocculate, coalesce; **—уемость** *f.* coagulability; **—уемый** *a.* coagulable; **—ующий** *a.* coagulating; coagulant; **—ующий реагент,** **—ующее средство** coagulant.

коагул/юм, **—ят** *m.* coagulum, clot; coagulate; **—янт,** **—ятор** *m.* coagulator; coagulant; coagulating agent; **—яция** *f.,* **—яционный** *a.* coagulation, coagulating.

коадаптация *f.* coadaptation.

коаксиальный *a.* coaxial.

коала *f.* (mam.) koala; *pl.* Phascolarctidae.

коалесценция *f.* coalescence.

коалит *m.* coalite, semicoke.

коалиция *f.* coalition.

коаптация *f.* coaptation.

коарктация *f.* coarctation, stricture.

коата *f.* (mam.) spider monkey (*Ateles*).

коати *m.* (mam.) coatimundi (*Nasua*).

коацерв/ат *m.* coacervate; **—атный** *a.* coacervate, densely clustered; **—ация** *f.* coacervation.

кобаламин *m.* cobalamin, vitamin B_{12}.

кобальт *m.* cobalt, Co; **закись —а** cobaltous oxide; **соединение закиси —а** cobaltous compound; **землистый к.** (min.) earthy cobalt, asbolite; **—окись —а** cobaltic oxide; **соединение окиси —а** cobaltic compound; **синий к.** cobalt blue; **хлористый к.** cobaltous chloride; **хлорный к.** cobaltic chloride.

кобальт/амин, **—иак,** **—иамин** *m.* cobaltammine, cobaltiac; **—ил** *m.* cobaltyl; **—ин** *m.* (min.) cobaltite, cobalt glance.

кобальтиров/ание *n.* cobalting, cobalt plating; **—ан-ный** *a.* cobalt-plated; **—ать** *v.* (plate with) cobalt.

кобальтисто— *prefix* cobalto—, cobaltous; **—синеро-дистый калий** potassium cobaltocyanide; **—синеро-доводородный** *a.* cobaltocyanic (acid).

кобальт/истый *a.* cobaltous, cobalto—, cobalt; **—ит** *see* **кобальтин; —ицианид** *m.* cobalticyanide, hexa-cyanocobaltate; **—о—** *prefix* cobalti—, cobaltic; cobalto—; **—оазотистоводородный** *a.* cobaltoni-trous (acid); **—оазотистокалиевая соль** potassium cobaltinitrite.

кобальтов/ый *a.* cobalt(ic), cobalti—, cobaltiferous; **к. блеск** (min.) cobalt glance, cobaltite; **к. зелёный** cobalt green, cobalt zincate, Rinmann's green; **к. колчедан** (min.) cobaltpyrite, linnaeite; **к. купорос** cobalt vitriol, cobaltous sulfate; **к. обмёт, —ые цветы** (min.) co-balt bloom, erythrite; **к. шпат** (min.) spherocobaltite; **—ая синь** cobalt blue; **—ое синее стекло** cobalt glass.

кобальто/кальцит *m.* (min.) cobaltocalcite; **—марган-цовая руда** (min.) cobaltiferous wad, asbolan, as-bolite; **—менит** *m.* (min.) cobaltomenite; **—никеле-вый колчедан** *m.* cobaltpyrite; **—рганический** *a.* organocobalt.

кобальтосинеродист/ая кислота, —оводородная кислота cobalticyanic acid; **—ый калий** potassium cobalticyanide.

кобамид *m.* cobamide, vitamin B_{12}.

кобеллит *m.* (min.) kobellite.

кобель *m.* male dog; (ichth.) gudgeon (*Gobio g.*).

коби/евые *pl.* (ichth.) Rachycentridae; **—я** *f.* cobia (*Rachycentron*).

кобка *f.* bucket.

коблик *see* **кобель** (ichth.).

кобловый *a.* pollard, pollarded (tree).

кобол *m.,* **КОБОЛ** *abbr.* (comp.) COBOL, common business-oriented language.

кобра *f.* (herp.) cobra (*Naja*).

кобрез/иевник *m.* Kobresia meadow; **—иевый** *a.,* **—ия** *f.* (bot.) Kobresia, Cobresia.

коброtoксин *m.* cobra toxin.

кобура *f.* leather case, holster.

кобчик *m.* (orn.) falcon (*Falco vespertinus*).

кобыл/а *f.* mare; (ichth.) asp (*Aspius a.*); **—ий** *a.* mare's; **—ица** *f.* filly; bridge (of string instrument); (ent.) acri-dian; **—ятина** *f.* horse meat.

ковала *f.* (ichth.) Kowala.

ковалентн/ость *f.* covalence; **—ый** *a.* covalent.

ковалла *f.* (ichth.) king mackerel (*Scomberomorus caval-la*).

ков/ало *n.* forge hammer; **—аль** *m.* blacksmith; **—аль-ня** *f.* forge, smithy; **—ание** *see* **ковка; —анность** *f.* hammered surface; **—ан(н)ый** *a.* forged, beaten, ham-mered; wrought (iron); shod (horse).

ковар *m.* Kovar (alloy).

ковари/антное *n.,* **—антный** *a.* (math.) covariant; **—антность** *f.,* **—анция** *f.* covariance; **—ационный** *a.* covariation, covariant; **—ация** *f.* covariation, covari-ance.

ковать *v.* forge, beat, hammer; swage; (fatigue testing) shot peen; shoe (a horse).

ковбой *m.,* **—ский** *a.* cowboy.

ковдозеровый *a.* (geog.) Lake Kovdo.

ковелл/ин, —ит *m.* (min.) covellite.

ковёр *m.* carpet, rug; (anat.; bot.) tapetum.

коверк/ание *n.* distortion; **—ать** *v.* distort, mangle, twist, mutilate; mispronounce.

коверкот *m.* (text.) covert coat; covert cloth.

коверсинус *m.* (math.) coversed sine.

ковк/а *f.* forging, etc., *see* **ковать; к. под молотом** drop forging; **сварка —ой** hammer welding; **—ий** *a.* ductile, malleable, forgeable, flexible, supple; **—ий чугун** wrought iron; **—ость** *f.* ductility, malleability, forgeability, flexibility.

ковок *sh. m. of* **ковкий.**

коволюм *m.* covolume, incompressible volume.

ковочн/о-штамповочный *a.* drop-forging; **—ый** *a.* forging, etc., *see* **ковать.**

ковра *gen. of* **ковёр.**

ковр/ига *f.* round loaf; **—ижка** *dim. of* **коврига;** (geol.) kovrizhka (hydrolaccolith or other permafrost hum-mock).

коврик *dim. of* **ковёр;** mat.

ковро/вый *a.* carpet; braided (cable); (biol.) tapetal; tap-estry (forest); **—вая материя** carpeting; **—вые рас-тения** ground cover; **—дел** *m.* carpet maker; **—делие** *n.* carpet making; **—ткачество** *n.* carpet weaving.

ковры *pl. of* **ковёр;** carpet-like meadow.

ковш *m.* dipper, scoop, shovel; (feed) hopper; bucket; port, harbor; (casting) ladle; **—евой** *see* **ковшовый;** *m.* ladle man; **—ик** *dim. of* **ковш; к.-ложка** *m.* ladle; **к.-лопата** *m.* excavator bucket; **—ово-ленточный** *a.* bucket and belt; **—овый** *a. of* **ковш; —овый транс-портёр** bucket conveyer; **—овая проба** (min.) pan-ning(s); (met.) ladle sample; **—овая тележка** (foun-dry) ladle car; **—овая турбина** Pelton wheel, Pelton turbine.

ковыл/ёк, —ь *m.,* **—ьный** *a.* feather grass (*Stipa*).

ковылять *v.* limp, hobble.

ковыр/нуть, –ять *v.* pick (at).

когда *adv. and conj.* when, while, as; where; **к. . . . к. . . .** sometimes . . . sometimes; **к. бы** if; **к. бы ни** whenever; **к. как** it depends; **к.-либо, к.-нибудь** sometime, some day, any time; ever; **к.-так** if so, in that case; **к.-то** formerly, once, sometime.

когез/ионный *a.,* **—ия** *f.* cohesion.

когенит *m.* (min.) cohenite.

когер/ент *m.* coherent; **—ентно-импульсный** *a.* (radar) coherent-pulse(d); **—ентность** *f.* coherence; **—ент-ный** *a.* coherent; **—ер** *m.* (rad.) coherer; **—ирование** *n.* cohesion, coherence; **—ировать** *v.* cohere.

когия *f.* (mam.) sperm whale (*Kogia*).

кого *acc. and gen. of* **кто,** whom.

когомо/логия *f.* (math.) cohomology; **—топический** *a.* cohomotopy, cohomotopic.

когорта *f.* (taxonomy) cohort, contingent.

ког/отковый *a. of* **коготок; —отный** *a.* claw, un-guiculate; **—оток** *dim. of* **коготь;** unguiculus; **—оть** *m.* (anat.) unguis, nail, claw, talon; catch; (hinge) knuckle.

кограница *f.* (math.) coboundary.

когт/евидный, —еобразный *a.* claw-like, hooked, un-guiform; **—евой** *a. of* **коготь; —еносный** *a.* un-guiculate; **—еходящий** *a.* (zool.) unguligrade; **—ти** *pl. of* **коготь;** claws, grapplers, pole climbers; **—ис-тые** *pl.* (mam.) Unguiculata; **—истый** *a.* sharp-clawed; unguiculate; **—ить** *v.* claw (at), grapple (with); maul; **—я** *gen. of* **коготь.**

код *m.* code, key, cipher, notation; **к. числа** number.

кодак *m.* (phot.) Kodak; **—ром** *m.* Kodachrome (color film).

кодамин *m.* codamine.

кодас *m.* (mam.) yak (*Poëphagus grunniens*).

коде/гидр(оген)аза *f.* codehydr(ogen)ase; **—ин** *m.* co-deine, methylmorphine; **—инизм** *m.* codeine addic-tion; **—иновый** *a.* codeine; codeic (acid).

кодекс *m.* code; statute.

код/ер *m.* (en)coder; **—ирование** *n.* (en)coding, codification; **—ированно-десятичный** *a.* (comp.) coded-decimal; **—ированный** *a.* (en)coded, in code; **—ировать** *v.* (en)code; **—ировщик** *m.* (en)coder; **—ирующий** *a.* (en)coding; **—ирующий диск** disk coder; **—ирующее устройство** (en)coder.

кодистилляция *f.* codistillation.

кодиум *m.* (bot.) Codium (algae).

код/ификационный *a.*, **—ификация** *f.* codification, coding; **—ифицировать** *v.* codify, systematize; **—ово-импульсный** *a.* pulse-code; **—овый** *a.* code(d); **—овая группа** (comp.) word.

кодоминантный *a.* (gen.) codominant.

кодон *m.* (gen.) codon.

кодопреобразователь *m.* decoder.

кодор/ииский *a.* (geog.) Kodori; **—ский** *a.* Kodor.

кое *pron. n.* which, that; **к.-где** *adv.* somewhere; **—го** *gen. of* **кой.**

коек *gen. pl. of* **койка.**

кое-как *adv.* anyhow, somehow, haphazardly; with difficulty; **к.-какой** *a.* some, any; **к.-когда** *adv.* sometimes, occasionally; **к.-кто** *pron.* somebody, some(one); **к.-куда** *adv.* somewhere.

коечный *a. of* **койка;** bed (patient).

кое-что *pron.* something; a little.

кож/а *f.* skin; (anat.) cutis, derma; integument; hide, leather; peel, paring, rind; **болезнь —и** cutaneous disease; **—ан** *m.* leather coat; (mam.) *see* **кожанок; —анка** *f.* leather jacket; hop tree (*Ptelea trifoliata*); **—ановые, —аны** *pl.* (mam.) plainnose bats (*Vespertilionidae*); **—ано-жёлтый** *a.* leather-colored; alutaceous; **—анок** *m.* (mam.) bat (*Eptesicus; Vespertilio*); **—аный** *a.* leather(y).

кожвинский *a.* (geog.) Kozhva.

кож/галантерейный *a.* leather and haberdashery; **—евенник** *see* **кожевник; —евеннообувный** *a.* leather-shoe (industry); **—евенный** *a.* tanning; leather; **—евенный завод** tannery; **—евенное дерево** (bot.) sumac (*Rhus*); **—евник** *m.* tanner, currier, leather-dresser; (bot.) sumac; **—евнический, —евничий** *a.* tanner's; **—евня** *f.* tannery; **—едёр** *m.* hide stripper; **—еед** *m.* (ent.) skin beetle (*Dermestes; Anthrenus,* etc.); **—еедина** *f.* beetle damage; **—еедовые, —еды** *pl.* (ent.) Dermestidae; **—ерез** *m.* (zool.) wood tick (*Dermacentor*); **—езавод** *m.* leather factory; **—заменитель** *m.* artificial leather; **—имит** *m.* artificial (sole) leather.

кожимский *a.* (geog.) Kozhim.

кож/истокрылые *pl.* (ent.) earwigs (*Dermaptera*); **—истолистный** *a.* leathery-leaved, scytophyllous; **—истый** *a.* leathery, leather-like, coriaceous; **—ица** *f.* film, pellicle; peel, husk, outer skin; (anat.) cuticle, cuticula; (biol.) epidermis; **—ицесниматель** *m.* peeler; **—ник** *m.* (med.) dermatologist; **—но-гальванический** *a.* cutaneogalvanic; **—нолоскутный** *a.* cutaneous (amputation); **—но-мышечный** *a.* skin-muscular; **—но-слизистый** *a.* mucocutaneous; **—носочленовный** *a.* dermarticular (bone); **—ный** *a.* skin, cutaneous, dermal; **—ная пластика** (med.) skin grafting; **—суррогат** *m.* artificial leather; **—сырьё** *n.* hides; **—ура** *f.* coat, rind, hull, skin; cortex; husk, pod.

кожух *m.* case, casing, housing, enclosure; cover(ing); sheath(ing); mantle, hood, cowl, jacket; shell (of boiler); leather coat; **заключённый в к.** *a.* jacketed; **—озмеевиковый** *a.* shell-and-coil (cooler); **—отрубный, —отрубчатый** *a.* shell-and-tube (heat exchanger).

коза *f.* (mam.) nanny goat (*Capra*); crate; (brick) hod; (min.) timber cart; **снежная к.** mountain goat (*Oreamnos americanus*).

козалит *m.* (min.) cosalite.

козачка *f.* plow handle.

коз/ёл *m.* goat (male); (met.) sow, salamander, bear (furnace scale); (av.) bounce; (ichth.) young bream (*Abramis brama*); surmullet (*Upeneus prayensis*); *gen. of* **козлы; болотный к., водяной к.** (mam.) kob, waterbuck (*Kobus*); **горный к.** Siberian ibex (*Capra sibirica*); **дикий к.** roe deer (*Capreolus c.*); **чёрный к.** chamois (*Rupicapra r.*); **—елец** *m.* (bot.) Scorzonera; **—елковый** *a.* (anat.) tragal; **—елок** *m.* horse, trestle; (screw) jack; morocco leather; (anat.) tragus; **—ерог** *m.* (astr.) Capricorn; **—ий** *a.* goat, caprine; **—ья ива** (bot.) goat willow (*Salix caprea*); **—инец** *m.* (vet.) knee-sprung condition.

козимаза *f.* cozymase, coenzyme I.

козл/а *gen. of* **козёл; —ение** *n.* (zool.) yeaning; **—ёнок** *m.* kid; kid leather; **—ик** *dim. of* **козёл; —ина** *f.* goatskin; kid; **—иные** *pl.* sheep and goats (*Caprinae*); **—иный** *a.* goat('s), goatlike, hircine; **—ить** *v.* (av.) bounce; **—иться** *v.* (zool.) kid, yean; **—обородник** *m.* (bot.) Tragopogon; **—овый** *a. of* **козёл, козлы; —ы** *pl.* trestle, (saw) horse, bench; gantry (of crane); (mam.) Caprinae; **—як** *m.* mushroom (*Boletus bovinus*); **—ята** *pl. of* **козлёнок; —ятина** *f.* goat meat; **—ятник** *m.* goat house; (bot.) goat's rue (*Galega*).

козовод *m.* goat breeder; **—ство** *n.*, **—ческий** *a.* goat breeding.

козод/оивые, —ои *pl.* (orn.) Caprimulgidae; **—ой** *m.* nightjar (*Caprimulgus*).

козочки, морские *pl.* (crust.) Caprellidae.

козуля *see* **косуля.**

козыль(ник) *m.* (bot.) ambrosia.

козыр/ёк *m.*, **—ьковый** *a.* visor; deflector, baffle plate; ledge, overhang; lip (of scoop); (wind) shield, screen; hood.

козья *f. of* **козий.**

козяв/ка *f.* (ent.) small beetle, spec. Lochnaea; **—очка** *f.* Pyrrhalta.

коизогенный *a.* (gen.) coisogenic.

коикс *m.* (bot.) Job's tears (*Coix*).

коилия *f.* (ichth.) Coilia.

коинциденция *f.* coincidence.

коипу *m.* (mam.) nutria, coypu (*Myocastor coypus*).

коитус *m.* coitus, copulation.

кой *pron. m.* who, which, that; *see under* **кое** for idioms.

койбагарский *a.* (geog.) Koibagar.

койевая кислота kojic acid.

койка *f.* cot, bed, berth, bunk; hammock.

койл/ание *n.* coiling; **—ер** *m.* (text.) coiler; **—ия** *see* **коилия.**

койот *m.* (mam.) coyote (*Canis latrans*).

койр *m.* coir, coconut fiber.

койский *a.* (geog.) Koi.

кок *m.* (av.) spinner (of propeller); (nose or tail) cone; (ship's) cook.

кока *f.*, **—иновый куст** (bot.) coca (*Erythroxylon coca*); **—евая кислота** cocaic acid; **—ин** *m.*, **—иновый** *a.* cocaine; **—инизировать** *v.* cocainize; **—инизм** *m.* cocaine addiction; **—инист** *m.* cocaine addict; **—иновые** *pl.* (bot.) Erythroxylaceae; **—ис** *m.* (geobot.) cocais; **к.-кола** *f.* Coca Cola.

кокарбоксилаза *f.* cocarboxylase.

кокард/а *f.* cockade, badge; **—овая руда** (min.) cockade ore, cockscomb pyrite.

кокарциноген *m.* (med.) cocarcinogen.

кокать *see* **кокнуть.**

кокейрос *m.* coconut palm grove.

кокил/ь *m.,* **—ьный** *a.* (foundry) chill mold, permanent mold; **отливать в —ях** *v.* cast cold; **отливка в —ях, —ьное литьё** chill casting; **—ьнооотлитый** *a.* chill-cast.

кокимбит *m.* (min.) coquimbite.

кокк *m.* (bact.) coccus; *pl.* cocci; **—о—** *prefix* cocco— (grain, seed, berry); **—овый** *a.* coccus, coccal; **—оидный** *a.* coccoid, spherical; **—олит** *m.* (min.) cocolite; (prot.) cocolith; **—олоба** *f.* (bot.) Coccoloba; **—офаг** *m.* (ent.) Coccophagus; **—улин;** cocculin; cocculine.

коклюш *m.* (med.) whooping cough.

коклюш/ечный *a.,* **—ка** *f.* bobbin.

коклюшный *a. of* **коклюш;** pertussoid.

ко-кнедер *m.* co-kneader.

кокнуть *v.* hit, strike; crack (egg).

кокон *m.,* **—ный** *a.* cocoon, chrysalis, pupa, follicle; **—оводство** *n.* silkworm rearing; **—оморилка** *see* **коконосушилка; —омотание** *n.* (silk) reeling; **—опряд-колечник** *m.* (ent.) tent caterpillar (*Malacasoma neustria*); **—опрядовые, —опряды** *pl.* (ent.) Lasiocampidae; **—оразмоточный** *a.* reeling; **—осушилка** *f.* cocoon drying room, coccoon roaster.

кокор *m.* (cartridge) box.

кокора *f.* (timber) knee; tree with stump.

кокорыш *m.* (bot.) fool's parsley (*Aethusa*).

кокос *m.,* **—овый** *a.* coconut; **—овая пальма** coconut palm (*Cocos nucifera*).

кок(-)пек *m.* (bot.) Atriplex cana.

кокпит *m.* (av.) cockpit.

кокс *m.* coke.

кокс— *prefix* (med.) cox— (hip joint).

кок-сагыз *m.* (bot.) kok-saghyz (*Taraxacum kok-saghyz*) (source of rubber).

коксальный *a.* (anat.) coxal.

коксик *m.* coke fines, coke breeze.

коксит *m.* (med.) coxitis.

коксо— *prefix* coke; (anat.) coxo— (hip joint); **—бензольный** *a.* benzene; coal-tar chemical (plant); **—брикет** *m.* coked briquette.

коксов/альный *a.* coke, coking; **—альная печь, —альное стойло** coke oven; **—альщик** *m.* coke oven operator; **—ание** *n.* coking; charring; **—ание в кучах** batch coking; **—ать** *v.* coke, carbonize, char; **—ик** *m.* (cer.; met.) sagger; cokeplant worker.

коксов/ый *a.* coke; coke oven (gas); coal (tar); **—ая мука** powdered coke; **—ая печь** coke oven; **—ые числа** coking values.

коксо/выталкиватель *m.* coke discharger; **—дробилка** *f.* breaker; **—дробильный** *a.* coke-breaking; **—обжигательная печь** coke oven; **—образование** *n.* coke formation, coking; gumming; (oil) carbonization; **—образующий** *a.* coke-forming.

коксоподит *m.* (crust.) coxopodite.

коксо/подобный *a.* coke-like; **—сортировка** *f.* coke sorter, coke screen.

коксотомия *f.* (med.) coxotomy.

кокс/отушильный *a.* coke-quenching; **—охимический** *a.* by-product of coke; **—охимия** *f.* by-product coke industry; **—уемость** *f.* coking capacity.

коксуйский *a.* (geog.) Koksu.

коксующий(ся) *a.* coking, charring.

коктальский *a.* (geog.) Koktal.

кокум *m.* kokum butter.

кокушник *m.* (bot.) Gymnadenia.

кокц/ерил *m.* cocceryl; **—ериловый** *a.* cocceryl; cос-

cer(yl)ic (acid); **—ида** *f.* (ent.) coccid; **—идий** *m.* (prot.) Coccidium; **—идиоз** *m.* (med.) coccidiosis, Coccidia infection; **—идиоидный** *a.* (prot.) coccidioidal; **—идовые, —иды** *pl.* scale insects (*Coccidae*); **—ин** *m.* coccin; **—инелиды** *pl.* (ent.) Coccinellidae; **—иновый** *a.* coccin; coccineous, bright red; coccinic (acid).

кок/четавский *a.* (geog.) Kokchetav; **—шаговый** *a.* Kokshaga; **—шалтауский** *a.* Kokshaal Tau; **—шаровит** *m.* (min.) koksharovite; **—шенгский** *a.* (geog.) Kokshenga.

кол *m.* stake, picket; peg; post, pole; (agr.) dibble.

кол. *abbr.* (**колебание**).

Кола способ Cole's method.

кола *f.* (bot.) cola; **—мин** *m.* colamine, 2-aminoethanol; **—с** *m.* colas (road tar); **—ста** *f.* colasta (plastic).

колатитуда *f.* (maps) colatitude.

колба *f.* flask; retort; shell, envelope; (elec.) bulb; (ichth.) goby; gudgeon (*Gobio g.*); **коническая к.** Erlenmeyer flask.

колбас/а *f.,* **—ный** *a.* sausage, bologna; bustle pipe (of blast furnace); **—(к)овидный** *a.* sausage-shaped, botuliform, allantoid; **—ное дерево** (bot.) Kigelia.

колб/невые *pl.* (ichth.) gobies (*Gobiidae*); **—нещука** *f.* clingfish (*Gobiesox*); **—нещуковые** *pl.* Gobiesocidae; **—ни** *see* **колбневые; —овидный** *a.* flask-shaped, ampulliform, ampullaceous; **—одержатель** *m.* flask clamp; **—онагреватель** *m.* flask heater; **—ообразный** *see* **колбовидный; —очка, —очковый** *a., dim. of* **колба;** (anat.) cone, conus (of retina).

колвинский *a.* (geog.) Kolva.

кол-во *abbr.* (**количество**) quantity.

колгуевский *a.* (geog.) Kolguyev.

колд-крем *m.* cold cream.

колдобина *f.* small pit; (road) pot hole.

колдоговор *m.* collective agreement.

колдун/ова трава, -трава *f.* (bot.) Circaea.

колеантус *m.* (bot.) Coleanthus.

колебан/ие *n.* oscillation; swinging, etc., *see* **колебать(ся)**; range, changes; (modulated) wave; perturbation (of orbit); frequency; voltage; (stat.) scattering, spread; **—ия** *pl.* oscillation; vibrations; (naut.) surging; **вид —ий** (rad.) mode; **генератор —ий** oscillator.

колебательность *f.* tendency to oscillate.

колебательн/ый *a.* oscillatory, oscillating, fluctuating; vibrating, vibratory, vibration(al); **к. контактор** vibrating contactor, chopper; **к. контур** (rad.) oscillatory circuit; **к. процесс** oscillation, vibration; **волна —ого движения** vibrational wave.

колеб/ать *v.* shake, agitate, vibrate; swing, rock; **—аться** *v.* oscillate, fluctuate, vary, range; vibrate; falter, hesitate, waver; flicker (of flame); vacillate; undulate, sway, swing, rock; hunt; wobble; **—аться в пределах** fluctuate, vary, range; **—лющийся** *a.* oscillating, etc., *see v.*; oscillatory, vibratory; variable, mutable; versatile; labile, unstable, wobbly; floating (rib); **—нуть** *v.* (give a) push, start swinging.

колебистый *a.* deep-rutted.

колеманит *m.* (min.) colemanite.

коленка *dim. of* **колено.**

коленкор *m.,* **—овый** *a.* (text.) calico.

колен/но— *prefix* (anat.) knee; genu—; **к.-рычажный механизм** toggle; **к.-рычажное соединение** toggle joint; **—ный** *a. of* **колено;** (anat.) genual; patellar; knee-jerk (reflex); **—ная чашка** patella, knee cap; **—о** *n.* (anat.) knee, genu; elbow, bend; offset; (shaft) crank; (manometer) arm; (barometer) leg; tribe, race, line, generation; (bot.) joint, node, knot, geniculum;

(geol.) limb, slope; curvature; **—це** *dim. of* **колено;** **—чатка** *f.* (bot.) loment(um); **—чатый** *a.* geniculate; **—чатоногие** *pl.* (zool.) sea spiders (*Pantopoda*).

коленчат/ый *a.* knee-like, geniculate; elbow(ed), angular, bent, crank(ed); angle (thermometer, etc.); jointed, articulate(d); **к. вал, —ая ось** crankshaft; **к. рычаг** crank; **—ая труба** elbow (pipe); **—ое соединение** elbow joint.

колео— *prefix* coleo— (sheath); **—птер** *m.* (av.) coleopter; **—птерология** *f.* (ent.) coleopterology; **—птиле, —птиль** *m.* (bot.) coleoptile; **—риза** *f.* coleor(r)iza, root sheath.

колер *m.* color (scheme); tint, shade; caramel, sugar coloring; (vet.) staggers.

колерябия *see* **кольраби.**

колёсико *n.* small wheel, caster, roller.

колёсн/ик (*or* **колесник**) *m.* wheelwright; **—о-гусеничный** *a.* half-track (tractor); **—о-токарный станок** wheel lathe; **—ый** *a.* wheel(ed); paddle-wheel (steamer); axle (grease).

колес/о *n.* wheel; impeller (of compressor, etc.); (squirrel) cage; *prefix* (biol.) troch(o)—; **метод —а** (geobot.) wheel point method; **пассивное к.** caster; **рабочее к.** rotor; (compressor) impeller; **к.-топчак** treadmill; **—овидный** *a.* wheel-shaped, rotiform; (anat.) trochoid; **—отокарный станок** wheel lathe.

колет *m.* collar; *pr. 3 sing. of* **колоть.**

колеть *v.* freeze; (zool.) die.

колеус *m.* (bot.) Coleus.

кол/ец *gen. pl. of* **кольцо; —ечко** *dim. of* **кольцо;** eye, ring; annulet, link; (anat.) anulus; **—ечный** *a. of* **колесо.**

колея *f.* rut, track; wheel span; (rr.) gage; (bridge) tread(way); **узкая к.** narrow gage.

коли *adv.* when; *conj.* if, since, as.

коли— *prefix* coli— [colon; coli (bacteria)]; **—бацил-лёз** *m.* (med.) colibacillosis.

колибри *m. or f.* (orn.) hummingbird; *pl.* Trochilidae.

коли/индекс *m.* (bact.) coli(form) index; **—ка** *f.,* **—ки** *pl.* colic, abdominal pain; **—мицин** *m.* colimycin.

колинеарность *f.* (gen.) colinearity.

коли/подобный *a.* (bact.) coliform; **—статин** *m.* colistatin; **—стин** *m.* colistin (antibiotic); **—т** *m.* (med.) colitis; **—титр** *m.* coliform count; **—цин** *m.* colicin (antibiotic).

количественн/о *adv.* quantitatively; **к. измеримый** *a.* quantifiable; **к.-неизмеримый** *a.* non-quantifiable; **—ый** *a.* quantitative; numerical (ratio); cardinal (number).

количеств/о *n.* quantity, amount, number, count; content; capacity; tonnage; body; large proportion; **к. движения** momentum; **в —е** in amounts (of), to the extent (of), at the rate (of); **в большом —е** in quantity.

колк/а *f.* splitting, cleaving, cleavage, fission; chopping (of wood); *gen. of* **колок; —и** *pl. of* **колок; —ий** *a.* split, fissured, cracked; cleavable, fissile; **—ость** *f.* cleavability.

колкотар *m.* colcothar, Prussian red, rouge.

колл. *abbr.* (**коллоидный**) colloidal.

коллаген *m.* collagen; **—ный, —овый** *a.* collagen(ous); **—оз** *m.* (med.) collagenosis.

коллапс *m.,* **—ный** *a.* collapse.

колларгол *m.* collargol, colloid silver.

коллатераль *f.,* **—ный** *a.* collateral.

колле/га *m.* colleague, associate; **—гиально** *adv.* collectively, jointly; **—гиальность** *f.* joint leadership; **—гиальный** *a.* collegiate, joint; **—гия** *f.* staff, board, college; **—(д)ж** *m.* college.

коллектив *m.* association, organization, group; collective (body); staff, personnel, crew, team; (opt.) collecting lens; **рабочий к.** all hands; **—изировать** *v.* collectivize, share; **—ный** *a.* collective, cooperative; community; shared; **—ный доступ** (comp.) multiaccess.

коллект/ирование *n.* collection; **—ировать** *v.* collect; **—ор** *m.* collector, receiver, receptacle, reservoir; collecting main; drum (of boiler); trap; sewer; (mach.) manifold, header; (elec.) commutator; (flotation) promoter; (library) pool; **—орный, —орский** *a. of* **коллектор;** collecting.

коллеку/ионер *m.* collector (of specimens); **—ионирование** *n.* collection; **—ионировать** *v.* collect; **—ионный** *a.* collection; sample, plot; **—ия** *f.* collection, set, complex.

колл/ема *f.* (bot.) Collema (lichen); **—емболы** *pl.* (ent.) springtails (*Collembola*); **—енхима** *f.* (bot.) collenchyma; (zool.) collenchyme; **—ет(ес)** *m.* (ent.) a bee (*Colletes succinta*); **—и** *m.* collie (dog); **—ибия** *f.* (bot.) Collybia; **—идин** *m.* collidine; **—изия** *f.* collision; **—иквационный** *a.* (med.) colliquative, colliquation.

коллим/атор *m.* (opt.) collimator; **—аторный** *a.* collimator; collimating, collimation; **—ационный** *a.,* **—ация** *f.* collimation; **—ированный** *a.* collimated; **—ировать** *v.* collimate, render parallel.

коллине/арность *f.* collinearity; **—арный** *a.* collinear; **—ация** *f.* collineation.

коллирит *m.* (min.) collyrite.

коллирия *f.* (ent.) Collyria.

колло— *prefix* coll(o)— (glue).

коллод/иальный, —ийный, —ионный *a.* collodion; **—иальная вата** collodion cotton, soluble guncotton, pyroxylin; **—ий, —иум** *m.* collodion.

коллоид *m.* colloid; **—альныий, —ный** *a.* colloid(al); **—альное движение** colloidal movement, Brownian movement; **—ное вещество** colloid; **—но-осмотический** *a.* colloid-osmotic, oncotic; **—но-растворимый** *a.* colloid-soluble; **—окластический** *a.* (med.) colloidoclastic (shock); **—ообразование** *n.* colloid formation.

колло/квиум *m.* (educ.) colloquium, academic conference; oral test; **—ксилин** *m.* colloxylin, pyroxylin; **—морфный** *a.* (geol.) colloform; **—типия** *f.* (phot.) collotype; **—фан** *m.* (min.) collophanite; **—химия** *f.* collochemistry, colloid chemistry.

коллюв/иальный *a.* (geol.) colluvial; **—ий** *m.* colluvium, colluvial deposit(s).

коло— *prefix* (anat.) colo— (colon).

колоб, —ок *m.* round loaf; (oil)cake; consolidated ice; **—няк** *m.* ball ice.

колобома *f.* (med.) coloboma.

коловдавливатель *m.* (agr.) stake press.

коловорот *m.* brace (and bit).

коловрат/ки *pl.* (zool.) rotifers, wheel animalcules (*Rotatoria*); **—ность** *f.* vicissitude, mutability, inconstancy.

коловратн/ый *a.* circular, rota(to)ry, revolving, gyrating; **к. насос** rotary pump; **к. сустав** (anat.) trochoid joint; **—ое движение** gyration.

коловращение *n.* circular motion, rotation, revolution.

коловый *a. of* **кол;** pole (bean).

кологарифм *m.* (math.) cologarithm.

колода *f.* block, log, chunk; trough; pack, deck (of cards); **к.-улей** *f.* beehive.

колод/езник *m.* well driller; **—езный** *a.,* **—езь, —ец** *m.* well, pit, shaft, sump; manhole; **—езная печь,**

—ец-печь *m.* (met.) soak(ing) pit; **отстойный —ец** drain, sink, sewer.

колод/ка *f.* (mech.) shoe, block, check; (wheel) chock; terminal block; (pressure) plate; last (of shoe); shoe tree; **контактная к.** receptacle, connector; **тормозная к.** brake shoe, brake block; (av.) chock; **к.-гайка** *f.* link block; **—ный** *a. of* **колода;** **—очный** *a. of* **колодка;** **—очный тормоз** block brake, shoe brake.

колодце/вый *see* **колодезный;** **—копатель** *m.* well driller.

колок *m.* peg, pin; game refuge; isolated grove (of birch or aspen); *gen. pl. of* **колка;** *sh. m. of* **колкий.**

колоказия *f.* (bot.) Colocasia.

колоквинт *see* **колоцинт.**

колокол *m.* bell; bell jar; (exhaust) hood; hopper; (av.) whipstall; (biol.) umbel; (zool.) umbrella; **плавательный к.** (zool.) nectophore; **—ец** *dim. of* **колокол;** **—ообразный, —оподобный** *a.* bell(-shaped), funnel-shaped, funneled, cupped; **—ьный** *a. of* **колокол;** bell (metal); **—ьчато—** *prefix,* **—ьчатый** *a.* campanulate, bell-shaped; **—ьчик** *dim. of* **колокол;** (bot.) Campanulaceae.

коломазь *f.* (axle) grease.

коломб/ин *m.* columbin; **—о** *n.* calumba root; **—ье** *n.* (paper) colombier.

коломенка *f.* kind of barge.

коломянка *see* **каламянка.**

колон/иальник *m.,* **—иальный домик** summer-range poultry house; **—иальный** *a.* colonial, colony; **—из(ир)овать** *v.* colonize, settle; **—ия** *f.* colony, settlement; culture; (cell) family.

колон/ка *dim. of* **колонна;** core (sample); (petrol.) casing, section; (gas) pump; geyser; band (of drops); small pile; (bot.) columella; *gen. of* **колонок; на —ках** *a.* column (chromatogram); **—ки** *pl. of* **колонка, колонок; —ковидный** *a.* columnar; columniform; **—ковый** *a. of* **колонка, колонок;** core (drill); **—кообразный** *a.* columnar; **—на** *f.* column, pillar, shaft; (stripping; distillation) tower; (elec.) pile; (cryst.) prism; **ионизация —нами** columnar ionization; **на —не** pillar type; **—нада** *f.* colonnade; **—на-стабилизатор** *f.* (petrol.) stabilizer; **—новидный, —нообразный** *a.* columnar; columniform; **—ный** *a.* column(ar); split, cleaved; **—ного типа** column (dissolver, etc.).

колоно— *prefix* (anat.) colono—, colon.

колонок *m.* (mam.) Siberian weasel, kolinsky (*Mustela sibirica*).

колоноскоп *m.* (med.) colo(no)scope.

колон/титул *m.* (typ.) running title, (running) headline, catchword; (page) header; **нижний к.** footer; **—цифра** *f.* (page) number, folio; **—чатый** *see* **колонновидный; —штейн** *m.* (horol.) jewel pin.

колорад/оит *m.* (min.) coloradoite; **—ский** *a.* (geol.) Coloradoan; **—ский жук** Colorado potato beetle.

колор/изация *f.* coloration, coloring; **—иметр** *m.* colorimeter; **—иметрировать** *v.* determine calorimetrically; **—иметрический** *a.* colorimetric; **—иметрия** *f.* colorimetry, colorimetric analysis; **—ист** *m.* (text.) dye specialist; (typ.) color matcher; **—ит** *m.* color(ing); **—итный** *a.* color(ful), vivid; **—ическая** *f.* (typ.) ink room; **—ический** *a.* coloristic; dyeing, tinctorial; **—эквивалент** *m.* color equivalent; **—эксцесс** excess color.

колос *m.* (bot.) ear, spike; **—еница** *f.* psyllium seed; **—ик** *dim. of* **колос; —истый** *a.* spicate, spiked; heavy-eared (corn, etc.); **—иться** *v.* ear, form ears, head; **—овидный** *a.* spiculiform; **—овый** *a. of* **ко-**

лосок; spicate, spiked; *suffix* —spiculate; **—коносный** *a.* spiculiferous.

колоскопия *f.* (med.) colo(no)scopy.

колосник *m.,* **—овый** *a.* grate bar, (fire) bar; **—и** *pl.* **—овая решётка** (fire) grate, grating; **—овый грохот** (min.) grizzly.

колосняк *m.* (bot.) wild rye (*Elymus*).

колосо— *prefix* stachy(o)—, spici— (spike, ear); **—видный** *a.* spike-shaped, spiciform, spicate; herringbone (design); **—вка** *f.* hummeler; **—вой** *a.* ear(ed), spike(d); **—вая трава** (bot.) Herniaria; **—вые** *pl.* cereal crops; **—к** *m.* spikelet; **душистый —к, пахучий —к** sweet-scented vernal grass (*Anthoxanthum odoratum*); **—носный** *a.* spiciferous; **—образный** *see* **колосовидный; —образование** *n.* ear formation, earing; **—подборщик** *m.* ear retriever; **—подъёмник** *m.* grain guard; lifter; **—приёмник** *m.* ear feeder; **—уборщик** *m.* ear stripper.

колоссальный *a.* colossal, huge.

колостомия *f.* (med.) colostomy.

колос/ый *a. suffix* —spicate; **—ья** *pl. of* **колос; —янка** *f.* (ichth.) Atherina mochon; **—яной** *a. of* **колос; —ящийся** *a.* earing.

колот/ило *n.* mallet, beater, rammer; bumper, buffer; **—ить** *v.* beat, knock, thrash, pound; mill, thresh; break, smash; **—иться** *v.* beat, pound (of heart); tremble, shake; **—овка** *f.* beater; **—ушка** *f.* beetle, beater, knocker.

колот/ый *a.* split, etc., *see v.*; lump (sugar); **—ая рана** (med.) puncture; **—ь** *v.* split, cleave; chop (wood); cut; prick, pierce, puncture; stab, slaughter; husk, crack; **—ье, —ьё** *n.* stitch, stab (of pain); colic pains; splitting, etc., *see v.*; **—ься** *v.* prick; be prickly; split, be fissile.

колоф/оловый, —оновый *a.* colopholic, colophonic (acid); **—оний** *m.* colophony, rosin; **—онит** *m.* (min.) colophonite.

колоцинт *m.* (bot.) colocynth (*Citrullus colocynthis*); **—ин** *m.* colocynthin.

колочный *a. of* **колок.**

колоша *f.* (met.) charge, batch; (blow-in) burden; (coke; fuel) bed.

колошение *n.* (bot.) heading, ear formation.

колошник *m.* (furnace) mouth, throat, top; **—овый** *a.* (met.) charge; charging (platform, etc.); blast furnace (dust, gas, etc.).

колп— see кольп—.

колпа/к *m.* cap, cover, cowl, hood, bell, helmet; cupola; dome (of furnace); globe, shade; (air) chamber, box; (foundry) cope; (agr.) hotcap; **колёсный к.** hub cap; **кольчатый к.** mushroom (*Rozites capaeata*); **паровой к.** steam collector; **стеклянный к.** bell jar; **к.-колокол** *m.* (furnace) crown; bell, cone (of blast furnace); **—ковидный** *a.* (biol.) galericulate; **—ковый** *a.* bell-shaped; bell-type (furnace); **—чковидный** *a.* mitriform; clyptriform; **—чковый** *a. of* **колпак; —чковая гайка** screw cap; **—чковая колонна** bubble tower, bubble-plate column; **—чковая тарелка** bubble (-cap) plate; **—чок** *dim. of* **колпак;** cap; bubble cap; head; (incandescent) mantle; (bot.) calyptra, covering; mitra.

колп/ик *m.,* **—ица** *f.* (orn.) spoonbill (*Platalea,* spec. *P. leucorodia*).

колповый *a.* (geog.) Kolp.

кол/сек *abbr.* (**колебания в секунду**) oscillations per second.

колтун *m.* (vet.) plica polonica.

колтунник *m.* (bot.) club moss (*Lycopodium clavatum*).

колумб/ат *see* **ниобат;** **—иевый** *a.* Columbia; *see also* **ниобиевый;** **—ий** *m.* columbium (now niobium); **—ийский** *a.* (geog.) Colombia(n); Columbia(n); **К. округ** District of Columbia; **—ин** *see* **колумбин;** **—ит** *m.* (min.) columbite, niobite; **—ова трава** Columbian grass (*Sorghum almum*).

колумелла *f.* (biol.) columella; stylus.

колун *m.* ax, wood chopper, cleaver.

колуп/ать, —нуть *v.* pick at (scab, etc.).

колхидский *a.* (geog.) Colchian.

колхиц/еин *m.* colchiceine; **—ин** *m.* colchicine; **—иновый** *a.* colchicinic (acid).

колхоз *m.,* **—ный** *a.* kolkhoz, collective farm; **—ник** *m.,* **—ница** *f.* kolkhoznik, collective farmer.

колчедан *m.* (min.) pyrite(s); **волосистый к.** millerite; **гребенчатый к.** cockscomb pyrite; **железный к., серный к.** iron pyrites, pyrite; **копьевидный к.** spear pyrite; **лучистый к.** marcasite; **—ный, —овый** *a.* pyrite, pyritic; **—ные огарки** (met.) pyrite cinders; roasted pyrites; **—осодержащий** *a.* pyritiferous.

колченогий *a.* lame (with one leg shorter).

колыбель *f.* cradle, origin.

колыванский *a.* (geog.) Kolyvan.

колымский *a.* (geog.) Kolyma.

колых/ание *n.* rocking, swaying; fluctuation; **—ать, —нуть** *v.* rock, sway, shake, swing; **—аться, —нуться** *v.* rock, sway, swing; fluctuate; waver; stir; heave.

колышек *dim. of* **кол;** peg, picket, prop; pin; (hort.) dibble.

колышка *f.* (text.) heald; kink (in rope).

коль *conj.* if, when, though; *adv.* how much, how many; *m.* (geol.) col.

Кольбе реакция Kolbe reaction.

Кольби печь Colby furnace.

кольд-крем *m.* cold cream.

кольев *gen. pl. of* **кол.**

кольз/а *f.,* **—овый** *a.* (bot.) colza, rape.

колькотар *see* **колкотар.**

кольм *m.* kolm (Swedish coal).

кольмат/аж *m.,* **—ация** *f.* silt deposition, silting, sedimentation; (petrol.) mud grouting; clogging.

кольник *m.* (bot.) Phyteuma.

кольнуть *see* **колоть.**

кольп/ит *m.* (med.) colpitis; **—о—** *prefix* (anat.) colp(o)— (vagina); **—оскоп** *m.* (med.) colposcope.

коль/раби, —ряби *f.* (bot.) kohlrabi.

Кольрауша закон Kohlrausch's law.

кольский *a.* Kola (peninsula).

коль-скоро *conj.* as soon as, as.

кольт *m.* colt (revolver).

кольтер *m.* coulter (of plow).

кольц/а *gen. and pl. of* **кольцо;** anuli; **—евание** *n.* ringing, etc., *see v.;* cyclization; (elec.) completion of circuit; (av.) cross-feed; **—еватость** *f.* (phyt.) ring-spot disease; **—евать** *v.* ring, girdle (trees); notch; band (poultry); **—евидный** *a. see* **кольцеобразный.**

кольцев/ой *a.* ring(-shaped), annular, circular, circumferential; cyclic; link (chain); collar-step, ring thrust (bearing); peripheral (flooding); **к. ватер** (text.) ring-spinning machine; **к. грохот** (min.) ring grizzly; **к. зазор** (mach.) radial clearance; (nucl.) annular gap; **к. счётчик** (nucl.) ring counter; **—ая втулка** packing sleeve; **—ая гора** crater; **—ая обмотка** (elec.) ring winding, Gramme winding; **—ая печь** (cer.) annular kiln; (met.) annular furnace; **—ая трубка** (nucl.) donut; **—ое соединение** ring compound, cyclic compound.

кольце/крутильный *a.* (text.) ring-twisting; **—образ-**

—ный *a.* ring-shaped, annular, circular; cyclic; **—пряд** *m.* (ent.) tent caterpillar (*Malacosoma neustria*); **—прядильный** *a.* (text.) ring-spinning; **—хвостый** *a.* ring-tailed.

кольц/о *n.* ring, collar; coil; link (of chain); washer; eye, hoop; ferrule; belt, girdle, band; (elec.) circuit; (ball bearing) race(way); (anat.) anulus, ring; **замыкание в к.** cyclization; **метод —а и шара** ring and ball method; **разрыв —а, расщепление —а** ring cleavage, cyclic cleavage; **срезать на к.** *v.* girdle (a tree); **—овка** *f.* unit train.

кольч/атка *see* **кольчец;** (bot.) fruit-bearing spur; **—атоуп(н)иковые** *pl.* (ent.) Annulipalpia; **—атый** *a.* ring(-shaped), annular, annulate(d); cyclic (compound); cockade (ore); **—атый червь, —ец** *m.* segmented worm, annelid.

колья *pl. of* **кол.**

колюр *m.* (astr.) colure; **—ия** *f.* (bot.) Coluria.

колют *pr. 3 pl. of* **колоть.**

колютик *m.* (bot.) Chamaepeuce.

колюче— *prefix* acantho— (thorny); echin(o)— (spiny); **—головые** *pl.* (zool.) Acanthocephala; **—головый** *a.* prickly-headed; *m.* acanthocephalan; **—зонтичник** *m.* (bot.) Echinophora; **—кустарниковый** *a.* thorn(y) bush; **—листник** *see* **колючник; —листный** *a.* prickly-leaved; **—носные** *pl.* (ichth.) Acanthuroidea; **—пёр** *m.* spiny-rayed fish; **—пёрые** *pl.* (ichth.) Acanthopterygii; Trachipteridae; **—пёрый** *a.* spiny-rayed; **—подушечник** *m.* thorn cushion plant formation; **—соневые** *pl.* (mam.) Platacanthomyidae; **—сть** *f.* prickliness; **—травник** *m.* thorny grass plot; **—чка** *dim. of* **колючка;** spinule; **—шиншилловые** *pl.* (mam.) Echimyidae.

колючий *a.* prickly, thorny, spiny, spinose.

колючинский *a.* (geog.) Kolyuchin.

колюч/ка *f.* prickle, spine, thorn, needle; spicule; burr, barb; (ichth.) *see* **колюшка; —овидный** *a.* spiniform, spine-shaped; **—ник** *m.* (bot.) carline thistle (*Carlina*).

колюшк/а *f.* (ichth.) stickleback; **—овые** *pl.* Gasterosteidae.

колющ/е-сосущий *a.* (ent.) piercing-sucking; **—ий** *a.* splitting, etc., *see* **колоть;** stinging; shooting (pain).

коляска *f.* carriage; wheelchair; (motorcycle) sidecar.

ком *m.* clot, lump, chunk, wad, ball, clod; *prepos. of* **кто;** *abbr.* (**килоом**) kilohm.

ком— *prefix* communist; communal; command; master; *suffix* committee; commissar(iat); commission.

кома *f.* (astr.; med.; opt.) coma.

комагматический *a.* (geol.) comagmatic.

команд/а *f.* command, order, instruction; signal; squad, crew, team, detail, party; **—ир** *m.* commander; leader; **—ировать** *v.* send on a mission; **—ировка** *f.* mission, out-of-town job or assignment; business trip; **—ировочные** *pl.* expense money; **—но-диспетчерский пункт** air traffic control tower; **—но-топливый** *a.* fuel-control; **—ный** *a.* command, order; instruction; control, master; guiding, supervising; (comp.) batch (file); **—о-аппарат** *m.* signalling device; master control switch; **—ование** *n.* commanding, etc., *see v.;* **—овать** *v.* command, order, give orders; be in command; tower (above); **—оконтроллер** *m.* master switch; **—ующий** *a.* commanding, etc., *see v.;* in command; **—ы** *pl.* instructions.

комановая кислота comanic acid, pyrone-alpha-carboxylic acid.

команчи *n.* (geol.) Comanchean series.

комар *m.* (ent.) mosquito (*Anopheles, Culex,* etc.); hollow punch, blank-cutting machine; **—ик** m. (ent.) midge; **—ики** pl. Cecidomyidae; **—иные** pl. Culicidae; **—иный** a. of **комар**; mosquito-borne (disease).

комарихинский a. (geog.) Komarikha.

комар/ник m. mosquito net; **—овка** f. (ent.) Bittacus; **—овковые** pl. scorpionflies (*Bittacidae*).

коматозный a. (med.) comatose.

коматулида f. (zool.) Comatulida.

комбайн m. (agr.; min.) combine (mobile, multipurpose machine); **—ер, —ёр** m. combine operator; **—ирование** n. combining; combine harvesting; **—ировать** v. (harvest by) combine; **—овый** a. combine; **—остроение** n. combine building; **—оуборка** f. combine harvesting.

комбат m. (mil.) battalion commander; **—ант** m. combatant.

комби— prefix combined, combination; **—жир** m. mixed fat; **—корм** m., **—кормовый** a. mixed feed, formula feed, concentrate.

комбин/антный a. (math.) combinant; **—ат** m. combine, concern; plant, mill; integrated works, group, complex; (training) center; **—атор** m. combiner; **—аторика** f. (math.) combinatorial analysis; **—аторный** a. combinatorial; **—атский** a. of **комбинат**; **—ационный** a. combination; (gen.) hybrid (variability); **—ационного рассеяния** (phys.) Raman (lines, spectrum, etc.); **—ационного типа** coincidence-type (adder); **—ация** f. combination, pattern, arrangement; set-up; compromise; **—езон** m. (c)overalls; union suit; **—ирование** n. combination; **—ированный** a. combined, combination; composite, compound; multiple (-unit); multiple-function; coincidence (adder); hybrid (computer); integrated (display); polarized neutral (relay); mixed-flow (compressor); **—ировать** v. combine, arrange; scheme, contrive.

комбретовые pl. (bot.) Combretaceae.

комедон m. (med.) comedo, blackhead.

комель m. butt, base (of tree trunk); end (of rope or cable).

коменаминовый a. comenamic (acid).

комендант m., **—ский** a. superintendent, official in charge; (mil.) commandant; **—ский час** curfew.

комендор m. (naut.) seaman-gunner.

комет/а f. (astr.; ichth.) comet; **—арный** a. comet-shaped; **—ный** a. comet; **—ография** f. cometography; **—оискатель** m. comet seeker or finder; **—ообразный, —оподобный** a. comet-shaped.

КомиАССР Komi Autonomous Soviet Socialist Republic.

комингс m. (naut.) coaming; (door) sill.

комисс/ар m. commissar, commissioner; **—ариат** m. commissariat; **—ионер** m. commissioner, agent, middleman, broker, jobber; **—ионный** a., **—ия** f. commission, committee, board; **—ура** f. commissure, joint, seam; **—уральный** a. commissural.

комитет m. committee, bureau.

комический a. comical, ridiculous.

комка gen. of **комок**; **—ть** v. crumple.

комко/вание n. caking, clotting; (met.) nodulizing; **—ватость** f. lumpiness; **—ватый** a. lumpy, lumped, clotted; cloddy, glebous; (soil) crumb (structure); **—одробитель** m. clod crusher; **—оламатель** m. roll breaker (for tea leaves); **—образный** a. cloddy; **—образование** n. clod formation.

комл/евый a. of **комель**; **—истый** a. having a thick butt; **—я** gen. of **комель**.

комма-бацилла f. (biol.) comma bacillus.

коммасация f. consolidation (of land).

коммелин/а f. (bot.) Commelina; **—овые** pl. spiderwort family (*Commelinaceae*).

коммеморативный a. commemorative.

комменсал m., **—ьный** a. (biol.) commensal; **—изм** m. commensalism; **—ист** m. commensal(ist).

коммент/арий m. comment(ary), remarks; **—атор** m., **—аторский** a. commentator; **—ирование** n. comment(ing); **—ировать** v. comment, remark, observe; annotate.

коммер/сант m. merchant, dealer; **—ция** f. commerce, trade; **—ческий** a. commercial, mercantile; business; **ставить на —ческую ногу** v. commercialize, put on a commercial basis.

коммивояжёр m. traveling salesman.

коммоция f. (med.) commotio, concussion.

коммун/а f. commune; **—ально-бытовой** a. communal-general (service); **—альный** a. communal, public, municipal; **—альная канализация** sewage system; **—альная служба** public utility; **—альная техника** municipal engineering; civil engineering; **—альное хозяйство** municipal service(s); **—альные предприятия, —альные сооружения** public utilities; **—изм** m. communism.

коммуника/тор m. communicator; **—ционный** a., **—ция** f. communication(s); pipelines, supply lines; **—ции** pl. (service) lines; **лабораторные —ции** laboratory services, utilities.

коммунист m., **—ический** a. communist.

коммунхоз m. municipal services.

коммут/ант m., **—антный** a. (math.) commutant, commutator group; **—ативность** f. commutativity; **—ативный** a. (math.) commutative; **—атор** m., **—аторный** a. (elec.) commutator; switch; (tel.) switchboard; **—ационный** a., **—ация** f. commutation; switching; **—ационный аппарат, —ационный механизм, —ационный прибор** switch; **—ационный шланг** patch cord; **—ационный щит, —ационная доска** switchboard; control panel; **—ационное устройство** switchgear; **—ирование** see **коммутация**; **—ированный** a. commutated; switched; **—ировать** v. commut(at)e, change over, reverse, switch; carry (to), terminate (at); **—ируемый** a. commutatable; commutated; switchable, switched (current); keyed (amplifier); **—ирующий** a. commutating, etc., see v.

коммюнике m. communique.

комнат/а f. room, apartment; **—ка** dim. of **комната**; **—ный** a. room; indoor; house (fly).

комовой a. of **ком**; ball, clot, lump(y).

комод m. chest of drawers; **шлаковый к.** ash pit.

комодский a. (geog.) Komodo.

ком/ок dim. of **ком**; lump, clump, clot, chunk, clod; cake; nodular deposit; (anat.) glomus; globus, sphere, ball, mass; (bot.) gleba; congylus; **пищевой к.** mouthful; **—ками, в —ках** in lumps, lumpy, clotted; **осадок —ками** nodular deposit.

комол m. Comol (alloy).

комол/ость f. absence of horns; **—ый** a. hornless, polled, acerous; **—ое животное** pollard.

коморский a. (geog.) Comoro (Islands).

комоч/ек dim. of **комок**; aggregate; (anat.) glomerulus, tuft, cluster.

компакт m. (math.) compact (set); **—ификация** f. compactification; **к.-кассета** f. casette; **—ность** f. compactness, density; compressibility (of information); cohesion; **—ный** a. compact, dense, tight, space-saving, low-bulk; concise; rugged; massive; **—ный в себе** (math.) absolutely compact; **—ор** m. compactor.

компанд/ирование *n.* (tel.) companding; **—ор** *m.* compandor.

компания *f.* company, partnership; party, crew; (air) line, carrier.

компан/овать *see* **компон(ир)овать; —ьон** *m.* companion, partner, associate.

компар/аскоп *m.* (med.) comparascope; **—атор** *m.* comparator; colorimeter; **—ирование** *n.* comparison, calibration, standardization; **—тимент** *m.* compartment.

компартия *f.* Communist party.

компас *m.,* **—ный** *a.* compass; **наземный к.-эталон** (av.) landing compass.

компаунд *m.* compound, filler; (elec.) insulation compound; compound engine; **заливать —ом** *v.* pot; **к.-жир** *m.* combined fats; **—ирование** *n.* compounding; (elec.) compound excitation; **—ированный** *a.* compound(ed); compound-wound; **—ировать** *v.* compound; **—ирующий** *a.* compounding; **к.-машина** *f.* compound engine; **—ный** *a.* compound(-wound); **к.-обмотка** *f.* compound winding; **к.-ядро** intermediate nucleus.

компенди/й, —ум *m.* compendium, digest; (cinema) special-effect device.

компенс/атор *m.* compensator, balancer, equalizer; expansion piece; expansion tank; surge chamber (of pump); (elec. eng.) condenser; (art.) replenisher; **—аторный, —аторующий** *a.* compensatory; **—ационный** *a.* compensation, compensating, expansion (piece); relief (valve); null (method); **—ационный токовый** torque-balance (telemetry); **—ация** *f.,* **—ирование** *n.* compensation, balancing, etc., *see v.;* (error) reduction; **—ированный** *a.* compensated, etc., *see v.;* **—ировать** *v.* compensate (for), make up (for); (counter)balance, offset, equalize, neutralize; cancel out; **—ирующий** *a.* compensating, etc., *see v.;* **—ованный** *a.* compensated; compensating.

компетен/тность, —ция *f.* competence, ability; jurisdiction; **—тный** *a.* competent, able.

компил/ирование *n.,* **—яция** *f.* compilation; **—ированный** *a.* compiled; **—ировать** *v.* compile, collect; **—ятивный** *a.* compiled, compilation; **—ятор** *m.* (comp.) compiler, compiling program.

компланарный *a.* coplanar.

комплекс *m.* complex, unit, set; system, structure; sum total, package; combination, association, sequence; (pal.) assemblage; **—ант** m. (chem.) complexing agent, sequestering agent; **—ирование** *n.* organization, integration; (comp.) grouping; **—ность** *f.* complexity; (soil) heterogeneity; **—ный** *a.* complex, comprehensive, complete; combined, joint, collective; overall, integrated (plan), multiobjective (planning), multi-(ple-)purpose, multiple (approach, etc.); compound; many-sided, inclusive; packaged; (comp.) system (debugging); multimodal (therapy); **—ная установка** package; **внутренный —ный** (chem.) chelate.

комплексо/н *m.* complexone; **—(но)метрический** *a.* complexometric; **—(но)метрия** *f.* complexometry; **—образование** *n.* complexing, complex formation; **внутреннее —образование** chelation; **—образователь** *see* **комплексант; —образующий** *a.* complexing.

комплект *m.* (complete) set, kit, outfit, assembly; batch; bank (of machines); complement (of personnel), specified number; **—ация** *f.* making up a set, etc., *see v.;* list of equipment or parts for a single order; **—но** *adv.* complete(ly), as complete units, in sets, in batches; **—ность** *f.* completeness of set(s), completed units;

batching; **—ность поставки** delivery in full; **—ный** *a.* complete; (in) sets, (in) units; (in a) batch; unitized; **—ование** *n.* making up a set, etc., *see v.;* acquisition, procurement; **—овать** *v.* make up (a set); complete; replenish; furnish, supply (as part of); stock (with spare parts); fulfill (a special order); acquire, procure (books); build up, bring up to strength; staff; **—овка, —овочный** *see* **комплектование; —овочная ведомость** list of standard equipment.

комплекция *f.* constitution, build.

комплемент *m.* (immun.) complement; **—арный** *a.* complementary; **—ация** *f.* (gen.) complementation.

компо/зит *m.,* **—зитный** *a.* composite (material); **—зиционный** *a.,* **—зиция** *f.* composition, compound, material; arrangement; **—зиционный материал** composite; **—нент** *m.,* **—нента** *f.* component, constituent, ingredient; (food) item; **—н(ир)овать** *v.* compose, group, arrange, lay out, put together, assemble; (comp.) bind, link; design; package (equipment); **—нование** *n.* composing, etc., *see v.;* **—новка** *f.* composition, grouping, arrangement, configuration, layout; design; linkage; **снаряд самолётной —новки** aircraft-type vehicle.

компост *m.* (agr.) compost.

компостер *m.* punch, ticket stamper.

компостиров/ание *n.* (agr.) composting; **—анный** *a.* composted; **—ать** *v.* (enrich with) compost; punch; date.

компот *m.* stewed fruit.

компр/емирование *n.* compression; **—есс** *m.* (med.) compress; **—ессиметр, —ессометр** *m.* compression gage; **—ессионный** *a.,* **—ессия** *f.* compression; **—есный** *a.* compress; **—ессор** *m.* compressor; **—ессорная** *f.* compressor house; **—ессорный** *a.* compressor; air-injection (engine); (petrol.) repressuring (production); **—имирование** *n.* compression; **—имированный** *a.* compressed; **—имировать** *v.* compress.

компром/етировать *v.,* **—исс** *m.* compromise, trade off; **не идущий на —исс** *a.* uncompromising.

комптон/ит *m.* (min.) comptonite; **—овское смещение** (radiation) Compton shift; **—овское явление, -эффект** Compton effect; **граница —овского поглощения** Compton edge.

компьютер *m.,* **—ный** *a.* computer.

комсомол *m.,* **—ьский** *a.* Komsomol, Young Communist League.

кому *dat. of* **кто,** to whom.

комфорт *m.,* **—ный** *a.* comfort; **температура —а** (zool.) preferred temperature; **—абельный** *a.* comfortable.

комфрей *m.* (bot.) comfrey (*Symphytum*).

комхоз *m.* municipal economy.

комья *pl. of* **ком.**

конваллотоксин *m.* convallotoxin.

конвейер *m.* conveyer; (comp.) pipeline; **зелёный к.** continuous supply of green fodder; **—изация** *f.* pipelining; **—ный** *a.* conveyer, conveying, traveling; conveyer-type (furnace); conveyorized (assembly); assembly line (work); **—ный режим** pipelining; **к.-штабелеукладчик** *m.* stacking conveyer.

конвек/тивный, —ционный *a.* convective, convection(al), by convection; **—тор** *m.* convector; **—ция** *f.* convection.

конвенц/иональный *a.* conventional; **—ия** *f.* convention; agreement.

конверг/ентность, —енция *f.* convergence; **—ентный** *a.* convergent; **—ировать(ся)** *v.* converge; **—ирующий** *a.* converging.

конверс/ия *f.,* **—ионный** *a.* conversion.

конверт *m.* envelope, cover.

конверт/ер *m.,* **—ерный** *a.* (met., nucl.) converter; vessel; **—ин** *m.* (coagulation) convertin, factor VII; **—ирование** *n.* conversion; **—ированный** *a.* converted; **—ировать** *v.* convert, bessemerize.

конверт/оплан *m.* (av.) convertiplane; **—ор** *see* **конвертер;** reformer.

конвицин *m.* convicine.

конв/оир *m.,* **—оировать** *v.,* **—ой** *m.,* **—ойный** *a.* convoy, escort.

конвольвулин *m.* convolvulin, rhoderetin; **—(ол)овый** *a.* convolvul(inol)ic acid.

конволюта *f.* (zool.) Convoluta.

конвульс/ант *m.* convulsant; **—ивный** *a.* convulsive; **—ия** *f.* convulsion.

Конвэя чашка (chem.) Conway dish.

конген/иальный *a.* congenial; **—итальный** *a.* congenital, inborn.

конгер *m.* (ichth.) conger eel; **—иевый** *a.,* **—ия** *f.* (mal.) Congeria; **—овые, —ы** *pl.* (ichth.) Congridae.

конгестивный *a.* congestive.

конгиоподовые *pl.* (ichth.) Congiopodidae.

конгидрин *m.* conhydrine.

конгломер/ат *m.,* **—атный** *a.* conglomerate; **—ация** *f.* conglomeration.

конглютин *m.* conglutin; **—ация** *f.* (med.) conglutination; **—ин** *m.* conglutinin.

конго *n.* Congol (dye); **к.-бумага** *f.* Congo (filter) paper; **—вый** *a.* Congo; congoic (acid); **к.-голубой** *m.* Congo blue; **к.-краситель** *m.* Congo dye; **к.-красный, —рот** *m.* Congo red; **—лезский** *a.* (geog.) Congo(ese), Congolese; **—лли** *a.* (ichth.) congolli (*Pseudaphritis bursinus*); **—ни** *a.* (mam.) kongoni (*Alcelaphus buselaphus*); **к.-спирт** *n.* Congo red solution in alcohol.

конгревный *a.* Congreve, relief (embossing).

конгревые *see* **конгеровые.**

конгрегация *f.* congregation.

конгресс *m.* congress, convention; **—ия** *f.* (gen.) congression.

конгрио *m.* (ichth.) congrio (*Genypterus*).

конгруэн/тность, —ция *f.* congruence; **—тный** *a.* congruent, corresponding.

конгсбергит *m.* (min.) kongsbergite.

кондёвка *f.* (ichth.) Siberian cisco (*Coregonus sardinella*).

конденсат *m.* condensate; **—ный** *a.* condensate; (petrol.) condenser (tube); **—оотводчик** *m.* steam trap; **—опровод** *m.* condensate pipe; **—ор** *m.* condenser; (elec.) capacitor; **—ор-испаритель** *m.* condenser-evaporator; **—орный** *a.* condenser; capacitor; **—орный горшок** moisture trap; **—осборник** *m.* hot well.

конденсационн/ый *a.* condensation, condensing; dew-point (hygrometer); **к. аппарат** condenser; **к. горшок** moisture trap, steam trap; **к. змеевик** spiral condenser; condenser coil; **к. продукт** condensate; **—ая вода** water of condensation.

конденс/ация *f.,* **—ирование** *n.* condensation; **температура —ации** dew point; **—ированный** *a.* condensed; **—ировать** *v.* condense; **—ируемый** *a.* condensable, compressible; precipitable; **—ирующий** *a.* condensing; **—ор** *m.,* **—орный** *a.* condenser, condensing lens.

кондестилляция *see* **кодистилляция.**

кондило— *prefix* condyl(o)— (knuckle, joint, knob); **—ма** *f.* (med.) condyloma.

кондилятры *pl.* (mam.) Protungulata.

кондинский *a.* (geog.) Konda.

кондитер *m.* confectioner; **—ские изделия** confectionery, candy; pastry.

кондиционер *m.* conditioner; air conditioner.

кондици/онирование *n.* conditioning, humidity control; **к. воздуха** air conditioning; **—онированный** *a.* conditioned; artificial; **—онировать** *v.* condition; cure (compost); **—онность** *f.* standard quality; meeting specifications; **—онный** *a.* conditional; conditioned; quality standard(ized), certified (seed); **—я** *f.* condition, requirement; (seed) standard; quality; clause.

кондовый *a.* tall, high, full-grown (forest); sound, vigorous; hard (wood).

кондом *m.* (med.) condom.

кондоминант *m.,* **—ный** *a.* (bot.) codominant.

конд/омский *a.* (geog.) Kondoma; **—опожский** *a.* Kondopoga; **—ор** *m.* (orn.) condor (*Vultur gryphus*); **—о-сосьвинский** *a.* (geog.) Konda-Sosva.

конд-р *abbr.* **конденсатор.**

кондрашка *f.* (med.) stroke.

кондуит *m.* conduit.

кондукт/ивность *f.* conductivity; **—ивный** *a.* conductive; **—ограмма** *f.* conductogram; **—ометр** *m.* conductivity bridge; **—ометрический** *a.* conductometric; **—ометрия** *f.* conductometric analysis.

кондуктор *m.,* **—ный** *a.* conductor; (mech.) jig; conductor pipe; template; **дисковый к.** plate jig; **—носверлильный станок** jig borer.

кондукци/онный *a.* conduction, conductive; **—я** *f.* conduction.

кондуран/гин *m.* condurangin; **—го** *n.* condurango (bark).

коне— *prefix* horse(-breeding); **—бойня** *f.* horse slaughter house; **—ведение, —водство** *n.,* **—водчески** *a.* horse breeding; **—завод** *m.* stud farm; **—й** *gen. of* **конь.**

конёк *dim. of* **конь;** (roof) ridge; (ice) skate; hobby; (ent.) grasshopper (*Chorthippus*); (orn.) pipit (*Anthus*); (ichth.) regional name for sucker, pilotfish, and others; **морской к.** (anat.) hippocampus; (ichth.) seahorse (*Hippocampus*).

конель *m.* Konel metal.

коне/матка *f.* brood mare; **—поголовье** *n.* horse population; **—ферма** *f.* horse-breeding farm; **племенная —ферма** stud farm.

кон/ец *m.* end, termination, finish, close; extreme, outer edge; end point (in titration, etc.); point, tip; extremity, tail; terminal; purpose, aim; distance, journey; length (of rope); outflow, issue, discharge; (elec.) lead; **—цом** end on; **острым —цом** edgewise; **—цы** *pl.* ends, butts, waste, scrap; **—цамн** at the ends; **в один к.** one-way (trip); **в оба —ца** round trip; **в —це —цов** finally, eventually; **вид с —ца** end view; **на худой к.** at the worst; **под к.** toward the end, finally; **положить к.** *v.* make an end (of), put a stop (to); **сводить —цы с —цами** *v.* make both ends meet; **толстый к.** butt; **тонкий к.** tip.

коне-час *m.* horse-hour (of work).

конечнеротые *pl.* (ichth.) Teleostomi.

конечно *introd. word* of course, certainly, naturally, surely, no doubt; (math.) (it) is finite; **к.-мерный** *a.* (math.) finite-dimensional; **к.-разностный** *a.* finite-difference; **—ротые** *pl.* (prot.) Telosporidia; **—сть** *f.* finiteness; limb, extremity, appendage.

конечн/ый *a.* final, ultimate, terminal, end, last, extreme, apical; terminating; trailing (e.g., zeros); resulting, finished (product); (math.) finite; *suffix* —end(ed); **к.**

мозг (anat.) telencephalon, endbrain; **к. момент** end point (in titration, etc.); **к. продукт** end product; **к. ряд** finite series; **—ая скорость** outlet velocity; **—ая температура** end temperature; outlet temperature; **—ая функция** finite function; **—ой точки** a. endpoint (method); **в —ом итоге** ultimately; **в —ом счёте** all things considered; eventually.

кон/завод m. stud horse farm; **—и** pl. of **конь.**

кониакский a. (geol.) Coniacian.

конид/иеносец m. (bot.) conidiophore; **—иеносный** a. conidi(i)ferous; **—ий** m., conidium; **—иоспора** f. conidiospore; **—ия** f. conidium; pl. conidia.

кониин m. coniine, 2-propylpiperidine; **—овый** a. coni(c)ic (acid).

коник dim. of **конь.**

кони/метр m. (min.) konimeter (for measuring dust); **—н** see **кониин.**

конина f. horse meat; horse hide.

конинкит m. (min.) koninckite.

конио— prefix coni(o)— (dust); **—з** m. (med.) coniosis; **—метр** m. coniometer.

конит m. (min.) konite.

конифер/ил m., **—иловый** a. coniferyl; **—иловый спирт, —ол** m. coniferyl alcohol, coniferol; **—ин** m. coniferin.

конихальцит m. (min.) conichalcite.

кониц/еин m. coniceine; **—ин** m. conicine.

коническ/ий a. conic(al), cone; bevel(ed); tapered, tapering; **к. клапан** cone valve; **—ая колба** Erlenmeyer flask; **—ая шестерня, —ое (зубчатое) колесо** bevel gear; **—ое сечение** (geom.) conic section.

коничность f. conicity, angle of taper; conic shape.

кон/катенация f. concatenation, linking (of sets); **—каулесценция** f. concaulescence; **—климакс** m. (bot.) conclimax; **—кордантность, —кордация** f. concordance.

конкр/емент m. concrement, concretion; **—есценция** f. concrescence.

конкрет/изация f. concrete definition; **—из(ир)овать** v. concretize, define concretely, specify; **—нее** adv. more specifically; **—ность** f. concreteness; **—ность руководства** specific management; **—ный** a. concrete, specific, particular.

конкреци/онный a. concretionary, nodular; **—я** f. concretion, nodule.

конкский a. (geog.) Konka.

конкур/ент m., **—ентка** f. competitor, rival; **—ент(н)оспособный** a. aggressive, competitive; **—ентность** f. competitiveness; **—ентный** a. competitive; concurrent, associated; **—ентная борьба** competition; **—ентная способность** aggressiveness; **—енция** f. competition; **вне —енции** unrivaled; **—ирование** n. competition; **—ировать** v. compete, be competitive (with); **—ирующий** a. competing, competitive; rival; **—с** m. competition; **—сный** a. competitive.

коннарит m. (min.) connarite.

коннект/ив m., **—ива** f. (anat.) connective, bridge; **—ор** m. connector.

коннелит m. (min.) connellite, footeite.

конн/о— prefix horse(-drawn); **—озаводство** n., **—озавод(че)ский** a. stud farming; **—о-моторный** a. horse-drawn and motor-driven (sprayer); **—ый** a. horse(-drawn); riding; bridle (path).

коновал m. horse veterinarian.

Коновалова закон Konowaloff rule.

коно/вод m. horse breeder; **—вязь** f. picket rope; **—гон** m. horse driver.

коно/д m. conode, tie line (in phase diagram); **—донт** m.

(pal.) conodont; **—ид** m., **—идальный** a. (geom.) conoid; (mach.) three-dimensional cam; (text.) cone drum.

коноконо m. (mam.) toro (*Isothrix*).

конометр see **конометр.**

коноп/атить v. calk, stop up, pack; **—атка** f. calking; calking iron; **—атный** a. calking; **—атый** a. (med.) pitted; **—ать** f. oakum; **—ачение** n. calking; **—ачен(н)ый** a. calked.

конопиды pl. (ent.) Conopidae.

конопл/е— prefix hemp; **—евидный** a. hemp-like, cannabinous; **—евод** m. hemp grower; **—еводный** a., **—еводство** n., **—еводческий** a. hemp growing; **—ёвые** pl. (bot.) Cannabinaceae; **—ежатка** f. hemp cutter; **—емолотилка** f. hemp thresher; **—емялка** f. hemp-crushing mill; **—етеребилка** f. hemp puller; **—еуборочный** a. hemp-harvesting; **—я** f. hemp; **—яник** m. hemp field; **—янка** f. (orn.) linnet (*Acanthis cannabina*); **—яный** a. hemp(en); hempseed (oil); linoleic (acid).

конорыл m. (ichth.) beaked salmon (*Gonorhynchus*); **—ые** pl. Gonor(h)ynchidae.

коносамент m. (com.) bill of lading.

коносир m. (ichth.) Konosirus.

коно/скоп m. (micros.) conoscope; **—цефал** m. (bot.) conocephalum; **—цефаловые** pl. Conocephalaceae (mosses).

коношский a. (geog.) Konosha.

конподвид m. (biol.) consubspecies.

конрингия f. (bot.) Conringia.

консек/вентность f. consequence; **—вентный** a. consequent; **—утивный** a. consecutive.

консерв/ант m. preservative; (tanning) curing agent; **—ативность** f. conservative nature; **—ативный** a. conservative; conserving (species); **—атизм** m. conservatism; **—атор** m. conserver; conservative (person); (oil) conservator; expansion tank; **—ация** see **консервирование.**

консервир/ование n. preserving, etc., see v.; conservation; **—ованный** a. preserved, etc., see v.; **—овать** v. preserve, can, tin; conserve; corrosion-proof, slush; close down temporarily; put in dead storage, mothball; **—овка** see **консервирование; —ующий** a. preserving, etc., see v.; **—ующее вещество** preservative; inhibitor.

консерв/ный a. preserving, canning; **к. завод** cannery; **к. нож** can opener; **—ы** pl. preserves, canned food; safety glasses; **мясные —ы** canned meat; **фруктовые —ы** canned fruit.

консертальный a. (cryst.) consertal.

консигнация f. (com.) consignment.

консилиум m. consultation, council.

консист/ентный a. consistent; thick; **—ентная смазка** (lubricating) grease; **—енция** f. consistence, density; consistency, body; composition; coherence; **—ометр** m. consistometer.

конск/ий a. horse, equine; **к. боб** (bot.) broad bean (*Vicia faba*); **—окаштановые** pl. buckeye family (*Hippocastanaceae*).

консолид/ация f. consolidation; **—ированный** a. consolidated; **—ировать** v. consolidate.

консоль f. cantilever, bracket, arm; console; (milling machine) knee; **к. крыла** (outer) wing; (plane) cell(ule); **—но** adv. in cantilever, as a cantilever; **—ный** a. of **консоль;** cantilever(ed), overhanging; **—ный подшипник** bracket bearing; **—ная балка, —ная ферма** cantilever.

консоме n. (food) consomme.

консон/анс *m.* consonance; **—антный** *a.* consonant; **—ирующий** *a.* consonating.

консор/т *m.* (biol.) consort, associate organism; **—тизм** *m.* consortism, symbiosis; **—ций, —циум** *m.,* **—ция** *f.* consortium, mutual association.

консоц/иация *f.* (biol.) consociation; **—ион** *m.* consocion; **—иула** *f.* consociule; **—ия** *f.* consocies.

конспект *m.* synopsis, conspectus, abstract, summary, compendium; **—ивность** *f.* brevity, conciseness; **—ивный** *a.* brief, concise; **—ирование** *n.* abstracting; **—ированный** *a.* abstracted; **—ировать** *v.* abstract, summarize; outline.

конспецифичный *a.* (biol.) conspecific.

констант/а *f.* constant; **—ан** *m.* constantan (alloy); **—инопольский** *a.* (geog.) Constantinople; **—ность** *f.* (biol.) constancy, immutability; **—ный** *a.* constant.

констат/ация *f.,* **—ирование** *n.* statement; establishment; **—ировать** *v.* state; establish, ascertain; certify; find, take note.

констелляция *f.* (astr.) constellation.

конститу/ировать *v.* constitute; **—тивный** *a.* constitutive; **—циональный** *a.* constitutional; **—ционный** *a.* constitution; constitutional (formula); **—ционная вода** water of constitution; **—ция** *f.* constitution, make-up; conformation; (chem.) configuration.

констрик/тивный *a.* constrictive; **—тор** *m.* (anat.) constrictor; **—ционный** *a.,* **—ция** *f.* constriction.

конструиров/ание *n.* construction, building, etc., *see v.*; development; elaboration (of logarithms); **принципы —ания** design philosophy; **—ать** *v.* construct, build, make; engineer, devise, design; develop.

конструк/тивно *adv.* mechanically, structurally; **—тивный** *a.* constructive, construction(al), structural; design; **—тивные особенности** design philosophy; **—тор** *m.* constructor, designer; **—торский** *a.* constructor, designer; structural; designing; size-and-mass (model); **—ционный** *a.* construction(al), structural; **—ция** *f.* construction, structure, formation; design, make, build; **последней —ции** of recent design.

консул *m.,* **—ьский** *a.* consul.

консульт/ант *m.* consultant; consulting physician; tutor; **—ативный** *a.* consultative, consulting, advisory; **—ационный** *a.,* **—ация** *f.,* **—ирование** *n.* consultation; consultation office; dispensary, clinic; guidance clinic; expert advice; (educ.) tutorial; **—ировать** *v.* advise, give advice, consult; **—ироваться** *v.* consult, ask advice.

консумент *m.* consumer.

контаг/ий *m.* (med.) contagion; **—иозность** *f.* contagiousness; **—иозный** *a.* contagious.

контакт *m.* contact, connection, terminal, (connector) pin; catalyst, interface; **к. (Петрова)** spec. a detergent mixture of sulfonaphthenic acids; **граница —а** interface; **находиться в —е** *v.* be exposed (to); **—ирование** *n.* contacting; engagement; **—ировать** *v.* (make) contact, come in contact; **—ирующий участок** (chem.) binding site; **—но-каталитический** *a.* contact-catalytic; **—но-разрывный** *a.* (elec.) make-and-break; **—ность действия** contact action.

контакт/ный, —овый *a.* contact; contacting (section of column); resistance (welding); **к. способ** contact process (for sulfuric acid manufacture); **—ная поверхность** contact surface; interface; **—ная пружина** (electron.) catwhisker; **—ное вещество, —ное средство** contact agent, catalyst; **—ор** *m.* (elec.) contractor, switch.

контаминация *f.* contamination.

контарь *m.* steelyard (a weighing device); quintal (100 kg).

контейнер *m.,* **—ный** *a.* container, capsule; tank; (nucl.) rabbit, can; **—овоз** *m.* container carrier; **к.-прицеп** *m.* container trailer; **к.-цистерна** *m.* tank container.

контекст *m.* context; (comp.) scope (of procedure).

контингент *m.,* **—ный** *a.* contingent, quota, share; **—ирование** *n.* quota (system); **—ность** *f.* (stat.) contingency table.

континент *m.* continent; **—альность** *f.* continentality; **—альный** *a.* continental.

контину/альный *a.* continuous; **—ум** *m.* (math.) continuum; **состояние —ума** continuous state.

контия *f.* (herp.) Contia.

контокоррент *m.,* **—ный счёт** (com.) account current.

контор/а *f.* office, bureau, board; **—ка** *f.* desk; small office building; river pier; **—ский** *a.* office; **—ская книга** account book, ledger; **—щик** *m.* clerk.

контр/(а)— *prefix* counter— (opposite, against); **—абанда** *f.* contraband; **—авалентность** *f.* contravalence; **—авариантный** *a.* (math.) contravariant.

контраг/ент *m.* contractor; **—ированный** *a.* contracted (dimensionally).

контрадик/торный *a.* contradictory; **—ция** *f.* contradiction.

контражур *m.* (phot.) back-lit exposure.

контракт *m.* contract, agreement, terms; **—ант** *m.* contractor; **—ационный** *a.* contracting; delivery, supply (contract); **—ация** *f.* contract(ing); **—ильность** *f.* contractility; **—ильный** *a.* contractile; **—ный** *a.* contract(ed), agreed; **—овать** *v.* contract.

контрак/тура *f.* (med.) contracture; **к. запястья** (vet.) popped knee, carpitis.

контральто *n.,* **—вый** *a.* contralto.

контра/поляризованный *a.* contrapolarized; **—прош** *m.* counterapproach.

контраст *m.* contrast; contrast medium; **—ировать** *v.* contrast, compare; **—ность** *f.* (degree of) contrast, contrastiness; contrast range; (optical storage devices) on/off ratio; **—ный** *a.* contrast(ing); sharp (color change).

контр/атака *f.,* **—атаковать** *v.* counterattack; **—атип** *m.* (phot.) duplicate negative; **—атипировать** *v.* duplicate a negative, dupe; **—афакция** *f.* infringement; **—афорс** *m.* stud (of chain link); **—ацекоз** *m.* (vet.) Contracaecum infestation; **—ацептивный** *a.* contraceptive; **—балансир** *m.* counterweight; **—букса** *f.* bottom box; (mach.) keep; **—винт** *m.* contrapropeller; **—гайка** *f.* lock nut.

контргруз *m.* counterweight, balance weight, counterbalance, counterpoise.

контр/-давление *n.* back pressure; **—диск** *m.* relief plate; **—ейлер** *m.* contrailer, mobile container; **—ела** *f.* opposite member of a friction pair; **—ибуция** *f.* contribution; **—ить** *v.* lock, secure; **—калибр** *m.* master gage, reference gage; **—клин** *m.* counterwedge; tightening key; gib (and cotter); **—кривошип** *m.* fly crank; **—мера** *f.* countermeasure; **—мина** *f.* (mil.) countermine; **—минирование** *n.* countermining; **—миноносец** *m.* (torpedo boat) destroyer; **—образец** *m.* reference sample; **—оверза** *f.* controversy, dispute.

контров/ка *f.* locking, securing; lock(-wire), safety wire; **проволочная к.** safety wire; **—очный** *a.* lock (washer, wire); retaining (rivet); **—ый** *a.* locking; safety (bolt).

контролёр *see* **контроллер;** inspector, supervisor, checker, monitor; **—ский** *a. of* **контролёр.**

контролир/ование *n.* controlling, etc., *see v.*; control, supervision; **—ованный** *a.* controlled, etc., *see v.*; control; **—овать** *v.* control, supervise, superintend, monitor; inspect, check, verify; **—овка** *see* **контролиро-вание;** **—уемый** *a.* controlled, etc., *see v.;* controllable; guided (missile); **—уемая величина** checked variable; **—ующий** *a.* controlling, etc., *see v.;* control, modifying (agent).

контроллер *m.,* **—ный** *a.* (elec.) controller, control unit; **главный к.** master switch.

контроль *m.* control, check(ing), checkout; inspection, supervision, monitoring; verification; follow-up; sampling; testing; blank test, standard; (seed) certification; (sanitary) surveillance; **к. за качеством** quality control; **к. на точность** precision control; **—ная** *f.* control room; **—ник** *m.* (comp.) verifier.

контрольно-/браковочный *a.* inspection; **к.-выпрямительное устройство** monitoring rectifier.

контрольно-измерительн/ый *a.* control and measuring; **—ые приборы** instrumentation, instruments; **произродственная —ая аппаратура** process instrumentation; **снабжён —ыми приборами** *a.* instrumented.

контрольно-инспекторский *a.* control and inspection; **к.-испытательный** *a.* checkout (equipment); **к.-кассовый аппарат** cash register; **к.-проверочный** *a.* control and check; **к.-пропускной** *a.* check (point), entry-control (point); **к. распределительный** *a.* checking and clearing; **к.-ревизионный** *a.* control and inspection; **к.-семенной** *a.* seed-testing; **к.-сортировочный** *a.* inspecting and sorting.

контрольн/ый *a. of* **контроль;** test, supervisory; audit (trail); check (digit); file (copy); master, reference, standard, sample, specimen (copy); planned, scheduled; routine (test); guide (line); pilot (light, etc.); final, revised (proof); **к. анализ** check analysis; **к. образец** control; **к. прибор** monitor; **к. редактор** reviser; **к. щиток** control panel; dashboard, instrument board; **—ая книга** log; **—ая нормаль** counter-sample; **—ая сумма** (comp.) checksum; **—ая точка** reference point; **—ое устройство** monitor.

контр/отбор *m.* (biol.) contraselection; **—оттяжка** *f.* (mech.) stub guy.

контрпар *m.* countersteam, back steam; **—ить** *v.* countersteam.

контр/перевод *m.* double transfer; **—поршень** *m.* counterpiston; **—предложение** *n.* counter-offer; **—пресс** *m.* transfer press; **—привод** *m.* countershaft; **—проверка** check determination; **пружина** *f.* counterspring; **—пуансон** *m.* counterpunch; **—разведка** *f.* counterintelligence; **—ракля** *f.* (text.) lint doctor; **—рельс** *m.* guard rail; **—рефлектор** *m.* subdish (of antenna); **—руль** *m.* contra-rudder; **—тело** *n.* partner, matching part; counterface; **—титул** *m.* duplicate title; **—ток** *m.* countercurrent, counterflow; **—фиксатор** *m.* counterstop; **—фланец** *m.* counterflange.

контрфорс *m.* counterfort, buttress, abutment; **—ный** *a.* buttress(ed).

контр/шлюз *m.* countersluice; **—штамп** *m.* counterdie, female die; **—шток** *m.* (art.) counterrecoil buffer; control plunger; **—ящий** *a.* locking, lock (nut); clamp, grip.

конту/женный *a.* contused, bruised; **—зионный** *a.,* **—зия** *f.* contusion, bruise; concussion; **—ить** *v.* contuse, bruise.

контур *m.* contour, outline, profile; (elec.; nucl.) loop, circuit; (rad.) network; duct (of jet engine); tank circuit, resonant circuit; boundary (of well); **анодный к.** plate tank; **линия —а** contour (line); **набрасывать к.** *v.* outline; **сеточный к.** grid tank; **—ный** *a.* contour, (in) outline, lineament(al); planimetric (survey); (elec.) loop (analysis).

конуляр/иды, **—ии** *pl.* (pal.) Conularia.

конура *f.* dog kennel.

конурбация *f.* conurbation (of cities).

конус *m.* cone; bevel, taper; clutch, coupling; (blast) nozzle; wind sock; target sleeve; (gripping) jaw; bell (of blast furnace); (growth) apex, point; (anat.) conus, cone; (mal.) cone shell (*Conus*); **к. выноса** (geol.) alluvial fan; **сводить** or **сходить на к.** *v.* taper; **угол —а** angle of taper; **усечённый к.** frustum; **к.-классификатор** *m.* cone classifier.

конусн/ость *f.* conicity, (angle of) taper; **—ый** *a.* cone, conic(al); bevel; taper(ed).

конус-обтекатель *m.* exhaust cone.

конусо/видность, **—образность** *f.* cone shape, conicity, taper; **—видный,** **—образный** *a.* cone-shaped, coniform, conoid, conical; taper(ed); **—головые** *pl.* (ent.) Conocephalinae; **—образование** *n.* coning.

конус-сгуститель *m.* cone thickener.

конфек/та *see* **конфета;** **—цион** *m.* ready-made clothes store or business; confection; **—ционировать** *v.* make; formulate; build up, piece (together); assemble; **—ционный** *a.* confection; ready-made (clothes); **—ция** *f.* making, etc., *see v.;* assembly.

конфервоидный *a.* (bot.) confervaceous.

конференция *f.* conference.

конфет/а *f.,* **—ный** *a.* candy; **—ка** *dim. of* **конфета;** **—ное дерево** honey tree (*Hovenia dulcis*); **—ти** *pl.* (punched card) chads; **—ы** *pl.* confectionery.

конфигурац/ионный *a. of* **конфигурация;** configurational; **—ия** *f.* configuration, profile, outline, contour, shape; layout; pattern, arrangement; (comp.) gulp; **со сложной —ией** complex shaped.

конфиденциальн/ость *f.* confidentiality, privacy; **—ый** *a.* confidential, private.

конфирмовать *v.* confirm.

конфиск/ация *f.* confiscation; **—овать** *v.* confiscate, seize.

конфликт *m.* conflict; (generation) gap; **—ность** *f.* pugnacity; **—ный** *a.* conflicting; **—овать** *v.* (run into) conflict.

конфлюэн/тность, **—ция** *f.* (math.) confluence; **—тный** *a.* confluent.

конфокальный *a.* (math.) confocal.

конфорка *f.* (stove) burner, ring.

конформ/ационный *a.* conformational (analysis); **—ация** *f.* conformation; **—ер** *m.* conformer, conformational isomer; **—ность** *f.* conform(al)ity; **—ный** *a.* (math.) conformal.

конфуз *m.* embarrassment; **—ить** *v.* embarrass, confuse; **—ный** *a.* embarrassing, awkward; **—ор** *m.* confuser, reducer, converging tube.

конх/(и) *prefix* conch(i)—, concho— (shell); **—иолин** *m.* conchiolin; **—ит** *m.* (min.) conchite; **—о—** *see* **конхи—;** **—оида** *f.* (geom.) conchoid; **—оидальный** *a.* conchoidal, shell-like; **—ология** *f.* (mal.) conchology; **—остраки** *pl.* (crust.) clam shrimps (*Conchostraca*).

конц/а *gen. of* **конец;** **—евой** *a. of* **конец;** end, terminal; extreme, outermost; tail; pin, rod (gage); **—евой зажим** (elec.) terminal (clamp); **—евой отдел** end.

концентр/ат *m.* concentrate; extract; concentrated feed; **—атомер** *m.* concentration meter; (paper) consistency meter; **—атор** *m.,* **—ационный аппарат** concentrator; **—ационный** *a.,* **—ация** *f.,* **—ирование** *n.,* **—ированность** *f.* concentration, density; strength; **—ированный** *a.* concentrated, etc., *see v.;* strong; **—ировать** *v.* concentrate; focus, center; (mil.) mass; **—ирующий** *a.* concentrating, etc., *see v.*

концентр/ически *adv.* concentrically; **—ический, —ичный** *a.* concentric; coaxial (cable); **—ичность** *f.* concentricity; **—ы** *pl.* (geom.) concentric circles.

концепция *f.* concept(ion), idea.

конце/равнитель *m.* trimming saw; **—резка** *f.* cut-off saw; **—резной** *a.* cut-off.

концерн *m.* (com.) concern.

концерт *m.* concert, recital; **—ный** *a.* concert; concerted.

концессия *f.* concession, grant.

кон-ция *abbr.* (концентрация).

концкорм *m.* (agr.) concentrated feed, concentrate.

конц/овка *f.* (typ.) tailpiece, end piece; conclusion (of article); runout (of film).

конц-т *abbr.* (концентрат).

концы *pl. of* конец; waste.

конч/ать *v.* finish, end, complete, conclude, terminate; **—аться** *v.* come to an end, expire, lapse; result, end (in), terminate (in); conclude (with), draw to a close, stop, finish; **—ая** *pr. ger.* ending (with); **начиная . . . и —ая** from . . . to; **—ен(н)ый** *a.* finished, etc., *see v.*

кончик *m.* tip, point, end; apex, apicule; nose.

кончить *see* кончать.

конш *m.,* **—ировать** *v.,* **—машина** *f.* conche (for chocolate).

коньектура *f.* conjecture.

коньюг/ант *m.* (gen.) conjugant; **—ат** *m.* conjugate; **—ата** *f.* (anat.) conjugate, conjugata; **—ационный** *a.* conjugative, conjugation(al); **—ация** *f.,* **—ирование** *n.* conjugation, pairing, union; **—ированный** *a.* conjugate(d), paired, coupled; **—ированные двойные связи** conjugate double bonds; **—ировать** *v.* conjugate, pair; **слабо —ирующий** *a.* loosely paired (chromosomes).

конъюнк/тива *f.* (anal.) conjunctiva; **—тивальный** *a.* conjunctival; **—тивит** *m.* (med.) conjunctivitis; **—тор** *m.* (electron.) AND gate, AND circuit; **—тура** *f.* (con)juncture; (business) conditions, state of affairs; **—ция** (electron.) conjunction, AND function.

конь *m.* horse, stallion; (ichth.) Hemibarbus, Catostomus and others.

коньк/а *gen.;* **—и** *pl. of* конёк; (ice) skates; (ichth.) seahorses (*Syngnathidae*); **—обежный** *a.* skating; **—овые** *see* коньки (ichth.); **—овый** *a. of* конёк.

конь-рыба *see* конь (ichth.).

конья/к *m.,* **—чный** *a.* cognac, brandy; **—чное масло** ethyl oenanthate.

конюга *f.* (orn.) auklet (*Aethia*).

коню/х *m.* stable boy, groom; **—шенный** *a.,* **—ня** *f.* stable.

ко/образ *m.* (math.) coimage; **—объём** *m.* covolume.

коопер/атив *m.* cooperative (store); **—ативно-общественный** *a.* cooperative; **—ативный** *a.* cooperative; **—атор** *m.* cooperator; collaborator; **—ация** *f.,* **—ирование** *n.* cooperation; collaboration; cooperative organization; **—ированный** *a.* affiliated; **—ировать** *v.* organize in a cooperative; collaborate; **—ироваться** *v.* cooperate; collaborate.

кооптировать *v.* coopt.

координ/ата *f.* (math.) coordinate; (point) reference; **система —ат** frame of reference; **—ативный** *a.* coordinate; **—атник** *m.* (elec.) coordinate spacer; **—атно-расточный** *a.* jig-boring (machine); **—атный** *a.* coordinate(d), correlative, multiple-aspect (indexing); coordination (number); variable (recorder); (photogrammetry) fiducial (marks); **—атный искатель, —атный соединитель** circuit selector and switch, crossbar switch; **—атная ручка** (comp.) joystick; **—атограф** *m.* (surv.) coordinatograph; **—ато-**

ме(т)р *m.* coordinate protractor; **—атор** *m.* (av.) position indicator; **—ационный** *a.* coordination; **—ационная связь** coordination link(age); coordinate bond; **—ация** *f.,* **—ирование** *n.,* **—ированность** *f.* coordination; trade-off; scheduling, timing; **—ированный** *a.* coordinate(d); scheduled; **—ировать** *v.* coordinate; schedule.

коориентация *f.* coorientation.

коп. *abbr.* (копейка) kopeck.

копа *f.* pile, heap.

Копа перегруппировка Cope rearrangement.

копа/еноска, —айба, —айва *f.* (bot.) copaiba (*Copaifera officinalis*); **—йский** *a.* copaiba; copaivic (acid); **—йский бальзам** copaiba; **—йфера** *f.* (bot.) Copaifera.

копал *m.* copal (resin); **к. каури** kauri gum, kauri resin; copal; **—ин** *m.* (min.) copaline, copalite; copalin (resin); **—иновая кислота** copalinic acid.

копалка *f.* digger, mattock, grubbing hoe.

копал/овый *a.* copal; copalic (acid); **—овая смола** copal (resin); **—оносный** *a.* copaliferous; **—уха** *f.* (orn.) grouse (*Tetrao urogallus*); **—ьный** *a.* copal.

коп/анец *m.* pond, pool; **—ание** *n.* digging, excavation; **—анный** *a.* dug; **—ань** *see* копанец; **—анье** *see* копание; **—атель** *m.* digger, excavator; **—ательный** *a.* digging; (zool.) fossorial; **—ать** *v.* dig, excavate; delve; loosen; **—аться** *v.* dig; rummage; probe, delve (into); **—ач** *m.* (root crop) digger, lifting plow.

копеечн/ик *m.* (bot.) Hedysarum; **—ый** *a. of* копейка.

копеина *f.* (ichth.) Copeina.

копей *gen. pl. of* копь.

коней/ка *f.* kopeck; **—на** *see* копеина.

копеллидин *m.* copellidine.

копель *m.* Copel (alloy).

копён *gen. pl. of* копна.

копенгагенский *a.* (geog.) Copenhagen.

копеподы *pl.* (crust.) Copepoda.

коп/ёр *m.* pile driver, ram, drop hammer; impact tester; (min.) headframe, headwork; **вертикальный к., испытательный к.** impact(-testing) machine; **испытание на —ре** drop test.

коперник/анский, —овский *a.* Copernican.

копетдагский *a.* Kopet Dagh.

копи *pl. of* копь.

копиапит *m.* (min.) copiapite.

копил/ка *f.* receptacle; (coin) box; **—ьник** *m.* (met.) forehearth receiver.

Копингера радикал Coppinger's radical, galvinoxyl.

копир *m.* copy, master form; former; copying device, contour follower, feeler mechanism; **изготовлять по —у** *v.* (mach.) profile.

копирин *m.* copyrine, 2, 7-benzodiazine.

копир/ка *f.* carbon paper; **—ный** *a.* copy.

копировально-/множительный *a.* duplicating; **к.-фрезерный** *a.* duplicate-milling, profile-milling, profiling, profile and contour milling (machine); **к.-шлифовальный** *a.* profile-grinding.

копир/овальный *a.* copying, etc., *see v.;* carbon or tracing (paper); transfer (color); **к. аппарат** duplicating machine, duplicator; (phot.) printer; **—овальщик** *m.* copier; **—ование** *n.* copying, etc., *see v.;* **—овать** *v.* (make a) copy, duplicate; trace, track; profile, machine to a template; imitate; (phot.) print; **—овка** *see* копирование; **—овочный** *a.* copying, etc., *see v.;* **—овщик** *m.* copier; **—одержатель** *m.* template holder; **—ующий** *a.* copying, etc., *see v.;* slave (unit); master-slave (manipulator).

копит/ель *m.* storer, accumulator; **—ь(ся)** *v.* accumulate, store up, save up, lay up, amass; build up.

коп/ия *f.* copy, transcript, duplicate, counterpart; tracing; (phot.) print; **снимать —ию** *v.* (make a) copy, duplicate.

копка *f.* digging (up), harvesting (of root crop); excavation.

копланарн/о-сеточный *a.* (comp.) coplanar grid (effect); **—ый** *a.* coplanar.

копн/а *f.* rick (of hay), shock (of wheat); heap, pile; **—ение** *n.* stacking, piling up; **—итель** *m.* stacker, piler, shocker; **—ить** *v.* stack, pile up, shock; **—овоз** *m.* sweep rake.

копнуть *see* **копать.**

коповичок *m.* (ichth.) parr, young salmon.

кополимер *see* **сополимер.**

копотливый *a.* sluggish; tedious, laborious.

копот/ный *a.* sooty, smoky; **—ь** *f.* soot, lampblack; smoke, fume; fly ash.

копошиться *v.* dart about; swarm.

Коппа закон Kopp's law.

коппит *m.* (min.) koppite.

копр *m.* (ent.) dung beetle; *prefix see* **копро—**; **—а** *f.* copra; *gen. of* **копёр; —о** *prefix* copr(o)— (feces).

копров/ой, —ый *a. of* **копёр**; pile-driving; hardness drop (test); **—ая прочность** impact strength.

копро/лит *m.* coprolite, fossil excrement; (med.) coprolith; **—порфирин** *m.* coproporphyrin; **—стаз** *m.* (med.) coprostasis, fecal impaction; **—станол, —стерин** *m.* coprostanol, coprosterol; **—фаг** *m.* coprophage; **—фаговый** *a.* coprophagous, dung-eating; **—фильный** *a.* coprophilous, dung-inhabiting.

копт/еть *v.* smoke; **—илка** *f.* oil lamp; smokehouse; **—ильный** *a.* smoking, curing; **—ильня** *f.* smokehouse.

коптис *m.* (bot.) Coptis.

копт/ить *v.* smoke, cure; (cover with) soot; **—ящий** *a.* smoking, etc., *see* **—еть.**

копул/ирование *n.*, **—ировка** *f.* (hort.) (whip)grafting; (zool.) copulation; **—ировать** *v.* (whip)graft; copulate; **—ятивный** *a.* copulatory, copulative; **—яция** *f.* copulation, coupling, union.

копунктальный *a.* (math.) copunctal.

копчение *n.* smoking, curing; fumigation.

коп/чён(н)ый *a.* smoked; soot-covered; **—чённости, —чёнье** *n.*, **—ченья** *pl.* smoked food(s).

копчик *m.* (anat.) coccyx, tailbone; (amph.) urostyle; (orn.) pygostyle; **—овый** *a.* coccygeal.

копчушка *f.* small smoked fish.

копыл *m.* (launching) poppet.

копыт/ень *m.* (bot.) Asarum; **—ка** *f.* (orn.) sandgrouse (*Syrrhaptes*); **—ник** *m.* Asarum; **—ные** *pl.* (mam.) Ungulata; **—ный** *a.* hoof(ed), ungulate; coffin (joint); **—ный жир, —ная мазь, —ное масло** neat's foot oil; **—о** *n.* hoof; **—овидный, —ообразный** *a.* hoof-shaped, unguliform, ungulate; **—оходящие** *pl.* (mam.) Ungulata; **—охождение** *n.* unguligrade walking; **—це** *dim. of* **копыто**; dewclaw; **—чатый** *see* **копытовидный.**

копь *f.* mine, pit.

копьё *n.* spear, lance; guard pin, prong.

копье/(видно)листный *a.* (bot.) lancifolious; **—видный** *a.* spear-shaped, spicular, lanceolate, hastate; **—нос** *m.* (mam.) spear-nosed bat; **—носец** *m.* (ent.) Acropedellus; (ichth.) spearfish (*Tetrapturus*); **—носка** *f.* (ent.) Gomphoceripppus; **—носые** *pl.* (mam.) Megadermatidae.

копьё/-рыба *f.*, **—рыл** *m.* billfish; **—рылые** *pl.* (ichth.) Istiophoridae.

копье/уска *f.* (ent.) Myrmeleotettix; **—ца** *pl.* fruit-bearing spurs.

кор *m.* core.

кора *f.* bark, rind; (anat.) cortex; (geol.) crust; (casting) skin.

кораб/ельный *a.* ship, marine; ship-borne; naval; mast (tree); **—ельщик** *m.* ship builder; (ent.) ship timber beetle; **—ельщики** *pl.* Lymexylidae; **—левождение** *n.* navigation; **—лекрушение** *n.* shipwreck.

кораблестро/ение *n.* **—ительный** *a.* shipbuilding; **—итель** *m.* ship builder.

корабл/ик *dim. of* **корабль**; (mal.) Argonauta; **—ь** *m.* ship, vessel; airship; (space) vehicle; (arch.) nave; **космический —ь-спутник** manned satellite.

кора/зол *m.* Corazol, pentylenetetrazol; **—коид** *m.*, **—коидный** *a.*) coracoid; **—коидно-плечевой, —коплечевой** *a.* coracobrachial.

коралл *m.* coral; **—ин** *m.* corallin, aurin; **—ина** *f.* (bot.) Corallina; **—ит** *m.* corallite; **—овидный** *a.* coralloid, coral-like; coralline; **—овые** *pl.* (zool.) Anthozoa; **—овый** *a.* coral(line), coral-red; **—ообразный** *see* **коралловидный.**

корамин *m.* Coramine, nikethamide.

корац/идий *m.* (zool.) coracidium; **—ин** *m.* (ichth.) black bream (*Coracinus*); **—иновые** *pl.* Coracinidae; **—ит** *m.* (min.) coracite.

корб/а *see* **корбус; —икула** *f.* (mal.) Corbicula; **—ула** *f.*, **—улевый** *a.* (mal.) Corbula; **—улевые, —улы** *pl.* Corbulidae; **—ус** *m.* (ichth.) dace (*Leuciscus l.*).

корги *pl.* korgi (small river bars; shoals in the Arctic Ocean).

коргонский *a.* (geog.) Korgon.

корд *m.* cord; **—а** *f.* tether; **гонять на —е** *v.* lunge (a horse).

кордаит/овые, —ы *pl.* (pal.) cordaitaleans.

кордиамин *m.* Cordiamin, nikethamide.

кордиерит *m.* (min.) cordierite, iolite.

кордил/ина *f.* (bot.) Cordyline; **—ит** *m.* (min.) cordylite; **—офора** *f.* (zool.) Cordylophora; **—ьера** *f.* cordillera, mountain range.

кордит *m.*, **—овый** *a.* (expl.) cordite.

кордицепин *m.* cordycepin (antibiotic).

корд/ия *f.* (bot.) Cordia; **—ный** *a.* cord.

Кордо резьба Cordeaux (screw) thread.

кордовская кожа *see* **кордуан.**

кордовый *a.* cord.

кордол *m.* cordol, tribromsalol.

кордон *m.*, **—ный** *a.* cordon.

кордриль *m.* (min.) core drill.

корд-суровьё *m.* untreated cord; **к.-ткань** *f.* cord fabric.

кордуан *m.*, **—ский сафьян** cordovan (leather).

кордулегастры *pl.* (ent.) Cordulegasteridae.

корд-шнур *m.* cord.

коре/видный *a.* morbilliform, like measles; **—вой** *a. of* **корь.**

корёжить(ся) *v.* bend, warp; twist out; writhe, double up (with).

кореит *m.* (min.) koreite, agalmatolite.

корейка *f.* breast of pork (or veal).

корейский *a.* (geog.) Korea(n).

корен/астый *a.* thickset, stumpy, stocky; (bot.) strong-rooted; **—иться** *v.* root, be rooted (in); be founded (on).

коренник *m.* shaft horse.

коренн/ой *a.* root; radical, fundamental, basic, trunk, main; native, indigenous, autochthonous; aboriginal (population); thorough; basement (clay); deep-well (brine); foundation (pile); shaft (horse); **к. вал** crankshaft; **к. выход** (geol.) bedrock; **к. зуб** (anat.) molar; cheek tooth; **малый к. зуб** premolar; **к. обитатель**

aborigine; **к. подшипник** crank(shaft) bearing; **—ая порода** bedrock; **—ые железы** molar glands.

кор/ень *m.* root; radix; (math.) radical; **вырывать с —нем** *v.* uproot, eradicate; **знак —ня** (math.) radical sign; **квадратный к.** (math.) square root; **кубический к.** cube root; **метод распределения —ней** root-locus method; **на —ню** standing, growing (crop); **пускать —ни** *v.* take root; **расположение —ней** radication, rooting pattern; **к.-прицепка** *m.* holdfast; **к.-человек** *m.* (bot.) ginseng (*Panax schinseng*).

кореопсис *m.* (bot.) Coreopsis.

ко-репрессор *m.* corepressor.

корец *m.* dipper, scoop.

кореш/ки *pl. of* **корешок;** (anat.) radices; **—ковидный** *a.* radiciform, root-shaped; **—ковый** *a. of* **корешок;** root, radicular; *suffix* —rhizous, -rooted; **—ок** *dim. of* **корень;** rootlet, radicle; stub (of receipt); butt (end); back, spine (of book); **—очек** *m.* rhizel; tiny root.

Корея (geog.) Korea.

корж *m.* (cer.) filter cake, cast; pancake; rock jutting from roof of mine.

корз *m.* coarse (low-grade rubber).

корзин/а *f.* basket, crate, crib; bucket; (centrifuge) bowl; (av.) nacelle, car; **—ка** *f.* basket; (art.) mount, holder; (bot.) calathidium, anthodium; capitulum; **—ковидный** *a.* calathiform, basket-shaped; **—очка** *dim. of* **корзинка;** (bot.) conceptacle; **—(оч)ный** *a. of* **корзина;** pancake (coil); (zool.) corbiculate; **—чатый** *a.* basket(-like); **—щик** *m.* basket weaver.

корзит *m.* (petr.) corsite, napoleonite.

Кори эфир Cori ester, glucose-1-phosphate.

кориамиртин *m.* coriamyrtin.

кориандр *m.,* **—овый** *a.* (bot.) coriander (*Coriandrum*); **—ол** *m.* coriandrol, linalool.

кори/бульбин *m.* corybulbine; **—далин** *m.* corydaline; **—далы** *pl.* (ent.) Corydalidae; **—дин** *m.* corydine.

коридор *m.* corridor, passage(way), alley(way); **—ный** *a. of* **коридор;** tunnel (dryer); **в —ном порядке** unstaggered; **—чик** *dim. of* **коридор.**

кори/кавамин *m.* corycavamine; **—кавидин** *m.* corycavidine; **—кавин** *m.* corycavine; **—кса** *f.* (ent.) Corixa; **—лофилин** *m.* corylophiline; **—не** *n.* (zool.) Coryne; **—небактерий** *m.* Corynebacterium; **—нин** *m.* corynin (a hydroxy acid) corynine, yohimbine; **—нит** *m.* (min.) corynite.

коринка *f.* currant(s).

коринфский *a.* (geog.) Corinthian.

кориолисовый *a.* Coriolis (force).

кори/пальмин *m.* corypalmine; **—туберин** *m.* corytuberine.

корить *v.* reproach, take to task.

кориум *m.* (anat.) corium, true skin.

кориф/ей *m.* coryphaeus, leader; **—елла** *f.* (mal.) Coryphella; **—ена, —ень** *f.* (ichth.) dolphin fish (*Coryphaena*); **—еновые** *pl.* Coryphaenidae.

корица *f.* cinnamon (bark).

коричне/ватый *a.* brownish; **—во-каштановый** *a.* chestnut brown; **—вый** *a.* brown; **—вая земля, —зём** *m.* korichnezem, cinnamonic soil.

коричник *m.* (bot.) cinnamon (*Cinnamomum*).

коричио/карбоновый *a.* carboxycinnamic (acid); **—кислый** *a.* cinnamic acid; cinnamate (of); **—кислый натрий, —натриевая соль** sodium cinnamate; **—кислая соль** cinnamate; **—этиловый эфир** ethyl cinnamate.

коричн/ый *a.* cinnamon; cinnamic (acid, alcohol); **к. альдегид** cinnamic aldehyde, cinnamaldehyde; **к. камень** (min.) cinnamon stone, essonite; **к. лавр, —ое**

дерево *see* **коричник; к. цвет** cinnamon flowers, cassia buds; **—ое масло** cinnamon oil; **китайское —ое масло** cassia oil; **соль —ой кислоты** cinnamate.

корка *f.* crust, incrustation, scale, scab; cake; bark; peel, rind; (met.) scum; (casting) skin; (biol.) cortex.

коркит *m.* (min.) corkite.

корков/атый *a.* suberous; **—идный** *a.* bark-like, crusty; crustaceous, crust-like; **—о—** *prefix* (anat.) cortico— (cortex); **—о-мостовой** *a.* corticopontine; **—о-спинномозговой** *a.* corticospinal; **—о-ядерный** *a.* corticonuclear; **—ый** *a. of* **корка;** (anat.) cortical; crustaceous, crustate; scabby; **—ый слой** (steel ingot) skin layer; (anat.) cortex; **—ая пробка** cork, stopper, plug.

коркодоновый *a.* (geog.) Korkodon.

корко/дробитель *m.* soil crust breaker; **—носный** *a.* corticose; **—образный** *a.* corticoid; **—образование** *n.* crust formation; cortication.

Корлиса клапан Corliss valve.

корм *m.* feed, forage, fodder; feeding, nutrition; nutriment.

корм/а *f.* (naut.) stern; **на —е** abaft.

кормёж/ка *f.,* **—ный** *a.* feed(ing), food.

кормидий *m.* (zool.) cormidium.

корм/илец *m.* provider; **—илица** *f.* wet nurse; **—ильщик** *m.* feeder; **—ить** *v.* feed, nourish; **—иться** *v.* feed (on), eat, graze; live (on), be sustained (by); **—ление** *n.* feeding, nourishment, nutrition; food supply; **—ленный** *a.* fed, nourished; **—ность** *f.* feeding capacity; food supply; food consumption; **—ный** *a. of* **корм;** feeding.

кормо— *prefix* feed. fodder; cormo— (tree trunk); **—вой** *a. of* **корм, корма;** food, feed(ing); nutrient (yeast); fodder, forage (grass); (naut.) stern, aft(er); tail, rear; **—вой коэффициент** feeding ration; **—вой продукт** fodder; feed; **—вая база** food or forage resources; **—вая единица** feed unit; **—вая продуктивность** carrying capacity (of pasture); **—вая смесь** feed, mash; **—вая соль** salt lick; **—вое угодье** grassland.

кормо/вочная *f.* feed (preparing) room; **—дробилка** *f.* feed or fodder grinder; **—завод** *m.* feed-processing plant; **—загрузчик** *m.* feed loader; **—запарник** *m.* feed steaming plant, fodder steamer; **—запар(оч)ный** *a.* feed- or fodder-steaming; **—запарочный агрегат** *see* **кормозапарник; —измельчитель** *m.* food chopper; **—кухня** *f.* feed-processing room; **—мешалка** *f.* feed mixer; **—мялка, —плющилка** *f.* feed crusher; **—подготовительная** *see* **кормокухня; —подготовительный** *a.,* **—подготовка** *f.* feed processing, fodder preparation; **—раздатчик** *m.* (bunk) feeder, feed dispenser; **—резка** *f.* fodder chopper; food cutter; **—смеситель** *m.* feed mixer.

кормофит *m.* (bot.) cormophyte.

кормо/хранение, —хранилище *n.* feed or fodder storage; **—цех** *see* **кормокухня.**

кормус *m.* (bot.; zool.) corm, cormus.

кормушка *f.* feed box, feeder, trough, rack, manger, crib.

корналин *m.* (min.) carnelian.

корнать *v.* cut short, crop.

корнвалл/ийский *a.* (geog.) Cornwall, Cornish; **—ит** *m.* (min.) cornwallite.

корне— *prefix* root, rhizo—.

корнеальный *a.* (anat.) corneal.

корне/видный *a.* radicine, root-like, rhizoid; radiciform; **—вище** *n.* (bot.) rhizome, rootstock, tap root; **—вищевый, —вищный** *a. of* **корневище;** rhizomatous (grass), rootstock-bearing; **—вой** *a.* root, radical; deepwell (salt); **—вой зачаток** radicle; **—вая шейка** crown; **—вые подвои** rootstock; **—головые** *pl.*

(zool.) Rhizocephala; **—грыз** *m.* (ent.) Rhizotrogus; **—дёр-вертелка** *m.* stump puller; **—душитель** *m.* (phyt.) Rosellinia; **—ед** *m.* (phyt.) root rot; (ent.) root borer (*Dorcadion*); **—еды** *pl.* (ent.) swifts (*Hepialidae*); **—жгутиковые** *pl.* (prot.) Rhizomonadina; **—жил** *m.* (ent.) bark beetle (*Hylastes*).

корне/измельчитель *m.* root shredder; **—искатель** *m.* (math.) root solver, root calculator; **—й** *gen. pl. of* **корень; —клубнемойка** *f.* vegetable washer; **—клубнемялка** *f.* root pulper; **—клубнеплод** *m.* root crop; **—листный** *a.* rhizophyllous; **—мойка** *f.* root washer; **—ножки** *pl.* (prot.) Rhizopoda; **—носец** *m.* (bot.) rhizophore; **—обитаемый** *a.* root-inhabited; **—обитаемый слой** root zone, root system layer; **—образование** *n.* root formation; **—отпрыск** *m.* (bot.) sobole, sucker, offset; **—отпрысковый** *a.* soboliferous; **—плод** *m.* root crop; tap root; **—плодный** *a.* root crop; rhizocarpous; **—плодохранилище** *n.* root cellar; **—резка** *f.* root cutter; **—родный** *a.* rhizogenic, root-producing; **—родный слой** pericycle; **—рождение** *n.* rhizogenesis; **—рот** *m.* (zool.) Rhizostoma.

корнерупин *m.* (min.) kornerupine.

корн/есобственный *a.* (bot.) self-rooted, true-rooted; **—ечистка** *f.* root peeler; **—и** *pl. of* **корень.**

корни/кулярия *f.* (bot.) Cornicularia; **—н** *m.* cornin; cornine (alkaloid).

Корнинга стекло Corning glass.

корнишон *m.* gherkin, small cucumber.

корнпапир *m.* granulated paper.

корнубианит *m.* (petr.) cornubianite.

корнуэльский *a.* (geog.) Cornwall, Cornish.

корнцанг *m.* (med.) packer; **—и** tongs.

Корню спираль (math.) Cornu's spiral, clothoid.

корнюры *pl.* gas conduits (of coke oven).

корня *gen. of* **корень.**

короб *m.* box, chest, case, container; (agr.) flat; basket, hamper; duct; (annealing) pot; body (of car); (loading) hopper.

коробить(ся) *v.* warp, deform, buckle.

коробка *f.* box, case, chest; housing, compartment, capsule; casing; (wing) cell(ule); (valve) cage; tank, header; hopper; (cable) junction; (door) frame; (building) shell; **к. передач, к. скоростей** gear box, transmission; **к. подач** feed gear box; **черепная к.** (anat.) cranium.

коробление *n.* warping, buckling, distortion.

короб/оватость *f.* warpage, camber (of rolled sheet); **—овая кривая** (arch.; math.) basket(-handle) curve; **—ок** *gen. pl. of* **коробка;** *dim. of* **короб; —очка** *dim. of* **коробка;** (bot.) boll, pod, capsule; (av.) box pattern; **—очко** *prefix* (biol.) theci— (theca); capsuli—, capsul(o)— (capsule); **—очковидный** *a.* theciform; capsuliform; **—очник** *m.* corn earworm (*Chloridea obsoleta*); **—очный** *a. of* **коробка; —чатый** *a.* box(-type), box-like, box-shaped; channel (iron); quadrant (valve); case (lock); (bot.) capsular; **—чатая отливка** box casting.

корова *f.* cow; **морская к., стеллерова к.** (mam.) Steller's sea cow (*Hydrodamalis stelleri*); **морская к.** (ichth.) stargazer (*Uranoscopus scaber*).

коровай *m.* round loaf.

коровальт *m.* Corowalt (abrasive).

коров/а-рекордистка *f.* record-holding cow; **—ий** *a.* cow, bovine; **—ье масло** butter; **—ка** *dim. of* **корова;** (ent.) ladybird (*Coccinella*); (bot.) edible boletus; **божья —ка** *see* **коровка** (ent.); **морская —ка** (ichth.) stargazer; **(божьи) —ки** *pl.* (ent.) Coccinellidae; **морские –ки** (ichth.) Uranoscopidae; **—ник** *m.,* **—ня** *f.* cow barn.

коров/ой, —ый *a.* crust(ed); cortical.

коров/ы, морские (mam.) sea cows (*Hydrodamalidae*); **—як** *m.* (liquid) cow manure; (bot.) mullein (*Verbascum*).

короед *m.* bark beetle (*Ips,* etc.); **—овые** *pl.* (ent.) Ipidae.

корок *gen. pl. of* **корка.**

корол/ева *f.* (ent.) queen bee; **—евский** *a.* king's, royal; **—евская желть** king's yellow, orpiment; **—евые** *pl.* oarfishes (*Regalecidae*); **—ёк** *m.* (met.) regulus, assay button, bead; (orn.) kinglet (*Regulus*); **—ь** *m.* king; **—ь шлюза** pointing sill; **—ьки, —ьковые** *pl.* (orn.) Regulidae; **—ьковый** *a. of* **королёк;** (met.) reguline; assay (balance).

коромандельский *a.* (geog.) Coromandel.

коромысло *n.,* **—вый** *a.* yoke, balance arm, balance beam, rocker, rocking shaft; (weight) lever; bascule; (ent.) dragonfly (*Aeschna*); *pl.* Aeschnidae, Aeshnidae.

корон/а *f.* crown, corona; **—адит** *m.* (min.) coronadite; **—адо(-сериола)** *f.* (ichth.) greater amberjack (*Seriola dumerili, S. lalandi*); **—альный** *a.* (astr.) coronal; **—арный** *a.* (anat.) coronary; **—ен** *m.* coronene; **—ий** *m.* (astr.) coronium.

корон/ирование *n.,* **—ирующий разряд** (dielectrics) corona (discharge); **—ировать** *v.* display corona; **—ка** *f.* crown, corona; (drill) bit; **—ковидный** *a.* coroniform, crown-shaped; **—ник** *m.* winter cutworm (*Agrotis segetum*); **—ный** *a.* corona; crown (drill, wheel, etc.); castle (nut); **—ный разряд** corona discharge; **—овать** *v.* crown; **—ограф** *m.* coronograph; **—остойкость** *f.* corona resistance; **—чатый** *a.* crown, castellate(d).

коро/обдирка *f.* (paper) (de)barking; barker, spudder; **—обдирочник** *m.* barker; **—обдир(оч)ный, —очистка** *f.,* **—очистный** *a.* barking, bark peeling.

короста *f.* (vet.) scab, mange; (phyt.) scurf; **—вник** *m.* (bot.) scabious (*Knautia*).

коростель *m.* (orn.) corn crake (*Crex c.*).

коротк/ий *a.* short, brief, quick; **—ое замыкание** shorting; **—о** *adv.* shortly, briefly; **—о говоря** in short, in brief, in a few words.

коротко — *prefix* brevi—, brachy—, short; **—ватый** *a.* rather short; **—ветвистый** *a.* short-branched, breviramose; **—волновый** *a.* short-wave; **—волокнистый** *a.* short-staple, short-fibered; **—волос(ист)ый** *a.* short-haired; **—выдержанный** *a.* briefly exposed; seasoned for a short time; (nucl.) short-decayed; **—главы** *pl.* (amph.) Microhylidae.

короткоголов *m.* (amph.) Brachycephalus; **—ость** *f.* (anat.) brachycephaly; **—ые** *pl.* (amph.) Brachycephalidae; **—ый** *a.* brachycephalic, short-headed, broadheaded.

коротко/действующий *a.* short-range; **—дневный** *a.* short-day; **—живущий** *a.* short-lived; **—замедленный** *a.* short-delay (blasting); **—замкнутый** *a.* (elec.) short-circuit(ed), shorted; squirrel-cage (motor); **—замыкатель** *m.* short-circuiting device; **—замыкающий** *a.* short-circuiting; **—звеньевой** *a.* short-link (chain); **—клювый** *a.* short-billed brevirostrate.

короткокрыл *m.* (ent.) Necydalis; **—ка** *f.* Podismopsis; **—ые** *pl.* rove beetles (*Staphylinidae*); **—ый** *a.* short-winged, brachypterous.

коротко/листный *a.* short-leaved, brachyphyllous; **—метражный** *a.* short (film); **—надкрылые** *see* **коротокрылые; —ногий** *a.* short-legged, breviped; short-stalked, brachypodous; **—ножка** *f.* (bot.) Brachypodium; **—ножковый** *see* **коротконогий; —носый** *a.* short-nose(d); **—опушённый** *a.* puberulent, minute-

277

ly downy; —**остистый** *a.* short-awned; —**палый** *a.* brachydactylic, short-fingered, short-toed; —**пламен-ный** *a.* short-flame; —**плечий** *a.* short-arm (balance); —**пробежный** *a.* short-range; —**проволочный** *a.* short-wire; —**рогий** *a.* short-horned; —**рылый** *a.* short-nosed; —**ствольный** *a.* short-stemmed, brevisca-pous; short-boled (forest); —**стебельный**, —**стеб-ельчатый** *a.* short-stalked, short-stemmed; —**столб-чатый** *a.* (min.) short-columnar; —**сть** *f.* shortness, brevity; —**телый** *a.* short(-bodied); —**узлие** *n.* (phyt.) fanleaf; —**усые** *pl.* (ent.) Brachycera; —**усый** *a.* brachycerous, short-horned; —**ухий** *a.* short-eared; —**фокусный** *a.* short-focus.

короткохвост *m.* (herp.) a lizard (Trachyurus rugosus); —**ка** *f.* (orn.) short-tail bush warbler (*Urosphena squameiceps*); —**ый** *a.* short-tail(ed), brachyuric, brachyural.

коротко/цикловый *a.* short-lived; —**шеий** *a.* short-necked; —**шёрст(н)ый** *a.* short-wooled; short-haired; —**штамбовый** *a.* bush(-form); —**язычный** *a.* short-tongued, brevilingual.

короток *sh. m. of* **короткий**.

коротоксигенин *m.* corotoxigenin.

корот/ыш *m.,* —**ышка** *f.* short person; —**ьё** *n.* (branch) wood, (short) cuts, ends.

корофий *m.* (crust.) Corophium.

короче *comp. of* **короткий, коротко.**

корочка *dim. of* **корка.**

корпеть *v.* sweat (over), drudge (at).

корпинчо *n.* (mam.) capybara (*Hydrochaeris h.*).

корпия *f.* lint.

корпора/тивный *a.* corporate; —**ция** *f.* corporation, body.

корпулентный *a.* corpulent, fat.

корпус *m.,* body, carcass, frame(work), chassis; housing, case, casing, shell, envelope; building, structure; (evaporator) effect; hull (of ship); (shipbuilding) body plan, section lines; (reactor) vessel; base (of plow); (typ.) long primer (10 points); (anat.) corpus; (mil.) corps; (elec.) chassis ground; (comp.) package; **монтаж в —е** packaging.

корпускул/а *f.* corpuscle; —**ярный** *a.* corpuscular; particulate, particle-sized.

корпусн/ой *a.* (mil.) corps; —**ый** *a. of* **корпус;** box-type (bit); cabinet (furniture).

корр/азия *f.* (geol.) corrasion; —**егирование** *see* **коррекция;** –**егировать** *see* **корригировать;** —**екс** *m.* apron (for film).

коррект/ив *m.* corrective; correction, amendment; —**ирование** *n.* correction, adjustment; (comp.) updating; proofreading; —**ировать** *v.* correct, adjust; update; proofread; —**ировка** *see* **корректирование;** —**ировочный** *a.* (error-)correcting, corrective; adjusting; proofreading; (beam-)guiding; positioning; —**ировщик** *m.* proofreader; (mil.) spotter; —**ирующий** *see* **корректировочный;** —**ность** *f.* correctness; —**ный** *a.* correct, proper; —**ор** *m.* corrector, adjuster; (altitude) compensator; proofreader; —**орская** *f.* proofroom; —**орский** *a.* proofreading; proofreader's; —**ура** *f.* correction(s); proof (page); proofreading; —**урный** *a.* proofreader's; —**урный оттиск** proofsheet.

коррекци/онный *a.,* —**я** *f.* correction; —**онная величина** extent of correction.

коррел/ированность *f.* correlation; —**ированный** *a.* correlated; —**ировать** *v.* correlate; —**ограмма** *f.* correlogram, correlation curve; —**ограф, —ометр** *see* **коррелятор;** —**ят** *m.* correlate; —**ятивный** *a.* correlative, correlation; —**ятор** *m.* correlator; —**яцион-ный** *a.,* —**яция** *f.* correlation; relationship.

корреспонден/т *m.* correspondent, reporter; (rad.) distant station; —**тский** *a. of* **корреспондент;** press (card) —**ция** *f.* correspondence, mail; (news) report; (tel.) traffic.

корригиров/ание *n.* correction; (correlation) adjustment; —**ать** *v.* correct, adjust, fix.

корродир/ование *n.* corrosion; —**ованный** *a.* corroded; —**овать** *v.* corrode; —**уемость** corrodibility; —**уемый** *a.* corrodible; corroded; —**ующий** *a.* corroding, corrosive; —**ующее средство** corrosive.

коррозие/стойкий, —устойчивый *a.* corrosion-resisting, noncorroding, rust-resisting, rustproof; stainless (steel); —**устойчивость** *f.* resistance to corrosion.

корроз/ийность *f.* corrosiveness; —**ийный** *see* **коррозионный;** —**ионностойкий, —ио(нно)устойчи-вый** *see* **коррозиестойкий;** —**ионный** *a.* corrosion; corrosive; —**ировать** *see* **корродировать;** —**ия** *f.* corrosion; **местная —ия** pitting.

корругатор *m.* (anat.) corrugator.

корсак *m.* (mam.) corsac (*Vulpes corsac*).

корсаковский *a.* (med.) Korsakoff's (syndrome); (geog.) Korsakov.

корсет *m.,* —**ный** *a.* corset; (ent.; ichth.) corselet; —**ность** *f.* corset shape.

корсиканский *a.* (geog.) Corsica(n).

корсогастеровые *pl.* (ichth.) Korsogasteridae.

корт *m.* court, yard; tennis court.

кортадерия *f.* (bot.) Cortaderia.

кортекс *m.* (anat.; bot.) cortex; —**ный** *a.* cortical; —**он** *m.* cortexone.

кортиев орган (anat.) Corti's organ.

кортиз/ол *m.* cortisol, hydrocortisone; —**он** *m.,* —**оновый** *a.* cortisone.

кортик *m.* dirk, short dagger.

корти/кальный *a.* (anat.) cortical; —**коид** *m.,* —**коид-ный** *a.* corticoid; —**костероид** *m.,* —**костероидный гормон** corticosteroid; —**костероидогенез** *m.* corticosteroid production; —**костерон** *m.* corticosterone; —**н** *m.* cortin; —**цин** *m.* corticin.

корток *m.* short-circuit(ing) current.

кортолон *m.* cortolone.

корточк/и: на —ах *a.* squatting; **опуститься на к., сидеть на —ах** *v.* squat.

кортуза *f.* (bot.) Cortusa.

корунд, —из *m.,* —**овый** *a.* (min.) corundum; **красный к.** ruby; **синий к.** sapphire.

корча *f.* spasm, cramp; stump with root.

корчага *f.* large pot, earthenware pot.

корчев/алка *see* **корчеватель;** —**альный** *a.,* —**ание** *n.* grubbing, uprooting, stump pulling; **взрывное —ание** stump blasting.

корчёванный *a.* uprooted.

корчев/атель *m.* grubber, stump puller; **к.-бульдозер** *m.* tree-dozer; —**атый** *a.* root-filled (ground); —**ать** *v.* grub, uproot, pull stumps.

корчёвка *see* **корчевание.**

корчи *pl.* convulsions; —**иться** *v.* convulse, writhe, squirm.

коршун *m.,* —**ий** *a.* (orn.) kite, hawk.

корыст/ный *a.* mercenary; profitable, advantageous; —**ь** *f.* profit; advantage.

корыт/ный *a.* trough(-shaped); U-, channel (iron); —**о** *n.* trough, pan, tray; vat; hod; —**овидный, —ообраз-ный** *a.* trough-shaped, U-shaped; —**це** *dim. of* **коры-то;** (ball bearing) race; saddle.

корь *f.* (med.) measles.

корьё *n.* (tan) bark.

корье/вой *a.* of **кора**; **—дроьилка** *f.* bark mill; **—ломка** *f.* bark breaker; **—резка** *f.* bark cutter or chopper.

корю/ха, —шка *f.*, **—шковый** *a.* (ichth.) smelt (*Osmerus*, spec. *O. eperlanus*); **—шки, —шковые** *pl.* Osmeridae.

коряв/ость *f.* roughness; **—ый** *a.* rough, uneven; rough-skinned, pitted, pimpled; (bot.) tortuose, tortuous; **—ый лес** dwarf growth.

коря/га, —жина *f.* snag, deadhead.

корякский *a.* (geog.) Koryak.

кос *sh. m. of* **косой.**

кос— *prefix* indirect; oblique.

коса *f.* scythe; (sand)spit, bar, tongue; plait, braid; (anat.) falx; (tanning) doctor blade; *sh. f. of* **косой**; **к.-бар** *f.* bay bar, barrier beach; **—рик** *m.* pincers; **—рь** *m.* mower; chopper.

косатк/а *f.* (mam.) killer whale (*Orcinus orca*); (orn.) falcated teal (*Anas falcata*); (ichth.) catfish [*L(e)iocassis*]; **—и, —овые** *pl.* (ichth.) Bagridae.

косач *m.*, **—иный** *a.* (orn.) black grouse (*Lyrurus tetrix*).

косвенн/о *adv.* indirectly, obliquely; **—овозбуждаемый** *a.* indirectly excited; **—одействующий** *a.* indirect; **—ый** *a.* indirect; oblique, cross; circumstantial (evidence); overhead (expenses).

косейсмический *a.* (geol.) coseismal.

косеканс *m.*, **—ный** *a.* (math.) cosecant; **—оида** *f.* cosecant curve.

косен *sh. m. of* **косный.**

косец *m.* mower; hay maker, hay cutter.

косил/ка *f.* mower, mowing machine; **к.-силосорезка** *f.* forage harvester; **—очный** *a.* mowing.

косина *f.* obliquity; (med.) strabismus.

косинский *a.* (geog.) Kosa.

косинус *m.* (math.) cosine; **к.-версус** *m.* versed cosine; **—оида** *f.* cosine curve.

косить *v.* mow, cut down; slant; squint, be cross-eyed; **—ся** *v.* be mowed; slope, slant; look askance (at); squint.

косица *f.* braid, rope; (wool) staple.

косма *f.* tangle (of hair); **—тить** *v.* make shaggy; **—тка** *f.* soft brush, mop; **—то—** *prefix* dasy—, lasi(o)—, shaggy; **—тый** *a.* shaggy, hairy, bristly; (biol.) crinite; **—ч** *m.* shaggy animal.

космети/ка *f.* cosmetic(s); cosmetology; **—ческий** *a.* cosmetic; **—ческие изделия** cosmetics.

косминский *a.* (geog.) Kosma.

космическ/ий *a.* cosmic; space (ship); outer (space); **к. (летательный) аппарат** spacecraft, space vehicle; **установленный на —ом корабле** *a.* space-borne; **—ая навигация** astronavigation; **—ое пространство** (outer) space.

космо— *prefix* cosm(o)— (universe); **—видение** *n.* space television; **—гонический** *a.* cosmogonic; **—гония** *f.* cosmogony; **—графия** *f.* cosmography; **—дром** *m.* spaceport, space-launch(ing) complex; **—лин** *m.* cosmoline, petroleum jelly; **—логический** *a.* cosmological; **—логия** *f.* cosmology; **—навигация, —навтика** *f.* astronautics, interplanetary navigation; **—навт** *m.* astronaut; **—полит** *m.* (biol.) cosmopolite, cosmopolitan species; **—политический, —(ич)ный** *a.* cosmopolitan, world-wide, widely distributed; **—с** *m.* cosmos; (outer) space; (bot.) Cosmos; **—трон** *m.* (nucl.) cosmotron, proton-synchrotron; **—химия** *f.* astrochemistry, cosmochemistry.

косналог *m.* indirect tax, hidden tax.

косн/еть *v.* stagnate; stiffen; **—ость** *f.* stagnation; lethargy, sluggishness; nonprogressiveness.

косноязыч/ие *n.* (med.) ankyloglossia, tongue-tie; **—ный** *a.* tongue-tied.

коснуться *see* **касаться.**

косный *a.* inert, stagnant, sluggish; backward, non-progressive.

косо *adv.* obliquely slantwise, slanting, on a bias, sideways, askance, askew; *prefix* lox(o)—, plagi(o)—, oblique; **к. поставленный** *a.* offset; **—бокий** *a.* lopsided, crooked; **—вато** *adv.* somewhat obliquely; **—ватый** *a.* somewhat oblique.

косовица *f.* haymaking; haying season.

косовичн/ик *m.*, **—ый ходок** (min.) crosscut, back entry.

косовище *n.* scythe handle.

косовый *a.* of **коса**; river bar (gold).

косоглаз/ие *n.*, **—ость** *f.* (med.) strabismus, squint; **—ый** *a.* cross-eyed.

косогольский *a.* (geog.) Kosogol.

косо/гон *m.* (mach.) pitman, connecting rod; **—гор** *m.* slant, incline, declivity, slope, hillside; **—горник** *m.* (bot.) Prenanthes; **—горный** *a.* of **косогор**; **—зуб(чат)ый** *a.* spiral, helical (gear).

кос/ой *a.* slanting, sloping; diagonal, transverse; sidelong, skew; oblique (angle); spiral, helical (gear); **—ая отточка** beveling; **—ая оптика** glancing incidence optics; **—ок** *m.* cushion (in heel of shoe).

косолап/ить *v.* (med.) toe in; **—ость** *f.* talipes, clubfoot; (vet.) winging (in or out); **—ый** *a.* talipedic, club (foot); pigeon-toed.

косо/нарезанный *a.* (text.) bias-cut; **—плодный** *a.* (bot.) loxocarpous; **—прицельный** *a.* oblique; **—рот** *m.* (ichth.) sole (*Solea*); **—ротые** *pl.* Soleidae; Cynoglossidae; **—рукость** *f.* (med.) talipomanus, clubhand; **—свет** *m.* oblique lighting fixture; **—симметричный** *a.* skew-symmetric; **—слоистый** *a.* (geol.) obliquely laminated; **—слой** *m.* cross grain, curly grain; (geol.) oblique bed; **—слойность** *f.* spiral growth (of tree); **—слойный** *a.* cross-fibered, cross-grained; (geol.) transversely or diagonally cross-bedded; ramp(-function) (wave); **—сть** *f.* obliquity, bias; **—угольный** *a.* oblique-angled; canted, bevel(ed); **—ур** *m.* bridgeboard, string (of stairs).

КОСПАС *abbr.* (**космическая система поиска аварийных судов**) (naut.) search and rescue satellite (SARSAT).

коссаит *m.* (min.) cossaite.

коссирит *m.* (min.) cossyrite.

костальный *a.* (anat.) costal, rib.

косте— *prefix* osteo—, osseo—, bone; **—видный** *a.* osteoid; **—держатель** *m.* bone forceps; **—дробилка** *f.* bone grinder; **—неть** *v.* ossify; grow numb; stiffen; **—нец** *m.* (bot.) Asplenium; Holosteum; **—неющий** *a.* ossifying, etc., *see v.*; **—носный слой** (geol.) bone bed; **—образование** *n.* osteogenesis, bone formation; **—образовательный, —образующий** *a.* osteogenetic, bone-forming; **—подобный** *a.* osteoid.

костёр *m.* bonfire, wood fire; mound, heap, stack, pile (in charcoal burning); (min.) chock, cog; (bot.) brome grass (*Bromus*).

костеразрушитель *m.* (med.) osteoclast; **—ный** *a.* osteoclastic, bone-destroying.

костерок, костёрчик *dim. of* **костёр.**

костерь *m.* (ichth.) sturgeon (*Acipenser baeri*; *A. gueldenstaedti*).

костеязычные *pl.* (ichth.) Osteoglossidae.

кости *gen., pl., etc. of* **кость**; ossa.

кости/азис, —оз *m.* (vet.) Costia infection.

кост/истая *f.* bony fish, teleost; **—ость** *f.* boniness; **—истые** *pl.* (ichth.) Teleosti; **—лявый** *a.* bony, gaunt; **—но—** *prefix* osteo—, osseo—, bone; **—но-пузырные** *pl.* (ichth.) Ostariophysi; **—но-суставной** *a.* (anat.) osteoarticular; bone and joint (disease); **—но-хрящевой** *a.* osteochondrous; **—нощёкие** *pl.* (ichth.) Cottoidei; **—нощитковые** *pl.* (pal.) Osteostraci; **—ноязыкие** *see* **костеязычные; —ный** *a.* bone, bony, osseous; **—ный клей** ossein, glutin.

косто— *prefix* bone; costo—, rib; **—еда** *f.* (med.) caries; **—прав** *m.* osteopath, bone setter.

косточк/а *dim. of* **кость**; (anat.) ossicle; (bot.) pyrena, stone, pit, seed, kernel; (elec.) bushing; **—овыбиватель, —овыниматель** *m.* pitter, pit remover; **—овые** *pl.* stone fruits, drupes; **—овый** *a. of* **косточка**; *suffix* -seeded; -pyrenous; **—овый плод, —овый фрукт** drupe.

костр/а *gen. of* **костёр; —ец** *m.* (meat) rump, leg; **—(ик)а, —ица** *f.,* **—ичный** *a.* (paper; text.) shive, boon; scutch, woody fiber; **—ище** *n.* campfire site; **—овый** *a. of* **костёр; костра;** pile, heap (charring); **—овая крепь** (min.) chock, cog.

костромской *a.* (geog.) Kostroma.

костросборник *m.* scutch collector.

костус *m.* (bot.) Costus.

костыл/езабивщик *m.* spike driver; **—едёр** *m.* spike puller; **—ёк, —ик** *dim. of* **костыль; —ь** *m.,* **—ьный** *a.* spike, cramp, peg, pin; (med.) crutch; (av.) (tail) skid; **—ять** *v.* walk on crutches.

кость *f.* (anat.) bone, os; **жжёная к.** bone black; **играль-ная к.** die; *pl.* dice; **к.-сырьё** *f.* unprocessed bones.

костюм *m.* costume, suit, outfit.

костяк *m.* skeleton, framework.

костян/ик *m.* (ent.) wireworm, Agriotes larva; **—ика** *f.,* **—ичный** *a.* (bot.) stone bramble (*Rubus saxatilis*); **—ка** *f.* (bot.) drupe; (zool.) centipede (*Lithobius*); **—ки** *pl.* (zool.) Lithobiidae; **—ковые** *pl.* drupaceous plants; **—ковый** *a.* drupaceous.

костян/ой *a.* bone; **к. уголь, —ая чернь** bone black, bone charcoal; **—ая зола** bone ash (tricalcium phosphate); **—ая мука, —ое удобрение** bone meal; **—ое масло** bone oil, Dippel's oil; **чёрная —ая** ivory black; **—очка** *f.* (bot.) drupelet.

косуля *f.* inclined arch; plow; (mam.) roe deer (*Capreolus c.*)

косын/ка *f.,* **—очный** *a.* gusset plate, corner plate, junction plate; kerchief; **—очный** *a.* triangular (bandage).

косьба *f.* mowing, cutting.

кось/винский *a.* (geog.) Kosva; **—инский** *a.* Kosyu.

косяк *m.* (door) jamb; stand, pillar; herd (of cattle); drove (of horses); flock (of birds); shoal, school (of fish); run (of salmon); wedge (of land); **промысловый к.** stock (of fish).

косяком *adv.* at an angle, obliquely.

косяч/ный *a.;* **—ок** *dim. of* **косяк**.

кот *m.* (mam.) cat (*Felis*); **морской к.** (mam.) fur seal (*Callorhinus*); (ichth.) stingray (*Dasyatis pastinaca*); *Scyliorhinus;* humantin (*Oxynotus centrina*).

кота *f.* (fishing) weir, fence.

котангенс *m.* (math.) cotangent; **—оида** *f.* cotangent curve.

котарнин *m.* cotarnine.

котёл *m.* kettle; boiler, heater; (nucl.) reactor; (geol.) kettle, pot hole; **к.-карлик** *m.* small boiler.

котел/ок *dim. of* **котёл**; pot; (compass) bowl; (mil.) mess tin; **к.-регенератор** *m.* recovery boiler; **к.-утилизатор** *m.* waste-heat boiler; **—ьная** *f.* boiler room, boiler house.

котель/ный *a. of* **котёл**; boiler flue (gas); **к. агрегат** boiler unit; **к. завод, к. цех** boiler works, boiler shop; **к. камень** boiler scale; **—ное железо** boiler plate; **—щик** *m.* boiler maker.

котёнок *m.* kitten.

котец *see* **кота**.

Котиаса способ (met.) Cothias method.

котик *dim. of* **кот**; sealskin; **морской к.** *see* **кот, морской** (mam.); **—и** *pl.* (bot.) clover (*Trifolium arvense*); **морские —и, —овые** *pl.* (mam.) Otariidae; **—овый** *a. of* **котик**.

котиледон *m.* (anat.; bot.) cotyledon.

котилозавр *m.* (pal.) cotylosaur.

котинг/и, —овые *pl.* (orn.) Cotingidae.

котип *m.* (biol.) cotype.

котиров/ать *v.* (com.) quote; **—аться** *v.* be quoted; be in demand; be regarded; **—ка** *f.,* **—очный** *a.* quotation.

котиться *v.* (zool.) bear young.

котла *gen. of* **котёл**.

котлет/(к)а *f.,* **—ный** *a.* cutlet; chop.

котло/агрегат *m.* boiler unit; **—ван** *m.* foundation pit, trench, ditch; **—вина** *f.,* **—винный** *a.* depression; (geol.) hollow, basin, crater, trough, kettle(hole); **—винная рубка** gap felling; **—вый** *a. of* **котёл; —надзор** *m.* boiler inspection; **—образный** *a.* kettle-shaped; **—образный провал** (geol.) cauldron; **—строение** *n.* boiler construction; reactor construction; **—турбинный** *a.* boiler and turbine.

котная *a.* pregnant (ewe), in lamb.

кото *see* **кото-кора**.

котовник *m.* (bot.) catnip (*Nepeta*).

кото/ин *m.* cotoin; **-кора** *f.* coto bark.

котомка *f.* backpack.

котон/изатор *m.* (text.) cottonizer; **—изация** *f.* cottonizing; **—изировать** *v.* cottonize; **—ин** *m.* cottonized fiber.

который *a. and pron.* which? what? which, that, who; **к.-нибудь** some, any; **к.-то** some (unknown).

котрель *m.* Cottrell precipitator; **Котреля процесс** Cottrell precipitation.

Котса земля (geog.) Coats Land.

котский *a.* (geog.) Cottian.

коттигит *m.* (min.) köttigite.

коттокомефорус *m.* (ichth.) Cottocomephorus.

Коттона-Мутона эффект (phys.) Cotton-Mouton effect.

коттонпикер *m.* (agr.) cotton picker.

Коттрелля аппарат *see* **котрель**.

коттункул/овые *pl.* (ichth.) tadpole sculpins (*Cottunculidae*); **—(юс)** *m.* Cottunculus.

котуй/канский *a.* (geog.) Kotuikan; **—ский** *a.* Kotui.

котуннит *m.* (min.) cotunnite.

коты *pl. of* **кот; морские к.** (ichth.) stingrays (*Dasyatidae*).

коуз *m.* pit, cistern.

коума *f.* (bot.) Couma.

Коупа перегруппировка Cope rearrangement.

коупер *see* **каупер**.

коуш *m.* dead eye, eyelet, thimble.

кофактор *m.* cofactor.

кофе *m.* coffee; **—варка** *f.* coffee maker; **—дубильный** *a.* caffetannic (acid).

кофеин *m.* caffeine, 1,3,7-trimethylxanthine; **—изм** *m.* caffeinism, caffeine poisoning; **—ка** *f.* coffee bean.

кофей *see* **кофе; —ник** *m.* coffee pot; **—ница** *f.* coffee grinder; coffee jar; coffee lover; **—новый** *a.* caffeine.

кофейнокисл/ый *a.* caffeic acid; caffeate (of); **—ая соль** caffeate.

кофейн/ый *a.* coffee; **—ая кислота** caffeic acid, 3,4-dihydroxycinnamic acid; **соль —ой кислоты** caffeate.

кофе/молка *f.* coffee grinder; **—подобный** *a.* coffee-like.

кофермент *m.* coenzyme; coferment.

кофий *see* **кофе.**

кофобелемнон *m.* (zool.) Kophobelemnon.

кофта *f.* blouse; jacket.

кофункция *f.* (math.) cofunction.

кофф/еин *see* **кофеин;** **—ердам** *m.* cofferdam; **—инит** *m.* (min.) coffinite.

Коха колба Koch flask.

кохе/зия *f.* cohesion; **—рер** *see* **когерер.**

кохинхинский *a.* (geog.) Cochin China.

кохия *f.* (bot.) Kochia.

кохл/еарный *a.* (anat.) cochlear; **—иокопа** *F.* (mal.) Cochliocopa; **—оспермовые** *pl.* (bot.) Cochlospermaceae.

Кохо Cohoe (name).

кохова палочка Koch's bacillus.

Кохрена критерий Cochran test.

кохун *m.* cohune (nut).

коцебуский *a.* (geog.) Kotzebue.

коцинин *m.* cocinin.

кочан *m.,* **—ный** *a.* head (of cabbage or lettuce); (corn) cob.

кочев/ание *n.* wandering, etc., *see v.;* nomadic life; **—ать** *v.* wander, roam, lead a nomad's life; (zool.) migrate.

кочёвка *see* **кочевание;** excursion; nomad's camp.

кочев/ник *m.,* **—ница** *f.* nomad; **—ой** *a.* nomad(ic); migratory; traveling, mobile; **—ье** *see* **кочёвка.**

кочегар *m.* stoker, fireman; **—ка,** **—ня** *f.* stokehole, stokehold, boiler room; **—ный** *a.* firing, stoking.

кочедыжник *m.* (bot.) Athyrium.

кочек *gen. pl. of* **кочка.**

коченеть *v.* grow numb; stiffen.

кочень *see* **кочан; кочерыжка.**

кочер/га *f.* poker, fire iron, (furnace) rake, rabble; **—ёжка** *dim. of* **кочерга.**

кочеры/га, **—жка** *f.* cabbage stalk, stump; **—говысверливатель** *m.* stump corer.

кочет *m.,* **—иный** *a.* rooster, cock.

кочечумский *a.* (geog.) Kochechum.

кочешок *dim. of* **кочень, кочан.**

кочк/а *f.* hummock, hillock, tussock; mound, knoll; (ant, mole) hill; **травяная к.** tussock; **—арник** *m.* hummocky marsh; **—арный,** **—оватый** *a.* hummocky, tussocky, hill(ock)y; **—оватое болото** everglade; **—орез** *m.* mound grader, hill(ock) cutter.

кочкорский *a.* (geog.) Kochkorka.

кочн/а *gen. of* **кочан;** **—я** *gen. of* **кочень.**

кочубеит *m.* (min.) kotschubeite.

кочумдекский *a.* (geog.) Kochumdek.

кочующий *see* **кочевой;** (bot.) free-growing.

кош *m.* corncrib; trap.

кошар/а *f.* sheep pen; **—ование** *n.* folding.

кошач/ий *a.* cat, feline; **к. глаз** (min.) cat's eye; (ent.) a butterfly (*Aglia tau*); **—ье серебро** cat silver, silvery mica; **—ьеакуловидные** *pl.* (ichth.) Scyliorhinoidei; **—ьи** *pl.* (mam.) Felidae; (ichth.) catfishes; **—ья лапка** (bot.) Antennaria; **—ья мята** catnip.

кошек *gen. pl. of* **кошка.**

кошелевский *a.* (geog.) Koshelev(k)a.

кошелёк *m.* purse, wallet.

кошёлка *f.* basket, woven bag.

кошель *m.* purse, wallet; basket, woven bag; (fishing) purse seine; net; (logging) boom, barrier; **—ки** *pl.* (bot.) Calceolaria; **—ковый** *a. of* **кошель.**

кошение *n.* mowing.

кошенил/евый *a.* cochineal; cochenillic (acid); **—еносный** *a.* cochenilliferous; **—ь** *f.* (ent.) cochineal (*Dactylopius coccus*); **—ьно-красный** *a.* cochineal red; **—ьный** *a.* cochineal.

кошен/ина *f.* mowed grass; mowing; **—(н)ый** *a.* mowed.

кошеч/ий *see* **кошачий;** **—ка** *dim. of* **кошка.**

кошиновое масло cochin (grass) oil.

Коши-Римана уравнения (math.) Cauchy-Riemann equations.

кошк/а *f.* (female) cat; drag; grapnel, grab; grapple fork; car, trolley, carriage (of crane); (air) hoist; (geol.) spit, bar; **к.-сом** *f.* catfish; **—и** *pl.* (climbing) grapplers; (mam.) Felidae; **—и-сомы** *pl.* catfishes (*Ictaluridae*).

кошлак *m.* year-old sea otter.

кошма *f.* felt(ing).

кошмар *m.,* **—ный** *a.* nightmare.

кошмить *v.* felt.

коэненит *m.* (min.) koenenite.

коэнзим *m.* coenzyme.

коэрци/тивность *f.,* **—тивная сила** coercivity, coercive force; **—тивный** *a.* coercive; **—(ти)метр** *m.* coercimeter.

коэф., коэф-т *abbr.* (**коэффициент**).

коэффициент *m.* coefficient, factor; ratio; rate; (respiratory; utilization) quotient; (stat.) index; degree (of polymerization): **к. полезного действия** efficiency, output; **к. при** the coefficient of; *look up idioms under more descriptive words, e.g.,* **расширения, коэффициент.**

коэхлинит *m.* (min.) koechlinite.

коядро *n.* (math.) cokernel.

кп *abbr.* (**килопонд**) kilogram-weight; (**кислородный потенциал**) oxygen potential; **КП** (**компенсатор поляризации**) polarization compensator.

кпд, к.п.д., К.П.Д. *abbr.* (**коэффициент полезного действия**) efficiency.

кпереди *adv.* to the front.

кпс *abbr.* (**килопарсек**) kiloparsec; **кпс.** (**капсула**) capsule; **КПС** (**коэффициент продуктивности скважины**) productivity index of a well.

кр *abbr.* (**кюри**) curie; **к-р** *abbr.* (**конденсатор**) condenser, capacitor; **кр.** (**край**), (**критический**); **Кр** (**кристаллизация**).

краб *m.* (crust.) crab; **—овидный** *a.* crab(-like); **—овый** *a.* crab; **—оед** *m.* (mam.) crab-eating macaque (*Macaca irius*); **—оконсервный** *a.* crab(-canning); **—олов** *m.* crabber; crab boat; **—оловный** *a.* crab-catching; **—оядный** *a.* crab-eating; **—ы-плавунцы** *pl.* (crust.) Portunidae.

кравчик *m.* (ent.) Lethrus.

кравший *past act. part. of* **красть.**

краги *pl.* leggings, leather gaiters.

краденный *past pass. part. of* **красть.**

краевед *m.* regional specialist; **—ение** *n.,* **—ческий** *a.* regional study.

краевик *m.* (ent.) squash bug (*Coreus*); **—и** *pl.* Coreidae.

крае/вой *a. of* **край;** region(al), district; rim, edge, margin(al), fringe; end (effect); contact (angle); outer (zone); corner (stone); (math.) boundary; **к. поток** (elec.) fringing; **—глазка** *f.* (ent.) Pararge; **—корешковый** *a.* (bot.) pleurorhizal; **—кучник** *m.* Cheilanthes; **—угольный** *a.* corner (stone); **—шек** *dim. of* **край;** border; tip.

кража *f.* theft; larceny; (elec.) tampering.

кра/й *m.* edge, rim, border, margin, periphery; fringe, side, verge, extremity, tip, end; limb (of celestial body); boundary; brim; lip (of wound) side (of beef); (anat.

limbus; krai, territory, region, land, country; **вы-ливаться через к.** *v.* overflow; **на —ях, с —ю** at the edge, marginal; **—йздрав** *m.* regional department of public health.

крайне *adv.* extremely, very, highly.

крайн/ий *a.* extreme, utmost, urgent; last, end, on the end, terminal; border, limiting; rock-bottom (price); outer, outside; far (north, etc.); **к. член** (math.) extreme; **—ее значение** extreme; limit; **—ее положение** extreme; **—ие пластинки** (zool.) marginalia; **—яя величина** extreme; **—яя необходимость** emergency; **в —ем случае** as a last resort, in an emergency, failing this; **по —ей мере** at least.

крайност/ь *f.* extreme, extremity, need, exigence, emergency; excess; opposite; **впадать в —и** *v.* run to extremes; **до —и** in the extreme, to excess.

крайт *m.* (herp.) krait (*Bungarus*).

кракен *m.* crackene.

краковский *a.* (geog.) Krakow.

краксы *pl.* (orn.) Cracidae.

крал *past m. sing. of* **красть.**

крамбе *f. or m.* (bot.) Crambe.

крамерия *f.* (bot.) rhatany (*Krameria*).

крамповать *see* **кардовать.**

кран *m.* (stop)cock, tap, faucet, valve, spigot; (fire) hydrant; crane; **водомерный к.** gage cock; **поворотный к.** jib crane, swing crane; **подвижный к.** traveling crane; **подъёмный к.** crane; **к.-балка** *f.* (crane) jib; overhead track hoist; (naut.) cat davit, cat crane; **к.-брызгалка** *m.* spray cock.

крандаллит *m.* (min.) crandallite.

кран-двунога *m.* (hoisting) sheers; **к.-дозатор** *m.* metering cock.

кранец *m.* (naut.) fender.

крани— *see* **кранио—;** **—альный** *a.* (anat.) cranial.

краник *dim. of* **кран;** cock.

кранио— *prefix* crani(o)— (cranium, skull); **—логический** *a.* craniological; **—логия** *f.* craniology; **—метр** *m.* (med.) craniometer; **—метрия** *f.* craniometry.

кранный *a. of* **кран;** cock, faucet.

кранов/щик *m.* crane operator; **—ый** *a.* crane; **—ая балка** jib, boom.

кран-смеситель *m.* mixing faucet, blender; **к.-стогометатель** *m.* crane hay stacker; **к.-столбостав** *m.* pole-setting derrick; **к.-тренога** *m.* tripod crane; **к.-трубокладчик** *m.* pipe-laying crane; **к.-укосина** *m.* wall-mounted derrick crane.

кранцеводитель *m.* (leather) rand guide.

кранцит *m.* (min.) krantzite.

кран-штабел/ёр, —еукладчик *m.* stacking crane.

крап *m.* specks, speckles; (bot.) madder (*Rubia tinctorum*); **—ать** *v.* spot, speckle; sprinkle, dizzle, trickle.

крапив/а *f.* (bot.) nettle (*Urtica*); **китайская к.** ramie (*Boehmeria*); **—ник** *m.* nettle thicket; (orn.) wren (*Troglodytes*); **—ники, —никовые** *pl.* Troglodytidae; **—ница** *f.* (med.) nettle rash, urticaria; (ent.) nettle butterfly (*Vanessa urticae*); **—ные** *pl.* (bot.) Urticaceae; **—ный** *a.* nettle, urticaceous; **—ная капсула** (zool.) nematocyst, urticator; **—ная клетка** nematoblast; **—ная лихорадка, —ная сыпь** nettle rash.

крапин/а, —ка *f.* speck(le), spot, macula; tracer, identification thread.

краплак *m.* madder lake.

крап/ление *n.* spotting, etc., *see* **крапать;** **—ленный** *a., —лёный** *part.* spotted, etc., *see* **крапать.**

крап/п *m., —(п)овый** *a.* madder.

краппи *m.* (ichth.) crappie (*Pomoxis*); *pl.* Centrarchidae.

крапплак *m.* madder lake.

крапчат/ость *f.* mottling; **—ый** *a.* spotted, speckled, mottled, marbled; maculate.

краруп/изация *f.* (tel.) Krarup loading; **—изированный** *a.* continuously loaded; **—изировать** *v.* load continuously; **—овский** *a.* Krarup.

красав/ица *f.* beauty; **дневная к.** (bot.) Convolvulus tricolor; **ночная к.** jalap (*Mirabilis jalapa*); Hesperis mationalis; **снежная к.** snowberry (*Symphoricarpus*); **—ка** *f.* belladonna (*Atropa belladonna*); (orn.) small crane (*Anthropoides virgo*); (ichth.) male minnow (during spawning).

крас/ен *sh. m. of* **красный;** **—иво—** *prefix* calli—, cal(o)— (beautiful); **—ивоплодный** *a.* (bot.) callicarpous; **—ивый** *a.* beautiful, fine.

красильн/ый *a.* dye, tinctorial; **к. бак** dye vat; **к. завод** dye works; **к. камень** (min.) dyestone, Clinton ore; **к. корень** (bot.) *see* **крап; к. лак** (color) lake; **к. отвар** dye liquor; **—ая барка** dye vat; **—ое вещество** dye(stuff); **—ое дерево** dyewood; **—ые материалы** dyestuffs.

красиль/ня *f.* dye works; **—щик** *m.* dyer.

красина *f.* (phyt.) red rot.

красит/ель *m.* dye(stuff); coloring, pigment; stain; **—ь** *v.* dye, color, paint, stain; improve; **—ься** *v.* take dye; run, stain; make up (face).

краск/а *f.* paint; dye(stuff); color, stain, pigment; (printer's) ink; dyeing, painting; **к. смешанного цвета** secondary color; **масляные —и** oil paints; **сухая к.** pastel color; **—о—** *prefix see* **краска; —овар** *m.* colorist; **—оварка** *f.* (text.) color room; dye preparation; **—одувка** *f., —омёт, —опульт** *m., —ораспылитель** *m.* paint sprayer; **—оёмкость** *f.* (paper) coloring power; **—омешалка** *f.* paint agitator; **—отёр** *m., —отёрка** *f.* color mill, color grinder; paint grinder; **—оустранитель** *m.* paint remover.

красн/ая *f.* red (color); (ichth.) salmon (*Oncorhynchus nerka, O. kisutch*); **—еть** *v.* redden, turn red; flush; blush; **—еться** *v.* show red; **—еющий** *a.* reddening, (e)rubescent; **—ина** *f.* (phyt.) red rot.

красно— *prefix* erythr(o)—; red; **—армейский** *a.* Red Army; **—бородка** *f.* (ichth.) red mullet (*Mullus barbatus*); **—брюхий** *a.* red-bellied; **—бурый** *a.* reddish brown, russet; **—ватый** *a.* reddish; **—водский** *a.* (geog.) Krasnovodsk; **—волосистый** *a.* red-haired; **—волоска** *f.* (bot.) Callitriche; **—волосковые** *pl.* Callitricheae; **—глазка** *f.* (ichth.) roach, rudd, redeye, etc.; **глазковые** *a.* (ichth.) Emmelichthyidae; **—головый** *a.* red-headed, erythrocephalous; **—горский** *a.* (geog.) Krasnaya Gor(k)a; **—дарский** *a.* (geog.) Krasnodar; **—деревец** *m.* cabinetmaker; **—днев** *m.* (bot.) Hemerocallis; **—дублёный** *a.* tanned to a russet color.

красно/зём *m., —зёмный** *a.* terra rossa, red earth; krasnozem, red soil, lateritic soil; **—зобик** *m.* (orn.) redcrop (*Calidris testacea*); **—зобый** *a.* red-throated; **—калильный** *a.* red-hot, red-heat; red (heat); **—клоп** *m.* (ent.) Pyrrhocoris; **—клоповые** *pl.* Pyrrhocoridae; **—клювый** *a.* red-billed; **—кожий** *a.* red-skinned; **—корковый** *a.* red-barked; **—крыл** *m.* (orn.) flamingo; **—крылка** *f.* (ichth.) roach (*Rutilus r.*); redeye; **—крылки** *pl.* (ent.) cardinal beetles (*Pyrochroidae*); **—крылый** *a.* red-winged; **—лесье** *n.* coniferous forest; redwood forest; **—листный** *a.* red-leaved, rubrifolious; **—ловье** *n.* sturgeon fishery.

красноломк/ий, —остный *a.* (met.) red-short, hot-short, hot-brittle; **—ость** *f.* red-shortness, hot-brittleness.

красно/морский *a.* (geog.) Red Sea; **—ногий** *a.* red-legged; —**ножка** *f.* (orn.) redshank (*Tringa totanus*); —**носый** *a.* red-nosed; —**пёр** *m.,* —**пёрка** *f.* (ichth.) regional name for redfin, dace, minnow, rudd and others; —**пёрый** *a.* red-finned; —**плодный** *a.* (bot.) erythrocarpous; —**пузырниковые** *pl.* Celastraceae; —**пятнистый** *a.* red-spotted, red-stained; —**рыбица** *f.* (ichth.) Atlantic salmon (*Salmo salar*); —**спинный** *a.* red-backed; —**стебельный** *a.* red-stemmed; —**стойкость** *f.* (met.) red hardness; —**та** *f.* redness; (med.) erythema; —**тал** *m.* willow (*Salix acutifolia*); —**тел** *m.* (ent.) Calosoma; —**телки,** —**телковые** *pl.* (zool.) red mites (*Trombidiidae*); —**флотский** *a.* Red navy; —**хвост** *m.* (ent.) Dasychira; —**цветковые** *pl.* red-flowered; —**цветный** *a.* red(-colored); —**цветы** *pl.* (geol.) red beds; —**шапочный** *a.* red-capped; —**шейка** *f.* (orn.) redthroat; —**щёкий** *a.* red-cheeked; —**щёчка** *f.* (ichth.) black-backed shad (*Alosa kessleri*); —**ядерно-спинномозговой** *a.* (anat.) rubrospinal; —**ярский** *a.* (geog.) Krasnoyarsk.

краснуха *f.* (med.) German measles, rubella; (vet.) erysipelas (of swine); infectious ascites (of carp); (phyt.) red rot; (ichth.) salmon; roach.

красн/ый *a.* red; top-quality; vegetable (tanning); cartilaginous (fish); coniferous, softwood (forest); —**ое дерево** mahogany.

красоднев *m.* (bot.) Hemerocallis.

красок *gen. pl. of* **краска**.

красо/ля *f.* (bot.) nasturtium (*Tropaeolum majus*); —**та** *f.* beauty; —**тел** *m.* (ent.) Calosoma; —**тка** *f.* Calopteryx; —**тки** *pl.* Calopterygidae.

красочн/ость *f.* brilliance; (typ.) number of color inks; —**ый** *a.* brilliant; colorful.

краспе/дакуста *f.* (zool.) Craspedacusta; —**досома** *f.* Craspedosoma.

крассик *m.* (geol.) krassyk (decomposed ferruginous schist).

красть *v.* steal; (elec.) tap (a wire); —**ся** *v.* steal, sneak, creep (up to).

красу/ля *f.,* —**н** *m.* (ent.) cereal chafer (*Anisoplia segetum*).

красящ/ий *a.* dyeing, coloring, staining; inking (roll); —**ая сила,** —**ая способность** dyeing power, tinting power; —**ее вещество** dye(stuff), coloring, pigment, stain.

крат *m.* (commun.) arm; **во много к.** many times; —**ен** *sh. m.* **кратный.**

кратер *m.,* —**ный** *a.* (geol.) crater.

кратк/ий *a.* short, brief, concise; abridged (book); —**о** *adv.* briefly, concisely.

кратковременн/ость *f.* short time; briefness; —**ый** *a.* short(-lived), of short duration, short-term, brief; temporary, transient, momentary; short-time (strength); (comp.) volatile (memory); acute (toxicity); **испытание на** —**ую прочность** (met.) short-time creep test, rupture test.

кратко/дневный *a.* short, brief; —**срочный** *a.* short (-term), short-range; —**сть** *f.* shortness, brevity.

кратн/о *adv.* multiply; divisible (by); —**ое** *n.* (math.) multiple; **общее наименьшее** —**ое** least common multiple; —**ость** *f.* multiplicity, ratio; rate, frequency; (light filter) factor; —**ость превышения** number of times by which . . . exceeds . . . ; —**ый** *a.* multiple; divisible (by); *suffix* —**fold;** —**ое число** multiple; **закон** —**ых отношений** law of multiple proportions.

краток *sh. m. of* **краткий.**

кратон *m.* craton, shield.

кратчайший *superl. of* **краткий.**

краун-эфир, крауновый эфир crown ether.

краурит *m.* (min.) kraurite, dufrenite.

крафт/-бумага *f.,* **к.-пепер** *m.* kraft paper; **к.-мешок** *m.* paper bag; **к.-целлюлоза** *f.* kraft pulp.

крах *m.* (com.) crash, failure, bankruptcy.

крахмал *m.* starch; **животный к.** animal starch; glycogen; —**ение** *n.* starching; —**енный** *a.* starched; —**истость** *f.* starchiness; starch content; —**истый,** —**оподобный** *a.* starchy, amyloid, amylaceous; —**ить** *v.* starch; —**о**— *prefix* starch, amylo—; —**ометр** *m.* amylometer; —**онос** *m.* amyliferous plant; —**оносный** *a.* amyliferous, starch-producing; —**орасщепляющий** *a.* starch-splitting; —**осодержащий** *a.* starch-containing; **к.-сырец** *m.* raw starch.

крахмаль/ный *a.* starch, amylaceous; **к. клей** sizing; —**ная патока** starch syrup, glucose; —**щик** *m.* starch manufacturer.

крац/бюрст *m.* (met.) scratch(ing) brush; —**евальный** *a.* scratch(ing); —**евание** *n.* scratching, scratch-brushing; scratch finish; —**овка** *f.* scratching; scratch(ing) brush; —**эйзен** *m.* scraper.

крачка *f.* (orn.) tern (*Sterna*).

крашен/ие, —**ье** *n.* dyeing, etc., see **красить;** —**ный** *a.* dyed, etc., *see* **красить.**

края *gen. and pl. of* **край.**

креат/ин *m.* creatine, guanidine methylglycine; —**инин** *m.* creatinine; —**иновый** *a.* creatine; —**инурия** *f.* (med.) creatinuria; —**инфосфорная кислота** creatinephosphoric acid, phosphocreatine; —**отоксин** *m.* creatotoxin, meat poison or ptomaine.

Кребса цикл Krebs cycle.

кребы *pl.* (bot.) crab apples.

креветка *f.* (crust.) shrimp, prawn.

кредит *m.* credit; —**ный билет** bank note; —**овать** *v.* credit (with); —**оваться** *v.* get credit; —**овый** *a.* credit; —**ор** *m.* creditor; —**оспособность** *f.* credit status; —**оспособный** *a.* solvent.

креедиевые *pl.* (ichth.) Creediidae.

креднерит *m.* (min.) crednerite.

крез/атин *m.* cresatin, *m*-cresyl acetate; —**идин** *m.* cresidine, aminocresol.

крезил *m.,* —**овый** *a.* cresyl; —**ат** *m.* cresylate; —**ен** *m.* cresylene, tolylene; —**ит** *m.* (expl.) cresylite; —**овая кислота,** —**овый спирт** *see* **крезол.**

крезокси—*prefix* cresoxy—, toloxy—.

крезол *m.,* —**овый** *a.* cresol, cresylic acid; —**сульфо- кислота** *f.* cresolsulfonic acid; —**ьный** *a.* cresol; —**ят** *m.* cresolate.

крезорцин *m.* cresorcin(ol).

крезотиновая кислота cresot(in)ic acid, hydroxytoluic acid.

Крейза испытание Kreis test.

крейс/ер *m.* (naut.) cruiser; **к.-разведчик** scout; —**ерский** *a.* cruising; cruise-control (curve); —**ирование** *n.* cruising; —**ировать** *v.* cruise, patrol.

крейт *m.* crate; —**ер** m. crater, crating machine.

крейттонит m. (min.) kreittonite.

крейц/копф *m.,* —**копфный** a. (mach.) crosshead, slide block; —**мейсель** *m.* groove chisel, cross chisel, gouge.

крекер *m.* cracker; cracking plant; **к.-вальцы** cracker mill.

крек/инг *m.,* —**инговый** *a.* (petrol.) cracking; cracking plant; (shale) retorting; **подвергать** —**ингу** *v.* crack; **к.-бензин** *m.* cracked gasoline; **к.-битум** *m.* cracked asphalt; **к.-газ** *m.* cracked still gas; **к.-мазут** *m.* cracked fuel oil; **к.-остаток** *m.* cracking residue; **к.-печь** *f.* cracking still; **к.-процесс** *m.,* —**ирование** *n.* cracking (process); **к.-установка** *f.* cracking plant;

—ированный *a.* cracked; **—ировать** *v.* crack; **—ируемость** *f.* crackability; **—ируемый** *a.* crackable; cracked; **—ирующий** *a.* cracking.

крелосный *a.* Krelius, core (drilling).

крем *m.* cream.

кремальер/а *f.* rack and pinion; **—ный** *a.* rack (mechanism).

кремастер *m.* (anat.) cremaster (muscle).

крема/торий *m.* crematory, incinerator; **—ция** *f.*, **—ционный** *a.* cremation; **—ционная печь** incinerator.

кременецкий *a.* (geog.) Kremenets.

кременчугский *a.* (geog.) Kremenchug.

кремень *m.* (min.) flint; chalcedony.

Кремера проба Cramer's (sucrose) test.

кремерзит *m.* (min.) kremersite.

кремериевые *pl.* (ichth.) Kraemeriidae.

кремешок *dim. of* **кремень.**

кремл/ёвский *a.*, **—ь** *m.* fortress; Kremlin.

кремне— *prefix* silico—; silicate (of); **—алюминиевая соль** aluminum silicate; **—борокальцит** *m.* (min.) silicoborocalcite.

кремнёвка *f.* kremnyovka (kaolinic refractory clay).

кремне/во **—see кремне—**; **—водород** *m.* silicon hydride; silicohydride, silane; **—вокарбидный** *a.* silicon carbide; **—вольфрамовый** *a.* silicotungstic (acid); **соль —вольфрамовой кислоты** silicotungstate; **—вомолибденовый** *a.* silicomolybdic (acid); **—вомолибденовая соль** silicomolybdate.

кремнев/ый *a.* silicon, silicic, siliceous, flinty, *see also* **кремнистый**; **к. ангидрид** silicic anhydride, silica, silicon dioxide; **к. гель** silica gel; **—ая галька** flint, flint pebble; **—ая кислота** silicic acid; **гель —ой кислоты, студенистая —ая кислота** silica gel; **золь —ой кислоты** silica sol; **соль —ой кислоты** silicate; **—ое ружьё** flintlock, firelock; **—ые водоросли** *pl.* (bot.) Diatomaceae.

кремнегел/ит, —ь *m.* silica gel.

кремнезём *m.* silica, silicon dioxide; **водный к., гидрат —а** hydrated silica; silicic acid; **гель —а** silica gel, colloidal silica; **—истый, —ный** *a.* siliceous, silicic, siliciferous.

кремне/зол *m.* silica sol; **—калиевая соль** potassium silicate; **—каучук** *m.* silicone rubber; **—кислота** *f.* silicic acid, silicon dioxide, silica; **—кислый** *a.* silicic acid; silicate (of); **—кислый алюминий** aluminum silicate, **—кислая соль** silicate; **—любивое растение** (bot.) silicole; **—натриевая соль** sodium silicate; **—носный** *a.* siliciferous; **—органический** *a.* organosilicon; **—содержащий** *a.* silicon-containing, siliceous, siliciferous; **—фил** *m.* (bot.) silicole; **—фосфат** *m.* silicophosphate.

кремнефтор/ид *m.* silicofluoride, fluosilicate; **—(ист)оводородная кислота** fluosilicic acid; **соль —(ист)оводородной кислоты** fluosilicate, silicofluoride; **—истый** *a.* fluosilicate (of); **—истый калий** potassium fluosilicate.

кремн/ехлороформ *m.* silicochloroform; **—ецинковая соль** zinc silicate; **—иевый** *see* **кремневый.**

кремн/ий *m.* silicon, Si; **водородистый к.** silicon hydride, hydrogen silicide; **двуокись —ия** silicon dioxide, silica; **карбид —ия, углеродистый к.** silicon carbide, carborundum; **к.-каучук** *m.* silicone rubber; **—ийорганический** *a.* organosilicon, silicone; **—ийсодержащий** *a.* siliceous, silicon-containing.

кремнисто— *prefix* silico—; **—зеркальный чугун** (met.) silicon spiegel, ferrosilicomanganese; **—сть** *f.* siliceousness; silicon content.

кремнист/ый *a.* siliceous, flinty, gravelly; silicide (of);

flint (corn); **к. водород** hydrogen silicide, silicon hydride; **к. малахит** (min.) chrysocolla; **к. марганец** manganese silicide; (min.) manganese spar, rhodonite; **к. металл** metallic silicide; **к. сланец** (petr.) chert; **к. туф, —ая накипь** (min.) siliceous sinter; geyserite; **—ая медь** copper silicide; (met.) cuprosilicon; (min.) chrysocolla; **—ая сталь** silicon steel; **—ое железо** iron silicide; (met.) ferrosilicon.

кремницкие белила Kremnitz white, Crems white (white lead pigment).

кремня *gen. of* **кремень.**

кремовый *a.* cream, cream-colored.

кремортартар *m.* cream of tartar, potassium bitartrate.

кремские белила *see* **кремницкие белила.**

крен *m.* (naut.) heel(ing), list(ing); (av.) bank(ing), roll(ing); **боковой к.** rolling, **при отсутствии —а** when level; **продольный к.** pitching.

кренат *m.* crenate.

кренгов/ание *n.* (naut.) careening, heeling; **—ать** *v.* careen, heel.

крендель *m.*, **—ный** *a.* pretzel.

креневый *a. of* **крень**; compression (wood).

крен/ение *see* **крен**; **—ить** *v.* (naut.) heel over; **—иться** *v.* list, heel over, careen; (av.) bank, roll.

кренкит *m.* (min.) kröhnkite.

креннерит *m.* (min.) krennerite.

креновать *see* **кренговать.**

креноме(т)р *m.* (naut.) (in)clinometer.

кренул/ированный *a.* crenulate; **—яция** *f.* crenulation.

крень *f.* compression wood.

креодонты *pl.* (pal.) Creodonta.

креозол *m.* creosol, methoxycresol.

креозот *m.*, **—овый** *a.* creosote.

крео/лин *m.* Creolin (disinfectant); **—льский** *a.* Creole; **—филюс** *m.* (ent.) Creophilus.

креп *m.* (rubber; text.) crepe; *past m. sing. of* **крепнуть.**

крепа *f.* support.

крепдешин *m.* (text.) crepe de Chine.

крепёж *m.* fasteners, mounting hardware; **—ный** *a.* fastening, holding, mounting; reinforcing; **—ный лес** (min.) supports, props; **—ные детали** industrial holders and fasteners, clamps.

креп/еукладчик *m.* timber placer; **—и** *gen., pl., etc. of* **крепь**; **—ильщик** *m.* timberman.

крепирование *n.* (paper) creping, crimping.

крепитация *f.* (med.) crepitation, crackling.

крепитель *m.* binder, bond; **—ный** *a.* strengthening, etc., *see* **крепить;** confirming, corroboratory; (med.) astringent.

крепитирующий *a.* crepitant, crackling.

крепить *v.* strengthen, fortify; concentrate (solution); reinforce, buttress, brace, support, prop; attach, mount, clamp, bind, fix, make fast, fasten, lash, secure, anchor, staple; case (well); (min.) timber, roof; fortify (wine); (med.) constipate; **—ся** *v.* restrain oneself, hold out; be strengthened, etc.

креп/кий *a.* strong, solid, firm, fast; sturdy, tough, robust, vigorous; concentrated (solution); sound (sleep); **—ко** *adv.* firmly, tight(ly); *prefix* strong; **—коногий** *a.* strong-legged; **—коплодник** *m.* (bot.) Euclidium; **—котелый** *a.* strong-bodied; **—ление** *n.* strengthening, etc., *see* v.; attachment, linkage; mounting; fixture; fortification (of wine); (min.) timber(work); **прочность —ления** holding power; **с кольцевым —лением** ring-mounted; **—лён(н)ый** *a.* strengthened, etc., *see* v.; **—нуть** *v.* get stronger; harden, stiffen.

креповый *a.* crepy; (text.) crepe.

крепок *sh. m. of* **крепкий.**

крепост/ной *a. of* **крепость;** serf (labor); **—ь** *f.* strength, toughness, tenacity, stability, rigidity, solidity; hardness; concentration (of solution): fortress, stronghold; **—ь на разрыв** tensile strength.

креп/чайший *superl. of* **крепкий; —чать** *v.* grow stronger; get more severe; blow harder; **—че** *comp. of* **крепкий; —ь** *f.* (min.) timber(ing), support(s), props, lining; overgrown thicket; **—ящий** *a.* strengthening, etc., *see* **крепить.**

кресельный *a. of* **кресло.**

крескограф *m.* crescograph, growth recorder.

кресл/о *n.* seat; (arm)chair; chair (configuration of stereoisomers); **форма —a** chair conformation; **к.-каталка** *n.* wheelchair.

кресс *m.* (bot.) cress; **водяной к.** water cress (*Nasturtium officinale*); **огородный к., посевной к., садовый к., к.-салат** *m.* garden cress (*Lepidium sativum*).

крест *m.* cross, four-way (junction) piece; **к. на к.** crosswise, crisscross; **к. нитей** cross hairs; **—ец** *m.* (anat.) sacrum; crosswise stack; **сложный —ец** (orn.; pal.) synsacrum; **—ик** *dim. of* **крест**; check(mark).

крестовидн/ый *a.* cross-shaped, cruciform, cruciate; **—ая муфта** four-way connection, crossing box.

крестов/ик *m.* (min.) chiastolite; (zool.) Epeira; **—ин(к)а** *f.* cross (piece), cross pipe, crosshead, cross beam; (mach.) spider, center-piece, four-way union; swing-out rotor (of centrifuge); (rr.) frog; turnstile; **связывающая —ина** *f.* cross bond, cross brace; **—ичка** *f.* (ent.) Dociostaurus or Notostaurus; **—ичок** *m.* (zool.) Gonionemus; **—ка** *f.* (amph.) Pelodytes; **—ки** *pl.* Pelobatidae; **—ник** *m.* (bot.) groundsel (*Senecio*); **—ница** *f.* Crucianella; **—ый** *a. of* **крест.**

кресто/мотальный *a.* (text.) cone-winding; **—носец** *m.* (ent.) Anisoplia agricola; **—носный** *a.* cruciferous; **—образно** *adv.* cross-wise; **—образный** *see* **крестовидный; —цветные** *pl.* (bot.) Cruciferae.

крестц/а *gen. of* **крестец; —ово—** *prefix* (anat.) sacro—, sacrum; **—ово-бугорный** *a.* sacrotuberal; **—ово-копчиковый** *a.* sacrococcygeal; **—ово-остистый** *a.* sacrospinal; **—ово-подвздошный** *a.* sacroiliac; **—ово-поясничный** *a.* sacrolumbar; **—ово-тазовый** *a.* sacropelvic; **—овый** *a.* sacral; **—овая кость** sacrum.

крестьян/ин *m.,* **—ский** *a.* peasant, farmer; **—ка** *f.* peasant woman; **—ствовать** *v.* farm for a living.

кретин *m.,* **—ка** *f.* (med.) cretin; **—изм** *m.* cretinism; **—ический** *a.* cretinous; **—овидный** *a.* cretinoid.

кретон *m.,* **—ный** *a.* (text.) cretonne.

крец *m.,* **—a** *f.* waste metal (dross, cuttings, sweepings, etc.).

кречет *m.* (orn.) gyrfalcon (*Falco gyrfalco*).

кречётка *f.* (orn.) plover (*Chettusia*).

крешер *m.* crusher; crusher gage.

крещенские морозы January freeze.

крибральный *a.* cribral, sieve-like.

крив *sh. m. of* **кривой; —ая** *f.* (math.) curve; **—ая в координатах давления и температуры, —ая зависимости давления от температуры** temperature-pressure curve; **—ая напряжение-удлинение** stress-strain curve; **кривизна —ой, наклон —ой** degree of curvature; **температурная —ая давления** temperature-pressure curve.

Кривбасс *m.* (geog.) Krivoi Rog basin.

криветь *v.* go blind in one eye.

крив/изна *f.* curvature, curve, flexure; crookedness, warping; bend(ing), slope; (wing) camber; **вторая к.** torsion; **измеритель —изны линий** rotameter; **с двойной —изной** *a.* double-curved; **—ить** *v.* curve, flex, bend; twist, distort; **—иться** *v.* curve, bend; go out of

shape; twist; cant, tilt; **—ки** *pl.* (orn.) oystercatchers (*Haematopinae*); **—ляться** *v.* grimace; **—o** *adv.* crookedly; on a slope; **—обокий** *a.* lopsided, one-sided; **—оглазый** *a.* one-eyed; **двенадцатиперстная —оголовка** (zool.) hookworm (*Ancylostoma duodenale*); **—озуб** *m.* (ichth.) Charax; **—ой** *a.* crooked, curve(d), bent; blind in one eye; **—ая линия** curve.

криво/лесье *n.* elfin woodland, dwarf growth; **—линейность** *f.* curvature; **—линейный** *a.* curvilinear, curvilineal, curved; **—листный** *a.* (bot.) curvifolious; **—ногий** *a.* crooked-legged; **—ножка** *f.* crooked-legged creature; **—нос** *m.* (orn.) wrybill (*Anarhynchus frontalis*); **—носый** *a.* crooked-nosed; wry-billed; **—рожский** *a.* (geog.) Krivoi Rog; **—рот** *m.* (ichth.) wrymouth; **—ротые** *pl.* Cryptacanthodidae; **—ротый** *a.* crooked-mouthed, wry-mouthed; **—ствольный** *a.* crooked (tree); **—хвостка** *f.* razorfish; **—хвостки, —хвостые** *pl.* Centriscidae; **—цвет** *m.* (bot.) Lycopsis; **—шеий** *a.* crooked-neck(ed); **—шея** *f.* (med.) torticollis, wryneck.

кривошип *m.* crank(-handle); **ось —a** crankshaft; **—нобалансирный** *a.* oscillating crank (drive); **—но-камерный** *a.* crankcase; **—но-шатунный** *a.* crank (drive, gear); **—ный** *a.* crank; **—ный вал** crankshaft; **—ный механизм** crank gear; **—ная** crankcase.

кривощек *m.* (ichth.) Chondrostoma nasus.

криз/(ис) *m.,* **—исный** *a.* crisis; *pl.* crises; critical state; **к. сопротивления, волновой к.** critical region (of Reynolds numbers).

кризо— *see* **хризо—.**

крик *m.* cry, shout, scream; (geol.) creek; **—ливый** *a.* clamorous, noisy; **—нуть** *v.* shout, call out, cry out.

крико— *prefix* crico— (cricoid, cartilage).

кримин/алистика *f.* criminal law; **—альный** *a.* criminal; **—ология** *f.* criminology.

кринин *m.* (physiol.) crinin.

криница *f.* well, spring.

кринка *f.* milk jug.

криноид *m.,* **—ный** *a.* (zool.) crinoid.

кринолин *m.* (naut.; text.) crinoline.

кринум *m.* (bot.) Crinum.

крио— *prefix* cryo— (cold, freezing); **—биология** *f.* cryobiology; **—ген** *m.* cryogen, freezing mixture; **—геника** *f.* cryogenics; **—генин** *m.* Cryogenine, phenicarbazide; **—глобулин** *m.* cryoglobulin; **—генный** *a.* cryogenic; **—гидрат** *m.* cryohydrate; **—гидратный** *a.* cryohydric (point); **—кинеграф** *m.* glaciometer; **—конт** *m.* cosmic dust; **—лиз** *m.* cryolysis.

криолит *m.* (min.) cryolite, Greenland spar; **—ионит** *m.* cryolithionite; **—овый** *a.* cryolite, cryolitic.

крио/логия *f.* cryology; **—метр** *m.* cryometer, low-temperature thermometer; **—планктон** *m.* (biol.) cryoplankton; **—сар** *m.* (electron.) cryosar; **—скоп** *m.* cryoscope; **—скопический** *a.* cryoscopic; **—скопия** *f.* cryoscopy; **—стат** *m.* cryostat; **—сушка** *f.* freeze drying; **—сфера** *f.* cryosphere; **—трон** *m.* (electron.) cryotron; **—физика** *f.* cryophysics; **—фил** *m.* cryophilic organism; **—филлит** *m.* (min.) cryophyllite; **—фильный** *a.* cryophilic, cold-loving; **—фит** *m.* (bot.) cryophyte; **—хирургия** *f.* cryosurgery.

крип *m.* (met.) creep; **—оустойчивость** *f.* creep resistance; **—оустойчивый** *a.* creep-resistant.

крипта *f.* crypt(a), follicle, pit; **—нд** *m.* cryptand; **—т** *m.* cryptate; **—тация** *f.* cryptation.

криптический *a.* cryptic, concealed, hidden; protective (coloration).

крипто— *prefix* crypt(o)— (hidden, concealed; crypt);

—**биоз** *m.* (vet.) cryptobiosis; —**валентность** *f.* cryptovalence, abnormal valence.

криптогам/ист *m.* (bot.) cryptogamist; —**ия** *f.* cryptogamy; —**ный** *a.* cryptogamic; —**ное растение** cryptogam.

крипто/генетический, —**генный** *a.* cryptogen(et)ic; —**грамма** *f.* (bot.) Cryptogramma; —**графия** *f.* cryptography; —**депрессия** *f.* (geol.) cryptodepression; —**кластический** *a.* cryptoclastic, compact; —**коккоз** *m.* cryptococcosis, Cryptococcus infection; —**кристаллический** *a.* cryptocrystalline, microcrystalline; —**ксантин** *m.* cryptoxanthin.

криптол *m.* Kryptol (resistance material).

крипто/лит *m.* (min.) cryptolite; (med.) cryptolith; —**мер** *m.* (gen.) cryptomere; —**мерия** *f.* (bot.) Cryptomeria; —**мерный** *a.* cryptomerous; —**мерный ген** cryptomere; —**метр** *m.* (paints) cryptometer; —**митоз** *m.* (gen.) cryptomitosis; —**монады** *pl.* (prot.) Cryptomonadina; —**морфит** *m.* (min.) cryptomorphite.

криптон *m.* krypton, Kr.

крипто/пертит *m.* (min.) cryptoperthite; —**пин** *m.* cryptopine; —**пиррол** *m.* cryptopyrrole; —**подзол** *m.* (soil) semipodzol; —**порный** *a.* cryptoporous; —**пс** *m.* (zool.) Cryptops; —**псар** *m.* (ichth.) Cryptopsarus.

крипторх/(ид) —**идовый** *a.* (med.) cryptorchid; —**изм** *m.* cryptorch(id)ism.

крипто/скоп *m.* cryptoscope, fluoroscope; —**тил** *m.* (min.) kryptotile; —**фит** *m.* (bot.) cryptophyte; —**фтальм** *m.,* —**фтальмия** *f.* (med.) cryptophthalmos; —**хитон** *m.* (mal.) Cryptochiton; —**цианин** *m.* cryptocyanine.

крисмес-фактор *m.* (med.) Christmas factor.

криста *f.* crista, crest, ridge.

кристадин *m.* (rad.) crystal detector.

кристалл *m.* crystal; (electron.) chip; —**виолет** *m.* (pharm.) crystal violet, gentian violet; **к.-вкрапленник** *m.* phenocryst; **к.-гость** *m.* chadacryst; **к.-двойник** *m.* twin crystal.

кристаллиз/атор *m.* crystallizer, crystallizing basin, crystal pan; —**ация** *f.,* —**ационный** *a.* crystallization, crystallizing; —**ационная вода** water of crystallization; —**(ир)ованный** *a.* crystallized; —**(ир)овать(ся)** *v.* crystallize; —**уемость** *f.* crystallizability; —**ующийся** *a.* crystallizing, crystallizable.

кристалл/ик *dim. of* **кристалл**; crystal(line) particle; (electron.) chip, die; —**иновый** *a.* crystallinic (acid); —**ит** *m.* (geol.) crystallite, crystalline grain.

кристаллич/еский *a.* crystal(line), crystallized; granulated (sugar); —**еская решётка** crystal lattice; **неясно к., скрытно к.** cryptocrystalline; —**ность** *f.* crystallinity; —**ный** *a.* crystal(line).

кристалло/бластический *a.* (geol.) crystalloblastic; —**видный** *see* **кристаллообразный;** —**вый** *a.* crystal; —**генезис** *m.* crystallogenesis; —**генический** *a.* crystallogenic; —**гения** *f.* crystallogeny; —**гидрат** *m.* crystal hydrate; —**гобиус** *m.* (ichth.) crystal goby (*Crystallogobius*); —**грамма** *f.* crystallogram.

кристаллограф *m.* crystallographer; —**ический** *a.* crystallographic; —**ия** *f.* crystallography.

кристалло/держатель *m.* crystal mount; —**за** *f.* crystallose; —**ид** *m.,* —**идальный** *a.* crystalloid; —**логия** *f.* crystallology; —**люминесценция** *f.* crystalloluminescence; —**метрический** *a.* crystallometric; —**н** *m.* crystallon, seed crystal; —**номия** *f.* crystallonomy; —**носный** *a.* containing crystals, crystalliferous; —**образный** *a.* crystal-like, crystalloid, crystalline; —**образование** *n.* crystallization; —**оптика** *f.* crystal optics; —**подобный** *see* **кристаллообразный;**

—**раститель** *m.* crystallizer; —**физика** *f.* crystal physics; —**химия** *f.* crystal chemistry.

кристалл-фантом *m.* phantom crystal; **к.-хозяин** *m.* host crystal.

кристальн/о *adv.* crystal; **к. чистый** *a.* crystal clear; —**ость** *f.* clearness, clarity; —**ый** *a.* crystal, clear.

крист/ианит *m.* (min.) christianite, anorthite; —**ивомер** *m.* (ichth.) Cristivomer; —**мас** *see* **крисмес;** —**обалит** *m.* (min.) cristobalite.

кристофит *m.* (min.) christophite.

крит *m.* (nucl.) crit (critical mass); crith (unit of density).

критер/иальный *a.* criterion(al); (phys.) standard; dimensionless; —**ий** *m.* criterion; (dimensional analysis) number; standard; measure, test; guideline; (reliability) index; *pl.* criteria; —**ий качества** figure of merit, performance criterion.

критик *m.* critic, reviewer —**а** *f.* criticism, censure; review (of book); **подвергать** —**е** *v.* challenge; —**овать** *v.* criticize; review.

критическ/и *adv.* critically; —**ий** *a.* critical, crucial, ultimate; priority; marginal; minimum (requirement); —**ий предел** critical limit, breaking-down point; —**ий элемент** bottleneck; —**ое обстоятельство** emergency; —**ое состояние** criticality; **константа** —**ой точки** critical constant.

крит/ичность *f.* criticality; —**ичный** *a.* critical; —**масса** *f.* (nucl.) critical mass.

критмум *m.* (bot.) Crithmum.

критрадиус *m.* critical radius.

критск/ий *a.* (geog.) Crete, Cretan; —**ая лихорадка** (med.) brucellosis.

крифал *m.* (ent.) Cryphalus.

крица *f.* (met.) ball, bloom, pig, bar.

крич/ать *v.* shout, yell, call (out), cry (out), scream, shriek; —**ащие** *pl.* (orn.) Clamatores.

кричн/ый *a. of* **крица;** (met.) refinery; bloom(ery); ball, refined (iron); **к. горн** refinery hearth; bloomery; **к. мастер** refiner; **к. сок** slag.

кричтонит *m.* (min.) crichtonite.

кров *m.* shelter, roof; home.

кровав/ик, —**ник** *m.* (min.) bloodstone; —**о**— *prefix* hem(at)o—, blood; blood-red, hematine; —**оцветковый** *a.* (bot.) hemanthous; —**ый** *a.* bloody, bloodstained; blood-red; sanguineous; —**ый пот** (med.) hematidrosis, bloody sweat; —**ая моча** hematuria.

кроват/ка *f.* cot; —**ный** *a.,* —**ь** *f.* bed.

крове— *see also under* **крови**—; —**заменитель** *m.* blood substitute; —**замещение** *n.* blood substitution; —**й** *gen. pl. of* **кровь.**

кровель *gen. pl. of* **кровля;** —**ка** *f.* (bot.) aril; —**ный** *a. of* **кровля;** —**ный жёлоб** gutter; —**ный картон** roofing paper, tar paper; —**ный материал** roofing (material); —**щик** *m.* roofer.

крове/мозговой *a.* (physiol.) blood-brain (barrier); —**наполнение** *n.* (med.) plethora; —**неть** *v.* become bloodied; —**носный** *a.* sanguiferous; blood (vessel); vascular, circulatory (system); —**носные органы** vasculature; —**пятнистая болезнь** (vet.) thrombo(cyto)penic purpura; —**споровики** *pl.* (prot.) Haemosporidia; —**творный** *see* **кровотворный;** —**щелочная соль** *see* **кровяная соль.**

крови *gen., pl., etc. of* **кровь;** —**е** *n. suffix* (med.) —emia; —**нка** *f.* blood particle.

кровл/еобразный *a.* tectiform, roof-like; —**ля** *f.* roofing; (min.) roof, top, hanging wall, back; (biol.) tectum.

кровн/ость *f.* consanguinity, kinship; thoroughbred qualities; —**ый** *a.* blood (relative), consanguineous; thoroughbred, pure bred; closely related; deep, significant;

—ое разведение inbreeding; **—ое родство** consanguinity.

крово— *prefix* hemo—, blood; *see also under* **крове—**; **—жадный** *a.* sanguinolent, blood-thirsty; sanguivorous, blood-eating; **—извлечение** *n.* blood discharge; **—излияние** *n.* (med.) hemorrhage; extravasation; apoplexy; **—излияние в почку** renal apoplexy; **—мочка** *f.* hematuria; **—образование** *see* **кровотворение; —образующий** *a.* hematopoietic; **—обращение** *n.* circulation; **—освежение** *n.* (blood) rejuvenation; **—останавливающий** *a.* styptic, hemostatic, antihemorrhagic; **—останавливающее средство** hemostat; **—очистительный** *a.* hemocatheretic; **—очищение** *n.* hem(at)ocatharsis, blood lavage.

крово/переливание *n.* blood transfusion; **—подтёк** *m.* bruise, black-and-blue, ecchymosis; **—потеря** *f.* hemorrhage; hematozemia; **—пролитие** *n.* bloodshed; **—пускание** *n.,* **—пускательный** *a.* bloodletting; bleeding; **—смесительный** *a.* incestuous; **—смесительство, —смешение** *n.* incest; inbreeding; **—снабжение** *n.* blood donation; **—сос** *m.* (mam.) vampire bat (*Desmodus*); (herp.) Calotes versicolor; **—соска** *f.* (zool.) tick; mite; **—соски** *pl.* (ent.) Hippoboscidae; **—сосный, —сосущий** *a.* blood-sucking; **—сосы** *pl.* Desmodontidae; **—творение** *n.* hematopoiesis, blood formation; **—творный** *a.* hematopoietic, hematogenic, blood-producing; **—течение** *n.* hemorrhage, bleeding; **остановка —течения** hemostasis.

кровото/к *m.* blood stream; **—чащий** *a.* bleeding; **—чивость** *f.* (med.) hemophilia; **—чивый** *a.* hemophilic, (free-)bleeding; **—чить** *v.* bleed.

крово/харканье *n.* (med.) hemoptysis; **—харкать** *v.* spit blood; **—хлёбка** *f.* (bot.) Sanguisorba; **—хлёбковый** *a.* sanguisorbous.

кров/ь *f.* blood; breed; **болезнь —и** hemopathy; **истекать —ью** *v.* bleed; **сушёная к.** blood meal; **—янистый** *a.* sanguinolent; bloody (meat); **—янка** *f.* (mal.) Sanguinolaria.

кровян/ой *a.* blood(y), sanguineous; **к. шарик, —ое тельце** blood corpuscle, hemocyte; **белый к. шарик** leucocyte; **красный к. шарик** erythrocyte; **—ая пластинка** thrombocyte, blood platelet; **подсчёт —ых телец** blood count; **жёлтая —ая соль** potassium ferrocyanide; **красная —ая соль** potassium ferricyanide; **—окрасный** *a.* blood-red.

кроен/ие *n.* cutting (by pattern); **—ный** *a.* cut (out).

кроет *pr. 3 sing. of* **крыть.**

кро/ильный *a.* cutting (by pattern); **—йть** *v.* cut (out); **—й** *m.* cutting; cut, style; **—йка** *f.* cutting out.

кройте *imp. of* **крыть.**

крокер *m.* (ichth.) croaker (*Macrodon opercularis; Micropogon undulatus*).

кроки *n. or pl.* rough sketch, field sketch.

крокидолит *m.* (min.) crocidolite, blue asbestos.

крокиров/ание *n.,* **—ка** *f.* sketch(ing), outlining; **—ать** *v.* sketch, outline; draw a sketch map (of).

крокодил *m.,* **—ий, —овый** *a.* (herp.) crocodile (*Crocodylus*).

крок/о(из)ит *m.* (min.) croco(is)ite; **—ус** *m.* (bot.) crocus; (min.) crocus, rouge; **—оснабжение** *n.* rouge distribution.

крол/ик *m.* (mam.) rabbit (*Oryctolagus*); **—ики и зайцы** *pl.* hares and rabbits (*Leporidae*); **—иковод** *m.* rabbit breeder; **—иководство** *n.,* **—иководческий** *a.* rabbit breeding; **—ичий** *a.* rabbit.

кроль *m.* (swimming) crawl.

крольч/атина *f.* rabbit meat; **—атник** *m.* rabbit hutch; **—иха** *f.* doe; **—онок** *m.* baby rabbit, young rabbit.

кроме *prep. gen.* except (for), with the exception (of), save, apart from, aside from, other than; besides, in addition (to); **к. того** besides, also, moreover, furthermore, what is more.

кромериевые *pl.* (ichth.) Cromeriidae.

кромерский *a.* (geol.) Cromerian.

кром/ка *f.* edge, border, hem; rim, brim; bead, shoulder; (text.) list, selvage; (sonic) sweep; (ice) barrier, edge; **—ко(за)гибочный** *a.* edging, flanging; **—кообрезной** *a.* edging (saw); **—кообрубочный станок** trimmer; **—кострогальный** *a.* edge-planing; **—кофрезерный** *a.* edge-milling; **—очный** *a. of* **кромка.**

кромсать *v.* shred, cut to pieces.

крон *m.* crown (glass); chrome pigment, spec. chrome yellow; unit of time; **зелёный к., —а** *f.* chrome green; **красный к.** chrome red; **—а** *f.* corona; corolla; crown, crest, top (of tree).

Крона болезнь (med.) Crohn's disease.

крон/арциум *m.* (bot.) Cronartium; **—блок** *m.,* **—блочный** *a.* crown block; **—глас** *m.* crown glass; **—енпробка** *f.* crown closure, crown cap; **—ировка** *f.* formation of (tree) crown.

кроноцкий *a.* (geog.) Kronotsky.

кронфлинт *m.* crown flint glass.

крон/циркуль *m.* calipers; **к.-толщиномер** *m.* outside calipers; **—шнеп** *m.* (orn.) curlew (*Numenius*); **—штедтит** *m.* (min.) cronstedtite; **—штейн** *m.* cantilever, bracket, arm; support, holder, stand.

кропать *v.* botch, bungle; scribble.

кроп/ить *v.* sprinkle, spray; batch (jute); **—ление** *n.* sprinkling, etc., *see v.*

кропотливый *a.* tedious, painstaking, minute, detailed, meticulous.

кросс *m.* (commun.) distributing frame; terminal room; cross-country race; **—бридинг** *m.* (gen.) crossbreeding; **—инг** *m.* crossing; **—инговер** *m.* (gen.) crossing-over; **—ировка** *f.* (commun.) cross connection, cross-strapping; **—ит** *m.* (min.) crossite; **—овер** *m.,* **—оверный** *a.* (gen.; electron.) crossover.

крот *m.* (mam.) mole (*Talpa*).

кротал/изм *m.* (vet.) crotalism; **—ин** *m.* crotaline; **—отоксин** *m.* crotalotoxin; **—ярия** *f.* (bot.) Crotalaria.

кротдрена *f.* mole drain.

кроткий *a.* mild, gentle, meek.

крот/машина *f.,* **—ователь** *m.* mole plow; **—ование** *n.* mole plowing, mole draining; **—овина** *f.* molehill, mole run, tunnel; **—овые** *pl.* (mam.) Talpidae; **—овый** *a. of* **крот; —одренажный** *a.* mole drainage; **—оземлеройка** *f.* (mam.) mole shrew.

кроток *sh. m. of* **кроткий.**

кротон *m.* (bot.) Croton; **—аза** *f.* crotonase; **—ат** *m.* crotonate; **—ил** *m.,* **—иловый** *a.* crotonyl; **—илен** *m.* crotonylene, 2-butyne.

кротонов/ый *a.* croton(ic); **к. альдегид** crotonaldehyde, 2-butenal; **—ая кислота** crotonic acid, 2-butenoic acid; **соль —ой кислоты, —окислая соль** crotonate; **—ое масло** croton oil.

кротоноил *m.* croton(o)yl.

кротплуг *m.* mole plow.

кроукер *see* **крокер.**

кроха *f.* crumb, grain.

крохаль *m.* (orn.) merganser (*Mergus*).

крох/и *pl.* remains, scrap; **—кий** *a.* friable, crumbly; **—отка** *f.* crumb, pinch, a little bit; miniature; **—отный** *a.* midget, miniature.

кроц/еиновая кислота croceic acid, 2-naphthol-8-sulfonic acid; **—етин** *m.* crocetin; **—ин** *m.* crocin.

крош/ащийся *a.* crumbling, crumbly, friable; **—ево** *n.*

chopped food; **—ение** *n.* crumbling, etc., *see v.*; **—ен(н)ый** *a.* crumbled, etc., *see v.*; **—ечка** *f.* crumb, grain, very small particle; **—ечный** *a.* very small, minute; **—ить** *v.* crumble, break up; chop up, mince; chip (of gear tooth); **—иться** *v.* crumble, be friable; **—ица** *f.* (ichth.) river or lake trout; **—ка** *f.* crumb; (ent.) Atomaria; *suffix* meal, dust; **—коватость** *f.* friability.

кро́ю/т *pr. 3 pl.* of **крыть**; **—щие** *pl.* (orn.) tectrices, (wing) coverts; **—щий** *a.* covering, coating; protective; (anat.) tectorial; **—щая спосо́бность** covering power, hiding power, body (of paint); **—щие перья** *see* **кро́ющие.**

кроя́ *gen.* of **крой**; *pr. ger.* of **кроить.**

КРП, К.Р.П. *abbr.* (**конта́ктная ра́зность потенциа́лов**) contact potential difference.

КРС *abbr.* (**комбинацио́нное рассе́яние све́та**) Raman effect.

круг *m.* circle, ring, disk, wheel, orbit, circumference; range, scope, compass; period, cycle; round; group; (potter's) wheel; (circulatory) system; (sports) lap; (anat.) circulus; **к. кровообраще́ния** blood circulation; **второ́й к.** (av.) go-around; **на к.** on the average; **опи́сывать к.** *v.* (av.) circle; **поворо́тный к.** turntable; **ско́рость по —у** peripheral speed; **к.-иска́тель** *m.* (geod.) finder-circle.

круги́т *m.* (min.) krugite.

кру́гл/ая *f.* (elec.) quad; (typ.) em; **—ение** *n.,* **—ильный** *a.* rounding; **—еть** *v.* become round; **—ить** *v.* make round, round off.

кругло́ *adv.* round(ly); *prefix* (bot.) rotundi—, round; cycl(o)— (circle); sphaer(o)— (sphere); **—брю́шка** *f.* (ichth.) round herring (*Etrumeus teres*); **—ватый** *a.* roundish; **—вяза́льный** *a.* circular-knitting; **—годи́чный, —годово́й** *a.* year-round; continuous; **—голо́вка** *f.* (herp.) Phrynocephalus; **—голо́в(чат)ый** *a.* round-headed, sphaerocephalous; **—гу́бцы** *pl.* roundnose pliers; **—до́нный** *a.* round-bottomed; **—кле́точный** *a.* round-cell; **—ли́стный** *a.* (bot.) rotundifolious; **—ли́цый** *a.* round-faced; **—ло́бый** *a.* rounding (hammer); **—ме́р** *m.* out-of-round gage; **—обра́зный** *a.* circinate, ring-shaped; orbiculate, circular; **—па́лочка** *f.* dowel; **—пёр** *m.* (ichth.) lumpsucker; **—пёры(е)** *pl.* Cyclopteridae; **—пи́льный стано́к** circular saw; **—пло́дный** *a.* (bot.) cyclocarpous; **—поляризо́ванный** *a.* (circularly polarized).

кругло́/ресни́чные *pl.* (prot.) Peritricha; **—ро́тые** *pl.* (zool.) Cyclostomata; **—се́точный** *a.* (paper) cylinder; **—су́точно** *adv.* (a)round the clock, on a 24-hour basis, 24 hours a day; **—су́точный** *a.* twenty-four-hour, continuous; **—та́** *f.* roundness, round shape; **—тка́цкий** *a.* circular-weaving; **—у́гольный** *a.* round-cornered; **—фре́зерный** *a.* circular-milling; **—шлифова́льный стано́к** cylindrical grinder, circular grinder; **—шо́вные** *pl.* (ent.) circular-seamed flies (*Cyclorrhapha*); **—щёкий** *a.* round-cheeked; **—язы́чные** *pl.* (amph.) Discoglossidae.

кру́гл/ый *a.* round, circular, annular, globular, spherical; round-bar (iron); teres (muscle); **к. год** the year round; **—ыш, —як, —яш** *m.* round(ed) stone; round timber, rough log; (ichth.) Harvest fish (*Peprilus alepidotus*); round goby (*Neogobius melanostomus*); silver bream (*Blicca bjoerkna*); **—яки́** *pl.* (ent.) Clambidae.

кругови́на *f.* zonule, zonula, little belt.

кругов/о́й *a.* circular, round, ring, circling; cyclic; endless (conveyer); continuous (drive); mutual (guarantee); circumferential (weld seam); angular (frequency); (comp.) end-around (carry); orbicular (muscle); **к. но́ниус** dial; **к. ого́нь** (elec.) ring fire; **к. полёт** (av.)

circuit; **к. проце́сс** cycle; **—ая диагра́мма** circle diagram; **—ая кача́лка** rotary shaker; **—ая систе́ма** circulating system; **—ое враще́ние** rotation; **—ое движе́ние** circular motion, rotary motion, rotation, circling, circle; circulation; **дава́ть —ое движе́ние, име́ть —ое движе́ние** *v.* rotate; circulate; **—ое обраще́ние** circulation, circuit; **—ые фу́нкции** inverse trigonometric functions.

круго/воро́т *m.* rotation, turnover, circulation; cycle; whirlpool, vortex; **к. азо́та** nitrogen cycle; **—враща́тельный** *a.* rotary, gyrating, circular, circulatory; **—враще́ние** *n.* rotation, circular motion; circling; circulation; **—зо́р** *m.* scope, horizon, views, mental outlook; range (of vision); **—м** *adv. and prep. gen.* (a)round, about; (mil.) about face; in a ring, in a circle; **—напра́вленный** *a.* omnidirectional (antenna); **—оборо́т** *m.* circuit; circulation; rotation; circulating load (of impurities); cycle; **—обра́зность** *f.* roundness, round shape, circularity; **—обра́зный** *a.* round, circular; orbicular; **—обраще́ние** *see* **круговраще́ние; —поля́рный** *a.* circumpolar; **—ресни́чные** *pl.* (prot.) Peritricha; **—све́тный** *a.* round-the-world, world-wide.

кружа́л/о *n.,* **—ьный** *a.* (building) centering, bow member, curve piece; rotating screen; **—ьное ребро́** curve piece.

кружа́щийся *a.* circling, gyrating.

кружев/ни́ца *f.* (text.) lace maker; (ent.) lace bug; **—ни́цы** *pl.* Tingi(ti)dae; **—но́й** *a.* lace; heavily puddled (ice); **—о, —це, —цо,** *n.* lace; **—ови́дный** *a.* lace-like, lacy.

кру́жек *gen. pl.* of **кру́жка.**

круже́ние *n.* turning, etc., *see* **кружи́ть(ся)**; vertigo, dizziness.

круже́ч/ка *dim. of;* **—ный** *a.* of **кру́жка.**

кружи́ть *v.* turn, spin, rotate; circle; wander; **—ся** *see* **кружи́ть;** revolve around; whirl, rise (of dust); wander, be lost; **у него́ кру́жится голова́** he is dizzy.

кру́жка *f.* mug, jug, jar; (spinning) pot; (med.) irrigator.

кружко́вой *a.* of **кружо́к.**

круж/ны́й *a.* circuitous, roundabout; **—о́к** *dim. of* **круг;** disk, washer; tablet, cake; association, society, circle; area; (anat.) areola; orbiculus; **—о́чек** *dim. of* **кружо́к.**

крук/ези́т *m.* (min.) crookesite; **—о́вое тёмное простра́нство** Crookes dark space.

круно́да *f.* (geom.) crunode.

круп *m.* (med.; zool.) croup.

круп/а́ *f.* groats, grit(s); soft hail, graupel, (snow) pellets; **перло́вая к.** pearl barley.

кру́пен *sh. m.* of **кру́пный.**

круп/и́нка *f.* grain, granule; **—и́тчатый** *a.* grainy, granular, grumose; wheaten; **—и́ца** *f.* grain, crumb; **—и́чатый** *a.* fine-grained; **—ка** *dim. of* **крупа́;** grit; middlings, grist; (bot.) whitlow grass (*Draba*); **—не́е** *comp. of* **кру́пно, кру́пный.**

крупе́ть *v.* grow larger, grow heavier.

кру́пно *adv. and prefix* coarse(ly); macro— (large); on a large scale; **—би́тый** *a.* patch, lumpy (ice); **—бло́чный** *a.* large-block, large-panel, prefabricated slab (construction); coarse-grained; **—волокни́стый** *a.* coarse-fiber(ed); **—габари́тный** *a.* large(-sized); **—голо́вчатый** *a.* microcephalous, big-headed; **—заводски́й** *a.* large-scale (industry); **—зём** *m.* coarse earth; **—зерни́стость** *f.* coarseness; **—зерни́стый, —зёрный** *a.* coarse(-grained), large-grain(ed), coarsely granular; **—зла́чник** *m.* tall grass community; **—ка́дровый** *a.* large-frame; **—кали́берный** *a.* large-caliber; **—кле́точный** *a.* large-celled; **—кле́тчатый** *a.* wide-mesh(ed); **—ко́лос(ков)ый** *a.* (bot.) megastachyous, large-spiked; **—кристалли́ческий** *a.* coarsely crystalline, macrocrystalline; **—кусковой** *a.* lumpy, large-sized, in large pieces.

крупно/листный *a.* large-leaved, macrophyllous; **—масштабный** *a.* large-scale; **—молотый** *a.* coarsely ground; **—ноздреватый** *a.* coarse-pored; **—очаговый** *a.* macrofocal; **—панельный** *a.* (large-)panel (construction); **—плодник** *m.* (bot.) Megacarpaea; **—плодность** *f.* high yield; **—плодный** *a.* (bot.) macrocarpous, large-fuited; **—пористый** *a.* macroporous, coarse-pored; **—порфировый** *a.* (geol.) magnophyric; **—размерный** *a.* large-size(d); **—разнотравник** *m.* tall herb community; **—семянный** *a.* large-seeded, macrospermous; **—серийный** *a.* large-lot, large-series, large-scale (production); **—сланцеватый** *a.* (geol.) platy; **—слойный** *a.* wide-layered; wide-ringed (wood); **—сортный** *a.* (large-size), heavy; large sections (mill).

крупно/сть *f.* size, magnitude; coarseness, thickness; fineness; particle size; **гидравлическая к.** fall or sinking velocity; **разделять по —сти** *v.* size, classify; **—та** *f.* (degree of) fineness; **—товарный** *a.* large-scale; **—тоннажный** *a.* large(-capacity), large-tonnage; **—травье** *n.* tall herbaceous vegetation; **—цветковый** *a.* large-flowered; **—чешуйчатый** *a.* coarse-scaled; **—ягодный** *a.* large-berried; **—ячеистый** *a.* large-mesh(ed).

крупный *a.* big, coarse; large(-scale); major; strong, significant, important, prominent; large-sized; closeup (view); heavy-duty (machine); high, tall; standing (timber); lump (coal).

крупо— *prefix see* **крупа; —вейка** *f.* middlings cleaner; **—дёрка, —дёрный станок** hulling mill, scourer.

крупозный *a.* (med.) croupous.

крупон *m.,* **—ировать** *v.* (leather) crop, butt.

крупо/пропариватель *m.* groats parboiling unit; **—резка** *f.* groats grinder; **—рушка** *f.* hulling mill, sheller; **—сортировка** *f.* groats grader.

крупповский *a.* (met.) Krupp.

круп/чатка *f.* grainy wheaten flour, semolina; wheat-grinding mill; **—чатый** *a.* grainy, large-grained, coarse; **—яной** *a. of* **крупа.**

крустацеоз *m.* Crustacea-induced sickness.

крустифи/кация *f.* (geol.) crustification; **—цированный** *a.* crustified.

крут *sh. m. of* **крутой; —ай** *m.* (bot.) Echinops; **—ец** *m.* twisted flax tow.

крутизна *f.* steepness, steep slope, drop; gradient; characteristic slope; tangent, derivative; rate (of change); (electron.) transconductance.

крут/ило *n.* twisting pliers; **—ильный** *a.* torsion(al), twisting; **—ильный ватер, —ильная машина** (text.) twisting frame, doubling frame; **—ильные весы** torsion balance; **—ильщик** *m.* twister; **—ить** *v.* twist, wring; turn, whirl; (elec.) reverse; **—иться** *v.* turn, revolve, gyrate; spin around, eddy, swirl; squirm; **—ка** *f.* twist(ing); **положительная —ка** (av.) wash-in; **—комер** *m.* twist counter; **—нуть** *v.* give a turn or twist.

крут/о *adv.* steeply, abruptly, sharply, severely; tightly; **—обокий** *a.* steep-sided; **—ой** *a.* steep, precipitous, abrupt, sharp, sudden; severe, tough; stiff (dough); vigorously boiling; hard-boiled (eggs); **—ая характеристика** steepness (of curve).

круток *m.* coarse linen.

круто/падающий *a.* steeply dipping, steep(-grade); vertically linear; **—сть** *f.* steepness, abruptness, sharpness; slope; gradient; pitch (of roof); (stat.) kurtosis; **—яр** *m.* steep bank.

крутящ/ий *a.* torsion(al), twisting; **к. момент** torque; **измеритель —его момента** torquemeter.

круча *f.* steep slope, steepness.

кручак *m.* sheep bot fly (*Oestrus ovis*).

круче *comp. of* **круто, крутой; —ние** *n.* twisting, etc., *see* **крутить(ся);** twist; torsion; rotation; (mach.) running; **измеритель —ния** torsionmeter; **момент —ния** torque; **ползучесть при —нии** torsional creep.

круч/енный *part.,* **—ёный** *a.* twisted, spun; thrown (silk).

крушение *n.* wreck, ruin; accident; breakdown, collapse.

крушень-древоточец *m.* (ent.) goat moth, carpenter moth (*Cossus c.*).

крушилка *f.* disintegrator, disintegrating mill, crusher, grinder.

крушин/а *f.* (bot.) buckthorn (*Rhamnus*); **американская к.** cascara sagrada (*R. purshiana*); **—ник** *m.* buckthorn thicket; (bot.) Frangula; **—ница** *f.* brimstone butterfly (*Gonepteryx rhamni*); **—ные, —овые** *pl.* (bot.) Rhamnaceae; **—ный, —овый** *a.* buckthorn.

крушить *v.* shatter, destroy, wreck.

крыж *m.* (naut.) lashing, seizing (of rope).

крыжов/енный *a.,* **—ник** *m.* (bot.) gooseberry (*Grossularia*); **—никовые** *pl.* Grossulariaceae.

к-рый *abbr.* (**который**) who, which.

крыктытауский *a.* (geog.) Kryktytau.

крыл *past m. sing. of* **крыть.**

крылан *m.* (mam.) fruit bat; **—овые, —ы** *pl.* Pteropodidae, Megachiroptera.

крылат/ка *f.* wing nut; vane; (bot.) samara, winged fruit, winged seed; (mam.) ribbon seal (*Histriophoca fasciata*); (ichth.) butterfly fish (*Pterois*); grayling (*Thymallus*); **—ковидный** *a.* (bot.) samaroid; **—ые** *pl.* (ent.) Pterygota; **—ый** *a.* winged, alate; hydrofoil (boat).

крыл/ач *m.* fan, rotor, impeller; **—ечко** *dim. of* **крыльцо.**

крыл/о *n.* wing; blade, vane, impeller; (automobile) fender; (bridge) leaf; (semaphor) arm; (geol.) limb, side, leg, flank; (anat.) ala; **подводное к.** hydrofoil; **придаточное к.** (ent.) alula; **с —ьями** *a.* winged; *prefix* pter(o)—, pteryg(o)— (wing, fin).

крыло/ватость *f.* (timber) twist; **—видно—** *prefix* pterygo—; **—видно-верхне-челюстной** *a.* (anat.) pterygomaxillar; **—видно-ушная** *a.* (anat.) pterotic (bone); **—видный** *a.* pterygoid, wing-shaped, aliform; alar (ligament); (ichth.) cycloid (scales); **—жаберные** *pl.* (zool.) Pterobranchia; **—нёбный** *a.* (anat.) pterygopalatine; **—ногие** *pl.* (mal.) Pteropoda.

крыло-оболочка *f.* (av.) wing shell.

крылообразный *see* **крыловидный;** valley (iceberg).

крыло-остистый *a.* (anat.) pterygospinous.

крыло/пёрые *pl.* (ichth.) Dactylopteridae; **—плодный** *a.* (bot.) pterocarpous; **—семянный** *a.* pterospermous; **—ухие** *pl.* (ent.) Pterygota; **—хвостка** *f.* (ent.) Urapteryx.

крылышко *dim. of* **крыло;** (orn.) alula.

крыльный *a. of* **крыло;** alar.

крыльцо *n.* porch, flight of steps, perron.

крыльчатка *f.* impeller; vane; wing.

крыльчат/ый *a.* wing, vane; butterfly (damper); **к. движитель** rotating-blade propeller; **к. насос** vane pump; **—ая гайка** wing nut; **—ое колесо** blade wheel, impeller; paddle wheel.

крылья *pl. of* **крыло;** (anat.) alae.

Крым Crimea.

крымза *f.* zinc sulfate.

крым/-сагыз *m.* (bot.) krym-saghyz (*Taraxacum gymnanthum* or *T. hybernum*); **—ский** *a.* (geog.) Crimea(n).

крын/ка *f.* earthenware crock, milk jug; **—очка** *dim. of* **крынка;** (bot.) pyxidium; **—очковидный** *a.* pyxidate.

крыс/а *f.,* **—ий, —иный** *a.* (mam.) rat (*Rattus*); **серая к.** Norway rat; **—ёнок** *m.* baby rat; **—ид** *m.* rat poison; **—иношиншилловые** *pl.* (mam.) chinchilla rats (*Abrocomidae*); **—оистребление** *n.* rat extermination; **—оловка** *f.* rat trap; rat catcher; **—ы и мыши** *pl.* Murinae.

крыт/ый *a.* covered, etc., *see v.;* closed (car); closed-top (trailer); **—ь** *v.* cover, cap; roof, shingle; shelter, house; coat (with paint); clad (with metal); conceal; seal, cap (honey); (zool.) sire; **—ье** *n.* covering; **—ься** *v.* be covered, etc.; hide; lie in, consist in.

крыш/а *f.* roof, top; (biol.) tegmen, cover; (anat.) tectum; **—евидный, —еобразный** *a.* tectiform, roof-like; **—евый** *a.* roof(-shaped); mesh-roof (antenna); **—ечка** *dim. of* **крышка;** lid, cover(ing), operculum; **—ечная** *f.* (ichth.) opercle; **—ечный** *a.* of **крышка;** (ichth.) opercular; **—ка** *f.* cover, lid, cap; hood, end shield; plate; door, gate; (cylinder) head; end, finish; (anat.) tegmen, roof; operculum, lid; **—коделательный** *a.* (typ.) case-making.

крэб *m.* crabapple; **—триевый** *a.* Crabtree.

Крюгера элемент Krüger cell.

крюйт-камера *f.* ammunitions storeroom.

крюк *m.,* **—овой** *a.* hook, crook, crotch; grapple, cramp iron; staple; pick(ax); clinch, clench; detour.

крюсспеленг *m.* (geod.) cross bearing.

крючиться *v.* be doubled up (with pain).

крюч/ко— *prefix* unci—, unco— (hook); **—коватый** *a.* uncinate, hooked; jagged, hackly (fracture); hamate (bone); **—коватый ключ** spanner, wrench; **—ковидный** *see* **крючкообразный;** hamate (bone); **—ковый** *a. of* **крючок;** barbed; **—кообразный** *a.* hook-like, hooked, crooked; unciform, uncinate; **—корог** *m.* (ichth.) hookear sculpin (*Artediellus*); **—ник** *m.* carrier, stevedore; **—ничать** *v.* work with a grapple; **—ок** *m.* hook, catch, claw; lifting handle; (grip) pawl, dog; (anat.) hamulus; (surgical) retractor; **—очек** *dim. of* **крючок;** **—очный** *a. of* **крючок;** **—ья** *pl. of* **крюк.**

крюшон *m.* white wine blend.

кряду *adv.* together, running.

кряж *m.,* **—евый** *a.* block, log; ridge, crest; (mountain) range, chain; (hort.) local strain; **—истый** *a.* sturdy (tree).

кряк *m.,* **—анье** *n.* quack(ing); **—ать, —нуть** *v.* quack; **—ва** *f.,* **—овая утка, —уша** *f.* mallard duck (*Anas platyrhynchos*).

крях/еть *v.* groan; **—ун** *m.* (orn.) woodcock (*Scolopax rusticola*).

КС *abbr.* (**кажущееся сопротивление**) apparent resistivity; (**камера сгорания**) combustion chamber; (**катодное свечение**) cathode glow; (**кипящий слой**) fluidized bed; (**компрессорная станция**) compressor station; (**кривая сопротивления**) resistivity curve.

ксант— *prefix* xanth(o)— (yellow); **—алин** *m.* xanthaline; **—ат** *m.* xanthate; **—атбарабан** *m.* xanthation churn; **—атин** *m.* xanthathin; **—гидрол** *m.* xanthydrol, 9-hydroxyanthene; **—еин** *m.* xanthein.

ксантен *m.,* **—овый** *a.* xanthene, diphenylmethane oxide; **—он** *m.* xanth(en)one.

ксантил *m.* xanthyl; **—ий** *m.* xanthylium; **—овый** *a.* xanthyl; xanthylic (acid).

ксантин *m.,* **—овый** *a.* xanthine, 2,6-purinedione; **—оксидаза** *f.* xanthinoxidase; **—урия** *f.* (med.) xanthi(n)uria.

ксантит *m.* (min.) xanthite.

ксанто— *prefix* xantho— (yellow); **—арсенит** *m.* (min.) xantharsenite.

ксантоген *m.* xanthogen; **—амид** *m.* xanthogenamide, thiourethan; **—ат** *m.* xanthate; **—ератор** *m.* (text.) xanthator; **илцеллюлоза** *f.* cellulose xanthate; **—ирование** *n.* xanthation; **—ировать** *v.* xanthate.

ксантогеново/кислый *a.* xanthic acid; xanthate (of); **к. калий** potassium xanthate; **—кислая соль** xanthate; **—натриевая соль** sodium xanthate; **—этиловый эфир** ethyl xanthate.

ксантогенов/ый *a.* xanthogen(ic); **к. эфир** ethyl xanthate; **—ая кислота** xanthic acid, ethyloxydithiocarbonic acid; **соль —ой кислоты** xanthate.

ксанто/зин *m.* xanthosin, xanthinriboside; **—з(ис** *m.* (vet.) xanthosis; **—зома** *f.* (bot.) Xanthosoma; **—кон(ит)** *m.* (min.) xanthoconite; **—ксилин** *m.* xanthoxylin; **—силум** *m.* (bot.) Xanthoxylum; **—ма** *f.* (med.) xanthoma; **—мицин** *m.* xanthomycin (antibiotic); **—мный** *a.* xanthomatous.

ксантон *m.* xanthone, 9-xanthenone; **—овый** *a.* xanthone; xanthonic (acid).

ксантопротеин *m.* xanthoprotein; **—овый** *a.* xanthoprotein; xanthoproteic (acid).

ксанто/псин *m.* xanthopsin, visual yellow; **—птерин** *m.* xanthopterin; **—пу(к)цин** *m.* xanthopuccine; **—пурпурин** *m.* xanthopurpurin, purpuroxanthene; **—рамнин** *m.* xanthorhamnin; **—рия** *f.* (bot.) Xanthoria; **—ртит** *m.* (min.) xanthorthite; **—сидерит** *m.* xanthosiderite; **—токсин** *m.* xanthotoxin.

ксантофил/л *m.* xanthophyll; **—лит** *m.* (min.) xanthophyllite; **—ьный** *a.* xanthophyllous, yellow-leaved.

ксант/офор *m.* (cyt.) xanthophore; **—охелидоновый** *a.* xanthochelidonic (acid); **—уреновый** *a.* xanthurenic (acid); **—урия** *f.* (med.) xanthuria.

ксб *abbr.* (**кило-стильб**) kilostilb.

к.с.в., КСВ *abbr.* (**коэффициент стоячей волны**) standing wave ratio; **к.с.в.н., КСВН** *abbr.* (**коэффициент стоячей волны напряжения**) voltage standing wave ratio.

КСД *abbr.* (**компрессор среднего давления**) medium pressure compressor.

ксен— *see* **ксено—**; **—ийность** *f.* (gen.) xenia; **—ил** *m.* xenyl; **—иламин** *m.* xenylamine, *p*-biphenylamine; **—ия** *f.* (gen.) xenia; (zool.) Xenia; **—ный** *a. suffix* —xenous (host).

ксено— *prefix* xen(o)— (guest, host, stranger; foreign, strange); **—гамия** *f.* (gen.) xenogamy, cross fertilization; **—генез** *m.* xenogenesis; **—генит** *m.* (geol.) xenogenite; **—генозный** *a.* (gen.) xenogenous; **—конгеровые** *pl.* (ichth.) Xenocongridae; **—кристалл** *m.* (geol.) xenocryst; **—лит** *m.* (min.) xenolite; (geol.) xenolith, inclusion; **—морфный** *a.* (min.) xenomorphic; **—н** *m.* xenon, Xe; **—паразитный** *a.* xenoparasitic; **—тим** *m.* (min.) xenotime; **—трансплантат** *m.* (med.) xenograft, heterograft; **—фобия** *f.* xenophobia; **—цианин** *m.* xenocyanine.

ксерический *a.* xeric, with scanty moisture.

ксеро— *prefix* xero— (dry); **—гель** *m.* xerogel; **—граф** *m.* xerographic recorder; **—графия** *f.* xerography; **—дерма** *f.* (med.) xeroderma; **—з** *m.* xerosis; **—лл** *m.* (soils) xeroll; **—морфный** *a.* xeromorphic; **—новый** *a.* xeronic (acid); **—радиография** *f.* xeroradiography; **—термический** *a.* xerothermic, drought- and heat-resistant; **—термическое растение** (bot.) xerotherm; **—фил** *m.* xerophilous organism; **—фильный** *a.* xerophilous, drought-resistant; **—фит** *m.* (bot.) xerophyte; **—фитный** *a.* xerophytic; **—фобный** *a.* xerophobous; —**форм** *m.* xeroform, bismuth tribromophenate; —**фтальмия** *f.* (med.) xerophthalmia.

ксиелиды *pl.* (ent.) Xyelidae.

ксил/ан *m.* xylan; —**ема** *f.* (bot.) xylem; —**ен** *m.* (coal) xylain; —**енол** *m.* xylenol; —**идин** *m.* xylidine, dimethylaniline; —**идиновый** *a.* xylidine; xylidic (acid).

ксилил *m.* xylyl; —**ен** *m.* xylylene; —**овый** *a.* xylyl; xylic (acid).

ксили/н *m.* xylin; —**т** *m.* xylite, xylitol.

ксило— *prefix* xylo— (wood); —**бетонный камень** a type of concrete block; —**гравюра** *f.* woodcut, wood engraving; —**графия** *f.* xylography, wood engraving; —**за** *f.* xylose, wood sugar; —**зид** *m.* xyloside; —**зиевый** *a.* xylosic (acid); —**идин** *m.* xyloidin; —**ил** *m.* xyloyl; —**карпный** *a.* (bot.) xylocarpous; —**кокус** *m.* (ent.) Xylococcus; —**копа** *f.* Xylocopa.

ксилол *m.* xylene, dimethylbenzene; —**ин** *m.* xyloline (yarn); —**ит** *m.* xylolith, wood-stone; a compressed sawdust block; —**огия** *f.* (bot.) xylology; —**сульфокислота** *f.* xylenesulfonic acid.

ксилометр *m.* xylometer.

ксилон *m.* xylon, wood cellulose; —**ит** *m.* xylonite, celluloid; —**овый** *a.* xylon; xylonic (acid).

ксило/пал *m.* xylopal, wood opal; —**рсин**, —**рцин** *m.* xylorcinol, dimethylresorcinol; —**та** *f.* (ent.) Xylota; —**томия** *f.* (bot.) xylotomy; —**фаг** *m.* xylophage; —**фаговый** *a.* xylophagous, wood-eating, wood-destroying; —**фильный** *a.* xylophilous; —**фит** *m.* xylophyte; —**хинон** *m.* xyloquinone, dimethylquinone.

ксилулоза *f.* xylulose.

кси/мения *f.* (bot.) Ximenia; —**рис** *m.* xirid (*Xyris*); —**рисовые** *pl.* Xyridaceae.

КСК *abbr.* (**корреляционный сейсмический каротаж**) correlational seismic logging.

ксо, КСО *abbr.* (**конденсатор, слюдяной опрессованный**) pressed-mica capacitor.

ксонотлит *m.* (min.) xonotlite.

КСП *abbr.* (**кабина слепого полёта**) instrument-flight simulator.

КСР *abbr.* (**счётно-решающий компенсатор**) computing compensator.

КССВ *abbr.* (**константа спин-спинового взаимодействия**) spin-spin coupling constant.

КССР *abbr.* Kazakh Soviet Socialist Republic; Kirgiz Soviet Socialist Republic.

кстати *adv.* to the point, to the purpose, opportunely; at the same time; incidentally, by the way.

КСЭ *abbr.* (**комплексная сейсмологическая экспедиция**) joint seismological expedition.

кт *abbr.* (**килотонна**) kiloton; **к-т** *abbr.* (**комбинат**) kombinat; (**комитет**) committee; (**концентрат**) concentrate.

к-та *abbr.* (**кислота**) acid.

ктен/идий *m.* (zool.) ctenidium; —**иевидный** *a.* ctenoid; —**о—** *prefix* cten(o)— (ctenoid); —**оидный** *a.* ctenoid; —**омиды** *pl.* (mam.) Ctenomyidae; —**офоры** *pl.* (zool.) Ctenophora.

ктетосома *f.* (gen.) ctetosome.

ктипеит *m.* (min.) ktypeite.

КТК *abbr.* (**керамический трубчатый конденсатор**) tubular ceramic capacitor.

кто *pron.* who, who? **к. бы ни** whoever; **к.-либо, к.-нибудь** somebody, someone, anybody; **к.-то** somebody.

к.т.п. *abbr.* (**коэффициент теплопередачи**) coefficient of heat transfer.

КТР *abbr.* (**кодовое трансмиттерное реле**) code transmitter relay; (**коэффициент теплового расши-**

рения) coefficient of thermal expansion; (**критическая температура растворения**) critical solution temperature.

ктыр/евидки *pl.* (ent.) Therevidae; —**и** *pl.* Asilidae; —**ь** *m.* robber fly (*Asilus*).

к-ть *abbr.* (**кислотность**) acidity.

Ку; лихорадка Ку (med.) Q fever.

куб *m.* (math.) cube; block; vat; still; **в —е** cubed; **возводить в к.** *v.* cube, raise to the third power; **перегонный к.** still; distilling flask.

куб. *abbr.* (**кубический**) cubic.

Куба (geog.) Cuba.

кубанит *m.* (min.) cubanite, chalmersite.

кубанка *f.* (bot.) wheat (*Triticum durum*).

кубанский *a.* (geog.) Kuban.

кубаревидный *a.* turbinate, top-shaped.

кубарка *f.* rake (used with tractor).

кубар/чатый *see* **кубаревидный**; —**ь** *m.* (spinning) top.

кубатур/а *f.* cubic capacity, volume, bulk; cubature, volume determination; —**ник** *m.* volumetric table.

куб. дм *abbr.* (**кубический дециметр**) cubic decimeter; **куб. дм.** *abbr.* (**кубический дюйм**) cubic inch.

кубеб/а *f.* (pharm.) cubeb; —**ин** *m.* cubebin, 3,4-dimethylene-oxy-*p*-oxystyrone; —**овый** *a.* cubeb; cubebic (acid).

кубель *m.* box.

кубенский *a.* (geog.) Kubena.

кубик *dim. of* **куб**; cube; (glass) brick.

кубинский *a.* (geog.) Cuba(n).

куб-испаритель *m.* still.

кубитальный *a.* (anat.) cubital, forearm.

кубицит *m.* (min.) cubicite, cubic zeolite.

кубич/еский, —**ный** *a.* cubic(al); **к. корень** (math.) cube root; —**еское уравнение** cubic equation.

куб. км *abbr.* (**кубический километр**).

кубко/видный, —**образный** *a.* cyathiform, poculiform, cup-shaped.

куб. м *abbr.* (**кубический метр**); **куб. мм** (**кубический миллиметр**).

кубовидн/о-ладьевидный *a.* (anat.) cuboideonavicular; —**ый** *a.* cubical, cube-shaped; cuboid, cubiform.

кубо/вой *a. of* **куб**; **к. остаток**, —**вая жидкость** bottoms; —**вая руда** (min.) cube ore, pharmacosiderite; —**вщик** *m.* still operator.

кубо/вый *a.* indigo blue; still; **к. краситель** vat dye; **к. процесс** vat dyeing; —**глав** *m.* (ichth.) cigarfish (*Cubiceps*); —**золь** *m.* vat sol.

кубок *m.* goblet, cup; beaker; (bot.) scyphus.

кубо/медузы *pl.* (zool.) Cubomedusae; —**метр** *m.* cubic meter; —**нит** *m.* cubic boron nitride; —**образный** *see* **кубовидный**; —**силицит** *m.* (min.) cubosilicite; —**хвост(ов)ые** *pl.* (ichth.) square-tails (*Tetragonuridae*).

кубрик *m.* cockpit; (naut.) crew's quarters; lower deck.

куб. см *abbr.* (**кубический сантиметр**) cubic centimeter, cc.

кубычанье *n.* somersault(ing).

кубышк/а *f.* jug; coin box; egg sac, egg capsule, egg pod; saccule; (bot.) Nuphar; **морские —и** (zool.) Holothur(i)oidea.

кувалда *f.* sledge hammer.

кувез *m.* (med.) incubator.

кувейтский *a.* (geog.) Kuwait.

кувел/яж, -яция *see* **кювеляж**.

куверт *m.* envelope.

кувшин *m.* pitcher, jug, jar; —**ка** *f.* (bot.) water lily (*Nymphaea*); —**ковые** *pl.* Nymphaeaceae; —**ный** *a. of* **кувшин**; —**чатый** *a.* urceolate, ascidiform, pitcher-shaped; **—чик** *dim. of* **кувшин;** (biol.) ascidium.

кувырк/ать, —нуть *v.* turn upside down, turn over, upset; tumble; **—аться** *v.* somersault; **—ающийся** *a.* somersaulting, tumbling; **—ом** *adv.* head over heels.

кувырнуть *see* **кувыркнуть.**

куга *f.* (bot.) cattail (*Typha*).

кугуар *m.* (mam.) cougar (*Felis concolor*).

куд *m.* elbow.

куда *adv.* where? in what direction? **к. бы ни** wherever; **к. как** how very; **к. либо, к.-нибудь** somewhere, anywhere; **к-то** somewhere.

кудахтать *v.* cackle, gabble.

кудбер *m.* (dyes) cudbear, orchil.

куделеприготов/итель *m.* flax (or hemp) tow maker; **—ительный** *a.* tow-making; **—ление** *n.* tow processing.

кудель *f.,* **—ный** *a.* (text.) tow, oakum.

кудр/еватый *a.* somewhat curly; crispate, crisp(ed); **—епёр** *m.* (ichth.) curlfin; **—епёр(ов)ые** *pl.* Cirrhitidae; **—и** *pl.* curls; (bot.) Ballota; **—явиться** *v.* curl; **—явый** *a.* curly, curled, frizzly, crimped; crisp, wavy, cincinnal; **—яш** *m.* (bot.) crown flax (*Linum usitatissimum*); **—яшки** *pl.* curls.

куду *m.* (mam.) kudu (*Tragelaphus*).

кудцу *m.* (bot.) kudzu (*Dolichos hirsutus*).

куенкский *a.* (geog.) Cuenca.

куеста *f.* (geol.) cuesta.

куёт *pr. 3 sing. of* **ковать.**

кузбасс *m.* Kusnetsk coal fields; **к.-лак** *m.* coaltar varnish.

куз/ен *m.,* **—ина** *f.* cousin; **—иния** *f.* (bot.) Cousinia.

куз/ка *see* **кузька; —мичёва** *see* **кузьмичёва.**

кузнец *m.* blacksmith, smithy; (ichth.) regional name for goby, grayling, John dory; **к.-инструментальщик** *m.* toolsmith; **—кий** *a.* (geog.) Kuznetsk.

кузнечик *m.* (ent.) grasshopper (*Tettigonia*); (orn.) chiffchaff (*Phylloscopus collybita*); **—и, —овые** *pl.* Tettigoni(i)dae.

кузнечно-прессов/ый *a.* press-forging; **—ое дело** forging; **—ое производство** (press) forging.

кузнечно-штамповочный *a.* forging.

кузн/ечный *a.* forge, forging; (black)smith's; sledge (hammer); hammer (welding); **к. цех** *see* **кузница; к. шлак** hearth cinder, forge cinder; **—ая мастерская, —ица, —я** *f.* smithy, blacksmith shop; forge (shop), hammer press shop.

кузов *m.* basket; body (of vehicle); **—ица** *f.* (bot.) osier willow (*Salix longifolia*); **—ки, —ковые** *pl.* (ichth.) Ostraciidae; **—ной** *a. of* **кузов; —ок** *dim. of* **кузов;** (bot.) pyxidium; trunkfish, boxfish (*Ostracion*); **—остроение** *n.* body building, body work; **к.-фургон** *m.* van body; **к.-холодильник** *m.* refrigerator body; **—ый** *a. of* **кузов.**

кузу *m.* (mam.) possum (*Trichosurus,* spec. *T. vulpecula*).

кузька *m.* (ent.) grain beetle (*Anisoplia austriaca*).

кузьмичёва трава (bot.) Ephedra distachya.

куйбышевский *a.* (geog.) Kuibyshev.

куйтозёрский *a.* (geog.) Lake Kuyto.

Кука пролив (geog.) Cook strait.

кукаль *m.* (orn.) coucal (*Centropus*).

куканг *m.* (mam.) slow loris (*Nycticebus coucang*).

кукарек/анье *n.* crow(ing) (of rooster); **—ать, —нуть** *v.* crow.

кукеит *m.* (min.) cookeite.

кукельван *see* **кукольван.**

кукерс/ит *m.,* **—кий сланец** (petr.) kukersite, Kukruze oil shale.

кукла *f.* doll, puppet.

куклоро/дные *pl.* (ent.) Pupipara; **—дный, —ждающий** *a.* pupiparous.

куковать *v.* (orn.) cuckoo.

куколеотборник *see* **кукольник.**

кукол/ка *dim. of* **кукла;** (ent.) chrysalis, pupa, nymph, cocoon; **—кообразный** *a.* pupiform; **—очный** *a. of* **куколка.**

куколь *m.* (bot.) corncockle (*Agrostemma*); **—ван** *m.* Cocculus; **—ник** *m.* cockle cylinder, cockle separator; **—ный** *a. of* **кукла, куколь.**

кукурбитацин *m.* curcurbitacin.

кукуруз/а *f.,* **—ный** *a.* corn, maize (*Zea*); **к. в початках** corn on the cob; **—ный экстракт** corn steep; **—о—** *prefix,* **—овый** *a.* corn; **—овод** *m.* corn grower; **—оводство** *n.,* **—оводческий** *a.* corn growing; **—одробилка** *f.* corn crusher; **—олущилка** *f.* corn sheller; **—осажалка, —осеялка** *f.* corn planter; **—оуборочная машина** corn picker; **—охранилище** *n.* corn crib.

кукуш/ечий *a.,* **—ка** switcher; (min.) dinky; (orn.) cuckoo (*Cuculus*); **—ки** *pl.* Cuculidae; **—кин цвет** cuckoo flower (*Coronaria flos-cuculi*); **—кины слёзки** (bot.) Orchis; **—ковые** *pl.* (orn.) Cuculidae; **—ник** *m.* (bot.) Gymnadenia; **—онок** *m.* young cuckoo.

куку-яман *m.* (mam.) bharal (*Pseudois nayaur*).

кукша *f.* (orn.) jay (*Perisoreus*).

кукшинский *a.* (geog.) Kuksha.

кул, кул. *abbr.* (**кулон**) coulomb.

кулаж *m.* loss, waste.

кулак *m.* (mach.) cam, knuckle; *see also* **кулачок;** (min.) hammer (of crusher); (min.) кер, keep; (anat.) fist; kulak (rich peasant).

кулан *m.* (mam.) kulan (*Equus hemionus*).

куландинский *a.* (geog.) Kulandy.

куланутпесский *a.* (geog.) Kulan-Utpes.

кулачество *n.* kulak class of farmers.

кулачко/во-стержневой *a.* cam and pushrod; **—вый** *a. of* **кулачок;** hammer (mill); sheep's foot (roller); **—вый вал** camshaft; **—вый механизм, —вый привод** cam gear; **—образный** *a.* cam-shaped.

кулачник *m.* round coal.

кулачн/ый *a. of* **кулак; к. патрон** jaw chuck; **—ая муфта** jaw clutch.

кулачок *dim. of* **кулак;** cam; ram (blowout preventer); claw, dog; block; jaw (of chuck); pawl, catch, detent, check(ing) device; tappet; **приводной к., рабочий к.** actuating cam; **сгибающий к.** bending block.

кулебяка *f.* meat or vegetable pie.

кулевой *a.* sac, packaged in sacks.

кулёр, сахарный caramel.

кулеш *m.* thin gruel, paste.

Кулея-Тьюки алгоритм Cooley-Tukey algorithm.

Кули анемия (med.) Cooley's anemia.

кулига *f.* (orn.) flock; (ent.) swarm.

Кулиджа трубка Coolidge tube.

кулиевые *pl.* (ichth.) Kuhliidae.

кулик *m.* (orn.) sandpiper; **—и** *pl.* Limicolae.

куликойдэс *m.* (ent.) Culicoides.

кулинарный *a.* culinary.

кулировать *v.* (text.) sink the loops.

кулис/а *f.,* **—ный** *a.* link; rocker (arm); slot (hole), guide (slot), slideway; sector; windbreak, strip (of trees); **—ный камень** slide block, link block; die block; guide shoe; **—ный механизм, —ный привод** link gear; (elec.) rocker gear; **—ная рубка** alternate (clear) strip felling; **—ообразное строение** echelon structure.

кулитка *f.* flax bundle.

Ку-лихорадка *f.* (med.) Q fever.

кулич *m.* cake.

кулия *f.* (ichth.) flagtail (*Kuhlia*).

куло/метр, —н(о)метр *m.* (elec.) coulometer, coulomb meter; **—н** *m.* coulomb; **—новский** *a.* Coulomb('s).

култук *m.* kultuk (deeply indented shallow bay).

култышка *f.* (med.) amputated stump.

кулуар *m.* chute, conduit; lobby.

кулумысский *a.* (geog.) Kulumys.

кулундинский *a.* (geog.) Kulunda.

куль *m.* bag, sack; pocket, pouch.

кульбаба *f.* (bot.) Leontodon.

кульверт *m.* culvert.

кульгардит *m.* (min.) coolgardite.

кульдо– *prefix* culdo— (cul-de-sac).

кульм *m.* culm, anthracite coal.

кульман *m.* Kuhlman drafting unit.

кульмановский *a.* Kuhlmann's (green).

кульмин/ационный *a.,* **—ация** *f.* culmination, culminating; **к. пуикт** climax; **—ировать** *v.* culminate, end, terminate.

культ *m.* cult; *prefix see* **культурный.**

культи *gen and pl. of* **культя.**

культивар *m.* (hort.) cultivar.

культиватор *m.* cultivator; **к.-груббер** *m.* grubber; **к.-косилка** *m.* tiller mower; **—ный** *a.* cultivator; cultivating, hoeing; **к.-окучник** *m.* hilling cultivator; **к.-планет** *m.* hand cultivator; **к.-плоскорез** *m.* subsurface tiller; **к.-попольник** *m.* weeder; **к.-рыхлитель** *m.* scarifier; **к.-скарификатор, к.-экстирпатор** grubber.

культив/ационный *a.,* **—ация** *f.,* **—ирование** *n.* cultivation, cultivating; **—ированный** *a.* cultivated, etc., *see v.;* **—ировать** *v.* cultivate, till; raise, grow; **—ировка** *see* **культивация; —ируемый** *a.* cultivated.

культиген *m.* (bot.) cultigen.

культ/работа *f.* cultural and educational work; **—товары** *pl.* cultural and educational material.

культур/а *f.* culture, cultivation; crop; cultivar; **к. бацилл** bacilliculture; **ведущая к., главная к.,** **основная к.** staple (crop); **—альный** *a.* culture; **—бытовой** *a.* cultural and domestic; **—но-воспитательный** *a.* cultural and educational; **—но-поливной** *a.* cultivated and irrigated; **—но-просветительный** *a.* cultural and educational; **—ность** *f.* (standard of) culture; **—но-технический** *a.* cultural and professional; **—ный** *a.* culture(d), cultural; cultivated, tilled; arable (soil); **—техник** *m.* (agr.) ameliorator; **—техника** *f.* amelioration, soil improvement.

культя, —пка *f.* (med.) amputated stump.

кульцита *f.* (zool.) sea star (*Culcita*).

кумай *m.* (orn.) snow griffon (*Gyps himalayensis*).

кумалин *m.* coumalin, 1,2-pyrone; **—овая кислота** coumalic acid.

куман/ика *f.,* **—ичный** *a.* bramble (*Rubus* spec. *R. fruticosus*).

кумар/ан *m.* coumaran, dihydrocoumarone; **—ат** *m.* coumarate; **—ил** *m.* coumaryl; **—иловая кислота** coumarilic acid, 1-benzofurancarboxylic acid; **—ин** *m.* coumarin, 1,2-benzopyrone; **—инкарбоновая кислота** carboxycoumaric acid; **—(ин)овая кислота** coumar(in)ic acid; **—овый альдегид** coumaraldehyde; **—он** *m.,* **—оновый** *a.* coumarone, benzofuran; **—ун** *m.* coumarouna bean, tonka bean.

кумарчик *m.* (bot.) Agriophyllum.

кумач *m.,* **—ный, —овый** *a.* red calico.

Кумбса проба (immun.) Coombs' test.

кумен *see* **кумол.**

куменгеит *m.* (min.) cumengeite.

кумен/ил *m.* cum(en)yl; **—ол** *see* **куминол.**

куметр *m.* (elec. comm.) Q-meter.

кумжа *f.* (ichth.) salmon trout (*Salmo trutta*).

кумидин *m.* cumidine, cumenylamine; **—овая кислота** cumidic acid, dimethylphthalic acid.

кумил *m.,* **—овый** *a.* cum(en)yl; **—овая кислота** cumylic acid, durylic acid.

кумин/ал(ь) *m.* cuminal(dehyde); **—амид** *m.* cuminamide; **—амовый** *a.* cuminamic (acid).

куммингтонит *m.* (min.) cummingtonite.

кумин/ил *m.* cuminyl; cuminil, dikuminoketone; **—илиден** *m.* cuminylidene; **—овый** *a.* cumin, cum(in)ic; **—овый альдегид** cumic aldehyde, cumaldehyde; **—овая кислота** cum(in)ic acid, *p*-isopropylbenzoic acid; **—ол** *m.* cuminol, cumic alcohol.

куминский *a.* (geog.) Kuma.

кумкват *m.* (bot.) kumquat (*Fortunella*).

куммеровия *f.* (bot.) Kummerovia.

куммингтонит *m.* (min.) cummingtonite.

кумо/вые *pl.* (crust.) cumaceans (*Cumacea*); **—ил** *m.* cumoyl; **—л** *m.* cumene, *l*-propylbenzene; **—нитрил** *m.* cumonitrile, cumenyl cyanide; **—тиазон** *m.* cumothiazone; **—фенамид** *m.* cumophenamide, cumanilide; **—хинон** *m.* cumoquinone.

кумрочовый *a.* (geog.) Kumroch.

кумский *a.* (geog.) Kuma.

кумул/ен *m.* cumulene; **—ированный** *a.* cumulated; **—иты** *pl.* (petr.) cumulites; **—огия** *f.* cumulogy; **—юс** *m.* cumulus, little mound, heap; **—офировый** *a.* (geol.) cumulophyric; **—ятивность** *f.* cumulative effect or action; **—ятивный** *a.* cumulative; pile-up (pulse); hollow, shaped (charge); (geol.) cumulose (deposits); **—яция** *f.* (ac)cumulation.

кумы *pl.* kumy (quicksands in Central Asia).

кумыс *m.,* **—ный** *a.* koumiss (an alcoholic drink from milk); **—олечение** *n.* koumiss therapy.

кунак *m.* (bot.) Italian millet (*Setaria italica*).

кунаширский *a.* (geog.) Kunashir.

кунг/ей-алатауский *a.* (geog.) Kungei-Alatau; **—урский** *a.* Kungur; **—усский** *a.* Kungus.

кунджа *f.* (ichth.) char (*Salvelinus* spec. *S. leucomaenis*); *see* **кумжа.**

Кундта закон Kundt's rule.

кунжут *m.,* **—ный** *a.* (bot.) sesame (*Sesamum*); **—ные, —овые** *pl.* Pedaliaceae.

куниаль *m.* Cunial (copper-base alloy).

куний *a. of* **куница;** sable (fur).

кунико *n.* Cunico (alloy).

кунина *f.* (zool.) Cunina.

кунифе *n.* Cunife (alloy).

куниц/а *f.* (mam.) marten (*Martes*); **к.-рыболов** *f.* fisher (*Martes pennanti*); **—ы** *pl.* Mustelidae; **сумчатые —ы** Dasyuridae.

куннингамия *f.* Chinese fir (*Cunninghamia*).

кунокта(н)та *f.* (zool.) Cunoctantha.

кунцит *m.* (min.) kunzite.

куньи *pl. of* **куница;** (mam.) Mustelidae.

кунь/инский *a.* (geog.) Kunia; **—луньский** *a.* Ku(e)nlun, Shan.

купа *f.* cluster, group; **—в(к)а** *f.* (bot.) globe flower (*Trollius*).

купаж *m.,* **—ирование** *n.* mixing (of liquids); mixture, blend; blending (of wines, etc.); dilution: **—ированный** *a.* blended; **—ный барабан** blender.

купальница *f.* globe flower (*Trollius*).

куп/альный *a.* bath(ing); **—альня** *f.* bath (house); **—альщик** *m.* bather; **—ание** *n.* bathing, swimming; bathing place; **—ать(ся)** *v.* bathe.

купе *n.* coupe; (rr.) compartment; **—йный** *a.* divided into compartments.

купел/ирование *n.* (met.) cupellation; **—ировать** *v.* cupel; **—ь** *f.* cupel; (typ.) font; **—яционный** *a.* cupel(lation); **—яция** *f.* cupellation.

купена *f.* (bot.) Solomon's seal, sealwort (*Polygonatum*).

купер/ит *m.* (med.) cowperitis; (min.) cooperite; **—овы железы** (anat.) Cowper's glands.

Купер/с-Крик (geog.) Cooper's Creek; **-Юитта лампа** Cooper-Hewitt lamp.

куп/ец *m.* merchant, tradesman; **—еческий** *a.* mercantile; **—ечество** *n.* trade; merchants.

купировать *v.* mix, blend; dilute, cut; arrest, stop, cut short; (med.) cup; (rr) divide into compartments.

куп/ить *v.* buy, purchase; **—ленный** *a.* bought, purchased; **—ля** *f.* buying, purchase.

купок *m.* belly, side (of smoked fish).

купол *m.* cupola, dome, bowl, bell, crown (of furnace); canopy (of parachute); (min.) pot; (geol.) boss; (anat.) cupula; **—овидный, —ообразный** *a.* dome-shaped, domed, cupola-shaped, cupuliform; arched; (geol.) quaquaversal, domal (structure); **—ообразование** *n.* dome-formation, doming; **—ьный** *a.* of **купол**; arched; (anat.) cupular.

купон *m.*, **—ный** *a.* coupon.

купорос *m.* vitriol; **белый к.** white vitriol, zinc sulfate; **железный к., зелёный к.** green vitriol, copperas, ferrous sulfate heptahydrate; **медный к., синий к.** blue vitriol, copper sulfate; **свинцовый к.** lead vitriol, lead sulfate; **цинковый к.** *see* **купорос, белый**; **—ить** *v.* vitriolate.

купоросн/ый *a.* vitriol(ic); **—ое масло** oil of vitriol, commercial sulfuric acid.

купр/аммониевый *a.* cuprammonium; **—ат** *m.* cuprate; **—еин** *m.* cupreine.

купрей *m.* (mam.) kouprey (*Bos sauveli*).

купр/ен *m.* cuprene; **—еол** *m.* cupreol; **—ессоидный** *a.* cupressoid; **—и—** *prefix* cupri—, cupric; **—ин** *m.* cuprine; **—ит** *m.* (min.) cuprite, red copper ore.

купро— *prefix* cupr(o)— (copper, cuprous); **—адамит** *m.* (min.) cuproadamite; **—бисмутит** *m.* cuprobismuthite; **—деклуазит** *m.* cuprodescloizite.

купрокс *m.*, **—ный** *a.* (rad.) copper oxide rectifier; cuprous oxide; **—ный выпрямитель** copper oxide rectifier.

купро/магнезит *m.* (min.) cupromagnesite; **—марганец** *m.* (met.) cupromanganese; **—н** *m.* cupron, α-benzoinoxime; (elec.) cupron cell; **—никель** *m.* cupronickel (alloy); **—нин** *m.* cupronine; **—новый аккумулятор, —нэлемент** *m.*, cupron cell, copper oxide cell; **—отунит** *m.* (min.) cuproautunite; **—пирит** *m.* (min.) copper pyrites; **—плюмбит** *m.* (min.) coproplumbite; **—склодовскит** *m.* (min.) cuprosklodowskite; **—тунгстит** *m.* cuprotungstite; **—уранит** *m.* (min.) cuprouranite; **—хлорид** *m.* cuprous chloride; **—шеелит** *m.* (min.) cuproscheelite.

купул/а (anat.) cupula, cupule, cup; **—ярный** *a.* cupular.

купфер/меритоль *m.* a copper-calcium arsenate insecticide and fungicide; **—никель** *m.* (min.) copper nickel, niccolite.

купферовский *a.* Kupffer's (cells).

купфер/он *m.* cupfer(r)on; **—онат** *m.* cupferonate; **—штейн** *m.* (met.) copper matte.

купца *gen. of* **купец**.

купыр/ник *m.* (bot.) hedge parsley (*Torilis*); **—ь** *m.* chervil (*Anthriscus*).

купюра *f.* cut, abridgement; deletion; (com.) note, bond; denomination; bill (e.g., ten-dollar bill).

кура-араксинский *a.* (geog.) Kura-Arax.

курага *f.* dried apricots.

курай *m.* (bot.) Russian thistle (*Salsola ruthenica*).

курак *m.* cotton boll; **—осборник** *m.* cotton boll picker.

курант *m.* (paints) grinder.

куранты *pl.* chimes.

курар/е *n.* or *m.* curare; **—еподобный** *a.* curariform, curare-like; **—изация** *f.* curarization; **—ин** *m.* curarine.

куратор *m.* curator, custodian; chairman of sectional meeting at a congress; observing medical student.

курба *f.* (vet.) curb.

курбель *m.* knob.

курвиметр *m.* curvometer, map measurer.

курган *m.* burial mound; barrow, hill, mound, clamp, tumulus; **—ник** *m.* (orn.) burial mound buzzard (*Buteo*, spec. *B. rufinus*); **—ный** *a.* of **курган**.

курганский *a.* (geog.) Kurgan.

кургуз/ить *v.* curtail, cut back; **—ый** *a.* dock-tailed; too short and tight.

курдистанский *a.* (geog.) Kurdistan.

курдский *a.* (geog.) Kurd(ish).

курдю/к *m.* fat tail (of sheep); **—чный** *a.* fat-tail(ed); Kurduyk (fat).

курево *n.* smoke, haze; smoky fire; smoking tobacco; fumigant.

курейковый *a.* (geog.) Kureyka.

курение *n.* smoking, etc., see **курить**; fumigant.

кур/ёнок *m.* chick; **—ий** *see* **куриный**.

курень *m.* house, hut, booth.

курил/ка, —ьная *f.* smoking room; **—ьня** *f.* (opium) den.

курильский *a.* (geog.) Kuril(ian).

курильщ/ик *m.*, **—ица** *f.* smoker.

куриматовые *pl.* (ichth.) Curimatidae.

курин *m.* curine.

**кур
инский** *a.* (geog.) Kura.

курин/ые *pl.* gallinaceous birds; **—ый** *a.* gallinaceous; chicken, hen's; **—ая слепота** (med.) night blindness, nyctalopia; (bot.) Chelidonium.

курировать *v.* cure, treat.

курит/ельная *f.* smoking area or compartment; **—ельный** *a.* fumigating; smoking; **—ельное вещество** fumigant; **—ь** *v.* smoke, cure; fumigate; distil; **—ься** *v.* be smoked; give off fumes; appear, rise, swirl (of fog).

кури/ца *f.*, **—чий** *a.* hen, chicken.

курка *gen. of* **курок**.

куркасовое масло curcas oil.

курковые *pl.* (ichth.) Aluteridae.

курков/ый *a.* of **курок**; trigger (circuit); **к. механизм** hammer action; **—ая коробка** (torpedo) starting gear.

куркум/а *f.* (bot.) tumeric (*Curcuma*); **—ин** *m.*, **—овый жёлтый** curcumin, tumeric yellow; **—овый** *a.* tumeric, curcuma; curcumic (acid).

курлатиров/ание *n.* (paper) curling, etc., see *v.*; **—ать** *v.* curl, crepe, crinkle.

курлык/ать, —нуть *v.* (orn.) whoop, trumpet.

курмак *m.* (bot.) coarse-grain millet (*Echinochloa macrocarpa*); barnyard grass (*E. crus-galli*).

курнакит *m.* (min.) kurnakite.

курник *m.* chicken coop.

курной *a.* smoky.

курносый *a.* pug-nosed, snub-nosed.

курнуть *v.* inhale (smoke); take a puff.

куро/вод *m.* poultry man; **—водство** *n.*, **—водческий** *a.* poultry or chicken farming; **—ед** *m.* (herp.) Spilotes pullatus.

курок *m.* lever, trigger, cock, hammer (of gun); (ichth.) triggerfish (*Balistes*).

курол *m.* (orn.) cuckoo-roller (*Leptosomus*); **—ы** *pl.* Leptosomatidae.

куронгит *m.* (min.) coorongite.

куропат/ка *f.,* **—ковый** *a.* (orn.) partridge (*Perdix*); **белая к.** grouse (*Lagopus*); **—очка** *dim. of* **куропатка; —очья трава** (bot.) Dryas.

курорт *m.,* **—ный** *a.* health resort; **—ник** *m.* resort resident; **—ология, —отерапия** *f.* treatment at health resorts.

курослеп *m.* one of several yellow-flowered plants, spec. Ranunculus.

курочка *dim. of* **курица;** (orn.) crake (*Porzana*).

курри порошок curry powder.

Курроля соль Kurrol salt, potassium polyphosphate.

курс *m.* heading, course, direction; track, path; policy; (com.) rate of exchange; (educ.) course; **брать к. на** *v.* head for; **—ант** *m.,* **—антка** *f.,* **—антский** *a.* student; trainee; (mil.) cadet.

курсив *m.* italic type; italics; **выделять —ом, набирать —ом** *v.* italicize; **—ный** *a.* italic, italicized.

курсировать *v.* course, ply, run (between).

курск/ий *a.* (geog.) Kursk; Kura (river); **—ит** *m.* (min.) kurskite.

курсовка *f.* resort certificate.

курсо/вертикаль *m.* attitude and heading reference (system); **—вой** *a. of* **курс;** directional; azimuth (gyroscope); (ballistics) target (angle); (med.) protracted (treatment); **—глиссадный** *a.* (av.) course and glide; **—грамма** *f.* course recording; **—граф** *m.* avigraph, course recorder; **—прокладчик** *m.* course plotter.

курсор *m.* cursor; **—ный** *a.* cursory.

курсо/указатель *m.* (av.) position indicator; **—централь** *f.* heading reference.

куртаж *m.,* **—ный** *a.* (com.) brokerage.

куртина *f.* flower bed; grove (of trees).

куртка *f.* jacket.

куртовые *pl.* (ichth.) hump-heads (*Kurtidae*).

куртозис *m.* (stat.) kurtosis.

курточка *f.* jacket.

куртус *m.* (ichth.) hump-head (*Kurtus*); **—овые** *see* **куртовые.**

куртушибинский *a.* (geog.) Kurtushib(a).

куру *f.* (mam.) forest mouse (*Grammomys*).

курум *m.* stone stream, rock stream.

курупр *m.* administration of health resorts.

Курциуса реакция Curtius reaction.

курчав/иться *v.* curl; **—ка** *f.* (bot.) Atraphaxis; **—оволосистый** *a.* ulotrichous, curly-haired; **—олистный** *a.* curly leaved; **—ость** *f.* curliness; (phyt.) leaf curl; crimp (of wool); **—ый** *a.* curly; eriocomous, wooly-haired.

курчатовий *m.* kurtchatovium, Ku.

курчонок *m.* chick.

курчумский *a.* (geog.) Kurchum.

куршабский *a.* (geog.) Kurshab.

куры *pl. of* **курица.**

курьёз *m.* curiosity, curious phenomenon, oddity, strange thing; **—но** *adv.* curiously, in a strange way; **—ный** *a.* curious, strange, odd.

курьер *m.* messenger; **—ский** *a.* express.

курьинский *a.* (geog.) Kuria.

курья *f.* kurya (long narrow oxbow, detached from river at upper end).

курят/ина *f.* chicken (meat); **—ник** *m.* chicken coop; predator.

курящий *a.* smoking, fuming.

кус *see* **кусок; —ание** *n.* biting, etc., *see v.;* **—ать** *v.* bite; (ent.) sting; (orn.) peck; nibble; (frost) nip; (seasoning) be hot; **—ачка** *f.* (ichth.) spined loach (*Cobitis taenia*); **—ачки** *pl.* wire cutter, cutting pliers, nippers; **—ачки-плоскогубцы** *pl.* flatnose (cutting) pliers; **—ающий** *a.* biting, etc., *see v.;* pungent; **—ающийся** *a.* snapping (turtle).

кусинский *a.* (geog.) Kusa.

куск/и *pl. of* **кусок; —оватость** *f.* lumpiness; **—оватый, —овой** *a.* lump(y).

кусковский *a.* (geog.) Kuskovo.

куско/гигрин *m.* cuscohygrine; **—нидин;** **—нин** *m.* cusconidine; **—нин** *m.* cusconine.

кускус *m.* (mam.) cuscus (*Phalanger*).

кускута *f.* seed grader; (bot.) Cuscuta.

куснуть *v.* take a bite.

кус/ок *m.* piece, lump, block, chunk fragment; length, segment; cut, slice; **—камн, в —ках** in pieces, lumpy; **в —ке** piece (dyed); **в —ки** piecemeal; **из одного —ка** one-piece; **на —ки** to pieces, apart; **одним —ком** in block, whole; **по —кам** piece by piece, piecemeal; **—очек** *dim. of* **кусок;** fragment; (med.) section.

кусочн/о *adv.* piecewise; sectionally; **к.-гладкий** *a.* (math.) piecewise smooth; **к.-линейный** *a.* piecewise-linear; **к.-непрерывный** *a.* piecewise continuous; **к.-постоянный** *a.* piecewise constant; **—ый** *a. of* **кусок;** piecewise; sectional.

куспар/идин *m.* cusparidine; **—ин** *m.* cusparine; **кора —ия** cusparia bark, angostura bark.

куспид/ария *f.* (mal.) Cuspidaria; **—ин** *m.* cuspidine.

куссо *n.,* **цветы к.** kousso.

куст *m.* bush, shrub; bunch, cluster, group; section; pocket (of ore); battery (of wells); **отводка —ом** (hort.) layer(ing).

кустанайский *a.* (geog.) Kustanai.

кустарн/ик *m.* bush, shrub(bery); brushwood, scrub, undergrowth, thicket; (bot.) frutex; **—ики** *pl.* shrubbery; **—иковый** *a.* bushy, shrubby, fruticose; dwarf (tree); brush (fire); **—иковый плуг** ripper; **—иковые птицы** (orn.) Atrichornithidae; **—иковые растения** shrubs, bushes; **—ица** *f.* (orn.) shrub thrush (*Garrulax*); **—ицы** *pl.* (orn.) Timaliidae.

кустар/ничать *v.* do handicraft work at home; use primitive methods; **—ничек** *dim of* **кустарник; —ничество** *n.* handicrafts; amateurish work; (hort.) shrub culture; **—ничковый** *a.* dwarf-shrub, low-bush; **—ный** *a.* homemade, handicraft; cottage (industry); primitive, amateurish; (bot.) *see* **кустарниковый; —щина** *f.* haphazard work; **—в** *m.* handicraftsman.

куст/ик *dim. of* **куст;** (bot.) fruticulus; **—истость** *f.* bushiness; (bot.) tillering capacity, layering capacity; **—истый** *a.* fruticulose, bushy, shrubby; **—иться** *v.* bush (out); (bot.) tiller; cluster; **—ование** *n.* (biol.) tuft formation; (elec.) interconnection; **—ованный** *a.* interconnected; (tel.) bank; **—оватый** *a.* shrubby, bushy, tufted; **—овой** *a. of* **куст;** bushy, tuft, bunch (grasses); data-collecting (station); cluster, multiple (drilling); **—оизмельчитель** *m.* scrub slasher; **—орез** *m.* scrub or brush cutter; **—охвостый** *a.* bushy-tailed.

кустпром *m.* cottage industry.

кусцы *see* **кусачки.**

кутан *m.* sheep pen, sheep fold.

кут/ан(н)ый *a.* wrapped (up), muffled; **—ать** *v.* wrap (up) muffle.

кутема (ichth.) grayling (*Thymallus t.*).

кутец *m.* (fishing) pot (of fyke net).

кутиа *f.* (mam.) agouti (*Dasyprocta aguti*).

кутикул/а *f.* (biol.) cuticula, cuticle; **—яризация** *f.* (med.) cuticularization; **—ярный** *a.* cuticular.

кут/ин *m.* cutin; **—инизация** *f.* (cyt.) cutinization, cutin formation; **—иновый** *a.* cutin; cutic (acid); **—иреакция** *f.* (med.) cutireaction, cutaneous reaction; **—ис** *m.* (anat.) cutis, dermis.

кутка *gen. of* **куток.**

куткутия *f.* pufferfish (*Tetraodon cutcutia*).

куток *m.* (min.) heel; cod end (of trawl).

кутора *f.*, **водяная к.** (mam.) water shrew (*Neomys*, spec. *N. fodiens*).

кутр/а *f.*, **—овый** *a.* (bot.) Indian hemp (*Apocynum*); **—овые** *pl.* Apocynaceae.

куттер *m.* (food) chopper, mincer; (naut.) cutter; **к.-мешалка** *m.* mincer and blender.

кутум *m.* (ichth.) roach (*Rutilus frisii kutum*); ide (*Leuciscus idus*).

куфия *f.* (herp.) Trimeresurus.

куфта *f.* (text.) cut; reel; knot of yarn.

кух/арка *f.*, **—арь** *m.* cook; **—ить, —ничать** *v.* (be a) cook.

кухлянка *f.* deer-skin shirt.

кух/ня *f.* kitchen; (naut.) galley; cooking, cuisine; **—онный** *a.* kitchen, cooking; **—онька** *dim. of* **кухня.**

кухтыль *m.* large net float.

куцак *m.* (ichth.) Black Sea shad (*Alosa*).

куцый *a.* (too) short, stumpy.

куч/а *f.* pile, heap, mass, cluster, congestion, congregation, group, clump; dump; (ant) hill; **в —е** in a pile, collectively, as a group; **обжиг в —ах** heap roasting; **—евое облако** cumulus; **—еводождевое облако** cumulonimbus; **—еобразный** *a.* cumuliform (cloud); **—ек** *gen. pl. of* **кучка.**

кучер *m.*, **—ский** *a.* driver, teamster.

кучеряв/иться *v.* curl; **—ый** *a.* curly.

кучерявчик *m.* (geol.) underclay.

кучеукладчик *m.* stacker.

кучиевые *pl.* (ichth.) Amphipnoidae.

кучина *f.* (bot.) mahaleb (*Prunus mahaleb*).

кучинский *a.* (geog.) Kuchino.

кучиться *v.* cluster, crowd (together).

кучичингский *a.* (geol.) Coutchiching.

кучия *f.* (ichth.) cuchia (*Amphipnous*, spec. *A. cuchia*).

куч/ка *dim. of* **куча**; handful; group (of people): (anat.) cumulus; (bot.) sorus; **—ной** *a.* heap, mound; **—ность** *f.* density, compactness, concentration; close grouping, close planting; cluster; (art.) accuracy; **—ный** *a.* dense, compact, concentrated; (petr.) glomeroplasmatic.

кучукский *a.* (geog.) Kuchuk.

кучурганский *a.* (geog.) Kuchurgan.

кушак *m.* belt, girdle, sash.

куш/анье *n.* food, dish; **—ать** *v.* eat.

кушетка *f.* couch.

Кушинга синдром (med.) Cushing's disease.

кушкинский *a.* (geog.) Kushka.

кушмурунский *a.* (geog.) Kushmurun.

кущ/а *f.* crown (of tree); foliage; **—ение** *n.* tillering, bushing (out); layering.

куэпия *f.* (bot.) Couepia.

куэст/а *f.*, **—овый** *a.* (geol.) cuesta.

кують *pr. 3 pl. of* **ковать.**

кх, кХ *abbr.* (**килоикс**) kilo-X (1.00202 Å.).

КЦ *abbr.* (**кислотоупорный цемент**) acid-resistant cement; **КЦВ** *abbr.* (**кислотоупорный и водонепроницаемый цемент**) acid-resistant and waterproof cement.

к-ция *abbr.* (**концентрация**) concentration.

КЧ *abbr.* (**ковкий чугун**) wrought iron; (**частотный корректор**) frequency corrector; (**чёрный карбид кремния**) black silicon carbide; **к/ч** (**километров в час**) kilometers per hour; **к.ч.** (**координационное число**) coordination number; (**кислотное число**) acid number.

КШ *abbr.* (**кольцо и шар**) ring and ball (method).

кызасский *a.* (geog.) Kyzas.

кызыл— *prefix* (geog.) Kyzyl, Kizil; **—кумский** *a.* Kyzyl-Kum; **—суский** *a.* Kyzylsu.

кыновский *a.* (geog.) Kyn.

кырлык *m.* (bot.) Tartary buckwheat (*Polygonum tataricum*).

кыспак *m.* kyspak (isolated table mountain made up of sandstones).

кыштымит *m.* (petr.) kyschtymite.

Кьел/даля колба Kjeldahl flask.

Кьёлен (geog.) Kjølen Mountains.

Кьеллина печь (met.) Kjellin furnace.

кьельдализация *f.* Kjeldalization.

к.э. *abbr.* (**крахмальный эквивалент**) starch equivalent; (**каломельный электрод**) calomel electrode.

КЭАМ *abbr.* (**концентрированная эмульсия антраценого масла**) Carbolineum, concentrated emulsion of anthracene oil.

кэб *m.* cab.

Кэв *abbr.* (**килоэлектрон-вольт**) kiloelectron volt, keV.

КЭД *abbr.* (**кожная эритемная доза**) erythema dose (of radiation).

кэк *m.*, **—и** *pl.* (sinter) cake.

к. экв. *abbr.* (**крахмальный эквивалент**) starch equivalent.

КЭМС *abbr.* (**коэффициент электромеханической связи**) coefficient of electromechanical coupling.

КЭП *abbr.* (**катэлектронический потенциал**) cat-electronic potential.

кэпрок *m.* (min.) cap rock.

к-эрг *abbr.* (**килоэрг**) kilo-erg.

кэш *m.* cache; **—ирование** *n.* caching; **—ировать** *v.* cache.

кэшью *m.* cashew nut.

кюбель *m.* (excavator) bucket.

кювел/яж *m.*, **—яция** *f.* (eng., min.) tubbing, lining.

кювет *m.* (drainage) ditch, gutter; cell, vessel; **—(к)а** *f.* cell, container, vessel, tank; bulb; (phot.) tray; (glass) cuvette; **—одержатель** *m.* cuvette holder; **—окопатель** *m.* ditch digger.

кювьер/а *f.* (bot.) Cuviera; **—овый** *a.* Cuvier's (ducts); Cuvierian (organs).

кюльдо— *see* **кульдо—.**

кюльшиф *m.* (brewing) cooler.

кюммель *m.* kümmel (liqueur).

Кюммеля болезнь (med.) Kümmell's disease, spondylitis.

кюмпель-пресс *m.* circular flanging press.

кюрасао *n.* curacao.

кюрет/аж *m.* (med.) curettage; **—ка** *f.* curet.

кюри *m.* curie, Curie unit (of radioactivity); **К. температура, К. точка** Curie point; **—грамма** *f.* curiegram; **—граф** *m.* curiegraph; **—й** *m.* curium, Cm; **—т** *m.* (min.) curite; **—терапия** *f.* Curie therapy, radium therapy; **к.-эквивалент** *m.* curie-equivalent.

кяль *m.* castrated buffalo.

кяр(г)из *m.* kyariz (underground water-collecting gallery).

Л

л *abbr.* (**литр**) liter; **л.** (**левый**) left; (**люмен**) lumen, lm; **Л.** (**лейкоциты**) leucocytes.

ЛА *abbr.* (**летательный аппарат**) aircraft.

лаб. *abbr.* (**лаборатория, лабораторный**).

лабаз *m.* granary; feed store; (fodder) shed; —**ник** *m.* (bot.) Filipendula.

лабария *f.* (herp.) fer de lance (*Bothrops atrox*).

лабарраковый *a.* Labarraque (solution).

лабео *m.* (ichth.) Labeo.

лабиал/изация *f.* (phonetics) labialization; —**ьный** *a.* (anat.) labial.

лабильн/ость *f.,* —**ое состояние** lability, labile state; —**ый** *a.* labile, unstable.

лабинский *a.* (geog.) Laba.

лабио— *prefix* (anat.) labio—, lip; —**ментальный** *a.* labiomental.

лабиринт *m.* labyrinth, maze; (mach.) labyrinth (packing); —**ит** *m.* (med.) labyrinthitis; —**ный, —овый** *a.* labyrinth(ine); —**овые** *pl.* (ichth.) Anabantidae; —**одонт** *m.* (pal.) labyrinthodont; —**ообразный** *a.* labyrinthiform.

лабор/ант *m.* laboratory worker or assistant; research man; —**атория** *f.* laboratory; facility; (phot.) darkroom; —**аторный** *a.* laboratory, bench (testing).

лабрадор *m.* (min.) labrador(ite); —**ит** *m.,* —**овая порода** (petr.) labradorite; —**овый, —ский** *a.* (geog.) Labrador.

лабурнин *m.* laburnine.

лабфермент *m.* chymosin, rennin.

лав/а *f.* (geol.) lava; (min.) longwall, face; **волнистая л.** ropy lava, pahoehoe; **выемка** —**ами** longwall system; **поток** —**ы** lava flow; **стекловидная л.** volcanic glass, obsidian.

Лаваля сопло Laval's nozzle.

лаванд/а *f.,* —**ный, —овый** *a.* (bot.) lavender (*Lavandula*).

лава-этаж *f.* (min.) horizon face.

лавдан *see* **ладан.**

лавендулин *m.* lavendulin.

лавенит *m.* (min.) lâvenite.

лавер *m.* (sugar) washer.

Лавеса фазы (met.) Laves phases.

лавзон — *see* **лавсон—.**

лавин/а *f.* avalanche; —**ный** *a.* avalanche; cumulative (ionization); cascade (theory); —**ообразный** *a.* avalanche-like; —**ообразование** *n.* avalanching.

лавировать *v.* maneuver; (naut.) tack, put about, shift one's course.

лавис *m.* (typ.) copperplate (engraving).

лавка *f.* store, shop; bench.

лавливать *see* **ловить.**

лаво— *prefix,* —**вый** *a.* (geol.) lava, lav(at)ic.

лавок *gen. pl. of* **лавка.**

лаво/пад *m.* lava cascade; —**подобный** *a.* lava-like, lav(at)ic.

лавоч/ка *dim. of* **лавка;** bench; —**ник** *m.* retail merchant; —**ный** *a.* bench.

лавр *m.* (bot.) laurel (*Laurus*); *prefix, see also* **лаур—.**

лаврак *m.* (ichth.) bass (*Morone,* spec. *M. labrax; Roccus saxatilis*).

лаврен/тийский, —тьевский *a.* (geog.; geol.) Laurentian; —**ций** *m.* lawrencium, Lr.

лавро/вишенник *m.,* —**вишневый** *a.,* —**вишня** *f.* (bot.), cherry laurel (*Laurocerasus*); —**вые** *pl.* laurel family (*Lauraceae*); —**вый** *a.* laurel; lauric; *see also under* **лауриновый;** —**листный** *a.* laurel-leaved, laurifolious.

LAWSAN *m.* Lavsan (polyethylene terephthalate fiber).

лавсон/ит *m.* (min.) lawsonite; —**ия** *f.* henna plant (*Lawsonia inermis* or *alba*).

Лавуазье Lavoisier (French chemist).

лаг *m.* (naut.) log; recorder; broadside; lag; **стать —ом** *v.* turn broadside.

лага *f.* sleeper; bolster.

лаггар *m.* (orn.) laggar (*Falco jugger*).

лагер *m.* (geod.) bearing.

лагер/ный *a.,* —**ь** *m.* camp (site); —**ная стоянка** camp site.

лаглинь *m.* (naut.) log line.

лаго/зерис *m.* (bot.) Lagoseris; —**трикс** *m.* (mam.) wooly monkey (*Lagothrix*); —**хилин** *m.* lagochilin; —**хилус** *m.* (bot.) Lagochilus.

лагранж/евый *a.,* —**иан** *m.* (math.) Lagrangian.

лагун *m.* (naut.) water tank.

лагун/а *f.,* —**ный** *a.* lagoon, pool.

лагута *f.* (bot.) cowpea (*Vigna sinensis*).

лаг(-)фаза *f.* lag phase, lag period.

лад *m.* harmony, concord; way, manner, style, type; (music) stop, fret; **идти на л.** *v.* go well; **не в —у, не в —ах** in disagreement (with), at variance, at odds.

ладакский *a.* (geog.) Ladak(h).

ладан *m.,* —**ный** *a.* la(b)danum; **росный л.** gum benzoin; —**ник** *m.* rock rose (*Cistus*); —**никовые** *pl.* Cistaceae.

ладен *sh. m. of* **ладный.**

ладинский век (geol.) Ladinian stage.

лад/ить *v.* agree, be on good terms (with); fit, adapt, adjust; —**иться** *v.* go well, succeed; —**но** *adv.* well, in concord; successfully; all right, very well!; —**ный** *a.* harmonious, in accord, on good terms; in tune; suitable, good.

ладовый *a. of* **лад.**

ладожск/ий *a.* (geog.) Ladoga; —**ие свиты** (geol.) Ladogian stage.

ладо/нно— *prefix* (anat.) palmo—; —**нный** *a.* palm(ar), volar; —**нчатый** *a.* (biol.) palmate; —**нь** *f.* palm, vola; —**ши** *pl.* palms.

ладье— *prefix* cymbi—, cymbo—, scaph(o)— (boat); —**видный, —образный** *a.* keel-shaped, carinate; boat-shaped, scaphoid; cymbiform; (anat.) navicular; —**листный** *a.* scaphoid-leaved; —**ногие** *pl.* (mal.) Scaphopoda; —**образная складка** (geol.) carinate fold, isoclinal fold.

ладья *f.* (anat.) navicular; scapha.

ладьян *m.* (bot.) Corallorhiza.

лаек *gen. pl. of* **лайка.**

лает *pr. 3 sing. of* **лаять.**

лаж *m.* (currency exchange) agio.

лаз *m.* manhole; crawlway; —**анье** *n.* climbing.

лазаревый *a.* (geog.) Lazarev.

лазарет *m.,* —**ный** *a.* hospital, infirmary; **плавучий л.** hospital ship.

лаз/ательный, —ающий *a.* climbing; scansorial (feet); —**ать** *v.* climb, crawl; —**ейка** *f.* manhole; gap, opening.

лазер *m.,* —**ный** *a.* (phys.) laser, optical maser; **генерация в —е** lasing; **л.-дальномер** *m.* laser range finder; —**ный локатор** laser radar, lidar.

лазея *see* **лазейка.**

лазий *m.* (ent.) Lasius.

лазить *v.* climb; clamber; scale; get into; **л. вверх** ascend; **л. вниз** descend.

лаз/оревка *f.* (orn.) blue tit (*Parus,* spec. *P. caeruleus*); —**оревый** *see* **лазурный;** —**оревый шпат, —улит** *m.* (min.) lazulite, azure spar; —**улитовый** *a.* lazulitic.

лазур/евый see **лазурный; л. камень, —ик** m. (min.) azure stone, lapis lazuli; **—ит** m. lazurite; **—ник** m. (bot.) laserwort (*Laserpitium*); Laser; **—ный** a., **—ь** f. azure, sky blue; **Л-ный берег** (geog.) French Riviera; **берлинская —ь** Prussian blue.

лазящ/ие pl. scansorial birds; **—ий** a. scansorial, climbing, scandent.

лай m. bark(ing).

лайда f. laida (treeless part of a forest and tundra landscape; low seacoast plain dissected by tortuous rills).

лайк/а f., **—овый** a. kid (leather); Husky (dog).

лайлинский a. (geog.) Laila.

лайм m. (bot.) lime (*Citrus aurantifolia*).

лайма f. lima bean (*Phaseolus lunatus*).

лаймановский a. Lyman.

лайнер m. liner.

лайский a. (geog.) Laya.

ЛАК abbr. (**лаборатория акустического каротажа**) acoustic logging laboratory.

лак m. lac; lake; varnish; lacquer.

лак/ать v. lap (up), drink; lick; **—ающий** a. lapping, etc., see v.

лак-дей m. lac dye.

лакедра f. (ichth.) amberjack (*Seriola*).

лакиров/альный a., **—ание** n. lacquering; varnishing; **—анный** a. lacquered; varnished; patent (leather); **—ать** v. lacquer; varnish; **—ка** f., **—очный** a. see **лакирование.**

лакка f. lacca (gum), lac; **—за** f. laccase; **—иновый** a. lacca(in)ic (acid).

лакколит m. (geol.) laccolith, laccolite.

лак-лак m. lac lake.

лакмоид m. lacmoid, resorcinol blue.

лакмус m., **—овый** a. litmus.

лакнуть see **лакать.**

лако/бумага f. varnished paper; **—вар** m. varnish boiler; **—варка** f. varnish or lacquer boiling room.

лаков/ый a. lacquer(ed); varnish(ed); patent (leather); **—ое дерево** lac tree; spec. lacquer tree (*Rhus vernicifera*).

лако/ёмкость f. varnish need; **—красочный** a. paint and varnish; **—лента** f. varnished (insulation) tape.

лаком/ство n. delicacies; **—ый** a. tasty.

лаконич/еский, —ный a. laconic, brief, concise.

лако/нос m., **—носка** f. (bot.) Phytolacca; **—носные, —носовые** pl. Pytolaccaceae; **—носный** a. lacciferous; **—образный** a. varnish-like; **—образование** n. varnish or lacquer formation; varnishing; (oils) lacquer deposition; **—образующий** a. varnish or lacquer-forming; **—пленочный** a. lacquer-film.

лак-опоек m. patent calf leather.

лако/стеклоткань f. varnished glass cloth; **—тканевый** a. cambric (insulation); **—тканевая лента** varnished tape; **—ткань** f. varnished cambric (or fabric).

лакрим/альный a. lacrimal, tear; **—атор** m. lacrimator; **—аторный, —огенный** a. lacrimatory, tear-producing; **—ация** f. lacrimation.

лакри/ца f., **—чник** m., **—чный** a. (bot.) licorice (*Glycyrrhiza glabra*).

лакруазит m. (min.) lacroixite.

лаксативное средство laxative.

лаксит m. laxite, fragmental rocks.

лаксманнит m. (min.) laxmannite.

лакт— prefix lact(o)— (milk); **—аза** f. lactase; **—альбумин** m. lactalbumin; **—амид** m. lactam, lactan; **—амид** m. lactamide, 2-hydroxypropanamide; **—ан** see **лактам; —ар(ий)** m. whitefish (*Lactarius l.*);

—ариновый a. lactarinic (acid); **—аровые** pl. (ichth.) Lactariidae; **—аровый** a. lactaric (acid); **—аррея** see **лакторея; —ат** m. lactate; **—ационный** a. lactation(al), lactiferous; **—ация** f. lactation; **—ид** m. lactide; **—икодегидрогеназа** f. lactate dehydrogenase, LDH; **—ил** m. lactyl; **—илмочевина** f. lactylurea; **—иловый** a. lactylic (acid); **—им** m. lactim; **—ирующий** a. lactating, milking.

лакто— prefix lact(o)— (milk); **—альбумин** m. lactalbumin; **—бацилла** f. lactobacillus; **—бациллин** m. lactobacillin; **—бионовый** a. lactobionic (acid); **—бутирометр** m. lactobutyrometer; **—генный** a. lactogenic; **—глобулин** m. lactoglobulin; **—денсиметр** m. lactometer; **—за** f. lactose, milk sugar; **—зурия** f. (med.) lactosuria; **—ил** m. lactoyl; **—л** m. lactol, naphthyl lactate; **—лит** m. lactolite (a casein plastic); **—метр** m. lactometer; **—н** m. lactone; **—наза** f. lactonase; **—нитрил** m. lactonitrile; **—новая связь** lactonic linkage; **—нокислота** f. lactonic acid; **—пероксидаза** f. lactoperoxidase; **—рея** f. (med.) (ga)lactorrhea; **—скоп** m. lactoscope; **—тропин** m. lactotropin, prolactin; **—тропный** a. lactotropic; **—флавин** m. lactoflavine, riboflavine, vitamin B$_2$.

лакту/карий m. lactucarium (juice of *Lactuca virosa*); **—кон, —церол** m. lactucon, lactucerin, taraxasterol acetate; **—цин** m. lactucin.

лакуна f. lacuna, gap; **—рный** a. lacunar.

лакфиоль m. (bot.) Cheiranthus.

лакц/ерол m. laccerol; **—ин** m. laccin; **—иновый** a. laccinic (acid).

лак-шевро m. patent kid (leather).

Лаланда злемент (elec.) Lalande cell.

лаллеманция f. (bot.) Lallemantia.

лало— prefix lal(o)—(speech; babbling); **—патия** f. lalopathy, speech disorder.

лама f. (mam.) llama (*Lama glama*).

ламантин m. (mam.) manatee (*Trichechus*); **—овые, —ы** pl. Trichechidae.

Ла-манча, Ламанш (geog.) English Channel.

ламаркизм m. (biol.) Lamarck's theory.

ламбд/а f. lambda; **—овидный** a. lamboid.

ламберт m. lambert (unit of brightness); **—ит** m. (min.) lambertite, uranophane; **—овский** a. Lambert's, Lambertian.

ламел/ла f. lamella; **—либранхиаты** pl. (mal.) lamel-libranchs; **—лярииды** pl. Lamellari(i)dae; **—лярный, —ьный** a. lamellar, lamellate, scale-like; **—ь** m. lamella, lamina; (elec.) commutator segment, bar, strip; (diaphragm) blade; (weaving) dropper, drop wire.

лами/ация f. (bot.) lamiation; **—на** f. lamina; **—нальный** see **ламинарный.**

ламинар/ан see **ламинарин; —иевые, —ии** pl. (bot.) Laminariaceae; **—иевый** a. laminarian; **—изация** f. laminarization; **—ин** m. laminarin; **—ия** f. (bot.) Laminaria; **—ность** f. laminarity; **—ный** a. laminar, laminal; **—ный поток, —ное движение, —ное течение** laminar flow, streamline flow; **—овый** a. laminaric (acid).

ламин/ация f., **—ирование** n. lamination; **—ированный** a. laminated, laminary, lamellar; **—ировать** v. laminate.

лам/ия f. (bot.) lamies; **—новые** pl. (ichth.) mackerel sharks (*Lamnidae*).

Ламонта закон (phys.) Lamont's law.

лампа f. lamp, light; (elec.) bulb; (rad.) tube; **л.-вспышка** f. (phot.) flash (bulb); **—дит** m. (min.) lampadite; **л.-желудь** f. acorn tube; **л.-малютка** f. miniature tube; **л.-молния** f. a very bright kerosene lamp;

—никт *m.* (ichth.) Lampanyctus; **л.-преобразова-тель** *m.* converter-tube; **—ра** *f.* lampara net; **л.-фара** *f.* floodlight.

ламpetra *f.* (ichth.) lamperon (*Lampetra*).

лампион *m.* lantern.

лампов/ая *f.* (min.) lamp room; **—щик** *m.* lamp man; lamp maker; **—ый** *a. of* **лампа**; vacuum-tube (potentiometer); **—ая копоть, —ая сажа, —ая чернь** lampblack; **—ое стекло** lamp chimney.

лампо/вынииматель *m.* lamp or tube extractor; **—держатель** *m.* lamp or tube holder; **—испытатель** *m.* tube tester; **—чка** *dim. of* **лампа**; pilot light.

ламп/ридовые *pl.* (ichth.) opahs [*Lamprid(id)ae*]; **—рофир** *m.* (petr.) lamprophyre; **—силин** *m.* (mal.) Lampsilis.

ланаркит *m.* (min.) lanarkite.

ланатозид *m.* lanatoside.

ланациловый *a.* lanacyl (violet).

ланберийский *a.* (geol.) Llanberis.

ланг/ас *m.* (bot.) Languas; **—бейнит** *m.* (min.) langbeinite; **—ергансовый** *a.* (anat.) Langerhans (islets); **—ит** *m.* (min.) langite.

лангобардский *a.* (geog.) Lombard(ic).

лангур *m.* (mam.) langur (*Presbytis*, spec. *P. entellus*).

лангуст *m.,* **—а** *f.* (crust.) spiny lobster (*Palinurus vulgaris*).

ландак *m.* (mam.) porcupine (*Thecurus*).

Ланде множитель (phys.) Lande (splitting) factor, g-factor.

ландкарт/а *f.* map; **—ообразный** *a.* maplike.

ландоверский *a.* (geol.) Llandovery.

Ландольта реакция Landolt's reaction.

ландольфия *f.* (bot.) Landolphia.

ландшафт *m.,* **—ный** *a.* landscape, topography, country; district, region; **уход за —ом** landscape maintenance.

ланды *pl.* (bot.) landes, heath.

ландыш *m.,* **—евый** *a.* (bot.) lily of the valley (*Convallaria*).

Ланжевена ион Langevin ion.

лан/и *gen., pl., etc. of* **лань**; **—ка** *f.* doe.

ланкаширский *a.* (geog.) Lancashire.

лано/лин *m.,* **—линовый** *a.* lanolin, hydrous wool fat; **—стерин** *m.* lanosterol.

лансфордит *m.* (min.) lansfordite.

лантан *m.* lanthanum, La; **—иды** *pl.* lanthanides; **—ит** *m.* (min.) lanthanite; **—овый** *a. of* **лантан**; (med.) lanthanic, symptom-free; **—оид** *m.* lanthanoid, *formerly* lanthanide.

лант/ионин *m.* lanthionine; **—опин** *m.* lanthopine, lantol.

лануго *n.* (anat.) lanugo, down.

ланцет *m.* (med.) lancet; **—ник** *m.* (zool.) lancelet; (ichth.) lancet (*Branchiostoma*); **—ники** *pl.* Branchiostomidae; **—но—** *prefix,* **—ный** *a.* lancet; lanceolate; **—овидный** *a.* lanceolate, lance-like; **—олистный** *a.* (bot.) lancifolious; **—онос** *m.* (mam.) mouse-tailed bat (*Rhinopoma*); **—оносы** *pl.* Rhinopomidae.

лань *f.* (mam.) fallow deer (*Dama d.*)

лап/а *f.* foot, paw; dovetail, tenon; lug, boss, claw; clamp, clutch, grip; leg (of bit); flange, lap (of slide valve); (cylinder) base; tine, tooth (of cultivator); fluke (of anchor); shank, share, blade; (cultivator) shovel, sweep; (anat.) pes, foot; (zool.) pad; (bot.) long-stemmed leaf; evergreen branch; **л.-сковородень** dovetail; **сборка в —у** dovetailing.

лапаро— *prefix* (med.) lapar(o)— (loin, flank, abdominal wall); **—томия** *f.* laparotomy, abdominal section.

лапа/тин *m.* lapathin; **—ховая кислота, —хол** lapachoic acid, lapachol.

лапач *m.* (ichth.) mullet (*Mugil auratus*).

лапилли *pl.* (geol.) lapilli (pieces of lava).

лапина *f.* (bot.) wing nut (*Pterocarya*).

лапингование *see* **лаппингование.**

лапи *see* **ляпис.**

лапистый *a.* big-pawed; paw-like (leaf).

лапис *see* **ляпис.**

лапк/а *f. dim. of* **лапа**; boss, lug, pawl; tongue, tenon; grip; draw vise, eccentric clamp or grip, toggle; tooth (of cultivator); (anat.) carpus, wrist; (ent.) tarsus; **спинная л.** (mal.) notopodium; **—и** *pl.* draw tongs; (typ.) double quotes.

Лапландия (geog.) Lapland.

лапландский *a.* Lapland(ian), Lappish.

Лапласа преобразование (math.) Laplace transform.

лаплас/иан *m.* (math.) Laplacian (operator); (nucl.) buckling; **—овский** *a.* Laplace, Laplacian.

лаплатский *a.* (geog.) La Plata.

лапник *m.* (hort.) brushwood mulch.

лапо/видный, —образный *a.* paw-shaped; **—вый** *a. of* **лапа.**

лапорты *pl.* doors (of coke oven).

лаппаконитин *m.* lappaconitine.

лаппинг/ование *n.* lapping (process); **—овать** *v.* lap; **—станок** *m.* lapping machine.

лапсердак *m.* (text.) gabardine.

Лаптевых море (geog.) Laptev Sea.

лапундер *m.* (mam.) Macaca nemestrina.

лапчат/ка *f.* (bot.) cinquefoil (*Potentilla*); **—оног** *m.* (orn.) finfoot (*Heliornis*); **—оногие** *pl.* Heliornithidae; **—ый** *a.* palmate, paw-shaped; (bot.) digitate; (zool.) web-footed; tooth (harrow).

лапш/а *f.* noodles; **—аной** *a.* noodle; **л.-рыба** *f.* (ichth.) glass fish (*Salangichthys microdon*); **л.-рыбы** *pl.* Salangidae; **—евник, —енник** *m.* noodle dish; **—ерезка** *f.* noodle cutter; **—овый** *a.* noodle.

лар *m.* (mam.) lar gibbon (*Hylobates lar*).

ларамийский *a.* (geol.) Laramian.

ларв/альный *a.* larval; **—ицид** *m.,* **—ицидный** *a.* larvicide; **—отрема** trematode larva.

ларга *f.* (mam.) seal (*Phoca vitulina largha*).

лардит *m.* (min.) lardite, agalmatolite.

лар/евой *a.* chest, bin; **—ёк** *m.* stall; **—ец** *m.* small chest, trunk; **—ёчный** *a. of* **ларёк, ларь.**

лариксин *m.,* **—овая кислота** larixine, larixinic acid.

ларинг/ит *m.* (med.) laryngitis; **—о—** *prefix* laryng(o)-(larynx); **—ология** *f.* laryngology; **—оскоп** *m.* laryngoscope; **—отрахеальный** *a.* (anat.) laryngotracheal; **—офон** *m.* laryngophone, throat microphone.

ларицин *m.* laricin, coniferin.

ларич *m.* (ichth.) immature mullet.

ларморовский *a.* (phys.) Larmor.

ларнит *m.* (min.) larnite.

лар/чик *dim. of* **ларь; —ь** *m.* bin, bunker, chest; hopper; pit, cistern; booth, stall; (ore) pocket.

ласк/а *f.* caress, kindness; (mach.) lap, scarf; (mam.) weasel (*Mustela,* spec. *M. nivalis*); **сваривать в —у** *v.* lap-weld; **л.-рыба** *f.* weaselfish (*Brotula*); **—ательный** *a.* tender; (pet) name; **—ать** *v.* caress, pet, fondle.

ласкир/ка, —ь *f.* (ichth.) bream.

лас/ковый *a. of* **ласка**; affectionate; **—ок** *gen. pl. of* **ласка.**

ласт *m.* (biol.) pinna, fin; flipper; paddle; (naut.) unit load.

ластик *m.,* **—овый** *a.* eraser; (text.) ribbed goods, lasting; elastic.

ластичная игла dial needle.

ласто/вень *m.* (bot.) Asclepias; Vincetoxicum; Anti-toxicum; —**видный** *a.* pinniform, fin-shaped; —**вица** *f.* gore; (bot.) celandine (*Chelidonium majus*); —**вневые** *pl.* milkweed family (*Asclepiadaceae*); —**вник** *m.* Cynanchum; —**ногие** *pl.* (mam.) pinnipeds; —**ногий** *a.* pinniped(ian), fin-footed; —**образный** *see* **ластовидный;** —**хвост** *m.* (herp.) Hydrophis.

ласточ/ка *f.* (orn.) swallow (*Hirundo*); **морская л.** damsel-fish (*Chromis c.*); **соединение в —ку** dovetailing; **л.-касатка** *f.* barn swallow; —**ки** *pl.* Hirundinidae; —**кин хвост** swallowtail, dovetail (joint); (rolling) fishtails; (min.) swallowtail crystal; —**ковые** *pl.* (orn.) Hirundinidae; —**ник** *m.* (bot.) Asclepias.

лат. *abbr.* (**латвийский; латинский**).

лата *see* **латина.**

латания *f.* (bot.) Latania.

лат/ан(н)ый *a.* patched; —**ать** *v.* patch, mend.

латвийский *a.* Latvian; **Латвия** Latvia.

ЛатвССР *abbr.* (**Латвийская Советская Социалистическая Республика**) Latvian Soviet Socialist Republic.

латекс *m.,* —**ный** *a.* latex; —**оподобный** *a.* latex-like, latex.

латен/сификация *f.* (phot.) latensification, latent-image intensification; —**тность** *f.* latency; quiescence; dormancy; abeyance; —**тный** *a.* latent; quiescent; dormant; in abeyance.

латеральный *a.* lateral.

латерит *m.* (geol.) laterite; —**изация** *f.* lateritization; —**изированные породы** laterites; —**иин** *m.* lateritiin (antibiotic); —**ный** *a.,* —**овый** *a.* lateritic.

латеро—_prefix_ (anat.) latero—[lateral(ly); to one side]; —**спорин** *m.* laterosporin (antibiotic).

лат/ес *m.* (ichth.) perch (*Lates calcarifer*); —**илус** *m.* Latilus; —**имериевые** *pl.,* —**меровые** *pl.* Latimeriidae; —**имерия** *f.* Latimeria, spec. L. chalumnae.

латина *f.* lath, batten.

латин/ица *f.* Roman type; —**оамериканский** *a.* Latin-American; —**ский** *a.* Latin.

латит *m.* (petr.) latite.

латка *f.* patch, piece; earthenware pan.

л-атм *abbr.* (**литро-атмосфера**) liter-atmosphere.

латок *gen. pl. of* **латка.**

латорфский *a.* (geol.) Lattorfian.

латук *m.,* —**овый** *a.* lettuce (*Lactuca*); **л.-ромэн** *m.* Romaine or cos lettuce; **л.-салат** *m.* garden lettuce; —**овый опий** lactucarium.

латунелитей/ная *f.,* —**ный завод** brass foundry; —**щик** *m.* brass founder.

латун/ирование *n.* brass plating; —**ировать** *v.* brass-plate; —**ный** *a.,* —**ь** *f.* brass.

латынь *f.* Latin.

латышский *a.* (geog.) Latvian.

лаубанит *m.* (min.) laubanite.

лаудан/идин *m.* laudanidine, tritopine; —**ин** *m.* laudanine; —**озин** *m.* laudanosine, N-methyltetrahydropapaverine.

лаундерометр *m.* launderometer.

лаур/ат *m.* laurate; —**елин** *m.* laureline.

лауренсит *m.* (min.) lawrencite.

лаурентский *a.* (geol.) Laurentian.

лаур/ил *m.,* —**иловый** *a.* lauryl; —**иловый спирт** lauryl alcohol, 1-dodecanol; —**ин** *m.* laurin, glyceryl laurate; —**иновая кислота** lauric acid, dodecanoic acid; —**иновокислый** *a.* lauric acid; laurate (of); —**иновый альдегид** lauric aldehyde; —**ит** *m.* (min.) laurite.

лауро—_prefix_ lauro—; —**ил** *m.* lauroyl; —**н** *m.* laurone, 12-tricosanone; (pharm.) Lauron; —**ноловый** *a.* lau-

ronolic (acid); —**стеариновый** *a.* laurostearic, lauric (acid); —**тетанин** *m.* laurotetanine.

лаусонит *m.* (min.) lawsonite.

Лаута стан Lauth (rolling) mill; **Л. фиолетовый** Lauth's violet, thionine.

лаут/аль *m.* Lautal (alloy); —**арит** *m.* (min.) lautarite; —**ит** *m.* (min.) lautite.

лауэ/вский *a.* Laue; —**грамма** *f.* Laue diffraction pattern, Laue photograph.

лафет *m.* carriage, gun mount; **л.-двунога** *m.* bipod mount; —**ный** *a. of* **лафет;** —**ная жатка** (agr.) windrower; **л.-тумба** *m.* column mount.

лахар *m.* lahar, volcanic mudflow.

лахтак *m.* (mam.) bearded seal (*Erignathus barbatus*).

лацерация *f.* laceration.

лацертиды *pl.* (herp.) lizards (*Lacertidae*).

лац(-)порт *m.* (naut.) (side) port.

ЛАЧХ *abbr.* (**логарифмическая амплитудно-частотная характеристика**) logarithmic frequency response characteristic.

ла/ющий *a.* barking; hoarse (voice); —**я** *gen. of* **лай;** —**яние** *n.* barking; —**ять** *v.* bark, bay.

лб *abbr.* (**ламберт**) lambert.

лба *gen. of* **лоб.**

ЛБВ *abbr.* (**лампа бегущей волны**) traveling wave tube.

ЛВЖ *abbr.* (**легковоспламеняемая жидкость**) inflammable liquid.

ЛВТ *abbr.* (**линейно-вращающийся трансформатор**) linear rotary transformer.

лг/аньё *n.* lying, deception; —**ать** *v.* lie, deceive; —**ущий** *a.* lying, deceptive.

ЛД *abb.* (**летальная доза**) lethal dose.

лебеговый *a.* (math.) Lebesgue.

лебеда *f.* (bot.) Atriplex; Chenopodium.

леб/едёнок *m.* (orn.) cygnet; —**еди** *pl.* cygnidae; —**единый** *a. of* **лебедь;** sygneous; —**ёдка** *f.* female swan; (mech.) hoist, winch, windlass; jack.

лебедов/ые *pl.* (bot.) Chenopodiaceae; —**ый** *a. of* **лебеда.**

лебёд/очный *a. of* **лебёдка;** —**чик** *m.* hoist operator.

лебедь *m.* (orn.) swan (*Cygnus*); (astr.) Cygnus; **л.-трубач** *m.* trumpeter swan (*C. buccinator*); **л.-шипун** *m.* mute swan (*C. olor*).

лебиасиновые *pl.* (ichth.) Lebiasinidae.

лебия *f.* (ent.) ground beetle (*Lebia*).

леблановский *a.* Le Blanc (soda).

лебоит *m.* (min.) lebeauite.

лебяжий *a. of* **лебедь.**

лев *m.* (mam.) lion (*Leo leo*); (astr.) Leo; **морской л.** sea lion (*Zalophus*).

левада *f.* paddock, enclosed pasture; shore forest.

леван *m.* levan.

левант(ий)ский *a.* (geog.) Levant(ine).

левеит *m.* (min.) löweite.

Левенгерц Löwenherz (name).

левероид *see* **летероид.**

леверьерит *m.* (min.) leverrierite.

леветь *v.* go left; be on the left.

левзея *f.* (bot.) Leuzea.

левиафан *m.* wool-washing machine.

Левига способ Löwig's process.

левигит *m.* (min.) löwigite.

левизит *m.* (min.) lewisite, romeite.

левин(ит) *m.* (min.) levyn(it)e.

левинштейновский *a.* Levinstein.

левкания *f.* (ent.) army worm (*Leucania*).

левкена *f.* (bot.) Leucaena.

левко— *see* **лейко—;** **—донт** *m.* (ent.) leucodont.

левкой *m.* (bot.) stock (*Matthiola*).

левкорриниа *f.* (ent.) Leucorrhinia.

лево, на л. *adv.* (to the) left.

лево— *prefix* levo—, left; **—бережный** *a.,* **—бережье** *n.* left bank; **—вращающий** *a.* levorotatory; **—завернутый, —закрученный, —извитой** *a.* laeotropous, leiotropic; **—мицетин** *m.* Levo-mycetin, chloramphenicol; **—пимаровый** *a.* levo-pimaric (acid); **—поляризованный** *a.* polarized counterclockwise; **—правосторонний** *a.* left-to-right (shunt); **—режущий** *a.* left-hand (tool); **—рукий, —ручной, —сторонний** *a.* lefthand(ed).

левул/ёза, —оза *f.* levulose, fructose; **—ин** *m.* levulin, fructosin; **—иновая кислота** levulinic acid, oxopentanoic acid; **—иновокислый** *a.* levulinic acid; levulinate (of); **—иновый альдегид** levulinaldehyde.

левция *f.* (bot.) Leuzia.

левша *m.* or *f.* lefthanded person.

лев/ый *a.* left(-hand), counterclockwise, levo—; wrong, reverse (side); **—ого направления** left-handed; **—ое вращение** (opt.) levorotation; **с —ым ходом** left(handed) (screw, etc.).

лёг *past m. sing. of* **лечь.**

легавая собака pointer, setter.

легализ(ир)овать *v.* legalize; **—ся** *v.* become legal.

легальн/о *adv.* legally; it is legal; **—ость** *f.* legality; **—ый** *a.* legal, lawful.

легаш *see* **легавая собака.**

леггорн *m.* Leghorn (chicken).

легенда *f.* legend, marginal note; **—рный** *a.* legendary; unlikely, improbable.

легир/ование *n.* (met.) alloying; doping (of catalyst or semiconductor); **—овать** *v.* alloy; dope; **—ующий** *a.* alloy(ing); **—ующий элемент** component (of alloy).

легитим/изовать, —ировать *v.* legitimize; **—ный** *a.* legitimate, legal.

лёгк/ие *pl.* (anat.) lungs; **воспаление —их** pneumonia.

лёгк/ий *a.* light(-weight); easy, simple; thin, slight; light-textured (soil); sandy (loam); fly (ash); mild (laxative); facile (reaction); **—ого типа** light-duty (machine).

легко *adv.* lightly; easily, readily, with ease, freely; it is easy; **л. доступный** easily accessible, readily available; **л. растворимый** readily soluble, very soluble; **—верный** *a.* credulous, gullible; **—вес** *m.* lightweight brick; **—весность** *f.* lightness, light weight; **—весный** *a.* light(-weight); **—вик** *m.* auto(mobile), car; **—водный** *a.* light-water (reactor); **—водолазный** *a.* aqualung diving; **—водяной** *a.* light-water; **—вой** *a.* passenger (car); **—воспламеняющийся** *a.* highly inflammable, deflagrable; **—доступный** *a.* easily accessible.

лёгкое *n.* (anat.) lung, pulmo.

легко/зольный *a.* light-ash; **—кипящий** *a.* low-boiling, having a low boiling point; **—крылый** *a.* light-winged; **—летучий** *a.* highly volatile; **—мысленный** *a.* light, frivolous; thoughtless; **—ногий** *a.* light-footed; **—обнаруживаемый** *a.* readily detectable; **—окисляемый** *a.* readily oxidizable.

легкоплавк/ий *a.* (easily) fusible, low-melting; **—ая вставка** (elec.) fuse; **—ость** *f.* low melting point, ready fusibility.

легко/подвижный *a.* mobile; **—полимеризующий** *a.* readily polymerizing; **—прессованный** *a.* (mach.) wringing (fit); **—проницаемый** *a.* readily permeable; **—раненый** *a.* (s)lightly wounded; **—растворимый** *a.* readily soluble; **—сжижающийся** *a.* readily liquefiable; **—силосующийся** *a.* (agr.) fermentable; **—спе-**

кающийся *a.* readily sintering; **лёгкость** *f.* lightness, light weight; easiness, ease, facility; **лёгкость ухода** accessibility; **—суглинистый** *a.* sandy loam; **—сульфируемый** *a.* readily sulfonated; **—усвояемый** *a.* readily available; readily assimilable; **—ходовой** *a.* smooth-running, free(-running); **—язвимый** *a.* fragile, vulnerable.

легли *past pl. of* **лечь.**

лёгок *sh. m. of* **легкий.**

лёгочн/ики, —ые *pl.* (mal.) Pulmonata; **—ица** *f.* (bot.) lungwort (*Pulmonaria*); **—о—** *prefix* (anat.) pulmo—, lung(s); **—о-сердечный** *a.* cardiopulmonary; cardiopneumatic; **—ый** *a.* pulmonary, lung.

леграндит *m.* (min.) legrandite.

легуаны *pl.* (herp.) Iguanidae.

легумин *m.* legumin.

легч/айший *superl. of* **лёгкий;** **—ать** *v.* lighten, abate; (med.) improve; **—е** *comp. of* **лёгкий, легко.**

легший *past act. part. of* **лечь.**

лёд *m.* ice; **грунтовый л., донный л., почвенный л.** ground ice, anchor ice.

ЛЕД *abbr.* (**лягушечья единица действия**) (physiol.) frog unit.

ледгиллит *m.* (min.) leadhillite.

ледебурит *m.* (met.) ledeburite.

леден/ение *n.* freezing, congelation; **—еть** *v.* freeze, congeal, turn to ice; ice up; go numb (with cold); **—ец** *m.* hard candy; **—истый** *a.* icy, ice-like; **—ить** *v.* freeze, chill, ice; **—цовый** *a. of* **леденец;** **—ящий** *a.* freezing.

ледерин *m.* imitation leather, leatherette.

ледиды *pl.* (mal.) nut clams (*Nuculanidae*).

лёд-камень *m.* ground ice.

ледник *m.* refrigerator, icebox; refrigerator car; icehouse; (geol.) glacier; **—овый** *a. of* **ледник;** ice; (geol.) glacial.

ледничник *m.* (ent.) snow flea (*Boreus*); **—и** *pl.* Boreidae.

ледо— *prefix, see also under* **льдо—;** ice; **—витоморский** *a.* (geog.) Arctic Ocean; **—витый** *a.* ice, icy; **—вый** *see* **ледяной; —генератор** *m.* ice maker; **—делательный** *a.* ice-making; **—делка** *f.* ice maker; **—дробилка** *f.* ice crusher; **—к** *dim. of* **лёд; —кол** *m.,* **—кольный** *a.* ice breaker; **—кол-буксир** *m.* icebreaking tug; **—лом** *m.* (bridges) ice apron; **—мерный** *a.* glacial (survey); **—пад** *m.* ice fall; **—рез** *m.* ice breaker, ice cutter; (bridges) ice apron; **—руб** *m.* ice pick; **—сброс, —скат, —спуск** *m.* ice chute; **—став** *m.* freeze-up, complete freezing; **—стойкий** *a.* sleetproof; **—техника** *f.* ice technology; **—форма** *f.* ice mold; **—ход** *m.,* **—ходный** *a.* ice drift, ice flow.

лёд-сало *m.* ice slush.

ледуксит *m.* (min.) ledouxite.

ледышка *f.* small piece of ice, chip.

Ледюка эффект (phys.) Leduc effect.

ледян— *see under* **леден—;** **—ка** *f.* ice boat.

ледян/ой *a.* ice(-cold), freezing; glacial; **л. кабан, —ая голова** ice block; **л. камень** (min.) ice stone, cryolite; **л. песок** corn snow; **л. шпат** (min.) ice spar, sanidine; **—ая гора** iceberg; **—ая каша** (ocean.) brash; **—ая корка** brackish ice crust; **—ая уксусная кислота** glacial acetic acid; **—ое сало** slush; **—ые красители** ice colors (azo dyes); **—ые поля** ice floes.

ледяшка *see* **ледышка.**

леек *gen. pl. of* **лейка.**

леер *m.,* **—ный** *a.* (naut.) handrail; manrope, handrope.

леерсия *f.* (bot.) Leersia.

лееч/ка *dim. of* **лейка; морская л.** (mal.) Brechites giganteus; **—ный** *a. of* **лейка.**

лёжа *adv.* lying down.

лежа/к *m.* bedstone; recumbent log or other object; **—лый** *a.* stale, not fresh; **—н** *see* **лежень.**

Лежандра полином (math.) Legendre polynomial.

леж/ание *n.* lying, etc., *see v.*; **—ать** *v.* lie, rest; be (situated); fall (within); form (the foundation); lead to (of route); (med.) be down (with), be laid up; **—ать на** have bearing on; be the function of.

лежа/чий, —щий *a.* lying, recumbent, horizontal, prostrate, prone; (bot.) procumbent, trailing; sessile (drop); **л. бок** under side; lower wall, footwall; **л. в** embedded; **л. вне** extra—, e.g., **л. вне сердца** extracardial; **л. внутри** internal; **л. возле** para—, e.g. **л. возле носа** paranasal; **л. выше** superincumbent; **л. между** interjacent; **л. над** epi—, supra—, e.g. **л. над грудиной** episternal; **л. ниже** underlying; **л. около** para—, peri—; **л. под** infra—, sub—, e.g. **л. под бедром** subfemoral.

лежбище *n.* (seals) rookery, grounds; (ichth.) resting place.

леж/ень *m.* foundation beam, sill; (anchor) log; footpiece; ground plate; sleeper, tie; *see* **лежняк.**

лёж/ка *f.* ground plate; foot board; keeping quality; lying around (of produce, etc.); seasoning, aging; *see* **лежбище; —кий** *a.* storable, durable, lasting; **—кость** *f.* storability, keeping quality, shelf life.

леж/невая дорога log road; **—ни** *pl. of* **лежень;** stillage; **—няк** *m.* bottom millstone, bedstone, bedder.

лезв/ие *n.*, **—ийный** *a.* (cutting) edge, blade; bit; **острое л.** knife edge.

лезть *v.* climb, scale; creep; get in(to), penetrate; fit; meddle, interfere; (hair) come out, fall out.

лей *imp. of* **лить.**

лейас *m.* (geol.) Lias(sic).

лейденская банка (elec.) Leyden jar.

лейдиговый *a.* Leydig's (duct; organ).

лейк— *see* **лейко—.**

лейка *f.* funnel; watering can, sprinkler; (boat) bailer; Leica (camera).

лейкем/ический *a.* (med.) leukemic; **—ия** *f.* leukemia.

лейко— *prefix* leuc(o)—, leuk(o)— (white, colorless); **—анилин** *m.* leucoaniline, triaminotriphenylmethane; **—ворин** *m.* leucovorin; **—ген** *m.* leucogen; **—дендрон** *m.* (bot.) leucodendron; **—дерма** *f.* (med.) leukoderma; **—дрин** *m.* leucodrin, proteacin; **—з** *m.* (med.) leucosis; **—зин** *m.* leucosin; **—индиго** *n.* leuco-indigo, indigo white; **—кратовый** *a.* (petr.) leucocratic; **—ксен** *m.* (min.) leucoxene; **—лиз** *m.* (med.) leuko(cyto)lysis; **—лин** *m.* leucoline, *i*-quinoline; **—ма** *f.* (med.) leukoma; **—мицин** *m.* leucomycin.

лейкон leucone; (zool.) leucon; **—овый** *a.* leucon; leuconic (acid).

лейко/основание *n.* leuco base; **—пения** *f.* (med.) leukopenia; **—пирит** *m.* (min.) leucopyrite; **—пласт** *m.* (bot.) leucoplast; **—пластырь** *m.* adhesive bandage or tape; **—производное** *n.* leuco derivative; **—птерин** *m.* leucopterin; **—р(р)ея** *f.* (med.) leukorrhea; **—скоп** *m.* (opt.) leucoscope; **—соединение** *n.* leuco compound; **—сфенит** *m.* (min.) leucosphenite; **—токсический** *a.* leukotoxic; **—троп** *m.* leucotrope; **—туровая кислота** leucoturic acid; **—фан** *m.* (min.) leucophan(ite); **—феницит** *m.* (min.) leucophoenicite; **—фир** *m.* (petr.) leucophyre; **—хальцит** *m.* (min.) leucochalcite.

лейкоцит *m.* leukocyte, white blood cell; **гранулярный**

л. granulocyte; **негранулированный л., незернстый л.** lymphocyte; **—оз** *m.* leukocytosis.

лейна/-селитра *f.* leuna saltpeter; **—фос** *m.* leunaphos (fertilizer).

лейнер *m.* liner.

лейо— *prefix* leio— (smooth).

лейпцигский *a.* (geog.) Leipzig.

лейст/а *f.* lath; **—овидный** *a.* lath-like.

лейстерский *a.* (geog.) Leicester.

лейте *imp. of* **лить.**

лейфит *m.* (min.) leifite.

лейхтенбергит *m.* (min.) leuchtenbergite.

лейц/ил *m.* leucyl; **—илглицин** *m.* leucylglycine; **—ин** *m.* leucine; **—инаминопептидаза** *f.* leucine aminopeptidase; **—иновый** *a.* leucine; leuc(in)ic (acid).

лейцит *m.* (min.) leucite, amphigene; **—ит** *m.* (petr.) leucitite; **—овый** *a.* leucitic; **—оэдр** *m.* (cryst.) leucitohedron.

лейшман/ий *m.*, **—ия** *f.* (prot.) Leishmania; **—иоз** *m.* (med.) leishmaniasis.

лекаж *m.* leakage.

лекал/о *n.* (French) curve; mold, form, pattern, templet, template; standard, gage; **—ьный** *a. of* **лекало;** gaged; **—ьщик** *m.* gage maker, gager.

леканор/а *f.* (bot.) Lecanora; **—овый** *a.* Lecanora; lecanoric (acid).

лекарственн/оустойчивый *a.* drug-resistant; **—ый** *a.* medicinal; medicated; drug-induced; **—ый препарат, —ое вещество, —ое средство, —о** *n.* medicine, drug.

лек(в)ерелла *f.* (bot.) Lesquerella.

Лекланше элемент (elec.) Leclanché cell.

леконтит *m.* (min.) lecontite.

лекпом *m.* surgeon's assistant.

лекс/ема *f.* lexeme (word in context); **—ика** *f.* glossary, vocabulary; **—икограф** *m.* lexicographer; **—икография** *f.* lexicography; **—икология** *f.* lexicology; **—икон** *m.* vocabulary; dictionary; **—ический** *a.* lexical, lexicographic, vocabulary.

лёксостэгэ *n.* (ent.) Loxostege.

лектин *m.* (phyto)lectin.

лектор *m.*, **—ский** *a.* lecturer, speaker; **—ий** *m.* lecture room, auditorium.

лёкуста *f.* (ent.) Locusta.

лекц/ионный *a.*, **—ия** *f.* lecture, discourse; **читать —ии** *v.* lecture.

леллингит *see* **лоллингит.**

лёмаспилис *m.* (ent.) Lomaspilis.

леме/х *m.*, **—шный** *a.* plowshare.

Леминга способ (gas) Laming process.

лемма *f.* (math., bot.) lemma.

лемминг *m.* (mam.) lemming (Lemmus).

лемниск *m.* (anat.) lemniscus, band, bundle; **—ата** *f.* (geom.) lemniscate.

лемносская земля (geol.) Lemnian earth.

лемонграсовое масло lemongrass oil.

леморан *m.* lemoran, levo-dromoran.

лемпач *m.* adobe.

лемур *m.* (mam.) lemur (Lemur); **—иды, —овые** *pl.* Lemuridae.

лён *m.* (bot.) flax (Linum); (ichth.) taimen (Hucho taimen); tench (Tinca t.).

ленгенбахит *m.* (min.) lengenbachite.

ленгмюровский *a.* Langmuir.

ленд-лиз *m.* (com.) lend-lease.

лён-долгунец *m.* fiber flax.

ленец *m.* (bot.) bastard toadflax (Thesium).

лензин *m.* (paints) ground gypsum.

ленив/ец *m.* idler; idle wheel, idling sprocket; (mam.) sloth (*Bradypus*); **—о** *adv.* sluggishly, lazily; **—цы** *pl.* Bradypodidae; **—ый** *a.* sluggish, slow, lazy.

леникс *m.* tension roller, pinch roller.

ленин/аканский *a.* (geog.) Leninakan; **—градский** *a.* Leningrad; **—ский** *a.* Lenin.

лениться *v.* be idle, be (too) lazy.

ленки *pl. of* **ленок; морские л.** (ichth.) greenlings (*Hexagrammidae*).

ленкоранский *a.* (geog.) Lenkoran.

лён/-кудряш *m.* crown flax; **л.-межеумок** *m.* intermediate flax; **л.-моченец** *m.* water-retted flax; **—овые** *pl.* (bot.) Linaceae.

ленок *m.* (ichth.) lenok (*Brachymystax lenok*); taimen; greenling; (bot.) Linosyris.

лён-прыгунец, л.-скакунец *m.* dehiscent flax; **л.-рогач** *m.* crown flax.

ленский *a.* (geog.) Lensk; Lena (river).

лён-стланец *m.* dew-retted flax; **л.-сырец** *m.* raw flax.

лент/а *f.* tape, band, strip, ribbon, string, lace; belt(ing); column; (recorder) chart; (saw) blade; (text.) sliver; (anat.) tenia; lemniscus, band; stria, streak; **диаграммная л.** strip chart; **обматывать —ой** *v.* tape up; **л.-сетка** *f.* screening conveyer.

лентец *m.* (zool.) tapeworm (*Diphyllobothrium*); cestode; **—ы** *pl.* Diphyllobothridae.

лентикулярный *a.* lenticular, lens-shaped.

ленто/бычковые *pl.* (ichth.) Taenioididae; **—направитель** *m.* (text.) sliver guide; **—видный, —образный** *a.* t(a)eniform, tape-like, ribbon-like; **—обмоточный** *a.* taping; **—остник** *m.* (bot.) Taeniatherum; **—протяжный** *a.* tape-winding, tape-transport; feed; **—протяжный механизм** (comp.) tape drive; **—ткацкий станок** ribbon loom; **—ткачество** *n.* ribbon or tape weaving; **—телые** *pl.* bandfishes (*Cepolidae*); **—укладчик** *m.* (text.) coiler (can); **—хвостые** *pl.* (ichth.) ribbontails (*Taeniophoridae*); **—чка** *dim. of* **лента**; margin (of drill); **—чник** *m.* (ent.) Limenitis; **—чница** *f.* catocalid (Catocala); **—чнопильный станок** band saw.

ленточн/ый *a. of* **лента**; conveyer-type, traveling-belt (dryer, etc.); continuous; flat (cable); varved (clay); continuous-weighing (scales); taeniate, ribbon-like; **л. грохот** belt screen; **л. конвейер** belt conveyer; **л. масштаб** tape measure; **л. посев** (agr.) strip cropping; **л. рекордер** tape recorder; **л. тормоз** band brake; **л. червь** (zool.) tapeworm; **—ая машина** (text.) drawing frame; **—ая муфта** belt coupling; **—ая пила** band saw; **—ая подача** belt feed; **—ое железо** strip iron.

Ленца закон (elec.) Lenz's law.

ленчик *m.* (saddletree) pommel.

лень *f.* idleness, laziness; (ichth.) regional name for minnow, taimen, tench.

леон/гардит *m.* (min.) leonhardite; **—ит** *m.* (min.) leonite; **—тица** *f.* (bot.) Leontice.

леопард *m.,* **—овый** *a.* (mam.) leopard (*Leo pardus*); **морской л.** leopard seal (*Hydrurga leptonyx*).

леопольдия *f.* (bot.) Leopoldia.

леотропный *a.* l(a)eotropic (left).

ЛЕП *abbr.* (**линия злектропередачи**) line (of) route.

лепест/ковидный *a.* petal-shaped, petaliform; **—ковый** *a.* petal(ed), petalous; lobed; (phot.) leaf-type (shutter); **—ный** *suffix* —petalous; **—ок** *m.* petal; (antenna) lobe; (mach.) tab; (ichth.) filament (of gill); (mal.) palp.

лепёшк/а *f.* (pan)cake; pellet, lump; (pharm.) tablet, lozenge; **—овидный, —ообразный** *a.* in tablet form; oblate; (zool.) placoid, plate-like.

лепидин *m.* lepidine, 4-methylquinone.

лепидо—*prefix* lepido— (scale, flake); **—дендрон** *m.* (pal.) Lepidodendron; **—завры** *pl.* (herp.) Lepidosauria; **—зафес** *m.* (ent.) Lepidosaphes; **—крокит** *m.* (min.) lepidocrocite; **—лит** *m.* lepidolite, lithia mica; **—мелан** *m.* lepidomelane; **—н** *m.* lepidone, hydroxylepidine; **—новые** *pl.* (ichth.) Lepidopidae; **—птерология** *f.* (ent.) lepidopterology; **—сирен** *m.* (ichth.) Lepidosiren; **—сиреновые** *pl.* Lepidosirenidae.

леп/ить *v.* model, sculpture, shape, mold; build, make; stick (on); **—иться** *v.* be molded, etc.; adhere, cling, stick (to); hold on (to); crawl, creep; **—ка** *f.* modeling, molding; molded object; form, shape; **—кий** *a.* sticky; **—ной** *a.* plastic; modeled; stucco (molding); **—ная работа** modeling.

лепо— *prefix* lepo— (husk, rind, scale).

лепонтинский *a.* (geog.) Lepontine.

лепоспондил/ы, —ьные *pl.* (herp.) Lepospondyli.

лепр/а *f.* (med.) leprosy; **—озный** *a.* leprous; **—озорий** *m.* leper colony.

лепт/агон *m.* (ichth.) Leptagus; **—идиа** *f.* (ent.) Leptidia; **—(ин)ит** *m.* (petr.) lept(yn)ite; **—инотарза** *f.* (ent.) Leptinotarsa.

лепто— *prefix* lepto— (small, weak, thin, fine, slender); **—боция** *f.* (ichth.) Leptobotia; **—гиум** *m.* (bot.) Leptogium; **—дора** *f.* (crust.) Leptodora; **—клаз** *m.* leptoclase, minor fracture; **—м** *m.,* **—ма** *f.* (bot.) leptome; **—менингеальный** *a.* (anat.) leptomeningeal; **—н** *m.* (phys.) lepton; **—нема** *f.* (gen.) leptonema; **—пел** *m.* leptopel (suspension); **—спироз** *m.* (med.) leptospirosis; **—тена** *f.* (gen.) leptotene; **—фильный** *a.* (bot.) leptophyllous; **—хлорит** *m.* (min.) leptochlorite; **—цефал** *m.* (ichth.) eel larva, leptocephalus.

лептура *f.* (ent.) Leptura.

лепчица *f.* (bot.) catchweed (*Galium*).

лепщик *m.* modeler, molder.

лер *m.* (glass) lehr, annealing furnace.

лербахит *m.* (min.) lehrbachite.

лерз— *see under* **лерц—**.

лерка *f.* (threading) die, thread chaser, die chaser; gage.

лерне/ид *m.* (crust.) Lernaea; **—оз** *m.* (vet.) lernaeosis.

лерок *gen. pl. of* **лерка**.

лерцолит *m.* (petr.) lherzolite.

лес *m.* woods, forest; timber; **вырубка —ов** deforestation; **круглый л.** logs; **—а** *pl.* woodland, forests; scaffold(ing); trestle; *f.* fish line; **строительные —а** scaffolding.

лесби/анка *f.,* **—йский** *a.* lesbian.

лесенка *dim. of* **лестница.**

лес/ина *f.* felled tree; **—исто-болотистый** *a.* marshy-wooded; **—истость** *f.* (extent of) forestland; **—истый** *a.* wooded, woody, sylvan, forested, forest-clad.

леска *f.* fishing line; *gen. of* **лесок.**

лескеевые *pl.* (bot.) Leskeaceae.

лесни/к *m.* forester, forest ranger; **—на** *f.* wild apple; **—чество** *n.* forestry; ranger station; **—чий** *a.* forest ranger's, forestry; *m. see* **лесник.**

лесн/ой *a.* wood(land), forest; lumber, timber; **л. массив** woodland; **л. материал** lumber, timber; **л. орех** *see* **лещина; л. склад** lumberyard; **—ая шерсть** pine needle batting; **—ое дело, —ое хозяйство** forest management, forestry; **—ые земли, —ые участки** timberland.

лесо— *prefix* silvi—, forest, woods; timber; sawmill; **—автопоезд** *m.* lumber truck; **—вал** *m.* windfall; **—ведение** *n.* silviculture, forest science; **—вик** *m.* bark beetle (*Dryocoetes*).

лесовод *m.* forester; **—ственный** *a.* forestry; **—ство** *n.*, **—ческий** *a.* forestry, silviculture, tree growing.

лесо/воз *m.* timber carrier; lumber ship; log(ging) truck; **—возный** *a.* lumber-hauling, timber-carrying; logging; **—возвращение, —обновление, —восстановление** *n.* re-forestation, forest regeneration; **—вой** *a.* wood, forest; **—гон** *m.* raftsman; **—завод** *m.*, **—заводский** *a.* sawmill.

лесозаготов/итель *m.* lumberjack, woodsman; **—ительный** *a.*, **—ка** *f.* lumbering, logging; **—ительные работы** logging.

лесо/защита *f.*, **—защитный** *a.* forest conservation; **—инвентаризация** *f.* forest survey(ing); **—использование** *n.* forest utilization; **—истребление** *n.* forest devastation; **—к** *dim. of* **лес**; grove; **—катка** *f.* log roller; **—комбинат** *m.* logging and sawmill operation; **—луговой** *a.* forest-meadow; **—любивый** *a.* forest-loving, hylophilous; **—материал** *m.* lumber, timber, wood.

лесомелиор/ативный, —ационный, *a.*, **—ация** *f.* forest (a)melioration, forest reclamation, forest improvement.

лесо/нарушение *n.* unlawful forest exploitation; **—насаждение** *n.* forest planting, forest cover; tree farm(ing); stand, standing crop; **товарное —насаждение** timber; **—образующий** forest-forming; **—охрана** *f.*, **—охранение** *n.* forest conservation, forest protection; **—парк** *m.* forest park; **—перевалочный** *a.* timber-handling.

лесопил/ение *n.* sawmill operation; **—ка** *f.* sawmill; power saw; **—ьный** *a.* sawing, sawmill(ing); **—ьный завод** sawmill; **—ьная рама** gang mill, gang saw, frame saw; **—ьня** *f.* sawmill.

лесо/питомник *m.* tree nursery; **—погрузка** *f.*, **—погрузочный** *a.* timber loading; **—погрузчик** *m.* logger; **—покрытый** *a.* wooded, forest(-clad); **—полоса** *f.* forest belt; **—посадка** *f.*, **—посадочный** *a.* tree planting; **—посадочная база** forest nursery; **—провод** *m.* logway.

лесопромы/словый *a.* lumber; **—шленник** *m.* lumberman, lumber dealer; **—шленность** *f.*, **—шленный** *a.* lumber industry.

лесо/пропускное сооружение log sluice; **—разработка** *f.* forest exploitation, logging; logging site; **—рама** *f.* saw frame; frame saw; **—расчистка** *f.* clearance, slash disposal.

лесоруб *m.* lumberjack, feller; **—ка** *f.*, **—(оч)ный** *a.* felling, wood cutting; **—очные остатки** slash.

лесо/сека *f.*, **—сечный** *a.* felling, cut(ting); felling site; clearing; felling rate; **—скат**, **—спуск** *m.* timber slide, chute, flume; **—сплав** *m.*, **—сплавный** *a.* (log) rafting; **—сплавное сооружение** log sluice; **—степной** *a.*, **—степь** *f.* forest steppe; **—сушилка** *f.* lumber kiln.

лесо/таска *f.* log hauler, log chain; **—технический** *a.* wood technology; **—торговец** *m.* lumber dealer; **—торговля** *f.* lumber business; **—транспортер** *m.* log conveyer; **—тундра** *f.*, **—тундровый** *a.* forest tundra; **—укладчик** *m.* lumber stacker; **—управление** *n.* forest management; **—устроитель** *m.* forest manager; forest surveyor; **—устроительный** *a.*, **—устройство** *n.* forest management; **—химический** *a.* wood chemical, wood chemistry; **—химия** *f.* wood chemistry; **—хозяйственный** *a.*, **—хозяйство** *n.*

forest management, forestry; **—эксплуатационный** *a.*, **—эксплуатация** *f.* forest utilization.

леспеде/за, —ца *f.* (bot.) Lespedeza.

леспром *m.* lumber industry; **—хоз** *m.* industrial forestry.

лесс *m.* (geol.) loess (wind-blown silt).

лессингит *m.* (min.) lessingite.

лессир/овать *v.* (paints) scumble; glaze; **—овка** *f.*, **—ующий** *a.* scumbling; glazing.

лёссо/видный *a.* (geol.) loess-like; **—вый** *a.* loess; **—вая кукла** loess kindchen.

лестерский *a.* (geog.) Leicester.

лестни/ца *f.* staircase, stairs; ladder; (fire) escape; (hydr.) flight (of locks); scale; (anat.) scala; **движущаяся л.** escalator; **складная л., л.-стремянка** *f.* stepladder; **—чатый столб** H-pole; **—чный** *a. of* **лестница**; scalar(iform); scalene (muscle); **—чная жила** (geol.) ladder vein; **—чная клетка** stairwell; **—чная площадка** landing.

лес/хим— *see* **лесохимический**; **—хоз** *m.*, **—хозный** *a.* regional forestry (administration); forest enterprise.

лет *gen. pl. of* **лето**; **лёт** *m.* flight, flying; **на лету** flying, on the wing, in flight; **лета** *gen. of* **лето**; years, age; **лёта** *gen. of* **лёт.**

леталь *f.* lethal factor; lethal gene; **—ность** *f.* lethality; death rate, mortality (rate); fatality (rate); **коэффициент —ности** lethal range; **—ный** lethal, deadly, mortal, fatal; **—ный исход** death.

летание *n.* flight, flying.

летарг/ический *a.* lethargic; **л. сон, —ия** *f.* lethargy.

лета/тельный *a.* flying; **л. аппарат** aircraft; **—ть** *v.* fly; (av.) pilot; **—ющий** *a.* flying.

летероид *m.* leatheroid.

лететь *v.* fly, volatilize; hasten.

летига *f.* Indian summer.

летка *gen. of* **леток**; **лётка** *f.* (met.) taphole, notch (of furnace); (foundry) gate; bee gate.

летнаб *m.* aerial observer.

летн/езелёный *a.* deciduous (forest); **—ий** *a.* summer, estival; softwood (cutting); *suffix* —year, —ennial; **—ик** *m.* (bot.) annual; summer road; summer cottage.

летница *f.* (ichth.) Salmo letnica.

лётн/о-испытательный *a.* test-flight; **—оподъёмный состав** flight crew; **—о-технические данные** flight performance; **—ый** *a.* flying, flight; aviation; landing (field); **—ое дело** aviation, aeronautics.

лет/няк *m.* summer camp, herdsman's hut; **—о** *n.* summer; **ему пять лет** he (or it) is five years old; **средних лет** middle-aged; **—ование** *n.* estivation; **—овать** *v.* estivate; **—овка** *f.* nomads' (summer) camp; **—овье** *n.* estivation; summer quarters.

леток *m.* (hive) entrance; **лёток** *gen. pl. of* **лётка.**

летом *adv.* in the summer.

летопис/ь *f.*, **—ный** *a.* chronicle, annals, yearbook, annual.

леторосль *f.* (bot.) shoot, sprout, sucker.

летосчисл/ение *n.* chronology; era; **—ительный** *a.* chronological.

леточная масса ball (of puddled iron).

летошка *f.* psalterium, third stomach.

летрин *m.* (ichth.) scavenger (*Lethrinus*); **—овые** *pl.* Lethrinidae.

леттсомит *m.* (min.) lettsomite.

летун *m.* flier; habitual job changer; **—ья** *f.* (ent.) Aiolopus; Epacromius.

летуч/есть *f.* volatility; fugacity; **—ие** *pl.* volatile matter; **—ий** *a.* volatile, fugaceous; flying; brief, short; light (ash); **—а мышь** (mam.) bat; **—ка** *f.* flier, leaflet; short meeting; briefing; emergency team or measure; light truck; (bot.) pappus, thistledown; samara, winged seed; flying fish (*Exocoetus*); **ремонтная —ка** mobile repair shop; **—ки, —ковые** *pl.* (ichth.) Exocoetidae; Dactylopteridae.

летующий *a.* estivating, summering.

лётчик *m.* aviator, flyer, pilot; **л.-испытатель** *m.* test pilot; **л.-космонавт** *m.* astronaut; **л.-наблюдатель** *m.* aerial observer; **л.-планерист** *m.* glider pilot.

летя/га *f.* (mam.) flying squirrel (*Pteromys volans*); **—ги, —говые, —жьи** *pl.* Pteromyidae; **—щий** *a.* flying.

леуко— *see* **лейко—**; **—бриевые** *pl.* (bot.) Leucobryaceae; **—рриния** *f.* (ent.) Leucorrhinia.

лефуа *f.* (ichth.) Lefua.

лёффлеровский *a.* Loffler's.

лехеровский *a.* (elec.) Lecher (wire).

лецид/ея *f.* (bot.) Lecidea; **—овый** *a.* lecidic (acid).

лецит/ин *m.* lecithin; **—иназа** *f.* lecith(in)ase, phospholipase; **—ол** *m.* lecithol.

лечебн/ик *m.* medical manual; **—ица** *f.* clinic, infirmary; hospital; **—о—** *prefix* medical; treatment; **—о-профилактический** *a.* preventive medicine; **—о-процедурный** *a.* treatment and regimen; **—ый** *a.* medic(in)al; therapeutic, curative; treatment (procedure); immune (serum); **—ое воздействие** therapy; **—ое питание** dietetic treatment.

леч/ение *n.* (medical) treatment, therapy; **—енный** *a.* treated, etc., see *v.*; **—ить** *v.* treat, cure; be under a doctor's care; **—ить от** treat for; **—иться** *v.* undergo treatment; **—у** *pr. 1 sing.* of **лечить; лететь.**

лечь *v.* lie (down), rest (on); fall (into position); (av.; naut.) take a (course); spread, cover; go (to hospital).

лешательевский *a.* Le Chatelier (principle).

лещ *m.* (ichth.) bream (*Abramis,* spec. *A. brama*); **морской л.** pomfret (*Brama*).

лещад/ка *f.* (bricks) split; **—ная плита** coping; **—ь** *m.* slab, flagstone; (met.) hearth bottom (of blast furnace); bed (plate).

лещётки *pl.* (vet.) castration clamp(s).

лещи pl. of **лещ; морские л.** (ichth.) Bramidae; **—к** *dim. of* **лещ.**

лещин/а *f.,* **—овый** *a.* (bot.) filbert, hazel nut (*Corylus*); **—овые** *pl.* Corylaceae.

лже— *prefix* pseudo—, false; **—акация** *f.* (bot.) locust (*Robinia pseudoacacia*); **—апельсин** *m.* osage orange (*Maclura pomifera*); **—блошка** *f.* (ent.) Scirtes; **—грибница** *f.* (bot.) pseudomycelium; **—жерех** *m.* (ichth.) Pseudaspius; **—короеды** *pl.* (ent.) Bostrychidae; **—ктыри** *pl.* Therevidae; **—лиственница** *f.* (bot.) Pseudolarix; **—лопатонос** *m.* (ichth.) Pseudoscaphirhynchus; **—научный** *a.* pseudo-scientific; **—пескарь** *m.* (ichth.) Pseudogobio; **—пестрянка** *f.* (ent.) Syntomis; **—сельдевые** *pl.* (ichth.) Bathyclupeidae; **—тсуга** *f.* (bot.) Douglas fir (*Pseudotsuga*); **—ц** *m.* liar.

лжи *gen., etc., of* **ложь; —вый** *a.* false, lying, misleading, deceptive.

ЛЗП *abbr.* (**линия заданного пути**) (av.) course (line).

ЛЗС *abbr.* (**лесозащитная станция**).

ли *conj.* whether, if; *interrogative particle not translated,* e.g., **возможно ли?** Is it possible? **ли. . . ли** whether. . . or.

лиаза *f.* lyase.

лиалис *m.* (herp.) legless lizard (*Lialis*).

лиан/а *f.,* **—овый** *a.* (bot.) liana, vine; **—овидный** *a.* lianoid.

либеллюля *f.* (ent.) Libellula.

либенерит *m.* (min.) liebenerite.

либеральный *a.* liberal.

либер/ийский *a.* (geog.) Liberia(n); **—кюновый** *a.* Lieberkuhn's (glands); **—мановский** *a.* Liebermann.

либетенит *m.* (min.) libethenite.

Либига охладитель Liebig condenser.

либигит *m.* (min.) liebigite, uranothallite.

либидиби *m.* (leather) divi-divi (hulls).

либо *conj.* or; **л. . . . л.** either . . . or.

либрация *f.* (astr.; chem.) libration.

либриформ *m.* (bot.) libriform, wood fiber.

Ливан (geog.) Lebanon.

ливанский *a.* Lebanese, Lebanon.

ливеингит *m.* (min.) liveingite.

ливень *m.* shower, downpour, cloudburst; (snow) flurry.

ливер *m.,* **—ный** *a.* pluck (of animal); transfer pipet; siphon (tube); pump; crane.

ливийский *a.* (geog.) Libyan.

ливингстонит *m.* (min.) livingstonite.

ливистона *f.* (bot.) Livistona.

ливия *f.* (ent.) Livia; **Л.** (geog.) Libya.

ливне/вый *a. of* **ливень;** torrential (rain); flash (flood); **л. дождь** downpour; **—провод** *m.* storm water conduit; **—сборник** *m.* drain(age) well; **—спуск** *m.* catch basin.

ливший *past act. part. of* **лить.**

лига *f.* league.

лигаза *f.* ligase, synthetase.

лигамент *m.,* **—ный** *a.* ligament.

лиганд *m.* (chelation) ligand.

лигатур/а *f.,* **—ный** *a.* ligature; (met.) master alloy, hardener.

лигировать *v.* (med.) ligate.

лигн— *see* **лигно—**; **—ин** *m.,* **—иновый** *a.* lignin; **—ит** *m.* lignite, brown coal; **—итовый** *a.* lignite, lignitic, lignitiferous; **—итизировать** *v.* lignitize; **—ификация** *f.* lignification; **—ифицировать** *v.* lignify.

лигно— *prefix* lign(o)—(wood); **—лит** *m.* a plywood; **—стон** *m.* a laminated wood; **—сульфоновый** *a.* ligno-sulfonic (acid); **—фоль** *m.* laminated wood; **—цериновый** *a.* lignoceric (acid).

лигосома *f.* (herp.) Lygosoma.

лигрис *m.* (ent.) Lygris.

лигроин *m.,* **—овый** *a.* (petrol.) ligroin.

лигул/а *f.* (anat.; ent.) ligula; (bot.) ligule; (zool.) Ligula; **—ёз** *m.* (med.) ligulosis.

лигурийский *a.* (geog.) Ligurian.

лигустрин *m.* ligustrin, syringin.

лидар *m.* (elec.) lidar, optical radar.

лиддит *m.* (expl.) lyddite.

лидер *m.* leader; pacemaker (enzyme).

лидийский камень *see* **лидит.**

лидировать *v.* lead, head, be in front.

лидит *m.* (min.) Lydian stone, touchstone.

лидол *m.* Lydol, meperidine hydrochloride.

Лидс (geog.) Leeds.

лиды *pl.* false webworms (*Lydidae*).

лиеврит *m.* (min.) lievrite, ilvaite.

лиен/альный *a.* (anat.) lienal, splenic; **—ит** *m.* (med.) lienitis; **—о—** *prefix* lieno—, splen(o)—(spleen).

лижерьен *m.* (geol.) Ligerian substage.

лижущ/е-сосущий *a.* licking-sucking (mouth part); **—ий** *a.* licking.

лиз/алка *see* **лизунец; —альный** *a.,* **—ание** *n.* licking.

лизат *m.* (cyt.) lysate.

лизать *v.* lick.

лизергиновая кислота lysergic acid.

лизи— *see* **лизо—**; **—генный** *a.* (cyt.) lysigenous; **—дин** *m.* lysidine, methyldihydroimidazole; **—л** *m.* lysyl; **—метр** *m.* lysimeter; **—н** *m.* lysine, 2,6-diaminohexanoic acid; lysin (antibody); **—ровать** *v.* lyse, undergo lysis; **—с** *m.* lysis, dissolution.

лизнуть *v.* lick.

лизо— *prefix* lyso— (lysis, dissolution); **—ген** *m.* (immun.) lysogen; **—генизация** *f.* (bact.) lysogenization; **—гения, —генность** *f.* lysogeny; **—генный** *a.* lysogenic; **—кефалин** *m.* lysocephalin; **—л** *m.* lysol; **—лецитин** *m.* lysolecithin; **—сома** *f.* (cyt.) lysosome; **—цим** *m.* lysozyme.

лизу/нец *m.* salt lick (for cattle); salt spring; **—ха** *f.* (vet.) allotriophagy.

лик *m.* face, countenance, appearance.

ликаконитин *m.* lycaconitine.

ликания *f.* (bot.) Licania.

ликват *m.* segregated material.

ликвац/ионный *a.* (met.) liquating, liquation; **—ия** *f.* liquation, segregation.

ликвидамбар *m.* (bot.) sweet gum (*Liquidambar,* spec. *L. styraciflua*).

ликвид/атор *m.* (av.) destructor (mechanism); sterilizer; **—ационный** *a.,* **—ация** *f.,* **—ирование** *n.* liquidation, etc., *see v.*; **—ированный** *a.* liquidated, etc., *see v.*; **—ировать** *v.* liquidate, put an end (to), do away (with), abolish, eliminate, eradicate, get rid (of); dismantle, abandon; overcome, remedy; **—ироваться** *v.* go out of business, close down; **—ность** *f.* (com.) liquidity, solvency; **—ный** *a.* liquid; **—ные средства** liquid assets; **—ус** *m.* (met., etc.) liquidus.

ликвировать *v.* (met.) liquate, segregate.

ликвор *m.,* **—ный** *a.* (body) liquor; cerebrospinal fluid; **—ея** *f.* (med.) liquorrhea.

ликер *m.,* **—ный** *a.* liqueur; **—о-водочный** *a.* liqueur and vodka.

лико— *prefix* lyc(o)— (wolf); **—д** *m.* (ichth.) eelpout (*Lycodes*); **—довые, —ды** *pl.* Lycodidae; **—ктонин** *m.* lycoctonine; **—маразмин** *m.* lycomarasmine; **—пен** *m.* lycopene; **—персицин** *m.* lycopersicin, tomatine; **—пин** *m.* lycopine; **—подиевые** *pl.* (bot.) Lycopodiaceae; **—ий** *m.* club moss (*Lycopodium*); lycopodium powder; **—подовый** *a.* lycopodic (acid); **—рин** *m.* lycorine, narcissine; **—трисса** *f.* (ichth.) Lycothrissa.

ликсоза *f.* lyxose.

ликтрос *m.* (naut.) boltrope.

лил *past m. sing. of* **лить.**

лилацин *m.* lilacin, syringin.

лилейн/ик *m.* (bot.) Hemerocallis; Antherium; **—ые** *pl.* Liliaceae; **—ый** *a.* lily(-like).

лили *past pl. of* **лить.**

лил/ии *pl. of* **лилия; морские л.** (zool.) Crinoidea; **—оцерис** *m.* (ent.) Lilioceris.

лилипут *m.,* **—ский** *a.* dwarf, pigmy; (min.) small locomotive.

лилия *f.* (bot.) lily (*Lilium*); (zool.) crinoid.

лиллианит *m.* (min.) lillianite.

лило *past n. sing. of* **лить.**

лилов/атый, —еющий *a.* lilac-colored; **—еть** *v.* turn lilac or mauve; **—ый** *a.* lilac(-colored).

лилось *past n. sing. of* **литься.**

лима *see* **лайма;** (mal.) Lima.

лиман *m.* liman (drowned river valley); lagoon, pool, pond.

лиманда *f.* (ichth.) dab (*Limanda*).

лиманный *a. of* **лиман;** limanous.

лимантрия *f.* (ent.) Lymantria.

лима/понция *f.* (mal.) Limapontia; **—цид** *m.* limacide, slug poison; **—циды** *pl.* (mal.) Limacidae; **—цина** *f.* Limacina.

лимб *m.* limb; dial, graduated circle; (anat.) limbus, border, fringe.

лимбургит *m.* (petr.) limburgite.

лиметт/а *f.,* **—овый** *a.* (bot.) lime (*Citrus limetta*); **—ин** *m.* limettin.

лимит *m.* limit, maximum; quota; allocation; **—ация** *f.,* **—ирование** *n.* limitation; **—ировать** *v.* (set a) limit; restrict; **—ирующий** *a.* limiting; rate-determining (factor); **—ный** *a. of* **лимит;** extreme.

лимн/атис *m.* (zool.) Limnatis; **—играф** *m.* limnigraph; **—ит** *m.* (min.) limnite; **—ихтовые** *pl.* (ichth.) Limnichth(y)idae; **—ический** *a.* limnetic, lacustrine; **—о—** *prefix* limn(o)— (pool, lake; marsh; fresh water); **—обиотический** *a.* (zool.) limnobiotic, fresh-water; **—одрил** *m.* (zool.) Limnodrilus; **—олог** *m.* limnologist; **—ологический** *a.* limnologic(al); **—ология** *f.* limnology; **—опланктон** *m.* limnoplankton; **—офил** *m.* limnophilous organism; **—фит** *m.* limnophyte, pond plant.

лимон *m.* (bot.) lemon (*Citrus limonia*); **морской л.** (mal.) sea slug (*Doris*); **сладкий л.** *see* **лиметта; —ад** *m.,* **—адный** *a.* lemonade; fruit drink; **—ен** *m.* limonene; **—ин** *m.* limonin; **—ит** *m.* (min.) limonite, brown hematite; **—ник** *m.* (bot.) Schizandra; **—ница** *f.* brimstone butterfly (*Gonepteryx rhamni*).

лимонно— *prefix* lemon; citrate; **—борнокислая соль** borocitrate; **—бутиловый эфир** butyl citrate; **—жёлтый** *a.* lemon yellow; **—кислый** *a.* citric acid; citrate (of); **—кислый магний, —магниевая соль** magnesium citrate; **—кислая соль** citrate; **—растворимый** *a.* (fertilizers) citrate-soluble; **—этиловый** *a.* ethyl citrate.

лимонн/ый *a.* lemon; citric (acid); **соль —ой кислоты** citrate; **—ая корка** lemon peel; **—ая мята** (bot.) Melissa.

лимоно/видный, —образный *a.* citriform, lemon-shaped; **—вый** *a.* lemon.

лимский *a.* (geog.) Lima.

лимузин *m.* limousine.

лимурит *m.* (petr.) limurite.

лимф/а *f.* (physiol.) lymph; **—аденит** *m.* (med.) lymphadenitis; **—аденоз** *m.* lymphadenosis; **—ангио—** *prefix* (anat.) lymphangio— (lymphatic vessel); **—анг(о)ит** *m.* (med.) lymphangitis; **—атический** *a.* lymph(atic); **—атическая клетка, —атическое тельце** lymphocyte; **—огенный** *a.* lymphogenous, lymph-producing; **—оидный** *a.* lymphoid; **—оидная клетка** lymphocyte; **—ома** *f.* (med.) lymphoma; **—ообразование** *n.* lymphopoiesis; **—ообращение** lymph circulation; **—оузел** *m.* lymph node; **—оцит** *m.* lymphocyte.

лимы *pl. of* **лима;** (mal.) Limidae.

лина/лил *m.,* **—лиловый** *a.* linalyl; **—илацетат** *m.* linalyl acetate; **—лоол** *m.* linalool, coriandrol; **—марин** *m.* linamarin; **—рин** *m.* linarin; **—рит** *m.* (min.) linarite.

лингвист/ика *f.* linguistics; **—ический** *a.* linguistic.

линдакерит *m.* (min.) lindackerite.

линдан *m.* Lindane (insecticide).

линдгренит *m.* (min.) lindgrenite.

Линде способ Linde process.

линд/енский *a.* (geog.) Linde; **—ерния** *f.* (bot.) Lindernia; **—ор** *m.* (ent.) Lindorus; **—охит** *m.* (min.) lyndochite.

линеариз/ация *f.* linearization; **—(ир)ованный** *a.* lin-

линевать *see* **линовать.**

линеевский *a.* (biol.) Linnaean.

линей *gen. pl. of* **линь.**

линейк/а *f.* rule(r), straightedge; gage, dipstick; (piercing mill) liner; **в —y** ruled (paper); **—о —** *see* **линейно —**; **—орубилка** *f.* (typ.) rule cutter.

линейно *adv.* linearly, as a linear function (of); **л.-изменяющийся** *a.* linearly variable; **л.-нарастающий** *a.* increasing linearly; **л.-независимый** *a.* linearly independent; **л.-падающий** *a.* decreasing linearly; **л.-поляризованный** *a.* linearly polarized; **—построенный, л.-пропорциональный** *a.* linear (with); **л.-растущий** *a.* increasing linearly; **—сть** *f.* linearity; **л.-упакованные** *pl.* linear-stacked polymers.

линейн/ый *a.* linear, line; enumerative, unidimensional (classification); in-line (cryotron); slide-wire (bridge); distribution (power transformer); forked (lightning); specific (ionization coefficient); straight (knife); (gen.) purebred; **л. корабль** battleship; **л. монтёр, л. рабочий** lineman; **—ая потеря энергии** linear stopping power.

линей/чатость *f.* lineation; **—чатый** *a.* linear; ruled; lineate(d); (bright-)line (spectra); **—щик** *m.* lineman.

линёк *dim. of* **линь.**

линза *f.* (opt.) lens; (geol.) lens, lenticle.

линзенштихель *m.* engraver's tool.

линзо/видный, —образный *a.* lentiform, lens-shaped, lenticular; **—вый** *a. of* **линза; —вый компенсатор** corrugated expansion joint; **—чка** *dim. of* **линза;** (geol.) lenticule.

лини *pl. of* **линь.**

линиатура *f.* (screen) line number, size.

линиевыбиратель *m.* (tel.) selecting switch.

линимент *m.* liniment.

линин *m.* linin, oxychromatin.

линифии *pl.* (zool.) Linyphiidae.

лин/ия *f.* line, curve; mark; path, direction; row; (gen.) line, strain, lineage; (anat.) linea; **л.-анализатор** *f.* tester strain; **—ии** *pl.* (flow) pattern.

линкер *m.* (sausage) linker.

линкомицин *m.* Lincomycin (antibiotic).

линкор *m.* battleship.

линкруст *m.* Lincrust (a wall covering).

линне/евский *a.* (biol.) Linn(a)ean; **—он** *m.* linn(a)on; **—я** *f.* (bot.) Linnaea; **—ит** *m.* (min.) linnaeite.

линобатист *m.* (text.) lawn.

линов/альный *a.,* **—ание** *n.* ruling; **—ан(н)ый** *a.* ruled, lined; **—ать** *v.* rule, line (off); **—ка** *f.* ruling.

линогравюра *f.* linoleum engraving, linocut.

лино/зит *m.* (min.) linosite; **—ксин** *m.* linoxyn (solid, oxidized linseed oil).

линоле/ат *m.,* **—вокислая соль** linoleate; **—вая кислота** linoleic acid, 9,12-octadecadienoic acid; **—ум** *m.,* **—умный, —умовый** *a.* linoleum, floor covering.

линоотделитель *m.* delinter.

линотип *m.,* **—ный** *a.* linotype (machine); **—ист** *m.* linotypist, linotype setter.

линофировый *a.* (petr.) linophyric.

линочный *a. of* **линька;** (med.) desquamative.

линсанг *m.* (mam.) linsang (*Prionodon*).

линт/(ер) *m.* (text.) linters; **—ер(-машина)** (cotton) gin; delinterer; **—ерный** *a.* linters; **—ерование** *n.,* **—еровка** *f.* (de)lintering; **—отделитель, —уловитель** *m.* delinter.

линь *m.* (naut.) line; (ichth.) tench (*Tinca t.*); taimen; carp.

лин/ька *f.* (zool.) shedding, molting; (ent.) ecdysis; **—ючесть** *f.* fugitiveness; **—ючий** *a.* fugitive, fading (color); molting, shedding.

линя *gen. of* **линь.**

лин/ялый *a.* faded, etc., *see* *v.*; **—яние** *see* **линька; —ять** *v.* fade, lose color; (zool.) molt, shed, cast, slough; **—яющий** *a.* fading, etc., *see* *v.*; fugitive (color).

лио— *prefix* lyo— (solution, solvent); l(e)io— (smooth); **—гель** *m.* lyogel; **—гнатовые** *pl.* (ichth.) jennies (*Leiognathidae*); **—золь** *m.* lyosol; **—нзия** *f.* (mal.) Lyonsia; **—нский** *a.* (geog.) Lyons; **—пельма** *f.* (amph.) Liopelma; **—сорбция** *f.* lyosorption; **—тропный** *a.* lyotropic; **—фермент** *m.* lyoenzyme.

лиофил/изация *f.* lyophilization, freeze-drying; **—изировать** *v.* lyophilize; **—ьность** *f.* lyophilic nature; **—ьный** *a.* lyophilic; **—ьный раствор** lyophil.

лио/фобность *f.* lyophobic nature; **—фобный** *a.* lyophobic; **—хром** *m.* lyochrome.

лип *past m. sing. of* **липнуть.**

липа *f.* (bot.) linden, lime (*Tilia*).

лип/аза *f.* lipase; **—арис** *m.* (bot.; ichth.) Liparis; **—ар(ис)овые** *pl.* snailfishes (*Liparidae*); **—арит** *m.* (petr.) liparite, rhyolite; **—арский** *a.* (geog.) Lipari; **—емия** *f.* (med.) lipemia.

липец *m.* linden blossom honey or drink.

липецкий *a.* (geog.) Lipetsk.

лип/ид, —ин *m.* lipid, lipin.

липистиевые *pl.* (zool.) Lip(h)istiidae.

липиц(ц)анский *a.* Lipizzan (horse).

липк/ий *a.* sticky, tacky, gummy, viscid; clammy (skin); **—ометр** *m.* tackiness meter; **—опластырный** *a.* adhesive plaster; **—ость** *f.* stickiness. etc., *see* *a.*; oiliness.

липник *m.* linden tree grove.

липнуть *v.* adhere, stick; be sticky.

липняк *m.* linden grove; linden (tree).

липо— *prefix* lip(o)— (fat; lipid); (bot.) *see* **липа; —вка** *f.* linden honey cask; **—вые** *pl.* (bot.) Tiliaceae; **—вый** *a. of* **липа; —генный** *a.* lipogenous, fat-producing; **—евая кислота** lipoic acid, thioctic acid; **—ид** *m.* lipoid; **—идный** *a.* lipoid(al), fat-like; **—идоз** *m.* (med.) lipoidosis; **—иодин** *m.* lipoiodine.

липок *sh. m. of* **липкий.**

липо/каик, —каин *m.,* **—каическая субстанция** lipocaic (hormone); **—кластический** *a.* lipoclastic, lipopolytic; **—ксидаза** *f.* lipoxydase; **—лиз** *m.* lipolysis; **—листный** *a.* (bot.) tiliaefolious; **—литический** *a.* lipolytic, fat-cleaving; **—ма** *f.* (med.) lipoma; **—протеид, —протеин** *m.* lipoprotein; **—сома** *f.* (cyt.) liposome; **—сцелис** *m.* (ent.) Liposcelis; **—тропный** *a.* lipotropic; **—фильный** *a.* lipophilic, lipid-soluble; **—фусцин** *m.* lipofuscin; **—хром** *m.,* **—хромовый пигмент** lipochrome.

липпия *f.* (bot.) Lippia.

липуч/есть *f.* stickiness; **—ий** *a.* sticky, adhesive; **—ка** *f.* anything sticky; (bot.) stickseed (*Lappula*).

лира *f.* lyre, harp; spring clip; lira (money); (astr., anat.) lyra; (carpentry) apron; **л.-рыба** *f.* (ichth.) dragonet (*Callionymus lyra*).

лирио/дендрон *m.* tulip tree (*Liriodendron,* spec. *L. tulipifera*); **—пе** *f.* (bot.) Liriope.

лиро/видно— *prefix* lyrati—, lyrately; **—видный** *a.* lyrate, lyre-shaped; **—вые** *pl.* (ichth.) Callionymidae.

лиросонит *m.* (min.) liroconite.

лиро/образный *see* **лировидный; —хвост** *m.* (ichth.) lyretail (*Aphyosemion*); (orn.) lyrebird (*Menura*); *pl.* Menuridae.

лиса *see* **лисица.**

Лисабон (geog.) Lisbon.

лис/ёнок *m.* fox cub; **—ий, —иный** *a.* fox('s), vulpine; **—ица** *f.* (mam.) fox (*Vulpes v.*); (astr.) Vulpecula; **морская —ица** (ichth.) thornback ray (*Raja clavata*); thresher shark (*Alopias,* spec. *A. vulpinus*); **морские —ицы** Alopiidae; **—ичка** *f.* young fox; (astr.) Vulpecula; (bot.) chanterelle (*Cantharellus cibarius*); (mach.) thread chaser, (screw) die; **морские—ички, —ичковые** *pl.* (ichth.) sea poachers (*Agonidae*); **—овин** *m.* male fox; **—оводство** *n.* fox breeding; **—охвост** *m.,* **—хвостовый** *a.* (bot.) foxtail (*Alopecurus*); **—хвостник** *m.* foxtail meadow; foxtail.

Лиссажу фигуры (phys.) Lissajous figures.

лиссо— *prefix* (med.) lysso- (rabies).

лист *m.* leaf; sheet (of metal, paper, etc.); plate; page; lamina, scale; foil; terminal node, leaf node (of logic tree); record sheet; (anat.) folium; **в л.** in folio; **корющий л.** (bot.) bract; **резина в —ах** sheet rubber; **—аж** *m.* number of sheets or pages; **—ать** *v.* leaf through; **—ва** *f.* leaves, foliage, verdure.

лиственн/ица *f.,* **—ичный** *a.* (bot.) larch (*Larix*); **—ичный гриб, —ичная губка** (bot.) purging agaric (*Polyporus officinalis*); **—ичник** *m.* larch forest.

лиственн/ый *a.* leaf(y), foliate; deciduous, broadleaf; **—ая древесина** hardwood.

листв/яг *see* **лиственничник; —яжий** *a.* (geog.) Listvyaga; **—янский** *a.* Listvyanka.

листер *m.* lister(-plow); **—еллёз, —иоз** *m.* (vet.) listeriosis; **—ия** *f.* (bact.) Listeria; **л.-культиватор** *m.* (agr.) lister(-cultivator); **—ный** *a.* lister.

листик *dim. of* **лист; leaflet, blade.**

листинг *m.* (comp.) listing.

лист/ки *pl. of* **листок;** (anat.) folia; **—ный** *a. suffix* **—phyllous, —folious, -leaved, -leaf; -sheet; —о—** *prefix* leaf, phyllo—, foli—; sheet, plate; **—бит** *m.* (met.) flattener; **—блошка** *f.* (ent.) leaf hopper (*Psylla*); **—облошки** *pl.* Psyllidae; **—обойня** *f.* (met.) flatting mill; **—оборот** *m.* (mam.) leaf-nose bat (*Mormoops megalophylla*); **—овальный** *a.* sheeting; **—ование** *n.* sheeting(-out), sheet formation; **—оватость** *f.* lamination, foliation; fissility; **—оватый** *a.* leaf-like, foliate(d), scaly, laminated, lamellate, lamellar; **—овать** *v.* sheet out; **—овёртки** *pl.* (ent.) leaf rollers (*Tortricidae*); **—оветвь** *f.* (bot.) phylloclade; **—овидки** *pl.* leaf insects (*Phyllidae*); **—овидный** *a.* leaf-like, foliate(d), foliaceous, foliiform, leaf-shaped; single (cockscomb); **—овик** *m.* (bot.) Phyllitis; **—овка** *f.* (typ.) leaflet; (biol.) follicle; (bot.) Parmelia; **—овковые** *pl.* (orn.) leafbirds (*Irenidae*).

листов/ой *a.* leaf, foliated; sheet, in sheet form; sheet-metal; foliar, foliaceous, leafy; sheet-fed (press); loose-leaf (notebook); flat (printing); lamellar, flake; (elec.) plate (condenser; frame); **л. материал** *m.* sheet; **л. металл** sheet (metal); metal foil; **л. покров** foliage; **л. стан** plate mill, sheet (rolling) mill; **—ая заготовка** sheet bar; **—ая резина** sheet rubber; **—ая рессора** laminated spring, plate spring; **—ая сварка** sheet welding, plate welding; **—ая сталь** steel plate, sheet steel; **—ая структура** (geol.) book structure; **—ая фибра** fiberboard; **—ая щётка** (elec.) laminated brush; **—ое золото** gold leaf.

листо/гибочный *a.* sheet-bending; **—грызы** *pl.* (ent.) leaf miners (*Tineoidea*); **—еды** *pl.* leaf beetles (*Chrysomelidae*); **—к** *dim. of* **лист;** leaf(let); record sheet, chart; foil; (anat.) folium; **—колосник** *m.* (bot.) Phyllostachys; **—лаз** *m.* (amph.) tree toad (*Phyllobates*); **—ногие** *pl.* (crust.) Phyllopoda; **—нос** *m.* (mam.) leaf-

nose bat; **—носный** *a.* (bot.) foliferous; **—носы(е)** *pl.* (mam.) Phyllostomatidae; **—образный** *a.* leaf-shaped, foliform, foliate, lamellar; **—образующий** *a.* phyllogenetic, leaf-producing; sheet-forming; **—отделение** *n.,* **—отделительный** *a.* sheet separating.

листопад *m.,* **—ение** *n.* defoliation, leaf fall; (phyt.) leaf drop; **—ка** *f.* (ichth.) grilse; **—ный** *a.* defoliation; deciduous (tree).

листо/подборочный *a.* (typ.) collating; **—правильный** *a.* (met.) plate-straightening; **—прокатка** *f.,* **—прокатный** *a.* sheet rolling; **—расположение** *n.* (bot.) phyllotaxy; **—резка** *f.* sheet cutter; **—резный станок** (met.) shearing machine; **—сложение** *n.* (bot.) vernation; **—сортировочный** *a.* sheet-classifying; **—сос** *see* **листоблошка; —стебельный** *a.* (bot.) caulescent; **—телы** *pl.* (ent.) Phyllidae; **—уборный** *a.* leaf-sweeping; **—укладчик** *m.* sheet stacker; **—чек** *dim. of* **листок;** leaflet, foliole; **—чки** *pl.* (gill) filaments; **—чковый** *a.* leaflet, foliolate; **—чный** *a.* leaf; **—ядный** *a.* phyllophagous, leaf-eating; browsing.

листья *pl. of* **лист,** leaves, foliage; **бродящие л.** (ent.) Phyllidae.

лисья *see* **лисий.**

лит *sh. m. of* **литый.**

Литва (geog.) Lithuania.

литейн/ая *f.* (met.) foundry; **—о-механический** *a.* foundry and machine.

литейн/ый *a.* (met.) foundry, founding, casting, pouring; **л. двор** casting bed; casting yard; **л. завод** foundry; **л. лом** cast(ing) scrap; **—ая воронка** pouring funnel; **—ая канава, —ая яма** casting pit, foundry pit; **—ая лихорадка** (med.) spelter's fever; **—ая форма** (ingot) mold; **—ое дело, —ое производство** foundry work.

литейщик *m.* foundry hand, founder.

литера *f.* (typ.) letter, type, character.

литератур/а *f.* literature; **—ный** *a.* literature, literary; **—ная собственность** copyright.

литерный *a. of* **литера.**

литзея *f.* (bot.) Litsea.

лит/иаз *m.* (med.) lithiasis; **—иевый** *a.,* **—ий** *m.* lithium, Li; **—иевая слюда** lithia mica, lepidolite; **карбонат —ия, углекислый —ий** lithium carbonate; **окись —ия** lithium oxide, lithia; **—ийорганический** *a.* organolithium; **—ийсодержащий** *a.* lithium-containing.

лити/н *m.* lithia, lithium oxide; **едкий л.** lithium hydroxide; **—нистый** *see* **литиевый; —онит** *m.* (min.) lithionite, lithia mica; **—офилит** *m.* lithiophilite; **—фицировать** *v.* lithify, petrify.

литический *a.* (biol.) lytic, cell-destroying.

литмоцидин *m.* litmocidin (antibiotic).

литник *m.* (foundry) gate, pouring gate, sprue, runner; **—овый** *a. of* **литник;** pouring; pouring head (system); **—овая чаша** pouring basin.

лито— *prefix* litho— (stone, calculus).

литовский *a.* (geog.) Lithuanian.

литоген/ез(ис) *m.* (geol.; med.) lithogenesis; **—етический** *a.* lithogenetic; lithogenic, stone-producing.

литограф *m.* lithographer; **—ирование** *n.* lithography; **—ированный** *a.* lithographed; **—ировать** *v.* lithograph; **—ический** *a.* lithographic; **—ия** *f.* lithography; lithograph; **—ский** *a.* lithographic.

лито/зиа *f.* (ent.) lithosid (*Lithosia*); **—идит** *m.* (petr.) lithoidite; **—идный** *a.* lithoidal, stony.

лит/ой *a.* (foundry) cast; molded; poured; floated (asphalt); **—ые трубы** pipe castings; **в —ом виде** as cast.

литоклаз *m.* (geol.) lithoclase.

литолог/ический *a.* lithologic; **—ия** *f.* lithology, petrology.

литопон *m.* lithopone (white pigment).

литораль *f.,* **—ная зона** littoral (zone); **—ный** *a.* littoral, coastal, shore.

литорина *f.* (mal.) periwinkle (*Littorina*).

литоринх *m.* (herp.) Lythorhynchus.

лито/сфера *f.* lithosphere, earth's crust; **—томия** *f.* (med.) lithotomy; **—фага** *f.* (mal.) Lithophaga; **—фаг-ный** *a.* lithophagous, rock-burrowing; **—физа** *f.* (petr.) lithophysa; **—фильный** *a.* lithophile (elements); (geol.) lithophylic; (biol.) lithophilous; **—фит** *m.* (bot.) lithophyte; **—холевый** *a.* lithocholic (acid); **—циста** *f.* (biol.) lithocyst.

литр *m.* liter (unit of volume).

лит-ра *abbr.* (**литература**) literature.

литраж *m.* (mach.) displacement, capacity; volume in liters.

литровать *v.* refine, purify.

литров/ка *f.* one-liter container; **—ый** *a.* (per) liter, volumetric.

ЛитССР *abbr.* (**Литовская Советская Социалистическая Республика**) Lithuanian Soviet Socialist Republic.

литторина *see* **литорина**.

литцендрат *see* **лицендрат**.

лит/ый *a.* poured; (met.) cast; **—ь** *v.* pour; found, cast, run, teem; mold.

литьё *n.* founding, casting; cast (material); pouring; **л. в землю, л. в песке** sand casting; **л. в сырую форму** green-sand casting; **л. под давлением** pressure-die casting, injection molding; **стальное л.** cast steel; steel casting.

литься *v.* pour, run, flow, stream, course.

лифт *m.,* **—овой** *a.* elevator, lift; (min.) cage; pump; **—ёр** *m.* elevator operator; lifter; guide; (grain) guard; **л.-экспресс** *m.* express elevator.

лифчик *m.* brassiere.

лихачество *n.* recklessness; reckless driving.

лихвинский *a.* (geol.) Likhvin.

лихен *m.* (med.) lichen; **—аза** *f.* lichenase, cellulase; **—изировать** *v.* lichenize; **—ин** *m.* lichenin, lichen starch; **—иформин** *m.* licheniformin; **—оидный** *a.* lichenoid; **—ология** *f.* (bot.) lichenology.

лихия *f.* (ichth.) garrick (*Lichia*).

лихнис *m.* (bot.) Lychnis.

лихой *a.* daring; agile; hard (times).

лихорад/ить *v.* run a fever, have a temperature; **—ка** *f.* fever; **—очник** *m.,* **—очная трава** (bot.) hedge hyssop (*Gratiola officinalis*); **—очность** *f.* feverishness; **—очный** *a.* feverish, febrile.

лихтенберговский *a.* Lichtenberg.

лихтер *m.,* **—ный** *a.* (naut.) lighter (barge); **—ный сбор, —овка** *f.* lighterage.

лиц/а *f.* (text.) heald, heddle; *gen. and pl. of* **лицо**; **—евальный** *a.,* **—евание** *n.* turning, etc., *see v.*; **—евать** *v.* turn (clothing); face; strip.

лицев/ой *a.* face, facial, front; personal (account); **—ая отделка** facing; **—ая поверхность** face; **—ая сторона** face, front; right side (of material).

лицемерный *a.* hypocritical.

лицендрат *m.* (electron.) litz, Litz wire.

лиценз/иат *m.* license holder; **—ионный** *a.,* **—ия** *f.* license.

лиценхел(ис) *m.* (ichth.) eelpout (*Lycenchelis*).

лицетол *m.* lycetol, lupetazine tartrate.

лиций *m.* (bot.) Lycium.

лиц/о *n.* face, side; (anat.) facies; person; (leather) grain; (text.) right side; **—овка** *f.* smooth-cut file; **—ый** *a.* *suffix* -faced.

личи *n.* (bot.) Litchi; (mam.) waterbuck (*Kobus lechwe*).

личин/ка *f.* larva, grub, maggot; (art.) bolt head; elevator; **земляная л.** cutworm (*Agrotis*); **—ковый** *a.* larva(l); **—коед** *m.* (orn.) Pericrotus; Crotophaga; **—едовые, —еды** *pl.* Campephagidae; **—кообразный** *a.* larviform, larva-shaped; **—коуловитель** *m.* larva trap; **—кохордовые, —очнохордовые** *pl.* (mal.) Tunicata, Urochordata; **—коядный** *a.* larvivorous, larva-eating; **—ник** *m.* caterpillar (*Scorpiurus*); **—очный** *a.* larval; (med.) larvate, masked; immature.

лично *adv.* personally, in person.

личной *a.* facial, face; smooth-cut (file).

личн/ость *f.* personality; person; **удостоверение —ости** identification card; badge; **—ый** *a.* personal, individual, private, particular; **—ый состав** personnel, staff.

лишаевидный *a.* resembling lichen; (med.) herpetic, herpetiform.

лишай *m.* (bot.; med.) lichen; (med.) herpes; **морской л.** (bot.) alga; **опоясывающий л.** (med.) shingles; **стригущий л.** (med.) ringworm; **чешуйчатый л.** (med.) psoriasis.

лишайн/ик *m.,* **—иковый** *a.* (bot.) lichen; **исландский л.** Iceland moss (*Cetraria islandica*); **красильный л., лакмусовый л.** orchilla weed (*Rocella tinctoria*); **—иковидный** *a.* lichenoid, lichen-like; **—ицы** *pl.* (ent.) Lithosiidae; **—ый** *a.* (bot.) lichen; (med.) herpetic.

лишать *v.* deprive (of), take away, withdraw, remove, eliminate; strip (vegetation); **—ся** *v.* be deprived (of), lose, forfeit.

лишек *m.* surplus, excess.

лиш/ение *n.* deprivation, loss, forfeiture; removal; *pl.* hardship; **—ённый** *a.* deprived (of), devoid (of); **—less, e.g., ённый волос** hairless; **—ить** *see* **лишать**.

лишн/ий *a.* superfluous, unnecessary, supernumerary, surplus, extra, excess(ive); spare, odd; overtime; **л. раз** once more, yet again; **не —ее** it wouldn't hurt, it would be useful; **с —им** plus; **сто с —им** a hundred odd.

лишь *adv. and conj.* only, but, even, merely; no(t) more than, not until, no sooner than, as soon as; **л. бы** provided, if only; **л. только** as soon as.

лия *pr. ger. of* **лить**.

лияльная ложка (foundry) casting ladle.

лк *abbr.* (**люкс**) lux.

ЛКАО *abbr.* (**линейная комбинация атомных орбит**) linear combination of atomic orbit(al)s, LCAO.

ЛКП *abbr.* (**лакокрасочная промышленность**) paint and varnish industry.

лк-сек *abbr.* (**люкс-секунда**) lux-second.

лл. *abbr.* (**листы**) sheets, pages.

ллан— *see also under* **лан—**.

лландейльский *a.* (geol.) Llandeilian.

ллойдия *f.* (bot.) Lloydia.

лм *abbr.* (**люмен**) lumen.

ЛМ *abbr.* (**лейкоцитная масса**) leucocytes; (**линейный мост**) slide balance, slide-wire bridge; (**лунный модуль**) lunar module, LM.

лмб *abbr.* (**ламберт**) lambert.

л/мин *abbr.* (**литров в минуту**) liters per minute.

лм-с *abbr.* (**люмен-секунда**) lumen-second; **лм-ч** (**люмен-час**) lumen-hour.

л.н.с., ЛНС *abbr.* (**линия наименьшего сопротивления**) line of least resistance.

лоаоз *m.* (med.) loaiasis, Loa infection.

лоб *m.* (anat.) forehead, frons; front, face; **под лбом** *a.* subfrontal; **—ан** *m.* person or animal with a high forehead; (ichth.) striped mullet (*Mugil cephalus*); any large mullet; bream; shad; **—анчик** *dim. of* **лобан.**

лобар/ия *f.* (bot.) Lobaria; **—ный** *a.* lobar; **—ь** *m.* (ichth.) sturgeon.

лоб/астый *a.* with a high forehead; **—ач** *see* **лобан.**

лобел/анидин *m.* lobelanidine; **—анин** *m.* lobelanine; **—идин** *m.* lobelidine; **—иевые** *pl.* (bot.) Lobeliaceae; **—ин** *m.* lobeline; **—иновый** *a.* lobelic (acid); **—ия** *f.* (bot.) Lobelia.

лобзик *m.,* **—овый** *a.* scroll saw, fret saw, keyhole saw; **механический л., —овый станок** jig saw.

лобик *dim. of* **лоб.**

лобин/ин *m.* lobinine; **—ол** *m.* lobinol.

лобия *f.* hyacinth bean (*Dolichos lablab*).

лобков/о— *prefix* (anat.) pubo— (pubis); **л.-бедренный** *a.* pubofemoral; **л.-пузырный** *a.* pubovesical; **—ый** *a.* pubic; **—ая кость** pubis.

лобненский *a.* Lobnya (works).

лоб/но—, —о— *prefix* (anat.; zool.) fronto— (forehead; frontal); **—задний** *a.* frontoposterior; **л.-носовой** *a.* frontonasal; **—ный** *a.* forehead, frontal; head (lamp); **—ный пузырь** (ent.) ptilinum; **—ный шип** (zool.) rostrum; **—овина** *f.* forehead, frontal bone.

лобов/ой *a.* front(al), face; facing (cutter); head-on (impact); primary (turbine); (elec.) end (winding); (anat.) frontal; **л. (токарный) станок** (sur)facing lathe; **л. фонарь** headlight; **—ая доска** faceplate, face chuck (of lathe); **—ая поверхность** face; **—ая стенка** top cover (of cylinder); **—ое сопротивление** (aero.) head resistance, drag; **коэффициент —ого сопротивления** head drag coefficient; **сила —ого сопротивления** drag (force).

лобогрейка *f.* (agr.) reaper, harvester.

лобок *m.* (anat.) pubis.

лобопод/ий *m.,* **—ия** *f.* (biol.) lobopodium.

лобот *m.* (ichth.) tripletail (*Lobotes*); **—овые** *pl.* Lobotidae.

лоботокарный станок (sur)facing lathe.

лоботомия *f.* (med.) lobotomy.

лобофиллия *f.* (zool.) Lobophyllium.

Л-образный *a.* inverted-U-shaped.

лобулярный *a.* lobular.

лов *m.* catching, capture; hunting; trapping; catch; **л. рыбы** fishing; fishery.

лов, ЛОВ *abbr.* (**лампа обратной волны**) backward-wave tube.

ловатьский *a.* (geog.) Lovat.

Лове волна (seismology) Love wave.

ловель *gen. pl. of* **ловля.**

ловеров бугорок (anat.) Lower's tubercle.

ловеттия *f.* (ichth.) Lovettia.

ловец *m.,* **—кий** *a.* fisherman, angler; trapper, hunter; catcher.

ловиль/ный *a.* catch(ing); **л. инструмент** (min.) grab (iron); **л. колокол** bell socket; **—ные работы** (oil wells) fishing; **—щик** *m.* catcher.

ловит/ель *m.* catch, stop; grab; catcher; (core) lifter; guide pin; (min.) extractor; **—ить** *v.* catch, capture, seize, recover; hunt, trap; **—ть рыбу** fish.

ловк/ий *a.* clever, skillful, adroit; **—ость** *f.* cleverness, skill, knack, dexterity.

ловля *see* **лов.**

ловозёрский *a.* (geog.) Lovozero.

ловок *sh. m. of* **ловкий.**

ловушк/а *f.* trap, snare, pitfall; catcher; (chem.) entrainment trap; absorption column; catch basin, retainer; **л.-**

пескоотделитель *f.* sand trap; **—о-сутки** *pl.* (zool.) trap day.

ловче *comp. of* **ловкий.**

ловч/ий *a.* catching, trap(ping); hunting; prehensile; **—ая полоса** insect trap.

лог *m.* ravine, valley, hollow; (math.) log, logarithm; *m. suffix* **—log**(ist) (specialist).

логаниевые *pl.* (bot.) Loganiaceae.

логарифм *m.* (math.) logarithm, log; **десятичный л.** common logarithm, Briggs' logarithm; **—ика** *f.* logarithmic curve; **—ирование** *n.* taking the logarithm; **—ировать** *v.* take the logarithm; **—ирующий** *a.* logarithmic-computing; **—ический** *a.* logarithmic; slide (rule).

логгерхед *m.* loggerhead turtle (*Caretta c.*).

логи/ка *f.* logic; **—стика** *f.* logistics; **—стический** *a.* logistic(al); **—ческо, —чно** *adv.* logically; **—ический, —чный** *a.* logical; Boolean; **—чность** *f.* logic(ality).

лого— *prefix* logo— (word, speech).

логов/ище, —о *n.* (zool.) burrow, lair, den; slough, mudhole; covert, shelter.

логометр *m.* (elec.) ratiometer.

лого/патия *f.* logopathy, speech disturbance; **—педия** *f.* logopedics, speech therapy.

лог-уошер *m.* (min.) log washer.

лодал *m.* lodal.

лоджия *f.* (arch.) loggia.

лодикула *f.* (bot.) lodicule.

лод/ка *f.* boat; (glass) debiteuse; **подводная л.** submarine; **—коклюв** *m.* (orn.) boat-tailed flycatcher (*Megarhynchus pitangua*); **—кообразный** *a.* scaphoid, boat-shaped; **—кохвостый** *a.* boat-tailed; **—очка** *dim. of* **лодка;** (analysis) combustion boat; (anat.) scapha; (bot.) carina; **—очный** *a. of* **лодка.**

лодыга *f.* (art.) trunnion plate.

лодыж/ечный *a.,* **—ка** *f.* cam, catch; (folding) platform; (anat.) ankle, malleolus, talus; **—ковый** *a.* malleolar.

ложа *f.* (gun) stock; *gen. of* **ложе.**

лож/бина *f.* hollow, cavity; trough, ravine; **—бинка** *dim. of* **ложбина;** stria; **—бинный** *a. of* **ложбина; —биночный** *a.* vallecular; **—бистый** *a.* pitted; **—е** *n.* **—евой** *a.* (river) bed, channel; runway; (gun) stock; (anat.) matrix; **—е соцветия** (bot.) receptacle.

ложек *gen. pl. of* **ложка.**

ложемент *m.* lodgings; bed, cradle, support.

ложен *sh. m. of* **ложный.**

ложеобразователь *m.* scraper bar.

ложеч/ка *dim. of* **ложка;** scoop; sleeker; **морская л.** (mal.) Periploma; **—ник** *m.,* **—ница** *f.,* **—ная трава** (bot.) spoonwort (*Cochlearia*); **—ный** *a.* spoon; shell; post-hole (auger).

ложить *v.* lay; **—ся** *v.* lie down, fall; form (the basis of).

ложк/а *f.,* **—овый** *a.* spoon; (met.) ladle; skimmer; sleeker; (med.) curet(te), scraper, scoop; **—овидный, —ообразный** *a.* cochlear(iform), spoon-shaped; **—овый бур** post-hole auger; **—овый питатель** (concrete) channel feeder.

ложно *adv.* false(ly); *prefix* pseudo—; *see also under* лже—; **—блинчатый** *a.* plate (ice); **—гусеница** *f.* caterpillar-like larva; **—долгохвост(ов)ые** *pl.* (ichth.) Ateleopidae; **—жабра** *f.* (ichth.) pseudobranch, false gill; **—кокон** *m.* (ent.) puparium; **—коренный зуб** premolar; **—короеды** *pl.* (ent.) Bostrychidae; **—куколка** *f.* pseudopupa; **—луковица** *f.* (bot.) pseudobulb; **—мучнеросные грибы, мучнисторосяные** *pl.* (phyt.) downy mildews (*Peronosporaceae*); **—ногие** *pl.* (herp.) Boidae.

ложно/ножка *f.* (prot.) pseudopod(ium); **лопастная л., пальцевидная л.** lobopodium; **—очиток** *m.* (bot.) Pseudosedum; **—паразит** *m.* pseudoparasite; **—покровница** *f.* (bot.) Notholaena; **—проволочники** *pl.* (ent.) tenebrionid and alleculid larvae; **—сетчатокрылые** *pl.* Odonata; **—скорпион** *m.* (zool.) pseudoscorpion; **—слон(н)иковые** *pl.* (ent.) Anthribidae; **—сть** *f.* falsity; **—угревые** *pl.* (ichth.) swamp eels (*Synbranchidae*); **—щитовка** *f.* (ent.) scale.

лож/ный *a.* untrue, false, spurious; erroneous, fallacious; pseudo—, mock; fault, ghost (image); (aut.) parasitic (circuit); decoy (warhead); **л. вывод** fallacy.

ложок *m.* stretcher.

ложь *f.* falsehood, untruth, deception.

лоза *f.* vine, cane, runner; willow.

лозаннский *a.* (geog.) Lausanne.

лоз/ник, —няк *m.* willow bush; willow thicket; **—овидный** *a.* pampiniform, tendril-like; **—овый** *a. of* **лоза;** **—оподобный** *a.* vine-like.

лозьвинский *a.* (geog.) Lozva.

лойальный *a.* loyal.

Лока раствор Locke's solution.

локаин *m.* locaine (dye).

локал/изатор *m.* localizer, finder, detector; indicator; **—изация** *f.* localization; containment; site, abode; **—из(ир)ованный** *a.* localized; **—(из)ировать** *v.* localize; bring under control; **—изуемый** *a.* localizable; **—итет** *m.* locality; **—ьность** *f.* locality; restriction; **—ьный** *a.* local; autochthonous, indigenous; **—ьный режим кипения** torpid boiling.

локатор *m.* locator, detector, probe; radar; (petrol.) tracer; **звуковой л.** sonar.

локаут *m.,* **—ировать** *v.* (labor) lock out.

локация *f.* detection and ranging; location.

локва *f.* (bot.) loquat (*Eriobotrya japonica*).

локер *m.* locker; **л.-морозильник** *m.* freezer locker; **л.-холодильник** *m.* refrigerated locker.

локомо/биль *m.* locomobile; **—бильный** *a.* locomobile; portable; **—тив** *m.,* **—тивный** *a.* locomotive, engine; **—торный** *a.* locomotor; **—моция** *f.* locomotion, movement.

локон *m.* lock (of hair); (geom.) witch.

локот/ник *m.* arm rest; **—ной** *a.,* **—ь** *m.* (anat.) elbow, cubitus; forearm, ulna; cubit, ell (approx. 0.5 m.).

локсо— *prefix* lox(o)— (oblique).

локсодром *m.,* **—а, —ия** *f.* loxodrome, loxodromic curve, rhumb (line); **—ический, —ный** *a.* loxodromic.

локсоклаз *m.* (min.) loxoclase.

локт/евой *a.* (anat.) ulnar, elbow; anconeal (muscle); **—евая кость** ulna.

локтевский *a.* (geog.) Loktevka.

локте— *prefix* (anat.) ulno— (ulnar and); **—запястный** *a.* ulnocarpal.

локула *f.* locule, cavity.

локус *m.* (gen.; math.) locus; *pl.* loci.

лола *f.* Lola (a flame-resistant fiber).

лолиго *m.* (mal.) Loligo.

лолинь *m.* (naut.) lead line.

лом *m.* (crow)bar, pinch bar; scrap, waste; dull ache; *suffix* —break; **железный л.** scrap iron.

лома *f.* (geobot.) loma (littoral desert).

лом/аная *f.* broken line; **—ание** *n.* breaking, etc., *see v.;* **—ан(ный)** *a.* broken, etc., *see v.;* bent; irregular; **—анье** *see* **ломание;** **—ать** *v.* break (up), crush, fracture, smash; demolish, wreck, pull down; quarry (stone); rack (one's brain); change, alter; hurt, ache; butcher (a language); **—ться** *v.* break, crack, collapse,

fail, get out of order; be breakable; **—ающийся** *see* **ломкий.**

ломбардский *a.* (geog.) Lombardy, Lombard(ic).

ломик *dim. of* **лом;** pinch bar, wrecking bar.

лом/ить *v.* break (up, through); smash, crush; push up (price); hurt, ache; **—иться** *v.* break, snap; be jampacked; **—ка** *see* **ломание;** (stone) quarry.

ломк/ий *a.* brittle, friable, frangible, fragile, breakable; short; snap (bean); crack (willow); **—околосник** *m.* (bot.) Psathyrostachys; **—ость** *f.* brittleness, friability; fragility; **—ость в холодном состоянии** cold shortness.

ломов/ик *m.* draft horse; driver; **—ой** *a. of* **лом;** scrap (iron); draft (horse).

ломозубы(е) *pl.* (icth.) snaggletooths (*Astronesthidae*).

ломок *gen. pl. of* **ломка;** *sh. m. of* **ломкий.**

ломонос *m.* (bot.) Clematis.

ломонтит *m.* (min.) laumontite.

ломот/а *f.,* **—ный** *a.* ache, dull pain.

лом/оть *m.* slice, chunk; **—терезка** *f.* slicer; **—тик** *dim. of* **ломоть.**

Лонг-Айленд (geog.) Long Island.

лонг/волл, —уолл *m.* (min.) longwall.

лондо/ковский *a.* (geog.) Londoko; **—нский** *a.* London.

лонжа *f.* cord.

лонжерон *m.,* **—ный** *a.* (av.) longeron, spar, beam; side rail, side member.

лонн/о— *prefix* (anat.) pubo— (pubic and); **л.-бедренный** *a.* pubofemoral; **—ый** *a.* pubic; **—ая кость** pubis.

лонсдалеоидный *a.* (pal.) lonsdaleoid.

лонсдейлит *m.* lonsdalite (a form of carbon).

лонхокарпус *m.* (bot.) Lonchocarpus.

лопание *n.* bursting, cracking, breaking.

лопарит *m.* (min.) loparite.

лопар/ский *a.* (geog.) Lapland(ian); **—ь** *m.* Lapp, Laplander; lifting rope; (naut.) fall (tackle).

лопаснинский *a.* (geog.) Lopasnya.

лопасте/видный, —образный *a.* lobiform; **—носные** *pl.* (zool.) Lobata; **—пёрые** *pl.* lobe-finned fishes (*Sarcopterygii*).

лопаст/инка *f.* lobule; **—инчатый** *a.* lobulate; **—ники** *pl.* (ent.) Dascillidae; **—но—** *prefix,* **—ной** *a.* lobate, lob(ul)ar; **—но-колёсный** *a.* bucket-wheel (excavator); **—но-регулируемый** *a.* blade-regulated; **—ность** *f.* (biol.) lobation; **—ный** *a.* blade, vane, paddle; turbo—; rotary, centrifugal (pump); (biol.) laciniate, lobed, lobate; **—ная машина** turbomachine; **—ное колесо** paddle wheel; (pump) rotor, impeller; **—ь** *f.* blade, vane, paddle; fan; (biol.) lobe.

лопат/а *f.* shovel, spade; rabble; scraper, scoop; **обратная л.** back hoe; **—ень** *m.* (orn.) shoveler shorebird (*Eurynorhynchus pygmeum*); **—ить** *v.* shovel, spade, turn (over); **—ка** *dim. of* **лопата;** trowel; scoop; (debarking) knife; skimmer; blade, paddle, vane (of turbine); (anat.) scapula, shoulder blade; (med.) spatula, depressor; **—ки-рыбы** *pl.* batfishes (*Oncocephalidae*).

лопаткинский *a.* (geog.) Lopatka.

лопато/видный *a.* (biol.) paliform; **—ног** *m.* (amph.) Scaphiopus; **—ногие** *pl.* (mal.) Scaphopoda; **—нос** (orn.) *see* **лопатень;** (ichth.) shovelnose sturgeon (*Scaphirhynchus*); **—образный** *see* **лопатовидный;** **—чка** *dim. of* **лопата;** trowel; scoop, spatula; **—чно—** *prefix* (anat.) scapulo—; **—чно-ключичный** *a.* scapuloclavicular; **—чный** *a. of* **лопата;** (anat.) scapular; *see also under* **лопастный.**

лопатчатый *a.* spathulate, spatula-shaped.

лоп/аться *v.* burst (open), dehisce; crack, break, split, snap; **—ающийся** *a.* bursting, etc., *see v.*; dehiscent; pop (corn); **—нуть** *see* **лопаться.**

лополиты *pl.* (geol.) lopoliths.

лопу/х *m.*, **—ховый** *a.*, **—шник** *m.* (bot.) burdock (*Arctium*); **—шистый** *a.* burdock-like; broad-leaved.

Лорана кислота Laurent's acid, 1-naphthylamine-5-sulfonic acid.

лорандит *m.* (min.) lorandite.

лордоз *m.* (med.) lordosis.

лоренсия *f.* (bot.) Laurencia.

Лоренца сила Lorentz force.

лоренценит *m.* (min.) lorenzenite.

лоретин *m.* loretin, yatren.

лори *m.* (orn.) lory; (mam.) loris; *pl.* (orn.) Loriidae; **—евые**, **—зиды** *pl.* (mam.) lorises, pottos (Lorisidae); **—кариевые** *pl.* loricariid catfishes (*Loricariidae*).

лосанджелесский *a.* (geog.) Los Angeles.

лос/ёвый, **—ий**, **—иный** *a. of* **лось**; **—ёнок** *m.* elk calf; **—ина** *f.* buckskin; elk meat; **—иха** *f.* elk cow.

лоск *m.* gloss, luster, glaze; (text.) sheen.

лоскут *m.* shred, rag, scrap; (anat.) panniculus; (med.) flap, graft; **—ки** *pl.* (anat.) carunculae; **—ный** *a. of* **лоскут**; pannicular; patch (work); flap, closed (amputation); **—ок** *m.* (allergy) patch; (anat.) caruncle; **—ье** *n.* rags.

лосн/истый *a.* glossy, sleek; **—иться** *v.* be glossy, lustrous or shiny, shine; **—няк** *m.* (bot.) Liparis; **—ящийся** *a.* shining, glossy, lustrous.

лосос/ёвые *pl.* (ichth.) Salmonidae; **—ёвый**, **—ий**, **—иный** *a.* salmon(-colored); **—еокуневые** *pl.* Percopsidae; **—ина** *f.*, **—инный** *a.* (food) salmon; **—ь** *m.* salmon (*Salmo*, spec. *S. salar*); **—ь-таймень** *m.* sea trout (*S. trutta*).

лось *m.* (mam.) elk, moose (*Alces a.*).

лосьон *m.* lotion.

лосят/ина *f.* elk meat; **—ник** *m.* elk barn; elk hunter.

лот *m.* plumb (line), plummet, sounding lead; **механический л.** sounder.

лотарингский *a.* (geog.; geol.) Lorraine, Lotharingian.

лотелла *f.* (ichth.) Lotella.

лотер/ейный *a.*, **—ея** *f.* lottery.

лотк/а *gen.*, **—овый** *a. of* **лоток**; pan (conveyer); launder-type (classifier); **—ообразный** *a.* trough-shaped.

лот-линь *m.* (naut.) lead-line.

лоток *m.* trough, tray, pan (for gold washing); (min.) launder; cradle, mold; hod; (ball bearing) race; (mill) course, race; chute, flume, channel; gutter; (drainage) ditch, gully; cup (of nest); booth, stall; **охлаждающий л.** (glass) leer pan, lehr pan.

лотос *m.*, **—овый** *a.* (bot.) lotus (*Nelumbo*).

лоточ/ек *dim. of* **лоток**; (nest) cup, cavity; **—ный** *see* **лотковый.**

лотошить *v.* speak rapidly and incoherently.

лотрит *m.* (min.) lotrite.

лоттия *f.* (mal.) limpet (*Lottia*).

лотурин *m.* loturine, harman.

лоуренсий *m.* lawrencium, Lr or Lw.

Лоусона критерий Lawson criterion.

лоф/ин *m.* lophine, 2,4,5-triphenylimidazole; **—о—** *prefix* loph(o)— (crest, tuft); **—одонтный** *a.* lophodont (teeth); **—озиевые** *pl.* (bot.) Lophoziaceae; **—от** *m.* crestfish (*Lophotus*).

лофотенский *a.* (geog.) Lofoten.

лофо/товые *pl.* (ichth.) Lophotidae; **—трихный** *a.* (biol.) lophotrichous; **—фор** *m.* (zool.) lophophore;

—форин *m.* lophophorine, methoxyanhalonine; **—хелия** *f.* (zool.) Lophohelia.

лох *m.* (bot.) oleaster (*Elaeagnus*); (ichth.) male salmon (during spawning).

лохан/ка *f.*, **—ный**, **—очный** *a.*, **—ь** *f.* pan, tub, basin; (anat.) pelvis.

лох/ио— *prefix* (med.) lochi(o)—[lochia(l)]; **—ия** *f.* lochia.

лохм/атиться *v.* become matted, get mussed up; **—атый** *a.* shaggy; pannose, ragged; **—ач** *m.* shaggy creature; **—оток** *m.* scrap, piece; **—отья** *pl.* rags, tatters; **—ы** *pl.* (fur) tangle(s).

лохов/ые *pl.* (bot.) Elaeagnaceae; **—ый** *a. of* **лох.**

лохштейн *m.* jewel (bearing).

лоц/ировать *v.* detect, locate, find; (echo) sound; **—ия** *f.* navigational direction(s); (ecol.) locies.

лоцман *m.*, **—ский** *a.* pilot; pilotfish (*Naucrates ductor*); **—ство** *n.* piloting.

лошад/и(ные) *pl.* (mam.) Equidae; **—иный** *a.* horse, equine; **—иная сила** horsepower; **—ка** *dim. of* **лошадь**; pony; **—ник** *m.*, **—ница** *f.* horse breeder; **—ь** *f.* horse (*Equus caballus*).

лошак *m.* (mam.) hinny (*Equus hinnus*).

лош/алый *a.* (ichth.) spawned out, spent; **—ание** *n.* post-spawning condition.

лошачий *a. of* **лошак.**

Лошмидта число Loschmidt number.

лошок *m.* (ichth.) parr, young salmon; brook trout; gudgeon; minnow.

лошонок *m.* colt, foal.

лощалый *see* **лошалый.**

лощ/ение *n.* glossing, etc., *see* **лощить**; **—ён(н)ый** *a.* glossed, etc., *see* **лощить**; glossy; **—илка** *f.*, **—ило** *n.* burnisher; slicker.

лощильный *a.* glossing, polishing, burnishing; glazing; **л. зуб** burnisher; **л. пресс** (paper) rolling press, calender.

лощина *f.* hollow, depression; ravine, gulch, gully, draw; (forest) glen, dell.

лощить *v.* gloss, polish, burnish, smooth, finish; (paper) calender, glaze.

л.с., ЛС *abbr.* (лошадиная сила) horsepower; **ЛС, л/с, л./с.** (личный состав) personnel, staff.

л/сек *abbr.* (литров в секунду) liters per second.

Л-система *f.* laboratory system.

ЛССР *see* **ЛатвССР; ЛитССР.**

л.с.-ч *abbr.* (лошадиная сила-час) horsepower-hour.

ЛТ *abbr.* (ленточный транспортёр) conveyer belt; (лучевой тетрод) beam tetrode.

лу—*see also under* **лю—.**

луарский *a.* (geog.) Loire (river).

луб *m.* (bot.) bast (fiber); **—ка** *gen. of* **лубок; —ковый** *a.* bast-fiber.

лублинит *m.* (min.) lublinite.

лубо/вой *a.* bast (fiber); **—волокнистый** *a.* bast-fiber(ed); **—вый** *a.* bast(-fiber); **—еды** *pl.* bark beetles (*Ipidae*); **—к** *m.*, **—чный** *a.* bast (fiber); (med.) splint; **—отделитель** *m.* defibrer.

лубрикатор *m.* lubricator, oil can.

луб/ья *pl. of* **луб; —яной** *a.* bast-fiber.

лувар/евые, **—овые** *pl.* (ichth.) Luvaridae; **—ь** *m.* louvar.

луг *m.* meadow, grassland.

луганский *a.* (geog.) Lugan; Lugansk.

луго—*prefix* meadow; **—ведение** *n.* grassland ecology; **—вик** *m.* (bot.) hairgrass (*Deschampsia*); (ent.) crane fly (*Limonia*); **—вина** *f.* small meadow, glade; short-grass meadow; **—водство** *n.* meadow culture, grassland management; —**вой** *a.* meadow; sod (plow); prairie (dog); —**вой клин** hay fields, meadows; —**вая руда** meadow ore, bog iron ore; —**во-серозёмный** *a.* prairie gray (soil); —**мелиоративный** *a.;* —**мелиорация** *f.* meadow reclamation or development; —**пастбищный** *a.* pasture land, grassland; —**пастбищное угодье** grassland; —**рез** *m.* sod cutter, scarifier.

луда *f.* luda (a rocky littoral shoal or islet); (met.) tinning alloy.

луд/ильный *a.* (met.) tinning; tinplating (plant); —**ильщик** *m.* tinsmith; —**ить** *v.* tin(-plate), tin-coat.

лудламит *m.* (min.) ludlamite.

лудловские свиты (geol.) Ludlovian series, Ludlow beds.

лудо/га *f.,* —**жный,** —**жский** *a.* (ichth.) Ludoga whitefish (*Coregonus lavaretus ludoga*).

лужа *f.* puddle, pool.

лужайка *f.* lawn, grass plot, glade, green.

луж/айник *m.* (bot.) Limosella; —**анка** *f.* (mal.) freshwater snail; —**анки** *pl.* Viviparidae.

луж/ение *n.* (met.) tinning, tinplating; —**ё(н)ный** *a.* tinned, tinplated; —**ёное листовое железо** tinplate.

лужица *f.* pool, puddle.

лужицкий *a.* (geog.) Luzicke.

луж/ник *m.* (ent.) diving beetle (*Laccophilus*); —**ница** *f.* (bot.) Limosella; —**ок** *dim. of* **луг.**

лужский *a.* (geog.) Luga.

луз/га *f.* husk, shell, chaff; —**гать** *v.* husk, shell, shuck; —**говейка** *f.* hull aspirator; —**жистый** *a.* husky.

лузитанский *a.* (geol.) Lusitanian.

лузский *a.* (geog.) Luza.

луизианский *a.* Louisiana(n).

лук *m.* bow; (bot.) onion (*Allium*); **морской л.** squill (*Urginea maritima*).

лука *f.* bend, curve; saddle bow; pommel.

лукавый *a.* sly, cunning.

лук-арпаджик *m.* seed onion; **л.-батун** *m.* Welsh onion (*Allium fistulosum*).

лукит *m.* (min.) luckite.

луковиц/а *f.* (bot.) bulb; (anat.) bulb(us); (taste) bud; —**евидный,** —**еобразный,** —**еподобный** *a.* bulbiform, bulboid; —**еносный** *a.* bulbiferous, bulb-bearing.

лукович/ка *dim. of* **луковица;** bulbil, bulblet; —**но** *prefix* bulbo—; —**но-мочеиспускательный** *a.* (anat.) bulbourethral; —**ный** *a.* bulb(ous), bulbiferous; onion; bulbourethral (gland).

луко/вка *see* **луковичка;** —**возелёный** *a.* leek-green; —**вый** *a. of* **лук;** alliaceous; —**образный** *a.* bulbshaped, bulbiform; arched, bow-shaped.

лукошко *n.* bast basket.

лук-перо *m.* scallion; **л.-пор(р)ей** *m.* leek (*Allium porrum*); **л.-резанец** *m.* chives (*A. schoenoprasum*); **л.-репка** *m.* common onion (*A. cepa*); **л.-севок, л.-сеянец, л.-сеянчик** *m.* seed onion, onion set; **л.-скорода** *see* **лук-резанец.**

лукс/улианит *m.* (petr.) luxullianite; —**ириантный** *a.* luxuriant, lush, profuse.

лук-татарка *see* **лук-батун.**

лук-черемша *m.* (bot.) ramson (*Allium ursinum*); **л.-чернушка** *see* **лук-севок; л.-чеснок** *m.* garlic (*A. sativum*); **л.-ша(р)лот** *m.* shallot (*A. ascalonicum*); **л.-шнит(т)** *see* **лук-резанец.**

лум—*see also under* **люм**—.

лумп *m.* lump sugar.

луна *f.* moon; satellite; (geom.) lune; **л.-рыбы** *pl.* sunfishes (*Molidae*); moonfishes (*Lamprididae*).

лунат/изм *m.* somnambulism, sleepwalking; —**ик** *m.* somnambulist.

лунация *f.* (astr.) lunation.

Лунге нитрометр Lunge nitrometer.

луни *pl. of* **лунь.**

лунк/а *f.* hole, pit; crater(let), indentation, hollow; (turbine) bucket; (anat.; bot.) alveolus; (zool.) lunule; (antibiotic testing) well; (ent.) Phalera; —**оделатель,** —**окопатель** *m.* hole digger; dibbler.

лунник *m.* (bot.) Lunaria.

лунн/ый *a.* moon, lunar; lunitidal (interval); **л. камень** moonstone (gem); **л. пепельный свет** earthshine; **л. цирк** lunar ring formation; **л. экспедиционный модуль** lunar excursion module, LEM; —**ое молоко** agaric mineral.

лунок *gen. of* **лунка.**

луно/образный *see* **луновидный;** —**семянник** *m.* (bot.) moonseed (*Menispermum*); —**семянниковые** *pl.* Menispermaceae; —**трясение** *n.* moonquake; —**ход** *m.* lunokhod, moon vehicle, moon rover.

луноч/ка *dim. of* **лунка;** (anat.) alveole; lunula; (geom.) lune; —**ковый** *a. of* **луночка;** —**ный** *a. of* **лунка;** alveolar.

лунуляриевые *pl.* (bot.) Lunulariaceae.

лунчат/озубые *pl.* thecodont reptiles; —**ый** *a.* alveolate; selenodont (teeth).

луны-рыбы *see* **луна-рыбы.**

лунь *m.* (orn.) harrier (*Circus*).

луньевский *a.* (geog.) Lunyevka.

луня *gen. of* **лунь.**

лупа *f.* magnifier, magnifying glass.

луп/анин *m.* lupanine; —**еол** *m.* lupeol; —**етазин** *m.* lupetazine, dimethylpiperazine; —**етидин** *m.* lupetidine; —**етидиновый** *a.* lupetidinic (acid).

лупин *m.* (bot.) lupine (*Lupinus*); —**идин** *m.* lupinidine; —**ин** *m.* lupinin (glucoside); lupinine (alkaloid); —**оз** *m.* (vet.) lupinosis; —**оутомление** *n.* (soil) lupine sickness.

луп/ить *v.* peel, pare, strip; —**иться** *v.* peel, scale, flake (off), come off, break away; —**ка** *f.,* —**ление** *n.* peeling, etc., *see v.;* —**леный** *a.* peeled, etc., *see v.*

лупоглазый *a.* bug-eyed.

лупу/ин *m.,* lupulin; —**иновый** *a.* lupulin; lupulinic (acid); —**он** *m.* lupulone.

лупящийся *a.* peeling, etc., *see* **лупиться.**

лускать *v.* shell, husk, hull.

лускач *m.* (corn) sheller.

лусонский *a.* (geog.) Luzon.

лут *m.* leatherback turtle (*Dermochelys coriacea*).

луте/ин *see* **лютеин; —о**—*see* **лютео**—.

лут/еций *see* **лютеций; —идин** *m.* lutidine, dimethylpyridine; —**идиновый** *a.* lutidinic (acid); —**идон** *m.* lutidone, 2,4-dimethyl-3-oxypyridine.

луток *m.* (orn.) smew (*Mergus albellus*).

лутьян *see* **луциан.**

луфар/евые, —**и** *pl.* (ichth.) Pomatomidae; —**ь** *m.* bluefish (*Pomatomus saltatrix*).

Луффа раствор Luff's solution.

лухский *a.* (geog.) Lukh.

луциан *m.* (ichth.) snapper (*Lutjanus*); —**овые** *pl.* Lutjanidae.

луци/дол *m.* lucidol, benzoyl peroxide; —**нит** *m.* (min.) lucinite; —**фераза** *f.* luciferase (enzyme); —**ферин** *m.* luciferin.

луцонит *m.* (min.) luzonite.

луч *m.* ray, beam, shaft (of light); path (in phase diagram);

wire; (biol.) arm; (zool.) ray; **испускать —и** v. radiate, emit rays; **—e** *prefix* actin(o)—, radio—[ray(s); radiated structure]; **—евидный** *see* **лучеобразный**; **—евики** *pl.* (prot.) Radiolaria; **—евод** *m.* light (wave)guide.

лучев/ой *a.* ray, radial; radiation (pressure; sickness); beam; electron beam (tetrode); beam-type (maser); *suffix* —radiate, -rayed; **—ая диаграмма** wave-front chart; **—ая кость** (anat.) radius.

луче/запястный *a.* (anat.) radiocarpal; **—зарность** *f.* radiance; **—зарный** *a.* radiant, bright; **—звуковой** *a.* radiophonic.

лучеиспуск/ание *n.* radiation; irradiation; **поверхность —ания** radiating surface; **—ательный, —ающий** *a.* radiating; **—ать** *v.* emit rays, radiate.

луче/локтевой *a.* radio-ulnar; **—ние** *n.* fishing by flashlight; **—образующий** *a.* beam-forming; **—преломление** *see* **лучепреломление**; **—пёрые, —плавниковые** *pl.* (ichth.) Actinopterygii; **—плечевой** *a.* (anat.) radiohumeral; **—поглощение** *n.* radiation absorption.

лучепреломл/ение *n.* refraction, refringence; **двойное п.** birefringence; **—яемость** *f.* refractility, refractivity; **—яющий** *a.* refractive.

луче/приёмник *m.* radiation detector; **—прозрачный** *a.* diathermic; **—расщепитель** *m.* beam splitter.

лучи *pl. of* **луч**; radiation; **—к** *dim. of* **луч**.

лучин/(к)а *f.*, **—(оч)ный** *a.* splinter, chip, shaving; (typ.) pin, finger.

лучисто— *see* **луче—**; **л.-волокнистый** *a.* (geol.) radiating columnar; **—симметричный** *a.* actinomorphous; **—сть** *f.* radiance; radiation, radiant energy.

лучист/ый *a.* radiant, radial, radiating, radiate(d); radiation; radiative (transfer of energy); **л. грибок** (bact.) Actinomyces; **л. камень** (min.) actinolite; **л. поток** radiant flux; **л. разряд** (elec.) brush and spray discharge; **—ая сфера** (gen.) astrosphere; **—ые животные** (zool.) Radiata.

луч/ить *v.* fish by flashlight; **—иться** *v.* shine, beam; **—ицы** *pl.* (bot.) Charophyta.

луч/ковый *a.* bow (saw); **—ок** *dim. of* **лук**; bow (of saw); drill bow.

лучш/е *comp. of* **хороший, хорошо**, better, superior; **л. всего** best; **как можно л.** as well as possible; **тем л.** so much the better, all the better; **—ий** *a.* the best; the better; **в—ем случае** at best, at most; **к—ему** for the best.

лущ/ёвка *f.*, **—ение** *n.* shelling, etc., *see v.*; **—ён(н)ый** *a.* shelled, etc. *see v.*; **—илка** *f.* sheller, huller; **—ильник** *m.* stubble breaker, surface plow; **—ильный** *a.* shelling, etc., *see v.*; shell (beans); **—ить** *v.* shell, hull, husk; strip, peel (off), take off; break (soil, stubble); **—иться** *v.* peel off, come away.

луяврит *m.* (petr.) lujavrite.

ЛФЧХ *abbr.* (**логарифмическая фазочастотная характеристика**) logarithmic phase-frequency characteristic.

лыж/а *f.*, **—ный** *a.* ski; (elec.) shoe.

лыко *n.*, **—вый** *a.* bast (fiber); **—дёр** *m.* bast (fiber) peeler.

лыс/ач *m.* (ichth.) pike asp (*Aspiolucius esocinus*); **—еть** *v.* grow bald; **—еющий** *a.* calvescent; balding; **—ина** *f.* bald spot; (med.) alopecia, baldness; **—ка** *f.* flat, flattened spot; **—о—** *prefix* phalacro—(bald); psilo—(bare); **—огорский** *a.* Bald Mountain; **—осемянник** *m.* Phalacrachena; **—ун** *m.* (ichth.) bald goby (*Pomatoschistus*); (mam.) Greenland seal (*Pagophilus groenlandica*); **—уха** *f.* (orn.) coot (*Fulica atra*); **—ый** *a.* calvous, bald.

лыч/ко *dim.*, **—ный** *a. of* **лыко**.

ль *see* **ли.**

льв/а *gen. of* **лев**; **—ёнок** *m.* lion cub; **—инка** *f.* (ent.) soldier fly (*Stratiomys*); **—инки, —инковые** *pl.* Stratiomidae; **—ино—***prefix* leonto—, lion; **—иноголовка** *f.* lionhead (goldfish); **—иность** *f.* (med.) leontiasis.

льви/ный *a.* leonine, lion; **л. зев** (bot.) snapdragon (*Antirrhinum*); **л. зуб** dandelion (*Taraxacum dens-leonis*) **—ная голова** (ichth.) flying gurnard (*Dactylopterus volitans*); **—ное лицо** *see* **львиность**; **—ца** *f.* lioness.

львовский *a.* (geog.) L'vov.

льв/ы *pl. of* **лев**; **морские л.** (mam.) Otariidae; **—ята** *pl. of* **львёнок.**

льгот/а *f.* privilege, exemption, advantage; **—ный** *a.* preferential; cut, reduced (rate).

льд/а *gen. of* **лёд**; **—ина** *f.* ice cake, ice floe; **—инка** *dim. of* **льдина**; small piece of ice; icicle; **—истость** *f.* ice content; **—истый** *a.* icy.

льдо— *prefix* ice; **—генератор** *m.* ice maker; **—дробилка** *f.* ice crusher; **—завод** *m.* ice-making plant; **—камень** *m.* ground ice; **—образование** *n.*, **—подобный** *a.* ice-like, icy; **—производство** *n.* ice manufacture; **—скат** *m.* ice chute; **—удаление** *n.* de-icing; **—удалитель** *m.* de-icer; **—хранилище** *n.* ice house.

льды *pl. of* **лёд**; **серые л.** winter ice.

льежский *a.* (geog.) Liege.

льёт *pr. 3 sing. of* **лить.**

льна *gen. of* **лён.**

льно— *prefix* flax; linen; linseed; **—водство** *n.*, **—водческий** *a.* flax growing; **—волокно** *n.* flax fiber; **—вые** *pl.* (bot.) Linaceae; **—головка** *f.* flax boll; **—завод** *m.* flax-processing plant; **—комбайн** *m.* flax harvester; **—комбинат** *see* **льнозавод**; **—коноплемялка** *f.* flax and hemp breaker; **—кудель** *f.* flax tow; **—молотилка** *f.* flax thresher; **—мялка** *f.* flax breaker; scutcher; **—обрабатывающий** *a.*, **—обработка** *f.* flax processing.

льноочиститель *m.* flax (seed) cleaner; **—ный** *a.* flax cleaning.

льнопряд/ение *n.*, **—ильный** *a.* flax spinning; **—илка, —ильня** *f.* flax mill.

льно/семеноводство *n.* flaxseed culture; **—сеялка** *f.* flaxseed drill; **—солом(к)а** *f.* flax straw; **—сушилка** *f.* flax dryer; **—теребилка** *f.* flax puller; **—тёрка** *f.* linseed huller; **—трепалка** *f.* flax scutcher; **—трещётка** *f.* linseed sorter; **—триер** *m.* flax seed cylinder grader; **—уборка** *f.*, **—уборочный** *a.* flax harvesting; **—утомление** *n.* (soil) flax sickness; **—чесалка** *f.* flax-hackling machine.

льнуть *v.* cling, stick, adhere (to).

льнянка *f.* (bot.) toadflax (*Linaria*).

льнян/ой *a.* flax(en); linen; linseed (meal, oil, cake); **л. холст** linen; **—ая кислота** linoleic acid; **соль —ой кислоты** linoleate; **—ая трава** *see* **льнянка**; **—ое семя** linseed, flaxseed.

льняно/кислый *a.* linoleic acid; linoleate (of); **л. кальций, —кальциевая соль** calcium linoleate; **—кислая соль** linoleate; **—масляная кислота** *see* **льняная кислота.**

льстить *v.* flatter; **—ся** *v.* be tempted.

льюи/зит, —сит *m.* (mil.; min.) lewisite; **—совский, —совый** *a.* Lewis (acid).

льющий *pres. act. part. of* **лить.**

льял/а *f.*, **—о** *n.* (naut.) bilge(way); (foundry) mold; **—ьный** *a. of* **льяло**; bilge (water).

льяносы *pl.* (geobot.) llanos.

лэмбовский сдвиг (phys.) Lamb shift.

Лэнгмюра теория Langmuir theory.

ЛЭП *abbr.* (**линия электропередачи**) power transmission line.

лэптоп *m.* (comp.) laptop.

любезн/ичать *v.* be considerate, be nice (to); **—ость** *f.* kindness, courtesy; **—ый** courteous, obliging, polite; **с —ого согласия** courtesy (of).

люберецкий песок Lyubertsy sand.

любим/ец *m.,* **—ица** *f.,* **—ый** *a.* favorite.

любисток *m.* (bot.) lovage (*Levisticum*).

любитель *m.,* **—ский** *a.* amateur, fan; **л.-коротковолновик** *m.* short-wave radio ham.

любить *v.* like, love; require, need.

любка *f.* (bot.) Platanthera.

люблинский *a.* (geog.) Lublin.

любоваться *v.* admire.

любовина *f.* lean (beef).

любов/ник *m.,* **—ница** *f.* lover; **—ный** *a.,* **—ь** *f.* love, liking; **—ная стрела** (zool.) dart.

любознательн/ость *f.* intellectual curiosity; **—ый** *a.* curious, inquiring.

любой *a.* any; either; all; arbitrary.

любопыт/ничать, —ствовать *v.* be curious; **—ный** *a.* curious, inquiring; **—ство** *n.* curiosity.

любящий *pr. act. part. of* **любить.**

люлер(с) *m.* louver; (naut.) eyelet.

люд *m.* people, nation.

людвигит *m.* (min.) ludwigite.

Людерса линии (met.) Lüders (flow) lines.

люд/и *pl.* people, men; **без —ей** unmanned (satellite); **заселённый —ьми, с —ьми** manned; populated.

людийский ярус (geol.) Ludian stage.

людн/ость населения population density; **—ый** *a.* crowded, thickly populated.

люд/оед *m.,* **—оедский** *a.* cannibal; (ichth.) man-eater shark (*Carchar(h)inus glaucus*); **—оедство** *n.* cannibalism, anthropophagy; **—ской** *a.* human; manpower; **—ской материал** manpower; **—ской состав** personnel, staff.

люизит *see* **льюизит.**

люк *m.,* **—овый** *a.* manhole, hatch, trap door; (min.) chute; **—овой** *m.* chute drawer.

люкс *m.* (illum.) lux, meter-candle; **—ембургскин** *a.* (geog.) Luxembourg; **—метр** *m.* lux(o)meter; **—метр-свеча** *see* **люкс; л.-секунда** *f.* lux-second; **—урировать(ся)** *v.* luxuriate, grow exuberantly.

люл/ечный *a.,* **—ька** *f.* cradle, cage; basket, bucket; (foundry) ingot chair; swing bolster; swinging tray; (smoking) pipe; **—ечная балка** swing bolster.

люма/хель, —шель *m.* lumachel(le), fire marble.

люмб/аго *n.* (med.) lumbago; **—альный** *a.* (anat.) lumbar; **—о—** *prefix* lumbo— (loins); **—рикулюс** *m.* (zool.) Lumbriculus; **—рициды** *pl.* earthworms (*Lumbricidae*); lumbricides, lumbrici-destroying agents.

люмен *m.* lumen (unit of luminous flux); **—(о)метр** *m.* lumen meter; **л.-секунда** lumen-second; **л.-час** lumen-hour.

люминал *m.* Luminal, phenobarbital.

люминесц/ентно-битумный *a.* (geol.) bitumen-luminescence; **—ентный** *a.* luminescent; fluorimetric (analysis); fluorescent (lamp); scintillation, track (chamber); **—енция** *f.* luminescence; **—ировать** *v.* luminesce; **—ирующий** *a.* luminescent.

люми/ноген *m.* phosphorogen, luminogen; **—носкоп** *m.* luminoscope; **—нофор** *m.* (phys.) phosphor; (chem.) luminophore; **твёрдый —нофор** (opt.) luminescent solid; **—родопсин** *m.* lumirhodopsin; **—стерин** *m.* lumisterol, irradiated ergosterol; **—флавин** *m.* lumiflavin; **—хром** *m.* lumichrome.

люмнит *m.* lumnite (shielding material).

люмпен *m.,* **—а** *f.,* **—ус** *m.* lumpfish, snake blenny (*Lumpenus*); **—овые** *pl.* Lumpenidae.

люнебургит *m.* (min.) lüneburgite.

люнет *m.* lunette (opening); sighthole; (glass) linnet hole; (mach.) steady(rest); **—одержатель** *m.* steady holder.

люнкерит *m.* (met.) lunkerite.

люп/ин *see* **лупин; —озорий** *m.* lupus-treating hospital; **—оидный** *a.* (med.) lupoid; **—оидная клетка** LE cell; **—ус** *m.* lupus, spec. lupus erythmatosus.

люр *m.* (ichth.) pollack (*Pollachius*).

люрик *m.* (orn.) little auk (*Plautus alle*).

люсайт *m.* (plastics) lucite.

люстр *m.* (cer.) luster (color), luster glaze; brilliance; flash.

люстра *f.* chandelier; **проходческая л.** cluster floodlight.

люстр/ин *m.,* **—иновый** *a.* (text.) lustrine; **—ировать** *v.* luster, make lustrous.

люстровый *a. of* **люстра.**

люте/ин *m.,* **—иновый** *a.* lutein; **—инизация** *f.* luteinization; **—инизирующий** *a.* luteinizing, lutein-stimulating (hormone); **—оза** *f.* luteose; **—оид** *m.* luteoid; **—олин** *m.* luteolin; **—ома** *f.* (med.) luteoma; **—омицин** *m.* luteomycin (antibiotic); **—ол** *m.* luteol; **—осоединение** *n.* luteo compound; **—остерон** *m.* luteosterone, progesterone; **—остимулирующий** *a.* luteinizing; **—отропин** *m.* luteotropin; **—отропный** *a.* luteotropic (hormone).

лютер *see* **люттер.**

лютетский ярус (geol.) Lutetian stage.

лютеций *m.* lutecium, Lu.

лютианиды *pl. see* **луциановые.**

лютик *m.,* **—овый** *a.* (bot.) crowfoot (*Ranunculus*); **—овые** *pl.* Ranunculaceae.

лютк/а *f.* (ent.) Lestes; **—и** *pl.* damsel flies (*Lestidae*).

люттер *m.* (distilling) low wine, first run; **—ная колонна** continuous distillation column; low-wine still.

лютый *a.* strong (wind); severe (frost); bloodthirsty (animal).

люф/а, —овый *see* **люффа.**

люфт *m.* gap, clearance; slack, free play, backlash, freedom; dead stroke.

люфф/а *f.,* **—овый** *a.* (bot.) luffa, dishcloth gourd (*Luffa*).

люцерн/а *f.,* **—овый** *a.* (bot.) alfalfa (*Medicago*); **—ария** *f.* (zool.) Lucernaria; **—ик** *m.,* **—ище** *n.* alfalfa field; **—оводство** *n.* alfalfa growing; **—оутомление** *n.* (soil) alfalfa sickness.

люци— *see under* **луци—; —ниды** *pl.* (mal.) Lucinidae; **—т** *m.* lucite.

люч/ина *f.* (naut.) hatch board; **—ок** *dim. of* **люк;** hatch; (access) hole, peep hole.

ля *n.* (music) A.

лябиидэ *pl.* (ent.) Labiidae.

лягавая собака pointer; setter.

лягать *v.* kick (out); paw (the ground); spurn, injure, hurt.

лягв/а *f.* frog; **л.-рыболов** *f.* (ichth.) anglerfish (*Lophius piscatorius*); **—оголов** *see* **лягушкоголов; —ы-рыболовы** *pl.* Lophiidae.

лягнуть *see* **лягать.**

лягут *fut. 3 pl. of* **лечь.**

лягуш/атник *m.* ranarium, frog terrarium; **—ачий, —ечий, —ечный, —иный** *a.* frog; (elec.) frog-leg (winding); (med.) saltatory (gait); **—ечная трава** (bot.) water pepper (*Polygonum hydropiper*); **—ечник** *m.* frogbit (*Hydrocharis morsus-ranae*); **—ка** *f.* (amph.) frog (*Rana*); draw vise, tongs, grip, toggle; **—ка-бык, —ка-вол** *f.* bull frog (*Rana catesbeiana*);

—ка-рыба *f.* (ichth.) lumpsucker (*Cyclopterichthys*); **—ки** *pl.* (amph.) Ranidae; **—ко—** *prefix* batrach(o)—, frog; **—коголов** *m.* (ichth.) tadpole fish (*Raniceps raninus*); **—коедка** *f.* (ent.) Lucilia bufonivora; **—ко-зуб** *m.* (amph.) Ranodon; **—корот** *m.* (orn.) frogmouth; **—вороты** *pl.* Podargidae; **—онок** *m.* young frog.

ляда *f.* (geol.) overgrown depression; gully, ravine; clearing; (min.) trap door.

лядвенец *m.* (bot.) trefoil (*Lotus*); **рогатый л.** bird's foot trefoil (*Lotus corniculatus*).

лядина *see* **ляда.**

лядник *m.* (bot.) Hierochloe.

ляжет *fut. 3 sing. of* **лечь.**

ляжка *f.* (ent.) thigh, haunch; shank.

лязг *m.,* **—ать** *v.* clank, clang, jingle.

Ляймана серия (phys.) Lyman series.

ляллеманция *f.* (bot.) Lallemantia.

лямд/а *f.* lambda, microliter; **—овидный** *a.* lambdoid.

лямбл/иоз *m.* (med.) lambliasis, giardiasis; **—ия** *f.* (prot.) Lamblia, Giardia.

Ляме параметр Lamé's constant.

лямель *see* **ламель.**

лямиа *f.* (ent.) Lamia.

лямингова масса (gas) Laming's mass.

ляминария *f.* (bot.) sea tangle (*Laminaria*).

лям/ка *f.,* **—очный** *a.* strap; (parachute) riser.

ляо/дунский *a.* (geog.) Liaotung; **—хэский** *a.* Liao.

ляп/ать *v.* botch, bungle; **—нуть** *v.* blurt out; **—нуться** *v.* plop down, fall.

ляпис *m.* lunar caustic, silver nitrate; **л.-лазурь** *m.* lapis lazuli.

ляпсусы *pl.* (typ.) corrigenda.

лярд *m.,* **—овый** *a.* lard; **л.-ойль** *m.* lard oil.

ляринго— *see* **ларинго—.**

лятентный *see* **латентный.**

лятимерия *see* **латимерия.**

ляфрия *f.* (ent.) Laphria.

ляховский *a.* (geog.) Lyakhov.

ляцинулярия *f.* (zool.) Lacinularia.

М

м, М *abbr. for many terms, most commonly used of which are:* **м** *abbr.* (**метр**) meter; (**милли-**) milli-; **м., М** *abbr.* (**масштаб**) scale; (**минута**) minute; (**море**) sea; **М** *abbr.* (**мега-**) mega-; (**металл**) metal; (**молярность**) molarity; (**молярный**) molar; (**число Маха**) Mach number; (**метод**) method; **М.** (**мультиплет**) multiplet; *abbr.* (**Москва**) Moscow.

м- *see* **мета—.**

ма *abbr.* (**миллиампер**) milliampere.

Ма *abbr.* [**Мах (число)**] Mach (number).

маар *m.* maar (a type of volcanic crater).

мавзолей *m.* mausoleum.

маврешок *m.* (ichth.) ombre (*Sciaena umbra*).

маври/кийский *a.* (geog.) Mauritius, Maurice; **—танский** *a.* Mauritanian; Moorish.

мавролик *m.* (ichth.) Maurolicus.

МАГА *abbr.* (**магнитногидродинамическая аналогия**) magnetohydrodynamic analog method.

магаданский *a.* (geog.) Magadan.

магазин *m.* store; warehouse; (feeder) bin; box; magazine; hopper, dispenser; (comp.) stack; **м. ёмкости** (elec.) capacitor box; **м. сопротивлений** (elec.) resistance box; **—ирование** *n.* storing; (min.) stoping; shrinkage; recharge (of sewage or underground water); **—ка** *f.* magazine rifle; **—ный** *a. of* **магазин; —ный список** (comp.) pushdown stack; **—ного типа** stack (memory); last-in, first-out (stack).

маггемит *m.* (min.) maghemite.

магеллан/овый, —ский *a.* Magellan(ic).

магента *f.* magenta, fuchsin.

магист/ерский *a.* (educ.) Master's; **—ерство** *n.* Master's degree; **—р (точных) наук** Master of Science, M.S.

магистрал *m.* (met.) magistral (a roasted copper pyrite).

магистраль *f.* main line, trunk line, artery; (gas, water) main; manifold; (elec.) main circuit, bus; highway, turnpike; **—ный** *a. of* **магистраль;** main; arterial; long-distance, long-haul; **—ная труба** main.

магистрант *m.* undergraduate.

магический *a.* magic.

магма *f.* (geol.) magma, molten rock; (pharm.) magma; **—тизм** *m.* magmatism; **—тический** *a.* magma(tic).

магн *m.* magne (magnetic unit).

магнавольт *m.* two-stage rotary amplifier.

магнал/ий, —иум *m.* magnalium (alloy); **—ит** *m.* magnalite (alloy).

магнамицин *m.* Magnamycin, carbomycin.

магнезиальный *a.* magnesia(n); **м. цемент** magnesian cement, Sorel's cement.

магнезиоферрит *m.* (min.) magn(esi)oferrite.

магнезит *m.,* **—ный, —овый** *a.,* **—овый шпат** (min.) magnesite; **—охромитовый** *a.* magnesite-chromite.

магнезия *f.* magnesia, magnesium oxide; **белая м.** magnesia alba, hydrated magnesium carbonate; **водная м.** magnesium hydroxide; **жжёная м.** magnesia; **лимоннокислая м.** citrate of magnesia; **сернокислая м.** magnesium sulfate.

магне/зон *m.* (analysis) Magneson; **—син** *m.* (elec.) Magnesyn (synchro).

магнетиз/ёр *m.* magnetizer; **—ирование** *n.* magnetization; **—ированный** *a.* magnetized; **—ировать** *v.* magnetize; **—м** *m.* magnetism.

магнетик *m.* magnetic substance.

магнетит *m.,* **—овый** *a.* (min.) magnetite, magnetic iron ore.

магнет/ический *a.* magnetic; **—о** *n.* (elec.) magneto (generator); **—ометр** *m.* magnetometer; **—он** *m.* magneton (unit of magnetic moment); **—охимия** *f.* magnetochemistry; **—рон** *m.,* **—ронный** *a.* (electron.) magnetron.

магниев/ый *a.* magnesium, magnesia(n); **м. известняк** (min.) magnesian limestone, dolomite; **—ая лента** magnesium ribbon; **—ая слюда** (min.) magnesium mica, phlogopite; **—ые квасцы** magnesia alum, pickeringite.

магниетермический *a.* magnesium-reduced.

магн/ий *m.* magnesium, Mg; **окись —ия** magnesium oxide; **сернокислый м., сульфат —ия** magnesium sulfate; **хлористый м.** magnesium chloride.

магний/алкильное соединение magnesium alkyl compound; **—бромэтил** *m.* ethyl-magnesium bromide; **—галоидалкилы** *pl.* alkylmagnesium halides; **—катионирование** *n.* magnesium zeolite softening process (of water); **—органический** *a.* organomagnesium (compound); Grignard (reaction); **—фосфат** *m.* magnesium phosphate.

магни/ко *n.* Magnico (alloy); **—стор** *m.* (electron.) Magnistor (reactor).

магнит *m.* magnet; **брусковый м.** magnetic bar, bar magnet; **естественный м.** (min.) natural magnet, lodestone.

магнит/изм *m.* magnetism; **—ить** *v.* magnetize.

магнитно/активный *a.* magnetic; **—жёсткий** *a.* magnetically hard; **—ионный** *a.* magnetoionic; **—мягкий** *a.* magnetically soft; high magnetic permeability; **—полупроводниковый** *a.* transistor-magnetic; **—сть** *f.* magnetization; magnetizability; **—электроразрядный** *a.* magnetic-electric discharge.

магнит/ый *a.* magnetic; **м. железняк** (min.) magnetic iron ore, magnetite; **м. колчедан** (min.) magnetic pyrites, pyrrhotite; **м. поток** magnetic flux; **измеритель —ого потока** fluxmeter; **—ая восприимчивость** (magnetic) susceptibility; **—ая диаграмма** magnetogram; **—ая запись** tape recording; **—ая индукция** (magnetic) induction, flux density; **—ая лента** magnetic tape; **—ая подвижность** magnetic fluctuation; **—ая проводимость** (elec.) permeance; **—ая проницаемость** permeability; **—ая сила** magnetic force; **—ая стрелка** magnetic needle; **—ая цепь** magnetic circuit; **—ое дутьё** magnetic drive; **—ое наклонение** angle of dip, magnetic dip; **—ое поле** magnetic field; **—ое притяжение** magnetic attraction; **—ое сопротивление** (elec.) magnetic resistance, reluctance; **удельное —ое сопротивление** (elec.) reluctivity; **—ые элементы** (aut.) magnetics.

магнито— *prefix* magneto—, magnet(ic); **—газодинамика** *f.* magnetogas dynamics; **—газодинамический** *a.* magnetogas dynamic.

магнитогидро/динамика *f.* magnetohydrodynamics; **—динамический** *a.* magnetohydrodynamic; **—механика** *f.* magnetohydromechanics; **—статический** *a.* magnetohydrostatic.

магнито/горский *a.* (geog.) Magnitogorsk; **—грамма** *f.* magnetogram; **—граф** *m.* magnetograph, recording magnetometer; **—графия** *f.* electromagnetic printing; **—движущая сила** magnetomotive force; **—держатель** *m.* magnet support, magnet cradle; **—диэлектрик** *m.* ferrite; **—звуковой** *a.* magnetosonic; **—ионный** *see* **магнитоионный**; **—ла** *f.* combination radio-tape recorder; **—лог** *m.* magnetologist.

магнитометр *m.* magnetometer; **—ический** *a.* magnetometric; magnetic (measurement); **—ия** *f.* magnetometry.

магнито/механический *a.* magnetomechanic(al); **—мягкий** *a.* magnetically soft; **—оптика** *f.* magnetooptics; **—оптический** *a.* magneto-optical; **—пирит** *m.* (min.) magnetic pyrites, pyrrhotite; **—писец** *m.* magnetic recorder; **—плазмодинамический** *a.* magnetoplasmodynamic; **—провод** *m.* magnetic circuit; core; yoke; **—разведка** *f.* magnetic prospecting; **—резистор** *m.* magnetoresistor; **—скоп** *m.* magnetoscope; **—сопротивление** *n.* magnetoresistance; **—статика** *f.* magnetostatics; **—статический** *a.* magnetostatic.

магнитострик/тор *m.* (geol.) magnetostrictive drill; **—ционный** *a.* magnetostrictive; **—ция** *f.* magnetostriction.

магнито/твёрдый *a.* magnetically hard, magnetically rigid (alloy); **—теллурический** *a.* magnetotelluric; **—уловитель** *m.* magnetic detector; **—упругий** *a.* magnetoelastic; **—фон** *m.* magnetic tape recorder; magnetophone; **—фонный** *a.* tape recorder; tape recording; **—фонная лента** magnetic tape; **—химия** *f.* magnetochemistry.

магнитоэлектричес/кий *a.* magnetoelectric; permanent-magnet (generator); **м. измерительный прибор** moving-coil instrument; **—кая машина** magneto; **—тво** *n.* magnetoelectricity.

магни/т-уничтожитель *m.* magnetic compensator, corrector; **—ченность** *f.* degree of magnetization; **—ченный** *a.* magnetized.

магно/лиевые *pl.* (bot.) Magnoliaceae; **—лиевый** *a.* magnolia; **—лин** *m.* magnolin; **—лит** *m.*, **—литовый** *a.* xylolith (a building material); **—лия** *f.* magnolia; **—феррит** *m.* (min.) magn(esi)oferrite; **—хромит** *m.* magn(esi)ochromite.

Магнуса соль Magnus salt, tetrammine-platinum(II) chloroplatinate.

магогани *n.* mahogony (wood).

магония *f.* (bot.) Mahonia.

магот *m.* (mam.) macaque monkey (*Macaca invus*).

мадагаскарский *a.* (geog.) Madagascar.

мадаке *m.* (bot.) Phyllostachys.

мадаполам *m.*, **—овый** *a.* (text.) madapolam.

мадер/а *f.* Madeira (wine); **—изация** *f.* maderization.

мад/иевый *a.*, **—ия** *f.* (bot.) Madia.

мадрепор/а *f.* madrepore (coral); **—ит** *m.* (zool.) madreporite; **—овый** *a.* madreporic.

мадука *f.* (bot.) Madhuca.

мадурский *a.* (geog.) Madura.

маек *gen. pl.* of **майка.**

мажет *pr. 3 sing.* of **мазать.**

мажеф *m.* manganese ferric phosphate (corrosion inhibitor).

мажор *m.* (music) major key.

мажор/анта *f.*, **—антный** *a.* (math.) majorant; **—ирование** *n.* majorization; **—ированный** *a.* majorized, dominated; **—ировать** *v.* majorize, dominate; **—ирующий** *a.* dominant; **—итарный** *a.* majority; **—ный** *a.* major, greater.

мажущий *a.* smearing, etc., *see* **мазать;** **—ся** *a.* greasy, slippery; creamy, spreadable (food).

мазама *m.* (mam.) brocket deer (*Mazama*).

мазан/ие, **—ье** *n.* smearing, etc., *see* **мазать;** **—ка** *f.* mud hut; mud wall; **—(н)ый** *a.* smeared, etc.

мазариды *pl.* (ent.) Masaridae.

маз/ать *v.* smear, daub, spread, apply; grease, oil; soil; **—евый** *a.* of **мазь;** **—еобразность** *f.* greasiness; (paper) softness, wetness; **—еобразный,** **—еподобный** *a.* smeary, greasy, slippery; salve-like, paste-like, pasty.

мазер *m.*, **—ный** *a.* (phys.) maser, molecular activator.

маз/и *gen., pl., etc., of* **мазь;** **—илка** *f.* brush; **—ка** *see* **мазание; метод —ков** smear technique; **—ница** *f.* tar pot; **—нуть** *see* **мазать;** **—ня** *f.* smear, blur; **—ок** *m.* dab, stroke (of brush); smear; coat(ing).

мазонит *m.* masonite (fiberboard).

мазу *f.* (ichth.) masu salmon (*Oncorhynchus masu*).

мазут *m.* residual fuel oil, boiler fuel; atmospheric resid; **—охранилище** *n.* fuel oil storage tank.

мазь *f.* ointment, salve, cream; lubricant; **жидкая м.** liniment.

маиевский *a.* Mach (number).

маис *m.*, **—овый** *a.* (bot.) maize, corn (*Zea mays*); **—овая каша** hominy, grits.

май *m.* May; **м.-балык** *m.* (ichth.) regional name for shad, shemaya, etc.

майдан *m.* tar pit; tar distillery; (market) square; **—(ник)** *m.* rapids.

Майера *see* **Мейера.**

майка *f.* (ent.) Meloe.

майкельсоновский *a.* Michelson.

майк/и, —овые pl. (ent.) Meloidae.

майконг m. (mam.) a fox (*Cerdocyon thous*).

майллардовый a. (agr.) Maillard (reaction).

Майн (geog.) the Main.

майна f. lane; crack or hole in ice; (orn.) myna (*Acridotheres*).

майник m. (bot.) Majanthemum.

майолика f. majolica (earthenware).

майонез m. mayonnaise.

майоран m. (bot.) marjoram (*Majorana*).

майорановский a. (nucl.) Majorana.

майский a. May; (geog.) Maya.

майснеровский a. Meissner (oscillator).

майсорский a. (geog.) Mysore.

майтицид m. miticide.

майтландит m. (min.) maitlandite.

майцена f. cornstarch.

майшфильтр m. (food) mash filter.

мак m. (bot.) poppy (*Papaver*); **снотворный м.** opium poppy.

МАК abbr. (**метакриловая кислота**) methacrylic acid.

макадам m. macadam(ized) road; **—изация** f. macadamization; **—ия** f. (bot.) Macadamia.

макак m., **—а** f. (mam.) macaque (*Macacus*).

мак/альный a. dipping; **м. пруток** dipstick; **—ание** n. dip(ping); **—аный** a. dipped; seamless.

макаровский a. (geog.) Makarov(o).

макарон/ный a., **—ы** pl. macaroni.

макассаровое масло Macassar oil.

макат/ельный a. dipping; **—ь** v. dip.

Мак Бэна центрифуга McBain centrifuge.

маквис m. maquis, evergreen shrub thicket.

македонский a. (geog.) Macedonian.

макензийский a. (geog.) Mackenzie.

макет m., **—ный** a. model, mock-up; prototype; pattern, set-up; (typ.) layout, makeup, dummy, copy, sample; design, format; (flight) simulator; (comp.) breadboard model; **—ирование** n. breadboarding; prototyping.

маки m. (mam.) Lemur.

макинтош m. mackintosh, raincoat.

макинтошит m. (min.) mackintoshite.

макитра f. earthenware pot.

Макки дистрибутор, Мак Ки д. (met.) McKee distributor.

Мак-Кинли (geog.) Mount McKinley.

маккия see **маквис**.

Мак Кормика жатвенная машина (agr.) McCormick reaping machine.

маклейин m. macleyine, protopine.

Мак Леода манометр McLeod gage.

маклер m. (com.) (stock)broker; **—ствовать** v. job, be a broker.

маклок m. (anat.) tuber coxae.

Маклорена теорема (math.) Maclaurin's theorem.

макл/урин, —юрин m. maclurin; **—юра** f. (bot.) osage orange (*Maclura*).

макнуть see **макать**.

маков/ка f. poppy head; crown, top, summit, cupola; **—ые** pl. (bot.) Papaveraceae; **—ый** a. poppy; poppy-seed (oil); **—ая текстура** (petr.) pelitic structure.

макома f. (mal.) Macoma.

макрел/евые pl. (ichth.) Scombridae; **—евый** a. of **макрель**; **—ещука** f. Scomberesox; **—ещуки, —ещуковые** pl. skippers, etc. (*Scomberesocidae*); **—и** see **макрелевые; —ьный** see **макрелевый**.

макрель f. mackerel (*Scomber scombrus*); **—ьный** see **макрелевый**.

макро— prefix macr(o)—, (long, large); broad-scale, large-scale; **—биотический** a. macrobiotic, long-

lived; life-prolonging; **—возмущение** n. broadscale perturbation; **—гамета** f. (gen.) macrogamete; **—гамия** f. macrogamy; **—генератор** m. (comp.) macrocommand generator; **—глобулин** m. macroglobulin; **—деталь** f. macrodetail; **—зейгерование** n. (met.) macrosegregation.

макрозерн/истость f. (phot.) graininess; **—истый** a. grainy, coarse(-grained); **—о** n. macroscopic grain.

макро/индикатор m. high-speed indicator; **—киносъёмка** f. macrofilming; **—климат** m. macroclimate; **—команда** f. (comp.) macroinstruction, macro(command); **—концентрация** f. macroscopic concentration; **—коньюгант** m. (gen.) macroconjugant; **—коррозия** f. macrocorrosion; **—косм(ос)** m. (astr.) macrocosm(os); **—кристаллический** a. macrocrystalline; **—ликвация** f. (met.) macrosegregation; **—мер** m. (gen.) macromere; **—метр** m. macrometer; **—мир** m. macroworld; **—мия** f. (ent.) dragonfly (*Macromia*).

макромолекул/а f. macromolecule; **—ярный** a. macromolecular.

макро/мутация f. (gen.) macromutation; **—напряжение** n. macrostress; **—нуклеус** m. (prot.) macronucleus; **—организм** m. macroorganism; **—ось** f. (cryst.) macroaxis; **—пара** f. macrocell; **—пиннодовые** pl. (ichth.) Macropinnidae; **—планктон** m. (biol.) macroplankton; **—плёнка** f. macrofilm; **—под** m. paradise fish (*Macropodus*); **—подовые** pl. (ichth.) Anabantidae; **—полость** f. macrocavity, macrovoid; **—пора** f. macropore; **—процесс** m. large-scale process; **—радикал** m. macroradical; **—с** m. (comp.) macro(command); **—сейсмический** a. (geol.) macroseismic; **—сейсмы** pl. macroseisms; **—система** f. macrosystem.

макроскоп/ический a. macroscopic; overall (reaction); (petr.) megascopic; **—ия** f. macroscopy.

макро/снимок m. macro(photo)graph; **—сома** f. (biol.) macrosome; **—состав** m. gross composition.

макроспор/а f. (bot.; prot.) macrospore; **—ангий** m. macrosporangium; **—иоз** m. (phyt.) macrosporiosis; **—офилл** m., **—офилла** f. (bot.) megasporophyll, macrosporophyll.

макро/спутник m. macrosatellite; **—структура** f. macrostructure, macroscopic structure; **—схема** f. macrocircuit; **—съёмка** f. macrophotography, ultra-close-up photography; **—твёрдость** f. macrohardness; **—течение** n. broad-scale flow; large-scale (air) current; **—травление** n. macroetching; **—фаг** m. (cyt.) macrophage; **—филл** m. macrophyllous plant; **—фил(л)ьный** a. macrophyllous, large-leaved; **—фировый** a. (geol.) macrophyric; **—флора** f. macroflora; **—фотография** see **макросъёмка; —фотоснимок** m. macrophotograph, enlargement; photomacrograph; **—химия** f. macrochemistry; **—цепь** f. macrochain; **—цефалический** a. macrocephalic, large-headed; **—цит** m. (cryst.) macro(erythro)cyte; **—частица** f. macroparticle; **—шлиф** m. macrosection; **—эволюция** f. (gen.) macroevolution; **—элемент** m. macroelement, macronutrient; macrocell; **—энергический** a. high-energy; **—эрг** m. high-energy compound; **—эргический** a. macroergic, high-energy.

макрур/онус m. (ichth.) Macruronus; **—ус** m. grenadier, rattail; **—усовые** pl. Macruridae.

мак-самосейка m. corn poppy (*Papaver rhoeas*).

максвелл m. (elec.) maxwell (unit of magnetic flux); **м.-виток** m. maxwell-turn; **—метр** m. maxwellmeter, fluxmeter; **—овский, —овый,** a. Maxwell, maxwellian (distribution).

максилл/а f. (anat.; zool.) maxilla; **—ярный** a. maxillary.

максим/ально *adv.* at most, at a maximum; as much as possible; **м. возможный** *a.* the ultimate, the maximum, the greatest possible; **м. использовать** *v.* make the most (of), make the best use (of); **—альнодопустимый** *a.* permissible; **—альный** *a.* maximum, highest, greatest, largest; top, ceiling, peak; the most, extreme; **—изировать** *v.* maximize, magnify; **—ум** *m.* maximum, peak, high; extreme (range); as a maximum, at most; **—ум до** to a maximum; **в —уме** at a maximum; **обеспечивать —ум** *v.* maximize.

максун *see* муксун.

мактра *f.* (mal.) Mactra.

макула *f.* macula, macule, stain, spot.

макулатур/а *f.* waste paper, spoilage; paper stock, mixed paper; **—ный** *a.* waste; common, low-quality; chip (board).

макул/ёза *f.* (ichth.) poison toadfish (*Thalassophryne maculosa*); **—о—** *prefix* maculo—, macular; **—ярный** *a.* macular, maculate.

макуха *f.* oil cake, mill cake.

макуш/а *f.*, **—ечный** *a.*, **—ка** *f.* crown, top, summit, apex.

макфлуктуация *f.* macroscopic fluctuation.

мал *sh. m. of* **малый.**

мал/абарский *a.* (geog.) Malabar; **—ага** *f.* Malaga (wine); **—агасийский** *a.* (geog.) Malagasy; **—айский** *a.* Malay(an); **—акантовые** *pl.* (ichth.) Malacanthidae; **—аккский** *a.* (geog.) Malacca.

малако— *prefix* malaco—(soft; mollusca); **—(зоо)логия, ** *f.* malacology, study of mollusks; **—лит** *m.* (min.) malacolite; **—метрия** *f.* determination of degree of softness; **—н** *m.* (min.) malacon; **—сома** *f.* (ent.) Malacosoma; **—стеевые, —стовые** *pl.* (ichth.) loosejaws (*Malacosteidae*); **—ст(ей)** *m.* Malacosteus.

маламид *m.* malamide, malic amide.

малармат *m.* (ichth.) malarmat (*Peristedion*).

малат *m.* malate; **—дегидрогеназа** *f.* malate dehydrogenase; **—(и)он** *m.* Malathion (insecticide).

малахит *m.*, **—овый** *a.* (min.) malachite, basic cupric carbonate.

малахра *f.* (bot.) Malachra.

малашки *pl.* (ent.) Malachiidae, Melyridae.

Малая Азия (geog.) Asia Minor.

малеат *m.* maleate.

малевать *v.* paint roughly.

малеилацетоуксусный *a.* maleylacetoacetic.

малеиновокисл/ый *a.* maleic acid; maleate (of); **—ая соль** maleate.

малеинов/ый *a.* maleic; **м. альдегид** maleic aldehyde, malealdehyde; **—ая кислота** maleic acid, *cis*-butanedioic acid; **гидразид —ой кислоты** maleic hydrazide; **соль —ой кислоты** maleate.

малейший *a.* least, slightest.

малёк *m.* young fish, fry, fingerling; **м.-покатник** *m.* smolt.

маленовые *pl.* (bot.) Rubiaceae.

маленький *a.* small, little.

малеоил *m.* maleoyl.

малийский *a.* (geog.) Mali.

маликофермент *m.* malic enzyme.

малин/а *f.* raspberry (*Rubus*); **—ник** *m.* raspberry garden, raspberry canes; (ent.) raspberry fruit-worm (*Byturus*); **—ники** *pl.* Byturidae; **—ный** *a.* raspberry; **—овка** *f.* (orn.) robin (*Erithacus rubecula*); **—овый** *a.* raspberry(-colored), crimson.

мали-скраб *m.* (geobot.) mallee-scrub.

малк/а *f.* bevel (square), bevel protractor; **в —у** askew, obliquely.

малковый *a.* (geog.) Malka.

маллардит *m.* (min.) mallardite.

маллеин *m.* (vet.) mallein; **—изация** *f.* malleinization, mallein test.

мало *adv.* little, few, not enough; slightly; **м. кто знает** few (people) know; **м. ли что** it does not matter (that); what of it! **м. по малу** little by little, gradually, by degrees; **м. того** moreover.

мало— *prefix* low, little; slightly, weakly, poorly, insufficiently; rarely; not very; pauci—, olig(o)— (few); (geog.) Little; **—азиатский, —азийский** *a.* (geog.) Asia Minor; **—активный** *a.* low-activity; inactive, non-reactive, inert; slow; low-level; (nucl.) cold; **—алкалоидный** *a.* low-alkaloid; **—алкогольный** *a.* low-alcohol; **—амперный** *a.* (elec.) low-amperage, low-current; **—белковой** *a.* low-protein.

малоберцов/ый *a.* (anat.) fibular; peroneal (artery); **—ая кость** fibula.

малобуферный *a.* weakly buffered.

маловажн/ость *f.* insignificance; **—ый** *a.* insignificant, unimportant.

маловат/о *adv.*, **—ый** *a.* rather little.

маловаттный *a.* (elec.) low-watt.

маловероятн/о *adv.* (it is) unlikely, highly improbable; **—ость** *f.* unlikelihood, improbability; **—ый** *a.* unlikely, improbable, doubtful.

маловесный *a.* light(-weight), not heavy.

маловлажный *a.* low-moisture, low-humidity.

маловод/ность *f.*, **—ье** *n.* (geol.) shortage of water, low water level; insufficient irrigation; **—ный** *a.* low-water, with little water; poorly irrigated; dry (year).

мало/вразумительный *a.* unclear, not (very) comprehensible; unconvincing; **—всхожий** *a.* poorly germinating (seed); **—выгодный** *a.* not (very) profitable; **—вязкий** *a.* low-viscosity, light (oil); **—габаритный** *a.* small(-scale), small-size(d), compact, miniature, pigmy, pocket; midget (tube); (microelectronics) small-outline (package); low-weight; (text.) narrow; **—глазый** *a.* small-eyed; **—говорящий** *a.* saying or explaining little; **—головый** *a.* microcephalous, small-headed; **—грамотный** *a.* uneducated; unskilled; **—дебитный** *a.* low-yield, marginal (well); **—действенный, —действительный** *a.* ineffective; **—дисторсионный** *a.* low-distortion; **—дойка** *f.* (agr.) poor milker; **—дойный** *a.* low-milk-yielding (cow); **—доказательный** *a.* unconvincing; **—достоверный** *a.* unreliable, untrustworthy.

малодоступн/ость *f.* inaccessibility; **—ый** *a.* (rather) inaccessible, hard to reach; unavailable.

малодоходный *a.* not very profitable.

мал/ое *n.* little; **без—ого** almost.

малоезж/еный, —ий *a.* little used, unfrequented (road); untried (horse).

малоёмк/ий *a.* low-capacity, small-size; **—остный** *a.* small-capacitance.

мало/енисейский *a.* (geog.) Little Yenisei; **—заметный** *a.* unobtrusive, inconspicuous, barely perceptible; ordinary; **—заселённый** *a.* sparsely populated; **—земелье** *n.* shortage of arable land; **—земельный** *a.* land-poor; small (farmer); **—знакомый** *a.* unfamiliar, strange.

малознач/ащий, —ительный, —ущий *a.* insignificant, unimportant; **—ительность** *f.* insignificance.

мало/зольный *a.* low-ash; high-carbon (coke); **—изведанный** *a.* little-investigated; **—известный** *a.* little-known; **—изученный** *a.* little-studied.

малоил *m.* maloyl.

мало/имущий *a.* poor, needy; **—инерционный** *a.* low-inertia; quick-response; high-speed (memory); —**интенсивный** *a.* low-intensity, weak; low (flux); —**интересный** *a.* of little interest, unattractive; —**исследованный** *a.* little-investigated; —**кавказский** *a.* (geog.) Little Caucasus; —**калиберный** *a.* small-caliber, small-bore; subcaliber (rocket); —**калорийный** *a.* low-calorie; —**квалифицированный** *a.* poorly qualified; unskilled (labor); —**кисл(отн)ый** *a.* weakly acid; —**компетентный** *a.* not very competent; —**комплектный** *a.* small; —**крахмалистый** *a.* low-starch; —**кремнистый** *a.* low-silicon; —**кровие** *n.* (med.) anemia; oligemia; —**кровный** *a.* anemic; oligemic.

малол *m.* malol, ursolic acid.

мало/легированный *a.* (met.) low-alloy; —**лесный** *a.* forest-poor; —**лесье** *n.* scarcity of forests; sparsely wooded country; —**летка** *f.* infant, baby; —**летние** *pl.* preteen-age children; —**летний** *a.* young, under age, minor; —**летники** *pl.* (bot.) annuals and perennials; —**леток** *m.* infant, baby; (zool.) young stock; —**летство** *n.* childhood; —**летучий** *a.* low-volatile, slightly volatile; —**листный** *a.* (bot.) oligophyllous.

малолитраж/ка *f.* economy car; —**ный** *a.* economy, fuel-efficient; small-capacity, small-displacement.

малолюд/ие *n.*, —**ность** *f.*, —**ство**, —**ье** *n.* sparse population; —**ный** *a.* sparsely populated, unfrequented.

мало/марганцовистый *a.* low-manganese; —**масличный** *a.* low-oil; low-fat; —**масштабный** *a.* small-scale; —**мерный** *a.* scanty, short; undersized; small (-size); —**метражный** *a.* small, short; —**молочная** *a.* low-milk-yielding (cow); —**мощность** *f.* low power, weakness; —**мощный** *a.* low-power, low-capacity, low-duty (machine); weak, poor; shallow, thin (soil); petty (business); —**надёжный** *a.* not (very) reliable; —**наезженный** *a.* little-used (road).

малонамид *m.* malonamide.

мало/наполненный *a.* low-charged (stock); —**направленный** *a.* broad (beam); —**населённый** *a.* sparsely populated.

малон/ат *m.* malonate; —**ил** *m.* malonyl; —**илмочевина** *f.* malonylurea.

малоново/кислый *a.* malonic acid; malonate (of); **м. натрий** sodium malonate; —**кислая соль** malonate; —**этиловый эфир** ethyl malonate.

малоно/вый *a.* malonic; **м. ангидрид** malonic anhydride; **м. эфир** malonic ester, diethyl malonate; —**вая кислота** malonic acid, propanedioic acid; **соль** —**вой кислоты** malonate; —**нитрил** *m.* malononitrile.

мало/ношеный *a.* little-worn; —**обитаемый** *a.* little-inhabited; —**облачный** *a.* with few clouds; —**облиственный** *a.* with scanty foliage; —**облучённый** *a.* slightly irradiated; —**обогащённый** *a.* slightly enriched; —**оборотный** *a.* low-speed (engine); —**обоснованный** *a.* poorly grounded; —**обработанный** *a.* insufficiently processed; —**образованный** *a.* poorly educated; —**объёмный** *a.* low-volume, small-capacity; —**опасный** *a.* low-hazard, safe; —**опытный** *a.* inexperienced, with little experience; —**основательный** *a.* with a poor foundation; —**ответственный** *a.* with few responsibilities; low-duty.

мало/пёрый *a.* (ichth.) shortfin(ned); —**питательный** *a.* not very nourishing; —**плодный** *a.* (bot.) oligocarpous; —**плодородный** *a.* not very productive; poor (soil); —**подвижность** *f.* moderate mobility; —**подвижный** *a.* moderately mobile, slow-moving, lethargic; sedentary (life); stiff (joint); —**подготовленный** *a.* poorly prepared; —**полярный** *a.* low-polarity.

мало-помалу *adv.* little by little, gradually.

мало/поместительный *a.* small, cramped; —**понятный** *a.* abstruse, difficult to understand; —**пористый** *a.* low-porosity; —**потерный** *a.* low-loss; —**прибыльный** *a.* not (very) profitable; —**пригодный** *a.* of little use, not very suitable; —**применимый** *a.* not very applicable; —**приспособленный** *a.* little suited, not well adapted; —**продуктивный** *a.* inefficient, wasteful, low-yield(ing); not very productive; —**производительный** *a.* low-output, unproductive; —**процентный** *a.* low-grade, low-percentage; —**прочный** *a.* not very durable.

мало/радиоактивный *a.* weakly radioactive; —**развитой**, —**развитый** *a.* un(der)developed; —**распространённый** *a.* little-distributed, rare; —**растворимый** *a.* difficultly soluble; —**реакционн(оспособн)ый** *a.* weakly reactive, inactive, inert; —**ресничные** *pl.* (prot.) Oligotricha; —**ресурсный** *a.* short-life (engine); —**рослый** *a.* stunted, undersized, dwarf; —**рот** *m.* (ichth.) small-mouthed flounder; —**рот(ков)ые** *pl.* Microstomatidae; —**ротый** *a.* microstom(at)ous, small-mouthed.

мало/светосильный *a.* slow (lens); —**семейный** *a.* having a small family; —**семянный** *a.* (bot.) oligospermous; —**серистый** *a.* low-sulfur, low-sulfide; —**сильный** *a.* weak, feeble; low-powered; —**скоростной** *a.* low-velocity, low(-speed); —**смолистый** *a.* low-rosin (paper); —**снежность** *f.*, —**снежье** *n.* dearth of snow; —**снежный** *a.* with little snow; —**содержательный** *a.* superficial, shallow; —**сознательный** *a.* little aware; —**соль** *f.* lightly salted caviar; —**сольный** *a.* fresh-salted, freshly pickled; not very salty; —**состоятельный** *a.* not conclusive; poor; —**споровый** *a.* poorly sporulating; —**способный** *a.* slow (learner); —**стебельчатый** *a.* short-stemmed; —**стойкий** *a.* not (very) stable; (hort.) non-hardy, tender; —**строчный** *a.* low-definition, coarse; —**сть** *f.* insignificant amount, a little; trifle; *adv.* a bit, somewhat; —**существенный** *a.* insignificant, unimportant; —**съедобный** *a.* not very edible; —**теплопроводный** *a.* with poor thermal conductivity; —**тиражный** *a.* limited (edition); —**токсический** *a.* weakly toxic; —**тычинковый** *a.* (zool.) multispined; (bot.) oligandrous.

мало/убедительный *a.* unconvincing, not conclusive; —**углеродистый** *a.* low-carbon; —**угловой** *a.* small-angle, low-angle; —**удойная** *a.* low-yield (cow); —**употребительный** *a.* rarely used, rare; —**упожайный** *a.* low-yield (crop); —**усадочность** *f.* (text.) low shrinkage; —**успевающий**, —**успешный** *a.* not (very) successful; —**устойчивый** *a.* not (very) stable; —**форматный** *a.* compact (camera); —**фосфористый** *a.* low-phosphorus; —**ходный** *a.* low-profit (farm); —**цветковый** *a.* (bot.) oliganthous; —**цветущий** *a.* poorly flowering; —**ценный** *a.* poor, inferior, of small value; lean (gas).

малочисленн/ость *f.* small number; —**ый** *a.* scanty, few; (biol.) oligomerous.

малочник *m.* bevel board, beveler.

мало/чувствительный *a.* low-sensitivity, not (very) sensitive; —**шёрстный** *a.* shorthair; —**шумный**, —**шумящий** *a.* quiet, noiseless; low-noise (amplifier); —**щелочной** *a.* low-alkali; —**щетинковые** *pl.* (zool.) Oligochaeta; —**этажный** *a.* low (building); —**ядовитый** *a.* mildly toxic, low-toxicity.

малхит *m.* (petr.) malchite.

мал/ый *a.* little, low, minor; small(-scale); low-power (magnification); slow (rate); semi-minor (axis); minor (surgery); (anat.) lesser; **весьма м.** minute, tiny; **баллистическая ракета —ой дальности** short-range ballistic missile, SRBM; **под —ым углом** glancing, grazing.

малыш *m.* infant, youngster.

мальабсорбция *f.* (med.) malabsorption.

мальбрук *m.* (mam.) Cercopithecus cynosurus.

мальв/а *f.,* **—овый** *a.* (bot.) mallow (*Malva*); **—идин** *m.* malvidin; **—ин** *m.* malvin; **—овые** *pl.* Malvaceae.

маль/гашский *a.* (geog.) Malagasy; **—дивский** *a.* Maldive; **—донит** *see* **малдонит.**

мальк/и *pl.;* **—овый** *a.* of **малёк.**

малькольмия *f.* (bot.) Malcolmia.

мальм *m.* (cer.) malm, washed clay.

мальма *f.* (ichth.) malma (*Salvelinus malma*).

мальпиг/иевые *pl.* (bot.) Malpighiaceae; **—иевый** *a.* (anat.) Malpighian; **—ия** *f.* (bot.) Malpighia.

мальсекко *n.* (phyt.) malsecco.

мальта *f.* (geol.) maltha, mineral tar.

мальтаза *f.* maltase (enzyme).

мальтацит *m.* (min.) malthacite.

мальтены *pl.* malthenes, petrolenes.

мальтийск/ий *a.* (geog.) Malta, Maltese; **м. механизм** (mech.) Maltese-cross intermittent transmission; **—ая лихорадка** (med.) brucellosis.

мальтин *m.* maltine, extract of malt.

мальто— *prefix* malto—; **—биоза** *f.* malto(bio)se; **—бионовая кислота** maltobionic acid; **—декстрин** *m.* maltodextrin, amyloin; **—за** *f.* maltose, malt sugar; **—зурия** *f.* (med.) maltosuria; **—л** *m.* maltol; **—мобиль** *m.* malt plow; **—новый** *a.* maltonic (acid).

мальтузианский *a.* Malthusian (law).

мальхит *m.* (petr.) malchite.

мальц-экстракт *m.* malt extract.

мальчик *m.,* **—овый** *a.* boy.

Малюса закон (phys.) Malus' law.

малю/сенький *a.* tiny, miniature; **—тка** *f.* miniature; pigmy; baby, infant; **подводная лодка-малютка** minisubmarine.

малявка *f.* fry, young fish.

маляр *m.* (house or sign) painter.

маляр/ийный *a.* (med.) malarial; **—ик** *m.* malaria patient; **—иолог** *m.* malariologist.

малярить *v.* paint.

малярия *f.* (med.) malaria.

малярн/ая *f.* paint store; **—ичать** *v.* paint; be a house-painter; **—о-технический** *a.* painting technology; **—ый** *a.* of **маляр;** (anat.) malar, cheek; **—ое дело** painting.

мамалыга *f.* hominy, grits.

мамб/а *f.* (herp.) mamba (*Dendroaspis*); (ichth.) mamba (*Protopterus*); **—овые** *pl.* Protopteridae.

маметр *see* **махметр.**

мамилл/а *f.* mamilla, nipple; **—ярия** *f.* (bot.) Mamillaria; **—ярный** *a.* mamillary.

маммея *f.* (bot.) mammee tree (*Mammea*).

мамм/ит *m.* (med.) mammitis, mastitis; **—о—** *prefix* mammo— (breast; mammary gland); **—отропин** *m.* mammotropin, prolactin.

мам(м)ут/-насос *m.* air lift; **м.-растворитель** *m.* air-lift mixer.

мамонт *m.,* **—овый** *a.* mammoth; **—овое дерево** big tree (*Sequoia gigantea*).

мамский *a.* (geog.) Mama.

мамура *f.* (bot.) arctic bramble, dewberry (*Rubus arcticus*).

мамут *see* **маммут.**

манакин/овые, —ы *pl.* (orn.) Pipridae.

мангал *m.* brazier.

манган/ат *m.* manganate; **—ин** *m.,* **—иновый** *a.* manganin (alloy); **—ит** *m.,* **—итовый** *a.* (chem.; min.) manganite.

мангано/за *f.* manganese carbonate fertilizer; **—зит** *m.* manganosite, manganese protoxide; **—кальцит** *m.* manganocalcite; **—лит** *m.* (petr.) manganolite; **—стибиит** *m.* (min.) manganostibiite; **—сферит** *m.* manganospherite; **—танталит** *m.* manganotantalite; **—филлит** *m.* manganophyllite; **—фильный** *a.* manganophilous, manganese-requiring.

мангеймский *a.* Mannheim (gold).

мангл/евый *a.,* **—ь** *m.* (bot.) mangrove.

манго *n.* (bot.) mango (*Mangifera*).

мангобей *m.* (mam.) mangabey (*Cercocebus*).

манговый *a.* of **манго.**

мангольд *m.* (bot.) Swiss chard (*Beta vulgaris var. cicla*).

мангост/ан *m.* (bot.) mangosteen; **—ин** *m.* mangostin; mangosteen.

мангров/а *f.,* **—ый** *a.* (bot.) mangrove.

мангуст *m.,* **—а** *f.* (mam.) mongoose (*Herpestes*).

мангустан *see* **мангостан.**

мангут *m.* (mam.) raccoon dog (*Nyctereutes*).

мангышлакский *a.* (geog.) Mangyshlak.

мандарин *m.* (bot.) mandarin (*Citrus reticulata*); mandarine, β-naphthol orange (dye); **—ка** *f.* (ichth.) mandarin fish (*Synchiropus splendidus*); (orn.) mandarin duck (*Aix galericulata*); **—ник** *m.* mandarin grove; **—ный, —овый** *a.* of **мандарин.**

мандат *m.,* **—ный** *a.* mandate, order.

манделат *m.* mandelate.

мандельштейн *m.* (petr.) almond rock, amygdaloid, amygdule.

мандибул/а *f.* (anat.; zool.) mandibula, mandible; **—ярный** *a.* mandibular.

мандрагор/а *f.,* **—овый** *a.* (bot.) mandrake (*Mandragora*); **—ин** *m.* mandragorine.

мандрен *m.* (med.) mandrin, catheter guide.

мандрил *m.* (mam.) mandrill (*Mandrillus sphinx*).

манеб *m.* Maneb (fungicide).

манебахский *a.* (cryst.) Manebach (law).

ман/ёвр *m.,* **—ёвренный** *a.* maneuver; **—ёвренная способность, —ёвренность** *f.* maneuverability; **—еврирование** *n.* maneuvering, etc., *see v.;* **—еврировать** *v.* maneuver, manipulate, manage, work, operate; (rr.) switch, shunt; **—евровый** *a.* maneuvering; shunting, switching; **—евроспособность** *f.* maneuverability; **—евроспособный** *a.* maneuverable; **—ёвры** *pl.* switching, shunting; maneuvers, field exercise.

манеж *m.* riding academy or school; training, breaking in; **—ить** *v.* train; **—ный** *a.* of **манеж;** incessant (movements).

манекен *m.* mannequin; model, mock-up, dummy.

манер *m.,* **—а** *f.* manner, way, form, fashion, method; (behavior) pattern; **—а** *f.* (printing) stencil; **на м.** in the manner (of), like; **таким —ом** in this fashion, in this way, thus.

манерка *f.* screw-top flask; (ichth.) tugun (*Coregonus tugun*).

манетка *f.* lever, throttle.

манжет *m.,* **—а** *f.* (packing) gland, gasket, ring, seal(ing) ring, collar, cuff, sleeve; (piston) cup; (tire) patch; (blood pressure) cuff; **—ка** *dim.* of **манжета;** (bot.) Alchemilla; **—ный** *a.* of **манжета.**

маниак *m.* (med.) maniac; **—ально-депрессивный** *a.* manic-depressive; **—альный** *a.* maniacal.

маникюр *m.,* **—ный** *a.* manicure.

манил/л(к)а Manila hemp, abaca; **—ьский** *a.* (geog.) Manila.

ман/иок *m.,* **—иока** *f.,* **—иот** *m.* (bot.) manioc, cassava (*Manihot*).

манипул/ирование *n.* manipulation, handling, treatment; operation; (telegraphy) keying; **—ированный** *a.* manipulated, etc., *see v.;* **—ировать** *v.* manipulate, handle, treat; operate; key; position; **—ятор** *m.* manipulator, positioner; signaling key; operator; **—ятор ближнего действия** (nucl.) handler; **—ятор-кантователь** *m.* (met.) universal manipulator; (ingot) tipper; **—яционный, —яция** *see* **манипулирование.**

манить *v.* attract, lure, entice.

манифест/ация *f.* manifestation; **—ировать** *v.* manifest, demonstrate.

манифольд *m.* manifold.

маниха *f.* slack tide, ebb tide.

манихот *see* **маниок.**

манишка *f.* (orn.) bib.

мания *f.* (med.) mania; **м. величия** megalomania.

манка *f.* bird call, lure; (food) semolina.

манкировать *v.* neglect, miss.

манлийская эпоха (geol.) Manlius epoch.

манна *f.* manna; **—за** *f.* mannase; **—н** *m.* mannan; **—я** *f.* (food) semolina.

маннеотетроза *f.* stachyose (tetrasaccharide).

маннесмановский *a.* Mannesmann.

манни/к *m.,* **—ковый** *a.* (bot.) manna grass (*Glyceria*); **—т(оль)** *m.* mannitol.

Манниха основание Mannich base.

манно/гептоза *f.* mannoheptose; **—за** *f.* mannose; **—замин** *m.* mannosamine; **—зид** *m.* mannoside; **—зидострептомицин** *m.* mannosidostreptomycin, streptomycin B; **—зофосфат** *m.* mannose phosphate; **—лит** *m.* mannolite, chloramine-T; **—метилоза** *f.* mannomethylose; **—новый** *a.* mannonic (acid); **—пираноза** *f.* mannopyranose.

маннуроновый *a.* mannuronic (acid).

манн/ый *a.* of **манна;** **—ая крупа** semolina.

мано— *prefix* mano—(thin, rare); **—вакууммстр** *m.* vacuum manometer, vacuum gage; **—граф** *m.* manograph, recording manometer; **—детандер** *m.* pressure regulator, reducing valve.

манок *m.* bird call, lure.

манометр *m.* manometer, pressure gage; **—ический** *a.* manometric; gage, over-(pressure); **—ия** *f.* manometry.

маностат *m.* manostat, pressure control instrument; **—ирование** *n.* manostatting.

мансард/а *f.* mansard, attic; mansard roof; **—ный** *a.* mansard; **—ное помещение** attic, garret.

манский *a.* (geog.) Mana.

мансонеллёз *m.* (med.) mansonelliasis.

мант/а *f.* (ichth.) manta (*Manta birostris*); **—ийная** *f.* mantle; **—ийный** *a.* mantle; (mal.) pallial, palliate; **—исп(ид)ы** *pl.* (ent.) mantis flies (*Mantispidae*); **—исса** *f.* (math.) mantissa; **—ия** *f.* mantle; (anat.; mal.) pallium; **—овые** *pl.* (ichth.) devilrays (*Mobulidae*).

Манту реакция (med.) Mantoux test.

манубр/ий **—иум** *m.* (biol.) manubrium.

манул *m.* (mam.) Pallas' cat (*Felis manul*).

мануфактур/а *f.,* **—ный** *a.* fabrics, dress goods; obs. textile mill; manufacture.

ман/хаттанский *a.* (geog.) Manhattan; **—хеймский** *a.* Mannheim; **—честер** *m.* (text.) velveteen; **—честерский** *a.* (geog.) Manchester.

маншон *m.* (paper) jacket.

манычовый *a.* (geog.) Manych.

маньчжурский *a.* (geog.) Manchurian.

маньяк *see* **маниак.**

манящий *a.* luring, tempting.

мара *f.* thick fog; (mam.) Patagonian cavy (*Dolichotis patagonum*).

марабу *m.* (orn.) marabou stork, adjutant stork (*Leptoptilus*).

маразм *m.* (med.) marasmus, progressive waste; **—атический** *a.* marasmic.

маракайбовский *a.* (geog.) Maracaibo.

марал *m.,* **—ий** *a.* (mam.) maral (*Cervus elaphus maral*); **—оводство** *n.,* **—оводческий** *a.* maral breeding; **—уха** *f.* maral doe; **—ьник** *m.* maral park, Siberian deer park.

маранта *f.* (bot.) arrowroot (*Maranta*).

марантический *see* **маразматический.**

марантов/ые *pl.* (bot.) Marantaceae; **—ый** *a.* arrowroot (starch).

маранье *n.* dirtying, etc., *see* **марать.**

мараскин *m.* maraschino (liqueur).

марат/ор *m.* (blast furnace) supporting ring; **—орный** *a.,* **—ра** *f.* mantle.

марать *v.* dirty, soil, smear; scribble; strike out; **—ся** *v.* get dirty; lose color.

марафонский *a.* marathon.

марашка *f.* (typ.) slur, mottle, smear.

марган/ец *m.* manganese, Mn; **закись —ца** manganous oxide; **соль закиси —ца** manganous salt; **закись-окись —ца** manganomanganic oxide; **окись —ца, чёрный м.** manganic oxide, manganese (sesqui-)oxide; **соль окиси —ца** manganic salt; **сернокислая закись —ца** manganous sulfate; **сернокислая окись —ца** manganic sulfate; **хлористый м.** manganous chloride; **хлорный м.** manganic chloride; **—изировать** *v.* add manganese salts.

марган/о— *prefix* mangano—; **—цево—** *see* **марганцово—;** **—цевый** *see* **марганцовый.**

марганцовисто— *prefix* mangano—, manganous; **—калиевая соль** potassium manganate; **—кислый** *a.* manganic acid; manganate (of); **—кислая соль** manganate; **—синеродоводородная кислота** manganocyanic acid.

марганцовист/ый *a.* manganous, manganese, manganiferous; **м. ангидрид** manganese trioxide; **м. доломит** (min.) mangandolomite; **м. купорос** manganous sulfate; **м. шпат** *see* **марганцовый шпат; —ая кислота** manganic acid; **соль —ой кислоты** manganate; **—ая соль** manganous salt; **—ая сталь** (met.) manganese steel; **—ое железо** (met.) ferromanganese.

марганцовка *f.* potassium permanganate.

марганцово— *prefix* mangani—, manganic, manganese; **—калиевая соль** potassium permanganate; **—кислый** *a.* permanganic acid; permanganate (of); **—кислая соль** permanganate; **—рудный** *a.* manganese ore; **—синеродоводородный** *a.* manganicyanic (acid).

марганцов/ый *a.* manganic, manganese; **м. ангидрид** permanganic acid anhydride, manganese heptoxide; **м. блеск** (min.) manganese glance, alabandite; **м. купорос** manganese sulfate; **м. шпат** (min.) manganese spar, rhodochrosite; **—ая кислота** permanganic acid; **соль —ой кислоты** permanganate; **—ая обманка** (min.) mangan-blende, alabandite; **—ая пена** (min.) bog manganese, earthy manganese, wad; **—ая соль** manganic salt.

маргарин *m.,* **—овый** *a.* margarine (butter substitute); **—овая кислота** margaric acid, heptadecanoic acid; **—овокислый** *a.* margaric acid; margarate (of); **—ое масло** margarine oil.

маргарит *m.* (min.) margarite.

маргаритка *f.* (bot.) daisy (*Bellis*).

маргаритовая кислота margaritic acid.

маргаросанит *m.* (min.) margarosanite.

маргинал/ии *pl.* marginal notes; **—ьный** *a.* marginal.

маргозовое масло margosa oil.

марев/о *n.* haze; mirage; looming; **—ые** *pl.* (bot.) Chenopodiaceae; **—ый** *a. of* **марь;** swampy.

марей *m.* (ichth.) round herring (*Etrumeus teres*).

мареканит *m.* (petr.) marekanite.

марен/а *f.,* **—ный, —овый** *a.* (bot.) madder (*Rubia,* spec. *R. tinctorum*); (ichth.) barbel (*Barbus b.*); minnow (*Phoxinus p.*); **—овые** *pl.* (bot.) Rubiaceae.

мареограф *m.* depth gage, tide gage.

марзан *m.* (typ.) clump, slug.

марзанка *f.* (bot.) Asperula cynanchica.

мари *gen., pl., etc., of* **марь;** (geol.) mari (sparse larch forests with peat moss litter; shallow, often hummocky, bog; horizontal or sloping stretches with numerous small knolls or ridges with swampy patches between).

мари/алит *m.* (min.) marialite; **—анский** *a.* (geog.) Mariana; **—инский** *a.* Mariinsk; **—йский** *a.* Mari.

мари/культура *f.* mariculture, aquiculture, sea farming; **—на** *f.* seascape; (ichth.) *see* **марена.**

маринад *m.* marinade; pickles.

маринка *f.* (ichth.) marinka (*Schizothorax*).

маринов/ание *n.* marinating; pickling; **—анный** *a.* marinated; pickled; **—ать** *v.* marinate; pickle; put off, shelve.

Мариотта закон (phys.) Mariotte's law.

марипозит *m.* (min.) mariposite.

марита *f.* (zool.) marita; fluke.

мариуполит *m.* (petr.) mariupolite.

марихуана *f.* marihuana.

марка *f.* stamp, mark, brand, make; quality, sort, type; (load) line; (cable) designation; (typ.) front lay; type symbol; (coal) rank; (postage) stamp; **заводская м., фабричная м.** tradename, brand, nameplate.

марказит *m.* (min.) marcasite, white iron pyrites; **гребенчатый м.** coxcomb pyrites; **—овый** *a.* marcasite, marcasitic.

маркак/ольский, —ульский *a.* (geog.) Markakul.

маркёр *m.* marker, tag; index; (comp.) label; (radioactive) tracer; **—ный** *a. of* **маркёр;** identification (signal); **м.-следоуказатель** *m.* marker.

маркетинг *m.* marketing.

марки *pl.* (surv.) markers.

маркиза *f.* awning, canopy, marquee.

маркизет *m.* (text.) marquisette, voile.

маркизский *a.* (geog.) Marquesas.

маркий *a.* readily soiled; bleeding (color).

маркир/овальный *a.,* **—ование** *n.* marking, etc., *see v.;* **—ованный** *a.* marked, etc., *see v.;* gene-tagged (chromosome); **—овать** *v.* mark, stamp; tag, label, identify; grade; lay out; stencil; trace (lines); **—овка** *f.,* **—овочный** *a.* marking, etc., *see v.;* layout; (color) code; **—овщик** *m.,* **—ующии горизонт** marker; **—ующий** *a.* marking, etc., *see v.*

марковский *a.* Markoff (process).

Маркони когерер (rad.) Marconi coherer.

маркость *f.* (text.) ready soilability; **м. окраски** marking off.

маркшейдер *m.* (mine) surveyor; **—ия** *f.,* **—ская съёмка, —ское дело** mine surveying, underground surveying; **—ский** *a.* surveyor's, surveying; miner's.

марлат *see* **метоксихлор.**

марлевый *a.* gauze; cheesecloth.

марлин *m.* (ichth.) marlin (*Makaira*); **—овые, —ы** *pl.* Istiophoridae.

марлит *m.* (petr.) marlite, stony marl; **—овый** *a.* marlitic.

марлон *m.* Marlon (alkylbenzene sulfonate).

марля *f.* (med.) gauze; cheesecloth.

марматит *m.* (min.) marmatite.

мармелад *m.* fruit-paste candy.

мармит *m.* food warmer; **—ница** *f.* warmer container; **—ный** *a.* hot food.

мармозетка *f.* (mam.) marmoset (*Callithrix*).

мармолит *m.* (min.) marmolite.

марморировать *see* **мраморировать.**

марок *gen. pl. of* **марка;** *sh. m. of* **маркий.**

марок/ен *m.,* **—еновый** *a.* (text.) marocain; Morocco (leather); **—(ан)ский** *a.* (geog.) Morocco(n).

марочный *a. of* **марка.**

марс *m.* (naut.) top; Mars pigment; **М.** (astr.) Mars; **—а желть** Mars yellow; **—ала** *f.* Marsala (wine).

марсель *m.* (naut.) top sail.

марсельский *a.* (geog.) Marseilles; castile (soap); Kenya (fever).

марсианский *a.* (astr.) Mars, Martian.

марсилиевые *pl.* (bot.) Marsileaceae.

марсо/вой *a. of* **марс; —ход** *m.* Mars rover.

марсупиализация *f.* (med.) marsupialization.

март *m.* March.

мартен *m.* (met.) open-hearth furnace; open-hearth steel; **—зит** *see* **мартенсит; —ование** *n.* open-hearth refining; **—овец** *m.* open-hearth worker.

мартеновск/ий *a.* (met.) Martin, open-hearth; **м. передел** (Siemens-)Martin process, open-hearth process; **м. цех** open-hearth (steel) mill; **—ая ванна** molten bath in open-hearth process.

мартенсит *m.* martensite (steel); **—ный, —овый** *a.* martensite, martensitic.

мартенщик *m.* (met.) open-hearth worker.

март/ингал *m.* martingale; **—иниевые** *pl.* (bot.) Martyniaceae; **—иникский** *a.* (geog.) Martinique; **—инит** *m.* (min.) martinite; **—иния** *f.* (bot.) Martynia; **—ит** *m.* (min.) martite, iron sesquioxide.

мартовик *m.* (ichth.) toad goby (*Mesogobius batrachocephalus*).

мартовский *a.* March.

марты/н *m.,* **—шка** *f.* (orn.) river tern (*Sterna hirundo*); **—шка** *f.* (mam.) guenon (*Cercopithecus*); **—шковые** *pl.* Cercopithecidae.

МАРУ *abbr.* (мгновенная автоматическая регулировка усиления) instantaneous automatic gain control, IAGC.

марулька *f.* (ichth.) Sebastes.

марухский *a.* (geog.) Marukha.

марховый *a.* (geog.) Markha.

мархур *m.* (mam.) markhor (*Capra falconeri*).

марципан *m.,* **—ный, —овый** *a.* marzipan (confection).

Марциуса жёлтый Martius yellow (salt of 2,4-dinitro-1-naphthol).

марчеван *m.* (building) forepole.

марчита *f.* marcita, irrigated meadow.

марш *m.* march; flight (of stairs); marsh (land).

Марша проба Marsh test (for arsenic).

маршал/ит *m.* (met.) marshalite; **—лагиоз** *m.* (vet.) Marshallagia infection; **—ловый** *a.* (geog.) Marshall.

маршанц/иевые *pl.* (bot.) Marchantiaceae; **—ия** *f.* liverwort (*Marchantia*).

маршев *see under* **марша.**

маршевый *a. of* **марш;** cruise, sustainer (engine); cruising, sustaining; **м. двигатель** sustainer.

марши *pl.* marsh, morass, swamp.

маршировать *v.* march.

маршит *m.* (min.) marshite.

маршрут *m.* route, itinerary, course; (geod.) traverse route, line route; (aerial surveying) flight line, strip, pass; track; (rr.) block train; (comp.) path; **—изация** *f.* routing; running traffic in blocks; **—ный** *a. of* **маршрут**; **—ный поезд** through freight train.

марыйский *a.* (geog.) Mary.

марь *f.* mist; (bot.) goosefoot (*Chenopodium*); (geol.) *see* **мари; белая м.** lamb's quarters, pigweed (*C. album*); **—ин корень** Ural peony (*Paeonia anomala*).

марьянник *m.* cow wheat (*Melampyrum*).

масел *gen. pl. of* **масло.**

маска *f.* mask, disguise; face guard, face shield; (mil.) screen, net; (ent.) mask; **защитная м.** face guard.

масканьит *m.* (min.) mascagnite.

маска-перекрытие *f.* cover, drape net.

маскаренский *a.* (geog.) Mascarene.

маска-штора *f.* camouflage blind.

маскег *m.* muskeg (wet grassland).

маскир/ование *n.* masking, etc., *see v.*; **—ованный** *a.* masked, etc., *see v.*; under the guise (of); **—овать** *v.* mask, disguise, camouflage; conceal, cover, screen; **—овка** *see* **маскирование**; disguise, camouflage; concealment; deception; **световая —овка** black-out; **—овочный** *a.* masking, etc., *see v.*; deceptive, camouflage; **—овщик** *m.* camouflage specialist; **—ующий** *see* **маскировочный.**

маско/держатель *m.* mask holder; **—образный** *a.* mask-like.

масксеть *f.* (mil.) camouflage net.

маскулиниз/ация *f.* masculinization, virilization; **—ировать** *v.* masculinize.

масленка *f.* lubricator, oil can; lubricating valve; oil cup; oiler; grease cup; butter dish; pasteboard paper.

маслен/ый *a.* oiled, lubricated; **—ная нефть** crude oil rich in lube oil fractions.

масленок *see* **масляник.**

масленый *see* **масляный.**

маслин/а *f.,* **—ный, —овый** *a.* (bot.) olive (*Olea*); **—ные, —овые** *pl.* Oleaceae.

маслить *v.* oil, grease, lubricate; butter.

масличн/ость *f.* oil content; **—ые** *pl.* oil-producing plants; **—ый** *a.* oleaginous, oil-bearing; oil(-yielding); olive (tree); **—ая пальма** oil palm (*Elaeis guineensis*).

масло *n.* oil; butter; **м. какао** cacao butter; **коровье м.** butter; **—бак** *m.* oil tank; **—бензостойкий** *a.* resistant to oil and gas; **—бензостойкость** *f.* resistance to oil and gas.

маслобой/ка *f.* butter churn; oil mill; **—ножировой** *a.* butter and fats; oil and fats; **—ный** *a.* oil (mill); oil-extracting (industry); **—ный завод, —ня** *f.* oil mill; **—ный станок** oil press; **—щик** *m.* oil manufacturer.

масло/влагоуловитель *m.* oil and moisture trap; **—вместилище** (bot.) oil-storing organ; **—выделитель** *m.* oil extractor; **—выпускное отверстие** oil drain.

маслодел *m.* butter maker; **—ие** *n.* butter making; **—ьный** *a.* butter-making, butter (industry); creamery; **—ьный завод, —ьня** *f.* butter factory; creamery.

масло/добывание *n.* oil manufacture; oil extraction; **—добывающий** *a.* oil-extracting; **—ёмкость** *f.* oil absorption, oil number (of pigment); **—жировой** *a.* oil and fats; **—завод** *m.* creamery, butter dairy; oil mill; **—заправщик** *m.* oil(-servicing) tanker; **—изготовитель** *m.* butter churn; **—манометр** *m.* oil pressure gage; **—мер** *m.,* **—мерное стекло** oil gage; **—мерный** *a.* oil-measuring; dip (stick); **—наливной** *a.* oil-filling; **—наполненный** *a.* oil-extended, oil-filled;

—насос *m.* oil pump; **—непроницаемый** *a.* oiltight, oilproof, oil-resistant; greaseproof; **—носный** *a.* oleaginous, oily; oil-bearing; (rub.) oil-extended; **—обработник** *m.* butter kneader.

маслообраз/ный *a.* oily, greasy; **—ование** *n.* butter formation; **—ующий** *a.* oil-forming, olefiant.

масло/отбойное кольцо oil wiper; **—отводное кольцо** oil scraper.

маслоотдел/ение *n.* oil extraction; **—итель** *m.* oil separator, oil trap; grease trap, grease interceptor; **—яющий** *a.* oil-separating; grease (filter).

масло/отражатель *m.* oil deflector; oil seal; **—отстойник** *m.* oil sump; **—охладитель** *m.* oil cooler.

маслоочист/итель *m.* oil purifier, oil filter; **—ительный завод** oil refinery; **—ка** *f.* oil purification.

масло/перепускной *a.* oil overflow (valve); **—поглощаемость** *f.* oil-absorbing capacity, oil absorption; **—подобный** *a.* oily; **—подогреватель** *m.* oil heater; **—поставка** *f.* oil delivery, oil supply; **—приёмник** *m.* oil header.

маслопровод *m.* oil (pipe)line; **—ный** *a.* oil-conducting, oil-piping.

масло/прокачивающий *a.* oil-priming; **—прочный** *a.* oil-resistant; **—радиатор** *m.* oil cooler (assembly); **—разбрызгиватель** *m.* oil thrower, oil splasher; **—разбрызгивающий** *a.* oil-splashing; oil (ring); **—раздаточный** *a.* oil-dispensing; **—распределитель** *m.* oil distributor, oil dispenser; **—распределительный** *a.* oil-dispensing; **—распылитель** *m.* oil splasher, lubricator; **—растворимый** *a.* oil-soluble; **—расширитель** *m.* (transformer) oil conservator; **—родный** *a.* olefiant.

масло/сбиватель *m.* butter churn; **—сборник** *m.* drip pan, sump, oil collector, oil trap; **—сбрасывающий** *a.* oil throwing, oil flinging; **—сгонное кольцо** obturator ring, wiper ring; **—семя** *n.* oil seed; **—система** *f.* lubrication system; **—слив** *m.* oil drain; **—собирательное кольцо** oil wiper; **—содержащий** *a.* oil-containing; oily (waste); **—спускной** *a.* oil-drain(ing); **—стойкий** *a.* oil-resistant, oilproof; **—счётчик** *m.* oil meter; oil gage; **—сырзавод** *m.* butter and cheese factory; **—сыроваренный** *a.* butter and cheese making; **—съёмное кольцо** oil (piston) ring, oil scraper.

маслотта *f.* ring pot.

масло/указатель *m.* oil gage; **—уловитель** *see* **маслосборник; —уловительный** *a.* oil-catching; lubricating (ring); **—упорный** *see* **маслостойкий; —фильтр** *m.* oil filter; **—хранилище** *n.* oil storage tank; **—щуп** *m.* oil gage (stick), oil (level) dipstick.

масл/уха *f.,* **—яник** *m.* (bot.) butter mushroom (*Boletus luteus*); **—юк** *m.* butterfish, gunnel (*Pholis*); **—юки, —юковые** *pl.* (ichth.) Pholidae.

маслянист/ость *f.* oiliness; lubricity, lubricating property; oil content; fat content; (wine) ropiness; (phyt.) greasy pod; **—ый** *a.* oily, oleaginous; butyrous, buttery; emulsive; ropy (wine); viscous; unctuous; **—ая взвесь** emulsion; **—ая смола** oleoresin.

маслянка *see* **масленка.**

масляно/кислый *a.* butyric acid; butyrate (of); **м. кальций, —кальциевая соль** calcium butyrate; **—кислая соль** butyrate; **—кислое брожение** butyric (acid) fermentation; **—метиловый эфир** methyl butyrate; **—растворимый** *a.* fat-soluble; **—смоляной** *a.* oleo-resinous (varnish); **—сть** *f.* oiliness, greasiness, fatness.

маслян/ый *a.* oil(-base) (paints); oily, greasy; butyrous, butyric; **м. альдегид** butyraldehyde, butanal; **м. ангидрид** butyric anhydride; **м. газ** oil gas; **—ая**

загрунтовка coat of oil paint; **—ая кислота** butyric acid, butanoic acid; **соль—ой кислоты** butyrate; **—ая пальма** (bot.) oil palm (*Elaeis guineensis*).

маслята *see* **масляник.**

масок *gen. pl. of* **маска.**

масс/а *f.* mass, bulk, volume; heap; a great many, a host (of); stuff, stock; matter, substance, compound, composition, material; the masses; shoal, swarm; block; body; (paper) pulp; (cer.) paste, slip; pith (of tree); **м. на единицу площади** mass-area ratio; **м. покоя** (nucl.) rest mass; **в (общей) —е** for the most part; **дефект —ы** mass defect; **единица —ы** unit of mass, unit of measure; (nucl.) atomic mass unit, amu; **закон действия масс** law of mass action; **испытание —ы** bulk test; **перенос —ы** mass transfer; **собственная м.** rest mass.

массаж *m.,* **—ировать** *v.,* **—ный** *a.* massage; **—ист** *m.* masseur; **—истка** *f.* masseuse.

массайский *a.* (geog.) Masai.

масса-светимость *f.* (astr.) mass-luminosity.

масс. ед. *abbr.* (**массовая единица**) mass unit; atomic mass unit.

массив *m.* solid mass, body; main part; block, group; large tract, area, district; (cards) deck, pack, stack; (ice) pack; file, collection, array; (furnace) shell; (geol.) massif, mountain mass; **м. данных, м. информации** (comp.) data array; data file; **битовый м.** (comp.) bitmap; **большой м. данных** (comp.) mass data; **жилищный м.** development, tract (of houses); residential district; **лесной м.** forest range, forest tract; **пастбищный м.** pastures; **состояние —а** state of aggregation; **—ность** *f.* massiveness, solidity; **—ный** *a.* massive, bulky, substantial, sturdy, heavy, compact; solid (tire, etc.).

массикот *m.* massicot, lead monoxide.

массиров/ание *n.,* **—ка** *f.* massaging; massing; **—анный** *a.* massaged; massed; **—ать** *v.* massage, rub, knead; (mil.) mass, concentrate.

масскуит *m.* (sugar) massecuite.

массов/ик *m.* mass organizer; **—ка** *f.* mass meeting; excursion; **—ость** *f.* mass, quantity; **—ый** *a. of* **масса;** mass, assembly-line, wholesale (manufacture); large-tonnage (product); high-volume; abundant, widespread, popular; aggregate, collective; **—ая единица** (nucl.) atomic mass unit, amu; **—ая операция** queueing operation; **—ое обслуживание** queueing; **—ое число** (nucl.) mass number; **средний —ый** weighted mean.

массо/гон *m.* (paper) propeller-type agitator; **—мер** *m.* basis weight gage; **—мойка** *f.* pulp washer; **—обмен** *m.,* **—обменный** *a.* mass exchange; **—передача** *f.* mass transfer; **—провод** *m.* (paper) pulp pipeline; **—проводность** *f.* mass conductivity; **—содержание** *n.* mass content.

масс-сепаратор *m.* mass separator.

масс-спектр *m.,* **—альный** *a.* mass-spectrum; **—ограф** *m.* mass spectrograph; **—ометр** *m.* mass spectrometer; **—ометрия** *f.* mass spectrometry.

масс-эквивалент *m.* mass equivalent.

мастакс *m.* (zool.) mastax, gizzard.

мастей *gen. pl. of* **масть.**

мастер *m.* foreman; master, expert, skilled workman; maker, manufacturer; **м.-беч** *m.* (rubber) master batch; **—ить** *v.* make, contrive, rig up, fix up; **м.-карта** *f.* master card; **—ко—** *prefix* (bot.) trulli—; **м.-копир** *m.* master cam; **—овой** *a.* skilled, experienced; *m.* craftsman; **—ок** *m.* trowel, float; **м.-пуансон** *m.* master punch; **—ская** *f.* (work)shop, repair shop; **—ские**

pl. works; **—ский** *a. of* **мастер;** **—ской** *a.* skillful; **м.-станок** *m.* master tool; **—ство** *n.* skill, mastery, workmanship; trade, craft; **м.-штамп** *m.* master die.

масти *gen. of* **масть.**

мастика *f.* mastic, cement, composition, paste, compound; **—тор** *m.* masticator, (breakdown) mill; **—ция** *f.* mastication, breakdown.

маст/иковый *a. of* **мастика;** **—икс** *see* **мастика;** **—ит** *m.* (med.) mastitis.

мастихин *m.* spatula.

мастицин *m.* masticin.

мастицировать *v.* masticate, break down.

мастичный *a.* mastic.

масто— *prefix* (anat.) mast(o)— (breast; mastoid process).

мастодонт *m.* (pal.) mastodon.

мастоидит *m.* (med.) mastoiditis.

мастурбация *f.* masturbation.

масть *f.* (zool.) color.

мастэктомия *f.* (med.) mastectomy.

масштаб *m.* scale, gage, rule; degree, quantity, measure; rate; **м. скольжения** sliding scale; **большого —а** large scale; **в —е** to scale; **в —ах** in quantities; **в маленьком —е** on a small scale; **в промышленных —ах** on an industrial scale; **в уменьшенном —е** scaled down; **истинный м. времени** (comp.) real time; **по —у** to scale; **сводить к определённому —у** *v.* bring to scale; **складной м.** folding rule; **уменьшать м.** *v.* scale down; **чертить в —е** *v.* to draw to scale; **—ирование** *n.* scaling; multiplex(ing); **—ировать** *v.* scale; **—ность** *f.* extent; **—ный** *a. of* **масштаб;** **—ная линейка** scale, measuring rule.

мат *m.* mat, dull finish; (floor) mat, rug; **наводить м.** *v.* mat, produce a mat finish; grind, frost (glass); **протрава для —а** (met.) dull pickling; **стравлять на м.** *v.* dull (pickle).

матамата *f.* (herp.) Chelus fimbriata.

мате *see* **матэ.**

мателот *m.* adjacent ship (in convoy).

математи/зировать *v.* mathematize; **—к** *m.* mathematician; **—ка** *f.* mathematics; **—чески** *adv.* mathematically; **—ческий** *a.* mathematical; complete (induction); logical (memory); **—ческая машина** mathematical machine; computer; **—ческое обеспечение** (comp.) software; **—ческое ожидание** mathematical expectation, expected value.

матереть *v.* harden; grow (out).

матери *gen., pl., etc., of* **мать.**

материал *m.* material, goods, stock; data; fabric, cloth, stuff; substance; **м. для изучения** test(ing) material; **сырой м.** raw material; **м.-заменитель** *m.* substitute material; **м.-носитель** *m.* carrier material.

материало/вед *m.* materials technologist, materials man; **—ведение** *n.* materials technology, materials science; **—ёмкий** *a.* material-intensive; **—ёмкость** *f.* materials consumption.

материалы *pl. of* **материал;** data; conference papers.

материальн/о-технический *a.* materials and equipment, materiel; **—ый** *a.* material, physical; mass (point); **—ая база** material resources, storage base; **—ая выгода** tangible effect; **—ая часть** equipment, materiel; **—ая обеспеченность** financial security; **—ое хозяйство** materials control.

материга *f.* contribution (to).

материк *m.* continent, (main)land; subsoil; (hydr.) horizon D; (petr.) bedrock; (biol.) parent tissue; mature animal; **—овый** *a. of* **материк;** continental; bed (rock); land (ice).

материнс/кий *a.* maternal, mother(ly); (brood) cell; parent, source; inherent, intrinsic; bed (rock); **—тво** *n.* maternity, motherhood; parentage.

материя *f.* material, fabric; matter, substance; pus.

мат/ерка, —ёрка *f.* (bot.) pistillate hemp.

матерой *a.* (zool.) mature; experienced; deep, navigable (water).

матерчатый *a.* cloth, fabric.

матёрый *see* **матерой.**

матико *n.* matico (leaves).

матильдит *m.* (min.) matildite.

матиров/ание *n.* dull finish; producing dull finish; frosting (glass); **—анный** *a.* mat, dull; ground, frosted; **—ать** *v.* dull, deaden, tarnish; give a mat surface (to), produce a dull finish; frost, etch; **—ка** *see* **матирование.**

матиссеновый *a.* Mathiessen's (rule).

мати/ца *f.,* **—чный** *a.* girder, beam, joist; templet; bag, sac.

матка *f.* (anat.) uterus, womb; (geol.) matrix; (zool.) dam, female parent; queen bee; (aircraft) carrier; master batch (of rubber); (text.) printing roller; (met.) rising gate, mother ship, base; master compass; **искусственная м.** brooder (house); **м.-кормилица** *f.* lactating ewe; **м.-рекордистка** *f.* champion dam.

матко/вод *m.* (bees) queen breeder; **—возка** *f.* ewe and lamb cart; **—выводной** *a.* queen-breeding; **—уловитель** *m.* queen trap.

матлокит *m.* (min.) matlockite.

матлот *see* **мателот.**

матов/ание *n.* (glass) frosting, etching; **—опозолочённый** *a.* dead-gilded; **—ость** *f.* dullness, etc., *see* **матовый.**

матов/ый *a.* dull, lusterless, tarnished, dead, mat, mat-finish; ground, frosted, etched (glass); (bot.) opaque; **м. блеск** dull finish, mat finish; **—ая отделка** dull finish(ing); **—ая позолота** dead-gilding; **—ая протрава** (met.) pickle for giving a dull surface; **—ое место** dead spot.

матовязальный *a.* mat-weaving.

мато/к *gen. pl. of* **матка;** **—чка** *f.* (anat.) utriculus, utricle; **—чковый** *a.* utricular.

маточник *m.* mother liquor; master tap; lead screw; master batch; manifold; (hort.) parent plant; seed plot; nursery; (agr.) pen for dams; queen bee egg; (bot.) Ostericum; dragonhead (*Dracocephalum moldavicum*); **м.-свинарник** *m.* (agr.) sow pen.

маточно— *prefix* (anat.) utero—(uterus); **м.-влагалищный** *a.* uterovaginal; **м.-трубный** *a.* uterotubal; **м.-шеечный** *a.* uterocervical.

маточн/ый *a. of* **матка;** mother, parent, source; master (batch); brood, spawning (stock); stock (pond; nursery); breeding; (apid.) royal (jelly); (anat.) uterine; **м. лист** (met.) starting sheet; **м. метчик** master tap; **м. рассол, м. раствор** mother liquor; **м. чан** (vinegar) mother vat.

матр/ас *m.* separating flask; **—ас, —ац** *m.* mat(tress); (inflatable) bed; (thermal) blanket; (geol.) pillow lava; **—асик** *dim. of* **матрас;** mat; **—асник** *m.* mattress cover; **—асный** *a. of* **матрас;** **—ацевидный** *a.* pillow (cleavage); **—ацный** *a. of* **матрац.**

матрикария *f.* (bot.) Matricaria.

матриархальный *a.* matriarchal.

матрик/альный *a.* matrical, matrix; **—с** *m.* matrix; *pl.* matrices.

матрин *m.* matrine, isolupanine.

матри/ца *f.* (math.; typ.) matrix; array; (stamping die,

female die; template, transcription code; *pl.* matrices; **битовая м.** bitmap; **м.-образец** *f.* master die; **литьёв—цах** die casting; **—цедержатель** *m.* die holder; **—цирование** *n.* matrixing, matrix making; **—цировать** *v.* make matrices; **—чный** *a. of* **матрица;** master (card, etc.); (gen.) messenger (RNA); **—чная телекамера** (robotics) matrix array television camera; **—чное печатающее устройство** dot-matrix printer.

матроклин/ия, —ность *f.* (gen.) matrocliny; **—ный** *a.* matroclinal, matroclinous.

матрос *m.,* **—ский** *a.* sailor, seaman.

матт, белый white metal.

маттиола *f.* (bot.) Matthiola.

матчинский *a.* (geog.) Matcha.

матчасть *f.* materiel, physical plant.

мать *f.* mother.

Матьё функция (math.) Mathieu's function.

мать-(и-)мачеха *f.* (bot.) coltsfoot (*Tussilago farfara*).

матэ *n.* (bot.) maté, Paraguay tea (*Ilex paraguariensis*).

маун *m.,* **—ный** *a.* (bot.) Valeriana.

Маунт— *prefix* (geog.) Mount.

маухерит *m.* (min.) maucherite.

мауцелиит *m.* (min.) mauzeliite.

мауэрлат *m.* wall plate.

маф/ит *m.* (min.) mafite; **—ический** *a.* mafic, ferromagnesian.

мафурское сало mafura tallow.

мах *m.* motion, move, stroke, wave; swing, oscillation; gait; Mach number.

Маха число (phys.) Mach number.

махагони *see* **махогани.**

махайроды *pl.* (pal.) Machairodontidae.

мах/альный *a.* signaling, etc., *see* **махать;** *m.* signal man; **—альщик** *m.* signal man; **—ание** *n.* signaling, etc., *see* **махать.**

махаон *m.* (ent.) swallow-tail butterfly (*Papilio machaon*).

махать *v.* signal, brandish, wave; beat, flap (wings); wag (tail).

махе *n.,* **М. единица** (nucl.) Mache unit.

махи *pl.* (orn.) remiges.

махил/иды, —исы *pl.* (ent.) Machilidae; **—ин** *m.* machiline, coclaurine; **—ис** *m.* (ent.) Machilis.

махметр *m.* machmeter, Mach indicator.

махнуть *see* **махать.**

махов/ик *m.,* **—иковый, —ичный** *a.* flywheel; handwheel; knob; **м.-регулятор** *m.* flywheel governor; **—ичок** *dim. of* **маховик;** **—ое** *see* **маховик;** **—ой** *a. of* **маховик;** fly (wheel); **—ое перо** (orn.) oar feather, remex; *pl.* remiges.

махогани *n.* mahogany (wood).

махор/ка *f.,* **—очный** *a.* (bot.) makhorka, common tobacco (*Nicotiana rustica*); **—коведение, —ководство** *n.* makhorka culture.

махорчатый *a.* heavily fringed.

махотка *f.* clay pot.

махра *see* **махорка.**

махров/ость *f.* (bot.) doubleness; **—ый** *a.* double (-flowering); shaggy.

махсир *m.* (ichth.) mahseer (*Tor tor*).

маца *f.* matzoth, unleavened bread.

македонский *a.* (geog.) Macedonia(n).

мацерал *m.* (coal) maceral.

мацер/атор *m.* macerator; **—ация** *f.,* **—ирование** *n.* maceration; **—ировать** *v.* macerate, soak to a pulp.

мациленовая кислота macilenic acid.

мацис *m.,* **—овый** *a.* mace (spice).

мац/они, —ун *m.* matzoon (fermented milk).

мачёк *m.* (bot.) horn poppy (*Glaucium*).

мачет/а, —е *f.* (ichth.) menhaden (*Brevoortia*); machete (*Elops*).

мачт/а *f.* mast, column, post, pole, tower, support; spar tree; **м.-антенна** *f.* tower-type antenna; **—овка** *f.* spar tree; **—овник** *m.* spar tree forest; **—овый** *a.* of **мачта;** high-standing (timber); spar (tree); street (lamp); **—овый выключатель** (elec.) pole switch; **—отруба** *f.* mack.

мачу/ела, —эла *f.* (ichth.) thread herring (*Opisthonema,* spec. *O. oglinum*).

маш *m.* (bot.) mung bean (*Phaseolus aureus*).

машет *pr. 3 sing. of* **махать.**

машин/а *f.* machine, engine; car, automobile, vehicle; computer; (smoke) generator; **—ер,** *e.g.,* **опрыскивающая м.** sprayer; **—ы** *pl.* machines, machinery; **м.-аналог** *f.* analog computer; **м.-двигатель** *f.* engine; **м.-компаунд** *f.* compound engine.

машинальн/ость *f.* mechanicalness; **—ый** *a.* mechanical, automatic.

машина-орудие *f.* machine tool, power tool; **м.-чиститель** *f.* purifier.

машин/изация *f.* mechanization; **—изировать** *v.* mechanize; equip with machinery; **—ист** *m.* machine operator; mechanic; driver; (rr.) engineer; **—истка** *f.* typist; **—ка** *dim. of* **машина;** typewriter.

машинно— *prefix* machine; **м.-дорожный** *a.* road machinery; **м.-рыболовецкий** *a.* mechanized fishing; **м.-сенокосный** *a.* hay-cutting machine; **м.-тракторный** *a.* implement and tractor.

машинн/ый *a.* machine, engine; power (driven); mechanical; automatic; operating (time); machine-made; typing (office); computer(-aided, -assisted or -based); absolute (code); **м. журнал** logbook of machine performance; **м. зал** machine shop; engine room; **—ое оборудование** machinery, mechanical equipment; **обрабатывать —ым способом** *v.* machine.

машино— *prefix* machine; **—вед** *m.* mechanic, mechanical engineer; **—ведение** *n.* mechanical engineering, machine science; **—вооруженность** *f.* (farm) machinery; **—испытательный** *a.* machine-testing; **—писный** *a.* typewritten; **—пись** *f.* typing; **—поделочный** *a.* structural (steel); **—прокатный** *a.* machine-hiring; **—ремонтный** *a.* machine repair(ing); **—смена** *f.* machine shift; **—строение** *n.* machine building, engineering industry; equipment design.

машиностроитель *m.* mechanic; mechanical engineer; **—ный** *a.* machine-building, mechanical(-engineering); machine (industry, shop).

машиносчётный *a.* computer (center).

машино-час *m.* machine hour.

машистый *a.* with a wide swing.

машпром *m.* machine industry.

машуковый *a.* (geog.) Mashuk.

машущий *pr. act. part. of* **махать.**

мая *gen. of* **май.**

маяк *m.* lighthouse, beacon, signal tower; buoy; (forestry) standard; (plastering) screed; **плавучий м.** lightship; **м.-ответчик** *m.* transponder-beacon.

маятник *m.* pendulum; **—овый** *a.* pendulum, oscillating; floating; swing (saw); **—овый копёр** impact tester; pendulum hammer; **—овая дорога** single-span cableway; **—овая миграция** commuting; **—овое колебание** (spectroscopy) rocking vibration; **—ообразный** *a.* penduliform.

маятничек *dim. of* **маятник.**

маяться *v.* suffer; drudge.

маячить *v.* show (up), be visible; shimmer, shine.

маяч/ковый, —ный *a. of* **маяк;** dominant, standard (tree).

мб, мбар *abbr.* (**миллибар**) millibar; **м-б** *abbr.* (**масштаб**) scale; **м.б.** *abbr.* (**может быть**) perhaps.

мбарн *abbr.* (**миллибарн**) millibarn.

мбр *see* **мб; МБР** *abbr.* (**межконтинентальная баллистическая ракета**) intercontinental ballistic missile, ICBM.

МБС *abbr.* (**межконтинентальный баллистический снаряд**) intercontinental ballistic missile, ICBM.

МБТ *abbr.* (**меркаптобензотиазол**) mercaptobenzothiazole, MBT.

мбу *m.* (ichth.) puffer (*Tetraodon mbu*).

мбуга *f.* (geobot.) mbuga (acacia woodland).

мбэр *abbr.* (**миллибэр**) millirem.

мв *abbr.* (**милливольт**) millivolt; **мв, м.в., МВ** *abbr.* (**молекулярный вес**) molecular weight; **м.в.** *abbr.* (**меры веса**) measures of weight; **Мв** *abbr.* (**мегавольт**) megavolt; **М/В** *abbr.* (**масло/вода**) oil-water emulsion, O/W.

Мва *abbr.* (**мегавольтампер**) mega-volt-ampere.

МВР *abbr.* (**магнито-вариационная разведка**) magnetic-variation surveying; (**молекулярно-весовое распределение**) molecular weight distribution.

мвт *abbr.* (**милливатт**) milliwatt; **Мвт** *see* **мгвт.**

мг *abbr.* (**миллиграмм**) milligram; (**мега-**) mega-; **мГ** *abbr.* (**миллиграм-сила**) milligram force; **Мг** (**мегаграмм**) megagram.

мга *see* **мгла.**

мгб *abbr.* (**мегабар**) megabar.

мгв *see* **Мв.**

мгвт *abbr.* (**мегаватт**) megawatt; **мгвт-ч** *abbr.* (**мегаватт-час**) megawatt-hour.

МГГ *abbr.* (**Международный геофизический год**) International Geophysical Year.

мггц *abbr.* (**мегагерц**) megahertz, MHz.

МГД *abbr.* (**магнитогидродинамический**) magneto-hydrodynamic, MHD; **МГД-генератор** *m.* MHD generator.

мгдж *abbr.* (**мегаджоуль**) megajoule.

мгд(и)н *abbr.* (**мегадина**) megadyne.

М-ген *m.* (gen.) M-gene.

мгинский *a.* (geog.) Mga.

мгкал *abbr.* (**мегакалория**) megacalorie.

мгл/а *f.* mist, haze; **дымная м.** smog; **—истый** *a.* misty, hazy.

мгм *abbr.* (**мегаметр**) megameter.

мгн *abbr.* (**миллигенри**) millihenry.

мгновен/ие *n.* instant, moment; **—но** *adv.* instantaneously, instantly; momentarily; **—но-критический** *a.* prompt-critical; **—но-упругий** *a.* Hookean (deformation); **—ность** *f.* instantaneousness; **—ный** *a.* instant(aneous), prompt; momentary, brief; flash (freezing, etc.); **—ного действия** instantaneous.

мго *see* **мо; мгом** *abbr.* (**мегом**) megohm.

Мгт *abbr.* (**мегатонна**) megaton.

Мгц *see* **мггц.**

мгэв *abbr.* (**мегаэлектрон-вольт**) million electron-volts, MeV.

мг-экв *abbr.* (**миллиграмм-эквивалент**) milligram-equivalent.

м.д. *abbr.* (**миллионная доль**) part per million, ppm.

МДК *abbr.* (**максимальная допустимая концентрация**) maximum permissible concentration.

МДП *abbr.* (**металл-диэлектрик-полупроводник**) metal-insulator-semiconductor, MIS.

м.д.с. *abbr.* (**магнитодвижущая сила**) magnetomotive force.

ме, МЕ *abbr.* (**массовая единица**) mass unit; **МЕ** *abbr.* (**международная единица**) international unit.

меандр *m.* meander, winding; loop (of river); fret, key pattern; meander, crenulated molding; **—ирующий, —ический** *a.* meandering, winding.

меато— *prefix* (anat.) meato— (meatus, opening, passageway).

мебел/евоз *m.* moving van; **—ь** *f.* furniture; **—ьностолярный** *a.* furniture (factory); **—ьный** *a.* furniture; cabinet (work); **—ьная моль** (ent.) clothes moth (*Tineola bisseliella*); **—ьщик** *m.* furniture maker.

мёбиусовый *a.* Möbius' (syndrome, etc.).

меблиров/ание *n.* furnishing; **—анный** *a.* furnished; **—ать** *v.* furnish; **—ка** *f.* furniture; furnishing.

мевалоновый *a.* mevalonic (acid).

мега— *prefix* mega(a)— (10⁶, million; large); **—байт** megabyte (2²⁰ byte); **—бар** *m.* megabar; **—варметр** *m.* (elec.) megavarmeter; **—ватт** *m.* megawatt; **—ватт-час** megawatt-hour; **—вольт** *m.* megavolt; **—вольтампер** *m.* mega-volt-ampere; **—гамета** *f.* (gen.) megagamete, the egg; **—гаусс** *m.* (elec.) megagauss; **—герц** *m.* megahertz, megacycle(s) per second; **—дермы** *pl.* (mam.) Megadermatidae; **—джоуль** *m.* megajoule; **—дина** *f.* megadyne; **—калория** *f.* megacalorie; **—кариоцит** *m.* (cyt.) megacaryocyte; **—кулон** *m.* megacoulomb; **—кюри** *m.* megacurie.

мегало— *prefix* megalo— (large, great); **—бласт** *m.* (blood) megaloblast; **—миктеровые** *pl.* (ichth.) Megalomycteridae; **—па** *f.* (crust.) megalopa, megalops; **—цит** *m.* (blood) megalocyte.

мега/мега— *prefix* megamega—, tera— (10¹²); **—метр** *m.* megameter; **—ом** *see* **мегом; —перм** *m.* megaperm (alloy); **—рад** *m.* (nucl.) megarad; **—резерфорд** *m.* megarutherford; **—рентген** *m.* megaroentgen; **—сейсмы** *pl.* (geol.) megaseisms.

мегаскоп *m.* megascope; **—ический** *a.* megascopic, visible to the naked eye.

мега/спора *f.* (bot.) megaspore; **—спороцит** *m.* (embr.) megasporocyte; **—терий** m. (pal.) Megatherium; **—терм** *m.* megatherm, tropical plant; **—тонна** *f.* megaton; **—трон** *m.* (electron.) megatron; **—троф** *m.* megatrophic plant; **—фарада** *f.* (elec.) megafarad, macrofarad; **—фон** *m.* megaphone; **—хилины** *pl.* (ent.) Megachilidae; **—цикл** *m.* (elec.) megacycle; **—электронвольт** *m.* megaelectron volt, million electron volt, MeV; **—эрг** *see* **мегэрг.**

меггер *m.* (elec.) megger, megohmmeter.

мегдым *m.* (ichth.) Siberian dace (*Leuciscus l. baicalensis*).

мегом *m.,* **—ный** *a.* (elec.) megohm; **—метр** *see* **меггер.**

мегр/ельский *a.* (geog.) Megrel; **—инский** *a.* Megri.

мегэрг *m.* (phys.) megerg.

мёд *m.* honey; **падевый м., росовый м.** honey dew.

мед, МЕД *abbr.* (**международная единица действия**) international unit of activity.

мед— *prefix* (**медицинский**) medic(in)al.

медал/ист *m.* prize winner; **—ь** *f.,* **—ьный** a. medal, coin; **—ьерное искусство** coin casting; **—ьон** *m.* medallion.

медбрат *m.* male nurse.

медведевский *a.* (geog.) Medvedka.

медвед/и *pl. of* **медведь;** (mam.) Ursidae; **—иха, —ица** *f.* she-bear, sow; **большая —ица** (astr.) Ursa Major; **малая —ица** Ursa Minor; **—ицы** *pl.* (ent.) tiger moths (*Arctiidae*).

медведк/а *f.* truck; (art.) truck carriage; wood block; (carpentry) two-man plane; die, stamp, punch press; (ent.) mole cricket; **—и** *pl.* Gryllotalpidae.

медведь *m.* (mam.) bear (*Ursus*).

медвеж/атина *f.* bear meat; **—атки** *pl.* bear animalcules (*Tardigrada*); **—атник** *m.* bear hunter; bear trainer; bear house; **—ачий** *see* **медвежий.**

медвеж/ий *a.* bear, ursine; **м. виноград, —ья толокнянка, —ьи ягоды** (bot.) bearberry (*Arctostaphylos uva ursi*); **—ье ухо** mullein (*Verbascum*); **—ья лапа** bear's breech (*Acanthus*); **—ина** *f.* bear meat; **—онок** *m.* bear cub; **—ьи** *see* **медведи.**

медвуз *m.* institution of higher medical education.

медвян/о-жёлтый *a.* honey-colored; **—ый** *a.* honey, melleous; **—ая роса** (aphid) honeydew.

Медгиз State Medical Publishing House.

медгородок *m.* medical center.

меде— *prefix* copper; **—литейная** *f.* copper foundry; **—носный** *a.* copper-bearing; cupriferous; **—обжигательная печь** copper furnace; **—очистительный завод** copper refinery; **—плавильный** *a.* coppersmelting; **—содержащий** *a.* copper-bearing, cupriferous; **—электролитный завод** electrolytic copper refinery.

меди *gen., pl., etc., of* **медь.**

меди/альный *a.* medial, middle; (stat.) median; **—ан** *m.,* **—ана** *f.,* **—анный** *a.* median; **—астинит** *m.* (med.) mediastinitis; **—астино—** *prefix* (anat.) mediastino— (mediastinum); **—атор** *m.,* **—аторный** *a.* mediator, messenger; (physiol.) transmitter; **—атриса** *f.* (math.) midperpendicular; **—ация** *f.* mediation.

медик *m.* medical man; **—амент** *m.* medicine, medicinal, medicament, remedy; **—аментозный** *a.* medicinal; drug-induced; **—о-инструментальный** *a.* medical instrument; **—о-механический** *a.* medicomechanical; **—о-санитарный** *a.* (mil.) medical; public health; **—о-санитарная часть** public health organization.

мединал *m.* Medinal, barbital sodium.

мединститут *m.* medical institute.

медист/о— *prefix* cupro—, cuprous, copper; honey; **—осинеродистый** *a.* cuprocyanide (of); **—ость** *f.* honey-producing capacity; **—ый** *a.* cuprous, copper; cupriferous.

медицин/а *f.* medicine, medical science; **—ский** *a.* medic(in)al; medicated (honey, etc.); clinical (thermometer); registered (nurse); surgical (gloves).

медкомиссия *f.* medical commission.

медл/енно *adv.* slowly; **—еннодействующий** *a.* slow (-acting); **—енность** *f.* slowness; **—енный** *a.* slow, sluggish; low-speed, low-velocity; slowly varying (function); low-rate (filter); **—ительность** *f.* sluggishness; **—ительный** *a.* sluggish, slow, tardy; **—ить** *v.* be slow, delay, hang back, hesitate; **—яки** *pl.* (ent.) darkling beetles (*Tenebrionidae*).

медн/ение *n.* copper plating; **—еный** *a.* copper-plated; **—ик** *m.* copper smith; **—ить** *v.* copper-plate; **—ицкая** *f.,* **—ицкий** *a.* copper smithy.

медно— *prefix* cupri, cupric, copper; **—аммиачный шёлк** cuprammonium rayon; **—винная кислота** cupritartaric acid; **—закисный** *a.* cuprous oxide; copper oxide (cell; rectifier); **—кислый** *a.* cupric acid; cuprate (of); **—кислая соль** cuprate; **—котельная** *f.* copper smithy; **—красный** *a.* copper-colored.

меднолитей/ная *f.* copper foundry, brass foundry; **—ный** *a.* copper founding; **—щик** *m.* copper founder.

медно/плавильный *a.* copper-smelting; **—прокатный** *a.* copper-rolling; **—рудный** *a.* copper ore; **—сере-**

бряный блеск (min.) stromeyerite; —**синеродистый** *a.* cupricyanide (of); —**цинковый** *a.* copper-zinc.

медн/ый *a.* cupric, copper; **м. блеск** (min.) copper glance, chalcocite; **м. дождь** (met.) copper rain; **м. изумруд** (min.) copper emerald, dioptase; **м. колчедан** (min.) copper pyrites, chalcopyrite; **м. купорос** blue vitriol, copper sulfate; **м. уранит** (min.) copper uranite, torbernite; **м. штейн** (met.) copper matte, blue metal; —**ая зелень** copper rust, verdigris; (min.) malachite; —**ая кислота** cupric acid; **соль** —**ой кислоты** cuprate; —**ая лазурь** (min.) azurite; —**ая синь** (min.) blue verditer, azurite; —**аз смоляная руда** (min.) copper pitch ore; —**ая чернь** (min.) melaconite, black copper oxide; —**ое индиго** (min.) copper indigo, covellite.

медо— *prefix* honey; nectar.

медобслуживание *n.* medical service.

медов/ар *m.* mead brewer; —**арение** *n.,* —**ар(ен)ный** *a.* mead brewing; —**еды** *pl.* (orn.) honey guides (*Indicatoridae*); —**ик** *m.* strong bee colony; (bot.) nectary; Melianthus; —**иковые** *pl.* Melianthaceae; —**ка** *f.* (ent.) apple psylla; —**ник** *m.* nectary; hemp nettle (*Galeopsis*); —**о—** *prefix* meli—, honey.

медов/ый *a.* honey; mellitic (acid); **м. камень** (min.) honeystone, mellite; **м. уксус** oxymel; —**ая вода** hydromel; —**ая патока** liquid honey; —**ая роса** (aphid) honeydew; —**ое вино** mead, mulse.

медо/гонка *f.,* —**гонная машина** honey extractor, honey centrifuge; —**ед** *m.* (mam.) honey badger (*Mellivora*); —**качание** *n.* honey extraction; —**качка** *see* **медогонка;** —**нос** *m.* nectar(iferous) plant; —**носность** *f.* nectar-bearing capacity; —**носный** *a.* nectariferous, melliferous; honey (bee); —**отстойник** *m.* honey tank; —**сбор** *m.* honey flow, honey yield.

мед/осмотр *m.* medical inspection, medical examination; —**осос** *m.* meliphagous bird, honey eater; —**ососовые** *pl.* Meliphagidae; —**ососущий** *a.* meliphagous, honey-sucking; —**оуказчики** *pl.* (orn.) honeyguides (*Indicatoridae*); —**персонал** *m.* medical staff; —**помощь** *f.* medical assistance; —**препарат** *m.* drug; —**пункт** *m.* medical center; —**работник** *m.* medical worker.

мёд-самотек *m.* liquid honey.

медсестра *f.* registered nurse.

медуз/а *f.* (zool.) medusa, jellyfish; —**овидный,** —**оидный,** —**ообразный** *a.* medusoid.

медулл/а *f.* (anat.) medulla, marrow; —**ярный** *a.* medullary.

медун/ица *f.* (bot.) lungwort (*Pulmonaria*); —**ка** *f.* medick (*Medicago*); lungwort (*Pulmonaria*); hemp nettle (*Galeopsis ladanum*).

медфак *m.* faculty of medicine.

мед/ь *f.* copper, Cu; **белая м.** white copper, German silver (alloy); **гидрат закиси** —**и** cuprous hydroxide; **гидрат окиси** —**и** cupric hydroxide; **жёлтая м.** (met.) brass; **закись** —**и** cuprous oxide; **соль закиси** —**и** cuprous salt; **красная м.** cuprite, red copper ore; **окись** —**и** cupric oxide; **соль окиси** —**и** cupric salt; **подовая м.** (copper) bottoms; **сернокислая м.,** **сульфат** —**и** copper sulfate; **сернокислая закись** —**и** cuprous sulfate; **сернокислая окись** —**и** cupric sulfate; **хлористая м.** cuprous chloride; **хлорная м.** cupric chloride; **чёрная м.** (met.) black copper, coarse copper; (min.) black copper ore; **черновая м.** black copper; blister copper.

медь/органический *a.* organocopper; —**содержащий** *see* **медесодержащий.**

медян/ица *f.* (ent.) Psylla; (herp.) blind worm (*Anguis*

fragilis); —**ицы** *pl.* (ent.) Psyllidae; —**ка** *f.* verdigris, green copper rust; (herp.) *see* **медяница;** grass snake (*Coronella austriaca*); (phyt.) anthracnose; —**ки** *pl.* (ent.) Buprestidae.

меж— *see* **между—.**

межа *f.* bound(ary), landmark, limit.

меж/американский *a.* inter-American; —**атомный** *a.* interatomic; —**библиотечный** *a.* interlibrary; —**бугорковый** *a.* (anat.) intertubercular; —**ведомственный** *a.* interdepartmental, interagency; —**видовой** *a.* (biol.) interspecific, interspecies; —**вузовское совещание** conference of schools of higher education; —**галактический** *a.* (astr.) intergalactic; —**генный** *a.* (gen.) intergenic; —**глазничный** *a.* (anat.) interocular, interorbital; —**глазье** interocular space; —**годов(н)ой** *a.* year-to-year; —**горный** *a.* (geol.) intermontane; —**групповой** *a.* between groups, external (variance); —**дендритовый** *a.* interdendritic; —**долевой** *a.* (anat.) interlobar; —**дольковый,** **дольчатый** *a.* interlobular.

междо/молекулярный *a.* intermolecular; —**узельный,** —**узловой** *a.* internodal; (cryst.) interstitial; —**узлие** *n.* internode; interstice.

между *prep. instr. and gen.* between, among; **м. прочим** by the way, among other things; **м. тем** meanwhile; **м. тем как** while, whereas; **м. центрами** center-to-center.

между— *prefix* inter—, between; *see also under* **меж—;** —**антный** *a.* (instrumentation) interdee; —**блочный** *a.* interunit; —**ведомственный** *a.* interdepartmental; —**венцовый зазор** rim clearance; —**видовой** *see* **межвидовой;** —**витковый** *a.* turn-to-turn; —**гнездье** *n.* the space in between; —**городный** *a.* interurban; intercity; (tel.) long-distance, toll; —**гранулярный** *a.* intergranular; —**железное пространство** air gap, clearance; —**звёздный** *a.* (astr.) interstellar; —**зернистый** *a.* intergranular; —**клеточный** *a.* intercellular; —**кристаллический** *a* intercrystalline; —**ледниковый** *a.* (geol.) interglacial; —**лежащий** *a.* intermediate; —**линзовый** *a.* between-the-lens; —**молекулярный** *a.* intermolecular.

международн/ый *a.* international, standard; —**ое право** international law.

между/национальный *a.* international; —**осный** *a.* interaxial; —**парный** *a.* pair-to-pair; —**парье** *n.* (agr.) period between spring and summer field work; —**планетный** *a.* interplanetary; —**полюсный** *a.* interpolar; —**проводный** *a.* wire-to-wire (capacitance); —**путье** *n.* track spacing; —**рёберный** *a.* (anat.) intercostal.

междуречный *a.* interfluvial; —**ье** *n.* interfluve, interfluvial area.

междуряд/ие, —**ье** *n.* (inter-)row spacing; —**ный** *a.* inter-row, inter-crop.

между/слойный *a.* interlayer, interlaminar; —**союзнический** *a.* inter-associate; —**строчие** *n.* (typ.) interlinear space; —**строчный** *a.* interlinear; —**узлие** *n.* internode; interstice; —**фазный** *a.* interphase, phase-to-phase; —**цепной** *a.* intermolecular; —**этажный** *a.* between floors.

межев/альный *a.,* —**ание** *n.* surveying.

межёванный *a.* surveyed; with fixed boundaries.

межев/ать *v.* survey; fix boundaries; measure (land); —**ик** *m.* surveyor.

межёвка *see* **межевание.**

межевой *a.* surveying; boundary; land (e.g., landmark); mile (e.g., milestone); *m.* surveyor.

мёжевский *a.* (geog.) Myozha.

межевщик *m.* surveyor.

межен/ный *a.* low; **—ь** *f.* low water (level or period); drought period; limit; (ichth.) summer salmon; **в —ь** as a limit, at the outside.

межеум/ок *m.* intermediate (breed or variety); **—очный** *a.* intermediate, in-between, transitional.

меж/жаберный *a.* (ichth.) interbranchial; **—желудочковый** *a.* (anat.) interventricular; **—заводский, —заводской** *a.* interplant; **—запястный** *a.* (anat.) intercarpal; **—звёздный** *a.* (astr.) interstellar; **—зернный, —зернистый** *a.* intergranular; **—извилистый** *a.* (anat.) intergyral; **—ионный** *a.* inter-ion; **—каскадный** *a.* interstage; **—клетник** *m.* (bot.) intercellular space or duct; **—клет(оч)ный** *a.* intercellular; **—клиновидный** *a.* (anat.) intercuneiform; **—ключичный** *a.* interclavicular; **—колхозный** *a.* interkolkhoz; **—континентальный** *a.* intercontinental; **—корневой** *a.* interradicular; **—костный** *a.* (anat.) interosseous; **—кочье** *n.* space between hummocks; **—кристаллический, —кристаллитный, —кристальный** *a.* intercrystalline; intergranular (corrosion); **—крышечная** *a.* (ichth.) interopercle.

межледников/ый *a.* (geol.) interglacial; **—ье** *n.* interglacial period.

меж/лопаточный *a.* (anat.) interscapular; **—молекулярный** *a.* intermolecular; **—мочеточниковый** *a.* (anat.) interureteric; **—мышечный** *a.* intermuscular; **—мыщелковый** *a.* intercondylar; **—национальный** *a.* international; **—нёбный** *a.* (anat.) interpalatine; **—ник** *m.* boundary strip or stone; **—ножковый** *a.* (anat.) intercrural; interpeduncular; **—носовой** *a.* internasal; **—няк** *m.* (ent.) Cicindela; **—областной** *a.* (inter)regional; **—обмоточный** *a.* interwinding; **—оболочечный** *a.* intermembranous; **—операционный** *a.* interoperational; **—осевой, —осный** *a.* interaxial; center(-to-center).

межост/истый *a.* (anat.) interspinal; **—ный** *a.* interosseous (artery).

меж/островный *a.* inter-island; **—отраслевой** *a.* interindustry; **—офазовый** *a.* phase-transfer (catalysis); **—пещеристый** *a.* (anat.) intercavernous; **—планетный** *a.* interplanetary; outer (space); space (vehicle); **—плодник** *m.* (bot.) mesocarp; **—плоскостный** *a.* interplanar; **—плюсневой** *a.* (anat.) intertarsal; **—позвоночный** *a.* intervertebral; **—половой** *a.* intersexual; **—полосный** *a.* interstrip; **—поперечный** *a.* intertransverse; **—породный** *a.* interbreed; cross (breeding); interracial; **—почечный** *a.* (anat.) interrenal; **—правительственный** *a.* intergovernmental; **—предсердный** *a.* (anat.) interatrial; **—приступный** *a.* (med.) interictal; **—пучковый** *a.* interfascicular; **—радиальный** *a.* interradial; **—районный** *a.* (inter)regional, (inter)district; **—расовый** *a.* interracial; **—рёберный** *a.* (anat.) intercostal; **—ремонтный** *a.* between servicing; overhaul (life); **—родовой** *a.* (biol.) intergeneric.

меж/сегмент(ар)ный *a.* intersegmental; **—сетевой** *a.* (comp.) internet; **—сортовой** *a.* intervarietal; **—союзнический** *a.* inter-associate; **—стадийный** *a.* interstage; **—станционный** *a.* (tel.) interexchange; zonal (seed testing); **—тарелочный** *a.* interplate; **—теменной** *a.* (anat.) interparietal; **—течка** *f.* (zool.) dioestrus; **—трапповый** *a.* (geol.) intertrappean; **—трубный** *a.* intertubular; **—узел** *m.* crosslink; **—уточный** *a.* intermediary, intermediate; (anat.) interstitial; **—учрежденческий** *a.* interagency; **—фазный, —фазовый** *a.* interphase; interfacial (tension); **—фаланговый** *a.* (anat.) interphalangeal; **—формационный** *a.* (geol.) interformational; **—хрящевой** *a.* (anat.) interchondral; **—центровый** *a.* center-to-

center; **—цепной** *a.* interchain (reaction); **—цеховой** *a.* interplant; **—цикловые** *pl.* between-batch time; **—частичный** *a.* interparticle; (anat.) intermaxillary; **—ъядерный** *a.* internuclear; **—ъязыковой** *a.* interlanguage; multilingual; **—этажный** *a.* between floors.

меза *f.* (geol.) mesa; plateau, terrace.

меза/коновая кислота mesaconic acid, methylfumaric acid.

меза/-область *f.* (geol.) mesa; **—структура** *f.* mesa (structure); **—транзистор** *m.* mesa transistor.

мезг/а *f.,* **—овый** *a.* (vegetable) pulp; **—оловушка** *f.* pulp trap.

мездр/а *f.* scrapings, shreds (of hide), glue stock; flesh side (of hide); **—ение** *n.,* **—ильный** *a.* fleshing, etc., *see v.;* **—ина** *f.,* **—инный** *a.* flesh side; **—ить** *v.* flesh, scrape, scour; **—овый, —яной** *a. of* **мездра;** flesh (side); hide (glue); **—як** *m.* scraping knife.

мезембрин *m.* mesembrine.

мезенский *a.* (geog.) Mezen.

мезен/терий *m.* (anat.) mesentery; **—терический** *a.* mesenteric; **—хима** *f.* (embryology) mesenchyme.

мези/дин *m.* mesidine, 2,4,6-trimethylaniline; **—л** *m.* mesyl; **—тен** *m.* mesitene.

мезитил *m.,* **—овый** *a.* mesityl; **—ен** *m.* mesitylene; **—еновый, —иновый** *a.* mesityl(en)ic (acid); **—овый спирт** *see* **мезитол.**

мезит/ин *m.,* **—ит** *m.* (min.) mesitine spar, mesitite; **—ол** *m.* mesitol, trimethylphenol; **—оновая кислота** mesitonic acid, dimethyllevulinic acid.

мезо— *prefix* mes(o)— (middle, intermediate); **—атом** *m.* mesonic atom; **—биливиолин** *m.* mesobiliviolin; **—билирубин** *m.* mesobilirubin; **—бласт** *m.* (embr.) mesoblast; **—винный** *a.* mesotartaric (acid); **—глея** *f.* (zool.) mesogl(o)ea; **—дерма** *f.* (embr.) mesoderm; **—диалит** *m.* (min.) mesodialyte; **—динамика** *f.* mesodynamics; **—зои, —иды** *pl.* (zool.) Mesozoa; **—зой** *m.,* **—зойская эра** (geol.) Mesozoic era; **—инозит** *m.* meso-inositol; **—карп(ий)** *m.* (bot.) mesocarp; **—котиль** *m.* mesocotyl; **—кратовый** *a.* (petr.) mesocratic.

мезоксал/евая кислота mesoxalic acid, oxopropanedioic acid; **—евокислый** *a.* mesoxalic acid; mesoxalate (of); **—ил** *m.* mesoxalyl; **—(ил)мочевина** *f.* mesoxalylurea, alloxan.

мезо/лит *m.* (min.) mesolite; (geol.) Mesolithic; **—логия** *f.* mesology, ecology.

мезомер *m.* mesomer, meso-form; **—ия** *f.* mesomerism; **—ный** *a.* mesomeric.

мезо/митоз *m.* (gen.) mesomitosis; **—молекула** *f.* mesomolecule; **—морф** *m.* (biol.) mesomorphic organism.

мезон *m.* (nucl.) meson; **—ий** *m.* mesonium.

мезонин *m.,* **—ный** *a.* mezzanine.

мезонный *a.* (nucl.) meson(ic).

мезо/пауза *f.* (meteor.) mesopause; **—пик** *m.* mesopeak; **—плазма** *f.* (cyt.) mesoplasm; **—подий** *m.* (biol.) mesopodium; **—положение** *n.* mesoposition; **—породы** *pl.* mesorocks, medium colored rocks; **—порфирин** *m.* mesoporphyrin; **—птиль** m. (orn.) mesoptile; **—сома** f. (gen.) mesosome; **—среда** *f.* mesic environment; **—стазис** *m.* (petr.) mesostasis, basis, base; **—сфера** *f.* mesosphere; **—тан** *m.* mesotan; ericin; **—тарзальный** *a.* (anat.) mesotarsal, midtarsal; **—телий** *m.* (embr.) mesothelium; **—терм** *m.* (bot.) mesotherm; **—термальный** *a.* mesothermal; **—тип** *m.* (min.) mesotype; **—торий** *m.* mesothorium, MsTh; **—трон** *see* **мезон; —трофный** *a.* mesotrophic, moderately nutritious; **—филл** *m.* (bot.) mesophyll; **—фит**

m. (bot.) mesophyte; —**форма** *f.* mesoform;—**хилий** *m.* (bot.) mesochil(ium).

мейбомиевый *a.* meibomian (glands).

Мейгса синдром (med.) Meigs' syndrome.

Мейера закон Meyer's law.

мейергофферит *m.* (min.) meyerhofferite.

меймацит *m.* (min.) meymacite.

мейо— *prefix* meio— (lesser, smaller); —**з** *m.* (gen.) meiosis; —**нит** *m.* (min.) meionite; —**мерный** *a.* meiomerous; —**тический** *a.* (gen.) meiotic; —**цит** *m.* meiocyte.

мейснеровы тельца (anat.) Meissner's corpuscles.

мекамин *m.* mec(amyl)amine.

меккелев хрящ Meckel's cartilage.

меккский бальзам Mecca balsam.

мекленбургский *a.* (geog.) Mecklenburg.

мекон/ат *m.* meconate; —**иевый** *a.*, —**ий** *m.* (embr.) meconium; —**ин** *m.* meconin; —**иновый** *a.* meconinic (acid); —**овый** *a.* meconic (acid).

мекоптеры *pl.* (ent.) scorpion flies (*Mecoptera*).

мекоцианин *m.* mecocyanin.

Мексика Mexico.

мексиканский *a.* Mexican.

мел *m.* chalk; (geol.) Cretaceous (period); (acous.) mel (unit); **красный м.** red chalk, red bole; **отмученный м.** prepared chalk, whiting; **чёрный м.** slate black.

мёл *past m. sing. of* **мести.**

мелаконит *m.* (min.) melaconite.

мелаксума *f.* (phyt.) melaxuma, black sap.

мелальгия *f.* (med.) melalgia, sciatica.

мелам *m.* melam; *dat. pl. of* **мел;** —**ин** *m.*, —**иновый** *a.* melamine, cyanuramide; —**фаевые** *pl.* (ichth.) Melamphaidae; —**фай** *m.* melamphid (*Melamphaes*).

меланезийский *a.* (geog.) Melanesia(n).

меланелла *f.* (mal.) Melanella.

меланж *m.* blend; —**евый** *a.* blend(ed), mixed; —**ёр** *m.* blender, mixer; —**ировать** *v.* blend, mix.

мелан/изм *m.* (med.) melanism; —**илин** *m.* melaniline; diphenyl guanidine; —**ин** *m.* (biol.) melanin; —**ист** *see* **меланоид.**

меланит *m.* (min.) melanite; —**овый** *a.* melanite, melanitic.

мелано— *prefix* melan(o)— (black, dark); —**вый** *a.* melanic, dark-colored; —**ген** *m.* melanogen; —**дерма** *f.* (med.) melanoderma; —**з** *m.* (med.) melanosis; (physiol.) melanism; (phyt.) melanose; —**ид** *m.* melanoid, melanistic animal; —**идин** *m.* melanoidin; —**ма** *f.* (med.) melanoma; —**кратовый** *a.* (petr.) melanocratic, dark-colored; —**новые** *pl.* (ichth.) Melanonidae; —**солод** *m.* melanoidin malt; —**стомиевые** *pl.* (ichth.) Melanostomiatidae; —**тениевые** *pl.* Melanotaeniidae; —**тический** *a.* melanotic, melanin; —**тропин** *m.*, —**тропный гормон** melanotropin, melanocyte-stimulating hormone; —**флогит** *m.* (min.) melanophlogite; —**фор** *m.* (cyt.) melanophore; —**форный** *a.* melanocyte-stimulating (hormone); —**хальцит** *m.* (min.) melanochalcite; —**церит** *m.* melanocerite; —**цетовые** *pl.* (ichth.) Melanocetidae; —**цит** m. (cyt.) melanocyte; —**цитостимулирующий** *a.* melanocyte-stimulating.

мелан/терит *m.* melanterite, mineral copperas; —**уровый** *a.* melanuric (acid).

меланхолия *f.* (med.) melancholy.

меласс/а *f.*, —**овый** *a.* molasses; —**овая кислота** melassic acid; —**образователь** *m.* molasses-producing substance; —**отворный** *a.* molasses-producing, melassigenic.

мелась *past f. sing. of* **местись.**

мелатонин *m.* (hormone) melatonin.

мелафир *m.* (petr.) melaphyre.

мелегет/(т)а *f.*, —**ский церец** Melegueta pepper, grains of paradise.

мелем *m.* melem (amide of cyanuric acid).

мелен *m.* melene, triacontylene.

мел/ение *n.* chalking; —**ёный** *a.* chalked.

мелет *pr. 3 sing of* **молоть.**

мелетин *m.* meletin, quercetin.

мелеть *v.* shoal, grow shallow.

мелёфагус *m.* (ent.) Melophagus.

мелецитоза *f.* melezitose, melicitose.

мелеющий *a.* shoaling, growing shallow.

мели *past pl. of* **мести;** *gen., etc., of* **мель.**

мели/бе *m.* (mal.) Melibe; —**биоза** *f.* melibiose, glucose-α-galactoside; —**бионовый** *a.* melibionic (acid); —**гетэс** *m.* (ent.) Meligethes; —**евые** *pl.* (bot.) Meliaceae; —**лит** *m.* (min.) melilite.

мелилотовая кислота melilotic acid, hydroxyhydrocinnamic acid.

мелинит *m.*, —**овый** *a.* (expl.) melinite.

мелинофан *m.* (min.) melinophane.

мелиоидоз *m.* (vet.) melioidosis.

мелиор/ант *m.* improver; (soil science) amendment; —**ативномашинный** *a.* machine and tractor reclamation; —**ативный** *a.* meliorative; (land) reclamation; conservation (district); —**атор** *m.* ameliorator, improver; (land) reclaimer; —**ационный** *a.*, —**ация** *f.* (a)melioration, improvement, development; reclamation (of land); —**ировать** *v.* (a)meliorate, improve, develop; reclaim.

мелипона *f.* (ent.) Melipona.

мелис *m.* granulated sugar.

Мелиса тельца (zool.) Mehlis' glands.

мелисс/а *f.* (bot.) balm (*Melissa officinalis*); —**ил** *m.* melissyl; —**(ил)овый спирт**, —**ин** *m.* melissyl alcohol, myricyl alcohol; —**иновая кислота** melissic acid; —**овый** *a.* melissa, balm.

мелистый *a.* shelvy, shoaling.

мелит *m.* (med.) melitis.

мелите *imp. of* **молоть.**

мелит(ри)оза *f.* melitose, raffinose.

мелить *v.* chalk; make fine, grind.

мелицитоза *see* **мелецитоза.**

мелкий *a.* shallow, shoal; small(-sized), fine(ly divided); unimportant, second-rate.

мелко *adv.* fine, in small particles; *prefix* small, fine; shallow; —**брюх** *m.* (ent.) Apanteles; —**ватый** *a.* smallish; somewhat shallow; —**ветвистый** *a.* ramulose; —**вильчатый** *a.* furcellate; —**вкраплённый** *a.* disseminated (ore); —**водие**, —**водье** *n.* shoal water, shallow water; shoal; —**водный** *a.* shoal, shallow; —**волокнистый** *a.* fine-grained, close-grained; (biol.) fibrillate; —**городчатый** *a.* crenulate; —**дерновинный** *a.* bunch-grass; —**дисперсный** *a.* finely divided; —**дольчатый** *a.* lobular; —**донный** *a.* shallow-bottomed; —**зазубренный** *a.* crenulated, serrate; —**зём** *m.* melkozem, fine earth; silt; —**зёмистый** *a.* agrill(ace)ous; silt (talus).

мелкозернист/ость *f.* fineness (of grain), compact grain structure; —**ый** *a.* fine(-grained), close-grained; microgranular.

мелкозуб/ка *f.* smooth(-cut) file; fine-tooth saw; —**(чат)ый** *a.* fine-tooth(ed); denticulate, crenulate, serrulate.

мелко/калиберный *a.* small-bore, small-caliber; —**каменистый** *a.* (med.) calculous; —**капельный** *a.* fine-droplet; mist (irrigation); —**клеточный** *a.* parvicellular, microcellular; —**клетчатый** *a.* fine-mesh close-mesh, close-weave; —**клочковатый** *a.* flocculose; —**колосый** *a.* small-spiked; —**колючковый** *a.* echinulate; —**комковатый** *a.* crumbly (soil); —**крестьянский** *a.* small peasant (farming); —**кристаллический** *a.* finely crystalline; —**крупичатый** *a.* finely grumose; —**крыл** *m.* (ent.) Micropteryx; —**крючковатый** *a.* hamulate; —**кусковой** *a.* small-sized, fine; —**лепестник** *m.* (bot.) fleabane (*Erigeron*); —**лесный** *a.*, —**лесье** *n.* low forest, scrub forest, brushwood, coppice; (under)growth; new forest growth; —**лист(вен)ный** *a.* small-leaved, microphyllous; —**масштабный** *a.* small-scale; —**молотый** *a.* finely ground; —**морье** *n.* shallow (sea); shelf; —**нарезанный** *a.* finely cut; —**осоковый** *a.* low sedge (fen); —**очаговый** *a.* areolar, pitted; —**пильчатый** *a.* serrulate, finely notched; —**плодный** *a.* small-fruit(ed), microcarpous; —**пористый** *a.* fine-pore, finely porous; —**порошковый, —раздробленный, —размолотый, —распылённый** *a.* pulverized; finely divided; —**распылённая среда** fog.

мелко/рослый *a.* small, short; —**семянный** *a.* microspermous, small-seed(ed); —**серийный** *a.* small-scale, small-batch, small-lot, job-lot, short-run; —**сидящий** *a.* shallow; —**слойный** *a.* fine-grain (wood); —**сопочник** *m.* undulating plain, hillocky area; —**сортный** *a.* light-section, small-section (steel); jobbing, merchant (mill); —**сть** *f.* shallowness; smallness, fineness, mesh; —**та** *f.* smallness; small objects; —**товарный** *a.* small(-scale), semicommercial; —**толчённый** *a.* finely ground, pulverized; —**травье** *n.* (area of) low grass; —**трещинный** *a.* (cer.) crackle; —**укореняющийся** *a.* shallow-rooted; —**фокусный** *a.* shallow-focus (earthquake); —**хвойность** *f.* (phyt.) littleleaf; —**хвостник** *m.* (bot.) Psilurus; —**цветковый** *a.* micranthous, small-flower(ed); —**чешуйчатый** *a.* squamulose, minutely squamous; —**шёрстный** *a.* short-haired; —**щелистый** *a.* rimulose; —**щетинистый** *a.* setulose; —**ягодный** *a.* microcarpous, small-berried; —**ямчатый** *a.* foveate, finely pitted; —**ячеистый** *a.* fine-mesh(ed), close-mesh(ed).

меллас *see* **меласса.**
меллеин *m.* mellein.
мёллеровский *a.* Möller (scattering).
меллит *m.* (min.) mellite, honeystone; (pharm.) mellite, medicated honey; —**иловый** *a.* mellityl (alcohol); —**овый** *a.* mellitic (acid); —**овокислая соль** mellitate.
мелло/н *m.* mellon(e); —**новодородная кислота** hydromellonic acid; —**фановая кислота** mellophanic acid.
мелляса *see* **меласса.**
мело *past n. sing. of* **мести.**
меловальный *a.* (paper) coating.
меловая *f.* (rubber) compounding room.
меловка *f.* melovka (white clay produced by the action of organic acids).
мелов/ой *a.* chalk(y); (geol.) Cretaceous (period); —**ая нитка** chalk line; —**ые свойства** chalkiness.
мелод/ический *a.* melodious; —**ичность** *f.* melody, melodiousness; —**ия** *f.* melody, tune.
мелозирование *n.* (met.) mellosing.
мелок *m.* piece of chalk; *sh. m. of* **мелкий.**
мелонит *m.* (min.) melonite, tellurnickel.
мелоподобный *a.* chalky, chalk-like.
мелореостоз *m.* (med.) melorheostosis.
мелось *past n. sing. of* **местись.**
мелочной *a.* retail; small, petty.
мелочн/ость *f.* triviality, pettiness; —**ый** *a.* trivial, petty.

мелочь *f.* trifle, detail; fines, smalls, shorts; (money) small change; undersized fish; **каменная м.** grit; **рудная м.** (min.) fines.
мел-рухляк *m.* chalk marl.
мёлся *past m. sing. of* **местись.**
мелубрин *m.* melubrin.
мель *f.* shallow, shoal; **сесть на м.** *v.* run aground.
мельдолы голубой meldola blue, naphthol blue (dye).
мельк/ание *n.* flashing, etc., *see v.*; flicker; (color) break-up; —**ать, —нуть** *v.* flash, sparkle, gleam, appear for an instant, flicker; —**ом** for a moment, in passing.
мельник *m.* miller.
мельниковит *m.* (min.) melnikovite.
мельни/ца *f.* mill, grinder; (paper) pulper; **м.-циклон** cyclone mill; —**чный** *a.* mill(ing), grinding; —**чный камень** millstone.
мельхиор *m.*, —**овый** *a.* German silver, cupronickel (alloy).
мельч/айший *a.* smallest, finest, minute, almost imperceptible; —**ать** *v.* grow smaller, diminish in size; get shallower; —**е** *comp. of* **мелкий, мелко;** —**ить** *v.* make fine, pulverize, grind.
мельштоф *m.* (paper) flour, fines.
мел/ют *pr. 3 pl. of* **молоть;** —**ющий** *a.*, —**я** *pr. ger.* milling, grinding.
меляс, —са *see* **меласса.**
мембран/а *f.* membrane, film, diaphragm; (carbon) microphone, transmitter; —**ный** *a.* membrane, membranous; diaphragm (pump); push-bottom (oil can).
мем/истор *m.* memistor, resistor with memory; —**носкоп** *m.* memnoscope; —**орандум** *m.* memorandum; —**ориальный** *a.* memorial; —**отрон** *m.* memotron; —**уары** *pl.* memoirs.
мена *f.* exchange, barter.
менак(к)анит *m.* (min.) menaccanite, ilmenite.
менафтил *m.* menaphthyl.
менгадин *see* **менхеден.**
менделе/вий *m.* mendelevium, Md; —**(е)вит** *m.* (min.) mendeleevite; —**евский** *a.* Mendeleev.
менделизм *m.* (biol.) Mendelism.
мендипит *m.* (min.) mendipite.
мендо/зит *m.*, —**цит** *m.* (min.) mendozite.
менев(иен)ский *a.* (geol.) Menevian.
менегинит *m.* (min.) meneghinite.
менеджер *m.* manager.
менее *comp. of* **мало,** less; under, below; **м. всего** least of all; **м., чем** under, less than; **не м.** no less; **тем не м.** nevertheless, for all that.
менёк *m.* (ichth.) tusk (*Brosme b.*); burbot (*Lota l.*)
мензул/а *f.*, —**ьный** *a.* (surv.) plane table; —**ьная съёмка** plane tabling.
мензурка *f.* graduate, graduated cylinder, measuring glass.
мениантин *m.* menyanthin, celastin.
менидия *f.* (ichth.) silverside (*Menidia*).
менилит *m.* (min.) menilite.
менинг/еальный *a.* (anat.) meningeal; —**ит** *m.* (med.) meningitis; —**о—** *prefix* mening(o)— (meninges, membrane); —**ококк** *m.* (bact.) meningococcus.
менинкс *m.* (anat.) meninx, membrane.
мениск *m.* (anat.; phys.) meniscus; —**о(-)бедренный** (anat.) meniscofemoral; —**овый** *a.* meniscus; —**оцитоз** *m.* meniscocytosis, sickle cell anemia.
менисpermовый *a.* menispermic (acid).
мено— *prefix* (physiol.) meno— (menses).
меновой *a.* barter, (in) exchange, exchangeable.
меновые *pl.* moonfishes (*Menidae*).
менопауза *f.* (physiol.) menopause.

менопон *m.* (ent.) Menopon.

меноррагия *f.* (med.) menorrhagia.

менотропин *m.* menotropin (hormone).

менстру/альный *a.* (physiol.) menstrual; **—ация** *f.* menstruation; **—ировать** *v.* menstruate.

мент/адиен *m.* menthadiene; **—адиенон** *m.* menthadienone; **—ан** *m.* menthane, hexahydrocymene; **—андиол** *m.* menthanediol; **—анол** *m.* menthanol; **—анон** *m.* menthanone; **—ен** *m.* menthene.

ментенер *m.* road scraper.

ментен/ол *m.* menthenol; **—он** *m.* menthenone.

ментил *m.,* **—овый** *a.* menthyl; **—амин** *m.* menthylamine; **—овый спирт** menthanol; **—овый эфир валериановой кислоты** menthyl valerate.

менто/л *m.,* **—ловый** *a.* menthol; **—ментен** *m.* menthomenthene; **—н** *m.* menth(an)one.

ментор *m.* educator, instructor; (genetics) mentor.

менх/аден, **—еден** *m.* (ichth.) menhaden [*Brevo(o)rtia*].

мень *m.* (ichth.) burbot (*Lota l.*)

Меньера болезнь (med.) Meniere's disease.

менька *see* **мень;** *gen. of* **менёк.**

меньш/е *comp. of* **мало, малый** smaller; less (than), under, below; **м. всего** the least; **вдвое м.** half (as much or as big); **—ий** *comp. of* **малый,** lesser, smaller, minor, least; lower, inferior; **—инство** *n.* minority.

меню *n.* menu.

меня *gen. and acc. of* **я,** me.

мен/яльный *a.* (ex)change; **—ять** *v.* change, vary, shift, alter(nate), affect; reverse (direction); **—ять местами** trade places, interchange; **не —ять** leave unaltered; retain (properties); **—яться** *v.* change, vary, shift, fluctuate; exchange; alter; go (from. . . to); **—яющийся** *a.* changing, etc., *see* v.; variable; intermittent; live (load).

мепазин *m.* mepazine, lacumin.

мер/а *f.* measure, dimension, size; standard, gage; degree, extent; modulus (of precision); **без —ы** immeasurably, a great deal; **в —у** sufficiently, moderately; **в значительной —е** largely, to a considerable extent; **не в —у, сверх —ы, через —у** excessively, immoderately; **единица —ы** unit of measure; **не знать —ы** *v.* be immoderate; **ни в коей —е не** by no means, in no way, not at all; **по —е** in proportion to, according to, as, so far as, with (use); **по —е возможности** as far as possible; **по —е необходимости** as needed, as required; **по —е того как** as; **по большей —е** at most, at the utmost; **по крайней —е, по меньшей —е** at least, at any rate; **принимать —ы** *v.* take measures, provide, arrange; make sure (that), see to it (that), take care (to), take precautions (to); **соблюдать —ы** *v.* keep within limits or bounds, restrict oneself.

мерв/а *f.,* **—оск** *m.* wax residue.

мергел/евание *n.* marling, marl application; **—евый, —истый, —ьный** *a.* (geol.) marl(y), marlaceous; **—ь** *m.* marl.

мерёжа *f.* seine, drag net.

мере/йный *a. of* **мерея;** (met.) blistered; **—йчатый** *a.* grained.

мерен *sh. m. of* **мерный.**

меренга *f.* (food) meringue.

меренхима *f.* (bot.) merenchyma.

мереть *v.* die (off), perish.

мерещиться *v.* seem, appear dimly.

мерея *f.* (leather) grain.

мерзкий *a.* repulsive.

мёрзлость *f.* frozen state, congealment.

мерзлот/а frozen state, congealment; frozen ground; **вечная м.** permafrost, perennially frozen ground; **—ный** *a. of* **мерзлота;** permafrost (research); **—ове-**

дение *n.* geocryology, permafrost study; **—омер** *m.* cryopedometer, frost-depth meter.

мёрзлый *a.* frozen, congealed, solidified; cryogenic.

мерз/ляк *m.* frozen turf; person sensitive to cold; **—лятина** *m.* and *f.* anything frozen (spec. food spoiled by freezing); *see* **мерзляк.**

мёрзнуть *v.* freeze, congeal.

мери— *prefix* meri— [a part, a share; (chem.) parti—, partly].

меризия *f.* (zool.) Moerisia.

мерикарпий *m.* (bot.) mericarp.

мерикгиппус *m.* (pal.) Merychippus.

мериклинальный *a.* mericlinal (chimera).

мерил/о *n.* standard, criterion, gage, measure, scale; **—ьный** *a.* measuring.

мерин *m.* gelding (horse).

мерингия *f.* (bot.) Moehringia.

меринос *m.,* **—овый** *a.* merino (sheep or wool).

мерист— *prefix* merist(o)— (divided, divisible); **—ела** *f.* (bot.) meristele; **—ема** *f.* meristem, formative tissue; **—ический** *a.* meristic, segmented; **—ома** *f.* (phyt.) meristoma.

меритель *m.* measurer; **—ный** *a.* measuring; **—ная ножка** calipers.

мерить *v.* measure, gage; fit, try on.

мерихинон *m.* meriquinone.

мерк/а *f.* measure; (art.) grid; **снимать —у** *v.* measure.

мерка/золил *m.* Mercazole, methimazole; **—мин** *m.* mercamine, Cysteamine.

меркантильный *a.* mercantile, commercial.

меркапт/ал(ь) *m.* mercaptal, thioacetal; **—ан** *m.,* **—ановый** *a.* mercaptan; **—ид** *m.* mercaptide, metal mercaptan; **—о—** *prefix* mercapto— (indicating thiol group); **—огруппа** *f.* mercapto group; **—ол** *m.* mercaptol; **—опроизводное** *n.* mercapto derivative; **—опурин** *m.* mercaptopurine; **—осоединение** *n.* mercapto compound; **—оускоритель** *m.* mercapto accelerator; **—офос** *m.* mercaptophos, Demeton (insecticide).

меркаторский *a.* Mercator (projection).

меркелевское тельце, Меркеля клетка (anat.) Merkel's corpuscle.

мерк/лый *a.* dull, dim; **—нуть** *v.* darken, grow dim, fade.

меркузал *m.* Mercusal, mersalyl.

меркуриал/изм *m.* (med.) mercury poisoning; **—ьный** *a.* mercurial, mercury.

меркуриаммоний *m.,* **—ный** *a.* mercuriammonium, mercuric ammonium.

меркуризация *f.* mercur(iz)ation.

меркурий *see* **ртуть;** (astr.) Mercury.

меркури/метрия *f.* mercurimetry; **—рование** *see* **меркуризация;** **—рованный** *a.* mercurized, mercurated; **—соединение** *n.* Hg (II) compound; **—соль** *f.* Hg (II) salt; **—я желть** king's yellow, arsenic trisulfide.

меркуроаммоний *m.,* **—ный** *a.* mercuroammonium, mercurous ammonium.

меркуро/соединение *n.* Hg (I) compound; **—соль** *f.* Hg (I) salt; **—хром** *m.* Mercurochrome.

меркурэтил *m.* diethyl mercury.

мерлан/(г) *m.* (ichth.) whiting (*Merlangius m.*); **—ка** *f.* Black Sea whiting.

мерлуз/а *f.* (ichth.) hake (*Merluccius*); **—овые** *pl.* Merluciidae; Gadidae.

мерлушк/а *f.,* **—овый** *a.* lambskin.

мермисы *pl.* (zool.) Mermithidae.

мерн/ик *m.* measuring tank, calibrating tank, gaging tank; batcher, batch meter; hopper; **—ость** *f.* regularity, rhythm, uniformity; **—ый** *a.* measuring, gaging; volumetric, graduated (flask); good-sized (fish); orifice (coefficient); surveyor's (chain); measured, uniform, rhythmic, (slow and) regular; *suffix* —dimensional; —merous.

меро— *prefix* mer(o)—, (part, fraction; (anat.) thigh); **—бластический** *a.* meroblastic, partially dividing; **—гамия** *f.* (gen.) merogamy; **—генез** *m.* merogenesis; **—гония** *f.* merogony; **—зигота** *f.* (gen.) merozygote; **—зоит** *m.* (prot.) merozoite.

мерок *gen. pl. of* **мерка.**

меро/ксен *m.* (min.) meroxene; **—миза** *f.* (ent.) Meromyza; **—миксис** *m.* (gen.) meromixis; **—миозин** *m.* meromyosin.

мероморф/изм *m.* (math.) meromorphism, meromorphic mapping; **—ность** *f.* meromorphy; **—ный** *a.* meromorphic, fractional.

меро/определение *n.* metric, measure, criterion; **—приятие** *n.* (control) measure; procedure, practice; treatment; meeting; social event; **—приятия** *pl.* measures, arrangement; (preventive) action.

меростомовые *pl.* (zool.) Merostomata.

мероу *m.* (ichth.) grouper (*Epinephelus*).

мерохром *m.* (cryst.) merochrome.

мерочка *dim. of* **мера, мерка.**

мероэдрический *a.* merohedral.

мерсериз/ация *f.,* **—ирование** *n.* (text.) mercerization; **—ированный** *a.* mercerized; **—(ир)овать,** *v.* mercerize.

мертв/енность *f.* numbness; (vet.) flasheria; **—енный** *a.* numb, lifeless; **—еть** *v.* grow numb; **—ец** *m.* corpse, cadaver; **—ецкая** *f.* morgue; **—ечина** *f.* carrion, dead flesh; **—оеды** *pl.* carrion beetles (*Silphidae*); **—орождённость** *f.* (med.) stillbirth; **—орождённый** *a.* stillborn.

мёртв/ый *a.* dead, lifeless; useless, idle, dummy; inert; stagnant (water); dead-ripe; *m.* cadaver, corpse; **м. виток** (elec.) idle turn; **м. груз** dead weight, dead load; **м. запас** unavailable water; **м. покров** litter, mulch; **м. ход** free motion, play, backlash; **—ая голова** caput mortuum, colcothar; butterfly (*Acherontia atropos*); **—ая зона** stagnant air; (rad.) skip distance; **—ая точка,** **—ое положение** dead point, dead center; (chem., phys.) inversion point; anchoring point (of pipeline); **—ое пространство** dead space, dead spot; **—ящий** *a.* killing, destroying, eradicating.

мертель *m.* mortar.

мертензия *f.* (bot.) Mertensia.

мерц/ание *n.* flicker, glimmer, scintillation, shimmer, twinkling, gleam, flashing, blinking; (med.) fibrillation; **—ательный** *see* **мерцающий;** flame (cell); ciliary (motion); ciliated (epithelium); **—ать** *v.* flicker, glimmer, scintillate, shimmer, glitter, glint, gleam, flash, blink; (biol.) flagellate; **—ающий** *a.* flickering, etc., *see v.;* flicker (photometer); **—ающий свет** glitter, gleam, glint.

мерцанария *f.* (mal.) quahog (*Mercenaria*).

мер/ы *gen., etc., of* **мера; —ять** *see* **мерить.**

мес. *abbr.* (**месяц**) month.

месдоза *f.* dynamometer; load cell; hydraulic capsule.

мес/иво *n.* mash; **—илка** *f.* kneading machine, kneader, mixer, malaxator; masticator; **—илка-взвивалка** *f.* kneader-mixer; **—ильный** *a.* kneading, etc., *see v.;* **—ильщик,** **—итель** *m.* kneader; knead, work up, puddle (clay); malax, mix, blend.

мескалин *m.,* **—овый** *a.* mescaline.

мескитный *a.* mesquite (tree).

месниковатый песок (min.) gold-bearing sand with high clay content.

месонит *m.* masonite (fiberboard).

месопотамский *a.* (geog.) Mesopotamia(n).

мёссбауэровский *a.* Mössbauer (effect).

мессдоза *see* **месдоза.**

месселит *m.* (min.) messelite.

месс/енджер *m.* messenger; **—ерштихель** *m.* knife-shaped graver; **—инский** *a.* (geog.) Messina, Messinese; **—коффер** *f.* measuring set; **—ур** *m.* dial gage.

мест/ами *instr. pl. of* **место;** in some places, here and there; **посев м.** spot seeding; **—ечко** *dim. of* **место;** township, small town, settlement.

мести *v.* sweep; **—сь** *v.* be swept (along), rush.

местник *m.* permanent echo.

местн/о *adv.* locally; **—оанестезирующий** *a.* local anesthetic; **—ость** *f.* locality, district, region, place, site; ground, land, terrain, country, area; landscape; **определять на —ости** *v.* locate; **—ый** *a.* local, regional; locally available; partial; domestic, native, indigenous, home; (biol.) endemic; country (rock); spot (check); topical (treatment); vernacular (term); common (name); **—ый житель** native; **—ый предмет** landmark, feature (of terrain); **—ого значения** local (forest); **—ое действие** local action; **—ой породы** (biol.) indigenous.

мест/о *n.* place, spot, locality, location, site, seat, position, point (of entry, etc.); scene (of action); (genetics) locus; (av.) fix; space, room, situation, job; (feeding) ground; **м. положения** position, locus; **м. присоединения, м. связи** (chem.) binding site; **м. разрыва** break; **геометрическое м.** (math.) locus; **занимать м.** *v.* replace; **занимать первое м.** *v.* come first, head the list; **иметь м.** *v.* take place, occur; exist, prevail; be the case, be true; (math.) obtain, hold; **на м.** into position, into place, to location; **класть не на м.** *v.* misplace, mislay; **установка на м.** *f.* positioning; **на —е** on the spot, in situ, at (the) site; spot (check); in place; locally (available); **на видном —е** in plain view, prominently; **находящийся на —е** *a.* on site; **установленный на —е** *a.* field-erected; **на —ах** on site; **с —а** straightway; **трогаться с —а** *v.* start; **угол —а** elevation angle, position angle.

место— *prefix* place, location; space; **—жительство** *n.* residence; **—имение** *n.* (gram.) pronoun; **—м** *instr. of* **место; —м** *m.,* **—ма** *f.* (bot.) mestom(e); **—нахождение, —обитание** *see* **местоположение;** occurrence; **—положение** *n.* location, locality, site, position, seat; situation; station; (bot.) habitat; **—пребывание** *n.* residence, dwelling place; seat, location; **—произрастание** *n.* (biol.) habitat; **—происхождение** *n.* origin, source; **—расположение** *n.* location, situation, position, locus; **—рождение** *n.* birthplace; (geol.) layer, bed, deposit, formation; site; occurrence; (coal) field; pool; **карта —рождения** (geol.) field map.

месть *f.* vengeance, revenge.

меся/ц *m.* month; moon; **—цами** *adv.* for months at a time; **—цевидный** *a.* lunar, lunate; crescent; **—чник** *m.* month's campaign (for); one month's time; **—чногонное средство** (med.) emmenagogue; **—чные (регулы)** (physiol.) menstruation, menses; **—чный** *a.* monthly; lunar; *suffix* -month, -mestral; everbearing (strawberry).

мет— *prefix* meth—, methyl.

мета *f.* mark.

мета— *prefix* met(a)— (with, among, between; after, behind, following; a change); **в положении мета** in the metaposition; **—антимонат** *m.* metaantimonate; **—арсенат** *m.* metaarsenate; **м.-атом** *m.* meta-atom; **—биоз** *m.* (ecol.) metabiosis; **—бисульфит** *m.* metabisulfite.

метабол/(из)ировать *v.* metabolize; **—изм** *m.* metabolism; **деструктивный —изм** catabolism; **конструктивный —изм** anabolism; **—ит** *m.* (biol.; petr.) metabolite; **—ический** *a.* metabolic; **—он** *m.* (nucl.) metabolon.

мета/борнокислый *a.* metaboric acid; metaborate (of); **—ванадиевокислый** *a.* metavanadic acid; metavanadate (of); **—висмутовокислый** *a.* metabismuthic acid; metabismuthate (of); **—вольтин** *m.* (min.) metavoltine; **—вольфрамовокислый** *a.* metatungstic acid; metatungstate (of); **—галактика** *f.* (astr.) metagalaxy; **—генез(ис)** (gen.) metagenesis; **—гиния** *f.* (bot.) metagyny; **—дин** *m.,* **—динный** *a.* (elec.) metadyne; **—железистокислый** *a.* ferric (III) acid; metaferrite (of); **—замещение** *n.* meta substitution; **—замещённое** *n.* meta substituted product; **—зо(е)а** *f.* (crust.) metazoaea; **—иодный** *a.* metaperiodic (acid); **—карпальный** *a.* (anat.) metacarpal; **—кинез** *m.* (gen.) metakinesis; **—кремнекислый** *a.* metasilicic acid; metasilicate (of).

метакрил/ат *m.* methacrylate; **—атное органическое стекло** plexiglas; **—овый** *a.* methacrylic (acid).

мета/кристалл *m.* (petr.) metacryst, porphyroblast; **—ксенический** *a.* metoxenous (parasites); **—ксения** *f.* metaxenia; metoxeny; **—ксит** *m.* (min.) metaxite; **—лепсия** *f.* metalepsis, substitution; **—лин** *m.* metaline (lubricant).

металл *m.* metal; **белый м.** white metal, babbit; **—ат** *m.* metallate; **м.-заменитель** *m.* emergency metal; **—ид** *m.* intermetallic compound.

металлиз/атор *m.* metal spray gun; **—ация** *f.,* **—ирование** *n.* metallization, metallic coating, plating; bonding (of metal parts); (min.) metallization, mineralization; **—ация распылением** pulverization (of a metal); **—(ир)ованный** *a.* metallized; **—(ир)овать** *v.* metallize, coat with metal, spray coat; plate.

металлирование *n.* metallation.

металлист *m.* metal worker.

металлическ/ий *a.* metal(lic); **—ое полотно** wire gauze; **—ие изделия** hardware.

металличность *f.* metallicity, metallic properties.

металл-микроскоп *m.* metallographic microscope.

металло— *prefix* metallo—, metal; **—бумажный** *a.* metallized-paper, metal-foil; **—вед** *m.* metal scientist; **—ведение** *n.* science of metals, physical metallurgy; **—видка** *f.* (ent.) Phytometra, etc.; **—видность** *f.* metallicity; **—видный** *a.* metallic, metalline, metalliform; **—выделение** *n.* metal deposition; **—генический** *a.* (geol.) metallogenic; **—гения** *f.* metallogeny.

металлограф *m.* metallographer; **—ический** *a.* metallographic; **—ия** *f.* metallography.

металло/делательный завод metal works; **—ёмкий** *a.* with high metal content; **—ёмкость** *f.* metal content; **—ид** *m.,* **—идный** *a.* metalloid, non-metal; **—изделия** *pl.* hardware, metal ware; **—изол** *m.* waterproof foil; **—индикатор** *m.* metal indicator; **—искатель** *m.* metal detector; **—капиллярный** *a.* dispenser (cathode).

металлокерам/ика *f.* metal ceramics; metal-reinforced ceramic, metal-ceramic composite; powder metallurgy; **—ический** *a.* metal-ceramic; **—ический материал** cermet (material); **—ический твёрдый сплав,** **—ическое изделие** sintered carbide.

металло/комплексообразователь *m.* (metal)-chelating agent; **—конструкция** *f.* metalwork, steelwork; **—корд** *m.* metal cord; **—лом** *m.* metal scrap; **—магнитный** *a.* metallomagnetic; **—метр** *m.* metallometer; metal tester; **—метрический** *a.* metallometric;

—носность *f.* metal content; **—носный** *a.* metalliferous, metal-bearing.

металлообраб/атывающий *a.,* **—отка** *f.* metal working.

металло/образный *see* **металловидный;** **—оптика** *f.* metal optics; **—органический** *a.* metalloorganic, organometallic; **—очистительный** *a.* metal-refining; **—плавильный** *a.* smelting; **—плакирование** *n.* metal cladding; **—пласт** *m.* metal-base laminate; **—подобный** *a.* metallic, metalline, metal-like; **—подъёмник** *m.* (foundry) riser (of mold); **—покрытие** *n.* metallic coating; **—полимер** *m.* metal-containing polymer; **—пористый** *a.* dispenser (cathode); **—приёмник** *m.* (furnace) well; **—прокатный** *a.* metal-rolling.

металлопромышленн/ость *f.,* **—ый** *a.* metal industry.

металло/протеид *m.* metalloprotein; **—пульверизатор** *m.* metal spray gun.

металло/режущий *a.* metal-cutting; **м. станок** machine tool; **—рукав** *m.* flexible metal pipe or hose.

металлосодержащий *a.* metal-containing, metalliferous; metallic (ore).

металло/струйная обработка grit blasting; **—термия** *f.* thermal reduction methods; **—ткацкий** *a.* wire cloth; **—ткачество** *n.* wire cloth weaving; **—тропия** *f.* metallotropy; **—физика** *f.* metal physics; **—флавопротеин** *m.* metalloflavoprotein; **—химия** *f.* chemistry of metals; **—хром** *m.* metallochrome; **—хромия** *f.* metallochromy, tinting of metal; **—цен** *m.* metallocene; **—цикл** *m.* metallocycle.

металлург *m.* metallurgist; **м.-сталеплавильщик** steel metallurgist; **—ический** *a.* metallurgic(al); **—ия** *f.* metallurgy.

металл-ферментный *a.* metal-enzyme (complex).

метальдегид *m.* metaldehyde.

метамер *m.* metamer(ide); **—ия** *f.* metamerism; **—ный** *a.* metameric, segmented.

метамикт/изация *f.* (min.) metamictization; **—ный** *a.* metamict.

метаморф/изация *f.* (geol.) metamorphization; **—изировать** *v.* metamorphize; **—изм** *m.* metamorphism; **—изованный** *a.* metamorphized, converted; **—ический,** **—ный** *a.* metamorphic; **—оз** *m.,* **—оза** *f.* (geol.; biol.) metamorphosis.

метамышьяков/истокислый *a.* metaarsenous acid; metaarsenite (of); **—окислый** *a.* metaarsenic acid; metaarsenate (of).

метан *m.* methane; **—ал(ь)** *m.* methanal, formaldehyde; **—амид** *m.* methanamide, formamide.

мета/направляющий *a.* meta-directing; **—дикарбоновый** *a.* methanedicarboxylic, malonic (acid).

метанефр/идий *m.* (zool.) metanephridium; **—ический** *a.* (embr.) metanephric; **—ос** *m.* metanephros, hindkidney.

метание *n.* throwing, etc., *see* **метать.**

метанил/(ин)овая кислота metanilic acid, aniline-*m*-sulfonic acid; **—овый** *a.* metanil (yellow).

метаниобиевокислый *a.* metaniobic acid; metaniobate (of).

метанкислота *f.* methanoic acid, formic acid.

метанный *past pass. part. of* **метать.**

метан/ный, **—овый** *a.* methane; **—овая кислота** methanoic acid, formic acid; **—оген** *m.* methanogen; **—оил** *m.* methanoyl, formoyl; **—окислородный** *a.* methane-oxygen; **—ол** *m.* methanol, methyl alcohol; **—ол-сырец** *m.* crude methanol; **—тенк** *m.* anaerobic digester; **—тиол** *m.* methanethiol, methyl mercaptan.

мета/оловяннокислый *a.* metastannic acid; metastannate (of).

мета/-ориентат *m.* meta director; **м.-ориентирующий** *a.* meta-directing; **—плазия** *f.* (cyt.) metaplasia; **—плазма** *f.* metaplasm; **—положение** *n.* meta-position; **—производное** *n.* meta-derivative; **м.-ряд** *m.* meta series; **—самка** *f.* (gen.) metafemale, superfemale; **—свинцовокислый** *a.* metaplumbic acid; metaplumbate (of); **—соединение** *n.* metacompound.

метасомат/изм, —оз *m.* (geol.) metasomatism, replacement; **—ический** *a.* (geol., zool.) metasomatic.

метаспециальный *a.* (math.) metaspecial.

метастабильн/ость *f.* metastability; **—ый** *a.* metastable.

метаста/з *m.* (biol.; med.; petr.) metastasis; **образовать —зы, —зировать** *v.* metastasize; **—тический** *a.* metastatic.

метастирол *m.* metastyr(ol)ene.

метасульфит *m.* metasulfite, pyrosulfite.

метасурьмян/истокислый *a.* metaantimonous acid; metaantimonite (of); **—окислый** *a.* metaantimonic acid; metaantimonate (of).

мета/тарзальный *a.* (anat.) metatarsal; **—теза** *f.* (chem.) metathesis.

метатель *m.* thrower, launcher.

метатель/ный *a.* throwing, etc., *see* **метать;** launching; propellant (charge); **м. снаряд** projectile; **м. станок** launcher, launching ramp; **—ая установка** launcher, launching device.

мета/тип *m.* (biol.) metatype; **—титановокислый** *a.* metatitanic acid; metatitanate (of).

метаторбернит *m.* (min.) metatorbernite.

метать *v.* throw, fling, cast, project; (missiles) launch; pitch (hay); bring forth; (ichth.) spawn; baste, sew; **—ся** *v.* rush about, dart.

мета/устойчивый *a.* metastable; **—фаза** *f.* (biol.) metaphase; **—фен** *m.* Metaphen, nitromersol; **—фенилен** *m.* metaphenylene; **—физ** *m.* (anat.) metaphysis; **—флоэма** *f.* (bot.) metaphloem; **—фос** *m.* metaphos, methyl parathion (insecticide).

метафосфор/истокислый *a.* metaphosphorous acid; metaphosphite (of); **—нокислый** *a.* metaphosphoric acid; metaphosphate (of); **—нонатриевая соль** sodium metaphosphate.

мета/хлорит *m.* (min.) metachlorite; **—холин** *m.* methacholine; **—хромазия** *f.* metachromasy; **—хроматический** *a.* metachromatic; **—цейнерит** *m.* (min.) metazeunerite; **—центр** *m.* metacenter; **—центрический** *a.* (gen.) metacentric; **—цетин** *m.* methacetin, *p*-methoxyacetanilide; **—цид** *m.* metacide (insecticide).

метацимол *m.* metacymene.

метаязык *m.* meta-language.

метгемоглобин *m.* methemoglobin.

мётел *gen. pl. of* **метла.**

метел/емер *m.* snowdrift gage; **—истый** *a.* stormy; **—ица** *f.* storm, blizzard; (ent.) beet webworm (*Loxostege sticticalis*).

метёлк/а *f.* whisk broom, brush; (bot.) panicle, head (of grass); **—овидный, —образный** *a.* paniculiform.

метеллаговая кислота metellagic acid.

метелоидин *m.* meteloidine.

метёлоч/ка *dim. of* **метёлка;** (elec.) brush; **—ный** *a. of* **метёлка.**

метель *f.* snowstorm, blizzard; **—ник** *m.* (bot.) Spartium; **—ный** *a. of* **метла; метель.**

метельчатый *a.* (bot.) paniculate.

метён *sh. m. of* **метённый.**

метен *m.* meth(yl)ene; **—амин** *m.* methenamine, hexamethylenetetramine.

метение *n.* sweeping.

метенил *m.,* **—овый** *a.* methenyl.

метён(н)ый *past pass. part. of* **мести.**

метенцикло— *prefix* methenecyclo—.

метео— *prefix* meteorologic(al), weather; **—аэробюллетень** *m.,* **—донесение** *n.* weather report; **—данные** *pl.* weather data; **—зонд** *m.* meteorological sounding balloon; **—минимум** *m.* (av.) weather minimum; **—наблюдение** *n.* weather observation; **—обстановка** *f.* weather conditions; **—прибор** *m.* meteorological instrument.

метеор *m.* (astr.) meteor.

метео/радиолокатор *m.* meteorological radar; **—разведка** *f.* weather reconnaissance; **—ризм** *m.* (vet.) meteorism, bloat.

метеор/ит *m.* (min.) meteorite; **—итика** *f.* (astr.) meteoritics; **—итный, —итовый** *a.* meteorite, meteoritic; meteoric (iron); **—ический, —ный** *a.* meteor(ic); **—ношлаковый** *a.* meteor-slag.

метеорограф *m.* meteorograph; **—ический** *a.* meteorographic; **—ия** *f.* meteorography.

метеоролог *m.* meteorologist; **—ический** *a.* meteorologic(al); **—ическая станция** weather bureau; **—ия** *f.* meteorology.

метеороподобный *a.* meteor-like, meteoric.

метеоротропный *a.* meteorotropic, influenced by weather conditions.

метео/сводка *f.* weather report; **—служба** *f.* meteorological service; **—сообщение** *n.* weather report; **—спутник** *m.* meteorological satellite; **—станция** *f.* weather bureau; **—условия** *pl.* weather conditions; **—центр** *m.* meteorological office.

метёт *pr. 3 sing. of* **мести.**

метизация *see* **метисация.**

метиз/ный *a.,* **—ы** *pl.* hardware, metalware.

метик *m.* (silv.) starshake (flaw).

метил *m.* methyl; **—акрилат** *m.* methyl acrylate; **—аллен** *m.* methyl allene, butadiene; **—ал(ь)** *m.* methylal, dimethoxymethane; **—амиловый эфир** methyl amyl ether; **—амин** *m.* methylamine, aminomethane; **—анилин** *m.* methylaniline; **—арсиновая кислота** monomethylarsenic acid, arrhenic acid; **—ат** *m.* methylate, methoxide; **—ацетат** *m.* methyl acetate; **—бензол** *m.* methylbenzene, toluene; **—бромид** *m.* methyl bromide; **—бутадиен** *m.* methyl butadiene, isoprene; **—бутанон** *m.* methyl butanone; **—винилпиридин** *m.* methylvinylpyridine; **—виолет** *m.* methyl violet; **—гепт—** *prefix* methylhept—; **—глиоксаль** *m.* methylglyoxal, pyruvic aldehyde; **—гуанидин** *m.* methylguanidine.

метилен *m.,* **—овый** *a.* meth(yl)ene; **—блау, —овая синь(ка), —овый голубой, —овый синий** methylene blue.

метил/замещённый *a.* methyl-substituted; **—изо—** *prefix* methyliso—.

метилиров/ание *n.* methylation; **—анный** *a.* methylated; **—ать** *v.* methylate.

метил/карбинол *m.* methylcarbinol, ethanol; **—каучук** *m.* methyl rubber; **—крахмал** *m.* methyl starch; **—малонил-КоА** *m.* methylmalonyl-CoA; **—меркаптан** *m.* methylmercaptan; **—метакрилат** *m.* methyl methacrylate; **—нитрат** *m.* methyl nitrate; **—овоспиртовой** *a.* methanol.

метиловый *a.* methyl; **м. альдегид** methyl aldehyde, formaldehyde; **м. спирт** methyl alcohol, methanol; **м. фиолетовый** methyl violet; **м. эфир** methyl ether; **м. эфир серной кислоты** methyl sulfate.

метил/оранж *m.* methyl orange (indicator); **—предни-**

золон *m.* methylprednisolone; **—производное** *n.* methyl derivative; **—рот** *m.* methyl red; **—салицилат** *m.* methyl salicylate; **—стирол** *m.* methylstyrene; **—сульфат** *m.* methyl sulfate; **—тестостерон** *m.* methyltestosterone; **—трансфераза** *f.* methyltransferase; **—трихлорсилан** *m.* methyltrichlorosilane; **—фенилдихлорсилан** *m.* methylphenyldichlorosilane; **—целлюлоза** *f.* methyl cellulose; **—цикло—** *prefix* methylcyclo—; **—ьный** *a.* methyl; **—этилкетон** *m.* methyl ethyl ketone.

метин *m.*, **—овый** *a.* methine.

метион/ил *m.* methionyl; **—ин** *m.* methionine, 2-amino-4-methylthiobutanoic acid; **—овая кислота** methionic acid, methanedisulfonic acid.

метис *m.* hybrid, halfbreed, mongrel; **—ация** *f.* interbreeding, hybridization; miscegenation; **—ный** *a. of* **метис.**

метистицин *m.* methysticin, kavain; **—овая кислота** methysticinic acid.

мет/ить *v.* mark; label, tag (with tracers); brand (livestock); band (fowl); aim (at), have in view; **—ка** *f.* mark(er), marking; sign; stamp, brand; (isotopic) label, tag, tracer; score; (timber) blaze, blazing; calibration mark; *sh. f. of* **меткий.**

метк/ий *a.* accurate, well-aimed; apt; **—ость** *f.* accuracy, exactness.

метла *f.* broom, brush; (bot.) Apera.

метлахская плитка ceramic (floor) tile.

метлица *f.* (bot.) Apera, spec. bent grass (*Apera spica venti*); (ent.) caddis fly.

метловидный *a.* scopiform, brush-like.

мётлы ведьмины (phyt.) witch's brooms.

метнуть *see* **метать.**

метод *m.* method, process, procedure, practice, technique, approach; way, means, mode, manner; system; **м. стратификации** stratified sampling; **—ом** by (the method), by the process; **—ом погружения** via immersion technique; **вносить м.** *v.* methodize; **—ика** *f.* method(s), procedure, technique; philosophy; **—ика работы** procedure; **—ист** *m.* (educ.) methodologist, methods instructor; **—ический, —ичный** *a.* methodical, orderly, deliberate; methodological; continuous (furnace); **—ично** *adv.* methodically; **—ичность** *f.* methodicalness; **—ология** *f.* method(ology).

меток *gen. pl. of* **метка;** *sh. m. of* **меткий.**

метоксазин *m.* metoxazine.

метокси/бензальдегид *m.* methoxybenzaldehyde; **—д** *see* **метилат;** **—л** *m.* methoxyl; **—лировать** *v.* methoxylate; **—хлор** *m.* methoxychlor (insecticide).

метол *m.* (phot.) Metol, *p*-methylaminophenol sulfate.

метонал *m.* methonal.

метопический *a.* (anat.) metopic, frontal.

метоха *f.* (ent.) Methocha.

метохинон *m.* metoquinone.

метоцин *m.* metozine, antipyrine.

метр *m.* meter (unit of length); *suffix* **—meter** (measuring device); *prefix see* **метро—;** **складной м.** folding rule; **—аж** *m.* meterage; measurement; metric area; length in meters; capacity.

метралгия *f.* (med.) metralgia.

метраппаж *m.* (typ.) maker-up.

метре/кон, **—хон** *m.* metrechon, half-picture storage tube.

метридий *m.* (zool.) Metridium.

метриз/ация *f.* metrization; **—овать** *v.* metrize; **—уемый** *a.* metrizable.

метрика *f.* metrics; birth certificate.

метрит *m.* (med.) metritis.

метрическ/и *adv.* metrically; **—ий** *a.* metric; *suffix* **—metric(al);** **—ая книга** birth, marriage and death register; **—ая мера** metric system; **—ое свидетельство** birth certificate.

метро *see* **метрополитен.**

метро— *prefix* metr(o)— (measure; uterus; mother); **—вка** *f.* folding rule; meter-long board; measurement in meters; **—вый** *a.* meter, metric; **—изол** *m.* metroizol (bitumen-impregnated cloth); **—логический** *a.* metrological; **—логия** *f.* metrology, science of weights and measures.

метрон/овая кислота methronic acid; **—ол** *m.* methronol.

метроном *m.* metronome.

метропатия *f.* (med.) metropathy.

метро/политен *m.* subway, underground railway; **—строевский** *a.*, **—строй** *m.* subway-building organization.

метроэндометрит *m.* (med.) metroendometritis.

метр/-рулетка *f.* tape measure; **м.-свеча** *f.* meter-candle (unit of illuminance); **—шток** *m.* sounding rod.

мет/сеть *f.* meteorological network; **—станция** *see* **метеостанция.**

метущий *pr. act. part. of* **мести.**

метчик *m.* (screw) tap, tap borer; marker; **ловильный м.** (oil-well drilling) grab.

метэлемент *m.* weather constituent.

Меуле реакция Mäule reaction.

меум *m.* (bot.) Meum.

мефенезин *m.* mephenesin.

мефитический *a.* mephitic, foul, noxious.

мех *m.* fur, pelt; bellows; water skin; **воздуходувный м.,** **—а** *pl.* bellows.

мех— *prefix* mechanical, mechanized; **—анайт** *m.* (met.) mechanite.

механиз/атор *m.* mechanic; machine operator; machinery maintenance man; **—ация** *f.* mechanization, powering; device; **—ация крыла** (av.) high-lift devices; **училище —ации** engineering school; **—ирование** *see* **механизация;** **—ированный** *a.* mechanized, power(ed), power-driven; **—ировать** *v.* mechanize, power.

механизм *m.* mechanism, works, movement, gear; device; **—er; м. (воз)действия** mode of action; **подающий м.** feeder; **—ы** machinery.

механик *m.* mechanic, operator; engineer; **м.-водитель** *m.* driver; **м.-конструктор** *m.* machine designer; **—а** *f.* mechanics; mechanism, machinery; **—о-термальный** *a.* thermomechanical.

механически *adv.* mechanically.

механическ/ий *a.* mechanical, machine, power-driven, power-operated, power (tool); by impact; stress-strain (properties); screen (analysis); **м. завод, м. цех** machine shop; **м. молот** power hammer; **м. момент** momentum; **м. состав** mechanical composition, texture (of soil); **м. станок** machine tool; **—ая обработка** machining; **—ая отдача** mechanical efficiency; **—ая свалка** junk yard; **—ая связь** ganging; **—ая отдача** mechanical efficiency (of engine); **—ие примеси** particulate contaminant, insoluble matter; **—ое оборудование** machinery; **с —им приводом** power-driven, power-operated.

механичный *a.* mechanical.

механо— *prefix* mechano— (mechanical; machine); **—монтажный** *a.* machine-assembling; **—прочность** *f.* (soils) crushing strength; **—рецептор** *m.* (biol.) (elec.) mechanoreceptor; **—сборочный** *a.* assembly (plant); **—стрикция** *f.* (phys.) mechanostriction; **—терапия** *f.* (med.) mechanotherapy, exercise therapy; **—трон** *m.*

mechanotron, movable-electrode electron tube; **—химия** *f.* mechanochemistry.

мехводитель *m.* (mil.) tank driver.

мехи *pl.* bellows; *pl. of* **мех.**

Мехико *m.* (geog.) Mexico City.

мехо/вой *a.* of **мех; —вщик** *m.* furrier; **—ед** *m.* carpet beetle (*Attagenus*); **—еды** *pl.* bird lice (*Mallophaga*).

мехом *m.* mechanical ohm; *instr. of* **мех.**

мехообразный *a.* furry; bellows-type.

мех/соединение *n.* (mil.) mechanized unit; **—состав** *m.* texture (of soil); **—часть** *f.* (mil.) motorized unit.

мецкалин *m.* mescal (liquor).

меццо-тинто *n.* (typ.) mezzotint.

меч *m.* sword; tree-planting tool; **—евидно-грудинный** *a.* (anat.) xiphosternal; **—евиднолистный** *a.* sword-leaved, xiphophyllous; **—евидный** *a.* ensiform, xiphoid, sword-shaped; **—елистный** *see* **мечевиднолистный.**

мечен/ие *n.* marking, etc., *see* **метить; —(н)ый** *a.* marked, etc., *see* **метить;** labeled (molecule); tagged, tracer (atom); **метод —ых элементов** tracer technique.

меченос *see* **меч-рыба; —ец** *m.* (ichth.) Xiphophorus; **—ница** *f.* (bot.) Securigera; **—овые** *see* **мечерылые.**

мече/ротые *pl.* (ichth.) Xiphostom(at)idae; **—рылые** *pl.* sword fishes (Xiphiidae); **—образный** *see* **мечевидный.**

мечет *pr. 3 sing. of* **метать.**

мечехвосты *pl.* (crust.) Xiphosura.

мечник *m.* (ent.) Conocephalus.

меч-рыб/а *f.* sword fish (*Xiphias,* spec. *X. gladius*); **—ы** *pl.* Xiphiidae.

мечта *f.* dream, hope; **—ть** *v.* dream.

меч-трава *f.* (bot.) Cladium.

мечущий *pr. act. part. of* **метать.**

меш *m., —а f.* mesh (of screen).

мешалка *f.* mixer, agitator, stirrer, stirring rod; churn; kneading machine; **м.-кристаллизатор** *m.* agitated crystallizer; **м.-охладитель** *f.* mixing-and-cooling tank; **механическая м.** rabble; **стеклянная м.** stirring rod.

меш/альный *a.* mixing, stirring; **—ание** *n.* mixing, etc., *see v.;* **—анина** *f.* mixture; **—анка** *f.* mixed crop, mixed feed; **—атель** *m.* mixer; **—ать** *v.* mix, stir, agitate; hinder, impede, interfere, be a handicap (to); inhibit, prevent, be a barrier (to); clog, stop; encumber; disturb; **—ающий** *a.* mixing, etc., *see v.;* **—ающее действие** interference; **—енный** *past pass. part. of* **месить.**

мешетчатые крысы (mam.) pocket gophers (*Geomyidae*); pocket mice (*Heteromyidae*).

мешечницы *see* **мешочницы.**

мешка *gen. of* **мешок;** *f.* blending, mixing.

мешкать *v.* delay, procrastinate.

мешко/вание *n.* bagging; **—ватость** *f.* bagginess; **—ватый** *a.* baggy; awkward; **—видный** *a.* bag-shaped, sacculate; **—вина** *f.* sackcloth, burlap, sacking; **—выбиватель** *m.* bag beater; **—вый** *a. of* **мешок; —вытряхиватель** *m.* bag shaker; **—вязатель** *m.* bag closer; **—грудые** *pl.* (zool.) Ascothoracica; **—держатель** *m.* bag holder; **—жаберниковые** *pl.* (ichth.) Heteropneustidae; **—жаберные** *pl.* Cyclostomata; **—зашиватель** *m.* bag-closing machine, sack stitcher; **—наполнитель, —насыпатель** *m.* bag filler; **—носы** *pl.* (ent.) Psychidae; **—образный** *see* **мешковидный; —погрузчик** *m.* sack loader; **—ротые** *pl.* (ichth.) gulpers (*Saccopharyngidae*); **—спуск** *m.* sack chute; **—таска** *f.* sack conveyer.

мешкотн/ость *f.* sluggishness; **—ый** *a.* sluggish, slow, unhurried; tedious.

меш/ок *m.* sac, pouch; bag; packet; pocket; receptacle; bursa; **—отчато—** *prefix* utriculo—; **—прыгуновые** *pl.* (mam.) pocket mice (*Heteromyidae*); **—отчатый** *a.* saccular; utricular (nerve); **—очек** *dim. of* **мешок;** kit; (biol.) follicle, utricle, saccule; **—очковидный** *a.* utriculiform, sacculate; **—очковый** *a.* saccular; **—очницы** *pl.* bagworms (*Psychidae*); **—очный** *a. of* **мешок; —очная ткань** sacking, burlap.

мещёрский *a.* (geog.) Meshchera.

МЖС *abbr.* (**машинно-животноводческая станция**) livestock-breeding and machine station.

МЗТ *abbr.* (**метод заряжённого тела**) charged body method.

МЗУ *abrr.* (**магнитное запоминающее устройство**) magnetic memory unit.

Ми рассеяние (light) Mie scattering.

миаз(ис) *m.* (med.) myiasis.

миазм/а *f., —ы pl.* miasma; effluvium, noxious exhalation; **—атический** *a.* myasmatic.

миальгия *f.* (med.) myalgia, muscle pain.

миаргирит *m.* (min.) miargyrite.

миаролитовый *a.* (geol.) miarolitic.

миарсенол *m.* myarsenol, sulfarsphenamine.

миаскит *m.* (petr.) miascite.

миассовый *a.* (geog.) Miass.

миастения *f.* (med.) myasthenia.

миастор *m.* (ent.) Miastor.

мибора *f.* (bot.) Mibora.

миг *m.* moment, instant.

миг/алка *f.* flicker device; flashing signal; distributing plate, discharge disk (of dust catcher); flap valve; **—ание** *n.* blinking, flicker(ing); nictitation, winking; flashing; **—атель** *m.* blinker, flasher; **—ательный** *a.* blinking, blinker, flicker(ing); nictitating, winking; **—ать** *v.* blink, flicker; wink, nictate; flash; **—ающий** *see* **мигательный;** pulsed (beam, etc.); **—ающий фонарь** blinker, flasher.

мигмат/изация *f.* (geol.) migmatization; **—ит** *m.* (petr.) migmatite.

миг/нуть *v.* blink, flash; wink; **—ом** *adv.* instantly, in a flash.

мигр/ант *m.* migrant; (geol.) allochthon; **—ационный** *a.* migratory; **—ация** *f.* migration.

мигрен/евый *a., —ь f.* (med.) migraine.

мигрир/овавший *a.* migrated, migratory; **—ование** *n.* migration; **—овать** *v.* migrate, travel; **—ующий** *a.* migratory; (geol.) allochthonous; wandering, ambulant; **далеко —ующий** wide-ranging (species).

мидель *m.* (naut.) maximum midsection; **м.-шпангоут** *m.* midship frame; mid-station; (av.) middle frame.

мидия *f.* (mal.) marine mussel (*Mytilus*).

Мидлсбро (geog.) Middlesbrough.

мидриа/зин *m.* Mydriasine; **—зис** *m.* (med.) mydriasis; **—тин** *m.* mydriatine; **—тический** *a.* mydriatic, pupil-dilating.

Мидуэй острова (geog.) Midway Islands.

миел/ин *m.* (anat.) myelin; **—инизация** *f.* (physiol.) myelin(iz)ation; **—иновый** *a.* myelinic; **—ит** *m.* (med.) myelitis; **—о—** *prefix* myel(o)— (bone marrow; spinal cord); **—област** *m.* (cyt.) myeloblast, granuloblast; **—огенный** *a.* myelogenic, myelogenous; **—оз** *m.* myelosis; **—ома** *f.* myeloma; **—оцит** *m.* myelocyte, marrow cell.

миерсит *m.* (min.) miersite.

мизерный *a.* miserable, meager, scanty.

мизид/ные, —овые *pl.* (crust.) Schizopoda; **—ный** *a.* mysidean; **—ы** *pl.* Mysidaceae.

мизинец *m.* (anat.) little finger; little toe.

мизо— *prefix* mis(o)— (hatred; aversion).

мизо/пода *f.* (mam.) Myzopoda, **—стомиды** *pl.* (zool.) Myzostomidae.

мии *pl.* (mal.) Myidae.

мииаз *see* **миазис.**

мийо— *prefix* myi(o)— (fly).

мика/лекс *m.* Mycalex (insulating material); **—лента** *f.* mica tape; **—нит** *m.,* **—нитовый** *a.* micanite (insulator).

микания *f.* (bot.) Mikania.

микарта *f.* micarta (insulator).

микижа *f.* Kamchatka trout (*Salmo mykiss*).

микки *n.* (comp.) mickey, unit of mouse movement.

мико— *prefix* myc(o)— (fungus; mucus, mucous membrane); **—дерма** *f.* (bact.) mycoderm; **—з** *m.* (med.) mycosis; **—за** *f.* mycose; **—литический** *a.* (phyt.) mycolytic; **—лог** *m.* (bot.) mycologist; **—логия** *f.* mycology; **—мицин** *m.* mycomycin; **—плазма** *f.* (phyt.) mycoplasm; **—протеинизация** *f.* (immun.) mycoproteination; **—риза** *f.* (bot.) mycorhiza; **—стерин** *m.* mycosterol; **—тический** *a.* (med.) mycotic; **—трофный** *a.* mycotrophic; **—фаговый** *a.* mycophagous, mushroom-eating; **—феноловый** *a.* mycophenolic (acid); **—цидин** *m.* mycocidin.

микрат *m.,* **—ная плёнка** Mikrat film.

микрит *m.* (geol.) micrite.

микро— *prefix* micro— (10^{-6}); small(-scale); microscopic; **—ампер** *m.* (elec.) microampere; **—амперметр** *m.* microammeter; **—анализ** *m.* microanalysis; **—анализатор** *m.* microanalyzer; **—аналитический** *a.* microanalytical; **—атмосфера** *f.* artificial atmosphere (of spaceship); **—афанитовый** *a.* (petr.) microaphanitic.

микроб *m.* microbe, bacterium.

микро/бар *m.* (acous.) microbar, barye; **—барн** *m.* (nucl.) microbarn; **—барограф** *m.* microbarograph.

микробиолог *m.* microbiologist; **—ический** *a.* microbiological; **—ия** *f.* microbiology.

микробный *a.* microbe, microbic.

микро/бромит *m.* (min.) microbromite; **—бюретка** *f.* microburet; **—ватт** *m.* (elec.) microwatt; **—весы** *pl.* microbalance; **—вид** *m.* microspecies; **—включённый** *a.* contained in microscopic foci; **—волна** *f.,* **—волновый** *a.* (rad.) microwave; **—волокнистый** *a.* very finely fibrous, microfiber; **—вольт** *m.* (elec.) microvolt; **—вольтметр** *m.* microvoltmeter; **—вплавление** *n.* microalloying; **—выключатель** *m.* microswitch; **—вязкость** *f.* microviscosity; **—гамета** *f.* (gen.) microgamete; **—гамма** *f.* microgamma; **—генри** *m.* (elec.) microhenry; **—геометрия** *f.* (study of) microirregularities; **—глия** *f.* (med.) microglia; **—горелка** *f.* microburner; **—грамм** *m.* microgram, gamma; **—гранитный** *a.* (petr.) microgranitic.

микрограф *m.* micrograph; (ent.) Pityophthorus; **—ический** *a.* micrograpic; **—ия** *f.* micrography.

микро/группировка *f.* microcommunity; **—гэс** *m.* small automatic hydroelectric power unit; **—двигатель** *m.* micromotor, miniature motor; (cosm.) thruster, reaction control jet; **—десмовые** *pl.* (ichth.) Microdesmidae; **—дефектность** *f.* microflaw, microimperfection; **—деформация** *f.* (met.) microstrain; **—диорит** *m.* (petr.) microdiorite; **—доза** *f.* microdose; **—дозировка** *f.* microdosage, micrometering; **—дюйм** *m.* microinch; **—животное** *n.* animalcule; **—загрязнитель** *m.* trace pollutant; **—запись** *f.* microrecording; **—зернистость** *f.* (phot.) fine grain; **—зернистый** *a.* fine-grain(ed); **—зонд** *m.* microprobe; **—измерение** *n.* micrometry; **—изображение** *n.* microimage; **—интерферометр** *m.* interference microscope; **—исследование** *n.* microanalysis, microexamination; **—калория** *f.* microcalorie, small calorie; **—камера** *f.* microchamber; (welding) glove box; **—канал** *m.* pin hole; **—капилляр** *m.,* **—капиллярный** *a.* microcapillary; **—каротаж** *m.* micrologging; **—карта** *f.* microcard; **—катор** *see* **микромер; —киносъёмка** *f.* (phys.) motion micropicture; **—кипение** *n.* microboiling; **—климат** *m.* microclimate; **—клин** *m.* (min.) microcline; **—книга** *f.* microfilmed book.

микрококк *m.* micrococcus (round bacterium); **—ин** *m.* micrococcin.

микро/количество *n.* microquantity, trace; **—компонент** *m.* microconstituent; microcomponent; **—конденсатор** *m.* microcapacitor; **—концентрация** *f.* trace concentration; **—копирование** *n.* microcopying; **—копия** *f.* microcopy; **—корм** *m.* micronutrient; **—коррозия** *f.* microcorrosion.

микрокосм *m.* microcosm; **—ический** *a.* microcosmic; **—ическая соль** microcosmic salt, sodium ammonium hydrogen phosphate; **—ос** *m.* microcosmos.

микрокристалл/ический *a.* (min.) microcrystalline, cryptocrystalline; **—ография** *f.* microcrystallography; **—о-скопия** *f.* crystalline microchemical analysis.

микро/кулон *m.* (elec.) microcoulomb; **—кюри** *m.* (nucl.) microcurie; **—легировать** *v.* add trace metals to alloy.

микролит *m.* (min.) microlite; (petr.) microlite, microcrystal; (med.) microlith, minute concretion; **—овый** *a.* microlitic; microlithic.

микро/литр *m.* microliter, lambda; **—логия** *f.* micrology; **—м** *see* **микроом; —манипулятор** *m.* (micros.) micromanipulator; **—манометр** *m.* micromanometer, micropressure gage; **—масштаб** *m.* microscale; **в —масштабах** on the tracer scale; **—мер** *m.* outside micrometer; (embr.) micromere; **—меритный** *a.* micromeritic, microcrystalline; **—мерия** *f.* (bot.) Micromeria; **—мерол** *m.* micromerol; **—местообитание** *n.* microhabitat; **—метеорит** *m.* micrometeorite; **—метод** *m.* micromethod, microprocedure.

микрометр *m.* micrometer (gage or caliper); **—ический** *a.* micrometer, micrometric; **—ия** *f.* micrometry.

микро/микро— *prefix* micromicro—, pico— (10^{-12}); **—микрон** *m.* micromicron; **—миллиметр** *m.* micromillimeter, millimicron; **—миниатюризация** *f.* microminiaturization; **—мир** *m.* microscosm; **—мо** *n.* (elec.) micmho; **—модификация** *f.* microanalytical modification; **—модуль** *m.,* **—модульный** *a.* micromodule; **—моль** *f.* micromole; **—мутация** *f.* (gen.) micromutation, genovariation; **—н** *m.* micron (10^{-3} mm); **—напряжение** *n.* microstress; **—население** *n.* (soil) microfauna; **—неровность** *f.* microscopic unevenness; **—нный** *a. of* **микрон; —нуклеус** *m.* (gen.) micronucleus; **—обломок** *m.* microfragment; **—обработка** *f.* microprocessing, micromachining; **—объектив** *m.* microscope objective; **—объёмный** *a.* microvolumetric; **—ом** *m.* (elec.) microhm; **—омметр** *m.* microhmmeter; **—определение** *n.* microdetermination, microchemical assay; **—организм** *m.* microorganism, microbe; **—остатки** *pl.* microfossils; **—острие** *n.* microinhomogeneity, whisker; **—очко-**

вый *a.* microaugen; **—пайка** *f.* microsoldering; **—пара** *f.* (elec.) microcell.

микропегматит *m.* (petr.) micropegmatite, microscopic pegmatite; **—овый** *a.* micropegmatitic, micrographic.

микро/перегонка *f.* microdistillation; **—переключатель** *m.* microswitch; **—пертит** *m.* (petr.) microperthite; **—печь** *f.* microfurnace; **—пиле** *n.* (biol.) micropyle; **—пипетка** *f.* micropipet(te); **—пирометр** *m.* micropyrometer; **—план местности** (radar) Micro-B scan; **—планктон** *m.* microplankton; **—плёнка** *f.* microfilm; **—подвид** *m.* microsubspecies; **—ползучесть** *f.* microcreep; **—полость** *f.* microcavity; **—пористый** *a.* microporous, microcellular; **—препарат** *m.* (micros.) mount, slide; **—привод** *m.* microdrive; **—примесь** *f.* trace contaminant; **—принтирование** *n.* microprinting; **—пробирка** *f.* microtube; **—провод** *m.* microwire; **—программный** *a.* microprogrammed; **—профилометр** *m.* microprofilometer; **—пучок** *m.* microbeam; **—район** *m.* microdistrict; **—растрескивание** *n.* (plastics) crazing; **—реакция** *f.* microreaction; **—реле** *n.* microrelay; **—рельеф** *m.* microrelief, microtopography; **—рентген** *m.* (nucl.) microroentgen; **—сварка** *f.* miniature welding; **—световод** *m.* microguide.

микросейсм/ический *a.* (geol.) microseismic; **—ы** *pl.* microseisms.

микросекунд/а *f.,* **—ный** *a.* microsecond.

микро/серия *f.* (bot.) serule; **—сеть** *f.* (anat.) microrete; **—сжигание** *n.* microincineration; **—сито** *n.* microscreen; **—складчатость** *f.* (geol.) microfoliation.

микроскоп *m.* microscope; **—ирование** *n.* microscopy; **—ировать** *v.* (use the) microscope; **—ический, —ичный** *a.* microscopic(al); micro—; **—ическая флора** (bot.) microflora; **—ия** *f.* microscopy; **—ный** *a.* microscope.

микро/скрытокристаллический *a.* microcryptocrystalline; **—словарь** *m.* microvocabulary; **—снимок** *m.* (photo)micrograph; **—сома** *f.* (biol.) microsome; **—соммит** *m.* (min.) microsommite; **—состояние** *n.* microstate.

микроспектро/скоп *m.* microspectroscope; **—скопия** *f.* microspectroscopy; **—фотометрия** *f.* microspectrophotometry.

микроспор/а *f.* (bot.) microspore; **—ангий** *m.* microsporangium; **—идии** *pl.* (prot.) microsporidia; Myxosporidia; **—идиоз** *m.* (vet.) microsporidosis; **—ия** *f.* (med.) microsporosis, ringworm infection; (bot.) microspory; **—огенез** *m.* microsporogenesis.

микро/сплавление *n.* microalloying; **—спутник** *m.* microsatellite; **—среда** *f.* microhabitat, microenvironment; **—срез** *m.* microsection; **—строение** *n.,* **—структура** *f.* microstructure; (cyt.) ultrastructure, fine structure; **—сферический** *a.* microspheric; **—сферулитовый** *a.* (petr.) microspherulitic; **—схема** *f.* microcircuit; **—схемотехника** *f.* microcircuitry; **—съёмка** *f.* photomicrography; **—таст** *m.* a minimeter; **—твердомер** *m.* microhardness tester; **—твёрдость** *f.* microhardness; **—текстиль** *m.* textile microscope; **—тепловидение** *n.* microthermography.

микротелефон *m.,* **—ная трубка** microtelephone, hand set; **—ный** *a.* microtelephone, microtelephonic.

микро/терм *m.* (bot.) microtherm; **—типия** *f.* microprinting; **—ток** *m.* microcurrent; **—том** *m.* (micros.) microtome, electron cyclotron; **—трещина** *f.* microfissure; **—трон** *m.* microtron, electron cyclotron; **—удобрение** *n.* trace-element fertilizer; **—узел** *m.* microassembly; **—укол** *m.* microinjection; **—фаг** *m.* (cyt.) microphage;

—фарада *f.* (elec.) microfarad; **—фауна** *f.* (zool.) microfauna.

микрофельзит *m.* (petr.) microfelsite; **—овый** *a.* microfelsitic.

микро/фибрилла *f.* microfibril; **—физика** *f.* microphysics.

микрофильм *m.* microfilm; **—ирование** *n.* microfilming; **—ировать** *v.* microfilm; **—ирующий** *a.* microfilm(ing); **—отека** *f.* microfilm library.

микро/фильный *a.* microphyllous, small-leaved; **—фировый** *a.* microphyric; **—фитоценоз** *m.* (bot.) microcommunity; **—фиша** *f.* microfiche, transparent microcard; **—флора** *f.* (bot.) microflora; **—флюидальный** *a.* (petr.) microfluidal.

микрофон *m.,* **—ная чашка** microphone; **—ный** *a.* microphone, microphonic.

микрофот *m.* (illum.) microphot.

микрофото/графирование *n.* photomicrography; microphotographing; **—графический** *a.* photomicrographic; **—графия** *f.* photomicrography; photomicrograph; **—копирование** *n.* microphotocopying, microfilming; **—метр** *m.* (opt.) microphotometer; **—метрирование** *n.* microphotometering; **—насадка** *f.* photomicrographic attachment; **—снимок** *m.* photomicrograph; **—съёмка** *f.* photomicrography; **—установка** *f.* photomicrographic set-up.

микро/химический *a.* microchemical; **—химия** *f.* microchemistry; **—хирургия** *f.* microsurgery; **—цебус** *m.* (mam.) mouse lemur (*Microcebus*); **—центр** *m.* (gen.) microcentrum, centrosome; **—цефалия** *f.* (med.) microcephaly; **—цидин** *m.* Microcidin, β-naphthol sodium; **—цит** *m.* (biol.) microcyte; **—частица** *f.* microparticle; **—чешуйчатый** *a.* finely foliated, finely squamous, scaly; **—шлиф** *m.* microsection; **—шприц** *m.* microsyringe; **—штатив** *m.* microscope stand; **—эволюция** *f.* microevolution; **—электрод** *m.* microelectrode; **—электроника** *f.* microelectronics; **—элемент** *m.* microelement, microcomponent; (elec.) microcell; (chem.) trace element; **—явление** *n.* microeffect, microphenomenon; **—ядро** *n.* (cyt.) micronucleus.

микрургия *f.* micrurgia, microdissection.

микседема *f.* (med.) myxedema.

миксер *m.* mixer, blender; (met.) holding furnace.

миксин/а *f.* hagfish (*Myxine*); **—овые** *pl.* Myxinidae; **пиявкоротые —ы** borers (*Bdellostomidae*).

миксит *m.* (min.) mixite.

миксо— *prefix* myx(o)— (mucus, slime); mixo— (mixed); **—бактерии** *pl.* myxobacteria; **—болиоз** *m.* (vet.) myxoboliosis; **—вариация** *f.* (gen.) mixovariation; **—ма** *f.* (med.) myxoma; **—мицеты** *pl.* (bot.) myxomycetes; **—плоид** *m.* (gen.) mixoploid; **—соматоз** *m.* (vet.) whirling sickness; **—споридиоз** *m.* myxosporidiosis; **—трофный** *a.* mixotrophic, partly parasitic; **—циприн** *m.* (ichth.) Myxocyprinus.

микстура *f.* (pharm.) mixture, potion.

миктофовые *pl.* lanternfishes (*Myctophidae*).

миктероперка *f.* (ichth.) Mycteroperca.

микшер *m.* (rad.) mixer, fader; monitor (operator).

мил *m.* mil(limeter) (unit of length); *sh. m. of* **милый.**

миланский *a.* (geog.) Milan.

миларит *m.* (min.) milarite.

милдью *see* **мильдью.**

мили *gen., pl., etc. of* **миля.**

милиарный *a.* miliary, millet-like.

мили/таризация *f.* militarization; **—ционер** *m.* militia man; policeman; **—ционный** *a.,* **—ция** *f.* militia.

миллепора *f.* (zool.) Millepora.

миллер/ит *m.* (min.) millerite; —**овский** *a.* Miller (index).

милли— *prefix* milli— (10^{-3}); —**ампер** *m.* (elec.) milliampere.

миллиард *m.* billion (10^9).

милли/бар *m.* (meteor.) millibar; —**барн** *m.* (nucl.) millibarn; —**ватт** *m.* (elec.) milliwatt; —**вольт** *m.* millivolt; —**гамма** *f.* milligamma, millimicrogram; —**генри** *m.* millihenry; —**грамм** *m.,* —**граммовый** *a.* milligram; —**дарси** *m.* (phys.) millidarcy; -E (enzymes) milli-unit; —**кюри** *m.* (nucl.) milli-curie; —**ламберт** *m.* (illum.) millilambert; —**литр** *m.* milliliter; **единица** —**массы** millimass unit, mamu.

миллиметр *m.* millimeter; —**овка** *f.* graph paper (with 1 sq. mm. squares); —**овый** *a.* (one-)millimeter; graph (paper).

милли/микро— *prefix* millimicro—, nano—(10^{-9}); —**микрон** *m.* millimicron (10^{-9} meter); —**моль** *f.* millimole.

миллион *m.* million; —**ный** *a.* millionth; —**ная доля** parts per million, ppm.

милли/осмол(ь) *m.* milliosmol(e) (unit of osmotic pressure); —**пьеза** *f.* millipieze; —**рад** *m.* (nucl.) millirad; —**резерфорд** *m.* (nucl.) millirutherford; —**рентген** *m.* milliroentgen; —**секунда** *f.* millisecond; —**стильб** *m.* (illum.) millistilb; —**фот** *m.* milliphot; —**эквивалент** *m.* milliequivalent, milligram-equivalent.

Миллона основание Millon's base.

милонит *m.* (petr.) mylonite; —**изация** *f.* mylonitization; —**овый** *a.* mylonitic.

милори, —евая синь *f.* Milori blue.

милость *f.* favor, kindness.

милошит *m.* (min.) miloschite.

милу *m.* (mam.) Father David's deer (*Elaphurus davidianus*).

Милуоки (geog.) Milwaukee.

мил-фут *m.* (elec.) mil-foot.

милый *a.* kind, pleasant.

миль *m.* mil (unit of length); *gen. pl. of* **миля;** (bot.) pearl millet (*Pennisetum tiphoides*).

мильбарс *m.* (met.) mill bar, flat bar, puddle(d) bar.

мильд/иу, —ью *f.* (bot.) mildew.

мильтон *m.* (text.) melton.

мильтохриста *f.* (ent.) Miltochrista.

мил/я *f.* mile; **количество** —**ь, расстояние в** —**ях, число** —**ь** mileage.

милябрис *m.* (ent.) Mylabris.

МИМ *abbr.* (**металлографический микроскоп**) metallographic microscope.

мимариды *pl.* (ent.) Mymaridae.

мимас *m.* (ent.), a genus of hawk moths (*Mimas*); (astr.) Mimas.

мимезис *m.* mimesis, mimicry.

мимеограф *m.,* —**ический** *a.* mimeograph, duplicating machine.

мимет/(ез)ит *m.* (min.) mimet(es)ite; —**изм** *m.* mimetism, mimicry; —**ирующий, —ический** *a.* mimetic, imitative; mimic, simulating.

мими/ка, —крия *f.* (biol.) mimicry; —**ческий** *a.* mimic, camouflaging.

мимо *adv. and prep. gen.* past, by; wide of (the mark); **проходить м.** *v.* bypass; —**ездом** *adv.* while passing by; —**езжий** *a.* passing by.

мимоз/а *f.,* —**овый** *a.* (bot.) mimosa; —**овые** *pl.* Mimosaceae.

мимолёт/ность *f.* transience; —**ный** *a.* transient, passing, momentary, fugitive, short-lived; —**ом** *adv.* (while) flying past; momentarily.

мимоходом *adv.* in passing, by the way, on the way; at the same time.

миму/люс *m.* (bot.) Mimulus; —**сопс** *m.* Mimusops.

мин. *abbr.* (**минимум**) minimum; (**минута**) minute.

мина *f.* mien, look, appearance, aspect; (mil.) mine; torpedo; **м.-ловушка** *f.* booby mine, booby trap.

минасрагрит *m.* (min.) minasragrite.

мина-сюрприз *see* **мина-ловушка.**

мингечаурский *a.* (geog.) Mingechaur.

мингуетит *m.* (min.) minguétite.

миндал/евидный *a.* almond-shaped, amygdaloidal; —**евидная пустота** (geol.) amygdule, geode; —**евидные железы** (anat.) tonsils; —**евые** *see* **миндальные;** —**евый** *a.* almond; —**екаменный, —еобразный** *see* **миндалевидный;** —**ик** *m.* tonsil; —**ина** *f.* almond; (geol.) amygdule, geode; (anat.) tonsil; —**ь** *m.* (bot.) almond (*Amygdalus*); **земляной** —**ь** chufa (*Cyperus esculentus*); —**ьник** *m.* (geol.) amygdaloid; —**ьные** *pl.* (bot.) Amygdalaceae; —**ьный** *a.* almond; (anat.) amygdaline; tonsillar; amygdalic, mandelic (acid).

минёр *m.* (ent.) miner; (mil.) miner, mine specialist; torpedo specialist.

минераграф/ический *a.* (min.) mineral(o)graphic; —**ия** *f.* minera(lo)graphy.

минерал *m.* mineral; **удаление** —**ов** demineralizing.

минерализ/атор *m.* (geol.) mineralizer; —**ация** *f.* mineralization; —**(ир)ованный** *a.* mineralized; —**(ир)овать** *v.* mineralize; petrify; —**ующий** *a.* mineralizing; —**ующее средство** mineralizer, mineralizing agent; —**ующийся** *a.* mineralizable.

минералит *m.* an asbestos cement.

минералог *m.* mineralogist; —**ический** *a.* mineralogical; —**ия** *f.* mineralogy.

минерало/графия *f.* mineralography; —**керамика** *f.* powdered ceramic material; —**кортикоидный гормон** mineralocorticoid; —**металлокерамика** *f.* cer(a)met, metal-ceramic; —**образование** *n.* mineral formation.

минерал-спутник *m.* accessory mineral.

минеральнокислый *a.* mineral acid.

минеральн/ый *a.* mineral; **м. воск** mineral wax, ozocerite; **м. дёготь** mineral tar, brea; —**ая бель** mineral white, permanent white; —**ая вата** slag cotton; —**ая шерсть** rock wool, mineral wool; —**ые ископаемые** minerals.

минёрный *a. of* **минёр.**

минетта *f.* minette, oölitic iron ore.

Минздрав *m.* Ministry of public health.

миниатюр/а *f.* miniature; —**изация** *f.* miniaturization; —**изировать** *v.* miniaturize; —**ность** *f.* miniature nature, smallness; —**ный** *a.* miniature, midget, peanut; micro—.

миний *see* **миния.**

минимакс *m.* (math.) minimax, saddle point.

минимальн/о *adv.* minimally; **м. эффективный** *a.* marginal; —**ость** *f.* minimum, minimality; **м.-фазовый** *a.* minimum-phase; —**ый** *a.* minimum, minimal, least, smallest; —**ое значение** minimum; —**ое количество** a minimum, as few as possible.

миниметр *m.* minimeter, mechanical comparator; **м.-наездник** *m.* straddle gage.

миним/изация *f.* minimization; —**изировать** *v.* minimize; —**ум** *m.* minimum; low(est) point; **в первом** —**уме** indispensable; **от** —**ума до максимума** peak to peak; **сводить к** —**уму** *v.* minimize, keep to a minimum.

минир/ование *n.* mining, mine laying; **—ованный** *a.* mined; **—овать** *v.* mine, lay mines, plant mines; undermine; **—ующий** *a.* mining, etc., *see v.*; **—ующие мухи, —ующие мушки** (ent.) leaf-miner flies (*Agromyzidae*).

минист/ерский *a.* ministerial; **—ерство** *n.* ministry; office, board, department; **—р** *m.* minister; Secretary.

мини/ум *m., —я f.* minium, red lead; **-ЭВМ** minicomputer.

минн/ый *a.* mine; torpedo; blasting (powder); **м. горн** bursting chamber; **м. заградитель** mine layer; **—ое заграждение, —ое поле** mine field.

миновать *v.* pass, elapse, run out, end; avoid, be rid (of); detour, by-pass.

миновылавливатель *m.* torpedo catcher.

мино/га *f., —говый а.* (ichth.) lamprey (*Lampetra*); **—говые** *pl.* Petromyzonidae; **—жий** *a.* lamprey.

мино/искатель *m.* mine detector; **—мёт** *m.* mine thrower; mortar; torpedo tube; mortar; **—мётание** *n.* aerial mine laying; **—носец** *m., —носка f., —носный а.* torpedo boat, destroyer.

минор *m.* (math.) minor (determinant); minor key.

минорка *f.* Minorca (hen).

миносбрасыватель *m.* mine rack.

минреп *m.* mooring cable.

Минсельхоз *m.* Ministry of Agriculture.

минский *a.* (geog.) Minsk.

минтай *m.* (ichth.) pollack (*Theragra*).

минуартия *f.* (bot.) chickweed (*Minuartia*).

минувш/ее *n.* the past; **—ий** *a.* past, elapsed, last (year).

минус *m.* (math.) minus, negative sign; shortcoming, disadvantage,, drawback, negative side, defect; minus, less, below; exclusive (of).

минусинский *a.* (geog.) Minusinsk.

минусовый *a. of* **минус**; negative; disadvantageous.

минут/а *f.* minute; moment, instant; **в данную —у** at the given moment, just now, for the moment; **сию —у** immediately, at once.

минутник *m.* a fine abrasive powder.

минутный *a.* minute; momentary; instantaneous; **м. объём** (cardiac) output.

мину/ть *see* **миновать; —я** *pr. ger. of* **минуть;** omitting, by-passing.

миньон *m.* (typ.) minion.

миньярский *a.* (geog.) Minyar.

мио— *prefix* myo— (muscle); mio— (smaller); **—биды** *pl.* (ent.) Myobiidae; **—ген** *m.* myogen; **—гиппус** *m.* (pal.) Miohippus; **—глобин** *m.* myoglobin; **—графия** *f.* myography; **—з(ис)** *m.* (med.) miosis; **—зин** *m.* myosin; **—зит** *m.* (med.) myositis; **—кард** *m.* (anat.) myocardium; **—кардит** *m.* (med.) myocarditis; **—киназа** *f.* myokinase; **—клония** *f.* (med.) myoclonia; **—логия** *f.* myology; **—ма** *f.* (med.) myoma; **—мбо** *m.* miombo (open xerophilic woodland); **—мер** *m.* (embr.) myomere; **—нема** *f.* (prot.) myoneme; **—патия** *f.* myopathy, muscle disease; **—пия** *f.* myopia, nearsightedness; **—септа** *f.* myoseptum, muscle segment; **—тено—** *prefix* myoteno— (muscle and tendon); **—тический** *a.* miotic, myotic; **—том** *m.* myotome; **—тония** *f.* (med.) myotonia; **—фибрилла** *f.* (anat.) myofibril; **—цен** *m.* (geol.) Miocene epoch; **—ценовый** *a.* Miocene; **—цит** *m.* myocyte, muscle cell.

мипора *f.* Mipora, microporous rubber.

мир *m.* world, planet; universe; (outer) space; peace; **во всем —е** world-wide, throughout the world; **животный м.** fauna; **растительный м.** flora.

мира *f.* (aerial surv.) target; (geod.) mark, mire.

мирабел/евый *a., —ь f., —ьный а.* cherry plum (*Prunus cerasifera*).

мирабил/ис *m.* (bot.) Mirabilis; **—ит** *m.* (min.) mirabilite, Glauber salt.

мираж *m.* mirage; candling (of eggs).

мирапинновые *pl.* (ichth.) Mirapinnidae.

мирацидий *m.* (zool.) Miracidium.

мирбанов/ая эссенция, —ое масло mirbane oil, nitrobenzene.

Мир. Вр. *abbr.* (**мировое время**) universal time, Greenwich time.

мириа— *prefix* myria— (10⁴); **—ватт** *m.* (elec.) myriawatt; **—да** *f.* myriad; **—литр** *m.* myrialiter; **—метр** *m.* myriameter.

мирика *f.* myrica, bayberry.

мирикария *f.* (bot.) Myricaria.

мирики *f.* (mam.) wooly spider monkey (*Brachyteles*).

мирикина *f.* (mam.) night ape (*Aotus*).

миринг(о)— *prefix* (anat.) myring(o)— (tympanic membrane).

мирио— *prefix* myri(o)— (countless).

мирист/ил *m., —иловый а.* myristyl; **—ин** *m.* myristin, glyceryl myristate; **—иновая кислота** myristic acid, tetradecanoic acid; **—он** *m.* myristone, myristic ketone.

миритизаль *m.* miritisal, Mauritia palm forest.

мирить *v.* reconcile, mediate; **—ся** *v.* reconcile oneself (with), tolerate, put up (with), accept, make the best (of).

мирихт *m.* (ichth.) Myrichthys.

мириц/етин *m.* myricetin, hydroxyquercetin; **—ил** *m.* myricyl; **—иловый спирт** myricyl alcohol, melissyl alcohol; **—ин** *m.* myricin, myricyl palmitate.

мирмекит *m.* (petr.) myrmekite.

мирмеко— *prefix* myrmeco— (ant); **—фил** *m.* (ent.) myrmecophil; myrmecophilous plant, myrmecophyte.

мирн/о *adv.* peacefully, quietly, without any disturbance; in harmony (with); **—ый** *a.* peaceful, quiet; peace (treaty); (zool.) non-predatory.

миробалан *m.* (bot.) myrobalan.

мировоззрен/ие *n., —ческий а.* world outlook, attitude, ideology.

миров/ой *a.* world; universal (time); peaceful; Pacific (Ocean); **—ое пространство** (outer) space.

мироздание *n.* the universe, cosmos.

миро/зин *m.* myrosin, myrosase; **—ксил** *m.* myroxyl; **—ксилон** *m.* (bot.) Myroxylon; **—новый** *a.* myronic (acid).

мирон(чик) *m.* (ichth.) barbel (*Barbus b.*).

миро/описание *n.* cosmography; **—понимание, —созерцание** *see* **мировоззрение; —творческий** *a.* peacemaking.

мирр *m., —а f., —овый а.* myrrh; **—ис** *m.* (bot.) myrrh (*Myrrhis*).

мирт *m.* (bot.) myrtle (*Myrtus*); **—енал** *m.* myrtenal, myrtenic aldehyde; **—еновая кислота** myrtenic acid; **—енол** *m.* myrtenol; **—иллин** *m.* myrtillin; **—овые** *pl.* Myrtaceae; **—овый** *a.* myrtle.

мирц/ен *m.* myrcene; **—ия** *f.* (bot.) Myrcia.

МИС *abbr.* (**машинноиспытательная станция**) machine testing center.

мисес *m.* (math.) mises; **условия пластичности —а** mises yield conditions.

миси *n.* (min.) misy, copiapite.

мис/ка *f.* pan, basin, dish; **—кообразный** *a.* dish(-pan), dish-shaped; **—очка** *dim. of* **миска;** (apid.) queen-cell cup.

миспикель *m.* (min.) mispickel, arsenopyrite.

миссисипский *a.* (geog.) Mississippi.

миссия *f.* mission, assignment.

миссурийский *a.* (geog.) Missouri.

мист *m.* (ichth.) Mystus; —акокариды *pl.* (crust.) Mystacocarida.

мист/ерия *f.* mystery; —ифицировать *v.* mystify, puzzle.

мистраль *m.* mistral (wind.)

мисцелла *f.* miscella (oil-containing extractant).

митигация *f.* mitigation, abatement.

митил/ит *m.* mytilitol, methylinositol; —отоксин *m.* mytilotoxin.

митинг *m.,* —овый *a.* meeting; —овать *v.* attend a meeting.

миткал/ь *m.,* —евый, —ьный *a.* (text.) calico; cambric.

мито— *prefix* mito— [thread(-like), rod]; —генетический *a.* (biol.) mitogenetic; —з *m.* mitosis; —тический *a.* mitotic; —тический коэффициент (cyt.) mitotic index; —хондрия *f.* mitochondrion; *pl.* mitochondria.

митр/а *f.* (biol.) mitra; (anat.) mitral valve; —агинин mitragynine; —альеза *f.* multibarrel shotgun; —альный *a.* (anat.) mitral; —он *m.* voltage-tunable magnetron.

миттель *m.* English type, 14-point type.

Митчелля грохот Mitchell screen.

миусский *a.* (geog.) Mius.

миф *m.* myth; —ический *a.* mythical.

михайловский *a.* Mikhailov.

Михаэл/иса константа Michaelis constant; —я реакция Michael reaction.

михелия *f.* (bot.) Michelia.

Мих/ельсона актинометр Michelson actinometer; —лера кетон Michler ketone.

мицел/ий *m.* mycelium, (mushroom) spawn; —ин *m.* mycelin; —ла *f.* micelle; —лярный *a.* micellar.

миц/етин *m.* mycetin; —ето— *prefix* myceto— (fungus); —етология *f.* my(cet)ology; —етома *f.* (med.) mycetoma; —етофаг *m.* mycetophage, fungivore; —етофаговый *a.* mycetophagous, fungi-eating.

мицуевые *pl.* (ichth.) Scombropidae.

миц(ц)онит *m.* (min.) mizzonite, dipyre.

Мичелля подшипник Michell bearing.

мичиганский *a.* (geog.) Michigan.

мичка *f.* (bot.) matgrass (*Nardus*).

мичуринский *a.* (gen.) Mitchurin.

мишен/евидный *a.* (med.) target (cell); —ый *a.,* —ь *f.* target; ток на —ь target current.

Мишера пипетка (biol.) Miescher pipet.

мишметалл *m.* mischmetal.

мишур/а *f.* tinsel, spangle, shining platelet; metallic thread; Dutch metal; —ный *a.* tinsel; deceptive.

миэ—*see* мие—.

мк *abbr.* (микро—) micro—; (микрон) micron; (милликулон) millicoulomb.

мка *abbr.* (микроампер) microampere.

Мкал *abbr.* (мегакалория) megacalorie.

мкб, мкбар *abbr.* (микробар) microbar.

МКБС *abbr.* (межконтинентальный баллистический снаряд) intercontinental ballistic missile, ICBM.

мкбэр *abbr.* (микробэр) microrem.

мкв *abbr.* (микровольт) microvolt; м. кв. (квадратный метр) square meter; МКВ (микровыключатель) microswitch.

мквт *abbr.* (микроватт) microwatt.

мкг *abbr.* (микрограмм) microgram.

мкгн *abbr.* (микрогенри) microhenry.

мкгсс, МКГСС *abbr.* (метр-килограмм-сила-се-

кунда) meter-kilogram (force)-second (system of units).

мкдм *abbr.* (микродюйм) microinch.

МКЗ *abbr.* (максимальное каротажное зондирование) maximum departure curves.

мкк *abbr.* (микрокулон) microcoulomb.

мкккюри *abbr.* (микрокюри) microcurie.

мкл *abbr.* (микролитр) microliter.

мкмк *abbr.* (микромикро—) micro-micro—, pico—; (микромикрон) micromicron; мкмкв *abbr.* (микромикровольт) micromicrovolt, picovolt; мкмквт *abbr.* (микромикроватт) micromicrowatt; мкмкг *abbr.* (микромикрограмм) micromicrogram; мкмкф *abbr.* (микромикрофарада) micromicrofarad.

мкмоль *abbr.* (микромоль) micromole.

мкн *abbr.* (микрон) micron.

мком *abbr.* (микроом) microhm.

мкр *abbr.* (микрорентген) microroentgen.

мкрад *abbr.* (микрорад) microrad.

мкс *abbr.* (максвелл) maxwell; МКС *abbr.* (метр-килограмм-секунда) meter-kilogram-second, MKS (system of units); МКСА *abbr.* (метр-килограмм-секунда-ампер) meter-kilogram-second-ampere (MKSA system).

мксек *abbr.* (микросекунда) microsecond.

МКСК *abbr.* (метр-килограмм-секунда-кулон) meter-kilogram-second-coulomb (system of units); МКСС *abbr.* (метр-килограмм-секунда-свеча) meter-kilogram-second-candle.

мкф *abbr.* (микрофарада) microfarad; (микрофот) microphot.

МКФ *abbr.* (монокальцийфосфат) monocalcium phosphate.

мкюри *abbr.* (милликюри) millicurie; Мкюри *abbr.* (мегакюри) megacurie.

мл *abbr.* (миллилитр) milliliter; Мл *abbr.* (моляльность) molality (of a solution); МЛ *abbr.* (магнитная лента) magnetic tape; (микроскоп люминесцентный) luminescence microscope.

МЛА *abbr.* (межпланетный летательный аппарат) interplanetary vehicle.

млад/енец *m.* infant, baby; —енческий *a.* infantile; immature; —енчество *n.* infancy; охрана—енчества child welfare; —ший *a.* younger, junior (partner); (comp.) low-order; *m.* the youngest.

млат-рыба *f.* (ichth.) smooth hammerhead (*Sphyrna zygaena*).

млб *abbr.* (миллиламберт) millilambert.

млд *abbr.* (миллиард) billion; МЛД *abbr.* (минимальная летальная доза) minimum lethal dose.

млеконосный *a.* lactiferous, lacteal.

млекопитающ/ее *n.,* м. животное mammal; —ий *a.* mammalian.

млекотечение *n.* (vet.) galactorrhea.

млеть *v.* be overcome; become numb.

млечн/ик *m.* bot.) sea milkwort (*Glaux*); milk duct; (bot.) lactiferous duct; milk vessel; —ый *a.* milk(y), lacteal, lacteous, lactic; —ый путь (astr.) Milky Way; —ый сок milky juice; (bot.) latex; (physiol.) chyle.

млн. *abbr.* (миллион) million.

млодарка *f.* (mam.) ribbon seal (*Histriophoca fasciata*).

млрд. *abbr.* (миллиард) billion.

млынок *m.* grain blower and sorter.

мм *abbr.* (миллиметр) millimeter; Мм *abbr.* (мегаметр) megameter; мМ *abbr.* (миллимолярность) millimolarity.

м.м.в. *abbr.* (максимальная молекулярная влагоёмкость) maximum molecular moisture-absorbing capacity.

мм вод. ст. *abbr.* (**миллиметр водяного столба**) millimeter(s) of water column.

ММД *abbr.* (**магнитомодуляционный датчик**) magnetic modulation sensor.

М-метр *m.* Machmeter, Mach indicator.

м/мин *abbr.* (**метров в минуту**) meters per minute.

ммк *abbr.* (**миллимикрон**) millimicron; **ммкг** *abbr.* (**миллигамма**) milligamma.

ммоль *abbr.* (**миллимоль**) millimole.

ММР *abbr.* molecular weight distribution.

мм рт. ст. *abbr.* (**миллиметр ртутного столба**) millimeter(s) of mercury column.

ММС *abbr.* (**машинно-мелиоративная станция**) machine reclamation center.

ММ(Т)Ф *abbr.* (**мясо-молочная товарная ферма**) meat and dairy farm.

мн. *abbr.* (**многие**) many.

Мн *abbr.* (**меганьютон**) meganewton.

МНА *abbr.* (**метод наведённой активности**) induced activity method.

мн. др. *abbr.* (**многие другие**) many others.

мне *dat. of* **я**, me, to me.

мнемо/зина *f.* (ent.) Parnassius mnemosyne; **—код** *m.* mnemonic code; **—ника** *f.* mnemonics; **—нический** *a.* mnemonic, memory; **—ническая схема, —схема** *f.* mimic flowsheet; graphic panel; **—техника** *f.* mnemonics; **—технический** *a.* mnemonic.

мнен/ие *n.* opinion, judgment; **по их—ию** according to them, they hold (that).

мнёт *pr. 3 sing. of* **мять.**

м-ние (**месторождение**) deposit.

мни/евые *pl.* (bot.) Mniaceae; **—й** *m.* Mnium.

мним/оумерший *a.* (med.) comatose; **—ый** *a.* seeming, imaginary, supposed; simulated, false; virtual (image); **—ая величина** imaginary number.

мнить *v.* think, imagine, suppose, be of the opinion; **—ся** seem, appear.

мниум *m.* (bot.) Mnium.

мн-к *abbr.* (**многоугольник**) polygon.

МНК *abbr.* (**многозондовый нейтронный каротаж**) multi-probe neutron logging.

мног/ие *pl.* (a great) many; **—ий** *a.* numerous, many, in large numbers.

много *adv.* much, many, a great deal, considerably; **на м.** by far, much.

много— *prefix* poly—, multi—, many, multiple; **—адресный** *a.* multiple-address (system); **—актный** *a.* multi-event; **—амперный** *a.* heavy-current; **—анодный** *a.* multianode; **—арочный** *a.* multiple-arch; **—аспектный** *a.* multi-dimensional, relative (classification); **—атомный** *a.* polyatomic; polyhydric (alcohol); **—баковый** *a.* multitank; **—блочный** *a.* multibank (engine); **—бородник** *m.* (bot.) beard grass (*Polypogon*); **—бородковый** *a.* multiple (punch); **—бороздный** *a.* multisulcate; **—брат(ствен)ный** *a.* (bot.) polyadelphous; **—брачие** *n.* polygamy; **—брачный** *a.* polygamous; **—бугорчатые** *pl.* (pal.) Multituberculata; **—бугорчатый** *a.* (anat.) multitubercular.

многовалентн/ость *f.* multivalence; **—ый** *a.* multivalent, polyvalent.

много/валковый *a.* (met.) multiple-roll, cluster (mill); **—вариантный** *a.* multivariant; **—вато** *adv.* a little too much; **—ваттный** *a.* (elec.) high-watt; **—венного действия** *a.* flash (pasteurizer); **—вершинный** *a.* polyconic; **—ветвистокишечные** *pl.* (zool.) Polycladida; **—ветвистый** *a.* polycladous, many-branched;

—вибраторный *a.* multidipole, multiunit (antenna); **—витковый** *a.* (elec.) multiturn, multiloop.

многовод/ный *a.* full of water, high-water; well irrigated; wet (year); polyhydrate (compound); **—водье** *n.* excess water (in stream, lake); flood season; (med.) hydramnion.

много/волновой *a.* multiwave; **—главый** *a.* polycephalous, multiceps; **—глазка** *f.* (zool.) Polycelis; **—глазый** *a.* many-eyed; **—гнёздный** *a.* multiple-cavity, multi-impression (mold); (biol.) multilocular; **—говорящий** *a.* meaningful, saying much; **—головчатость** *f.* polycephalitis (of beet); **—голов(оч-н)ый, —головчатый** *a.* polycephalous, many-headed; **—голосый** *a.* polyglot(tous).

многогранн/ик *m.* (geom.) polyhedron; **—ый** *a.* polyhedral, faceted; varied, many-sided, complicated; multangular.

много/групповой *a.* multigroup; **—дебитный** *a.* prolific (well); **—диапазонный** *a.* multirange; **—дисковый** *a.* gang (saw); **—дневный** *a.* lasting many days, prolonged; **—дольчатый** *a.* multilobular; **—домный** *a.* (bot.) polygamous.

многодыр/очный *a.* multihole; **—чатый** *a.* (multi)perforated.

мног/ое *n.* much; many things; **во —ом** in many respects; **—ожгутиковые** *pl.* (prot.) Polymastigina; **—ожгутиковый** *a.* multiflagellate; **—оженство** *n.* (biol.) polygyny.

многожильный *a.* multiple-strand, multiple-wire, multiple (cord); multi(ple)-core, compound (cable); **м. провод** cable wire.

много/забойный *a.* multihole (drilling); **—задачность** *f.*, **—задачный** *a.* multitasking; **—зажимный** *a.* multiterminal; **—замещённый** *a.* polysubstituted; **—зарядный** *a.* multi(ple)-charge, highly charged; **—заходный** *a.* multiple (thread); multiple-thread (screw); (phys.) multifilar (helix); **—звенный** *a.* ladder-type; multi-section; **—звучный** *a.* polyphonic.

многоземель/е *n.* large property; **—ный** *a.* rich in land.

многознаменательн/ость *f.* significance; **—ый** *a.* significant.

многознач/ащий, —ительный *a.* significant, influential; **—ность** *f.* multivalence, polyvalence; multiple meaning, polysemy; ambiguity; **—ный** *a.* multivalent, polyvalent; multiple-value(d); multiple-digit (number); polyhydric (alcohol).

много/зольность *f.* high ash content; **—зольный** *a.* high-ash; **—зондовый** *a.* multiprobe; **—зонный** *a.* multiregion; **—зуб(ец)** paddlefish (*Polyodon spatula*); **—зубчатый** *a.* multidentate; **—зубы** *pl.* (ichth.) Polydontidae; **—иглый** *a.* multiple-spined; **—игольчатый** *a.* multipin (cathode); **—инерционный** *a.* multilag; **—искровой** *a.* multipoint (ignition); **—камерные** *pl.* (prot.) Polythalamia; **—камерный** *a.* multiple-chamber, multichambered, multicellular; (biol.) multilocular; (zool.) polythalamous, aggregate, collective; multi(ple)-cavity, multisectional, multi-resonator (magnetron); compartment (mill).

многоканальн/ость *f.* multichanneling; **—ый** *a.* multichannel; multiplex, multiconductor (line); (rockets) multiperforate (grain).

много/каскадный *a.* multistage; **—катодный** *a.* polycathode; **—квартирный** *a.* apartment (house); **—километровый** *a.* (of) many kilometers; **—кислотный** *a.* polyacid; **—клемешник** *m.* multiple-furrow plow.

многоклеточн/ые *pl.* (zool.) Metazoa; **—ый** *a.* multicellular, many-celled; multicage (elevator).

много/клиновый *a.* multiple-wedge (bearing); **—ков-**

шовый *a.* (multi)-bucket, chain(-and-)bucket (excavator); ladder-type; **—колейный** *a.* multiple-track; **—коленчатые** *pl.* (zool.) sea spiders (*Pantopoda*); **—колёсный** *a.* multiple-impeller (pump); **—колосник** *m.* (bot.) Agastache; **—колпачковый** *a.* bubblecap (tower); **—кольчатый** *a.* polycyclic; **—колючник** *m.* (ichth.) Polycentrus schamburgkii; **—компонентный** *a.* multi(ple)-component; multiple (phase); **—контактный** *a.* multiple-contact; **—контурный** *a.* multicircuit, multiloop; multistage; multivariable (systems); **—коренник** *m.* (bot.) duckweed (*Spirodela*); **—корневой** *a.* multirooted; **—корпусный** *a.* multiple, multiple-unit; multiple-effect (evaporator); multiple-furrow, gang (plow); **—красочный** *a.* polychrom(at)ic, many-colored, multicolor(ed).

многократ *m.* multiple; **—но** *adv.* repeatedly, over and over, many times; **—но отражённая волна** (seismology) multiple reflection; **—ность** *f.* frequency, multiplicity; repetition, recurrence; (commun.) multiplex(ing); **—ный** *a.* multiple, frequent, numerous, repeated, manifold, multi—, multiplex, multistage; plural (scattering); many-valued; (comp.) iterative (addition); (wire drawing) multiple-draft; **—ная связь** multiple bond; **—ное число** multiple; **—ного действия** re-usable, recoverable.

много/кремниевый *a.* polysilicon; **—ламповый** *a.* (rad.) multitube; **—лезвийный** *a.* multiple-blade; **—лемешный** *a.* multiple, gang (plow); **—лепестковый** *a.* (bot.) many-petaled, polypetalous; **—лесный** *a.* rich in forests.

многолет/ие *n.* longevity, long life; **—немёрзлый** *a.,* **—немёрзлый грунт** permafrost; **—ний** *a.* of many years, old; long-term, secular; (bot.) perennial; **—ник** *m.* perennial.

много/линейный *a.* multicircuit; **—листник** *m.* multifoil; **—листный** *a.* many-leaved; (bot.) polyphyllous; multifold; **—литниковый** *a.* (met.) multigate; **—лонжеронный** *a.* multispar (wing); **—лопастный** *a.* multilobate, multilobed; **—лошадный** *a.* multiple horse; **—лучевой** *a.* multi(ple)-beam; many-pronged; multipath; multiblade (knife); **—людный** *a.* highly populated, dense; crowded; **—мерный** *a.* multidimensional; multiple; multiscale, multirange; (stat.) multivariate; **—местный** *a.* (math.) multiple, many-place(d); composite; multiple-cavity (mold); multiseater (plane); multiple (jig).

многомод/альный *a.* (math.) multimodal; **—овый** *a.* multimode; **—улирующий** *a.* analog (computer).

много/моторный *a.* multiple-motor; **—мужие** *n.* (bot.) polyandry; **—мужний** *a.* polyandrous; **—накальный** *a.* multifilament; **—надрезный** *a.* multifid; **—направленный** *a.* multidirectional, omnidirectional; **—нарезной** *a.* polygrooved; **—нитный** *a.* multifilament; **—ниточный** *a.* multiple(-thread); multiple (thread); multistrand; multiple-train (rolling).

многонож/ка *f.* (bot.) polypody (*Polypodium*); (zool.) myriapod; **—ки-броненосцы** *pl.* (zool.) Oniscomorpha; **—ковые** *pl.* (bot.) Polypodiaceae; **—ник** *m.* polypody.

много/обещающий *a.* promising, hopeful; challenging; **—обещающие возможности** challenge; **—оборотный** *a.* repeated; high-speed (engine); returnable (container); **—оборотное использование** *n.* recycling.

многообраз/ие *n.* diversity, variety, spectrum; multiformity; **—ия** *pl.* (math.) manifolds; (Jacobian) varieties; **—нозубые** *pl.* (mal.) Adapedonta; **—ность** *f.* diversity; **—ный** *a.* diverse, varied, multiform, polymorphous, manifold.

много/обходный *a.* multipoint; **—объективный** *a.* multiple(-lens); **—оплеточный** *a.* multibraided; **—опорный** *a.* multiple-seated (valve); **—опытный** *a.* highly experienced.

многоосновн/ость *f.* polybasicity; **—ый** *a.* polybasic.

много/отверстный *a.* multihole; **—отраслевой** *a.* multibranch, varied, diversified, mixed; integrated (economy); **—отростчатый** *a.* multipolar (cells); **—очковый** *a.* multiple-block (die); **—пазовый** *a.* multislot(ted); **—палый** *a.* (anat.) polydactylous; **—парный** *a.* (bot.) multijugate; large-capacity (cable); **—пёр** *m.* (ichth.) bichir (*Polypterus*); **—переходный** *a.* multipass (operation); **—пёровые** *pl.* (ichth.) Polypteridae; **—пестичный** *a.* (bot.) polygynous; **—петлевой** *a.* multiple-loop; compound (cycle); **—пламенный** *a.* (welding) multiple-torch, multiple-burner; multiple-jet (burner); multiflame (torch); **—плановый** *a.* with many plans; **—пластинный, —пластинчатый** *a.* multiplate; **—пластовый** *a.* multilayer, multiple-zone; **—плечий** *a.* multiple(-arm).

многоплод/ие *n.* superfecundation, multiple pregnancy; (zool.) prolificacy; **—ник** *m.* (bot.) polycarp; **—никовый** *a.* polycarpic; **—ный** *a.* prolific, polytocous.

много/подовый *a.* multiple-hearth; **—позиционный** *a.* multistation (machine); **—полосный** *a.* multiband; **—полосье** *n.* (agr.) multi-strip land use.

многополь/е *n.* multiple-field crop rotation; **—ный** *a.* multiple-field, multiple-crop.

много/полюсник *m.* (elec. comm.) network, multiport; multipole; **—полюсный** *a.* multipolar, multipole; **—постовой** *a.* multioperator (machine); **—предельный** *a.* multirange; **—проводный** *a.* (elec.) multiple-wire, multiple (line); **—пролётный** *a.* multispan (bridge); **—профильный** *a.* multiple-discipline, polytechnical; general (publication); **—пуансонный** *a.* gang (die, punch); **—раздельный** *a.* multipartite; (bot.) multifid; **—размерный** *a.* multidimensional; **—разовый** *a.* nonexpendable, re-usable, nondisposable; **—разрезной** *a.* slotted (wing); multislot, multisegment (magnetron); **—разрядный** *a.* (comp.) multi(ple)-digit; **—раскосная решётка** multiple latticework.

много/режимность *f.* multiplicity of operating levels; **—режимный** *a.* multimode; **—резонаторный** *a.* multi(ple)-cavity (magnetron, etc.); **—резцовые** *pl.* (mam.) Polyprotodonta; **—резцовый** *a.* multiblade, multicut(ting), multiple-tool; gang (tool); (mam.) polyprotodont.

много/рожковый *a.* multiple-jet; **—роты** *see* **многоусты**; **—рупорный** *a.* multiple-horn; **—ручьевой** *a.* multiple-pass (crystallizer); multiple-strand (casting); **—рядник** *m.* (bot.) Polystichum; **—рядный** *a.* polyserial, multiserial, multibank, multirow; multilane (road); multiple (riveting); gang (cultivator).

много/связ(ан)ный *a.* (math.) multiply connected; **—связы** *pl.* (zool.) Polydesmidae; **—секционный** *a.* segmented (roller); **—семянник** *m.* (bot.) Hymenolobus; **—семянный** *a.* (bot.) polyspermous; **—сернистый** *a.* polysulfide (of); **—сеточный** *a.* multigrid; **—сильный** *a.* (mach.) high-duty, strong, powerful; **—скачковый** *a.* multishock (diffuser); **—скоростной** *a.* multi(ple-)speed, multivelocity; **—сложный** *a.* complicated, complex, intricate; **—слойный** *a.* multilayer, multistratal; multi(ple)-ply; multiwall (bag); multiple (belting); **—сменный** *a.* multishift; polylophyodont (teeth); **—сопловой** *a.* multiple-jet (turbine); **—сочный** *a.* succulent; **—срезный** *a.* multiple-shear; **—стадийность** *f.* multistage nature; **—стадийный** *a.* multistage, multiphase.

многостаночн/ик *m.* operator of several machines; **—ый** *a.* multiple-machine.

много/ствольный *a.* multibarreled; multiple-stemmed; **—степенный** *a.* multistage; multigrade (equation); **—стержневой** *a.* multirod.

многосторонн/ий *a.* (geom.) polygonal, multilateral; many-sided, versatile; multi—; multiple, compound; combined (fertilizer); **—ость** *f.* versatility, variety.

много/стрендовый *a.* multiple-strand; **—стрингерный** *a.* multispan (structure); **—строчный посев** strip cropping; **—струйный** *a.* multiple(-jet); **—ступенный** *a.* multiple (operation); **—ступенчатый** *a.* multi(ple-)stage, multistep, multiple-phase, compound; multiple-speed (gearbox); multiple-runner (turbine); **—танковый** *a.* multitank; **—тигельный** *a.* multiple-crucible (furnace); **—тиражный** *a.* large (edition).

многотомн/ик *m.* many-volumed set; **—ый** *a.* in many volumes.

много/тоннажный, —тонный *a.* large-tonnage; **—топливный** *a.* multifuel; **—точечный** *a.* multiple-point; multiple-projection (weld); **—точие** *n.* dotted line; **—трубный** *a.* multitubular; **—тычинковый** *a.* (bot.) polyandrous; **—уважаемый** *a.* highly respected, Dear (in letter).

многоугольн/ик *m.* (geom.) polygon; **—ый** *a.* polygonal; multiangular.

много/узловой *a.* multinode; **—уровневый** *a.* multilevel; stacked (transistor); **—ус** *m.* (ichth.) Cirrhibarbis; **—усты** *pl.* (zool.) Polystomeae; **—усый** *a.* multiwhiskered; **—фабричный** *a.* multiple-plant; **—фазный** *a.* (elec.) polyphase, multiphase; compound (cable); multicoil (winding); complex (process); **—факторный** *a.* multiple-factor, complex; **—формность** *f.* polymorphism; **—фотонный** *a.* multiquantum (radiation); **—функциональный** *a.* multifunctional.

многоходовой *a.* multi(ple)-pass (converter); multishift (engine); multiple-start, multiple-turn, multiway; multi(ple-)thread (screw); multiple (thread); **м. червяк** helical gear.

много/хозяйный *a.* heteroecious, heteroxenous (parasites); **—хромосомность** *f.* (gen.) polyploidy.

многоцвет/ковость *f.* (bot.) multiflorous nature; **—ковый** *a.* multiflorous, polyanthous; **—ницы** *pl.* (ent.) Vanessidae; **—ость** *f.* polychromy; **—ый** *a.* polychromatic, polychrome, multicolored, full-color; (bot.) multiflorous.

много/целевой *a.* multipurpose, general-purpose; multimission (fighter); **—цилиндровый** *a.* multicylinder; (paper) multivat; **—частичный** *a.* many-particle; many-body (force); **—частотный** *a.* multifrequency; **—челночный станок** multiple-shuttle loom; **—черпаковый** *a.* multibucket; chain-and-bucket (excavator); ladder-type (ditcher); **—четверочный** *a.* multiquad (cable).

многочисленн/ость *f.* multiplicity; **—ый** *a.* multiple, numerous, manifold, many, myriad.

многочлен *m.* (math.) polynomial; **—ный** *a.* polynomial; polymerous.

много/шаговый *a.* multistep; **—шамот** *m.* ceramic ware containing a high percentage of chamotte; **—шашечный** *a.* multi(ple-)grain (charge); **—шиповые** *pl.* (ichth.) Polycentridae; **—шкальный** *a.* multiscale; multirange; **—шкальный (измерительный) прибор** multimeter; **—шлейфовый** *a.* multichannel, multiloop; (rad.) branched (line); **—шпиндельный** *a.* multi(ple) spindle, gang (tool); **—шпиндельный станок** multiple drill; **—шпоночный** *a.* sliding (shaft);

—штанговый *a.* (comp.) multibar; **—штемпельный** *a.* multiple, gang (die); **—штыревой** *a.* multiple-rod, polyrod (antenna); **—щелочной** *a.* alkali-rich; **—щетинковые** *pl.* (zool.) Polychaeta.

много/электродный *a.* multielectrode; **—элементный** *a.* multiple-unit; multioutlet (source); **—эмиттерный транзистор** multiemitter transistor, overlay transistor; **—этажный** *a.* many-storied; multi(ple-)stage; stagger (antenna); **—ядерный** *a.* polynuclear, polynucleate, multinuclear; polycyclic (compound); polymorphonuclear (leucocyte); **—ядность** *f.* (med.; zool.) polyphagia; **—ядные** *pl.* (ent.) Polyphaga; **—ядный** *a.* polyphagous; **—язычный** *a.* polyglot, multilingual; **—ярусный** *a.* multi(ple-)stage; multistory; multi-tier; many-layered.

многояч/еистый, —ейковый *a.* multicellular, multi(ple)-cell; **—ейный** *a.* multi(ple)-chambered.

множественн/ость *f.* plurality, multiplicity; **—ый** *a.* plural, multiple.

множеств/о *n.* great number, multitude, host, many, a great deal, numbers; mass; set (of numbers); class, collection, assemblage; **осреднённый по —у** *a.* ensemble-averaged.

множ/имое *n.* (math.) multiplicand; **—итель** *m.* multiplier, multiple, factor; (comp.) ier; **общий —итель** common multiple; **разложение на —ители** factorization; **—ительно-делительный** *a.* (aut.) multiplier-divider; **—ительный** *a.* multiplying, duplicating; (comp.) calculating (punch); **—ительный аппарат** duplicator; **—ительное устройство** multiplier; **—ить** *v.* multiply.

мной, мною *instr.* of **я,** by me.

МНР *abbr.* (**Монгольская Народная Республика**) Mongolian People's Republic.

мн/ут *pr. 3 pl.*; **—ущий** *pr. act. part.*; **—я** *pr. gerund of* **мять.**

мо *n.* (elec.) mho (unit of conductance).

МО *abbr.* (**молекулярная орбита**) molecular orbit.

моа *f.* (pal.) moa (*Dinornis*).

мобилиз/ационный *a.,* **—ация** *f.* mobilization; **—(ир)овать** *v.* mobilize; stimulate, activate; **—ованный** *a.* mobilized; *m.* mobilized soldier.

мобильн/ость *f.* mobility; **—ый** *a.* mobile; (mach.) locomotive.

мобула *f.* (ichth.) Mobula.

МОВ *abbr.* (**метод отражённых волн**) reflected wave method.

мовеин *m.* mauveine, aniline purple.

мовравый *a.* mowra; mowric (acid).

мог *past m. sing. of* **мочь,** could.

могар *m.* Italian millet (*Setaria italica*).

могаукит *m.* (min.) mohawkite.

могер *m.* mohair.

могера *f.* (mam.) talpa (*Mogera*).

могила *f.* grave, tomb.

могилёвский *a.* (geog.) Mogilev.

могиль/ник *m.* burial ground, graveyard; (bot.) harmel (*Peganum harmala*); **—ный** *a.* grave, tomb; **—щик** *m.* (ent.) burying beetle (*Necrophorus*); grave digger.

могли *past pl. of* **мочь,** could.

мого *n.* (geol.) Moho (strata between earth's crust and mantle).

могойтуйский *a.* (geog.) Mogoitui.

могу/т *pr. 3 pl. of* **мочь; —честь** *f.* strength; **—чий** *a.* strong, vigorous; **—щественный** *a.* potent, powerful, strong; **—щество** *n.* potency, power; **—щий** *a.* powerful, strong; he who can.

могший *past act. part. of* **мочь.**

мод *abbr.* (**модулятор**) modulator.

мода *f.* style, fashion; (math., stat.) mode; **м. колебаний** mode; —**льность** *f.* (math.) modality; —**льный** *a.* modal.

модел/изм *m.* work with models; —**ирование** *n.* modeling, etc., *see v.*; miniature-scale operation; (comp.) simulation, (software) prototyping; —**ировать** *v.* model, simulate, represent; build models, operate models; (hort.) shape, train; —**ировка** *see* **моделирование;** —**ируемый** *a.* prototype; —**ирующая вычислительная машина, —ирующее устройство** analog computer, simulator.

модел/ь *f.* mock-up, model; pattern, shape, form, standard; make, type; simulator; (comp.) analog; prototype; **испытание на —ях** mock-up testing; **м.-аналог** *f.* analog; **м.-болванка** *f.* mock-up; —**ьер** *m.* model maker; pattern maker; —**ьная** *f.,* —**ьностолярная мастерская** model shop; pattern shop; —**ьный** *a. of* **модель;** molding (board); —**ьщик** *see* **модельер; м.-эталон** *f.* master pattern.

модем *m.* (comp.) modem.

моден *sh. m. of* **модный.**

модер *m.* (silv.) duff mull.

модератор *m.* (mach.) moderator, speed regulator.

модерниз/атор *m.* modernizer; —**ация** *f.,* —**ирование** *n.* modernization, updating; —**(ир)ованный** *a.* modernized, updated; —**(ир)овать** *v.* modernize, update, bring up to date, renovate.

модильон *m.* modillion (a bracket).

модиола *f.* (mal.) Modiolus.

модифи/катор *m.* modifier, modifying agent; (met.) inoculant; —**кационный** *a.* modifying; —**кация** *f.,* —**цирование** *n.* modification; (modified) version, derivative, development; adaptation; —**цированный** *a.* modified, etc., *see v.*; —**цировать** *v.* modify, adapt, vary, update, change; inoculate (cast iron); —**цируемый** *a.* modifiable.

модный *a.* fashionable, stylish.

модулир/ование *n.* modulation; —**ованный** *a.* modulated; —**овать** *v.* modulate; —**ометр** *m.* modulation meter; —**ующий** *a.* modulating; —**ующего типа** analog (computer); —**ующийся** *a.* modular.

модуль *m.* (math.) modulus, coefficient; (bath or liquor) ratio; module, standard; **м. при кручении** torsional modulus; **м. сдвига** shear modulus; **м. упругости** modulus (of elasticity); —**ный** *a.* module, modular; worm (thread); —**ная фреза** gear cutter.

модуля/рный *a.* modular; —**тор** *m.* modulator; —**тор лазера** shutter; —**торный** *a.* modulator; modulating; —**ционный** *a.,* —**ция** *f.* modulation.

модус *m.* modus, mode of procedure.

моё *n.* *pronoun* my.

моёвка *f.* (orn.) kittiwake (*Rissa*).

мое/к *gen. pl. of* **мойка; —т** *pr. 3 sing. of* **мыть;** —**чный** *a.* washing, wash (water); —**чная машина** washer.

можа *pr. ger. of* **мочь.**

можайский *a.* (geog.) Mozhaisk.

может *pr. 3 sing. of* **мочь;** he can; is liable, is apt to, is likely to be; **м. быть** perhaps, maybe; **а м. быть** if not; **не м. быть** it is impossible; **м. использоваться** usable, operable.

можжевёлов/ый *a.* juniper; —**ая кислота** juniperic acid, 16-hydroxy-hexadecanoic acid; —**ая смола** juniper tar, cade oil; —**ое масло** juniper oil; **пригорелое —ое масло** cade oil, juniper tar.

можжевельн/ик *m.,* —**ый** *a.* juniper.

можжуха, болотная (bot.) Lycopodium.

можно *v.* it is possible, one may, one can; —able, *e.g.,* **м. регулировать** be adjustable.

мозазавр *m.* (pal.) Mosasaurus.

мозаи/ка *f.* mosaic; inlay; (phyt.) mosaic, brindle; **набирать —ку** *v.* inlay; —**ческий** *a.* mosaic; —**чно распределённый** *a.* tesselated (stresses); —**чность** *f.* patchiness; (cryst.) mosaic structure; (gen.) mosaicism; —**чный** *a.* mosaic, inlaid; tile; tesselated; patchy; —**чная болезнь** (phyt.) mosaic; —**чная особь** (gen.) mosaic.

мозамбикский *a.* (geog.) Mozambique.

мозандрит *m.* (min.) mosandrite.

мозг *m.* brain; (anat.) cerebrum; marrow, medulla; (spinal) cord; **головной м.** encephalon, cerebrum, brain; **задний м.** metencephalon; **конечный м.** telencephalon; **костный м.** marrow; **продолговатый м.** myelencephalon; **средний м.** mesencephalon.

мозглый *a.* damp and penetrating; rancid, rotten; thin, meager.

мозгов/атый *a.* pithy; —**ик** *m.* (zool.) Multiceps; —**ина** *f.* pulp; (bot.) pith.

мозгов/ой *a.* brain, cerebral; myeloid; medullary; cerebric (acid); marrow (bone); **м. придаток** (anat.) hypophysis, pituitary body; —**ая оболочка** meninx, mater; **мягкая —ая оболочка** pia mater; **твёрдая —ая оболочка** dura mater.

мозезит *m.* (min.) mosesite.

мозжеч/ково— *prefix* (anat.) cerebello—; **м.-бугорный, м.-таламический** *a.* cerebellothalamic; —**ко-вый** —**ок** *m.* cerebellum.

Мозли закон (phys.) Moseley's law.

мозол/евидный *a.* callus-like; —**еногие** *pl.* (mam.) Tylopoda; —**исто—** *prefix* tyl(o)—(knob); —**истость** *f.* callosity; —**истый** *a.* callous(ed); —**ь** *f.,* —**ьный** *a.* callosity, callus, corn.

МОЗУ *abbr.* (**магнитное оперативное запоминающее устройство**) magnetic memory device; processing, unit core storage; random-access memory, RAM.

мой *a.* my, mine.

мойва *f.* (ichth.) capelin (*Mallotus villosus*).

мой/ка *f.* washing; washer; —**ный** *a.* washing; —**щик** *m.* washer.

мокайа масло mocaya butter.

мокас(с)ины *pl.* moccasins.

моквинский *a.* (geog.) Mokva.

мокко *n.,* **кофе м.** mocha (coffee).

мокну/ть *v.* become wet, get soaked; soak, steep; (med.) fester, weep; —**щий** *a.* soaking; weeping (eczema).

моко *n.* (mam.) rock cavy (*Kerodon rupestris*).

мокой *m.* (ichth.) blue shark (*Prionace glauca*).

мокр *sh. m. of* **мокрый.**

мокра *f.* sprinkling brush.

мокрец *m.* (vet.) malanders (eczema); —**ы** *pl.* biting midges (*Heleidae; Ceratopogonidae*).

мокриц/а *f.* (ent.) wood louse; (bot.) chickweed (*Stellaria media*); —**ы** *pl.* (ent.) Cochlidiidae; (crust.) Oniscoidea.

мокро *adv.* wet; —**ватый** *a.* wettish, moist; —**воздушный** *a.* wet-air; —**воздушный насос** water-jet air pump; —**коллодионный** *a.* (phot.) wet-plate; —**молотый** *a.* wet-ground; —**погодица** *f.* rainy weather; —**соление** *n.* brine curing.

мокр/ота *f.* wet(ness), moisture, humidity; phlegm, mucus, sputum; —**отный** *a.* mucous; —**уха** *f.* (zool.)

slug (*Limax*); (bot.) Gomphidius; **—уховые** *pl.* Gomphidiaceae; **—ый** *a.* wet, moist, damp; fluid (vacuum pump); **анализ —ым путём** wet analysis; **—ядь** *f.* dampness; rainy weather.

моксостома *f.* (ichth.) Moxostoma.

моксун *see* **муксун.**

мокт *abbr.* (**миллиоктава**) millioctave.

мокчегор *m.* mochegor whitefish (*Coregonus lavaretus pidschian mokschegor*).

мокшанский *a.* Moksha (river).

мол *m.* pier, jetty, breakwater.

мол. *abbr.* (**молекулярный**) molecular.

моляльный *see* **моляльный.**

моланна *f.* (ent.) Molanna.

моласса *f.* (geol.) molasse.

мол. в. *abbr.* (**молекулярный вес**).

молва *f.* rumor; fame, reputation.

молдав/(ан)ский *a.* (geog.) Moldavian; **—ит** *m.* (petr.) moldavite.

молдинг *m.* molding.

молдовский *a.* (geog.) Moldova, Moldavian.

МолССР *abbr.* Moldavian Socialist Soviet Republic.

молевой *a.* of **моль;** loose (log drift); **м. (лесо)сплав** drift(ing), driving, floating.

молеед *m.* (ent.) Ageniaspis fuscicollis.

молекс *m.* molecular sieve.

молектроника *f.* molecular electronics.

молекул/а *f.* molecule; **м.-акцептор** *f.* acceptor molecule; **м.-гигант** *f.* macromolecule; **м.-донор** f. donor molecule; **м.-основа** *f.* parent molecule; **—ярнодисперсный** *a.* molecular-disperse; **—ярность** *f.* molecularity.

молекулярн/ый *a.* molecular; **м. вес** molecular weight; **—ая сила** molecular force; **—ая теплоёмкость** molecular heat.

молелистовертки *see* **моли-листовертки.**

молем *adv.* loosely, separately; **сплавлять м.** *v.* drift, drive, float (logs).

моле/образные, —подобные *pl.* (ent.) Tineoidea.

молескин *m.,* **—овый** *a.* (text.) moleskin.

молестойкий *a.* mothproof.

молета *f.* (typ.) rowel.

молеточина *f.* moth hole (in cloth).

молзавод *m.* dairy plant.

моли *gen., pl., etc., of* **моль; настоящие м.** clothes moths, etc. (*Tineidae*); **морские м.** (ichth.) sea moths (*Pegasidae*).

молибдат *m.* molybdate.

молибден *m.* molybdenum, Mo; **двуокись —а** molybdenum dioxide; **окись —а** molybdenum oxide, specif. molybdenum monoxide; **хлористый м.** molybdenum chloride; **—ил** *m.* molybdenyl.

молибденист/ый *a.* molybdenum, molybdenous; **—ое железо** ferromolybdenum.

молибден/ит *m.* (min.) molybdenite; **—о—** *prefix* molybdeno—.

молибденово/кислый *a.* molybdic acid; molybdate (of); **—кислая соль** molybdate; **—свинцовистая соль** lead molybdate.

молибденов/ый *a.* molybdenum, molybdic; **м. ангидрид** molybdic anhydride, molybdenum trioxide; **м. блеск** (min.) molybdenite; **—ая кислота** molybdic acid; **соль —ой кислоты** molybdate; **—ая обманка** molybdenite; **—ая охра** (min.) molybdic ocher, molybdite.

молибд/енсодержащий a. molybdenum-containing; **—ил** *m.* molybdyl.

молибдит *m.* (min.) molybdite.

молибдо/менит *m.* (min.) molybdomenite; **—содалит** *m.* molybdosodalite; **—филлит** *m.* molybdophyllite.

молиды *pl.* (ichth.) molas (*Molidae*).

молизация *f.* molization, formation of molecules (from ions, etc.).

молизит *m.* (min.) molysite.

моли-листовертки *pl.* (ent.) Glyphipterygidae; **м.-малютки** *pl.* Nepticulidae.

молин/иевый *a.,* **—ия** *f.* (bot.) Molinia.

моли-пестрянки *pl.* (ent.) Gracilariidae.

молисмология *f.* molismology (study of ocean pollution).

молить *v.* pray, beg, entreat.

моли-чехлоноски *pl.* (ent.) Incurvariidae.

Молиша проба Molisch test.

моллеруп *m.* mechanical plunger lubricator.

молли(енезия) *f.* (ichth.) Mollienesia.

моллиров/ание *n.* (glass) sagging; **—ать** *v.* sag, sink, subside, settle; lower, reduce, depress.

моллюго *m.* (bot.) Mollugo.

моллюск *m.* (mal.) mollusk; (med.) molluscum; **—овидный** *a.* molluscoid(al); **—овый** *a.* molluscous, mollusk; **—оза** *f.* mollusk-induced disease; **—оцид** *m.* molluscicide; limacide, slug poison.

молмаш *m.* dairy machinery.

молние/видный *a.* lightning-like; **—вый** *a.* lightning; **—защита** *f.* lightning protection; **—носный** *a.* quick (as lightning); (med.) fulminant; **—отвод** *m.* lightning rod, lightning conductor; **—подобный** *a.* lightning-like.

молнийный *a.* lightning.

молния *f.* lightning; priority telegram; urgent flyer; zipper; danger arrow (on signs); *suffix* express, fast; **зигзагобразная м., линейная м.** forked lightning, lightning stroke; **расплывчатая м., сплошная м.** sheet lightning.

молод/ёжный *a.,* **—ёжь** *f.* youth, young people; **—енький** very young; **—еть** *v.* be rejuvenated; **серобелый —ик** young winter ice; **серый —ик** young ice; **—ило** *n.* (bot.) house leek (*Sempervivum*); **—ить** *v.* make young again, rejuvenate; **—ка** *f.* pullet; **—няк** *m.* underbrush, undergrowth; young stock; younger generation; **—ой** *a.* young, youthful, immature; green, raw, unseasoned; fresh, recent; new (moon); **—ость** *f.* youth(fulness); **—ь** *f.* (zool.) young ones, brood; young fish, fingerlings, fry; (bot.) new growth.

моложавый *a.* young-looking, youngish.

моложе *comp. of* **молодой,** younger.

молозив/ник *m.* colostrum-fed stock; **—ный** *a.,* **—о** *n.* colostrum, first milk.

молокан *m.* (bot.) lettuce (*Lactuca*); Mulgedium; **—ка** *see* **молочан.**

молоки *pl.* soft roe, milt (of fish); sperm.

молок/о *n.* milk; milky solution; (cement) grout; **выделение —а** lactation.

молоко/ведение *n.* milk technology; **—воз** *m.* milk truck; **—выделение** *n.* lactation; **—гонный** *a.,* **—гонное средство** (ga)lactagogue; **—мер** *m.* lacto-(denso)meter, measuring pail; **—носный** *a.* lactiferous; **—образование** *n.,* **—отдача** *f.* **—отделение** *n.* lactation; **—отсос** *m.* breast pump; drawing off milk; **—охладитель** *m.* milk cooler; **—очиститель** *m.* milk separator; **—подобный** *a.* milk-like; **—сборник** *m.* milk can; **—сливная** *f.* milk-collecting center; **—содержащий** *a.* lactiferous.

молон *m.* molon (moles/kg of solution).

молот *m.* hammer; beater; **ковка —ом** hammer forging.

молот/илка *f.* (agr.) thresher; (corn) sheller; **м.-тёрка** *f.*

hulling thresher; —**ило** *n.* chain (of flail); —**ильный** *a.* threshing; shelling; —**ильщик** *m.*, —**ильщица** *f.* threshing operator; —**ить** *v.* thresh; shell.

молотко/видный *a.* hammer-shaped; —**вый** *a.* hammer; —**вый перфоратор** jack hammer; —**образный** *a.* hammer, mallet (finger or toe).

молото/боец *m.* hammerman; —**боина** *f.*, —**вая окалина** (met.) forge scale, (hammer) scale; —**вая** *f.* forge shop; —**вище** *n.* hammer handle; —**вой** *a.* hammer; percussive (welding); —**глав** *m.* (mam.) Hypsignathus; (orn.) hammerhead (*Scopus umbretta*); —**главовые** *pl.* Scopidae; —**главый**, —**головый** *a.* hammerhead; —**головые** *see* **молот-рыбы.**

молото/к *m.* hammer; mallet; beater; **м.-перфоратор** *m.* jack hammer; **м.-ручник** hand hammer; —**чек** *dim. of* **молоток;** (anat.) malleus; clapper (of bell); **морской** —**чек** (mal.) Malleus; —**чковый**, —**чный** *a.* hammer.

молот-рыб/а *f.* (ichth.) hammerhead shark (*Sphyrna zygaena*); —**ы** *pl.* Sphyrnidae.

молот/ый *a.* milled, ground; —**ь** *v.* mill, grind, stamp (ore).

молотьба *f.* (agr.) threshing.

молотянка *f.* (bot.) Elymus arenarius.

молох *m.* (herp.) Moloch.

молочай, —**ник** *m.* (bot.) spurge (*Euphorbia*); —**ная камедь** euphorbium; —**ные** *pl.* Euphorbiaceae; —**ный** *a.* spurge.

молочен(н)ый *a.* (agr.) threshed.

молоч/ко *dim. of* **молоко;** (apid.) royal jelly; (paper) rosin size; —**ная** *f.* dairy; milk house; —**ник** *m.* dairyman, milkman; milk can; suckling; milt fish; —**ница** *f.* dairy woman; (med.; vet.) aphtha, thrush.

молочно/белый *a.* milk-white; opal (glass); —**е** *n.* dairy products; —**кальциевая соль**, —**кислый кальций** calcium lactate; —**кислый** *a.* lactic acid; lactate (of); —**кислый ряд** lactic acid series; —**кислая соль** lactate; —**кислое брожение** lactic fermentation; —**кислые бактерии**, —**кислые палочки** lactic acid bacteria, Lactobacillaceae; -**консервный** *a.* milk-processing (plant); -**мясной** *a.* dairy and meat; beef and dairy (cattle); —**сть** *f.* milkiness, lactescence; productivity (of cow); —**товарный** *a.* commercial dairy.

молочнофосфорно/кальциевая соль calcium lactophosphate; —**кислая соль** lactophosphate.

молочн/ый *a.* milk, lactic; milk-white, milky, lacteal, lactescent; opal (glass); cream (separator); dairy (cattle); butter (fat); mammary (gland); (zool.) milk-fed, suckling; **м. альбумин** lactalbumin; **м. завод** dairy; **м. камень** (min.) galactite; **м. сахар** milk sugar, lactose; —**ая кислота** lactic acid; **соль** —**ой кислоты** lactate.

молпром *m.* dairy industry.

молуккск/ий *a.* (geog.) Molucca(n); —**ие острова** Moluccas, Spice Islands.

молуранит *m.* (min.) moluranite.

молча *adv.* silently; —**ливый** *a.* silent, uncommunicative, tacit; —**ние** *n.* silence; **зона** —**ния** (rad.) blind spot, dead band; —**ть** *v.* be silent; —**щий** *a.* silent; idle, quiescent; nontransmitting (satellite).

моль *f.* mole, gram-molecule; (ent.) moth; (log) drift, float, drive; (ichth.) smelt; owsianka; minnow; **морская м.** (ichth.) sea moth (*Pegasus volitans*).

мольберт *m.* easel.

мольва *f.* (ichth.) ling (*Molva*).

Молье диаграмма Mollier's chart.

моль-малютка *f.* (ent.) pigmy moth (*Stigmella*).

мольность *f.* molarity.

мольный *a.* molar; mole (fraction).

моль-чехлоноска *f.* (ent.) Incurvaria.

молью *see* **молем.**

молюскоцид *see* **моллюскоцид.**

моляльн/ость *f.* molality; —**ый** *a.* molal.

моляр *m.* (anat.) molar tooth; —**изация** *f.* (chem.) recombination; —**ность** *f.* (chem.) molarity; —**ный** *a.* molar; —**ная доля** mole fraction.

мом *abbr.* (**миллиом**) milliohm; **Мом** *abbr.* (**мегом**) megohm.

момбин *m.* (bot.) mombin (*Spondias*).

момент *m.* moment; momentum; feature, point; factor; torque; numerical value, level; *look for idioms under more descriptive words, e.g.*, **инерции, момент** moment of inertia; **м. времени** instant; **м. количества движения** angular momentum; **в м. вылета** at the instant it leaves, as it leaves; **механический м.** momentum.

моментальн/о *adv* instantly, at once, immediately; —**ый** *a.* instantaneous; (phot.) snap(shot); —**ого действия** instantaneous, immediate.

момент/ный *a. of* **момент;** —**омер** *m.* torque meter; —**ометр** *m.* (stat.) planimeter; —**оскоп** *m.* (mach.) ignition tester.

момордика *f.* (bot.) Momordica.

момот *m.* (orn.) motmot (*Momotus*); —**овые** *pl.* Momotidae.

момский *a.* (geog.) Moma.

мон— *see* **моно—.**

монада *f.* monad, simple organism.

монаднок *m.* (geol.) monadnock.

монаксонный *a.* monaxonic, elongate.

монам/ид *m.* monamide; —**ин** monamine.

монард/а *f.* (bot.) horsemint (*Monarda*); —**ин** *m.* monardin.

монархный *a.* (bot.) monarch.

монастер *m.* (gen.) monaster.

монах *m.* monk; (geol.) pinnacle, earth pillar, column; (ichth.) damselfish (*Chromis ch.*); **морской м.** skilfish (*Erilepis zonifer*).

монац/етин *m.* monacetin, glyceryl monacetate; —**ит** *m.* (min.) monazite.

монаш/енка *f.* (ent.) nun moth (*Lymantria monacha*); —**ка** (ent.) *see* **монашенка;** (ichth.) *see* **монах.**

монгеймит *m.* (min.) monheimite.

монгол/изм *m.* (med.) mongolism, Down's syndrome; —**о(в)идный** *a.* mongoloid; —**ьский** *a.* (geog.) Mongolian.

монгумовая кислота mongumic acid.

Монда газ Mond gas, semi-water gas.

монезия *f.* (bot.) Monesia.

монель-металл *m.* Monel metal (alloy).

монера *f.* (prot.) Monera.

монета *f.* coin.

монетит *m.* (min.) monetite.

монет/ница *f.* coin box; —**ный** *a.* monetary; coin; troy (weight); —**ный двор** mint; —**овидный**, —**ообразный** *a.* nummular, coin-shaped.

монж/у, —**ю(с)** *m.* montejus, air lift; (sugar) juice pump.

мониез/иоз *m.* (vet.) Moniezia infection; —**ия** *f.* Moniesia (tapeworm).

монил/иаз *m.* (med.; phyt.) moniliasis, Monilia infection; —**иальный** *a.* monilial; —**иоз** *m.* (phyt.) brown rot; —**иевые** *pl.* Moniliaceae (fungi); —**ия** *f.* Monilia.

монимолит *m.* (min.) monimolite.

монит *m.* (min.) monite.

монитор *m.* monitor; —**инг** *m.* monitoring.

моно— *prefix* mono— (one, single); —**азокраситель**

m. monoazo dye; **—азосоединение** *n.* monoazocompound; **—алкилировать** *v.* monoalkylate; **—амин** *m.* monoamine; **—аминокислота** *f.* monoamino acid; **—аммонии** *m.* monoammonium; **—атомный** *a.* monatomic; monovalent; monohydric (alcohol); **—ацетат** *m.* monoacetate; **—ацилировать** *v.* monoacylate; **—бластический** *a.* (embr.) monoblastic; **—блок** *m.*, **—блочный** *a.* monoblock unit; (respirator) feed gear; (av.) monocoque.

монобром— *prefix* monobrom(o)—; **—ид** *m.* monobromide; **—камфора** *f.* monobromated camphor; **—уксусный** *a.* monobromoacetic (acid).

моно/вакуумметр *m.* compound gage; **—валентный** *a.* monovalent; **—волокно** *n.* monofilament; **—галогенопроизводное** *n.* monohalogen derivative; **—гам** *m.* monogamist; **—гамический** *a.* monogamous; **—гамия** *f.* monogamy; **—ген** *m.* (chem.; immun.) monogen; **—генез** *m.* monogenesis; **—генный** *a.* (gen.; math.) monogenic; monofactorial; (geol.) monogene; **—геноидоз** *m.* (vet.) Monogenea infection; **—гибрид** *m.*, **—гибридный** *a.* (gen.) monohybrid; **—гидрат** *m.* monohydrate; **—гира** *f.* (cryst.) monogyre; **—гнатовые** *pl.* (ichth.) Monognathidae; **—гония** *f.* monogony, asexual reproduction; **—графия** *f.* monograph; **—дисперсный** *a.* monodisperse; **—доминантная ассоциация** (bot.) consociation; **—доминантное сообщество** plant community; **—за** *f.* monose, monosaccharide; **—замещённое** *n.* monosubstituted product; **—зиготный** *a.* (gen.) monozygotic.

моно/импульс *m.* single giant pulse (of laser); **—иодид** *m.* monoiodide; **—иод(о)** —monoiod(o)—; **—калий** *m.* monopotassium; **—кальций** *m.* monocalcium; **—карбоновый** *a.* monocarboxylic (acid); **—карпий, —карпик** *m.*, **—карпическое растение** monocarpic plant; **—кись** *f.* monoxide.

моноклин/аль *f.*, **—альная складка** (geol.) monocline, monoclinal fold; **—альный** *a.* monoclinal; **—ический**, **—ный** *a.* (cryst.) monoclinic; **угол —ности** axial angle.

монокок *m.* (av.) monocoque.

монокристалл *m.* monocrystal, single crystal; **—ический** *a.* monocrystalline.

моноксенический *a.* monoxenous (parasites).

моно/культура *f.* one-crop system, monoculture; **—куляр** *m.*, **—кулярный** *a.* (opt.) monocular.

монолит *m.* monolith; (soil) core sample; slab; (geod.) marker; **—ность** *f.* solidity, impermeability, density; homogeneity, uniformity; **—ный**, **—овый** *a.* monolithic; glacier (iceberg); slab; (concrete) cast in place.

моном *m.* (math.) monomial.

мономагний *m.* monomagnesium.

мономер *m.* monomer; **—ность** *f.* monomerism; **—ный** *a.* monomeric.

монометаллический *a.* monometallic.

монометил *m.*, **—овый** *a.* monomethyl; **—ировать** *v.* monomethylate.

мономолекулярный *a.* monomolecular; **м. слой** monolayer.

мономор/иум *m.* (ent.) Monomorium; **—фный** *a.* monomorphous, monomorphic.

моно/надсерная кислота permonosulfuric acid, Caro's acid; **—натриевый** *a.* monosodium; **—непредельный** *a.* monounsaturated; **—нитрировать** *v.* mononitrate; **—нитропроизводное** *n.* mononitro derivative; **—нить** *f.* (plastics) monofilament; **—нуклеарный** *a.* mononuclear; **—нуклеоз** *m.* (med.) mononucleosis.

мононх *m.* (zool.) Mononchus.

моно/окись *f.* monoxide; **—плакофоры** *pl.* (mal.) Monoplacophora; **—план** *m.* (av.) monoplane; **—плегия** *f.* (med.) monoplegia; **—плоид** *m.*, **—плоидный** *a.* (gen.) monoploid; **—подий** *m.* (bot.) monopode.

монопол/изация *f.* monopolization; **—изировать** *v.* monopolize; **—ия** *f.* monopoly; exclusive domain; **—ь** *m.* monopole; **—ьный** *a.* monopolistic, exclusive; **—ярный** *a.* monopolar.

монопропил *m.*, **—овый** *a.* monopropyl.

монорельс *m.*, **—овый** *a.* monorail, monorail overhead transporter.

моно/сахарид *m.* monosaccharide; **—силан** *m.* monosilane, silicomethane; **—симметрический** *a.* monosymmetric; **—скоп** *m.* monoscope; **—слой** *m.* monolayer; **—сомик** *m.* (gen.) monosome; **—спермия** *f.* (embr.) monospermy; **—спиросоединение** *n.* monospiro compound; **—споровый** *a.* monosporous, singlespore; **—сульфировать** *v.* monosulf(on)ate; **—терпен** *m.* monoterpene.

монотип *m.* (biol.; typ.) monotype; **—ист** *m.* monotype operator; **—ный** *a.* monotypic; monotype (metal).

монотонн/о *adv.* monotonically, uninterruptedly; monotonously, steadily; **—ость** *f.* monotony; **—ый** *a.* monotonous, uniform, steady; (math.) monotonic, monotone.

монотопливо *n.* monopropellant.

монотрихи *pl.* (bact.) Monotricha.

монотроп/изм *m.*, **—ия** *f.* monotropism; **—ный** *a.* monotropic.

моно/фаг *m.* monophage, monophagous parasite; **—фактор(иаль)ный** *a.* (gen.) unifactorial; **—фенолоксидаза** *f.* monophenoloxidase; **—филетический** *a.* (gen.) monophyletic; **—фосфат** *m.* monophosphate; **—фторид** *m.* monofluoride; **—хазий** *m.* (bot.) monochasium; **—хамус** *m.* (ent.) Monochamus; **—хлорид** *m.* monochloride; **—хлоруксусный** *a.* monochloroacetic; **—хорд** *m.* (phys.) monochord.

монохром/атизация *f.* monochromatization; **—атический** *a.* monochromatic; **—атичность** *f.* monochromatism; **—атор** *m.* monochromator; **—ный** *a.* monochrome.

моно/циклический *a.* monocyclic; **—цит** *m.* (anat.) monocyte; **—эдр** *m.* (cryst.) monohedron; **—эдрический** *a.* monohedral; **—энергетический** *a.* monoenergetic; **—энергетичность** *f.* energy homogeneity.

моноэтил *m.*, **—овый** *a.* monoethyl.

моноэфир *m.* monoester; monoether.

монпа/нсье, —сье *n.* drops, lozenges.

Монреаль (geog.) Montreal.

монроэнский подъярус (geol.) Monroan or Monroe substage.

монстера *f.* (bot.) Monstera.

монтаж *m.* assembling, etc., *see* **монтировать;** assembly; erection; (aerial) mosaic; (phot.) montage; **м. на стойке** rack mounting; **сварка на —е** field welding; **схема —а** hook-up; **м. проводов** (elec.) wiring; **—ная** *f.* assembly room; (cinematography) clipping room.

монтажн/ик *see* **монтёр; —о-наладочный** *a.* installation and check-out (work); **—ый** *a. of* **монтаж; —ая схема** (elec.) wiring diagram, hook-up.

монтан/а-воск, —вакс *m.*, **—ский воск** montan wax; **—иловый спирт** montanyl alcohol, nonacosanol; **—ит** *m.* (min.) montanite; **—овая кислота** montanic acid; **—селитра** *f.* ammonium sulfate-nitrate; **—ский слой** (geol.) Montanan subdivision.

монте *n.* (bot.) monte, xerophytic scrub.

монтебразит *m.* (min.) montebrasite.

монтеж/у, —ю *see* **монжу.**

Монте-Карло метод (nucl.) Monte-Carlo method.

монтёр *m.* assembler, erector, mounter, rigger, adjuster; (engine) fitter; repairman, mechanic; electrician; (cable) splicer; **линейный м., м.-линейщик** *m.* line(s)man; **м.-эксплуатационник** *m.* maintenance man; —**ский** *a.* fitter's, lineman's; tool (case).

монтжюс *see* **монжу.**

монтипора *f.* Montipora (coral).

монтиров/ание *n.* assembling, etc., *see v.;* assembly; —**анный** *a.* assembled, etc., *see v.;* —**ать** *v.* assemble, erect, mount, install, arrange, fit, fit up, build up, rig up, set (up); connect up, wire; compile; (cinema) edit; —**ка** *f.,* —**очный** *a.* assembling, etc., *see v.;* —**щик** *see* **монтёр.**

монт/ицеллит, —**ичеллит** *m.* (min.) monticellite; —**мориллонит** *m.* montmorillonite; —**ройдит** *m.* montroydite.

Монтье синий Monthier's blue.

монумент *m.* monument; —**альный** *a.* monumental.

монурон *m.* Monuron (herbicide).

монц/ия *f.* (bot.) Montia; —**онит** *m.* (petr.) monzonite; —**онитовый** *a.* monzonitic.

мончикит *m.* (petr.) monchiquite.

Монье свод Monier's arch.

Моора фильтрпресс Moore filter press.

Мооса шкала *see* **Моса шкала.**

мопед *m.* moped.

МОП-транзистор *m.* metal-oxide semiconductor transistor, MOS-transistor.

мор *m.* pestilence, plague, epidemic.

мора *f.* (ichth.) Mora; mora (*Mora excelsa* tropical rain forest).

Мора соль Mohr's salt, ferrous ammonium sulfate (hexahydrate).

моравский *a.* (geog.) Moravian.

мораль *f.* morals, ethics; —**ный** *a.* moral, ethical; mental; —**ный износ,** —**ное изнашивание** (mach.) obsolescence; —**ное состояние** morale.

мораторий *m.* (com.) moratorium.

морвонговые *pl.* (ichth.) morwongs (*Cheilodactylidae*).

морг *m.* morgue; unit of land measurement (approx. 0.5 hectares); blink.

морганида *f.* (gen.) morgan (unit).

моргание *n.* blinking; flickering.

морганит *m.* (min.) morganite.

морг/ать, —**нуть** *v.* blink; flicker.

морда *f.* muzzle, snout.

МордАССР *abbr.* Mordvinian Autonomous Soviet Socialist Republic, Mordovian ASSR.

морденит *m.* (min.) mordenite.

мордовник *m.* (bot.) globe thistle (*Echinops*).

мордовский *a.* (geog.) Mordovian.

мор/е *n.* sea; —**ем** by sea, by water; **к** —**ю** seaward; **каменное м.** (geol.) extensive stone placer; **удалённый от** —**я** inland; —**еведение** *n.* oceanography.

море— *prefix* thalass(o)—, sea; —**любивый** *a.* thalassophilous.

морена *f.* (geol.) moraine.

морен/ие *n.* starving, etc., *see* **морить;** —**ный** *a.* starved, etc., *see* **морить;** (geol.) morainic.

моренозит *m.* (min.) morenosite.

морён/ый *a.* thin, starved; treated, seasoned; steeped, stained, fumed; —**ые изделия** fumed unglazed earthenware.

мореперестрковые *pl.* (zool.) Pennatulaceae.

мореплав/ание *n.* navigation, seafaring; —**атель** *m.* navigator, seaman; —**ательный** *a.* nautical.

морепродукты *pl.* seafood.

моретрясение *n.* seaquake.

мореход, —**ец** *m.* seaman; —**ность** *f.* seaworthiness; —**ный** *a.* seaworthy, seagoing, seafaring; —**ство** *n.* navigation, seafaring.

морж *m.,* —**овый** *a.* (mam.) walrus (*Odobenus rosmarus*); —**и,** —**овые** *pl.* Odobenidae; —**иха** *f.* walrus cow; —**онок** *m.* walrus calf.

Морзе азбука Morse code.

морз/ист *m.* Morse code operator; —**янка** *f.* Morse code.

морил/ка *f.* (wood) stain; (dyeing) mordant; specimen jar, insect-killing jar; (sericulture) stoving room; —**ьный** *a.* mordant; stoving, stifling.

морин *m.* morin, pentahydroxyflavone.

моринг/а *f.* (bot.) Moringa; —**адубильный** *a.* moringatannic (acid); —**иевые,** —**овые** *pl.* (ichth.) worm eels (*Moringuidae*); (bot.) Moringaceae; —**уа** *f.* (ichth.) Moringua.

моринд/а *f.* (bot.) Morinda; —**овый** *a.* ben (oil); —**ин** *m.* morindin.

морион *m.* (min.) morion.

мористый *a.* far out at sea.

морить *v.* starve, exhaust; exterminate, kill; fume; stain (wood).

моричаль, морича-лес *m.* (silv.) morichales.

морка *f.* (sericulture) mortifying.

морков/ка *f.* carrot; —**ник** *m.* carrot dish; (bot.) Silaum; —**ница** *f.* Astrodaucus; —**ь** *f.* carrot (*Daucus*).

мормир/овые *pl.* snoutfishes (*Mormyridae*); —**опс** *m.* Mormyrops; —**ус** *m.* Mormyrus.

мормышка *f.* (fishing) artificial lure.

моров/ой *a.* pestilential; —**ая язва,** —**ое поветрие** pestilence, plague.

моровые *pl.* (ichth.) Moridae.

мороду/нка *f.* (orn.) terek (*Xenus cinereus*); —**шка** *f.* Baikal teal (*Anas formosa*).

морожен/ица *f.* ice cream freezer; —**ный** *a.* frozen; —**ое** *n.* ice cream; —**ый** *a.* frozen, frost-bitten.

мороз *m.* frost; frosted finish; silvering (glass defect); **наводить м.** *v.* frost; **побить** —**ом** *v.* freeze; —**ик** *m.* light frost; —**илка** *f.,* —**ильный аппарат** freezer; —**ильный** *a.* freezing; refrigerated, refrigerator; —**ильщик** *m.* refrigerator ship; —**ить** *v.* freeze, congeal, chill; —**ник** *m.* (bot.) hellebore (*Helleborus*); —**ный** *a.* frost(y); —**обоина,** —**овина** *f.* (geol.) frost cleft, frost fissure; (bot.) frost crack; —**обой** *m.* winter-killing; —**обойность** *f.* frost damage; —**бойный** *a.* frost damaged; frost (crack); —**обойная котловина** frost pocket; —**овыносливый** *a.* frostproof.

морозостойк/ий *a.* antifreeze, nonfreezing, cold-resistant; (bot.) winter-resistant, hardy, —**ость** *f.* resistance to cold; hardiness.

морозо/упорный *a.* frost-resisting, frost-proof, —**устойчивый** *see* **морозостойкий.**

морос/ить *v.* drizzle; —**ь,** —**ящий дождь** drizzle, light rain.

морошка *f.* (bot.) cloudberry (*Rubus chamaemorus*).

морруиновый *a.* morrhuic (acid).

морс *m.* fruit juice.

морск/ой *a.* sea, marine, maritime; nautical; naval; beach (sand); offshore (drilling); **м. ангел** monkfish; **м. воробей** lumpfish; **м. желудь** (zool.) barnacle; **м. клей** marine glue; **м. конёк** sea horse; **м. лук** (bot.) squill (*Scilla maritima*); **м. путь** shipping lane, seaway; **м. сухарь** hardtack, ship's biscuit; **м. флот** merchant marine; **м. шёлк** byssus silk; —**ая болезнь** seasickness; —**ая звезда** starfish; —**ая капуста** *see* **ка-**

тран; **—ая пенка** (min.) sea foam, sepiolite; **—ая свинка** (mam.) guinea pig; **—ая свинья** porpoise; **—ая синь** marine blue; **—ая трава** (bot.) grass wrack (*Zostera marina*); **—ие лилии** (zool.) sea lilies (*Crinoidea*); **—им путём** by sea; **—ое дело** maritime industry; **—ое ухо, —ое ушко** (mal.) abalone.

мортир/а *f.* (mil.) mortar; bossing (of propeller shaft); **—ка** *f.* rifle grenade discharger; **—ный** *a. of* **мортира.**

мортук *m.* (bot.) Eremopyron.

морула *f.* (embr.) morula.

морф/а *f.* (taxonomy) morphe, form; **—изм** *m.* (math.) (poly)morphism; **—ий, —ин** *m.* morphine; **—инизм** *m.* morphine addiction; **—инист** *m.* morphine addict; **—инный, —иновый** *a.* morphine.

морфо— *prefix* morph(o)— (shape, form, structure); **—вид** *m.* morphological species; **—генез** *m.* morphogenesis; **—з** *m.* morphosis, tissue formation; **—лин** *m.* morpholine.

морфолог *m.* morphologist; **—ический** *a.* morphological; **—ия** *f.* morphology.

морфометр/ический *a.* morphometrical, form-measuring; **—ия** *f.* morphometry.

морфотроп/изм *m.* (cryst.) morphotropism; **—ия** *f.* morphotropy; **—ный** *a.* morphotropic.

морщ/ина *f.* wrinkle, crease, fold, pucker, crinkle, furrow, ridge; (casting) lap; **—инистость** *f.* rugosity, wrinkle; **—инистый** *a.* wrinkled, creased; rugose; **—инить** *see* **морщить;** **—инка** *dim. of* **морщина; —инник** *m.* (ent.) Helophorus; **—ины** *pl.* ridges, rugae; **—ить** *v.* wrinkle, pucker, gather, crinkle, crumple; corrugate; **—иться** *v.* wrinkle up, shrivel; crumple.

моря *gen. and pl. of* **море; —к** *m.* seaman.

морянка *f.* (met.) blister steel; (orn.) marine duck (*Clangula hyemalis*).

МОС *abbr.* (**Международная организация для стандартизации**) International Organization for Standardization.

Моса шкала твёрдости (min.) Mohs hardness scale.

москатель *f.,* **—ный товар** commercial chemicals such as paints, oils, glues.

Москва Moscow.

москвич *m.* Muscovite; make of car; **—а** *f.* Muscovite.

москит *m.,* **—ный** *a.,* **м.-переносчик** *m.* (ent.) sandfly (*Phlebotomus*).

москов/ка *f.* (orn.) coal tit (*Parus ater*); **—ский** *a.* (geog.) Moscow; (geol.) Moscovian.

мос/лак, —ол *m.* (anat.) fetlock joint; protruding (hip) bone.

моссит *m.* (min.) mossite.

мост *m.* bridge; deck; (car) axle; (steering) linkage; (anat.) pons; **задний м.** rear-axle assembly; **построить м. через** *v.* bridge, span; **—ик** *dim. of* **мост;** footbridge, walkway, catwalk; (naut.) bridge; (welding) junction; cross bar; (polymer) cross link; **—иковый** *a.* bridge, bridging; cross-linkage; bridgehead (atoms); **—ообразующий** *a.* bridging.

мостить *v.* pave.

мостки *pl.* cat walk, gangway, footpath; bridge, platform, scaffold; (pipe) rack.

мосто/вая *f.* pavement, paved road; **—видный** *a.* (hist.) pavement (epithelium); **—вина** *f.* bridge board; **—вой** *a.* bridge; pavement; (anat.) pontine; overhead, traveling (crane); **—вые весы** platform scales or balance, weigh bridge; **—вщик** *m.* paver, road worker.

мостовье *n.* (leather) crust.

мосток *dim. of* **мост;** *see* **мостик.**

мосто/-мозжечковый *a.* (anat.) pontocerebellar; **—строение** *n.* bridge building.

мост-подмости *m.* scaffold bridge; **м.-транспортёр** *m.* transporter bridge; **м.-трубопровод** *m.* aqueduct (bridge).

мостящий *a.* paving; bridging; make-before-break (contact).

мот/алка *f.* reel(er), winder, coiler, coiling machine; (film) rewinder; **—альница** *f.* reel, winder; **—альный** *a.* reeling, winding; **—ание** *n.* reeling, etc., *see v.*; **—анный** *a.* wound, coiled; **—ать** *v.* reel, wind, coil; shake, wag; waste; **—аться** *v.* dangle, hang loose; hurry about.

мотель *m.* motel.

мотив *m.* motive, reason, cause, ground; **—ировать** *v.* motivate; justify; **—ировка** *f.* motivation, motives, reason, justification; (min.) motifs.

мотил *m.* antiknock motor fuel containing iron pentacarbonyl.

мот/ка *see* **мотание;** *gen. of* **моток; —нуть** *see* **мотать; —ня** *f.* (fishing) bag (of a seine); belly (of a trawl).

мото— *prefix* motor, power; mechanical; motorized; motorcycle; **—бур** *m.* power drill; portable drilling rig.

мотовил/о *n.* reel, reeling frame, swift, coiler; **—ьный** *a.* reeling.

мото/воз *m.* motor trolley; diesel switcher, switch engine; **—гондола** *f.* (av.) pod; engine nacelle; **—дрезина** *f.* motorized handcar; **—дром** *m.* motorcycle racing and testing grounds; **—инструмент** *m.* power tool.

моток *m.* skein, hank, bundle, cut; reel; *gen. pl. of* **мотка.**

мото/коляска *f.* motorized wheelchair; side car (of motorcycle); **—компрессор** *m.* engine compressor unit.

мотолин *m.* antiknock motor fuel containing 0.1% iron pentacarbonyl.

мото/лодка *f.* motorboat; **—лопата** *f.* power shovel, excavator; **—мех** *m.* (mil.) mechanized forces; **—механизированный** *a.* mechanized; **—нарты** *pl.* snowmobile; **—неврон** *m.* (cyt.) motoneuron; **—пехота** *f.* motorized infantry; **—пила** *f.* power saw; **—планёр** *m.* powered glider; **—помпа** *f.* motor-driven pump.

мотор *m.* motor, engine; car, automobile; **—ама** *f.* (av.) engine mount(ing); **м.-вагон** *m.* motor coach; **м.-вентилятор** *m.* blower, blast engine; **м.-генератор** *m.* (elec.) dynamo, generator; **м.-насос** *see* **мотопомпа.**

мото/ресурс *m.* motor potential, motor capacity; service life; **межремонтный м.** overhaul period; **—ризация** *f.* motorization; **—ризованный** *a.* motorized; **—ризовать** *v.* motorize; **—рика** *f.* (zool.) motor system; **—рист** *m.* motor mechanic, driver; **—рка** *f.* motor boat; (embr.) movement; **—рыболовный** *a.* motorized fishing (station); **—рный** *a. of* **мотор; —ролер** *m.* motor scooter; **—р-редуктор** *m.* geared motor; **—рчик** *dim. of* **мотор; —строение** *n.,* **—строительный** *a.* motor building.

мототерапия *f.* exercise therapy.

мотоцикл, —ет *m.,* **—етка** *f.,* **—етный** *a.* motorcycle.

моточасть *f.* (mil.) motorized division.

моточек *dim. of* **моток.**

мотошина *f.* motorcycle tire.

моттовский *a.* (phys.) Mott (scattering).

моты/га *f.* (agr.) hoe, mattock; scraper; (horse-drawn) cultivator; **вращающаяся м.** rototiller; **—жение** *n.* hoeing, hacking; **—жить** *v.* hoe; hack; **—жный** *a. of* **мотыга.**

мотыл/ёк *m.* (ent.) moth, butterfly; (ichth.) Pantodon; **кукурузный м., стеблевой м.** European corn borer (*Pyrausta nubilalis*); **луговой м.** beet webworm (*Loxostege sticticalis*); **—и** *pl.* midges (*Tendipedidae*);

—ица f. bee moth (*Galleria mellonella*); —ь m. crank, handle; (ent.) midge larva; —ьки pl. pyralid moths (*Pyralid(id)ae*).

мотыльков/ые pl. (bot.) Papilionaceae; (ichth.) Pantodontidae; —ый a. butterfly, papilionaceous; —**образ-ный** a. butterfly(-shaped).

мофетта f. (geol.) mofette.

мох m. (bot.) moss (*Muscus*); **болотный м.** peat moss, sphagnum; **дубовый м.** oak moss (*Evernia orunastii*); **исландский м.** Iceland moss (*Cetraria islandica*).

Мохаве (geog.) Mohave (desert).

мохарр/а f. (ichth.) mojarra; —**овые** pl. Gerridae.

мохиловый a. mochyl (alcohol).

мохнат/ка f. (ent.) Lagria; —**ки** pl. Lagriidae; —**оголов(чат)ый** a. shaggy-headed; —**ость** f. shagginess; —**ый** a. hairy, shaggy, long-napped; Turkish (towel); (bot.) pilose.

мохноногий a. shaggy-legged; (orn.) feather-legged.

мохо see **мого**.

мохо— prefix bry(o)— (moss); —**видные** pl. bryophytes; —**видный** a. mossy, muscoid, moss-like; —**вина** f. (bot.) mushroom (*Boletus circinans*); (min.) moss agate; —**вой** a. moss(y); —**головый** a. mossy-head(ed).

мохол m. (geol.) mohole, Mohorovicic hole.

мохообразн/ые pl. (bot.) Bryophyta; —**ый** a. moss-like, mossy, bryophytic.

моцион m. walk (for exercise).

моч/а f. urine; **анализ —и** urinalysis; **выделение —и** urinary secretion.

моча/га, —жина f. swampy hollow, pool (in bog).

мочал/ина f. filament, fiber; —**истый** a. fiber-like; —**ить** v. separate into fibers; —**ка** f. mop; —**о** n., —**ьный** a. (soaked) bast, fiber.

моче— prefix ur(in)o—, urine; —**вина** f. urea, carbamide; —**вина-корм** a high-protein feed; —**вино-альдегидный полимер** amino plastic; —**винофор-мальдегидный** a. ureaformaldehyde; —**воаммоние-вая соль** ammonium urate.

мочев/ой a. urine, urinary; **м. камень** (med.) urolith; **м. канал** (anat.) ureter; **м. пузырь** bladder; **воспаление —ого пузыря** (med.) cystitis; —**ая кислота** uric acid, trioxypurine; **соль —ой кислоты** urate.

мочево/калиевая соль, —кислый калий potassium urate; —**кислый** a. uric acid; urate (of); —**кислая соль** urate.

моче/выделение n. urination; —**гон** m. (bot.) Melittis; —**гонный** a., —**гонное средство** diuretic.

моче/гор see **мокчегор**; —**жина** see **мочажина**.

мочеизнурение n. (med.) diabetes.

мочеиспуск/ание n. urination; —**ательный** a. urinating; —**ательный канал** (anat.) urethra.

мочек gen. pl. of **мочка**.

моче/каменная болезнь (med.) urinary calculosis, urolithiasis; —**кислый** see **мочевокислый**; —**кровие** n. (med.) uremia.

мочен/ец m. retted flax; —**ие, —ье** n. wetting, etc., see **мочить**; urination; preservation (of fruit); —**ный, мочёный** a. wetted, etc., see **мочить**; water-retted (flax).

моче/образование n. urine formation, uropoiesis; —**об-разующий** a. urine-producing, uropoietic; —**отделе-ние** n. urinary excretion; —**отделительный** a. excretory; urinary (organs); —**половой** a. ur(in)ogenital; venereal (disease); —**приёмник** m. urinal; —**сбор-ник, —собиратель** m. cesspool; —**точник** m. (anat.) ureter; —**точниково—** prefix uretero—, ureter; —**точниково-пузырный** a. ureterovesical; —**точни-ковый** a. ureteral, ureteric.

мочил/ище, —о n. soaking pit, retting box; —**ьный** a. wetting, steeping, soaking, retting; —**ьня** see **мочило**.

мочить v. wet, moisten, soak, steep, drench, macerate; ret (fiber); —**ся** v. get wet; urinate.

моч/ище see **мочало**; —**ка** see **мочение;** lobe (of ear), lobulus; filament, thread, fiber; —**коватый** a. fibrous, filamentous, fascicular, tufty; —**ливый** a. very moist, wet.

мочь v. be able; f. strength, might.

мошек gen. pl. of **мошка**.

мошенничество n. swindle, fraud.

мошк/а f. (ent.) gnat, black fly (*Simulium*); (glass) seed; —**ара** f. swarm of midges; —**и** pl. Simuliidae.

мош/на f. pouch, bag; —**онка** f. (anat.) scrotum; —**он-ковидный** a. scrotiform, pouch-shaped; —**оночный** a. scrotal.

мощен sh. m. of **мощный**.

мощ/ение n. paving; —**ён(н)ый** a. paved.

мощи gen., pl., etc., of **мощь**.

мощность f. power, force, vigor; horsepower; duty (of engine), efficiency, output, capacity; yield (of nuclear explosion); rating; (dose) rate; potency; (elec.) potential, capacity; numerical abundance; girth (of tree); (geol.) width, depth, thickness, magnitude; (acous.) volume; thrust (of rocket); (math.) cardinal number (of a group); —**и** pl. industrial plants, machinery, etc.; **м. в лошадиных силах** horsepower; **м. на выходе** output; **м. установки** plant capacity; **большой —и** high-power, high-duty; **коэффициент —и** (elec.) power factor; **малой —и** low-power, low-duty; **на полную м.** at (full) capacity, at full power, in full operation; **отбор —и, отъём —и** (mach.) power take-off, p.t.o.; **переданная м., подведённая м., поглощённая м., сообщённая м.** power input; **полной —ью** full power; **с повышенной —ью** up-rated; **с пониженной —ью** down-rated.

мощный a. powerful, vigorous, energetic; high-power, high-duty, heavy-duty; thick, sturdy; potent; strong, dominant; heavy, big (run of fish); deep (soil); aggressive (root system); (rad.) power, output (tube); **м. си-ловой** a. superpower.

мощь f. power, vigor, strength.

МОЭ abbr. (**медноокисный элемент**) copper oxide cell.

мо/ют pr. 3 pl. of **мыть**; —**ющий** a. washing; —**ющая способность** detergency; —**ющее средство** detergent, cleanser; —**ющийся** a. washable; —**я** pr. ger. washing; pron. my.

МПА abbr. (**мясопептонный агар**) beef-extract agar; **МПБ** (**мясопептонный бульон**) beef-extract broth.

мПВ abbr. (**морской полярный воздух**) maritime polar air; **МПВ** abbr. (**малая постоянная времени**) small time constant; (**метод полей времён**) time fields method; (**метод преломлённых волн**) refraction method; **МПВО** (**местная противовоздушная оборона**) local air defense.

мпз abbr. (**миллипуаз**) millipoise; (**миллипьеза**) millipieze; **МПЗ** abbr. (**магнитное поле земли**) magnetic field of the earth.

МПП abbr. (**метод переходных процессов**) transient processes method.

м. пр. abbr. (**между прочим**) by the way.

МПУ abbr. (**магнитный путевой угол**) magnetic track angle; (**максимальный подпорный уровень**) top water level; (**матричное печатающее устройство**) dot-matrix printer.

мпуаз abbr. (**миллипуаз**) millipoise.

мр abbr. (**миллирентген**) milliroentgen.

м.р. *abbr.* (**малорастворимый**) slightly soluble; **Мр.** (**месторождение**) (oil) field.

мрад *abbr.* (**миллирад**) millirad.

мрак *m.* darkness, gloom, obscurity; —**обесный** *a.* (educ.) anti-progress, obscurant(ic).

мрамор *m.* marble; **под м.** marbled (surface); —**ировать** *v.* marble, marbelize; —**ник** *m.* (ichth.) cabezon (*Scorpaenichthys marmorata*); —**никовые** *pl.* Scorpaenichthyidae; —**ность** *f.* (phyt.) marbling; mottling (of teeth); —**ный** *a.* marble; —**овидный, —оподобный** *a.* marble-like, marbly, marbled, marmoreal, marmoric; —**щик** *m.* marble worker.

мрасский *a.* (geog.) Mras-Su.

мрач/иться *v.* grow despondent; —**неть** *v.* darken; —**ный** *a.* gloomy, dark, dismal, dim; —**ное помешательство** (med.) melancholia.

МРВ *abbr.* (**метод рефрагированных волн**) refringent wave method.

мрг *abbr.* (**мириаграмм**) myriagram.

МРГИ *abbr.* (**метод рассеянного гаммаизлучения**) gamma-ray scattering method.

мрд, мрезерфорл *abbr.* (**миллирезерфорд**) millirutherford.

МРЗ *abbr.* (**морозостойкость**) frost resistance; (**моторно-ремонтный завод**) motor repair plant.

мригал/а, —ь *f.* (ichth.) mrigala (*Cirrhina mrigala*).

мрм *abbr.* (**мириаметр**) myriameter; **МРМ** *abbr.* (**машиноремонтная мастерская**) machine repair shop.

МРС *abbr.* (**машиноремонтная станция**) machine repair station; (**механизм регулирования скорости**) speed control mechanism.

мрячная кость cartilage bone.

мсб *abbr.* (**миллистильб**) millistilb.

м-св *abbr.* (**метр-свеча**) meter-candle.

МСГ *abbr.* (**меланоцитостимулирующий гормон**) melanocyte-stimulating hormone, MSH.

мсек *abbr.* (**миллисекунда**) millisecond; **м/сек** *abbr.* (**метров в секунду**) meters per second.

МСК *abbr.* (**метод скользящих контактов**) sliding contact method; Scratcher electrode logging method; **МСКП** (**морской санитарно-контрольный пупкт**) maritime disease control point.

МСН *abbr.* MSN, copolymer of methyl methacrylate, styrene and acrylonitrile.

МССР *see* **МолССР.**

МСт, МСТ *abbr.* (**метеорологическая станция**) weather station; **мст** (**миллистокс**) millistoke.

мстить *v.* revenge oneself.

МСУ *abbr.* (**международная система уравнений**) IFC Formulation.

МСХ *abbr.* (**Министерство сельского хозяйства**) Ministry of Agriculture.

Мт *abbr.* (**мегатонна**) megaton.

МТЗ *abbr.* (**магнитотеллурическое зондирование**) magnetotelluric sounding; (**машинно-тракторная мастерская**) machine and tractor shop.

МТКК *abbr.* (**многоразовый транспортный космический корабль**) space shuttle.

МТМ *abbr.* (**машинно-тракторная мастерская**) machine and tractor shop.

МТП *abbr.* (**магнитотеллурическое профилирование**) magnetotelluric profiling.

МТР *abbr.* (**магнитный термоядерный реактор**) magnetic thermonuclear reactor.

МТС *abbr.* (**материально-техническое снабжение**) materials and equipment supply; (**машинотрактор-**

ная станция) machine and tractor service station; (**метр-тонна-секунда**) meter-ton-second; (**междугородная телефонная станция**) long-distance exchange.

МТТ *abbr.* (**метод теллурических токов**) telluric current method.

МТФ *abbr.* (**молочно-товарная ферма**) commercial dairy farm.

Муавра формула (math.) Moivre formula.

муар *m.* moire, watered fabric; moiré, watered effect; wrinkle finish, ripple finish; **фигура —а** (cryst.) moire pattern; —**ировать** *v.* water, moiré (fabric); —**овый** *a.* moiré.

муассан/ит *m.* (min.) moissanite; —**овский** *a.* Moissan (process).

мУВ *abbr.* (**морской умеренный воздух**) maritime moderate air.

мугилоидовые *pl.* (ichth.) Mugiloididae.

мугожарский *a.* (geog.) Mugozharyi.

мударовая кислота mudaric acid.

мудрено *adv.* ingeniously, subtly; it is difficult; **м. ли, не м.(, что)** no wonder (that).

мудрёный ingenious, clever; difficult, abstruse, complicated; strange, incomprehensible; astonishing, surprising; tricky.

мудр/ость *f.* wisdom; **зуб —ости** wisdom tooth; —**ый** *a.* wise, sage.

муж *m.* husband; —**еподобность, —естественность** *f.* masculinity (in a female), virilism; —**еподобный, —естественный** *a.* masculine, manly, virile.

муж/ик *m.* peasant; —**ской** *a.* masculine, male; (bot.) staminate (hemp); —**ская особь** male; —**ская половая клетка** sperm(atozoon); —**чина** *m.* man, male; —**чинский** *a.* male.

музарин *m.* musarin (antibiotic).

муз/еевед *m.* curator; —**ей** *m.*, —**ейный** *a.* museum; —**ейный штам** (biol.) stock strain.

музыка *f.* music; —**льный** *a.* musical.

муйский *a.* (geog.) Muya.

мука *f.* flour, meal; (potato) starch; (stone) dust; suffering, torture; **известковая м.** ground limestone; **торфяная м.** powdered peat; **м.-крупчатка** *f.* superfine flour.

муко— *prefix* muco— (mucus); flour, meal; —**вещество** *n.* mucoid substance; —**ед** *m.* grain beetle (*Laemophloeus*); —**за** *f.* mucosa, mucous membrane; —**ид** *m.* mucoid; —**итинсерный** *a.* mucoitin sulfuric (acid); —**комплекс** *m.* mucocompound; —**лактоновый** *a.* mucolactonic (acid); —**липид** *m.* mucolipid; —**мешалка** *f.* flour or meal mixer.

мукомол *m.* miller; —**ье** *n.*, —**ьный** *a.* flour-milling, grinding; —**ьный постав, —ьная мельница, —ьня** *f.* flour mill.

муко/новая кислота muconic acid, 2,4-hexadienedioic acid; —**полисахарид** *m.* mucopolysaccharide; —**просеиватель** *m.* flour sifter, flour classifier; —**протеид, —протеин** *m.* mucoprotein; —**рин** *m.* mucorin; —**ровые** *pl.* (bot.) Mucoraceae; —**смеситель** *m.* flour blender, meal mixer; —**соединение** *n.* muco compound; —**филёз** *m.* (vet.) mucophilosis; —**хлоровый** *a.* mucochloric (acid).

муксун *m.*, —**ий** *a.* whitefish (*Coregonus muksun*).

мул *m.* (mam.) mule, hinny.

мулат *m.*, —**ка** *f.* mulatto.

мулинетка *f.* (av.) club or dummy propeller; fan brake.

мулл/евый *a.* mull (soil); —**ит** *m.* (min.) mullite; —**ицит** *m.* mullicite.

мул/(л)ь *m.* mull, soft humus; (dyeing) mull madder; —**ьга-скраб** *m.* (bot.) mulga scrub; —**ьгедиум** *m.* (bot.) Mulgedium.

мульда *f.* (met.) mold, charging box, pan, basin; (geol.) trough, syncline.

мульденпресс *m.* (text.) cylinder press.

мульти— *prefix* multi—, poly—; *see also under* **много—**; —**валентный** *a.* multivalent; —**вариантный** *a.* multivariant; —**вибратор** *m.* (elec.) multivibrator; —**граф** *m.* (typ.) multigraph; —**группа** *f.* multigroup; —**модальный** *a.* (math.) multimodal; —**номи-(н)альный** *a.* multinomial; —**план** *m.* (av.) multiplane; —**плексный** *a.* multiplex.

мультиплет *m.,* —**ный** *a.* (phys.) multiplet; —**ность** *f.* multiplicity.

мультиплика/тивный *a.* (math.) multiplicative; —**тор** *m.* (phys.) multiplier, intensifier; (gas pressure) booster; metering pump; duplicating machine; multiple-lens camera; —**ция** *f.,* —**ционный** *a.* multiplication; animation; —**ционная коносъёмка** animation.

мультиплицировать *v.* gear up.

мультиполь *m.,* —**ный** *a.* multipole; —**ность** *f.* multipolarity.

мульти/полярный *a.* multipolar; —**программирование** *n.* multiprogramming; —**процессор** *m.* multiprocessor; —**ротация** *f.* multirotation, mutarotation; —**струг** *m.* multiplow; —**устойчивость** *f.* multistability; —**целлулярный** *a.* multicellular; —**цепс** *m.* (zool.) Multiceps (tapeworm); —**циклон** *m.* multistage cyclone (dust extractor); —**энзимный** *a.* multienzyme (complex).

мультфильм *m.* animated cartoon.

мульч/а *f.,* —**ировать** *v.* mulch; —**бумага** *f.* paper mulch; —**ер** *m.* mulcher; —**ирование** *n.* mulching; —**материал** *m.* mulching.

мулэн *m.* (geol.) moulin.

муляж *m.* mold(ing), cast(ing).

муметалл *m.* Mu Metal (alloy).

муми/фикация *f.* mummification; —**фицированный** *a.* mummified; —**фицировать** *v.* mummify; —**я** *f.* mummy; colcothar, Prussian red, rouge.

мунго *m.* mung bean (*Phaseolus aureus*); (mam.) banded mongoose (*Mungos mungo*).

мундир *m.* uniform; **картофель в —е** potato cooked in jacket.

мунду *m.,* —**шка** *f.* (ichth.) minnow (*Phoxinus percnurus*).

мундшту/к *m.,* —**чный** *a.* bit, mouthpiece; nozzle, jet, spout, tip; (extrusion) die; spinneret (for rayon).

Муни пластичность Mooney plasticity.

муниципальн/ый *a.* municipal; —**ые предприятия** public utilities.

мунский *a.* (geog.) Muna.

мунтжак *m.* (mam.) muntjac (*Muntiacus*).

мунц-металл *m.* Muntz metal.

мур *m.* (geol.) rock glacier.

мурава *f.* young grass; (cer.) glaze, enamel; **свинцовая м.** glazier's lead.

муравей *m.* (ent.) ant; **белый м.** termite; —**ник** *m.* ant hill.

мурав/ить *v.* (cer.) glaze; —**ление** *n.* glazing; —**лен-(н)ый** *a.* glazed.

муравье/видка *f.* (ent.) Sepsis; —**видки** *pl.* Sepsidae; —**д** *m.* (mam.) anteater (*Myrmecophaga*); —**жук** *m.* (ent.) ant beetle (*Thanasimus formicarius*); —**ловки,** —**ловковые** *pl.* (orn.) Formicariidae; —**любы** *pl.* (ent.) Myrmecophilidae.

муравьи *pl.* (ent.) ants (*Formicidae*).

муравьино/кислый *a.* formic acid; formate (of); **м. натрий, натриевая соль** sodium formate; —**кислая соль** formate; —**этиловый эфир** ethyl formate.

муравьин/ый *a.* (ent.) ant; formic; **м. альдегид** formaldehyde; **м. лев** (ent.) ant lion (*Myrmeleon*); **м. спирт** mixture of formic acid, alcohol and water; —**ая кислота** formic acid; **соль —ой кислоты** formate.

мураш *m.,* —**ка** *f.* small ant; —**еед** *m.* (mam.) banded anteater (*Myrmecobius fasciatus*); —**ееды** *pl.* Myrmecobiidae.

мургабский *a.* (geog.) Murgab.

муреин *m.* murein, peptidoglycan.

мурекс *m.* (mal.) Murex; —**ан** *m.* murexan, uramil; —**ид** *m.,* —**идный** *a.* murexide.

мурен/а *f.* (ichth.) moray eel (*Muraena helena*); —**овые** *pl.* Muraenidae; —**ощуковые** *pl.* congerpikes (*Muraenesocidae*); —**ы** *see* **муреновые.**

муретия *f.* (bot.) Muretia.

муреш-венгерский *a.* Hungarian Maros (river).

мурза *f.,* —**к** *m.* (ichth.) barbel (*Barbus*).

мурлыкать *v.* (zool.) purr.

мурманит *m.* (min.) murmanite.

мурманский *a.* (geog.) Murmansk.

муровать *v.* do masonry work; lay (brick).

муррайин *m.* murrayin.

мурский *a.* (geog.) Mura.

мур/уз *m.,* —**узка** *f.,* —**ца** *f.* (ichth.) barbel (*Barbus lacerta cyri*).

мурчисонит *m.* (min.) murchisonite.

муры *pl.* mud flow.

мусанг *m.* (mam.) Paradoxurus.

мусивный *a.* mosaic.

мускадин *n.* muscadine grape.

мускардина *f.* (vet.) muscardine, calcino.

мускарин *m.* muscarine; —**изм** *m.* muscarine poisoning; —**овый** *a.* muscarinic.

мускат *m.* nutmeg; muscatel (wine); muscadine (grape); —**ель** *m.* muscatel; —**ник** *m.* (bot.) Myristica; —**ные** *pl.* Myristicaceae.

мускатн/ый *a.* nutmeg; muscatell (wine); **м. бальзам, жирное —ое масло** nutmeg butter; **м. орех** nutmeg; **м. цвет** mace; —**ая дыня** muskmelon; —**ое дерево** nutmeg; —**ое масло** nutmeg oil; myristica oil; mace oil.

мусковит *m.* (min.) muscovite, potash mica, common mica.

мускон *m.* muscone, muskine.

мускул *m.* (anat.) muscle; —**атура** *f.* muscles, musculature; —**истость** *f.* muscularity; —**истый** *a.* muscular, sinewy, brawny; —**ы-открыватели,** —**ы отмыкатели** *pl.* divaricators; —**ьный** *a.* muscle, muscular.

мускус *m.,* —**ный** *a.* musk; **м.-амбрет** musk seed, musk-brette; —**ник** *m.* (ent.) musk beetle (*Aromia moschata*); —**ница** *f.* (bot.) Adoxa moschatellina. —**ная крыса** (mam.) muskrat (*Ondatra zibethica*).

муслин *m.,* —**овый** *a.* (text.) muslin.

мусор *m.* rubbish, trash, debris, refuse, sweepings; garbage; fines; **убирать м.** (comp.) scavenge; —**ить** *v.* litter; —**ник** *m.* (bot.) ruderal plant; —**ница** *f.* garbage bin; —**ный** *a. of* **мусор;** —**ная горловина** mud hole (of boiler); —**овоз** *m.* garbage truck; —**одробилка** *f.* macerator, shredder; —**оприёмник** *m.* refuse receptacle; —**опровод** *m.* rubbish chute; —**осжигатель** *m.,* —**осжигательная печь** incinerator; —**осжигательная установка** incinerator, garbage disposal plant; —**оуборочный** *a.,* —**оудаление** *n.* garbage or refuse disposal; —**щик** *m.* garbage man; (zool.) scavenger.

мусс *m.* (food) mousse.

муссивный *see* **мусивный.**

муссировать *v.* effervesce, foam, froth; whip (cream); (plastics) expand; spread (rumors).

муссон *m.,* **—ный** *a.* monsoon, trade wind.

муст *m.* must (of grapes).

мустанг *m.* (mam.) mustang.

мустье *m.,* **—рская культура** (pal.) Mousterian.

мут/абильность *f.* (gen.) mutability; **—абильный** *a.* mutable; **—аген** *m.* mutagen; **—агенировать** *v.* mutagenize; **—агенность** *f.* mutagenicity; **—агенный** *a.* mutagenic; **—аза** *f.* (chem.) mutase; **—ант** *m.,* **—антный** *a.* (gen.) mutant; **—аротация** *see* **мультиротация;** **—ационный** *a.,* **—ация** *f.* mutation.

мут/ен *sh. m. of* **мутный; —и** *gen., etc., of* **муть.**

мутиллиды *pl.* velvet ants (*Mutillidae*).

мутиляция *f.* mutilation.

мутир/ование *n.* mutation; **—овать** *v.* mutate; **—ующий** *a.* mutating.

мут/ить *v.* disturb, make turbid, make muddy, stir up; **—иться, —неть** *v.* grow turbid, get muddy, get cloudy.

Мутмана жидкость Muthmann liquid, acetylene tetrabromide.

мутманнит *m.* (min.) muthmannite.

мутн/оватый *a.* slightly turbid; **—омер** *m.* turbidimeter; **—ость** *f.* turbidity, muddiness, cloudiness; suspended load (in water); (opt.) dimming; **—ый** *a.* turbid, thick, muddy; slimy, sludgy; cloudy, hazy.

мутов/ка *f.* churn staff, beater; (biol.) verticil, whorl; **—чато** *adv. and prefix* verticilli-, verticillate; **—чатый** *a.* verticillate, whorled.

мутон *m.,* **—овый** *a.* (leather) mouton; (gen.) muton.

мутуал/изм *m.* (biol.) mutualism, symbiosis; **—истический** *a.* mutual(istic).

муть *f.* turbidity, suspension, cloud; mud, sludge, slime, sediment.

МУФ *abbr.* (**микроскоп ультрафиолетовый**) ultraviolet microscope.

муфель *m.,* **—ный** *a.* muffle.

муфлон *m.* (mam.) mouflon (*Ovis musimon*).

муфт/а *f.* coupling, connecting piece, connection, sleeve (pipe), socket, union; clutch; junction box (for cables); muff; (horol.) collet; (screw) cap; **м. сцепления, зубчатая м., кулачная м.** clutch; **м. с нарезкой** screw socket; **соединение —ой, —овое соединение** sleeve joint, socket joint; **соединительная м.** coupling box, union; **стяжная м.** turnbuckle; **—овый** *a. of* **муфта; —очка** *dim. of* **муфта.**

мух/а (ent.) fly (*Musca*); (astr.) Musca; **м.-жигалка, м.-кусалка** *f.* stable fly (*Stomoxys calcitrans*); **—и** Muscidae; **—и-кровохлебки** *pl.* louse flies (*Hippoboscidae*); **—и-сирфиды** *pl.* flower flies, hover flies (*Syrphidae*); **—ицветочницы** *pl.* Anthomyid flies; **—оловка** *f.* fly trap; (bot.) Venus' flytrap (*Dionaea muscipula*); (orn.) flycatcher (*Muscicapa*); (zool.) centipede (*Scutigera*); **—оловки, —оловковые** *pl.* (orn.) Muscicapidae; **—оловный** *a.* fly-catching; **—омор** *m.* (bot.) fly agaric (*Amanita muscaria*).

мухортый *a.* brown, bay.

мухусский *a.* (geog.) Muhu.

муцин *m.,* **—овый** *a.* mucin; **—оз** *m.* (med.) mucinosis.

муч/ение *n.* suffering, torment, pain, agony; **—ительный** *a.* acutely painful; **—ить** *v.* worry, torment; **—иться** *v.* suffer.

мучка *f.* low-grade flour or meal.

мучнист/оросяные грибы (bot.) Erysiphaceae; **—ость** *f.* mealiness; flour content; **—ые** *pl.* farinose plants;

—ый *a.* mealy, floury, farinaceous; **—ая роса** (phyt.) powdery mildew.

мучн/ой *a.* flour, meal(y), farinaceous; **—ая роса** *see* **мучнистая роса.**

мушек *gen. pl. of* **мушка.**

муш/иный *a.* (ent.) fly; **—ка** *f.* little fly, midge, gnat; (pharm.) cantharides; (front sight (of gun).

мушкель *m.* mallet, wooden hammer.

мушкетовит *m.* (min.) muschketowite.

мушловка *f.* (mam.) dormouse (*Muscardinus*).

мушмула *f.* (bot.) medlar (*Mespilus*).

муштабель *m.* maulstick, rest stick.

муштр/а *f.,* **—овать** *v.,* **—овка** *f.* (mil.) drill.

муюнкумский *a.* (geog.) Muyun-Kum.

мф *abbr.* (**миллифот**) milliphot; (**миллифарада**) millifarad.

мхи *pl. of* **мох;** (bot.) Bryophyta.

м-ц *abbr.* (**месяц**) month.

м/ч *abbr.* (**метров в час**) meters per hour.

мчать *v.* rush; **—ся** *v.* hurry, rush.

МЧЗ *abbr.* (**магнитное частотное зондирование**) magnetic frequency sounding.

М-число *n.* (aero.) Mach number.

мш/аник *m.* (apid.) moss-calked shed; **—анка** *f.* (bot.) pearlwort (*Sagina*); **—анки** *pl.* (zool.) Bryozoa; **—ара** *f.* mshara (mossy swamp forest); **—истый** *a.* mossy, moss-covered.

МШТ *abbr.* (**международная шкала температуры**) international temperature scale.

мщение *n.* revenge.

мы *pron.* we.

мывший *past act part. of* **мыть.**

мыз/а *f.,* **—ный** *a.* farm(stead).

мык/алка, —аница *f.* hatchel; **—ать** *v.* hatchel, hackle, ripple (hemp, flax); pluck (wool).

мыл *past m. sing. of* **мыть;** *gen. pl. of* **мыло.**

мыл/ение *n.* soaping, lathering; **—енный** *a.* soaped, lathered; **—истый** *a.* soapy; **—ить** *v.* soap, lather; **—кий** *a.* soapy, freely lathering; **—кость** *f.* soapiness.

мыло *n.* soap; lather; *past n. sing. of* **мыть; горное м.** (min.) saponite; **зелёное м.** soft soap, potash soap.

мыловар *m.* soap manufacturer; **—ение** *n.* soap manufacture; **—енный** *a.* soap(-making); **—ня** *f.* soap works.

мыловка *f.* (text.) soaping.

мылок *sh. m. of* **мылкий.**

мыло/нафт *m.* naphtha soap; **—подобный** *a.* soapy, saponaceous; **—резка** *f.* soap cutter; **—штамп** *m.* soap embossing press.

мыльница *f.* soap dish, soap box.

мыльн/ый *a.* soap(y), saponaceous; **м. камень** (min.) soapstone, steatite; **м. корень** soaproot; **—ая кора** soapbark, quillaia bark; **—ая пена** soapsuds, lather; **—ое дерево** (bot.) soapberry tree (*Sapindus*); Koelreuteria; **—я** *f.* wash room; **—янка** *f.* (bot.) Saponaria.

мыльце *dim. of* **мыло;** (med.) suppository.

мыс *m.* (geog.) cape, promontory, cusp; (anat.) promontory, promontorium; **М. Горн** Cape Horn; **М. Доброй Надежды** Cape of Good Hope.

мысл/енный *a.* mental; imaginary, ideal; **—имый** *a.* thinkable, conceivable; **—ительный** *a.* intellectual, thinking; **—ить** *v.* think, conceive.

мысль *f.* thought, idea, notion, conception; **ему пришло на м.** it occurred to him; **наводить на м., подавать м.** *v.* suggest, give an idea.

мыслящий *a.* thinking, intellectual.

мысок *m.* toe.

мыт *m.* (vet.) strangles; (poultry) molt; *sh. m. of* **мытый;** **—иться** *v.* molt.

мытник *m.* (bot.) Pedicularis.

мыт/ый *a.* washed; **—ь** *v.* wash (out), rinse, elute; **—ьё** *n.* washing.

мычать *v.* low, bellow, moo.

мышатник *m.* (bot.) Thermopsis.

мыш/е— *prefix* my(o)— (muscle; mouse); **—евидки** *pl.* (mam.) Phascogalinae; marsupial mice (*Dasyuridae*); **—евидный** *a.* mouse-like, murine; **—ёвка** *see* **мышовка; —ей** *gen. pl. of* **мышь;** *m.* bristle grass (*Setaria*); **—елов** *m.* (ichth.) chub (*Leuciscus cephalus*); (orn.) rough-legged buzzard (*Buteo lagopus*); **—еловка** *f.* mouse trap; **—еобразные** *pl.* (mam.) Myomorpha; **—еобраный** *see* **мышевидный; —ехвостник** *m.* (bot.) Myosurus; **—ехвостый** *a.* myurous; **—ецветный** *a.* myochrous, mouse-colored.

мышечно— *prefix* musculo—, my(o)—, muscle; **—кишечный** *a.* myenteric; **—скелетный** *a.* musculoskeletal.

мышечн/ый *a.* muscle, muscular, myo— myogenous; **м. сахар** inositol; **—ая оболочка** (anat.) myometrium; **—ое волоконце** myofibril.

мыш/и *pl.* (mam.) Muridae; **летучие м.** bats (*Chiroptera*); **морские м.** (ichth.) Callionymidae; frogfishes (*Antennariidae*); **—ий, —иный** *a. of* **мышь; —иносерый** *a.* mouse-gray; **—иные** *pl.* Muridae; **—ка** *dim. of* **мышь; под —кой** under one's arm; **—ковать** *v.* hunt for mice.

мышлен/ие *n.* thinking, thought; **—ный** *a.* thought, conceived.

мыш/овка *f.* (mam.) birch mouse (*Sicista*); **—овковые** *pl.* Zapodidae; **—онок** *m.* baby mouse.

мышца *f.* (anat.) muscle; **м.-вращатель** *f.* rotator; **м.-втягиватель** *f.* retractor; **м.-замыкатель** *f.* sphincter; **м.-напрягатель** *f.* tensor (muscle); **м.-разгибатель** *f.* extensor; **м.-расширитель** *f.* dilator; **м.-сгибатель** *f.* flexor; **м.-сжиматель** *f.* constrictor.

мышь *f.* (mam.) mouse (*Mus*); **летучая м.** bat; **морская м.** frogfish (*Antennarius*); (ichth.) Callionymus; (zool.) Aphrodite; **морская м.-лира** (ichth.) dragonet (*Callionymus*); **м.-малютка** harvest mouse (*Micromys*); **м.-полёвка** *f.* field mouse.

мышьяк *m.* arsenic, As; **белый м.** white arsenic (arsenous oxide); **жёлтый м.** yellow arsenic, arsenic trisulfide; **красный м.** red arsenic, arsenic disulfide; **хлористый м.** arsenous chloride, arsenic trichloride; **хлорный м.** arsenic pentachloride.

мышьяковисто/кальциевая соль, —кислый кальций calcium arsenite; **—кислый** *a.* arsenous acid; arsenite (of); **—кислая соль** arsenite; **—свинцовая соль** lead arsenite.

мышьяковист/ый *a.* arsenic, arsenous, arsenical, arsenide (of); **м. ангидрид** arsenous acid anhydride, arsenic trioxide; **м. водород** hydrogen arsenide, arsine; **м. колчедан** (min.) arsenopyrite; **м. цинк** zinc arsenide; **—ая кислота** arsenous acid; **соль —ой кислоты** arsenite; **хлорангидрид —ой кислоты** arsenyl chloride.

мышьяководород *m.* arsenic hydride, arsine.

мышьяково/кальциевая соль calcium arsenate; **—кислый** *a.* arsenic acid; arsenate (of); **—кислая соль** arsenate; **—свинцовистая соль** lead arsenate.

мышьяков/ый *a.* arsenic(al); **м. ангидрид** arsenic pentoxide; **м. колчедан** (min.) arsenopyrite; **—ая кислота** arsenic acid; **соль —ой кислоты** arsenate.

мышьякорганический *a.* organoarsenic.

мыщел/ка *f.,* **—ок** *m.* (anat.) condyle; **—ковый** *a.* condylar, condyloid.

Мэ *abbr.* (**мега-эрг**) mega-erg.

Мэв *abbr.* (**мегаэлектрон-вольт**) million electron-volts, MeV.

МЭК *abbr.* (**метилэтилкетон**) methylethyl ketone.

мэкв, м.-экв. *abbr.* (**миллиэквивалент**) milliequivalent.

Мэн (geog.) Maine; Man.

мэнджэк *m.* manjak (natural bitumen).

мэнх/еден, —эден *see* **менхаден.**

МЭП *abbr.* (**метод электродных потенциалов**) logging method using two SP electrodes.

мэр *m.* mayor.

Мэриленд (geog.) Maryland.

МЭС *abbr.* (**машинноэкскаваторная станция**) excavator station.

Мэтисона процесс Matheson process.

МЭЧЗ *abbr.* (**магнитоэлектрическое частотное зондирование**) magneto-electrical frequency sounding.

Мэя соль May's salt (benzene-diazonium chloride and antimony trichloride).

мю *n.* mu (μ).

мюллеров канал (anat.) müllerian duct; **—ский** *a.* Müller's, müllerian.

мюль *m.,* **м.-машина** *f.* mule, spinning jenny.

мю-мезон *m.* (nucl.) mu-meson, muon.

Мюнке насос Muencke (filter) pump.

мюнстерский *a.* (geog.) Münster.

мюнхенский *a.* (geog.) München.

мюон *see* **мю-мезон.**

мюрг *m.* (min.) unit of resistance to ventilation.

мюретия *f.* (bot.) Muretia.

мю-частица *see* **мю-мезон.**

мягк/ий *a.* soft, mild, mellow; pliant, supple; upholstered (furniture); clement (weather); weak (base; wine); gentle; **—ая прослойка** pad.

мягко *adv.* softly, mildly; *prefix* malac(o)— (soft; Mollusca); **—волосник** *m.* (bot.) starwort (*Malachium*); **—кожий** *a.* malacodermous, soft-skinned; **—кожистый** *a.* soft-shelled (turtle); **африканские —перосомовые** *pl.* (ichth.) Amphiliidae; **—пёрый** *a.* soft-finned; **—рисующий** *a.* soft-focus (lens); **—скорлуповые** *pl.* soft shell animals; **—тел** *m.,* **—телка** *f.* (ent.) Cantharis; **—телки** *pl.* Cantharididae; **—телые** *pl.* (mal.) Mollusca; **—телый** *a.* soft-bodied; **—тянутый** *a.* soft-drawn; **—шёрст(н)ый** *a.* soft-furred, soft-wool.

мяг/ок *m.* (min.) nontronite; *sh. m. of* **мягкий; —онькая** *f.* (ichth.) smooth lumpsucker (*Aptocyclus glaber*).

мягч/айший *a.* softest, very soft; **—е** *comp. of* **мягкий, мягко,** softer, more softly; **—ение** *n.* softening; **—еть** *v.* soften; **—ильный** *a.* softening; mellowing; **—итель** *m.,* **—ительное (средство)** softener, softening agent; plasticizer; (pharm.) emollient, demulcent; (tanning) bate; **—ительный** *a.* softening; plasticizing; emollient, demulcent; **—ить** *v.* soften; (tanning) bate.

мязга *see* **мезга.**

мяздра *see* **мездра.**

мяк *past m. sing. of* **мякнуть.**

мякин/а *f.* chaff, husk; **—ный** *a.* chaff, chaffy; (bot.) paleaceous; **—ная оболочка** hull.

мяк/иш *m.* pulp; (anat.) pad, cushion; **—лый** *a.* soft, pulpy; **—нуть** *v.* soften, grow pulpy; **—отница** *f.* (bot.) Malaxis; **—отный** *a.* pulp(y), flesh; (cyt.) myelinic; —**отная оболочка** myelin sheath; —**оть** *f.* (cyt.) myelin; flesh; (dental) pulp.

мял *past m. sing. of* **мять.**

мял/ица, —ка *f.,* —**о** *n.* brake (for fiber); —**ка** *f.* crusher, crushing mill, pulper; —**ьно-трепальная машина** breaker and scutcher; —**ьный** *a. suffix* (fiber) breaking; crushing; —**ня** *f.* rettery, retting room.

мясист/о— *prefix* sarc(o)— (meat, flesh); —**окорешковый** *a.* fleshy-rooted; —**ость** *f.* fleshiness, pulpiness; meat contents; —**ый** *a.* fleshy, pulpy, meaty; carnose, sarcoid; flesh (side of leather); —**ая оболочка** (anat.) tunica dartos.

мясная *f.* butcher shop.

мяснига *f.* myasniga (viscous clay in an auriferous placer).

мясник *m.* butcher.

мясника *see* **мяснига.**

мясн/ое *n.* meat dish; —**ой** *a.* meat; flesh(y), pulpy, carneous, carnose, flesh-colored; muscular; beef (cattle); mutton (sheep); —**ой сахар** inositol; —**ого направления** beef (cattle); —**ые мухи** (ent.) Calliphoridae; —**ость** *f.* fleshiness, meatiness, beefiness.

мясо *n.* meat, flesh; pulp (of fruit); *prefix* meat; sarc(o)— (flesh); **дикое м.** (med.) proud flesh; —**ведение** *n.* meat science or technology; —**едка** *f.* (ent.) Coprosarcophaga; —**заготовительный** *a.* meat-preparing; —**комбинат** *m.* meat-packing plant; —**консервный** *a.* meat-packing; —**молочный** *a.* meat and dairy (farm); dual purpose (cattle); sarcolactic (acid); —**пептонный** *a.*

beef extract (agar); —**продуктивный** *a.* commercial meat; —**пункт** *m.* slaughter house; —**резка** *f.* meat cutter; —**рубка** *f.* meat grinder; —**товарный** *a.* meat product(s); —**хладобойня** *f.* refrigerated meat-packing plant; —**шёрстный** *a.* wool-and-meat producing (sheep).

мясцо *n.* (anat.) caruncula, caruncle.

мят *sh. m. of* **мятый.**

мята *f.* (bot.) mint (*Mentha*); **английская м., перечная м.** peppermint (*M. piperita*); **зелёная м., колосовая м.** spearmint (*M. viridis*); **конская м.** horehound (*Marrubium vulgare*); **кошачья м.** catnip (*Nepeta cataria*); **лимонная м.** Melissa; **холодная м.** *see* **мята, английская.**

мятеж *m.* mutiny, revolt, rebellion.

мятие *see* **мятьё.**

мятина *f.* hollow, dent, nick.

мятка *f.* (oil extraction) seed pulp.

мятлик *m.* meadow grass (*Poa*); **луговой м.** Kentucky blue grass (*Poa pratensis*).

мятлица *f.* sunflower moth.

мятличник *m.* blue grass meadow.

мятный *a.* (pepper)mint.

мят/ый *a.* crumpled, etc., *see v.*; crumbled (microstructure); exhaust, spent (steam); —**ь** *v.* crumple, crease; brake, break (fiber); work up, knead (clay); dip (leather); throttle (steam); —**ьё** *n.* crumpling, etc., *see v.*

мяук/ать, —нуть *v.* mew (of cat).

мяч(ик) *m.* ball.

Н

н *abbr.* (**нано**) nano— (10^{-9}); (**ньютоя**) newton; **н., Н** *abbr.* (**нормальный**) normal.

на *prep. acc. to indicate motion; prepos. to indicate location;* at, by (up)on; in(to); for, per (unit); over, across; to, toward, as of (date); onto (conveyer); against (background); **на 10%** by 10%; **на 360°** through 360°; **на вес** by weight, in weight, **на другой день** next day; **на заказ** to order; **на запад** to the west, westward; **на зиму** for the winter; **на куски** (in)to pieces; **на полном ходу** at full speed; **на фут короче** a foot shorter; **на что?** what for? why?

на— *prefix used before verbs to denote completed action;* onto, toward.

набав/ить, —лять *v.* add, increase, raise; —**ка** *f.* increase; —**ленный** *a.* increased; —**очный** *a.* additional.

набалтывать *v.* add while agitating.

набат *m.,* —**ный** *a.* alarm (bell).

набег *m.* raid, invasion; incursion.

набе/гание *n.* running against, etc., *see v.*; climb (of belt); —**гать** *v.* run against, run on, hit, strike; invade; start up (of wind); creep, climb; run in, flow in; impinge (of flow); —**гающий** *a.* running against, etc., *see v.*; leading; inflowing; incident (wave); —**гающий поток** approach stream, windstream, drag; —**жать** *see* **набегать.**

набел/ить *v.* whiten, bleach; —**о** *adv.* clean, final; **переписанное —о** clean copy.

набережн/ая *f.* embankment, quay, pier, wharf; shore road; —**ый** *a.* quay, dock, harbor (crane).

наберёт *fut. 3 sing. of* **набрать.**

набив/ание *n.* packing, etc., *see v.*; —**ать** *v.* pack, fill, stuff; pad, line; tamp, stamp (in), ram; (text.) print; nail on; raise (price); —**ка** *see* **набивание;** filler; (filter) pad; seal, gasket; **с —кой** packed.

набивн/ой *a.* tamped, rammed; packed, stuffed; padded; (text.) printed, printing; **н. лёд** (ocean.) massive rafting of blocks and brash; —**ая футеровка** rammed lining; —**ые доски** print stamps, engraving plates.

набивочн/ый *a.,* **н. материал** packing, stuffing, padding; —**ая камера** stuffing box; —**ое кольцо** gasket.

набир/ание *n.* collecting, etc., *see v.*; (av.) climb; —**ать** *v.* collect, gather, accumulate; (typ.) compose, set up; dial (a number); contract (workers); pick up (speed); gain (height); fill up (with fuel); —**аться** *v.* accumulate, collect, gather.

набит/ый *a.* packed, etc., *see* **набивать;** —**ь** *see* **набивать.**

набла *f.* (math.) nabla, del operator.

наблюдаемый *a.* observable; under observation, observed, seen; apparent.

наблюдатель *m.* observer, spectator; overseer, supervisor; lookout, spotter; surveyor; —**ность** *f.* keenness of observation; —**ный** *a.* observant; observation; supervisory; —**ный пункт** observation post, lookout.

наблюд/ать *v.* observe, watch, survey; supervise, superintend, control; inspect; spot, detect, track, note; —**аться** *v.* be evident, be observed, occur; —**ающий** *a.* observing, etc., *see v.*; —**ающийся** *a.* observed, noted; —**ение** *n.* observation, study; supervision, superintendence, control; inspection; (visual) examination; monitoring, (statistical) survey; sampling data; lookout; **выборочное —ение** representative sampling; **контрольное —ение** monitoring; —**ённый** *a.* observed, etc., *see v.*

набоечный *a. of* **набойка.**

набой *m.* (vet.) gall.

набой/ка *f.* packing, stuffing; printed cloth; lining, facing, fettling (of furnace, etc.); heel tap; —**ник** *m.* stick;

calking tool; **—ный** *a.* (text.) printing; **—щик** *m.* printer; packer.

набок *adv.* on one side, sideways.

наболтать *v.* mix in.

набор *m.* outfit, kit, set, pack; collection, assembly; series, bank (of cells); aggregate; selection; recruitment (of labor); variety, array; arrangement (of chromosomes); framing (of ship); (typ.) composition, typesetting; (tel.) dialing; **н. высоты** ascent, climb; **н. ферментов** enzymatic pattern or equipment; **—ка** *f.* gathering, assembly; **—ная** *f.* typesetting room; **—но-печатный** *a.* composing and printing; **—но-пишущая машина** typewriter; **—но-фотографирующий** *a.* phototypesetting.

наборн/ый *a.* typesetting, composing; (mach.) gang(ed); inlay (work); **—ая машина** typesetter; **—ая строкоотливная машина** linotype machine; **—ое коммутационное поле** patching panel.

наборон/ить, —овать *v.* (agr.) harrow.

набортный *a.* shipborne; on board.

наборщик *m.* compositor, typesetter.

наботовый *a.* (anat.) Naboth's, nabothian.

набраков(ыв)ать *v.* reject.

набранный *a.* collected, gathered; (typ.) composed, set up.

набрасыв/ание *m.* throwing on; sketching; **—ать** *v.* throw on; sketch, draw, outline; **—аться** *v.* fall on, attack.

набрать *see* **набирать**.

набрести *v.* come across, happen upon.

набро/санный *a.* thrown on; sketched, outlined; **—сать, —сить** *see* **набрасывать**; **—ска** *f.* throwing on; (constr.) fill; (geol.) talus; **—сной** *a.* thrown up, heaped up; fill; stone rubble (dam); **—сок** *m.* sketch, layout, draft, rough copy; **—шенный** *past pass. part. of* **набросить**.

набрызг *m.* (constr.) sprayed plaster base; **—(ив)ать** *v.* sprinkle, spray.

набрюшник *m.* abdominal band or binder.

набрякнуть *v.* swell (from dampness).

набур/(ав)ить, —авливать *v.* drill, bore.

набутить *see* **набучивать**.

набух/аемость *f.* swelling ability; swelling; **—ание** *n.* swelling, etc., *see v.*; turgescence; **—ать, —нуть** *v.* swell, turgesce; distend, expand; (leather) plump; **—ший** *a.* swollen, turgid.

набучи(ва)ть *v.* line with stone or rubble; (text.) buck, steep.

набыль *f.* (geol.) thrust.

набьёт *fut. 3 sing. of* **набить**.

навага *f.* (ichth.) navaga (*Eleginus*).

наваждение *n.* obsession.

наважий *a. of* **навага**.

навал *m.* heap(ing), bulk; **—енный** *a.* heaped up, etc., *see v.*; **—ивание** *n.* heaping up, etc., *see v.*; **—и(ва)ть** *v.* heap up, pile, accumulate; fill, load, charge; (text.) felt, full; **—и(ва)ться** *v.* fall on, lean; **—ка** *see* **наваливание**; **—ом** *adv.* unpacked, bulk (cargo); **—оотбойка** *f.* coal hewing; **—оотбойщик** *m.* getter, hewer; **—очник** *m.* bulk carrier; **—очный** *a.* loading; **—очная машина** loader.

навальцованный *a.* rolled on.

навалять *v.* (text.) felt, full.

навар *m.* welded on metal; built up metal; scum; broth; cooking, brewing; **—енный** *a.* welded on, built up, etc., *see v.*; **—енный сталью** steel-faced, steel-tipped; **—ивание** *n.* welding on, etc., *see v.*; **—и(ва)ть** *v.* weld on, build up (metal); face, tip, paint, edge, overlay

(with); recap (tire); hard-face; sinter, fettle, frit (hearth bottom); boil, prepare, brew; cook (in quantity); **—истый** *a.* rich (food); **—ка** *see* **наваривание**; bead weld; **—ной** *a.* weld(ed), welding; sintered.

навастривать *v.* sharpen.

наващивать *v.* wax; (apid.) embed (comb foundation).

навевать *v.* drift, heap up, blow together; stack, load; roll on; evoke, bring on.

наведаться *see* **наведываться**.

наведение *n.* directing, etc., *see* **наводить**; guidance; application; induction (of synthesis); production (of slag); (radar) vectoring; pointing (of spacecraft telescope).

наведённый *a.* directed, etc., *see* **наводить**.

наведываться *v.* visit; inquire about.

наведя *pr. ger. of* **наводить**.

навезти *v.* bring in.

навеивать *see* **навевать**.

навеки *adv.* forever.

навёл *past m. sing. of* **навести**.

навербов(ыв)ать *v.* enroll, recruit.

наверно(е) *adv.* certainly, surely; most likely, probably; it is likely.

наверняка *adv.* undoubtedly, for sure.

навернут/ый *a.* turned on, twisted on; screwed on; **—ь** *see* **навёртывать**.

наверстать, навёрстывать *v.* make up, catch up; compensate; **навёрстывание** *n.* making up; recovery; compensation.

навертеть *see* **наверчивать**.

навёрт/ка *see* **навёртывание**; **—ный** *a.* twist, screw (cap); **—ывание** *n.* turning, on etc., *see v.*; **—ывать** *v.* turn on, twist on, wind; screw on.

наверх *adv.* up(ward); upstairs; **—у** *adv.* above, aloft, at the top (of), on top of; upstairs.

наверч/енный *a.* drilled, etc., *see v.*; **—ивать** *v.* drill, wind up; screw; churn up.

навес *m.* shed, hangar; awning; (geol.) overhang; roofing; (biol.) umbraculum; **ледяной н.** hanging glacier; **—истый** *a.* overhanging.

навес/ить *see* **навешивать**; **—ка** *f.* hanging; suspension, dispersion; weighed portion, batch, charge; specimen, sample; increment; linkage, hitch; hinge; fitting, mounting; **—ной** *a.* hinged; attached, inserted; (tractor-)mounted; **—ная петля** hinge; **—ный** *a. of* **навес**; high, steep (trajectory).

навести *see* **наводить**.

навестить *see* **навещать**.

навесу *adv.* (over)hanging; in suspension.

навес-хранилище *m.* storage shed.

наветренный *a.* upwind (side), windward, exposed to the wind.

навечно *adv.* forever.

навеш/енный *a.* hung (on), etc., *see v.*; **—ивание** *n.* hanging on, etc., *see v.*; suspension; **—(ив)ать** *v.* hang (on, up), suspend; mount; weigh (out).

навещать *v.* visit, see.

наве/яние *n.* (agr.) winnowing; **—ять** *see* **навевать**; winnow (a quantity of).

навзничь *adv.* backwards, on one's back; **лежащий н.** *a.* (med.) supine.

навив/альный *a.,* **—ание** *n.* winding, etc., *see v.*; **—ать** *v.* wind (on), roll (on), reel (in), coil; wrap; drift in (of snow); make (rope); **—аться** *v.* be wound; climb (of belt); **—ка** *see* **навивание**; wound material; reel, coil; layout, arrangement; **—ной, —очный** *see* **навивальный**.

навиг/атор *m.* navigator; **—ационный** *a.* navigation(al), nautical; —**ационный координатор** ground-position indicator; —**ация** *f.* navigation; shipping season.

навильник *m.* (agr.) pitch fork; forkfull.

навин/тить, —чивать *v.* screw on; —**ченный** *a.* screwed on; —**чивающийся** *a.* screw(-on), threaded.

навис/ание *n.* hanging over, impendence; —**ать, —нуть** *v.* hang over, overhang, project; impend; —**ающий, —лый, —ший** *a.* overhanging; impending, imminent; —**ь** *f.* overhang.

навит/ый *a.* wound on, rolled on, etc., *see* **навивать;** —**ь** *see* **навивать.**

361навле/кать, —чь *v.* bring on, cause, incur.

навод/ить *v.* direct, point (at), aim (at), position, set, sight (a telescope); (rockets) guide; bring on, lay on, apply; cover, coat (with); veneer; build up, form (slag); (elec.) induce; make (inquiries); (bring into) focus; erect, build (a bridge); bridge; **н. глянец** polish, gloss, **н. критику** criticize; **н. на фокус** focus; —**ка** *f.* directing, etc., *see v.*; adjustment.

наводн/ение *n.* flood, inundation, submersion, overflow; —**ённый** *a.* flooded, etc., *see v.*; —**ить, —ять** *v.* flood, inundate, submerge, overflow, deluge, swamp; —**ой** *a.* floating (bridge).

наводор/ажеваемость *f.* (met.) tendency to absorb hydrogen; —**аживание, —ожение, —оживание** *n.* hydrogen absorption; —**оженный** *a.* hydrogen-charged.

навод/чик *m.* gunner sighter; —**ящий** *a.* directing, etc., *see* **наводить;** guidance, controlling; guide, homing (beam); leading (question).

навоз *m.* manure, dung; —**ить** *v.* bring, carry, convey; manure, dung; —**ник** *m.* dung beetle (*Geotrupes, Pentadon, etc.*); (bot.) Coprinus mushroom; manure pit; —**ник-землерой** *m.* Geotrupes; —**ники** *pl.* Scarabaeidae; Geotrupidae; —**никовые** *pl.* (bot.) Coprinaceae; —**ница** *f.* manure wagon; manure-spreading (season); —**ницы** *pl.* (ent.) Cordyluridae; —**ничек** *m.* (ent.) Aphodius; —**ный** *a.* manure(d), dung; —**ная жижа** liquid manure; —**о—** *prefix* copr(o)— (dung, excrement); —**олюбивый** *a.* coprophilous; —**онагрузчик, —опогрузчик** *m.* manure loader; —**оразбрасыватель** *m.* manure spreader; —**охранилище** *n.* manure pit; **н.-сыпец** *m.* pulverized manure.

навой *m.* (text.) warp beam, back beam; winder; winding; wound material.

наволекив/ание *n.* (met.) galling; —**ать** *see* **наволочь.**

наволо/к *m.* (geol.) overthrust folding, nappe; low river bank; cloud, fog; —**ка** *f.* pillowcase; —**чить** *see* **наволочь;** —**чка** *f.,* —**чный** *a.* pillowcase; —**чь** *v.* drag (on, over); draw (wire).

навонять *v.* smell up.

навор/ачивать, —отить *v.* pile up, heap up, roll on; overfill.

наворс/ить, —овать *v.* (text.) tease.

навостр/ённый *a.* sharpened; —**ить** *v.* sharpen.

навощ/ённый *a.* cerated, waxed; —**ить** *see* **наващивать.**

навредить *v.* harm, injure, damage.

навряд(ли) *particle* hardly; it is unlikely.

навсегда *adv.* forever; **раз н.** once for all.

навстречу *adv.* toward; **итти н.** *v.* meet.

навыворот *adv.* wrong side out, inside out.

навык *m.* habit, practice, experience; know-how, knack, skill; **практический н.** skill.

навылет *adv.* (right) through.

Навье-Стокса уравнение Navier-Stokes equation.

навьючи(ва)ть *v.* load, burden.

навяз/анный *a.* fastened, etc., *see v.*; —**ать** *see* **навязывать;** —**ка** *f.* fastening; —**ной** *a.* tied on; knitted;

—**нуть** *v.* stick, cling; get stuck; —**чивость** *f.* obtrusiveness, importunity; —**чивый** *a.* obtrusive; fixed, obsessive; —**чивая идея** obsession; —**ывание** *n.* fastening, etc., *see v.*; attachment; —**ывать** *v.* fasten, attach, tie on, bind; impose, force, obtrude, press (advice); knit (a quantity of); —**ываться** *v.* intrude, thrust oneself (upon).

навяли(ва)ть *v.* sun-cure, jerk.

нагадать *v.* foretell, prophesy.

нага/дить *v.* foul, dirty, soil, —**женный** *a.* fouled, dirtied, soiled.

наган/а *f.* (vet.) nagana (tripanosomiasis); —**ин** *m.* naganin, suramin.

нагар *m.,* —**ный** *a.* carbon (deposit), soot; caking, fouling, scale, residue; (combustion chamber) deposits (in engines); hard carbon; —**ник** *m.* combustion chamber deposit collector; —**ообразование** *n.* carbon formation, carbonization; —**ообразующая способность** tendency to soot.

нагартов/анный *a.* (met.) cold-hardened, etc., *see v.*; —**ка** *f.,* —**очный** *a.* cold hardening, etc., *see v.*; —**ывать** *v.* cold-harden, cold-work, peen; ball up, gather (soil).

нага/тить, —чивать *v.* build a dike.

нагель *m.* pin, dowel, peg; nail.

нагельфлю *m.* (petr.) nagelfluh, gompholite, pudding stone.

нагиагит *m.* (min.) nagyagite.

нагиб/ание *n.* bending, bowing down; —**ать** *v.* bend, bow, down.

наглазн/ик *m.* eyeshade, eye-shield; —**ый** *a.* eye (shield).

наглазурить *v.* glaze.

наглухо *adv.* hermetically, tightly; permanently.

нагляд/еться *v.* observe, see (enough); —**но** *adv.* visually, by eyesight; by demonstration, graphically, pictorially; **представлять —но** *v.* visualize; —**ность** *f.* clearness, obviousness; use of visual aids; **сохранять —ность** *v.* keep in evidence; —**ный** *a.* graphic, descriptive, pictorial; dramatic, striking; visual (aids); intuitive; obvious, clear, object (lesson).

наглянцевать *v.* gloss, polish.

нагнаивать *v.* decompose, rot; —**ся** *v.* (med.) suppurate.

нагн/анный *a.* driven together, *etc., see* **нагонять;** —**ать** *see* **нагонять.**

нагнести *see* **нагнетать.**

нагнет *m.* (vet.) gall, sore.

нагнет/ание *n.* forcing, etc., *see v.*; injection; delivery; **камера —ания** discharge chamber; **ход —ания** pressure stroke; —**атель** *m.* blower, (force) pump; (mach.) supercharger; booster, compressor; —**атель наддува** supercharger; —**ательный** *a.* force(d), pressure; delivery (pump); discharge (nozzle; pipe); Plenum (air conditioning system); injection (well); —**ать** *v.* force, press, squeeze; deliver, feed, supply, provide; pump, charge, inject; increase (pressure); pump feed, discharge under pressure; —**ающий** *a.* forcing, etc., *see v.; see also* **нагнетательный;** —**ённый** *a.* forced, etc., *see v.*

нагно/ение *n.* suppuration; **вызвать н.** *v.* fester; —**ить** *see* **нагнаивать.**

нагнут/ый *a.* bent; —**ь** *see* **нагибать.**

нагой *a.* naked; bare, uncovered.

наголо *adv.* bare; entirely.

наголоватка *f.* (bot.) Jurinea.

наголовник *m.* cap.

наголодаться *v.* starve (a long time).

нагольный *a.* fur-lined leather (coat).

нагон *m.* driving together, etc., *see v.*; (hydr.) rising, blowing up, pileup, surge; **—ка** *f.* driving on, fitting; **—ный** *a.* piled-up (water); **—ять** *v.* drive together, drive on, fit; cause, bring on (condition); overtake, catch up (with); save (time); distil; **—яющий** *a.* driving together, etc., *see v.*; overlapping (travel-time curve).

на-гора *adv.* (min.) up (to the surface).

нагораживать *v.* pile up, stack up; divide into compartments; erect (fence).

нагор/ать, —еть *v.* be consumed (of fuel, etc.); smoke.

нагорец *m.* (ichth.) Schizopygopsis.

нагорно-карабахский *a.* (geog.) Nagorno-Karabakh.

нагорный *a.* upland, highland, raised; mountainous, high (land); hillside.

нагородить *see* **нагораживать.**

нагорье *n.* upland, highlands.

нагота *f.* bareness, nakedness.

нагот/авливать, —овить, —овлять *v.* prepare, make ready; store, stock up; **—ове** *adv.* ready, in readiness, on call; **стоящий —ове** *a.* standby.

нагофрировать *v.* corrugate, crimp.

награбить *v.* rake together.

награвировать *v.* engrave.

наград/а *f.* reward, recompense; premium, prize, award; **—ить** *see* **награждать.**

наградка *f.* back saw, tenon saw.

наградн/ой *a. of* **награда; —ые** *pl.* bonus.

награжд/ать *v.* reward, recompense; award; **—ение** *n.* reward; **—ённый** *a.* rewarded, etc., *see v.*

награнить *v.* cut, facet.

награфить *v.* rule; graph.

нагребать *v.* rake together, rake up.

нагрев *see* **нагревание;** degree of heat, temperature; heat build-up; heated surface; **степень —а** temperature; **—ание** *n.* heating (up), warming (up); **—атель** *m.* heater; radiator.

нагревательн/ый *a.* heating; (being) heated; hot (plate); warming; **н. колодец** (met.) soaking pit, pit furnace; **н. прибор** heater; **—ая печь** heating furnace; (met.) soaking pit.

нагрев/ать *v.* heat, warm up; **—ающий** *a.* heating, warming; **—остойкий** *a.* heat-resistant, thermostable; **—остойкость** *f.* heat resistance, thermostability, thermal endurance.

нагрести *see* **нагребать.**

нагрет/ость *f.* heated state, warmth; **—ый** *a.* heated, warm(ed); **—ь** *see* **нагревать.**

нагрешить *v.* make errors.

нагромо/ждать, —здить *v.* pile (up), accumulate, build up; **—ждение** *n.* pile, piling, heaping, packing; **—ждённый** *a.* piled, heaped.

нагрубо *adv.* rough(ly).

нагрудн/ик *m.* breastplate; safety vest; **—ый** *a.* breast.

нагру/жаемость *f.* load capacity; **—жать** *v.* load, charge; ballast; **—жающий** *a.,* **—жение** *n.* loading, charging; **—женный, —жённый** *a.* loaded, charged; supporting (surface); **—зить** *see* **нагружать.**

нагрузк/а *f.* load(ing), charge; force; stress, tension; burden, weight; rate; (tel.) traffic; lading, shipment, freight; details (of map); **н. глюкозой** (med.) glucose tolerance; **н. на разрыв** tensile stress; **н. по жидкости** liquid rate; **н. по отношению к мощности** power loading (pounds per horsepower); **без —и** empty; at no load, off load; **ёмкость —и** (elec.) load capacity; **коэффициент —и** load factor; **наибольшей —и** peak-load; **нести —у** *v.* have import; **под —ой** on load; **полная н.** full load; full-time job; **проба**

с —ой (med.) tolerance test; **чрезмерная н.** overstocking.

нагруз/ное сопротивление load impedance; **—очный** *a.* load(ing), charge; **—очное сопротивление** (elec.) load resistance; **—чик** *m.* loader.

нагрунтовать *v.* prime (surface).

нагрянуть *v.* take by surprise, come unawares (upon); happen suddenly; occur (unexpectedly).

нагул *m.* pasturing; fattening (of livestock); **—ивать, —ять** *v.* pasture; forage, feed and grow; fatten; **—ивающийся** *a.* fattening; foraging, growing; **—ьный** *a.* fattening, grazing, foraging; **—ьщик** *m.* herdsman.

нагыш *m.* (ichth.) smelt (*Osmerus*).

над *prep. instr.* above, over, on, upon.

над— *prefix* over—, super—, hyper—, epi—, above; per— (acid, salt).

надав/ить, —ливать *v.* press, squeeze.

НАД-аза *f.* NADase (nicotinamide adenine dinucleide enzyme).

надазотная кислота pernitric acid.

надаивать *v.* (get) milk.

надалбливать *v.* chisel (out).

надатмосферный *a.* outer (space).

надбав/ить, —лять *v.* add, increase; **—ка** *f.* increase, rise; allowance; bonus; surcharge, markup; **—ленный** *a.* increased, raised; **—очный** *a.* additional.

над/барабанный *a.* (anat.) epitympanic; **—барабанье** *n.* (tech.) upper drum jacket; **—бензойный** *a.* perbenzoic (acid); **—бережный** *a.* above the bank; **—би(ва)ть** *v.* crack, damage; **—блоковый** *a.* (anat.) supratrochlear.

надборн/ая кислота perboric acid; **соль —ой кислоты, —окислая соль** perborate; **—окислый** *a.* perboric acid; perborate (of).

над/бровный *a.* (anat.) supercilliary; **—брюшный** *a.* epigastric; **—бугорная область, —бугорье** *n.* epithalamus.

надвесный *a.* overhung, overhanging.

надвивать *v.* twist on, add, lengthen.

надви/г *m.* thrust; (geol.) (over)thrust, overlap; **крутой н.** upthrust; **—гание** *n.* moving up(on), etc., *see v.*; encroachment; **—гать** *v.* move up(on), move against, push on, thrust; slide (over), override; **—гаться** *v.* move upon, slide (over); approach, draw near; (geol.) overthrust; **—гающийся** *a.* approaching, impending, imminent; **—гообразование** *n.* thrusting; **—жной** *a.* sliding, movable; **—нутый** *a.* moved up(on), etc., *see v.*; **—нуть** *see* **надвигать.**

надвид *m.* (biol.) superspecies.

надви/жной *a.* sliding, movable; **—нутый** *a.* moved up(on), etc., *see* **надвигать; —нуть** *see* **надвигать.**

над/височный *a.* (anat.) supratemporal; **—вить** *see* **надвивать; —влагалищный** *a.* supravaginal.

надводный *a.* above-water, emergent; floating; surface (ship).

надвое *adv.* in two, in half; ambiguously; **деление н.** (biol.) binary fission.

надвольфрамовый *a.* pertungstic (acid).

надвор/ный *a.* outdoor, yard; out (building); exterior; **—ье** *n.* yard.

надвяз/анный *a.* knitted on, etc., *see v.*; **—ать** *see* **надвязывать; —ка** *f.* addition; **—ывание** *n.* knitting on, etc., *see v.*; **—ывать** *v.* knit on, add; tie on.

надгибать *v.* bend, fold.

надглазничный *a.* (anat.) supraorbital; ophthalmic (reflex).

надглазурный *a.* overglaze(d).

надглоточник *m.* (zool.) epipharynx.

надгни(ва)ть *v.* start decaying.

надгортанн/ик *m.* (anat.) epiglottis; **—ый** *a.* epiglottal.

надгроб/ие *n.* burial mound, tumulus; **—ный** *a.* funeral; tomb (stone).

надгруд/инник *m.* (anat.) episternum; **—инный** *a.* episternal, suprasternal; **—ный** *a.* above the breast; **—ная пластинка** (herp.) plastron.

надгруппа *f.* (math.) supergroup.

надгрыз(а)ть *v.* gnaw at, nibble at.

надда/(ва)ть *v.* add (more); accelerate, quicken, increase (speed); **—ча** *f.* addition.

наддув *m.* supercharge, supercharging, boosting; pressure charging, pressure feed, pressurization; **н. на взлёте** takeoff boost; **автомат —а** supercharger control; **компрессор —а** supercharger; **с —ом** supercharged.

надев/аемый *a.* female (gage); **—ание** *n.* putting on; **—ать** *v.* put on, slip on; don; gear, harness.

надежд/а *f.* hope, expectation; **возлагать —ы на** *v.* count (on), pin our hopes on, look (to).

надёжн/ость *f.* safety, security, reliability, dependability, assurance; **запас —ости** safety margin; **—ый** *a.* safe, secure, sure, reliable, dependable, trustworthy; sound, foolproof.

надел *m.* share, portion; plot (of land).

наделать *v.* make in large quantity, produce in mass; cause.

надел/ение *n.* dispensation, allotment, consignment; **—ить** *v.* impart, dispense, allot, consign.

наделка *f.* addition, added structure.

надельный *a.* of **надел**; allotted, assigned.

надельфейль *m.* needle file.

наделять *see* **наделить.**

надёрг(ив)ать *v.* pull up, pull out.

надерёт *fut. 3 sing. of* **надрать.**

надёрнуть *v.* pull on.

надет/ый *a.* put on, slipped on; **—ь** *see* **надевать.**

надеяться *v.* hope (for), look forward (to), rely (upon), have confidence (in).

наджаберный *a.* (ichth.) epibranchial.

наджелезно/кислая соль perferrate; **—синеродоводородная кислота** perferricyanic acid.

надзаголовочный *a.* before the title.

надземный *a.* above ground; overhead, aerial; elevated (railroad).

надзир/атель *m.* inspector, supervisor, superintendent, overseer; **—ательство** *n.* supervision, overseeing; **—ать** *v.* supervise, superintend, inspect.

надзор *m.* supervision, superintendence, inspection, control, oversight; surveillance; servicing.

надзрительный *a.* (anat.) supraoptic.

надизан *m.* Nadisan, carbutamide.

надилов/ый *a.,* **—ая жидкость** supernatant.

надир *m.* nadir, lowest possible point.

надирать *v.* tear up; raise; strip (off).

надкалывать *v.* pierce slightly, prick; split slightly, cleave, crack.

надкислот/а *f.,* **—ный** *a.* per acid.

надкласс *m.* (biol.) superclass.

надкле/ивание *n.* gluing on; **—и(ва)ть** *v.* glue on, lengthen, add; **—йка** *f.* gluing on; glued on part.

надклепать *see* **надклёпывать.**

надклёп/ка *f.* riveting on; riveted addition; **—ывание** *n.* riveting on, etc., *see v.;* **—ывать** *v.* rivet on, lengthen; unrivet slightly.

надклювье *n.* (orn.) maxilla.

надключичный *a.* (anat.) supraclavicular.

надков(ыв)ать *v.* forge on, lengthen.

над/кожица *f.* (biol.) epidermis; (bot.) cuticle; **—козелковый** *a.* (anat.) supratragal.

надкол *m.* cleft, crack; prick(ing).

надколенн/ик *m.* (anat.) patella, kneecap; **—ый** *a.* (supra)patellar.

надколот/ый *a.* (slightly) split, cracked; pricked; **—ь** *see* **надкалывать.**

надкостни/ая плева, —ица *f.* (anat.) periosteum; **—ичный** *a.* periosteal.

надкраевой *a.* supramarginal.

надкритич/еский, —ный *a.* above-critical, supercritical; **—ность** *f.* supercriticality.

надкрылье *n.* (ent.) elytron, wing sheath.

надкус *m.* bite; biting; **—(ыв)ать** *v.* bite (in several places); **—ить** *v.* take a bite.

надламывать *v.* break partway, crack.

надлёдный туман advection fog over ice.

надлеж/ать *v.* be necessary; want, need; **—ит это сделать** it must be done.

надлежащ/ий *a.* proper, fit, due, expedient, appropriate, pertinent, suitable; correct (size); **—им образом** properly, suitably.

над/лобковый *a.* (anat.) suprapubic; **—лобный** *a.* suprafrontal; **—лодыжковый** *a.* supramalleolar.

надлом *m.* incipient fracture or break; **—ать, —ить** *see* **надламывать; —ленность** *f.* fractured state; **—ленный** *a.* partly broken, cracked.

надлопаточный *a.* (anat.) suprascapular.

над/масляный *a.* perbutyric (acid); **—мозговой** *a.* (anat.) subpial; **—молекулярный** *a.* permolecular; supramolecular; **—молибденовый** *a.* permolybdic (acid); **—муравьиный** *a.* performic (acid).

надмыщел/ковый *a.* (anat.) supracondylar; **—ок** *m.* epicondyle.

НАДН *abbr.* NADH (reduced nicotinamide adenine dinucleotide).

на-днях *adv.* before long, one of these days; lately, the other day.

надо *v.* it is necessary; *prep., see* **над; ему н.** he must, he needs.

надо— — *see* над—.

надоблачный *a.* above the clouds.

надобн/ость *f.* necessity, requirement, need, want; **иметь н.** *v.* require, need; **нет —ости** there is no need; **—ый** *a.* necessary, requisite; useful.

надобьёт *fut. 3 sing. of* **надбить.**

надое/дать, —сть *v.* bore, annoy, worry, bother; **—дливый** *a.* irksome, tiresome, tedious.

над/оить *v.* milk; **—ой** *m.* milk yield.

надоконный *a.* over the window.

надолбить *v.* chisel (out).

надолбы *pl.* (mil.) obstacle, barrier, blocks, pillars, posts.

надолго *adv.* for a long time, for long.

надомн/ик *m.* home worker; **—ый** *a.* (at) home, domestic, cottage (industry).

надорв/анный *a.* slightly torn; strained; **—ать** *see* **надрывать.**

надорит *m.* (min.) nadorite.

надосад/ка *f.,* **—ок** *n.* supernatant (liquid); **—очный** *a.* supernatant.

над/основный *a.* superbasic; **—остный** *a.* (anat.) supraspinal; **—отдел** *m.* supersection; **—отряд** *m.* (biol.) superorder.

надо/умить, —умливать *v.* advise, help solve; **—шьёт** *fut. 3 sing. of* **надшить.**

надпазушный *a.* (bot.) supra-axillary.

надпалубный *a.* above the deck.

надпарывать *v.* rip a little or lightly.

надперекись *f.* superoxide, hyperoxide.

надпереносье *n.* (anat.) glabella.

надпестичный *a.* (bot.) epigynous.

надпил *m.* saw cut, notch; notching; **—енный** *a.* notched; **—ивание** *n.* notching; **—и(ва)ть** *v.* saw a little, notch; **—(ов)ка** *f.* notching.

надпис/анный *a.* inscribed; **—ать, —ывать** *v.* inscribe, superscribe; letter; **—ка** *f.,* **—ывание** *n.* inscription, etc., see v.; **—ь** *f.* inscription, superscript(ion); lettering; heading; legend; endorsement; superstructure, social structure; (anat.) intersectio.

надплодник *m.* (bot.) epicarp.

надподъязычный *a.* (anat.) suprahyoid.

надпойменный *a.* above the flood plain.

надполе *n.* (math.) overfield.

надпороть *v.* rip a little or slightly.

надпочвенный *a.* surface, above ground.

надпочечн/ик *m.* (anat.) adrenal gland; **—(иков)о-корковый** *a.* adrenocortical; **—(иков)ый** *a.* adrenal, suprarenal.

надпропионовый *a.* perpropionic (acid).

над/проходный *a.* (anat.) suprameatal; **—пузырный** *a.* supravesical; **—пяточный** *a.* talar.

надраи(ва)ть *v.* (naut.) polish, clean.

надрамочный *a.* (apid.) upper (space).

надрать see **надирать.**

надрез *m.* cut, incision, notch, gash, tap (on tree); cutting; **с —ом** notched; **—ание** *n.* cutting, incision; **—анный** *a.* cut, etc., see v.; *f.* score; **—ный** *a.* slit; *suffix* (bot.) —fid (lobed; cleft); **—(ыв)ать** *v.* cut (into), incise; slit, score, notch; tap; slash, blaze (tree).

надрениевая кислота perrhenic acid.

надробить *v.* crush, grind up.

надрод *m.* (biol.) supergenus.

надруб *m.* notch(ing), gash; blaze, cut, slash; **—ание** *n.* notching; **—ать, —ить** *v.* notch, gash, mark; **—ка** *f.* notch(ing), gash.

надрыв *m.* (surface) tear, rupture; (casting) shrinkage crack; strain, overstraining; **—ать** *v.* begin to tear, tear slightly, rupture, lacerate; strain, overdo; **—истый** *a.* tearing (cough); **—ный** *a.* strained.

надса/д *m.,* **—а** *f.* overexertion; **—живать** *v.* (over)-strain, overexert.

надсверли(ва)ть *v.* drill partway; drill.

надсек/ание *n.* gashing, incision; **—ать** *v.* gash, notch, cut, make incisions.

надсемейство *n.* (biol.) superfamily.

надсем/енодольное, —ядольное колено (bot.) epicotyl; **—ядольный** *a.* epicotyledonary.

надсерия *f.* (biol.) superseries.

надсерн/ая кислота persulfuric acid; **соль —ой кислоты, —окислая соль** persulfate; **—ый** *a.* persulfuric acid; persulfate (of); **—ый ангидрид** sulfur heptoxide.

надсеч/ённый *a.* gashed, notched, cut; **—ка** *f.* gash(ing); (zone) punching; **—ь** see **надсекать.**

надсинхронный *a.* hypersynchronous.

над/склеральный *a.* (anat.) episcleral; **—скорлупная плёнка** egg-shell cuticle.

надслоевой *a.* upper layer.

надслуховой *a.* supersonic, ultraphonic.

надсматривать *v.* supervise, look after, control, inspect.

надсмольная вода (resins) supernatant water, flushing liquor; tar water.

надсмотр *m.* supervision, inspection, control; **—щик** *m.* supervisor, overseer.

надсоль *f.* persalt.

надсосудистый *a.* (anat.) suprachorioid.

надстав/ить see **надставлять; —ка** *f.* extension (piece), extension arm; adapter; (crucible) top; **кольцевая —ка** extension ring; **—ленный** *a.* extended, etc., see v.; **—лять** *v.* extend, lengthen, add on; **—ной** *a.* extension; **—ная труба** adapter.

надст/ой *m.,* **—оящий** *a.* supernatant.

надстрагивать *v.* shave off, plane lightly.

надстраив/ание *n.* building on, superstructing; **—ать** *v.* build on, superstruct.

надстрогать see **надстрагивать.**

надстро/ечный *a.* superstructural; **—ить** see **надстраивать; —йка** *f.* superstructure; superstructing.

надстрочный *a.* superlinear; **н. элемент** (typ.) ascender, riser; **н. индекс** superscript.

надструг(ив)ать see **надстрагивать.**

надсульфоновый *a.* persulfonic (acid).

надсып/ать *v.* raise, pour more; **—ка** *f.* raising, addition.

над/твердооболочечный *a.* (anat.) epidural; **—тепловой** *a.* epithermal; **—тёс** *m.* cutting off; cut; **—тесать, —тёсывать** *v.* cut off (a little).

надтехнециевокислая соль pertechnetate.

надтиоугольн/ая кислота perthiocarbonic acid; **соль —ой кислоты, —окислая соль** perthiocarbonate.

надтональный *a.* supersonic.

надтреснутый *a.* slightly cracked.

надтриба *f.* (biol.) supertribe.

надуб/ить *v.* tan; **—лённый** *a.* tanned.

надув *m.* inflation, blowing up; drift (of hard, packed snow); **—ание** *n.* inflating, etc., see v.; inflation; **—ательный** *a.* inflation; **—ать** *v.* inflate, blow (up), fill (with air), distend; cheat, deceive; **—аться** *v.* swell, puff up; **—ка** *f.* inflation; **—ной** *a.* inflatable; air (cushion); pneumatic (boat); **—очный** *a.* inflating.

надугловой *a.* (anat.) supra-angular.

надугольн/ая кислота percarbonic acid; **соль —ой кислоты, —окислая соль** percarbonate; **—окислый** *a.* percarbonic acid; percarbonate (of).

надуксусн/ая кислота peracetic acid; **—окислая соль** peracetate; **—окислый** *a.* peracetic acid; peracetate (of).

надульник *m.* (art.) compensator; barrel mouthpiece.

надум/анный *a.* farfetched, exaggerated; **—(ыв)ать** *v.* devise, contrive; make up one's mind, decide.

надут/ый *a.* inflated, blown up, bloated; exaggerated; **—ь** see **надувать.**

надуш/енный, —ённый *a.* perfumed, scented; **—ить** *v.* perfume, scent; fumigate.

надфиль *m.* needle file, rat-tail file.

надфосфорный *a.* perphosphoric (acid).

надфюзеляжный *a.* (av.) dorsal.

надхвост/овой *a.* (anat.) suprapygal; **—ье** *n.* (orn.) upper tail coverts.

надхромовый *a.* perchromic (acid).

надхрящ/евая оболочка, —евая плева, —ница *f.* (anat.) perichondrium.

над/царство *n.* (biol.) superkingdom; **—циркониевый** *a.* perzirconic (acid); **—челюстной** *a.* supermaxillary; **—черепной** *a.* epicranial; **—чревный** *a.* epigastric; **—чревная область, —чревье** *n.* apigastrium; **—шахтный** *a.* above the mine shaft; head (house).

надши(ва)ть *v.* sew on, piece on, lengthen.

надшишковидный *a.* (anat.) suprapineal.

надъ— see **над—** (used before е, ю and я); **—яичниковый придаток** (anat.) epoophoron, parovarium.

надымить *v.* smoke up.

надымский *a.* (geog.) Nadym.

наедине *adv.* in private, alone.

наезд *m.* incursion; quick visit; **—ить** *v.* ride; train, break in (a horse); **—ник** *m.* rider, horseman; rider (of analytical balance); (ent.) ichneumonid fly (*Ichneumon*); **—ники** *pl.* Ichneumonidae.

наезж/ать *v.* run into, hit, collide (with); come, arrive; visit (occasionally); pack down (road); break in (horse); **—ивать** *see* **наездить**; **—ий** *a.* visiting; nonresident.

наём *m.* hire, rent(ing), lease; **брать в н.** *v.* rent (from); **отдавать в н., сдавать в н.** *v.* let, lease; **—ник** *m.* hired man; **—ный** *a.* hired.

наесться *v.* eat enough.

наехать *see* **наезжать**.

нажалить *v.* sting (all over).

нажаловаться *v.* complain (of).

нажари(ва)ть *v.* fry, roast; heat up.

нажат/ие *n.* pressing, pressure, depression; (telegr.) mark (condition); (comp.) click (of mouse button); **—ый** *a.* pressed down, depressed; reaped, harvested; **—ь** *see* **нажимать, нажинать**.

нажгут *fut. 3 pl. of* **нажечь**.

наждак *m.* emery (impure corundum).

нажадаться *v.* wait a long time.

наждачн/ый *a.* emery; **н. круг** emery wheel; **н. холст, —ая шкура, —ое полотно** emery cloth.

нажевать, нажёвывать *v.* chew (a given quantity).

наж/ечь *v.* burn, consume (fuel); warm up, heat up; **—жённый** *a.* burned, etc., *see v.*

нажив/а *f.* gain, profit; (fish) bait; **—ать** *v.* gain, acquire, get; contract (disease); **—ить, —лять** *v.*, **—ка** *f.*, **—ной** *a.* bait.

нажигать *see* **нажечь**.

нажим *m.* push, thrust, pressure, stress, emphasis; depression (of push button); squeeze (of bulb); clamp, pinchcock; **—ание** *n.* pushing, etc., *see v.*; **—ать** *v.* push, press (down), bear down, depress; punch; clamp, pinch; squeeze (juice); **—ать и отпустить** *v.* (comp.) click; **—ающее усилие** pressure.

нажимн/ой *a.* pressure; clamp(ing); push (button); **н. валик** press(ing) roller, pressure roller; printing roller; **н. механизм** (slabbing mill) screwdown; **н. стержень** push bar, press rod; **—ая планка** cleat; **—ое приспособление** printing device; clamp.

нажимчнк *m.* stuffing box.

нажин *m.* yield of harvested grain; **—ать** *v.* harvest, reap.

нажирание *see* **нажор**.

нажиров/ка *f.*, **—очный** *a.* (agr.) fattening.

нажить *see* **наживать**.

нажмёт *fut. 3 sing. of* **нажать**.

нажнёт *fut. 3 sing. of* **нажать**, reap.

нажор *m.* (tanning); steeping, stuffing, swelling, plumping; plumpness.

наз *m.* astronaut's emergency kit.

назавтра *adv.* (for) tomorrow.

назад *adv.* back(wards); **брать н.** *v.* back up, retract; **взгляд н.** retrospect; **год тому н.** a year ago; **движение н.** return; **ход н.** reverse running, backing; return stroke (of piston); **отогнутый н.** retroflexed; **—и** *adv.* in back, behind.

назализ(ир)овать *v.* (ling.) nasalize.

назв/ание *n.* name, designation; title; **носить н.** *v.* be called, be identified as; **—анный** *a.* named, called; **—ать** *see* **называть**.

назём *m.* dung, manure.

наземники *pl.* ground bugs (*Lygaeidae*).

наземн/ый *a.* land(-based), overland, ground, terrestrial;

surface (rock, water, etc.); **н. предмет** landmark; **—ая подготовка** (av.) ground training.

наземь *adv.* to the ground, down.

назидательный *a.* instructive, edifying.

назло *adv.* in spite of, in defiance of, out of spite; **как н.** unfortunately.

назнач/ать *v.* appoint, nominate, name, designate, assign; grant; predetermine, fix, set; prescribe (treatment); specify, call for; **—енец** *m.* appointed person.

назначен/ие *n.* appointing, etc., *see* **назначать**; appointment, assignment; function, purpose, designation, destination; (pharm.) prescription; **двойного —ия** dual purpose; **место —ия** destination; **общего —ия** general purpose, general duty; **особого —ия** special purpose; **по —ию врача** on doctor's orders; **станция —ия** receiving station, receiving end.

назнач/енный *a.* appointed, etc., *see* **назначать**; **—ить** *see* **назначать**.

назо— *prefix* naso— rhino—, nose.

назовёт *fut. 3 sing. of* **назвать**.

назойливый *a.* tiresome, importunate, insistent, troublesome, obtrusive.

назофарингеальный *a.* (anat.) nasopharyngeal.

назре/вание *n.* ripening, maturing; **—вать** *v.* ripen, mature; be about to happen; gather head (of abscess); become imminent; **—вающий** *a.* ripening, etc., *see v.*; **—вший** *a.* present, urgent (problem); **—лый** *a.* ripe, mature; **—ть** *see* **назревать**.

назубок *m.* file.

назубр/енный *a.* indented, etc., *see v.*; **—и(ва)ть** *v.* indent, notch, nick; learn by rote.

назыв/аемый *a.* called, etc., *see v.*; **так н.** so-called, what is known as; **—ание** *n.* calling, etc., *see v.*; **—ать** *v.* call, name, designate, term, refer (to), denote, describe, identify (as), mean (by).

назьма *gen. of* **назём**.

наи— *prefix* the most; **—более** *adv.* the most, utmost; best; **—больший** *a.* greatest, maximum, most, peak; worst (wear); overall (dimension); **—вероятнейший** *a.* most probable.

наивный *a.* naive, simple.

наи/выгоднейший *a.* most advantageous, most favorable, best; **—высший** *a.* highest, maximum, ceiling.

наидиды *pl.* (zool.) Naididae.

наизволок *adv.* uphill.

наизнанку *adv.* inside out, wrong side out.

наизусть *adv.* by heart, by rote.

наил/ивание *n.* silt deposition; **—ок** *m.* (agr.; geol.) warp.

наилучш/ий *a.* the best, optimal; **—им образом** to (the) best advantage, best, most efficiently.

наименее *adv.* the least; less.

наименов/ание *n.* name, denomination; item; **привести к одному —анию** *v.* (math.) reduce to one denomination; **—анный** *a.* named, etc., *see v.*; **—ать** *v.* name, call, denominate, designate.

наи/меньший *a.* the least, smallest, minimum; **н. общий** (math.) least common; **—низший** *a.* lowest, minimum.

наирит *m.* Nairit, chloroprene rubber.

наискос/ок, —ь *adv.* diagonally, obliquely, on a slant, skew; **располагать н.** *v.* skew.

наихудший *a.* the worst.

найден/ный *a.* found, etc., *see* **находить**; **—о, что** found to be.

Найквиста критерий Nyquist criterion.

найлон *m.* nylon.

найма *gen. of* **наём**.

наймёт *fut. 3 sing. of* **нанять**.

найти *see* **находить.**

найтов *m.* (naut.) lashing; **—ить** *v.* lash down.

НАК *abbr.* (**нитрил акриловой кислоты**) acrylonitrile.

наказ *m.* order; instructions; **—ание** *n.* punishment, penalty; **—анный** *a.* punished; **—(ыв)ать** *v.* punish.

накал *m.* incandescence, (intense) heat, glow; **батарея —а** filament battery, A battery; **белый н.** white heat, incandescence; **напряжение —а** (elec.) filament voltage; **нить —а** filament; **тело —а** luminous element; filament (of lamp); **ток —а** filament current, heating current; **цепь —а** heater power circuit.

накалённ/ость *f.* heat, incandescence; **—ый** *a.* incandescent, glowing, hot; thermionic (cathode).

накалив/ание *n.* heating, incandescence, glowing; **н. добела** incandescence, white heat; **лампа —ания** incandescent lamp; **—ать** *v.* heat, incandesce; bring to (white or red heat); **—аться** *v.* incandesce, get hot, glow; **—ающийся** *a.* incandescent.

накал/ить *see* **накаливать; —ка** *see* **накаливание.**

накалывать *v.* prick; split, break; pin on; slaughter, butcher.

накалять *see* **накаливать.**

накануне *adv.* the day before; *prep. gen.* before, on the eve of.

накапать *v.* drip, pour in drops.

накаплив/ание *n.* accumulation; **—ать** *see* **накоплять; —ающий** *a.* accumulating; **—ающий сумматор, —ающий счётчик** (comp.) accumulator; **—ающий энергию элемент** energy reservoir.

накапчивать *v.* smoke (up).

накапывать *v.* drip; dig (up).

накарбиживание *n.* carbide formation.

накат *m.* rolling (in); (paper) roller; (rolling) scab; subfloor(ing), dead floor, false ceiling; layer; (art.) counterrecoil; (wave) run-up; wash, uprush (of water); (auto.) coasting; application (of ink); **—анный** *a.* rolled, etc., *see* **накатывать; —ать** *see* **накатывать.**

накатина *f.* (trim) joist, trimmer.

накат/ка *see* **накатывание;** knurl, knurling tool; knurled surface; **винт с —кой** knurled screw; **—ник** *m.* flooring boards; (art.) counterrecoil mechanism; **—ный** *a.* rolling; board; **—ом** *adv.* (by) rolling; **движение —ом, езда —ом** coasting, free wheeling; **—чик** *m.* roller.

накатыв/ание *n.* rolling, etc., *see* v.; **—ать** *v.* roll (in, on); roll-thread; knurl, mill; pack (road); **—ающий** *a.* rolling, etc., *see* v.

накач/анный *a.* pumped, etc., *see* v.; **—ать** *see* **накачивать; —енный** *a.* rolled, etc., *see* **накатывать; —ивание** *n.* pumping, etc., *see* v.; inflation; **—ивать** *v.* pump (up), fill, inflate; feed, supply, deliver; **—ка** *see* **накачивание;** excitation (of laser, etc.).

накашивать *v.* (agr.) mow.

накерни(ва)ть *v.* prick-punch, center(-punch), mark, indent.

наки/дать *see* **накидывать; —дка** *f.* throwing on; cover, mantle, cloak, cape; increase (in price); **—дной** *a.* throw; additional; sleeve, coupling, union (nut); **—дывание** *n.* throwing on etc., *see* v.; **—дывать** *v.* thrown on, cover; add; **—дываться** *v.* attack; **—нутый** *a.* thrown on; covered; **—нуть** *see* **накидывать.**

накип/ать *see* **накипеть; —елый** *a.* deposited, incrusted; **—еобразование** *n.* scale formation; **—еочиститель** *m.* scaler; **—еть** *v.* boil up to the surface; be deposited, be incrusted; **—еудаление** *n.* scale removal; **—ной** *a. of* **накипь;** crustaceous, crust-like; **—ь** *f.* (boiler) scale, incrustation; deposit, sediment,

dregs, lees; sinter; scum; **—ятить** *v.* boil (up); **—ячённый** *a.* boiled (up).

накислороживание *n.* oxygenation.

накладк/а *f.* laying on top (of); overlapping; covering, (cover) plate, butt strap, gusset, patch; (brake) lining; (suction) cup; (typ.) sheet feed; (geol.) superposition, (over)lap; **с —ой** strap lap (joint).

накладная *f.* (com.) bill of lading, invoice.

накладн/ой *a.* laid on, put on, superposed; overlying; applied, plated; false (hair); **н. металл** metal plating; **—ое серебро** silver plate; **—ые расходы** overhead.

накладчик *m.* (typ.) hand feeder.

накладыв/аемый *a.* superposable; **—ание** *n.* laying on, etc., *see* v.; superposition; **—ать** *v.* lay on, put on, super(im)pose; apply, coat, plate; overlap; interfere; put in (stitches); fill (with); mount (on); telescope; **—ать сверху** superimpose; **—ающийся** *a.* superposable; superimposed.

наклёв *m.* (orn.) pecking, pipping; **—анный** *a.* pecked, pipped; **—ывание** *n.* pipping; (bot.) sprouting, germination.

наклёвать *see* **наклёвывать.**

наклёвывать *v.* peck (at), pip (eggshell); **—ся** *v.* begin sprouting.

накле/иваемый *a.* bonded (strain gage); **—ивание** *n.* gluing, pasting (on); **—и(ва)ть** *v.* glue, paste (on); **—йка** *f.* label, tag, sticker, nameplate; patch; gluing (on); veneering.

наклеймить *v.* brand, stamp.

наклейн/ой *a.* glued on; adhesive; **—ый пластинчатый тензометр** resistance-strip strain gage; **—ый угольный тензометр** carbon-strip strain gage.

наклёп *see* **наклёпывание; —анный** *a.* rivted on, etc., *see* v.

наклепать *see* **наклёпывать.**

наклёп/ка *f.* riveting on; riveted-on part; dressing (of scythe); **—ывание** *n.* riveting on, etc., *see* v.; cold work(ing); **—ывать** *v.* rivet on; (met.) cold-harden, cold-work, hammer-harden, wear-harden.

наклон *m.* slope, incline, inclination, slant, pitch, gradient, grade; tilt, cant, dip; (tool) rake; drift (of bore hole); **н. орбиты** orbital inclination; **в н.** at an incline; **механизм —а** tilting gear; **с —ом** inclined, tilted, at a slant; **—ение** *n.* inclination, dip, tilting, pitch; (gram.) mood; **—ение назад** (med.) retroversion; **магнитное —ение** magnetic dip; **стрелка —ения** (geol.) dip needle; **—ённый** *a.* inclined, etc., *see* **наклонять;** dip; **—ить** *see* **наклонять; —ная** *f.* inclined line.

наклонн/о *adv.* obliquely, slantingly, aslant; **—ость** *f.* inclination, leaning, tendency, bent, propensity, proclivity; **—ый** *a.* inclined, sloping, slanted, slanting, tilting, oblique; canted (fins); directional (drilling); **—ая линия** incline.

наклон/омер *m.* tiltmeter; **—яемый** *a.* inclinable; **—ять** *v.* incline, slant, slope, lean, tilt, tip; depress, decline; **—яться** *v.* slope, incline, lean (over).

наклю/ёт *fut. 3 sing. of* **наклевать; —нувшийся** *a.* slightly sprouted; **—нутый** *a.* (orn.) chipped, pipped; **—нуть** *v.* peck through; **—нуться** *v.* peck through, pip; happen upon; appear (of buds, sprouts).

наковальн/е-молоточковый *a.* (anat.) incudomalleal; **н.-стременной** *a.* incudostapedial; **—я** *f.* anvil; (anat.) incus, anvil; (meteor.) anvil cloud.

наков/анный *a.* forged on; **—(ыв)ать** *v.* forge on.

накожн/ик *m.* (zool.) scab mite (*Psoroptes*); **—ый** *a.* (epi)cutaneous, dermal, skin.

накоксовать *v.* coke.

накол *m.* pinhole.

наколачивать *v.* drive on, hammer on (or in); break; beat up.

наколенный *a.* knee; (comp.) laptop.

наколка *f.* pinning on; pricking out.

наколотить *see* **наколачивать.**

наколот/ый *a.* pinned on; pricked; split; **—ь** *see* **накалывать.**

наколоченный *a.* driven on; broken.

накол/ы-проколы *pl.* pricks; **—юшка** *f.* awl.

накомарник *m.* mosquito veil.

накомкать *v.* crumple up; lump.

наконец *adv.* at last, at length, finally.

наконечник *m.* tip, point, nose, end (piece); nozzle, spout, mouth(piece); nipple; adapter; head, cap; terminal, clip, clamp; top, extension; tag; ferrule; ring lug; (pole) shoe; **н.-распылитель** *m.* pulverizer, atomizer.

накоп/анный *a.* dug up (or out); **—ать** *v.* dig up (or out).

накопировать *v.* copy, duplicate.

накоп/итель *m.* accumulator; storage (unit), store, file; holding lagoon; tank; (comp.) memory; **н. прерываний** interrupt stacker; **н. на магнитной ленте** tape drive; **—ительный** *a.* accumulating; storing, storage; **—ительный блок** (comp.) pooling block; **—ить** *see* **накоплять; —ление** *n.* accumulation, accretion; storage, storing; build-up, pile-up; stockpiling; (energy) conservation; background (of experience); (med.) congestion; **коэффициент —ления** build-up factor; **—ленный** *a.* accumulated, etc., *see v.*; cumulative; **—лять** *v.* accumulate, gather, heap up, stack, pile up, stock up; build up, gain; store up; concentrate, enrich; **—ляться** *v.* accumulate, collect, gather; **—ляющийся** *a.* cumulative.

накоп/тить *v.* smoke; **—чённый** *a.* smoked.

накорм/ить *v.* feed; **—ленный** *a.* fed.

накоротк/е *adv.* at a short distance, nearby; for a short time; **—о** *adv.* quickly, in a short time; (elec.) short; **замкнуть —о** *v.* short (out), short-circuit.

накос *m.* mowed grass, mowed grain; **—ить** *v.* mow.

накостница *f.* (vet.) exostosis, bony lump.

накось *adv.* on a slant, on a bias.

накошенный *a.* mowed, cut.

накрадываться *v.* steal up to, creep up.

накраивать *v.* cut (patterns).

накрапывать *v.* spatter (of rain).

накрас/ить *see* **накрашивать; —ка** *f.* paint(ing); pigment film; dyeing.

накрахмалить *v.* starch.

накрашив/аемость *f.* dyeability; **—ать** *v.* paint; dye.

накрен/ённый *a.* tilted, lopsided; **—ить, —ять** *v.* tilt, tip (to one side).

накрепко *adv.* firmly, fast, tightly; very.

накрест *adv.* cross(wise); **н. лежащий** *a.* alternate (angles).

накрит *m.* (min.) nacrite.

накро/енный *a.,* **—ить** *v.* cut (patterns).

накрой *m.* lap (joint), overlapping.

накромс/анный *a.* shredded; **—ать** *v.* shred.

накрошить *v.* crumble; litter with crumbs.

накру/тить, —чивать *v.* wind, coil, twist (on); screw on; **—ченный** *a.* wound, coiled, etc., *see v.*

накры/вание *n.* covering; **—вать, —ть** *v.* cover; hit, strike (target); **—вка** *f.* finish coat (of plaster); **—тие** *n.* cover(ing); hitting; **—тый** *a.* covered.

нактоуз *m.* binnacle (of compass).

накуп/ать *v.* buy; bathe; **—ить** *v.* buy, purchase; **—ленный** *a.* purchased.

накури(ва)ть *v.* smoke (up); distill.

накус/анный *a.* bitten up; **—(ыв)ать** *v.* bite or sting all over.

накушаться *v.* eat enough.

накуют *fut. 3 pl. of* **наковать.**

налавливать *v.* catch, trap.

налагать *v.* impose, inflict; put on, superimpose, lay over; set (limits).

нала/дить *see* **налаживать; —дка** *f.,* **—дочный** *a.* fixing, etc., *see v.*; adjustment, alignment, tune-up, set-up (of lathe); **—дчик** *m.* repairman, troubleshooter, field engineer; (tool) setter-up; **—женность** *f.* (state of) good repair; **—женный** *a.* fixed, etc., *see v.*; **—живание** *see* **наладка; —живать** *v.* fix, repair, put right, put in order; (comp.) debug (a computer), troubleshoot; set up, adjust, tune up, align; create, organize.

налакиров(ыв)ать *v.* lacquer, varnish.

наламывать *v.* break up.

налево *adv.* (to the) left, on the left.

налег/ание *n.* superposition; overlap; **—ать** *v.* overlie; lean on; apply oneself; urge, make do; further (a cause); **—ающий** *a.* overlying, superimposed, incumbent.

налегке *adv.* unloaded, without baggage; lightly dressed; (traveling) light.

налед/енелый *a.* iced, covered with ice; **—енеть** *v.* get covered with ice, freeze over.

на/лёдный *a.,* **наледь** *f.* ice coating, ice crust, icing; water on top of ice.

належать *see* **налёживать.**

налёж/ивать *v.* acquire (bed sores); **—ка** *f.* (text.) defective spot (acquired while lying).

налез(а)ть *v.* get in or on; fit; climb on.

налепестный *a.* (bot.) epipetalous.

налеп/ить, —лять *v.* stick on, glue on; **—ленный** *a.* glued on; **—ь** *f.* clinging snow.

налёт *m.* deposit, incrustation, coating; bloom, tarnish, film, residue; accrued flying time; raid, inroad; sudden attack, onslaught, invasion (of insects); swoop (of bird); condensate, "sweat".

налет/ать *v.* fly (on, against; a given time or distance); (av.) log flying hours; strike, collide; come (of wind); drift in; rush at, fall upon; swoop down; **—ающий** *a.* flying, etc., *see v.*; incident, impinging, colliding, bombarding (particle); **—еть** *v.* fly against, fly to; encounter; attack; appear suddenly, start (of storm); arrive; settle down.

налёт/ный *a.* (orn.) migratory; **—образный** *a.* (biol.) pruinose, frosty; **—ывать** *see* **налетать.**

налечь *see* **налегать.**

налив *see* **наливание;** fullness, sap, juice; juiciness; filling, formation (of fruit, grain); bulk; **—ание** *n.* pouring in, etc., *see v.*; infusion; **—ать** *v.* pour in, introduce, fill (up); cast; **—аться** *v.* be poured in, run in; ripen (of fruit); form (of grain); **—ка** *see* **наливание;** fruit liqueur; **—ная** *f.* filling station, fuel pump; **—ники** *pl.* (prot.) Ciliata.

наливн/ой *a.* pouring, filling; molded; juicy (fruit); liquid (cargo); inlet (pipe); overshot (wheel); tank (car); water (mill); wet (dock); ripe, juicy (fruit); (anat.) full, firm; **—ое отверстие** inlet; **—ое судно** tanker.

наливочные *pl.* (zool.) Infusoria.

налим *m.,* **—ий** *a.* (ichth.) burbot (*Lota l.*); **усатый н.** rockling (*Ciliata; Gaidropsarus*).

налинов(ыв)ать *v.* rule, line.

налип/аемость *f.* adhesiveness; adhesion; **—ание** *n.* adhering, etc., *see v.*; adhesion; adherence (of soil); **—ать, —нуть** *v.* adhere, stick, cling; cake.

налитографировать *v.* lithograph.

налит/ой *a.* ripe, juicy; full (grain); firm, solid (body); **—ый** *a.* poured in, filled; swollen; *see* **налитой; —ь** *see* **наливать.**

нали/цо *adv.* present, available, on hand; **—чествовать** *v.* be present; **—чие** *n.* presence, availability; occurrence; **быть в —чии** *v.* be (present), be on hand, be in stock; **имеющийся в —чии** *a.* on hand, available, at our disposal; **при —чии** given, with; **при —чии возможности** where(ver) possible, when(ever) possible, if possible.

наличник *m.* (arch.) platband, crosspiece; (door, window) frame, case; weather strip; liner; (anvil) face, plate; face, flat side (of hammer); (ent.) clypeus, shield; **—овый** *a.* clypeal; **—ообразный** *a.* clypeiform.

наличн/ость *f.,* **—ые** *pl.* cash; goods on hand; presence; **в —ости** present, ready, on hand, available; **за —ые** cash (payment).

наличн/ый *a.* present, on hand, available; effective; **н. расчёт** cash payment; **н. состав** personnel; **—ые деньги** cash, ready money.

налобн/ик *m.* headrest; front (bridle) strap; **—ый** *a.* (on the) forehead; head.

налов/ить *v.* catch, trap; **—ленный** *a.* caught, trapped.

наловчиться *v.* become dextrous, become skilful, learn, get the know-how.

налог *m.,* **—овый** *a.* tax, assessment, charge, duty; **до вычета —а** before taxes; **облагать —ом** *v.* tax, assess; **—овый инспектор** assessor; **—ообложение** *n.* taxation; **—оплательщик** *m.* taxpayer; **—оспособный** *a.* taxable.

налож/ение *n.* laying on, imposition, superposition, superimposing; overlap; application; **—енный** *a.* laid on, laid over, (super)imposed; **—енный платёж** (com.) cash on delivery, C.O.D.; **—имость** *f.* applicability; **—ить** *see* **налагать, накладывать.**

налокотник *m.* elbow guard.

наломать *v.* break (up).

налорфин *m.* Nalorphine, allorphine.

налощить *v.* shine, polish, gloss.

налу/дить *v.* tin; **—женный** *a.* tinned.

налущи(ва)ть *v.* shell, husk.

нальёт *fut. 3 sing. of* **налить.**

нальчикин *m.* nalchikin, Nalchik clay.

наляжет *fut. 3 sing. of* **налечь.**

нам *dat. of* **мы,** (to) us, for us.

намагни/тить *v.* magnetize; **—ченность** *f.* (degree of) magnetization; **—ченный** *a.* magnetized; **—чиваемость** *f.* magnetizability; **—чиваемый** *a.* magnetizable; **—чивание** *n.* magnetization; **—чивать** *v.* magnetize; **—чивающий** *a.* magnetizing; **—чивающее устройство** magnetizer; **—чивающийся** *a.* magnetizable.

намаз/анный *a.* smeared, etc., *see v.;* **—ать** *see* **намазывать; —ка** *f.,* **—ный** *a.* smearing; paste, filler; (leather) depilatory-applying (machine); **—ывание** *n.* smearing, etc., *see v.;* **—ывать** *v.* smear, daub, paste, coat, cover, spread; **—ь** *f.* (leather) depilatory paste.

намалывать *v.* mill, grind.

намасл/енный *a.* greased, oiled; **—ивание** *n.* greasing, oiling, lubrication; **—и(ва)ть** *v.* grease, oil, lubricate.

наматыв/ание *n.* winding, etc., *see v.;* **—ать** *v.* wind, reel, coil; take up, wrap; **—ающий** *a.* winding, etc., *see v.;* take-up (reel).

намачив/ание *n.* wetting, etc., *see v.;* **—ать** *v.* wet, moisten; soak, steep, macerate; pack, preserve, pickle.

намащивать *v.* pave.

намбаты *pl.* (mam.) numbats (*Myrmecobiidae*).

намеж/евать, —ёвывать *v.* mark limits, bound.

намёк *m.* hint, allusion, insinuation.

намек/ать, —нуть *v.* hint, insinuate, allude (to), suggest, indicate.

намёл *past m. sing. of* **намести.**

намели(ва)ть *v.* chalk.

намельчить *v.* pulverize, crush.

намен/ивать, —ять *v.* exchange; appear, emerge, take shape.

намер/еваться *v.* intend, propose, design, consider; **—ение** *n.* intention, purpose, design; **—енный** *a.* intentional, deliberate, premeditated.

намерз/ание *n.* freezing over; **—ать** *v.* freeze over.

намёрз/нуть *see* **намерзать; —ший** *a.* frozen over.

намери(ва)ть *v.* measure.

намертво *adv.* dead; very firmly; permanently; **обжигать н.** *v.* deadburn.

намерять *see* **намеривать.**

намесить *see* **намешивать.**

намести *v.* sweep up; drift, carry.

намёт *m.* drift, landing net; (plaster) scratch coat; gallop, canter; **—анный** *a.* carried, etc., *see v.;* experienced.

наметать *v.* carry, drift; sweep up; throw, pitch (unto); spawn, breed; baste.

наметить *see* **намечать.**

намёт/ка *f.,* **—очный** *a.* mark(ing), outline, outlining, preliminary plan, rough draft; basting (thread); clamp; landing net; measuring rod, sounding rod; (art.) trunnion cap.

намётывать *v.* throw, spawn; baste.

намеч/ать *v.* mark, locate, spot; note, appoint, fix, decide (on); outline, plan, project, designate, schedule, slate; contemplate, have in view; set (a course); aim (a gun); **—аться** *v.* be outlined, begin to show; **—енный** *a.* marked, etc., *see v.;* target (date).

намеш/анный *a.* kneaded, mixed in, added; **—(ив)ать** *v.* knead, mix in, add.

нами *instr. of* **мы,** (by) us.

намин *m.* (vet.) inflamed sore; **—ать** *v.* knead, work; rub sore; **—ка** *f.* (vet.) capellet, bruised heel.

намного *adv.* (by) far, much, a great deal, considerably, well, vastly; many (fewer).

намогильный *a.* sepulchral, burial.

намоет *fut. 3 sing. of* **намыть.**

намозолить *v.* form a callus.

намок/аемость *f.* wettability; water absorption; **—ание** *n.* wetting; **—ать, —нуть** *v.* get wet; **—ший** *a.* wet, soaked.

намол *m.* milling; yield of milled flour; **—ачивание** *n.* threshing; **—ачивать** *v.* thresh (out); **—от** *m.* threshing; grain yield; **—отить** *see* **намолачивать; —отый** *a.* milled, ground; **—оть** *v.* mill, grind; **—оченный** *a.* threshed out.

намораживать *v.* freeze (on); build up (tips of thermocouples).

намордник *m.* muzzle.

наморить *v.* exterminate; stain (wood).

наморо/женный *a.* frozen; **—зить** *see* **намораживать.**

наморось *f.* condensation from a drizzle fog.

наморщи(ва)ть *v.* wrinkle up.

намостить *v.* pave; floor.

намота *f.* wrap-up.

намот/анный *a.* wound, coiled; **—ать** *see* **наматывать; —ка** *f.* winding, coil; **станок для —ки** coil winder; **—очный** *a.* (coil-)winding, reeling.

намоч/енный *a.* wet(ted); soaked, steeped; **—ить** *see* **намачивать.**

намощённый *a.* paved; floored.

намоющий *pr. act. part. of* **намыть.**

намусорить *v.* litter.

намутить *v.* make turbid, cloud up.

намучиться *v.* suffer (a great deal).

намушник *m.* (art.) protector.

намыв *see* **намывание;** inwash; (geol.) alluvium; (filter) precoat; **—ание** *n.* washing up, etc., *see v.;* alluviation, deposition, aggradation (of stream); **—ать** *v.* wash up, wash in (soil); build up (bank); deposit, alluviate, aggrade; pan out (gold); **—ка** *see* **намывание; —ной** *a.* alluvial; washed in, wave-built; washed up; built up; hydraulic fill (dam).

намыл/енный *a.* soaped, lathered; **—и(ва)ть** *v.* soap, lather.

намыть *see* **намывать.**

намять *see* **наминать.**

нанайский *a.* (geog.) Nanaian.

нанашивать *v.* carry, bring (in).

нанд/ер *m.* (ichth.) Nandus; **—инин** *m.* nandinine; **—иния** *f.* (mam.) Nandinia; **—овые** *pl.* leaffishes (*Nandidae*); (orn.) Rheidae; **—у** *m.* Rhea; *pl.* Rheidae.

нанес/ение *n.* applying, etc., *see* **наносить;** application; infliction; **н. делений** graduation; **н. покрытия** coating; **—ённый** *a.* applied, etc., *see* **наносить;** wrought (damage); brought; drawn; **—ти** *see* **наносить.**

на-нет: сойти н. *v.* come to nothing.

нанизм *m.* nanism, dwarfishness.

наниз(ыв)ать *v.* thread, string (on).

наниматель *m.* employer; tenant, lessee.

нанимать *v.* hire, engage, employ; rent; **—ся** *v.* apply for work; be hired.

нанк/а *f.* (text.) nankeen; **—инский** *a.* (geog.) Nankin; **—овый** *a.* nankeen.

нанно— *prefix* nan(n)o— (dwarf); **—перка** *f.* (ichth.) pigmy perch (*Nannoperca*); **—стом** *m.* pencilfish (*Nannostomus*).

нано— *prefix* nano— (10^{-9}; dwarf); **—ампер** *m.* (elec.) nanoampere.

наново *adv.* again.

наногенри *m.* nanohenry.

нанопланктон *m.* (biol.) nanoplankton.

нанос *m.* (geol.) alluvium; alluviation, deposition, aggradation, accretion; silt; deposit, load, drift; overburden (of rock); (sand) bar; **—ы** *pl.* detritus, drift, sediment(s); (river) load.

наносекунда *f.* millimicrosecond.

наноситель *m.* draftsman.

наносить *v.* apply (to), coat (with); bring; heap, drift; deposit, build up; aggrade; plot, draw, map; insert, inscribe, enter; punch (data on cards); mark (off), calibrate; inflict (damage).

наносн/ый *a.* (geol.) alluvial, drift; alien, superficial; **н. слой, —ая земля, —ое отложение** alluvium, alluvion; **—ая почва** alluvial deposit, silt, transported soil.

наносо/перехватывающий, —улавливающий *a.* desilting (area); sediment-detention (basin); **—перехватывающее устройство** sediment or silt excluder.

нанофарада *f.* (elec.) nanofarad.

нанофин *m.* Nanofin, 2, 6-lutidine.

наношенный *see* **нанесённый.**

нансук *m.,* **—овый** *a.* (text.) nainsook.

нантокит *m.* (min.) nantokite.

нантский *a.* (geog.) Nantes.

нанят/ой *a.* hired; rented; **—ь** *see* **нанимать.**

наоборот *adv.* inversely, the opposite way; wrong side out; conversely, vice versa; on the contrary, on the other hand.

наобум *adv.* at random, haphazardly.

наоконный *a.* (on the) window.

наострить *v.* sharpen, grind.

наотический *a.* naotic.

наоткос *adv.* aslant, slantwise, obliquely.

наоткрывать *v.* open (in quantity).

наотрез *adv.* flatly, point-blank.

наохри(ва)ть *v.* coat with ocher.

напавший *a.* having fallen, etc., *see* **нападать.**

напад *see* **нападение; —ать** *v.* fall (on, out), accumulate; attack, invade, infest, encounter, run into, find; find fault (with), criticize; **—ающий** *a.* falling, etc., *see v.;* **—ение** *n.* attack, invasion, infestation; **—ки** *pl.* criticism, attacks, accusations.

напа/ивать *v.* solder on, fuse on; water (livestock); **—йка** *f.* soldering on, building up (metal); soldered piece.

напаковка *f.* filling, packing.

напалечник *m.* (lab.) fingerstall.

напалм *m.,* **—овый** *a.* (mil.) Napalm.

напалывать *v.* weed.

напари(ва)ть *v.* steam.

напарник *m.* partner, associate.

напарье *n.* auger, (screw) drill.

напас/ать, —ти *v.* save (up).

напасть *see* **нападать;** *f.* disaster, misfortune.

напах(ив)ать *v.* plow.

напахтать *v.* churn (up).

напачкать *v.* dirty, soil.

напая/нный *a.* soldered on, fused on; **—ть** *see* **напаивать.**

НАПВ *abbr.* (**несинхронное автоматическое повторное включение**) asynchronous automatic reclosing.

напев *m.* tune, melody; **—ать** *v.* sing; hum; **—ный** *a.* melodious.

напекать *v.* bake, roast.

напеллин *m.* napelline, benzaconine.

напени(ва)ть(ся) *v.* foam up, froth up.

наперво *adv.* first (of all).

наперебой *see* **наперерыв.**

наперевес *adv.* atilt, tilting.

наперёд *adv.* in advance, beforehand; in front; first.

напере/кор *adv. and prep. dat.* in defiance (of), counter (to); **—крест** *adv.* crosswise; **—рез** *adv.* across (path of travel); **—рыв** *adv.* vying (with each other); interrupting (one another).

напереть *see* **напирать.**

наперечёт *adv.* thoroughly, without exception; there are few.

наперст/ковый *a.,* **—ок** *m.,* **—очный** *a.* thimble; (detonator) well.

наперстянка *f.* (bot.) digitalis.

напетлять *v.* loop; tangle up.

напеть *see* **напевать.**

напечат/анный *a.* printed, published; **—ать** *v.* print, publish.

напеч/ённый *a.* baked, roasted; **—ь** *v.* bake, roast.

напиваться *v.* quench one's thirst; get drunk.

напил/и(ва)ть *v.* saw (out, up); file; **—ок, —ьник** *m.,* **—очный** *a.* file; **—ьник-брусовка** *m.* coarse file.

напирать *v.* (de)press.

напис/ание *n.* writing; **—анный** *a.* written; **—ать** *v.* write (down); paint.

напит/анный *a.* impregnated, saturated; engorged; **—ать** *see* **напитывать.**

напиток *m.* drink, beverage; liquor.

напитыв/ание *n.* saturation, etc., *see v.;* **—ать** *v.* saturate, impregnate, soak, steep; infiltrate; satiate.

напиться *see* **напиваться.**

напих(ив)ать *v.* stuff, pack, fill.

напишет *fut. 3 sing. of* **написать.**

наплав *m.,* **—ать** *v.* float; **—ить** *see* **наплавливать; —ка** *f.* fusing, etc., *see v.;* (met.) surfacing; hard-facing; bead(ing), weld seam; **—ление** *n.* fusing, etc., *see v.;* **—ленный** *a.* fused, etc., *see v.;* **—ливать, —лять** *v.* fuse, (s)melt; weld on, build up; face, surface, overlay; hard-face; float.

наплав/ной, —очный *a.* fused; fusing; smelting; welding (metal); surfacing (alloy); floating; **н. материал** (welding) filler.

напластать *v.* slice up.

напластов/ание *n.* (geol.) stratification, deposition, bedding; super(im)position, overlap(ping); **—ания** *pl.* strata; **—анный** *a.* stratified; super(im)posed; unconformity (iceberg); **—(ыв)ать** *v.* arrange in layers; super(im)pose; overlap; deposit (sediments); **—(ыв)аться** *v.* stratify.

наплевать *v.* spit (out).

наплескать, наплёскивать *v.* splash, spatter (on).

наплечный *a.* (on the) shoulder.

наплодить *v.* bring forth, produce; **—ся** *v.* multiply, breed.

наплы/в *m.* floating, etc., *see v.;* influx, abundance, accumulation; extension; excrescence, burl, swelling, wart; curly grain (wood defect); (cinematography) dissolve; bead(ing); roll, collar, scab; **—(ва)ть** *v.* float, drift, sail (against, over, together); spread (of smell, sound); **—вной** *a.* floating; (geol.) alluvial.

наплюёт *fut. 3 sing. of* **наплевать.**

наплющи(ва)ть *v.* flatten.

наповал *adv.* on the spot, outright.

наподда(ва)ть *v.* strike (upward); increase, add (steam).

наподобие *prep. gen.* like, resembling.

напо/енный *a.* watered (stock); **—ённый** *a.* saturated (with); **—ить** *v.* saturate, drench; water.

напой *m.* soldered-on piece.

напоказ *adv.* for show, for demonstration.

наполаскивать *v.* rinse.

наполеонит *m.* (petr.) napoleonite, corsite.

наполз/ать, —ти *v.* creep (in on, over).

наполиров(ыв)ать *v.* polish.

наполн/ение *n.* filling, etc., *see v.;* admission; charge; inflation; fullness; (concrete) aggregate; **коэффициент —ения** coefficient of charge; **недостаточного —ения** weak (pulse); **хорошего —ения** strong (pulse); **—енность** *f.* fullness; **—енный** *a.* filled, etc., *see v.;* full; **—енный газом** gas-filled; **—итель** *m.* filler; extender; additive; sealer; feeder, charger; **—ительный** *a.* filling, etc., *see v.;* **—ить, —ять** *v.* fill (up), pack, stuff; load, charge; feed, admit; extend; seal; inflate; **—яющий** *a.* filling, etc., *see v.*

наполовину *adv.* (in or by) half; twice (as low); semi—.

наполоскать *v.* rinse.

наполоть *v.* (agr.) weed.

наполу: насыщать н. half-saturate.

напольный *a.* low-ground, ground-type; outdoor, field; floor.

напом/инание *n.* reminding, reminder; **—инать** *v.* remind, recall, suggest, resemble, be like; **—инающий** *a.* reminding, etc., *see v.;* reminiscent; **—им, что** recall, it will be recalled; **—нить** *see* **напоминать.**

напополам *adv.* in half.

напор *m.* (hydr.) head; pressure; thrust; stress; **высота —а** head; **—истый** *a.* energetic, assertive; **—ноструйный** *a.* pressure, reaction (turbine); **—ный** *a.* pressure; delivery (conduit); ascending, rising, stand

(pipe); discharge (nozzle); **—ный бак** header, supply tank; gravity tank; **—ная флотация** pressurized air flotation; **—ное движение** crowding motion (of bulldozer); **—омер** *m.* pressure gage.

напороть *v.* gore; rip; **—ся** *v.* run up (against); get pierced.

напорошить *v.* powder, sprinkle, sift.

напор/тить *v.* spoil, damage; **—ченный** *a.* spoiled, damaged, reject.

напослед/ках, —ок *adv.* at the end, in conclusion, finally; after all.

напочвенный *a.* ground.

напоют *fut. 3 pl. of* **напеть; напоить.**

напр. *abbr.* (**например**) for example.

направ/итель *m.* guide; **—ительный** *a.* guiding, directing; **—ительное тельце** (gen.) polar body, polocyte; **—ить** *see* **направлять; —ка** *f.* adjustment, setting.

направлен/ие *n.* direction; trend; tendency, leaning; bearing, set; alignment; course, route; guidance, guiding; specialization; sense (of lines, rotation, etc.); line, field, avenue (of research); type, e.g., **сального —ия** lard-type; order, permit; (job) assignment; **код —ия** (comp.) routing code; **основное н.** basic concept; main trend; **переменить н.** *v.* reverse; **по —ию** in the direction (of), toward, with; **побочное н. реакции** side reaction; **следовать в —ии** *v.* (av.) be bound (for); **—ноискривлённый** *a.* controlled directional (well); **—ность** *f.* directivity; trend; **диаграмма —ности** beam pattern; directional pattern; **—ный** *a.* directed, etc., *see* **направлять;** directional, directive; pointing; purposeful, intentional, target; **—ный вверх** upward; **—ный вниз** downward; **—ный внутрь** inward(ly); **—ный наружу** outward.

направл/яемый *a.* guided; **—ять** *v.* direct, guide, lead, channel (into); control, regulate; focus (on); aim, point; set, adjust, fix; train (on), project; send, refer; **—яться** *v.* set out, head (for); straighten out; **—яющая** *f.* guide, rail, runner, slide(way); (lathes) slide guide; carriage; (math.) directrix.

направляющ/ий *a.* guiding, guide, directive, directing; control(ling), regulating; leading, leader; pilot(ing); key (word); set, adjusting (screw); deflecting (wall, etc.); (chem.) determinative (group); **н. лист** baffle plate, deflector; **н. лоток** baffle; **н. ролик** guide (pulley), idler; **н. стержень** steering bar, guide; **н. экран** baffle; **—ая поверхность** sliding track, slide; **—ая проводка** (rolling) guard; **—ая связка** (anat.) gubernaculum; **—ая сила** controlling force; **—ее колесо** idle wheel, idler; steering wheel; **—ее поле** (nucl.) guide field; **—ее устройство** guide.

направо *adv.* (to the) right, on the right.

напрактиковаться *v.* get (enough) practice.

напрасн/о *adv.* in vain, to no purpose, uselessly; **не н.** to some purpose; **—ый** *a.* useless, vain, purposeless.

напрашиваться *v.* thrust oneself (upon); ask (for); suggest itself.

напревать *v.* decay; become inflamed.

напрессов(ыв)ать *v.* press onto, press-fit; emboss.

напрёт *fut. 3 sing. of* **напереть.**

напреть *see* **напревать.**

например *adv.* for example, for instance, to illustrate; **так н.** for instance; thus.

напринимать *v.* accept, take.

напрокат *adv.* on hire, for hire; **сдавать н.** *v.* hire out, let.

напрол/ёт *adv.* through, without interruption; **—ом** *adv.* right through; **идти —ом** *v.* stop at nothing; break through.

напроситься *see* **напрашиваться.**

напротив *adv. and prep. gen.* opposite, counter, facing, across; *adv.* on the contrary; on the other hand.

напрочь *adv.* altogether, entirely.

напружини(ва)ть *v.* spring (over, into); tense up (for springing over).

напружи(ва)ться *v.* strain oneself.

напрут *fut. 3 pl. of* **напереть.**

напрыск *m.* sprinkling, dispersion; **—(ив)ать** *v.* sprinkle.

напряг/атель *m.* (anat.) tensor; **—ать** *v.* stress, strain, exert, force, tax; **—ающий** *a.* stressing, etc., *see v.*; tensor (muscle).

напрядать *v.* spin.

напряжен/ие *n.* stress, pressure, tension, strain; (elec.) voltage; (electrode) potential; exertion, effort; **н. в отливке** casting stress; **н. на зажимах** terminal voltage; **н. на поверхности** surface tension; **н. от** *or* **при кручении** torsional stress; **н. при изгибе** bending stress; **н. печи** furnace voltage; **н. при разрыве** breaking stress; **н. разложения** decomposition voltage; **н. смещения сетки** (electron.) grid bias; **н. тока** voltage; **без —ия** (elec.) dead; **высокого —ия** (elec.) high-voltage (line); high-pressure; **механическое н.** mechanical stress; **наложение н.** stressing; **низкого —ия** low-voltage (line); low-pressure; **поверхностное н.** surface tension; **повышать н.** *v.* (elec.) boost; **под —ием** (elec.) live, charged; **подавать н. на** *v.* energize; **постоянного —ия** constant-voltage; constant-pressure; **предельное н.** breaking load, maximum stress; **ряд —ий** electromotive series; **температурное н., тепловое н.** thermal stress; **узел —ия** (elec.) potential node; **чрезмерное н.** overstrain.

напряжённ/о *adv.* tensely, under tension; **—о-армированный** *a.* prestressed reinforced (concrete); **—ость** *f.* intensity, strength; tension; strain; (mech.) stress level; (biol.) competition (for food); **—ость поля** (elec.) field intensity; **—ый** *a.* tense, strained, taut; intense, intensive; stressed; tight (fit); **—ое состояние** stress; **предварительно —ый** *a.* prestressed (concrete).

напрям/ик, —ки *adv.* straight; point-blank.

напрясть *v.* spin.

напрятать *v.* hide, conceal.

напрячь *see* **напрягать.**

напугать *v.* frighten, scare.

напудри(ва)ть *v.* dust, powder.

напульсник *m.* wrist band.

напус/к *m.* letting in, etc., *see v.*; admission; irrigation, flood(ing); bleeding-in; leak-in; lap (joint); overlap; projection; **в н.** *adv.* lap, overlapping; **полив —ком** (agr.) flooding; flood irrigation; **сросток в н.** lap joint; **—кание** *see* **напуск; —кать** *v.* let in, admit, run in fill (with), flood; (over)lap; let down; **—кной** *a.* let in, admitted; assumed, put on; overlapping; **—тить** *see* **напускать.**

напут/анный *a.* confused, entangled; **—(ыв)ать** *v.* confuse, entangle, make a mess (of); make a mistake.

напух/ание *n.* swelling; **—ать, —нуть** *v.* swell.

напущенный *a.* let in, admitted, run in; (over)lapped.

напыжи(ва)ться *v.* strain, exert oneself.

напыл/ение *n.* raising dust, etc., *see v.*; (plasma) spraying, spray-coating, deposition; **—ённый** *a.* spray-coated; **—и(ва)ть** *v.* raise dust; spray, dust; deposit; (electron microscopy) sputter, shadow; **—ьник** *m.* dust screen.

напяли(ва)ть *v.* pull on, don, stretch on.

нар *m.* (mam.) a hybrid camel, nar.

нар— *prefix* (**народный**) the people's.

нараб/атывать, —отать *v.* produce, turn out; earn, make; operate; **—отаться** *v.* be exhausted by work; **—отка** *f.* (accrued) operating time, running time; **—отка на отказ** full (operating) time.

наравне *adv.* on a level (with), flush (with), on a par (with), just as, like.

наральник *m.* tip, point (of cultivator).

нараст/ание *n.* growth, growing, rise; (math.) slope; enhancement, augmentation; accumulation, building up; increment; build-up, increase (of pressure); rate (of current); (min.) accretion; **коэффициент —ания** growth factor; **—ать** *v.* grow on, be formed on; increase, accumulate; build up; enhance, augment; **—ающий** *a.* growing, etc., *see v.*; incremental; cumulative; progressive; **—и** *see* **нарастать; —ить** *see* **наращивать.**

нарасхват *adv.* in great demand.

наращ/ающий *see* **нарастающий; —ение** *see* **наращивание;** (math.) increment; **—ённый** *a.* accumulated, etc., *see v.*; **—ивание** *n.* accumulating, etc., *see v.*; accumulation, increment, accretion; connection, joint, splicing; **—ивание хромированием** chrome plating; **—ивать** *v.* accumulate; grow, cultivate, raise; graft, join, splice, connect, scarf; lengthen, add (pipe); increase; pick up, gather (speed); extend, advance; build up, plate; feed (drill tools); **—иваться** *v.* increase.

нарбоннский *a.* (geog.) Narbonne.

нарвал *m.* (mam.) narwhal (*Monodon monoceros*).

нарвать *v.* tear off, gather, pick; shred, tear up; dig up; swell and fester; **—ся** *v.* encounter, meet.

нарвский *a.* (geog.) Narva.

нара *m., —овый a.* citronella (grass or oil).

нардосмия *f.* (bot.) Nardosmia.

нарёберный *a.* (on the) rib.

нарез *see* **нарезка;** groove; **—ы** *pl.* rifling; **—ание** *n.* cutting, etc., *see* **нарезывать; —анный** *a.* cut, etc., *see* **нарезывать; —ать** *see* **нарезывать.**

нарезвиться *v.* develop further.

нарезк/а *f.* cut, incision, indentation; cutting, threading; thread (of screw), worm; rifling; division; allotment (of land); (min.) development; (leather) embossing; **н. борозд** (agr.) ridging, (deep) furrowing; **с —ой** serrated; threaded; **с правой —ой** right-handed (screw).

нарез/ной *a.* cut; threaded, tapped; rifled; **—ывание** *n.* cutting, etc., *see v.*; **—ывать** *v.* cut (up); thread, tap; chase; groove, rifle; hob; slaughter; **—ывать под** thread for, tap for.

наречие *n.* dialect; (gram.) adverb.

нарзан *m., —ный a.* Narzan mineral water.

наринг/енин *m.* naringenin, 4,5,7-trihydroxyflavanone; **—ин** *m.* naringin.

нарисов/анный *a.* drawn, sketched; **—(ыв)ать** *v.* draw, sketch, delineate, depict.

нарифл/ение *n.* rifle, rifling, grooving; (min.) rifle; **—ённый** *a.* rifled, grooved; **—ять** *v.* rifle, groove.

нарицательный *a.* nominal; common, generic; face (value).

нарко(гнюсо)вые *pl.* numbfishes (*Narkidae*).

наркоз *m.* (med.) narcosis, anesthesia.

нарколан *m.* Narcolan, tribromoethanol.

нарком *m.* People's commissar.

наркоман *m.* drug addict; **—ия** *f.* drug addiction; **алкогольная —ия** alcoholism.

наркотиз/ация *f.* narcotization, anesthetization; **—(ир)овать** *v.* narcotize, anesthetize; **—м** *m.* narcotism, addiction.

наркот/ик *m.* narcotic; drug addict; **—ин** *m.* narcotine, noscapine; **—ический** *a.,* **—ическое средство** narcotic.

наровский *a.* (geog.) Narva.

народ *m.* people, nation; **—ить** *v.* give birth (to), bear; **—ность** *f.* nationality; national character; people; **—нохозяйственный** *a.* national economy; **—ный** *a.* popular, people's, national, public; common (name); folk (medicine); **—ное здравие** public health; **—ное хозяйство** national economy; **—онаселение** *n.* population; **—оисчисление** *n.* census.

нароет *fut. 3 sing. of* **нарыть.**

нарож/(д)ать *v.* give birth to, bear; **—даться** *v.* be born, be a large crop (of); **—дённый** *a.* born; newborn.

нарожник *m.* (arch.) jack rafter, jack timber, jack rib.

нарос *past m. sing. of* **нарасти.**

нарост *m.* excrescence, (out-)growth; tuber(cle); knot, node (on tree); wart; (met.) scab; (metal-cutting) built-up edge; build-up; protuberance, bump; (slag) crust; **костный н.** (med.) exostosis; **—ить** *see* **наращивать; —ок** *dim. of* **нарост.**

наросший *past act. part. of* **нарасти.**

нароч/итый *a.* intentional, deliberate, studied; **—но** *adv.* on purpose, intentionally; **—ный** *a.* intentional; *m.* express messenger; **—ным** by express; by special delivery.

нарощенный *a.* accumulated, etc., *see* **наращивать.**

нароют *fut. 3 pl. of* **нарыть.**

нарпит *m.* public eating facilities.

НАРС *abbr.* (**неуправляемый авиационный ракетный снаряд**) unguided aircraft rocket.

нарсарсукит *m.* (min.) narsarsukite.

нарский *a.* (geog.) Nara.

нарсуд *m.* People's court.

нарта *f.* sledge.

нартеций *m.* (bot.) Narthecium.

нарт/овый *a.,* **—ы** *pl.* sledge.

наруб/ание *n.* chopping, cutting; **—ать, —ить** *v.* chop, cut; hew, fell (trees); **—ка** *f.* chopping, cutting; cut, incision, notch; **—ленный** *a.* chopped, cut.

наружи *adv.* (on the) outside; apparently.

наружн/о *adv.* externally; apparently; **—ое** (med.) for external use; **—осекреторный** *a.* (physiol.) exocrine; **—ораковинные** *pl.* (mal.) Ectocochlia; **—ость** *f.* exterior, outward aspect, appearance; **—ый** *a.* external, exterior, outer, outside; surface; extraneous; outdoor; male (thread); circumambient, surrounding; ecto-, *e.g.* **—ый паразит** ectoparasite; **—ая часть** exterior.

наружу *adv.* out(side), outwards, outgoing.

нарукавный *a.* on the sleeve.

наручн/ики *pl.* handcuffs; **—ый** *a.* (on the) hand; wrist (watch).

наруш/ать *v.* break, infringe, transgress, violate; infract; force out (of parallel); disturb, upset, disrupt; trouble; strip (land); **—ение** *n.* break(ing), breach, infringement, infraction, violation; disturbance, dislocation; distortion, perturbation; (structural) rupture; deterioration (of vacuum); disorder, irregularity; injury, impairment, derangement, breakdown; disruption, trouble; offense; (climatic) accident; **—ение деятельности** (med.) disorder; **—ение всасывания** malabsorption; **—ение обмена** error in metabolism; **—енность** *f.* degree of disturbance; **—енный** *a.* broken, infringed, etc., *see v.*; shear (zone); **—итель** *m.* transgressor, violator; **—ить** *see* **нарушать.**

нархозплан *m.* plan of national economy.

нарц/еин *m.* narceine; **—еиновая кислота** narceonic acid; **—ил** *m.* narcyl, ethylnarceine hydrochloride; **—илен** *m.* narcylene; **—исс** *m.* (bot.) narcissus; **—ис(с)ин** *m.* narcissine.

нары *pl.* sleeping platform, bunk.

нарыв *m.* abscess, boil; **—ание** *n.* suppuration, gathering, festering; **—ать** *v.* tear off, gather; tear up, shred; dig up; fester, form an abscess; **—ник** *m.* blister beetle; **—ники** *pl.* (ent.) Meloidae; **—ной, —ный** *a.* abscess; blister-producing, vesicant; **—ное средство** vesicant.

нарынский *a.* (geog.) Naryn.

нарыть *v.* dig up.

наряд *m.* order; (mil.) detail, duty; dress, attire, coat; (orn.) plumage; **брачный н.** nuptial plumage; **гнездовой н., промежуточный н.** mesoptile (coat); **—ить** *v.* order; assign; dress up; **—ный** *a.* assigned; showy.

наряду *adv.* equally (to), together (with), along (with), alongside, concurrent (with), parallel (with), at the same time; as well as, in common (with).

нарядчик *m.* work assigner.

наряжать *see* **нарядить.**

нас *gen., prepos., acc. of* **мы,** us.

насада *f.* small fry, two-year fish.

насад/ить *see* **насаждать, насаживать; —ка** *f.* putting on, setting, fitting on; filling, packing (of column); nozzle, cap(ping), headpiece; hood; building up (of metal); built-up part; adapter, attachment, extension (piece); mouthpiece, jet; still head; fin (of drum dryer); bed (of demineralizer); (gas) checker; checker-(work) (of regenerator); fish bait; (agr.) planting; **башня без —ки** packless tower; **башня с —кой** packed tower; **заполнять —кой** *v.* pack; **—ка-лежень** cap sill; **—ок** *m.* probe; nozzle; **—очный** *a. of* **насадка;** packed (column).

насажать *see* **насаживать.**

насажд/ать *v.* plant, set; implant; spread, propagate; introduce; **—ение** *n.* planting, etc., *see v.*; plantation; stand (of trees); cultivation; **парковое —ение** park; **—ённость** *f.* density of tree stand; **—ённый** *a.* planted, etc., *see v.*

насаж/енный *a.* planted, etc., *see v.*; **—ивание** *n.* planting, etc., *see v.*; **—ивать** *v.* plant; fit, put (on), slip (over); force, clamp (on); set, mount; fill (with), pack (column); build up (metal).

насаливать *v.* grease; salt, pickle.

насасыв/ание *n.* pumping (up); vacuum molding; **—ать** *v.* pump (up), suck (up).

насахари(ва)ть *v.* sugar, sweeten.

насбивать *v.* knock off.

насбирать *v.* gather, pick up.

насверли(ва)ть *v.* drill (out).

насевать *v.* sow; sift.

насевший *past act. part. of* **насесть.**

насед *m.* (orn.) brood patch; **—ать** *v.* press; settle on; **—ка** *f.* setting hen, brood hen; **искусственная —ка** incubator; **—ное пятно** brood patch; **—очник** *m.* brooder house.

насеивать *v.* sow; sift.

насек/альный *a.,* **—ание** *n.* cutting, etc., *see v.*; **—альщик** *m.* cutter; **—ать** *v.* cut, incise, slot, slit, notch; scratch; frost, hatch; damaskeen (with gold, silver); emboss.

насеком/ое *n.* insect; **н.-вредитель** *m.* insect pest; **порошок от —ых** insect powder, insecticide; **—оопыляемый** *a.* (bot.) entomophilous; **—оуловитель** *m.* insect trap; **—оядные** *pl.* (mam.) Insectivora; **—оядный** *a.* insectivorous, insect-eating; **—ые** *pl.* Insecta, Hexapoda; **бескрылые —ые, низшие —ые** Apterygota; **высшие —ые, крылатые —ые** Pterygota.

насел *past m. sing. of* **насесть.**

насел/ение *n.* population, inhabitants; stock (of reservoirs); **—ённость** *f.* (density of) population; occupanсу; —**ённый** *a.* (thickly) populated; inhabited; habitable; —**ённый пункт** population center, community, settlement; —**ять** *v.* populate, settle, inhabit; —**яющий** *a.* inhabiting; *m.* inhabitant, resident.

насест *m.* (poultry) roost, perch.

насесть *v.* settle (on); sit down; press on.

насеч/ённый *a.* cut, incised; frosted, hatched (steel); —**ка** *f.* incision, notch; cut (of file) (file) teeth; cutting (of file teeth); (steel) hatch; (text.) embossing; (med.) scarification; **с крупной** —**кой** coarse (file); —**ник** *m.* (ent.) Bidessus; —**ь** *see* **насекать.**

насеять *v.* sow; sift.

наси/деть, —живать *v.* sit (on eggs), brood, hatch, incubate; (med.) get (hemorrhoids from sitting); —**живание** *n.* sitting, etc., *see v.*

насил/ие *n.* coercion, violence; —**овать** *v.* coerce, force; violate, rape; —**у** *adv.* with difficulty, hardly; —**ьник** *m.* violator, rapist; —**ьно** *adv.* by force; —**ьственный** *a.* forced, compulsive; violent.

насини(ва)ть *v.* (dye) blue.

наскабливать *v.* grate; scrub, scrape.

наскак(ив)ать *v.* run against, strike, attack; collide (with), smash (into).

наскальн/ый *a.* (on a) cliff; (bot.) rupestrine, saxatile; —**ые изображения** hieroglyphics, pictographs.

насквозь *adv.* (right) through, to the core; **проходить н.** *v.* penetrate, pierce.

наскоблить *see* **наскабливать.**

наскок *m.* collision; attack.

насколько *adv.* (for) how much? to what extent? as far as; **н. возможно** as far as possible; **н. нам известно** to (the best of) our knowledge, as far as we know.

наскоро *adv.* hastily, hurriedly.

наскочить *see* **наскакивать.**

наскре/бать, —сти *v.* scrape up.

наскучить *v.* bore, annoy.

насла/диться, —ждаться *v.* enjoy, take pleasure (in); —**ждение** *n.* pleasure, enjoyment.

наслаив/ание *n.* stratifying, etc., *see v.*; stratification, bedding; superposition; deposition; epitaxy; —**ать** *v.* stratify, arrange in layers, laminate; cover with a layer, superpose; overlap; add; —**аться** *v.* stratify.

насластить *v.* sweeten.

наслать *v.* send.

наслащивать *v.* sweeten.

наслед/ие *n.* inheritance, heritage, legacy; —**ить** *v.* leave traces; —**ник** *m.,* —**ница** *f.* heir, successor; legatee; —**овать** *v.* inherit, succeed (to); —**ственность** *f.* heredity, inheritance; —**ственный** *a.* hereditary; genetic; —**ственный фактор** gene; —**ственная вариация** genovariation, gene mutation; —**ственная масса** genetic material; —**ство** *n.* heritage, inheritance, legacy; **передающийся по** —**ству** *a.* hereditary; —**уемость** *f.* heritability; —**уемый** *a.* heritable, hereditary; genetic (sign).

насло/ение *see* **наслаивание;** stratum, strata, layer(s); overlay; (cyt.) apposition; —**ённый** *a.* stratified, etc., *see* **наслаивать;** rafted (ice); —**ить** *see* **наслаивать.**

наслуд *m.* glimmer ice.

насмаливать *v.* tar.

насмерть *adv.* to death, fatally, mortally.

насме/хаться *v.* mock, deride, ridicule; —**шка** *f.* mockery, ridicule, derision.

насмолить *v.* tar.

насморк *m.* (med.) rhinitis, head cold.

насобирать *v.* gather, pick (up).

насов(ыв)ать *v.* push in or on.

насолаживать *v.* (min.) make sweet.

насолить *v.* salt, pickle.

насолодить *v.* malt.

насонит *m.* (min.) nasonite.

насорить *v.* litter.

насортиров(ыв)ать *v.* sort, classify.

насос *m.* pump; (astr.) Antlia; **подавать** —**ом** *v.* pump (up); —**анный** *a.* sucked (up); pumped (up); —**ать** *v.* suck (up); pump (up).

насос/-дозатор *m.* controlled-volume pump, metering pump; **н.-дробилка** disintegrating pump; —**ик** *dim. of* **насос; н.-качалка** *f.* pump jack; **н.-лягушка** *m.* diaphragm pump; **н.-мамут** *m.* air lift; —**ная** *f.* pump house; —**ный** *a.* pump; —**ная станция** water works; —**ное колесо** impeller; —**отурбина** *f.* pump turbine, reversible turbine; **н.-смеситель** *m.* pump mixer; **н.-ускоритель** booster pump; **н.-форсунка** *m.* force pump; **н.-эжектор** *m.* jet pump.

насох/нуть *v.* dry (on); —**ший** *a.* dried.

наспех *adv.* hurriedly.

наспинный *a.* (on the) back.

наспиртов/анный *a.* alcoholized; —**ывание** *n.* alcoholization; —**(ыв)ать** *v.* alcoholize; saturate with alcohol.

насса *f.* (mal.) Nassa.

Насс/ау, —о (geog.) Nassau.

нассула *f.* (prot.) Nassula.

наст *m.* snow crust, ice scum.

наст. *abbr.* (**настоящий**) real, true.

наставать *v.* approach, come (of time).

настав/ительный *a.* instructive; —**ить** *v.* instruct, direct; piece, add, extend, lengthen; set up; —**ка** *f.* piecing, addition, extension; enlargement; extension rod; adapter; —**ление** *n.* directions, instructions, guidance; manual; admonition; —**ление по эксплуатации** service manual; —**лять** *see* **наставить;** put (on); aim, point (at); admonish; teach; —**ной** *a.* pieced, added, set on; extension (pipe, etc.).

настаив/ание *n.* digestion, infusion, steeping; persistence, insisting; —**ать** *v.* digest, infuse, steep; persist, insist, urge, press; —**ать на том, что** insist that; —**ающий** *a.* digesting, etc., *see v.*; insistent.

настал/енный *a.* steel-faced; —**ивание** *n.* steel facing; —**ивать** *v.* steel, face, plate, edge or point with steel.

настан/авливать, —овить *v.* set, place.

настать *see* **наставать.**

настегать, настёгивать *v.* quilt, stitch; lash.

настежь *adv.* (wide) open.

настелить *v.* lay, put down, spread.

настельный *a.* (biol.) imbricate.

настенный *a.* wall(-type); bracket; mural.

настиг/ать, —нуть *v.* overtake, catch up.

настил *m.* floor(ing), deck(ing), boarding, planking; layer; bridging; plating; **половой н.** flooring; —**ание** *n.* laying, etc., *see v.*; —**ать** *v.* lay, plank, board, pave (with); floor, deck; roof; bridge (over); —**ка** *f.* laying, etc., *see v.*; —**оукладочный** *a.* mat-laying; —**очный** *a. of* **настилка;** —**ьность** *f.* (math.) flatness; —**ьный** *a.* flat, low-angle (firing); laid.

настир(ыв)ать *v.* wash, launder.

настический *a.* (bot.) nastic (movement).

настичь *see* **настигать.**

настия *f.* (bot.) nastic movement.

настлать *see* **настилать.**

настовый *a.* (covered with a) frozen crust.

настой *m.* infusion, tincture, extract; **н. на травах** herb infusion; *imp. of* **настоять;** —**ка** *f.* liqueur; (pharm.) tincture, infusion; —**ники** *pl.* (prot.) Ciliata; Infusoria.

настойчив/ость *f.* persistence, insistence; urgency; —**ый** *a.* persistent, insistent, unremitting; urgent, pressing.

настолько *adv.* so; so far, thus far, so much; **н. же** every bit as . . . as; **н. . . . . что** so . . . that; **н., что** to an extent that; **н. насколько** as much as.

настольный *a.* table, desk-top; bench (lathe); reference (book).

настор/аживать, —ожить *v.* alert; **—оже** *adv.* on the alert, on the lookout (for); **—ожение** *n.* arousal; **—оженный, —ожённый** *a.* alert(ed), watchful; **—ожность** *f.* alertness.

настоян/ие *n.* insistence, persistence; **по его —ию** at his urgent request.

настоянный *a.* infused, steeped, digested.

настоятельн/о *adv.* urgently, strongly; **—ость** *f.* urgency, insistence; **—ый** *a.* urgent, pressing insistent.

настоять *see* **настаивать**.

настоящ/ее *n.* the present; **—ий** *a.* real, actual, genuine, natural, regular, true; present, current, contemporary; **в —ее время** at present, now, currently, at this time, in modern practice; **до —его времени** heretofore, previously, to date.

настрагивать *v.* plane, shave.

настрадаться *v.* suffer, go through (much).

настраив/аемый *a.* adjustable; **—ание** *see* **настройка; —ать** *v.* adjust, align, tune (up), tool (machine); (rad.) tune in, set; add, build (on), construct; (comp.) customize; incite, instigate; **—ающий** *a.* adjusting, etc., *see v.*

настрачивать *v.* stitch, sew on; scribble.

настрел/ивать, —ять *v.* shoot (down, up).

настри/г *m.* clip (of wool); shearing; **—гать, —чь** *v.* shear, cut.

настрог/анный *a.* planed; **—ать** *v. plane.*

настрого *advs.* strictly.

настроение *n.* frame of mind, mood.

настро/енный *a.* adjusted, etc., *see* **настраивать; —ечный** *a. of* **настройка; —ить** *see* **настраивать; —йка** *f.* adjustment; alignment; (rad.) tuning in, setting; tooling; addition, superstructure; **—йка на частоту** tuning; **—йщик** *m.* tuner, adjuster.

настрочить *see* **настрачивать**.

наструг(ив)ать *v.* plane, shave.

насту/дить, —ж(ив)ать *v.* chill, cool off.

наступ/ательный *a.* offensive; **—ать** *v.* approach, advance, come; encroach; set in (of reaction); step on; **—ает момент** there comes a point (when); **—ающий** *a.* approaching, etc., *see v.;* **—ление** *n.* approach, advance, onset; attack, invasion, encroachment; occurrence (of event); progradation (of shore line); (mil.) offensive; **с —лением дня** at daybreak; **с —лением ночи** at nightfall.

настуран *m.* (min.) pitchblende, uraninite.

настурц/ий *m., —ия* *f.* (bot.) nasturtium (*Tropaeolum*).

настывать *v.* freeze on; cool off.

настыль *f.* (met.) crust, incrustation, accretion, build-up; skull (oxidized metal) (coke) tree.

насты(ну)ть *see* **настывать**.

насунуть *v.* push on, slide on.

насухо *adv.* dry.

насучи(ва)ть *v.* spin, twist.

насуш/енный *a.* dried; **—и(ва)ть** *v.* dry.

насущный *a.* daily (bread); urgent.

насчёт *prep. gen.* of, about, concerning, as regards, with regard to.

насчит(ыв)ать *v.* count; add; contain, have; encounter; **—ся** *v.* be, number, run into; there are.

насшибать *v.* knock off.

насылать *v.* ship, send.

насып *m.* hopper, feed bin; **—ание** *n.* filling, etc., *see v.;* **—ать** *v.* fill, pour (in); build (dike, etc.); **—ка** *f.* fill-(ing); **—ной** *a.* filled, poured; bulk; **—ной вес** bulk weight; **—ная дорога** causeway.

насыпь *f.* bank, embankment, terrace, mound; dam, dike; fill; causeway; *imp. of* **насыпать; —ю** in bulk; **груз —ю** bulk freight.

насыт/имый *a.* saturable; **—ить** *see* **насыщать**.

насыхать *v.* dry (on).

насыщ/аемость *f.* saturability; **—аемый** *a.* saturable; saturated; **—ать** *v.* saturate, impregnate; satiate, satisfy; **—ать кислородом** oxygenate; **—аться** *v.* be-(come) saturated; **—ающий** *a.* saturating; **—ающее средство** saturator; **—ающийся** *a.* saturable; being saturated.

насыщен/ие *n.* saturation, impregnation; satiation; **предел —ия, точка —ия** saturation point; **—ность** *f.* (degree of) saturation; satiety; richness (in species); **—ный** *a.* saturated, impregnated; satiated, satisfied; deep (color); **—ный бромом** bromine-laden; **—ный водой** water-saturated; **—ный роботами** robotized (plant).

насыщный *a.* full (of).

насядет *fut. 3 sing. of* **насесть**.

натаивать *v.* melt, thaw out.

наталкивать *v.* push (on); direct, suggest; **—ся** *v.* encounter, run into, meet.

натамицин *m.* natamycin (antibiotic).

натапливать *v.* heat; melt.

натаск/а *f., —ивание* *n.* training (of dogs); **—(ив)ать** *v.* train, teach; drag, bring in; get.

натачать *v.* stitch (on), add.

натачивать *v.* sharpen; turn (on lathe).

натащить *v.* bring in, drag in; pull on.

натаять *see* **натаивать**.

натворить *v.* do; make, prepare.

натёк *m.* leakage; (geol.) sinter, incrustation; (paints) sag, run, drip; *past m. sing. of* **натечь**.

натек/ание *n.* leaking, etc., *see v.;* inleakage, leak-in; **—атель** *m.* flow regulator; leak (for mass spectrometers, etc.); **—ать** *v.* leak, drip (down, on); infiltrate; flow, run (into); accumulate.

нательный *a.* (worn) next to the skin.

натеребить *v.* (agr.) pull, pick.

натереть *see* **натирать**.

натёртый rubbed; coated by rubbing; grated.

натесать, натёсывать *v.* hew, cut.

натечка *f.* fine-calibrated orifice.

натеч/ник *m.* (med.) wandering abscess; **—ный** *a.* wandering, hypostatic; formed by dripping; (geol.) sinter; **—ь** *see* **натекать**.

нативный *a.* native; crude, untreated.

натика *f.* (mal.) Natica.

натир/ание *n.* rubbing, etc., *see v.;* touch(ing); **—ать** *v.* rub, polish; grate; touch; **—ка** *see* **натирание;** ointment; **—очный** *a.* rubbing, polishing.

натиск *m.* (in)rush, onslaught, onset; impact; impression; **—(ив)ать** *v.* impress; pack (in).

наткать *v.* weave.

наткнут/ый *a.* driven in, set out; **—ь** *see* **натыкать**.

натолкнуться *see* **наталкиваться**.

натолочь *v.* crush, grind, pulverize.

натопить *see* **натапливать**.

натор/елый *a.* experienced, skillful; **—еть** *v.* get the hang (of), get know-how.

наточ/енный *a.* sharpened, ground; **—ить** *v.* sharpen; run, let pour (in); **—иться** *v.* accumulate.

натощак *adv.* on an empty stomach.

натр *m.* soda (sodium oxide); **едкий н.** caustic soda, sodium hydroxide; **сернокислый н.** sodium sulfate.

натрав/ить *see* **натравлять; —ка** *f.* etching; **—лива-**

ние *n.* etching, etc., *see v.*; **—ливать, —лять** *v.* etch; poison, exterminate; set (at, on), instigate, incite; **—очный** *a.* etching.

натренированный *a.* trained, experienced.

натрепать *v.* scutch, swingle, beat (fibers).

натрёт *fut. 3 sing. of* **натереть.**

натриево/-водяной *a.* sodium-to-water (heat exchanger); **н.-катионитовый** *a.* sodium-cation.

натриев/ый *a.* sodium, soda; sodium-vapor (lamp); *see also under* **натронный; н. полевой шпат** (min.) soda feldspar, albite; **—ая селитра** Chile saltpeter, sodium nitrate; **—ая соль** sodium salt; **—ое растворимое стекло** water glass, sodium silicate; **—ые квасцы** soda alum, aluminum sodium sulfate.

натрие/кальциевый *a.* soda lime; **—термический** *a.* sodium-reduced (titanium).

натр/ий *m.* sodium, Na; **гидроокись —ия** sodium hydroxide; **едкий н.** caustic soda; **углекислый н.** sodium carbonate; **хлорид —ия, хлористый н.** sodium chloride, common salt; **—ийамид, —ийамин** *m.* sodamide, sodium amide; **н.-бутадиеновый каучук** synthetic butadiene rubber; **н.-катионирование** *n.* sodium zeolite softening process; **—ийксилолсульфо-кислота** *f.* xylenesulfonic acid sodium salt; **н.-метил** *m.* sodium methyl, sodium methide; **н.-натриевый** *a.* sodium-to-sodium (heat exchanger); **—ийорганиче-ский** *a.* organosodium; **н.-этил** *m.* sodium ethyl, sodium ethide.

натриодиуретический *a.* sodium diuretic.

натристый *see* **натриевый, натронный.**

натро/борокальцит *m.* (min.) natroborocalcite, ulexite; **—вый** *see* **натриевый.**

натрое *adv.* into three parts.

натро/кальцит *m.* (min.) natrocalcite, gaylussite; **—лит** *m.* natrolite.

натронн/ый *a.* soda; **н. щёлок** soda lye, caustic soda solution; **—ая известь** soda lime; **—ая селитра** Chile saltpeter, sodium nitrate; **—ое мыло** soda soap, hard soap; **—ое стекло** soda glass; **—ые квасцы** *see* **натриевые квасцы.**

натро/филит *m.* (min.) natrophilite; **—хальцит** *m.* (min.) natrochalcite.

натру/дить, —живать *v.* tire out, exhaust.

натру/сить *v.* sprinkle, scatter; shake (in, out); pour (in, out); **—ска** *f.* sprinkling, etc., *see v.*

натрут *fut. 3 pl. of* **натереть.**

натрушенный *a.* sprinkled, etc., *see* **натрусить.**

натрясти *v.* shake out, spill out, scatter.

нату/га *f.* effort, strain; **—го** *adv.* tight(ly); **—женный** *a.* stretched, strained; **—жи(ва)ть** *v.* stretch, strain, tighten; **—жи(ва)ться** *v.* make an effort, strain; **—жливый, —жный** *a.* strained, forced.

натур/а *f.* nature, character; weight of 1 liter (of grain); **измерение в —е** actual measurement; **платить —ой** *v.* pay in kind; **по —е** by nature, naturally; **—ализа-ция** *f.* naturalization; domestication; **—алист** *m.* naturalist.

натуральн/о *adv.* naturally; **—ость** *f.* naturalness; **—ый** *a.* natural; real; life (size); virgin (wool); crude (rubber); **—ый налог** tax in kind; **в —ную величину, —ых размеров** full-scale, full-size.

натурный *a.* full-scale; hectoliter (weight).

натуроза *f.* pasteurized grape juice.

натуроплата *f.* payment in kind, payment in produce.

натушить *v.* extinguish, put out (fire); slake, quench; suppress, put down; (food) stew, braize.

натыкать *v.* stick in, set out; **—ся** *v.* meet, encounter, run into.

натяг *m.* pull, tension, tightness; interference, obstruction; clearance (of roll); taper (of wedge); **предвари-тельный н.** preload; **—ивание** *n.* pulling, etc., *see v.*; **—ивать** *v.* pull (up), draw up, tighten, stretch; strain; string; fix, fasten; **—ивающий** *a.* pulling, etc., *see v.*; **—ивающая мышца** (anat.) tensor; **—ивающая сила, —ивающее усилие** tensile stress.

натяжен/ие *n.* tension, strain, stress; adjustment; pulling, (pull)-up, tightening; (med.) intention, closing (of wound); **поверхностное н.** surface tension; **пред-варительное н.** prestressing; **сила —ия** tensile stress; **степень —ия** tautness, tightness.

натяж/ка *see* **натягивание; —ник** *m.* stretcher.

натяжн/ой *a.* tightening, tension, strain; stretching; pull; guy (rope); draw (spring); **н. болт** adjuster bolt, draw-in bolt; strain pin; **н. выключатель** (elec.) pull switch; **н. груз** counterweight; **н. люк** (min.) access window; **н. прибор** tightening device; stretcher, stretching device; **н. ролик** tension roller; **н. стер-жень** tension rod; **—ого действия** pull-action, trip-wire (mine).

натянут/ость *f.* tension, tenseness; tightness; **—ый** *a.* tense, tight, drawn, stretched; strained; **в —ом состо-янии** in tension; **—ь** *see* **натягивать.**

наугад *adv.* by guesswork, by rule of thumb, haphazardly, at random.

науглерож/енный *a.* carbonized; (met.) carburized; **—ивание** *n.* carbonization; carburization; cementation; **—иватель** *m.* carburizer; **—ивать** *v.* carbonize; carburize; **—ивающий** *a.* carbonizing; carburizing.

наугольн/ик *m.* square, bevel, corner iron; (astr.) Norma; **—ый** *a.* angular; corner.

наудачу *adv.* haphazardly, at random.

наузник *m.* (bees) decoy hive.

наука *f.* knowledge, science; **академия наук** academy of sciences; **инженерная н.** engineering.

наукатский *a.* (geol.) Naukat.

наукоёмкий *a.* high-tech.

науманит *m.* (min.) naumannite.

наупли/альный, —усовый *a.* (crust.) nauplial.

наутил(о)идеи *pl.* (mal.) Nautiloidea.

наутофон *m.* nautophone, fog horn.

наутро *adv.* the next morning.

наутюжи(ва)ть *v.* iron, press.

науч/ать, —ить *v.* teach, instruct, direct; **—аться, —иться** *v.* learn; **—ение** *n.* education; **—енный** *a.* taught.

научно *adv.* scientific(ally); **н.-информационный** *a.* scientific information; **н.-исследовательский** *a.* research; **н.-исследовательская деятельность** *or* **работа** research; **н.-методический** *a.* scientific method; guidance (work); **н.-обоснованный** *a.* based on scientific data; **н.-популярный** *a.* popular science; **—сть** *f.* scientific nature; **н.-технический** *a.* scientific and technical, scientific and engineering; **н.-техниче-ская интеллигенция** brainpower.

научн/ый *a.* scientific; **—ые кадры** *or* **работники** brainpower; scientific *or* technical staff.

наушник *m.* ear muff, ear cap; headphone; **—и** *pl.* head set.

нафабриковать *v.* manufacture, produce.

наформов(ыв)ать *v.* form, mold; make molds.

нафт — *prefix* naphth(o)—; **—а** *f.* naphtha; **—азарин** *m.* naphthazarine, alizarin black; **—ан** *m.* naphthalane.

нафталанский *a.* (geog.) Naftalan.

нафтал/ат *m.,* **соль —евой кислоты** naphthalate; **—евая кислота** naphthalic acid, naphthalenedicar-boxylic acid; **—изировать** *v.* naphthalize, enrich with нафтальдегид   начинание

naphthalene; **—ин** *m.,* **—инный, —иновый** *a.*
naphthalene.

нафт/альдегид *m.* naphthaldehyde, naphthalenecarbo-
nal; **—амин** *m.,* **—аминовый** *a.* naphthamine; **—ан**
m. naphthane; **—ацен** *m.* naphthacene.

нафтен *m.* naphthene; **—ат** *m.* naphthenate; **—овый** *a.*
naphthenic.

нафтил *m.* naphthyl; **—амин** *m.* naphthylamine; **—ен**
m., **—еновый** *a.* naphthylene; **—овый** *a.* naphthyl;
—овый спирт naphthyl alcohol, naphthol; **—овый**
эфир naphthyl ether; **—овый эфир уксусной кисло-**
ты naphthyl acetate; **—уксусный** *a.* naphthylacetic
(acid).

нафт/ионовый *a.* naphthionic (acid); **—о—** *prefix* naph-
tho—; **—оил** *m.* naphthoyl; **—ойный** *a.* naphthoic
(acid, aldehyde); **—окси—** *prefix* naphthoxy—.

нафтол *m.,* **—овый** *a.* naphthol, naphthyl alcohol; **—ат**
m. naphtholate.

нафтохин/олин *m.* naphthoquinoline; **—он** *m.* naphtho-
quinone.

нахаль/ный *a.* arrogant, insolent; **—ство** *n.* arrogance,
insolence.

нахвали(ва)ть *v.* extol, praise.

нахват/анный *a.* snatched, etc., *see v.*; **—(ыв)ать** *v.*
snatch, grab, pick up; get.

нахичеванский *a.* (geog.) Nakhichevan.

нахколит *m.* (min.) nahcolite.

нахкур *m.* (med.) aftercare.

нахлебаться *v.* choke; (distillation) flood.

нахлебн/ик *m.* (biol.) commensal; **—ичество** *n.* commensalism; (micros.) stage community.

нахлёст/нуть, **—ать** *see* **нахлёстывать.**

нахлёст/ка *f.* (joint), overlap(ping); **в —ку** lap; **шов в**
—ку lap joint; **—ывание** *n.* (over)lapping, etc., *see v.*;
—ывать *v.* (over)lap; lash, whip; make a chalk line.

нахлынуть *v.* rush, flood; invade.

нахмури(ва)ться *v.* frown; be overcast.

находить *v.* find, locate, come upon, strike (oil, etc.);
detect, spot, discover; seek; determine, arrive at (solution), develop; **—ся** *v.* be, occur, exist; be found; **—ся**
под underlie.

находка *f.* find(ing); windfall, discovery; (geol.) occurrence.

находкинский *a.* (geog.) Nakhodka.

находчив/ость *f.* resourcefulness, readiness; **—ый** *a.* resourceful.

находящий *a.* finding, etc., *see* **находить; incumbent,**
lying upon; **—ся** *a.* found, being, occurring; placed,
situated; **—ся вне extra—,** external; **—ся вне сердца**
(anat.) extracardial; **—ся внутри endo—,** internal;
—ся возле para—; —ся между interposed between;
—ся над epi—, supra—; —ся над остью supraspi-
nal; **—ся под underlying; sub—, infra—; —ся под**
действием under; —ся под ребром (anat.) subcostal.

нахождение *n.* finding, locating, detecting; trouble-
shooting; being, occurrence; calculation.

нахохли(ва)ть *v.* (orn.) ruffle up.

нахрапник *m.* cavesson (of training halter).

нахур *m.* (mam.) blue sheep (*Pseudois nayaur*).

нахыст *m.* catching (fish), capturing.

нацарап(ыв)ать *v.* scratch (on); scribble.

наце/дить, **—живать** *v.* strain, filter.

нацел/енный *a.* aimed, etc., *see v.*; **н. на** targeted to;
—ивание *n.* aiming, etc., *see v.*; **—и(ва)ть** *v.* aim (at);
point, focus (on); **—и(ва)ться** *v.* aim (at), point; be
focused; get ready (to).

нацело *adv.* completely, wholely; **делиться н.** *v.* (math.)
divide evenly.

нацен/и(ва)ть *v.* (com.) raise the price; **—ка** *f.* price
increase.

нацеп/ить, **—лять** *v.* attach, fasten, hook on; **—ленный**
a. attached, etc., *see v.*

национал/изация *f.* nationalization; **—изировать** *v.* na-
tionalize; **—ьность** *f.* nationality; **—ьный** *a.* national.

нацист *m.,* **—ский** *a.* Nazi.

нация *f.* nation, people.

нацменьшинство *n.* national minority.

нач. *abbr.,* **нач—** *prefix* (начало; начальный; начальник; начальствующий).

начавший *past act. part. of* **начинать.**

начадить *v.* smoke up.

начал/о *n.* beginning, start, outbreak, onset; commence-
ment, initiation, inception; origin(ation), source;
(math.) principle, basis; (biol.) germ; (gen.) disposition;
(av.) approach end (of runway); (comp.) home; **—а** *pl.*
principles, elements (of subject); **н. истечения** (petrol.) initial point; **н. координат** origin; **н. процесса**
start-up; **брать н.** *v.* spring, rise (from), originate;
быть под —ом *v.* be in subordination (to); **вести н.** *v.*
originate; date (from), stem (from); **вести своё н. от** *v.*
date back to; **давать н.** *v.* give rise (to); **действу-**
ющее н. primary nutrient; active principle; **для —а** to
start, to begin (with); **на кредитных —ах** on credit
basis; **на равных —ах** on a par (with); **положить н.**
v. initiate, give rise (to).

начальник *m.* head, chief, superior.

начальн/ый *a.* initial, original, first; starter; elementary,
rudimentary; primary (school); feed (plate; liquor);
(comp.) leading (zero); home (position); **н. загрузчик**
m. (comp.) bootstrap; **н. угол** angle of impulsion;
—ая точка origin, source; starting point; **—ые ядра**
(cyt.) nuclei of origin.

начальство *n.* superiors, management; **—вать** *v.* be in
charge, manage; command.

начат/ки *pl.* rudiments, elements; **—ый** *a.* started; **—ь**
see **начинать.**

начекани(ва)ть *v.* stamp; coin.

начеку *adv.* on the alert, ready.

начеркать, начёркивать *v.* sketch; jot down.

начернить *v.* paint or dye black, blacken.

начерно *adv.* rough(ly), coarse(ly); in draft form; **об-**
делка н. rough finish(ing), roughing; **обрабатывать**
н. *v.* rough-finish, rough (out); **шлифовать н.** *v.*
rough-grind.

начернять *see* **начернить.**

начерп/ать, **—ывать** *v.* scoop up.

начер/тание *n.* sketch, outline, plan; trace, tracing; representation, design; **—тательный** *a.* graphic; descriptive (geometry); **—тать, —тить, —чивать** *v.* draw,
trace, outline, draft; **—ченный** *a.* traced, outlined.

начёс *m.* carding, etc., *see* **начёсывать;** (text.) nap, pile;
(med.) irritation.

начесать *see* **начёсывать.**

начёсный *a.* napped.

начесть *see* **начитывать.**

начёсывать *v.* card (wool); hackle (fiber); raise (nap).

начёт *m.* deficit; **—истый** *a.* disadvantageous, unprofitable.

начётнический *a.* dogmatic.

начин/ание *n.* beginning, start; undertaking; **—атель** *m.*
originator, initiator, author; founder; **—ательный** *a.*
(gram.) inceptive; **—ать** *v.* begin, start, initiate, set in;
come into (use); set up; undertake; **—ать действо-**
вать *v.* come into play; **начнём с того, что** to begin
with; **успешно —ать** make a good start; **—аться** *v.*
begin, start, set in; originate; **—ающий** *m.* beginner,

novice; *a.* beginning, initial; —**ающийся** *a.* incipient; —**ая** *pr. ger.* beginning, etc., *see v.*; —**ая . . . и кончая** (ranging) from . . . to; —**ая от . . . и кончая** anywhere from . . . to; —**ая с этого момента** from this time on.

начин/ивать *v.* fix, repair; —**ить** *v.* fix, repair; stuff, fill; sharpen; —**ка** *f.*, —**очный** *a.* stuffing, filling; —**ок** *m.* (text.) cop base; —**ять** *v.* stuff, fill.

начисл/ение *n.* (extra) charge; entry; counting (up); —**ить,** —**ять** *v.* charge extra; enter, put down; count (up); set, impose (a fine).

начистить *see* **начищать.**

начисто *adv.* clean(ly); thoroughly, completely; openly; cold (drawn); **обрабатывать н.** *v.* finish (off); —**ту** *adv.* openly, frankly.

начитанный *a.* well-read.

начитывать *v.* charge extra; find a deficit.

начищать *v.* clean; peel, shell; polish.

начнёт *fut. 3 sing. of* **начинать.**

начсостав *m.* executive staff.

начтённый *past pass. part. of* **начесть.**

начхим *m.* chief of chemical warfare department.

наш *pron.* our(s).

нашатыр/ный спирт aqua ammonia, ammonium hydroxide; —**ь** *m.* sal ammoniac, ammonium chloride.

нашвыр/ивать —**ять** *v.* throw, fling, pile.

нашедший *past act. part. of* **найти.**

нашейник *m.* collar.

нашёл *past m. sing. of* **найти.**

нашелушить *v.* hull, husk, shell.

нашест *m.* roost, perch.

нашествие *n.* attack, invasion, infestation, outbreak (of pests).

нашив/ать *v.* sew (on); —**ка** *f.* sewing on; (mil.) stripe, tab; —**ной** *a.* sewn on.

нашильник *m.* breeching (of harness).

нашинков(ыв)ать *v.* shred, chop, cut.

нашит/ый *a.* sewn on; —**ь** *see* **нашивать.**

нашла *past f. sing. of* **найти.**

нашлёт *fut. 3 sing. of* **наслать.**

нашло *past n. sing. of* **найти.**

нашлют *fut. 3 pl. of* **наслать.**

нашпигов(ыв)ать *v.* lard, grease.

нашпили(ва)ть *v.* pin on, set on.

наштампов(ыв)ать *v.* stamp, punch.

нашуметь *v.* make noise.

нашьёт *fut. 3 sing. of* **нашить.**

нащёлк(ив)ать *v.* crack, shell (nuts).

нащёльники *pl.* (constr.) battens.

нащепать *v.* split, cleave, chip.

нащип(ыв)ать *v.* pinch; gather, pluck.

нащуп/ать, —**ывать** *v.* feel, probe; find; —**ыватель** *m.* feeler, probe.

наэкономить *v.* economize.

наэлектризов/ание *n.* electrification; —**анный** *a.* electrified; —**(ыв)ать** *v.* electrify.

наяву *adv.* when awake, in reality.

наяд/а *f.*, —**овый** *a.* (ent.) naiad; (bot.) Najas; —**овые** *pl.* Najadaceae.

нб, н/б *abbr.* (**не был**) not found; **НБ** (**научная библиотека**) scientific library; (**нижний бьеф**) (hydr.) tail water.

НБП *abbr.* (**нижняя боковая полоса**) lower sideband; **НБПДЧ** (**нижняя боковая полоса доплперовских частот**) lower sideband of Doppler frequencies.

н/в *abbr.* (**низковольтный**) low-voltage.

н.в.э. *abbr.* (**нормальный водородный эквивалент**) normal hydrogen equivalent; **НВЭ** *abbr.* (**нормаль-**

ный водородный электрод) standard hydrogen electrode.

нгайовый *a.* ngai (camphor).

НГГК *abbr.* (**нейтронный гамма-гамма каротаж**) neutron gamma-gamma logging.

НГДУ *abbr.* (**Нефтегазодобывающее управление**) Oil and Gas Production Administration.

НГК *abbr.* (**нейтронный гамма-каротаж**) neutron-gamma logging.

НГМ *abbr.* (**нейтронный гамма-метод**) neutron-gamma logging.

НГН *abbr.* (**наногенри**) nanohenry.

НДАР *abbr.* Algerian People's Democratic Republic.

не *particle* not, no, none; *prefix* un—, in—, non—, mis—, dis—; **не . . . , а** not . . . but, rather than; **не в** off, out of (phase, etc.); **не зная** without knowing; —**абелевый** *a.* (math.) non-Abelian; —**автоматический** *a.* nonautomatic, manual; —**автономный** *a.* (comp.) on-line; —**аддитивный** *a.* nonadditive; —**адэкватный** *a.* inadequate, insufficient; —**аккуратный** *a.* careless, sloppy; inaccurate.

неактив/ированный *a.* non-activated; —**ность** *f.* inactivity; —**ный** *a.* inactive, passive, inert; idle.

неактуальный *a.* not of current importance.

неаллельный *a.* (gen.) non-allelic.

неаналитический *a.* nonanalytic.

неандертальский *a.* Neanderthal (man).

неанический *a.* (zool.) neanic.

неаполитанск/ий *a.* (geog.) Neapolitan, Naples; —**ая болезнь** (med.) brucellosis.

неаппаратное оборудование (comp.) software.

неаппетитный *a.* unappetizing.

неармированный *a.* plain (concrete).

неароматический *a.* nonaromatic.

неассоци/ативный *a.* nonassociative; —**ированный** *a.* nonassociated.

неастазированный *a.* static, stable-type.

неатом(ар)ный *a.* nonatomic.

неба *gen. of* **небо.**

небаланс *m.* imbalance; —**ный** *a.* unbalanced.

небалиевые *pl.* (crust.) Nebaliidae.

небез— *prefix* not without; somewhat, rather; —**вредный** *a.* rather harmful; —**выгодный** *a.* somewhat profitable; —**надёжный** *a.* not hopeless; —**опасный** *a.* not safe, unsafe, hazardous, insecure; —**основательный** *a.* not unfounded; —**различный** *a.* not indifferent; relevant; fairly important; —**результатный,** —**успешный** *a.* more or less successful; —**ызвестный** *a.* fairly well known; —**ынтересный** *a.* not without interest, (fairly) interesting.

небелёный *a.* unbleached, crude, raw.

небелковый *a.* non-protein, non-albuminous.

небереговой *a.* offshore.

небережливый *a.* careless, wasteful.

небес— *see* **небез—.**

небес/а *pl. of* **небо;** —**ноголубой** *a.* sky-blue; —**ный** *a.* sky; celestial.

небес/плодный *a.* not fruitless, not useless; —**полезный** *a.* fairly useful.

небитдагский *a.* (geog.) Nebit-Dag.

неблаго/дарный *a.* ungrateful, thankless; unsatisfactory; —**звучный** *a.* unpleasant (sound); —**получный** *a.* unsuccessful, unfortunate; defective; unhealthy, infected, infested.

неблагоприятн/о *adv.* adversely; **н. влиять** *v.* be detrimental (to), impair; —**ый** *a.* unfavorable, adverse, disadvantageous; difficult (conditions).

неблаго/разумный *a.* unreasonable, imprudent, ill-advised; —**склонный** *a.* unfavorable; ill-disposed; —**устроенный** badly organized; uncomfortable, ill-equipped; undeveloped (land).

неблестящий *a.* insignificant.

нёбн/о— *prefix* (anat.) palat(o), palate; **н. глоточный** *a.* palatopharyngeal; **н.-решётчатый** *a.* palatoethmoidal; **н.-язычный** *a.* palatoglossal; —**ый** *a.* palatine; —**ая занавеска** velum palatinum; —**ая щель** (med.) palatoschisis, cleft palate.

небо *n.* sky, heaven, firmament; crown (of furnace); (ice) blink.

нёбо *n.* (anat.) palate.

небогатый *a.* poor, scanty, limited.

небоеспособный *a.* disabled, unfit for action.

неболезнетворный *a.* (med.) nonpathogenic.

небольш/ой *a.* small, little, minor; low (altitude); light (load); **сто с —им** one hundred odd.

небо/свод, —**склон** *m.* firmament; horizon, sky; —**скрёб** *m.* skyscraper.

небрежн/ость *f.* carelessness, negligence; —**ый** *a.* careless, negligent, slipshod.

небул/арин *m.* nebularine (antibiotic); —**ярный** *a.* nebular.

небывалый *a.* unprecedented.

небытие *n.* nonexistence.

небьющийся *a.* unbreakable, shatterproof, safety (glass).

невад/ит *m.* (petr.) nevadite; —**ский** *a.* (geog.) Nevada.

неважн/о *adv.* insignificantly; poorly; it is not important; **это н.** it does not matter; —**ый** *a.* unimportant, insignificant; poor, indifferent.

невалидный *a.* invalid, void, null.

неварёный *a.* raw.

невдал/еке, —**и** *adv.* not far, near.

невдо/гад, —**мёк** *adv.* having no idea; **ему н.** it never occurred to him.

неве/дение *n.,* —**жественность** *f.,* —**жество** *n.* ignorance; —**домый** *a.* unknown, unfamiliar; —**жественный** *a.* ignorant, uneducated.

невежливый *a.* impolite, discourteous.

невез/ение *n.* bad luck, failure; —**учий** *a.* unfortunate, unsuccessful, unlucky.

невейка *f.* unwinnowed, ground grain.

невеликий *a.* not great, small.

неверн/о *adv.* incorrectly, wrong; **н. рассчитать** *v.* miscalculate; —**ость** *f.* inaccuracy; —**ый** *a.* inaccurate, incorrect, invalid, wrong; untrue, false, mis—; unsure, uncertain, weak (light); —**ый нуль** false zero.

невероятн/о *adv.* incredibly; it is improbable; —**ость** *f.* incredibility; improbability; —**ый** *a.* incredible, unbelievable, inconceivable; improbable, unlikely.

невесом/ость *f.* imponderability, zero gravity, weightlessness; —**ый** *a.* imponderable, weightless, trace.

неветвящийся *a.* non-branching, tufted.

невзаим/ный *a.* nonmutual; —**одействующий** *a.* non-interacting; —**озаместимый** *a.* non-interchangeable.

невзгода *f.* adversity, misfortune.

невзирая *see* **несмотря**.

невзначай *adv.* accidentally, by chance.

невзнос *m.* nonpayment.

невз/орвавшийся *a.* unexploded; **н. снаряд** dud; —**рываемость** *f.* nonexplosiveness; —**рываемый,** —**рывчатый** *a.,* —**рывающийся** *a.* nonexplosive; —**рывоопасный** *a.* explosion-proof.

невзыскательный *a.* unexacting.

невианскит *m.* (min.) nevyanskite.

невид/анный *a.* unheard of, unusual; unprecedented; —**имость** *f.* invisibility; —**имый** *a.* invisible; (biol.) latent; far (side of moon); hidden (line); —**ный** *a.* in-

significant, inconspicuous; —**ящий** *a.* unseeing, unobservant.

невинный *a.* innocent, not guilty; harmless.

невихревой *a.* irrotational, noncircuital.

невключённый *a.* disconnected, off.

невкусный *a.* bad-tasting, unpalatable.

невменяемый *a.* irresponsible.

не/вмешательство *n.* non-intervention, non-interference; —**вмоготу,** —**вмочь** *adv.* unbearable, intolerable; —**внимательный** *a.* inattentive, absentminded; careless; —**внятный** *a.* indistinct, unintelligible, inarticulate.

невод *m.* seine, sweep net, casting net; —**ник** *m.* seine-hauling boat.

неводный *a.* nonaqueous; anhydrous.

неводостойкий *a.* hydrolabile.

невозбуждённый *a.* unexcited.

невозврат/имый, —**ный** *a.* irrevocable, irretrievable, irreversible.

невозделанный *a.* raw, crude, untreated; virgin (soil), unworked, uncultivated, untilled; undeveloped (land).

невоздерж(ан)ный *a.* intemperate, immoderate, uncontrolled, unrestrained.

невозможн/о *adv.* impossibly; it is impossible; **если это н.** failing this; —**ость** *f.* impossibility; —**ый** *a.* impracticable, impractical.

невозмущённый *a.* unperturbed, undisturbed; quiescent (value); free (stream).

невозобновл/яемый, —**яющийся** *a.* nonrenewable, irreplaceable.

невозрастающий *a.* nonincreasing (sequence).

неволить *v.* force, compel.

неволокнистый *a.* nonfibrous.

невол/ьный *a.* involuntary, unintentional; forced; —**я** *f.* captivity; necessity.

не/вообразимый *a.* unimaginable, inconceivable; —**вооружённый** *a.* unarmed; unaided, naked (eye).

невоспламеняющийся *a.* incombustible, nonflammable; safety (film).

невосполнимый *see* **невозобновляемый.**

невоспри/имчивость *f.* immunity, resistance; insensibility; —**имчивый,** —**нимающий** *a.* immune, resistant, non-susceptible; insensible.

невоспроизводимость *f.* nonreproductivity.

невосстанавливаемый *a.* nonrecoverable.

невосстановленный *a.* unreduced.

невостребованный *a.* unclaimed, dead (mail).

невоюющий *a.* non-warring, nonbelligerent.

невпопад *adv.* inopportunely, out of place, irrelevantly.

невпроворот *adv.* very much, excessively.

невр— *prefix* neur(o)— (nerve), *see also under* **нейр**—.

невразумительный *a.* incomprehensible.

невр/алгический *a.* (med.) neuralgic; —**алгия** *f.* neuralgia; —**астеник** *m.* neittrastheni(a)c; —**астенический** *a.* neurasthenic; —**астения** *f.* neurasthenia.

невращающийся *a.* irrotational, nonrotatory, nonrotating.

невред/имый *a.* unharmed, unhurt, safe, intact; —**но** *adv.* harmlessly, safely; it is safe; —**ный** *a.* harmless, innocuous, safe.

неври/лемма *f.* (anat.) neurilemma; —**т** *m.* (med.) neuritis; (anat.) neurite, axon.

невро— *prefix* neuro— (nerve).

неврождённый *a.* not inborn, acquired.

невро/з *m.* (med.) neurosis; —**зный** *a.* neurotic; —**лиз(ис)** neurolysis; —**лог** *m.* neurologist; —**логический** *a.* neurological; —**логия** *f.* neurology; —**ма** *f.* neuroma; —**мер** *m.* (embr.) neuromere, neural segment; —**н** *m.* neuron, nerve cell; **двигательный** —**н** motoneuron; —**патология** *f.* neuropathology; —**подий** *m.* (cyt.) neuropodium; —**темис** *m.* (ent.) Neurothemis; —**тик** *m.*, —**тический** *a.* neurotic; —**фибрилла** *f.* (cyt.) neurofibril; —**цель** *m.* (anat.) neurocoel; —**эпителиома** *f.* (med.) neuroepithelioma.

невский *a.* (geog.) Neva.

невручение *n.* non-delivery.

невскрывающийся *a.* (bot.) indehiscent.

невспаханный *a.* unplowed, untilled.

невспененный *a.* unfoamed, expanded.

невставленный *a.* unmounted, loose.

невстон *m.* neuston, floating vegetation.

невсхожий *a.* non-germinating; blind (bud).

невтяжной *a.* non-retractile (claws).

невулканизированный *a.* uncured.

невус *m.* nevus, birthmark; *pl.* nevi.

невшательский *a.* (geog.) Neuchatel.

невыветривающийся *a.* weatherproof.

невыводимый *a.* indelible (ink).

невыгод/а *f.* disadvantage; loss; —**но** *adv.* disadvantageously; it is not profitable; it is useless; —**ный** *a.* disadvantageous, unfavorable, unprofitable, uneconomical; **в** —**ном положении** at a (great) disadvantage.

невыделанный *a.* raw, crude, unfinished; undressed (hide).

невыдержанный *a.* new, insufficiently aged.

невыдыхающийся *a.* nonvolatile.

невызрев/ающий *a.* non-maturing; —**ший** *a.* unripe(ned), softwood (cutting).

невыколашивание *n.* non-earing (of grain).

невыложенный *a.* (zool.) ungelded.

невымол/от *m.* incomplete thrashing(s); —**оченный** *a.* unthrashed.

невымывающийся *a.* indelible (stain); fast (dye).

невынос/имый *a.* intolerable, unbearable, excruciating (pain); —**ливый** non-hardy.

невыполн/ение *n.* nonperformance, nonfulfillment, failure; —**енный** *a.* unfulfilled, outstanding; —**имость** *f.* impracticability; —**имый** *a.* impracticable.

невырождённый *a.* nondegenerate (laser); nonsingular (matrix).

невыс/окий *a.* not high, low(-grade); moderate; —**отный** *a.* low-altitude, sea-level.

невысыхающий *a.* nondrying (oils).

невыход *m.* absence, nonappearance.

невыцветающий *a.* nonfading, fast (dye).

невычет *m.* (math.) nonresidue.

невыясненный *a.* unexplained, obscure, unclarified, unanswered.

невьянскит *m.* (min.) nevyanskite.

невязка *f.* (geod.) discrepancy, (error of) closure, misclosure, error of connection.

невязкий *a.* nonviscous, inviscid.

невязь *f.* unbound stalks (of grain).

негабарит *m.* oversize, outsize; —**ность** *f.* bulkiness; —**ый** *a.* outsize, oversize, bulky, off-gage.

негаданный *a.* unexpected.

негармонический *a.* nonharmonic.

негасимый *a.* unquenchable; nonslaking (lime).

нега/скоп *m.* (phot.) negative viewer; —**тив** *m.* negative; —**тивность** *f.* negativeness; —**тивный** *a.* negative; —**тивное изображение** negative (image); —**тоскоп** *m.* X-ray film viewer.

негатрон *m.* negatron (vacuum tube); (nucl.) negative electron.

негашёный *a.* unslaked, quick (lime).

негде *adv.* there is no room, there is no place, there is nowhere (to).

негемовый *a.* (biochem.) nonheme (iron).

негентропия *see* **негэнтропия.**

негермет/изированный *a.* unsealed; —**ический**, —**ичный** *a.* nonhermetic, leaking; —**ичность** *f.* leaking, seepage, seal failure.

негибк/ий *a.* inflexible, stiff, rigid; —**ость** *f.* inflexibility, stiffness, rigidity.

негигиенический *a.* unsanitary.

негигроскопичный *a.* nonhygroscopic.

негидр/ированный *a.* unhydrogenated; —**оксилированный** *a.* hydroxyl-free.

негистоновый *a.* (biochem.) nonhistone.

негладкий *a.* uneven, rough, jagged.

неглазурованный *a.* unglazed.

негласный *a.* secret; private.

неглубокий *a.* not deep, shallow; mild.

негн/июучка *f.* (bot.) arbor vitae (*Thuja occidentalis*); —**иющий** *a.* rot-resistant; —**ой** *m.*, —**ой-дерево** *n.* English yew (*Taxus baccata*).

негнущийся *a.* unbending, inflexible, rigid.

него *gen. and acc. of* **он, оно** *after prep.*

негодн/ость *f.* unfitness, unsuitability; worthlessness; **приходить в н.** *v.* get out of order; —**ый** *a.* unsuitable, unfit, improper, useless, worthless; refuse, waste; faulty, defective.

неголономн/ость *f.* (math.) nonholonomicity; —**ый** *a.* nonholonomic.

негомогенн/ость *f.* inhomogeneity; —**ый** *a.* inhomogeneous, nonhomogeneous.

негорюч/есть *f.* incombustibility; —**ий** *a.* incombustible, non-combustible, nonburning, fire-resistant.

негорящий *a.* nonburning.

неготовый *a.* not ready, unprepared.

негр *m.* negro.

неграмотный *a.* illiterate.

негранёный *a.* rough, uncut (jewel).

негрит/ёнок *m.* negro child; —**янка** *f.* negro woman; —**янский** *a.* negro, black.

негромкий *a.* quiet.

негрообразный *a.* negroid.

негустой *a.* thin, watery, dilute.

негэнтропия *f.* (phys.) negentropy.

нед— *prefix* sub—, below; un—.

недавн/ий *a.* recent, late, new; —**о** *adv.* recently, lately, of late; the other day; —**о прибывший** *a.* newly arrived; *m.* newcomer.

недалёкий *a.* near, not far, not distant; recent; limited; short (distance).

недалеко *adv.* near (at hand), not far.

недальний *a.* near, not far.

недаром *adv.* not in vain, not without reason; no wonder.

недатированный *a.* undated.

недвиж/имость *f.* immovability; real estate; —**имости** *pl.* immovables; real estate; —**имый** *a.* immovable, immobile; fixed (capital); —**ный** *a.* motionless; —**ущийся** *a.* stationary.

недвусмысленный *a.* unambiguous, clear.

недееспособный *a.* incompetent.

недейственный *a.* inactive, inert.

недействительн/ость *f.* ineffectiveness, inefficiency; invalidity; —**ый** *a.* ineffective, inefficient, inoperative; inefficacious (medicine); invalid, null and void; **делать** —**ым** *v.* invalidate, nullify, cancel, neutralize.

недействующий *a.* inactive, passive, inert; nonoperating, inoperative, idle.

неделим/ость *f.* indivisibility; **—ый** *a.* indivisible; prime (number).

неделовой *a.* unbusinesslike.

недел/ьный *a.* week(ly); **—я** *f.* week.

неделящийся *a.* (nucl.) nonfissionable.

недемпфированный *a.* undamped.

недержание *n.* nonretention, irretention; (med.) incontinence.

недетерминированный *a.* indeterminate.

недетонирующий *a.* nonknocking, knock-free, antiknock (gasoline).

недефицитный *a.* readily available.

недеформированный *a.* undistorted.

недёшево *adv.* not cheap(ly).

недеятель/ность *f.* inactivity, inertness, inertia, passivity; ineffectiveness, inefficiency; **—ый** *a.* inert, inactive; slow to react; passive; inoperative, idle; dormant; ineffective, inefficient.

недислоцированный *a.* undisturbed.

недиссоциированный *a.* undissociated.

недисциплинированный *a.* undisciplined.

недифференцированн/ый *a.* undifferentiated, indifferent (tissue); **—ая клетка** clasmatocyte.

недиффундирующий *a.* nondiffusing.

недо — *prefix* under—, incompletely; **—бирать, —брать** *v.* not get enough, get a low yield; **—бор** *m.* (harvest) deficiency, (yield) shortage; shortfall, deficit; incomplete collection; (money) arrears; **—брод** *m.* underfermentation.

недобро/желательный *a.* hostile, antagonistic; **—качественность** *f.* poor quality; **—качественный** *a.* inferior, low-grade; **—совестный** *a.* not conscientious, careless (work).

недобрый *a.* unkind; not good, bad.

недовальцовка *f.* underexpansion.

недовар *m.* undercooking; **—енный** *a.* undercooked; parboiled; **—и(ва)ть** *v.* undercook; parboil.

недоверчивый *a.* suspicious, distrustful.

недове/с *m.* short weight, underweight; **—сить, —шивать** *v.* give short weight.

недовозбуждённый *a.* underexcited.

недоволь/ный *a.* discontent, dissatisfied; **—ство** *n.* discontent, dissatisfaction.

недовосстановленный *a.* incompletely reduced.

недовулканиз/ация *f.* undervulcanization, undercure; **—ировать** *v.* undercure.

недо/вымолот *m.* (agr.) underthrashing; **—пас** *m.* undergrazing; **—выполнение** *n.* underfulfillment; **—выполнить, —выполнять** *v.* underfulfill; **—выработка** *f.* underproduction; **—глядеть** *v.* overlook, miss; neglect; **—гон** *m.* unfertile stem; **—грев** *m.* underheating.

недогру/жать, —зить *v.* underload; **—з** *m.,* **—зка** *f.* underload(ing); idle capacity.

недода/(ва)ть *v.* not give enough; underproduce; **—ча** *f.* deficiency in delivery.

недодел/анный *a.* unfinished, incomplete; **—ать** *v.* not finish; **—ка** *f.* unfinished state; omission, lack; imperfection, defect; substandard work.

недодерж/анный *a.* (phot.) underexposed; **—ивание** *n.,* **—ка** *f.* underexposure; insufficient treatment; **—(ив)ать** *v.* underexpose; not treat long enough.

недо/едание *n.* malnutrition; **—едать, —есть** *v.* suffer from malnutrition.

недожать *see* **недожинать.**

недож/ечь, —игать *v.* (cer.) underfire; burn incompletely; roast incompletely; **—жён(н)ый** *a.* underfired, etc., *see v.*

недожин *m.* poor crop; unharvested section; **—ать** *v.* get a poor crop.

недожог *m.* underburning; underfiring; unburned combustible matter; **н. топлива** carbon loss; **химический н.** incomplete combustion.

недозамедленный *a.* unmoderated.

недозрелый *a.* unripe, immature, green.

недоимка *f.* arrears.

недойный *a.* dry (period of cow).

недоказ/анный *a.* unproved, unconfirmed; **—ательный** *a.* failing to prove, unconvincing; **—уемый** *a.* unprovable.

недокал *m.* underheating.

недокармливать *v.* underfeed.

недокат *m.* (rolling) unfinished section.

недокись *f.* suboxide.

недоконченный *a.* unfinished, incomplete.

недокорм *m.* underfeeding; **—ить** *v.* underfeed.

недокрытие *n.* underlap.

недолгий *a.* brief, temporary.

недолго *adv.* for a short period, briefly; **—вечный** *a.* short-lived, transient; **—временный** *a.* brief, short-term.

недолёт *m.* falling short; undershot.

недол/ив *m.* underfilling, incomplete filling; short run (casting), misrun; shortage; **—ивание** *n.* underfilling; **—и(ва)ть** *v.* underfill, fill short of the top; **—ивка** *f.* underfilling; **—итый** *a.* underfilled.

недолов *m.* poor catch (of fish).

недомачивание *see* **недомочка.**

недомер *m.* short measure; offsize; **—и(ва)ть** *v.* give short measure; **—ок** *m.* undersize.

недомес *m.* undermixing, underkneading.

недоминирующий *a.* nondominant, subordinate.

недомог/ание *n.* poor health, malaise, indisposition; **—ать** *v.* be unwell.

недомол *m.* undermilling, undergrinding.

недомолвка *f.* reservation, omission.

недо/молот *m.* (agr.) underthrashing; **—молоченный** *a.* underthrashed; **—моченный** *a.* undersoaked, etc.; **—мочка** *f.* undersoaking, understeeping, underretting; **—напряжение** *n.* understress(ing); **—насыщенный** *a.* undersaturated.

недоно/сок *m.* premature baby; miscarriage; (zool.) slink; **—шенный** *a.* premature.

недообожжённый *a.* underburned, underbaked.

недоокис/лённый *a.* incompletely oxidized; **—ь** *f.* suboxide.

недооклейка *f.* incomplete clarification.

недоотверждение *n.* incomplete hardening.

недоохлаждение *n.* undercooling.

недооцен/ивать *v.* underestimate, underrate, undervalue; **—ка** *f.* underestimation, underestimate, underrating.

недо/паивать *v.* not solder completely; not water sufficiently; **—пал** *m.* incompletely burned material; **—паять** *v.* not solder completely; **—пекать, —печь** *v.* underroast, underbake; (met.) undersinter; **—пивать** *v.* not finish drinking; **—писанный** *a.* unfinished, incomplete (entry); **—пить** *see* **недопивать; —плата** *f.* underpay(ment); arrears; **—платить, —плачивать** *v.* underpay.

недоплодовитый *a.* sterile.

недопоить *v.* not water sufficiently.

недополуч/ать, —ить *v.* not get enough; **—ение** *n.* deficiency.

недопрессов/анный *a.* short; **—ка** *f.* shortness, undermolding.

недопроизводство *n.* underproduction.

недопроявление *n.* underdevelopment.

недопу/стимый *a.* inadmissible, intolerable, not to be tolerated; (comp.) invalid; **—щение** *n.* nonadmission; banning.

недораб/атывать *v.* not finish work (on); treat incompletely; **—отанность** *f.* unfinished state; **—отанный** *a.* unfinished; **—отать** *see* **недорабатывать**; **—отка** *f.* incomplete work; incomplete treatment; omission.

недоразв/ивающийся *a.*, **—ившийся** *a.* abortive; **—итие** *n.* underdevelopment; (mental) deficiency; (med.) aplasia; **—итость** *f.* underdeveloped state; **—итый** *a.* underdeveloped, rudimentary; imperfect, abortive; stunted, dwarfish; juvenile, immature; backward, retarded.

недо/разложившийся *a.* incompletely decomposed; **—разумение** *n.* misunderstanding; **—расширение** *n.* underexpansion.

недорог/о *adv.* inexpensively; **—ой** *a.* inexpensive, cheap, moderately priced.

недо/род *m.* crop failure, poor crop; **—руб** *m.* incomplete felling; **—саливать** *v.* not salt enough; **—сатурированный** *a.* undersaturated; **—се(и)вать**, **—сеять** *v.* not sow enough; **—сека** *f.* (text.) miss of weft; **—сказанный** *a.* left unsaid; **—сланный** *a.* short-shipped; **—слышать** *v.* not hear clearly.

недосмотр *m.* oversight, slip, error; **—еть** *v.* overlook, miss, slip up.

недосол *m.* insufficient salting; insufficient pickling; **—ить** *v.* not salt enough.

недоспать *v.* not get enough sleep.

недоспелый *a.* unripe, green, immature.

недоста/вать *v.* be wanting, be insufficient, fall short, run short, lack, miss; be needed, be required; be absent; **ему —ёт** he lacks, he is short (of).

недостат/ок *m.* deficiency, shortage, lack, scarcity; defect, fault, blemish, flaw, imperfection; disadvantage, drawback, shortcoming; limitation; deficit; (structural) weakness; **из-за —ка** for lack of, for want of; **иметь н.** *v.* have the disadvantage; be short, want, lack; need; **испытывать н.** *v.* be short (of), be in short supply.

недостаточн/о *adv.* insufficiently; it is insufficient; (it is) deficient (in); under—; imperfectly (understood); **н. напряжённый** *a.* understressed; **—ость** *f.* insufficiency, inadequacy, inefficiency; incompetence; shortage, deficiency, lack; imperfection; (heart) failure; **—ость витаминов** vitamin deficiency; **состояние —ости** deficiency; **—ый** *a.* insufficient, inadequate, under—, meager, deficient, scarce, poor; defective, faulty, imperfect, inefficient; **—ое питание** malnutrition; **—ое развитие** underdevelopment; **быть —ым** *v.* fall short.

недоста/ть *see* **недоставать**; **—ча** *f.* deficiency, shortage, lack; **—ющий** *a.* deficient, lacking, missing.

недостижим/ость *f.* inaccessibility; **—ый** *a.* inaccessible, unattainable.

недостоверный *a.* doubtful, uncertain; inexact; unauthentic.

недостойный *a.* unworthy.

недостроенн/ость *f.* incompleteness; **—ый** *a.* unfinished, incomplete; unfilled (electron shell).

недоступн/ость *f.* inaccessibility; unavailability; **—ый** *a.* inaccessible, unapproachable, impenetrable; unavailable; out of reach; prohibitive (cost); difficult (to understand).

недосчит(ыв)аться *v.* find a deficit, find something missing.

недо/сылать *v.* ship short; **—сылка** *f.* short shipment; **—сыпать** *v.* not fill completely; not sleep enough; **—сыщение** *n.* undersaturation.

недосягаем/ость *f.* unattainability; **—ый** *a.* unattainable, inaccessible, beyond the reach.

недотрав *m.* underpickling.

недотрога *f.* (bot.) Impatiens.

недотя/гивать, **—нуть** *v.* not reach.

недоуздок *m.* (livestock) halter.

недоум/евать *v.* be perplexed, be at a loss; **—ение** *n.* perplexity, quandary; **—енный** *a.* perplexed, baffled.

недоуч/есть, **—итывать** *v.* not take into sufficient account.

недохват *m.*, **—ка** *f.* shortage, deficiency.

недоходный *a.* unprofitable.

недочёт *m.* deficiency, deficit; mistake, error; shortcoming, defect.

недоэкспонированный *a.* underexposed.

недра *pl.* depths, interior (of the earth); midst; mineral resources; **богатства недр** mineral wealth; **в —х** in situ, in place; in the midst of.

недренируемый *a.* non-drainable.

недружелюбный *a.* unfriendly, ill-disposed.

недуализируемость *f.* (math.) nondualizability.

недуб/ящее *n.* non-tannin; **—лёный** *a.*, **—ленный** *part.* untanned, raw (hide).

неду/г *m.* illness, ailment, sickness; **—жный** *a.* ailing, infirm, sick.

недурной *a.* not bad.

недюжинный *a.* unusual, outstanding.

нее *gen. and acc. of* **она** *after prep.*, her.

неевклидовый *a.* (math.) non-Euclidean.

неезженый *a.* little used (road).

неенхеловые *pl.* (ichth.) Neenchelidae.

неестественный *a.* unnatural, abnormal.

нежарк/ий *a.* not hot, temperate (climate); **—о** *adv.* (it is) not hot.

нежвачные *pl.* (mam.) nonruminants.

нежданный *a.* unexpected.

нежелательн/о *adv.* (it is) undesirable; **—ость** *f.* undesirability; **—ый** *a.* undesirable, objectionable, unwanted; (rad., etc.) parasitic.

нежелезный *a.* (met.) nonferrous.

нежели *conj.* than.

нежен *sh. m. of* **нежный.**

нежёстк/ий *a.* flexible, not rigid; loose; soft (water); mild; (comp.; math.) fuzzy; **—о соединённый** *a.* loosely connected, loose.

нежи/вой *a.* abiotic, non-living; dead, lifeless, inanimate; inorganic; **—зненный** *a.* abiotic; impractical; **—знеспособный** *a.* nonviable; **—лой** *a.* uninhabited, non-residential.

нежир/ный *a.* lean; **—овой** *a.* fat-free.

нежн/ик *m.* (bot.) Helianthemum; **—о** *adv.* tenderly, gently; **—ость** *f.* gentleness, delicacy, tenderness, softness; **—ый** *a.* gentle, delicate, fine, tender, soft; sensitive; pleasant (taste).

незабивающийся *a.* nonclog(ging).

незабрушенный *a.* uncapped (honey).

незаб/удка *f.* (bot.) Myosotis; **—удочник** *m.* Eritrichium; **—ываемый** *a.* unforgettable.

незавер/енный *a.* uncertified; **—шёнка** *f.* work in progress; **—шённый** *a.* unfinished, incomplete; in process.

незавидный *a.* poor, insignificant, mediocre.

независим/о *adv.* independently; **н. от** regardless of, disregarding, whatever, no matter what; **н. от того** no matter how, whether or not, be it; **—ость** *f.* independence; freedom (of movement); **—ый** *a.* independent, individual, self-contained, separate, insulated, isolated; foreign (body).

независящий *a.* not depending, independent.

незагруж/енный, —ённый *a.* unloaded, uncharged; idle (machine).

незагрязн/енность *f.* noncontamination, purity; **—ённый** *a.* uncontaminated, pure; **—яющийся** *a.* nonfouling.

незадействованный *a.* idle, vacant, dead.

незадемпфированный *a.* undamped.

незадержанный *a.* undelayed.

незадерн/елый, —ованный *a.* unsodded, bare.

незадолго *adv.* shortly, not long (before).

незадросселированный *a.* unthrottled.

незадымляемая лестничная клетка fire tower.

незаживающий *a.* slow-healing.

незаземлённый *a.* (elec.) ungrounded.

незаиляющий *a.* nonsilting.

незаинтересованный *a.* disinterested.

незакалённый *a.* (met.) untempered.

незаклинённый *a.* unfastened, loose.

незаконн/омерный *a.* irregular; **—ый** *a.* illegal, unlawful; unjustified.

незаконтрактованный товар consignment.

незаконченн/ость *f.* unfinished state; **—ый** *a.* unfinished, incomplete, partial.

незакреплённ/ость *f.* looseness; **—ый** *a.* loose, unfastened, unmounted; loose-running, mobile, floating.

незалупа *f.* (med.) phimosis.

незамедл/енный *a.* (nucl.) unmoderated; **—ительный** *a.* prompt, immediate.

незаменим/ость *f.* irreplaceability; indispensability; **—ый** *a.* irreplaceable, not interchangeable; indispensable; essential (amino or fatty acid).

незамерзающ/ий *a.* non-freezing; **н. раствор, —ая жидкость** antifreeze.

незаметн/о *adv.* unnoticeably, imperceptibly; it is not noticeable; **—ый** *a.* unnoticeable, imperceptible, inconspicuous; insignificant; indistinct.

незамеченный *a.* unnoticed, overlooked.

незамещённый *a.* unsubstituted.

незаминированный *a.* mine-free.

незамкнутый *a.* unlocked, open.

незамужний *a.* unmarried, single.

незанятый *a.* unoccupied, idle, free, available; vacant, unfilled, empty.

не/запечатанный *a.* unsealed; uncapped (honey); **—запланированный** *a.* (comp.) ad hoc (query); **—заполнение** *n.* (met.) underfilling; **—заполненный** *a.* underfilled; unfilled, blank; **—заработанный** *a.* unearned.

незара/жённый *a.* noninfected; uncharged (particle); **—зный** *a.* noncontagious.

незаращ/ение *n.* (med.) patency, nonclosure; persistence (of fontanel); **—ённый** *a.* patent, open, unobstructed.

незарегистрированный *a.* unauthorized.

незарегулированный *a.* natural (flow).

незаросший *a.* not overgrown.

незаряж/енный, —ённый *a.* uncharged, unloaded.

незасекреченный *a.* unclassified.

незаслуженный *a.* undeserved, unfair.

незасорённый *a.* unobstructed, clear; clean; weed-free (garden).

незастеклённый *a.* unglazed.

незастроенный *a.* vacant, open, unbuilt; undeveloped (land).

незатейливый *a.* simple, plain.

незатопл/енный *a.* (hydr.) free(-fall); **—яемый** *a.* not inundated.

незатухающий *a.* continuous, (self-)sustained, undamped.

незаурядный *a.* superior, above average.

незачем *adv.* unnecessarily; there is no need.

незащищённый *a.* unprotected, unsheltered, exposed; (nucl.) unshielded; open, bare (ground).

незвязывающий *a.* nonbinding.

нездешний *a.* not local, outside.

нездоров/ый *a.* unwholesome, unsanitary; sick, unwell, **—ье** *n.* ill health.

неземной *a.* nonterrestrial, celestial.

незеркальный *a.* non-reflecting.

незернистый *a.* nongranular, agranulo—; **н. лейкоцит** (immun.) agranulocyte.

незимующий *a.* (bot.) summer (annuals).

незлоб/ивый, —ный *a.* gentle, mild.

незнаком/ый *a.* unknown, unfamiliar, unacquainted, strange; **—ая область** terra incognita.

незнание *n.* ignorance, lack of knowledge.

незнач/ащий *a.* insignificant, unimportant; (math.) nonsignificant; **—имость** *f.* (stat.) nonsignificance.

незначительн/ость *f.* insignificance; **—ый** *a.* insignificant, negligible, trivial, imperceptible; small, little, low, slight, minor, modest.

незокия *f.* (mam.) pest rat (*Nesokia*).

незрел/овылупляющийся *a.* (orn.) altricial; **—ость** *f.* immaturity, greenness, **—ый** *a.* immature, unripe, green.

незр/имый *a.* invisible; **—ячий** *a.* blind.

незыблем/ость *f.* firmness, immovability; **—ый** *a.* firm, steady, secure, stable, immovable; hard-and-fast (rule).

неидеальный *a.* imperfect.

неидент/ифицированный *a.* unidentified; **—ичность** *f.* non-identity.

неидиды *pl.* (ent.) Neididae.

неизбежн/о *adv.* inevitably, of necessity, (it is) bound to; **—ость** *f.* inevitability, imminence; **—ый** *a.* inevitable, imminent, unavoidable.

неизбирательный *a.* nonselective.

неизбывный *a.* hard to get rid of.

неизведанный *a.* untried, unexplored.

неизвестн/о *adv.* it is unknown, it is not known; **—ое** *n.* the unknown; unknown (quantity); **—ость** *f.* certainty, ignorance, obscurity; **быть в —ости** *v.* be uncertain; **—ый** *a.* unknown, undetermined, uncertain, obscure.

неизвлекаемый *a.* nonremovable.

неизгладимый *a.* indelible, lasting.

неизданный *a.* unpublished.

неизлечим/ость *f.* incurability; **—ый** *a.* incurable, irremediable.

неизлучающий *a.* nonradiating.

неизменн/о *adv.* invariably; **—ость** *f.* invariability, changelessness, inalterability, immutability; **—ый** *a.* invariable, unchangeable, unalterable, immutable; invariant (shape); constant, fixed, permanent, stable, stationary; unfailing.

неизменя/емость *f.* inalterability, stability; **н. на** resistance (to); **—емый** *a.* unalterable, immutable, permanent, constant; **—ющийся** *a.* unchanging; insensitive.

неизмерим/о *adv.* immeasurably, very; **—ый** *a.* immeasurable, very great.

неизолированный *a.* uninsulated, bare.

неизотермический *a.* anisothermic.

неизотопный *a.* nonisotopic; heterotopic.

неизотропн/ость *f.* anisotropy, anisotropism; **—ый** *a.* anisotropic.

неизученный *a.* uninvestigated, unexplored.

неизъясимый *a.* inexplicable.

неимен/ие *n.* lack, want; **за —ием, по —ию** for want (of), for lack (of).

неименованный *a.* indeterminate, abstract.

неимоверный *a.* incredible, very great.

неимущий *a.* poor, indigent; *m.* the poor, the have-nots.

неиндуктивный *a.* noninductive.

неинтегрируемый *a.* nonintegrable.

неинтересный *a.* uninteresting.

неион/изирующий *a.* nonionizing; **—(оген)ный** *a.* nonionic.

неискаж/аемый, —ённый *a.* undistorted, distortion-free; **—ающий** *a.* undistorting, distortionless.

неискоренимый *a.* hard to eradicate.

неискренний *a.* insincere.

неискрящийся *a.* nonsparking, sparkless; (elec.) non-arcing.

неиску/сный *a.* inexpert, unskilled; **—шённый** *a.* with little know-how.

неисповедимый *a.* incomprehensible.

неисполн/ение *n.* non-performance, non-fulfillment; **—енный** *a.* unfulfilled, unrealized; **—имость** *f.* impracticability; **—имый** *a.* impracticable; **—ительный** *a.* careless (worker).

неиспольз/ованный *a.* unutilized, untapped; idle (land); **—уемый** *a.* non-utilizable.

неиспорченный *a.* unspoiled, sound.

неисправ/имый *a.* irreparable, incorrigible; **—ленный** *a.* uncorrected; **—ность** *f.* fault, trouble, defect, bug; malfunction, failure, disrepair; carelessness; **поиск —ностей** (comp.) trouble shooting; **—ный** *a.* damaged, defective, inoperative, useless; careless, improper; inaccurate.

неиспробованный *a.* untested, untried.

неиспытанный *a.* untested, untried.

неисследованный *a.* unexplored, uninvestigated, untapped, virgin.

неиссякаемый *a.* inexhaustible.

неистощим/ость *f.* inexhaustibility; **—ый** *a.* inexhaustible.

неистребимый *a.* impossible to get rid of.

неисцелимый *see* **неизлечимый.**

неисчезающий *a.* non-vanishing, lasting, durable, permanent, persistent; stable, fast (color).

неисчерпаемый *a.* inexhaustible.

неисчислимый *a.* innumerable, countless.

ней *dat., etc., of* **она** *after prep.*

нейбергский *a.* Neuberg (blue).

нейблау *m.* new blue (dye).

нейва *f.* (ichth.) char (*Salvelinus neiva*).

нейвидский *a.* Neuwied (blue).

Нейгофа диаграмма Neuhoff diagram.

нейдорфит *m.* (min.) neudorfite.

нейзильбер *m.,* **—овый** *a.* German silver, nickel silver.

нейлон *m.,* **—овый** *a.* nylon.

нейманоовый *a.* Neumann('s).

нейр *—see* **невр—;** **—аминовый** *a.* neuraminic (acid); **—ин** *m.* neurine, amantine; **—истор** *m.* (electron.) neuristor; **—ит** *see* **неврит; —овирулентность** *f.* neurovirulence; **—оглия** *f.* (anat.) neuroglia; **—огуморальный** *a.* (physiol.) neurohumoral; **—озин** *m.* neurosin, calcium glycerophosphate; **—окератин** *m.* (histol.) neurokeratin; **—олимфоматоз** *m.* (vet.) neurolymphomatosis; **—он** *m.* neuron, nerve cell; **—онал** *m.* neuronal, diethyl-bromacetamid; **—опиль** *m.* (anat.) neuropil(e); **—осекрет** *m.,* **—осекреция** *f.* (physiol.) neurosecretion; **—осекреторный** *a.* neurosecretory; **—отоксический** *a.* neurotoxic, nerve-poisoning; **—офизиология** *f.* neurophysiology; **—охирургия** *f.* neurosurgery; **—ула** *f.* (embr.) neurula.

нейский *a.* (geog.) Neya.

нейстон *m.* (biol.) neuston (floating organisms).

нейтр. *abbr.* (**нейтральный**) neutral; (**нейтрон, нейтронный**) neutron.

нейтрализ/атор *m.* neutralizer, neutralizing tank; detoxifier; catalytic converter (for exhaust gas); **—ационный** *a.,* **—ация** *f.* neutralization; **—ованный** *a.* neutralized; **—овать** *v.* neutralize; counteract, balance out, equalize; detoxify; **—ующий** *a.* neutralizing; **—ующее средство** neutralizing agent, neutralizer.

нейтралитет *m.* neutrality.

нейтраль *f.* (elec.) neutral wire or conductor; neutral (point); (mach.) neutral line.

нейтральн/о *adv.* neutrally; **—ость** *f.* neutrality; **—ый** *a.* neutral; inert (gas); nontoxic (smoke); uncharged (particle); neutral-density (filter).

нейтрет(т)о *n.* neutreto, neutral meson.

нейтрин/ный *a.,* **—о** *n.* (nucl.) neutrino.

нейтродин *m.,* **—ный, —овый** *a.* (rad.) neutrodyne (amplifier).

нейтрон *m.* (nucl.) neutron; **на быстрых —ах** fast-neutron (cycle); fast (reactor fission); **на медленных —ах** slow; **поток —ов** neutron flux; **—ный** *a.* neutron; **—ограмма** *f.* neutron diffraction pattern; **—ограф** *m.* neutron diffraction camera; **—ография** *f.* neutron diffraction analysis; **—одефицитный** *a.* neutron-deficient; **—озахватывающий** *a.* neutron-capture; **—ометрия** *f.* neutron logging; **—онепроницаемый** *a.* neutron-tight.

нейтро/пения *f.* (med.) neutropenia; **—фил** *m.* neutrophil; **—фильный** *a.* neutrophilic.

нейтр/сек *abbr.* (**нейтронов в секунду**) neutrons per second.

нейтр-ция *abbr.* (**нейтрализация**).

нейуротропин *m.* new urotropine.

некавитирующий *a.* subcavitating.

некальцинированный *a.* uncalcined, unroasted, raw.

неканализованный *a.* without sewers.

некаптированный *a.* wild (oil well).

некастрированный *a.* uncastrated, ungelded, entire.

некатороз *m.* (med.) necatoriasis.

некачественный *a.* unsound, poor (quality).

неквалифицированный *a.* unqualified; inexpert, unskilled (labor).

неквантов(анн)ый *a.* nonquantized.

некий *a.* one, some, a certain.

некк *m.* (geol.) neck, plug.

неклассическое название (biol.) common name.

неклён *m.* (bot.) box elder (*Acer negundo*).

неклеточный *a.* acellular; noncellular.

некоаксиальный *a.* misaligned.

нековкий *a.* not malleable.

некогда *adv.* there is no time; formerly, once, long ago, in the past.

некогерентн/ость *f.* (phys.) noncoherence; **—ый** *a.* incoherent; scrambled (speech).

некого *pron.* there is no one.

некодированный *a.* not coded, nonsymbolic.

некоксующийся *a.* noncoking, noncaking.

неколючий *a.* (bot.) thornless.

некомпактный *a.* (math.) noncompact.

некомпенсированный *a.* uncompensated.

некомпетентн/ость *f.* incompetence; **—ый** *a.* incompetent.

некомплект *m.* shortage, deficiency; **—ность** *f.* incompleteness; **—ный** *a.* incomplete (set).

неконгениальный *a.* incongenial.

неконденсирующийся *a.* noncondensing.

некондиционный *a.* substandard, below standard, off-grade.

неконкурентный *a.* noncompetitive.

неконстантный *a.* inconstant, fickle.

неконтрастный *a.* not contrasty, soft.

неконтролируемый *a.* uncontrolled.

неконченный *a.* unfinished, incomplete.

некоптящий *a.* sootless, nonsmoking.

некорнев/ой *a.* (agr.) foliar, spray (feeding); **—ое удоб-рение** leaf-feeding spray.

некорректный *a.* incorrect, improper, false.

некоррелированный *a.* uncorrelated.

некорро/дируемый, —зийный, —зионный, —зируемый *a.* noncorrodible, corrosion-resistant, rustless; **—дирующий** *a.* noncorroding, nonrusting, stainless.

некоторый *a.* some, certain; given, limited.

некошеный *a.* uncut, unmowed (grass).

некрасивый *a.* unattractive.

некрасящий *a.* nonstaining, nondyeing.

некратный *a.* (math.) aliquant.

некредитоспособный *a.* (com.) insolvent.

некрепкий *a.* not strong, weak.

некристаллический *a.* noncrystalline, amorphous, structureless.

некритический *a.* uncritical, noncritical.

некро— *prefix* necro— (dead); **—бациллёз** *m.* (vet.) necrobacillosis; **—биоз** *m.* (med.) necrobiosis; **—биотический** *a.* necrobiotic; **—гормон** *m.* necrohormone; **—з** *m.* (med.) necrosis; **—лиз** *m.* necrolysis; **—лог** *m.* obituary; **—спермия** *f.* (med.) necrospermia.

некроссоверный *a.* (gen.) noncrossover.

некротиз/ация *f.,* **—ирование** *n.* (med.) necrotization; **—ированный** *a.* necrotic, necrotized; **—ировать** *v.* necrotize.

некро/томия *f.* necrotomy, autopsy; **—фаг** *m.* necrophage; **—фаговый** *a.* necrophagous, saprophytic; **—фильный** *a.* necrophilous; **—цитоз** *m.* (med.) necrocytosis.

некруглый *a.* noncircular, out-of-round.

некрупный *a.* not large, middle-sized.

некрутой *a.* not steep, easy (climb).

нек-рый *abbr.* (**некоторый**).

некрытый *a.* uncovered, roofless.

некстати *adv.* inopportunely, untimely, irrelevantly.

нектар *m.* (bot.) nectar; **—ий, —ник** *m.* nectary, nectar gland; **—ин** *m.* nectarine (fruit); **—ницы** *pl.* sunbird family (*Nectariniidae*); **—ность** *f.* nectar-forming capacity; **—ный** *a.* nectar(iferous), nectar-secreting; **—овыделение** *n.* nectar secretion; **—онос** *m.* nectariferous plant; **—оносность** *f.* nectar capacity (of area); **—оносный** *a.* nectariferous, nectar-producing; **—охранилище** *n.* nectarotheca.

некто *pron.* somebody, someone.

некто— *prefix* necto— (swimming); **—зома** *f.* (zool.) nectosome; **—н** *m.,* **—нный** *a.* nekton; **—фор** *m.* nectophore, nectocalyx.

нектрия *f.* (phyt.) coral spot.

некуда *adv.* (there is) nowhere (to).

некульт/ивированный *a.* uncultivated, untilled, natural; **—урный** *a.* uncultured, rough-mannered; (bot.) wild, uncultivated.

некурящий *a.* non-smoking; *m.* non-smoker.

нелад/ный *a.* bad, wrong; out of order; unsuccessful; **—ы** *pl.* misunderstanding, discord.

нелегальный *a.* illegal.

нелегированный *a.* (met.) unalloyed.

нелёгкий *a.* fairly heavy; difficult, not easy; **нелегко** *adv.* with difficulty; it is difficult.

нелеп/ость *f.* absurdity; **—ый** *a.* absurd, preposterous; incongruous.

нелетающий *a.* nonflying, flightless.

нелётный *a.* (av.) unfavorable (weather).

нелетущий *a.* nonvolatile, fixed.

неликвид *m.* property subject to liquidation.

нелин/еаризированный *a.* nonlinearized; **—ейность** *f.* nonlinearity; **—ейный** *a.* nonlinear.

нелиняющий *a.* unfading, fast.

нелишний *a.* not superfluous; useful.

неловкий *a.* awkward, clumsy.

нелогичный *a.* illogical.

нелокализ/ованный *a.* delocalized (electrons); **—уемый** *a.* nonlocalizable.

неломкий *a.* (met.) tenacious, tough.

нельзя *adv.* it is impossible, cannot (be); **н. отличить** be indistinguishable.

нельм/а *f.,* **—овый** *a.* (ichth.) nelma (*Stenodus leucichthys nelma*); Aspius; Elopichthys bambusa; **—ушка** *f.* whitefish (*Coregonus lavaretus nelmuschka*).

нелюдимый *a.* unpopulated; unsociable.

нем *sh. m.* of **немой**; *m.* nem (unit of nutrition).

нём *prepos.* of **он, оно,** him, it.

нем. *abbr.* (**немецкий**) German.

немагический *a.* nonmagic (nucleus).

немагнитный *a.* nonmagnetic.

немалит *m.* (min.) nemalite.

немал/о *adv.* much, many; very; **—оважный** *a.* important; **—ый** *a.* fairly big; considerable, fairly long (time).

неманский *a.* (geog.) Neman, Niemen.

нематалоза *f.* (ichth.) Nematalosa.

нематериальный *a.* intangible (loss, etc.).

немато— *prefix* (biol.) nemato— (thread; nematode); **—бластический** *a.* (petr.) nematoblastic; **—да** *f.* (zool.) nematode (*Nematoda*); **—доз** *m.* nematode infection, nematodiasis; **—доустойчивый** *a.* resistant to nematodes; **—морфы** *pl.* hairworms (*Nematomorpha*); **—цид** *m.* nematocide.

немафилит *m.* (min.) nemaphyllite.

нембутал *m.* Nembutal, pentobarbital sodium.

немедленн/о *adv.* immediately, instant(aneous)ly, directly, at once, without delay; **—ый** *a.* immediate, instant(aneous), prompt, fast.

немезонный *a.* (nucl.) nonmesonic.

немертины *pl.* (zool.) nemertines.

неместный *a.* ecdemic, not native.

неместриниды *pl.* (ent.) Nemestrinidae.

неметаболичный *a.* ametabolic.

неметалл *m.* nonmetal; metalloid; **—ический** *a.* nonmetallic.

неметизированный *a.* (gen.) uncrossed.

неметь *v.* grow numb.

немеханизированный *a.* manual.

немец *m.,* **—кий** *a.* German; long-link (chain); Manheim (gold).

немеченый *a.* (radiochem.) unlabelled.

немигающий *a.* unwinking, unblinking.

немигрирующий *a.* nonmigratory, resident.

неминуем/ость *f.* inevitability, unavoidability; **—ый** *a.* inevitable, unavoidable, inescapable; impending.

немиптеровые *pl.* (ichth.) Nemipteridae.

немихтовидные *pl.* (ichth.) Nemichthyoidei.

немки *pl.* velvet ants (*Mutillidae*).

немног/ие *pl.* (a) few, not many; **—ий** *a.* few, some; **—о** *adv.* not much, slightly, somewhat; some, (some) few; *prefix* pauci— (few); olig(o)— [few; scant; (med.) deficiency]; **—осемянный** *a.* (bot.) oligospermous; **—ое** *n.* little; **—ословный** *a.* brief; **—очисленный, —очленный** *a.* few, not numerous; **—очисленность** *f.* scarcity.

немнущийся *a.* (text.) noncrushable.

немодулированный *a.* unmodulated.

немой *a.* dumb, mute; silent; outline (map); (geol.) barren; *m.* mute.

немолодой *a.* mature, middle-aged.

немоно/кристаллический *a.* polycrystalline; —тонный *a.* undulatory; —хроматический *a.* polychromatic.

немонтированный *a.* unmounted; unassembled.

неморальный *a.* (biol.) nemoral; nemorose.

немота *f.* dumbness, muteness.

немотивированный *a.* unprovoked, unjustified.

немотин *m.* Nemotin (antibiotic); —овый *a.* Nemotin; nemotinic (acid).

немочёный *a.* raw (flax).

немочь *see* немощь.

немощёный *a.* unpaved, dirt (road).

немощ/ность *f.* infirmity; —ный *a.* infirm, weak; (math.) nilpotent; —ь *f.* infirmity, illness; бледная —ь chlorosis.

нему *dat.* of он, оно *after prep.*, him, it.

немунасовый *a.* (geog.) Nemunas, Niemen.

немыслимый *a.* unthinkable, impossible.

ненаблюдаемый *a.* unobservable.

ненабухающий *a.* nonswelling.

ненави/деть *v.* hate, detest; —стный *a.* hateful, odious; —сть *f.* hatred.

ненагруж/енный, —ённый *a.* empty, idle.

ненадёжн/ость *f.* unreliability, insecurity; —ый *a.* unreliable, insecure, unsafe, untrustworthy.

ненадкевит *m.* (min.) nenadkevite.

ненадлежащий *a.* undue, excessive.

ненадобность *f.* uselessness.

ненадолго *adv.* for a short time.

ненамеренный *a.* unintentional.

ненамного *adv.* a little, not much.

ненаполненный *a.* unadulterated, pure; unfilled, unloaded, filler-free; non-pigmented (rubber).

ненаправленный *a.* nondirectional.

ненапряжённый *a.* relaxed; unstressed, unstrained; (elec.) dead.

ненароком *adv.* accidentally, inadvertently.

ненарушенный *a.* undisturbed, intact.

ненасиженный *a.* unhatched (egg).

ненаследственный *a.* (gen.) nonhereditary.

ненастный *a.* rainy, inclement, foul, bad (weather).

ненастоящий *a.* not genuine, artificial, not real, pseudo—, false.

ненастроенный *a.* untuned, unadjusted.

ненастье *n.* bad weather, rainy weather.

ненасытный *a.* insatiable.

ненасыщ/ающийся *a.* unsaturable; —еннополиэфирный *a.* unsaturated polyester; —енность *f.* nonsaturation, undersaturation; insatiability; —енный *a.* unsaturated; unsatiated, unsatisfied.

ненатуральный *a.* artificial; unnatural.

ненатянут/ость *f.* looseness, slack; —ый *a.* loose, slack, flaccid, flabby.

ненаучный *a.* unscientific.

ненесущий *a.* nonbearing, nonsupporting.

ненецкий *a.* (geog.) Nenets.

неноздреватый *a.* nonporous, dense, compact.

ненормальн/ость *f.* abnormality; anomaly, irregularity; н. в работе faulty performance, erratic operation; —ый *a.* abnormal; off (color).

ненормированный *a.* unregulated (price).

ненужн/о *adv.* unnecessarily; it is unnecessary; —ый *a.* unnecessary, redundant; useless, needless, superfluous.

ненулевой *a.* nonzero, nontrivial.

ненумерованный *a.* unnumbered.

неньютоновский *a.* non-Newtonian.

нео— *prefix* neo— (new, recent); —абиетиновый *a.* neoabietic (acid); —аймалин *m.* (neo)ajmaline, rauwolfine; —арсфенамин *m.* neoarsphenamine.

необделанный *a.* unfinished, rough.

необдуманный *a.* rash, ill-considered.

необеспеченн/ость *f.* deficiency, lack; —ый *a.* unprovided (for), needy.

необесшламленный *a.* (min.) undeslimed.

необитаемый *a.* uninhabited; unmanned.

необлавливаемый район virgin ground.

необлесённый *a.* (silv.) unstocked.

необлицованный *a.* unlined.

необлучаемый *a.* radiation-free.

необмока *f.* (bot.) Adiantum.

необнародованный *a.* unpublished.

необнаружив/аемый *a.* undetectable; —ающийся *a.* cryptic, hidden.

необогащённый *a.* (met.) unconcentrated, undressed, crude (ore).

необожжённый *a.* unburnt, unroasted, raw (ore); (cer.) unfired.

необозначенный *a.* not indicated.

необозрим/ость *f.* vastness, immensity; —ый *a.* vast, immense, boundless.

необоснованный *a.* groundless, baseless, unfounded, without proof.

необработанн/ость *f.* crude state; —ый *a.* crude, raw, untreated, unrefined, coarse; unfinished, rough; unprocessed (data); uncultivated (field).

необразованный *a.* uneducated.

необрастающий *a.* nonfouling; antifouling (paint).

необратим/ость *f.* irreversibility; —ый *a.* irreversible, nonreversible.

необрушенный *a.* unhusked, unhulled.

необсаженный *a.* uncased, open (hole).

необслуживаемый *a.* unattended, unwatched.

необстоятельный *a.* superficial.

необученный *a.* untrained, unskilled.

необходим/о *adv.* necessarily; it is necessary, it should be, needs to be; —ое *n.* requisite, necessaries; —ость *f.* necessity, need, indispensability; в силу —ости of necessity; в случае —ости if need be, if required, if necessary; вызвать —ость *v.* necessitate; нет —ости there is no need (for); первой —ости essential; по —ости of necessity; when or if necessary; to suit requirements; по мере —ости, при —ости as needed, as (may be) required, as the need arises.

необходим/ый *a.* necessary, needed, required, requisite, indispensable, essential, imperative; делать —ым *v.* necessitate; заранее н. prerequisite; крайне н. urgent, imperative.

необшитый *a.* unlined, unfaced.

необъезженный *a.* unbroken (horse).

необъявленный *a.* (tel.) unlisted.

необъясним/о *adv.* inexplicably; it is inexplicable; —ость *f.* inexplicability; —ый *a.* inexplicable, unaccountable.

необъятный *a.* immense, unbounded.

необыкновенн/о *adv.* unusually; it is unusual; —ость *f.* unusualness, singularity; —ый *a.* unusual, singular, uncommon, rare, extraordinary.

необыч/айный *a.* unusual, remarkable; not characteristic (of); —ный *a.* different, unconventional, exceptional.

необязательный *a.* not obligatory, optional; unrequired, elective (course); dispensable, nonessential; facultative (parasite).

нео/витамин *m.* neovitamin; **—гексан** *m.* neohexane, 2,2-dimethylbutane; **—ген** *m.* (geol.) Neogene system; Neogen (alloy); **—генез** *m.* (biol.) neogenesis, regeneration; **—генный** *a.* (geol.) Neogenic; **—гея** *f.* (biogeog.) Neogaea, Neogaean realm.

неогнеопасный *a.* fireproof, fire-resistant.

неогороженный *a.* unfenced, open.

неограниченн/о *adv.* unreservedly, without restriction, beyond all bounds, indefinitely; **—ый** *a.* unrestricted, unbounded, indefinite, unlimited, absolute (power); unheard-of (yield); immense, limitless; complete (solubility).

неодарвинизм *m.* (zool.) Neo-Darwinism.

неодевон *m.* (geol.) Neodevonian period.

неодетый *a.* undressed, bare; unsheeted (slope).

неодим, —ий *m.* neodymium, Nd; **окись —ия** neodymium oxide, neodymia.

неодинаков/ость *f.* dissimilarity; **н. свойства** different properties; **—ый** *a.* different, dissimilar; not uniform, not homogeneous; unequal; (met.) differential (aeration).

неоднозначн/ость *f.* ambiguity; polyvalence; **устранение —ости** disambiguation; **—ый** *a.* ambiguous.

неодно/имённый *a.* unlike, opposite, dissimilar; **—кратно** *adv.* repeatedly, time and again; **—кратный** *a.* repeated, reiterated; **—образный** *a.* irregular.

неоднородн/ость *f.* heterogeneity, inhomogeneity, nonuniformity; discontinuity, irregularity; **—ый** *a.* heterogeneous, inhomogeneous, nonuniform.

неодобр/ение *n.* disapproval; **—ительный** *a.* disapproving.

неодолимый *a.* insurmountable, irresistible.

неодревесневший *a.* softwood.

неодушевлённый *a.* inanimate.

неожид/аемый *a.* unpredictable; **—анно** *adv.* suddenly, unexpectedly, abruptly; **—анность** *f.* suddenness; surprise; **—анный** *a.* sudden, surprising, unexpected.

неожижаемый *a.* noncondensable.

неозвученный *a.* silent (moving picture).

неозой *m.* (geol.) Neozoic group; **—ский** *a.* Neozoic, Cenozoic.

неокаймлённый *a.* immarginate.

неокаин *m.* neocaine, procaine.

неокисл/ённый *a.* unoxidized; **—яемость** *f.* inoxidizability; **—яемый** *a.* inoxidizable, nonoxidizable; **—яющий** *a.* nonoxidizing; **—яющийся** *a.* nonoxidizing; nonoxidizable.

неоком *m.* (geol.) Neocomian stage.

неоконч/ательный *a.* inconclusive, not final; **—енный** *a.* unfinished, incomplete.

неокоренный *a.* unpeeled, not peeled.

неокраш/енный *a.* colorless; unpainted, unfinished; **—ивающийся** *a.* chromophobe, non-stainable.

нео/купферон *m.* neo-cupferron; **—ламаркизм** *m.* (gen.) Neo-Lamarckism; **—лин** *m.* Neolin, benzathine penicillin G.

неолит *m.* (geol.) Neolithic stage; **—ический** *a.* Neolithic, stone age.

неологизм *m.* neologism, new term.

нео/мения *f.* (mal.) Neomenia; **—ментол** *m.* neomenthol; **—мицин** *m.,* **—мициновый** *a.* neomycin; **—морф** *m.* (biol.) neomorph.

неомыл/яемый *a.* unsaponified; **—яемый, —яющийся** *a.* unsaponifiable.

неон *m.* neon, Ne; (ichth.) neon (*Paracheirodon innese*); **—ал** *m.* Neonal, butethal; **—овый** *a.* neon.

неопадающий *a.* (bot.) nondeciduous, evergreen; persistent (leaf).

нео/палеозойский *a.* (geol.) Neopaleozoic; **—пальмитиновый** *a.* neopalmitic.

неопасн/о *adv.* safely; it is safe; **—ый** *a.* safe, harmless.

неопентан *m.* neopentane.

неопер/ённый *a.* unfinned, finless (rocket); (orn.) featherless, bare; **—ившийся** *a.* not feathered, unfledged.

неопёртый *a.* unsupported.

неопилина *f.* (mal.) Neopilina.

неопин *m.* neopine, β-codeine.

неопис/анный *a.* not yet described; **—уемый** *a.* indescribable.

неоплазма *f.* (med.) neoplasm, tumor.

неопла/тный *a.* irredeemable; insolvent; **—ченный** *a.* unpaid.

неоплодотворённый *a.* unfertilized.

не/опознанный *a.* unidentified, questionable; **—оправданный** *a.* unjustified, unwarranted.

неопределён/о *adv.* indefinitely; it is not definite; **—ость** *f.* indefiniteness, uncertainty, vagueness, indeterminacy; ambiguity; (math.) indeterminate form; **принцип —ости** (quantum mechanics) indeterminacy principle, uncertainty principle; **—ый** *a.* indefinite, uncertain, vague, indeterminate (function); undefined, undetermined.

неопредел/имый, —яемый *a.* undefinable, indeterminate; undefined (concept).

неопрен *m.,* **—овый** *a.* neoprene.

неопробованный *a.* untested, untried.

неопровержим/ость *f.* irrefutability; **—ый** *a.* irrefutable, indisputable, incontrovertible, undeniable.

неоптиль *m.* (orn.) neoptile, down feather.

не/оптимальный *a.* non-optimal; **—опубликованный** *a.* unpublished; **—опушённый** *a.* (bot.) hairless, glabrous, bald.

неопытн/ость *f.* inexperience; **—ый** *a.* inexperienced, unpracticed, unskilled.

неорганизованн/ость *f.* lack of organization; **—ый** *a.* disorganized.

неорганический *a.* inorganic.

неориентированный *a.* unoriented.

неорошаемый *a.* unirrigated, dry (farming).

неосальварсан *m.* neosalvarsan, neoarsphenamine.

неосахаренный *a.* unsweetened.

неосведомлённ/ость *f.* ignorance, lack of information; **—ый** *a.* ignorant, uninformed.

неосвоенный *a.* unassimilated, unprocessed; undeveloped (land, resources).

не/осевой *a.* off-axis; **—оседающий** *a.* nonsettling; **—осёдланный** *a.* unsaddled (horse); **—оседлый** *a.* nomad, wandering.

неоскопеловые *pl.* (ichth.) Neoscopelidae.

неослабный *a.* unremitting, unabated.

неослепляющий *a.* nonglare, antiglare.

неоснователь/о *adv.* groundlessly, without foundation; **—ость** *f.* groundlessness, lack of foundation; **—ый** *a.* groundless, unfounded; superficial.

неоснов/ой/, ой *a.* minor(ity), auxiliary.

неособый *a.* (math.) nonsingular (matrix).

неоспоримый *a.* indisputable.

неостаток *m.* nonresidue.

неостетовые *pl.* (ichth.) Neostethidae.

неосторожн/о *adv.* carelessly; **—ость** *f.* carelessness, negligence; **—ый** *a.* careless, negligent, unwary, incautious, imprudent, ill-advised.

неосуществим/ость *f.* impracticability; **—ый** *a.* impracticable, not feasible.

неосыпаемый *a.* resistant to shedding.

неосязаем/ость *f.* intangibility; **—ый** *a.* intangible, imperceptible, impalpable.

неотверждаемый *a.* nonhardening.

неотвесный *a.* out of plumb.

неотвратимый *a.* inevitable, unavoidable.

неотделанный *a.* unfinished, rough; undressed, uncut (stone); raw.

неотделимый *a.* inseparable.

неотектоника *f.* (geol.) neotectonics.

неотен/ин *m.* neotenin, juvenile hormone; **—ический** *a.* neotenic; **—ия** *f.* neoteny.

неотёсанный *a.* rough, uncut (stone).

неотип *m.* (min.; pal.) neotype.

неоткатывающийся *a.* nonrolling, stay.

неотклоняющий(ся) *a.* undeflecting, nondeviating.

неоткуда *adv.* (from) nowhere.

неотличимый *a.* indistinguishable.

неотложн/ость *f.* urgency; emergency; **—ый** *a.* urgent, pressing, emergency.

неотлучный *a.* always present, permanent, continuous.

неотожжённый *a.* unannealed, raw.

неотокит *m.* (min.) neotocite.

неотома *f.* (mam.) pack rat (*Neotoma*).

неотпадающий *a.* adeciduate.

неотпущенный *a.* (met.) untempered.

неотравленный *a.* unpoisoned; (nucl.) uncontaminated, clean.

неотраж/ающий *a.* nonreflective, nonreflecting; nonreverberatory; **—ённый** *a.* nonreflected, direct.

неотразимый *a.* irresistible; insurmountable; irrefutable.

неотрицательный *a.* (math.) non-negative.

неотропический *a.* (biogeog.) neotropical.

неотрывный *a.* continuous, uninterrupted.

неотсортированный *a.* unsorted, unculled.

неотст/аивающийся *a.* nonsettling; **—оявшийся** *a.* unsettled, turbid.

неотступный *a.* importunate, urgent, persistent.

неотчётливый *a.* distinct, vague.

неотчуждаемый *a.* (law) inalienable.

неотъемлемый *a.* integral, inherent; permanent (sovereignty).

неофит *m.* (bot.) neophyte.

неофициальный *a.* unofficial, informal.

неоформленный *a.* not official, not accepted.

неохватный *a.* very large, huge.

неохлаждаемый *a.* uncooled.

неохотный *a.* unwilling, reluctant.

неохраняемый *a.* unprotected (by law).

неоцен *m.* (geol.) Neocene.

неоценимый *a.* inestimable, invaluable.

неоцидин *m.* neocidin.

неоцинкованный *a.* (met.) ungalvanized.

неочётливый *a.* vague, indistinct.

неочищенный *a.* unpurified, unrefined, crude, raw; sour (gasoline); untreated (sewage); commercial (grade).

неоштукатуренный *a.* unplastered, unfinished.

неощут/имый, —ительный *a.* impalpable, imperceptible, inappreciable.

неоэндем *m.* neoendemic plant.

неп *abbr.* (**непер**) neper, nep.

непалин *m.* nepaline.

непальский *a.* (geog.) Nepal.

непарн/ик *m.* (ent.) gypsy moth (*Lymantria dispar*); **—окопытные, —опалые** *pl.* (mam.) perissodactyls; **—окопытный, —опалый** *a.* perissodactyl, odd-toed; **—оперистый** *a.* (bot.) odd-pinnate.

непарный *a.* unpaired, unmatched; azygous, odd; odd-numbered; single; median (fin).

непахотопригодный *a.* nonarable (land).

непахучий *a.* odorless.

непентес *m.* (bot.) Nepenthes.

непер *m.* (acous.) neper (unit).

непере/варенный *a.* undigested; **—вар(ив)аемый** *a.* indigestible; **—водимый** *a.* untranslatable; **—гружающийся** *a.* antisaturation (amplifier); **—крывание** *n.*, **—крывающийся** *a.* nonoverlapping.

непереноc/имость *f.* intolerance; idiosyncracy; **—имый** *a.* intolerable, unbearable; **—ный** *a.* nonportable, stationary.

непересе/кать *v.* not cross, not intersect; not overlap; **—кающий(ся)** *a.* noncrossing, nonintersecting, disjoint; nonoverlapping; **—чённый** *a.* not crossed, etc., *see v.*

непере/тачиваемый *a.* disposable, throw-away (blade); **—ходный** *a.* (gram.) intransitive.

непериодич/еский *a.* nonperiodical, aperiodic(al), noncyclic; **—ность** *f.* aperiodicity.

неперовый *a.* (math.) Napier(ian).

неписаный *a.* unwritten (rules).

непищевой *a.* inedible.

неплав/кий *a.* infusible, nonmelting; **—кость** *f.* infusibility; **—ящийся** *a.* nonmelting, nonconsumable.

непластифицированный *a.* unplasticized.

неплатёж *m.* nonpayment, default; **—еспособность** *f.* (law) insolvency; **—еспособный** *a.* insolvent.

неплод/(ород)ие *n.*, **(ород)ность** *f.* sterility, infertility, barrenness; **(ород)ный, —отворный, —ущий** *a.* sterile, infertile, barren; unproductive (land).

неплоск/ий *a.* not flat, uneven, irregular, nonplanar; hilly; **—остность** *f.* nonflatness, etc., *see a.*

неплотн/о *adv.* loosely; **—ость** *f.* looseness; leakiness, leakage; unsoundness; **—ый** *a.* loose, not compact; low-density; leaky, leaking; unsound; not firm.

неплох/о *adv.* not badly, rather well; **—ой** *a.* not bad, satisfactory.

не/победимый *a.* unconquerable, invincible; **—поворотимый** *a.* irrotational, nonrotatory; **—поворотливый** *a.* clumsy, awkward, slow, sluggish; **—повреждённый** *a.* unimpaired, intact, sound, undamaged.

неповтор/имый, —яемый *a.* unique.

непогашеный *a.* unslaked, quick (lime).

непоглощающий *a.* nonabsorbing.

непого/да, —дь *f.* bad weather; **—жий** *a.* bad, foul (weather).

непогрешимый *a.* infallible.

неподалёку *adv.* near, not far.

неподатливый *a.* tenacious, unyielding; unmanageable, stubborn.

неподвижн/о *adv.* motionlessly; immovably, securely, fast; genuinely, really; **—огрудые** *pl.* (herp.) Firmisternia; **—ость** *f.* immobility, fixity; stiffness, rigidity; (med.) akinesia; **—ый** *a.* immobile, immovable, stationary, fixed; tight, rigid; motionless, resting, at rest, standing, quiescent; stagnant; still (air; water); sessile (drop); fixed-bed (catalyst); (elec.) static; dead (center); **—ая точка** point of rest; fulcrum; pause.

непод/готовленный *a.* unprepared; **—дающийся действию** *a.* resistant; **—дельный** *a.* unadulterated, pure; genuine, real, authentic.

неподеленный *a.* unshared, lone.

неподлежащий *a.* not subject (to), not liable (to), exempt, free (from).

неподменяемый *a.* noninterchangeable.

неподобный *a.* dissimilar, unlike.

неподражаемый *a.* inimitable.

неподрессор(ен)ный *a.* unsprung, springless.

неподходящий *a.* unsuitable, unsuited, inappropriate, inadequate, unfitted.

непозвол/ительный *a.* not permissible, nonpermissible; inadmissible; **—яющий** *a.* nonpermissive.

непозвоночное *n.* (zool.) invertebrate.

непоколебимый *a.* firm, unyielding.

непокрытый *a.* uncoated, uncovered.

неполад/ка *f.* shutdown, failure, breakdown, disrepair, malfunction, maladjustment; trouble, fault, hitch, bug, kink; **выявление —ок, нахождение —ок** troubleshooting; **устранять —ки** *v.* debug.

неполег/аемость *f.* (agr.) standing power; **—ающий** *a.* not fallen, standing.

неполивной *a.* unirrigated, dry (farming).

неполированный *a.* unpolished.

неполно *adv.* incompletely; **—зубые** *pl.* (mam.) Edentata; **—зубый** *a.* edentate; intermittent (gear); **—крыл** *m.* (ent.) Molorchus; **—мерный** *a.* short, scanty; undersized; **—обожжённый** *a.* incompletely burned; **—сть, —та** *f.* incompleteness, imperfection; **—стью** incompletely.

неполноценн/ость *f.* defect, inferiority, insufficiency; (mental) deficiency; **—ый** *a.* inferior, defective; abnormal, substandard; deficient (diet); handicapped (person); **—ое питание** malnutrition.

неполный *a.* incomplete, partial, unfinished; not full; below standard; low-order (detonation); short (measure); light (load); imperfect, defective.

неполов/озрелый *a.* (sexually) immature, preadult; **—ой** *a.* asexual.

неположительнйи *a.* nonpositive.

неполяр/изованный *a.* nonpolarized; **—ный** *a.* nonpolar, apolar.

непомерный *a.* exorbitant, excessive.

непоним/ание *n.* incomprehension; misunderstanding; **—ающий** *a.* uncomprehending.

непонят/ливый *a.* uncomprehending, slow-witted, dull, dense; **—но** *adv.* incomprehensibly; it is incomprehensible; **—ность** *f.* incomprehensibility; **—ный** *a.* incomprehensible, unintelligible, obscure; **—ый** *a.* misunderstood.

непопадание *n.* miss(ing).

непоправим/о *adv.* beyond repair; **—ость** *f.* irreparability; **—ый** *a.* irreparable.

непораждённый *a.* unaffected.

непористый *a.* nonporous, compact, dense.

непородистый *a.* common, with no pedigree.

непорченный *a.* unspoiled, sound.

непорядок *m.* disorder, chaos, confusion.

непосвящённый *a.* uninitiated.

непоседливый *a.* restless, fidgety.

непосещение *n.* non-attendance (at lecture).

непосильный *a.* excessive; too difficult.

непоследовательн/о *adv.* inconsistently, not in order; **—ость** *f.* inconsistency, inconsequence; **—ый** *a.* inconsistent, inconsequent, irrelevant, irregular, nonconsecutive.

непоспелый *a.* unripe, immature.

непосредственн/о *adv.* immediately, directly, next; just; **н. перед тем как** just before; **н. после того как** just after; as soon as; **—ость** *f.* immediateness; spontaneity; **—ый** *a.* immediate, direct; spontaneous; **—ого действия** direct-action.

непостижимый *a.* incomprehensible.

непостоян/ный *a.* inconstant, unstable, labile, changeable, variable; unsteady, unsettled; (gen.) mutable; **—ство** *n.* inconstancy, instability, etc., *see a.;* variation(s).

не/потопляемый *a.* unsinkable; **—похожий** *a.* dissimilar, unlike; **—початый** *a.* entire, untouched; **—появ-**

—ление *n.* nonappearance, failure; (math.) nonoccurrence.

неправд/а *f.* falsehood, lie; **—оподобный** *a.* improbable, unlikely.

неправильн/о *adv.* incorrectly, etc., *see a.;* improperly (designed); it is not correct, it is wrong; **н. расположенный** *a.* misplaced; **—ость** *f.* inaccuracy, mistake, error; irregularity; **—ый** *a.* incorrect, inaccurate, untrue, false, wrong; defective; irregular, erratic; mis—, mal—; improper, in error; off (color); **—ый запал** misfire; **—ый термин** misnomer; **—ая дробь** (math.) improper fraction; **—ая работа** malfunction; **—ая форма** irregular shape; **—ое питание** malnutrition; **—ое развитие** malformation; **—ое сращение** (med.) vicious union; **—ое употребление** misuse.

неправ/имый *a.* (med.) irreducible; **—ленный** *a.* unreduced; **—омерный** *a.* unfair, unjust; illegal; **—омочный** *a.* incompetent.

неправоспособн/ость *f.* incompetence; **—ый** *a.* incompetent, disqualified.

неправ/осудный *a.* illegal; **—ый** *a.* wrong.

непрактичн/ость *f.* impracticability; **—ый** *a.* impracticable.

непревзойдённый *a.* unsurpassed, second to none, supreme.

непревращённый *a.* unreacted, not used up.

непредвиденный *a.* unforeseen, unlooked for, unexpected.

непредельный *a.* unlimited, unbound; nonlimiting; (chem.) unsaturated.

непред/намеренный *a.* unpremeditated; **—отвратимый** *a.* unavoidable; **—охранённый** *a.* unprotected; (elec.) without a fuse; **—положительный** *a.* (math.) nonconjectural; **—убеждённый** *a.* unprejudiced, unbiased; **—усмотренный** *a.* unforeseen, unprovided (for).

непре/клонный *a.* inflexible, unbending, rigid, firm; **—кращающийся** *a.* ceaseless, incessant; **—ложный** *a.* immutable, unalterable; indisputable.

непременн/о *adv.* without fail, for certain; necessarily; **—ый** *a.* unfailing, certain; indispensable, necessary.

непреодолимый *a.* insurmountable; invincible.

непререкаемый *a.* unquestionable, indisputable; sure, certain.

непрерывно *adv.* uninterruptedly, without interruption, continuously; at all times, ever, steadily; **—действующий, —поточный** *a.* continuous; **—сть** *f.* continuity, persistence; (phys.) continuum; **нарушение —сти** discontinuity.

непрерывн/ый *a.* continuous, uninterrupted, unbroken, constant, permanent, steady, unabated; continued (fraction); perpetual (inventory); (math.; stat.) moving (averages); **—ого действия** continuous (operation); **—ого излучения** continuous(-wave) (laser).

непрестанный *a.* ceaseless, unremitting.

непреходящий *a.* permanent.

неприбыльный *a.* unprofitable, profitless; noncommercial.

непривар *m.* nonfusion (of welded metals); cold welding; **—ка** *f.* failure to weld.

неприветливый *a.* unfriendly.

неприводимый *a.* irreducible.

непривлекательный *a.* unattractive.

неприводной *a.* (typ.) out-of-register.

непривы/кший *a.* unaccustomed (to); **с —чки** for want of habit; **—чный** *a.* unaccustomed, unused (to); uncommon, strange, unusual.

неприглядный *a.* unsightly, unattractive.

непригодн/ость *f.* inadequacy, unsuitability; **—ый** *a.* inadequate, unsuitable, unfit, impractical, impracticable; useless, unserviceable; (mil.) ineligible.

неприемлемый *a.* unacceptable.

непризнанный *a.* unacknowledged.

неприкосновенный *a.* emergency (supply); reserve (funds); (law) protected, immune; **н. запас** reserve funds; (mil.) emergency rations or stock.

неприкреплённый *a.* unattached, free.

неприкрытый *a.* slightly open, ajar; uncovered, unprotected.

неприличный *a.* not respectable, unseemly.

неприложимый *see* **неприменимый.**

неприменим/ость *f.* inapplicability; irrelevance; **—ый** *a.* inapplicable, unusable, unworkable; irrelevant.

неприметный *a.* imperceptible, indiscernible, inconspicuous.

непримиримый *a.* irreconcilable; implacable; uncompromising; incompatible.

непринуждённый *a.* unconstrained, free.

непринятие *n.* rejection, refusal.

неприродный *a.* artificial, unnatural.

неприспособ/ительный *a.* inadaptive; **—ленность, —ляемость** *f.* inadaptability; maladjustment; **—ленный, —ляемый** *a.* inadaptable, inapplicable, inadequate.

неприступн/ость *f.* inaccessibility; **—ый** *a.* inaccessible, unapproachable.

неприученный *a.* untrained.

неприхотливый *a.* simple, unpretentious; undemanding, modest; frugal (diet).

неприят/ель *m.* enemy; **—ельский** *a.* enemy, hostile; **—но** *adv.* unpleasantly; it is unpleasant; **—ность** *f.* unpleasantness, trouble, nuisance; **—ный** *a.* unpleasant, disagreeable, troublesome, objectionable; obnoxious; off (odor, taste); **—ное чувство** disorder; **—ные явления** nuisance.

непрободённ/ые *pl.* (prot.) Imperforata; **—ый** *a.* imperforate(d).

непробудный *a.* sound (sleep).

непровар *m.* (welding) incomplete fusion, poor penetration; (glass) incomplete melting; (paper) undercooked pulp; **—енный** *a.* undercooked; incompletely fused.

непровод/ник *m.* nonconductor; **—ящий** *a.* nonconducting.

непроглядный *a.* dense, impenetrable (fog).

непродиффундированный *a.* not diffused.

непродолжительн/ость *f.* short duration; brevity, briefness; **—ый** *a.* short, brief, transient, temporary; intermittent, discontinuous.

непродуб *m.* insufficiently tanned leather; **—ленный** *a.* undertanned; underdone.

непродуваемость *f.* wind impenetrability.

непродуктивн/ость *f.* nonproductivity; **—ый** *a.* unproductive, barren.

непроезжий *a.* impassable.

непрозрачн/ость *f.* opacity, nontransparency; **коэффициент —ости** (astr.) opacity; **—ый** *a.* opaque, nontransparent, impervious; cloudy (liquid).

непроизводительн/о затраченный *a.* wasted; **—ость** *f.* nonproductivity; **—ый** *a.* nonproductive, unproductive, barren, poor (land); wasteful.

непроизводственный *a.* low-productivity.

непроизвольн/о *adv.* involuntarily, unintentionally; **—ый** *a.* involuntary, unintentional; **—ое движение** involuntary movement, reflex.

непрокалывающийся *a.* puncture-proof.

непролазный *a.* impassable.

непромокаем/ость *f.* impermeability, imperviousness; **—ый** *a.* impermeable, impervious, nonwettable, waterproof; **делать —ым** *v.* waterproof.

непромы/словый *a.* noncommercial; unexploited (population); **—шленный** *a.* nonindustrial, noncommercial; unprofitable.

непроникаемость *see* **непроницаемость.**

непроницаем/ость *f.* impermeability, impenetrability, tightness; (opt.) opacity; **—ый** *a.* impermeable, impervious, impenetrable, tight; hermetic (seal); opaque; **—ый для воздуха** airtight; **—ый для звука** soundproof.

непропечатка *f.* missing type.

непропитанный *a.* unimpregnated.

непропорциональн/о *adv.* disproportionately, out of proportion; **—ость** *f.* disproportion(ality); **—ый** *a.* disproportionate, out of proportion.

непропускающий *a.* impervious, tight.

непрореагировавший *a.* unreacted.

непрореженный *a.* unpruned, unthinned.

непрорезывающийся *a.* unerupted (tooth).

непро/свечивающий *a.* opaque; **—свещённый** *a.* uneducated, unenlightened; **—сеянный** *a.* unsifted, whole (meal); **—стительный** *a.* inexcusable.

непросушенный *a.* unseasoned, undried.

непротивореч/ащий *a.* (math.) consistent; **—ивость** *f.* consistency.

непро/точный *a.* standing, still, dead, stagnant (water); **—травленный** *a.* untreated (seeds); **—фессиональный** *a.* nonoccupational; **—фильный** *a.* nonspecialized, general.

непроход/имость *f.* impermeability, imperviousness, etc., *see a.*; obstruction, impaction, blockage; **—имый** *a.* impermeable, impervious, impassable; obstructed; **—ной** *a.* impassable; no-go (gage); nonmigratory, nonanadromous (fish).

непрочн/о *adv.* loosely (bound).

непрочн/ость *f.* instability; flimsiness; perishability; **—ый** *a.* unstable, labile, changeable, inconstant; flimsy, insecure, unreliable; fragile, not strong, not durable; fugitive (color); perishable (food).

непрощупываемый *a.* impalpable, intangible.

непроявление *n.* (phot.) nondevelopment; failure to appear.

непрям/ой *a.* indirect; (med.) mediate; **—ое деление** (cyt.) karyokinesis; **—олинейный** *a.* nonrectilinear.

Нептун (astr.) Neptune.

нептун/ат *m.* neptunate; **—ий** *m.* neptunium, Np; **—ит** *m.* (min.) neptunite; **—ический** *a.* (geol.) neptunic, neptunian; **—ия** *f.* (mal.) Neptunea; **—овый** *a.* Neptune.

непуит *m.* (min.) nepouite.

непуст/ой *a.* (math.) nonvoid; **—отелый** *a.* solid.

непьющий *a.* nondrinking, sober.

неработ/ающий *a.* idle, standing, nonoperating; **—оспособность** *f.* working disability, disablement, invalidity; **—оспособный** *a.* inoperative; disabled, unfit to work.

нерабоч/ий *a.* idle, not working, inactive; down (time); off (position); **н. день** day off.

неравенств/а *pl.* (astr.) perturbations; **—о** *n.* inequality, disparity.

неравно— *prefix* aniso— (unequal, dissimilar); inequi— (of unequal size); impari— (odd); **—бокий** *a.* inequilateral; (geom.) scalene; **—великий** *a.* of different sizes; **—весие** *n.,* **—весный** *a.,* **—весное состояние** nonequilibrium.

неравногранн/ик *m.* (cryst.) scalenohedron; **—ый** *a.* scalenohedral.

неравно/значный *a.* inequivalent; **н. телеграфный код** Morse code; **—крылые** *pl.* (ent.) dragon flies (*Anisoptera*); **—крылый** *a.* anisopterous; **—листный** *a.* anisophyllous; **—лопастный** *a.* inequilobate, heterocercal (tail).

неравномерн/о *adv.* irregularly, not uniformly; **—ость** *f.* irregularity, nonuniformity, inequality; **коэффициент —ости** (illum.) variation factor; **—ый** *a.* irregular, erratic, uneven, not uniform, nonuniform, unequal; differential (heating).

неравно/мускульные *pl.* (mal.) Anisomyaria; **—осный** *a.* heteraxial; **—плечий** *a.* (gen.) heterobrachial, pericentric; **—правный** *a.* inequitable; **—сторонный** *a.* inequilateral; **—ценный** *a.* inequivalent; heterodynamic.

неравный *a.* unequal, uneven, unlike.

нерад/ение *n.*, **—ивость** *f.* negligence, carelessness; **—ивый** *a.* negligent.

нерадиоактивный *a.* nonradioactive, cold.

неразбавленный *a.* undiluted, concentrated; raw (alcoholic beverage).

неразбор/ный *a.* nonseparable; fixed(-frame) (hive); one-piece (syringe); **—чивость** *f.* unintelligibility, etc., *see a.*; unintelligible, undecipherable, illegible; unscrupulous; undiscriminating.

неразбуренный *a.* undeveloped (oil field).

неразведённый *a.* undiluted.

неразвертывающийся *a.* undevelopable.

неразветвлённый *a.* linear, unbranched.

неразви/вшийся зачаток (anat.) rudiment; **—той** *a.* undeveloped; **—тость** *f.* un(der)development, undeveloped state; backwardness; **—тый** *a.* undeveloped; backward; juvenile (erosion, etc.).

неразглашённый *a.* undisclosed.

неразделённый *a.* undivided.

неразделимый *a.* indivisible, inseparable.

нераздельнокипящий *a.* azeotropic.

нераздельн/ость *f.* inseparability, indivisibility; **—ый** *a.* inseparable, indivisible; unseparated, undivided; **—ая часть** integral part.

неразжимный *a.* tight (nut).

неразлагаем/ый *a.* undecomposable, simple; indivisible; **—ое вещество** element.

неразличимый *a.* indiscernible, indistinguishable, undecipherable.

неразлож/енный, —ившийся *a.* undecomposed; **—имый** *see* **неразлагаемый.**

неразлучник *m.* African lovebird (*Agapornis*).

неразлучный *a.* inseparable.

неразмывающий *a.* noneroding, nonscouring.

неразобранный *a.* unsorted.

наразрезной *a.* continuous, solid.

неразреш/ённый *a.* unauthorized; forbidden; un(re)solved; **—имый** *a.* insoluble (problem).

неразруш/аемый *a.* indestructible; **—ающий** *a.* nondestructive; **—енный** *a.* intact; **—имость** *f.* indestructibility; **—имый** *a.* indestructible.

неразрывн/о *adv.* indissolubly, inseparably, intimately; **—ость** *f.* indissolubility; continuity; **—ый** *a.* indissoluble, inseparable; strong, indestructible; continuous.

неразумный *a.* unreasonable, unwise.

неразъед/аемый, —ающийся *a.* noncorrodible, corrosion-resistant; **—ающий** *a.* noncorroding, noncorrosive.

неразъёмный *a.* nondetachable, solid, one-piece, continuous; permanent.

неразъяснимый *a.* inexplicable.

нерал(ь) *m.* neral, citral.

нерас/кисленный *a.* unreduced; **—крывающийся** *a.* (bot.) indehiscent; **—крытый** *a.* unopened, closed; undisclosed (secret); **—падающийся** *a.* nondisintegrating, intact; **—паханный** *a.* unplowed, virgin (land); **—плавленный** *a.* unfused, unmelted; **—плывающийся** *a.* nondeliquescent; **—познаваемый** *a.* undecipherable; **—пространение** *n.* nonproliferation (of nuclear weapons); **—пустившийся** *a.* (bot.) unopened; **—сортированный** *a.* unsorted.

нераствор/ённый, —ившийся *a.* undissolved; **—имость** *f.* insolubility; **—имый** *a.* insoluble, nonsoluble.

нерас/трескивающийся *a.* (bot.) indehiscent; **—ходуемый** *a.* permanent (electrode); **—ходящийся** *a.* nondiverging, nondisjunctive; **—хождение** *n.* nondisjunction; **—цепной** *a.* sleeve-type (clutch).

нерасчётлив/ость *f.* extravagance, wastefulness; **—ый** *a.* extravagant, wasteful, not economical.

нерас/членённый *a.* inarticulate, not segmented; whole; undifferentiated; **—членимый** *a.* indivisible; **—членный** *a.* intact, solid; **—щепляемый** *a.* nonfissionable, nonsplitting.

нерационал/изированный *a.* nonrationalized; **—ьный** *a.* irrational, not rational; wasteful; **—ьное использование** abuse.

нерв *m.* (anat.) nerve; (leaf) vein, rib; **—ация** *f.* (bot.) nervation, venation; **—изм** *m.* nervousness; **—ничать** *v.* be nervous; **—но** *adv.* nervously; *prefix* neur(o)— (nerve); **—нобольной** *a.* and *m.* neurotic; **—номышечный** *a.* neuromuscular; **—нососудистый** *a.* neurovascular; **—ность** *f.* nervousness.

нервн/ый *a.* nervous; nerve, neural; *suffix* (bot.) -veined; **н. узел** (anat.) ganglion; **—ая клетка** neuron; **—ая пластинка** (embr.) medullary plate; (anat.) medullary lamina; **—ое волокно** nerve fiber, axon.

нер-во *abbr.* (**неравенство**).

нерво/зность *f.* nervousness; irritability; **—зный** *a.* nervous, high-strung; irritable; **—н** *m.* nervon; **—овый** *a.* nervonic (acid); **—сосудистый** *a.* neurovascular.

нервюра *f.* (arch.) nerv(ur)e; (av.) rib.

нереагирующий *a.* nonreacting.

нереальный *a.* unreal; impracticable.

нереверберирующий *a.* anechoic.

нереверс/ивный *a.* nonreversing; **—ируемый** *a.* nonreversible.

нерегенерир/ованный *a.* unreclaimed (rubber); **—уемый** *a.* nonregenerable.

нерегистрирующий *a.* discrete-reading.

нерегул/ируемый *a.* (aut.) unregulable; unadjustable; wild, uncontrolled (flood); **—ярность** *f.* irregularity; **—ярный** *a.* irregular, occasional, random, erratic.

нередк/ий *a.* not uncommon, not infrequent, ordinary, common; **—о** *adv.* not infrequently, often; it is not unusual.

нередуцированный *a.* unreduced.

нерезк/ий *a.* blurred (image); soft (sound); **—ость** *f.* blurriness; softness.

нерезонансный *a.* nonresonance.

нереи/ды *pl.* (zool.) Nereidae; **—с** *m.* clam worm (*Nereis*).

нерекуррентный *a.* nonrecurrent.

нерелятивистский *a.* nonrelativistic.

нерентабельный *a.* unprofitable.

нерест *m.*, **—овый** *a.* (ichth.) spawning; **—илище** *n.* spawning ground(s), breeding area; **—иться, —овать** *v.* spawn; **—овик** *m.* hatchery pond.

нерешённый *a.* unsolved, undecided, pending.

нерешительн/ость *f.* indecision, irresolution; **быть в**

—ости, проявлять н. *v.* hesitate; **—ый** *a.* undecided, indecisive, irresolute, dubious, hesitating.

нержавеющий *a.* nonrusting, rustproof, rust-resisting; stainless (steel).

нери/антин *m.* neriantin; **—ин** *m.* neriin.

неритмичный *a.* ar(r)hythmic, uneven.

нерит/ический, —овый *a.* neritic, shore(ward), coastal.

нер/иус *m.* (ichth.) char (*Salvelinus lepechini*); **—ка** *f.* red salmon (*Oncorhynchus nerka*).

Нернста лампа (elec.) Nernst lamp.

неровн/о *adv.* unevenly, etc., *see a.*; **—ость, —ота** *f.* unevenness, roughness, irregularity, wrinkle; protuberance; inequality; (abrasion and friction) asperity; (comp.) jaggy (*pl.* jaggies); **—ый** *a.* uneven, rough, irregular, rugged, ragged, jagged; bumpy; unequal; odd (number).

неродственн/ый *a.* unrelated, alien; **—ое разведение** outbreeding.

нерок *gen. pl. of* **нерка.**

нерол *m.* nerol; **—идол** *m.* nerolidol; **—иевый** *a.* neroli; **—ин** *m.* nerolin.

неросёный *a.* raw (flax).

нерофис *m.* (ichth.) Nerophis.

нерп/а *f.,* **—ичий, —овый** *a.* (mam.) seal (*Phoca*).

нерский *a.* (geog.) Nera.

нерудный *a.* (min.) nonmetalliferous, nonvaluable; nonmetal(lic).

нерушим/ость *f.* inviolability; **—ый** *a.* inviolable, indestructible.

нерчинский *a.* (geog.) Nercha; Nerchinsk.

нерыночный *a.* not marketable.

неряшливый *a.* careless, sloppy, negligent.

нёс *past m. sing. of* **нести.**

несамо/гасящийся *a.* non-self-quenching; **—изливающий** *a.* non-flowing (well); **—сопряжённый** *a.* (math.) not self-adjoint, not self-conjugate; **—стоятельный** *a.* non-independent, dependent; **—ходный** *a.* not self-propelled.

несанкционированный *a.* unauthorized.

несахар *m.* nonsugar; **—ный** *a.* insipid (diabetes).

несбалансиров/ание *n.* imbalance; **—анный** *a.* unbalanced; inadequate (diet).

несброженный *a.* unfermented.

несбыточн/ость *f.* impossibility of realization; **—ый** *a.* unrealizable, unachievable, impossible, vain.

несварение *n.* indigestion.

несведущий *a.* inexpert, unskilled.

несвеж/есть *f.* staleness; **—ий** *a.* stale, not fresh, spoiled; stagnant; soiled, dirty.

несвёртываемый *a.* incoagulable.

несветящийся *a.* nonluminous.

несвободный *a.* restricted, constrained, bound, not free; combined (element).

несводка *f.* (maps) misfit, misregistration.

несвоевременн/ость *f.* inopportuneness; **—ый** *a.* inopportune, untimely, ill-timed; late, out of season.

несвойственный *a.* not characteristic (of), unnatural, extrinsic, alien; unusual.

несвязанный *a.* uncombined, free, available; unbound, loose; unbonded; noncohesive, incoherent, disconnected, unconsolidated (deposits); isolated (case).

несвязн/ость *f.* incoherence; **—ый** *a.* incoherent, noncohesive, cohesionless.

несгиб/аемый, —ающийся *a.* inflexible, rigid, stiff.

несгор/аемость *f.* incombustibility; **—аемый** *a.* incombustible, noncombustible, fireproof, refractory; **—аемый шкаф** safe, strongbox; **—ающий** *a.* incombustible, nonburning; **—евший** *a.* unburned.

несгущаемый *a.* noncondensable.

несдавливаемый *see* **несжимаемый.**

несдержанн/ость *f.* lack of restraint; incontinence; **—ый** *a.* unfulfilled; unrestrained, violent; incontinent.

несегментированный *a.* unsegmented.

несекретный *a.* unclassified.

несельскохозяйственный *a.* urban, nonrural.

несение *n.* performance (of duties).

несённый *a.* carried.

несенсибилизированный *a.* nonsensitized.

несерийный *a.* custom-built, custom-made.

несерьёзный *a.* unimportant, insignificant.

несессер *m.* case, container.

несестринский *a.* (gen.) nonsister.

несёт *pr. 3 sing. of* **нести.**

несеянный *a.* unsifted.

несжимаем/ость *f.* incompressibility; **—ый** *a.* incompressible, noncondensable.

несимбатный *a.* (math.) reciprocally proportional.

несимметр/ический, —ичный *a.* unsymmetrical, asymmetric(al), unbalanced; irregular; **—ичность, —ия** *f.* dissymmetry, asymmetry, lack of symmetry.

несинерирующий *a.* nonbleeding.

несинусоидальный *a.* (elec.) nonsinusoidal (wave), distorted.

несинхронный *a.* asynchronous, nonsynchronous.

несистематический *a.* nonsystematic, erratic, accidental, random (error).

несите *imp. of* **нести.**

неск. *abbr.* (несколько) several.

нескандиеносный *a.* scandium-free.

несквашинный *a.* unfermented, unleavened.

несквегонит *m.* (min.) nesquehonite.

несквозной *a.* blind (passage).

нескладный *a.* clumsy; incoherent.

нескладчатый *a.* (geol.) unfolded.

нескользящий *a.* nonskid(ding), skidproof, antiskid, nonslip.

несколько *adv.* somewhat, to some extent, slightly, just; some, few, several.

нескончаемый *a.* endless, interminable.

нескоропортящийся *a.* nonperishable.

нескрещиваемый *a.* (gen.) nonhybridizable.

нескрывающийся *a.* nondisappearing.

неслепящий *a.* nondazzling.

несли *past pl. of* **нести.**

неслия *f.* (bot.) Neslia.

несложн/о *adv.* simply; **—ость** *f.* simplicity; **—ый** *a.* simple, uncomplicated.

неслоистый *a.* unstratified.

неслучной *a.* (zool.) noncoupling.

неслы/ханный *a.* unheard of; **—шный** *a.* inaudible.

несмачив/аемость *f.* nonwettability; **—аемый, —ающийся** *a.* nonwettable, moisture-repellent, water-repellent; **—ание** *n.* nonwetting.

несменяемый *a.* irremovable, noninterchangeable; (law) constant.

несмертельный *a.* nonlethal.

несмесимость *see* **несмешиваемость.**

несметный *a.* infinite, innumerable.

несмеш/анный *a.* unmixed, unblended; **—иваемость** *f.* immiscibility; **—иваемый, —ивающийся** *a.* immiscible, nonmiscible.

несмещённый *a.* not out of place; (math.) unbiased.

несминаемый *a.* crease-resistant.

несмотря (на) *prep. acc.* in spite of, despite, notwithstanding, regardless of; **н. на всё** for all that; **н. на то,**

что despite the fact that, even though; **н. на это** in spite of this, nevertheless.

несмываемый *a.* indelible, permanent.

несносный *a.* unbearable, intolerable.

несоблюдение *n.* nonobservance, infringement (of patent law); violation.

несобранный *a.* unassembled, dismantled; ungathered; unable to concentrate.

несобственн/ый *a.* improper (integral); **—ая прямая** (math.) ideal line, line at infinity.

несовершенно *adv.* imperfectly; **—летие** *n.* minority; **—летний** *a.* minor, under age; *m.* minor.

несовершен/ный *a.* imperfect, defective; incomplete, inadequate, deficient (number); submerged (weir); (gram.) imperfective; **—ная работа** work in process; **—ство** *n.* imperfection, irregularity; nonideality.

несовме/стимость, —стность *f.* incompatibility, inconsistency; **—стимый, —стный** *a.* incompatible, inconsistent, incongruous; **попарно —стимый** mutually exclusive; **—щение** *n.* misfit, mismatch; nonregistration (of colors).

несовпадение *n.* noncoincidence, disagreement, discrepancy, variance; nonconcurrence, nonconformity; misalignment (of axis); (electron.) anticoincidence; mismatch.

несовременный *a.* not contemporary.

несоглас/ие *n.* disagreement, variance, difference, unconformity, nonconformity; **—но** *adv.* in disagreement (with), at variance (with); **—ность** *f.* disagreement; **—ный** *a.* disagreeing, differing, discordant; inconsistent, incompatible; (geol.) unconformable; **—ованность** *f.* inconsistency, disagreement, noncoordination; **—ованный** *a.* uncoordinated; not in agreement.

несодержащий *a.* not containing; **н. хлора** chlorine-free.

несознательн/ость *f.* irresponsibility; **—ый** *a.* irresponsible, unreasonable.

несозре/вший, —лый *a.* unripe, immature; **—лость** *f.* immaturity.

несоизмерим/ость *f.* (math.) incommensurability; **—ый** *a.* incommensurable.

несократимый *a.* nonreducible (fraction).

несокрушимый *a.* firm, steady; indestructible, invincible.

несол/ёный *a.* not saline, not salty; **—еобразующий** *a.* nonsalt-forming; **—ожёный** *a.* unmalted.

несомненн/о *adv.* undoubtedly, no doubt, certainly, decidedly, assuredly; **—ый** *a.* doubtless, indubitable, definite, absolute, unquestionable, obvious.

несомый *pr. pass. part. of* **нести.**

несообразн/ость *f.* incompatibility, incongruity, absurdity; **—ый** *a.* incompatible, incongruous (with), absurd.

несоосность *f.* misalignment.

несоответств/енный, —ующий *a.* conflicting, incongruous, contrary, inappropriate, irrelevant, unsuitable, inadequate, inexpedient, undue; **—ие** *n.* noncorrespondence, conflicting, nonconformity, discrepancy, disparity, inadequacy, incompatibility; unbalance; gap, misfit, failure to meet, mismatch.

несопряжённый *a.* disconnected, unlinked, unmated, uncombined.

несоразмерн/ость *f.* disproportion; incommensurability; inadequacy; **—ый** *a.* disproportionate; incommensurable; inadequate; (chem.; math.) asymmetric.

несорт/ированный *a.* un(as)sorted, run-of-mine, run-of-mill; **—ный** *a.* low-quality, second-rate; **—овой** *a.* low-quality; mixed (varieties).

несостоявшийся *a.* not taken place.

несостоятельн/ость *f.* insolvency, failure; groundlessness; unsoundness; **—ый** *a.* insolvent, bankrupt; groundless, unfounded; flimsy, unsound; indigent; (stat.) inconsistent.

несохранение *n.* nonconservation.

не/сочленённый *a.* inarticulate, disjointed; **—спаренный** *a.* unpaired, single; **—спасаемый** *a.* nonrecoverable, expendable; **—спекающийся** *a.* noncaking, noncoking, nonsintering; **—спелый** *a.* unripe, immature.

неспециал/изированный *a.* nonspecialized; **—ист** *m.* nonspecialist, layman; **—ьный** *a.* general-purpose, nonspecialized, universal.

неспецифический *a.* nonspecific, unspecific.

неспешный *a.* slow, unhurried; not urgent.

несплавление *see* **непровар.**

несплошн/ость *f.* discontinuity; **—ой** *a.* not continuous, broken.

несподручн/о *adv.* inconveniently, it is inconvenient; **—ый** *a.* inconvenient.

неспокойный *a.* restless, erratic; stormy.

неспоро/вый, —образующий *a.* asporogenic.

неспособн/о *adv.* (it is) inconvenient, it does not suit; **—ость** *f.* incapacity, inability, incapability, incompetence; failure; (sexual) impotence; **—ость к свёртыванию** incoagulability; **—ость реагировать** nonreactivity; **—ый** *a.* incapable, unable, incompetent; difficult, inconvenient.

несправедливый *a.* unjust, wrong.

неспроста *adv.* not without purpose, it is not for nothing, no wonder.

несрабатывание *n.* nonoperation.

несравн/енный, —имый *a.* incomparable, matchless, perfect.

несродный *a.* heterogeneous; uncongenial.

несслер/изировать *v.* nesslerize; **—ов реактив** Nessler reagent.

нессорамфовые *pl.* (ichth.) Nessorhamphidae.

нёсся *past m. sing. of* **нестись.**

нестабил/изированный *a.* unstabilized; unregulated; **—ьность** *f.* instability; **—ьный** *a.* unstable, labile, changeable.

неста/дный, —иный *a.* nongregarious, lone.

нестандартн/ый *a.* nonstandard, irregular, atypical; rogue (value); optional, custom-built; out of range (content); **—ой формы** odd-shaped; **—ых размеров** off-dimension.

нестар/еющий *a.* non-aging; **—ый** *a.* not old, comparatively young.

нестационарн/ость *f.* transient state; **—ый** *a.* transient, transitional, unsteady; nonstationary, portable; nonsteady (process).

нестерильный *a.* nonsterile.

нестерпимый *a.* unendurable, intolerable.

нести *v.* carry, bear, support; have, be equipped (with); suffer, sustain, incur (losses); smell, reek (of); lay (eggs); perform (duties); fulfill (obligation).

нестир/аемый, —ающийся *a.* indelible (stain); (comp.) nonerasable.

нестись *v.* rush (along); be carried, drift; lay eggs.

нестойк/ий *a.* unstable, labile, inconstant; (bot.) nonhardy, nonpersistent; fragile, decomposable (matter); **—ость** *f.* instability, etc., *see v.*

нестор *m.* (orn.) kea (*Nestor*).

нестреловидный *a.* unswept, straight (wing).

нестроганый *a.* rough (lumber).

нестроевой *a.* (mil.) noncombatant; nonbuilding (timber).

нестройный *a.* discordant; disordered.

несудоходный *a.* nonnavigable.

несульфидный *a.* sulfide-free (mineral).

несуразный *a.* absurd; awkward.

несут *pr. 3 pl. of* **нести.**

несушка *f.* laying hen.

несущая *f.* carrier.

несущественный *a.* unessential, minor, unimportant, immaterial, neglible.

несущ/ий *a.* bearing, supporting, carrying, carrier; *suffix* —phorous, —ferous, —gerous; **н. винт** (av.) rotor; **н. элемент** carrier; **—ая волна** (rad.) carrier wave; **—ая поверхность** supporting surface, lifting surface; (av.) airfoil; **—ая способность** (load-)carrying capacity; **—ая частота** carrier frequency; **ее устройство** carrier.

несфокусированный *a.* unfocused.

несхватывающийся *a.* green (concrete).

несход/имость *f.* divergence; **—имый** *a.* divergent; **—ный** *a.* dissimilar, unlike, diverse; unsuitable; **—ство** *n.* dissimilarity, difference, discrepancy; **—ящийся** *see* **несходимый.**

несцементированный *a.* loose (rock).

несчаст/ливый, —ный *a.* unlucky, unfortunate; unhappy; **—ный случай** accident, mishap; **—ье** *n.* misfortune, accident, disaster, ill luck; **к —ью, на —ье** unfortunately.

несчётный *a.* innumerable, countless.

несший *past act. part. of* **нести.**

несъедобный *a.* inedible.

несъёмный *a.* fixed, permanent.

неся *pr. ger. of* **нести.**

несяк *m.* floeberg, floe.

нет *adv.* no; there is not, there are no; **свести на нет** *v.* reduce to zero, offset.

нетабельный *a.* improvised, expedient.

нетабличный *a.* abnormal.

нетан(н)ид *m.* nontan(nin).

нетвёрдый *a.* unsteady, shaky; soft.

нетекучий *a.* stagnant, still (water).

нетель *f.* pregnant heifer.

нетемнеющий *a.* nondarkening; nonbrowning (glass).

нетепло/проводный *a.* non-heat-conducting, impervious to heat; **—прозрачный** *a.* atherm(an)ous; **—стойкий, —устойчивый** *a.* not heat-resistant.

нетер/евой, —овый *a.* (math.) Noether(ian).

нетерп/еливый *a.* impatient; **—ение** *n.* impatience; **—имый** *a.* intolerable; intolerant.

нетёсаный *a.* rough, uncut (stone).

нетипичный *a.* atypical, not typical.

нетканый *a.* (text.) nonwoven.

нетождеств/енно *adv.* not identically; **—о** *n.* nonidentity.

нетоксичный *a.* nontoxic.

нетолерантный *a.* incompatible.

нетональный *a.* unpitched (sound).

нетопливый *a.* nonfossil (fuel).

нетопыр/евые *pl.* batfishes (*Ogcocephalidae*); **—и** *pl.* (mam.) Vespertilionidae; **морские —и** batfishes; **—ь** *m.* bat (*Pipistrellus*); batfish, spadefish.

неторопливый *a.* slow, unhurried.

неточн/о *adv.* not exactly, inaccurately; **—ость** *f.* inaccuracy, error, discrepancy; **—ый** *a.* inexact, inaccurate.

нетребовательный *a.* not exacting, undemanding, modest.

нетрезвый *a.* intoxicated, drunk.

нетронут/ый *a.* untouched, undisturbed, intact, whole; untapped, virgin; **—ая территория** wilderness.

нетропсин *m.* netropsin.

нетрудн/о *adv.* without difficulty; it is not difficult, it is easy; **—ый** *a.* easy.

нетрудоспособн/ость *f.* disability; **—ый** *a.* disabled; invalid.

нетрудящийся *a.* nonworking.

неттастомовые *pl.* (ichth.) Nettastomidae.

нетто *adv.* net; **вес н.** net weight.

неубедительн/ость *f.* unconvincing nature; **—ый** *a.* unconvincing, inconclusive.

неубранный *a.* unharvested, unpicked.

неубывающий *a.* nondecreasing.

неуверенн/ость *f.* uncertainty, conjecture; **—ый** *a.* uncertain, unsure, hesitant.

неувлажнённый *a.* unmoistened, unhumidified.

неувяд/аемый, —ающий *a.* unfading; nonwilting.

неувязка *a.* discrepancy, disagreement; lack of coordination.

неугасимый *a.* inextinguishable, unquenchable.

неуглеродный *a.* non-carbon.

неугодный *a.* objectionable, unsuitable.

неуда/вшийся *a.* unsuccessful; **—ча** *f.* failure, misfortune, lack of success; **—чливый** *a.* unlucky; **—чник** *m.,* **—чница** *f.* failure; **—чно** *adv.* unsuccessfully; **—чный** *a.* unsuccessful, unfortunate, unlucky; absurd, inappropriate.

неудерж/имый, —ный *a.* uncontrollable, irresistible, irrepressible.

неудивительн/о *adv.* not surprisingly; it is not surprising; **—ый** *a.* not surprising, ordinary.

неудобн/о *adv.* inconveniently; it is inconvenient; **—ый** *a.* inconvenient, awkward, embarrassing; unsuitable, unfit; barren, useless, unproductive (land).

неудобо— *prefix* inconvenient(ly); with difficulty; **—варимый** *a.* indigestible; **—исполнимый** *a.* impracticable; **—понятный** *a.* unintelligible; **—проходимый** *a.* (almost) impassable; **—читаемый** *a.* illegible.

неудобренный *a.* (agr.) unfertilized.

неудобство *n.* inconvenience; drawback, difficulty, disadvantage.

неудобь *f.* unfit or unsuitable land.

неудовлетвор/ение *n.* refusal, noncompliance; **—ённость** *f.* dissatisfaction; **—ённый** *a.* dissatisfied; **—ительно** *adv.* unsatisfactorily; (it is) unsatisfactory; **—ительный** *a.* unsatisfactory, poor, insufficient, inadequate; **—яющий** *a.* not satisfying; **—яющий стандартам** substandard.

неуёмный *a.* untiring; incessant (pain).

неужели *adv.* is it possible? indeed?

неузнаваемый *a.* unrecognizable.

неуклонн/о *adv.* steadily, ever; **—ый** *a.* steady, constant; infallible.

неуклюж/есть *f.* clumsiness, awkwardness; **—ий** *a.* clumsy, awkward.

неукореняющийся *a.* non-rooting.

неукоснительный *a.* strict, unfailing.

неукротимый *a.* indomitable, uncontrollable; pernicious (vomiting).

неулавливаемый *a.* inappreciable, imperceptible; elusive.

неулетучивающийся *a.* nonvolatile, fixed.

неуловимый *see* **неулавливаемый.**

неулучшенный *a.* unimproved.

неуме/лый *a.* unskillful, incompetent; **—ние** *n.* lack of skill, incompetence.

неумеренн/о *adv.* immoderately, in excess; **—ый** *a.* immoderate, excessive.

неуместный *a.* misplaced, out of place, irrelevant, uncalled for, superfluous.

неумол/каемый, —чный *a.* ceaseless, incessant (sound).

неумышленный *a.* unintentional, inadvertent.

неуничтожаем/ость *f.* indestructibility; **—ый** *a.* indestructible.

неуплата *f.* nonpayment.

неуплотн/ённый *a.* noncompacted, loosely spread; unconsolidated (rock); **—яемость** *f.* incompressibility; **—яемый** *a.* incompressible.

неупомянутый *a.* omitted, not mentioned.

неупорядоченный *a.* disordered, disorderly.

неупотреб/ительный *a.* not in use, not used, unused; **—ление** *n.* disuse.

неуправка *f.* trouble, problem.

неуправляемый *a.* unguided, random, uncontrolled, out of control, free(-flight).

неупражнение *n.* lack of exercise, disuse.

неупругий *a.* inelastic, rigid.

неуравновешенн/ость *f.* imbalance; **—ый** *a.* unbalanced, out of balance, out of alignment.

неурожай *m.* crop failure, poor crop; **—ный** *a.* unproductive, barren.

неурочный *a.* unseasonable; inopportune.

неусвояемый *a.* unassimilable; unavailable; nonappropriable.

неусидчивый *a.* restless; nonpersevering.

неусиленный *a.* nonreinforced.

неуспе/ваемость *f.* poor progress; **—вающий** *a.* poor; backward, slow; **—х** *m.* failure, lack of success; **—шный** *a.* unsuccessful.

неустанный *a.* relentless, tireless.

неустанов/ившийся *a.* unsettled, unsteady(-state); irregular, interrupted; transient, transitional; **н. режим** transient; **—ленный** *a.* undetermined, unestablished; unmounted.

неусто/ечный *a.,* **—йка** *f.* forfeit, fine, penalty; failure; **—ечные проценты** interest in arrears.

неустойчив/ость *f.* instability, unsteadiness, fluctuation; **—ый** *a.* unstable, labile; unsteady, fluctuating, variable, shifting; precarious (position); versatile (reproduction); **—ый к кислотам** acid-labile; **—ый к нагреванию** thermolabile.

неустранимый *a.* unavoidable, irremovable; (comp.) fatal (error).

неустро/енный *a.* poorly organized; (socially) handicapped; **—йство** *n.* disorder, lack of organization.

неутилизированный *a.* nonrecycled.

неутолимый *a.* unquenchable; unappeasable.

неутомимый *a.* tireless, indefatigable.

неучёный *a.* uneducated.

неуч/ёт *m.* neglect, failure to take into account; **—итываемый** *a.* negligible; **—тённый** *a.* unaccounted for.

неуязвимый *a.* invulnerable, immune, safe.

неф— *prefix* neph(o)— (cloud).

нефазовый *a.* unphased, nonphasic.

нефелин *m.* (min.) nepheline, nephelite; **—ит** *m.* (petr.) nephelinite; **—овый** *a.* nepheline, nephelinic.

нефело— *prefix* nephel(o)— [cloud(iness)]; **—гилея** *f.* mountain rain forest.

нефелометр *m.* nephelometer, turbidimeter; **—ировать** *v.* determine by nephelometric analysis; **—ический** *a.* nephelometric, turbidimetric; **—ия** *f.* nephelometry, nephelometric analysis.

нефермент/ативный *a.* nonenzymatic; **—ированный** *a.* unfermented.

нефиксированный *a.* indefinite, indeterminate, uncertain; unrestrained.

нефильтрованный *a.* unfiltered.

нефитоцидный *a.* nonphytocidal.

нефлуктуирующий *a.* nonfluctuating.

нефо— *see* **неф—**; **—скоп** *m.* nephoscope.

нефр— *prefix* nephr(o)— (kidney).

нефранкированный *a.* unstamped.

нефр/идиальный *a.* (anat.; zool.) nephridial; **—идий** *m.* nephridium; **—ит** *m.* (min.) nephrite, jade; (med.) nephritis; **—итный, —итовый** *a.* nephritic; **—о—** *see* **нефр—**; **—оз** *m.* (med.) nephrosis.

нефро/логия *f.* (med.) nephrology; **—ма** *f.* nephroma; (bot.) Nephroma; **—микоз** *m.* (vet.) nephromycosis; **—миксий** *m.* (anat.; zool.) nephromixium; **—н** *m.* (anat.) nephron; **—патия** *f.* nephropathy, kidney disease; **—склероз** *m.* nephrosclerosis; **—стом** *m.* (embr.) nephrostome.

нефрэктомия *f.* (med.) nephrectomy.

нефте— *prefix* petroleum, oil; **—база** *f.* bulk plant, petroleum base, oil tank farm; **—бак** *m.* petroleum tank; **—вать** *v.* petrolize, treat with petroleum; **—водяное зеркало** (geol.) oil-water table; **—воз** *m.* tanker; **—вытеснение** *n.* petroleum displacement.

нефтегазо/вый *a.* oil and gas; **—каротаж** *m.* oil and gas logging; **—носный** *a.* oil and gas bearing; **—провод** *m.* oil and gas pipeline.

нефте(де)гиль *m.* (min.) neft(de)gil.

нефтедобы/вающий *a.* petroleum(-extracting); **—ча** *f.* oil output, oil production.

нефте/завод *m.,* **—заводский** *a.* oil refinery; **—залежь** *f.* oil pool; **—кокс** *m.* petroleum coke; **—колонка** *f.* fuel pump; **—ловушка** *f.* oil trap; **—материнский** *see* **нефтепроизводящий**; **—мер** *m.* oil meter; **—накопление** *n.* oil accumulation.

нефтеналивн/ой *a.* bulk oil; **—ое судно** tanker, tank ship.

нефтенепроницаемый *a.* oil-tight.

нефтеносн/ость *f.* oil content, oil pool, oil zone; **—ый** *a.* oil-bearing, petroliferous; **—ый район** oil field.

нефте/образование *n.* oil formation; **—образующий** *a.* oil-forming, oil-generating; **—отдача** *f.* oil recovery; **конечный козффициент —отдачи** ultimate petroleum recovery; **—отделитель** *m.* oil separator; **—очистительный** *a.,* **—очистка** *f.,* **—перегонный** *a.* oil refining; **—перегонный завод** refinery.

нефтеперераб/атывающий *a.* petroleum processing, oil refining; **—отка** *f.* petroleum processing, oil refining; **—отчик** *m.* oil refiner.

нефте/поиски *pl.* oil exploration; **—провод** *m.* (oil) pipeline; **—продукты** *pl.* petroleum products; **—производящий** *a.* petroleogenetic, oil-yielding, source (rocks).

нефтепромы/сел *m.,* **—словый** *a.* oil field; **—словое дело** petroleum industry; **—шленник** *m.* oil worker; **—шленность** *f.,* **—шленный** *a.* petroleum industry.

нефте/проявление *n.* oil show, oil seepage; **—разведка** *f.* oil prospecting, oil exploration; **—сборник** *m.* storage tank; **—склад** *m.* petroleum warehouse; **—содержащий** *a.* oil-containing, oily (waste); **—топливо** *n.* fuel oil.

нефтехим/икат *m.* petroleum chemical; **—ический** *a.* petrochemical, petroleum chemical; **—ия** *f.* petroleum chemistry.

нефте/хозяйство *n.* fuel economy; **—хранилище** *n.* oil (storage) tank, petroleum storage; **—шлам** *m.* oil sludge.

нефт/ь *f.* petroleum, oil, crude; mineral oil; **сернистая н.** sour crude; **—яник** *m.* oilman; petroleum specialist; **—янка** *f.* gasoline engine, semidiesel engine; tanker.

нефтян/ой *a.* petroleum, oil; gasoline (engine); **н. источник** oil well; **н. эфир** petroleum ether; **—ое месторождение** oil field; **—ое топливо** fuel oil; **—ые остатки** petroleum residue, mazut.

нефункциональный *a.* nonfunctional.

нехарактерный *a.* uncharacteristic.

нехват/ать *see* **недоставать; —ка** *f.* shortage, deficit, dearth, scarcity, lack, absence; deficiency; (gen.) deletion.

неходовой *a.* unmarketable, not in demand; inoperative, out of order.

нехолодостойкий *a.* noncold-resistant.

нехорош/ий *a.* bad, poor, low (yield); **—о** *adv.* badly; it is bad, it is wrong.

нехотя *adv.* unwillingly, reluctantly.

нехрущ *m.* (ent.) Amphimallon.

нецелесообразн/о *adv.* to no purpose; it is inexpedient; **—ый** *a.* inexpedient, unsuitable.

нецел/ое *n.* noninteger; **—очисленный, —ый** *a.* nonintegral, fractional.

нецентр/альный *a.* off-center, side; noncentral; **—ированный** *a.* eccentric.

нециклический *a.* acyclic, noncyclic.

нечаст/о *adv.* infrequently; **—ый** *a.* infrequent; not dense, not thick.

нечаянн/о *adv.* accidentally, by accident; **—ость** *f.* unexpectedness; unforeseen accident; **—ый** *a.* unexpected, inadvertent, accidental, unintentional, random.

нечего there is nothing (to); **н. и говорить, что** it goes without saying that; **больше н.** no(thing) more; **нечему удивляться** it is no wonder.

нечеловеческий *a.* superhuman.

нечему *neg. dat. of* **что;** *see* **нечего.**

нечернозёмный *a.* (agr.) poor in chernozem, nonchernozem.

нечестный *a.* dishonest.

нечет *m.* odd number.

нечётк/ий *a.* illegible, indistinct; (comp.; math.) fuzzy; **—ое ожидание** fuzzy expected value, FEV.

нечётн/о-нечётный *a.* odd-odd; **—о-чётный** *a.* odd-even; **—ый** *a.* odd, uneven (number); **с —ым количеством** odd-numbered.

нечисто *adv.* not cleanly; **—кровный** *a.* half-breed; **—та** *f.* dirtiness, impurity; **—ты** *pl.* impurities; sewage.

нечистый *a.* unclean, impure.

нечлен/истый, —ораздельный *a.* inarticulate, not segmented.

нечто *pron.* something, somewhat.

нечувствительн/ость *f.* insensitivity; **зона —ости** dead zone; **—ый** *a.* insensitive, dead, inert; insensible, imperceptible.

неширокий *a.* (fairly) narrow.

нешлакующийся *a.* nonclinkering.

нешлифованный *a.* unpolished, brown (rice).

нещелевой *a.* simple, plain (flap).

неэвклидовый *a.* (geom.) non-Euclidean.

неэкви/валентный *a.* inequivalent, nonequivalent; **—потенциальный** *a.* nonequipotential.

неэконом(ич)ный *a.* uneconomical, wasteful.

неэкранированный *a.* unshielded.

неэластичн/ость *f.* inelasticity, rigidity, stiffness; **—ый** *a.* inelastic, rigid.

неэлектролит *m.* nonelectrolyte.

неэндемический *a.* ecdemic, not native.

неэнзиматический *a.* nonenzymatic.

неэстерифицированный *a.* unesterified (acid).

неэтилированный *a.* unleaded (gasoline).

неэффективный *a.* ineffective, inefficient.

нею *instr. of* **она** *after prep.,* her.

неяв/ка *f.* non-appearance, absence; **—ственный** *a.* indistinct; **—ный** *a.* (math.) implicit (function); implied (addressing).

неядовитый *a.* nontoxic, nonpoisonous.

неярк/ий *a.* dull, subdued, pale, soft (color); **—ость** *f.* dullness.

неярусный *a.* intabulated, not tabulated.

неясн/о *adv.* vaguely, it is not clear; *prefix* adel(o)— (not apparent, concealed); aphan(o)— (obscure, invisible); **—ость** *f.* vagueness, obscurity, confusion; **—оусатый, —оустьицевый** *a.* adelostomous; **—ый** *a.* vague, obscure, indistinct, blurred, hazy, nebulous, foggy, turbid; confused, not clear.

неясыть *f.* (orn.) owl (*Strix*).

н.з.ч. *abbr.* (**низкая звуковая частота**) low audio frequency.

ни *neg. particle, conj.* neither, nor; not a; **ни . . . ни** neither . . . nor; **ни за что** on no account; **ни один** none, nobody; **чтобы ни случилось** whatever may happen.

НИ *abbr.* (**научный институт**) scientific institute; *see also* **НИИ; н.-и.** *abbr.* (**научно-исследовательский**) scientific-research.

ниагарский *a.* Niagara (Falls); (geol.) Niagarian (series).

ниайе *m.* (geobot.) niaye.

ниацин *m.* niacin, nicotinic acid.

нива *f.* lowland meadow, lea.

нивал/ин *m.* nivalin, galanthamine; **—овый** *a.* nivalic (acid).

нивальный *a.* nival, snow.

нивация *f.* (geol.) nivation.

нивелир *m.* (surveyor's) level; **—ный** *a.,* **—ование** *n.* leveling, alignment; grading; **—овать** *v.* level, align; grade; **—овка** *f.,* **—овочный** *a. see* **нивелирование; —овщик** *m.* leveler; **—ующий** *a.* leveling, etc., *see v.;* **—ующийся** *a.* (gen.) obsolete (character).

нивенит *m.* (min.) nivenite.

нивский *a.* (geog.) Niva.

нивян/ик *m.,* **—ка** *f.* (bot.) Leucanthemum.

НИГ *abbr.* (**научно-исследовательская группа**) scientific research group.

нигде *adv.* nowhere.

Нигер (geog.) Niger; **—ия** Nigeria.

нигеровое масло nigerseed oil.

нигр— *prefix* nigr(o)— (black); **—анилин** *see* **нигрозин; —изин** *m.* nigrisine (dye); **—ин** *m.* (min.) nigrine; (elec.; min.) nigrite; **—ита** *f.* (ichth.) cobia (*Rachycentron*); sergeant fish (*Elacata nigra*); Warsaw grouper (*Epinephelus nigritus*); **—итовые** *pl.* Rachycentridae; **—озин** *m.* nigrosine, analine black; **—ол** *m.* nigrol (gearbox oil); **—ометр** *m.* nigrometer (for carbon blacks); **—оспороз** *m.* (phyt.) Nigrospora infection; **—отовая кислота** nigrotic acid.

нидация *f.* (biol.) nidation, implantation.

нидерландский *a.* Netherland, Dutch.

Нидерланды Netherlands.

нижайший *superl. of* **низкий.**

ниже *comp. of* **низкий, низко,** lower; *prep. gen.* below, beneath, under; beyond; minus; down (stream); sub (-zero); *prefix* infra—, hypo—; **—изложенный** *a.* given below, set forth below; **—кипящий** *a.* lower-boiling; **—лежащий** *a.* underlying; **—означенный** *a.* mentioned below; **—подписавшийся** *a.* the undersigned.

нижеприв/едённый, —одимый *a.* mentioned below, given below, following.

нижерот *see* **нижнерот.**

нижеследующ/ий *a.* following, next; **сказал —ее** said as follows.

нижестоящий *a.* lower.

нижет *pr. 3 sing. of* **низать.**

нижеупомянутый *a.* mentioned below.

нижне— *prefix* lower; (geog.; geol.) Lower; —**альпийский** *a.* alpestrine, subalpine; —**амурский** *a.* (geog.) Lower Amur; —**боковой** *a.* (anat.) inferolateral; —**волжский** *a.* (geog.) Lower Volga; —**глазничный** *a.* infraorbital (nerve); —**глоточный** *a.* lower pharyngeal, infrapharyngeal (teeth); —**днепровский** *a.* (geog.) Lower Dnieper; —**дунайский** *a.* Lower Danube; —**жаберные** *pl.* (ichth.) Hypotremata; —**жаберный** *a.* hypotrematic; (crust.) hypobranchial; —**калифорнийский** *a.* (geog.) Baja California; —**латеральный** *a.* (anat.) inferolateral; —**лицевой** *a.* basifacial; —**меловой** *a.* (geol.) Lower Cretaceous; —**плиоценовый** *a.* Lower Pliocene; —**подъязычный** *a.* (anat.) hypohyal, infrahyoid; —**рёберный** *a.* costoinferior; infracostal; —**рот** *m.* (ichth.) Hypostomus; —**сторонний** *a.* lower, bottom; —**челюстной** *a.* (anat.) mandibular; —**челюстная кость** mandible, mandibula, lower jaw bone; —**четвертичный** *a.* (geol.) Lower Quaternary.

нижн/ий *a.* lower, bottom, inferior, under; down (draft); downhand (welding); ground (floor); first-stage (rocket); (geol.) Lower, Early; **н. задний** inferoposterior; **н. индекс** subscript; —**ик** *m.* bottom part, bottom section; **Н.-Новгород** Nizhni-Novgorod; **н. слой** substratum; —**яя часть,** bottom.

нижут *pr. 3 pl. of* **низать.**

низ *m.* bottom, base; lower part, bottom half; (autom.) underbody; (casting) drag; (geol.) lowermost stratum; *prefix* down(ward).

низать *v.* string, thread.

низбегающий *a.* running down, decursive, decurrent.

низвед/ение *n.* lowering; —**ённый** *a.* lowered, reduced, brought down.

низвер/гать, —**гнуть** *v.* precipitate, throw down; —**жение** *n.* precipitation.

низ/вести, —**водить** *v.* bring down, reduce.

низин *m.* nisin.

низин/а *f.* depression, lowland, floodplain, low place, flat, hollow, swale; —**ный** *a. of* **низина;** low(-lying), down-river.

низка *f.* stringing, threading.

низк/ий *a.* low, short, undersized, inferior; early; deep (sound); low-temperature (treatment); —**ая малая вода** (ocean.) lower low water; —**ая полная вода** lower high water.

низко *adv.* low; *prefix* chamae— (low); nan(o)— (dwarf); —**активный** *a.* low-activity, low-level (waste); —**валентный** *a.* low-valence; —**водный** *a.* low-level (bridge); —**вольтный** *a.* (elec.) low-voltage; —**вязкий** *a.* low-viscosity; —**головый** *a.* platycephalous, flat-headed; —**горье** *n.* low mountain relief; —**злачник** *m.* short grass meadow; —**калорийный** *a.* low-calorie; —**качественный** *a.* low-grade; —**кипящий** *a.* low-boiling; —**клиренсный** *a.* low-clearance; —**кубический** *a.* pavement (epithelium); —**легированный** *a.* low-alloy; —**лесье** *see* **мелколесье;** —**летающий** *a.* low-flying; —**молекулярный** *a.* low-molecular; —**нагружаемый** *a.* standard-rate (filter); —**напорный** *a.* low-pressure; —**оборотный** *a.* slow-speed; —**омный** *a.* (elec.) low-resistance; —**организованный** *a.* poorly organized; —**плавкий** *a.* low-melting, easily fusible; —**план** *m.* low-wing monoplane; —**потенциальный** *a.* low-potential, low-level, low-grade.

низкопробн/ость *f.* inferior quality; —**ый** *a.* poor-quality, base (alloy).

низко/продуктивный *a.* poor (pasture); —**проходный** *a.* (rad.) low-pass; —**процентный** *a.* low-percentage,

low-grade, inferior; —**рамный** *a.* low-built, low-bed (trailer); —**расположенный** *a.* low(-set); —**режущий** *a.* low-cutting.

низкоросл/ость *f.* dwarfism, stunted growth; —**ый** *a.* dwarf(ish), nanous, low-(growing), low-sized, stunted, short.

низко/сидящий *a.* low; —**скоростной** *a.* low-speed; —**сортность** *f.* poor or inferior quality; —**сортный** *a.* poor quality, low grade; —**ствольник** *m.* coppice, brushwood; —**стебельный** *a.* low-stemmed; —**сучный** *a.* bushy, stunted (tree).

низкотемпературный *a.* low-temperature; deep (freezing); **н. шкаф** freezer.

низко/травный *a.* short grass; —**углеродистый** *a.* low-carbon; —**удойная** *a.* low-production (milk cow); —**фонный** *a.* low-background (counter); —**частотный** *a.* low-frequency; —**шёрстный** *a.* (zool.) short-haired; —**широтный** *a.* low-altitude; —**энергетический** *a.* low-energy.

низменн/ость *f.* lowness; lowland, bottom land; —**ый** *a.* low(-lying).

низмянка *f.* (bot.) Centunculus.

низов/ой *a.* bottom, sedimentary (fermentation); lowland, situated downstream; ground, surface, wild (fire); basal, basilar; —**ье** *n.* lower course, lower part (of river); **в** —**ьях** down stream.

низ/ок *m.* bottom; *sh. m. of* **низкий;** —**ом** *adv.* along the bottom, at the bottom; —**ший** *superl. of* **низкий;** lowest; (educ.) primary; —**ь** *f.* low place.

НИИ *abbr.* (**научно-исследовательский институт**) scientific research institute.

никак *adv.* by no means, in no way; —**ой** *a.* no, not any, none, no . . . whatsoever.

никандра *f.* (bot.) Nicandra.

никеле— *prefix* nickeli—, nickel(ic); —**восурьмяный блеск** (min.) ullmannite.

никелев/ый *a.* nickel; **н. блеск** (min.) nickel glance, gersdorffite; **н. изумруд** (min.) emerald nickel, zaratite; **н. купорос** nickel vitriol, nickel sulfate; —**ая соль** nickel salt (usually nickelous salt); —**ое железо** (met.) ferronickel; —**ые цветы** (min.) nickel bloom, annabergite.

никелесинеродоводородная кислота nickelicyanic acid.

никелин *m.,* —**овый** *a.* nickeline (alloy); (min.) nickeline, niccolite.

никелиров/ание *n.* (met.) nickel plating; —**анный** *a.* nickel-plated; —**ать** *v.* nickel-plate; —**ка** *f.,* —**очный** *a.* nickel plating.

никелисто— *prefix* nickelo—, nickel(ous); —**синеродоводородная кислота** nickelocyanic acid.

никел/ь *m.* nickel, Ni; **закись** —**я** nickelous oxide, nickel monoxide; **соль закиси** —**я** nickelous salt; **карбонил** —**я** nickel carbonyl (gas); **молибденистый н.** nickel-molybdenum; **окись** —**я** nickel oxide; **хлористый н.** nickel(ous) chloride.

никель/аммоний *m.* nickel ammonium; —**марганцевый** *a.* nickel-manganese; —**содержащий** *a.* nickel-containing; —**шпейс** *m.* (met.) nickel speiss, —**штейн** *m.* nickel matte.

никем *instr. of* **никто.**

никитский *a.* (geog.) Nikita.

никкол/ат *m.* nickelate; —**ит** *m.* (min.) niccolite, nickeline.

ник/лый *a.* wilted; —**нуть** *v.* wilt.

никогда *adv.* never, at no time.

никого *gen. and acc. of* **никто.**

никодуст *m.* lime-nicotine sulfate insecticide.

никоим образом *adv.* by no means, in no way; not at all.

николаевский *a.* (geog.) Nikolaevsk.

никол/аит *m.* (min.) nicolayite; **—ин** *m.* nicoline; **—ит** *see* **никколит.**

николь *m.* (opt.) nicol, Nicol prism.

никольсонит *m.* (min.) nicholsonite.

Николя призма *see* **николь.**

никому *dat. of* **никто.**

никот/еин *m.* nicoteine; **—еллин** *m.* nicotelline; **—иа-нин** *m.* nicotianine.

никотин *m.,* **—ный, —овый** *a.* nicotine; **—амид** *m.* nicotinamide; **—амидадениндинуклеотид** *m.* nicotinamide adenine dinucleotide, NAD; **—изм** *m.* nicotinism, nicotine poisoning; **—овая кислота** nicotinic acid, niacin, antipellagra vitamin.

никотирин *m.* nicotyrine.

никоторый *m. pron.* none.

никр/ал *m.* Nicral (alloy); **—осилал** *m.* Nicrosilal (cast iron).

никт—, —и— *prefix* nyct(i)— (night); **—агиновые** *pl.* (bot.) Nyctaginaceae; **—алопия** *f.* (med.) nyctalopia, night blindness; **—ериды** *pl.* (mam.) Nycteridae.

никто *pron.* nobody, no one, none.

никтурия *f.* (med.) nycturia.

никуда *adv.* nowhere, in no direction; **н. не годный** *a.* useless, worthless.

никчёмный *a.* no good, useless.

Нил Nile (river).

НИЛ *abbr.* (**научно-исследовательская лаборатория**) scientific research laboratory.

Ниландера реактив Nylander reagent.

нилас *m.* newly formed ice; **светлый н.** young ice; **тёмный н.** ice rind.

ниль *m.* nil, null, zero; **—гау** *m.* (mam.) nylghaie, blue bull (*Boselaphus tragocamelus*); **—гирийский** *a.* (geog.) Nilgiri; **—группа** *f.* (math.) nil-group; **—потентный** *a.* nilpotent; **—радикал** *m.* nil-radical; **—ряд** *m.* nil-series; **—ский** *a.* (geog.) Nile.

ним *instr. of* **он(о)** *after prep.; dat. of* **они** *after prep.*

Ним (geog.) Nimes.

нимало *see* **нисколько.**

нимб *m.* nimbus (of lunar crater); halo.

ними *instr. of* **они** *after prep.*

нимф/а *f.* (ent.) nymph; (anat.) nympha; **—алиды** *pl.* (ent.) Nymphalidae; **—ея** *f.* (bot.) water lily (*Nymphaea*); **—о—** *prefix* (anat.; med.) nympho—.

нингидрин *m.,* **—ный** *a.* ninhydrin.

ниоб/ат *m.,* **—иевокислая соль** niobate, columbate; **—иевокислый** *a.* niobic acid; niobate (of); **—иевый** *a.* niobium, columbium; niobic, columbic (acid); **—ий** *m.* niobium, Nb, columbium; **—ит** *m.* (min.) niobite, columbite.

ниобовое масло niobe oil, methyl benzoate.

НИОКР *abbr.* (**научно-исследовательские и опытно-конструкторские работы**) research and development, R&D.

ниоткуда *adv.* from nowhere.

нипа *f.* (geobot.) nipa-palm brake.

нипагин *m.* Nipagin, ethyl- or methyl-*p*-hydroxybenzoate.

нипекотовая кислота nipecotic acid, 3-piperidinecarboxylic acid.

нипочём *adv.* very cheaply; it is nothing; never.

ниппель *m.,* **—ный** *a.* nipple, sleeve, adapter, union; (hose) fitting; **соединительный н.** connector, union nipple.

НИР *abbr.* (**научно-исследовательская работа**) scientific research; **НИР и ОКР** research and development.

нирван/ин *m.* nirvanine; **—ол** *m.* nirvanol.

нирезист *m.* Niresist (alloy).

нис— *prefix* down(ward).

нисколько *adv.* not at all, not in the least; **н. не меньше** none the less.

ниспа/дать, —сть *v.* fall down.

ниспровергающий *a.* subversive.

нисса *f.* (bot.) tupelo (*Nyssa*).

Ниссля тельце (cyt.) Nissl granule.

нистагм(ус) *m.* (med.) nystagmus.

нистатин *m.* Nystatin, fungicidin.

нисход/ить *v.* descend, go down; **—ящеперистый** *a.* (bot.) decursively pinnate.

нисходя/щий *a.* descending, down(ward), downcast, downtake; top-down; drain, waste (pipe); (med., meteor.) catabatic; **н. дымоход** downtake; **н. канал** (min.) downcast (shaft); **н. сброс** (geol.) downcast fault, downthrow fault; **—ее скольжение** downslide.

нисхождение *n.* descent.

нит *m.* (illum.) nit (1 candle/m²); (ent.) nit (louse egg).

ниталь *m.* nital (pickling reagent).

нитбанк *m.* riveting stock.

ните—, —видно— *prefix* fili—, nemat(o)—, thread; **—видный** *a.* threadlike, filar, filiform, capillary, filament, filamentary; filamentous; nematoic; straight-chain (molecule); thready (pulse); **—видный кристалл** whisker; **—видное образование** filament; **—видные перья** (orn.) filoplumes; **—вод(итель)** *m.* thread guide, thread carrier; **—жаберные** *pl.* (mal.) Filibranchia; **—й** *gen. pl. of* **нить; —крылка** *f.* Nemoptera.

нителла *f.* (bot.) Nitella.

ните/ловка *f.* thread picker, thread extractor; **—льсы** *pl.* netting, cargo net; **—носец** *m.* (ichth.) threadfin (*Trichogaster*); **—носный** *a.* filiferous; **—образный** *see* **нитевидный;** thread (worm); **—образователь** *m.* (text.) spinneret, spinning jet; **—пёры** *pl.* (ichth.) Nemipteridae; **—проводник** *m.* (text.) thread guide; **—разделитель** *m.* thread separator; **—резка** *f.* thread cutter; **—стебельный** *a.* (bot.) filicauline; **—хвостые** *pl.* (ichth.) Nemichthyidae; **—хвостый** *a.* (orn.) wire-tailed; **—щупиковые** *pl.* (ent.) Filipalpia.

нит/и *gen. pl. of* **нить;** (anat.) fila; (achromatic) figure; **—ка** *f.* thread, fiber, filament; string, twine, line; stream, train (of process); (colored) tracer; branch (of pipeline); (anat.) filum; **в две —ки** two-stream (plant, etc.).

нитон *m.* niton, Nt, radon, Rn.

ниточ/ка *f. dim. of* **нитка:** filament; **—ник** *m.* (text.) thread board; **—ный** *a.* thread, filar.

нитр— *prefix* nitr(o)—; **—агин** *m.* nitragin (bacterial fertilizer); **—азин** *m.* nitrazine; **—ал(л)ой** *m.* Nitralloy (steel); **—амид** *m.* nitramide; **—амин** *m.* nitramine, tetranitromethylaniline; **—амино—** *prefix* nitramino—.

нитранил/ин *m.* nitraniline; **—овая кислота** nitranilic acid.

нитрат *m.* nitrate; **н. калия** potassium nitrate; **—ин** *m.* (min.) nitratine, sodium nitrate; **—ный** *a.* nitrate; **—ные бактерии** nitro-bacteria; **—ор** *m.* nitrator; **—редуктаза** *f.* nitrate reductase.

нитр/ационный *a.* nitrating; **—ация** *f.* nitration; **—ен** *m.* nitrene; **—ид** *m.* nitride; **—ил** *m.,* **—иловый, —ильный** *a.* nitrile; **—илотриуксусный** *a.* nitrilotriacetic (acid); **—ин** *m.* nitrin(e).

нитрир/ование *n.* nitration; (met.) nitriding; **—ованный** *a.* nitrated; nitrided; **—овать** *v.* nitrate; nitride; **—ующий** *a.* nitrating; nitriding.

нитрит *m.* nitrite; **н. натрия** sodium nitrite; **—о—** *prefix* nitrito—.

нитрифи/катор *m.* nitrifying agent; **—кация** *f.* nitrification; **—цировать** *v.* nitrify; **—цируемый, —цирующийся** *a.* nitrifiable; **—цирующий** *a.* nitrifying.

нитро— *prefix* nitro—; **—амин** *m.* nitramine; **—амино-соединение** *n.* nitro-amino compound; **—анилин** *m.* nitro-aniline; **—бактерии** *pl.* nitro-bacteria; **—бензойный** *a.* nitrobenzoic (acid); **—бензол** *m.* nitrobenzene.

нитров/альная смесь nitrating mixture; **—ание** *n.* nitration; nitriding; **—анный** *a.* nitrated; nitrided; **—ать** *v.* nitrate; nitrify; nitride.

нитро/винная кислота nitrotartaric acid; **—глауберит** *m.* (min.) nitroglauberite; **—гликоль** *m.* glycol dinitrate; **—глицерин** *m.* nitroglycerin; **—группа** *f.* nitro group; **—гуанидин** *m.* nitroguanidine; **—желатин** *m.* (expl.) nitrogelatin; **—за** *f.* nitrose; **—замещение** *n.* nitrosubstitution; **—замещённое** *n.* nitrosubstituted product; **—замещённый** *a.* nitro(substituted).

нитрозил *m.,* **—овый** *a.* nitrosyl; **сернокислый н.** nitrosyl sulfate, nitrososulfuric acid; **—овая кислота** nitrosylic acid (hyponitrous acid); **—серная кислота** nitrosylsulfuric acid.

нитроз/ирование *n.* nitrosation; **—ит** *m.* nitrosite; **—ный** *a.* nitrose; nitrous.

нитрозо— *prefix* nitroso—; **—амин** *m.* nitrosoamine; **—бензол** *m.* nitrosobenzene; **—группа** *f.* nitroso group; **—краситель** *m.* nitroso dye; **—мочевина** *f.* nitrosourea; **—производное** *n.* nitroso derivative; **—соединение** *n.* nitroso compound; **—толуол** *m.* nitrosotoluene.

нитро/ил *m.* nitroyl; **—кальцит** *m.* (min.) nitrocalcite; **—кислота** *f.* nitro acid.

нитроклетчат/ка *f.,* **—очный** *a.* nitrocellulose.

нитро/краситель *m.* nitro dye; **—краска** *f.* nitrocellulose enamel; **—крахмал** *m.* (expl.) nitro starch; **—ксил** *m.* nitroxyl; **—л** *m.* nitrol; **—лак** *m.* nitrolacquer; **—ловый** *a.* nitrolic (acid); **—магнезит** *m.* (min.) nitromagnesite; **—маннит** *m.* (expl.) nitromannite, mannitol nitrate; **—метан** *m.* nitromethane; **—метр** *m.* nitrometer; **—мочевина** *f.* nitrourea.

нитрон *m.,* **—овый** *a.* (chem.; text.) nitron, nitrone.

нитро/нафталин *m.* nitronaphthalene; **—ний-ион** *m.* nitronium ion; **—новый** *a.* nitronic (acid); **—олеум** *m.* nitro-oleum (nitrogen peroxide in nitric acid); **—плёнка** *f.* nitrate film; **—покрытие** *n.* collodion final coat; **—поташ** *m.* potassium nitrate; **—производное** *n.* nitro derivative.

нитропруссид *m.* nitroprusside; **—водородный** *a.* nitroprussic (acid); **—ный натрий** sodium nitroprusside.

нитро/сахар *m.* nitrosugar; **—серный** *a.* nitrosulfuric (acid); **—смесь** *f.* mixed acid, nitrosulfuric acid; **—смолы** *pl.* nitro resins; **—соединение** *n.* nitro compound; **—спирт** *m.* nitro alcohol, nitrated alcohol; **—стирол** *m.* nitrostyrene; **—сульфоновая кислота** nitrosulfonic acid, nitrosyl sulfuric acid; **—тело** *n.* nitro compound; **—толуол** *m.* nitrotoluene; **—фенол** *m.* nitrophenol; **—фил, —фит** *m.* nitrophyte, nitrogen-loving plant; **—фильный** *a.* nitrophilous; **—форм** *m.* nitroform, trinitromethane; **—фоска** *f.* nitrophoska (fertilizer); **—фос(фат)** *m.* nitrophosphate; **—фталевый** *a.* nitrophthalic (acid); **—хлорбензол** *m.* nitrochlorobenzene; **—целлюлоза** *f.,* **—целлюлозный** *a.* nitrocellulose; **—цементация** *f.* (met.) cyanide casehardening, cyanidation; **—цементировать** *v.* cyanide, carbonitride; **—шёлк** *m.* nitrocellulose rayon;

—эмаль *f.* nitrocellulose enamel; **—эфир** *m.* nitric acid ester, ethyl nitrate.

нитрующ/ий *a.* nitrating; nitrifying; (met.) nitriding; **—ийся** *a.* nitratable; nitrifiable; nitridable.

нитчат/ка *f.* (zool.) Filaria; (bot.) Conferva; **—ки** *pl.* nematode parasites (*Filariae*); **—жаберные** *pl.* (mal.) Filibranchia; **—ый** *a.* filament(ous), filiform; (bot.) confervoid; **—ые перья** *pl.* (orn.) filoplumes.

нит/ь *f.,* **—яный** *a.* thread, filament, fiber; (anat.) chorda; filum; ligament; (tires) cord; (med.) suture; **н. гриба** (bot.) hypha; **—яный крест** (micros.) cross-hairs.

НИУИФ-1 an ethylmercury phosphate fungicide; **НИУИФ-2** *see* **гранозан; НИУИФ-100** *see* **паратион.**

нифарг(ус) *m.* (crust.) Niphargus.

нифе *n.* Ni-Fe (nickel-iron core of earth).

них *gen., acc., and prepos. of* **они** *after prep.,* them.

нихром *m.,* **—овый** *a.* Nichrome (alloy).

Ницца (geog.) Nice.

ничего *gen. of* **ничто,** nothing, not anything; it does not matter.

ничей(ный) *a.* nobody's, no man's (land).

ничем *instr. of* **ничто;** in no way.

ничто *pron.* nothing; **н. иное как** nothing less than, nothing but.

ничтож/но *adv.* insignificantly; **н. малый** *a.* negligible; **—ность** *f.* insignificance; **—ный** *a.* insignificant, slight, faint, negligible, infinitesimal; minute, micro (quantity); **—ное количество** trace.

ничуть *see* **нисколько.**

ниша *f.* niche, recess, housing, bay; shelter, dugout, pit; (min.) hole.

нищ/ета *f.* poverty; **—ий** *a.* poor; *m.* beggar, pauper.

НИЭР *abbr.* (**низкочастотная индуктивная электроразведка**) low-frequency inductive electrical surveying.

НК *abbr.* (**натуральный каучук**) natural rubber; (**низкокипящий компонент**) low-boiling component.

НКС *abbr.* (**Непрерывный сейсмографический каротаж скорости**) sonic logging.

н.к.т. (**нижняя критическая температура**) lower critical temperature; **НКТ** (**насосно-компрессорный трубы**) tubing.

Н.К.Э. *abbr.* (**нормальный каломельный электрод**) standard calomel electrode, SCE.

н/м *abbr.* (**ньютон на метр**) newton(s) per meter.

нм³ *abbr.* (**м³ пересчитанный на нормальные условия**) normal cubic meter.

НМВ *abbr.* (**низкая малая вода**) lower low water, LLW.

нмт, н.м.т. *abbr.* (**нижняя мёртвая точка**) lower dead center.

н.н., НН *abbr.* (**низкое напряжение**) low voltage; low pressure.

ННД *abbr.* (**дисковый номеронабиратель**) rotary telephone dial; **ННК** (**кнопочный номеронабиратель**) pushbutton telephone dial.

но *conj.* but; yet.

нобел/евский *a.* Nobel; **—ий** *m.* nobelium, No.

нов *sh. m. of* **новый.**

новаин *m.* novain, carnitine.

новакулит *m.* (petr.) novaculite.

нов/альгин *m.* Novalgin; **—арсенол** *m.* neoarsphenamine; **—асекит** *see* **новачекит.**

новатор *m.* innovator; **—ство** *f.* innovations.

нов/атофан *m.* Novatophan, neocinchophen; **—атропин** *m.* Novatropin, homoatropine methyl bromide; **—ация** *f.* (gen.) novation, new combination; **—ачекит** *m.* (min.) novacekite.

новая *f.* (astr.) nova; *a.* (geog.) New; **Н. Англия** New England.

нов/городский *a.* (geog.) Novgorod; **—ейший** *a.* newest, latest, most recent, up-to-date; **—и** *gen., etc.,* of **новь; —изна** *f.* novelty; innovation; **—ина** *see* **новь: —инка** *f.* novelty; **—ичок** *m.* novice, beginner, apprentice.

ново *adv.* newly; recently, just; *prefix* neo—, new(ly); nov(o)—; **—английский** *a.* (geog.) New England; **—биоцин** *m.* novobiocin (antibiotic); **—введение** *n.* innovation, novelty; **—гвинейский** *a.* (geog.) New Guinea; **—годний** *a.* new year's; **—е** *n.* new data, advances; **—зеландский** *a.* (geog.) New Zealand; **—изобретённый** *a.* newly invented, recent; **—каин** *m.* Novocaine, procaine hydrochloride; **—кастильский** *a.* (geog.) New Castile; **—крылые** *pl.* (ent.) Neoptera.

новола/ки, —чные смолы *pl.* novolacs (soluble phenol-formaldehyde resins).

ново/ледниковье *n.* (geol.) New Glacial Period; **—луние** *n.* new moon.

новоль *m.* (paints) a drying oil.

ново/межледниковье *n.* (geol.) New Interglacial Period; **—мексиканский** *a.* (geog.) New Mexican; **—населённый** *a.* newly settled; **—нёбные птицы** (orn.) Neognathae.

новообразован/ие *n.* new formation; (med.) neoplasm, new growth; regeneration; **—ный** *a.* newly formed; neogenic, neogene.

ново/освояемый *a.* newly broken (soil); **—пахотный** *a.* newly plowed; **—прибывший** *a.* newly arrived; *m.* newcomer; **—приобретённый** *a.* newly acquired; **—рождённый** *a.* neonatal, newborn; this year's; *m.* infant, neonate; **—садка** *f.* novosadka (one season's deposit of salt in lake); **—светский** *a.* (geog.) New World; **—сибирский** *a.* Novosibirsk, New Siberian; **—стройка** *f.* new building project; **—сть** *f.* news; novelty; **—тельная** *a.* newly calved, fresh (cow); **—цератиевые** *pl.* (ichth.) Novoceratiidae; **—циллин** *m.* novocillin (antibiotic).

новумбра *f.* (ichth.) Novumbra.

новшество *n.* innovation, novelty.

новые *pl.* (astr.) novae.

нов/ый *a.* new, novel, modern, recent, fresh; virgin (land); (geog.) New; neo— *e.g.* **н. мозг** (anat.) neoencephalon; **Н. Орлеан** New Orleans; **—ая звезда** (astr.) nova, **—ая область** frontier; **Н-ые гебриды** New Hebrides.

новь *f.* virgin soil; new grain crop.

ног/а *f.* (anat.) pes, foot; footing, basis; stand, brace; **идти в —у** *v.* keep pace (with); **на твёрдую —у** on a sure footing; **—авка** *f.* leg band.

ногайский *a.* (geog.) Nogaisk.

ног/и *pl.* of **нога;** pedes, feet; **—ие** *pl. suffix* (zool.) —poda; **—овидный** *a.* pediform, foot-shaped.

ноголистник *m.* (bot.) Podophyllum; **—а смола** podophyllin (resin).

ного/образный *see* **ноговидный; —пёры(е)** *pl.* goosefishes (*Lophiidae*); **—плодник** *m.* (bot.) Podocarpus.

ногот/ки *pl.* claws; (bot.) Calendula; **—ковидный** *a.* unguiculate; **—ковый** *a.* of **ноготки; —ница** *see* **нокотница; —ок** *m. dim.* of **ноготь;** claw; **—ь** *m.* (anat.) unguis, nail.

ногохвост *m.* (ent.) Tomocerus; **—(и)ки, —ы(е)** *pl.* springtails (Collembola).

ного/челюсть *f.* (zool.) maxilliped; **—щупалец** *m.* pedipalp; **—щупальцы** *pl.* whip scorpions (*Pedipalpi*).

ногт/е— *prefix* (anat.) onych(o)—, ungui— (nail, claw);

—видный *a.* onychoid; **—евой** *a.* unguicular, ungual; unguiculate, clawed; **—еобразный** *a.* onychoid; **—образующий** *a.* onychogenic, nail-forming; **—ти** *pl. of* **ноготь; —оеда** *f.* (med.) whitlow, felon, onychia.

ноет *pr. 3 sing.* of **ныть.**

нож *m.* knife, blade, cutter; (can) opener; **—ебрюшков**ые *pl.* razorfishes (*Centriscidae*); **—евидный** *a.* knifeshaped, cultriform.

ножев/ой *a.* of **нож; н. клинок** knife blade; **н. патрон, —ая головка** cutter block; **н. товар** cutlery; **н. штамп** shearing die; **—ая коррозия** intergranular corrosion; weld decay; **—ая опора** knife-edge (bearing).

ноже/держатель *m.* knife or blade holder; **—зубые** *pl.* (ichth.) Oplegnathidae.

ножек *gen. pl.* of **ножка.**

нож/енки *dim.* of **ножницы; —еобразный** *see* **ножевидный; —етелки, —етелые** *pl.* knife-fishes (*Rhamphichthyidae*); **—ик** *dim.* of **нож.**

ножк/а *f. dim.* of **нога;** leg, foot; support, base; shank, stem; (anat.; bot.; ent.) stalk, pedicle, pedicel; (instr.) jaw; (mech.) shoe; (mach.) root; arm, tine (of tuning fork); **белая н.** (phyt.) rhizoctoniosis; **чёрная н.** black leg; **установочный н.-винт** levelling screw; **—и** *pl. of* **ножка;** penduculi, crura, brachia; *suffix* (zool.) **—poda; —о—** *prefix* pod(o)— (foot; stalk, peduncle); **—овидный** *a.* stipi(ti)form, stalklike; **—овый** *a.* underlying; podal; peduncular.

нож/-корнерез *m.* root-cutter knife; **—литом** *m.* (med.) lithotome; **—ницевидный, —ницеобразный** *a.* scissor(-shaped), forfic(ul)ate; **—ницы** *pl.* scissors, shears, clippers, cutter; **—ницы-кусачки** *pl.* cutting pliers; **—ничный** *a.* of **ножницы;** scissoring (vibration).

ножно— *prefix* cole(o)— (sheath).

ножн/ой *a.* foot, pedal; **с —ым приводом** pedaloperated; **н. рычаг** pedal.

ножны *pl.* case, sheath, scabbard.

ножов/ка *f.* hack saw; handsaw; **узкая н.** keyhold saw; **—очный** *a.* of **ножовка;** hack (file); **—очный станок** power hack saw; **—ый** *a.* of **нож.**

нож-резец *m.* cutting knife, milling tool; **н.-рыхлитель** *m.* ripper knife, hoeing tool; **н.-скребок** *m.* scraper; **н.-шпатель** *m.* knife-spatula.

ноздреват/ость *f.* porosity, sponginess; **—ый** *a.* porous, spongy; blown, blistered; flawy.

ноздр/евой *a.* (anat.) narial; **—евые волосы** vibrissae; **—и** *pl.* nares, nostrils; **—ица** *f.* (bot.) agaric; **—я** *f.* (anat.) naris, nostril; eye (in cheese).

нозеан *m.,* **—овый** *a.* (min.) nosean, noselite; **—ит** *m.* (petr.) noseanite.

нозема *f.* (prot.) Nosema; **—тоз** *m.* Nosema infection, nosematosis; pebrine disease (of silkworms).

нозо— *prefix* noso— (disease); **—токсический** *a.* nosotoxic; **—фен** *m.* Nosophene, iodophthalein.

нокард/амин *m.* nocardamin; **—ии** *pl.* (bot.) Nocardia.

нок/даун *m.* knockdown, KD (pest poison); **—метр** *m.* knock indicator.

нокотница *f.* spiny dogfish (*Squalus acanthias*).

ноктал *m.* Noctal, Nostal.

нол/евой *see* **нулевой; —ик** *see* **ноль.**

нолит *m.* (min.) nohlite.

ноль *m.,* **—ный** *a.* zero; naught, cipher; **—ный уступ** (min.) lower level.

нома *f.* (med.) noma.

номад *m.* nomad; **—ный** *a.* nomad(ic).

ном/еевые, —еи *pl.* man-of-war fishes (*Nomeidae*); **—ей** *m.* Nomeus.

номенклатур/а *f.,* **—ный** *a.* nomenclature; system of notations; letter, number, designation; list, range; **—ный** *a.* top-level (post).

номер *m.* number; issue, copy (of journal); size, gage (of wire); mesh (of screen); count (of yarn); item; (hotel) room; **с чётным —ом** even-numbered; **—ация** *see* **нумерация;** **—ник** *m.* (tel.) switchboard; drop indicator; wire gage; **—ной** *a.* number, numerical; **—ное сверло** wire drill; **—овать** *see* **нумеровать; —ок** *dim. of* **номер;** tally, tag; **—онабиратель** *m.* (tel.) dial; **—оуказатель** *m.* call indicator.

номинал *m.* rating, rated value.

номинальн/ый *a.* nominal; rated; face, par (value); **н. параметр** (mach.) rating (factor); **н. режим работы** rated duty; **н. режим разряда** rated discharge; **н. ток** current rating; **—ая мощность** (elec.) rated output, power rating; **—ое напряжение** voltage rating(s); **меньше —ого размера** undersize; **снижение —ых параметров** derating.

номо— *prefix* nomo— (usage, law); **—генез** *m.* (evolution) nomogenesis; **—грамма** *f.* nomogram, nomographic chart; **линейная —грамма** alignment chart; **механическая —грамма** calculating board; **—графический** *a.* nomographic; **—графия** *f.* nomography.

нона/декан *m.* nonadecane; **—дециловый спирт** nondecyl alcohol, nonadecanol; **—козан** *m.* nonacosane.

нонан *m.* nonane; **—аль** *m.* nonyl aldehyde; **—овая кислота** nonanoic acid, pelargonic acid; **—оил** *m.* nonanoyl; **—ол** *m.* nonanol; **—он** *m.* nonanone.

нонвариантный *a.* nonvariant.

нон/дециловый *a.* nonadecylic (acid); **—ен** *m.* nonene, nonylene; **—ея** *f.* (bot.) Nonea.

нонил *m.* nonyl; **—амин** *m.* nonylamine; **—ен** *m.* non-(yl)ene; **—овая кислота** nonylic acid, pelargonic acid; **—овый альдегид** nonyl aldehyde, pelargonaldehyde; **—овый** *a.* nonyl.

нонин *m.* nonine, *n*-heptylacetylene.

нониус *m.* nonius, vernier.

ноннея *f.* (bot.) Nonnea.

ноноза *f.* nonose (a monosaccharide).

нонпарель *f.* (typ.) nonpareil.

нонтронит *m.* (min.) nontronite.

ноо— *prefix* noo— (mind); **—сфера** *f.* sphere of practical human action.

нопин/ен *m.* nopinene; **—овый** *a.* nopinic (acid); **—ол** *m.* nopinol.

нор— *prefix* nor—.

нора *f.* burrow, hole, lair.

нор/адреналин *m.* noradrenaline, norepinephrine; **—бергит** *m.* (min.) norbergite; **—билин** *m.* norbiline, hexadiphane.

норв. *abbr.* (**норвежский**).

норвалин *m.* norvaline.

Норвегия Norway.

норвежский *a.* Norwegian.

нор/гваяксмоляной *a.* norguaiaretic (acid); **—гераниевый** *a.* norgeranic (acid).

норд *m.* (naut.) north; north wind; **н.-вест** *m.,* **н.-вестовый** *a.* northwest; northwest wind.

нордгаузенск/ая серная кислота, —ое купоросное масло Nordhausen acid, fuming sulfuric acid, oleum.

норденшельд/ин, —ит *m.* (min.) nordenskiöldine.

норд/капский *a.* (geog.) Nordkapp; **—манновский** *a.* Nordmann's; **—маркит** *m.* (min., petr.) nordmarkite; **—овый** *a.* of **норд;** **—ост** *m.,* **—остовый** *a.* northeast; northeast wind.

Норидж (geog.) Norwich.

нор/ийский *a.* (geol.) Norian; **—ильский** *a.* (geog.) Norilsk; **—ит** *m.* (petr.) norite; Norit (activated carbon).

норичник *m.* (bot.) figwort (*Scrophularia*); **—овые** *pl.* Scrophulariaceae.

нория *f.* bucket elevator, bucket conveyer, bucket chain; noria, irrigating wheel.

норка *dim. of* **нора;** (mam.) Old World mink (*Mustela lutreola*); **американская н.** mink (*M. vison*).

норкамф/ан *m.* norcamphane, 1,2,2-bicycloheptane; **—ора** *f.* norcamphor.

норкарен *m.* norcarene, bicycloheptene.

норковый *a. of* **норка** (mam.).

норлейцин *m.* norleucine, glycoleucine.

норм. *abbr.* (**нормальный**) normal.

норм/а *f.* norm, standard; rate, quota; number, quantity; ration; normal range, standard range; (filter precoat) load; **н. расхода** consumption rate; dose (of pesticide); **возвращать(ся) к —е** *v.* normalize; **—алемер** *m.* gear tooth micrometer.

нормализ/атор *m.* (math.) normalizer; **—ация** *f.* normalization, standardization; (met.) normalizing; **—ованный** *a.* normalized, standardized; **—овать** *v.* normalize, standardize.

нормаль *f.* (tech.) standard (specification); (math.) normal, perpendicular; **—ность** *f.* normality; **—ный** *a.* normal, standard, regulation, conventional; regular; natural; forward (motion of cathode spot); perpendicular (to axis); **—ный раствор** normal solution; **—ное завершение работы** (comp.) orderly close-down; **—ной величины** full-size; **—ные технические условия** standard specifications.

норман/дский *a.* (geog.) Norman, Normandy; **—ихтовые** *pl.* (ichth.) Normanichthyidae.

норматив *m.* norm, standard(s), quota, unit output; specification; **—ный** *a.* normal, standard(ized), normative; **—ный состав** norm; **—ы** *pl.* regulations.

нормир/ование *n.* normalization, etc., *see v.*; rating, rate fixing; proration; **н. потребления** rationing (of water); **твёрдое н.** establishment of strict standards; **—ованный** *a.* normalized, etc., *see v.*; standard; fixed, set; legal; (math.) normed; **—овать** *v.* normalize, standardize, set standards; fix rates; calibrate; ration, control; (agr.) thin out; **—овка** *f.,* **—овочный** *a. see* **нормирование;** **—овщик** *m.* standardizer; rate fixer; **—овщик-хронометражист** *m.* time and motion study expert; **—уемость** *f.* (math.) normability; **—ующий** *a.* normalizing, etc., *see v.*

нормо— *prefix* (normal, usual); **—бласт** *m.* (cyt.) normoblast; **н.-день** *m.* working day standard; **н.-час** *m.* norm-hour, working hour standard.

нормы *pl.* regulations, specifications, standards.

норникотин *m.* nornicotine.

норов *m.* (vet.) restiveness (of horse), affliction with staggers; **—истый** *a.* restive, jibbing, balking; afflicted with staggers; **—ить** *v.* hurry, strive; aim (at).

нор/ок *gen. pl. of* **норка;** **—олюбы** *pl.* (ent.) Leptinidae; **—оточина** *f.* burrow.

норпин/ан *m.* norpinane, 1,1,3-bicycloheptane; **—овый** *a.* norpinic (acid).

норсульфазол *m.* norsulfazole, sulfathiazole.

Нортона теорема (elec.) Norton's theorem.

нортроп/ан *m.* nortropane; **—инон** *m.* nortropinone.

Нортрупа печь (elec.) Northrup furnace.

нортупит *m.* (min.) northupite.

Норфолк (geog.) Norfolk (Island).

норэфедрин *m.* norephedrine.

нос *m.* (anat.) nose, nasus; (orn.) bill, beak; (pouring) lip, spout; (geog.) cape; (geol.) headland, promontory, point; (anvil) horn; (naut.) bow, prow; **область —а** nasal region.

НОС *abbr.* (**нестойкое органическое соединение**) decomposable organic matter, DOM.

носарь *m.* (ichth.) Don ruffe (*Acerina a.*)

нос/астый *a.* large-nosed; (orn.) big-billed; **—атик** *m.* (mam.) proboscis monkey (*Nasalis*); **—атка** *f.* (ent.) nettle-tree butterfly (*Libythea celtis*); **—атки** *pl.* Libytheidae; Dictyopharidae; **—атый** *see* **носатый**; with a large spout; **—ач** *see* **носатик**; big-billed bird; big-nosed person.

носик *dim. of* **нос**; spout; tip; toe (of shoe); (anat.; zool.) rostrum; (bot.) rostellum; **—овидный** *a.* rostriform, beak-shaped.

носил/ки *pl.* handbarrow; stretcher, litter; skids; **н.-каталка** *pl.* gurney; **—очный** *m.* stretcher bearer; **—ьный** *a.* carrying; for wearing; **—ьное бельё** underwear; **—ьщик** *m.* carrier, porter; stretcher bearer.

носител/ь *m.* carrier, vehicle, bearer, support; (comp.) medium; **н. гена** (gen.) trait; **н. записи** recording medium; **н. заразы, н. инфекции** (med.) vector; **н. информации** storage device; **без —я** carrier-free; **—ство** *n.* carrier state.

носить *v.* carry, bear; wear; lay (eggs); **—ся** *v.* drift, float, ride, be borne; rush (about); wear.

носк/а *f.* carrying, bearing; wear(ing); *gen. of* **носок**; **—ий** *a.* durable, lasting, long-wearing; high egg-producing, productive (layer); **—овый** *a. of* **носок**; **—ость** *f.* durability, wearing qualities; productivity.

носо— *prefix* (anat.) naso— (nose, nasal); rhin(o)— (nose); rostri— (beak); **—верхнечелюстной** *a.* nasomaxillary; **—вой** *a. of* **нос**; nasal; **—вая качка** (naut.) pitching; **—вая раковина** (anat.) nasal concha; **—глотка** *f.* (anat.) nasopharynx; **—губный** *a.* nasolabial.

носок *m.* spout, nozzle; point, bill; (rocket) nose, cone; (rocket fin) cuff; leading edge (of wing); (pouring) lip; toe (of shoe); sock.

носо/лобный *a.* (anat.) nasofrontal; **—нёбный** *a.* nasopalatine.

носорог *m.* (mam.) rhinoceros; (ent.) rhinoceros beetle; **—и, —овые** *pl.* (mam.) Rhinocerotidae; **—и-птицы** *pl.* (orn.) Bucerotidae; **—овый** *a. of* **носорог**; **н.-рыба** *f.* unicorn fish (*Naso literatus*).

носорожий *a. of* **носорог**.

носослёзный *a.* (anat.) nasolacrimal.

носочный *a. of* **носок**; front; sock(s).

ностоковые *pl.* (bot.) Nostocaceae.

носуха *f.* (mam.) coatimundi (*Nasua*).

носчик *m.* carrier, bearer.

НОТ *abbr.* (**научная организация труда**) industrial engineering.

нота *f.* note; tone.

нотабен/а *f.,* **—е** *n.* nota bene, N.B.

нотакантовые *pl.* spiny eels (*Notacanthidae*).

нотальный *a.* (anat.; geog.) notal.

нотариус *m.* notary public.

нотатин *m.* notatin.

нот/ация *f.* notation, system of notations; instruction(s); **—ификация** *f.* notification; **—ифицировать** *v.* notify.

нотный *a.* note; music.

ното— *prefix* (anat.) noto— (back); (biol.) notho— (illegitimate, spurious); **—бранх** *m.* (ichth.) Nothobranchius; **—граптовые** *pl.* Notograptidae; **—латеральный** *a.* (anat.) dorsolateral; **—лепис** *m.* (ichth.) Notolepis.

нотопечатание *n.* music printing.

нотоптер *m.* (ichth.) featherback (*Notopterus*); **—овые** *pl.* Notopteridae.

ното/скопел *m.* (ichth.) Notoscopelus; **—тениевые, —тенииды** *pl.* Nototheniidae; **—тения** *f.* Antarctic cod (*Notothenia*).

ноу-кау, н.-хау *m. or n.* know-how.

ноцерин *m.* (min.) nocerine, nocerite.

ночва *f.* tray, shallow trough.

ноч/евать *f.* spend the night, sleep; **—ёвка** *f.* overnight stay; sleep, night's rest; tray; **—есветка** *f.* (prot.) Noctiluca; **—ецветные** *pl.* (bot.) Nyctaginaceae; **—ецветный** *a.* night-blooming; **—лег** *m.* night's lodging, overnight stay; **место —лега** sleeping place; **—лежный** *a.* overnight; **—ник** *m.* night worker; night light; **—ница** *f.* (mam.) bat (*Myotis*); (ent.) noctuid, night moth; **—ницы** *pl.* (ent.) Noctuidae; **—ное** *n.* night watch; **—ной** *a.* night(ly), nocturnal; **—ь** *f.* night; **по —ам** at night, nights; **—ью** at night.

нош/а *f.* load, burden, charge; kit; (apid.) honey and pollen gathering; **—ение** *n.* carrying; wearing; **—енный** *a.* carried, borne; **—еный** *a.* worn.

ноющий *pr. act. part. of* **ныть.**

ноябрь *m.,* **—ский** *a.* November.

нп *abbr.* (**непер**) neper.

НПВ *abbr.* (**низкая полная вода**) lower high water, LHW.

НПВЧ *abbr.* (**наименьшая применимая высокая частота**) lowest applicable high frequency.

нпз, НПЗ *abbr.* (**нефтеперерабатывающий завод**) petroleum refinery, oil refinery; (**носимый прибор заражения**) portable contamination apparatus.

НПП *abbr.* (**наставление по производству полётов**) flight manual.

НПУ *abbr.* (**нормальный подпорный уровень**) normal pool elevation.

нр. *abbr.* (**нерастворимый**) insoluble.

НР *abbr.* (**нормаль**) standard.

НРА *abbr.* (**Народная Республика Албания**) People's Republic of Albania.

нрав *m.* disposition, temper; character; way (of life); **—иться** *v.* please; **ему не —ится** he does not like; **—ственность** *f.* integrity, morals; **—ственный** *a.* moral.

НРБ *abbr.* (**Народная Республика Болгария**) People's Republic of Bulgaria.

НРВ *abbr.* (**нефтяное ростовое вещество**) petroleum growth stimulant.

НРТ *abbr.* (**нетто-регистровый тоннаж**) net registered tonnage.

Н.с., н. сек. *abbr.* (**ньютон-секунда**) newton second.

НСМО *abbr.* (**низшая свободная молекулярная орбиталь**) lowest unoccupied molecular orbital, LUMO.

НСУ *abbr.* (**непрерывная система управления**) continuous control system.

нт *abbr.* (**нит**) nit.

н-то *abbr.* (**нетто**) net; **НТО . . .** *abbr.* (**научно-техническое общество . . .**) Scientific and Technical Society (of).

НТС *abbr.* (**научно-технический совет**) scientific and technical council.

ну *particle* (well) now; why.

нуазетовый *a.* (hort.) Noisette.

нубийский *a.* (geog.) Nubian.

нубук *m.* buffed-grain leather.

нувистор *m.* (rad.) nuvistor.

нуг *m.* (bot.) Guizotia.

нуга *f.* nougat.

нугушский *a.* (geog.) Nugush.

нудный *a.* tedious.

нудовая кислота nudic acid.

нужд/а *f.* need, necessity, want; **без —ы** unnecessarily; **по —е** emergency (feeding); **расход энергии на собственные —ы** auxiliary power; **—аемость** *f.* need, requirement; **—аться** *v.* need, require, want, be in want (of), lack; **—ающийся** *a.* needing, needy, destitute.

нужн/о *adv.* (it is) necessary, it needs (to), it must be; **—ый** *a.* necessary, requisite, required, essential, wanted.

нук *see* **нуг;** **—ас** *m.* (ichth.) Rhodeus sericeus amarus.

нукле/аза *f.* nuclease (enzyme); **—арный** *a.* nuclear; **—ация** *f.* nucleation.

нуклеин *m.,* **—овый** *a.* nuclein; **—овая кислота** nucle(in)ic acid.

нуклео/альбумин *m.* nucleoalbumin; **—бионт** *m.* nucleobiont; **—генез(ис)** *m.* nucleogenesis; **—гистон** *m.* nucleohistone; **—зид** *m.* nucleoside; **—зидаза** *f.* nucleosidase; **—зидфосфат** *m.* nucleoside phosphate; **—ид** *m.* (gen.; cyt.) nucleoid; **—ла** *f.,* **—ль** *m.* nucleolus; **—м** *m.* (cyt.) nucleome; **—н** *m.* see **нуклон; —ника** *f.* nucleonics; **—плазма** *f.* (cyt.) nucleoplasma; **—протеид, —протеин** *m.* nucleoprotein; **—сома** *f.* (gen.) nucleosome; **—тид** *m.,* **—тидный** *a.* nucleotide; **—тидаза** *f.* nucleotidase; **—фил** *m.* nucleophile, nucleophilic agent; **—фильный** *a.* nucleophilic.

нукл/еус *m.* nucleus; queen cell (of bees); **—ид** *m.* nuclide; **—он** *m.* nucleon, nuclear particle; **—онный** *a.* nucleon(ic).

нукула *f.* (mal.) nut clam (Nucula).

нулбенгер *m.* (mam.) honey possum (Tarsipes spenserae).

нулев/ой *a.* zero, zero-point, zero-order, null, neutral; (comp.) base-band (modem); **н. отсчёт** zero reading; **н. прибор** null indicator; **н. провод** (elec.) neutral wire; **—ая группа** (gases) inert element group; **—ая линия** (math.) zero line, base line; **—ая мощность** zero power; **—ая поверхность** (surv.) datum level; **—ая точка** zero (point); origin; **смещение —ой точки** zero creep; **—ая черта, —ое деление** zero mark; **—ое положение** zero position, standby position.

нулик *see* **ноль.**

нуллиплекс *m.,* **—ный** *a.* (gen.) nulliplex.

нуллипор/а *f.* (bot.) nullipore; **—овый** *a.* nullipore, nulliporous.

нуллисомик *m.* (gen.) nullisomic organism.

нуллифицировать *v.* nullify, annul.

нуллосомик *see* **нуллисомик.**

нул/ь *m.* zero (point), null, nil, naught; cipher; origin; **н. высот** (geod.) datum level; **н. глубин** (ocean.) chart datum, reference level; **н. поста** (hydr.) gage datum; **время возврата на н.** reset time; **обращающийся в н.** *a.* vanishing, disappearing; **отличный от —я** *a.* nonvanishing.

нуль/-валентность *f.* zero valence; **—индикатор** *m.* null indicator; **н.-корпус** *m.* pre-evaporator; (sugar) pre-cooker; **—мерный** *a.* zero-dimensional; **н.-орган** *m.* null detector; **н.-прибор** *m.* zero reader, flight director; **—пункт** *m.* zero point; **—указатель** *m.* null indicator.

н.у.м. *abbr.* (**над уровнем моря**) above sea level.

нуме(а)ит *m.* (min.) noumeite, garnierite.

нумер *see* **номер; —атор** *m.* numerator, numbering machine; annunciator, indicator; **—ационный** *a.* numerical; **—ация** *f.* (e)numeration; numbering, number system; **—ический** *a.* numerical; **—ник** *m.* (wire) gage plate; **—ной** *a.* numerical; **—ной аппарат** indicator;

—ная доска (wire) gage plate; **—овальный** *a.* numbering; **—ование** *see* **нумерация; —ованный** *a.* numbered; quantized; **—овать** *v.* number; index; **—овка** *see* **нумерация.**

нуммулит *m.* (zool.) nummulite; **—овый** *a.* (geol.) nummulitic.

нунатак *m.* nunatak (hill or peak).

Нупа твёрдость (met.) Knoop hardness.

нуп/тиальный, —циальный *a.* (biol.) nuptial.

НУрВ *abbr.* (**нижний уровень воды**) lower water level.

нуринский *a.* (geog.) Nura.

нут *m.* (bot.) chick-pea (Cicer arietinum).

нут/ационный *a.* nutant, nodding; **—ационное движение, —ация** *f.* (astr.; bot.; mech.) nutation; **—ировать** *v.* nutate.

нутканский *a.* (geog.) Nootka.

нутревики *pl.* (bot.) Gasteromycetes.

нутриев/ые *pl.* (mam.) Capromyidae; **—ый** *a.* nutria.

нутри/ент *m.* nutrient; **—тивный** *a.* nutritious.

нутрия *f.* (mam.) nutria, coypu (Myocastor coypus).

нутро *n.* inside, interior; **—вка** *f.* evisceration, gutting.

нутромер, н.-калибр *m.* inside calipers, inside micrometer, internal gage.

нутря/к *m.* inner fat; **—ной** *a.* internal, inner, inward.

нутталлиоз *m.* (vet.) nuttalliosis.

нутч(-фильтр) *m.* Nutsch filter, suction filter.

нуфарин *m.* nupharine.

нухальный *a.* (anat.) nuchal.

нуц/еллус, —еллюс *m.* (bot.) nucellus; **—еллярный** *a.* nucellar; **—ин** *m.* nucin, juglone.

нуч *see* **нутч.**

НЦУ *abbr.* (**непосредственное цифровое управление**) direct digital control.

НЧ *abbr.* (**низкочастотный**) low-frequency; **Н.Ч.** *abbr.* (**низкая частота**) low frequency.

НЧК *abbr.* (**нейтрализованный чёрный контакт**) neutralized black contact medium, deemulsifying agent.

ныл *past m. sing. of* **ныть.**

нын/е *adv.* now, at present; **н. живущий** *a.* recent, living now; **—ешний** *a.* present, this (year, etc.); contemporary, modern; **—че** *adv.* today; now(adays); **—че утром** this morning.

ныр/ки *pl. of* **нырок; —ковый** *a.* diving; **—ковая утка** *see* **нырок; —нуть** *see* **нырять; —ок** *m.* diver; (orn.) diving duck (Aythya); **—ялка** *f.* (ent.) Hydroporus; **—яло** *n.* ram, plunger; **—яльщик** *m.* diver; **—яние** *n.* diving, etc., *see v.;* dip; galloping motion; **—ять** *v.* dive, plunge, dip, pitch; **—яющий** *a.* diving, etc., *see v.*

ныть *v.* ache; whine, complain.

Нью New (in geographic names).

ньюар(к)ский *a.* (geol.) Newark (series).

ньюбериит *m.* (min.) newburyite.

Нью/-брансуик (geog.) New Brunswick; **Н.-гемпшир** New Hampshire; **Н.-джерси** New Jersey; **Н.-Йорк, нью-йоркский** *a.* New York; **—касл** Newcastle.

ньютон *m.* newton (unit of force).

Ньютона цветные кольца (phys.) Newton's rings.

ньютон/ианский, —овский *a.* Newton(ian); **—ит** *m.* (min.) newtonite.

ньюфаундленд *m.* Newfoundland dog; **—ский** *a.* (geog.) Newfoundland.

Нью-/Хейвен (geog.) New Haven; **Н.-хэмпшир** New Hampshire.

ньяла *f.* (mam.) nyala (Tragelaphus).

ньясский *a.* (geog.) Nyasa.

н.э. *abbr.* (**нашей эры**) A.D.

нэк *m.* (geol.) neck, chimney; strait.

нэп *m.* new economic policy.
ню — *see also under* **нью**—.
нюанс *m.* nuance, shade.
нюйский *a.* (geog.) Niuya.
нюкжинский *a.* (geog.) Niukzha.
нюрнбергский *a.* (geog.) Nürnberg.
нюрольковый *a.* (geog.) Niurolka.

нюх *m.* (sense of) smell; scent; —**а(те)льный** *a.* smelling, olfactory; —**ательный табак** snuff; —**ать,** —**нуть** *v.* smell, sniff, take (snuff).
няндомский *a.* (geog.) Nyandoma.
нян/чить *v.* nurse, tend; —**ька,** —**я** *f.* nurse; **карибская** —**ька** (ichth.) nurse shark (*Ginglymostoma cirratum*).
няша *f.* soil humus.

О

о *prep. acc.* against; *prepos.* about, concerning, (up)on, of, dealing with.
о. *abbr.* (**область**) oblast, region; (**остров**) island.
о— *prefix* circum—, about, around.
оазис *m.,* —**ный** *a.* oasis.
ОАР *abbr.* (**Объединённая Арабская Республика**) United Arab Republic.
об *see* **о; об**— *see* **о**—.
об *abbr.* (**оборот**) revolution; **об. %** *abbr.* (**объёмный процент**) percent by volume.
оба *m. and n. numeral* both.
обабок *m.* (bot.) birch mushroom.
обагр/ённый *a.* bloodstained; —**ить,** —**ять** *v.* stain with blood; redden.
обанкротиться *v.* go bankrupt.
обапол *m.* slab, lag(ging).
обарыченный *a.* irrigated (land).
оббе/гать *see* **обегать;** —**жать** *see* **обежать.**
обби(ва)ть *see* **оби(ва)ть.**
обборка *f.* (min.) knocking down loose rock from ceiling.
об. в. *see* **об. вес.**
обвал *m.* collapse, cave-in, slump, subsiding; crumbling; drop (in mold); slide, avalanche; —**енный** *a.* collapsed, caved in, fallen; —**и(ва)ть** *v.* knock down, cave in; heap around, bank; —**и(ва)ться** *v.* collapse, cave in, fall; crumble (down); —**истый** *a.* easily caving in.
обвалка *f.* (de)boning (meat), stripping.
обвалов/ание *n.* banking, etc., *see v.;* embankment; —**ать** *v.* bank (up), build, construct (levee, etc.); dam up.
обвалять *v.* roll in; dust (with).
обвар/и(ва)ть *v.* scald, blanch; —**ка** *f.* scalding; shoulder, collar, seam.
обвевать *v.* winnow, fan.
обвед/ение *n.* enclosing, encircling, surrounding; outline, contour; —**ённый** *past pass. part. of* **обвести;** enclosed, within (a circle).
обвеивать *see* **обвевать.**
обвёрнутый *a.* wrapped up, etc., *see* **обвернуть;** (bot.) involucrate.
обвер/нуть, —**теть** *v.* wrap up, bind up, envelop; entwine, twist around.
обвёр/тка *see* **обёртка;** —**тка соцветия** (bot.) spathe; —**тковидный** *a.* involucral; —**точка** *f.* involucel; —**точный** *a. of* **обвёртка;** involucral.
об. вес *abbr.* (**объёмный вес**) volumetric weight, density.
обвес *m.* false weight, short weight; screen, shield; —**ить** *see* **обвешивать.**
обвести *see* **обводить.**
обветр/енный *a.* weather-beaten, weathered; windblown; —**еть,** —**иваться** *v.* become weathered; —**ить** *v.* erode, weather, dry out; —**иться** *v.* be eroded; dry out.
обветш/алый *a.* decrepit; —**ать** *v.* become decrepit, deteriorate.

обвеш/анный *a.* hung, covered (with); —**ать** *see* **обвешивать;** —**енный** *a.* marked with stakes; —**ивание** *n.* hanging, etc., *see v.;* —**ивать** *v.* hang, cover (with); give short weight; mark with stakes; —**ить** *v.* mark with stakes.
обвеять *see* **обвевать.**
обвив/ание *n.,* —**ка** *f.* winding around; whipping (of cable); —**ать(ся)** *v.* wind around, twist around; whip.
обвин/ение *n.* accusation, charge; —**итель** *m.* accuser, prosecutor; —**ить,** —**ять** *v.* accuse, charge (with); —**яемый** *m.* the accused, defendant.
обвис/ать, —**нуть** *v.* droop, hang; —**лый** *a.* drooping, hanging, flabby, flaccid.
обвит/ый *a.* wound around, etc., *see* **обвивать;** obvolute; —**ь** *see* **обвивать.**
об-во *abbr.* (**общество**) society.
обвод *m.,* —**ка** *f.* surrounding, etc., *see v.;* encirclement; (out)line, contour, profile; by-pass, detour; —**ить** *v.* surround, encircle, enclose, encompass; outline, contour; lead around, by-pass; ink (a drawing); —**ка** *f.* (met. rolling) repeater.
обводн/ение *n.* flooding, etc., *see v.;* water supply development; water encroachment; —**ённость** *f.* rate of water supply; water content; (petrol.) degree of flooding; —**ённый** *a.* flooded, etc., *see v.;* —**ительно-оросительный** *a.* water supply and irrigation; —**ительный** *a.* flooding, etc., *see v.;* water-supply; —**ить** *v.* flood, inundate, drown; irrigate; convey water, supply with water; develop water supply; invade, encroach (of water).
обводн/ый *a.* encircling, surrounding; leading around; by-pass; detouring; **о. канал, о. провод** by-pass (canal), by-pass conduit; —**ая стена** enclosure; —**ые аппараты** (rolling) delivery guides.
обводнять *see* **обводнить.**
обвойник *m.* (bot.) Periploca.
обвол/акивание *n.* wrapping, etc., *see v.;* obvolution; —**акивать,** —**очь** *v.* wrap (up, around), envelop, cover (in, up), coat; encapsulate; drag around.
обвяз/ать *see* **обвязывать;** —**ка** *f.* binding, etc., *see v.;* bandage, binder; connections; brace, framework; (pump) manifold; hoop; system of piping; —**очный** *a.,* —**ывание** *n.* binding, etc., *see v.;* —**ывать** *v.* bind, fasten, tie, bandage; hoop (barrel); —**ь** *f.* frame(work); hoop.
обвянуть *v.* wilt; dry slightly.
обгар *m.* combustion loss.
обгибать *v.* bend around; by-pass.
обгладить *see* **обглаживать.**
обглаживать *v.* pick off, gnaw; browse.
обглаживать *v.* smooth out.
обглод/анный *a.* gnawed; bare (bone); —**ать** *see* **обглаживать;** —**ок,** —**ыш** *m.* gnawed left-over.
обглядывать *see* **оглядывать.**
обгни(ва)ть *v.* spoil on the surface.
обгон *m.,* —**ка** *f.* overtaking, etc., *see v.;* detour; —**ный**

a. overtaking, passing; by-pass, detour; **—ять** *v.* overtake, pass, outstrip, outdistance.

обгор/ание *n.* charring, etc., *see v.;* **—ать, —еть** *v.* char, scorch; burn (around); **—елый** *a.* charred, etc., *see v.*

обгрыз(а)ть *see* **огрыз(а)ть.**

обгул/иваться, —яться *v.* (zool.) conceive.

обда(ва)ть *v.* scald; drench, pour over.

обдел/ать *see* **обделывать; —ка** *f.,* **—очный** *a.,* **—ывание** *n.* working, etc., *see v.;* **—ывать** *v.* work, fashion, shape, form; polish, finish; jacket, case, face; dress (leather); set (jewels).

обдёрг(ив)ать *v.* pull off, rip off.

обдер/нить, —нять *v.* (put down) sod.

обдир *see* **обдирка; плодовый —ало** (ent.) mottled umber moth (*Erannis defoliaria*); **—ание** *see* **обдирка; —ать** *v.* strip, peel, bark; rip off, skin, flay; hull, shell (corn); rough (out); **—ка** *f.* stripping, etc., *see v.;* rough-working; **—ный** *a.* hulling; hulled; **—очнообточный** *a.* stripping; **—очный** *a.* stripping, etc., *see v.;* abrasive; rough (grinding); **—очный камень** abrasive; **—очный постав** huller, sheller; **—очный резец** roughing tool; **—очная шкурка** coarse emery cloth.

обдув *see* **обдувка;** blower; **—аемый** *a.* blown off, etc., *see v.;* **—ание** *see* **обдувка; —ать** *v.* blow off, blow out, blast; ventilate; **—ка** *f.,* **—очный** *a.* blowing off, etc., *see v.;* blow out; (petrol.) air cooling, air-blast cleaning; (av.) airflow.

обдум/анно *adv.* with careful planning; **—анный** *a.* well-planned, carefully thought out; deliberate; **—(ыв)ать** *v.* consider, think over, weigh.

обдуть *see* **обдувать.**

обе *see* **оба.**

обег/ать *v.* run around, run past, by-pass; circulate; **—ающий** *a.* by-pass; circulating; scanning; multiple switching (check).

обед *m.* dinner; **—ать** *v.* dine; **—енный** *a.* dinner, dining.

обеди/евший, —елый *a.* poor, impoverished; **—ение** *n.* impoverishment, exhaustion, depletion; stripping; degradation, deterioration; **—ённый** *a.* impoverished, depleted; depletion (layer); stripped; underfit, misfit (river); **—ённый гликогеном** glycogen-poor; **—еть** *v.* become poor, become depleted; **—ик** *m.* southeast wind; **—ить, —ять** *v.* impoverish, deplete, strip; **—яющий** *a.* stripping (column).

обежать *v.* run around, (by-)pass.

обез— *prefix* be—, de—.

обезболив/ание *n.* anesthetization; **—ать** *v.* anesthetize; **—ающее средство** anesthetic; analgesic.

обезвершинивать *v.* top, pollard.

обезвкусить *v.* deprive of flavor.

обезвод/еть *v.* become dehydrated; **—ить** *see* **обезвоживать.**

обезводоро/дить *v.* dehydrogenate; **—жение** *n.* dehydrogenation.

обезвоженный *a.* dehydrated, desiccated; anhydrous.

обезвожив/ание *n.* dehydration, desiccation; water loss; **—атель** *m.* dehydrator, desiccator; **—ивать** *v.* dehydrate, desiccate; dewater; **—аться** *v.* be dehydrated, become anhydrous; **—ающий** *a.* dehydrating; **—ающее вещество, —ающее средство** drying agent, desiccant; dehydrating agent, dehydrant.

обезвоздушивать *v.* deaerate.

обезволашив/ание *n.* (hides) depilation, unhairing; **—ать** *v.* depilate, unhair.

обезволи(ва)ть *v.* brainwash.

обезволосить *see* **обезволашивать.**

обезвре/дить *see* **обезвреживать; —женный** *a.* rendered harmless, etc., *see v.;* **—живание** *n.* rendering harmless, etc., *see v.;* disposal; decontamination, detoxi(fi)cation; processing, sterilization (of waste); remediation; **—живать** *v.* render harmless, render safe, make innocuous, neutralize; dispose of (explosives); decontaminate, detoxify; **—живать яд** detoxify; **—живающий** *a.* rendering harmless, etc., *see v.;* decontamination; **—живающий синтез** detoxi(fi)cation.

обезга/живание *n.* degassing, etc., *see v.;* degasification; **—живать, —зить** *v.* degas(ify), deaerate; (vacuum system) outgas.

обезглав/ить, —ливать *v.* decapitate, behead; **—ление, —ливание** *n.* decapitation; **—ленный** *a.* decapitated, beheaded.

обезголосить *v.* lose one's voice.

обезгорч/еть *v.* lose bitter taste; **—ивать** *v.* remove bitter taste.

обездвиж/енный *a.* immobilized, restrained; **—ивание** *n.* immobilization, restraint; **—и(ва)ть** *v.* immobilize, restrain.

обездубливать *v.* (leather) free from tannic acid, detan.

обезжелез/ивание *n.* deferrization, iron removal; **—ненный** *a.* iron-free.

обезжир/енный *a.* degreased, nonfat, fat-free; skim (milk); (text.) scoured; **—ивание** *n.* degreasing, etc., *see v.;* fat extraction; **—иватель** *m.* degreasing agent, degreaser; scouring agent; **—и(ва)ть** *v.* degrease, defat, extract the fat; skim; scour; clean; **—ивающий** *a.* degreasing, etc., *see v.*

обеззара/женность *f.* sterility; **—женный** *a.* sterile, disinfected, antiseptic; **—живание** *n.* disinfection, etc., *see v.;* **—живать, —зить** *v.* disinfect, sterilize; (bact.) inactivate; decontaminate; purify (water); **—живающий** *a.* disinfecting, disinfectant, antiseptic, germicidal; decontaminating; **—живающее средство** disinfectant, germicide.

обеззземели(ва)ть *v.* dispossess of one's land, expel from the land.

обеззол/енный *a.* ashless, ash-free; decalcified; **—ивание** *n.* de-ashing, ash removal; decalcification; **индекс —ивания** deashability index; **—ивать** *v.* de-ash; decalcify, delime; **—ивающий** *a.* de-ashing, etc., *see v.*

обеззубеть *v.* lose one's teeth.

обезиливать *v.* desilt, deslime.

обезлес/ение *n.* deforestation; **—енный** *a.* deforested, clear (land); **—еть** *v.* become deforested; **—ить** *v.* deforest, clear (land), cut down forests.

обезлиств/ение *a.* defoliate(d); **—ить** *v.* defoliate; **—ление** *n.* defoliation.

обезлич/енный *a.* depersonalized; without personal responsibility; general-purpose, standard; **—и(ва)ть** *v.* depersonalize; do away with personal responsibility; **—ка** lack of personal responsibility.

обезлю/дить, —живать *v.* depopulate.

обезмасл/ивание *n.* deoiling; grease removal; **—и(ва)ть** *v.* deoil; degrease.

обезматоч/еть *v.* lose the queen bee; **—ный** *a.* queenless (hive).

обезме/дивание, —живание *n.* decoppering, copper extraction; **—женный** *a.* decoppered.

обезметилировать *v.* demethylate.

обезножеть *v.* lose the use of one's legs.

обезобра/женный *a.* mutilated, etc., *see v.;* unsightly; **—живание** *n.* mutilation, etc., *see v.;* disfigurement; pollution (of environment); **—живать, —зить** *v.* mutilate, disfigure, deform, cripple.

обезопасить *v.* secure (against).

обезоруж/ение, —ивание *n.* disarmament; **—и(ва)ть** *v.* disarm.

обезрепеив/ание *n.,* **—ающий** *a.* (text.) deburring, burr-extracting.

обезроживать *v.* cast off horns of antlers.

обезрыб/еть *v.* become fish-free; **—ление** *n.* fish depletion; **—ленный** *a.* fish-free, made free of fish; **—ливание** *n.* fish removal.

обезуглеро/дить, —живать *v.* decarbonize; decarburize; **—женный** *a.* decarbonized; **—живание** *n.* decarbonization.

обезуметь *v.* lose one's head or mind.

обезшламленный *a.* slime-free, sludge-free.

обезызвествление *n.* (med.) decalcification.

обезыливать *v.* desilt, deslime.

обезьян/а *f.* (mam.) monkey, ape; **—ий** *a.* simian; primate; **—ка** *dim. of* **обезьяна;** **—ник** *m.* monkey house; **—оед** *m.* (orn.) monkey-eating eagle (*Pithecophaga jefferyi*); **—олюди** *pl.* ape men; **—оподобный** *a.* ape-like, simian; **—очеловек** *m.* ape man, anthropoid; **—ы** *pl.* Simiae.

обелённый *a.* whitened, etc., *see* **обелить.**

обелиск *m.* obelisk, spine, needle.

обел/ить, —ять *v.* whiten, bleach; (law) acquit, clear; whitewash.

обепин *m.* aubepine, anisaldehyde.

обер— *prefix* chief.

оберег/атель *m.* protector, defender; **—ать** *v.* protect, defend, guard.

оберёт *fut. 3 sing. of* **обобрать.**

оберечь *see* **оберегать.**

обер-мастер *m.* overseer, foreman.

обёрнутый *a.* wrapped, enveloped; (bot.) involucrate.

обернуть *see* **обёртывать.**

оберон *m.* (astr.) Oberon.

обёртка *f.* wrapper, wrapping, envelope, cover, casing, sheath; (book) jacket; (corn) husk; (bot.) involucre.

обертон *m.* (acous.) overtone; (seism.) mode.

обёрточ/ка *dim. of* **обёртка;** (bot.) involucel; **—ный** *a. of* **обертка;** involucral; packing (material).

обертух *m.* (paper) overfelt.

обёртыв/ание *n.* wrapping, etc., *see v.;* **о. с льдом** (med.) ice pack; **—ать** *v.* wrap (up, around), envelop, cover; turn; **—аться** *v.* be wrapped; turn (around, out); manage; **—ающий** *a.* wrapping, etc., *see v.*

оберут *fut. 3 pl. of* **обобрать.**

обес— *see* **обез—.**

обескислоро/дить *v.* deoxygenate, deprive of oxygen; **—женный** *a.* oxygen-free; **—живание** *n.* deoxygen(iz)ation, oxygen removal.

обескле/енный *a.* (text.) degummed; with glue removed; **—ивание** *n.* degumming, desizing; glue removal; (wine) fine; **—ивать** *v.* degum, desize; unglue, detach.

обес/коривание *n.* decortication, barking, peeling; **—кремнивание** *n.* desilic(oniz)ation, silicon removal; **—кремнивать** *v.* desilicify.

обескров/ить, —ливать *v.* bleed, exsanguinate, blanch; dehematize; **—ление, —ливание** *n.* bleeding, exsanguination, etc., *see v.;* **—ленный** *a.* exsanguinated, etc., *see v.;* bloodless; lifeless.

обес/крыли(ва)ть *v.* pinion, trim the pinions; **—памятеть** *v.* lose memory; lose consciousness; **—паривать** *v.* devaporate, condense from vapor; **—пененный** *a.* defoamed.

обеспеч/ение *n.* security, guarantee, warrant, assurance, collateral; provision, supply; support; control; **о. кислородом** oxygen supply; **для —ения** for; **мате-** матическое о., программное о. (comp.) software; социальное о. social security; техническое о. (comp.) hardware; **—енность** *f.* provision, providing (with); security; frequency; (food) supply; **коэффициент —енности** (power plants) utilization factor; **—енный** *a.* provided, etc., *see v.;* secure; **—ивание** *n.* providing, etc., *see v.;* **—и(ва)ть** *v.* provide, supply, furnish, give; equip, fit (with); assure, guarantee, warrant, ensure, secure, safeguard, make sure (of); offer, permit; achieve, effect; control, establish a control base; **—и(ва)ть возможность** make possible; **—ивающий** *a.* providing, etc., *see v.;* safety.

обеспло/деть, —диться *v.* become sterile; **—дить, —живать** *v.* sterilize; **—женный** *a.* sterile, sterilized; **—живание** *n.* sterilization.

обеспоко/енный *a.* anxious, concerned (about); **—ить** *v.* trouble, bother; **—иться** *v.* become anxious or uneasy.

обеспузыривание *n.* (glass) bubble removal.

обеспыл/енный *a.* dust-free; **—ивание** *n.* dust removal, dust control; dedusting; **—иватель** *m.* dust remover, deduster; **—и(ва)ть** *v.* remove dust, dedust; **—ивающий** *a.* dust-removing, dedusting; dust-laying.

обессахар/енный *a.* sugar-free; **—ивание** *n.* desaccharification, sugar extraction; **—ивать** *v.* desaccharify, extract sugar.

обес/свинцевание *n.* deleading, lead extraction; **—серебрение** *n.* desilverization, silver extraction.

обессер/ение, —ивание *n.* desulfurization, desulfurizing; **—енный** *a.* desulfurized; **—иватель** *m.* desulfurizer; **—ивать** *v.* desulfurize, free from sulfur; **—ивающий** *a.* desulfurizing, sulfur-removing.

обессил/еть *v.* become weak, lose strength; **—и(ва)ть** *v.* weaken, debilitate.

обессмерченный *a.* immortalized.

обессмолив/ание *n.* resin extraction, deresination; detarring; (paper) pitch removal; **—ать** *v.* extract resin, deresinate; detar; remove pitch.

обессол/енный *a.* salt-free; **—ивание** *n.* salt elimination; desalinization; demineralization; **глубокое —ивание** (ultrafiltration) high rejection (ratio); **—и(ва)ть** *v.* free from salt; salt out.

обессталивать *f.* (met.) soften.

обесточ/енный *a.* (elec.) dead; de-energized; **—и(ва)ть** *v.* disconnect, cut off current; de-energize.

обесфеноливание *n.* dephenolization.

обесфосфор/енный *a.* dephosphorized; **—ивание** *n.* dephosphorization; **—ивать** *v.* dephosphorize, free of phosphorus.

обесфторенный *a.* defluorinated.

обесхлорить *v.* dechlorinate.

обесцветить *see* **обесцвечивать.**

обесцвеч/ение *see* **обесцвечивание;** **—енный** *a.* decolorized, etc., *see v.;* **—ивание** *n.* decolorization, bleaching, color removal; discoloration, stain, blemish; (bot.) etiolation; fading; **—иватель** *m.* decolorant, bleach; **—ивать** *v.* decolorize, bleach; (leather) tone down; discolor, stain; **—и(ва)ться** *v.* lose color, fade; **—ивающий** *a.* decolorizing, etc., *see v.;* **—ивающее средство** decolorizing agent, decolorant.

обесцен/ение, —ивание *n.* depreciation; **—енный** *a.* depreciated; **—и(ва)ть** *v.* depreciate; cheapen.

обесцинкование *n.* (met.) dezincing, zinc extraction.

обесшкуривать *v.* skin.

обесшламлив/ание *n.,* **—ающий** *a.* desliming, desludging, deslurrying.

обес/шумливание *n.* noise reduction, noise control; **—щелачивание** *n.* dealkalization.

обетонирование *n.* concrete fixation (of wastes); removal from concrete.

обечайка *f.* shell (of boiler), hood; (diffuser) cowl(ing).

обещ/ание *n.,* **—ать** *v.* promise.

обжаловать *v.* appeal a case.

обжар/и(ва)ть *v.* roast; brown, sear (meat); **—ка** *f.* searing.

обжат/ие *n.* squeezing, etc., *see* **обжимать;** (rolling) reduction; compression; **единочное о.** (rolling) draft; **степень —ия** shrinkage; **черновое о.** roughing; **чрезмерное о.** overdraft; **—ый** *a.* squeezed, etc., *see* **обжимать; —ь** *see* **обжимать;** reap.

обжечь *see* **обжигать.**

обжиг *m.* roasting, etc., *see v.;* **печь для —а** roasting furnace; kiln; **—аемый** *a.* calcinable; calcined; for roasting; **—ание** *n.,* **—а(те)льный** *a.* roasting, etc., *see v.;* calcination; combustion; **—ательная печь** roasting furnace; kiln; **—ательная установка** roasting plant; (nucl.) calciner; **—ать** *v.* roast, sinter (ore); burn (bricks); fire (pellets, etc.); calcine; kiln, bake; **—овый** *a. of* **обжиг.**

обжим *see* **обжимка;** crush (in mold); **процесс —а** (met.) reducing, necking; **—ание** *n.* squeezing, etc., *see v.;* **—ать** *v.* squeeze, (com)press, wring out; (met.) shingle; upset, swage; crimp; (rolling) cog (down), reduce; **—ка** *f.* squeezing, etc., *see v.;* crimper, crimping tool; (riveting) die; **—ки** *pl.* residue; **—ной, —(оч)ный** *a.* squeezing, etc., *see v.;* pinch, roughing (roll); set (hammer); **—ной стан** (rolling) cogging mill; roughing mill; **—ные щипцы** crimper.

обжин *m.,* **—ка** *f.* reaping; **—ать** *v.* reap.

обжитый *a.* permanently inhabited.

обжог *m.* (phyt.; vet.) (sun)burn, scald, scorch.

обжор *m.,* **—а** *m. and f.* glutton; (ichth.) great sturgeon (*Huso h.*); **лайковый о.** emulsion, nourishing, paste; **—ливость** *f.,* **—ство** *n.* gluttony; **—ливый** *a.* gluttonous, greedy.

обжум *m.* drying (of grapes).

обзав/едение *n.* acquisition; fitting out, equipment; **—естись, —одиться** *v.* acquire.

обзол *m.* (timber) wane (defect).

обзол/ение, —ивание *n.* calcination, etc., *see v.;* combustion; ashing; **—енный** *a.* calcined, etc., *see v.;* **—и(ва)ть** *v.* calcine, incinerate, char; reduce to ashes; ash (molds).

обзольный *a.* dull-edged; (timber) wany.

обзор *m.* survey, review, synopsis, summary, outline, digest; coverage; (field of) view, vision; (rad.) scanning; **о. вниз** downward view; **о. назад** rear view; **краткий о., реферативный о.** abstract, résumé; **—ность** *f.* field of vision, visibility; **—ный** *a. of* **обзор;** survey (instrument); surveillance (radar); with a good view; summarized; correlated (abstract); general (map); **—ная площадка** scenic viewpoint.

обизвест/вление, —ковывание *n.* calcification.

обилие *n.* abundance, affluence, plenty; **о.-преобладание** *n.* (geobot.) total estimate (of cover and density).

обильн/о *adv.* liberally, heavily; **—ость** *f.* abundance, etc., *see v.;* **—оцветущий** *a.* (bot.) floribund, heavy-flowering; **—ый** *a.* abundant, plentiful, copious, ample, liberal, profuse, voluminous; prolific; rich, generous; heavy (dose); flood (lubrication).

обирать *v.* gather, pick.

обит/аемость *f.* habitability; **—аемый** *a.* habitable, inhabited, populated; manned (satellite); **—ание** *n.* habitation; (biol.) habitat; **ареал —ания, место —ания, район —ания** habitat; **—атель** *m.* inhabitant, resi-

dent, dweller, inmate; **—ать** *v.* inhabit, reside, dwell, live (in); **—ающий** *a.* inhabiting; *suffix* **—**dwelling; (zool.) **—**philous, loving.

обит/ый *a.* upholstered, padded, covered; **—ь** *see* **обивать.**

обиход *m.* custom, habit, practice; use; **входить в о.** *v.* become popular; become customary; **выйти из —а** *v.* become obsolete; **—ный** *a.* common, usual, everyday; household; colloquial (term).

обкалывать *v.* pin, prick around; break (out), chip out; cleave around.

обкап/ать *v.* spatter; **—ывание** *n.* spatter(ing); digging around; **—ывать** *v.* spatter; dig around, hoe.

обкармлив/ание *n.* overfeeding; **—ать** *v.* overfeed; **—аться** *v.* overeat.

обкат *m.* rolling out; wearing smooth; road test, test run; (gear) generation; (typ.) inking failure; **—анный** *a.* rolled (out); worn smooth; road-tested, test-run; **—ать** *see* **обкатывать; —ить** *v.* roll around; drench; **—ка** *f.* rolling out; (steel) cold rolling, cold finish; generating, hobbing (of gears); burnishing, cladding; (rivets) spinning; running(-in), breaking in; **—ка в холостую** idle run, idling; **—ной, —ный** *a. of* **обкат(ка); —очный** *a. of* **обкатка; —ывание** *see* **обкатка; —ывать** *v.* roll (out) smooth; wear smooth; burnish; generate (gear teeth); spin (rivet heads); run in, break in, road-test, test-run; **—ываться вокруг** *v.* revolve around.

обкачивать *v.* drench, sluice.

обкашивать *v.* mow around.

обкид(ыв)ать *v.* pile on, bank (with); cover (with a rash).

обклад/ка *f.,* **—очный** *a.* facing, etc., *see v.;* coat; (capacitor) plate; casing; sheath(ing); **—ывание** *n.* facing, etc., *see v.;* **—ывать** *v.* face, line, edge, coat, cover, lay around, surround; impose (a tax).

обклевать, обклёвывать *v.* peck.

обклеивать *see* **оклеивать.**

обкол/ачивать, —отить *v.* knock, chip (off, out); **—ка** *f.* chipping (off, out).

обколоть *see* **обкалывать.**

обком *m.,* **—овский** *a.* district committee.

обкопать *v.* dig around.

обкорачивать *v.* shorten, clip.

обкорм *m.,* **—ка** *f.* overfeeding; **—ить** *v.* overfeed; **—ленный** *a.* overfed.

обкорнать *v.* cut, clip.

обкоротить *v.* shorten, curtail, crop.

обкосить *v.* mow around.

обкрошиться *v.* crumble at the edges.

обкру/тить, —чивать *v.* wind around.

обкури(ва)ть *v.* smoke; smoke out (bees); fumigate; season (a pipe).

обкус(ыв)ать *v.* bite, gnaw (around); trim.

обл. *abbr.* **(областной, область); обл—** *prefix see* **областной.**

облав/а *f.* (hunting) battue, beat; chase; **—ливать** *v.* hunt, fish or catch (in a given area); seine.

облаг/аемый (налогом) *a.* taxable, assessable; **—ать** *v.* impose (a tax).

облагор/аживание *n.* refining, etc., *see v.;* improvement; enrichment; (wood) modification; (paper) surface treatment; **—аживать, —одить** *v.* refine, purify; improve, upgrade, enrich; (agr.) cultivate; (text.) finish, dress; **—ожение** *see* **облагораживание; —оженный** *a.* refined, etc., *see v.*

облад/ание *n.* possession; **—атель** *m.* possessor, owner, proprietor; **—ать** *v.* possess, own, have, include, embody, incorporate; feature, offer, display, exhibit.

облак/о *n.* cloud; (vapor) plume; **вне —ов** (av.) clear of clouds; **затянутый —ами** overcast; **—омер** *m.* cloud-range meter.

обламыв/ание *n.* breaking off, chipping off, truncation; calving (of glacier); **—ать** *v.* break off, chip off; truncate; calve; **—ающийся** *a.* fragile.

област/ной *a.* district, regional, territorial; **—ь** *f.* region, sphere, area, zone, field, domain; range, band, spectrum; district, territory; (biol.) realm, kingdom, circle; (administration) oblast; **—ь спектра** spectrum; **в —и** in; over area; **температурная —ь** temperature range.

облат/ка *f.,* **—очный** *a.* wafer; capsule.

облач/ение *n.* (anat.; biol.) indusium; **—ко** *dim. of* **облако; —ность** *f.* cloudiness, cloud cover, clouds, overcast sky; nebulosity; **—ный** *a.* cloudy, clouded, overcast; nebulous; ceiling (light); **—ное знамя** banner cloud.

облег/ание *n.* surrounding, etc., *see v.;* encirclement; outline; **—ать** *v.* surround, encircle, encompass, enclose; cover (with fog); outline; cling, fit closely; **—ающий** *a.* surrounding, etc., *see v.*

облегч/ать *v.* alleviate, lighten, relieve, ease (up), make easier, facilitate; aid, assist, promote; reduce; simplify (design); **—ающий** *a.* alleviating, etc., *see v.;* **—ение** *n.* alleviation, lightening, etc., *see v.;* relief; **—ённый** *a.* alleviated, etc., *see v.;* light(-weight), light-duty; **—ённого типа** light-duty; **—ительный** *see* **облегчающий; —ить** *see* **облегчать.**

облед/ене(ва)ть *v.* ice over, ice up, freeze; **—енелый** *a.* iced, icy, ice-covered; **—енение** *n.* ice formation, icing (up), freezing, congelation; glaze; **—ить** *v.* ice over, cover with ice; **—ь** *f.* icing, ice deposit.

облез/ать, —ть *v.* peel (off), come off; come out, fall out, shed; creep around; **—лый** *a.* shabby, bare; sparse; peeling (paint).

облей(те) *imp. of* **облить.**

облек/ание *n.* enveloping; (geol.) mantle; **—ать** *v.* envelop, shroud; invest (with power); express, formulate.

облеп/ить, —лять *v.* stick around, glue around; **—иха** *f.* (bot.) sea buckthorn (*Hippophae*); **—ишник** *m.* sea buckthorn scrub; **—ленный** *a.* stuck around; incrusted; **—ли(ва)ть, —лять** *v.* stick all over.

облес/ение *n.* (af)forestation; **—енный** *a.* (af)forested; **—ительный** *a.* forest-planting; **—ить** *v.* (af)forest, establish a forest, plant forests.

облёт *m.* fly(ing) off, fly(ing) by, fly(ing) over, circling; (trail) flight, pass; play flight (of bees); **о. препятствий** terrain following.

облет/ать *v.* fly around, circle; test (in flight); hover around; overtake; spread (of news); **—аться** *v.* become accustomed to flying; **—елый** *a.* bare (tree); **—еть** *v.* fly around, fly past; fall off (of leaves); be bare (of trees).

облётывать *v.* fly over; test, make a trial flight.

облеч/ённый *a.* invested (with); **о. доверием** entrusted (with); **—ь** *see* **облекать.**

облив *m.,* **—ание** *n.* drenching, etc., *see v.;* **окраска —ом** (paints) flow coating; **—ать** *v.* drench, douse; pour around or over; cast around; (med.) perfuse; **—аться** *v.* become drenched; **—ка** *see* **обливание;** (cer.) glaze, glazing; **—ной** *a.* drenched, wet; glazed.

облигатный *a.* (biol.) obligate, obligatory; natural (self-pollination).

облигаци/я *f.,* **—онный** *a.* (com.) bond.

облиз/ать, —ывать *v.* lick (all over).

облик *m.* appearance, look, aspect; outlook; (min.) habit; **—ва** *f.* penguinfish (*Thayeria obliquus*).

облин/ялый *a.* faded; molted; **—ять** *v.* fade; molt, shed.

облип/ание *n.* coating; **—ать, —нуть** *v.* stick all around.

облиств/(ен)еть *v.* be covered with foliage; **—(л)ение** *n.* foliation, leafing, leafage, foliage; **—енность** *f.* leafiness, foliage, leafage; **—енный** *a.* leafy, verdant, foliated, leaf-clad, frondose.

облитер/ация *f.,* **—ирование** *n.* obliteration, complete removal; **—ированный** *a.* obliterated; **—ировать** *v.* obliterate.

облит/ый *a.* drenched, covered (with a liquid); **—ь** *see* **обливать.**

облиц/евать *see* **облицовывать; —ованный** *a.* faced, etc., *see v.;* **—ованный свинцом** lead-lined; **—овка** *f.,* **—овочный** *a.* facing, etc., *see v.;* coat; revetment; (radiator) shell, frame, case; finish; **без —овки** unlined; **—овывание** *n.* facing, etc., *see v.;* **—овывать** *v.* face, line, coat, cover, jacket, (in)case; revet; (met.) fettle.

облич/ать, —ить *v.* discover, reveal, display; expose; convict.

облический *a.* oblique.

обличье *n.* appearance; contour.

облов *m.* catch(ing); fishing (off), removal; seining; **—ить** *see* **облавливать.**

облог *m.,* **—а** *f.* fallow, overgrown field.

облож/ение *n.* facing, etc., *see* **обкладывать;** taxation, assessment; **подлежать —ению** *v.* be subject (to); **—енный** *a.* faced, etc., *see* **обкладывать;** coated (tongue); **—ечный** *a.,* **—ка** *f.* (book) cover; folder, envelope; (bot.) involucrum; **—ить** *see* **обкладывать; —ной** *a.* steady (rain).

облой *m.* (molding) fin, flash, projection; **—ник** *m.* flash (recess).

облом *m.* break, breaking (off); mold(ing); cross-section; **—анный** *a.* broken off; truncated; **—ать** *see* **обламывать; —ка** *f.* break, breaking (off); **—ок** *m.* broken piece, fragment, splinter, chip; **—ки** *pl.* cuttings; rubble, scrap, debris, waste; wreckage; (volcanic) ejecta; (geol.) detritus, rock waste; **—очный, —чатый** *a.* rubbly; (geol.) detrital, clastic, fragmental.

облоно *m.* regional division of national education.

облопа/тывание, —чивание *n.* (turbines) blading, blades.

облу/дить, —живать *v.* tinplate.

облуп *m.* (phyt.) rhizina root rot; **—ить** *v.* peel (off), pare, strip, decorticate; shell, hull; **—иться** *v.* peel off, come off; **—ленный** *a.* peeled, etc., *see v.;* **—ливание** *n.* peeling, etc., *see v.;* **—ливать** *see* **облупить.**

облуха *f.* (ichth.) roach (*Rutilus r.*).

облуч/атель *m.* irradiator, radiation source; (antenna) feed, exciter; **—ать, —ить** *v.* irradiate, expose (to radiation); **—аться** *v.* get a dose of radiation, be treated with radiation; **—ение** *n.* irradiation, exposure; **анализ до —ения** prebombardment analysis; **мощность —ения** radiation power; **—ённость** *f.* irradiance, irradiancy; **—ённый** *a.* irradiated, exposed.

облучок *m.* driver's seat.

облушка *f.* (ichth.) rudd (*Scardinius erythrophthalmus*).

облущи(ва)ть *v.* shell, hull.

облыс/евший, —елый *a.* bald; **—ение** *n.* baldness; balding; **—еть** *v.* get bald.

обляжет *fut. 3 sing. of* **облечь.**

обмаз/анный *a.* daubed, etc., *see v.;* **—ать** *see* **обмазывать; —ка** *f.* daubing, etc., *see v.;* daub; (first) coat; putty, lute, plaster; **—ывание** *n.* daubing, etc., *see v.*; **—ывать** *v.* daub, smear, coat (with), cover; putty, plaster, cement; render (plaster); grease.

обмак/ивать, —нуть *v.* dip, steep.

обмалывать *v.* grind (into flour).

обман *m.* fraud; deception, illusion; spoof; **о. зрения** optical illusion.

обманка *f.* (min.) blende; spec. zinc blende.

обман/ный *a.* fraudulent; misleading; **—уть, —ывать** *v.* deceive, mislead; **—чивость** *f.* fallacy, illusion; **—чивый** *a.* deceptive, delusive, illusory.

обмасл/ивание *n.* oiling, lubrication; **—и(ва)ть** *v.* oil, lubricate.

обматыв/ание *see* **обмотка; —ать** *v.* wind (around), coil, wrap (around), tape, encircle; sheathe, cover, insulate.

обмах/ивать, —нуть *v.* brush away; fan.

обмачивать *v.* steep, dip, soak, wet.

обмеднение *see* **омеднение.**

обмежевать, обмежёвывать *v.* stake out, set boundaries.

обмел *past m. sing. of* **обмести.**

обмел/ение *n.* shoaling; **—еть** *v.* shoal, (grow) shallow; run around.

обмели(ва)ть *v.* outline in chalk.

обмелить *v.* make shallow.

обмельчать *v.* become smaller; grind.

обмен *m.*, **—а** *f.* exchange, interchange, change; barter; (physiol.) metabolism; (elec. comm.) traffic; (meteor.) austausch; (biochem.) balance; (comp.) swapping; input-output; **о. азота** nitrogen balance; **о. белков** protein balance; **о. веществ** metabolism; **болезни —а веществ** metabolic diseases; **о. газов** gas exchange; **о. жира** lipid metabolism; **о. кальция** calcium metabolism; **о. покоя, основной о.** basal metabolic rate; **о. РНК** RNA turnover; **о. теплоты** heat exchange, heat transfer; **коэффициент —а** metabolic rate; **продукт —а (веществ)** metabolite; **реакция —а** exchange reaction; **ток —а** (electrochem.) diffusion current.

обмен/иваемый *a.* exchangeable; **—и(ва)ть** *v.* exchange, interchange; substitute, replace; **—иваться** *v.* metabolize; react; **—ивающийся** *a.* exchangeable; **—ник** *m.* exchanger, interchanger; **—но-связанный, —оспособный** *a.* exchangeable (catalysts); **—ный** *a.* exchange, exchangeable; metabolic; double (decomposition); converted, composite (wave); **—ный баланс** metabolic equilibrium; **—ная способность** exchange capacity; **—ное взаимодействие** exchange reaction; **—ное разложение** metabolization; **—о** *see* **обменно—; —ять** *see* **обменивать.**

обмер *m.* measure(ment), measuring; **—енный** *a.* measured.

обмереть *v.* become numb; faint.

обмерз/ание *n.* freezing (over, up), etc., *see v.*; frost damage; **—ать** *v.* freeze (over, up), get frozen; ice over; frost up; **—ающий** *a.* freezing, etc., *see v.*

обмёрз/лый iced over; frosted; **—нуть** *see* **обмерзать.**

обмер/ивание *n.* measurement; short measure; **—и(ва)ть** *v.* measure; give short measure; **—иться** *v.* make a mistake in measuring; **—ка** *f.*, **—ный** *a.* measurement; **—ок** *m.* short weight; **—ять** *see* **обмеривать.**

обмести *v.* sweep off.

обмёт *m.* sweepings, contaminated flour; trapping net.

обметать *v.* sweep off; overstitch, overcast; (med.) cover (with a rash).

обметить *v.* label, mark.

обмётывать *v.* overcast, overstitch.

обмечать *v.* label, mark.

об/мин. *abbr.* [оборот(ы) в минуту] revolutions per minute, r.p.m.

обмин *m.* pressing down, packing; **—ать** *v.* press down, pack, trample down.

обмирать *see* **обмереть.**

обмоет *fut. 3 sing. of* **обмыть.**

обмок/ать, —нуть *v.* get wet.

обмол *m.* grinding (into flour); yield of ground grain.

обмол/ачивание *n.* (agr.) threshing; **—ачивать** *v.* thresh; **—от** *m.* threshing; yield of threshed grain; thresh; **—отить** *v.* thresh; **—отки** *pl.* chaff; **—оточный** *a.* threshing.

обмолоть *v.* grind (into flour).

обмолоченный *a.* (agr.) threshed.

обмор/аживание, —ожение *n.* freezing; frostbite; **—аживать, —озить** *v.* freeze.

обмор/ок *m.* (med.) syncope, faint; **падать** or **упасть в о.** *v.* faint, lose consciousness; **—очный** *a.* syncopal, syncopic.

обмот/анный *a.* wound, coiled, wrapped, taped, covered; insulated (wire); **—ать** *see* **обматывать; —ка** *f.* winding, coiling, wrapping, taping, sheath(ing), cover(ing); tape; (elec.) winding, coil, armature; **—ки** *pl.* puttees, leggings; **—очный** *a. of* **обмотка;** spun (yarn); *suffix* -wound; **—чик** *m.* winder.

обмочить *see* **обмачивать.**

обмоющий *pr. part. of* **обмыть.**

обмундиров(ыв)ать *v.* equip, fit out.

обмуров/анный *a.* brick-lined, bricked; **—ать** *see* **обмуровывать; —ка** *f.* walling up, bricking; brickwork, masonry, covering, casing, setting; lining (of furnace); **—ывать** *v.* wall up, brick(-line).

обмыв *m.*, **—ание** *n.* washing; (med.) lavage; **—ать** *v.* wash (out or off), elute, rinse; **—ка** *see* **обмыв; —очно-дезактивационный** *a.* bath and decontamination; **—очный** *a. of* **обмывание.**

обмыл/и(ва)ть *v.* soap all over; **—ок** *m.* remnant of soap; **—ки** *pl.* soapy wash water.

обмыть *see* **обмывать.**

обмяк/ать, —нуть *v.* get flabby or soft.

обмять *see* **обминать.**

обнадёжи(ва)ть *v.* reassure, encourage.

обнаж/ать *v.* (lay) bare, uncover, strip; reveal, disclose; expose; **—аться** *v.* become exposed, appear; (geol.) crop out; lose foliage; **—ение** *n.* baring, denudation; uncovering, exposure; erosion; outcrop (of rock); dereliction (of shore); scalping (of vegetation); barking, rossing (of wood); **—ённый** *a.* bare, uncovered, exposed, naked; eroded; outcropped; defoliated; **—ённая порода** outcrop; **—ить** *see* **обнажать.**

обнародов/ание *n.* publication; **—ать** *v.* publish, promulgate.

обнаруж/ение *n.* uncovering, discovery, finding, disclosure, detection; development, appearance; display; estimation, determination, assay; identification; test (for); proof, evidence; occurrence; **—ение белка** protein test; **—ение дефектов** troubleshooting; **—енный** *a.* uncovered, etc., *see v.*; **—иваемый** *a.* detectable; detected, sensed; **—ивание** *see* **обнаружение; —ивать** *v.* uncover, discover, disclose, detect, reveal, identify, find, trace, locate; expose; strike (oil); develop, display; observe; estimate, determine, measure, assay; prove, ascertain; **—иваться** *v.* develop, appear; be found; **—итель** *m.* feeler, detection, finder; **—ительный** *a.* detector, warning; **—ить** *see* **обнаруживать.**

обн/ашивать, —ести *see* **обносить**; **—есённый** *a.* enclosed, surrounded.

обнимать *v.* embrace, hug, envelop, include.

обнищ/алый *a.* impoverished; **—ать** *v.* grow poor, become impoverished.

обнов/а *f.* new acquisition; **—итель** *m.* restorer, regenerator; **—ительный** *a.* restoring, etc., *see v.*; **—ить** *see* **обновлять**; **—ление** *n.* restoration, etc., *see v.*; renewal; innovation; (comp.) updating; recruitment; (chem.) resynthesis; **—лённый** *a.* restored, etc., *see v.*; **—ляемость** *f.* renewability; interchangeability; **—ляемый** *a.* renewable; interchangeable; **—лять** *v.* restore, regenerate, renew, refresh; rejuvenate; renovate; repair; update, bring up to date; resynthetize, resynthesize.

обнож/ка, —ь *f.* (apid.) pollen load; **—ки** *pl.* breech (low grade wool).

обнос *m.* enclosure; (naut.) overhang; **—ить** *v.* enclose, surround, encompass; wall, fence, rail (in); carry around; **—ка** *f.,* **—ный** *a.* encloosing, etc., *see v.*

обнул/ение *n.* null, zero output; **—ивающий** *a.* (comp.) nulling.

обнять *see* **обнимать.**

обо *see* **о**; **обо—** *see* **о—**.

обобрать *see* **обирать.**

обобщ/ать *v.* generalize, infer, theorize; combine, correlate (data); **—ение** *n.* generalization, etc., *see v.*; general conclusion; extension (of theory); **—ённый** *a.* generalized, etc., *see v.*; composite (index of water quality); **—ествить, —ествлять** *v.* collectivize, communalize, socialize; **—ествление** *n.* collectivization, etc., *see v.*; **—ествлённый** *a.* collectivized, etc., *see v.*; **—ить** *see* **обобщать.**

обобьёт *fut. 3 sing. of* **обить.**

обовьёт *fut. 3 sing. of* **обвить.**

обога/тимый *a.* capable of concentration, dressable; **—титель** *m.* enriching additive; (min.) dresser; **—тительный** *a.* enriching; (met.) concentration; **—тить, —щать** *v.* enrich; concentrate; treat, process, prepare; separate, clean, dress, wash; beneficiate; **—щаемый** *see* **обогатимый**; **—щение** *n.* enriching, etc., *see v.*; enrichment; concentration; **коэффициент —щения** (nucl.) enrichment factor; **—щённый** *a.* enriched, etc., *see v.*; forced (blast).

обогн/анный *a.* outdistanced, passed; **—ать** *see* **обгонять.**

обогнуть *v.* bend around; by-pass.

обогр/ев *m.* heating, warming; heater; **—еваемый** *a.* heated, warmed; **—евание** *n.* heating, warming; **—еватель** *m.* heater; **—евательный** *a.* heating, warming; **—евать** *v.* heat, warm; **—етый** *a.* heated, warmed; **—еть** *see* **обогревать.**

обод *m.* rim (of wheel); hoop, ring, circle; **—ковый** *a. of* **обод**; ring-shaped, annular; **—ок** *m.* margin, border, edge, rim; ring, circle, ferrule; (anat.) an(n)ulus; limbus, labrum; **—очнокишечный** *a.* (anat.) colic; **—очный** *a. of* **обод**; (anat.) colonic; **—очная кишка** colon.

ободр/анный *a.* peeled, etc., *see v.*; **—ать** *v.* peel, skin, strip, rip off.

ободр/ить, —ять *v.* encourage, inspire; **—яться** *v.* take courage; **—яющий** *a.* encouraging, promising.

ободья *pl. of* **обод.**

обоеполый *a.* bisexual, androgynous, hermaphroditic; (bot.) monoecious.

обоечн/ый *a.* grain-cleaning, hulling; **—ая машина** huller, scourer.

обождать *v.* wait (for; for a while).

обожжённый *a.* burnt, calcined, roasted; (bot.) sphacelate, dead, withered; **окончательно о.** dead-burned.

обожмёт *fut. 3 sing. of* **обжать.**

обоз *m.* train, transport, convoy.

обознач/ать *v.* designate, denote, indicate, specify, define; label, mark, identify; signify, stand for, mean, represent; **детально о.** specify; **—ающий** *a.* designating, etc., *see v.*; **—ая X через Y** letting Y represent X; **—ение** *n.* designation, etc., *see v.*; mark(ing), labeling; notation, nomenclature; symbol(s), sign, index, criterion; formula; **система —ений** nomenclature; **условные —ения** legend; **—енный** *a.* designated, etc., *see v.*; **хорошо —енный** well-defined; **чётко —енный** sharply defined, clear-cut; **—ить** *see* **обозначать.**

обозный *a. of* **обоз**; draft (horse).

обозр/еватель *m.* reviewer; **—е(ва)ть** *v.,* **—ение** *n.* review, survey; **—имый** *a.* visible; foreseeable (future).

обозчик *m.* transport driver.

обо/и *see* **оба**; *pl.* wallpaper; **оклеить —ями** *v.* paper.

обой *m.* windfall (fruit).

обойдённый *a.* by-passed.

обойка *f.* huller; scourer; upholstering.

обойма *f.* ring, band, girdle, yoke, holder; (spring, cartridge) clip; casing, housing; (bearing) race, cage; magazine (of pistol); (nozzle) jacket; (roller) draw plate; brush box; seal cage (of stuffing box); stirrup; fork.

обоймёт *fut. 3 sing. of* **обнять.**

обоймица *f.* block, hanging hook.

обойный *a.* upholstery; wallpaper; tack (hammer); **о. гвоздь** tack.

обой/ти *see* **обходить**; **—тись** *see* **обходиться**; **все —дётся** everything will be all right.

обойщик *m.* upholsterer; paper hanger.

обок *adv. and prep. gen.* beside, near.

оболвани(ва)ть *v.* (foundry) roughhew, rough-work, rough out.

оболовый *a.* obolus (phosphorite).

оболонь *f.* (bot.) alburnum, sapwood.

оболоч/ечный *a.* shell; **—ка** *f.,* **—ковый** *a.* shell, envelope, cover, sheath(ing), case, casing; (nucl.) jacket, can; (gas) blanket; mantle, crust (of earth); film, coating; (anat.) membrane; tunic(a); (cell) wall; cladding (of optical fiber); (reactor) containment; **—ка нервов** myelin; **—ка семени** spermoderm, seed coat; **внутренняя —ка** (anat.) tunica interna; tunica intima; (ent.) endochorion; **внутренняя —ка сердца** endocardium; **водная —ка** (embr.) amnion; **выпуклая —ка** convex hull; **мягкая —ка** (anat.) pia mater; **наружная —ка** tunica externa, outer coat; **покрытие —кой** filming (over); jacketing, canning; **с резиновой —кой** rubber-covered; **твёрдая —ка** (anat.) dura mater; **теория —ек** (mech.) shell theory; **—ко—** *prefix* chlamyd(o)— (mantle); **—ковый** *a. of* **оболочка;** chlamydate; (bot.) chlamydeous; **—ковое литьё** (met.) casting in shell molds; **—косеменные** *pl.* (bot.) Chlamydospermae; **—ники, —никовые** *pl.* (zool.) Tunicata; **—ный** *a.* shell; **—ь** *v.* wrap around, cover, envelop.

оболтка *f.* tumbling (in drum).

обольёт *fut. 3 sing. of* **облить.**

обомнёт *fut. 3 sing. of* **обмять.**

обон/яние *n.* (sense of) smell, olfaction; **органы —яния** olfactory organs; **—ятельный** *a.* olfactory; **—ятельный мозг** (anat.) rhinencephalon; **—ятельная кость** ethmoid (bone); **—ять** *v.* smell.

обопре(ва)ть *v.* get moldy.

обопрёт(ся) *fut. 3 sing. of* **опереть(ся).**

обор *m.* (text.) coarse abb; refuse clinker; **—а** *f.* cord, lace.

оборачив/аемость *f.* turnover; (book) circulation, cycle;

—ание *n.* turning; **—атель** *m.* turner; **—ать** *v.* turn (over); ted (hay).

оборв/анный *a.* torn, broken, cut short; broken (line); **—ать** *see* обрывать.

оборка *f.* flounce, trimming.

оборон/а *f.* defense; **—ительный** *a.* defens(iv)e, defended; **—ить, —ять** *v.* defend; **ный** *a.* defense; **—оспособность** *f.* (physiol.) defensive function; **—оспособный** *a.* prepared (for defense), defensive.

оборот *m.* revolution, rotation, turn; orbit (of satellite); (chem.) recycle; cycle; turning (round), circulation; (pipe) elbow; (com.) turnover; convolution; change of direction; reverse (side), back; (гг.) turn-around; **жиклёр быстрых —ов** accelerating nozzle; **—ы** *pl.* (engine) speed; **—ы в минуту** revolutions per minute, rpm; **на . . . о.** by . . . a revolution; **на —е** on the reverse (side); overleaf; **поступать в о.** *v.* be recycled; **пускать в о.** circulate; **работать на малых —ах** *v.* idle; **работать на полных —ах** *v.* run at full power; **с малым числом —ов** slow-speed; **сбавить —ы, сбросить —ы** *v.* slow down; **счётчик —ов** speedometer; **увеличить —ы** *v.* accelerate (engine); **число —ов** rotation speed.

оборотистый *a.* resourceful, clever.

оборотить *see* оборачивать.

оборотливый *see* оборотистый.

обороти/ость *f.* (mach.) speed, revolutions per unit time; **—ый** *a. of* оборот; reverse, back, wrong (side); verso, left-hand (page); reusable (solution); recycled, recycling, return (water); utilizable (waste); **—ый капитал** current assets, circulating or floating capital, turnover fund; **—ый котёл** Scotch boiler, marine boiler; **—ый продукт** recycled product; **—ая система** circulation system.

оборудов/ание *n.* equipment, machinery; apparatus, instrumentation; facilities; plant, outfit; (out)fitting, installation; experiment; arrangement, system; **о. для сварки** welding equipment; **о. паром** steam working, steam driving; **о. транзисторами** transistorization; **машинное о.** machinery; **—анный** *a.* equipped, etc., *see v.*; featuring, incorporating; **—анный приборами** instrumented; **—ать** *v.* equip, provide, fit (with); supply; install; arrange.

оборыш *m.* (agr.) culls, rejects.

обосабливать *see* обособлять.

обоснов/ание *n.* basis, ground; reason; rationale; control; survey, study; **высотное о.** (geod.) vertical control; **—анность** *f.* validity, soundness; **—анный** *a.* valid, sound; substantiated, well-founded; **—(ыв)ать** *v.* base, ground; prove, substantiate.

обособ/ить *see* обособлять; **—ление** *n.* isolation, etc., *see v.*; **—ленно** *adv.* apart, by oneself or itself; **—ленность** *f.* isolation, etc., *see v.*; independence, individualism; **—ленный** *a.* isolated, etc., *see v.*; solitary; autonomous; individual, single, separate; **—лять** *v.* isolate, separate, segregate, set apart; detach; insulate; **—ляться** *v.* separate, stand out.

обостр/ение *n.* aggravation, sharpening, etc., *see v.*; (med.) exacerbation; (electron.) peaking; **—ённость** *f.* intensity, acuteness; **—ённый** *a.* aggravated, etc., *see v.*; acute, sharp; keen (interest); **—ённый выборочный контроль** (math.; stat.) tighten sampling; **—итель** *m.* sharpener; peaker; **—ить, —ять** *v.* aggravate, sharpen, intensify, enhance, increase, strengthen; accentuate; strain; **—иться, —яться** *v.* become sharp; grow acute; **—яющий** *a.* aggravating, etc., *see v.*; peaking (circuit).

оботрёт *fut. 3 sing. of* обтереть.

обоч/ина *f.* berm, shoulder (of road); roadside, wayside; border, edge; **—ный** *a.* roadside.

обошедший *past act. part. of* обойти.

обошьёт *fut. 3 sing. of* обшить.

обоюд/но *adv.* mutually, reciprocally; **—ность** *f.* mutuality; reciprocity; **—ный** *a.* mutual, reciprocal; **—о-** *prefix* mutually; **—овогнутый** *a.* concavo-concave, biconcave; **—овыпуклый** *a.* convexo-convex, biconvex; **—оострый** *a.* double-edged; **—осторонний** *a.* mutual.

обр. *abbr.* (образец) sample, specimen.

обрабатываем/ость *f.* workability, etc., *see a.*; **о. на станках** machinability; **—ый** *a.* workable, processable; treatable; machinable; in process; processed, worked, tilled, plowed, arable, crop (land); **—ая деталь** work, job.

обраб/атывание *see* обработка; **—атывать** *v.* process, treat, digest; work, machine, tool; turn (on lathe); size, cut, trim; finish, dress; face, surface; process, handle (data); adapt, condition; prepare, manufacture; develop, elaborate (plans); (agr.) cultivate, till, farm; **—атывать гепарином** (med.) heparinize; **—атывать на станке, механически —атывать** machine, tool; **—атывать начисто** finish; **—атывать паром** steam; **—атывать предварительно** pretreat, prepare; condition; **—атываться** *v.* be processed, etc.; be in process; **—атывающий** *a.* processing, etc., *see v.*; process (industry); **—отанный** *a.* processed, etc., *see v.*; **—отать** *see* обрабатывать.

обработк/а *f.* treatment; digestion; adaptation; manufacture, preparation; (information) retrieval; (stat.) analysis; evaluation (of data), processing, (agr.) tillage, cultivation; **о. давлением** mechanical working; **о. данных** data processing; **о. кислотой** acid treatment; **о. резанием** machining; **подвергать механической —и** *v.* machine, tool; **поточная о.** bath processing, in-line processing; **предварительная о.** pretreatment, preparation; conditioning.

обработ/очный *a. of* обработка; **—чик** *m.* handler.

обрадоваться *v.* be glad, be pleased.

обравнивать *v.* level, even up, trim.

образ *m.* shape, form; manner, way; image representation; pattern; trend (of thought); **о. действия** procedure; policy; **о. жизни** (mode of) life, habit(s), pattern; **каким —ом** how, in what manner; **некоторым —ом** in a way, after a fashion, somehow; **никоим —ом** by no means; **таким —ом** thus, in this way, by this means, so.

образ/ец *m.* specimen, sample, model, example, prototype; test piece; (met.) test specimen, test bar; pattern, shape, form, type; standard, original; **о. для испытаний** test piece, specimen; **взятие —цов, выбор —ца, забор —ца, отбор —цов** sampling; **опытный о.** prototype, test specimen; **сделать по —цу** *v.* duplicate, pattern (after); **о.-кубик** *m.* (concrete) test cube; **о.-свидетель** *m.* control sample.

образн/ость *f.* imagery, vividness, color; **—ые** *pl. suffix* (biol.) **—(i)formes**; **—ый** *a.* descriptive; figurative; graphic; *suffix* -shaped, **—form**, -resembling, **—oid**; **—ый камень** (min.) figure stone, agalmatolite.

образов/авшийся *see* образованный; **—ание** *n.* formation, etc., *see* образовывать; origin, genesis; development; occurrence; (chem.) gelation; **—ание гелf** gelation; **—ание жира** lipogenesis; **—ание зародышей** (phys.) nucleation; **—ание корки** crusting; **—ание осадка** precipitation; **—ание пены** foaming; **высшее —ание** higher education, college education; **в момент —ания** nascent, in the nascent state; **неправильное**

—ание malformation; **с —анием** forming, yielding, giving; educated; **—анность** *f.* education; **—анный** *a.* formed, etc., *see* **образовывать;** educated.

образов/атель *m.* organizer, creator; **—ательный** *a.* forming, etc., *see* v.; formative (cell); educational; **—а-тельная ткань** (bot.) nascent tissue, meristem; **—(ыв)ать** *v.* form, produce, make, combine (into); give, yield; evolve, generate (gas, heat); constitute, make up, comprise; compose; organize, establish, originate, develop; educate, teach, instruct; **—ать пузырь-ки** bubble; **—ать складки** fold; **—(ыв)аться** *v.* form, develop, originate, arise, appear; be educated.

образ/ующая *f.* (math.) generatrix; generator (of cone); element (of cylinder); **высота по —ующей** slant height (of cone); **—ий** *a.* forming, etc., *see* **образовы-вать; —ийся (при этом)** *a.* resulting, resultant; **—уя** *pr. ger. of* **образовывать,** forming, etc.

образцов/ый *a.* sample, model, exemplary, classical, standard, master, original; perfect, best, optimum; reference, calibrating (instrument); check (gage); proof (coin); **—ая гиря** standard weight; **—ая мера** standard (measure); **—ое сопротивление** calibration resistance; comparison rheostat.

образчик *m.* sample, specimen; pattern.

обральдрук *m.* duplicating process.

обрам/ить *v.* frame; **—ление** *n.* framing, framework; housing, box; mask; (geol.) rimrock; **—лённый** *a.* framed; **—лять** *v.* frame.

обраст/ание *n.* overgrowing; fouling (of ship, etc.); (marine) growth; **—атель** *m.* fouling organism; (biol.) epibiont; **—ательный** *a.* epibiotic; **—ать, —и** *v.* overgrow (with); foul, cover, surround; be encrusted with marine growth.

обрат *m.* skimmed milk; usable waste.

обрати/мость *f.,* **о. хода** reversibility; **—мый** *a.* reversible; (math.) invertible (group); **—мая связь** feedback; **—ть** *see* **обращать.**

обратная *f.* inverse, converse.

обратно *adv. and prefix* back, inversely, conversely, reversibly; as a reciprocal of; vice versa; counter—; ob-(reversely, in an opposite direction); **о. пропорцио-нально** as the reciprocal of, inversely with; **о. пропор-циональный** *a.* inversely proportional; **о. текущий** *a.* returning (liquid), reflux; **идти о.** *v.* return, retrace one's steps.

обратно/е *n.* inverse, reverse, opposite; **—идущий** *a.* retrograde, retrogressive; returning; **—квадратиче-ский** *a.* inverse-square-law; **—коничиский** *a.* obconic, inversely conical; **—ланцетный** *a.* (bot.) oblanceolate; **—сердцевидный** *a.* obcordate, inversely heart-shaped; **—ступенчатый** *a.* backstep (welding); **—яйцевидный** *a.* obovate, inversely egg-shaped.

обратн/ый *a.* reverse, return, back(ward); counter, opposite; (math.) inverse; retrograde (condensation, etc.); far (side of moon); check, no-return (valve); negative (correlation); re—, *e.g.* **—ая абсорбция** reabsorption; **о. вход** re-entry; **о. ом** (elec.) reciprocal ohm, mho; **о. поток** reflux; **о. преобразователь** (elec.) inverter; **о. удар** kick(back), recoil; backfire (of motor); **о. удар пламени** flashback; **дать о. удар** *v.* kick back; **о. ход** return (motion), reverse running, backing, back stroke of piston); **дать о. ход** *v.* reverse, back (up); **—ого хода** reverse (lever, etc.); **с —ым ходом** reversing, reflux; **о. холодильник** reflux condenser; **о. час** (nucl.) inverse hour, inhour; **—ая величина, —ая дробь** (math.) reciprocal; **—ая вспышка** back-fire, flashback; **—ая ёмкость** (comp.) stiffness; **—ая продувка** (gas chromatography) back purge; **—ая ре-**

акция back reaction; **—ая связь** feedback; **цепь —ой связи** feedback circuit; **—ая сторона** reverse; **—ая эмульсия** water-in-oil emulsion; **—ое влия-ние, —ое действие** re(tro)action; имеющий **—ое действие** retroactive; **—ое движение** return movement, back stroke (of piston); retrograde motion (of cathode spot); **—ое добывание** recovery (from waste); **—ое положение** converse (of theorem); **—ое течение** reflux; **—ое титрование** back titration; **—ое управление** feedback control; **—ого направления** reverse; **—ой волны** reverse-wave (tube); **—ой пос-ледовательности** negative-sequence (reactance); **—ой почтой** by return mail; **на —ом пути** on the way back, while returning.

обращаемость *f.* circulation; turnover.

обращать *v.* turn, change, convert, transform; reduce; reverse; invert (sugar); circulate; give (consideration); call, draw, direct, pay (attention); **о. в нуль** make . . . vanish; **—ся** *v.* turn, rotate, circle, revolve (around); circulate; return, revert; address, refer (to), apply, appeal, turn (to); handle, manipulate, treat; be transformed (into), turn into, become; **—ся вокруг** circulate, recycle; rotate; **—ся к** direct attention; **—ся плохо** maltreat, abuse.

обращающий *a.* turning, etc., *see* **обращать; —ся** *a.* rotating; circulating.

обращен/ие *n.* revolution, rotation, turn; circulation; application, appeal; treatment, usage, handling, manipulation, care (for); distribution; transformation, conversion, reduction; reversal; inversion; (comp.) reference, access; call (to a subroutine); **о. фаз** phase inversion; **время —ия** access time; **пустить в о.** *v.* issue, circulate, put in circulation; **температура —ия** transition point.

обращённый *a.* turned (to), exposed, facing, presented (to); reversed; inverse, inverted; invert (sugar) **о. вверх** supine.

обрез *m.* cut, gash; edge (of paper); recess (in wall); (ingot) crop; (rolling) crop shear; discard; (half-)tub; sawed-off shotgun; **в о.** barely enough; **—ание** *n.* cutting (off), etc., *see* v.; cut-off; **—анный** *a.* cut (off), etc., *see* v.; **—атель** *m.* (pulse) chopper; **—ать** *v.* cut (off, back, short); (hort.) clip, crop, trim, prune; lop, top; (cryst.) truncate; (med.) amputate; circumcise.

обрезин/енный *a.* rubberized, rubber-coated; **—ивание** *n.,* **—ка** *f.* rubberizing, rubber coating; **—и(ва)ть** *v.* rubberize, coat with rubber.

обрез/ка *see* **обрезание;** edging; **—ковый** *a.* scrap; **—ной** *a.* cut(-off), trimming; rip (saw); **—ной станок** trimmer; **—ок** *m.* piece, cut, length, end; **—ки** *pl.* ends; cuttings, clippings, shavings, scrap; **—очный** *a.* cut (off), trimmed; scrap; **—чик** *m.* trimmer; **—ыва-ние** *see* **обрезание; —ывать** *see* **обрезать; —ь** *f.* cuttings, crop ends, scrap, discard.

обремен/ение *n.* overloading, etc., *see* v.; **—ительный** *a.* burdensome, overwhelming, heavy; **—ить, —ять** *v.* overload, (over)burden, overtax; encumber; clog.

обре/сти, —тать *v.* find, discover; **—тение** *n.* finding, discovery; **—тённый** *a.* found, discovered.

обреше/тина *f.* (roof) purlin; lathwork; **—тить** *v.* board, sheath (roof); provide with a grate.

обрешёт/ка boarding, sheathing; bracing; grate; lathwork, lattice; (constr.) furring; **—ник** *m.* lathing; **пе-реплёт —ника** latticework.

обрешечивать *see* **обрешетить.**

обрив/ание *n.* shaving; **—ать** *v.* shave.

обрисов/ать, —ывать *v.* sketch, outline; **—ка** *f.* sketch, outline, outlining.

обрить *see* **обривать.**

обровн/енный *a.* evened out, smoothed; **—ять** *v.* even out, smooth.

обронить *v.* drop, let fall, lose.

оброс/лость *f.* overgrowth (with hair); **—т** *see* **обрастание; —ший** *a.* overgrown (with); (naut.) foul.

оброт/ать *v.,* **—ь** *f.* halter.

обруб *m.* trimming, etc., *see v.*; trimmed end; log framework; **—ание** *see* **обрубка; —ать, —ить** *v.* trim, cut (off), clip, prune (trees); chop off, lop off, crop, shorten; knock off, chip off; **—ка** *f.* trimming, etc., *see v.*; **—ленный** *a.* trimmed, etc., *see v.*; **—ная** *f.* (foundry) cleaning shop; fettling shop; **—ной** *a.* trimming, etc., *see v.*; **—ок** *m.* block, trunk, stump; lump, piece; **—ки** *pl.* scrap, chippings; **—очный** *see* **обрубной; —щик** *m.* fettler.

обруч *m.,* **—ный** *a.* hoop, band, collar; (vet.) exostosed ring-bone; **—еосадочный** *a.* hoop-driving.

обруш/ать *see* **обрушивать; —ение** *n.* caving (in), etc., *see v.*; cave-in, collapse; demolition; **—енный** *a.* caved in, etc., *see v.*; fallen, collapsed; **—ивание** *see* **обрушение; —и(ва)ть** *v.* cave in, knock down, breaks down, demolish; peel, husk, scour, shell, hull, decorticate, debark; **—и(ва)ться** *v.* cave in, come down, collapse, fall (down), break down, crumble; **—ившийся** *see* **обрушенный; —ка** *see* **обрушивание.**

обрыв *m.* precipice, cliff, bluff, escarpment, (e)scarp; (down)fall; drop (in mold); break(ing) off, breakage; termination (of reaction); torque failure, twist-off; deletion (of chromosome); **реле —а** line break relay; **—ание** *n.* breaking, etc., *see v.*; **—атель** *m.* plucker, picker; **—ать** *v.* break; pluck, pick, tear off; intercept, cut off; dig around; **—аться** *v.* break, tear (off); fall; stop suddenly.

обрывист/ость *f.* steepness, abruptness; **—ый** *a.* steep, abrupt, precipitous; clipped, scamping (speech).

обрыв/ность *f.* breaks, breakage; tears; (text.) end-breakage rate; **—ный** *a. of* **обрыв; —ок** *m.* scrap, fragment, bit; patch; **—очный** *a.* patched, pieced.

обрызг *m.* sprinkle, spray(ing); (plaster) scratch coat; **—ганный** *a.* sprinkled, etc., *see v.*; **—гивание** *n.* sprinkling, etc., *see v.*; **—гиватель** *m.* sprinkler, sprayer; **—ги(ва)ть** *v.* sprinkle, spray, splash; perfuse; wet, moisten.

обрыскать *v.* search everywhere, hunt.

обрыт/ый *a.* dug up; **—ь** *v.* dig up.

обрюзг/лый, —ший *a.* edematous, fat and flabby; **—нуть** *v.* grow fat and flabby.

обряд *m.* ceremony, rite; **—ка** *f.* trussing (of bird carcass); **—овый** *a.* ritual, ceremonial.

обса/дить *see* **обсаживать; —дка** *f.* compression, shortening, etc., *see v.*; swage; (min.) casing; **—дный** *a.,* **—дные трубы** casing; **—дочный** *a.* drive; **—женный** *a.* compressed, etc., *see v.*; thickly sown; **—живание** *n.* compressing, etc., *see v.*; **—живать** *v.* compress, shorten, upset, swage; case (a well); plant (around).

обсаливать *v.* salt (all over).

обсасывать *v.* suck around.

обсахаривать *v.* sugar, candy; saccharify.

обсев *m.* sowing, seeding; bare spot; standing crop; **—ать** *v.* sow, seed; **—ки** *pl.* chaff, siftings; **—ок** *m.* bare spot.

об/сек. *abbr.* [оборот(ы) в секунду] revolutions per second, rps.

обсекать *v.* cut off, trim.

обсемен/ение *n.* sowing, seeding; **искусственное о.** artificial insemination; **—ённость** *f.* dissemination; bacterial contamination; **—ённый** *a.* sown, seeded; disseminated; **—ительный** *a.* sowing, seed(ing); **—ить, —ять** *v.* sow, seed, plant; inseminate; disseminate; **—иться** *v.* go to seed, shed seeds.

обсерва/тория *f.,* **—торский** *a.* observatory; **—ционный** *a.* observation; observatory; **—ция** *f.* observation.

обсеребрение *n.* silvering, silver-plating.

обсеч/ение *n.,* **—ка** *f.* cutting off, trimming; **—ки** *pl.* trimmings, scrap; **—ь** *v.* trim, cut off.

обсея/нный *a.* sown; **—ть** *v.* sow.

обсидиан *m.* (petr.) obsidian, volcanic glass, rhyolite glass; **—иты** *pl.* obsidianites, obsidian pebbles.

об/ск. *see* **об/сек.**

обскабливать *v.* scrub, scour, scrape off.

обский *a.* (geog.) Ob.

обскоблить *see* **обскабливать.**

обследов/ание *n.* inspection, etc., *see v.*; test (run); analysis; operating test (of process unit); survey; (med.) examination; **о. на выбор** screening; **—анный** *a.* inspected, etc., *see v.*; **—атель** *m.* inspector; **—ательский** *a.* inspector's, inspection; **—ать** *v.* inspect, investigate, examine, check.

обследуемый *a.* examined; *m.* examinee.

обслуженный *a.* serviced, maintained.

обслужив/аемый *a.* service(d), served; attended; **—ание** *n.* servicing, etc., *see v.*; service(s), maintenance, care, attendance; operation; accommodation; **массовое о.** (comp.) queuing; **техническое —ание** maintenance; **машина технического —ания** maintenance vehicle; **—ать** *v.* service, maintain, care (for), take care (of), attend (to); operate, handle, serve, cover; cater (to, for); accommodate (with); **—ающий** *a.* servicing, etc., *see v.*; service, maintenance; auxiliary; *m.* attendant, service man; **—ающий персонал** attendants; **—ающее лицо** attendant, servicer.

обслужить *see* **обслуживать.**

обсм/атривать, —отреть *v.* examine, inspect.

обсолить *v.* salt (all over).

обсос/анный *a.* sucked around; **—ать** *v.* suck around; **—ки** *pl.* (anode) scrap; **—чик** *m.* suction nozzle.

обсохнуть *see* **обсыхать.**

обсоюзка *f.* (leather) foxing.

обста/вить, —влять *v.* surround, encircle, enclose; furnish; set up, arrange; **—новка** *f.* furniture, furnishings; setting, arrangement; circumstances, conditions, situation.

обстипация *f.* (med.) obstipation.

обстоятель/но *adv.* thoroughly, in detail; **—ный** *a.* circumstantial, detailed, exhaustive; thorough, reliable; **—ство** *n.* circumstance, case; (gram.) adverb; **—ства** *pl.* condition, situation; **имея в виду это —ство** with this in mind; **по —ствам** as appropriate, as the condition may require.

обсто/ять *v.* be, get along; **иначе —ит дело с** not so with, it is different with.

обстрагивать *see* **обстругать.**

обстраив/ание *n.* building; **—ать** *v.* build (around), construct.

обстрачивать *v.* hem.

обстрел *m.* fire, firing, bombardment; **—ивать, —ять** *v.* fire on, bombard.

обстри/гание *n.* cutting, etc., *see v.*; **—гать** *v.* cut, crop, shear, clip; **—женный** *a.* cut, etc., *see v.*, shorn.

обстро/гать *see* **обстругать; —жка** *see* **обстругивание.**

обстро/ить *v.* build (around); **—йка** *f.* building.

обстроч/ить *v.* hem; **—ка** *f.* hemming.

обструг/ивание *n.* planing, etc., *see v.*; **—(ив)ать** *v.* plane, smooth off, clean off, trim.

обструк/тивный *a.* obstructive; **—ция** *f.* obstruction, obstacle.

обстук/ать, —ивать *v.* knock (all around); (cold hardening) bombard (with steel balls); **—ивание** *n.* knocking; bombardment; tap test.

обступ/ать, —ить *v.* surround.

обсу/дить *see* **обсуждать**; **—ждаемый** *a.* under discussion; **—ждать** *v.* discuss, consider, treat, cover, go into, review (a situation); dispute, debate; **—ждаться** *v.* be discussed; discuss, be concerned (with), cover, deal (with); **—ждение** *n.* discussion, dispute; consideration; (design) review; **предмет —ждения** the issue; **—ждённый** *a.* discussed, etc., *see v.*; **—живать** *see* **обсуждать**.

обсуш/енный *a.* dried; **—ивание** *n.,* **—ка** *f.* drying, desiccation; **—и(ва)ть** *v.* dry.

обсч/ёт *m.* miscount, miscalculation; **—ит(ыв)ать** *v.* short-change; estimate, assess; **—ит(ыв)аться** *v.* miscount, miscalculate.

обсып/ать *see* **осыпать**; **—ка** *f.* sprinkling; cushioning layer.

обсыхать *v.* get dry, dry (up).

обтаивать *v.* thaw, melt around.

обтаптывать *v.* trample, pack.

обтач/ать *v.* stitch around; **—ивание** *n.* turning, etc., *see v.*; **—ивать** *v.* turn (on lathe), machine, round off; dress, face; grind; stitch around; **—ка** *f.* stitching around, overcasting.

обтаять *see* **обтаивать**.

обтек/аемость *f.* streamlining; **—аемый** *a.* streamline(d); **—ание** *n.* flowing around, etc., *see v.*; flow (-around), flow-past; **картина —ания** streamline flow; **—атель** *m.* deflector, shield; cowl, fairing; (av.) cowl(ing); (propeller) cone; (sonar) dome; (antenna) cap; **—ать** *v.* flow around, circumvent, pass around, by-pass; stream past, flow past; **—ающий** *a.* flowing around, etc., *see v.*; circumvent, circumfluent.

обтереть *see* **обтирать**.

обтёртый *a.* wiped, etc., *see* **обтирать**; worn.

обтёсанный *a.* rough-hewn, squared, etc., *see v.*; **грубо о.** rough-finished.

обтесать, обтёсыв/ать *v.* rough-hew, rough-work, chip, square; dress, trim; **—ка** *f.,* **—ивание** *n.* rough-hewing, etc., *see v.*

обтечь *see* **обтекать**.

обтир/ание *n.* wiping, etc., *see v.*; rub(bing); **—ать** *v.* wipe, swab, clean; dry; rub; wear (away, out); **—ка** *see* **обтирание**; swab cloth; **—очный** *a.* wiping, etc., *see v.*

обтоптать *v.* trample, pack.

обточ/енный *a.* turned (on lathe), machined; **—ить** *see* **обтачивать**; **—ка** *f.,* **—ный** *a. see* **обтачивание**; **лобовая —ка, поперечная —ка, торцовая —ка** (sur)facing.

обтрёп/анный *a.* worn out, frayed; **обтрепать, —ы-вать** *v.* wear out, fray; swingle (flax); **обтрепаться, —ываться** *v.* get worn, fray.

обтрескаться *v.* crackle, crack all over.

обтрясти *v.* shake off.

обтузиловая кислота obtusilic acid.

обтуратор *see* **обтюратор**.

обтыкать *v.* stick all around.

обтюр/атор *m.,* **—аторный** *a.* obturator, seal, cut-off; baffle plate, shield; diaphragm, stop; (phot.) shutter; spec. rotating shutter; **—ационный** *a.* obturation, ob-

structive; occlusive (ileus); **—ация** *f.* obturation, closing, stopping, sealing.

обтя/гивание *n.* stretching, etc., *see v.*; **—гивать** *v.* stretch (over), cover, jacket, coat; **—жечный** *a.* stretching; **—жка** *f.* cover(ing); **в —жку** tight-fitting; **—жной** *a.* covering; covered; **—нуть** *see* **обтягивать**.

обув/ать *v.* provide with shoes; **—ной** *a.* shoe; **—щик** *m.* shoemaker; **—ь** *f.* footwear, shoes.

обугл/енный *a.* carbonized, charred; **—ероживание** *n.* carbonizaton; (met.) carburization, carburizing; **—ива-емый** *a.* carbonizable; **—ивание** *n.* carbonization, charring; **—и(ва)ть** *v.* carbonize; char; **—ивающий** *a.* carbonizing; **—ивающийся** *a.* carbonizing, carbonizable.

обуж/ение *n.* narrowing, tightening; **—енный** *a.* narrow(ed), tight; **—ивать** *v.* (make) narrow, make tight, tighten.

обузд(ыв)ать *v.* bridle; restrain, repress, curb, (keep in) check, control.

обузить *see* **обуживать**.

обуревать *v.* agitate, shake.

обусл/авливать, —овить *see* **обусловливать**; **—ов-ленность** *f.* dependence; stipulation; **—овленный** *a.* caused, etc., *see v.*; due to, resulting (from), stemming (from); conditional; **—овливать** *v.* cause, be responsible (for); specify, stipulate, define, determine, dictate, govern; make conditions; condition; **—овливаться** *v.* depend (on), be determined (by), result, spring, stem, arise (from).

обут/ый *a.* shod; (bot.) booted, peronate; **—ь** *see* **обу-вать**.

обух *m.* butt, head (of axe); back (edge); (naut.) eye-bolt, lug.

обуч/аемость *f.* rate of learning; trainability; **—аемый** *a.* taught; learning (machine); *m.* trainee; **—ать** *v.* teach, instruct, train; **—аться** *v.* be taught, learn; **—а-ющий** *a.* teaching, training; tutorial; **—ение** *n.* teaching, instruction, training; schooling, education, learning; **—енный** *a.* taught, trained; **—ить** *see* **обучать**.

обушок *m.* back (edge); pick; eye bolt.

обхаживать *see* **обходить**.

обхват *m.* clasp(ing), hold, engagement, encompassing, girth; circumference; grasp; strap; (math.) perimeter; **угол —а** angle of contact; **—ить, —ывать** *v.* clasp, hold, embrace, girth, surround, envelop; **—ывающий** *a.* clasping, etc., *see v.*; (mech.) female.

обход *m.* by-pass, diversion; pass(ing) around, circumvention; avoidance; alternate route, detour; beat, round, patrol(ling); (commun.) alternative trunking; **о. кон-тура** (math.) path tracing; **в о.** bypassing, indirectly; **направлять в о.** *v.* divert, reroute (traffic).

обходить *v.* visit, make the rounds, go round; by-pass, circumvent, pass by or over, disregard, avoid, evade; deprive (of); **—ся** *v.* cost, come to; manage, do; treat; get used to; **—ся без** do without, dispense with; omit.

обходн/ый *a.* roundabout, circuitous, alternate, indirect; by-pass; (aut.) transfer (bus); **о. канал** by-pass; **о. путь** detour; **о. способ** makeshift, indirect method; **—ые выработки** (min.) by-passes, detour shafts.

обходчик *m.* inspector, patrolman.

об. ч. *abbr.* **(объёмная часть)** part by volume.

обчесать *see* **очесать**.

обчесться *see* **обсчитаться**.

обчи/стить, —щать *v.* clean, scour; peel, pare; **—стка** *f.* cleaning, etc., *see v.*

обшив/ание *n.* facing, etc., *see v.*; **—ать** *v.* face, line, sheathe, cover, case, jacket, coat; board, plank, panel, veneer, trim; sew around, edge, border; **—ка** *f.* facing, etc., *see v.*; sheath(ing); lagging, revetment; jacket; plating, shell, housing; board, plank, panel, veneer; (av.) skin, outer casing; edging, trim, border; **пояс —ки** strake (of ship); **—ной** *a.* of **обшивка;** sewn around; sewing; **—очный** *a.* of **обшивка;** cover (plate).

обширн/ость *f.* spaciousness, magnitude, vastness, expanse, latitude, field; **—ый** *a.* spacious, big, vast, broad, wide, ample, voluminous; comprehensive, extensive; **—ая мышца** (anat.) musculus vastus.

обшит/ый *a.* faced, etc., *see* **обшивать; о. сталью** steel-plated; **—ь** *see* **обшивать.**

обшкури(ва)ть *v.* grind, polish.

обшла/г *m.,* **—жный** *a.* cuff.

общ *sh. m.* of **общий.**

общаться *v.* associate, mix (with).

обще— *prefix* general(ly), widely, common(ly), universal(ly); All-.

общедоступн/ость *f.* accessibility; popularity; **—ый** *a.* accessible; popular.

обще/е *n.* the general; **—житие** *n.* home, hostel, boarding house; society, community; **—заводский** *a.* (common to the whole) plant; **—значимый** *a.* of general importance.

общеизвестн/о *adv.* commonly known; it is common knowledge; **—ость** *f.* common knowledge; **—ый** *a.* of common knowledge, well-known, universally known.

обще/народный *a.* general, public, people's, national; **—ние** *n.* association, intercourse, contact; **—образовательный** *a.* general instruction, nonspecialized; **—обязательный** *a.* compulsory, obligatory.

общеполезн/ость *f.* universal utility, world-wide use; **—ый** *a.* generally useful, universally beneficial.

обще/пользовательный *a.* general-purpose; **—понятный** *a.* popular, readily comprehensible, obvious, clear; **—признанный** *a.* generally acknowledged; **—принятый** *a.* generally accepted, universally adopted; universal, world-wide, standard; conventional (method); current; working (standard); **—производительный** *a.* overhead (expenses); **—равномерно** *adv.* equally, uniformly; **—распространённый** *a.* widespread, universally distributed. **—соматический** *a.* general (hospital); **—союзный** *a.* All-Union.

обществен/ик *m.* public worker; **—оживущий** *a.* social, gregarious; **—о-полезный** *a.* useful to the community; public; public opinion; **—о-экономический** *a.* social-economic; **—ый** *a.* social, public, common; mass (transportation); **—ая гигиена** public health; **—ого пользования** public access (area).

обще/ство *n.* society; community; association, company; **—ствоведение** *n.* social science; **—токсический** *a.* generally toxic; systemic (insecticide).

общеупотребительн/ость *f.* general use; **—ый** *a.* in general use, general-purpose, generally applicable, commonly used, current, customary; conventional (method).

обще/установленный *a.* common, standard; **—хирургический** *a.* surgical; **—хозяйственный** *a.* overhead (expenses); **—ядовитый** *see* **общетоксический.**

общ/ий *a.* general, common, public; total, aggregate, overall (length); combined, collective; output (information); universal; basic (problems); joint, mutual; communal, common; shared; generalized (infection); systemic (disease); integral (dose); secular (succession); (silv.) clear (cutting); miscellaneous; **о. азот** total nitrogen content; **о. для всех** in common; **о. делитель**

(math.) common divisor; **о. итог** total; lump sum; **о. остаток** total residue; **—ая мощность** unit capacity; total capacity; **—ая реакция** (biol.) systemic reaction; **—ее место** generality, commonplace; **—ее свойство рода** generic feature, peculiarity, property; **—ие определители** auxiliary subdivisions (of time, place, etc.); **—его действия** total; **—его назначения** multipurpose, universal; **в —ем** on the whole, in general.

общин/а *f.* community, society; common (pasture); **земельная о., крестьянская о.** common land.

общин/ывание *n.* plucking, etc., *see v.*; **—(ыв)ать** *v.* pluck, pick, pinch (off); nibble, browse.

общительный *a.* sociable, convivial.

общност/ь *f.* generality; community; unity, continuity; conformity, similarity; affinity; common character; common conditions; **коэффициент —и** index of similarity.

объ— *see* **о** (used before **е, ю, я**).

объед/ать *v.* eat around; corrode; **—аться** *v.* overeat; **—ение** *n.* overeating; **—енный** *a.* eaten (around, up); corroded.

объедин/ение *n.* union, joining, amalgamation, consolidation, unification; (math.) combination (of subgroups); building (of compound members); firm; society, association; (ecol.) consociation; conjunction; congregation, pool(ing); complex; integration, fusion, merger; (chem.) compound; **—ённый** *a.* united, etc., *see v.*; joint, associate; **—ительный** *a.* uniting; **—ить, —ять** *v.* unite, join, combine, pool, consolidate, amalgamate, unify; integrate; assemble; associate; merge; tie together; **—ять в себе** combine with; **—яться** *v.* unit, incorporate.

объед/ки *pl.* leavings, left-overs, remains; **—ья** *pl.* left-over fodder.

объез/д *m.* circuit, round; by-pass, detour, roundabout way; range; **—дить** *v.* make the rounds, inspect; visit (around); by-pass, detour; break in (horse); **—дка** *f.* going around, etc., *see v.*; **—дник** *m.* (forest) ranger; **—дной** *a.* detour, bypassing; visiting; **—дной путь** detour; **—дчик** *m.* watchman; (silv.) district officer; horse trainer; **—жать** *see* **объездить; —жий путь** detour.

объект *m.* object, item; entity; (research) subject, specimen, species; substance; objective, target; facility, installation, plant, station; member; (water) body; **о. регулирования** (comp.) controlled system.

объектив *m.* (opt.) objective (lens); **о.-анастигмат** *m.* anastigmat(ic lens); **—ация** *f.* (med.) objectivation; exteriorization; **—ность** *f.* objectivity; **—ный** *a.* objective; direct-observation; unbiased, unprejudiced; **—ное стекло** lens.

объект-микрометр *m.* stage micrometer.

объектно-характеристический *a.* plant characteristic (table).

объект/ный *a.* of **объект; о. код** compiled code (in machine language); **—одержатель** *m.* (micros.) slide.

объём *m.* volume, size, magnitude, quantity; amount; bulk, space, capacity, contents; weight; size; compass, extent, amplitude, scope; range (of hearing); body (of data); (drilling) footage, meterage; **о. материала** bulk; **о. работы** work load; **в —е** in bulk; **в процентах —а** per cent by volume; **измеритель —а** volu(meno)-meter; **испытание на о.** (nucl.) bulk test; **коэффициент —а** volumetric efficiency; **кубический о.** capacity; **мёртвый о.** dead storage (of reservoir); **полезный о.** effective capacity (of reservoir); **равные —ы** in equal shares; **соотношение —ов** volume ratio;

увеличиваться в —е *v.* expand; **удельный о.** specific volume.

объёмист/ость *f.* bulk(iness); **—ый** *a.* bulky, voluminous, capacious; unwieldy.

объёмл/ет *fut. 3 sing. of* **обнимать**; **—ющая** *f.* envelope; **—ющий** *a.* enveloping; envelope (curve); (bot.) equitant.

объёмно *adv.* volumetrically; in volume; **—аналитический** *a.* volumetric; titration, titrimetric; **о.-весовой** *a.* weight-space; **—сть** *f.* volume, capacity; (test.) bulking; (phot.) three-dimensional state; **—центрированный** *a.* (cryst.) body-centered.

объёмн/ый *a.* volume, volumetric, bulk; by volume; voluminous, bulky; three-dimensional; space (charge, velocity, etc.); cavity (resonator); positive-displacement (pump, etc.); dilute (phase of fluidized bed); **о. анализ** volumetric analysis; **о. блок** (building) module; **о. вес** specific weight, density; (soil) volume weight, apparent density; **о. контур** (electron.) cavity circuit; **о. коэффициент** (ionization) rate; volume ratio; **о. к.п.д.** ratio of actual to theoretical capacity (of pump); **о. процент** percent by volume; **о. центрированный** (cryst.) body-centered; **—ая волна** (seism.) body wave; **—ая доза** (nucl.) volume dose, integral dose; **—ая масса** density; **—ая плотность** volume density; **—ая производительность** volumetric efficiency; **—ая пряжа** bulk yarn; **—ая скорость потока** (chem.) flux rate; (phys.) flow rate; **—ая упругость** compressibility; **—ая часть** part by volume; **—ое количество** volume; **—ое отношение** volume ratio; **—ое число** specific volume; **—ым путём** volumetrically.

объёмометр *m.* volumenometer.

объесть *see* **объедать.**

объехать *see* **объезжать.**

объизвествл/ение *n.* calcification, lime deposition; **—ённый** *a.* calcified; **—ять** *v.* calcify.

объяв/итель *m.* advertiser; announcer; **—ить, —лять** *v.* advertise, announce; state, notify, declare; **—ление** *n.* advertisement, announcement; statement, declaration; bill, poster, notice; **доска для —лений** bulletin board.

объягниться *v.* (zool.) lamb.

объярь *f.* moire, watered silk.

объясн/ение *n.* explanation, comment, legend (of diagram); **—ённый** *a.* explained, etc., *see v.*; **—имый** *a.* explicable; explained; **—ительный** *a.* explanatory; **—ить, —ять** *v.* explain, elucidate, demonstrate, clear up; account (for), be responsible (for); **—иться, —яться** *v.* be explained (by); depend (upon); result, stem, arise, come (from); be due (to), be caused (by).

объяче/нный *a.* enmeshed, caught (in a net); **—иваться** *v.* become enmeshed or entangled; **—ивающий** *a.* gill (fishing net).

обыденн/ость *f.* commonness, usualness; **—ый** *a.* common, usual, everyday, ordinary.

обызвест/вление *n.* calcification; (agr.) liming; **—влённый** *a.* calcified; limed; **—влять** *v.* calcify; lime; **—кование** *n.* (physiol.) calcification; liming; (geol.) calcitization.

обыкновен/ие *n.* habit, custom, way; **по —ию** as usual.

обыкновенн/о *adv.* usually, ordinarily, as a rule; **как о.** as usual; **—ый** *a.* usual, customary, normal, regular, common, ordinary, simple, plain.

обымет *fut. 3 sing. of* **обнять.**

обындеветь *v.* get covered with frost.

обыск *m.,* **—(ив)ать** *v.* search.

обыскривание *n.* sparking.

обычай *m.* custom, usage, use, habit.

обычн/о *adv.* usually, etc., *see a.*; it is common (practice), it is customary; as a rule, more often than not; **—ый** *a.* usual, normal, regular, typical, ordinary, common(place), conventional, customary, routine, standard; plain; straight (text); (biol.) common (name); fixed-wing (aircraft); **—ое дело** commonplace; **—ым путём** in the usual fashion, as usual, routinely.

обэ, ОБЭ *abbr.* (**относительная биологическая эффективность**) relative biological effectiveness, RBE.

обязанн/ость *f.* duty, obligation, charge, responsibility; **—ый** *a.* obligated, under obligation, indebted; owe (to); **он обязан** he must, he has (to).

обязатель/но *adv.* without fail; be sure (to); certainly; by all means; of necessity; **—ый** *a.* obligatory, compulsory, mandatory, a must; legal; indispensable, required; helpful, cooperative; **—ная принадлежность** a must, indispensable; **—ство** *n.* obligation, engagement, commitment, contract; (law) liability; (socialist) pledge.

обяз(ыв)ать *v.* bind, oblige, engage.

ОВ *abbr.* (**отравляющее вещество**) toxic agent; **о-в** (**остров**) island; **о-ва** (**острова**) islands.

овал *m.* oval.

овалевое масло owala oil.

овал/огубцы *pl.* roundnose pliers; **—оцитоз** *m.* (med.) elliptocytosis; **—ьбумин** *m.* ovalbumin, egg-white albumin; **—ьно-** *prefix* ovato—, ovate; oval; **—ьно-ланцетовидный** *a.* (bot.) ovate-lanceolate; **—ьно-округлый** *a.* ovate-orbicular; **—ьность** *f.* ovalness, out-of-roundness; **—ьнотокарный станок** lathe for oval pieces; **—ьный** *a.* oval, out-of-round; (bot.) ovate.

овар/иальный *a.* (biol.) ovarian; **—ио—** *prefix* (anat.) ovario— (ovary); **—иолы** *pl.* (ent.) ovarioles; **—иотомия** *f.* (med.) ovariotomy; **—ит** *m.* ovaritis, oophoritis.

овевать *v.* (agr.) winnow, fan.

овер/драйв *m.* (automobile) overdrive; **—хенг** *m.* overhang; **—шот** *m.* (oil-well drilling) overshot.

овёс *m.* (bot.) oats (*Avena*).

овец *gen. pl. of* **овца.**

овеч *m.* (ichth.) sockeye salmon (*Oncorhynchus nerka ovetsch*).

овеч/ий *a.* sheep, ovine, **о. жиропот** wool grease; **о. копытный жир** sheep's-foot oil; **—ка** *f.* ewe lamb; (bot.) Boletus piperatus.

овеществ/ить, **—лять** *v.* reify; **—лённый** *a.* reified.

овеять *v.* (agr.) winnow, fan.

овивать *v.* coil, wind, twist (around).

овин *m.,* **—ный** *a.* (drying) barn.

овить *see* **овивать.**

ови/ум *m.* (biol.) ovium, mature ovum; **—цид** *m.* ovicide.

овлад/евать, **—еть** *v.* seize, take possession (of); master; **—ение** *n.* seizing; mastering.

о-во *abbr.* (**общество**) society.

ово— *prefix* (biol.) ovo— (ovum, egg cell); **—альбумин** *m.* ovalbumin; **—вителлин** *m.* (ovo)vitellin; **—генез** *m.* o(v)ogenesis, ovulation.

овод *m.* (ent.) gadfly, botfly; **желудочный о.** botfly (*Gasterophilus*).

оводн/ение *n.* irrigation; soaking, steeping; (chem.) hydration; **—енность** *f.* water content; degree of swelling; **—ять** *v.* irrigate; soak, steep; hydrate.

овод/овые *pl.* (ent.) Oestridae; **—ы** *pl.* tachinid flies (*Tachinidae*).

ово/идный *a.* ovoid, egg-shaped; **—клор** *see* **овотран; —мукоид** *m.* ovomucoid; **—скоп** *m.* ovoscope, candler; **—скопировать** *v.* candle (eggs); **—тран** *n.*

Ovotran (miticide); —**флавин** *m.* ovoflavin, D-riboflavin; —**фор(о)** *prefix* oophor(o)— (ovary); —**цит** *m.* (embr.) o(v)ocyte.

овощ *m.* vegetable; —**евод** *m.* vegetable grower, truck farmer; —**еводство** *n.* vegetable growing, truck farming; —**еводческий** *a.* vegetable-growing; truck (farm); —**езаготовка** *f.* vegetable supply; —**емойка** *f.* vegetable washer; —**ерезка** *f.* vegetable slicer; —**есушилка** *f.* vegetable dehydrator; —**есушильный** *a.* vegetable-drying; dehydrated vegetable (industry); —**етёрка** *f.* vegetable grater; —**ехранилище** *n.* vegetable storage pit or cellar; —**ечистка** *f.* vegetable peeler; —**и** *pl.*, —**ь** *f.* vegetables, greens; —**ной** *a.* vegetable; —**ные растения** vegetables.

ОВП *abbr.* (**окислительно-восстановительный потенциал**) oxidation-reduction potential, redox potential; (**каротаж относительных вызванных потенциалов**) constant current-induced potential logging.

овра/г *m.* gully, gulch, ravine, gorge; —**гозакрепительный** *a.* gully control (planting); —**гообразование** *n.* gullying, gully formation; ravine formation; —**жек** *dim. of* **овраг**; (mam.) suslik, gopher (*Citellus*); —**жистый** *a.* gullied; —**жность** *f.* extent of gully formation; degree to which area is subjected to gullying; —**жный** *a. of* **овраг**; pit (sand).

ОВС *abbr.* (**окислительно-восстановительная среда**) oxidation-reduction medium.

овс/а *gen. of* **овес**; —**ец** *m.* perennial oat (*Avenastrum*); —**инка** *f.* single oat stalk or grain; —**о** *prefix* oat; —**одробилка** *f.* oat grinder; —**озавод** *m.* oat mill; —**орушка** *f.* oat huller or clipper; —**осушилка** *f.* oat dryer; —**ошелушитель** *m.* oat huller; —**юг** *m.*, —**южный** *a.* wild oat (*Avena fatua*); —**южница** *f.* wild oat separator; —**яница** *f.* fescue (*Festuca*); —**янище** *n.* oat field; —**янка** *f.* oatmeal; (orn.) bunting (*Emberiza*); (ichth.) owsianka (*Leucaspius delineatus*); dace (*Leuciscus l.*); —**янки**, —**янковые** *pl.* (orn.) Emberizidae; —**овидный** *a.* oat-shaped; oat (cell); —**яной**, —**яный** *a.* oat; —**яной корень** (bot.) oyster plant, salsify (*Tragopogon porrifolius*); —**яноклеточный** *a.* (med.) oat cell (carcinoma).

овуляция *f.* (physiol.) ovulation.

овц/а *f.* sheep, ewe (*Ovis*); —**ебык** *m.* (mam.) musk-ox (*Ovibos moschatus*); —**евод** *m.* sheep breeder; —**еводство** *n.* sheep breeding; —**еводческий** *a.* sheep breeding; —**ематка** *f.* ewe; —**ферма** *f.* sheep farm.

овч/ар *m.* shepherd; —**арка** *f.* sheep dog; —**арник** *m.*, —**арня** *f.* sheep pen; —**ина** *f.*, —**инный** *a.* sheepskin; —**ина-голяк** *f.* sheared sheepskin.

Огайо (geog.) Ohio.

огар/ок *m.* cinder, ash; (met.) calcine; zinc cinders; **водочный о.**, **кислотный о.** niter cake, sodium bisulfate; —**ки** *pl.* cinders, esp. pyrite cinders; skimmings, scoria, discarded metal (of electrode); —**ь** *m.* (orn.) ruddy duck (*Tadorna* or *Casarca ferruginea*).

огболт *m.* eye bolt, eye ring.

огиб/ание *n.* rounding; diffraction (of waves); —**ать** *v.* round; bend round; —**ающая** *f.*, —**ающая кривая** (math.) envelope; —**ающий** *a.* rounding; circumflex (artery, veins).

огива *f.* (stat.) ogive.

ОГК *abbr.* (**окончательный газовый каротаж**) final mud logging.

оглавл/ение *n.* (table of) contents; index; —**енный** *a.* indexed; —**ять** *v.* index, prepare the table of contents.

огла/дить, —**живать** *v.* smooth out.

оглазури(ва)ть *v.* glaze.

огланлинский *a.* (geog.) Oglanly.

огла/сить, —**шать** *v.* publish, announce; —**ска** *f.* publicity; —**шение** *n.* publicizing; **не подлежащий** —**шению** confidential.

оглеен/ие *n.* (soil) gleization, gleying; —**ный** *a.* gley(ed).

оглинение *n.* argillization; claying (of soil).

оглоб/ельный *a.*, —**ля** *f.* shaft; poppet stringer (of launch).

оглох/нуть *v.* get deaf; —**ший** *a.* (growth) deaf.

оглум *m.* (med.) hydrocephalus.

оглуп/еть *v.* become stupid; —**ить**, —**лять** *v.* make stupid.

оглуш/ать, —**ить** *v.* deafen; stun, stupefy; —**ающее средство** stupefacient; —**ённый** *a.* deafened; stunned, dazed; —**ительный** *a.* deafening; stunning.

огля/деть *see* **оглядывать**; —**дка** *f.* looking back; care, caution; mistake, oversight; —**дывание** *n.* looking around, etc., *see* v.; —**дывать**, —**нуть** *v.* look around; look over, examine; —**дываться** *v.* look around; look back; proceed with caution.

огне— *prefix* pyro—, fire; —**видный** *a.* fire-like; (geol.) igneous, plutonic; —**вица** *f.* fever; (bot.) pellitory (*Anacyclus pyrethrum*).

огнёвка *f.* (ent.) pyralid moth; (mam.) red fox.

огнев/ой *a.* fire; (art.) firing; flame-colored; (geol.) pyrogenous, igneous; **о. ход** (flame) flue; —**ая зачистка** scarfing; —**ая камера**, —**ая коробка** firebox; combustion chamber; —**ая рафинировка** pyrorefining; —**ая точка** (art.) emplacement; —**ые работы** (min.) firing.

огнегаситель *m.*, —**ный прибор** fire extinguisher; —**ный** *a.* fire-extinguishing.

огнедышащ/ий *a.* active (volcano); —**ая гора** volcano.

огне/задерживающий *a.*, fire-retardant; —**задерживающее вещество** fire retardant; —**защита** *f.* fire barrier; —**защитный** *a.* fireproof(ing); flameproof (clothing); —**защитное средство** fire retardant.

огнемёт *m.* (mil.) flame thrower, flame projector; —**нозажигательный** *a.* flame and incendiary; —**ный** *a.* flame-throwing; fire-throwing, igneous.

огненно— *prefix* pyr(o) (fire); phlogi—, phlog(o); flame; —**водный** *a.* (geol.) igneo-aqueous; —**жидкий** *a.* molten, fused; —**красный** flame-colored; red hot; **о.-полированный** fire-polished.

огненный *a.* fire, igneous.

огнеопасн/ость *f.* inflammability, fire risk, fire hazard; —**ый** *a.* inflammable, subject to fire risk.

огне/постоянный *a.* fire-resistant, heat-stable; —**припасы** *pl.* (mil.) ammunition; —**провод** *m.* portfire, time fuse; —**проводный шнур** fuse; —**родный** *a.* (geol.) pyrogenous, igneous; —**смесь** *f.* burning mixture.

огнестойк/ий *a.* refractory, fireproof; heat-stable; noncombustible; —**ость** *f.* refractoriness; fire or flame resistance.

огнестрельн/ый *a.* firing; gunshot; bullet (wound); —**ое оружие** firearm(s); —**ые припасы** ammunition.

огне/сушилка *f.* open fire dryer; —**телки** *pl.* (zool.) Pyrosomida; —**трубный** *a.* fire-tube (boiler).

огнетушитель *m.*, —**ный прибор**, —**ное средство** fire extinguisher; —**ный** *a.* fire-extinguishing.

огнеупор *m.* refractory (material); —**ность** *f.* refractoriness, resistance to fire.

огнеупорн/ый *a.* fireproof, refractory; heat-resisting (metals); **о. кирпич** firebrick, refractory brick; —**ая глина** fire clay, refractory clay; —**ая набойка**, —**ая футеровка** refractory lining; brasque, steep.

огнецветк/а *f.* (ent.) cardinal beetle (*Pyrochroa*); —**и** *pl.* Pyrochroidae.

огни *pl. of* **огонь**; **—во** *n.* flint(stone); hanging line (of fish net); (min.) cap; **—стый** *a.* flame-colored; **—ще** *n.* bonfire (site).

огов/аривать, —орить *v.* stipulate, specify, mention; blame, accuse; **—орка** *f.* stipulation, reservation, clause.

огол/ение *n.* uncovering, etc., *see v.;* **—ённость** *f.* bareness; **—ённый** *a.* uncovered, etc., *see v.;* bare, naked, nude; bald, glabrate; **—ить** *v.* uncover, expose, strip, bare, denude; defoliate.

оголов/ник *m.* (tower) cap, assembly; **—ок** *m.,* **—ь** *f.* head(piece), cap, end; **—ье** *n.* headband; (bridle) halter, frontstall.

огол/ять *see* **оголить; —яющийся** *a.* (biol.) glabrescent; calvescent.

огонёк *dim. of* **огонь;** light; (bot.) globe flower (*Trollius asiaticus*).

огонь *m.* fire, flame; light; **разводить о.** *v.* fire up, kindle; **—ки** *pl.* (bot.) *see* **огонёк;** Adonis.

огоражив/ание *n.* enclosing, etc., *see v.;* enclosure; **—ать** *v.* enclose, fence in, rail in.

огород *m.* (truck) garden; **—ина** *f.* vegetables; **—ить** *see* **огораживать; —ник** *m.* gardener; **—ничать** *v.* garden; **—ничество** *n.* truck gardening; horticulture; **—ничий** *a.* garden(er's); **—ный** *a.* vegetable garden, kitchen garden.

огорож/а *f.* fence, enclosure; **—енный** *a.* enclosed, etc., *see* **огораживать.**

огорч/ать *v.* distress, vex, annoy; **—ение** *n.* distress, vexation, concern, annoyance; **—ённый** *a.* distressed, concerned; **—ительный** *a.* distressing, irritating; **—ить** *see* **огорчать.**

ОГП *abbr.* (**определение границ пласта**) reservoir limit test.

огра *f.* Ogra (Soviet thermonuclear mirror machine).

ограда *f.* fence, fencing, enclosure, wall; (anat.) cancellus; claustrum (of brain).

оградитель *m.* protector, guard; fender; **—ный** *a.* protecting, guard; enclosing **—ный щит** guard, fender; **—ные сооружения** (hydr.) breakwater, protecting structure.

оград/ить *see* **ограждать; —ка** *dim.;* **—ный** *a. of* **ограда.**

огражд/ать *v.* defend, guard, protect; enclose, fence; **—а-ющий** *a.* safety, security; enclosing; **—ение** *n.* guard-(ing), guardrail, safeguard, protection, safety device; enclosing, enclosure, fence, fencing, screen, barrier; locking.

огран/ённый *a.* cut; edged (crystal); **—и(ва)ть** *v.* cut (facets).

огранич/ение *n.* restriction, etc., *see v.;* (de)limitation, restraint, constraint; (petrol.) proration; (birth) control; **время —ения** clipping time; **—енность** *f.* limitedness; (math.) boundedness; scantiness; shortness (of time); **—енноядный** *a.* (zool.) oligophagous; **—енный** *a.* restricted, etc., *see v.;* meager, scanty; short (time); narrow(-minded); **—енный полом** sex-limited; **—ивание** *see* **ограничение; —ивать** *v.* restrict, bound, limit, set limits, confine, restrain; terminate; circumscribe, enclose (area); narrow; (electron.) clip; **—иваться** *v.* restrict, confine (oneself); be restricted, etc.; **—ивающий** *a.* restricting, etc., *see v.;* **—ивающий скорость** rate-limiting; **—ивающийся** *a.* restricted, confined.

ограничитель/ь *m.* stop, stop piece, stopping device, catch, arresting device; (electron.) (de)limiter; clipper; **о. импульсов, цепь —я импульсов** (instrumentation) clipping circuit; **о. тока** current limiter; **о. хода** stop, arrester; restraining arm; **постоянная времени**

—я clipping time; **—ьный** *a.* restricting, etc., *see* **ограничивать;** restricted; check (ring).

ограничить *see* **ограничивать.**

огранка *f.* cut(ting), faceting; (crystal) faces.

огребать *v.* rake around; take (swarm of bees).

огрёбки *pl.* rakings, scraps, remnants.

огревать *see* **обогревать.**

огрести *see* **огребать.**

огрех *m.* blemish, flaw, lapse, fault; gap, bare spot; (agr.) balk.

огромн/ость *f.* vastness; **—ый** *a.* vast, big, huge, immense, tremendous, great; paramount, prime; overwhelming (majority).

огрохочение *n.* screening.

огрский *a.* (geog.) Ogre.

огруб/е/(ва)ть *v.* coarsen, roughen; **—елость** *f.* roughness; **—елый** *a.* coarse(ned), rough; **—ение** *n.* coarsening; **—ить, —лять** *v.* roughen; desensitize.

огрудок *m.* gravel.

огрыз/(а)ть *v.* gnaw (all around); **—ок** *m.* remnant; (apple) core; (pencil) stub.

ОГТ *abbr.* (**общая глубинная точка**) common depth point.

огузок *m.* buttock, rump; rump hide.

огул/ом *adv.* wholesale, in a lump; all together; **—ьный** *a.* groundless, unfounded; indiscriminate.

огулявшийся *a.* fertilized (queen bee).

огур/ец *m.,* **—ечный** *a.* cucumber (*Cucumis,* spec. *C. sativus*); **бешеный о.** squirting cucumber (*Ecballium elaterium*); **—ечник** *m.* (ichth.) pond smelt (*Hypomesus olidus*); Arctic smelt (*Osmerus mordax dentex*); **—еч-ник, —ечная трава** (bot.) borage (*Borago officinalis*); **—цевидный, —цеобразный** *a.* cucumiform, cucumber-shaped; **морские —цы** (zool.) sea cucumbers (*Holothuroidea*).

одабривать *see* **одобрить.**

одалживать *v.* lend.

одарённый *a.* talented, gifted.

оде/вание *n.* dressing, etc., *see v.;* **—вать** *v.* dress, clothe; put on, cover, coat; face, revet; **—вать на** slip over, fit, mount on.

одёжка *see* **одежда.**

одежавель *m.* Javel water.

одежда *f.,* **одёжный** *a.* clothes, clothing; jacket, lining, insulation; (mach.) replaceable parts; facing, revetment; cover, surface, surfacing, topping, pavement.

одеколон *m.,* **—ный** *a.* eau de Cologne.

одел/ить, —ять *v.* give, present, endow (with); distribute, share.

одёргивать *v.* jerk down.

одеревен/евший, —елый *a.* lignified, etc., *see v.;* woody; **—елость** *f.* lignification; **—елость позвоночника** (med.) Strümpell-Marie disease; **—ение** *n.* lignification; **—еть** *v.* lignify, become woody; stiffen, harden.

одерж(ив)ать *v.* gain, win; **о. верх** overcome, get the upper hand, get the advantage (of).

одержим/о-навязчивый *a.* (med.) obsessive-compulsive; **—ость** *f.* obsession; **—ый** *a.* obsessed; afflicted (with); seized, overcome.

одерн/ение *n.,* **—овка** *f.* sodding, turfing; **—ованный** *a.* sodded, turfed.

одёрнуть *v.* jerk down.

одесский *a.* (geog.) Odessa.

оде/тый *a.* dressed, clothed, clad, coated; reveted, faced (slope); **о. снегом** snow-clad; **—ь** *see* **одевать; —я-ло** *n.* blanket, quilt; **—яние** *n.* (bot.) indumentum, hairy covering.

одз, ОДЗ *abbr.* (**ослепляющая дымовая завеса**) blinding smoke screen.

од/ин *m., a., pron.,* —**на** *f.,* —**но** *n.* one; a certain; a, an; alone, only, single; like (sign); **о. другого** one another, each other; **о. за другим** one after another; —**но и тоже** (it is) one and the same thing; **все до** —**ного** everyone; **по** —**ному** one by one, singly.

одинаков/о *adv.* in like manner, alike, equally; —**окрылые** *pl.* (ent.) termites (*Isoptera*); Homoptera; —**ость** *f.* sameness, identity, equality; homogeneity, uniformity; (color) match; —**ый** *a.* (the) same, identical, duplicate, equal, (a)like; uniform, homogeneous; common (to).

одинарный *a.* single; single-thickness, single-ply; one-piece; unitary; (chem.) unary; simple; (gen.) haploid.

одинец *m.* (navigation) rock, reef.

одиннадцати— *prefix* hendeca—, undecim— (eleven); —**плоскостной** *a.* (cryst.) hendecahedral; —**угольник** *m.* (geom.) hendecagon; —**угольный** *a.* hendecagonal; —**шарнирный** *a.* (comp.) eleven-pivot.

одиннадцат/ый *a.* eleventh; —**ь** eleven.

одино/кий *a.* single, solitary, unique, only, lone; lonely; —**чество** *n.* solitude, isolation; —**чноплодный** *a.* single-fruited; —**чный** *a.* single, separate, self-contained; solitary, isolated, sole, lone, only; individual, simple; **насос** —**очного действия** single-acting pump.

одиозный *a.* odious, repulsive, offensive.

одич/авший, —**алый** *a.* (run) wild, feral; savage; —**алость** *f.* wildness; —**ание** *n.* running wild, etc., *see v.;* —**ать** *v.* run, go, or grow wild.

одна *f.* of **один.**

однажды *adv.* once, one day.

однако *conj.* but, however, nevertheless, yet, still.

одн/и *pl.* of **один;** —**о** *n.* of **один.**

одно— *prefix* mono—, uni—, one-, single-; hapl(o)— (single, simple); —**адресный** *a.* single-address (computer); —**анодный** *a.* single-anode; —**аспектный** *a.* unidimensional, linear (classification); —**атомность** *f.* monovalency; —**атомный** *a.* monovalent, monatomic; monohydric (alcohol); —**базовый** *a.* single-base; —**бокий** *a.* lopsided; one-sided; —**бромистый** *a.* monobromide (of); monobromated (camphor); —**братственный** *a.* (bot.) monadelphous; —**брачие** *n.* (biol.) monogamy: —**брачный** *a.* monogamous; —**брусный** *a.* (agr.) single-cutterbar.

одновалентн/ость *f.* univalence; —**ый** *a.* univalent, monovalent.

одно/вальный *a.* single-shaft; —**ванный** *a.* single-bath; —**вариантный** *a.* monovariant, univariant; —**вершинный** *a.* single-vertex; unicuspid; (math.) unimodal; —**ветвистый** *a.* uniramous, one-branched; —**вибратор** *m.* (electron.) univibrator, one-shot multivibrator; —**винтовой** *a.* single-screw; —**витковый** *a.* (elec.) single-turn, single-coil; —**водный** *a.* monohydrate; —**возрастный** *a.* of the same age, even-aged, coeval, uniform.

одновременн/о *adv.* simultaneously, at the same time, concurrent(ly) (with); **существовать о.** *v.* coexist; —**ость** *f.* simultaneousness, synchronism, coincidence; —**ый** *a.* simultaneous, synchronous.

одно/генный *a.* (gen.) monogenic; —**главый** *a.* one-headed, monocephalous; —**глазый** *a.* one-eyed, monophthalmic; —**гнёздный** *a.* one-celled, unicellular, unilocular, monothalamous; single-chambered; monomerous; —**годичный** *a.* one-year; annual; —**годок** *m.* yearling; —**горбый** *a.* single-humped, unigibbous; —**горловый** *a.* single-neck(ed); single-die (tubing machine); —**губый** *a.* unilabiate; —**декадный** *a.*

(comp.) one-digit decimal; —**дерёвка** *f.* dugout (boat); —**диапазонный** *a.* single-band; —**дневка** *f.* (ent.) May fly, ephemerid; —**дневки** *pl.* Ephemeridae; —**дневный** *a.* one-day, ephemeral.

однодольн/ые *pl.* (bot.) monocotyledons; —**ый** *a.* monocotyledonous.

одно/домность *f.* (bot.) monoecism; —**домный** *a.* monoecious; —**дуантный** *a.* one-dee (cyclotron); —**жгутиковый** *a.* (zool.) uniflagellate, monociliated; —**желобчатый** *a.* single-groove; —**женство** *n.* monogamy; —**жильный** *a.* single-core, single (cable).

однозамещённ/ые *pl.* monoderivatives; —**ый** *a.* monosubstituted; —**ый фосфат кальция** monocalcium phosphate.

одно/зародышевый *a.* single-germ (seed); —**зарядно-положительный** *a.* with a single positive charge; —**зарядный** *a.* single-charged; —**заходный** *a.* single-thread, single-cut (screw); single (thread); —**звучный** *a.* monotone, monotonous.

однозёрный *a.* one-grained, monospermous.

однозернянка *f.* einkorn (*Triticum monococcum*).

однознач/ащий *a.* synonymous, identical; —**но** *adv.* unambiguously, uniquely, in a unique manner; —**ность** *f.* unambiguity; uniqueness; single-valuedness; univocacy; —**ный** *a.* unambiguous, unequivocal, clear, well-defined; single-value(d), one-valued (function, etc.); univocal; monovalent; synonymous; —**ное число** simple number, digit.

одно/зуб *m.* (zool.) Mononchus; —**зубчатый** *a.* monodont; —**иглистый** *a.* monacanthous, one-spined; —**имённый** *a.* homonymous, like(-named); similar, analogous, of the same kind; —**й** *gen., etc.* of **одна;** —**йодистый** *a.* monoiodide; —**калиберный** *a.* of the same caliber; —**калиевый** *a.* monopotassium.

однокамерн/ые *pl.* (prot.) Monothalama; —**ый** *a.* single-chamber, single-compartment; single-stage; single-bed (jig); (biol.) unilocular, unicamerate, monothalamous; simple (stomach).

одно/канальный *a.* single-channel; —**каскадный** *a.* single-stage, single-step; single-spool, single-rotor (compressor); —**катушечный** *a.* single-coil; —**качественный** *a.* (math.) isomorphic; —**квантовый** *a.* one-quantum; —**керновый** *a.* unipivot (instrument); —**кислотный** *a.* monoacid; —**клапанный** *a.* single-valved, one-valve; —**классник** *m.,* —**классница** *f.* classmate.

одноклеточн/ые *pl.* protozoa, one-celled animals; —**ый** *a.* unicellular, one-celled; —**ый организм** protozoon.

одно/клетьевой прокатный стан single-stand (rolling) mill; —**клиномерный** *a.* monoclinic; —**кнопочный** *a.* single-button, single-knob; —**ковшовый экскаватор** *m.* payloader; back hoe; —**колейка** *f.* single-track railroad; —**колейный** *see* **однопутный;** —**коленчатый** *a.* single-jointed, single-throw; —**колерный** *a.* monochromatic; —**колонный** *a.* single-column; open-side (machine); —**кольчатый** *a.* monocyclic; —**комнатный** *a.* one-room.

однокомпонентн/ый *a.* single-component; —**о, —ое топливо** (rockets) monopropellant.

одно/конный *a.* one-horse; —**контурный** *a.* single-circuit; —**координационный** *a.* (chem.) monodentate, unidentate; —**копытные** *pl.* whole-hoofed animals, solid ungulates; —**копытный** *a.* whole-hoofed, solid-ungulate; perissodactyl; —**корзиночный** *a.* (bot.) monocephalous; —**корпусный** *a.* single-unit; single-effect (evaporator); single-hull (ship); single-furrow (plow); —**косточковый** *a.* (bot.) monopyrenous; —**янка** *f.* unidrupe; —**красочный** *a.* monochromatic.

однократн/о *adv.* once, one time; **о. используемый** *a.* disposable; one-shot (rocket); **—оцветущий** *a.* (bot.) hapaxanthic; **—ый** *a.* single(-stage); once through; one-shot; single-pass (cracking); (wire drawing) single-draft; flash (distillation); shock (compression); **—ого действия** single-acting.

одно/кристальный *a.* single-crystal; (electron.) single-chip; **—крылый** *a.* single-blade; (bot.) monopterous, one-winged; single-leaf (bridge); **—крышечковые** *pl.* (mal.) Monoplacophora; **—курсник** *m.* classmate; **—ламповый** *a.* (rad.) single-tube; **—лёгочн(иков)-ые** *pl.* lung fishes (*Ceratodidae*); **—лемешный** *a.* single-furrow (plow); **—лепёстный** *a.* (bot.) monopetalous.

однолет/ка *f.* year-old seedling; **—ний** *a.* one-year (old), yearly, annual; **—нее растение, —ник** *m.* (bot.) annual; **—ок** *m.* yearling; seedling.

одно/линейный *a.* unilinear, single-line; **—листность** *f.* (math.) univalence; **—листный** *a.* single-leaved, monophyllous; (math.) one-sheeted; univalent, schlicht (function, etc.); **—листное отображение** univalent mapping; **—лонжеронный** *a.* single-spar (wing); **—лопастный** *a.* single-lobed, unilobate; **—лучевой** *a.* single-beam, single-ray; **—мастный** *a.* monochromic, solid-color; **—мерный** *a.* unidimensional, linear (flow); univariate; **—мерные временные ряды** (stat.) simple time series; **—местный** *a.* single seat (vehicle); (comp.) single-place; single-position; **—микросекундный** *a.* one-microsecond; **—модовый** *a.* supermode (laser); **—мозерский** *a.* (geog.) Odnomozero; **—молекулярный** *a.* monomolecular; **—моментный** *a.* instantaneous; one-stage (operation); **—моторный** *a.* single-motor; **—мужие** *n.* (biol.) monandry; **—мундштучный** *a.* single-die; **—мускульные** *pl.* (mal.) Monomyaria; **—направленный** *a.* unidirectional; **—натриевый** *a.* monosodium; **—нит(оч)-ный** *a.* unifilar monorail (conveyer); single-thread (screw); **—ногий** *a.* one-legged; **—носковый** *a.* single-spout; **—оборотный** *a.* single-cut, single-thread (screw).

однообраз/ие *n.* monotony, equality; similarity, uniformity; **—ный** *a.* monotonous, alike, equal, uniform; unchanging; monotonic (function).

одно/объективный *a.* single-lens; **-однозначный** *a.* one-to-one; **—окись** *f.* monoxide; **—осевой** *a.* uniaxial.

однооснóвн/ый *a.* monobasic; monohydric (alcohol); monofunctional (compound); **—ая карбоновая кислота** monocarboxylic acid.

однооснóсть *f.* (cryst.) uniaxiality; **—ый** *a.* uniaxial, monoaxial; single-axle.

одноотверстн/ые *pl.* (ichth.) deepsea eels (*Synaphobranchidae*); **—ый** *a.* single-entry.

одно/отказный *a.* fail-passive, fail-soft; **—палубный** *a.* single-deck; **—палые** *pl.* fingerfishes (*Monodactylidae*); **—палый** *a.* unidactyl, monodactylous; **—пальцевый** *a.* fingertip (control); **—парнорезцовые** *pl.* (mam.) Simplicidentata; **—парный** *a.* unijugate; **—перегородчатый** *a.* uniseptate; **—периодный** *a.* single-phase; sequential (key punch); **—перистый** *a.* unipennate; **—пёрый** *a.* single-finned; **—пестичный** *a.* (bot.) monogynous; **—пламенный** *a.* single-flame; **—платный** *a.* single-board (computer) **—плечий** *a.* (biol.) monobrachial; **—плодный** *a.* monocarpous; single (pregnancy); **—подкосный** *a.* single-lock (bridge); **—подовый** *a.* single-hearth (furnace); **—покровный** *a.* (bot.) monochlamydeous; **—полосный** *a.* single-band; **—полостный** *a.* (math.)

of one sheet; **—полупериодный** *a.* half-wave (circuit); **—полый** *a.* unisexual.

однополюсн/ость *f.* unipolarity; **—ый** *a.* unipolar; single-pole, monopolar; single-throw (switch).

одно/полярный *a.* single-pole, monopolar, unipolar; **—породный** *a.* monogenetic; uniform breed; **—порые** *pl.* (ent.) Monotrysia; **—постовый** *a.* (mach.) single-operator; **—поточный** *a.* single-flow; **—предельный** *a.* solid (gage); single-range (instrument); **—предсердные** *pl.* (mal.) Monotocardia, Pectinibranchia; **—преломляющий** *a.* singly refracting, **—проводный** *a.* single-wire, single-line; **—проволочный** *a.* unifilar; **—пролётный** *a.* single-span; **—проходные** *pl.* (mam.) Monotremata; **—проходный** *a.* monotrematous; single-pass (welding).

однопут/ка *f.* single-track railroad; **—ный** *a.* single-track, single-gage; single-line; one-way (street).

одно/размерный *a.* of equal dimensions; **—разовый** *a.* single, one-time, one-shot; disposable, expendable; **—разового пользования** disposable, throw-away (container); **—разрядный** *a.* one-column, single-digit (adder); **—реданный** *a.* (av.) single-step; **—реечный** *a.* simplex (classifier); **—резонаторный** *a.* single-cavity (laser); **—рельсовый** *a.* monorail, single-rail; **—ремешковый** *a.* single-belt; **—рогий** *a.* one-horned, monocerous; single (hook).

однородн/ость *f.* homogeneity, homogeneousness, uniformity, similarity; evenness (of fibers); **—ый** *a.* homogeneous, uniform, even, monotonous; similar, of the same kind; pure (notation).

одно/ростковый *a.* (bot.) monogerm, single-seed; **—рукий** *a.* one-handed; **—ручный** *a.* single-handled; **—рядный** *a.* single(-row), one-row, uniserial, unilinear; (chem.) single-stranded; (bot.) monostichous; single-file; **—связный** *a.* singly or simply connected; **—сегментовый** *a.* monomerous; **—селенистый** *a.* monoselenide (of); **—сельчанин** *m.* native (of).

односем/енодольные *pl.* (bot.) monocotyledons; **—енодольный, —ядольный** *a.* monocotyledonous; **—янка** *f.* monachenium; **—янный** *a.* single-seeded, monospermous.

одно/сернистый *a.* monosulfide (of); **—скатный** *a.* lean-to (roof); single-ended (discriminator); **—скачковый** *a.* single-shock; **—слойный** *a.* single-layer, single-ply, one-ply; **—сменный** *a.* single-shift (work); **—сортный** *a.* monovarietal, same variety; **—споровый** *a.* one-spore, monosporous; **—срезный** *a.* (in) single shear; **—стадийный** *a.* single-step, single-stage; one-pass (classification); **—станинный** *a.* open-side (machine); overhanging (hammer); **—станочный** *a.* single-machine.

одноствол/ка *f.* single-barrel gun; **—ьный** *a.* single-barrel(ed); single-trunk (tree).

одностворчат/ые *pl.* (mal.) Gastropoda; **—ый** *a.* univalve, single-valved; single(-leaf) (door); **—ый моллюск** gastropod.

одно/стебельный *a.* single-stemmed; **—стенный** *a.* single(-wall); **—стоечный** *a.* single-column; single-frame (forging hammer); overhanging (hammer); open-side (machine); (av.) single-strut.

односторонн/е *adv.* unilaterally; *prefix* secundi— (unilateral, secund); **—ецветковый** *a.* (bot.) secundiflorous; **—ий** *a.* unilateral, one-sided, single(-ended); single-headed (stud); one-way, unidirectional; linear (pressure); open-side (machine); (text.) not reversible; on one side, anopisthographic (edition); (bot.) secund; simple (fertilizer); prejudiced, biased; **—яя память** (comp.) read-only storage.

одно/стриг *m.* single clip; **—стрига** *f.* single-clip wool; **—строечный** *a.* single-frame; **—струнный** *a.* one-stringed; **—ступенный** *a.* single (filtration); **—ступенчатый** *a.* single-stage, single-step, one-stage, one-step; single-reduction (axle); simple (process); **—суставной** *a.* single-jointed; **—счётный** *a.* (numerical program control) single word-step system; **—тактный** *a.* single-cycle, single-pulse; (electron.) single-ended; **—тёс** *m.* plank nail.

однотип/(ич)ный *a.* monotypic, homotypic, single-type, of the same type; uniform, similar; **—ность** *f.* homotypy; uniformity.

однотомн/ик *m.* one-volume edition; **—ый** *a.* one-volume, in one volume.

одно/тонный *a.* monotonous; monochromatic; uniform; **—точечный** *a.* single-point, one-point; degenerate (set); **—трубка** *f.* single (tube); **—трубный** *a.* tubeless (tire); **—тычинковый** *a.* (bot.) monandrous; **—тяжный** *a.* (chem.) single-stranded; **—углеродный** *a.* one-carbon; **—угольный** *a.* one-angled; **—ударный** *a.* single-stoke; **—укосный** *a.* single-crop, once cut; **—утробные** *pl.* (mam.) Eutheria; Monodelphia; **—утробный** *a.* monodelphian; **—ухий** *a.* one-eared.

одно/фабричный *a.* one-plant; **—фазный** *a.* single-phase, monophase, uniphase; **—факторный** *a.* single-factor; (gen.) unifactorial; **—фосфористый** *a.* monophosphide (of); **—фтористый** *a.* monofluoride; **—футовый** *a.* one-foot (length); **—хвостка** *f.* (zool.) Monura; **—хлористый** *a.* monochloride (of); **—ходовой** *a.* single-pass, one-pass, straight-through (flow); single-thread (screw); simplex (winding); rat-tail (burner); **—хозяй(ствен)ность** *f.* (bot.) autoecism; **—хозяй(ствен)ный** *a.* autoecious.

одноцвет/ка *f.* (bot.) Moneses; **—ковый** *a.* single-flowered, uniflorous; **—ный** *a.* monochromatic.

одно/целевой *a.* single-purpose; **—центровый** *a.* concentric; **—цеп(оч)ный** *a.* (chem.) single-stranded, one-chain; (elec.) single-circuit; **—цилиндровый** *a.* single-cylinder; **—цокольный** *a.* single-end(ed) (magnetron); **—часовой** *a.* one-hour; **—частичный** *a.* single-particle; **—частотный** *a.* single-frequency; **—челюстные** *pl.* (ichth.) Monognathidae; **—черпаковый** *a.* one-way scoop (feeder); **—член** *m.* (math.) monomial; **—членный** *a.* monomial; (biol.) monomerous; **—шахтный** *a.* single-shaft; **—шкивный** *a.* single-pulley; **—шпиндельный** *a.,* **—шпорцевый** *a.* unicalcarate, one-spurred; **—щелевой** *a.* single-slot(ted); single-port (slide valve); **—этажный** *a.* single-stage, single-deck; one-story; **—этапный** *a.* single-stage; **—ягодник** *m.* (bot.) herb Paris (*Paris quadrifolia*); **—ядерный** *a.* mononuclear, uninuclear; **—ядность** *f.* (zool.) monophagy; **—ядный** *a.* monophagous; **—яйцовый** *a.* (biol.) monozygotic, identical; **—якорный** *a.* single-armature; rotary (converter); **—ярусник** *m.* one-story stand; **—ярусный** *a.* one-story, one-deck; one-layered; **—ячейковый** *a.* unicellular, one-celled.

одобр/ение *n.* approval; recommendation; **—енный** *a.* approved, etc., *see v.*; **—ительный** *a.* approving; **—ить, —ять** *v.* approve, endorse, favor, sanction, recommend.

одограф *m.* (naut.) odograph, dead-reckoning computer; (math.) hodograph.

одоле(ва)ть *v.* overcome, surmount, master, conquer; overrun.

одолж/ение *n.* favor, service; loan; **—ать, —ить** *v.* lend, loan.

одомашн/ение *n.* domestication, taming; **—енный** *a.* domesticated, tamed; **—и(ва)ть** *v.* domesticate, tame.

одометр *m.* odometer, distance gage.

одонто— *prefix* odonto— (tooth); **—бласт** *m.* (anat.) odontoblast; **—граф** *m.* odontograph; **—лит** *m.* odontolith, dental calculus; (pal.) odontolite; **—лог** *m.* odontologist, dentist; **—логия** *f.* odontology; **—ма** *f.* (med.) odontoma; **—патия** *f.* odontopathy; **—стом** *m.* (ichth.) Odontostomus; **—хирургический** *a.* dental surgery.

одор/ант *m.* (mal)odorant; **—изатор** *m.* odorizer; **—изация** *f.* imparting odor (to gases); **—иметрия** *f.* odorometry; **—ин** *m.* odorin.

одревесн/е(ва)ть *v.* lignify, become wood(y); **—евший** *a.* lignified; woody (cutting), hardwood; **—ение** *n.* lignification; **—еть** *v.* lignify.

одряхл/ение *n.* aging, decrepitation; **—еть** *v.* age, become decrepit.

одсадочный *a.* single, individual.

одубина *f.* (leather) tannery waste, spent tan; (fuel) wood extraction chips.

одуванчик *m.* (bot.) dandelion (*Taraxacum*); **—олистный** *a.* taraxifolious.

одум(ыв)аться *v.* think better of it, reconsider, change one's mind.

одур/елый *a.* stupefied; **—еть** *v.* become stupefied; **—манить** *v.* stupefy; **—ь** *f.* stupor; **сонная —ь** (bot.) belladonna (*Atropa belladonna*); **—ять** *v.* stupefy; **—яющий** *a.* stupefying.

одутловатый *a.* puffy, bloated.

одутыш *m.* porcupinefish (*Diodon hystrix*).

одушев/ить, —лять *v.* animate; **—ление** *n.* animation; **—лённый** *a.* animated.

одышка *f.* shortness of breath, panting; (med.) dyspnea, labored breathing.

одюбоновский *a.* Audubon (Society).

ожгут *fut. 3 pl. of* **ожечь.**

Оже эффект (phys.) Auger effect.

ожеледь *f.* glaze, ice-crust(ed ground).

ожелезнен/ие *n.* iron plating; (soils) iron accumulation; ferrugination; **—ный** *a.* iron-plated; ferruginous.

оже-переход (phys.) Auger transition.

ожеребиться *v.* foal.

ожерелье *n.* necklace; collar.

ожесточ/ать, —ить *v.* harden, embitter; increase (in) rigidity; **—ённый** *a.* embittered, bitter; fierce, violent; desperate.

ожечь *v.* roast, calcine; kiln, fire, bake, burn off, scorch.

оже-эффект *m.* (electron.) Auger effect.

ожжённый *a.* roasted, etc., *see* **ожечь.**

оживал *m.* (arch.; stat.) ogive; **—ьный** *a.* ogival.

ожив/ание *n.* revival; **—ать** *v.* revive, regain consciousness, come to life; **—ающий** *a.* reviving; **—ить** *see* **оживлять; —ка** *f.* revival; regeneration; **—ление** *n.* regeneration, etc., *see v.*; revival, (re)vivification; **—лённый** *a.* regenerated, etc., *see v.*; lively, animated; **—лять** *v.* regenerate; revivify, revive, resuscitate; animate, enliven; brighten, freshen (color); **—ляющий кислородный аппарат** pulmotor, resuscitator.

ожига *see* **ожика.**

ожигать *see* **ожечь.**

ожид/аемость *f.* expectancy; **—аемый** *a.* expectant; expected; **—аемый срок службы** (mach.) life expectancy; **—ание** *n.* expectation, waiting; expectancy, anticipation; **в —ании** pending; (av.) hold(ing); **время —ания** latency; **математическое —ание** expectation value, mean value; **обмануть —ание** *v.* disappoint, come short of one's expectations; **—ать** *v.* expect, wait (for); anticipate; **как и следовало —ать** as one would expect; **—ающий** *a.* awaiting; **—ающий выполнения** outstanding, pending.

ожиж/аемый *a.* liquefiable; **—ать** *v.* liquefy; fluidize; **—ающий** *a.* liquefying; **—ающийся** *a.* liquefiable; **—ение** *n.* liquefaction (of gas); (met.) thinning; liquation; destructive hydrogenation (of coal) **—енный** *a.* liquefied; fluidized; **—итель** *m.* liquefier.

ожика *f.* (bot.) wood rush (*Luzula*).

ожина *f.* dewberry (*Rubus caesius*).

ожинок *m.* unharvested stalk.

ожир/евший, —елый *a.* fat(ty), obese; **—ение** *n.* obesity, adiposity, adiposis, corpulence; fatty degeneration (of heart); lipo(mato)sis; seasoning (of wine); **—енный** *a.* fat(ty), oily; **—еть** *v.* get fat.

ожить *see* **оживать**.

ожог *m.* (phyt.; vet.) burn, scald, scorch(ing); (chem.; med.) combustion; (phyt.) blight; scab; **о. от трения** (med.) rope burn; **—овый** *a.* of **ожог**.

оз *m.* (geol.) os, esker.

оз. *abbr.* (**озеро**) lake.

озабо/тить, —чивать *v.* occupy, busy; **—титься, —чиваться** attend (to), take care (of); **—ченность** *f.* preoccupation, anxiety, concern; **—ченный** *a.* preoccupied, anxious, concerned, troubled.

озаглав/ить, —ливать *v.* entitle; **—ленный** *a.* entitled.

озадач/енный *a.* perplexed, puzzled; **—и(ва)ть** *v.* perplex, puzzle.

озазон *m.* osazone, diphenyl hydrazone.

озаннит *m.* (min.) osannite.

озарить *see* **озарять**.

озаркит *m.* (min.) ozarkite.

озарять *v.* illuminate, light(en); dawn.

ОЗВ *abbr.* (**определение загрязности воздуха**) determination of air pollution.

озвуч/ание, —ение, —ивание *n.* sonication; sound recording; scoring; public address system; **—енный** *a.* sonicated, etc., *see* *v.*; sound (movie); **—и(ва)ть** *v.* sonicate; record sound; produce with sound; expose to sonic waves; score.

оздоров/еть *v.* become healthier; **—ительный** *a.* health-improving; sanitation, sanitary; **—ить, —лять** *v.* improve sanitary conditions, sanitize; normalize, standardize, refresh (air); **—ление** *n.* sanitation; improvement, enhancement (of environment); rehabilitation, restoration.

озелен/ение *n.* landscape gardening; **—итель** *m.* landscape gardener; **—ительный** *a.* landscaping; greenbelt; **—ить, —ять** *v.* landscape, plant with trees and shrubs, beautify.

оземь *adv.* to or on the ground.

озена *f.* (med.) ozena.

озёрк/а *f.* (ichth.) Manchurian lake minnow (*Phoxinus percnurus mantschuricus*).

озерко *n.*, *dim. of* **озеро**; puddle; small bay.

озернённость *f.* grain content in ear.

озёрно-речной *a.* (geol.) fluvio-lacustrine.

озёрн/ый *a.* lake, lacustrine; (biol.) limnetic; **о. планктон** limnoplankton; **—ая руда** (min.) bog (iron) ore.

озер/о *n.* lake; (anat.) lacus, lacuna; **растение озер** (bot.) limnophyte; **—оведение** *n.* limnology; **о.-старица** *n.* oxbow lake; **—цо** *dim. of* **озеро**.

озим/о-яровой *a.* winter-and-spring (crop); **—ые** *pl.* winter crops; **—ый** *a.* winter, hibernal, hiemal; **—ь** *f.* winter crop.

озираться *v.* look around, observe.

озиритин *m.* osyritin.

озлоб/ить, —лять *v.* embitter; **—ление** *n.* bitterness, animosity; **—ленный** *a.* bitter, resentful, hostile.

ознак/амливать *see* **ознакомлять**; **—омительный** *a.* familiarizing; introductory; **—омить** *see* **ознакомлять**; **—омление** *n.* acquaintance; familiarization; **—омлять** *v.* acquaint, familiarize (with), introduce (to); **—омляться** *v.* become familiar, get acquainted.

ознаменов/ание *n.* commemoration; sign; **в о.** in honor (of), to mark the occasion; **—(ыв)ать** *v.* signalize, mark; celebrate, commemorate.

означ/ать *v.* mean, stand for, denote, indicate, imply, be taken to mean; specify, designate; mark, note; **—енный** *a.* indicated; above(-mentioned), the aforesaid; **—ить** *see* **означать**.

озноб *m.* (med.) algor, chill, rigor; **—ить, —лять** *v.* chill; **—ление** *n.* chilling; frostbite, chilblain, pernio.

озо/бензол *m.* ozobenzene; **—бром** *m.* (phot.) ozobrome.

озокерит *m.* (min.) ozocerite, ozokerite, mineral wax, fossil wax.

озоление *n.* calcination; combustion; incineration; ashing; **аналнз мокрым —м** wet assaying; **анализ сухим —м** blow-pipe analysis.

озол/енный *a.* ashed; **—ить** *see* **озолять**.

озолотить *v.* gild.

озолять *v.* incinerate, (reduce to) ash; **о. сухим путем** dry-ash.

озон *m.* ozone; **—ат, —ид** *m.* ozonide; **—атор** *m.* ozonator, ozone generator; **—изация** *f.* ozonization, ozone treatment.

озониоз *m.* (phyt.) Texas root rot.

озониров/ание *see* **озонизация**; **—анный** *a.* ozonized; **—ать** *v.* ozonize.

озон/ный, —овый *a.* ozone; **—ная бумага** ozone test paper; **—олиз** *m.* ozonolysis.

озонометр *m.* ozonometer; **—ический** *a.* ozonometric; **—ия** *f.* ozonometry.

озоно/стойкий *a.* ozone-resistant; **—стойкость** *f.* resistance to ozone; **—сфера** *f.* ozonosphere.

озотипия *f.* (phot.) ozotype (process).

ОЗРА *abbr.* (**отдел защиты растений**) plant protection department.

ОЗУ *abbr.* (**оперативное запоминающее устройство**) random access memory, RAM.

ОЗЦ *abbr.* [**ожидание затверде(ва)ния цемента**] waiting on cement, W.O.C., setting time.

озы *pl.* (geol.) osar (*pl. of* os), eskers.

озябнуть *v.* get chilled.

оид/ий, —иум *m.*, **—ия** *f.* (phyt.) oidium, powdery mildew; **—иоспора** *f.* oidiospore; **—иофор** *m.* oidiophore.

ойкокристалл *m.* (petr.) oikocryst.

ойльдаг *m.* Oildag (lubricant).

оймяконский *a.* (geog.) Oimyakon.

ойтиковое масло oiticica oil.

ок. *abbr.* (**около**) approximately; (**океан**) ocean.

ока, ОКА *abbr.* (**оживляющий кислородный аппарат**) pulmotor, resuscitator.

оказ/ание *n.* offering, etc., *see* *v.*; **—ать** *v.* offer, give; have, produce (effect); exert (pressure); show, render; **—ать влияние** affect; **—ать действие** influence, act (on); operate, work; **—аться** *v.* find oneself, be found, occur, appear; happen; turn out, prove to be; **—ываемый** *a.* offered, etc., *see* *v.*; brought to bear (upon); **—ывать** *see* **оказать**.

окайм/ить, —лять *v.* edge, border, flange; **—ление** *n.* edging, bordering, margination; flange, burr; **светлое —ление** halo, halation; **—лённый** *a.* edged, etc., *see* *v.*; marginate; limbate; **—ляющий** *a.* edging, etc., *see v.*

окалин/а *f.* scale; cinder, sinter; slag, dross, scoria; **образование —ы** (met.) high-temperature scaling; **рыхлая о.** loose oxide; **—оломатель** *n.* descaler, scale breaker; **—ообразование** scaling, scale formation; **—остойкий** *a.* scale-resistant; **—остойкость** *f.* resistance to scaling, resistance to oxidation.

окалывать *v.* break away, split round; cut, hew; pin (round).

окамен/е(ва)ть, —ять *v.* petrify, silicify, lithify, calcify, fossilize; **—евший, —елый** *a.* petrified, etc., *see v.*; fossil; **—елый плод** (med.) lithopedion; **—елость** *f.* petrification, etc., *see v.*; fossil; **—ение** *n.* petrification, etc., *see v.*; muscardine, dying off (of silkworms).

окантов/ка *f.* framing, edging; frame; edge former, shaping strip; **—(ыв)ать** *v.* edge, border, frame; (phot.) mount.

оканчивать *v.* finish, end, terminate; graduate; **—ся** *v.* (come to an) end, stop, cease, desist; run out, disappear.

окапать *v.* spatter.

окапи *m.* (mam.) okapi (*Okapia johnstoni*).

окапыв/ание *n.* spattering, etc., *see v.*; **—ать** *v.* spatter; dig around, entrench, bank up (earth); hoe, till.

окараванивать *v.* pile (peat).

окарбоначивание *n.* carbonate accumulation (in soils).

окармливать *see* **обкармливать.**

окат/анность *f.* roundness; **—анный** *a.* rolled, rounded; nodulized; capsized (iceberg); **—ать** *v.* (make) round.

окатить *see* **окачивать.**

окат/ывание *n.* nodulizing, etc., *see v.*; agglomeration by tumbling; **—ывать** *v.* nodulize, pelletize, (make) round; hose down (with water); **—ыш** *m.* (met.) pellet; **приготовление —ышей** pelletizing.

окачивать *v.* drench, sluice.

окашивать *v.* mow around.

окварц/евание *n.* silification; **—еваться** *v.* silicify; **—ованный** *a.* silicified.

ОКГ *abbr.* (**оптический квантовый генератор**) laser.

океан *m.* ocean; **—ариум** *m.* ocean aquarium; **—ический** *a.* ocean(ic); **—ичность** *f.* (meteor.) oceanity; **—ограф** *m.* oceanographer; **—ографический** *a.* oceanographic; ocean station (vessel); **—ография, —ология** *f.* oceanography, oceanology; **—ский** *a.* ocean (ic).

окенит *m.* (min.) okenite (a zeolite).

ОКЗ, О.К.З. *abbr.* (**отношение короткого замыкания**) short-circuit ratio.

окилен/ие *n.* (biol.) carina; **—ный** *a.* carinate(d), keel-shaped.

окинский *a.* (geog.) Oka.

окис/ание *see* **окисление; —ать** *see* **окиснуть; —ел** *m.* oxide; **—и** *gen., pl., etc.,* of **окись.**

окислен/ие *n.* oxidation; souring; **о.-восстановление** *n.* oxidation-reduction, reduction-oxidation, redox; **—ность** *f.* degree of oxidation, oxidation number.

окислённый *a.* oxidized; soured.

окислитель *m.* oxidizing agent, oxidant, oxidizer; acidifier; **—но-восстановительный** *a.* reduction-oxidation, redox; **—ный** *a.* oxidizing, oxidative.

окисл/ить *see* **окислять; —ость** *f.* sourness; **—ый** *a.* oxide; sour(ed); **—яемость** *f.* oxidizability; **—яемый** *a.* oxidizable; oxidized; **—ять** *v.* oxidize; sour; **—ять-ся** *v.* oxidize; turn sour; **—яющий** *a.* oxidizing; souring; **—яющийся** *a.* oxidizable; oxidizing, oxidative, oxidation.

окисн/о-ртутный *a.* mercury-mercurous oxide (electrode); **—оуглеродный** *a.* carbon monoxide; **—уть** *v.*

oxidize; turn sour; **—ый** *a.* oxide; higher or **—ic** (salt); **—ое железо** ferric iron.

окис/ь *f.* oxide (higher or **—ic** oxide); **о. железа** ferric oxide; **азотнокислая о. железа** ferric nitrate; **о. меди** cupric oxide; **сернокислая о. меди** cupric sulfate; **о. углерода** carbon monoxide; **безводная о.** anhydride; **водная о., гидрат —и** hydroxide.

окичобийский *a.* (geog.) Okeechobee.

ОКК *abbr.* (**Общество Красного Креста**) Red Cross Society.

окклю/дирование *n.,* **—зия** *f.* occlusion, obstruction; trapping (of liquid or gas); **неправильная —зия** (med.) malocclusion; **—дированный** *a.* occluded; **—дировать** *v.* occlude; **—зометр** *m.* (med.) occlusometer, gnathodynamometer.

оккультный *a.* occult, obscure.

оккуп/ант *m.* (mil.) occupying force, invader; **—ация** *f.* occupation; **—ированный** *a.* occupied; **—ировать** *v.* occupy.

оклагомский *a.* (geog.) Oklahoma.

оклад *m.* tax; salary, pay; setting, frame(work); (min.) set.

окладка *f.* lining.

окладной *a.* of **оклад**; steady (rain); **о. венец** sole timber.

оклахомский *a.* (geog.) Oklahoma.

окле/енный *a.* glued (around), etc., *see v.*; laminated (board); **—ечный** *a.* backing (board); **—ивание** *n.* gluing (around), etc., *see v.*; **—и(ва)ть** *v.* glue (around), paste, plaster; cover (over, with); clarify (juice); purify, refine (wine); **—йка** *see* **оклеивание;** cover(ing); **—йка обоями** papering.

оклендский *a.* (geog.) Oakland (USA); Auckland (New Zealand).

окно *n.* window; opening, rift; aperture; port; (charging) hole; (anat.; zool.) fenestra; (forest) glade.

око *n.* eye; (ichth.) humpback salmon (*Oncorhynchus gorbuscha*).

оковалок *m.* loin end (of beef).

оков/анный *a.* iron-bound; **—ка** *f.,* **—ывание** *n.* binding, etc., *see v.*; fittings, ironwork; **—ы** *pl.* fetters; **—(ыв)ать** *v.* bind, fit, mount, hammer.

околачив/ание *n.* (leather) hammering; knocking off; **—ать** *v.* hammer; knock off, chip off.

околица *f.* (village) outskirts; detour.

околка *f.* breaking (a)round, chipping; dressing (of stone).

около *prep. gen. and adv.* near, toward; around, about, by; approximately, in the neighborhood of; *prefix* near, para—, peri—; circum—; **—верхушечный** *a.* periapical; **—водный** *a.* near the water; **—глазничный, —глазной** *a.*(anat.) periocular; **—глоточный** *a.* peripharyngeal; **—горизонтальный** *a.* circumhorizontal; **—двенадцатиперстнокишечный** *a.* (anat.) paraduodenal; **—док** *m.* (rr.) line section; **—жаберный** *a.* (zool.) peribranchial; **—звуковой** *a.* (acous.) transonic; **—земный** *a.* near (the) earth; **—зенитный** *a.* circumzenithal; **—зубный** *a.* (anat.) paradental; **—конечный** *a.* paraterminal; **—лепестный** *a.* (bot.) peripetalous; **—лунный** *a.* circumlunar; **—маточный** *a.* (anat.) parametric; **—медицинский** *a.* paramedical; **—ногтевой** *a.* (anat.) periungual; **—носовой** *a.* (para)nasal; **—пестичный** *a.* (bot.) perigynous.

околоплод/ие *n.* (bot.) pericarp, seed vessel; **—ник** *m.* (bot.) pericarp; (anat.) fetal, amniotic (fluid); **—ная оболочка** amnion; **—ные воды** amniotic fluid.

околопол/юсный, —ярный *a.* (astr.) circumpolar; polar (region); **—юсное плато** Antarctica.

около/почечный *a.* (anat.) paranephric; **—пупочный** *a.* paraumbilical; **—ротовой** *a.* adoral, circumoral; **—семянник** *see* **околоплодник.**

околосерд/ечно-сумочно-диафрагмальный *a.* (anat.) pericardiacophrenic; **—ечносумочный** *a.* sternopericardial; **—ечный** *a.* pericardial; **—ечная оболочка, —ечная сумка, —ие** *n.* pericardium.

около/сосудистый *a.* (anat.) perivascular; **—срединный** *a.* (med.) paramedian; **—ствольный** *a.* (min.) shaft; **—стыковой** *a.* boundary, junction (zone).

околот/ить *see* **околачивать; —ок** *m.* (rr.) line section; **—ь** *see* **окалывать.**

около/устье *n.* (biol.) peristome; **—ушный** *a.* (anat.) parotid (gland); **—цветник** *m.* (bot.) perianth; **—цветниковый** *a.* perianthal; chlamydeous; **—центральный** *a.* pericentral; **—шовный** *a.* (welding) near the seam; **—щитовидный** *a.* parathyroid (gland); **—ядерный** *a.* perinuclear; **—яичник** *m.* paraophoron.

околыш *m.* cap band.

окольный *a.* roundabout, indirect, tortuous, devious; oblique (electron); (anat.) collateral; para—; **о. мочеиспускательный** *a.* paraurethral; **о. путь** indirect route; detour.

окольц/евать, —овывать *v.* ring, band, girdle; **—ованный** *a.* ringed, etc., *see* v.

окомков/ание *n.* (met.) pelletizing, etc., *see* v.; **—атель** *m.* pelletizer; **—ать** *v.* pelletize, nodulize; lump, clot.

окон *gen. pl. of* **окно.**

оконечн/ик *m.* terminator; **—ость** *f.* extremity, end, tip; tail; edge, border; **—ый** *a.* terminal, end, final; output (stage); **—ое устройство** (comp.) terminal, termination.

оконн/ица *f.* window frame; **—ый** *a.* window.

оконоп/атить, —ачивать *v.* calk, stop up; **—атка** *f.,* **—ачивание** *n.* calking.

оконтур/енный *a.* outlined, etc., *see* v.; **—ивание** *n.* outlining, etc., *see* v.; delineation; **—и(ва)ть** *v.* outline, delineate, delimit, contour; enter (into a graph); (min.) map; **—ивающий** *a.* outlining, etc., *see* v.; extension, outpost (well).

оконце *dim. of* **окно.**

оконцев/ание *n.* termination; **—атель** *m.* (elec.) end terminal.

окончание *n.* end(ing), completion, finishing, termination, conclusion, consummation, closing, expiration; (anat.) end plate; (bot.) tip, apicule; **о. работы** (rockets) thrust cutoff, cutout.

окончательн/о *adv.* finally, definitively, conclusively; again; **о. обработанный** (completely) finished; **—ый** *a.* final, finishing, closing, definitive; **—ая отделка** finishing.

окончат/ый *a.* fenestrated, having apertures; **—ое отверстие** (anat.) fenestra; **—ые мотыльки** *pl.* (ent.) Thyrididae.

оконч/енный *a.* finished, completed; **—ивающий** *a.* finishing, etc., *see* v.; **—ить** *v.* finish, complete, terminate.

окоп *m.* trench, emplacement, foxhole; **—ать** *v.* trench, dig around; till, cultivate; **—ка** *f.* trenching, etc., *see* v.

окопник *m.* (bot.) comfrey (Symphytum).

окоп/ный *a. of* **окоп; —окопатель** *m.* trench digger; **—чик** *m.* pit.

окорачивать *v.* shorten, curtail, crop.

окорен/ие *n.* rooting, etc., *see* v.; **—иться** *v.* root, take or strike root.

окоренный *a.* decorticated, barked, peeled, stripped.

окорёнок *m.* small basin or tub.

окор/ивание *n.,* **—ка** *f.* barking, etc., *see* v.; **—и(ва)ть** *v.* bark, peel, decorticate, strip, scrape.

окорм *m.* overfeeding; **—ить** *v.* overfeed; poison (with bait or food); **—ка** *f.* overfeeding; poisoned bait.

окорн/ать *v.* cut, clip, cut too short; **—ик** *m.* spudder.

окорок *m.,* **—овый** *a.* ham, haunch; leg (of lamb).

окоротить *see* **окорачивать.**

окорочный *a. of* **окорка; окорок.**

окорчёвка *f.* uprooting.

окор/щик *m.* barker; **—ять** *see* **окори(ва)ть.**

окосить *v.* mow around.

окостен/е(ва)ть *v.* ossify; harden, stiffen; become numb; **—елость** *f.* ossification; hardness, stiffness; rigidity; numbness; **—елый** *a.* ossified; hard(ened), stiff; numb(ed); **—ение** *n.* ossification; hardening, etc., *see* v.

окот *m.* bearing young, spec. lambing; **—иться** *v.* give birth; lamb.

окочен/евший, —елый *a.* numb, stiff; **—ение** *n.* stiffness, rigidity; **трупное —ение** rigor mortis; **—еть** *v.* get numb, grow stiff.

окошенный *a.* mowed around.

окош/ечко, —ко *n.* little window, aperture; **—ечный** *see* **оконный.**

ОКП *abbr.* (**обратный компасный пеленг**) reciprocal compass bearing; (**оптический квантовый прибор**) laser; (**отсчёт компасного пеленга**) compass bearing reading.

ОКР *abbr.* (**опытно-конструкторская работа**) research and development, R&D.

окр. *abbr.* (**округ, окружной**).

окра *f.* (bot.) okra (Abelmoschus esculentus).

окраин/а *f.,* **—ный** *a.* outskirts, edge; remote area; (bot.) peristome; **—ные моря** landlocked seas.

окрайка *f.* (anat.) corner incisor.

окра/с *m.* color, tint; **—сить** *see* **окрашивать; —ска** *f.,* **—сочный** *a.* coloring, etc., *see* v.; color; (protective) coloration; (nuptial) dress, attire; discoloration; **—шение** *n.* coloring, etc., *see* v.; **—шенно—** *prefix* chromat(o)—, chrom(o)—, color; **—шенный** *a.* colored, etc., *see* v.; **—шиваемость** *f.* colorability; **—шиваемый** *a.* colorable; **—шивание** *n.* coloring, etc., *see* v.; pigmentation; coat, coloration; tinge, tint; **реакция —шивания** color reaction; **—шивать** *v.* color, tint, dye, stain; paint; **—шиваться** *v.* color; turn, change (color); **—шивающий** *a.* coloring, etc., *see* v.; **—шивающее средство** pigment.

окреа *f.* (bot.) oc(h)rea.

окремн/евать *v.* silicify; **—ение** *n.* sili(cifi)cation; **—енный** *a.* silicified.

окрепнуть *v.* become stronger.

окрест *adv. and prep. gen.* around; **—ность** *f.,* **—ности** *pl.* neighborhood, vicinity, environment, environs, surroundings; **—ный** *a.* neighboring, adjacent, surrounding.

Ок-Ридж (geog.) Oak Ridge.

окристаллизов/анность *f.* crystallinity; **—ать(ся)** *v.* crystallize.

окров/авленный *a.* blood-stained, bloody; **—енеть** *v.* get blood-stained.

окрол *m.* (rabbits) giving birth.

окроп/ить, —лять *v.* sprinkle, spray.

округ *m.* okrug, district, region; (hunting) ground; circuit, circle; **—а** *f.* vicinity.

округление *n.* rounding (off), making round.

округлённо *adv.* round; in round numbers; **—ость** *f.* roundness.

округлённоуглеват/ость *f.* subangularity; **—ый** *a.* subangular.

округл/ённый *a.* rounded (off), blunt; **о. до минуты** to the nearest minute; **—еть** *v.* become round(ed); **—ить** *see* **округлять;** **—ость** *f.* roundness; circle; curve; **—оугловатость** *see* **округлённоугловатость;** **—ый** *a.* round(ed), rotund(ate); curved; orbicular, spheroidal; dome-shaped; **—ять** *v.* round (off), make round; approximate.

округж/ать *v.* surround, encircle, enclose, envelop, embrace, encompass; **—ающее** *n.* environment, surroundings; **—ающий** *a.* surrounding, etc., *see v.;* circumjacent, circumfluent; circumflex (arteries); peripheral, distal; environmental; ambient (temperature, etc.); **—ающий рот** circumoral; **—ающая среда** environment; **—ающей среды** environmental; **—ение** *n.* surrounding, etc., *see v.;* surroundings, environment, medium; vicinity, circle; (biol.) habitat, background; **—ённый** *a.* surrounded, etc., *see v.;* **—ной** *a. of* **округ.**

окружн/ость *f.* circumference, periphery, circle; circuit; surrounding region, neighborhood, district; **сила на —ости** circumferential force; **—ый** *a.* circumferential, peripheral, circling, circular; surrounding.

окру/тить, —чивать *v.* wind, coil (around); **—ченный** *a.* wound, coiled.

окрыл/ённый, —ившийся *a.* winged, alate; **—иться, —яться** *v.* grow wings.

оксаз/идин *m.* oxazidine; **—ин** *m.,* **—иновый** *a.* oxazine; **—ол** *m.,* **—оловый** *a.* oxazole; **—олин** *m.* oxazoline, ethylene urea; **—он** *m.* oxazone.

оксал/амид *m.* ox(al)amide; **—ат** *m.* oxalate; **—ный** *a.* oxalate(d); **—атосодержащая моча** (med.) oxaluria; **—ацетат** *m.* oxaloacetate; **—ен** *m.* oxalene; **—ил** *m.* oxalyl; **—илхлорид** *m.* oxalyl chloride; **—он** *m.* oxalon (fiber); **—уровый** *a.* oxaluric (acid).

оксам/ид *m.* oxamide, ethanediamide; **—ил** *m.* oxamyl; **—(ин)овая кислота** oxam(in)ic acid; **—иновокислая соль** oxamate; **—иновокислый** *a.* oxamic acid; oxamate (of); **—иновометиловый эфир** methyl oxamate.

оксан *m.* oxane, ethylene oxide; **—илид** *m.* oxanilide; **—иловая кислота** oxanilic acid, phenyloxamic acid.

окс/антранол *m.* oxanthranol; **—афенамид** *m.* oxaphenamide; **—афор** *m.* oxaphor, 3-hydroxycamphor.

окси— *prefix* oxy— (sharp, quick, sour; oxygen-containing); (more frequently) hydroxy—; **—азокраски** *pl.* hydroxyazo dyes; **—азосоединение** *n.* (hydr)oxyazo compound; **—алкильный** *a.* alkoxy(l); **—альдегид** *m.* hydroxyaldehyde; **—аминокислота** *a.* hydroxyamino acid; **—аммиак** *m.* oxyammonia, hydroxylamine; **—антраниловый** *a.* hydroxyanthranilic (acid); **—ацетиленовый** *a.* oxyacetylene (welding); **—ацетон** *m.* hydroxyacetone, 1-hydroxy-2-propanone; **—ацетофенон** *m.* hydroxyacetophenone; **—ацил** *m.* hydroxyacyl; **—бензойный** *a.* hydroxybenzoic (acid); **—биотин** *m.* oxybiotin (vitamin); **—биотический** *a.* oxybio(n)tic, aerobic; **—бутират** *m.* hydroxybutyrate; **—газ** *m.* oxygen gas; **—гемоглобин** *m.* oxyhemoglobin, hematoglobulin; **—гемометр** *m.* (med.) oximeter; **—цианин** *m.* oxyhemocyanine; **—геназа** *f.* oxygenase; **—генатор** *m.* (med.) oxygenator; **—ген(из)ация** *f.* oxygenation; **—ген(о)терапия** *f.* oxygen therapy; **—гидрохинон** *m.* hydroxyhydroquinone, 1,2,4-trihydroxybenzene; **—графис** *m.* (bot.) Oxygraphis; **—группа** *f.* hydroxy group.

оксид *m.* oxide; **—аза** *f.* oxidase; **—ат, —ационит** *m.*

oxidation product; **—атор** *m.* oxidant; **—ация** *f.* oxidation.

оксидендрон *m.* (bot.) Oxydendron.

оксидиметрия *f.* oxidimetry.

оксидиров/ание *n.,* **—ка** *f.* oxidation; (met.) oxide coating; **—анный** *a.* oxidized; **—ать** *v.* oxidize.

оксид/ная плёнка oxide film; **—оредуктаза** *f.* oxidoreductase; **—оредукция** *f.* oxidoreduction, oxidation-reduction, redox.

окси/женная соль tin tetrachloride; **—замещённый** *a.* hydroxy substituted; **—изомераза** *f.* isomerase; **—индолуксусная кислота** hydroxyindole acetic acid, HIAA; **—иодид** *m.* oxyiodide; **—карбидный** *a.* oxycarbide; **—карбоновый** *a.* hydroxycarboxylic (acid); **—керченит** *m.* (min.) oxykertschenite; **—кетон** *m.* hydroxy ketone; **—кислота** *f.* hydroxy acid; **—коричная кислота** hydroxycinnamic acid, coumaric acid; **—кортизон** *m.* hydroxycortisone; **—кортикостероид** *m.* hydroxycorticosteroid; **—лактон** *m.* hydroxylactone; **—лизин** *m.* hydroxylysine, Hyl; **—ликвит** *m.,* **—ликвитный** *a.* (expl.) Oxyliquit; **—лит** *m.* (welding) oxylith; **—лофит** *m.* (bot.) oxylophyte; **—льный** *a.* —oxyl (compounds); **—м** *m.* oxime; **—малоновый** *a.* hydroxymalonic (acid); **—масляный** *a.* hydroxybutyric (acid); **—мель** *m.* oxymel (medicated honey).

оксимет/ил *m.* hydroxymethyl; **—илен** *m.* oxymethylene, formaldehyde; **—иловый, —ильный** *a.* hydroxymethyl; **—окси** *prefix* hydroxymethoxy—; **—р** *m.* (med.) oximeter; **—рия** *f.* oximetry.

оксим/ид *m.* oximide; **—идосоединение** *n.* oximido compound; **—ирование** *n.* oximation; **—ный** *a.* oxime.

оксин *m.* oxine, 8-hydroxyquinoline; **—дол** *m.* oxindol, 2-ketoindoline.

окси/нервоновый *a.* oxynervonic (acid); **—нитрил** *m.* (hydr)oxynitrile; **—новый** *a.* oxine, oxinic; **—олеиновый** *a.* hydroxyoleic (acid); **—патия** *f.* (med.) oxypathia, hyperesthesia; **—пиридин** *m.,* oxypyridine, pyridone; **—порамфовые** *pl.* (ichth.) Oxyporamphidae; **—производные** *pl.* hydroxy compounds; **—пролин** *m.* hydroxyproline; **—пропионовый** *a.* hydroxypropionic (acid); **—пурин** *m.* oxypurine; **—ран** *m.* oxirane; **—соединение** *n.* hydroxy compound; **—соль** *f.* oxide salt; **—стероид** *m.* hydroxysteroid; **—сульфид** *m.* oxysulfide; **—тенк** *m.* oxygen tank; **—тетрациклин** *m.* oxytetracycline, Terramycin; **—тоцин** *m.* oxytocin (hormone); **—триптофан** *m.* hydroxytryptophan; **—уксусный** *a.* hydroxyacetic (acid).

оксиур/ицид *m.* (med.) oxyuricide, anti-oxyurid agent; **—ия** *f.,* **—оз** *m.* oxyuriasis; **—овые** *pl.* oxyurids, pinworms (*Oxyuridae*).

окси/фер *m.* (met.) ferrite; **—фил** *m.* (cyt.) oxyphil; **—фильный** *a.* oxyphil(ous), oxyphilic; **—фторидный** *a.* oxyfluoride; **—хинон** *m.* hydroxyquinone; **—хлоридный** *a.* oxychloride; **—хроматин** *m.* (cyt.) oxychromatin; **—целлюлоза** *f.* hydroxycellulose; **—циан** *m.* oxycyanogen; **—этил** *see* **оксэтил;** **—янтарная кислота** hydroxysuccinic acid, malic acid.

окск/ий *a.,* **—о—** *prefix* (geog.) Oka.

оксо/группа *f.* oxo group; **—д** *see* **оксилит;** **—замещённый** *a.* oxo-substituted; **—зон** *m.* oxozone; **—зонид** *m.* oxozonide; **—кислота** *f.* oxo(carbonic) acid.

оксоль *m.* a drying oil (for paints).

оксон/иевый *a.* oxonium; **—ий** *m.* oxonium compound; **—ит** *m.* (expl.) oxonite.

оксосинтез *m.* oxo synthesis, hydroformylation.

оксфорд *m.* (geol.) Oxfordian stage.

оксфордск/ий *a.* Oxford; **о. отстойник** Oxford settler; **о. ярус** (geol.) Oxfordian stage; **—ая единица** Oxford unit, Florey unit (for penicillin).

оксэтил *m.* ethoxy, hydroxyethyl.

окт. *abbr.* (**октябрь, октябрьский**).

окт—, —а— *prefix* oct(a)— (eight); **—ава** *f.* octave; **—агон** *m.* (geom.) octagon.

октадекан *m.* octadecane; **—овая кислота** octadecanoic acid, stearic acid; **—ол** *m.* octadecanol.

окта/деценовый *a.* octadecenic (acid); **—децил** *m.*, **—дециловый** *a.* octadecyl; **—диен** *m.* octadiene, conylene.

октальдегид *see* **октиловый альдегид.**

окта/льный *a.* octal, scale-of-eight; **—мер** *m.* octamer; **—метил** *m.* octamethyl pyrophosphoramide (insecticide); **—н** *m.* octane; **—н-корректор** *m.* octane selector.

октан/овая кислота octanoic acid, caprylic acid; **—овое число** octane number, octane rating (of gasoline); **—ол** *m.* octanol, octyl alcohol; **—он** *m.* octanone.

окта/нт *m.* octant; (astr.) Octans; **—хлор** *m.* Chlordan(e) (insecticide).

октаэдр *m.* (cryst.) octahedron; **—ит** *m.* (min.) octahedrite; **—ический** *a.* octahedral.

окт/ен *m.* octene, caprylene; **—ет** *m.* octet (group of 8 valence electrons).

октиббенит *m.* (min.) octibbenite.

октил *m.* octyl; **—амин** *m.* octylamine; **—ен** *m.* octylene, octene; **—еновая кислота** octylenic acid; **—овый** *a.* octyl; octylic (acid); **—овый альдегид** octyl aldehyde, caprylic aldehyde; **—овый спирт** octyl alcohol, octanol; **—овый эфир уксусной кислоты** octyl acetate; **—ьон** *m.* octillion (number).

октин *m.* octyne, hexylacetylene.

окто— *prefix* octo—; **—д** *m.* (electron.) octode; **—за** *f.* octose; **—л** *m.* Oktol (low molecular weight polybutene); **—митоз** *m.* (vet.) octomitosis, Octomitus infection; **—плоид** *m.*, **—плоидный** *a.* (gen.) octoploid; **—пусы** *pl.* (mal.) octopuses (*Octopoda*).

октуполь *m.* (phys.) octupole.

октэстрол *m.* Oestrol, benzestrol.

октябрь *m.*, **—ский** *a.* October.

ОКУ *abbr.* (**оптический квантовый усилитель**) laser amplifier.

окуба воск ocuba wax.

окуёт *pr. 3 sing. of* **оковать.**

окукл/ение, —ивание *n.* (ent.) pupation; **—и(ва)ться** *v.* pupate.

окулиров/ание *see* **окулировка; —анный** *a.* inoculated; (hort.) budded, grafted; **—ать** *v.* inoculate; bud, graft; **—ка** *f.*, **—овочный** *a.* inoculation; budding, grafting; **—щик** *m.* grafter.

окул/ист *m.* (med.) oculist; **—о—** *prefix* oculo— (eye); **—оназальный** *a.* (anat.) oculonasal.

окульт/ивировать *see* **окультуривать; —уренность** *f.* soil under cultivation; **—уренный** *a.* cultivated, etc., *see v.*; tame; **—уривание** *n.* cultivation; (biol.) selective breeding; domestication; (landscape) development; **—ури(ва)ть** *v.* cultivate (by selection); improve; tame, domesticate.

окулянт *m.* budded plant, grafted plant.

окуляр *m.* ocular, eyepiece (of microscope); eye glass; **о.-микрометр** *m.* ocular micrometer; **—ный** *a.* ocular.

окун/ание *n.* dipping, etc., *see v.*; **—ать(ся)** *v.* dip, plunge, immerse.

окун/евидные *pl.* (ichth.) perches and basses; **—ёвые** *pl.* Percidae; **—евый** *a.,*; **—ёк** *dim. of* **окунь; —образные** *pl.* Perciformes; **—и** *pl.* Percidae; **каменные —и** sea basses (*Serranidae*) **ушастые —и, чёрные —и** sunfishes (*Centrarchidae*).

окунуться *see* **окунать(ся).**

окунь *m.* (ichth.) perch (*Perca*, spec. *P. fluviatilis*); **морской о.** ocean perch (*Sebastes marinus*).

окуп/аемость *f.* reimbursement, pay-back, recovery (of expenses); **—ать, —ить** *v.* compensate, repay; justify, warrant (expenses); **—аться, —иться** *v.* pay (for itself), be worth.

окур/енный *a.* fumigated, etc., *see v.*; **—ивание** *n.* fumigation; curing, smoking; **—иватель** *m.* fumigator; **—и(ва)ть** *f.* fumigate, disinfect; cure, smoke; **—ивающий** *a.* fumigating; smoking; **—ивающее средство** fumigant; **—ок** *m.* (cigarette) butt, stub.

окусков/ание *n.* lumping, etc., *see v.*; **—(ыв)ать** *v.* lump, clot, agglomerate; sinter, cake.

окут/анный *a.* wrapped, etc., *see v.*; **—(ыв)ать** *v.* wrap (up), envelop, blanket, shroud.

окуч/ивание *n.* (agr.) hilling, etc., *see v.*; **—и(ва)ть** *v.* hill, ridge; bank, cover (with earth); **—ивающий** *a.* hilling, etc., *see v.*; **—ивающая лапа, —ник** *m.* hiller, ridger; **—ка** *see* **окучивание.**

окуют *pr. 3 pl. of* **оковать.**

окципитальный *a.* (anat.) occipital.

окшар *m.* a white lead-lead sulfate pigment; **цинковая —а** blue powder (zinc dust).

оладья *f.* pancake.

олакациевые *pl.* (bot.) Olacaceae.

олафит *m.* (min.) olafite.

Олбани (geog.) Albany.

Олбрайта синдром (med.) Albright's syndrome.

Олдем (geog.) Oldham.

олеандомицин *m.* oleandomycin.

олеандр *m.* (bot.) oleander (*Nerium oleander*); **—ин** *m.* oleandrin.

олеа/нол *m.* oleanol; **—ноловая кислота** oleanolic acid; **—т** *m.* oleate.

оледен/евать *see* **оледенеть; —елый** *a.* frozen, congealed, iced, covered with ice; **—(ен)ие** *n.* freezing, etc., *see v.*; congelation; (geol.) glaciation; **—еть** *v.* freeze, congeal, be covered with ice, ice over, glaciate.

оле/иловый *a.* oleyl (alcohol); **—ин** *m.* olein.

олеиново/калиевая соль, —кислый калий potassium oleate; **—кислый** *a.* oleic acid; oleate (of); **—кислая соль** oleate.

олеинов/ый *a.* olein, oleic; **—ая кислота** oleic acid, 9-octadecanoic acid; **соль —ой кислоты** oleate.

олёкм/инский *a.*, **—о—** *prefix* (geog.) Olekma; Olekminsk.

олекранон *m.* (anat.) olecranon.

олене/бык *m.* (mam.) Taurotragus; **—вод** *m.* reindeer breeder; **—водство** *n.*, **—водческий** *a.* reindeer breeding.

олен/ёк *m.* (ent.) lesser stag beetle (*Dorcus*, spec. *D. parallelopipedus*); (mam.) mouse deer (*Tragulus*); **—ёкский** *a.* (geog.) Olenek; **—ёнок** *m.* fawn; **—и** *pl.* deer (*Cervidae*).

олен/ий *a.* deer, cervine; **о. лишай** (bot.) reindeer moss (*Cladonia rangiferina*); **о. рог, спирт —ьего рога** (spirit of) hartshorn (ammonia water); **—ья кожа** buckskin; **—ина** *f.* venison; deerskin.

олёнка (ent.) chafer, spec. rose chafer (*Oxytherea, Epicometis hirta*, etc.).

олен/тинский *a.* (geog.) Olentyi; **—уха** *f.* doe; **—ь** *m.* deer (*Cervus*); (ichth.) minnow (*Phoxinus ph.*); **благо-**

родный —**ь** red deer (*Cervus elaphus*); **пятнистый** —**ь** sika deer (*Cervus nippon*); —**ьи** *see* **олени;** —**ь-ки** *pl. of* **оленёк;** mouse deer (*Tragulidae*); —**ь-самка** *f.* hind; —**ята** *pl. of* **оленёнок; fawns.**

олео— *prefix* oleo— (oil); —**гранулёма** *f.* (med.) oleogranuloma; —**графия** *f.* (typ.) oleography; —**зома** *see* **олеосома;** —**ма** *f.* (med.) oleoma; —**маргарин** *m.* (oleo)margarine; —**метр** *m.* oleometer, oil hydrometer; —**нафт** *m.* a lubricating oil; —**сома** *f.* (cyt.) oleosome, lipidoplast; —**стеарин** *m.* oleostearin, beef stearin; —**стеариновый** *a.* oleosteric; —**торакс** *m.* (med.) oleothorax; —**фильность** *f.* oleophilic nature; oil receptivity, water repellance; —**фильный** *a.* oleophilic, hydrophobic; —**фобный** *a.* oleophobic, hydrophilic.

олесковский *a.* (geog.) Olesko.

олеум *m.* oleum, fuming sulfuric acid.

олефин *m.,* —**овый** *a.* olefin.

олешник *m.* alder grove, alder stand.

олибанум *m.* olibanum, frankincense.

олив/а *f.* olive (tree); (anat.) olive, olivary body; (mal.) olive shell (*Oliva*); —**енит** *m.* (min.) olivenite, wood copper; —**ин** *m.* (min.) olivine; —**инит** *m.* (petr.) olivinite; —**иновый** *a.* olivine.

оливк/а *f.,* —**овое дерево** olive (tree) (*Olea europaea*); —**оватый** *a.* olivascent; —**овидный** *a.* olive-shaped; —**ово-зелёный** *a.* olive green; —**овый** *a.* olive, olive-colored.

олив/ный *a.* (anat.) olivary, olive-shaped; —**омозжечковый** *a.* olivocerebellar; —**оспинномозговой** *a.* olivospinal.

олиго— *prefix* oligo— [few, scant; (med.) deficiency]; —**амин** *m.* oligoamine; —**ген** *m.* (gen.) oligogene, key gene; —**генный** *a.* oligogenic; —**дендроглиома** *f.* (med.) oligodendroglioma; —**дендроглия** *f.* oligodendroglia; —**динамический** *a.* oligodynamic; —**дон** *m.* (herp.) Oligodon; —**карбонатакрилат** *m.* oligocarbonate acrylate; —**кардия** *f.* (med.) oligocardia, bradycardia; —**клаз** *m.* (min.) oligoclase; —**ксенный** *a.* oligoxenous (parasite).

олигомер *m.* (chem.) oligomer; —**изация** *f.* oligomerization; —**ия** *f.* (bot.) oligomery; —**ный** *a.* oligomerous.

олиго/мицин *m.* oligomycin (antibiotic); —**нит** *m.* (min.) oligonite, oligon spar; —**нуклеотид** *m.,* oligonucleotide; —**пептид** *m.* oligopeptide; —**пиренный** *a.* (gen.) oligopyrene; —**пноэ** *n.* (med.) oligopnea, hypoventilation; —**сапробный** *a.* (ecol.) oligosaprobic; —**термный** *a.* oligothermic; —**троф** *m.* oligotrophic plant; —**трофный** *a.* oligotrophic; —**фаг** *m.* oligophagous organism; —**френия** *f.* oligophrenia, mental defiency; —**френопедагогика** *f.* special education; —**хеты** *pl.* (zool.) Oligochaeta; —**цен** *m.,* —**ценовые слои** (geol.) Oligocene (epoch); —**ценовый** *a.* Oligocene; —**цитемия** *f.* (med.) oligocythemia.

олигурия *f.* (med.) oliguria.

олимпийский *a.* Olympian, Olympic.

олировые *pl.* (ichth.) Olyridae.

олиственный *a.* leafy, foliated.

олиф/а *f.* drying oil, boiled oil, paint vehicle; —**ить** *v.* treat with drying oil.

олицетвор/ить, —**ять** *v.* personify; embody.

олов/о *n.* tin, Sn; **гидрат закиси** —**а** stannous hydroxide; **гидрат окиси** —**а** stannic hydroxide; **закись** —**а** stannous oxide, tin monoxide; **соль закиси** —**а** stannous salt; **листовое о.** tin foil; **(одно)сернистое о.** stannous sulfide; **окись** —**а** tin oxide, now spec. tin monoxide; **сернокислая закись** —**а** stannous sul-

fate; **сернокислая окись** —**а** stannic sulfate; **хлористое о.** stannous chloride; **хлорное о., четырёххлористое о.** stannic chloride, tin tetrachloride.

олово/водород *m.* tin hydride; —**носный** *a.* tinbearing, stanniferous; —**органический** *a.* organotin; —**плавильный** *a.* tin-smelting; —**содержащий** *see* **оловоносный;** —**тетраметил** *m.* tetramethyl tin; —(2)-**фтористоводородный** *a.* fluostannous (acid); —(4)-**фтористоводородный** *a.* fluostannic (acid); —(4)-**хлористоводородный** *a.* chlorostannic (acid).

оловянисто/кислый *a.* stannous acid; stannite (of); **о. натрий, —натриевая соль** sodium stannite; —**кислая соль** stannite.

оловянист/ый *a.* stannous, tin; —**ая кислота** stannous acid, stannous hydroxide; **соль** —**ой кислоты** stannite; —**ая соль** stannous salt.

оловянно/кислый *a.* stannic acid; stannate (of); **о. натрий, —натриевая соль** sodium stannate; —**кислая соль** stannate; —**фтористый калий** potassium fluostannate; —**фтороводородный** *a.* fluostannic (acid); —**хлористый аммоний** ammonium chlorostannate; —**хлороводородный** *a.* chlorostannic (acid).

оловянн/ый *a.* stannic, tin; **о. ангидрид** stannic anhydride, stannic oxide; **о. камень** (min.) tinstone, cassiterite; **о. колчедан** *m.* (min.) tin pyrites, stannite; **о. пепель, —ая зола** tin ash, stannic oxide; —**ая кислота** stannic acid; **соль** —**ой кислоты** stannate; —**ая соль** stannic salt; *commercially* stannous chloride; —**ая чума** "tin pest" (allotropic transformation); —**ое дерево** dendritic crystals of tin; —**ое масло** butter of tin, stannic chloride.

олометр *m.* holometer, altitude gage.

олонецкий *a.* (geog.) Olonets.

олуговение *n.* meadow formation.

олуш/а *f.* (orn.) gannet (*Sula*); **о.-глупыш** *f.* gannet (*Sula bassana*); —**евые,** —**и** *pl.* Sulidae.

ольгинский *a.* (geog.) Olga('s); Olgi.

ольдгамит *m.* (min.) oldhamite.

ольденбургский *a.* (geog.) Oldenburg.

оль/нея *f.* (bot.) Olneya; —**пидий** *m.* Olpidium; —**с** *m.* (geobot.) ols (alder swamp forest); —**ский** *a.* (geog.) Ola.

ольслайминг *m.* all-sliming (of ore).

ольфакт/а *f.* olfacty (unit of smell); —**ометр** *m.* olfactometer; —**ометрия** *f.* olfactometry, odorimetry.

оль/ха *f.* (bot.) alder (tree) (*Alnus*); —**ховник** *m.* alder grove; —**ховый** *a.* alder; alderwood (charcoal); —**холистный** *a.* alder-leaved; —**хонский** *a.* (geog.) Olkhon; —**ша(т)ник,** —**шняк** *m.* alder grove.

олюторский *a.* (geog.) Olyutorka, Olyutorsky.

оляпк/а *f.* (orn.) dipper (*Cinclus*); —**овые** *pl.* Cinclidae.

ом *m.* ohm (unit of electrical resistance); **обратный о.** reciprocal ohm, mho.

Ома закон (elec.) Ohm's law.

омад *m.* (elec.) ohmad.

омаин *m.* Omaine, colchamine.

оманский *a.* (geog.) Oman.

омар *m.* (crust.) lobster (*Homarus vulgaris*).

омасливание *n.* oil treatment.

Омаха (geog.) Omaha.

омачивать *v.* wet, moisten.

омбро— *prefix* ombro— (rain); —**граф** *m.* recording rain gage; —**метр** *m.* ombrometer, rain gage; —**фил** *m.* ombrophil(e), ombrophilous plant; —**фильный** *a.* ombrophilous, rain-loving; —**фит** *m.* (bot.) ombrophyte; —**фобный** *a.* ombrophobous, rain-disliking; —**фобное растение** ombrophobe.

омгаз *m.* an enriched water gas.

омег *m.* (bot.) hemlock (*Conium*).

омега *f.* omega (ω).

омегатрон *m.* (spectrography) omegatron.

омедн/ение *n.* coppering, copper plating; **—ённый** *a.* copper-plated, copper-clad; **—ить, —ять** *v.* copper (plate).

омежник *m.* (bot.) Oenanthe.

омела *f.* (bot.) mistletoe (*Viscum*).

омелеть *v.* grow shallow.

омент/альный *a.* (anat.) omental; **—o—** *prefix* omento— (omentum).

омертв/евший, —елый *a.* stiff, numb; (med.) necrotic, gangrenous; **—елость** *f.* stiffness, numbness; necrosis; **—еть** *v.* grow stiff or numb; become gangrenous, mortify; **—ить, —лять** *v.* necrotize, mortify; **—(л)ение** *n.* numbness; necrosis; gangrene, mortification.

омёт *m.* stack.

омическ/ий *a.* (elec.) ohmic; Ohm's (law); **—ое сопротивление** resistance.

омлет *m.* omelet.

омматидий *m.* (ent.) ommatidium, facet.

омметр *m.* (elec.) ohmmeter.

омни— *prefix* omni— (all); **—бус** *m.* bus; **—потентность** *f.* omnipotence; **—потентный** *a.* omnipotent.

омнопон *m.* (pharm.) omnopon, pantopon.

омов/ский, —ый *see* **омический**.

омограф *m.* homograph.

омоет(ся) *fut. 3 sing. of* **омыть(ся)**.

омозол/евший *a.* callous(ed); **—елость** *f.,* **—ение** *n.* callosity; **—елый** *a.* callous.

омол/аживание, —ожение *n.* rejuvenation, regeneration, renewal, rejuvenescence; reduction in average age (of population); **—аживать, —одить** *v.* rejuvenate, regenerate, renew; **—ожённый** *a.* rejuvenated, etc., *see v.*; (zool.) neanic.

омол/ойский *a.* (geog.) Omoloi; **—онский** *a.* Omolon.

омоним *m.* homonym; **—ический, —ичный** *a.* homonymic, homonymous.

омосуд/ис *m.* (ichth.) hammerjaw (*Omosudis*); **—овые** *pl.* Omosudidae.

омоч/енный *a.* wetted, moistened; **—ить** *v.* wet, moisten.

омоют(ся) *fut. 3 pl. of* **омыть(ся)**.

ОМП *abbr.* (**обратный магнитный пеленг**) reciprocal magnetic bearing; (**отсчёт магнитного пеленга**) magnetic bearing reading.

ОМПА *see* **октаметил**.

омрач/ать, —ить *v.* obscure, darken.

омский *a.* (geog.) Omsk; Om (river).

омул/евый *a.,* **—ь** *m.* (ichth.) omul (*Coregonus*); Arctic cisco (*C. autumnalis*).

омут *m.* deep hole on lake or river bottom; (whirl)pool; chasm; **—истый** *a.* pitted with such holes; **—ник** *m.* (ent.) Helochares; **—нинский** *a.* (geog.) Omutninsk.

омфал/ит *m.* (med.) omphalitis; **—(o)—** *prefix* (anat.) omphal(o)— (navel, umbilicus); **—одес** *m.* (bot.) Omphalodes; **—одий** *a.* omphalo(i)dium, hilum (of seed); **—оцеле** *n.* (med.) omphalocele.

омфацит *m.* (min.) omphacite.

омшаник *m.* apiary house.

омыв/аемый *a.* washed, reached (by stream, etc.); **—ание** *n.* washing; flow(ing) about, around, over or past; **—атель** *m.* washer, squirter; **—ать** *v.* wash; flow about, around, over or past; pass over; **—ающий** *a.* washing, etc., *see v.*; circumambient, surrounding.

омыл/ение, —ивание *n.* saponification; **—ивающий** *a.* saponifying; **—ивающее средство, —итель** *m.* saponifier, saponifying agent; **—ить** *see* **омылять**;

—яемость *f.* saponifiability; **—яемый, —яющийся** *a.* saponifiable; **—ять(ся)** *v.* saponify; hydrolyze.

омыть *see* **омывать**.

он *m. pron.* he; it; **—a** *f. pron.* she; it.

онагр *m.* (mam.) onager (*Equus hemionus onager*); **—(ик)овые** *pl.* (bot.) Onagraceae.

онанизм *m.* onanism, masturbation.

онгстрем *m.* (phys.) angstrom (unit).

ОНД *abbr.* (**общий наибольший делитель**) greatest common divisor.

ондатр/а *f.,* **—овый** *a.* (mam.) muskrat (*Ondatra zibethica*).

ондограф *m.* (elec.) ondograph.

ондомозерский *a.* (geog.) Ondomsky Lakes.

ондул/ировать *v.* undulate; **—ятор** *m.* (elec.) undulator, telegraphic register; **—яция** *f.* undulation.

онегит *m.* (min.) onegite.

онежский *a.* (geog.) Onega.

онейро— *prefix* oneir(o)— (dream); **—диния** *f.* oneirodynia, nightmare; **—довые** *pl.* (ichth.) dreamers (*Oneirodidae*); **—логия** *f.* oneirology.

онем/елость *f.,* **—ение** *n.* torpor, sluggishness; numbness; mutism; **—елый** *a.* numb; **—еть** *v.* grow numb; become mute or dumb.

ОНЗ *abbr.* (**общий наименьший знаменатель**) least common denominator.

Онзагера уравнение Onsgager equation.

они *pron.* they.

ониевый *a.* onium (compound).

они/кс *m.,* **—ксовый** *a.* (min.) onyx; **—хит** *m.* onychite, onyx marble; **—хит** *m.,* **—хия** *f.* (med.) onychia, onychitis; **—хо—** *prefix* onych(o)— (nail, claw); **—хомикоз** *m.* (med.) onychomycosis; **—хофагия** *f.* onychophagy, nailbiting; **—хофары** *pl.* (zool.) Onychophora.

онко— *prefix* onc(h)o— (tumor, swelling, mass; barb, hook); **—генный** *a.* (med.) oncogenic, tumor-inducing; **—граф** *m.* oncograph; **—лог** *m.* oncologist; **—логический** *a.* oncological; **—логия** *f.* oncology.

онколь *m.,* **—ный счёт** (com.) on call, current account.

онко/ринх *m.* (ichth.) Oncorhynchus; **—рнавирус** *m.* (med.) oncornavirus; **—сфера** *f.* (zool.) oncosphere; **—тический** *a.* (med.) oncotic, swelling; colloidosmotic (pressure); **—цефаловые** *pl.* batfishes (*Ogcocephalidae, Oncocephalidae*); **—цит** *m.* (cyt.) oncocyte.

онлайн-обработка *f.* (comp.) on-line processing.

оно *n. pron.* it.

оно/кол *m.* onocol, onocerin; **—мато—** *prefix* onomato— (name, nomenclature, word); **—матопея** *f.,* **—матопоэз** *m.* onomatopoeia, onomatopoiesis; **—нин** *m.* ononin; **—нский** *a.* (geog.) Onon; **—сма** *f.* (bot.) Onosma; **—фрит** *m.* (min.) onofrite; **—церин** *see* **онокол**.

онто— *prefix* onto— (being, existence); **—генез** *m.,* **—гения** *f.* (biol.) ontogenesis, development; **—генетика** *f.* developmental biology; **—генетический** *a.* ontogenetic.

онхоцерк/а *f.* (zool.) Onc(h)ocerca; **—оз** *m.* (vet.) onchocerciasis, Onchocerca infestation.

онцилла *f.* (mam.) Felis pardinoides.

оо— *prefix, see also under* **ово—**; **оо—** (egg, ovum); **—бласт** *m.* (embr.) ooblast.

О-образный *a.* bandy, bow (legs).

ООВ *abbr.* (**оптически отбеливающее вещество**) optical brightening agent.

оогам/ета *f.* (gen.) oogamete, female gamete; **—ия** *f.* oogamy; **—ный** *a.* oogamous.

оо/генез *m.* (gen.) oogenesis; **—гоний** *m.,* **—гония** *f.* oogonium, oogone; **—диноз** *m.* (vet.) oodinosis, Oodinium infection; **—кинез** *m.* (gen.) ookinesis; **—кинета** *f.* (prot.) ookinete, vermicule; **—лит** *m.* (petr.) oolite; oolith; **—литовый** *a.* oolitic, like fish roe; **—мицеты** *pl.* (bot.) Oomycetes.

ООН *abbr.* (**Организация Объединённых Наций**) United Nations, UN(O).

оо/плазма *f.* (embr.) ooplasm; **—порфирин** *m.* ooporphyrin.

ООС *abbr.* (**охрана окружающей среды**) environmental protection.

оо/спора *f.* (biol.) oospore; **—спороз** *m.* (vet.) oosporosis; **—сфера** *f.* (gen.) oosphere; **—тека** *f.* ootheca; **—тида** *f.* ootid(e); **—тип** *m.* ootype; **—фит** *m.* (bot.) oophyte; **—форит** *m.* (med.) oophoritis; **—форо—** *prefix* (anat.) oophor(o)— (ovary); **—цит** *m.* oocyte.

оп. *abbr.* (**опытный**) experimental.

ОП-7, ОП-10 emulsifiers and wetting agents (mixtures of mono— and dialkyl ethers of polyethyleneglycol).

опа/вший *a.* fallen, etc., *see v.;* **—д** *m.* falling, shedding; (forest) floor; **—дание, —дение** *n.* falling (off), etc., *see v.;* defoliation; (med.) ptosis; **—дать** *v.* fall off, come down; shed; collapse; do down, subside (of swelling); **—дающий** *a.* falling off, etc., *see v.;* deciduous.

опаздыв/ание *n.* lateness, delay, retardation; **—ать** *v.* be late, come too late; be slow (of clock).

опаивать *v.* solder; overwater (livestock).

опак *m.* opaque, opacity; white kaolin; dishware of fine kaolin; **о.-иллюминатор** *m.* (micros.) vertical or direct-light illuminator; **—овый** *a.* opaque; (bot.) dull.

опал *m.* (min.) opal; *past m. sing. of* **опасть.**

опалённый *a.* singed, burned.

опалесц/енция *f.* opalescence; **—ировать** *v.* opalesce; **—ирующий** *a.* opalescent.

опалив/ание *n.* singeing, burning; **—ать** *v.* singe, burn, sear, scorch.

опалин *m.* opaline (glass), fusible porcelain, milky glass; **—а** *f.* (prot.) Opalina; **—овые** *pl.* opalinids.

опал/ить *see* **опаливать;** **—ка** *f.* singeing, burning.

опало/вый *a.* opal(ine), opalescent; **—подобный** *a.* opal-like, opaline.

опалуб/ить *v.* sheathe, incase, jacket; **—ка** *f.,* **—очный** *a.* sheathing, casing, lining; timbering; (concrete) form(s); **подвижная —ка, передвижная —ка** slipform; **—очные работы** preparation of forms.

опалыв/ание *n.* weeding, hoeing; **—ать** *v.* weed, hoe.

опалять *see* **опаливать.**

опар/а *f.* leavened dough; (dyeing, tanning) bran drench, bran steep; earthenware bowl; **—ник** *m.* earthenware bowl; **—ный** *a. of* **опара.**

опаршиветь *v.* (vet.) become mangy.

опас/аться *v.* fear, apprehend; avoid, guard against; **—ение** *n.* fear, apprehension, misgiving; anxiety, alarm; **—ка** *f.* caution; **с —кой, —ливо** *adv.* warily, cautiously; **—ливость** *f.* wariness, caution, circumspection; **—ливый** *a.* wary, cautious, watchful, guarded.

опасн/о *adv.* dangerously; it is dangerous; **—ость** *f.* danger, risk, hazard; **вне —ости** out of danger, safe, secure; **находящийся в —ости** *a.* endangered; **—ый** *a.* dangerous, unsafe, hazardous; critical (section); **—ое положение** hazard.

опасть *see* **опадать.**

опах *m.* (ichth.) opah (*Lampris regius*).

опах/ало *n.,* **—альный** *a.* fan; (orn.) web, vane, vexillum; (bot.) rhipidium; **—анный** *a.* plowed around; **—ать** *v.* plow around; **—ивание** *n.* plowing around,

circular plowing; **—ивать** *v.* plow around; fan; **—нуть** *v.* fan.

опаховые *pl.* (ichth.) opahs (*Lampridae*).

опацит *m.* (petr.) opacite.

опашка *see* **опахивание.**

опаять *v.* solder.

опек/а *f.* custody, guardianship; **—ать** *v.* watch (over), take care (of); **—ун** *m.* custodian, guardian; tutor.

опенер *m.* opener.

опёнок *m.* (bot.) honey mushroom (*Armillaria*).

опер/абильный *a.* operable; **—анд** *m.* (comp.) operand.

оператив/ка *f.* staff meeting; **—но-производственный** *a.* schedule (planning); **—ность** *f.* efficiency.

оперативн/ый *a.* operative, operational, operation(s); prompt, expeditious, effective, practical; short-term (memory); on-line (system); rapid (information); active (stock); **—ая память** random-access memory, RAM; **—ая сводка** summary of operations; **—ое совещание** staff meeting.

оператор *m.* operator; administrator, controller; statement; cameraman; (med.) surgeon; (comp.) instruction; (gen.) operator gene; **—ный** *a. of* **оператор;** operational.

операц/ионализм *m.* (phys.) operationalism; **—ионная** *f.* (med.) operating room; **—ионный** *a.* operation(al), operating; (comp.) interpretive (version); fiscal (year); surgical (instrument); scrub (nurse); **—ионная доска** (elec.) switchboard; **—ия** *f.* operation, working; (laboratory) step, run; **компонент —ии** (math.) operand; **сделать —ию** *v.* operate.

опере/дить, —жать *v.* lead, outstrip, outrun; anticipate, be ahead (of); **—жающий** *a.* leading; (comp.) lookahead (buffer); **—жающий угол** (elec.) angle of lead; **—жающая связь** (robotics) feedforward; **—жение** *n.* leading, etc., *see v.;* lead, advance; anticipation; (rolling) forward slip; **—жение на** leading by.

опер/ение *n.* feathering, feathers, plumage; (av.) empennage, tail assembly, tail (unit), fin assembly, fin(s); **—ённый** *a.* feathered, plumose, fledge(d); finned; **—ье** *see* **оперение.**

опереться *see* **опираться.**

оперившийся *see* **оперённый.**

опериров/ание *n.* operation, operating; **—ать** *v.* operate; work, perform, do.

оперить *see* **оперять.**

оперкул/ум, —юм *m.* (biol.) operculum, opercle, lid; **—ярный** *a.* opercular.

оперон *m.* (biochem.; gen.) operon.

оперофтера *f.* (ent.) Operopht(h)era.

опёртый *a.* supported.

оперять *v.* feather; (av.) equip with fins; **—ся** *v.* fledge, acquire feathers.

опесчан/енный *a.* arenated; **—иваться** *v.* become sandier.

опечатать *see* **опечатывать.**

опечатка *f.* typographical error, misprint.

опечатыв/ание *n.* sealing; **—ать** *v.* seal (up).

опечек *m.* (glass) muffle lehr.

опеченение *n.* (med.) hepatization.

опешивание *n.* clipping (of queen bees).

опиа/нил *m.* opianyl, meconine; **—нин** *m.* opianine; **—новая кислота** opianic acid, 5,6-dimethyoxyphthalaldehydic acid; **—т** *m.* opiate, narcotic; **—товый** *a.* opiatic, narcotic.

опивки *pl.* dregs, sediment.

опиевый *see* **опийный.**

опизометр *m.* (surv.) opisometer, map measurer.

опий *m.,* **—ный** *a.* opium.

опил/ивание *see* опиловка; —и(ва)ть *v.* trim, saw (off); file; —ка *see* опиловка; —ки *pl.* filings, turnings; (wood) sawdust; —ковидный, —кообразный *a.* scobicular, ramentacous; —овка *f.,* —овочный *a.* trimming, filing; —очный *a.* sawdust.

опио/курение *n.* (med.) opium smoking; —мания *f.* opiomania; —фагия *f.* opiophagy.

опирать *v.* support; rest, push; —ся *v.* be supported (by), be carried (by); rest (on), lean (against), bear up (against); be based (on).

опис/ание *n.* description, account, report; (patent) specification; entry; (comp.) declaration; —анный *a.* described, etc., *see v.;* —атель *m.* describer; (comp.) descriptor; —ательный *a.* descriptive; loose (translation); —ать *see* описывать; —ка *f.* clerical error, slip of the pen; —ной *a. of* опись.

описто— *prefix* opisth(o)— (back, backward); —гнат *m.* jawfish (*Opisthognathus*); —гнатический *a.* (anat.) opisthognatous; —гнатовые *pl.* (ichth.) Opisthognathidae; —нема *f.* Opisthonema; —прокт *m.* Opisthoproctus; —проктовые *pl.* Opisthoproctidae; —рх(ис) *m.* (zool.) liver fluke (*Opisthorcis*); —рхоз *m.* (vet.) opisthorchiasis; —цельный *a.* (anat.) opisthocoelous.

опис/ывать *v.* describe, depict, set forth, explain; report, (re)present; discuss; cover; govern; trace out, outline; list, inventory; circumscribe; —ываться *v.* be described, etc.; describe, cover, deal (with), be concerned (with); have, be given (by equation); —ь *f.* list, catalog, schedule; note (of contents); —ь дел inventory.

опиум *m.,* —ный *a.* opium.

ОПЛ *abbr.* (**оборотное поворотнолопастное рабочее колесо**) reversible adjustable-blade runner (of hydraulic turbine).

оплав/ить *see* оплавлять; —ление *n.* (partial) fusion, melting; softening roasting; (welding) flashing off, flash-off, burning off; sweating; (glass) fire polishing; (cer.) vitrification; **сварка —лением** flash welding; —ленный *a.* (partially) fused; —лять *v.* melt (at edges), partially fuse; smelt out; sweat.

опла/та *f.* pay(ment), wages, remuneration; **о. по труду** contract or piece work; **о. труда** pay; —тить, —чивать *v.* pay, remunerate, reimburse; cash (check); meet (costs); settle (account); —ченный *a.* (post)paid; **с —ченным ответом** prepaid; —чиваемый *a.* paying; **хорошо —чиваемый** profitable; —чивание *n.* paying, etc., *see v.*

оплегнат *m.* (ichth.) Oplegnathus.

оплескать, оплёскивать *v.* splash, spatter.

оплеснев/елый *a.* moldy, musty; —еть *v.* become moldy, get musty.

оплеснуть *v.* splash, spatter.

опле/сти, —тать *v.* braid; cover, insulate (wire); entwine; —тающий *a.* braiding, etc., *see v.;* —тённый *a.* braided, etc., *see v.;* basket-covered (carboy).

оплёт/ка *f.* braid(ing); **с —кой** braided (cable); —очный *a.* braid(ing); covering; basket.

оплешиветь *v.* grow bald.

оплодотвор/ение *n.* impregnation, etc., *see v.;* **близкородственное о.** inbreeding; **взаимное о.** cross fertilization; —ённый *a.* impregnated, etc., *see v.;* pregnant; —итель *m.* impregnator, fecundator; —ительный *a.* impregnating, etc., *see v.;* —ить, —ять *v.* impregnate, fecundate, inseminate, fertilize; fructify; engender; —яющий *a.* impregnating, etc., *see v.;* —яющая **спора** androspore.

опломбиров/ание *n.* sealing; filling; —анный *a.* sealed; filled; —ать *v.* seal; fill (tooth).

оплот *m.* bulwark, stronghold; —ник *m.* boom.

оплош/ать *v.* make a mistake, fail; —ка, —ность *f.* mistake, oversight.

оплы/в *m.,* —вание *n.* circumnavigation; guttering (of candle); collapse, creep, slip(ping); —(ва)ть *v.* circumnavigate; swim around; gutter, run; grow over (with fat); creep, slip, flow down; —вина *f.* mudflow.

опобальзам *m.* opobalsam.

опове/ститель *m.,* —стительное устройство signal device; annunciator; —стить, —щать *v.* inform, notify, advise, let know; signal; —щение *n.* announcement; reporting, warning.

оповожение *n.* breaking in (of horses).

оподельдок *m.* (pharm.) opodeldoc.

оподзол/енный *a.* podsolized (soil); —ивание *n.* podsolization; eluviation, chemical denudation; —ивать *v.* podsolize; leach, eluviate.

опоек *m.* calf leather, calfskin; **о.-велюр** *m.* suede calf; **о.-слизок** *m.* slink; **о.-сосунок** *m.* sucking calf.

опоён(ный) *a.* drunk, intoxicated.

опоечный *a. of* опоек.

опозд/ание *n.* being late, tardiness, delay; —ать *see* опаздывать.

опозн/авание *see* опознание; —аватель *m.* identifier; —авательный *a.* identifying, etc., *see v.;* identify (code); distinctive, episematic (coloration); —а(ва)ть *v.* identify, recognize, spot; —аки *pl.* (photogrammetry) photo(point) control, picture points; —ание *n.* identification, recognition; discrimination.

опоить *v.* overwater (stock).

опой *m.* (vet.) rheumatic pododermatitis.

опойковый *a.* calfskin.

опока *f.* (foundry) flask, mold box, mold frame, casting box; *pl.* (petr.) opoka, gaize; **верхняя о.** (foundry) cope; **нижняя о.** drag; **средняя о.** cheek.

ополаскив/ание *n.* rinsing; washing up; —атель *m.* rinser; —ать *v.* rinse; wash up.

ополз/ание *n.* creep(ing), slump(ing), slip(ping), sliding; —ать *v.* creep, slump, slip, slide; —ень *m.,* —невый *a.* (land)slide, rock slide, earth creep; slump; —невая **почва** soil creep; —неопасный *a.* subject to creep; —ти *see* оползать.

ополовник *m.* (orn.) long-tailed tit (*Aegithalos caudatus*).

ополос/кать, —нуть *see* ополаскивать; —ки *pl.* rinse water.

ополоть *see* опалывать.

ополч/аться, —иться *v.* take up arms (against); assail; —енец *m.* militia man, home guard; —ение *n.* militia.

опользень *see* оползень.

опомиза *f.* (ent.) Opomyza florum.

опомниться *v.* regain consciousness.

опопанакс *m.,* —овый *a.* (bot.) opopanax.

опор: **во весь о.** at full speed.

опор/а *f.* bearing, support, rest, carrier, prop, bracing, backing, mount(ing); base, foot(ing), leg; holder, seat, chair; (leveling) control (base); trestle; (floating) pier; mast, pole, pillar, buttress, abutment (of arch); foothold, fulcrum; (anat.) sustentaculum; **катковая о.** roller bearing; **клиновидная о., ножевидная о., призматическая о.** knife edge; **точка —ы** point of rest; bearing; fulcrum, prop.

опоражн/ивание *n.* emptying, etc., *see v.;* evacuation; discharge; —ивать, —ять *v.* empty, evacuate, discharge, drain, dump, unload; deflate.

опорно-двигательный *a.* (anat.) locomotor (system); **о.-показательный** *a.* model, exemplary.

опорн/ый *a.* bearing, supporting; index, guide, key, reference (value); exploratory, research, orientation (well); mounting, base; backing-up (rolls); (av.) fundamental (frequency); bracket (insulator); marker (horizon); fulcrate, fulcral; benchmark (basin); (anat.) sustentacular; **о. изолятор** stub insulator (of coaxial cable); **о. каток** trunion; **о. фланец** bearing flange; **—ая конструкция** supporting structure; **—ая плита** bearing disk, step; foundation plate, bed plate; **—ая плоскость** (math.) plane of reference; **—ая площадь, —ая поверхность** bearing (surface), seat; **—ая подушка** support, cushioning; **—ая призма** fulcrum; knife edge; **—ая свая** bridge pile; **—ая стойка** support, stand; **—ая точка** reference point; (leveling) control point; **—ое давление** bearing pressure; counter-pressure; **—ое значение** reference input; **—ое кольцо** supporting ring, ring support; bracket rim (of furnace); bearing race; **—ое напряжение** reference voltage; **—ое трение** friction of rest, static friction.

опорожн/ение see **опоражнивание; —ённый** a. empty, evacuated, clear; **—ить, —ять** see **опоражнивать.**

опорос m. farrowing (of pigs); **—иться** v. farrow, have a litter.

опосред/ованный, —ственный a. indirect; mediated, through (the agency of); **—(ств)овать** v. mediate, attain indirectly.

опоссум m. (mam.) opossum; **—ы** pl. Didelphiidae.

опотерапия f. (med.) opotherapy.

опочный a. of опока.

опояс/анный a. encircled, etc., see v.; **—(ыв)ать** v. encircle, surround, girdle, span; **—ывающий** a. encircling, etc., see v.; girdle; **—ывающий лишай** (med.) shingles.

оппанол m. Oppanol (a synthetic polyisobutylene rubber).

Оппенгеймера-Филлипса процесс (nucl.) Oppenheimer-Phillips process.

ОППИР abbr. (переносный оптический пирометр) portable optical pyrometer.

оппо/зитный a. opposite, contrary; **—зиционный** a., **—зиция** f. opposition; **—нент** m. opponent; **—нировать** v. oppose.

оправа f. case, holder; mount(ing), setting; (eyeglass) frame, rim; mandrel.

оправд/ание n. excuse, justification; (law) acquittal; **—анный** a. excused, etc., see v.; in line (with), proper; **—ательный** a. justificatory; **—ательный документ** voucher; **—(ыв)ать** v. excuse, justify, warrant, live up to; offset (cost); vindicate; acquit; **—(ыв)ать себя** pay (to), pay for itself; **—(ыв)аться** v. justify oneself; prove to be correct; pay, be worthwhile; be confirmed; be realized.

оправ/ить see **оправлять; —ка** f. mandrel, holder, arbor, drift; (seamless tube rolling) mandrel rod; (boring) bar; (tube) expander; (lathe) chuck; setting, etc., see v.; adjustment; **—лять** v. set, mount; set right, arrange, adjust; straighten out; **—ляться** v. recover, recuperate; **—очный** a. of оправка.

опрашивать v. interrogate, examine, question; get a report (on); (tel.) answer; poll.

определение n. determination, identification; detection, finding, location; definition; decision; appointment; computation, calculation, estimation; measurement; evaluation; judgment; proof, evidence; analysis, assay; test; **о. весовым способом** gravimetric determination; **о. твёрдости** hardness test.

определённ/о adv. definitely, positively, absolutely; **о. одно** one thing is certain; **—ость** f. definiteness; definability; determinacy; **со всей —остью** conclusively, convincingly; **—ый** a. determined; definite, specific, fixed, certain, given, particular; well-defined,

specified; precise, distinct, sharp; concrete, absolute; (math.) determinate; **за —ое время** in a unit of time; **заранее —ый** preset; **совершенно —ый** distinct.

определим/ость f. (math.) determinateness, definability; **—ый** a. determinate, determinable, definable.

определ/итель m. finder, locator, detector; guide, index, key; analyzer; (math.) determinant, discriminator; (information) subdivision, table, class; handbook, manual; **—ительная таблица** (identifying) key; **—ить** see **определять; —яемый** a. determinable, etc., see v.; determined, etc., see v.; unknown; **—ять** v. determine, establish, ascertain, define; dictate, control, govern; specify, fix, place, set (limit); assess, appraise, evaluate, estimate, compute; calculate, measure, assay; define, identify; detect, locate; find, arrive (at); settle, decide (on); allot, assign, appoint; judge, infer (from); **—ять положение** locate; **—яющий** a. determining, etc., see v.; determinant, determinative, decisive, master; indicating, indicial; characteristic; pacemaking (reaction).

опрелость f. (med.) intertrigo.

опресн/ение n. freshening, etc., see v.; distillation; **—ённый** a. freshened, etc., see v.; sweet, fresh (water); **—итель** m., **—ительная установка** demineralizer, distiller, desalter; (water) softener; **—ительный** a. freshening, etc., see v.; **—ить, —ять** v. freshen, desalt, demineralize; distil; soften (water); **—оки** pl. unleavened bread.

опрессов/анный a. molded, etc., see v.; **—ка** f., **—ывание** n. molding, etc., see v.; **—ывать** v. mold, press (around), press-fit, shape; pressure-mold; pressure-test; pressurize.

опробков/ание, —ение n. (bot.) suberization; (phyt.) suberification, corking; **—еть** v. suberize.

опробов/ание n. sampling, etc., see v.; test(ing), try-out, trial, examination, check; assay(ing); **—атель** m. sampler; tester; **—ательный** a. sampling, etc., see v.; **—ать** v. sample, try out, test(-operate); check; analyze, assay.

опровер/гать, —гнуть v. refute, disprove; dispute, argue (against), be at variance (with); reject **—жение** n. refutation, disproof, denial, rejection.

опроки/дной a. dump(ing); **—дывание** n. overturning, etc., see v.; reversal (of phase); **время —дывания** triggering time; **схема —дывания** (aut.) flip-flop; **—дыватель** m. dumper, tipper, kick-up; trip(per); tripping gear; (rad.) reverser, inverter; **—дывать** v. overturn, turn over, tip (over), dump, tumble, upset, disturb; trip; destabilize; invert, reverse (phase); stall (of asynchronous motor); (naut.) capsize; (mil.) overrun; **—дываться** v. tip over; snap over, flip back; capsize; stall; **—дывающий(ся)** a.overturning, etc., see v.; tilting, dump; reversing (thermometer); (rad.) flip-flop; **—нутый** a. overturned, etc., see v.; (bot.) resupinate(d); **—нуть** see **опрокидывать.**

опрол m. (hydr.)oxyproline.

опромет/чивый a. rash, hasty, precipitate, imprudent, indiscreet; **—ью** adv. headlong.

опрос m. inquiry, interrogation; question; request; scan; polling, survey; sensing; (value) sampling; **—ить** v. inquire; interrogate, examine; **—ный** a. interrogatory, inquiry; **—ный лист** form, questionnaire.

опростать v. empty.

опростить v. simplify.

опросчик m. interrogator.

опротестов/ание n. protest, complaint; **—(ыв)ать** v. protest, complain; appeal.

опрощать v. simplify.

опрыс/канный *see* **опрыснутый;** **—кать** *see* **опрыскивать;** **—кивание** *n.* spraying, etc., *see v.;* **—киватель** *m.* sprayer; **—кивать** *v.* spray, sprinkle, wet, moisten; **—кивающий** *a.* spraying, etc., *see v.;* **—нутый** *a.* sprayed, etc., *see v.;* **—нуть** *see* **опрыскивать.**

опрятный *a.* neat, clean, orderly.

ОПС *abbr.* (**однополосный сигнал**) (electron.) single sideband signal, SSB.

опс/ин *m.* (biochem.) opsin; **—иноген** *m.* (immun.) ops(in)ogen; **—ия** *f. suffix* —opsia, —opsy (kind or condition of vision); **—онизация** *f.* (bact.) opsonization; **—онизировать** *v.* opsonize; **—онин** *m.* (immun.) opsonin; **—онический** *a.* opsonic; **—онофагоцитарный** *a.* opsonocytophagic.

опт. *abbr.* (**оптика, оптический**); (**оптимальный**).

оптация *f.* (com.) op(ta)tion.

оптик *m.* optician; **—а** *f.* optics; **—атор** *m.* optical gage; **—окинетический** *a.* (med.) opt(ic)okinetic; **—о-механический** *a.* optical instrument.

оптимальный *a.* optimum, optimal, best, most favorable.

оптиметр *m.* optical caliper.

оптимиз/атор *m.* optimizer; **—ация** *f.* optimizing, optimization.

оптим/изм *m.* optimism; **—ированный** *a.* optimized; **—истический, —истичный** *a.* optimistic; **—истичность** *f.* optimism; **—ум** *m.* optimum, the best, ideal.

оптич/ески *adv.* optically; **—еский** *a.* optic(al), visual; light (microscope); **—еский (квантовый) генератор, —еский квантовый прибор** laser; **—еская деятельность** *see* **оптичность; —еская ось** optic axis; **угол —еских осей** (optic) axial angle; **—ность** *f.* opticity, optical activity, rotatory power.

опто/вик *m.* wholesale dealer; (text.) converter; **—вый** *a.,* **—м** *adv.* wholesale; **торгующий —м** wholesaler.

оптометр *m.* (med.) optometer.

опторг *m.* wholesale business.

опто/техника *f.* technical optics; **—транзистор** *m.* optoelectronic transistor; **—фон** *m.* optophone; **—хин** *m.* (pharm.) Optochin, ethylhydrocupreine; **—электроника** *f.* optoelectronics.

оптрон *m.* (electroluminescence) optron.

опубликов/ание *n.* publication; **—анный** *a.* published, etc., *see v.;* available; **—(ыв)ать** *v.* publish, issue, release; report, make public, put on record.

опудрив/ание *n.* dusting, powdering; **—ать** *v.* dust, powder.

опунция *f.* (bot.) Opuntia.

опуск *m.* omission; **—ание** *n.* lowering, etc., *see v.;* (geol.) subsidence; depression; descent, downstroke (of piston); omission; (nuclear testing) emplacement; **—атель** *m.* depressor; **—ать** *v.* lower, let down, drop, sink; depress; dip, plunge, immerse; apply; omit, bypass, skip, leave out; **—аться** *v.* descend, sink, subside, settle; drop, fall, collapse; diminish; **—ающий** *a.* lowering, etc., *see v.;* **—ающая мышца** (anat.) depressor; **—ающийся** *a.* descending, etc., *see v.;* **—ной** *a.* lowering, drop; trap (door); down (pipe); **—ной колодец** caisson.

опуст/елый *a.* empty, deserted, desolate; **—еть** *v.* become empty; be depopulated.

опуст/ившийся *a.* sunken, submerged; **—ить** *see* **опускать.**

опустош/ать, —ить *v.* destroy, lay waste; empty; **—ение** *n.* destruction, devastation, havoc; exhaustion, depletion; **—ительный** *a.* devastating, destructive, disastrous.

опустын/ение *n.* encroachment of the desert; **—и(ва)ться** *v.* become a desert.

опут(ыв)ать *v.* bind, enmesh, entangle.

опух/ание *n.* swelling, (in)tumescence, puffiness; **—ать** *v.* swell, intumesce, puff up; **—лость** *f.* puffiness, intumescence; **—лый** *a.* swollen, distended, puffed up; **—нуть** *see* **опухать; —олевый** *a.,* **—оль** *f.* tumor; **—ший** *see* **опухлый.**

опуш/ать *v.* cover with down; trim, edge (with fur); sprinkle, powder (with snow, etc.); **—ение** *n.* covering with down, etc., *see v.;* down(niness), pubescence, indumentum; (corn) silking; **—ённо—** *prefix* (bot.) downy; hebe— (pubescent); ptil(o)— (down, feather); **—ённолистный** *a.* downy-leaved; **—ённоплодный** *a.* (bot.) hebecarpous; **—ённость** *f.* pubescence, downiness, nappiness; **—ённый** *a.* covered with down, etc., *see v.;* downy, pubescent, tomentose; **—ечный** *a.,* **—ка** *f.* (forest) edge, margin, border, skirt; (fur) trimming; selvedge (of net).

опущен/ие *see* **опускание;** (med.) ptosis, prolapse; **о. желудка** gastroptosis; **—ный** *a.* lowered, etc., *see* **опускать;** ptosed, prolapsed.

опыл/ение *n.* dusting, spraying; (bot.) pollination; **—ённый** *a.* dusted; pollinated; **—ивание** *see* **опыление; —и(ва)тель** *m.* duster; pollinator; **—и(ва)ть, —ять** *v.* dust, spray; pollinate; **—ительный** *a.* dusting; pollinating.

опыт *m.* experiment, test, trial, run; know-how, experience, practice; **о. на замерзание** freezing test; **в порядке —а** tentatively; **в пределах ошибок —а** in the range of experimental error; **делать —ы, производить —ы** *v.* experiment; **на —е** experimentally; in practice; **на основании —а** a posteriori; **ошибка —а** experimental error; **производственный о.** know-how; **условия —а** experimental conditions; **—ник** *m.* research worker; **—нический** *a.* research, experimental; **—ничество** *n.* experimentation, experimental work; innovation.

опытно *adv.* expertly; experimentally; *prefix* experimental; **о.-заводский** *a.* pilot-plant; **о.-конструкторская работа** development work; experimental designing; **о.-механический** *a.* experimental-mechanical; **о.-показательный** *a.* experimental model; **о.-статистический** *a.* empirical-statistical; **—сть** *f.* experience, proficiency, know-how.

опытн/ый *a.* experienced, practiced, expert, competent, skillful, skilled; experimental, tentative, test, trial (run); research; experiment (station); pilot (plant); empirical (formula, etc.); **о. образец** prototype; **доводка —ого образца** engineering development; **разработка —ого образца** advanced development; **о. участок** pilot area; **—ая установка** pilot plant; **—ая эксплуатация** beta test; **—ое дело** experimentation, experimental work; **—ое исследование** pilot study; **—ые работы** development; **программа —ых работ** development effort; **—ым путём** by experimentation, experimentally; empirically.

опьян/елый, —ённый *a.* intoxicated; **—ение** *n.* intoxication; **—еть** *v.* become intoxicated; **—ить, —ять** *v.* intoxidate, inebriate; **—яющий** *a.* intoxicating; **—яющее средство** intoxicant.

опята *pl. of* **опёнок.**

опять *adv.* again, once more; **—же** besides; **о.-таки** (but) again, besides.

ора *f.* ora, margin.

орало *n.* plow share, cultivator.

оральн/о— *prefix,* **—ый** *a.* (anat.) oral.

орангутан(г) *m.* (mam.) orangutan (*Pongo pygmaeus*).

оранж *m.* orange (dye); **—ад** *m.* orangeade; **—евожёл-тый** *a.* orange-yellow; **—евый** *a.* orange(-colored), aurantiacous.

оранжер/ея *f.*, **—ейный** *a.* greenhouse, hothouse, conservatory.

оранжит *m.* (min.) orangite.

оранье *n.* yelling, shouting.

оратор *m.* orator, public speaker; **—ское искусство** oratory.

орать *v.* yell, shout.

орафлон *m.* (geol.) oraphlon.

орбикулярный *a.* (bot.) orbicular, circular; (petr.) orbicular, spheroidal.

орбит/а *f.* orbit(al), trajectory; **на —е** orbiting; **по —е** orbital; **движущийся по —е** in orbit; **—аль** *f.* orbital(e); **—ально** *prefix* (anat.) orbito—; **—альный** *a.* orbital, planetary; **—ирование** *n.* orbiting.

орвиллит *m.* (min.) orvillite.

орг— *prefix*, **орг.** *abbr.* (**организационный**; **органический**).

оргазм *m.* (physiol.) orgasm.

орган *m.* organ, member; device, tool, instrument; element, unit; institution, department; (executive) body; **земельный о.** land registry office; **рабочий о.** (agr.) tool; **—ы управления** controls.

органелла *f.* (biol.; prot.) organelle.

организ/атор *m.* organizer; **—ационноуправленче-ская техника** industrial engineering; **—ационный** *a.* organization(al); constitutional (type); **—ационная техника** clerical or managerial aids; **—ация** *f.* organization, management, regulation, entity; constitution, structure.

организ/м *m.* organism; **о.-индикатор** *m.* indicating organism; **о.-концентратор, о.-накопитель** *m.* magnifier; **о.-обрастатель** *m.* fouling organism; **—ован-ность** *f.* discipline; **—ованный** *a.* organized, etc., *see v.*; **—ов(ыв)ать** *v.* organize, establish; manage, arrange; **—ов(ыв)аться** *v.* get organized.

органика *f.* organic matter; organic chemistry.

органист *m.* (orn.) organist (*Euphonia*).

органическ/и *adv.* organically: **о. присущий** *a.* intrinsic; **—ий** *a.* organic; **—ое стекло** organic glass, polymethyl methacrylate.

органичный *a.* intrinsic.

орган/ка *f.*, **—ная крепь** (min.) organpipe supporting structure; **—орган-мишень** *f.* (physiol.) target organ; **—ный** *a.* organ (pipe).

органо— *prefix* organo—, organic; **—ген** *m.* (chem.) organogen; **—генез** *m.*, **—гения** *f.* (embr.) organogenesis, organogeny; **—генный** *a.* organogen(et)ic; (petr.) organogenic, biogenic; **—гидридсилан** *m.* (chem.) organosilane; **—графия** *f.* (anat.) organography; **—золь** *m.* (chem.) organosol; **—ид** *m.*, **—идный** *a.* (biol.) organoid; **—лептический** *a.* (physiol.) organoleptic; **—логия** *f.* (biol.) organology; **о.-ми-неральный** *a.* organic and mineral; **—образование** *n.* organogenesis; **—терапия** *f.* (med.) organotherapy.

орган/-род *m.* (biol.) organogenus; **—чик** *dim. of* **орган**; *m.* (zool.) organpipe coral (*Tubipora*).

орг/(а)техника *f.* office equipment or facilities; **—на-бор** *m.* organized recruitment; **—раф** *m.* directed graph; **—стекло** *see* **органическое стекло.**

орг-ция *abbr.* (**организация**).

орд/ен *m.*, **—енский** *a.* order; decoration; **—енская лента** (ent.) Catocala; **—ер** *m.* order; warrant, writ; authorization.

ординальный *a.* ordinal (number).

ординар *m.* zero water level, normal water level; **—ность** *f.* ordinariness; **—ный** *a.* ordinary, common; single, plain.

ордината *f.* (math.) ordinate; **ось ординат** axis of ordinates, Y-axis.

ордин/атор *m.* staff physician, resident physician, intern; **—атура** *f.* appointment as staff physician, etc.; clinical studies; **—ация** *f.* (ecol.) ordination.

ордов/икский период, —иций, —ич *m.* (geol.) Ordovician (period).

ореальный *a.* (silv.) oreal.

оребрен/ие *n.* finning, ribbing, fins; **—ный** *a.* finned, ribbed.

орегонский *a.* (geog.) Oregon.

оредежский *a.* (geog.) Oredezh.

орёл *m.* (orn.) eagle (*Aquila*); (astr.) Aquila; **морской о.** (ichth.) meagre (*Sciaena aquila*); **о.-курганник, о.-мо-гильнык** *m.* Imperial eagle (*Aquila heliaca*).

орельский *a.* (geog.) Orel.

оренбургский *a.* (geog.) Orenburg.

орео— *prefix* ore(o)— (mountain).

ореол *m.* aureole, corona, halo, halation, nimbus; **—ооб-разование** *n.* halation.

орео/питек *m.* (pal.) oreopithecus; **—фильный** *a.* oreophilous, mountain-loving; **—фит** *m.* (bot.) oreophyte.

орёт *pr. 3 sing. of* **орать.**

орех *m.* nut, spec. walnut (*Juglans*); **австралийский о.** macadamia nut (*Macadamia ternifolia*); **американ-ский о., бразильский о.** Brazil nut (*Bertholletia*); **болотный о., водяной о.** water chestnut (*Trapa natans*); **волошский о., грецкий о.** English walnut (*Juglans regia*); **волшебный о.** witch hazel (*Hamamelis*); **земляной о.** peanut (*Arachis*); chufa (*Cyperus esculentus*); **китайский о.** Chinese walnut (*Juglans sinensis*); **лесной о.** filbert (*Corylus*); **ломбард-ский о.** giant filbert (*C. maxima*); **медвежий о.** Turkish filbert (*C. colurna*); **серый о.** butternut (*Juglans cinerea*); **чёрный о.** black walnut (*J. nigra*).

орехо— *prefix* nuci—, nut; kary(o)— (nut, kernel); **—ватость** *f.* (soil) nut structure; **—видка** *f.* (mal.) nut clam (*Nucula*); **—видный** *a.* nuciform, nut-shaped; **—видный сустав** (anat.) enarthrosis; **—вка** *f.* (orn.) nutcracker (*Nucifraga caryocatactes*); **—во-зуевский** *a.* (geog.) Orekhovo-Zuyevo; **—вобурый** *a.* nut-brown; **—вые** *pl.* walnut family (*Julandaceae*); **—вый** *a. of.* **орех;** **—носный** *a.* nuciferous, nut-bearing; **—плодные** *pl.* nut trees, nuciferous plants; **—творка** *f.* (ent.) gall wasp (*Cynips*, etc.).

ореш/ек *dim. of* **орех;** nut(let), nucule; (stone pine) seed; (lime tree) capsule, achene; nut coal; **мелкий о.** pea coal; **—ина** *see* **орешник.**

орешко/видный *a.* (bot.) nuculiform, nucamentaceous; **о. плод** nucament(um), ament(um), catkin; **—вый** *a. of* **орешек;** gallic (acid); *suffix* (bot.) **—coccous,** **—coccoid;** **—дубильный** *a.* tannic (acid).

орешник *m.* nut tree, spec. filbert (*Corylus*); (min.) coarse-grain ore; nut coal; nut tree grove; **лесной о., обыкновенный о.** filbert (*Corylus avellana*); **мелкий о.** peat(-grade) coal; **—овые** *pl.* (bot.) Juglandaceae; **—овый** *a. of* **орешник.**

ориб/атиды *pl.* (zool.) mites (*Oribatidae*); **—и** *m.* (mam.) oribi (*Ourebia*).

оригинал *m.* original (copy), manuscript; eccentric (person); **о.-макет** *m.* layout, make-up page, camera-ready copy; **—одержатель** *m.* copy holder; **—ьно** *adv.*

originally, etc., *see a.*; —**ьность** *f.* originality, etc., *see a.*; —**ьный** *a.* original, singular, peculiar, eccentric, unique.

оригинатор *m.* originator; selection breeder.

ориент/ант *m.* (chem.) orienting substituent; —**атор** *m.* (av.) autonavigator, tracker; attitude control unit; —**ационный** *a. of* **ориентация;** key (plan); —**ация** *f.* orientation, guidance; (av.) attitude control; exposure (of building); (geol.) attitude (of beds) **параметры** —**ации** attitude parameters.

ориентир *m.* reference point, check point; marker, indicator; landmark; **естественный о.** landmark; **о.-буссоль** *m.* declinometer; —**ный** *a.* orienting, directing, guiding; reference; —**ование** *n.* orientation, control, direction; —**ованный** *a.* oriented, etc., *see v.*; —**о-вать** *v.* orient, direct, position; —**оваться** *v.* orientate, get one's bearings, be guided (by); lie, run, extend (in a given direction); —**овка** *see* **ориентирование;** (inertial navigation) attitude; —**овочный** *a.* reference (point); approximate, preliminary, rough, tentative (plan); examination (test); —**уемость** *f.* orientability; —**уемый** *a.* orientable; swiveling; —**ующий** *see* **ориентировочный;** orienting.

ориз/ацидин *m.* oryzacidin (antibiotic); —**иевые** *pl.* (ichth.) Oryziatidae; —**эфилюс** *m.* (ent.) Oryzaephilus.

орикс *m.* (mam.) oryx; —**ы** *pl.* Hippotraginae.

орикто— *prefix* orycto— (fossil, mineral; dug); —**гнозия** *f.* oryctognosy.

оринокский *a.* (geog.) Orinoco.

ориньяк *m.,* —**ская культура** (archeol.) Aurignacian (culture).

орион *m.* (astr.) Orion.

ориск/анский ярус, —**эни** (geol.) Oriskany stage.

орицикл *m.* (math.) oricycle, horocycle.

оркестр *m.,* —**овый** *a.* orchestra, band.

оркета *see* **оркуета.**

оркиш *f.* (bot.) Triticum monococcum.

оркнейский *a.* (geog.) Orkney (Islands).

оркуета *f.* (ichth.) Pacific bumper (*Chloroscombrus orqueta*).

орла *gen. of* **орёл.**

орлайя *f.* (bot.) Orlaya.

орлан *m.* (orn.) bald eagle (*Haliaeetus*).

орлеан *m.* orlean, annatto (dye); —**овые** *pl.* (bot.) Bixaceae.

орлёнок *m.* (orn.) eaglet, young eagle.

орлец *m.* (min.) rhodonite.

орлики *pl.* (bot.) columbine (*Aquilegia*).

орли/ные *pl.* (orn.) Aquilidae, Accipitridae; —**ный** *a.* aquiline; eagle; —**ный камень** (min.) eaglestone, aetite; —**ца** *f.* eagless, female eagle; —**чки** *see* **орлики.**

орловский *a.* (geog.) Orel; Orlovka; Orlov (printing); Orloff (horse).

орлон *m.* (chem.) nitron; (text.) orlon.

орлы *pl. of* **орёл.**

орляк *m.* (bot.) bracken (*Pteridium*); (ichth.) eagle ray (*Myliobatis*); —**и,** —**овые** *pl.* Myliobatidae.

ормозинин *m.* (chem.) ormosinine.

орнамент *m.* ornament(ation), decorative pattern; —**(аль)ный** *a.* ornamental, decorative; —**ация** *f.,* —**ирование** *n.,* —**ировка** *f.* ornamentation, decoration; —**ировать** *v.* ornament, decorate.

орнитин *m.,* —**овый** *a.* ornithine, 2,5-diaminopentanoic acid.

орнито— *prefix* ornitho— (bird); —**гамный** *a.* (bot.) ornithogamous; —**з** *m.,* —**за** *f.* (vet.) ornithosis, psittacosis; —**лог** *m.* ornithologist; —**логия** *f.* orni-

thology; —**птер** *m.* (aero.) ornithopter; —**фауна** *f.* avifauna, bird life; —**фил** *m.* ornithophilous plant; —**фильный** *a.* ornithophilous.

орнитуровая кислота ornithuric acid.

оро— *prefix* oro— (mountain).

ороген/ез(ис) *m.* (geol.) orogenesis, orogeny; —**ический** *a.* orogenic.

орогов/евать *v.* (anat.) keratinize; —**евающий** *a.* keratinizing; —**евший,** —**елый** *a.* cornified, horny, keratoid; —**ение** *n.* keratinization, keratosis; cornification; —**еть** *v.* keratinize, harden; —**икованный** *a.* (petr.) metamorphosed to hornfels.

орограф/ический *a.* (geol.) orographic, mountain; —**ия** *f.* orography.

орология *f.* (geol.) orology, orography.

оронго *m.* (mam.) Tibetan antelope (*Pantholops hodgsoni*).

оропон *m.* (leather) Oropon.

ороситель *m.* irrigator, sprinkler; irrigating ditch; (met.) feeder; —**ный** *a.* irrigating, irrigation; sprinkling, trickling, spray, trickle (cooler); —**ный аппарат** sprinkler, sprayer; —**ного типа** trickle (dissolver).

оросить *see* **орошать.**

орот/идиловый *a.* orotidylic (acid); —**идин** *m.* orotidine; —**овый** *a.* orotic (acid).

орофит *m.* orophyte, mountain plant.

ороченский *a.* (geog.) Orochen.

орош/аемый *a.* irrigated, etc., *see v.*; reflux (tower); —**атель** *see* **ороситель;** —**ать** *v.* irrigate, sprinkle, spray; —**ающий** *see* **оросительный;** —**ение** *n.* irrigation, sprinkling, spraying, trickling; (distillation) reflux; **внутрипочвенное** —**ение, подповерхностное** —**ение, подпочвенное** —**ение** subirrigation; —**ённый** *a.* irrigated, etc., *see v.*

орро— *prefix* orrho— (serum).

ОРС *abbr.* (**отдел рабочего снабжения**) Supply Section.

Орса прибор (gas analysis) Orsat apparatus.

орс/еин *m.* (chem.) orcein; —**еллиновый** *a.* orsellinic (acid); —**ин** *m.* orcin(ol), methylresorcinol.

орский *a.* (geog.) Orsk; Or (river).

орсудан *m.* (pharm.) Orsudan.

орт *m.* (math.) unit vector; (min.) crosscut, cross drift, breakthrough.

ортант *m.* (bot.) volunteer.

орт/анта *f.* (bot.) Orthanta; —**езии** *pl.* (ent.) Ortheziidae; —**етрум** *m.* Orthetrum.

орт/занд *m.* ortsand (calcium carbonate-containing sand); —**изон** *m.* (chem.) Ortizon.

ортикон *m.* (telev.) orthicon.

ортит *m.* (min.) orthite, allanite.

орто— *prefix* ortho— (straight, upright, perpendicular; correct, normal); —**алюминиевый** *a.* orthoaluminic (acid); —**арсенат** *m.* orthoarsenate; —**борнокислый** *a.* orthoboric acid; orthoborate (of); —**ванадиевокислый** *a.* orthovanadic acid; orthovanadate (of); —**водород** *m.* (nucl.) ortho hydrogen.

ортовый *a. of* **орт.**

орто/гелий *m.* (chem.) ortho helium; —**генез(ис)** *m.* (biol.) orthogenesis; —**гнатический** *a.* orthognathic, straight-jawed; —**гнейс** *m.* (petr.) orthogneiss.

ортогональн/ость *f.* (geom.) orthogonality; —**ый** *a.* orthogonal, right-angled.

орто/доксальный *a.* orthodox; —**дома** *f.* (cryst.) orthodome; —**донтический** *a.* (med.) orthodontic; —**донтия** *f.* orthodontics.

ортодром/ический *a.* (navigation) orthodromic, great circle; —**ия** *f.* orthodromic (line), great circle course or track.

орто́/з *m.* (med.) orthosis (orthopedic support); **—замещённый** *a.* (chem.) ortho-substituted; **—изомер** *m.* ortho isomer; **—кислота́** *f.* ortho acid; **—клаз** *m.,* **—клазовый** *a.* (min.) orthoclase; **—кремнекислый** *a.* orthosilicic acid; orthosilicate (of); **—метрический** *a.* (geod.) orthometric, absolute (height); **—муравьи́ный** *a.* orthoformic (acid).

ортомышьяко́в/истокислый *a.* orthoarsenious acid; orthoarsenite (of); **—окислый** *a.* orthoarsenic acid; orthoarsenate (of).

орто/норми́рованный *a.* orthonormal; **—ось** *f.* (cryst.) orthoaxis, orthodiagonal.

ортопе́д *m.* (med.) orthopedist; **—и́ческий** *a.* orthopedic; **—ия** *f.* orthopedics.

орто/пло́ид *m.,* **—пло́идный** *a.* (gen.) orthoploid; **—плумба́т** *m.* (chem.) orthoplumbate; **—пноэ́** *n.* (med.) orthopn(o)ea; **—положе́ние** *n.* (chem.) ortho position; **—пте́роидные** *pl.* (ent.) Orthopteroidea; **—располо́женный** *a.* in ortho position; **—ромби́ческий** *a.* (cryst.) orthorhombic, prismatic; **о.-ря́д** *m.* (chem.) ortho series; **—свинцовоки́слый** *a.* orthoplumbic acid; orthoplumbate (of); **—селе́кция** *f.* (biol.) orthoselection; **—силика́т** *m.* (chem.) orthosilicate; **—сифо́н** *m.* (bot.) Orthosiphon.

ортоско́п *m.* (med.; phot.) orthoscope; (art.) aim corrector; **—и́ческий** *a.* (opt.) orthoscopic; distortion-free (lens); **—ия** *f.*

орто/соедине́ние *n.* (chem.) ortho compound; **—стати́ческий** *a.* (med.) orthostatic; **—стиха́** *f.* (bot.) orthostichy.

ортосурьмя́н/истокислый *a.* orthoantimonious acid; orthoantimonite; **—окислый** *a.* orthoantimonic acid; orthoantimonate.

орто/те́ст *m.* outside micrometer; **—титановоки́слый** *a.* orthotitanic acid; orthotitanate (of); **—толиди́н** *m.* orthotolidine; **—то́нус** *m.* (med.) orthotonos; **—тропный** *a.* (bot.) orthotropic; **—у́гольный** *a.* orthocarbonic (acid); **—уксусный** *a.* orthoacetic (acid); **—фи́р** *m.* (petr.) orthophyre; **—фи́ровый** *a.* orthophyric; **—фони́ческий** *a.* (acous.) orthophonic; **—фори́я** *f.* (med.) orthophoria.

ортофосф/а́т *m.* (chem.) orthophosphate; **—ори́стокислый** *a.* orthophosphorous acid; orthosphosphate (of); **—орнокислый** *a.* orthophosphoric acid; orthophosphate (of).

орто/хлори́т *m.* (min.) orthochlorite; **—хромати́ческий** *a.* (phot.) orthochromatic; **—эфи́р** *m.* (chem.) ortho ester.

орштейн *m.,* **—овый горизо́нт** (geol.) ortstein, iron pan.

оруден/е́лость *f.* mineralization; protore; **—е́лый** *a.* (geol.) mineralized; **—е́ние** *n.* mineralization.

ору́д/ие *n.,* **—и́йный** *a.* instrument, tool, implement; (fishing) gear; gun, piece.

оруднéние *n.* mineralization.

орудовать *v.* manage, handle, run.

оруже́йн/ый *a.* gun, armament; **о. заво́д,** **—я** *f.* arsenal, armory; **о. мастер,** **—ик** *m.* gunsmith, armorer.

ору́жие *n.* weapon; *pl.* arm(s).

ору́ссиды *pl.* (ent.) Orussidae.

ору́т *pr. 3 pl. of* **ора́ть.**

орфа́ *f.* (ichth.) orfe (*Leuciscus idus*).

орфографи́ческий *a.* orthographic.

Орфорда спо́соб (met.) Orford process.

орх/иде́я *f.* (bot.) orchid; **—идные** *pl.* Orchidaceae; **—(о)** *prefix* (anat.) orchi(o)— (testes); **—и́т** *m.* (med.) orchitis.

орц/е́лла *f.* (mam.) Irawadi dolphin (*Orcaella*); **—ин** *see* **орсин.**

орша́д *m.* a cooling drink made from barley or almonds.

орь-иле́кский *a.* (geog.) Or-Ilek.

оря́сина *f.* long rod, pole.

оса́ *f.* (ent.) wasp.

оса́да *f.* seige.

осади́тель *m.* precipitator, precipitant, precipitating agent; settler; **—ный** *a.* precipitation, precipitating; settling; (fibers) coagulation (bath); **—ный аппара́т** precipitator; settler.

оса́д/ить *v.* settle, precipitate; beseige, ply (with questions); check, rein in; **—ка** *f.* settling, settlement, set(ting); sag(ging); subsidence (of soil); yielding (of foundation); sinking, immersion; sedimentation; (forging) upsetting, shortening, swaging; camber (of spring); (naut.) draft; (nucl.) pressurizing; charge slip; **—ка ко́нуса** (concrete) slump; **—ки** *pl. of* **оса́дка, оса́док;** sediments, deposits; sedimentary rock; rainfall, precipitation; (acid) sludge; (radioactive) fall-out; **атмосфе́рные —ки** rainfall; **выпаде́ние —ка** precipitation; **дождевы́е —ки, жи́дкие —ки** rainfall; **ка́рта —ков** (meteor.) isohyetal map; **—коме́р** *m.* rain gage; (naut.) draft gage; **—конакопле́ние** *n.* sedimentation; **—кообразова́ние** *n.* sedimentation; sludging.

оса́дный *a. of* **оса́да.**

оса́д/ок *m.* residue, dregs, tails; sediment, mud, sludge; deposit(ion), precipitate; **выпаде́ние —ка** (chem.) precipitation.

оса́доч/ный *a. of* **оса́дка;** sedimentation (tank); sedimentary (rock); plating (bath); sludge (superphosphate); **о. чехо́л** (geol.) sedimentary mantle; **—ая маши́на** upsetter; jolt-ramming machine; **—ые кольца** Liesegang rings.

осажда́ем/ость *f.* precipitability; sedimentation capacity; **—ый** *a.* precipitable; precipitated.

осажда́ть *v.* precipitate, deposit, settle (out), separate out; upset; (mil.) lay siege; **—ся** *v.* precipitate (out), settle out, fall out, be deposited; set; sink, sag.

осажда́ющ/ий *a.* precipitating, settling; **о. реакти́в, —ее сре́дство** precipitant, precipitating agent; coagulant; **—ийся** *a.* precipitating, settling; precipitable.

осажде́н/ие *n.* precipitation, precipitating, settling (out), deposition, sedimentation; precipitate, deposit, sediment; condensation; (concentration) jigging; (met.) plating, coat(ing).

осаждённый *a.* precipitated, etc., *see* **осажда́ть;** sedimentary.

осажи́в/ание *n.* checking, etc., *see v.*; set; **—ать** *v.* check; press back; clench, clinch (rivet); jolt, (up)set, jump (up), swage; tap (down), settle; **—ающий** *a.* checking, etc., *see v.*; jolt-ramming (machine).

осал/ива́ние *n.* fattening (of livestock); going rancid; **—ивать** *v.* fatten; grease; **—и(ва)ться** *v.* fatten up; go rancid.

оса́нка *f.* posture, attitude.

осарсо́л *m.* (pharm.) Osarsol, acetarsone.

осаха́р/ивание *n.* saccharification; hydrolysis (of wood); **—иватель** *m.* saccharifier; (starch) converter; hydrolyzer; **—и(ва)ть** *v.* saccharify; hydrolyze; sugar, candy.

осборни́т *m.* (min.) osbornite.

осва́г *m.* information agency.

осваи́в/ание *n.* familiarization; **—ать** *v.* assimilate; familiarize; adopt, utilize, appropriate; perfect, master, cope (with); reclaim; develop (land); accept, tolerate; **—аться** *v.* become familiar (with), get used (to), adapt; feel comfortable (in a situation); **—аться с кли́матом** become acclimated.

осведом/итель *m.* informer; (rad.) commentator; **—и-тельный** *a.* informative; information (agency); **—ить, —лять** *v.* inform, notify; **—иться, —ляться** *v.* inquire, ask about, question; **—ление** *n.* information, notification; inquiry; **—лённость** *f.* information, knowledge; **—лённый** *a.* (well-)informed.

освеж/ать *v.* refresh, freshen; air (room); regenerate, renew, strengthen; bring up to date; brush up (on data); recondition, restore, rejuvenate; rebond (molding sand); **—ающий** *a.* refreshing, etc., *see v.*; **—евать** *v.* skin and eviscerate (animal); **—ение** *n.* refreshing, etc., *see v.*; refreshment; renewal; **—ённый** *a.* refreshed, etc., *see v.*; **—итель** *m.* (re)freshener, etc., *see v.*; **—ительный** *see* **освежающий; —ить** *see* **освежать.**

освейский *a.* (geog.) Osveya.

осветитель *m.* illuminator, illuminant; reflector; (laser) pump; (micros.) condenser; cleaning agent; **—ный** *a.* illuminating, illumination, lighting; lamp (oil); **—ная арматура** (elec.) fixtures; **—ная ракета** (av.) flare; **—ное средство** illuminant; **—ные приборы** fixtures.

осветить *see* **освещать.**

осветл/ение *n.* clarifying, etc., *see v.*; clarification, purification; brightening effect (of detergents); **—ённый** *a.* clarified, etc., *see v.*; **—итель** *m.* clarifier, clarification tank; **—ить, —ять** *v.* clarify, clear, settle; purify; strain, filter; clean; bleach (butter, etc.); defecate (sugar); fine (glass); (hort.) thin (out), open (up or out); **—яющий** *a.* clarifying, etc., *see v.*

освечивание *n.* illumination; candela-second (unit); **энергетическое о.** watt-second/steradian.

освещ/ать *v.* light, illuminate; irradiate, expose (to light); throw light (upon), interpret, elucidate; cover (a subject); **—ающий** *a.* lighting, etc., *see v.*; pilot (bomb); **—ение** *n.* light(ing), illumination; (phot.) exposure; interpretation; **количество —ения** exposure; **—ён-ность** *f.* (intensity of) illumination; illuminance; **коэффициент естественной —ённости** daylight factor; **реле —ённости** lighting control relay; **—ённый** *a.* lit, illuminated, etc., *see v.*; **—ённый луной** moonlit; **—ённый солнцем** sunlit.

освидетельствов/ание *n.* examination, survey; **—ать** *v.* examine, survey, inspect.

освинц/евание, —ов(ыв)ание *n.* lead sheathing, lead plating, lead coating; treatment with lead; **—ованный** *a.* lead-sheathed, lead-plated, lead-coated, lead-lined; **—ов(ыв)ать** *v.* sheathe, plate, coat or line with lead; (treat with) lead.

освободит/ель *m.* liberator; **—ельный** *a.* liberating, freeing, emancipating; **—ь** *see* **освобождать.**

освобожд/ать *v.* (set) free, release, liberate; emancipate; disengage, unlock; get rid (of), eliminate; clear (a line); vacate (premises); relieve; exempt; loose(n), ease, slacken; drain, empty; **о. от** de—, *e.g.,* **о. от яда** detoxify; **—аться** *v.* get rid (of), get free (of); become empty or vacant; (math.) eliminate; **—ающий** *a.* setting free, etc., *see v.*; **—ающий механизм** release.

освобождён/ие *n.* setting free, etc., *see* **освобождать;** liberation; release; riddance, elimination; exemption; **о. от серы** desulfurization; **вызывать о.** *v.* set free, release, liberate.

освобождённый *a.* set free, freed, etc., *see* **освобождать;** exempt.

осво/ение *n.* assimilation, etc., *see* **осваивать;** acceptance; mastering, coping (with) management; opening up, development (of land); reclamation (of bogs); (bot.) land invasion; introduction (of crop rotation); (oil wells) completion; startup and operation (of a plant);

—енный *a.* assimilated, etc., *see* **осваивать;** completed (well); **—ить** *see* **осваивать.**

осевки *pl.* chaff, siftings.

осев/ой *a.* axial; axle; axial-flow (pump, etc.); **о. цилиндр, —оцилиндрический отросток** (cyt.) (neur)axon, axis cylinder; **—ое давление** end thrust.

осевший *a.* precipitated, settled, deposited.

оседаем/ость *f.* precipitability; **—ый** *a.* precipitable; precipitated.

осед/ание *n.* settling, etc., *see v.*; settlement; subsidence, depression; sag(ging); collapse; precipitation, sedimentation; deposition, lodging; (nucl.) fall-out; shrinkage; **скорость —ания эритроцитов** (med.) sedimentation rate; **—ать** *v.* settle (down or out); subside, sink; sag, yield, collapse; precipitate; deposit, lodge (on); set; **—ающий** *a.* settling, etc., *see v.*

оседж *m.,* **—енский** *a.* (geol.) Osagean.

осёдланный *a.* saddle (horse).

оседлать *v.* saddle; straddle; dominate, override.

оседлость *f.* residency; settled way of life; permanence.

осёдлывать *v.* saddle.

оседлый *a.* settled down, resident; stationary; stable; non-migratory (fish).

осей *gen. pl. of* **ось.**

осел *past m. sing. of* **осесть.**

осёл *m.* (mam.) ass (*Equus asinus*).

осел/едец(ь) *m.,* **—ёдка** *f.,* **—ец** *m.* (ichth.) shad, spec. Black Sea shad (*Alosa kessleri pontica*).

осел/ок *m.,* **—очный** *a.* whetstone, hone.

осемен/ение *n.* sowing, etc., *see v.*; (zool.) insemination, impregnation; **—ённый** *a.* sown, etc., *see v.*; **—итель-ный** *a.* sowing, etc., *see v.*; artificial insemination (station); **—ить, —ять** *v.* sow, seed, plant; (bot.) fertilize, pollinate; (zool.) inseminate (artificially).

осен/не-зимний *a.* autumn-winter; **—ний** *a.* autumn, fall; **—ник** *m.* (bot.) autumn saffron (*Colchicum autumnale*); **—чук** *m.* beard grass (*Andropogon*); **—ь** *f.* autumn, fall; (ichth.) Atlantic salmon (*Salmo salar*); **—ью** *adv.* in autumn.

осеребр/ить, —ять *v.* silver(-plate).

осерёдок *m.* alluvial islet (in stream).

осер/енный *a.* sulfured, fumigated with sulfur; **—нение** *n.* sulfuring; **—нять** *v.* sulfur, fumigate with sulfur.

осерчать *v.* get angry, be angry.

осесимметрич/еский, —ный *a.* axisymmetric, axially symmetric.

осесть *see* **оседать.**

осетинский *a.* (geog.) Ossetian.

осетокарный станок shafting lathe.

осётр *m.* (ichth.) sturgeon (*Acipenser*).

осетр/ина *f.,* **—инный** *a.* (food) sturgeon; **—овые** *pl.* Acipenseridae; **—овый** *a.* sturgeon.

осецентробежный *a.* axial-centrifugal, mixed-flow (compressor).

осечённый *a.* truncated, shortened.

осечка *f.* miss, misfire, hangfire.

оси *gen., pl., etc., of* **ось;** axes.

осили(ва)ть *v.* overcome, get the better (of), prevail (upon).

осин/а *f.* (bot.) aspen (*Populus tremula*); **—ка** *f.* young aspen; **—ник** *m.* aspen grove; **—овик** *m.* aspen mushroom (*Boletus rufus*); **—овый** *a.* asp(en).

осинский *a.* (geog.) Osa.

осин/ые *pl.* (ent.) wasps (*Vespidae*); **—ый** *a.* wasp.

осип/лость *f.* hoarseness; **—лый** *a.* hoarse; **—нуть** *v.* get hoarse.

осиять *v.* illuminate.

оскабливать *v.* scrape, scour.

оскали(ва)ть *v.* bare one's teeth.

оскальзываться *v.* slip, skid, slide.

оскоблить *see* оскабливать.

оскол/ок *m.* splinter, sliver, fragment, chip, scale; **—ки** *pl.* chippings, debris; **—ки деления** (nucl.) fission fragments; **разрыв на —ки** fragmentation; **—оченный** *a.* splintered; comminuted (fracture); **—очно-фугасный** *a.* high-explosive (bomb); **—очный** *a. of* осколок; fragmentation(-type); fission-produced (isotope); **—очный элемент** fission product.

оскольз/аться, —нуться *v.* slip, skid.

оскольский *a.* (geog.) Oskol.

оскольчатый *a.* (med.) splintered, comminuted (fracture).

оскомин/а *f.* astringent taste; **набить —у** *v.* set the teeth on edge.

оскоп/ить, —лять *v.* castrate; **—ление** *n.* castration.

оскорб/ительный *a.* offensive; **—ить, —лять** *v.* offend, insult; **—ление** *n.* offense; **—лённый** *a.* offended.

оскре/бать, —сти, —сть *v.* scrape off; **—бки** *pl.* scrapings.

оскуд/е(ва)ть *v.* become poor; grow scarce, die off; **—елый** *a.* scanty; poor; **—ение** *n.* impoverishment, exhaustion (of soil).

оскул/ум *m.,* **—ярная трубочка** (zool.) osculum.

осла *gen. of* осёл.

ослаб/евание *n.* weakening, etc., *see v.;* **—е(ва)ть** *v.* weaken, grow weaker; diminish, lessen, decrease; subside, abate, fade away (of noise); decline; slacken, relax, loosen, work loose; **—евший, —елый** *a.* weakened, etc., *see v.;* debilitated, weak, feeble; loose; **—итель** *m.* (phys.) attenuator; (phot.) reducer; **—ить** *see* ослаблять.

ослабл/ение *n.* weakening; dilution; deterioration, attenuation (of signal); fall (in), reduction, decrease, abatement; decay (of sound); relief (of pain); relaxation, loosening, slack(ening), laxity; debilitation, weakness; (light) absorption; reducing, reduction (of negatives); **коэффициент —ения** (nucl.) attenuation factor; (acous.) reduction factor; (immun.) coefficient of extinction; **слой двухкратного —ения, слой половинного —ения** (nucl.) half-thickness, half-value layer; **цепочка —ения** *see* ослабитель; **—енный** *a.* weakened, etc., *see v.;* weak, infirm, feeble; loose, lax; **—ять** *v.* weaken, debilitate, enfeeble; dilute; attenuate, reduce, decrease, abate, diminish; release, back up (screw); allay, ease, relieve (pain); loosen, relax, slacken, ease up; reduce (negative); **—яться** *v.* weaken; decrease, fall off; **—яющий** *a.* weakening, etc., *see v.;* **—яющий раствор** (phot.) reducer; **—яющая цепочка** *see* ослабитель; **—яющее средство** diluent; debilitant.

ослаб/(нув)ший *a.* weak(ened); loose, slack; **—нуть** *see* ослабевать.

осланцев/ание *n.* (min.) stone or rock dusting (with shale); **—атель** *m.* stone duster.

ослёнок *m.* foal (of donkey).

ослепительный *a.* blinding, glaring, dazzling; **о. свет** glare.

ослеп/ить, —лять *v.* blind, dazzle; **—ление** *n.* blinding; glare; **—лённый** *a.* blinded, dazzled; **—нуть** *v.* go blind.

ослиз/лый *a.* slimy; **—нение** *n.* sliming; **—нуть** *v.* get slimy; get wet and slippery.

ослик *dim. of* осёл; **водяной о.** (crust.) water sow bug (*Asellus aquaticus*).

ослинник *m.* (bot.) Oenothera.

осли/ный *a.* asinine, ass; **—ха, —ца** *f.* female ass, jenny ass.

осложн/ение *n.* complication; **—ённый** *a.* complicated, complex; **—ить, —ять** *v.* complicate, aggravate.

ослуш(ив)ать *v.* (med.) listen, sound; **—ся** *v.* disobey, not follow (directions).

ослы *pl. of* осёл.

ослышаться *v.* hear incorrectly.

ослюден/елые *pl.* (geol.) micatized rocks; **—ение** *n.* mica formation; micatization.

ослянский *a.* (geog.) Oslyanka.

осмалив/ание *n.* resinification; pitching, tarring; **—ать** *v.* resinify; pitch, tar; **—аться** *v.* resinify, become resinous; gum (of oil).

осман *m.* (ichth.) osman (*Diptychus*).

осмат *m.* (chem.) osmate.

осматрив/ание *n.* examination, inspection, survey; **—ать** *v.* examine, inspect, survey, look over, scan; search; see view; **—аться** *v.* look around, get one's bearings.

осмеливаться *v.* dare, have the courage.

осмелит *m.* (min.) osmelite, pectolite.

осмелиться *see* осмеливаться.

осмеять *v.* ridicule, laugh at.

осмиев/окислый *a.* osmic acid; osmate (of); **—ый** *a.* osmium, osmic.

осм/ий *m.* (chem.) osmium, Os; **закись —ия** osmious oxide, osmium monoxide; **иридистый о.** *see* осмирид; **окись —ия** osmic oxide, osmium dioxide.

осм/илы *pl.* (ent.) Osmylidae; **—ирид(ий)** *m.* (min.) osmiridium; **—истый** *a.* (chem.) osmium, osmious, osmium-containing; **—ия** *f.* (ent.) Osmia.

осмо— *prefix* osm(o)— (push, thrust; smell, odor); **—з** *see* осмос; **—зировать** *v.* osmose, subject to osmosis.

осмол *m.* resinous (pine) wood; tarry residue; (chem.) osmol; **пнёвый о.** resinous stump; **—альность** *f.* (chem.) osmolality; **—ение** *n.,* **—ка** *f.* resinification; gumming, gum formation; tarring, pitching; **—ённый** *a.* resinified, etc., *see v.;* **—ить** *v.* resinify, pitch, tar; **—яемость** *f.* tar value.

осмолярн/ость *f.* (chem.) osmolarity; **—ый** *a.* osmolar (solution).

осмолять *v.* resinify, pitch, tar.

осмометр *m.* (chem., phys.) osmometer.

осмондит *m.* (met.) osmondite.

осмо/регулирующий *a.* (physiol.) osmoregulatory; **—регуляция** *f.* osmoregulation; **—с** *m.* osmosis; **—таксис** *m.* osmotaxis (of cells); **—тически** *adv.* by osmosis; **—тический** *a.* osmotic.

осмотр *m.* examination, inspection; survey, review, search; **производить о.** *v.* inspect, check; **—енный** *a.* examined, etc., *see* осматривать; **—еть** *see* осматривать, **—ительность** *f.* discretion, caution, care, circumspection, wariness; **—ительный** *a.* cautious, careful, circumspect, wary; **—щик** *m.* examiner, inspector.

осмофор *f.* (chem.) osmophore.

осмысл/ение, —ивание *n.* comprehension, understanding; interpretation; **—енный** *a.* comprehended, understood; intelligent, sensible; **—и(ва)ть, —ять** *v.* comprehend, understand; interpret.

осна/стить, —щать *v.* equip, fit out (with), rig, furnish, provide, supply; apply; (mach.) tool; instrument; **—стка** *see* оснащение; rig, assembly, outfit; holding device; **—щение** *n.* equipping, etc., *see v.;* equipment; **—щения** *pl.* equipment, rigging, instrumentation;

attachments; —**щённый** *a.* equipped, etc., *see v.*; —**щённый приборами** instrumented.

оснежённый *a.* snow-covered.

основ/а *f.* base, basis, foundation, groundwork, substrate; origin, starting point; framework, backing; principle, element; (met.) starting sheet; (text.) warp; stem (of word); (anat.) stroma, matrix, tela; —**ы** *pl.* essentials, fundamentals, principles; **лежать в —е** *v.* be the basis (for), underlie; **металл —ы** base metal, parent metal; **на —е** on the basis (of), based (on), starting (from), using . . . as the base; in terms (of); **на —е латекса** latex (paint); **на водной —е** water-base; **на свинцовой —е** lead-based (paint); **набирать —у** *v.* (text.) warp.

основан/ие *n.* foundation, basis; (chem.; geom.) base; foot (of perpendicular); foot(ing), bed(ding), ground-(work), bottom, substructure; pedestal, mount(ing); characteristic; principle; origin, starting point; founding, establishment; motive, reason; **о. системы счисления** radix; **о. степени** base number; **всё о.** good reason; **давать о.** *v.* give grounds (for); **ион —ия** basic ion; **лежать в —ии** *v.* underlie; **на —ии** on the basis of, based (on), on the strength (of), from; **не без —ия** with reason; —**ный** *a.* based, etc., *see* **основывать;** depending (on).

основатель *m.* founder, establisher; —**но** *adv.* fully, thoroughly, soundly; —**ность** *f.* soundness; —**ница** *f.* (ent.) fundatrix, stem-mother; —**ный** *a.* solid, sound, well-grounded, thorough, substantial, firm.

основать *see* **основывать.**

основн/ой *a.* fundamental, basic, principal, essential, chief, main, primary, dominant, leading, foremost, key, major, overriding; master; base (metal); (welding) parent (metal); foundation, bed (plate); ground, normalized (state of nucleus, etc.); primary (color); stock (solution); fixed (capital); pacing (factor, item); fixed (point); staple (commodity); flat (rate); sustainer (engine); full-flow (condensate); full (title); (anat.) basilar; **о. двигатель** sustainer; **о. носитель заряда, о. носитель тока** majority carrier; **о. обмен** (physiol.) basal metabolism; **о. пласт** (min.) mother lode, source vein; **о. уровень** standard level datum; (nucl.) ground level; —**ая** *see also under* **основный;** —**ая жила** *see* **основной пласт;** —**ая масса** bulk; matrix; —**ая плоскость** (cryst.) basal plane; —**ая система отсчёта** system of fixed axes; —**ая часть** the bulk, the greater part; —**ое вещество** matrix; (med.) ground substance; —**ое количество** the bulk; —**ое направление** guideline; —**ое состояние** (biol., chem., phys.) ground state, normal state; —**ые законы** see **принципы** philosophy; —**ые носители** (semiconductors) majority carriers; —**ые средства** fixed assets; **в —ом** basically, mainly, principally, essentially, primarily, for the most part; on the whole; much (as).

основно-нёбный *a.* (anat.) sphenopalatine.

основность *f.* basicity, alkalinity.

основно-челюстной *a.* (anat.) sphenomaxillary.

основн/ый *a.* basic, alkaline; sub— (salt); (text.) warp; **о. силикат** subsilicate; —**ая соль углекислоты** subcarbonate.

основовязание *n.* (text.) warp or tricot knitting.

основопол/агающий *a.* basic; **о. принцип** guideline; —**ожник** *m.* founder, initiator, establisher.

основывать *v.* base (on), found, establish, create, set up, constitute, erect; —**ся** *v.* be based (on), proceed (from) start.

ОСО *abbr.* (**отделение санитарной обработки**) decontamination section.

особ/а *f.* person; —**енно** *adv.* especially, particularly, unusually; —**енность** *f.* feature, characteristic, property; distinction, peculiarity, specialty; quality; pattern, habit; (math.) singularity; —**енности питания** eating habits; **в —енности** in particular, particularly, especially; **характерная —енность** characteristic.

особенный *a.* special, singular, peculiar, particular, specific.

особняк *m.* detached house; —**ом** *adv.* by oneself; **стоять —ом** *v.* be single, be alone; occupy a special position.

особо *adv.* apart, separately; especially, particularly; extra; *prefix* idio— [personal, separate, distinct; (chem.; med.) self-produced]; —**пестичный** *a.* (bot.) idiogynous; —**чувствительный** *a.* hypersensitive.

особ/ый *a.* peculiar, distinct(ive), singular, own; particular, special; separate, single, individual; —**ая ситуация** exception; —**ого назначения** special-purpose; —**ь** *f.* individual, specimen; (biol.) species.

осов *m.* (geol.) slough, slip.

осов/елый *a.* dazed, torpid; —**еть** *v.* fall into a dazed state.

осовремени(ва)ть *v.* bring up to date, modernize.

осо/вые *pl.* (ent.) wasps (*Vespidae*); —**ед** *m.* (orn.) honey buzzard (*Pernis*, spec. *P. apivorus*).

осозн/а(ва)ть *v.* realize, become aware (of), become cognizant; —**аемый** *a.* conscious; —**ание** *n.* realization; —**анный** *a.* realized; deliberate.

осок/а *f.* (bot.) sedge (*Carex*); —**ово-злаковый** *a.* sedge-grass; —**ово-кочкарный** *a.* sedge (bog); —**ово-пушицевый** *a.* sedge-cotton grass; —**овые** *pl.* Cyperaceae; —**овый** *a.* sedge.

осокор/ник *m.* (bot.) black poplar grove; —**ь** *m.* black poplar (*Populus nigra*).

осолажив/ание *n.* malting; —**атель** *m.* malting extract; —**ать** *v.* add malt.

осолод/евать *v.* solodize (soil); —**елый** *a.* solodized; —**ение** *n.* solodization.

осолон/цевание *n.* salinization (of soils); solonetzization, alkalization; —**чакование** *n.* salinization; development of solonchak.

осот *m.* (bot.) thistle; spec. sow thistle (*Sonchus*); **розовый о.** Canada thistle (*Cirsium arvense*).

осочник *m.* sage meadow.

осп/а *f.* (med.) smallpox, variola; (vet.) pox; (phyt.) anthracnose (of grapes), wart disease (of potatoes); (met.) pock marks; **о.-дифтерит** *m.* (vet.) avian diphtheria, fowl pox; **ветряная о.** chicken pox; **натуральная о.** smallpox; **прививать —у** *v.* vaccinate; **телячья о.** cow pox.

оспаривать *v.* dispute, call in question; contest, contend (for); **можно о.** it is open to argument.

оспенн/ый *a.* variolous, variolate; (petr.) variolitic; **о. камень** (petr.) variolite; —**ая коррозия** (met.) pitting.

оспина *f.* pock mark; (met.) skin hole.

оспиртованный *a.* alcoholized.

осповидн/ый *a.* pock-marked; —**ое разъедание** (met.) pitting.

оспопривив/ание *n.,* —**ательный** *a.* (med.) vaccination.

оспор/имый *a.* disputable, debatable, questionable; —**ить** *see* **оспаривать.**

ОСР *abbr.* (**орган сравнения**) comparator, discriminator.

осредн/ение *n.* averaging, smoothing; (chem.) neutralization; **о. по времени** time averaging; —**ённый** *a.* averaged, mean; faired (curve); —**итель** *m.* averager; —**ять** *v.* average; neutralize.

ОСС *abbr.* (**опытно-селекционная станция**) experimental selection station.

оссе/ин *m.* (bioch.) ossein, collagen; **—омукоид** *m.* osseomucoid.

оссифи/кация *f.* (med.) ossification; **—цирующий** *a.* ossifying, ossification; **—цирующийся** *a.* ossific.

ост *m.* east.

ОСТ *abbr.* (**общесоюзный стандарт**) All-Union Standard.

остав/аться *v.* remain, be left over; stay, stop; persist; **—ить** *v.* leave, give up, abandon, desert, quit, relinquish; keep, retain, preserve; lay down; **—ить за собой** reserve; **—ить у себя** keep, retain; **—ление** *n.* leaving, etc., *see v.*; abandonment; **—ленный** *a.* left, etc., *see v.*; **—лять** *see* **оставить; —ляющий** *a.* leaving, etc., *see v.*

остаётся *pr. 3 sing. of* **оставаться**; it (now) remains.

осталивать *v.* (met.) steel, electroplate with iron; acierate, convert to steel.

остальн/ое *n.* the remainder, the rest, the balance; **—ой** *a.* remaining, residual; **—ые** *pl.* the rest; **в —ом** as to the rest, in other respects.

останавлив/ать *v.* stop, discontinue, close, shut down, put out of service; check, arrest; bring to a stop; switch off, turn off; restrain; inhibit; stunt (growth); **быстро о.** (nucl.) scram; **—аться** *v.* stop, cease, come to rest, come to a halt; shut down; dwell (on subject); **—ающий** *a.* stopping etc., *see v.*; **—ающее приспособление** stop, arrester.

остан/ется *fut. 3 sing. of* **остаться; —ец** *m.* remnant, relic; (geol.) outlier, monadnock, residual mountain, hill or rock; **—ки** *pl.* remains.

останов *m.* stop, check(ing device), detent, catch, lock, dog; shut-down, outage; **—ившийся** *a.* stopped, at rest; dead (engine); **—ить** *see* **останавливать; —иться на** *v.* decide (on); **—ка** *f.* stop(ping), stoppage, halt(ing), cessation, standstill; closing, shutdown; outrage; intermission, pause; disturbance, interruption; slowdown, delay; (engine) failure; blowing out (of blast furnace); station, terminal; (cardiac) arrest; **аварийная —ка, быстрая —ка** (nucl.) scram, emergency shutdown; **—ленный** *a.* stopped, standing; **—очный** *a.* of **остановка**; check(ing), arresting.

останцовый *a.* of **останец**; residual.

остареть *v.* age.

остат/ковый *see* **остаточный; —ний** *a.* the last, the remaining.

остат/ок *m.* residue, remains, remnant, vestige, trace; surplus, balance, the rest, carry-over; (chem.) radical, group; (math.) remainder; (coking, etc.) char; **о. воды** hydroxyl; **—ки** *pl.* scraps, leftovers, fragments, refuse, waste, bottoms; debris (of cells).

остаточн/ый *a.* residual, remaining, left-over, carry-over; remanent (magnetization); permanent; irreducible; unrecovered (oil); (geol.) detrital, indigenous; rudimentary, vestigial; relict (species); nonprotein (nitrogen); **о. член** (math.) remainder; **явление —ого магнетизма** remanence; magnetic after-effect; **—ая теплота** after-heat; **—ого действия** residual (insecticide); **—ое воздействие** residual effect, carry-over effect.

остаться *see* **оставаться**.

осташи *pl.* rough, undyed leather boots.

остающийся *see* **остаточный**; lasting, durable, stable; persistent; staying, stopping.

Оствальда закон Ostwald law.

осволение *n.* (bot.) trunk formation.

остей *gen. pl. of* **ость**.

остекл/е(ва)ние *n.* glazing; vitrification, hardening; windows; transparency; **—(ен)еть** *v.* become glassy (of eyes); **—ённый** *a.* glazed, glass-enclosed; vitrified; **—ить** *v.* glaze, glass in; **—ованный** *see* **остеклённый; —ов(ыв)ание** *see* **остекление; —ов(ыв)ать** *v.* glaze; vitrify; **—ов(ыв)аться** *v.* vitrify, become vitreous, become glassy; **—янелый** *a.* vitreous, glassy; **—янеть** *see* **остеклов(ыв)аться; —ять** *see* **остеклить**.

остео— *prefix* (anat.) osteo— (bone); **—бласт** *m.* (cyt.) osteoblast.

остеоген *m.* (physiol.) osteogen, **—ез** *m.* osteogenesis, bone formation; **—ный** *a.* osteogenic, osteogenous; **—ная клетка** osteoblast.

остео/дентин *m.* (ichth.; med.) osteodentin; **—дистрофия** *f.* (med.) osteodystrophy; **—идный** *a.* osteoid, bone-like; **—класт** *m.* osteoclast, giant cell; **—лиз** *m.* osteolysis, bone dissolution; **—лит** *m.* (min.) osteolite, earthy apatite; **—лог** *m.* (anat.) osteologist; **—логия** *f.* osteology; **—ма** *f.* (med.) osteoma; **—маляция** *f.* osteomalacia; **—миелит** *m.* osteomyelitis; **—миело—** *prefix* osteomyelo—; **—н** *m.* (anat.) osteon(e); **—патия** *f.* osteopathy, bone disease; **—пороз** *m.* osteoporosis; **—саркома** *f.* osteosarcoma; **—склероз** *m.* osteosclerosis; **—склеротический** *a.* osteosclerotic; **—скоп** *m.* osteoscope.

остеотделитель *m.* (agr.) hummeller.

остео/томия *f.* (med.) osteotomy; **—тропный** *a.* osteotropic; **—тропное вещество, —фил** *m.*, **—фильный изотоп** bone seeker; **—фильный** *a.* bone-seeking; **—фит** *m.* osteophyte, bony escrescence; **—фон** *m.* osteophone (a hearing aid); **—хондрит** *m.* (med.) osteochondritis; **—цит** *m.* osteocyte, bone cell.

остепн/ение *n.* steppization, transformation into steppe; **—ённый** *a.* steppe (meadow); **—ённая местность** steppe heath.

остёр *sh. m. of* **острый.**

остер/егание *n.* warning, admonition; **—егать, —ечь** *v.* warn, caution; **—егаться** *v.* be careful, be on guard, guard against, avoid.

остестригальный *a.* (leather) plucking.

ости *gen., etc., of* **ость;** spinae, spines.

Ост-Индия (geog.) East Indies.

ост-индский *a.* East Indian.

остировать *v.* standardize to All-Union specifications.

остист/о— *prefix* (bot.) arist(o)—, athero— (arista, awn); **—ый** *a.* awned, bearded, aristate; (anat.) spinal; **—ый отросток** (anat.) spinous process.

ост/ит *m.* (med.) osteitis; **—ия** *f.* (biol.) ostium.

остный *a. of* **ость;** aristate, awned.

остов *m.* skeleton, frame(work), shell, hull, body, casing; (tire) carcass; core (of atom); (math.) spanning set; (chromatin) network; (hist.) stroma; **костный о.** (anat.) skeleton; **—ный** *a. of* **остов.**

остож/ина *f.,* **—ье** *n.* (agr.) haystack area.

остоз *m.* (physiol.) ost(e)osis.

остойчив/ость *f.* stability, equilibrium; **—ый** *a.* stable.

остол *m.* (biochem.) osthole.

остолбен/елый *a.* stupefied; **—ение** *n.* stupor, stupefaction, daze, torpor.

остолбить *v.* stake out.

осторожн/о *adv.* carefully, with care, cautiously, gently; **—ость** *f.* care, (pre)caution, heed; **—ый** *a.* careful, cautious, delicate (adjustment); conservative (estimate).

остр *sh. m. of* **острый.**

острагивать *v.* plane.

остракод/а *f.,* **—овый** *a.* (crust.) ostracod.

остр/ее *see* **острие;** *comp. of* **острый; —ейший** *superl. of* **острый; —ение** *n.* pointing, sharpening.

остреогрицин *m.* ostreogrycin (antibiotic).

острец *m.* (bot.) Agropyron; Carex.

остригать *v.* shear, cut, crop.

остр/ие *n.* (cutting) edge, point; peak, cusp; pivot; **о. кривой** (math.) cusp; **разряд с —ия** (elec.) point discharge.

остриженный *a.* cropped, sheared, cut.

остр/ийный *a. of* **острие**; **о. счётчик** (nucl.) Geiger counter; **—ильный** *a.* pointing; **—ильная машина** pointer; **—ица** *f.* (zool.) pinworm (*Oxyuris vermicularis*); (bot.) Asperugo.

остричь *see* **остригать**.

остро *adv.* sharply, etc., *see* **острый**; *prefix* acuti—, acr(o)— (tip, end, extreme); oxy— (sharp, keen, acute).

остров *m.* island; (anat.) insula.

остро/ватый *a.* acutate, slightly sharpened; **—верхий** *a.* peaked; **—вершинность** *f.* peakedness; **—вершинный** *a.* peaked.

остров/итянин *m.* islander; **—ковый** *a.* islet; insular; **—ковый аппарат** (anat.) islands of Langerhans; **—ной** *a.* island, insular; **—ок** *dim. of* **остров**; islet; (safety) island; *pl.* (anat.) insulae.

острога *f.* spear, harpoon, gaff.

острогать *v.* plane, pare down.

остро/глазый *a.* sharp-eyed, sharp-sighted; **—головка** *f.* (herp.) vine snake (*Oxybelis*); **—головки, —головковые** *pl.* (ent.) Acridinae; **—головый** *a.* (med.) acrocephalic; **—губцы** *pl.* cutting pliers, nippers; **—дефицитный** *a.* very scarce; **—заразный** *a.* highly contagious; **—зуб** *m.* (ichth.) Pristipomoides; **—зубый** *a.* sharp-toothed; **—кильница** *f.* (bot.) Lembotropis.

остроконеч/ие *n.* sharp point, cusp, spine; **—ный** *a.* sharp(-pointed), (fine-)pointed, acuminate, acute, acicular, tapered, tapering; (biol.) cuspidate; peaked (wave); ridged, gable (roof).

острокрыл/ки *pl.* (ent.) Lonchopteridae; **—ый** *a.* sharp-winged; sharp-finned.

остролист/(ник) *m.* (bot.) holly (*Ilex*); **—(н)ый** *a.* sharp-leaved, oxyphyllous.

остро/лицый *a.* sharp-faced; **—лодочник** *m.* (bot.) Oxytropis; **—лучевой** *a.* pencil-beam; **—лучка** *f.* (ichth.) Capaetobrama (spec. *C. kuschakewitschi*); **—направленный** *a.* narrow, pointed, sharp; pencil (beam); pencil-beam, high-directional (antenna); **—нос-(ик)** *m.* (ichth.) gray mullet (*Mugil saliens*); **—носый** *a.* sharp(-nosed), pointed, taper(ed); **—пёстр** *m.,* **—пёстро** *n.* milk thistle (*Silybum marianum*).

остропили(ва)ть *v.* secure (with) rafters.

остро/пить *v.* strop; **—плодный** *a.* (bot.) oxycarpous; **—рылый** *a.* (zool.) sharp-faced, sharp-nosed; **—та** *f.* sharpness, etc., *see* **острый**; pungency (of taste); acuity.

остроугольн/ик *m.* (geom.) acute-angled figure; **—ость** *f.* acuteness; **—ый** *a.* acute-angled; acute (triangle).

остроум/ие *n.* wit, ingenuity; **—ный** *a.* witty, ingenious, clever.

остро/ух *m.* (mam.) painted bat (*Kerivoula*); **—ухий** *a.* sharp-eared; **—фокусный** *a.* sharp(-focused); **—хвостые** *pl.* (ichth.) snake eels (*Ophichthidae*); **—хвостый** *a.* sharp-tailed; **—шиповатый** *a.* (bot.) oxyacanthous; **—щетинистый** *a.* exasperate.

остру́г(ив)ать *v.* plane, pare off.

оструктур/енный *a.* aggregated, structurized (soil); **—ивание** *n.* aggregation; conditioning; **—ивать** *v.* aggregate, structurize; condition.

острутин *m.* (biochem.) ostruthin.

остр/ый *a.* sharp, keen, fine, edged, pointed, acicular; (geom.; med.) acute; critical; forced (draft); strong, pungent (taste), acrid (odor); live (steam); short-term (experiment); **о. конец** point; **—як** *m.* (rr.) tongue, point.

остудить *see* **остужать**.

остуднев/ание *n.* gelatinization; **—ать** *v.* gelatinize, gelate.

остуж/ать *v.* cool, chill; **—енный** *a.* cooled; **—ивание** *n.* cooling, chilling.

остук(ив)ать *v.* knock (loose; all around).

осты/вание *n.* cooling (down, off); **—вать, —(ну)ть** *v.* cool (down, off); congeal; **—вший** *a.* cool(ed), cold; congealed.

ост/ь *f.* (biol.) arista, awn, beard, seta, barb; (zool.) kemp, coarse hair; guard hair; (anat.) spina, spine; **относящийся к —и** *a.* spinal.

осу/дить, —ждать *v.* criticize, blame, censure; condemn, convict; **—ждение** *n.* blame, censure; conviction; **—ждённый** *a.* condemned.

осумкован/ие *n.* (biol.) encystment; (en)capsulation; **—ный** *a.* encysted, (en)capsulate(d); sacculated.

осунуться *v.* become gaunt-looking.

осуш/аемый *a.* being drained; drainage (area); **—ать** *see* **осушивать**; **—ающий** *a.* drying, etc., *see v.*; **—ение** *n.* drying, etc., *see v.*; desiccation; drainage, reclamation (of land); **—енный** *a.* dried, etc., *see v.*; **—ивание** *n.* *see* **осушение**; **—ивать** *v.* dry, desiccate, dehumidify, dewater; drain, reclaim (land); **—итель** *m.* dehumidifier, desiccator; drier, drying agent, desiccant, siccative; drainage channel, surface drain; **—ительный** *a.* *see* **осушающий**; **—ить** *see* **осушивать**; **—ка** *see* **осушение**; accretion (of shore); **—ка летом** pond estivation; **зона —ки** intertidal zone.

осуществ/имость *f.* feasibility, practicability; **—имый** *a.* feasible, practicable, realizable; **—ить** *see* **осуществлять**; **—ление** *n.* carrying out, etc., *see v.*; realization, accomplishment, achievement; **—лённый** *a.* carried out, etc., *see v.*; **—ляемый** *a.* under way; **—лять** *v.* carry out, realize, accomplish, bring about, achieve, attain; implement, put into effect, put into practice; complete; handle, conduct, run, perform, do; **—лять управление** management is the function (of); **—ляться** *v.* be carried out, etc.; be (in progress), be under way; take place, occur, happen.

осфрадий *m.* (mal.) osphradium.

осцилл/атор *m.* oscillator; **—ирование** *n.* oscillation; **—ировать** *v.* oscillate; **—ирующий** *a.* oscillating; **—ограмма** *f.* oscillogram; **—ограф** *m.* oscillograph; **—ометр** *m.* oscillometer; **—оскоп** *a.* oscilloscope; **—ятор** *m.* oscillator; **—яторный** *a.* oscillator(y), oscillating; **—яционный** *a.*, **—яция** *f.* oscillation.

осцин *m.* (biochem.) oscine, scopoline.

ос. ч. *abbr.* (**особой чистоты**) very pure.

осы *pl.* (ent.) wasps (*Vespidae*); **о.-блестяник** *pl.* Chrysididae; **о.-землерои** *pl.* digger wasps (*Sphecidae*).

осып/аемость *f.* collapsibility; (bot.) deciduousness; **—ание** *n.* falling (down, off), etc., *see v.*; **—анный** *a.* fallen, crumbled, etc., *see v.*; strewn; **—ать** *v.* sprinkle, dust, strew (with), scatter; cast (seed); shed (leaves); heap, bank; **—аться** *v.* fall (down, off); crumble, collapse, slip (down); (min.) slough; shed (of leaves); shatter (of grain); **—ающийся** *a.* falling, etc., *see v.*; (bot.) deciduous.

осы-пескорои *see* **осы-землерои**.

осып/ка *see* **осыпание**; **—ь** *f.* mound, heap, bank; (geol.) debris, talus, scree.

ос/ь *f.* axis; axle, shaft, spindle, pin, pivot; center line; **о. вращения** pivot; **о. первого порядка** (bot.) main stem, ascending axis; **о. соцветия** rachis; **боковая о.** (cryst.) secondary axis; **имеющий общую о.** *a.* coaxial; **малая о.** minor axis (of ellipse); **на одной —и** in line (with), in alignment (with), aligned; **по —и** axially, endwise.

осьми— *see* **восьми—**; **—зубые** *pl.* (mam.) Octodontidae; **—ног** *m.* (mal.) octopus; **—ножиха** *f.* female octopus.

осядет *fut. 3 sing. of* **осесть.**

осяз/аемость *f.* tangibility, tactility; **—аемый** *a.* tangible, tactile; **—ание** *n.* (sense of) touch, taction, feel; tactus; **чувство —ания** tactus, touch; **—ательный** *a.* tactile, palpable; sensitive, sensible; noticeable; **—а-тельные волосы** (zool.) vibrissae; **—ать** *v.* touch, feel; perceive.

от *prep. gen.* from, off, out of, of, for; against; **от . . . до** (ranging) from . . . to; between . . . and; **от и до;** from point to point; **день ото дня** from day to day.

от— *prefix* de—, ab—, away from.

отава *f.* aftermath, aftergrowth.

отавит *m.* (min.) otavite.

отавный *a. of.* **отава.**

отакелажи(ва)ть *v.* rig out.

отальгия *f.* (med.) otalgia, earache.

отаплив/аемый *a.* heated; fired; **—ание** *n.* heating; firing; **—ать** *v.* heat; fire.

отаптывать *v.* tread down, trample.

отар/а *f.* flock; **—щик** *m.* shepherd.

отбав/ить *v.* decrease, diminish, take away, subtract; **—ка** *f.,* **—ление** *n.* decrease, diminution, taking away, subtraction; removal; **—лять** *see* **отбавить.**

отбалансировать *v.* balance, equilibrate.

отбе/г *m.* (bot.) stolon, runner; **—гать, —жать** *v.* run off or away.

отбей(те) *imp. of* **отбить.**

отбел *m.* chill, hard spots, formation of cementite; **—ён-ный** *a.* whitened, etc., *see v.;* chilled (cast iron); **—и-вание** *n.* whitening, etc., *see v.;* brightening effect (of detergent); **—иватель** *m.* bleach; **—ивательный** *a.* whitening, etc., *see v.;* **—ивать** *v.* whiten, bleach, blanch, decolorize; (met.) refine; chill (cast iron); **—и-вающий** *see* **отбеливательный; —ивающее вещество** whitener, bleach; **—ить** *see* **отбеливать; —ка** *f.,* **—очный** *a.* whitening, etc., *see v.;* **—ьная** *f.* bleachery; **—ьный** *a.* bleaching; bleached; **—ьная земля** bentonite; **—ьщик** *m.* bleacher.

отбензин/ённый *a.* topped, lean (oil); stripped, dry (gas); **—ивание** *n.* topping; stripping; **—и(ва)ть** *v.* top; strip (gas); **—ивающий** *a.* topping; stripping; cycling (plant); **—ование** *see* **отбензинивание.**

отберёт *fut. 3. sing. of* **отобрать.**

отбив *see* **отбивание; —аемый** *a.* repelled, etc., *see v.;* **с —аемым концом** break-seal (tube); **—ание** *n.* repelling, etc., *see v.;* **—ать** *v.* repel, ward off, drive away; beat, fag (fiber); beat off, strike off; break away; break off; hammer out, straighten; hammer free (from); measure out, strike (a line); take away, remove; recapture, retake; liberate (prisoners); whet (scythe); (zool.) wean, separate; **—ать запах** deodorize; **—аться** *v.* repel; stop, cease; fall behind; break off, chip off; **—ка** *see* **отбивание;** (typ.) spacing; **—ной** *a.* beating; beaten.

отбир/ание *n.* taking away, etc., *see v.;* withdrawal; **—ать** *v.* take away, confiscate; remove, (with)draw, run off; take off, tap, bleed (off); extract; take (sam-

ples); select, choose, pick, sort (out), screen, cull; bevel (edge).

отбит/ие *see* **отбивание; —ь** *see* **отбивать.**

отблеск *m.* reflection, gleam; (ice) blink; **—ивать** *v.* reflect.

отбликовать *v.* tarnish, grow dull.

отбой *see* **отбивание;** stop; (hydr.) apron; backsweep (of waves); ringing (of signal); all-clear signal; clearing, release; (tel.) ring-off; **о. паром** steam cushioning; **бить о.** *v.* back down; **давать о.** *v.* ring off; **—ка** *f.* (min.) breaking (down, out, up), cutting; **—ник** *m.* (petrol.) baffle; **—но-вызывной** *a.* (tel.) calling; **—ный** *a.* repelling, recoil; guard; (tel.) supervisory, clearing, ring-off, release; (petrol.) baffle, deflecting (plate); (min.) breaking, cutting; fast (current); **—ный мо-лоток** pick; pneumatic hammer; **—ная перегородка** baffle; **—щик** *m.* (min.) cutter, breaker.

отболеть *v.* undergo an illness.

отбомбить *v.* bomb, finish bombing.

отбор *m.* selection, choice; withdrawal, bleeding, extraction, removal; recovery (of drilled core); yield; (distillation) overhead, takeoff; sampling; picking, separating, sorting, screening; (power) take-off; (isotope separation) outgoing materials; (ichth.) grayling (*Thymallus th.*); **о. образцов, о. проб** sampling; **правило —а** (nucl.) selection rule; **—ка** *f.* withdrawal; molding plane: **—ник** *m.* separator, sorter; sifter; sampler; **—но-навалочная машина** (min.) cutter-loader; **—ный** *a.* choice, select, the best; picked, screened, culled, high-grade; **—очный** *a.* selecting, selection, screening, qualifying.

отбортов/анный *a.* flanged, etc., *see v.;* **—ка** *f.* flanging, etc., *see v.;* flange, crimp; **—щик** *m.* flanger; **—ывать** *v.* flange, bead, crimp.

отбоя *gen. of* **отбой.**

отбраков/ать *see* **отбраковывать; —ка** *f.* rejection; grading, etc., *see v.;* **—очный** *a. of* **отбраковка;** quality-control; **—щик** *m.* inspector; **—ывать** *v.* reject; grade, sort (out), cull.

отбрасыв/аемый *a.* rejected, etc., *see v.;* expendable; **—ание** *n.* rejection, discarding, etc., *see v.;* kick; repulsion; spatter; **—ать** *v.* reject, discard, throw away, throw aside; drop, omit, suppress, (comp.) delete, eliminate; (math.) truncate; reflect, throw (image); repel, repulse, drive back; kick; spatter; centrifuge; (chem.) decant.

отбро/д *m.* degree of end fermentation; **—дить** *v.* finish fermenting; **—женный** *a.* fermented (completely).

отбро/с *m.* residue, waste product, rejected material; deflection; **—сы** *pl.* waste, refuse, garbage, sweepings, scrap; (min.) tail(ing)s, dross; **—сы производства** industrial waste; **твёрдые —сы** refuse; **—санный** *see* **отброшенный; —сать; —сить** *see* **отбрасы-вать; —ска** *see* **отбрасывание; —сный, —совый** *a.* waste; **—шенный** *a.* rejected, etc., *see* **отбрасы-вать.**

отбудет *fut. 3 sing. of* **отбыть.**

отбуксировать *v.* tow (away); float.

отбурить *v.* drill through; finish drilling.

отбучи(ва)ть *v.* (text.) buck, scour.

отбы/вать, —ть *v.* depart, set off; **—тие** *n.* departure.

ОТВ *abbr.* (**общая точка взрыва**) common shot point.

отва/га *f.* courage, bravery; **—дить, —живать** *v.* drive off; break (a habit); **—живаться** *v.* dare, venture; **—жный** *a.* brave, courageous, fearless.

отвал *m.* pushing aside; dump(ing ground), (rubbish) heap; tail(ing)s, spent material; (min.) bank, terrace;

furrow; moldboard (of plow); (bulldozer) blade; (naut.) departure; **идти в о.** *v.* go to the dump, go to waste; **—ивание** *n.* pushing aside, etc., *see v.*; **—ивать** *v.* push aside, push away; heap, bank; dump, throw aside; (naut.) depart, set off; **—иваться** *v.* fall off, come off; **—ивающийся** *a.* falling off; (bot.) caducous, deciduous; **—ить** *see* **отваливать;** **—ка** *see* **отваливание.**

отвалообразов/ание *n.* piling, dumping, refuse disposal; **—атель** *m.* swing chute; spreader, stoker; stacker; **передвижной двусторонний ленточный —атель** reversible shuttle conveyor.

отвальн/ый *a.* dump, waste; nonutilizable (waste); banking; stacking, stockpile (conveyer); **о. плуг** terracer, terracing plow, blade grade; **—ая доска** moldboard (of plow).

отвалять *v.* (text.) full; finish fulling.

отвар *m.* decoct(ion), broth, extract; (dye) liquor; (barley) water; (soup) stock; **—ивание** *n.* boiling, etc., *see v.*; (text.) boil-off; **—и(ва)ть** *v.* boil, digest, cook; decoct; (text.) scour; (welding) separate; **—ка** *see* **отваривание;** **—ной** *a.* boiled, etc., *see v.*

отвед/ение *n.* drawing off, etc., *see* **отводить;** removal, elimination; (physiol.) abduction; (ECG or EEG) lead; **—ённый** *a.* removed, etc., *see* **отводить;** knock (knees).

отвезти *see* **отвозить.**

отвеив/ание *n.* winnowing; elutriation; **—ать** *v.* winnow, blow away; elutriate.

отверг/ать, —нуть *v.* reject, refuse, repudiate; vote down; delete, discard; **—нутый** *a.* rejected, etc., *see v.*

отверд/е(ва)ние *n.* hardening, etc., *see v.*; induration, etc., *see v.*; **—е(ва)ть** *v.* harden, grow hard, congeal, set, solidify; consolidate; **—елость** *f.* hardness, callosity; **—елый** *a.* hardened, etc., *see v.*; **—итель** *m.* hardener, curing agent; **—ить** *see* **отверждать.**

отвержд/аемый *a.* hardenable; **—ать** *v.* harden, set, cure; solidify, consolidate, strengthen; **—ение** *see* **отвердевание;** **—ённый** *a.* hardened, etc., *see v.*

отверженный *a.* rejected, repudiated.

отвёрнутый *a.* unscrewed, etc., *see* **отвёртывать;** (bot.) revolute.

отвернуть *see* **отвёртывать.**

отверст/ие *n.* opening, aperture, hole, perforation, mesh (of screen); orifice, mouth, vent, passage, inlet, outlet, port; break, gap; eye, loop; duct; bore; span (of bridge); (photometry) slit; (anat.) foramen, *pl.* foramina; ostium, entry; hiatus; **выходное о.** outlet; exit hole (of wound); **сто —ий на 1 дм.** 100-mesh.

отвер/теть *see* **отвёртывать.**

отвёрт/ка *f.* screw driver; **—ывать** *v.* unscrew, loosen; twist off; screw off; unfasten; open (valve); turn (away, off), avert; make a turn (of river, road); **—тываться** *v.* unscrew, come off; open; turn away (from), reject.

отверченный *a.* unscrewed, etc., *see* **отвёртывать.**

отвес *m.* plumb (line, bob); vertical slope or drop; **груз —а** bob; **ставить о.** *v.* keep plumb; **ставить по —у** *v.* plumb; **уклонение —а** (astr.) deflection of the vertical; **—ить** *see* **отвешивать.**

отвесн/о *adv.* sheer, plumb, perpendicular; **—ость** *f.* perpendicularity, verticality, steepness; **—ый** *a.* perpendicular, vertical, upright, plumb; steep, abrupt, sheer, precipitous; **—ый берег** bluff; **—ая доска** plumb rule.

отвести *see* **отводить.**

ответ *m.* answer, reply, response; (commun.) answerback; **время ожидания —а** response time.

ответвитель *m.* coupler.

ответвительн/ый *a.* branching, distributing; branch (terminal); **—ая коробка** (elec.) distributing box, distributor.

ответвить *see* **ответвлять.**

ответвлен/ие *n.* branch(ing), parting, arm, offset, offshoot, leg; branch pipe; side drain; derivation, tap(ping), take-off; spur line; (elec.) shunt(ing); (biol.) ramus, branch, *pl.* rami; (bot.) shoot, sprout; **сделать о.** *v.* branch off.

ответвлённый *a.* branch(ed); (elec.) shunt, derived (circuit).

ответвл/ять *v.* branch off, turn off; take off, tap, derive; (elec.) shunt; **—яться** *v.* branch out, bifurcate; **—яющий** *a.* branching, etc., *see v.*

ответ/ить *see* **отвечать;** **—ный** *a.* reply, answering, in answer; reciprocal, return; **—ная реакция** response.

ответств/енность *f.* responsibility, liability; **—енный** *a.* responsible, liable (for), answerable (for); essential, important, critical, vital; demanding (application); **—енный орган** competent body, agency having jurisdiction; **—енный работник** executive, senior official; **—енного назначения** critical (component); **—овать** *v.* reply, answer; be responsible (for).

ответчик *m.* (rad.) transponder; (rockets) responder beacon; (law) defendant.

отвечать *v.* answer, reply, respond; correspond (with), conform (to), comply (with), fit, (ful)fill, satisfy (requirements); meet (specifications); be in full accord (with); **о. перед** be responsible to.

отвеш/енный *a.* weighed (out), etc., *see v.*; **—ивание** *n.* weighing (out), etc., *see v.*; **—ивать** *v.* weigh (out, off); plumb, make vertical.

отвеять *v.* (agr.) winnow; finish winnowing.

отвивать *v.* unwind; finish spinning.

отвин/тить *see* **отвинчивать;** **—ченный** *a.* unscrewed, etc., *see v.*; **—ивание** *n.* unscrewing, etc., *see v.*; **—чивать** *v.* unscrew, screw off; turn off; undo, loosen, withdraw, extract, take out, remove (screw); take off (nut); dismantle, take down; **—чиваться** *v.* unscrew, work loose.

отвис/ать, —нуть *v.* hang down, sag; **—лый, —ший** *a.* sagging, pendant, pendulous; flaccid.

отвить *see* **отвивать.**

отвле/каемость *f.* distractibility, inability to concentrate; **—каемый** *a.* distractible; **—кать** *v.* distract, divert; draw off, withdraw; (med.) derive; abstract; **—каться** *v.* be distracted; digress, ignore, turn from; **—кающее** *n.* (med.) derivative; **—кающий** *a.* distracting, etc., *see v.*; **—чение** *n.* distraction, diversion; digression; abstraction; discharge, removal; **—чённый** *a.* abstract (quantity); distracted; removed, drawn off; **—чь** *see* **отвлекать.**

отвод *m.* branch (pipe), offset; bend, elbow; tap, drain, outlet, run-off, by-pass flue; tapping, drawing off, take-off; withdrawal, extraction, removal, discharge, elimination (of heat); disposal; diversion (of river); derivation (of water); assignment, allocation allotment, distribution; (patent) claim; objection; diffuser (of centrifugal compressor); edge, border; (hort.) layering; **делать о.** *v.* object, take exception (to); **полоса —а** freeway.

отвод/имый *a.* outgoing, exit; withdrawable; **—итель** *m.* outlet; baffle; otter (of mine sweeper); **—ить** *v.* remove, eliminate, draw off, drain off, run off, discharge; lead away, lead off, take (away), carry (away, off); branch, divert, take aside, deflect; swing (arm); derive (water); back away (from); reject, refuse; allocate, assign; (elec.) shunt; (hort.) layer; (physiol.) abduct, draw away; **—ить назад** run back; **—ить от** withdraw; **—иться** *v.* be removed, etc.; play (a role); **—ка** *f.* diversion; branch; (elec.) tap(ping); (belt) shifter; release lever; connection; edge, border; (cer.) banding; (hort.) layering; **—ник** *m.* drain; remover; **—ник тока** (elec.) brush.

отводн/ой, —ый *a. of* **отвод**; deflecting (nozzle); diversion (ditch); layer (cutting); **о. канал** diverter, diversion cut, spillway; **о. кран** drain (cock).

отвод/ок *m.* (hort.) layer, cutting; (apid.) swarm; **разводить —ками** *v.* layer.

отводящ/ий *a.* deflecting, diverting, diversion; discharge, outlet; (anat.) abducent, deferent; **о. канал** offtake; **о. трубопровод** drain (pipe); **—ая мышца** (anat.) abductor; **—ая труба** exhaust (pipe).

отво/евать, —ёвывать *v.* fight; win over, win back; **—еваться, —ёвываться** *v.* finish the war.

отвоз *m.,* **—ка** *f.* transportation; **—ить** *v.* transport, take away.

отволаживать *v.* steep, soak; soften (food); moisten, damp(en) humidify.

отволакивать *v.* drag away.

отвол/гнуть *v.* become damp; **—ожить** *v.* steep, soak; **—ожка** *f.* (leather) rehydration.

отволочь *v.* drag away.

отворачивать *see* **отвёртывать, отворотить.**

отвор/енный *a.* open(ed); **—ить** *see* **отворять.**

отвор/от *m.* fold, flange; flap, top (of boot); **—отить** *v.* turn up; turn away, turn aside, avert; **—оченный** *a.* turned up, etc., *see v.*; recurvate; revolute.

отворять *v.* open.

отвра/тительный *a.* disgusting, repulsive; foul, fetid; **—тить, —щать** *v.* disgust; avert, ward off; bend back; **—щение** *n.* disgust, aversion, distaste, repulsion; **—щённый** *a.* disgusted, etc., *see v.*; (bot.) averse.

отв./см² *abbr.* **(отверстий в сите на 1 см²)** openings/cm² in screen.

отвык /ать, —нуть *v.* lose the habit, be out of practice.

отвяз/ать *see* **отвязывать; —ка** *f.,* **—ывание** *n.* untying, etc., *see v.*; **—ывать** *v.* untie, unbind, unfasten, loosen, disengage; **—ываться** *v.* come loose, separate (from); get rid (of).

отгад(ыв)ать *v.* guess.

отгиб *m.* fold, flange; bend (along axis); (biol.) lamina, blade, limbus, ligule; **—ание** *n.* bending (aside), etc., *see v.*; deflection; diffraction; **—атель** *m.* (coil) opener; **—ать** *v.* bend (aside, up, down); deflect; diffract; bend off, snap off; turn back, turn down, fold; unbend, straighten; **—ка** *see* **отгибание** flanging (of edges).

отглагольный *a.* (grammar) verbal.

отгла/дить, —живать *v.* iron, press, smooth (out); **—живаться** *v.* come out smooth.

отгл/атывать, —отнуть *v.* swallow, take a mouthful.

отгни(ва)ть *v.* rot off.

отгов/аривать, —орить *v.* dissuade; **—ариваться** *v.* excuse oneself; **—орка** *f.* pretext, pretense, excuse.

отголосок *m.* echo, response.

отгон *m.* distillate; distillation, distilling off; (agr.) drive to range; **—ка** *f.* driving off, elimination; distillation; evaporation; sublimation (of volatile substances); (petrol.) flashing-off, topping; stripping; **аппарат для —ки** still; **—но-пастбищный** *a.* distant-pasture; **—ный** *a. of* **отгон**; distant, remote (pasture); range (breeding); **—ная часть** (distillation) stripping section; **—ять** *v.* drive (off, away, out), eliminate, remove, run off; distill off, top, strip; cut off; drive back, repel.

отгораживать *see* **отгородить.**

отгор/ать, —еть *v.* burn off; stop burning.

отгоро/дить *v.* partition off, fence off, shut off, cut off, stop; screen off, enclose; **—женный** *a.* partitioned off, etc., *see v.*; **—женное место** enclosure.

отградуировать *v.* graduate.

отграни(ва)ть *v.* facet, cut facets.

отгранич/ение, —ивание *n.* dividing, etc., *see v.*; **—енность** *f.* differentiation, demarcation; **—енный** *a.* divided, etc., *see v.*; definite, distinct; circumscribed, focal; **—(ив)ать** *v.* divide, separate, delimit, fix limits, demarcate, set boundaries, define.

отгре/бать, —сти *v.* rake aside, rake off, rake away, scrape; row away.

отгру/жать, —зить *v.* unload; ship, dispatch, send off; **—зка** *f.* unloading; dispatch, shipment; **—зочный** *a.* shipping (weight).

отгрыз(а)ть *v.* gnaw or bite off.

отгул *m.* (agr.) range fattening; compensatory leave, flex time; **—ивать, —ять** *v.* take compensatory leave; **—иваться** *v.* fatten on the range.

отд. *abbr.* **[отдел(ение), отдельный].**

отдаваемый *a.* output.

отдавать *v.* give (away), donate, lose, give up, liberate, release; deliver, yield, give off, lose; smell (of); give back, return, restore; recoil, rebound, reverberate; loosen (bolt), unfasten, slacken, unscrew, turn back; place (in job); pay (debt); issue (an order); cast (anchor); **о. назад** give back, return; recoil, kick back; **—ся** *v.* devote oneself (to); resound, ring, echo.

отдав/ить, —ливать *v.* squeeze, crush.

отдаивать *v.* strip (cow); **—ся** *v.* go dry.

отдал/ение *n.* distance; removal; alienation; postponement; **в —ении** at a distance, distant, remote; **—ённость** *f.* remoteness; distance; **—ённый** *a.* distant, remote, far, alienated; postponed; indirect; ab— (away from) *e.g.,* **—ённый от рта** (anat.) aboral; **самый —ённый** outermost (planet); **—ить, —ять** *v.* move off, remove; estrange, alienate; postpone; **—иться, —яться** *v.* move away; shun.

отда/ние *n.* giving; **—нный** *a.* given back, returned; given off, yielded; **—ть** *see* **отдавать.**

отдач/а *f.* delivery, output, yield; (chem., phys.) donation; evolution, emission (of heat); extraction (of oil); loss (of electron); (mach.) performance, efficiency; release, return; recoil, kick (of gun), rebound, repercussion, spring back, springiness; deflection (of structure or machine); payment (of debt); **о. мощности** efficiency; **весовая о.** load ratio; **коэффициент —и** efficiency; (elec.) output coefficient; **кривая —и** efficiency curve; **промышленная о.** efficiency; **удельная о.** (elec.) specific output; **частица —и** (nucl.) recoil particle.

отдви/гать *see* **отодвигать; —жной** *a.* (re)movable, sliding.

отдел *m.* section, division, branch, department; class; step, stage; (geol.) formation, series; (taxonomy) phylum.

отдел/анный *a.* finished, etc., *see* **отделывать; —анная поверхность** finish; **—ать** *see* **отделыбать.**

отдел/ение *n.* division, branch, department, section, compartment, partition; room, chamber, shop; separation; separating out, isolation, segregation; removal, elimination, release; secretion, excretion; evolution, emission; precipitation; recovery (from waste); cutting, cleaving, severance; detachment; **—ённый** *a.* separated, etc., *see* **отделять;** disjunct, disconnected; **—ённый осаждением** precipitated out.

отдел/ившийся *a.* separated, loosened; **—имость** *f.*

separability; **—имый** *a.* separable; detachable; **—и-тель** *m.* separator, divider; eliminator; (liquid) trap; isolating switch; **—ительный** *a.* separating; **—ить** *see* **отделять.**

отдел/ка *f.* finishing, etc., *see v.*; finish; structure; **о. начисто** polishing; **—очная** *f.* finishing shop; **—очно-расточный** *a.* fine-boring; **—очный** *a. of* **отделка; —ывать** *v.* finish (off), dress, trim, clean; planish; decorate; work up, fashion; set (gem); align, adjust; (mil.) spoil; **—ывать под** finish in; **—ывать-ся** *v.* be finished, etc.; finish (with), get rid (of).

отдельно *adv.* separately, apart, singly; **о. стоящий** independent, separate, detached.

отдельност/ь *f.* individuality, separateness; (geol.) cleavage, parting, rift, jointing; structure; (structural) unit; **в —и** separately; **по —и** singly.

отдел/ьный *a.* separate, discrete, individual; detached, independent, isolated, single; partial, divided; specific (case); scattered (clouds); **—яемое** *n.* discharge, secretion; **—яемость** *f.* separability; **—яемый** *a.* separable, etc., *see v.*; escape (module) ejection (capsule); **—ять** *v.* separate (out), extract, recover; single out, isolate, segregate; divide, part; partition; sever, cut off, detach, disengage; drive off, eliminate, liberate, free, release; eliminate, remove; secrete, excrete; pick, soft (ore); **—яться** *v.* separate (out); secrete; break away; **—яющий** *a.* separating, etc., *see v.*; (physiol.) secretory; apocrine (glands); **—яющийся** *a.* separable; **с —яющейся косточкой** freestone (peach).

отдёргив/ание *n.* drawing back, withdraw, jerk back. **—ать** *v.* draw back, withdraw, jerk back.

отдерёт *fut. 3 sing. of* **отодрать.**

отдёрнуть *see* **отдёргивать.**

отдиализовать *v.* dialyze.

отдир/ание *n.* tearing off, etc., *see v.*; **—ать** *v.* tear off, rip off, peel off, skin.

отд. л. *abbr.* (**отдельный лист**) separate sheet; **отд-ние** (**отделение**).

отд/оить *v.* strip (cow); **—оиться** *v.* go dry; **—ой** *m.* stripping.

отдохнуть *see* **отдыхать.**

отдраи(ва)ть *v.* (naut.) open.

отдубина *f.* tan waste, spent tanbark.

отдув/ать *v.* blow (off, away); strip; **—аться** *v.* pant; **—ка** *f.* blowing, etc., *see v.*

отдулина *f.* bulge, bulging, blister.

отдум(ыв)ать *v.* reconsider.

отдуть *see* **отдувать.**

отдух *see* **отдушина.**

отдушивать *v.* perfume.

отдуш/ина *f.*, **—ник** *m.* (air) vent, air hole, drain; exhaust pipe; ventilator; **—истость** *f.* (leather) break; **—ка** *f.* additive perfume, odoriferous substance.

отдых *m.* rest, repose, recreation, relaxation; time off; (tech.) recovery; **без —а** incessantly; **дом —а** rest home; **зона —а** recreation area; **—ать** *v.* rest; be on vacation; **—ающий** *a.* resting; *m.* vacationer.

отдышаться *v.* catch one's breath.

отёк *m.* (med.) edema, dropsy; (paints) sag; *past m. sing. of* **отечь; о. лёгких** (med.) emphysema.

отек/ание *n.* swelling, etc., *see v.*; (med.) edematization; **—ать** *v.* swell; become dropsical; drip, flow off, run.

отёк/лый, —ший *a.* swollen; (o)edematous.

отёл *m.* calving.

отелиться *v.* calve.

отель *m.*, **—ный** *a.* hotel.

отенит *m.* (min.) autunite.

отен/ить, —ять *v.* shade.

отепл/ение *n.* warming, etc., *see v.*; heat insulation; **—ительный** *a.* warming, etc., *see v.*; **—ить, —ять** *v.* warm, heat; defrost; protect from cold.

отереть *see* **обтирать.**

отесать, отёсывать *v.* rough-work; dress, trim.

оте/ц *m.* father; **—ческий** *a.* paternal.

отечеств/енный *a.* native, home; domestic (industry); Soviet-made; patriotic (war); indigenous; **—о** *n.* fatherland, native country.

отёч/ность *f.* (med.) intumescence; **—ный** *a.* edematous, dropsical; **—ная болезнь** edema; **—ная жидкость** transudate; **—ь** *see* **отекать.**

отешет *fut. 3 sing. of* **отесать.**

отжари(ва)ть *v.* finish roasting, finish frying.

отжат/ие *see* **отжим;** release (telecom.) space; **—ый** *a.* squeezed (out), etc., *see* **отжимать; —ь** *see* **отжимать;** finish harvesting.

отжечь *see* **отжигать.**

отжив/ать *v.* become obsolete; **—ающий** *a.* obsolescent; **—ший** *a.* obsolete.

отжиг *m.*, **—ание** *n.*, **—ательный** *a.* annealing, etc., *see v.*; **—ать** *v.* anneal; (electron.) fire; burn off, bake off, roast.

отжим *m.*, **—ание** *n.* squeezing (out), etc., *see v.*; **—ать** *v.* squeeze (out), press out, force out; wring out; centrifuge; detach, pry off; separate; **—аться** *v.* be squeezed (out), etc.; become detached, get loose; **—ка** *see* **отжим;** centrifuge; wringer; **—ки** *pl.* residue, scrap; **—ный** *a.* squeezing (out), etc., *see v.*; centrifugal; drying (press); **—ная машина** centrifuge, wringer; **—ное течение** offshore current, undertow.

отжинать *v.* finish harvesting.

отжит/ый *a.* obsolete; **—ь** *see* **отживать.**

отзаторивание *n.* mashing.

отзв/анивать, —енеть, —онить *v.* ring (off); stop ringing; **—ук** *m.* repercussion, echo; **—учание** *n.* sonification; **—учать** *v.* echo, resound; stop, die away (of sound); **—ученный** *a.* subjected to ultrasonic vibrations; **—учивание** *n.* application of ultrasonic vibrations.

отзейгерованный *a.* (met.) liquated, melted out; liquation (lead).

отзимовать *v.* (spend the) winter.

отзовёт *fut. 3 sing. of* **отозвать.**

отзол *m.* (leather) liming; lime solution; **—ить** *v.* lime; **—ка** *f.*, **—ьный** *a.* liming.

отзыв *m.* testimonial, reference; review; response; comment; recall; report, echo; **—ать** *v.* call away, summon back, recall; revoke, countermand; smell, taste (of); **—аться** respond; echo; **—ающийся** *a.* resonant; **—ной** *a.* recall; **—чивость** *f.* response, effect, reaction; responsiveness (of instrument); **—чивый** *a.* effective; responsive, sympathetic.

отиатр *m.* (med.) otologist, ear specialist; **—ический** *a.* otological; **—ия** *f.* otology.

ОТИЗ *abbr.* (**отдел технической информации и изобретательства**) division of technical information and invention.

отирать *see* **обтирать.**

отит *m.* otitis, inflammation of ear.

ОТК *abbr.* (**отдел технического контроля**) quality control department.

отказ *m.* refusal, denial, rejection, repudiation; malfunction, nonoperation, breakdown, failure; (pile driving) resistance; **о. в работе** breakdown; **о. от** abstention (from): **о. от участия** non-participation; **без —а** (mach.) normally, smoothly; **до —а** to the limit, as far as possible; to capacity, full; (mach.) home, tight, all the way in; **полный до —а** heaping full; **—оустой-чивый** *a.* fault-tolerant; fail-safe; **—чик** *m.* conscientious objector; **—(ыв)ать** *v.* refuse, forbid, deny, reject; break down, fail; **—(ыв)аться** *v.* refuse, decline, give up, abandon, drop; renounce; resign (from a position); **—(ыв)аться действовать** *v.* fail, break down, get out of order; **—(ыв)аться от** discard, discontinue, drop, rid oneself (of), abandon, give up.

откалыв/ание *n.* breaking off, etc., *see v.;* **—ать** *v.* break off, split off, chip off, flake off, spall; cut off, chop off; detach, separate, exfoliate; unfasten, unpin; **—аться** *v.* split off, chip, spall, splinter; come apart.

откапыв/ание *n.* exhumation; **—ать** *v.* exhume, dig up, disinter, unearth.

откармлив/аемость *f.* fattening capacity; **—аемый** *a.* fattened; **—ание** *n.* fattening; nutrition; **—ать** *v.* fatten, feed up.

откат *see* **откатывание**; (art.) recoil; backrush (of wave); (comp.) undo; **—ать** *v.* roll back, roll away; **—ить** *see* **откатывать**; **—ка** *see* **откатывание**; (min.) haulage; **—но-подъёмный** *a.* rolling-lift (bridge); **—ный** *a.* rolling, roller; pull-back, retractable, draw (bridge); drag (reel); **—очный** *a.* (min.) haulage; **—чик** *m.* hauler, haulage man; **—ывание** *n.* rolling away, etc., *see v.;* **—ывать** *v.* roll away, aside or off; wheel off; (min.) haul; **—ываться** *v.* roll away; roll back (of waves); (art.) recoil; **—ывающийся** *a.* rolling away, etc., *see v.;* sledge (carriage).

откач/анный *a.* pumped out, etc., *see* **откачивать**; **—ать** *see* **откачивать**.

откаченный *past pass. part. of* **откатить**.

откач/ивание *n.* pumping out, evacuation, etc., *see v.;* withdrawal; **—(ив)ать** *v.* pump out, evacuate, exhaust, withdraw, draw away; purge, scavenge; resuscitate; (comp.) swap (out); **—ивающий** *a.* pumping out, etc., *see v.;* discharge (pump); **—ка** *see* **откачивание**; (honey) extraction; (comp.) roll-out.

откачнуть *v.* swing away.

откачный *a.* exhaust, discharge.

огкашивать *v.* mow; finish mowing.

откашл/ивание *n.* expectoration, spitting; **—ивать(ся)** *v.* expectorate, spit; **—ивающее** *n.* expectorant; **—я-нуть** *v.* cough up; **—ять** *v.* cough up; finish coughing.

отакваска *f.* steep, drench.

откид/анный *a.* thrown back, thrown aside; **—ать** *see* **откидывать**; **—ка** *f.* (blade) rake; **—ной** *a.* folding (-back), hinged, flap, drop (valve); collapsible; reversible; tipping, dumping; swing, swivel(ing); slip (hook); deflecting (nozzle).

отки/лывать, **—нуть** *v.* throw off, aside or away; throw back, fold back, open, lift (lid); disregard; drain; tilt; **—дыш** *m.* (bot.) brood bud, bulbil.

откип/ать, **—еть** *v.* boil off; stop boiling.

откисл/енный *a.* deacidified, neutralized; **—ить** *v.* deacidify, neutralize.

отклад/ка *f.,* **—ывание** *n.* putting off, etc., *see v.;* postponement; (zool.) oviposition; **о. икры** (ichth.) spawning; **—ывать** *v.* put off, postpone, defer, delay, shelve (a project, etc.); adjourn, call off; put aside, set aside, put away, reserve, put by, lay up; settle, deposit, precipitate; plot (curve), lay off; oviposit, lay (eggs).

отклевать, **отклёвывать** *v.* peck off; stop pecking.

откле/енный *a.* unglued, etc., *see v.;* **—ивание** *n.* ungluing, etc., *see v.;* **—и(ва)ть** *v.* unglue, degum, take off, remove; **—и(ва)ться** *v.* come off; **—йка** *see* **отклеивание**.

отклик *m.* response; echo; **—аться**, **—нуться** *v.* re-

spond; comment; echo; **поверхность —а** (math.) response surface.

отклонен/ие *n.* deviation, departure, divergence, difference, discrepancy, error; digression, aberration, variation, diversion, anomaly; deflection, declination (of needle); diffraction (of rays); throw (of point); tilt, bias; **о. кзади, о. назад** retroversion; **о. от круглой формы** out-of-roundness; **о. шага** difference in pitch; **вертикального —ия** Y-axis (amplifier); **предел —ия** play; **сила —ия** deflecting force.

отклонённый *a.* deflected, etc., *see* **отклонять**; divergent; (anat.) clinoid (process).

отклон/итель *m.* deflector; (petrol.) deflection tool; **—ить, —ять** *v.* deflect, decline, turn aside, divert, deviate; alter, send off (course); avert; derive; **—иться, —яться** *v.* be deflected, etc.; deflect, decline, divert, deviate, digress, aberrate, vary, diverge; swerve, go off (course); slant, tilt; **—яться от круглой формы** be out of round; **—яющий** *a.* deflecting, etc., *see v.;* beam-deflection (tube); sweeping (magnet); **—яющие отображения** (math.) perturbation mappings; **—яющийся** *a.* deflecting, etc., *see v.;* divergent, aberrant.

отключ/аемый *a.* detachable; **—атель** *m.* disconnector; **—ать** *v.* detach, disconnect, disengage; unplug, switch off, cut off, turn off, turn out; isolate; throw off (switch); deactivate; **—ающий** *a.* detaching, etc., *see v.;* cut-off; **—ение** *n.* detaching, etc., *see v.;* detachment, disengagement; **—ённый** *a.* detached, etc., *see v.;* off; **—ить** *see* **отключать**.

отков/анный *a.* forged; **—(ыв)ать** *v.* forge; finish forging; knock off.

отковыр/ивать, **—нуть**, **—ять** *v.* pick out or off; chip off.

откол *m.* splitting off, break(ing)-away; **—ачивать** *v.* knock off; **—ка** *f.* (glass) burn-off, flame cut-off; **—отить** *v.* knock off; **—отый** *a.* split off; unpinned, unfastened; **—оть** *see* **откалывать**; **—оченный** *a.* knocked off; **—ьный** *a. of* **откол**; (seismic surveying) split-off, break-away.

откомандиров(ыв)ать *v.* send, assign, dispatch.

откомлёвывать *v.* (forestry) jump-butt.

отконопа/тить, **—чивать** *v.* caulk; uncaulk, remove caulking.

отконтролировать *v.* check.

откоп/ать *see* **откапывать**; **—ка** *f.* exhumation, digging out; (hort.) uncovering.

откорм *m.,* **—ка** *f.* fattening; **ставить на о.** *v.* start fattening; **—ить** *v.* fatten (up), batten, (flush-)feed; **—ленность** *f.* fattened condition; **—ленный** *a.* fattened, well-fed; enriched; **—очник** *m.* feed lot; sow being fattened; **—очный** *a.* fattening; finishing, flush-feeding; feeder, mast-fed (cattle); **—очное хозяйство** feed lot; **—щик** *m.* feeder.

откорректированный *a.* corrected.

откос *m.* slant, slope, declivity, inclination, dip, incline; (met.) bank (of furnace); (window) jamb; prop; back (of dam); **с —ом** sloped; **угол естественного —а** angle of rest or repose.

откосить *v.* finish mowing.

откос/ник *m.* (road) backsloper; **—ный** *a. of* **откос**; sloping, inclined; **—опланировщик** *m.* slope grader.

откоч/евать, **—ёвывать** *v.* migrate; **—ёвка** *f.* migration.

откраивать *v.* cut by pattern.

откреп/ительный *a.* unfastening; **—ить, —лять** *v.* unfasten, detach; untie, loosen; strike off (the list).

откровен/ие *n.* revelation; **—ность** *f.* frankness, candor; **—ный** *a.* frank, outspoken

откроет *fut. 3 sing. of* **открыть.**

откроить *see* **откраивать.**

откру/тить, —чивать *v.* unscrew, take off (nut); twist off, untwist (rope); turn off (flow); open (valve); **—титься** *v.* turn off; come loose; get out (of); **—ченный** *a.* unscrewed, etc., *see v.*

открыв/аемый *a.* detectable; **—ание** *n.* opening, etc., *see v.*; **—атель** *m.* opener; discoverer; **—ать** *v.* open (up), force open, push open; uncover, reveal, disclose, detect; turn on (valve); clear (path); offer (a challenge); unlock; **—аться** *v.* open (up); **—ающийся** *a.* opening; (bot.) dehiscent.

открылок *m.* (building) lean-to.

открытие *n.* opening; disclosure, finding; detection, identification; proof, evidence; breakthrough, discovery, development, invention; inauguration (of operation).

открытка *f.* post card.

открыто *adv.* openly, publicly; *prefix* chasmo— [open-(ing)]; **—плодные** *pl.* (bot.) Discomycetes; **—пузырный** *a.* (ichth.) physostomous; **—угольный** *a.* open angle; **—цветущий** *a.* (bot.) chasmogamic, open-flowered; **—ячеистый** *a.* open-pored, open-cell (plastic).

открыт/ый *a.* open, exposed, uncovered, unprotected; mid-(ocean); open-top (trailer); (min.) open-pit, open-cut; flat, platform (car); uncapped (honeycomb); straightforward, frank; (comp.) active (file); **о. разрез** open-cut mine; **о. способ** open-cut mining; **—ое письмо** post card; **—ые работы** open-cut mining; stripping; **на —ом воздухе** in the open, outdoors; open-air (method); **—ь** *see* **открывать.**

откуда *adv.* from where, from which, whence, how; **о.-либо, о.-нибудь** from somewhere or other; **о. следует** whence it follows, it therefore follows; **о.-то** from somewhere.

откуёт *fut. 3 sing. of* **отковать.**

откуп: отдавать на о. *v.* farm out; **—ать, —ить** *v.* buy up; **—аться, —иться** *v.* pay off.

откупор/енный *a.* uncorked, etc., *see v.*; **—ивание** *n.*, **—ка** *f.* uncorking, etc., *see v.*; **—и(ва)ть** *v.* uncork, unstop, uncap, unseal, open.

отку/санный *see* **откушенный; —сить** *see* **откусывать; —сывание** *n.* biting off, etc., *see v.*; **—сывать** *v.* bite off, cut off, snap off, (s)nip off, trim off; **—шенный** *a.* bitten off, etc., *see v.*

отлавливать *v.* catch, trap.

отлаг/ательство *n.* delay, procrastination; **—ать** *v.* delay, put off; set aside; (geol.) deposit; **—аться** *v.* separate, settle out, precipitate, deposit; lodge (on).

отла/дить *see* **отлаживать; —дка** *f.* fixing, etc., *see v.*; (program) checkout, debugging; **система —дки** test bed; **—дочная программа** debugger; **—дочная система** test envelope; **—женный** *a.* fixed, etc., *see v.*; **—живать** *v.* fix, adjust, tune up; debug, rectify, repair (a program).

отлакировать *v.* lacquer, varnish.

отламывать *v.* break off, chip off.

отлежаться *see* **отлёживаться.**

отлёж/иваться *v.* rest; lie around; **—ка** *f.* resting; wetting off, softening; **—ь** *f.* sediment, deposit.

отлеп/ить, —лять *v.* take off, unglue; mold, fashion.

отлёт *m.* flying away, take-off, departure; **быть на —е** *v.* be about to leave.

отлет/ать, —еть *v.* fly away or off, take off, depart; come off; have completed a flight; **—ающий** *a.* flying away, etc., *see v.*

отлётный *a.* departing (plane); migrating (birds).

отлив *m.* reflux, return flow, discharge; outlet; pouring off, etc., *see v.*; play (of colors); (arch.) drip mold; ebb, low tide; **о. цветов** iridescence, opalescence; **прилив и о.** ebb and flow; **с —ом** iridescent, opalescent, chatoyant; shot (with a color); **—аемость** *f.* flowability; **—ание** *see* **отливка** discard; pump out, bail out; (met.) cast, found; (plastics) cast, mold; (ocean) ebb; be shot (with a color); **—ать всеми цветами радуги** iridesce, be iridescent; **—ка** *f.* pouring off, etc., *see v.*; cast (material); (plastics) injection molding; (paper) pulp handsheets; **—ка в песке** sand casting; **—ка в почве** casting in the open; **чугунная —ка** cast iron.

отливн/ой *a.* founded, cast; founding, casting; decanting; discharge (jet, gate); delivery (pipe); (ocean) ebb-tide; **—ая печь** founding furnace; **—ая рама** casting box; **—ое течение** ebb.

отлив/ный *a.* (ocean.) ebb; **—ок** *m.* cast(ing); **—очный** *a. of* **отливка.**

отлинять *v.* (zool.) finish shedding or molting.

отлип *m.* adhesion, tack(iness); **—ание** *n.* ungluing, etc., *see v.*; **зазор —ания** residual gap (of relay); **—ать, —нуть** *v.* unglue, come off, become detached, peel off.

отлит/ый *a.* cast, founded; poured off, decanted; **—ое отверстие** core hole; **в —ом виде** as cast; **—ь** *see* **отливать.**

отлич/ать *v.* distinguish, discriminate, differentiate, discern; **—аться** *v.* differ, be distinguished (by), be characterized (by); surpass, outdo, excel; feature, be noted (for); **—ающийся** *a.* differing, etc., *see v.*; different, distinct, dissimilar, unlike; **—ённый** *a.* distinguished (from); **—ие** *n.* difference differentiation, distinction; contrast; nature, variety; honors; **в —ие от** in contrast to, by contrast, unlike, as opposed to, as distinguished from; **крупных —ий** *a.* large-scale.

отличительн/ый *a.* distinctive, distinguishing, identification, characteristic, peculiar, special; **о. знак** distinctive mark, distinction; **о. признак** (distinguishing) feature, characteristic; **—ая черта** characteristic.

отлич/ить *see* **отличать; —ник** *m.* outstanding worker, outstanding student; **рабочий —ник** outstanding worker; **—но** *adv.* excellent(ly), very well; it is fine; **—ный** *a.* excellent, very good, first-rate, superior, exceptional; different, distinct (from); unlike; **о. от других** unique, distinctive, peculiar.

отлов *m.* catch, take, harvesting (of wildlife); **—ить** *v.* catch, trap; fish out; **—ленный** *a.* caught, trapped; fished out.

отлог *m.* inclination, slope; **—ий** *a.* sloping, shelving, gentle (climb); flat, low-angle (trajectory); **—о** *adv.* at a slope; **—о спускаться** *v.* slope, slant, shelve; **—ость** *f.* slope, sloping, declivity.

отлож/ение *n.* precipitation, precipitate, sediment; formation; accretion (of ice); accumulation, store; (geol.) deposit(ion), sedimentation, blanket, incrustation; laying aside, postponing; **—енный** *a.* precipitated, etc., *see v.*; **—ившийся** *a.* precipitated, deposited, settled; **—ить** *v.* precipitate; (geol.) deposit; lay aside, set aside; postpone, put off; open, unlock; unharness.

отлом/ать, —ить *see* **отламывать; —ка** *f.*, **—очный** *a.* cracking, breaking off; **—очное железо** (glass) cutter.

отлуп *m.* (forestry) cup shake, ring shake; **—ить(ся), —лять(ся)** *v.* peel off.

отлуч/аться, —иться *v.* absent oneself, be absent; **—ение от матки** weaning; **—ка** *f.* absence.

отмаз(ыв)ать *v.* finish greasing; unlute.

отмани(ва)ть *v.* lure away.

отмарывание *n.* (dyeing) mark off.

отмастка *f.* shading, shade (of fur).

отматыв/ание *n.* unwinding, etc., *see v.*; **—ать** *v.* unwind; rewind; (typ.) offset, set off.

отмах/(ив)ать, —нуть *v.* fan away, wave away; swing away; cover (distance); dispatch, hurry through; (naut.) signal.

отмачив/ание *n.* soaking, etc., *see v.*; **—атель** *m.* steeping tank; **—ать** *v.* soak (off); steep, ret; wet (off or out).

отмаш/ет *fut. 3 sing. of* **отмахать**; **—ка** *f.* (naut.) signal(ing).

отмеж/евание *n.* marking off, etc., *see v.*; **—ёванный** *a.* marked off, etc., *see v.*; **—евать** *see* **отмежёвывать; —ёвка, —ёвывание** *see* **отмежевание; —ёвывать** *v.* mark off, draw a boundary, fix boundaries; measure off, survey; **—ёвываться** *v.* dissociate, isolate oneself; be separate.

отмёл *past m. sing. of* **отмести.**

отмель *f.* bank, shoal (water); shallow, shelf; (sand) bar.

отмен/а *f.* abolition, etc., *see v.*; repeal; (comp.) undo; cancel; **—ённый** *a.* abolished, etc., *see v.*; **—ить** *v.* abolish, cancel, annul; repeal, revoke, rescind, reverse, countermand.

отменный *a.* superior, excellent.

отменять *see* **отменить.**

отмереть *see* **отмирать**

отмерз/ать *v.* freeze off; (agr.) be killed by frost; thaw.

отмёрз/лый frozen (off); frostbitten; thawed out; **—нуть** *see* **отмерзать.**

отмер/ивание *n.* measuring off; (pharm.) dosage; **—и(ва)ть** *v.* measure off, mark off; dose.

отмерший *a.* atrophied, dead; extinct.

отмерять *see* **отмери(ва)ть.**

отмести *see* **отметать.**

отмёт *m.* shedding, extrusion (of larvae).

отметать *v.* sweep aside or away; give up, reject.

отмет/ина *f.* mark(ing), notch, nick; **—ить** *see* **отмечать; —ка** *f.* mark(er), notch; (reference) mark, check point, control point; (leveling) elevation, vertical control point; (zero) datum; elevation, level, grade; sign, indication; label; marking; **высотная —ка** elevation, level; **на рабочей —ке** at operating level; **на —ке 17 м** at the 17-meter level; **—чик** *m.* marker, indicator, recorder; **—чик времени** timer.

отмеч/ать *v.* record, register, note, mark (down); take (readings); label; plot; list, quote; point out, indicate, mention, observe; emphasize, stress; **—ающий** *a.* recording, etc., *see v.*; distinct; **—ающий автоматически** self-recording; **—енный** *a.* recorded, etc., *see v.*

отмин *m.* (leather) break; **—ать** *v.* knead, work.

отмир/ание *n.* dying off, necrosis, atrophy; disappearance (of species); **—ать** *v.* die off; disappear; **—ающий** *a.* moribund; rudimentary.

отмобилизовать *v.* (mil.) mobilize.

отмоет *fut. 3 sing. of* **отмыть.**

отмок/а *f.* soak(ing), steeping, softening; **—ать, —нуть** *v.* soak (off), steep; come off; get wet, get damp; **—ший** *a.* soaked off; wet.

отмол/ачивать, —отить *v.* (agr.) thresh; finish threshing.

отмолоть *v.* grind, mill; finish milling.

отмор/аживание *n.* freezing, frostbite; **—аживать** *v.* freeze (off), be frostbitten; **—ожение** *see* **отмораживание; —оженный** *a.* frozen, frostbitten; **—озить** *see* **отмораживать.**

отмостка *f.* blind area.

отмотать *see* **отматывать.**

отмоч/енный *a.* soaked (off); **—ить** *v.* soak (off); **—ка** *f.* soaking; **—ный** *a.* soaking; soaked.

отмоющий *pr. part. of* **отмыть.**

отму/тить *see* **отмучивать; —тка** *see* **отмучивание; —ченный** *a.* elutriated, etc., *see v.*; **—чивание** *n.* elutriation, etc., *see v.*; **—чивать** *v.* elutriate, clarify, wash; decant; (min.) buddle; deposit (starch); (soil) separate in layers (by washing).

отмучиться *v.* finish suffering.

отмыв/ание *n.,* **—ка** *f.* washing (away), etc., *see v.*; **—ать** *v.* wash (away, off, out), rinse; (chem.) elute; tint, shade (drawing).

отмык/ание *n.* unlocking, etc., *see v.*; **—ать** *v.* unlock, unbolt, open; **—ающий** *a.* unlocking, etc., *see v.*; **—ающая мышца** (anat.) divaricator.

отмылив/ание *n.* rinsing; **—ать** *v.* rinse, free from soap, cleanse from soap.

отмыт/ый *a.* washed, washed off, washed out; **—ь** *see* **отмывать.**

отмычка *f.* skeleton key, master key.

отмяк/ать *v.* soften, grow soft; **—лость** *f.* softening; **—лый, —ший** *a.* soft(ened); **—нуть** *see* **отмякать.**

отмять *see* **отминать.**

ОТН *abbr.* (**отделение технических наук**) Division of Technical Sciences.

отн. ед. *abbr.* (**относительная единица**) relative unit.

отнерестившийся *a.* spent, spawned out (fish).

отнес/ение *n.* taking away; referral; **—ённый** *a.* taken away, carried away; **—ённый к** referring to, in terms of; **—ти** *see* **относить.**

отниз(ыв)ать *v.* unstring, separate.

отникелировать *v.* nickel-plate.

отним/ать *v.* take away, confiscate; rob (of), deprive (of); take (off), withdraw, remove, eliminate; consume (time); cut off, amputate; **—аться** *v.* be taken away; be paralyzed, lose the use (of); **—ающий** *a.* taking away, etc., *see v.*; **—ающий воду** dehydrating.

отнога *f.* (bot.) aerial root.

относ *m.* delivery; taking away, carrying away; referral; deviation.

относ. *abbr.* (**относительный**).

относимость *f.* reference; relationship.

относительн/о *adv.* comparatively, relatively; *prep. gen.* relative to, regarding, with regard to, concerning, with reference to, in relation to, with respect to, as to, about, from; **—ость** *f.* relativity, relation; **теория —ости** theory of relativity; **—ый** *a.* relative, comparative; percentage (error); specific (volume); clinical (death); **—ая система отсчёт** system of relative coordinates, system of moving axes; **—ое отверстие** aperture ratio, *f*-number (of lens).

относ/ить *v.* take, move, carry (away); deliver; postpone; refer; deviate; **о. к** class(ify) with, group with; place in (category); attribute to; direct; **—иться (к)** *v.* concern, be concerned (with), pertain, belong (to), fall (in); refer, relate (to), apply (to), be true, hold true (for); treat, behave, act (toward); date back (to); **к ним —ятся** among these are; **—ка** *see* **относ; —чик** *m.* (glass) feeder; **—ящий** *a.* taking, etc., *see v.*; (anat.) deferent; **—ящийся (к)** *a.* concerning, etc., *see v.*; relative to, regarding, as regards; pertinent to; being considered; **—ящийся к аорте** (anat.) aortic; **—ящийся к ним** associated; **не —ящийся** unrelated.

отношен/ие *n.* relation(ship), connection; (math.) ratio, proportion; attitude, bearing, behavior; reaction, response; (psychology) involvement; regard, consideration; treatment, care; reference; rate; official document; **о. к известном** in a sense; **о. массы к**

площади mass-area ratio; **о. мощности** power ratio; **быть в хорощих —иях** *v.* be on good terms (with); **в —ии** in regard (to), as regards, as (to), in respect (to), in reference (to); in the ratio; **в других —иях** in other respects, otherwise; **во всех —иях** in every respect, in every way; **во многих —иях** in many respects; **весовое о.** ratio by weight; **закон кратных —ий** law of multiple proportions; **закон постоянства весовых —ий** law of constant proportions; **иметь о.** *v.* pertain (to), concern, apply, affect; have a bearing (on), have to do (with), be related (to); **не имеющий —ия** unrelated, not pertinent, beside the point; **обратное о.** inverse ratio; **оператор —ия** relational operator; **по —ию** as regards, concerning, with reference (to), relative (to), with respect (to), to, about.

отныне *adv.* henceforth, henceforward.

отнюдь *adv.* by no means, not at all; **о. не** far from, not nearly so . . . as.

отнят/ие *n.* taking away, removal, withdrawal; elimination; (oxygen) deprivation; **о. от матки** weaning; **о. серы** desulfurization; **—ый** *a.* taken away, removed, eliminated; **—ь** *see* **отнимать**.

ото *see* **от**.

ото— *see* **от—**; *prefix* oto— (ear).

отобит *m.* otobite (from otoba wax).

отобра/жать *v.* reflect, mirror, represent; map; depict; transform; **—жающий** *a.* reflecting, etc., *see v.*; transformation (function); **—жение** *n.* reflection, etc., *see v.*; mapping, display; **—жение в себя** self-mapping; **побитовое —жение** bitmap(ping); **устройство —жения** display unit; **—жённый** *a.* reflected, etc., *see v.*; reflex (angle); **—зить** *see* **отображать**.

отобр/анный *a.* taken away, withdrawn; selected, chosen; **—ать** *see* **отбирать**.

отобьёт *fut. 3 sing. of* **отбить**.

отовари/вание *n.* bartering; **—(ва)ть** *v.* barter; have a contract (for).

отовсюду *adv.* from everywhere.

отогенный *a.* (anat.) otogenic.

отогн/анный *a.* driven off; distilled; **—ать** *see* **отгонять**.

отогнут/ый *a.* bent (back, aside, up, down); recurved; retroflexed, backward; straightened out; **о. назад** replicate(d), retrorse, retroflexed; **—ь** *see* **отгибать**.

отогре/вание *n.* warming; **—(ва)ть** *v.* warm, take the chill off; thaw out.

отодви/гание *n.* removing, etc., *see v.*; removal; **—гать, —нуть** *v.* remove, move away, move aside, set aside; postpone; relegate (to background); **—гаться, —нуться** *v.* draw aside; **—нутый** *a.* removed, etc., *see v.*; remote.

отодрать *see* **отдирать**.

отожгут *fut. 3 pl. of* **отжечь**.

отож(д)еств/ить, —лять *v.* identify; **—ление** *n.* identification.

отожжённый *a.* annealed.

отож/мёт *fut. 3 sing. of* **отжать**, squeeze out; **—нёт** *fut. 3 sing. of* **отжать**, finish harvesting.

отозв/ание *n.* recall(ing); **—ать** *v.* recall; **—аться** *v.* respond; react.

отойти *see* **отходить**.

отоларинголог *m.* (med.) otolaryngologist, ear, nose and throat specialist.

отолит *m.* (zool.) otolith, ear stone; **—ический, —овый** *a.* otolithic; **—оидес** *m.* (ichth.) Otolithoides.

отология *f.* (med.) otology.

отольёт *fut. 3 sing. of* **отлить**.

отомкнут/ый *a.* unlocked, open; **—ь** *see* **отмыкать**.

отомрут *fut. 3 pl. of* **отмереть**.

отомстить *v.* revenge; avenge.

ото/пёрка *f.* (ichth.) gray grunt (*Otoperca aurita*); **—пиор(р)ея** *f.* (med.) otopyorrhea.

отоп/итель *m.* heater; **—ительный** *a.* heat(ing); **—ить** *v.* heat; fire; **—ка** *f.* heating; (glass) fusion, sealing; **—ленец** *m.* heat specialist.

отоплен/ие *n.* heating; warming; firing; **водяное о.** hot-water heating; **воздушное о.** hot-air heating; **паровое о.** steam heat; **с нефтяным —ием** oil (furnace); **—ный** *a.* heated; warmed; fired.

отопревать *v.* become damp or soft after thawing; come off from heat or damp.

отопрёт *fut. 3 sing. of* **отпереть**.

отопреть *see* **отопревать**.

отоптать *v.* tread down, trample.

оторачивать *v.* edge, border, trim.

оторв/анность *f.* separation; **—анный** *a.* torn off, severed, separated; distracted; **—ать(ся)** *see* **отрывать(ся)**.

оторг *m.* chief organizer.

оториноларингология *f.* (med.) oto(rhino)laryngology.

отороп/елый *a.* frightened, confused; **—ь** *f.* extreme confusion.

отороч/енный *a.* edged, etc., *see v.*; marginate; **—ить** *v.* edge, border, trim; **—ка** *f.* edge, edging, border; (geol.) margin, fringe.

ото쉰рагия *f.* (med.) otorrhagia.

оторфов/анный *a.* turned peaty; **—(ыв)ание** *n.* peat formation.

оторцовка *f.* (forestry) cross cutting, trimming.

ото/склероз *m.* (med.) otosclerosis; **—скопирование** *n.*, **—скопия** *f.* otoscopy.

отослать *see* **отсылать**.

отоспаться *v.* get enough sleep, sleep off.

ототкнуть *v.* unstopper, open.

ототрёт *fut. 3 sing. of* **оттереть**.

ото/фон *m.* (med.) otophone, hearing aid; **—цинкл** *m.* (ichth.) Otocinclus; **—цист** *m.* (embr.; zool.) otocyst, otic vesicle.

отошедший *past act. part. of* **отойти**.

отошлёт *fut. 3 sing. of* **отослать**.

отошьёт *fut. 3 sing. of* **отшить**.

отощ/авший, —алый *a.* lean, emaciated; **—ать** *v.* grow lean, become emaciated; **—ающий** *a.* leaning; inert (component); **—ение** *n.* leaning; (cer.) grog addition; **—ённый** *a.* leaned; lean (coal); **—итель** *m.* leaning material; (cer.) shortening material, grog.

отпад *m.* falling off; (silv.) slash, waste, scrap; **—ание** *n.* falling off, etc., *see v.*; drop; disconnection; **—ать** *v.* fall off, drop off; drop out (of organization); trip, be disconnected; become superfluous; **—ающий** *a.* falling off, etc., *see v.*; (biol.) deciduous; **—ающая оболочка** (anat.) decidua; **—ение** *see* **отпадание**.

отпа/ивание *n.* unsoldering; sealing off; liquid intake; **—ивать** *v.* unsolder; seal off; give (to drink); (elec.) tap (a line); **—иваться** *v.* come off; **—ика** *f.* unsoldering, separation.

отпал/ка *f.,* **—очный** *a.* firing, blasting.

отпар/ивание *n.* steaming (off); pressing (of clothes); **—и(ва)ть** *v.* steam (off); press; (petrol.) strip; **—ный** *a. of* **отпаривание**; **—ная колонна** stripper, stripping tower.

отпарывать *v.* rip, rip off, rip out.

отпасть *see* **отпадать**.

отпахать *v.* plow; finish plowing.

отпая/нный *a.* unsoldered; sealed off; **—ть** *see* **отпаивать**.

отпенсационный *a.* compensating.

отпер/еть *see* **отпирать;** **—тый** *a.* unlocked, etc., *see* **отпирать.**

отперфорировать *v.* punch, key (into).

отпескоструить *v.* sandblast.

отпечат/анный *a.* printed, etc., *see v.;* **—ок** *m.* print; impression, imprint, stamp, seal; mark; dent, indentation; mold, cast; **метод —ка пальцев** fingerprint method; **цветной —ок** color print; **—(ыв)ание** *n.* printing, etc., *see v.; see* **отпечаток;** **—ать** *v.* print; type; imprint, impress, stamp; tape; unseal, open up; **—(ыв)аться** *v.* leave an impression (on).

отпивать *v.* take a sip; finish drinking.

отпил/ивание *n.,* **—ка** *f.* sawing off; **—и(ва)ть** *v.* saw off, cut off, trim.

отпир/ание *n.* unlocking, etc., *see v.;* **—ать** *v.* unlock, open, unfasten, unbolt; unblock; (electron.) trigger; drive into conduction; **—аться** *v.* fire (of thyratron); **—ающий** *a.* unlocking, etc., *see v.;* trigger, gate-opening.

отпит/ый *past pass. part. of* **отпивать;** **—ь** *see* **отпивать.**

отпих/ивать, —нуть *v.* push off.

отпла/та *f.* repayment, return; **в —ту** in return; **—тить, —чивать** *v.* repay; recompense, reward, reciprocate.

отплёвывать *v.* expectorate.

отплёс/кивать, —нуть *v.* splash back, splash out, spatter.

отпле/сти, —тать *v.* untwist, undo; finish braiding; **—стись, —таться** *v.* come undone.

отплодоносивший *a.* after having borne fruit.

отплы/(ва)ть *v.* swim away, float away; (naut.) depart; **—тие** *n.* departure.

отплюнуть *v.* expectorate.

отпоить *see* **отпаивать.**

отполаскивать *v.* rinse (out).

отполз/ать, —ти *v.* crawl away or back.

отполиров(ыв)ать *v.* polish off.

отполоскать *v.* rinse out; finish rinsing.

отпор *m.* repulse, resistance; rebuff; **—ный** *a.* repulsing; dog (hook).

отпороть *see* **отпарывать.**

отпот/евание *n.* sweat(ing), dew, condensate; **—е(ва)ть** *v.* sweat, perspire; fog, mist (up); **—елый** *a.* covered with sweat or condensate.

отпочков(ыв)/ание *n.* (biol.) propagation by gemmation; **—аться** *v.* gemmate.

отправ/итель *m.* sender, transmitter; shipper, dispatcher, consignor; (commun.) originator; initiator; **—ительный** *a.* transmitting, transmission; **—ить** *see* **отправлять;** **—ка** *f.,* **—ление** *n.* sending, etc., *see v.;* transmission; shipment, consignment; departure, start; performance; function(ing); **точка —ления** starting point; source; **—ленный** *a.* sent, etc., *see v.;* **—ляемый** *a.* sent, etc., transmittable; transmitted (wave); **—лять** *v.* send, transmit, forward, dispatch; ship, consign (goods); perform (duties); **—ляться** *v.* set off, set forth, depart, proceed, start; **—ляющийся** *a.* setting forth, etc., *see v.;* **—ной** *a.* starting (point); **—очный** *a. of* **отправка;** shipping.

отпрепарировать *v.* prepare.

отпрессов/анный *a.* pressed, etc., *see v.;* **—ать** *v.* press, squeeze (out); force out, expel, express; (plastics) extrude; **—ка** *f.,* **—(ыв)ание** *n.* pressing, etc., *see v.;* extrusion.

отпречь *v.* unharness, unhitch.

отпрыг/ивать, —нуть *v.* jump aside; rebound, recoil, spring back.

отпрыск *m.* spur, branch; (bot.) shoot, sprout, sucker; descendant, offspring; **корневой о.** sobole, root sucker; **—овый** *a.* sprouting, soboliferous.

отпря/гание *n.,* **—жка** *f.* unharnessing, unhitching; **—гать** *v.* unharness, unhitch; **—жённый** *a.* unharnessed, unhitched.

отпрянуть *v.* rebound, recoil, spring back.

отпрячь *v.* unharness, unhitch.

отпуг/ивание *n.* frightening off; **о. дымом** fumigation, smoking out; **—иватель** *m.,* **—ивающее средство** repellent; **—ивать, —нуть** *v.* frighten off, scare away; repel.

отпус/к *m.* leave (of absence), furlough, vacation, holiday; issue, distribution, delivery, dispatching; (met.) tempering; **о. в масле** oil tempering; **высокий о.** high-temperature tempering; **низкий о.** low-temperature tempering; **нормальный о.** (silv.) planned felling; **—кание** *n.* letting go, etc., *see v.;* release; (comp.) drop-out; **—кать** *v.* let go, dismiss, release, give leave; slacken, unfasten, loosen, ease, slack off, back off; release (brake); unscrew; supply, allot, allocate, issue, distribute; (met.) temper; dispense (medicine); grow (hair); **—кник** *m.* vacationer; **—кной** *a. of* **отпуск;** dismissive; release (spring); temper (brittleness); selling (price); **—тить** *see* **отпускать.**

отпут(ыв)ать *v.* disentangle, untie.

отпущенный *a.* dismissed, released; slackened, loosened; (met.) tempered.

отпыл/итель *m.* (paper) duster; **—овка** *f.* (de)dusting.

отраб/атывать *v.* serve (one's term); fulfill (one's task); work for or through; work off (debt); try out; develop; perfect, optimize; minimize (errors); (comp.) follow to indicate; **—отавший, —отанный** *a.* worked out, used up, exhausted, depleted, spent (solution); waste, stripped, exhaust (gas); developed; **—отать** *see* **отрабатывать;** **—отка** *f.* working off; finishing off.

отрав/а *f.,* **—итель** *m.* poison, toxin, venom; **—ить** *see* **отравлять;** **—ление** *n.* poisoning, toxic effect; contamination; **—ленный** *a.* poisoned; contaminated; **—лять** *v.* poison, intoxicate; contaminate; **—ляющий** *a.* poisonous, toxic; poisoning; contaminating; **—ляющее вещество** poison, toxic agent; contaminant; (war) gas.

отрадный *a.* comforting, gratifying.

отраж/аемость *f.* reflectivity; **—атель** *m.* reflector; mirror; repeller; ejector; deflector; extractor (of gun); repeller electrode.

отражательн/ый *a.* reflecting, reflection, reflective, reflector; reverberatory (furnace); deflecting, baffle; repeller (electrode); **о. козырёк, о. лист, о. свод, о. щиток, —ая заслонка, —ая плита** deflector, deflecting plate, baffle (plate); **—ая способность** reflecting power, reflectivity; (nucl.) albedo; reflectance.

отраж/ать *v.* reflect, mirror, reverberate; indicate, represent, display; rebound; repel, repulse, ward off; refute (charge); take into account, make allowance (for); echo (sound); **—аться** *v.* reflect, reverberate; rebound, impinge; echo; affect, have an effect (on); **—ающий** *a.* reflecting, reverberatory; deflecting.

отражен/ие *n.* reflection, reverberation; (mirror) image; repercussion, rebound, impingement; repulsion; echo(ing); display, indication, representation; **о. от местности** (radar) terrain echo; **о. от местных предметов** ground clutter; **о. от морских волн** sea return or clutter; **коэффициент —ия** reflection coefficient, reflectance, reflectivity; return loss (of current); **метод —ия** backscatter method (for determining ash content).

отражён/ный *a.* reflected, etc., *see* **отражать**; indirect (light); reciprocal (rhythm of heart); —**ный звук** echo; —**ное рассеяние** (nucl.) backscattering.

отразить *see* **отражать.**

отрапортов(ыв)ать *v.* report.

отрасл/евой *a. of* **отрасль**; special(ized), subject (catalog, etc.); sectional; branch-wide; industry-wide; trade (association); —**ь** *f.* field, area, division, segment, branch; sphere, department; industry; (bot.) sprout.

отра/стание *n.* growing (up, out); regrowth, new growth; maturing; —**стать, —сти** *v.* grow (up, out); regrow, grow anew; sprout; mature; —**стить, —щивать** *v.* let grow; raise; —**щивание** *n.* growth; growing, cultivation.

отрегулиров/ание *n.* adjustment; —**анный** *a.* adjusted, set; —**ать** *v.* adjust, set, regulate.

отредактировать *v.* edit.

отрез *m.* cut; piece, length; cutting (off); tear strip, perforated line; (plow) colter, cutter; —**ание** *see* **отрезывание**; —**анный** *a.* cut (off), severed; —**ать** *see* **отрезывать.**

отрезв/еть *v.* become sober; —**ить, —лять** *v.* make sober; —**иться, —ляться** *v.* sober up; —**ление** *n.* sobering up.

отрез/ка *see* **отрезывание**; section; *gen. of* **отрезок**; —**ковый** *a.* segmental; —**ной** *a.* cut-off, cutting, slicing; shearing (die); detachable, tear-off; —**ок** *m.* piece, length, stretch, distance; section; fragment, remnant, scrap, chip; —**очный** *a.* shear; cutting-off; —**ывание** *n.* cutting (off), etc., *see v.*; severance; —**ывать** *v.* cut (off), sever; (hort.) clip, trim, prune; crop; divide off.

отрекаться *v.* deny, repudiate.

отрекомендов(ыв)ать *v.* introduce; recommend.

отремонтиров/анный *a.* repaired, etc., *see v.*; —**ать** *v.* repair, fix, mend; overhaul, refit, recondition.

отрепать *v.* wear out, fray; swingle (flax).

отрёпки *pl.* hemp or flax residue.

отрепье *n.* rags.

отрёт *fut. 3 sing. of* **отереть.**

отречься *see* **отрекаться.**

отреш/аться, —иться *v.* renounce, give up; dismiss, get rid (of).

отриц/ание *n.* negation, denial; negative; **о. импликации** (math.) nonimplication; **о. переноса** (comp.) nocarry; **знак —ания** minus sign; —**ательно** *adv.* negatively; adversely; —**ательногеотропический** *a.* (biol.) negative geotropic; —**ательный** *a.* negative (charge, etc.), minus; adverse, bad, unfavorable, detrimental; damaging, destructive; —**ательная сторона** disadvantage, drawback; —**ательная температура** temperature below 0° C.; —**ательное ускорение** deceleration; —**ать** *v.* negate, deny, contradict.

отрог *m.* spur, branch, offshoot; (meteor.) ridge.

отрод/у *adv.* never (in one's life); —**ье** *n.* offspring; spawn; variety; breed.

отрое/к *m.* new swarm (of bees); —**ние** *n.* swarming.

отроет *fut. 3 sing. of* **отрыть.**

отрождение *n.* hatching (of eggs).

отроить(ся) *v.* (bees) form a new swarm.

отрос *past m. sing. of* **отрасти;** —**ток** *m.* sprout, sprig, (off)shoot; branch, side arm; outlet, tap; prolongation, extension, projection; (anat.) process; (med.) appendix; (geol.) apophysis.

отроют *fut. 3 pl. of* **отрыть.**

отруб *m.* (saw) cut; butt, end (of tree); —**ание** *n.* chopping off, etc., *see v.*; —**ать** *v.* chop off, cut off, chisel off; clip.

отруб/евидный *a.* pityroid, furfuraceous, bran-like; —**и** *pl.* bran; siftings; —**истость** *f.* bran content.

отрубить *see* **отрубать.**

отрубной *a.* cutting; chipping.

отруб/ный, —яной *a. of* **отруби.**

отрубыш *m.* ocean sunfish (*Mola mola*).

отрули(ва)ть *v.* (av.) taxi; backtrack.

отрут *fut. 3 pl. of* **отереть.**

отрухляветь *v.* disintegrate.

отрыв *m.* break(-off), break(ing)-away, separation, detachment, removal; termination; escape; ejection (of electron); (av.) take-off, lift-off; distraction (of attention); abstraction, fission (of atoms from molecules); **зажигание на о.** make-and-break ignition; **скорость —а** escape velocity; —**ание** *see* **отрыв**; —**ать** *v.* break (off, away), tear (off, away), separate, detach; distract; dig up, unearth, disinter, excavate, trench; —**аться** *v.* break (away, off), tear away, come off, separate, lose contact (with); leave, escape; (av.) lift off, become airborne; —**ающий** *a.* breaking, etc., *see v.*; —**ающая сила** pull.

отрывист/ость *f.* abruptness, etc., *see a.*; —**ый** *a.* abrupt, sudden, jerky.

отрыв/ка *f.* digging up, trenching; *gen. of* **отрывок**; —**ной** *a. of* **отрыв**; detachable; tear-off (notebook); (elec.) contact-breaking; —**ок** *m.* fragment, piece; excerpt, extract, passage; —**очность** *f.* fragmentary nature, spottiness; —**очный** *a.* fragmentary; interrupted; spotty (information).

отры/г(ив)ание *n., —жка* *f.* eructation, belching; regurgitation; —**г(ив)ать, —гнуть** *v.* eruct, belch; regurgitate.

отрыть *v.* dig up, excavate.

отря/д *m.* (biol.) order; brigade, team, group; (rescue) party; unit, detachment; —**дить** *v.* detach, assign, dispatch, send (on assignment); appoint, order; —**дный** *a. of* **отряд**; —**жать** *see* **отрядить.**

отря/сать, —сти, —хивать, —хнуть *v.* shake off.

Отса берег (geog.) Oates Coast.

отса/дить *see* **отсаживать**; —**дка** *f.* separation; weaning (of young stock); transplanting; (min.) jigging; —**док** *m.* (hort.) transplant; layer, slip, scion, cutting; —**дочный** *a. of* **отсадка**; jig(ging); —**дочный чан** buddle; —**дочная машина** jigging machine, jig(ger); —**живание** *see* **отсадка**; —**живать** *v.* plant out, transplant; (hort.) layer; separate; jig.

отсалив/ание *n.* salting out; —**ать** *v.* salt out, grain, cut (soap).

отсасыв/ание *n.* sucking off, etc., *see v.*; suction, aspiration; —**атель** *m.* suction pump, aspirator; —**ать** *v.* suck off, aspirate, draw off, exhaust; filter by suction; press dry; —**ающий** *a.* suction; outgoing, outlet; exhaust (fan, hood).

отсве/т *m.* reflection, sheen, shine; —**тить** *v.* stop shining; —**чивание** *n.* brilliancy, glare; reflection; —**чивать** *v.* reflect; shine, gleam.

отсев *m.* sifting, etc., *see v.*; siftings, screenings, residue; —**ание** *n.* sifting; —**ать** *v.* sift, screen, riddle; eliminate, drop out; —**ки** *pl.* siftings; —**ной** *a.* sifted.

отседать *v.* settle, precipitate.

отсеив/ание *n.* sifting, etc., *see v.*; —**ать** *v.* sift, screen (out); select, cull.

отсек *m.* compartment, cubicle, cell, chamber, bay, section; bin; (freight) hold; *past m. sing. of* **отсечь; о. КЛА** spacecraft module; —**ание** *see* **отсечение: —а-тель** *m.* cutter, splitter; cut-off; cut plate, harrow (of reclaimer); —**ательный** *a.* intercepting, etc., *see v.*; cut-off (valve); —**ать** *v.* intercept, cut off, chop off, detach, sever; (comp.) clip; split off, cleave; shut off, close; —**ающий** *see* **отсекательный; о.-убежище**

m. escape compartment; **о.-хранилище** *m.* storage bay.

отселектировать *v.* choose, select.

отсепарировать *v.* separate; dissect away.

отсеч/ение *n.* interception, cutting off, etc., *see* **отсекать**; pruning; scissoring (part of graphic image); **—ённый** *a.* intercepted, etc., *see* **отсекать**; **—ка** *see* **отсечение**; cut-off; (typ.) serif; **время —ки** intercept time; **—ный** *a.* cut-off, shut-off (valve); **—ь** *see* **отсекать**.

отсеять *see* **отсевать**.

отсигналить *v.* signal.

отси/деться, —живаться *v.* grow numb from sitting; sit out; **—живать** *v.* stay (for); serve (one's time); make numb by sitting.

отсинённый *a.* blued.

отсифон/и(ро)вание *n.* siphoning off; **—и(ро)вать** *v.* siphon off.

отскаблив/ание *n.* scraping off; **—ать** *v.* scrape off.

отскакать *see* **отскакивать**; gallop off.

отскакив/ание *n.* recoiling, etc., *see v.*; recoil, kick, rebound, spring back, jump back; break-away; **упругое о.** resilience; **—ать** *v.* recoil, rebound, kick, spring back, jump back, bounce; jump (aside, away, off), fly off, slip off; break away, peel off, come off; gallop away.

отскоблить *see* **отскабливать**.

отско/к *see* **отскакивание**; recoil, rebound; **—чить** *see* **отскакивать**.

отскребать *v.* scrape off, scrub off.

отскрёбки *pl.* scrapings.

отскрести *see* **отскребать**.

обслаив/ание *n.* exfoliation, scaling, etc., *see v.*; (med.) desquamation; flake, scale; peel; **—ать** *v.* exfoliate, scale, flake; peel, strip; separate; deposit in layers; **—аться** *v.* exfoliate, scale (off), flake (off); desquamate; peel (off); separate; settle in layers; **—ающий** *a.* exfoliative; **—ающийся** *a.* (radiometry) stripping (film).

отслежива/ние *n.* (mech.) servoing; **контур —ния** servoloop; **—ть** *v.* follow up, track; servo.

отсло/ение *see* **отслаивание**; *pl.* (concrete) blisters; **—ённый** *a.* exfoliated, etc., *see* **отслаивать**; **—ить(ся)** *see* **отслаивать(ся)**; **—йка** *see* **отслаивание**; removal; detachment (of retina).

отслужи(ва)ть *v.* serve (one's or its) time; become obsolete.

отснять *v.* film, photograph.

отсоедин/ение *n.* disconnecting, disconnection, etc., *see v.* detachment; disengagement; **—ённый** *a.* disconnected, etc., *see v.*; **—ить, —ять** *v.* disconnect, detach, disengage; trip; switch off, turn off; isolate; interrupt.

отсол/ённый *a.* salted out; **—ить** *v.* salt out; **—ка** *f.* salting out.

отсортиров/ание *n.* sorting (out), etc., *see v.*; **—анный** *a.* sorted (out), etc., *see v.*; **—ка** *see* **отсортирование**; **—(ыв)ать** *v.* sort (out), cull; classify, grade; pick, select; reject.

отсос *m.* suction; exhaust; **—анный** *a.* sucked off, drawn off, filtered by suction; **—ать** *see* **отсасывать**; **—ный** *a.* of **отсос**.

отсохнуть *see* **отсыхать**.

отсроч/енный *a.* postponed, etc., *see v.*; **—и(ва)ть** *v.* postpone, put off, delay, defer; (law) adjourn; extend; **—ка** *f.* postponement, delay, deferment, extension; adjournment; respite.

отстав *m.* (typ.) lining.

отстав/ание *n.* lag(ging), creep; delay, retardation; arrears, backlog (of work); loosening, peeling, exfoliation; **о. по фазе, о. фаз** phase lag; **зона —ания** (rolling) zone of creep; **промежуток —ания** time lag; **—ать** *v.* lag (behind), fall behind, not keep pace (with), be outstripped (by); creep; be slow (of clock); be backward; loosen, come off, peel, exfoliate, break away; **—ать по срокам** slip; **не —ать от** keep pace with.

отстав/ить *v.* set aside, remove; dismiss, discharge; **—ка** *f.*, **—ление** *n.* setting aside, removal; dismissal; resignation; retirement; **в —ке** retired; **выйти в —ку** *v.* resign, retire; **—ленный** *a.* set aside, etc., *see v.*; distant; **—лять** *see* **отставить**; **—ник** *m.* retired serviceman; **—ной** *a.* retired; movable.

отстаёт *pr. 3 sing. of* **отставать**.

отстаив/ание *n.* settling, clarification, etc., *see v.*; sedimentation; standing; **—ать** *v.* settle, clarify; deposit, precipitate; thicken; (rubber) cream; let stand, allow to settle; fight (for), defend, stand up (for); uphold (principle); champion (a cause); **—аться** *v.* settle, precipitate; stand; thicken; (naut.) ride out, ride at anchor, **—ающийся** *a.* settling, etc., *see v.*

отстал/ость *f.* retardation, backwardness; **—ый** *a.* backward, retarded; underdeveloped; out of date, outdated.

отст/ать *see* **отставать**; **—ающий** *a.* lagging, slow, backward; late.

отстёгивать, отстегнуть *v.* unfasten, unhook, unbutton.

отстир(ыв)ать *v.* wash out, launder out.

отстование *see* **отставание**.

отстой *m.* precipitate, sediment; dregs, bottoms, residue, sludge, deposit; (wine) lees; period of settling; **—ник** *m.* settler, settling tank; sedimentation tank, precipitation tank; thickener; sump; retainer; mud drum; (slurry) pond; (sugar) clarifier, clarifying tank; **о.-ловушка** *m.* gravity separator; **о.-сгуститель** *m.* thickening tank; **—ный** *a.* settling, sedimentation (tank); decanting (flask); **о. бак, о. бассейн, о. резервуар, о. чан** *see* **отстойник**.

отсто/яние *n.* distance, range; **—ять** *see* **отстаивать**; be (apart), be spaced, be separate; stay to the end; **—ящий** *a.* distant, remote; open, exposed.

отстрагивать *v.* plane (off).

отстраив/ание *n.* building up, construction; **—ать** *v.* build up; **—аться** *v.* be built up; (rad.) tune out.

отстран/ение *n.* putting aside, etc., *see v.*; removal, discharge, dismissal; **—ить, —ять** *v.* put or push aside, set aside; suspend; remove; discharge, dismiss; **—яться** *v.* move away, keep away (from).

отстрел *m.* fire, firing, shooting; (art.) test(ing); harvesting, take (of game); (fuse) calibration; **—и(ва)ть** *v.* shoot off, fire; **—ять** *v.* shoot; use up (ammunition).

отстри/гать, —чь *v.* clip, shear, cut off.

отстрогать *v.* plane; finish planing.

отстро/ить *see* **отстраивать**; **—йка** *f.* building up; (rad.) tuning (out).

отстрочить *v.* stitch on, stitch up.

отструг(ив)ать *see* **отстрогать**.

отстук(ив)ать *v.* tap out; type.

отступ *m.* indent(ation); **обратный о.** hanging indent; **—ание** *see* **отступление**; loss (of land); **—ательный** *a.* retreating; **—ать** *v.* fall back, give way, withdraw, recede, retreat; digress, depart; **—аться** *v.* give up, renounce; **—ающий** *a.* falling back, etc., *see v.*; retrograde; divergent; **—ить** *see* **отступать**; **—ление** *n.* falling back, withdrawal, recession, retreat, regression, retrogression; departure, deviation, variation, divergence, digression, difference; **—ник** *m.* apostate, turncoat; —**ный** *a.* receding, retreating; —**я** *adv.* at a distance, off.

отстучать *see* **отстукивать.**

отсутств/ие *n.* absence, freedom, (from); deficiency, lack (of); **быть в** —**ии** *see* **отсутствовать; за** —**ием** for lack (of), for want (of); in the absence (of); —**овать** *v.* be free (of, from), be lacking, be unavailable; be missing, be absent, be nonexistent; (law) default; —**ующий** *a.* missing, absent; nonexistent; not found; *m.* absentee.

отсуши(ва)ть *v.* kiln-dry, cure.

отсчёт *m.,* —**ный** *a.* reading; read-out, display; indication; reference; count(ing off); metering; sample; **о. на нуль, о. от нуля** zero reading; **о. по прибору** instrument reading; **о. показаний** reading; **основная система** —**а** system of absolute coordinates, system of fixed axes; **ось** —**а** a reference axis; **относительная система** —**а** system of relative coordinates, system of moving axes; **прямого** —**а, с непосредственным** —**ом** direct-reading; **система** —**а** frame of reference, reference system; **точка** —**а** reference point.

отсчит/анный *a.* read (off), etc., *see v.;* —**ывание** *n.* reading, etc., *see v.;* —**(ыв)ать** *v.* read (off), take a reading; measure, count off, reckon.

отсыл/ать *v.* send off, dispatch, post, mail, forward; refer (to); remit (money); —**ка** *f.,* —**очный** *a.* sending off, etc., *see v.;* reference.

отсып/ание *n.* pouring off, etc., *see v.;* —**ать** *v.* pour off or out; discharge (part of); measure off; —**аться** *v.* be poured off; catch up on sleep; —**ка** *see* **отсыпание;** (min.) fill; dry dumping.

отсыр/е(ва)ть *v.* become damp or moist; —**елый** *a.* damp(ened); —**ение** *n.* damp(en)ing.

отсых/ание *n.* drying up or off; —**ать** *v.* dry up, wither; dry off.

отсюда *adv.* from here, hence; as a result, owing to this; **о. следует** from this it follows, it therefore follows, this suggests.

оттаив/ание *n.* thawing (out), defrosting; —**ать** *v.* thaw (out), defrost, melt.

отталкив/ание *n.* repulsion; **сила** —**ания,** —**ательная сила** repulsive force; —**ать** *v.* repel, push away, drive back, resist; alienate, antagonize; —**аться** *v.* push off; depart; —**ающий** *a.* repellent, repelling, repulsive.

оттаптывать *v.* trample (down).

оттарт(ыв)ать *v.* bail (out), bail down.

оттаск/а *f.,* —**ивание** *n.* dragging away; —**(ив)ать** *v.* drag away, pull aside.

оттачив/ание *n.* sharpening, etc., *see v.;* —**ать** *v.* sharpen, whet, grind; point.

оттащить *see* **оттаскивать.**

отта/янный *a.* thawed out, defrosted; —**ять** *see* **оттаивать.**

оттвейлерские слои (geol.) Ottweilian series.

оттёк *see* **отток;** syrup.

оттекание *n.* backflow, draining; flow back, run back, run off, drain, drip.

оттен/ение *n.* shading, etc., *see v.;* —**ённый** *a.* shaded, etc., *see v.;* —**ить,** —**ять** *v.* shade, tint, tinge; shadow; set off, emphasize; —**ок** *m.* shade, shading, hue, tinge, tint, tone; gradation; discoloration; **с** —**ком** tinged (with); —**яться** *v.* be shaded; stand out.

оттепель *f.* thaw; **стоит о.** it is thawing; —**ный** *a.* thaw(ing).

оттеребить *v.* finish plucking (fiber).

оттереть *see* **оттирать.**

оттертрал *m.* (hunting) otter trawl.

оттесать *see* **оттёсывать.**

оттесн/ить, —**ять** *v.* force back; supplant.

оттёсывать *v.* chop off, lop off.

оттечь *see* **оттекать.**

оттешет *fut. 3 sing. of* **оттесать.**

оттир/ать *v.* rub (away, down, off, out), abrade; remove (stain); wipe away; —**ка** *f.* rubbing (away), etc., *see v.;* attrition.

оттис/к *m.* impression, imprint; indentation, dent; print, copy; printing; **отдельный о.** offprint, reprint; **пробный о.** proof; —**кивание** *n.* pressing back, etc., *see v.;* —**кивание краски** set-off; —**кивать** *v.* press back, push aside; impress, (leave an) imprint; print; —**кная ложка** (med.) impression tray; —**нуть** *see* **оттискивать.**

оттитров(ыв)ать *v.* titrate (back).

Отто цикл otto cycle (of engine).

оттого *adv.* therefore, therefrom.

отток *m.* outflow, efflux; flow-off, run-off; backflow, drain; (lava) withdrawal.

оттолк/ать, —**нуть** *see* **отталкивать.**

оттопить *v.* stop heating.

оттоптать *see* **оттаптывать.**

оттопыр/енный *a.* protruding, bulging; bristling; (biol.) squarrose; —**и(ва)ть(ся)** *v.* protrude, bulge, stick out; bristle (up).

оттор *m.* strong offshore wind.

оттор/гать, —**гнуть** *v.* tear away, separate, detach; split; —**женец** *m.* detached mass; —**жение** *n.* tearing away, separation, detachment; splitting; repulsion, casting off; rejection (reaction).

отторировать *v.* calibrate; tare (off).

оттормаживать *v.* release the brake.

отточ/енный *a.* sharp(ened), pointed; —**ие** *n.* (typ.) row of dots, leader; —**ить** *v.* sharpen, whet, grind; point; —**ка** *f.* sharpening, etc., *see v.*

оттрелит *m.* (min.) ottrelite, chloritoid.

оттрепать, оттрёпывать *v.* scutch, beat (fiber).

оттря/сать, —**сти,** —**хивать,** —**хнуть** *v.* shake out (dust).

оттуда *adv.* from there, thence.

оттушевать *see* **оттушёвывать.**

оттушёв/ка *f.* shading; —**ывать** *v.* shade.

оттыкать *v.* unstopper, open.

оттягать *v.* gain by lawsuit.

оттягив/ание *n.* drawing off, etc., *see v.;* removal; retraction; —**атель** *m.* retractor; —**ать** *v.* draw off, divert; draw out, stretch; pull back, pull away, retract; remove; clarify (liquid); delay, prolong, extend, procrastinate; span; —**ать молотом** hammer out; —**ающий** *a.* drawing off, etc., *see v.;* release (spring); —**ающая мышца** (anat.) retractor.

оття/жка *f.* drawing out, stretching; delay, procrastination; span, guy (line), guy rope, guy wire; tension member, stay, strut, brace; (wire drawing) pointing; withdrawal (of liquor); **о. из проволок** guy wire; —**жной** *a.* drawing out; set, adjusting (screw); guy (rope); —**нутый** *a.* drawn off, etc., *see* **оттягивать;** attenuate, tapered, narrowed; —**нуть** *see* **оттягивать.**

оттяп/нуть, —**(ыв)ать** *v.* chop off, cut off; gain by lawsuit.

отумани(ва)ть *v.* fog (up), cloud; blur, dim; confuse; obscure.

отунит *m.* (min.) autunite.

отуп/евший, —**елый** *a.* dull, torpid, apathetic; —**ение** *n.* torpor, apathy; —**еть** *v.* become apathetic; —**ить,** —**лять** *v.* make apathetic, make dull.

отуч/(ив)ать *v.* break (a habit); —**ить** *v.* break (a habit);

educate; **—иться** *v.* lose (a habit); finish one's education.

отучнеть *v.* get fat.

отушёвывать *v.* shade off.

отфильтров/ание *n.* filtration; **—анный** *a.* filtered (off, out); **—(ыв)ать** *v.* filter (off, out).

отфлан/жированный, —цованный *a.* flanged.

отформов(ыв)ать *v.* model, mold, shape.

отфрезеров(ыв)ать *v.* mill.

отфугов(ыв)ать *v.* centrifuge.

отхаживать *v.* nurse back to health, cure, heal; tire from walking.

отхарк/ивание *n.* expectoration, spitting; **—(ив)ать, —нуть** *v.* expectorate, spit; **—ающее** *n.,* **—ающий** *a.* expectorant.

отхват/ить, —ывать *v.* take off, cut off, snip off; acquire, get, obtain.

отхлебнуть, отхлёбывать *v.* take a swallow, take a sip.

отхлынуть *v.* rush back.

отход *m.* setting off, departure, start; withdrawal, removal; drop-out; waste, scrap; residue; death loss (of young stock); deviation; **—ы** *pl.* waste (products), refuse, rejects; (metal) scrap; by-product; (min.) tailings, tails; siftings, screenings; bottoms; **бытовые —ы** garbage; **твёрдые —ы** refuse.

отходить *v.* go off, leave, depart, withdraw; fall back; disappear (of stain); come loose, break away; deviate, digress, diverge (from); branch out; attend, be (on job); return to normal; nurse to health.

отходни/к *m.* seasonal migratory worker; **—чество** *n.* seasonal work.

отхо/дный *a.* of **отход**; **—дчивый** *a.* easily appeased; **—ды** *pl.* of **отход**; **—дящий** *a.* outgoing, exit, waste, exhaust (gas); off; **—ждение** *n.* departure, digression, deviation; **—жий** *a.* seasonal (work); **—жее место** latrine.

отхромировать *v.* chrome-plate.

отца *gen.* of **отец**.

отцве/сти, —тать *v.* finish blooming; blossom fall; defloration; **—тший** *a.* (bot.) deflorate.

отце/дить, —живать *v.* filter, strain (off); draw off; **—живание** *n.* filtering, etc., *see v.;* **—живатель** *m.* strainer; straining tank; **—живаться** *v.* filter, pass through.

отцентр(ир)овать *v.* center.

отцеп *m.* release, uncoupling; uncoupler; **—ить** *see* **отцеплять; —ка** *f.,* **—ление** *n.* uncoupling, etc., *see v.;* release; **—ляемый** *a.* uncoupled, etc., *see v.;* detachable; **—лять** *v.* uncouple, unhook, unhitch, detach, release, disengage; **—ной** *a.* detachable; **—щик** *m.* uncoupler.

отцифров(ыв)ать *v.* digitize.

отцовс/кий *a.* paternal; **—тво** *n.* parentage.

отчаиваться *v.* despair, lose courage.

отчал *m.,* **—ивание** *n.* (naut.) casting off; **—и(ва)ть** *v.* cast off, push off.

отчасти *adv.* partly, in part, partially, to some extent, to a degree.

отча/яние *n.* despair; **—янный** *a.* desperate; **—яться** *v.* despair.

отчего *adv.* why, for what reason; **о.-либо, о.-нибудь, о.-то** for some reason.

отчекани(ва)ть *v.* stamp (out); coin.

отчеренковать *v.* (hort.) plant cuttings.

отчёркивать, отчеркнуть *v.* mark off.

отчерп/ать, —нуть *see* **отчёрпывать.**

отчёрпывать *v.* bail out, ladle out.

отчер/тить, —чивать *v.* sketch, outline.

отчёт *m.* account, report, record, minutes; **о. о ходе работ** progress report; **отдавать себе о.** be aware (of), realize; **—ы** *pl.* proceedings.

отчётлив/о *adv.* distinctly; **о. выраженный** *a.* distinct; **—ость** *f.* distinctness; intelligibility, comprehensibility; precision; **—ый** *a.* distinct, clear, sharp; intelligible, comprehensible; articulate, well-enunciated.

очётн/ость *f.* accounts, accounting, bookkeeping, paperwork; accountability; **—ый** *a.* account; report; current, accountable; fiscal (year); under review, under consideration; **—ый доклад** report.

отч/изна *f.* native land, fatherland; **—им** *m.* stepfather.

отчисл/ение *n.* deduction, writing off; assignment, allotment, allocation, allowance; dismissal; charge; **—енный** *a.* deducted, etc., *see v.;* **—ить, —ять** *v.* deduct, write off; assign, allot, allocate; dismiss, discharge, transfer.

отчистить *see* **отчищать.**

отчит(ыв)ать *v.* finish reading; rebuke; **—ся** *v.* report.

отчищ/ать *v.* clean off, scour; free (from); purify; **—енный** *a.* cleaned, etc., *see v.*

отчлен/ение *m.* separation, detachment, dismemberment; **—ить, —ять** *v.* separate, detach, dismember.

отчу/дить, —ждать *v.* alienate, estrange; confiscate, dispossess; **—ждение** *n.* alienation, estrangement; confiscation, dispossession, expropriation; **полоса —ждения** right-of-way; freeway; **—ждённый** *a.* alienated, etc., *see v.*

отшаги(ва)ть *v.* pace off; step back.

отшат/нуться, —ываться *v.* shrink back, recoil; renounce, forsake.

отшвартов(ыв)ать *v.* (naut.) cast off.

отшвыр/енный *a.* thrown away, rejected; **—ивать, —нуть** *v.* throw away, fling away; reject.

отшельник *m.* solitary (animal), hermit.

отшествие *n.* (naut.) departure.

отшиб *m.;* **на —** by oneself, alone; at a distance; **—ать, —ить** *v.* strike off, knock off, crack off, break off; hurt; **у него —ло память** his memory failed him.

отши/(ва)ть *v.* rip off; finish sewing; panel; box off; **—тый** *a.* ripped off, etc., *see v.*

отшлаков/ывание *n.* slag removal; **—(ыв)ать** *v.* tap off slag, clear from slag.

отшлифов/анный *a.* ground, polished; **—ка** *f.* grinding, etc., *see v.;* **—(ыв)ать** *v.* grind, polish, buff; cut (gems).

отшнуров/ание *n.* pinch, constriction; contraction, shrinkage; **—анный** *a.* pinched; **—ать** *v.* pinch, constrict; snare.

отшпили(ва)ть *v.* unpin, unfasten, undo.

отштампов(ыв)ать *v.* stamp out.

отштукатур/енный *a.* plastered; **—и(ва)ть** *v.* plaster.

отшуметь *v.* stop making noise.

отщёлк/ивать *v.* click off; **—нуть** *v.* click open.

отщем/ить, —лять *v.* pinch (off).

отщеп *m.* flake; **—ать** *see* **отщеплять; —енец** *m.* (biol.) deviate; **—енство** *n.* deviation; **—ить** *see* **отщеплять; —ление** *n.* splitting off, separation, etc., *see v.;* cleavage; detachment, removal; **—ление воды** dehydration; **—лённый** *a.* split off, etc., *see v.;* **—лять** *v.* split off, chip off, spall; separate, detach; remove, eliminate, abstract; **—ляться** *v.* split (off, out), come off.

отщип/нуть, —(ыв)ать *v.* pinch off.

оть— *see* **от—** (used before **е, ю, я**).

отъедать *v.* eat off, gnaw off; eat away; finish eating; **—ся** *v.* be well fed.

отъедин/ение *n.* disconnecting, switching off; **—ённый**

a. disconnected; **—ять** *v.* disconnect, switch off; separate.

отъез/д *m.* departure, leaving, setting off; pull-back; **—дить** *v.* cover (a given distance): **—жать** *v.* drive or ride off, depart, leave, set off; **—жающий** *a.* departing; *m.* departing person.

отъём *m.* removal, withdrawal; (zool.) weaning; take-off; tripper (of conveyer); **о. мощности** power take-off, p.t.o.; **—ка** *f.* detachment; taking away; confiscation; **—ный** *a.* of **отъём**; removable, detachable; **—ыш** *m.* (zool.) weanling; weaner.

отъесть(ся) *see* **отъедать(ся).**

отъехать *see* **отъезжать.**

отыгр/(ыв)ать(ся) *v.* win back; **—ыш** *m.* retrieved losses.

отым/ать *see* **отнять; —ённый** *a.* (gram.) denominative.

отыск/ание *n.* searching, etc., *see v.*; detection, etc., *see v.*; discovery; **о. повреждений** troubleshooting; **—анный** *a.* searched (for), etc., *see v.*; **—ивание** *see* **отыскание; —(ив)ать** *v.* search (for), look (for), seek, track down; detect, locate, determine, find, discover; **—иваться** *v.* come up, turn up, appear.

отэкзаменовать *v.* examine; finish examining.

отэнит *m.* (min.) autunite.

отяг/отить, —ощать, —чать, —чить *v.* weigh down, burden, aggravate; **—ощённость** *f.* (gen.) tendency, hereditary predisposition; **—ощённый** *a.* tainted.

отяжел/евший, —елый *a.* heavy; **—ение** *n.* growing heavy; (text.) weighting; **—еть** *v.* grow heavy; **—ить, —ять** *v.* make heavier; weight.

ОУА *abbr.* (**относительная удельная активность**) relative specific activity.

Оуена процесс Owen (flotation) process.

Оук Ридж (geog.) Oak Ridge.

о.у.р. *abbr.* (**относительная удельная радиоактивность**) relative specific radioactivity.

офайстон *m.* (bot.) Ophaiston.

ОФБО *abbr.* (**оксифенилбензоксазол**) hydroxyphenylbenzoxazole.

офелиевая кислота ophelic acid.

оферт *m.*, **—а** *f.* (com.) offer.

офи—, —д— *prefix* ophi(d)—, ophio— (snake, serpent); **—дизм** *m.* (med.) ophidism; **—дический** *a.* ophidic, snake; **—кальцит** *m.* (petr.) ophicalcite; **—оксилин** *m.* (chem.) ophioxylin; **—олит** *m.* (petr.) ophiolite; **—олитовый** *a.* ophiolitic; **—он** *m.* (ent.) Ophion; **—опогон** *m.* (bot.) Ophiopogon; **—токсемия** *f.* (med.) ophiotoxemia; **—отрикс** *m.* (zool.) Ophiothrix.

офит *m.* (petr.) ophite; **—овый** *a.* ophitic, biabasic, lath-shaped.

офиуры *pl.* (zool.) Ophiuroidea.

офицер *m.* officer; **—ский** *a.* officer's; **—ство** *n.* officers.

официальный *a.* official, formal.

официант *m.* waiter; **—ка** *f.* waitress.

официнальный *see* **оффицинальный.**

официоз *m.* semiofficial publication or organ; **—ный** *a.* semiofficial.

офлюсование *n.* fluxing.

оформ/итель *m.* (book) designer; **—ить** *see* **оформлять; —ление** *n.* shaping, etc., *see v.*; appearance, design (of book); makeup, get-up; official registration; presentation (of results); execution (of forms); **аппаратурное —ление** implementation, instrumentation, mechanization (of process); **архитектурное —ление** styling; **—ленный** *a.* shaped, etc., *see v.*; **—лять** *v.* shape; design, make up, get up; mount; register offi-

cially, make official, legalize; put in order; draw up (a document); put on the staff; execute (records); implement (a process); **—ляться** *v.* shape up; **—ляющий** *a.* shaping, etc., *see v.*

офорт *m.*, **—ный** *a.* etching, copper-plate engraving; aqua fortis, nitric acid.

офриосколекс *m.* (prot.) Ophryoscolex.

офрис *m.* (bot.) Ophrys.

офсет *m.*, **—ный** *a.* (typ.) offset.

офтальм/ический *a.* ophthalmic; **—ия** *f.* (med.) ophthalmia; **—о—** *prefix* ophthalmo— (eyes); **—олог** *m.* (med.) ophthalmologist; **—ологический** *a.* ophthalmologic(al); **—ология** *f.* ophthalmology; **—опатия** *f.* ophthalmopathy, eye disease; **—оплегия** *f.* ophthalmoplegia.

офтальмоскоп *m.* (med.) ophthalmoscope; **—ировать** *v.* examine with an ophthalmoscope; **—ия** *f.* ophthalmoscopy.

офтальмохирургия *f.* (med.) eye surgery.

офферта *f.* (com.) offer.

оффицинальн/ый *a.* officinal, medicinal; **—ые травы** medicinal herbs.

оффретит *m.* (min.) offretite.

оха-бланка *f.* (phyt.) oja-blanca disease.

охапка *f.* bunch, bundle, armful.

охарактеризовать *v.* characterize, determine; describe.

охва/т *m.* reach, range, coverage, compass, scope, girth; envelopment; overlapping; conformance (of flooded area); wrap (of cable); (mil.) outflanking; **коэффициент —та** conformance factor; **угол —та** included angle; **—тить** *see* **охватывать; —тываемый** *a.* embraced, etc., *see v.*; male (contact); **—тывание** *see* **охват; —тывать** *v.* embrace, envelop, encompass, cover; include, comprise, involve; enclose, surround, encircle; touch (upon); wrap (of cable, chain); grip, seize; grasp, comprehend; bracket; **—тывающий** *a.* embracing, etc., *see v.*; surrounding, ambient; female (contact); **—ченный** *a.* embraced, etc., *see v.*

охвостье *n.* tailings, tails; (agr.) chaff.

охинский *a.* (geog.) Okha.

охлад/евать, —еть *v.* become cool; become indifferent (to).

охладитель *m.* cooler, refrigerator; condenser; coolant; cooling agent, refrigerant; (met.) quenching medium; cooling plant; **башенный о.** cooling tower; **обратный о.** reflux condenser; **—ный** *a.* cooling; freezing (mixture); **—ная коробка** (met.) chill box, chill mold, cooler.

охла/дить *see* **охлаждать; —ждаемый** *a.* cooled; **—ждаемый водой** water-cooled; **—ждать** *v.* cool, chill, reduce the temperature (of); refrigerate; condense (steam); **—ждаться** *v.* cool (off).

охлаждающ/ий *a.* cooling, etc., *see* **охлаждать;** freezing (mixture); refrigerant; **о. прибор** cooler, refrigerator; **о. цилиндр** condenser; **—ая жидкость** coolant; **—ее вещество** cooling agent, coolant, refrigerant; (met.) quenching compound; **—ее пространство** condensation chamber.

охлажден/ие *n.* cooling, chilling, refrigeration; condensation; (met.) quenching; (med.) hypothermia; **глубокое о.** deep freeze; subzero treatment (of steel); **искусственное о.** air conditioning; **коэффициент —ия** (meteor.) chill factor; **поверхность —ия** cooling surface; condensing surface; **пространство —ия** cooling jacket; condensation chamber; **с водяным —ием** water-cooled; **с воздушным —ием** air-cooled; **система —ия** cooling system.

охлаждённый *a.* cooled, etc., *see* **охлаждать.**

охлоп/ок *m.* tow, stuffing, combing(s); **—ки** *pl.,* **—ье** *n.* waste.

охмел/ение *n.* hopping (of wort); **—еть** *v.* become intoxicated; **—ить, —ять** *v.* add hops, hop; **—яющий** *a.* intoxicating.

ОХН *abbr.* (**отделение химических наук**) Division of Chemical Sciences.

охоло/стить *v.* castrate; **—щение** *n.* castration.

охот/а *f.* desire, will, inclination; hunt(ing), chase; (zool.) oestrus, rut, heat; **о. у него отпала** he no longer wanted (to); **отбивать —у** *v.* discourage; **половая о.** oestrus; **приходить в —у** *v.* come into heat; **—инспектор** *m.* game warden; **—иться** *v.* hunt, chase, shoot; want; **—ливый** *a.* willing; **—ник** *m.* hunter, trapper, sportsman; amateur, lover; volunteer; (submarine) chaser; **—ничий** *a.* hunter's, hunting; **—ничий лес** (game) preserve; **—ничье-промысловый** *a.* game (animal); **—но** *adv.* willingly, readily; **—ное дело** hunting; **—овед** *m.* wildlife biologist.

охот/оморский *a.* (geog.) Okhotsk Sea; **—ский** *a.* Okhotsk; Okhota (river).

охра *f.* ocher (mineral pigment); **бурая о.** (min.) brown (iron) ocher; **жёлтая о.** yellow ocher; **красная о.** red (iron) ocher; **чёрная о.** black ocher, wad.

охран/а *f.* guard, escort, custody; conservation, preservation; safeguarding, security; care, protection; (child) welfare; (fire) prevention; (environmental) control; **о. труда** industrial hygiene; job safety; **—ение** *n.* (safe)guarding, etc., *see v.;* security; **сторожевое —ение** (mil.) outpost; **—ённый** *a.* (safe)guarded, etc., *see v.;* **—итель** *m.* guard(ian), protector; preserver; **—ительный** *a.* protective, guard; preservative; safety (device); **—ить** *see* **охранять; —ник** *m.* guard; **—ный** *a.* safety; (microelectronics) collar (ring); protective, buffer (zone); restricted (area); **—яемый** *a.* protected; **район —яемых почв** soil conservation district; **—ять** *v.* (safe)guard, protect, keep watch (over); preserve; cover (with a patent); **—яющий** *a.* (safe)guarding, etc., *see v.;* protective.

охренный *see* **охристый.**

охридский *a.* (geog.) Ohrid.

охрип/лость *f.* hoarseness; **—лый** *a.* hoarse; **—нуть** *v.* get hoarse.

охр/истый, —овый *a.* ocherous, ocher-colored; **—ить** *v.* paint with ocher.

охрома *f.* (bot.) Ochroma.

охрометь *v.* grow lame.

охро/ноз *m.* (med.) ochronosis; **—подобный** *a.* ochroid, ocherous, ocher-colored.

охрупчив/ание *n.* (met.) embrittlement; **—аться** *v.* embrittle.

охряный *see* **охристый.**

охрящевение *n.* (physiol.) chondrification.

оцарап/нуть, —(ыв)ать *v.* scratch.

оцар/ка *f.,* **—ок** *m.* pen, trapping corral.

оцеживать *v.* strain, filter.

оцеллярный *a.* (petr.) ocellar.

оцелот *m.* (mam.) ocelot (*Felis pardalis*).

оцен/ённый *a.* appraised, etc., *see v.;* **—ивание** *see* **оценка; —и(ва)ть** *v.* appraise, evaluate, assess, estimate, judge, gage, grade, rate, price; define, determine; value, appreciate; **—и(ва)ть из точки зрения** rate; **—ка** *f.* appraising, evaluation, etc., *see v.;* appraisal, estimate, assessment; analysis, study, interpretation; rating, rate; value; (integral) criterion; (livestock) judging; **вне —ки** non-grade (grain); **давать —ку** *see* **оценивать; —очный** *a. of* **оценка;** appraised; **—щик** *m.* appraiser, estimator; **—ять** *see* **оценивать.**

оцепен/елость *f.* numbness, torpor, rigidity; **—елый** *a.* numb, torpid; **—ение** *n.* numbness, torpor; catalepsy, rigor; **зимнее —ение** dormancy; **—еть** *v.* grow numb or torpid; **—ить, —ять** *v.* make numb, benumb, torpify.

оцеп/ить, —лять *v.* surround, encompass; **—ление** *n.* surrounding, encompassing.

оцимен *m.* ocimene, 2,6-dimethyl-1,5,7-octatriene.

оцинков/ание *n.* zincing, zinc-plating, zinc-coating, galvanization; **—анный** *a.* zinc-plated, zinc-coated, galvanized; **—ать** *see* **оцинковывать; —ка** *f.,* **—очный** *a. see* **оцинкование; —щик** *m.* galvanizer; **—ывание** *see* **оцинкование; —ывать** *v.* zinc(-plate), coat with zinc, galvanize.

оципода *f.* (crust.) Ocypode.

оцифров/ка *f.* numbering; **—(ыв)ать** *v.* number, assign numerical values.

ОЦК *abbr.* (**объёмноцентрированная кубическая решётка**) body-centered cubic lattice, bcc; (**определение цементного кольца**) cement top determination.

оч. *abbr.* (**очень**) very; **ОЧ, о.ч.** *abbr.* (**октановое число**) octane number.

оча/г *m.* focus, focal point, seat, center, site, point, place, location; source, origin; zone (of deformation); (magma) chamber; hearth, fireplace; **о. обтания** pocket; **—говый, —жный** *a. of* **очаг;** focal (med.) insular (sclerosis); local (reaction); **—жок** *dim. of* **очаг.**

очанка *f.* (bot.) eyebright (*Euphrasia*).

очаровательный *a.* charming.

очевид/ец *m.* eyewitness; **—но** *adv.* apparently, evidently, obviously; it is obvious; **—ность** *f.* evidence, obviousness; reality, tangibility; **в силу —ности** ipso facto; **—ный** *a.* evident, obvious, apparent, clear.

очей *gen. pl. of* **око.**

очекан/ивание *n.* calking; chiseling; **—и(ва)ть** *v.* calk; chisel (around).

очень *adv.* very, greatly, highly, much **о. плохо, о. трудно** poorly, with difficulty, barely (soluble).

очервиветь *v.* become wormy.

очерёдно *adv.* alternately; *prefix* alterni—.

очередной *a.* in turn, the next, immediate, successive; regularly scheduled (meeting, etc.); (bot.) alternate.

очерёдно/листный *a.* alternifoliate; **—расположенный** *a.* regularly arranged; **—сть** *f.* sequence, succession; priority, order (of priority).

очеред/ь *f.* turn, course; line, queue; phase (of work); (art.) salvo, burst; **в первую о.** first (of all), primarily; **в свою о.** in turn; **вставать в о.** *v.* queue; **по —и** in turn.

очерет *m.* (bot.) bog rush, reed (*Schoenus*); **—ник** *m.* Rhynchospora; **—ный, —овый, —яный** *a. of* **очерет.**

очерк *m.* outline, sketch, essay; synopsis, abridgement; tabulation.

очёркивать, очеркнуть *v.* outline.

очерковый *a. of* **очерк.**

очерствелый *a.* hard, stale (bread).

очер/тание *n.* outline, contour, configuration, form, profile, shape, cut-out; **—тить, —чивать** *v.* trace, outline, draw a line, describe, define; delineate; circumscribe; **—ченный** *a.* traced, etc., *see v.*

очёс *m.* combings, waste, noil(s); (flax) tow; (peat) dust.

очесать *see* **очёсывать.**

очёс/ка *f.* combing; **—ки** *pl.* combings, waste; (silk) floss; **—ывание** *n.* combing; deseeding (of flax); **—ыватель** *m.* combing maching; **—ывать** *v.* comb; deseed.

очехловка *f.* jacketing, canning.

очечн/ик *m.* eyeglass case; **—ый** *a.* of **очки.**

очешет *fut. 3 sing. of* **очесать.**

очи *pl. of* **око.**

очин *m.* (biol.) calamus, scapus, stem.

очини(ва)ть *v.* sharpen (pencil).

очиститель *m.* purifier, clean(s)er, (gas) scrubber; separator; rectifier; (nucl.) decontaminator, scavenger.

очистительн/ый *a.* purifying, etc., *see* **очистить; о. аппарат** purifier; rectifier; **о. бак** (sugar) clarifier, clearing pan; **о. завод, —ая установка** refinery; **—ое средство** purifying agent, purifier; clean(s)er, detergent; decontaminant; (pharm.) purgative.

очист/ить *v.* purify, refine; clean(se); clarify; clear (away, of, off, up); free, get rid (of), remove; scrape off, trim; peel, husk, hull; (casting) fettle; rectify; scrub (gas); (nucl.) decontaminate, scavenge; (met.) scour, pickle; (sand-)blast; (concentration) separate; **—ка** *f.* purifying, purification, etc., *see v.*; refinement; removal, de—; cleanup; treatment (of waste); cleaning unit; (nucl.) scavenger; **—ка от загрязнений** decontamination; **—ка от кожуры** peeling; **—ка от накипи** or **окалины** scale removal, descaling; **—ка от семян** (de)seeding; **—ка растворителем** solvent refinement; **мокрая —ка** (gas) scrubbing; **подвергать —ке** *v.* purify; **показатель —ки** decontamination index; **тонкой —ки** secondary (filter); **—ка сортировка** *f.* cleaner-grader; **—ки** *pl.* siftings, screenings, waste; peelings; **—ная** *f.* cleaning room; **—ной, —ный** *a.* purifying, etc., *see v.*; clear (felling); **—ный забой** (min.) productive working; **—ная станция, —ная установка, —ное сооружение** (sewage) treatment plant, waste disposal plant; **—ные работы** (min.) stoping, extraction of minerals.

очиток *m.* (bot.) stonecrop (*Sedum*).

очищ/аемость *f.* treatability (of sewage): **—ать** *see* **очистить; —ающий** *see* **очистительный;** sweeping (electrode); **—ение** *see* **очистка; —енный** *a.* purified, etc., *see* **очистить;** net (rate).

очк/и *pl.* glasses, spectacles; eyepiece; (protective) goggles; (contact) lenses; (zool.) ocelli, eye spots; **—о** *n.* eye(let), eyepiece; (zool.) ocellus; (screen) mesh; aperture, hole, peephole; cavity, pocket; (typ.) face; (sports) point.

очковать *v.* (hort.) graft.

очков/ый *a.* of **очки, очко;** (petr.) augen; **—ая змея** (herp.) cobra (*Naja*); **—ая печь** (met.) spectacle furnace.

очной *see* **очный.**

очнуться *v.* regain consciousness.

очн/ый *a.* ocular, eye; **о. цвет** (bot.) pimpernel (*Anagallis*); **—ая ставка** (law) confrontation; **—ая трава** (bot.) eyebright (*Euphrasia officinalis*).

ОЧТ *abbr.* (**октановое число топлива**) octane number of fuel.

очувств/итель *m.* sensitizer; **—ление** *n.* sensitization; **—ленный** *a.* sensitized.

очутиться *v.* appear, find oneself.

ошак *m.* (bot.) Dorema.

ошва *f.* (naut.) sheathing.

ошвартовать *v.* (naut.) make fast, moor.

ошев *m.* calcar, fritting furnace.

ош/еек *m.* (meat) neck; **—ейник** *m.* (choke) collar; (mech.) bush; **—ейниковый** *a.* collared; (zool.) ring-necked.

ошелом/ить, —лять *v.* stupefy, stun.

ошелудиветь *v.* grow scabby, get mangy.

ошелуш/ённый *a.* shelled, husked; **—ивать** *v.* shell, husk.

ошибаться *v.* make a mistake, err.

ошибень *m.* (ichth.) cusk eel (*Ophidion*).

ошиб/иться *v.* make a mistake, err; **—ка** *f.* mistake, error, inaccuracy; blunder, oversight, fault; **—ка анализа** analytical error; **—ка взвешивания** weighing error; **—ка в расчёте** miscalculation; **—ка по дальности** range error; **—ка при отсчёте** reading error; **—ка счёта** miscount; **выявлять —ки** *v.* debug; **код —ки** (comp.) error code; **по —ке** by mistake, erroneously.

ошибн/евые, —и *pl.* (ichth.) Ophidiidae.

ошибочн/о *adv.* by mistake, erroneously; **—ость** *f.* inaccuracy; fallibility; **—ый** *a.* mistaken, wrong, erroneous, in error, inaccurate, incorrect, faulty; anomalous, abnormal; mis— *e.g.* **—ый диагноз** misdiagnosis.

ошинов/ка *f.,* **—ывание** *n.* putting on a tire, etc., *see v.*; (elec.) leads; busbars; bus arrangement; **—ывать** *v.* put on a tire; (elec.) equip with busbars.

ошипов/анный *a.* lugged (furnace shell interior); **—ать** *v.* lug; **—ка** *f.* lugging.

оширенный *a.* broadened, extended.

ошкуй *m.* (mam.) polar bear (*Ursus maritimus*).

ошкур/енный *a.* decorticated, etc., *see v.*; **—ивать** *v.* decorticate, peel, bark; sand, rub with emery.

ошлаков/анный *a.* scorified; **—атель** *m.* scorifier; **—(ыв)ание** *n.* (met.) slagging, scorification; (coal) clinkering; **—(ыв)ать** *v.* slag, form slag, scorify, clinker; **—(ыв)аться** *v.* slag, form slag or clinker.

ошламование *n.* slime formation.

ошмёток *m.* lump; rag.

ошмыгивание листьев *n.* defoliation.

ошмянский *a.* (geog.) Oshmyanka.

ошорский *a.* (geog.) Oshoro.

ошпар/енный *a.* scalded; **—ивание** *n.,* **—ка** *f.* scalding; **—иватель** *m.* scalding vat; **—ивать** *v.* scald; (text.) bowk, kier(-boil).

ошский *a.* (geog.) Osh.

оштрафов(ыв)ать *v.* fine.

оштукатур/енный *a.* plastered; **—ивание** *n.* plastering; (outside) stucco work; **—и(ва)ть** *v.* plaster; stucco.

ощелачив/ание *n.* alkalization, alkalizing; **—ать** *v.* alkalize.

ощен/ение *n.* (zool.) whelping, etc., *see v.*; **—ить(ся)** *v.* whelp, pup, cub, litter.

ощетини(ва)ть(ся) *v.* (zool.) bristle.

ощип/ка *f.,* **—ывание** *n.* plucking, etc., *see v.*; **—(ыв)ать** *v.* pluck, pick; dress (poultry).

ощупники *pl.* (ent.) Pselaphidae.

ощуп/(ыв)ание *n.* feeling, etc., *see v.*; (med.) palpation; **—(ыв)ать** *v.* feel, finger, examine manually, touch, probe, sound; palpate; **—ывающее средство** feeler, probe; **—ь** *f.* feel, touch; **на —ь** to the touch, by feel; **—ью** *adv.* by touch; **искать —ью** *v.* grope (for).

ощу/тимо *adv.* perceptibly, etc., *see a.*; **—тимость** *see* **ощутительность; —тимый** *see* **ощутительный; —тительность** *f.* perceptibility, tangibility, palpability; **—тительный** *a.* perceptible, tangible, palpable; appreciable, material; **—тить, —щать** *v.* feel, perceive, be(come) aware (of), sense; **—щаться** *v.* make itself felt; be observed; **—щение** *n.* feel(ing), perception, sensation; sense; (med.) esthesia; **—щение холода** cryesthesia; **—щённый** *a.* felt, perceived.

оэция *f.* (zool.) ooecium, ovicell.

оягниться *v.* (zool.) lamb.

П

п *abbr.* (**пико—**) pico— (10^{-12}); (**пуаз**) poise; (**пьеза**) pieze.

ПАБК *abbr.* (**парааминобензойная кислота**) *p*-aminobenzoic acid, PABA.

ПАВ *abbr.* (**поверхностная акустическая волна**) surface acoustic wave, SAW; (**поверхностно-активное вещество**) surfactant.

пава *f.* (orn.) peahen.

павиан *m.* (mam.) baboon (*Papio, Cynocephalus*).

павильон *m.*, **—ный** *a.* pavilion; hall; (bee) house.

павинол *m.* pavinol (a leather substitute).

павлин *m.* (orn.) peafowl, peacock (*Pavo*); **—ий, —ный, —овый** *a.* peacock, pavonine; **—ий глаз** (ent.) peacock butterfly (*Vanessa*); **—ово-голубой** *a.* peacock blue; **—овые** *pl.* peacockfishes (*Nematistiidae*); **—о-глазка** *f.* (ent.) Saturnia; **—оглазки** *pl.* saturnid moths (*Saturniidae*); **—ьи** *pl.* (orn.) Phasianidae; **—ья руда** (min.) peacock ore, bornite.

павло/вния *f.* (bot.) Paulownia; **—вский** *a.* (geog.) Pavlovsk; (med.) Pavlov; **—дарский** *a.* (geog.) Pavlodar.

павод/коаккумулирующий *a.* detention (basin); **—коведение** *n.* study of floods; **—ковый** *a.*, **—ок** *m.*, **—очный** *a.*, **—ье** *n.* flood (water), flood tide, high water, freshet; flood(ing), overflow, inundation; flash flood.

павой *m.* (bot.) Periploca.

павш/ие *pl.* (mil.) the fallen; **—ий** *a.* fallen, etc., *see* **падать**; (mil.) killed.

пагелл, —ь, —юс *m.* (ichth.) sea bream (*Pagellus*).

пагинация *f.* (typ.) pagination, page numbering.

пагод/ит *m.* (min.) pagodite, agalmatolite; **—овый** *a.* pagoda.

паголенок *m.* leg (of stocking).

пагон *m.* (biol.) anabiotically frozen organisms living in ice.

пагр(ус) *m.* (ichth.) sea bream (*Pagrus*).

пагуб/а *f.* ruin, destruction; **—но отражаться** *v.* have a pernicious effect (on); **—ный** *a.* pernicious, noxious, deleterious, detrimental, malignant, destructive, fatal.

пагума *f.* (mam.) palm civet (*Paguma*).

пада/леяды *pl.* carrion eaters; **—лица** *f.* windfall, fallen fruit, fallen seed or grain; **—ль** *f.* carrion, offal; cadaver, carcass; **—льница** *f.*, **—льная муха** (ent.) Calliphora, Lucilia.

паданг *m.* (geobot.) padang.

падан/ец *m.* fallen fruit; **—ие** *see* **падение**.

пад/ать *v.* fall, drop, diminish, decrease, decline, sink; fall off or out; (geol.) dip; strike, impinge (on), be incident (on); **п. на** be due to, be made up, be comprised, be accounted for; **—ающий** *a.* falling, etc., *see v.*; incident (rays, etc.); incoming (particle); shooting (star); drop, trip (hammer); gravity (stamp).

падди *m.* paddy (unmilled rice).

паддок *m.* paddock, enclosure, pen.

падев/ость *f.* honeydew content; **—ый мёд** honeydew.

падёж *m.*, **—ный** *a.* (vet.) epizootic (disease); murrain; epidemic; mortality, die-off; loss(es) (from disease).

падеж *m.* (gram.) case.

падемелон *m.* (mam.) scrub wallaby (*Thylogale*).

паден/ие *n.* fall(ing), drop(ping), sinking, decrease, decline, diminution, reduction, lowering, depression; loss (of weight); incidence (of rays); (geol.) dip(ping); gradient (of curve), slant, slope, descent, incline, inclination, grade; precipitation; collapse; (river) profile; (bal.) impact; **п. на поверхность** incidence; **высота —ия** drop height; **сброс по —ию** (geol.) dip fault; **угол —ия** angle of incidence; (geol.) angle of dip.

падёт *fut. 3 sing. of* **пасть**.

падзол *m.* tannery waste (fertilizer).

падин/а *f.*, **—ный** *a.* ravine, gorge, crevice; (bot.) Padina.

падкий *a.* inclined, having a weakness (for), susceptible (to).

падуб *m.* (bot.) holly (*Ilex*); **—овый** *a.* ilicaceous; **—олистный** *a.* ilicifolious, holly-leaved.

пад/учая *f.*, **п. болезнь** (med.) epilepsy; **—учий** *a.* falling; **—учка** *f.* (ent.) grape rootworm (*Adoxus obscurus*); **—ший** *a.* fallen; **—ь** *f.* honeydew (from aphids); (geol.) ravine, creek valley.

па/ёв *gen. pl. of* **пай**; **—евой** *a. of* **евпай**; **—ой взнос** share.

паёк *m.* allowance, ration.

паёл *m.* (meteor.) overhead, ceiling.

паженый *a.* grooved.

пажитник *m.* (bot.) Trigonella.

пажит/ный *a.*, **—ь** *f.* pasture.

ПАЗ *abbr.* (**противоатомная защита**) antinuclear defense.

паз *m.* groove, mortise, slot, rabbet, channel(ing), flute, recess, notch; (welding) gap; (longitudinal) seam (in ship); **п. под обмотку** slot; **п. под шип** (building) mortise.

пазания *f.* (bot.) tan oak (*Pasania, Lithocarpus*).

пазанка *f.* hare's pad.

паз/ить *see* **пазовать**; **—ник** *m.* grooving plane, groover; (bot.) cat's-ear (*Hypochaeris*); **—ный** *a.* grooved, slotted; **—овальный** *a.* slotting, groove-cutting; **—овать** *v.* groove, mortise; join by tenon and mortise; **—овик** *m.* notching tool; boaster, drove chisel (for masonry); **—овочный** *a.* grooving, mortising.

пазо/вый *a. of* **паз**; grooving, slotting; slotted; **п. нож** grooving tool, slotting tool; **—вая фреза** slot mill; **—резный, —фрезерный** *a.* slot-milling; **—штамповочный пресс** notching machine.

пазу/ха *f.* bosom; pocket, recess; spandrel (of arch); gullet (of saw); (anat.) sinus, antrum, bursa, cavity; (bot.) axil; **—шный** *a.* axillary.

паивать *v.* water (livestock).

па/й *m.* part, portion; share, interest; (chem.) equivalent (weight), combining weight; **вес —я** weight equivalent.

Пайерлса-Набарро силы Peierls-Nabarro force.

пайза *f.* (bot.) Japanese millet (*Echinochloa frumentacea*)

пайк/а *f.* solder(ing); seal; *gen. of* **паёк**; **п. мягким припоем** soldering; **п. твёрдым припоем** brazing; **п.-сварка** *f.* braze welding; **—овый** *a. of* **паёк**.

пайлер *m.* (rolling) piler.

пайн *m.* pine (lumber).

пайол *m.* bilge boards, bottom ceiling.

пайрекс-трубки *see* **пирекс-трубки.**

пайсбергит *m.* (min.) paisbergite.

пайщик *m.* shareholder; solderer.

пак *m.* pack; pack ice.

пака *f.* (mam.) (al)paca; **—рановые** *pl.* pacaranas, false pacas (*Dinomyidae*).

пакгауз *m.* warehouse, storehouse.

пакеляж *see* **паклаяж.**

пакер *m.* (oil-well drilling) packer.

пакет *m.* packet, package, parcel, pack, bale; (met.) fagot, pile; (lumber) stack; bundle, bank; (comp.) batch; (software) package; kit; (mach.) block; (milk) carton; (paper) bag; (registered) letter; **п. битов** (comp.) bit cluster; **прокатка —ами** (met.) pack rolling; **—бот** *m.*

packet boat; **—(из)ированный** *a.* packed, etc., *see v.;* **—ик** *dim. of* **пакет; —ирование** *n.,* **—ировка** *f.,* **—ировочный** *a.* packing, etc., *see v.;* palletization, containerization; **—ировать** *v.* pack, package, bale; stack; palletize; (met.) fagot, pile.

пакет/ный *a. of* **пакет;** pack (rolling); stack (cutting); fagot(ed) (iron); packet-type, rotary (switch); batch (processing); **—ная связка** fagot, pile; **—овидный** *a.* sarciniform, packet-like; **—онаполнитель** *m.* bag filler; **-пресс** *m.* (met.) baling press, packing press.

паки *pl. of* **пака.**

пакистанский *a.* (geog.) Pakistan.

паклевидный *a.* tow-like, wooly.

паклён *m.* (bot.) field maple (*Acer campestre*); **—ок** *m.* Tartar maple (*A. tataricum*).

паклун *m.* (bot.) germander (*Teucrium*).

пакля *f.* tow, oakum, fiber packing.

пакляж *m.* stone base (of pavement).

пакляный *a.* tow, oakum.

паков/ание *see* **пакетирование; —ать** *see* **пакетировать; —ка, —очный** *see* **пакетировка, пакетировочный; —щик** *m.* packer; **—ый** *a.* pack.

пакпресс *m.* packpress.

пакт *m.* pact, agreement.

пакфонг *m.* (met.) German silver.

пак-хой *m.* (bot.) Chinese cabbage (*Brassica napus* var. *chinensis*).

пал *m.* ridge; (mach.) pawl; (naut.) bollard, mooring post; steppe *or* forest fire; burned out site; *past m. sing. of* **пасть.**

палагонит *m.* (petr.) palagonite; **—овый** *a.* palagonite, palagonitic.

паламедеи *pl.* (orn.) screamers (*Anhimidae*).

палас *m.* reversible rug.

палата *f.* chamber, board; house (of representatives); bureau, department; (hospital) ward.

палатальный *a.* (phonetics) palatal.

палатин/ит *m.* (petr.) palatinite; **—овый красный** Palatin Red (dye); **—ол** *m.* palatinol; **—охромовый чёрный** Palatinchrome Black.

палат/ка *f.* tent; stall, stand, booth; (anat.) tentorium; **—ный** *a. of* **палата;** head (nurse).

палато— *prefix* (anat.) palato— (palate).

палаточный *a. of* **палатка; п. городок** camp, camp site, encampment.

палахеит *m.* (min.) palacheite.

пал/гед *m.* (mach.) pawl head; **—гун, —гуп** *m.* pawl bed, pawl ring.

палеарктический *see* **палеоарктический.**

палевый *a.* pale yellow, straw-colored.

пален/ие *n.* burning, etc., *see* **палить; —ина** *f.* singed object.

палё(н)ный *a.* burned, etc., *see* **палить.**

палео— *prefix* paleo— (old, ancient; early, primitive); **—арктический** *a.* (biogeog.) Pal(a)earctic; **—биология** *f.* paleobiology; **—ботаника** *f.* paleobotany, fossil botany; **—ген** *m.,* **—геновый период** (geol.) Paleogene; **—завр** *m.* palaeosaur; **—зой** *m.* (geol.) Paleozoic era; **—зойский** *a.* Paleozoic; **—зоология** *f.* paleozoology; **—лит** *m.* (archeology) paleolith; **—нтолог** *m.* paleontologist; **—нтология** *f.* paleontology; **—терий** *m.* (pal.) palaeothere; **—тропический** *a.* (bot.) paleotropic; **—фитология** *f.* paleophytology, fossil botany; **—цен** *m.,* **—ценовый период** (geol.) Paleocene period; **—ценоз** *m.* paleo(bio)coenosis.

палестинский *a.* (geog.) Palestinian.

палета *f.* (horol.) pallet.

палетка *f.* template, pattern; standard curve, (set of) master curves; graticule; surveyor's plane; transparency.

палет/ный *a. of* **палета; —очный** *a. of* **палетка; —та** *see* **палета.**

пал/ец *m.* finger; (crank)pin, pin, peg; (stud) bolt; dog, detent; spindle; cam, cog, tooth, catch; guard; lifter; (anat.) digit, dactyl; **п. кисти** finger; **п. стопы** toe; **большой п.** thumb; big toe; **область —ьца** digital region; **отпечаток —ьца** fingerprint.

пали *past pl. of* **пасть;** *gen., pl., etc., of* **паль.**

паликурин *m.* (bioch.) palicourine.

палильный *a.* burning, etc., *see* **палить.**

палимбия *f.* (bot.) Palimbia.

палин— *prefix* palin— (again, back again); **—генез(ис)** *m.* (biol.) palingenesis.

палинолог/ический *a.* (bot.) palynological; **—ия** *f.* palynology, pollen analysis.

палинурихт *m.* (ichth.) Palinurichthys.

палисад *m.,* **—ный** *a.* palisade, paling; (mil.) stockade; **—ник** *m.* fence; yard.

палисандр *m.,* **—овый** *a.,* **—овое дерево** palissander, Brazilian rosewood.

палит *m.* palite, chloromethyl chloroformate (poison gas).

палитра *f.* palette.

палить *v.* burn, scorch, singe; fire, discharge, shoot; blast.

палиц/а *f.* stick, club; **—евидный** *a.* claviform.

палия *f.* (ichth.) char (*Salvelinus*).

палка *f.* stick, staff, cane; segment.

паллад/а *f.* (astr.) Pallas; **—иевый** *a.* (chem.) palladium; palladic (acid); **—(из)ированный** *a.* palladized, palladium-coated; **—ий** *m.,* **—ийный** *a.* palladium, Pd; **закись —ия** palladous oxide; **соль закиси —ия** palladous salt; **окись —ия** palladic oxide; **соль окиси —ия** palladic salt; **—ирование** *n.* palladium coating; **—истый** *a.* palladous, palladium; **—ит** *m.* (min.) pallad(in)ite.

палла/зина *f.* (ichth.) tubenose poacher (*Pallasina*); **—сит** *m.* (petr.) pallasite, Pallas iron.

паллет *m.,* **—а** *f.* pallet.

паллиатив *m.,* **—ный** *a.* palliative.

паллид/о— *prefix* (anat.) pallido—; **—ум** *m.* pallidum, globus pallidus; **—умальный** *a.* pallidal.

пало *past n. sing. of* **пасть.**

палоделатель *m.* (agr.) checker, ridge maker.

палок *gen. pl. of* **палка.**

палоло *m. or n.* (zool.) palolo worm (*Eunice*); **—вые** *pl.* Eunicidae.

палоч/ка *dim. of* **палка;** rod, stick, wand, baton; (bact.) bacillus, (rod-shaped) bacterium; **—ко—** *prefix* bacilli— (bacillus); bactro— (rod); **—ковидный, —кообразный** *a.* bacilliform, bacillary, rod-shaped; interhyal (bone); **—ковиды** *pl.* (ent.) stilt-bugs (*Berytinidae*); **—ковый** *a. of* **палочка; —кохвост(ов)ые** *pl.* (ichth.) tubeeyes (*Stylophoridae*); **—коядерный** *a.* (biol.; nucl.) stab, rod (neutrophil); stab-nuclear; **—ник** *m.* pole(stage) forest, poles; (bot.) Typha; **—ники** *pl.* (ent.) walkingsticks (*Bacillidae, Phasmatidae*); **—ный** *a. of* **палка.**

палтус *m.* (ichth.) halibut (*Hippoglossus*).

палуб/а *f.* deck; **—ный** *a.* deck, shipboard; carrier-borne (plane); covered (lighter); *suffix* -decker, e.g. **двухпалубный** *a.* two-decker.

палудрин *m.* (pharm.) Paludrine, proguanil hydrochloride.

ПАЛФ *abbr.* (**пиридоксальфосфат**) pyridoxal phosphate, PALP.

палы *pl. of* **паль;** burning.

палыгорскит *m.* (min.) palygorskite.

палый *a.* fallen.

паль *f.* burned-out area; —**ба** *f.* firing.

пальм/а *f.* palm (tree); **кавказская п.** (bot.) boxwood (*Buxus*); —**арозовый** *a.* palmarosa (oil); —**атин** *m.* (chem.) palmatine.

пальмер *m.* micrometer calipers or gage.

пальмерит *m.* (min.) palmerite.

пальмер-фосфат *m.* a phosphate fertilizer.

пальметка *see* **пальмер.**

пальмиерит *m.* (min.) palmierite.

пальмирский *a.* (geog.) Palmyra.

пальмит/ат *m.* (chem.) palmitate; —**иловый спирт** palmityl alcohol, cetyl alcohol; —**ин** *m.* palmitin; —**иновокислый** *a.* palmitic acid; palmitate (of); —**иновый** *a.* palmitin; palmitic, hexadecanoic (acid); —**(о)ил** *m.* palmit(o)yl; —**олевый** *a.* palmitolic, 7-hexadecynoic (acid); —**он** *m.* palmitone, 16-hentriacontanone; —**онитрил** *m.* palmitonitrile, hexadecanenitrile.

пальмо/видный *a.* palm-shaped; —**вник** *m.* palm grove; —**вые** *pl.* (bot.) Palmaceae; —**вый** *a.* palm; —**керновый**, —**ядерный** *a.* palm (kernel) (oil).

пальн/ик *m.* (blasting) cap; (orn.) black grouse (*Lyrurus tetrix*); —**уть** *v.* discharge, fire.

пальп/а *f.* (zool.) palp(us), feeler; —**ация** *f.* (med.) palpation; —**ебральный** *a.* (anat.) palpebral, eyelid; —**ировать** *v.* palpate; —**итация** *f.* (med.) palpitation.

пальто *n.*, —**вый** *a.* coat.

пальц/а *gen. of* **палец**; —**е** *prefix* dactyl(o)— (finger; toe); digiti— (finger); —**евиднораздельный** *a.* (biol.) palmatipartite; —**ивидный** *a.* digitiform, finger-shaped, dactylate; finger(ed), digitate; —**евидное образование** (anat.) digitation; —**евой, —евый** *a.* finger, digital; finger-action (tool); —**евые фрезы** end mills, end-milling cutters; —**екопытоходящий** *a.* (zool.) digitungulograde; —**екрыл** *m.* (ichth.) flying gurnard (*Dactylopterus volitans*); —**екрылки** *pl.* (ent.) Alucitidae; Pterophoridae; —**е-носовой** *a.* (med.) pointing (test); —**еобразный** *see* **пальцевидный.**

пальце/пёр *m.* (ichth.) threadfin; —**пёрые** *pl.* Polynemidae; —**ходящие** *pl.* digitigrade animals; —**ходящий** *a.* digitigrade.

паль/цы *pl. of* **палец**; —**чатка** *f.* (bot.) hairy crabgrass (*Digitaria sanguinalis*).

пальчато— *see* **пальце—**; palm(at)i—, palmate; —**видный** *a.* digitiform; —**жильный, —нервный** *a.* (bot.) digitinervate, palminerved; —**лопастный** *a.* palmatilobate; —**перистый** *a.* digitate-pinnate; —**раздельный** *a.* palmatipartite; —**рассечённый** *a.* palmatisect; palmatifid (wing); —**сложный** *a.* palmately compound.

пальчат/ый *a.* finger, prong, pin; toothed; dactylate, fingerlike, digitate; (anat.) tubular (gland); (bot.) palmate; —**ая трава** Bermuda grass (*Cynodon dactylon*).

пальч/ашка *see* **пальчатка**; —**ик** *dim. of* **палец**; —**иковый** *a.* bantam, miniature, peanut, mini—.

пальщик *m.* firer, blaster, discharger.

палья *see* **палия.**

палюдозный *a.* paludous, marsh(y).

палюстр/ин *m.* (chem.) palustrine, equisetine; —**овый** *a.* palustric (acid).

паля *f.* stake.

Паля-Кнорра синтез Paal-Knorr synthesis (of pyrrole derivatives).

палящий *a.* burning, etc., *see* **палить.**

пама *f.* (herp.) krait (*Bungarus fasciatus*).

памбакский *a.* (geog.) Pambak.

памирский *a.* (geog.) Pamir.

памп *m.* (ichth.) pomfret (*Pampus*).

памп/а *f.* pampa (prairie); —**асный, —асовый, —асский** *a.*, —**ы** *pl.* pampas; —**асная трава** pampas grass (*Cortaderia*).

пампельмус *m.* (bot.) grapefruit, shaddock (*Citrus maxima*).

памфагиды *pl.* (ent.) Pamphagidae.

памфлет *m.*, —**ный** *a.* pamphlet.

памят/ка *f.* memorandum; instructions, directions; leaflet; —**ливость** *f.* retentive memory; —**ливый** *a.* having a retentive memory; —**ник** *m.* monument, memorial; memoir; —**ник природы** nature sanctuary; —**ный** *a.* memorable; note (book); —**ная записка** memorandum; —**уя** *pres. ger.* remembering, bearing in mind; —**ь** *f.* memory, recollection; (comp.) storage, store; —**ь большой ёмкости** mass storage; —**ь на конденсаторах** capacitor memory; **быстродействие —и** access time; **восстанавливать в —и** *v.* remember, recollect; **заучить на —ь** *v.* memorize; **машинная —ь** memory, file, storage, store; **объём —и** storage capacity; **распределение —и** storage allocation.

пан— *prefix* pan— (all).

панакс *m.* (bot.) Panax.

панам/а *f.* Panama bark, quillaia bark; panama hat; —**ериканский** *a.* (geog.) Pan-American; —**ский** *a.* Panama.

панариций *m.* (vet.) panaris, felon, whitlow.

панацея *f.* panacea, cure-all, universal remedy.

панаширия *f.* (bot.) panachure, mottling.

панбархат *m.* (text.) panne.

пангазиевые *pl.* (ichth.) Schilbeidae.

пангамовая кислота pangamic acid, vitamin B_{15}.

панген *m.* (gen.) pangen, hypothetical unit; —**ез(ис)** *m.* pangenesis.

панголин *m.* (mam.) pangolin (*Manis*); —**ы** *pl.* scaly anteaters (*Pholidota*).

панда *f.* (mam.) panda (*Ailurus*, spec. *A. fulgens*); (geobot.) panda.

пандажметр *m.* (min.) pendage *or* dip meter.

пандан(ус) *m.* (bot.) screw pine (*Pandanus*); —**овые** *pl.* Pandanaceae.

пандатив *m.* (arch.) pendant; pendentive.

пандем/ический *a.* (med.) pandemic, widely epidemic; —**ия** *f.* pandemic (disease).

пандермит *m.* (min.) pandermite, priceite.

пандора *f.* (mal.) Pandora.

пандус *m.* (fixed) ramp.

панель *f.*, —**ный** *a.* panel, wainscot, bay; (switch) board; footpath, sidewalk; **п. набора** switchboard panel; **обшивать —ю** *v.* panel; —**ная обшивка** paneling, wainscoting.

панзоот/ический *a.*, —**ия** *f.* (vet.) panzootic.

панидиоморфный *a.* (petr.) panidiomorphic.

паник/а *f.* panic, fear, fright; —**ер** *m.* alarmist; —**(ерств)овать** *v.* panic.

паниров/ать *v.* (cooking) bread; —**очный** *a.* breaded.

панический *a.* panic; panicky.

пан/кардит *m.* (med.) pancarditis; —**кластит** *m.* (expl.) panclastite; —**климакс** *m.* (geobot.) panclimax; —**кратический** *a.* pancratic (eyepiece); zoom (lens); —**краций** *m.* (bot.) Pancratium.

панкреа/с *m.* (anat.) pancreas; —**тико—** *prefix* pancreatico— (pancreatic duct); —**тин** *m.* (pharm.) pancreatin; —**тит** *m.* (med.) pancreatitis; —**тический** *a.* pancreatic; —**тическая железа** pancreas; —**то—**

prefix pancreato— (pancreas); **—топептидаза** *f.* pancreatic peptidase (enzyme).

панкреоцимин *m.* pancreozymin (hormone).

панмик/сис *m.*, **—сия** *f.* (biol.) panmixis, panmixia, random mating; **—тический, —т(ич)ный** *a.* panmictic.

панникулит *m.* (med.) panniculitis.

панно *n.* (wall) panel; picture.

паннонский *a.* (geog.) Pannonian, Pannonic.

паннус *m.* (med.) pannus.

паноген *m.* Panogen (insecticide).

панорам/а *f.* panorama; (opt.) panoramic sight; **—ирование** *n.* (phot.) panning; panorama; scanning; **—ировать** *v.* pan; scan; **—ный** *a.* panorama, panoramic.

панорповые *pl.* scorpion flies (*Panorpidae*).

пан/остит *m.* (med.) panosteitis; **—отит** *m.* panotitis; **—офтальмит** *m.* panophthalmitis; **—плегия** *f.* panplegia, total paralysis.

пансион *m.*, **—ный, —ский** *a.* boarding house; boarding school; board and lodging; **—ат** *m.* guest house, inn, resort; lodging; **—ер** *m.* boarder, guest.

пантаналь *m.* pantanal (seasonal marsh).

пантеле/граф *m.* (elec. comm.) pantelegraph; **—графия** *f.* pantelegraphy, facsimile telegraphy; **—фон** *m.* pantelephone, microtelephone.

пантера *f.* (mam.) panther (*Panthera*).

пант/етеин *m.* (chem.) pantetheine; **—о—** *prefix* pant(o)— (all, whole, complete, entire).

пантовый *a. of* **панты**; antlered.

панто/граф *m.* pantograph (copier); **—дон** *m.* butterfly fish (*Pantodon buchholtzi*); **—евый** *a.* pantoic (acid); **—карены** *pl.* (naut.) cross curves of stability; **—крин** *m.* (pharm.) pantocrine; **—логия** *f.* pantology; **—метр** *m.* pantometer; **—морфизм** *m.* (cryst.) pantomorphism; **—поды** *pl.* (zool.) sea spiders (*Pantopoda*); **—пон** *m.* (pharm.) Pantopon; **—скоп** *m.* pantoscope, panoramic camera; **—тен** *m.*, **—теновая кислота** pantothenic acid, vitamin B₅; **—терии** *pl.* (pal.) Pantotheria; **—фаг** *m.* pantophage, omnivore; **—цид** *m.* (chem.) Pantocid, halazone.

пантропический *a.* pantropic(al) (virus).

панты *pl.* (zool.; pharm.) velvet antlers.

пан/фобия *f.* (med.) pan(o)phobia; **—хроматический** *a.* (phot.) panchromatic.

панцирн/ик *m.* (ichth.) gar (*Lepisosteus*); **—иковые** *pl.* Lepisosteidae; **—оголовые** *pl.* (herp.) Stegocephalia; **—ость** *f.* incrustation, crustification; **—ощёкие** *pl.* (ichth.) sculpins (*Cottidae*); **—ые** *pl.* (ichth.) placoderms; poachers (*Agonidae*); (zool.) Loricata; (prot.) Dinoflagellata.

панцир/ный *a.* armor(ed), armorclad; (zool.) loricate; (med.) jacket (cancer); **—ь** armor, case, shell; (zool.) lorica; **в медном —е** copperclad.

панцитопения *f.* (med.) pancytopenia.

панцырный *see* **панцирный**.

панэндем *m.* panendemic plant.

папавер/альдин *m.* (bioch.) papaveraldine; **—ин** *m.* papaverine; **—иновый** *a.* papaverine; papaveric, rhoeadic (acid).

папа/евые *pl.* (bot.) Caricaceae; **—(йот)ин** *m.* papain, papayotin, vegetable pepsin; **—йя** *f.* (bot.) papaya (*Carica papaya*).

папаноковые *pl.* (ichth.) Cheimarrhichthyidae.

папилл/а *f.* (biol.) papilla; **—ит** *m.* (med.) papillitis; **—овидный** *a.* papilliform; **—озный** *a.* papillose; **—ома** *f.* (med.) papilloma; **—ярный** *a.* papillar, nipple-shaped.

папильон/аж *m.* silkworm breeding in small bags; **—ирование** *n.* (hydr.) cross dredging.

папирос/а *f.*, **—ный** *a.* cigarette; **—ная бумага** tissue paper; cigarette paper.

папирус *m.* papyrus (paper); **—ный** *a.* papyrus, papyraceous.

папк/а *f.*, **—овый** *a.* portfolio; file (folder); (comp.) folder (icon); cardboard, (mill)board; (roofing, etc.) paper; pulp; **п.-планшет** *m.* map case.

пап-машина *f.* constructionboard machine, millboard machine.

папоротник *m.* (bot.) fern; **—и** *pl.* Felicinae; Polypodiophyta; **вод(я)ные —и** Hydropteridinae; **—о—** *prefix* pterido—, filici— (fern); **—овидный** *a.* filiciform, fern-like; **—овые** *pl.* Pteridophyta; **—овый** *a.* fern; **—олистный** *a.* fern-leaved.

папоч/ка *dim.*; **—ный** *a. of* **папка.**

паппатачи лихорадка (med.) pappataci fever, phlebotomous fever.

паппус *m.* (anat.; bot.) pappus.

паприк/а *f.*, **—овый** *a.* paprika.

папуасский *a.* (geog.) Papua.

папула *f.* (med.) papule.

папуш/а *f.* bundle, sheaf, stack; **—овка** *f.* bundling; **—овочная** *f.* (tobacco) bundling room.

папшер *m.* cardboard cutter.

папье-маше *n.* papier-maché.

пар *m.* steam, vapor; fumes; (agr.) fallow; *gen. pl. of* **пара**; **—ы** *pl.* vapor; fumes; **водяной п.** steam; water vapor; **давление —а** vapor pressure; **земля под —ом** fallow (land); **обрабатывать —ом** *v.* steam; **очищать —ами** *v.* fumigate; **перегонка —ом** steam distillation; **плотность —а** vapor density; **поднять —ы** *v.* fire up (boiler), raise steam; **полным —ом** full steam, full power; **продутый —ом** steam-treated; **температура образования —а** vaporization point.

пар/а *f.* pair, couple, dyad; set; suit, outfit; team of four; para rubber; **п. сил** (mech.) couple; **без —ы** unpaired, odd; **винтовая п.** screw gage, micrometer; **образование —ы** (nucl.) pair production.

пара— *prefix* para— (near, at the side of; wrong, faulty; to ward off); (chem.) para-; **в положении пара** in the para position; **—аминосалициловый** *a.* paraaminosalicylic (acid); **—бановый** *a.* parabanic (acid); **—бельский** *a.* (geog.) Parabel.

парабио/з *m.* (biol.) parabiosis; **—нт** *m.* parabiont; **—тический** *a.* parabiotic.

парабол/а *f.* (geom.) parabola; **—ический** *a.* parabolic; **—оид** *m.* paraboloid.

пара/бронх *m.* (orn.) parabronch; **—вагинальный** *a.* (anat.) paravaginal; **—ван** *m.* (naut.) paravane; **—вертебральный** *a.* (anat.) paravertebral; **—винный** *a.* paratartaric, racemic (acid); **—водород** *m.* para hydrogen; **—вольфрамат, —вольфрамовокислая соль** (chem.) paratungstate; **—выпуклый** *a.* paraconvex; **—ганглий** *m.* (cyt.) paraganglion; *pl.* paraganglia; **—гастральная полость** (zool.) paragaster; **—гвайский** *a.* (geog.) Paraguay; **—гелий** *m.* (chem.) para helium; **—гематин** *m.* (bioch.) parahematin.

параген/езис *m.* (min.) paragenesis; **—етический** *a.* paragenetic.

пара/гинный *a.* (gen.) paragynous; **—гоним** *m.* (zool.) Paragonimus; **—гонимоз** *m.* (med.) paragonimiasis; **—грас** *m.* (bot.) Para grass (*Panicum barbinode*).

параграф *m.* paragraph, section, clause.

парад *m.* parade, show, display; (mil.) review.

парадиазин *m.* (chem.) paradiazine.

парадигма *f.* paradigm (conjugation or declension); example, model; **—тический** *a.* paradigmatic.

парадизка *f.* paradise apple.

парад/ировать *v.* parade; **—ное** *n.* front door; **—ный** *a.* of **парад**; gala; front, main.

парадокс *m.* paradox; **—альный** *a.* paradoxical; **—ит** *m.* (min.) paradoxite.

пара-замещённ/ое *n.* (chem.) para-substitution product; **—ый** *a.* para-substituted, in the para position.

паразит *m.* parasite; parasitic oscillation; (bot.) epiphyte; (mech.) idler wheel, idle gear, idler; **внутренний п.** (zool.) endoparasite; **животный п.** zooparasite; **наружный п.** ectoparasite; **—арный** *a.* parasitic; **—изм** *m.* parasitism; **—ировать** *v.* parasitize, be a parasite; **—ические** *pl.* (ent.) Parasitica; **—ический, —ный** *a.* parasitic; spurious, stray; idle (gear); hitch-hiker (satellite); **—ная связь** (elec.) stray coupling; **—ник** *m.* (orn.) Arctic skua (*Stercorarius parasiticus*); **—ное колесо** idler.

паразито/з *m.* parasitosis, parasite infestation; **—лог** *m.* parasitologist; **—логия** *f.* parasitology; **—носитель** *m.* parasite carrier or host; **—носительство** *n.* parasitosis; **—подобный** *see* **паразитный**; **—убивающий** *a.* parasiticidal; **—устойчивость** *f.* resistance to parasites; **—цид** *m.* parasiticide; **—цидный** *a.* parasiticidal.

пара/изомер *m.* (chem.) para isomer; **—казеин** *m.* paracasein; **—каучук** *m.* para rubber; **—кислота** *f.* para acid; **—клаза** *f.* (geol.) paraclase; **—кме** *n.* (biol.) paracme, phylogerontic period; **—колит** *m.* (med.) paracolitis; **—кольпит** *m.* paracolpitis; **—компактный** *a.* (math.) paracompact; **—коновый** *a.* paraconic (acid); **—коттус** *m.* (ichth.) Paracottus; **—красный** *a.* para red (dye); **—ксиальный** *a.* paraxial (beam); **—ксонный** *a.* paraxonic; **—лаврионит** *m.* (min.) paralaurionite; **—лалия** *f.* paralalia, speech disturbance; **—лепис** *m.* (ichth.) Paralepis.

парали/затор *m.* paralyzer; (chem.) inhibitor; **—зация** *f.*, **—зование** *n.* paralyzation; **—зованный** *a.* paralyzed, paralytic; **—зовать** *v.* paralyze, petrify; **—тик** *m.*, **—тический** *a.* paralytic.

паралихт *m.* (ichth.) bastard halibut (*Paralichthys*); **—овые** *pl.* Bothidae.

паралич *m.* paralysis, palsy; **—plegia**, e.g. **п. нижних конечностей** paraplegia; **неполный п.** paresis; **—ный** *a.* paralytic.

параллак/с *m.* parallax; **—сный, —тический** *a.* parallactic, parallax; **—тический ход** (surv.) trig traverse.

параллел/епипед *m.* (geom.) parallelepiped; **—изировать** *v.* parallel(ize); match; **—изм** *m.* parallelism, parallel evolution; overlap(ping); concurrency; **—ограмм** *m.* parallelogram.

параллель *f.* parallel; **проводить п.** *v.* draw a parallel; contrast, compare; **—но** *adv.* parallel (with); (elec.) in parallel; **—но(-)жилковатый, —нонервный** *a.* (bot.) parallelinervate; **—но-последовательно** *adv.* (elec.) in parallel-series; **—но-последовательный** *a.* parallel-serial; **—ность** *f.* parallelism; (wheel) alignment.

параллельн/ый *a.* parallel; collateral; cocurrent (flow); shunt (excitation); aligned (wheels); **п. перенос координат** (math.) translation of axes; **—ое включение** (elec.) connection in parallel; **—ого действия** parallel-action (computer); **гравировать —ыми линиями** *v.* hatch, shade; **с —ыми пластинами** parallel-plate.

пар/альдегид *m.* (chem.) par(acet)aldehyde; **—альдол** *m.* paraldol; **—алюминит** *m.* (min.) paraluminite.

парамагн/етизм *m.* paramagnetism; **—етик** *m.* paramagnet(ic), paramagnetic substance; **—итный** *a.*, **—итное тело** paramagnetic.

парамер *m.* (anat.; ent.) paramere.

параметр *m.* (math.) parameter; argument; (comp.) qualifier; **—ы** *pl.* parameters, variables; characteristics, properties; values; (working, etc.) conditions; (mach.) performance; **—ы трансляции** (comp.) compiler toggles *or* options; **номинальные —ы** (mach.) rating; **—иальный** *a.* (anat.) parametrial, parametric; **—изация** *f.* parametrization; **—ий** *m.* (anat.) parametrium; **—ит** *m.* (med.) parametritis; **—ически** *adv.* parametrically; **задаваться —ически** *v.* be represented parametrically; **—ический** *a.* parametric; **—ический ряд** parametric series; **—он** *m.* parametron, parametric subharmonic oscillator.

парамец/ин *m.* paramecin (antibiotic); **—ия** *f.* (prot.) paramecium.

парами *adv.* in pairs.

пара/мид *m.* (chem.) paramide, mellimide; **—миксина** *f.* (ichth.) Paramyxine; **—миносалициловый** *a.* p-aminosalicylic (acid); **—миозин** *m.* paramyosin (a protein); **—миотония** *f.* (med.) paramyotonia; **—митоз** *m.* (gen.) paramitosis; **—молибдат** *m.*, **—молибдовокислая соль** (chem.) paramolybdate; **—мо** *m.* (geobot.) paramo; **—молочный** *a.* p-lactic, sarcolactic (acid).

параморф/а *f.* paramorph, variant form; **—изм** *m.* (min.) paramorphism; **—ный** *a.* paramorphic; **—оз** *m.*, **—оза** *f.* paramorph (crystal).

парамуширский *a.* (geog.) Paramushir.

парандра *f.* (ent.) Parandra.

пара/некроз *m.* (med.) paranecrosis; **—нема** *f.* (biol.) paranema, paraphysis; **—нефральный** *a.* (anat.) paranephric; **—нефрит** *m.* (med.) paranephritis; **—нитротолуол** *m.* (chem.) p-nitrotoluene.

парано/ид, —ик *m.* (med.) paranoiac; **—идный** *a.* paranoid; **—ия** *f.* paranoia.

парантез *m.* parenthesis.

парантиселена *f.* (astr.) parantiselene.

паранукл/еарный *a.* (cyt.) paranuclear; **—еин** *m.* (bioch.) paranuclein.

пара/офорон *m.* (anat.) paroophoron; **—перкис** *m.* (ichth.) Parapercis; **—перковые** *pl.* smelts (*Mugiloididae*).

парапет *m.* parapet, balustrade; coping.

пара/плазма *f.* (med.) paraplasm; **—план(ёр)** *m.* (av.) paraglider, paraplane; **—плегия** *f.* (med.) paraplegia; **—подий** *m.*, **—подия** *f.* (zool.) parapodium; **—положение** *n.* (chem.) para position; **—польский** *a.* (geog.) Parapol; **—пофиз** *m.* (anat.; zool.) parapophysis; **—пристипома** *f.* (ichth.) Parapristipoma; **—проктит** *m.* (med.) paraproctitis; **—протеин** *m.* (immun.) paraprotein; **—процесс** *m.* (phys.) para-process; **—псориаз** *m.* (med.) parapsoriasis; **—пузырный** *a.* (anat.) paravesical.

пара/ректальный *a.* (anat.) pararectal; **—розоловая кислота** p-rosolic acid, aurin; **—ряд** *m.* (chem.) para-series; **—сакральный** *a.* (anat.) parasacral; **—сахариновый** *a.* p-saccharic (acid); **—сексуальный** *a.* (gen.) parasexual; **—селена** *f.* paraselene, mock moon; **—сепиолит** *m.* (min.) parasepiolite; **—симпатический** *a.* (anat.) parasympathetic; **—синдес(ис)** *m.* (gen.) parasyndesis; **—скаридоз** *m.* (vet.) parascaridosis, Parascaris infection; **—соль** *m.* (av.) parasol; **—сорбиновый** *a.* parasorbic (acid); **—стернальный** *a.* (anat.) parasternal; **—стихтис** *m.* (ent.) Parastichtis; **—судис** *m.* (ichth.) Parasudis; **—сфеноид** *m.*, **—сфеноидная кость** (anat.) parasphenoid.

пара/такамит *m.* (min.) paratacamite; **—тгормон** *m.* parathormone, parathyroid hormone; **—теций** *m.* (bot.) parathecium; **—тион** *m.* Parathion (insecticide); **—тип**

m. (gen.) paratype; —**тиреоидин** *m.* (bioch.) parathyroidin; —**тиреоидный** *a.* parathyroid (gland, hormone); —**тиф** *m.* (med.) paratyphoid (fever); —**тормон** *see* **паратгормон;** —**трофный** *a.* paratrophic (nutrition); —**туберкулёз** *m.* (med.) paratuberculosis; —**уретральный** *a.* (anat.) paraurethral; —**физ** *m.* (embr.) paraphysis, paraphyseal body; —**физа** *f.* (bot.) paraphysis; —**фимоз** *m.* (med.) paraphimosis.

парафин *m.* paraffin (wax), wax; **жидкий п.** liquid paraffin, mineral oil; —**ёр** *m.* paraffiner, paraffin tank; —**изация** *f.*, —**ирование** *n.* paraffin treatment; —**ированный** *a.* paraffined, paraffin-coated; —**ировать** *v.* paraffin(ize); —**истость** *f.* wax content; —**истый** *a.* paraffin-containing, paraffin-rich; —**ный, —овый** *a.* paraffin, wax; paraffin-base (petroleum); paraffinic (acid); **п.-сырец** *m.* crude paraffin.

парафировать *v.* initial.

пара/форм(альдегид) *m.* (chem.) paraform(aldehyde); —**фталевый** *a.* p-phthalic, terephthalic (acid); —**фуксин** *m.* parafuchsin (dye); —**хлортолуол** *m.* (chem.) p-chlorotoluene; —**хор** *m.* parachor (expression of molecular volume); —**центез** *m.* paracentesis, surgical puncture; —**центральный** *a.* paracentral; —**центрический** *a.* paracentric; —**цетамол** *m.* (pharm.) paracetamol, acetaminophen; —**циан** *m.* (chem.) paracyanogen; —**цимол** *m.* p-cymene; —**цистит** *m.* (med.) paracystitis.

парашют *m.* parachute; —**изм** *m.*, —**ирование** *n.* parachute jumping, parachuting; —**ировать** *v.* parachute; —**ист** *m.* parachutist, parachute jumper; —**ист-перворазник** *m.* parachutist on his first jump; —**но-десантный** *a.* airdrop (container); (mil.) paratroop; —**ный** *a.* parachute.

паращитовидный *a.* parathyroid (gland).

пар/волин *m.* (chem.) parvoline; —**газит** *m.* (min.) pargasite; —**гелий** *m.* parhelion, mock sun; —**гелический** *a.* parhelic.

пардус *m.* (mam.) cheetah (*Acinonyx*).

парез *m.* (med.) paresis, incomplete paralysis; **п. желудка** gastroparesis.

парей/азавр *m.* (pal.) Pareiasaurus; **корень —ры** pareira (root).

парен/ец *m.* flax fiber; —**ие** *n.* steaming, etc., *see* **парить;** (frost) smoke; soaring, flight; —**ие моря** steam fog; —**ина** *f.* (agr.) perennial fallow; —**(н)ый** *a.* steamed, etc., *see* **парить.**

парентеральный *a.* (med.) parenteral.

паренхим/а *f.* (biol.) parenchyma; **листовая п.** (bot.) mesophyll; **первичная п.** meristem; —**альный** *a.* (anat.) parenchymal; —**(атоз)ный** *a.* parenchymatous.

пареный *see* **парен(н)ый.**

парень *m.* young man, fellow.

паре/стезия *f.* (med.) paresthesia, abnormal sensation; —**тический** *a.* paretic.

пари *n.*, **держать п.** *v.* bet, wager.

париан *m.* Parian porcelain; —**ит** *m.* (min.) parianite.

париетальный *a.* (biol.) parietal.

париет/ин *m.* parietin, physcion; —**овая кислота** parietic acid, chrysophanic acid.

парижск/ий *a.* Paris, Parisian; **п. жёлтый** Paris yellow, lead chromate; —**ая зелень** Paris green (insecticide); —**ая синь** Paris blue, ferric ferrocyanide.

паризит *m.* (min.) parisite.

парик *m.* wig; —**махер** *m.* barber; —**махерская** *f.* barbershop; hairdresser's; —**овый** *a.* wig; —**овое дерево** (bot.) smoke tree (*Rhus cotinus; Cotinus*).

парилка *f.* steamer; steam(ing) room.

парилл/ин *m.*, —**овая кислота** parillin, parillic acid.

париль/ный *a.* steaming; —**ня** *f.* steam(ing) room; —**щик** *m.* steamer.

паринаровая кислота parinaric acid.

парировать *v.* parry, counter(act), arrest.

паритель *m.* (av.) glider pilot.

паритет *m.* parity, equality; —**ный** *a.* parity; parity-check(ing) (code); **на —ных началах с** on a par with.

парить *v.* steam, stew; scald; evaporate; soar, hover, glide; (agr.) let lie fallow.

парицин *m.* (chem.) paricine.

парк *m.* park, yard; garage, depot; fleet, stock; inventory; (tank) farm; (oyster) bed; **п. подвижного состава** rolling stock; **п. путей** switch yard; **мостовой п.** bridging train.

парка *f.* parka (coat); *see* **парение;** *gen. of* **парок.**

паркеризация *f.* parkerizing, parkerization (rustproofing process).

паркесирование *see* **Паркса способ.**

паркет *m.* parquet (floor); rabbit warren; —**ина** *f.* parquet block; —**ники, —никовые** *pl.* (ichth.) Muraenolepidae; —**но-строгальный** *a.* floor-finishing; —**но-шлифовальный** *a.* floor-polishing; —**ный** *a.* parquet; —**чик** *m.* parquet layer.

паркинсон/изм *m.* (med.) parkinsonism; **болезнь П-а** Parkinson's disease; —**ик** *m.*, —**ческий** *a.* parkinsonian.

парковый *a.* *of* **парк; п. лес** parkland; **п. пояс** greenbelt.

Паркса способ (met.) Parkes process.

парламент *m.* parliament.

парлифт *m.* steam lift (for liquids).

парма *f.* (geobot.) parma; —**ч** *m.* (ent.) snout beetle (*Rhynchites auratus*).

парм/езан *m.* Parmesan cheese; —**елиевые** *pl.* (bot.) Parmeliaceae; —**елия** *f.* Parmelia (a lichen); —**ский** *a.* (geog.) Parma; —**ы** *pl.* parmy (low, wooded ridges flanking the Ural Mountains).

парнассиус *m.* (ent.) Parnassius.

парная *f.* steam room.

парник *m.* hotbed, seed bed; steamer; **в —е** under glass; **холодный п.** coldframe; —**овый** *a.* hotbed, hothouse (plants).

парно *adv.* humid(ly); it is humid.

парно — *prefix* gemini— (paired, double); dipl(o)— (twice, double, twin); zyg(o)— (yoke, pair); pari— (equal).

парнокопытн/ые *pl.* (mam.) Artiodactyla; —**ый** *a.* artiodactyl, even-toed.

парнолистник *m.* (bot.) bean caper (*Zygophyllum*); —**(ов)ые** *pl.* Zygophyllaceae.

парно/палые *see* **парнокопытные;** —**перистый, —перистосложный** *a.* (bot.) paripinnate, abruptly pinnate.

пар-носитель *m.* (distillation) steam.

парно/сть *f.* paired state; (math.) twoness; —**усые** *pl.* (zool.) tracheata; Antennata; —**цветковый** *a.* (bot.) geminiflorous.

парн/ый *a.* twin, pair, sister, geminate; in pairs, in couples; dual; even-numbered; paired (electron); conjugate (leaves); fuming, steam(ing), humid; *suffix* (biol.) —jugate, —jugous, —geminate (paired); —**ая деталь** mate; —**ое взаимодействие** pair interaction.

паро — *prefix* steam; vapor; (agr.) fallow; paro—; —**вание** *n.* steaming; fallowing; —**варий** *m.* (anat.) parovarium, epoophoron; —**вать** *v.* steam; (let lie) fallow; —**вик** *m.* steam boiler; steam engine; —**вичная** *f.* boiler room; —**вичный** *a.* steam; boiler; —**вичок** *m.* boiler, steam generator.

паровка *f.* pairing, mating, copulation.

паро/водоструйный насос steam-operated water ejector; **—водяной** *a.* steam-and-water; steam, water vapor; **—воз** *m.* locomotive, steam engine; **—воздушный** *a.* gas-vapor (mixture); **—возник** *m.* steam engine mechanic; **—возный** *a. of* **паровоз; —возостроительный** *a.* locomotive(-building).

паров/ой *a.* steam(-driven); vapor(ous); (agr.) fallow; (hort.) hot house; **п. котёл** steam generator, boiler; **—ая машина** steam engine; **—ая мельница** power mill; **—ая пробка** vapor lock; **—ое отопление** steam heat; **—ое поле** fallow.

паро/впуск *m.,* **—впускная труба** steam admission pipe; **—выпускной** *a.* exhaust; **—выхлопной** *a.* steam (pipes); **—газ** *m.,* **—газовой** *a.* steam and gas; vapor-gas; **—газовая полость** cavity (in cavitation); **—газогенератор** *m.* steam-gas generator; **—генератор** *m.* steam generator; **—гидравлический** *a.* steam-hydraulic; **—динамо** *n.,* **—динамомашина** *f.* steam dynamo, steam-driven generator.

пародонт *m.* (anat.) parodontium; **—ит** *m.* (med.) parodontitis, periodontitis.

паро/занимающий *a.* (agr.) fallow(-grown); **—запорный** *a.* (steam) cut-off; **—изоляция** *f.* vapor seal; **—к** *dim. of* **пар;** vapor; **—компрессионный** *a.* vapor compression (distillation).

пароконный *a.* two-horse (team); team (harness); team-drawn.

пароксизм *m.* (med.) paroxysm, seizure.

пароль *m.* (comp.) password.

паром *m.* ferry (boat); raft; *instr. of* **пар; подвесной п.** transporter bridge; **п. амфибия** *m.* amphibious ferry.

паро/масляный *a.* oil-diffusion (pump); **—ме(т)р** *m.* steam (flow) meter; vaporimeter.

паром/-ледокол *m.* icebreaking ferry; **—ный** *a. of* **паром.**

паромомицин *m.* Paromomycin (antibiotic).

паром/-самолёт *m.* current-operated ferry; **—щик** *m.* ferryboat operator.

паро/нагреватель *m.* steam heater; **удельное —напряжение котла** rate of evaporation per unit of heating surface; **—непроницаемый** *a.* steamproof, steamtight; vaportight.

паронит *m.* Paronite (rubberized asbestos fabric).

паронихия *f.* (med.) paronychia.

парообработ/ка *f.* (agr.) fallow tillage; **—ник** *m.* weeder.

парообраз/ный *a.* vaporous, in vapor form; volatile; steamlike; **—ование** *n.* steam generation; evaporation, vaporization; **теплота —ования** heat of evaporation.

парообразователь *m.,* **—ный прибор** steam generator; evaporator, vaporizer; **—ный** *a.* steam-generating, steam-producing; evaporative (capacity).

паро/осушитель *m.* steam dryer; **—отвод** *m.* steam discharge pipe, exhaust pipe; **—отделитель** *m.* steam separator or trap.

пароотсек/атель *m.* steam cut-off valve; **—ающий** *a.* steam cut-off.

паро/охладитель *m.* steam attemperator; (mach.) desuperheater; **—очиститель** *m.* steam purifier; (agr.) field cultivator; **—перегрев** *m.* (steam) superheating; **—перегреватель** *m.* superheater; **—пескоструйный аппарат** steam sand blast(er); **—подвод** *m.* steam supply; **—преобразователь** *m.* desuperheater; **—привод** *m.,* **—приводная труба** steam supply line; **—приёмник** *m.* steam receiver; **—провод** *m.,* **—проводная труба** steam pipe, steam line; **—прогрев** *m.* steaming; steam curing (of concrete).

паропроизвод/ительность *f.* (boiler) rating, efficiency;

steam(-generating) capacity; **—ительный** *a.* steam-producing; evaporating; evaporative (capacity); **—ство** *n.* generation of steam.

паропроницаемость *f.* water vapor or steam permeability, steam penetrability.

парораспредел/ение *n.* steam distribution; **—итель** *m.* steam distributor, steam header; (locomotives) steam chest; **—ительный** *a.* steam-distributing, steam-supply (line).

парораспыл/ение *n.* steam atomization; **—итель** *m.* steam atomizer.

паро/ртутный *a.* mercury-jet; **—сборник** *m.* steam collector; dome (of boiler); **—светный** *a.* vapor-discharge; **—сепаратор** *m.* steam separator; steam or vapor dryer; **—силовая установка** steam power plant; **—смеситель** *m.* steam or vapor mixer; **—собиратель** *m.* steam collector; steam header; **—содержание** *n.* steam content; vapor content.

паросский *a.* Parian (marble; porcelain).

паро/стойкий *a.* steam-resistant; vapor-proof; **—струйный** *a.* steam-jet; blast; **—сушение** *n.* steam drying; **—сушитель** *m.* steam dryer; **—съём** *m.* steam production; **—терма** *f.* (geol.) steam jet.

парот/ида *f.,* **—идный** *a.* (anat.) parotid gland; **—(ид)ит** *m.* (med.) parotitis.

паротурб/ина *f.* steam turbine; **—инный** *a.* steam power (plant); **—овоз** *m.* steam turbine locomotive; **—огенератор** *m.* steam turbine generator.

паро/увлажнение *n.* steam humidification; **—уплотнительный** *a.* steam-stuffing (box); **—фазный** *a.* vapor-phase.

пароход *m.,* **—ный** *a.* steamship, steamer; (ocean) liner; **—ик** *dim. of* **пароход; —ная труба** smoke stack; **—ство** *n.* steamship line; steam navigation.

пароэлектр/ический *a.* steam-electric; **—оцентраль** *m.* steam power plant.

Парри архипелаг (geog.) Parry Islands.

парсек *m.* (astr.) parsec, parallax-second.

парсонсит *m.* (min.) parsonsite.

парта *f.* (school) desk; (arch.) part.

партгрупорг *m.* party group organizer.

партено— *prefix* (biol.) partheno— (asexual); **—гамия** *f.* (gen.) parthenogamy; **—генез** *m.* parthenogenesis; **—генетический** *a.* parthenogenetic; **—карпий** *m.* (bot.) parthenocarp; **—карпия** *f.* parthenocarpy; **—миксис** *m.* (gen.) parthenomixis; **—спора** *f.* (bot.) parthenospore; **—т** *m.* (gen.) parthenote.

партер, —ный *a.* (hort.) parterre; (theatre) pit, stalls.

парти/ец *m.* (Communist) Party member; **—занский** *a.* guerrilla (warfare); **—йно—** *prefix* Party; **—йность** *f.* Party membership or spirit; **—йный** *a.* Party, communist.

партикул/а *f.* particle; **—яция** *f.* particulation.

партионный *a.* batch(wise).

партитура *f.* (music) score.

партия *f.* party, group, crew; (com.) parcel, consignment; lot, shipload; set; run, batch; cut (of flax); (music) part; set, game; **п. груза** consignment; **—ми** in lots.

партнёр *m.,* **—ша** *f.* partner, mate.

парторг *m.* Party organizer.

парубни *pl.* longitudinal bars of hotbed sash.

парус *m.* sail, canvas; flag, banner, standard; (bot.) vexillum, wing, vane; (anat.; zool.) velum, veil; (arch.) pendentive; (scythe) cradle; **—а** *pl.* (astr.) vela; **—ина** *f.,* **—инный, —иновый** *a.* canvas, duck, sailcloth; tarpaulin; **—ить** *v.* sail; fill out (with wind); **—ник** *m.* sailboat; (ichth.) sailfish; (ent.) swallowtail; (zool.) Velella; (mal.) veliger; **—ники** *pl.* (ent.) Papilionidae; **—ники, —никовые** *pl.* (ichth.) Istiophoridae; **—ность** *f.* sailing capacity (of seeds); (naut.) sail area; **—ный, —овый** *a.* of **парус**; velate, veiled; **—ая личинка** (mal.) veliger; **—оносный** *a.* vexillary, standard.

парующий *a.* (agr.) fallow (land).

парфорс *m.*, **—ный** *a.* choke collar.

парфюмер *m.* perfumer; **—изация** *f.* imparting odor (to gas); **—ия** *f.* perfumery; **—ный** *a.* perfumery; perfume (manufacture); **—ное искусство** perfumery; **—ные товары** perfumes, perfumery.

парфюмировать *v.* perfume, scent.

парц. *abbr.* (**парциальный**) partial.

парцел/ла *f.* parcel, lot; **—лировать** *v.* parcel (out), allot; **—ьный, —лярный** *a.* parcel(led), lot; small-acreage (farming); **—ляция** *f.* parceling (out), allotment.

парциальный *a.* partial, fractional.

парч/а *f.*, **—евая ткань** (text). brocade; **—евой, —евый** *a.* brocade(d).

парш/а *f.* (med., vet.) favus, mange, scab; (phyt.) scab; **—иветь** *v.* grow mangy; **—ивый** *a.* mangy, scabby.

пары *pl.* of **пар**; *gen.* and *pl.* of **пара**.

парэнтеральный *a.* (anat.) parenteral.

паря *pr. ger.*; **—щий** *pr. act. part.* of **парить.**

пас *m.* (sports, games) pass.

пасека *f.* apiary, beehives.

пас/ение *n.* grazing, pasturing; **—ённый** *a.* pastured; **—ётся** *pr. 3 sing.* of **пастись.**

пасечн/ик *m.* bee keeper; **—ый** *a.* of **пасека.**

пасик *m.* round drive belt.

паск *m.*, **ПАСК** *abbr.* (**параминосалициловая кислота**) p-aminosalicylic acid.

паскаль *m.* pascal (unit of pressure).

Паскаля закон Pascal's law.

паскоит *m.* (min.) pascoite.

паслён *m.* (bot.) nightshade (*Solanum*); **—овые** *pl.* Solanaceae.

паслись *past pl.* of **пастись.**

пасм/а *f.*, **—о** *n.* (text.) lea, length; (phyt.) septoriosis (of flax).

пасмурн/ость *f.* mist, haze; gloominess, gloomy weather; **—ый** *a.* cloudy, dull, overcast; gloomy, dismal.

пасока *f.* (bot.) exuding or bleeding sap.

паспалум *m.* (bot.) Paspalum.

паспарту *n.* passe-partout, mount; master key; (typ.) paste-in.

паспорт *m.* pass(port); record, certificate (of technical and operational data); license; testimonial; name plate, rating (plate); chart; log(book), traveler; (steel) test log, test coupon; (livestock) pedigree; **—изация** *f.* certification, registration, recording (of data); rating, assessment, estimation; classification; conditioning (of machines, etc.); **—ный** *a.* of **паспорт; —ная таблица** nameplate, rating plate.

пасс *m.* pass; **—аж** *m.* passage; (shopping) arcade; transition; **—ажир** *m.*, **—ажирный** *a.* passenger, occupant; **—ажировместимость** *f.* passenger capacity; (number of) seats; **—ажирскотоварный** *a.* passenger and freight; **—ажный** *a.* of **пассаж;** (astr.) transit (instrument).

пассалиды *pl.* (ent.) Passalidae.

пассаметр *m.* outside snap gage.

пассант *m.* (bot.) passant; passer-by.

пассат *m.* tradewind.

пассатижи *pl.* cutting pliers.

пассатный *a.* of **пассат; п. ветер** tradewind.

пассет *m.* bubble cap (in distillation or absorption tower).

пассив *m.* (com.) liabilities; (gram.) passive voice.

пассив/атор *m.* (met.) passivator; (chem.) inhibitor, retarder, anticatalyst; **—ационный** *a.*, **—(из)ация** *f.*, **—ирование** *n.* passivating, etc., *see v.*; inhibition; **—ированный** *a.* passivated, etc., *see v.*; **—ировать** *v.* passivate; deactivate, block; inhibit, retard; (min.) depress; **—ирующий** *a.* passivating, etc., *see v.*

пассивн/о *adv.* passively; **—оплавающий** *a.* floating passively, drifting; (zool.) planktonic; **—оплавающее население** plankton; **—ость** *f.*, **—ое состояние** passiveness, passivity, inertness; **—ый** *a.* passive, inert; parasitic; (com.) adverse (balance); **—ый полёт** (rockets) coasting, free flight.

пассиметр *m.* indicating plug gage.

пассиров/ание *n.*, **—ать** *v.* passage.

пассифлора *f.* (bot.) Passiflora.

паста *f.* (polishing) paste, compound.

паст/бище *n.*, **—бищный** *a.* pasture(land), grassland, range; **ёмкость** *or* **производительность —бища** grazing capacity; **—бищеоборот** rotation grazing; **—бищное угодье** range; **—ва** *f.* flock, herd; pasture (grazing).

пастель *f.*, **—ный** *a.* pastel crayon.

пастер/елла *f.* (bact.) Pasteurella; **—еллёз** *m.* (med.) pasteurellosis; **—еллоз птиц** fowl cholera; **—изатор** *m.* pasteurizer; **—изация** *f.*, **—(ир)ование** *n.* pasteurization; **—из(ир)ованный** *a.* pasteurized; **—из(ир)овать** *v.* pasteurize.

пастернак *m.* (bot.) parsnip (*Pastinaca*).

пастеровский *a.* Pasteur.

пасти *v.* tend, herd, shepherd; pasture; *gen., etc.*, of **пасть.**

пастила *f.* fruit candy; lozenge, pastille.

пастилаж *m.* (cer.) ornamentation in relief.

пастиров/ание *n.* pasting; **—анный** *a.* pasted; **—ать** *v.* paste.

пастись *v.* graze, pasture.

пасто/зность *f.* pastiness; **—зный, —образный** *a.* pasty, dough-like; **—образная смесь** slurry; **—смеситель** *m.* paste mill.

пасту/х *m.*, **—шеский, —ший** *a.* herdsman, cowherd, swineherd, shepherd; (electric) fence; (orn.) *see* **пастушок; —шество** *n.* herding; **—шки, —шковые** *pl.* (orn.) rails (*Rallidae*); **—шок** *m.* (orn.) rail (*Rallus*); (ichth.) man-of-war fish (*Nomeus gronovii*).

пастушья сумка, п. трава (bot.) shepherd's purse (*Capsella bursa pastoris*).

пасть *see* **падать;** *f.* mouth, orifice; trap, snare; **волчья п.** (med.) cleft palate.

пастьба *f.* pasturage, grazing.

пасын/кование *n.* (agr.) sucker removal; **—ковать** *v.* remove suckers *or* side shoots; **—ок** *m.* sucker, side shoot; stub (of post support); stepson; outcast.

пасьма *f.* (text.) cut, lea, skein.

пасюк *m.* (mam.) Norway *or* brown rat (*Rattus norvegicus*).

пат *m.* paste; marmalade; (chess) stalemate.

пат. *abbr.* (**патент; патологический; патология**).

патагонский *a.* (geog.) Patagonian.

патана *f.* patana, mountain savanna.

патанатомия *f.* pathologic anatomy.

патат *m.* sweet potato (*Ipomoea batatus*).

пателл/а *f.* (mal.) Patella; **—о—** *prefix* (anat.) patello— (patella).

патент *m.* patent; license; **владелец —а** patentee; **заявлять п.** *v.* (apply for a) patent; **—(ир)ование** *n.* patenting; **—никель** *m.* copper-nickel alloy; **—ный** *a.* patent(ed); **—ование** *n.* (wire industry) patenting; **—ованный** *a.* patented; patent (blue, yellow); **—овать**

v. patent; **—овед** *m.* patent practitioner; **—обладатель** *m.* patent holder; **—оспособный** *a.* patentable.

патер/гия *f.* (med.) pathergy; **—ния** *f.* paternia, gray alluvial soil; **—ностер** *m.* paternoster (elevator).

патефон *m.,* **—ный** *a.* phonograph.

патин/а *f.* patina (metal oxide film); **—ирование** *n.,* **—ировка** *f.* patination; **—ировать** *v.* patinate.

патинсонировать *v.* (met.) pattinsonize.

патиссон *m.* (bot.) summer squash, pumpkin (*Cucurbita pepo*).

патла *f.* long tangle (of hair); **—(с)тый** *a.* shaggy.

патматериал *m.* pathological material.

пато— *prefix* patho—, pathological; **—анатомия** *f.* pathologic anatomy.

патоген *m.* (med.) pathogen; **—ез** *m.* pathogenesis; **—етический** *a.* pathogen(et)ic; **—ность** *f.* pathogenicity; **—ный** *a.* pathogenic, disease-producing.

паток/а *f.* molasses; syrup; **сахарная п.** syrup; **чёрная п.** molasses; **—ообразование** *n.,* **—ообразующий** *a.* molasses-forming; **—оователь** *m.* molasses-forming substance.

патолог *m.* pathologist; **—ический** *a.* pathologic; **—ия** *f.* pathology.

патомский *a.* (geog.) Patom.

пато/физиология *f.* (med.) pathophysiology; **—химия** *f.* pathochemistry.

паточный *a.* syrupy; molasses; **п. песок** brown sugar.

патринит *m.* (min.) patrinite, aikinite.

патриния *f.* (bot.) Patrinia.

патриотичный *a.* patriotic.

патрица *f.* (typ.) patrix.

патро— *prefix* patro— (father); **—клиния, —клинность** *f.* (gen.) patrocliny; **—клинный** *a.* patroclinous; **—морфный** *a.* patromorphic.

патрон *m.* chuck (of drill, lathe), hold(er), holding device; jig; cartridge, case, shell; extractor thimble; (elec.) receptacle; (lamp) socket; pattern, stencil; patron; **зажимной п.** chuck; **плавкий п.** (elec.) cartridge fuse; **полный п.** (molding) core barrel.

патрон/аж *m.* public health service; medical attendance; home nursing; patronage; **—ажный** *a. of* **патронаж;** visiting (nurse); **—ат** *m.* foster care (of children).

патрон-боевик *m.* (expl.) primer.

патронит *m.* (min.) patronite.

патронник *m.* cartridge chamber.

патронн/ый *a. of* **патрон;** sleeve (coupling); socket (wrench); chucking (lathe); ammunition (factory, etc.); **п. захват** socket tool; **п. предохранитель** (elec.) cartridge fuse; **—ая гильза** cartridge case; **—ая лента** cartridge belt.

патрон/осушитель *m.* dehydrator plug; -**пальник** *m.* igniter; **—таш** *m.* cartridge belt; **—чик** *dim. of* **патрон.**

патрубок *m.* nipple, nozzle, outlet; socket, sleeve, connection, connecting piece, connecting pipe; branch pipe; (thermometer) boss; **впускной п., всасывающий п.** inlet (pipe); **выпускной п., нагнетательный п.** outlet, discharge (pipe).

патруль *m.,* **—ный** *a.* patrol.

паттерн *m.* pattern.

Паттинсона белила Pattinson's white (pigment); **П. процесс** (met.) Pattinson process.

паттинсониров/ание *n.* (met.) pattinsonization; **—ать** *v.* pattinsonize.

патулектор *m.* (ecol.) patulector.

патулин *m.* patulin (antibiotic).

патэковые *pl.* (ichth.) Pataecidae.

паужняк *m.* southwest wind.

пауз/а *f.* pause, break, interval, spacing (interval), intermission, rest; delay; blank; **длительность —ы** resting time.

пауз/ить *v.* load onto a flat-bottomed river boat; **—ка** *f.* loading.

паузный *a. of* **пауза.**

паузок *m.* flat-bottomed river boat.

паук *m.* (zool., mech.) spider; basket; compressed-air distributor; distillation "pig" (fraction distributor); **—и** *pl.* (zool.) spiders, arachnids; **морские —и** Pantopoda; **—и-бокоходы, —и-крабы** *pl.* crab spiders (*Thomisidae*); **—и-волки** *pl.* tarantulas (*Lycosidae*); **—и-птицееды** *pl.* Mygalomorphae; **—и-сенокосцы** *pl.* Pholcidae; **—и-скакуны** *pl.* Salticidae; **—и-тенётники** *pl.* Theridiidae; **п.-каракурт** *m.* black widow (*Latrodectus*); **—ообразные** *pl.* arachnids; **—овидный, —ообразный** *a.* arachnoid, spider-like, cobweb-like; (cyt.) spider (cell); **—ообразная опора** (mech.) spider.

Паули принцип (phys.) Pauli (exclusion) principle; **П. реакция** (chem.) diazoreaction.

паул/(л)иния *f.* (bot.) Paullinia; **—овня** *f.* Paulownia.

паундаль *m.* poundal (unit of force).

пауроподовые *pl.* (zool.) Pauropoda.

пауссиды *pl.* (ent.) Paussidae.

паут *m.* (ent.) gadfly.

паутин/а *f.* (cob)web; (anat.) tela; **—исто—** *prefix* araneose; **—истый** *a.* araneose, cobwebby; **—ка** *f.* thread of web; **—ный** *a.* spiderweb, arachnoid, cobweb-like; silk (gland); **—ная оболочка** (anat.) arachnoid (membrane); **—оносный** *a.* arachniferous.

паутка *f.* (ent.) horse tick (*Hippobosca equina*).

пауцин *m.* (chem.) paucine.

пауч/ий *a. of* **паук; птичьи —ки** (zool.) red mites (*Dermanyssidae*); **—ник** *m.* (bot.) Cleome; **—ок** *dim. of* **паук.**

паушальный *a.* total, lump (sum).

пауэлловский *a.* Powell.

пах *m.* (anat.) groin, inguen.

пах/ание *n.* plowing; **—ан(н)ый** *a.* plowed; **—арь** *m.* plowman; **—ать** *v.* plow.

пахи— *prefix* pachy— (thick); **—дермический** *a.* pachydermatous, thick-skinned; **—дермия** *f.* (med.) pachyderma; **—дискус** *m.* (pal.) Pachydiscys; **—карпин** *m.* (bioch.) pachycarpine; **—каулический, —каульный** *a.* (bot.) pachycaul(us); **—мененгит** *m.* (med.) pachymeningitis; **—нема** *f.* (gen.) pachynema; **—ноз** *m.* (bot.) pachynosis; **—тена** *f.* (gen.) pachytene.

пахнолит *m.* (min.) pachnolite.

пахн/уть *v.* smell, reek (of); puff, gust; **—ущий** *a.* smelling, redolent.

пахов/о— *prefix* (anat.) inguino—; **—о-половой** *a.* genitoinguinal; **—ой, —ый** *a.* inguinal, groin.

пахот/а *f.* tillage, plowing; arable land; **под —ой** *a.* arable; **—нопригодный, —(н)оспособный** *a.* arable, tillable; **—ный** *a.* arable, tillable; top (soil); plow and tractor (unit); **—ные земли** plowed field.

пахт/а *f.* buttermilk; **—алка** *f.* churn; **—анье** *n.* churning; buttermilk; **—ать** *v.* churn; **—оотделитель** *m.* churning machine.

пахуч/еколосник *m.* (bot.) Anthoxanthum; **—есть** *f.* fragrance, scent, odoriferousness; **—ий** *a.* fragrant, sweet-scented, odor(ifer)ous, aromatic, redolent; **—ий колосок** Anthoxanthum; **—ее вещество** perfume; **—ка** *f.* (bot.) woodruff (*Asperula odorata*); Calamintha; Clinopodium; savory (*Satureia*).

пациент *m.,* **—ка** *f.* (med.) patient.

пацифист *m.*, **—ка** *f.*, **—ский** *a.* pacifist.

пач/ек *gen. pl.*; **—ечный** *a. of* **пачка.**

пачиниевы тельца (anat.) Pacinian corpuscles.

пачка *f.* pack(et), parcel, bundle; batch, block; (met.) fagot, pile, stack; (stratigraphy) member; (pulse) burst; band, bench (of coal).

пачк/ание *n.* soiling, contamination; **—ать** *v.* soil, contaminate, dirty.

пачковязальный *a.* bundle-tying.

Пачука чан (min.) Pachuca tank.

пачул/ен *m.* (chem.) patchoulene; **—и** *pl.*, **—(и)евый** *a.* (bot.) patchouli (*Pogostemon patchouli*); **—ин** *m.* patchoulin.

Пашена ряд (spectroscopy) Paschen series.

паш/енный *a.* plowed; **—ет** *pr. 3 sing. of* **пахать; —ня** *f.* plowed field.

паштет *m.*, **—ный** *a.* (food) pâté; paste.

пашущий *a.* plowing.

паюсный *a.* pressed (caviar).

пая *gen. of* **пай.**

паяльник *m.* soldering iron.

паяльн/ый *a.* soldering; **п. свинец** lead solder; **—ая вода** soldering fluid; **—ая горелка, —ая лампа, —ая трубка** blowpipe; (blow) torch.

пая/льщик *m.* solderer; **—ние** *n.* soldering; **—ние мягким припоем** soldering; **—ние твёрдым припоем** brazing; **—(н)ный** *a.* soldered; **—ть** *v.* solder; braze.

ПБВ *abbr.* (**полимер-битумный вяжущий**) polymer-bitumen binder.

ПБГ *abbr.* (**порфобилиноген**) porphobilinogen, PBG.

ПБК *abbr.* (**передвижная барокамера**) mobile pressure chamber.

ПБМА *abbr.* (**полибутилметакрилат**) polybutyl methacrylate.

ПБС *abbr.* (**пожаровзрывобезопасный состав**) insensitive high explosive, IHE.

ПБФМА *abbr.* (**полибутилметилфенилметакрилат**) polybutylmethylphenyl methacrylate.

ПВД *abbr.* (**подогреватель высокого давления**) high-pressure heater; (**приёмник воздушных давлений**) pressure head, Pitot-static tube; *see also* **ПВРД.**

ПВК *abbr.* (**пировиноградная кислота**) pyruvic acid.

ПВЛ *abbr.* (**повальное воспаление лёгких**) epidemic pneumonia.

ПВМ *abbr.* (**перфорационная вычислительная машина**) punched-card computer; (**персональная вычислительная машина**) personal computer, PC; (**прессовыдувная машина**) press-and-blow machine.

ПВО *abbr.* (**противовоздушная оборона**) air defense; **п-во** (**производство**) production, manufacture.

ПВП *abbr.* (**правила визуального полёта**) visual flight rules, VFR.

ПВРД *abbr.* (**прямоточный воздушнореактивный двигатель**) ramjet engine.

ПВС *abbr.* (**поливиниловый спирт**) polyvinyl alcohol, PVA.

пвт *abbr.* (**пиковатт**) picowatt.

ПВФЗ *abbr.* (**планетарная высотная фронтальная зона**) planetary high-altitude frontal zone.

ПВХ *abbr.* (**поливинил хлорид**) polyvinyl chloride; **ПВХО** (**противовоздушная и противохимическая оборона**) air and chemical defense.

пг *abbr.* (**пикограмм**) picogram.

ПГКС *abbr.* (**полуавтоматическая газокаротажная станция**) semi-automatic mud-logging unit.

пдд, ПДД *abbr.* (**предельно допустимая доза**) maximum permissible dose, MPD; tolerance level.

пдк, ПДК *abbr.* (**предельно допустимая концентрация**) maximum permissible concentration, MPC.

ПДМ *abbr.* (**прибор дегазации местности**) ground decontamination device.

ПДУ *abbr.* (**пневматическое дистанционное управление**) pneumatic remote control system; (**предельно допустимый уровень**) maximum permissible level.

пеан *m.* (med.) Pean's forceps.

пебрина *f.* pébrine (silkworm disease).

пев/ец *m.*, **—ица** *f.* singer; **—ун** *m.* (orn.) warbler; **—учий** *a.* melodious; **—чие** *pl.* songbirds (*Oscines*); **—чий** *a.* (orn.) osc(in)ine, singing; song (birds).

пеганин *m.* (bioch.) peganine, vasicine.

пеганит *m.* (min.) peganite, variscite.

пеганка *f.* (orn.) shield-duck (*Tadorna t.*).

пегас *m.* (astr.) Pegasus; (ichth.) sea moth (*Pegasus*); **—овые** *pl.* Pegasidae.

пегель/мессер *m.*, **—ная установка** transmission level meter.

пегий *a.* dappled, spotted, mottled; piebald, pied (horse); brindle(d) (cattle).

пегмат/изация *f.* (geol.) pegmatization; **—ит** *m.* (petr.) pegmatite, giant granite; **—итовый** *a.* pegmatitic; **—оидный** *a.* pegmatoid.

пегость *f.* dappled coloring, piebaldness.

пед— *prefix* ped(i)— (child; foot).

педагог *m.* pedagogue, teacher; **—ика** *f.* pedagogy, education; **—ический** *a.* pedagogical, education(al), teaching (methods); **—ичный** *a.* educationally correct.

педал/ь *f.*, **—ьный** *a.* pedal, foot lever, treadle; **от —и, с —ьным приводом** pedal-driven; **работать —ью** *v.* pedal; **с управлением от —и** pedal-operated; **тормоз с —ью** foot brake; **—ьное коромысло** foot lever, pedal.

педантичный *a.* pedantic, punctilious.

педвуз *m.*, **—овский** *a.* school of secondary education.

педерастия *f.* (med.) pederasty.

Педжета болезнь (med.) Paget's disease.

педи— *see* **пед—.**

педиальный *a.* (cryst.) pedial.

педиатр *m.* (med.) pediatrician; **—ический** *a.* pediatric; **—ия** *f.* pediatrics.

педигри *n.* (gen.) pedigree.

педикул/ёз *m.* pediculosis, infestation with lice; **—ицид** *m.* pediculicide; **—иды** *pl.* (zool.) Pediculidae.

педикюр *m.* (med.) pedicure, chiropody; **—ша** *f.* pedicurist.

педил/антус, —янтус *m.* (bot.) Pedilanthus.

пединститут *m.* teachers' college.

педи/он *m.* (cryst.) pedion; **—палец** *m.*, **—пальпа** *f.* (zool.) pedipalp; **—пальпы** *pl.* whip scorpions (*Pedipalpi*); **—плен** *m.* (geol.) pediplain; pediplane; **—цел** *m.* (biol.) pedicel, stem; **—целлярия** *f.* (zool.) pedicellaria.

педо— *prefix* ped(o)— (foot; child); **—гамия** *f.* (gen.) p(a)edogamy; **—генез** *m.* pedogenesis; (geol.) soil formation; **—климакс** *m.* pedoclimax, soil climax.

педолог *m.* pedologist, soil specialist; **—ический** *a.* pedological; **—ия** *f.* pedology, soil science; pedology, child study.

педо/метр *m.* pedometer, step counter; **—морфоз** *m.* (evolution) paedomorphosis; **—филический** *a.* pedophilic, child-loving.

пед/практика *f.* student teaching; **—училище** *n.* school of primary education; **—фак** *m.* education department.

пежина *f.* different colored spot on fur.

пезиза *f.* (bot.) Peziza.

пей *imp. of* **пить.**
пейеровы бляшки (anat.) Peyer's patches.
пейзаж *m.*, **—ный** *a.* landscape.
пейцеданин *m.* (bioch.) peucedanin.
пек *m.* pitch (distillation residue); peck (measure).
пёк *past m. sing. of* **печь.**
пекан *m.* (bot.) pecan (*Carya pecan*); (mam.) fisher (*Martes pennanti*).
пекари *m.* (mam.) peccary (*Tayassu*); *pl.* Tayassuidae.
пекар/ня *a.* baking; **—ня** *f.* bakery; **—ь** *m.* baker.
пекинский *a.* (geog.) Peking.
пек-кокс *m.* pitch coke.
пекла *past f. sing. of* **печь.**
Пекле число Peclet number.
пекл/еванный *a.*, **—ёванный** *part.* finely ground, esp. rye flour; **—евать** *v.* grind fine and sift; **—ёвка** *f.* grinding fine; fine rye flour.
пекло *n.* scorching heat; *past n. sing. of* **печь.**
пеко/вый *a.* pitch; **—коксовый** *a.* pitch coke.
пект/аза *f.* (bioch.) pectase; **—ат** *m.* pectate; **—енин** *m.* pectenine; **—ены** *pl.* (mal.) pectens, scallops; **—изация** *f.* pectization, gelatinization; **—изировать** *v.* pectize, gelatinize.
пектин *m.* (bioch.) pectin; **—аза** *f.* pectinase; **—овокислый** *a.* pectic acid; pectate (of); **—овый** *a.* pectin; pectic (acid); **—оза** *f.* pectinose, arabinose; **—офора** *f.* (ent.) Pectinophora.
пектовентральный *a.* (ichth.) pectoral to pelvic fin (distance).
пекто/лиз *m.* (chem.) pectolysis; **—лит** *m.* (min.) pectolite; **—литический** *a.* pectolytic, pectinhydrolyzing.
пекторилоквия *f.* (med.) pectoriloquy.
пекульнейский *a.* (geog.) Pekul'ney.
пекулярный *a.* (astr.) peculiar.
пек/ут *pr. 3 pl. of* **печь;** **—ущий** *a.* baking, roasting; **—ший** *past act. part. of* **печь.**
пел *past m. sing. of* **петь.**
пелаг/иаль *f.* (ocean.) pelagic zone; **—ит** *m.* (min.) pelagite; **—ический** *a.* pelagic, pelagian, deep-sea; **—ия** *f.* (zool.) Pelagia; **—отурии** *pl.* Pelagothurida; **—оциклус** *m.* (ichth.) Pelagocyclus.
пеламид/а *f.* (ichth.) bonito (*Sarda s.*); **—овые, —ы** *pl.* Scombridae.
пеларгон/ат *m.* (chem.) pelargonate; **—идин** *m.* pelargonidin; **—ий** *m.*, **—ия** *f.* (bot.) Pelargonium; **—ин** *m.* pelargonin; **—овокислый** *a.* pelargonic acid; pelargonate (of); **—овоэтиловый эфир** ethyl pelargonate; **—овый** *a.* pelargonic (acid); **—овый альдегид** pelargonaldehyde, nonanal.
Пеле волосы (min.) Pele's hair.
пелеа *f.* (mam.) rhebok (*Pelea capreolus*).
пеледуйский *a.* (geog.) Peledui.
пеледь *see* **пелядь.**
пелейский *a.* peléan (eruption).
пелена *f.* shroud, cover(ing), cloth, sheet; roof edge; (bot.) hymenium; mantle (of snow); **чёрная п.** (av.) blackout; **—ние** *n.* swaddling; (med.) sparganosis; **—ть** *v.* swaddle, wrap.
пеленг *m.* bearing, direction; **—атор** *m.*, **—аторный** *a.* direction finder; **—ация** *f.*, **—(ир)ование** *n.* direction finding; **—(ир)овать** *v.* set, bear, take a course, take bearings; **—овый** *a. of* **пеленг; —уемый радиозонд** radarsonde.
пелёнка *f.* diaper, swaddling cloth.
пелерина *f.* pelerine, cape, cloak.
пелециподы *pl.* (mal.) Pelecypoda.
пели *past pl. of* **петь.**

пелик/ан *m.*, **—аний** *a.* (orn.) pelican (*Pelecanus*); **—ановые, —аны** *pl.* Pelecanidae; **—озавры** *pl.* (pal.) Pelycosauria.
пелингас *see* **пиленгас.**
пелит *m.* (geol.) pelite, mudstone; **—овый** *a.* pelitic; **—оморфный** *a.* pelitomorphic.
пеллагр/а *f.* (med.) pellagra; **—ик** *m.* pellagra patient; **—озный** *a.* pellagrous.
пеллет/айзер *m.* pelletizer; **—иерин** *m.* (chem.) pelletierine; **—иериновый** *a.* pelletierine; pelletieric (acid).
пеллидол *m.* (pharm.) Pellidol.
пеллиевые *pl.* (bot.) Pelliaceae.
пелликул/а *f.* pellicle, membrane, film; **—ярный** *a.* pellicular.
пеллотин *m.* (chem.) pellotine.
пело— *prefix* pelo— (mud); **—идотерапия** *f.* (med.) pelotherapy, mud therapy; **—медузовые** *pl.* (herp.) Pelomedusidae; **—н** *m.* organisms living in dried-up mud; **—рей** *m.* (ent.) Sceliphron.
пелор/ический *a.* (bot.) peloric; **—ус** *m.* (naut.) pelorus, dummy compass.
пелотерапия *see* **пелоидотерапия.**
пелофильный *a.* (biol.) pelophilous.
пелымский *a.* (geog.) Pelym.
пельвеция *f.* (bot.) Pelvetia.
пельви— *prefix* (anat.) pelvi— (pelvis).
пельгеровский *a.* (gen.) Pelger('s).
пель-компас *m.* bearing compass.
пельмен/ный *a.*, **—ь** *m.* meat dumpling.
пельтатный *a.* (bot.) peltate, shield-shaped.
пельтигера *f.* (bot.) Peltigera.
Пельтона турбина Pelton wheel.
пельтуровый ярус (geol.) Peltura stage.
Пельтье явление Peltier effect.
пельтьерин *see* **пеллетиерин.**
пелюшка *f.* maple pea (*Pisum arvense*).
пеля/дь, —тка, —ть *f.* (ichth.) whitefish (*Coregonus peled*).
пембский *a.* (geog.) Pemba.
пемз/а *f.* pumice (stone); **—обетон** *m.* pumice concrete; **—овальный** *a.*, **—ование** *n.*, **—овка** *f.* pumicing, etc., *see v.*; **—овать** *v.* pumice, polish with pumice, buff, rasp; **—овидный, —ообразный** *a.* pumiceous; **—овый** *a.* pumice.
пемфер/иды, —овые *pl.* (ichth.) sweepers (*Pempheridae*).
пемфиг *m.* (ent.) poplar gall aphid (*Pemphigus*); **—ус** *m.* (med.) pemphigus.
пен/а *f.* foam, froth, spume; head (on beer); scum, skimmings, dross; **образование —ы** foaming, frothing; **переходить в —у** *v.* froth.
пенал *m.* box, case, container; tank; (isotope) can.
пендельфедер *m.* (horol.) pendulum spring.
пен(д)жабский *a.* (geol.) Penjabian.
пендин/ка *f.*, **—ская язва** (med.) Penjdeh ulcer, cutaneous Leishmaniasis.
пендус *m.* mshara (mossy swamp forest).
пене— *prefix* pen(e)— (almost).
пенёк *dim. of* **пень;** (barrel) pin; (mushroom) stalk, stipe.
пенелопа *f.* (orn.) Penelopa.
пенение *n.* foaming, frothing.
пенеплен *m.* (geol.) peneplain.
пенесейсмический *a.* (geol.) peneseismic.
пенетр/ант *m.*, **—анта** *f.* penetrant; **—антность** *f.* (gen.) penetrance; **—ация** *f.* penetration; **—ировать** *v.* penetrate; **—ирующий** *a.* penetrating; **—ометр** *m.* penetrometer.

пенжинский *a.* (geog.) Penzhina.

пензенский *a.* (geog.) Penza.

пение *n.* singing; (bees) piping; song; crowing (of cock).

пенис *m.* (anat.) penis.

пенист/ость *f.* foaminess, frothiness; effervescence; **—ый** *a.* foamy, frothy; foam (rubber); effervescent; froth (fermentation); **—ый шпат, —ая земля** (min.) aphrite, foaming earth, foam spar; **—ый камень** foamstone.

пенитенциарный *a.* (law) penitentiary.

пенить *v.* make foam, churn up; **—ся** *v.* foam, froth; effervesce, bubble.

пеницилл *m.* (bot.) Penicillium; **—ин** *m.* penicillin; **—иназа** *f.* penicillinase; **—иноустойчивый** *a.* penicillin-fast (bacteria); **—овый** *a.* penicillic (acid); **—оиновый** *a.* penicilloic (acid).

пенка *f.* foam, froth, scum, skimmings, skin (on hot liquid); (orn.) *see* **пеночка; морская п.** (min.) meerschaum, sepiolite.

пенкатит *m.* (min.) pencatite.

пенко/вый *a.* of **пенка; —снимание** *n.* skimming; **—сниматель** *m.* skimmer.

пенн/атула *f.* (zool.) sea pen (*Pennatula*); **—ин** *m.* (min.) pennin(it)e; **—инский** *a.* (geog.) Pennine; **—ирояловый** *a.* pennyroyal (oil); **—исетум** *m.* (bot.) Pennisetum.

пенницы *pl.* (ent.) spittlebugs (*Cercopidae*).

пенн/ый *a.* foam(y), froth(y); **—ая флотация** froth flotation; **—ое число** lather value (of detergent).

пено— *prefix* foam, cellular; froth; **—аккумулятор** *m.* (fire fighting) foam generator; **—бетон** *m.,* **—бетонный** *a.* foam concrete; **—бетономешалка, —бетоньерка** *f.* froth concrete mixer; **—гаситель** *m.* foam suppressor, froth breaker, antifoam agent; **—гасительный** *a.,* **—гашение** *n.* foam quenching; **—генератор** *m.* foam generator; **—гипс** *m.* gypsum insulation board; **—графит** *m.* cellular graphite; **—заполнитель** *m.* foam filler; **—измеритель** *m.* froth meter; **—керамический** *a.* foam ceramic; **—кокс** *m.* coked foam; **—лёд** *m.* Penolyod (heat-insulation material); **—ловитель** *m.,* **—ловушка** *f.* foam catcher, foam collector; **—магнезит** *m.* magnesite-gypsum insulation board; **—материал** *m.* foam; foamed plastic.

пенообраз/ный *a.* foamy, frothy; **—ование** *n.* foaming, frothing, foam generation; **—ователь** *m.,* **—ующее вещество** foaming agent, frothing agent; foam generator; (flotation) frother; **—ующий** *a.* froth-forming.

пеноотдел/ение *n.* froth separation, skimming; **—итель** *m.* froth separator, skimmer.

пенопласт *m.,* **—ический** *a.* foam plastic; **—масса** *f.* expanded plastic; **—ный, —овый** *a.* of **пенопласт.**

пенополи/винилхлорид *m.* polyvinyl chloride foam; **—стирол** *m.* polystyrene foam; **—уретан** *m.* polyurethane foam; **—эпоксид** *m.* epoxy resin foam.

пено/приёмник *m.* foam-collecting chamber; **—реагент** *m.* foaming agent; **—резина** *f.* foam rubber; **—сборник** *m.* froth trap or collector; **—силикат** *m.* cellular silicate (a porous concrete); **—смеситель** *m.* (fire fighting) foam mixer; **—сниматель** *m.* skimmer; **—стекло** *n.,* **—стекольный** *a.* foam glass; **—стойкость** *f.* froth resistance; **—структура** *f.* foam structure; **—тушение** *n.* foam quenching; foam fire fighting; **—уловитель** *m.* foam trap; **—уретан** *m.* urethane foam.

пеночка *dim. of* **пенка;** (orn.) warbler (*Phylloscopus*).

пенс *m.* (com.) penny; *pl.* pence.

пенсильванский *a.* (geog.) Pennsylvania(n).

пенс/ионер *m.,* **—ионерка** *f.* retiree; pensioner; **—ия** *f.* pension; **выйти на —ию** *v.* retire, be pensioned off; **выход на —ию** retirement.

пентстемон *m.* (bot.) Pentstemon.

пента— *prefix* penta— (five); **—бром—** *prefix* (chem.) pentabrom(o)—; **—бромид** *m.* pentabromide; **—гидрат** *m.* pentahydrate; **—гон** *m.* (geom.) pentagon; **—гональный** *a.* pentagonal; **—грамма** *f.* pentagram; **—грид** *m.* (electron.) pentagrid, heptgrid; **—грид-преобразователь частоты** pentagrid converter.

пентада *f.* pentad, five-day period; pentalogy.

пентадекан *m.* pentadecane; **—овый** *a.* pentadecanoic (acid); **—ол** *m.* pentadecanol, pentadecyl alcohol.

пента/децил *m.* (chem.) pentadecyl; **—диен** *m.* pentadiene; **—диенон** *m.* pentadienone, divinyl ketone; **—дный** *a.* pentad; five-day; **—зол** *m.* (chem.) pentasol; **—йодид** *m.* pentaiodide; **—козан** *m.* pentacosane; **—козановый** *a.* pentacosanic (acid); **—кринусовый** *a.* (zool.) pentacrinoid; **—л** *m.* (chem.) pental, trimethylene; **—мерный** *a.* pentamerous.

пентаметил *m.* (chem.) pentamethyl; **—ен** *m.* pentamethylene, cyclopentane; **—ендиамин** *m.* pentamethylenediamine, cadaverine.

пента/мин *m.* (pharm.) Pentamin, azamethonium bromide; **—мицин** *m.* pentamycin.

пентан *m.* (chem.) pentane; **—диол** *m.* pentanediol; **—ол** *m.* pentanol, amyl alcohol; **—он** *m.* pentanone.

пента/пептид *m.* (chem.) pentapeptide; **—пирамида** *f.* pentagonal pyramid; **—плоид** *m.* (gen.) pentaploid; **—подовые** *pl.* (ichth.) Pentapodidae; **—призма** *f.* (opt.) pentaprism; **—рит** *see* **пентрит; —сульфид** *m.* (chem.) pentasulfide; **—тионовокислый** *a.* pentathionic acid; pentathionate (of); **—тоника** *f.* (acous.) pentatonic scale; **—фенилэтан** *m.* (chem.) pentaphenyl ethane; **—фторид** *m.* pentafluoride; **—хлор—** *prefix* pentachlor(o)—; **—хлорбензол** *m.* pentachlorobenzene; **—хлорид** *m.* pentachloride; **—цер** *m.* (ichth.) boarfish (*Pentaceros*); **—церовые** *pl.* Pentacerotidae; **—циклический** *a.* pentacyclic, five-membered; **—эдр** *m.* (geom.) pentahedron; **—эдрический** *a.* pentahedral; **—эритрит** *m.* (chem.) pentaerythritol; **—этил** *m.* pentaethyl.

пент/диопент *m.* (chem.) pentdyopent; **—ен** *m.* pentene; **—енил** *m.* pentenyl; **—еновый** *a.* penten(o)ic (acid); **—ил** *m.* pentyl, amyl; **—илен** *m.* pentylene, pentadiene; **—ин** *m.* pentyne; **—ит** *m.* pentitol.

пентландит *m.* (min.) pentlandite.

пенто/барбитал *m.* (pharm.) pentobarbital; **—д** *m.* (electron.) pentode; **—дная сетка** suppressor grid; **—дон** *m.* (ent.) Pentodon; **—за** *f.* (chem.) pentose; **—зан** *m.* pentosan; **—зазон** *m.* pentosazon; **—зный** *a.* pentose; **—зурия** *f.* (med.) pentosuria; **—ксил** *m.* pentoxyl, 5-hydroxymethyl-4-methyluracil; **—ксим** *m.* pentoxime; **—л** *m.* pentol; pentaerythritol oleate; **—н** *m.* pentone; **—новый** *a.* pentonic (acid).

пентрит *m.* (expl.) penthrite (PETN), pentaerythritol tetranitrate.

пенфильдит *m.* (min.) penfieldite.

пены *gen., pl., etc., of* **пена.**

пень *m.* stump, stub, trunk (of tree).

пеньк/а *f.* hemp; **п.-сырец** *f.* raw hemp; **—овый** *a.* hemp(en); **—озавод** *m.* hemp-processing mill; **—опрядение** *n.,* **—опрядильный** *a.* hemp-spinning, hemp-processing; **—опрядильня** *f.* hemp-spinning mill; **—отрепальный** *a.,* **—отрепание** *n.,* **—очесальный** *a.* hemp scutching.

пен/я *f.* penalty, fine; **брать —ю** *v.* fine; **—ять** *v.* reproach, blame.

пенящийся *a.* frothing, frothy, foaming, foamy; effervescent, sparkling (wine).

пеон *m.* (bot.) peony (*Paeonia*); **—ин** *m.* peonin, aurine; peonine (alkaloid); **—ол** *m.* peonol.

пепел *m.* ash(es), cinder(s); **—истый** *a.* ashen; **—ить** *v.* turn to ash(es); **—ица** *f.* (phyt.) powdery mildew; **—ище** *n.* site of fire; **—ьник** *m.* (bot.) Cineraria; **—ьница** *f.* ashtray; (ent.) cabbage aphid (*Brevicoryne brassicae*); **—ьно—** *prefix* spod(o)— (ashes); tephr(o)— [ash-gray; (med.) gray matter]; **—ьноплодный** *a.* (bot.) tephrocarpous; **—ьно-серый** *a.* ash-gray, tephreous, cinereous; **—ьный** *a.* ash(en), ash-colored, tephreous, ciner(ac)eous; **—ьный свет** (lunar) earthshine; **—ьная ива** (bot.) gray willow (*Salix cinerea*).

пеперин *m.* (min.) peperino, leucite tuff.

пепермент *m.* peppermint.

пеперомия *f.* (bot.) Peperomia.

пепл/а *gen. of,* **—овый** *a. of* пепел; ash(y), cinereous; **—опад** *m.* ashfall.

пепсин *m.* pepsin (enzyme); **—образующий** *a.* pepsinogenous, pepsin-producing; **—овый** *a.* peptic, pepsin; **—оген** *m.* pepsinogen.

пептид *m.* (bioch.) peptide; **—аза** *f.* peptidase; **—ный** *a.* peptide.

пептиз/атор *m.* (chem.) peptizer, peptizing agent; **—ация** *f.,* **—ирование** *n.* peptization; **—ировать** *v.* peptize; **—(ир)ованный** *a.* peptized.

пептич/еский, —ный *a.* (bioch.) peptic.

пептоли/з *m.* peptolysis, peptone hydrolysis; **—тический** *a.* peptolytic.

пептон *m.* (bioch.) peptone; **—изация** *f.* peptonization; **—изировать** *v.* peptonize; **—изующий** *a.* peptonizing; **—ный, —овый** *a.* peptone, peptonic; **—урия** *f.* (med.) peptonuria.

пёр *past m. sing. of* **переть.**

пер. *abbr.* (**перевод**) translation; (**период**) period, cycle; (**периодический**) periodic; batch.

пер— *prefix* per— (through, all over, completely); (chem.) per—; **—акариды** *pl.* (crust.) Peracarida; **—бензойный** *a.* perbenzoic (acid); **—борат** *m.* perborate; **—бромат** *m.* perbromate; **—бунан** *m.* Perbunan (synthetic rubber).

перв/ак *m.* (bees) prime swarm; **—ач** *m.* top-quality goods; **—ейший** *a.* very first; first-rate; **—енец** *m.* first-born; firstling.

первенств/о *n.* priority, precedence; (sports) championship; **—овать** *v.* take priority (over), take precedence; take first place; **—ующий** *a.* top-priority, most important, first.

первер/зия, —сия *f.* perversion.

первибр/атор *m.* (constr.) pervibrator; **—ация** *f.* pervibration, inside vibration.

первинка *f.* something new.

первитин *m.* (pharm.) Pervitin.

первично *adv.* primarily, initially, first; *prefix see* **прото—**; **—бескрылые** *pl.* (ent.) Apterygota; **—бесхвостые** *pl.* (amph.) Proanura; **—жаберные** *pl.* (mal.) Protobranchia; **—монадные** *pl.* (prot.) Protomonadina; **—покровный** *a.* (bot.) archichlamydeous; **—полостной** *a.* protocoelous; **—почечный** *a.* (embr.) mesophrenic; **—ресничные** *pl.* (prot.) Protociliata; **—ротые** *pl.* (zool.) Protostomia; **—сть** *f.* originality; primariness; **—трахейные** *pl.* (zool.) Protracheata; **—хордовые** *pl.* Hemichord(at)a.

первичн/ый *a.* primary, initial, first, original, fundamental; primordial, primeval, virgin, natural (community); prime (mover); starting (reaction); raw (material);

source (information); parent; virgin (neutron); **п. спирт** primary alcohol.

перво— *prefix* first, primary; proto— (first, original); **—беременная** *a.* (med.) primigravid.

первобытн/ообщинный *a.* (anthropology) primitive communal; **—ость** *f.* primitiveness, primitive state; **—ый** *a.* primitive, primeval, original.

перво/годок *m.* animal or child in its first year; **—гон** *m.* (distillation) first runnings; **—е** *n.* the first; first course; **—животное** *n.* primitive animal; **—зародыш** *m.* primary embryo; **—звери** *pl.* (mam.) Prototheria; **—зданный** *a.* first-existing, earliest; (geol.) protogenic; **—зимье** *n.* beginning of winter; **—источник** *m.* (primary) source, original source, source material, origin, background material; **—классник** *m.* (educ.) first-grader; **—классный** *a.* first-class, first-rate; **ярка —котка** *f.* primiparous ewe lamb; **—курсник** *m.,* **—курсница** *f.* first-year student, freshman; **—майский** *a.* May first, May day.

первоначал/о *n.* beginning; **—ьно** *adv.* originally, initially, at first; **—ьный** *a.* elementary, primary, primitive, primeval, primordial; original, initial; incipient; parent (substance); raw (material); prime (number, factor).

первообраз *m.* prototype, protoplast, original; **—ный** *a.* protoplastic, original; primitive (function); **—ование** *n.* incipience, inception, beginning.

перво/описание *n.* original description; **—опороска** *f.* (vet.) primiparous sow; **—основа** *f.* fundamental principle; **—открыватель** *m.* discoverer, pioneer; **—открывательство** *n.* pioneering.

первоочередн/ой, —ый *a.* first, primary, immediate; (top-)priority; **—ость** *f.* (top) priority; **право —ости** right of way.

перво/печатный *a.* early-printed; first (edition); **—почва** *f.* primary soil; **—причина** *f.* original cause, origin, source; **—птица** *f.* (pal.) Archaeornis; Archaeopteryx; **—разник** *m.* first timer; **—разрядник** *m.* (sports) first-class participant; **—разрядный** *a.* first-rate.

перворо/дный, —ждённый *a.* primogenital; original; **—дство** *n.* primogeniture; **—дящая** *f.* (med.) primipara, primiparous female.

перво/сортность *f.* top quality; **—сортный** *a.* top-grade, high-grade, first-rate, first-class; **—степенный** *a.* paramount, foremost, overriding, chief; prime, first, critical, vital, fundamental.

первотёлка *f.* (vet.) primiparous heifer.

первотельная *a.* primiparous.

перво/ткань *f.* primary tissue; **—укосный** *a.* first-cut (hay); **—цвет** *m.,* **—цветный** *a.* (bot.) primrose (*Primula*); early-blooming plant; **—цветные** *pl.* Primulaceae.

перв/ый *a.* first; chief, main, primary; early; former; raw, starting (material); front (page); maiden (voyage); **—ая помощь** first aid; **—ого порядка** *a.* primary; **—ым делом** first of all; **—ым долгом** primarily; **в п. раз** the first time; **во —ых** in the first place, to begin with.

перга *f.* bee bread.

пергамент *m.,* **—ный** *a.* parchment; **—ирование** *n.* parchmentizing; **—ировать** *v.* parchmentize; **—ный** *a.* pergament(aceous); **—овидный, —ообразный** *a.* parchment-like.

пергамин *m.* pergamyn, artificial paper parchment; tracing paper; glassine paper; asphalt roofing paper.

пергидр/ат *m.* (chem.) perhydrate; **—ид** *m.* perhydride; **—оль** *m.* perhydrol; hydrogen peroxide.

пергола *f.* pergola, arbor.

пергонос *m.* pollen-bearing plant.

пердоминант *m.* (biol.) perdominant species.

пере—*prefix* afresh, again, anew, re—; over, super—; out—; inter—; trans—, across; back and forth.

переадрес/ация, —овка *f.*, **—овывание** *n.* address change; (comp.) address modification; **—ов(ыв)ать** *v.* re-address; change or substitute the address.

пере/алкилирование *n.* (chem.) transalkylation; **—амидирование** *n.* transamidation; **—аминирование** *n.* transamination; **—ассигнов(ыв)ать** *v.* reassign.

перебазиров/ание *n.*, **—ка** *f.* move; **—ать(ся)** *v.* move, shift (base), relocate.

перебалансиров/ать *v.* overbalance; (av.) retrim; **—ка** *f.* overbalance.

перебалтыв/ание *n.* agitation, thorough mixing; **—ать** *v.* agitate, mix thoroughly.

перебе/г *m.*, **—гание** *n.* crossing, etc., *see v.*; (instr.) overtravel; (honing stones) travel, stroke; desertion, defection; **—гать, —жать** *v.* cross, run over; overrun; go over (to), defect, desert; **—жка** *see* **перебег**; **—жчик** *m.*, **—жчица** *f.* defector, deserter.

перебел/и(ва)ть *v.* overbleach; whitewash (again); make a final copy; **—ка** *f.* overbleaching, etc., *see v.*

переберёт *fut. 3 sing. of* **перебрать**.

перебеситься *v.* (vet.) go rabid, go mad.

перебив/ание *n.* interrupting, etc., *see v.*; **—ать** *v.* interrupt, intercept, break in; break up; renail; reupholster; overcome; (mil.) kill; outbid; spoil (appetite); **—аться** *v.* get by; **—ка** *see* **перебивание**; (commun.) break-in operation.

перебинтовать *v.* (med.) dress, (re)bandage.

перебирать *v.* look over or through, sort out; (mach.) overhaul; (typ.) reset; recall, touch (upon); **—ся** *v.* get over, move.

перебить *see* **перебивать**.

переб/ой *m.* intermission, interruption, stop, delay, standstill, stoppage, breakdown, trouble, failure, disturbance; omission; missing (of engine); misfire, misfiring; (service) irregularity; **без —оев** *a.* trouble-free; **давать п.** *v.* fail, stop; miss; **работать с —оями** *v.* miss; **с —оями, —ойный** *a.* intermittent.

переболеть *v.* suffer (an illness).

переболт/анный *a.* agitated, thoroughly mixed; **—ать** *see* **перебалтывать**.

перебор *m.* (mach.) gear(ing), gear train, reduction gearing; excess, surplus; (math.) exhaustive search; (filter) grading, set; **зубчатый п.** gear train, gearing.

переборанивать *v.* harrow again.

перебор/ка *f.* sorting, looking over; overhaul(ing); bulkhead, partition, diaphragm, wall, baffle; (typ.) resetting; **тарелка с —ками** baffle plate; **—ный** *a. of* **перебор**.

переборон/ить, —овать *v.* harrow again.

перебороть *v.* overcome, subdue.

перебор/очный *a. of* **переборка**; **—щик** *m.* sorter; overhauler.

перебражив/ание *n.* (over)fermentation; **—ать** *v.* overferment; ferment completely.

перебраков(ыв)ать *v.* reject; re-evaluate.

перебранный *a.* sorted out, etc., *see* **перебирать**.

перебрасыв/ание *n.* throwing over, etc., *see v.*; transfer; **—ать** *v.* throw or fling over; transfer, shift; reshovel; **—аться** *v.* get (over), jump (over); exchange (words); spread (of fire, etc.).

перебрать *see* **перебирать**.

перебрести *v.* ford (a river).

перебро/дивший, —женный *a.* (over)fermented; **—дить** *v.* (over)ferment.

перебро/с *m.* throw-over, change-over, transfer, carryover; splashing over; surge (of gas); (elec. comm.) flipflop; (geol.) overthrust; **—сать, —сить** *see* **перебрасывать**; **—ска** *see* **перебрасывание**; transport, transfer(ence), conveyance; diversion (of flow); **—ска по воздуху** air lift; **—ска стока** water importation; **—шенный** *a.* thrown over; transferred; overthrust.

пере/будить *v.* rouse; **—буксовка** *f.* (comp.) thrashing; **—буривать** *v.* redrill; overdrill; **—бы(ва)ть** *v.* stay, be, have called (on); **—бьёт** *fut. 3 sing. of* **перебить**.

перевал *m.* passing, crossing; (mountain) pass; dam, bridgewall (of furnace); (min.) cave-in; (agr.) trenching, deep plowing; (math.) saddle point; **—ивание** *n.* transferring, etc., *see v.*; **—и(ва)ть** *v.* transfer, shift, reload, handle; cross, be past, be over, exceed; drag over; turn over; (hort.) repot, replant; **—и(ва)ться** *v.* fall over; **—ка** *f.* transfer, reloading, transshipment; (freight) handling; (roll) changing; **—очный** *a. of* **перевалка**; storage (terminal); **—ьный** *a. of* **перевал**; handling.

перевальцов/анный *a.* (rubber) remilled; dead-milled; **—ывать** *v.* remill; overmill.

перевалять *v.* dump out; (text.) re-full.

перевар *m.* recooking, reboiling; overcooking; broth; **мясной п.** (bact.) infusion medium; **—енный** *a.* overdone, overcooked; digested; **—и(вае)мость** *f.* digestibility; **—и(вае)мый** *a.* digestible; **—ивание** *n.* overcooking, etc., *see v.*; digestion; **—и(ва)ть** *v.* overcook, overboil; recook, reboil; melt (wax, etc.); digest; overcure (varnish); **—ка** *see* **переваривание**.

перевев/ание *n.* (agr.) rewinnowing; shifting (of sand); **—ать** *v.* rewinnow.

переведение *n.* transfer; transformation.

перевез/ённый *a.* conveyed, etc., *see* **перевозить**; **—ти** *see* **перевозить**.

пере/вёрнутый *a.* upset, turned over, upside down, inverted; reverse; (biol.) resupinate; **—вернуть** *see* **перевёртывать**.

переверстать *see* **перевёрстывать**.

перевёрст/ка *f.*, **—ывание** *n.* (typ.) re-imposition; **—ывать** *v.* re-impose.

перевертеть *v.* turn over; strip, damage (thread); rewind; replace (screw).

перевёрт/ка *f.*, **—ывание** *n.* turning over, etc., *see v.*; inversion, resupination; **—ывать** *v.* turn over, upset, invert; reverse; stir, rabble; ted (hay); overwind; **—ываться** *v.* turn over; (naut.) capsize.

перевес *m.* overweight, overbalance; preponderance; advantage; reweighing; **п. в его пользу** the odds are in his favor; **иметь п.** *v.* overbalance; **численный п.** majority, numerical superiority; **—ить** *see* **перевешивать**; **—ка** *f.* reweighing; rehanging.

перевести *see* **переводить**.

перевеш/ать *v.* hang; weigh; **—енный** *a.* reweighed, etc., *see v.*; **—ивание** *n.* reweighing, etc., *see v.*; **—ивать** *v.* reweigh; outweigh, overbalance; overcome; rehang; **—иваться** *v.* lean over; overhang; **—ивающий** *a.* preponderant, top-heavy.

перевеять *see* **перевевать**.

перевив/аемый *a.* interweavable; transplantable; **—ание** *n.*, **—ка** *f.* interweaving, etc., *see v.*; (microbiol.) (re)inoculation; transplantation; **—ать** *v.* interweave, intertwine, intertwist; (re)wind; regraft; (re)inoculate; transplant (tumor); **—ной** *see* **перевитый**.

перевин/тить, —чивать *v.* replace (screw); damage, strip (thread).

перевис/ать, —нуть *v.* overhang.

перевит/ый *a.*, interwoven, etc., *see* **перевивать; —ь** *see* **перевивать.**

перевод *m.* transfer, change-over, switch(-over), shift-(ing); conversion, transformation; reaction; transference; (com.) remittance; (money) order; waste, squandering; translation, interpretation; **п. строки** (typ.) line feed; **бледный п.** (typ.) outlining; **в —е на** in terms of; **коэффициент —а** conversion factor.

переводина *f.* crossbeam, joist.

переводительный *a.* transferring, etc., *see* **переводить;** (comp.) interpretive.

переводить *v.* transfer, change (over), switch over, shift; carry over, convey; convert, recalculate, reduce; translate, interpret; remit (money); use up, squander; exterminate; **—ся** *v.* be transferred, etc.; convert, react; change; die out.

переводка *f.* shifter.

переводник *m.* adapter; substitute.

переводн/ой, —ый *a.* transfer(ing), shift(ing), switch(ing); conversion; translation, translated; reversing; bypass (pipe); striking (pin); carbon (paper); reversing; **п. коэффициент** conversion factor, reduction factor; (chem.) transference number, transport number; **п. механизм** shifter; **п. рельс** switch rail; **—ая картина** decalcomania; **—ая муфта** reducer; **—ая надпись** (com.) indorsement; **—ая таблица, —ая шкала** conversion table.

переводч/еский *a.* translation; **—ик** *m.* translator; interpreter; (art.) fire control lever; **—ик-инженер** *m.* specialist translator; **—ик-неспециалист** *m.* non-specialist translator; **—ик-предохранитель** *m.* safety lock and fire selector; **—ик-совместитель** *m.* part-time translator.

перевод/ящий *a.* transfering, etc., *see* **переводить;** target (language).

перевоз *see* **перевозка;** ferry.

перевозбужд/ение *n.* (elec.) overexcitation; **—ённый** *a.* overexcited.

перевоз/имый *a.* transportable; **п. по воздуху** airborne; **—ить** *v.* convey, carry, cart, haul, move, transfer, transport, ship; **—ка** *f.* conveyance, carting, hauling, haulage, transfer, transport(ation), shipment; **—ки** *pl.* transportation; freightage; traffic; **при —ке** in transit; **—оч)ный** *a.* transporting, conveying; delivery; **—чик** *m.* carrier; ferryman; (mam.) *see* **перевязка;** (orn.) sandpiper (*Actitis* or *Tringa hypoleucos*).

переволакивать *v.* carry, transport.

переволновать *v.* upset, alarm, excite.

перевол/ок *m.*, **—ока** *f.* portage; **—очить, —очь** *v.* make portage, carry.

перевооруж/ать, —ить *v.* re-arm; re-equip; **—ение** *n.* re-arming; re-equipment; **—ённость** *f.* re-armament.

переворачив/ание *see* **перевёртывание;** flipping; (image) inversion; (med.) conversion; **—атель** *m.* turner; (agr.) tedder; **—ать** *see* **перевёртывать.**

перевор/ашивать *v.* turn over, disturb, stir up; change; **—от** *m.* upheaval, overturn; turnover; (geol.) cataclysm; (av.) half-roll; **двойной —от** roll; **—ошить** *see* **переворашивать.**

перевоспит(ыв)ать *v.* re-educate.

перевулканиз/ация *f.* overvulcanization, overcure, reversion; **—ованный** *a.* overvulcanized, overcured; **—овывать** *v.* overvulcanize, overcure.

перевыпас *m.* overgrazing.

перевыполн/ение *n.* overfulfillment, surpassing; **—ить, —ять** *v.* overfulfill, exceed, surpass.

перевяз/ать *v.* bind, tie up, bandage, dress; **—ка** *f.*, **—очный** *a.* binding, dressing, bandage; bond(ing);

ligature; (anat.) vinculum, *pl.* vincula; (mam.) marbled polecat (*Vormela peregusna*); **—очная** *f.* dressing station or room; **—очный материал** dressing; **—очная вата** sterile cotton; **—ывание** *n.* binding; dressing; **—ывать** *see* **перевязать;** tie up again; knit again; **—ь** *f.* binding, band; shoulder belt, crossbelt; (med.) sling; (anat.) fascia.

перевясло *n.* straw binder.

перегазовка *f.* (mach.) throttling, choking.

перегар *m.*, **—ный** *a.* burning (out, through); odor of burning; combustion product; (sod) decomposition.

перегас/ить, —нуть *v.* put out, quench.

перегиб *m.* bend(ing), fold(ing); twist(ing), kink(ing); excessive bend, reverse bend; (curve) knee, discontinuity; inflection; immoderacy, excess, extreme; (naut.) hog(ging); (physiol.) flexion; **п. вперёд** (med.) anteflexion; **п. назад** retroflexion; **точка —а** (math.) inflection point; **—ать** *v.* bend, fold, double (on itself); twist, kink; go to extremes; **—ный** *a. of* **перегиб;** inflectional.

перегла/дить, —живать *v.* iron (again).

перегласовка *f.* (linguistics) mutation.

переглотать *v.* swallow (all or many).

переглушить *v.* deafen; kill, exterminate.

перегля/деть, —дывать *v.* (re-)examine; look over; **—дываться, —нуться** *v.* exchange glances.

перегна/нный *a.* distilled; **—ать** *see* **перегонять.**

перегни/вание *n.* decaying, rotting, decomposition; (anaerobic) digestion; **—ватель** *m.* digester, digestion tank, septic tank; **—(ва)ть** *v.* rot, decay, decompose (completely).

перегной *m.* humus, mulch, compost; **—но—** *prefix* humus; **—ный** *a.* hum(o)us, humic; **п.-сыпец** *m.* aged loose manure.

перегнут/ый *a.* bent, etc., *see* **перегибать; —ь** *see* **перегибать.**

перегов/аривать, —орить *v.* talk over, discuss; **—ор** *m.* conversation; (tel.) call; **—оры** *pl.* negotiations; **вести —оры** *v.* negotiate; **—орный** *a.* intercommunication; negotiatory; (tel.) call; telephone (booth); **—орное устройство** intercom(munication system).

перегодка *f.* (filter) medium.

перегон *see* **перегонка;** distillate; stretch, section, leg (of road); trip; stage, span (between stations); run; (rr.) open line.

перегонк/а *f.* distillation; driving over, transfer; (av.) ferry(ing); retorting (of shale); **п. в вакууме** vacuum distillation; **п. водяным паром** steam distillation; **вторичная п.** rerun; **дробная п.** fractionation; **продукт —и** distillate.

перегон/ный, —очный *a.* distillation, distilling, distilled; (av.) ferry(ing); (text.) warp rebeaming, taping (machine); **п. завод** distillery; **п. куб** still; **—ная колонна** distillation column, fractionating column; **—щик** *m.* distiller; (av.) ferry pilot; **—яемость** *f.* distillability; **—яемый** *a.* distillable; **—ять** *v.* distill, drive over; sublimate; outspeed, outstrip, outrun, (sur)pass; outdistance; drive (cattle); (av.) ferry; (text.) wind, spool.

перегоражив/ание *n.* partitioning, enclosure; **—ать** *v.* partition (off).

перегор/ание *n.* burning (out, through), etc., *see v.*; combustion; decomposition; blowout (of fuse); **—ать, —еть** *v.* burn (out, through); blow out; rot, decay; corrode through; **—елый** *a.* burnt out, etc., *see v.*

перегород/ить *see* **перегораживать; —ка** *f.* partition, bulkhead, barrier, screen, (dividing) wall, diaphragm, membrane; compartment, closure; baffle (plate), deflector; (slag) bridge; (anat.) septum, *pl.* septa; (biol.) (dis)sepiment; septum, filter leaf; **горизонтальная —ка** (anat.) tentorium; **мышечная —ка** myoseptum; **через —ку** barrier (diffusion); **—ковидный** *a.* septiform; **—очка** *dim.* of **перегородка**; (anat.) septulum; *pl.* septula; **—очно-краевой** *a.* septmarginal; **—очный** *a.* of **перегородка**; dividing; (biol.) septal; sept(ul)ate; **—чатожаберные** *pl.* (mal.) Septibranchia; **—чатый** *see* **перегородочный.**

пере/горчить *v.* make too bitter; **—градуировать** *v.* recalibrate; **—граждать** *v.* lock.

перегранич(ива)ть *v.* fix other limits, change the boundaries.

перегребат/ель *m.* (met.) rake, rabble arm; **—ь** *v.* rake over, rabble.

перегрев *m.* excess heat, superheat(ing), overheat(ing); **местный п.** hot spot; **—ание** *m.* superheating, overheating; **—атель** *m.* superheater; **—ать** *v.* superheat, overheat; reheat; **—аться** *v.* overheat, run hot.

перегрест/и, —ь *see* **перегребать.**

перегрет/ый *a.* superheated, overheated; (met.) overrefined; hot (spot); **—ь** *see* **перегревать.**

перегру/жаемость *f.* overload capacity; **—жатель** *m.* (re)loader; **—жающий** *a.* overloading, etc., *see v.*; (min.) cross (conveyer); **—женность** *f.* overload, overwork; **—женный** *or* **—жённый** overloaded, etc., *see v.*; **—ж(ив)ать** *v.* overload, overwork, strain, force; surcharge, overcharge; transship, transfer (cargo or load), reload, handle; **—з** *see* **перегрузка**; **—зить** *see* **перегруживать**; **—зка** *f.* overloading, etc., *see v.*; overload, excess load; surcharge; overwork, strain; transshipment, transfer; (min.) flooding, spillover; (road) congestion, blocking; (av.) load factor, G-force; (comp.) thrashing; **—зка пастбища** overstocking; **—зка по запросу** over-interrogation; **—зка по току** (elec.) current overload; **допустимая —зка** permissible overload, G tolerance; **—зной** *a.* transshipped; **—зочный** *a.* of **перегрузка**; **—зочный костюм** G suit, antiblackout suit.

перегрунтов(ыв)ать *v.* prime again (in painting).

перегруппиров/анный *a.* rearranged; **—ка** *f.* rearrangement, regrouping; recongregation; change, conversion; **—(ыв)ать** *v.* rearrange, regroup, reorder.

перегрыз(а)ть *v.* gnaw (through).

перегуд *m.* (acous.) continuous rumbling.

перегу/стить, —щать *v.* make too thick.

перед *prep. instr.* before, in front of, ahead of; prior to, preliminary to; upstream from; against; to; *m.* front, forepart.

передав/аемый *a.* transmitted, etc., *see v.*; transferable; negotiable; **—ать** *v.* transmit, transfer, pass (on, to); relay, convey, impart, give (over), turn over (duties); deliver, hand; report, communicate; broadcast; refer, remit; **—аться** *v.* be transmitted, etc.; (med.) be catching, be contagious, be caught.

передав/ить, —ливать *v.* crush; force over, convey, transfer (by pressure); (plastics) eject; (typ.) offset.

перед/анный *a.* transmitted, etc., *see* **передавать**; trans(information); **—аточность** *f.* transmissibility.

передаточн/ый *a.* transmitting, transmission, transfer, conveying, carrier; driving; intermediary; distance-velocity (lag); **п. вагон** transfer car; **п. вал** countershaft; **п. механизм** driving gear, drive; **п. путь** delivery line; **п. ремень** driving belt; **п. стержень** transmission lever; **п. червяк** worm conveyor; **—ая волна** transmission wave; **—ое колесо** carrier; **—ое отношение, —ое число** gear ratio; (illum.) transmission ratio; **—ые рычаги** transmission gear.

передатчик *m.* transmitter, transferrer, carrier; (heat) conductor; (elec. comm.) transmitter, transmitting station, sending set, sender; (chain) transfer agent; **п. кислорода** oxygen carrier.

передать *see* **передавать.**

передач/а *f.* transmission, transmittal, transfer(ring); (comp.) (parameter) passing; passage, conveyance, delivering, delivery, sending; (data) communication; gearing, (driving) gear, gear ratio; drive, driving; assignment; mission; signalling; (biochem.) transport; **п. данных** data transfer; **п. энергии** energy transfer; power transmission; **большая п.** high gear ratio; **вести —у** *v.* send, transmit; **винтовая п.** screw gear; **высота единицы —и** height of transfer unit, HTU (of packed column); **колёсная п.** gearing; **коробка передач** gear box, transmission; **коэффициент —и** transmittivity, transmission factor; transfer constant (of network); (electron.) propagation ratio; transfer ratio; gain (factor); (mach.) gear ratio; **малая п.** low gear (ratio); **механизм силовой —и** transmission; **на . . . —е** in . . . gear; **ось —и** drive center line; **первая п.** first gear; **повышенная п.** overdrive; **цепная п.** chain drive.

передающ/ий *a.* transmitting, etc., *see* **передавать**; **п. аппарат** transmitter; **—ее приспособление** carrier; gearing.

передваивать *v.* plow again.

передвиг/ание *see* **передвижение**; **—атель** *m.* mover, shifter; **—ать** *v.* move, shift, transfer; slip, slide; **—аться** *v.* move, travel; **—аться по** traverse; **—ающий** *a.* moving, etc., *see v.*; feed (magnet); push (rod); **—ающий механизм** thrust gear.

передвиж/ение *n.*, **—ка** *f.* travel, progression, moving, movement, locomotion; removal, transfer, transport(ation); shift(ing); (ionic) migration; (bot.) translocation; **средства —ения** means of transportation.

передвижн/ой *a.* traveling, mobile, field, vehicular; skidbase (machine); movable, (trans)portable; sliding, adjustable; shifting, displaceable; **п. ковш** (foundry) ladle car; **п. кран** traveling crane, traveler; **—ая лестница** escalator; **—ая платформа** elevator car; **—ая установка** mobile unit, vehicle.

передвинут/ый *a.* moved, shifted, slid; **—ь** *see* **передвигать.**

передвоить *v.* plow again.

передел *m.* redistribution, reallotment, repartition, redivision; (met.) conversion; **—анный** *a.* altered, etc., *see* **переделывать**; **—ать** *see* **переделывать**; **—ённый** *a.* redistributed, etc., *see* **переделять**; **—ить** *see* **переделять**; **—ка** *f.*, **—очный** *a.*, **—ывание** *n.* alteration, remodeling, remaking; conversion, transformation, changing; **—ывать** *v.* alter, remodel, remake; convert, transform, change; **—ьный** *a.* conversion (cast iron); **—ять** *v.* redistribute, reallot, repartition, redivide.

передемпфировать *v.* overdamp.

передёргивать *v.* pull, tug, jerk (through); cheat, misrepresent.

передерж/анный *a.* held over, etc., *see v.*; **—ивание** *n.*, **—ка** *f.* holding over, etc., *see v.*; re-examination; misrepresentation; (phot.) overexposure; **—(ив)ать** *v.* hold over, keep too long; overdo, overcook; (phot.) overexpose; repeat (exam).

передёрнуть *see* **передёргивать.**

передифференцировать *v.* (cyt.) dedifferentiate.

передковый *a.* of **передок.**

передне— *prefix* pro— (before, in front of); (anat.) antero— (anterior, front); **—азиатский** *a.* (geog.) Near

East, Near Asia(n); —**боковой** *a.* (anat.) anterolateral; —**бороздчатые** *pl.* (herp.) Proteroglypha; —**брюшие** *n.* (zool.) preabdomen; —**верхний** *a.* (anat.) anterosuperior; —**височный** *a.* anterotemporal; —**грудь** *f.* (ent.) prothorax; —**жаберные** *pl.* (mal.) Prosobranchia(ta); —**задний** *a.* (anat.) anteroposterior; —**клиновидная кость** presphenoid; —**коренной** *a.* premolar (teeth); —**крыловидная кость** (anat.) presphenoid; —**лапка** *f.* (zool.) pretarsus; —**латеральный** *a.* (anat.) anterolateral; —**лобная кость** prefrontal (bone); —**моторные** *pl.* (ent.) front-wing powered insects; —**навесной** *a.* (mach.) front-mounted; —**нижний** *a.* (anat.) anteroinferior; —**носовой** *a.* prenasal (bone); —**порошицевые** *pl.* (zool.) Prosopygia; —**расположенный** *a.* (at the) front; nose, fore; —**ротые** *pl.* (zool.) Prosostomata; —**спинка** *f.* (ent.) pronotum; —**ушная (кость)** pro-otic (bone).

передне/шовные, —щёчные *pl.* (pal.) Proparia; —**шовный, —щёчный** *a.* proparian.

передн/ий *a.* front, fore, anterior, forward, leading, leader, head; live (center); preceding (spot); (anat.) pre—, anterior; **п. план** foreground; **п. фронт** leading edge; **п. ход** forward running; —**яя грань** face (of tool); —**яя сторона, —яя часть** front, forepart; —**ее стекло** (automobile) windshield.

перед/ник *m.* apron; (bot.) thorowort pennycress (*Thlaspi perfoliatum*); —**няя** *f.* entrance hall, lobby, vestibule; —**о** *see* **перед**; —**овая** *f.* leading article, editorial; (mil.) front line.

передовер/енный договор subcontract; —**ить, —ять** *v.* subcontract; delegate.

передов/ик *m.* leader; progressive man; *pl.* foremost people; **п. труда** outstanding worker; —**ица** *f.* leading article, editorial; —**ой** *a.* leading, foremost, top-level; progressive, forward, advanced, fore(most); front.

передозиров/ать *v.* overdose. —**ание** *n.*, —**ка** *f.* overdose, overdosage.

передо/ить *v.* milk (all or many); —**йка** *f.* superlactating cow; —**йность** *f.* superlactation, prolongation of the lactation period.

передок *m.* forecarriage (of plow); (art.) limber; vamp (of shoe).

передохнуть *v.* die off; take a breath; take a short rest.

передубить *v.* (leather) overtan.

передув/ать *v.* overblow; —**ка** *f.* overblowing; (met.) afterblow.

передум(ыв)ать *v.* think over.

передутый *a.* overblown.

передушить *v.* strangle, smother, kill.

переды/хать *v.* stop and rest; —**шка** *f.* respite, rest.

переезд/ание *n.* corrosion; overeating; —**ать** *v.* corrode (through); eat up; overeat.

пере/езд *m.*, —**ездной, —ездный** *a.* passage, crossing, transit; journey; transfer; moving; —**езжать** *v.* cross, come over; move; run over; —**езжающий** *a.* crossing, etc., *see v.*; mobile.

переесть *see* **переедать**.

переехать *see* **переезжать**.

пережари(ва)ть *v.* fry roast (all; too much); —**ся** *v.* get overdone; get too hot (from sun).

пережать *v.* pinch; (agr.) reap.

пережгут *fut. 3 pl. of* **пережечь**.

переждать *v.* wait (for).

пере/жёванный *a.* masticated, chewed; —**жевание, —жёвывание** *n.* mastication, chewing; rumination; —**жевать, —жёвывать** *v.* masticate, chew well; ruminate.

пережелтить *v.* make too yellow.

переж/ечь *see* **пережигать**; —**жённый** *a.* burnt, burned, overroasted.

пережив/аемость *f.* survivability; —**аемый** *a.* survivable; —**ание** *n.* survival; experience; sensation, emotion, excitement; —**ать** *v.* survive; experience, undergo, endure, suffer.

пережиг *m.*, —**ание** *n.* burning, combustion; calcination, roasting; excessive consumption (of fuel); —**ать** *v.* burn (through, up); calcine, roast.

пережидать *v.* wait (for).

пережим *m.* narrowing, contraction; constriction, pinch(ing); (forging) fullering; gorge (of rolls); nick, pinch (by rolls); knuckle (of furnace arch); —**ать** *v.* pinch, constrict; squeeze again; —**ка** *f.* (forging) fuller; —**ный баллон** intermediate vessel.

пережировать *v.* (leather) overstuff.

пережит/ое *n.* past experience; —**ок** *m.*, —**очный** *a.* survival; remnant, vestige.

пережог *m.* burning (through), burn-out; overburning; (met.) overheating; hot spot (of furnace shell); overconsumption (of fuel); burnt ground.

пережующий *pr. act. part. of* **пережевать**.

перезаключ/ать, —ить *v.* renew (a contract); —**ение** *n.* renewal; —**ённый** *a.* renewed.

перезагру/жать *v.* (comp.) reboot; —**зка** *f.* reboot(ing); **холодная —зка** cold boot.

перезаливать *v.* (mach.) overprime, choke.

перезапис/(ыв)ать *v.* rewrite, (re)record, transcribe; recirculate (information); —**ывающее устройство** rewriting device, transcriber; —**ь** *f.* rewriting, etc., *see v.*; regeneration.

перезапуск *m.* (comp.) restart(ing).

перезаразить *v.* infect (all; many).

перезаря/д *m.* overcharge; recharge; —**дить** *see* **перезаряжать**; —**дка** *f.* overcharging, etc., *see v.*; overcharge; recharge; (nucl.) charge exchange, charge transfer; —**дный** *a. of* **перезарядка**; charge-exchange (injection); (comp.) capacity-discharge (reading); —**жание** *see* **перезарядка**; —**жать** *v.* overcharge, supercharge; overload; recharge, reload; —**жение** *see* **перезарядка**; —**женный** *or* —**жённый** *a.* overcharged, etc., *see v.*

пере/затачивать *v.* regrind (tools); —**заточка** *f.* regrinding; —**звон** *m.* ringing, chime(s); —**звонить** *v.* call up; call again, call back.

перезимов/авший *a.* hibernated; —**ка** *f.*, —**(ыв)ание** *n.* hibernation, wintering; —**(ыв)ать** *v.* hibernate, winter (over).

перезнакомить *v.* re-acquaint.

перезол *m.*, —**ение** *n.*, —**ка** *f.* (leather) overliming; —**ить** *v.* overlime.

перезолотить *v.* gild (all; many); regild.

перезон *m.* perezone, pipitzahoic acid.

перезре/вание *n.* overripening; —**(ва)ть** *v.* overripen, become overmature; —**вший, —лый** *a.* overripe, too ripe; overmature; hypermature (cataract); —**лость** *f.* overripeness, overmaturity.

пере/зябнуть *v.* get chilled; —**игр(ыв)ать** *v.* (re)play; overdo; —**избыток** *m.* excess; —**известкование** *n.* (agr.) overliming; —**изд(ав)ать** *v.*, —**издание** *n.* reprint; —**именов(ыв)ать** *v.* rename; —**имчивый** *a.* imitative, adaptable; —**иначи(ва)ть** *v.* change, alter; misinterpret.

переизлуч/ать *v.* re-emit; —**ение** *n.* re-emission; release (of energy).

переирин *m.* (bioch.) pereirine.

пере/искать *v.* look or search all over; —**испытать** *v.* experience, suffer; —**исследовать** *v.* reinvestigate.

перейдённый *past pass. part. of* **переходить.**

перейма *f.* (geol.) double tombolo.

переймёт *fut. 3 sing. of* **перенять.**

перейоподы *pl.* (crust.) pereiopods.

перейти *see* **переходить;** (comp.) GOTO (command).

перекал *m.* overheating, overrunning, hot shot (of vacuum tubes); (met.) overtempering; **—ённый** *a.* overheated, burnt; overtempered.

перекалечить *v.* cripple, maim (all; many).

перекалибровка *f.* recalibration.

перекал/ивание, —ка *see* **перекал; —и(ва)ть** *v.* overheat, overrun; (met.) overtemper.

перекалывать *v.* break up, split up; repin; puncture; stab, spear, kill.

перекал/ьный *a. of* **перекал; —ьная печь** (glass) calcar; **—ять** *see* **перекаливать.**

пере/капать *v.* drop in too much; **—капчивать** *v.* oversmoke; (re)smoke; **—капывать** *v.* dig (again; up); drop in too much; **—кармливание** *n.* overfeeding; **—кармливать** *v.* overfeed.

перекат *m.* rolling, moving; rift, bar, shallow, shoal, crossing; thunderclap, peal, roll (of thunder); (met.) rerolled products; **—ать** *v.* (re)roll; move (over); **—и-поле** *n.* (bot.) baby's breath (*Gypsophila paniculata*); **—ить** *see* **перекатывать; —ка** *f.* (re)rolling; **—ный** *a.* rolling; **—чик** *m.* roller; **—ывание** *n.* rolling, etc., *see v.*; **—ывать** *v.* roll, move; reroll; roll over, turn over; leapfrog.

перекач/анный *a.* pumped (over), transferred; **—ать** *see* **перекачивать.**

перекаченный *a.* rolled (over); rerolled.

перекач/ечный *a.*, **—ивание** *n.*, **—ка** *f.* pumping, transfer, delivery; overinflation, overfilling; **—ивать** *v.* pump (over), transfer, deliver; overinflate, overfill; **—ивающий** *a.* pumping, etc., *see v.*; transfer (pump).

перекачнуться *v.* tilt (over).

перекашив/ание *n.* distortion, buckling, warping, twisting, torsion; **—ать** *v.* warp, twist, bend, slant, cant; mow (again); **—аться** *v.* twist, distort, run out of true, get out of alignment.

переквалифи/кация *f.* training for a new occupation; **—цированный** *a.* retrained; overqualified; **—цировать** *v.* train (for a new profession or occupation).

переква/сить, —шивать *v.* let get too sour.

перекид/анный *a.* turned over; thrown over, spanned; **—ать** *see* **перекидывать; —ка** *see* **перекидывание;** (overhead) span; rehandling, transfer; reversal (of valves).

перекидн/ой *a.* reversing, reversible; tipping, dumping; knife (switch); break(-before)-make (contact); short-gap (bridge); (elec. comm.) flip-flop; **п. механизм** tumbler; **п. рычаг** reverse lever; **—ая схема** flip-flop.

переки/дывание *n.* turning over, etc., *see v.*; **—дывать, —нуть** *v.* turn over; throw over, fling over, span; throw too far; tip over; move (earth), reload; reverse (valve); **—нутый** *a.* turned over, etc., *see v.*

перекип/ать, —еть *v.* overboil, overcook; boil over; **—ятить** *v.* boil again.

перекис/ать *v.* turn sour; become too acid; **—ление** *n.* overacidification; peroxidation, overoxidation; **—лён-ный** *a.* overacidified, etc., *see v.*; too acid, too sour; **—лить, —лять** *v.* overacidify; peroxidize, over-oxidize; **—новодородный** *a.* hydrogen peroxide; **—нуть** *see* **перекисать; —ный** *a.* peroxide; per- (salt); **—ь** *f.* peroxide; **—ь водорода** hydrogen peroxide.

переклад *m.* cross bar; (min.) cap, (ceiling) girder; **—ина** *f.* crossbeam, cross bar, tie beam, joist, brace; slat, rung (of ladder); spar; transom; (anat.) trabecula;

—инка *dim. of* **перекладина; —ка** *see* **переклады-вание; —ной** *a.* relay; reversible (telescope); **—ча-тый** *a.* (biol.) cross-barred, trabeculate; **—чик** *m.* re-stacker; handler; **—ывание** *n.* transferring, etc., *see v.*; transposal; rearrangement; **—ывать** *v.* transfer, transpose; restack, rearrange, reset, relay; interlay; over-stack; resurface (road); (typ.) interleave.

переклассификация *f.* reclassification.

переклевать *v.* peck (up, all over).

перекле/ивание *n.* (re)gluing; **—и(ва)ть** *v.* (re)glue; **—йка** *f.* (re)gluing; plywood.

переклеймить *v.* (re)stamp, replace (stamp).

переклепать *v.* (re)rivet.

переклёп/ка *f.*, **—ывание** *n.* (re)riveting; **—ывать** *v.* (re)rivet.

перекли/к *m.* call(ing); **—каться, —кнуться** *v.* call (to one another); have something in common; agree (with); resemble; **—чка** *f.* calling; roll call.

переключ/аемый *a.* reversible; switch-selectable; switched; **—атель** *m.* (change-over) switch, toggle (switch), selector switch, reverser, commutator; (pole) changer; (TV) tuner; **—атель газа** (oil wells) periodic gas feeder; **—атель рода работы** function switch; **—атель управления** control switch; **—ательный** *see* **переключающий; —ать** *v.* switch (over), change over, reverse, commutate; throw switch (over), flip switch, set switch; move; shift (gears, etc.); **—ать на обратное** reverse; **—ающий** *a.* switching, etc., *see v.*; throw-over, change-over, switch-over; **—ающийся** *a.* reversing; shifting; bridging, make-before-break (contact).

переключен/ие *n.* (elec.) switching, etc., *see* **пере-ключать;** change(-over), commutation; shift, move; reversal; transfer; **п. кода** (comp.) escape; **п. скоро-стей** gear shifting; **п. строки** (comp.) line spacing, line feed; **порог —ия** switching threshold; **рычаг —ия** shift lever; **—ный** *a.* switched, etc., *see* **переклю-чать.**

пере/ключить *see* **переключать; —ковать** *see* **пере-ковывать; —коверк(ив)ать** *v.* distort.

переков/ка *f.*, **—ывание** *n.* reforging; (re)shoeing (of horses); **—ывать** *v.* reforge, rework; (re)shoe.

пере/колачивать, —колотить *v.* break up; renail; **—колоть** *see* **перекалывать; —комбинация** *f.* re-combination; **—комкать** *v.* crumple up.

перекомпаундирован/ие *n.* (elec.) overcompounding; **—ный** *a.* overcompounded, heavily compounded.

перекомпенс/ация *f.* overcompensation, overbalancing, overbalance; (semiconductors) overdoping; **—ировать** *v.* overcompensate, overbalance.

пере/компоновка *f.* re-arrangement; **—компрессия** *f.* overpressure, excess pressure; **—конденсировать** *v.* recondense.

переконопа/тить, —чивать *v.* (re)caulk.

переконструиров/ание *n.* redesigning, etc., *see v.*; **—ать** *v.* redesign, remodel, rebuild.

перекоп *m.* cross ditch; **—ать** *v.* dig up; redig; make a ditch across; **—ка** *f.* digging up, etc., *see v.*

перекопский *a.* (geog.) Perekop.

перекоп/тить *see* **перекапчивать; —чённый** *a.* (re)-smoked; oversmoked.

перекорм *m.*, **—ка** *f.* overfeeding; **—ить** *v.* overfeed; **—ленный** *a.* overfed.

перекоробить(ся) *v.* warp, twist (badly).

перекос *m.* warping, etc., *see* **перекашивать;** skewness, warp, cant (of shaft); defect, fault; slant, angularity; bias, misalignment, mismatch; stratification (of temperature); **—ить** *see* **перекашивать.**

перекочевать *see* **перекочёвывать.**

перекочёв/ка *f.*, **—ывание** *n.* (trans)migration; **—ывать** *v.* (trans)migrate; move on.

перекошенн/ость *f.* warped condition, skewness; angularity; misalignment; **—ый** *a.* warped, twisted, skew; distorted; out of alignment.

перекраивать *v.* alter, recut (pattern).

перекра/сить *see* **перекрашивать; —ска** *f.*, **—шивание** *n.* (re)dyeing; (re)painting; **—шивать** *v.* (re)dye; (re)paint; **—шиваться** *v.* change color.

перекреп/ить, —лять *v.* refasten.

перекрест *m.* crossing over; (anat.; gen.) chiasm(a), decussation; *pl.* chiasmata; crux (of heart); intersection; (bot.) cross pollination; **п. петель** (anat.) decussation of lemniscus; **—ие** *n.* cross lines; crosshairs; **—ить** *see* **перекрещивать.**

перекрёст/ник *m.* cross-pollinating plant; **—но-диагональный** *a.* diagonal (sowing); **—ноклеточный** *a.* (bot.) diacytic; **—нонервный** *a.* (geol.) cross-veined; **—нонесовместимость** *f.* (gen.) cross-incompatibility.

перекрестноопыл/ение *n.* (bot.) cross pollination; **—итель** *see* **перекрестник; —яемый** *a.* cross-pollinated; **—яющий** *a.* cross-pollinating; **—яющийся** *a.* self-pollinating.

перекрёстнослоистый *a.* cross-bedded.

перекрёст/ный *a.* cross; cruciate, cross-shaped; crossed; decussate; crossing; **—ное оплодотворение** cross fertilization, allogamy; **—ок** *m.* crossing, crossroads, intersection; crossover; **—омышечные** *pl.* (ent.) Chiastomyaria.

перекрестье *n.* (opt.) crosshairs; cross.

перекрещённый *a.* crossed, etc., *see* **перекрещивать.**

перекрещива/ние *n.* crossing, etc., *see v.*; **—ть** *v.* cross (over), intersect; transpose; rename; **—ться** *v.* cross, intersect; **—ющийся** *a.* crossing, intersecting, crosscross; **гравировать —ющимися линиями** *v.* crosshatch.

перекрив/ить, —лять *v.* twist.

перекристаллиз/ация *f.*, **—ование** *n.* recrystallization; **—ов(ыв)ать** *v.* recrystallize.

перекр/оить *v.* alter, revise; **—ой** *m.*, **—ойка** *f.* alteration; revision.

перекромсать *v.* shred, chop fine.

перекрошить *v.* crumble up.

перекру/тить *see* **перекручивать; —тка** *f.*, **—чение, —чивание** *n.* twist(ing), (dis)tortion; (gen.) torsion; **обратное —чивание** detorsion; **—чивать** *v.* twist (too far); overwind; skew, distort; bind; **—чиваться** *v.* twist; rotate.

перекры/вание *n.* (over)lapping, etc., *see v.*; lap; **—вать** *v.* (over)lap, imbricate, overlie, superimpose; mask, override; spark, arc or flash over; (re)cover, reproof; cap, cope (a wall); span, bridge (over); cross (of belt); duplicate (data); stop, shut off, cut off, shut down; intercept, block (passage); dam (river); outdo, exceed; **—вающий** *a.* (over)lapping, etc., *see v.*; **—вающий ряд** coping; **—вающие породы** (min.) overburden; **—вной** *a.* shut-off (valve); **—тие** *see* **перекрывание;** cover(age); ceiling, roof; floor; span; enclosure; (elec.) sparkover, arcover, flashover; (gear) engagement; **—тие частот . . . до** frequency range; **коэффициент —тия** engagement factor; **—тый** *a.* (over)lapped, etc., *see v.*

перекрыш/а, —ка *f.* overlap(ping), lap, imbrication; ceiling, cover.

перекуп/ать *v.* outbid; bathe (all; too long); **—ить** *v.* outbid; **—ной** *a.* bought for resale; **—щик** *m.* secondhand dealer.

перекур *m.* smoke break; **—и(ва)ть** *v.* take a smoke break; smoke too much, suffer from smoking; **—ка** *f.* smoke break; distillation.

перекус/ать *v.* bite (all; many); **—ить, —ывать** *v.* bite through.

пере/кут(ыв)ать *v.* wrap (too warmly); **—кушать** *v.* overeat; **—куют** *fut. 3 pl. of* **перековать; —лавливать** *v.* catch, trap; **—лагать** *see* **перекладывать; —ладить, —лаживать** *v.* fix, adjust; **—лакиров(ыв)ать** *v.* (re)varnish; **—ламывать** *v.* break apart, break in two; fracture; overcome, master; **—лежать** *v.* lie (too long); spoil in storage; **—лез(а)ть** *v.* crawl or climb (over); **—лепить, —леплять** *v.* repaste; reshape.

перелес/ка *f.* (bot.) Hepatica; **—ок** *m.* grove, small woods; **—ье** *n.* glade.

перелёт *m.* flight, passage; overshoot(ing); (orn.) (trans)migration; **маршрут —а** (orn.) flyway.

перелет/ание *n.* flying (across); **—ать, —еть** *v.* fly (across, over); overshoot (the mark).

перелёт/ный *a.* migratory; adventive, exotic, peregrine; **—ная птица** bird of passage, migrant, transient, visitor; **—ывать** *v.* migrate.

пере/лечи(ва)ть *v.* (med.) treat; treat unsuccessfully; **—лечь** take another position, change one's position, move.

перелив *m.*, **—ание** *n.* pouring over, etc., *see v.*; transfer (of liquid); overflow(ing); spillover; **—ать** *v.* pour over, decant; transfer; overfill; transfuse; (met.) recast; play (of colors); **—аться** *v.* overflow, run over; play, iridesce; (acous.) modulate; **—ающий** *a.* pouring over, etc., *see v.*; flowing (well); iridescent (colors); **—ка** *f.* transfer; recasting; **—ница** *f.* (ent.) Apatura.

переливн/ой *a.* pouring; overflow; (foundry) recast(ing); **п. ствол** overflow lip; **—ая труба** overflow (pipe); **—ое отверстие** overflow, outlet.

переливчат/ость *f.* iridescence; **—ый** *a.* iridescent, chatoyant, opalescent.

пере/линивать, —линять *v.* (zool.) shed, molt; **—линов(ыв)ать** *v.* (re)line; **—лист(ыв)ать** *v.* turn (pages), look through, scan.

перелит/ый *a.* poured over, decanted; (foundry) recast; **—ь** *see* **переливать.**

перелиц/евать, —овывать *v.* turn, reverse; alter; **—ованный** *a.* turned, etc., *see v.*

пере/лов *m.* overtrapping; overfishing; overexploitation; **—ловить** *v.* catch, trap; **—лог** *m.*, **—логовый** *a.* (agr.) fallow (land), lea; waste land.

перелож/ение *n.* transposition; **—енный** *a.* transposed; **—ить** *see* **перекладывать.**

переложный *a.* (agr.) fallow.

перелой *m.* (med.) gonorrhea.

перелом *m.* break, discontinuity; rupture, breakage, breaking (apart); turning point, crisis, (sudden) change, sudden transition; (med.) fracture; **до точки —а** breakpoint; **—ать** *v.* break (up); **—ить** *see* **переламывать; —ный** *a.* transition(al); critical, crucial; **—ный момент** turning point; **—ный сдвиг** (math.) inflection point; **—овывих** *m.* (med.) dislocation fracture.

перелопа/тить, —чивать *v.* shovel (up), spade, dig up, scoop; mix (with shovel), turn; reblade (turbine); **—чивание** *n.* shoveling, etc., *see v.*; **—чиватель** *m.* shoveler; (fermentation) floor plow.

перельёт *fut. 3 sing. of* **переливать.**

перемагни/тить, —чивать *v.* reverse the magnetism; **—чение, —чивание** *n.* magnetic reversal, remagnetization.

перемаз(ыв)ать *v.* smear (up); soil.

перемалыв/ание *n.* (re)grinding, etc., *see v.*; **—атель** *m.* grinder; (number) cruncher; **—ать** *v.* (re)grind, mill, crush, pulverize.

перемани(ва)ть *v.* entice, lure, win over.

перемасли(ва)ть *v.* lubricate (excessively).

перематыв/ание *n.* (text.) rewinding; **—атель** *m.* rewind(er); **—ать** *v.* (re)wind; reel.

перемачив/ание *n.* soaking, etc., *see v.*; **—ать** *v.* soak, wet; oversteep (malt).

перемащивать *v.* (re)pave.

перемеж/аемость *f.* alternation; **—ать** *v.* alternate; intermit; (comp.) interleave; **—аться** *v.* alternate; intermit, occur intermittently; **—ающийся** *a.* alternate, alternating (with); alternating direction (method); intermittent; intermediate; (geol.) interbedded, interstratified; permutation (code); (elec.) alternating; (med.) remittent (fever).

перемеж/евать, —ёвывать *v.* (re)survey, (re)set boundaries.

перемелет *fut. 3 sing. of* **перемолоть.**

перемен/а *f.* change, alteration, mutation, transformation, conversion; exchange; alternation; variation; interval, recess, break; reversal; move, shift; **п. движения, п. направления, п. хода** reversal, reversing; **поддающийся —е** alterable; **рычаг —ы хода** reverse lever; **—ённый** *a.* changed, etc., *see* **переменять; —ить** *see* **переменять; —ка** *f.* recess, break; **—ная** *f.* (astr.; math.) variable.

переменно *adv.* alternately; *prefix* allag(o)—; **п. действующий** *a.* alternating; **п.-возвратный** *a.* reciprocal (motion); **—е** *n.* (math.) variable; **—листный** *a.* (bot.) allagophyllous; **—полярный** *a.* (elec.) heteropolar; **—поточный** *a.* variable-flow.

переме́ниость *f.* variability, changeability, mutability, instability.

переменн/ый *a.* variable, varying, (inter)changeable, alternative; alternate; (elec.) alternating; live (load); intercepting (valve); **генератор —ого тока** alternator; **—ая величина, —ое** *n.* (math.) variable; **—ой массы** *a.* variable-mass; **с —ым ходом** *a.* reversible.

переменчив/ость *see* **переменность; —ый** *a.* variable, changeable, mutable, alterable; inconstant, unstable; shifting.

переменять *v.* change, vary, alter, transform; shift; exchange, interchange; **п. направление** reverse; **—ся** *v.* (ex)change; take turns.

перемер *m.* (re)measuring, measurement.

пере/мерзать, —мёрзнуть *v.* freeze (over, up).

перемер/ивание *n.*, **—ка** *f.* (re)measuring, measurement; **—и(ва)ть, —ять** *v.* (re)measure.

перемесить *see* **перемешивать.**

перемести *v.* sweep (again); drift (of snow).

переместит/ельность *f.* (math.) commutativity; **—ельный** *a.* transposing, transposable; commutative; **—ь** *see* **перемещать.**

пере/мёт *m.* seine, net; cross beam; (snow) drift; **—метать** *v.* sweep again; drift; (re)stack; (re)baste.

пере/метилирование *n.* (chem.) transmethylation; **—метить** *see* **перемечивать.**

пере/мётка *f.* (re)stacking; (text.) (re)basting; **—метнуть** *v.* fling (over); **—мётный** *a. of* **перемёт; —мётная сумка** saddle bag; **—мётывать** *v.* (re)stack; (re)baste.

перемеч(ив)ать *v.* (re)label, mark, tag.

перемеш/анный *a.* mixed, etc., *see v.*; **—ивание** *n.* mixing, etc., *see v.*; randomization; (comp.) hashing; (radial) dispersion; agitation; confusion; **—иватель** *m.* mixer; (rad.) scrambler; **—(ив)ать** *v.* mix, stir, agitate,

rabble; intermingle, intersperse, intermix, blend; scramble; mix up, confuse; **—иваться** *v.* be stirred; get confused.

перемещ/аемость *f.* movability; transportability; **—аемый** *a.* movable, mobile; transportable; **—ать** *v.* transpose, transfer, transport, move, shift, displace; (comp.) scroll; convey, drive; **—ать вперёд** advance; **—аться** *v.* move, slip, slide, migrate, travel; **—ающий** *a.* moving, motive; **—ающийся** *a.* moving, movable, mobile, adjusting, sliding; traversing, shifting, heaving (sand); migratory, traveling.

перемещ/ение *n.* translocation, relocation, displacement; transfer(ence); transposition; shift(ing), moving, movement, motion, travel, migration; adjustment, sliding; (tape) advance; (comp.) scrolling; (math.) permutation; **прямолинейное п.** (mech.) translation.

перемещённый *a.* transposed, etc., *see* **перемещать;** displaced (person).

переминать *v.* knead, work.

перемирие *n.* truce, armistice.

перемнож/ать *v.* multiply; **—ающий** *a.* multiplying; **—ение** *n.* multiplication; **—ить** *v.* multiply.

перемогать *v.* overcome.

перемод/ифицирование *n.* remodification; overmodification; **—уляция** *f.* overmodulation.

перемоет *fut. 3 sing. of* **перемыть.**

перемок/ать, —нуть *v.* get wet, get drenched; soak too long.

перемол *m.* (re)grinding, (re)milling.

перемол/ачивание *n.*, **—от** *m.* (agr.) (re)threshing; **—ачивать, —отить** *v.* (re)thresh.

перемолоть *v.* (re)grind, (re)mill.

перемолоченный *a.* (agr.) (re)threshed.

перемонт/аж *m.*, **—ирование** *n.*, **—ировка** *f.* reassembly; rewiring; remounting; **—ировать** *v.* reassemble; rewire; remount.

перемор/аживать, —озить *v.* (re)freeze.

перемостить *v.* (re)pave.

перемот/анный *a.* (re)wound; **—ать** *v.* (re)wind; **—ка** *f.*, **—(оч)ный** *a.* (re)winding, rewind.

перемоч/енность *v.* (degree of) oversoaking; **—енный** *a.* wet; oversoaked, oversteeped; drenched; **—ить** *v.* wet; oversoak, oversteep; **—ка** *f.* oversoaking, oversteeping.

пере/мочь *v.* overcome; **—моют** *fut. 3 pl. of* **перемыть; —мутить** *v.* cloud, make turbid; **—мучиться** *v.* suffer; **—мы(ва)ть** *v.* (re)wash.

перемы/кание *n.* connecting, etc., *see v.*; **—кать** *v.* connect, bridge (over); (elec.) strap, short; **—чка** *f.* connector, connecting strip, link; crosspiece, tie plate, bridge; (aircraft) bonding wire; (hydr.) cofferdam; dam, dike; straight arch; (door) lintel; (elec.) jumper, strap, bypass; (min.) stopping; (anat.) intersection; **коммутирующая —чка** contact junction.

перемягч/ать, —ить *v.* (leather) overbate.

перемят/ый *a.* crumpled, etc., *see v.*; **—ь** *v.* crumple, deform; (re)knead.

перенала/дить, —живать *v.* readjust; **—дка** *f.* readjustment.

перенапря/гать *v.* overstrain; **—жение** *n.* overstrain, excessive strain; overstress, overtension; (elec.) overvoltage; **волна —жения** surge; **—чь** *v.* overstrain.

перенасел/ение *n.*, **—ённость** *f.* overpopulation, overcrowding, congestion; **—ённый** *a.* overpopulated, congested; **—ить, —ять** *v.* overpopulate.

перенастр/аивать *v.* readjust, retune; change over; **—ойка** *f.* readjustment, retuning; change-over.

перенасы/тить, —щать *v.* supersaturate; oversaturate;

—щение *n.,* **—щенность** *f.* supersaturation; over-saturation; **—щенный** *a.* supersaturated; oversatu-rated.

пере/нашивать *see* **переносить; —нейтрализация** *f.* (leather) overneutralization.

перенес/ение *n.* transfer(ence), transportation, removal; postponement; endurance, bearing; **—ённый** *a.* trans-ferred, etc., *see* **переносить; —ти** *see* **переносить.**

перенимать *v.* imitate, borrow; intercept, catch; take over.

перенормиров/анный *a.* renormalized; **—ка** *f.* renor-malization.

перенос *m.* transfer, transport(ation); transmission; trans-position; conversion, transformation; migration (of ions); (comp.) hyphenation; (comp.; math.) carry; (med.) metastasis; vection; **п. вещества, п. массы** (phys.) mass transfer; **п. копии** (typ.) laying; **п. тепла** heat transfer; **единица —а** transfer unit (of column); **постоянная —ов** migration constant (of ions); **реак-ция —а** (chem.) transfer reaction; **схема —ов** (cryst.) translation pattern; **уравнение —а** transport equation; **фермент —а** (bioch.) transferase; **цепь —а** (comp.) carry circuit; **число —а** transport number, trans-ference number; **чистый п.** (isotopes separation) net transport; **—имость** *f.* (comp.) portability (of pro-gram); **—имый водой** water-borne; **—имый объём** carrying capacity; **—имый по воздуху** airborne.

переноситель *m.* carrier; transferrer, transporter, trans-mitter; **п. галогена** halogenating agent.

перенос/ить *v.* transfer, carry (over), convey, take, trans-mit, transport, relay, shift; (chem.) convert; (math.) transpose; extrapolate; (comp.) port (a program to another machine); put off, postpone; endure, bear, stand, tolerate; undergo (operation); **—иться** *v.* be car-ried, etc.; (chem.) migrate; **—ица** *f.* (anat.) bridge of nose; **—ка** *see* **перенесение;** carrier; portable lamp; **—ность** *f.* portability; **—ный** *a.* transferable, (trans)-portable, moving, (re)movable; applicable; figurative; translational; anastatic (printing); **—ное движение** transport(ation).

переноспор/овые *pl.* (bot.) Perenosporaceae; **—оз** *m.* (phyt.) Perenospora mold.

перенос/чик *m.* carrier, vector, transmitting agent, trans-mitter; transfer agent; (conveyer) shifter; **теория —чиков** (bioch.) carrier theory; **—ье** *see* **переноси-ца; —ящий** *a.* transferring, etc., *see* **переносить.**

пере/ночевать *v.* spend the night; **—ношенный** *a.* trans-ferred, etc., *see* **переносить;** overmature (fetus).

перенумер/ация *f.* (re)numbering; relabeling (of coordi-nates); **—ов(ыв)ать** *v.* (re)number; relabel.

перенюх(ив)ать *v.* smell, sniff over.

перенять *see* **перенимать.**

переоблучение *n.* overirradiation, overexposure (to radi-ation).

переобогащение *n.* rewashing, reconcentration; **п. го-рючей смеси** use of an over-rich air-fuel mixture.

переоборудов/ание *n.* retooling, etc., *see* *v.;* re-equip-ment; conversion; **—ать** *v.* retool, re-equip, engineer; remodel, convert, adapt.

переобуч/ать, —ить *v.* (re)train, (re)educate; **—ение** *n.* (re)training, conversion training.

переоде(ва)ть *v.* change (clothes); disguise.

переокисл/ение *n.* peroxidation; **—ять** *v.* peroxidize, overoxidize.

переокле/еный *a.* (wine) overfined, overclarified; **—йка** *f.* overfining.

переописание *n.* redescription; new description.

переоподы *pl.* (crust.) pereiopods.

переопредел/ение *n.* redefinition; (gen.) change, trans-formation; **—ять** *v.* redefine.

переопыл/ение *n.* (bot.) cross pollination; repollination; **—ивать** *v.* repollinate; (phyt.) dust again.

переорганизов(ыв)ать *v.* reorganize.

переориент/ация *f.,* **—ирование** *n.,* **—ировка** *f.* reor-ientation; overcorrection; flipping (of spins); **—иро-вать** *v.* reorient; overcorrect.

переоса/дить, —ждать *v.* reprecipitate; **—ждение** *n.* reprecipitation.

пере/освидетельствовать *v.* re-examine; **—оснас-тить, —оснащать** *v.* re-equip, fit out anew; **—от-клонение** *n.* overshoot(ing), overswing; **—отливка** *f.* (met.) recasting; **—отложение** *n.* redeposition.

переохла/дитель *m.* subcooler; (mach.) aftercooler; **—дить, —ждать** *v.* supercool, undercool; subcool, overcool; **—ждение** *n.* supercooling, etc., *see* *v.;* surfu-sion; **—ждённый** *a.* supercooled, etc., *see* *v.;* freezing (rain).

переоцен/ённый *a.* overrated, etc., *see* *v.;* **—ивание** *n.,* **—ка** *f.* overrating, overestimation, etc., *see* *v.;* reap-praisal; **—и(ва)ть** *v.* overrate, overestimate; over-emphasize; emphasize strongly; reevaluate, reappraise.

перепад *m.* drop, jump; (pressure) differential, drop, dif-ference; (temperature) drop, gradient; steep declivity, sudden decline, slant; lapse rate; (hydr.) overfall; (blast furnace) skimmer; **п. напряжения** (elec.) change of voltage, pulse; **—ать** *v.* fall (one after another); fall intermittently (of rain); pass, elapse.

перепа/ивание *n.,* **—йка** *f.* (re)soldering; **—ивать** *v.* (re)solder; overwater (stock).

пере/палзывать *v.* creep over; **—палить** *v.* burn, use (fuel); **—палывать** *v.* (re)weed; **—пари(ва)ть** *v.* (over)steam; **—пасть** *see* **перепадать; —пахи-(ва)ть** *v.* (re)plow; cut a furrow across; **—пачкать** *v.* soil, dirty; **—пашка** *f.* (re)plowing, second plowing; **—паять** *v.* (re)solder. **—пекать** *v.* (over)bake.

пере/пел *m.,* **—пелиный** *a.* (orn.) quail (*Coturnix*); **—пелка** *f.* (ichth.) quail wrasse (*Crenilabrus quin-quemaculatus*); **—пёлка** *f.* (orn.) quail hen; **—пелят-ник** *m.* (orn.) sparrow hawk (*Accipiter nisus*).

перепечат/анный *a.* reprinted; retyped; **—ка** *f.,* **—ыва-ние** *n.* reprint(ing); retyping; **—(ыв)ать** *v.* reprint; (re)type, transcribe.

перепечь *v.* (over)bake.

перепивать *see* **перепить.**

перепил *m.* (leather) oversplitting; **—енный** *a.* sawed up; sawed in half; **—ивание** *n.,* **—ка** *f.* sawing up; sawing in half; **—и(ва)ть** *v.* saw up; saw in half.

перепис/ать *see* **переписывать; —ка** *f.* copying, etc., *see* *v.;* correspondence; **—ной** *a.* census; inventorial; **—чик** *m.* copyist; typist; **—ывание** *see* **переписка; —ывать** *v.* copy, rewrite; type, transcribe; list; **—ываться** *v.* correspond; **—ь** *f.* census; inventory, list.

перепит/ка *f.* overfeeding (of boiler); **—ь** *v.* drink exces-sively, outdrink; **—ься** *v.* get drunk.

перепих/ивать, —нуть *v.* push over, move.

переплав *see* **переплавка; —ить** *see* **переплавлять; —ка** *f.,* **—ление** *n.* remelting, etc., *see* *v.;* **—ленный** *a.* remelted, etc., *see* *v.;* **—лять** *v.* remelt; (met.) smelt, refine; float, drift, raft.

перепланиров/ание *n.,* **—ка** *f.,* **—ывание** *n.* replan-ning; **—(ыв)ать** *v.* replan.

перепла/та *f.* surplus payment; **—тить, —чивать** *v.* overpay.

пере/плеск *m.* splashing over; **—плёскивать, —плес-нуть** *v.* splash over.

переплести *see* **переплетать.**

переплёт *m.* (book) binding, cover; (chair) caning; casement, frame; (window) sash; **в материчатом —е** cloth-bound; **мягкий книжный п.** paper back; **твёрдый книжный п.** hard cover.

переплет/ание *n.* interweaving, etc., *see v.;* **—ать** *v.* interweave; bind (a book); cane (chair); **—аться** *v.* interweave, intertwine, interlace, interlock; get entangled; (chem.) crosslink; **—ающийся** *a.* interwoven, interlaced, interlocked; **—ение** *n.* interweaving, etc., *see v.;* interdigitation; (text.) weave; (chem.) crosslinking; **—ённый** *a.* interwoven, etc., *see v.;* entangled; bound (book).

переплёт/ная *f.* bindery; **—ный** *a.* (book)binding; sparlock (bridge); **—ное дело** bookbinding; **—чик** *m.* bookbinder.

переплы(ва)ть *v.* cross, swim across.

переподгот/авливание *n.,* **—овка** *f.* retraining; refresher courses; **—авливать, —овить, —овлять** *v.* retrain; give a refresher course, update.

переподъём *m.* (min.) overwind.

пере/поить *v.* give too much to drink; get drunk; **—поласкивать** *v.* (re)rinse.

переполз/ание *n.* creeping over; climb; (gen.) rearrangement; **—ать, —ти** *v.* creep or crawl over.

переполн/ение *n.* overfilling, overcrowding; (comp.) overflow; **—енный** *a.* overfull, overcrowded, overflowing; **—ить, —ять** *v.* overfill, overcrowd; **—иться, —яться** *v.* get too full, overflow.

пере/полоскать *v.* (re)rinse; **—полоть** *v.* (re)weed; **—полюсовать** *v.* reverse the polarity, change the poles.

перепон/ка *f.,* **—очный** *a.* membrane, film, web(bing), diaphragm; **—очка** *dim. of* **перепонка;** (prot.) membranella; membranula; **—чато** *adv. and prefix* membran(ace)ous; **—чатокрылые** *pl.* (ent.) Hymenoptera; **—чатокрылый** *a.* hymenopterous, membranouswinged; **—чатопалый** *a.* web-footed; **—чатый** *a.* membranous, webbed, velar; **—чатый покров** (anat.) tentorium.

пере/портить *v.* spoil, ruin; **—поручать, —поручить** *v.* turn over (duties); farm out; **—пояс(ыв)ать** *v.* gird(le), encircle, surround.

переправ/а *f.* passage, crossing, ferry(ing); fording; **—ить** *see* **переправлять; —ка** *f.* ferrying, etc., *see v.;* revision; **—лять** *v.* ferry, take across, convey; send, ship; revise, correct; **—ляться** *v.* cross; **—очно-мостовой** *a.* crossing; bridge (train); **—очный** *a. of* **переправка.**

перепре/вание *n.* rotting, etc., *see v.;* **—(ва)ть** *v.* rot, decay, decompose, disintegrate; overcook, get overdone; **—вший, —лый** *a.* rotten, decayed, putrid.

пере/прививка *f.* (hort.) regrafting; transplant(ation); **—приём** *m.* (commun.) retransmission, relay operation; **—приёмник** *m.* transducer; **—пробовать** *v.* taste, try out; **—проверять** *v.* double check; **—программировать** *v.* reprogram; **—прода(ва)ть** *v.* resell; **—проектировать** *v.* redesign; **—производство** *n.* overproduction; **—промысел** *m.* overexploitation, overkill; **—проявление** *n.* (phot.) overdevelopment; **—прудить, —пруживать** *v.* dam; **—пруженный** *a.* dammed; **—прыгивать, —прыгнуть** *v.* jump (over); **—прягать** *v.* reharness, change (horses); **—прясть** *v.* (text.) spin; **—прячь** *see* **перепрягать.**

перепуг *m.* scare, fright; **—анный** *a.* frightened; **—ать** *v.* scare, frighten.

перепуск *m.,* **—ание** *n.* by-passing, etc., *see v.;* crossover; by-pass; gradual transfer; blow-off (of compressor); **—ать** *v.* by-pass; let (go) across; let overflow; transfer slowly; flush through (mold); slacken (rope); render (fat); **—ной** *a.* by-pass; passage; release (valve), relief (cock); overflow (pipe); (art.) regulator (valve); **—ной канал** by-pass, passageway, spillway; **—ное устройство** by-pass.

перепустить *see* **перепускать.**

перепут/анный *a.* (en)tangled, etc., *see v.;* intricate; **—(ыв)ать** *v.* (en)tangle; mix up, confuse; **—ье** *n.* crossroads.

перепущенный *past pass. part. of* **перепускать.**

перераб/атываемый *a.* processable, workable, machinable; **—атывание** *see* **переработка; —атывать** *v.* (re)process, (re)treat, work over; digest; refine (oil); refabricate, remake, redo, redesign; make over, convert (to); recover (fuel); revise (book); (rr.) reclassify (trains); overwork, work overtime; **—атывающий** *a.* (re)processing, etc., *see v.;* **—отанный** *a.* (re)processed, etc., see v.; **—отать** *see* **перерабатывать; —отка** *f.,* **—оточный** *a.* (re)processing, etc., *see v.;* treatment; recovery; conversion; revision; handling (of loads); overtime work.

переразвит/ие *n.,* **—ость** *f.* overdevelopment, gigantism; **—ый** *a.* overdeveloped.

переразряд/ить *v.* (elec.) run down; **—ка** *f.* running down; **—ок** *m.* overload(ing).

перераспредел/ение *n.* redistribution, rearrangement; transposition; (chem.) disproportionation; **—ённый** *a.* redistributed; **—ить, —ять** *v.* redistribute.

перераст/ание *n.* overgrowing, etc., *see v.;* **—ать, —и** *v.* overgrow; develop, grow (into); build up (into); outgrow, outstrip.

перерасход *m.,* **—ование** *n.* overexpenditure, (cost) overrun; overspending; excessive consumption; (com.) overdraft; **—овать** *v.* spend too much; overdraw.

пере/расчёт *m.* recalculation; conversion; **—расширение** *n.* overexpansion; **—рвать** *v.* tear (apart), break; **—регистрировать** *v.* (re)register, (re)record; **—регулирование** *n.* overcontrol; overshooting, overswing; resetting of controls; excessive correction.

перерез *m.* (cross)cut; cutting apart; tub; **на п.** at right angles; **—анный** *a.* cut apart, etc., *see v.;* cutthroat (trout); **—ка** *f.,* **—ывание** *n.* cutting apart, etc., *see v.;* (med.) (dis)section, operation, —tomy (incision); **—ка сухожилия** tenotomy; **—(ыв)ать** *v.* cut apart, cut up; dissect; block, cut off (access); intersect, cross; slaughter, kill.

перереш/ать, —ить *v.* change one's mind, alter one's decision; solve.

пережав/елый *a.* rusted; **—еть** *v.* get rusty, rust apart.

перерисов(ыв)ать *v.* (re)draw, copy.

перерод *m.* (agr.) degenerative crop; **—дить** *see* **перерождать.**

перероет *fut. 3 sing. of* **перерыть.**

перерож/ать *v.* (zool.) bear one after another; **—дать** *v.* regenerate; revive; transform; **—даться** *v.* be regenerated; degenerate; **—денец** *m.* degenerate; **—дение** *n.* regeneration; transformation, conversion, change; degeneration; **—дённый** *a.* degenerative, degenerate(d).

перерос *past m. sing. of* **перерасти; —ток** *m.* overgrown youngster; **—ший** *a.* overgrown.

переруб *see* **перерубание;** cut, gash; beam, joist; **—ание** *n.,* **—ка** *f.* chopping (apart, off, up), etc., *see v.;* **—ать, —ить** *v.* chop (apart, off, up); (forestry) clear cut, overcut, superfell.

перерыв *m.* interruption, break, discontinuity, disturbance; delay; gap, pause, stop, interval, intermission, rest period; **с —ами** intermittent, interrupted.

пере/рывать *v.* tear apart, break; dig up, dig across;

—рывчатый *a.* intermittent, interrupted; **—рытый** *a.* dug up, turned over; **—рыть** *v.* dig up, turn over; dig across.

переса/дить *see* **пересаживать;** **—дка** *f.,* **—дочный** *a.* transplanting, etc., *see v.;* transfer; (med.) transplant(ation), graft(ing); **—жать** *v.* plant (all, many); **—живание** *see* **пересадка;** **—женный** *a.* transplanted, etc., *see v.;* **—живатель** *m.* (trans)planter; **—живать** *v.* transplant, replant, repot, reset; graft; transfer, transship; **—живаться** *v.* be transplanted, etc.; change (trains); exchange seats.

пере/саливать *v.* oversalt; (re)salt; pickle, corn; **—сасывать** *v.* pump over, transfer; suck over; **—сасывающий вал** (paper) pick-up roll; **—сатурированный** *a.* oversaturated; **—сахари(ва)ть** *v.* oversweeten; **—сверлить** *v.* (re)drill, (re)bore; **—свист** *m.,* **—свистнуться, —свистываться** *v.* (orn.) call notes; **—сд(ав)ать** *v.* retake, repeat (exam); sublet.

пересе/в *m.,* **—(и)вание** *n.* (re)seeding, re-sowing, replanting; (bact.) (re)inoculation; (re)shifting; **—вка** *f.* summer and winter sown wheat; **—(и)вать** *v.* (re)seed, (re)sow; (re)sift.

пересек *m.* tub; *past m. sing. of* **пересечь; —ать** *v.* intersect, intercept, cut (across); traverse; interlace; **—аться** *v.* cross, intersect; meet; overlap; **—ающий** *a.* intersecting, etc., *see v.;* transverse (axis); (opt.) crossed (beam); **—ающая линия** (geom.) secant; **—ающийся** *a.* intersecting, crossing; collision (course); concurrent (axes; forces); interlaced (structure).

пересел/енец *m.* migrant; immigrant, incomer; colonist; **—ение** *n.* migration, etc., *see v.;* resettlement; move; **—ить, —ять** *v.* move; resettle, relocate; **—иться, —яться** *v.* migrate, transmigrate; immigrate; move, relocate.

пересесть *v.* change (trains); change seats.

пересеч/ение *n.* intersection, crossing, crossover, traversal; traverse; interlacing; overlap; **—ённый** *a.* intersected, etc., *see* **пересекать;** broken, rugged (terrain); (astr.) barred (spiral); **—ь** *see* **пересекать.**

пересея/нный *a.* sown again; (re)sifted; **—ть** *v.* sow again, (re)sow; (re)sift.

пересили(ва)ть *v.* overpower, override.

пересини(ва)ть *v.* blue (again; too much).

переск/акать *see* **перескакивать;** **—акивание** *see* **перескок;** **—акивание искр** sparking over; **—акивать** *v.* jump over, hop (over); skip, omit; **—акивающий** *a.* jumping over, etc., *see v.*

перескиа *f.* (bot.) Pereskia.

переск/ок *m.* jump(-over), skip; transfer, transition, passage; migration (of atoms); nonlinear buckling, transient buckling; **п. искры** sparkover; **п. частоты** (commun.) (frequency) hopping; **—очить** *see* **перескакивать.**

переславский *a.* (geog.) Pereslav(ic).

переслаив/ание *n.* (geol.) interstratification, interbedding; (chem.) superposition, covering; layers, beds; **взаимное п.** (geol.) interfingering; **—ать** *v.* alternate (layers); (chem.) overlay; **—аться** *v.* interstratify, alternate, intercalate; **—ающийся** *a.* interstratified, interbedded, interbanded, alternating.

пересланный *a.* sent, transmitted.

пересластить *v.* oversweeten.

переслать *see* **пересылать.**

переслащ/енный *a.* oversweetened; **—ивать** *v.* oversweeten.

пересло/ённый *a.* interstratified, interbedded; **—ить** *see* **переслаивать.**

пересматрив/ание *see* **пересмотр; —ать** *v.* inspect, look over, (re)examine, review; reconsider; revise.

пересмен(к)а *f.* shift change.

пересмеш/ка *f.* (orn.) warbler (*Hippolais*); **—ник** *m.* mockingbird (*Mimus polyglottos*); **—ники, —никовые** *pl.* Mimidae.

пересмотр *m.* inspection, (re)examination; review; revision; **—енный** *a.* inspected, etc., *see* **пересматривать;** **—еть** *see* **пересматривать.**

пересн/имать, —ять *v.* rent again; (phot.) copy; rephotograph.

пересовывать *v.* move over, shift.

пересоедин/ить, —ять *v.* (inter)change the connections, reconnect.

пересозда(ва)ть *v.* recreate.

пересол *m.* excess salinity; **—ен(н)ый** *a.* oversalted; **—ить** *see* **пересаливать;** **—ка** *f.* salting; pickling.

пересорт/ирование *n.,* **—ировка** *f.* (re)sorting; **—иров(ыв)ать** *v.* (re)sort; **—ица** *f.* regrading (of goods).

пересосать *see* **пересасывать.**

пересостав/ить, —лять *v.* revise.

пересох/лость *f.* aridity, dried up condition; **—лый, —ший** *a.* dried up, dry, parched; **—нуть** *see* **пересыхать.**

переспать *v.* (over)sleep; sleep over.

переспе/вание *n.* overripening; **—(ва)ть** *v.* overripen, get too ripe, overmature; **—лость** *f.* overripeness, overmaturity; **—лый** *a.* overmature(d), overripe; (met.) overrefined; dry (copper).

переспр/ашивание *see* **переспрос; —ашивать** *v.* question; repeat (a question), ask (again), ask to repeat; **—ос** *m.* questioning; (comp.) request for repetition; **—осить** *v.* see **переспрашивать.**

переспуск полос (typ.) reimposition.

перестав/ать *v.* cease, stop, discontinue, end; **не —ая** incessantly.

перестав/ить *see* **переставлять;** **—ленный** *a.* transposed, etc., *see v.;* **—ляемый** *a.* adjustable; (math.) permutable; **—лять** *v.* transpose, rearrange, (inter)change; reset, readjust, regulate; displace, move, shift; (math.) permute; rotate (tires); **—ной** *a.* adjustable.

перестаив/ание *see* **перестой;** overripening, overmaturity; **—аться** *v.* stand too long; spoil from standing, deteriorate.

перестан/авливать, —овить *see* **переставлять;** **—овка** *f.* transposition, transposing, etc., *see* **переставлять;** rearrangement; (ex)change, interchange; readjustment; (math.) permutation; (byte) swap; **угол —овки** angle of displacement; **—овочнолопастный** *a.* hand-adjustable (turbine); **—овочность** *f.* (math.) permutability; **—овочный** *a.* permutable.

пере/стать *see* **переставать;** **—стилать** *v.* (re)lay, (re)floor; board; (re)make (a bed); **—стир(ыв)ать** *v.* (re)launder, (re)wash; **—стлать** *see* **перестилать.**

пересто/й *m.* deterioration (from standing too long); overripe crop; (silv.) overmatured or declining stand; overripening, overmaturity; **—йный** *a.* overripe, ripe, overmature(d); declining (stand); **—явшийся, —ялый** *a.* overripe, overmature; deteriorated; **—ять** *v.* get overripe; deteriorate in storage.

пере/страгивать *v.* (re)plane; **—страдать** *v.* suffer, undergo; **—страивать** *v.* rebuild, reconstruct; overhaul; reorganize, change over, rearrange; revise; (rad.) (re)tune; **—страховка** *f.* reinsurance; **—страхов(ыв)аться** *v.* get reinsured; play safe.

перестрел/иваться *v.* (mil.) exchange fire; **—ка** *f.* exchange of fire; **—ять** *v.* shoot; use up (ammunition).

пере/стрига *f.* second clip (of sheep); **—стригать, —стричь** *v.* shear (again); cut apart; **—строгать** *v.* (re)plane.

перестро/ение *see* **перестройка;** —**оенный** *a.* rebuilt, etc., *see* **перестраивать;** —**оить** *see* **перестраивать;** —**йка** *f.* rebuilding, reconstruction, etc., *see* **перестраивать;** restructuring; rearrangement, adjustment; (chem.) conversion, change, transformation; (chromosome) aberration; —**йка программы** reprogramming; **структурная** —**йка** structural change.

переструг(ив)ать *v.* plane (again).

пересту/дить, —**живать** *v.* overcool.

перестук *m.* knocking; —**ивать(ся)** *v.* knock; communicate by tapping.

переступать *v.* cross, step over; overstep, exceed; transgress; **едва п.** move slowly.

переступень *m.* (bot.) bryony (*Bryonia*).

переступить *see* **переступать.**

пересты(ва)ть *v.* cool off completely.

пере/суд *m.* retrial; —**сульфитировать** *v.* (chem.) oversulfurize; —**сунуть** *v.* shove, move over; —**сучи-(ва)ть** *v.* spin (again).

пересуш/енный *a.* overdried, etc., *see v.;* —**ивание** *n.,* —**ка** *f.* overdrying, excessive drying; —**и(ва)ть** *v.* overdry, parch; (re)dry.

пересчёт *m.* conversion, translation; recalculation; scaling; counting; **п. на два** scale of two; **в** —**е на** in terms of; on an; **в** —**е на год** on an annual basis; **вести п. на** *v.* (comp.) scale by; **двоичный п.** binary scaling; **коэффициент** —**а** scaling factor; conversion factor; **при** —**е на** on conversion to; **таблица (для)** —**а** conversion table; —**ка** *f.* scaler, scaling circuit; —**ный** *a. of* **пересчёт;** —**ный бинарный** *a.* scale-of-two (circuit); —**ный десятичный** *a.* scale-of-ten; —**ный прибор,** —**ная установка,** —**ное устройст-во** (radiation counting) scaler, scaling unit; counter (of electric pulses); —**ная схема** scaler, scaling circuit; counter system; **кольцевая** —**ная схема** ring scaler; —**чик** *m.* register, director; translator.

пересчит/анный *a.* recounted, etc., *see v.;* —**ать** *see* **пересчитывать;** —**ываемый** *a.* countable; —**ыва-ние** *n.* recounting, etc., *see v.;* —**ывать** *v.* recount, count over; (re)calculate; scale; convert.

пересъёмка *f.* copying; rephotographing.

пересылатель *m.* sender; —**ать** *v.* send, forward; transport, convey; remit (money); (comp.) move; —**ка** *f.* sending, etc., *see v.;* remittance; transfer; —**ьный** *a.* transit.

пересып *m.,* —**ание** *see* **пересыпка;** —**ать** *v.* transfer, pour over; overfill; intersperse; —**ка** *f.* transfer; overfilling, interspersion; charge, fill; (coke) booster; —**ь** *f.* (geol.) bay barrier, sandbar, spit.

пересытить *see* **пересыщать.**

пересых/ание *n.* drying up, etc., *see v.;* desiccation; —**ать** *v.* dry up, dry out, parch; overdry, get too dry; —**ающий** *a.* drying up, etc., *see v.;* intermittent (stream).

пересыщ/ать *v.* supersaturate; surfeit; —**ение** *n.* supersaturation; satiety; —**енный** *a.* supersaturated; surfeited.

пересядет *fut. 3 sing. of* **пересесть.**

переталкив/ать *v.* push over, move over; —**ающий** *a.* reciprocating (feed).

пере/тапливать *v.* heat up; reheat; overheat; use up (fuel); (re)melt; —**таптывать** *v.* trample; —**таски-(ва)ть** *v.* carry; drag across.

перетасов/ка *f.,* —**ывание** *n.* (re)shuffling (of cards), randomization; —**(ыв)ать** *v.* (re)shuffle, mix up, randomize.

перетачив/аемый *a.* regrindable; —**ать** *v.* (re)sharpen, regrind; turn (on lathe); reface (valve).

перетащить *v.* drag across, carry.

перетек/ание *n.* overflow(ing), run-over, spillover; leakage; —**ать** *v.* (over)flow, run over, spill over; leak, bleed (from into).

пере/тереть *see* **перетирать;** —**терпеть** *v.* undergo, endure; —**терять** *v.* lose (one after another); —**те-сать,** —**тёсывать** *v.* cut, hew (again); —**течь** *see* **перетекать.**

перетир *m.,* —**ание** *n.,* —**ка** *f.* wearing (through), etc., *see v.;* pulverization; scarification (of seeds); —**ать** *v.* wear (out or through); grind, mill; rub, wipe; —**аться** *v.* wear through, fray.

перетишь *f.* (meteor.) brief calm.

пере/тле(ва)ть *v.* decay, rot; compost; —**ток** *m.* overflow; (elec.) overcurrent; tapping, draining, redrawing (of wine); transfer; **обратный** —**ток** reflux.

перетолк/ать, —**нуть** *see* **переталкивать.**

пере/толков(ыв)ать *v.* misinterpret; discuss a matter; —**толочь** *v.* (re)grind; —**томить** *v.* oversteam.

перетоп/ить *see* **перетапливать;** —**ка** *f.* (re)melting; —**ки** *pl.* dregs.

перетоптать *v.* trample.

переточ/ить *v.* (re)grind, (re)sharpen, (re)bore; turn (on lathe); tap, drain; —**ка** *f.* (re)grinding, etc., *see v.;* —**ный** *a. of* **переток.**

перетрав *m.* overpickling; —**ить,** —**ливать** *v.* overpickle; poison.

пере/тратить, —**трачивать** *v.* overconsume, use too much; —**тревожить** *v.* alarm, disturb; —**трепать** *v.* (agr.) scutch, beat, swingle; —**трескаться** *v.* crack all over, crackle; —**трёт** *fut. 3 sing. of* **перетереть.**

перетря/сать, —**сти** *v.* shake out; look over; —**хива-тель** *m.* shaker; —**хивать,** —**хнуть** *v.* shake up, toss (hay).

перетуп/ить, —**лять** *v.* blunt, dull.

перетушить *v.* extinguish; slake; stew.

переть *v.* press, push, thrust; —**ся** *v.* push ahead, push on.

перетя/гивание *n.* stretching, etc., *see v.;* —**гивать** *v.* stretch, draw, (re)tighten; overwind (spring); bind, constrict, strangle; pull across, tow; pump over; —**желе-ние** *n.* overweight; —**желённый** *a.* overweight(ed), heavy; —**жка** *see* **перетягивание;** intake; constriction, neck(ing), narrowing; sausage-type instability (in a plasma column); (chromosomal) strangulation; —**ну-тость** *f.* tightness; —**нутый** *a.* stretched, etc., *see v.;* —**нуть** *see* **перетягивать.**

переувлажн/ение *n.* waterlogging, excessive moisture; —**ённый** *a.* water-logged, wet; —**ённые земли** wetlands.

переугл/ероживание *n.* (met.) excessive carburization; recarburization; —**ивание** *n.* carbonization, charring.

переудобренность *f.* overfertilization.

переукладка *f.* restacking, repiling.

переуло/к *m.,* —**чный** *a.* lane, alley.

переуплотнение *n.* overcrowding (of population); overstocking.

переуспокоение *n.* overdamping.

переустр/аивать, —**оить** *v.* rebuild; reorganize; —**ойст-во** *n.* rebuilding; reorganization, rearrangement; reconstruction; overhaul.

переуступ/аемый *a.* negotiable; —**ать,** —**ить** *v.* cede, give up; recede.

переутом/ить *v.,* —**ление** *n.,* —**лять** *v.* overfatigue; overstrain; overwork; —**лённый** *a.* overfatigued, etc., *see v.*

переуч/есть *v.* take stock (of); —**ёт** *m.,* —**ётный** *a.* stock-taking, inventory; registration.

переучивать *v.* reteach; relearn; —**ся** *v.* relearn.

переучитывать *v.* take stock (of).

переучить *see* **переучивать.**

переучтёт *fut. 3 sing. of* **переучесть.**

переформ/ирование *n.*, **—ировка** *f.* re-forming; **—ов-(ыв)ать** *v.* re-form; **—улировать** *v.* reformulate.

пере/фосфорилирование *n.* (chem.) transphosphorylation; **—фразировать** *v.* rephrase, paraphrase.

перехва/т *see* **перехватывание;** capture, beheading (of river); (embr.) cervical sinus; (histol.) isthmus; **—тить** *see* **перехватывать;** overshoot the mark; **—тчик** *m.* interceptor; **—тывание** *n.* interception, etc., *see v.*; (med.) strangulation, constriction; **—тывать** *v.* intercept; tap (a wire); (med.) strangle, constrict; bind; behead, capture (a river); borrow (for a short time); pass (a rope) hand over hand; **—ченный** *a.* intercepted, etc., *see v.*

пере/хитрить *v.* outwit, outsmart; **—хлестнуть, —хлёстывать** *v.* gush (over); go too far, overlap.

перехлорирован/ие *n.* superchlorination (of water), excess chlorination; **—ный** *a.* after-chlorinated, post-chlorinated.

переход *m.* passing (into, over), etc., *see v.*; transition, change(-over), conversion; exchange, switch(ing); transfer, transit, passage; swing (to); jump; (semiconductors) junction; reducer, adapter; (mil.) march; (comp.) branch(ing), GOTO (command), call; **п. к подпрограмму** subroutine call; **диаграмма —ов** transient graph; **пешеходный п.** pedestrian overpass *or* underpass; **при—е от . . . к** in going from . . . to; **таблица —ов** (comp.) jump table; **точка —а** transition point; (chem.) end point; **фазовый п.** change of phase, (phase) transition; **—ить** *v.* pass (into, over), cross, go over; go (into solution); migrate (of ions); change, convert, be converted, transform, turn (into); shift, switch; develop, proceed; exceed, go beyond; stop, end, come (to); blend, shade (of colors); turn (attention); **—ить из . . . в** go over into; **—ник** *m.* reducer, adapter; **—ной** *see* **переходный; —ноклеточный** *a.* (med.) transitional cell (carcinoma).

переходн/ый *a.* transition(al), transient, passing, intermediate; connecting, crossover; junction (box); reducing (nipple); make-before-break (contact); (math.) transient (function); transition (matrix); tie-line (triangular phase diagram); (gram.) transitive; **п. конденсатор** isolating or blocking capacitor; **п. коэффициент** conversion factor; **п. патрон, п. патрубок** adapter, reducer; **п. профиль** (gear teeth) inflection contour region; **п. процесс** transient (process); **построение —ых процессов** transient evaluation; **п. режим кипения** transition boiling; **—ая втулка** adapter, reducer; **—ая колодка** tube adapter; **—ая муфта** adapter, reducer; **—ая полоса** transition zone; **—ая труба** reducer; **—ая характеристика** transient response; **—ое положение** transition; **—ое сопротивление** contact resistance; **—ое состояние** transient state, transition state; **—ое явление** transient; **время —ого режима** transient period.

перехо/дящий *a.* passing (into, over), etc., *see* **переходить; —ждение** *n.* transition, crossing over.

пер/ец *m.* (bot.) pepper (*Piper*); **водяной п.** smartweed (*Polygonum hydropiper*); **горький п., жгучий п., острый п.** hot pepper; **зерно —ца** peppercorn; **стручковый (красный) п., турецкий п.** red pepper (*Capsicum annuum*); **ямайский п.** pimento.

перецарап(ыв)ать *v.* scratch up.

переце/дить, —живать *v.* (re)filter, strain, pour over; **—живание** *n.* (re)filtration, straining.

перецеп/ить, —лять *v.* (re)hook.

перечекани(ва)ть *v.* (re)stamp.

перечень *m.* enumeration, list(ing), check list; repertory, catalog, index; inventory; sum, total; summary, contents.

пере/черкать, —чёркивать, —черкнуть *v.* strike out, cross out, cancel.

перечерн/ить, —ять *v.* (over)blacken.

перечерпать *v.* bail out.

перечерстветь *v.* get too stale.

перечер/тить, —чивать *v.* copy, (re)draw.

пере/чесать *v.* (re)comb; (text.) (re)hackle; **—честь** *v.* count; (re)-read; **—чёсывать** *see* **перечесать; —чёт** *see* **пересчёт; —чини(ва)ть** *v.* mend, fix, repair; (re)sharpen; **—чиркать** *see* **перечеркать.**

перечисл/ение *n.* enumeration, listing, inventory; (com.) transfer; **—енный** *a.* enumerated, etc., *see v.*; **—имый** *a.* (math.) (d)enumerable; countable; **—ить, —ять** *v.* enumerate, list, tabulate, give; transfer; (math.) convert.

перечист/ить —щать *v.* clean (again; up); (re)purify; **—ка** *f.* (re)purification, afterpurification, final cleaning; **—ный** *a.* (re)purifying.

пере/чит(ыв)ать *v.* (re)read; **—чить** *v.* contradict; **—чищать** *see* **перечистить.**

перечневый *a.* abridged, brief.

перечник *m.* (bot.) candytuft (*Iberis*).

перечн/ица *f.* pepper pot; **—ые** *pl.* (bot.) Piperaceae; **—ый** *a.* pepper(y).

перечтёт *fut. 3 sing. of* **перечесть.**

перешаг/ивать, . . . —нуть *v.* step over, cross.

перешвыр/ивать, —нуть, —ять *v.* fling over, toss over, throw over.

перешедший *past act. part. of* **перейти.**

перешеек *m.* isthmus, neck; vent.

перешёл *past m. sing. of* **перейти.**

перешиб *m.* fracture; **—ать, —ить** *v.* fracture, break.

пере/ши(ва)ть *v.* alter; sew; repanel; gage, adjust (track); **—шлёт** *fut. 3 sing. of* **переслать; —шлифо-в(ыв)ать** *v.* (re)grind; **—шло** *past n. sing. of* **перейти.**

перешнуров/анный *a.* constricted, etc., *see v.*; **—ка** *f.*, **—ывание** *n.* constriction, strangulation; **—(ыв)ать** *v.* constrict, strangulate, strangle.

пере/штемпелевать, —штемпелёвывать *v.* (re)stamp; **—штукатури(ва)ть** *v.* (re)plaster; **—шьёт** *fut. 3 sing. of* **перешить; —щелачивать** *v.* overlime (sugar); **—щипать** *v.* pluck; pinch; **—щуп(ыв)ать** *v.* feel, probe (all over); **—экзаменов(ыв)ать** *v.* re-examine; **—эксплуатация** *f.* overexploitation; **—э(с)терификация** *f.* (chem.) (trans)esterification, ester interchange.

переяр/ка *f.*, **—ок** *m.* yearling.

пери— *prefix* peri— [near, (a)round]; **—ант(ий), —анций** *m.* (bot.) perianth; **—артер(и)ит** *m.* (med.) periarteritis; **—астр(он)** *m.* (astr.) periastron; **—бласт** *m.* (embr.) periblast; **—блема** *f.* (bot.) periblem; **—брон-хиальный** *a.* (anat.) peribronchial; **—васкулярный** *a.* perivascular; **—галактий** *m.* (astr.) perigalactica; **—гастрит** *m.* (med.) perigastritis; **—гей** *m.* (astr.) perigee; **—гелий** *m.*, **—гельный** *a.* perihelion; **—ге-патит** *m.* (med.) perihepatitis; **—гиний** *m.* (bot.) perigynium; **—гляционный** *a.* (paleogeog.) periglacial; **—дерма** *f.* (biol.) periderm; **—дий** *m.* (bot.) peridium; **—динеи** *pl.* (prot.) Peridinea, Dinoflagellata; **—диола** *f.* (bot.) peridiole; **—дот** *m.* (min.) peridot; **—дотит** *m.* (petr.) peridotite.

перикард, —ий *m.* (anat.) pericardium; **—ит** *m.* (med.) pericarditis; **—ический** *a.* pericardial, pericardiac.

перикарпий *m.* (bot.) pericarp.

пери-кислота *f.* 1-naphthylamine-8-sulfonic acid.

перикл/аз *m.* (min.) periclase, magnesia; **—ин** *m.* (min.) pericline; **—инальный** *a.* (bot.; geol.) periclinal; **—иновый** *a.* pericline.

пери/колит *m.* (med.) pericolitis; **—краний** *m.* (anat.) pericranium.

перила *f.* (hand)rail, railing, balustrade, guard rail, bar, barrier, parapet.

перилен *m.* (chem.) perylene.

перилимфа *f.* (anat.) perilymph; **—тический** *a.* perilymphatic.

перилл/а *f.* (bot.) Perilla; **—овый** *a.* perilla; perillic (acid); **—овый альдегид** perillaldehyde.

periль/ный *a. of*, **—ца** *dim. of* **перила.**

периметр *m.* (geom.; ophth.) perimeter; **—ий** *m.* (anat.) parimetrium; **—ийный** *a.* perimetric; **—ит** *m.* (med.) perimetritis; **—ический** *a.* (geom.) perimetric.

пери/мидин *m.* (chem.) perimidine; **—мизий** *m.* (anat.) perimysium; **—морфоза** *f.* (min.) perimorph.

перина *f.* featherbed; (bot.) perine.

пери/натальный *a.* perinatal, near birth; **—нафто—** *prefix* (chem.) perinaphtho—; **—неальный** *a.* (anat.) perineal; **—нео—** *prefix* perineo— (perineum); **—нефрит** *m.* (med.) perinephritis; **—ний** *m.* (bot.) perine.

перин/ка *dim. of*, **—ный** *a. of* **перина.**

период *m.* period, time, phase, stage; age, era; life; (breeding or growing) season; interval; (operating) cycle; (lattice) spacing, pitch; spell (of weather); **п. в десятичной дроби** repeating decimal; **п. в секунду** cycles per second; **п. задержки** delay; **п. повторения импульсов** pulse repetition time; **п. решётки** (cryst.) lattice spacing *or* constant; (nucl.) lattice pitch; **п. роста** growing period; **за п.** over a period (of), during; **измеритель —а** (nucl.) period meter.

периодат *m.* (chem.) periodate.

период/изатор *m.* (comp.) iterator; **—изация** *f.* division into periods; **—ика** *f.* periodical(s); periodicity rhythm; **—ически** *adv.* periodically, at regular intervals; intermittently.

периодическ/ий *a.* periodic(al), recurrent; alternating, intermittent; batch (process); cycle (storage); routine (inspection); **п. закон** periodic law, Mendeleyev's law; **—ая дробь** (math.) repeating decimal; **—ая литература, —ая печать** periodicals; **—ая система** periodic system (of elements); **—ого действия** batch(-operated); **с —им профилем** stepped (shaft).

периодичн/ость *f.* periodicity; frequency; interval, spacing; batch nature, noncontinuity; (feed) rate; **—ый** *see* **периодический.**

периодонт *m.* (anat.) periodontium; **—ит** *m.* (med.) periodontitis; **—овый** *a.* periodontal.

периодопреобразователь *m.* frequency changer.

пери/онихий *m.* (anat.) perionychium; **—оральный** *a.* perioral; **—орбита** *f.* periorbit(a); **—орбитальный** *a.* periorbital; **—орхит** *m.* (med.) periorchitis; **—ост** *m.* (anat.) periosteum; **—остит** *m.* (med.) periostitis; **—остракум** *m.* (mal.) periostracum; **—плазма** *f.* (biol.) periplasm; **—плазмодий** *m.* (bot.) periplasmodium; **—пласт** *m.* (cyt.; prot.) periplast; **—плоцин** *m.* (bioch.) periplocin; **—плома** *f.* (mal.) spoon shell (*Periploma*).

пери-положение *n.* (chem.) peri-position.

пери/прокт *m.* (anat.) periproct; **—сарк** *m.* (zool.) perisarc; **—селение** *n.* (astr.) perilune; **—скоп** *m.* periscope; **—скопический** *a.* periscopic; **—сперм(ий)** *m.* (bot.) perisperm; **—спленит** *m.* (med.) perisplenitis; **—спорий** *m.* (bot.) perispore.

периссо— *prefix* perisso— (odd, uneven).

перистаз *m.* peristasis, environment.

перистальт/ика *f.* (physiol.) peristalsis; **—ин** *m.* (bioch.) peristaltin; **—ический** *a.* peristaltic, compressive; **—ическое сокращение** peristalsis.

перистед/иевые *pl.* (ichth.) Peristediidae; **—ион** *m.* Peristedion.

перистерит *m.* (min.) peristerite.

перистиль *m.* (arch.) peristyle.

перисто— *prefix* pinni— (feather, fin); (bot.) penni—, pinnately; **—головник** *m.* (bot.) Pterocephalus; **—жаберные** *pl.* (zool.) Pterobranchia; **—жилковатый** *a.* feather-veined, penninerved; **—крылки, —крылковые** *pl.* (ent.) caddis flies (*Trichoptera*); **—кучевое облако** cirrocumulus, mackerel sky; **—лист(н)ый** *a.* (bot.) pinnate, feather-leaved; **—лопастный** *a.* (bot.) pinnately lobed.

перистом *m.*, **—а** *f.* (biol.) peristome.

перисто/надрезной *a.* (bot.) pinnatifid; **—нервный** *a.* penninerved; **—образный** *a.* featherlike; cirriform (cloud); **—раздельный** *a.* (bot.) pinnatipartite; **—рассечённый** *a.* pinnatifid, pinnatisect; **—сложный** *a.* pinnately compound; **—слоистое облако** cirrostratus; **—сть** *f.* plumosity; **—уски** *pl.* (ent.) Chaoboridae, Corethridae; **—усый** *a.* feather-barbelled.

перист/ый *a.* feather(y); (biol.) plumose, feathered; pinnate, feather-like; feathered (structure); cirrous (clouds); **—ое облако** cirrus.

перитекти/ка *f.* (chem.; met.; petr.) peritectic system; **—ческий** *a.* peritectic.

пери/телий *m.* (anat.) perithelium; **—тендиний** *m.* peritendineum; **—тендинит** *m.* (med.) peritendinitis; **—теций** *m.* (bot.) perithecium.

перитон/еальный *a.* (anat.) peritoneal; **—ео—** *prefix* peritoneo— (peritoneum); **—изировать** *v.* peritonize; **—ит** *m.* (med.) peritonitis.

пери/трихальный *a.* (biol.) peritrichous; **—трихи** *pl.* (prot.) Peritricha; **—трофический** *a.* (ent.) peritrophic; **—уретральный** *a.* (anat.) periurethral.

перифер/ийный, —ический *a.* peripheral, circumferential; outlying (district); **—ия** *f.* periphery, peripheral region; outlying district; circumference.

пери/физ *m.*, **—физа** *f.* (bot.) periphysis; **—фитон** *m.* periphyton (fouling organisms); **—фокальный** *a.* perifocal; **—фокус** *m.* perifocus; **—фолликулит** *m.* (med.) perifolliculitis.

перифраз *m.*, **—а** *f.* periphrasis, redundancy; **—ировать** *v.* periphrase.

пери/хеций *m.* (bot.) perichaetium; **—холецистит** *m.* (med.) pericholecystitis; **—хондр(ий)** *m.* (anat.) perichondrium; **—хондрит** *m.* (med.) perichondritis; **—хорда** *f.* (anat.) perichord; **—хордальный** *a.* perichordal; **—цементит** *m.* (med.) pericementitis.

перицентр *m.* (astr.) pericenter; **—альный** *a.* pericentral; **—ический** *a.* (gen.) pericentric.

пери/цикл *m.* (bot.) pericycle; **—циклический** *a.* pericyclic; **—цит** *m.* (cyt.) pericyte.

перйодат *m.*, **—ный** *a.* (chem.) periodate.

пёрка *f.* (drill) bit, flat bit, flat drill.

перкал/ь *m.*, **—евый** *a.* (text.) percale.

перкамфорный *a.* percamphoric (acid).

перкарбонат *m.* (chem.) percarbonate.

перкарина *f.* (ichth.) Percarina.

Перкина реакция Perkin's reaction.

перкислота *f.* peracid.

перкнит *m.* (petr.) perknite.

пёрковый *a. of* **пёрка.**

перкол/ировать *v.* percolate; **—ирующий** *a.* percolating; **—ят** *m.* percolate, leachate; **—ятор** *m.* percolator, percolation vat; trickling filter; **—яционный** *a.*, **—яция** *f.* percolation.

перко/псовые *pl.* (ichth.) trout perches (*Percopsidae*); **—фис** *m.* Percophis; **—фисовые** *pl.* flatheads (*Percophiidae*).

перку/ссионный *a.*, **—ссия** *f.* percussion; **—тировать** *v.* percuss; **—торный** *a.* percussive, percussion; **—торный звук** resonance.

перл *m.* pearl, bead; (typ.) pearl (5 points).

пёрла *past f. sing. of* **переть.**

перламутр *m.* mother-of-pearl, nacre; **—енница, —овка** *f.* (ent.) pearl butterfly (*Argynnis*); **—овый** *a.* mother-of-pearl, nacreous, pearly, margaritaceous.

перл/аш *m.* (chem.) pearl ash (a potassium carbonate); **—вейс** *m.* pearl white (white lead).

пёрли *past pl. of* **переть.**

перлинь *m.* (naut.) hawser, tow line.

перлит *m.* (petr.) perlite; (met.) pearlite; **—ный, —овый** *a.* perlitic, spherulitic; **—обетон** *m.* perlite concrete; **—ообразный** *a.* pearl-shaped, bead-shaped.

пёрло *past n. sing. of* **переть.**

перлов/ица *f.* pearl shell; pearl oyster; (mal.) Unio; **—ицы** *pl.* Unionidae; **—ка** *f.* pearl barley; **—ник** *m.* melic grass (*Melica*); **—ый** *a.* pearl; **—ая крупа** pearl barley.

перлон *m.* (synthetic fibers) perlon.

перл/(о)полимеризация *f.* (chem.) pearl polymerization; **—ь** *see* **перл.**

перлювий *m.* (geol.) perluvium.

пермаллой *m.* Permalloy (alloy).

перманган/ат *m.* (chem.) permanganate; **п. калия** potassium permanganate; **—(ат)ометрия** *f.* permanganometry, permanganate titration.

перманентн/ость *f.* permanence, permanency; **—ый** *a.* permanent, lasting; continuous; **—ая белая** permanent white, precipitated barium sulfate.

перм/атрон *m.* (electron.) permatron; **—еабильный** *a.* permeable; **—еаза** *f.* (bioch.) permease, transport agent; **—еаметр** *m.* permeameter; **—ендюр** *m.* Permendur (alloy).

перм/мин *abbr.* **(периодов в минуту)** cycles per minute.

перм/инвар *m.* Perminvar (alloy); **—иссивный** *a.* permissive; **—ский** *a.* (geog.) Perm; (geol.) Permian, Permic.

пермут/ационный *a.* permutation(al); rotational (index); **—ация** *f.*, **—ирование** *n.* permutation; transmutation; Permutit process; **—ит** *m.* permutite (artificial zeolite); **—итный процесс** Permutit process (for water purification).

пермь *f.* (geol.) Permian (period).

пернамбуковое дерево (dyeing) pernambuco.

пернат/ые *pl.* birds; **—ый** *a.* feathered, plumigerous; full-fledged; **—ая дичь** game bird.

пернигранилин *m.* pernigranilin (dye).

пернитрид *m.* (chem.) pernitride.

пернициозный *a.* (med.) pernicious.

Перно печь Pernot furnace (for steel).

Перо лампа Pérot lamp.

перо *n.* feather, penna, plume; (anat.) pinna; (writing) pen; blade, vane; fin (of fish, rocket); (rail) tongue; (onion) leaf, top; **лук на п.** bunch onion; **морское п.** (zool.) sea pen (*Pennatula*); **нитевидное п.** (orn.) filoplume; **охота по —у** fowling; **писчее п.** (anat.) calamus scriptorius; **придаточное п.** (orn.) aftershaft; **—овидный** *a.* featherlike; penniform; **—овой** *a.* of **перо;** pointed.

перо/вскит *m.* (min.) perovskite; **—гнат** *m.* (mam.) pocket mouse (*Perognathus*); **—диктикус** *m.* potto (*Perodicticus*).

пероеды *pl.* (ent.) bird lice (*Mallophaga*).

пёрок *gen. pl. of* **пёрка.**

перокрылк/а *f.* (ent.) ptilium; **—и, —овые** *pl.* Ptiliidae.

перокс/ид *m.* (chem.) peroxide; **—идаза** *f.*, **—идазный** *a.* peroxidase; **—о** *prefix* peroxo—, per(oxy)—; **—оборат** *m.* perborate; **—одисерный** *a.* peroxydisulfuric, persulfuric (acid); **—окарбонат** *m.* percarbonate; **—омоносерный** *a.* permonosulfuric (acid); **—осульфат** *m.* peroxysulfate.

перонин *m.* (pharm.) peronine, benzylmorphine hydrochloride.

пероносный *a.* (biol.) pennigerous.

пероноспороз *m.* (phyt.) downy mildew, Peronospora infection.

перообразный *see* **перовидный.**

пероральный *a.* (med.) peroral, by mouth.

перохвостый *a.* (biol.) feather-tailed.

перочинный ножик pocketknife.

перпендикуляр *m.* perpendicular; **—но** *adv.* perpendicularly, perpendicular (to); **—ность** *f.* perpendicularity; **—ный** *a.* perpendicular, normal; square (with axis).

перпетуум мобиле *n.* perpetual motion.

перрадиальный *a.* (zool.) perradial.

перренат *m.* (chem.) perrhenate.

перрон *m.*, **—ный** *a.* (building) perron; (rr.) platform; (av.) ramp, apron.

перрутенат *m.* (chem.) perruthenate.

перс/еверация *f.* (med.) perseveration; **—еиды** *pl.* (astr.) Perseids (meteors); **—ей** *m.* Perseus.

пер/сек *abbr.* **(периодов в секунду)** cycles per second.

персептрон *n.* perceptron (learning device).

персея *f.* (bot.) Persea; **приятнейшая п.** avocado (*P. americana*).

персидск/ий *a.* Persian, Iranian; **п. порошок** pyrethrum dust; **—ая камедь** sagapenum.

персик *m.* (bot.) peach (*Persica*); **—овидный** *a.* peach-like; **—овый** *a.* peach(-colored), persicine; peach kernel (oil); **—олистный** *a.* peach-leaved, persicaefolious.

персилит *m.* (min.) percylite.

персимон *m.* (bot.) persimmon (*Diospyros*).

персист/ентность *f.*, **—енция** *f.*, **—ирование** *n.* persistence; **—ентный, —ирующий** *a.* persistent, persisting; (bot.) evergreen; **—ор** *m.* (comp.) persistor.

Персия (geog.) Persia, Iran.

Персо раствор Persoz solution (of basic zinc chloride).

персоль *f.* (chem.) persalt.

персон/а *f.* person(age); **—ал** *m.* personnel, staff; **—альный** *a.* personal; **—атный** *a.* masked, disguised; **—ификация** *f.* personification; **—ифицировать** *v.* personify.

перспекс *m.* Perspex (plastic).

перспектив/а *f.* perspective, vista, outlook, prospect, aspect; challenge; **—ы** *pl.* horizons; outlook; **в —е** in the future, in the long term; **—ность** *f.* long-term outlook; **—ный** *a.* perspective, prospective; promising, showing promise, challenging; exploratory, advanced (research); long-range, long-term (plan); oblique (aerial surveying, etc.); **—ное сокращение** foreshortening.

перст/ень *m.* (signet) ring; **—не** *prefix* (anat.) crico—, cricoid; **—невидноклеточный** *a.* signet-ring cell; **—не(видно)щитовидный** *a.* cricothyroid; **—невидный** *a.* cricoid; **—неглоточный** *a.* cricopharyngeal; **—непищеводный** *a.* cricoesophageal; **—нетрахеальный** *a.* cricotracheal; **—нечерпаловидный** *a.* cricoarytenoid.

пер/сульфат *m.* (chem.) persulfate; **—тио—** *prefix* perthio—.

пертит *m.* (min.) perthite; **—овый, —оподобный** *a.* perthitic.

пертофит *m.* (bot.) perthophyte.

пертубация *f.* (med.) pertubation.

перту/и, —й *m.* (ichth.) small cod.

пертулинь *m.* (naut.) cat(head) stopper.

пертурбац/ионный *a.* perturbation; perturbative (function); **—ия** *f.* perturbation.

пертуссин *m.* (pharm.) Pertussin.

пертуя *see* **пертуй.**

Перу (geog.) Peru.

перу/виан *m.* a Peruvian rubber; **—(ви)анский** *a.* (geog.) Peruvian; **—виол** *m.* (chem.) peruviol, nerolidol; **—ген** *m.* perugen, synthetic Peru balsam.

пер/угольный *a.* percarbonic (acid); **—уксусный** *a.* peracetic (acid).

перфо/жетон *m.* punch badge; **—карта** *f.* card, punch(ed) card; **—лента** *f.* punched tape, perforated tape, perforator tape.

перфоратор *m.*, **—ный** *a.* perforator, punch(er); punch-card machine; (pneumatic) drill; drill press; **п. результатов** output punch; **считывающий п.** card-reader punch; **—ий** *m.* (zool.) perforatorium, acrosome; **п.-репродуктор** *m.* (comp.) reproducing punch, reperforator.

перфор/ационный *a.* perforation, punching; punched (card); punched-card, punched-tape; **—ационное отверстие** perforation; **—ация** *f.*, **—ирование** *n.* perforation (pattern), punching, etc., *see v.*; hole; punch; **ведущая —ация** sprocket holes; **—ированный** *a.* perforated, etc., *see v.*; **—ировать** *v.* perforate, punch, key(-punch); drill, bore; **—ирующий** *a.* perforating, etc., *see v.*; **—ирующая коррозия** pitting.

перфосфат *m.* (chem.) perphosphate.

перфтор— *prefix* (chem.) perfluoro—; **—бензол** *m.* perfluorobenzene; **—пропилен** *m.* perfluoropropylene, hexafluoropropylene; **—углеводород** *m.* perfluorohydrocarbon; **—этан** *m.* perfluoroethane.

перфуз/ионный *a.* perfusion, perfused; **—ировать** *v.* perfuse; **—ия** *f.* perfusion.

перхать *v.* cough from throat irritation.

перхлор— *prefix* (chem.) perchlor(o)—; **—ат** *m.* perchlorate; **—(ат)ирование** *n.* perchloration; **—бутадиен** *m.* perchlorobutadiene; **—ид** *m.* perchloride; **—метан** *m.* perchlormethane, carbon tetrachloride; **—(о)винил** *m.*, **—(о)виниловый** *a.* perchlorovinyl, vinyl perchloride; **—этан** *m.* perchloroethane, hexachloroethane.

перхота *f.* dry tickling in throat.

перхоть *f.* dandruff, scurfy particles.

перхромат *m.* (chem.) perchromate.

перц/а *gen. of* **перец**; **—евые** *pl.* (bot.) pepper family (*Piperaceae*).

перцеп/трон *m.* (comp.) perceptron; **—ция** *f.* perception.

перцеяды *pl.* (orn.) Ramphastidae.

перцилит *see* **персилит.**

перцина *f.* (ichth.) Percina.

перцов/ка *f.* pepper brandy or vodka; **—ый** *a. of* **перец.**

перчат/ка *f.*, **—очный** *a.* glove; sleeve; (cables) joint; **—очная камера** (nucl.) glove box.

перчинка *f.* peppercorn.

перчить *v.* (season with) pepper.

першерон *m.*, **—ский** *a.* Percheron (horse).

першить *v.* tickle (throat).

пёрышко *dim. of* **перо;** plumule; (bot.) pinnule.

пер/ышковидный *a.* plumuliform; **—ьевой** *a. of,* **—ья** *pl. of* **перо;** plumage; **—янка** *f.* (ichth.) fin.

пёс *m.* dog, hound; (astr.) Canis.

песен *gen. pl. of,* **—ный** *a. of* **песня.**

песец *m.* (mam.) Arctic fox (*Alopex lagopus*).

песига *f.* breech wool, birth wool.

пёсий *a.* canine, dog('s); **п. язык** (bot.) hound's tongue (*Cynoglossum officinale*).

песка *gen. of* **песок.**

пескар/и *see* **пескарковые; —ка** *f.* (ichth.) dragonet (*Callionymus*); **—(к)овые** *pl.* Callionymidae; **—ь** *m.* gudgeon (*Gobio g.*).

песк/и *pl. of* **песок;** sands, desert; **—о—** *prefix* sand, (ps)amm(o)— stratification (of seeds); **—оватый** *a.* (rather) sandy; **—овый** *a.* sand(y); **—одувка** *f.* sandblast(er); **—одувный** *a.* sandblast(ing); **—ожил** *m.* (zool.) lugworm (*Arenicola*); **—ожилые** *pl.* (ichth.) sand eels (*Trichonotidae*); **—озоб** *m.* (ichth.) loach; **—озоб(ч)ик** *see* **пескарь; —окат** *m.* troutperch (*Percopsis*); **—олов(уш)ка** *f.* sand trap; (wastewater treatment) grit chamber; **—олюб** *m.* (bot.) Ammophila; **—олюбивый** *a.* psammophilous, sand-loving; **—омёт** *m.* (foundry) sand slinger; **—омойка** *f.* sand washer.

песко/отделитель *m.* desander; sand trap; **—разбрасыватель** *m.* sander; **—разбрасывать** *v.* sand; **—рои** *pl.* (mam.) African mole rats (*Bathyergidae*); **—рой** *m.* (mam.) Bathyergus; Cryptomys; (ent.) sand wasp (*Ammophila*); (ichth.) sand eel (*Ammodytes*); **—ройка** *f.* (ichth.) lamprey larva, ammocoete; **—сортировка** *f.* sand screen(ing).

пескостру/ить *v.* sandblast; **—й** *m.* sandblast(er); **—йный** *a.* sandblast(ing); **—йная очистка** sandblasting.

пескосушилка *f.* sand dryer.

пескоукреп/итель *m.* sand binder; **—ительный, —ляющий** *a.* sand binding.

песко/уловитель *m.* sand trap; **—черпалка** *f.* sand dredger.

песня *f.* song.

песобой *m.* (bot.) meadow saffron, autumn crocus (*Colchicum autumnale*).

песо/к *m.* sand; (med.) gravel; **мозговой п.** sand bodies, acervulus; **п.-плывун** *m.* running sand; **—чек** *dim. of* **песок; —чина** *f.* (met.) sand hole, sand mark; *pl.* sand; **—чник** *m.* sandbox; (orn.) sandpiper (*Calidris*); (ichth.) goby; dace; **—чница** *f.* sand box; (rr.) sander; (paper) riffler, sand trap.

песочн/ый *a.* sand(y), arenaceous; (biol.) arenicolous; short (pastry); **п. насос** sand pump, suction bailer; **—ая бумага** sandpaper; **—ая ванна** sand bath; **—ая раковина** sand hole (in casting); **—ая шкурка** sandpaper; **—ые часы** hourglass; **отливка в —ой форме** (foundry) sand casting.

пессарий *m.* (med.) pessary.

пессимистич/еский, —ный *a.* pessimistic.

пест *m.* pestle, beater, rammer, stamp; **—ик** *dim. of* **пест;** pestle, pounder; pin; (bot.) pistil; **—иковый** *a.* pistillate, pistillary.

пестицид *m.*, **—ный** *a.* (agr.) pesticide.

пестичн/ый *a.* (bot.) pistillate; *suffix* **—gynous; —ая ножка** gynopodium.

пестовой молот drop hammer.

пестр/ак *m.* (ent.) Gnorimus; Valgus; **—еть** *v.* appear variegated; **—ец** *m.* (bot.) Boletus variegatus; Hierochloe borealis; **—ить** *v.* variegate; **—ица** *f.* (phyt.) first stage of mosaic disease.

пёстро *adv.* variegatedly.

пестро— *prefix* poecil(o)— (variegated; various; pied); **—ватый** *a.* somewhat variegated; **—глазка** *f.* (ent.) Melanargia; **—головый** *a.* spotty-headed; **—грудка** *f.* (orn.) spotty-breasted warbler (*Bradypterus*); **—грудый**

a. spotty-breasted; —**крылка** *f.* (ichth.) a sculpin (*Batrachocottus multiradiatus*); —**крылки** *pl.* (ent.) fruit flies (*Trypetidae*); —**крылый** *a.* (orn.) variegatedwinged; (ichth.) variegated-finned; —**крыльница** *f.* (ent.) Araschnia.

пестролистн/ость *f.* (phyt.) leaf variegation, mottling; —**ый** *a.* motley leaved; having variegated leaves.

пестро/овсяничник *m.* (geobot.) variegated fescue subalpine meadow; —**полье** *n.* irregular sowing; —**польный** *a.* irregularly cultivated; —**та** *f.* variegation, diversity of colors; —**тканый** *a.* (text.) striped, checked; —**ткань** *f.* tapestry; —**тность** *f.* mosaic structure.

пестр/уха *f.* (ichth.) minnow (*Phoxinus Ph.*); sevruga (*Acipenser stellatus*); brown trout (*Salmo trutta*); —**ушка** *f.* variegated animal such as spotted hen, brindle cow, piebald horse; (mam.) lemming (*Lagurus l.*); (ent.) Neptis; (ichth.) brook trout, rainbow trout.

пёстр/ый *a.* variegated, motley, speckled, particolored; blended.

пестр/ядёвый *a.*, —**ядина** *f.*, —**ядинный** *a.*, —**ядь** *f.* coarse varicolored cloth; —**як** *m.* (ent.) Chrysops; (ichth.) one of seven species; —**яки** *pl.* (ent.) checkered beetles (*Cleridae*); —**яковые** *pl.* (ichth.) rabbitfishes (*Siganidae*); —**янки** *pl.* (ent.) Zygaenidae; —**ятка** *f.* (ichth.) parr (*Salmo salar*).

пестун *m.*, —**ья** *f.* yearling bear cub.

песц/овый *a.*, —**ы** *pl.* of **песец.**

песчан/ик *m.*, —**иковый** *a.* (petr.) sandstone; (mam.) souslik (*Lepus tolai; Citellus fulvus*); (ent.) Trox; (ichth.) goby; gudgeon; minnow; —**ики** *pl.* (ent.) Trogiidae; —**истость** *f.* sandiness; —**истый** *a.* sandy, arenaceous; —**ка** *f.* (ent.) Hyalorrhipis; (ichth.) sand eel (*Ammodytes*); (mam.) gerbil (*Gerbillus*); (orn.) sanderling (*Crocethia* or *Calidris alba*); (bot.) sandwort (*Arenaria*); —**ки** *pl.*, —**ковые** *pl.* (ichth.) Ammodytidae; (mam.) Gerbillinae.

песчано— *prefix* sand(y), arenaceous; —**вые** *see* **песчанковые;** —**глинистый** *a.* sandy-argillaceous; —**струйный** *see* **пескоструйный.**

песчан/ый *a.* sand(y), arenaceous, sabulose, gritty, gravelly; *see also* **песочный;** —**ая буря** sandstorm; —**ая коса** sandbar.

песчинка *f.* grit, particle of sand.

песь *f.* (med.) vitiligo.

песья *f.* of **песий; п. вишня** (bot.) Physalis.

петалит *m.* (min.) petalite.

петал/оидный *a.* petaloid, petal-like; —**ьный** *a. and suffix* petaled, —petalous.

петарда *f.* (mil.) petard; firecracker; (rr.) detonator; (powder) pellet.

петель *gen. pl.*, —**ка** *dim.* of **петля;** eyelet, mesh; —**ный** *a.* loop; —**чатый** *a.* net(ted); (min.) reticulate, mesh (texture).

петехиальный *a.* (vet.) petechial (fever).

петзит *m.* (min.) petzite.

Пети *see under* **Дюлонг и Пти.**

петигреновое масло petitgrain oil.

петикот *m.* (rr.) petticoat pipe.

петинка *f.* (text.) hank.

петиотизовать *v.* petiotize (wines).

петит *m.* (typ.) brevier (8 points).

петитов канал (anat.) Petit's canal.

петиция *f.* petition.

петл/евание *n.* looping; —**евидный** *a.* loop(-shaped), ansiform; —**евой** *a.* of **петля;** looping (mill); loopmill (rolling); ansa(ted); lap (winding); —**евой вибратор** folded antenna, bent dipole; —**едержатель** *m.* (met. rolling) looper; —**ение** *n.* kinking (of line); —**еобмёточный** *a.* buttonhole (machine); —**еобраз-**

ный *see* **петлевидный;** lap (winding); —**еобразование** *n.* looping; —**еобразователь** *m.* looper; —**еотвод** *m.* drop looper; —**истый** *a.* loop(ed), ansate; —**ица** *f.*, —**ичный** *a.* buttonhole; tab.

петл/я *f.* loop, kink; noose, slip knot; mesh (of net); eye; hinge (of door); (elec.) loop; collar; sling; cycle; (anat.) lemniscus; ansa; buttonhole; (surgical) snare; (knitting) stitch; **на** —**ях** hinged; **образование петель** looping; **свернуться в** —**ю** *v.* kink; —**ять** *v.* loop; kink.

Петри чашка Petri dish.

петриссаж *m.* petrissage (type of massage).

петрифи/кация *f.* petrification; —**цирующийся** *a.* petrifying.

петро— *prefix* petro—, stone, rock.

Петров крест (bot.) Lathraea; —**а контакт** (chem.) Petrov catalyst (surfactant).

петроген/езис *m.* (petr.) petrogenesis; —**етический** *a.* petrogenetic; —**ия** *f.* petrogeny.

петрограф *m.* petrographer; —**ический** *a.* petrographic; —**ия** *f.* petrography.

петрозёрский *a.* (geog.) Lake Peter.

петрозит *m.* (med.) petrositis.

петрол/ат(ум) *m.* petrolatum; —**ейный** *a.* petroleum; —**ейный эфир** petroleum ether; —**еум** *m.* petroleum.

петролог/ический *a.* petrologic(al); —**ия** *f.* petrology.

петроль *m.* petrol (British term for gasoline); petroleum ether.

петро/селиновый *a.* petrosel(in)ic (acid); —**симония** *f.* (bot.) Petrosimonia; —**физика** *f.* petrophysics; —**фильный** *a.* petrophilous, rock-dwelling; —**фит** *m.* petrophyte, rock plant; —**химия** *f.* petrochemistry.

петруш/ечница *f.* (ent.) orange-tip butterfly (*Anthocaris cardamines*); —**ечный** *a.*, —**ка** *f.* (bot.) parsley (*Petroselinum*); **собачья** —**ка** fool's parsley (*Aethusa cynapium*).

петр. эф. *abbr.* (**петролейный эфир**).

петсай *m.* (bot.) Chinese cabbage (*Brassica pekinensis*).

петтикот *m.* (elec.) petticoat.

петун/идин *m.* (chem.) petunidin; —**ин** *m.* petunin; —**ия**, —**ья** *f.* petunia.

петух *m.* rooster, cock; (ichth.) goby; gurnard (*Trigla*); **морской п.** Trigla; sea robin (*Prionotus*); **морские** —**и** Triglidae.

петуш/ий, —**иный** *a.* of **петух;** gallinaceous; **п. гребень** cockscomb; **п. гребешок** (bot.) cock's comb (*Celosia cristata*); —**ки** *pl.* of **петушок;** (bot.) iris; —**ник** *m.* (bot.) hemp nettle (*Galeopsis*); —**ок** *m.* cockerel; weathercock; (elec.) riser, neck (of commutator); (orn.) ruff (*Philomachus pugnax*); —**каменный** —**ок** cotingid (*Rupicola*); **морской** —**ок** (ichth.) Alectrias; **сиамский п.** Siamese fighting fish (*Betta splendens*); —**ье просо** (bot.) barn grass (*Echinochloa crus-galli*).

петцит *m.* (min.) petzite.

пет/ый *a.* sung, etc. *see v.*; —**ь** *v.* sing, hum; pipe; warble; crow (of cock).

пеун *m.* (ent.) Zabrus.

пехлевийский *a.* (geog.) Pekhlevi.

пехмановский *a.* Pechmann (dyes).

пехот/а *f.* (mil.) infantry; **морская п.** marines; —**инец** *m.* infantry man; —**ный** *a.* infantry.

пехтерь *m.* crate, osier basket.

пехштейн *m.* (petr.) pitchstone.

пецек *m.* (ichth.) mud minnow (*Umbra krameri*).

пецил/иевые, —**ии** *pl.* (ichth.) livebearers (*Poeciliidae*); —**о—** *prefix* poecil(o)— (variegated).

пеци/а *f.* (bot.) Peziza; —**овые** *pl.* Pezizaceae.

печаль *f.* grief, sorrow; —**ница** *f.* (ent.) Anthrax; —**ный** *a.* sad, mournful; regrettable, unfortunate.

печат/ание n. printing; typing; imprint; sealing; capping (of honeycomb); **—анный** a. printed; **—ать** v. print; type; stamp, seal, imprint, impress; **—ающий** a. printing; **—ающее устройство** printer; printing device; **—ка** f. signet, seal; stamped article; (honeycomb) cappings; **—ник** m. printer; **—но** adv. in print.

печат/ый a. printed, published; printing; press; stamped, sealed, marked; **п. лист** quire; **п. станок** printing press; **—ая копия** hard copy; **—ая схема** (electron.) printed circuit.

печат/очный a. stamped (with tradename); (biol.) sigillate, seal-like; **—ующее устройство** printer; **—ь** f. stamp, seal; print(ing), printed matter; press, printer; (instr.) reading, setting; (comp.) print-out; **выйти из —и** v. come out, appear, come off the press; **вышло из —и** published; **глубокая—ь** intaglio; **золотая —ь** (bot.) golden seal (*Hydrastis canadensis*); **накладывать —ь** v. stamp.

печ/ево n. baked goods; **—ей** gen. pl. of **печь**; **—ек** gen. pl. of **печка**; **—ение** n. baking.

печёнка see **печень**.

печёнков/ый see **печёночный**; **п. колчедан** (min.) liver pyrites; **—ая руда** (min.) liver ore.

печённый a. baked, roasted.

печёно— see **печёночно—**.

печёночн/ик m., **—ица** f. (bot.) liverwort (*Hepatica*); **—о—** prefix (anat.) hepat(o)— (liver); **—о-двенадцатиперстн(окишечн)ый** a. hepatoduodenal; **—ожелудочный** a. hepatogastric; **—о-ободочн(окишечн)ый** a. hepatocolic; **—о-поджелудочный** a. hepatopancreatic; **—о-почечный** a. hepatorenal; **—о-селезёночный** a. hepatolienal; **—ый** a. hepatic, liver; **—ый мох** see **печёночник**; **—ый сахар** liver sugar, glycogen; **—ая ворвань** fish-liver oil, spec. cod-liver oil.

печёный a. baked, roasted.

печень f. (anat.) liver; **серная п.** (chem.) potassium sulfide.

печенье n. pastry; baked goods.

печерица f. (bot.) Psalliota campestris.

печ/и gen., pl., etc. of **печь**; **—ка** see **печь**; **—коуступная система** (min.) stoking; **—ник** m. furnace service man; (orn.) ovenbird (*Furnarius*); **—ники, —никовые** pl. Furnariidae.

печ/ой a. furnace, stove; kiln (brick); coke-oven (coke); **п. агрегат** furnace unit; **п. камень** ovenstone; **п. сок, п. шлак** (furnace) slag; **—ая труба** chimney, flue; **—ое стекло** glass that has run down into the hearth.

печорский a. (geog.) Pechora.

печурка f. small stove.

печ/ь f. furnace, kiln, oven, stove; (min.) cut-through, breakthrough, bord; heading; raise; v. bake, roast; **п. с мешалкой** rabble furnace; **п. сопротивления** resistance furnace; **высушенный в —и** kiln-dried; **п.-компаунд** f. combination (coke) oven.

пеш/еход m. pedestrian; **—еходный** a. pedestrian; hand (tractor); foot (bridge); **—еходный туризм, —еходная прогулка** hiking; **—ий** a. pedestrian; (mil.) foot; bush (bean); **—ком** adv. on foot; **идти —ком** v. walk.

пешня f. crowbar, lever; ice chisel.

пещер/а f. cave, cavern; (anat.) antrum, cavity, cavern(a); pl. antra; **—истый** a. cavernous; spongy; **—ный** a. cave; interstitial (water); **—ный человек** cave-dweller; **—оведение** n. speleology.

пещур m. basket, backpack.

ПЖР abbr. (**плотномер жидкости радиоактивный**) radioactive fluid densitometer.

пз abbr. (**пьеза**) pièze; (**пуаз**) poise; **ПЗ** (**полоса заражения**) contamination zone; (**переходная зона**) transition zone.

ПЗС abbr. (**прибор с зарядовой связью**) (semicond.) charge-coupled device, CCD.

ПЗУ abbr. (**постоянное запоминающее устройство**) (comp.) read-only memory, ROM.

пи (math.) pi, π; **ПИ** abbr. PI (proportional-plus-reset) control.

пиазолин m. (pharm.) piazoline.

пиала f. drinking bowl.

пиан m. (typ.) platen.

пиан/ино n. upright piano; **—иссимо** adv. pianissimo; **—ист** m., **—истка** f. pianist.

пиартроз m. (med.) pyarthrosis.

пиас(с)ава f. palm fibers for rope.

пиаузит m. (min.) piauzite.

пивал/ил m. pivalyl; **—иновая кислота** pivalic acid, trimethylacetic acid.

пивн/ой a. beer; brewer's (yeast); **—ая гуща** brewer's grains, spent malt.

пиво n. beer; ale; **варить п.** v. brew.

пивовар m. (beer) brewer; **—ение** n. brewing; **—ен(н)ый** a. brewing; **—енный завод** brewery; **—ничать** v. brew (beer or ale); **—ня** f. brewery.

пивохранилище n. beer tank.

пивший past act. part. of **пить**.

пигалица f. (orn.) lapwing, plover (*Vanellus v.*, etc.).

пигатрикс m. (mam.) Pygathrix.

пигид/иальный щит, **—ий** m. (zool.) pygidium; **—ий, —ия** f. (ichth.) Pygidium.

пигмей m. pygmy, dwarf.

пигмент m. pigment, coloring agent; **—ация** f., **—ирование** n. pigmentation; **—ированный** a. pigmented, colored; **—ировать** v. pigment, color; **—ный** a. pigment(ary), pigmented; **—ное пятно** (med.) mole, nevus pigmentosus; (ent.) stigma, ocellus; **—ообразование** n. chromogenesis, color production; **—ообразующий** a. chromogenic; **—офаг** m. (cyt.) pigmentophage.

пигмолит m. (geol.) pigmolite (dome-like magma massif resembling a fist).

пиго— prefix pygo— (buttocks); **—паг** m. (med.) pygopagus; **—стиль** m. (orn.) pygostyle, ploughshare bone.

пиджа/к m., **—чный** a. coat, jacket.

пиджонит m. (min.) pigeonite.

пидмонт m. (geol.) piedmont.

пиезмы pl. (ent.) Piesmidae.

пиезо— see **пьезо—**.

пие/лит m. (med.) pyelitis; **—ло—** prefix (anat.) pyel(o)— (renal pelvis); **—лография** f. (med.) pyelography; **—лонефрит** m. pyelonephritis; **—мия** f. pyemia.

пижам/а f., **—ный** a. pajamas.

пижемский a. (geog.) Pizhma.

пижма f. (bot.) tansy (*Tanacetum*).

пижонит m. (min.) pigeonite.

пиз/анит m. (min.) pisanite; **—олит** m. pisolite, peastone; **—олитовый, —олитоподобный** a. pisolitic, pea-like.

пиин m. (bioch.) pyin.

пик m. peak, pinnacle, cusp, crest; spire; spike; **час п.** rush hour.

пика f. pike, lance, spear; pick; poker; (hort.) dibble; (med.) pica.

пикаковый a. picacic (acid).

пикантный a. piquant (flavor).

пикап m. pickup (truck).

пикать v. squeak; cheep, peep.

пик-вольтметр *m.* (elec.) peak voltmeter.

пике *n.* (text.) piqué; (av.) dive; —**йный** *a.* pique.

пикел/евание *n.* (leather) pickling; —**евать** *v.* pickle; —**ь** *m.* pickle, pickling solution.

пикер *see* **пиккер.**

пикет *m.* picket; stake, peg; (rr.) 100-meter mark; station (distance); (art.) ranging point; —**аж** *m.*, —**ажный** *a.* picketing; stationing; staking out; —**ажная книжка** fieldbook; —**ировать** *v.* (labor) picket; —**ный** *a.* of **пикет;** —**чик** *m.* picketer.

пики *pl.* of **пик;** (work) peaks.

пикир/овальный *a.,* —**ование** *n.* (av.) diving, dive; (hort.) transplanting, pricking out; **п. колышек** dibble; —**ованный** *a.* transplanted, pricked out; —**ованная рассада** transplants; —**овать** *v.* dive; transplant, prick out; single; —**овка** *f.* transplanting, pricking out; —**овщик** *m.* dive bomber; —**ующий** *a.* diving, dive.

Пикквика синдром (med.) pickwickian syndrome.

пиккер *m.* (agr.) picker.

пиккерингит *m.* (min.) pickeringite, magnesia alum.

пиккер-хескер *m.* (corn) picker-husker; **п.-шеллер** *m.* picker-sheller.

пикколо *n.* piccolo.

пиклевать *see* **пикелевать.**

пикн— *see* **пикно—**; —**ида, —идия** *f.* (bot.) pycnidium; —**иды** *pl.* Pycnidia; —**ий** *m.* pycnium.

пикник *m.* picnic.

пикнит *m.* (min.) pycnite.

пикнический *a.* picnic.

пикно— *prefix* pycn(o)—, pykn(o)— (thick, dense, compact, close); —**з** *m.* (cyt.) pyknosis, thickening; —**конидия** *f.* (bot.) pycnoconidium, pycnidiospore; —**метр** *m.* (phys.) pycnometer, specific gravity bottle; —**подия** *f.* (zool.) Pycnopodia; —**спора** *f.* (bot.) pycnospore; —**троп** *m.* (min.) pycnotrope; —**хлорит** *m.* pycnochlorite.

пикнуть *v.* let out a sound; squeak.

пико— *prefix* pico—, micromicro— (10^{-12}); —**ватт** *m.* (elec.) picowatt.

пико/видный *a.* spiculate; —**вые** *pl.* spadefishes (*Ephippidae*); —**вый** *a.* of **пик;** peak-load; —**вое острие** spear point; —**держатель** *m.* pick holder.

пикол/ил *m.* picolyl; —**ин** *m.* picoline, methylpyridine; —**иновая кислота** picolinic acid, 2-pyridinecarboxylic acid.

пи-комплекс *m.* π-complex.

пико/образный *a.* pointed; pinnacled (iceberg); —**ограничитель** *m.* peak limiter.

пикотаж *m.* making mine tubing watertight with wedges.

пикотит *m.* (min.) picotite, chrome spinel.

пикофарад/а *f.,* —**ный** *a.* (elec.) picofarad, micro-microfarad.

пикрасмин *m.* (chem.) picrasmin, isoquassin.

пикраль *m.* picral (etching reagent).

пикрам/ид *m.* picramide, 2,4,6-trinitroaniline; —**иновая кислота** picramic acid, 2-amino-4,6-dinitrophenol.

пикр/ат *m.,* —**иновокислая соль** *m.* picrate; —**ил** *m.* picryl; —**илхлорид** *m.* picryl chloride; —**иновокислый** *a.* picric acid; picrate (of); —**иновая кислота** picric acid, trinitrophenol; —**ит** *m.* (petr.) picrite.

пикро— *prefix* picr(o)— [bitter; (chem.) picric; (min.) containing magnesium]; —**амозит** *m.* (min.) picroamosite; —**ильменит** *m.* picroilmenite; —**кроцин** *m.* (chem.) picrocrocin; —**л** *m.* picrol; —**лит** *m.* (min.) picrolite; —**лихениновый** *a.* picrolichenic (acid); —**лоновый** picrolonic (acid); —**мерит** *m.* (min.) picromerite; —**мерус** *m.* (ent.) Picromerus; —**мицин**

m. (pharm.) picromycin; —**подофиллин** *m.* picropodophyllin; —**тефроит** *m.* (min.) picrotephroite; —**тин** *m.* (chem.) picrotin; —**тиновый** *a.* picrotinic (acid); —**титанит** *m.* (min.) picrotitanite; —**токсин** *m.* (chem.) picrotoxin; —**токсинин** *m.* picrotoxinin; —**фармаколит** *m.* (min.) picropharmacolite.

пиксел(ь) *m.* (comp.) pixel.

пиксидий *m.* (bot.) pyxidium.

пикто— *prefix* picto— (pictorial); —**грамма** *f.* pictogram; (comp.) icon; —**графический** *a.* (archeol.) pictographic; —**графия** *f.* pictograph; pictography.

пик-трансформатор *m.* (elec.) peak(ing) transformer.

Пиктэ-Шпенглера реакция (chem.) Pictet-Spengler reaction.

пикули *pl.* pickles, gherkins.

пикульник *m.* hemp nettle (*Galeopsis*).

пикфактор *m.* (elec.) peak factor.

пикш/а *f.* (ichth.) haddock (*Melanogrammus aeglefinus*); —**уй** *m.* small haddock.

пил *past m. sing.* of **пить;** *gen. pl.* of **пила.**

ПИЛ *abbr.* (**прибор для измерения липкости почвы**) soil adhesiveness meter.

пила *f.* saw; *sometimes* file; (bot.) Pila; *past f. sing. of* **пить; п. одноручка** handsaw; **п. по дереву** wood saw; **круглая п.** circular saw, disk saw.

пилав *m.* pilaf, stewed rice.

пила-дровянка *f.* two-man crosscut saw; **п.-ножовка** *f.* hack saw; **п.-рыба** *f.* (ichth.) sawfish (*Pristis,* spec. *P. pectinatus*); **п.-рыбы** *see* пилы-рыбы.

пиленгас *m.* (ichth.) mullet (*Mugil so-iuy*).

пил/ение *n.* sawing; filing; —**ё(н)ный** *a.* sawed, precut; filed; lump (sugar).

пилефлебит *m.* (med.) pylephlebitis.

пилея *f.* (bot.) Pilea.

пили *past pl.* of **пить.**

пилиганин *m.* (chem.) piliganine.

пилигримовый стан *see* пильгер-стан.

пилидий *m.* (bot.; zool.) pilidium.

пилиль/ный *a.* saw(ing); filing; —**щик** *m.* sawyer; (ent.) sawfly; (zool.) slug (*Caliroa*); —**щики** *pl.* (ent.) Tenthredinidae; **злаковые, стеблёвые** *or* **хлебные** —**щики** (ent.) Cephidae; **паутинные** —**щики, щик-ткачи** *pl.* Pamphili(i)dae; —**щик-минер** *m.* Hoplocampa.

пилиров/ание *n.* milling; —**ать** *v.* mill, grind (soap).

пилит *m.* (min.) pilite.

пил/ить *v.* saw; file; —**ка** *f.* sawing; filing; fret saw; file.

пиллерс *m.* (naut.) pillars, (deck) stanchion.

пиллинг *m.* (text.) pilling.

пило— *prefix* pilo— (hair); saw; —**аррекции** *pl.* (med.) piloerection; —**боловые** *pl.* (bot.) Pilobolaceae; —**брюхие** *pl.* (ichth.) Pristigasterinae; —**видный** *see* **пилообразный; —вочник** *m.* saw log; —**вочный** *a.* saw, for sawing; —**заточный** *a.* saw-sharpening; —**зубые** *pl.* lancetfishes (*Alepisauridae*).

пилозин *m.* (bioch.) pilosine.

пилокарп/ин *m.* pilocarpine; —**иновый** *a.* pilocarpic (acid); —**ус** *m.* (bot.) Pilocarpus.

пилолит *m.* (min.) pilolite.

пило/материал *m.* lumber, (sawn) timber; —**машина** *f.* power saw.

пиломоторный *a.* (physiol.) pilomotor.

пилон *m.* pylon, tower; pillar; pier.

пилонасекательный *a.* file-cutting.

пилонный *a.* of **пилон.**

пило/нос *m.* (ichth.) saw shark (*Pristiophorus*); —**носы** *pl.* Pristiophoridae; —**образный** *a.* sawtooth, serrate, saw-like, dentate, notched; shed (roof).

пилоповый *a.* pilopic (acid).

пило/прав *m.* saw fitter; **—продукция** *f.* sawn timber; **—рама** *f.* frame saw; saw frame.

пилор/ит *m.* (med.) pyloritis; **—ический** *a.* (anat.; zool.) pyloric; **—ические придатки** (zool.) pyloric caeca; **—о—** *prefix* pylor(o)— (pylorus); **—оспазм** *m.* (med.) pylorospasm.

пило/рот *m.* (ichth.) Serrivomer; **—руб** *m.* file cutter.

пилорус *m.* (anat.) pylorus.

пило/рыл *see* **пила-рыба**; **—сошниковые** *pl.* (ichth.) deep-sea eels (*Serrivomeridae*).

пилот *m.* pilot; pilotfish (*Naucrates ductor*); **—аж** *m.*, **—ажный** *a.* piloting, flying; acrobatics, aerobatics; **—ажно-навигационный** *a.* flight, navigation (instruments); **—ажно-проекционный** *a.* head-up (display).

пилотакситовый *a.* (petr.) pilotaxitic.

пилотир/ование *n.* piloting, etc., *see v.*; **—овать** *v.* pilot, fly; man, handle; **—уемый** *a.* piloted, etc., *see v.*; **—ующий** *a.* piloting, etc., *see v.*

пилотка *f.* (mil.) field cap.

пилотная установка pilot plant.

пилоточный *a.* saw-sharpening.

пилот/-сигнал *m.* pilot signal; **—ский** *a.* pilot's(s).

пило/усы *pl.* (ent.) Heteroceridae; **—хвост** *m.* Paecilimon; (ichth.) dogfish (*Pristiurus melanostomus*); **—штамп** *m.* saw swage (shaping tool).

пилоцереин *m.* (chem.) pilocereine.

пилы *pl., gen., etc. of* **пила**; **п.-рыбы** *pl.* sawfishes (*Pristidae*).

пильбарит *m.* (min.) pilbarite.

пильгер-стан *m.* pilger mill (for pipes).

пильный *a.* saw(ing); file; lump (sugar); **п. мастер** saw-sharpener; file cutter; **п. станок** bench saw; filing machine.

пильпеля *m.* pilpelya (mud volcano in Transcaucasia).

пильчард *m.* (ichth.) pilchard, sardine (*Sardina pilchardus*).

пиль/чато— *prefix* serrato—, serrate; prion(o)— (saw); **—чатозубчатый** *a.* (bot.) serrate-dentate; **—чатость** *f.* serration; **—чатый** *a.* sawtooth(ed), serrate, notched; **—щик** *m.* sawyer.

пилэ *n.* crushed sugar.

пилюл/ька *dim. of* **пилюля**; pellet; **—ьник** *m.* (ent.) pill bug; **—ьница** *f.* (bot.) Pilularia; **—ьный** *a. of* **пилюля**; **—ьщик** *m.* pill bug; **—ьщики** *pl.* Byrrhidae; **—я** *f.* pill, capsule, globule, pellet.

пилястр *m.*, **—а** *f.* pilaster, column.

пилящий *a.* sawing; filing.

пимаровая кислота pimaric acid.

пи-мезон *m.* (nucl.) pi-meson, pion.

пимел/(ин)ат *m.* (chem.) pimelate; **—инкетон** *m.* pimelic ketone, cyclohexanone; **—иновокислый** *a.* pimelic acid; pimelate (of); **—ит** *m.* (min.) pimelite; **—од** *m.* (ichth.) pimelodid catfish; **—одовые** *pl.* Pimelodidae.

пимент *m.*, **—овый** *a.* pimento; **—овая кислота** pimentic acid.

пи-месон *see* **пи-мезон**.

пимпинеллин *m.* (chem.) pimpinellin.

пимпла *f.* (ent.) Pimpla.

пимы *pl.* deerskin boots.

пинавердол *m.* pinaverdol (dye).

пинагор *m.* (ichth.) lumpfish (*Cyclopterus*, spec. *C. lumpus*); **—овые**, **—ы** *pl.* Cyclopteridae.

пинакиолит *m.* (min.) pinakiolite.

пинакоид *m.* (cryst.) pinacoid, pinakoid; **—альный** *a.* pinacoid(al).

пин/акол *see* **пинакон**; **—аколил** *m.*, **—аколиловый** *a.* (chem.) pinacolyl; **—аколин** *m.*, **—аколиновый** *a.* pinacolin, 3,3-dimethyl-2-butanone; **—акон** *m.*, **—аконовый** *a.* pinacol, pinacone, 2,3-dimethyl-2,3-butanediol; **—альдегид** *m.* pinaldehyde; **—ан** *m.* pinane, bicyclo-(2:4)-heptane; **—ацианол** *m.* pinacyanol.

пинг/вин *m.* (orn.) penguin; (chem.) pinguin, alantol; **—виновые**, **—вины** *pl.* (orn.) Spheniscidae; **—понг-механизм** *m.* (bioch.) ping-pong mechanism.

пинеальн/ый *a.* (anat.) pineal; **—ая железа** pineal gland, pineal body.

пинежский *a.* (geog.) Pinega.

пин/ен *m.*, **—еновый** *a.* (chem.) pinene; **—еоловый** *a.* pineolic (acid); **—иновый** *a.* pininic (acid); **—иолы** *pl.* pine nuts; **—ит** *m.* pinitol, cyclohexanepentol; (min.) pinite; **—ия** *f.* (bot.) stone pine (*Pinus pinea*).

пинк *m.* (cer.) pink (tin and chromium oxides); **—зальц** *m.* pink salt, ammonium stannic chloride.

пинктада *f.* (mal.) Pinctada.

пинн/а *f.* (mal.) pen shell (*Pinna*); **—оит** *m.* (min.) pinnoite; **—ула** *f.* (bot.; zool.) pinnule.

пино/вый *a.* pinic (acid); **—л** *m.* pinol, pine camphor; **—лин** *m.* pinoline, rosin spirit; **—лит** *m.* (petr.) pinolite; **—ловый** *a.* pinolic (acid).

пиноль *m.* tail spindle (of lathe).

пинон *m.*, **—овый** *a.* pinone, 6-oxypinol; **—овая кислота** pinonic acid.

пиноцит *m.* (cyt.) pinocyte; **—оз** *m.* pinocytosis.

пинский *a.* (geog.) Pinsk.

пинта *f.* pint (measure); (med.) pinta, azul.

пинтадилья *f.* (ichth.) Cheilodactylus variegatus.

пинтадоит *m.* (min.) pintadoite.

пинц/ет *m.* pincers, nippers, forceps, tweezers; extractor; **—етка** *f.* forceps, tweezers; **—ирование** *n.*, **—ировка** *f.* pinching (off), nipping.

пинче *m.* (mam.) a marmoset (*Leontocebus oedipus*).

пинчер *m.* Doberman pinscher (dog).

пинч-эффект *m.* pinch effect.

пинь/ейро *n.* (geobot.) pinheiro (subtropical forest); **—ола** *f.* pine nut; **—яда** *f.* (geobot.) pinada; **—яль** *m.* pinal.

пио— *prefix* pyo— (pus); **—бациллёз** *m.* (vet.) pyobacillosis; **—генный** *a.* pyogenic; **—дермия** *f.* pyoderm(i)a; **—ксантин** *m.* pyoxanthine (pigment); **—ктанин** *m.* pyoktanin, gentian violet; **—липовый** *a.* pyolipic (acid); **—метра** *f.* (med.) pyometra; **—миозит** *m.* pyomyositis.

пион *m.* (bot.) peony (*Paeonia*); (nucl.) pi-meson, pion.

пионер *m.*, **—ка** *f.*, **—ный**, **—ский** *a.* pioneer, fore runner, precursor; pioneer plant.

пионефроз *m.* (med.) pyonephrosis.

пионов/ые *pl.* (bot.) Paeoniaceae; **—ый** *a.* peony.

пио/пневмо— *prefix* (med.) pyopneumo—; **—поэз** *m.* pyopoiesis, pus formation; **—(р)рея** *f.* pyorrhea.

пиоскоп *m.* pioscope (for estimating fat content of milk).

пио-соединение *n.* Pyo (antibiotic).

пиотин *m.* (min.) piotine, saponite.

пиоторакс *m.* (med.) pyothorax, empyema.

пиоуйский *a.* (geog.) Piaui, Piauhy.

пиофилиды *pl.* (ent.) Piophilidae.

пио/цефалия *f.* (med.) pyocephalus; **—цианин** *m.* pyocyanin, cyopin; **—цианиновый** *a.* pyocyanic; pyocyanogenic; **—цистит** *m.* (med.) pyocystitis.

пипа *f.* (amph.) Pipa.

пипеколин *m.* (chem.) pipecline, methyl piperidine; **—овый** *a.* pipecol(in)ic (acid).

пипер/аз(ид)ин *m.* (chem.) piperaz(id)ine, diethylene diamine; **—амид** *m.* piperamide, piperic acid amide.

пиперид/ил *m.* (chem.) piperidyl; **—ин** *m.*, **—иновый** *a.* piperidine, hexahydropyridine; **—иниевые соединения** piperidinium compounds; **—инкарбоновый** *a.* piperidinecarboxylic (acid); **—овый** *a.* piperidic (acid).

пипер/ил *m.* (chem.) piperyl; **—илен** *m.* piperylene, pentadiene; **—ин** *m.* piperine, piperylpiperidine; **—иновая кислота** piperic acid; **—итон** *m.* piperitone; **—онал** *m.* piperonal, heliotropin; **—онил** *m.* piperonyl; **—ониловый** *a.* piperonylic (acid).

пипет/ировать *v.* (chem.) pipet(te); **—ка** *f.* pipet(te); (medicine) dropper; **—ка без градуировки, —ка с одной меткой** transfer pipet; **обыкновенная —ка, простая —ка** calibrated pipet; **—очный** *a.* pipet(te).

пипитзаоиновый *a.* pipitzahoic (acid).

пиповые *pl.* (amph.) Pipidae.

пипра *f.* (orn.) manakin (*Pipra*).

пир *m.* (ichth.) grayling (*Thymallus th.*).

ПИР *abbr.* (**привод, индивидуальный на ротор**) individual transmission of the rotary table.

пир— *prefix* pyr(o)— (fire, heat); **—авста** *f.* (ent.) Pyrausta; **—азин** *m.* (chem.) pyrazine.

пиразол *m.* (chem.) pyrazole, 1,2-diazole; **—идин** *m.* pyrazolidine, tetrahydropyrazole; **—идон** *m.* pyrazolidone, ketopyrazolidine; **—ил** *m.* pyrazolyl; **—ин** *m.* pyrazoline, dihydropyrazole; **—овый** *a.* pyrazole, pyrazolic; **—ол** *m.* pyrazolol; **—он** *m.*, **—оновый** *a.* pyrazolone, ketopyrazoline.

пира/йя *see* **пиранья; —канта** *f.* (bot.) Pyracantha; **—конитин** *m.* (chem.) pyraconitine; **—ллолит** *m.* (min.) pyrallolite; **—меис** *m.* (ent.) Pyrameis.

пирамид/а *f.* pyramid; rack, frame; (anat.) pyramis; **—ально-метельчатый** *a.* (bot.) thyrsoid; **—альный** *a.* pyramidal, taper(ed); **—альный куб** tetrahexahedron; **—ка** *dim. of* **пирамида; (bot.) thyrse; —ный** *a.* pyramid(al); **—он** *m.* (pharm.) Pyramidon, aminopyrine.

пиран *m.* (chem.) pyran.

Пирани манометр Pirani gage.

пиран/ил *m.* (chem.) pyranyl; **—ограф** *m.* (phys.) pyranograph; **—оза** *f.*, **—озный** *a.* (chem.) pyranose; **—озид** *m.* pyranoside; **—ометр** *m.* pyranometer (for measuring solar radiation); **—трен** *m.* (chem.) pyranthrene; **—ьевые** *pl.* (ichth.) piranhas (*Serrasalmidae*); **—ья** *f.* piranha.

пираргирит *m.* (min.) pyrargyrite.

пират/-окунь *m.* (ichth.) pirate perch (*Aphredoderus sayanus*); **—оокуневые** *pl.* Aphredoderidae; **—ство** *n.* piracy.

пир/ацин *m.* (chem.) pyracine; **—гелиометр** *m.* (meteor.) pyrheliometer; **—геометр** *m.* pyrgeometer; **—гоморфиды** *pl.* (ent.) Pyrgomorphidae; **—екс-трубки** *pl.* Pyrex (glass) tubes; **—ен** *m.* (chem.) pyrene, benzo(*def*)phenanthrene; *prefix see* **пирено—**.

Пиренеи the Pyrenees.

пиренейский *a.* (geog.) Pyrenean.

пирен/о— *prefix* pyren(o)— (fruit stone); **—овый** *a.* pyrenic (acid); **—оид** *m.*, **—оидный** *a.* (bot.; prot.) pyrenoid; **—омицеты** *pl.* (bot.) Pyrenomycetes.

пирет/огенный *a.* (med.) pyretogenic, fever-producing; **—ол** *m.* solution of pyrethrin in alcohol; **—рин** *m.* (chem.) pyrethrin; **—рум** *m.* (bot.) Pyrethrum.

Пири Peary (explorer).

пирибол *m.* (petr.) pyribole.

пиридаз/ин *m.* (chem.) pyridazine, 1,2-diazine; **—инон** *m.* pyridazinone; **—он** *m.* pyridazone, 3-ketopyridazine.

пиридил *m.* (chem.) pyridyl.

пиридин *m.* (chem.) pyridine; **—зависимый** *a.* pyridine-

linked; **—иевый** *a.*, **—ий** *m.* pyridinium; **—нуклеотид** *m.* pyridine nucleotide; **—овый** *a.* pyridine; **—фермент** *m.* pyridine enzyme.

пиридокс/алевый *a.*, **—аль** *m.* (bioch.) pyridoxal; **—альфосфат** *m.* pyridoxal phosphate; **—амин** *m.* pyridoxamine; **—иловый, —иновый** *a.* pyridoxic (acid); **—ин** *m.* pyridoxine, vitamin B$_6$.

пир/идон *m.* (chem.) pyridone, ketopyridine; **—илиевый** *a.*, **—илий** *m.* pyrylium (cation).

пирит *m.* (min.) pyrite; pyrites; **—изация** *f.* pyritization; **—изировать** *v.* pyritize; **—ный, —овый** *a.* pyritic; **—ная плавка** (met.) pyritic smelting; **—ные огарки** pyrite cinders.

пирито/ид *m.* (cryst.) pyritoid, pyritohedron, pentagonal dodecahedron; **—логия** *f.* pyritology; **—подобный** *a.* pyritiform, resembling pyrite; **—содержащий** *a.* pyritiferous; **—эдр** *see* **пиритоид; —эдрический** *a.* pyritohedral.

Пирке реакция (med.) Pirquet('s) reaction.

пиро— *prefix* (fire, heat; fever); **—антимонат** *m.* (chem.) pyroantimonate; **—арсенат** *m.* pyroarsenate; **—аурит** *m.* (min.) pyroaurite; **—белонит** *m.* (min.) pyrobelonite; **—бензол** *m.* pyrobenzol (high-octane gasoline additive); **—битум** *m.* (min.) pyrobitumen; **—болт** *m.* (rockets) explosive bolt; **—борат** *m.* (chem.) pyroborate, tetraborate; **—борнокислый** *a.* pyroboric acid, tetraboric acid; pyroborate, tetraborate (of); **—ванадат** *m.* pyrovanadate; **—ванадиевокислый** *a.* pyrovanadic acid; pyrovanadate (of).

пировин/ная кислота pyrotartaric acid; **—нокислый** *a.* pyrotartaric acid; pyrotartrate; **—оградная кислота** pyroracemic acid, pyruvic acid.

пирог *m.* pie; mass; (sinter) cake.

пирогаз *m.* pyrolysis gas.

пирогалл/овая кислота, —ол *m.* pyrogallic acid, pyrogallol; **—овокислый** *a.* pyrogallic acid; pyrogallate (of).

пирогелит *m.* (min.) pyrogelite.

пироген *m.* (dyes) pyrogene; (med.) pyrogen; **—етический** *a.* pyrogenetic, heat-producing, heat-produced; **—(из)ация** *f.* pyrolysis; **—ный** *a.* (geol.) pyrogenic, igneous; (med.) pyrogenic; **—овый** *a.* pyrogene (dye).

пиро/глобулин *m.* (bioch.) pyroglobulin; **—гностика** *f.* (min.) pyrognostics; **—головка** *f.* explosive cap; **—графит** *m.* pyrolytic graphite; **—дин** *m.* (chem.) pyrodin, acetylphenylhydrazine.

пирож/ное *n.* pastry; **—ный** *a.* of; **—ок** *dim. of* **пирог.**

пиро/замок *m.* (rockets) separation charge; **—запал** *m.* cartridge igniter, squib; **—заряд** *m.* explosive charge; **—катехин** *m.* (chem.) pyrocatechol, 1,2-benzenediol; **—керам** *m.* Pyroceram (microcrystalline glass); **—кислота** *f.* pyro acid; **—клапан** *m.* pyrotechnic valve, explosive valve; **—кластический** *a.* (petr.) pyroclastic; **—колл** *m.* (chem.) pyrocoll; **—коллодион** *m.* pyrocollodion, nitrocellulose; **—коэффициент** *m.* pyroelectric coefficient; **—кремнекислый** *a.* pyrosilicic acid; pyrosilicate (of).

пироксен *m.* (min.) pyroxene; **—ит** *m.* (petr.) pyroxenite; **—овый** *a.* pyroxene, pyroxenic.

пироксилин *m.*, **—овый** *a.* (expl.) pyroxylin, guncotton; **—овый порох** pyropowder.

пироксмангит *m.* (min.) pyroxmangite.

пиро/лигнит *m.* (chem.) pyrolignite; **—лиз** *m.* pyrolysis, decomposition by heat; steam cracking (of ethane or naptha); **потери при —лизе** loss on ignition, L.O.I.; **—литический** *a.* pyrolytic; **—логия** *f.* pyrology, blowpipe analysis; **—люзит** *m.* (min.) pyrolusite; **—магнетизм** *m.* pyromagnetism; **—магнитный** *a.*

pyromagnetic; —**мекаин** *m.* (pharm.) pyromecaine; —**меллитовый** *a.* pyromellitic (acid); —**металлургия** *f.* pyrometallurgy; —**метаморфизм** *m.* (geol.) pyrometamorphism.

пирометр *m.* pyrometer; —**ический** *a.* pyrometric, pyrometer; **огнеупорность по —ическому конусу** pyrometric cone equivalent, PCE; —**ия** *f.* pyrometry.

пироморф/ит *m.* (min.) pyromorphite; —**ный** *a.* pyromorphous.

пиромышьяков/истокислый *a.* pyroarsenous acid; pyroarsenite (of); —**окислый** *a.* pyroarsenic acid, diarsenic acid; pyroarsenate (of).

пирон *m.* pin, dowel; (chem.) pyrone.

пиронафт *m.* lighthouse lamp kerosene.

пирон/ин *m.* (histol.) pyronine; —**карбоновый** *a.* pyronecarboxylic (acid).

пироп *m.* (min.) pyrope.

пиропатрон *m.* flare cartridge, pyrotechnic cartridge, squib, explosive charge.

пирописсит *m.* (min.) pyropissite.

пиропистолет *m.* explosive gear.

пироплазм/а *f.* (prot.) Piroplasma, Babesia; —**оз** *m.* piroplasmosis, babesiasis, Babesia infection; —**оцидный** *a.* piroplasmicidal.

пиропроводимость *f.* pyroconductivity.

пироретин *m.* pyroretin (a coal resin).

пиросвеча *f.* igniter, squib.

пиросерн/ая кислота pyrosulfuric acid, disulfuric acid; **хлорангидрид —ой кислоты** pyrosulfuryl chloride; —**истокалиевая соль** potassium pyrosulfite; —**истокислый** *a.* pyrosulfurous acid; pyrosulfite (of); —**о-кислый** *a.* pyrosulfuric acid; pyrosulfate, disulfate (of).

пиросиликат *m.* (chem.) pyrosilicate.

пироскоп *m.* (phys.) pyroscope, Seger (polymetric) cone.

пирослизев/ая кислота pyromucic acid, furan-2-carboxylic acid; —**окислая соль** pyromucate.

пиро/смалит *m.* (min.) pyrosmalite; —**стат** *m.* pyrostat, high-temperature thermostat; —**стартер** *m.* cartridge starter; —**стильпнит** *m.* (min.) pyrostilpnite; —**сульфат** *m.* (chem.) pyrosulfate; —**сульфит** *m.* pyrosulfite; —**сульфурил** *m.* pyrosulfuryl; —**сурьмянокислый** *a.* pyroantimonic acid; pyroantimonate (of).

пиросфера *f.* (geol.) pyrosphere, barysphere.

пиротехни/ка *f.* pyrotechnics; —**ческий** *a.* pyrotechnic; —**ческие изделия** fireworks.

пироуксусн/ая кислота pyroligneous acid, pyracetic acid; —**окислая соль** pyrolignite; —**окальциевая соль** calcium pyrolignite.

пирофан *m.* (min.) pyrophane; —**ит** *m.* (min.) pyrophanite.

пирофиллит *m.* (min.) pyrophyllite.

пирофит *m.* pyrophyte, fire-resistant plant; —**овые водоросли** Pyrophyta.

пирофор *m.* (chem.) pyrophore; (ent.) Pyrophorus; —**ный** *a.* pyrophoric, spontaneously igniting.

пирофос *m.* (chem.) tetraethyl monothiopyrophosphate; —**фат** *m.* pyrophosphate; —**фатаза** *f.* pyrophosphatase; —**фит** *m.* pyrophosphite; —**форил** *m.* pyrophosphoryl.

пирофосфор/илаза *f.* (chem.) pyrophosphorylase; —**истокислый** *a.* pyrophosphorous acid; pyrophosphite (of); —**нокислый** *a.* pyrophosphoric acid; pyrophosphate (of); —**нонатриевая соль** sodium pyrophosphate; —**ный** *a.* pyrophosphoric (acid); pyrophosphate (bond).

пиро/химия *f.* pyrochemistry; —**хлор** *m.* (min.) pyrochlore; —**хроит** *m.* (min.) pyrochroite; —**хромат** *m.* (chem.) pyrochromate, dichromate.

пироэлектричес/кий *a.* (cryst.) pyroelectric; —**тво** *n.* pyroelectricity.

пироэффект *m.* pyroelectric effect.

пирр— *prefix* pyrr— (flame-colored); —**иа** *f.* (ent.) Pyrrhia; —**ил** *m.* (chem.) pyrrolyl; —**ит** *m.* pyrrhite.

пирро— *prefix* pyrr(h)o—; —**диазол** *m.* (chem.) pyrrodiazole; —**ил** *m.* pyrroyl; —**колин** *m.* pyrrocoline, 8-pyrrolopyridine.

пиррол *m.* (chem.) pyrrole, azole; —**енин** *m.* pyrrolenine; —**идил** *m.* pyrrolidyl; —**идин** *m.* pyrrolidine, tetrahydropyrrole; —**идон** *m.* pyrrolidone; —**илен** *m.* pyrrolylene, 1,3-butadiene; —**ин** *m.* pyrroline, dihydropyrrole; —**овый** *a.* pyrrole, pyrrolic; —**рот** *m.* pyrrole red; —**ьный** *a.* pyrrole.

пирро/тин, —тит *m.* (min.) pyrrhotine, pyrrhotite, magnetic pyrite.

пиррулина *f.* (ichth.) Pyrrhulina.

пире *m.* (naut.) pier.

Пирса печь Pearce (turret) furnace.

пирсинг-процесс *m.* (roll-)piercing process; **стан пирсинг** piercing mill.

Пирсона коэффициент Pearson's coefficient.

пирссонит *m.* (min.) pirssonite.

пирув/ат *m.* (chem.) pyruvate; —**атдекарбоксилаза** *f.* pyruvate decarboxylase; —**аткиназа** *f.* pyruvate kinase; —**овый** *a.* pyruvic (acid); —**одекарбоксилаза** *see* **пируватдекарбоксилаза.**

пирула *f.* (mal.) fig shell (*Pyrula*).

пирцеит *m.* (min.) pearceite.

писание *n.* writing.

писанит *see* **пизанит.**

писанный *a.* written.

писар/ка *f.* (ichth.) Alburnoides bipunctatus, spec. A. b. rossicus; —**ский, —ской** *a.* clerk's; —**ь** *m.* clerk.

писасфальт *m.* (min.) pissasphalt.

пис/атель *m.* writer, author; —**ательство** *n.* writing; —**ать** *v.* write; type.

пи-связь *f.* pi-bond.

писем *gen. pl. of* **письмо.**

писк *m.* squeak; peep, chirp.

пискарь *see* **пескарь.**

писк/ливый, —лявый *a.* squeaky, squeaking; —**нуть** *see* **пищать;** —**отня** *f.* squeaking; peeping, chirping; —**улька** *f.* (orn.) peeping goose (*Anser erythropus*); —**ун** *m.* (ent.) water beetle (*Berosus*); (ichth.) loach; gudgeon; lamprey; —**уны** *pl.* (ent.) Culicidae; —**унья** *f.* Syritta pipiens.

Пис-Ривер (geog.) Peace River.

писсуар *m.* urinal.

пистаколовая кислота pistacolic acid.

пистацит *m.* (min.) pistacite, epidote.

пистиллодий *m.* (bot.) pistillode.

пистолет *m.* pistol; (welding) gun; nozzle; **п.-напылитель, п.-распылитель** *m.* paint sprayer or spray gun; —**ный** *a. of* **пистолет; п.-пулемёт** *m.* submachine gun.

пистомезит *m.* (min.) pistomesite.

пистон *m.* (percussion) cap, blasting cap; primer; piston, valve; grommet; —**чик** *m.* eyelet.

писци/диновый *a.* piscidic (acid); —**дия** *f.* (bot.) Piscidia; —**кола** *f.* (zool.) Piscicola; —**колёз** *m.* (vet.) piscicolosis, fish leech infestation; —**культура** *f.* (ichth.) pisciculture.

писч/ебумажный *a.* stationery, paper; **п. товар,** —**ебумажная бумага** writing paper, stationery; —**ий** *a.* writing; —**ая судорога** writer's cramp; —**ее перо** (anat.) calamus scriptorius.

пис/ывать *v.* write; —**ьмена** *pl.* characters, letters;

—**ьменно** *adv.* in writing, by letter; —**ьменность** *f.* written language.

письменн/ый *a.* writing, written, recorded; (petr.) graphic; **п. стол** desk; —**ая руда** (min.) graphic ore, sylvanite; —**ые принадлежности** stationery.

письмо *n.* letter; writing; script; —**водитель** *m.* clerk; —**водство** *n.* clerical work; —**носец** *m.* mailman, mail carrier.

питаемый *a.* fed.

питан/ие *n.* feed(ing), nourishment, nutrition, sustenance, food; loading, charging; (power) supply; source; alimentation (of river); recharge (of ground water); **блок** —**ия, источник** —**ия** (elec. comm.) power pack; **изучение по** —**ию** nutritional study; **линия** —**ия** feed line; **народное п., общественное п.** public eating facilities; —**недостаточность** —**ия** malnutrition; **обратное п.** feedback; **продукты** —**ия** foodstuffs; **резервуар** —**ия** feed tank; **с двойным** —**ием** dual-feed; **с** —**ием от батареи** battery-operated; **химия** —**ия** food chemistry.

питатель *m.* feeder; supply unit; (casting) gate, runner; **п.-дозатор** *m.* batcher; —**ность** *f.* food value, nutritive value.

питательн/ый *a.* feed(ing), feeder; nourishing, nutritious, food, dietary; alimentary, nutritional, nutrient; culture (medium); storage (tank); foliage (spraying); **п. кран** feed cock; **п. микроэлемент** micronutrient; **п. прибор** feeder; —**ая труба** feed pipe, supply pipe; —**ая установка** source; —**ая ценность** food value; —**ое вещество** nutriment, nutrient, food(stuff); —**ые соки** (bot.) sap.

пит/ать *v.* feed, deliver, supply; load, charge; nourish; maintain; —**аться** *v.* feed (on), live (on); be fed, draw current (from), be powered (by), operate (from); —**ающий** *a.* feed(ing); nourishing; power supply; supply (tank); nurse (cell); —**ающий механизм** feeder; —**ающий провод** (elec.) power lead; —**ающая оболочка** (embr.) trophamnion; —**ающая труба** feed pipe, feed line; —**ающийся** *a.* feeding (on); operated, powered (by).

питек— *prefix* pithec— (ape); —**антроп** *m.* Pithecanthropus.

питиевые *pl.* (bot.) Pythiaceae.

питириаз *m.* (med.) pityriasis.

питкарлодер *m.* (min.) pit car loader.

Пито трубка Pitot tube, Pitot's gage.

питометр *m.* (hydr.) pitometer.

питом/ец *m.,* —**ица** *f.* foster child, ward, charge; pupil; alumnus; —**ник** *m.* (hort.) nursery; (zool.) vivarium; **селекционный** —**ник** breeding farm; —**никовод** *m.* nursery man; —**ниководство** *n.* nursery work, plant rearing; —**ниководческое** *or* —**ническое хозяйство** nursery.

пито/н *m.* (herp.) python; (pharm.) Piton; (orn.) common shearwater (*Puffinus p.*); —**цин** *m.* (pharm.) Pitocin, oxytocin.

питский *a.* (geog.) Pit.

питт/а *f.* (orn.) Pitta; —**ер** *m.* (oil) Petter (engine); —**инг** *m.,* —**инговый** *a.* pitting (corrosion); —**инит** *m.* (min.) pittinite; —**ицит** *m.* pitticite; —**овые** *pl.* (orn.) Pittidae.

питуит/арный *a.* (anat.) pituitary; —**арная железа** pituitary gland, hypophysis; —**рин** *m.* Pituitrin (extract).

питч *m.,* —**евой** *a.* pitch (of gear); —**евая резьба** worm thread.

Питчера насос Pitcher pump.

пить *v.* drink; —**ё** *n.* drink, beverage; drinking; **годный для** —**я,** —**евой** *a.* potable, drinking (water).

пиурия *f.* (med.) pyuria.

пифагорский *a.* Pythagorean (proposition).

пи-фотомезон *m.* (nucl.) photo-pion.

пих/ать, —**нуть** *v.* push, shove; stuff.

пихт/а *f.* (bot.) fir (*Abies*); —**арник,** —**ач** *m.* fir grove; —**овый** *a.* fir, abietic; —**ообразный** *a.* abietinous, fir-like.

пиц/еин *m.* (chem.) picein; —**ен** *m.* picene; —**еновый** *a.* picenic (acid); —**ит** *m.* (min.) picite, pizite.

Пичи способ (rub.) Peachey process.

пич/ковый *a.,* —**ок** *dim. of* **пик;** spike, spiking.

пичу/га, —**жка** *f.* little bird.

пич-пайн *m.* (bot.) pitch pine, yellow pine (*Pinus australis*).

Пише испаритель Piché evaporimeter.

пишет *pr. 3 sing. of* **писать.**

пишущ/ий *a.* writing; recording; printing (wheel); —**ая машинка** typewriter.

пищ/а *f.* food(stuff), nutriment, nourishment, nutrition, sustenance; **годный в** —**у** edible.

пищать *v.* squeak, peep; buzz.

пищевар/ение *n.* digestion; **плохое п.** indigestion; —**ительный** *a.* digestive, peptic; alimentary (canal).

пищевик *m.* worker in food industry.

пище/вкусовой *a.* flavoring; —**вод** *m.* (anat.) esophagus; gullet; —**водно**— *prefix* esophago—; —**водно-слюнный** *a.* esophagosalivary (reflex); —**водный** *a.* esophageal; —**вой** *a.* food (industry, etc.); dietary; nutritional; edible, table; alimentary, nutritive; —**вой продукт** foodstuff; —**вой рацион,** —**вой режим** diet; —**вой сок** (physiol.) chyle; —**вая кашица** chyme; —**концентратный** *a.* food concentrate; —**пром** *m.* food industry; —**промышленный** *a.* food-processing.

пищик *m.* buzzer, ticker; (car) horn.

пищух/а *f.* (mam.) pika, whistling hare (*Ochotona*); (orn.) creeper (*Certhia*); —**и,** —**овые** *pl.* (mam.) Ochotonidae; (orn.) Certhiidae.

пиэ— *see also under* **пие**—; —**лит** *m.* (med.) pyelitis; —**мия** *f.* pyemia.

пиявк/а *f.* (zool.) leech; —**и** *pl.* Hirudinea(e); **хоботные** —**и** Rhynchobdellae; —**орот** *m.* (ichth.) hagfish (*Eptatretus*).

ПК *abbr.* (**персональный компьютер**) personal computer, PC.

ПКБ *abbr.* (**проектно-конструкторское бюро**) planning and design office.

ПКЖ *abbr.* (**крупнопанельная железобетонная плита**) large reinforced concrete slab.

ПКО *abbr.* (**противокосмическая оборона**) astrodefense, antisatellite defense.

пл, ПЛ (*abbr.* (**подводная лодка**) submarine; **ПЛ** (**подвижная лаборатория**) mobile laboratory; **ПЛ** (**плёнка**) film; **пл.** (**плавление; плоскость; площадь**); **п.л.** (**печатный лист**) printer's sheet.

ПЛА *abbr.* (**подводная лодка, атомная**) nuclear(-powered) submarine.

плав *m.* float(ing), drift(ing); melt, fusion; (chem.) fusion cake; **засыпать на** —**у** *v.* (leather) lay away; **на** —**у** *adv.* afloat; —**ание** *n.* floating, etc., *see v.;* navigation; voyage, trip, run; **в** —**ании** *adv.* at sea; **выходить в** —**ании** *v.* put to sea; —**ательный** *a.* floating, flotation, non-sinkable; swimming, natatorial; —**ательный пузырь** (ichth.) swim(ming) bladder, air bladder; —**ательная перепонка** (zool.) web; —**ать** *v.* float, swim; navigate, sail, ply; —**ающие** *pl.* natators, swimmers; (amph.) Nectridia; —**ающий** *a.* floating, etc., *see v.;* amphibious (vehicle); (nucl.) swimming-pool

(reactor); —**ающий автомобиль** amphibian; —**ающая запятая**, —**ающая точка** (comp.) floating
point; —**база** *f.* floating base, mother ship; —**ёж** *m.*
(ichth.) surface feeders.

плавен *sh. m. of* **плавный.**

плавень *m.* flux, fusing agent.

плавик *m.,* —**овый шпат** (min.) fluorspar, fluorite;
—**овый** *a.* fluoric; —**овая кислота** hydrofluoric
acid; —**овый соль** —**овой кислоты** fluoride.

плавильник *see* **плавильный горшок.**

плавильн/ый *a.* melting; (met.) smelting; **п. горшок**
crucible, melting pot; **п. жар** fusion temperature; **п.
завод** *see* **плавильня; п. журнал** (met.) charge book;
—**ая печь** smelting furnace, smelter; —**я** *f.* foundry,
smelter(y).

плав/ильщик *m.* founder, smelter, furnace operator;
—**итель** *m.* melter; —**ить** *v.* melt, fuse, flux; (met.)
smelt; float; —**иться** *v.* melt, fuse; blow out (of fuse);
float; —**ка** *f.* melting, fusing, fusion; smelting; melt,
heat, tap, cast, charge; **доводка** —**ки** heat finishing.

плавк/ий *a.* fusible, meltable; liquefiable; (met.) smelt-
able; melting; **п. камень** (min.) mizzonite, dipyre; **п.
предохранитель, п. штепсель,** —**ая вставка,**
—**ая пробка** (elec.) fuse; —**ая проволока** (elec.)
fuse (wire); —**ость** *f.* fusibility, meltability; fusion;
liquescence.

плавлен/ие *n.* fusion, melting, liquefaction; (phys.) melt;
(met.) smelting; (open-hearth process) melting down
period; **сварка** —**ием** fusion welding; **сырое п.** ore
smelting; **температура** —**ия, точка** —**ия** melting
point; **теплота** —**ия** heat of fusion; —**(н)ый** *a.*
melted, etc., *see* **плавить;** sintered; floated; processed
(cheese).

плавн/евый *a.,* —**и** *pl.* flood plain, flooded areas.

плавни/к *m.,* —**ковый** *a.* (ichth.) fin; (zool.) flipper;
driftwood; **брюшной п.** pelvic fin; **спинной п.** dorsal
fin; —**ковидный,** —**кообразный** *a.* pinniform, fin-
shaped; —**чок** *m.* (ichth.) finlet.

плавн/о *adv.* gradually, etc., *see a.;* step by step, little by
little; —**ой** *a.* drift (net); —**опеременный** *a.* continuously variable; —**орегулируемый** *a.* continuously adjustable; —**ость** *f.* smoothness, evenness, continuity;
facility; —**ый** *a.* gradual, smooth, even, continuous;
fluent, flowing.

плав/ок *gen. pl. of* **плавка;** *sh. m. of* **плавкий;**
—**очный** *see* **плавильный.**

плавт *m.* (ent.) saucer bug (*Ilyocoris cimicoides*); —**ы** *pl.*
Naucoridae.

плавун *m.* quicksand; driftwood; (ent.) *see* **плавунец;**
(mam.) beaked whale (*Berardius*); water opossum
(*Chironectes minimus*); —**ец** *m.* (ent.) diving beetle
(*Dytiscus*); —**цы** *pl.* Dytiscidae; —**чик** *m.* (ent.) Hali-
plus; (orn.) phalarope (*Phalaropus*); —**чики** *pl.* (ent.)
Haliplidae; (orn.) Phaloropididae; —**ы** *pl.* (mam.)
beaked whales (*Ziphiidae*).

плавуч/есть *f.* floatability, buoyancy; —**ий** *a.* buoyant;
floating; pontoon (crane); —**ий рыбозавод** fish-
processing ship; —**ая база** tender, depot ship.

плавь *f.* pig iron for steel making.

плавящий *a.* melting, etc., *see* **плавить;** —**ся** *v.* melting; consumable (electrode).

плагиат *m.* plagiarism, plagiarizing.

плагио— *prefix* plagio— (slanting, oblique); —**гедри-
ческий** *a.* plagiohedral; —**гранит** *m.* (petr.) pla-
giogranite; —**клаз** *m.* (min.) plagioclase; —**клазовый** *a.* plagioclastic; —**нит** *m.* plagionite; —**сланец** *m.*
plagioslate, diopsidic slate; —**тропный** *a.* (bot.) pla-

giotropic; —**хила** *f.* (bot.) Plagiochila; —**хиловые** *pl.*
Plagiochilaceae.

плагировать *v.* plagiarize.

плаз *m.* (shipbuilding) mold loft.

плазм/а *f.* plasma; **физика** —**ы** plasma physics; —**аген**
m. (gen.) plasmagene; —**алемма** *f.* (cyt.) plasmalem-
ma, plasma membrane; —**алоген** *m.* (bioch.) plasmal-
ogen; —**атические** *pl.* (prot.) Plasmadroma; —**атический** *a.* plasm(at)ic; —**атрон** *m.* plasma generator;
—**ацитоклеточный** *a.* (med.) plasma cell; —**ачувст-
вительный** *a.* plasma-sensitive; —**енный** *a.* plasma;
plasma-filled (diode); plasma jet (spraying); —**енный
ракетный** *a.* plasmajet (engine); —**енный сгусток**
plasmoid; —**енный шнур** (nucl.) plasma column,
pinch; —**ид** *m.* (gen.) plasmid; —**ин** *m.* (bioch.) plas-
min, fibrinolysin.

плазмо— *prefix* plasmo—, plasma; —**гамия** *f.* (cyt.)
plasmogamy; —**ген** *m.* (gen.) plasmagene; (cyt.) plas-
mogen; —**генератор** *m.* plasma generator; —**десма** *f.*
(cyt.) plasmodesm(a); —**дий** *m.* (prot.) Plasmodium;
—**диофора** *f.* (bot.) Plasmodiophora; —**замещающий** *a.* plasma-substituting; —**клеточный** *a.* (med.)
plasma cell; —**лиз** *m.* (cyt.) plasmolysis; —**литический** *a.* plasmolytic; —**н** *m.* (gen.) plasmon; —**образование** *n.* plasma formation; —**сома** *f.* (cyt.) plasmosome; —**трон** *m.* plasmotron, plasma gun, (low-
temperature) plasma generator; —**химический** *a.*
plasma chemical; —**хин** *m.* (pharm.) Plasmochin,
pamaquine; —**цид** *m.* plasmocid, antimalarine; —**цит**
m. (cyt.) plasmocyte, plasma cell.

плайя *f.* (geol.) playa, salt pan.

плакат *m.,* —**ный** *a.* placard, poster, bill; **учебный п.**
wall chart; —**ный** *a.* lithographic (color).

плакать *v.* weep, cry; drip; get covered with condensate.

плакиров/ание *n.,* —**ка** *f.* cladding, etc., *see v.;* —**анный** *a.* clad, etc., *see v.;* —**ать** *v.* clad, plate; turf, sod.

плакода *f.* (embr.) placode.

плакоидный *a.* placoid, plate-shaped.

плак/орная трава, —**ун** *m.* (bot.) purple loosestrife
(*Lythrum salicaria*).

плакуна *f.* (mal.) Placuna.

плак/ун-трава *see* **плакун;** —**учий** *a.* drooping, weeping, pendant; —**учая ива** (bot.) weeping willow (*Salix
pendula*).

пламегаситель *m.* flame damper, flame-quenching additive; flash suppressor.

пламен/еть *v.* flame, blaze; —**еющий** *a.* flaming, blazing; ignescent, inflammatory; —**и** *gen. etc. of* **пламя;**
—**ник** *m.* torch; (bot.) phlox; —**нокрасный** *a.* fiery
red; —**но-фотометрический** *a.* (chem.) flame-
photometric.

пламенн/ый *a.* flame, flaming, fiery, ardent; warm (col-
or); bituminous (coal); **п. порог** fire bridge; —**ая печь**
reverberatory furnace; —**ая сажа** lamp black; —**ая
труба** flue.

плам/ень *see* **пламя;** —**еотражатель** *m.* flame deflector, blast shield; —**естойкий** *a.* flameproof; —**еуловитель** *m.* flame trap; —**я** *n.* flame, fire, blaze, flare,
flash; **мерцательное** —**я, ресничное** —**я** (zool.)
flame cell; **выбрасывание** —**ени** flareback; —**яфо-
тометр** *m.* (chem.) flame photometer.

план *m.* plan, scheme, proposal, project; design, layout;
draft; device; schedule, program; plane, surface; **в** —**е**
in terms of; proposed; **задний п.** background; **на первый п.** in the forefront; **передний п.** foreground;
составлять п. *v.* plan, design; —**аксиальный** *a.*
plane-axial.

план/а́рия *f.* (zool.) planarian (*Planaria*); **—а́рный** *a.* planar; **—а́ция** *f.* planation, stream erosion; flattening.

планге́рд *m.* (min.) racking table.

план-гра́фик *m.* schedule; Gantt chart.

планёр *m.* (av.) glider; airframe (of airplane).

планер/и́зм *m.* glider flying; **—и́ст** *m.* glider pilot.

планери́т *m.* (min.) planerite.

планёрный *a.* of **планёр**; glider-borne; **п. полёт** gliding.

планеродро́м *m.* glider airfield.

планёр-пари́тель *m.* sailplane.

плане́т *m.* (agr.) cultivator.

плане́та *f.* planet; **ма́лая п.** asteroid; **п.-гига́нт** *f.* giant planet; **—рий** *m.* planetarium; **—р(н)ый** *a.* planet(ary); global (climate); **—рный механи́зм, —ая переда́ча** planetary gear.

плане́тка *see* **плане́т**.

планзи́фтер *m.* plansifter (screen).

планиме́тр *m.* (geom.) planimeter; **—и́рование** *n.*, **—и́я** *f.* planimetry, plane geometry; planimetric measurement; **—и́ровать** *v.* compute area; **—и́рующий** *a.* integrating (indicator); **—и́ст** *m.* planimeter operator; **—и́ческий** *a.* planimetric.

плани́р *m.* leveler; (coke oven) leveling bar.

плани́р/ование *n.* planning, etc., *see v.*; (experiment) design; **—ова́ть** *v.* plan, project, propose; schedule (to start), program; design, lay out, systematize; grade, level, smooth, plane; glide, soar; size (paper); **—о́вка** *f.*, **—о́вочный** *a.* planning, etc., *see v.*; lay-out, design; (experimental) procedure; **—о́вщик** *m.* planner; (road) grader; leveler, smoother; scheduler, programmer; **—у́емый** *a.* planned, etc., *see v.*; **—у́ющий** *a.* planning, etc., *see v.*; gliding, glide; **—у́ющий полёт** hovering.

планисфе́р/а *f.*, **—ный** *a.* (astr.) planisphere.

пла́нка *f.* plank, lath, strip; cleat; (mach.) gib; plate, strap; (measuring) rod; (slide) bar; (hitch) rail; (paper) bedplate, beater plate; **закрепля́ть —ми** *v.* cleat; **п.-га́йка** *f.* (met.) lifting plate.

Пла́нка постоя́нная Planck's constant.

планкообра́зный *a.* (cryst.) lath-shaped.

планкт/и́ческий *a.* (biol.) plankton(ic); **—о́н** *m.* plankton; **озёрный —о́н, пресново́дный —о́н** limnoplankton; **оса́дочный —о́н** seston; **—о́нер** *m.* plankton organism; **—о́нный** *a.* plankton(ic); **—о́ноед** *m.* planktophage; **—о(но)ло́гия** *f.* planktology; **—о(но)я́дный** *a.* plankton-eating, planktotrophic; **—офа́г** *m.* planktophage, plankton eater.

пла́но— *prefix* plano— [plane (and); flatly; roaming, wandering, motile].

пла́нов/ать *see* **плани́ровать**; **—и́к** *m.* planner; **—о-предупреди́тельный** *a.* (scheduled) preventive, regular, routine; **—о-произво́дственный** *a.* planning and production; **—о-распреди́тельный** *a.* planning and distribution; **—о-сетево́й гра́фик** decision tree (in PERT); **—ость** *f.* plans; development according to plan; **—ый** *a.* planned, systematic, scheduled; planning; mapping (photography); vertical (aerial photograph); **—ое зада́ние** target, goal, plan, quota; **—ое хозя́йство** planned economy.

пла́но/гаме́та *f.* (gen.) planogamete; **—зиго́та** *f.* (bot.) planozygote; **—зо́л** *m.* planosol (group of soils).

плано́к *gen. pl.* of **пла́нка**.

планоме́рн/о *adv.* systematically; according to plan; **—ость** *f.* development according to plan; regularity; **—ый** *a.* systematic, according to plan; regular, planned.

пла́но/со́ма *f.* (gen.) planosome; **—спо́ра** *f.* planospore; **—фе́ррит** *m.* (min.) planoferrite; **—фи́ровый** *a.* (petr.) planophyric; **—ци́т** *m.* planocyte, wandering cell.

плано́чный *a.* of **пла́нка**.

план-схе́ма *m.* plan; map.

планта́ж *m.* deep plowing, trenching; **—ный** *a.* of **планта́ж**; subsoil.

планта́рный *a.* (anat.) plantar.

плант/а́тор *m.* plantation owner; planter, grower; **—а́ция** *f.* plantation; field.

плану́ла *f.* (zool.) planula.

план(-)фи́льтр *m.* horizontal filter.

планхеи́т *m.* (min.) plancheite.

пла́нчатый *a.* plank, lath, strip.

планша́йба *f.* (lathe) faceplate; surface plate, disk chuck.

планше́т *m.* (surv.) plane table, plotting board, clip board; chart (board); map case; (comp.) (graphic) tablet, (graphics) pad; (instr.) base table; topographic map; aerial survey; planchet, small dish; **наноси́ть на п.** *v.* plot; **—ка** *dim.* of **планше́т**; **—ный** *a.* of **планше́т**; plotting (board) flatbed (plotter); **—ный цифра́тор** (comp.) digitizing pad; **п.-постро́итель** *m.* plotting board; **п.-преобразова́тель** *m.* conversion table.

планши́р(ь) *m.* (naut.) rail; covering board.

пласку́н *m.* (ichth.) shad (*Alosa caspia tanaica; A. kessleri pontica*); **—е́ц** *m.* Danube shad (*A. caspia nordmanni*).

плассо́н *m.* (cyt.) plasson.

пласт *m.* layer, sheet; (geol.) stratum, bed, seam, reservoir; blanket, shell; (agr.) furrow (slice), sod; **в —е** in situ; **объёмный коэффицие́нт —а** formation volume factor, F.V.F.; **то́нкий п.** lamina; **—а́ть** *see* **пластова́ть**.

пластбето́н *m.* plastic concrete.

пласти́/да *f.*, **—дный** *a.* (bot.) plastid; **—дный ген** (gen.) plastogene; **—до́м** *m.* plastidome; **—дообра́зный** *a.* plastid-like; **—зо́ль** *m.* (chem.) plastisol.

пласти́к *m.* plastic (material); **—а** *f.* laminated plastic; plastic art; (med.) plastic surgery, —plasty, e.g. **—а вен** phleboplasty; **—а ко́жи** skin graft; **—ат** *m.* plasticized or masticated rubber; plastic compound; flexible polyvinyl chloride; **—а́тор** *m.* plasticizer, plasticizing agent, masticator, kneader; **хими́ческий —а́тор** peptizing agent, peptizer; **—а́ция** *f.* plasticization, mastication, breakdown.

пластили́н *m.* plasticine, modeling clay.

пласти́н/а, —ка *f.* plate, disc, lamina, lamella; membrane; slab, sheet; wafer, tablet, flake(let), leaf; (leaf) blade; scale; (zool.) plastron; scute; (mushroom) gill; (blood) platelet; (phonograph) record, disc; (radiator) fin; **—ы** *pl.* (battery) grid; **ме́тод —ок** plate count; **ни́жняя —ка** (herp.) hypoplastron; **рези́на в —ах** sheet rubber; **—какомпенса́тор** *m.* (av.) fixed trim tab; **—ка-подло́жка** *f.* membrane support; **—ковидный** *a.* lamelliform, plate-like; **—кожа́берные** *see* **пластиножа́берные**; **—коно́сный** *a.* lamelliferous; **—кообра́зный** *see* **пластинкови́дный**.

пластинн/и́ковые *pl.* (bot.) Agaricaceae; **п. грибы́** Agaricales; **—ый** *a.* plate, laminar, lamelliform.

пластино/жа́берные *pl.* (ichth.) Elasmobranchii; Chondrichthyes; **—жа́берный** *a.* elasmobranch; bivalve (mollusk); **—кры́л** *m.* (ent.) Phaneroptera; **—о́бразный** *a.* plate-like, lamellar, lamelliform, tabular; **—хво́ст** *m.* (ent.) cricket (*Leptophyes albovittata*); **—чка** *dim.*, **—чный** *a.* of **пласти́нка**; (med.) platelet.

пластинчато/жа́берные *pl.* (mal.) Lamellibranchia, Bivalvia; **—зу́бая кры́са** (mam.) Nesokia; **—клю́вые** *pl.* (orn.) Anseriformes; **—о́бразный** *a.* lamelliform; **—сть** *f.* lamination, foliation; **—у́сые** *pl.* (ent.) Scarabaeidae.

пластинчат/ый *a.* lamellar, lamellate, laminar, laminated, foliated, scaly, flaky, flaked; plate(-type); platelike, tabular; leaf, plate and frame (filter); vane (pump); finned (cooler); platform, apron (conveyer); sheet (-like); gill (fungi); (blood) platelet; (anat.) splenial; **п. конденсатор** plate condenser; **—ая отдельность** lamination; **—ая слюда** sheet mica; **—ая структура** slaty structure, lamination; **—ые грибы** (bot.) Agaricales.

пласти/фикатор *see* **пластикатор; —фикация** *f.*, **—(фи)цирование** *n.* plasticization; mastication; **—(фи)цированный** *a.* plasticized; masticated, broken down; **—(фи)цировать** *v.* plasticize; masticate, break down.

пластич/еский *a.* plastic, moldable, pliable; soft (clay, rubber); **п. материал, —еская масса** plastic; **—еская обработка** shaping, molding; **—еская смазка** lubricating grease; **—еское последействие** relaxation; **—но-вязкий** *a.* yielding (material); **—ность** *f.* plasticity, pliability, elasticity, flexibility; ductility; (rock) flowage; **—ный** *see* **пластический.**

пласткожа *f.* an artificial leather.

пласт-коллектор *m.* (geol.) reservoir bed.

пластмасс/а *f.*, **—овый** *a.* plastic; **—овый корпус** molded case.

пластов/ание *n.* stratification, lamination, bedding; **—ать** *v.* stratify; **—ой** *a.* stratified, sheet, layer; formation (gas); formational, reservoir (pressure); stratal, deposit (water); blanket (deposit); **—ая культура** crop on newly broken soil, sod crop; **геометрическая —ая карта** stratigraphic map; **—ой-газовый фактор** gas-oil ratio.

пласто/гамия *f.* (cyt.) plastogamy; **—ген** *m.* (gen.) plastogene; **—граф** *m.* plastograph; **—конт** *m.* (cyt.) plastocont, chondriocont; **—мер** *m.* (chem.) plastomer, thermoplast; **—метр** *m.* plastometer.

пластообраз/ный *a.* sheet(-like), in sheets; **—ователь** *m.* (agr.) sod former.

пласто/рез *m.* (agr.) sod cutter; **—сома** *f.* (cyt.) plastosome; **—хинон** *m.* (bioch.) plastoquinone; **—эластичный** *a.* plasto-elastic.

пласт-проводник *m.* (geol.) carrier bed.

пластрон *m.* (zool.) plastron.

пласт-спутник *m.* (min.) guiding bed.

пластун *m.* (ichth.) Azov shad (*Alosa caspia tanaica*); **—ец** *see* **пластун;** Black Sea shad.

пласты *pl. of* **пласт;** strata.

пластыр/ный *a. of* **пластырь;** (anat.) splenial; **—ь** *m.* plaster, patch; splenium.

пласть *f.* face (of lumber).

плата *f.* pay(ment); charge, fee; card, sheet, plate, board; (sub)assembly; (detector) array.

платакс *m.* (ichth.) Platax; **—овые** *pl.* batfishes (*Platacidae*).

платан *m.*, **—овый** *a.* (bot.) plane tree, sycamore (*Platanus*); **—овые** *pl.* Platanaceae.

плата-основание *f.* baseplate.

платёж *m.* payment; **наложенным —ом** cash on delivery, C.O.D.; **расписка в —е** receipt; **—еспособный** *a.* (com.) solvent; **—ный** *a.* payment.

плательный *a.* dress (fabric).

плательщик *m.* payer.

плати— *prefix* platy— (flat, broad); **—гастер(ид)ы** *pl.* (ent.) Platygasteridae; **—зма** *f.* (anat.) platysma; **—метр** *m.* (elec.) platymeter.

платин/а *f.* (chem.) platinum, Pt; (horol.) plate; (text.) sinker; *prefix see* **платино—; закись —ы** platinous oxide, platinum monoxide; **окись —ы** platinic oxide,

platinum dioxide; **иридистая п.** (min.) platiniridium; **—аорганический** *a.* organoplatinum; **—ат** *m.* platinate; **—иак** *m.* platinammine.

платиниров/ание *n.*, **—ка** *f.* platinization, platinum plating; **—анный** *a.* platinized, platinum-plated; **—ать** *v.* platinize.

платинисто— *prefix* (chem.) platino—, platinous.

платинистосинерод/истый натрий sodium platinocyanide; **—оводородная кислота** platinocyanic acid; **соль —оводородной кислоты** platinocyanide.

платинистохлор/истый натрий sodium platinochloride; **—оводородная кислота** chloroplatinous acid; **соль —оводородной кислоты** platinochloride.

платинистый *a.* platinous, platinum.

платинит *m.* (min.) platynite; (chem.; met.) platinite.

платино— *prefix* platini—, platinic.

платиново/кислый *a.* platinic acid; platinate (of); **—кислая соль** platinate; **—синеродистая кислота** platinicyanic acid.

платинов/ый *a.* platinic, platinum; **п. лист** platinum foil; **—ая кислота** platinic acid; **соль —ой кислоты** platinate; **—ая лодочка** platinum boat (for analysis); **—ая сетка** platinum gauze; **—ая чернь** platinum black.

платино/ид *m.* platinoid, platinum metal; **—носный** *see* **платиносодержащий; -родий** *m.* platinum-rhodium; **—подобный** *a.* platinoid, like platinum; **—селеносинеродоводородная кислота** selenocyanoplatinic acid; **—сернистый** *a.* sulfoplatinate (of); **—синеродистый** *a.* platinocyanide (of); **—синеродоводородный** *a.* platinicyanic (acid); **—содержащий** *a.* platiniferous, platinum-containing; **—трон** *m.* (electron.) platinotron.

платинохлор/(ист)оводородный *a.* chloroplatinic (acid); **—истый** *a.* chloroplatinate, platinichloride (of).

плати/пецилия *f.* (ichth.) platy (*Xiphophorus*); **—подия** *f.* (med.) platypodia, flatfoot; **—пус** *m.* (mam.) platypus (*Ornithorhynchus anatinus*).

платить *v.* pay.

плати/филлин *m.* (chem.) platyphylline; **—цефальный** *a.* platycephalous, wide-headed.

платнерит *m.* (min.) plattnerite.

платный *a.* requiring payment; paying; paid; toll (road).

плато *n.* (geol.) plateau, upland, tableland, elevated plain; (math.) plateau; **п.-базальт** *n.* plateau basalt.

плато/к *m.*, **—чный** *a.* (hand)kerchief.

платтнерит *m.* (min.) plattnerite.

платформ/а *f.* platform, stage; flatcar; (geol.) platform, continental plateau; (off-shore) bench; **п.-лафет** *f.* platform mount; **—енный** *a. of* **платформа; —инг** *m.* (petrol.) platforming.

плат/ье *n.*, **—ьевой, —яной** *a.* clothes, clothing, dress, garment.

плаун *m.*, **—ный, —овый** *a.* (bot.) club moss (*Lycopodium*); **—овые** *pl.* Lycopodiaceae.

плафон *m.*, **—ный** *a.* (elec.) ceiling fixture, dome light, ceiling light; lampshade; plafond, decorated ceiling.

плаха *f.* (silv.) block, chunk, billet.

пласт/а *f.*, **—овый** *a.* heavy striped or checkered fabric.

плацдарм *m.* (mil.) bridgehead; beachhead; springboard, jumping-off ground; base.

плацебо *n.* (pharm.) placebo.

плацент/а *f.* (biol.) placenta, afterbirth; **—арные** *pl.* (mam.) placentals (*Eutheria, Placentaria*); **—арный** *a.* placental, placentary; **—ация** *f.* placentation; **—оносный** *a.* placentiferous.

плацкарт/а *f.* reserved seat ticket; **—ный** *a.* reserved (seat).

плач *m.* weeping; (bot.) bleeding, sap exudation; —**евный** *a.* deplorable, sorry, poor; sad; —**евный исход** failure.

плаченный *a.* paid.

плачущий *pr. act. part. of* **плакать.**

плаш/ечный *a.,* —**ка** *f.* (mach.) (threading) die; (drawing) nib; (chuck) jaw; (bending) block; ram (in blowout preventer); (typ.) solid; (oil) slip; —**кодержатель** *m.* die stock.

плашкоут *m.* (naut.) scow; —**ный** *a.* pontoon (bridge).

плашмя *adv.* flat(wise), prone; **п.-направленный** *a.* broadside directional (antenna).

плашник *m.* split billet (firewood).

плащ *m.,* —**овый** *a.* mantle, blanket; cloak, raincoat; (tectonics) veneer; (anat.; pal.; zool.) pallium; —**еносец** *m.* (ichth.) frill(ed) shark (*Chlamydoselachus anguineus*); (mam.) armadillo (*Burmeisteria; Chlamyphorus*); **слизистая** —**еноска** (mal.) Amphipeplea glutinosa; **п.-палатка** *m.* poncho, groundsheet.

плева *f.* membrane, film, coat, pellicle; (anat.) tunica, cuticle, covering; (bot.) aril; **девственная п.** (anat.) hymen.

плев/альница *f.* spittoon; —**ание** *n.* spitting, etc., *see v.;* —**ать** *v.* spit, expectorate; splutter (of arc); shrug off.

плевел *m.* weed; (bot.) rye grass (*Lolium*).

плевок *m.* spittle; (med.) sputum.

плевр/а *f.* (anat.) pleura; —**альный** *a.* pleural; —**ит** *m.* (med.) pleurisy; (zool.) pleurite; —**итический,** —**итный** *a.* pleuritic; —*prefix* pleur(o)— (pleura, rib, side); —**обрахия** *f.* (zool.) Pleurobrachia; —**огенный** *a.* pleurogenous, growing from the side; —**одонтный** *a.* (anat.; zool.) pleurodont; —**олёгочный** *a.* pleuropulmonary; —**он** *m.* (zool.) pleuron; —**опищеводный** *a.* (anat.) pleuroesophageal; —**отиф** *m.* (med.) pleurotyphoid; —**отомарииды** *pl.* (zool.) Pleurotomariidae; —**оцистида** *f.* (bot.) pleurocystidium, lateral cystidium.

плёвый *a.* trivial, trifling.

плед *m.* rug; plaid.

плёдиа *f.* (ent.) Plodia.

плезанский *a.* (geol.) Plaisancian (stage).

плезио— *prefix* plesio— (near, close to); —**завр** *m.* (pal.) plesiosaur(us); —**морфный** *a.* (cryst.) plesiomorphous; —**псовые** *pl.* (ichth.) roundheads (*Plesiopidae*) —**тип** *m.* plesiotype, supplementary type.

плеи *pl.* (ent.) Pleidae.

плейасы *pl.* (geol.) playas.

плейо— *prefix* ple(i)o— (more); —**морфный** *a.* (biol.) pleomorphic; —**н** *m.* (meteor.) pleion; —**тропность** *f.* (gen.) pleiotropy; —**тропный** *a.* pleiotropic; —**хазий** *m.* (bot.) pleiochasium.

плейр/ит (zool.) pleuron; —**о—** *see* **плевро—.**

плейсто— *prefix* pleisto— (most).

плейстон *m.* pleuston, free-floating plants.

плейстофировый *a.* (petr.) pleistophyric.

плейстоцен *m.,* —**овый** *a.* (geol.) Pleistocene.

плекси/глас(с) *m.* Plexiglas; —**гум** *m.* Plexigum (plastic); —**т** *m.* (med.) plexitis; —**формный** *a.* (anat.) plexiform, network-like.

плект/енхима *f.* (bot.) plectenchyma; —**остела** *f.* plectostele; —**ропом** *m.* (ichth.) Plectropomus.

плёл *past m. sing. of* **плести.**

плем/ён *gen. pl. of* **племя;** —**енник** *m.* pedigreed sire; —**енной** *a.* pedigree(d), pure strain; breeding; stud (horse); —**енной рассадник** breeding station, stud farm; —**енная заводская работа** stud breeding; —**енная книга** breeding register, herdbook; —**енное**

дело pedigree animal breeding; —**енное хозяйство** breeding farm; —**енные рыбы** brood fish, breeders; —**хоз** *m.* pedigreed stock farm; breeding of pedigreed stock; —**я** *n.* tribe, race; breed; generation; —**янник** *m.* nephew; —**янница** *f.* niece.

плен *m.* captivity.

плена *f.* (ingot casting) scab; (rolling) sliver; (teeming) lap; skin.

пленарный *a.* plenary, complete.

пленение *n.* capture.

пленистая полоса (met.) blister bar.

плёнк/а *f.* film, layer, pellicle, coating; skin, membrane; (bot.) glume, husk, hull; (biol.) cuticle; tarnish; skimmings, scum, dross; (phot.) film; **в** —**ах** *a.* unhusked, hull (rice); —**овидный** *a.* chaffy, paleaceous; —**одержатель** *m.* (phot.) film holder; —**оносный** *a.* membraniferous.

плёнкообраз/ование *n.* film formation, skinning; —**ователь** *m.* film-forming substance; —**ующий** *a.* filmforming.

пленн/ик *m.,* —**ый** *a.* captive, prisoner.

плён/ок *gen. pl. of,* —**очка** *dim. of* **плёнка;** (bot.) paleola, lodicule; (anat.) panniculus; stratum, layer; —**очно-ручьевой режим** film-rivulet condensation; —**очный** *a. of* **плёнка;** pellicular; film-type (condensation); —**очный дозиметр** (nucl.) film badge; —**очная форсунка** hollow-cone spray nozzle.

пленум *m.* plenum, plenary session.

плёнчат/о— *prefix* hymen(o)—, membrane, film; —**овидный** *a.* membrane-like; (bot.) hymenoid; —**ость** *f.* filminess; chaffiness; —**ый** *a.* membranous; filmy; laminate, scaly; (bot.) glumaceous; hulled, husk(ed).

плёны *pl., etc., of* **плена.**

плео— *prefix* ple(i)o— (more than usual); —**морфизм** *m.* (cryst.) pleomorphism; —**морфный** *a.* pleomorphic; —**наст** *m.* (min.) pleonaste, ceylonite; —**под** *m.* (crust.) pleopod; —**споровые** *pl.* (phyt.) Pleosporaceae.

плеохрои/зм *m.* (cryst.) pleochroism; —**ческий,** —**чный** *a.* pleochro(mat)ic; —**чные дворики,** —**чные кольца,** —**чные оболочки** (min.) pleochroic halos.

плеро/ма *f.* (bot.) plerome; —**церкоид** *m.* (zool.) plerocercoid (larval tapeworm).

плёс *m.* reach, stretch (of water); pool.

плесен/естойкий *a.* mildew-resistant; —**ный** *a.* mold(y), musty; —**ь** *f.* mold, must; (bot.) mildew (*Mucor*); efflorescence; **водяные** —**и** Phycomycetes.

плеск *m.* splash, splatter; —**ание** *n.* splashing; —**ать** *v.* splash, splatter; flutter.

плесне/велый *a.* moldy, musty; —**вение** *n.* molding, etc., *see v.;* mold; —**(ве)ть** *v.* mold, get moldy, grow musty; effloresce; —**видный** *a.* mucid, moldy; mucoid; —**вица** *f.* (med.) mycosis; —**вой** *a. of* **плесень;** —**вые грибки** mold (fungus); —**еды** *pl.* (ent.) Endomychidae; —**стойкий** *a.* mold-resistant.

плеснуть *see* **плескать.**

плёсо *see* **плёс.**

Плесси зелень Plessy's green, chromic phosphate.

плессиметр *m.* (med.) plessimeter, pleximeter.

плессит *m.* (min.) plessite.

плести *v.* braid, plait; spin; weave, wattle; net; twine.

плете/видка *f.* (herp.) Dryophis; —**видный** *a.* flagelliform, whip-like; —**й** *gen. pl. of* **плеть;** —**льный** *a.* braiding, weaving; —**льщик** *m.* weaver.

плетение *n.* network, plexus; net(ting), fencing; braiding, plaiting, weaving; wickerwork, basketwork; wattle.

плетён/ка *f.* plexus, network; mat; braid; basket; —**ый** *a.* woven, wicker; mesh.

плетень *m.* wattle; net, fencing; **—ье** *see* **плетение**.

плетёт *pr. 3 sing. of* **плести**.

плетизмо— *prefix* plethysmo— (enlargement); **—граф** *m.* (med.) plethysmograph.

плётка *f.* lash.

плетнёвый *a. of* **плетень**; basket-weave.

плетора *f.* (med.) plethora.

плетостатический *a.* plethostatic.

плет/ушка *f.* basket; **—ущий** *a.* braiding, etc., *see* **плести**; **—ь** *f.* vine, runner, flagellum; length (of pipe); (ichth.) Ussuri catfish (*Leiocassis ussuriensis*); **—юха** *f.* basket.

плеуро/погон *m.* (bot.) Pleuropogon; **—томария** *f.* (mal.) Pleurotomaria.

плече— *prefix* (anat.) omo—, shoulder; brachio— (arm); humero— (humerus); **—вой** *a.* shoulder, humeral, brachial; pectoral (fin); **—вой отросток** acromial process, acromion; **—евой пояс** pectoral girdle; **—вая кость** humerus; **—вое крыло** (ent.) parapterum; **—вые** *pl.* (orn.) scapulars; **—головной** *a.* (anat.) brachiocephalic; **—локтевой** *a.* humeroulnar; **—лопаточный** *a.* humeroscapular; **—лучевой** *a.* humeroradial; **—мышечный** *a.* humeromuscular; **—ногие** *pl.* (crust.) Brachiopoda.

плеч/ико *dim. of* **плечо**; shoulder strap; (coat) hanger; shoulder padding; (typ.) shoulder; **—истый** *a.* broad-shouldered; **—о** *n.* (anat.) shoulder, humerus; brachium, arm; (mech.) arm, leg; length; **область —а** brachial region.

плешанка *f.* (orn.) black-eared wheatear (*Oenanthe hispanica*).

плеш/иветь *v.* get bald; become bare; **—ивость** *f.* baldness; (med.) alopecia; **—ивый** *a.* bald(ing); **—ина** *f.* bald spot, bare place; lapse; balk (in plowing); **—ь** *f.* bald spot or patch.

плещет *pr. 3 sing. of* **плескать**.

плеяда *f.* pleiad.

плиенсбахский *a.* (geol.) Pliensbachian.

плик/ат(ив)ный *a.* plicative, plicate(d), folded, plaited; **—ативная дислокация** (geol.) folding; **—ация** *f.* plication, folding.

плимутрок *m.* Plymouth rock (chicken).

плин/ианский *a.* (geol.) Plinian; **—сбахский** *a.* Pliensbachian.

плинт *m.* plinth, skirting, baseboard; (tel.) plinth, terminal or distributing block; **—ит** *m.* (min.) plinthite.

плинтов/ать *v.* smooth, level, clean off; **—ка** *f.* surface levelling.

плинтус *see* **плинт**.

плио— *prefix* plio— (more); *see also* **пле(й)о—**; **—трон** *m.* (electron.) pliotron.

плиоцен *m.*, **—овая эпоха** (geol.) Pliocene (epoch); **—овый** *a.* Pliocene.

плис *m.* (text.) plush, velveteen.

плис/ка *f.* (orn.) yellow wagtail (*Motacilla flava*); **—овый** *a. of* **плис**.

плисс/е *n.* (text.) plisse; **—ированный** *a.* gathered, plaited.

плистофороз *m.* (vet.) Plistophora infection.

плит/а *f.* plate, slab, tile; flag(stone); (continental) platform; sheet (of ice); (wall) board; (turn) table; range, stove, hot plate; **в —ах** *a.* slab (iron); **проверочная п.** (mach.) gage block; **—ка** *f.* slab, cake, block; (candy) bar; tile, tablet, plate; (semiconductors) chip; (conveyer) pallet; scale, flake; hot plate; **измерительная —ка**, **—ка-калибр** gage block.

плитко/ватый *a.* laminated; **—образный** *a.* plate-like, tabular; (elec.) batch (winding).

плитный *see* **плиточный**.

плитняк *m.*, **—овый** *a.* flagstone; plate coal; platy (structure).

плито/видный *see* **плитообразный**; **—к** *gen. pl. of* **плитка**; **—ломня** *f.* quarry; **—образный** *a.* plate-like, tabular, slab-shaped.

плит/очный *a.* plate, laminated; cake, brick; apron, slat (conveyor); tile; block (gage); **п. пресс** slab-molding machine; **—чатый** *a.* (geol.) platy.

плица *f.* shoe, cleat; float; bailing device; (wheel) paddle.

плов *m.* (food) pilaf.

плов/ец *m.* swimmer; floater; (crust.) nauplius; **—учесть** *f.* floatability, buoyancy; **—учий** *a.* floating, buoyant.

плод *m.* fruit, offspring; (med.) fetus, embryo; **смерть —а** fetal death; **п.-зерновка** *m.* (bot.) caryopsis; **—ик** *m.* mericarp; **—иться** *v.* procreate, (re)produce, generate, propagate; **—иться** *v.* multiply, breed, propagate; spawn; **п.-коробочка** *m.* (bot.) capsule, boll, pod; **п.-костянка** *m.* drupe; **—ник** *m.* (bot.) pistil; *suffix* **—carp**; **—ный** *a.* (fruit-)bearing; fertile (egg); fetal; *suffix* **—carpous, -fruited; —ный пузырь** (anat.) amnion; **—ное поле** embryonic or germinal area; **—ные воды** amniotic fluid.

плодо— *prefix* fructi—, carp(o)—, fruit; (med.) fetus; **—вед** *m.* (hort.) pomologist; **—ведение** *n.* pomology; carpology; **—витость** *f.* fruitfulness, fertility, fecundity; birth rate; **—витый** *a.* fruitful, fertile, fecund, prolific, productive; **—вместилище** *n.* uterus; **—вод** *m.* fruit grower; **—водство** *n.*, **—водческий** *a.* fruit growing; **—вый** *a.* fruit(-bearing); fetal (sac); **—вый сахар** fruit sugar, fructose; **—вая оболочка** (bot.) pericarp; **—вая моль** (ent.) ermine moth (*Hyponomeuta padella*); **—вое тело** (bot.) carposoma, fruit body, ascocarp, receptacle; **—вые мушки** (ent.) fruit flies (*Drosophilidae*).

плодо/головка *f.* (bot.) carpocephalum; **—гонный** *a.* (med.) abortive; **—дробилка** *f.* fruit mill; **—жил** *m.* (ent.) snout beetle (*Curculio*); **—жорка** *f.* Laspeyresia; **яблочная —жорка** codling moth (*L. pomonella*); **—жорки** *pl.* (ent.) Laspeyresinae; Tortricidae; **—изгнание** *n.* (med.) fetal expulsion; **—корм** *m.* mast (nuts collectively); **—листик** *m.* (bot.) carpel; **—мер** *m.* fruit-sizing device; **—мойка** *f.* fruit washer; **—ножка** *f.* fruit stem, pedicel; **—нос(ец)** *m.* carpophore, stalk; **—носить** *v.* bear fruit; **—носность** *f.* fruit-bearing capacity, fruitfulness; **—носный** *a.* fruit-bearing, fruitful, productive; rich, fertile (soil); **—носящий** *a.*, **—ношение** *n.* fruit bearing, fruiting, fructification; **—образование** *n.* fruit formation, fructification.

плодоовощ/е— *prefix* fruit and vegetable; **—евод** *m.* fruit and vegetable grower; **—еводство** *n.* truck and fruit farming; **—епереработка** *f.* fruit and vegetable processing; **—и** *pl.* fruits and vegetables; **—ной** *a.* fruit and vegetable.

плодо/переменность *f.* (agr.) crop rotating system; **—переменный** *a.* crop-rotating; **—переработка** *f.* fruit processing; **—питомник** *m.*, **—питомнический** *a.* fruit-tree nursery; **—резка** *f.* fruit chopper.

плодород/ие *n.*, **—ность** *f.* fertility, productivity; (diminishing) return; **—ный** *a.* fertile, fecund, productive, prolific; rich (soil).

плодо/сбор *m.* fruit harvest(ing); **—смен** *m.*, **—сменная система** (agr.) crop rotation; **—сниматель** *m.* fruit picker; **—сортировка** *f.* fruit grading; fruit grader or sorter; **—сумчатые** *pl.* (bot.) Carpoascomycetidae; **—сушилка** *f.* fruit (and vegetable) dryer; **—сушильня** *f.* drying building; **—съём(ник)** *m.* fruit picker; **—съёмочный** *a.* fruit-picking; **—творный** *a.*

fruitful, productive, rewarding; —**хранилище** n. fruit storage (place); produce warehouse; —**ягодный** a. fruit and berry; —**ядный** a. fruit-eating, frugivorous.

плод/-семянка m. (bot.) achene; —**уха, —ушка** f. fruit spur; —**ущий** a. fruiting, fruit-bearing, fertile.

пло/ение n. folding, plaiting; —**ён(н)ый** a. folded, plaited, plicated.

плоид/ия, —ность f. (gen.) ploidy.

плоить v. fold, plait.

плойчат/ость f. (geol.) plication, fold(ing), corrugation; —**ый** a. plicated, folded together, puckered.

пломб/а f. stamp, seal, label; (dental) filling, inlay; —**ир** m. stamp, seal; ice-cream (with fruit, etc.); —**ирный** a. sealing (compound); —**ирование** n. sealing, etc., see v.; —**ированный** a. sealed, etc., see v.; —**ировать** v. seal, stamp, stop, plug; fill (tooth); —**ировка** see **пломбирование;** —**овый** a. of **пломба.**

плоск/ий a. flat, plane; planar (structure); two-dimensional; parallel-plate (capacitor); disk (valve); sheet (film); flat-bar (iron); flat-bed (printing); flush; laminar (flow); (hist.) squamous (epithelium); **п. скачок** (phys.) step shock; —**ая поверхность** plane (surface).

плоско adv. flat(ly), on a plane; prefix plani—, plano—; platy— (broad, wide, flat); —**бимсовый** a. flat-bulb (iron); —**бокорезы** pl. sidecutting pliers; —**брюхий** a. flat-bellied; —**бульбовый** a. flat-bulb; —**верхний** a. flat-top; —**вогнутый** a. planoconcave; —**выпуклый** a. planoconvex; —**вытянутый** a. (cryst.) lathlike; —**вязальный** a. flat-bed knitting (machine); —**голов** m. (ichth.) flathead (Platycephalus); —**головость** f. (med.) platycephaly; —**головые** pl. (ichth.) Platycephalidae; —**головый** a. platycephalous, flat-head(ed).

плоскогорье n. tableland, upland, highland; (high) plateau; **столовое п.** mesa.

плоско/грудый a. flat-chested; —**грудые птицы** cursorial birds (Ratitae); —**губцы** pl. flat(-nosed) pliers; —**донка** f. flat-bottomed boat; —**донный** a. flat-bottom(ed); —**звенный** a. flat-link; —**зубые** pl. (herp.) Placodontia; —**камерный** a. plate-and-frame (system); —**клеточный** a. (cyt.) planocellular; —**компаундированный** a. (elec.) flat-compounded; —**листный** a. flat-leaved, planifolious; —**лоб** m. (ichth.) flathead (Neoplatycephalus macropterus); —**ножка** f. (ent.) Platycnemis; —**ножки** pl. Platycnemididae; —**нос(ик)** m. (ichth.) flatnose (Bathydraco); —**носы** pl. Bathydraconidae; —**носый** a. platyrhine, broad-nosed; —**параллельный** a. plane-parallel; parallel-plate (electrode, etc.); —**пёрые** pl. torrentfishes (Homalopteridae); —**печатная машина** flatbed (printing) press; —**плавниковые** see **плоскопёрые;** —**пламенный** a. laminar-flame; —**плодник** m. (bot.) Meniocus; —**плодный** a. platycarpic; —**поляризованный** a. plane-polarized; —**рёберный** a. flat-ribbed; —**режущая** or —**резная лапа** (agr.) blade; —**раз** m. subsurface cultivator; —**спиральный** a. (zool.) planispiral; —**стебельный** a. flat-stalked; —**стной** a. plane, planar; junction (transistor); —**стность** f. planeness, levelness, flatness; **до —стности** adv. flat; —**стопие** n. (med.) platypodia, flatfoot; —**стручковый** a. flat-podded.

плоскост/ь f. plane, surface, level, flatness; area; layer (of charge); pad, sheet; face, facet (of crystal); (floor) line; **геометрия на —и** plane geometry.

плоско/тел m., —**тёлка** f. (ent.) cucujid beetle; —**тёлки** pl. Cucujidae; —**телый** a. flat(-bodied); —**хвост** m. (herp.) Laticauda; —**хвостый** a. flat-tailed; —**ходы** pl. (ent.) Platypodidae; —**цилиндрический** a. plane-

cylindrical; —**шлифовальный станок** (sur)face grinder; —**шляпный** a. flat-headed (nail); —**электронный** a. flat-plate (tube).

плоск/унец m. (ichth.) Azov shad (Alosa caspia tanaica); —**уша** f. silver bream (Blicca bjoerkna).

плосок sh. m. of **плоский.**

плот m. raft, float; (math.) plot; —**бище** n. rafting site; **п.-брандер** n. firefloat.

плотв/а f., —**ичный** a. (ichth.) roach (Rutilus r.); also refers to five other species.

плотен sh. m. of **плотный.**

плотик m. (min.) firm; (geol.) bedrock.

плотильщик m. raft maker.

плотин/а f., —**ный** a. dam, weir, dike, embankment, barrier; causeway.

плотить v. make into a raft.

плот/ица see **плотва;** —**ич(к)а** dim. of **плотва.**

плотн/ейший superl. of **плотный;** (cryst.) face-centered; —**еть** v. get dense(r).

плотни/к m. carpenter; (zool.) shipworm, borer; —**чать** v. do carpentry work; —**ч(еск)ий** a. carpenter's; —**чество** n., —**чье дело** carpentry; —**чный** a. carpentry.

плотно adv. densely, etc., see **плотный; п. лежащий, п. пригнанный, п. прилегающий** snug, tight; —**ватый** a. rather tight or dense; —**дерн(ов)инный** a. firm-bunch (grasses); —**зернистый** close-grained, compact; —**колосый** a. (bot.) dense-eared; —**кустовой** a. densely tufted; —**лежащий** a. dense, close; —**рогие** pl. (mam.) Cervidae; —**(сте)мер** m. densimeter, density gage; —**стный** a. density; dense.

плотность f. density, specific gravity; consistency; solidity, compactness, impenetrability, tightness; closeness; close weave (of cloth); (population) concentration, crowding; **п. вязкости** (petrol.) viscosity gravity constant, v.g.c.; **п. орошения** flooding velocity; **п. тока** (elec.) current density.

плотноупакованный a. close-packed.

плотн/ый a. dense, thick, consistent, solid, compact, close, thickset; sound, hard, tough; (air-)tight, leak-proof, leak-free; close, intimate; hard-textured (filter paper); closely woven (cloth); (min.) massive, close-grained; strong (constitution); cubic (meter); **п. слой** packed bed.

плото— prefix raft; —**вод** m. raft tug; raftsman; —**вой** a. raft, float; —**вщик, —гон** m. raftsman.

плотозиды pl. (ichth.) Plotosidae.

плото/спуск, —ход m. raft, log or timber chute; rafting canal.

плотоядн/ые pl. (zool.) Carnivora; (ent.) Adephaga; —**ый** a. carnivorous, flesh-eating; —**ые зубы** carnassial teeth, cutting teeth, canine teeth, fangs.

плоть f. (anat.) corpus, body; **крайняя п.** prepuce, preputium.

плох/о adv. bad(ly), etc., see a.; weakly (soluble); n. (educ.) bad mark; **п. обусловленный** a. ill-conditioned; —**оватый** a. rather poor; —**ой** a. bad, poor, inferior; inadequate; ill, detrimental, adverse; off (color); mal—; —**ая настройка** maladjustment; —**опроводящий** a. poorly conducting; —**орастворимый** a. poorly soluble.

плошать v. make a mistake, slip up.

плошка f. earthen saucer; lampion.

площад/ка f. platform, stand, stage, landing; area, site, place; ground(s), yard; (sample) plot; (landing) field; (launching) pad; plateau (of graph); (anat.) planum; (bot.) cicatrix; **посев —ками** seeding on plots; —**ной** a. area; —**очка** dim. of **площадка;** —**ь** f. area, acreage; surface, plane; space, section; square; **—ь в плане** plan area; **—ь основания, —ь устройства** (comp., robotics) footprint; **единица —и** unit of area; **закон —ей** law of areas; **по —и** areal.

площе *comp. of* **плоский.**

площица *f.* (ent.) crab louse (*Phthirus pubis*).

плувиометр *see* **плювиометр.**

плуг *m.* (agr.) plow; (brush) breaker, cutter; **—(ат)арь** *m.* plowman; (ichth.) plugar (*Gymnodraco acuticeps*); **п.-канавокопатель** *m.* trenching plow; **п.-корчеватель** *m.* grubbing plow, grubber; **п.-лущильник** *m.* stubble breaker; **—овой** *a.* plow; **п.-окучник, п.-распашник** *m.* ridging plow, ridger, hiller; **п.-сеялка** *m.* drill plow.

плуж/ный *a.* plow; **—ок** *dim. of* **плуг.**

плумб/агин *m.* (chem.) plumbagin; **—аго** *n.* plumbago, native graphite; **—ан** *m.* plumbane; **—ат** *m.* plumbate; **—ит** *m.*, **—итный** *a.* plumbite; **—о—** *see* **плюмбо—.**

плумиер/ин *m.* plumierin, asonidin; **—овая кислота** plumieric acid.

плумозит *m.* (min.) plumosite.

плунжер *m.*, **—ный** *a.* plunger, ram, piston; **—ный поршень** plunger, piston.

ПЛУР *abbr.* [противолодочная управляемая (торпедо-)ракета] antisubmarine rocket, ASROC; submarine-launched rocket, SUBROC.

плут *m.* cheat, swindler; (net) float, cork.

плутеус *m.* (zool.) pluteus.

плутон *m.* (petr.) pluton; (astr.) Pluto; **—иевый** *a.*, **—ий** *m.* plutonium, Pu; **—ил** *m.* plutonyl; **—ический** *a.* (petr.) plutonic, intrusive, of igneous origin.

плыв/ёт *pr. 3 sing. of* **плыть; —ун** *m.*, **—унный** *a.* quicksand; floating layer; **—учесть** *f.* fluidity, deliquescence; slushiness; **—учий** *a.* flowing, deliquescent; quick, running (rock).

плыть *v.* navigate; float, swim; run (of melted candle).

плювиальный *a.* pluvial, rain.

плювио— *prefix* pluvio—, rain; **—граф** *m.* pluviograph, recording rain gage; **—метр** *m.* pluviometer, rain gage; **—метрический** *a.* pluviometric.

плюёт *pr. 3 sing. of* **плевать.**

Плюккер (math.) Plücker.

плюмаж *m.* plumage, plume.

плюмб— *see* **плумб—.**

плюмбо/гуммит *m.* (min.) plumbogummite; **—кальцит** *m.* plumbocalcite; **—куприт** *m.* plumbocuprite; **—ниобит** *m.* plumboniobite; **—станнит** *m.* plumbostannite; **—стибит** *m.* plumbostibite; **—феррит** *m.* plumboferrite; **—ярозит** *m.* plumbojarosite.

плюм/ерицин *m.* (chem.) plumericin; **—ерия** *f.* (bot.) Plumeria; **—ула** *f.* plumule.

плюнуть *see* **плевать.**

плюр *m.* onionskin (paper).

плюри/ворный *a.* plurivorous (parasite); **—гландулярный** *a.* (anat.) pluriglandular.

плюс *m.* (math.) plus, positive sign; advantage; (surv.) plus station.

плюск/а *f.* (bot.) cupule, cup; **—овидный** *a.* cupuliform, cup-shaped; **—оносные** *pl.* Cupuliferae; **—оносный** *a.* cupuliferous, catkin-bearing.

плюс-минус either way, plus or minus.

плюсн/а *f.* (anat.) metatarsus; **кость —ы** metatarsal (bone); **—евой** *a.* metatarsal; **—ефаланговый** *a.* metatarsophalangeal.

плюсов/альный *a.*, **—ание** *n.* (leather; text.) padding; **—ать** *v.* pad, soak; add; **—ка** *f.* padding; padding machine.

плюсовой *a.* plus, positive.

плюсов/очный *see* **плюсовальный; —щик** *m.* padder; **—ый** *a. of* **плюс; плюсование.**

плюсский *a.* (geog.) Plyusa.

плютелля *f.* (ent.) Plutella.

плюхея *f.* (bot.) Pluchea.

плюхнуть(ся) *v.* flop down, splash.

плюш *m.* (text.) plush, velour; **—евание** *n.* (leather) polishing; **—евый** *a. of* **плюш; —ка** *f.* (food) roll, bun; **льняная —ка** (bot.) knotweed (*Polygonum linicola*).

плющ *m.*, **—евый** *a.* (bot.) ivy (*Hedera*); **—евидный** *a.* ivy-like, hederaceous; **—елистный** *a.* ivy-leaved.

плющ/ение *n.* flatt(en)ing, etc., *see v.*; spread; **—енный** *a.* flatt(en)ed, etc., *see v.*; **—илка** *f.* flatt(en)er; roller, crusher; **—ильный** *a.* flattening, etc., *see v.*; flatting (mill); planing (hammer); edging (roll); pressure (calender); **—ильня** *f.* flatting mill; **—ить** *v.* flat(ten), upset; (rolling) spread, laminate, roll out; compress, crush.

пляж *m.*, **—евой, —ный** *a.* beach, strand.

пляс *m.* dance; **—ание** *n.* dancing; (med.) saltation; **—ать** *v.* dance; **—ка** *f.* dance, dancing; (carotid) shudder; **—ка св. Витта, виттова —ка** (med.) chorea; St. Vitus' dance; **—овой** *a.* dance; saltatory; **—ун** *m.*, **—унья** *f.* dancer; **—уны** *pl.* (ent.) dance flies (*Empididae*).

пляти— *prefix* plat(y)— (broad, wide, flat); **—пецилиус** *m.* (ichth.) Platypoecilius.

ПММА *abbr.* (**полиметилметакрилат**) polymethyl methacrylate.

ПМР *abbr.* (**протонный магнитный резонанс**) proton magnetic resonance; paramagnetic resonance control.

п.н. *abbr.* (**порядковый номер**).

ПНД *abbr.* (**подогреватель низкого давления**) low-pressure heater; (**поправка наклонной дальности**) slant-range correction.

пневма *f.* pneuma, breath(ing); **—тизация** *f.* (physiol.) pneumatization; **—тизированный** *a.* (zool.) pneumatized; **—тик** *m.* (pneumatic) tire; **—тика** *f.* pneumatics; **—тический** *a.* pneumatic; air-operated; air (lift); compressed-air (drive); percussion; diffused-air (aeration); **—тический элеватор** blower; **—тичность** *f.* (orn.) pneumaticity.

пневмато— *prefix* pneuma(to)— (air, gas; respiration); **—да** *f.* (bot.) pneumat(h)ode; **—з** *m.* (med.) pneumatosis; **—лиз** *m.* (geol.) pneumatolysis; **—лит** *m.* pneumatolith; **—литический** *a.* pneumatolytic; **—логия** *f.* (phys.) pneumatology, pneumatics; **—фор** *m.* (bot.) pneumatophore; **—форус** *m.* (ichth.) Pneumatophorus; **—целе** *n.* (med.) pneumatocele.

пневмеркатор *m.* pneumercator, pneumatic (liquid-level) gage.

пневмо— *prefix* pneumo— (lung); pneumatic; air-operated, pressure-operated; **—автоматика** *f.* pneumatic control (components); **—агент** *m.* carrier gas; **—аппарат** *m.* valve; **—бетон** *m.* gunite (concrete); **—вибратор** *m.* pneumatic vibrator; **—граф** *m.* (med.) pneumograph; **—датчик** *m.* pressure pickup; **—забойник** *m.* air-operated tamper; **—заброс** *m.* pneumatic spreading; **—золоудаление** *n.* pneumatic ash removal.

пневмо/клапан *m.* pneumatic valve; **—кокк** *m.* (bact.) pneumococcus; **—колёсный** *a.* pneumatic-tire(d); **—колонка** *f.* air column; **—мельница** *f.* pneumatic mill, flash pulverizer; **—метр** *m.* (med.) pneum(at)ometer, aspirometer; **—механический** *a.* pneumatic; **—микоз** *m.* (vet.) pneumomycosis, mycotic pneumonia; **—молот(ок)** *m.* pneumatic hammer; **—насос**

m. pneumatic pump, air-lift pump; **—ника** *f.* pneumonics; **—нический** *a.* (med.) pneumonic; **—ния** *f.* pneumonia; **—оборудование** *n.* pneumatic equipment.

пневмо/погрузчик *m.* blower-loader; **—подушка** *f.* pneumocushion, air cushion; **—подъём** *m.* air lifting; **—подъёмник** *m.* air lift; **—почта** *f.*, **контейнер —почты** (nucl.) (pneumatic) rabbit, shuttle; **—привод** *m.* pneumatic actuator; **—разгрузчик** *m.* discharge blower; **—раскрепитель** *m.* pneumatic uncoupler; **—распределитель** *m.* air distributor; **—силикоз** *m.* (med.) (pneumo)silicosis; **—склероз** *m.* pneumosclerosis; **—смеситель** *m.* compressed air mixer; **—сопротивление** *n.* fluidic or pneumonic resistor; **—сушилка** *f.* pneumatic dryer; **—тахограф** *m.* (med.) pneumotachograph; **—торакс** *m.* pneumothorax; **—трамбовка** *f.* compressed air rammer; **—транспорт(ёр)** *m.* pneumatic conveyer, blower; **—установка** *f.* pneumatic device; **—формование** *n.* (plastics) compressed air molding; **—шинный** *a.* rubber-tired; **—шлем** *m.* pneumatic helmet; **—электроклапан** *m.* electropneumatic valve.

пн/ёвый *a. of* **пень**; stump(y), stubby; **—ёвая поросль** (bot.) soble; **—екорчеватель** *m.* stump extractor; **—и** *pl. of* **пень**.

ПНР *abbr.* (**Польская Народная Республика**) Polish People's Republic.

пня *gen. of* **пень**.

по *prep. dat.* on, by, at, over, through, via, by the method of; from; regarding, with respect to; according to; along (the length); at the rate of; **по всему** throughout; **по двое** two at a time, in pairs; **по дороге** on the way, in passing; **по капле** drop by drop; **по Кариусу** by the Carius method; according to Carius; **по масштабу** to scale; **по нашему** by our method; in our opinion; **по одному** one at a time; *prep. acc.* as far as, up (to), till; **с 1920 по 1928 г.** from 1920 to 1928; *prep. prepos.* on, after; for; **по рассмотрении** on examination; **диаграмма по времени** time diagram.

ПО *abbr.* (**программное обеспечение**) (comp.) software.

по— *prefix with verbs signifying action which is weak or continues for a short or unknown length of time, usually translated as* "a little"; *prefix with adjectives and adverbs meaning* "somewhat more, as possible," *e.g.,* **поинтереснее** somewhat more interesting; as interesting as possible; *prefix with certain adverbs meaning* "in," *e.g.,* **по-английски** in English; **говорить по-английски** *v.* speak English.

побагроветь *v.* become purple.

побайтовый *a.* (comp.) byte-serial.

побаливать *v.* ache *or* hurt occasionally.

побалтывать *v.* agitate periodically.

побег *m.* escape, flight; (bot.) shoot, sprout, sucker, runner, stolon; scion, graft; **п. кущения** sucker; **водяной п.** water sprout; **корневой п.** soble; **плетевой п.** runner; **подземный п.** soble; **пускать —и** *v.* sprout; **—ать** *v.* run (a little); **—овьюн** *m.* (ent.) Evetria; **—овьюн-смолёвщик** *m.* pine resin-gall moth (*E. resinella*); **—оносный** *a.* (bot.) stoloniferous; **—ообразование** *n.* stolon formation.

победа *f.* victory, conquest, triumph.

победит *m.* pobedite (USSR alloy).

побед/итель *m.* winner, victor; **—ить** *see* **побеждать**; **—ный**, **—оносный** *a.* victorious, triumphant.

побежал/ость *f.* (met., min.) iridescence, iridescent tarnish, heat tinting; **цвет —ости** temper color, oxidation tint; **—ый** *a.* iridescent; temper (color).

побежать *v.* run; pass; start to run.

побежд/ать *v.* conquer, overcome, get the better (of); **—ённый** *a.* overcome.

побежка *f.* pace, gait (of horse); treadmill.

побей(те) *imp. of* **побить.**

побел *m.* whitewashing; **—а** *f.* (cer.) engobe; **—ение** *n.* whitening; **—еть** *v.* grow white, turn pale, blanch; **—ить** *v.* whiten, whitewash; **—ка** *f.* whitening, whitewashing.

побереж/ный *a. of* **побережье**; littoral; **—ье** *n.* seaboard, seaside, (sea)coast, shore.

поберечь *v.* save, conserve, keep.

побеспокоить *v.* disturb; **—ся** *v.* see to.

поби/вать *v.* beat; bruise; break; kill; **—тость** *f.* bruising (of produce); **—тый** *a.* beaten; bruised; broken; killed; **—ть** *see* **побивать.**

поблагодарить *v.* thank.

побледнеть *v.* turn pale.

поблёк/лый *a.* faded, etc., *see v.*; **—нуть** *v.* fade, dull, tarnish, (bot.) wither.

побл/ёскивать *v.* glimmer, gleam; **—естеть** *v.* shine for awhile.

поблизости *adv.* near (at hand), close by.

поблуждать *v.* stray for a while.

побоище *n.* slaughter, carnage.

побоку *adv.* to the side, away.

поболее *comp. of* **большой, много,** larger; more.

поболеть *v.* be sick or ache for a while.

поболтать *v.* agitate for a while; chat.

побольше *adv.* a little larger; a little more.

побор *m.* excessive tax *or* fee.

поборник *m.* advocate, supporter.

побороть *v.* overcome, conquer, subdue.

побочн/ый *a.* secondary, side, by—, subsidiary, subordinate, incidental; indirect; accessory, collateral, supplementary, adjoining; false, ghost, spurious (image, etc.); extraneous (wave); **п. вопрос** side issue; **п. продукт** by-product; **п. путь** (railroad) siding; **п. счёт** spurious count; **—ая валентность** auxiliary valence, secondary valence; **—ая ось** (cryst.) secondary axis; **—ая работа** sideline; **—ая реакция** side reaction; (med.) adverse reaction, side effect; **—ое действие** side effect; **—ое производство** sideline; **—ое ядро** (cyt.) paranucleus.

побрасывать *v.* throw from time to time.

побриться *v.* shave.

побродить *v.* wander for a while; ferment.

побросать *v.* throw haphazardly; abandon.

побрызг/ать *v.* sprinkle a little; **—ивать** *v.* sprinkle from time to time.

побудет *fut. 3 sing. of* **побыть.**

побудитель *m.* stimulus, stimulator, motivator; (elec.) booster; agitator (of batcher); **—ный** *a.* stimulating, motivating, inciting; **—ная причина** incentive, motive.

побудить *see* **побуждать.**

побужд/ать *v.* stimulate, impel, induce, prompt, spur (on), urge; force (circulation); **—ающий** *a.* stimulating, etc., *see v.*; **—ение** *n.* stimulation; incentive, motive, inducement; **—ённый** *a.* stimulated, etc., *see v.*

побуквенный *a.* character (printer).

побур/евший, —елый *a.* brown(ed); darkened (wine); **—ение** *n.* browning; (phyt.) brown rot; damping off (of seedlings); russeting (of fruit); (leaf) scorch; infuscation, darkening; **—еть** *v.* turn brown.

побыв/ать *v.* visit, be for a while; **—ка** *f.* leave of absence; (mil.) furlough.

побыть *v.* stay for a time.

побьёт *fut. 3 sing. of* **побить**.

п-ов *abbr.* (**полуостров**) peninsula.

повагонный груз carload.

повад/ить *v.* train; **—иться** *v.* get into the habit (of); **—ка** *f.* habit, custom, usage; **—ки** *pl.* behavior, conduct.

повал/енный *a.* thrown down, etc., *see v.;* **—ить** *v.* throw down, overthrow; tip over, overturn; knock down; fell (tree); start to fall (of snow, etc.); go or come in hordes; **—иться** *v.* fall; **—ка** *f.* throwing down, etc., *see v.;* turn(ing)-down (of converter); (vet.) epidemic pneumonia; **в —ку** huddled together, crowded.

повальн/о *adv.* without exception, all; **—ое** *n.*, **—ое воспаление лёгких** (vet.) pleuropneumonia; **—ый** *a.* general, collective, mass, wholesale; (med.) epidemic, epizootic; **—ая болезнь** mass epidemic.

повалять *v.* roll (in flour, etc.).

повар *m.* cook; **—енный** *a.* culinary, cooking; **—енная соль** common salt, sodium chloride; **—ить(ся)** *v.* cook for a while, digest for a while.

по-вашему *adv.* in your opinion; your way.

повевать *v.* fan from time to time.

поведать *see* **поведывать**.

поведен/ие *n.* conduct, behavior, performance; habit; procedure; **п. по времени** time behavior; **—ческий** *a.* behavioral.

поведённый *past pass. part. of* **повести**.

поведывать *v.* tell, communicate.

повезти *v.* take, deliver.

повёл *past m. sing. of* **повести**.

повелительный *a.* commanding, imperative.

повеллит *m.* (min.) powellite.

повенецкий *a.* (geog.) Povenets.

повер/енный *a.* entrusted; *m.* agent; attorney; **—ить** *v.* (en)trust; believe; check, verify; **—ка** *f.* check(ing), verification; inspection, examination; control (test); (math.) proof; (mil.) roll call; **на —ку** in actual fact.

повёрнутый *a.* turned, etc., *see* **повернуть**.

повернуть *v.* turn, rotate, swing (through); displace.

поверочн/ый *a.* of **поверка**; **п. анализ** check analysis; **—ая проба** umpire assay; **—ое испытание** check test; aptitude test.

повёрстный *a.* (by the) verst.

повертеть(ся) *v.* rotate for awhile.

повёртыва/ние *n.* turning; **—ть(ся)** *v.* turn (around); swivel; **—ться кругом** face about.

поверх *prep. gen. and adv.* over, above.

повехностно *adv.* on the surface, superficially; **п.-активный** *a.* surface-active; **п.-активное вещество** surfactant; **п.-барьерный** *a.* surface-barrier; **—сть** *f.* superficiality.

поверхностн/ый *a.* surface, superficial; skin (effect); shell-and-tube-type (desuperheater); (agr.) top (dressing); exposed (wire); **п. разряд** (elec.) surface discharge; **—ая закалка** (met.) case hardening; **—ая плотность** surface density; **—ое натяжение** surface tension; (oil/water) interfacial tension.

поверхност/ь *f.* surface, area, plane; face; (anat.) facies, superfacies, outer surface; topography; (water) table; **п. нагрева** heating surface; **п. раздела (фаз)** interphase, boundary surface; **п. разрыва** breakdown surface; shock front (of plasma); **п. среза** cut, section; **п. срыва** separation surface; **выход слоя на п.** (geol.) outcrop; **задняя п.** flank face (of tool); **нагрузка на единицу —и** load per unit area; **опорная п.** (robotics, comp.) footprint; **охлаждаемый с —и** surface-cooled; **передняя п.** rake face (of tool); **сожжение**

под —ью submerged combustion; **удельная п.** specific surface (area); (concrete) fineness.

поверху *adv.* on top, along the surface.

поверченный *a.* rotated a few times.

повершить *v.* top off.

повер/ье *n.* belief, superstition; **—ять** *v.* (en)trust; verify, check.

повеселить *v.* cheer up.

повесить *v.* hang (up), suspend.

повести *v.* lead, conduct, take (to); move.

повестка *f.* notice, summons, subpoena; **п. дня** agenda.

повесть *f.* story, account, report.

поветрие *n.* epidemic; infection; craze.

поветь *f.* (storage) shed.

повечереть *v.* become dusk.

повешен/ие *n.* hanging; **—ный** *a.* hung; hanged; *m.* hanged man.

повеять *v.* begin to blow.

повзрослеть *v.* grow up, mature.

повив *m.* lay(er) (of cables).

повивать *v.* (en)twine; spiral.

повидаться *v.* see each other, meet.

по-видимому *introd. word* probably, likely to be; seemingly, apparently; it seems, it appears.

повидло *n.* fruit paste; (apple) butter.

повили/ка, —ца *f.,* **—чный** *a.* (bot.) dodder (*Cuscuta*); **—ковые** *pl.* Cuscutaceae.

повинн/ость *f.* duty, obligation, compulsory service; **—ый** *a.* guilty.

повинов/аться *v.* obey, comply (with); **—ение** *n.* obedience, compliance.

повис/ать *v.* hang, droop, be suspended; **—ающий** *a.* hanging, etc., *see v.;* dependent; **—еть** *v.* hang for a while; **—лый** *a.* drooping, dependent; flaccid, flabby; **—нуть** *see* **повисать**.

повитель *m.* (bot.) bindweed.

повитуха *f.* (med.) midwife; (amph.) obstetrical toad (*Alytes obstetricans*).

повить *v.* (en)twine; spiral.

повлажнеть *v.* get damp.

повлечь *v.* involve, entail, necessitate, occasion, bring on; drag (along).

повлиять *v.* influence, affect.

повод *m.* rein; occasion, reason, ground, cause; **давать п.** cause, occasion, give rise (to); **по —у** in connection (with), apropos (of).

поводень *m.* (ent.) Graphoderes.

поводец *m.* (fishing) ganglion, snood.

поводить *v.* conduct, lead around, walk; move.

повод/ка *f.* distortion, deformation, warpage, buckling; shrinkage; **—ковый** *a.* of **поводка, поводок; п. патрон** carrier or catch plate; **—ковая рамка** tool-bar frame; **—ок** *m.* carrier, guide; lead, leash, line, rein; tenon, tongue; drawbar, towbar; inundation; (anat.) habenula; **—ырь** *m.* guide (of blind); **—ья** *pl. of* **повод;** reins.

повоз/ить *v.* (take for a) drive; **—иться** *v.* fuss, bother (with); **—ка** *f.,* **—очный** *a.* vehicle, conveyance, cart, carriage, wagon, car.

повой *m.* (bot.) glorybind (*Calystegia*); **—ни(че)к** *m.* waterwort (*Elatine*); **—ничковые** *pl.* Elatinaceae.

поволжье *n.* (geog.) Volga region.

поволока *f.* (bot.) involucre, spathe.

поволоч(ит)ь *v.* drag (for a while).

поворачива/ние *n.* turning, etc., *see v.;* **—ать** *v.* turn (round), swing, swivel, slew; turn over, tilt; change; divert, turn aside, deflect; (elec.) reverse; **—ать на**

себя pull; —ать от себя push; —аться v. turn, swing, swivel; rotate, work, run; —ающий a. turning, etc., see v.; rotator (muscle); —ающая внутрь мышца (anat.) pronator; —ающая наружу мышца supinator; —ающийся a. turning, etc., see v.; swivel; reversible.

поворот m. turn(ing), turning about, swinging around; bend, curve, corner(ing); reversal; see also **поворачивание**; (med.) version (of foetus); **п. координатной системы** (math.) rotation of axes; **механизм —а** tilting gear, swivelling mechanism; **муфта —а** steering clutch; **ось —а** pivot axis; **угол —а** deflection angle; —ить see **поворачивать.**

поворотлив/ость f. maneuverability, turning ability; handiness, agility; —ый a. maneuverable, handy, agile.

поворотно-/кратковременный a. continuously running; —лопастный a. adjustable-blade, Kaplan (turbine).

поворотн/ый a. turning, steering; rotating, rotatable, rotary, revolving, revolvable; swing(ing), traversing, deflection; swivel(ing), tilting, pivoted, slewing, slewable; reversing, reversible; hinged, articulated; rotational (isomerism); **п. кран** slewing crane, swing crane; **п. круг** turntable, turnplate; **п. момент** turning point; **п. свод** swing roof; —ая головка swivel head.

поворошить v. stir up a little.

повре/дить see **повреждать**; —ждаемость f. damageability, damage susceptibility, sensitivity to damage; —ждаемый a. damageable; —ждать v. damage, break, spoil, impair; injure, harm, hurt, wound; —ждаться v. get damaged, get out of order, break down, fail; —ждение n. damage, injury, harm, impairment, breakage, failure; accident; fault, defect; —ждение нейтронами neutron-induced damage; без —ждений a. undamaged, intact; биологическое —ждение biodeterioration; —ждённый a. damaged, etc., see v.; broken down.

повремен/ить v. put off, wait a little; —но adv. at regular intervals, periodically; —ный a. periodic(al), regular; (labor) by the hour/day/week/month; —ное издание periodical; —щик m. worker paid by time.

повседневн/о adv. daily, every day; —ость f. daily occurrence; —ый a. daily, everyday, routine.

повсеместн/о adv. universally, everywhere; —ый a. universal, ubiquitous, general; (biol.) common.

повсюду adv. everywhere, throughout.

повтор m. repetition; replica; —ение n. repetition, recurrence, (re)iteration; overlap(ping); (comp.) retry, recycling; replica(te), replication; —ённый a. repeated, etc., see **повторять**; —итель m. repeater; follower; —ительный a. repeating, reiterative; —ить see **повторять.**

повторн/о adv. repeatedly, (over) again; **использовать п.** v. reuse; —обеременная a. multigravid; —овходимый a. re-entrant (program); **п.-кратковременный** a. intermittent; recurring short-time; —ородящий a. multiparous; —ость f. repeatedness; (gen.) number of replications; —оцветущий a. (bot.) remontant, everblooming; —ый a. repeated, repetitive, reiterated, re—; recurrent (disease); after-(treatment); repeat (order); iterative (impedance); new (edition); several, multiple, duplicate; —ое замерзание refreezing.

повтор/яемость f. repetition, reiteration; recurrence, frequency; return period; redundancy; **п. импульсов** pulses per second; —яемый a. repetitive, repeating; repeatable; —ять v. repeat, reiterate, replicate; follow,

track; read back; (comp.) recycle; —яться v. recur; repeat, be repeated; —яющийся a. recurrent, reiterative; repeating, repetitive.

повы/дергать, —дёргивать v. pull out (all, many).

повым/ереть, —ирать v. die out.

повыс/итель m. booster, augmenter; (elec.) step-up transformer; —ительный a. boosting; step-up; —ить see **повышать**; —отный a. (surv.) upward.

повыть v. howl for a while.

повыш/ать v. raise, increase, heighten, augment, elevate; up(grade), enhance, improve, build up; promote, advance, boost; (elec.) step up; —аться v. rise, increase; improve; —ающий a. raising, etc., see v.; step-up; —е adv. somewhat higher; above; —ение n. raising, etc., see v.; rise, rising, increase, gain; build-up; —енный a. raised, etc., see v.; better, higher than usual; hyper—, super—, over—; —енная кислотность hyperacidity; —енное раздражение overstimulation; —енного типа advanced.

повьёт fut. 3 sing. of **повить.**

повядать v. wilt, wither.

повяз/ка f. band(age), dressing; (anat.) fascia; (plaster) cast; —(ыв)ать v. tie, bind; bandage; knit.

повянуть v. wilt, wither.

погадать v. guess, surmise.

погад/ить v. mess up, dirty; —ка f. (orn.) regurgitated pellet; —ки pl. ejection.

поган/ка f. (bot.) toadstool; **бледная п.** death cup (Amanita phalloides); (orn.) loon (Gavia); grebe (Podiceps); (ichth.) gudgeon (Gobio g.); —ковые pl. (orn.) Podicipedidae; —ый a. bad, unclean; poisonous (mushroom); garbage (can); —ь f. filth; dregs.

пога/сание n. extinction, extinguishment; (flame) failure; optical density; —сать, —снуть v. go out, be extinguished; —сить see **погашать**; —сший a. extinguished; extinct; —шаемый a. liquidating (e.g., loan); **автоматически —шаемый** a. self-liquidating; —шать v. extinguish, put out, quench; darken; pay off, liquidate, discharge (debt), amortize; cancel; —шение n. extinguishing, etc., see v.; extinction, extinguishment; (re)payment; —шенный a. extinguished, etc., see v.; out.

погектарный a. (per) hectare.

погиб/ать, —нуть v. perish, be killed, be lost; —ельный a. ruinous, disastrous; —ший a. lost, ruined, perished, defunct.

погибь f. (deck) camber.

погла/дить, —живать v. pat, stroke; iron a little; —живание n. patting, etc., see v.

поглот/ать v. swallow up; —итель m. (ab)sorbent, absorber; —ительный a. absorptive; dissipative (attenuator); accumulation (crossbreeding); —ительная башня absorption tower; —ительная способность absorptivity; —ительное вещество absorbent; —ить see **поглощать.**

поглощ/аемость f. absorptivity; —аемый a. absorbable; absorbed; —ательный see **поглотительный;** —ать v. absorb; swallow (up), take up, pick up, consume, engulf; capture (neutrons); —аться v. be absorbed; merge; be lost (to); —ающий see **поглотительный;** —ающая сила absorptivity.

поглощен/ие n. absorption; uptake, take-up, pick-up; capture (of neutrons); retention; input, consumption (of power); **коэффициент —ия** absorption coefficient; **сила —ия** absorptive power.

поглощённый a. absorbed, etc., see **поглощать.**

поглубже adv. somewhat deeper.

погляд/еть *v.* look, see; **—ывать** *v.* look from time to time.

пог. м. *abbr.* (**погонный метр**).

погнать *v.* drive; (chem.) distill; **—ся** *v.* ran (after), give chase; strive (for); be distilled.

погнёт *fut. 3 sing. of* **погнуть.**

погн(о)ить *v.* rot, decay.

погну/вшийся *a.* bent; **—тость** *f.* (slight) curvature; **—тый** *a.* bent, curved; **—ть** *v.* bend, curve.

поговорить *v.* talk (of), discuss.

погода *f.* weather.

погодить *v.* wait a little.

погодки *pl.* siblings with a year's difference.

погодо/о *adv.* annually, yearly, per year; **—ый** *a.* annual, yearly; weather.

погодо— *prefix* weather; **—стойкий, —устойчивый** *a.* weatherproof, weather-resistant; **—стойкость, —устойчивость** *f.* weather(ing) resistance.

погожий *a.* (meteor.) fine.

поголов/но *adv.* without exception, all; one by one; **—ный** *a.* general; by the head; **—ье** *n.* livestock (population), stock, number; **недостаточное —ье** understocking.

поголодать *v.* starve for a while.

поголубеть *v.* turn blue(r).

погон *m.* distillate, fraction; pursuit; (ball) race; (mil.) shoulder strap; **—ит** *fut. 3 sing. of* **погнать.**

погонофоры *pl.* (zool.) Pogonophora.

погон/щик *m.* driver, drover; **—ыш** *m.* (orn.) crake (*Porzana p.*); **—ыш-крошка** *m.* tiny crake (*P. pusilla*); **—я** *f.* quest (for); pursuit, chase; **—ялка** *f.* (text.) picking stick; **—ять** *v.* drive, urge on; (chem.) distill.

погор/ать, —еть *v.* burn (down, out; for a while); fail; **—елый** *a.* burned.

пограничн/ик *m.* frontier guard; **—ый** *a.* border(line), bordering (upon), adjacent, adjoining; frontier (area); boundary; interdisciplinary; **—ый слой** boundary layer; **—ая область** border zone; **—ая пластинка** (anat.) terminal plate.

погранохрана *f.* frontier guards.

погреб *m.* cellar; vault; (powder) magazine; (petr.) vug; *past m. sing. of* **погрести; —ать** *v.* bury, inter; **—ение** *n.* burial, interment; **—ённый** *a.* buried, interred; blind (placer); connate (water); **—ной** *a. of* **погреб; —ное хозяйство** wine cellar(s); **—ок** *m.* recess; wine shop.

погрем/ок *m.*, **—ушка** *f.* rattle; *n.* (bot.) yellow rattle (*Rhinanthus, Alectophorophus*).

погрести *v.* bury; rake for a while; row for a while.

погреть *v.* heat up, warm up.

погреш/ать, —ить *v.* err, make mistakes; **—имость** *f.* fallibility; **—имый** *a.* fallible; **—ность** *f.* error, mistake; fault, defect; (stat.) uncertainty; **—ность инструмента** instrument(al) error; **—ность округления** (comp.) rounding error; **—ность отбрасывания** truncation error; **абсолютная —ность** accuracy (of reading).

погруб/елый *a.* roughened, coarse, grown hard; **—еть** *v.* roughen, grow hard.

погруж/аемый *a.* submergible, submersible; immersion, immersed; **—ать** *v.* plunge, dip, immerse, submerge, bury, embed, sink; load; **—аться** *v.* plunge, dive; dip, sink (into), (sub)merge; cave in; settle down; **—аю-щий(ся)** *a.* plunging, etc., *see v.*; **—ение** *n.* plunging, etc., *see v.*; plunge, dive, dip; immersion, submersion, submergence; **—ение свай** pile driving; **испытание при —ении** (met.) immersion test; **—ённость** *f.* sub-

mergence; **—ённый** *a.* plunged, etc., *see v.*; hidden, concealed; swimming-pool (nuclear reactor); **—ённый в масло** oil-immersed; **—ной** *a.* immersion, immersible, submersible; subsurface; deep-well, underwater (pump); dipping (refractometer).

погруз/ившийся *a.* sunken, buried; **—ить** *see* **погружать; —ка** *f.* load(ing), shipping, freight handling; **—ка жидкостей** liquid cargo; **—очно-разгрузочный** *a.* handling, loading and unloading; **—очно-разгрузочные устройства** handling facilities; **—очный** *a.* load(ing), charging; **—очная установка** handling equipment; **—чик** *m.* loader; **вильчатый —чик** forklift; **грейферный —чик** clam-type loader; **—чик-зернопульт** *m.* (grain) blower; **—чик-штабелёр** *m.* loader-stacker.

погрыз *m.* trace of gnawing; **—ть** *v.* gnaw (for a while; up); **—ы** *pl.* toothmarks.

погряз/ать, —нуть *v.* get stuck, mire.

погуб/ить, —лять *v.* ruin, destroy.

погулять *v.* take a walk; play (for a while).

погустеть *v.* thicken.

под *m.* (furnace) hearth, bottom; depression; **печь с вращающим —ом** rotary-hearth furnace.

под *prep. acc. denoting direction: instr. denoting position:* under(neath), below; to, toward, near; to receive, to accommodate, to fit; at (an angle); in (latitude); open to (question); in imitation of; **п. гору** down hill; **п. землёй** underground; **п. красное дерево** in imitation of mahogany; **п. рукой** near at hand.

под— *prefix* sub—, hypo—, infra— (under, below); (geog.) near; *with verbs indicating* under, up to, close; *also* up, *as in* **подсчитать** *v.* count up.

подав/аемый *a.* fed, etc., *see v.*; feed (water); **—аль-щик** *m.* feeder, server; waiter; supplier, delivery man; **—ание** *n.* feeding, etc., *see v.*; **—атель** *m.* feeder, feeding device, feeding carriage; (art.) magazine platform; (spring) elevator; **—ать** *v.* feed, supply, provide, convey, deliver, conduct; discharge, release; serve, give, present; submit, hand in (application); set (an example); **—аться** *v.* be fed, etc.; feed (into), enter; draw, move; give way, yield.

подав/итель *m.* suppressor; attenuator (of oscillation); (flotation) depressant, depressing agent; depressor; **—ить** *see* **подавлять; —иться** *v.* choke; **—ление** *n.* suppression, etc., *see v.*; quenching, etc.; depression, decrease; **—ление по протонам** proton decoupling (NMR); **—ленный** *a.* suppressed, etc., *see v.*; (med.) latent; **—лять** *v.* suppress, repress, restrain; (chem.) inhibit; overwhelm, crush; quench; (de)press; eliminate; (mil.) neutralize; **—ляющий** *a.* suppressing, etc., *see v.*; overwhelming (majority); **—ляющий фаг** phage-inhibiting.

подавно *adv.* all the more.

подагр/а *f.* (med.) podagra, gout; **—ик** *m.* podagra patient; **—ический** *a.* podagric, podagral, gouty; (bot.) podagricous.

подазотистый *a.* hyponitrous (acid).

подалирий *m.* (ent.) Papilio podalirius.

подальше *adv.* somewhat farther on.

подапшеронский *a.* (geog.) near Apsheron.

подар/енный *a.* donated; **—ить** *v.* donate, give; **—ок** *m.*, **—очный** *a.* gift, donation.

податель *m.* bearer, petitioner.

податлив/ость *f.* pliability, flexibility, pliancy, ductility; give, yielding; (min.) bearing strength; (acous.) compliance; **п. эрозии** erodibility (of soil); **—ый** *a.* pliable, flexible, pliant, yielding, workable.

подать *see* **подавать;** *f.* tax, duty.

подач/а *f.* giving, presenting; supply, feed(ing), introduction, injection; delivery, delivering; conveyance, admission, inflow, input; motion, travel, approach; advance, advancing; capacity (of pump); (steam) flood; **п. воздуха** air feed, air supply; **п. насосом** pumping; **высота —и** lift (of pump); **коробка подач** gear box; feed unit, feeder; **механизм —и** feed mechanism; **объём —и** delivery volume (of pump); **с автоматической —ей** self-feeding; **с верхней —ей** *a.* top-fed; **с нижней —ей** *a.* bottom-fed, underfeed.

подающ/ий *a.* feed(ing), conveying, supply, delivery (pump, pipe); **п. механизм** feeder; **п. червяк** worm conveyer; screw conveyer; **—ая лента** feed belt.

подбаб/ник *m.* driving cap (for pipe); **—ок** *m.* follower; driving cap.

подбав/ить, —лять *v.* add (a little); **—ка** *f.* adding, addition.

подбадривать *v.* encourage.

подбал/ка *f.* bolster, support; trimmer; **—очник** *m.* trimmer.

подбалтывать *v.* beat in, mix in, stir in.

подбарабанье *n.* (mech.) concave.

подбегать *v.* run up to.

подбедренный *a.* (anat.) subfemoral.

подбежать *v.* run up to.

подбей(те) *imp. of* **подбить.**

подбел *m.* (bot.) Petasites; Andromeda.

подбел/ивание *n.*, **—ка** *f.* whitening, bleaching; (calico) branning; **—и(ва)ть** *v.* whiten, bleach.

подбережник *m.* (bot.) purple loosestrife (*Lythrum salicaria*).

подберёзовик *m.* birch mushroom.

подберёт *fut. 3 sing. of* **подобрать.**

подбив/ать *v.* line, pad; pack; drive under; nail up; instigate; disable (a gun); resole (shoes); **—аться** *v.* damage (soles of hoof); injure (pads of dog); **—ка** *f.* lining, etc., *see v.*

подбир/ание *n.* gathering, etc., *see v.*; selection; **—ать** *v.* gather, glean, collect, pick up; select, sort (out), collate, assort, match, fit, blend (colors); **—аться** *v.* be gathered, etc.; steal up to.

подбить *see* **подбивать.**

подблоковый *a.* (anat.) infratrochlear.

подбодр/ить, —ять *v.* encourage.

подб/оечный *a. of* **подбойка;** **—ой** *m.* lining; nailing (on); knocking down; (min.) cut(ting); (shoes) sole leather; **—ойка** *see* **подбой;** set hammer; tamper; swage; (min.) (under)cutting; **—ойник** *m.* swage; **—ойный** *a. of* **подбой;** **—ойщик** *m.* (min.) cutter.

подболт/ать *v.* mix in, add; **—ка** *f.* mixing in, addition; additive.

подбор *m.* selection, choice; collection, assortment, set; matching, fitting; proportioning; grading; (biol.) breeding; **п. состава** proportioning, mix design; **в п.** (typ.) run on; set flush; **путём —а** by trial and error; **на п.** selected, assorted.

подбора *f.* (fishing) seine rope, line.

подборка *see* **подбирание;** collection.

подбород/ник *m.*, **—ный ремень** throatband (of halter); **—ок** *m.* (anat.) mentum, chin; (biol.) mentum.

подбородочн/о— *prefix* (anat.) mento—, genio— (chin); **п.-губной** *a.* mentolabial; **п.-задний** *a.* mentoposterior; **п.-челюстной** *a.* mentomandibular; **—ый** *a.* mental, chin; submental (artery).

подборочн/о-раскладочная машина collator; **—ый** *a. of* **подборка.**

подборщик *m.* picker, collector; sorter; (agr.) pick-up attachment; **п.-волокуша** *m.* pick-up hay rake; **п.-**измельчитель *m.* pick-up chopper; **п.-копнитель** *m.* pick-up hay shocker.

подбр/асывать, —осить *v.* throw up, toss up; throw (under); abandon; add; **—ос** *m.* (geol.) underthrust fault; **—оска** *f.* throwing up, etc., *see v.*; addition; **—ошенный** *a.* thrown up, etc., *see v.*

подбрюш/ина *f.* (zool.) underbelly; **—инный** *a.* (anat.) subperitoneal; **—ник** *m.* (harness) belly band; (boiler) cradle, saddle; (naut.) packing (timbers).

подбугор/ный *a.* (anat.) subthalamic; **—ье** *n.* subthalamus, hypothalamus.

подбур/ок *m.*, **—очный** *a.* (min.) block or plug hole.

подбутка *f.* inferior concrete.

подвал *m.* basement, cellar; vault; (newspaper) lower part, feuilleton.

подвали(ва)ть *v.* come en masse; heap up, add; roll under; float (up to), moor; **—ся** *v.* fall under.

подвальн/ый *a. of* **подвал;** **п. этаж** basement; **—ая мушка** (ent.) vinegar fly (*Drosophila*).

подвальцовка *f.* rerolling.

подвар/и(ва)ть *v.* weld on, reweld; cook, digest or boil again or more; **—ка** *f.* welding on, etc., *see v.*; (welding) backing run; **—очный** *a.* back(ing), sealing.

подващивать *v.* wax (more).

подвед/ение *n.* leading up to etc., *see* **подводить** supply; **п. фундамента** underpinning; **—ённый** *a.* led up to, etc., *see* **подводить.**

подведомственный *a.* in charge (of); within the jurisdiction (of).

подвез/ти *v.* deliver, haul, transport; **ему —ло** he had a stroke of luck.

подвер/гаемый *a.* subjected (to), etc., *see v.*; under; **—гать** *v.* subject, submit, put through, impose, place (strain on); treat (with); expose (to); **—гать анализу** analyze; **—гать гидролизу** hydrolyze; **—гать действию** expose (to the action of); treat; **—гать испытанию** test, experiment (with); **—гаться** *v.* be subjected, etc.; undergo, experience, go through; run into (danger); be open (to question); **—гающий** *a.* subjecting, etc., *see v.*; **—гающийся действию** exposed (to); **—гнуть** *see* **подвергать;** **—жение** *n.* subjection, etc., *see v.*; **—жение изгибу** bending load; **—женность** *f.* susceptibility; liability; **—женный** *a.* subjected (to), etc., *see v.*; subject, liable (to), susceptible, prone (to); **—женный нагреву** heat-affected.

подвёрнутый *a.* tightened, etc., *see* **подвёртывать;** involute.

подвернуть *see* **подвёртывать.**

подв/ерстать, —ёрстывать *v.* (typ.) make up additionally.

под/вертеть *see* **подвёртывать; —вёртка** *see* **подвёртывание;** second wrapper.

подвертлужный *a.* (anat.) hip (joint).

подвёртыв/ание *n.* tightening, etc., *see v.*; **—ать** *v.* tighten, screw; fold or turn under; slip or thrust under; **—аться** *v.* slip under; turn up, appear.

подверх/ний, —ушечный *a.* (biol.) subapical.

подвес *m.* suspension; suspension device, carrier arm, hanger; **точка —а** point of support; **—ить** *see* **подвешивать; —ка** *f.* suspension, hanging; suspension support, arm or member; suspender, hanger, hinge, bracket; (engine) mounting; **система —ок** supporting structure; **точка —ки** slinging point.

подвесн/ой, —ый *a.* suspension, suspended, hanging, hanger, supporting; overhead, overhung, aerial; underslung; swinging, pendant; mounted, attached; midmounted (implement); outboard (motor); trolley (conveyer); pod-type (ramjet engine); **п. мост** suspension bridge; **—ая дорога** ropeway, overhead trolley, monorail; **—ая дуга** bracket rim (of furnace); **—ая кривая** (math.) catenary; **—ая рейка** leveling rod; **—ая рессора** supporting spring; **—ая система** supporting structure; (parachute) harness; **—ая стенка** breastwall.

подвесо/к *m.* (biol.) suspensor; **—чный** *a.* suspensory, suspended; hyomandibular (bone).

подвести *see* **подводить.**

подветренный *a.* (naut.) lee(ward).

подвеш/енный *a.* suspended, pendent, perched (rock); **—енный на пружинах** spring-mounted; **—ивание** *n.* suspension, hanging; **—ивать** *v.* suspend, hang (up); hook; mount (on springs); **—ивающий** *a.* suspending, etc., *see v.*; suspensory.

подвздошн/о — *prefix* (anat.) ilio— (ilium); **п.-бедренный** *a.* iliofemoral; **п.-гребешковый** *a.* iliopectineal; **п.-копчиковый** *a.* iliococcygeal; **п.-крестцовый** *a.* iliosacral; **п.-лобковый** *a.* iliopubic; **п.-ободоч-(нокишеч)ный** *a.* ileocolic; **п.-паховый** *a.* ilioinguinal; **п.-подчревный** *a.* iliohypogastric; **п.-поясничный** *a.* iliolumbar; **п.-рёберный** *a.* iliocostal; **п.-слепокишечный** *a.* ileocecal; **—ый** *a.* iliac; **—ая кишка** ileum; **—ая кость** ilium; **—ая область** inguen, groin.

подвивать *v.* curl slightly.

подвиг *m.* exploit, feat.

подвиг/ание *n.* advance; **—ать** *v.* move (on), advance, promote; **—аться** *v.* advance, make progress, get ahead; **—аться вперёд** *v.* progress.

подвид *m.*, **—овой** *a.* (biol.) subspecies.

подвижка *f.* movement, shift; (tectonics) shove; (ore) adjustment; (ice) push, debacle.

подвижник *m.* mover; zealot, devotee.

подвижногрудые *pl.* (amph.) Arcifera.

подвижн/ой, —ый *a.* mobile, movable, moving; (trans)portable; migratory; traveling, sliding, traversing; loose, free, floating; vagile, wandering, free-floating; active, lively; flexible; live (center); dynamic (equilibrium); moving-bed (catalyst); **п. контакт** (elec.) sliding contact; **п. кран** traveling crane; **п. состав** (rr.) rolling stock; **—ая (теле)камера** (robotics) agile camera; **—ая счётная таблица** sliding scale; **—ая щека** swing jaw (of crusher); **—ое топливо** (nucl.) circulating fissionable material; **—ость** *f.* mobility, maneuverability; fluidity; liveliness; portability; availability (of nutrients); (zoogeog.) vagility; (chem.) migration speed; **—ость ионов** ionic mobility; **терять —ость** *v.* get sluggish.

подвинтить *see* **подвинчивать.**

подвинут/ый *a.* progressive, advancing; **—ь** *see* **подвигать.**

подвинчивать *v.* screw up or down, tighten.

подвисание *n.* hanging, suspension; hold-up (in distillation); **п. шихты** (met.) bridging-over of stock.

подвисочный *a.* (anat.) infratemporal.

подвить *v.* curl slightly.

подвишен/ник *m.*, **—ь** *f.* (bot.) subcherry mushroom (*Clitopilus prunulus*).

подвластный *a.* subject (to), dependent (on).

подвод *see* **подводка;** input; admission; feed line; (elec.) lead; (comp.) positioning; underpinning prop; **п. тепла** heat supply; **линия —а** supply line.

подвода *f.* wagon, cart.

подвод/имый *a.* fed, supplied; **п. воздух** air supply; **—имая мощность** power input; **—имое количество** input; **—ить** *v.* lead up to, conduct, bring into contact (with); deliver, feed, supply, provide; place under;

—ка *f.* leading up to, etc., *see v.*; delivery, feed(ing), supply.

подводник *m.* submariner; diver; aqualung; (ent.) dytiscid beetle (*Coelambus*).

подводной *a.* of **подвод;** feed.

подводн/ый *a.* subaqueous; submarine; submerged; sunk(en); submersible (instrument); undersea; underwater; (bot.) submersed; wagon; **—ая лодка** submarine, U-boat; **—ая мина** depth charge; **—ое крыло** (hydrodyn.) hydrofoil; **—ое плавание** scuba diving; **—ое течение** undercurrent.

подводчик *m.* feeder; wagon driver.

подводящ/ий *a.* leading up to, conveying, feed(ing), supply, delivery; inlet; tributary (ditch); **п. канал** head race, feeder; (intake) conduit; **п. провод** (elec.) supply main, feeder; **—ее сопло** feed nozzle, distributing nozzle.

по-двое *adv.* in pairs, two at a time.

подвоз *m.* supply; transport(ation), hauling, conveyance.

подвозбудитель *m.* (elec.) pilot exciter.

подвозить *v.* bring, carry; transport.

подвоз/ка *f.* hauling, transportation, delivery; **—ный** *a.* imported; **—чик** *m.* hauler, transporter, delivery man.

подвой *m.* (hort.) rootstock.

подволакивать *v.* haul (by portage).

подволок *m.* attic; **—а** *f.* attic; (naut.) ceiling, deckhead.

подволоч/ить, —ь *v.* haul (by portage).

подворачивать *v.* turn under.

подворный *a.* per farm.

подворотить *v.* turn under.

подворотня *f.* gate baseboard; gateway.

подвощить *v.* wax slightly.

подвпрыск *m.* secondary injection (of fuel).

подвулканиз/ация *f.* (rubber) prevulcanization, precuring, scorch(ing); **—ировать** *v.* burn (stock); **—овывать** *v.* prevulcanize, precure, scorch.

подвывих *m.* (med.) subluxation.

подвыпить *v.* sip; have a few drinks.

подвяз/ать *see* **подвязывать;** **—ка** *f.* binding; suspender; garter; **—ной** *a.* suspended; **—очный** *a.* of **подвязка;** **—ывание** *n.* binding, tying (up); **—ывать** *v.* bind, tie (up); **—ь** *f.* binding, cord(ing).

подвял/ивание *n.*, **—ка** *f.* wilting, withering; open-air drying; **—и(ва)ть** *v.* cure slightly; cure more; expose to air.

подгаечник *m.* (mech.) lock nut.

подгар *m.* scorch(ing), burn-off; (elec.) burning; (nucl.) burn-up.

подгиб *m.* (met.) bended form; **—ать** *v.* bend under or back; **—ной** *a.* bendable.

подглаз/н(ичн)ый *a.* (anat.) suborbital, infraorbital; **—ье** *n.* suborbital depression.

подглазурный *a.* (cer.) underglaze.

подглоточн/ик *m.* (anat.) hypopharynx; **—ый** *a.* hypopharyngeal, suboesopharyngeal.

подгн/ивание *n.* rotting; **—и(ва)ть** *v.* start decaying, rot slightly; **—оить** *v.* rot, decay.

подгов/аривать, —орить *v.* incite, instigate.

подголов/ник *m.* head rest; **—ный** *a.* under the head; **—ок** *m.* neck (of bolt).

подголосовой *a.* (anat.) infraglottic.

подгон *see* **подгонка;** (bot.) second growth; **—ка** *f.* driving on, etc., *see v.*; adjustment, fit, alignment; **—ный** *a.* of **подгон;** **—ообразование** *n.* sprouting; **—очный** *a.* of **подгон;** **—щик** *m.* driver; beater; **—ять** *v.* drive on, fit, match, adjust, adapt, work into place; trim, reduce (to one size); drive up to or under; speed up, hurry, urge on.

подгор/ание *n.* scorching, burning; gumming up (of piston rings); **—ать, —еть** *v.* scorch, burn; catch fire; **—елый** *a.* scorched, burnt.

подгоризонт *m.* subhorizon.

подгорный *a.* (geol.) submontane.

подгородный *a.* near a city, suburban.

подгорье *n.* foothills.

подготавлив/ание *see* **подготовка**; **—ать** *see* **подготовлять**.

подготовитель *m.* preparator; **—но-заключительный** *a.* set-up and clear (work); preparation and finishing-up (time); **—ный** *a.* preparatory, preliminary; roughing (mill); **—ная работа** preliminary work, development (work).

подготов/ить *see* **подготовлять**; **—ка** *f.* preparation, preparing, etc., *see v.*; (hort.) treatment; **—ка текстов** word processing; **без —ки** unprepared, impromptu; **—ление** *see* **подготовка**; **—ленность** *f.* preparedness; readiness; fitness; **—ленный** *a.* prepared, etc., *see v.*; ready, fit (for); **—лять** *v.* prepare, (make) ready; train, school; prime (engine).

подгр/ебание *n.* raking up; **—ебать** *v.* rake (up to), scrape up; row (up to); **—ёбка** *f.* raking up; **—ёбки** *pl.* rakings; **—ебной** *a.* raked up; **—ести** *see* **подгребать**.

подгруд/инный *a.* (anat.) substernal, infrasternal; **—ной** *a.* subpectoral; **—ный ремень** breastband; **—ок** *m.* (zool.) dewlap, jowl, wattles.

подгрузд/ок *m.* (bot.) Russula; **—ь** *m.* Lactarius scrobiculatus.

подгруз/ить *v.* load more, add; **—ка** *f.* additional load(ing), additional charge.

подгруппа *f.* subgroup, subunit.

подгрушевидный *a.* (anat.) infrapiriform.

подгрыз(а)ть *v.* gnaw under, undermine.

подд/авать *v.* increase, reinforce; throw up, kick; subdue, subjugate; **—аваться** *v.* yield, give in, give way; be prone, be susceptible, be amenable, lend itself (to); **—аваться ремонту** be repairable; **не —аваться действию** be unaffected (by), be resistant (to); **—анный** *a.* increased, etc., *see v.*; *m.* subject; **—анство** *n.* citizenship; **—ать** *see* **поддавать**; **—ача** *f.* increasing, etc., *see v.*; increase, reinforcement.

поддающийся *a.* yielding (to); **—able**; e.g., **п. обработке** machinable; **п. ремонту** repairable; **не п.** unyielding, resisting; **не п. анализу** unanalyzable.

поддвиг *m.* (geol.) underthrust.

под/дёв *m.* (fishing) hand line, jig; **—девать** *v.* lift up; hook, snag; wear (underneath); **—девный** *a.* long-line (fishing).

поддел/ать, —ывать *v.* forge, falsify; imitate, counterfeit; adulterate; **—ка** *f.* imitation, counterfeit; adulteration; adulterant; **—ывание** *n.* imitation, counterfeiting; adulteration; **—ьный** *a.* counterfeit, forged (signature); fake, imitation; artificial, synthetic; false, dummy; adulterated, impure.

поддельтовидный *a.* (anat.) subdeltoid.

поддёргивать *v.* tug, pull, jerk (up).

поддерж/ание *n.* supporting, etc., *see v.*; maintenance, upkeep; (chem.) stabilization; **—анный** *a.* supported, etc., *see v.*; **—ать** *see* **поддерживать**; **—иваемый** *see* **поддержанный**; sustainable; **—ивание** *see* **поддержание**; **—ивать** *v.* support, hold (up), bear, carry; sustain, keep; maintain, keep up; service; advocate, back up, favor; **—ивающий** *a.* supporting, etc., *see v.*; supportive; maintenance, sustenance (ration); lifting (force); (anat.) suspensory (ligament); trailing, balancer (wheel); **—ивающее устройство** carrier; **—ка** *see*

поддержание; support, prop, rest, holder, carrier, stay; (riveting) dolly; (reel) post; (anat.) sustenaculum.

поддёрнуть *see* **поддёргивать**.

поддёсенный *a.* (anat.) subgingival.

поддеть *see* **поддевать**.

поддиапазон *m.* subrange, sub-band.

поддиафрагмальный *a.* (anat.) subdiaphragmatic, subphrenic.

поддир *m.* (min.) cutting wedge.

поддолевой *a.* (anat.) infralobar.

поддоменник *m.* (met.) furnace house.

поддомкрачивать *v.* jack (up).

поддон *m.* tray, (drip) pan; sump; (cargo) pallet; (ingot) stool.

поддуб/ица *f.* oak-forest soil; **—ливание** *n.* (leather) pretannage; **—овик** *m.* (bot.) Boletus pachypurus.

подду/вало *n.*, **—вальный** *a.* (furnace) ash pit; **—вание** *n.* heaving, etc., *see v.*; heave; creep(ing) (of soil); **—(ва)ть** *v.* heave, swell; blow (under); **—вающийся** *a.* heaving.

поддуговой *a.* (anat.) subarcuate.

подевать *v.* put, dispose (of).

подействовать *v.* act, have an effect (on); work, operate.

подекадно *adv.* every ten days.

поделать *v.* make, do, perform.

подел/ённый *a.* shared; **—ить(ся)** *v.* share.

подел/ка *f.* odd job; article; manufacture, fabrication; **—очный** *a.* manufacturing, fabricating; commercial (timber).

подён/ка *f.* day work; (ent.) May fly; **—ки** *pl.* Ephemeridae; **—но** *adv.* daily, by the day; **—ный** *a.* daily, day; *m.* day laborer; **—щик** *m.* day laborer; **—щина** *f.* day labor, manual labor; **—щица** *f.* working woman.

подера *f.* (geom.) pedal curve.

подёрг/ивание *n.* twitch(ing), jerk(ing); **—(ив)ать** *v.* twitch, jerk, pull (at).

подерж/ание *n.* holding, keeping; **взять на п.** *v.* borrow; **дать на п.** *v.* lend; **—анный** *a.* secondhand, used; kept, held; **—ать** *v.* hold for some time, keep for a while.

подёрнуть *v.* jerk or tug lightly; cover (with mist or ice).

подеций *m.* (bot.) podetium.

подешеветь *v.* get cheaper.

поджаберный *a.* (embr.) hypobranchial.

поджар/енный *a.* roasted; fried; **—ивание** *n.* roasting; frying; **—и(ва)ть** *v.* roast (a little); toast; fry; broil; **—ка** *f.* frying; fried meat.

поджарый *a.* lean, thin, wiry; flat (stomach).

поджат/ие *see* **поджим**; adjustment; waisting (of fuselage); **—ь** *see* **поджимать**.

поджелудочн/о— *prefix* (anat.) pancreatico— (pancreatic duct); **п.-селезёночный** *a.* pancreaticosplenic; **—ый** *a.* pancreatic; subventricular; **—ая железа** pancreas.

поджечь *see* **поджигать**.

подживать *v.* heal, be healing.

поджиг *m.* ignition; **—ание** *n.* ignition, firing; **—атель** *m.* incendiary; igniter; instigator; **—ательный** *a.* inflammatory; **—ать** *v.* set fire (to), ignite, light, kindle; **—ающий** *a.* incendiary; trigger, keep-alive (electrode).

поджидать *v.* wait (for), watch (for).

поджилки *pl.* (anat.) hough, hock.

поджим *m.*, **—ание** *n.* drawing in, etc., *see v.*; contraction; **—ать** *v.* draw in, contract; tighten, adjust; precompress (air); **—ающий** *a.* drawing in, etc., *see v.*; preliminary (compressor).

поджить *see* **подживать**.

поджог *m.* setting fire (to); arson.

подзаголов/ок *m.*, **—очные сведения** subtitle, subhead(ing).

подзар/яд *m.* (elec.) boost charge, recharge, recharging; **—ядить, —яжать** *v.* recharge; replenish; **—ядка** *see* **подзаряд.**

подзатылочный *a.* (anat.) suboccipital.

подзащитный *m.* client (of lawyer).

подзвуковой *a.* (acous.) subsonic.

под/зём *m.* subsoil; **—земелье** *n.*, **—земельный** *a.* cave, vault; **—земка** *f.* subway.

подземный *a.* underground, subterranean, subsurface; buried; ground (water, ice); subsoil; (coal gasification) in situ; subway (train); **п. толчок, п. удар** earthquake shock; **п. ход** subway, tunnel.

подзёмок *m.* subway; small heater.

подзимний *a.* late fall, early winter.

подзовёт *fut. 3 sing. of* **подозвать.**

подзол *m.* (soil) podzol; (leather) lime slurry, tanning lime; **—изация** *f.* podzolization; **—исто-болотный** *a.* podzolic boggy; **—истость** *f.* podzol content; **—истый** *a.* podzolic; **—ообразование** *n.* podzol formation; **—ообразовательный** *a.* podzol-forming.

подзона *f.* subzone.

подзор *m.* trim, edging; (naut.) counter, overhang.

подзорн/ый *a.* observation; sight (glass); **—ая труба** telescope, field glass.

подзывать *v.* call up, call over.

подизвестковистый *a.* subcalcareous.

подий *m.* podium.

подин/а *f.* furnace bottom, hearth, sole; fettling (of open-hearth furnace); **подготовка —ы** fettling, fritting.

подинтегральн/ый *a.* (math.) subintegral; **—ая функция** integrand.

подкалиберный снаряд (mil.) sabot.

подкали(ва)ть *v.* heat (slightly; more).

подкалывать *v.* split, cleave, break (a little); pin up; puncture, prick.

подкаменщик *m.* (ichth.) sculpin (*Cottus*); *also the common name for 8 other species;* **—овые** *pl.* Cottidae.

подканал *m.* subchannel.

подкапать *v.* drip in more.

подкапливать *v.* accumulate (slowly; more); store up.

подкапчивать *v.* smoke (lightly; more).

подкапывать *v.* undermine, dig under, dig down, excavate; plow out; add (by drops).

подкараули(ва)ть *v.* be on the watch (for).

подкармлив/ание *n.* supplementary feeding; **—ать** *v.* feed up, fatten; dress (plants).

подкасательный *a.* (geom.) subtangent.

подкассетник *m.* spool holder (of tape recorder).

подкат *see* **подкатка;** (met.) semifinished rolled stock; **—ить** *see* **подкат(ыв)ать; —ка** *f.* rolling, etc., *see v.;* fullering, rounding-up; **—чик** *m.* (min.) drawer; **—(ыв)ать** *v.* roll (up to, under); drive up.

подкач/анный *a.* pumped; added; **—енный** *past pass. part. of* **подкатить; —ивание** *n.*, **—ка** *f.* pumping, etc., *see v.;* addition; excitation (of laser, etc.); (comp.) roll-in, swap-in, swap(ping); **файл —ки** swapfile; **—(ив)ать** *v.* pump (up to; more); add; (comp.) spool (data); boost; **—ивающий** *a.* pumping, etc., *see v.;* booster (pump).

подкашивать *v.* mow (down, more).

подква/сить, —шивать *v.* inoculate with ferment; acidulate.

подки/д(ыв)ать, —нуть *see* **подбрасывать.**

подкипятить *v.* boil (lightly; more).

подкисл/ение *n.* acidification; acidulation; **—енный** *a.*

(slightly) acidified, acidulous; **—ить, —ять** *v.* acidify; acidulate; **—яющий** *a.* acidifying.

подкишечный *a.* (anat.) subintestinal.

подклад *m.* (poultry) dummy eggs; **—ка** *f.* lining, back(ing), pad(ding), cushion(ing), pillow; packing, strip, washer; base, foundation; block; **—ки** *pl.* blocking; **—ной** *a.* (laid) under, base, sub—; subpress, self-guiding (die); **—очный** *a.* lining; **—ывание** *n.* lining, etc., *see v.;* **—ывать** *v.* line, pad; put under, lay under; add.

подкласс *m.* subdivision; (biol.) subclass.

подкл/евать, —ёвывать *v.* peck, pick up.

подкле/ивание *n.*, **—йка** *f.* pasting, etc., *see v.;* **—и(ва)ть** *v.* paste (up, more); glue under.

подклёп/ка *f.*, **—ывание** *n.* riveting, etc., *see v.;* **—(ыв)ать** *v.* rivet (under; more).

подклинивать *v.* wedge up, shim.

подклювье *n.* (orn.) mandible.

подключ/ать, —ить *v.* connect up, attach; (elec.) switch in *or* on; **—ение** *n.* connecting, etc., *see v.;* connection; **—ённый** *a.* connected, etc., *see v.;* on; (comp.) on-line.

подключичн/ый *a.* (anat.) subclavian; **—ая кость** infraclavicle.

подков/а *f.* horseshoe; **—анный** *a.* shod; **—ать** *v.* shoe; **—ка** *f.* shoe(ing); **—ник** *m.* (bot.) Hippocrepis; **—ный** *a.* horseshoe; **—огуб** *m.* (mam.) Hipposideros; **—огубые** *pl.* leaf-nosed bats (*Hipposideridae*); **—онос** *m.* horseshoe bat (*Rhinolophus*); **—оносовые, —носы** *pl.* Rhinolophidae; **—ообразный** *a.* horseshoe-shaped; horseshoe (magnet); **—ывание** *n.* shoeing, etc., *see v.;* **—(ыв)ать** *v.* shoe (horses); fit (runners); ground, give grounding (in).

подкож/ица *f.* (anat.) hypoderm(is); **—ник** *m.* (ent.) Oedemagena; **—ный** *a.* subcutaneous, hypodermic; **—ная клетчатка** subcutis.

подколачивать *v.* nail on (or under).

подколен/ки *pl.* (anat.) back of the knees; **—ник** *m.* poples; **—никовый** *a.* infrapatellar; **—ный** *a.* popliteal; **—ная чашка** patella.

подколено *n.* (biol.) subtribe.

подколка *f.* pinning up; pricking.

подколонник *m.* column footing, base.

подколотить *v.* nail up.

подколоть *see* **подкалывать.**

подкольцо *n.* (math.) subring.

подкомитет *m.* subcommittee.

подконтрольный *a.* under control.

подкоп *m.* undermining; underground passage; **—ать** *v.* undermine, dig under.

подкопить *see* **подкапливать.**

подкоп/ка *f.*, **—ный** *a.* undermining.

подкоптить *see* **подкапчивать.**

подкорачивать *v.* shorten a little.

подкоренн/ая *f.*, **п. величина, —ое выражение, —ое число** (math.) radicand; **—ой** *a.* subradical; under the radical sign; (bot.) under the root(s).

подкор/ка *f.* (anat.) subcortex; **—(к)овый** *a.* subcortical; under the crust; **—(к)овые пузыри** (met.) subcutaneous blowholes.

подкорм *m.*, **—ка** *f.*, **—очный** *a.* feed(ing); (agr.) top dressing; supplementary feeding, supplements; subnutrition, defective nutrition; **—ить** *v.* feed up, fatten; **—очное опрыскивание** (hort.) spray feeding; **—очное удобрение** top dressing; **—щик** *m.* feeder; fertilizer spreader.

подкорники *pl.* (ent.) flatbugs (*Aradidae*).

подкоровый *a.* subcortical; (geol.) subcrustal.

подкоротить *v.* shorten a little.

подкорье *n.* (bot.) sapwood, alburnum.

подко/с *m.* strut, stay, prop; (angle) brace; (agr.) mowing; mowed meadow; —**сить** *v.* mow; —**сный** *a. of* **под-кос;** strut-braced; —**шенный** *a.* mowed.

подкрадыв/аться *v.* steal up to; —**ающийся** *a.* insidious (disease).

подкраевой *a.* submarginal.

подкраивать *v.* cut to pattern.

подкрановое поле reach of crane.

подкрас/ить *see* **подкрашивать;** —**ка** *f.* tint(ing).

подкрасться *see* **подкрадываться.**

подкраш/енный *a.* tinted, etc., *see v.;* —**ивание** *n.* tinting, etc., *see v.;* —**ивать** *v.* tint, color, touch up, retouch; stain, dye.

подкреп/ить, —**лять** *v.* fortify, strengthen, reinforce; support, sustain; straighten, stiffen; reward; —**ление** *n.* fortification, reinforcement; support; —**ляющий** *a.* fortifying, etc., *see v.;* nourishing, wholesome.

подкритич/еский *a.* subcritical; below-critical; —**ность** *f.* subcriticality.

подкроить *v.* cut to pattern.

подкругл/ить, —**ять** *v.* round off slightly.

подкру/тить, —**чивать** *v.* screw, turn, twist (lightly; more).

подкрыл/ок *m.* (wing) flap; —**ье** *n.* (orn.) inside of wing; —**ьный** *a.* under the wing; —**ьцовый** *a.* (anat.) axillary.

подкрыш/ечная, —**ка** *f.* (ichth.) subopercle; —**ечный** *a.* subopercular; —**ник** *m.* cover, top (of beehive).

подкупать *v.* bribe; buy more.

подкуривать *v* smoke; fumigate.

подкус/ить, —**ывать** *v.* cut (wire).

подлавливать *v.* catch.

подладанник *m.* (bot.) Cytinus.

подла/дить, —**живать** *v.* fit, adapt; suit; (rad.) tune; —**живание** *n.* fitting, etc., *see v.*

подлакиров(ыв)ать *v.* lacquer, varnish.

подламывать(ся) *v.* break, crack, split.

подлап/ок *m.* bracket; —**ки** *pl.* blocking.

подле *adv. and prep. gen.* near, by, beside, by the side of, side by side.

подлегарс *m.* (shipbuilding) rising.

подледн/ик *m.* under-ice fishing tackle; —**иковый** *a.* (geol.) subglacial.

подлёдный *a.* under ice.

подлеж/ать *v.* depend (on), be subject (to), be under the jurisdiction (of); —**ащее** *n.* subject; —**ащий** *a.* subject, liable; applicable, relevant; —**ащий измерению** to be measured; —**ащий уплате** payable.

подлез(а)ть *v.* creep under, get under.

подлес/ник *m.* (bot.) Sanicula; —**ок** *m.,* —**ье** *n.* underbrush, undergrowth.

подлет/ать, —**еть** *v.* fly up to; rush up to.

подлечи(ва)ть *v.* (med.) treat.

подлещ/(ик) *m.* (ichth.) bream (*Abramis brama*); *also refers to three other species;* —**ник** *m.* young bream.

подлив *see* **подливание;** —**а** *f.* sauce; —**ание** *n.* addition (of liquid); —**ать** *v.* pour (more), add; —**ка** *f.* addition; mortar, grout; sauce, gravy; —**ной** *a.* mortar, grout; undershot (wheel).

подлинн/ик *m.* original (copy), manuscript; —**о** *adv.* in truth, really, authentically; —**ость** *f.* authenticity; identity (of seeds); **удостоверять** —**ость** *v.* authenticate; —**ый** *a.* authentic, original, real, genuine, true.

подлинь *f.* bird in eclipse phase.

подлисок *m.* young fox; fox-dog hybrid.

подлистный *a.* (bot.) hypophyllous.

подлит/ый *a.* added; —**ь** *see* **подливать.**

подлобковый *a.* (anat.) subpubic.

подловить *v.* catch.

подлодка *f.* submarine.

подлож/ечка *f.* (anat., zool.) epigastrium; —**ечный** *a.* epigastric; —**ить** *see* **подкладывать;** —**ка** *f.* foundation, support; base (layer), back(ing); underlying material, bed; core; (catalyst) carrier; bottom plate; substrate, substratum; (cryst.) sublayer; **без** —**ки** unsupported; **на** —**ке** backed (emulsion).

подложный *a.* false, counterfeit.

подлокотник *m.* arm rest.

подлом *m.* break(ing); —**ать,** —**ить** *see* **подламывать;** —**ленный** *a.* broken (underneath).

подлонный *a.* (anat.) subpubic.

подлопаточный *a.* (anat.) subscapular.

подлунный *a.* sublunar, terrestrial.

подлый *a.* mean, base.

подмагнич/енный *a.* magnetized, biased; —**ивание** *n.* magnetizing; magnetic biasing; **обмотка** —**ивания** bias winding; —**ивать** *v.* magnetize, bias.

подмаз/ать, —**ывать** *v.* grease, oil; smear; paint; —**ка** *f.,* —**ывание** *n.* greasing, etc., *see v.;* first coat (of paint).

подмал/евать, —**ёвывать** *v.* paint, tint, touch up.

подмалывать *v.* grind more.

подман/енный, —**ённый** *a.* lured, etc., *see v.;* —**ивание** *n.* luring, etc., *see v.;* —**и(ва)ть** *v.* lure, entice, decoy; beckon.

подмаренник *m.* (bot.) Galium.

подмасли(ва)ть *v.* oil (lightly; more).

подмастерье *m.* apprentice, assistant.

подматывать *v.* wind (more; under).

подмачивать *v.* wet, moisten, dampen.

подмащивать *v.* put under.

подмезривать *v.* (leather) (re)flesh.

подмёл *past m. sing. of* **подмести.**

подмен *m.,* —**а** *f.* substitute, substitution; —**ён(н)ый** *a.* substitute(d); —**ивание** *n.* substitution; —**и(ва)ть,** —**ять** *v.* substitute, exchange, replace, switch.

подмера *f.* submeasure.

под/мерзать, —**мёрзнуть** *v.* freeze (a little), get frostbitten; —**мёрзлый** *a.* slightly frozen, frostbitten.

подмес/ить *v.* mix in, add, knead in; —**ка** *f.* mixing in, etc., *see v.;* addition.

подмести *v.* sweep up.

подмесь *f.* adulteration, admixture, additive; (biol.) rogue.

подмет/альн(о-уборочн)ый *a.,* —**ание** *n.* sweeping; —**альная машина** sweeper; —**ать** *v.* sweep; baste, tack.

подметить *see* **подмечать.**

подмёт/ка *f.* basting, tacking; sole (of shoe); —**очный** *a.* sole; —**ывать** *v.* baste, tack.

подмеч/ать *v.* notice, observe; —**енный** *a.* noted, observed.

подмеш/анный, —**енный** *a.* mixed in, etc., *see v.;* —**ивание** *n.* mixing in, etc., *see v.;* —**и(ва)ть** *v.* mix in, add, knead in, stir in; adulterate.

подминать *v.* tread, trample (on).

подмножество *n.* (math.) subset.

подмога *f.* help, aid; (building) header.

подмодель *f.,* —**ный** *a.* (casting) master pattern, double contraction pattern; —**ая плита** bottom board.

подмодул/ь *m.* (math.) submodule; —**ятор** *m.* (radar) driver.

подмоет *fut. 3 sing. of* **подмыть.**

под/мозговая железа (anat.) hypophysis, pituitary gland; —**мозолистый** *a.* subcallous.

подмок/ать, —нуть v. get slightly wet.

подмолаживание n. fermentation.

подмолоть v. grind (some more).

подмолочник m. (bot.) Lactarius volemus.

подмор m. dying (of bee colony); dead bees.

подмор/аживать, —озить v. freeze (a little); chill, refrigerate; **—оженный** a. frozen, etc., see v.; frostbitten.

подмосков/ный a. (geog.) (near) Moscow; **—ье** n. districts near Moscow.

подмост/и, —ки pl. scaffold(ing), platform, staging, stage; trestle; supporting structure; **—ить** v. put under.

подмот/ать v. wind (more; under); **—ка** f. winding (more; under); (text.) underwinding.

подмоч/енный a. wet, moistened, damp; **—ить** see **подмачивать.**

подмошник m. (bot.) Boletus subtomentosus.

подмыв m., **—ание** n. washing, etc., see v.; undercut(ting), erosion; **—ать** v. wash (away; up); scour; undermine, undercut, erode; (pile driving) jet.

подмыл/и(ва)ть v. soap (a little; more); **—ьный щёлок** spent lye, underlye.

подмыт/ый a. washed, etc., see **подмывать; —ь** see **подмывать.**

подмыш/ечный a. (anat.) axillary; **—ечная впадина, —ечная ямка, —ка** f. axilla, armpit; **—ечнйе перья** (orn.) axillars; **—ник** m. dress shield.

подмять see **подминать.**

поднадвиг m., **—овый** a. (geol.) underthrust.

поднадзорный a. under surveillance.

поднад/коленниковый a. (anat.) infrapatellar; **—костничный** a. subperiosteal.

поднаж(им)ать v. apply more pressure.

поднакапливать v. save up, accumulate.

поднаковальн/ик m., **—я** f. anvil bed, anvil block, anvil stand.

поднакопить v. save up, accumulate.

поднала/дить see **подналаживать; —дка** f. adjustment; **—дчик** m. automatic adjuster; **—живать** v. adjust, set.

поднаряд m. (shoe) pad, insert sole.

поднасадочный a. rider (regenerator arch).

поднатужи(ва)ть v. tighten, tense (more).

подневольный a. dependent; forced (labor).

поднес/ение n. presentation; **—ти** see **подносить; —ущая** f., **—ущий** a. (elec. comm.) subcarrier.

поднижнечелюстной a. (anat.) submandibular.

подним/ание n. raising, etc., see v.; **—атель** m. lift(er), elevator; (anat.) levator; arrector, raiser; **—ать** v. raise, lift, hoist, pull up; elevate, jack (up); pick up; get up (steam); turn up (flame); increase, improve, enhance, build up; (elec.) step up; open up, plow up (new land), break up, turn over (soil); rouse, flush (game); **—аться** v. rise, go up, climb, ascend, get up; increase, grow; improve; **—ающий** a. raising, etc., see v.; **—ающая мышца** (anat.) levator; **—ающийся** a. rising, etc., see v.

поднов/ить, —лять v. renovate, renew, repair, alter; **—ление** n. renovation; **—лённый** a. renovated.

подногтев/ой a. (anat.) subungual, hyponychial; **—ая пластинка** hyponychium.

поднож/ие n. foot (of hill, etc.), pedestal; **—ка** f. step, footboard, running board (of automobile); **—ный** a. underfoot; **—ный корм** green fodder, pasture.

поднормаль f. (math.) subnormal.

поднос m. bringing near; tray; **—ить** v. bring near, bring into contact, carry up to; offer, present; **—ка** f., **—ный** a. bringing near, etc., see v.

подносовой a. (anat.) subnasal; nasolabial; **п. желобок** philtrum.

подно/счик m. carrier; **—шение** n. gift, tribute, offering.

поднутр/ение n. undercut(ting); **угол —ения** undercut; **—енный** a. undercut; **—ять** v. undercut, recess.

подныр/ивать, —нуть v. dive under.

поднят/ие n. rise, rising, ascent, lift; (geol.) unheaval, elevation, uplift; upwelling; reclamation (of land); **—ый** a. raised, etc., see **поднимать;** upright, erect; **—ь** see **поднимать.**

подо see **под.**

подоб/ать v. suit, befit; **—ающий** a. suitable, fitting, proper, due.

подоб/ие n. similarity, similitude, likeness, resemblance; analog; **по —ию** in the image (of), resembling; **теория —ия** similarity theory, similitude theory.

подобласть f. subregion, subdomain.

подоблачный a. under the clouds.

подобн/о adv. (much) like, just as; **п. тому, как** just as (. . . so); **—ый** a. similar, like; similarity; scaled (model); suffix **—like, —oid,** resembling; **—ым образом** in like manner, similarly, likewise; **и тому —ое** and the like; **ничего —ого** nothing of the kind.

подоболочка f. subshell (of electrons).

подобр/анный a. gathered, etc., see **подбирать;** adjusted; **плохо п.** ill-assorted; **—ать** see **подбирать.**

подобьёт fut. 3 sing. of **подбить.**

подов/ой, —ый a. of **под; п. материал** (met.) bottoms; **п. шлак** hearth cinder, slag; **—ая медь** copper bottoms; **—ая плита** hearth plate.

подовьют fut. 3 pl. of **подвить.**

подогн/анный a. driven on, fitted, etc., see **подгонять; —ать** see **подгонять.**

подогнут/ый a. bent under or back; **—ь** v. bend under or back; fold over.

подогре/в m., **—вание** n. (pre)heating; warming up; **ток —ва** heater current; **—ватель** m. (pre)heater, economizer; reboiler (of distillation unit); **—вательный** a. (pre)heating; maintaining, holding (furnace); soaking (pit); **—вать** v. preheat; warm up, heat up; **—вный** a. heating, warming; indirectly heated (cathode); **—тый** a. preheated; warmed up, heated up; **—ть** see **подогревать.**

пододви/гать, —нуть v. push up.

подоенный a. milked.

подождать v. wait (for).

подожжённый past pass. part. of **поджечь.**

подожмёт fut. 3 sing. of **поджать.**

подозвать see **подзывать.**

подозре/вать v. suspect, doubt, mistrust; **—ние** n. suspicion, distrust.

подозрительн/о adv. suspiciously, with suspicion; it is suspicious; **—ость** f. suspiciousness; **—ый** a. suspicious, suspect(ed); suggestive.

подо/ить v. milk; **—йник** m. milk pail.

подойти see **подходить.**

подокарп/иновая кислота podocarpic acid; **—(ус)** m. (bot.) Podocarpus.

подокеанный a. suboceanic.

подоконн/ик m., **—ый** a. window sill.

подол m. hem; lowland near hill.

подолбить v. chip for a while.

подолгу adv. for a considerable time.

подолит m. (min.) podolite.

подольёт fut. 3 sing. of **подлить.**

подольский a. (geog.) Podol'sk.

подонема f. (ichth.) Podonema.

подонки pl. sediment, residue, dregs.

подоплёка f. underlying reason or motive; inside information; real state (of affairs).

подопочный *a.* bottom.

подопревать *v.* spoil, decay slightly.

подопределитель *m.* (math.) minor of an element in a determinant.

подопрелый *a.* spoiled, slightly decayed.

подопрёт *fut. 3 sing. of* **подпереть.**

подопреть *see* **подопревать.**

подопытный *a.* experimental, test, trial; laboratory (animals).

подорв/анный *a.* undermined, etc., *see* **подрывать**; depleted (resources); **—ать** *see* **подрывать.**

подорожать *v.* become more expensive.

подорешник *m.* (bot.) Lactarius volemus.

подорлик *m.* (orn.) spotted eagle (*Aquila*).

подорожник *m.* (bot.) plantain (*Plantago*); (orn.) bunting (*Calcarius*); **—овые** *pl.* (bot.) Plantaginaceae.

подорожный *a.* along the road, roadside.

подосиновик *m.* (bot.) Boletus rufus; Leccinum aurantiacum.

подослать *see* **подсылать.**

подоснова *f.* true basis; (text.) underwarp.

подоспе(ва)ть *v.* come or arrive in time.

подоспермум *m.* (bot.) Podospermum.

подостлать *see* **подстилать.**

подостный *a.* (anat.) infraspinous.

подостр/ить *v.* sharpen (a little; additionally); **—ый** *a.* subacute.

под/отдел *m.* subdivision, subsection, branch; **—отрасль** *f.* (sub-)branch; (sub-)industry; **—отряд** *m.* (biol.) suborder.

подотчётный *a.* accountable (to).

подофилл *m.* (bot.) Podophyllum; **—ин** *m.* podophyllin (resin); **—овая кислота** podophyllic acid.

подохнуть *v.* die off (of animals).

подоходный налог income tax.

подоцит *m.* (cyt.) podocyte.

подошв/а *f.* foot(ing), base(ment), bottom; (min.) floor; hollow, trough (of wave); (dam) foundation, toe; (subsoil) layer; (rail) flange; (anat.) planta, sole; **—енный** *a. of* **подошва**; (anat.) plantar; bottom (water); **—енная мышца** (anat.) plantaris; **—овидный, —ообразный** *a.* soleiform, slipper-shaped; **—оприщивный** *a.* sole-stitching.

подошлёт *fut. 3 sing. of* **подослать.**

подошьёт *fut. 3 sing. of* **подшить.**

подпаивать *v.* solder up.

подпазушный *a.* (bot.) subaxillary.

подпал *m.* reddish yellow *or* whitish spot on fur; *past m. sing. of* **подпасть.**

подползать *v.* creep (under, up to).

подпал/и(ва)ть *v.* singe, scorch; set on fire; **—ина** *see* **подпал**; scorched place, burn.

подпарывать *v.* rip (a little, up).

подпасок *m.* shepherd boy, herdsboy.

подпасть *see* **подпадать.**

подпаутинный *a.* (anat.) subarachnoid.

подпах/(ив)ать *v.* plow (a little more); **—отный** *a.* sub(soil), subsoil.

подпаять *see* **подпаивать.**

подпекать *v.* bake brown, bake longer.

подпергамент *m.* imitation parchment.

подпереть *see* **подпирать.**

подпёртый *a.* propped, supported; back (water).

подпестичн/ик *m.* (bot.) podogynium, gynopodium; **—ый** *a.* hypogynous.

подпечат(ыв)ать *v.* print a little more.

подпечёночный *a.* (anat.) subhepatic.

подпечь *see* **подпекать.**

подпивка *f.* (met.) pumping, rod feeding.

подпил *m.*, **—ивание** *n.*, **—ка** *f.* sawing, etc., *see v.*; **—и(ва)ть** *v.* saw (off; under); file; **—ок** *m.* file.

подпир/ание *n.* propping, etc., *see v.*; **—ать** *v.* prop, brace, stay, back, shore, steady, stiffen, sustain, bear, support; underpin (wall); back up (water); **—ающий** *a.* propping, etc., *see v.*

подпис/ание *n.* signing; subscription; **—ан(ный)** *a.* signed; **—ать** *v.* sign; **—ка** *f.* signature; subscription; signed statement; **—ной** *a.* signed; subscribed; subscription (publication); final (proof); **—чик** *m.* subscriber; **—ывание** *see* **подписание**; **—ывать** *v.* sign; **—ываться** *v.* sign; subscribe; **—ь** *f.* signature; subscript; (typ.) legend; **за—ью** signed (by).

подпит/ка *f.* makeup, additional feeding, replenishment; feed maintenance; water-level maintenance (in boiler); field current, magnetization current; (elec.) additional charging; **—очный** *a.* makeup; feed; **—ывание** *see* **подпитка**; **—ывать** *v.* make up, replenish.

подпих/и(ва)ть, **—нуть** *v.* push under.

подпищеводный *a.* (anat.) subesophageal.

подпланширный *a.* gunwale.

подпласток *m.* substratum.

подплевральный *a.* (anat.) subpleural.

подплетина *f.* (text.) tangle.

подплодный *a.* (bot.) hypocarpogean.

подплы(ва)ть *v.* swim, float, sail or drift up to or under.

подповерхностный *a.* subsurface, under(current).

подподбородо/к *m.* (ent.) submentum; **—чный** *a.* (anat.) submental, beneath the chin.

подподъязычный *a.* (anat.) infrahyoid.

подпокровный *a.* catch (crop); cover crop (sowing).

подполе *n.* (phys.) subfield.

подполз/ать, **—ти** *v.* creep under.

подполковник *m.* (mil.) lieutenant colonel.

подполь/е *n.* cellar, basement; underground work; underground organization, resistance; **—ный** *a.* under the floor; underground; illegal; **—щик** *m.* member of an underground organization.

подпор *m.* (hydrostatic) head, backwater; affluent (of river); rising (of ground waters); (av.) overpressure.

подпор/а, **—ка** *f.* prop, support, brace, strut, stay; stand; foundation, pillar, post, shore, buttress; bracket, rest, bearer; packing, chock, wedge, block; foothold; (anat.) sustentaculum; **—ный** *a. of* **подпора**; supporting; backwater (level); retaining (wall); **—ный насос** booster pump; **—ная стена** bulkhead.

подпороговый *a.* subliminal, below threshold; inadequate (stimulus).

подпорядок *m.* suborder.

подпочв/а *f.* subsoil, undersoil, subsurface, substratum; **—енный** *a.* subsoil, subsurface, subterranean; ground, underground (water); **—енная порода** bedrock.

подпояс(ыв)ать *v.* strap up, put on a belt.

подправ/ить *v.* touch up, retouch, correct, rectify; **—ленный** *a.* corrected; **—лять** *see* **подправить.**

подпревать *v.* decay a little, spoil.

подпрессов/ка *f.*, **—очный** *a.* premolding (press), prepressing.

под/программа *f.* (comp.) subprogram, subroutine; **п. исправления** (comp.) patch; **—пространство** *n.* (math.) subspace; **—протектор** *m.* undertread (of tire); **—пруга** *f.* girth, bellyband (of harness).

подпруж/иненный *a.* spring-loaded, spring-operated, spring-controlled; **—инивать** *v.* spring-load; **—ный ремень** *see* **подпруга.**

подпрыг *m.*, **—ивание** *n.* jumping, etc., *see v.*; jump; (med.) saltation; **—ивать**, **—нуть** *v.* jump (up), hop, bounce, bob (up and down), spring; (tools) chatter.

подпрямой *a.* (math.) subdirect.

подпункт *m.* subparagraph.

подпупочный *a.* (anat.) infraumbilical.

подпус/к *m.* fishing line; **—кать, —тить** *v.* admit, let (in); allow to approach; add.

подпут(ыв)ать *v.* mix up, entangle (a little).

подпух/ать *v.* swell a little, puff up; **—лость** *f.* puffiness; **—нуть** *see* **подпухать.**

подпуш/ек *m.* fluff, down, fuzz; (text.) linter; **—ить** *v.* powder lightly; trim with fur; **—ка** *f.* fur trim(ming); selvage (of fabric); edge, border; **—коотделитель** *m.* delinter; **—ок** *m.* linter, fuzz.

подпятник *m.* (mach.) step bearing, thrust bearing; (rr.) center plate; heel (of derrick, etc.); **кольцевой п.** collar (step) bearing.

подраб/атывать, —отать *v.* prepare; earn overtime; have a second job, moonlight; go over again; (min.) chip away; **—отаться** *v.* (mach.) wear out; **—отка** *f.* (min.) underworking, robbing (pillars).

подравн/ивать, —ять *v.* level, make even, fit together, trim.

подрагивать *v.* twitch; tremble intermittently.

подраж/ание *n.* imitation; **—атель** *m.* imitator; **—ательность** *f.* mimicry; **—ательный** *a.* imitative, mimetic; **—ать** *v.* imitate, mimic, follow; **—ающий** *a.* imitative.

подразбиение *n.* (math.) subdivision.

подраздел *m.*, **—ение** *n.* subdivision; section; (mil.) subunit, element; **—ённый** *a.* (sub)divided, etc., *see v.*; split (winding); **—ительный** *a.* (sub)dividing, etc., *see v.*; **—ить, —ять** *v.* (sub)divide, distribute; class(ify); graduate; **—яющийся** *a.* divisible.

подразновидность *f.* (bot.) subvariety.

подразумев/аемое *n.* inference; **—ание** *n.* implication; **—ать** *v.* imply, mean; understand, suppose; **—аться** *v.* be implied, be meant, be implicit (in).

подрам/ник, —ок *m.* (under)frame; stretcher; (engine) casing; **—очный** *a.* bottom (space of beehive).

подран/енный *a.* slightly wounded; **—и(ва)ть** *v.* wound slightly, wing; **—ок** *m.* wounded game; winged bird.

подра/стание *n.* growing up; **—стать** *v.* grow up; **—стающий** *a.* rising (generation); **—сти** *v.* grow up; **—щенный** *a.* grown, cultivated; **—щивание** *n.* growing, cultivation; **—щивать** *v.* grow, raise; breed.

подрёбер/ный *a.* (anat.) subcostal (nerve); hypochondrial (reflex); **—ье** *n.* hypochondrium.

подрегулиров/ание *see* **подрегулировка; —ать** *v.* (re)adjust; **—ка** *f.* (re)adjustment, fine adjustment.

под ред. *abbr.* (**под редакцией**) edited by.

подрез *m.* cut, gash; undercut(ting) (of gear teeth); trimming; runner; blade (of skate); flaw (in welding); **—ание** *n.* cutting, etc., *see* **подрезывать; —анный** *a.* cut, etc., *see* **подрезывать; —ать** *see* **подрезывать; —ающий** *a.* cutting, etc., *see* **подрезывать;** clipper (tube).

подрез/ка cutting, etc., *see* **подрезывать;** (under)cut, notch; machining; **—ной** *a.* cut(ting), trimming; undercutting; recessing (tool); coping (saw); **—ные шуровки** (boilers) prickets, blades; **—ывание** *see* **подрезание; —ывать** *v.* cut, clip, trim, prune, shorten; undercut; face; notch; **—ывать торец** (mach.) face (a workpiece); **—ывать уступы** shoulder (a workpiece); **—ь** *f.* cut, gash; blade (of skate).

подремонтировать *v.* do minor repairs.

подрессор/(ен)ный *a.* spring (wheel); spring-loaded, spring-mounted; **—ивание** *n.* cushioning; **—ивать** *v.* mount on springs, cushion; spring-load.

подрешетина *f.* counterlathing.

подрешёт/ка *f.* sublattice, lathing; **—ный** *a.* undersize.

подрисов(ыв)ать *v.* touch up, retouch, draw or paint in; make up (face).

подробн/о *adv.* in detail, at length, comprehensively; **—ость** *f.* detail; particularity; **—ости** *pl.* minutiae; **—ый** *a.* detailed, minute, comprehensive, thorough; painstaking; **—ый перечень, —ое обозначение, —ое определение** specification.

подровнять *see* **подравнивать.**

подрод *m.* (biol.) subgenus; **—овой** *a.* infrageneric.

подрост *m.* seedlings, seedling growth; regrowth; undergrowth; **—ковый** *a.*, **—ок** *m.* adolescent, teenager, juvenile, youngster, youth; **труд —ков** juvenile labor.

подруб/ание *n.*, **—ка** *f.* hewing, etc., *see v.*; **—ать, —ить** *v.* (min.) hew, (under)cut; chop (under; more); cut off, hack.

по-другому *adv.* otherwise, by a different method.

подруд/ный *a.*, **—ок** *m.* (min.) smalls, slack.

подружиться *v.* make friends.

подрули/вать *v.* steer, drive; **—вающий** *a.* auxiliary steering; **—ть** *see* **подруливать.**

подрумян/и(ва)ть *v.* flush, redden; (cooking) brown.

подрусловый *a.* under a river bed; underground (river or stream); **п. сток** underflow; (geol.) infrabed.

подручн/ик *m.* (tool) rest; hand rest, arm rest; **—ый** *a.* handy, available; assisting; improvised, makeshift; *m.* apprentice, assistant.

подрыв undermining, etc., *see v.*; demolition; detriment; injury; popping (of valve); **автомат —а** (rockets) self-destruction unit; **—ание** *n.* undermining, etc., *see v.*; demolition; **—атель** *m.* underminer, undercutter; **—ать** *v.* undermine, sap; dig under; explode, blast, blow up, demolish, dynamite; fire (mines); **—аться** *v.* dig under; blow up, explode; **—ка** *see* **подрывание; —ник** *m.* demolition specialist, firer; (mil.) member of demolition squad; **—ной** *a.* blasting, exploding; detonation (device); subversive; **—ные работы** demolition work, blasting.

подрыт/ый *a.* undermined, etc., *see* **подрывать;** sunken, depressed; **—ь** *see* **подрывать.**

подря/д *adv.* in succession, without interruption, at a time, on end; *m.* contract; subseries; **несколько дней п.** several days running; **—дить** *v.* hire, contract; **—дный** *a.* contract; **—дческий** *a.* contractor's; **—дчик** *m.* contractor; **—жать** *v.* hire, contract.

подса/д *m.* supplementary planting; **—дить** *see* **подсаживать; —дка** *f.* introduction; additional planting; (biol.) implantation; **—дный** *a.* (hunting) decoy; **—живание** *n.* setting out, etc., *see v.*; supplementary planting; **—живать** *v.* set out, plant (in addition); supplement; introduce; add, recharge; help mount (a horse); **—живаться** *v.* take a seat, sit down.

подсак *m.* fish net, hand net.

подсал/ивать *v.* add more salt; grease lightly; **—ить** *v.* grease lightly.

подсанки *pl.* (logging) sloop, sled.

подсасыв/ание *n.* drawing in, sucking in, inflow; **—ать** *v.* draw in, suck in, drain; **—ающий** *a.* drawing in, etc., *see v.*; offset (well).

подсахари(ва)ть *v.* (add) sugar.

подсачив/ание *n.* tapping, etc., *see v.*; **—ать** *v.* tap, gash (trees); net, catch.

подсборка *f.* subassembly.

подсвежка *f.* fresh river water in salt water.

подсвекольник *m.* beetroot, pigweed (*Amaranthus retroflexus*).

подсве/т *m.* illumination; (art.) dimmer; **лампа —а** instrument panel light; **—тить** *see* **подсвечивать;** **—тка** *f.* illuminating, etc., *see v.*; bias lighting; **—тка развёртки** (radar) brightening, intensity gate; **полоса —тки** (comp.) highlight bar; **—тник** *m.* instrument panel light; **—ченный** *a.* illuminated, etc., *see v.*; **—чивание** *see* **подсветка;** bottom illumination; unblanking; **—чивать** *v.* illuminate, light (up; from below); intensify, brighten, highlight, strobe; **—чивающий** *a.* illuminating, etc., *see v.*; intensifier; **—чник** *m.* candlestick; (petrol.) pipe setback.

подсвинок *m.* (agr.) gilt, immature sow.

подсев *m.*, **—ание** *n.* (agr.) undersowing; interplanting; additional sowing; **—ать** *v.* sow more; interplant; undersow; **—ной** *a.* sown in addition; undersown.

подсевок *m.* (min.) smalls, fines, slack.

подсегментарный *a.* (anat.) infrasegmental.

подсед *m.* (bot.) sprout(s), undergrowth; downy wool; (leather) scud; (vet.) malanders; scratches; foot rot; grease heel; **—ал** *m.* (vet.) dourine.

под/седельник *m.* girth, bellyband; **—седельный** *a.*, **—седлать**, **—сёдлывать** *v.* saddle.

подсеива/ние *n.* undersowing, reseeding, interplanting; **—ть** *v.* sow more; interplant.

подсек/а *f.* clearing; **—ание** *n.* clearing, etc., *see v.*; **—ать** *v.* clear, chop down; tap, gash; strike, set the hook (angling).

подсекция *f.* subsection, subdivision.

подсемейство *n.* (biol.) subfamily.

подсемядольное колено (bot.) hypocotyl.

подсеребрить *v.* silver (more; lightly).

подсерия *f.* subseries.

подсернисто/кислый *a.* hydrosulfite (of); **—натриевая соль** sodium hydrosulfite.

подсерозный *a.* (anat.) subserous.

подсеточный *a.* (paper) tray (water).

подсеч/ение *see* **подсекание;** undercutting; interruption; (ore) intersection; **—ённый** *a.* cleared, etc., *see* **подсекать;** **—ка** *f.* clearing, chopping down; cutting, incision, tapping; cutter; strike (setting the hook in the fish's mouth); anvil chisel, hardie (forging tool); **—ноогневая вырубка** slash-and-burn opening; **—ный** *a.* clearing; undercutting; **—ное хозяйство** resin tapping; **—ь** *see* **подсекать.**

подсеять *see* **подсевать.**

подсин/ивание *n.* bluing; **—и(ва)ть** *v.* blue, use bluing; **—ька** *f.* bluing.

подсинхронный *a.* hyposynchronous.

подсистема *f.* subsystem.

подскабливать *v.* scrape; rub off, erase; shave, plane lightly.

подсказ/анный *a.* prompted (speech); **—ать** *see* **подсказывать;** **—ка** *f.* prompting, suggestion; (comp.) prompt; **диалоговая —ка** (comp.) help; **—чик** *m.*, **—чица** *f.* prompter; **—ывание** *n.* prompting; **—ывать** *v.* prompt, suggest.

подскак/ать, **—ивать** *v.* jump up, spring up, gallop up to; **—ивающий** *a.* (med.) collapsing (pulse), water-hammer (pulse).

подскальник *m.* (text.) warp beam rod.

подскирд/ник *m.*, **—ье** *n.* hay straddle.

подсклеральный *a.* (anat.) subscleral.

подскоблить *see* **подскабливать.**

подско/к *m.* upward jump; **—чить** *see* **подскакивать.**

подскорлуп/ная плёнка outer-egg membrane; **—овая оболочка** putamen, shell membrane (of egg).

подскре/бать, **—сти** *v.* scrape.

подскуловой *a.* (anat.) subzygomatic.

подслаива/ние *n.* undercoating; **—ть** *v.* (chem.) underlay.

подсла/стить, **—щивать** *v.* sweeten; **—щённый** *a.* sweetened; **—щивание** *n.* sweetening.

подследственный *a.* (law) under investigation.

подслеповатый *a.* having poor vision.

подслизистый *a.* (anat.) submucous.

подсло/евище *n.* (bot.) hypothallus; **—евищный** *a.* hypothalline; **—ение** *see* **подслаивание;** **—еный** *a.* underlaid, undercoated; **—й** *m.* substratum, substrate, sublayer, underlayer, undercoat(ing), precoat; **—йка** *f.* (bot.) subiculum.

подслуш/ать *see* **подслушивать;** **—ивание** *n.* listening, (wire) tapping; **—ивать** *v.* listen in, intercept, eavesdrop, bug.

подсм/аливать, **—олить** *v.* tar; **—олок** *m.*, **—ольная вода** tar water.

подсм/атривать *v.* observe (stealthily), spy.

подсменный *a.* shift, auxiliary (worker).

подсмотреть *see* **подсматривать.**

подснежн/ик *m.* (bot.) snowdrop (*Galanthus*); **—ый** *a.* under the snow.

подсоб/ить *v.* help, give a hand; **—ка** *f.* storeroom; **—ник** *m.* helper, shop hand.

подсоб/ный *a.* secondary, by—; auxiliary, subsidiary, ancillary; additional; helping; labor-saving; branch (works); utility (building); servo (motor); **п. материал** intermediate; **п. продукт** by-product; **п. рабочий** helper, shop hand; **—ное хозяйство** garden attached to a factory, sanatorium, etc.

подсобрать *v.* collect gradually.

подсов(ыв)ать *v.* push under.

подсоедин/ение *n.* connection, junction; **—ённый** *a.* connected; **—ить**, **—ять** *v.* connect (up), switch (into); (comp.) log on.

подсозна/ние *n.*, **—тельный** *a.* subconscious.

подсокра/тить, **—щать** *v.* shorten; decrease.

подсол *see* **подсолка;** **—евой** *a.* (geol.) subsalt; **—енный** *a.* salted; **—ить** *v.* add salt; pickle some more; **—ка** *f.* additional salting; additional pickling.

подсолн/ечник *m.* sunflower (*Helianthus*); **—ечниковая моль** sunflower moth; **—ечный** *a.* sunflower; subsolar; **—ух** *m.* sunflower (seeds).

подсортиров/ка *f.*, **—ывание** *n.* sorting out; **—(ыв)ать** *v.* sort out.

подсос *m.* inflow, inleakage, influx, suction; sucking; **—ать** *see* **подсасывать;** **—ок** *m.* (zool.) suckling; **—ный** *a.* inflow; lactating, suckling.

подсостояние *n.* substate.

подсохнуть *see* **подсыхать.**

подсоч/(еч)ный *a.* (resin) tapping, gashing; **—и(ва)ть** *v.* tap, gash; **—ка** *f.* tapping, turpentine extraction.

подспорангиатный *a.* subsporangial.

подспорье *n.* help, assistance, aid.

подспудный *a.* latent, hidden.

подспутниковый *a.* subsatellite.

подстава *f.* tray, trough; (shipbuilding) stopping up.

подстав/имость *f.* (math.) substitutability; **—ить** *see* **подставлять;** **—ка** support, prop, brace, strut, stay; subiculum, fulcrum; post, mounting; stand, base, rest, bracket; chock, block; substitution; **—ленный** *a.* substituted, etc., *see v.*; **—лять** *v.* substitute; place under; hold up; **—ной** *a.* substitute; false, dummy; **—очный** *a.* of **подставка.**

подстановка *f.* substitution; (comp.) stuffing.

подстанция *f.* substation, local telephone exchange; satellite office.

подстволок *m.* (min.) sump, pit.

подст/егать, **—ёгивать** *v.* pad, line; quilt.

подстелить *see* **подстилать.**

подстен/ный *a.* wall; **—ок** *m.* buttress, prop; **—ье** *n.* foundation.

подстере/гать, —чь *v.* be on the lookout (for), be on the watch.

подстил *see* **подстилка; —ать** *v.* lay under, place under; **—ающий** *a.* underlying, subjacent; under (layer); basement (rock); **—ающий слой** pedicularium; underlayer, base; **—ающая порода** bedrock, base or basement rock; **—ающая поверхность** substratum; **—ка** *f.* laying (under); bedding, litter; flooring; (forest) floor; substratum; (naut.) dunnage; **—очный** *a. of* **подстилка.**

подстирание *n.* gradual fading.

подстожье *n.* hay straddle.

подстолбие *n.* (biol.) stylopod.

подстолье *n.* table frame and legs.

подстрагивать *v.* plane, smooth off.

подстраив/ание *n.* building on, etc., *see v.*; (re)adjustment, fine adjustment, alignment; fine tuning; **—ать** *v.* build on, add; (re)adjust, trim, align; tune; arrange secretly, contrive.

подстрахов/ать *v.* secure (against); **—ка** *f.* securing (against).

подстрачивать *v.* stitch on.

подстрек/ать, —нуть *v.* instigate, incite; excite.

подстрели(ва)ть *v.* wound with a gunshot, wing.

подстрел/ина *f.* angle brace; **—ьник** *m.* cross bar.

подстри/гание *n.* cutting, etc., *see v.*; **—гать** *v.* cut, shear, clip, crop; trim, prune (trees); **—женный** *a.* cut, etc., *see v.*; shorn; **—жка** *see* **подстригание; —чь** *see* **подстригать.**

подстрогать *see* **подстрагивать.**

подстро/ечный *a.* tuning, aligning; trimming (capacitor); (constr.) additional; **—ить** *see* **подстраивать; —йка** *see* **подстраивание;** (frequency) control.

подстропильный *a.* under the rafters.

подстрочить *v.* stitch on.

подстрочн/ик *m.* interlinear translation; **—ый** *a.* interlinear; below the line; footnote; word-for-word (translation); **—ый индекс** subscript; **—ый элемент** (typ.) descender; **—ое примечание** footnote.

подструги(ва)ть *v.* plane, smooth off.

подструктура *f.* substructure.

подстуживание *n.* (steel) interim cooling.

подступ *m.* approach, advance; access; (min.) bench; **—ать, —ить** *v.* approach, advance, come near; **—енок** *m.* (stair) riser.

подсуд/имый *m.* (law) defendant; **—ность** *f.* cognizance; jurisdiction; competence; **—ный** *a.* under or within the jurisdiction (of).

подсумо/к *m.* cartridge pouch; **—чный** *a. of* **подсумок;** (bot.) basilar (cells).

подсунуть *see* **подсовывать.**

подсуставной *a.* (anat.) infraglenoid.

подсухожильный *a.* subtendinous.

подсучи(ва)ть *v.* twist on.

подсуш/енный *a.* dried (off); **—ивание** *n.,* **—ка** *f.* drying (off), predrying; **—и(ва)ть** *v.* dry (off), predry.

подсч/ёт *m.* calculation, etc., *see v.*; data compilation; (math.) measuring, counting; estimate; **—ит(ыв)ать** *v.* calculate, figure out, determine; count (up), compute, estimate; tabulate.

подсып/ание *n.,* **—ка** *f.* addition; (partial) filling; fill; (met.) cushion fill; chip packing (of ballast); **—ать** *v.* add, fill (with more); pile up, heap up.

подсыреть *v.* get a little damp.

подсых/ание *n.* drying; **—ать** *v.* get dry, get a little drier; exsiccate, desiccate.

подтазиковый *a.* (crust.) precoxa.

подтаивать *v.* thaw, melt.

подталамическ/ий *a.* hypothalamic; **—ая область** (anat.) hypothalamus; **—ое ядро** subthalamic nucleus.

подталина *f.* thawed spot.

подталкив/атель *m.* plunger; ram; push rod; **—ать** *v.* push, shove, nudge, jostle; instigate; encourage; **—ающий** *a.* pushing, actuating.

подтангенс *m.* (geom.) subtangent.

подтапливать *v.* heat a little; thaw out some more.

подтаранный *a.* (anat.) subtalar.

подтаскивать *v.* drag up to.

подтачив/ание *n.* sharpening, etc., *see v.*; (geol.) erosion; **—ать** *v.* sharpen, give an edge (to); undercut; gnaw, bore; erode; sew on; (cinema) dub.

подтащить *see* **подтаскивать.**

подтаять *see* **подтаивать.**

подтвер/дительный *a.* confirming, corroborating; **—дить** *see* **подтверждать; —дооболочечный** *a.* (anat.) subdural; **—ждать** *v.* confirm, corroborate, bear out, attest (to), assert; support; acknowledge (receipt); **—ждать установление связи** (commun.) handshake; **—ждаться** *v.* be corroborated, be borne out; **—ждение** *n.* confirmation, etc., *see v.*; **—ждение подлинности, —ждение права на доступ** authentication; **—ждение связи** (commun.) handshake, handshaking; **символ —ждения** acknowledge character; **—ждённый** *a.* confirmed, etc., *see v.*

под/тёк *m.,* **—текание** *n.* inflow, leakage, seepage; (med.) bruise, suffusion (of blood); (paint) drip; dribble; **—текать** *v.* flow under, leak, seep; dribble; **—текающий** *a.* leaking.

подтекст *m.* implication.

подтёлок *m.* yearling calf.

подтеменной *a.* (anat.) subparietal.

подтепловой *a.* subthermal.

подтереть *see* **подтирать.**

под/тесать, —тёсывать *v.* cut off (a little; more).

подтечь *see* **подтекать.**

подтип *m.* subtype; (biol.) subphylum.

подтирать *v.* wipe up, dry.

подтоварник *m.* dunnage; (goods handling) pallet; odd sizes of lumber.

подток *m.* inflow, seepage.

подтолк/ать, —нуть *v.* push, nudge.

подтолочь *v.* crush, grind (more).

подтональный *a.* (acous.) subsonic, subaudio, infrasonic.

подтоп/ить *see* **подтапливать, подтоплять; —ка** *f.* additional firing; additional heating; small heater; **—ление** *n.* rise (of ground water); waterlogging; **—лять** *v.* flood, submerge (partially); waterlog; **—ок** *m.* auxiliary heater.

подторм/аживать, —озить *v.* brake lightly.

подточ/енный *a.* sharpened, etc., *see* **подтачивать; п. червями** worm-eaten; **—ить** *see* **подтачивать; —ка** *f.* sharpening; recess, groove.

подтрав/ить *see* **подтравливать; —ливание** *n.* etching; **—ливать** *v.* pickle, etch (more).

подтриб *m.,* **—а** *f.* subtribe.

подтроп/ики *pl.* subtropics; **—ический** *a.* subtropical.

подтумок *m.* (ichth.) Black Sea shad.

подтуш/евать, —ёвывать *v.* shade slightly.

подтыкать *v.* tuck under.

подтынник *m.* (bot.) Polypodium.

подтя/гивание *n.* tightening, etc., *see v.*; pull; **—гивать** *v.* tighten, pull (up; under), draw up; adjust, reset; screw up, screw tighter; (mil.) bring up, move up; **—ги-**

ваться *v.* pull (oneself) up, tighten, pull oneself together; catch up (with the rest); **—жка** *see* **подтягивание; —жки** *pl.* suspenders; **—нутый** *a.* tightened, etc., *see v.*; **—нуть** *see* **подтягивать.**

поду *see* **под.**

подузел *m.* subassembly, subunit; **—ковый** *a.* subassembly; subnodal.

подуклонка *f.* sloping, inclination, canting.

подуключина *f.* crutch socket, rowlock socket (of rowboat).

подум/авши *adv.* on second thought; **—ать** *v.* reflect, consider; think; **—ывать** *v.* think (of), contemplate.

подуровень *m.* sublevel; substate.

подуры *pl.* (ent.) springtails (*Poduridae*).

подуст *m.* (ichth.) undermouth, nase (*Chondrostoma nasus*).

подуть *v.* start blowing; blow a while.

подуч/ать, —и(ва)ть *v.* instruct, teach; **—иться** *v.* learn.

подуш/ечка *f.* cushion; (stamp) pad; (finger) pad; (zool.) torulus, antennifer; (ent.) pulvillus; **листовая —ечка** pulvinus; **—ечницы** *pl.* scale insects (*Coccidae*); **—ечный** *a. of* **подушка; —ечный слой** cushion, padding; **—ить** *v.* spray with perfume; **—ка** *f.* cushion, pillow, pad; bearing; chock; saddle, cradle; slab, plate; (gas) blanket; (distillation) carrier liquid, chaser; (concrete) raft; (anat.) pulvinar; (bot.) pulvinus; **—ковидный, —кообразный** *a.* pillow (like), cushion-shaped, pulvinate.

подушный *a.* per capita, poll (tax).

подфарник *m.* parking light, side light.

подфасциальный *a.* (anat.) subfascial.

подферменник *m.* foundation stone.

под/фракция *f.* (chem.) subfraction; **—функция** *f.* minorant (function).

подфюзеляжный *a.* (av.) ventral, under.

подхват *m.* cross support, carrier arm; tow net; catching up, picking up; pickup; **реакция —а** (nucl.) pickup (reaction); **—ить, —ывать** *v.* take up, catch up, snatch up, pick up, seize (up); **—цы** *pl.* tongs; forceps, tweezers; **—чик** *m.* pickup.

подхвост/ник *m.* (harness) crupper; **—овой** *a.* (zool.) subcaudal; anal (fin); **—ье** *n.* (orn.) under-tail coverts.

подход *m.* manner, (method of) approach; point of view; access; run (of salmon); **охота с —а** (game) stalking; **—ы** *pl.* access; **—ить** *v.* approach, come near, draw near, arrive (at); attack (a problem); be adequate; near (completion); come (to an end); fit, match (up); suit, be suited (for), be adequate; **—ка** *f.* (leather) fleshing knife, scraping knife; **—ный** *a.* approach, access; **—ящий** *a.* suitable, fitting, appropriate, adequate, proper (to occasion), right, expedient, pertinent, advantageous; approaching, incoming.

подхомутник *m.* horse undercollar.

под/хордовый *a.* (anat.) sub(noto)chordal; **—хрящевой** *a.* (anat.) subchondral.

подцапфенник *m.* trunnion bearing.

подцарство *n.* (biol.) subkingdom.

подцвет/ка *f.* dyeing, etc., *see v.*; azuring (of paper); **—ковый** *a.* (bot.) hypanthial; **—ник** *m.* (bot.) hypanthium; **—очный** *see* **подцветковый.**

подцвеч(ив)ать *v.* dye, color, paint; tint, shade.

подцензурный *a.* censored.

подцеп/ить, —лять *v.* hook (up); pick up, catch; **—ка** *f.* hooking, etc., *see v.*

подцикл *m.* (mach.) minor cycle.

подчали(ва)ть *v.* (naut.) moor (to).

подчас *adv.* sometimes, at times.

подчасник *m.* watch or clock stand.

подчасок *m.* (mil.) relief sentry.

подчаш/ечный *a.* (bot.) calycular, cup-shaped; **—ие** *n.* outer calyx, calycle, epicalyx, involucel.

подчекан/енный *a.* calked; **—и(ва)ть** *v.* calk; **—ивающий** *a.* calking.

подчелюстной *a.* (anat.) submaxillary.

подчерепная оболочка (anat.) pericranium.

подчёрка *f.* (typ.) serif.

подчёрк/ивание *n.* underlining, emphasis, accentuation, stress; **—ивать** *v.* underline, underscore; stress, emphasize, point out, accentuate; **—нутый** *a.* stressed, emphasized, accentuated.

подчеркнуть *see* **подчёркивать.**

подчернить *v.* blacken.

подчер/тить, —чивать *v.* add (to drawing).

подчин/ение *n.* subordination, compliance; **—ённость** *f.* subordination; **—ённый** *a.* subordinate(d); (comp.) slave; (bot.) second-grade (stand of trees); secondary, overtopped; (zool.) recessive; (mil.) under the command (of); *m.* subordinate; **—ительный** *a.* (grammar) subordinating; **—ить, —ять** *v.* subordinate, subdue; **—ить себе** override; **—иться, —яться** *v.* submit, obey, comply, conform, adhere (to), follow, be governed (by); come under, satisfy; acquiesce, give way; surrender (to).

подчист/ить *see* **подчищать; —ка** *f.* cleaning up; erasing, erasure; trimming.

подчит/ать, —ывать *v.* (typ.) read copy, proofread; read aloud; **—ка** *f.* copyholding; **—чик** *m.* copyholder; proofreader.

подчищать *v.* clean, erase, rub out.

подчрев/ный *a.* (anat.) hypogastric; **—ная область, —ье** *n.* hypogastrium.

подшабри(ва)ть *v.* scrape (up).

подшашка *f.* (min.) sprag, gib, brob.

подше/ек, —йник *m.* (harness) throatband, throatlatch.

подшёрсток *m.* (zool.) underfur, undercoat; downy wool (of sheep); (embr.) lanugo, down.

подшефный *a.* under the patronage (of), supported by, sponsored.

подшиб/ать, —ить *v.* injure, hit, knock down.

подшив/ание *n.* sewing, etc., *see v.*; **—ать** *v.* sew (on, up); line; fasten together; nail from underneath; sole; hem; file (papers); **—ка** *see* **подшивание;** lining; filing; file, set, packet; hemming; soling; (ceiling) boarding; **—ной** *a.* lining; **—очный** *a. of* **подшивка.**

подшипник *m.*, **—овый** *a.* bearing, bush(ing); collar; chock; **п. скольжения** slide bearing, plain bearing; **шариковый п.** ball bearing.

подшить *see* **подшивать.**

подшлемник *m.* helmet liner.

подшлифов/анный *a.* sueded (leather); **—ывать** *v.* grind, polish.

подштукатури(ва)ть *v.* patch up.

подштурман *m.* navigator's assistant.

подщелачив/ание *n.* alkalization; caustic treatment; **—ать** *v.* alkalize, make alkaline.

подщелоч/ение *n.* alkalization; **—енный** *a.* alkalized; **—ить** *v.* alkalize.

подщитиковый *a.* (ent.) subscutal.

подъедать *v.* eat up, finish off.

подъезд *m.* approach, access; entrance; arrival; **—ной, —ный** *a. of* **подъезд;** driveway; **—ная аллея** driveway.

подъезжать *v.* drive up, approach; arrive; get around (someone).

подъельник *m.* (bot.) Indian pipe (*Monotropa hypopitys*).

подъём *m.* ascent, rise, (up)lift; hoisting, lifting, raising, elevation; enhancement; (mech.) pitch; (constr.) camber; (rr.) grade, gradient; (av.) ascent, climb; lever, hand screw, jack; telescope (of lift truck); (anat.) instep; (econ.) development, growth; enthusiasm, animation; (agr.) plowing; (math.) slope; (mil.) reveille; **п. зяби** fall plowing; **высота —а** lift; **—ка** *f.* hoisting, hauling up; **—ник** *m.* hoist, lift, elevator; jack; **самоходный —ник** lift truck.

подъёмно/-маршевый *a.* lift-cruise, vectored-thrust (engine); **п.-откатный** rolling lift (bridge); **п.-поворотный** *a.* (art.) elevating and traversing; **п.-раскрывающийся** *a.* semilift bascule (bridge); **п.-транспортный** *a.* hoisting and transport, material-handling.

подъёмные *pl.* traveling expenses; moving expenses.

подъёмн/ый *a.* lifting, hoisting, elevating, raising; swing; vertical-lift (bridge), leveling (screw); overhead (irrigation); traveling (expenses); **п. механизм** hoisting mechanism, hoist; **п. мост** drawbridge; **п. мост лафета** erector, erecting rail; **п. противовес** sash weight (of window); **п. стол** lifting platform, lift; **—ая башня** derrick tower; **—ая вагонетка** lift truck, telescoping truck; **—ая заслонка** drop door; **—ая машина** elevator, lift; **—ая мощность, —ая сила** lifting force, lifting power; (rr.) carrying capacity; (av.) lift; buoyancy; leverage; **—ая труба** uptaking pipe, riser; **—ое приспособление, —ое устройство** lifting device, hoisting equipment, hoist; **коэффициент —ой силы** lift coefficient.

подъём/овязатель *m.* lifting and binding apparatus (of combine); **—опреодолеваемость** *f.* climbing ability (of car); **—щик** *m.* lifter.

подъесть *see* **подъедать;** gnaw.

подъехать *see* **подъезжать.**

подъэтаж *see* **подэтаж.**

подъязок *m.* (ichth.) ide, orfe (*Leuciscus idus*); (ichth.) roach (*Rutilus rutilus*).

подъязык *m.* (anat.) sublingua, hypoglottis; (ent.) hypoglossis.

подъязычн/о— *prefix* (anat.) hyo— (hyoid, U-shaped); **п.-глоточный** *a.* hyopharyngeal; **п.-нижнечелюстной** *a.* hyomandibular; **п.-щитовидный** *a.* hyothyroid; **п.-язычный** *a.* hyoglossal; **—ый** *a.* sublingual, hypoglossal; hyoid (bone).

подъяремный *a.* (anat.) subjugular.

подъярус *m.* (geol.) substage.

подымать *see* **поднимать.**

подымет *fut. 3 sing. of* **поднять.**

подымить *v.* smoke a little.

подынтегральн/ая функция, —ое выражение (math.) integrand.

подыск/(ив)ание *n.* searching, etc., *see v.;* **—(ив)ать** *v.* search, seek, try to find, look for something suitable.

подытож/ивание *n.* summation; **—и(ва)ть** *v.* sum up, add up, total.

подыхать *v.* die off (of animals).

подышать *v.* breathe, blow (on a lens, etc.).

подэпителиальный *a.* (med.) subcuticular (suture).

подэра *see* **подера.**

подэтаж *m.,* **—ный** *a.* (min.) sublevel; shortwall.

поед/аемость *f.* palatability; **—ание** *n.* devouring, eating (up); **—ать** *v.* eat up, devour; corrode; **—аться** *v.* be eaten (by); **—енный** *a.* eaten, devoured.

поедет *fut. 3 sing. of* **поехать.**

поедят *fut. 3 pl. of* **поесть.**

поезд *m.* train; **автомобильный п.** tractor-trailer unit; **—ить** *v.* travel; **—ка** *f.* trip, journey, voyage; **—ной**

a. train; (med.) railroad (nystagmus); optokinetic; **—ограф** *m.* railway traffic recorder.

поём *see* **пойма;** **—истый** *a.* flooding extensively; **—ные луга** water meadows; **—ный** *a.* flooded, inundated.

поение *n.* watering (of stock).

поесть *v.* eat.

поёт *pr. 3 sing. of* **петь.**

поехать *v.* go; set off, depart; take (a train); ride; slide, glide.

пож. *abbr.* **(пожарный)** fire.

пожалеть *v.* regret, be sorry (for).

пожалова/ние *n.* award, grant; **—ть** *v.* grant, confer, present; **—ться** *v.* complain.

пожалуй *intr. word* maybe, perhaps, very likely; **—ста** *particle* please, kindly; you are welcome.

пожар *m.* fire, conflagration; **верховой п.** (forestry) crown fire; **низовой п.** ground fire.

пожарить *v.* roast, fry.

пожар/ище *n.* site after a fire; burn; **—ник** *m.* fireman.

пожар/ный *a.* fire; fire-fighting; *m.* fireman; **п. кран** fire hydrant; **п. автомобиль, п. насос** fire engine; **п. сарай** firehouse; **—ная вышка** firewatching tower; **—ная машина** fire engine; **—ная цепочка** bucket brigade; **—овзрывобезопасный** *a.* insensitive (high explosive); **—овзрывоопасность** *f.* fire and explosion hazard; **—оопасность** *f.* fire hazard; inflammability; **—отушение** *n.* fire fighting.

пожат/ие *n.* pressing, squeezing, clasp; **п. руки** handshake; **—ь** *see* **пожимать, пожинать.**

пожевать *v.* chew, masticate.

пожел/ание *n.,* **—ать** *v.* wish.

пожелт/евший, —елый *a.* yellowed, flavescent; **—ение** *n.* yellowing; (phyt.) flavescence; **—еть** *v.* turn yellow; **—ить** *v.* color yellow.

пожертвова/ние *n.* donation; **—ть** *v.* sacrifice, give up; offer; make a donation.

пож/ечь *v.* burn up; **—жённый** *a.* burned up.

пожива *f.* gain, profit.

пожив/ать *v.* live; feel (well or ill); **—ший** *a.* experienced.

пожигать *v.* burn up.

пожиже *adv.* more dilute, weaker.

пожизненный *a.* life(long).

пожилой *a.* middle-aged, elderly.

пожимать *v.* press, squeeze; shake (hands); shrug (shoulders); **—ся** *v.* huddle.

пожинать *v.* reap, harvest; earn, receive (rewards, etc.).

пожира/ние *n.* devouring; **—тель** *m.* (ichth.) swallower; **—ть** devour (of fire, animals); **—ющий** *a.* greedy (algorithm; solution); **—ющая клетка** (hemat.) phagocyte.

пожитки *pl.* belongings, things.

пожить *v.* live, stay.

пожмёт *fut. 3 sing. of* **пожать** (press).

пожн/ёт *fut. 3 sing. of* **пожать** (reap); **—ивный, —ивной** *a.* after-harvest; late-summer (crop); catch (crop); stubble(field); **—иво, —ивье** *n.* stubble field; **—я** *f.* (reaped) field.

пожог *m.* burnt out site.

пожует *fut. 3 sing. of* **пожевать.**

пожух/лый *a.* dulled (color); **—нуть** *v.* get dull.

поза *f.* pose, posture, stance, attitude.

позаботиться *v.* look after, take care (of), see to, exercise care, make sure.

позабы(ва)ть *v.* forget.

позавчера *adv.* day before yesterday.

позади *adv. and prep. gen.* behind; (naut.) astern, abaft; *prefix* retro—; **—челюстной** *a.* retromandibular.

позаимствовать *v.* adopt, borrow.

позаказный *a.* to order, custom-made.

позамёрзнуть *v.* freeze (to death).

позаниматься *v.* study for a while.

позапрошлый *a.* last but one; **п. год** the year before last.

позарастать *v.* gradually overgrow (with).

позванивать *v.* ring from time to time.

позвать *v.* call, summon.

позвенеть *v.* ring for a while.

по-зверски *adv.* brutally, etc., *see* **зверский**.

позвол/ение *n.* permission, leave; **—енный** *a.* permitted, allowed; **—ительный** *a.* permissible; **—ить, —ять** *v.* permit, allow, let, give leave; make possible, enable; **не —ять** prevent; **—яющий** *a.* permitting, permissive.

позвонить *v.* ring; (tel.) call up.

позвон/ки *pl.* (anat.) vertebrae; **истинные п.** vertebrae verae; **ложные п.** vertebrae spuriae; **—ковый** *a.* spinal, vertebral, spondylous; **—о** *prefix* vertebro— (vertebra, vertebral column); **—обедренный** *a.* vertebrofemoral; **—ок** *m.* (anat.) vertebra, spondyl; **выступающий —ок** vertebra prominens; **—очник** *m.* spine, backbone, spinal column; **—очники** *see* **позвоночные**; **—очные** *pl.* (zool.) vertebrates, vertebrata; **—очный** *a.* vetebral; spinal column; (zool.) vertebrate; **—очный столб** spine, spinal column.

позвучать *v.* sound, be heard.

поздн/е— *prefix* late; **—ее** *comp. of* **поздно**, later; **—ейший** *a.* last, latest, posterior; (more) recent; younger.

позднеледников/ый *a.* late-glacial (period); **—ье** *n.* late glaciation.

поздн/еспелый *a.* late(-ripening); **—етретичный** *m.* (geol.) Late Tertiary; **—ецветущий** *a.* late-flowering, tardiflorous; **—ий** *a.* late, tardy, retarded; (geol.) recent, young; (bot.; zool.) serotinous, serotinal; **—ика** *f.* deadly nightshade (*Solanum nigrum*); **—о** *adv.* late; **—о** *prefix* tardi— (slow), opsi— (late); **—овато** *adv.* rather late; **—оцветущий** *a.* (bot.) tardiflorous.

поздороветь *v.* improve (in health).

поздрав/ительный *a.* congratulatory; **—ить, —лять** *v.* congratulate; greet; **—ление** *n.* congratulation(s); good wishes, greetings.

позелен/елый *a.* (turned) green(ish), viriscent; **—ение** *n.* greening, turning green, viriscence; **—еть** *v.* turn green(ish); **—ить** *v.* make green.

позём *m.* manure.

поземельн/ый *a.* land, territorial; **—ая книга** land use register.

позём/ка *f.*, **—ок** *m.* drifting snow.

позже *adv.* later on, at a later time; *comp. of* **поздний**.

по-зимнему *adv.* as in winter; in winter clothes.

позитив *m.* (phot.) positive; **—ность** *f.* empiricism; **—ный** *a.* (phot.) positive; empirical.

позитрон *m.*, **—ный** *a.* positron, positive electron; **—ий** *m.* positronium; **—ноактивный** *a.* positron-emitting.

позиц/ионер *m.* (mach.) positioner; **—ионный** *a.* position; syntactical (analysis); trench (warfare); **—ионное положение** (math.) local value; (naut.) trimmed position of submarine; **—ия** *f.* position, site; attitude; item (of estimate, etc.).

познабливание *n.* light chill.

познава/емый *a.* comprehensible; **—тельный** *a.* cognitive; **—ть** *v.* (get to) know, experience; grasp (ideas), comprehend.

познакомить *v.* acquaint, introduce; **—ся** *v.* become acquainted, become familiar (with); meet.

позн/ание *n.* knowledge, conception; perception; (AI) cognition; experience; **—ать** *see* **познавать**.

позовёт *fut. 3 sing. of* **позвать**.

позоло/та *f.* gilding, gilt, gold-plating, gold leaf; **—тить** *v.* gild; **—ченный** *a.* gilded, gilt, gold-plated.

позондировать *v.* sound, probe.

позонный *a.* zone(d), compartmented.

позор *m.* disgrace, dishonor, shame, infamy, ignominy; **—ить** *v.* disgrace; **—ный** *a.* disgraceful, shameful.

позумент *m.* trimming, galloon, braid.

позыв *m.* inclination, urge; (med.) tenesmus, straining; attack, onset; **п. на мочеиспускание** vesical tenesmus.

позыв/ать *v.* call, summon; **—ной** *a.* (rad.) call; **—ные** *pl.* call letters, station identification letters.

позябнуть *v.* perish from cold.

поиздержать *v.* spend; **—ся** *v.* overspend.

поизноситься *v.* wear out gradually.

поилка *f.* fountain; drinking bowl; water trough.

поимен/но *adv.* by name; **—ный** *a.* nominal; **—овать** *v.* name, designate, mention.

поимка *f.* catching, capture, seizure.

поимущественный *a.* property (tax).

по-иному *adv.* otherwise, differently.

поиск *m.* search; scan(ning); sweep; (mil.) raid; reconnaissance; (information) retrieval; **осуществлять п.** (comp.) retrieve; **—ать** *v.* seek, search; explore; **—и** *pl.* search(ing), hunt, quest, pursuit; (trouble-)shooting; research; (min.) prospecting, exploration; **—овик-геолог** *m.* geologist prospector; **—ово-спасательный** search and rescue; recovery (ship); **—овый** *a. of* **поиск**; basic (research); **—овый шум** irrelevant information; **—овая работа** prospecting.

поистине *adv.* indeed, in truth.

поить *v.* water (animals).

поищет *fut. 3 sing. of* **поискать**.

пойдёт *fut. 3 sing. of* **пойти**.

пойкило— *prefix* poikil(o)— (varied); **—бласт** *m.* (hemat.) poikiloblast; **—гидрический** *a.* (bot.) poikilohydrous (becoming dormant in the dry season); **—дермия** *f.* (med.) poikiloderma; **—термный** *a.* (zool.) poikilothermous, cold-blooded.

пойло *n.* swill, hogwash.

пойма *f.* bottom land, floodplain.

пойм/анный *a.* caught, captured; **—ать** *v.* catch, capture, catch hold (of), seize, trap; pick up (signal); lock on (radar).

пойменный *a. of* **пойма;** tidal (marsh); alluvial; backwater (swamp); flood-plain.

поймёт *fut. 3 sing. of* **понять**.

пойти *v.* go; come; start.

Пойнтинга эффект (chem.) Poynting effect.

пока *adv. and conj.* while, so long as; until (now), so far, as yet, for the present, for now; **п. ещё** while still; **п. что** for the time being, meanwhile.

покадров/ый *a.* (by the) frame; **—ая киносъёмка** time-lapse filming; **режим —ой выборки** frame-access mode.

показ *m.* show(ing), demonstration, exhibition, presentation; illustration; **на п.** for show, on display; **—ан** *sh. m. of* **показанный**.

показани/е *n.* reading; indication; showing, exhibiting, (compass) bearing; aspect (of signal); (law) deposition, testimony, evidence; affidavit; **давать п.** *v.* bear witness, testify; **снимать —я** read, take a reading.

показанный *a.* shown, exhibited, etc., *see* **показывать; не п.** not shown, omitted.

показатель *m.* indicator, pointer; property, characteristic; showing; number, figure, value, factor, term, parameter, coefficient; (phys.) quantity; degree; rate; (math.) power, exponent, index; (intelligence) quotient; **п. достоверности** (stat.) confidence coefficient; **п. качества** quality index; **п. степени** (math.) exponent, power; **п. твёрдости** hardness number; penetration index (of soil); **это —но** it is significant; **—ный** *a.* exponential; characteristic, demonstrative, representative, symptomatic, model, demonstration; potential; significant; **—ная функция** (math.) exponential function; **—ство** *n.* example, illustration.

показ/ать *see* **показывать; —ной** *a.* display; **—ывание** *n.* showing, etc., *see v.*; **—ывать** *v.* show, exhibit, demonstrate, display, set forth, disclose, reveal; read, register; indicate, suggest; direct, instruct, show how; illustrate, depict, portray, picture; point (at), point to the fact (that); (law) testify, give evidence, bear witness; **—ываться** *v.* show itself, appear, emerge, seem; **—ывающий** *a.* showing, etc., *see v.*; **—ывающий прибор** indicator.

покалечить *v.* cripple, mutilate.

покалить *v.* heat (a while; lightly).

покалыва/ние *n.* pricking, tingling; **—ать** *v.* prick; feel occasional pain.

покамест *see* **пока.**

покап(ыв)ать *v.* drop in; drip (a while).

покараулить *v.* watch (for a while).

покат *m.* slope, slant, incline; **—ить** *v.* roll, set rolling; **—иться** *v.* roll, start rolling; roll away; **—ник** *m.*, **—ная (рыба)** *f.* (ichth.) downstream migrant; **—о** *adv.* slopingly, at a slope; **—ость** *f.* slope, declivity, descent, inclination, grade, pitch, gradient; **—ывать** *v.* roll little by little; **—ый** *a.* slope, sloping, slanting, inclining, declivous; drooping; **—ый настил** chute; **—ое место** grade.

покач/анный *a.* swung, rocked, etc., *see* **покачать; —ать** *v.* swing, rock, shake (a little); pump (a little); **—енный** *a.* rolled, etc., *see* **покатить; —ивание** *n.* swinging, etc., *see* **покачивать; —ивать** *v.* keep swinging lightly; shake, vibrate, agitate; **—нуть** *v.* shake, unsettle; tilt.

покашл/ивание *n.* (med.) tussiculation, hacking cough; **—ивать, —ять** *v.* cough sporadically.

поквартальн/о *adv.* quarterly; **—ый** *a.* (per) block.

поквартирный *a.* per tenant, per residence.

поквитаться *v.* fully repay, get even (with).

поки/дание *n.* (av.) (emergency) exit; **—дать, —нуть** *v.* forsake, abandon, quit, desert, leave, vacate; **—нутый** *a.* deserted, vacated; desolate.

покип/еть *v.* boil for a while; **—ятить** *v.* (let) boil for a while.

покладистый *a.* complaisant, obliging.

поклажа *f.* load, freight; placing.

поклевать *v.* peck (at), nibble.

поклёв/ка *f.* peck; bite, strike (of fish); **—ывать** *v.* peck occasionally.

поклон *m.* greeting, salute; regards.

поков/ать *v.* forge; **—ка** *f.* forging; forged piece; **—ки** *pl.* forge work; **—очный** *a.* of **поковка.**

покоиться *v.* rest, lie, repose.

пок/ой *m.* rest, quiet, peace, repose, stand-still, quiescence; state of rest; (bot.) dormancy; estivation; hibernation; (hospital) room, ward; **в —ое** at rest; **в состоянии —оя** at rest; (bot.) dormant; **масса (в состоянии) —оя** (nucl.) rest mass; **на —ое** in seclusion, retired; **находящийся в —ое** at rest, idle; **обмен —оя** basal metabolism; **оставить в —ое** *v.* let alone,

let be; **период —оя** quiescent stage, dormancy; **рак в —ое** cancer in situ; **состояние —оя** state of rest; dormant state; quiescence; **стадия —оя** lag-phase, resting stage; **точка —оя** point of rest; fulcrum; pause; **трение в —ое** static friction; **угол —оя** angle of repose; **энергия массы —оя** rest-mass energy; **энергия —оя** potential energy.

покойн/ик *m.* corpse; the deceased; **—ицкая** *f.* mortuary; morgue; **—о** *adv.* quietly, peacefully, restfully; **—ый** *a.* quiet, calm, peaceful, at rest; dead, deceased, late; defunct; (phys.) rest, quiescent; *m.* the deceased.

поколачив/ание *n.* tapotement, tapping (in massage); **—ать** *v.* tap.

поколебать *v.* shake, vibrate, swing; **—ся** *v.* hesitate, waver; heave (of ocean).

поколени/е *n.* generation; **ряд —й, последовательность —й** lineage; **чередование —й** heterogenesis.

поколоть *v.* prick; slaughter; split.

поколых(ив)ать(ся) *v.* fluctuate.

покомкать *v.* crumple.

покончить *v.* finish (off; with), cut short.

покопать(ся) *v.* dig (for a while).

покоптить *v.* smoke.

покор/ение *n.* subjugation, conquest; **—ить** *see* **покорять.**

покормить *v.* feed.

покорн/ость *f.* obedience; **—ый** *a.* submissive, obedient, acquiescent, resigned.

покороб/ившийся *a.* warped, buckled; **—ить** *v.* warp, bend, buckle; **—ленность** *f.* warpage; **—ленный** *see* **покоробившийся.**

покороче *adv.* somewhat shorter.

покорять *v.* subdue; **—ся** *v.* submit, yield, give in, surrender, acquiesce, resign oneself.

покос *m.* hay field; haying season; haymaking, mowing; **второй п.** aftermath; **—ившийся** *a.* lopsided; rickety; **—ить** *v.* slope, slant; mow; **—иться** *v.* be lopsided, heel over; **—ный** *a.* of **покос.**

покоссин *m.* pocossin, swamp forest.

покошенный *a.* slanted, sloping; mowed.

покоя *gen.* of **покой; —щийся** *a.* quiescent, at rest, stationary; (cyt.) resting; **—щаяся спора** resting spore.

покрап(ыв)ать *v.* sprinkle, drizzle; spot, speckle.

покрас/ить *v.* paint, dye, color; **—ка** *f.* painting, dyeing; coat (of paint).

покрасн/евший *a.* reddened; **—ение** *n.* reddening, rubescence; **—ение кожи** (biol.) erythema; **—еть** *v.* redden, get red.

покра/сочный *a.* of **покраска; —шенный** *a.* colored, tinted, dyed.

покрепч/ать *v.* get stronger; **—е** *adv.* stronger.

покрив/ить *v.* warp, twist, bend, distort; **—иться** *v.* warp, buckle, become crooked; **—лённый** *a.* warped, twisted.

покров *m.* cover, envelope, case, shell; tegmentum; sheath(ing); coat(ing); deposit; (earth's) mantle; (geol.) nappe, sheet, cap, blanket; (lava) bed, flow; canopy (of clouds); (anat.) integument; **п. воздушных корней** (bot.) velamen, root sheath; **п. цветка** perianth, floral envelope; **внешний п.** (bot.) exothecium; **внутренний п.** endothecium; **волосяной п.** hair coat; hair side (of hide); **кожный п.** (biol.) epidermis; integument; **листовой п.** foliage; **плодовый п.** (bot.) induvia; **почечный п.** perule; **твёрдый п.** crust.

покровитель *m.* patron, sponsor; **—ственный** *a.* protective; **—ство** *n.* patronage, protection, support, sponsorship; **—ствовать** *v.* patronize, protect; sponsor, support, promote.

покровн/о— *prefix* chiton(o)— (coat); chlaen(o)—, chlamyd(o)— (mantle); **—окрылый** *a.* (bot.) chlaenopterous; **—оплодный** *a.* chlamydocarpous; **—оцветковый** *a.* chitonanthous; **—ый** *a. of* **покров;** cover(ing), tectorial; tegmental; dermal, cutaneous; (biol.) integumentary; (bot.) induviate (covered with old and withered parts); (agr.) cover-crop; (geol.) blanket (deposit); **—ая кость** (anat.) dermal bone; **—ая перепонка** (anat.) tectorial membrane; **—ое стекл(ышк)о** (micros.) cover glass; **—ые культуры, —ые растения** (agr.) cover crop.

покрово— *see* **покровно—;** **—листик** (bot.) perianthial leaf.

покровский *a.* (geog.) Pokrovsk.

покроенный *a.* cut (by pattern).

покроет *fut. 3 sing. of* **покрыть.**

покр/оить *v.* cut (by pattern); **—ой** *m.* cut, style.

покромка *f.* (text.) selvage.

покромсать *v.* shred.

покрош/енный *a.* crumbled; **—ить** *v.* crumble.

покружить(ся) *v.* turn round and round, spin; fly around, circle.

покрупнеть *v.* get bigger, increase.

покру/тить(ся) *see* **покручивать(ся); —чивать(ся)** *v.* rotate, spin, turn, twist.

покрыв/ало *n.* cover, spread, blanket, veil; (bot.) spathe; involucre; **—альце** *n.* (bot.) involucre; indusium, membranous covering; **—ание** *n.* covering, etc., *see v.;* **—ать** *v.* cover, cap; roof (over); house, shelter; sheathe, envelop, blanket; insulate (wire); drown (noise); overlay, deposit, apply, give a coat (of), coat (with); (met.) plate, clad; span, bridge; wipe out (deficit); pay (debt); offset (cost), defray (expenses); **—ать лаком** varnish, lacquer; **—ающий** *a.* covering, etc., *see v.;* tectorial; **—ающий слой** coat(ing); **—ной** *a. of* **покрыть.**

покрытие *see* **покрывание;** cover(ing); roof; pavement, floor; facing, lining, dressing; vestiture; (astr.) occultation; coat(ing) (of paint); layer, film, deposit; blanket; insulation (of wire); payment, discharge (of debts, etc.), defrayment (of expenses); mulching (of soil).

покрыто— *prefix* steg(o) (roof); angi(o)— (vessel); **—головый** *a.* (zool.) stegocephalous; **—жаберные** *pl.* (mal.) sea slugs, etc. (*Tectibranchia*); **—плодный** *a.* (bot.) angiocarpous; **—семенные, —семянные** *pl.* (bot.) Angiospermae; **—семянный** *a.* angiospermous.

покрыт/ый *a.* covered, etc., *see* **покрывать;** clothed; overgrown (with); (ent.) obtect; **п. медью** copper-plated; **—ь** *see* **покрывать;** strike (target); set (a table); sire.

покрыш/ечно— *prefix* tecto— (roof); **—ечноспинномозговой** *a.* tectospinal; **—ечный** *a. of* **покрышка;** coping (stone); **—ка** *f.* cover(ing); lid, cap; hood, mantle, jacket(ing), case, casing; tire (casing); (hotbed) frame; (geol.) caprock; (anat.) tegmentum; operculum; **—ка среднего мозга** operculum.

покуда *see* **пока.**

покуёт *fut. 3 sing. of* **поковать.**

покупатель *m.* buyer, purchaser; customer, client; **—ный** *a.* purchasing; **—ский** *a.* consumer; buyer's.

покуп/ать *v.* buy, purchase; bathe; **—аться** *v.* be bought; take a bath; **—ка** *f.* buying, purchasing, purchase; **—ной** *a.* purchased, bought.

покурить *v.* smoke.

покусать *v.* bite, sting (all over).

покуситься *see* **покушаться.**

покушать *v.* eat.

покуш/аться *v.* attempt; encroach (on); **—ение** *n.* attempt.

пол *m.* floor(ing); ground; sex; **сцепление с —ом** (biol.) sex linkage.

пол— *see* **полу—.**

пол. *abbr.* (**половина; поляризация**).

пола *f.* skirt, flap; (leather) belly, flank.

полаг/ается it is usual, it is the custom; **—ать** *v.* think, believe, feel; suppose, assume, imagine; expect, count (on); (math.) let; **можно п.** it seems, presumably; **—аться** *v.* rely, depend (on); **—ают** it is assumed, it is claimed; **—ающийся** *a.* due.

поладить *v.* come to terms, agree.

полазить *v.* crawl around.

полакать *v.* lap up.

поламывать *v.* break from time to time; hurt a little.

полат/а *f.* crow's nest; **—и** *pl.* (raised) platform.

полб/а *f.,* **—енный** *a.* spelt wheat (*Triticum spelta*); emmer wheat (*Triticum dicoccum*); **—овидный** *a.* speltoid.

полбяной *a. of* **полба.**

пол/века *m.* half a century; **—года** *m.* half a year; **—день** *m.,* **—дневный** *a.* noon, midday, meridian; **—дник** *m.* (afternoon) snack; **—дничать** *v.* snack; **—дня** *m.* half-day; **—дороги** *f.* halfway; **—дюжины** *f.* half a dozen.

пол/е *n.* field, ground, area, campo; zone (of tolerance); (filtration) bed; (ice) flow; margin (of book); brim (of hat); **заметки на —ях** marginal notes.

полеви/ца *f.* bentgrass (*Agrostis*); **белая п.** (redtop) fiorin (*Agrostis alba*); **—цевый** *a. of* **полевица; —чка** *f.* love grass (*Eragrostis*); **—чник** *m.* bentgrass meadow.

полёвка *f.* (bot.) Myagrum.

полёвк/а *f.* (mam.) vole; **—и, —овые** *pl.* field mice, voles, muskrats, etc. (*Microtinae*).

полевод *m.* field-crop grower, agronomist; **—ство** *n.,* **—ческий** *a.* field-crop cultivation.

полев/ой *a.* field; unipolar, field-effect (transistor); hunting (dog); **в —ых условиях** in the field, field (-proven); **—ошпатовый** *a.* feldspar, feldspathic.

полег/аемость *f.* lodgeability (of grain crop); **—ание** *n.* lodging; **—ать** *v.* lodge, beat down; **—аться** *v.* fall; **—лый** *a.* lodged, downed, fallen.

полег/оньку *adv.* by easy stages; **—чать** *v.* improve, become easier; **—че** *adv.* (somewhat) easier.

полежать *v.* lie for a while.

полезащитн/ый *a.* field-protecting, windbreak; **—ая лесная полоса** windbreak, shelter belt.

полезно *adv.* usefully; it is useful, it is good practice; **—сть** *f.* usefulness, utility.

полезн/ый *a.* useful, of use, helpful, beneficial, advantageous; serviceable; available; active, effective; profitable, valuable; net, pay (load); residence, living (space); good (for); **п. груз** payload; **п. сигнал** (TV) desired signal; **—ая лошадиная сила** effective horsepower; **—ая мощность** (elec.) net power, power output; (rad.) output; (rockets) thrust output; удельная **—ая мощность** specific output; **—ая нагрузка** payload; **—ая площадь** (phot.) image space; usable area; **—ая работа** useful work, efficiency; **—ое действие** (useful) effect, efficiency; (mach.) duty; **коэффициент —ого действия** efficiency, performance.

полезть *v.* start climbing.

полей *m.* (bot.) pennyroyal (*Mentha pulegium*); *gen. pl. of* **поле; —те** *imp. of* **полить.**

полеми/зировать *v.* dispute, argue; **—ка** *f.* controversy, polemic(s); **—ческий** *a.* controversial, polemical.

полемохорный *a.* (bot.) polemochorous.

поленика *f.* arctic bramble (*Rubus arcticus*).

полениться *v.* be (too) lazy.

поленница *f.* stack (of firewood).

полен/о *n.* log, billet, chump, block; **—це** *dim. of* **полено.**

полесовщик *m.* forest ranger.

полесье *n.* wooded district, forest area; polessie (vast alluvial plain).

полёт *m.* flight; travel, voyage, trip; space vehicle; shot, test firing (of a projectile); *pr. 3 sing. of* **полоть; п. краски** (typ.) ink flying, ink misting; **длина —а** range (as of water jet); **скорость —a** flying speed, velocity.

полет/ай *m.* (bot.) northern wild oat; **—ать** *v.* fly (for a while); **—еть** *v.* fly (off), take off.

полёт/ный *a.* flying; airborne; **—опригодный** *a.* airworthy; **полёт-соло** *m.* solo flight; **—ы** *pl.* flying.

полечить *v.* (med.) treat (for a while).

полечь *v.* lie (down); fall, be killed; (grains) get lodged.

полешко *n.* small log.

полз/ание *n.* creeping, etc., *see v.*; **—ать, —ти** *v.* creep, crawl, slide, glide; peel off; (text.) ravel; **—ком** *adv.* on all fours; by creeping.

ползун *m.* slide block, slide bar, slide(r), runner, slipper, (guide) shoe, crawler; crosshead (of engine); sliding bearing; selector rod (of gear box); (zool.) caterpillar; (ichth.) *see* **ползуновые; —ковый** *a. of* **ползунок; —овые** *pl.* (ichth.) climbing perches (*Anabantidae*); **—ок** *dim. of* **ползун;** (elec.) sliding contact, slider; cursor; carrier (of lathe); crawler (child); (ichth.) *see* **налим.**

ползуче/прочность *f.* creep strength; **—сть** *f.* (met.) creep; **удельная —сть** creep rate.

ползуч/ий *a.* creeping; viscous; slow (fever); (med.) serpiginous; (bot.) repans; **—ая лихорадка** (med.) slow fever, brucellosis; **—ая скорость** (rate of) creepage (of electrolytes); **—ее растение** vine.

ползучка *see* **плаун.**

ползушка *see* **ползун;** cursor (of slide rule).

ползущий *a.* creeping; (biol.) benth(on)ic; (med.) serpiginous (lesion).

поли— *prefix* poly—, many, multiple; **—авитаминоз** *m.* (med.) multiple vitamin deficiency; **—ада** (chem.) polyad; **—аденит** *m.* (med.) polyadenitis; **—аденома** (med.) polyadenoma; **—аза** *f.* polyase; **—азокрасители** *pl.* polyazo dyes.

полиакрил/амид *m.* polyacrylamide; **—ат** *m.* polyacrylate; **—овый** *a.* (poly)-acrylic (plastics); **—онитрил** *m.* polyacrylonitrile, Orlon.

полиакролеин *m.* (chem.) polyacrolein.

полиакси/альный *a.* polyaxial; (cyt.) polyaxon.

полиамид *m.*, **—ный** *a.* polyamide.

полиаминотриазол *m.* polyaminotriazole, PAT.

полиандри/ческий *a.* (biol.) polyandrous; **—я** polyandry.

полиантовый *a.* (bot.) polyanthous.

поли/арилзамещённый *a.* polyaryl substituted; **—арильный** *a.* polyaryl(ated); **—артериит** *m.* (med.) polyarteritis; **—артрит** *m.* (med.) polyarthritis; **—архический, —архный** *a.* (bot.) polyarch; **—атомный** *a.* polyatomic; polyhydric (alcohol).

полибласт *m.* (cyt.; med.) polyblast, histiocyte, macrophage; **—ический** *a.* (bot.) polyblastic.

полибут/адиен *m.* polybutadiene.

полив *m.* watering, irrigation; casting; (phot.) coating.

полива *f.* glaze, glazing, enamel.

поливаксина *f.* (med.) polyvalent vaccine.

поливалентный *a.* (chem.) multivalent; polyvalent.

полив/алка *f.* watering can; **—альщик** *m.* sprinkler, irrigator; **—ание** watering, etc., *see* **поливать;** flood.

поливариантный *a.* polyvariant.

поливать *v.* water, irrigate; hose, flush; sprinkle, shower, pour on, wet.

поливенный *a.* glazed, enameled; (phot.) coated.

поливинил/ацетат *m.* polyvinyl acetate; **—карбазол** *m.* polyvinyl carbazole; **—овый** *a.* polyvinyl; **—овый спирт** polyvinyl alcohol; **—пирролидон** *m.* polyvinylpyrrolidone; **—спиртовый** *a.* polyvinyl alcohol; **—хлоридный** *a.* polyvinyl chloride, PVC.

поливитамин *m.* multivitamin.

полив/ка *f.* watering, etc., *see* **поливать;** glazing; **—ной** *a.* irrigated, requiring irrigation; **—ный** *a.* glazed, enameled.

поливольтинный *a.* (biol.) polyvoltine (producing several broods in a season).

поливочн/ая машина (street) sprinkler; **—ый** *a. of* **поливка; —ая жидкость** cooling mixture, coolant.

поли/галит *m.* (min.) polyhalite; **—гамический** *a.* (biol.) polygamous; **—гамия** *f.* polygamy; **—гамный** *a.* polygamous; **—гаплоид** *m.* (gen.) polyhaploid; **—гексоза** *f.* polyhexose; **—ген** *m.* (biol.) polygene; **—гения** *f.* (gen.) polygeny; **—генный** *a.* polygenous, polygenic, polygene (system); **—гибрид** *m.*, **—гибридный** *a.* polyhybrid; **—гидроксильный** *a.* (chem.) polyhydroxylated; **—гидроксисоединение** *n.* polyhydroxy compound; **—гиния** *f.* (biol.) polygyny; **—гинный** *a.* polygynous; **—гирия** *f.* (anat.) polygyria; **—глобулия** *f.* polyglobulia; **—глюкин** *m.* polyglucin, dextran.

полигон *m.* (geom.) polygon; (art.) (test) range, proving ground; (geod.) traverse; **—альный** *a.* polygonal; (bot.) patterned (soil); **—изация** *f.* polygonization; **—ный** *a. of* **полигон; —ометрия** *f.* traversing, survey traverse.

полиграф *m.* polygraph (copying machine); (physiol.) polygraph; **пушистый п.** a bark beetle (*Polygraphus poligraphus*); **—ист** *m.* printer; polygraph operator; **—ический** *a.* graphic arts; **—ическое производство** printing; **—ия** *f.* graphic arts.

полигубка *f.* (plastics) polyfoam.

полидактилия *f.* (med.) polydactyly.

поли/дериваты *pl.* poly derivatives; **—дерма** (bot.) polyderm; **—дисперсность** *f.* polydispersion; **—дисперсный** *a.* polydispersion(al).

полиев пузырь (zool.) Polejaeff's vesica; Polian vesicle.

полиен *m.*, **—овый** *a.* polyene.

полизамещённый *a.* (chem.) polysubstituted.

полизать *v.* lick.

полизиготный *a.* (bot.) polyzygotic.

полиизо/бутилен *m.* polyisobutylene; **—прен** *m.* polyisoprene; **—цианат** *m.* polyisocyanate.

полиин *m.* polyine, polyacetylene.

полик *m.* floor.

поли/капроамид, —капролактам *m.* polycaprolactam, nylon-6; **—карбонат** *m.* polycarbonate; **—карбоновая кислота** polycarbonic acid; **—карио—** *prefix* polykaryo—; **—кариоцит** *m.* (cyt.) polykaryocyte; **—карпий** *m.* (bot.) polycarp; **—карпический** *a.* (bot.) polycarpic; **—кислота** *f.* poly acid; **—кистозный** *a.* (med.) polycystic; **—клиника** *f.* (med.) polyclinic, out-patient clinic, dispensary; **—клония** *f.* (med.) polyclonia.

поликонденс/ат *m.* polycondensate; **—ационный** *a.* (poly)condensation (plastics); **—ация** *f.* polycondensation, condensation polymerization.

поли/коричный *a.* polycinnamic (acid); **—кория** *f.* (med.) polycoria; **—кремнёвый** *a.* polysilicic (acid).

поликристалл *m.* polycrystal; **—ический** *a.* polycrystalline.

поли/кросс *m.* (bot.) polycross; **—кротический** *a.* (med.) polycrotic (pulse).

поли/ксенный *a.* (zool.) polyxenous (parasites); **—ксилический** *a.* (bot.) polyxylic; **—ктениды** *pl.* (ent.) Polyctenidae; **—лизин** *m.* (bioch.) polylysine; **—линеарный** *a.* (math.) multilinear.

поли/мастия *f.* (anat.) polymastia; **—мегалия** *f.* polymegaly; **—мелия** *f.* (med.) polymelia.

полимент *m.* gilding size, gold size.

полимер *m.* polymer; **—аза** *f.* (enz.) polymerase; **п.-аналог** *m.* polymer analog; **п.-гомолог** *m.* polymer-homolog; **—изат** *m.* polymerization product; **—изатор** *m.* polymerization reactor; **—изационный** *a.*, **—изация** *f.* polymerization; **блочная —изация** block (co)polymerization; bulk polymerization; **—изация в объёме** bulk polymerization; **—изованный** *a.* polymerized; **—изовать(ся)** *v.* polymerize; **—ия** *f.* (chem.) polymerism; (bot.) polymery; **—ный** *a.* polymer(ic); **—ное соединение** polymer; **—обетон** *m.* organic concrete, polymer-impregnated concrete.

полиметакрил/ат *m.* polymethacrylate; **—овый** *a.* polymethacrylic.

поли/металлический *a.* polymetallic; complex (ore); **—метиленовый** *a.* polymethylene; **—метилметакрилат** *m.* polymethyl methacrylate; **—метиновый** *a.* polymethine (dyes); **—метр** *m.* polymeter.

поли/микробный *a.* (med.) polymicrobial; **—микроудобрение** *n.* (agr.) fertilizer containing several trace elements; **—миксиевые** *pl.* (ichth.) barbudos (Polymixiidae); **—миксин** *m.* polymixin (antibiotics); **—миктный, —миктовый** *a.* (geol.) polymict(ic); **—митоз** *m.* (cyt.) polymitosis; **—молибдат** *m.* polymolybdate.

полиморф *m.* (cyt.) polymorph, polymorphonuclear leucocyte; **—изм** *m.* polymorphism; **—ический** *see* **полиморфный**; **—ноклеточный** *a.* polymorphocellular; **—ный** *a.* polymorphous, polymorphic.

полимочевина *f.* polyurea.

полиневрит *m.* (med.) polyneuritis.

полинезийский *a.* (geog.) Polynesian.

полином *m.*, **—иальный** *a.* (math.) polynomial.

полинуклеотид *m.* (bioch.) polynucleotide.

полин/ялый *a.* faded, discolored; **—ять** *v.* fade, lose color; molt, shed.

полиовирус *m.* (med.) polio(myelitis) virus.

полиодонтия *f.* (med.) polyodontia.

полиоз *m.* (med.) poliosis, premature grayness; **—а** *f.* (biochem.) polyose, polysaccharose.

поли/окись *f.* polyoxide; **п. пропилена** polypropylene oxide; **—окси-** *prefix* (chem.) poly(hydr)oxy—; **—оксиальдегид** *m.* polyhydroxyaldehyde; **—оксиметилен** *m.* polyoxymethylene, polyformaldehyde; **—олефин** *m.* polyolefin.

полиомиелит *m.* (med.) poliomyelitis.

полиопия *f.* (ophth.) polyopia, double vision.

полиорганосилоксан *m.* polyorganosiloxane, silicone.

полиорхизм *m.* (med.) polyorch(id)ism (having more than two testes).

полиоэнцефалит *m.* (med.) polioencephalitis.

полип *m.* (med.; zool.) polyp(us); **простейший п.** (zool.) hydrula.

поли/пептид *m.* polypeptide; **—пептидаза** *f.* (bioch.) polypeptidase; **—пептидемия** *f.* (med.) polypeptidemia; **—пептин** *m.* polypeptin; **—планетический** *a.* (biol.) polyplanetic; **—пластический** *a.* polyplastic, capable of assuming many forms.

полиплоид *m.* (gen.) polyploid; **—изация** *f.* (gen.) poly-ploidization; **—ия** *f.* (biol.) polyploidy; **—ный** *a.* polyploid.

полипноэ *n.* (med.) polypnea, hyperpnea.

полип/ный *a. of* **полип**; **—няк** *m.* (zool.) polypary; **коралловый —няк** coral colony; **—одий** *m.* (bot.) Polypodium; **—оз** *m.* (med.) polyposis; **—озноязвенный** *a.* ulceropolypous; **—ообразный** *a.* polypoid, polypous.

поли/порин *m.* polyporin; **—поровидные** *pl.* (bot.) pore-bearing fungi (Polyporaceae); **—прагматизм** *m.* polypharmacy, administration of excessive medication; **—прен** *m.* polyprene; **—прион** *m.* (ichth.) bass (Polyprion); **—присоединение** *n.* (chem.) polyaddition, addition polymerization; **—пропилен** *m.*, **—пропиленовый** *a.* polypropylene.

полипы *pl.* (zool.) Anthozoa; **гидроидные п.** Hydrozoa.

полирадикулит *m.* (med.) polyradiculitis, inflammation of nerve roots.

поли/рекомбинация *f.* polyrecombination; **—решётка** *f.* composite lattice; **—рибонуклеотид** *m.* (bioch.) polyribonucleotide; **—рибосома** *f.* (gen.) poly(ribo)-some.

полировально-шлифовальный станок honing machine.

полировальн/ый *a.* polishing, buffing, burnishing; **п. материал** polish; **—ая бумага** sandpaper; **—ая жидкость** liquid polish; **—ая работа** polishing, buffing.

полиров/ание *n.* polishing, buffing, burnishing; **—анный** *a.* polished, burnished; plate (glass); **—ать** *v.* polish, buff, burnish, brighten; **—ка** *f.* polishing, buffing; polish, gloss, finish; **—ник** *m.* polisher, burnisher; burnishing stick; **—очная** *f.* polishing room, polishing department; **—очный** *a. of* **полировка**; **—щик** *see* **полировник**.

полирующий *a.* polishing; **—ся** *a.* capable of taking on a polish.

полис *m.* (insurance) policy.

поли/сапроб *m.* (zool.) polysaprobe; **—сапробный** *a.* polysaprobic, thriving on decomposable organic material; **—сахарид** *m.* polysaccharide; **—серозит** *m.* (med.) polyserositis; **—силикат** *m.* polysilicate; **—силоксан** *m.* (chem.) polysiloxane, polysilicone; **—симметричный** *a.* polysymmetric(al); **—синтетический** *a.* polysynthetic; **—соль** *f.* poly salt.

полисом *m.*, **—а** *f.* (bioch.; cyt.) polysome; **—атия** *f.* (cyt.) polysomaty; **—ия** *f.* (gen.) polysomy; (embr.) polysomia; **—ный** *a.* (gen.) polysomic; (cyt.) polysomatic.

полиспаст *m.* compound pulley, pulley block, block and tackle; (crane) pulley.

поли/спермия *f.* (biol.) polyspermy; **—спондилия** *f.* (embr.) polyspondyly; **—спора** *f.* (bot.) polyspore; **—спороз** *m.* (phyt.) Polyspora disease; **—стирол** *m.* polystyrene; **—стихин** *m.* polystichin; **—стихинол** *m.* polystichinol; **—стихоцитрин** *m.* polystichocitrin.

полистный *a.* (per) sheet.

полистэс *m.* (ent.) paper wasps (Polistes).

полисульфид *m.*, **—ный** *a.* polysulfide.

полит *sh. m. of* **политый.**

поли/телия *f.* (anat.) polythelia; **—тен** *see* **полиэтилен**; **—тения** *f.* (gen.) polyteny; **—тенный** *a.* polytene (chromosome); **—терпен** *m.* (chem.) polyterpene; **—тетрафторэтилен** *m.* polytetrafluoroethylene, Teflon.

политехни/зация *f.* introduction of polytechnic education; **—зм** *m.* system of polytechnic education; **—ка** *f.* polytechnics, polytechnology; **—кум** *m.* polytechnic school; **—ческий** *a.* polytechnic(al).

полит/заключённый *m.* political prisoner; **—ик** *m.* politician, political figure; **—ика** *f.* politics; policy.

поли/тионовый *a.* polythionic (acid); **—тиоцепь** *f.* (chem.) polythio chain; **—типаж** *m.* (typ.) duplicated ornament; **—типический** *a.* polytypic, having several species; **—типный** *a.* polytypic (species or genus).

политический *a.* political.

политом/ный *a.* (bot.) polytomous; **—ия** *f.* polytomy.

политональность *f.* (music) polytonality.

политоп *m.* (math.) polytope; **—изм** *m.* (biol.) polytopism, polygenesis; **—ный** *a.* polytopic, occurring in many places.

политрих/ия *f.* (med.) polytrichia, excessive hairiness; **—овые** *pl.* (bot.) Polytrichaceae; **—ум** *m.* haircap moss (*Polytrichum*).

политроп/а *f.*, **—ическая кривая** polytropic curve; **—ический,** **—ный** *a.* polytropic; **—ия** *f.* polytropy.

политро/фический *a.* (bact.; zool.) polytrophic; **—хный** *a.* (zool.) polytrochal.

политура *f.* polish; lac varnish.

Политцера проба (med.) Politzer's test.

полит/ый *a.* watered, irrigated; poured; **—ь** *v.* water, irrigate; start pouring.

политэн *m.* (chem.) polyethylene.

поли/уретан *m.*, **—уретановый** *a.* polyurethane; **—урия** *f.* (med.) polyuria; **—фаг** *m.* (zool.) polyphage; **—фагия** *f.* (biol.) polyphagy, ability to subsist on various kinds of food; (med.) polyphagia, excessive eating; **—фазный,** **—фазовый** *a.* polyphase; **—факторный** *a.* (gen.) multifactorial; **—фалангия** *f.* (med.) polyphalangia; **—фенилен** *m.* (chem.) polyphenyl; **—фения** *f.* (gen.) pleiotropy; **—фенол** *m.* (chem.) polyphenol; **—фенолоксидаза** *f.* (enz.) polyphenoloxydase; **—фермент** *m.* multienzyme; **—филетический** *a.* (biol.) polyphyletic, convergent; **—филия** *f.* (biol.) polyphyly; **—филла** *f.* (ent.) Polyphylla; **—фиодонт** *m.*, **—фиодонтный** *a.* (zool.) polyphyodont; **—фобия** *f.* (psych.) polyphobia; **—формальдегид** *m.* (chem.) polyformaldehyde, polyoxymethylene, POM; **—фторопрен** *m.* polyfluoroprene; **—хазий** *m.* (bot.) polychasium; **—хеты** *pl.* (zool.) marine worms (*Polychaeta*); **—хилия** *f.* (med.) polychylia; **—хирия** *f.* (med.) polycheiria, supernumerary hands.

полихлор/винил *m.*, **—виниловый** *a.* polyvinyl chloride, PVC; **—ид** *m.* polychloride; **—ированный** *a.* polychlorinated; **—опрен** *m.* polychloroprene; **—трифторэтилен** *m.* polytrifluorochloroethylene; **—урия** *f.* (med.) polychloruria.

поли/холия *f.* (med.) polycholia; **—хондрит** *m.* polychondritis.

полихроизм *m.* (cryst.) polychroism, pleochroism.

полихром *m.* polychrom, esculin; **—азия** (med.) polychromasia, polychromatophilia; **—атический** *a.* polychrom(at)ic, multicolored; **—атофильный** *a.* polychromatophilic; **—ия** *f.* polychromy; multicolor printing; **—овая кислота** polychromic acid.

полихронный *a.* polychronic.

полицейский *a.* police; *m.* policeman.

поли/центрический *a.* (gen.) polycentric; **—центропиды** *pl.* (ent.) Polycentropidae; **—циклический** *a.* polycyclic; **—цитемия** *f.* (med.) polycythemia.

полиция *f.* police (force).

поли/эдр *m.* (geom.) polyhedron; **—эдрический** *a.* polyhedral; **—эдрия** *f.*, **—эдроз** *m.* (vet.) grasserie, polyhedrosis; **—экран** *m.* (comp.) split screen; **—электролит** *m.* polyelectrolyte; **—эмбриония** *f.* (embr.) polyembryony; **—энергетический** *a.* polyenergetic, heteroenergetic; **—энергидный** *a.* (cyt.) polyenergid;

—эстезия *f.* (med.) polyesthesia; **—эстричный** *a.* (zool.) poly(o)estrous; **—этерификация** *f.* (chem.) polyesterification; **—этилен** *m.* polyethylene; **—этиленгликол** *m.* polyethylene glycol; **—этилентерефталат** *m.* polyethylene terephthalate.

полиэфир *m.* polyester; polyether; **простой п.** polyether; **сложный п.** polyester; **—акрилат** *m.* polyester acrylate; **—ный** *a. of* **полиэфир;** **—опласт** *m.* polyester resin.

полиэция *f.* (bot.) polyoecism.

полк *m.* (mil.) regiment.

полка *f.* shelf, rack; ledge; tray; wing, flange (of beam); seat (of rim); (agr.) weeding.

полков/ник *m.* colonel; **—ой** *a.* regimental.

Полкский пролив Palk Strait.

поллак *m.* (ichth.) pollack; **—и—** *prefix* pollaki— (frequent, often); **—идипсия** *f.* (med.) pollakidipsia, abnormally frequent thirst.

полл/антин *m.* (pharm.) pollantin; **—ен** *m.* (bot.) pollen; **—енин** *m.* pollenine; **—инарий** *m.* pollinarium; **—иний** *m.* pollen mass; pollinium; **—иноз** *m.* (med.) pollinosis, seasonal hay fever.

поллопас *m.* Pollopas (synthetic resin).

полл/укс *m.* (astr.) Pollux; **п.,** **—уцит** *m.* (min.) pollucite, pollux.

поллюция *f.* (med.) pollution, spermatorrhea.

поллярдированный *a.* (agr.) pollarded, polled.

пол/месяца *f.* half a month; **—миллиона** *m.* half a million; **—минуты** *f.* half a minute.

полнейший *a.* fullest, utmost, utter.

полнеть *v.* grow stout, gain weight.

полно *adv.* full, completely; that is enough; *prefix* holo—; **—ватый** *a.* rather full; **—весный** *a.* full-weight; heavy-eared (grain); **—властный** *a.* sovereign; **—водный** *a.* high (river); full (lake); deep; **—водье** *n.* high water level; flood; **—возрастной** *a.* full grown, adult; **—габаритный** *a.* full-size(d); **—гранник** *m.* (cryst.) holohedron; **—гранный** *a.* holohedral; **—древесный** *a.* nontapering (tree); **—звучный** *a.* sonorous; **—зернистый** *a.* full-grained; **—кристаллический** *a.* holocrystalline.

полнокров/ие *n.* (med.) plethora, hyperemia, engorgement; **—ный** *a.* full-blooded; (med.) plethoric.

полно/луние *n.* full moon; **—масштабный** *a.* full-scale; **—мерный** *a.* full(-sized); **—метражный** *a.* full-length, feature (film); **—мочие** *n.* authority, power; (law) proxy; **—мочный** *a.* plenipotentiary; authorized, empowered; **—осный** *a.* (cryst.) holoaxial; **—поточный** *a.* full-flow; **—правный** *a.* competent; enjoying full rights; **—проходной** *a.* flush (joint); **—размерный** *a.* full-scale; **—сборный** *f.* prefabricated (construction).

полностью *adv.* completely, totally, fullly, wholly, in full; throughout; at (full) length; all-, e.g. **п. электрический** *a.* all-electric.

полнот/а *f.* fullness; completeness; amplitude; (sound) volume; (forestry) density; corpulence, stoutness; **коэффициент —ы давления** pressure coefficient; **коэффициент —ы сгорания** combustion efficiency.

полноценн/ость *f.* full value; **—ый** *a.* full-value, face-value; optimum; complete (protein); wholesome, nutritious; valuable; full-fledged.

полноциклический *a.* (biol.) holocyclic.

полноч/ный *a.*, **—ь** *f.* midnight.

полношаговый *a.* full-pitch (winding).

полн/ый *a.* full, complete, holo— (complete, whole); absolute; total, gross, overall; thorough, comprehensive, exhaustive (information); full-length; maximum (capacity); high (water); deep (sound); stout, corpulent; **п. вес** gross weight; (chem.) combining weight; **п. излучатель** (ideal) black body; **п. эллиптический интеграл** complete elliptic integral; **—ое орошение** (distillation) total reflux; **—ое смещение** complete mixing; back mixing; **в —ой мере** fully, completely.

пол-оборота *m.* half turn; (mil.) half-face.

полова *f.* chaff.

половик *m.* (floor) mat, runner.

половин/а *f.* (one) half; **п. на —у** half and half; **в —у** half as much; **на —у** (in) half; **—ка** *f.* half; **—ник** *m.* semibeam, semigirder; **—ный** *a.* half; **—чатый** *a.* halved, (half and half), split; folding; mottled (iron); dimidiate; indeterminate; **—щик** *m.* partner.

половить *v.* catch, trap.

половица *f.* floor board.

половн/ик *m.* ladle; **—як** *m.* (constr.) bat, half-brick.

полово— *prefix* (anat.) genito—, genital; **—бедренный** *a.* (anat.) genitofemoral.

половод/ный *a.*, **—ье** *n.* (spring) flood, high water.

половзрел/ость *f.* (sexual) maturity, puberty; **—ый** *a.* mature.

полов/ой *a.* sex(ual); reproductive; venereal (disease); genital; estrous (cycle); pudendal (canal); floor; **п. аппарат** genitalia; **п. фактор** (gen.) F-factor; **п. член** (anat.) penis; **—ая губа** (anat.) labium pudendi; **—ая железа** (anat.) reproductive gland, gonad; **—ая зрелость** puberty; **—ая клетка** gamete; **—ая область** (anat.) external genitalia, pudendum; **—ая холодность** frigidity; **—ая щель** (anat.) pudendal fissure; **—ое бессилие** impotence; **—ые органы** genitals, genitalia; **женская —ая железа** ovarium; **мужская —ая железа** testis; **пластика —ого члена** (med.) phalloplasty; **ядро п. клетки** germ nucleus.

полово/собиратель, —уловитель *m.* chaff collector.

полог *m.* canopy, cover, screen.

полог/ий *a.* gently sloping; flat(tened) (curve); shallow (slope); low-angle (trajectory); tapered (wing shell); **—оскладчатый** *a.* gently undulating; **—ость** *f.* slope, declivity; **—охолмистый** *a.* gently rolling.

полодия *f.* (phys.) polhode, centrode.

пологовый *m.* chaff fan, chaff blower.

положен/ие *n.* position, situation, location, locality, place; layout, (spatial) distribution; state, condition, status, aspect; circumstances, case; stand, conclusion, assumption; **—ия договора** provisions of a treaty; **в —ии включения** on; **в должном —ии** in place, in position; **высота в —ии стоя** standing height; **место —ия** position, locus; **рефлекс —ия** postural reflex; **эффект —ия** position effect; **—ный** *a.* placed, put, set, fixed; appointed (hour); allotted (time); assumed.

полож/ивший *a.* having placed, (on) putting, having set; **—им** *see* **положить**.

положительно *adv.* positively; decidedly; **п.-определённый** *a.* (math.) positive-definite; **—сть** *f.* positiveness.

положительн/ый *a.* positive, plus, above-zero; affirmative; favorable; good, beneficial; absolute; **п. знак** (math.) plus, positive sign; **п. столб** positive column (of arc); **—ое качество** feature, advantage.

положи/ть *see* **полагать**; place, set; **—м** let us assume (that).

полоз *m.* runner, slide, skid; (plow) sole; (herp.) racer (*Coluber*).

полоз/ок *m.* (foundry) sleeker, smoother; strip; **—ья** *pl.* runners, skids, slide.

полоида *see* **полодия**.

полок *m.* loading platform, shelf; scaffold; (min.) suspended platform; platform cart; *gen. pl. of* **полка**.

пололепестник *m.* (bot.) Coeloglossum.

половль/ник *m.* hoe; cultivator; **—ный** *a.* weeding; **—щик** *m.* weeder.

полом/анный *a.* broken (down); **—ать(ся)** *v.* break (down); **—ка** *f.* break(ing), breakdown, failure, collapse; breakage, damage.

поломоечный *a.* floor-washing.

полон *sh. m. of* **полный**.

полони/й *m.*, **—евый** *a.* polonium, Po; **—ны** *pl.* polonines (high mountain pastures).

полоопределяющий *a.* sex-determining.

полопаться *v.* burst (of tires, etc.).

полороги/й *a.* (zool.) hollow-horned; **—е** *pl.* (mam.) Bovidae.

полорыл *m.* (ichth.) Coelor(h)ynchus.

полос/а *f.* band; strip, stripe, border; (met.) skelp; piece, stock; streak; zone, belt; stretch, width; period, interval; lane (of road); rail; (cutter) bar; (valence) band; (typ.) page; (anat.) tenia; fascia; stria; **метод полос** schlieren method; **п. частоты** frequency band; **—атик** *m.* (mam.) rorqual (*Balaenoptera*); (ichth.) *see* **боопс**; **малый —атик** (mam.) lesser rorqual; **синий —атик** (great) blue whale; **—атость** *f.* striature, banding; **—атый** *a.* band(ed); striped, ribbed, striated, streaky; fasciated; (biol.) vittate; **—атый спектр** band spectrum; **—атое тело** (anat.) striate body, corpus striatum; **—ка** *f. dim. of* **полоса**; (narrow) band, strip, streak; (biol.) stria.

полоск/ание *n.* rinse, rinsing; gargle; wash; **—ательный** *a.* rinsing; **—ать** *v.* rinse; gargle; **—аться** *v.* dabble, splash; flap (of flags, sails, etc.).

полосков/идный *a.* striiform; **—ый** *a.* band, strip(line).

полоскун *m.* (mam.) raccoon; (ent.) water beetle (*Acilius*).

полосн/о-заграждающий *a.* (elec.) band-stop; **—ой** *see* **полосовой**; **–опропускающий** *a.* band-pass; **—уть** *v.* slash; **—ый** *see* **полосовой**; (typ.) full-page.

полосо/бульб *m.*, **—бульбовый** *a.* (met.) bulb bar; **—вать** *v.* make into bars; cut into strips; stripe; **—видный** *a.* ribbon-like, striiform; **—вой** *a.* band, strip; bar (metal); band-pass (filter); **—посадка** *f.* (silv.) strip planting.

полост/вольный *a.* (bot.) hollow-stemmed; **—ебельчатый** *a.* (bot.) hollow-stalked; **—ной** *a.* cavity(-type); (zool.) cavitary; (anat.) perivisceral (fluid).

полость *f.* hollow, cavity, void, lacuna; recess, housing, chamber; cage; (anat.) cavum, caverna; cavitas, space, pocket, antrum; (cryst.) vacancy; **п. зуба** cavum dentis, nerve cavity; **п. коронки зуба** cavum coronale; **п. тела** coelom, body cavity; **большая п.** (catalysts) supercage; **вторичная п.** (embr.) metacoeloma.

полосчат/ость *f.* banding, striation; (phyt.) streak; **вирусная кукурузная п.** (agr.) corn streak; **—ый** *a.* banded, banding, striped, streaky, striated; ribbon; lamellar, laminated; **—ая руда** band(ed) ore.

полотен/ечный *a.*, **—це** *n.* towel; (constr.) sling (plate).

полотёр *m.* floor sander; floor polisher (worker); **—ный** *a.* floor-polishing.

полотнище *n.* (text.) breadth, length, strip; panel, leaf (of door); (tool) blade; plating (of bulkhead); gore (of parachute); bolt (of canvas).

полотн/о *n.* fabric, cloth, spec. linen or canvas; (tool) blade; (ax) head; (road) bed; (conveyer) belt; deck (of distillation tray); (paper) web, sheet; **земляное п.** roadbed; **—яный** *a.* linen.

полоть *v.* (agr.) weed; **—ье** *n.* weeding.

полоумный *a.* insane, half-witted.

полоцит *m.* (gen.) polocyte, polar body.

полоч/ка *dim. of* **полка; —ный** *a. of* **полка;** shelved; tray (dryer); multiple-hearth (reactor).

полощет *pr. 3 sing. of* **полоскать.**

пол/пути *m.* halfway (mark); **—румба** *m.* half (point); **—сотни** *num.* fifty.

пол. ст. *abbr.* (**полевой стан**) field camp; (**полярная станция**) polar station.

полтавский *a.* (geog.) Poltawa.

полтор/а *m. and n.* *num.,* **—ы** *f.* *num.* one and a half, sesqui—; **—аста** *num.* one hundred and fifty.

полу— *prefix* semi—, demi—, hemi—, half—; sub—.

полуавтомат *m.* semiautomatic device; **токарный п.** semiautomatic lathe; **—ический** *a.* semiautomatic.

полу/активный *a.* semiactive; **—альдегид** (chem.) semialdehyde; **—амплитуда** *f.* half range; **—ацеталь** *m.* hemiacetal; **—байт** *m.* (comp.) nibble, half-byte, four bits; **—бархат** *m.* (text.) velveteen; **—батанчик** *m.* rack (of loom); **—бездымный** *a.* semi-smokeless; **—белый** *a.* off-white; **—бесконечный** *a.* (math.) semi-infinite; **—бимс** *m.* half-beam; **—битуминозный** *a.* semibituminous; **—блестящий** *a.* semi-lustrous; **—ботинки** *pl.* low shoes, slippers; **—блок** *m.* (elec.) (battery plate) group; **—бочка** *f.* (av.) half roll; **—бутылка** *f.* half bottle.

полу/вагон *m.* (rr.) gondola car; **—вал** *m.* (half-)sole leather; **—валик** *m.* (arch.) bead, fillet; **—вальмовый** *a.* gambrel (roof); **—вальный** *a. of* **полувал; —вар** *m.* pitch and tar; **—вареный** *a.* half-cooked, half-digested; souple(d) (silk); **—ватманская бумага** machine-made Whatman paper; **—ватт** *m.* (elec.) half-watt; **—вековой** *a.* half-century; **—вид** semi-species; **—винтовый** *a.* half-turn; **—влажный** *a.* semihumid; **—водяной** *a.* semiwater (gas).

полуволн/а *f.,* **—овой** *a.* half-wave; **—истый** *a.* (met.) semicorrugated.

полу/вращающийся *a.* semirotatory; **—вулканизация** *f.* (rubber) precuring; **период —выведения** (nucl.) half-life; **—гайка** *f.* half nut; **—гидрат** *m.* semihydrate, hemihydrate.

полугармоника *f.* harmonic of one-half frequency; **—гнёздный** *a.* (bot.) semilocular.

полугод/ие *n.* half year; **—ичный, —овальный** *a.* semiannual; six-month-old; **—овой** *a.* semiannual.

полугранн/ик *m.* (cryst.) hemihedron; **—ый** *a.* hemihedral.

полугрузовик *m.* pickup (truck).

полугрупп/а *f.,* **—овый** *a.* (math.) semigroup.

полугусеничный *a.* half-track.

полуда *f.* tin (plate); tinning.

полу/денный *a.* midday, noontide, meridional; **—дерево** *n.* large shrub; **—диаметр** *m.* semidiameter, radius; **—дизель** *m.* semi-Diesel engine; **—дикий** *a.* half wild; **—дислокация** *f.* (phys.) semidislocation, half-displacement; **—дистанционный** *a.* semiremote.

полудить *v.* tin(-plate).

полу/дня *gen. of* **полдень; —древесный** *a.* semi-arboreous; **—дремота** *f.* half-dreaming state.

полудюйм *m.,* **—овый** *a.* half-inch; **—овка** *f.* half-inch plank.

полужабра *f.* (zool.) gill arch, hemibranch.

полужёстк/ий *a.* semirigid; **—окрылые** *pl.* (ent.) Hemiptera.

полу/жидкий *a.* semiliquid, semifluid; **—жирный** *a.* (typ.) bold; semithick; **—забытый** *a.* half-forgotten; **—забытье** *n.* semiconsciousness; **—заводский** *a.* pi-

---

lot plant; **—закалка** *f.* semihardening; **—закрытый** *a.* semi(en)closed; **—закрыть** *v.* semi(en)close; **—залом** *see* **черноспинка; —замкнутый** *a.* partially enclosed (sea); **—запруда** *f.* dike, etc., *see* **буна; —засушливый** *a.* semi-arid; **—затемнённый** *a.* semishade(d); **—затопленный** *a.* waterlogged; **—защищённый** *a.* semiprotected; **—звезда** *f.* semistar; **—зонтик** *m.* (bot.) cyme; **—зонтиковый** *a.* (bot.) cymose; **—зрелый** *a.* half-ripe, green; **—зубатка** *f.* (ichth.) chum salmon (*Oncorhynchus keta*); **—зубки, —зубые** *pl.* (ichth.) Hemiodontidae; **—известковистый** *a.* semicalcareous; **—инструментальный** *a.* semi-instrument(al), approximate; **—ископаемый** *a.* partly fossilized.

полу/канал *m.* (anat.) semicanal, semicanalis; **—карбид** *m.* semicarbide; **—кардан** *m.* semicardan joint; **—картон** *m.* thin (card)board; **—кашка** coarse grindings; **—квадрат** *m.* (typ.) en; **—квалифицированный** *a.* semiskilled; **—кегельная** *f.* (typ.) en; **—кислый** *a.* semiacid; **—клевер** *m.* (bot.) yellow trefoil (*Medicago lupulina*); **—клетка** *f.* (bot.) semicell; **—кожистый** *a.* subcoriaceous (approaching a leathery texture); **—кожник** *m.* kip (undressed hide of a young animal); **—козёл-тар** *m.* (mam.) tahr (*Hemitragus*).

полукокс *m.* semicoke; **—ование** *n.* semicoking, low-temperature carbonization; **—овый** *a.* semicoke.

полу/количественный *a.* (chem.) semiquantitative; **—коллоид** *m.* hemicolloid; **—кольцевой** *a.* channel (wing); semi-annular; **—кольцо** *n.* half circle; (math.) semi-ring (of sets); **верхнее —кольцо** (zool.) tergite; **нижнее —кольцо** (zool.) sternite; **—коммутативный** *a.* (math.) semicommutative; **—комплект** *m.* subassembly; subset; **—консервы** *pl.* (food) preserves; **—коронирующий разряд** (dielectrics) semicorona discharge; **—котельное железо** (met.) boiler plate; **—кочевник** *m.* semimigrant; **—кочевой** *a.* semimigratory; **—кристаллический** *a.* semicrystalline; **продувка —крицы** (met.) first refining.

полукров/ка *f.,* **—ный** *a.* (gen.) halfbreed.

полукруг *m.* semicircle; **—лая** *f.* (typ.) en; **—лый** *a.* semicircular; semispherical, half-round; (bot.) cupshaped.

полукруж/ие *see* **полукруг; —ный** *a.* (anat.) semicircular (canals).

полу/кубический *a.* semicubical; **—кустарник** *m.* (bot.) semishrub, subshrub; **—кустарниковый** *a.* (bot.) suffrutescent, slightly shrubby; **—лапчатый** *a.* (orn.) semipalmate, half-webbed; **—лежать** *v.* recline; **—летальный** *a.* semilethal; **—лечь** *v.* recline; **—линза** *f.* hemilens; **—литровый** *a.* half-liter; **—логарифмический** *a.* (math.) semilog(arithmic) (scale); **—локальный** *a.* (math.) semilocal; **—лунниковые** *pl.* (ichth.) halfmoons (*Scorpididae*); **—лунный** *a.* half-moon, crescent(-shaped); semilunar; lunate (bone); **—лунное образование** (anat.) falx; **—лучевой** *a.* semiradiate; **—ляжет** *fut. 3 sing. of* **полулечь; —мак** *m.* gentle-lemur (*Hapalemur*); **—максимальный** *a.* half-maximum; **—масса** *f.* (paper) mixed-fiber pulp, half stuff; **—матовый** *a.* semigloss, semimatte; **—мгла** *f.* partial darkness, twilight, dusk, dawn; **—мезга** *f.* vegetable pulp; **—мера** *f.* half measure; palliative; **—мёртвый** *a.* dying, half-dead; **—месяц** *m.* half-moon; (ichth.) anglefish; **—месячный** *a.* half-month, fortnightly.

полуметалл *m.* semimetal; **—ический** *a.* semimetallic; (min.) submetallic.

полу/микроаналитический *a.* semimicroanalytical; **—мрак** *m.* semidarkness, gloom; **—мутовка** *f.* (bot.)

false whorl, semiverticillaster; —**муфта** *f.* (mech.) half-coupling; **лесная** —**мышь** woodland jumping mouse (*Napaeozapus insignis*); —**навесной** *a.* semimounted; —**надкрыло** *n.* (ent.) hem(i)elytron; —**надпестичный** *a.* (bot.) semi-epigynous; —**непарный** *a.* (anat.) hemiazygos (vein); —**непрерывный** *a.* semicontinuous; —**непроницаемый** *a.* semitight; —**нижний** *a.* (ichth.) subterminal (mouth); (bot.) perigynous; half-inferior (ovary); —**ница** *f.* (bot.) hill strawberry (*Fragaria viridis*); —**нормальный** *a.* half-normal; —**ночный** *see* **полночный.**

полу/обезьяны *pl.* (mam.) Lemuroidea; **период** —**обмена** (chem.) half-time of exchange; —**обнажённый** *a.* half-bare; —**оборот** *m.* half turn; **на** —**оборот** halfway around; —**обработанный** *a.* semifinished; semiprocessed; —**обращёный** *a.* (bot.) hemitropous; —**обтекаемый** *a.* semistreamlined; —**объемлющий** *a.* (bot.) equitant, overlapping; —**овальный** *a.* semioval; —**ограниченный** *a.* (math.) semirestricted, semifinite; —**однородный** *a.* semihomogeneous; —**окаймлённый** *a.* (bot.) semimarginate; —**окатанный** *a.* subangular; —**округлый** *a.* hemispherical; nearly circular; —**окружность** *f.* semicircumference; —**опушённый** *a.* (bot.) hemitrichous; —**освещённый** *a.* half-lit, poorly illuminated; —**осевой насос** mixed-flow pump; —**осёл** *m.* Asiatic wild ass (*Equus hemionus*); —**основный** *a.* (chem.) weakly basic; —**остистый** *a.* (anat.) semispinalis (muscle); (bot.) semiawned.

полуостров *m.* peninsula; —**ной** *a.* peninsular.

полу/ось *f.* semiaxis; semiaxle, split axle, axle shaft; **большая п.** semimajor axis; **малая п.** semiminor axis; —**отворенный** *a.* partly open, ajar; —**отделанный** *a.* semifinished; rough-finished; unfinished (furniture); —**открытый** *a.* semienclosed; partly open, ajar; —**охватывающий** *see* **полуобъемлющий;** —**очищенный** *a.* (chem.) partially purified; —**пальто** *n.* jacket; —**пар** *m.* (agr.) bastard fallow; —**параболический** *a.* semiparabolic; —**паразит** *m.* (bot.) hemiparasite; —**паралич** *m.* (med.) paresis; hemiplegia; —**перекрёстный** *a.* quartertwist (belt); —**переменный** *a.* semivariable; —**переносный** *a.* semiportable; —**перепончатая мышца** (anat.) semimembranosus.

полупериод *m.* half period, half-cycle; (nucl.) half-life; **п. распада** half-life; **п. реакции обмена** (chem.) half-time of exchange; **биологический п.** biological half-life.

полуперистый *a.* (bot.) imperfectly pinnate, semipinnate.

полу/петля *f.* (text.) half-stitch; —**пирамида** *m.* semipyramid; —**плод** *m.* (bot.) hemicarp; —**плоскость** *f.* half-plane; (optics) half-fringe; —**поверхность** *f.* (bot.) semifacies; —**погружённый** *a.* semi-immersed; emerging (above water); —**подвал** *m.,* —**подвальный** *a.* semibasement; —**подвижный сустав** (anat.) amphiarthrosis; —**подкисленный** *a.* semiacidified; —**покровный** *a.* (bot.) hemichlamydeous; —**полба** *see* **полба;** —**полярный** *a.* (chem.) semipolar; —**послед** *m.* semiplacenta; —**потайной** *a.* half-countersunk; —**призма** *f.* (cryst.) hemiprism; —**прилегающий** *a.* semi-adherent; —**приросший** *a.* (bot.) semiadnate, partly grown together; —**прицеп** *m.* semitrailer.

полупровод/ник *m.* (elec.) semiconductor; —**никовый** *a.* semiconductor; semiconductive; (comp.) transistor(ized); —**никовый триод,** —**никовый усилитель** transistor; —**ящий** *a.* semiconducting.

полу/продукт *m.* semifinished article, intermediate

product; **п. гормона** (bioch.) prohormone; —**прозрачный** *a.* translucent; —**промышленный** *a.* semicommercial; pilot(-plant); —**проницаемый** *a.* semipermeable; —**просвечивающий** *a.* semitranslucent; —**простой** *a.* (math.) semisimple; —**пространство** *n.* half space; —**профиль** *m.* half section; —**проходной** *a.* semimigratory; (ichth.) semianadromous; —**прямая** *f.* (math.) ray, half line; —**прямостоячий** *a.* (bot.) semi-erect; —**пустынный** *a.* semiarid; —**пустыня** *f.* semiarid land, semidesert; —**пуховидные перья** (orn.) semiplumes.

полу/равнина *f.* (geol.) peneplain; —**размах** *m.* amplitude; (av.) semispan; —**разрез** *m.* semisectional view; —**разрушенный** *a.* half demolished, partially collapsed; —**разъём** (connector) plug, receptacle; —**раковистый** *a.* subconchoidal; —**раскос** *m.* (constr.) knee brace; —**раскрытый** *a.* partly open.

полураспад *m.* (nucl.) half-decay, half-life; half-value (layer, etc.); **период** —**а** half-life, half-value period.

полу/расплавленный *a.* semifused, semimolten; —**реплика** *f.* half-replicate (of a full factorial design in experiment planning); —**рогие** *pl.* (mam.) Bovoidea; —**рыловые** *pl.* halfbeak fishes (*Hemiramphidae*); —**саванна** *f.* semisavanna; —**сапрофит** *m.* (bot.) hemisaprophyte; —**сварить** *v.* parboil, partially boil; —**свет** *m.* weak illumination; twilight; —**светящийся** *a.* semiluminous; —**свод** *m.* semivault; —**связанный** *a.* semifixed; —**сердцевидный** *a.* (bot.) semicordate; —**сёстры-полубратья, сибсы** *pl.* half-siblings; —**сидячий** *a.* (zool.) semisessile; —**синкарпный** *a.* (bot.) hemisyncarpous; —**скоростной** *a.* half-velocity; —**слово** *n.* (comp.) half-word; —**смертельный** *a.* semilethal; —**смола** *f.* resinoid; —**сознательный** *a.* semiconscious; —**сон** *n.* doze; somnolence; —**сонный** *a.* drowsy; —**сотня** *f.* half a hundred; —**спёкшийся** *a.* semisintered, partly caked; —**спелый** *a.* half-ripe, green; —**спокойный** *a.* (met.) semi-killed.

полу/стационарный *a.* semifixed; semiportable; —**стеблеобъемлющий** *a.* (bot.) semiamplexicaul; —**стекловатый** *a.* semivitreous; —**стекловидный** *a.* vitreous (grain); —**степь** *f.* semisteppe; **горная** —**степь** semisavanna; —**стойкий** *a.* semipersistent (toxic agent); semistable; —**сток** *m.* semiflow; —**стреловидный** *a.* (bot.) semisagittate; —**строб** *m.* (half) gate; —**структура** *f.* semilattice; —**стык** *m.* half joint; —**сумеречный** *a.* (biol.) semivespertine; —**сумма** *f.* average; —**сумматор** *m.* (comp.) half adder, two-input adder; —**сумрак** *m.* semitwilight; —**суперфосфат** *m.* semisuperphosphate; —**сустав** *m.* (anat.) hemiarthrosis; —**суточный** *a.* semidiurnal, 12-hour; —**сухожильная мышца** (anat.) semitendinosus; —**сухой** *a.* semiarid; semidry; —**сушка** *f.* partial drying; —**сфера** *f.* hemisphere; —**сферический** *a.* hemispherical.

полу/тарифный *a.* half-rate; —**твёрдый** *a.* semisolid; medium hard; —**тело** *n.* half body; —**тёмный** *a.* poorly lit; —**теневой** *a.,* —**тень** *f.* (opt.) penumbra; light shade; —**толщина** *f.* (nucl.) half thickness; —**томпак** *m.* (met.) low brass; —**тон** *m.,* —**тоновый** *a.* half-tone, semitone; (comp.) gray-scale.

полутор/а *see* **полуторный—**; —**аокись** *f.* sesquioxide; —**асернистое соединение** sesquisulfide; —**ка** *f.* one and a half-ton truck.

полуторно— *prefix* sesqui— (one and a half); —**сернистый** *a.* sesquisulfide (of); —**углекислая соль** sesquicarbonate; —**угленатриевая соль** sodium sesquicarbonate; —**хлористый** *a.* sesquichloride (of); —**хромовокислая соль** sesquichromate.

полуторн/ый *a.* one and one half, sesqui—; tripartite (pontoon); **—ая окись** sesquioxide; **—ая соль** sesquisalt; **соль —ой окиси металла** salt of a trivalent metal.

полу/точный *a.* half-exact; **—трава** *f.* semigrass; **—травянистый** *a.* (bot.) semiherbose; **—трубчатый** *a.* semitubular; **—туникатный** *a.* (bot.) semitunicate; **—тьма** *f.* semidarkness; **—убирающийся** *a.* (av.) semiretractable.

полууг/ловатость *f.* (geol.) subangularity; **—ол** *m.* semi-angle.

полу/уравновешенный *a.* semibalanced; **—утопленный** *a.* semiflush, semirecessed; **—фабрикат** *m.* semifinished product, intermediate product; convenience food; **—фарфор** *m.* semiporcelain; **—ферма** *f.* semitruss; **—форма** *f.* half mold, mold section; **—фуганок** *m.* (carpentry) long plane.

полухлорист/ый *a.* (—ous) chloride; **—ая медь** cuprous chloride; **—ая сера** sulfur monochloride.

полу/хордовые *pl.* (zool.) Hemichordata; **—цветочковый** *a.* (bot.) semifloscular; **—целлюлоза** *f.* (paper) hemicellulose, semichemical pulp, half stuff; **—целый** *a.* half-integral, semi-integral; half-integer (momentum); **—целое число** half integer; **—центр** *m.* half center; **—циклический** *a.* (bot.) hemicyclic; **—цилиндр** *m.* semicylinder; **—цилиндрический** *a.* (bot.) hemicylindrical; semiterete; **—циркуль** *m.* semicircle; **—циркульный** *a.* semicircular.

получаем/ый *a.* received, etc., *see* **получать**; resulting, resultant; available; **—ая энергия** (elec.) input.

получас *m.* half hour; **—овой** *a.* half hourly.

получ/атель *m.* recipient; **—ать** *v.* receive, obtain, get, acquire, secure; derive, extract, draw; take in; gain, win; isolate; make, produce, fabricate; generate; **—ать обратно** recover; **—аться** *v.* be received, etc.; turn out, result, happen; work, succeed; **—ение** *n.* receiving, reception, etc., *see v.*; receipt; acquisition; availability; preparation, extraction, recovery; output, crop; **обратное —ение** recovery; **—енный** *a.* received, etc., *see v.*; resultant.

полу/чёрный *a.* half-rough; **—черпак** *m.* (leather) half-butt; **—чешуйник** *m.* (ichth.) Irish lord (*Hemilepidotus*); **—чистый** *a.* semifinished; partly contaminated.

получ/ить *see* **получать; можно п.** can be had, is available; **—ка** *f.* sum; pay.

получленик *m.* (bot.) article, joint of stem or fruit body.

получше *adv.* somewhat) better.

полу/шар *m.*, **—шарие** *n.* hemisphere; (anat.) cerebrum; **—шаровидный, —шарообразный** *a.* hemispheric(al); (bot.) semiglobose; **—шёлковый** *a.* part-silk; **—шёрстный** *a.* sparsely covered with hair; **—шерстяной** *a.* part-wool; **—ширина** *f.* half width; (phys.) full width at half height (of a pulse); half thickness (of absorber); **—широта** *f.* (naut.) half-breadth plan.

полушник *m.* (bot.) quillwort (*Isoëtes*).

полушубок *m.* short sheepskin coat, short winter coat.

полу/щелевой *a.* half-slot; **—эдрический** *a.* hemihedral; **—элемент** *m.* (elec.) half cell; **—элитр** *m.* (ent.) hem(i)elytron; **—эллиптический** *a.* semielliptic(al), half-elliptic; **—эмпирический** *a.* semiempirical; **—эпифит** *m.* hemiepiphyte; **—этаж** *m.* half story; **—ют** *m.* (naut.) poop; **—явный** *a.* semiexplicit (differential equation); **—яйцевидный** *a.* (bot.) semiovate.

пол/фунта *m.* half a pound; **—цены** *f.* half price; **—часа** *m.* half an hour; **—чок** *m.* (mam.) dormouse (*Glis glis*).

полы *gen. sing.* of **пола**; *pl.* of **пол, пола.**

пол/ый *a.* hollow, tubular; cored; concave; core (drill); shell (circuit); bare, uncovered, open; **—ая вена** (anat.) vena cava; **—ая вода** high water in spring.

полым *m.* river channel; **—я** *n.* (fishing) hole in the ice.

полын/ный *a.* of **полынь; —ная водка, —овка** *f.* absinthe (liqueur); **—ное масло** oil of wormwood; **—ок** *m.* wormwood; gold poppy (*Elsholtzia*); **—ь** *f.* (bot.) wormwood, absinthe, sagebrush (*Artemisia*); **горькая —ь** wormwood; **эстрагонная —ь** tarragon.

полынья *f.* open lead, air hole (in ice).

полысеть *v.* get bald.

полыхать *v.* blaze.

польдер *m.* polder, diked land.

полье *f.* (geol.) polje; *suffix* -field (*or* -year) crop rotation, e.g. **двуполье** *n.* two-field crop rotation.

польёт *fut. 3 sing.* of **полить.**

польз/а *f.* use, good, profit, benefit, advantage; **в —у** on behalf (of); **извлекать —у** *v.* benefit (from), put to good use; **—ование** *n.* use; **—ователь** *m.* user; **—овательный** *a.* commercial; **—оваться** *v.* make use (of), put to use, employ, profit (by); rely (on); have, enjoy.

польский *a.* (geog.) Polish; **п.-китайский** (agr.) Poland China (pigs).

польщённый *a.* satisfied, pleased.

полья *pl.* (geol.) poljes.

полюс *m.* pole, terminal; (anat.) polus, extremity; **поверхность —а** polar surface; **шаг —ов** (elec.) pole pitch.

полюсн/ый *a.* polar, pole; **п. зажим** pole terminal; **п. магнитный поток** polar flux; **п. стержень** contact bar; **п. шаг, —ое деление** pole pitch.

полюсо— *prefix* polar; **—определитель** *m.* (elec.) polarity indicator.

поля *gen. and pl.* of **поле.**

поляжет *fut. 3 sing.* of **полечь.**

полян/а *f.* glade, meadow; **—ка** *dim. of* **поляна.**

поляр/а *f.* (math.) polar; **—изатор** *m.*, **—изационная призма** (opt.) polarizer; **—изационный** *a.*, **—изация** *f.* polarization; **—из(ир)уемый** *a.* polarizable; **—изование** *n.* polarization; **—изованный** *a.* polarized; polarization; **—изовать** *v.* polarize; **—изуемость** *f.* polarizability; **—изуемый** *a.* polarizable; polarized; **—изующий** *a.* polarizing.

поляриметр *m.* (opt.) polarimeter; **—ический** *a.* polarimetric; **—ия** *f.* polarimetry.

полярископ *m.* (opt.) polariscope.

полярник *m.* polar research worker; polar explorer.

полярность *f.* polarity.

полярн/ый *a.* polar; arctic; **п. пояс** frigid zone; **—ая звезда** North Star, Polaris; **—ая клетка** (gen.) polar body, polar cell; **—ая ось** (cryst.) polar axis; **—ая связь** polar bond; **—ое сияние** aurora polaris, aurora; **—ое тельце** *see* **полярная клетка.**

полярограмма *f.* (phys., chem.) polarogram.

полярограф *m.* (electroanalysis) polarograph; **—ирование** *n.* polarography, polarographic analysis; **—ический** *a.* polarographic; **—ическая кривая** polarogram; **—ия** *f. see* **полярографирование; амальгамная —ия с накоплением** stripping polarography.

поляр/оид *m.* Polaroid (light-polarizing sheet material); (opt.) polarization filter; **—он** *m.* polaron.

пом. *abbr.* **(помощник)** assistant.

помад/а *f.* pomade, salve, ointment; **—азиевые** *pl.* (ichth.) grunts (*Pomadasyidae*); **—ить** *v.* put on salve, grease.

помаз/(ыв)ать *v.* anoint, smear, apply; oil, grease; **—ок** *m.* brush; (foundry) bosh, swab.

помак/ать, —нуть *v.* dip, soak.

помаленьку *adv.* little by little, gradually.

помарка *f.* blot, blur; (pencil) mark, correction.

помаслить *v.* oil, lubricate.

поматосхистус *m.* (ichth.) goby (*Pomatoschistus*).

помах(ив)ать *v.* wave, swing; wag (tail).

помацентр/иды, —овые *pl.* damselfishes (*Pomacentridae*).

помедлить *v.* delay, put off.

помеднённый *a.* copperplated.

помелеть *v.* grow shallow.

помело *n.* hearth broom.

помельчать *v.* become finer or smaller.

поменьше *adv.* (a little) less, (a little) smaller.

поменять(ся) *v.* exchange.

померан/ец *m.*, **—цевый** *a.* bitter orange, Seville orange (*Citrus aurantium*); **—цевая трава** citronella grass (*Cymbopogon nardus*); **—цевое дерево** osage orange (*Maclura*); **—цеволистный** *a.* aurantifolious (having golden leaves).

помереть *v.* die.

помёрз/лый *a.* frostbitten; **—нуть** *v.* be frostbitten; be killed by frost.

померить *v.* measure, fit; **—ся** *v.* contend (with); measure (against).

померк/лый *a.* dimmed, tarnished; **—нуть** *v.* grow dim, get tarnished; be eclipsed, disappear.

помертвелый *a.* lifeless, numb; deathly pale.

помесить *v.* knead (for a while).

помесный *a.* crossbred.

поместительн/ость *f.* roominess; **—ый** *a.* capacious, roomy, spacious.

поместить *see* **помещать.**

поместье *n.* estate.

помесь *f.* mixture; adulteration; (biol.) cross(breed); hybrid.

помесячн/о *adv.* per month, once a month; **—ый** *a.* monthly.

помёт *m.* dung, excrement, droppings, manure; litter, brood.

помет/ить *v.*, **—(к)а** *f.* mark, note.

помётохранилище *n.* dunghill.

помех *gen. pl. of* **помеха.**

помех/а *f.* interference, disturbance; hindrance, impediment, obstacle, barrier, handicap; difficulty, trouble, kink, (comp.) bug; **—и** *pl.* (rad.) interference, noise, static; jamming; **атмосферные —и** static; **наводка помех** (elec.) stray pick-up; (rad.) noise induction; **передатчик помех** jamming transmitter, jammer; **служить —ой** *v.* hinder, impede, stand in the way; **создавать —и** *v.* disturb; **—овый** *a. of* **помеха;** jamming; **—оглушитель** *m.* (rad.) squelch circuit.

помехо/защитный *a.* (comp.) error-detecting, error-correcting; **—защищённость** *f.* interference-killing feature, anti-jamming, noise immunity; **—защищённый** *a.* anti-noise, anti-interference; **—подавляющий** *a.* noise-eliminating, noise-suppressing; **—стойкий** *a.* anti-static, anti-interference; **—устойчивость** *f.* interference-killing feature, noise-proof feature; invulnerability to jamming; noise stability; performance (of data transmission system); **—устойчивый** *a.* jamproof, antijamming; noise-suppressing, interference-suppressing; (comp.) error-correcting.

помеч/ать *v.* mark, annotate, label; (nucl.) tag; point out; **—енный** *a.* marked, etc., *see v.*

помеш/анный *a.* mixed, stirred; obsessed; insane, psychotic, deranged; *m.* psychotic; **—ательство** *n.* insanity, mania, derangement, psychosis; **однопредметное**

—ательство monomania; **—ать** *v.* mix, stir, agitate; be in the way (of), prevent, hinder; **—аться** *v.* be mixed; be obsessed (by); become mentally ill; **—енный** *a.* kneaded; **—ивание** *n.* mixing, stirring, agitation; **—ивать** *v.* stir occasionally.

помещ/ать *v.* place, put, set, install, insert; set up, establish, locate, situate, position; interpose (between); enclose, house, accommodate, arrange; (com.) invest, deposit; **—аться** *v.* be placed, etc.; sit, rest, fit, occupy; **—ение** *n.* placing, etc., *see v.*; room, apartment, quarters, space, compartment, chamber; place, accommodation(s); (com.) investment; **жилые —ения** living quarters; **находящийся в —ении** the occupant; **рабочие —ения** office space; **—ённый** *a.* placed, etc., *see v.*; **—ик** *m.* landlord.

помзав *m.* assistant manager.

помиги(ва)ть *v.* blink, flicker.

помидор *m.*, **—ный** *a.* tomato.

помимо *prep. gen.* apart from, with the exception of, except for, besides, aside from, over and above, in addition to; without the knowledge (of); **п. того** moreover.

поминутн/о *adv.* every minute; **—ый** *a.* per minute; frequent.

помирать *v.* die, be dying.

помириться *v.* be(come) reconciled (to).

помнёт *fut. 3 sing. of* **помять.**

помнить *v.* remember, keep in mind.

помногу *adv.* much, in large quantities.

помнож/ать *v.* multiply; **—ение** *n.* multiplication; **—енный** *a.* multiplied; **—ить** *v.* multiply.

помнут *fut. 3 pl. of* **помять.**

помогать *v.* help, assist, aid; relieve, ease; favor, promote.

помоет *fut. 3 sing. of* **помыть.**

пом/ои *pl.* slops, swill, dishwater; **—ойка** *f.* slops pit; **—ойница** *f.* wash hole; drain; **—ойный** *a.* slops, swill; **—ойная яма** drain pit, sink, cesspool.

помокнуть *v.* soak for a time.

помоксис (ichth.) *see* **краппи.**

помол *m.* grist; grinding; milling; (paper) pulp, stock; **степень —а** (paper) pulp freeness.

помолоб(ус) *m.* (ichth.) alewife (*Pomolobus*).

помолог *m.* (agr.) pomologist, fruit grower; **—ия** *f.* (agr.) pomology.

помолодеть *v.* be rejuvenated, grow or look younger.

помолотить *v.* (agr.) thresh.

помолот/ый *a.* ground, milled; **—ь** *v.* grind (up), mill.

помолоченный *a.* (agr.) threshed.

помольный *a.* grinding, milling.

помор *m.*, **—ка** *f.* coast dweller.

поморники *pl.* (orn.) jaegers and skuas (*Stercorariidae*).

поморозить *v.* freeze, congeal.

поморосить *v.* drizzle.

помор/ский *a.* seashore, coast; **—ье** *n.* seashore, coast, coastal region, littoral.

помост *m.* raised platform, stage, dais, rostrum; gallery, scaffold, bridging.

помотать *v.* wind; wag, wave, shake.

помоха *f.* pomokha (haze of dust from deflation over chernozem); hot-wind burn.

помоч/енный *a.* wetted; **—и** *pl.* supporting straps; suspenders; **—ить** *v.* wet, moisten.

помочь *see* **помогать.**

помощ/ник *m.*, **—ница** *f.* helper, assistant, (naut.) mate; **—ь** *f.* help, assistance, aid; use; relief; favor, service; **—ью, при —и, с —ью** with the help (of), by means (of); **оказ(ыв)ать —ь, подавать —ь** *v.* help, assist, treat; **первая —ь, скорая —ь** first aid.

помоют *fut. 3 pl. of* **помыть**.

помпа *f.* pump; **—ж** *m.* pumpage; (mach.) pulsation, surging, surge, hunting; (jet engines) compressor stalling, stall.

помпано *m.* (ichth.) pompano (*Trachinotus*).

помпейский *a.* Pompeian (color).

помпельмус *m.* (bot.) shaddock.

помрач/ать, —ить *v.* darken, obscure.

помум *m.* (bot.) pome.

помут/ить *v.* make turbid; **—иться** *v.* become turbid, get cloudy, fog; get dim, blear; blur; **—нение** *n.* turbidity, cloudiness; dimness, blur; fogging; (corneal) opacity; **—нение воздуха** atmospheric turbidity; **испытание на —нение** cloud test; **проба —нения** (bioch.) turbidity test; **точка —нения** (petroleum) cloud point; **—нённый** *a.* (made) turbid, cloudy; fogged; **—неть** *v.* become turbid.

помуч/ать, —ить *v.* torment.

помчаться *v.* rush, dart.

помыл/и(ва)ть *v.* soap, lather; **—ки** *pl.* suds, lather.

помыт/ый *a.* washed; **—ь(ся)** *v.* wash.

помят/ый *a.* crumpled, creased; flabby; **—ь(ся)** *v.* crumple, crease, wrinkle; trample (grass); knead (dough); brake (flax).

понаблюдать *v.* observe (for a while).

понабрать(ся) *v.* collect gradually.

понавезти *v.* import, bring in.

понадобиться *v.* be necessary.

понапрасну *adv.* in vain.

по-настоящему *adv.* in earnest; in the right way, properly.

поначалу *adv.* from (or at) the beginning.

по-нашему *adv.* in our opinion; in our way, according to our custom.

понгиды *pl.* anthropoid apes (*Pongidae*).

понд *m.* gram force.

пондеромоторное притяжение (elec.) pondermotive force.

поневоле *adv.* against one's will, by force, perforce, necessarily.

понедельн/ик *m.* Monday; **—о** *adv.*, **—ый** *a.* weekly, per week.

по-немецки *adv.* (in) German.

понемногу *adv.* little by little, gradually.

понести *v.* carry (along); **—сь** *v.* rush off.

пони *m.* (mam.) pony.

понижать *v.* reduce, decrease, diminish, cut down; lower, let down; relieve (pressure); depress (a constant); (elec.) step down; **—ся** *v.* fall, go down, drop, lower, diminish; settle, subside.

понижающий *a.* reducing, depressing (constant); (elec.) step-down; **—ся** *a.* falling, dropping, downward.

пониже *adv.* somewhat lower, a little below; a little shorter; **—ние** *n.* reduction, lowering, recession, drop (in pressure, temperature), abatement, decrease, decline, loss, fall, falling down, subsiding, settling; depression (of constant); (elec.) stepping down; (wage) cut; (geol.) subsidence; **—ние в рельефе** (meteor.) low, trough; **период —ния** period of decline; **—нный** *a.* reduced, etc., *see* **понижать**; partial (thrust); degraded; impaired; sunken, low-lying; sub—, hyp(o)—; **—нная кислотность** (med.) hypoacidity.

пониз/итель *m.* reducer; (elec.) step-down transformer; **п. вязкости** thinner; **п. частоты** (elec.) scaling circuit; **—ительный** *a.* reducing; (elec.) step-down; negative (booster); **—ительный редуктор** reduction gear; **—ить** *see* **понижать; —у** *adv.* low, along the surface, close to the ground.

поник/ать *v.* droop, wilt; **—ающий** *a.* drooping, nutant; **—лость** *f.* wilting; **—лый** *a.* drooping, bent; **—нуть** *see* **поникать; —ший** *a.* falling over, falling forward.

поним/ание *n.* understanding, comprehension, insight, awareness, grasp, conception, sense, interpretation; **—ать** *v.* understand, comprehend, realize, recognize; grasp, seize; gain some insight (into); **—ать неправильно** misunderstand, misinterpret.

понов(к)а *f.* (apid.) renewal, renovation activities.

по-новому *adv.* in a new way; **рассматривать п.** *v.* take a new view (of).

понограф *m.* (med.) ponograph.

понор *m.* (geol.) sink (hole), swallow hole.

понос *m.* (med.) diarrhea, dysentery.

поно/сить *v.* carry (for a while); wear; abuse, revile; **—шенный** *a.* carried; worn, shabby.

понравиться *v.* appeal (to).

понселет *m.* Poncelet (water) wheel.

понсировка *f.* rubbing with pumice.

понсо *n.* ponceaux (a group of dyes).

понт *m.* bridge (in oil well); (geol.) Pontian.

понтианак *m.* pontianac (resin).

понтинный *a.* (anat.) pontile, pontine.

понтический *a.* (geol.) Pontian; (obs.) Black Sea.

понтия *f.* (glass) pontil, punty.

понтол *m.* pontol (alcohol denaturant).

понтон *m.* pontoon; scow; **—ёр** *m.* pontoon specialist; **—ный** *a.* pontoon; floating (crane).

понтоп *m.* Pontop (rubberized cloth).

понудитель *m.* compeller; **—ный** *a.* compelling, coercive, impellent, forced.

пону/дить, —ждать *v.* compel, force, drive, impel, urge, press; **—ждение** *n.* compulsion, coercion; **—ждённый** *a.* compelled, etc., *see* *v.*

понур *m.* (hydr.) upstream floor, fore apron.

понцирус, трёхлисточковый (bot.) trifoliate orange (*Poncirus trifoliata*).

пончик *m.* doughnut.

пончо *n.* poncho; (mam.) capybara.

поныне *adv.* up to the present (time), until now, heretofore.

понырять dive (for a while).

понюх(ив)ать *v.* sniff, smell.

понят/ие *n.* concept(ion), idea, notion; **—ийный** *a.* (math.) conceptual; **—ливость** *f.* comprehension; **—ливый** *a.* comprehending readily, quick; **—но** *adv.* clearly, plainly, intelligibly; naturally, of course; **—ность** *f.* clearness, intelligibility; **—ный** *a.* clear, intelligible, comprehensible, understandable, apparent; **—ой** *m.* witness; **—ый** *a.* understood; **—ь** *see* **понимать; позволять —ь** *v.* give an insight (into).

пообещать *v.* promise.

пооб/сохнуть *v.* dry off gradually; **—тереться** *v.* wear off, rub off.

поодаль *adv.* at some distance, removed.

поодиночке *adv.* one by one, singly.

пооперационный *a.* (per) operation, step-by-step.

поостыть *v.* cool off gradually.

по-отрядно *adv.* (av.) by flights.

поотстать *v.* fall somewhat behind.

поотсыреть *v.* grow slightly damp.

поотягивать *v.* tug.

поочерёдн/о *adv.* by turn(s), alternately, successively; **—ый** *a.* by turn, alternate.

поощр/ение *n.* encouragement, incentive; promotion; **средство —ения** incentive; **—ительный** *a.* encouraging, stimulating, inspiring; **—ить, —ять** *v.* encourage, stimulate, spur, inspire; promote, favor, advance.

поп *m.* (ichth.) *see* **подкаменщик;** priest.

попад/ание *n.* hit, impact; entry, ingress, penetration; entrapment; **предотвращать п.** *v.* keep clear or free (of); —**ать** *v.* hit, strike; get (in)to, fall (on, within); come (into view); —**аться** *v.* get into, get caught, fall into; meet, run across.

попало *past n. of* **попасть; как п.** carelessly, haphazardly, anyhow; **куда п.** at random, anywhere.

попарить *v.* steam; soar.

попарно *adv.* in pairs, two by two; mutually.

попаромно *adv.* by rafts.

попасти *v.* pasture; —**сь** *v.* graze.

попасть(ся) *see* **попадать(ся).**

попахать *v.* plow (for a while).

попахивать *v.* give off a slight odor.

попёк *past m. sing. of* **попечь.**

поперёк *adv. and prep. gen.* transverse (to), across, crosswise; at right angles to; (naut.) athwart(ship); **разрезание п.** cross-cutting.

попеременн/о *adv.* by turns, in turn, alternately; **п.-возвратный** *a.* alternate, reciprocating (motion); —**ый** *a.* alternate; alternative, alternating.

попереть *v.* push forward, make one's way; drive out; fire (from work).

попереч/ина *f.* (cross) beam, transverse beam, cross bar, cross tie, cross piece, tie beam, sleeper, joist; crosshead (of engine); boom, jib (of crane); —**ка** *f.* crosscut saw; —**ник** *m.* diameter; girth; cross section; cross beam.

поперечно *adv.* transversely; *prefix* trans—; **п.-направленный** *a.* broadside; **п.-овальный** *a.* (anat.) brachypellic (pelvis); **п.-остистый** *a.* (anat.) transversospinal (muscle); **п.-полосатый** *a.* striated; striped (muscles); **п.-поляризованный** *a.* cross-polarized; **п.-рёберный** *a.* transversocostal (muscle); **п.-резальная машина** (typ.) rotary cross cutter; —**ротые** *pl.* (ichth.) sharks, rays, etc. (*Selachii*).

поперечн/ый *a.* transverse, cross, diametrical; cross-sectional; lateral; variable-area (recording); cross-cut (saw); **п. отросток** (anat.) transverse process, diapophysis (of spine); true rib; **п. разрез** cross section; —**ая кость** (anat.) os transversum; —**ая связь** crosslink; —**ая сила** transverse force, shearing force; —**ое отверстие** (anat.) transverse foramen; —**ое ребро** tie; —**ое сечение** cross section; **в —ом направлении** across; **коэффициент —ой деформации** Poisson's ratio; **образование —ых связей** crosslinking, crosslinkage.

поперхнуться *v.* choke.

попеч/ение *n.* care, charge (of); management; —**итель** *m.,* —**ница** *f.* trustee, guardian, curator, manager.

попечь *v.* bake, roast (for a while).

попилить *v.* saw (for a while; up).

попирать *v.* trample (on), tread (underfoot), flout; violate (rights).

попискивать *v.* peep, cheep.

поплавать *v.* swim, float.

поплав/ковый, —очный *a.* floating, float; **п. клапан** float valve, ball valve; **п. кран** ball cock; **п. шар** ball float; —**ок** *m.* float, buoy; pontoon; flask, vial; —**ок-интегратор** *m.* float gage; **уровень** —**ка** float level.

поплатиться *v.* pay (for); pay the consequences.

поплести *v.* braid, weave; —**сь** *v.* meander.

поплин *m.,* —**овый** *a.* (text.) poplin.

поплотнеть *v.* become denser.

поплыть *v.* swim, float; start swimming, start floating.

поповник *m.* (bot.) ox-eye daisy (*Chrysanthemum leucanthemum*).

попозже *adv.* (a little) later.

пополам *adv.* in two, in half.

пополз/ать *v.* creep (for a while); —**ень** *m.* (orn.) nuthatch; —**ти** *v.* creep, slide; start creeping; —**ушка** *f.* slide (contact); runner; radius link (of link gear).

пополн/ение *n.* supplement; replenishment, recharge, enrichment, addition, completing; reinforcement, replacement; recruitment, (mil.) draft; —**енный** *a.* supplemented, etc., *see v.;* —**итель** *m.* replenisher; —**ить, —ять** *v.* supplement, add, fill up, refill, replenish; enrich, widen, enlarge; (mil.) reinforce.

пополоскать *v.* rinse (for a while); gargle.

пополоть *v.* weed (for a while).

пополу/дни *adv.* post meridiem (P.M.); —**ночи** *adv.* ante meridiem (A.M.).

по-польски *adv.* (in) Polish.

попона *f.* (horse) blanket.

попонтонно *adv.* by successive pontoons.

попор/тить *v.* spoil; damage; —**ченный** *a.* spoiled; damaged.

поправ/имый *a.* remediable, repairable; —**ить** *see* **поправлять;** drive (for a while); —**ка** *f.* correction, etc., *see v.;* repair(ing), readjustment; allowance; amendment; (med.) recovery; —**ка на** correction for; **вводить —ку на** *v.* correct for; —**ление** *see* **поправка; —ленный** *a.* corrected, etc., *see v.;* —**лять** *v.* correct, rectify; modify, alter, amend; allow (for); repair, mend, readjust, put in order; —**ляться** *v.* recover, improve; —**очный** *a. of* **поправка; —очный коэффициент** correction factor.

попрактиковаться *v.* practice.

по-прежнему *adv.* as before, as usual.

попрек/ать, —нуть *v.* reproach, reprove.

попреть *v.* mildew, damp off, decay.

поприще *n.* area, field; course.

попробовать *v.* try out.

попросить *v.* ask, request.

попросохнуть *v.* dry gradually.

попросту *adv.* simply.

попрочнеть *v.* become stronger.

попрыгать *v.* jump, hop.

попрыск(ив)ать *v.* sprinkle.

попрятать *v.* hide, conceal.

попуга/евые *pl.* parrot fishes (*Scaridae*); —**и** *pl.* parrots (*Psittacidae*); —**йная болезнь** (med.) parrot fever, psittacosis; —**й-рыбы** *see* **попугаевые;** —**йчик** *m.* (orn.) parakeet.

попудно *adv.* by the pood (36 pounds).

популин *m.* populin, salicin benzoate.

популяр/изация *f.* popularization; —**изировать** *v.* popularize; —**ность** *f.* popularity; —**ный** *a.* popular.

популяция *f.* (biol.) population.

попуск *m.* (hydr.) drawdown; flush.

попуст(ом)у *adv.* in vain, to no purpose.

попут/но *adv.* in passing, by the way; incidentally; at the same time; —**ный** *a.* passing; accompanying, associated; on the way; fair, tail (wind); casing-head (gas); side, by-product; —**ный поток** side flow; (naut.) wake; —**ная струя** (ocean.) backwash; —**чик** *m.,* —**чица** *f.* companion.

попытать(ся) *v.* try, attempt, undertake; —**ка** *f.* trial, attempt, endeavor, venture.

попыхивать *v.* puff; emit smoke or steam.

попятиться *v.* move backwards; back up.

пор. *abbr.* (**пороги**) rapids.

пора *f.* pore, porus, cell; (ent.) stigma; (zool.) osculum; (bot.) stoma; (met.) freckle; (gas) pocket; (lunar) craterlet.

пор/а *f.* time, season, period; it is time (to); **в —у** at the right time, opportunely; **вечерней —ой** in the evening;

глухая п. slack season, off season; давно п. it is high time; до —ы up to a certain time; до каких пор how long? until when? до сих пор until now, hitherto, up to this point, so far, thus far, to date; до тех пор, пока until; до этих пор thus far, till now, hitherto; с тех пор since then; с этих пор hence, in future, from now on.

поработать v. work (for a while).

порабо/титель m. oppressor; —тить, —щать v. enslave, subjugate.

поравнять v. equate, make equal; —ся v. equal; come up to.

порадент m. (med.) poradenitis.

пораж/аемость f. vulnerability, susceptibility; —аемый a. vulnerable, endangered; —ать v. affect, afflict; overcome; contaminate; infest (with pests); strike, hit; astonish, surprise; —аться v. be surprised; —ающий a. affecting, etc., see v.; harmful, injurious; —ающее действие, —ающие факторы nuclear (weapon) effects; —ение n. affection, etc., see v.; disease, infection; blow, injury, damage; (lightning) stroke; (med.) lesion; destruction; defeat; —осис, —пафи; —ение желёз adenosis, adenopathy; зона —ения killing zone, effective zone; местное —ение local lesion; оружие массового —ения weapon of mass destruction; —ённость f. development (of hairline cracks); —ённый a. affected, etc., see v.

пораз— double prefix for verbs, see under раз—, рас—; —ведать v. make an extensive survey; find out; —гонять v. scatter about.

поразит/ельно adv. remarkably, astoundingly, amazingly; it is remarkable; —ельный a. remarkable, astounding, amazing, dramatic; —ь see поражать.

поразному adv. differently, in different ways.

поразогнать v. scatter about.

поразряд/ный a. (comp.) step-by-step, bit-by-bit, bitwise; cascaded (carry); —ое дополнение radix-minus-one complement.

поразузнать v. investigate gradually.

порайонный a. by districts, regional.

поран/ение n. wound(ing); —енный a. wounded; —ить v. wound.

пораньше adv. a little earlier.

порас— see пораз—; —кидать v. scatter gradually; —спросить v. inquire around.

пораст/ать v. overgrow (with); —и v. grow (for a while); overgrow (with); —ить v. raise.

поратный a. (bot.) porate, set with pores.

порв/анный a. torn, broken; —ать v. break (off), tear (up), disrupt (communications); —ать(ся) v. tear, break.

порги (ichth.) porgy (Sparidae).

поребрик m. border (stone).

пореде/вший, —лый a. grown thinner, grown sparse; —ть v. thin out; become sparse.

порез m. cut, slash, wound; cutting; —ать v. cut, slash, wound; slice; slaughter; —ник m. (bot.) libanotis.

порей m. (bot.) leek (Allium porrum).

порекомендовать v. recommend, suggest.

порет pr. 3 sing. of пороть.

пореч/ник m. (bot.) Athamanta; mountain parsley (Peucedanum oreoselinum); —ный a. riverside; —ье n. river country.

порешня f. (mam.) otter.

поржаветь v. get rusty, corrode.

пориомания f. (psych.) poriomania.

порист/ость f. (bot.) porosity, sponginess; п. костей osteoporosis; —ый a. porous, spongy, blown, foam (rub-

ber), vesicular, cellular, pitted; timely, ready; —ая перегородка (chem.) diffusion barrier; —ая перепонка, —ая стенка porous diaphragm.

порит(ес) m. coral (Porites).

пориц/ание n. blame, censure; —ать v. blame, censure, reprove, reproach.

поркуп/айн, —ин m. porcupine.

поровну adv. equally, in equal parts.

поровнять v. even out, smooth out.

поров/ость f. porosity; —ый a. pore, poral; interstitial (water).

порог m. threshold, limen; baffle (plate), bridge, sill; (overflow) lip, edge; (spillway) ramp, crest; п. чувствительности detection threshold; —амия f. (bot.) porogamy; —и pl. rapids; sill; (physiol.) limina; —и реки rapids; —овый a. of порог; liminal, barely perceptible; cut-off (input); —овый ток threshold current; —овое значение threshold (value); —овое устройство (elec.) gate; —овое переключение threshold switching.

порода f. breed, stock, race, strain, species, variety, kind; (geol.) rock.

породиновый a. porodic, amorphous.

пород/истый see породный.

породить see порождать.

породный a. thoroughbred, pedigreed; kept for breeding; rock; п. делитель (rock) refuse pulper.

породо/испытание n. breed testing, breed trials; —образование n. breed formation; rock formation; —образующий a. rock-forming; —отборка f., —отборный a. picking, sorting, inspection; —составляющие pl. rock constituents.

пороет fut. 3 sing. of порыть.

порожд/ать v. produce, generate, give rise (to); breed, give birth (to), beget; —ающий a. producing, etc., see v.; origin (frequency); —ение n. result, outcome, product.

порожек dim. of порог.

порожистый a. full of rapids.

порожн/ём see порожняком; —ий a. empty, vacant, unladen, without load; —ий ход idling; —ый a. of порог; —як m. empty (car); —яком adv. empty, without load.

пороз m. (med.) porosis.

порозиметр m. porosity meter.

порознь adv. separately, apart, severally; вместе и п. all and sundry.

порозоветь v. turn rose-colored.

пороидный a. (bot.) poroid, resembling or having pores.

порой adv. now and then, occasionally; m., —ка f. (apid.) afterswarm.

порок m. flaw, blemish, defect, imperfection, fault; vice; (shrinkage) cavity; (wine) nonbacterial disorder; п. сердца heart disease, valvular disease.

порокератоз m. (med.) porokeratosis.

поролой m. polyurethane, foam rubber.

порометр m. porosimeter.

пороносный a. (bot.) poriferous.

поронот m. (ichth.) butterfish (Poronotus triacanthus).

порообраз/ование n. pore formation, (plastics) blowing; —ователь m. blowing agent; —ующий a. blowing.

поропласты pl. foam(ed) plastics; porous plastic.

порос past m. sing. of порасти.

порос/ение n. (zool.) farrowing; —ёнок m. piglet; —иться v. farrow.

порос/левый a. shoot, sprout; п. лес coppice (wood), underbrush; п. побег (bot.) soboleь; —левое размножение sprout, sucker propagation; —ль f. shoot, sprout; undergrowth; **корневая —ль** sobole, root sucker; **—ли** *pl.* undergrowth, scrub, brush; **—ший** *a.* overgrown.

порося/та *pl.* young pigs; **—чий** *a.* pig.

пороть *v.* rip, undo.

порофор *m.* blowing agent.

порох *m.* (gun)powder; (rockets) propellant; **—овой** *a.* powder; solid-fuel, solid-propellant; **—овой аккумулятор давления** solid-propellant gas generator; **—овая шашка** (rockets) grain; **—острельная работа** blasting.

пороцефалёз *m.* (med.) porocephaliasis.

пороцит *m.* (zool.) porocyte, pore cell.

пороч/ить *v.* defame, discredit; **—ный** *a.* defective, faulty; fallacious; depraved; vicious (circle); **—ное развитие** (med.) teratism (monstrosity).

порош/а *f.* powdery new snow; **—ечный** *a.* powder(ed); **—инка** *f.* grain (of powder or dust); **—ить** *v.* powder, dust; fall (of snow).

порошицевый *a.* (zool.) proctal, anal.

порошко/вание *n.* trituration, reduction to a powder; **—ватый, —видный** *a.* powdery, powder-like, powdered, pulvurulent; meal(y); **—вый** *a. of* **порошок;** **—вый пух, —вые перья** (orn.) powder down; **—грамма** *f.* (spectr.) powder pattern; **—образный** *see* **порошковидный.**

порош/ник *m.* powder particle; **—ок** *m.* powder, dust; **в —ке** in powder form; **превращать в —ок** *v.* powder, pulverize; **—очный** *a.* powder(ed).

порощица *f.* (cyt.) cytoproct, cell anus.

порою *see* **порой.**

поррей *see* **порей.**

порт *m.* port, harbor; porthole; **район —а** waterfront.

порт. *abbr.* (**португальский**) Portuguese.

портакавальный *a.* (anat.) portacaval.

портал *m.* portal, doorway; gantry (of crane); (anat.) porta; **—ьный** *a. of* **портал;** straddle (trailer).

портативн/ость *f.* portability; **—ый** *a.* portable, handy; (comp.) laptop.

портвейн *m.* port (wine).

портер *m.,* **—ный** *a.* porter (beer).

портик *m.* portico, porch; port.

портить *v.* spoil, damage, ruin, waste, impair; corrupt; **—ся** *v.* spoil, be damaged, get out of order; decay, rot; deteriorate; become corrupt.

порткаустик *m.* portcaustic (handle for holding a caustic substance).

портланд/ский *a.* Portland; **—цемент** *m.* Portland cement.

портниха *f.* long-tailed tailor-bird (*Orthotomus*).

портн/ой *m.* tailor; **—яжный** *a.* tailor(ing); **—яжная мышца** (anat.) sartorius.

портов/ик *m.,* **—ый грузчик** longshoreman; **—ый** *a.* port, harbor.

портография *f.* (med.) portography.

Порто-Рико Puerto Rico.

порто-франко free port.

портплед *m.* hold-all, carry-all.

портрет *m.* portrait.

портсигар *m.* cigar or cigarette case.

портсмутский *a.* (geog.) Portsmouth.

португальский *a.* Portuguese, Portugal.

портулак *m.,* **—овый** *a.* (bot.) Portulaca, **—овые** *pl.* purslane family (*Portulacaceae*).

португ/ейный *a.,* **—ея** *f.* shoulder strap.

портфель *m.* portfolio, briefcase.

портьера *f.* curtain.

портэзия *f.* (ent.) Porthesia.

портящийся *a.* spoiling, etc., *see* **портиться;** perishable.

поруб/ить *v.* chop, fell; cut, slash; chop up; **—ка** *f.* felling section; (illegal) felling; **—очные станки** slash, logged area of forest strewn with debris; **—щик** *m.* lumberjack; **—ь** *f.* felling section.

порука *f.* pledge, guarantee, bail.

по-русски *adv.* (in) Russian.

поручать *v.* commission, commit, entrust (with), charge (with).

поручейник *m.* (bot.) water parsnip (*Sium*); (orn.) marsh sandpiper (*Tringa stagnatilis*).

поручен/ец *m.* special messenger; (mil.) aide-de-camp **—ие** *n.* assignment, commission, charge; mission, errand; message; **по —ию** on the instructions of; **—ный** *a.* commissioned, etc., *see* **поручать.**

поручень *m.* handrail, guardrail, railing; (grab) handle.

поручит/ель *m.* guarantor; **—ельство** *n.* guarantee, bail; **—ь** *see* **поручать.**

поручн/евая скоба handle; **—и** *pl. of* **поручень;** railing.

порушить *v.* destroy.

порфин *m.* (biochem.) porphin(e).

порфир *m.* (petr.) porphyry; *prefix* porphyr— (purple); **—а** *f.* purple; (bot.) Porphyra.

порфир/изация *f.* porphyrization, pulverization; **—ин** *m.* porphyrin; porphyrine (alkaloid); **—иновый** *a.* (chem.) porphyrin; **—ит** *m.* (petr.) porphyrite; **—ический** *a.* porphyritic; **—ия** *f.* (med.) porphyria; **—област** *m.* porphyroblast; **—областический** *a.* porphyroblastic; **—овидный** *a.* porphyritic, porphyraceous; **—овый** *a.* (petr.) porphyr(it)ic (acid); (bot.) porphyraceous; **—оид** *m.* porphyroid; **—оксин** *m.* porphyroxine; **—оподобный** *see* **порфировидный; —опсин** *m.* (bioch.) porphyropsin.

порфобилиноген *m.* (bioch.) porphobilinogen, PBG.

порх/ать, —нуть *v.* flap, flutter, flit.

порционн/о *adv.* in portions, in batches, in small amounts; **—о-периодического действия** repeated-batch (dryer); **—ый** *a.* portion, batch, lot; (food) à la carte; **—ое испытание** batch testing.

порция *f.* portion, batch, lot.

порч/а *f.* damage, injury, breakage, waste; spoiling, putrefaction; corruption; deterioration, wear and tear; failure, trouble; defect, flaw; contamination; **—енный** *a.* damaged, injured; spoiled, putrefied, decomposed; tainted (meat).

поршень *m.* piston, plunger (of pump); **п.-буфер** *m.* buffer piston.

поршневание *n.* (petrol.) swabbing.

поршнев/ой, —ый *a.* piston; piston-cylinder (balance); wrist (pin); **п. насос** reciprocating pump; piston pump; **п. привод** piston drive; **п. стержень, п. шток** piston rod.

поршнеобразование *n.* (chem.) slugging (in a fluidized bed).

порыв *m.* gust (of wind), puff, fit, inrush; break(ing); **—ание** *n.* breaking; **—ать** *v.* break (off), interrupt; **—аться** *v.* endeavor; **—истость** *f.* gustiness; impetuosity, violence; **—истый** *a.* gusty, violent, impetuous; percussive, jerky, irregular.

порыж/евший, —елый *a.* grown rust-colored, reddish, brownish; **—еть** *v.* turn brown.

порыть(ся) *v.* dig (around), rummage, search.

порычать *v.* growl, snarl, roar.

порэнцефалия *f.* (med.) porencephalia.

порют *pr. 3 pl. of* **пороть.**

порядить *v.* contract; **—ся** *v.* bargain, make a deal (with).

порядка *gen. of* **порядок.**

порядков/ый *a.* ordinal; index, entry, filing (word); sequence (code); rank, serial (correlation); **п. номер, —ое число** ordinal number; serial number; atomic number; **—ое числительное** (grammar) ordinal.

порядком *adv.* rather; thoroughly.

порядовка *f.* (masonry) straight line.

поряд/ок *m.* order, rank, (math.) power; form; sequence, series, succession, course, arrangement; (biol.) order; (shut-down or start-up) procedure; line (of nets); **п. величины** order of magnitude; **п. подчинённости** (mil.) chain of command; **—ка** on the order (of), in the neighborhood (of), in the region (of); **в полном —ке** in running order; all right; under control; **второго —ка** (cyt.) secondary (oocyte); **высших —ков** higher; **изменение —ка** rearrangement; **на два п.** by a factor of 10^2; **не в —ке** out of order, irregular; **обыкновенным —ком** ordinarily; **первого порядка** (cyt.) primary (oocyte); **по —ку** in order, in succession, one after the other; **делать по —ку** *v.* proceed in order, do things systematically; **приводить в п.** *v.* set in order, set right, arrange, adjust; **смотреть за —ком** *v.* keep order; **это в —ке вещей** that is as it should be, that is normal.

порядоченная насадка (phys.) stacked packing, ordered packing.

порядочн/о *adv.* rather; pretty well; honestly; **—ость** *f.* decency, honesty; **—ый** *a.* honest, respectable, decent; sizable, considerable (price).

посад *m.* charge; settlement; suburb.

посадить *v.* set (down), put, seat; (av.) land; (agr.) plant.

посадк/а *f.* setting, putting; (mach.) fit; boarding (vehicle); (av.) landing; (agr.) planting; plants; stocking (fish); seat (of rider); (min.) collapse; checkered brickwork; **п. по прибором** instrument landing; **п. роя** (apid.) hiving (a swarm); **аварийная п.** crash landing; **вынужденная п.** emergency landing, forced landing; **глухая п.** tight fit, close fit; **горячая п.** shrink fit; **итти на —у** *v.* make a landing, land; **планирующая п.** dead-stick landing; **слепая п.** blind approach; **тугая п.** tight fit, close fit; **ударная п.** hard landing; **ячейка —и** checker opening.

посадочн/о-рулежный *a.* landing-taxiing (light); **—ый** *a. of* **посадка;** seed (potato); **—ый курс** landing pattern; **—ый материал** stock; **—ая машина** (met.) charging machine; (agr.) plant setter, transplanter; **—ая площадка** landing field.

посапывать *v.* wheeze, breathe heavily.

посасывать *v.* draw in at intervals.

посвеж/елый *a.* (grown) fresh; **—еть** *v.* get fresher, get cooler; brighten.

посвет/ить *v.* give some light; **—леть** *v.* grow light(er).

по-своему *adv.* in one's own way.

посвя/тить, —щать *v.* devote; dedicate; **—щение** *n.* devotion; dedication; **—щённый** *a.* devoted; dedicated.

посев *m.* sowing, seeding, planting; culture; inoculation; young crop; seed; **—ать** *v.* sow, plant; **—ной** *a.* sowing; seed; (bot.) sown, cultivated, common (*sativus*); **—ной материал** seed(s); (immun.) inoculum; **—ные семена** seed(s).

посед/евший, —елый *a.* (grown) gray; **—ение** *n.* graying, canities; (hist.) achromatosis; **—еть** *v.* turn gray.

посезонный *a.* seasonal.

посек *past m. sing. of* **посечь.**

посел/енец *m.* settler; **—ение** *n.* settlement, habitation, colony; **—ить(ся)** *see* **поселять(ся); —ковый** *a. of* **посёлок.**

посёлок *m.* settlement, village; **рабочий п.** factory housing, company town.

поселять *v.* settle, colonize, establish; **—ся** *v.* settle, take up residence.

посеребр/ённый *a.* silver-plated, silvered; **—ить** *v.* silver(-plate).

посереди(не) *adv. and prep. gen.* in the middle (of); halfway.

посереть *v.* grow gray.

посетит/ель *m.* visitor; **—ь** *see* **посещать.**

посечь *v.* chop up; notch, cut.

посещ/аемость *f.* attendance; **—аемый** *a.* frequented, attended; **—ать** *v.* frequent, visit, attend; **—ение** *n.* attendance.

посе/янный *a.* sowed, planted; **—ять** *v.* sow, plant.

посигналить *v.* signal a few times.

посидеть *v.* sit for a while.

посизение *n.* darkening (of wine).

посильный *a.* within one's powers, feasible.

посин/елый *a.* turned blue; **—еть** *v.* turn blue; **—ить** *v.* (color) blue.

поскальзываться *v.* slip, slide.

поскоблить *v.* scrape (for a while).

поскок *m.* jump, hop.

поскользнуться *v.* slip, slide.

поскольку *conj.* in so far as, inasmuch as, so long as; as, since, because, considering that; **п. . . . постольку** just as . . . so.

поскон/ина *f.* hemp cloth; **—ник** *m.* (bot.) Eupatorium; **—ный** *a.* hemp(en); **—ь** *f.* Cannabis sativa; hemp cloth.

поскорее *adv.* faster.

поскрёбки *pl.* scrapings; scraps.

поскрести *v.* scrape a little.

послаб/еть *v.* weaken; slacken, relax; **—ление** *n.* relaxing, loosening; indulgence; **—ляющий** *a.* relaxing; (med.) remittent (fever); relief (incision).

посл/анец *m.* messenger; **—ание** *n.* message; **—анник** *m.* envoy; **—анный** *a.* sent; *m.* messenger; **—ать** *v.* send.

после *prep. gen. and adv.* after(wards), later, subsequently, since, following, (up)on, within (a given time); *prefix* post—, after, subsequent, additional, supplementary, secondary; **п. чего** whereupon, then, after which; **—военный** *a.* postwar; **—всходовый** *a.* postemergence; **—гнездовая линька** (orn.) juvenal molt.

послед *m.* remainder, rest; (med.) afterbirth; (anat.) placenta; **—ить** *v.* look after, watch; **—ки** *pl.* remainder, residue, leavings.

последействи/е *n.* secondary action, reaction; aftereffect, residual effect; (phys.) hysteresis; (pulse) tail; **ток —я** (elec.) aftercurrent.

последки *pl.* remnants.

последн/ий *a.* last, closing, finishing, final, conclusive, terminal; recent, latest, latter, last-mentioned; *m.* the latter; **—им пришёл, первым обслужен** (comp.) last in, first out (LIFO); **в —ее время** lately, of late; recently; **за —ее время** lately, recently.

последование *n.* following.

последователь *m.*, **—ница** *f.* follower; **—но** *adv.* in succession, in sequence, in tandem, one after another; (elec.) in series; **—но расположенный** in series; in-line, tandem (booster); **—нопараллельный** *a.* (elec.) series-parallel; **—ность** *f.* sequence, succession, series, order, coherence, continuity; graduation; (wave, pulse) train; **—ность во времени** distribution in time; **—ность операции** flow sheet; **—ность переключения кода** (comp.) escape sequence; **—ность поколений** lineage, pedigree.

последовательн/ый *a.* successive, consecutive, sequential; consequent; gradual, step-by-step; consistent, coherent, systematic, orderly; follow-up; (elec.) series-connected, (in) series; serial (adder); **п. порядок** consecutive order, sequence, succession; **п. образ** (physiol.) afterimage; **—ая обмотка** (elec.) series winding; **—ое деление** consecutive indexing; **—ого типа** serial-type (adder); **машина —ого действия** serial computer; **—ые приближения** iteration.

послед/овать v. follow; **—овые** (mam.) see **плацентарные; —овый** a. (anat.) placental; (med.) afterbirth; **—ствие** n. consequence, result, aftereffect; **—ствия** pl. effect.

последующ/ий a. following, subsequent, consequent, ensuing, next, successive, follow-up, post—, after—; succeeding (tide); **—ая обработка** aftertreatment; **и п.** and subsequent, followed by; **с —им** attended by, followed by.

последыш m. the youngest, last-born.

послежелтушный a. (med.) posticital.

после/завтра adv., **—завтрашний** a. day after tomorrow; **—зародышевый** a. postembryonic; **—изображение** n. image retention; afterimage; **—импульс** m. afterpulse; **—импульсы** pl. afterpulsing; **—кризисный** a. epicritic; **—ледниковый** a. (geol.) postglacial; **—лётный** a. (av.) postflight; **—лечение** n. (med.) aftercare; **—лихорадочный** a. (med.) postfebrile; **—лог** m. (linguistics) postposition; **—наркозный** a. (med.) postanesthetic; **—нерестовый** a. (ichth.) postspawning; **—операционный** a. (med.) postoperative; recovery (room); **—охладитель** m. aftercooler, recooler; **—очиститель** m. repurifier.

после/полётный a. (av.) postflight; **—полуденный** a. afternoon; **—радиационный** a. postradiation; **—ремонтный** a. (tires) after recapping; **—родовой** a. postnatal; puerperal (fever); postpartum.

послесвечен/ие n. afterglow, phosphorescence; persistence; **с —ием** persistent (phosphor); **с длительным —ием** long-persistence, longlag; **с коротким —ием** short-persistence, rapid-decay.

после/словие n. concluding remarks, afterword; epilogue; **—счётный** a. (comp.) postmortem; **—теплота** f. afterheat; **—течка** f. (zool.) metoestrus; **—третичный** a. (geol.) post-Tertiary; **—уборочный** a. (agr.) post-harvest; **—узловой** a. postganglionic; **—ускорение** n., **—ускоряющий** a. postacceleration; **—фокусировка** f. secondary focusing.

послов/ица f. proverb, saying; **—ный** a. literal, word-for-word; per word; **—ичный** a. proverbial.

послойн/о adv., **—ый** a. in layers; lit-parlit; graded (cultivation); multistage (plowing); **—ая рентгенография** (med.) tomography; **—ое движение** laminar flow, viscous flow, streamline flow.

послуж/ить v. serve or work for a while; be employed; act (as); be used (for); **—ной список** service record.

послуш/ание n. obedience; **—ать** v. listen; (med.) auscultate; **—аться** v. obey; **—ивать** v. listen from time to time; **—ность** f. (missiles) tractability; **—ный** a. tractable, controllable, manageable, obedient, responsive.

посматривать v. glance at occasionally, observe from time to time.

посменн/о adv. by turns, alternately, in shifts; **—ый** a. in shifts.

посмертн/ый a. posthumous; postmortem; **—ая ригидность** rigor mortis.

посметь v. dare.

посметюшка f. (orn.) crested lark (*Galerida cristata*).

посмеяться v. laugh (for a while).

посмотреть v. (take a) look, examine; look (after), watch; see; **не п.** disregard.

поснимать v. take off.

пособ/ие n. help, assistance, aid; grant, allowance; wages, pay; guide, manual, textbook; **п. по безработице** unemployment compensation; **—ить, —лять** v. help, aid, relieve; **—ник** m., **—ница** f. accomplice; **—ничество** n. complicity.

посоветовать v. advise; **—ся** v. consult.

посовещаться v. confer (for a while).

посодействовать v. help, assist, promote, further, contribute (to); cooperate.

посол m. ambassador; see **посолка; —ить** v. salt; pickle, corn; **—ка** f. salting; pickling, corning; **—овелый** a. bleary; **—оветь** v. glaze (of eyes); **—очный** a. of **посолка; —ьский** a. ambassadorial; embassy; **—ьство** n. embassy.

пососать v. suck, draw (for a while).

посотенно adv. by hundreds, by the hundred.

посох m. staff, (shepherd's) crook; past m. sing. of **посохнуть; —нуть** v. dry up, wither.

поспать v. sleep (for a while), (take a) nap.

посп/евать, —еть v. ripen, mature; be ready, arrive in time; keep up, keep pace (with); **п. за** keep up with.

поспеш/ать, —ить v. hurry; **—но** adv. hurriedly, in a hurry, hastily; **—ность** f. hurry, haste, speed; **—ный** a. hurried, hasty; prompt; rash, thoughtless; (med.) premature.

поспорить v. argue, dispute, contend (with).

поспособствовать v. promote, aid.

поспр/ашивать, —осить v. interrogate.

посреди(не) adv. and prep. gen. in the middle (of), halfway between, midway between.

посредни/к m. negotiator, intermediary, agent; broker, middleman; umpire, arbitrator; messenger RNA; **—ческий** a. of **посредник;** intercessory, interceding, intervening; **—чество** n. intervention; agency; mediation.

посредственн/ость f. mediocrity; **—ый** a. mediocre, fair, adequate.

посредство n. means, agency, medium; **через п., —м** adv. through, via, by (means of), by the utilization of; **—м которого** by means of which, whereby; **—м рейки** rack (feed); **—м этого** thereby.

посредствующий a. intermediate.

поссум m. (mam.) phalanger; **кольцехвостый п.** ringtail possum (*Pseudocheirus*); **—ы** pl. (mam.) Phalangeridae.

пост m. post, station; pulpit; (bench) mark; (diet) fast(ing); prefix post— (after, behind); **п. управления** control room, control station.

пост. abbr. (**постоянный**) constant.

постав m. (text.) loom; mill, huller; set of millstones; (body) posture.

поставить v. put, place, set; erect, set up, raise; regulate; conduct (experiment); supply, deliver; **п. под угрозу** jeopardize.

постав/ка f. supply(ing), delivery; procurement; **—ки** pl. supplies; **—ленный** a. placed, set; **—ленная цель** goal, objective; **—лять** v. supply, furnish, deliver; **—лять на нуль** set to zero; **—ляться** v. come; be obtainable; **—щик** m. contractor, supplier, vendor, outfitter; maker.

постадийно adv. in stages.

постаивать v. stand around.

постамент m. pedestal, base, support; boom table, mast table, mast house.

постан/авливать, —овить see **постановлять.**

постановка f. erection, raising; laying; planting; definition; statement, formulation; organization (of work, etc.); putting (a question); arrangement, set-up.

постановл/ение *n.* decision, resolution, decree, ordinance; **—ять** *v.* decide, fix, stipulate, establish, decree, enact.

постантеннальный орган (zool.) postantennal organ, organ of Tömösvary.

постараться *v.* try, make an effort.

постар/евший, —елый *a.* aged; **—ение** *n.* aging, senility; **—еть** *v.* age.

по-старому *adv.* as of old, as before.

постатейн/о *adv.*, **—ый** *a.* by paragraphs, clause by clause; **—ая пагинация** separate pagination of articles; **—ая роспись** bibliography of papers.

пост/ганглионарный *a.* (anat.) postganglionic; **—гастр(о)эктомический** *a.* (med.) postgastrectomy, dumping (syndrome); **—геморрагический** *a.* posthemorrhagic; **—генеративный** *a.* postgenerative; **—гипнотический** *a.* posthypnotic; **—дефинитивный** *a.* post-permanent (teeth); **—дифтеритный** *a.* (post)diphtheric (paralysis); **—дорсальное расстояние** (ichth.) post-dorsal distance, distance from end of dorsal fin to base of caudal fin.

постел/ить *see* **постилать; —ь** *f.*, **—ьный** *a.* bed; layer; (geol.) bed, substratum; bottom, sole; foot (of seam).

постенн/ица *f.* (bot.) pellitory (*Parietaria*); **—ый** *a.* (biol.) parietal.

постепенно *adv.* gradually, by degrees, little by little, by stages, step by step, progressively; **—сть** *f.* gradualness, grad(u)ation; course.

постепенн/ый *a.* gradual, progressive, step-by-step; (forestry) successive (felling); fractional (crystallization); graceful (degradation); **п. переход** gradation.

постеречь *v.* watch for a while.

постериорный *a.* posterior.

постзигот/ический, —ный *a.* (biol.) postzygotic.

пости/гать, —гнуть *v.* understand, comprehend, grasp; strike, overtake, reach; **—жение** *n.* understanding, comprehension; **—жимый** *a.* understandable, comprehensible, conceivable.

постил/ать *v.* spread, lay; **—ка** *f.* spreading, laying, covering; litter, bed.

постирать *v.* wash, launder.

постит *m.* (med.) posthitis.

поститься *v.* fast.

постичь *see* **постигать.**

постклимак/с *m.* (bot.) postclimax (relict of a former climax community); **—терический** *a.* postclimacteric, postmenopausal.

постлать *see* **постилать.**

постличиночный *a.* postlarval.

постнатальный *a.* postnatal.

постн/ичать *v.* fast; **—ичество** *n.* fasting; **—отум** *m.* (zool.) postnotum, acrotergite; **—ый** *a. of* **пост**; fast(ing); lenten; lean (meat); meat- and milk-free (diet), vegetable; **—ое масло** vegetable oil.

постовой *a. of* **пост**; posted.

постольку *conj.* in so far as, inasmuch as.

посторбитальный *a.* postorbital.

посторожить *see* **постеречь.**

посторониться *see* **сторониться.**

посторонн/ий *a.* strange, foreign, alien, outside, exogenous, ectogenic, extraneous; *m.* stranger, outsider, unauthorized person, bystander; **—ее включение, —яя примесь** foreign matter, contaminant, impurity.

постостный *a.* (anat.) postglenoid.

постоянн/ая *f.* (math) constant; **—о** *adv.* constantly, continually, always, at all times, steadily; permanently;

uniformly; **—ожаберные** *pl.* (herp.) salamanders, etc. (*Perennibranchiata*); **—окипящий** *a.* azeotropic (mixture); **—о-направленный** *a.* constant (field).

постоянн/ый *a.* constant, invariable, steady, uniform; stable, permanent, fixed, stationary, dead (center); perpetual, persistent, lasting, continuous, sustained; unavoidable (impurities); (elec.) direct(-current); regular (train); (comp.) read-only (memory); **п. белый** permanent white, precipitated barium sulfate; **п. магнит** permanent magnet; **п. ток** (elec.) direct current; **двигатель —ого тока** direct-current motor, d.c. motor; **—ая величина** constant; **—ая точка** fixed point; **—ое запоминающее устройство** (comp.) read-only memory, ROM; **—ое напряжение** (elec.) direct-current voltage; **—ые белила** *see* **постоянный белый.**

постоянств/о *n.* constance, stability, steadiness, uniformity; continuity, continuance, persistence; **п. отношений** constant proportions; **закон —а весовых отношений, закон —а состава** law of definite proportions.

постоять *v.* stand for a while.

постплиоценовая эпоха (geol.) Post-Pliocene epoch.

пост/программа *f.* (comp.) post-mortem program; **—процессор** *m.* (comp.) postprocessor, backend processor.

пострад/авший *a.* having suffered; having undergone; *m.* victim, casualty; **—ать** *v.* suffer, come to harm; undergo.

постраничный *a.* per page, paginal.

постредактирование *n.* post-editing.

постредукци/онный *a.*, **—я** *f.* (med.) postreduction.

пострелять *v.* shoot.

построгать *v.* (carp.) plane.

постро/ение *n.* construction; building up, synthesis; structure; (curve) plot(ting); order, formation; **п. потока** flux plot; **масштаб —ения** plotting scale; **—енный** *a.* constructed, built; composite; plotted (against); **—ечный** *a.* building; **—итель** *m.* plotter, plotting device; **—ить** *v.* construct; build (up), synthesize; devise; plot (curve); **—йка** *f.* building, structure, construction.

постромка *f.* trace (of harness).

построчный *a.* (by the) line; line-by-line; line-a-time (printing).

постругать *v.* (carp.) plane.

постсинаптический *a.* (biol.) postsynoptic.

постскриптум *m.* postscript.

пост/травматический *a.* posttraumatic, postconcussional (syndrome); **—трансфузионный** *a.* (med.) (post)transfusion (hepatitis).

постукив/ание *n.* tapping; (med.) percussion; **—ать** *v.* tap, knock, rap.

постул/ат *m.* postulate, axiom; **—ировать** *v.* postulate, assume.

поступательно-возвратн/ый *a.* reciprocating; **—ое движение** reciprocation, alternating motion.

поступательно-циркуляционный *a.* combined rectilinear-circulatory (flow).

поступательн/ый *a.* progressive, forward, advancing; translational (energy; movement); step (function); sliding (pair); **—ое движение** forward motion, advance, headway; (mech.) translation; **—ое сгущение** livering (of paint).

поступ/ать *v.* act, deal, treat; behave, conduct oneself; proceed, do; originate, come (from); be drawn (from), be derived (from); appear (on the market); join; arrive, enter, go in, be admitted; enlist; go to work (for); **—аться** *v.* give up, waive; **—ающий** *a.* acting, etc., *see v.*; incoming, feeding (into); available, drawn (from); **—ивший** *a.* admitted (patent**); —ить** *see* **поступать; —ление** *n.* entrance, entering, entry, penetration, infiltration, arrival, admission, ingress, intake, inflow; supply; return, receipt (of profits); enlistment, joining; accession; **—ление заданий** (comp.) job entry; **—ок** *m.* action, act, step; conduct, behavior; procedure; **—ь** *f.* advance (of screw); step; gait; entrance.

постучать *v.* knock, tap.

пост/флоральный *a.* (bot.) postfloration; **—центральный** *a.* (anat.) postcentral.

постыдить *v.* put to shame; **—ся** *v.* be ashamed.

пост/эмбриональный *a.* (med.) postembryonic, fetal; **—енцефалитический** *a.* postencephalitic.

посуд/а *f.* dish(ware), utensils, glassware, (lab.) equipment; **фарфоровая п.** chinaware; **—ина** *f.* vessel, container; **—ник** *m.* cupboard; dishwasher; **—ный** *a. of* **посуда; —омоечный** *a.* dish-washing; **—омойка** *f.* dishwasher.

посуточн/о *adv.,* **—ый** *a.* per day, per diem, daily, every 24 hours.

посу/ху *adv.* by dry land; **—шить** *v.* dry.

посчастлив/иться *v.* succeed; thrive; progress; be lucky; **ему —илось** he is lucky, he happened (to).

посчитать *v.* count; consider; (mis)take for; charge (price).

посыл/атель *m.* sender, transmitter; **—ать** *v.* send, mail, post; **—ка** *f.* sending, consignment; parcel, package; (elec. commun.) sample, (im)pulse; errand; **нерабочая —ка** (commun.) space; **—очный** *a. of* **посылка;** mail-order; **—ьный** *m.* messenger.

посып/ание *n.* sprinkling, etc., *see v.*; **—анный** *a.* sprinkled, etc., *see v.*; **—ать** *v.* sprinkle, strew, powder, dust; pour; **—ка** *see* **посыпание;** grit.

посяг/ание *n.,* **—ательство** *n.* encroachment, infringement; **—ать** *v.,* **—нуть** *v.* encroach, infringe; attempt; **—ающий** *a.* encroaching, infringing.

пот *m.* perspiration, sweat, sudor; suint, yolk (of wool); **мочевой п.** (med.) ur(h)idrosis; **обильный п.** hyper(h)idrosis; **профузный п.** hidrosis; **скудный п.** anhidrosis.

пота/ить *v.* hide, conceal; **—й** *m.* countersink, depression; **—йник** *m.* submerged rock; **—йной** *a.* (counter)sunk, flush; hidden, secret.

поталь *m.* (met.) Dutch gold.

потамо— *prefix* potamo—, river; **—логия** *f.* potamology; **—планктон** *m.* potamoplankton, river plankton.

потанс *m.* (constr.) gibbet, jib.

потапливать *v.* heat (on and off); warm.

потаск/анный *a.* dragged; worn; shabby, frayed; **—ать** *v.* drag; tow, pull.

потассий *see* **калий.**

поташ *m.* potash, potassium carbonate; **едкий п., каустический п.** caustic potash, potassium hydroxide; **—ник** *m.* Russian thistle (*Salsola kali*); **—ный** *a.* potash, potassic.

потащить *v.* drag, start dragging; tow, pull.

потаять *v.* melt, thaw (out).

потворствовать *v.* indulge, cater (to), be lenient.

потвердеть *v.* harden.

П-отделимый *a.* (math.) P-separable.

потёк *m.* (paints) drip(ping); streak(ing); *past m. sing. of* **потечь.**

потёмки *pl.* darkness, obscurity.

потем/невший *a.* dim, dark(ened); **—нение** *n.* darkening, dimness, dullness; fogging (of film); **—неть** *v.* darken, grow dark.

потен *sh. m. of* **потный; —ие** *n.* perspiration, sweating.

потенциал *m.* potential; voltage; **п. зонд** potential sonde (used in well logging); **разность —а, скачок —а** potential difference; **—опроводность** *f.* (mass transfer) potential diffusivity; **—оскоп** *m.* potentialscope, storage tube; **п.-регулятор** *m.* potential regulator; **—ьно** *adv.* potentially; **—ьность** *f.* potentiality; **—ьный** *a.* potential; **—ьная ёмкость** carrying capacity (of ecosystem).

потенциодинамический *a.* (elec.) potential cycling, linear potential sweep.

потенциометр *m.* (elec.) potentiometer; **п. смещения** bias bleeder; **—ический** *a.* potentiometric (titration, etc.); **—ический датчик** resistive transducer, potentiometric pick-up; **—ия** *f.* potentiometry.

потенц/ирование *n.* (math.) taking antilogarithms; **—ировать** *v.* take antilogarithms, raise to a higher power; (pharm.) potentiate; **—ирующий** *a.* antilogarithmic; **—ия** *f.* potential, hidden capacity; potency, generative power; potentiality.

потепл/ение *n.* warming up, rise in temperature; **—еть** *v.* get warmer.

потереть *v.* rub, chafe, wear (out).

потери *gen., pl., etc., of* **потеря.**

потерна *f.* (mil.) underground or fortified corridor.

потерп/евший *a.* having suffered, having undergone; *m.* victim, sufferer; **—еть** *v.* suffer, undergo, endure.

потёрт/ость *f.* chafe, chafing, abrasion; **—ый** *a.* chafed, rubbed, worn, abraded, threadbare.

потер/я *f.* loss; disappearance, waste, escape (of gas, etc.), leak(age); depletion; deterioration (of quality); (mil.) casualty; death; **п. в весе** weight loss; **п. воды** dehydration, loss of water; **п. вследствие поглощения** absorption loss; **п. на испарение** loss by evaporation; **—и в, —и за счёт, —и из-за, —и на, —и от, —и при** *pl.* loss(es) (by, due to, from, etc.), e.g. **—и на трение** friction loss, loss by friction; **—и при переработке** processing loss; **с —ей энергии** energy-consuming.

потер/явший *a.* having lost; **—янный** *a.* lost, dissipated; **—ять** *v.* lose.

потесать *v.* hew, trim, cut or dress with an adz.

потеснить(ся) *v.* crowd, push together.

потесь *f.* large paddle.

потеть *v.* perspire, sweat; become covered with condensate.

потечь *v.* (start to) flow.

потешный *a.* comical, amusing.

потирать *v.* rub slightly.

потихоньку *adv.* little by little, slowly; noiselessly, silently, quietly; by stealth, stealthily.

поткать *v.* weave (for a while).

пот/ливость *f.* tendency to perspire; **—ливый** *a.* perspiring readily; sweaty; **—ник** *m.* (horse) blanket; **—ница** *f.* (med.) heat rash, miliaria; **—ный** *a.* perspiring, sweaty; covered with condensate; **—о** *m.* honey bear, kinkajou (*Potos flavus*); **—овой** *a. of* **пот;** sudatory, sudorific, sudoral; **—овой жир** (wool) suint, yolk; **—огонный** *a.* sudorific, diaphoretic, sweat-inducing; **—огонное (средство)** sudorific; **—озадерживающее средство** antiperspirant.

поток *m.* stream, current, torrent, flow; (magnetic) flux; (astr.) shower; (rr.) traffic; run, race, duct; **п. с разрядом** discharge flow; **в —е газа** (gasification) entrained flow (e.g. of coal); **вверх по —у** upstream; **линия —а** streamline; **ниже по —у** downstream; **обратный п.** reflux; **отношение —ов** flux ratio; **по —у** downwind; downstream; **скорость —а** flow rate; **фильтрация поперечного —а** cross-flow filtration;

—о— *prefix* rhyac(o)— (torrent, stream); **—овый** *a.* *of* **поток; —овый граф** flow graph; **—овое растение** (bot.) rhyacad; **—олюбивый** *a.* (bot.) rhyacophilous; **—ообразный** *a.* torrential; **—осцепление** (elec.) flux linkage.

потолкать *v.* push (several times).

потолкоуступн/ый *a.* overhead; **—ая выемка** (min.) overhand stoping.

потол/ок *m.* ceiling; crown (of furnace); (min.) ridge, back; *past m. sing. of* **потолочь; —очина** *f.* ceiling beam; block (of ore); **—очка** *f.* tabula, dissepiment (in corals), **—очки** *pl.* tabulae; **—очный** *a. of* **потолок;** ceiling, overhead; inverted (compass).

потолочь *v.* crush, break up.

потолстеть *v.* become fat(ter), gain weight.

потом *adv.* then, next, subsequently, later on, afterwards, after this.

потомакский *a.* (geog.) Potomac.

потомер *m.* (bot.) potometer.

потомок *m.* descendant, offspring.

потомств/енный *a.* hereditary; **—о** *n.* posterity, descendants, progeny.

потому *adv.* therefore, consequently; **п. что** because, on account of.

потон/увший *a.* drowned, sunk(en), submerged; **—уть** *v.* drown, sink, go down.

потоотделение *n.* (med.) diaphoresis; **повышенное п.** hyper(h)idrosis.

потоп *m.* flood, inundation, deluge; **—ить** *v.* flood; sink; heat for a while; **—ление** *n.* flooding; sinking, submersion; **—ленность** *f.* submergence; **—ленный** *a.* flooded, etc., *see v.;* **—лять** *v.* flood; drown, sink, submerge, immerse; **—нуть** *v.* drown, sink.

потоптать *v.* trample (down); tread.

поторапливать *v.* hasten, hurry, push, speed up.

поторговать(ся) bargain, trade (for a while).

поторопить *see* **потарапливать.**

потору *m. and pl.* rat kangaroo, potoroo (*Potoroinae*).

поточечн/о *adv.* pointwise, point-by-point; **—ный** *a.* point.

поточить *v.* sharpen (a little).

поточн/о-автоматический *a.* transfer (line); **п.-бригадный** *a.* mobile crew flow-type (production method); **п.-массовый** *a.* continuous mass (production); **п.-раздельный** *a.* sectionalized flow-line (method); **п.-транспортный** *a.* conveyor (system); **—ость** *f.* continuity; **—ый** *a. of* **поток;** continuous, flow(-line), in-line, line-flow, line (production), production-line; **—ый камер** tunnel (burner) section; **—ая линия** (rolling) rolling train; flow line, production line.

потрав/а *f.* crop damage from grazing; **—ить** *v.* spoil (crops); poison, exterminate; **—ленный** *a.* eaten up, consumed; **—лять** *v.* spoil (crops), overgraze.

потра/тить *v.* spend, use up, consume, waste; **—ченный** *a.* spent, used (up), consumed.

потреб/итель *m.* user; consumer; **—ительный** *a.* consumer's, consumption; **—ительский** *a.* consumers'; cooperative (store); subsistence (farming); **—ить** *see* **потреблять; —ление** *n.* consumption, use, expenditure; uptake, intake; requirement, demand; **—ляемый** *a.,* **—ляемая мощность** input, intake; **—лять** *v.* use, consume, expend; **—ляться** *v.* be used; **—ляющий** *a.* using, etc., *see v.*

потребн/ость *f.* necessity, need, requirement, demand, want; **п. кислорода, п. в кислороде** oxygen requirement, demand; **—ый** *a.* necessary, needful, required; **—ая мощность** (elec.) demand; **—ое количество** demand.

потребовать *v.* demand, request.

потрёпанный *a.* frayed; shabby.

потрепаться *v.* fray.

потреск/авшийся *a.* cracked, rimose, fissured; **—аться** *v.* crack (up), be covered with cracks; **—ивание** *n.* (de)crepitation, crackling; **—ивать** *v.* (de)crepitate, crack(le); **—ивающий** *a.* (de)crepitating, crackling.

потрёт *fut. 3 sing. of* **потереть.**

потрещать *see* **потрескивать.**

потро/ха *pl.* viscera, entrails; **—шёный** *a.* disemboweled, etc., *see v.;* **—шить** *v.* disembowel, gut, eviscerate, clean (fish), draw (poultry).

потруд/иться *v.* work (for a while); make an effort, take the trouble; **—нее** *comp. of* **трудно, трудный** (a little) more difficult.

потрут *fut. 3 pl. of* **потереть.**

потряс/ать *v.* shake (up), concuss; shock, amaze, astound; **—ающий** *a.* concussive; tremendous, of utmost importance; staggering, stupendous; startling; **—ение** *n.* shock, **—ённый** *a.* shaken; shocked; **—ти** *see* **потрясать.**

потряхивать *v.* shake from time to time, jolt.

потсдамский *a.* (geog.) Potsdam.

Потта костоеда (med.) Pott's disease, tuberculosis of the spine; **Потта параплегия** Pott's paralysis.

поттиевые *pl.* (bot.) Pottiaceae.

потто *m.* (mam.) potto, softly-softly (*Perodicticus potto*).

потуги *pl.* (muscle) spasms, contractions.

потускн/елый *a.* dull; dim; **—ение** *n.* tarnishing, etc., *see v.;* **—еть** *v.* tarnish, become dull, lose luster; fog, cloud.

потух/ание *n.* extinction; **—ать, —нуть** *v.* be extinguished, go out; **—ший** *a.* extinct, out; discolored, faded, dull, lackluster.

потушить *v.* extinguish, put out; slake; simmer.

Потье реактивное сопротивление (elec.) Potier's reactance.

потька *see* **карп.**

потяг *m.* pull; rein, leash, strap; **—ивание** *n.* pull(ing); pandiculation, stretching and yawning; **—ивать** *v.* pull (occasionally); draw in; sip.

потяжелеть *v.* become heavy, gain weight.

потянуть *v.* pull; **—ся** *v.* stretch.

поубавить *v.* lessen, diminish.

поуби(ва)ть *v.* kill.

поубыть *v.* decrease a little; go away.

поузловой *a.* unit, module, assembly, component; **п. ремонт** unit repair.

поукосный *a.* post-harvest.

поурочн/о *adv.* by the piece; **—ый** *a.* piecework (pay); (per) lesson.

поутру *adv.* in the morning.

поуч/ение *n.* instruction; **—ительный** *a.* instructive; **—ить** *v.* teach (for a while); give a lesson (in); **—иться** *v.* learn.

пофразовый *a.* sentence-for-sentence.

по-французски *adv.* (in) French.

похвал/а *f.,* **—и(ва)ть** *v.* praise, commend; **—иться** boast, brag; **—ьный** *a.* praiseworthy, commendable; **—ьная грамота** certificate of merit, commendation.

похватать *v.* snatch up.

похлестать, похлёстывать *v.* whip, lash.

похлопать *v.* slap, clap, tap; flap (wings).

похмелье *a.* hangover.

поход *m.* expedition, trip, cruise; hike, march; campaign; overweight; iter, passage, canal; **—ить** *v.* walk a little; resemble; **—ка** *f.* walk, gait; **—ный** *a.* expeditionary; camp(ing); mobile, field; traveling; temporary (plant); **—я** *adv.* on the move, hurriedly, in passing.

похож/е *introd. word* it looks, it appears; **—ий** *a.* like, similar, resembling.

похолод/ание *n.* cooling off; cold spell, temperature drop; **—ать, —еть** *v.* cool off.

похорон/ить *v.* bury, inter; **—ный** *a.*, **—ы** *pl.* funeral, burial services.

похорошеть *v.* improve in appearance.

похот/ливость *f.* libido, nymphomania, lust; **—ливый** *a.* lascivious; **—ник** *m.* (anat.) clitoris; **—ь** *see* **похотливость.**

похуде/ние *n.* thinning; (med.) emaciation; **—ть** *v.* become thin(ner), lose weight.

поцарапать *v.* scratch, mar.

поцедить *v.* strain.

поцел/овать(ся) *v.,* **—уй** *m.,* **—уйный** *a.* kiss.

поззина *f.* pozzine (peatbog meadow).

почас/но *adv.,* **—овой** *a.* per hour, by the hour, hourly.

почат/ковидный *a.* (bot.) spadiciform; **—ковый** *a.* (bot.) spadiceous; **—кодробилка** *f.* (agr.) cob crusher; **—кообрыватель, —коотделитель, —косрыватель** *m.* (corn) picker-husker; **—коочиститель** *m.* corn husker; **—коцветные** *pl.* spadix-forming plants (*Spadiciflorae*); **—ок** *m.* (bot.) spadix; (corn) cob; (text.) cop; **—очный** *a.* spadiceous; cob; cop.

почаще *adv.* more often, more frequently.

почв. *abbr.* (**почвенный**) soil, pedological.

почв/а *f.* soil, ground, earth, land; foot(wall); (min.) floor, bottom, bed; **п. на мелах** chalky soil; **на —е** resulting from, due to; **—енно—** *prefix* soil, edapho—, ped(o)—; **—енный** *a. of* **почва;** edaphic; **—енная вода** ground water; **—ые организмы** (biol.) edaphon.

почво/вед *m.* soil scientist, pedologist; **—ведение** *n.* soil science, pedology, edaphology; **—ведческий** *a.* pedological; **—грунт** *m.* ground, soil and subsoil; **—закрепляющий** *a.* soil-conserving, soil-stabilizing; **—зацеп** *m.* lug, cleat, grouser (of track); **—защитный** *a.* soil-protecting, soil-stabilizing; **—истощающий** *a.* soil-depleting; **—обрабатывающая машина** cultivator; **—обработка** *f.* cultivation; **—образование** *n.* soil formation, pedogenesis; **—образующий** *a.* pedogenic; **—образующий фактор** soil former; **—покровный** *a.* ground-cover; **—углубитель** *m.* (agr.) subsoil plow, deep plow; **—углубление** *n.* subsoil plowing; **—укрепляющий** *a.* soil-stabilizing, soil-fixing (plant); **—улучшение** *n.* soil reclamation, soil conditioning; **—уплотнитель** *m.* packer; **—уступный** *a.* (min.) underhand (stope); bench-cut; **—утомление** *n.* soil depletion; **—фреза** *f.* rototiller.

почек *gen. pl. of* **почка.**

почём *adv.* how much? what is the price?

почему *adv.* why; **п.-то** for some reason; **вот п.** that is why.

почерк *m.* handwriting; (spectrum) signature.

почерн/евший, —елый *a.* blackened, grown black; **—ение** *n.* blackening; (phot.) density; **—ение стебля** (phyt.) black stem; **плотность —ения** density; **—еть** *v.* turn black; **—ить** *v.* blacken.

почерп/ать, —нуть *v.* draw up, fetch, get; scoop, dip out; pick up (information).

почерстветь *v.* get stale, harden.

почесать *v.* comb, card; scratch.

почесть *f.* honor(s); respect, esteem; *v. see* **почитать.**

почесуха *f.* (med.) prurigo; itching.

почёсывать(ся) *v.* scratch (occasionally).

почёт *m.* honor, respect; **—ный** *a.* honorable, honorary, complimentary.

почечка *f.* (biol.) gemmule, small bud, plumule.

почечно— *prefix* reno—, nephr(o)— (kidney); **—каменная болезнь** (med.) renal calculosis, kidney stones.

почечн/ый *a. of* **почка;** kidney, renal, nephritic; (biol.) bud, gemmaceous; **п. камень** (med.) kidney stone; **п. покров** (bot.) perule; **п. чай** Java tea (*Orthosiphon stamineus*); **эффективный п. кровоток** effective renal blood flow, ERBF; **—ая лоханка** (anat.) renal pelvis; **—ое сало** suet.

почечу/й *m.,* **—я** *pl.* (med.) hemorrhoids; **—йный** *a.* hemorrhoidal; **—йная трава** (bot.) persicary (*Polygonum persicaria*).

почин *m.* beginning; initiative.

почин/ить *v.* mend, repair, fix; **—ка** *f.* mending, repair(ing), fixing.

почин/очный *a. of* **починка; —ять** *v.* repair, fix, mend (several times).

почистить *v.* clean (up); purify.

почитать *v.* read a little; honor, respect.

почихать *v.* sneeze (several times).

почище *adv.* cleaner; **—нный** *past pass. part. of* **почистить;** cleaned, etc.

поч/ка *f.* (bot.) bud, gemma; (min.) druse, nodule, (clay) ball; (anat.) kidney; caliculus; **воспаление —ек** (med.) nephritis; **вторичная п.** (anat.) metanephros; **выводковая п.** (bot.) bulblet; **головная п.** (anat.) pro(to)nephros; **задняя п.** (anat.) metanephros; **зимняя п.** (bot.) hibernaculum; **первичная п., туловищная п.** (anat.) mesonephros.

почко— *prefix* reni—, nephr(o)— (kidney); **—вание** *n.* (biol.) budding, gemm(ul)ation; **—ватый** *see* **почковидный; —ваться** *v.* bud; sprout; **—видный** *a.* kidney-shaped, reniform, nephroid, nodular; **—вый** *a.* gemmate, bud; **—клей** *m.* (bot.) blastocolla; **—луковица** *f.* bulbogemma, bulbil; **—носный** *a.* gemmiferous; **—образный** *see* **почковидный; —образование** *n.* bud formation; **—рез** *m.* scarab beetle (*Lethrus apterus*); **—сложение** *n.* (bot.) (a)estivation, pr(a)efloration; pr(a)efoliation, vernation; **листовое —сложение** prefoliation, vernation; **цветочное —сложение** pr(a)efloration.

почленн/о *adv.,* **—ый** *a.* (math.) termwise, term-by-term.

почт/а *f.* mail, post; post office; (nucl.) rabbit; **по —е** by mail; **—альон** *m.* mailman, postman; messenger; **—амт** *m.* post office.

почтен/ие *n.* respect, esteem, consideration, honor; **—ный** *a.* respectable, honorable; considerable.

почти *adv.* nearly, almost, at the point (of); *prefix* near—, almost, sub—; quasi—; **п. или совсем не** little or no; **п. как** very similarly to; **п. таким же образом** in much the same manner; **п. фиолетовый** (bot.) subviolaceous.

почти-равнина *f.* (geol.) peneplain.

почти что *see* **почти.**

почтов/ый *a.* mail, post(al), postage; carrier (pigeon); **п. перевод** money order; **п. штемпель** postmark; **—ая марка** stamp; **—ое отделение** post office.

почувствовать *v.* (start to) feel, experience.

пошаговый *a.* step-by-step.

пошат/ать, —нуть *v.* push, sway, rock slightly; **—нуться** *v.* stagger; lean to one side, cant; **—ывать** *see* **пошатать.**

пошедший *past act. part. of* **пойти;** converted (to); consumed (in).

пошёл *past m. sing. of* **пойти.**

пошелушить *v.* shell, hull, husk.

пошерстный *a.* (rr.) trailing.

пошив *m.,* —**ка** *f.,* —**очный** *a.* sewing.

поширеть *v.* become wider, widen.

пошить *v.* sew.

пошлёп(ыв)ать *v.* slap.

пошлёт *fut. 3 sing. of* **послать.**

пошли *past pl. of* **пойти.**

пошлин/а *f.,* —**ный** *a.* duty, customs, tax; **оплаченный —ой** duty paid; —**ы** *pl.* costs, expenses.

поштучн/о *adv.,* —**ый** *a.* by the piece, piecemeal, by the job; item by item; —**ая плата** piecework pay.

пошуметь *v.* make noise (for a while).

пошьёт *fut. 3 sing. of* **пошить.**

пощад/а *f.* pity, mercy, compassion; —**ить** *v.* pity; spare.

пощёлк(ив)ать *v.* click, snap; crack (nuts).

пощёчина *f.* slap, box on the ear.

пощип/ать *v.* pinch, pluck; nibble; —**ывание** *n.* tingling, prickling; —**ывать** *see* **пощипать.**

пощуп/ать, —**ывать** *v.* feel, handle; (med.) palpate; —**ывание** *n.* palpation.

ПОЭ *abbr.* (**полиоксиэтиленгликоль**) polyoxyethylene glycol.

поэкзаменовать *v.* examine.

поэтажный *a.* floor, story; per floor.

поэтапно *adv.* in stages.

поэтому *adv. and conj.* therefore, that is why, consequently, and so, because of this.

поют *pr. 3 pl. of* **петь.**

поющий *a.* singing, humming.

появ/иться *see* **появляться;** —**ление** *n.* appearance, emergence, emersion, advent, occurrence; (**внезапное**) **массовое —ление** (biol.) outbreak; **потенциал —ления** appearance potential; —**ляться** *v.* appear, make its appearance, show itself, emerge, originate, develop; —**ляющийся** *a.* appearing, etc., *see v.;* forthcoming; collapsible, bobbing (target).

пояр/ок *m.,* —**ковый** *a.* lamb's wool.

поярусно *adv.* stepped, tiered, etc., *see* **ярусный.**

пояс *m.* belt, band, girdle; zone, region; flange, collar, hoop; chord (of girders); ring, course (of vertical tank); (geol.) series (of veins); (anat.) cingulum; (met.) double teem; **п. верхней конечности** (anat.) shoulder girdle; **п. конечности** (anat.) cingulum membri; **п. низней конечности, задний п.** pelvic girdle; **зелёный п.** (bot.) greenbelt; **передний п.** shoulder girdle; —**ковые** *pl.* (zool.) Clitellio; —**ковый** *a.* (zool.) clitellar; connectivalis; zonular.

поясн/ение *n.* explanation, elucidation; —**ительный** *a.* explanatory; —**ить** *see* **пояснять.**

поясни/ца *f.* (anat.) loin(s), lumbus; (orn.) rump; **область —цы** lumbar region; —**чно—** *prefix* lumbo—, lumbar; —**чно-крестцовый** *a.* lumbosacral; —**чно-рёберный** *a.* lumbocostal; —**чно-спинной** *a.* lumbodorsal; —**чный** *a.* lumbar; psoas (muscle); —**чный прокол** (med.) lumbar puncture.

поясн/ой *a. of* **пояс;** zonal; flange (plate; rivet); necklace (charge); **п. слой** (anat.) zonal layer; —**ая плацента** zonular placenta; annular placenta.

поясность *f.* zonality; **вертикальная п.** (bot.) altitudinal zonality.

пояснять *v.* explain, elucidate, expound, comment, illustrate.

пояс/овое сложение (geol.) ribbon structure; **п. строение** (geol.) girdle fabric; —**ок** *dim. of* **пояс;** collar, band; strap; (zool.) clitellum; zonula; —**ок-противоомеднитель** *m.* decoppering ring; —**охвосты** *pl.* (herp.) Cordylidae.

поят *pr. 3 pl. of* **поить.**

пп. *abbr.* (**параграфы**) paragraphs.

п/п *abbr.* (**подлинник подписан**) original signed; (**по порядку**) in order; serial number.

ПП *abbr.* (**пакет программ**) software package; (**перегретый пар**) superheated steam; (**пищевая промышленность**) food industry; (**полипропилен**) polypropylene; (**постоянная память**) (comp.) read-only memory, ROM.

ППБУ *abbr.* (**полупогружаемая буровая установка**) semisubmersible drilling vessel.

ППЗ *abbr.* (**процессор с плавающей запятой**) (comp.) floating-point processor.

ППЗУ *abbr.* (**программируемое постоянное запоминающее устройство**) (comp.) programmable read-only memory, PROM.

ППК *abbr.* (**противоперегрузочный костюм**) G-suit.

ППМ *abbr.* (**промежуточный пункт маршрута**) checkpoint.

п.п.п. *abbr.* (**потери при прокаливании**) calcination loss.

ППТ *abbr.* (**процессор с плавающей точкой**) (comp.) floating-point processor.

ППУ *abbr.* (**пенополиуретан**) polyurethane foam.

пр. *abbr.* (**прочее, прочий**) the rest; (**порошок**) powder; (**правый**) right(-hand); (**прошлый**) past, last.

пра— *prefix* great—; —**бабушка** *f.* great-grandmother.

права *pl. of* **право;** license.

правд/а *f.* truth, fact; justice; (it is) true; —**ивость** *f.* truthfulness, fidelity; —**ивый** *a.* truthful, honest.

правдинский *a.* (geog.) Pravdinsk.

правдоподоб/ие *n.* probability, likelihood, plausibility; **функция —ия** likelihood function; —**ный** *a.* probable, likely, plausible.

правил/о *n.* rule, maxim, principle; law; regulation, specification; straightedge, guide bar; float; (trail) handspike; **п. отбора** (phys.) selection principle; **п. правой руки** (phys.) right-hand rule; —**а** *pl.* instructions, specifications, rules, regulations; code; practice; —**а безопасности** safety regulations; **как п.** as a rule.

правильнее *adv.* more correctly, more accurately.

правильно *adv.* right, accurately, correctly, properly; —**сть** *f.* accuracy, correctness, validity; principle (of process); regularity, basic pattern.

правильн/ый *a.* accurate, correct, proper; true; normal, sound, regular, legitimate; straightening; straightedge; guiding; rectilineal (polygon); **п. вал** (paper) guide roll; **п. раствор** (chem.) regular solution; —**ая доска** straightedge, ruler; —**ая дробь** (math.) proper fraction; —**ые перья** (orn.) retrices, tail feathers.

правильщик *m.* straightener.

правитель *m.* ruler, administrator, manager; **п. делами** head clerk; —**ственный** *a.,* —**ство** *n.* government; —**ствующий** *a.* ruling, governing.

прав/ить *v.* govern, rule, manage, direct, guide, administer; steer, drive; drive (car); correct; set (saw); grind (cutting tools); straighten, dress, trim; —**ка** *f.* correcting, correction(s), revision; adjustment, trueing; straightening, dressing, trimming, leveling; setting.

правлен/ие *n.* government; direction, administration, management; board (of directors); —**ный** *part.* corrected; straightened; —**ый** *a.* corrected, edited.

правну/к *m.,* —**чка** *f.* great-grandchild.

прав/о *n.* right; privilege, priority; law; claim, title (to); *introd. word* really, truly, indeed; *prefix* law; right (-hand); (naut.) starboard; **п. прохода** right of way; **авторское п.** copyright; **доктор прав** doctor of laws (degree); **неотъемлемое п.** inalienable right; **по —у** rightfully, legally; **поплатиться —ом** *v.* forfeit (the right); **предъявлять —а** *v.* lay claim, assert one's claims (to).

право/винтовой *a.* right-handed screw; **—вой** *a.* legal; law.

правовращающ/ий *a.* dextrorotatory; **—ее соединение** dextrorotatory compound, dextro-compound.

правоза/вёрнутый *a.* (bot.) dextrorse-involute; **—крученный** *a.* (bot.) dextrorse; clockwise.

право-левосторонний *a.* (med.) right-to-left (shunt).

право/мерность *f.* justification; (math.) legitimacy; **—мерный** *a.* rightful; lawful; **—мочие** *n.* competence; **—мочный** *a.* competent; **—нарушение** *n.* infringement of the law, breaking of a law, offense; **—писание** *n.* orthography, spelling; **—поляризованный** *a.* polarized clockwise; **—порядок** *m.* law and order; **—рукий** *a.* right-handed; **—способность** *f.* capacity; **—способный** *a.* capable, competent; **—сторонний** *a.* righthand; **—судие** *n.* justice; **—та** *f.* correctness; legitimacy; justice; integrity; **—ходовой** *a.* right-hand.

правщик *m.* straightener.

прав/ый *a.* right(-hand), clockwise, dextro—; (naut.) starboard; (political) right-wing; right(ful); **—ая винная кислота** dextrotartaric acid; **—ое вращение** (opt.) dextrorotation; **быть —ым** *v.* be right; **на —ую сторону** to the right, on the right hand.

правящий *a.* governing, ruling.

Прага, пражский *a.* Prague.

прадед, —ушка *m.* great-grandfather; **—ы** *pl.* ancestors, forefathers.

праздн/ик *m.* holiday, celebration, (book) festival; **—ичный** *a.* of **праздник**; festive; **—овать** *v.* celebrate; **—ость** *f.* idleness, inactivity; **—ый** *a.* idle, inactive.

празелень *f.* bluish green color.

празеодим *m.*, **—иевый** *a.* praseodymium, Pr; **окись —ия** praseodymium oxide; **сернокислый п.** praseodymium sulfate; **—иевая земля** praseodymia, praseodymium trioxide; **—ий** *see* **празеодим.**

Прайса-Джонса кривая (hemat.) Price-Jones curve.

практик *m.* practical person; practitioner; skilled worker; **—а** *f.* practice, training; experience; **на —е** in practice; **—ант** *m.* practician; probationer; trainee; **—овать** *v.* practice; **—оваться** *v.* (be in common) practice; **—ум** *m.* laboratory course; practicum; practical work; laboratory manual; **—ующий** *a.* practicing.

практицизм *m.* practicality.

практич/ески *adv.* practically, essentially; in practice; **п. возможный** *a.* practical, feasible; **п. применимый** *a.* useful, usable; **—еский, —ный** *a.* practical, useful, applied; operating; **—ность** *f.* practicality, usefulness.

Прандтля число Prandtl number.

прапра— *prefix* great-great—; **—баб(уш)ка** *f.* great-great-grandmother.

прародитель *m.* ancestor, progenitor.

ПРАС *abbr.* (**программа работы аппаратного средства**) (comp.) firmware program.

пратенсол *m.* pratensol.

прачечн/ая *f.*, **—ый** *a.* laundry.

пращ *m.*, **—а** *f.* sling; **—евидный** *a.* fundiform, sling-shaped, loop-shaped; **—евой** *a.* sling; **—ник** *see* **баллист.**

пра/щур *m.* ancestor, forefather; **—язык** *m.* parent language.

пр-во *abbr.* (**правительство; производство**).

пр/г *abbr.* (**прошлого года**) last year.

ПРД *abbr.* (**пороховой ракетный двигатель**) solid-fuel rocket engine; (**прямоточный реактивный двигатель**) ramjet engine.

пре— *prefix* very, most; *prefix with verbs* sur—, over—;

through; **—адаптация** (biol.) preadaptation; **—анальный** *see* **преданальный; —антенна** *f.* (zool.) preantenna.

пребы/вание *n.* stay, residence; tenure (in office); **место —вания** residence; **—(ва)ть** *v.* stay, reside; continue, be.

превен/тивный *a.* preventive; **—торий** *m.* (med.) preventorium; **—ция** *f.* prevention.

превзой/дённый *a.* surpassed; **—ти** *see* **превосходить.**

превозмо/гать, —чь *v.* overcome, master.

превозн/ести, —осить *v.* overrate; praise.

превосход/ить *v.* surpass, excel, outdo, top, exceed, be more than; **п. числом** outnumber; **—но** *adv.* excellently, superiorly; **—ный** *a.* excellent, superior, first-class, splendid; (grammar) superlative; **—ство** *n.* excellence, superiority, preeminence; preponderance; advantage; **—ствовать** *see* **превосходить; —ящий** *a.* surpassing, etc., *see v.*

преврат/имый *see* **превращаемый; —ить** *see* **превращать.**

преврат/но *adv.* wrongly; **п. истолковать** *v.* misinterpret, misunderstand; **—ый** *a.* wrong; changeful, inconstant.

превращ/аемый *a.* convertible, transformable; **—ать** *v.* convert, transform, transmute, change, turn (into), alter; (math.) reduce; **—аться** *v.* be converted, change, turn, become, pass over, pass into, go over (to another form), metamorphose.

превращен/ие *n.* conversion, transformation, metamorphosis, change, transmutation (of elements); inversion (of sugar); (zool.) metaboly, euglenoid movement; **интервал —ия** (chem.) transition range, transition interval; **неполное п.** hemimetabolism, partial metamorphosis; **полное п.** holometabolism, complete metamorphosis; **реакция —ия** conversion (reaction); **точка —ия** transition point, critical point; **число —ий** (enz.) turnover number.

превращённый *a.* converted, transformed, changed; invert (sugar).

превы/сить, —шать *v.* exceed, be more than, be over; surpass, outdo, excel; **—шающий** *a.* exceeding, etc., *see v.*; greater (than); **—ше** *adv.* much higher, much greater; **—шение** *n.* excess, exceeding, surpassing; (geog.) elevation, difference in height; vertical interval; **—шение стоимости** (cost) overrun; **—шенный** *a.* exceeded, etc., *see v.*

прегаллюкс *m.* (anat.) prehallux, calcar.

прегаустория *f.* (bot.) prehaustorium.

прегенеративный *a.* pregenerative.

прегетерокинез *m.* (biol.) preheterokinesis.

прегн/ан *m.* (biochem.) pregnane; **—андиол** *m.* pregnan(e)diol; **—ен** *m.* pregnene; **—енолон** *m.* pregnenolone; **—ин** *m.* pregneninolone, ethisterone.

прегра/да *f.* obstacle, obstruction, barrier, bar, barricade, block, impediment; interception; fender; **грудобрюшная п.** (anat.) diaphragm; **действие —ды** (phys.) screening effect; **—дить, —ждать** *v.* obstruct, block up, impede, bar; intercept, interrupt; **—ждать доступ** seal (off); **—ждающий** *a.* obstructing, etc., *see v.*; blocking (capacitor); **—ждение** *n.* obstruction, blocking up, etc., *see v.*; **—ждённый** *a.* obstructed, etc., *see v.*

пред *see* **перед**; *prefix* pre—; pro—; ante—; (geog.) Cis— (on this side of).

предавать *v.* betray, give up; hand over; consign; **—ся** *v.* devote oneself (to); give oneself up.

предагональный *a.* (med.) preagonal.

предальпийский *a.* cisalpine.

преданальный *a.* (anat.) preanal (region).

преданн/ость *f.* devotion, loyalty; **—ый** *a.* devoted, attached, loyal; **—ый вам** yours truly.

предать *see* **предавать**.

предаццит *see* **предаззит**.

предбрачный *a.* prenuptial.

предбрюшинный preperitoneal.

предварен/ие *n.* precedence; advance, lead; anticipation, forestalling; **п. впуска** preadmission; **угол —ия** (elec.) angle of lead.

предварительн/о *adv.* preliminarily, first, beforehand, previously; **pre—**, **fore—**; **п. напряжённый** *a.* prestressed (concrete); **п. образованный** preformed; **п. охлаждать** *v.* precool; **п. сжатый** precompressed; **—ый** *a.* preliminary, previous, pre—; preparatory; provisional, tentative (conclusion); introductory (remark); **—ый оттиск** preprint (of an article); **—ая обработка** preprocessing, pretreatment; **—ое нагревание** preheating; **—ое условие** prerequisite.

предвар/ить, —ять *v.* (fore)warn; precede, anticipate, forestall.

предвесенний *a.* late-winter.

предвест/ие *n.,* **—ник** *m.* forerunner, sign, indication; (med.) prodrome, precursor; **—ить** *see* **предвешать**.

предвечерний *a.* before evening.

предвещать *v.* predict, foretell, foreshadow, warn (of); forerun.

предвзят/ый *a.* preconceived; **—ое мнение** preconception, prejudice.

предвид/ение *n.* foresight; **—еть** *v.* foresee, visualize, forecast; **—имый** *a.* predictable, foreseeable.

предвку/сить, —шать *v.* anticipate; **—шение** *n.* anticipation, expectation.

предводитель *m.* leader, commander; **—ство** *n.* leadership; **—ствовать** *v.* lead, head, command.

предвоенный *a.* prewar.

предвулканизация *f.* scorching, precuring.

предвосхи/тить, —щать *v.* anticipate; **—щение** *n.* anticipation.

пред/выделение *n.* advanced precipitation; **—вычисление** *n.* precomputation; (navig.) prediction; **—вычислять** *v.* precompute, predict; advance (ship's position); **—глабелярный** *a.* preglabellar (furrow, field); **—глазничный** *a.* (anat.) preorbital; preocular (scuta); **—глоточный** *a.* prepharyngeal; **—горный** *a.* (geol.) piedmont; **—горье** *n.* piedmont, foothills; **—грозовой** *a.* prestorm; **—грозье** *n.* period before a storm; **—грудина** *f.,* **—грудинник** *m.* (anat.) omosternum; presternum.

преддвер/ие *n.* threshold; (anat.) vestibule, vestibulum; antrum, atrium (of heart); **п. гортани** vestibule of the larynx; **вена —ия** vestibular vein; **поле —ия** vestibular area; **—но-улитковый** *a.* vestibulocochlear, auditory (nerve); **—ный** *a.* vestibular.

пред/движение *n.* premovement; **—детонация** *f.* preknock; predetonation; **—дипломный** *a.* undergraduate; **—дождевой** *a.* prerain.

предел *m.* limit, bound(ary), end, termination, limitation; capacity, extent, compass, range; point; (fatigue; creep) strength; **п. насыщения** saturation point; **п. прочности** (ultimate) strength; **п. регулировки** range of adjustment; **п. скорости** speed limit; **—ы** *pl.* range; margin (of error); **—ы кипения** (chem.) distillation range, cut points; **—ы колебания температуры** temperature range; **в —ах** within (the boundaries or limits of), in the range; **в —ах от 30 до 40** from 30 to 40; **вне —ов видимости** out of sight; **в температурных —ах** in the temperature range; **выходить за —ы** *v.*

exceed; lie outside (of); be beyond the scope (of); **за —ами** extra—, outside; **не выходить за —ы** *v.* be confined (to); **достигать —а** *v.* range; attain; **за —ы** outside of, beyond; **положить п., ставить п.** *v.* limit, terminate.

предельно *adv.* utterly; to the extreme; **—допустимый** *a.* maximum (permissible); **—допустимая доза** tolerance level.

предельн/ый *a.* limit(ing), boundary, threshold; extreme, terminal, end (point, position); difference, limit (gage); maximum (permissible), critical, ultimate, full, overall (dimension); (chem.) saturated; **п. возраст** age limit; **п. срок** deadline, time limit; **п. угол** critical angle; **—ая величина** threshold (value); **—ая грань** termination; **—ая дальность** effective range, operating range; **—ая кривая** limit(ing) curve; **—ая линия** boundary (line); border; **—ая плоскость** (cryst.) end plane, base; **—ая поверхность** boundary surface, surface of contact, interface; **—ая скорость** speed limit; top speed; **—ое напряжение сдвига** yield value; **—ое соединение** saturated compound; **точка —ого значения** yield point.

предентин *m.* predentin.

предетерминация *f.* (gen.) predetermination.

пред/жаберный *a.* (zool.) prebranchial; **—желтушный** *a.* (med.) preicteric.

пред/желудок *m.* (zool.) rumen; proventriculus; (ent.) gizzard; **—зажигание** *n.* (elec.) prestrike (of an arc); keep-alive discharge; **—зажигатель** *m.* trigger electrode, keep-alive electrode; **—закатный** *a.* before sunset; **—зародыш** *m.* proembryo; **—зародышевый** *a.* proembryonic; **—затылочный** *a.* (anat.) preoccipital; **—зимний** *a.* late-fall; **—знаменование** *n.* foreboding, omen.

предик/ат *m.* (math.) predicate; **—тивный** *a.* predictive, predicting.

предисловие *n.* preface, foreword, introduction; **служить —м** *v.* preface.

предкавказский *a.* (geog.) Ciscaucasian.

Предкавказье Ciscaucasia.

предкамер/а *f.,* **—ный** *a.* antechamber, precombustion chamber; **—ное горение** precombustion.

предкарпатский *a.* (geog.) cis-Carpathian.

предки *pl.* of **предок**; ancestry, parentage.

предклимакс *m.* (bot.) preclimax.

предклинье *n.* (anat.) precuneus.

предковый *a.* ancestral.

предкоренной зуб premolar.

предкрыл/овой бугорок (orn.) prealar callus; wing spur; **—ок** *m.* (av.) (leading-edge) flap.

предкрыш/ечный *a.* (anat.) pretectal; **—ка** *f.* (ichth.) preopercle.

предкуколка *a.* (ent.) prepupa.

предлагать *v.* offer, propose, put forward, propound, suggest, advance.

предлапка *f.* (zool.) pretarsus.

предлежа/ние *n.* (med.) presentation; **п. плаценты** placental presentation; **роды при ягодичном —нии** breech delivery; **—щая плацента** placenta previa.

предлист *m.* (bot.) prophyllum.

предлихорадочный *a.* (med.) prefebrile.

предличинка *f.* (ichth.) alevin.

предлоб/ковый *a.* (anat.) prepubic; **—ный** *a.* prefrontal.

предлог *m.* pretext, pretense, excuse; grounds (for); (gram.) preposition.

предлож/ение *n.* offer, proposal, proposition, suggestion; (com.) supply; sentence, clause; statement; **вспомогательное п.** (math.) lemma; **делать п.** *v.* propose;

спрос и п. supply and demand; **—енный** *a.* offered, etc., *see* **предлагать;** **—ить** *see* **предлагать; —ный** *a.* (grammar) prepositional.

пред/лонный *a.* (anat.) prepubic; **—лопаточный** *a.* suprascapular; **—менструальный** *a.* (med.) premenstrual.

предместье *n.* suburb, outskirts.

предмет *m.* subject, topic, feature; object; product, article, commodity, item; piece of work; **местный п.** (surv.) feature (of terrain), landmark; **—ы** *pl.* goods, supplies; **п. (широкого) потребления** commodity; **на п.** for; **—изация** *f.* subject cataloging, subject indexing, featuring; **—изировать** *v.* catalog by subject, assign subject headings; **—но-замкнутый** *a.* finished-product manufacturing; **—ность** *f.* objectivity.

предметн/ый *a.* of **предмет;** object(ive); impersonal (account); **п. столик** (micros.) stage, stand; **п. указатель** subject index; **п. урок** object lesson; **—ое стекло** (micros.) slide.

предметодержатель *m.* (micros.) stage, stand; slide, mount.

предмолочный *a.* prelacteal (tooth).

предмост/ный *a.* in front of a bridge; **—ное укрепление** (mil.) bridgehead; **—ье** *n.* bridge entrance.

преднадколенниковый *a.* (anat.) prepatellar.

предназнач/ать, —ить *v.* intend, reserve (for); designate, set aside, earmark (for); design; **—ение** *n.* destination; design; purpose; **—енный** *a.* destined, intended; to, bound for.

преднамерен/ие *n.,* **—ность** *f.* premeditation, forethought; **—но** *adv.* on purpose, by design; **—ный** *a.* premeditated, aforethought, preconceived, intentional, deliberate.

преднапряжённый *a.* prestressed.

предначерт/ание *n.* outline, plan, design; **—ать** *v.* outline in advance.

предниз/олон *m.* (pharm.) prednisolone; **—он** *m.* prednisone.

пред/ночной *a.* before nightfall; **—ок** *m.* progenitor, predecessor, ancestor, forefather; antecedent; **—оконечный** *a.* penultimate; driver (tube).

предоминирующий *a.* predominant.

предоперационный *a.* preoperative.

предоперкулярн/ый *a.* (ichth.) preopercular; **—ая кость** preopercle.

предоплата *f.* prepayment.

предопредел/ение *n.* predetermination; **—ённый** *a.* predetermined; **—ить, —ять** *v.* predetermine.

предосенний *a.* late-summer.

предостав/ить *v.,* **—лять** *v.* leave, submit; let, allow; make available; give, grant; inform; offer, supply; **п. уведомление** notify; **—ление** *n.* leaving, submitting; giving; assignment, allocation.

предостере/гательный *a.* warning, cautionary; **—гать** *v.* warn, caution, admonish, put on guard; **—гающий** *a.* (biol.) allosematic (coloration); **—жение** *n.* warning, caution, notice; **—чь** *see* **предостерегать.**

предостный *a.* (anat.) supraspinal.

предосторожност/ь *f.* precaution, safeguard; **мера —и** precautionary measure, precaution.

предотвра/тимый *a.* avoidable; **—тить** *see* **предотвращать; —щаемый** *a.* preventable; **—щать** *v.* prevent, avert, avoid, ward off, keep from, (safe)guard against, preclude, suppress; **—щение** *n.* prevention, averting, etc., *see v.;* avoidance; **—щённый** *a.* prevented, etc., *see v.*

предотъездный *a.* before departure.

предохладитель *m.* precooler.

предохран/ение *n.* protection, security; (mach.) safety device; preservation, conservation; prevention; **—ённый** *a.* protected, shielded; preserved.

предохранитель *m.* protector, safety device, safety catch, (safe)guard; preserver, preservative; (elec.) fuse, cutout; **п. от обледенения** (av.) deicer; **—новзводящий** *a.* safety and arming; **—ность** *f.* (explosives) safety.

предохранительн/ый *a.* protective, protecting, protection; safety, security, guard; preservative; precautionary (measures); (elec.) fuse (box, wire); relief (cock); (med.) prophylactic, preventive; (biol.) anticryptic (coloration); (nucl.) shut-off, scram (rod); **п. клапан** safety valve; **п. кожух** (nucl.) shield; **п. штепсель, —ая вставка** (elec.) fuse; **п. щит** (mach.) fender, guard; **—ая маска** face guard; **—ая плита** baffle plate; screen; **—ая пробка** (elec.) fuse; **—ая трубка** safety tube; **—ое приспособление** safeguard; **—ое средство** preservative; (med.) prophylactic; **—ое устройство** precaution; protector, safety device.

предохран/ить, —ять *v.* protect, (safe)guard, keep safe, keep (away) from, insulate (from), cushion (against shock); prevent, preserve, conserve; **—яющий** *see* **предохранительный.**

предочаговый *a.* preliminary (deformation).

предочистка *f.* pretreatment.

предпис/ание *n.* order, regulation, instruction, direction(s), injunction, prescription; **согласно —анию** by order; **—анный** *a.* prescribed, specified; **—ать, —ывать** *v.* prescribe, order, decree; instruct, direct; assign.

пред/пламенный *a.* pre-ignition; **—пластида** *f.* (bot.) proplastid; **—плата** *f.* prepayment; **—плечевой** *a.* (anat.) antebrachial; **—плечье** *n.* antebrachium, forearm; **область —плечья** antebrachial region; **—плодие** *n.* (bot.) procarp; **—плужник** *m.* (agr.) skim colter, (skim) jointer.

предплюсн/а *f.* (anat.) tarsus; **кости —ы** tarsalia; **связки —ы** tarsal ligaments; **—евой** *a.* tarsal; **—е-плюсневой** *a.* tarsometatarsal.

предпобег *m.* (bot.) protocorm.

предпод/бородок *m.* (ent.) prementum.

предпозвоночный *a.* (anat.) prevertebral (lamina).

предполаг/аемый *a.* proposed, etc., *see v.;* hypothetical, conjectural, probable, prospective; **п. срок жизни** life expectancy; **—ать** *v.* propose, suggest, infer; assume, take as, presume, suppose, surmise, conjecture; anticipate, expect; intend; **предположим, что** if we assume that, let (us assume that), suppose; **—аться** *v.* be proposed, etc., *see v.;* **—ая** *pr. ger.* proposing, etc., *see v.*

предполётный *a.* preflight.

предполимеризация *f.* prepolymerization.

предполож/ение *n.* supposition, surmise, hypothesis, assumption, premise; plan, project, scheme, proposal; **исходя из —ения** assuming (that); **при —ении** with (or under) the assumption; **—енный** *a.* supposed, assumed; proposed; **—им, что** if we assume that, let (us assume that), suppose; **—ительно** *adv.* supposedly, presumably, hypothetically; tentatively; **—ительность** *f.* hypothetical nature; **—ительный** *a.* hypothetical, conjectural; tentative (value); **—ить** *see* **предполагать.**

предполье *n.* (mil.) security zone; no man's land.

пред/полярный *a.* subarctic; **—посадочный** *a.* (av.) prelanding, approach; (agr.) preplanting; **—посевной** *a.* presowing; **—послать** *see* **предпосылать; —последний** *a.* penultimate, next to last.

предпосыл/ать *v.* precede, preface (with), introduce;

send in advance; **—ка** *f.* prerequisite; premise; reason, ground.

предпоч/есть *see* **предпочитать; —итаемый** *a.* preferred, preferable, selected; **—итать** *v.* prefer, favor, like better; **—итаться** *v.* be preferable.

предпочка *f.* (embr.) pro(to)nephros.

предпочтение *n.* preference.

предпочтительн/о *adv.* preferably, in preference, rather; **—ость** *f.* preferableness; **—ый** *a.* preferable; preferential.

предпошлёт *fut.* 3 *sing. of* **предпослать.**

предприватниковый *a.* (anat.) prepyloric (vein).

предприимчив/ость *f.* enterprise; **—ый** *a.* enterprising.

предприн/иматель *m.* industrialist, owner (of firm or business); entrepreneur; employer; **—имательский** *a.* owner's, employer's; **—имательство** *n.* (free) enterprise; **—имать, —ять** *v.* undertake, launch, initiate.

предприяти/е *n.* undertaking, enterprise; concern, business; plant, works; **п.-тень** (mil.) skeleton factory, standby plant; **стандарт —я** factory standard.

пред/прядение *n.* (text.) roving, preparatory spinning; **—прятокрылые** *pl.* (zool.; pal.) Protorthoptera; **—пузырный** *a.* (anat.) prevesical, precystic; **—пусковой** *a.* preliminary, pre-operational; **—раковый** *a.* (med.) precancerous.

предраспол/агать *v.* predispose; **—ожение** *n.* predisposition; (med.) diathesis; (gen.) disposition; **—оженный** *a.* predisposed, susceptible, liable; **—ожить** *v.* predispose.

пред/распределительный *a.* predistributing; **—рассветный** *a.* predawn; **—рассудок** *m.* prejudice; **—рёберный** *a.* (anat.) precostal; **—революционный** *a.* prerevolutionary; **—редактирование** *n.* pre-editing.

предре/кать, —чь *v.* predict, foretell.

предреш/ать, —ить *v.* predetermine, decide beforehand; **—ённый** *a.* predetermined.

пред/родовой *a.* prenatal; antepartal; **—росток** *m.* (bot.) protonema; **—ротовой** *a.* (anat.) preoral; **—ротовая лопасть** (zool.) prostomium.

председатель *m.* chairman; speaker; president; **—ствовать** *v.* preside; **—ствующий** *a.* presiding; *m.* chairman.

предсерд/ечный *a.* (anat.) precardiac, precordial; **—ие** *n.* (anat.) auricle, atrium; precordium; **—иевый** *a.* atrial; **—но—** *prefix* (anat.) atrio—; **—но-желудочковый** *a.* atrioventricular; **—но-пазуховый** *a.* sinoatrial; **—ный** *a.* atrial.

предсерийный *a.* preproduction.

предсказ/ание *n.* prophecy, prediction; prognosis; (weather) forecast; **—анный** *a.* predicted; (comp.) look-ahead (carry); **—атель** *m.* forecaster; **—ывание** *see* **предсказание; —(ыв)ать** *v.* predict, foretell; forecast.

предсмертный *a.* (before) death; terminal (state), antemortem.

предсошник *m.* (anat.) prevomer, paradoxical bone.

представ/ать *v.* appear; **—имый** *a.* (math.) representable (by or as); **—итель** *m.* representative, one (of); example; species, kind; (faunal or floral) form; **—ительный** *a.* representative; impressive, showy; **—ительство** *n.* representation; **—ительствовать** *v.* represent.

представ/ить *see* **представлять; —ление** *n.* presentation, etc., *see v.*; representation; concept, idea, notion; **—ленный** *a.* presented, etc., *see v.*; **—лять** *v.* present, show, exhibit, display; offer, introduce, submit (plan); represent, describe, depict; be (of interest); constitute (a

threat); **—лять себе** *v.* imagine, visualize, picture, think of (as); **—лять собой** *v.* be; represent, comprise, constitute; **—ляться** *v.* be presented, etc.; seem, appear.

предстартовый *a.* prefiring, prelaunch.

предстарческ/ий *a.* (med.) presenile; **—ое слабоумие** presenile dementia, Alzheimer's disease.

предстательн/ый *a.* (anat.) prostatic; **—ая железа** (anat.) prostate gland.

предстать *v.* appear, come before.

предстепье *n.* (geol.) pre-steppe.

предсто/ять *v.* be imminent, be coming; remain (to); **ему —ит** he has (to); he faces; **—ящее** *n.* future, fate; (math.) coefficient; **—ящий** *a.* future, impending, (forth)coming, ahead.

предсудорожный *a.* (med.) preconvulsive.

предсуществующий *a.* pre-existing.

пред/съездовский *a.* preconference, preconvention; **—тазик** *m.* (zool.) pretarsus; **—тамбур** *m.* fore air lock; **—теча** *m. and f.* forerunner, precursor; **—течка** *f.* (zool.) preheat, pro-oestrus.

предтопок *m.* precombustion chamber, preliminary chamber (of furnace).

предтрахеальный *a.* (anat.) pretracheal.

предубежд/ать *v.*, **—ение** *n.* prejudice; **—ённый** *a.* prejudiced, biased.

предубойный *a.* before slaughter.

предуборочный *a.* preharvest(ing).

предуведом/ить, —лять *v.* (fore)warn, notify, advise; **—ление** *n.* notification, notice, forewarning.

предугад(ыв)ать *v.* predict, foresee.

предузловой *a.* antenodal; preganglionic.

предумышленн/ость *f.* premeditation; **—ый** *a.* premeditated.

предупредительн/ый *a.* preventive, precautionary; alerting, warning (signal); (med.) prophylactic; courteous, attentive; **—ая мера, —ое средство** preventive.

предупредить *see* **предупреждать.**

предупрежд/аемый *a.* preventable; **—ать** *v.* prevent; forestall, anticipate; notify (in advance), warn, caution (against); **—ающий** *a.* preventing, etc., *see v.*; (biol.) sematic (coloration); premonitory (symptoms); precautionary, preventive; **—ающее устройство** warning device, alarm; **—ение** *n.* prevention, preventing, etc., *see v.*; control; **—ение беременности** (med.) contraception; **—ение смерзания** freeze-proofing; **—ённый** *a.* prevented, etc., *see v.*

Предуралье (geog.) Cis-Ural region.

предуральский *a.* Cis-Ural.

предусилитель *m.* preamplifier.

предускорение *n.* preacceleration.

предусм/атривать *v.* provide (for), specify, call (for); foresee, envisage; involve, include, incorporate; **п. возможность** make provision (for), allow (for); **—отренный** *a.* provided, etc., *see v.*; built-in; **—отреть** *see* **предусматривать; —отрительность** *f.* foresight, forethought; prudence; **—отрительный** *a.* foresighted; prudent.

пред/установленный *a.* predetermined, preestablished; **—устье** *n.* pro-estuarine region, region of a lake or sea just outside the estuary of a river; **—утренний** *a.* before dawn, daybreak; **—ушной** *a.* (anat.) pro-otic; **—фаза** *f.* (gen.) prophase; **—фильтр** *m.* prefilter; **—фронтальный** *a.* (meteor.) prefrontal, squall-line; **—фронтальная зона пляжа** shoreface; **—холодильник** *m.* precooler; preliminary condenser, precondenser; **—хрящ** *m.* (embr.) precartilage; **—хрящевой** *a.* prochondial.

пред/центральный *a.* (anat.) precentral; **—чашечный** *a.* (anat.) prepatellar; **—челюстной** *a.* premaxillary; **—чувствие** *n.* premonition.

предшеств/енник *m.* predecessor, forerunner, precursor; **—ие** *n.* precedence; **—овавший** *see* **предшествующий**; **—овать** *v.* precede, forego, forerun; antedate; **—ующий** *a.* preceding, precedent, antecedent, foregoing, prior, previous, former.

предщит *m.* (ent.) prescutum; **п. среднегруди** (ent.) dorsulum, mesonotum.

предъ— *see* **пред—**.

предъяв/итель *m.* bearer; **—ительный** *a.* presenting; **—ить, —лять** *v.* present, produce, show, set forth; place, impose, make (demands); **—ление** *n.* presentation, etc., *see v.*; **по —лении** on sight.

предъядерный *a.* (gen.) prokaryotic.

предыдущий *a.* preceding, foregoing, previous, former, earlier, above; **п. член отношения** (math.) antecedent.

предынфарктный *a.* (med.) pre-infarctate.

пред/ыонизация *f.* pre-ionization; **—ыскажение** *n.* (rad.) pre-emphasis, predistortion; **—ыскание** *n.* preselection; **—ыскатель** *m.* preselector, line switch; **групповой —ыскатель** master switch; **—ыстория** *f.* past history.

предэклампсия *f.* (med.) preeclampsia.

предэкспонен/т *m.* pre-exponential function; **—циальный** *a.* pre-exponential.

преем/ник *m.* successor; **—ственность** *f.* continuity, succession; heredity; **—ственный** *a.* successive; hereditary; **—ство** *n.* succession.

прежде *adv.* before, previously, formerly, heretofore; *prep. gen.* before; **п. всего** first of all, to begin with; primarily, chiefly, mainly; **п. чем** before, prior to, previous to.

преждевременн/о *adv.* prematurely; **—ость** *f.* prematurity; precocity; **—ый** *a.* premature, early; pre—.

прежн/ее *n.* the past; **—ий** *a.* previous, preceding, prior, former, earlier; **по —ему** as before.

презентация *f.* presentation.

презерв/атив *m.* preservative; (med.) condom; **—ация** *f.* preservation; **—ы** *pl.* preserved foods.

прези/дент *m.* president; **—диум** *m.* presidium.

през/ирать *v.* scorn, disdain; **—рение** *n.* contempt; **—реть** *see* **презирать**; **—рительный** *a.* contemptuous.

презумпция *f.* (law) presumption.

преизбыток *m.* superabundance, excess.

преим. *abbr.* **(преимущественно)**.

преимагинальный *a.* (ent.) preimaginal.

преимуществ/енно *adv.* in preference, preeminently; mostly, principally, chiefly, mainly, for the most part; **—енный** *a.* primary; preferred; advantageous; **—енное право** preference; pre-emption; **—о** *n.* advantage, asset, virtue, merit; preference; superiority; privilege; odds in favor; **по —у** *see* **преимущественно**.

преисполн/енный *a.* full, filled; **—ить, —ять** *v.* fill.

прейскурант *m.* price list, price current.

прекан/кроз *m.* (med.) precancrum; **—крозный** *a.* precancerous; **—цер** *m.* precancer.

прекапиллярный *a.* (biol.) precapillary.

прекар/диальный *a.* (anat.) precardiac; **—циноматозный** *a.* (med.) precarcinomatous.

преклонный *a.* advanced (years); **п. возраст** old age.

прекома *f.*, **—тозное состояние** (med.) precoma; **—тозный** *a.* precomatose.

прекордиальный *a.* (anat.) precordial; chest (lead).

прекостальный *a.* (ent.) praecostal.

прекрасн/о *adv.* excellently, very well; *prefix* cal(l)o—, calli— (beautiful); **—оголовчатый** *a.* (bot.) calo-

cephalous; **—окрылый** *a.* calopterous; **—олистный** *a.* calophyllous; **—ый** *a.* excellent, fine, superior; beautiful.

прекра/тившийся *see* **прекращённый**; **—тить, —щать** *v.* discontinue, cease, stop, put a stop (to), terminate, finish, end, break off, cut off, shut off, turn off; close down, shut down; suspend; **—щаться** *v.* discontinue, cease, stop, come to an end, terminate; die away; **—щение** *n.* discontinuance, ceasing, etc., *see v.*; cessation; suspension; (commun.) blackout; **аварийное —щение** (power) failure; **—щение работ, —щение производства** phase-out; **—щённый** *a.* discontinued, etc., *see v.*

прекурсорный *a.* precursory, preceding.

прелактеальный *a.* prelacteal (tooth).

прелест/ный *a.* charming, attractive; **—ь** *f.* charm, allure(ment).

прелиминар/ии *pl.* preliminaries; **—ный** *a.* preliminary.

прелом/имый *see* **преломляемый**; **—итель** *m.* refractor; **—ить** *see* **преломлять.**

преломл/ение *n.* breaking; (phys.) refraction; **двойное п.** (cryst.) double refraction, birefringence; **измеритель —ения** refractometer; **показатель —ения** index of refraction, refractive index; **—ённый** *a.* refracted.

преломл/яемость *f.* refractability, refractivity, refrangibility; **—яемый** *a.* refractable, refrangible; **—ять** *v.* break; refract; diffract, deflect; **—яться** *v.* be broken; be refracted, deflect; **—яющий** *a.* refracting, refractive.

прел/ость *f.* rottenness, putrescence; moldiness; fustiness; (med.) intertrigo; **п. стрелки** (vet.) rotten frog, thrush; **—ый** *a.* rotten; fusty; **—ь** *f.* rot, decayed spot; mold(iness); (bot.) sclerotinia.

премаксиллярный *a.* premaxillary (bone).

премейотический *a.* (gen.) premeiotic.

прементум *m.* (ent.) prementum.

премиальный *a.* premium; bonus.

преминуть: не п. *v.* not fail to.

премиров/анный *a.* prize (cattle, etc.); rewarded; **—ать** *v.* award a prize or bonus.

премитотический *a.* (biol.) premitotic.

премия *f.* premium, prize, bonus; **п.-надбавка** supplementary bonus.

премоляр *m.* (anat.) premolar tooth.

премутаци/онный *a.*, **—я** *f.* premutation.

пренатальный *a.* prenatal.

пренебре/гаемый *a.* negligible; **—гать** *v.* disregard, ignore, overlook, neglect; discard, omit; scorn (advice, etc.); **—гая** *pr. ger.* disregarding, etc., *see v.*; barring; **—жение** *n.* disregard, neglect; disdain; **—жимо малый, —жимый** *a.* negligible; **—чь** *see* **пренебрегать.**

прение *n.* rotting, putrefaction; sweating; stewing.

прениламин *m.* (pharm.) prenylamine.

пренит/ен *m.* (chem.) prehnitene, 1,2,3,4-tetramethylbenzene; **—иловый** *a.* prehnitilic (acid); **—овый** *a.* prehnitic (acid).

прения *pl.* debate; discussion.

преоблад/ание *n.* predominance, prevalence; (commun.) bias; **—ать** *v.* (pre)dominate, prevail; **—ающий** *a.* (pre)dominant, prevailing, preponderant.

преобра/жать *v.* transform, change; **—жающая** *f.* (math.) transform; **—жение** *n.* transformation.

преобраз *m.* (math.) inverse image; **—ить** *see* **преображать**; **—ование** *n.* transformation, etc., *see v.*; (math.) transform; processing, reduction (of information); conversion; **волновое —ование** (wave guides) mode conversion; **—ованный** *a.* transformed, etc., *see v.*;

—**ованная функция** (math.) transform; —**ователь** *m.* transformer, converter, inverter, changer; (elec. comm.) transducer; (image) translator; —**ователь цикла Ранкина** Rankine cycle engine; —**ователь частоты** frequency converter; **измерительный** —**ователь** transducer; —**овательный** *a.* transforming, etc., *see v.*; converter (substation); —**ов(ыв)ать** *v.* transform, convert, change, turn (into), modify, alter; translate; transpose (equation, etc.); transduce; reorganize, reform; process, reduce (information); —**ующий** *a.* transforming, etc., *see v.*; transfer (function).

преодол/е(ва)ние *n.* overcoming, etc., *see v.*; passage; —**е(ва)ть** *v.* overcome, surmount, cross, get over, master, meet, defeat; negotiate (curve); clear (obstruction); —**имый** *a.* surmountable.

преостный *a.* (anat.) preglenoid.

препакт-бетон *m.* prepact concrete.

препарат *m.* preparation, compound; (micros.) specimen; (med.) drug; —**ивный** *a.* preparative; —**(ив)ная соль** preparing salt (sodium stannate); —**одержатель** *m.* mounting screen (in electron microscope); —**ор** *m.* lab assistant.

препар/ирование *n.* preparation; —**ировать** *v.* prepare, make; (med.) dissect; cut a section; —**ировка** *f.*, —**ировочный** *a.* preparation; —**овальный, овочный** *a.* dissecting (instruments); —**овочная** *f.* specimen-preparing laboratory.

препилорический *a.* (anat.) prepyloric.

препинание *n.* punctuation.

препод/авание *n.* instruction, teaching; —**аватель** *m.* teacher, instructor; —**авательский** *a.* teacher's, teaching; —**авать** *v.* teach, instruct, lecture.

преподн/есение *n.* presentation; —**ести, —осить** *v.* present, offer.

преполлекс *m.* (anat.) prepollex.

препона *f.* difficulty, hindrance, obstacle.

препотен/тность *f.* (gen.) hereditary capacity; prepotency (domination of characteristics); —**ция** *f.* prepotency.

препрег *m.* prepreg, partially cured impregnated fabric.

препринт *m.* preprint, advance sheets.

препрово/дительный *a.* accompanying; —**дить, —ждать** *v.* forward, send, dispatch, convey.

препуци/альные железы (med.) Tyson's glands, preputial glands; —**й** *m.* (anat.) prepuce.

препятств/ие *n.* obstacle, impediment, difficulty, obstruction, barrier, hindrance, drawback, deterrent, handicap; check, stop; (chem.) inhibition; **облако —ия** crest cloud; **условное п.** (av.) screen; —**овать** *v.* prevent, stop, inhibit, obstruct, hinder, impede, hamper, block; interfere, interrupt, oppose, cross; —**ующий** *a.* inhibiting; —**ующий росту** growth-inhibiting.

прерв/анно *adv., prefix* abruptly; —**аннопористый** *a.* (bot.) abruptly pinnate; —**анный** *a.* interrupted, etc., *see* **прерывать**; discontinuous; rejected (takeoff); —**ать** *see* **прерывать.**

прередукци/онный *a.*, —**я** *f.* (gen.) prereduction.

прерия *f.* prairie.

прерогатива *f.* prerogative.

прерыв *m.*, —**ание** *n.* interrupt(ion), interrupting, etc., *see v.*; break, discontinuity; —**ание беременности** abortion; —**атель** *m.* interrupter; (contact) breaker, cut-out, switch; (instruments) chopper; disconnector; —**атель-распределитель** *m.* distributor and contact-breaker unit; —**ать** *v.* interrupt, break (off), intercept, stop, discontinue, cut off, cut out, switch off; (elec.) chop (a signal); suspend; —**ающий** *a.* interrupting, etc., *see v.*; disruptive; make-and-break, chopper (disk);

—**ающий контакт** chopper; —**ающийся** *a.* intermittent, discontinuous.

прерыв/истопористый *a.* (bot.) interruptedly pinnate; —**исторядный** *a.* interruptedly serial; —**истость** *see* **прерывность**; —**истый** *see* **прерывный**; —**ность** *f.* intermittency; discontinuity; —**ный** *a.* discontinuous, noncontinuous, interrupted, intermittent, jerky; gusty (wind); broken (line); (math.) discrete; —**ного действия** intermittent; —**чатый** *see* **прерывный.**

пресакральный *a.* (anat.) presacral (nerve).

пресби— *prefix* presby— (old; old age); —**опия** *f.* (med.) presbyopia.

пресекать *see* **пресечь.**

пресен *sh. m. of* **пресный.**

пресенильный *a.* presenile.

пресервы *pl.* canned foods.

пресеч/ение *n.* stopping, etc., *see v.*; —**ённый** *a.* stopped, etc., *see v.*; —**ь** *v.* stop, suppress, interrupt, cut short.

пресистол/а *f.* (physiol.) presystole; —**ический** *a.* presystolic.

прескверный *a.* very bad.

прескутум *see* **предщит.**

преслед/ование *n.* pursuit, persecution; (law) prosecution; —**овать** *v.* pursue, chase, follow; persecute; prosecute; —**ующий** *a.* pursuing.

пресмык/аться *v.* creep, crawl, —**ающиеся** *pl.* (zool.) reptiles.

пресн/оводность *f.* freshness (of water); (ichth.) fresh-water phase (time spent in fresh water before going to sea); —**оводный** *a.* fresh-water, limnetic; —**ость** *f.* freshness; insipidity, flatness (of taste); —**осухой** *a.* air-dried; —**ый** *a.* fresh; insipid, flat, unflavored; unleavened (bread).

пресперматида *f.* (zool.) prespermatid, secondary spermatocyte.

пресс *m.* press; (agr.) baler; **склеечный п.** splicing machine; —**а** *f.* (journalism) press; **п.-автоклав** *m.* autoclave press; —**борд** *m.* pressboard; **п.-изделие** *n.* molded article; **п.-композиция** *f.* molded material; **п.-котёл** *m.* autoclave press; **п.-литьё** *n.* die-casting; **п.-маслёнка** *f.* grease gun; pressure lubricator; **п.-масса** *f.*, **п.-материал** *m.* molding material.

прессо/вальный *a.* press(ing), molding; (agr.) baling; —**вальщик** *m.* presser; baler; —**вание** *n.* pressing, etc., *see v.*; (met.) extrusion; (agr.) baling; (plastics) compression molding; **горячее —вание** hot pressing; —**вание выдавливанием** extrusion; —**ванный** *a.* pressed, etc., *see v.*; compression-molded; —**ванный картон** pressboard; —**ванные дрожжи** yeast cake; —**вать** *v.* press; mold; squeeze, extrude; compress, compact (powder); bale; —**вка** *f.*, —**вочный** *a. see* **прессование**; —**вщик** *m.* presser; pressman; —**выдувной** *a.* (glass) press and blow; —**вый** *a. of* **пресс**; force(d), drive (fit); —**рецептор** *m.* (physiol.) pressoreceptor.

пресс/-папье *n.* paper weight; —**пат** *m.* (paper) pulp-drying machine; **п.-подборщик** *m.* (agr.) pickup baler; **п.-порошок** *m.* molding powder; —**уемость** *f.* moldability; (metal powders) compactability; —**уемый** *a.* moldable, extrudable; molded; extruded; —**утяжка** *f.* (met.) pipe, extrusion defect; —**ующий** *a.* press(ing); molding; extrusion; injection (plunger); —**фильтр** *m.* press filter; —**форма** *f.* (press) mold; —**шпан** *m.* pressboard.

престабитоль *m.* Prestabitol (detergent).

престарел/ость *f.* old age; —**ый** *a.* very old, ancient.

престиж *m.* prestige.

преступ/ать, —ить *v.* transgress, overstep, pass; **—ление** *n.* crime, offense; **—ник** *m.*, **—ница** *f.*, **—ный** *a.* criminal.

пресы/тить, —щать *v.* satiate; supersaturate; surcharge.

пресыщен/ие *n.* satiation; supersaturation; **—ность** *f.* satiety, surfeit; **—ный** *a.* satiated; supersaturated.

прёт *pr.* 3 *sing. of* **переть**.

претарсус *see* **предлапка**.

претвор/ить, —ять *v.* transform, change, transmute; translate; **—ять в дело** put into practice, carry out.

претен/довать *v.* pretend, claim, lay claim (to); **—зия** *f.* pretension, claim; grievance.

претерпе(ва)ть *v.* undergo, experience, endure, bear, suffer; **п. гидрацию** be hydrated.

претибиальн/ый *a.* (anat.) pretibial; **—ая лихорадка** pretibial fever, Fort Bragg fever.

претоксемия *f.* (med.) incipient toxemia.

преть *v.* sweat; simmer, stew; rot.

преувелич/ение *n.* exaggeration, overstatement, overestimation; **—енный** *a.* exaggerated; **—ивать, —ить** *v.* exaggerate, overstate.

преуменьш/ать, —ить *v.* minimize, understate, underestimate; **—ение** *n.* understatement; **—енный, —ённый** *a.* minimal.

преумножение *n.* augmentation, increase.

преуспе/вать *v.* succeed, prosper; flourish, thrive; **—вающий** *a.* successful, flourishing; **—ть** *see* **преуспевать**.

преференциальный *a.* preferential.

префикс *m.* (gram.) prefix.

префильтр *m.* first filter, coarse filter.

преформ/ационный *a.* preformistic; **—ация** *f.* (embr.) preformation; **—изм** *m.*, **теория —изма** (gen.) preformation theory; **—ированный** *a.* preformed; **—ист** *m.* preformationist.

префронтальный *a.* prefrontal.

преход/имость *f.* temporary nature; **—ить** *v.* pass; **—ный** *a.* transition (metals); **—ящий** *a.* passing, transient, temporary.

пре/хондральный *a.* (anat.) prechondral; **—хордальный** *a.* (anat.) prechordal.

прецедент *m.* precedent.

процесс/ионный *a.* precessional; **—ировать** *v.* precess; **—ия** *f.* precession.

прецизионн/ость *f.* precision, accuracy; **—ый** *a.* precision; precise.

преципит/ат *m.* precipitate; spec. dicalcium phosphate (fertilizer); **белый п.** white precipitate, ammoniated mercuric chloride; **—ационный** *a.*, **—ация** *f.* precipitation; **—ин** *m.* precipitin; **—иноген** *m.* precipitinogen; **—ировать** *v.* precipitate.

прецирроз *m.* (med.) precirrhosis.

прешпан *m.* pressboard.

преэклампсия *f.* (med.) preeclampsia.

Пржевальск/ий Prz(h)ewalski; **лошадь —ого** Prz(h)ewalski's horse (*Equus przewalskii*).

при *prep. prepos.* in, at, by, near; in the presence of; (up)on; by (means of); when, while, during, under; with; attached to, affiliated with; when suffering from (a disease); in case of; **п. анализе** on analysis; **п. вращении** as . . . rotates; **п. всём том** for all that; **п. нагревании** (up)on heating, on being heated, when heated; **п. нём** in his presence; **п. определённых условиях** under certain conditions; **п. прочих условиях** other conditions being. . .; **п. цифре** followed by a figure; **п. этом** in this case, here; at the same time, simultaneously; as this takes place; in so doing, in the

process; therewith; **напряжение п. сжатии** compression stress.

при— *prefix* ad—, toward; at, in the region of, in the vicinity of, near; sub— (under, less than normal); par(a)— (at the side of); **—азовский** *a.* (geog.) Azov Sea coastal (region).

приакантовые *pl.* (ichth.) bigeyes (*Priacanthidae*).

приальпийский *a.* alpestrine, subalpine.

Приамурье Amur river region.

прианодный *a.* anolyte (layer); near the anode.

приапизм *m.* (med.) priapism.

приапул *m.* (zool.) Priapulus.

Приаралье *n.*, **приаральский** *a.* Aral Sea coastal region.

приарктический *a.* subarctic.

приатлантический *a.* Atlantic coast.

прибав/ить *see* **прибавлять**; **—ка** *f.*, **—ление** *n.* increase, addition, supplement, annex, appendix; allowance; (com.) bonus, raise (in salary); **с —лением лимоннокислых солей** (chem.) citrated; **с —лением щавелевокислых солей** oxalated; **—ляемое** *n.* (math.) addend; **—лять** *v.* add, increase, augment, widen, lengthen, extend; **—лять на** allow for; **—ляться** *v.* increase; **—очный** *a.* additional; surplus; after—; **—очный труд** surplus labor.

Прибайкалье (geog.) Baikal region.

прибалтийский *a.* (geog.) Baltic.

Прибалтика (geog.) Baltic (Sea) region.

прибе/гать, —гнуть *v.* have recourse (to), resort (to), apply (to); fall back (on); **—гать, —жать** *v.* run (up to), come running; **не —гая** without recourse (to); **—жище** *n.* refuge, shelter, sanctuary.

приберегать *v.* save, keep, reserve.

прибереж/ёт *fut.* 3 *sing. of* **приберечь**; **—ный** *see* **прибрежный**; **—ье** *see* **прибрежье**.

приберёт *fut.* 3 *sing. of* **прибирать**.

приберечь *see* **приберегать**.

прибив/ание *n.*, **—ка** *f.* fastening, etc., *see v.*; **—ать** *v.* fasten, fix, attach; nail (on); knock down, lodge (grain); **—ной** *a.* fastened, nailed (on).

прибирать *v.* put in order, clean up; **п. к рукам** appropriate, claim; pilfer.

прибит/ый *a.* fastened, etc., *see* **прибивать**; **—ь** *see* **прибивать**.

прибл. *abbr.* (**приблизительно**).

приближ/ать *v.* draw nearer, approximate, approach; make earlier; **—аться** *v.* (draw) near, approximate, approach, converge; **не —аться** keep away (from); **—ающийся** *a.* approaching, forthcoming.

приближен/ие *n.* approximation, approach(ing), drawing near; **в первом —ии** roughly, as a first approximation; **датчик —ия** proximity sensor; **метод —ия** approximation method; **метод последовательных —ий** trial and error method; convergence method.

приближённо *adv.* approximately; **—околичественный** *a.* semiquantitative; **—ость** *f.* proximity, vicinity, nearness; approximateness, (degree of) approximation; **—ый** *a.* approximate(d), rough, coarse; close; approximation (method).

приблизительно *adv.* approximately, about, around, roughly, in the neighborhood of, in the vicinity of; **—ость** *f.* approximateness; approximation; **—ый** *a.* approximate, rough.

приблизить *see* **приближать**.

прибой *m.* surf, breakers, swash; **—ный** *a.* of **прибой**.

приболеть *v.* be a little sick, ail.

приболотный *a.* near a swamp.

прибор *m.* instrument, apparatus, equipment, appliance, unit; device, mechanism, implement; set, outfit; gear;

—ер, —or, e.g., **п. для испытания** tester; **п. для измерения, измерительный п.** meter; **оборудованный —ами** a. instrumented; **по —ам** instrument (flying); **погрешность —a** instrumental error; **регистрирующий п.** recorder; plotter; **с измерительными —ами, снабжён —ами** instrumented; **установка —ов** instrumentation.

пребореальный a. (meteor.) subboreal, very cold.

приборка f. putting in order, clean-up.

прибор/ный a. of **прибор**; instrument(al); instrumentation (equipment); **—ная доска** instrument panel; **—остроение** n., **—остроительный** a. instrument making.

прибортовой a. near the side of (a boat).

прибор-указатель m. detection instrument.

прибранный a. put in order.

прибрасывать v. throw on (more), add.

прибрать see **прибирать**.

прибреж/ник m. (bot.) shoreweed (*Litorella*); **—ники** pl. (ent.) shore bugs (*Saldidae*); **—ница** f. (bot.) Aeluropus; **—номорской** a. coastal; **—ный** a. littoral, coastal, near shore, offshore; (naut.) inshore; neritic, tidal (marsh); riparian; **—ная мушка** (ent.) shore fly (*Ephydra*); **—ная полоса** strand, coastal strip; **—ье** n. coast, shore.

прибросить see **прибрасывать**.

прибудет fut. 3 sing. of **прибыть**.

прибуксировать v. tow in.

прибыв/ание n. increase, rise, rising; **—ать** v. increase; rise; arrive, come; wax (of moon); **—ающий** a. increasing, etc., see v.; waxing (moon).

Прибылова острова Pribilof Islands.

прибылой a. risen (water); (zool.) this year's (brood).

прибыль f. profit, gain; increase, rise; **—ность** f. profitableness; **—ный** a. of **прибыль**; profitable, lucrative; commercial.

прибыт/ие n. arrival; **—ь** see **прибывать**.

прибьёт fut. 3 sing. of **прибить**.

приваживать v. bait, lure.

привал m. halt; approach; (naut.) mooring; **—ивание пластов** (turning and) leaning furrow slices against each other by a plow; **—и(ва)ть** v. lean, rest (against); heap up; come, arrive, reach, approach; (naut.) come alongside; moor; **—ьный** a. mooring; **—ьный брус** (naut.) fender (guard).

привар see **приваривание**; **—енный** a. welded (on); **—ивание** n. welding (on); adhesion; **—и(ва)ть** v. weld (on); cook some more; **—и(ва)ться** v. adhere; **—ка** f. welding; adhesion; **—ной** a. welding, welded.

привар/ок m., **—очный** a. cooked food, hot meals; provisions.

приведени/е n. bringing, etc., see **приводить**; adduction; (math.) reduction; **температура —я** reference temperature.

приведённ/ый a. brought, led, etc., see **приводить**; given, shown; relative, adjusted (unit); derived; **п. центр** reduction point; **—ая величина выхода** (aut.) effective output; **—ая вязкость** reduced viscosity; **—ая чувствительность** factor of merit (of measuring instruments); **—ое О-образно колено** (anat.) bowleg.

привезённый a. brought (from), etc., see **привозить**.

привезти see **привозить**.

привёл past m. sing. of **привести**.

привенчик m. (bot.) corona, paracorolla.

привередливый a. demanding, fastidious, squeamish.

привержен/ец m. adherent, follower; **—ность** f. adherence; devotion; **—ный** a. attached; devoted, loyal.

привер/нуть, —теть see **привёртывать**.

привёрт/ка f. screwing, etc., see v.; **—ный** a. screwed on, screw; **—ывание** see **привёртка**; **—ывать** v. screw, tighten, clamp, fasten; turn down (flame); turn in.

привес m. gain in weight; overweight; **—ить** see **привешивать**; **—ка** f. hanging; increase (in weight); pendant; **—ки** pl. appendices; **—ной** a. hanging; **—ок** m. addition; overweight; pendant; appendage, appendix.

привести see **приводить**.

привет m. welcome; regards; **—ливый** a. friendly; **—ствовать** v. greet, welcome.

привешивать v. append, hang, suspend; make up the weight.

привив/ание n. grafting; inoculation, etc., see v.; **—ать** v. graft; (cryst.) inoculate, seed; (med.) inoculate, vaccinate; acclimate, accustom (to); twist together; **—аться** v. be grafted; take; **—ка** see **прививание**; graft; **—ка в корень** root grafting; **—ка в приклад(ку)**, **—ка сближением** (hort.) inarching; **полимеризация —кой** graft polymerization; **—ной** a. grafted; **—ок** m. graft, scion; **—очный** a. grafting; inoculating.

привиден/ие n. apparition, ghost; **—ьевые** pl. (ent.) Phasmodea.

привилег/ированный a. privileged, licensed; **—ия** f. privilege, exemption, license.

привин/тить see **привинчивать**; **—ченный** a. screwed on; **—чивание** n. screwing on; **—чивать** v. screw on (or to).

привит/ие see **прививание**; **—ый** a. grafted; graft (polymer); **—ь** see **прививать**.

привкус m. (after) taste.

привле/кательный a. attractive, alluring; **—кать** v. attract, draw, pull; arouse (interest); recruit, enlist; **—кающий** a. attracting, etc., see v.; **—кающие средства** (insect) lures; **—чение** n. attraction, drawing, pulling; **—чённый** a. attracted, etc., see v.; **—чь** see **привлекать**.

привн/ести, —осить v. introduce; **—ос** m. introduction, addition.

привод m. bringing; (av.) homing; (mach.) drive, gear; control (linkage); (brake) control; actuator; **п. от вала** shaft drive; **оборудованный —ом** a. powered, driven (by); **паровой п.** steam drive; **передача —ом** gear transmission; **ремённый п.** belt drive; **с —ом** driven by; **с —ом от мотора** motor-operated; **с механическим —ом** power-driven, power-operated; **с ножным приводом** pedal-operated; **с ремённым —ом** belt-driven; **с ручным —ом** hand-operated, hand-driven; **червячный п.** worm gear.

приводимый a. driven; reducible; cited (as an example); **п. здесь** accompanying; **п. мотором** motor-operated, motor-driven.

приводить v. bring, lead, direct; cause, give rise (to), result (in); (mach.) drive; quote, cite, refer, list, give, report; illustrate, depict, display, exhibit; adduce, bring forward; correct; (math.) reduce; set (in motion); put (in practice); (physiol.) adduct; **п. в действие** actuate, trigger, start; **п. к масштабу** scale; **п. к тому, что** mean, signify that; **—ся** v. be brought, be led, etc.; be powered (by); chance, happen; **—ся в состояние непригодности** be rendered unusable.

приводка f. (printing) registration.

приводнение n. water landing, splashdown.

приводн/ой a. driving, drive; power-driven, power-operated; supply; homing (radar); **п. вал** drive shaft; **п. механизм** driving gear; **п. насос** power pump; **п. шкив** driver, driving pulley; **—ая цепь** sprocket chain, chain drive.

приводняться *v.* land on water, splash down.

приводящ/ий *a.* bringing, etc., *see* **приводить**; (physiol.) adducent, adducting; **—ая мышца** (anat.) adductor; **—ая пора** ostium (in sponges).

привоз *m.* bringing, supply, delivery, shipment; import(ation); **—ить** *v.* bring, convey, deliver; import; **—ной, —ный** *a.* imported; delivered.

привой *m.* (bot.) graft, scion.

привокзальный *a.* at or near the station.

приволакивать *see* **приволоч(ит)ь.**

приволжский *a.* Volga.

Приволжье Volga region.

приволоч(ит)ь *v.* drag (over, to), haul.

привол/е *n.* large, open space; spaciousness; freedom; **—ный** *a.* extensive, wide; free.

приворот *m.* (bot.) cocklebur(r) (*Agrimonia*); **—ный** *a.* at, by or near the gate.

привратник *m.* gate keeper; porter; (elec.) door opener; (anat.) pylorus; **—овый** *a.* pyloric.

привск/акивать, —акнуть, —очить *v.* jump up; start.

привулканизация *f.* direct vulcanization.

привходящий *a.* attendant; supplementary.

привы/кание *n.* getting accustomed, acclimatization; habituation; **—кать, —кнуть** *v.* get accustomed (to), become used (to); become acclimated; **—чка** *f.* habit, custom, practice; **—чный** *a.* habitual, customary; recurrent, persistent.

привяда/ние *n.* wilting; **—ть** *v.* wilt slightly.

привяз/анность *f.* attachment; affection (for); **—анный** *a.* attached, fastened; bound, tethered, leashed; selective (species); tied, etc., *see v.*; **—ать(ся)** *see* **привязывать(ся)**; **—ка** *f.* tying, etc., *see v.*; attachment; connection, coupler, tie(-in); (TV) clamper; (gram.) conjunction; survey(ing); **—ной** *a.* tied, tying, etc., *see v.*; ground (cable); captive (balloon); **—чивый** *a.* affectionate; persistent, annoying; **—ывание** *n.* tying, etc., *see v.*; **—ывать** *v.* tie, bind, lash, restrain, leash; fasten, attach; (surv.) refer, fix; **—ываться** *v.* be tied, etc; become attached (to) (radio, radar) lock on; keep after, bother; correlate; **—ь** *f.* tie, band, strap, string, rope, leash, tether; stanchion (in cow barn); (anat.) retinaculum; **на —и** tethered.

привяли(ва)ть *v.* cure lightly, make into jerky.

привянуть *see* **привядать.**

пригар *m.*, **—ина** *f.* (forging) overheating, burning(-on); burn-on, fusion (of ore); sticking; pickup (of molding sand); **—ь** *f.* burned taste.

пригво/ждать, —здить *v.* nail down.

пригибать *v.* bend down, bow.

пригла/дить, —живать *v.* smooth down.

пригла/сительный *a.* inviting; **—сительная связь** paging system; **—сить, —шать** *v.* invite, ask, bid; call (a doctor, etc.); hire; **—шение** *n.* invitation; (job) offer.

приглуб/ость *f.* great depth; **—ый** *a.* very deep.

приглуш/ать, —ить *v.* damp down, choke (fire); suppress, muffle, deaden (sound).

пригляд/еть, —ывать *v.* look after, attend (to); **—ываться** *v.* look attentively (at), scrutinize; familiarize oneself.

пригн/анность *f.* fitting together; **—анный** *a.* fitted, etc., *see* **пригонять**; ground in; **—анная деталь** mate; **—ать** *see* **пригонять.**

пригнуть *see* **пригибать.**

пригов/аривать *v.* sentence; repeat; **—ор** *m.* sentence, verdict, decision; **—орённый** sentenced.

пригод/иться *v.* be of use, be useful; **—ность** *f.* usefulness, fitness, suitability, adaptability; **—ный** *a.* useful,

fit, suitable, adaptable, applicable, adequate, good (for); **—ный для** suited (for, to); rated; oriented; **—ный для использования** serviceable; **—ный для использования в космических условиях** space-rated; **—ный для использования человеком** man-rated; **—ный для разработки** workable; **не —ный** unsuitable.

приголовок *m.* first runnings.

пригон *m.* driving; shed, corral.

пригон/ка *f.* fitting, etc., *see v.*; fit; adjustment, alignment; **п. частей** assemblage, assembly; **—очный** *a. of* **пригонка**; **—щик** *m.* fitter, adjuster; **—ять** *v.* fit (in, on, together); match, align; adjust, adapt; work in, grind in, run in; join(t); reseat (valve); bring in, drive (livestock).

пригораживать *v.* enclose; build on.

пригор/ание *n.* scorching, etc., *see v.*; sticking, seizing (of piston rings); **—ать** *v.* scorch, burn; stick, gum up; seize by fusion; **—евший, —елый** *a.* scorched, etc., *see v.*; sticky (piston); empyreumatic, tarry; **—еть** *see* **пригорать.**

пригород *m.* suburb; **—ка** *f.* enclosure; annex; **—ный** *a.* suburban; (tel.) local.

пригорок *m.* hillock, knoll, elevation.

пригоршня *f.* handful.

пригот/авливать *v.* prepare, make ready, provide, arrange; make, produce; **—овительный** *a.* preparatory; *suffix* -processing; **—овить** *see* **приготавливать**; **—овление** *n.* preparation, etc., *see v.*; arrangement; **без —овления** extempore, on the spur of the moment; **—овленный** *a.* prepared, etc., *see v.*; **—овленный к** ready for; **—овленный на** made with; **—овлять** *see* **приготавливать.**

приграничный *a.* (near the) boundary.

пригребать *v.* rake up; row in.

пригрев *m.* warming up; warm spot; **—ание** *n.* warming up; **—ать** *v.* warm up.

пригрести *v.* rake up; row in.

пригрет/ый *a.* warmed up; **—ь** *v.* warm up.

пригрозить *v.* threaten, menace.

придавать *v.* give, add, confer, lend, impart; attach, adjoin; build on; **п. жёсткость** stiffen; **п. форму** form, shape, fashion.

придав/ить, —ливать *v.* press, squeeze; **—ленный** *a.* pressed, squeezed.

придан/ие *n.* giving, etc., *see* **придавать**; **—ный** *a.* given, added, etc., *see* **придавать.**

прида/тки *pl.* (anat.) adnexa, appendages, caeca.

придаток *m.* appendage; appendix; caecum; addition, supplement; adjunct, accessory; **п. привеска яичка** (anat.) paradidymis; **п. семенника, п. яичка** epididymis; **п. яичника** epoophoron; **верхний п. мозга** (zool.) epiphysis cerebri; **нижний п. мозга** hypophysis cerebri.

придат/очный *a.* additional, accessory; (bot.) adventive; (biol.) adventitious, secondary (root); appendicular; **п. орган** (anat.) appendix; **п. язычок** (zool.) paraglossa; (ent.) superlingua; **—ть** *see* **придавать**; **—ча** *f.* addition.

придви/гать *v.* move, draw, pull (nearer), bring closer; **—гаться** *v.* draw near, approach; **—жной** *a.* movable; set, adjusting (screw); **—нутый** *a.* moved, etc., *see v.*; **—нуть(ся)** *see* **придвигать(ся).**

придел/ать *see* **приделывать**; **—ка** *f.*, **—ывание** *n.* joining, etc., *see v.*; addition; **—ывать** *v.* join, add; fasten; put (on); adapt, fit.

придерж/анный *a.* held, etc., *see v.*; **—ивание** *n.* holding, etc., *see v.*; **—(ив)ать** *v.* hold (back, down), clamp (down); **—(ив)аться** v. hold, keep (to), adhere, follow; confine oneself (to); **—ка** see **придерживание**; clamp; stripper.

придёт fut. 3 sing. of **прийти**.

придир/аться v. find fault (with), nag; quibble; **—ка** f. frivolous objection, quibble; **—ки** pl. carping, nagging; **—чивый** a. overcritical.

приднепровный a. by or along the Dnieper.

Приднепровье Dnieper region.

придонн/ый a. (biol.) bottom-dwelling, benth(on)ic, demersal; **—ое растение** benthophyte.

придорожн/ый a. roadside, viatic; **—ая полоса** shoulder (of road).

придраться see **придираться**.

придум/анный a. devised, etc., see v.; **—ать** see **придумывать**; **—ка** f. invention; **—щик** m. inventive person; **—ывание** n. devising, etc., see v.; **—ывать** v. devise, contrive, think (of, up), invent, find; develop; **—ываться** v. come (to mind).

придушить v. choke, suppress, smother.

придыха/ние n. (linguistics) aspiration; **—тельный** a. aspirate.

придя pr. ger. of **прийти**.

приез/д m. arrival, coming; **—жать** v. arrive, come; **—жающий** a. arriving; m. newcomer, visitor; **—жий** a. on tour; m. nonresident, visitor.

приём m. reception, receiving, acceptance; (rad.) end of transmission, "over"; admission, intake; mode, way, manner, technique, method, (method of) procedure, process, dose (of medicine); (laboratory) step, run; (mil.) drill; (chem.) absorption; suffix practice, method; **п. калорий** caloric intake; **амбулаторный п.** (mil.) sick parade; **дежурный п.** (rad.) listening watch, standby (status); **ружейный п.** rifle drill; **—ы** pl. procedure; measures, steps; **акт —а** acceptance report; **в несколько —ов** in stages, by series; **первого —а** primary.

приёмистост/ь f. intake capacity, injectivity; response, responsiveness; (engine) pickup, acceleration; **автомат —и** automatic acceleration control; **клапан —и** acceleration control valve.

приём/ка f. reception, acceptance, adoption; inspection; takeover, take-up.

прием/лемость f. acceptability; **—лемый** a. acceptable, admissible, tolerable.

приёмн/ая f. reception room, waiting room; **—ик** m. receiver, (receiving) vessel, collector, receptacle, container, flask, tank, reservoir; hopper; (elec.) transducer; (radiation) detector; receiving center; radio (set); (chem., med.) acceptor; (comp.) stacker; (mil.) ammunition tray; **—ик воздушных давлений** Pitot tube, air-velocity tube; **—ик-передатчик** m. (radar) transponder; **—о-передающий** a. transceiving; **—о-усилительный** a. receiver-amplifier.

приёмн/ый a. reception, receiving, collecting, take-up, pick-up; adopted, adoptive, step—, foster; acceptance (certificate, test); office (hours); drawing-in, take-in (roller); suction (chamber, valve of pump); mixing (nozzle); (telev.) picture (tube); **п. калибр** purchase inspection gage; **п. покой** (med.) casualty ward; **п. отец** stepfather, foster father; **п. резервуар** holding pond or lagoon; **—ая воронка** (feed) hopper; charging hopper; **—ое отверстие** inlet, intake; **—ое устройство** intake.

приёмо/ответчик m. (radar) transponder; **—передаточный** a. (rad.) two-way; **—передатчик** m. transceiver, transmitter-receiver, two-way radio; **—сдаточный** a. acceptance (certificate, test); **—указатель** m.

finder; **—чно-технический** a. warranty (test); **—чный** a. receiving, accepting, acceptance (certificate, test).

приём-передача: переключатель п. transmit-receive switch, polyplexer.

приёмщик m. receiver, inspector.

приёмы pl. of **приём**.

приехать see **приезжать**.

прижат/ие see **прижимание**; **—о** adv. (bot.) appressedly; **—о-волосистый** a. appressedly-pilose; **—ый** a. pressed (down), etc., see **прижимать**; (bot.) appressed; low-altitude (beam); **—ь** see **прижимать**.

прижечь see **прижигать**.

прижив/аемость f. adaptability; **—аемый** a. adaptable; **—ание** n. acclimatization; (bot.) rooting; **—аться** v. get accustomed, get used (to), become acclimated; take root; adapt (to); naturalize, become as if native; **—иться** see **приживляться**; **—ление** n. fusion, coalescence, accretion; adaptation; **—лённый** a. fused, etc., see **приживляться**; **—ляться** v. grow together, fuse, coalesce.

прижиг/ание n. searing, cauterization; **—атель** m. (med.) cautery, cauterant; branding iron; **—ательный** a. (med.) caustic; **—ать** v. sear, cauterize, scorch; brand; **—ающий** a. searing, cauterizing, caustic; **—ающее средство** caustic; cauterant.

прижизненн/о adv. in vivo; **—ый** a. in one's lifetime, intravital; vital, living.

прижим see **прижимание**; clamp, clip; holder; tightening device, screw press; **—ание** n. pressing (down, against), etc., see v.; **—ать** v. press (down, against), force, squeeze (against); hold (down, up); tighten, clamp (down); **—ать к земле** (mil.) pin down; **—ающий** a. pressing (down, against), etc., see v.; **—ка** see **прижимание**; pressure; **—ный** a. of **прижим**; clamp(ing); hold-down; **—ная лапка** (hold-down) clip; **—ная планка** cleat; **—ное кольцо** snap ring, retaining ring.

прижиться see **приживаться**.

прижмёт fut. 3 sing. of **прижать**.

прижмурить v. squint, peer nearsightedly.

приз m. prize.

призабойный a. (petrol.) critical (zone), well-bore face; (min.) (at the) face.

призв/ание n. vocation, calling; **—анный** a. called (to, upon); for the purpose (of); **—ать** see **призывать**.

призвук m. additional sound.

приземистый a. thickset, squat, stocky, compact; (bot.) low-growing.

призем/ление n. (av.) landing; touchdown; (mil.) dropping flat, hitting the deck; **—лённый** a. landed; down; **—лившийся** a. fallen (rocket); **—лить(ся); —лять(ся)** v. land, touch ground; **—ной, —ный** a. surface, (near the) ground.

призма f. prism; knife-edge (bearing); (anat.) prisma; **упорная п.** shell (of an earth dam); **—ы** pl. prismata.

призматическ/ий a. prismatic; **—ая опора** knife-edge (bearing).

призм/атоид m. (geom.) prismatoid; **—енный** a. prism(atic); **—оид** m., **—оидный** a. prismoid; **—ообразный** a. prismoid(al); **—очка** dim. of **призма**.

признавать v. acknowledge, recognize, admit, own; spot, identify; **—ся** v. be acknowledged; confess, admit.

признак m. sign, indication, symptom, mark, index, criterion; feature, characteristic, attribute, trait, property; vestige, trace; (comp.) character; tag, marker, sentinel; **п. состояния** (comp.) flag; **—и** pl. of **признак**; evidence, pattern; **служить —ом** v. indicate, denote.

призн/ание n. acknowledgement, recognition, acceptance; **по общему —анию** it is generally acknowledged; it is recognized as one of; **—анный** *a.* acknowledged, accepted, established; well-known; **—ательный** *a.* grateful, thankful; **—ать** *see* **признавать; надо —аться, что** it must be admitted that.

призовёт *fut. 3 sing. of* **призвать.**

призовой *a.* prize.

призонный *a.* fitted (bolt); set, fitting (pin).

призра/к *m.* specter, phantom; illusion; **—чный** *a.* illusory, unreal.

призыв *m.* conscription; call, appeal; slogan; **—ать** *v.* call; call up, draft, conscript; **—ник** *m.* conscript; **—ной** *m.* draftee; *a.* draft; **—ный** *a.* vocative.

прииск *m.* mine, placer; (gold) field; **—ание** *n.* finding; **—атель** *m.* miner, prospector; **—ать** *v.* find; **—ивание** *n.* seeking; **—ивать** *v.* seek, look (for); **—овый** *a.* mine, mining, prospecting.

прийти *see* **приходить.**

Прикавказье (geog.) Caucasus region.

приказ *m.* order, command, injunction; **—ание** *n.* order, command, summons; direction, instruction; **—ной, —ный** *a. of* **приказ; —(ыв)ать** *v.* order, command, bid; direct, instruct.

прикалывать *v.* pin on.

Прикамье (geog.) Kama region.

приканчивать *v.* finish (up; off); kill.

прикапливать *v.* store up.

прикапывать *v.* add dropwise; (agr.) heel in.

прикарибский *a.* Caribbean.

прикармливать *v.* bait; give supplementary feeding.

прикарпатский *a.* Carpathian.

прикасат/ельный *a.* abutting; contact; **—ься** *v.* touch, abut, adjoin; **не п.** keep away (from).

прикаспийский *a.* Caspian Sea (region).

прикат/ать *v.* (agr.) roll down, pack; **—ить** *v.* roll (on; up to); arrive, come; **—ка** *f.* rolling on; arrival.

прикатодный *a.* at the cathode, cathodic; catholyte (layer).

прикат/очный *a.* rolling (on); **—чик** *m.* roller; **—ывание** *n.* (agr.) rolling, packing; **—ывать** *v.* roll, pack; roll up to.

прикач(ив)ать *v.* pump in, add.

прикачнуть *v.* swing near.

прики/дка *f.,* **—дывание** *n.* addition; estimation; **—дывать, —нуть** *v.* add, throw on more; estimate; try on.

прикип/ать, —еть *v.* scorch, stick.

приклад *m.* (art.) butt(stock); (silv.) butt end; (text.) trimmings; addition.

прикладной *a.* applied (chemistry, etc.); contact (goniometer); closed-circuit (television); (comp.) application (software).

прикладыв/ание *n.* application; **—ать** *v.* apply; add, annex, affix, join; set (next to, against); enclose; **—аться** *v.* be applied, etc.; come in contact (with); take aim.

прикле/енный *a.* glued, pasted (on); agglutinate(d); **—ивание** *n.* bonding, etc., *see* **приклеивать; —**adhesion; **—и(ва)ть** *v.* bond, glue, paste, stick; **—и(ва)ться** *v.* be glued; stick, adhere; **—йка** *see* **приклеивание;** glued-on object.

приклёпанный *a.* riveted on.

приклепать *see* **приклёпывать.**

приклёп/ка *f.* riveting; riveted section; **—ывание** *n.* riveting (on); **—ывать** *v.* rivet (on, to).

приклинок *m.* (mach.) gib.

приклон/ить, —ять *v.* lay, incline, lean (against); bend down (to).

приключ/ать, —ить *v.* (elec.) connect up; **—аться, —иться** *v.* happen, occur; **—ение** *n.* adventure; incident; (elec.) connection.

приков(ыв)ать *v.* forge (to); chain; rivet (attention).

прикол *m.* tie post; **—ачивать** *v.* nail on; **—ка** *f.* fastening, pinning on; pin; **—отить** *v.* nail on; **—отый** *a.* pinned on, etc., *see* **прикалывать; —оть** *see* **прикалывать; —ьный** *a. of* **прикол.**

прикомандиров(ыв)ать *v.* (mil.) attach.

приконтурный *a.* marginal (flooding).

прикончить *v.* finish up.

прикопать *v.* (agr.) heel in.

прикопить *v.* save up, store up.

прикопка *f.* (agr.) heeling in.

прикоплен/ие *n.* saving up; **—ный** *a.* saved up, stored up.

прикорм *m.,* **—ка** *f.* bait(ing).

прикорнев/ой *a.* radical; at the roots; hilar; **—ая зона** rhizosphere.

прикосновен/ие *n.* touch(ing), contact, tangency; contiguity; **—ность** *f.* contiguity, proximity; participation, implication; **—ный** *a.* contiguous, adjacent, adjoining; implicated (in).

прикоснуться *see* **прикасаться.**

прикошарный баз sheep pen, fold.

прикра/сить, —шивать *v.* embellish, adorn.

прикреп/итель *m.* fastener; **—ительный** *a.* fastening, etc., *see v.;* **—ительный орган** (biol.) appressor(ium), holdfast; **—ить** *see* **прикреплять; —ление** *n.* fastening, etc., *see v.;* insertion; implantation (of placenta); fixture, attachment; **—лённый** *a.* fastened, etc., *see v.;* adherent; (zool.) sessile, sedentary; **—лять** *v.* fasten, attach, (af)fix, secure, anchor, connect; **—ляться** *v.* become attached, adhere; **—ляющий** *a.* adherent, clinging.

прикроет *fut. 3 sing. of* **прикрыть.**

прикру/тить, —чивать *v.* tie, bind, fasten; turn down, tighten.

прикры/вание *n.* covering, etc., *see v.;* mulching (of soil); **—вать** *v.* cover, screen, shelter, protect; (agr.) mulch; close (partly); conceal; terminate; throttle (valve); **—ваться** *v.* hide; close up; **—вающий** *a.* covering, etc., *see v.;* **—тие** *n.* cover, screen, shield, protection, housing; escort, convoy; covering, etc., *see v.;* **—тый** *a.* covered, etc., *see v.;* **—ть** *see* **прикрывать.**

прикубанский *a.* (geog.) Kuban.

прикуёт *fut. 3 sing. of* **приковать.**

прикуп *see* **прикупка; —ать, —ить** *v.* buy more; **—ка** *f.* additional purchase; **—ной** *a.* bought in addition.

прикус *m.* (odontology) bite, occlusion; cog engagement; *also see* **прикуска; неправильный п.** malocclusion; **—ить** *v.* nip, nibble; **—ка** *f.* (vet.) air swallowing, wind sucking; (med.) aerophagy; **—очный** *a. of* **прикуска.**

прилавок *m.* (store) counter; (geol.) bench, ledge.

прилаг/аемый *a.* enclosed, attached, accompanying; **имя —ательное** (gram.) adjective; epithet; **—ать** *v.* add, append, enclose; apply; **—аться** *v.* approach; add; connect (with).

прила/дить *see* **прилаживать; —живание** *n.* fitting, etc., *see v.;* (med.) coaptation; **—живать** *v.* fit, adapt, adjust; **—дка** *f.* fitting; adjusting, adjustment.

прилёг *past m. sing. of* **прилечь.**

прилег/ание *n.* (ad)joining, etc., *see v.;* adjacency; abutment; fit; **—ать** *v.* adjoin, be adjacent (to), abut, butt (against), border; fit (snugly); **плотно —ать к** fit; be snug against; **—ающий** *a.* adjoining, adjacent, contiguous, neighboring, abutting; close-fitting; (bot.) adherent; accumbent.

приледниковый *a.* (geol.) periglacial.

прилежание *n.* diligence, application.

прилежать *v.* be adjacent, be contiguous (to), adjoin, abut.

прилежащ/ий *a.* adjacent, adjoining, contiguous; **п. угол** angle of contact; **—ие тела** *pl.* (ent.) corpora allata.

прилежный *a.* diligent, industrious.

прилез/ать, —ть *v.* crawl or creep up to.

прилеп/естник *m.* (bot.) corolla appendage; **—естнико-видный** *a.* (bot.) parapetalous; **—ить, —лять** *v.* stick, glue, attach (to); **—иться** *v.* stick, adhere.

при/лёт *m.* (av.) arrival; **—летать, —лететь** *v.* arrive, come (by air; flying); **—лётный** *a.* (orn.) migratory; **—лёточный** *a.* arriving.

прилечь *v.* lie down; settle (of dust).

прилив *m.* influx, flow, flood; congestion (of blood); rise, increase; (high) tide; surge; rib, tongue, boss, lug; cleat; **п. и отлив** ebb and flow; **—ы** *pl.* (med.) hot flash; **—ы и отливы** tides; **волна —а** tidal wave; **—ать** *v.* flow (to); rush (of blood); pour in, run in, add more (liquid); **—ающий** *a.* inflowing, affluent; **—ный** *a.* tidal, tide; cast on; **—ная полоса** tidelands; **—ообразующий** *a.* tide-generating; **—о-отливный** *a.* tidal (current); tidewater (region); **—чик** *m.* boss, rib, fillet.

прилиз/ать, —ывать *v.* lick smooth, smooth down.

прилип/аемость *f.* adherence; adhesiveness; **—аловые, —алы** *pl.* remoras, sharksuckers (*Echeneidae*); **—аль-це** *n.* (bot.) retinaculum; **—ание** *n.* adhesion, adherence, sticking, attachment; agglutination; (phys.) capture; **—атель** *m.* (insecticides) sticker; **—ать, —нуть** *v.* adhere, stick, cling, agglutinate, cohere; be communicated (of disease); **—чивость** *f.* stickiness; **—чивый** *a.* sticky, adhesive; (med.) contagious; persistent; bothersome, pesky (person); **—ший** *a.* adhesive, adherent; stuck.

прилистни/к *m.* (bot.) stipule; **—чек** *m.* stipel(lum); **—чный** *a.* stipular.

прилитие *n.* addition (of liquid); **п. крови** (agr.) introduction of new blood (in breeding).

прилит/ый *a.* added, run in; (foundry) cast on; **—ь** *see* **приливать**.

приличный *a.* decent, proper, good.

прилов *m.* incidental catch, something caught in net unintentionally.

приловчиться *v.* adapt oneself, get the knack.

прилож/ение *n.* application; enclosure; appendix, supplement, addition, annex; complement; (chem.) bond, linkage; (gram.) apposition; **точка —ения** (chem.) working point; **—енный** *a.* applied; **—ить** *see* **прикладывать**.

прилун/ение *n.* lunar landing; **—иться** *v.* land on the moon.

прилуч/ать, —ить *v.* lure, attract.

прильёт *fut. 3 sing. of* **прилить**.

приляжет *fut. 3 sing. of* **прилечь**.

прим *m.* (math., etc.) prime.

прим. *abbr.* (**примечание**) note.

примаз(ыв)ать *v.* paste, cement (on, down); **—ся** *v.* stick, hang on (to).

приман/ивать *v.* bait, lure, attract, entice, decoy (birds); **—ка** *f.* bait, chum, lure; decoy; **—ный, —очный** *a.* baiting, enticing, decoy; **—ная дудка** bird call.

примат *m.* pre-eminence, primacy; (mam.) primate; **—ология** *f.* (mam.) primatology.

приматы *pl.* (zool.) primates; **высшие п., человекоподобные п.** anthropoid apes.

приматывать *v.* wind on, add.

примахин *m.,* **—овый** *a.* (pharm.) primaquine.

примачивать *v.* bathe, moisten, wet; apply (lotion).

примащивать *v.* arrange, fit.

прим/вераза *f.* primverase; **—верин** *m.* primverin; **—еверин** *m.* primeverin; **—евероза** *f.* primeverose.

примеж/евать, —ёвывать *v.* (surv.) add.

примексиканский *a.* Mexican.

примен/ение *n.* application, etc., *see v.;* use, employment; **—ённый** *a.* applied, etc., *see v.;* **—имость** *f.* applicability; **—имый** *a.* applicable, usable, useful, suitable, practicable, appropriate; available; **—ительно** *adv.* as applied (to), to fit; **—ительный** *a.* applicable, suitable; **—ить(ся)** *see* **применять(ся);** **—яемость** *f.* applicability; scope, range of application; **—яемый** *a.* applied, etc., *see v.;* in use; applicable; **—ять** *v.* apply, use, utilize, employ, adapt, (put in) practice; **—яться** *v.* be applied, etc.; conform (to); be suitable; **—яя** *pr. ger.* (by) applying.

пример *m.* example, model, sample, instance; **—ом является** an example is; **по —у** in imitation of; **приводить в п.** cite as an example, illustrate (with).

примерз/ание *n.* freezing on, adhesion by freezing; **—ать** *v.* freeze (on, to, together).

примёрз/нуть *see* **примерзать; —лый** *a.* frozen.

пример/ивание *n.,* **—ка** *f.* trying on, fitting; **—и(ва)ть** *v.* try on, fit.

примерн/о *adv.* as an example; approximately, say, about, around, some; in the neighborhood of; **п. таким же образом** in much the same manner; **п. такой же** much the same; **—ый** *a.* exemplary; approximate, rough.

пример/очный *a.* fitting; **—очная** *f.* fitting room; **—ять** *see* **примеривать**.

примеси *pl. of* **примесь;** pollutant (in air).

примесный *a. of* **примесь;** extrinsic, doped (semiconductors).

примести *v.* sweep up to.

примесь *f.* admixture, addition, ingredient; foreign body, foreign matter, impurity, contaminant; adulteration, contamination; (met.) alloy; (semiconductors) dopant; **антикоррозийная п.** rust inhibitor; **побочная п., посторонняя п., случайная п.** secondary constituent; impurity, foreign matter; **с —ю** impure.

примет *fut. 3 sing. of* **принять**.

примет/а *f.* sign, indication, mark, index, criterion, characteristic; **—ы** *pl.* description, distinctive marks.

приметать *v.* sweep up to; tack, baste on; pack (hay, etc.).

приметить *see* **примечать**.

примётка *f.* (text.) tacking, basting.

примет/ливый *a.* observant; **—но** *adv.* perceptibly; **—ный** *a.* perceptible, noticeable; conspicuous; characteristic.

примётывать *v.* (text.) tack, baste; pack.

примеч/ание *n.* note, annotation, comment, remark, observation; footnote; **снабжать —аниями** *v.* annotate; **—ательность** *f.* notability, noteworthiness; **—ательный** *a.* notable, noteworthy, remarkable; **—ать** *v.* perceive, notice, take notice (of), observe.

примеш/анный *a.* admixed, etc., *see v.;* **—ивание** *n.* admixing, addition, introduction; impurity; **—(ив)ать** *v.* admix, add, introduce; (met.) alloy.

приминать *v.* crush, flatten, pack.

примир/ение *n.* reconciliation; pacification; settlement, arbitration; **—итель** *m.,* **—ительница** *f.* conciliator, peacemaker; arbitrator; **—ительный** *a.* conciliatory; **—ить, —ять** *v.* reconcile; conciliate; arbitrate; **—иться, —яться** *v.* reconcile oneself (to); make peace (with).

примите *imp. of* **принимать**.

примитив *m.* primitive; **—ный** *a.* primitive, early; simple, rough; raw (soil).

примкнут/ый *a.* placed against or next to; joined; (mil.) fixed (bayonet); secured (flanks); **—ь** *see* **примыкать.**

примоет *fut. 3 sing. of* **примыть.**

примоина *f.* (geol.) alluvium, river silt.

примораживать *v.* freeze on.

приморди/альный *a.* primordial; **—й** *m.* (biol.) primordium.

примороз/ить *see* **примораживать; —ок** *m.* light frost.

примор/ский *a.* maritime; seaside; tidal (marsh), coastal (swamp); sea (port); **п. объект** (mil.) coastal installation; **—ье** *n.* seaside, (sea-)shore; **Приморье** Maritime Territory.

примостить *v.* fit in, squeeze in; arrange.

примотать *v.* wind on, add.

примоч/ить *see* **примачивать; —ка** *f.* wash, lotion, fomentation; (med.) embrocation; application of wet compress; **глазная —ка** (med.) collyrium, eyewash.

примочная трава compact bellflower (*Campanula glomerata*).

прим. ред. *abbr.* (**примечание редактора**) editor's note.

примул/а *f.* (bot.) Primula; **—аверин** *m.* primulaverin; **—ин** *m.*, **—иновый** *a.* primulin; **—ит** *m.* primulite.

примус *m.* Primus (a Swedish stove).

примут *fut. 3 pl. of* **принять.**

примык/ание *n.* (ad)joining, etc., *see v.*; contiguity; **—ать** *v.* (ad)join, abut, border (on); fix (on); **—ающий** *a.* (ad)joining, etc., *see v.*; adjacent, neighboring; affiliated (organization).

примят/ый *a.* trampled, crushed, packed (soil); **—ь** *see* **приминать.**

принагнуть *v.* bend slightly; **—ся** *v.* stoop.

принадлеж/ать *v.* belong, (ap)pertain; fall (into classification); **—ность** *f.* belonging, affiliation; appurtenance; appliance, implement, fixture, fitting, accessory, attachment, part; **национальная —ность** (naut.) registry; **—ности** *pl.* outfit, equipment; tackle; parts, accessories, fittings; belongings; **по —ности** to the proper quarter.

принайтов/ать, —ить *v.* lash, bind with rope.

принакопить *v.* accumulate, save up.

приналечь *v.* lean on, recline on; tackle vigorously.

приневоли(ва)ть *v.* force, coerce.

принес/ение *n.* bringing; **—ти** *see* **приносить; —тись** *v.* drift; carry (of sound, smell).

прини/жать, —зить *v.* disparage, minimize; lower, debase; depreciate; mark down, discount.

принимаемый *a.* taken, received; assumed.

приним/ать *v.* take, receive, accept, admit; assume, put on, take on, take up, adopt; pick up (signal); inspect (merchandise); **п. за** mistake for; take as; **п. к сведению** take note; **п. на себя** assume, take upon oneself; **п. нулевое значение** vanish; **п. решение** decide; plan; **п. строевую стойку** (mil.) come to attention; **—аться** *v.* be taken, etc.; begin, get started, set to, set about; take (root); **—ающий** *a.* taking, etc., *see v.*; take-up (reel).

приноготовник *m.* (bot.) Paronychia.

принор/авливать, —овить, —овлять *v.* adapt, adjust.

прино/с *m.* bringing (in); **—сить** *v.* bring (in), fetch; bear, yield; **—ситься** *v.* be brought (in), etc.; drift; carry (of sound, smell); **—сный** *a.* brought in; drift; **—сящий** *a.* (physiol.) afferent; **—шение** *n.* gift, offering.

принудиловка *f.* compulsory labor.

принудит/ельный *a.* compulsory, coercive; forced; constrained, positive (motion); induced; drive (fit); **—ь** *see* **принуждать.**

принужд/ать *v.* oblige, constrain, force, compel, impel; **—ение** *n.* constraint, forcing, compulsion, coercion; **—ённо** *adv.* constrainedly, by force; **—ённый** *a.* constrained, forced.

принцип *m.* principle; rule; law; **п. максимума поля** (phys.) maximum-field principle; **в —е** in principle, basically; as a matter of principle; theoretically; **из —а** on principle; **технические —ы** engineering philosophy; **—иально** *adv.* in essence, fundamentally; **—иальный** *a.* principle, basic, key; schematic, circuit, line (diagram); conceptual (design); theoretical; **—иальная схема** schematic, flowsheet.

принюх(ив)аться *v.* get accustomed to an odor; recognize a scent.

принявшийся *a.* established (seedling).

принят/ие *n.* reception, acceptance, admission, adoption, assumption; **п. решений** decision making; **—о** it is assumed, it is customary; **это не —о** it is not done, it is not the custom; **—ый** *a.* taken, received, etc., *see* **принимать;** established; **—ое решение** *n.* plan; **—ь** *see* **принимать.**

приобре/сти *see* **приобретать; —татель** *m.* acquirer; purchaser; **—тать** *v.* acquire, get, obtain, take (on); assume; gain; purchase; **—тать вновь** resume; regain; **—тение** *n.* acquisition; purchase; **—тённый** *a.* acquired, etc., *see v.*

приобщ/ать, —ить *v.* unite, join, aggregate; acquaint, familiarize (with), accustom (to); **—ение** *n.* uniting, etc., *see v.*; junction; integration (into the mainstream).

приовраж/ный *a.* (by a) gully or ravine; gully-control (planting); **—ье** *n.* gully slope, gullied area.

при/озёрный *a.* (by a) lake; **—озерье** *n.* lake region.

прионус *m.* (ent.) longhorn beetles (*Prionus*).

приоритет *m.* priority; **—ный** *a.* first; previous; priority; (comp.) foreground (program).

приосновной *a.* basal.

приостан/авливание *see* **приостановка; —авливать, —овить** *v.* stop, suspend, cease (operation); cut off, turn off; close (down); delay; **—овка** *f.*, **—овление** *n.* stopping, etc., *see v.*; stop(page), cessation; pause, rest, delay; **период —овки** down time (of plant, etc.); **—овленный** *a.* stopped, etc., *see v.*

приострённый *a.* acuminate, tapering at the end.

пр. и от. *abbr.* (**прибытие и отправление**) arrival and departure.

приот/ворить, —ворять, —кры(ва)ть *v.* crack (open), open slightly.

приотста(ва)ть *v.* lag, fall behind.

припад/ать *v.* fall (down); press (against); limp slightly; **—ливость** *f.* (soil) subsidence; **—ок** *m.* fit, attack, seizure; **—очный** *a.* and *m.* epileptic; **—очное явление** seizure.

прип/аек *gen. pl. of* **припайка; —аиваемый** *a.* solderable; soldered, etc., *see v.*; **—аивание** *n.* soldering, etc., *see v.*; **—аивать** *v.* solder (on), braze (to); fix (on); **—ай** *m.* fast ice, shore ice, ocean ice frozen to the shore; **—айка** *see* **припаивание;** soldered-on part; **—айный** *a.* of **припай;** névé (iceberg).

припал/ённый *a.* burnt, singed; **—зывать** *v.* crawl or creep over; **—и(ва)ть** *v.* burn, singe, scorch.

припар/ивание *n.* fomentation, etc., *see v.*; **—и(ва)ть** *v.* steam, poultice, foment; **—ка** *f.* poultice.

припас *m.* store, supply, provision; **—ы** *pl.* supplies, provisions; **боевые —ы** ammunition; **—ать** *v.* lay up, store.

припасов/анный *a.* fitted; **—ать, —ывать** *v.* fit; align; **—ка** *f.* fitting; alignment.

припасти *see* **припасать.**

припасть *see* **припадать.**

припах/ивание *n.* extra plowing; **—ивать** *v.* smell slightly (of); **—(ив)ать** *v.* plow more, add to a field by plowing additional area.

припашка *see* **припахивание.**

припая *gen. of* **припай; —нный** *a.* soldered, brazed; (elec.) burned-on; **—ть** *see* **припаивать.**

прип/ёк *m.* heat; hot spot, sunny side; (sun) burn; gain in weight of bread on baking; **—екание** *n.* scorching, etc., *see v.;* coalescence; **—екать** *v.* scorch, burn; parch; get hot, be hot; (met.) sinter.

припереть *see* **припирать.**

приперчи(ва)ть *v.* pepper lightly.

припечат/ать, —ывать *v.* seal; (typ.) add; **—ка** *v.* sealing; addition.

припечь *see* **припекать.**

припивать *v.* drink up; drink (with food), wash down.

припирать *v.* press (against); (partly) close.

припис/анный *a.* added, etc., *see v.;* **—ать** *see* **приписывать; —ка** *f.* addition; postscript; codicil (to will); registration; **порт —ки** port of registry; **—ной** *a.* added, incorporated; registered; **—ывание** *n.* adding, etc., *see v.;* **—ывать** *v.* add (writing); ascribe, attribute, put down (to), credit (to), impute; assign; register; attach.

припла/та *f.* additional payment; **—тить, —чивать** *v.* pay in addition.

припле/сти, —тать *v.* weave, work, splice (in); implicate.

приплод *m.* issue, offspring; **деловой п.** surviving litter; **—ный скот** breeding cattle, breeding stock.

приплотинный *a.* (at or by the) dam.

приплы(ва)ть *v.* swim, float, sail, come (up to).

приплюснут/ый *a.* flat(tened); depressed; **—ь** *v.* flatten.

приплюсов(ыв)ать *v.* add.

приплющивать *v.* flatten.

приповерхностный *a.* near (or at) the surface.

приподн/иматель *m.* (anat.) arrector, erector; **—имать** *v.* raise (a little), uplift, elevate; **—иматься** raise (a little); heave; **—имающийся** *a.* assurgent, ascending, rising; **—ятие** *n.* raising, etc., *see v.;* **—ятость** *f.* elevation; **—ятый** *a.* raised, etc., *see v.;* **—ять** *see* **приподнимать.**

прип/ой *m.* solder; **крепкий п.** brazing solder; **паять крепким —оем** *v.* braze; **пайка мягким —оем** soft soldering.

приполярный *a.* circumpolar; polar.

припом/инание *n.* remembering, recollection; **—инать, —нить** *v.* remember, recollect, recall.

припор/ох *m.* stencil(ing) (with powder); **—ошить** *v.* powder, dust, sprinkle; **—ошка** *f.* stenciling.

припортовый *a.* (near a) port.

припосадочный *a.* preplanting, starter.

приправ/а *f.* seasoning, condiment; **—ить, —лять** *v.* season, flavor; (typ.) make ready; **—ка** *f.* making ready; **—очный** *a. of* **приправка;** seasoning.

припряж/ка *f.* harnessing (to); harness of a trace horse; **—ной** *a.* harnessed to; **—ная лошадь** trace horse.

припрят(ыв)ать *v.* conceal, store up, hoard.

припудренный *a.* powdered (with).

припудрив/ание *n.* dusting; powdering; **—ать** *v.* dust, sprinkle, powder.

припус/к *m.* admitting, etc., *see v.;* allowance, margin; **п. на** allowance for; **оставлять п.** *v.* allow (for); **—кать, —тить** *v.* admit, let approach, be accessible (to); let in; allow (for), add; (sewing) let out; make longer or wider; let run faster; couple, pair.

припух/ать, —нуть *v.* swell; **—лость** *f.* swelling, intumescence; **—лый** *a.* swollen, puffed up.

припущенный *a.* admitted, etc., *see* **припускать.**

припыл *m.*, **—ивающее вещество** (foundry) parting powder; **—ивание** *n.* powdering, dusting; **—ивать** *v.* powder, dust (molds).

прираб/атываемый *a.* adaptable to fitting; **—атывать** *v.* earn extra; break in (a machine); **—атываться** *v.* work in, run in (of bearing); be broken in; **—отавшийся** *a.* worn in; **—отанный** *a.* run in; broken in; **—отаться** *see* **прирабатываться; —отка** *f.* running in; breaking in; **—оток** *m.* extra pay; perquisite.

приравн/енный *a.* equated, etc., *see v.;* **—ивание** *n.* equating, etc., *see v.;* comparison; **—ивание кривой** (math.) curve fitting; **—ивать** *v.* equate, make equal; set (to zero, etc.); level, adjust; compare (with).

приразрывный *a.* fracture (cleavage).

прира/стание *n.* adnation, adhesion; **—стать, —сти** *v.* adhere; accrete, agglutinate; grow, increase, accrue; **—стить, —щивать** *v.* make adhere, attach; increase; **—щение** *n.* increment, increase, gain; attachment; adherence; **—щение на** (comp.) INCREMENT BY (command).

прирез *m.* plot, section (of land); **—ать** *see* **прирезывать; —ной** *a.* cut; sectioned-off; **—ок** *m.* section, plot; **—ывать** *v.* cut, fit (in); add, section off (land); slaughter, kill.

приречный *a.* on (or by) the river, riparian.

пририсов(ыв)ать *v.* add (to drawing).

прировнять *see* **приравнивать.**

природ/а *f.* nature, character; countryside; **дикая п.** wildlife; **испытатель —ы** naturalist; **по —е** by nature, inherently.

природн/ый *a.* natural, inborn, innate, congenital, inherent, intrinsic, indigenous, native, in the native state; naturally occurring; crude, raw; **п. житель** native; **в —ых условиях** (geol.) in situ.

природо/ведение *n.* natural history; **—охранный** *a.* environmental (design); **—пользование** *n.* resource management.

прирождённый *a.* inborn, innate, native, inherent, congenital, intrinsic; unconditioned (reflex).

прирос/т *m.* growth, increment, increase, gain; accretion; **—ток** *m.* excrescence; growth; (bot.) young shoot; paraphysis; **—ший** *a.* adnate; adherent; **—ший к** grown fast to.

прируб *m.* butt joint; log annex.

прирубежный *a.* frontier, border.

прирули(ва)ть *v.* drive, steer, pilot (up to).

прируслов/ый *a.* along the river bed; **—ье** *n.* river bed area.

прируч/ать *v.* domesticate, tame; **—ение** *n.* domestication; **—ённость** *f.* tameness; **—ить** *see* **приручать.**

Приса формула (elec.) Preece's formula.

присадистый *a.* stocky, compact.

приса/дить *see* **присаживать; —дка** *f.* addition, admixture; addition agent, additive; (welding) filler; supplement; (agr.) additional planting; **—дочный** *a.* additional; adding, additive, addition (agent); adjusting (device); **—женный** *a.* added, etc., *see v.;* **—живание** *n.* adding, etc., *see v.;* **—живать** *v.* add, introduce, fill (up); fasten, attach; plant more; **—живаться** *v.* sit down.

присаливать *v.* salt lightly, salt more.

присасыв/ание *n.* sucking, suction, indraft; **—ательный** *a.* suction; adhesive; **—ательная ямка** (zool.)

bothr(id)ium, sucker; **—ать** *v.* suck, pull, draw in; **—аться** *v.* attach itself (to), stick, adhere by suction; **—ающий** *a.* sucking.

присваива/ние *n.* assignment, allocation; **знак —ния** (comp.) assignment operator; **—ть** *v.* appropriate, adopt, assume; award, give, confer; assign, allocate.

присвист *m.* whistle (in breathing, etc.); sibilance.

присводовый *a.* crest.

присво/ение *n.* appropriation; awarding, conferment; attribution; **п. адресов** (comp.) address allocation; **п. значений параметров** (comp.) argument association; **—ить** *see* **присваивать**; (comp.) LET (command).

присев *m.* (agr.) additional sowing; **—ать** *v.* sow more, add.

присед/ание *n.* squatting; **—ать** *v.* squat; cower.

присем/енник *m.* (bot.) caruncle; **—янник** *m.* aril, seed covering.

присерия *f.* prisere, plant succession on area previously without vegetation.

присесть *see* **приседать**.

присеять *see* **присевать**.

прискак(ив)ать *v.* hop, gallop, skip (up to); arrive in a rush.

прискорб/ие *n.* sorrow, regret; **—ный** *a.* regrettable, sad.

присл/анный *a.* sent; **—ать** *v.* send.

прислон/ённый *a.* recumbent, leaning; **—ить, —ять** *v.* lean (against).

прислу/га *f.* attendant(s); (mil.) crew; **—живать** *v.* serve, attend.

прислуш(ив)аться *v.* listen (for).

присматривать *v.* look (for); **п. за** look after, keep an eye on, attend; supervise, oversee (work); **—ся** *v.* examine, scrutinize.

присмиреть *v.* calm down.

присмотр *m.* looking after, care, attendance; superintendence, supervision; **—еть** *see* **присматривать**.

приснеговой *a.* subniveal.

присниться *v.* dream; appear in a dream.

присовокуп/ительный *a.* additional; **—ить, —лять** *v.* add, annex, append; **—ление** *n.* addition.

присоедин/ение *n.* addition, annexation, joining, attachment; gain; (elec.) connection, contact; (chem.) bond; fusion; annellation; (phys.) acceptance (of electrons); **продукт —ения** addition compound; **продукт —ения брома** bromine addition product; **реакция —ения** addition (reaction); **—ённый** *a.* added, joined; augmented; associated, connected; apparent (mass).

присоедин/ительный *a.* connecting; **—ить, —ять** *v.* add, (ad)join, annex, attach, incorporate; gain, pick up, accept; (elec.) connect (up); (chem.) bind; link, combine, associate; **—яющийся** *a.* additive; (ad)joining; accessory; (biol.) annectent, linking.

присолить *see* **присаливать**.

присос *m.* suction; suction device; (biol.) sucker; **—анный** *a.* sucked, pulled, drawn; **—ать** *see* **присасывать**; **—ка** *f.* *see* **присосок**; clingfish; **брюшная —ка** (ichth.) ventral sucker; **передняя —ка** oral sucker; **—ковые, —копёрые** *pl.* clingfishes (*Gobiesocidae*); **—ный** *a.* of **присос**; **—ок** *m.* (biol.) sucker, sucking disk; acetabulum; **—ы** *pl.* (air) infiltration.

присохнуть *see* **присыхать**.

приспе/(ва)ть *v.* approach, come; mature, ripen; **—вающий** *a.* immature; green.

приспешн/ик *m.*, **—ица** *f.* helper; hireling.

приспос/абливать, —обить *see* **приспособлять**; **—обительный** *a.* adaptive.

приспособл/ение *n.* adaptation, acclimation, adjustment, fitting, accommodation, arrangement; device, appli-

ance, apparatus, contrivance, gadget, attachment, accessory, fixture; equipment, outfit; gear; **п. для —ер, —or**, e.g., **п. для пускания** launcher; **коэффициент —ения** accommodation coefficient; **соединительное п.** connector; **—енность** *f.* suitability, fitness; adaptability; **—енный** *a.* adapted, etc., *see* *v.*; rated; **—яемость** *f.* adaptability; **—яемый** *a.* adaptable, adjustable; applicable; **—ять** *v.* adapt, fit, tailor (to, for); convert; adjust, suit, accommodate, arrange; **—яться** *v.* adapt oneself, get accustomed (to).

приспус/кать, —тить *v.* lower (a little).

постав/ание *n.* adhesion, clinging, sticking; **—ать** *v.* adhere, cling, stick; join, side; worry, annoy; be caught (of disease); touch shore, beach.

пристав/ить *see* **приставлять**; **—ка** *f.* attachment, accessory; adapter; extension; prefix; **—ление** *n.* leaning; appointment; **—лять** *v.* lean, set, put (against); appoint; **—ной, —очный** *a.* added, attached; lean-to (ladder); **—ший** *a.* adherent.

пристальный *a.* fixed, intent, steady; **п. взгляд** stare.

пристанет *fut. 3 sing.* of **пристать**.

пристан/ище *n.* refuge, shelter; **—ный, —ский** *a.* of **пристань**.

пристанционный *a.* (at the) terminal or station.

пристань *f.* landing, pier, quay, wharf, dock; refuge.

пристатейный *a.* accompanying the article.

прист/ать *see* **приставать**; **—ающий** *a.* adhering, adhesive, adherent; tenacious.

приствольный *a.* (bot.) stem, stalk, trunk.

прист/егать, —ёгивать *v.* tack on; **—ёгивать, —егнуть** *v.* fasten (on); harness; add; **—ежной** *a.* detachable.

пристелла *f.* X-ray fish (*Pristella*).

пристен/ный *a.* boundary (layer); (biol.) parietal; **—очный** *a.* parietal.

присти/гастер *m.* (ichth.) Pristigaster; **—гение** *n.* (ichth.) catalufa (*Pristigenys*); **—мерин** *m.* pristimerin; **—помы** *pl.* (ichth.) grunts (*Pomadasyidae*).

пристрагивать *v.* plane to fit.

пристраив/ание *n.* adding, etc., *see* *v.*; **—ать** *v.* add, build on; arrange, settle, establish, place, fix; join up; **—аться** *v.* be added, etc.; find a place, settle; join up (with formation).

пристраст/ие *n.* addiction; predilection (for); **—иться** *v.* become addicted; **—ный** *a.* partial (to), biased.

пристрачивать *v.* stitch on.

пристрел *see* **пристрелка**; **—ивать(ся)** *v.* range (on); zero in; (mil.) target; **—ка** *f.* adjustment fire, ranging (fire); zeroing; **—очно-зажигательный** *a.* adjustment-incendiary; **—очный** *a.* of **пристрелка**; adjustment (fire); tracer (bullet); reference (piece); **—ьный** *a.* adjusted, corrected fire (range); **—янный** *a.* zeroed; **—ять** *see* **пристреливать(ся)**; shoot down; destroy.

пристрогать *v.* plane to fit.

пристро/енный *a.* added on, built on; **—ить** *see* **пристраивать**; **—йка** *f.* lean-to, shed, addition, annex.

пристрочить *see* **пристрачивать**.

пристуг(ив)ать *v.* plane to fit.

приступ *m.* fit, attack, paroxysm, seizure; spell, bout (of illness); assault, storm, rush; access; beginning; **к нему нет —а** he is inaccessible; **—ать, —ить** *v.* approach; set about, enter upon, begin, start, proceed.

приступ/ка *f.*, **—ок** *m.* step.

приступн/ый *a.* intermittent; **—ообразный** *a.* paroxysmal.

присты/дить, —жать *v.* (put to) shame; **—жённый** *a.* shamed.

пристяж/ка *f.* trace horse; **в —ке** in traces; **—ной** *a.*, **—ная** *f.* trace horse.

прису/дить, —ждать *v.* award; sentence; condemn; confer (a degree); **—ждение** *n.* awarding, conferment; sentencing.

присутств/ие *n.* presence, occurrence; attendance; **в п. или в отсутствие** with or without; **—овать** *v.* be present, attend, assist; **—ующий** *a.* present, attending, attendant, assisting.

присуч/ивание *n.* twisting together, piecing (of thread); **—и(ва)ть** *v.* twist together, piece on.

присуши(ва)ть *v.* dry out (a little).

присущ/ий *a.* inherent, innate, intrinsic, indigenous; typical, characteristic, peculiar (to); **—ность** *f.* inherence.

присч/ёт *m.* addition; **—ит(вы)ать** *v.* add (on); add incorrectly; take into account.

присыл/ать *v.* send; **—ка** *f.* sending.

присып/ать *v.* add, pour more; sprinkle, powder; **—ка** *f.* addition; sprinkling; powder.

присыхать *v.* dry on, adhere.

прися/га *f.* oath; **—гать, —гнуть** *v.* swear, take an oath; **—жный** *m.* juror.

приталкивать *v.* push over.

притаптывать *v.* trample, crush, pack (lightly).

притаскивать *v.* drag over, haul.

притачивать *v.* grind to fit; stitch on.

притащить *see* **притаскивать**.

притвор *m.* fold, flap; joint; **—ить** *see* **притворять**.

притвор/ный *a.* pretended, simulated; **—ство** *n.* pretense, simulation.

притвор/ять *v.* shut, close (partly); **—яться** *v.* close (partly); pretend, simulate; **—яшки** *pl.* (ent.) spider beetles (*Ptinidae*).

притек/ать *v.* flow (to), run; **—ающий** *a.* flowing, incoming.

притемн/ение *n.* shading, screening; **—ить, —ять** *v.* darken a little.

притен/ить, —ять *v.* (put in the) shade.

притереть *see* **притирать**.

притёртый *a.* ground (in, down); ground-glass (stopper); fitted in; chamfered (edge).

притесать *see* **притёсывать**.

притёс/ывать *v.* adz(e); cut to fit; **—ка** *f.* adzing; cutting.

притечь *see* **притекать**.

притир *m.* lap; lapping tool; grinding; grinding powder; **—ание** *see* **притирка; —ать** *v.* lap, polish; grind (in, down); fit (in); reseat, set (valve); chamfer (edge); rub (in, down), wear down, abrade; **—ка** *f.*, **—очный** *a.* lapping, etc., *see v.*; abrasion, attrition; **—очный станок** lapping machine.

притих/ать, —нуть *v.* quiet down.

приткнуть *see* **притыкать**.

приток *m.* tributary (of river), affluent; influx, inflow; delivery, admission, intake, feed, supply; rise, increase.

притолк/ать, —нуть *v.* push over.

притолка *f.* lintel (of door).

притом *conj.* besides, moreover.

притом/ить, —лять *v.* tire out; tire a little; **—лённый** *a.* tired out.

притон *m.* den, hide-out; **район —ов** skid row.

притонение *n.* haul (of a drag seine).

притоптать *see* **притаптывать**.

приторм/аживать, —озить *v.* slow down, brake.

приторный *a.* sugary, excessively sweet.

приточ/енный *a.* ground-in, fitted, machined (to size); **—ить** *v.* grind in, fit, machine; **—ка** *f.* grinding in, etc., *see v.*

приточн/о-вытяжной *a.* balanced (ventilation); **—ый** *a.* of **приток;** influent; **—ая трава** (bot.) Campanula glomerata.

притр/агиваться, —онуться *v.* touch.

притулиться *v.* press (against), nestle (against), cuddle; squeeze in.

притуп/ить *see* **притуплять; —ление** *n.* blunting, etc., *see v.*; **—ленный** *a.* blunted, etc., *see v.*; obtuse; retuse (leaves, shells); **—лять** *v.* blunt, dull, deaden; smooth, round; (cryst.) truncate; obtund (sensitivity, etc.).

приту/хать, —хнуть *v.* go down (of flame); **—шить** *v.* extinguish; lower (lights, etc.); damp (a fire).

притык *m.* joint; abutment, end; **сваривать в п.** *v.* butt-weld; **сросток в п.** butt joint; **—ать** *v.* stick, fasten (to); stop up; **—аться** *v.* touch, join.

притяг/ательный *a.* attractive; magnetic (force); **—ивать** *v.* attract, draw, pull; tighten.

притяжательный *a.* (gram.) possessive.

притяжен/ие *n.* attraction, gravitation; **взаимное п.** affinity; **земное п.** gravity; **сила —ия** gravitational force, gravity, pull; **—ность** *f.* gravity.

притяз/ание *n.* claim; **—ать** *v.* claim.

притянут/ый *a.* pulled, attracted, tightened; **—ь** *see* **притягивать**.

приукра/сить, —ш(ив)ать *v.* decorate, embellish.

приулечься *v.* die down (of wind, etc.).

приуменьш/ать, —ить *v.* decrease.

приумнож/ать, —ить *v.* increase, augment, multiply; **—ение** *n.* augmentation, multiplication.

Приуралье (geog.) Ural region.

приуроч/енность *f.* confinement; coherence; **—енный** *a.* confined, etc., *see v.*; coherent; **—и(ва)ть** *v.* confine; time, coordinate, relate, adapt; accustom; (geol.) refer to an epoch.

приусадебн/ый *a.* (at the) farm; private (plot of a collective farmer); **—ое землепользование** *n.* land tenure; **—ое хозяйство** (agr.) private plot.

приустать *v.* tire, become slightly weary.

приустьевой *a.* estuarine.

приутайки *pl.* (ent.) Byrrhidae.

приутих/ать, —нуть *v.* quiet down, abate.

приуч/ать *v.* train, school, coach; **—аться** *v.* get accustomed, get used (to); **—ение** *n.* training, etc., *see v.*; **—ить(ся)** *see* **приучать(ся).**

прифермский *a.* (near or at a) farm.

прифлянцованный *a.* flange-mounted.

приформовать *v.* mold on, vulcanize on.

прифронтовой *a.* (at the) front, front-line.

прифугов/ка *f.* joint(ing); **—ывать** *v.* joint.

прихварывать *v.* be sickly, ail.

прихв/ат *see* **прихватка; —атить** *see* **прихватывать; —атка** *f.* catching, etc., *see v.*; tack weld, temporary weld; clamp; **сварка с —атками** tack weld-(ing); **—атывание** *n.* catching, etc., *see v.*; **—атывать** *v.* catch, seize; stick, freeze; (tools) stall; drag (of brake); (welding) tack; strike (of disease); **—аченный** *a.* caught, stuck, frozen, etc., *see v.*

прихворнуть *see* **прихварывать**.

прихл/ебнуть, —ёбывать *v.* sip.

прихлоп/нуть, —ывать *v.* slam; slap; kill; nip, catch.

прихлынуть *v.* rush, gush, surge.

приход *m.* coming, arrival, advent; income; receipt; **—ить** *v.* come, arrive; appear; reach (conclusion); become (inoperative); **—ить в себя** recover consciousness; **—ить к** attain, reach (equilibrium); **—иться** *v.* fit; be; be obliged to, have to; exert, be exerted (of pressure); **—иться на** be due to; fall within; **ему —ится** he has to, he must; **—норасходный** *see* **при-**

ходорасходный; —ный *a.* coming, arriving; income (tax); receipt (book); **—овать** *v.* (com.) enter as income; **—орасходный** *a.* credit-debit; **—орасходная книга** account book, ledger; **—ящий** *a.* arriving, incoming; day, non-resident (pupil); out (patient); **—ящийся на** (math.) per; necessary (for).

прихожая *f.* entrance, vestibule.

прихот/ливый *a.* demanding; capricious; **—ь** *f.* whim.

прихрамыв/ание *n.,* **—ать** *v.* limp.

прицветни/к *m.* (bot.) bract; **вторичный п.** bractlet; **—ковидный** *a.* bracteiform; **—ковый** *a.* bracteal, bracteate; **—чек** *m.* bractlet, bracteola.

прицветный *a.* floral, involucral.

прицеит *m.* (min.) priceite.

прицел *m.* aim(ing); sight (of gun); **—ивание** *n.* aiming, sighting; **—и(ва)ться** *v.* (take) aim, point, sight.

прицельн/ый *a.* sighting; aimed (fire); collimating (telescope); **п. барабан** range dial; **—ая колодка** rearsight bed; **—ая линия** line of aim; **—ые нити** cross hairs; **—ые приспособления** sights.

прицеп *m.* trailer; coupling, hitching; hook; **п.-дача** (camper) trailer; **—ить** *see* **прицеплять; —ка** *see* **прицепление;** trailer; attachment; hook; (bot.) tendril, cirrus; (bot.) holdfast, hapteron; **с —ками** (bot.) uncinate; **п.-контейнер** *m.* box trailer; **—ление** *n.* coupling, etc., *see v.;* **—ленный** *a.* coupled, etc., *see v.;* adherent; **п.-лесовоз** *m.* straddle trailer; **—лять** *v.* couple, hitch, hook (on), connect, attach; **—ляться** *v.* couple, hook (on); adhere, stick; **—ник** *m.* hedgehog parsley (*Caucalis*); **—ной** *a.* trailer, pull-type; towed; **—ной брус** drawbar; **—ной вагон, —ная тележка** trailer; **п.-роспуск** *m.* pole trailer; **п.-самосвал** *m.* dump trailer; **—щик** *m.* (agr.) implement operator; tractor mechanic.

прицепыши *pl.* (ent.) water bugs (*Dryopidae*).

причал *m.* hawser, mooring rope; moorage, berth; **рейдовой п.** offshore mooring; **—ивание** *n.* mooring; **—и(ва)ть** *v.* moor, make fast; **—ка** *f.* alignment cord; **—ьный** *a.* mooring.

причастие *n.* (gram.) participle.

причастн/ость *f.* participation; **—ый** *a.* participating (in), implicated, involved, concerned; (gram.) participial.

причека *f.* (mach.) gib; tightening key.

причём *conj. and adv.* while, during which, whereupon; at the same time, also, and, with; **п. известно, что** it being known that.

причерноморский *a.* Black Sea coastal (region).

причесать *see* **причёсывать.**

причесть *v.* add.

причёсывать *v.* comb, brush.

причин/а *f.* reason, cause, source, origin, principle; **п. ошибки** source of error; **по —е** because (of), owing (to); **служить —ой** *v.* cause, be the cause (of).

причин/ение *n.* causing; **—ённый** *a.* caused; **—ить** *see* **причинять; —о-следственный** *a.* cause-effect; **—ность** *f.,* **—ная связь** causality; **—ный** *a.* causal, causative; **—о-средственный** *a.* genetic (relation); **—ять** *v.* cause, occasion, do.

причисл/ение *n.* reckoning; addition; attaching; **—ить, —ять** *v.* reckon, number, rank; add; attach.

причит/аться *v.* be due; **—ающийся** *a.* due.

причлен/ение *n.* (chem.) association, addition; articulation, joint, connection; **—ённый** *a.* articulated, jointed; attached; **—иться, —яться** *v.* articulate; connect.

причуд/а *f.* whim(sy), caprice; oddity, idiosyncrasy, eccentricity; **—ливый** *a.* whimsical, odd; freakish, extraordinary; **—ник** *m.,* **—ница** *f.* crank, eccentric.

причу/ивать, —ять *v.* (pick up a) scent.

пришабр/енный *a.* scraped; **п. к** scraped to fit; **—ивание** *n.* scraping off; **—и(ва)ть** *v.* scrape, scour (to fit).

пришвартов(ыв)ать *v.* moor, tie, fasten.

приш/едший *past act. part. of* **прийти; —ёл** *past m. sing. of* **прийти; первым —ёл, первым обслужен** (comp.) first come, first served; **—елец** *m.* stranger; immigrant, *m.* newcomer, tenderfoot; **—ествие** *n.* arrival, advent.

пришиб/ать, —ить *v.* strike dead; crush (to death); hurt (with a blow), bruise; depress; **—ленный** *a.* killed, etc., *see v.;* crestfallen, dejected.

приш/ивание *n.* fastening, etc., *see v.;* **—ивать** *v.* fasten, fix, make fast; sew on; **—ивка** *see* **пришивание; —ивной** *a.* fastened; sewed on; **—ить** *see* **пришивать.**

пришкольный *a.* (at the) school.

пришлёт *fut. 3 sing. of* **прислать.**

пришлифов/анный *a.* ground (down, in); **—(ыв)ать** *v.* grind (down, in, to fit).

пришл/о *past n. sing. of* **прийти; —ый** *a.* ecdemic, of foreign origin; (bot.) adventitious; newcomer, immigrant.

пришоссейный *a.* (along or on the) highway.

пришпили(ва)ть *v.* fasten, pin on.

пришьёт *fut. 3 sing. of* **пришить.**

прищем/ить, —лять *v.* pinch, catch, jam.

прищеп *m.* (bot.) graft; **—ить, —лять** *v.* graft (on); **—ок** *m.* scion to be grafted on; clothespin.

прищип/ка *f.* (hort.) pinching back; **—нуть** *see* **прищипывать; —ывание** *see* **прищипка; —ывать** *v.* (hort.) pinch back.

прищур *m.,* **—ивание** *n.,* **—ка** *f.* blinking, etc., *see v.;* **—и(ва)ть** *v.* blink, twinkle, wink, squint.

приэлектродный *a.* near the electrode.

приют *m.* shelter, refuge, asylum; **—ить** *v.* shelter, give refuge.

приямок *m.* areaway; pit, depression; reservoir; drain hole.

прият/ель *m.,* **—ельница** *f.* friend; **—ный** *a.* pleasant; **—ский** *a.* friendly.

прк, пр-к *abbr.* (**противник**) enemy.

пр. куб. *abbr.* (**простая кубическая решётка**) simple cubic lattice.

пр.м., пр/м *abbr.* (**прошлого месяца**) last month.

Прм *abbr.* (**приёмник**) receiver.

пр-ное *abbr.* (**производное**) (math.) derivative.

про *prep. acc.* of, about; for.

ПРО *abbr.* (**противоракетная оборона**) (anti)missile defense.

про— *prefix* per—, through, past; pro— (before, in front of; precursor of); *with verbs to indicate action over a definite period, or completed or thorough action.*

проазотировать *v.* nitride, nitrify.

проактиномицин *m.* proactinomycin.

проакцеллерин *m.* (hemat.) proaccelerin, Factor V.

проамнион *m.* (embr.) proamnion.

проанализировать *v.* analyze.

проатлант *m.* (anat.) proatlas.

проб/а *f.* trial, test, experiment; (test) sample, specimen; analysis; (met.) assay; purity (of gold); standard; **п. на** test for; **п. нагреванием** heat test; **брать —у** *v.* sample; **взять на —у** *v.* sample; take on trial; **взятие —ы, отбор —ы** sampling; **метод проб (и ошибок)** trial-and-error method.

пробазидия *v.* (bot.) probasidium.

пробактериофаг *m.* (bact.) probacteriophage.

пробалтывать *v.* agitate.

пробанд *m.* (gen.) propositus, proband.

пробанить *v.* brush out (flues).

пробег *m.* run, mileage; running through, flow, passage; race; (phys.) range, path (length); **п. поглощения** (nucl.) attenuation length; **время —а** running time; traveling time, transit time; **длина —а** range, reach, scope; path length (of particle); **измерение —ов** (aut.) range measurement; **испытание —ом** road test; **разброс —ов** range straggling; **соотношение п.-энергия** range-energy relation; **спектр —ов** range spectrum; **средняя длина свободного —а** (phys.) mean free path; **число миль —а на** miles per (gallon, etc.).

пробегать *v.* run for a while; *see also* **пробежать.**

пробежать *v.* run (over, through), traverse, pass over, skim.

пробеж/ка *f.* running, passing (over, through); range; **—но-ионизационный** *a.* range-ionization.

пробей(те) *imp. of* **пробить.**

пробел *m.* gap, blank, lacuna; omission, failure, lack, deficiency; spacing, interval; (typ.) white space; **—и(ва)ть** *v.* whiten, bleach; whitewash; **—ьная** *f.* bleaching department; **—ьный** *a. of* **пробел;** bleaching; **—ьный материал** (typ.) blanks, white space, leading.

проберёт *fut. 3 sing. of* **пробрать.**

пробертит *m.* (min.) probertite.

пробив/ание *n.* piercing, etc., *see v.*; puncture; (elec.) breakdown, rupture; **—ать** *v.* pierce, puncture, punch, perforate, make a hole (in); breach, break through, go through; break down; (foundry) tap; force open, clear; **—аться** *v.* break through, get through; (bot.) sprout; (physiol.) beat; **—ающий** *a.* piercing, etc., *see v.*; (elec.) disruptive; **—ка** *see* **пробивание;** (comp.) perforation, punch; caulking (material); **—ной** *a. see* **пробивающий;** break-through; penetrating (bullet); **—ной станок** punch; **—ная напряжённость электрического поля** dielectric strength; **—очный** *see* **пробивающий.**

пробирать *v.* go through, penetrate (of cold); (agr.) weed; reproach, reprimand; **—ся** *v.* get through.

пробир/ка *f.* test tube; **в —ке** in vitro.

пробир/ный *a.* test(ing); assay(ing); **п. цилиндр** test tube; **—ая игла** touch needle; **—ая склянка** test tube; **—ое искусство** assaying; **—ые весы** assay balance.

пробир/ование *n.* assay(ing); **—овать** *v.* assay; hallmark.

пробит/ие *see* **пробивание; —ый** *a.* pierced, etc., *see* **пробивать; —ь** *see* **пробивать.**

пробк/а *f.* cork; stopper, plug; tap, spigot; (elec.) fuse; plug gage, internal gage; block, lock (in pipe); (vapor) lock; bottleneck; (bot.) obturator; bung; (air) lock; **дульная п.** (mil.) tampion; **кровяная п.** (hemat.) thrombus; embolus; **—о—** *prefix* suberi—, phell(o)—; **—овидный** *a.* suberiform, suberose; (hemat.) emboliform; **—овидное ядро** (anat.) emboliform nucleus (of cerebellum).

пробковокислая соль suberate.

пробков/ый *a.* cork(-like), suberose, corky(-textured); stopper, plug; **п. уголь** burnt cork; **п. камбий** phellogen, cork cambium; **п. режим течения** plug-flow conditions; **—ая кислота** suberic acid, octanedioic acid; **соль —ой кислоты** suberate; **—ое вещество** suberin; **—ое дерево** cork oak (*Phellodendron*).

пробко/листный *a.* suberifolious; **—носный** *a.* suberiferous, cork-bearing; **—образовательная ткань** phelloderm.

проблема *f.* problem; challenge; crux (of matter); **—ти-**

ка *f.* problems; **—тический, —тичный** *a. a.* problematic.

проблемн/ый *a.* problem(-solving); (comp.) domain-specific; **—ая комиссия** task force; **—ая область** (comp.) domain.

проблес/к *m.*, **—кивать** *v.* gleam, flash; **—ковый** *a.* flashing, intermittent; **—нуть** *v.* gleam, flash.

проблеять *v.* bleat (for a time).

пробник *m.* sampler, sampling tube; test rod; probe; try cock, gage cock; (elec.) tester; (art.) proof plug; (agr.) sample sire, teaser ram.

пробн/ый *a.* experimental, test; trial, pilot; tentative (proposal); exploratory (operation); sample, specimen; proof (page, sheet); standard (gold, silver); **п. груз** test load; **п. залёт** trial flight; **п. заход** dry run; **п. кран** try cock, gage cock; **п. оттиск** proof; **п. спирт** proof spirit; **п. экземпляр** specimen; **—ая полоса** test strip; **—ая протолочка** mill run, mill test; **—ая серия** pilot run.

пробов/ание *n.* trying, etc., *see v.*; **—ать** *v.* try, test, sample; (met.) assay; experiment; attempt, endeavor; taste.

пробод/атель *m.* (zool.) perforatorium, head cap (of spermatozoon); **—ать** *v.* perforate, pierce, gore; **—ающий** *a.* perforating (ulcer); **—ение** *n.* perforation; (med.) tresis; **—ённый** *a.* perforated, foraminate(d), holed, pierced; **—ной** *a.* perforating; (med.) perforative (peritonitis).

пробоина *f.* hole, gap, rift; puncture.

проб/ой *m.* puncture, rupture, disruption; irruption; breakthrough; (elec.; phys.) breakdown; flash-over, sparkover; (eye) bolt, shackle; hasp; **п. меток в ушах** (agr.) earmarking; **напряжение —оя** breakdown voltage; **—ойка** *f.* piercing; clearing; punch; caulking material; **восковая —ойка** (apid.) slumgum, wax residue; **—ник, —чик** *m.* (hole) punch, drift.

пробок *gen. pl. of* **пробка.**

проболеть *v.* be sick (for a time).

проболтать *see* **пробалтывать.**

пробомбить *v.* bomb.

пробо/отбиратель, —отборник *m.* sampler, (sampling) probe; **—печатание** *n.* proof printing; **—разделочная машина** sample conditioner.

проборанивать *v.* (agr.) harrow.

пробор/ка *f.* (text.) drawing-in; (agr.) weeding; reprimanding; **—ный станок** drawing-in frame.

пробороздить *v.* leave a furrow.

проборон/ить, —овать *v.* (agr.) harrow.

пробо/укупорочный *a.* corking; **—чник** *m.* corkscrew; **—чный** *see* **пробковый;** plug (welding).

пробрасывать *v.* throw; screen, sift; err (by); miss.

пробраться *see* **пробираться.**

пробродить *v.* ferment; stroll.

пробрас/ать *v.* throw, finish throwing; **—ить** *see* **пробрасывать.**

пробудет *fut. 3 sing. of* **пробыть.**

пробу/дить, —ждать *v.* (a)waken, (a)rouse; **—диться, —ждаться** *v.* wake up.

пробуксовка *f.* slip(ping), skidding.

пробулькивать *v.* bubble (through).

пробурав/ить *see* **пробуравливать; —ленный** *a.* (bot.) terebrate; **—ливать** *v.* bore, perforate, drill (through); **—ливание** *n.* boring.

пробы *gen., pl., etc., of* **проба.**

пробыть *v.* stay, remain, be.

пробьёт *fut. 3 sing. of* **пробить.**

провал *m.* downfall; valley, trough; dip (of curve); cave-in; dip; gap, (air) pocket; (memory) lapse; failure; collapse; hole, pit; (geol.) subsidence; —**и(ва)ться** *v.* fall through, collapse, cave in; subside; break down; fail; disappear; —**ьный** *a. of* **провал**; downcomer; —**ьная тарелка** (distillation) downcomerless (shower-type) tray in tower, e.g. grid tray; —**ьная электроэнергия** electric power generated in off-peak periods.

провалять *v.* felt, full.

Прованс (geog.) Provence.

прованское масло olive oil (high grade).

провар *m.* (welding) penetration; (glass) complete melting; fusion; —**иваемость** *f.* (paper) pulpability; penetrability; —**ивание** *n.* boiling; cooking, digestion; penetration; —**и(ва)ть** *v.* digest, cook, boil thoroughly; penetrate; —**ка** *see* **проваривание;** scalding.

проваскулярный *a.* provascular.

Провацека тельце (med.) Prowazek's body.

проващивать *v.* wax.

провевать *v.* winnow; blow.

проведать *see* **проведывать.**

провед/ение *n.* conducting, etc., *see* **проводить; п. досуга** leisure activity; **порядок —ения** procedure; —**ённый** *a.* conducted, etc., *see* **проводить.**

проведывать *v.* find out, learn; visit.

провезти *see* **провозить.**

провеивать *v.* (agr.) winnow.

провёл *past m. sing. of* **провести.**

провентилировать *v.* ventilate, air.

провер/енный *a.* checked, etc., *see* **проверять;** —**ить** *see* **проверять;** —**ка** *f.* checking, verification, etc., *see* **проверять;** check(-up), follow-up, inquiry; test(ing); calibration; control; —**ка в составе комплекса** (comp.) online testing; —**ка на чётность** (comp.) parity check; —**ка на месте** spot check; —**ка по калибру** calibration, gaging; —**ка состояния** status check.

провернуть *v.* crank, turn (engine); drill, make (hole); grind (meat); work out (problem); do quickly.

проверочный *a. of* **проверка;** verifying; calibrating (gage, instrument); control (experiment).

про/вертеть *v.* bore, perforate, pierce; —**вертеться** *v.* turn (for a time); —**вёртывать** *see* **провернуть.**

провер/щик *m.* —**щица** *f.* checker, inspector; *a.* under examination; —**ять** *v.* check, verify, test; examine, inspect; calibrate; keep check, follow up; take (inventory); audit; —**яющий** *a.* checking, etc., *see v.;* *m.* checker, inspector.

провес *m.* wrong weight; short weight; weighed portion, given weight; slack, sag(ging), dip (of wire); **стрела** —**а** deflection, sag, dip; —**ить** *see* **провешивать.**

провесной *a.* air-dried, cured.

провести *see* **проводить.**

проветр/иваемый *a.* ventilated; —**ивание** *n.* ventilation, airing, aeration; —**и(ва)ть** *v.* ventilate, air, aerate.

провеш/енный *a.* aligned; plumbed; staked out, pegged, demarcated; stake (line); —**ённый** *a.* weighed; weighed short; cured, air-dried; —**ивание** *n.* aligning, etc., *see v.;* alignment; chain surveying; —**ивать** *v.* align; plumb; stake out, peg, demarcate; weigh; weigh short; cure, air-dry; —**иваться** *v.* be aligned, etc.; sag; make a mistake in weighing; dry.

прове/янный *a.* (agr.) winnowed; —**ять** *v.* winnow; blow.

провид/ение *n.* foresight; —**еть** *v.* foresee.

провизия *f.* provisions, food; provision.

провизор *m.* pharmacist, druggist; **п.-аналитик** *m.* analytical chemist.

провизорный *a.* provisional, temporary; preliminary; (med.) relaxation.

провин/иться *v.* be guilty (of), be at fault; —**ность** *f.* misdemeanor, offense.

провинция *f.* province.

провирус *m.* (gen.; med.) provirus.

провис/ание *n.* sag(ging), slack(ening), dip, deflection; —**ать** *v.* sag, go slack, dip, deflect; —**еть** *v.* hang (for a while); —**лый** *a.* sway (back); —**нуть** *see* **провисать;** —**ший** *a.* sagged, sagging, slack.

провитамин *m.,* —**ный** *a.* provitamin, vitamin precursor.

провод *m.* conductor, wire, cable; lead, conduit, duct; conducting; **п. с пущенным током** (elec.) live wire; **вводной п.** (elec.) lead; **монтировать —а** *v.* wire; **прокладка —ов** wiring; **по прямому —у** by direct contact.

проводим/ость *f.* conductivity, conduction; admittance (of servo system); **п. передачи** (aut.) transfer admittance; **активная п., ваттная п.** (elec.) conductance; **дырочная п.** p-type conduction, hole conduction; **полная п.** admittance; **удельная п.** conductivity; —**ый** *a.* conducted; in progress, under way.

проводить *v.* conduct, lead, carry; carry out (reaction); do, run, perform, make, accomplish, execute; institute (proceedings); install, lay, take through (cables); construct (road); drive (tunnel); draw, trace (line); lay out, mark; put (into operation); record, register; escort, send off; pursue (research); spend, pass (time); develop (idea); adopt; follow (policy); hold (meeting); —**ся** *v.* be conducted, etc.; be underway, be in progress.

проводка *f.* conducting, etc., *see* **проводить;** wires, wiring, conduit wire; leads; guide; circuit; supply system; drilling (oil well); (agr.) (stock) show; **п. управления** control circuit; **п. цели** tracking.

проводник *m.,* —**овый** *a.* conductor; leader; guide; vehicle (of infection); **п. звука** sound conductor; **п. под током** (elec.) current-carrying conductor; —**овый материал** conductor.

провод/ной *a. of* **провод;** line, wire (communication); —**ность** *see* **проводимость;** —**ный** *a.* conducting; wire; —**одержатель** *m.* hanger; -**рельс** *m.* contact rail, conductor rail; —**ящий** *a.* conducting, etc., *see* **проводить;** conductive; (anat.) conduction (path); vascular (system); —**ящий цилиндр** (bot.) stele; —**ящая жила** conductor.

провожать *v.* accompany, escort, convoy.

провоз *m.* conveying, carting, transport; conveyance; **стоимость —а** freight charge.

провозглашение *n.* proclamation.

провоз/ить *v.* convey, transport, carry; —**ной** *a. of* **провоз;** carrying (capacity); —**оспособность** *f.* capacity.

провока/торный *a.* provocative, exciting, stimulating; —**ционный** *a.* stimulating; —**ция** *f.* provocation; stimulation (of growth); irritation.

проволакивать *v.* drag along; draw (wire).

проволок/а *f.* wire; —**ообразный** *a.* wire-shaped, filiform; —**ошвейный** *a.* stapling; —**ошвейная машина** stapler.

проволочить *v.* drag along; draw (wire).

проволоч/ка *dim. of* **проволока;** delay; —**ник** *m.* wire specialist; (ent.) wireworm; —**ники** *pl.* (ent.) click beetles (*Elateridae*).

проволочно/-волочильный *a.* wire-drawing; **п.-канатный** *a.* wire-rope, cable; **п.-намоточный** *a.* wire-coiling; **п.-прокатный** *a.* rod-rolling; rod, wire (mill).

проволочн/ый *a.* wire; wire-wound (resistor); **п. штаг,** —**ая оттяжка** guy wire; —**ая ткань** wire fabric; —**ая сеть** wire netting, fencing.

проволочь *see* **проволочить.**

проворачив/ание *n.* (mach.) cranking, etc., *see v.;*

—ать *v.* crank, turn over; (av.) prop off, swing (propeller); accomplish quickly.

проворный *a.* quick, adroit, dexterous.

проворотить *see* **проворачивать.**

проворочать *v.* turn, roll (for a time).

проворство *n.* adroitness, dexterity.

провоцировать *v.* provoke; induce, stimulate (growth); (med.) excite, irritate.

провощить *v.* wax, impregnate with wax.

провя/ли(ва)ть *v.* sun-dry, jerk; **—нуть** *v.* dry out (somewhat).

прогад(ыв)ать *v.* miscalculate.

прогал *m.*, **—ина** *f.*, **—ок** *m.* (forest) clearing, glade; (ocean.) shore lead.

прогамный *a.* (biol.) progamic, before fertilization.

прогар *m.*, **—ина** *f.* burnout, burn(ing)-through, burnt place; hot spot; **—ный лист** baffle (plate).

прогастрин *m.* (biochem.) progastrin.

проген/ез *m.* (gen.) progenesis; **—ия** *f.* (orthodontics) progenia; (biol.) progeny.

прогерия *f.* progeria, premature old age.

прогест/ерон *m.* progesterone, luteal hormone; **—ин** *m.* Progestin.

прогиб *m.* sag(ging), deflection, flexure, camber; buckling, caving in, break; depression, trough; **краевой п., передовой п., предгорный п.** (geol.) foredeep; **стрела —а** deflection (of beams); opening (of spring); **—ание** *n.* deflection, sag(ging); **—ать** *v.* deflect; **—аться** *v.* deflect, sag, give; flex; yield, collapse, cave in; **—ающийся** *a.* deflecting, etc., *see v.*; **—омер** *m.* deflectometer.

прогла/дить, —живать *v.* iron, press, smooth out, plane, level; **—дка** *f.*, **—живание** *n.* ironing, etc., *see v.*; temper rolling.

прогл/атывание *n.* swallowing; **—атывать, —отить** *v.* swallow; **—оттида** *f.* (biol.) proglottid; **—оченный** *a.* swallowed.

прогля/деть, —дывать *v.* overlook, miss; glance through, scan; examine; **—дывать, —нуть** *v.* appear, show through.

прогнат/изм *m.* (med.) prognathism; **—ический** *a.* prognathous.

прогнать *see* **прогонять.**

прогн/ивание *n.* rotting through; **—и(ва)ть** *v.* rot through.

прогно/з *m.* forecast; prediction, prognosis; **ставить п., —зировать** *v.* predict, forecast, prognosticate; **—зирование** *n.* forecast(ing), prediction; projection; (comp.) look ahead; **—зист** *m.* forecaster; **—зный** *a.* predictive; **—стика** *f.* prognostication; **—стический** *a.* prognostic; forecast(ing).

прогнуться *see* **прогибаться.**

проголодать *v.* starve (for a time); hunger; **—ся** *v.* get hungry; fast.

прогон *m.* run, pass; drive; girder, main beam, span, stringer, baulk; bearer; (roof) purlin; (stair) well; **п. бумаги** (comp.) skip (in printing); **повторный п.** (comp.) rerun; **пробный п.** dry run; **холостой п.** (comp.) skip; **—ка** *f.* trial run; driving; screw die, threading die; **метод —ки** (comp.) elimination method; **—ять** *v.* drive (away, off, through); dismiss, fire; run, operate; pass (current, etc.); (mach.) drift; (comp.) skip (paper).

прогор/ание *n.* burning through; burn-out; **—ать, —еть** *v.* burn through, burn down; go bankrupt; **—елый** *a.* burnt through.

прогорк/ать *v.* get rancid; **—лость** *f.* rancidity; **—лый** *a.* rancid, rank; **—нуть** *see* **прогоркать.**

прогорчить *v.* make extremely bitter.

проградуирова/нный *a.* graduated, etc., *see v.*; **—ть** *v.* graduate, calibrate.

программ/а *f.* (comp.) program, routine; (educ.) schedule, curriculum; **составление —ы** programming; **п.-диспетчер** *m.* (comp.) supervisor (program); **п.-загрузчик** *m.* (comp.) loader; **—атор** *m.* programming device; programmer; **—ирование** *n.* programming, program writing, software development; **средства —ирования** software; **—ированный** *a.* programmed; **—ировать** *v.* program; **—ируемый** *a.* programmable; **—ирующий** *a.* programming; **—ирующая программа** (comp.) compiler; **—ирующее приспособление** programmer; **—но-аппаратные средства** firmware; **—ный** *a.* program(ming); preset (guidance; control); on the agenda, scheduled; **—ный механизм** programmer; **—ное обеспечение** software.

прогребать *v.* scrape (away), clean off.

прогрев *see* **прогревание; —аемость** *f.* heating capacity; extent of warm-up; **—ание** *n.* warming up, etc., *see v.*; warm-up; **—ать** *v.* warm up, warm thoroughly, heat.

прогреметь *v.* thunder.

прогресс *m.* progress, development, evolution; **—ивка** *f.* accelerating piece rate (of pay); **—ивно** *adv.* progressively, gradually, by degrees; **—ивно-горящий** *a.* progressive-burning; **—ивно-сдельная плата** *see* **прогрессивка; —ивность** *f.* progressiveness; **—ивный** *a.* progressive, progressing, gradual; accelerated; cumulative (depreciation); **—ировать** *v.* progress; **—ирующий** *see* **прогрессивный; —ия** *f.* progression; series.

прогрести *v.* scrape, clean off; row.

прогреть *see* **прогревать.**

прогрохо/тать, —тить *v.* screen, sift; **—чённый** *a.* screened, sifted.

прогрузить *v.* load, charge.

прогрыз/ать, —ть *v.* gnaw (through).

прогудеть *v.* buzz; hoot.

прогул *m.* absence from work; truancy, absenteeism; **—ка** *f.* walk; excursion; (bot.) shoot, scion; **—очный** *a. of* **прогулка;** promenade (deck); pleasure (boat); easy (pace); **—ьный** *a.* nonworking (day); **—ьщик** *m.*, **—ьщица** *f.* absentee, truant; shirker; **—ять** *v.* walk, stroll; be absent from work.

прод— *prefix* supply.

продав/ать *v.* sell, market; **—аться** *v.* sell, be on the market; **—ец** *m.* salesman, vendor.

продав/ить *see* **продавливать; —ливание** *n.* pressing through, etc., *see v.*; **—ливание на прессе** impact puncture (test); **сопротивление —ливанию** bursting strength; **—ливать** *v.* press through, force through, squirt; puncture, punch.

продавщица *f. of* **продавец.**

продаж/а *f.* sale, selling, marketing; **в —е** for sale, on sale, on the market; **имеющийся в —е** *a.* on the market, commercially available; **пустить в —у** *v.* (put on the) market; **—ный** *a.* selling, sales, marketing; commercial.

продалбливать *v.* chisel through, make a hole in.

проданный *a.* sold, marketed.

продать *see* **продавать.**

продви/гать *v.* move (forward), advance, promote; impel; extend; **—гаться** *v.* advance, move forward, get on, make way; **—жение** *n.* advance(ment), progress, headway; feed; **—нутый** *a.* progressive, etc., *see v.*; **—нуть(ся)** *see* **продвигать(ся).**

продев/ание *n.* passing through, etc., *see v.*; **—ать** *v.* pass through, run through, insert; thread.

продежурить *v.* watch, be on duty.

продезинфицировать *v.* disinfect.

продел *m.* cracked grain.

продел/ать *see* **проделывать;** **—ка** *f.* hole, opening; cutting; **—ывание** *n.* making, etc., *see v.;* execution; **—ывать** *v.* make; do, perform, execute; break through, open; cut (an opening); peel, shell; **—ьный** *a.* broken through; peeled, shelled; cracked (grain).

продельфин *m.* genus of dolphins (*Stenella*).

продемонстрировать *v.* demonstrate.

прод/ергать, **—ёргивать** *v.* pull through, thread; (agr.) thin out, pluck.

продержать *v.* keep, hold, detain; **—ся** *v.* hold out, stay.

продёржка *f.* pulling through, etc., *see* **продёргивать;** thinned seedling.

продёрнуть *see* **продёргивать.**

продеть *see* **продевать.**

продешев/ить, **—лять** *v.* sell below cost.

продигиозин *m.* prodigiosin(e).

продиктовать *v.* dictate.

продирать *v.* wear or tear holes (through), wear out; **—аться** *v.* be worn out; push through.

продифференцировать *v.* (math.) differentiate, take the derivative (of).

продиффундировавш/ий *a.* diffused; **—ее вещество** diffusate, dialyzate.

продком *m.* food committee.

продл/евать *see* **продлить;** **—ение** *n.* prolongation, extension; **—ённый** *a.* prolonged, extended; **—ить** *v.* prolong, extend, lengthen; **—иться** *v.* last.

прод/маг *m.* grocery; **—налог** *m.* tax in kind.

продовольств/енный *a.* supply, provision, food; ration (book, card); **п. склад** supply depot; **—енные товары** food(stuffs); **—ие** *n.* provisions, food(stuffs); rations.

продолбить *see* **продалбливать.**

продолговат/ость *f.* oblong form; **—ый** *a.* oblong; prolate, extended; elongated, prolonged; (anat.) oblongatal; **—ый мозг** (anat.) medulla oblongata.

продолж/атель *m.* continuer, successor; **—ать** *v.* continue, go on, go ahead, proceed; carry on, pursue, persist; resume; prolong, extend; elongate, lengthen, broaden; **—аться** *v.* be continued, etc.; continue, last, persist; be in progress; **—ающий** *a.* continuing, etc., *see v.;* **—ающийся** *a.* continuing; continued, serial (article); **—ение** *n.* continuation, etc., *see v.;* continuance; sequel; duration, course, space (of time), interval; **в —ение** in the course (of), during, throughout; **—енный** *a.* continued, etc., *see v.;* sustained; **—имость** *f.* extendibility; **—имый** *a.* extendible.

продолжительн/ость *f.* continuance, duration, length, period, time, cycle; endurance; (life) span; unbroken succession; **п. действия** (service) life; **п. жизни** life (expectancy), longevity; **п. круговорота** (biol.) life cycle; **п. полёта** lifetime (of satellite); **п. работы, п. службы** (useful) life; **полёт на п.** endurance flight; **—ый** *a.* continuous, lasting, prolonged, of long duration, long(-term), extended; persistent; chronic; **—ый режим работы** continuously rated operation; **на —ое время** for a long time.

продолжить *see* **продолжать.**

продольно *adv.* longitudinally, lengthwise; **—зубые** *pl.* (herp.) Mecodontia; **п.-овальный** *a.* (anat.) dolichopellic (pelvis); **п.-скользящий** *a.* sliding.

продольн/ый *a.* longitudinal, lengthwise, linear; drawn out; rip (saw); elevator, pitch (control); **п. изгиб** buckling; **п. набор** (aircraft) longitudinal framework; **п. профиль** long profile (of a river); **п. разрез** axial sec-

tion, longitudinal section; **—ая каретка** (mach.) saddle; **—ое движение** pitching; **—ое изменение** linear deformation; **в —ом направлении** lengthwise.

продорож/ённый *a.* slotted, etc., *see v.;* **—ивание** *n.* slotting, etc., *see v.;* **—ивать** *v.* slot; groove, rifle.

продпункт *m.* food supply depot.

продрейфовать *v.* drift.

продро/гнуть, **—жать** *v.* shiver; be chilled.

продром/а *f.*, **—альное явление** (med.) prodrome, premonitory symptom.

продтовары *pl.* foods, foodstuffs.

продуб/ить *v.* tan; **—лённый** *a.* tanned.

продувало *n.* ashpit.

продув/ание *see* **продувка;** **—ательный** *see* **продувочный;** **—ать** *v.* blow (through, off, out, or down); blast; scavenge, remove, exhaust (gases); purge, drain; bubble through; in(suf)flate; **—ка** *f.* blowing through, etc., *see v.;* blowout, blowoff; blowdown; blast cleaning; purge, drainage; (wind tunnel) test; (med.) insufflation; **—ной, —очный** *a.* blow-through, blow-out, blow-off, blast(ing); scavenging (air; pump); drain (cock).

продукт *m.* product, commodity, item; **—ате,** e.g. **п. адсорбции** adsorbate.

продуктивн/о *adv.* productively, efficiently, with good results; **—ость** *f.* productivity, efficiency; output, yield; **—ый** *a.* productive, fruitful, producing, efficient; commercial (livestock); active (vocabulary); -bearing, e.g. **—ые на флогопит пласты** phlogopite-bearing beds.

продуктовый *a.* produce, food.

продуктообмен *m.* barter.

продукц/ия *f.* production, productive capacity, output, manufacture; product(s), goods, manufactured articles; produce; **количество —ии** output.

продум/анный *a.* (well) thought out; **—(ыв)ать** *v.* think out, reason out; consider.

продут/ый *a.* blown (through), etc., *see* **продувать; —ь** *see* **продувать.**

продух *m.*, **—а** *f.* air hole.

продуц/ент *m.* producer; **—ирование** *n.* formation; **—ировать** *v.* produce, form; **—ирующий** *a.* producing, productive.

продушина *f.* air hole, vent; spiracle.

продушить *v.* permeate with a strong odor.

продымить *v.* smoke up.

продыряв/ить *see* **продырявливать; —ленный** *a.* perforated, etc., *see v.;* fenestrate; foraminous (tract); pitted, cribrose; **—ливание** *n.* perforation; **—ливать** *v.* perforate, puncture, pierce.

проед/ать *v.* eat away, corrode; **—енный** *a.* corroded.

проез/д *m.* passage(way); lane; thoroughfare, way; travel, journey; **—дить** *v.* ride, drive; **—дка** *f.* ride; **—дная плата** fare; **—дом** *adv.* in transit; passing through; **—жать** *v.* pass, drive, go (through), cover (a distance); **—жающий** *a.* passing (by, through); travelling; *m.* traveller, passerby; **—жая дорога** public road, highway, thoroughfare.

проект *m.* project, plan, scheme, layout, design; **п. стандарта** tentative standard; **составлять п.** *v.* plan, design; **технический п.** specification; **—ант** *m.* designer; **—ивность** *f.* (math.) projectivity; **—ивный** *a.* projective; **—ивное соответствие** projectivity.

проектиров/ание *see* **проектировка; п. на основе вычислительных машин** computer-aided design, CAD; **—анный** *a.* projected, etc., *see v.;* **—ать** *v.* project, design, plan, engineer; **—ка** *f.*, **—очный** *a.* projecting, etc., *see v.;* projection; design, layout; **—щик** *m.* designer; project engineer.

проектно/-конструкторские работы development; **п.-расчётный** *a.* preliminary estimation.

проектн/ый *a. of* **проект**; rated; theoretical; **—ая величина** (elec.) rating; **—ая мощность** (elec.) rated capacity; **—ая нагрузка** load rating; **—ая схема** layout.

проектор *m.* projector.

проекц/ионный *a.*, **—ия** *f.* projection; **вертикальная —ия** (arch.) front view, elevation; **горизонтальная —ия** plan view; **п. аппарат, п. фонарь** projector.

проём *m.* aperture, opening, embrasure; **п. двери** doorway; **—ный** *a.* through.

проесть *see* **проедать.**

проехать *see* **проезжать.**

проехидна *f.* long-billed anteater (*Proechidna*).

проецировать *v.* project (image).

прожар/енный *a.* thoroughly roasted; **—и(ва)ть** *v.* heat at a high temperature; roast thoroughly; fry.

прожать *see* **прожимать, прожинать.**

прождать *v.* wait.

прож/евать, —ёвывать *v.* masticate, chew thoroughly.

прожектор *m.* projector, searchlight, floodlight; (electron) gun; **—ист** *m.* projector operator; **—ный** *a. of* **прожектор**; beam (antenna); **—ное освещение** floodlighting.

прожелть *f.* yellowish tint.

прож/ечь *see* **прожигать; —жённый** *a.* burned (through, out).

проживать *v.* live, reside, stay; spend.

проживление *n.* refining.

прожиг/ание *n.* burning, etc., *see v.*; arc-over; (oxygen) lancing; **—ательный** *a.* burning (through, out); burn (bar), oxyacetylene (torch); **—ать** *v.* burn (through, out).

прожил/ка *f.* vein(let), fiber, filament; **—ково-вкраплённый** *a.* (geol.) vein-disseminated; **—ковый** *a.* streaky, veined; **—ок** *m.* vein(let), streak, stringer.

прожим/ание *n.* squeezing through (or out); trickling; **—ать** *v.* squeeze through (or out); **—аться** *v.* squeeze through (or out); trickle.

прожинать *v.* cut a swath.

прожир/енный *a.* greased, tallowed; **—овать** *v.* grease, tallow.

прожит/ие *n.* living, livelihood; **—ое** *n.* the past; **—очный** *a.* living; **индекс —очного минимума** cost of living index; **—ь** *see* **проживать.**

прожмёт *fut. 3 sing. of* **прожать.**

прожог *m.* (weld.) burn-through.

прожорливый *a.* voracious, gluttonous.

прожужжать *v.* buzz, drone.

прозама *f.* (foundry) mixer.

прозв/анивать *v.* test (a circuit) for continuity.

прозв/ание *n.* nickname; **—ать** *v.* (nick)name, call; **—енеть** *see* **прозвонить; —ище** *n.* cognomen, nickname.

прозв/онить *v.* ring, **—онка** *f.* continuity check.

прозвуч/ивание *n.* sounding; **—(ив)ать** *v.* sound, be heard.

проз/евать, —ёвывать *v.* miss, let slip.

прозект/ор *m.* prosector, dissector; **—орская** *f.* autopsy room, dissection laboratory; **—орский** *a.* dissecting; **—ура** *see* **прозекторская.**

прозелен/еть *v.* turn green; (bot.) stay green; **—ь** *f.* greenish tint.

прозенхима *f.* (bot.) prosenchyma.

прозерин *m.* proserine, neostigmine.

прозерпинус *f.* (ent.) hawk moths (*Proserpinus*).

прозимовать *v.* (spend the) winter.

прозо— *prefix* proso— (forward; anterior).

прозодежда *f.* work clothes.

прозопальгия *f.* (med.) prosopalgia, trigeminal neuralgia.

прозопиды *pl.* (ent.) Prosopidae.

прозопис *m.* (bot.) screw bean (*Prosopis*); **серёжкоцветный п.** mesquite (tree).

прозопо— *prefix* prosopo— (face); **—плегия** *f.* (med.) prosopoplegia, facial paralysis.

прозор *m.* space, gap.

прозорливый *a.* sagacious, discerning.

прозрачн/ость *f.* transparency; (optical) transmittance; (filter) transmission; **—ый** *a.* transparent, translucent, pellucid, limpid, clear; obvious; (biol.) hyaline; tracing (cloth).

прозр/е(ва)ть *v.* recover one's sight; **—ение** *n.* recovery of sight; enlightenment, insight.

прозубри(ва)ть *v.* file, sharpen (saw).

прозывать *see* **прозвать.**

прозэнцефалон *m.* (embr.) prosencephalon, forebrain.

прозяб *m.* (silv.) seedling growth; **—ание** *n.* vegetative life; **—ать** *v.* vegetate.

прозябнуть *v.* get thoroughly chilled.

проигра *f.* flight (of bees).

проигр/ать *see* **проигрывать; —ывание** *n.* losing; playback; simulation; rehearsal; **—ыватель** *m.* record player; **—ывать** *v.* lose (out); play (record); **—ыш** *m.* loss, failure; **коэффициент —ыша** disadvantage factor; **—ышный** *a.* disadvantageous, unfavorable.

произвед/ение *n.* production, work, composition; origination; (math.) product; **п. растворимости** solubility product; **ионное п.** (chem.) ionic product; **—ённый** *a.* produced, etc., *see* **проводить.**

произвести *see* **производить.**

произ-во *abbr.* (**производство**).

производимый *a.* producible.

производитель *m.* producer, generator; manufacturer, maker; grower; (breeding) sire, stud; **п. работ** works superintendent.

производительн/ость *f.* productivity, productiveness, production, productive capacity, output, yield, delivery, discharge (of pump); throughput; capacity, efficiency, effect, performance, duty (of machine); (elec.) rating; performance; **п. труда** output per man-hour; operating efficiency (of a plant); **—ый** *a.* productive, efficient; prolific.

производить *v.* produce, make, manufacture, turn out; form, build, construct; prepare; create, originate, fabricate; exert (pressure); generate (gas); derive; effect, perform, do; take (reading); set off (explosion); carry out (experiments); commission (an officer); **п. запрос** interrogate; challenge; **п. разведку** (mil.) reconnoitre; **п. ревизию** (comm.) audit; **п. экстраполяцию** (math.) extrapolate; **—ся** *v.* be produced, etc.; be in production, be available.

производн/ая *f.* (math.) derivative; **п. по** derivative with respect to; **брать —ую** *v.* differentiate, take the derivative (of); **—ое** *n.* (chem.) derivative; **—ые** *pl.* derivatives; **—ый** *a.* derivative, derived; secondary (forest).

производственн/ик *m.*, **—ица** *f.* industrial worker; **—о-контрольный** *a.* quality-control; **—о-технический** *a.* industrial-engineering.

производственн/ый *a.* industrial, manufacturing, production, commercial; process (control instrumentation); working (conditions, etc.), occupational (hazard, etc.); professional (skill); operative (staff); **п. контроль** plant supervision; **п. образец** prototype; **п. совет** work council; **—ая единица** production unit; **—ая**

мощность productive capacity; **—ая практика** industrial practice; **—ая стоимость** cost of production, operating cost.

производ/ство *n.* production, making, etc., *see* **производить;** manufacture; industry; factory, works, plant; output; **своего —ства** of domestic make; **—ящий** *a.* producing, etc., *see* **производить;** productive; producer; **—ящее колесо** (mach.) crown wheel; **—ящийся** *a.* being produced, in production, in process, in progress.

производьн/о *adv.* arbitrarily, at will; voluntarily; at random; **—ость** *f.* arbitrariness; randomness (of retrieval); **—ый** *a.* arbitrary; random; (geod.) assumed, undefined (scale); voluntary; **—ый доступ** random access; **—ая выборка** random access; **—ая постоянная** (math.) arbitrary constant; **—ое обращение** random access.

произн/ести, —осить *v.* pronounce, utter; make (a speech); **—ошение** *n.* pronunciation, articulation; utterance.

произойти *see* **происходить.**

произраст/ание *n.* growth, growing, springing (up); vegetation; **место —ания** habitat; **—ать** *v.,* **—и** *v.* grow, thrive; spring up, sprout; **—ающий** *a.* growing, etc., *see v.;* (bot.) native.

проиллюстрировать *v.* illustrate.

проинструктировать *v.* instruct.

проискать *v.* search (for).

происте/кать, —чь *v.* result, ensue, stem, arise, derive, spring (from); **—кающий** *a.* resulting, resultant.

происход/ившее *see* **происходящее; —ивший** *a.* having come (from), etc., *see v.;* **—ить** *v.* come (from), emanate, proceed, result, spring, arise, originate, be derived; descend, issue, stem (from); happen, occur, take place, be in progress, come about, come to pass; **—ящее** *n.* happening, past occurrence; **—ящий** *a.* coming (from), etc., *see v.;* under way, in progress.

происхождение *n.* origin(ation), genesis, birth, parentage, ancestry, descent; generation, procreation; derivation, extraction; emanation; **п. видов** (biol.) origin of species; **п. элементов** nucleogenesis.

происшедш/ее *n.* past occurrence(s), the past; **—ий** *past act. part. of* **произойти.**

происшествие *n.* incident, occurrence, event; accident, emergency.

пройденн/ое *n.* covered ground, material already covered; **—ый** *a.* passed, etc., *see* **проходить.**

пройма *f.* opening, aperture, hole.

пройти *see* **проходить; не п.** *v.* fail (a test).

прок *m.* use, benefit; **заготовлять в п.** *v.* cure (food); **запасать в п.** store.

прока/жённый *a.* (med.) leprous; *m.* leper; **—за** *f.* leprosy.

прокаин *m.* procaine, Novocaine.

прокал/ённый *a.* calcined, etc., *see v.;* **—иваемость** *f.* hardenability (of steel); penetration hardness; **—ивание** *n.* calcination, roasting, etc., *see v.;* **потеря при —ивании** ignition loss (of cement); **проба —иванием** fire assay; flame test; **—и(ва)ть** *v.* calcine, roast; bake, fire; ignite, burn; harden (steel); temper, anneal.

прокалыв/ание *n.,* **—ательный** *a.* puncturing, etc., *see v.;* **—ать** *v.* puncture, pierce, perforate; prick; punch.

прокамби/альный *a.* (bot.) procambial; **—й** *m.* (bot.) procambium.

прокапчивать *v.* smoke (up), cure.

прокапывать *v.* dig (out, through).

прокараулить *v.* stand guard.

прокарбоксипептидаза *f.* (enz.) procarboxypeptidase.

прокариот/ический, —ный *a.* (gen.) prokaryotic.

прокаркать *v.* (orn.) caw, croak.

прокармливать *v.* keep, feed.

прокарп(ий) *m.* (bot.) procarp.

прокат *m.* rolling; (met.) rolled products, (rolled) stock; lease, rent(ing); **—анный** *a.* rolled, laminated; **в —анном виде** as rolled; **—ать, —ить** *see* **прокатывать; —ка** *see* **прокатывание; —ный** *a.* rolling, milling; rolled; mill (scale); rented, rental; **—ный валок** roller; **—ный профиль** (met.) rolled shape.

прокат/чик *m.* roller, rolling mill operator; **—ывание** *n.* rolling, etc., *see v.;* **—ывать** *v.* roll, mill, flatten, laminate, draw out; drive, ride; **—ывать в холодном состоянии** cold-roll.

прокаченный *a.* rolled, etc., *see* **прокатить.**

прокач/иваемый *a.* pumpable; pumped, etc., *see v.;* **—ивать** *v.* pump (through); prime; bleed (brakes); **—ка** *f.* pumping, etc., *see v.;* injection; circulation.

прокашивать *v.* (agr.) mow.

проква/сить, —шивать *v.* (let) sour; leaven (bread); **—шенный** *a.* leavened.

прокип/ать, —еть *v.* boil thoroughly; **—ятить** *v.* (let) boil thoroughly; **—ячённый** *a.* boiled.

прокис/ать, —нуть *v.* (turn) sour, turn; **—лый, —ший** *a.* sour, rancid.

проклад/ка *f.* laying, etc., *see v.;* packing, pad(ding), cushion, lining, stuffing, filler, liner, seal; (inter)layer, washer, gasket; spacer, separator; (adjusting) shim; (biol.) trama, dissepiment; (naut.) plotting; **—ной** *a. of* **прокладка;** bearing (disk); **—ное кольцо** gasket; **—очный** *a.* laying, etc., *see v.;* **—чик** *m.* plotter (of course); **—ывать** *v.* lay (off, out); interlay, sandwich; run (a wire); plot (a course); break (a road); drive (a tunnel); pave (the way).

прокле/енный *a.* sized, etc., *see v.;* **—ивание** *n.* sizing, etc., *see v.;* **—и(ва)ть** *v.* (paper) size; paste, glue; **—йка** *see* **проклеивание;** size; sized product; **—йщик** *m.* sizer.

проклюнуться *v.* (orn.) peck through; emerge from egg; (bot.) sprout, appear.

проков/анный *a.* forged, etc., *see v.;* **—ать** *see* **проковывать; —ка** *f.,* **—очный** *a.* forging, etc., *see v.;* **—ывать** *v.* forge, hammer, peen.

проковыр/ивать, —ять *v.* pick through.

прокол *m.* prick(ing), puncture; (pin)hole; tap(ping); **напряжение —а** (elec.) punch-through voltage, collector-emitter breakdown voltage.

проколачивать *v.* break through.

проколка *f.* pricking, puncturing; (mach.) scrapless piercing.

проколлаген *m.* (pharm.) procollagen; **—аза** *f.* procollagenase.

проколот/ить *see* **проколачивать; —ый** *a.* bored, holed; perfossate, perforated, pierced.

проколоть *see* **прокалывать;** split.

прокомментировать *v.* comment, interpret.

прокомпостировать *v.* punch (a hole).

проконвертин *m.* (hemat.) proconvertin, Factor VII.

проконопа/тить, —чивать *v.* caulk (up).

проконспектировать *v.* summarize.

проконсультировать *v.* consult.

проконтролировать *v.* supervise, check; verify.

прокоп *m.* digging (out, through); dug-out; **—анный** *a.* dug (out, through); **—ать** *v.* dig (out, through); **—ка** *f.* digging.

прокопт/елый *a.* smoked, etc., *see v.;* sooty; **—еть** *v.* smoke; be smoked, be cured; **—ить** *v.* smoke (up), fumigate; smoke, cure.

прокорм *m.* feeding; nourishment; **—итель** *m.* host, donor; **—ить** *v.* feed; sustain; **—иться** *v.* subsist (on); **—ление** *n.* feeding, etc., *see v.*

прокорректировать *v.* correct, edit.

проко/с *m.* (agr.) swathe; **—сить** *v.* mow; **—шенный** *a.* mowed.

прокрадываться *v.* creep, get (through, by, past).

прокрас/ить *see* **прокрашивать;** **—ка** *f.* painting; dyeing.

прокрасться *see* **прокрадываться.**

прокраш/енный *a.* painted; dyed; **—ивание** *n.* painting; dyeing; (hist.) staining; **—ивать** *v.* paint; dye.

прокроить *v.* cut out (by pattern).

прокру/жить *v.* circle; spin around; **—тить** *see* **прокручивать;** **—титься** *v.* rotate, run, idle; **—тка** *f.* idling, motoring, cranking (of engine); (comp.) scrolling; **—ченный** *a.* rotated; scrolled; **—чивать** *v.* (comp.) scroll.

прокры(ва)ть *v.* prime, give a first coat.

проксазол *m.* (pharm.) proxazole.

проксимальный *a.* proximal.

проктальгия *f.* proctalgia.

прокт/ит *m.* (med.) proctitis; **—о—** *prefix* procto—(rectum); **—олог** *m.* (med.) proctologist; **—ополип** *m.* rectal polyp; **—оскопия** *f.* proctoscopy.

прокур(ат)ор *m.* procurator, agent; prosecuting attorney, public prosecutor; **военный п.** (mil.) judge advocate.

прокурсивный *a.* (pro)cursive (epilepsy).

прокуртка *f.* (comp.) scrolling.

проку/с *m.* bite (wound); **—сить,** **—сывать** *v.* bite through; **—шенный** *a.* bitten (through).

прол. *abbr.* **пролив.**

пролагать *see* **прокладывать.**

пролаз *m.* (crawl) hole, passage; **—ный** *a.* (for) access.

пролактин *m.* prolactin (hormone).

проламин *m.* prolamine, albumin.

проламывать *v.* break (through), cut open; fracture; **—ся** *v.* break through.

пролан *m.* prolan (hormone).

пролаять *v.* (zool.) bark.

прол/егать *v.* lie (of road); **—ежать,** **—ёживать** *v.* lie (around); **—ежень** *m.* (med.) bedsore; decubitus ulcer

пролёжка *f.* (leather) aging.

пролежневый *a.* (med.) decubital.

пролез(а)ть *v.* get through, wriggle through.

пролейкоцит *m.* (hemat.) proleucocyte.

пролей(те) *imp. of* **пролить.**

пролептический *a.* precocious; (med.) proleptic.

пролес/ка *f.* (bot.) squill (*Scilla*); (bot.) mercury (*Mercurialis*); **—ник** *m.* (bot.) mercury, **—ок** *m.* glade.

пролёт *m.* flight; span, spacing, bay, aperture, opening; aisle, runway; flight (of stairs), stairwell; transit (of electron); fly(ing)-by, fly(ing)-over; migration (of birds); **п. в свету** span, internal width; **время —а** transit time; flight time; **по времени —а** time of flight (spectrometer); **угол —а** transit angle.

пролетарский *a.* proletarian.

пролет/ать, **—еть** *v.* fly (past, over, through), cover (distance).

пролёт/ный *a. of* **пролёт;** (nucl.) drift, flight-path (tube); (orn.) migratory; **—ный путь** (orn.) flyway; **—ное строение** (bridge) span, bay; superstructure.

пролечь *v.* lie (of road).

пролив *m.* strait, sound, channel; spill(age).

пролив/ать *v.* spill; shed, throw (light); (foundry) cast on; **—ень** *m.* downpour; **—ка** *f.* spilling, etc., *see v.*; flow (test); **—ной** *a.* pouring (rain).

пролидаза *f.* (enz.) prolidase.

проликсин *m.* (pharm.) fluphenazine hydrochloride, Prolixin.

прол/ил *m.* prolyl; **—ин** *m.* proline, 2-pyrrolidinecarboxylic acid.

пролиназа *f.* (enz.) prolinase, iminadipeptidase.

пролит/ие *n.* shedding, spilling; **—ый** *a.* spilled; **—ь** *see* **проливать.**

пролифер/ативный *a.* proliferative; proliferating; **—ация** *f.* (biol.) proliferation; **—ировать** *v.* proliferate.

пролифи/кация *f.* (biol.) prolification; **—цировать** *v.* prolificate.

пролож/енный *a.* laid, etc., *see* **прокладывать;** sandwiched; interleaved; **—ить** *see* **прокладывать.**

пролом *m.* breach, gap, break; fracture; **—анный** *a.* breached, broken; **—ать,** **—ить** *see* **проламывать;** **—ник** *m.* (bot.) Androsace.

пролонг/ация *f.* prolongation; **—ировать** *v.* prolong.

пролыс/енный *a.* bared, denuded; bark-stripped; **—ина** *f.* bare spot, bald spot.

прольёт *fut. 3 sing. of* **пролить.**

пролювий *m.* (geol.) slopewash; proluvium.

проляжет *fut. 3 sing. of* **пролечь.**

пром. *abbr.* (**промышленность**).

пром— *prefix* industrial.

промаз/анный *a.* greased, etc., *see v.*; **—ать, —ывать** *v.* grease; smear, daub; coat; putty, fill up; **—ка** *f.* **—ывание** *n.* greasing, etc., *see v.*

промалывать *v.* mill.

промасл/енный *a.* oiled, etc., *see v.*; **—енная ткань** oilskin; **—ивание** *n.* oiling; lubrication; **—и(ва)ть** *v.* oil, treat with oil; lubricate.

промах *m.* miss, fault; blunder, slip, oversight, failure; **—иваться, —нуться** *v.* miss (the mark), miss one's aim.

промачив/ать *v.* wet thoroughly, drench, soak, steep; **—ающий** *a.* soaking.

промедл/ение *n.*, **—ить** *v.* delay.

промежност/но-влагалищный *a.* (anat.) perineo-vaginal; **—ный** *a.* (anat.) perineal; **—ь** *f.* perineum.

промежут/ки *pl.* (anat.) spatia; **—ок** *m.* interval, space, stretch, distance, gap, clearance, play; span; intermediate space, interspace; interstice; time interval, period, pause; **—ок времени** period, interval; **—ок встречи** collision gap.

промежуточн/ый *a.* intermediate; interjacent, interstitial; intervening (space; time); transfer (tank); secondary, auxiliary; relay (detonator); (comp.) half (adder); reheat (steam); catch (crop); intercalary, interposed; (chem.) connecting (link); false (bottom); scratchpad (memory); inter—, e.g. **п. холодильник** intercooler; **п. вал** communicator; **п. изолирующий слой** barrier layer (in semiconductors); **п. продукт** intermediate (product); **п. пункт маршрута** checkpoint; **п. слой** streak (in soil); **—ая кость** (anat.) intermedium, lunar bone; **—ая часть** spacer; **—ая шестерня** idler (gear); **—ое колесо** (mach.) cogwheel; **—ое кольцо, —ое тело** spacer.

промелет *fut. 3 sing. of* **промолоть.**

промелькнуть *v.* flash by, flash past.

промен *m.*, **—ивать,** **—ять** *v.* barter, exchange.

промер *m.* measurement, measuring; survey; error in measurement.

промерз/аемость *f.* freezing rate; **—ание** *n.* freezing; frost penetration; **глубина —ания, граница —ания, линия —ания** frost line; **—ать** *v.* freeze through.

промёрз/нуть *see* **промерзать;** **—лый** *a.* frozen.

промеривать *see* **промерять.**

промеристема *f.* (bot.) promeristem.

промер/ить *see* **промерять;** **—ный** *a.* measuring, surveying; sounding (line); **—ять** *v.* measure, survey; make a mistake in measurement.

промесить *v.* knead (thoroughly); puddle (clay).

промести *v.* sweep (out).

прометазин *m.* (pharm.) promethazine.

прометафаза *f.* (gen.) prometaphase.

прометий *m.* promethium, Pm.

промеш/анный *a.* thoroughly mixed; **—(ив)ать** *v.* mix well; knead well.

промикропс *m.* (ichth.) giant grouper (*Promicrops*).

промил/ле, —ь *adv.* pro mille, per thousand.

промин/ать *v.* knead, work; press in; exercise (an animal); **—ка** *f.* exercise (of horses).

промитоз *m.* (gen.) promitosis.

промодель *f.* master pattern.

промоет *fut. 3 sing. of* **промыть.**

промозглый *a.* damp, dank (weather); stagnant (air).

промои *pl.* wash water; **—на** *f.* washout, scour, gullied land; washed-out hole in ice.

промок/ание *n.* permeation, wetting; **—ательная бумага** blotting paper; **—ать, —нуть** *v.* get wet, get soaked, be permeated, be wetted; blot (of ink); **—ший** *a.* wet, soaked, permeated.

промол/ачивать —отить *v.* (agr.) thresh.

промолот/ый *a.* milled, etc., *see v.;* **—ь** *v.* mill, grind.

промолоченный *a.* threshed, thrashed.

промолчать *v.* keep quiet, not reply.

промораживать *v.* freeze through.

промороз/ить *промораживать;* **—ка** *f.* promorozka (natural freezing of the ground during the sinking of a pit in a water-bearing horizon).

промотать *v.* coil, wind; waste, misuse.

промо/тирование *n.* promotion; **—тировать** *v.* promote; **—тор** *m.* (catalyst) promoter, activator, accelerator.

промотыжить *v.* hoe, cultivate.

промоция *f.* promotion.

промочить *see* **промачивать.**

промоют *fut. 3 pl. of* **промыть.**

пром/предприятие *n.* industrial plant; **—продукт** *m.* intermediate product; (ore dressing) middlings; **—сток** *m.* industrial effluent.

пром-сть *abbr.* **(промышленность).**

промтовар/ный *a.,* **—ы** *pl.* dry goods.

промфинплан *m.* industrial and financial plan.

промчаться *v.* fly past, rush past.

промыв *m.* washout, channel; **—алка** *f.* washer; wash bottle; **—альщик руды** (min.) jig(ger); **—ание** *n.* washing, etc., *see* **промывать;** (med.) lavage, irrigation; leaching, elution; **—ание для ран** lotion; **—атель** *m.* washer, purifier, scrubber; **—ательный** *a.* washing; wash (bottle).

промыв/ать *v.* wash, rinse, flush (out); (chem.) elute, leach; scrub (gas); syringe (wound); **—ка** *f.* washing, etc., *see v.;* leaching operation (of soil); washer.

промывн/ой *a.* washing, flushing, rinsing.

промывочный *see* **промывной.**

промыс/ел *m.* trade, industry, business, profession; industrial enterprise; (oil) field, lease; catch, capture; **горный п.** mining.

промыслить *see* **промышлять.**

промысло/ведение *n.* technology; **—вик** *m.* professional trapper, hunter, or fisherman; miner; **—вый** *a.* industrial; commercial (fish); useful (plants); game (bird); fishing (e.g. boat, fleet); craft; **—вое свидетельство** (hunting, fishing, etc.) license.

промыт/ый *a.* washed, etc., *see* **промывать; —ь** *see* **промывать.**

промычать *v.* low, moo.

промышленн/ик *m.* manufacturer; industrialist; **—ость** *f.* industry.

промышленн/ый *a.* industrial, commercial; production; occupational (e.g. hazard); net (efficiency); pay (ore); **в —ом масштабе** on an industrial scale, industrially, commercially.

промышлять *v.* get, obtain, capture; hunt; fish; harvest; be engaged in a trade or industry.

промять *see* **проминать.**

прона/тор *m.,* **—торный** *a.* (anat.) pronator; **—ционный** *a.,* **—ция** *f.* (physiol.) pronation.

пронашивать *v.* wear out, wear through.

пронести(сь) *see* **проносить(ся).**

пронефрический *a.* (embr.) pronephric.

пронз/ать *v.* pierce; **—ённолистный** *a.* (bot.) perfoliate; **—ённый** *a.* (bot.) perfoliated (leaf); perforated; **—ить** *see* **пронзать; —ительный** *a.* piercing, sharp, shrill, acute.

пронз/(ыв)ать *v.* pierce, perforate; permeate; thread.

проник/ание *see* **проникновение; —ать** *v.* penetrate, permeate, find its way, pervade, infiltrate, filter through, percolate, impregnate; sink, work into, bore, pierce, pass through, gain access; **—ать взаимно** interpenetrate; **—аться** *v.* penetrate; be permeated; **—ающий** *a.* penetrating, etc., *see v.;* hard (radiation); thorough; (rockets) sweat (cooling); **—новение** *n.* penetration, etc., *see v.;* ingress; intrusion; insight; **двойники —новения** (cryst.) penetration twins.

проникнут/ый *a.* penetrated, etc., *see* **проникать; —ь** *see* **проникать.**

проницаем/ость *f.* penetrability, permeability, perviousness, porosity; transmittancy; (dielectric) permittivity; **вероятность —ости** penetration probability, transmission coefficient; **диэлектрическая п.** dielectric constant; **магнитная п.** permeability; **—ый** *a.* penetrable, permeable, pervious; passable, pellucid (light).

прониц/ание *n.* permeation; **—ательность** *f.* penetration, understanding, acumen, insight; penetrability; **—ательный** *a.* penetrating; acute, keen; shrewd, astute; **—ать** *see* **проникать.**

проно/с *m.* carrying; channel; **—сить** *v.* carry (along, past, through); wear; **—ситься** *v.* rush (along, past, through); wear (out); **—сный** *a.* purgative; **—шенный** *a.* worn out, worn through.

пронуклеус *m.* (gen.) pronucleus; **женский п.** egg nucleus.

пронумеров/(ыв)ать *v.* number.

проныр/ивать, —нуть *v.* dive under.

пронюх(ив)ать *v.* smell out.

прообраз *m.* prototype, standard; type, symbol, sign; **быть —ом** *v.* indicate.

пропавший *a.* lost, vanished, disappeared; fallen.

пропаганда *f.* propaganda.

пропага/тивный *a.* propagative, reproductive; **—ция** *f.* propagation.

пропагула *f.* (bot.) propagule.

пропада/ние *n.* loss; failure; (phys.) extinction; **—ть** *v.* be lost, vanish, disappear; (rad.) fade; perish; fall (a given distance).

пропа/диен *m.* propadiene, dimethylenemethane; **—езин** *m.* propaesin, propyl *p*-aminobenzoate.

пропажа *f.* loss; lost article.

пропазин *m.* (pharm.) Propazin (a herbicide).

пропаз/ить *v.* mortise, groove; **—ованный** *a.* mortised, grooved, slotted.

пропаивать *v.* solder; water (livestock).

пропаланин *m.* propalanine, aminobutyric acid.

пропали(ва)ть *v.* singe, burn (through).

пропалывать *v.* cultivate, weed.

пропан *m.* propane; **—ал(ь)** *m.* propanal, propionaldehyde; **—дикислота, —диовая кислота** malonic acid; **—овая кислота** propionic acid; **—ол** *m.* propanol, propyl alcohol; **—он** *m.* acetone.

пропар/ивание *n.,* **—ка** *f.* (low-temperature) steaming, steam-curing; **—иватель** *m.* steamer, sterilizer, autoclave; pressure cooker; **—ивать** *v.* steam (out); **—ина** *f.* proparina (open space in ice produced by subaqueous springs); **—очный** *a.* steaming.

пропарх/ивать *v.* dart, fly swiftly (past or between).

пропарывать *v.* rip, tear, cut (through).

пропасти *v.* pasture; **—сь** *v.* graze.

пропасть *see* **пропадать;** *f.* precipice, abyss, gulf; a great deal, a lot (of).

пропа/х(ив)ать *v.* plow (through); **—хнуть** *v.* become permeated with an odor; **—шка** *f.* (thorough) plowing; **—шник** *m.* furrow plow; cultivator; **—шной** *a.* tilling, cultivating; tilled, cultivated, row (crops).

пропащий *a.* ruined, lost, hopeless.

пропаять *v.* solder (thoroughly).

пропедевт/ика *f.* (educ.) introductory course; **—ический** *a.* introductory.

пропекать *v.* heat, bake (thoroughly).

пропеллер *m.* propeller; fan, impeller; **—ный** *a. of* **пропеллер;** propeller-type; agitator (mixer); axial-flow (pump).

пропен *m.* propene, propylene; **—ал(ь)** *m.* propenal, acrolein; **—ил** *m.* propenyl; **—илиден** *m.* propenylidene; **—иловый** *a.* propenyl; **—ол** *m.* propenol, allyl alcohol.

пропептон *m.* propeptone, hemialbumose.

пропердин *m.* properdin (serum protein).

пропечат(ыв)ать *v.* publish, print.

пропеч/ённый *a.* heated, baked (thoroughly); **—ь** *see* **пропекать.**

пропил *m.* kerf, (saw) cut, groove, gash, notch.

пропил *m.* propyl; **п. галлат** (pharm.) propyl gallate; **—амин** *m.* propylamine; **—бензол** *m.* propylbenzene.

пропилен *m.* prop(yl)ene; **—гликол** *m.* propylene glycol, propanediol.

пропиленный *a.* sawed (out, through, up to).

пропиливать *v.* saw (out, through, up to).

пропилиден *m.* propylidene.

пропилит *m.* (petr.) propylite; **—изация** *f.* propylitization; **—овый** *a.* propylite, propylitic.

пропил/ить *see* **пропиливать; —ка** *f.* sawing (out, through, up to).

пропилнитрит *m.* propyl nitrite.

пропиловый *a.* propyl; **п. спирт** propyl alcohol, propanol; **п. эфир уксусной кислоты** propyl acetate.

проп/ин *m.* propyne, allylene; **—инал(ь)** *m.* propynal, propioaldehyde; **—иновая кислота** propynoic acid, propiolic acid; **—инол** *m.* propynol, propargyl alcohol; **—иолактон** *m.* propiolactone; **—иолил** *m.* propiolyl; **—иоловый** *a.* propiolic; **—иоловый альдегид** *see* **припинал(ь).**

пропион *m.* propione, 3-pentanone; **—ат** *m.* propionate; **—ил** *m.* propionyl.

пропионитрил *m.* propionitrile, ethyl cyanide.

пропионово/кислый *a.* propionic acid; propionate (of); **п. натрий, —натриевая соль** sodium propionate; **—кислая соль** propionate; **—этиловый эфир** ethyl propionate.

пропионов/ый *a.* propionic; **п. альдегид** propionic aldehyde, propionaldehyde; **—ая кислота** propionic acid; **соль —ой кислоты** propionate.

пропиофенон *m.* propiophenone.

пропис/анный *a.* prescribed, etc., *see v.;* **—ать** *see* **прописывать; —ка** *f.* visa, registration; residence permit; inscription, entry; omission, erratum; **—ной** *a.* capital

(letter); common (truth); **—очный** *a.* visa, registration; **—ывание** *n.* prescribing, etc., *see v.;* prescription; **—ывать** *v.* prescribe, order; register, enter, record; **—ь** *f.* prescription, recipe; sample of writing; (preliminary) sketch, outline; **—ью** *adv.* in words, written out (of figures).

пропитание *n.* subsistence, livelihood.

пропит/анность *f.* (degree of) impregnation; **—анный** *a.* impregnated, etc., *see v.;* dipped; **—ать** *see* **пропитывать;** feed, nourish; **—ек** *m.* (mam.) sifaka (*Propithecus*); **—ка** *see* **пропитывание;** impregnating compound; (capillary) imbibition; **—очный** *see* **пропитывающий; —ываемость** *f.* impregnability; **—ываемый** *a.* impregnable, etc., *see v.;* **—ывание** *n.* impregnation, soaking, etc., *see v.;* treatment; **—ывать** *v.* impregnate; soak, saturate, permeate, steep, dip, treat; preserve (wood); **—ывать дёгтем** tar; **—ывающий** *a.* impregnating, etc., *see v;* **—ывающее вещество** impregnant.

пропих/(ив)ать, —нуть *v.* shove, push (through).

проплав *m.* fusion, melting; smelting rate.

проплавать *v.* swim, cruise, sail.

проплав/ить *see* **проплавлять; —ка** *see* **проплавливание; —ление** *n.* (weld) penetration; **—ливание** *n.* melting, fusion; **—ленный** *a.* melted, fused; **—ливать, —лять** *v.* melt, fuse, smelt; **—ной шов** transfusion weld.

пропластид *m., —а* *f.* (bot.) proplastid.

пропласток *m.* (geol.) intercalation, interstratification, parting; (gas) streak; (thrust) sheet.

проплесневеть *v.* become moldy.

пропле/сти *v. see* **проплестать; —стись** *v.* stagger along; **—тать** *v.* braid, weave (into).

проплешина *f.* bald spot, bare spot.

проплиопитекус *m.* (pal.) Propliopithecus.

проплы(ва)ть *v.* swim, float, sail, cruise (along, past, through).

проповед/ник *m., —овать* *v.* advocate.

пропод/еум *m.* (ent.) propodeon; **—ит** *m.* (crust.) propodite; **—иум** *m.* (mal.) propodium.

пропоить *v.* water (livestock).

пропокси— *prefix* propoxy—.

прополаскив/ание *n.* rinsing, flushing; **—ать** *v.* rinse, flush, gargle.

прополз/ать, —ти *v.* creep, crawl (past, through).

прополис *m.* propolis, bee glue.

прополка *f.* weeding.

прополоск/анный *a.* rinsed, flushed, etc., *see v.;* **—ать** *v. see* **прополаскивать.**

прополо/тый *a.* weeded; **—ть** *v.* weed (out); **—чный** *a.* weeding; **—ьник** *m.* weeder, hoe.

пропонал *m.* proponal, di-*iso*-propylbarbituric acid.

пропорхнуть *see* **пропархивать.**

пропорциональн/о *adv.* proportionally, in proportion, as; **изменяться п.** vary with or as; **обратно п.** inversely proportional (to); **прямо п.** directly proportional (to); **среднее —ое** mean proportion; **—ость** *f.* proportionality, ratio; **обратная —ость** inverse proportion, inverse ratio; **—ый** *a.* proportional, proportionate, in proportion; balanced.

пропорция *f.* proportion, ratio; degree, rate; **п. флегмы** reflux ratio.

пропот/евание *n.* transudation, etc., *see v.;* **—е(ва)ть** *v.* transude, exude through; perspire (heavily); **—елый** *a.* soaked with perspiration.

проприо— *prefix* proprio— (one's own); **—цептивный** *a.* (physiol.) proprioceptive.

пропрясть *v.* spin.

пропс *m.* prop; **—ы** *pl.* props.

пропудривание *n.* (rubber) dusting.

пропульсивный *a.* propulsive.

пропуск *m.* pass, permit; admission, passing, passage; omission, skip(ping), lapse, miss; (comp.) ignore; blank (space), gap, lacuna; absence, nonattendance; idle stroke (of piston); balk (in plowing); release (from reservoir); escapement (of salmon, etc.); leak(ing); (mil.) pass(word); **п. зажигания** misfire; **за один п.** in one operation; **регулирование —ами** hit and miss governing; **—аемость** *f.* transmittancy, transmissivity; throughput; **—аемый** *a.* transmitted; **—аемая полоса** (elec.) pass band, bandwidth.

пропускан/ие *n.* pass(ing through), passage; omission; (illum., elec. comm.) transmission; bubbling (gas); (comp.) gating; **п. через фильтр** filtration; **коэффициент —ия** transmission factor; **полоса —ия** pass band, bandwidth; **схема —ия** (comp.) gate, gating circuit.

пропу/скатель *m.* (elec.) bandpass filter; acceptor; **—скательный** *a.* transmitting, etc., *see v.*; **—скательная способность** transmissivity; **—скать** *v.* transmit, carry; (let) pass, pass through, run through, allow passage, conduct; bubble (gas); (comp.) gate; omit, leave out, miss, skip, ignore; rove (rope); leak; **—скать мимо** by-pass; **—скающий** *a.* transmitting, etc., *see v.*; by-pass; gating (impulse); acceptor (circuit); translucent, transparent; **не —скающий воды** watertight; **—скной** *a.* permeable; carrying, throughput (capacity); **—скная способность** throughput, carrying capacity; operating capacity; permeability; **—стить** *see* **пропускать;** **—щенный** *a.* transmitted, etc., *see v.*

пропылить *v.* (raise) dust; **—ся** *v.* get dusty.

прораб *m.* foreman, supervisor.

прораб/атывание *see* **проработка;** **—атывать, —отать** *v.* work (at, through, up); study, become familiar (with); criticize; treat, process; **—отка** *f.* working, etc., *see v.*; study, critical analysis.

проран *m.* (hydr.) boat passage (in dam); closure channel; wash-out.

прора/стание *n.* intergrowth; (geol.) penetration; (bot.) germination; **двойник —стания** (cryst.) penetration twin; **щель —стания** (pal.) germinal aperture; **—стать** *v.* (inter)grow; penetrate; germinate, sprout, shoot (up); appear; (med.) invade; **—стающий** *a.* intergrowing, etc., *see v.*; invasive (cancer); **—сти** *see* **прорастать; —стить** *v.* (make) germinate; **—щение** *see* **прорастание; —щённый** *a.* intergrown; penetrated, etc., *see v.*; **—щивание** *see* **прорастание; —щиватель** *m.* (agr.) germinator; **—щивать** *v.* let germinate.

прорва *f.* mud hole, swamp hole; narrow channel.

прорва/нный *a.* broken through, etc., *see v.*; **—ть** *see* **прорывать.**

прореагиров/авший *a.* reacted; converted; **—ать** *v.* react.

проредактировать *v.* edit.

проре/дить *see* **прореживать; —жённый** *a.* (agr.) thinned (out); **—живание** *n.* thinning (out); **—живать** *v.* thin (out).

прорез *m.* slot, slit, groove; notch, recess, cut, nick; perforation, aperture; section; cutting; **—ание** *n.* cutting, slotting; **—анный** *a.* slotted, slit; notched, cut; **—ать** *see* **прорезывать.**

прорезин/енный *a.* rubberized, etc., *see v.*; **—ивание** *n.* rubberizing, etc., *see v.*; **—и(ва)ть** *v.* rubberize, coat with rubber, treat with rubber; **—ка** *see* **прорезинивание.**

прорез/ка *f.* cutting, etc., *see v.*; **—ной** *a.* cutting, slit(ting); scroll, fret (saw); **—ной шов** slot lap weld;

—ная трава (bot.) mountain parsley (*Peucedanum oreoselinum*); **—ывание** *see* **прорезка;** dentition; **—ывание зубов** eruption (of teeth), teething; **—ывать** *v.* cut (through), slit, slot, notch; **—ывать канавки** *v.* groove; **—ывать пазы** *v.* slot; **—ь** *see* **прорез;** fishing boat for carrying live fish.

прореха *f.* hole, slit, tear; lapse, gap.

прорецензировать *v.* review, criticize.

прорешка *dim. of* **прореха.**

проржав/евший *a.* rusted through; **—еть** *v.* rust through.

прорис *m.* tracing; **—ованный** *a.* traced, drawn; **—о-в(ыв)ать** *v.* trace, draw; **—овка** *f.*, **—овывание** *n.* tracing, drawing.

пророет *fut. 3 sing. of* **прорыть.**

пророс *past m. sing. of* **прорасти; —тковый** *a.* germinal; **—ток** *m.* (bot.) plantule; germ; seedling; blastopore; **—ть** *f.* sprout; marbling (of fat in meat); (wood) defect; fibrous formation (in fruit); **—ший** *a.* germinated, sprouted; intergrown.

пророч/еский *a.* prophetic; **—ить** *v.* predict.

проруб/ать, —ить *v.* chop, break (through); **—ь** *f.* ice hole.

проруха *f.* mistake, oversight.

прорыв *m.* breaking through, etc., *see v.*; break(through), breach, gap; outbreak, (out)burst, rupture, blowout; (in)rush; debacle; leakage; **полный п.** breakdown; **—ать(ся)** *v.* break through, break out; tear, rupture, burst open; dig through; (agr.) thin; **—ка** *f.* digging; (agr.) thinning.

прорыскать *v.* hunt, search; (naut.) yaw.

прорыт/ие *n.* digging; **—ый** *a.* dug (out, through); **—ь** *v.* dig (out, through); burrow through.

прорычать *v.* growl, snarl.

просадить *see* **просаживать.**

просад/ка *f.*, **—очный** *a.* sag(ging), subsidence, slump.

просажать *v.* plant, set out.

просаж/енный *a.* broken through, etc., *see v.*; **—ивать** *v.* break through, pierce; waste, squander; **—иваться** *v.* settle (down).

просаливать *v.* salt down.

просали(ва)ть *v.* grease.

просапогенин *m.* prosapogenin.

просасыв/ание *n.* suction, draft; **—ать** *v.* draw through; suck through; filter; **—аться** *v.* be drawn through; infiltrate; seep through.

просачив/ание *n.* soaking (through), permeation, etc., *see v.*; seepage, leak(age), escape; exudation; **—аться** *v.* soak (through), permeate, impregnate, infiltrate, percolate; ooze (through), exude, seep, leak, escape; **—ающийся** *a.* soaking (through), etc., *see v.*

просверкать *v.* flash (of lightning).

просверл/ённый *a.* drilled, etc., *see v.*; **—ивание** *n.* drilling, etc., *see v.*; (med.) trephination; **—и(ва)ть** *v.* drill, bore, perforate, pierce.

просвет *m.* clearance, opening, gap, break, space; (rad.) gate; (anat.) lumen; beam (of light); **на п.** (micros.) by transillumination.

просветит/ельный *a.* instructive, enlightening; **—ь** *see* **просвещать.**

просветл/ение *n.* clarification; becoming paler; brightening; lucid interval; **—ённость** *f.* clearness; **—ённый** *a.* clarified; translucent; coated (lens); **—еть** *v.* clear up, become clear, clarify; become lucid; **—ить, —ять** *v.* clear, clarify; bleach; coat (a lens); **—яющий** *a.* clarifying, clearing; antireflection (coating).

просветн/ость *f.* translucence; **—ый** *a.* translucent, see-through.

просвеч/енный *a.* (trans)illuminated, etc., *see v.*; **—ива́емость** *f.* translucence; **—иваемый** *a.* translucent; **—ивание** *n.* (trans)illumination; translucence; radioscopy, X-raying; candling (of eggs); **—ивать** *v.* (trans)illuminate; shine through; X-ray, examine with X-rays; be translucent; **—ивающий** *a.* translucent, diaphanous, transparent; (micros.) transmitting, transmission-type.

просвещ/а́ть *v.* enlighten, educate, inform; **—е́ние** *n.* enlightenment, education; **—ённый** *a.* enlightened, educated, informed; expert (opinion); clarified.

просвинцо́ванный *a.* lead-impregnated.

просви́рн/ик, —я́к *m.* (bot.) Malva.

просе́в *m.* sifting; undersize (ore, etc.); gap (in sowing); balk (in plowing); **—а́льный** *a.*, **—а́ние** *n.* sifting, etc., *see v.*; **—а́ть** *v.* sift, screen, bolt, riddle, sieve; **—ка** *see* **просева́ние.**

просе́д/ание *n.* collapse, sag(ging), caving in, subsidence; **—а́ть** *v.* collapse, cave in, sag.

про́седь *f.* streaks of gray or white hair(s).

просе́ивать *see* **просева́ть.**

просе́к *m.*, **—а** *f.* cut-through, breakthrough; (min.) cross adit, cross hole; (forestry) ride, clearing, opening, gap, swath; **противопожа́рный п.** firebreak; **—а́ние** *n.* cutting through, breaking through; **—а́ть** *v.* cut through, break through.

просекрети́н *m.* prosecretin (hormone).

просёло/к *m.*, **—чная доро́га** country road, dirt road, side road.

просере́нный *a.* fumigated with sulfur.

просе́сть *see* **проседа́ть.**

просе́ч/ка *f.* breakthrough, gap; notching; punching; breaking through, cutting through; **—ь** *see* **просека́ть.**

просе́/янный *a.* screened, sifted, riddled; **—ять** *see* **просева́ть.**

просигнали(зирова́)ть *v.* signal, warn.

проси/де́ть, —жива́ть *v.* stay, sit (through).

проси́н/ить *v.* blue; **—ь** *f.* bluish color.

проси́т/ель *m.*, **—ельница** *f.* (law) petitioner; **—ь** *v.* ask, request, solicit; sue; intercede; **—ься** *v.* ask.

проси́ять *v.* brighten up, shine (through), irradiate.

проскабли́ть *v.* scrape through.

проска́к(ив)ать *v.* jump, spring, slip (in, past, through), get through.

проска́льзыв/ание *n.* slipping, etc., *see v.*; slip(page); **—ать** *v.* slip (past, through); channel, by-pass.

проскан(д)и́ровать *v.* scan, analyze.

проскобли́ть *see* **проскабли́вать.**

проско́к *m.* passage; getting through; breakthrough (in ion exchange); overshoot(ing); (mach.) missing, skip(ping); **п. и́скр** sparking; **п. перено́са** (comp.) carry skip; **п. пла́мени** flashback; **—ну́ть** *see* **проскаки́вать.**

проскользну́ть *see* **проска́льзывать.**

проскочи́ть *see* **проскаки́вать.**

проскре/ба́ть, —сти́ *v.* scrub thoroughly; scrub through.

проскули́ть *v.* whine (of dog).

проскурня́к *see* **просви́рник.**

прослаби́ть *v.* have loose bowels, have diarrhea.

просла́в/иться, —ля́ться *v.* become famous; **—ленный** *a.* famous, celebrated.

просла́ив/ание *n.* interlaying, etc., *see v.*; **—ать** *v.* interlay, interstratify, interbed, interleave; sandwich, insert (between); layer; (chem.) overlay.

просле/ди́ть *see* **просле́живать; —дова́ть** *v.* pass, proceed, go; **—женный** *a.* traced, followed; **—живание** *n.* tracing, etc., *see v.*; **—живать** *v.* trace, track, follow.

просло́/ек *see* **просло́й; —ённый** *a.* interlaid, etc., *see* **прослаивать; —ечный** *a.* *of* **просло́йка; —ить** *see* **прослаивать; —й** *m.*, **—йка** *f.* interlayer(ing); layer, sheet, lamina; pad(ding); insert(ion); (air) space; (geol.) intercalation, interstratification, interbed, band, parting; (soil) streak; separating layer; **с —йками** interlayered (with).

прослужи(ва)ть *v.* serve, be used; run, operate.

прослу́ш/ивание *n.* listening; (elec. commun.) crosstalk; (educ.) auditing, attendance; **п. перфора́ций** sprocket hum; **контро́льное п.** monitoring; **—(ив)ать** *v.* listen; audit, attend.

просма́ливать *v.* tar, coat with tar, impregnate with tar; treat with resin.

просма́тривать *v.* look through, look over, scan; (comp.) browse; overlook, miss; (rad.) sweep.

просмол/е́ние *n.* tarring, etc., *see* **просма́ливать;** resin exudation; **—ённый** *a.* tarred, etc., *see* **просма́ливать;** friction (tape); **—и́ть** *see* **просма́ливать.**

просмо́тр *m.* survey, review; (comp.) lookup; browse; scanning; omission, oversight, blunder; **п. вперёд** (comp.) look-ahead; **п. содержи́мого па́мяти** (comp.) storage scan; **предвари́тельный п.** look-ahead; **—енный** *a.* reviewed; revised, checked, looked over, examined; **—еть** *see* **просма́тривать.**

просну́ться *v.* wake up.

про́со *n.* millet (*Panicum*); **италья́нское п.** foxtail millet (*Setaria italica*); **кури́ное п.** barnyard millet (*Echinochloa crus-galli*); **обыкнове́нное п., посевно́е п.** broomcorn millet (*Panicum miliaceum*); **—ви́дный** *a.* miliary, like millet seeds; **—вод** *m.* millet grower.

просо́вывать *v.* push through, shove through, force through, extrude.

просо́вый *a.* millet.

просол/енный *a.* salted, preserved in salt; salt-impregnated; corned (beef); **—и́ть** *v. see* **проса́ливать.**

просору́шка *f.* millet mill.

прососа́ть *see* **проса́сывать.**

просо́х/нуть *v.* get dry, dry out; **—ший** *a.* dried.

просочи́ться *see* **проса́чиваться.**

проспа́ть *v.* sleep (through), miss; oversleep.

проспе́кт *m.* prospectus, pamphlet, brochure, folder; avenue, boulevard; **—ивный** *a.* prospective; advertising.

проспе́ктор *m.* (min.) prospector.

проспиртов(ыв)а́ть *v.* treat with alcohol.

просро́ч/енный *a.* overdue; **—ивать, —ить** *v.* be overdue; hold over, delay; **—ка** *f.* delay, expiration (of term).

прост *sh. m. of* **просто́й.**

проста́в/ить *see* **проставля́ть.**

простагланди́н *m.* (bioch.) prostaglandin, PG.

проста́в/ка *f.* spacer; **—ля́ть** *v.* enter, record; **—ок** *m.*, **—очный** *a.* spacer.

проста́ивать *v.* stand.

простано́вка *f.* specification (of tolerances).

проста́т/а *f.*, **—и́ческая железа** (anat.) prostate (gland); **—и́т** *m.* (med.) prostatitis; **—о—** *prefix* (anat.) prostat(o)— (prostate); **—оэктоми́я** *f.* prostatectomy.

прост/ега́ть, —ёгивать *v.* quilt; **—ёгивание** *n.*, **—ёжка** *f.* quilting.

просте́йш/ий *a.* the simplest; **—ие** *pl.*, **—ие живо́тные** (zool.) Protozoa.

простели́ть *v.* lay (over), spread.

просте́но/к *m.*, **—чный** *a.* partition, pier.

простере́ть *v.* stretch, extend.

простере́чь *v.* watch, guard; miss.

просто́ртый *a.* stretched, etc., *see* **простира́ть;** prostrate.

простетический *a.* prosthetic (group).

прост/еть *v.* become simpler; **—ец** *m.* uneducated person.

простилать *v.* lay, spread.

простир/ание *n.* stretch, extension, extent; spread(ing); (geol.) course, strike, trend; **п. пластов** direction of strata; **—анный** *a.* laundered, washed; **—ать** *v.* stretch, extend, reach (out); launder; **—аться** *v.* stretch, reach, range, spread, extend; (geol.) trend, run, strike; **—ывать** *v.* launder, wash.

простит/ельный *a.* pardonable, justifiable; **—ь** *v.* pardon, forgive.

просто *adv.* simply, merely, just; *prefix* hapl(o)— (single, simple); **—губый** *a.* (bot.) haplocheilic.

прост/ой *a.* simple, ordinary, plain, straightforward; bare, mere; prime (factor, number); main (UDC number); monovalent (bond); common (fraction); (rockets) single-stage; single-head (wrench); single-entry (bookkeeping); cotton (stockings); flat (rate); naked (eye); *m.* standstill, standing (time), (forced) inactivity, idle time, lost time; demurrage; **время —оя** downtime, idletime, waiting time; **иметь п.** *v.* be idle, be inactive; **—ая балка** freely supported beam; **—ого действия** single-action; **—ое вещество, —ое тело** element; **—ойный** *a.* idle(-time), downtime.

простокваша *f.* sour milk, clabber, yogurt.

простолистник *m.* (bot.) Haplophyllum.

простонать *v.* groan, moan.

простор *m.* spaciousness, ampleness, roominess, space, scope; **—ный** *a.* spacious, ample, roomy, capacious, open; spatial, steric.

просторожить *see* **простеречь.**

простота *f.* simplicity; ease (of operation); **п. обслуживания** easy servicing.

простоять *v.* stand, stay, remain.

прострагивать *v.* plane, shave.

пространн/о *adv.* extensively; at length, in detail; **—ость** *f.* extensiveness; **—ый** *a.* extensive, vast, ample; verbose; detailed.

пространственн/о-временной *a.* space-time; **п.-однородный** *a.* spatially homogeneous; **—оподобный** *a.* space-like; **—ый** *a.* space, spatial, steric, three-dimensional; solid (angle); directional (quantization); cross-linked (polymer); block, graphic (diagram); **—ый блок** (building) module; **—ый заряд** space charge; **—ая изомерия** stereoisomerism; **—ая решётка** (cryst.) space lattice; **—ая формула** spatial formula; **—ая химия** stereochemistry; **—ое затруднение,** **—ое препятствие** steric hindrance; **—ое размещение** spacing.

пространств/о *n.* space, spacing, expanse, scope, extent, range, amplitude; field, area; room, volume; distance; inside (of furnace); (anat.) spatium; (bot.) life span; **на широком —е** over a widespread area.

прострация *f.* prostration, exhaustion.

прострачивать *v.* stitch; machine-gun.

прострел *m.* (radiation) streaming, leakage; channeling; (med.) lumbago, myalgia; (bot.) anemone; pasque flower (*Pulsatilla*).

прострел/ивание *n.* firing, etc., *see v.*; (well) shooting; **—и(ва)ть** *v.* fire, shoot (through); clean, blow out (tubes); perforate; **—ка** *see* **прострeливание; —очно-взрывный** *a.* shooting; **—очный** *a.* firing, etc., *see v.*; **—ять** *see* **прострeливать.**

прострогать *v.* plane, shave.

простроить *v.* build.

прострочить *see* **прострачивать.**

простру́г(ив)ать *v.* plane, shave.

просту/да *f.* (med.) common cold; **—диться, —жаться** *v.* catch cold; **—дный** *a.* catarrhal.

простукивать *v.* rap, tap.

проступ/ать, —ить *v.* show (through), come out, appear; ooze, exude.

проступок *m.* fault; misdemeanor, breach of regulations.

проступь *f.* tread; going.

простучать *v.* tap (out); knock.

простывать *v.* cool off.

простынный *a.* sheet.

простынуть *v.* cool off.

простыня *f.* sheet.

просунуть *v.* push, shove (through).

просуш/енный *a.* dried, etc., *see v.*; **—ивание** *n.* drying, etc., *see v.*; **—и(ва)ть** *v.* dry (out, thoroughly), desiccate, dehumidify; season (timber); **—ка** *see* **просушивание.**

просуществовать *v.* exist.

просчёт *m.* calculation error; count-down, counting loss; checking.

просчит(ыв)ать *v.* check; count; miscount; **—ся** *v.* miscount; miscalculate.

просыпа/ние *n.* sifting, screening; **—ть** *v.* spill; oversleep; **—ться** *v.* wake up, awaken, rouse; be spilled, spill.

просыхать *v.* dry (up).

просьб/а *f.* request, petition, application; **обращаться с —ой** *v.* ask, request.

просянка *f.* (bot.) bristly foxtail grass (*Setaria*); (orn.) corn bunting (*Emberiza calandra*).

просяной *a.* millet.

просящий *a.* requesting, asking.

протагон *m.* protagon.

протаив/ание *n.* thawing; **—ать** *v.* thaw (out), melt (through).

протактин/иды *pl.* protactinides; **—ий** *m.* protactinium, Pa.

проталин/а *f.* thawed patch, puddle (in ice or snow); **—ка** *dim. of* **проталина.**

проталкив/ание *n.* pushing (through); **—ать** *v.* push, force (through).

проталлий *m.* (bot.) prothallium, prothallus.

протамин *m.* protamine (simple protein); **—аза** *f.* (enz.) protaminase.

протандрия *f.* (bot.) prot(er)andry.

протанопия *f.* (ophth.) protanopia.

протапливать *v.* heat.

протаптывать *v.* beat (a path).

протарг/ил *m.* protargyl, protyle; **—ол** *m.* Protargol.

протарс *m.* a calcium arsenite seed disinfectant.

протаск/а *f.* towing; **—ивать** *v.* drag, pull, run (through); tow.

протаспис *m.* (zool.) protaspis (trilobite larva).

протач/ать *v.* stitch; **—ивание** *n.* stitching, etc., *see v.*; **—ивать** *v.* stitch; turn (on lathe); erode, wash out; bore (of worm).

протащить *see* **протаскивать.**

протаять *see* **протаивать.**

протеаза *f.* protease, proteolytic enzyme.

протез *m.* (med.) prosthesis; (hearing) aid; **—ирование** *n.* prosthetics; **—ист** *m.* prosthetist; **—ный** *a.* prosthetic.

протеи *pl.* (zool.) Proteidae.

протеид *m.* proteide (protein).

протеин *m.* protein; **—аза** *f.* proteinase; **—овый** *a.* protein; proteic (acid); **—овое вещество** protein; **—оз** *m.* (med.) proteinosis; **—урия** *f.* (med.) proteinuria.

протей *m.* (zool.) Proteus; **американский п.** water lizard

(*Necturus*); **европейский п.** blind white salamander (*Proteus anguineus*).

протёк *m.* passage; drip, seepage.

протек/аемость *f.* leakage; **—ание** *n.* passing, etc., *see v.*; flow; course; occurrence; **потенциал —ания** streaming potential; **—ать** *v.* pass, flow, run (past, through); leak, seep; proceed, take place, occur; elapse; **—ать нормально** take a normal course; **—ающий** *a.* passing, etc., *see v.*; leaky.

протектированный *a.* protected; recapped (tire); self-sealing.

протектор *m.* protector, protective device, protective cover; (tire) tread; **—ный** *a. of* **протектор;** sacrificial (electrode); **—ная защита** (met.) cathodic protection.

протёкший *past act. part. of* **протечь.**

протел *m.* (mam.) aardwolf.

протеоли/з *m.* proteolysis; **—тический** *a.* proteolytic, protein-splitting.

протерандрия *see* **протандрия.**

протереть *see* **протирать.**

протеро— *prefix* proter(o)— (earlier, former); **—генез** *m.* proterogenesis; **—гиния** *f.* prot(er)ogyny; **—зой** *m.,* **—зойская эра** (geol.) Proterozoic era.

протерпеть *v.* endure, undergo.

протёртый *a.* rubbed (through), etc., *see* **протирать;** worn, threadbare; strained (food).

протёс *m.,* **—ка** *f.* cutting, etc., *see v.*

потесать *see* **потёсывать.**

потёсывать *v.* cut, hew, dress.

протеч/ка *f.* leakage, seepage; **—ный** *a. of* **протёк;** filter (paper); **—ь** *see* **протекать.**

против *prep. gen.* opposite, facing; (as) against, versus; to; anti—, counter—; contrary to, as compared with; **п. ветра** upwind; **за и п.** pro and con; **идти п.** *v.* oppose; **лекарство п.** medicine for.

противень *m.* drip pan; griddle; tray; baking tin.

противиться *v.* oppose, resist, object.

противн/ик *m.* adversary, opponent, enemy; **воздушный п.** enemy air forces; **—о** *prep. dat. and adv.* contrary to, against; disgustingly; **—ый** *a.* opposed, contrary, adverse, head (wind); alien; disgusting, repugnant; **в —ом случае** otherwise.

противо— *prefix* counter—, anti—; contra—; **—атомный** *a.* antinuclear; **—бактерийный** *a.* antibacterial; **—болевой** *a.* (med.) analgesic, antipain; **—борство** *n.* hostile encounter, conflict.

противобродильн/ый *a.* antifermentative, antizymotic; **—ое средство** antiferment.

противо/вес *m.* counterweight, counterpoise, balance weight; **—вирусный** *a.* (med.) antiviral; **—включение** *n.* (elec.) opposition, balancing; **—воздушный** *a.* anti-aircraft; air defense (training); **—воспалительный** *a.,* **—воспалительное средство** (med.) antiphlogistic; anti-inflammatory; **—вспениватель** *m.* foam suppressant; **—вспенивающий** *a.* antifoam(ing); **—вуалирующий** *a.* (phot.) antifogging; **—выбрасывающее устройство, —выбросовое устройство** (petrol.) blowout preventer; **—вытяжение** *n.* (med.) counterextension.

противогаз *m.,* **—овый шлем** gas mask, respirator; **—овый** *a.* gasproof, antigas.

противо/гельминтный *see* **противоглистный; —гидролокационный** *a.* antisonar; **—гистаминный** *a.* antihistaminic; **—глистный** *a.* (med.) anthelmintic, vermifuge.

противогнилостн/ость *f.* asepsis; resistance to rotting; **—ый** *a.* a(nti)septic; antiputrefactive; preservative; **—ое средство** preservative.

противо/градиент *m.* antigradient; **—грибковый** *a.* fungicidal, antifungal; **—гриппозный** *a.* influenza virus (vaccine), flu (vaccine); **—гусеничный** *a.* (mil.) tank-disabling; anti-track (mine); **—давление** *n.* counterpressure, back pressure, resistance.

противодейств/ие *n.* counteraction, reaction, resistance, opposition, counterforce; countermeasure; **оказывать п.** *v.* counteract; **радиоэлектронные —ия** electronic countermeasures, ECM; **—овать** *v.* counteract, react (against); oppose, resist; cross; destroy; **—ующий** *a.* counteractive, reactive; opposing, antagonistic; reactionary; **—ующий момент** antagonistic couple; **—ующая сила** counterforce, opposing force, thrust.

противо/десантный *a.* (mil.) beach-defense; anti-airborne; **—детонирующий** *a.* antiknock; **—динатронная сетка** (rad.) suppressor grid; **—дифтерийный** *a.* (med.) antidiphtherial; **—днищевый** *a.* (mil.) tank-killing, belly-attack (mine); **—дымный** *a.* smoke-suppressant, smoke (filter); **—естественный** *a.* unnatural, irregular, abnormal.

противо/завиток *m.* (anat.) ant(i)helix; **—задирный** *a.* antiscuff; antiscoring; **—законный** *a.* illegal; **—закручиватель** *m.* anti-twist device; **—замерзающий** *a.* antifreeze; **—заморозковая защита** frost control; **—зачаточное средство** contraceptive; **—зенитный** *a.* (mil.) anti-aircraft; evasive (action); **—змеиный** *a.* (med.) antivenous; **—змейное средство** antivenin; **—зудный** *a.* (med.) antipruritic; **—изгибатель** *m.* reinforcer; **—излучение** *n.* (meteor.) back radiation, counter-radiation; **—износный** *a.* wear-resistant; **—ион** *m.* counterion, gegenion.

противо/кашлевый *a.* antitussive, cough (remedy); **—кислотный** *a.* acidproof; (pharm.) ant(i)acid; **—коагулирующий** *a.* anticoagulant; **—козелок** *m.* (anat.) antitragus; **—коклюшный** *a.* (med.) antipertussis (serum); **—компаундный** *a.* differential compound; **—коревой** *a.* (med.) measles (vaccine); **—коррозионный** *a.* anticorrosive; **—космический** *a.* (mil.) antisatellite, antispacecraft; **—кражная сигнализация** burglar alarm; **—личиночный** *a.* larvicidal; **—лежать** *v.* (geom.) subtend, lie opposite; **—лежащий** *a.* (lying) opposite.

противолихорадочн/ый *a.* antifebrile; **—ое средство** febrifuge, antifebrile.

противо/лодочный *a.* antisubmarine; **—лодочная подводная лодка** hunter-killer submarine; **—ломотный** *a.* (med.) antiarthritic; **—луна** *f.* (meteor.) antiselene; **—малярийный** *a.* (med.) antimalarial; **—микробный** *a.* antimicrobic; **—мягчитель** *m.* stiffener; **—накипное средство** boiler compound; **—напряжение** *n.* counter-voltage; **—нитный** *a.* counterfilar.

противообледенитель *m.* de-icer; anti-icer; **—ный** *a.* de-icing; anti-icing.

противо/обрастающий *a.* antifouling; **—общественный** *a.* antisocial; **—озоностаритель** *m.* antiozonant; **—окислитель** *m.* antioxidant; **—опухолевый** *a.* (med.) antitumor(igenic); **—ореольность** *f.* antihalation; **—ореольный** *a.* antihalo; **—осколочный** *a.* splinterproof; **—отверстие** *n.* (med.) contra-aperture; **—откатный** *a.* (art.) counterrecoil; **—отражательный** *a.* antireflection, nonglare; **—паводковый** *a.* flood-control; **—параллельный** *a.* (geom.) antiparallel.

противо/перегрузочный *a.* antigravity; **п. костюм** G-suit; **—пехотный** *a.* (mil.) antipersonnel.

противопожарн/ый *a.* fireproof; fire-fighting; fire (break); **—ая техника** fire prevention.

противопоказ/ание *n.* contraindication; **—анный** *a.*

contraindicated; **—ующий, —ывающий** *a.* contraindicant.

противополагать *see* **противопоставить.**

противополож/ение *n.* contrast, antithesis, contradistinction; opposition; **—ить** *see* **противопоставить; —но** *adv.* contrarily, contrariwise, in contrast, oppositely; **—ное** *n.* the contrary, the reverse, counterpart; **—ность** *f.* opposition, contrast; converse, reverse (of); **в —ность** on the contrary, in contrast (to), unlike; as opposed (to); **—ный** *a.* contrary, opposite, opposed, contradictory, reverse, inverse, counter—, antithetic(al); incoherent (orientation); **диаметрально —ный** antipodal.

противопомпажный *a.* antisurge.

противопоносный *a.* antidiarrheal.

противопостав/ить *v. see* **противопоставлять; —ление** *n.* contrasting, etc., *see v.;* opposition; contraposition; **в —лении** versus; **—лять** *v.* contrast, set against, set off; oppose, object; **—ляющий** *a.* contrasting, etc., *see v.;* opposite; **—ляющая мышца** (anat.) opponens.

противопригарная краска (met.) mold wash, mold coating.

противо/пылевой *a.* dust (flap); **—пыльный** *a.* dustproof, dust-tight; **—радиолокационный** *a.* antiradar, radar (countermeasures); **—ракета** *f.,* **—ракетный** *a.* antimissile, antiballistic missile (defenses), ABM; **—раковый** *a.* (med.) anticarcinogenic; **—рвотный** *a.* (med.) antiemetic; **—регулирование** *n.* counterregulation.

противореч/иво *adv.* in contradiction; **—ивость** *f.* conflict, inconsistency, discrepancy; **—ивый** *a.* conflicting, discrepant, inconsistent, contradictory; **—ие** *n.* conflict, discrepancy, inconsistency, contradiction; variance; **устранение —ий** (comp.) disambiguation; **—ить** *v.* conflict, be in conflict (with), be at variance (with), contradict; contrast.

противоросник *m.* (astr.) dew cap.

противо/самолётный *a.* antiaircraft; **—свёртывающий** *a.* (hemat.) anticoagulative; **—связь** *f.* (constr.) counter-tie; (rad.) negative feedback; **—сибиреязвенный** *a.* (vet.) antianthrax (serum); **—сифилитический** *a.* (med.) antisyphilitic; **—сияние** *n.* (astr.) counterglow; **—скарлатинозный** *a.* (med.) antiscarlatinal; **—совпадающий** *a.,* **—совпадение** *n.* (nucl.) anticoincidence; **—средство** *n.* antidote, remedy; **—старитель** *m.* age resistor, antideteriorant, preservative; **—столбнячный** *a.* (med.) antitetanic.

противосто/яние *n.* resistance; (astr.) opposition; **—ять** *v.* resist, oppose, withstand, face; contradict, conflict (with); **—ящий** *a.* opposed, resisting; opposite.

противосудорожн/ый *a.,* **—ое средство** (med.) antispasmodic.

противо/сумеречный *a.* anticrepuscular; **—сырост-ный** *a.* dampproof, moisture-resistant; **—танковый** *a.* (mil.) antitank; **—тело** *n.* (immun.) antibody; **—течение** *n.* counterflow; **—тифозный** *a.* (med.) antityphoid; **—ток** *m.* countercurrent, counterflow; reflux; return flow; **—торпедный** *a.* antitorpedo; **—точный** *a. of* **противоток; —тральный** *a.* antiminesweeping; **—туберкулёзный** *a.* (med.) antitubercular; **—туманный** *a.* fog (lights); **—тяга** *f.* reverse thrust.

противо/угон *m.* (rr.) anticreeper, rail anchor; **—угонный** *a.* anticreep, antisliding; **—ударный** *a.* collision (protection); **—утомитель** *m.* antifatigue agent; **—фаза** *f.* antiphase, opposite phase; **в —фазе** out of phase; **—фильтрационный** *a.* impervious; **—флоккулирующий** *a.* antiflocculating; **—фоновый** *a.* (rad.) antibackground; antihum.

противохимическ/ий *a.* (mil.) antigas, antichemical (warfare), anti-CW; **—ая оборона** gas defense, chemical warfare (CW) defense.

противохолерный *a.* (med.) anticholeric.

противо/цинготный *a.* (med.) antiscorbutic; **—чумный** *a.* (anti)plague (vaccine, etc.); **—шёрстный** *a.* counter (course); (rr.) facing; **—штопорный** *a.* antispin (parachute); **—шум** *m.* earplug; **—шумовой** *a.* antinoise; **—эдс** *f.* (phys.) back emf; **—электродвижущий** *a.* counterelectromotive; **—эрозийный** *a.* soil conservation, erosion-preventive; **—эховый** *a.* anti-echo, antireflection; **—юзовый** non-skid; **—ядие** *n.* antidote; **—ядный** *a.* antidotal.

протий *m.* protium (hydrogen isotope).

протир/ать *v.* rub (through); grate; wear through; rub clean, wipe, sponge (clean, dry, off); **—ка** *f.,* **—очный** *a.* rubbing (through), etc., *see v.;* swab, slush brush; **—очная машина** triturator.

протис/кать, —кивать, —нуть *v.* press, squeeze (through, past).

протисты *pl.* (biol.) Protista.

проткать *v.* weave (a design).

проткнуть *see* **протыкать.**

прото— *prefix* proto— (first); **—актиний** *m.* protactinium, Pa; **—анемонин** *m.* (pharm.) protoanemonin; **—вератрин** *m.* protoveratrine; **—гем** *m.* (biochem.) (proto)heme; **—ген** *m.* (geol.) protogen; (chem.) protogen A, thioctic acid; **—генный** *a.* protogenic; **—зоа** *pl.* (zool.) protozoa; **—зойный** *a.* protozoan; **—исторический** *a.* prehistoric.

проток *m.,* **—a** *f.* canal, channel, branch (of river); bayou; tube; throat, neck (of furnace); (anat.) duct; dilution; **маленький п.** ductulus, ductule.

протокатех/овая кислота protocatechuic acid, 3,4-dihydroxybenzoic acid; **—ол** *m.* protocatechol.

протокла/з *m.* (petr.) protoclase; **—стический** *a.* protoclastic.

протококк/и *pl.,* **—овые зелёные водоросли** (bot.) Protococcaceae.

протокол *m.* (diplomacy; med.; commun.) protocol; log, report; **п. квитирования связи** (commun.) handshaking protocol; **—ировать** *v.* record; **—ы** *pl.* minutes, record(s), proceedings, transactions.

протоксилема *f.* (bot.) protoxylem.

протокурарин *m.* protocurarine.

протол/из *m.* protolysis; **—ит** *m.* protolyte; **—итический** *a.* protolytic.

протолк/ать, —нуть *see* **проталкивать.**

протолковать *v.* discuss.

протолоч/ка *f.* grinding, crushing; **—ь** *v.* grind, pulverize; break, crush.

протон *m.* proton.

протонема *f.* (bot.) protonema.

протонефть *f.* protopetroleum.

протон/изация *f.* (phys.) proton addition, proton acceptance.

протон/-мишень *m.* target proton; **—ный** *a.* proton(ic).

протоно/генный *a.* (chem.) protogenic; **—генный растворитель** proton donor, protogenic solvent; **—обменный ЯМР** (phys.) proton-enhanced nuclear magnetic resonance; **—фильный** *a.* (chem.) protophilic; **—фильный растворитель** proton acceptor, protophilic solvent.

протопин *m.* protopine, fumarine.

протопить *v.* heat (up); melt.

протоплазм/а *f.* (biol.) protoplasm; **—енный** *a.* protoplasmic.

протопласт *m.* protoplast.

протопорфирин *m.* protoporphyrin.

протоптать *see* **протаптывать.**

протоптер, —ус *m.* African lungfish (*Protopterus annectens*); **—овые, —усы** *pl.* (ichth.) Protopteridae.

протор/ить, —ять *v.* make, beat (a path).

прото/сома *f.* (gen.) protosome; **—така** (mal.) littleneck clam (*Protothaca*); **—тип** *m.* prototype.

прототроп/ия *f.* prototropy, proton transfer; **—ный** *a.* prototropic.

протофи/брилла *f.* (hist.) protofibril; **—льный** *a.* protophilic; **—фит** *m.* (bot.) protophyte; **—флоэма** *f.* (bot.) protophloem.

протоцилиаты *pl.* (zool.) Protociliata.

проточ/ек *m.* (anat.) ductule, ductulus; **—енный** *a.* turned, etc., *see v.;* **—енный червями** worm-eaten; **—ина** *f.* channel; eroded gully; worm hole; **—ить** *v.* turn, machine; wash out, erode; eat, gnaw, bore; **—ка** *f.* turning, etc., *see v.;* groove; **—ки** *pl. of* **проточек, проточка.**

проточн/ость *f.* flow(age); **—ый** *a.* flow(ing), flow-type, flow-through; circulating, continuous(-flow); running (water); production (line); entrained-flow (reactor); **—ый счётчик** flow-type counter; **—ая часть** casing (of pump).

протрав/а *f.* (met.) pickling, dip; (dyeing) mordant(ing); (wood) stain; **—итель** *m.* (seed) disinfectant; seed-treating apparatus; **—ить** *see* **протравливать; —ка** pickling, etching, staining; disinfection; **—ление** *see* **протравливание; —ленный** *a.* pickled, etc., *see v.;* **—ливание** *n.* pickling, etc., *see v.;* (seed) disinfection, treatment; **газовое —ливание** fumigation; **—ливатель** *see* **протравитель; —ливать** *v.* (met.) pickle, etch; soak, dip, steep; (dyeing) mordant; stain (wood) disinfect, treat (seeds); **—ливающий** *a.* pickling, etc., *see v.;* **—лять** *see* **протравливать.**

протрав/ной *a. of* **протрава; —очный** *see* **протравливающий;** mordant.

протрак/тор *m.* (instr.) protractor; **—ция** *f.* (anat.) protraction.

протрали(ва)ть *v.* sweep, trawl (for mines).

протратить *v.* spend, expend.

протрезв/еть, —иться, —ляться *v.* sober up.

протрёт *fut. 3 sing. of* **протереть.**

протромбин *m.* prothrombin, factor II; **—аза** *f.* (enz.) prothrombinase, factor V.

протрузия *f.* protrusion.

протуберан(е)ц *m.* (astr.) protuberance, prominence.

протух/ать *v.* become rotten, spoil; become moldy; **—лость** *f.* rottenness; mustiness; moldiness; **—лый** *a.* rotten; musty; spoiled (food); **—нуть** *see* **протухать.**

протык/алка *f.* pricker; **—альник** *m.* skewer; **—ать** *v.* prick through, pierce, puncture, punch.

протычка *f.* pricker.

протягив/ание *n.* extending, etc., *see v.;* **—ать** *v.* extend, stretch, draw out; pull through, draw through; run, lay; broach (holes); drag out, prolong; reach out; **—аться** *v.* extend, stretch out; last.

протяжен/ие *n.* extent, stretch, expanse; spread, expansion, extension, elongation; range, amplitude; field; space, area; distance, dimension, length; run; **п. времени** duration; **п. в длину** length; **п. в ширину** width; **на —ии** during; over a length (of); **на всём —ии** all the way from . . . to.

протяжён/ность *see* **протяжение; —ный** *a.* extended, etc., *see* **протягивать.**

протяж/ка *see* **протягивание;** (mach.) broach; (comp.) (tape) transport; (mach.) fullering; **устройство —и (бумаги)** (comp.) paper tractor; **—ной** *a. of* **протяж-**

ка; pull-through; broaching (lathe); **—ность** *f.* slowness, drawl (of speech); **—ный** *a.* drawn out, long-lasting, slow, lengthy; batch-type (furnace); pull-through (winding).

протянут/ый *a.* extended, etc., *see* **протягивать; —ь** *see* **протягивать.**

Проута гипотеза Prout hypothesis.

проучи(ва)ть *v.* teach (a lesson).

проушина *f.* lug, ear, eye, loop, ring.

проф. *abbr.* (**профессиональный; профессор; профсоюзный**).

проф— *prefix* trade-union; professional, vocational, occupational.

профаг *m.* (gen.) prophage.

профаза *f.* (biol.) prophase.

профермент *m.* proenzyme, zymogen.

профессиограмма *f.* job description.

профессионал *m.* professional, specialist; **—изация** *f.* specialization; **—ьно-технический** *a.* vocational; **—ьный** *a.* professional; vocational; occupational (disease, hazard); trade (union).

professс/ия *f.* profession, occupation, trade, business, function; **—ор** *m.* professor; **—орский** *a.* professorial; **—орско-преподавательский состав** faculty; **—орство** *n.* professorship.

профетин *m.* prophetin.

профзаболевание *n.* occupational disease.

профилакт/ика prophylaxis, preventive treatment; preventive measure; (fire) prevention; (mach.) preventive maintenance; **—ический** *a.* prophylactic; preventive, protective; routine (check); (comp.) marginal (checking); **—ический осмотр** preventive maintenance; **—ическая мера** prophylactic, preventive; **—ическая наладка** trouble shooting; preventive maintenance; **—ическое средство** *see* **профилактическая мера; —орий** *m.* dispensary; (mach.) preventive maintenance building.

профилизация *f.* specialization.

профилиров/ание *n.* profiling, etc., *see v.;* shape (of rolls); **—анный** *a.* profiled, etc., *see v.;* profile; **—ать** *v.* profile, cut a profile, shape, form; grade; **—ка** *see* **профилирование; —очно-гибочный** *a.* forming, shaping (mill); **—очный** *a.* profiling, etc., *see v.;* forming (mill).

профил/ирующий *see* **профилировочный;** *a.* profile; **п. зазор** die.

профилл *m.* (bot.) prophyl(lum).

профил/ограф *m.* surface roughness recorder.

профил/ь *m.* profile, shape, outline, contour, lines, design; cross section, side view; elevation; qualification, capability; **продольный п.** longitudinal section; **широкого —я** multiskilled (worker).

профильн/ый *a. of* **профиль;** profiling, forming, shaping, edging (tool); special-shape (tubes); specialized, occupational (publication); **п. фрезер** profile cutter; **—ая проекция** end view; **—ое железо** section(al) iron, sections.

профильтров/анный *a.* filtered (through or out); **—(ыв)ать** *v.* filter (through or out).

про/флавин *m.* proflavine, 3,6-diaminoacridine; **—форетин** *m.* prophoretin.

профондометр *m.* (med.) profondometer.

профориентация *f.* vocational guidance.

профрезированный *a.* milled.

проф/союз *m.,* **—союзный** *a.* trade union; **—техшкола** *f.* trade school, vocational school.

профундаль *f.* profundal zone (of body of water).

профшкола *see* **профтехшкола.**

прохаживать *see* **проходить.**

прохват/ить, —ывать *v.* penetrate; chill.

прохла/да *f.* coolness, freshness; **—дительный** *a.* cooling, refreshing; soft (drinks); refrigerating; **—дить** *see* **прохлаждать;** **—дно** *adv.* coolly; it is cool; **—дность** *f.* coolness, freshness; **—дный** *a.* cool, fresh; **—ждать** *v.* cool, chill; refresh; **—ждённый** *a.* cooled, etc., *see v.*

проход *m.* passage(way), conduit, canal, channel, duct, vent; pass; breach, gap, cut; passing (through); thoroughfare, way, lane, aisle, alley(way); aperture, opening, orifice, gate; (anat.) undersize; (screening) undersize; (drawing) draft; **за один п.** in one operation, per pass; **задний п.** (anat.) anus; **проделывание —ов** breaching; **слуховой п.** (anat.) acoustic meatus; **узкий п.** (anat.) isthmus.

проходим/ость *f.* passability, etc., *see a.*; trafficability; capacity (of vehicles) for cross-country travel; **—ый** *a.* passable, navigable; permeable, pervious.

проходить *v.* pass, go, walk, move, travel (across, past, by, through); traverse; run, extend; cross, cover (distance); go over, learn; penetrate, permeate; (min.) cut, drill; sink (shaft); drive (tunnel); undergo, be subjected (to); negotiate (curve); terminate, end, stop, be over, expire, elapse; run, operate, work; disregard, overlook; fall (of rain); be held (of meeting); take (a course); **не п.** hang on, linger.

проход/ка *f.* passing, etc., *see v.*; (drilling) footage, progress, penetration; tunneling; (met.) working, heading; **—ная** *f.* passage(way); **—ник** *m.* drill, auger; **—ной, —ный** *a.* through; straightway; transfer; continuous (furnace); flow-passage; go (gage); (ichth.) migratory, anadromous, transitory, transient; **—ной изолятор** bushing insulator, (feed-)through insulator; **—ной пункт** portal; **—ная рубка** (silv.) thinning; **—ом** *adv.* in passing; **—ческий** *a.* (min.) cutting, drilling, sinking; heading, tunneling; **—чик** *m.* tunneler, drift miner; **—ящий** *a.* passing, etc., *see v.*; transient; transmitted (light); *m.* passerby, transient; **—ящий сквозь** (anat.) emissary.

прохож/дение *n.* passing, etc., *see* **проходить;** passage, path; flow; transmission; traversal; (astr.) transit; **—ий** *a.* passing, transient; *m.* passerby, transient.

прохол/аживать, —одить *v.* chill.

прохолостение *n.* barrenness, dryness.

прохондральный *a.* (embr.) prochondral.

процарап(ыв)ать *v.* scratch (through).

процвета/ть *v.* prosper; thrive; flower; **—ющий** *a.* thriving, etc., *see v.*; prosperous, flourishing, vigorous.

процедить *see* **процеживать.**

процедура *f.* procedure; (court) proceedings; (med.) treatment.

процеж/енный *a.* strained, etc., *see v.*; **—ивание** *n.* straining, etc., *see v.*; **—ивать** *v.* strain, filter; percolate.

процельный *a.* (anat.) procoelous.

процент *m.* percent(age); incidence; interest rate; **п. влажности** moisture content; **в —ах** on a percentage basis; **в весовых —ах, весовой п.** percent by weight; **содержание в —ах** percentage, content; **число —ов** *n.* percentage; **—иль** *f.* (stat.) percentile; **—ность** *f.* percentage; degree.

процентн/ый *a.* of **процент;** interest-bearing; percent(age); **—ая квантиля** percentile; **—ое начисление** interest charge; **—ое отношение** percentage; **—ое отношение по весу** percent by weight; **—ое отношение по объёму** percent by volume; **—ое содержание** percentage, percent, content.

процеркоид *m.* (biol.) procercoid.

процесс *m.* process, operation; procedure; lawsuit; **вводить в п.** put on stream; **в —е** in the course (of), during.

процессия *f.* procession.

процессор *m.* processor; **п. базы данных** (comp.) back-end processor; **ассоциативный п.** content-addressable processor; **главный п.** host processor; **командный п.** shell; command processor; **служебный п.** server; **текстовой п.** word processor; **центральный п.** central processing unit, CPU.

процитировать *v.* quote.

прочекани(ва)ть *v.* stamp, punch (out); (hort.) pinch back.

прочен *sh. m.* of **прочный.**

прочёркивать *v.* draw a line.

прочер/кнуть *see* **прочёркивать;** **—тить, —чивать** *v.* draw.

прочёс *m.* combing(s); (text.) web, fleece; **—анный** *a.* combed.

прочесать *see* **прочёсывать.**

прочесть *see* **прочитать.**

прочёсыв/ание *n.* combing; hackling (of flax); **—ать** *v.* (text.) card, comb; hackle; (paper) brush; search.

проч/ий *a.* other, rest, remaining; sundry (accessories); **и —ее** and so on, et cetera; **и всё —ее** and all the rest of it; **кроме всего —его** among other things; **между —им** by the way, incidentally; **между —ими** among the rest, among others.

прочинить *v.* fix, mend, repair.

прочист/ить *see* **прочищать;** **—ка** *f.* scouring, cleansing; (med.) purging; (silv.) thinning (out), clearing; **—ной** *a.* of **прочистка.**

прочит(ыв)ать *v.* read, peruse; scan; (comp.) get.

прочить *v.* intend (for).

прочищ/ать *v.* scour, cleanse, clean (out), clear; (silv.) thin; (med.) purge; **—аться** *v.* clear up; **—ающий** *a.*, **—ение** *n.* scouring, etc., *see v.*

прочн/ист *m.* material-strength engineer; structures specialist; **—о** *adv.* firmly, etc., *see* **прочный;** securely, tightly, permanently (bound); **—о-плотный** *a.* composite (weld); **—оскелетный** *a.* (biol.) armored; **—остной** *a.* of **прочность;** strength.

прочност/ь *f.* strength, durability, toughness; firmness, rigidity, sturdiness, solidity, soundness, reliability; tenacity, endurance, lasting (quality), stability, permanence; resistance; fastness (of color); **п. конструкции** structural strength; **п. на** resistance to; **п. на изгиб** bending strength, transverse strength; **п. на износ** resistance to wear; **п. на кручение** torsional strength; **п. на разрыв** tensile strength; **п. на сдвиг, п. на срез** shearing strength; **п. на удар** resistance to impact; **длительная п.** endurance limit; **запас —и, коэффициент —и** strength factor; **испытание на п.** endurance test; **предел —и** (tensile) strength; **предел —и на сжатие** compression strength.

прочный *a.* firm, rigid, stable, solid, sturdy, robust, strong, firm (ice); secure, reliable; tough, rugged, high-strength; durable, lasting, permanent; wear-resisting; fast (color).

прочтение reading.

прочь *adv.* away, off; *imp.* go away, stand back; **он не п.** he is willing, he has no objection (to).

прошедш/ее *n.* the past; **—ий** *a.* past, previous; having passed, elapsed; last.

прошёл *past m. sing.* of **пройти.**

прошеллаченный *a.* shellacked.

прошен/ие *n.* application, petition; **—ный** *a.* requested, asked.

прошеств/ие *n.* lapse, expiration, end; **по —ии** on expiration (of), after.

прошиб/ать, —ить *v.* break through; penetrate (of cold, etc.).

прошив/ание *n.* sewing, etc., *see v.*; **—ать** *v.* sew, stitch; (med.) suture; (mach.) broach, punch; riddle (with holes); **—ень** *m.* punch, broach, drift; **—ка** *see* **прошивание;** (push) broach; (text.) insert.

прош/ивной *a.* sewn; trimmed; broached, broaching; **—ивочный** *a.* trimming; broaching, piercing (mill).

прошипеть *v.* hiss.

прошить *see* **прошивать.**

прошлифов/очный *a.,* **—ывание** *n.* honing; polishing; **—ывать** *v.* hone; polish.

прошлогодний *a.* last year's.

прошл/ое *n.* the past; **—ый** *a.* past, former; last (year, month, etc.).

прошнуров(ыв)ать *v.* lace, cord, tie.

прошпакл/евать, —ёвывать *v.* spackle, putty.

проштемпелевать *v.* stamp.

проштукатурить *v.* plaster.

прошуметь *v.* make noise.

прощальный *a.* farewell, final.

прощать *v.* pardon, excuse, overlook; **—ся** *v.* be excused; take one's leave.

проще *comp. of* **просто, простой,** easier, simpler; **п. говоря** put simply.

прощелина *f.* slit, slot, crack.

прощёлкивание *n.* snapping, popping.

прощение *n.* pardon, forgiveness.

прощуп/(ыв)ать *v.* feel (for), probe; (med.) palpate; **—ываемый** *a.* palpable; **—ывание** *n.* probing; (med.) palpation; fingering.

проэкзаменовать *v.* examine.

проэктировать *see* **проектировать.**

проэмбрио(н) *m.* (embr.) proembryo.

проэнзим *m.* proenzyme, zymogen.

проявит/ель *m.* (phot.) developer; **—ельный** *a.* developing; **—ь** *see* **проявлять.**

проявл/ение *n.* manifestation, display, exhibition, show; (phot.) development; **п. хрупкости** brittle behavior; **—енный** *a.* manifested, etc., *see v.*; **—ять** *v.* manifest, display, show, exhibit, exert, give rise (to); use (care); indicate; develop; express (interest); **—яться** *v.* develop, come through, appear; **—яющий** *a.* manifesting, etc., *see v.*; **—яющее вещество** developer.

проявочный *a.* (phot.) developing, processing.

проясн/ение *n.* clearing; **—еть, —и(ва)ть** *v.* clear up, brighten; **—ить, —ять** *v.* clear, clarify; elucidate, explain; **—яться** *v.* clear up.

пр. сч. *abbr.* (**пропорциональный счётчик**) proportional counter.

ПРУ *abbr.* (**передвижная рентгеновская установка**) mobile X-ray unit.

пруд *m.* pond, reservoir, pool; **—ить** *v.* dam; **—овик** *m.* pond snail (*Lymnaea*); **—овой** *a. of* **пруд;** (biol.) stagnicolous; **—ок** *m.* pool, puddle; **—охладитель** *m.* cooling pond.

пружин/а *f.* (coil) spring; **главная п.** mainspring; **п.-волосок** *f.* hairspring; **—ение** *n.* spring(ing), spring action; **—истый** *a.* springy, elastic; **—ить** *v.* spring, have a spring (in), be elastic, yield; **—ка** *dim. of* **пружина;** *f.* (bot.) elater; **—ность** *f.* springiness, elasticity; **—ный** *a.* spring(-actuated), spring-controlled; lock (washer); snap (hook); **—ное стопорное кольцо** retaining ring; **—одержатель** *m.* spring holder; **—онавивочный** *a.* spring-coiling; **—ящий** *a.* springy, elastic; spring (action); snap (ring); **—ящая способность** springiness.

прулауразин *m.* (chem.) prulaurasin.

пруназ/а *f.* prunase; **—ин** *m.* prunasin.

прун/етол *m.* prunetol, genistein; **—ол** *m.* prunol, ursolic acid.

пруриго *n.* (med.) prurigo.

прус, —ик *m.* (ent.) locust (*Calliptamus italicus*); **—ак** *m.* (German) cockroach.

Пруссия Prussia; **прусский** *a.* Prussian.

Пруста закон Proust's law, law of constant proportions.

прут *m.* rod, bar; stick, twig, switch; *pr. 3 pl. of* **переть; —ик** *dim. of* **прут; —ковый** *a.* rod(-shaped); **—няк** *m.* (bot.) Kochia; Vitex; **—овидный** *a.* rod-shaped, virgate; **—овидная ива** basket willow (*Salix viminalis*); **—ок** *m.* bar, rod; knitting needle; (ladder) rung; **—яной** *a. of* **прут;** osier.

прыг/ание *n.* jumping, etc., *see v.*; (med.; gen.) saltation; **—ательный** *a.* (biol.) saltatory; **—ать, —нуть** *v.* jump, leap, spring, bound, skip, jerk; knock (of valve); dance (of needle); **—ун** *m.* jumper; (ent.) skipper; (bot.) Impatiens; (mam.) klipspringer (*Oreotragus*); springbok (*Antidorcas marsupialis*); titi (*Callicebus*); **малый —ун** kangaroo mouse (*Microdipodops*); **—уновые** *pl.* (ichth.) mudskippers (*Periophthalmidae*); **—унчики** *pl.* (mam.) elephant shrews (*Macrosulididae*); (ent.) ground hoppers (*Tetrigidae*); **—гуны** *see* **прыгуновые; тушканчиковые —гуны** (mam.) kangaroo rats, etc. (*Heteromyidae*); **пребрежные —гуны** (ent.) shore bugs (*Acanthiidae*).

прыжок *m.* jump, leap, spring, bound; (med.; gen.) saltation; (gen.) mutation.

прыс/калка *f.* sprayer, syringe; **—кание** *n.* spraying; **—кать, —нуть** *v.* spray.

прыт/кий *a.* agile, nimble, quick; **—че** *comp. of* **прыткий; —ь** *f.* speed, quickness; **во всю —ь** at top speed.

прыщ *m.* pimple; (med.) pustule; **—авость** *f.* acne; **—ик** *see* **прыщ; —еватый** *a.* pimpled; pustular; **—инец** *m.* (bot.) banewort (*Ranunculus flammula*).

прюнель *f.* prunelle (prune); (text.) prunella.

пряд/ево *n.* tow; **—ение** *n.* spinning; **—еный** *a.* spun; **—ет** *pr. 3 sing. of* **прясть.**

пряди *pl. of* **прядь;** (anat.) flumina, streams.

прядиль/ный *a.* spinning; textile; **—ные насосики** (rayon) spinnerets; **—ня** *f.* spinning mill; **—щик** *m.* spinner.

пряд/ка *dim. of* **прядь; —ут** *pr. 3 pl. of* **прясть; —ущий** *a.* spinning; **—ь** *f.* strand, yarn; ply; (anat.) flumen, stream.

пряжа *f.* yarn, thread; (bot.) maidenhair.

пряж/ка *f.,* **—ечный** *a.* buckle, clasp.

пряжный *see* **прядильный.**

прял *past m. sing. of* **прясть; —ка** *f.* spinning wheel.

прям *sh. m. of* **прямой; —ая** *f. of* **прямой;** straight line; **по —ой** straight-line; **по одной —ой с** in line with; **—изна** *f.* straightness; **—ик** *m.* direct route; **—иком** *adv.* by a direct route, cross country; **—ить** *v.* straighten (out, up); **—лёный** *a.* straightened (out).

прямо *adv.* straight, directly; frankly; immediately; normally (magnetized).

прямо— *prefix* straight, rect(i)—; direct(ly); orth(o)—; **—бортный** *a.* beadless (tire); **—бочный** *a.* straight; **—возбуждаемый** *a.* directly excited; **—волновой** *a.* square-law (capacitor); **—гонный** *a.* directly distilled; straight-run; **—действующий** *a.* direct(-acting); **—ёмкостный** *a.* straight-line (capacitor).

прям/ой *a.* straight, direct, through; straightforward; upright, erect; right (angle); forward; linear (equation); primary, straight-run (distillation); positive (correlation); one-way (classification); open (belt); (geod.) polar (network); exact (opposite); normal (magnetization); roman (type); reef (knot); sheer (waste); **п. предок** (set theory) proper ancestor; **п. резец** straight-shank tool; **—ая кишка** (anat.) rectum; **—ая мышца** (anat.) rectus; **—ая призма** right prism; **—ая пропорция** direct proportion; **—ая связь** direct coupling; **—ая эмульсия** oil-in-water emulsion; **—ое выдавливание** forward extrusion, direct extrusion; **—ое действие** direct action, direct effect; **—ым путём** directly; **с —ым отсчётом** direct-reading.

прямозубое колесо spur gear.

прямокишечн/о— *prefix* (anat.) recto—; **—овлагалищный** *a.* rectovaginal; **—оматочный** *a.* rectouterine; **—опузырный** *a.* rectovesical; **—ый** *a.* (anat.) rectal.

прямо/крылые *pl.* (ent.) grasshoppers, crickets, etc. (*Saltatoria, Orthoptera*); **—крылый** *a.* straight-winged.

прямолинейно *adv.* rectilinearly; straight-forwardly; **п.-возвратный** *a.* reciprocating, moving to and fro.

прямолинейн/ость *f.* rectilinearity; **—ый** *a.* rectilinear, straight(-line), linear; plane (geometry).

прямо/пёры *pl.* (ichth.) featherbacks (*Notopteridae*); **—поточный** *a.* direct-flow; **—семянный** *a.* (bot.) orthospermous.

прямослойн/ость *f.* straight grain (of wood); **—ый** *a.* straight-grained.

прямо/ствольный *a.* (bot.) straight-boled, straight-stemmed; stately (tree); **—сторонний** *a.* straight-sided; **—стоячий, —стоящий** *a.* erect, upright; **—струйный** *a.* direct-spray, direct-jet; **—та** *f.* straightness, rectitude; **—ток** *m.* parallel(-current) flow, concurrent flow.

прямоточно/-ракетный *a.* ramjet-rocket (engine); **—сть** *f.* direct flow, straight-through feed; **п.-турбинный** *a.* turbo-ramjet (engine).

прямоточный *a.* direct-flow, straight-flow; once-through, single-pass, straight-through, flow-through, concurrent (boiler); downstream (injection); ram (jet engine); rocket); **п. воздушно-реактивный** *a.* ramjet (engine).

прямоугольн/ик *m.* rectangle; **—ый** *a.* right-angled, rectangular, quadrate, square; orthogonal; right (triangle); square-wave (modulation); **—ая кромка** straightedge.

прямо/частотный *a.* straight-line frequency; **—шовные** *pl.* straight-seamed flies (*Orthorrhapha*).

прямые *pl.* straight lines.

прян/ость *f.*, **—ое вещество** spice, condiment, seasoning; **—ый** *a.* spicy.

прясть *v.* spin.

пря/тание *n.* hiding; **—танный** *a.* hidden; **—тать** *v.* hide, conceal, cover; secrete; **—ча** *adv.* hiding, etc., *see v.;* **—чет** *pr. 3 sing. of* **прятать; —чущий** *a.* hiding, etc., *see v.*

пс *abbr.* (**параллакс-секунда**) (astr.) parallax-second, parsec; (**пенополистирол**) polystyrene foam; (**полистирол**) polystyrene.

псаммо— *prefix* psamm(o)— (sand); **—бионт** *m.* (biol.) psammobiont, sand dweller; **—ма** *f.* (med.) psammoma (granular tumor); **—фильный** *a.* (biol.) psammophilous, sand-loving; **—фит** *m.* (bot.) psammophyte.

псевдо— *prefix* pseud(o)— (false, imitating); **—аконитин** *m.* pseudoaconitine; **—аллелизм** *m.* (gen.) pseudoallelism; **—аллель** *m.* pseudoallele; **—ангина** *f.* (med.) false angina; **—бульба** *f.* tuberidium (of orchid); **—вакуоль** *f.* pseudovacuole; **—гамия** *f.* pseudogamy; **—жиженный** *see* **псевдоожиженный; —идиоморфный кристалл** idioblast; **—изомерия** *f.*

pseudoisomerism; **—индил** *m.* pseudoindyl; **—кислота** *f.* pseudo acid; **—код** *m.* pseudocode; **—команда** *f.* (comp.) instructional constant.

псевдокристалл *m.* pseudocrystal; **—ический** *a.* pseudocrystalline.

псевдо/кумол *m.* pseudocumene; **—линейный** *a.* pseudolinear; **—мерия** *f.* pseudomerism; **—миксис** *m.* (gen.) pseudomixis, pseudogamy.

псевдоморф *m.* (cryst.) pseudomorph; **—ия** *f.* pseudomorphy; **—ный** *a.* pseudomorphous; **—оза** *f.* pseudomorphosis.

псевдоним *m.* pseudonym, pen name; (comp.) alias.

псевдоожиж/аемость *f.* fluidizability; **—аемый** *a.* fluidizable; fluidized; **—ающий** *a.* fluidizing; **—ение** *n.* fluidization; **—енный** *a.* fluidized, quasi-liquid; **—енный слой** fluidized bed.

псевдо/опухоль *f.* pseudotumor, phantom tumor; **—основание** *n.* pseudobase; **—паралич** *m.* pseudoparalysis, false paralysis; **—период** *m.* (phys.) quasi-period; **—периодический** *a.* quasi-periodic; **—подий** *m.* (biol.) pseudopod(ium); **—равновесие** *n.* pseudo-equilibrium; **—раствор** *m.* pseudo solution; **—регулярный** *a.* pseudoregular; **—симметрия** *f.* pseudosymmetry; **—скалярный** *a.* (phys.) pseudoscalar; **—случайный** *a.* pseudorandom; **—совместимость** *f.* pseudocompatibility; **—соединение** *n.* pseudo compound; **—сфера** *f.* (geom.) pseudosphere; **—тройной** *a.* pseudoternary; **—холестен** *m.* pseudocholestene; **—цирроз** *m.* (med.) pseudocirrhosis; **—цифелла** *f.* (bot.) pseudocyphella (in lichens); **—чума** *f.* pseudopest, Newcastle disease (poultry disease); **—шар** *m.* pseudosphere.

псен *m.* (ichth.) Psenes; **—опс(ис)** *m.* Japanese butterfish (*Psenopsis*).

псеттод/овые, —ы *pl.* spiny-ray flatfishes (*Psettodidae*).

псефит *m.* (petr.) psephite; **—овый** *a.* psephitic, made up of pebbles.

псефур *m.* (ichth.) Psephurus.

пси *m.* (Greek letter) psi.

псикаин *m.* psicaine, *d-psi*-cocaine bitartrate.

псилловый *a.* psyllic (acid, alcohol).

псилл(ид)ы *pl.* (ent.) Psyllidae.

псило— *prefix* psil(o)— (mere, bare); **—з** *m.* psilosis, depilation; **—фит** *m.* (pal.) psilophyte, prairie plant.

псин/а *f.*, **—ый** *a.* dog('s).

пситтакоз *m.* (med.) psittacosis.

психиатр *m.* psychiatrist; **—ический** *a.* psychiatric; **—ия** *f.* psychiatry.

психи/ка *f.* psychics, psychology; psyche, mind, mentality; **—чески** *adv.* mentally (ill); **—ческий** *a.* mental (illness); psychic; *m.* mental patient; **—ческая болезнь** psychosis.

психо— *prefix* psycho— (psyche; mind), psychological; **—анализ** *m.* psychoanalysis; **—аналитик** *m.* psychoanalyst; **—вать** *v.* act deranged; be hysterical; **—генез** *m.* psychogenesis; mental development; **—генный** *a.* psychogenic; **—з** *m.* psychosis; **циркулярный —з** manic-depressive psychosis.

психолог *m.* psychologist; **—ический** *a.* psychological; **—ия** *f.* psychology.

психомоторный *a.* psychomotor.

психо/невроз *m.* (psycho)neurosis; **—невролог** *m.* neuropsychiatrist; **—пат** *m.* psychopath; **—патия** *f.* psychopathy; **—патология** *f.* psychopathology; **—приёмник** *m.* mental hospital; **—соматический** *a.* psychosomatic; **—терапия** *f.* psychotherapy; **—техника** *f.* psychotechnics, psychological testing; **—тический** *a.* psychotic; **—трин** *m.* psychotrine; **—физика** *f.* psychophysics; **—физический** *a.* psychophysical, psychological and physical; **—физиология** *f.* psychophysiology.

психро— *prefix* psychro— (cold); **—лютовые** *pl.* (ichth.) tadpole sculpins (*Psychrolutidae*); **—метр** *m.* (meteor.) psychrometer; **—метрический** *a.* psychrometric; **—метрия** *f.* psychrometry; **—метр-пращ** *m.* sling psychrometer; **—фильный** *a.* (biol.) psychrophilic, cold-loving; **—фит** *m.* (bot.) psychrophyte.

псковский *a.* (geog.) Pskov.

псов/еть *v.* grow up (of puppy); **—ина** *f.* feathers (on dog's legs and tail); **—ый** *a.* dog('s), canine; **—ые** *pl.* dogs.

псо/ит *m.* (med.) psoitis; **—риаз** *m.* (med.) psoriasis; **—ралея** *f.* (bot.) scurfy pea (*Psoralea*); **—роптоз** *m.* (vet.) psoroptic mange; **—роспермий** *m.* psorosperm, parasitic sporozoon; **—фометрический** *a.* (tel.) psophometric.

ПСП *abbr.* (**прибор слепой посадки**) instrument-landing device; (**промежуточный сборный пункт**) intermediate rendezvous point.

пст. *abbr.* (**пестик**) (bot.) pistil.

пт *abbr.* (**полупроводниковый триод**) semiconductor triode.

пт. *abbr.* (**пятница**) Friday.

ПТ *abbr.* (**полевой транзистор**) field-effect transistor, FET.

птармика *f.* (bot.) sneezewort (*Ptarmica*).

птелея *f.* hop tree (*Ptelea*).

птен/ец, —чик *m.* (orn.) fledgeling.

птенцов/ый *a.* (zool.) altricial; (orn.) nidicolous; **—ая птица** (orn.) altrice.

птеранодон *m.* (pal.) pteranodon.

птер/игий *m.* (zool.) pterygium; **—игоспермин** *m.* (pharm.) pterygospermin; **—идин** *m.* pteridine; **—идо-** *prefix* pterido—, fern; **—идология** *f.* pteridology; **—илии** *m.* (orn.) pterylae, feather tracts; **—иновый** *a.* pteroic (acid); **—ис** *m.* (bot.) brake (*Pteris*).

птеро— *prefix* ptero— (wing); **—дактил** *m.* (pal.) pterodactyl; **—завр** *m.* pterosaur; **—карпин** *m.* pterocarpin; **—малиды** *pl.* (ent.) Pteromalidae; **—подовый** *a.* (ocean.) pteropod (ooze).

Пти *see under* **Дюлонга-Пти закон.**

птиал— *prefix* ptyal(o)— (saliva); **—изм** *m.* (med.) ptyalism (excessive salivation); **—ин** *m.* ptyalin, ptyalase; **—о—** *see* **птиал—.**

птигматовый *a.* (geol.) ptygmatic.

птилихтовые *pl.* (ichth.) quillfishes (*Ptilichthyidae*).

птихо— *prefix* ptych(o)— (fold, layer); **—птериды** *pl.* (ent.) Ptychopteridae.

птиц/а *f.* bird; poultry, fowl; *see also under* **птицы; п. воловья** cowbird (*Molothrus*); **буйволова п.** oxpecker; **домашняя п.** poultry; **зонтичная п.** umbrellabird; **рисовая п.** ricebird, e.g. bobolink, Java sparrow; **теневая п.** hammerkop (*Scopus umbretta*); **—е—** *prefix* ornith(o)—, avi— (bird); poultry; **—ебойня** poultry processing plant; **—евод** *m.* poultry farmer; **—еводство** *n.* poultry farming; aviculture; **—еводческий** *a.* poultry (farm); **—езвери** *pl.* egg-laying mammals (*Monotremata*); **—екомбинат** *m.* poultry processing plant; **—еловство** *n.* bird catching, fowling; **—емлечник** *m.* (bot.) star of Bethlehem (*Ornithogalum*); **—ефабрика** *f.* poultry plant; **—еферма** *f.* poultry farm.

птицы *pl.* birds (*Aves*); **райские п.** birds of paradise, etc. (*Paradiseidae*); **сахарные п.** honey-eaters, etc. (*Promerops*); **синие п.** blue thrushes, etc. (*Myophonus*);

типичные п. Neognathae; **—лиры** *pl.* lyrebirds, etc. (*Menuridae*); **—мыши** *pl.* colies, mousebirds, etc. (*Coliidae*); **—носороги** *pl.* hornbills, etc. (*Bucerotidae*); **—секретари** *pl.* secretary birds, etc. (*Serpentariidae, Sagittariidae*).

птич/ий *a.* bird, avian; poultry (yard); **п. глаз** (bot.) birds-eye maple; **п. помёт** guano; **—ьи горы** (orn.) rookeries; **—ья гречиха** *see* **спорыш; —ья шпора** (anat.) calcar avis; **вид с —ьего полёта** birdseye view.

птич/ка *dim. of* **птица;** check(mark); **—ник** *m.* aviary; poultry house, coop; poultry man; **—ница** poultry woman; **—ьи** *pl.,* **—ья** *f. see* **птичий.**

ПТК *abbr.* (**переключатель телевизионных каналов**) TV tuner, channel selector.

птоз/(ис) *m.* (med.) ptosis; **—ный** *a.* ptotic.

птомаин *m.* ptomaine; **—отоксикоз** *m.* ptomaine poisoning.

ПТУ *abbr.* (**профтехучилище**) trade school.

ПТФЭ *abbr.* (**политетрафторэтилен**) polytetrafluoroethylene, Teflon.

ПУ *abbr.* (**пенополиуретан**) polyurethane foam; (**полиуретан**) polyurethane; (**програмное управление**) program control.

пуаз *m.* poise (unit of viscosity).

Пуазей(л)я закон Poiseuille's law.

Пуанкаре теорема Poincaré theorem.

пуансов способ (mech.) Poinsot's method.

пуансон *m.* punch; (top) die, plunger die, heading die; ram; (cutting) ring; **—одержатель** *m.* die stock.

пуассоновский *a.* (math.) Poisson.

пубертатный *a.* (med.) adolescent, puber(t)al.

пуберул/овый *a.* puberulic (acid); **—оновый** *a.* puberulonic (acid).

публик/а *f.* public; **—ация** *f.* publication; advertisement; **—овать** *v.* publish; advertise, announce.

публичный *a.* public, common, open.

ПуВРД *abbr.* (**пульсирующий воздушнореактивный двигатель**) pulse jet (engine).

пуга *f.* air pocket (in egg).

пуг/ало *n.* scarecrow; **—анный** *a.* frightened, timid; **—ать** *v.* frighten, scare, intimidate; appall; **—ач** *m.* (orn.) eagle owl; **—ливость** *f.* timidity; **—ливый** *a.* fearful, timid; **—нуть** *see* **пугать**

пугов/ица *f.,* **—ичный** *a.* button, stud; **—ичный транспортёр** (min.) a type of apron conveyer; **—ка** *f.* head, knob; button; sleeker; **—ковидный** *a.* bulliform, puckered; **—чатый** *a.* (med.) bulbous-end (probe); button (suture).

пуголовка *f.* (ichth.) Benthophilus.

пуд *m.* pood (16.38 kg).

пудинг *m.* pudding.

пудлингов/альный *a.,* **—ание** *n.* (met.) puddling; **—ать** *v.* puddle.

пудов/ой, **—ый** *a. of* **пуд.**

пудр/а *f.* (fine) powder; (met.) parting dust; **—ение** *n.* powdering; **—еный** *a.* powdered; **—ет** *m.* poudrette, fecal dust; **—ить** *v.* powder, dust; **—ообразный** *a.* powder-like.

пуерария, волосистая п. kudzu vine (*Pueraria hirsuta*).

ПУЗ *abbr.* (**постоянное запоминающее устройство**) (comp.) read-only memory, ROM.

пузанок *m.* (ichth.) shad (*Alosa*).

пуз/атый *a.* pot-bellied; **—о** *n.* belly, paunch; **—ула** *f.* (bot.) pusule.

пузыр/е— *prefix* cyst(o)— (bladder, cyst); phys(o)— (presence of gas); **—евидный** *a.* bubble-like; bladder-like, utricular; vesicular; **—ёк** *dim. of* **пузырь;** bubble;

blister; bead; phial, vial; ampulla; (biol.) vesicle, vesicula, vacuole; follicle; **—еногие** *pl.* (ent.) thrips (*Thysanoptera*); **—еплодник** *m.* (bot.) Physocarpus; **—ик** *dim. of* **пузырь;** **—истый** *see* **пузырчатый; —ить** *v.* blow out; **—иться** *v.* bubble; blister; effervesce; **—ник** *m.* (bot.) Colutea; **—но—** *prefix* (anat.) vesico— (bladder); **—номаточный** *a.* (anat.) vesicouterine; **—нопрямокишечный** *a.* (anat.) vesicorectal; **—ный** *a. of* **пузырь;** (anat.) vesical; cystic (artery, etc.); **—чатка** *f.* (med.) pemphigus; (bot.) bladderwort (*Utricularia*); **—чатник** *see* **пузыреплодник.**

пузырчат/ость *f.* vesiculation; (met.) blistered condition; (bot.; med.) pustule; **—ый** *a.* bubbly; blistered; (biol.) vesicular.

пузырь *m.* bubble, blister, air hole, blow hole, cavity; pocket, sac; (anat.) bladder; vesica, venter; (biol.) cyst; hotwater bottle; **жёлчный п.** gall bladder; **—ки** *pl. of* **пузырёк;** vesiculae; **—ки** *v.* bubble, effervesce; **—ковый** *a. of* **пузырь; —ковый барьер** air curtain (for oil spills); **—ковое кипение** nucleate boiling; **—коносный** *a.* vesiculiferous; (bot.) utriculiferous.

пук *m.* bunch, tuft; bundle; bulge.

пуку *m.* (mam.) waterbuck (*Kobus*).

пукатеин *m.* (chem.) pukateine.

пукциния *f.* (phyt.) Puccinia.

пул *m.* pool; (comp.) pooling block.

Пула феномен (med.) Pool's phenomenon.

пулевой *a. of* **пуля.**

пулегон *m.* pulegone.

пулек *gen. pl. of* **пулька.**

пулекс *m.* (ent.) fleas (*Pulex*).

пулемёт *m.*, **—ный** *a.* machine gun; **—чик** *m.* machine gunner, gunner.

пуленен *m.* pulenene.

пуле/непроницаемый, —стойкий *a.* bullet-proof; **—улавливатель, —уловитель** *m.* bullet trap.

пуллороз *m.* pullorosis (poultry disease).

пуловер *m.* pullover (e.g. sweater).

пульвериз/атор *m.* pulverizer; atomizer, sprayer; nebulizer; spray can; **—ационный** *a.* pulverization, pulverizing; atomizing, spray(ing); jet (pump); **—ация** *f.*, **—ирование** *n.* pulverization; atomization, spraying; (agr.) dusting; **—(ир)ованный** *a.* pulverized, etc., *see* *v.*; pulverulent; **—(ир)овать** *v.* pulverize, reduce to a powder; atomize, spray.

пульвилла *f.* (zool.) pulvillus.

пулька *dim. of* **пуля.**

пульман *m.*, **—овский** *a.* (rr.) Pullman car.

пульмо— *prefix* pulmo— (lungs); **—нальный** *a.* pulmonary.

пульмотор *m.* pulmotor.

пульп/а *f.* pulp; slurry; **—ер** *m.* pulper, pulping machine; **—ит** *m.* (med.) pulpitis; **—овидный** *a.* pulpy; **—омер** *m.* pulp density meter; **—ообразователь** *see* **пульпер; —отделяющий** *a.* depulping; **—опровод** *m.* pulp line, sludge line.

пульс *m.* (physiol.) pulse, pulsus; **—ар** *m.* (astr.) pulsar; **—атор** *m.* (med.) pulsator; pulser; (min.) pulsator jig; **—атрон** *m.* pulsatron; **—ация** *f.*, **—ирование** *n.* pulsation, fluctuation; throbbing; ripple, flutter; surging, surge; **—ионный** *a.* (med.) pulsion; **—ировать** *v.* pulse, pulsate; flash (repeatedly); beat; fluctuate, oscillate; flutter; **—ирующий** *a.* pulsating, etc., *see* *v.*; pulsatory; ripple (voltage); pulsed (ion source, etc.); variable, intermittent; (med.) pulsatile; **—ирующий воздушно-реактивный** *a.* pulse-jet (engine); **—ирующее кипение** bumping; **—овой, —овый** *a.* pulse; **—ометр** *m.*

pulsometer, vacuum pump; **п.-реле** *n.* relay-interrupter.

пульт *m.* desk; stand; panel, board; console; controller; (comp.) terminal; (av.) pedestal; **п. обучения** (robotics) teach box; **п. управления** switchboard; control panel, control console; **испытательный п.** tester; **клавишный п.** (comp.) keyboard.

пуля *f.* bullet, ball, shot; pellet.

пуляр/да, —ка *f.* spayed hen.

пума *f.* (mam.) puma.

пум/ит *m.* (min.) pumice; **—ицит** (min.) pumicite.

пуммело *see* **помпельмус.**

пумп/а *f.*, **—овый** *a.* pump.

пуна *f.* (geobotany) puna.

пуниц/ин *m.* punicine, pelletierine.

пункт *m.* point, spot, place, locality; paragraph, item, clause; (med.) dispensary; (observation) post; (service) station, center, unit; (ocean.) port; **проходной п.** portal.

пунктация *f.* stippling.

пунктир *m.* dotted line, broken line; stipple; **п. точка-тире, осевой п., фигурный п.** dot-and-dash line; **точечный п.** dotted line.

пунктирн/ый *a.* dotted, dashed, punctuate; dotting (needle); prick (wheel); spot (welding); (agr.) single-seed (drill); single-grain (sowing); **—ая линия** dotted line, broken line.

пунктиров/альный *a.*, **—ание** *n.* pricking, etc., *see* *v.*; prick (wheel); **—анный** *a.* pricked, etc., *see* *v.*; punctate; **—ать** *v.* prick, point, dot; stipple; **—ка** *see* **пунктирование.**

пунктуальн/о *adv.* punctually; **—ость** *f.* punctuality, exactness, accuracy; **—ый** *a.* punctual, precise, exact.

пунктуация *f.* punctuation.

пункция *f.* (med.) puncture; tapping, paracentesis.

пуночка *f.* (orn.) snow bunting (*Plectrophenax nivalis*).

пунсон *see* **пуансон;** symbol; (typ.) punch.

пунтиус *m.* (ichth.) barb (*Puntius*).

пунцовый *a.* crimson.

пунш *m.*, **—евый** *a.* punch (drink).

пунширов/ание *n.* punching; **—ать** *v.* punch, stamp.

пуня *f.* hay barn.

пуп *see* **пупок.**

пупавка *f.* (bot.) camomile (*Anthemis*).

пуларий *m.* (ent.) puparium.

Пупартова связка (anat.) Poupart's ligament, inguinal arch.

пупилло— *prefix* (anat.) pupillo— (pupil); **—метр** *m.* (ophth.) pupillometer; **—моторный** *a.* pupillary (reflex).

пупин/изация *f.* (elec. comm.) pupinization, coil loading; **шаг —изации** coil spacing; **—изированный** *a.* coil-loaded; **—овская катушка** Pupin coil, loading coil.

пупк/а *gen. of* **пупок; —о—** *prefix* umbilic(i)— (navel); omphal(o)— (navel, umbilicus); **—овидный** *a.* umbilicate; omphaloid.

пупо/вина *f.* (anat.) umbilical cord, funis, funiculus; **—к** *m.* (anat.) navel, umbilicus; omphalus; protuberance; knob; (orn.) ventriculus, gizzard; **—чно—** *prefix* (anat.) omphalo— (umbilical, navel); **—чнобрыжеечный** *a.* omphalomesenteric; **—чнокишечный проток** (embr.) urachus; **—чный** *a.* umbilical; **—чная грыжа** (med.) omphalocele.

пупыр/истый, —чатый *a.* pimply; papulose; **—ышек, —ь** *m.* pimple, blemish; papule; pustule.

пурбекский *a.* (geol.) Purbeckian.

пурга *f.* snowstorm, blizzard.

пурген *m.* phenolphthalein.

пуржить *v.* swirl (of snow).

пурин *m.*, **—овый** *a.* purine.

пурка *f.* grain-grading balance.

Пуркинье (med.; anat.) Purkinje('s) (cells, fibers, etc.).

пуромицин *m.* (pharm.) puromycin.

пурпур *m.* purple; **зрительный п.** (bioch.) rhodopsin, visual purple; **—а** *f.* (med.) purpura; **—ат** *m.* purpurate; **—есоединение** *n.* purpureo compound; **—ин** *m.* purpurin, trihydroxyanthraquinone.

пурпурно—, **пурпурово—** *prefix* purpur(o)—, porphyr(o)— (purple).

пурпур/ный, **—овый** *a.* purple; purpuric; **—овая кислота** purpuric acid; **—овеющий** *a.* purpurescent, becoming purple; **—овокислый** *a.* purpuric acid; purpurate (of); **—оксантен** *m.* purpuroxanthene, xanthopurpurin; **—оксантовый** *a.* purpuroxanthic (acid); **—сульфоновый** *a.* sulfopurpuric (acid).

пуррон *m.* purrone, euxanthone.

пуск *m.* start(ing), start-up; (rockets) launch(ing); release; admission (of a gas); **пробный п.** test run; **—ай** *see* **пусть**; **—ание** *n.* starting, etc., *see v.*; **—атель** *m.* starter; **—ать** *v.* start (up), set in motion; release; trigger; launch (rocket); turn on (water, gas); let, allow, permit; put (into service); set (to work); strike, take (root); put forth (sprouts); spread (rumor); **—ать в ход** start (up); **—аться** *v.* be started, etc.; start, set out.

пусков/ой *a.* starting, start-up, trigger(ing); actuating; tune-up (period); (rockets) launching; **п. контейнер** (rocket) pod; **п. механизм** starter; launcher; **п. момент** (elec.) starting torque; **п. прибор** starter; trigger; **п. станок** launcher; **п. стол** launch stand; **п. ток** (elec.) in-rush current; **—ая ракетная установка** launcher; **—ая рукоятка** crank; **—ая схема** trigger circuit; **—ая установка** launcher.

пускорегулирующий *a.* start-control.

ПуСО, ПУСО *abbr.* (**пункт специальной обработки**) decontamination station.

пуссули *see* **амур, чёрный**.

пуст *sh. m. of* **пустой**; **—а** *f.* puszta, grass steppe; *sh. f. of* **пустой**.

пустельга *f.* (orn.) kestrel.

пустер *m.* (dentistry) chip syringe.

пустеть *v.* (become) empty.

пустить *see* **пускать**.

пуст/о *adv.* empty, emptily; **—оватый** *a.* rather empty; **—овать** *v.* be empty, be vacant; **—ой** *a.* empty, unfilled, vacant, void, (math.; comp.) null; dummy; uninhabited, deserted; hollow (tube); blank; bare; vain, futile; (geol.) barren, dead; slight (wound, etc.); superficial (person); **—ой слиток** (met.) bootleg; **—ой узел** (cryst.) vacancy; **—ая порода** barren rock, (waste) gangue; **—ое место** blank; **—ое пространство** vacuum; void; **—опорожний** *a.* unpopulated, vacant; **—ота** *f.* emptiness, vacuum; interstice, void, empty space, pore, vacuity; (mach.; med.) cavitation; hollow(ness), cavity, blow hole (in casting); blankness; (cryst.) vacancy; **в —оте** in a vacuum; **коэффициент пустот** void factor.

пустотел/ость *f.* hollowness; **—ый** *a.* hollow.

пустотн/ость *f.* hollow(ness); vacuum; **—ый** *a.* hollow; vacuum; void (effect).

пустоцвет *m.* (bot.) sterile flower; **—ный** *a.* sterile flower(ed), ananthous.

пустош/ный *a.* wasteland; heath; insignificant; **—овка** *f.* hollow joint; **—ь** *f.* waste or idle land.

пустоягодник *m.* strawberry clover (*Trifolium fragiferum*).

пустул/а *f.* (med.) pustule; **—ёзный** *a.* pustulous, pustular.

пустын/е—, **—о—** *prefix* (bot.; zool.) erem(o)— (lonely, solitary); **—ница** *f.* (ent.) Sphingonotus; **—нокосник** *m.* (bot.) desert rod (*Eremostachys*).

пустынно-степной *a.* desert and steppe.

пустын/ный *a.* desert, arid; unpopulated; **—ное растение** (bot.) eremad, eremophyte, desert plant; **—я** *f.* desert, wilderness.

пустырник *m.* (bot.) Leonurus.

пустырь *f.* vacant land; waste land; vacant lot.

пусть *particle and conj.* let, assume (that), suppose (that); even if, though; **п. будет** let it be; **п. его, п. себе** let him (or it); **п. так** so be it; **п. это будет** be it, (no matter) whether it is.

пустя/к *m.* trifle; **—ковый, —чный** *a.* trivial, insignificant.

пусьера *f.* blue powder (a zinc dust).

пут/анина hemp or flax waste; **—аница** *f.* confusion, tangle, maze; mix-up; **—анный** *a.* confused, etc., *see v.*; **—ать** *v.* confuse, mix up; tangle; involve; hobble (horse); **—аться** *v.* be confused; get tangled; get involved, interfere.

путассу *f.* (ichth.) blue whiting, putassu.

путе— *prefix* course, path; (rr.) track.

путёвка *f.* pass, permit; voucher; schedule of duties; routing slip; assignment; appointment (to a job); start (in life).

путевод/итель *m.* guide(book), itinerary; **—ный** *a.* guide, guiding.

пут/евой *a. of* **путь**; traveling, itinerary; flight-path; ground (speed); directional (control); steering (compass); road (machinery); train, track; yawing (motion); **—еец** *m.* railroad worker; **—ей** *gen. pl. of* **путь**; **—ейский** *a.* railroad and highway.

путём *adv. and prep. gen.* through, via, by means of, with, by (way of), by. . . route; properly; *instr. of* **путь**; **п. отмера** by measuring.

путе/мер *m.* pedometer; **—обходчик** *m.* (rr.) track inspector; **—очиститель** *m.* track cleaner; **—передвигатель** *m.* track shifter; **—погрузчик** *m.* track-transporting car; **—подбивочный** *a.* track-packing; **—подъёмник** *m.* track lifter; **—провод** *m.* overpass; **—прокладчик** *m.* track layer; **—рихтовочный** *a.* track-lining; **—рихтовщик** *m.* track liner.

путеуклад/ка *f.*, **—очный** *a.* track-laying; **—чик** *m.* track layer.

путешеств/енник *m.* traveler; **—ие** *n.* travel, journey, trip; voyage; **—овать** *v.* travel.

пут/и *gen., pl., etc., of* **путь**; (anat.) tracts; viae; **—ина** *f.*, **—инный** *a.* fishing season; **—лище, —ло** *n.* stirrup strap; **—лять** *v.* wander; **—ник** *m.*, **—ница** *f.* traveller, passerby; **—ный** *a.* useful; sensible; *suffix* -lane; -way; -track.

путо *n.* hobble (for a horse); **—вой** *a.* hobbling, hobble; **—вой сустав** fetlock joint; coffin joint; (zool.) **—вая кость** first phalanx.

путорак *m.* (mam.) piebald shrew (*Diplomesodon pulchellum*).

путы *pl.* hobble, spancel, fetters.

пут/ь *m.* way, road, route, course, path(way); (nucl.; rr.) track; (supply) line; race, runway, passage; stretch (of water); (anat.) tractus, tract, via, duct; trajectory; distance, displacement; (highway) lane; means, ways, method; journey; **п. данных** (comp.) data path, data bus; **п. доступа** (comp.) path; **п. кровообращения** blood vessel; **п. направления, п. прохождения** path, course; **в —и** in transit; **вектор —и** distance vector;

водный п. waterway; **линия —и** (av.) flight path, course line; **мокрым —ём** wet (analysis, etc.); **на ложном —и** on the wrong track; **на обратном —и** on the way back; **на пол —и** halfway, midway; **опытным —ём** experimentally; **перехватить на —и** v. intercept; **сбиться с —и** v. lose one's way, stray; **ставить на —и** v. interpose, insert; **сухим —ём** by land; dry (analysis, etc.).

пуф(ф) m. (gen.) puff; **образование —ов** puffing.

пух m. down, fluff, fuzz; plumule, down feather; downy wool; undercoat; (cotton) linters; **растительный п.** kapok fibers.

пух/лость f. plumpness; puffiness; **—лый** a. puffed up, plump; fluffy; swollen; bulky; **—ляк** see **гаичка; —ляковый** a. swollen, turgid; **—нуть** v. puff up, swell; **—овки** pl. (orn.) puffbirds (Bucconidae); **—овник** see кендырь; **—овый** a. of пух; down(y), fluff(y); **—оеды** pl. (ent.) bird lice; **—онос** m. (bot.) nappy plant (Trichophorum); **—отделитель** m. (agr.) (de)linter.

пуццолан m., **—а** f., **—овая земля** (petr.) pozzuolana; **—овый** a. pozzuolanic.

пуч/еглазие n. (med.) exophthalmos; buphthalmos; **—ение** n. swelling; heaving; **—ение живота** (med.) flatulence; meteorism; **—ина** f., **—инный** a. (frost) heaving; gulf, abyss, chasm; depths (of water).

пучить v. swell, raise, inflate, distend; **—ся** v. swell, rise, heave.

пучк/а gen. of **пучок; —и** pl. of **пучок; основные —и, собственные —и** proper fascicles.

пучко/вание n. bunching; **—ватель** m. buncher; **—ватый** a. (bot.) fascicular; **—видный** a. clustered, tufted; **—вый** a. of **пучок; —жаберные** pl. pipefishes, seahorses (Syngnathidae).

пучность f. (phys.) antinode, loop.

пуч/ок m. cluster, tuft, bunch, bundle, sheaf, pile, nest; wisp; pencil (of rays); (rad., nucl., etc.) beam; (anat., bot.) fascicle; **п. проводов** (elec.) multiwire conductor; **п. спинного мозга** (anat.) funiculus (of spinal cord); **встречные —ки** colliding beams; **ленточный п.** strip beam.

пушек gen. pl. of **пушка.**

пуш/ение n. fluffing; (leather) buffing; **—ёный** a. fiberized (asbestos).

пушер m. pusher, ram.

пушечн/ый a. gun, cannon; (rockets) full-flow (start); **п. металл, —ая бронза** gun metal (alloy).

пушилка f. (leather) beam.

пуш/инка f. particle of fluff; flake, floc; (orn.) plumule; **—истолистный** a. wooly-leaved, dasyphyllous; **—истопестичный** a. (bot.) hebegynous; **—истость** f. fluffiness; downiness, hairiness, pubescence; **—истый** a. fluffy, downy, pubescent, hairy, fleecy, cottony.

пушиц/а f., **—евый** a. cotton grass (Eriophorum).

пушка f. cannon; (clay; electron) gun.

пушковые волосы (embr.) lanugo.

пушн/ина f. fur(s), pelt(s); **—ой** a. fur(-bearing); **—ой товар** furs, peltry.

пушок see **пух;** (bot.) bloom, down; (embr.) lanugo; (biol.) pubes.

пушонка f. slaked lime, calcium hydroxide; **асбестовая п.** flaked asbestos.

пушпул/л m., **—ьный** a. (rad.) push-pull.

пушта f. puszta, grass steppe.

пуща f. dense forest.

пущенный a. started, etc., see **пускать.**

пуэр/ария f. (bot.) kudzu; **—ильный** a. puerile, immature; **—перальный** a. (med.) puerperal.

Пуэрто-рико (geog.) Puerto Rico.

пф abbr. (**пикофарада**) picofarad; (**полярный фронт**) polar front.

пфейфка f. tube, pipe.

пфлюгеровский (anat.) Pflüger's (tube, etc.).

Пфунда серия Pfund series.

ПХВ abbr. (**полихлорвинил**) polyvinyl chloride.

ПХЗ abbr. (**противохимическая защита**); **ПХО** abbr. (**противохимическая оборона**) antigas (or chemical) defense.

ПХФ abbr. (**пентахлорфенол**) pentachlorophenol.

п. ч. abbr. (**потому что**) because; **ПЧ** abbr. (**промежуточная частота**) intermediate frequency.

пчел/а f. (honey)bee; **—иный** a. bee; **—иный воск** beeswax; **—иный клей** bee glue, propolis; **—иный яд** bee venom, apitoxin; **—иная смазка** propolis; **—оводство** n. apiculture, bee keeping; **—оед** m. (orn.) honey buzzard; **—оматка** f. queen bee; **—опыление** n. bee pollination.

пчёлы pl. bees (Apidae).

пчельник m. apiary.

пшени/ца f., **—чный** a. wheat (Triticum).

пш/ённый a., **—ено** n. millet (grain).

Пшорра синтез Pschorr synthesis.

пыж m. wad(ding), closing plug; (min.) stemming; **—ик** m. reindeer fawn; fur of reindeer fawn; (orn.) murrelet (Brachyrhamphus); **—ить** v. wad, plug; stem; **—иться** v. try very hard; behave pompously; **—овый** a. of пыж.

пылать v. flame, blaze; glow.

пыле— prefix dust; **—ватый** a. dusty, dust-like; silty (soil); **—видный** a. pulverulent, pulverized, powdered; dust, dust-like, dusty; **—влагонепроницаемый** a. dust- and moistureproof; **—водозащищённый** a. dust- and waterproof; **—вой** a. dust; dust-borne (infection); **—высасыватель** m. dust remover; **—защищённый** a. dustproof; **—ловка** f. dust catcher, filter; **—мер** m. (meteor.) dust counter; **—н** sh. m. of пыльный; **—непроницаемый** a. dustproof, dusttight; **—ние** n. pulverization; dusting.

пылеобраз/ный see **пылевидный; —ование** n. dust formation; **—ующий** a. dust-producing.

пылеосадитель m. dust extractor; (dust) precipitator; **центробежный п.** cyclone; **—ный** a. dust-extracting, dust-collecting; dust-settling.

пыле/осадочный see **пылеосадительный; —отделитель** m. dust separator; **—отсасывающий** a. dust-removing; vacuum; **—отстойный** see **пылеосадительный; —очиститель** m. dust remover; **—перекачивающий** a. pulverized-fuel (pump); **—подавление** n. dust suppression; **—приготовление** n. pulverization (of coal, etc.); **—сборник, —собиратель** m. dust collector; dust catcher; **—содержание** n. dust content; **—сожигательный** a. pulverized-fuel (burner); **—сос** m., **—сосный** a. vacuum cleaner; **—стойкий** a. dustproof.

пыле/угольный a. coal-dust; coal-pulverizing (mill); **—удаление** n. dust removal, dust elimination; **—улавливание** n. dust collecting; dust catching.

пылеуловитель m. dust catcher, dust collector, dust trap, deduster; **—ный** a. dust-catching, dust-collecting.

пыли gen., pl., etc., of **пыль; —мость** f. flaking; **—нка** f. particle (of dust), mote; (bot.) grain of pollen; **—ть** v. raise dust; **—ться** v. get dusty.

пылкий a. passionate, fervent.

пыль f. dust, powder; spray; (soils) silt; (bot.) pollen; **—ник** m. dust coat, smock; (bot.) anther; **—никовый**

a. (bot.) anther(al), stamineal; —**ность** *f.* dustiness; pulverulence; —**ный** *a.* dusty, dust-laden (air); pulverulent, powdery; —**ная буря** dust storm; —**ца** *f.*, —**цевой** *a.* (bot.) pollen; —**цевое зерно** pollen grain; —**цевход** *m.* (bot.) micropyle; —**цеголовник** *m.* (bot.) Cephalanthera; —**цееды** *pl.* (ent.) Alleculidae; —**целистик** *m.* (bot.) microsporophyll; —**ценосный** *a.* polliniferous.

пылящий *a.* raising dust, etc., *see* **пылить.**

пырей *m.* (bot.) Agropyron.

пытать *v.* attempt; (met.) assay; torture; —**ся** *v.* attempt, try, endeavor.

пытка *f.* torture, anguish.

пытливый *a.* inquisitive, searching.

пых/ать, —**нуть** *v.* blaze (up); puff (steam); glow (with health); —**теть** *v.* puff; pant.

пышен *sh. m. of* **пышный.**

пышет *pr. 3 sing. of* **пыхать.**

пышный *a.* luxuriant, rank (vegetation); opulent, lush.

пьедестал *m.* pedestal, stand, base.

пьедмонт *m.* (geol.) piedmont.

пьедра *f.* (med.) piedra.

пьеза *f.* pièze (unit of pressure equal to 1 kN/m²).

пьезо— *prefix* piezo— (pressure); piezoelectric; —**двупреломление** *n.* (opt.) piezobirefringence; —**диффузия** *f.* pressure diffusion; —**ид** *m.* piezoid; —**кварц** *m.* piezoelectric crystal; —**керамический** *a.* piezoceramic; —**кристалл** *m.* piezo (electric) crystal; —**кристаллизация** *f.* piezocrystallization; —**метр** *m.* piezometer, pressure gage; —**метрический** *a.* piezometric; —**метрическая высота** pressure head; —**переход** *m.* piezojunction; —**тензометр** *m.* piezoelectric strain gage; —**тропный** *a.* piezotropic; —**химический** *a.* piezochemical; —**химия** *f.* piezo chemistry.

пьезоэлектр/ик *m.* piezoelectric (crystal); —**ический** *a.* piezoelectric; —**ичество** *n.* piezoelectricity.

пьезоячейка *f.* piezocell, sound cell.

пьемонтит *m.* (min.) piedmontite.

пьёт *pr. 3 sing. of* **пить.**

Пьюджет-саунд (geog.) Puget Sound.

пьющий *pr. act. part. of* **пить.**

пьявица *f.* leaf beetle.

пьявка *see* **пиявка.**

пьян/еть *v.* get intoxicated; —**ить** *v.* intoxicate; —**ица** *f. and m.* alcoholic; (bot.) bog bilberry (*Vaccinium uliginosum*); —**ый** *a.* intoxicated; —**ый хлеб** bread made of contaminated grain; (phyt.) Gibberella rot, Fusarium blight, wheat scab; —**ая болезнь** (ichth.) staggers, ichthyosporidosis; —**ая трава** (bot.) Stellaria.

ПЭ *abbr.* (**полиэтилен**) polyethylene.

пэ-аш *p*H (hydrogen ion concentration).

ПЭВМ *abbr.* (**персональная электронная вычислительная машина**) personal computer, PC.

ПЭГ *abbr.* (**полиэтиленгликоль**) polyethylene glycol.

пюи *m.* (geol.) puy, small volcanic cone; **Пюи-де-Дом** (geog.) Puy de Dôme.

пюпитр *m.* desk, reading stand.

пюре *n.* puree, soup.

ПЯВ *abbr.* (**подземный ядерный взрыв**) underground nuclear explosion.

пяд/еницы *pl.* (ent.) Geometridae; —(**ен**)**ь** *f.* span; stretch.

пял/ить *v.* stretch, pull on; —**ка** *f.*, —**о** *n.* stretcher; —**ьцы** *pl.* stretching frame.

пяст/но— *prefix* (anat.) metacarpo—; —**ный** *a.* metacarpal; —**ь** *f.* metacarpus, shank.

пят/а *f.* (anat.) heel, calx; abutment (of arch), base, foot; pin, pivot (journal), thrust journal, vertical journal;

шарнир в —**е** pivot hinge; —**ачок** *m.* (zool.) snout (of pig, etc.); patch (of ground).

пятая *f.* (one) fifth.

пятен *gen. pl. of* **пятно.**

пят/еричный *a.* fivefold, quintuple; quinary (digit); —**ёрка** *f.* (set of) five; (educ.) excellent (grade), A; —**ерной** *a.* five-part, quinquepartite; quinary; —**ерня** *f.* five fingers of hand; —**еро** *num.* five; —**ёрочник** *m.*, —**ёрочница** *f.* excellent student, A student.

пяти— *prefix* penta—, quinque—, five; *gen. of* **пять**; —**аллюрный** *a.* five-gaited (horse); —**атомный** *a.* pentatomic; —**балльный** *a.* five-point; —**бромистый** *a.* pentabromide (of).

пятивалентн/ость *f.* pentavalence; —**ый** *a.* pentavalent.

пятивёрст/ка *f.* map with a scale of 5 versts to the inch; —**ный** *a.* 5-verst; 5-versts to the inch.

пятиводный гидрат pentahydrate.

Пятигорск (geog.) Piatigorsk.

пятигранн/ик *m.* (geom.) pentahedron; —**ый** *a.* pentahedral; pentagonal.

пяти/десяти— *prefix* fifty; —**десятилетие** *n.* fiftieth anniversary; 50-year period; —**десятый** *a.* fiftieth; —**дневка** *f.* five-day period; —**дневный** *a.* five-day; —**дорожечный** *a.* (comp.) five-channel; —**замещённые** *pl.* pentaderivatives; —**значный** *a.* five-digit; five-unit.

пятикант *m.* ashlar.

пяти/карбонил железа iron pentacarbonyl; —**кольчатый** *a.* pentacyclic, five-membered; —**компонентный** *a.* five-component, quinary; —**конечный** *a.* five-point(ed); —**кратный** *a.* five-fold, quintuple; —**лепестный** *a.* (bot.) pentapetalous.

пятилет/ие *n.* five-year period; fifth anniversary; —**ка** *f.* Five-Year Plan; five-year period; —**ний** *a.* five-year.

пяти/листный *a.* (bot.) pentaphyllous; —**лучевой** *a.* pentactinal, five-rayed; —**месячный** *a.* five-month; —**минутный** *a.* five-minute; —**объективный** *a.* five-lens; —**окись** *f.* pentoxide; —**основный** *a.* pentabasic; —**пал(ьчат)ый** *a.* (zool.) pentadactyl; —**пестичный** *a.* (bot.) pentagynous; —**полье** *n.*, —**польная система** (agr.) five-field crop rotation; —**раздельный** *a.* quinquepartite, divided into five parts; —**сернистый** *a.* pentasulfide (of); —**слойный** *a.* five-ply (veneer); —**сотлетний** *a.* quincentenary; —**сотый** *a.* five hundredth.

пятисторонн/ий *a.* five-sided; (geom.) pentahedral; —**ик** *m.* pentahedron.

пяти/тонка *f.* five-ton truck; —**тонный** *a.* five-ton; —**тысячный** *a.* five-thousand(th); —**тычинковый** *a.* (bot.) pentandrous; —**тычинковая ива** (bot.) *Salix pentandra.*

пятиться *v.* back up, move back.

пятиугольн/ик *m.* (geom.) pentagon; —**ый** *a.* pentagonal.

пяти/фазный *a.* five-phase; —**фтористый** *a.* pentafluoride (of); —**хлористый** *a.* pentachloride (of); —**членный** *a.* five-membered; (bot.) pentamerous; —**электродный** *a.* five-electrode (tube); —**этажный** *a.* five-story.

пятка *dim. of* **пята**; *f.* heel, calx, hock (of horse); tang (of tool); anvil, sole.

пяткоход *m.* (mam.) honey possum.

пятна *gen. and pl. of* **пятно**; maculae.

пятнадцат/икратный *a.* fifteenfold; —**ый** *a.* fifteenth; —**ь** *num.* fifteen.

пятнать *v.* spot, stain, blot.

пятнист/ость *f.* spottiness, mottling, patchwork; (electrochem.) spotting out; flecks (in wood); (phyt.) leaf spot, blight, mosaic disease; **кольцевая п.** ring spot; **—ый** *a.* spotty, spotted, mottled, speckled, dappled, stained; (biol.) punctate; maculose (structure), maculate; (med.) flecked (spleen).

пятнить *v.* spot, speckle.

пятница *f.* Friday.

пятн/о *n.* spot, stain, blotch, dab, patch; smear, blur; blot, blemish; (anat.; med.) macula; **п. контакта** (mach.) bearing pattern; **жёлтое п.** (anat.) macula lutea; **покрытый —ами** mottled, speckled, spotted; **—овывод-**

ящее средство stain remover, cleaner; **—ышко** *dim. of* пятно; speck(le), freckle.

пято/вый *a. of* пята; **—к** *gen. pl. of* пятка; *m.* five (of a kind).

пяточн/о— *prefix* (anat.) calcaneo—; **—о-кубовид-ный** *a.* calcaneocuboid; **—ый** *a.* calcaneal, heel; (anat.) soleus (muscle); **—ая кость** calcaneus.

пят/ый *a.* fifth; **—ая часть** (one) fifth; **—ь** *num.* five; **—ьдесят** *num.* fifty; **—ьсот** *num.* five hundred; **—ью** *adv.* multiplied by five.

Р

р *abbr.* **(рентген)** roentgen; **(радиан)** radian; **Р** *abbr.* **(температура по Реомюру)** (phys.) degree Réaumur.

раб *m.* slave, automaton.

рабарберон *m.* (chem.) rhabarberon.

рабатка *f.* border (of plants).

раббиттит *m.* (min.) rabbittite.

раббриг *m.* work brigade, crew; team.

рабдо— *see* **рабдо—.**

рабдит *m.* (zool.) Rhabditis; rhabdite.

рабдо— *prefix* rhabd(o)— (rod, stick); **—лит** *m.* (zool.) rhabdolith; **—м** *m.* rhabdome, optic rod.

рабелаизин *m.* rabelaisin.

рабирубия *see* **желтохвост.**

работ/а *f.* work, labor, task, job; employment; service (of equipment), duty, performance (of machine); working, running, operation, (biol.) function; procedure; effort; (cardiac) output; action (of wind, etc.); reference, study, paper; **—ы** *pl.* work, operations; **р. на изгиб** bending strain; **р. на клавиатуре** (comp.) key(board)ing; **в —е** at work, in operation; **загонять —ой** *v.* overwork; **многозадачная р.** (comp.) multitasking; **объём работ** effort; **освободить с —ы** *v.* discharge (a worker), fire, lay off; **при —е** when operating, with; **проведение работ, программа работ** effort; **режим —ы** procedure; operating conditions; **условия —ы** operating conditions, working conditions; **ход —ы** operation.

работ/авший *past act. part. of* **работать;** spent; **—ать** *v.* work, run, operate, be in operation, function, perform; serve, act (as); be active (in); **—ать от** operate from, be powered by; **не —ать** be idle, be inoperative, be out of order; **—ающий** *a.* working, etc., *see v.*; driven, powered (by); operational; **—ающий от батареи** battery-operated.

работни/к *m.*, **—ца** *f.* worker, laborer, hand; operator.

работодатель *m.* employer.

работоспособн/ость *f.* efficiency; working capacity, fitness for work, health (of an instrument); **испытание на р.** functional test; **—ый** *a.* efficient; able-bodied.

работы *pl., etc., of* **работа;** work(s), workings; (data) processing; **взрывные р.** blasting; **океанографические р.** oceanographic(al) survey.

работя/га *m. and f.* hard worker, slogger; **—щий** *a.* industrious.

рабоч/ий *m. see* **работник;** *a.* work(ing); workers', labor; running, operating, functioning; feed (tank); on (position); drive (pulley, etc.); power (stroke); draft (horse); active, actuating; useful, effective (area, range, volume, etc.); net (load); process (solution); live (steam); characteristic, performance (curve); service, official, staff (catalog); tabulating (punched card); time (card, sheet); detail (design); **р. диск** (comp.) temporary disk; **р. конус** (seamless tube rolling) mandrel; **р. прогон**

production run; **р. процесс** operation, procedure; **р. режим** performance; operating conditions; **р. цилиндр** main cylinder; **р. чертёж** blueprint; detail design; **—ая диаграмма** load-extension curve; **—ая жидкость** pressure fluid (of hydraulic press); **—ая лента** (comp.) scratch tape; **—ая нагрузка линии** (comp.; commun.) traffic; **—ая сила** labor, manpower; **—ая смена** shift, operating crew; **—ая смесь** (nucl.) working mixture; (engines) air-fuel mixture; **—ая станция** *see* **рабочее место; —ая функция выхода** work function (of electron); **—ая характеристика** (mach.) performance; **—ая часть** body; **—ее вещество** agent; **—ее колесо** impeller; **—ее место** work place; operator's position; (comp.) workstation; **—ее пространство** (furnace) combustion space; **—ее тело** working fluid; **—ие режимы** (comp.) execution states; **—ие руки** labor; **в —их условиях** under working conditions, in operation; performance (test).

рабочий-сдельщик *m.* worker paid on piece-work scale.

рабсила *f.* manpower, labor.

рабство *n.* slavery.

рабфак *m.* workers' preparatory school.

рав-во *abbr.* **(равенство).**

равен *sh. m. of* **равный.**

равен/дук, —тух *m.* (text.) duck.

равенство *n.* equality, parity; congruence; (chem.; math.) equation.

равн/ение *n.* leveling, equalization; **—ина** *f.*, **—инный** *a.* plain, flatland, flat country, lowland; **—итель** *m.* leveler, smoother; trimmer; (paper) dandy roll.

равно *adv.* equally, uniformly, alike; also; (it) is equal; *prefix* equi—, iso—, homo—; **р. как и** as are, as does, along with; **всё р.** all the same, it makes no difference; **ему всё р.** he does not care; **—бедренный** *a.* (geom.) isosceles; **—бокий, —бочный** *a.* equilateral; **—великий** *a.* equidimensional, equal-sized, equal-area, equivalent; **—вероятность** *f.* equal probability; **—вероятный** *a.* equally probable; **—вершинный** *a.* (bot.) fastigiate.

равновес/ие *n.* equilibrium, balance, equipoise; **отношение —ия** equilibrium ratio; **приводить в р.** *v.* balance, equilibrate; **—ность** *f.* state of equilibrium; **—ный** *a.* equilibrium; equiponderant; synchronous (ion); **—ных схем** indicator** null indicator.

равновильчатый *a.* (bot.) isotomous.

равновременн/ость *f.* isochronism; **—ый** *a.* isochronous; (math.) tautochronous.

равновысокий *a.* equal in height; (bot.) fastigiate.

равнодействующ/ая *f.*, **—ая сила** resultant, equivalent force; **—ий** *a.* equal, equally effective; resultant.

равноденств/енный *a.* equinox, equinoctial; equatorial; **—ие** *n.* equinox.

равно/доступный *a.* equally accessible, easily accessible; **—душие** *n.* apathy, indifference; **—душный** *a.* apathetic, indifferent, unconcerned.

равнозернист/ость *f.* even-grained texture; **—ый** *a.* even-grained.

равнознач/ащий *a.* equivalent; **—ность** *f.* equivalence (of propositions), (logic) bicondition; **—ный, —ущий** *a.* equivalent.

равнозубые *pl.* (mal.) Taxodonta.

равно/излучающий *a.* uniformly irradiating; equal-energy (dish); **—коррелированный** *a.* uniformly correlated; **—крылые** *pl.* (ent.) Homoptera; **—лепестный** *a.* isopetalous; **—листный** *a.* isophyllous; **—лопастный** *a.* (zool.) isocercal.

равномерн/о *adv. of* **равный**; uniformly, evenly; **р.-зернистый** *a.* even-grained; **—ость** *f.* uniformity, evenness, steadiness; proportionality; **—ый** *a.* uniform, even, steady; proportional; rhythmic, regular; linear (scale); balanced (lighting).

равно/молярный *a.* equimolar; **—мощность** *f.* equivalence; **—мощный** *a.* equipollent, equivalent; **—мускульный** *a.* (zool.) isomyarian; **—направленный** *a.* (elec.) rectified, unidirected, equidirectional; of like orientation; **—ногие** *pl.* (zool.) Isopoda; **—образие** *n.* homomorphism; **—осный** *a.* equiaxial; **—отстоять** *v.* be equidistant; **—отстоящий** *a.* equidistant, equally spaced.

равнопад/аемость *f.*, **—ающий** *a.* equal falling, equal settling; **коэффициент —аемости** settling ratio.

равно/плечий *a.* (elec.) equal-arm; (zool.) isobrachial; **р. анкер** circular pallet; **—площадный** *a.* equal-area; **—полярный** *a.* isopolar; **—потенциальный** *a.* equipotential; **—правный** *a.* having equal rights; equitable (contract); peer-to-peer; **—приливный** *a.* cotidal; **—пролётный** *a.* equal-span (beam); **—промежуточный** *a.* equidistant; evenly spaced; **—противоположный** *a.* equal and opposite; **—прочный** *a.* full-strength (weld); **—размерный** *a.* equal in size; **—распределение** *n.* equipartition.

равно/ресничные *pl.* (zool.) Holotricha; **—сигнальный** *a.* equisignal; **—силие** *n.*, **—сильность** *f.* equivalence; **—сильный** *a.* equivalent; equipotent; isodynamic; **—споровый** *a.* (bot.) homosporic; **—створчатый** *a.* (zool.) equivalved; **—степенный** *a.* (math.) equipotential; even-spaced (map); **—сторонний** *a.* equilateral; even-spaced (map); **—сть** *f.* equality; **—та** *f.* evenness; **—температурный** *a.* isothermal; **—точный** *a.* equally accurate; **—угольник** *m.* (geom.) isogon; **—угольный** *a.* isogonal, equiangular; conformal (projection); **—удалённый** *a.* equidistant, equispaced; **—ускоренный** *a.* uniformly accelerated; **—фазный** *a.* equiphase; **—ценность** *f.* equivalence; **—ценный** *a.* equivalent; **—частотный** *a.* equifrequent.

равночисленн/ость *f.* equality in number; **—ый** *a.* equal in number.

равночленный *a.* homonomous (growth, etc.).

равноэнергетический *a.* equal-energy.

равн/ый *a.* equal, (a)like, similar; even, uniform; (math.) equipollent (vectors); **р. азимут** isoazimuth; **—ым образом** equally, to the same extent; **на —ых основаниях, на —ых правах** interchangeably (with); **не имеющий себе —ого** *a.* having no equal, unrivaled, unparalleled.

равнять *v.* equalize, equate; even, smooth, level, flatten; compare; **—ся** *v.* be equal(ized); compare (to); (mil.) dress (e.g. a line of troops).

рад *m.* rad (radiation absorbed dose); *abbr.* (**радиан**) radian; *a.* glad, pleased.

радар *m.*, **—ный** *a.* radar (radio detection and ranging).

рад. ген. *abbr.* (**радиационная генетика**) radiation genetics.

ради *prep. gen.* for (the sake of), on account of; **р. чего** why, what for?

радиально *adv.* radially; **р. расходиться** *v.* radiate, diverge; **—волокнистый** *a.* radial-columnar, divergent-columnar; **—кольцевой, —круговой** *a.* radial-circular; **—лучистая структура** (cryst.) divergent structure, radiation; **р.-осевой** *a.* radial-axial, mixed-flow (turbine); **—ребристый** *a.* (pal.) radially striated; **—столбчатый** *see* **радиальноволокнистый**; **—упорный** *a.* radial thrust; **—фазовый** *a.* synchrotron (oscillation).

радиальный *a.* radial; radial-flow (turbine).

ради/ан *m.*, **—анный** *a.* (geom.) radian; **—ант** *m.*, **—антный** *a.* (astr.) radiant; **—атор** *m.* radiator; emitter; (oil) cooler; heat sink; **—ационно-химический** *a.* radiation-chemistry; radiochemical; **—ационный** *a.* radiation, radiative; solar (thermometer); **—ационный захват** (nucl.) radiative capture; **—ация** *f.* radiation; **—евый** *a.* radium(-bearing); **—ировать** *v.* radiate.

рад/ий *m.* radium, Ra; **излучение —ия, эманация —ия** radium emanation, radon, Rn; **лечение лучами —ия** radium therapy; **—ийсодержащий** *a.* radium-bearing, radium-containing.

радикал *m.* radical; **знак —а** (math.) radical sign.

радикальн/ость *f.* radicalness; efficiency, completeness; **—о-цепной** *a.* chain-radical; **—ый** *a.* radical; efficient, complete.

радикотомия *f.* (med.) rhizotomy.

радикул/а *f.* (anat.) (bot.) radicle; **—ит** (med.) radiculitis; **—о—** *prefix* radiculo— (root); **—опатия** *f.* (med.) radiculopathy; **—ярный** *a.* radicular, radicle, root.

радио *n.* radio; *prefix* radio—, radio-frequency; radiation, radioactive; radium; **—автограф** *see* **авторадиограф.**

радиоактив/ационный *a.* (radio)activation; **р. анализ** (chem.) activation analysis; **—ация** *f.* radioactivation; **—ировать** *v.* radioactivate; **—ность** *f.* radioactivity; **—ный** *a.* (radio)active; hot (waste); **—ный ряд** radioactive series; decay chain; **—ный углерод** radiocarbon; **—ный элемент** radioelement; **—ные осадки** fallout.

радио/актиний *m.* radioactinium, RaAc; **—акустический** *a.* radioacoustic; **—альтиметр** *m.* radio altimeter; **—аппарат** *m.* radio (receiving) set; **—аппаратура** radio equipment; **—аутография** *f.* autoradiography.

радиобиолог *m.* radiobiologist; **—ический** *a.* radiobiological; **—ия** *f.* radiobiology.

радио/блок *m.* radio unit; **—вещание** *n.*, **—вешательный** *a.* broadcast(ing); **—взрыватель** *m.* radio detonator, electronic fuze, radar fuze; **—видение** *n.* microwave imaging; **—вождение** *n.* radio aids to navigation; **—война** *f.* electronic warfare; **—волна** *f.* radio-wave; **частота —волн** radio frequency; **—волновод** *m.* radio waveguide; **—всплеск** *m.* radio burst (of sun); **—вызов** *m.* radio call; **—высотомер** *m.* radio(electronic) altimeter; **—вышка** *f.* radio tower.

радио/генный *a.* radiogenic; **—глушение** *n.* radio jamming; **—гониометр** *m.* radiogoniometer; **—гониометрический** *a.* radiogoniometric, radio direction-finding; **—горизонт** *m.* radio horizon, radar horizon; **—грамма** *f.* radiogram, radio message; X-ray (photograph).

радиограф *m.*, **—ировать** *v.* radiograph, photograph by X-rays, etc.; **—ический** *a.* radiographic; **—ия** *f.* radiography, X-ray photography; radiograph.

радио/данные *pl.* radio data; **—диагностика** *f.* X-ray diagnostics; **—завод** *m.* radio manufacturing plant; **—запросчик** *m.* (radar) interrogator, radar IFF; **—засечка** *f.* radio fix; **—зонд** *m.*, **—зондовый** *a.* (meteor.) radiosonde; **—излучение** *n.* radio (-frequency) emission; radio waves; **—изотоп** *m.* ra-dio(active) isotope; **—иммунитет** *m.* (med.) radio-immunity; **—индуцированный** *a.* radiation-induced; **—инженер** *m.* radio engineer; **—иод** *m.* (chem.) ra-dioiodine; **—источник** *m.* radiation source; (astr.) ra-dio source.

радио/канал *m.* radio channel; **—керамика** *f.* ceramic high-frequency insulation; **—коллоид** *m.* radiocol-loid; **—комбайн** *m.* combination television, radio, tape recorder and record player.

радио/лампа *f.* (rad.) tube; **—лечение** *n.* radiotherapy; **—лиз** *m.* radiolysis; radiolytic decomposition; **—ли-тический** *a.* radiolytic.

радиолог *m.* (med.) radiologist; **—ический** *a.* radiologi-cal; **—ия** *f.* radiology; **медицинская —ия** nuclear medicine.

радиолокатор *m.* radar (set); **р. обнаружения** surveil-lance radar; **р. сопровождения** tracking radar.

радиолокационн/ый *a.* radar, radiolocation; **р. пере-датчик помех** radar jammer; **р. обтекатель** radome; **—ая станция** radar; **—ое противодействие** elec-tronic countermeasures.

радиолокация *f.* radar (radio detection and ranging).

радио/лот *m.* sound-ranging altimeter; **—луч** *m.* radio beam; **—любитель** *m.* radio amateur, ham; **—люминесцентный** *a.* radioluminescent.

радиоляр/иевый *a.* radiolarian; **р. ил, —ит** *m.* (petr.) radiolarite, radiolarian ooze; **—ии** *pl.* (zool.) Radio-laria.

радио/маркёр *m.* (radio) marker beacon; **—мачта** *f.* radio mast, radio tower; **—маяк** *m.* radio range (bea-con), radiophare, (marker) beacon; **—маяк-ответчик** transponder.

радио/метеорология *f.* radiometeorology; **—метионин** *m.* radioactive methionine; **—метка** *f.* (radioactive) tracer.

радиометр *m.* radiometer, radiation meter; **—ист** *m.* radar operator; radio operator; **—ический** *a.* radio-metric; **—ия** *f.* radiometry.

радио/механик *m.* radio repairman; **—миметический** *a.* (immun.) radiomimetic; **—молчание** *n.* radio si-lence; **—мутация** *f.* radiomutation; **—наблюдение** *n.* radio observation, monitoring, interception; **—наведе-ние** *n.* radio guidance, electronic guidance; **—навига-ционный** *a.* radio navigational; **—навигация** *f.* radio navigation; **—наушники** *pl.* earphones.

радио/обмен *m.* radio traffic; **—обнаружение** *n.* radio detection; **—оборудование** *n.* radio equipment; **—опе-ратор** *m.* radio operator; **—отправитель** *m.* (radio) transmitter; **—отражение** *n.* radio reflection, radio echo.

радиопеленг *m.*, **—ация** *f.* (radio) direction finding, ra-dio bearing; **—атор** *m.* direction finder.

радиопереда/тчик *m.* transmitter; **—ча** *f.* transmission; **—ющий** *a.* transmitting.

радио/перекличка radio communication; **—перехват** *m.* radio interception; **—подслушивание** *n.* radio inter-ception; **—позывной** *m.* radio call sign; **—полуком-пас** *m.* radio compass; **—помехи** *pl.* radio interfer-ence.

радиоприём *m.* radio reception; **—ник** *m.* receiver, re-ceiving set; **—ный** *a.* receiving.

радио/прожектор *m.* searchlight(-control) radar; **—проз-рачный** *a.* radioparent; **—противодействие** *n.* elec-tronic countermeasures.

радио/разведка *f.* (mil.) signals intelligence; **—реле** *n.*, **—релейный** *a.* radio relay; **—рубка** *f.* radio room; **—свечение** *n.* radioluminescence; **—свинец** *m.* radio-lead; radium G, PbRa; **—связь** *f.* radio communica-tion; **линия —связи** radio link; **—сенсибилизация** *f.* radiosensitization; **—сеть** *f.* radio network; **—сигнал** *m.* radio signal.

радиоскоп *m.* radioscope; **—ический** *a.* radioscopic; **—ия** *f.* radioscopy, detection of radioactive substances.

радио/служба *f.* radio service; **—снимок** *m.* radio-graph; **—сопровождение** *n.* radio tracking; **—спек-троскопия** *f.* radiofrequency spectroscopy; **—стан-ция** *f.* radio station; **—стерилизация** *f.* radiation sterilization; **—стойкость** *f.* radioresistance; radiation hardness.

радиотелеграф *m.*, **—ировать** *v.* radiotelegraph; **—ист** *m.* wireless operator; **—ия** *f.* radiotelegraphy; **—ный** *a.* radiotelegraph(ic).

радиотеле/измерение *n.*, **—метрический** *a.* radiotele-metering; **—метрия** *f.* radiotelemetry; **—механика** *f.*, **—механический** *a.* radio control; **—скоп** *m.* (astr.) radio telescope; **—управление** *n.* radio remote con-trol; **—фон** *m.*, **—фонный** *a.* radio-telephone.

радиотень *f.* radio shadow.

радиотерап/евт *m.* radiotherapist; **—евтический** *a.* ra-diotherapeutic; **—ия** *f.* radiotherapy, radiation therapy.

радиотехн/ик *m.* radio engineer, radio technician; **—ика** *f.* radio engineering, electronics; **—ический** *a.* radio, electronic.

радиотокс/емия *f.* radiation sickness; **—икология** *f.* radiotoxicology; **—ичность** *f.* radiotoxicity.

радио/тор *m.* radiothor, radioactive indicator; **—торий** *m.* radiothorium, RaTh; **—трансляционный** *a.*, **—трансляция** *f.* rebroadcasting, radio relay (system); **—углерод** *m.* (chem.) radiocarbon; **—узел** *m.* radio center, broadcasting center; **—ульнарный** *a.* (anat.) ra-dioulnar; **—управление** *n.* radio control; **—управ-ляемый** *a.* radio-controlled, radio-guided.

радиоусилитель *m.* radio amplifier; **—ная лампа** am-plifying tube.

радио/установка *f.* radio set; radio plant; radio installa-tion; **—устойчивость** *f.* radioresistance; **—устройст-во** *n.* radio set; radio equipment; electronic device; **—физика** *f.* radiophysics; **—физический** *a.* radio-physical.

радиофи/кация *f.* radio installation; **—цированный** *a.* radio-equipped; **—цировать** *v.* install radio(s), equip with radios.

радио/фон *m.* radio telephone set; **—фосфор** *m.* (chem.) radiophosphorus; **—фотолюминесценция** *f.* radio-photoluminescence.

радиохим/ик *m.* radiochemist; **—икали** *pl.* radioactive chemicals; **—ический** *a.* radiochemical; **—ия** *f.* radio-chemistry.

радио/центр *m.* radio center; **—частота** *f.*, **—частот-ный** *a.* radio-frequency; **—чувствительность** *f.* ra-diosensitivity; **—шар-зонд** *m.* radio sounding balloon; **—шум** *m.* radio noise, radio interference.

радиоэлектрон/ика *f.* (radio)electronics, electronic en-gineering; **—ный** *a.* (radio)electronic.

радио/элемент *m.* radioactive element; **—эхо** *n.* radio echo; radar echo.

рад/ировать *v.* radio; **—ируемый** *a.* radioed; **—ист** *m.* radio operator.

радиус *m.* radius; **р. действия** range; reach (of robot); **р. инерции** (mech.) radius of gyration; **—ный** *a.* radius.

радлюкс *m.* radlux (photometric unit).

радовать *v.* gladden, rejoice.

радон *m.,* **—ный** *a.* radon, Rn.

радостный *a.* glad, joyous.

рад/сек *abbr.* (**радиан в секунду**) radians per second.

радуг/а *f.* rainbow; **переливающий всеми цветами —и** iridescent.

радуж/ина, —ка *f.* (anat.) iris; **—ница** *f.* long-horned leaf beetle; rainbow fish; **—но—** *prefix* (anat.) irido— (iris); **—нозелёный** *a.* iridescent green; **—нороговичный** *a.* (anat.) iridocorneal; **—носиний** *a.* iridescent blue; **—ность** *f.* iridescence; **—ный** *a.* rainbow (-hued), iridescent, opalescent; (anat.) iris; **—ная оболочка** (anat.) iris; **разрез —ной оболочки** (med.) iridotomy; **отливать —ными красками** *v.* iridesce, opalesce.

радула *f.* (zool.) radula.

радфот *m.* radphot (photometric unit).

раз *adv.* once; times, by a factor (of); *m.* time; *conj.* since; **р. навсегда** once for all; **в другой р.** some other time, another time; **р. в три года** (once) every three years, triennially; **в два —а больше** twice (as much), double; **в два —а меньше** half (as much); **в шесть р.** six times, sixfold; **ещё р.** once more, again; **за р.** at once, at one go; **как раз** just, exactly; **много р.** repeatedly, many times, often; **не р.** more than once; **пять р. по пять** five times five; **этот р.** this time.

раз— *prefix* un—, dis—; away, off; *with verbs to indicate intensified action, division into parts, cessation of action or reversal of action.*

разалеться *v.* become scarlet.

разарретировать *v.* uncage (a gyroscope), free; actuate.

разасфальтирование *n.* deasphalting.

разб. *abbr.* (**разбавленный**).

разбав/итель *m.* diluent; (paint) thinner; extender; **—ить** *v. see* **разбавлять**; **—ка** *f.,* **—ление** *n.* dilution, thinning, rarefaction; **—ленный** *a.* dilute(d), thin(ned); **—лять** *v.* dilute, thin, cut; rarefy (gas).

разбаза/р/и(ва)ть *v.* squander; —**ование** *n.* waste.

разбаланс *m.* unbalance; mismatch; **напряжение —а** out-of-balance voltage; **—ированный** *a.* out of balance, out of trim; **—ироваться** *v.* get out of balance.

разбаливаться *v.* start aching; ache more.

разбалластовать *v.* lighten, unload.

разбалтывать *v.* shake up; agitate; mix; **—ся** *v.* be shaken up; get loose.

разбе/г *m.* start(ing), warm(ing)-up, acceleration, racing (of motor); momentum; (av.) take-off run; (met.) beveling; **—гаться, —жаться** *v.* get started, warm up, accelerate, race; gather momentum; disperse, scatter; dart in all directions.

разбел *m.* brightening; lightening; **—ивающая способность** tinting strength (of white pigment); **—ительный** *a.* brightening.

разбередить *v.* irritate, chafe.

разберёт *fut. 3 sing. of* **разобрать**.

разбив/ание *n.* breaking, etc., *see v.*; **—атель** *m.* (paper) pulper; disintegrator; **—ать** *v.* break (down, into, up); smash, fracture; (sub)divide, split (up), group, classify; (mach.) dismantle, take apart; plan, lay out, mark off, peg out (a line); (typ.) space out; (mil.) defeat; **—ка** *f.* breaking, etc., *see v.*; breakdown, breakup; (sub)division; layout; **в —ку** retail; haphazardly; (typ.) spaced out; **—ной** *a.* separable; **—очный** *a.* marking, spacing; **—очный колышек** peg stake; **—чивый** *a.* brittle, frangible.

разбиение *n.* breakdown, decomposition, split(ting), fragmentation, break-up; partition(ing), subdivision; **р. на логические блоки** (comp.) logical partitioning; **р. на области** regionalization; **р. на слои** layering; **р. текста на страницы** pagination.

разбинтов(ыв)ать *v.* remove bandage; unwrap.

разбир/аемый *a.* in question, under discussion; **—ание** *n.* dismantling, etc., *see v.*; examination, discussion; **—ательство** *n.* examination, discussion; (law) trial; **—ать** *v.* dismantle, take apart, disassemble, strip, break down, knock down, take down, dismount; pull down, demolish, wreck; unpack; sort, pick, choose; discuss, analyze, examine; make out, discern, recognize, decipher; strike (center); (law) try; **—аться** *v.* be dismantled, etc.; dismantle, come apart; put in order; discriminate; unpack; figure out; investigate.

разбит/ый *a.* broken, smashed, etc., *see* **разбивать**; beaten; ruined; foundered (horse); **—ь** *see* **разбивать**.

разблокиров/ание *n.* unlocking, unblocking, deblocking (of data); enable (of signal); **—ать** *v.* unlock, uncouple; block out; gate (a pulse or signal).

разбогатеть *v.* get rich, become prosperous; **р. внезапно** boom.

разбой *m.* robbery; piracy.

разболеться *see* **разбаливаться**.

разболт/анный *a.* stirred, shaken up, loose; disorganized; (med.) flail (joint); **—ать** *see* **разбалтывать**.

разболчивать *v.* unbolt.

разбомбить *v.* bomb, destroy.

разбор *m.* choice, selection; analysis, examination (of problem); review, criticism (of book); (law) trial; *see also* **разборка**; **без —а** indiscriminately; **грамматический р.** parsing; **одного —а** of the same stamp.

разбор/ка *f.* dismantling, etc., *see* **разбирать**; disassembly; (agr.) singling; (apid.) manipulation; **—ный** *a.* collapsible, dismountable, knock-down, sectional, separable; prefabricated.

разборон/ить, —овать *v.* harrow (out).

разборочный *a. of* **разборка**.

разбортовка *f.* (mach.) inward flanging.

разборчив/о *adv.* clearly, plainly; **—ость** *f.* intelligibility; **—ый** *a.* clear, plain, legible; discriminating; fastidious.

разбраков/ка *f.* grading, etc., *see v.*; **—(ыв)ать** *v.* grade, sort, inspect, reject.

разбрасыв/ание *n.* scattering, etc., *see v.*; dispersion, dispersal; **—атель** *m.* disperser; dispenser; spreader, distributor; sower, broadcaster; **—ать** *v.* scatter, disperse, throw around; broadcast (seed); spread, distribute (fertilizer); waste; **—аться** *v.* be scattered, etc.; have no definite goal, dissipate (one's efforts); **—ающий** *a.* scattering, etc., *see v.*

разбр/едаться, —естись *v.* disperse, scatter; **—од** *m.* dispersion; disorder; dissension.

разброс *see* **разбрасывание**; scatter, spread; straggling; **р. по углам** angle spread; **случайный р.** straggling; **случайный р. пробега** range straggling; **—анность** *f.* dispersion; disconnectedness; **—анночешуйчатый** *a.* (ichth.) mirror (carp); **—анный** *a.* scattered, etc., *see* **разбрасывать**; loose (cargo); speckled, spotted; **—ать, —ить** *see* **разбрасывать**; **—ка** *see* **разбрасывание**; **—ной** *a. of* **разброс**; **—ной аппарат** dispenser; **—ной посев** (agr.) broadcasting.

разбрушивать *v.* (apid.) uncap.

разбрыз/ганный *a.* sprayed, etc., *see v.*; **—гать** *see* **разбрызгивать**; **—гивание** *n.* spraying, etc., *see v.*; **испытание при —гивании** (met.) spray test; **охлаждение —гиванием** spray cooling; **—гиватель** *m.* sprayer, etc., *see v.*; **—гивать** *v.* spray, sprinkle;

atomize, pulverize; spatter, splash; sputter; **—гив-ающий** *a.* spraying, etc., *see v.*; spray (nozzle); **—нуть** *see* **разбрызгивать.**

разбудить *v.* wake up, arouse.

разбур/ав *m.* countersink; **—авить, —авливать** *v.* countersink, widen; **—ённый** *a.* drilled (out); developed (field); **—ивание** *n.* drilling (out); development; **—и(ва)ть** *v.* drill (out); develop; **—овка** *f.* countersink (bit).

разбух/ание *n.* swelling, etc., *see v.*; **—ать, —нуть** *v.* swell, distend, intumesce, turgesce, bulge, inflate, expand; blow; **—ший** *a.* swollen, tumid, bloated.

развал *m.* disorganization, collapse, breakdown; breakup, split (of nucleus); flare; camber (of wheels); split log; **—енный** *a.* pulled down, etc., *see v.*; collapsed, broken down; loose (cargo); **—ивать** *v.* pull down, demolish, wreck; spoil, undo; disorganize, break up; scatter; roll out; **—иваться** *v.* fall apart, collapse; sprawl; **—ина** *f.* ruin, wreck; **—ины** *pl.* ruins, debris; **—ить(ся)** *see* **разваливать(ся).**

развалка *f.* spreading; rolling (out).

разваль/ный *a.* open; **—цевать** *see* **развальцовывать.**

развальцов/анный *a.* rolled out, etc., *see v.*; **—ка** *f.* rolling out, lamination, etc., *see v.*; breakdown; expander; **—ывать** *v.* roll out, laminate, expand; break down; bead; open out, flare.

развалять *v.* spread; roll out.

развар/енный, —ной *a.* cooked to a pulp; **—и(ва)ть** *v.* cook to a pulp, digest thoroughly.

разве *adv. and conj.* perhaps (. . . had better); if (not), unless; except; really?

развев/аемый *a.* drift (sand); **—ание** *n.* blowing, scattering; weathering; deflation (wind action) **—ать** *v.* blow, scatter.

развед/анный *a.* explored, tested, proved; **—ать** *see* **разведывать.**

разведен/ие *n.* dilution, thinning, etc., *see* **разводить;** (bact.) culture; **р. в себе, чист(олинейн)ое р.** pure breeding.

разведённый *a.* diluted, etc., *see* **разводить;** dilute, thin(ned), rare.

разведк/а *f.* search, exploration; survey(ing); reconnaissance; intelligence; (min.) prospecting; (sound) ranging; **предварительная р.** reconnaissance; **производить —у** *v.* reconnoiter; prospect.

разведочн/ый *a.* exploring, exploratory, reconnaissance; (min.) prospecting.

разведчик *m.* (min.) prospector, scout; intelligence agent; reconnaissance plane.

разведший *past act. part. of* **развести.**

разведыв/ание *n.,* **—ательный** *a.* searching, exploring; reconnaissance; (min.) prospecting; intelligence; **—ать** *v.* investigate, explore; inquire (about); scout, reconnoiter; prospect; exploit.

развезти *see* **развозить.**

развеивать *v.* scatter, blow away, disperse, dispel.

разверз/ание *n.* opening, etc., *see v.*; **—ать, —нуть** *v.* open wide, gape; **—аться, —нуться** *v.* open up, separate.

развериться *v.* get out of true, get out of alignment.

развёрнут/ый *a.* unfolded, etc., *see* **развёртывать;** total (length); straight (angle); expanded; detailed, comprehensive.

развернуть *see* **развёртывать.**

разверстать *see* **развёрстывать.**

развёрст/ывать *v.* divide, distribute, allot; **—ка** *f.* division, distribution, allotment; **—ка добыче** proration.

разверстый *a.* wide open, gaping, drawn apart.

развертеть *see* **развёрчивать.**

развёрт/ка *see* **развёртывание;** (geom.) involute, evolvent; deployment; resolution, analysis; development; (rad.) sweep; scan; trace; time base; reamer, broach (bit); **временная р.** countdown; time base; **генератор —ки** time-base generator, sweep generator; **зеркальная р.** (phot.) rotating-mirror scan; streak photography; **ось —ки** timing axis, time base; **—ывае-мый** *a.* (geom.) developable; developed; **—ывание** *n.* unfolding, etc., *see v.*; deployment; (bot.) efflorescence; frondescence; unrolling; scanning; (geom.) development; evolvement, evolution, build-up; presentation; extension; expansion (of hole); **—ывание по столбцам** (math.) column-major order; **—ыватель** *m.* scanner; **—ывать** *v.* unfold, open (up), unwrap, unroll, unwind, uncoil; expound; spread out, extend; deploy; straighten out, flatten, rectify; (geom.) develop; evolve; scan, analyze, explore; (electron.) sweep; expand, ream, broach; turn around, make a turn; get ready; **—ываться** *v.* be unfolded, etc.; develop, expand; unwind, run down (of spring); get ready; deploy; turn around; **—ывающий** *a.* unfolding, etc., *see v.*; **—ывающая кривая** involute; **—ывающее устройство** scanner; **—ывающийся** *a.* developing; developable; **—ывающаяся линия** involute.

разверчивать *v.* ream, expand, enlarge; unscrew; get rolling; **—ся** *v.* expand; unscrew, get loose; get rolling.

развес *see* **развеска; на р.** by weight.

развесистый *a.* spreading, branched, branchy, ramose, ramous; canopy (tree).

развес/ить *see* **развешивать; —ка** *f.* weighing; hanging; **—ной** *a.* sold loose by weight; **—очная** *f.* weighing room; (rubber) compounding room; **—очный** *a.* weighing.

развести *see* **разводить.**

разветв/итель *m.* bifurcating device, splitter; **—итель-ный** *a.* branching, etc., *see v.*; branch, splice (box); **—ить(ся)** *see* **разветвлять(ся); —ление** *n.* branching, ramification, etc., *see v.*; branch, fork; leg; **—лен-ность** *f.* (degree of) branching; ramified structure; **—лённый** *a.* branched, etc., *see v.*; branch; multipath (circuit); ramose; **—лять** *v.* branch (out), ramify; bifurcate, fork; subdivide; split (program); tap off; **—ляться** *v.* branch (out), fork; ramify; **—ляющийся** *a.* branching; manifold (flow).

развехованный *a.* marked.

развеш/ать, —ивать *v.* suspend, hang (around, up); **—енный** *a.* suspended; hung (around, up); weighed out; **—ивать** *v.* weigh out; spread (of tree).

развеять *see* **развевать.**

развив/аемый *a.* developed, etc., *see v.*; **—аемая мощность** output (of machine); **—ание** *n.* development, generation; **—ать** *v.* develop, generate, evolve; amplify, build up; exert, induce; untwist, unwind; **—ать скорость** accelerate; **—аться** *v.* develop, grow; unfold, evolve; **—ающий(ся)** *a.* evolving, etc., *see v.*; **—шийся** *a.* developed, etc., *see v.*

развил/ина *f.* fork, yoke, crotch; forking, bifurcation, divarication; (bot.) axil; dichotomy; **—истый** *a.* forked, (bi)furcate; **—ка** *f.* fork, yoke; **в —ку** Y-shaped.

развин/тить *see* **развинчивать; —ченность** *f.* enervation, restiveness; **—ченный** *a.* unscrewed, etc., *see v.*; unstrung; loose; **—чивание** *n.* unscrewing, etc., *see v.*; (drilling) back off, break out (of tool); **—чивать** *v.* unscrew, screw off, unfasten, loosen; enervate; **—чиваться** *v.* become unnerved; come unscrewed.

развит/ие *n.* development, growth, build-up, progress,

evolution; extension, spread, distribution; **биология —ия** developmental biology; ontogenesis; **индивидуальное р.** life history; ontogeny; **обратное р.** (med.) regression; **порок —ия** developmental defect; **—ой** *a.* mature, developed; high-level; widespread; **—ость** *f.* maturity; progressiveness; **—ый** *a.* developed, etc., *see* **развивать; —ь** *see* **развивать.**

развле/кать, —чь *v.* divert, distract; entertain; **—чение** *n.* recreation.

развод *m.* (agr.) raising, breeding; separation, divorce; set (of saw teeth); posting (of sentries); **—имый** *a.* cultivated (plants); **—ить** *v.* dilute, thin; rarefy (gas); breed, propagate, raise, cultivate; separate; dissolve; divorce; open, pull up, draw (bridge); set (saw teeth); get up, raise (steam); start, light (a fire); show (around); disperse (troops); spread (apart); **—иться** *v.* breed, multiply; separate, get divorced; **—ка** *f.* culture, propagation; separation; drawing (of bridge); displacement; saw set; wiring; **—ка питания** (elec.) power routing; **—ка соединений** wiring; **—ной** *a.* separating; draw (bridge); crescent (wrench); split (cotter); cotter (pin); saw-setting; **—ный** *a.* divorce.

разводы *pl.* designs.

разводье *n.* pool of open water in ice; spring flood.

разводящий *pr. act. part. of* **разводить;** transfer (manifold); distributing, distribution.

развожжать *v.* unbridle, unharness (a horse).

развоз *see* **развозка.**

развозбуждение *n.* de-excitation, de-energizing.

развоз/ить *v.* convey, transport, carry, deliver, distribute; **—ка** *f.* conveyance, transport(ation), delivery; **—ной** *a.* transportation, delivery; transported; **—чик** *m.* transport worker; delivery man.

разволакивать *v.* scatter (of clouds).

разволновать *v.* agitate, excite.

разволокняться *v.* separate (of fiber).

разволочь *see* **разволакивать.**

разворачив/ание *n.* unwrapping, etc., *see v.;* **—ать** *v.* unwrap, unfold, unroll; turn around; take apart; demolish, shatter, destroy, raise havoc; crack, split; **—аться** *v.* be unwrapped, etc.; unroll; expand, develop; speed up; turn around.

разворашивать *v.* scatter, stir up; strew, ted (hay).

развор/от *m.* turn; opening, unfolding; double-page spread; inside (of rolled or folded object); **—отить, —очать** *see* **разворачивать; —оченный** *a.* unwrapped, etc., *see* **разворачивать.**

разворошить *see* **разворашивать.**

разврат *m.* depravity, debauchery; **—итель** *m.* seducer; **—ный** *a.* lewd, depraved.

развращать *v.* corrupt, deprave.

развьючи(ва)ть *v.* unpack, unload.

развяз/анный *a.* untied, etc., *see v.;* **—ать** *v. see* **развязывать; —ка** *f.* untying; outcome, issue; bypass; overpass; (elec.) decoupling; isolation; isolator; **—ание** *n.* untying, etc., *see v.;* **—ывание цен** (comm.) unbundling (e.g. software cost from hardware cost); **—ывать** *v.* untie, unbind, undo, unfasten, uncouple, free; **—ываться** *v.* be untied, etc.; come loose; **—ывающий** *a.* untying, etc., *see v.*

разгад(ыв)ать *v.* guess, puzzle out, break (a code), solve.

разгар *m.* thermal erosion; burnout (of walls); (lining) wear; climax, height (of season); **в полном —е** in full swing; **—остойкость** *f.* resistance to thermal erosion.

разгерметизация *f.* depressurization; seal failure; leakage; rupture.

разгиб *m.*, **—ание** *n.* unbending, etc., *see v.;* crease; extension; **—атель** *m.* (anat.) extensor; **—ать(ся)** *v.* unbend, straighten (out, up); **—ающий** *a.* unbending, straightening; **—ающая мышца** extensor.

разгла/дить *see* **разглаживать; —женный** *a.* smoothed, etc., *see v.;* **—живание** *n.* smoothing, etc., *see v.;* **—живать** *v.* smooth (out), press, iron.

разгла/сить, —шать *v.* divulge, publish, make public; **—шение** *n.* divulgence; disclosure.

разгляд/еть, —ывать *v.* view, examine, scrutinize, consider; perceive.

разгнев/анный *a.* angry, incensed; **—ать** *v.* anger, infuriate; **—аться** *v.* lose one's temper.

разгов/аривать *v.* talk, speak; **—ор** *m.* talk, conversation; (tel.) call; **—орный** *a.* conversation(al), spoken (language); telephone (booth, station).

разгон *m.* acceleration, speeding up, racing; run, start; (missiles) boost; dispersal, dispersion; (typ.) spacing; (nucl.) excursion, divergence; **р. реактора** runaway; reactor excursion; **период —а** rise time; **—истый** *a.* (typ.) widely spaced; **—ка** *f.* acceleration, scattering, dispersal, distillation; flashing; (met.) spread, flattening; **—ный** *a. of* **разгон;** booster (stage); runaway (speed); **—ять** *v.* accelerate, speed up, race; start up (a reactor); distill; drive away, dispel, dissipate, disperse, scatter; (typ.) space; **—яться** *v.* pick up speed.

разгораживать *v.* fence, partition (off), separate; take down a partition.

разгор/аться, —еться *v.* start burning, flame up.

разгородить *see* **разгораживать.**

разгорячённый *a.* heated.

разгра/дить, —ждать (mil.) remove obstacles, clear.

разграждение *n.* (mil.) removal of obstacles; clearing.

разгранич/ение *n.* demarcation; boundary; **—енный** *a.* delimited, etc., *see v.;* **—ивание** *n.* delimiting, etc., *see v.;* **—ивать** *v.* delimit, demarcate, bound, mark limits, fix the limit; **—ивающий** *a.* delimiting, bounding; **—итель** *m.* (comp.) delimiter; **—ительный** *a.* boundary (line); **—ить** *see* **разграничивать.**

разграф/ить, —лять *v.* rule, draw lines; divide into columns.

разгре/бать, —сти *v.* rake (apart), spread out.

разгром *m.* destruction; **—ить** *v.* destroy.

разгру/жатель *m.* discharger, unloader; **—жать** *v.* discharge, unload, empty, dump, throw off, remove; relieve, ease; handle; **—жать давление** depressurize; **—жающий** *a.* discharging, etc., *see v.;* **—жённый** *a.* discharged, etc., *see v.;* balanced (valve); **—зитель** *m.* discharger, unloader; **—зить** *see* **разгружать; —зка** *f.* discharging, etc., *see v.;* discharge; relief; (comp.) dump; off-loading; **—зочно-обрывной** *a.* tension-release (mine); **—зочный** *a. of* **разгрузка;** relief (well); fasting (diet); **—зочный клапан** safety valve, relief valve; **—зочная шайба** balancing disk; **—зчик** *m.* discharger, unloader.

разгруппиров/ание *n.* debunching; **—аться** *v.* debunch; divide into groups.

разгрыз/ать, —ть *v.* gnaw (apart); bite in two.

разд. *abbr.* **(раздел)** section.

раздав/ание *n.* distribution, dispensation; **—ать** *v.* distribute, dispense, deal out; confer, grant; spread, widen, expand, open out, flare; **—аться** *v.* be distributed, etc.; give way; expand, grow wider, flare; gain weight; be heard, resound.

раздав/ить *see* **раздавливать; —ленный** *a.* crushed, (s)mashed; **—ливание** *n.* crush(ing), smash(ing), mashing; **—ливание нервов** (med.) neurotripsy; **—ливать** *v.* crush, (s)mash; **—ливаться** *v.* be crushed; (min.) jack-knife.

раздаивать *v.* (agr.) increase milk yield.

раздалбливать *v.* hollow out, groove; gouge out.

раздат/очный *a.* distributing; delivering; **р. механизм** dispenser; **р. штамп** bulging die; **—очная ведомость** pay roll; **—очное устройство** dispenser; **—чик** *m.* distributor; **—ь** *see* **раздавать**.

раздача *f.* distribution, allotment; delivery; spread, expansion, flare, flaring; bulging.

раздваивать *v.* bifurcate, split; **—ся** *v.* bifurcate, fork; split off, break down; bisect.

раздв/иг *see* **раздвижка**; release; (geol.) fault in which displacement is perpendicular to breakage surface; separation distance; **—игание** *see* **раздвижка**; **—игать** *v.* separate, part, draw apart, drive apart, force apart; disengage (coupling); extend, open; gage (track); **—игаться** *v.* separate, move apart; telescope; **—ижение** *n.*, **—ижка** *f.* separation, parting, etc., *see v.*; gaging (of tracks); **—ижной** *a.* extensible, extension-type, collapsible, telescopic, telescoping; slide (gage); sliding, roll-back (roof); retractor (spring); movable; adjustable (wrench); expansion (bit); expanding (reamer); **—инутый** *a.* separated, etc., *see v.*; distant; **—инуть** *see* **раздвигать**.

раздво/ение *n.* (bi)furcation, dichotomy, fork(ing), branching; splitting; **—енный** *a.* (bi)furcate, dichotomous, forked; split (in half), bifid; bicorn; swallow (tail); **—ить** *see* **раздваивать**.

раздвойникование *n.* untwinning.

раздев/алка *f.* changing room, locker room; **—ание** *n.* undressing; stripping; **—ать** *v.* undress; strip.

раздел *m.* division, allotment; section, chapter, heading; interface (between two media); partition; **р. вод** watershed; **граница —а** interface; (seism.) discontinuity; **линия —а** line of demarcation, dividing line; **поверхность —а** interface; interfacial area; (phase) contact area; **—ать** *see* **разделывать**.

разделени/е *n.* division, separation, partition; (chem.) fractionation; breaking (of chemical bond); (assaying) parting; distribution; cut; classification, classing, indexing; cleaving, cleavage, fission, splitting; segregation (of genes; losses, etc.); (sex) differentiation; **р. бумаги** (comp.) bursting; **р. времени** time sharing; **р. труда** division of labor; **временное р. каналов** time demultiplexing; **коэффициент —я** separation factor; (distillation) relative volatility; **схема —я** (comp.) buffer; **точка —я** separation point.

раздел/ённый *a.* divided, etc., *see* **разделять**; (comp.) split (screen); **—ённый на две части** bipartite; **—ившийся** *a.* divided, etc., *see* **разделять**; (nucl.) fissioned.

разделим/ость *f.* divisibility, separability; **—ый** *a.* divisible, separable; analyzable.

разделитель *m.* separator, separating agent; delimiter; divider, spacer; (assaying) parting agent; guide card; **—ный** *a.* dividing, etc., *see* **разделять**; partition (chromatography); blocking (capacitor); **—ная стенка** barrier; partition.

разделитель-сортировщик *m.* burster (for continuous-feed printer paper).

разделить *see* **разделять**.

раздел/ка *f.*, **—очный** *a.* finishing, etc., *see v.*; finish; baffle; **—ывание** *n.* finishing, etc., *see v.*; **—ывать** *v.* finish, dress; strip; do; prepare, lay out; cut (meat); gut (fish); dress (game); flense (whales); widen, expand; splice (cable); **—ывать под дуб** give an oak finish; **—ываться** *v.* be finished, etc.; part, be done (with), be free (of), settle (a bill).

раздельно *adv.* separately; *prefix* chori— (distinct);

dialy— (bot.) (separated); eleuther(o)— (free); **—двуполый** *a.* bisexual; **—лепестный** *a.* (bot.) choripetalous; **—листный** *a.* choriphyllous; **—полый** *a.* (biol.) dioecious; **р.-поточный** *a.* sectionalized flowline; **—пыльниковый** *a.* (bot.) eleutherantherous; **—сть** *f.* separateness, discreteness; **—чашелистиковый** *a.* (bot.) dialysepalous.

раздельный *a.* divided, separate, distinct, discrete; split (bearing); adjustable (charge); (petrol.) selective (cracking).

раздел/ять *v.* divide, separate; partition; split (up), break down; (assaying) part; sever, disjoint, dissociate; classify, grade, sort, pick (ore); class, index; analyze; fractionate; disintegrate; share, distribute; slot (brush); **—яться** *v.* be divided, etc.; separate, split, branch; **—яющий** *a.* dividing, etc., *see v.*; discernible, perceptible; (nucl.) fissionable; **—яющее приспособление** divider, separator.

раздергать, раздёр/гивать, —нуть *v.* pull apart, shred; let go (a rope).

раздет/ый *a.* undressed; stripped; **—ь** *see* **раздевать**.

раздир *m.* tear(ing); **—альный** *a.* tearing, etc., *see v.*; **—альная машина** disintegrator, shredder; **—ание** *n.* tearing, etc., *see v.*; **предел прочности при —ании** tear strength; **—ать** *v.* tear (apart; open; up; to shreds); lacerate; shred, disintegrate; dismember; open (a pack or package); separate (sheets); **—ающий** *a.* tearing, etc., *see v.*; unbearable; **—ка** *see* **раздирание**.

раздобреть *v.* gain weight.

раздобы(ва)ть *v.* get, obtain, procure.

раздо/енная корова cow at peak lactation; **—ить** *see* **раздаивать; —йка** *f.* (agr.) increasing milk yield.

раздолбить *see* **раздалбливать**.

раздоль/е *n.* spaciousness; freedom; **—ный** *a.* open (space); comfortable (living).

раздор *m.* quarrel, dissension.

раздрабливать *see* **раздроблять**.

раздраж/ать *v.* irritate, annoy; stimulate; **—ающий** *a.* irritating, acrid; **—ение** *n.* irritation; stimulation; **порог —ения** (physiol.) absolute threshold; **—имость** *f.* irritability; **—имый** *a.* irritable, sensitive; **—итель** *m.* irritant; (biol.) stimulus, stimulant; **болезненная —ительность** (med.) erethism; **—ительный** *a.* irritable; **—ить** *see* **раздражать**.

раздревеснение *n.* (bot.) delignification.

раздроб/ить *see* **раздроблять; —ление** *n.* shattering, etc., *see v.*; comminution; fragmentation; *suffix* —tripsy (crushing); **—ленность** *f.* state of comminution; **—ленный** *a.* shattered, etc., *see v.*; granulated; **—лять** *v.* shatter, break (to pieces; up), disintegrate, crush, grind, comminute, reduce; fractionate, split; splinter; break down, (sub)divide; mince; parcel (land); **—ляться** *v.* shatter, fall apart; **—ляющий** *a.* shattering, etc., *see v.*; **—ляющее приспособление** crusher.

раздув *m.* bulge; **—альный** *a.* blowing, inflating; **—альный мех** bellows; **—ание** *n.* blowing (up), etc., *see v.*; inflation; **—ать** *v.* blow (up), inflate, distend; swell, puff up; fan, blow away, disperse; **—аться** *v.* blow up; swell, bulge; **—ающий** *a.* blowing, etc., *see v.*; **—ающее вещество** blowing agent.

раздулка *f.* (bot.) water fennel, horsebane (*Oenanthe phellandrium*).

раздум/ать *v.* change one's mind; **—ывать** *v.* hesitate; ponder, deliberate; **—ье** *n.* hesitation; meditation.

раздут/ие *n.*, **—ость** *f.* swell(ing), distention, inflation; bulge, bulging; **—ый** *a.* inflated, swollen, bulging; (med.) balloon (cell); **—ь** *see* **раздувать**.

разевать *v.* gape, open wide.

разжат/ый *a.* unclasped, etc., *see* **разжимать;** slack; **—ь** *see* **разжимать.**

разж/евать, —ёвывать *v.* masticate, chew.

разжелобок *m.* (arch.; art.) valley.

разж/ечь *see* **разжигать; —иг** *m.,* **—игание** *n.* firing, etc., *see v.;* **—игать** *v.* fire, kindle, light up, start up (furnace); excite, stimulate; **—игаться** *v.* catch fire, blaze up.

разжи/дить *see* **разжижать; —жаемость** *f.* liquescence; **—жаемый** *a.* capable of dilution; liquefiable, liquescent; **—жать** *v.* dilute, thin; rarefy (gas); liquefy, dissolve; **—жающий** *a.* diluting, etc., *see v.;* **—жающее вещество** *see* **разжижитель; —жение** *n.* dilution, thinning, etc., *see v.;* **—жённость** *f.* fluidity, liquid state; **—жённый** *a.* diluted, etc., *see v.;* thin, rare; **—житель** *m.* diluent, thinner, thinning agent; liquefier.

разжим/ание *n.* unclasping, etc., *see v.;* release; **—ать** *v.* unclasp, open, release, unfasten, unclamp, unclench (fist); spread, expand; **—аться** *v.* open, unclamp, etc.; **—ной, —ный** *a.* releasing; expanding (mandrel, reamer); expansion (cam).

разжиреть *v.* grow fat.

раззенков/ка *f.* countersink; reamer; **—ывание** *n.* countersinking; reaming; **—ывать** *v.* countersink; ream (out).

раззуд/еться *v.* itch, smart; **—ить** *v.* irritate (a wound).

разинуть *see* **разевать.**

разительный *a.* striking, impressive.

разить *v.* smell, reek (of); strike, hit.

разлаг/аемый *a.* decomposable; analyzable; **—ать** *v.* decompose, dissociate, separate; break down (into), split up, resolve (into); decay, disintegrate; disperse; analyze; (rad.) scan, sweep; (math.) expand; **—аться** *v.* decompose, disintegrate, break up, break down, separate; dissolve; decay, rot; **—ающий** *a.* decomposing, etc., *see v.;* **—ающийся** *a.* decomposing; decomposable; analyzable.

разлад *m.* discord, dissension; disorder.

разла/дить *see* **разлаживать; —женность** *f.* state of disrepair; maladjustment, misalignment; **—женный** *a.* disordered; broken down (machine); **—живать** *v.* break up, upset, derange; (mach.) damage, break; **—живаться** *v.* break down, get out of order.

разламыв/ание *n.* breaking, etc., *see v.;* break, fracture; demolition; **—ать** *v.* break, fracture; break up, chip; break open, force open; demolish, wreck, pull down (building); **—ающийся** *a.* (bot.) ruptile.

разлез(а)ться *v.* come apart, tear; unravel.

разлеп/ить, **—лять** *v.* unglue, separate.

разлёт *m.* dispersion, scattering, spread; **угол —а** angle of divergence.

разлет/аться, —еться *v.* fly apart, scatter, disperse; come apart, disintegrate; accelerate.

разлив *see* **разливание;** overflow, inundation, flood(ing); high water; (oil) spill; **—ание** *n.* pouring, etc., *see v.;* diffusion; (paints) spread; **—ательный** *a.* *see* **разливочный; —ать** *v.* pour (out), ladle; run (in); spill; distribute, spread, diffuse; bottle, can, fill; (met.) cast; teem (steel); **—аться** *v.* be poured, etc.; overflow, spill; **—ающий** *a.* pouring, etc., *see v.;* **—ающийся** *a.* (over)flowing, spilling; **—ка** *see* **разливание;** (met.) casting; **—ка без корки** (met.) ice-free teeming; **—ной** *a.* bottling; draft (beer, etc.); bulk (milk); **—(очн)о-укупорочный** *a.* bottling and capping; **—очный** *a.* pouring, etc., *see v.;* ladle (crane); **—очный автомат** dispenser; **—очный пролёт** casting bay; **—щик** *m.* caster, pourer.

разлинзование *n.* (geol.) boudinage.

разлинов(ыв)ать *v.* rule, draw lines.

разлип/аться, —нуться *v.* come unglued, separate, open.

разлистов/ание *n.* foliation, cleavage; **зона —ания** (geol.) sheeted zone; **—анный** *a.* foliated, leaf-like, laminated; **—ать** *v.* foliate.

разлит/ие *see* **разлив; р. жёлчи** (med.) bilious attack; **—ой, —ый** *a.* poured, etc., *see* **разливать;** diffuse(d); confluent (hepatitis); diffuse (peritonitis); **—ь** *see* **разливать.**

различ/ать *v.* discern, distinguish, differentiate; discriminate; **—аться** *v.* differ, be unlike, be distinguished, deviate (from); **—ающийся** *a.* deviating, etc.; distinct; **—ение** *n.* distinction, discrimination; **порог —ение** (physiol.) differential threshold; **—ие** *n.* distinction, difference, diversity, discrepancy; variety; **—ие мнений** disagreement; **проводить —ие** *v.* distinguish; **—имость** *f.* discernibleness; (radiotelescopy) discrimination, resolution; **—имый** *a.* discernible; **—итель** *m.* discriminator; **—ительно** *adv.* in contradistinction (to); **—ительный** *a.* distinctive; **—ить** *see* **различать.**

различн/о *adv.* differently; **—ость** *f.* difference, unlikeness; **—ый** *a.* different, unlike, dissimilar, distinct, varied, variable, varying, various, diverse.

разложен/ие *n.* decomposition, disintegration, catabolism, separation, dissociation, splitting (up), breaking down (into), breakdown; analysis; (electron.) scanning, sweeping; resolution (of forces); putrefaction, decay, rotting; (geom.) development; *suffix* **—lysis; р. (в ряд)** (math.) expansion; **р. на множители** factorization; **гидролитическое р.** hydrolysis; **гнилостное р.** wet rot; **двойное р., обменное р.** double decomposition; metathesis; **продукт —ия** decomposition or dissociation product; **реакция —ия** (biol.) catabolic reaction, decomposition reaction.

разлож/енный *a.* decomposed, dissociated; analyzed; laid out; (math.) expanded; **—ившийся** *a.* putrefied, putrid, putrescent, rotten; **—имость** *f.* decomposability; **—имый** *a.* decomposable, dissociable, separable; analyzable; **—ить** *see* **разлагать, раскладывать; —ить в ряд** *v.* expand in . . . series.

разлом *see* **разламывание; —анный** *a.* broken, etc., *see* **разламывать; —ать** *see* **разламывать; —ить** *v.* break up; start aching; **—ка** *see* **разламывание.**

разлу/ка *f.* separation; **—чать, —чить** *v.* sever, separate, part.

размагни/тить *see* **размагничивать; —ченный** *a.* demagnetized; **—чивание** *n.* demagnetization; degaussing; **обмотка —чивания** (main) coil, degaussing coil (of ship); **—чивать** *v.* demagnetize; degauss; **—чивающий** *a.* bucking (field).

размаз/анный *a.* smeared (out); **—ать, —ывать** *v.* smear, spread; blur; **—ывание** *n.* smearing.

размалыв/аемость *f.* grindability; **—аемый** *a.* grindable; **—ание** *n.* grinding, etc., *see v.;* **—ать** *v.* grind, crush, break up, mill, pulverize; (paper) beat.

размаривать *v.* exhaust (from heat, etc.).

размасли(ва)ть *v.* (treat with) oil.

разматыв/ание *n.* unwinding, etc., *see v.;* **—ать(ся)** *v.* unwind, unreel, reel off, uncoil, unroll, pay out, run off.

размах *m.* swing, sweep, stroke; spread, span (of wings); range, scope; (electron.) amplitude; (mech.) throw; **р. напряжения** peak-to-peak voltage; **отношение —а к хорде** (aerodyn.) aspect ratio; **—ивание** *n.* swinging; **—ивать, —нуть** *v.* swing, sway; wave, brandish.

размачив/ание *n.* soaking, etc., *see v.;* saturation, maceration; **—ать** *v.* soak, steep, saturate, wet, macerate, soften; ret (flax, hemp).

размаш/истый *a.* sweeping (motion); **—ка** *f.* fast trotting.

размедитель *m.* (met.) decoppering agent.

размеж/евание *n.*, **—ёвка** *f.*, **—ёвывание** *n.* demarcation, etc., *see v.*; **—евать, —ёвывать** *v.* demarcate, delimit, bound, fix limits, mark by boundaries.

размёл *past m. sing. of* **размести.**

размелет *fut. 3 sing. of* **размолоть.**

размельч/ать *v.* crush, grind, break up, disintegrate, comminute, pulverize; mince; diminish, reduce; **—аться** *v.* break up, disintegrate; shrink, get smaller; **—ение** *n.* crushing, etc., *see v.*; (met.) refining (of grain); **—ённый** *a.* crushed, fix, *see v.*; **—итель** *m.* grinder, etc.; **—ить** *see* **размельчать.**

размен *m.*, **—ивать, —ять** *v.*, **—ный** *a.* (ex)change; **—ная монета** small coin, change.

размер *m.* dimension, size, gage, caliber; rate; quantity, amount; yield; grade (of particles); length; width; diameter; distance; format; dimension(al) figure (on drawing); **—ом с** the size of; **в р., по —у** to size; **не по —у** offsize; **точно по —у** to specifications; **—ение** *n.* measurement; **—ения** *pl.* dimensions; **—енный** *a.* measured, etc., *see v.*; **—ивание** *n.* measuring, etc., *see v.*; measurement; **—и(ва)ть** *v.* measure (off, out); determine; proportion; **—ность** *f.* dimension(s); dimensionality; scale; comparability; **уравнение —ности** (math.) dimensional equation; **—ный** *a.* measuring; dimensional; **—ная обработка** machining; **—ять** *see* **размеривать; —яющий** *a.* measuring, etc., *see v.*

размесить *see* **размешивать.**

размести *see* **размётывать.**

разместить *see* **размещать.**

размёт *m.* paddling, winging out (of horse); **с —ом** splay-footed.

размёт/анный *a.* effusive; scattered.

разметать *see* **размётывать.**

размет/ить *see* **размечать; —ка** *f.* marking, etc., *see* **размечать;** mark-up; mark, sign; layout; **—очно-сверлильный станок** jig borer; **—очный** *a.* of **разметка; —очные циркули** dividers; **—чик** *m.* marker, tracer.

размётывать *v.* toss, scatter, disperse, spread about; sweep away.

размеч/ать *v.* mark (off, out, up), lay off, lay out, prepare a layout; trace; graduate (a vessel); format (a disk); annotate; **—енный** *a.* marked, etc., *see v.*; **—ивание** *n.* marking, etc., *see v.*; **—ивать** *see* **размечать.**

размеш/анный *a.* mixed, etc., *see v.*; **—ать** *see* **размешивать; —ивание** *n.* mixing, etc., *see v.*; **—ивать** *v.* mix, stir, blend; churn; knead (clay); **—ивающий** *a.* mixing, etc., *see v.*

размещ/ать *v.* dispose, distribute, arrange, set, place, position, mount, lay out; allocate; invest (money); space; locate, site; accommodate, house; **—аться** *v.* (comp.) reside (in memory); **—ение** *n.* disposing, disposition, etc., *see v.*; disposal; order, arrangement, layout; planning; spacing; position; (math.) permutation; **—ённый** *a.* disposed, etc., *see v.*

размина/ние *n.* (massage) pétrissage; **—ть** *v.* knead, mash; soften; stretch, flex.

разминиров/ание *n.* (mil.) mine clearance; **—анный** *a.* mine-free; **—ать** *v.* clear mines.

разминка *f.* kneading, etc., *see* **разминать;** (sports) warmup.

размин/овка *f.* (rr.) by-pass, siding, turnout; **—уться** *v.* pass each other, cross (of letters).

размнож/ать *v.* multiply, propagate, reproduce; proliferate; replicate, duplicate, copy, manifold; **—аться** *v.* breed, propagate, spawn; proliferate; **—ающий** *a.* multiplying, etc., *see v.*; fertile (medium); breeder (reactor); **—ение** *n.* multiplication, etc., *see v.*; fission; (bact.) growth; proliferation; (nucl.) breeding; **—ение без оплодотворения** parthenogenesis; **—ение делением** (biol.) fission; **колья —ения** (hort.) cuttings; **—итель** *m.* breeder; **—ить** *see* **размножать.**

размоет *fut. 3 sing. of* **размыть.**

размозж/ение *n.* crush(ing); **—ённый** *a.* burst, smashed, crushed; **—ить** *v.* smash, crush, break.

размоина *f.* washout.

размок/ание *n.* soaking, etc., *see v.*; **—анный** *a.* soaked, sodden; **—ать, —нуть** *v.* soak, get wet, soften; **—ший** *see* **размоканный.**

размол *see* **размалывание;** grist, grind.

размолачивать *v.* (agr.) thresh, crush.

размолоспособность *f.* grindability.

размолотить *see* **размолачивать.**

размолот/ый *a.* ground, etc., *see* **размалывать; —ь** *see* **размалывать.**

размор/аживать *v.* thaw out, defrost; freeze out; **—ить** *see* **размаривать; —озить** *see* **размораживать.**

размот/анный *a.* unwound, etc., *see* **разматывать; —ать** *see* **разматывать; —ка** *f.*, **—очный** *a.* unwinding, etc., *see* **разматывать.**

размочал/енный *a.* shredded, etc., *see v.*; **—и(ва)ть** *v.* shred, separate into filaments or fibers; unravel; **—иваться** *v.* fray, come unravelled.

размоч/енный *a.* soaked, etc., *see* **размачивать; —ить** *see* **размачивать; —ка** *see* **размачивание.**

размыв *m.*, **—ание** *n.* washing, etc., *see v.*; (geol.) washout, erosion, corrasion; smearing (of lines, etc.); **—ание фронта** (meteor.) frontolysis; **—атель** *m.* scourer; **—ать** *v.* wash (away, off, out), scour; hollow out, erode; level, flatten; blur, smear; **—ающий** *a.* washing, etc., *see v.*

размык/ание *n.* opening, etc., *see v.*; cleavage, splitting; break, interruption; **быстрое р.** (mech.) quick release; **—атель** *m.* release, trip, disengager; (circuit) breaker; **—ать** *v.* open, unlock, unfasten, release, disengage, trip; split (up); break, interrupt, disconnect, turn off; **—ающий** *a.* opening, etc., *see v.*; release, trip (mechanism); break (contact).

размыслить *see* **размышлять.**

размыт/ие *n.* erosion; (image) blur; smearing; (meteor.) decay; spreading, blow-up (of beam); disassembly (of plasma); (astr.) speckle; **р. края зоны** (elec.) band-edge tailing; **—ость** *f.* fuzziness; **—ый** *a.* washed out, eroded; diffuse, blurred, fuzzy, broad(ened); **—ь** *see* **размывать.**

размычка *see* **размыкание.**

размышл/ение *n.* reflection, thought, deliberation; **—ять** *v.* reflect, consider, think over.

размягч/ать, —ить *v.* soften; soak (until soft); **—ающий** *a.* softening; (pharm.) emollient; **—ающее средство** softening agent; emollient; **—ение** *n.* softening; (med.) malacia, morbid softening; **—ение костей** (med.) osteomalacia; **температура —ения, точка —ения** softening point; **—итель** *m.* softener; plasticizer.

размяк/ать, —нуть *v.* soften.

размят/ие *n.* crumbling; kneading; (geol.) shearing; **—ый** *a.* crumbled; kneaded; sheared; **—ь** *see* **разминать.**

разнашивать *see* **разносить.**

разнарядка *f.* order, warrant.

разнес/ение *n.* carrying around, conveyance, delivery; separation, spacing; diversity; **—ённый** *a.* carried, etc., *see* **разносить;** spaced (winding); two-finned (tail); (rad.) diversity; **—ти** *see* **разносить.**

разнимать *v.* part, separate, dismember, disjoint, tear apart; take apart, take to pieces, dismantle, dismount.

разн/иться *v.* differ, vary, be unlike; **—ица** *f.* difference, distinction, contrast; variation, divergence, discrepancy; **—о** *adv.* differently, diversely, variously.

разно— *prefix* different, hetero—, diversi—; **—бой** *m.* disparity, disagreement; **—бойность** *f.* (art.) difference(s); **—вес** *m.* set of weights.

разновидн/ость *f.* variety; modification, version; **—ый** *a.* various, diverse, multiform, of different form, mutant.

разновозрастный *a.* varying in age.

разноволосый *a.* (bot.) heterotrichous.

разновременн/ость *f.* diversification; difference in time; heterochrony; difference in phase; **—ый** *a.* alternative; diverse; at different times; not contemporary.

разноглас/ие *n.,* **—ица** *f.* discord, difference of opinion, variance, discrepancy; **—ный** *a.* discordant, conflicting.

разноголосица *see* **разногласие.**

разнодомный *a.* polygamous; heteroecious.

разное *n.* variety, miscellany.

разнозернист/ость *f.* variation(s) in grain size; **—ый** *a.* with varying grain size; (petr.) inequigranular; sutured (texture); (geol.) consertal.

разно/значащий *a.* having a different meaning; **—зуб** *m.* (ichth.) California hornshark (*Heterodontus*); **—зубый** *a.* (zool.) heterodont(oid); **—имённый** *a.* of different kinds, unlike, opposite; (elec.) of opposite charge; **—калиберный** *a.* different-caliber, different-sized.

разнокачественн/ость *f.* heterogeneity; **—ый** *a.* qualitatively different.

разнолепест/ка *f.* (bot.) candytuft (*Iberis*); **—ковый, —ный** *a.* (bot.) heteropetalous.

разно/листный *a.* (bot.) heterophyllous, diversifolious; **—мастный** *a.* different(-colored); **—мыслие** *n.* difference of opinion, disagreement; **—мышечные** *pl.* (mal.) Anisomyaria; **—направленный** *a.* multidirectional.

разнообраз/ие *n.* variety, diversity, range; multiplicity; variability; **—ить** *v.* vary, diversify; **—ность** *f.* variety, diversity, heterogeneity; **—ный** *a.* various, varied, different, diversified, diverse, heterogeneous, variegated; miscellaneous.

разно/осный *a.* heteraxial; **—племённый** *a.* of different races, of different stock; **—плодный** *a.* (bot.) heterocarpous; **—покровный** *a.* (bot.) heterochlamydeous; **—полый** *a.* of different sexes; **—полярный** *a.* heteropolar; **—рабочий** *m.* handyman, unskilled worker; **—резонаторный** *a.* rising-sun (magnetron); **—ресничные** *pl.* (zool.) Heterotricha.

разнореч/ивый *a.* contradictory, inconsistent; **—ие** *n.* contradiction.

разнородн/ость *f.* heterogeneity; difference in kind; **—ый** *a.* heterogeneous, mixed, hybrid, unlike, different, dissimilar, diversified, various, manifold.

разнос *m.* carrying (around), etc., *see* **расносить;** delivery, distribution; dispersion; separation, spacing; diversity; (mach.) racing, overspeeding; open-cut mine, quarry.

разносемянный *a.* (bot.) heterospermic.

разнос/ить *v.* carry (around), convey, deliver, distribute, transport; disperse, scatter; spread (disease, etc.); separate; stretch; tear (apart); puff up, swell; race, speed; destroy; break in (shoes, etc.); **—иться** *v.* be carried, etc.; spread; resound; **—ка** *see* **разнос; —ный** *a. of* **разнос;** runaway (speed).

разно/споровый *a.* (bot.) heterosporous; **—стенность** variations of wall thickness; **—стеномер** *m.* pipe-thickness gage.

разности/о-дифференциальный *a.* difference-differential; **—ый** *a.* difference, different; differential; **—ые уравнения** difference equations.

разностолбиковый *a.* (bot.) heterostyled.

разносторонн/ий *a.* many-sided, comprehensive; versatile; (geom.) scalene; **—ость** *f.* comprehensiveness; versatility; multiplicity.

разноступенчатость *f.* (bot.) heterobathism.

разность *f.* difference; gradient, drop (in temperature, etc.); variety, diversity; mutant; (math.) remainder (after subtraction).

разносчик *m.* delivery man; peddler; (med.) carrier, vector.

разно/типность *f.* (biol.) type diversity; **—типный** *a.* different-type; (gen.) heterotypic; **—толщинный** *a.* of different thickness; **—тонный** *a.* different in tone; **—травный** *a.* (agr.) forb; **—травье** *n.* mixed grass, herbage, forbs; **—тычинковый** *a.* (bot.) heterostemonous; **—усые** *pl.* (zool.) Heterocera; **—форменность** *f.* heteromorphism; **—хозяйственный** *a.* (biol.) heteroecious.

разно/цветковый *a.* (bot.) diversiflorous; **—цветный** *a.* many-colored, multi-colored, varicolored, variegated, heterochromatic; **—центренный** *a.* eccentric; **—чтение** *n.* variant reading, alternative version; **—шенный** *a.* carried, etc., *see* **разносить; —шёрстный** *a.* different-colored; **—язычный** *a.* polyglot, multilingual; **—яйцевой, —яйцевый** *a.* (biol.) dizygotic, fraternal (twins).

разнузда/нный *a.* unbridled (horse); unruly; **—ть** *v.* unbridle.

разный *a.* different, unlike, dissimilar, diverse, various, miscellaneous.

разнять *see* **разнимать.**

разо— *see* **раз—.**

разоблагораживать *v.* downgrade.

разоблачение *n.* disclosure, exposure.

разоборудовать *v.* strip, dismantle, disassemble.

разобр/анный *a.* dismantled, etc., *see* **разбирать; —ать** *see* **разбирать.**

разобщ/ать *v.* disconnect, uncouple, disengage, release; sever; dissociate, separate; insulate (from); partition, section; interrupt, disturb; cut out; throw out of gear; **—ающий** *a.* disconnecting, etc., *see v.;* dissociative; cut-out; straddle (packer); **—ающий механизм** release (mechanism), trip; **—ающая муфта** uncoupler; **—ение** *n.* disconnecting, etc., *see v.;* disengagement, decoupling, release; separation; interruption, disturbance; partitioning (of faunas); **—ённость** *f.* separateness, discreteness; **—ённый** *a.* disconnected, etc., *see v.;* separate, discrete; **—итель** *m.* disconnector, release, cutout; **—ительный** *see* **разобщающий; —ить** *see* **разобщать.**

разобьёт *fut. 3 sing. of* **разбить.**

разовый *a.* single, one-time, disposable, expendable, throwaway; occasional.

разовьёт *fut. 3 sing. of* **развить.**

разогн/ание *see* **разгон; —анный** *a.* accelerated, etc., *see* **разгонять;** staggered, alternating; **—ать** *see* **разгонять.**

разогнуть *see* **разгибать.**

разогре/в *m.* warm-up, heat-up; reheating; self-heating; **—вание** *n.* warming up; evolution of heat (from reaction); **—(ва)ть** *v.* warm up; **—(ва)ться** *v.* warm up, get warm; **—тый** *a.* warmed up, heated.

разодр/анный *a.* torn, tattered; lacerated; **—ать** *see* **раздирать.**

разожжённый *past pass. part. of* **разжечь.**

разожмёт *fut. 3 sing. of* **разжать.**

разойтись *see* **расходиться.**

разок *dim. of* **раз.**

разольёт *fut. 3 sing. of* **разлить.**

разом *adv.* at once, at one stroke; simultaneously; **все р.** all together, simultaneously.

разомкнут/ый *a.* opened, etc., *see* **размыкать;** clear; open (circuit); **—ь** *see* **размыкать.**

разомнёт *fut. 3 sing. of* **размять.**

разопрёт *fut. 3 sing. of* **распереть.**

разорв/анно— *prefix* (meteor.) fracto— (ragged, broken); **р.-дождевое облако** fractonimbus; **р.-кучевое облако** fractocumulus; **р.-слоистое облако** fractostratus; **—анный** *a.* torn, ruptured; lacerated; blown up; disrupted, broken; (geol.) faulted; **—ать** *v.* tear, rupture; lacerate; blow up; disrupt, break; **—аться** *v.* tear, rupture, crack; explode, burst.

разор/ение *n.* ruin, destruction; **—ённый** *a.* ruined, destroyed; **—ительный** *a.* ruinous, destructive, wasteful; **—ить** *see* **разорять.**

разоруж/ать *v.* disarm; dismantle; **—ение** *n.* disarmament; dismantling.

разорять *v.* ruin, destroy, spoil, waste.

разослать *see* **рассылать.**

разостлать *see* **расстилать.**

разотравление *n.* removal of poison.

разотрёт *fut. 3 sing. of* **растереть.**

разочаров/ание *n.*, **—анность** *f.* disappointment; **—анный** *a.* disappointed; **—(ыв)ать** *v.* disappoint.

разочтёт *past pass. part. of* **расчесть.**

разошедшийся *past act. part. of* **разойтись;** exhausted, out of print.

разошлёт *fut. 3 sing. of* **разослать.**

разраб/атываемый *a.* workable, exploitable, capable of development; under development; **р. на** worked for; **—атывание** *see* **разработка;** **—атывать** *v.* develop, elaborate; work out, formulate, devise, evolve; lay out, draw up, map; exploit, work (a mine); treat, process; dress (ore); cultivate (soil); **—атываться** *v.* be developed, etc.; be under development; develop, evolve; run out of true; **—отанность** *f.* readiness (of plan); **—отанный** *a.* developed, etc., *see v.*; **—отать** *see* **разрабатывать;** **—отка** *f.* developing, elaboration, etc., *see v.*; development; treatment; (research) effort; study; (process) design; (systems) engineering; **горные —отки** mining; **срок —отки** lead time; **—отчик** *m.* developer.

разравнивать *v.* level, smooth out.

разра/жаться, —зиться *v.* break out, burst.

разра/стание *n.* growth, expansion; (bot.) excrescence; proliferation; **—статься, —стись** *v.* grow, expand; proliferate; **—щение** *n.* (abnormal) growth, enlargement; proliferation; (med.) vegetation.

разрегулиров/анность *f.* misalignment; **—анный** *a.* misaligned, maladjusted; **—ка** *f.* misalignment, maladjustment.

разре/дить, —жать *v.* rarefy, evacuate, exhaust; (agr.) thin (out), open out; **—жающий** *a.* rarefying, etc., *see v.*; vacuum (pump); **—жение** *n.* rarefaction, rarefying, etc., *see v.*; vacuum; **—жение костной ткани** (med.) osteoporosis; **камера —жения** vacuum space; **—жён-**

—ность *f.* rarefaction, rarity, thinness, tenuity; vacuum; dilution; **—жённый** *a.* rarefied, etc., *see v.*; thin; sparse (matrix); open-weave; dispersed, broken (ice); open (ice edge); **—жённое пространство** vacuum.

разрежет *fut. 3 sing. of* **разрезать.**

разрез *m.* cut, slit, slot; (med.) incision, discission, section; gash, slash, rip; profile, (cross) section, plan, cutaway view; (min.) open pit; layer; (drill) log; **—томы; р. печени** (med.) hepatotomy; **в р.** contrary; **вид в —е** sectional view, cut-away view; **горизонтальный р.** plan; **местный р.** broken section (on a drawing); **—альный** *a.*, **—ание** *n.* cutting, slitting; ripping; **—анно—** *prefix* incisi—, inciso— (deeply cut); **—анолистный** (bot.) incisifolious, cut-leaved; **—анный** *a.* cut, slit; dissected; incised; ripped; **—ать** *see* **разрезывать;** **—ка** *see* **разрезание;** **—ной** *a.* slit, cut, split, cut-away; slot (burner, magnetron, etc.); slotted (washer); gapped, discontinuous; detached (foundation); rip (saw); (bot.) laciniate(d), incised; **—ывание** *see* **разрезание;** **—ывать** *v.* cut (open), slit; rip; section.

разреш/ать *v.* permit, allow, authorize, enable; solve (problem); clear up, settle (question); (opt., etc.) resolve; **—аться** *v.* be permitted, etc.; be permissible; dissolve; **—ающий** *a.* permitting, etc., *see v.*; **—ающая сила, —ающая способность** resolving power, resolution; **—ающая способность по времени** time resolution; **—ающее время** resolving time (of counter); **—ающее устройство** (comp.) gate; **—ение** *n.* permission, authorization; (av.) clearance; permit, grant, license; solution (of problem); settlement (of question); (opt.) resolution; **—ение на взлёт** take-off clearance; **давать —ение** *v.* clear; **функция —ения** resolution function; **—ённый** *a.* permitted, etc., *see v.*; permissible.

разрешим/ость *f.* solvability; **проблема —ости** decision problem; **—ый** *a.* solvable, capable of solution, decidable.

разрешит/ельный *a.* absolving; permitting; **—ь** *see* **разрешать.**

разрисов/анный *a.* painted, etc., *see v.*; **—(ыв)ать** *v.* paint, decorate; **—ка** *f.* painting, decoration.

разровнять *see* **разравнивать.**

разроет *fut. 3 sing. of* **разрыть.**

разрозн/енный *a.* separated, etc., *see v.*; single, separate; odd, stray (volume); broken, incomplete (set); uncoordinated; **—и(ва)ть** *v.* separate; disconnect; break.

разрос/ть *f.* proliferation; **—шийся** *a.* grown, etc., *see* **разрастаться.**

разруб *see* **разрубание;** cut, gash; **—ание** *n.* chopping, etc., *see v.*; **—ать, —ить** *v.* chop, cut, slash, cleave, split; **—ка** *see* **разрубание;** **—ной нож** (mach.) shearing blade.

разруха *f.* collapse, ruin, devastation.

разруш/аемый *a.* destructible; (comp.) volatile (memory); **—ать** *v.* destroy, ruin, wreck, demolish; shatter, crush, break down, break up; rupture; corrode, attack; erode; (chem.) degrade, decompose; **—аться** *v.* be destroyed, etc.; go to ruin, collapse; fail; decompose, decay, disintegrate, crumble; **—ающий** *a.* destroying, etc., *see v.*; destructive, devastating, disruptive; ultimate (load); **—ающее напряжение** breaking point; (aerodyn.) ultimate (tensile) stress; (chem.) decomposition potential; **—ающийся** *a.* disintegrating; weathered (iceberg).

разрушен/ие *n.* destruction, demolition, wrecking; collapse, failure, breakdown, disintegration; rupture, shattering, crushing, break-up, breakage, disruption; damage, degradation; attack, corrosion, deterioration, decomposition; (fatigue) fracture; disaggregation (of soil); (med.) caries, decay; (biol.) catabolism; **р. пены** lather collapse, foam breakage; **без —ия** nondestructive; **время —ия** time to failure; **предел —ия** breaking point; **—ный** *a.* destroyed, etc. *see* **разрушать;** decayed, rotten, crumbling (rock).

разруш/ившийся *a.* decayed, crumbled; **—ительный** *a.* destructive, deleterious; **—ить** *see* **разрушать.**

разрыв *m.* rupture, break(age), breach; fracture, fissure, crack, gap, void; severance, breaking (off), disruption, discontinuity, interruption, disturbance; tear; parting; break(age); cleft, cleavage; disjunction; bursting, explosion, blow-out (of tire); (astrophysics) burst; (min.) fracturing; laceration; (heart) failure; (med.) —rrhexis; shear (of wind); (geol.) fault, joint, break; **р. вены** (med.) phleborrhexis; **р. непрерывности** discontinuity; **прочность на р.** tensile strength.

разрыв/ание *n.* tearing, etc., *see* v.; **—атель** *m.* (paper) pulper, pulp shredder, disintegrator; **—ать** v. tear, lacerate; split; shatter; blow up; rupture, break, disrupt, interrupt; dig up, unearth, excavate; turn upside-down; **—аться** v. tear, rupture, break; explode, burst; split, cleave; **—ающий** *a.* tearing, etc., *see* v.; ruptile; disruptive; **—ной** *a.* tearing; breaking (capacity, etc.); break (contact); ultimate (stress); explosive (force; shell); bursting (charge); disruptive; split, discontinuous; discontinuity (coefficient); broken, yawning (open); (met.) tensile-test (specimen); tensile-testing (machine); percussion, dumdum (bullet); **—ная прочность** breaking strength; **—ная трубка** fuse; **—ность** *f.* discontinuity.

разрывомер *m.* gap meter.

разрыв-трава *f.* (bot.) saxifrage.

разрывчатый *see* **разрывной.**

разрыт/ый *a.* dug up, excavated; **—ь** v. *see* **разрывать;** dig up, unearth, excavate.

разрыхл/ение *n.* loosening (up), etc., *see* v.; disintegration; fraying; (med.) mollities; —lysis (dissolution); distension, expansion; aeration; (blast furnace) slips; **р. ногтей** (med.) onycholysis; **—ённость** *f.* loose state, fluffy condition; **—ённый** *a.* loosened (up), etc., *see* v.; **—еть** v. break up, get loose; **—итель** *m.* (agr.) scarifier; **—итель теста** leavening agent; **—ительный** *a.* loosening, etc., *see* v.; **—ить, —ять** v. loosen (up), break up, stir up, fluff up, aerate; destabilize; pulverize, disintegrate; expand, distend; hoe, mellow (soil); **—яющий** *a.* loosening, etc., *see* v.; antibonding (electron level).

разряд *m.* order, class, category, rank, rate, rating; place, position; wage class; release, catch; (comp.) digit, bit; (elec.) discharge; **безразличный р.** don't-care bit; **двоичный р.** binary digit, bit; **информационный р.** data bit; **первого —а** first-class; **тёмный р., тихий р., тлеющий р.** (dielectrics) silent discharge, corona; **—итель** *m.* discharger; **—ить** *see* **разряжать;** (typ.) space; **—ка** *f.* discharging, discharge; unloading; relaxation; catharsis; deexcitation; (typ.) spacing, emphasis; **—ка (международной) напряжённости** détente; **набирать в —ку** v. space.

разрядн/ик *m.* (elec.) discharger; (lightning) arrester; (spark) gap; **—ость** *f.* (comp.) capacity; word length; width (of data bus); **—ый** *a. of* **разряд.**

разряж/ать v. discharge, unload, relieve; disarm (an explosive device); **—аться** v. discharge, run down; **—ающийся** *a.* discharging; **—ение** *n.* discharging, discharge, unloading; **—ённый** *a.* discharged.

разсеивание размеров variations in dimensions.

разслоение *n.* lamination.

разуб/едить, —еждать v. dissuade.

разубож/ивание *n.* impoverishment, depletion, exhaustion, working out (of ore); **—ивать** v. impoverish, deplete, exhaust, work out; down-grade; dilute; **—енный** *a.* lean, low-grade (ore).

разувер/ить, —ять v. dissuade; talk out of.

разуголка *f.* cornerpiece.

разузна(ва)ть v. inquire, investigate

разукра/сить, —шивать v. decorate.

разукрупн/ение *n.* subdivision; comminution; **—ить** v. subdivide; comminute.

разум *m.* reason, intelligence, mind; **—ение** *n.* understanding; **по моему —ению** to my mind, as I understand it; **—еть** v. understand; mean, imply; **—еется** it is understood; certainly, of course; **само собой —еется** it stands to reason, it is obvious, needless to say; **—но** *adv.* reasonably, sensibly; **—ный** *a.* reasonable, intelligent, judicious; smart (computer terminal).

разуплотнение *n.* thinning, dispersion; seal failure.

разупорядоч/ение *n.* disorder(ing); (comp.) missequencing; (biol.) randomization; **—енный** *a.* disordered; randomized; **—ивать** v. disorder; randomize; **—ный** *a.* disordered, disorderly.

разупрочн/ение *n.* weakening; (met.) softening; **временное р.** (steel) time yield; **—енный** *a.* weakened, softened; **—ять** v. weaken, soften.

разучи(ва)ть v. learn, study; practice; **—ся** v. unlearn, forget.

рацепить *see* **расцепить.**

разъ— *see* **раз—** (before е, ю, я).

разъед/аемость *f.* corrodibility; **—аемый** *a.* corrodible; **—ание** *n.* corrosion, attack, eating away, pitting; (geol.) erosion; **—ать** v. corrode, attack, eat away, etch, pit; erode; **—ающий** *a.* corroding, corrosive, caustic; erosive; (med.) phagedenic, perambulating (ulcer); **—ающее вещество** corrosive; **—ение** *see* **разъедание; —енный** *a.* corroded, etc., *see* v.

разъедин/ение *n.* separation, unfastening, etc., *see* v.; release; disengagement; **—ённый** *a.* separated, etc., *see* v.; separate, discrete; out of gear; **—итель** *m.* disconnector, cut-out switch, circuit breaker; **—ительный** *see* **разъединяющий; —ительная муфта** uncoupler; **—ить, —ять** v. separate, unfasten, detach, unlink, uncouple; sever, dissociate; release, disengage; throw out of gear; (elec.) disconnect, cut (out), break, interrupt; (commun.) clear; **—яющий** *a.* separating, etc., *see* v.; cut-off, cut-out; trip (hook); dissociative; **—яющий механизм** release (mechanism), trip.

разъез/д *m.* departure; separation; missing, passing; (rr.) siding; **—дной** *a.* traveling; passing; passenger (boat); **—дной путь** (rr.) siding; **—жать** v. travel around, drive around; **—жаться** v. (de)part; pass, miss (one another); separate, slide apart; come apart, fall apart; **—женный** *a.* travel-worn (road).

разъём *m.* parting, etc., *see* **разнимать;** separation, detachment; break; joint, junction, connector; (elec.) plug and socket unit; **—ный** *a.* detachable, separable, dismountable, snap, pop-off; disengaging; release; sectional, built-up; split (bearing, etc.).

разъесть *see* **разъедать.**

разъехаться *see* **разъезжаться.**

разъяр/ённый *a.* infuriated; **—ить, —ять** infuriate, drive to a frenzy.

разъясн/ение *n.* explanation, interpretation; **—ительный** *a.* explanatory; **—ить** v. (meteor.) clear up; **—ить, —ять** v. explain, interpret; make clear; **—яющий** *a.* explanatory.

разыск/ание *n.* (re)search, investigation; **—ать** v. find, discover; **—аться** *v.* be found, turn up; **—ивание** *see* **разыскание**; **—ивать** *v.* search, look for, hunt for, trace, investigate.

рай *m.* paradise.

РАИ *abbr.* **(радиоактивный изотоп)** radioactive isotope.

рай— *prefix* regional, district.

райграс *m.* (bot.) rye grass (*Lolium*).

рай/дерево *n.* (bot.) Venice sumac (*Rhus cotinus*); **—ка** *f.* paradise apple.

райком *m.* district committee.

раймовка *f.* residual slag in zinc distillation.

раймондит *m.* (min.) raimondite.

райол/енье *n.* trenching; **—ьная вспашка** (agr.) trenching, deep plowing.

район *m.* region, district, area, zone, field, locality; vicinity; (administrative) raion; (migratory) range; **р. действия** range; **в районе** near, in the neighborhood (of); **—ирование** *n.* zoning, etc., *see v.*; (sub)division (into regions, etc.); **—ированный** *a.* zoned, etc., *see v.*; **—ировать** *v.* zone, regionalize, divide into districts; lay out, break up (area); **—ный** *a.* regional, district.

райсемхоз *m.* district seed farm.

райск/ий *a.* paradise; **р. цвет** (bot.) bird of paradise (flower); **—ие зёрна** grains of paradise.

Райта прибор Wright's meter.

рак *m.* (med.) cancer, carcinoma; (phyt.) canker, cancerous growth; (zool.) crayfish; (astr.) Cancer; **р. клевера** (bot.) sclerotium disease of clover; **р. корней свёклы** crown gall in sugar beet.

ракель *m.* (typ.) doctor, wiper, squeegee; **—ная печать** gravure printing, rotogravure.

ракета *f.* rocket, (mil.) missile, projectile; probe; flare; (tennis) racket; **р. земля-орбита** earth-to-orbit rocket; **р. средней дальности** intermediate-range missile; **крылатая р.** cruise missile; **р.-болванка** *f.* dummy rocket; **р.-зонд** *f.* sounding rocket, probe; **р.-ловушка** *f.* decoy missile; **р.-мишень** *f.* missile target; **р.-носитель** *f.* launch vehicle, booster (rocket), carrier rocket; **р.-парашют** *f.* parachute flare; **р.-перехватчик** *f.* interceptor missile, anti-missile missile; **р.-спутник** *f.* orbital rocket, satellite; **р.-торпеда** *f.* rocket-assisted torpedo.

ракетка *f.* racket, paddle.

ракетн/ица *f.* flare pistol; **—о-прямоточный** *a.* rocket-ramjet (engine); **—о-турбинный** *a.* turborocket; **—о-ядерный** *a.* nuclear-missile (weapon).

ракетн/ый *a.* of **ракета**; rocket-propelled; rocket-borne; guided-missile (ship); jet (plane); **р. вспомогательный объект** missile support facility; **р. снаряд** rocket; **р. состав** rocket fuel, propellant; **—ая техника** rocketry; **—ое оружие** missiles; **—ые средства** missile systems; **с —ым двигателем** rocket-propelled.

ракето/держатель *m.* flare carrier; **—динамика** *f.* rocket dynamics; **—дром** *m.* rocket range, space launch center, launching site; **—носец** *m.* missile carrier; **—носный** *a.* missile-carrying; **—план** *m.* rocket glider.

ракетостро/ение *n.*, **—ительный** *a.* rocket building, rocket manufacture; rocket design; **—итель** *m.* rocket designer.

ракетчик *m.* flare signaler; rocketeer.

раки *pl.* of **рак.**

ракит/а *f.* willow, spec. goat willow; **—ник** *m.* willow thicket; (bot.) broom (*Cytisus*).

раккорд *see* **ракорд.**

раккурс *see* **ракурс.**

ракля *f.* (text.) doctor (blade), scraper.

раковидный *a.* (med.) cancerous.

раковин/а *f.* shell, carapace; pit, sink, basin; vesicle; (anat.) concha; earpiece (of stethoscope, etc.); **р. на поверхности** (met.) skin hole; **носовая р.** (anat.) concha nasalis; **ушная р.** concha of auricle; **—ка** *dim.* of **раковина**; **—ный** *a.* of **раковина**, **—ные амёбы** (zool.) Testacea; **—овидный** *a.* conchate, shell-shaped; **—ообразный** *a.* shell-like, conchoidal.

раковист/ый *a.* shell(y), shell-like, conchoidal (fracture, structure).

рак/овый *a.* of **рак**; (med.) cancerous, carcinomatous; **—ом** *instr.* of **рак**; *adv.* sideways; **—ообразный** *a.* cancerous; (zool.) crustacean.

ракообразные *pl.* (crust.) Crustacea; **десятиногие р.** Decapoda; **усоногие р.** barnacles (*Cirripedia*); **эвфаузиевые р.** krills (*Euphausiacea*).

ракорд *m.* leader (tape), trailer film.

рак-отшельник *m.* (zool.) hermit crab.

ракоустойчив/ость *f.* resistance to cancer; **—ый** *a.* cancer-resistant.

ракурс *m.* foreshortening; angle of approach; (target) aspect.

ракуша *f.* hempseed husk.

ракуш/ечник *m.*; **—ечниковый** *a.* coquina, shell rock; **—ечный** *a.* shell(y); **—ка** *f.* (zool.) mussel; **песчаная —ка** long-neck clam (*Mua arenaria*); **—ковые** *pl.* (zool.) Ostracoda; **—ник** *m.* crag (shell and sand rock).

рак/шевые *see* **ракши**; **—шеобразные** *pl.* hornbills, kingfishers (*Coraciiformes*); **—ши** *pl.* (orn.) rollers (*Coraciidae*).

рало *n.* plowshare, cultivator.

рама *f.* frame(work), casing, cradle, rack, (mounting) bracket; trestle (of bridge); chassis, carriage; extension; bed (plate); (casting) flask; (hotbed) sash; (geol.) enclosing rock.

раман/овский *a.* Raman; **—спектр** *m.* Raman spectrum.

рамбла *f.* rambla, dry ravine.

рамбулье *m.* Rambouillet (merino sheep).

рамен/ты *pl.* (bot.) ramenta; **—ь** *f.*, **—е** *n.* coniferous forest; forest border.

рамз/аевский *a.* Ramsay.

рами *f. or n.* (bot.) ramie (*Boehmeria*); **—котомия** *f.* (med.) ramisection.

рамификация *f.* ramification, branching.

рамк/а *dim.* of **рама; р. из припоя** (semicond.) brazing preform; **—и** *pl.* scope; **в —ах** within the scope, within the framework (of).

рамн/егин *m.* rhamnegin; **—етин** *m.* rhamnetin; **—оза** *f.* rhamnose; **—ол** *m.* rhamnol, ß-sitosterol.

рам/ный *a.* of **рама**; *see also* **рамочный.**

рамов/ание *n.*, **—ка** *f.* training (of vine).

рамо/зный *a.* ramose, branching; **—оборот** *m.* hotbed crop rotation.

рамочный *a.* of **рамка**; plate-and-frame (filterpress); gate (mixer); loop, coil (antenna); **р. гальванометр** moving-coil galvanometer.

рампа *f.* ramp; manifold.

рамул/и(о)спороз *m.* (phyt.) Ramulispora leaf spot; **—яриоз** *m.*, **—яриозная пятнистость** Ramularia leaf spot; **—ярный** *a.* ramular.

рамф/ихтовые *pl.* (ichth.) knifefishes (*Rhamphichthyidae*); **—окоттовые** *pl.* grunt sculpins (*Rhamphocottidae*); **—отека** *f.* (orn.) rhamphotheca, horny sheath of bill.

рана *f.* wound, injury, vulnus, sore, cut.

ранарекс *m.* automatic gas analyzer.

ранверсман *m.* (av.) re(n)versement.
Ранвье (anat.) Ranvier; **перехват Р.** nodes of Ranvier.
ранг *m.* rank, class, grade, order, range; **—ированный** *a.* ranked; **—овый** *a.* of **ранг**; ranked.
рангоут *m.*, **—ный** *a.* (naut.) masts and spars.
рандаль *m.* (agr.) disc cultivator.
рандеву *n.* rendezvous.
рандомизация *f.* (stat.) randomization; (comp.) hashing.
Рандю (med.) Rendu.
раневой *a.* of **рана.**
ранее *see* **раньше.**
ранен/ие *n.* wound(ing); **—ый** *a. and m.* wounded; **носилочный р.** stretcher case.
ранет *m.* (bot.) pippin.
ранец *m.* knapsack, pack, kit, satchel.
ранжир *m.* rank, range, order; **по —у** by size; **—овать** *v.* rank, range; **—овка** *f.* ranking, ranging.
ран/имый *a.* vulnerable; **—ить** *v.* wound, injure, cut; **—ка** *dim.* of **рана**; scratch.
Ранкина градус degree Rankine.
ранне— *prefix* pre—, prae—, early; **—весенний** *a.* (bot.) praevernal; **—спелость** *f.* early maturity; **—спелый** *a.* early(-ripening); **—третичный** *a.* (geol.) Early Tertiary.
ранн/ий *a.* early, previous, premature, precocious; initial, first; **р. детский возраст** infancy; **—ее обнаружение дефектов** incipient failure detection; **—ее слабоумие** dementia precox.
ранник *m.* polypody root.
рано *adv.* early, at an early hour, soon; **—опадающий** *a.* (bot.) caducous.
ранорасширитель *m.* (med.) retractor.
рант *m.*, **—овой, —овый** *a.* welt; ledge; **—овшивной** *a.* welt-sewing.
ранула *f.* (med.) ranula.
ранцания *f.* sunfish (*Ranzania*).
ранцевый *a.* of **ранец**; portable.
рань *f.* early morning.
раньше *comp.* of **ранний, рано** earlier, sooner; before, formerly, prior; **как можно р.** as soon as possible.
ранящий *a.* wounding, injuring.
рапа *f.* natural brine, saline water, bittern.
рапин *m.* rapine; **—овая кислота** rapinic acid, rapic acid.
рапира *f.* rapier, foil.
рапный *a.* of **рапа.**
рапонтик *m.* rhubarb.
рапорт *m.* report; **—ичка** report form; brief report; **—овать** *v.* report.
раппорт *m.* (text.) pattern repeat.
рапс *m.* (bot.) rape (*Brassica napus*); **—овое масло** rape(seed) oil.
рапунцель *m.* corn salad.
раритет *m.* rarity, curiosity.
рас— *see* **раз—.**
раса *f.* race, breed, strain.
расбора *f.* (ichth.) Rasbora.
рас/изм *m.* racism; **—ист** *a.*, **—истский** *a.* racist.
раскалённ/ость *f.* incandescence, glow; **—ый** *a.* incandescent, glowing, red hot; thermionic (cathode); **—ая нить** (elec.) filament.
раскали(ва)ть *v.* incandesce, bring to red heat; **—ся** *v.* get hot, begin to glow.
раскалываем/ость *f.* cleavability, cleavage; **—ый** *a.* cleavable.
раскалыв/ание *n.* cleaving, etc., *see v.*; chopping; cleavage; separation, division; scission; (nucl.) spallation; **—атель** *m.* splitter; **—ать** *v.* cleave, split (off, up),

crack, rift, fissure; slit, cut off; **—аться** *v.* cleave, split, crack; **—ающийся** *a.* cleavable, scissile, fissile; cleaving, splitting, rifting; **—ающийся пластами** fissile.
раскалять *see* **раскаливать.**
раскапыв/ание *n.* unearthing, etc., *see v.*; **—ать** *v.* unearth, excavate, dig out, dig up.
раскармливать *v.* feed up, fatten.
раскарстованный *a.* (geol.) karst, karstic.
раскат *see* **раскатывание**; acceleration, build-up; (rolling) feed(er); **—ать** *see* **раскатывать; —истый** *a.* resounding, rolling (sound); **—ить** *v.* set rolling; **—иться** *v.* roll off, swerve; accelerate, gather momentum; resound; **—ка** *see* **раскатывание**; burnishing tool; **время —ки** rise time (of signal); **—ник** *m.* burnisher; **—очный** *a.* of **раскатка**; take-off, pay-out; **—ывание** *n.* rolling (out), etc., *see* **раскатывать;** burnishing; **граница —ывания** plastic limit (of soil); **—ывать** *v.* roll (out), flatten, mangle, laminate, expand; unroll, unwind, pay out.
раскач/ать *see* **раскачивать; —ивание** *n.* swinging, etc., *see v.*; (av.) excessive rolling; rise, build-up (of current); **—ивать** *v.* swing, set swinging, sway, oscillate; shake loose, loosen; **—иваться** *v.* swing, sway, oscillate; loosen, get rickety; **—ивающий** *a.* swinging, etc., *see v.*; driving (potential); **—ка** *see* **раскачивание;** driving.
раскашивать *v.* prop up.
расквартиров(ыв)ать *v.* house, quarter, accommodate.
расква/сить, —шивать *v.* smash, squash.
расквитаться *v.* pay off, pay back.
раски/дать *see* **раскидывать; —дистый** *a.* scattered; sprawling; spreading (tree); **—дной** *a.* (un)folding, collapsible; **—дывание** *n.* spreading, etc., *see v.*; **—дыватель** *m.* (agr.) spreader; **—дывать** *v.* spread, scatter; unfold; **—нутый** *a.* spread, extended; **—нуть** *v.* spread, extend; pitch (tent); **—нуть умом** consider.
раскип/аться, —еться *v.* come to a vigorous boil.
раскисать *v.* rise, swell.
раскисл/ение *n.* deoxidation, reduction; **—енный** *a.* deoxidized, reduced; killed (steel); **—итель** *m.* deoxidizing agent, reducing agent, reducer; (met.) scavenger; **—ительный** *a.* deoxidizing, reducing; **—ить, —ять** *v.* deoxidize, reduce; **—яющий** *a.* deoxidizing, reducing.
раскиснуть *see* **раскисать.**
расклад/ка *see* **раскладывание; —ной** *a.* folding; **—очно-подборочная машина, —очная машина** (aut.) collator; **—очный** *a.* spreading, etc., *see v.*; **—чик** *m.* pickup, handler; depiler, separator; (mine) layer, planter; spreader; **—чик-питатель** *m.* pickup feeder; **—ывание** *n.* spreading, etc., *see v.*; distribution, allotment, allocation; arrangement, (page) layout; **—ывать** *v.* spread, lay out; distribute, allot, allocate, apportion; build (a fire); (chem.) decompose; analyze.
раскл/ёв *m.* (bird) cannibalism; **—евать, —ёвывать** *v.* peck to pieces.
расклеи(ва)ть *v.* unglue, separate, open; paste up, post; **—ся** *v.* come apart, fall apart.
расклепать *see* **расклёпывать.**
расклёп/ка *f.*, **—ывание** *n.* unriveting, etc., *see v.*; **—ывать** *v.* unrivet, unclench; rivet, clench; spread, drive, close up (a rivet); **—ываться** *v.* come apart.
расклин/ивание *n.* wedging, etc., *see v.*; cleavage; **—ивать, —ить** *v.* wedge, fasten with wedges; unwedge, loosen, unkey; split, cleave; **—ивающий** *a.* wedging, etc., *see v.*; disjoining (pressure); propping (agent); **—цовка** *f.* (masonry) galleting.
расков/ать *see* **расковывать; —ка** *f.* hammering out, etc., *see v.*; **испытание на —ку** hammer test;

—ывать *v.* hammer out, flatten, spread, draw out; jump (up), upset; unshoe (a horse); unshackle; **—ываться** *v.* expand, spread; lose a shoe.

расковыр/ивать, —ять *v.* scratch open, pick open.

раскодировать *v.* decode.

раскол *m.* splitting; cleft, crack, crevice.

расколачив/ание *n.* breaking up, etc., *see v.*; **—ать** *v.* break up; rap (mold); hammer flat, stretch.

расколка *f.* splitting, cleavage.

расколот *m.* (min.) bunton (timbers); **—ить** *see* **расколачивать;** **—о—** *prefix* schist(o)— (cleft, fissure), fissi—, schizo—(cleft, divided); **—олепестный** *a.* (bot.) schizopetalous; **—олистный** *a.* fissifolious; **—ый** *a.* split, cleaved; **—ь** *see* **раскалывать.**

расколыхать *v.* rock, set rocking.

расконоп/атить, —ачивать *v.* uncalk.

расконсервировать *v.* resume (operations); reactivate; take out of (long-term) storage.

раскоп/анный *a.* unearthed, excavated, dug up; **—ать** *see* **раскапывать;** **—ка** *see* **раскапывание.**

раскорм/ить *v.* fatten; **—ленный** *a.* fattened, well fed.

раскорч/евать, —ёвывать *v.* grub out, stub out (tree stumps); uproot; clean up.

раскорячи(ва)ть *v.* straddle.

раскос *m.* cross stay, angle brace, diagonal (strut), strut, truss, prop; **—ина** *f.* cross bar; angle iron; **—ить** *v.* brace, prop; slant; mow; **—ный** *a. of* **раскос;** truss (bridge); **—ная система** latticework; **—ость** *f.* slant; (ophth.) divergent strabismus; **—ый** *a.* slanting.

раскраивать *v.* cut out, lay out (pattern).

раскрай *m.* (fishing) trawl.

раскрас/ить *v.* color, etc., *see* **раскрашивать; —ка** *f.* painting, coloring, coloration.

раскрасн/евшийся *a.* red, crimson; **—еться** *v.* redden, flush, blush.

раскраш/енный *a.* painted, colored; **—ивание** *n.* painting, coloring; **—ивать** *v.* paint, color; crumble.

раскреп/ить *see* **раскреплять; —ление** *n.* unfastening, etc., *see v.*; **—лённый** *a.* unfastened, etc., *see v.*; **—лять** *v.* unfasten, undo, separate, take apart, loosen.

раскрепо/стить, —щать *v.* emancipate, (set) free; **—щение** *n.* emancipation, liberation; **—щённый** *a.* emancipated, liberated.

раскритиков(ыв)ать *v.* criticize severely.

раскроенный *a.* cut out, laid out (pattern).

раскроет *fut. 3 sing. of* **раскрыть.**

раскрой *m.* (pattern) cutting, laying out; cut out article; **—ка** *f.*, **—ный** *a.* cutting.

раскромс/анный *a.* shredded; **—ать** *v.* shred, cut to pieces.

раскрош/енный *a.* crumbled, broken; **—ить** *v.* crumble, break up, crush; **—иться** *v.* crumble, disintegrate.

раскружаливать *v.* (constr.) strike (centers).

раскру/тить *see* **раскручивать; —тка** *f.* overspeeding; **—ченный** *a.* untwisted, etc., *see v.*; **—чивание** *n.* untwisting, etc., *see v.*; back twist; **—чивать** *v.* untwist, unwind, uncoil; wind up, get going, start rotation, spin; **—чиваться** *v.* untwist, get untwisted, unwind, snap back; gather momentum, get going.

раскрыв *m.* aperture, opening; **—ание** *n.* bursting, dehiscence; **—ать** *v.* uncover, open, reveal, disclose, expose; detect; **—аться** *v.* open (up); become known; (bot.) dehisce; **—ающийся** *a.* opening; hinged; (bot.) dehiscent; **—ный** *a.* aperture.

раскрылка *f.* may disease (of bees).

раскрыт/ие *n.* uncovering, opening, deployment; disclosure, detection, exposure; aperture, mouth; (math.) expansion; removal (of brackets); splitting, cleavage; (ring) scission; **—ый** *a.* uncovered, etc., *see* **раскры-**

вать; open; patent; (bot.) ringent; detected; accessible; **—ь** *see* **раскрывать.**

раскряжёв/ка *f.* (logging) crosscutting, etc., *see v.*; **—ывать** *v.* buck, saw into logs, crosscut.

раскулачив/ание *n.* dispossession of kulaks; **—ать** *v.* dispossess kulaks; cannibalize (parts).

раскуп/ать, —ить *v.* buy up.

раскупор/и(ва)ть *v.* open, uncork, unplug, unseal; **—ка** *f.* opening, etc., *see v.*

раскуститься *v.* (bot.) bush out.

раскус/ить, —ывать *v.* bite through, open by biting; understand.

раску/т(ыв)ать *v.* uncover, unwrap; **—чивать** *v.* unearth, remove soil.

расовый *a.* race, racial; proli— (offspring).

расп. *abbr.* (**распад**).

распавшийся *a.* disintegrated, crumbled.

распад *m.* decomposition, breaking up, etc., *see v.*; break-up, breakdown, disintegration, *suffix* —lysis; catabolism; disruption; resolution; ruin, downfall, destruction; (nucl.) decay; (chem.) decomposition; precipitation (of emulsion); extinction; **р. белка** (physiol.) albuminolysis; **продукты —а** decomposition products; **реакция —а** catabolic reaction; **ряд —ов** (nucl.) decay chain, disintegration series; **скорость —а** disintegration rate; **теплота —а** heat of dissociation; **цепочка —ов** *see* **распадов, ряд; —аться** *v.* decompose, break down, disintegrate, break up, separate (into), dissociate; decay; fall apart, collapse; **—ающийся** *a.* decomposing, etc., *see v.*; separating (fruit); **—ение** *see* **распад.**

распадок *m.* creek valley, ravine.

распа/ивание *see* **распайка; —ивать** *v.* unsolder; seal off; **—йка** *f.* unsoldering; making soldered connections; (arrangement of) soldered connections, pin-out (of a connector).

распаков/ать, —ывать *v.* unpack, undo; **—ка** *f.*, **—очный** *a.* unpacking.

распалить *see* **распалять.**

распалуб/ить *v.* (concrete) strike, remove forms; **—ка** *f.* striking.

распалять *v.* kindle; heat to high temperature; inflame; **—ся** *v.* get very hot; be incensed.

распар *m.* (blast furnace) bosh extension.

распар/енный *a.* steamed, steam-softened; **—ивание** *n.* steaming, steam-softening; (med.) fomentation; **—и(ва)ть** *v.* steam, soften; **—ка** *f.*, **—очный** *a.* steaming, steam-softening.

распарывать *v.* rip open.

распасться *see* **распадаться.**

распатор *m.* (med.) raspatory, surgical file.

распах/анный *a.* tilled, etc., *see v.*; **—ать** *v.* plow up, till; **—ивание** *n.* plowing up; **—ивать** *v.* plow up; open wide; **—нуть** *v.* open wide, throw open.

распаш/ка *f.* plowing; **—ник** *m.* ridging plow, furrower, cultivator; **—ной** *a.* plowing; double-page (illustration); double (door, etc.).

распа/янный *a.* unsoldered; **—ять** *see* **распаивать.**

распереть *see* **распирать.**

распечат/ать *see* **распечатывать; —ка** *f.* (comp.) listing, printout; dump; **—ывание** *n.* opening, unsealing, uncapping (of honeycombs); **—ывать** *v.* open, unseal, break the seal; unlute; (comp.) print out, list.

распил *m.* saw cut; sawing; **—енный** *a.* sawed, cut (up); **—и(ва)ть** *v.* saw (apart), cut (up); **—(ов)ка** *f.*, **—овочный** *a.* sawing; **—овщик** *m.* sawyer.

распирать *v.* bulge out, push apart; burst.

расписание *n.* time table, schedule.

распис/ать *see* **расписывать; —ка** *f.* receipt; painting (of walls, etc.); —**ной** *a.* painted, decorated; —**ывание** *n.* entering, etc., *see* v.; analysis (of periodicals); —**ывать** *v.* enter, register; assign, fix; depict, describe; paint; transcribe; write (all over); —**ываться** *v.* sign; register.

распит *m.* (min.) raspite.

распих/(ив)ать, —**нуть** *v.* push (aside).

расплав *m.* melt; fusion; **шлаковый р.** melted slag; —**ить** *see* **расплавлять;** —**ка** *f.,* —**ление** *n.* melting, etc., *see* v.; fusion; (open-hearth process) working period, refining period; —**ление активной зоны** core meltdown (of a reactor); —**ленный** *a.* melted, etc., *see* v.; molten; —**ленный металл** smelt; —**ленная масса** melt, molten mass; —**лять** *v.* melt (down), fuse, liquefy; (met.) smelt; —**опровод** *m.* melt conduit.

распланиров/ать, —**ывать** *v.* plan out, lay out, mark out; level out; —**ка** *f.* planning out, etc., *see* v.; layout.

распласт/ать(ся) *see* **распластывать(ся);** —**овать** *v.* split in two; —**ывание** *n.* spreading, etc., *see* v.; (flood) subsidence; —**ывать** *v.* spread, flatten, stretch; split in two; stratify; —**ываться** *v.* stretch out, lie prone; sprawl, hug the ground.

распла/та *f.* pay(ment); —**титься,** —**чиваться** *v.* pay, settle (with).

распл/ескать, —**ёскивать,** —**еснуть** *v.* spill, splash out, spatter.

распле/сти, —**тать** *v.* untwist, unbraid; —**тание** *n.* untwisting; —**тённый** *a.* untwisted, etc., *see* v.

распло/д *m.* breeding, reproduction, procreation; breed; brood; —**дить,** —**жать** *v.* breed, propagate, reproduce; —**диться** *v.* breed, multiply, reproduce.

расплы/ваемость *f.* deliquescence; —**вание** *n.* spreading, etc., *see* v.; deliquescence; —**ваться** *v.* spread, run (of paint); streak, blend (of colors); diffuse, blur, smear; broaden; deliquesce; swell up, gain weight; swim or drift apart; —**ваться в растворе** (chem.) dissolve; —**вающийся** *a.* deliquescent; —**вчатость** *f.* blur(ring), smearing, diffuseness; —**вчатый** *a.* diffuse(d), blurred, smeared, indistinct, dim; —**вчатое пятно** circle of confusion; —**ться** *see* **расплываться.**

расплю/снуть *see* **расплющивать;** —**щенный** *a.* flattened, hammered out; —**щивание** *n.* flattening, hammering out; —**щи(ва)ть** *v.* flatten, hammer out; —**щи(ва)ться** *v.* expand, mushroom.

расп/мин *abbr.* (**распадов в минуту**) disintegrations per minute.

распозн/аваемый *a.* discernible, perceptible; —**(ав)ание** *n.* recognition, etc., *see* v.; discernment, perception; (med.) diagnosis; —**(ав)ать** *v.* recognize, identify; discern, perceive, distinguish, discriminate; diagnose; —**анный** *a.* recognized, etc., *see* v.; —**ающий** *a.* recognizing, etc., *see* v.

располаг/аемый *a.* available; net (thrust); —**ать** *v.* arrange, lay out, dispose, place, position, station (troops); post (guards), locate, set, put; space, distribute, group; have available; intend, propose; —**аться** *v.* be positioned, be located; —**ающий** *a.* arranging, etc., *see* v.; conducive (to).

располз/аться *v.,* —**тись** *v.* tear, come apart, deteriorate; diffuse; crawl (apart), scatter.

расположен/ие *n.* disposition, disposal, arrangement, layout, set-up; distribution, spacing, grouping, order; pattern, design; (phys.) geometry, configuration; position(ing), site, situation, location, locality, exposure (of building); (med.) situs; attitude (of fetus); inclination, tendency; mood; **р. местности** lay of the land; **р. нервов** nervation; **схема—ия** layout.

располож/енный *a.* arranged, etc., *see* **располагать;** inclined, having a tendency (to); predisposed (to); **р. близ** juxtaposed; **р. вблизи** (anat.) para—; **р. в, р. внутри** intra—; **р. внутри железы** intraglandular; **р. возле** peri—, para—; **р. возле грудины** parasternal; **р. за** retro—; **р. за языком** retrolingual; **р. между** inter—; **р. между предсердиями** interatrial; **р. на** epi—; **р. над** superposed; supra—; epi—; **р. над ухом** epiotic; **р. под** sub—; **правильно р.** in position; —**ить** *see* **располагать.**

располосов(ыв)ать *v.* cut into strips.

распор *m.* thrust; spread, expansion; —**ка** *f.* thrust; brace, cross bracing, strut, tie (beam), (stay) rod; spreader, spacer; (chain) stud; —**ный** *a.* thrust, brace; spacing; —**ная балка** brace; —**ная деталь** spacer; —**ная крепь** (min.) stull.

распороть *v.* rip open.

распорочный *see* **распорный.**

распорядитель *m.* manager, director, administrator; —**ность** *f.* good management, efficiency; **отсутствие —ности** mismanagement; —**ный** *a.* efficient, capable, active, administrative, control.

распоря/диться *see* **распоряжаться;** —**док** *m.* routine; arrangement, division (of work); regulations; (standing) order; —**жаться** *v.* dispose (of), deal (with), do, have done, see to, make arrangements; manage, be in charge; order.

распоряжен/ие *n.* disposition, disposal, arrangement; instruction(s), direction(s); order, decree; **в р.** under the management (of); **в —ии** at the disposal (of), at or on hand, available; **отдать р.** *v.* give orders, leave instructions; **управление —ия** (nucl.) configuration control.

расправ/илка *f.* (ent.) stretch board; —**итель** *m.* expander; —**ить** *see* **расправлять;** —**ление** *n.* expanding, etc., *see* v.; —**ленный** *a.* expanded, etc., *see* v.; —**лять** *v.* expand, spread; (text.) tenter; straighten out; set right; open; —**ляться** *v.* straighten out; deal (with), get done, settle, dispose (of).

распределен/ие *n.* distribution, etc., *see* **распределять;** allocation, assignment, allotment, division, apportionment; (comp.) mapping; (gene) assortment; assessment (of tax); pattern; timing; gearing; **р. во времени** time distribution; **р. выхода по массам** yield-mass distribution; **групповое р.** (bot.) hyperdispersion; **коэффициент —ия** (chem.) partition coefficient.

распределённый *a.* distributed, etc., *see* **распределять;** **тонко р.** finely divided.

распределитель *m.* distributor, spreader; timer; (bunker) marker block; —**ность** *f.* (math.) distributiveness, distributivity.

распределительн/ый *a.* distributing, distributive, distribution; regulating, control, timing (mechanism); partition (chromatography); **р. вал** camshaft; **р. клапан** regulating valve; **р. щит** (elec.) switchboard, panel; (automobile) dashboard; **р. щиток** dashboard; —**ая доска** *see* **распределительный щит;** —**ая коробка** (elec.) switch box; —**ая магистраль** (elec.) distributing main, distributor.

распределитель-трансмиттер *m.* distributor-transmitter; **р.-щит** *m.* switchboard.

распредел/ить, —**ять** *v.* distribute, allocate, assign, allot, apportion, dispense; divide, sort; spread, broadcast, diffuse, disseminate; regulate; assess (tax); —**яющий** *a.* distributing, etc., *see* v.

распред/пункт distribution center; —**щит** *m.* switchboard.

распрессов(ыв)ать *v.* press (off, out).

распрод/авать, —**ать** v. sell out, auction off; —**аваться** v. sell, have a market; —**ажа** f. sale, auction.

распрост/ереть see **распростирать;** —**ёртый** a. extended, etc., see v.; prostrate; (bot.) creeping, trailing; procumbent; —**ирать** v. stretch out, extend, spread, widen.

распространение n. propagation; spread(ing), proliferation, dispersion, dissemination, distribution; (gene) flow; extension; enlargement, amplification, expansion; diffusion, emission; convection (of heat); circulation; occurrence, frequency, prevalence; **динамическое р.** dispersal.

распространён/ность f. prevalence, extent, rate of occurrence, frequency, incidence; abundance (of isotopes, etc.); —**ный** a. spread, etc., see **распространять;** (med.) generalized (osteoporosis), universal (calcinosis); prevailing, prevalent, common, popular, widespread, abundant; controlling (influence, etc.); **широко** —**ный** widely distributed, widespread.

распростран/итель m. vector, spreader (of disease); —**ительный** a. extended; —**ить,** —**ять** v. circulate, spread, broadcast, propagate; publicize, make widely known; extend; disseminate, disperse; distribute, diffuse, radiate, emit; —**иться,** —**яться** v. spread, travel, become widely known; expand, broaden, extend, branch out; propagate; radiate, emit; pervade; occur; persist; —**яющийся** a. spreading, etc., see v.; pervasive; borne; —**яющийся в воде** waterborne.

распрыск(ив)ать v. spray, sprinkle.

распрягать v. unharness.

распрям/ить, —**лять** v. straighten, unbend; set upright; —**иться,** —**ляться** v. straighten out; —**ление** n. straightening, unbending.

распрячь see **распрягать.**

расп/сек abbr. (**распадов в секунду**) disintegrations per second.

распус/кание n. melting, etc., see v.; opening (of buds), sprouting; deliquescence; **р. цветков** (bot.) efflorescence; —**кать** v. melt, liquefy; let go, undo, untie, relax; spread, unfurl; disperse, diffuse; unravel; discharge (employees); —**каться** v. melt, dissolve, deliquesce; relax; become unraveled; get muddy (of road); (bot.) open, unfold, bud; —**кающийся** a. melting, etc., see v.; deliquescent; —**тившийся** a. unfolded, open, etc., see **распускаться;** —**тить** see **распускать;** —**тка** f. (zool.) heat, estrus.

распут/(ыв)ать v. disentangle, untangle, unravel, untwine; —**ный** a. depraved, dissolute; —**ье** n. intersection; poor road system; **на** —**ье** undecided, hesitant.

распух/ание n. swelling, inflation; intumescence; —**ать** v. swell, inflate, bulge, expand; —**ающий** a. swelling; intumescent; —**лый** see **распухший;** —**нуть** see **распухать;** —**ший** a. swollen, inflated, tumid.

распучи(ва)ть v. distend, inflate.

распуш/ённый a. fluffed up; —**ить** v. fluff up; —**иться** v. become fluffy.

распущенный a. relaxed, etc., see **распускать;** loose; undisciplined; untied; open (blossom).

распыл/ение n. spraying, sputtering, atomization, etc., see v.; **высушивание** —**ением** spray drying; —**ённый** a. sprayed, etc., see v.; pulverulent; **тонко** —**ённый** finely divided; —**ённое масло** oil spray; —**ивать** see **распылять;** —**ивающий** see **распыляющий;** —**ивающий абсорбер** spray chamber; —**итель** m. sprayer, atomizer, pulverizer, diffuser; spray gun, blow gun; air brush; (agr.) duster; —**ительный** see **распыляющий;** —**ительная головка** injector (of jet engine); —**ительная сушилка** spray drier; —**ить** see **распылять;** —**яемый** dispersible; —**яемый геттер** flash getter; —**ять** v. spray, atomize, diffuse, disperse; dissipate; pulverize, powder; (agr.) dust; (electron.) sputter; —**яться** v. be sprayed, etc.; disperse, scatter; turn to dust; —**яющий** a. spraying, etc., see v.; spray.

распял/и(ва)ть v. pull tight, stretch; —**ка** f. stretcher.

расса f. rasse (a civet) (*Viverricula indica*).

расса/да f. seedling(s), sprout(s); —**дить** see **рассаживать;** —**дка** f. planting; —**дник** m. nursery; seedbed, hotbed; breeding farm; breeding ground, source; —**допосадочный** a. transplanting; —**живание** n. (trans)planting; seating; —**живать** v. (trans)plant, set out; seat.

рассасыв/ание n. resorption; relaxation; (med.) resolution; —**ать** v. re(ab)sorb; —**аться** v. resolve; go down (of swelling).

рассверл/ённый a. bored; reamed; —**ивание** n. boring; reaming; —**и(ва)ть** v. bore, drill out; ream.

рассвести see **рассветать.**

рассвет m. dawn, daybreak; **на** —**е** at dawn, at daybreak; —**ать** v. dawn.

рассев m. sowing; dissemination, broadcasting; screening, separation (of powders); (screen) sizing; inoculation, seeding; sifter; —**ать** see **рассеивать;** sift.

рассадаться v. crack (on settling).

рас/седлать, —**сёдлывать** v. unsaddle.

рассеив/аемый a. dispersible, etc., see v.; —**аемая мощность** dissipated power; —**ание** n. dispersion, scattering, etc., see v.; dispersal; (stat.) spread; —**атель** m. disperser, diffuser, scatterer, scattering material; —**ать** v. disperse, scatter, dissipate, diffuse, leak, disseminate, dispel; sprinkle, strew; (stat.) vary; sift; (agr.) sow; —**аться** v. be dispersed, etc.; disperse, scatter, dissipate, diverge; leak, stray; —**ающий** a. dispersing, etc., see v.; dispersion, dispersive, dissipative; diffusion (factor); diffusing (power); scattering (filter); diverging (lens); —**ающая способность** dispersibility; diffusion factor; (electrolysis) throwing power.

рассек/ание n. cleaving, etc., see v.; split; —**атель** m. splitter; divider; dissector; —**ать** v. cleave, split, divide, bisect; dissect.

рассекре/тить, —**чивать** v. declassify, open (to the public); deny access (to classified documents, etc.).

рассел/ение n. settlement; dispersal, spreading (of a species); migration; —**ённый** a. dispersed, etc., see **расселять.**

расселина f. split, cleft, rift, crack, fissure.

расселить see **расселять.**

Расселя-Сондерса связь (nucl.) Russell-Saunders coupling.

расселять v. (re)settle; disperse; —**ся** v. expand, spread out.

рассердить v. anger, rile; —**ся** v. get angry.

рассесть see **рассаживать;** settle down; crack (on settling).

рассеч/ение n. dissection; (med.) —**томы;** (anat.) sectio; **р. влагалища** vaginotomy; —**ённость** f. articulation (of terrain); —**ённый** a. cleaved, cleft, split; dissected; *suffix* —sectional; —**ка** see **рассекание;** breaking (of circuit); (min.) crosscut; **в** —**ку** (elec.) in series; —**ь** see **рассекать.**

рассеян/ие n. dispersion, scattering, etc., see **рассеивать;** (magnetic) leakage; degradation (of energy); **р. пучка** beam divergence; **р. на сетке** grid dissipation; **р. света** light scattering; **р. тепла** heat dissipation; **комбинационное р.** Raman effect, Raman scattering; **коэффициент —ия** dispersion factor; **обратное р., отражённое р.** backscatter(ing); **—но** *adv.* here and there, sparsely; *prefix* sparsi—; absentmindedly; **—нопористый** *a.* diffuse-porous; **—ность** *f.* dispersity, diffusivity; distraction, absentmindedness; **—ноцветковый** *a.* sparsiflorous; **—ный** *a.* dispersed, etc., *see* **рассеивать;** diffuse, scattered (light); misdirected, stray; sparse; distracted, absent-minded; erratic (value); trace (element); (med.) multiple (sclerosis); **—ный обратно** back-scattered.

рассеять *see* **рассеивать.**

рассказ(ыв)ать *v.* tell, relate.

расслаб/е(ва)ть *v.* grow weak, weaken; **—ить** *see* **расслаблять; —ление** *n.* weakening, prostration; relaxing, lassitude; debilitation; incontinence (of sphincter); (med.) dilat(at)ion; **—ленность** *f.* (med.) asthenia; debility; **—ленный** *a.* weakened, atonic, enfeebled, prostrate; relaxed, slack; **—лять** *v.* weaken; relax; **—ляющий** *a.* weakening; relaxing; **—ляющее средство** relaxant.

расслаив/ание *n.* stratification, separating (into layers), etc., *see v.*; delamination; segregation, disintegration (of concrete); cleavage; phase separation; **—ать** *v.* stratify, separate (into layers), laminate, (ex)foliate, scale, flake; **—аться** *v.* stratify, form in strata; exfoliate, peel off, flake, scale; (concrete) disintegrate, segregate; **—ающий** *a.* stratifying, etc., *see v.*

рассланц/евание *n.* (geol.) schist formation; **—ованность** *f.* schistosity; **—ованный** *a.* schistose; **—овка** *see* **рассланцевание.**

расследов/ание *n.* investigation, inquiry, examination; (law) inquest; **—ать** *v.* investigate, inquire, look into.

рассло/ение *see* **расслаивание; —ённый** *a.* stratified, etc., *see* **расслаивать;** (math.) fibered (spaces).

рассло/ина *see* **расслой; —ить** *see* **расслаивать; —й** *m.* (met.) spill, seam (defect); **—йка** *see* **расслаивание;** (geol.) strata; **—яемый** *a.* (math.) stratifiable, fiber (space).

рассм/атриваемый *a.* under consideration, in question, being investigated, at hand; **—атривание** *see* **рассмотрение;** **—атривать** *v.* consider, discuss, cover, review; examine, inspect, screen, overhaul; observe, study, investigate, look at, scrutinize; treat; **—атриваться** *v.* be considered, etc.; be under consideration; **—отрение** *n.* consideration, etc., *see v.*; scrutiny; treatment; **направлять на —отрение** *v.* refer, submit (to); **—отренный** *a.* considered, etc., *see v.*; **—отреть** *see* **рассматривать.**

рассна/стить, —щивать *v.* (naut.) dismantle, remove rigging.

рассов(ыв)ать *v.* shove (into place); stuff (into pockets, etc.).

рассогласован/ие *n.* mismatch(ing), misalignment, discrepancy, unbalance; (displacement) error; error signal; **угол —ия** displacement angle.

рассол *m.* pickle, brine; (mother) liquor; (chem.) salt solution; **—ение** *n.* desalinization; **—одение** *n.* desolodization, reclamation of solod (soil); **—онение** *n.* dilution of brine; **—оносная зона** (geol.) zone of sedimentary rocks over salt deposit; **—онцевание** *n.* desolonetzization, dealkalinization, reclamation of solonetz (soil); **—ьный** *a.* of **рассол.**

рассортиров/ать, —ывать *v.* sort out, grade, classify; decollate; **—ка** *f.,* **—ывание** *n.* sorting out, classification.

рассос/анный *a.* re(ab)sorbed; **—ать** *v.* re(ab)sorb.

рассох/а *f.* forked tree, bifurcated stem; **—нуться** *see*

рассыхаться; —шийся *a.* cracked, split (from dryness).

расспр/ашивание *n.* questioning, interrogation, inquiry; **—ашивать, —осить** *v.* question, inquire, interrogate; **—ос** *m.* question, inquiry, interrogation.

рассредоточ/ение *n.* dispersal, distribution; **—енный** *a.* dispersed, distributed; **—и(ва)ть(ся)** *v.* disperse.

рассроч/и(ва)ть *v.* spread out (payments); **—ка** *f.* installment, part payment; **в —ку** on the installment plan.

расстав *m.* (bookbinding) turn-in; **—ание** *n.* parting, separation; **—аться** *v.* part, separate, leave; break (habit).

расстав/ить *see* **расставлять; —ленный** *a.* scattered, etc., *see v.*; remote, separated; (bot.) interrupted (inflorescence); **—лять** *v.* place, set, arrange; file; post (guards); move apart, spread; enlarge.

расстан/авливать, —овить *v.* place, arrange; post (guards); set (a trap); **—овка** *f.* arrangement, order; location, placement; filing; spacing; **функция —овки** (comp.) hashing function; **—овщик** *m.* file clerk, (book) shelver.

расстаться *see* **расставаться.**

расстёг/ивать, —нуть *v.* unfasten, unbuckle, unclasp, unhook, unbutton.

расстеклов/ание *n.* devitrification; **—анный** *a.* devitrified; **—ывать** *v.* devitrify.

расстелить *v.* spread.

расстил *m.* spreading, etc., *see v.*; dew retting (of flax); **—ание** *n.* spreading, etc., *see v.*; **—ать(ся)** *v.* spread, strew; unfold, extend; **—ка** *f.* spreading, etc., *see v.*; **—очный** *a.* spreading.

расстопоривание *n.* unlocking, release.

расстоя/ние *n.* distance, way; space, spacing, interval; separation; range; **измерение —ия** range measurement; **на р.** (by or for) a distance; **на —ии** at a distance, from a distance, distant; within . . . of; remote (control); **на одинаковом —ии** at regular intervals, regularly spaced; **на равном —ии (друг от друга)** evenly spaced, equidistant; **перевозка на дальнее р.** long-distance transportation; **управление на —ии** remote control.

растраив/ание *n.* unbalancing, etc., *see v.*; misalignment; **—ать** *v.* unbalance, unsettle, disorganize, upset, disturb, disrupt, disarrange; (mil.) break up (an attack); misalign; (rad.) detune; **—аться** *v.* be unbalanced, etc.; get out of tune; get upset.

расстрел *m.* execution; shooting; (art.) bore enlargement; (min.) bunton; **—ивать, —ять** *v.* execute; shoot; enlarge bore.

расстро/енный *a.* unbalanced, etc., *see* **расстраивать;** faulty (nutrition); **—ить** *see* **расстраивать; —йка** *see* **расстраивание.**

расстройство *n.* disorder, disorganization, derangement, disturbance, disruption; (psychiatric) breakdown; (med.) dysfunction; impairment; **р. желудка** (med.) indigestion; **р. памяти** dysmnesia, impaired memory; **р. хода** breakdown.

расстыков/ка *f.* undocking (of spacecraft); disengagement, separation; **—(ыв)ать** *v.* disengage, detach, move apart; **—(ыв)аться** *v.* undock.

рассудительн/ость *f.* common sense, reasonableness; **—ый** *a.* reasonable.

рассуд/ить *v.* think, decide, judge; **—ок** *m.* reason, intellect, mind, common sense; **—очно** *adv.* rationally; **—очность** *f.* rationality; **—очный** *a.* rational.

рассужд/ать *v.* reason, discuss, argue, debate; **—ение** *n.* reasoning; discussion, discourse.

рассунуть *see* **рассовывать.**

рассучи(ва)ть *v.* untwist, unravel, unlay (rope).

рассчит/анный *a.* calculated, etc., see *v.*; meant, deliberate; rated (at); —**(ыв)ать** *v.* calculate, compute, figure out, estimate; rate (equipment); expect, depend, count (on); (mil.) sound off; design (for), intend, mean; dismiss, discharge; —**(ыв)ать на** *v.* calculate for; depend on; —**(ыв)аться** *v.* be calculated, etc.; settle (accounts with); —**ывающий** *a.* calculating, etc., see *v.*; expectant.

рассыл/ание *see* **рассылка;** —**ать** *v.* send (away, around), dispatch; mail; distribute, circulate; —**ка** *f.*, —**очный** *a.* sending, etc., see *v.*; distribution; delivery; —**ьный** *a.* sent, circulated; *m.* messenger, delivery man.

рассып/ание *n.* scattering, etc., see *v.*; dispersal; —**анный** *a.* scattered, etc., see *v.*; loose (cargo); —**ать** *v.* scatter, spill, strew, sprinkle, disperse; pour; —**аться** *v.* scatter, spill; disperse; crumble (away), disintegrate, fall apart; —**ка** *see* **рассыпание;** loss in weight (of bulk products); —**ной** *a.* loose; **в** —**ную** loose(ly).

рассыпчат/ость *f.* friability; —**ый** *a.* friable, crumbly, powdery, grannular, arenaceous.

рассыхаться *v.* dry (out), parch.

Раста метод Rast's method.

растаивать *v.* thaw, melt; disappear.

расталкивать *v.* push apart; rap (mold).

растаплив/ание *n.* kindling, etc., see *v.*; —**ать** *v.* kindle, light, fire up; heat up; melt, fuse, liquefy; (met.) smelt.

растаптывать *v.* crush, trample, tread down; wear out (shoes).

растаривание *n.* unpacking (of bags).

растартывать *v.* (petrol.) bail, swab.

растаск(ив)ать *v.* pull apart, remove (piece by piece); pilfer.

растачивать *v.* bore (out), ream.

растащить *see* **растаскивать.**

раста/явший *a.* melted, thawed out; —**ять** *see* **растаивать.**

раствор *m.* solution; liquor, bath; paste, suspension; (drilling) mud; mortar, grout; (cement) slurry; gap, aperture, opening, span (of vise); range (of instrument); **белильный р.** bleach; **давление** —**а** solution pressure; **твёрдый р.** solid solution; **угол** —**а** aperture angle; flare angle.

раствор/ение *n.* solution, dissolving; (met.) diffusion; (physiol.) —lysis; **р. ядра клетки** karyolysis; —**ённый** *a.* dissolved; opened; —**ённое вещество** solute.

раствор/имое *see* —**имость** *f.* solubility; deliquescence; —**имый** *a.* soluble; —**имый в воде** water-soluble; —**имая РНК** transfer RNA; —**итель** *m.* solvent; (paint) vehicle; dissolver; (biol.) menstruum, solvent medium; —**ить** *see* **растворять;** —**яемость** *f.* solubility; —**яемый** *a.* soluble; dissolving, undergoing solution; —**ять(ся)** *v.* dissolve; open, unfasten; (physiol.) lyse; —**яющий** *a.* dissolving, etc., see *v.*; (physiol.) —lytic; —**яющий слизь** mucolytic.

растворяющ/ий *a.* dissolving, solvent; —**ая способность** solvent action; —**ее вещество, —ее средство** solvent; —**ийся** *a.* dissolving; soluble.

растек/аемость *f.* spreadability; spread, flow, spill; —**ание** *n.* spread(ing), flow, spill; —**атель** *m.* spreading agent, wetting agent; —**аться** *v.* spread, flow, spill, run; —**ающийся** *a.* spreading, etc., see *v.*; yielding (material).

рас/тёл *m.* calving; —**ели(ва)ться** *v.* calve.

растение *n.* plant, vegetation; **вредное р.** destructive weed; **высшее р.** higher plant, spermatophyte; **низшее**

р. thallophyte; —**ведение** *n.* botany; —**вод** *m.* plant grower; —**водство** *n.*, —**водческий** *a.* plant growing, agriculture; **р.-индикатор** *n.* soil-testing crop, indicator plant; **р.-краситель** *n.* dye crop; **р.-ксерофит** *n.* drought-resistant plant, xerophyte; —**любивый** *a.* phytophilous; **р.-перекрестник** *n.* cross-pollination plant; —**питатель** *m.* plant feeder; **р.-подушка** *n.* cushion plant; **р.-родоначальник** *n.* original plant; **р.-сухолюб** *n.* xerophyte; **р.-хозяйн** *n.* host plant; —**ядный** *a.* phytophagous, plant-eating; vegetarian.

растеньице *n.* (bot.) plantule (embryonic shoot or bud in seed).

растепление *n.* warming up, firing up.

растер/еть *see* **растирать;** —**з(ыв)ать** *v.* tear (to pieces); lacerate.

растёртый *a.* pulverized, etc., *see* **растирать.**

растер/янный *a.* lost, perplexed, confused; —**яться** *v.* be at a loss.

рас/тесать, —**тёсывать** *v.* chop open (in wood).

растечение *n.* (gene) flow.

растечься *see* **растекаться.**

расти *v.* grow, increase; develop; —**льня** *f.* germinator.

растинон *m.* Rastinon, tolbutamide.

растир/аемый *a.* pulverizable, friable; —**ание** *n.* pulverization, grinding, trituration; attrition, rubbing, massage; —**ательный** *a.* pulverizing, etc., see *v.*; —**ать** *v.* pulverize, grind, triturate, comminute, crush; rub up (paint); rub, massage; —**ающий зуб** molar; —**ка** *f.*, —**очный** *a.* pulverizing, etc., see *v.*

растис/к(ив)ать, —**нуть** *v.* push apart; split open, pierce; unclench, open.

растительно— *prefix* vegeto—, vegetable; herbi—; plant; —**животный** *a.* vegetoanimal; —**сть** *f.* vegetation, flora; —**ядный** *a.* (zool.) herbivorous, phytophagous; vegetarian.

растительн/ый *a.* plant, vegetable, phyto—; vegetative; natural (rubber); **р. жир** vegetable fat; —**ая земля** humus; —**ая химия** phytochemistry; **токсин** —**ого происхождения** phytotoxin.

растить *v.* grow, raise, breed.

растолкать *see* **расталкивать.**

растолков/ать, —**ывать** *v.* interpret, explain, expound; —**ывание** *n.* interpretation, explanation.

растолочь *v.* pound, grind, crush.

растолстеть *v.* gain weight, get fat.

растоп/итель *m.* melter, defroster; **судовый р. льда** ice melter for ships; —**ить** *see* **растапливать;** —**ка,** —**ление** *see* **растапливание;** —**ленный** *a.* kindled, etc., *see* **растапливать;** —**лять** *see* **растапливать;** —**очный** *a.* (for) kindling.

растоптать *see* **растаптывать.**

растопыр/енный *a.* bristling; (bot.) divaricate; —**и(ва)ть** *v.* spread wide; straddle; —**и(ва)ться** *v.* bristle.

расторг/ать, —**нуть** *v.* cancel, break.

расторжение *n.* cancellation, dissolution.

растормаживать *v.* release the brake; (physiol.) release an inhibition.

расторопша *f.* (bot.) milk thistle (*Silybum*).

расточ *see* **расточка;** —**ать** *v.* dissipate, waste, squander; —**енный** *a.* bored out, reamed; wasted; —**ительность** *f.*, —**ительство** *n.* waste(fulness), extravagance, profligacy; —**ительный** *a.* wasteful, extravagant, profligate; —**ить** *v.* bore, drill (out), ream; dissipate, waste; —**ка** *f.* bore, boring, drilling; —**ник** *m.* drill operator, borer; —**ный** *a.* boring, drilling, reaming.

растр *m.* (electron.; typ.) raster, grating, grill, screen; scanning pattern, scan, scanned area; (comp.) bit map; dot matrix; **точка** —**а** pixel.

растрав/ить, —ливать, —лять *v.* irritate, aggravate; corrode.

растра/та *f.,* **—чивание** *n.* spending; waste, dissipation, loss; embezzlement; **—тить, —чивать** *v.* spend; waste, dissipate; embezzle.

растревожи(ва)ть *v.* alarm, disturb.

растрёп/анный *a.* disarranged, etc., *see v.*; tousled, straggling (hair); **—ывание** *n.* disarranging, etc., *see v.*; **—(ыв)ать** *v.* disarrange; tatter, fray; fringe, untwist, unravel.

растрес/кавшийся *a.* (bot.) split, fissured, rimose; **—каться** *see* **растрескиваться; —кивание** *n.* cracking, etc., *see v.*; decrepitation, disintegration; (nucl.) spallation; (masonry) spalling; (biol.) dehiscence, bursting open; **осколок —кивания** spallation fragment; **—киваться** *v.* crack, burst, split, fissure, dehisce, gape; decrepitate, disintegrate; **—кивающийся** *a.* cracking, etc., *see v.*; friable.

растров/ый *a. of* **растр**; scanning (electron microscope); screen (printing); bit-mapped; half-tone (image); zebra-stripe (display); **—ое изображение** (maps) dot area.

раструб *m.* funnel, funnel-shaped opening, trumpet, bell, (bell) mouth; acoustic horn; cone bottom (of tank); socket (of pipe); (bot.) ocrea; **расходиться —ом** flare; **с —ом** bell-mouthed; **соединение —ом** bell-and-spigot, spigot and socket joint (of pipes); **—ный** *a. of* **раструб**; bell-mouthed; bell-shaped; **—овидный** *a.* (bot.) ocreate.

растр/усить *see* **раструшивать; —уска** *f.* weight loss (of bulk materials in shipping); spreading (of manure), etc.); **—ушивать** *v.* spill, scatter, spread; **—ясти, —яс(ыв)ать** *v.* scatter, strew; shake up.

растуш/евать *see* **растушёвывать; —ёвка** *see* **растушёвывание;** (drawing) stump; **—ёвывание** *n.* shading, etc., *see v.*; **—ёвывать** *v.* shade, stipple, stump.

растущий *a.* growing, rising, etc., *see* **расти.**

растык(ив)ать *v.* stick around; make holes (in); place, put away (haphazardly).

растягив/аемый *a.* stretchable; stretched, etc., *see v.*; **—ание** *n.* stretching, extension, etc., *see v.*; **—ать** *v.* stretch (out), extend, draw out, prolong, lengthen, elongate, distend, expand, dilate; (med.) sprain, strain, wrench; **—аться** *v.* stretch, extend, give; distend; spread; **—ающий** *a.* stretching, etc., *see v.*; **—ающий механизм** stretcher; **—ающая мышца** (anat.) tensor (muscle); **—ающая нагрузка** tension (load); **—ающая сила, —ающее усилие** tensile force, tension, pull.

растяжен/ие *see* **растягивание;** stretch; pull, tension; (med.) strain, sprain, wrench; distention, ectasia; dilation; **диаграмма —ия** stress-strain diagram; **прочность на р.** tensile strength; **работающий на р.** *a.* tension (joint); **рефлекс —ия** (physiol.) myotatic reflex, stretch reflex; **сила —ия** tensile force; **фиброзное р.** (anat.) aponeurosis; **—ный** *a.* (med.) ectatic, stretched, distended; **р.-сжатие** stress-strain.

растяжим/ость *f.* stretchability, elasticity; extensibility; expansibility; (met.) ductility; **—ый** *a.* stretchable, tensile, elastic; extensible; ductile.

растяж/ка *see* **растягивание;** tension member, brace, bracing (wire), strut; *see also* **крестовина; в —ку** at full length; **—ной** *a.* stretch(ing), extension; flexible; expansion (bolt).

растянут/ость *f.* lengthiness; **—ый** *a.* stretched (out), etc., *see* **растягивать;** lengthy, dragged out; **—ь** *see* **растягивать.**

расфазиров/ание *n.* phase shift; **—ка** *f.* (elec.) skew.

расфасов/ать *see* **расфасовывать; —ка** *f.,* **—очный** *a.* bagging, pack(ag)ing; transfusing; decanting; **—очно-упаковочный автомат** automatic bagger; **—щик** *m.* packager, bagger; **—ывание** *see* **расфасовка; —ывать** *v.* bag, pack(age).

расфокусиров/ание *see* **расфокусировка; —анный** *a.* defocused, etc., *see v.*; out of focus; **—ать** *v.* defocus, get out of focus; debunch (electrons); **—ка** *f.* defocusing, etc., *see v.*

расформиров/ание *n.* dissolution, breaking up; **—(ыв)ать** *v.* dissolve, break up, separate.

расхаживать *v.* work up and down, reciprocate.

расхвали(ва)ть *v.* praise.

расхват/ить, —(ыв)ать *v.* snatch up.

расхляб/анность *f.* looseness, shakiness; lack of discipline; **—анный** *a.* loose, slack; **—аться** *v.* get loose, work loose, get slack; get shaky; need tightening.

расход *m.* expense, expenditure, outlay, disbursement; flow (rate); discharge (of water); run-off; delivery (of pump); consumption, input; (nucl.) throughput; span (of vise); **р. на ступень** (nucl.) stage circulation, turnover; **р. энергии** power consumption; **план —ов** budget.

расход/имость *f.* divergence; **—иться** *v.* part, break up, disperse, diverge, go separate ways, separate; come apart, gape (open), open out, splay out; disagree, differ; spread, radiate; increase, pick up speed, gain momentum; be consumed, be spent; vanish, disappear (of clouds, etc.).

расходка *f.* (zool.) rut, period of sexual excitement.

расходник *m.* (bot.) quillwort (*Isoetes*).

расход/ный *a. of* **расход;** expendable; input-output (characteristic); service (tank); storage (tank); delivery (outlet of pump); **—ование** *n.* expenditure, consumption; **—овать** *v.* spend, consume, deplete, use up; **—омер** *m.* flowmeter; **—омерный** *a.* flow-measuring, flow-metering; **—ометрия** *f.* flow metering; **—уемый** *a.* expendable; consumable (electrode).

расходящийся *a.* divergent, diverging.

расхождение *n.* divergence, separation, gaping (of joints); gap, space; deviation, disagreement, discrepancy; disjunction (of chromosomes, etc.); segregation; (med.) diastasis; (bot.) divarication.

расхожий *a.* popular, in common use; utility; spending.

расхол/аживание *n.* residual heat removal, decay heat removal (of reactor); **—аживать, —одить** *v.* cool off; **—ожённый** *a.* cooled off.

расцарап(ыв)ать *v.* scratch.

расцве/сти *see* **расцветать; —т** *m.* blossom, bloom, flower; **—тание** *n.* blooming, blossoming, efflorescence, opening; **—тать** *v.* bloom, open, come to flower; flourish.

расцве/тить *see* **расцвечивать; —тка** *see* **расцвечивание;** colors; tint, hue; panachure, mottling; **—ченный** *a.* colored, etc., *see v.*; **—чивание** *n.* coloring, etc., *see v.*; **—чивать** *v.* color, paint, tint, tone; color-code, mark.

расцен/ивание *n.* estimation, evaluation, appraisal; **—и(ва)ть** *v.* estimate, evaluate, appraise, value; regard, consider; assess, tariff; **—ка** *f.* estimation, estimate, quotation, evaluation, appraisal; assessment; price, fee, rate; piece-rate price; tariff; cost sheet; **денежные —ки** daily wage; **—ок** *m.* rate of wages; **—очный** *a.* valuation; **—очная ведомость** cost sheet; **—щик** *m.* appraiser, assessor.

расцеп/(итель) *m.* trip, release, uncoupler; **—ить** *see* **расцеплять; —ка** *f.* uncoupling; release (catch); **—ление** *n.* uncoupling, etc., *see v.*; trip(ping); breaking (a chain); release; —**ленный** *a.* uncoupled, etc., *see v.*; out of gear; —**лять** *v.* uncouple, disconnect, unhook, unlink; trip, release; disengage, throw out of gear; —**ляющий** *a.* uncoupling, etc., *see v.*; —**ляющий автомат** (automatic) release; —**ляющий механизм** release (mechanism), trip; —**ной** *a.* detachable.

расчал/енный *a.* braced; —**и(ва)ть** *v.* brace, guy, —**ка** *f.* bracing (wire), guy wire; tension member; —**очный** *a.* (wire-)braced.

расчекан/енный *a.* calked; —**и(ва)ть** *v.* calk, tighten (seam); —**ка** *f.* calking.

расчеренковать *v.* (hort.) propagate by cuttings.

расчер/тить, —**чивать** *v.* trace, line, rule, delineate.

рас/чёсанный *a.* combed, etc., *see* **расчёсывать;** —**чесать** *see* **расчёсывать;** —**чёска** *see* **расчёсывание;** comb.

расчесть *v.* calculate, compute; dismiss.

расчёсыв/ание *n.* combing, etc., *see v.*; —**ать** *v.* comb; card, hackle (flax); scratch (up).

расчёт *m.* calculation, computation, estimation, estimate; sizing, rating (of equipment); account(ing); design, intention; economy; pay(ment); dismissal (from work); crew, team; **р. времени** timing; **р. мощности** capacity rating; **р. на прочность** strength analysis; **р. размеров** dimensioning, sizing; **в —е на** referred to, in terms of; **входить в р.** *v.* be taken into consideration; **из —а** taking into consideration, allowing (for); on the basis (of); at the rate (of); **неполный р.** skeleton crew; **не принимаемый в р.** *a.* negligible; **нет —а** it is not worth; **по его —у** according to him; **принять в р.** *v.* take into consideration, allow (for), take into account; **с таким —ом, чтобы** so that.

расчётлив/ость *f.* economy, thrift; —**ый** *a.* economical, careful, calculating.

расчёт/ность *f.* calculation; rating; design; —**ный** *a.* calculated, estimated, rated; calculating, computing; mathematical (formula); design(ed); slide (rule); budgetary (control); current (account); reference (point); effective (span); gage (length); —**ный стол** network analyzer; —**ная величина** (elec.) rating; —**чик** *m.* calculator, estimator; designer.

расчехл/ить, —**ять** *v.* uncover.

расчисл/ение *n.* calculation, computation, reckoning; —**ить**, —**ять** *v.* calculate, compute, reckon, figure out.

расчист/ить *see* **расчищать;** —**ка** *see* **расчищение.**

расчит/анный на referred to, in terms of; —(**ыв)ать** *v.* calculate; rate (at).

расчищ/ать *v.* clear (away), strip (off); free, open up; eradicate; —**ение** *n.* clearing, etc., *see v.*; —**енный** *a.* cleared, etc., *see v.*; clear, open.

расчлен/ение *n.* separation, breaking up, etc., *see v.*; disjunction; segmentation; **р. на модули** modularization; —**ённость** *f.* (bot.) articulation, lobation (of leaf); (geol.) ruggedness; —**ённый** *a.* separated, etc., *see v.*; (math.) disjoint (sets); mixed (heredity); —**ить**, —**ять** *v.* separate, break up, disconnect; part(ition); dismember, disjoint, disarticulate; analyze, dissect, bisect.

расшат/анность *f.* shakiness, instability; —**анный** *a.* loose(ned), shaky, unstable; shattered; —**ать** *see* **расшатывать;** —**ывание** *n.* loosening, etc., *see v.*; —**ывать** *v.* loosen, shake loose; impair, shatter, upset (health); —**ываться** *v.* get loose(ned); go to pieces.

расшвыр/ивать, —**ять** *v.* throw around, scatter.

расшевели(ва)ть *v.* rouse, stir up, disturb; —**ся** *v.* stir, start moving.

расшив/ание *n.* (masonry) pointing, etc., *see v.*; —**ать** *v.* point; joint; brace; rip, undo; embroider; —**ка** *see* **расшивание;** pointing trowel.

расширен/ие *n.* expansion, widening, etc., *see* **расширять;** spread; development; enlargement; broadening (of spectral lines); dilatation (of the heart); (med.) ectasia, dila(ta)tion, distention; (anat.) ampulla; bulb(us); **р. артерии** aneurysm; **р. артерий** arteriectasia; **р. вен** phlebectasia, varicosity; **р. возможностей** enhancement; **коэффициент —ия** coefficient of expansion; **машина с —ием пара** expansion engine; —**ный** *a.* expanded, etc., *see* **расширять;** flared; extensive.

расширитель *m.* dilator, widener, expander, stretcher, extender; (well drilling) (under)reamer; flash box; (med.) bougie, dilator; —**ный** *a.* expanding, etc., *see* **расширять;** expansion (bolt, tank, valve, etc.); extension (tube).

расшир/ить *see* **расширять;** —**яемость** *f.* expansibility, extensibility, dilatability; degree of expansion; —**яемый** *a.* expansible, extensible, expansive, dilatant, dilatable; —**ять** *v.* expand, widen, broaden, dilate, flare, spread; enlarge, amplify, increase; extend, elongate; develop; —**яться** *v.* expand; bulge out; dilate; flare; —**яющий** *a.* expanding, etc., *see v.*; —**яющая мышца** (anat.) dilator (muscle); —**яющийся** *a.* expansible, extensible, dilatable; expanding, spreading out; expansive (cement).

расшит/ый *a.* pointed, ripped, etc., *see* **расшивать;** —**ь** *see* **расшивать.**

расшифров/ать *see* **расшифровывать;** —**ка** *f.*, —**очный** *a.* decoding, etc., *see v.*; interpretation; expansion; analysis; —**очная машина** decoding machine, interpreter; —**щик** *m.* decoder, interpreter; —**ывание** *see* **расшифровка;** —**ывать** *v.* decode, decipher, interpret; identify (spectra); expand (abbreviation); —**ывать код** *v.* decode.

расшлихтов/ание *n.* (text.) desizing; —**анный** *a.* desized; —**ать** *v.* desize; —**ка** *f.* desizing; —**щик** *m.* desizer; —**ывать** *v.* desize.

расшнуров(ыв)ать *v.* unlace, untie.

расштыбовщик *m.* (min.) gummer.

расшуметься *v.* get noisy.

расщеб/ени(ва)ть *v.* crush; —**ёнка** *f.* crushing; rubble.

расщел/и(ва)ться *v.* crack, split; —**ина** *f.* crack, split, chink, cleft, rift, fissure, crevice, crevasse, interstice, gap, opening; (naut.) lead (in ice); (anat.) hiatus; —**ина неба** (med.) cleft palate; —**истый** *a.* (bot.) —rimose.

расщёлк/ать, —**ивать**, —**нуть** *v.* crack (seeds, nuts).

расщем/ить, —**лять** *v.* unclamp, release; —**лённый** *past pass. part. of* **расщемить.**

расщеп *m.* split, fixture, scissure; (ichth.) enlarged anal scales; **прививка в р.** (hort.) split grafting, cleft grafting; —**ать** *see* **расщеплять;** —**итель** *m.* (beam) splitter; (atom) smasher; —**ить** *see* **расщеплять.**

расщеплен/ие *n.* splitting, decomposition, etc., *see* **расщеплять;** break-up, fission, division, resolution (into); cleavage, (nucl.) spallation; (biol.) segmentation; (gen.) segregation; (chromosome) break; (chem.) breakdown, degradation; (hoof) cleft; fissure; (protein) catabolism; (bot.) dehiscence; —**olysis**, e.g. **р. жира** lipolysis; **постепенное р.** degradation; **продукт —ия** cleavage product, fission product.

расщеплённо— *prefix* schizo — (division, cleavage); —**листный** *a.* (bot.) fissifolious, split-leaved; —**ногие** *pl.* (zool.) Schizopoda.

расщепл/ённый *a.* split, cleaved, etc., *see v.*; extended (dislocation); bundle, multiple (conductor); bifid, forked; divergent; —**ённые ноги** (zool.) fissipeds; —**яемость** *f.* cleavability, fissility, fissionability; cleavage; —**яемый** *a.* cleavable, fissile, fissionable; cleaved, split, broken (bond); —**ять(ся)** *v.* split (up), cleave; separate, break down, decompose, disintegrate, dissociate; rend, fissure, crack, slit; foliate, laminate; splinter, shatter, chip; dehisce; (gen.) segregate; lacerate; —**яющий** *a.* splitting, etc., *see v.*; —lytic, e.g. —**яющий жиры** lipolytic; —**яющийся** *a.* splitting, etc., *see v.*; cleavable, fissile, fissionable, scissile; breaking up, disappearing; splintery (fracture).

расщепобрюхий *a.* (ent.) schizothoracic.

расщепывание *see* **расщепление.**

расщип(ыв)ать *v.* pick apart, shred.

ратан/ин *m.* rhatanin, angelin; —**ия** *f.* (bot.) rhatany (*Krameria triandra*); —**овая кислота** rhatanic acid, krameric acid.

ратели *pl.* (mam.) honeybadgers (*Mellivora*).

ратин *m.* (text.) ratteen, frieze; —**ировать** *v.* frieze, curl; —**ирующий** *a.* (text.) plush (machine).

ратифи/кация *f.* ratification; —**цировать** *v.* ratify, validate.

Ратке карман (embr.) Rathke's pouch.

раткеа *f.* (zool.) Rathkea.

Рато турбина Rateau turbine.

РАТУ *abbr.* (**расчётные атмосферные температурные условия**) rated atmospheric temperature conditions.

ратуфа *f.* giant squirrel (*Ratufa*).

раувольфия *f.* (bot.) Rauwolfia.

Рауля закон Raoult's law.

Рауса критерий Routh's criterion.

раухтопаз *m.* (min.) smoky quartz, smoky topaz.

рауш-наркоз *m.* (med.) etherrausch.

рафан/ин *m.* raphanin; —**ол** *m.* raphanol.

рафаэлит *m.* (min.) rafaelite.

рафе *n.* (anat.) raphe, seam.

рафид *m.,* —**а** *f.* (bioch.; bot.) raphide; —**аскаридоз** *m.* (ichth.) raphidascaridosis.

рафинад *m.* refined (lump) sugar; —**ный** *a.* refining; —**ный завод** sugar refinery.

рафин/аза *f.* raffinase; —**ат** *m.* raffinate.

рафин/ация *see* **рафинирование;** —**ер** *m.,* —**ерный** *a.* (paper) refiner; —**ировальщик** *m.* refiner; —**ирование** *n.* (re)fining, refinement, purification; —**ированный** *a.* refined, purified; cleared; —**ировать** *v.* refine, purify; clear; —**ировка** *f.,* —**ировочный** *a.* (re)fining; —**ировочный завод** refinery.

рафия *f.* raffia (fiber; palm).

раффин/ат *m.* raffinate; —**оза** *f.* (biochem.) melitose.

раффлезия *f.* (bot.) Rafflesia.

рахиальгия *f.* (med.) rachialgia, pain in vertebral column.

рахи/(о)— *prefix* rachi(o)— (spine); —**опатия** *f.* (med.) rachiopathy; —**с** *m.* rachis, vertebral column; —**схиз** *m.* (med.) rachischisis; **задний —схиз** spina bifida.

рахит *m.* (med.) rickets; —**изм** *m.* rachitism, tendency to rickets; —**ик** *m.* rickets patient; —**ический, —ичный** *a.* rachitic; —**огенный** *a.* rachitogenic, causing rickets.

рахитомия *f.* (med.) rachitomy, surgical opening of vertebral column.

рахицентровые *pl.* (ichth.) cobias (*Rachycentridae*).

рацем/аза *f.* (enz.) racemase; —**ат** *m.* (chem.) racemate; —**изация** *f.,* —**изирование** *n.* racemization; —**изировать** *v.* racemize; —**ический** *a.* racemic; —**ия** *f.* racemism; —**озный** *a.* (bot.) racemose.

рацефе/дрин *m.* (pharm.) racephedrine; —**мин** *m.* racefemine; —**н** *m.* racephen, phenamine.

рацион *m.* ration, food allowance.

рационализ/атор *m.* rationalizer; innovator; efficiency expert; —**аторский** *a.* efficiency; —**аторское пре**-**дложение** innovation, improvement; —**аторство** *n.* efficiency work; —**ация** *f.* (math.) rationalization; efficiency promotion; improvement (in production methods); simplification (of motion, work); —**(ир)овать** *v.* rationalize; innovate; improve, make more efficient, streamline.

рациональн/о *adv.* rationally; efficiently; it is sound practice;—**ость** *f.* (math.) rationality; efficiency; —**ый** *a.* rational (formula, number); efficient, expedient; sensible; —**ое использование** conservation, management (of resources).

рацион(«ров/ание *n.* rationing; —**анный** *a.* rationed; —**ать** *v.* ration.

рация *f.* radio station; hand-held radio transceiver, walkie-talkie.

рачий *a.* crayfish.

рачка *f.* ratchet; **сверлильная р.** ratchet drill.

рачки *pl. of* **рачок; ракушковые р.** *pl.* (crust.) Ostracoda.

рачок *dim. of* **рак.**

Рашига кольца Raschig rings.

рашкуль *m.* charcoal pencil.

рашпилевидный *a.* (bot.) raduliform, rasp-like.

рашпиль *m.* rasp (file), grate(r); (constr.) float; (zool.) radula.

рашплевые *pl.* (ichth.) angelsharks (*Squatinidae*).

рашпля *f.* angelshark, monkfish.

ращение *n.* raising, growing; roching (of alum).

ращённый *a.* raised, grown.

рб *abbr.* (**разбавленный**) diluted.

рб. *abbr.* (**рубль**) ruble.

РБ *abbr.* (**разнояйцовые близнецы**) fraternal, dizygotic twins.

РБМК *abbr.* (**реактор большой мощности канальный**) uranium graphite channel-type reactor, RBMK reactor.

рва *gen. of* **ров.**

рвал *past m. sing. of* **рвать.**

рван/ина *f.* fissure, crack; laceration, tear; flaw; transverse crack; (rolling) scab; —**уть** *v.* pull, jerk; —**ый** *a.* torn, lacerated; broken, ragged; —**ь** *f.* rag(s) (spinning) waste; (tech.) clamp; —**ьё** *n.* rag(s); tearing.

рват/ель *m.* (core) lifter, extractor; —**ь** *v.* tear, lacerate; sever, break; pull, extract, pick, gather; vomit; —**ься** *v.* tear; strain (at); break, snap; burst, explode; long (for).

рвение *n.* fervor, zeal.

рвет *pr. 3 sing. of* **рвать.**

рвота *f.* vomiting, emesis; (met.) flaw; **р. крови** (med.) hematemesis; **сухая р.** retching.

рвотное *n.* emetic.

рвотн/ый *a.* emetic; **р. камень** tartar emetic, antimonyl potassium tartrate; **р. корень** ipecac root, ipecacuanha; **р. орех** (bot.) nux vomica (seeds); —**ое средство** emetic.

рву/т *pr. 3 pl. of* **рвать; —шка** *f.* tension link; —**щий** *a.* tearing, etc., *see* **рвать;** breaking (stress).

РГА *abbr.* (**реакция гемагглютинации**) hemagglutination reaction.

РГЧ *abbr.* (**разделяющаяся головная часть**) reentry vehicle.

рд *abbr.* (**резерфорд**) rutherford; (**регулятор давления**) pressure regulator.

рде/лый *a.* red; —**ние** *n.* redness, glow.

рдест(ник) *m.* pond weed (*Potamogeton*).

рде/ть(ся) *v.* redden, glow; —**ющий** *a.* glowing.

РДО (**реакция на движущийся объект**) reaction to a moving object.

РДП *abbr.* (**ранцевый дегазационный прибор**) portable decontaminator; (**устройство для работы дви-гателя под водой**) snorkel.

РДС *abbr.* (**район диспетчерской службы**) control tower area.

РД(Т)Т *abbr.* (**ракетный двигатель твёрдого то-плива**) solid-propellant rocket engine.

рдяный *a.* scarlet, red.

ре *n.* rhe (unit of fluidity); (music) D; **Pe** *abbr.* (**число Рейнольдса**) Reynolds number.

ре— *prefix* re—, back, again.

реабилит/ация *f.* rehabilitation; **—ировать** *v.* rehabilitate.

реабсорб/ировать *v.* reabsorb; **—ция** *f.* reabsorption.

реагенин *n.* rhoeagenine.

реагент *m.* (chem.) (re)agent, reactant; **р.-коагулянт** flocculation chemical; **р.-регулятор** *m.* conditioning agent; (min.) modifier.

реагир/ование *n.* reacting, reaction, response; **скорость —ования** responsiveness; **—ованный** *a.* reacted; **—овать** *v.* react; respond; **неспособный —овать** *a.* (chem.) inert; **—ующий** *a.* reactive, reactive; responsive (to); **—ующее вещество** reactant; **быстро —ующий** sensitive; **не —ующий** nonreacting, nonreactive.

реадаптация *f.* readaptation.

реад/ин *m.* rhoeadine; **—овая кислота** rhoeadic acid, papaveric acid.

реакклиматизация *f.* reacclimatization.

реактан/с, —ц *m.* (elec.) reactance.

реактив *m.* (re)agent; **—ор**, e.g. **индикаторный р.** indicator; **р. на группу** group reagent; **—ация** *f.*, **—ирование** *n.* reactivation; **—ированный** *a.* reactivated; **—ировать** *v.* reactivate; revive; **—ность** *f.* reactivity; (elec.) reactance; **указатель —ности** reactimeter.

реактивн/ый *a.* reactive, reaction; recoil (force); reagent (bottle, solution, etc.); (elec.) reactive; reactance (tube); jet-propelled, jet-powered, jet (engine); rocket (motor); retrorocket (braking); **р. снаряд** rocket, missile; **р. цилиндр** test tube; **—ая катушка** (elec.) reactor, reactance coil; **—ая проводимость** (elec.) susceptance; **—ая сила** jet power; **—ая трубка** test tube; **—ое движение** jet propulsion; **—ое сопротивление** (elec.) reactance, reactive resistance; **—ое средство** reagent; **с —ым двигателем** jet-propelled.

реактиметр *m.* reactimeter.

реактогенный *a.* eliciting (stimulus).

реактопласты *pl.* thermosetting plastics.

реактор *m.* reaction vessel; (nucl., chem.) reactor; (elec.) reactor, reactance coil; **р. на тепловых нейтронах** thermal reactor; **р. с кольцевой активной зоной** annular core reactor; **тепловой р.** thermal reactor; **р.-двигатель** *m.* propulsion reactor; **р.-конвертер** *m.* converter; **—ная техника** reactor engineering; **—остроение** *n.* reactor construction; **р.-размножитель** *m.* breeder reactor; **р.-размножитель на быстрых нейтронах** fast breeder reactor.

реакционн/о-инертный *a.* reactionless; **—оспособность** *f.* reactivity; **—оспособный** *a.* reactive; **—ость** *f.* reactivity; **—ый** *a.* reaction; **—ая способность, —ые свойства** reactivity.

реакц/ия *f.* reaction; interaction, reciprocity; response; (elec.) reactance; **р. на** reaction for; **р. на воздействие** response; **р. на крахмал** starch reaction; **р. первого порядка** (chem.) first order reaction; **р. почвы** soil reaction, *p*H; **конец —ии** end point; **ответная р.** response; **отсутствие —ии** unresponsiveness; inertness; stolidity; **подвергнуть —ии** *v.* react; **продукты —ии** reaction products.

реал *m.* (typ.) composing frame, rack.

реализ/атор *m.* (gen.) sex differentiator; **—ация** *f.* realization; implementation; sale; **—(ир)ованный** *a.* realized; **—(ир)овать** *v.* realize; implement; convert to cash; **—(ир)оваться** *v.* be achieved; **—уемый** *a.* feasible; possible.

реалист *m.* realist; **—ический** *a.* realistic.

реальгар *m.* (min.) realgar.

реальн/ость reality; **—ый** *a.* real, tangible, concrete; workable, practicable; **в реальном (масштабе) времени** real-time.

Реамюра шкала (phys.) Réaumur scale.

реанимация *f.* resuscitation.

реассимилирование *n.* reassimilation.

реаэрация *f.* reaeration.

ребёнок *m.* child, infant.

рёбер *gen. pl. of* **ребро**; **—но—** *prefix* (anat.) costo—, rib; **—но-диафрагмальный** *a.* costodiaphragmatic; **—но-ключичный** *a.* costoclavicular; **—но-мечевидный** *a.* costoxiphoid; **—но-позвоночный** *a.* costovertebral; **—ный** *a.* rib, costal; **—ные пластинки** (zool.) costalia.

реборд/а *f.*, **—ный** *a.* flange, rim, bead.

ребра *gen. of* **ребро**.

рёбра *pl. of* **ребро**; costae; ribbing; **снабжён —ми** *a.* finned.

ребристо/призматический *a.* angularprismatic; **—сть** *f.* ribbing; **—трубчатый, —тубулярный** *a.* fin-tube.

ребрист/ый *a.* ribbed, costate, costal; finned, corrugated; gilled; sectional (roller); edge (point); (geol.) mullion, rodding (structure); **р. нагреватель** radiator; **р. плитчатый** *a.* plate fin; **—ая труба** grilled tube.

ребр/о *n.* rib, fin; edge, verge; (geol.) ridge; riffle; (arch.) arris; *see also* **рёбра**; **краевое р.** (pal.) marginal frill; **—оверхняя (кость)** *f.* (anat.) epipleural (bone); **—ом** edgewise; bluntly, point-blank; **поставить —ом** *v.* stand edgewise, stand on edge.

ребровый *a. of* **ребро**.

рёбрышко *dim. of* **ребро**; (biol.) costula.

ребя/та *pl. of* **ребёнок**; **—ческий** *a.* child's, childish; **—чество** *n.* childish behavior; **—чий** *a.* child's; immature; **—читься** *v.* behave childishly; **—чливый** *a.* childlike, childish.

рёв *m.* howl(ing), etc., *see* **реветь**.

ревакцинация *f.* (med.) revaccination.

ревальвация *f.* revaluation.

ревен/ный *a.*, **—ь** *m.* rhubarb.

ревербер *m.* reverberator; reverberatory furnace; reflecting lamp; **—ационный** *a.* reverberation, reverberative, reflective; **—ация** *f.* reverberation; **—ировать** *v.* reverberate; **—ирующий** *a.* reverberating, reverberative; **—ный** *a.* reverberatory (furnace); **—ометр** *m.* reverberometer.

реверзум *m.* (myc.) reversum.

реверс *m.* reverse, reversing gear; reversal; rundown (of nuclear reactor); **—ер** *m.* reverser; **—ивность** *f.* reversibility; **—ивный** *a.* reversible, reversing, reverse; sign-alternating; reversible-polarity (transducer); two-way (feeder); forward/backward (pulse counter); **—ивная коробка** reversing gear box; **—ир** *m.* reverser; **—ирование** *n.* reversing, reversal, reverse; **—ированный** *a.* reversed; **—(ир)овать** *v.* reverse; **—ируемость** *f.* reversibility; **—ируемый** *a.* reversible; **—ирующий** *a.* reversing, reverse; **—ирующее приспособление** reverser; **—ия** *f.* reversal; reversion, throwback, atavism; **—ор** *m.* reverser.

реветь *v.* howl (of dog, wolf); low, bellow (of cattle); bray (of donkey); roar (of lion); rage (of storm); squeal, howl (of radio).

ревивиф/айер *m.* revivifier; **—икация** *f.* revivification, reactivation.

ревиз/ионный *a.* revisionary, revisory; inspection; auditing (of accounts); **—ия** *f.* revision; examination, inspection; audit (of accounts); census (of population); **—овать** *v.* revise; examine, inspect, audit; test; **—ор** *m.* inspector, auditor.

ревильон *m.* Reveillon typeface.

ревм/артрит *m.* (med.) rheumatoid arthritis.

ревмат/альгия *f.* rheumatalgia, chronic rheumatic pain; **—изм** *m.* (med.) rheumatism; **мышечный —изм** *m.* muscular rheumatism, fibrositis rheumatism; **острый суставной —изм** acute articular rheumatism, rheumatic fever; **—ик** *m.*, **—ический** *a.* rheumatic; **—ический узелки** (med.) Aschoff's nodules; **—оидный** *a.* rheumatoid; **—олог** *m.* rheumatologist.

ревмокардит *m.* (med.) rheumatic carditis, rheumatic heart disease.

ревн/ивый *a.* jealous; **—ость** *f.* jealousy.

ревокация *f.* revocation; stopping payment (of check).

револьвер *m.* revolver; (micros.) nosepiece.

револьверн/ый *a.* revolving; revolver; **р. станок** turret lather.

револьверщик *m.* turret lathe operator.

револю/ионизировать *v.* revolutionize; **—ионный** *a.* revolutionary; **—ия** *f.* revolution.

ревун *m.* siren; foghorn; (zool.) howler (monkey) (*Alouatta*); bawling child.

рег. *abbr.* **(регистр; регистровый).**

рег *m.* (geog.) reg, desert region of North Africa.

регенерант *m.* regenerate.

регенерат *m.* reclaim, reclaimed rubber; regenerate; **—ивный** *a.* regenerative, regeneration; **—ивное считывание** (comp.) regenerative read, read and restore (cycle); **—ный** *a. of* **регенерат**; **—ор** *m.* reclaimer; regenerator.

регенер/ационный *a.*, **—ация** *f.*, **—ирование** *n.* regeneration, reclaiming, etc., *see v.*; (comp.) log-in; recovery; **счётчик —ации** (comp.) refresh counter; **—ированный** *a.* regenerated, etc., *see v.*; **—ировать** *v.* regenerate, reclaim, recover, restore, reestablish, revive; reprocess; reactivate; (comp.) retransmit (signal); refresh; **—ироваться** *v.* (comp.) log in; **—ируемый** *a.* regenerable, reclaimable, recoverable.

регион *m.* region; **—ализация** *f.* regionalization; **—альность** *f.* regionality; **—альный** *a.* regional, district; local (anaesthetic); **—арный** *a.* (med.) regional.

регистр *m.* register, list, index; damper; (typ.) case; **—атор** *m.* registrar, recorder; plotter; recording system; monitor; (pulse) storing device; **—атура** *f.* registry, registration office; **—ационный** *a.*, **—ация** *f.*, **—ирование** *n.* registration, recording, etc., *see v.*; (comp.) login, logon; **карта —ации** recording chart; **—(ир)ованный** *a.* registered, etc., *see v.*; **—ировать** *v.* register, record, enter, file; enroll; (comp.) log in; monitor, follow (with instrument); log, keep a record; (information) post, identify; detect; charge (library book); **—(ир)ующий** *a.* registering, etc., *see v.*; data-acquisition (equipment); **—ирующий прибор** recorder; **—овый** *a. of* **регистр**.

регитин *m.* Regitine, phentolamine.

регламент *m.* regulation, rule, (standing) order, procedure; **согласно —у** in order; **—ация** *f.* regulation; **—ированный** *a.* regulated; **—ировать** *v.* regulate, fix, control; stipulate; **—ный** *a. of* **регламент**; operational (check).

регма *f.* (bot.) regma.

реград/ация *f.* (soil) regradation; **—ировать** *v.* regrade.

регресс *m.* re(tro)gression, regress, return, retrogradation; **—ивность** *f.* regressivity; **—ивный** *a.* regressive; regression (analysis); **—ированный** *a.* re(tro)gressed; **—ировать** *v.* re(tro)gress, retrograde; **—ия** *f.* regression.

регулиров/ание *n.* regulation, control, governing, management; arrangement, setting, adjustment, tuning; alignment, line-up; monitoring; **р. по времени** time control; **—анный** *a.* regulated, etc., *see v.*; **—ать** *v.* regulate, control, govern, gage; set, adjust, tune; align, line up; **—ка** *see* **регулирование.**

регулир/овочный *see* **регулирующий; —овочное приспособление** adjuster; **—овщик** *m.* regulator; **—уемость** *f.* controllability; **—уемый** *a.* controllable, adjustable; controlled, regulated; variable-area (diffuser); (math.) variable (drive); **—уемый человеком** manipulated.

регулирующ/ий *a.* regulating, regulator, control(ling), governing, adjusting; **р. клапан** regulator valve, throttle (valve); **р. элемент** control(ler); **—ее воздействие** input variable; **—ее приспособление** control device, adjustment device, adjuster; governor; **—ийся** *a.* adjustable; controlled (by).

регулы *pl.* (physiol.) menstruation, menses.

регулярн/о *adv.* regularly, at regular intervals; **—ость** *f.* regularity, order; **—ый** *a.* regular, routine.

регуля/тивный *a.* regulating, controlling, guiding; **—тор** *m.* regulator, control(ler), adjuster; governor; **шаровой —тор** ball governor; **—торный** *a. of* **регулятор**; regulatory; **—торзаслонка** *m.* damper regulator; **—ционный, —ция** *see* **регулирование.**

регур *m.* (agr.) regur, black loam.

регургитация *f.* regurgitation.

ред. *abbr.* **(редактирован, редактор, редакционный, редакция).**

ред— *prefix* editorial; *m. suffix* editor.

редак/тирование *n.* editing; **—тирован(ный)** *a.* edited; **—тировать** *v.* edit; **—тор** *m.* editor; (comp.) word processor; **главный —тор** editor-in-chief; **—ториздатель** *m.* publisher; **—торский** *a.* editorial; **—торство** *n.* editorship, editorial work; **—торствовать** *v.* do editorial work; **—тура** *f.* editing; **—ционный** *a.* editorial; **—ция** *f.* editing; wording; editorship; editor's office; editorial staff; editorial board; **от —ции** editor's note; **под —цией** edited (by).

реддитивный *a.* restorative.

редек *gen. pl. of* **редька.**

редели *pl.* hay-drying rack.

редемаркация *f.* redemarcation.

редеть *v.* thin out, become less frequent; be depleted.

редечный *a. of* **редька.**

редина *f.* open-weave cloth; burlap, sacking; (silv.) thin forest.

Рединг *m.* (geog.) Reading.

рединный *a. of* **редина.**

редис *m.*, **—ка** *f.* garden radish.

редистилляция *f.* redistillation, rerun.

редия *f.* (zool.) redia, a trematode larva.

редк/ий *a.* rare, uncommon, infrequent, scarce, sparse; exotic (species); extraordinary; dispersed; drift (ice); loose, thin; loosely woven, open-weave; **—ая вещь** curiosity, rarity; **—ие земли** rare earths.

редко *adv.* rarely, seldom; *prefix* rare; oligo— (few, scant); (bot.) laxi— (scattered); span(o)— (scarce); **—вато** *adv.* rather rarely; moderately; economically; **—ватый** *a.* rather rare; **—волосый** *a.* (zool.) bare-skinned; **—земельный** *a.* rare-earth; **—зубый** *a.* with widely spaced teeth; **—колючковый** *a.* (bot.) sparsely thorned.

редкол *m.* editorial board.

редко/лесный *a.*, **—лесье** *n.* open woodland, thin forest; **—листный** *a.* (bot.) laxifoliate.

редколлегия *f.* editorial staff, editorial board.

редко/метальный *a.* rare-metal; **—населённый** *a.* sparsely populated; **—стный** *a.* rare, infrequent; **—стойный** *a.* thin, open (forest); **—столбчатый** *a.* oligobaculate (grain); **—сть** *f.* rarity, rareness, infrequency; **—цветковый** *a.* (bot.) rariflorous, spananthous.

редно *n.* coarse hempen cloth, sacking.

редокс *m.* redox, reduction-oxidation; **—аза** *f.* redoxase; **—(и)потенциал** *m.* redox potential.

редрессация *f.* redressing, correction.

редуктаза *f.* reductase (enzyme).

редукто— *prefix* reducto—.

редуктор *m.* reducer, reducing agent; reductor (apparatus); (pressure) regulator; (mech.) reducer; reduction gear; gearbox; reducing valve; speed reducer, decelerator; **—ный** *a. of* **редуктор**; geared; **р.-трансформатор** (elec.) step-down transformer.

редукци/онный *a. of* **редукция; р. вентиль** reducer, reducing valve, pressure regulator; **—онное деление** (biol.) meiosis; **—онное тельце** (gen.) polar body, polocyte; **—я** *f.* reduction, reducing; loss, dwindling; (gen.) segregation.

редунка *f.* (mam.) reedbuck (*Redunca*).

редупликация *f.* reduplication.

редуцир/ование *n.* reduction; loss, decrease; **—ованный** *a.* reduced; vestigial (structure); **—овать(ся)** *v.* reduce, decrease, diminish; dwindle; **—ующий** *a.* reducing; **—ующий фермент** reductase.

редчайший *superl. of* **редкий.**

редьк/а *f.* radish; **—овидный** *a.* (bot.) rapiform.

редюсинг *m.* reducing.

ре/ек *gen. pl. of* **рейка; —ёк** *m.* (naut.) yard.

реестр *m.*, **—овый** *a.* register, list, file, catalog; record.

реет *pr. 3 sing. of* **реять.**

реечн/ик *m.* (geod.) rodman; **—о-шестерёночный** *a.* rack and pinion; **—ый** *a. of* **рейка;** rack (and pinion) (gear); rack; rake, drag (classifier); shingle (nail).

режак *m.* (fishing) a type of trammel net.

реже *comp. of* **редкий;** rare, less common(ly).

режевый *a.* large-meshed (net).

режект/ирующий *a.* rejecting; trap; **—ор** *m.* rejector; **—орный** *a.* rejector, rejective; band-elimination (filter).

режет *pr. 3 sing. of* **резать.**

режим *m.* regime, system, practice(s), method(s), process; (normal) operation, routine, running, working, service, duty, performance; characteristics; behavior, mode; (operating) conditions, state; cycle, rate, schedule; rating (of engine); (reservoir) drive; (med.) regimen, treatment; *frequently not translated but absorbed in idiom;* **р. грунтовых вод** subterranean water system; **р. запуска** start-up conditions; **р. заряда** charging (rate); **р. кипения** boiling; **р. питания** diet; **р. потока** flow; **р. при заряде** charging load; **р. работы** routine, procedure; operating conditions; (comp.) operating mode; (mach.) performance, duty; service, operation, running; **в проточном —е** continuous-flow; **вихревой р. потока** turbulent flow; **водный р.** water balance; **многозадачный** (comp.) multitasking; **работа в критическом —е** critical operation; **с лёгким —ом** light-duty; **—ные параметры** process conditions.

режут *pr. 3 pl. of* **резать.**

режуха *see* **резуха.**

режущ/ий *a.* cutting, slicing; sharp (pain); (anat.) inci-

sive; secodont; **р. зуб** tool edge, blade; **р. инструмент** cutter; slicer; **р. орган** lancet (in nematodes); **—ое ребро** tool edge, blade; **хорошо р.** sharp, keen.

ре/жьте *imp. of* **резать; —з** *m.* cut; kerf.

резазурин *m.* resazurin, diazoresorcinol.

рез/ак *m.* cutter, knife, blade; chopper; forge chisel; (cutting) torch; plowshare, colter; lip (of scoop); butcher; (bot.) Falcaria; sedge (*Carex gracilis*); **—алка** *f.* cutter.

рез/альгин *m.* resalgin, antipyreticin; **—альдол** *m.* resaldol.

рез/альный *a.* cutting; **—альщик** *m.* cutter; **—ание** *n.* cutting, etc., see *v.*; **—ан(н)ый** *a.* cut, etc., see *v.*; **—ательный** *a.* cutting, etc., see *v.*; **—ать** *v.* cut, clip, sever; slice, slit; slaughter, butcher; engrave.

резацетофенон *m.* resacetophenone, 2,4-dihydroxyacetophenone.

резачок *m.* bit, point, tip.

резв/иться *v.* frolic, romp, play; **—ость** *f.* playfulness; speed (of horse); **—ый** *a.* playful, frisky; fast (horse).

резед/а *f.*, **—овый** *a.* (bot.) mignonette (*Reseda*).

резекция *f.* (med.) resection; (med.) **—ектомия**, e.g. **р. лёгкого** pneumonectomy.

резен *m.* resene.

резерв *m.* reserve, depot; margin; backup, redundancy; standby; drainage canal; dump hole; **р. мощности** reserve capacity; **холодный р.** cold standby; **—аж** *m.* (text.) resist, reserve; **—ат** *m.* reservation, sanctuary; **—ация** *f.*, **—ирование** *n.* reserve, reservation; redundancy; **—ировать** *v.* reserve, save; **—ный** *a.* reserve, spare, standby, stored (fat, etc.), emergency, subsidiary; backup, overflow (stock); **—ная установка** emergency service.

резервуар *m.*, **—ный** *a.* reservoir, receiver, receptacle, container, basin, cistern, tank, flask, vessel, well; source, seat (of disease); **р.-накопитель** *m.* impounding basin, retention basin; **р.-хранилище** *m.* storage tank.

резервы *pl. of* **резерв;** reserves, resources.

резерпин *m.* reserpine.

резерфорд *m.* rutherford (unit of radioactivity); **—овский** *a.* Rutherford.

резец *m.* cutter, (cutting) tool; knife, blade, chisel; (drill) bit; colter (of plow); (anat.) incisor.

резецировать *v.* (med.) resect, cut out.

резид *m.* remainder, residue.

резиден/т *m.* resident; **—тный** *a.* (comp.) (memory-)resident; **—ция** *f.* residence.

резидуальный *a.* residual.

резильянс *m.* resilience.

резина *f.* (vulcanized) rubber; rubber band.

резин/амин *m.* resinamine; **—ат** *m.* resinate.

резина-утиль *f.* scrap rubber.

резин/еон *m.* resineon; **—ировать** *v.* (wines) resinate.

резинка *f.* elastic, rubber band; eraser.

резино/вый *a.* rubber; **—вый клей** rubber cement; **—вая смесь** rubber stock; **—губчатый** *a.* foam rubber.

резиноид *m.* resinoid.

резинол *m.* resinol.

резино/подобный *a.* rubbery; **—смеситель** *m.* rubber mixer, masticator; **—содержащий** *a.* rubber-containing.

резинотаннол *m.* resinotannol.

резин/отехнический *a.* industrial rubber; **—отканевый** *a.* rubber(ized)-fabric; **—щик** *m.* worker in rubber industry.

резист *m.* resist, protective layer; (microelectronics) photoresist; **—ентность** *f.* resistance; **—ентный** *a.* resistant; **—ер** *m.* (elec.) resistor; resistance; **—ивность** *f.* (elec.) resistivity, specific resistance; **—ивный** *a.* resistive, resistance(-coupled); **—омицин** *m.* resistomycin; **—ор** *m.* (elec.) resistor; **бескорпусный р.** resistor chip; **интегральный р.** on-chip resistor; **навесной р.** off-chip resistor.

резит *m.* resite, C-stage resin; **—ол** *m.* (plastics) resitol.

резка *f.* cutting, etc., *see* **резать;** cuttings; slicing; *sh. f. of* **резкий.**

резк/ий *a.* sharp, abrupt, sudden, drastic, catastrophic, extreme, pronounced, marked; severe (scolding); acute, distinct, crisp (outlines); shrill, piercing (sound); pungent, acrid; **—о** *adv.* sharply, etc., *see a.;* **—о выраженный** *a.* clearly defined, marked, pronounced; **—о обозначенный** *a.* well-defined; **—ость** *f.* sharpness, etc., *see a.;* (phot.) definition; acuity; **наводить на —ость** *v.* (phot.) focus.

резнатрон *m.* (electron.) resnatron, high-power tetrode.

резн/ой *a.* cut, carved, fretted; **—ая работа** carving; **—уть** *v.* (make a) cut; **—я** *f.* slaughter.

резок *sh. m. of* **резкий;** *gen. pl. of* **резка.**

резол *m.* resol.

резольвент/а *f.,* **—ный** *a.* resolvent.

резольный *a.* resol.

резолюция *f.* resolution, decision.

резон *m.* reason; **—анс** *m.* (acous.) resonance; **—ансный** *a.* resonance; resonance; fluorescent (lamp); **—атор** *m.* resonator, vibrator; (resonant) cavity; **—аторный** *a.* cavity (magnetron); resonator (accelerator); **—ировать** *v.* resonate; **—ирующий** *a.* resonating, resonant.

резонный *a.* reasonable, rational.

резонон *m.* resonon.

резорб/ированный *a.* re(ab)sorbed; **—ировать** *v.* re(ab)sorb; **—тивный** *a.* resorptive; **—ция** *f.* resorption.

резорциловокислый *a.* resorcylic acid; resorcylate (of).

резорцилов/ый *a.* resorcyl; **—ая кислота** resorcylic acid, dihydroxybenzoic acid.

резорцин *m.,* **—овый** *a.,* **—ол** *m.* resorcin(ol); **—изм** *m.* resorcin poisoning; **—овый голубой** resorcin blue (microchemical stain).

резо/флавин *m.* resoflavin (dye); **—цианин** *m.* resocyanine.

резочный *a.* cutting.

результант *m.* (math.) resultant.

результат *m.* result, consequence, outcome, effect; yield; product; corollary; (foregone) conclusion; **—ом этого было** the result was (that); **в —е** as a result, in consequence; by, from, upon; **в —е чего** with the result that; **в —е этого** as a result, in consequence; **иметь —ом** *v.* result (in), give rise (to); **полученный —ом** *a.* resulting; **происходить в —е, явиться —ом** *v.* result, arise, stem (from), be due (to); **—ивный** *a.* result-producing, successful; effective; final, closing (balance); **—ный** *a.* resulting, resultant; **—ы** *pl.* data, findings.

результирующ/ий *a.* resulting, resultant; net (loss, etc.); composite (field); **—ая величина** (math.) resultant.

резус *m.* (zool.) rhesus (*Macaca mulatta*); **р.-фактор** *m.* rhesus factor, Rh-factor.

резу/ха *f.* (bot.) rock cress (*Arabis*); **—шка** *f.* a cress (*Arabidopsis*).

резца *f.* (anat.) incisor; *gen. of* **резец.**

резце— *prefix* cutter, tool; **—видный** *a.* (bot.) chisel-shaped, scalpriform; **—державка** *f.,* **—держатель** *m.* tool holder, tool post, tool clamp, tool block; tool box.

резцов/ый *a.* tool, cutter; incisor (tooth); incisive (suture); **—ая кость** (anat.) incisive bone; (embr.) premaxilla.

резче *comp. of* **резкий, резко.**

резч/ик *m.* cutter, engraver, carver; chisel; **—ицкий** *a. of* **резчик;** carving.

резь *f.* (med.) colic, sharp pain.

резьб/а *f.* carving, engraving, fretwork; (screw) thread; **нарезать —у** *v.* thread.

резьбов/ой *a.* thread(ing); threaded, screw (joint); **р. гребец** threading tool, chaser; **р. калибр** thread gage; **р. резец** chaser; **р. фрезер** thread-milling cutter; **—ая гребёнка** chaser; **—ые часы** thread indicator.

резьбо/измерительный инструмент, —мер *m.* thread gage, screw pitch gage; **—накат(оч)ный** *a.* thread-rolling; **—нарезной** *a.* threading, thread-cutting; **—рез** *m.* thread cutter; **—сверлильный** *a.* tapping; **—токарный станок** threading lathe; **—указатель** *m.* thread indicator; **—фрезерный** *a.* thread-milling; **—шлифовальный** *a.* thread-grinding.

резюм/е *n.* résumé, summary, synopsis; **—ировать** *v.* summarize, sum up.

реин *m.,* **—овая кислота** rhein, rheinic acid.

реинфекция *f.* (med.) reinfection.

рей *m.* (naut.) yard.

рейб/ал, —ол, —ор *m.* reamer, broach.

рейд *m.* raid; dash; (naut.) road(stead), harbor.

Рейда бомба Reid (vapor pressure) bomb.

рейд/ер *m.* raider; **—ировать** *v.,* **—овый** *a. of* **рейд;** coastal.

рейк/а *f.* lath, batten, cleat; edging, strip; (measuring) rod; stick, staff; (depth) gage; (graduated) rule; (mach.) rack; **передача зубчатой —ой** rack and pinion (gear); **—овый** *a. of* **рейка.**

рейлиев островок (anat.) insula of Reil.

Реймс (geog.) R(h)eims.

рейнвейн *m.* Rhine wine.

Рейно болезнь Raynaud's disease.

Рейнольдса число Reynolds number.

рейнск/ий *a.* (geog.) Rhine; **—ое** *n.* Rhine wine.

рейс *m.* run, stretch, (round) trip; flight; passage, voyage.

Рейса микрофон Reis microphone.

рейсм/ас, —ус *m.* scribing block, surface gage; marking tool; shifting gage; planer.

рейснерова перепонка (anat.) Reissner's membrane.

рейсовый *a. of* **рейс;** scheduled (flight).

рейстрек *m.* (phys.) race track.

рейс/федер *m.* drawing pen; pencil holder; **—шина** *f.* T-square.

рейтер *m.* rider (of analytical balance).

Рейтера синдром (med.) Reiter's syndrome.

рейтузы *pl.* tights, (diver's) drawers.

Рейхеля проток клоаки (anat.) Reichel's cloacal duct.

Рейхерт-Мейссля число (butter analysis) Reichert-Meissl number.

рейхс— *prefix* Reichs—.

рейян *m.* Reyan (solid propellant).

рек/а *f.* river, stream; **р.-захватчик** pirate river; **вверх по —е** upstream.

рекапитуляци/я *f.* (biol.) recapitulation; **теория —и** recapitulation theory, biogenetic law.

рекарбюриз/атор *m.* (met.) recarburizer; **—ация** *f.* recarburization; **—ировать** *v.* recarburize, recarbonize.

рекаталогизация *f.* recataloging.

рекаулесценция *f.* (bot.) recaulescence.

реквиз/ировать *v.,* **—иция** *f.,* **—иционный** *a.* requisition.

реки *gen., pl., etc., of* **река.**

реклам/а *f.* advertisement; publicity; **—ация** *f.* reclamation; protest, complaint; claim; **—ировать** *v.* advertise; make a claim; **—ный** *a.* advertising; publicity; **—ный листок** handbill, flyer; **—одатель** *m.* advertiser.

реклассификация *f.* reclassification.

Реклингаузена болезнь Recklinghausen's disease of the bone.

реко— *prefix* potam(o)—, river.

рекогносциров/ать *v.* reconnoiter, survey, explore, scout; **—ка** *f.*, **—очный** *a.* reconnoitering, etc., *see v.*; reconnaissance; **—очно-поисковые методы** (petrol.) reconnaissance prospecting; **—очный** *a.* baseline (studies).

рекой *adv.* in a stream, copiously.

реколюбивый *a.* potamophilous, river-loving.

рекомбин/атор *m.* recombiner; **—ационный** *a.*, **—ация** *f.* recombination; **—ированный** *a.* recombinant; **—ировать** *v.* recombine.

рекоменд/ательный *a.* recommendation, recommending; suggested (bibliography); **—ация** *f.* recommendation, advice, introduction, reference, testimonial; **—ованный** *a.* recommended, introduced; **—овать** *v.* recommend, advise, introduce; **—уемый** *a.* tentative; **—уется** it is advisable, it is good practice.

рекон *m.* (gen.) recon.

реконвалесцен/т *m.* convalescent; **—ция** *f.* (med.) convalescence, recuperation.

реконверсия *f.* reconversion.

реконстру/ировать *v.* reconstruct, rebuild, remodel, renovate, restore, overhaul, modernize, improve, redesign; rearrange; **—ктивный** *a.* reconstructive; **—кция** *f.* reconstruction, etc., *see v.*; rearrangement; regeneration, redevelopment, renovation, (urban) renewal.

реконцентрация *f.* reconcentration.

рекорд *m.* record; **—ер** *m.* recorder; **—ист** *m.* (agr.) record-breaking stock; champion; record holder; **—ный** *a.* record(-breaking); **—смен** *m.* record holder.

рекостав *m.* (river) freeze-up.

рекреация *f.* recreation.

рекристаллиз/ация *f.* recrystallization; **—ованный** *a.* recrystallized; remelt (junction).

рекрудесценция *f.* (med.) recrudescence, recurrence of symptoms.

рексигенный *a.* rhexigenous; (cyt.) lysigenous.

рексис *m.* (med.) rhexis, rupture; (gen.) chromosome fragmentation.

рексия *f.* (ichth.) king barracouta (*Rexea solandri*).

рект/альный *a.* rectal; **—ит** *m.* (med.) rectitis, proctitis.

ректифи/кат *m.* rectificate; rectified alcohol; **—катор** *m.* rectifier; **—кационный** *a.* rectification; fractionating; **—кационная колонна** fractionating column, fractionator; **—кация** *f.* rectification, etc., *see v.*; purification; fractional distillation; **—кованный** *see* **ректифицированный**; **—ковать** *see* **ректифицировать**; **—цированный** *a.* rectified, etc., *see v.*; **—цировать** *v.* rectify, redistill; fractionate.

ректо (typ.) recto.

ректо— *prefix* recto—, procto— (rectum); **—абдоминальный** *a.* rectoabdominal.

ректор *m.* rector, head (of university); **—ат** *m.* university administration; rector's office; **—ство** *n.* rectorate, rectorship.

ректо/скоп *m.* (med.) rectoscope, proctoscope; **—уретральный** *a.* (anat.) rectourethral; **—целе** *n.* (med.) rectocele, proctocele.

рекультивация *f.* reclamation, recultivation, restoration (of land).

рекупер/ативный *a.* recuperative, regenerative; recovery; **—атор** *m.* recuperator, regenerator; recovery unit; **—ация** *f.* recuperation, regeneration; recovery; **—ированный** *a.* recuperated, etc., *see v.*; **—ировать** *v.* recuperate, regenerate, restore; recover.

рекурвация *f.* (med.) recurvation.

рекуррентный *a.* recurrent, recurring; (math.) recurrence (formula); recursive.

рекурс/ивно *adv.* (math.) recursively; **р.-перечислимый** *a.* recursive-enumerable (set); **—ивный** *a.* recursive; fractal; **р. список** (comp.) recursive list, self-referent list; **—ия** *f.* recursion.

релакс/ант *m.* relaxant; **—атор** *m.* relaxation oscillator; **—ационный** *a.*, **—ация** *f.* relaxation; (stress) relief; **—ационная схема** trigger circuit, multivibrator; **—ин** *m.* relaxin (a hormone); **—ированный** *a.* relaxed; **—ировать** *v.* relax; **—ометр** *m.* relaxometer.

реле *n.* (elec.) relay; **р. времени** timer; **включающее р.** relay switch.

релевантный *a.* relieving, alleviating.

релеевский *a.* Rayleigh (scattering).

релейн/о-контактный *a.* relay-contact, relay-switching (circuit); **—ый** *a.* relay(-controlled); repeating; discontinuous-type; trigger (tube); **—ая защита** relay protection; **—ое устройство** relay system.

реле-клопфер *n.* sounding relay; **р.-повторитель** *n.* repeating relay; **р.-регулятор** *n.* generator regulator; **р.-счётчик** *n.* meter relay.

Релея интерферометр Rayleigh interferometer.

реликви/я *f.* reliquia, relic; **—и** *pl.* relics, organic remains, (bot.) induviae.

реликт *m.* relic(t), remnant, leftover; **—овый** *a.* relic(t); connate (waters); cliff (dwelling).

рёлка *f.* forest-covered ridge.

Рёло теория (mech.) Reuleaux theory.

релуктанц *m.* (elec.) reluctance.

рельеф *m.* relief, contour; topography; anaglyph; (ocean.) feature; (land) configuration; terrain; boss; projection; pattern; **р. кристалла** (electron.) chip pattern; **потенциальный р.** (comp.) charge pattern; **форма —а** topographic form; **—но** *adv.* in relief; **—ность** *f.* relief; **—ный** *a.* relief, embossed, raised, prominent, salient, projecting; topographic (map).

рельс *m.* rail; runway; **—о**— *prefix* rail; **—вый** *a.* rail; track(-borne); **—вый путь** track; **—ы** *pl.* rails, track.

релэ *see* **реле**.

релюктанц *see* **релуктанц**.

реляксатор *see* **релаксатор**.

релятив/изм *m.* relativity; **—ист(иче)ский** *a.* relativistic, relativity; **—истское уравнение массы** relativistic mass equation; **—ность** *f.* relativity; **—ный** *a.* relative.

реляционный *a.* relational (algebra, etc.).

рем— *prefix* repair, maintenance.

ремаковский *a.* (anat.) Remak's (band, fibers, etc.).

реманентн/ость *f.* (elec.) remanence, retentivity; **—ый** *a.* remanent.

ремарка *f.* remark, marginal note.

рембаза *f.* repair base, maintenance center.

ремез *m.* (orn.) Penduline tit (*Remiz pendulinus*).

ремённ/ый *a.* of **ремень**; (anat.) splenial; **—ая мышца** musculus splenius; **от —ого привода, с —ым приводом** belt-driven.

ремень *m.* belt(ing), strap, sling; **р. безопасности** safety belt, seat belt.

ремень-рыбы *pl.* oarfishes, king-of-the-herring (*Regalecidae*).

ременчатый *a.* of **ремень**.

Рёмер (astr.) Roemer.

ремесленн/ик *m.* workman, craftsman, artisan; **—ичество** *n.* workmanship; **—ый** *a.* trade, industrial, vocational (school).

ремесло *n.* trade, occupation; (handi)craft.

ремеш/ковый *a.*, **—ок** *dim. of* **ремень;** thong, tringle; watchband.

ремзавод *m.* maintenance plant, repair shop.

ремиз *m.* (com.) fine; payment.

ремиз *m.*, **—(к)а** *f.*, **—ный** *a.* (weaving) heald, heddle, harness, shaft, leaf.

ремингтон *m.* Remington typewriter.

реми/ссия *f.* remission; **—тировать** *v.* remit; **—тирующий** *a.* remittent.

рем/летучка *f.* mobile repair shop; **—тех** *m.* machine repair shop.

ремне— *prefix* lori—, belt, strap, band; **—видный** *a.* lorate, strap-shaped; **—зуб** *m.* beaked whale (*Mesoplodon*); **—листный** *a.* lorifolious; **—телые** *pl.* dealfishes (*Trachipteridae*); **—ткачество** *n.* belt weaving; **—цы** *pl.* tapeworms (*Ligulidae*); **—цветник** *m.* (bot.) Loranthus.

ремн/и *pl. of* **ремень;** **—я** *gen. of* **ремень.**

ремонт *m.* repair(s), repair work, reconditioning, overhaul; upkeep, maintenance, service; replacement (of stock); **р. и уход** care and maintenance; **в —е, при —е** under repair; **капитальный р.** (major) overhaul; **текущий р.** maintenance.

ремонтантный *a.* (bot.) remontant, everblooming, everbearing.

ремонтина *f.* (min.) temporary support.

ремонтиров/ание *n.* repairing, etc., *see v.*; repair, mending, maintenance; **—анный** *a.* repaired, etc., *see v.*; **—ать** *v.* repair, recondition, service, maintain, overhaul; recap (tires); replace (stock); refit; **—ка** *see* **ремонтирование.**

ремонтник *m.* repairman; **—и** *pl.* maintenance crew.

ремонтн/о-техническая станция service and supply center; **—ый** *a. of* **ремонт;** **—ый пункт** service station; **—ый слесарь** repairman, mechanic; **—ый цех** repair shop; **—ое обслуживание** remedial maintenance; **—ое стадо** (ichth.) replacement stock; **—ое хозяйство** maintenance.

ремонто/пригодность, —способность *f.* maintainability; accessibility (for repair).

ремора *f.* (ichth.) remora (*Remora remora*).

реморкер *m.* (hauling) truck.

рему *n.* remou (local atmospheric disturbances); (hydr.) swirl, wake.

рен *m.* (instr.) run.

ренальный *a.* (anat.) renal, kidney.

рендзина *f.* rendzina (group of soils).

рендомизация *see* **рандомизация.**

ренет *see* **ранет.**

Рене(я) никель Raney nickel.

рениев/ый *a.* rhenium; **р. ангидрид** rhenium heptoxide; **—ая кислота** perrhenic acid; **соль —ой кислоты, —окислая соль** rhenate.

рен/ий *m.* rhenium, Re; **двуокись —ия** rhenium dioxide; **хлористый р.** rhenium chloride.

ренин *m.* renin (kidney enzyme).

Ренкина *see* **Ранкина.**

ренклод *m.* greengage (plum).

Ренн (geog.) Rennes.

ренн/аза *f.*, **—ин** *m.* rennin, rennase.

Реннера комплекс (gen.) Renner complex.

рено— *prefix* (anat.) reno— (kidney); **—патия** *f.* (med.) renopathy, nephropathy.

ренод *m.* renode valve.

реноме *n.* fame, reputation, name.

ренормализация *f.* renormalization.

рента *f.* rent; annuity; return (on investment).

рентабельн/о *adv.* profitably; **—ость** *f.* profitableness, earning capacity; **коэффициент —ости** net profit ratio; **—ый** *a.* profitable, paying, commercial, economical.

рентген *m.* roentgen (unit of X-ray radiation); **р. в ткани** tissue roentgen; **биологический эквивалент —а** roentgen equivalent man, rem.

Рентгена лучи Roentgen rays, X-rays.

рентгенгониометр *m.* X-ray goniometer.

рентгениз/ация *f.* X-raying; **—ировать** *v.* X-ray; (med.) treat with X-rays.

рентген/-кубический сантиметр roentgens per cubic centimeter; **—ометр** *m.* roentgen meter.

рентгено— *prefix* Roentgen, X-ray, radio —; **—биология** *f.* radiobiology; **—вский, —вый** *a.* roentgen, X-ray; **—вский анализ** roentgen-ray analysis, X-ray (diffraction) analysis; **—вский снимок** roentgenogram, X-ray photograph; X-ray(diffraction) pattern; **—вская плёнка** radiographic film; X-ray film; **—вские лучи** roentgen rays, X-rays; **—вское излучение** *n.* X-rays, X-ray radiation; **—вское облучение** X-ray irradiation; **—вское просвечивание** fluoroscopy; **подвергать действию —вских лучей** *v.* X-ray; irradiate; **—грамма** *see* **рентгеновский снимок.**

рентгенограф *m.* roentgenograph, X-ray photograph; **—ический** *a.* roentgenographic, X-ray diffraction; X-ray (examination); **—ия** *f.* roentgenography, X-ray diffractometry, X-ray diffraction analysis; *suffix* —graphy; **—ия вен** venography, phlebography; **—ия металлов** radiometallography.

рентгено/дефектоскопия *f.* X-ray flaw detection; **—диагностика** *f.* X-ray diagnosis; **—кимограф** *m.* roentgen(o)kymograph; **—киносъёмка** *f.* X-ray cinematography; **—контрастный препарат** X-ray contrast medium; radiopaque.

рентгенолог *m.* radiologist; X-ray technician; **—ический** *a.* roentgenologic, X-ray; **—ия** *f.* radiology, roentgenology.

рентгено/метр *m.* roentgenometer; **—облучение** *n.* X-ray irradiation; **—прозрачный** *a.* radioparent; **—проницаемый** *a.* radiolucent; **—скоп** *m.* roentgenoscope, fluoroscope; **—скопический** *a.* fluoroscopic; **—скопия** *f.* roentgenoscopy, radioscopy, fluoroscopy, X-ray examination; **—снимок** *m.* roentgenogram, X-ray photograph; **—спектральный** *a.* X-ray spectral; **—структурный** *a.* X-ray diffraction; X-ray (analysis); **—терапия** *f.* radiotherapy, X-ray therapy; **—техник** *m.* X-ray technician; radiographer; **—техника** *f.* X-ray technology.

рентген-эквивалент *m.* roentgen equivalent; **биологический р.** roentgen equivalent man (rem); **физический р.** roentgen equivalent physical (rep).

Реньо (chem.; phys.) Regnault.

рео— *prefix* rheo— (current; flow); **—база** *f.* (physiol.) rheobase; **—вирус** *m.* (med.) reovirus, ether-resistant RNA virus; **—вискозиметр** *m.* rheoviscosimeter; **—гамеон** *m.* (biol.) rheogameon, polytypic species; **—графия** *f.* rheography.

реодорант *m.* (rubber) reodorant.

рео/дубильная кислота rheotannic acid, rhubarb tannin.

реокисление *n.* reoxidation.

рео/логия *f.* rheology; **—ометр** rheometer, flowmeter.

реомюр *m.* Réaumur thermometer; **Реомюра шкала** (phys.) Réaumur scale.

реономный *a.* time-dependent.

реопирометр *m.* resistance pyrometer, resistance temperature meter.

реоплетизмография *f.* impedance plethysmography.

реорганиз/ационный *a.* reorganization(al); **—ация** *f.* reorganization, rearrangement; **—ов(ыв)ать** *v.* reorganize, rearrange.

рео/скоп *m.* (elec.) rheoscope, current detector; **—сплав** *m.* high-resistivity alloy.

реостат *m.* (elec.) rheostat, variable resistor, potentiometer; control; **р. возбуждения** field rheostat; **р. накала** filament rheostat; **р. скорости** speed control; **—ноёмкостный** *a.* resistance-capacitance; **—ный** *a.* rheostat(ic); resistance (amplifier, transducer); resistor (coupling).

рео/стрикция *f.* (elec.) rheostriction, pinch effect; **—таксис** *m.* (biol.) rheotaxis; **—тахиграфия** *f.* (med.) rheotachygraphy; **—том** *m.* (elec.) rheotome (current breaker); **—тропный** *a.* (biol.) rheotropic; **—фильный** *a.* (biol.) rheophilic; **—фит** *m.* (bot.) rheophyte; **—хорд** *m.*, **—хорда** *f.* slide-wire rheostat; **—хризин** *m.* rheochrysin.

репа *f.* turnip.

репара/тивный *a.* reparative; **—торный фермент** repair enzyme, raparase; **—ционный** *a.*, **—ция** *f.* repair.

репей/(ник) *m.* (bot.) bur(r), spec. burdock; **засмёжка типа —ника** hook and loop fastener, Velcro; **—никовидный** *a.* prickly, hamate; **—ница** *f.* (ent.) painted lady; **—ничек** *m.* (bot.) Agrimonia; **—ный** *a. of* **репей**.

репеллент *m.* repellent.

репер *m.* reference point; (surv.) datum mark, datum (point), bench mark; **—ный** *a.* reference(-point); datum; bench (mark); calibration (curve); **—ная точка** reference point.

реперфоратор *m.* reperforator.

репет/ир *m.* (horol.) repeater (clock); **—ировать** *v.* rehearse; tutor, coach; **—итор** *m.* tutor, coach; self-teaching unit; **—иторство** *n.* tutoring, coaching; **—иторствовать** *v.* tutor, coach; **—иция** *f.* (horol.) striking mechanism; rehearsal; **—ичный** *a.* (naut.) signal-repeating; **—овать** *v.* repeat signals.

репешок *see* **репейничек.**

репитер *m.* repeater.

репица *f.* (zool.) tail head, dock (of horse).

репка *f.* carline thistle (*Carlina vulgaris*).

реплантация *f.* re(im)plantation.

репленишер *m.* replenisher.

реплика *f.* reply, retort, remark; (micros.) replica; **—ция** *f.* replication.

репликон *m.* (gen.) replicon.

реплум *m.* (bot.) replum.

реп/ница *f.* cabbage butterfly; **—ный** *a. of* **репа**; rape (seed); **—ная капуста** kohlrabi; **—овидный** *a.* turnip-shaped, napiform; **—овый** *see* **репный.**

репозиция *f.* (med.) reduction (of a fracture, etc.).

реполов *see* **коноплянка;** robin redbreast (*Erithacus rubecula*).

репообразный *see* **реповидный.**

репорт/аж *m.* reporting, account; **—ёр** *m.* reporter, representative of the press.

Реппе синтез (chem.) Reppe synthesis.

рёпперит *m.* (min.) roepperite.

репрезент/ант *m.*, **—ативный** *a.* representative; **—ация** *f.* representation.

репресс/ибельный *a.* repressible; **—ия** *f.* repression; **—ор** *m.* repressor.

репро/графия *f.* reprography, reproduction methods; **—дуктивный** *a.* reproductive; **—дуктор** *m.* reproducer; (comp.) reproducing punch, reperforator; (rad.) (loud)speaker; **—дукционный** *a.* reproduction; reproducing (punch); **—дукция** *f.* reproduction; reproduced

copy; **—дуцент** *m.* reproducer; **—дуцирование** *n.* reproduction, duplication, copying; **—дуцированный** *a.* reproduced, etc., *see v.*; **—дуцировать** *v.* reproduce, duplicate, copy.

репс *m.* (text.) repp; (bot.) rape; **—овый** *a. of* **репс**; rapeseed.

рептили/йный *a.* reptilian; **—я** *f.* (zool.) reptile.

репульпатор *m.* (flotation) repulper.

репульсионный *a.*, **—ия** *f.* repulsion.

репутация *f.* reputation, name.

репчатый *see* **реповидный;** turnip-like.

репьи *pl. of* **репей.**

Рёрига трубка Röhrig tube.

ресивер *m.* receiver.

ресинтез *m.* resynthesis.

ресинхронизированный *a.* resynchronized.

ресмус *see* **рейсмус.**

ресни/тчатый *a.* (biol.) ciliate; (anat.) ciliary; fringed; **—цевидный** *a.* ciliiform; **—ца** *f.* eyelash, cilium; **—чато-** *prefix* ciliate, fringe; **—чка** *f.* (biol.) cilium; **—чки** *pl.* cilia; **—чные** *pl.* (zool.) Ciliata; **—чный** *a.* eyelash, ciliary; (biol.) ciliate; **—чный покров** ciliary coat; **—чный эпителий** ciliated epithelium; **—чное кольцо** trochus (of rotifer discs); **—чные инфузории** Ciliata; **—чные черви** (zool.) Turbellaria.

ресорб/ированный *a.* re(ab)sorbed; **—ировать** *v.* re(ab)sorb; **—ция** *f.* re(ab)sorption.

респир/атор *m.* respirator, breathing apparatus, inhaler, mouthpiece; **—аторный, —ационный** *a.* respiratory; (med.) hyperventilation (tetany); **—ация** *f.* respiration; **—ометр** *m.* respirometer.

республика *f.* republic, commonwealth.

Ресселл, —а, рессело́ва (phys.) Russell.

рессор/а *f.* spring, spec. leaf spring; **—ный** *a.* spring; sprung.

реста *f.* (ichth.) silver bream (*Blicca*).

реставр/ация *f.*, **—ирование** *n.* restoration, renovation; repair; **—ированный** *a.* restored, etc., *see v.*; **—ировать** *v.* restore, rebuild, renovate, repair, mend.

рестант *m.* residue, remainder; (biol.) surviving species, restant species; **—ы** *pl.* (com.) leftovers, old stock.

рестарт *m.* (comp.) restart.

рестелий *m.* (bot.) roestelia.

рестинга *f.* (bot.) restinga; shrubby forest.

реституция *f.* (biol.) restitution, regeneration.

ресторан *m.*, **—ный** *a.* restaurant.

ресупинация *f.* (biol.) resupination.

ресургентный *a.* resurgent.

ресурс *m.* resource; (mach.) life(time), operating life, service; life; **—ы** *pl.* resources, reserve; (food or water) supply; provisions, supplies.

ресциннамин *m.* (pharm.) rescinnamine.

ретардация *f.* retardation.

ретен *m.* retene, methylisopropylphenanthrene.

ретенци/онный *a.*, **—я** *f.* retention.

Ретийские альпы (geog.) Rhaetian Alps.

ретивый *a.* zealous, fervent.

ретикул/ёз *m.* (med.) reticulosis; **—ин** *m.* reticulin; **—иновый** *a.* reticular, reticulate, net-like; **—оцит** *m.* (hemat.) reticulocyte; **—о-эндотелиальный** *a.* reticuloendothelial; **—ум** *m.* (zool.) reticulum; **—ярный** *see* **ретикулиновый.**

ретин/а *f.* (anat.) retina; **—акул(ум)** *m.* (bot.) retinaculum; **—аль** *m.* retinene, vitamin A aldehyde; **—альный** *a.* (anat.) retinal; **—ен, —ин** *see* **ретиналь;** (med.) retinitis; **—о-** (anat.) *prefix* retino— (retina); **—ол** *m.* retinol, rosin oil; retinol, vitamin A; **—опатия** *f.* retinopathy; **—ула** *f.* (cyt.) retinula.

ретипификация *f.* (bot.) retypification.

ретиров/аться *v.* retreat, retire, withdraw; **—ка** withdrawal.

ретовина *f.* rot.

ретоперителий *m.* (cyt.) retoperithelium.

реторт/а *f.*, **—ный** *a.* retort; boiler; **—ообразный** *a.* retort-shaped.

ретотелий *m.* (cyt.) retothelium; *a.* retothelial.

ретрак/тор *m.* retractor; (anat.) retractor muscle; **—ция** *f.* retraction.

ретранс/лировать *v.* retransmit, relay, rebroadcast, repeat; **—лирующий** *a.* retransmitting, etc., *see v.*; relay; **—лятор** *m.* (commun.) translator, relay station, retransmitter; (comp.) relay; **—ляционный** *see* ретранслирующий; **—ляция** *f.* retransmission, relaying, etc., *see v.*; **—миттер** *m.* retransmitter.

ретро— *prefix* retro— (back, backward; behind; retrograde); **—активность** *f.* retroaction; retroactivity; **—активный** *a.* retroactive; **—вакцина** *f.* (med.) retrovaccine; **—версия** *f.* (med.) retroversion; **—градация**, **—градность** *f.* retrogradation; **—градный** *a.* retrograde; reactionary; **—грессивный** *a.* retrogressive; **—девиация** *f.* (med.) retrodeviation, backward displacement.

ретронецин *m.* retronecine; **—овая кислота** retronecinic acid.

ретро/орбитальный *a.* (anat.) postorbital; **—перитонеальный** *a.* (anat.) retroperitoneal.

ретропинн/овые, **—ы** *pl.* (ichth.) Australian smelts (*Retropinnidae*).

реторзный *a.* (bot.) retrorse.

ретроспек/тивный *a.* retrospective; **—ция** *f.* retrospection.

ретрофлексия *f.* retroflexion.

ретур *m.* return(s); (chem.) recycle, return flow, reflux.

ретурнбенд *m.* (air) trap (of a drain); U-bend.

ретуш/ёвка *f.*, **—ирование** *n.*, **—ь** *f.* (phot.) retouching; **—ировать** *v.* retouch.

ретциево пространство (anat.) Retzius space.

реумэмодин *m.* rheum-emodin.

реутилизация *f.* reuse, reutilization.

реф. *abbr.* (**реферат**).

рефер/ат *m.*, **—ат(ив)ный** *a.* abstract, synopsis; reference; paper, report; **—ативный обзор** abstract, review; **—ендум** *m.* (political) referendum; **—ент** *m.* reader, reviewer; **—енция** *f.* reference; **—енцэллипсоид** *m.* (geod.) reference ellipsoid; **—и** *m.* (sports) referee; **—ирование** *n.* abstracting, etc., *see v.*; **—ировать** *v.* abstract; read, review; referee.

рефлек/с *m.* reflex; (phot.) (lens) flare; **условный р.** conditioned reflex; **—сивность** *f.* (math.) reflexivity; **—сивный** *see* рефлективный; **—сивное отношение** (math.) reflexive relation; **—сия** *f.* reflection; reflex action; **—сный** *a.* reflex; reflected (code); **—сная печать** reflex printing, contact copying; **—сная фотобумага** contact paper; **—сология** *f.* (zool.) reflexology; **—тивный** *a.* reflective; reflex; involuntary; **—тировать** *v.* reflex, reflect; react; **—тирующий** *a.* reflexing, reflecting; **—тометр** *m.* reflectometer; **—тор** *m.* reflector, mirror; reflecting telescope; reflector heating lamp; reverberator; (med.) speculum; **—торный** *a.* reflector, reflectory; reflex.

рефлюкс *m.* (fractional distillation) reflux, bottoms; backward flow; (physiol.) regurgitation.

рефокусировать *v.* refocus.

реформ/а *f.* reform; **—инг** *m.* (petrol.) reforming; **—ировать** *v.* reform.

рефракт/ерный *a.* (zool.) refractory (period); **—ометр**

m. (light) refractometer; **—ометрическая разница** refractivity intercept; **—ометрия** *f.* refractometry; **—ор** *m.* refractor; refracting telescope; **—орный** *a.* refractor(y); refracting, refractive.

рефракци/онный *a.*, **—я** *f.* refraction.

рефрижер/атор *m.* refrigerator; **—аторный** *a.* refrigerator (car, ship, or truck); cooler; refrigerated; **—ация** *f.* refrigeration.

рефуги/ум *m.*, **—я** *f.* refuge.

рефул/ёр *m.* hydraulic dredge; **—ирование** *n.* deposition, aggradation; conveyance (of grain, etc.) by suction tube.

рецбаниит *see* **резбаниит.**

рецедентность *f.* recedence.

реценз/ент *m.* critic, reviewer; **—ировать** *v.*, **—ия** *f.* review.

рецент *m. adv.* lately, recently; **—ный** *a.* new, fresh, recent.

рецепт *m.* prescription; recipe, mix, formula(tion).

рецептакул *m.*, **—а** *f.*, **—ум** *m.* (bot.) receptacle, receptaculum; **—ярный** *a.* receptacular.

рецеп/тар *m.* prescription clerk; **—тивный** *a.* receptive; **—тированный** *a.* formulated, etc., *see v.*; **—тировать** *v.* formulate, mix, compound; **—тный** *a.* of рецепт; **—тор** *m.* (anat.) receptor; **внешний —тор** (anat.) exteroceptor; **—тура** *f.* prescription (drugs); formula; compounding; **—турная** *f.* drug room; **—турный** *a.* of **рецептура; —туростроение** *n.* compounding; **—турщик** *m.* compounder; **—ция** *f.* reception; perception of a stimulus, sense; **слуховая —ция** sense of hearing.

рецессив *m.*, **—ный** *a.* (biol.) recessive.

рецессия *f.* (med.) recession.

рецидив *m.* relapse, setback; recurrence; **—изм** *m.* (law) recidivism; **—ирующий** *a.* (med.) recurring, relapsing (laryngitis); transition (tumor); **—ист** *m.*, **—истка** *f.* repeat offender; **—ный** *a.* recidive, relapsing.

рецикл *m.* recycle, recycling.

реципиент *m.*, **—ный** *a.* recipient; receiver, reservoir, container.

реципрокный *a.* reciprocal.

рециркул/ировать *v.* recirculate, recycle, feed back; **—яционный** *a.* recirculating, recycling; recycle (valve); **—яция** *f.* recirculation, recycling.

речевой *a.* speech; vocal, verbal.

речей *gen. pl. of* **речь.**

реч/ка *f.* river; **—ник** *m.* river gravel; river transport worker; **—ной** *a.* river(ine), fluvial; bank (sand); *prefix* potamo— (river); **—ной планктон** potamoplankton.

реч/ь *f.* speech, address; discourse; enunciation; **о котором идёт р.** referred to; **о чём р.?** what is the question? **органы —и** vocal organs; **паралич —и** (med.) laloplegia; **расстройство —и** dyslalia, alalia.

реш/ать *v.* decide, determine, settle, fix; resolve, make up one's mind; solve, work out; compute; **—аться** *v.* decide, determine, resolve, make up one's mind; dare, venture; be determined; **—ающий** *a.* deciding, etc., *see v.*; decisive, key, crucial; marginal; (comp.) decision (element); arbitration (analysis); **—ающий фактор** determinant; deciding factor; **—ающее устройство** resolver; computer; **—ение** *n.* decision, determination, resolution; derivation, working (out), solution (of problem); answer; design; conclusion; judgment, decree; award (in arbitration); **выносить —ение** deliver a verdict; adjudicate; **дерево —ений** (math.) decision tree; **принимать —ение** decide; **техническое —ение** design; **—ённый** *a.* decided, etc., *see v.*

решет/ина *f.* lath; bar (of a grating); **—ить** *v.* nail on laths, perforate, riddle; screen, sift.

реш/ётка *f.* lattice, grating; grate, grill, grid; framework; trellis; tube sheet (in heat exchanger); (aero.) cascade; crating; checker(work); (optical) array; louver(s); fencing; (bot.) clathrus; (anat.) cribrum; **р. с дополнениями** (math.) complemented lattice; **обратная р.** (cryst.) reciprocal lattice; **посадить за —ётку** *v.* jail, imprison; **постоянная —ётки** (cryst.) lattice constant; **р.-дробилка** macerater; **—ёткообразный** *a.* lattice (-like); **—етник** *m.* lathing; **—ётный** *a.*, **—ето** *n.* screen, sieve, sifter; (anat.) cribrum; **—етовидный,** **—етоподобный** *a.* (anat.) cribriform, ethmoid; **—еточный** *a.* screen; network.

решётчат/о— *prefix* cribrose; clathrate; **—осемянный** *a.* (bot.) clathrospermous; **—ый** *a.* grate, grill, grid; screen; meshed; latticed, lattice(-like); cribriform, sieve-like; (anat.) ethmoid(al); (bot.) clathrate; **—ый барабан** revolving screen; **—ый колосник** grid (bar); **—ый люк** grating; **—ая балка** lattice beam; **—ая жесть** perforated sheet; **—ая конструкция** lattice-work, lattice girder construction; framework; **—ая пластина** (elec.) grid plate; **—ая система** framework; **—ая структура** lattice structure, mesh structure; **—ая ферма** lattice girder; **—ое пятно** (anat.) macula cribrosa; **—ые трубки** (bot.) sieve tubes.

решимость *f.* resoluteness, resolution.

решительн/о *adv.* resolutely, determinedly, absolutely; **—ость** *f.* resolution, determination, decision, decisiveness, firmness; **—ый** *a.* resolute, determined, decisive, resolved; categorical; deciding, crucial; drastic (measures).

решить *see* **решать.**

решка *f.* tails (of a coin).

решофер *m.* reheater.

рештак *m.* (min.) chute; trough.

реэкстра/гирование *n.* re-extraction; **—гировать** *v.* re-extract; **—гит** *m.* re-extract, re-extracted solution; **—кция** *see* **реэкстрагирование.**

Реюньон (geog.) Reunion (Island).

реюшка *f.* small fishing boat.

реющий *a.* soaring, etc., *see* **реять.**

рея/ние *n.* soaring, etc., *see v.*; **—ть** *v.* soar, hover; rush, gush, flow.

ржав/еть *v.* rust, corrode; **—еющий** *a.* rusting, corroding, rusty; corrodible; **—ление** *n.* rusting, corrosion; **—ленный** *a.* rusted, corroded; **—окрасный** *a.* rust(y)-red, ferruginous; **—осерый** *a.* grey ferruginous (soil); **—ость** *f.* rustiness.

ржавчин/а *f.* rust, corrosion; (phyt.) rust, blight; **—ники** *pl.*, **—ные (грибы)** rust fungi; **—оустойчивый** *a.* rust-resistant.

ржавый *a.* rusty, rusted, corroded; rust-colored.

ржание *n.* neighing.

рж/анище *n.* rye field; **золотистая —анка** (orn.) European golden plover (*Charadrius apricarius*); **—анки** *pl.* (orn.) plovers, lapwings (*Charadriidae*); **белые —анки** (orn.) sheathbills (*Chionididae*); **—анковые** *pl. see* **ржанки;** **—анкообразные** *pl.* (orn.) Charadriiformes; **—аной** *a.* rye; **—ано-пшеничный** *a.* rye-wheat (hybrids).

ржать *v.* neigh.

рж/евидный *a.* rye-like; **—и** *gen., pl., etc., of* **рожь.**

РЗ *abbr.* (**радиоактивное заражение** *or* **загрязнение**) radioactive contamination.

Р.З. *abbr.* (**редкие земли**) rare earths.

риас *m.*, **—овый** *a.* (geol.) ria.

риацихтовые *pl.* (ichth.) loach gobies (*Rhyacichthyidae*).

рибекит *m.* (min.) riebeckite.

рибитол *m.* (chem.) ribitol.

рибоз/а *f.* ribose; **—ид** *m.* riboside; **—офосфат** *m.* ribose phosphate.

рибойлер *m.* reboiler.

рибо/новая кислота ribonic acid; **—нуклеаза** *f.* ribonuclease; **—нуклеиновая кислота** ribonucleic acid, RNA.

рибонуклеопрот/еид *m.*, **—еидный** *a.* ribonucleoprotein, RNP; **—ид** *m.* (biochem.) ribonucleotide.

рибо/сома *f.* (cyt.) ribosome; **—сом(аль)ный** *a.* ribosomal; **—флавин** *m.* riboflavin, vitamin B$_2$.

рибулозофосфат *m.* ribulose phosphate.

риванол *m.* Rivanol, ethodin.

ривотит *m.* (min.) rivotite.

Ривса процесс Reeves process.

Ривьера (geog.) Riviera.

рига *f.* threshing barn.

ригель *m.* cross bar, collar beam; hasp, clasp, cleat; **—ный** *a.* of **ригель;** mortise (chisel).

Риги диполь Righi doublet.

ригид/ность *f.* rigidity; (med.) rigor; **—ный** *a.* rigid, inflexible, stiff.

риголен *m.* (petrol.) rhigolene.

ригор/изм *m.*, **—истичность** *f.* rigor.

ридберг *m.* rydberg (spectroscopic unit).

Ридберга постоянная (nucl.) Rydberg constant.

рижский *a.* (geog.) Riga.

Риза процесс (met.) Reese river process.

ризавка *f.* (ichth.) Danube shad (*Alosa*).

ризин *m.*, **—а** *f.* (bot.) rhizine.

ризо— *prefix* rhizo— (root); **—генный** *a.* rhizogenic; **—дерма** *f.* rhizoderm; **—ид** *m.* (bot.) rhizoid; **—карпий** *m.* rhizocarp; **—карповая кислота** rhizocarpic acid; **—ктониоз** *m.*, **—ктония** *f.* (phyt.) rhizoctonia root and stem rot; **—м** *m.*, **—ма** *f.* rhizome, rhizoma, rootstock; **—мелический** *a.* (anat.) rhizomelic (spondylitis); **—мииды** *pl.* bamboo rats (*Rhizomyidae*); **—морфа** *f.* (bot.) rhizomorph; **—новая кислота** rhizonic acid; **—пласт** *m.* rhizoplast; **—поды** *pl.* (zool.) Rhizopoda; **—сфера** *f.* (soils) rhizosphere; **—фор** *m.* rhizophore; **—холевая кислота** rhizocholic acid.

риккетс/ии *pl.* Rickettsia (microorganisms); **—иоз** *m.* (med.) rickettsiosis.

рикошет *m.* ricochet, rebound(ing), bounce; **делать р.,** **—ировать** *v.* ricochet, rebound; **—ом** on the rebound; **—ный** *a.* rebounding.

Рим Rome.

рима *f.* tenter, stretcher.

риманов/ой, **—ский** *a.* (math.) Riemann(ian).

римоцидин *m.* rimocidin.

римск/ий *a.* Roman; **—ие весы** beam scale.

рин— *see* **рино—;** **—альгия** *f.* (med.) rhinalgia; **—альный** *a.* rhinal, nasal, nose; **—антин** *m.* rhinanthin; **—ит** *m.* (med.) rhinitis.

Рингельмана шкала (ecol.) Ringelman chart (for smoke density measurements).

Рингера раствор (physiol.) Ringer's solution.

рингтрал *m.* ring-trawl.

ринекант *m.* (ichth.) triggerfish (*Rhinecanthus*).

ринихт *m.* (ichth.) dace (*Rhinichthys*).

ринманов зелёный Rinmann's green.

рино— *prefix* rhin(o)— (nose); **—лит** *m.* (med.) rhinolith, nasal concretion; **—логия** *f.* (med.) rhinology; **—питек** *m.* (mam.) Rhinopithecus; **—пластика** *f.* rhinoplasty; **—преновые** *pl.* (ichth.) thread-fin scat (*Rhinoprenidae*); **—склерома** *f.* rhinoscleroma; **—скоп** *m.* rhinoscope.

ринохимеровые *pl.* (ichth.) Rhinochimaeridae.

ринуться *v.* dash, dart.

ринх/(о)— *prefix* rhynch(o)— (snout, beak); —**омис** *m.* (mam.) shrew rat (*Rhynchomys soricoides*); —**оспориоз** *m.* (phyt.) Rhynchosporium leaf scald.

РИО *abbr.* (**редакционно-издательский отдел**) editing and publishing division.

Рио-Гранде (geog.) Rio Grande.

Рио-де-жанейро (geog.) Rio de Janeiro.

риолит *m.* (petr.) rhyolite; —**овый** *a.* rhyolite, rhyolitic.

риометр *m.* riometer, relative ionospheric opacity meter.

риотрон *m.* (elec.) ryotron.

рипидомис *m.* (mam.) climbing mice (*Rhipidomys*).

риппер *m.* ripper.

рипу(к)с *m.* (ichth.) cisco (*Coregonus*).

рирпроектор *m.* (cinema) rear projector, background projector.

рис *m.* rice (*Oryza sativa*).

рис. *abbr.* (**рисунок**) figure, illustration.

Рис (math.) Riesz.

рисайкл *m.* (petrol.) recycle stock; —**инг** *m.* recycling.

рисберма *f.* (hydr.) down(stream) apron.

риск *m.* risk, hazard; **оценка** —**a** risk assessment.

риск/а *f.* graduation line, mark, notch, groove, scribe; (met.) sealing flange; **наносить** —**и** *v.* mark, scribe.

риск/нуть *see* **рисковать;** —**ованность** *f.* riskiness; —**ованный** *a.* risky, hazardous; speculative; —**овать** *v.* risk, hazard, venture.

рислинг *m.* Riesling (grape or wine).

рисов/альный *a.* drawing; lettering (pen); —**альщик** *m.* draftsman; —**ание** *n.* drawing, designing; (comp.) inking; —**ать** *v.* draw, design; depict.

рисо/видка *f.* mountain rice (*Oryzopsis*); —**вка** *f.* drawing, drafting; posing; (orn.) Java sparrow, ricebird (*Munia oryzivora*); —**вод** *m.* rice farmer; —**водство** *n.,* —**водческий** *a.* rice growing; —**вый** *a.* rice; —**завод** *m.* rice mill.

рисок *gen. pl. of* **риска.**

рисо/обдирочный *a.* rice-scouring, rice-husking; —**рушка** *f.* rice mill, rice husker.

рисс *m.,* —**кое оледенение** (geol.) Riss, Third Pleistocene glaciation.

риссвюрмский *a.* (geol.) Riss-Würm(ian).

рис-сырец *m.* unmilled rice; paddy.

ристо/мицин *m.* ristomycin (antibiotic); —**цетин** *m.* ristocetin.

рисун/ок *m.,* —**очный** *a.* drawing, picture, illustration, figure, diagram, representation; cut; draft, sketch; design, pattern, markings; layout; —**чатый** *a.* patterned, figured.

ритидом *m.* (bot.) rhytidome.

ритизма *f.* (phyt.) tar spot.

ритм *m.,* —**ика** *f.* rhythm; cycle, period; pace; **водитель** —**a** (med.) pacemaker; —**изованный** *see* **ритмический;** —**ика** *f.* periodicity; rhythmical recurrence; —**ический** *a.* rhythmic, smooth, even; periodic; —**ично** *adv.* rhythmically; **работать** —**ично** *v.* run steadily, hum along; —**ичность** *f.* rhythmicality, smoothness; rhythmical recurrence; —**ичный** *a.* rhythmic, smooth, even; —**ограф** *m.* rhythmograph.

ритрон *m.* retron (a gamma-ray spectrometer).

Риттера-Ролле феномен (med.) Ritter-Rollet phenomenon.

ритуал *m.* ceremony, ritual, rite; —**изация** *f.* ritualization; —**ьный** *a.* ritual.

ритурбент *see* **ретурнбенд.**

Ритца уравнение Ritz formula.

Риу-гранди *see* **Рио-Гранде.**

риф *m.* reef, ledge, shelf.

рифайнер *m.* (rubber) refiner.

рифейский *a.* (geol.) Riphean.

риф *m.* reef points (of a sail); (ocean.) reef; —**ель** *m.* riffle, ripple; grooves; —**ельная сталь** cutting steel; —**ить** *v.* reef (a sail).

рифл/евать *v.* channel, groove, rib, flute; corrugate, crimp; knurl, mill (nut); —**ение** *n.* channeling, etc., *see v.*; knurl(ing); —**ёный** *a.* channeled, etc., *see v.*; riffled; knurled; reefed (sail); checkered; diamond-tread (tire); —**ить** *see* **рифлевать;** —**уар** *m.* riffle file, riffler; —**я** *f.* riffle, groove, flute; —**и** *pl.* fluting.

рифо/вые *pl.* (ichth.) damselfishes (*Pomacentridae*); —**вый** *a. of* **риф;** —**вый узел** square knot, reef knot; —**генный** *a.* (geol.) of reef origin; —**образующий** *a.* reef-building.

рифт *m.* groove; (geol.) rift; **лихорадка долины Рифт** (vet.) Rift Valley fever, enzootic hepatitis.

рифтали *pl.* reeftackle.

рифтовать *see* **рифлевать.**

Рихтгофен Richthofen.

Рихтера закон Richter's law.

рихтов/альный *see* **рихтовочный; р. станок** straightener; —**альная линейка** straightedge, ruler; —**ать** *v.* straighten, true, align, level, adjust; dress; —**ка** *f.,* —**очный** *a.* straightening, etc., *see v.*; set, flatter (hammer).

рицин *m.* ricin; —**а** *see* **ризина;** —**ат** *m.* ricin(ole)ate; —**ин** *m.* ricinine; —**иновая кислота** ricininic acid; —**овокислый** *a.* ricinic acid; ricinate (of); —**овый** *a.* ricin; ricinic (acid); castor (oil).

рицинолев/ая кислота ricin(ole)ic acid; **соль** —**ой кислоты,** —**окислая соль** ricin(ole)ate; —**окислый** *a.* ricin(ole)ic acid; ricin(ole)ate (of); —**онатриевая соль** sodium ricinoleate.

рицино/леин *m.* ricinolein, glyceryl ricinoleate; —**л-(еин)овая кислота** *see* **рицинолевая кислота;** —**стеароловая кислота** ricinostearolic acid.

рицинус *m.* (bot.) castor plant (*Ricinus*); **семена** —**а** castor oil beans.

рицинэлаидин *m.* ricinelaidin; —**овая кислота** ricinelaidic acid.

рицовка *f.* scored line.

Рича теорема (chem.) Reech's theorem.

Ричардсона, ричардсоновый *a.* Richardson; **формула Р.-Дешмена** (phys.) Richardson-Dushman equation.

ричмондский *a.* (geol.) Richmond(ian).

Рише газ (wood distillation) Riché gas.

ришта *f.* parasitic worm (*Filaria medinensis*); (med.) dracunculosis.

РИЯИ *abbr.* (**радиоактивные изотопы и ядерные излучения**) radioactive isotopes and nuclear radiations.

РК *abbr.* (**растительный каучук**) natural rubber.

р.л., РЛ *abbr.* (**рентгеновские лучи**) X-rays.

рлк *abbr.* (**радиолокация**) radar; (**радлюкс**) radlux.

РН *abbr.* (**регулятор напряжения**) voltage regulator.

р-н *abbr.* (**район**) area, region.

РНК *abbr.* (**рибонуклеиновая кислота**) ribonucleic acid; **РНК-аза** *abbr.* (**рибонуклеаза**) ribonuclease; **РНК-переносчик** *m.* transfer RNA, tRNA; **РНК-посредник** *m.* messenger RNA, mRNA.

РНП *abbr.* (**рибонуклеопротеид**) ribonucleoprotein, RNP.

ро rho, ρ.

роба *f.* work clothes, coveralls.

робаловые (ichth.) *see* **снуковые.**

робастн/ость *f.* robustness; —**ый** *a.* robust.

робеть *v.* be timid, be fearful.

робин *m.* (chem.) robin; **—ин** *m.* robinin; **—оза** *f.* robinose.

робкий *a.* timid, shy.

роб/ок *sh. m. of* **робкий.**

робокар *m.* robotic vehicle.

робость *f.* shyness, timidity.

робот *m.* robot, automatic device; **—ехника** *f.* robotics.

робче *comp. of* **робкий.**

ров *m.* ditch, pit, trench; (anat.) fossa.

ровен *sh. m. of* **ровный.**

ровенский *a.* (geog.) Rovno.

ровесн/ик *m.,* **—ица** *f.* contemporary, person of same age.

ровик *dim. of* **ров;** pit, trench.

ровнитель *see* **равнитель;** (paper) drainer.

ровни/ца *f.,* **—чный** *a.* (text.) roving; (wool) carder; (cotton) flyer frame.

ровно *adv.* just, exactly, equally; smoothly, steadily, uniformly.

ровн/ость *f.* equality; uniformity; evenness, flatness, smoothness; **—ый** *a.* equal; uniform, steady; even, flat, smooth, level, plane; straight; exact (weight); **—я** *m. and f.* equal; **—ять** *see* **равнять.**

рог *m.* horn, cornu; beak (of anvil); (anchor) arm; **р. аммонов** (anat.) cornu Ammonis, hippocampus; **—астый** *a.* large-horned.

рогатик *m.* (bot.) Clavaria.

рогат/ка *f.* barrier, road block, obstacle; turnpike; (mil.) knife rest; slingshot; (ichth.) sculpin (*Myoxocephalus*); **—ковые** *pl.* sculpins, etc. (*Cottidae*).

рогатый *a.* horned, cornute; spurred; **р. скот** cattle.

рогач *m.* stag beetle; (bot.) Ceratocarpus; (ichth.) devilray, manta (*Mobula*); **—евые** *pl.* Mobulidae; **—и** *pl.* (ichth.) *see* **рогачевые;** (mam.) antler-bearing deer; **р.-олень** *m.* stag beetle.

рого— *prefix* cerat(o)—, corn(i)— (horn).

роговидн/ый *a.* horn(-shaped), corniculate, cornute; horny, corneous; **р. выступ** horn; **—ое образование** (med.) cutaneous horn.

роговик *m.,* **—овая порода** (petr.) hornfels; **—овый** *a.* horny, corneous; hornfels; chert(y).

рогови/на *f.* horn; **—ца** *f.* (anat.) cornea; **—чный** *a.* corneal.

рогов/ой *a.* horn(y), corneous, keratic; chert (gravel); **р. каучук** ebonite, hard rubber; **—ая оболочка** (anat.) cornea; **—ая ткань** (anat.) horny tissue; **—ое вещество** keratin.

роговообманков/ый *a.* (min.) hornblende; **—ая порода** (petr.) hornblendite.

рогож/(ин)а *f.,* **—ный** *a.* mat(ting); **—ка** *dim. of* **рогожа;** coarse cloth, hopsack(ing); (bot.) mattula.

рогоз *m.,* **—овый** *a.* (bot.) cat-tail (*Typha*).

рогозуб *m.* (ichth.) lungfish, barramunda; **—овые** *see* **рогозубы;** **—ообразные** *pl.* (ichth.) Ceratodiformes; **—ы** *pl. of* **рогозуб,** Ceratodidae.

роголистник *m.* (bot.) Ceratophyllum.

роголистный *a.* (bot.) ceratophyllous.

рогоклювы *pl.* (orn.) broadbills (*Eurylaimidae*).

рогонос *m.* triggerfish (*Balistes*); **—ный** *a.* corniferous, horn-bearing.

рого/образный *a.* horn-shaped, horn-type; horny; (bot.) corniform; valley (iceberg); **—образование** *n.* (physiol.) keratogenesis; **—плодный** *a.* (bot.) ceratocarpous; **—семянный** *a.* (bot.) ceratospermous; **—хвосты** *pl.* (ent.) horntails (*Siricidae*).

рогул/ька, —я *f.* fork, splitting; slingshot; (text.) flyer.

род. *abbr.* (**родился**) born.

род *m.* family, origin, race, species, stock, descent; gener-

ation; (biol.) genus; variety, sort, type, kind, nature; (gram.) gender; *suffix* (chem.) **—ген,** e.g. **водород** hydrogen; **р. действия** method of operation; type of action; **в некотором —е** in some way; **всякого —а** of all kinds, of every description; **второго —а** a secondary (recrystallization); (phys.) second-order (transition); **что-то в этом —е** something to that effect.

род— *prefix* rhod— (rose red).

Рода реакция (proteins) Rhode test.

род/аллин *m.* rhodalline, allyl sulfocarbamide; **—амин** *m.* rhodamine, 4-keto-2-thiothiazolidine.

родаммоний *m.* rhodammonium.

родан *m.* thiocyanogen; **—ат, —ид** *m.* thiocyanate.

роданин *m.,* **—овая кислота** rhodanine, rhodanic acid.

родан/ирование *n.* thiocyanation; **—ировать** *v.* thiocyanate; **—истоводородный** *a.* thiocyanic (acid).

роданист/ый *a.* thiocyanate, sulfocyanate (of); thiocyanic (acid); **р. аммоний** ammonium thiocyanate; **—ая соль** thiocyanate; **—ое железо** ferrous thiocyanate; **—ое соединение** thiocyanogen compound.

роданкалий *m.* potassium thiocyanate.

родано— *prefix* thiocyano—.

родановодород *m.,* **—ная кислота** thiocyanic acid; **соль —ной кислоты** thiocyanate; **—ный** *a.* thiocyanate (of).

роданов/ый *a.* thiocyanate, sulfocyanate (of); thiocyanic (acid); **—ая ртуть** mercuric thiocyanate; **—ое железо** ferric thiocyanate; **—ое число** thiocyanogen value.

роданометрия *f.* thiocyanometry.

родацен *m.* rhodacene.

роддом *m.* maternity hospital.

Родезия Rhodesia.

роде/ит *m.* rhodeite, rhodeol; **—оза** *f.* rhodeose; **—оретин** *m.* rhodeoretin, convolvulin.

родиев/ый *a.* rhodium; **—ая чернь** rhodium black (catalyst).

родиен *m.* rhodiene.

родизоновая кислота rhodizonic acid.

род/ий *m.* rhodium, Rh.

родильница *f.* (med.) puerpera, woman who has recently given birth.

родильный *a.* (med.) obstetric, maternity (hospital); birth; delivery (room); puerperal (fever).

роди/мый *a.* native, natal; **—мое пятно** birthmark, nevus; **—на** *f.* native country, birthplace; habitat.

родинал *m.* rhodinal, cintronellal; Rodinal, *p*-aminophenol.

родинка *f.* birthmark, mole.

родин/овая кислота rhodinic acid; **—ол** *m.* rhodinol.

родирование *n.* (met.) rhodium plating.

роди/стый *a.* rhodium; **—стое золото, —т** *m.* (min.) rhodium gold, rhodite.

родител/и *pl.* parents; parentage; **—ь** *m.* parent; **—ьный** *a.* (gen.) mother (cell); (gram.) genitive; **—ьский** *a.* parental; paternal; **—ьский узел** (math.) parent, father.

родить *see* **рождать.**

родич *m.* relative.

родник *m.* spring, well (head); **—о—** *prefix* creno— (spring); **—овый** *a. of* **родник;** **—олюбивый** *a.* (biol.) crenophilous.

родн/ить *v.* bring together; make related, make similar; **—ичок** *m.* (anat.) fontanel(le); **—ой** *a.* native, natal; own; *m.* relative.

Р-однолистный *a.* (math.) *R*-univalent.

родн/ые *pl.* relatives; **—ый** *a. suffix* **—genic;** **—я** *f.* relatives, relations.

родо—*prefix* rhod(o)— (rose red); birth; —**вибрен** *m.* rhodovibrene, rhodopurpurin.

родо-видовой *a.* generic-specific.

родовой *a.* ancestral, racial, tribal; generic (concept; name); birth, labor (pains), parturient; puerperal (fever).

родовспомо/гательный *a.* (med.) obstetric; —**жение** *n.* obstetrics.

рододендр/ин *m.* rhododendrin; —**овник** *m.* rhododendron thicket; —**ол** *m.* rhododendrol; —**он** *m.* (bot.) rhododendron.

родо/дубильная кислота rhodotannic acid; —**ксантин** *m.* rhodoxanthin, thujorhodin; —**л** *m.* rhodol, metol.

родолия *f.* Australian lady beetle (*Rodolia cardinalis*).

родология *f.* (bot.) rhodology, study of roses.

родомицин *m.* rhodomycin.

родоначальн/ик *m.* ancestor, progenitor, forefather; —**ый** *a.* ancestral; parental; (bot.) original.

родо/пласт *m.* rhodoplast; —**псин** *m.* rhodopsin, visual purple; —**пурпурин** *m.* rhodopurpurin, rhodovibrene.

родоразрешение *n.* (med.) delivery, parturition.

Родос *see* **Родс.**

родослов/ие *n.*, —**ная** *f.* genealogy, pedigree; —**ный** *a.* genealogical.

родосское дерево *see* **розовое дерево.**

родоускоряющий *a.* (med.) parturifacient, labor-inducing.

Родс (geog.) Rhodes.

родств/енник *m.* relative, kinsman; —**енность** *f.* relation; **кровная** —**енность** consanguinity; —**енный** *a.* related, relative, akin (to), allied; —**енный материал** (geol.) cognate; —**енное разведение** inbreeding; —**о** *n.* relation(ship), kinship, propinquity; affinity, alliance; (petr.) consanguinity; parentage; **в** —**е** related; **кровное** —**о** *see* **кровная родственность.**

родузит *m.* (min.) rhodusite.

родулин *m.* rhoduline (aniline dye).

роды *pl.* childbirth, labor, delivery, parturition; (biol.) genera.

роёвня *f.* container for carrying swarming bees, swarm box.

рое/вой *a. of* **рой;** —**ние** *n.* swarming; —**сниматель** *m.* swarm catcher.

роет *pr. 3 sing. of* **рыть.**

рожа *f.* (med.) erysipelas; **свиная р.** (vet.) swine erysipelas; **палочка свиной** —**и** swine rotlauf bacillus.

рож/авшая *a.* parous, having given birth; —**ать** *see* **рождать;** —**ающий** *a.* parturient, giving birth.

рожд/аемость *f.* birth rate, natality; breeding, propagation; **контроль** —**аемости, ограничение** —**аемости** family planning; —**ать** *v.* bear, give birth, beget, bring forth; cause; —**аться** *v.* be born; originate, rise (from); breed; —**ающийся** being born; nascent.

рожден/ие *n.* birth; parturition, delivery; labor; production; origination; **до** —**ия** prenatal; **место** —**ия** birthplace; **статистика** —**ий** vital statistics.

рождественский *a.* (bot.) Christmas (fern, etc.).

рожек *gen. pl. of* **рожок.**

роженица *f.* (med.) parturient, woman in labor.

рожист/ый *a.* (med.) erysipel(at)ous; —**ое воспаление** erysipelas.

рожк/и *pl. of* **рожок; р., маточные** —**ки, чёрные** —**ки** (phyt.) ergot; **ржаные** —**и** (phyt.) ergot; —**овидный** *a.* corniculate, having horns; —**ово** *prefix* cerato—; —**овоглоточный** (anat.) ceratopharyngeal; —**овый** *a. of* **рожок;** horn-type, pronged; —**овое дерево** carob tree (*Ceratonia siliqua*).

рож/ок *dim. of* **рог;** (gas) burner, jet; catch, prong; horn, siren; socket (of lamp); (music) cornet, French horn;

shoehorn; baby bottle; (bot.) pod; **сахарный р., сладкий р.** *see* **рожковое дерево.**

рожь *f.* rye.

роз— *see* **раз**—.

роза *f.* rose; rosette; (radar) permanent echoes; **р. ветров** (meteor.) wind rose.

роза/гинин *m.* rosaginin; —**лия** *f.* (mam.) golden lion marmoset (*Leontideus rosalia*); —**нилин** *m.* rosaniline; —**риум** *m.* rose bed, rose garden.

розвальни *pl.* low, wide sleigh.

розвязь *f.* (agr.) unbound grain.

розга *f.* rod; **золотая р.** *see* **золотарник.**

роздых *m.* brief rest, break.

роз/еин *m.* rosein; —**елла** *f.* (orn.) rosella, Australian parakeet; —**енмюллеров орган** (anat.) Rosenmüller's body, epoophoron.

Розен/стила зелень Rosensthiel's green, barium manganate; —**штейна способ** Rosenstein process.

розеола *f.* (med.) roseola (rash).

розеомицин *m.* roseomycin.

розет/ировать *v.* make into rosettes; —**ка** *f.* rosette; (elec.) socket, outlet, receptacle; —**ный** *a.* rosette; —**очность** *f.*, —**очная болезнь** (phyt.) rosette; —**очный** *a.* rosette, rosulate.

розжиг *m.* kindling, firing.

розин/дон *m.* rosindone, rosindulone; —**дулин** *m.* rosinduline (aniline dye); —**ол** *m.* rosinol, retinol.

розлив *m.* pouring; bottling.

розмарин *m.*, —**овый** *a.* rosemary.

розни/ца: продавать в —**цу** *v.*, —**чный** *a.* retail.

розн/ый *a.* odd, unmatched, incomplete; —**ь** *f.* difference, diversity.

рознял *past m. sing. of* **разнять.**

розов процесс *see* **Розе процесс.**

розо/ватый *a.* rose-tinted, pinkish; —**веть** *v.* turn pink; redden; —**видный** *a.* (bot.) rose-like, rosaceous; —**во**— *prefix* roseo— (rose-red), rhod(o)— (rose); —**вокрасный** *a.* rose-red; —**воцветковый** *a.* (bot.) pink-flowered; rhodanthous; —**вый** *a.* rose(-colored); pink; —**вое дерево** rosewood; —**вое масло** rose oil, attar of roses; —**ловая кислота** rosolic acid, corallin; —**цветковый** *see* **розововоцветковый;** rosaeflorous; —**цианин** *m.* rosocyanin.

розыск *m.*, —**ной** *a.* (re)search, inquiry, investigation; **служебная** —**ная собака** police dog.

роистый *a.* frequently swarming.

роиться *v.* swarm.

рой *m.* cluster; swarm (of bees); **р. ионов** ion cluster; —**ба** *f.* swarming.

ройка *f.* (silv.) fluting, groove.

ройер(-машина) *m.* (foundry) royer (loam- and sand-preparing machine).

рой/ливость *f.* swarming tendency (of bees); —**ник** *see* **роесниматель; р.-первак** *m.* prime swarm; **р.-порой** *m.* second swarm.

рокад/а *f.* (mil.) border roads; lateral line of communication; —**ный** *a.* belt, lateral, border (road).

рокамболь *m.* (bot.) rocambole (*Allium scorodoprasum*).

рокарий *m.* rock garden.

Роквелл: твёрдость по —**у** (met.) Rockwell hardness.

рок(к)ер *m.* (min.) rocker, cradle.

рокот *m.* growl, low rumble; murmer; —**ание** *n.* rumble, rumbling; —**ать** *v.* roar; murmur.

рокфор *m.* Roquefort cheese.

рол *m.* roll (of paper, etc.); roller, cylinder, shaft; *see* **ролл;** —**евой** *a. of* **рол;** reel-fed; web (press).

роландова борозда (anat.) rolandic fissure, fissure of Rolando.

роли *gen., pl. etc., of* **роль**.

ролик *m.* roller, caster; roll; pulley, sheave; (elec.) porcelain insulator; **р. холостой ветви** return idler; **холостой р.** idler.

ролико/вый *a.* of **ролик;** roller (bearing); roll (feed, etc.); **—вая опора** idler; **—подпятник** *m.* roller thrust bearing; **—подшипник** *m.* roller bearing.

ролитетрациклин *m.* (pharm.) rolitetracycline (antibiotic).

роль *f.* role, part, function; roll (of paper, etc.); **играть р.** *v.* act (as), serve (as); **играть важную р.** *v.* play an important part, be vital (to); **—ганг** *m.* roller conveyer, roll train; table (of rolling mill); **—ный** *a.* of **рол(л);** roll(ed); sheet (metal).

рольс *m.* bollard.

ром *m.* rum.

романоскоп *m.* (med.) sigmoidoscope.

романский *a.* Roman.

ромаш/ка *f.*, **—ковый** *a.* daisy, spec. Matricaria; **аптечная р., лекарственная р.** German camomile (*M. chamomilla*); **—ник** *m.* pyrethrum.

ромб *m.* (geom.) rhomb(us); diamond, lozenge; (ichth.) turbot; brill; **—еппорфир** *m.* (petr.) rhomb porphyry.

Ромберга проба (med.) Romberg test.

ромбик *m.* (ichth.) boarfish.

ромбический *a.* (ortho)rhombic.

ромбо— *prefix* rhomb(o)—; **—видный** *a.* rhomboid, rhombiform; diamond(-shaped), double-wedge; **—видный мозг** (anat.) rhombencephalon, hindbrain; **—вые** *see* **ромбы; —вый** *a.* rhombus, rhombic; **—вая призма** rhombohedron; **—гемиморфный** *a.* (cryst.) rhombohemimorphous; **—двупирамидальный** *a.* (cryst.) rhombobipyramidal; **—ид** *m.* (geom.) rhomboid; **—идальный** *a.* rhomboid(al); **—клаз** *m.* (min.) rhomboclase; **—образный** *see* **ромбовидный.**

ромбоэдр *m.* (cryst.) rhombohedron; **—ический** *a.* rhombohedral.

ромбы *pl.* (ichth.) left-eyed flounders (*Bothidae*).

ро-мезон (phys.) rho meson.

ромеит *m.* (min.) romeite.

рометалл *m.* Rhometal (alloy).

ромовый *a.* rum.

ромштекс *m.* (food) rump steak.

Рона Rhone (river).

ронгалит *m.*, **—овый** *a.* rongalite (formaldehyde sodium sulfoxylate).

ронделетиевые *pl.* (ichth.) Rondeletiidae.

рондик *m.* (agr.) head stall.

ронжа *f.* cross beam, tie beam; (orn.) Siberian jay (*Cractes infaustus*).

ронидаза *f.* (enz.) Ron(i)dase.

ронить *see* **ронять.**

ронка *f.* (ichth.) grunt (*Haemulon*).

ронский *a.* Rhone (river); **Ронская низменность** Rhone Valley.

ронять *v.* drop, lose, shed (leaves, etc.); fell (trees); discredit, run down.

ропак *m.* (ocean.) ropak, turret ice.

ропалий *m.* (zool.) rhopalium (of jellyfish).

ропа/сить, —чить *v.* form ice hummocks.

ропот *m.* grumble, murmured disapproval; rustling; **—ание** *n.* grumbling, etc., *see v.*; **—ать** *v.* grumble (about), murmur.

рораксий *a.* (geol.) Rauracian, Sequanian.

роринг *m.* (vet.) roaring (in horses), laryngeal hemiplegia.

рос *past m. sing. of* **расти.**

рос— *see* **роз—.**

рос/а *f.* dew; (phyt.) mildew; **ложная мучнистая р.**

downy mildew; **ложномучнистая р. табака** (agr.) blue mold of tobacco; **медвяная р.** honeydew; **мучнистая р.** (agr.) powdery mildew; (willow) blight; **точка —ы** dew point.

росглав— *prefix* main administration (for).

рос/ение *n.* dew-retting (of flax); **—инка** *f.* dewdrop; **—истый** *a.* dewy; **—иться** *v.* be covered with dew.

росичка *f.* crabgrass (*Digitaria*).

роскошь *f.* luxury; splendor; **—ный** *a.* luxurious, splendid; luxuriant (foliage); de luxe (edition).

роскоэлит *see* **росколит.**

росл/и *past pl. of* **расти; —ость** *f.* height; (met.) spongy top, rising top; **—ый** *a.* full-grown, tall.

росн/оладанная кислота benzoic acid; **—ый ладан** gum benzoin.

росома/ха *f.*, **—ший** *a.* (zool.) wolverine (*Gulo gulo*).

росомер *m.* (meteor.) drosometer.

роспашь *f.* plowed land, clearing.

роспись *f.* painting; catalog, list; **р. разъёма** (elec.) pin designation of a connector, pin-out.

росплывь *f.* loose drifting (of logs); scattering.

роспуск *m.* breaking up; dismissal, (mil.) disbandment; unraveling; unreeling; **—и** *pl.* log trailer.

Росса Джеймса пролив James Ross Strait; **Р. море** Ross Sea; **Р. шельфовый ледник** Ross Ice Shelf.

росс/биграмма *f.* (meteor.) Rossby diagram; **—еландо-вый** *a.* Rosseland (mean).

Росси кривая Rossi curve.

российский *a.* of **Россия,** Russian.

Россия Russia.

россия *f.* (mal.) small squid (*Rossia*).

россомаха *see* **росомаха.**

россып/ный *a.* (geol.) placer, alluvial; **—ь** *f.* scattering, spreading; pouring; (ocean.) bar, shallow; (com.) loss of weight; (geol.) placer (deposit), alluvial deposit; (rock) detritus; **—ью** *adv.* loose, in bulk; placer (deposit).

рост *m.* height, size, stature; build-up, increase, growth, development; (urban) sprawl; germination; **—ом** in height; **во весь р.** full length; **давать р.** *v.* germinate; **кривая** growth curve; **остановить р.** *v.* stunt (growth); **сила —а** germinative power; **функции медленного —а** slowly-increasing functions.

ростбиф *m.* (food) roast beef.

роствёрк *m.* grating, grill(age); foundation mat; **р. на сваях** pilework.

ростеллум *m.* (bot.) rostellum, little beak.

ростепель *f.*, **—ный** *a.* thaw.

рост/ец *m.* (bot.) thallus; **—ковый** *a.* of **росток;** germinative; apical (cell); **—ковая муха** seed corn maggot; **—о—** *prefix* auxano—, growth; **—овой** *a.* growth; **—овой побег** (bot.) turion, sucker; **—овое вещество** growth stimulant.

ростовский *a.* (geog.) Rostov.

ростов/щик *m.* money lender, loan shark; **—щичество** *n.* usury.

рост/ок *m.* seedling; sprout, shoot; embryo; (wheat) germ; **пускать —ки** *v.* germinate, sprout; **—омер** *m.* auxanometer.

росторнит *m.* (min.) rosthornite.

ростоустойчив/ость *f.* resistance to growth; **—ый** *a.* resistant to growth.

ростподавляющий *a.* growth-inhibiting.

ростр/альный *a.* (zool.) rostral; **—ум** *m.* rostrum, beak.

росчин *m.* leaven.

росчисть *f.* (agr.) clearing.

росший *past act. part. of* **расти.**

рос/ы *gen., pl., etc., of* **роса; —яника** *f.* dewberry; **—янка** *f.* (bot.) Drosera; **—яной, —яный** *a.* dew.

рот *m.* mouth, opening, os, stoma; **вторичный р.** (zool.) metastoma; **клеточный р.** cytostome; **полость рта** oral cavity; **через р.** oral (administration).

рота *f.* company; (med.) erysipelas; **р.-лаборатория** *f.* laboratory company.

ротаметр *m.* rotameter, float-type flow meter.

ротан (ichth.) *see* **головешка.**

ротанг *m.* (bot.) rattan (*Calamus*).

рота/плёнка *f.* rotary stencil paper; **—принт** *m.*, **—принтный** *a.* offset duplicator; **—ри** *n.* rotary system; **—тивный** *a.* rotative, rotary; **—тор** *m.* rotator; rotary press; rotary stencil duplicator, mimeograph; **—тории** *pl.* (zool.) rotifers (*Rotatoria*); **—торный** *a. of* **рота-тор;** **—ционнобарабанный** *a.* rotary-drum.

ротационн/ый *a.* rotation, rotary, rotating; **р. сустав** (anat.) pivot joint, rotary joint; **—ая газодувка** cycloid-al blower; **—ая радиотерапия** rotation therapy; **—ая сушилка** rotary dryer; **—ое движение** rotary motion, rotation.

ротация *f.* rotation; rotary (press).

ротенон *m.*, **—овый** *a.* rotenone.

ротик *dim. of* **рот;** (zool.) osculum.

ротлерин *m.* rottlerin, kamalin.

ротный *a. of* **рота.**

рото— *prefix* mouth, stomato—.

ротовая кислота rothic acid.

ротов/ой *a.* mouth, oral, stomatous, stomatic; **—ая щель** (anat.) rima oris, oral fissure; **—ая ямка** (embr.) stomodeum; foregut.

ротогравюра *f.* rotogravure.

ротограф *m.*, **—ия** *f.* (phot.) rotograph.

ротожелудочный *a.* (anat.) stomatogastric.

ротон *m.* (nucl.) roton, quantum of rotational energy.

ротоногие *pl.* (zool.) Stomatopoda.

ротор *m.* rotor; (centrifuge) basket; (math.) curl (of a vector function).

роторасширитель *m.* (med.) gag, device to hold mouth open.

роторный *a.* rotor; rotary; agitated (thin-film evaporator).

ротоскоп *m.* rotoscope.

рототерапия *f.* (med.) rotation therapy.

Роуланда значение (opt.) Rowland's value.

роульс *m.* (naut.) roller.

Роуса саркома (med.) Rous sarcoma.

рохл/евые, —и *pl.* (ichth.) guitarfishes (*Rhinobatidae*); **—я** *f.* guitarfish.

роху (ichth.) rohu (*Labeo rohita*).

роцелл/овая кислота roccelic acid; **—ин** *m.* roccelin, orseillin.

рошеллева соль Rochelle salt, potassium sodium tar-trate.

рошерит *m.* (min.) roscherite.

Рошона призма Rochon prism.

рошпан *m.* (min.) cross brace.

рощ/а *f.* grove, wood; **—ица** *dim. of* **роща.**

РОЭ *abbr.* (**реакция оседания эритроцитов**) erythro-cyte sedimentation rate.

роющий *pr. act. part. of* **рыть;** burrowing (spiders); (zool.) fossorial.

роя *gen. of* **рой.**

рояль *m.*, **—ный** *a.* piano.

Рп *abbr.* (**репер**) bench mark.

рр. *abbr.* (**реки**) rivers; (**роды**) species, kinds; **р-р** *abbr.* (**размер**) size; (**раствор**) solution.

рРНК *abbr.* (**рибосомная рибонуклеиновая кислота**) ribosomal RNA.

р-РНК *abbr.* (**растворимая РНК**) transfer RNA.

р/сек *abbr.* (**рентген в секунду**) roentgen per second.

РСК *abbr.* (**реакция связывания комплемента**) com-plement fixation test.

РСМ *abbr.* (**разбираемость, слышимость, качество модуляции**) clarity, audibility, and quality of modulation.

РСП *abbr.* (**рецессивный, сцепленный с полом**) re-cessive, sex-linked.

рств. *abbr.* (**растворимость**) solubility.

РСФСР *abbr.* Russian Soviet Federated Socialist Republic.

РСХ *see* **райсемхоз.**

РТ *abbr.* (**расчётная точка**) reference point; (**регуля-тор температуры**) temperature regulator; (**рентгеновская трубка**) X-ray tube.

рта *gen. of* **рот.**

РТГА *abbr.* (**реакция торможения гемагглютина-ции**) hemagglutination-inhibition test.

РТМ *abbr.* (**руководящие технические материалы**) technical reference data.

ртов *gen. pl. of* **рот.**

РТС *abbr.* (**ретрансляционная телевизионная стан-ция**) television relay station, translator; (**робототех-ническая система**) robot(ic) system.

рт. ст. *abbr.* (**ртутный столб**).

ртутист/о— *prefix* mercuro—, mercurous—; **—ый** *a.* mercurous, mercury.

ртутник *m.* mercury-arc rectifier.

ртутно— *prefix* mercuri—, mercuric—; **—кварцевый** *a.* mercury-quartz; mercury vapor (lamp); **—синеродо-водородный** *a.* mercuricyanic (acid).

ртутн/ый *a.* mercuric, mercury; (pharm.) mercurial; **р. выпрямитель** (elec.) mercury arc rectifier; **р. столб(ик), —ая нить** mercury column; **—ая лампа** (elec.) mercury (vapor) lamp; **—ая соль** mercuric salt.

ртут/ь *f.* mercury, Hg, quicksilver; **азотнокислая за-кись —и** mercurous nitrate; **азотнокислая окись —и** mercuric nitrate; **амидисто-хлористая р., белая осадочная р., двухлористо-амидистая р.** white precipitate, ammoniated mercury; **двухлористая р.** mercury bichlo-ride; **закись —и** mercurous oxide; **соль закиси —и** mercurous salt; (**жёлтая**) **иодистая р.** mercurous io-dide, yellow mercury iodide; **иодная р.** mercuric io-dide; **однохлористая р., полухлористая р.** mercu-rous chloride; **окись —и** mercuric oxide; **соль окиси —и** mercuric salt; **сернистая р.** mercury sulfide; **сер-нокислая закись —и** mercurous sulfate; **сернокис-лая окись —и** mercuric sulfate; **хлористая р.** mer-curous chloride; **хлорная р.** mercuric chloride, mer-cury bichloride.

ртутьорганический *a.* organomercuric.

рты *pl. of* **рот.**

РУ *abbr.* (**рентгеновская установка**) X-ray unit.

Ру сыворотка (med.) Roux's serum, diphtheria antitoxin.

Руан (geog.) Rouen.

Руанда (geog.) Ruanda.

руб. *abbr.* (**рубль**) ruble.

рубазоновая кислота rubazonic acid.

рубанок *m.* plane (tool).

рубануть *see* **рубить.**

рубатоксин *m.* rubatoxin.

руба/ха *f.* shirt; **водоплавная р.** diving dress; **—шеч-ный** *a. of* **рубаха;** **—шка** *f.* shirt; jacket, housing; casing, lining; color (of fur); (math.) lateral area; **вод-яная —шка** water jacket.

рубеано/водородная кислота, —вый водород ru-beanic acid, rubean hydride.

рубеж *m.* border, boundary, limit, line, verge; **р. атом-ной безопасности** (mil.) risk distance line; **за —ом** abroad; **—ная черта** boundary line.

рубежанский *a.* (geog.) Rubezhnoe.
руб/ен *m.* rubene; **—еоз** *m.* (med.) rubeosis; **—ероид** *m.*, **—ероидный** *a.* ruberoid, roofing material, roofing felt; **—ефакция** *f.* (med.) rubefaction.
руб/ец *m.* scar, seam; gash, notch, slash; hem; (biol., med.) cicatrix; (zool.) rumen, first stomach; (met.) teeming lap; **листовой р.** (bot.) leaf scar; **рассечение —цов** (med.) ulotomy.
рубиа/новая кислота rubianic acid, ruberythric acid; **—цеоидный** *a.* (bot.) paracytic; **—цин** *m.* rubiacin (a madder dye).
рубид/ий *m.* rubidium, Rb.
руби/дин *m.* rubidine; **—ервин** *m.* rubijervine; **—ксантин** *m.* rubixanthin; **—линовая кислота** rubilic acid.
рубильн/ик *m.* cleaver, chopper; (elec.) knife switch, cut-out; **—ый** *a.* chopping; **—ая машина** chopper.
рубин *m.* rubin, fuchsin; (min.) ruby; ruby glass; **—ный, —овый** *a.* ruby; (rubinic) acid; **—огорлый** *a.* ruby-throated.
рубит/ельная машина (paper) clipper; **—ь** *v.* chop, hack, chisel; cut, sever; hew, fell (trees); build, erect.
рубицен *m.* rubicene.
руб/ка *f.* chopping, etc., *see* **рубить;** cut, gash; chiseling; logging operation; (naut.) deck house, (pilot's) cabin, (operations) room, sail (of submarine); **боевая р.** conning tower; **ограждение —ки** fairwater (of submarine).
рублёвый *a.* one-ruble.
рублен(н)ый *a.* chopped, etc., *see* **рубить;** (silv.) cleared; log (wall); **р. шрифт** sans-serif font.
рубль *m.* ruble.
рубнуть *v.* chop, hack (at).
рубочный *a.* of **рубка;** conning tower.
рубракс *m.* Rubrax.
рубрен *m.* rubrene.
рубри/ка *f.* head(ing); column; entry; **типовая р.** subdivision; **—катор** *m.* list of classification headings; **—кация** *f.*, **—цирование** *n.* classification; system of headings; division into columns; **—цировать** *v.* classify; provide with headings; divide into columns.
рубро— *prefix* rubro— (red); (med.) red nucleus.
рубро/глауцин *m.* rubroglaucine (pigment); **—н** *m.* rubrone (a rubber compound); **—фития** *f.* (med.) tinea, ringworm.
руб/ца *gen.* of **рубец; —цевание** *n.* scarring, cicatrization; **—цеватый** *a.* scarred, seamed, rough, grained; **—цеваться** *v.* cicatrize, scar, form scar tissue; **—цовый** *a.* scar, seam; gash, notch; **—чатый** *a.* scar(red), cicatr(ic)ose; seamed, ribbed, fluted, wrinkled; **—чик** *dim.* of **рубец;** (bot.) hilum, eye (of seed); areola; cicatricle, navel; **—чиковый** *a.* (bot.) hilar.
рубщик *m.* woodcutter.
рубэритриновая кислота *see* **рубиановая кислота.**
рубящий *a.* chopping, etc., *see* **рубить;** knife (switch).
рувета *f.* (ichth.) oilfish (*Ruvettus pretiosus*).
руга *f.* (biol.) ruga, fold, wrinkle.
ругат/ельный *a.* abusive; **—ь** *v.* scold; criticize; **—ься** *v.* swear, curse.
руда *f.* (min.) ore; **болотная р.** marsh ore; **дерновая р.** meadow ore, bog iron ore.
рудбекия *f.* (bot.) rudbeckia.
рудеральный *a.* (bot.) ruderal.
рудерпост *m.* (naut.) rudder post.
рудимент *m.* rudiment; **—арный** *a.* rudimentary, vestigial.
рудисты *pl.* (geol.) Rudistes.
рудит *m.* (petr.) rudite, coarse sediments.
рудник *m.*, **—овый** *a.* mine, pit, quarry.

руднич/ый *a.* mine, mining, miner's; **р. воздух, р. газ** firedamp, mine methane; **р. лес** timber, pit props; **—ые машины** mining equipment.
рудноугольный *a.* ore-carbon.
рудн/ый *a.* mining; ore; metallic (mineral); **р. двор** stockyard; **р. ларь** ore pocket; **р. столб** shoot (of ore); **р. шлам** ore slime; **—ая мелочь** smalls, slack, fines; **—ая проба** assay; **—ая промышленность, —ое дело** mining industry; **—ое ископаемое** metallic mineral.
рудо— *prefix* ore; **—вмещающие породы** host rock; **—воз** *m.* ore carrier, ore freighter; **—дробилка** *f.* (ore) crusher.
рудоискатель *m.* (min.) prospector; **—ный** *a.* prospecting; dowsing (rod).
рудо/катка *f.* rolls; **—коп** *m.* miner; **—мойка** *f.* ore washer; **—носный** *see* **рудосодержащий.**
рудообжиг/альщик *m.* (met.) roaster, calciner; **—ательная печь** roasting furnace, roaster, calciner.
рудо/обогатительный *a.* ore-dressing (plant), ore-beneficiating; **—образующий** *a.* ore-forming; **—отделительный** *a.* ore-separating; **—отложение** *n.* ore deposition; **—подготовка** *f.* ore beneficiation; **—подъёмный** *a.* ore-lifting; **—проводящий** *a.* ore-bearing (channel).
рудопромыв/ательный, —очный *a.* ore-washing; **—очная машина** ore washer, specif. log washer.
рудоразбор/ка *f.*, **—(оч)ный** *a.* (min.) sorting, picking, screening.
рудораспределитель *m.* ore distributor; **—ный** *a.* ore-distributing.
рудо/содержащий *a.* ore-bearing, metalliferous; **—спуск** *m.* ore chute; **—управление** *n.* mine management; **—усреднительный** *a.* ore-neutralizing.
рудяк *m.*, **—овый горизонт** (geol.) hardpan.
руж/ейник *m.* gunsmith; **—ейный** *a.* gun, rifle; **—ейня** *f.* gunsmith's shop; **—ьё** *n.* gun, rifle.
руина *f.* ruin(s).
рук/а *f.* hand; arm; brachium; **держать в —ах** *v.* have in hand; **затягивать от —и** screw finger-tight; **из вторых рук** second-hand; **из первых рук** first-hand; **махнуть —ой** *v.* overlook; **морская р.** a soft coral (*Alcyonium*); **на скорую —у** in haste, offhand; **от —и** manually, by hand; freehand (sketch); **установка от —и** manual adjustment, hand adjustment; **под —ами, под —ой** at hand, handy; **сбыть с рук** *v.* rid oneself (of).
рукав *m.* hose, flexible pipe; sleeve, sheath; (zool.) reticulum, second stomach; (filter) bag; (feed) chute; (tuyere) pipe; (swivel) arm; arm (of sea); branch (of river); **маточный р.** (anat.) vagina; **—ица** *f.* mitten; gauntlet; **—ный** *a.* of **рукав;** (biol.) peristaltic (pump); **—ный фильтр** bag filter.
рукавообразный *a.* sleeve-like, sleeve-shaped; (geol.) channel (deposit).
рукав/чатый *a.* long-sleeved; manicate; **—чик** *dim.* of **рукав;** short sleeve.
рукзак *m.* backpack.
рукоблудие *n.* masturbation.
руковод, —итель *m.* guide, adviser, instructor, supervisor, manager; (flight) controller; **—ительство** *see* **руководство; —ительствовать** *see* **руководить.**
руководить *v.* guide, lead, conduct; instruct, direct, govern; supervise, manage, run, boss; **р. неправильно** mislead; **—ся** *v.* be guided, etc.; be influenced (by); follow (directions).
руководство *n.* guidance, lead(ership), direction, supervision, administration, management; instructions, guide-

line(s), handbook, manual, guide; —**вать(ся)** *see* **руководить(ся).**

руководящ/ий *a.* guiding, etc., *see* **руководить;** guide(line); indicative; reference, key; managerial; —**ие ископаемые, —ие формы** index fossils, guide fossils.

рукодел/ие *n.* handwork; needlework; —**ьный** *a.* handmade.

руко/крылые *pl.* (zool.) bats (*Chiroptera*); —**мойник** *m.* hand basin; —**ногие** *pl.* Brachiopoda; —**ножки** *pl.* (mam.) aye-ayes (*Daubentoniidae*).

рукопашный *a.* hand-to-hand (combat).

рукопёрые *pl.* (ichth.) goosefishes (*Lophiidae*).

рукопис/ь *f.,* —**ный** *a.* manuscript.

руко/плескать *v.* applaud, clap; —**пожатие** *n.* handshake.

рукоят/ка, —ь *f.* handle, shaft, haft, grip; knob; crank (handle); lever, arm; (anat.) manubrium; (ent.) stipes; **р. грудины** manubrium sterni; **р. управления** (comp.; robotics) joystick; **с —кой** ansa(ted).

рулев/ой *a.* steering, rudder, helm; control; quill (feather); *m.* pilot, helmsman; **р. горизонтальщик** planesman (on a submarine); **—ая машина** control actuator, (autopilot) servo; **—ое управление** steering (system); **—ые (перья)** *pl.* (orn.) tail flight feathers, rectrices.

рулёжный *a.* steering, piloting, guiding; (av.) taxiing.

рулёк семенника (anat.) gubernaculum (of the testis), mesocardial ligament.

рулён *m.,* **—а** *f.* (ichth.) wrasse (*Crenilabrus*).

руление *n.* steering, etc., *see* **рулить.**

рулет *m.* roll; (meat) loaf, cutlet.

рулет/ка *f.,* **—очный** *a.* tape (measure); reel; **—та** *f.* (geom.) roulette, roll curve.

рулить *v.* steer, pilot, guide; (av.) taxi.

рулон *m.,* **свёртывать в р.** *v.* roll, coil; **—ный** *a.* roll (film, etc.); **—ная бумага** (comp.) continuous-feed paper; **—ные кровли** roofing materials.

руль *m.* rudder, helm, (steering) wheel, control; (bicycle) handle bar; (av.) control surface; (air) vane; (anat.) gubernaculum; **р. высоты, р. глубины** elevator; **р. направления** rudder; **р. управления** control surface; **—ка** *f.* (zool.) shank.

рум. *abbr.* **(румынский)** Rumanian.

румб *m.,* **—овый** *a.* bearing, point (of compass); rhumb (line).

руминированный *a.* (bot.) ruminate(d), mottled and wrinkled (as if chewed).

румицин *m.* rumicin.

румпель *m.* (naut.) tiller.

Румыния Rumania.

румынский *a.* Rumanian.

румян/а *f.* rouge; **—еть** *v.* redden, blush; **—ец** *m.* blush; erubescence, bloom (on fruit); **—ить** *v.* redden, paint red; **—ка** *f.* (bot.) viper's bugloss (*Echium*).

румяный *a.* rosy, ruddy.

Рунге-Кутта метод (phys.) Runge-Kutta method.

рунду/к *m.,* **—чный** *a.* locker, bin.

рун/ец *m.* (ent.) sheep tick; **—истый** *a.* fleecy; **—ный** *a.* *of* **руно; —ный ход** mass migration; **—о** *n.* fleece; (ichth.) shoal.

рупельский *a.* (geol.) Rupelian.

рупия *f.* (med.) rupia.

рупор *m.* horn, funnel; (loud)speaker, megaphone; mouth(piece); **—нолинзовый** *a.* horn and lens (radiator); **—ный** *a.* *of* **рупор;** horn-type.

руппия *f.* (bot.) Ruppia.

Рур, рурский *a.* (geog.) Ruhr.

рус. *abbr.* **(русский)** Russian.

руса/к *m.,* **—чий** *a.* (zool.) European hare (*Lepus europaeus*); (ichth.) shad (*Alosa*).

русалка *f.* water nymph.

русло *n.* (river) bed, channel, waterway, race; course, direction; (anat.) alveus; **высохшее р.** arroyo; **кровяное р.** blood vessel; **селевое р., сухое р.** dry wash, arroyo; **—вой, —вый** *a. of* **русло;** fluvial; **—вой двигатель** water wheel; **—вые процессы** evolution of river bed; **—очистительный** *a.* channel-cleaning.

русо— *prefix* light-brown.

русский *a., m.* (ethnic) Russian.

русско— *prefix* Russo—, Russian.

русск. пат. *abbr.* **(русский патент)** Russian patent.

руст *see* **рустика.**

Руста феномен (med.) Rust's phenomenon.

руст/ик *m.,* **—ика** *f.* (masonry) rustic, bossage; **—овать** *v.* face with rough stone, rusticate; **—овка** *f.* rustic masonry.

русый *a.* light brown.

рута *f.* (bot.) rue (*Ruta*).

Рута аккумулятор Ruth's accumulator.

рутаекарпин *m.* rutaecarpine.

рутен/ат *m.* ruthenate; **—иевый** *a.* ruthenium, ruthenic; **—иевая кислота** ruthenic acid; **соль —иевой кислоты, —иевокислая соль** ruthenate.

рутен/ий *m.* ruthenium, Ru; **окись —ия** *f.* ruthenium oxide; **сернистый р., сульфид —ия** *f.* ruthenium sulfide; **хлорид —ия, хлористый р.** ruthenium chloride.

рутен/истый *a.* ruthenium, ruthen(i)ous; **—овый** *a. see* **рутениевый.**

рутер *m.* rooter, road plow.

рутидоз *m.* (med.) rhytidosis.

рутил *m.* (min.) rutile.

рутил/иден *m.* rutylidene, 1-hendecyne; **—ин** *m.* rutylin.

рутиловый *a.* (min.) rutile.

рутин *m.* rutin.

рутин/а *f.,* **—ный** *a.* routine.

рутиновая кислота rutinic acid.

рутиноза *f.* (biochem.) rutinose, rhamnosidoglucose.

рут/ный, —овый *a.* (bot.) rue; rutic (acid); **—онал** *m.* rutonal, methylphenylbarbituric acid.

Рутса вентилятор Roots blower.

рутьер *see* **рутер.**

руфи/ановая кислота rufianic acid, quinizarinsulfonic acid; **—галловая кислота, —галлол** *m.* rufigallic acid, rufigallol; **—н** *m.* rufin; **—опин** *m.* rufiopin, tetrahydroxyanthraquinone.

руфол *m.* Rufol, sulfamethizole.

рух *m.* (glass) devitrification; friable place.

рухл/ость *f.* friability; unsteadiness; **—ый** *a.* friable; unsteady.

рухляк *m.* (geol.) marl; **—овый** *a.* marly, marlaceous.

рухнуть *v.* crash down, fall to the ground; crumble away.

ручат/ельный *a.* guarantee(ing); **—ельство** *n.* guaranty, warrant, voucher; **—ься** *v.* guarantee, warrant, vouch (for), answer (for), certify; be sure.

руч/еёк *dim. of* **ручей;** streamlet, rill, rivulet; **—еистый** *a.* fluted, cracked; **—ей** *m.* brook, stream, creek; (anat.) rivus; groove; impression (of a die).

ручейники *pl.* caddis flies (*Trichoptera*).

ручек *gen. pl. of* **ручка.**

ручка *dim. of* **рука;** handle, knob, (hand) grip, shaft; crank (handle); (hand) lever; (control) stick; arm; pen; (anat.) brachium; **автоматическая р.** fountain pen; **координатная р.** (robotics) joystick.

ручнеть *v.* become tame.

ручник *m.* hand towel; hammer.

ручни́ст *m.* dispenser of non-prescription drugs.

ручн/о́й *a.* manual, hand(-operated), manually operated; handmade; hand-held (camera); portable; wrist (watch); tame, domestic; **р. ввод** (comp.) keyboard entry, manual input; **—ая погру́зка** freight handling; **—ая прода́жа** sale of non-prescription drugs; **—ая рабо́та** handiwork; manual labor; **—ой рабо́ты** handmade; **с —ым приводом, с —ым управле́нием** hand-operated.

ручьево́й *a.* of **ручей; р. режи́м** (chem.) rivulet condensation.

руш/е́ние *n.* husking, etc., see *v.*; pearling; collapse; **—и́ть** *v.* husk, shell, scour, hull; demolish, pull down; **—и́ться** *v.* collapse, fall down.

рф *abbr.* **(радфот)** radphot; **(реферат)** abstract, paper.

РФК *abbr.* **(рибозофосфорная кислота)** ribose-phosphoric acid.

р.Х., Р.Х. *abbr.* **(рождество Христово)** birth of Christ, B.C.; **РХ** *abbr.* **(рыбий хвост)** fishtail, two-way bit.

РХБС *see* **эфирсульфонат.**

р-ция *abbr.* **(реакция)** reaction.

р/час *abbr.* **(рентген в час)** roentgens per hour.

р-ы *abbr.* **(размеры)** dimensions, size; **(растворы)** solutions.

рыб/а *f.* fish; *see also* **рыбка, рыбы; белая р.** name used for a variety of fish; *see* **верховка, жерех, кижуч, омуль, каймановая р.** longnose gar (*Lepisosteus*); **королевская р.** *see* **базилихт; красная р.** any of several kinds of high-quality sturgeon; **майская р.** shad (*Alosa*); **мелкая р.** fry, young fish; **молочная р.** *see* **ханос; мягкая р.** *see* **лягушка-рыба; поющая р.** *see* **рыба-мичман; прометеевая р.** rabbitfish (*Promethichthys prometheus*); **рулевая р.** amberjack (*Seriola*); **сеачуб** (*Kyphosus*); **слепая р.** Mexican cavefish (*Anoptichthys*); **собачья р.** *see* **евдошка; солнечная р.** pumpkinseed (*Lepomis gibbosus*); opah (*Lampris regius*); *see also* **луна-рыбы; чёрная р.** *see* **даллия.**

рыба- *prefix* fish; (*if compound name cannot be found, check for second component, e.g.* **рыба-курок,** *see* **курок;** *or reversed form, e.g.* **рыба-бекас,** *see* **бекас-рыба;** *or plural form, e.g.* **рыба-бабочка,** *see* **рыбы-бабочки**).

рыба-/а́нгел angelfish (*Pomacanthus*); **—ба́ба** *see* **подкаменщик; —ехи́дна** *see* **хаулиодовые; —зе́ркало** *see* **зеркаловые.**

рыб/а́к *m.* fisherman, angler.

рыба́-ка́мень stonefish (*Synanceia horrida*); **р.-ка́торжник** sheepshead (*Archosargus probatocephalus*); **р.-ла́сточка** *see* **тригла; р.-лист** leaffish (*Monocirrhus polyacanthus*); **—лка** *f.* (sport) fishing; fishing hole; **р.-ло́цман** pilotfish (*Naucrates ductor*); **р.-ми́чман** (ichth.) midshipman (*Porichthys*); **р.-мотылёк** *see* **рыбы-бабочки; р.-пик** *see* **рыбы-лопаты; р.-ползу́н** *see* **анабас; р.-пятно́** spot (*Leiostomus xanthurus*); **р.-со́лнечник** *see* **солнечниковые; р.-труба́** *see* **флейтовые; р.-туз-пик** spadefish; **р.-фона́рь** lanternfish (*Myctophum*).

рыб/а́цкий, —а́чий *a.* fishing; fisherman's; piscatory; **—а́чество** *n.* fishing; **—а́чить** *v.* fish; **—а́чка** *f.* fisherwoman; **—а-ши́шка** *see* **рыцар-рыбы; —е́ц** *m.* (ichth.) vimba; **—е́шка** *f.* young fish, fry; **—заво́д** *see* **рыбозавод.**

рыб/и́й *a.* fish, piscine; **р. глаз** air bubble, fisheye (defect in plastics, printing, etc.); **р. жир** fish oil, spec. codliver oil; **р. клей** isinglass, fish glue; **—ья чешуя́** (med.) ichthyosis, xerodermia.

рыби/на *f.* *see* **рыбинс;** large fish; **—нс** *m.* (naut.) diago-

nal (line); (shipbuilding) rising line, ribband, batten; **—ца** *see* **рыбка; —ща** *f.* very large fish.

рыбка *f. dim.* of **рыба;** (wooden) lure; (ent.) silverfish (*Lepisma*); **бойцо́вая р.** fighting fish (*Betta splendens*); **жемчу́жная р.** *see* **рыбы-жемчужницы; золота́я р.** minnow (*Phoxinus p.*); goldfish (*Carassius auratus*); **лю́ме р.** (ichth.) Bombay duck (*Harpadon nehereus*); **нео́новая р.** neon tetra; **ра́дужная р.** rainbow fish (*Melanotaenia*).

рыбле́ние *n.* combing, hackling (of flax).

рыб/ник *see* **рыбовод;** worker in fish industry, pisciculturist; **—ница** *f.* fish tank; fish(ing) boat; **—ный** *a.* piscine; **—ный яд** ichthyotoxin; **—ное хозя́йство** fisheries; **—ные отбро́сы** fish scrap, pomace; **—о—** *prefix* pisci—, fish; **—ове́д** *m.* ichthyologist; pisciculturist; **—ове́дение** *n.* ichthyology; pisciculture; **—ове́дческий** *a.* piscicultural; **—ови́дный** *a.* streamlined; lenticular (beam); fish-bellied (girders, etc.); fish-shaped.

рыбово́д *m.* pisciculturist; **—ный** *a.*, **—ческий** *a.* piscicultural; **—ный заво́д** fish hatchery; **—ство** *n.* pisciculture, fish breeding.

рыбое́д *m.* fish-eater.

рыбо/заво́д *m.* fish cannery, fish-processing plant; **пла́вучий р.** factory ship; **се́тчатый —загради́тель** fish screen; **—к** *gen. pl.* of **рыбка; —комбина́т** *m.* fish-processing combine; **—консе́рвный заво́д** cannery; **—копти́льный** *a.* fish-smoking; **—ко́стный** *a.* fish gelatin (agar).

рыболо́в *m.* fisherman; (mam.) fisher (*Martes pennanti*); **большо́й р.** *see* **рыбояд; —ецкий, —ный** *a.* fishing; piscatory; **—ные ору́дия** fishing gear; **—ство** *n.* fishing (industry).

рыбо/лока́тор *m.* fish finder; **—лока́ция** *f.* ultrasonic trawling methods; **—насо́с** *m.* fish transfer pump; **—обраба́тывающий** *a.* fish-processing; **—обра́зные** *see* **бесчелюстные; —обра́зный** *see* **рыбовидный; —пито́мник** *m.* fish hatchery; **—подо́бный** *a.* ichthyoid; **—подъёмник** *m.* fish elevator; **—подъёмный** *a.* fish-lifting; **—поса́дочный** *a.* (fish) stock(ing).

рыбопроду́кция *f.* biomasss of fish in a body of water; **промысло́вая р.** annual yield (of fish).

рыбопромы/словый, —шленный *a.*, **—шленность** *f.* fish industry.

рыбопропускно́й *a.* fishway; **р. шлюз** fish-lock.

рыбо/разведе́ние *n.* pisciculture, fish breeding; **—хо́д** *m.*, **—хо́дный** *a.* fish ladder, fish pass; **—хозя́йство** *n.* fishing industry; **—чи́стка** *f.* fish scaler; **—яд** *m.* (mam.) fish-eating bat (*Noctilio leporinus*); **—я́дный** *a.* (zool.) fish-eating, ichthyophagous; **—я́щер** *m.* (pal.) ichthyosaur.

рыб/хоз *m.* fish hatchery; **—цы** *pl.* of **рыбец.**

рыбы *gen., pl., etc., of* **рыба;** (astr.) Pisces; **высшие р.** higher fishes (*Neopterygii*); **жабови́дные р.** toadfishes (*Batrachoididae*); **и́льные р.** bowfins (*Amiidae*); **кора́лловые р.** *see* **щетинозубые; кости́стые р., ко́стные р.** bony fishes (*Osteichthyes*); **ле́нточные р.** oarfishes (*Regalecidae*); **лету́чие р.** flying fishes (*Exocoetidae*); **пеще́рные р.** cavefishes (*Amblyopsidae*); **у́гольные р.** sablefishes (*Anoplopomatidae*); **хрящевы́е р.** cartilaginous fishes (*Chondrichthyes*).

рыбы/-ба́бочки *pl.* butterflyfishes (*Chaetodontidae, Pantodontidae*); **р.-дельфи́ны** *pl.* dolphinfishes (*Coryphaenidae*); **р.-жемчу́жницы** *pl.* pearlfishes (*Carapidae*); **р.-ле́нты** *pl.* ribbonfishes, dealfishes (*Trachipteridae*); **р.-лопа́ты** *pl.* spadefishes (*Ephippidae*); **р.-пятаки́** *pl.* deepbody boarfishes (*Cap-*

roidae); **р.-солдаты** *see* **белки-рыбы**; **р.-сосновые шишки** *see* **шишноковые**; **р.-спутники** *pl.* rudderfishes (*Kyphosidae*); **р.-топорики** *pl.* hatchetfishes (*Sternoptychidae*); **р.-тряпки** *see* **тряпичниковые**; **р.-ящерицы** *pl.* lizardfishes (*Synodidae*).

рыбья *f. of* **рыбий.**

рыв/ок *m.* jerk; **—ками** jerkily, in jerks; **—ки** *pl.* jerking.

рыг/ать, —нуть *v.* belch.

рыд/ание *n.* sobbing; **—ать** *v.* sob.

рыж/еватый *a.* reddish, rusty, rust-colored, ferrugineous; **—еть** *v.* become reddish, get rust-colored; **—еухий** *a.* (orn.) red-eared; **—ий** *a.* reddish, rust-colored; rufous; red (fox); chestnut (horse); red-haired.

рыжик *m.* (bot.) Camelina; an edible brown mushroom (*Lactarius deliciosus*); (ichth.) goby; **—овое масло** cameline (seed) oil.

рыкание *see* **рычание.**

рыл *past m. sing. of* **рыть.**

рыл/о *n.* nozzle, jet, spout, mouth; (zool.) muzzle, snout; (anat.) rostrum; (bot.) stigma; **—овидный** *a.* rostriform; **—ьце** *dim. of* **рыло**; rostellum; **—ьцевый** *a.* (bot.) stigmatic.

рым *m.* (eye) bolt, ring (bolt); **р.-болт** eye bolt.

рыно/к *m.* market (place); **—чный** *a.* market, commercial.

рысак *m.* trotter, race horse.

рыс/ёнок *m.* lynx cub; **—и** *pl. of* **рысь; —ий** *a.* (zool.) lynx.

рыси/стый *a.* trotting; **—ть** *v.* trot.

рыск *m.,* **—ание** *n.* yaw(ing), hunt(ing); **—ать** *v.* yaw, hunt; **—ливость** *f.,* **—ливый** *a.* yawing; **—нуть** *v.* yaw.

рыси/а *f.* (horse's) jog trot.

рысь *f.* (zool.) lynx; trot; **рыжая р.** bobcat, bay lynx; **степная р.** caracal; **—ю** *adv.* at a trot.

рыт/вина *f.* rut, groove, fossula, gully, ravine; excavation, hollow; **дорожная р.** pothole; **—ый** *a.* dug.

рыть *v.* dig, hollow out, burrow, excavate; trench; mine; **—ё** *n.* digging, excavation.

рыхл/ение *n.* cultivation, loosening (of soil); **—еть** *v.* become friable, get porous; **—итель** *m.* cultivator; (soil) aerator; ripper; **—ить** *v.* stir up, loosen, cultivate, mellow (soil); shatter (subsoil); **—окомковатый** *a.* loose-aggregate, loosely lumpy (soil); **—ость** *f.* friability, porousness, porosity; **—ота** *f.* (met.) microporosity; **—оцветковый** *a.* (bot.) laxiflorous; **—ый** *a.* friable, porous, loose, flocculent; incoherent, unconsolidated; light, mellow (soil); **—ящий** *a.* stirring up, etc., *see v.*

рыцарь-рыбы *pl.* pinecone fishes (*Monocentridae*).

рычаг *m.* lever, arm, crank; (av.) stick; (med.) vectis; hand spike, jack; **—и** *pl.* controls; **действие —а** leverage.

рычаж/но-шаровой *a.* ball and lever (valve); **—ный** *a. of* **рычаг**; beam (balance); linkage (differential); alligator (shears); **—ный механизм** leverage, linkage; **—ный реверс** reverse lever; **—ный считыватель** (comp.) swipe reader; **—ный указатель** joystick; **—ок** *dim. of* **рычаг**; rod; tumbler; trigger.

рыч/ание *n.* roaring, etc., *see v.*; **—ать** *v.* growl, snarl, roar, bellow.

рыщет *pr. 3 sing. of* **рыскать.**

рьян/о *adv.* zealously, enthusiastically; **—ость** *f.* zeal; passion; **—ый** *a.* zealous, fervent; passionate.

р. э. *abbr.* (**радиоактивный элемент**) radioactive element.

РЭБ *abbr.* (**биологический рентген-эквивалент**) roentgen-equivalent man, rem.

рэл *m.* rel (unit of magnetic resistance).

рэлеевский, Рэлей *see* **релеевский.**

Рэнкина *see* **Ранкина.**

рэомис *m.* (mam.) water rats (*Rheomys*).

РЭС *abbr.* (**рентгеноэлектронная спектроскопия**) X-ray photoelectron spectroscopy; (**ретикуло-эндотелиальная система**) reticulo-endothelial system.

рэт *m.,* **—ический ярус** (geol.) Rhaetian stage.

рэф *abbr.* (**физический рентгенэквивалент**) roentgen equivalent physical, REP.

рюжа *f.* (fishing) fyke (net).

рюкзак *m.* knapsack, back pack.

рюм *m.* (orn.) shore lark (*Eremophila alpestris*); **—ка** *f.,* **—очный** *a.* jigger, small glass.

рябизна *f.* pitted surface.

ряб/ина *f.* (bot.) mountain ash (*Sorbus*); pockmark; waviness, ripple; **—инник** *m.* mountain ash grove; (bot.) Sorbaria; (orn.) fieldfare (*Turdus pilaris*); **—инный, —иновый** *a.* mountain ash; reddish orange; **—ить** *v.* ripple, curl; **—ишник** *m.* (bot.) tansy (*Tanacetum vulgare*); **—ки, —ковые** *pl.* (orn.) sandgrouse (*Pteroclidae*); **—ой** *a.* pitted, pocked, pockmarked; spotted, speckled; variegated; *m.* (ichth.) sea-poacher; **—ок** *sing. of* **рябки; —уха** *f.* (phyt.) wildfire; **—чик** *m.* (bot.) Fritillaria; (ichth.) *see* **берш**; (orn.) hazel grouse (*Tetrastes bonasia*); **полевой —чик** partridge.

рябь *f.* ripple(s), ripple marks, rippled surface; dazzle; ground-swells.

рявк/ать, —нуть *v.* bellow, roar.

ряд *m.* row, series, line; range, order, sequence, succession; level, layer; (pulse, etc.) train; set, bank (of machines); chain, string, strand, number, variety, array; (arithmetic or geometric) progression; (mil.) rank, file; **—ами** in rows, in banks, in batteries; **на —у с** on a line with; **помещать в р., ставить в р.** *v.* range, put in a row, align; **ставить на —у с** *v.* class with; **упорядоченный р.** array; **целый р.** multitude, many.

рядн/ина *f.,* **—о** *n.* coarse hempen or linen cloth, sacking.

рядный *a.* in-line; *suffix* -row; (biol.) **—стихоус; —фарrious, —fold.**

рядов/ой *a.* ordinary, commonplace; (mil.) rank-and-file, private, rating, airman; unsorted, commercial (grade); consecutive, serial; in rows, drill (sowing); windrow (harvester); coursed (pavement); run-of-mine (coal); **—ая сеялка** (agr.) seed drill; **—ое замещение** adjacent substitution, neighboring substitution (in organic ring compounds).

ряд/ок *dim. of* **ряд; —ом (с)** *adv.* beside, near, next (to), alongside, adjacent (to); **—ы** *pl. of* **ряд**; (phys.) array.

ряж *m.,* **—евый** *a.* crib(work); **—евый бык** crib pier.

рязанский *a.* (geog.) Ryazan.

рям *m.* riam (mossy high bog).

ряпу/ха, —шка *f.* (ichth.) whitefish, cisco (*Coregonus sardinella*).

ряска *f.* (bot.) duckweed (*Lemna*).

С

с *prep. instr.* with, by (means of); and; *prep. gen.* for, from, on, over, since, down, off; *prep. acc.* for; about, approximately.

с— *abbr.* (**санти—**) centi—; **с.** *abbr.* (**северный**) north-(ern); (**секунда**) second; (**страница**) page; (**сын**) son; **С.** *abbr.* (**север**) north.

с— *prefix, particularly with verbs* de—, down from; con—, with.

САА *abbr.* (**сульфамат аммония**) ammonium sulfamate.

саамский *a.* Lapp(ish).

саарский уголь Saar coal.

сабадилл/а *f.* (bot.) sabadilla; **семена —ы** sabadilla, cevadilla (seeds); **—ин** *m.* sabadilline, cevadilline; **—овая кислота** sabadillic acid, cevadic acid.

сабадин *m.* sabadine; **—ин** *m.* sabadinine, cevine.

сабалол *m.* sabalol.

сабатрин *m.* sabatrine.

Сабатье процесс Sabatier process.

саббатин *m.* sabbatin, gentiopicrin.

сабеллиды *pl.* (zool.) peacock worms (*Sabellidae*).

сабель *gen. pl. of* **сабля.**

сабельн/ик *m.* (bot.) Potentilla; iris; **—ый** *a. of* **сабля.**

сабл/евидный *a.* acinaciform, scimitar-shaped; **—езубовые, —езубы** *pl.* (ichth.) ogrefish (*Anoplogasteridae*); (pal.) saber-toothed tiger (*Machairodontidae*); **—елистный** *a.* (bot.) acinacifolious, **—еобразный** *see* **саблевидный; —и-рыбы** *pl.* (ichth.) cutlassfishes, hairtails (*Trichiuridae*); *see also* **чехонь; —истость** *f.* (med.) bowleggedness; **—я** *f.* sword, saber.

сабо *n.* sabot.

сабот/аж *m.* sabotage; **—ажник** *m.* saboteur; **—ировать** *v.* sabotage.

сабромин *m.* Sabromin, calcium dibromobehenate.

сабур *m.,* **—ный** *a.* (bot.) aloe.

Сабуро среда (med.) Sabouraud's agar.

саванна *f.* savanna (grassland).

савки *pl.* (orn.) a genus of ducks (*Oxyura*).

савой *m.,* **—ская капуста** Savoy cabbage.

Савойя (geog.) Savoie, Savoy.

савош (ichth.) *see* **ёрш.**

саврасый *a.* light bay (horse).

сага/пенум *m.* sagapenum (gum resin); **—резитаннол** *m.* sagaresitannol.

сагенит *m.* (min.) sagenite.

сагиттальный *a.* (anat.) sagittal, arrow-like.

саго *n.* sago (starch).

саговник *m.* sago palm (*Cycas*); **—овый** *a.* cycadaceous.

саговый *a.* sago.

саграды, кора cascara sagrada.

сагуин *m.* (mam.) long-tusked marmoset (*Saguinus*).

сагыз *m.* sagyz (a growth of salt crystals in the silt of salt lakes); *see also* **кок-сагыз, крым-сагыз, тау-сагыз.**

сад *m.* orchard; garden; park; **—жа** (orn.) *see* **копытка.**

садизм *m.* sadism.

сад/ик *dim. of* **сад; —ильник** *see* **сажальник.**

садист *m.* sadist; **—истский** *a.* sadistic.

садить *see* **сажать.**

садиться *v.* settle (down); sink, go down (of level, etc.); run down (of battery); (text.) shrink; (av.) land; sit (down), board; set (of sun); set to (work); go (on a diet); run (aground).

садка *f.* setting, placing; sitting (down), boarding; (text.) shrinkage; settling, precipitation; thickening (of liquids); crystallization, solidification (of honey); (agr.)

planting; (met.) charge, melt, burden; mating, copulation; *gen. of* **садок; жидкая с.** molten charge.

садкий *a.* rapidly settling; (paper) free, fast; (text.) shrinking considerably.

садковый *a. of* **садок.**

садкость *f.* settling rate; (paper) freeness; (text.) degree of shrinkage.

саднить *v.* scratch, irritate; smart, burn.

садо/в *gen. pl. of* **сад; —вник** *m.,* **—вница** *f.* gardener; horticulturist; **лесной с.** beetle (*Myelophilus*); **—внический** *a.* gardening, pruning (tool); **—вод** *see* **садовник; —водство** *n.* horticulture, gardening; cultivation of orchards; **—водческий** *a.* horticultural; gardening; orchard-growing; **—во-огородный** *a.* orchard and garden; **—во-парковый** *a.* garden and park; landscape (gardening); **—вый** *a.* garden, cultivated; horticultural; orchard; pruning (knife); grafting (wax); **—защитный** *a.* orchard- or garden-protecting; **—защитная полоса** windbreak.

садок *m.* breeding place, breeding house; fish pond, live fish tank; oyster reef; enclosure, container, (retainer) cage, run; (rabbit) hutch; trap; *gen. pl. of* **садка; sh. m. of** **садкий.**

садо/разведение *n.* gardening; **—строительство** *n.* landscaping.

садочн/ый *a.* charging, charge; batch (furnace); precipitated; **—ая машина** charger; **—ое окно** door (of furnace), charge hole.

саек *gen. pl. of* **сайка.**

саёк *m.* second-year deer with plain antler.

сажа *f.* carbon black; (furnace) soot; **с. просят** (vet.) exudative epidermitis, greasy pig disease; **белая с.** highly dispersed amorphous silica, silica filler; **газовая с.** gas black; **ламповая с.** lamp black.

саж/алка *f.* (agr.) planter; small pond; **—альник** *m.* dibble, planting stick; **—альный** *a.* planting; **—альный кол** dibble; **—альщик** *m.* planter; **—ание** *n.* planting, etc., *see v.;* **—ать** *v.* plant, set out, pot; set, place, put; seat.

саже/вый *a. of* **сажа; —наполнение** *n.* carbon black content; **—наполненный** *a.* carbon black reinforced (rubber).

саженец *m.* nursery plant, slip; nursery tree, sapling.

сажен/ный *a.* planted, etc., *see* **сажать; саженный** *or* **сажённый** *a. of* **сажень; —цевый** *a. of* **саженец; —ый** *a.* nursery (stock).

сажень *f.* sagene (2.134 meters); **морская с.** fathom.

саже/образование *n.* carbon black formation; **—продуватель** *m.* soot blower.

саживать *see* **сажать.**

саж/ивый *a.* carbon-black reinforced (rubber); **—истый** *a.* soot(y); **с. грибок, —ка** *f.* (phyt.) smut; **—ный** *a.* soot(y).

саз *m.* high marsh.

сазан *m.,* **—ий** *a.* (ichth.) carp (*Cyprinus carpio*); **с.-усач** (ichth.) *see* **усач.**

сай *m.* gully, ravine.

сайбелиит *m.* (min.) szaibelyite.

санга *f.,* **—к** *m.,* **—ки** *pl.* (mam.) saiga (antelope) (*Saiga tatarica*).

Сайгон (geog.) Saigon.

сайда *f.* (ichth.) pollack (*Pollachius virens*).

сайзель *see* **сизаль.**

сайка *f.* (bread) roll; (ichth.) polar cod (*Boreogadus saida*).

сайлентблок *m.* (automobile) silent block.

саймен/ский *a.* (geog.) Saima.

саймири *f.* (mam.) squirrel monkey (*Saimiri*).

сайодин *m.* Sajodin, calcium monoiodobehenate.

сайр/а *f.* (ichth.) Pacific saury (*Cololabis saira*); **—обые** *pl.* (ichth.) sauries (*Scomberesocidae*).

сайт *m.* (gen.) site.

сак *m.* bag (net), purse net; sack.

саква *f.* feed bag (for horses).

саквояж *m.* traveling bag, suitcase.

саки *n.* saki (a Japanese beer); *pl.* (mam.) saki (monkey) (*Pithecia*).

сакр/альный *a.* (anat.) sacral; **—о—** *prefix* (anat.) sacro— (sacrum; sacral); **—ококсит** *m.* (med.) sacrocoxitis.

саксатовая кислота saxatic acid.

саксаул *m.* (bot.) saxaul (*Haloxylon*).

саксидомус *m.* (mal.) Saxidomus.

саксонский *a.* Saxon (blue); (geog.) Saxony; (geol.) Saxonian.

сакуранин *m.* sakuranin.

сакхульминовый *a.* sacchulmic acid.

салага *f.* (ichth.) bleak (*Alburnus*); dace (*Leuciscus*).

салаз/ки *pl.* skids, slide, (slide) rails; (launching) cradle; carriage; saddle, guide block; sled, toboggan; **подача —ками** sliding advancement; **—ковый, —очный** *a. of* салазки; sliding, skid-mounted.

салазолон *m.* salazolon, antipyrine salicylate.

салак/а, —ушка *f.* (ichth.) Baltic herring.

саламандр/а *f.* (zool.) salamander; **—ин** *m.* salamanderine (alkaloid).

саламид *m.* salamide, salicylamide.

саланганы *pl.* (orn.) swiftlets (*Collocalia*).

салан/гихтис, —кс *m.*, **—ксовые** *pl.* (ichth.) Salangidae.

салантол *m.* salantol, salacetol.

салат *m.* salad; lettuce; **—ный** *a.* lettuce(-green); **с.-ромен** *m.* cos lettuce.

сал/ацетол *m.* salacetol, acetosalicylic ester; **—ачный** *a. of* салака; **—гипнон** *m.* salhypnone, benzoylmethyl salicylate.

салда *f.* (agr.) hack hook.

сален *sh. m. of* **сальный.**

салеп *m.* salep (dried tubers).

салив/ация *f.* (physiol.) salivation; **—ин** *m.* salivin, ptyalin.

салиген/ин, —ол *m.* Saligenin, salicyl alcohol.

саликор *m.* salicor, blanquette (ash from soda plants).

салиметр *m.* salimeter.

салин *m.* ash from molasses.

салина *f.* salina, South American salt desert.

салинг *m.* (naut.) crosstree.

салинигрин *m.* salinigrin.

салинометр *m.* salinometer.

салипирин *m.* Salipyrine, antipyrine salicylate.

салить *v.* tallow, grease.

сали/фебрин *m.* Salifebrin, salicylanilide; **—формин** *m.* Saliformin, methenamine salicylate.

салицил *m.* salicyl; **—аза** *f.* salicylase; **—амид** *m.* salicylamide; **—анилид** *m.* salicylanilide; **—ат** *m.* salicylate; **—ид** *m.* salicylide; **—изм** *m.* (med.) salicylism, toxic effects of excess salicylic acid; **—ил** *m.* salicylyl; **—ированный** *a.* salicylated; **—(ир)овать** *v.* salicylate; **—ка** *f.* sodium salicylate.

салицилово/аммониевая соль ammonium salicylate; **—висмутовая соль** bismuth salicylate; **основная —висмутовая соль** bismuth subsalicylate; **—кальциевая соль** calcium salicylate.

салициловокисл/ый *a.* salicylic acid; salicylate (of); **с. хинин** quinine salicylate; **—ая соль** salicylate.

салицилово/метиловый эфир methyl salicylate; **—натриевая соль** sodium salicylate; **—этиловый эфир** ethyl salicylate.

салицилов/ый *a.* salicyl(ic); salicylated (fat); **с. альдегид** salicylal(dehyde); **с. натр** sodium salicylate; **с. спирт** salicyl alcohol; **—ая кислота** salicylic acid; **соль —ой кислоты** salicylate.

салицило/л *m.* salicylol; **—нитрил** *m.* salicylonitrile, *o*-hydroxybenzyl nitrile; **—салициловая кислота** salicylosalicylic acid, diplosal.

салицил/резорцинол *m.* salicylresorcinol; **—уровая кислота** salicyluric acid.

салицин *m.*, **—овый** *a.* salicin, saligenin.

салический *a.* (petr.) salic, containing alumina.

Салливан (geog.) Sullivan.

Салливена реакция Sullivan's test.

салмлеры (ichth.) *see* харациновые; полузубые **с.** *pl.* (ichth.) Hemiodontidae.

салмонсит *see* сальмонсит.

сало *n.* fat, grease; lard; tallow; suet; (physiol.) sebum; (ice) grease, slush.

салоколл *m.* salocoll, phenocoll salicylate.

салол *m.* salol, phenyl salicylate.

саломас *m.* hydrogenated fat.

салоникский (geog.) *a.* Salonica.

сало/носный *a.* sebiferous; **—образный** *a.* tallowy; (anat.) sebaceous.

салоп(ий)ский *a.* (geol.) Salopian.

салотоп *m.* (fat) renderer; **—енный** *see* салотопный; **—ка** *f.* rendering; rendering plant; **—ление** *n.*, **—ный** *a.* rendering; tallow-melting; **—ня** *f.* rendering plant.

сало/фен *m.* Salophen, acetamidosalol; **—хинин** *m.* Saloquinine, quinine salicylate.

салу/мин *m.* Salumin, aluminum salicylate; **—фер** *m.* Salufer, sodium silicofluoride.

салфет/ка *f.*, **—очный** *a.* napkin; filter cloth; **—очка** *dim. of* салфетка.

саль *f.* (geol.) sial.

сальвадорский *a.* El Salvador.

сальварсан *m.* salvarsan (arsphenamine).

сальви/анин *m.* salvianin, monardein; **—ния** *f.* (bot.) Salvinia; **—ол** *m.* salviol, thujone; **—я** *f.* (bot.) sage (*Salvia*).

сальд/ировать *v.* balance (an account); **—ирующий** *a.* balancing; rolling total (tabulator); **—о** *n.* balance.

сальз *m.*, **—а** *f.* salse, mud volcano.

сальмин *m.* salmine (a protamine).

сальмлеровые (ichth.) *see* харациновые; полузубые **с.** *pl.* (ichth.) Hemiodontidae.

сальмон/еллёз *m.* (med.) salmonellosis; **—еллы** *pl.* (bact.) salmonella.

сальник *m.*, **—овый** *a.* stuffing box; (packing) gland; gasket, oil seal; (anat.) omentum; **—овый компенсатор** slip-type expansion joint; **—овая коробка** stuffing box; **—овая крышка** gland.

сальность *f.* greasiness; obscenity.

сальн/ый *a.* greasy, fatty, sebaceous; lardaceous; tallow(y); (med.) bacon (spleen); obscene; **—ая железа** (anat.) sebaceous gland.

сальпинг/ит *m.* (med.) salpingitis; **—(о)—** *prefix* salping(o)— [trumpet; (med.) Fallopian tube, Eustachian tube]; **—оофорит** *m.* (med.) salpingo-oophoritis.

сальпы *pl.* (zool.) Thaliacea.

сальсол/идин *m.* salsolidine; **—ин** *m.* salsoline.

сальт/аторный *a.* saltatory, leaping, jumping; **—ация** *f.* saltation; **—о** leap, jump; **—о-мортале** *n.* somersault.

салют *m.*, **—овать** *v.* salute.

сам *pron.* self, himself, itself; in person; **с. по себе** alone, by itself, per se; **—а** *f.* herself; **—и** *pl.* themselves, yourselves; **—о** *n.* itself; **—о собой разумеется** it is self-evident.

самадерин *m.* samaderin.

саман *m.* adobe, sun-baked brick; chopped straw.

саманда/ридин *m.* samandaridine; **—трин** *m.* samandatrine.

саман/ка *f.* adobe building; **—ный** *a.* adobe.

самариевый *a.* samarium, samaric.

самар/ий *m.* samarium, Sm; **окись —ия** samarium oxide; **сернокислая закись —ия** samarous sulfate; **сернокислая окись —ия** samaric sulfate; **хлористый с.** samarous chloride; **хлорный с.** samaric chloride.

самаристый *a.* samarium, samarous.

самаркандский *a.* (geog.) Samarkand.

самарский *a.* Samara.

самарскит *m.* (min.) samarskite.

сама-состояние *n.* sama condition, no thermal flow.

самбар *m.* (mam.) sambar (deer).

самбо *abbr.* (**самозащита без оружия**) unarmed self-defense; karate, etc.

самбук *m.* (bot.) elder (*Sambucus*).

самбу/нигрин *m.* sambunigrin; **—цинин** *m.* sambucinin.

самглав *m.* (ichth.) ocean sunfish (*Mola mola*).

самец *m.* male; **с.-производитель** *m.* sire.

сами *pl. of* **сам.**

самин *m.* samin.

самка *f.* female; **с.-производительница** *f.* (ent.) fundatrix, stem-mother.

само *n. of* **сам;** *prefix* self-, auto—, automatic, spontaneous; the most, the very.

Самоа (geog.) Samoa.

само/активируемый *a.* self-activated; **—анализ** *m.* introspection, self-examination; **—балансный**, **—балансирующийся** *a.* self-balancing; **—бесплодие** *n.*, **—бесплодность** *f.* (bot.) self-sterility, self-incompatibility; **—блокирующий** *a.* (elec.) self-latching (relay); **—браковка** *f.* (bot.) natural culling of disease-prone varieties; **—брожение** *n.* (chem.) spontaneous fermentation.

самобытн/ость *f.* originality; independence; **—ый** *a.* original; independent; distinctive.

самовар *m.* samovar, tea urn.

самоввводящийся *a.* self-loading.

самовентил/ирующийся *a.* self-ventilating; automatically ventilated; self-cooling (generator); **—яция** *f.* self-ventilation, automatic ventilation.

само/взводной *a.* repeating (trip lock); **—взводный** *a.* (art.) self-cocking; **—взводный револьвер** double-action revolver; **—взрывный** *a.* self-firing; contact (mine); **—включающийся** *a.*, **—включение** *n.* self-coupling; (elec.) automatic reclosing; **—влюблённость** *f.* conceit; **—внушение** *n.* auto-suggestion.

самовозбужд/ающийся *a.* (elec.) self-exciting; self-excited; **—ение** *n.* self-excitation; generation of parasitic oscillations; **—ённый** *a.* self-excited; self-sustained.

самовоз/врат *m.* self-recovery, automatic reset(ting); **—горание** *see* **самовоспламенение;** **—никающий** *a.* spontaneous; **—обновление** *n.* spontaneous regeneration.

самовол/ие *n.* wilfulness; license; insubordination; **—ка** *f.* absence without leave; **—ьный** *a.* arbitrary; self-willed; insubordinate; unwarranted; unauthorized; **самовольная отлучка** absence without leave, AWOL.

самовоспламен/ение *n.* spontaneous combustion; spontaneous ignition, self-ignition; **—иться** *v. see* **самовоспламеняться;** **—яемость** *f.* spontaneous combustibility; **—яемый** *see* **самовоспламеняющийся;** **—яться** *v.* ignite spontaneously; **—яющийся** *a.* spontaneously inflammable, self-inflammable, self-igniting; hypergolic (rocket fuel).

самовоспроиз/ведение, —водство *n.* self-reproduction, spontaneous reproduction; replication; **—водящий** *a.* (nucl.) breeder (reactor); **—водящийся** *a.* self-reproducing.

само/восстанавливающийся *a.* self-restoring, self-healing; self-righting; self-reducing; **—вращение** *n.* (av.) autorotation; windmilling; **—всасывающий** *a.* automatic intake, self-feeding; self-priming (pump); liquid-piston (pump); **—вулканизующийся** *a.* self-vulcanizing, self-curing; **—выкладывающийся** *a.* self-releasing; **—выключение** *n.* (engine) failure; automatic disconnect(ion); **—выпрямляющийся** *a.* self-straightening, self-righting.

самовыравнив/ание *n.* self-regulation, self-alignment; **—ающийся** *a.* self-regulating, self-aligning, self-balanced.

само/гасящийся *a.*, **—гашение** *n.* self-quenching; **—генератор** *m.* self-oscillator; **—гидрирование** *n.* autohydrogenation; **—гипноз** *m.* autohypnosis.

самогон *m.*, **—ка** *f.*, **—ный** *a.* home brew; **—щик** *m.*, **—щица** *f.* bootlegger.

самогорание *n.* spontaneous combustion.

самогрузный *a.* self-weighted (shaft).

самодви/гатель *m.* automatic engine; **—жущийся** *a.* automatic, self-powered, self-propelled.

само/двойственный *a.* (math.) self-dual; **—действие** *n.* self-action; **—действующий** *a.* self-acting, automatic.

самодел/ка *f.* homemade product; **—ковый, —ьный** *a.* homemade, handmade.

самодеятельн/ость *f.* independent action; enterprise; initiative; self-help, self-service; **—ый** *a.* gainfully employed; independent.

само/дифференцировка *f.* (zool.) self-differentiation; **—диффузия** *f.* self-diffusion; **—довлеющий** *a.* self-sufficient, independent, self-contained; **—докование** *n.*, **—докующийся** *a.* self-docking; **—дополняющийся** *a.* self-complementing (code); **—дренирующийся** *a.* self-draining; **—дуальный** *a.* (math.) self-dual.

само/забвение *n.* selflessness, self-denial; **—завод** *m.*, **—заводящийся** *a.* self-winding; self-starting; **—загорание** *see* **самозажигание;** **—заготовка** *f.* laying in one's own stores; **—загружающийся** *a.* self-feed(ing); (comp.) self-loading; **—загрузка** *f.* (comp.) bootstrapping; **—заживление** *n.* self-healing; **—зажигание** *n.* self-ignition, spontaneous ignition; **—зажимающий** *a. a.* self-gripping.

самозакал/ивание *n.* (met.) self-hardening; **—иваться** *v.* self-harden; **—ивающийся** *a.* self-hardening; **—ка** *f.* self-hardening; self-hardened steel; air-hardening steel.

само/заклеивающийся *a.* self-sealing; **—законтривающийся, —закрывающийся** *see* **самозамыкающийся;** **—залечивание** *n.* self-healing; **—заливающийся** *a.* self-priming (pump); **—замыкающийся** *a.*, **—запирание** *n.*, **—запирающийся** *a.* self-closing, automatic closing, self-locking.

самозаписывающийся *a.* (self-)recording, graphic; **с. аппарат** automatic recorder.

само/заполняющийся *a.* self-priming; **—запорный** *see* **самозамыкающийся**; **—запуск** *m.*, **—запускающийся** *a.* self-starting, self-triggering; **—заражение** *n.* (med.) auto-infection; **—зарождение** *n.* (biol.) spontaneous generation; **—зарядный** *a.* self-loading, semi-automatic (weapon); **—затачивание** *n.*, **—затачивающийся** *a.* self-sharpening.

самозатух/аемость *f.*, **—ание** *n.* self-extinction, natural dying away; **—ающий(ся)** *a.* self-extinguishing.

самозатягивающийся *a.* self-sealing.

самозахватывающий *a.* self-gripping; **с. грейфер** automatic grab.

само/защита *f.* self-defense; self-protection; self-preservation; **—защищающий** *a.* (nucl.) self-protecting; **—зеркальный** *a.* self-mirrored (nucleus); **—изливающий** *a.* flowing, gushing; **—излучение** *n.* self-emission, spontaneous radiation; **—изменение** *n.* self-modification; **—изреживание** *n.* (silv.) self-thinning.

самоиндук/тивность *f.* (elec.) self-inductance; **—тивный,** **—ционный** *a.* (elec.) self-inductive; **—ция** *f.* self-induction, self-inductance; **реакция —ции** inductive reactance.

само/ионизация *f.* self-ionization; **—испарение** *n.* self-evaporation; **—испарительный** *a.* vacuum (crystallizer); **—истребление** *n.* self-destruction.

самок *gen. pl. of* **самка.**

само/кал *see* **самокалка; —калечение** *n.* (zool.) autotomy; **—калка** *f.* self-hardened steel; **—кальный** *a.* self-hardened; **—карбурация** *f.* self-carburation; **—касание** *n.* self-tangency; **—кат** *m.* bicycle; **—катный** *a. of* **самокат;** gravity; **—катная доска** skateboard; **—катом** *adv.* by gravity; **—катчик** *m.* (bi)cyclist; **—квас** *m.* natural souring (of milk); **—колебание** *n.* natural vibration.

самокомпенсир/ованный *a.* self-compensated, auto-compensated; **—ующийся** *a.* self-compensating, auto-compensating.

самоконтрол/ируемый, **—ирующийся** *a.* self-supervisory; **—ирующий** *a.* self-checking; **—ь** *m.* self-control; self-check(ing), self-test(ing); self-regulation.

само/контрящийся *a.* self-locking (nut); **—конъюгация** *f.* (gen.) autosyndesis; **—кормушка** *f.* self-feeder; **—корректирующийся** *a.* self-correcting; **—крепление** *n.* self-attachment.

самолёт *m.* (air)plane, aircraft; **с.-амфибия** *m.* amphibian; **с.-бомбардировщик** *m.* bomber; **с.-заправщик** *m.* refueling plane, tanker aircraft; **—ик** *m.* miniature plane; **с.-истребитель** *m.* combat plane, fighter; **с.-корректировщик** *m.* spotter plane, observation plane, forward air controller; **с.-матка** *see* **с.-носитель; с.-мишень** *m.* target drone; **с.-носитель** *m.* carrier plane; host aircraft.

самолётный *a. of* **самолёт;** airborne, flight.

самолёто/вождение *n.* aerial navigation; **—вылет** *m.* mission, sortie; **—пыливатель** *m.* crop duster.

самолётостро/ение *n.*, **—ительный** *a.* plane manufacturing, aircraft industry; **—итель** *m.* aircraft manufacturer.

самолёт-перехватчик *m.* interceptor (aircraft); **с.-постановщик** *m.* (electronic) countermeasures aircraft; **с.-разведчик** *m.* reconnaissance plane; **с.-ракетоносец** *m.* missile-carrier plane; **с.-снаряд** *m.* cruise missile; **с.-торпедоносец** *m.* torpedo carrier, torpedo bomber; **с.-фоторазведчик** *m.* photoreconnaissance plane; **с.-штурмовик** *m.* ground attack plane.

самолечение *n.* (physiol.) autotherapy.

самоликвид/атор *m.* self-destroying device; **—ация** *f.* self-destruction.

самоличн/о *adv.* in person, personally, oneself; **—ый** *a.* personal.

самолов *m.* automatic trap; **—ный** *a. of* **самолов;** barbless (hook).

само/лучший *a.* the (very) best; **—люб(ец)** *m.* egotist; **—любивый** *a.* proud; selfish; **—любие** *n.* self-esteem, pride; egotism; **—малейший** *a.* the (very) smallest; **—мнение** *n.* conceit; self-importance; **—модуляция** *f.* natural modulation, self-modulation; **—наблюдение** *n.* introspection.

самонав/едение *n.* (missiles) homing (guidance), self-guidance, target-seeking guidance; (elec.) self-induction; **—едённый** *a.* self-guided; (elec.) self-induced; **—одиться** *v.* home; **—одящийся** *a.* homing, self-guided, self-guiding; **—одящаяся головка** seeker head.

само/нагревание *n.* spontaneous heating; **—надеянность** *f.* self-confidence; presumption; conceit; self-reliance; **—накатывание** *n.* (art.) automatic counter-recoil; **—наклад(чик)** *m.* (printing) feeder; **—напряжение** *n.* (concrete) self-stress; **—настраивающийся** *a.* self-adjusting, (self-)adaptive; **—настройка** *f.* (comp.) bootstrapping; **—насыщение** *n.* self-saturation; **—несовместимость** *f.* self-sterility; **—новейший** *a.* newest, most recent; **—нужнейший** *a.* the most necessary, very necessary.

само/обеспечение *n.* (comp.) bootstrapping; **—обжигающий анод** self-baking anode, Soderberg anode; **—обладание** *n.* self-control; poise, composure; **—обман** *m.* self-deception; **—обольщение** *n.* self-deception; **—оборона** *f.* self-defense; **—образование** *n.* self-education; **—обращение** *n.* self-reversal.

самообслужив/ание *n.*, **—ающийся** *a.* self-service, self-help; **—ающаяся установка** self-contained plant.

самообуч/ающийся *a.* self-teaching, self-instructing, learning; **—ение** *n.* self-instruction.

само/ограничение *n.* self-restraint; **—окапывание** *n.* (mil.) digging in; **—окисление** *n.* autooxidation, self-oxidation; **—окрашенный** *a.* self-colored; **—окупаемость** *f.* self-support; recoupment (of expenditures); **—окупаемый** *a.* self-supporting; **—опирающийся** *a.* unsupported, independent; **—оплодотворение** *n.* (biol.) autogamy, self-fertilization; **—определение** *n.* self-determination; **—опрокидывающийся** *a.* self-dumping, automatic dumping; **—опыление** *n.* (bot.) self-pollination; **—организующийся** *a.* self-organizing; self-adjusting; training (system); **—ориентирующийся** *a.* self-orientating; swivel, caster (wheel); **—осадка** *f.* natural precipitation.

самоосвобожд/ающийся *a.* self-releasing; **—ение** *n.* self-release.

самоостан/авливающийся *a.* self-stopping, self-catching; **—ов** *m.*, **—овка** *f.* automatic stop.

самоотверд/евать *v.* self-harden; **—ение** *n.* self-hardening.

самоотверженность *f.* selflessness.

само/отжиг *m.* self-annealing; **—отпуск** *m.* self-tempering; **—отравление** *n.* self-poisoning, autointoxication; **—отталкивание** *n.* self-repulsion; **—охлаждающийся** *a.* self-cooling; self-refrigerating; **—охлаждение** *n.* self-cooling; self-refrigeration; **—охрана** *f.* self-defense; self-preservation; **—очевидный** *a.* self-evident.

самоочи/стка *see* **самоочищение; —щаться** *v.* self-purify; self-clean; **—щающийся** *a.* self-purifying;

self-cleaning; **—щение** *n.* self-purification; self-cleaning.

само/ошлаковывающийся *a.* self-fluxing; **—пад** *m.* free fall, free-falling drill; **—переваривание** *n.* self-digestion, autolysis; **—перегревание** *n.* self-super-heating; **—передвигающийся** *a.* self-moving, automatic; **—переливание** *n.* (med.) autotransfusion; **—пересечение** *n.* (math.) crunode; **—писец** *m.* self-recorder, (automatic) recorder; **—питатель** *m.* self-feeder.

самопишущ/ий *a.* (self-)recording, (self-)registering; **с. прибор** *see* **самописец; —ее перо** fountain pen.

само/плавкий *a.* self-fluxing; **—плавом** *adv.* by the current; by its own power; **—плодность** *f.* self-fertilization; **—поворот** *m.* spontaneous version (of fetus); **—повреждение** *n.* (zool.) autotomy; **—поглощение** *n.* self-absorption.

самопод/аватель *m.*, **—ающий механизм** self-feeder, automatic feeder; **—ающий** *a.* self-feeding.

само/подготовка *f.* independent preparation; **—поддерживающийся** *a.* self-maintaining, self-supporting, self-sustaining; self-propagating; **—поедание** *n.* (zool.) autophagy; **—пожертвование** *n.* self-sacrifice; **—пожирание** *see* **самопоедание; —поилка** *f.* drinking fountain; **—прерывание** *n.* (elec.) self-blocking (of an oscillator); **—прикосновение** *n.* (math.) self-tangency; **—приспосабливающий(ся)** *a.* adaptive, self-adapting, self-adjusting, self-aligning; goal-seeking (system); **—притирка** *f.* automatic lapping; **—программирующийся** *a.* self-programming.

самопроизвольн/о *adv.* spontaneously; **—ость** *f.* spontaneity; **—ый** *a.* spontaneous, involuntary; arbitrary; random (arc extinctions).

самопуск *m.* self-starter, automatic starter; self-starting, self-triggering; **—ающийся** *a.* self-starting, self-triggering.

саморазвивающийся *a.* spontaneous.

саморазгру/жающийся *a.* self-discharging, gravity-discharge, automatic unloading; **—зчик** *m.* dumping mechanism.

само/разложение *n.* spontaneous decomposition; **—размагничивание** *n.* self-demagnetization; **—размагничивающийся** *a.* self-demagnetizing; **—разогрев** *m.*, **—разогревание** *n.* self-heating, evolution of heat (from reaction); spontaneous heating; **—разрушение** *n.* spontaneous decomposition.

саморазря/д *m.*, **—жение** *n.* (elec.) self-discharge, local action; **—жающийся** *a.* self-discharging, running down; leaking.

само/раскрывающийся *a.* opening automatically; **—распад** *m.* (nucl.) spontaneous decay.

самораспростран/ение *n.* self-propagation; **—яющийся** *a.* self-propagating.

саморассеяние *n.* (nucl.) self-scattering.

саморастворение *n.* (biol.; chem.) autolysis.

саморасцепл/ение *n.* self-detachment, automatic uncoupling; **—яющийся** *a.* self-detaching, self-unlocking, disconnecting automatically.

само/реагирующий *a.* spontaneous ignition (engine); **—регистрирующий** *a.* self-registering, self-recording.

саморегулир/ование *n.*, **—овка** *f.* automatic regulation, self-regulation, (physiol.) autoregulation; self-adjustment, self-alignment; **—овать** *v.* regulate itself, adjust itself; **—уемость** *f.* self-stabilization; **—ующийся** *a.* self-regulating, self-adjusting, self-governing.

саморегуляция *see* **саморегулирование.**

само/резка *f.* cutter; **—реклама** *f.* self-advertisement; **—род** *m.* native phosphoric ore.

самород/ный *a.* natural; (min.) native; **—ок** *m.* native metal, native ore; prill, nugget (of gold).

саморубцующаяся эпителиома (med.) keratosis follicularis, Darier's disease.

самосад *m.*, **—ка** *f.* native salt; rustic tobacco; **—очная соль** (geol.) salt deposited in lakes, seas, etc.

само/сброска *f.* (agr.) automatically unloading reaper; **—свал** *m.* dump (truck), dumper; **—свальный** *a.* dump(ing); **—сварение** *n.* autodigestion; **—светящийся** *a.* self-luminous, self-luminescent; **—связывающийся** *a.* self-bonding; **—сгорание** *see* **самовоспламенение; —сев** *m.* self-seeding; self-sown plant; volunteer crop; **—севка** *f.*, **—сей** *m.*, **—сейка** *f.* self-sown plant, volunteer; **—сжатие** *n.* self-constriction; **—сжатый, —сжимающийся** *a.* self-constricted; **—сильно** *adv.* independently; **—син** *m.* autosyn, synchro (selsyn).

самосинхрон/изация *f.* self-synchronization, self-timing; self-locking; **режим —изации мод** mode locking (of laser); **—изирующий, —ный** *a.* self-synchronizing, selsyn.

само/скидка *see* **самосброска; —склеивающийся** *a.* self-sealing; self-adherent; **—скрепление** *n.* self-reinforcement; (art.) autofrettage; **—слипание** *n.* self-adhesion.

самосмаз/ка *f.* self-lubrication, automatic lubrication; **—очный** *a.* self-lubricating; **—чик** *m.* automatic lubricator; **—ывающий(ся)** *a.* self-lubricating.

само/снабжаемость *f.*, **—снабжение** *n.* self-provision, self-supply(ing); **—совместимость** *a.* (biol.) self-compatibility; **—соглас(ован)ный** *a.* (self-)consistent, self-congruent; **—согревание** *n.* spontaneous heating; **—сознание** *n.* (self-)consciousness, self-knowledge; **—сопротивляющийся** *a.* self-resistant; **—сопряжённый** *a.* self-conjugate; self-adjoint (equation); **—сохранение** *n.* self-preservation; **—спасатель** *m.* escape (breathing) apparatus; **—спекающийся** *a.* clotting; clotted, coagulated; hardened; self-baking (electrode); **—сплав** *m.* drift of logs; **—спуск** *m.* self-triggering.

самостерильность *f.* self-sterility; (bot.) self-incompatibility.

самостойный *a.* independent.

самостоятельн/о *adv.* independently; **—ость** *f.* independence; **—ый** *a.* independent, self-contained, separate; self-maintained (discharge); solo (flight); (bot.) autonomic, spontaneous.

само/стрел *m.* self-inflicted wound; (mil.) malingerer; cross-bow; **—стрельный** *a.* automatic (gun); **—стягивание** *n.* (phys.) pinch effect; **—суйка** *f.* shaping machine, shaper; **—схват** *m.* (crane) grab, clamshell; **—схватывающийся** *a.* automatic grapple (fork); **—таска** *f.* conveyer; drag, dragging device; pullover.

самотёк *m.* (gravity) flow, gravity feed; drift; natural course; honey (flowing from combs); laissez faire; **—ом** by gravity; of its own accord; **подача —ом** gravity feed.

самотёчный *a.* self-flowing, gravity-flowing; automatic, spontaneous; gravity (lubrication, circulation, etc.).

самотканый *a.* (text.) homespun.

самотормо/жение *n.* self-braking, automatic braking, self-locking; **—зиться** *v.* stop automatically; jam; **—зящий(ся)** *a.* self-braking, self-stopping, self-locking; irreversible.

само/тяга *f.* natural draft, chimney effect; **—убивающий пояс** insecticide-impregnated band; **—убийство** *n.* suicide, self-destruction; **—убийца** *m. and f.* (person who commits) suicide; **—уважение** *n.* self-esteem;

—**уверенный** *a.* (self-)confident, assured; —**уга-сание** *n.* self-extinction (of arc); —**углубленный** *a.* self-absorbed; —**удержание** *n.* latch(ing); —**укла-дывание** *n.* self-packing.

самоуничтож/ающий(ся) *a.* self-destruct(ive); —**ение** *n.* self-destruction.

самоуплотн/ение *n.* self-packing, self-sealing; voluntary sharing of one's living quarters; —**яющийся** *a.* self-packing, self-sealing.

самоуправл/ение *n.* self-government, autonomy; —**яем-ый** *a.* self-governing; (mil.) homing; —**яющийся** *a.* self-governing.

само/управный *a.* arbitrary; —**управство** *n.* vigilantism; —**упрочнение** *n.* self-reinforcement; self-hardening; —**уравновешивающийся** *a.* self-balancing; —**спокоиться** *v.* become complacent, be (self-)satisfied.

самоустанавлив/ание *n.* self-adjustment, automatic adjustment; —**ающийся** *a.* self-adjusting, automatically adjusting, self-aligning; floating; swivelling; adjustable, flexible; free-steering (axle); castor (wheel); (geod.) self-leveling; self-setting.

самоустанов/ка, —ление *see* **самоустанавливание.**

самоустойчивость *f.* autostability.

самоустран/ение *n.* aloofness, reserve, withdrawal; —**яющийся** *a.* transient (failure).

самоуч/итель *m.* manual of self-instruction, handbook; —**ка** *f.* self-education; *m. and f.* self-taught person.

само/фазировка *f.* autophasing; —**фертильность** *f.* (bot.) autogamy, self-fertilization; —**флюсующийся** *a.* self-fluxing; —**фокусировка** *f.*, —**фокусирую-щийся** *a.* self-focusing; —**хвал** *m.*, —**хвалка** *f.* braggart; —**хвальный** *a.* boastful; —**хват** *m.* grip; (automatic) grab; clamshell.

самоход *m.* power feed; self-acting; creeping (of meter); self-propelled machine, gun or ship; **с.-тягач** *m.* (agr.) truck tractor; —**ка** *f.* self-propelled machine, gun, or ship; —**но-артиллерийская установка** self-propelled gun, mechanized gun; —**ный** *a.* automotive, self-propelled, self-moving, self-acting, power-driven, power-operated, power-fed; —**ная подача** power feed; —**ом** *adv.* self-propelled; mechanically.

самохронирующийся *a.* (elec.) self-pulsed (oscillator).

самоцвет *m.* gem; —**ный** *a.* fine (gem).

самоцентр/ирование *n.* self-centering, self-alignment, self-adjustment; —**ирующий(ся)** *a.* self-centering, self-aligning; concentric-jaw (chuck); —**овка** *see* **самоцентрирование.**

само/черт *m.* pantograph; —**чувствие** *n.* state of health; —**шлакующийся** *a.* self-fluxing; —**экранирование** *n.* (nucl.) self-shielding.

самум *m.* (meteor.) simoon, sandstorm.

самшит *m.* (bot.) box (tree).

сам/ый *a.* the very; the most; (self)same; **с. верхний** the highest, the topmost, uppermost; **с. высококачест-венный** top-quality; **с. лучший** the very best, (by far) the best; **с. предмет** the subject itself; **с. факт, что** the very fact that; —**ое большое** at (the) most, at best; **до —ого** all the way (up) to; **на —ом деле** as a matter of fact, in fact, actually; **с —ого начала** from the very first; **этот же с.** the same, this (self)same.

сан., сан— *abbr., prefix* (**санитарный**).

санатоген *m.* Sanatogen.

санатор/ий *m.*, —**ный**, —**ский** *a.* sanatorium.

санатрон *m.* (electron.) sanatron.

санация *f.* (med.) sanitation; oral hygiene; (com.) improvement of economic conditions; *see* **санирование.**

сангвин *m.*, —**а** *f.* red chalk (drawing); —**арин** *m.* san-

guinarine; —**ический** *a.* sanguine, optimistic; blood-colored.

сандал *m.* sandalwood (dye); —**ета** *f.* sandal; —**иевид-ный** *a.* (bot.) soleiform, slipper-shaped; —**ин** *see* **сан-талин**; —**ия** *f.*, —**ьный** *a.* sandal; —**ка** *f.* (ichth.) European cisco; —**овое дерево, —ьное дерево** sandalwood.

сандарак *m.*, —**овый** *a.* sandarac, gum juniper; —**овая смола** sandarac (resin); —**олевая кислота** sandara-colic acid.

сандарацин *m.* sandaracin; —**овая кислота** sandara-cinic acid.

сандарачный *a. of* **сандарак.**

сандвич *m.* sandwich; **техника —а** (immun.) sandwich technique, indirect fluorescent antibody technique.

Сандвичевы острова Sandwich Islands, Hawaiian Islands.

сандов *m.* harpoon, spear.

сандотрен *m.* sandothrene (color).

сани *pl.* sledge, sleigh; sled.

санинструктор *m.* hygiene instructor.

саниров/ание *n.* sanitation; remediation of financial difficulties; —**ать** *v.* improve sanitary conditions; (med.) treat; clear up financial difficulties.

санитар *m.* orderly; hospital attendant; —**ия** *f.* sanitation; preventive medicine; public health; —**ка** *f. of* **сани-тар**; nurse's aide; —**но-гигиенический** *a.* public health; —**но-контрольный** *a.* disease-control; —**но-технические работы** sanitary engineering; —**но-техническое оборудование** plumbing fixture(s); —**но-транспортное судно** hospital ship.

санитарн/ый *a.* sanitary, sanitation; public health (service); health (education); (mil.) medical (service); hospital (train); **с. автомобиль** ambulance; **с. набор** first-aid kit; **с. транспорт** ambulance; **с. узел** public bathroom and laundry; —**ая обработка** decontamination; —**ая техника** sanitary engineering; —**ое дело** public health; —**ое управление** department of sanitation.

санки *pl.* sled.

санкциониров/анный *a.* sanctioned, authorized; —**ать** *v.* sanction, assent (to).

саннуазский *a.* (geol.) Sannoisian.

санный *a. of* **сани**; sliding (microtome).

саноформ *m.* sanoform, methyl diiodosalicylate.

саночн/ик *m.* (min.) drawer; —**ый** *a. of* **сан(к)и.**

Сан-паулу (geog.) São Paulo.

санпро/пускник *m.* decontamination center; —**свет** *m.* hygiene instruction; health education.

сансериф *m.* (typ.) sans-serif (font).

сантал *m.* santal(enic acid); sandalwood; —**ал** *m.* santalal; —**еновая кислота** *see* **санталин**; —**ил** *m.* santalyl; —**ин** *m.* santalin, santal(en)ic acid; —**овый** *a.* santal; santal(en)ic (acid); sandalwood; —**ол** *m.* santalol.

сантен *m.* santene; —**овая кислота** santenic acid; —**ол** *m.* santenol.

сантехника *f.* sanitary engineering; plumbing fixtures.

санти— *prefix* centi— (10^{-2}); —**бар** *m.* centibar; —**грамм** *m.* centigram.

сантил *m.* Santyl, santalyl salicylate.

сантилитр *m.* centiliter.

сантиметр *m.* centimeter; rule or tape marked in centimeters; —**овый** *a.* (one-)centimeter; marked in centimeters; —**овая волна** centimeter wave, microwave.

санти/милли— *prefix* centimilli—; —**нормальный** *a.* centinormal; —**пуаз** *m.* centipoise; —**секунда** *f.* centisecond; —**стокс** *m.* centistoke.

сантол *m.* santol.

сантонин *m.* santonin; **—ная полынь** (bot.) santolina (*Artemisia cina*); **—овая кислота** santoninic acid; **—овокислый натрий** sodium santoninate.

сантон/истый *a.* santonous; **—овый** *a.* santonic (acid); **—овокислый натрий** sodium santonate; **—он** *m.* santonone.

сантонский *a.* (geol.) Santonian.

санторин/иев проток (anat.) duct of Santorini; **—ит** *m.* (petr.) santorinite.

сантохлор *m.* santochlor, *p*-dichlorobenzene.

Сантьяго (geog.) Santiago.

сан/узел *m.* public bathroom and laundry; **—упр** *m.* department of sanitation.

Сан-франциско (geog.) San Francisco.

Сан-Хосе (geog.) San Jose; **Сан-хуан** San Juan.

санчасть *f.* medical unit.

сап *m.* (vet.) glanders; **кожный с.** farcy, cutaneous glanders.

САП *abbr.* (**система автоматического поиска**) automatic search system.

сапа *f.* (mil. eng.) sap, trench.

сапёр *m.* (mil.) sapper, field engineer, combat engineer; **—но-строительные работы** field construction; **—ный** *a.* sapper, sapping, (en)trenching; **—ная спичка** slow match; **—ное дело** field engineering.

сапетка *f.* (corn) crib; (apid.) skep, beehive; **с.-лежак** long skep; **с.-стояк** upright skep.

сапин *m.* sapine (isomer of cadaverine); **—овая кислота** sapinic acid.

сапировать *v.* (mil.) sap, undermine.

сапка *f.* (agr.) hoe.

сапн/ой, —ый *a.* of **сап**; glanderous.

сапогенин *m.* sapogenin, sapogenol.

сапог/и *pl.* boots; **—оваляльный** *a.* felt boot.

сапожн/ик *m.* shoemaker; **—ичество** *n.* shoe-making; **—ый** *a.* shoemaker's, cobbler's; **—ый вар** cobbler's wax; **—ый крем, —ая вакса, —ая мазь** shoe polish.

сапожок штока operating post.

сапон/арин *m.* saponarin; **—етин** *m.* saponetin; **—ин** *m.* saponin.

сапонификация *f.* saponification.

сапоподобная болезнь (med.) melioidosis.

сапо/тален *m.* sapotalene, trimethylnaphthalene; **—тин** *m.* sapotin; **—тинетин** *m.* sapotinetin; **—токсин** *m.* sapotoxin.

САПР *abbr.* (**система автоматизированного проектирования**) computer-aided design, CAD.

саприн *m.* saprine (a ptomaine).

сапро— *prefix* sapro— (rotten, putrid); **—бионт** *m.* (biol.) saprobiont; **—генный** *a.* (biol.) saprogenous; **—зои** *pl.* saprozoites; **—легния** *f.* water mold (*Saprolegnia*).

сапропел/евый *a.* (zool.) sapropelic; **с. уголь, —ит** *m.*, **—итовый** *a.* (geol.) sapropelite; **—ь** *m.* sapropel, organic mud.

сапротрофный *a.* (bot.) saprotrophic.

сапроф/аг *m.* (biol.) saprophage; **—ит** *m.* saprophyte.

сапсан *m.* peregrine falcon (*Falco peregrinus*).

сапун *m.* breather (pipe).

сапфир *m.*, **—ный, —овый** *a.* sapphire.

САР *abbr.* (**система автоматического регулирования**) automatic control system.

Саравак (geog.) Sarawak.

сарай *m.*, **—ный** *a.* barn, shed; garage, carhouse; hangar.

саранча *f.* (ent.) locust.

саратовский *a.* (geog.) Saratov.

сарга *f.* (ichth.) roach (*Rutilus rutilus*).

сарган *m.* (ichth.) garfish (*Belone belone*); **—овые** *pl.* Belonidae; **—ообразные** *pl.* Beloniformes; **—ы** *see* **саргановые**.

саргассово море (geog.) Sargasso Sea.

саргус *m.* (ichth.) sheepshead.

сардел/евое масло anchovy oil; **—ь** *f.* anchovy; **—ька** *f. see* **сардель**; (ichth.) sprat, kilka; a short, thick sausage.

Сарджента диаграмма Sargent diagram.

сардин/(к)а *f.* sardine; **—елла** *f.* Sardinella; **—овый** *a.* sardine; **—опс** *m.* (ichth.) Sardinops; **—очный** *a.* sardine.

сарептская горчица (bot.) Indian mustard (*Brassica juncea*).

сарж/а *f.*, **—евый** *a.* (text.) serge, twill.

сарианак *m.* (ichth.) mullet.

саркин *m.* sarkine, hypoxanthine.

сарко— *prefix* sarco— (flesh); **—да** *a.* (zool.) sarcode (protoplasm of one-celled animals); **—дерма** *f.* (bot.) sarcoderm; **—довые** *pl.* (prot.) Sarcodina; **—зин** *m.*, **—зиновый** *a.* sarcosine; **—идоз** *m.* (med.) sarcoidosis; **—карпий** *m.* (bot.) sarcocarp; **—колла** *f.* sarcocolla (gum); **—коллин** *m.* sarcocollin; **—моподобный** *a.* (med.) sarcoid; **—лемма** *f.* (anat.) sarcolemma; **—лизин** *m.* sarcolysine; **—ма** *f.* (med.) sarcoma; **—матозный** *a.* sarcomatous; **—мицин** *m.* sarcomycin; **—плазма** *f.* (zool.) sarcoplasm; **—псилла** *f.* genus of fleas; **—фаг** *m.* sarcophagus; **—фаги** *pl.* flesh flies (*Sarcophagidae*).

сарлык *m.* yak (*Bos grunniens*).

сармат *m.*, **—ский** *a.* Sarmatian; **—ский ярус** (geol.) Sarmatian stage.

саротамнин *m.* sarothamnine.

саррацен/ин *m.* sarracenine; **—ия** *f.* (bot.) Sarracenia; **—овый** *a.* Sarracenia; sarracenic (acid).

сарсапар/е(л)ль, —иль *f.* sarsaparilla.

сарса/повая кислота sarsapic acid; **—сапонин** *m.* sarsasaponin.

сарци/дин *m.* sarcidin (antibiotic); **—н** *see* **саркин; —на** *f.* (bact.) Sarcina.

сарыч *m.* (orn.) buzzard (*Buteo*).

сарьянак *m.* (ichth.) gray mullet (*Mugil*).

САС *abbr.* (**селитряно-аммиачный суперфосфат**) ammonium nitrate superphosphate.

Саскачеван (geog.) Saskatchewan.

Саскуэханна Susquehanna (river).

сасса *see* **сассой**.

сассапарел(л)ь *see* **сарсапарел(л)ь**.

сассафрас *m.* (bot.) sassafras.

сасси *n.* sassy bark, casca bark.

сассой *m.* (mam.) klipspringer.

сассолин *m.* (min.) sassoline, sassolite.

сателл/ит *m.* satellite; **—итовый** *a.* satellite; subordinate; planetary (gear); **—оид** *m.* satelloid (flying missile).

САТ-зона (gen.) SAT-zone (secondary zone of satellite chromosome).

сативин *m.* sativin; **—овая кислота** sativic acid.

сатин *m.* (text.) satin; **—ёр** *m.* (paper) glazer, plater, plating machine; **—ет** *m.*, **—етовый** *a.* (text.) satinet.

сатиниров/альный *a.*, **—ание** *n.* (paper) glazing, etc., *see v.*; **—анный** *a.* glazed, etc., *see v.*; plate-glazed; satin; **—ать** *v.* glaze, plate, satin, (super)calendar; **—очный** *a. see* **сатинировальный**.

сатинит *m.* satin white (pigment).

сатинов/ый *a.* satin; sateen; **—ое дерево** satinwood.

сатион *m.* (bot.) sation (subdivision of seasonal society).

сатириаз *m.* (med.) satyriasis.

сатия *see* **сатион.**

сатко *n.* Satco alloy.

САТ-перетяжка *see* **САТ-зона.**

сатура/тор *m.*, **—торный** *a.* saturator; (sugar; beverages) carbonator; **—ционный** *a.* of **сатурация; —ционная грязь** dregs, lies; **—ция** *f.* saturation; carbon(iz)ation.

сатурея *f.* (bot.) savory.

сатурирование *see* **сатурация.**

Сатурн *m.* (astr.) Saturn; **система —a** Saturnian system.

сатурн/изм *m.* (med.) saturnism, lead poisoning; **—ии** *pl.* (ent.) Saturniidae; **—ово дерево** arbor Saturni, lead tree.

сат-хромосома *f.* chromosome with satellite.

САУ *abbr.* (**самоходно-артиллерийская установка**) self-propelled gun; (**система автоматического управления**) automatic control system.

Саудовская Аравия (geog.) Saudi Arabia.

саур(о)— *prefix* saur(o)— (lizard).

Саут— *prefix* (geog.) South—; **—гемптон, —хемптон** Southampton.

сафизм *m.* (med.) sapphism, lesbianism.

сафир *see* **сапфир.**

сафлор *m.* (bot.) safflower (*Carthamus tinctorius*); **—овый** *a.* safflower.

сафой *see* **савойская капуста.**

сафр/анин *m.* safranine; **—анинол** *m.* safraninol; **—анол** *m.* safranol; **—ен** *m.* safrene; **—озин** *m.* safrosin; **—ол** *m.* safrole; **—он** *m.* saffron.

сафьян *m.*, **—овый** *a.* morocco (leather).

сах. *abbr.* (**сахар, сахарный**) sugar; **САХ** *abbr.* (**средняя аэродинамическая хорда**) mean aerodynamic chord.

Сахалин (geog.) Sakhalin.

сахалинка *f.* (ichth.) Arctic smelt.

сахалинский *a.* (geog.) Sakhalin.

сахар *m.* sugar; **виноградный с.** glucose; **жжёный с.** caramel; **мелкий с.** powdered sugar; **молочный с.** lactose; **образование —a** glycogenesis; **плодовый с.** fructose; **простой с.** monosaccharide; **фруктовый с.** fructose.

Сахара Sahara (desert).

сахар/аза *f.* saccharase; **—ан** *m.* saccharane; **—ат** *m.* saccharate, sucrate.

сахари/д *m.* saccharide; **—метр** *m.* saccharimeter; **—метрия** *f.* saccharimetry.

сахарин *m.* saccharin; **—овый** *a.* saccharin; saccharinic (acid).

сахарист/ость *f.* saccharinity; sugar content; **—ый** *a.* sugary, saccharine, sacchariferous; (geol.) saccharoid(al).

сахарить *v.* (sweeten with) sugar.

сахарно/кальциевая соль, —кислый кальций calcium saccharate; **—кислый** *a.* saccharic acid; saccharate (of); **—кислая соль** saccharate.

сахарн/ый *a.* sugar(y), saccharine; sweet (corn); **с. завод** sugar refinery; **с. обмен** saccharometabolism; **с. песок** granulated sugar; **с. тростник** sugar cane; **—ая болезнь** (med.) diabetes mellitus; **—ая голова** sugar loaf; **—ая кислота** saccharic acid; **—ая пудра** confectioner's sugar; **соль —ой кислоты** saccharate.

сахаро/биоза *f.* saccharobiose, sucrose; **—вар** *m.* sugar refiner; **—варение** *n.*, **—вар(ен)ный** *a.* sugar refining; **—видный** *a.* (geol.) saccharoidal (texture); **—за** *f.* saccharose, sucrose; **—метр** *see* **сахариметр; —мицеты** *pl.* (bot.) saccharomycetes; **—молочная кислота** saccharolactic acid, mucic acid; **—новая**

кислота saccharonic acid; **—нос** *m.* sugar-yielding plant; **—носный** *a.* sacchariferous; **—образование** *n.* formation of sugar, saccharification; (physiol.) glycogenesis; **—подобный** *a.* sugar-like, saccharine, saccharoid, sugary; **—рафинадный завод** sugar refinery; **—снижающий** *a.* (physiol.) hypoglycemic; **—содержание** *n.* sugar content; **—содержащий** *a.* sugar-containing, sacchariferous, saccharine, saccharated; **—содержащая моча** (med.) glycosuria.

сахар-песок *m.* granulated sugar; **с.-рафинад** *m.* refined sugar; **с.-сатурн** *m.* sugar of lead, lead acetate; **с.-сырец** *m.* unrefined sugar.

сахельский ярус (geol.) Sahelian stage.

сачок *m.* hand net, insect net.

саше *n.* sachet; small bag.

САЮ *abbr.* (**система активной юстировки**) active alignment system.

саянский *a.* (geog.) Sayan.

сб *abbr.* (**стильб**) stilb, unit of brightness; **сб.** *abbr.* (**сборник**) collection, symposium.

сбав/ить, —лять *v.* reduce, lower, cut, deduct, subtract; **—ка** *f.* reduction, lowering, cut (in price), deduction.

сбалансиров/анный *a.* balanced; equilibrium (population); **—ать** *v.* balance (out), neutralize.

сбалтывать *v.* stir, mix up, shake up.

сбалчивать *v.* bolt together.

сбе/г *m.* run-off; fall(ing) off; run-out (of thread); taper (of lumber); (naut.) scupper; **—гание** *n.* running off, etc., *see* *v.*; **—гать** *v.* run off, run down, flow off; run over, overflow, bubble over; run for; **—гаться** *v.* run together, gather, collect; **—гающий** *a.* running off, etc., *see* *v.*; trailing; (bot.) excurrent; **—гающий скат** falling edge; decay edge; **—жать** *see* **сбегать.**

сбежист/ость *f.* taper, decrease; **—ый** *a.* tapering, decreasing.

сбей(те) *imp.* of **сбить.**

сбере/гательный *a.* saving(s); **—гать** *v.* save, economize; stock, lay up; keep, (p)reserve, conserve; **—жение** *n.* economy, saving; preservation, upkeep, maintenance; **—жения** (text.) savings; **—чь** *see* **сберегать.**

сберкасса *f.* savings bank.

сбеситься *v.* become rabid; become furious.

сбив/альный *a.*, **—ание** *n.* knocking off, etc., *see* *v.*; (rad.) beating, heterodyning; **—ание накипи** scaling (off); **—ать** *v.* knock off, throw off (course), divert; knock down, decrease; put together, nail together; churn (butter), whip (cream), beat (eggs); confuse; shoot down (plane); **—аться** *v.* be knocked off, etc., *see* *v.*; go off (course); get out of position; get confused; contradict oneself; **—ка** *see* **сбивание; —ной** *a.* knocking off, etc., *see* *v.*; knocked off, etc., *see* *v.*

сбивчив/ость *f.* confusion; inconsistency; **—ый** *a.* confused, indistinct; conflicting.

сбирать *see* **собирать.**

СБИС *abbr.* (**сверхбольшая интегральная схема**) (electron.) very large-scale integrated circuit, VLSI circuit.

сбит/ый *a.* knocked off, etc., *see* **сбивать;** out of position, out of alignment; biased; linked (boreholes); compact (body); **—ь** *see* **сбивать.**

СБК *abbr.* (**стационарная барокамера**) stationary pressure chamber.

сбли/жать *v.* draw together, bring together; bind, connect; compare; **—жаться** *v.* approach, come closer together, draw together, converge; **—жение** *n.* drawing together, etc., *see* *v.*; convergence; rapprochement; approach; rendezvous; approximation; **прививка —жением** (hort.) inarching; **скорость —жения** approach velocity; **—женность** *f.* contiguity, proximity; conver-

сбли/жение — **женный** *a.* drawn together, etc., *see v.*; converging; contiguous, adjacent; approximate; (bot.) connivent; **—зить** *see* **сближать.**

сблокиров/анный *a.* assembled, etc., *see v.*; multiple (motor); **—ать** *v.* assemble, connect up; interlock, interlink.

СБМ *abbr.* (**сбоечно-бурная машина**).

сбое/к *gen. pl. of* **сбойка**; **—чно-бурная машина** (min.) crosscut drill; **—чный** *a. of* **сбойка.**

сбоина *f.* residue, cake; husks.

сбой *m.* malfunction(ing), trouble, failure, damage; disturbance, interruption, irregularity, missing; dislocation; reduction, lowering; fragments; head, feet and entrails of slaughtered animal; tripe; **с. в линии** (commun.) lineout; **с. травостоя** overgrazing; **фатальный с.** (comp.) crash.

сбойка *f.* joining, joint, mortising; (min.) connector, crosscut; linking.

сбойня *see* **сбоина.**

сбоку *adv.* at the side (of), on the side, from the side; **вид с.** side view.

сболт/анный *a.* shaken up, stirred; **—ать** *see* **сбалтывать.**

сбол/тить *see* **сболчивать;** **—ченный** *a.* bolted (together), etc., *see v.*; **—чивание** *n.* bolting (together), etc., *see v.*; **—чивать** *v.* bolt (together), fasten, secure.

сбор *m.* assembly, muster, gathering, collection, accumulation; picking, reaping, harvest(ing), yield; gate receipts; fee, charge, duty, toll, dues; (pharm.) species; tea; **с. данных** (comp.) data acquisition, data logging; **с. колосьев** gleaning; **быть в —е** *v.* be assembled; **масляный радиатор в —е** oil-cooler assembly; **—ище** *n.* crowd, mob.

сборка *f.* assembly, assembling, putting together, building up, setting up, erecting, erection, installation, setup, rigging, mounting, fitting, joining; package, packaging; (diode) pack; (comp.) integration (of program modules); (rubber) building; gather, crease (in cloth); (glaze) shivering; **с. подборкой** selective assembly; **с. схемы** (elec.) circuitry; **предварительная с., узловая с.** preliminary assembly, subassembly.

сборник *m.* collection; symposium; collector, accumulator, receiver, receptacle, (storage or collection) tank, sump; header, manifold; **с. конденсата** hotwell.

сборно/-монолитный *a.* precast (concrete); **—разборный** *a.* dismountable assembled (fittings); **—сть** *f.* construction with prefabricated parts or modules.

сборн/ый *a.* assembled, built-up, sectional, module, unit-construction; ready-made, prefabricated; precast (concrete); combined, mixed (fertilizer); multiple; accumulative, collective, collecting, aggregate, heterogeneous, miscellaneous; composite (map); assembly, rendezvous (point); bilge (well); syncarpous (fruit); holding (tank); **с. горшок** receiver; **с. лист** preliminary matter, preliminary pages; **—ая группа** assembly; **—ая таблица** index diagram; **—ая шина** (elec.) collecting bar; **—ое строение** prefabrication.

сборочн/ая *f.* assembly shop, assembly plant, fitting shop; **—о-автоматическая линия** automatic assembly line; **—ый** *a.* assembly, assembling, erecting; grouping; unitized, module; fastening (screw); **—ый конвейер** assembly belt.

сборщи/к *m.* assembler, fitter, erector, mounter; adjuster; collector, picker, scavenger; **—ца** *f.* (apid.) field bee.

сбоч/ениться *v.* lean, tilt, list; **—ить** *v.* move to the side; **—ку** *see* **сбоку.**

сбоя *gen. of* **сбой.**

сбражив/ание *n.* fermentation; digestion; **—ать** *v.* ferment, brew.

сбрасыв/аемый *a.* jettisonable, drop(pable), expendable; waste (heat); **—ание** *n.* dumping, etc., *see v.*; drop, release, discharge; disposal; dispersal; (commun.) cut-off; (geol.) faulting; detrusion; **кнопка —ания** (commun.) cancel key; **проба —анием** (met.) drop-shatter test; **синдром —ания** (med.) dumping syndrome; **—атель** *m.* tripper (device); release (mechanism); (mach.) kicker; (rr.) derailer; (geol.) fault fissure; **плужковый —атель** plow (of a belt conveyor); **—ать** *v.* dump, drop, release, jettison, throw down; throw off, cast off, shed; discard, dispose (of); (comp.) clear, reset, erase, purge; relieve (pressure); decrease; (hydr.) run off, discharge; (rr.) derail; flood (the market); **—ающий** *a.* dumping, etc., *see v.*; (geol.) fault (fissure).

сбривать *v.* shave off, shear off.

сбрикетировать *v.* briquette.

сбрит/ый *a.* shaved off; **—ь** shave off.

сбро/дить *v.* ferment; **—женный** *a.* fermented, brewed; digested (sludge).

сброс *m.* drop; decrease; (stress) relief; release; (hydr.) run-off; disposal (of waste waters); dumping; jettison(ing); refuse pulp, effluent; (comp.) reset; (converter) burst; (phys.) fault (in line of creep); (geol.) fault, spec. normal (gravity) fault; **импульс —а** reset pulse; **откос —а, терраса —а, фас —а** fault scarp.

сброс/ать, —ить *see* **сбрасывать;** **—ка** *see* **сбрасывание;** **—ной, —ный** *a.* overflow, run-off, discharge, spillway; waste (water, etc.); **—овый** *a.* overflow, run-off; (geol.) fault; faulted (mountain; structure); **—овая глыба** fault block; **—овая деятельность** faulting; **—ообразование** *n.* (geol.) faulting; **—о-сдвиг** *m.* strike-slip normal fault.

сброшенн/ый *a.* dumped, etc., *see* **сбрасывать;** (geol.) faulted; **с. вниз** (geol.) downfaulted; **—ая котловина** fault basin.

сброшюрованный *a.* stitched (book).

сбру/йный *a.*, **—я** *f.* harness.

сбрыз/г *m.* sprayer, sprinkler; **—гивание** *n.* spraying, etc., *see v.*; **—гивать, —нуть** *v.* spray, sprinkle, wet.

сбы/вание *n.* sale, marketing; market; **—вать** *v.* sell off, market; dispose (of), get rid (of); go down (of water); **—ваться** *v.* happen, occur, turn out, be realized; **—т** *see* **сбывание; —тие** *n.* diminution; **—тный** *a.* marketable; **—товой** *a.* market(ing); **—ть** *see* **сбывать.**

св *abbr.* (**свеча**) candle; (**среднее время**) mean time; **св.** *abbr.* (**свыше**) over; (**святой**) saint; **с.в.** *abbr.* (**скорость ветра**) wind speed; **С.-В.** *abbr.* (**северо-восток**) northeast.

сваб/ирование *n.* swabbing (for starting oil wells).

свадебный *a.* nuptial.

свае/бойный *a.* pile-driving; **—выдёргиватель** *m.* pile extractor.

Свазиленд (geog.) Swaziland.

сва/и *gen., pl., etc.*; **—й** *gen. pl. of* **свая.**

свайка *f.* (naut.) fid, marline spike.

свайн/ик *m.* (zool.) strongyl(e), hookworm; **—обойный** *a.* pile-driving, ram; **—ый** *a.* pile(-supported); **—ые работы** piling, pile-driving.

свал *see* **сваливание;** dump; heap, pile; **—енный** *a.* dumped, etc., *see v.*; canted (rifle); **—ивание** *n.* dumping, etc., *see v.*; drop(ping); stall(ing) (of aircraft); **—и(ва)ть** *v.* dump, unload, discharge, drop, throw off; relieve (of); knock down, knock over, upset; fell (tree); overcome (with disease); attribute (to); heap up, pile up; felt, mat (together); decrease, abate, fall off, diminish; (av.) tilt; **—и(ва)ться** *v.* fall, collapse, tumble down; stall (of aircraft); fall ill; —**ка** see **сваливание;** dump; heap, pile; —**ка мусора** landfill; —**очный** *a. of* **свалка;** —**очное место** dump, dumping ground.

Свальбард (geog.) Svalbard.

свальный *a.* dump(ing).

свальцевать *v.* roll (into a given shape).

свальщик *m.* dumper; piler.

свал/яный, —явшийся *a.* felted, matted; —**ять** *v.* felt, mat.

Свана патрон (elec.) bayonet socket.

сванбергит *m.* (min.) svanbergite.

сваренный *a.* cooked, boiled; well-prepared (meal); welded, fused.

сварив/аемость *f.* weldability; bondability; —**аемый** *a.* weldable; —**ание** *n.* welding; (leather) shrinkage; —**ать** *v.* weld (together), weld up, fuse; solder; bond; —**ать в притык** butt-weld.

свар/ить *v.* boil, cook; weld; —**ка** *f.* welding; **термокомпрессионная с.** bonding; —**ной, —ный** *a.* welded; —**очный** *a.* weld(ing); welded; fused; —**очный порошок** welding flux.

Свартса реакция (chem.) Swarts reaction.

сварщик *m.* welder, welding operator.

свая *f.* pile, post, stilt; (mach.) spud; **с.-оболочка** *f.* tubular pile; **с.-стойка** *f.* end-bearing pile.

св-во *abbr.* (**свойство**) property, characteristic.

СВВП *abbr.* (**самолёт вертикального взлёта и посадки**) vertical take-off and landing (VTOL) aircraft.

св.г. *abbr.* (**световой год**) light year.

свевать *v.* blow (off, together); winnow.

сведа *f.* (bot.) seablite (*Suaeda*).

Свердберга правило (phys.) Svedberg rule.

сведен/ие *n.* knowledge, information; taking, etc., see **сводить(ся);** (med.) contraction, cramp; (beam) convergence; —**ия** *pl.* information, data; **с. в таблицу** tabulation; **доводить до —ия** *v.* notify; **принять к —ию** *v.* take into consideration; **сообщать —ия** *v.* instruct, inform.

сведённый *a.* taken, etc., see **сводить.**

сведущ/ий *a.* adept, versed (in), expert, skilled; experienced; —**ее лицо** expert.

свеет *fut. 3 sing. of* **свеять.**

свеж *sh. m. of* **свежий;** —**ак** *m.* strong, fresh wind; freshly caught fish; —**атина** *f.* fresh meat.

свеже *adv.,* **свеже—** *prefix* freshly, recently.

свежевать *v.* flay, dress (cattle).

свеже/вспаханный *a.* fresh-plowed; —**замороженный** *a.* quick-frozen; —**инфицированный** *a.* recently infected; —**испечённый** *a.* freshly baked; —**обнажённый** *a.* freshly uncovered; —**оплодотворенный** *a.* freshly fertilized; —**осаждённый** *a.* freshly formed; —**приготовленный** *a.* freshly prepared, fresh; —**просольный** *a.* freshly pickled; fresh-salted; —**разведённый** *a.* freshly diluted; fresh; —**распиленный** *a.* green, unseasoned (timber); —**скошенный** *a.* freshly mowed; —**смешанный** *a.* freshly mixed; —**снесённый** *a.* freshly laid (egg); —**срубленный** *a.* green(wood).

свеж/есть *f.* freshness; brilliance (of color); breeziness; crispness; —**еть** *v.* cool off; freshen, become stronger (of wind); —**еубранный** *a.* fresh-cut (flowers); fresh-picked (berries, etc.); —**ий** *a.* fresh, recent, new; brilliant, bright; live (steam); green (sand, coal, etc.); (med.) early (syphilis); virgin (neutron); —**о** *adv. and sh. n. of* **свежий;** it is chilly; —**ьё** *n.* fresh caught fish.

свез/ённый *a.* carried, conveyed, transported; —**ти** see **свозить.**

свеивать see **свевать.**

свёкла *f.* beet; **листовая с.** Swiss chard; **сахарная с.** sugar beet.

свекло— *prefix* beet; —**вица** *f.* beet, spec. sugar beet; —**вичник** *m.* Swiss chard; —**вичный** *a.* (sugar)-beet; —**вище** *n.* beet field; —**вод** *m.* beet grower; —**водство** *n.,* —**водческий** *a.* beet growing; —**комбайн** *m.* beet(root) combine; —**копатель** *m.* beet-(root) digger; —**мойка** *f.* beet washer; —**погрузчик** *m.* beet(root) loader; —**подъёмник** *m.* beet(root) digger, beet(root) harvester; —**резка** *f.* beet cutter or slicer; —**сахарный** *a.* beet-sugar; —**сеющий** *a.,* —**сеяние** *n.* beet growing; —**совхоз** *m.* sugarbeet state farm; —**уборка** *f.,* —**уборочный** *a.* beet harvesting; —**утомление** *n.* soil exhaustion from beets; —**хранилище** *n.* beet storage; root cellar.

свекольный *a.* beet(root); beet-red.

свёл *past m. sing. of* **свести.**

сверб/ёж *m.* itch(ing); —**еть** *v.* itch, be irritated.

сверби/га *f.* (bot.) Bunias; —**жница** *f.* Cephalaria.

сверг/ать *v.* throw down; overthrow; overcome; —**аться** *v.* fall (of water), cascade; —**нуть** see **свергать.**

свердловский *a.* (geog.) Sverdlovsk.

свер/ить see **сверять;** —**ка** *f.* collation, etc., see **сверять;** revise, revised proof, revision.

сверк/ание *n.* sparkle, sparkling, glitter, flash; —**ать, —нуть** *v.* sparkle, glitter, flash, gleam, scintillate; —**ающий** *a.* sparkling, etc., see *v.;* bright, radiant.

сверл/ение *n.* boring, drilling, piercing; —**илка** *f.* drill; —**ило(-корабельщик)** *n.* ship-timber beetle; —**ильник** *m.* borer, driller.

сверлильн/ый *a.* boring, drilling; **с. перфоратор** auger, rotary drill; **с. станок, —ая машина** drill (press); —**ая стружка** borings.

сверл/ильщик *m.* borer, driller; —**ить** *v.* bore, drill, perforate, pierce; —**ить под** drill (an opening or receptacle) for; nag.

сверло *n.* drill, borer, (boring) bit, auger.

сверло/вка *f.,* —**вочный** *a.* drilling, boring; —**вщик** *m.* driller, drill operator; —**заточный** *a.* drill-sharpening.

сверло-коронка *n.* core drill; **с.-развёртка** *n.* finishing drill.

сверл/янка *f.* (ent.) borer; —**ящий** *a.* drilling, boring; nagging; piercing (pain).

сверну/вшийся see **свернутый;** —**тость** *f.* convolution; —**тый** *a.* coagulated, etc., see **свёртывать;** convolute; contorted; (chem.) coiled, twisted, wound; refolded; —**ть** see **свёртывать.**

свёрст/ка *f.* (typ.) made up matter, make-up.

сверстать see **сверстывать.**

сверстн/ик *m.,* —**ица** *f.* person of the same age, peer.

свёрстывать *v.* (printing) impose; make up (into pages).

сверт/еть see **свёртывать.**

свёртка see **свертывание;** *gen. of* **свёрток.**

свёртн/ый *a.* screwed on; **с. вал** built-up shaft; —**ая гайка** *, —*ая муфта** screw cap; cap screw.

свёрток *m.* pack(et), package, parcel; roll; coagulum, clot, thrombus; *gen. pl. of* **свертка.**

свёртыв/аемость *f.* coagulability; **фактор —аемости** (hemat.) clotting factor, coagulation factor; —**аемый** *a.* coagulable.

свёртывани/е *n.* coagulation, curdling, etc., see *v.;* (math.) convolution; (comp.) folding (operating system); closure, wrap-up, phase-out; **с. кода** (comp.) code compression; **с. строк** (comp.) line folding; **фактор —я крови** (hemat.) coagulation factor; **фактор —я крови I** (hemat.) Factor I, fibrinogen; **фактор —я корви II** Factor II, prothrombin.

свёртыва/ть *v.* coagulate, curdle; turn (aside, off);

knock aside; twist; convolve; unscrew; strip (thread); roll up, wrap up; strike (tents); close down, phase out; break (camp); cut back, curtail; convert, reduce (information); **с. с дороги** turn off the road; **—ться** *v.* coagulate, curdle, clot; (chem.) flocculate; roll up, curl up, fold up; kink, twist; turn (to); cut back; **—ющийся** *a.* coagulating, etc., *see* v.

сверх *prep. gen.* above, over, on top of, in excess of, beyond; besides, in addition to; **с. того** moreover, over and above, besides.

сверх— *prefix* super—, hyper—, ultra—, extra—, excessively; **—адиабатический** *a.* superadiabatic; **—атмосферный** *a.* superatmospheric; **—баллон** *m.* balloon tire; **—барометрический** *a.* superatmospheric; **—быстродействующий** super fast, ultra-high-speed; super (computer); **—быстроходный, —быстрый** *a.* super fast, extra fast, ultra-high-speed; flash (freezing); **—вид** superspecies; **—восприимчивость** *f.* supersensitivity; **—возбуждение** *n.* superexcitation.

сверхвысок/ий *a.* superhigh, extremely high; super—; **—овольтная сеть** (elec.) supergrid; **—отемпературный** *a.* extreme-temperature; **—очастотный** *a.* microwave (discharge, maser, etc.).

сверх/гаплоид *m.* (gen.) hyperhaploid; **—глубокий** *a.* subsoil (plowing); **—густитель** *m.* superthickener; **—давление** *n.* excess pressure; **—дальний, —дальнобойный** *a.* ultra long-range; **—действие** *n.* peak output; **—диплоид** *m.* hyperdiploid; **—дозирование** *n.* overdosing; **—доминирование** *n.* superdominance; **—женщина** *see* **сверхсамка; —живучий** *a.* (bot.) hyperazoic; **—зарождение, —зачатие** *n.* (physiol.) superfetation; **—звуковой** *a.* (acous.) supersonic, ultrasonic; Laval (nozzle); **—излучение** *n.* super-radiation; **—кислотность** *f.* (med.) hyperacidity, excessive acidity; **—кислотный** *a.* strongly acid; **—компенсация** *f.* overcompensation; **—комплексный** *a.* supercomplex; **—комплектный** *a.* supernumerary, superfluous, extra, excess; accessory, supplemental (e.g., teeth).

сверхкритич/еский *a.* supercritical, above critical; **—ность** *f.* supercriticality.

сверх/легирование *n.* over-alloying; over-doping; **—лёгкий** *a.* superlight; supereasy; **—летальный** *a.* superlethal; **—лимитный** *a.* over the limit; excessively expensive, over-budget; **—мерный** *a.* oversize; **—микроскоп** *m.* electron microscope; **—миниатюрный** *a.* subminiature, subminiaturized.

сверх/мощный *a.* superpower; super—; **—мощная сеть** (elec.) supergrid; **—мягкий** *a.* extra soft; **—нагрузка** *f.* overloading; **—направленный** *a.* ultra-directional; **—натуральный** *a.* supernatural; **—неравноплечий** *a.* (biol.) hyperheterobrachial; **—низкий** *a.* extra low, ultralow; super-low (friction); **—никель** *m.* supernickel (alloy); **—новая** *f.* (astr.) supernova; **—нормальный** *a.* supernormal; **—обменный** *a.* superexchange (interaction); **—окись** *f.* superoxide, hyperoxide; **—оперативная память** (comp.) cache (memory); **—оплодотворение** *n.* (physiol.) superfecundation; **—отжиг** *m.* (met.) overannealing.

сверх/паразит *m.* (biol.) superparasite; **—плавкий** *a.* hyperfusible; **—плановый** *a.* exceeding the plan, more than planned (for); **—плоскость** *f.* (math.) hyperplane; **—подвижный** *a.* hypermobile; **—пороговый** *a.* (physiol.) supraliminal; **—прибыль** *f.* excess profit.

сверхпровод/имость *f.* superconductivity; **—ник** *m.* superconductor; **—ящий** *a.* superconducting.

сверх/прочный *a.* ultrastrong; superstrength (alloy);

—ранний *a.* (agr.) extra early; **—регенеративный** *a.* super-regenerative; self-quenching (detector); **—редкий** *a.* extremely rare; trace (element); **—рефракция** *f.* superrefraction.

сверхсам/ец *m.* (gen.) supermale; **—ка** *f.* (gen.) superfemale, triploid-X female.

сверх/световой *a.* faster than light; **—сжатие** *n.* overcompression; **—скоростной** *a.* super(-high)-speed, ultra high-speed, extra fast; **—соприкосновение** *n.* (geom.) superosculation; **—сопряжение** *n.* (chem.; phys.) hyperconjugation; **—срочник, —срочнослужащий** *m.* (mil.) reenlisted man; regular, career military man; **—срочный** *a.* very urgent; extended; (mil.) reenlisted; regular, career; **—стимуляция** *f.* overstimulation; **—структура** *f.* superstructure; (cryst.) superlattice; **—сходимость** (math.) superconvergence; **—счётный** *a.* odd; **—твёрдый** *a.* superhard, extra hard.

сверхтекуч/есть *f.* superfluidity; **—ий** *a.* superfluid.

сверх/ток *m.* (elec.) overcurrent, excess current; **—тонкий** *a.* ultrafine; (phys.) hyperfine; submicron (particle); **—точный** *a.* very precise, super— (regulator); high-precision; **—тяжёлый** *a.* superheavy, extra heavy.

сверху *adv.* (from) above; at the top (of); **с. до низу** from top to bottom; **вид с.** top view; **загрузка с.** top charging.

сверх/упругий *a.* hyperelastic, superelastic; **—урочные** *pl.* overtime pay; **—урочный** *a.* overtime (work); **—усиление** *n.* overamplification; **—устойчивость** *f.* superstability, overstability; **—фильтр** *m.* ultrafilter; **—фоторегистрация** *f.* moving-image photography; **—центрифуга** *f.* supercentrifuge; **—человеческий** *a.* superhuman; **—чистый** *a.* ultra-pure; **—чувствительный** *a.* supersensitive; **—широкоугольный** *a.* (phot.) superwide-angle; **—штатный** *a.* supernumerary; **—ъестественный** *a.* supernatural, preternatural; **—ядро** *n.* supernucleus.

сверчок *m.* (ent.) cricket; (orn.) grasshopper warbler (*Locustella*).

сверш/ать(ся), —ить(ся) *see* **совершать(ся); —ение** *see* **совершение.**

сверять *v.* collate, compare, check (against); **—ся** *v.* check.

свес *m.* overhang, jut, projection, extension; shed; **—ить** *v.* suspend; weigh; weigh down.

свести *see* **сводить.**

свет *m.* light; world; clearance; **в —е** in the light (of), considering; **в —у** (in the) clear, inside; **высота в —у** inside height, clearance; **выходить в с.** *v.* appear, come out, be published; **диаметр в —у** inside diameter, bore; **появляться на с.** appear, come into being; **преломление —а** optical refraction; **проливать с. на** *v.* illuminate, clarify, shed light on; **проливающий с.** luminous; **пропускающий с.** translucent; **сила —а** *see* **светосила.**

светать *v.* dawn, grow light.

светел *sh. m. of* **светлый.**

светил/о *n.* star, luminary, light; **—а** *pl.* heavenly bodies.

светильн/ик *m.* lamp, lighting fixture; **—ый** *a.* illuminating; **—я** *f.* lamp; wick.

светимость *f.* luminosity, luminance; radiance; transmission (of spectrometer).

светить *v.* (give) light; **—ся** *v.* shine, gleam, glisten, sparkle; glow, fluoresce.

светлее *comp. of* **светло, светлый;** paler.

светлеть *v.* lighten, grow light, brighten; clear up, clarify.

светлить *v.* give light; shine, polish.

светло *adv. and prefix* pallidi— (pale); light, bright, clear; it is light; **—вина** *f.* bright spot; **—волосый** *a.* blond; **—зем** *m.* light-colored soil; **—клеточный** *a.* (med.) clear cell (adenoma); **—коричневый** *a.* light brown; **—красный** *a.* light red, bright red; **—окрашенный** *a.* light(-colored); **—полый** *a.* (opt.) bright-field; **—сть** *f.* lightness, brightness; clearness, lucidity; **—та** *f.* luminosity; brightness; albedo, reflection factor; **—тянутый** *a.* bright-drawn (steel).

светлые *pl.* (petrol.) light products.

светлый *a.* light, luminous; clear, lucid; pale.

свет/лынь *f.* brightness, light; **—ля(чо)к** *m.* (ent.) firefly, glow-worm; **—ность** *f.* luminosity; highlight.

свето— *prefix* light, photo—; **—адаптированный** *a.* light-adapted; **—блик** *m.* light pattern; **—боязливый** *a.* photophobic, heliophobic; **—боязнь** *f.* (med.) photophobia; **—вод** *m.* (nucl.) light guide, (wavebeam) guide; optical cable; **—водный** *a.* fiber-optic; **—водная техника** fiber optics; **—возвращатель** *m.* cat's eye.

светов/ой *a.* light, luminous; illuminance (sensitivity); photo—; **с. год** light year; **с. заряд** flashpowder charge, flare; **с. поток** luminous flux; **с. пучок** pencil of light; **с. сигнал** flare; **—ая волна** light wave; **—ая дуга** luminous arc, (electric) arc; **—ая копия** *see* **светокопия**; **—ая мощность** luminosity, luminescence; **—ая чувствительность** *f.* photosensitivity; **—ое лечение** phototherapy; **—ое перо** (comp.) light pen; **—ое раздражение** *n.* (med.) photoirritation.

световоспринимающий *a.* (zool.) photoreceptive.

свето/выход *m.* light output; **—дальномер** *m.* (geod.) phototachymeter; **—диод** *m.* light-emitting diode, LED; **—закалка** *f.* (agr.) light hardening (of tubers); **—излучение** *n.* radiation of light; **—измерительный** *a.* photometric; **—испускающий** *a.* light-emitting, luminous.

светокоп/ир(оваль)ный *a. of* **светокопирование, светокопия**; **—ировальня** *f.* blueprint or photostat room; **—ирование** *n.*, **—ировка** *f.* blueprinting; photostating; diazotypy; **—ия** *f.* blueprint; photostat; diazotype; **синяя —ия** blueprint.

свето/культура *f.* (hort.) artificial-light culture; **—лечение** *n.* (med.) phototherapy, light treatment; **—ловушка** *f.* insect trap (using light); **—люб** *m.* (bot.) heliophyte; **—любивый** *a.* light-requiring, heliophil(ous), sun-loving; **—любие** *n.* (bot.) heliophilia; **—маскировка** *f.*, **—маскировочный** *a.* blackout; **—масса** *see* **светосостав**; **—маяк** *m.* (light) beacon; **—мер** *m.* photometer; **—мерный** *a.* photometric; **—метрический** *a.*, **—метрия** *f.* (mil.) flash ranging; **—модулятор** *m.* light modulator.

светонепроницаем/ость *f.* opacity; **—ый** *a.* lightproof, light-tight; opaque.

свето/носный *a.* luminiferous; **—обозначенный** *a.* marked with lights (of roads, exits, etc.); **—ориентация** *f.* (biol.) phototropism; **—отдача** *f.* light output; (light) source efficiency; **—отражательный** *a.* light-reflecting; **—ощущение** *n.* light perception; **—печатание** *n.* photographic printing; **—писное копирование** *see* **светокопирование**; **—пись** *f.* photography; **—поглощение** *n.* light absorption; **—потеря** *f.* loss of light.

светопреломл/ение *n.* refraction of light; **—яющий** *a.* light-refracting.

свето/провод *see* **световод**; **—проём** *m.* light aperture (in building).

светопрозрачн/ость *f.* translucence, light transmission; **—ый** *a.* translucent, light-transmitting.

светопроницаем/ость *f.* transparency; **—ый** *a.* transparent; translucent.

светопропуска/емость *f.* permeability to light; **—ние** *n.* light transmission.

светопрочн/ость *f.* fastness to light, photostability; **—ый** *a.* fast to light, photostable.

светорассе/ивание, —яние *n.* light diffusion, light scattering; **—иватель** *m.* diffusing screen; **—ивающий** *a.* light-diffusing.

светосигнал *m.* light signal; **—изатор** *m.* (av.) pilot light; **—изация** *f.* light signaling; **—ьный** *a.* light signal; signal(ling) (lamp).

светосил/а *f.* luminosity, lumen (output), candlepower; (phot.) aperture ratio; (lens) speed; transmission (of spectrometer); **—ьный** *a.* wide-aperture (lens).

свето/состав *m.* phosphor, luminescent substance, fluorescent substance; **—стабилизатор** *m.* light stabilizer (for plastics); **—старение** *n.* light aging.

светостойк/ий *a.* light-resistant, fast to light, photostable; **—ость** *f.* light resistance, fastness to light, photostability.

свето/схема *f.* illuminated chart; **—теневой** *a.* black and white (picture); **—тень** *f.* light and shade; **—теплостарение** *n.* light and heat aging; **—техника** *f.*, **—технический** *a.* illumination engineering; **—устойчивость** *see* **светостойкость**.

светофильтр *m.* light filter, color filter; **—ирующий** *a.* light-filtering, color-filtering; light-absorbing (pigment).

свето/фон *m.* optical telephone; **—фор** *m.*, **—форный** *a.* traffic light, light signal.

светочувствительн/ость *f.* sensitivity to light, photosensitivity; speed (of film); **—ый** *a.* light-sensitive, photosensitive; photographic, printing (paper); **—ая проводимость** (elec.) photoconductivity; **—ое сопротивление** photoresistance.

светоэлектрический *a.* photoelectric.

светский *a.* world(ly), secular, temporal.

светящ/ийся *a.* luminous, luminescent, phosphorescent, shining; noctilucent (cloud); **с. разряд** (elec.) glow discharge; **с. состав** luminophore; **—аяся лампа** (electron.) glow tube; **—аяся точка** luminous point, bright spot; focus.

свеч/а *f.* candle; spark plug; blow-off pipe (of gas well); bleeder (of blast furnace); (av.) vertical climb; (med.) suppository; **зажигательная с., запальная с.** spark-plug; (expl.) fuse lighter; **новая с.** candela, 0.995 international candle; **нормальная с.** *see* **стандартная с.**; **продувочная с.** gas vent; **стандартная с.** standard candle; **сила света в —ах, число —ей** candlepower; **с.-секунда** *f.* candle-second; **с.-час** candle-hour.

свечение *n.* luminescence, luminosity, brightness, glow, phosphorescence; (eximer) emission; lighting; **белое с.** incandescence, white heat; **красное с.** red heat.

свеч/еобразный *a.* candle-shaped; **—ка** *see* **свеча**; **—ной** *a. of* **свеча**; **—ность** *f.* candlepower.

свеш/ать *v.* weigh; **—ивать** *v.* weigh down; hang down; **—иваться** *v.* overhang; **—ивающийся** *a.* overhanging.

свеять *see* **свевать**.

свив/ание *n.*, **—ка** *f.* coil(ing), twist(ing), etc., *see v.*; **—ать** *v.* coil, twist, spin, wind, twine; unwind; weave (into); build (nest); **—аться** *v.* interweave; **—ка** *f.* coil(ing), etc., *see v.*; lay (of rope).

свидание *n.* meeting, appointment.

свидетел/ь *m.* witness, onlooker; (analysis) blank sample, control; (chromatography) reference spot, marker;

(geol.) outlier, monadnock; **быть —ем** *v.* witness, be a witness (to); **—ьское показание** (court) evidence.

свидетельств/о *n.* evidence, attestation, affirmation; testimony; document, certificate, license; record; bill (of sale); **—ование** *n.* witnessing, etc., *see v.*; **—овать** *v.* witness, attest, bear witness (to), testify; indicate, suggest, point (to the fact that); give evidence (of); **—ова-ться у доктора** get a health certificate; **—ующий** *a.* significative, indicating.

свизировать *v.* sight, level.

свил *past m. sing. of* **свить.**

свилеват/ость *f.* (bot.) curly grain, cross grain; **—ый** *a.* cross-grained; wavy-fibered; twisted, tortuous, knotty, gnarled.

свиливать *v.* swerve.

свило *past n. sing. of* **свить.**

свил/ь *f.* (timber) knot, snag, burr, curl; (cer.; glass) cord, waviness, ripple; (opt.) stria, schliere; streak, smear; (geol.) flow layer; **метод —ей** (opt.) schlieren method.

свильнуть *v.* swerve.

свинар/ка *f.* pig tender; **—ник** *m.* pigsty; **—ник-маточник** *m.* farrowing house; **—ня** *f.* pigsty; **—ь** *m.* swineherd.

Свинбурна испытание (elec.) Swinburne test.

свиневодство *n.* swine breeding.

свиней *gen. pl. of* **свинья.**

свин/ец *m.* lead, Pb; **мышьяковокислый с.** lead arsenate; **окись —ца** lead oxide, spec. lead monoxide; **соль окиси —ца** lead salt, spec. a salt of bivalent lead; **сернокислый с., сульфат —ца** lead sulfate; **уксуснокислый с.** lead acetate; **хлористый с.** lead chloride, plumbous chloride; **хлорный с.** lead tetrachloride, plumbic chloride; **хромат —ца, хромово-кислый с.** lead chromate.

свинец/алкил *m.* lead alkyl; **—арил** *m.* lead aryl; **—ди-алкил** *m.* lead dialkyl; **—диметил** *m.* lead dimethyl; **—диэтил** *m.* lead diethyl; **органический** *a.* organolead; **—содержащий** *a.* lead-containing; (min.) lead-bearing, plumbiferous; **—тетраэтил** *m.* lead tetraethyl.

свинина *f.* pork (meat).

свинк/а *f. dim. of* **свинья;** piglet; (mam.) porpoise (*Phocaena*); (met.) pig, ingot, bar; (mercury) switch; (med.) mumps; (ent.) beet weevil; **морская с.** (zool.) Guinea pig (*Cavia porcellus*); **патагонская с.** (zool.) Patagonian cavy; **чугун в —ах** pig iron; **—овые** *pl.* cavies, guinea pigs (*Caviidae*).

свиновод *m.* pig farmer; **—ство** *n.,* **—ческий** *a.* swine breeding.

свин/ой *a.* swine, pig; pork (meat); **с. жир, —ое сало** lard; **—ая рожа** (med.) erysipeloid; **—окопчёности** *pl.* smoked pork products; **—оматка** *a.* sow with litter, brood sow; **—орой** *m.* (bot.) Cynodon; **пальчатый —орой** Bermuda grass; **—орыловые** *pl.* (ichth.) scavengers (*Lethrinidae*); **—отоварный** *a.* commercial swinebreeding; **—хозяйство** *n.* pig(-breeding) farm.

свинтить *see* **свинчивать.**

свин/ух *m.,* **—уха** *f.* mushroom (*Agaricus violaceus*); **—ушка** *f.* mushroom (*A. placomyces, Paxillus involutus*); **—ушник** *m.* pigsty.

свинц/а *gen. of* **свинец; —евание** *n.* leadplating, leading; **—евать** *v.* lead(-plate); **—ованный** *a.* lead-plated, leaded.

свинцовисто/кислая соль plumbite; **—кислый на-трий, —натриевая соль** sodium plumbite.

свинцовист/ый *a.* lead(ed), plumbous; **—ая кислота** plumbous hydroxide; **соль —ой кислоты** plumbite.

свинцовка *f.* (bot.) leadwort (*Plumbago*).

свинцово/висмутовый *a.* lead-bismuth (alloy); **—во-**

дород *m.* lead hydride; **—кальциевая соль** calcium plumbate.

свинцовокисл/ый *a.* plumbic acid; plumbate (of); **с. натрий** sodium plumbate; **—ая соль** plumbate.

свинцово/медный штейн lead-copper matte; **—натрие-вая соль** sodium plumbate; **—оловянный сплав** lead-tin alloy; **—плавильная печь** lead furnace; **—плавильный завод** lead works; **—серый** *a.* lead-colored; **—суриковая покраска** red-lead coating.

свинцов/ый *a.* lead, plumbic; lead-colored; leaden; **с. корень** *see* **свинцовка; с. крон** chrome yellow, lead chromate; **с. сахар** sugar of lead, lead acetate; **с. сур-ик** red lead (oxide), minium; **—ая вода** 2% lead acetate solution; **—ая жёлтая** lead yellow, lead chromate; **—ая зелень** chrome green; **—ая кислота** plumbic acid; **соль —ой кислоты** plumbate; **—ая охра** lead ocher; **—ая примочка** Goulard's extract (solution of basic lead acetate); **—ая решётка** (elec.) lead grid; **—ые белила** white lead, lead carbonate.

свинчатка *f.* lead weight.

свинч/енный *a.* screwed (together), etc., *see v.*; **—ива-ние** *n.* screwing (together), etc., *see v.*; **—ивать** *v.* screw (together), secure; screw off, unscrew, remove; damage, strip (thread).

свин/ые, —ьи *pl.* swine (*Suidae*); **—ья** *f.* pig, swine, hog (*Sus*); sow; **большая лесная —ья** giant forest hog (*Hylochoerus*); **дикая —ья** wild boar (*Sus scrofa*); **земляная —ья** aardvark (*Orycteropus afer*); **мор-ская —ья** porpoise (*Phocaena*); **речная —ья** red river hog (*Potamochoerus porcus*); **—юшник** *m.* pigsty; **—ячий** *see* **свиной.**

свип-генератор *m.* sweep-frequency generator.

свиреп/ствовать *v.* rage, be furious; **—ый** *a.* fierce; violent.

свиристел/евые, —и *pl.* (orn.) waxwings (*Bombycillidae*); **шелковистые —и** (orn.) silky flycatchers (*Ptilogonatidae*).

свис/ать *v.* hang loose, sag, trail, dangle; overhang; **—ающий** hanging, pendent; **—лозадость** *f.* drooping croup (of horse); **—лый** *a.* hanging, sagging, drooping; **—нуть** *see* **свисать.**

свист *m.* whistle, hiss(ing); (rad.) howl(ing); **—ать, —еть, —нуть** *v.* whistle, hiss; (naut.; orn.) pipe; howl; gush out (of liquids); **—ок** *m.* whistle; **—ульки, —ульковые** *pl.* (ichth.) cornetfishes (*Fistulariidae*); **—ун** *m.* (mam.) chamois (*Rupicapra*); (amph.) a tropical toad (*Leptodactylus*); **—унок** *m.* (orn.) teal; **—ящий** *a.* whistling, etc., *see v.*; sibilant; wheezing.

свит *sh. m. of* **свитый.**

свита *f.* suite, set; (geol.) suite, series, formation; **с. плас-тов** (series of) strata, series, formation.

свитер *m.* sweater.

свит/ок *m.* roll, scroll; (zool.) volute, whorl; **—ый** *a.* coiled, convoluted; **—ь** *see* **свивать.**

свихнуть *v.* put out of joint, dislocate; **—ся** *v.* lose one's mind.

свищ *m.* flaw, unsound spot, air hole, gas pocket, blowhole; (casting) bubble; (timber) knothole; worm hole; (med.) fistula; (anat.) sinus; **—еватый** *a.* flawed, defective; **—евой** *a.* fistular, fistulous.

свищет *pr. 3 sing. of* **свистать.**

свищи *pl. of* **свищ;** honeycombing.

свиязь *f.* (orn.) wigeon (*Anas penelope*).

свобода *f.* freedom, liberty; latitude.

свободно *adv.* free(ly), loose(ly), easily; **с. вращаю-щийся** *a.* loose, idle (roller); **с. движущийся** *a.* free-moving; **с. надетый** *a.* loose(-fitting); **с. сидящий** *a.* loose(-running).

свобо́дно— *prefix* free, loose; (bot.) chori—, dialy—, apo— (separated); **—вися́щий** *a.* cantilever; **—лепе́стный** *a.* (bot.) apopetalous; eleutheropetalous; **—молекуля́рный** *a.* free-molecule (flow); **—несу́щий** *a.* cantilever; **—па́дающий** *a.* free-falling; **—пести́чный** *a.* (bot.) apocarpous; **—пла́вающий** *a.* free-floating; **—пото́чный** *a.* free-flowing; **—радика́льный** *a.* free radical; **с.-свобо́дный** *a.* (nucl.) free-free; **—скользя́щий** loose, sliding (fit); **—стоя́щий** *a.* free-standing, stand-alone, self-supported; **—стру́йный** *a.* free-jet (turbine); **—теку́щий** *a.* free-flowing; **—хво́стые** *pl.* mouse-tailed bats (*Rhinopomatidae*); **—ходя́щий** *a.* free-wheeling, coasting; idling.

свобо́дн/ый *a.* free, loose(-fitting), easy; clear, open; available, vacant; independent, separate, discrete, detached, unsupported; (chem.) uncombined; devoid (of); smooth (idling); idle (gear); natural (oscillation); market (price); transient (component); nonlocalized (vector); not critical (dimension); moving-boundary (electrophoresis); (educ.) permissive; **с. от пы́ли** dust-free; **с. от слу́жбы** off-duty; **с. от тре́ния** frictionless; **с. прохо́д** free area; **с. ход** freewheeling, coasting; idling; (horol.) detached escapement; **—ая высота́** clearance; **—ого паде́ния** *a.* free-fall (velocity); **—ое паде́ние** free fall.

свод *m.* arc(h), vault, dome; (arch) roof, crown (of furnace); saddle, crest; hang-up, bridge (in hoppers, feeders, etc.); (geol.) anticline; upfold; (anat.) (bot.) fornix, arcus; taking, etc., *see* **своди́ть**; collection, compendium, thesaurus, code (of laws); inventory, contents; summary, digest; **выводи́ть —ом** *v.* arch.

сво́дик *dim. of* **свод.**

свод/имость *f.* (math.) reducibility; **—и́ть** *v.* take, lead, conduct; bring together, draw together, converge; match; join, combine, assemble; reduce (to); take down; hold, keep (to a minimum); remove, eradicate, take out (stain, etc.); copy, trace; fell, clear (woods); settle, close (deal); square (accounts); contract (muscle); **—и́ть в табли́цу** tabulate; **—и́ть лес** deforest; **—и́ть на нет** reduce to zero, bring to nothing, nullify, neutralize; **—и́ться** *v.* lead, come, amount, boil down (to); be reduced (to); **всё э́то —и́тся к** the net result is.

сво́дка *f.* résumé, abstract, summary, compendium, table; report, bulletin; bringing together, combining; copying, tracing; felling, clearing; (typ.) revise, proof; **операти́вная с.** (mil.) situation report; **разве́дывательная с.** intelligence summary.

сво́дн/о-аналити́ческий *a.* synoptic analysis (sheet); **—ой** *a.* traceable; copied; capable of being fitted; **—ый** *a.* compound, composite, combined, consolidated; cumulative, collective, collected; summary, general; synoptic; multiple (correlation); union, joint; serial (publication); master (catalog, file); step— (mother, etc.); half— (brother, etc.); **—ая табли́ца часто́т** frequency correlation chart.

свод/-оболо́чка *m.* (arch.) shell; **—о́вый** *a. of* **свод;** center to edge (flooding); **—о́вые кисло́родные фу́рмы** roof oxygen lances (of open hearth furnace); **—ообра́зный** *a.* (biol.) fornicate, arching over; **—чатосемянно́й, —чатосемя́нный** *a.* (bot.) hollow-seeded, coelospermous; **—чатый** *a.* arched, vaulted, cambered; (biol.) fornicate; **—ящие му́скулы** (anat.) adductors.

своё *see under* **свой.**

своевре́менн/о *adv.* timely, opportunely, at the proper time; it is appropriate; **—ость** *f.* opportuneness; **—ый** *a.* on schedule, prompt; (med.) at full term; opportune, timely, well-timed.

своенра́вный *a.* willful, capricious, whimsical.

своеобра́з/ие *n. see* **своеобра́зность; —но** *adv.* characteristically; **—ность** *f.* originality, peculiarity; **—ный** *a.* characteristic; original, unusual, peculiar, unique, specific, out of the ordinary, distinctive.

своз *see* **сво́зка; —и́ть** *v.* take (down, in, away); bring (down, together); convey; transport; **—ка** *f.* taking, etc., *see v.*; conveyance, transport(ation).

сво/й *a. and possessive pron.* my, his, her, its, our, your, their; one's own; (mil.) friend(ly); domestic, home; in-house; **—его́ произво́дства** of domestic manufacture; **—и́ми глаза́ми** first-hand; **в —ё вре́мя** at one time, formerly; **настоя́ть на —ём** *v.* insist; **по —ему́** in one's own way.

свойла́чива/емость *f.* (text.) felting property; **—ть** *v.* interweave; **—ться** *v.* felt.

сво́йства *pl. of* **сво́йство;** behavior; (chem.; phys.) condition, state; **реакцио́нные с.** reactivity.

сво́йственн/ик *m.* relative by marriage; **—о** *adv.* naturally; it is natural; **—ость** *f.* peculiarity, singularity; **—ый** *a.* peculiar, distinctive, characteristic, typical, natural, native, indigenous, inherent, intrinsic.

сво́йств/о *n.* property, characteristic, trait, quality, attribute, feature, aspect; nature, character; capacity; habit; relationship (by marriage), alliance; **с. сцепле́ния** cohesiveness; **в —е** related; **вку́совое с.** palatability; **физи́ческие —а** physical properties; **хими́ческие —а** chemical properties.

свой-чужо́й (mil.) identification friend or foe, IFF.

свол/а́кивать, —о́чить, —о́чь *v.* drag (off, over, together); rake together.

сво́пинг: файл —а (comp.) swap file.

свора́ *f.* leash, lead; pack (of wolves, etc.); gang.

свора́чив/ание *n.* turning, etc., *see v.*; unfolding (of molecules); **—ать** *v.* turn, bend (aside), deflect; take off, remove, unscrew; displace, dislodge; roll up; curtail, cut back.

свор/ка *f.* lead, leash; **—ный** *a.* leashed, on a leash.

своро́т *m.* bend, turn (in road); **—и́ть** *v.* turn, swing (right or left); turn over, knock over; dump off, remove.

своя́/к *m.* brother-in-law; **—чени́ца** *f.* sister-in-law.

св. сек. *abbr.* (свеча́-секу́нда) candle-second.

СВЧ *abbr.* (сверхвысо́кая частота́, сверхвысокочасто́тный) ultra-high frequency, UHF (300 MHz–3 GHz); superhigh frequency, SHF (3–30 GHz); microwave (frequency) (roughly 1 GHz and above).

свы́к/аться, —нуться *v.* accustom oneself (to), become accustomed.

свы́ше *prep. gen.* above, beyond, upwards (of), over, in excess of, more than, plus.

свя́занно/-свобо́дный *a.* (nucl.) bound-free (transition); **—сть** *f.* combined state; coherence.

свя́зан/ный *a.* combined, bound, fixed, linked, tied, coupled, connected (up), associated, affiliated, allied, related, involving; bonded (to); constrained; due (to); attendant (upon), incident (to); latent (neutron); localized, fixed (vector); (mach.) gang(ed); (av.) body (axis); coherent; **с. с белко́м** protein-bound; **с. с произво́дством** production-oriented; **с. с ним** allied, related; **не с.** free; **хими́чески с.** (chemically) combined, fixed; **—ная переме́нная** (comp.) apparent variable; **—о с** (it) involves.

связа́ть *see* **свя́зывать.**

свя́зевый *a. of* **связь.**

свя́зи *gen., pl., etc., of* **связь.**

связи́ст *m.* signaler, signal man.

свя́з/ка *f.* bundle, roll, sheaf, pack, bunch, batch, fagot, bale; binding, band; bond; binder; (anat.) ligament; retinaculum; (vocal) cord; (math.) connective; **с. входа** input bundle; **с. И** (comp.) AND connective; **жёлтые —ки** (anat.) ligamenta flava; **обильный —ками** *a.* ligamentous; **пластика (суставных) —ок** (med.) syndesmoplasty; **поражение —ок** (med.) desmopathy; **с.-удерживатель** *m.* (anat.) retinaculum.

связник *m.* (bot.) connective; commissure, suture.

связной *a.* binding, fastening; communications, liaison; (mil.) runner, messenger; **с. грунт** cohesive soil.

связ/ость *f.* coherence; cohesion; (comp.) coupling (of system modules); tenacity (of soil); (math.) compendency, connectedness, connectivity; **—ый** *a.* connected, coherent, cohesive; compendent; ground-to-plane (radio); **—ый список** (comp.) threaded list; **—ое устройство** communicator.

связочн/ый *a.* bundle, bunch; (anat.) ligamentous, ligamental.

связ/ующее *n.* binder; (biol.; chem.) vehicle, medium; adhesive, cement; **—ующий** *a.* binding, etc., *see v.*; connective, conjunctive; (surv.) turning (point); **—ую- щее вещество** binder, cement, agglutinant; **—ыва- ние** binding, etc., *see v.*; combination; fixation (of nitrogen, etc.); (chem.) junction; association; **реакция —ывания комплемента** (immun.) complement fixation test, C.F.T.; **угол —ывания** (chem.) bond angle; **—ывать** *v.* bind, tie (together, up), bundle, link, couple, connect (up); combine, fix, take up; bond, cement; relate (to); affiliate, consolidate; brace, stay; strap (multiple-cavity magnetron); **—ываться** *v.* be bound, etc.; combine; get involved (with); associate, affiliate (with); **—ывающий** *a.* binding, etc., *see v.*; (anat.) communicating; **—ывающий камень** (masonry) bonder.

связ/ь *f.* communication(s); bond, tie, connection, coupling, link(age), join(t)ing, (con)junction, bonding, binding; (elec.) coupling; contact, association, relation-(ship), closeness, cohesion, coherence, continuity; binder; connector, tie piece, tie rod, stay, brace, bracing, strut, truss; belt(ing); (anat.) commissure; (stimulus-response) synapse; (chem.) bond; (bilateral) constraint; (naut.) member; **с. через излучение** radiation coupling; **в —и** in connection (with); in the context (of); because (of); **в непосредственной —и** directly connected (with); **двойная с.** double bond; **канал —и** communications channel; **константа —и** coupling constant; **корпус —и** signal corps; **коэффи- циент —и** coupling factor; **обратная с.** (elec.) feedback; **поддерживать с.** *v.* keep in touch; **порвать с.** *v.* sever a connection; **редактор —ей** (comp.) linkage editor; **служба —и** communication service; **с обрат- ной —ю** (phys.) regenerative; **сопротивление —и** (elec.) coupling resistance; **средство —и** means of communication; **установить с.** *v.* establish communication; (elec.) connect up; **энергия —и** (nucl.) binding energy; **эффект химической —и** (nucl.) chemical binding effect.

свясло *n.* bandage; straw binder.

свя/той *a.* saint, holy; **—щенный** *or* **—щённый** *a.* sacred.

сг *abbr.* **(сантиграмм)** centigram.

с.г. *abbr.* **(сего года)** this year.

СГГ-К *abbr.* **(селективный гамма-гамма каротаж)** selective gamma-gamma logging.

сгиб *m.* bend, flexure, fold, crimp; curvature, camber; lap; (anat.) flexion; **—аемость** *f.* pliability, flexibility; **—аемый** *a.* pliable, flexible, bendable; collapsible; **—ание** *n.* bending etc., *see v.*; flexure, flection; (robotics) yaw (of a manipulator); **—атель** *m.* (anat.) flexor;

—ательный *a.* bending, flexing; flexor; **—ать** *v.* bend, flex, fold; curve, crook; deflect; **—аться** *v.* bend (down), bow down, stoop; swerve; **—ающиеся** *pl.* (zool.) Kamptozoa; **—ающий** *a.* (anat.) flexor (muscle); **—ающийся** *a.* flexible; folding.

сгинуть *v.* vanish, disappear.

сгла/дить *see* **сглаживать;** **—жение** *see* **сглажива- ние;** **—женный** *a.* smoothed, etc., *see v.*; (bot.) levigate; subdued; **—живание** *n.* smoothing, etc., *see v.*; **—живатель** *m.* smoother, flattener; **—живать** *v.* smooth (off, out, over); burnish; scrape, plane, level (down), flatten; obliterate; reconcile; **—живаться** *v.* wear smooth; be smoothed, etc.; **—живающий** *a.* smoothing, etc., *see v.*

сгло/дать *v.* gnaw (at); **—тать** *v.* eat greedily, gulp.

сгн/аивать *v.* let rot, let spoil; **—ивание** *n.* dry rot; **—и(ва)ть** *v.* rot, spoil, decay; **—оённый** *a.* spoiled; **—оить** *see* **сгнаивать.**

сговариваться *v.* arrange (for), make arrangements (with), agree (upon).

сговор *m.* agreement, arrangement, deal; **—иться** *see* **сговариваться;** **—чивый** *a.* tractable, compliant.

сгодиться *v.* be useful, serve.

сгон *see* **сгонка;** (pipe) sleeve; drop in water level due to wind; **—ы и нагоны** (hydr.) water surges, off-and-on water; **—ка** *f.* driving together, etc., *see v.*; **—но- нагонный** *a.* (ocean.) tide (crack); **—ный** *a.* driven together, joined; rafting; **—ная гайка** screw cap; **—ная муфта** (pipe) sleeve, union; **—щик** *m.* fitter; raft driver; **—ять** *v.* drive together, join, fit; round up (cattle); drive away, drive off; eradicate, eliminate; raft, float.

сгораем/ость *f.* combustibility, inflammability; **—ый** *a.* combustible, inflammable, non-fireproof; **—ые ве- щества** combustibles.

сгоран/ие *n.* combustion, burning; (nucl.) burn-up; **с. жиров** (chem.) lipid oxidation; **камера —ия, прос- транство —ия** combustion chamber; **двигатель внутреннего —ия** internal-combustion engine.

сгор/ать *v.* burn (away, out, up), be consumed; **—аю- щий** burning; combustible.

сгорб/ить *v.* arch, hunch; **с. спину** hunch one's back or shoulders; **—иться** *v.* stoop; **—ленный** *a.* hunched; crooked.

сгор/евший *a.* burnt; **—еть** *see* **сгорать;** spoil (from heat or storage).

сготовить *v.* prepare, make.

сгре/балка *f.* rake; **—бание** *n.* raking, etc., *see v.*; **—бать, —сти** *v.* rake (together, up); shovel; skim; push off (slag); strike off.

сгру/дить *see* **сгруживать;** **—жать** *v.* unload; load (on); **—женный** *or* **—жённый** *a.* unloaded; loaded (on); heaped up, piled up; **—живать** *v.* heap up, pile up; **—зить** *see* **сгружать;** **—зка** *f.* unloading; loading (on).

сгруппиров/анный *a.* grouped, etc., *see v.*; belonging to a herd or flock; **—(ыв)ание** *n.* grouping, etc., *see v.*; **—(ыв)ать** *v.* group (together), bunch; classify; bank; assemble.

сгрыз(а)ть *v.* gnaw away completely; chew up.

СГС *abbr.* **(сантиметр-грамм-секунда)** centimeter-gram-second (system of units), cgs.

сгустившийся *see* **сгущённый.**

сгуститель *m.* thickener, coagulant, condenser; clarifier; settler; (paper) decker; **—ный** *a.* thickening, coagulating; **—ное средство** coagulant; **с.-центрифуга** *m.* centrifugal thickener.

сгуст/ить *see* **сгущать;** **—ок** *m.* (hemat.) coagulum, curd, clot; (med.) thrombus; cake; (chem.) coagulate;

bunch (of particles or ions), cluster; blob (in photo-emulsion); sheaf (of rays); **образование —ков** bunching, clustering; **плазменный с.** (phys.) plasmoid.

сгущаем/ость *f.* condensability, etc., *see a.*; **—ый** *a.* condensable; compressible; coagulable.

сгущ/ать *v.* thicken, condense, concentrate; compress, liquefy; coagulate, clot, curdle; bunch (in cyclotron); **с. выпариванием** boil down, concentrate; **—аться** *v.* be thickened, etc.; thicken; coagulate, clot, curdle; **—ение** *n.* thickening, condensation, etc., *see v.*; closeness, crowding (of contour lines); **—ение жёлчи** (med.) pachycholia; **—ёнка** *f.* curdled milk; **—ённость** *f.* thickness, density; **—ённый** *a.* thickened, etc., *see v.*; evaporated (milk); close, heavy, dense (sowing); crowded.

с/д *abbr.* (сегодня); (суточная дача) daily ration.

с.д. *abbr.* (сегодня).

СД *abbr.* (смертельная доза) lethal dose, LD.

сдабрива/ние *n.* flavoring; **—ть** *v.* flavor, season.

сдавать *v.* give up, yield; surrender, turn over, relinquish; be relieved (of duty); hand in (paper); deliver; take (exam); be weakened; rent, lease; check (baggage); **—ся** *v.* give in, surrender, yield, give way, acknowledge defeat; be for rent; seem, appear.

сдав/ить *see* **сдавливать**; **—ление** *see* **сдавливание**; **—ленный** *a.* squeezed, etc., *see v.*; depressed; constrained; **—ливание** *n.* squeezing, compression, etc., *see v.*; **—ливать** *v.* squeeze, (com)press, condense; pinch, constrict, contract; constrain; mash, crush; throttle; **—ливающий** *a.* constrictive (pericarditis).

сдадут *fut. 3 pl. of* **сдать**.

сдаива/ние *n.* milking dry, stripping (of cow); **—ть** *v.* milk.

сдалбливать *v.* chisel off, scrape.

сдаст *fut. 3 sing. of* **сдать**.

сда/точный *a.*, **—ча** giving up, etc., *see* **сдавать;** delivery; lease; change (in small coin); **—ть** *see* **сдавать**.

сдваив/ание *n.* doubling, duplication, etc., *see v.*; **период —ания** (nucl.) doubling time; **—ать** *v.* double, duplicate; pair, couple, join, combine; re—; **—ать пашню** *v.* replow, plow again; **—ающий** *a.* doubling, etc., *see v.*

сдвиг *m.* displacement, shift, slip; shear, shearing (action); (geol.) fault, spec. strike-slip fault; upheaval, heave; offset; (math.) translation (of structures); deviation; improvement, progress (in work, etc.); **с. фаз(ы), с. по фазе** (elec.) phase displacement, phase shift; **коэффициент —а** coefficient of shear; **на быстрый с.** dynamic shear (test); **напряжение —а** shear stress; **осевой с.** (bot.) concaulescence (of buds); **предельное напряжение —а** yield stress; **работающий на с.** under shear stress; **сила —а** (phys.) shearing; **сопротивление —у** shear strength, resistance to shear; **угол —а** angle of displacement; **угол —а фаз** phase angle; **элифилльная с.** (bot.) recaulescence.

сдвиг/ание *n.* shifting, etc., *see v.*; displacement; **—ать** *v.* shift, displace, slide, move, translate; shear; draw together, move closer; put away; **—ать назад** *v.* push back; **—аться** *v.* shift, move (out of position); shear; come together; **—ающий** *a.* shifting, etc., *see v.*; **—ающее напряжение** shear(ing) stress; **—ающее усилие** shear(ing) force; **—овый** *a. of* **сдвиг;** (acous.) thickness-sheer (vibrations of a plate); transverse (wave).

сдвиж/ение, —ка *see* **сдвигание**; **—ной** *a.* movable; collapsible, telescopic; slip (cover).

сдвинут/ый *a.* displaced, shifted, (re)moved, offset; out

of line, out of alignment, skew(ed); **с. по фазе** out of phase, phase shifted; **—ь** *see* **сдвигать**.

сдво/ение *n.* doubling, duplication; **—енный** *a.* double(d), duplex; twin(ned); binary, paired, combined in pairs, matched, coupled; (bot.) geminate; side-by-side (turbine); back-to-back; straddle (packer); **—ить** *see* **сдваивать**.

сдел/анный *a.* made, etc., *see v.*; **—ать** *v.* make, do, manufacture; accomplish, carry out; take (a reading); **—аться** *v.* become; happen.

сдел/ка *f.*, **—очный** *a.* agreement, transaction, deal, bargain; arrangement.

сдельн/о *adv.* by the piece, by the job; **с.-премиальная плата** piecework rate with bonuses; **с.-премиальная система** contract-bonus system; **с.-прогрессивная заработная плата** progressive (differential) piece rates; **—ый** *a.* (by the) piece, (by the) job; piece-rate (pay); piece, contract (work); **—ая заработная плата** piece rate.

сдельщи/к *m.* pieceworker, workman paid by the piece; **—на** *f.* piecework.

сдёргивать *v.* pull off, tear off, pull down.

сдерёт *fut. 3 sing. of* **содрать**.

сдерж/анно *adv.* with restraint; discreetly; **—анность** *f.* reserve, restraint; discretion; **—анный** *a.* reserved, discreet, composed, restrained; circumspect; **—ать** *see* **сдерживать;** **—ивание** *n.* check, restraint, suppression; (mil.) containment; **—ивать** *v.* (keep in) check, restrain, repress, deter, moderate; contain, support, sustain; **—иваться** *v.* control oneself; **—ивающий** *a.* restrictive.

сдернуть *see* **сдёргивать**.

сдир *m.* silk cocoon.

сдир/ание *n.* stripping, etc., *see v.*; **—ать** *v.* strip (off), peel, flay, skin; bark; **—аться** *v.* peel, flake, come off; **—ка** *f.*; **—очный** *a.* stripping; top layer, removable layer.

сдобный *a.* rich (pastry).

сдобрить *see* **сдабривать**.

сдоить *see* **сдаивать**.

сдор *m.* beef lard.

сдохнуть *v.* die (off).

сдрейф/ить, —овать *v.* drift.

сду/в *see* **сдувка;** **—ваемый** *a.* (geol.) fugitive; **—вка** *f.* blowing (away, off); (paper) relief; **делать —вку** *v.* release, relieve; **—(ва)ть** *v.* blow (away, off).

сдыхать *v.* die (off).

сеанс *m.*, **—овый** *a.* session; **с. связи** (commun.) contact.

себац/ил *m.* sebacyl; **—иновая кислота** sebacic acid, decanedioic acid; **соль —иновой кислоты** sebacate.

себе *dat. and prepos. of* **себя**.

себель *m.* (ichth.) bleak (*Alburnus*).

себестоимость *f.* net cost, cost price, (manufacturing) cost.

себо— *prefix* sebo— (sebum, suet); **—лит** *m.* (med.) sebolith; **—ррея** *f.* (med.) seborrhea.

Себу (geog.) Cebu.

себха *f.* sebkha (a salt-clay soil depression with steppe-like vegetation).

себя *gen. and acc. reflexive pron.* oneself, myself, himself, herself, itself, ourselves, yourselves, themselves.

сев *m.* (agr.) sowing, planting; seed; young crop, seedlings.

сев. *abbr.* (северный).

севал/ка *f.* (bot.) pod, husk; **—ьщик** *m.* sower.

севанский *a.* (geog.) Sevan.

севастопольский *a.* (geog.) Sevastopol.

сев.-вост. *abbr.* **(северо-восточный).**

север *m.* north; **—нее** *comp.* further north.

северн/ый *a.* north(ern), northerly, boreal; **С. ледовитый океан** Arctic Ocean; **с. полярный** Arctic; **Северная Америка** North America; **—ое сияние** aurora borealis, northern lights.

северо/-американский *a.* North American; **С.-Американские Соединённые Штаты** United States of America; **с.-атлантический** *a.* North Atlantic; **с.-африканский** *a.* North African; **с.-байкальский** *a.* North Baikal; **с.-восток** *m.*, **—восточный** *a.* northeast; **с.-запад** *m.*, **—западный** *a.* northwest; **с.-кавказский** *a.* North Caucasian; **с.-китайский** *a.* North Chinese; **с.-корейский** *a.* North Korean; **с.-крымский** *a.* North Crimean; **—магнитный** *a.* north magnetic; **с.-осетинский** *a.* North Ossetian; **с.-сибирский** *a.* North Siberian; **с.-тихоокеанский** *a.* North Pacific.

серверянин *m.* northerner.

севец *see* **сеяльщик.**

севзап— *prefix,* **сев.-зап.** *abbr.* **(северозападный).**

Севилья *(geog.)* Seville.

севин *m.* Sevin, Arylam.

севморпуть *m.* Northern Sea Route.

севооборот *m.* (agr.) crop rotation.

севр *m.* (geog.) Sèvres; (cer.) Sèvres ware.

севрю/га *f.* starred sturgeon (*Acipenser stellatus*); **—жина,** **—жка** *f.* sturgeon meat.

севчик *m.* sower.

сегеровский *a.* Seger (cone).

сегмент *m.* segment, section, (ent.) somite; **мышечный с.** (zool.) myomere; **—арный** *a.* (zool.) segmentary, segmental; **—ационный** *a.* segmentary; **—ационная клетка** (embr.) blastomere, cleavage cell; **—ация** *f.* segmentation; fission; **—ирование** *n.* segmentation; **—ированный** *a.* segmented; **—ироваться** *v.* segment, undergo cleavage; **—ный,** **—ообразный** *a.* segmental, segmentary, metameric; sectional; laminated (piston ring).

сегнерово колесо Segner's wheel.

сегнетиэлектрик *m.* ferrielectric.

сегнето/активный *see* **сегнетоэлектрический; —ва соль** Seignette salt, potassium sodium tartrate; **—керамика** *f.* ferroelectric ceramics; **—магнетик** *m.* magnetoelectric.

сегнетоэлектри/к *m.* ferroelectric; **—ческий** *a.* ferroelectric; **—чество** *n.* ferroelectricity.

сего *gen. of* **сей.**

сегодня *adv.* today, this day; **с. утром** this morning; **—шний** *a.* today's.

сегозерский *a.* (geog.) Seg (lake).

сеголет/ка *f.*, **—ок** *m.* this year's brood; **—ний** *a.* this year's.

сегрега/т *m.* segregate, segregant; **—тивный** *a.* segregative; **—ционное включение** (met.) segregate, segregant; **—ционный** *a.* segregation, segregated; **—ция** *f.* segregation; liquation.

сед *sh. m. of* **седой;** sed(d), sudd (floating mass of decaying vegetable matter).

седалищ/е *n.* (anat.) ischium; buttocks; **—но—** *prefix* ischio—; **—но-прямокишечный** *a.* (anat.) ischiorectal; **—ный** *a.* ischial; sciatic (nerve); **—ная болезнь** sciatica; **—ная кость** ischium.

седан *m.* sedan.

седан/олид *m.* sedanolid; **—оновый ангидрид** sedanonic anhydride; **—ский чёрный** Sedan black.

седативный *a.* sedative.

седатин *m.* sedatin, valeridin; Sedatine, antipyrine.

сёдел *gen. pl. of* **седло.**

седёл/ка *f.*, **—ковый,** **—очный** *a.* (saddle) pad.

седель/ник *m.* saddler; **—ный** *a. of* **седло;** (anat.) sellar; **—ный прицеп** semi-trailer; **—це** *dim. of* **седло; —чатый** *a.* saddle-shaped.

седение *n.* graying; bloom (on chocolate).

Седерберга *see* **Содерберга.**

седе/ть *v.* turn gray, get gray hair; **—ющий** *a.* (bot.) canescent; grayish-white; turning gray.

седиль *m.* (print.) cedilla.

седимент/ационный *a.* sedimentation; sedimentometric (analysis); **—ация** *f.*, **—ирование** *n.* sedimentation.

седиментометр *m.* sedimentometer; **—ический** *a.* sedimentometric; **—ия** *f.* sedimentometry.

седина *f.* gray hair; gray cast, grayish-white film; (met.) flaw.

седл/а *gen. of* **седло; —ание** *n.* saddling; **—ать** *v.* saddle.

седлистый *a.* swaybacked (horse).

седло *n.* saddle, seat (of tractor, etc.); seat (of valve); collar beam; (meteor.) col; (geol.) anticline, saddleback; (math.) saddle point; (anat.) sella; **возвращаться в седло** *v.* reseat (valve); **садиться на с.** *v.* seat (of valve); **турецкое с.** (anat.) sella turcica; **—ватость** *f.* saddle shaping; swayback (of horse); sheer (of ship deck); **—ватый** *a.* saddle-shaped; swayback(ed); weak (back); **—видный** *see* **седлообразный; —вина** *f.* saddle; saddle point (of a surface); col; valley, trough; saddleback; swayback; (anat.) sella; **—вка** *f.* saddling; **—образный** *a.* saddle-shaped; (anat.) sellar; (med.) straddling (embolus); **—образное соединение** (welding) saddle joint.

сёдлышко *n.* (bot.) gynobase; (crust.) ephippium.

седобородый *a.* gray-bearded.

седо/ватый *a.* grayish; hoary, canescent, grizzly; **—власый** *a.* gray-haired; **—волосый** *a.* gray-haired.

седогепт/оза *f.* (biochem.) sedoheptose; **—улоза** *f.* sedoheptulose.

седой *a.* gray-haired, hoary.

седок *m.* rider.

седопептоза *f.* (biochem.) sedopeptose.

седьмой *a.* seventh.

сеет *pr. 3 sing. of* **сеять.**

сежа *f.* fish net; (ecol.) ceja (forest).

сезаль *see* **сизаль.**

сезам *m.* (bot.) sesame; **—ин** *m.* sesamin; **—овый** *a.* sesame; **—о(в)идный** *a.* sesamoid; **—ол** *m.* sesamol; **—олин** *m.* sesamolin.

Сезерланда уравнение *n.* (phys.) Sutherland's equation.

сезон *m.* season, period; **по —у** in season; **—ник** *m.*, **—ница** *f.* seasonal worker; **—ность** *f.* seasonal fluctuation; **—ный** *a.* seasonal, periodic.

сей *pron. m.* this; *gen. of* **сия; за сим** after this, next; **до сих пор** up to now; **при сём** herewith.

Сейболта секунда (phys.) Saybolt (universal) second.

сейвал *m.* sei whale, coalfish whale (*Balaenoptera borealis*).

сейгнетова соль *see* **сегнетова соль.**

сеймурит *m.* (met.) Seymourite (alloy).

сейн/а *f.* seine; **—ер** *m.* seiner (fishing boat).

сейроспора *f.* (bot.) seirospore.

сейсм *m.* seism, earthquake; **—ика** *f.* seismic surveying; **—ический** *a.* seismic, earthquake; **—ическое явление** seism; **—ичность** *f.* seismicity.

сейсмо— *prefix* (geol.) seismo—, earthquake; **—грамма** *f.* seismogram; **—граф** *m.* seismograph, earthquake-shock recorder; **—графический** *a.* seismographic; **—графия** *f.* seismography; **—запись** *f.* seismogram; **—каротаж** *m.* seismic (well) logging, sound logging;

—**логия** *f.* seismology; —**метр** *m.* seismometer; —**метрия** *f.* seismometry; —**настический** *a.* (bot.) seismonastic; —**приёмник** *see* **сейсмограф**; seismic detector; —**профилирование** *n.* profile shooting; —**разведка** *f.* seismic prospecting or survey(ing); —**скоп** *m.* seismoscope; —**стойкий** *a.* aseismic, earthquakeproof; —**стойкость** *f.* seismic stability.

сейте *imp. of* **сеять.**

сейф *m.* safe, vault.

сейчас *adv.* now, immediately, at once, presently; just now.

сейша *f.* seiche (apparent tide in lake).

Сейшельские острова (geog.) Seychelles.

сек *past m. sing. of* **сечь.**

сек. *abbr.* (**секанс**); (**секунда**) second.

секал/ин *m.* secaline, trimethylamine; —**оновая кислота** secalonic acid.

секанс *m.* (math.) secant.

секатор *m.* cutter, pruning shears.

секач *m.* chopper; (peat) cutter; (mam.) young boar; young male fur seal.

секван *m.,* —**ский** *a.* (geol.) Sequanian.

секвестр *m.* (med.) sequestrum; (law) sequestration; —**ант** *m.* sequestering agent; —**ация** *f.* sequestration; —**ировать** *v.* sequester.

секвой/ен *m.* sequoiene; —**ное дерево, —я** *f.* (bot.) sequoia.

секировидный *a.* hatchet-shaped, securiform.

секи(те) *imp. of* **сечь.**

секли *past pl. of* **сечь.**

секодонтный *a.* (zool.) secodont.

секрет *m.* secret; (mil.) listening post; (physiol.) secretion; (ichth.) pikeperch; **по —у** secretly, confidentially.

секретар/и *pl.* (orn.) secretary birds (*Sagittariidae*); —**ский** *a.* secretarial; —**ь** *m.* secretary, clerk.

секретин *m.* (physiol.) secretin.

секретн/ичать *v.* keep confidential, classify; —**о** *adv.* in secret, covertly; —**ость** *f.* secrecy, confidential nature; privacy; security; —**ый** *a.* secret, confidential, classified; covert; uncooperative (satellite); combination (lock); **совершенно —ый** top secret.

секре/торный *a.* (physiol.) secretory, secreting; —**ция** *f.* secretion; **внешней —ции** *a.* exocrine (glands); **внутренней —ции** *a.* endocrine (glands).

секс— *prefix* sex—, six-; —**агональный** *a.* hexagonal; —**дукция** *f.* (gen.) sexduction; —**ифенил** *m.* sexiphenyl, hexaphenyl; —**ология** *f.* (med.) sexology; —**та** *f.* (music) sixth; —**тан(т)** *m.* (av.; naut.) sextant; —**тет** *m.* sextet; —**тиллион** *num.* sextillion.

сексуал/ьность *f.* sexuality; —**ьный** *a.* sexual.

секс-фактор *m.* (gen.) sex-factor, F-factor.

сектор *m.* (math.) sector; quadrant, segment, section, zone, area; arc; —(**и**)**альный** *a.* sector(ial); areal (velocity); —**ный** *a.* sector; sectoral (wave); off-centered (display); —**ный прицел** ramp sight (of pistol).

секун *m.* (ichth.) spined loach (*Cobitis*).

секунд/а *f.* second; —**ант** *m.* second, assistant; —**ный** *a.* (one-)second, per second; —**омер** *m.* stopwatch; —**омерный** *a.* timing.

секуринин *m.* securinine.

секут *pr. 3 pl. of* **сечь.**

секущ/ая *f.,* —**ая линия** (math.) secant; —**ий** *a.* cutting, intersecting, secant; —**ая жила** (geol.) cross vein.

секцион/ирование *n.* section(aliz)ing, etc., *see v.*; —**ированный** *a.* section(aliz)ed, etc., *see v.*; step(ped); —**ировать** *v.* section(alize), subdivide; grade, graduate; —**ный** *a.* section(al), (sub)divided; articulated; ali-

quot; dissecting; (med.) autopsy; pan (conveyer); separated-gang (cultivator).

секция *f.* section; (comp.) region; unit, cell; step, stage; (roller) gang; workshop; dissection, autopsy; **с. якоря** (elec.) armature coil.

сел *past m. sing. of* **сесть.**

сёл *gen. pl. of* **село.**

сел. *abbr.* (**селекционный**).

села *past f. sing. of* **сесть.**

сёла *pl. of* **село.**

селагинелла *f.* (bot.) Selaginella.

селах/иловый спирт selachyl alcohol; —**олеиновая кислота** selacholeic acid, 6,15-tetracosenoic acid.

селбенин *m.* Celbenin, methicillin sodium.

селевиниевые *pl.* (mam.) Seleviniidae.

селевой *a. of* **сель**; mud flow; **с. поток** mud flow, mud stream.

селедец *m.* (ichth.) shad (*Alosa*).

селёд/ка *f.,* —**очный** *a.* herring (*Coregonus*).

селезён/ка *f.* (anat.) spleen; —**очно—** *prefix* lien(o)—; —**очный** *a.* spleen, splenic, lienal; —**очный заворот** (anat.) splenic recess.

селезень *m.* (orn.) drake.

селек/тивность *f.* selectivity; discrimination; —**тивный** *a.* selective, discriminative, discriminatory; —**тор** *m.,* —**торный** *a.* selector; sorter; (time) gate; tuner; —**торная схема** (comp.) gating circuit, gate; —**трон** *m.* (elec.) selectron; —**ционер** *m.* breeder; selector; —**ционный** *a. of* **селекция**; —**ционный отлов, —ционный отстрел** culling; —**ция** *f.* selection; (biol.) breeding; indication (of moving target); (comp.) gating.

селен *m.* selenium, Se; **двуокись —а** selenium dioxide; **сернистый с.** selenium sulfide.

селен/ат *m.* selenate; —**ид** *m.* selenide.

селение *n.* settlement, village.

селенил *m.* selenyl.

селенисто/кислый *a.* selenious acid; selenite (of); —**кислый натрий, —натриевая соль** sodium selenite; —**кислая соль** selenite.

селенист/ый *a.* selenious, selenium; selenide (of); **с. ангидрид** selenious anhydride, selenium dioxide; **с. водород** hydrogen selenide; —**ая кислота** selenious acid; **соль —ой кислоты** selenite; —**ая соль** selenide.

селенит *m.* (chem.; min.) selenite; —**овый** *a.* selenitic.

селено— *prefix* selen(o)— (selenium; the moon).

селеноводород *m.* hydrogen selenide; **соль —ной кислоты** selenite.

селеново/кислый *a.* selenic acid; selenate (of); **с. натрий, —натриевая соль** sodium selenate; —**кислая соль** selenate.

селенов/ый *a.* selenium, selenic; seleniferous; selenide (of); **с. (фото-)элемент** selenium cell; —**ая кислота** selenic acid; **соль —ой кислоты** selenate.

селенограф *m.* selenographer, lunar cartographer; —**ический** *a.* selenographic, lunar; —**ия** *f.* selenography.

селено/донтный *a.* (zool.) selenodont; —**ид** *m.* (elec.) selenoid; —**лог** *m.* selenologist; —**логия** *f.* selenology; —**мочевина** *f.* selen(o)urea; —**рганический** *a.* organoselenium; —**содержащий** *a.* selenium-containing, seleniferous.

селенотопограф/ический *a.* selenotopographic; —**ия** *f.* lunar topography.

селено/углерод *m.* carbon selenide; —**физика** *f.* selenophysics, physics of the moon; —**центрический** *a.* selenocentric; —**циан** *m.* selenocyanogen.

селесброс *m.* flume.

сели *pl. of* **сель**; *past pl. of* **сесть.**

селин *m.* (bot.) Aristida.

селитебный *a.* development (land).

селитра *f.* saltpeter, niter, potassium nitrate; **аммиачная с.** ammonium nitrate; **воздушная с., известковая с.** calcium nitrate; **калиевая с.** potassium nitrate; **кальциевая с.** calcium nitrate; **кубическая с., натриевая с.** sodium nitrate; **норвежская с.** Norwegian saltpeter, calcium nitrate; **чилийская с.** Chile saltpeter, sodium nitrate.

селитр/енный *see* **селитряный;** **—оварня** *f.* niter works, saltpeter works; **—овый** *see* **селитряный;** **—ообразование** *n.* saltpeter formation; **—яница** *see* **селитроварня.**

селитрян/ый *a.* saltpeter, nitrous, nitric; **с. налет** niter efflorescence; **с. щёлок** saltpeter lye; **—ая земля** nitrous earth; **—ая известь** calcium nitrate; **—ая кислота** nitric acid; **—ые цветы** niter efflorescence.

селитьба *f.* developed land.

селиться *v.* settle, take up residence.

селище *n.* (archeol.) settlement site.

село *n.* village, settlement; *past n. sing. of* **сесть.**

сель *m.* mud stream, mud flow, mudslide.

сель— *prefix* agricultural; rural.

сельва(с) *m.* selva (rain forest).

сельвинит *m.* (min.) selwynite.

сельгэс *m.* rural hydroelectric power plant.

сельд/евидные *pl.* (ichth.) herrings, etc. (*Clupeoidei*); **—ёвые** *pl.* herrings (*Clupeidae*); **—ёвый** *a. of* **сельдь;** **—еобразные** *pl.* Clupeiformes; **—еподобные** *see* **сельдевидные.**

сельдерей *m.,* **—ный** *a.* celery.

сельди *pl. of* **сельдь; белые с.** bonefishes, ladyfishes (*Albulidae*); **большеглазые с.** tarpons, ten-pounders (*Elopidae*); **северо-западные с.** shad (*Alosa*).

сельдь *f.* herring (*Clupea*); shad (*Alosa*); cisco; **атлантическая с.** Atlantic herring (*Clupea harengus*); **волжская с.** blackbacked shad; **восточная с.** Pacific herring (*Clupea pallasi*); **многопозвонковая с., морская с., мурманская с.** Atlantic herring; **обская с.** Siberian cisco; **сос(ь)винская с.** tugun, Sosva cisco (*Coregonus tugun*); **тихоокеанская с.** Pacific herring; **черноморская с.** Black Sea shad.

сельдяные короли *pl.* (ichth.) oarfishes, king-of-the-herring (*Regalecidae*).

селькор *m.* rural correspondent, agricultural reporter.

сель/машстроение *n.* agricultural machine building; **—по** *n.* farmers' cooperative store.

сельсин *m.* (elec.) selsyn, synchro, autosyn; **с.-датчик** *m.* synchrotransmitter; **—ный** *a. of* **сельсин; с.-приёмник** *m.* selsyn receiver.

сельск/ий *a.* rural, country; **с. хозяин** farmer; **—ое хозяйство** agriculture, farming.

сельскохозяйственн/ый *a.* agricultural, farm; **с. инвентарь, —ое орудие** farm implements; **—ая промышленность** agriculture.

сельтерская вода seltzer water.

сельхоз— *prefix* agricultural, farm(ing); **—артель** *m.* collective farm; **—вуз** *m.* agricultural institute; **—заготовки** *pl.* State purchases of farm products; **—инвентарь** *m.* farming implements; **—продукты** agricultural products; **—пром** *m.* agricultural industry.

сельцо *dim. of* **село.**

селя *gen. of* **сель.**

селява *f.* (ichth.) cisco; bleak; shemaia.

сём *prepos. of* **сей.**

сем. *abbr.* (**семейство**).

сем— *prefix* seed.

семант/ика *f.* semantics; **—ический** *a.* semantic.

семафор *m.* semaphore, signaler; **—ить** *v.* signal; **—ный** *a.* semaphore, semaphoric; **—щик** *m.* signal man.

сёмг/а *f.,* **—овый** *a.* Atlantic salmon (*Salmo salar*).

семееды *pl.* (ent.) seed and stem chalcids (*Eurytomidae*).

сёмежно-красный *see* **сёмужно-красный.**

семезачаток *m.* ovule, seed bud.

семей *gen. pl. of* **семья; —но-наследственный** *a.* familial, hereditary; **—ный** *a.* family, familial; domestic; **—ственность** *f.* nepotism; **—ство** *n.* family; group, set; (chem.) series (of element); **—ство характеристик** performance characteristics.

семен/а *pl. of* **семя; —и** *gen. of* **семя; —истый** *a.* seedy, full of seeds; **—иться** *v.* go to seed; **—ник** *m.* seed plant; (anat.) testicle, testis; (bot.) ovary; seed pod; **—ники** *pl.* (ichth.) milt.

семенн/ой *a.* seed; (anat.; physiol.) seminal, spermatic; *suffix* (bot.) **—spermous; с. канатик** (anat.) spermatic cord; **с. пузырь, с. пузырёк** (anat.) seminal vesicle; **—ая жидкость** semen, sperm; **—ая камера** seed case; **—ая клетка** seminal cell, spermatozoön; **—ая коробка** (bot.) seed vessel; **—ая нить** (zool.) spermatozoön; **—ое ядро** male pronucleus; **—ые живчики, —ые нити** (anat.) spermatozoa.

семено— *prefix* seed; *see also under* **семя—; —вед** *m.* seed specialist; **—ведение** *n.* seed science; **—вод** *m.* seed grower; **—водство** *n.,* **—водческий** *a.* seed growing; **—ложе** *n.* (bot.) pericarp; seed bed; **—рушка** *f.* huller.

семе/отделитель *m.* seed separator; **—приёмник** *m.* (zool.) spermotheca; **—провод** *see* **семяпровод.**

сем/еричный *a.* septenary; **—ёрка** *see* **семеро; —ерной** *a.* sevenfold; (bot.) septenate; **—еро** *num.* (group of) seven.

семестр *m.,* **—овый** *a.* semester, term.

семечко *dim. of* **семя;** sunflower seed; pip, pit (of fruit); pome; **—вый** *a. of* **семечко.**

сёмжина *f.* flesh of salmon (for eating).

семи *gen. of* **семь.**

семи— *prefix* semi—; hepta—, sept(i)—, septem—, seven; **—атомный** *a.* heptatomic; heptavalent (alcohol), septivalent; **—бензол** *m.* semi-benzene.

семивалентн/ость *f.* heptavalence; **—ый** *a.* heptavalent, septivalent.

семиводный гидрат heptahydrate.

семигранн/ик *m.* (geom.) heptahedron; **—ый** *a.* heptahedral.

семидесяти— *prefix* seventy; **—летие** *n.* seventy-year period; seventieth anniversary; **—летний** *a.* seventy-year(-old); **—пяти—** *prefix* seventy-five; **—пятилетие** *n.* diamond anniversary.

семидесятый *a.* seventieth.

семиднев/ка *f.* seven-day period; **—ный** *a.* seven-day.

семи/дырка *f.* (ichth.) lamprey (*Lampetra*); **—жаберник** *m.* sevengill shark (*Heptranchias*).

семиинвариант *m.* (math.) semi-invariant.

семикарбаз/ид *m.* semicarbazide, aminourea.

семи/коллоид *m.* semicolloid; **—кратный** *a.* sevenfold, septuple; **—лепестный** *a.* (bot.) heptapetalous; **—летие** *n.* seven-year period; seventh anniversary; **—летка** *f.* seven-year-old; seven-year school; seven-year plan; **—летний** *a.* seven-year; septennial; **—листный** *a.* (bot.) heptaphyllous; **—листочковый** *a.* septemfoliolate; **—мерный** *a.* seven-dimensional; **—месячный** *a.* seven-month; **—метрический** *a.* (math.) semimetric; **—надрезной** *a.* (bot.) septemfid.

семинар *m.,* **—ский** *a.* seminar; workshop; **—ист** *m.* seminar student; seminarian.

семи/объективный *a.* seven-lens; **—окись** *f.* heptoxide.

семио/логия *f.* (med.) semiology, symptomatology; **—тика** *f.* semiotics, study of sign systems; (med.) symptomatology; **—тический** *a.* sem(e)iotic.

семипалатинский *a.* (geog.) Semipalatinsk.

семи/пестичный *a.* (bot.) heptagynous; **—плацента** (zool.) semiplacenta.

семиполь/е *n.*, **—ный** *a.* seven-field crop rotation system.

семи/полярный *a.* semipolar; **—раздельный** *a.* (bot.) septempartite; **—разрядный байт** (comp.) septet; **—сотый** *a.* seven-hundredth; **—стор** *m.* semistor (silicon resistor).

семитический *a.* Semitic.

семитысячный *a.* seven-thousandth.

семиугольн/ик *m.* (geom.) heptagon; **—ый** *a.* heptagonal.

семи/циклический *a.* semicyclic; heptacyclic; **—часовой** *a.* seven-hour; seven o'clock (flight, etc.); **—членный** *a.* seven-membered; heptamerous.

семматериал *m.* seed for sowing.

семнадцат/ый *a.* seventeenth; **—ь** *num.* seventeen.

семрассадник *m.* seed plot, nursery.

семсейит *m.* (min.) semseyite.

сёмуж/ий *a. of* **сёмга**; **—но-красный** *a.* salmon-red.

семфонд *m.* seed fund, seed stock.

семь *num.* seven; **—десят** *num.* seventy.

семь/и *gen., pl., etc., of* **семья**; **—сот** *num.* seven hundred; **—ю** *instr. of* **семь**; *acc. of* **семья**; *adv.* seven times, multiplied by seven.

семья *f.* family, household, kin; (bee) colony.

семя *n.* seed; grain; (anat.) sperm, semen; *see also under* **семено—**; **—вход** *m.* (bot.) micropyle; **—выбрасывающий** *a.* (anat.) ejaculatory (duct); **—выводящий проток, —выносящий проток** spermatic duct, vas deferens; **—дольный** *a.* (bot.) cotyledonous; **—доля** *f.* cotyledon; **—еды** *see* **семееды**; **—зачаток** *m.* (bot.) ovule; **—извержение, —излияние** *n.* (physiol.) ejaculation; **—истечение** *n.* (med.) spermatorrhea; **—ложе** *n.* seed bed; **—н** *gen. pl. of* **семя**; **—нка** *f.* (bot.) achene; **—нный** *a.* seed(-bearing); *suffix* —spermous, -seeded; **—ножка** *f.* (bot.) funicle, seed stalk; **—носец** *m.* placenta; **—носный** *a.* seed-bearing, seminiferous; **—носушилка** *f.* seed dryer; **—образование** *n.* (zool.) sperm(at)ogenesis; **—почка** *f.* seed bud, ovule; **—приёмник** *m.* (zool.) spermotheca; **—провод** *m.* seed tube; (anat.) spermaduct, vas deferens; **—сушилка** *f.* seed dryer; **—уловитель** *m.* seed trap; **—чко** *f.* seed; pip; pea (grade) coal.

Сен— *prefix* (geog.) Saint.

сена *gen. of* **сено**.

Сена the Seine.

сенбернар *m.* St. Bernard (dog).

сенег/а *f.* senega (snakeroot); **—альский** *a.* Senegal(ese); **—енин** *m.*, **—ениновая кислота** senegenin, senegeninic acid; **—ин** *m.* senegin.

сенекский ярус (geol.) Senecan stage.

сенеци/н *m.* senecine; **—онин** *m.* senecionine; **—оновая кислота** senecioic acid; **—филлин** *m.* seneciphylline; **—фолидин** *m.* senecifolidine; **—фолин** *m.* senecifoline.

сени *f.* entrance, passage, vestibule.

сен/илизм *m.* (med.) senilism, premature old age; **—ильность** *f.* senility; **—ильный** *a.* senile.

Сен-луи (geog.) Saint Louis.

сенна *f.* (bot.) senna (*Cassia*).

сенн/ик *m.* hay loft; **—ой** *a. of* **сено**; **сени**.

сено *n.* hay; **—вал** *m.* hay loft; **—волокуша** *f.* haysweep; **—ворошение** *n.* tedding; **—ворошилка** *f.*

tedder; **—вязалка** *f.* hay baler; **—дробилка** *f.* hay shredder; **—еды** *pl.* (ent.) Copeognatha.

сенозаготов/ительный *a.*, **—ка** *f.*, **—очный** *a.* haying, hay-making.

сенокопн/ение *n.* hay stacking; **—итель** *m.* stacker.

сеноко/с *m.* mowing; hay making, haying; haying season; hay field, meadow; **—силка** *f.* mower; **—силка-измельчитель** *m.* mower-shredder; **—сный** *a.* mowing; hay (field); **—сное угодье** grassland; hay field; **—сцы** *pl.* (zool.) Phalangida; **—шение** *n.* (hay) mowing, haying.

сеноман *m.*, **—ский ярус** (geol.) Senoman stage.

сенометатель *m.* hay stacker.

сенон *m.* (geol.) Senonian series.

сено/набиватель *m.* feed board (of baler); **—нагрузчик, —погружатель, —погрузчик** *m.* hay loader; **—пресс** *m.* baler; **—сгребание** *n.* hay raking; **—сгребатель** *m.* hay rake; **—скучиватель** *m.* hay-sweep; **—ставки** *pl.* (mam.) pikas (*Ochotonidae*); **—сушилка** *f.* hay dryer; **—таска** *f.* hay carrier; **—уборка** *f.*, **—уборочный** *a.* haying, hay making.

Сен-поль (geog.) Saint Paul.

сенс/ация *f.* sensation; **—ибилизатор** *m.* sensitizer; allergen; **—ибилизация** *f.* sensitization, sensitizing; **—ибилизированный** *a.* sensitized; **—ибилизирующий** *a.* sensitizing; **—илла** *f.* (zool.) sensilla; **—итивный** *a.* sensitive.

сенсито/грамма (phot.) sensitogram, control strip.

сенситометр *m.* (opt.) sensitometer; **—ический** *a.* sensitometric; **—ия** *f.* sensitometry.

сенсорный *a.* sensory; **с. экран** (comp.) touch-sensitive screen.

сент *m.* (acous.) cent (unit of pitch).

Сент- *see* **Сен-**.

сентябрь *m.*, **—ский** *a.* September.

сенцы *dim. of* **сени**.

сепалоидный *a.* (bot.) sepaloid.

сепар/абильность *f.* (math.) separability; **—абильный** *a.* separable; **—атный** *a.* separate, independent; separative; **—атор** *m.* separator; (bearings) retainer, cage; **—аторный** *a.* separation; skim (milk); **—атриса** *f.* separatrix; **—ационный** *a.* separation; separative (power); **—ационное пространство** disengagement space or height; freeboard; **—ация** *f.* separation (by centrifuge); dunnage; cushioning, packing material; **—ация по цвету** color separation; **—ирование** *n.* separation; **—ированный** *a.* separated; skim(med) (milk); **—ировать** *v.* separate, isolate; centrifuge.

сепия *f.* sepia (pigment); (zool.) cuttlefish; **коричневая с.** sepia brown.

сепс/ин *m.* sepsine (a yeast ptomaine); **—ис** *m.* (med.) sepsis.

септа *f.* (biol.) septum; **—льный** *a.* septal.

септаноза *f.* septanose.

септар/иевый *a.* (geol.) septarian; **—ии** *pl.* septaria, septarian nodules.

септация *f.* (bot.) septation.

септико— *prefix* septico—, septic; **—пиемия** *f.* (med.) septicopyemia.

септик-танк *m.* septic tank.

септильон *m.* septillion.

септима *f.* (music) seventh.

септи/рованный *a.* (bot.) septate; **—фрагный** *a.* septifragal.

септи/цемический *a.* (med.) septicemic; **—цемия** *f.* (med.) septicemia; **—цидный** *a.* (bot.) septicidal; **—ческий** *a.* septic, putrefactive, putrid.

септомаргинальный *a.* (anat.) septomarginal.

септориоз *m.* (phyt.) septoria leaf spot.

септотомия *f.* (med.) septotomy.

сер *sh. m. of* **серый**; *gen. pl. of* **сера.**

сер. *abbr.* (**середина; серийный, серия).**

сер— *see also* **цер—.**

сер/а *f.* sulfur, S; brimstone; *sh. f. of* **серый**; **двуокись —ы** sulfur dioxide; **ушная с.** (physiol.) cerumen, earwax.

сераделла *f.* (bot.) serradella (*Ornithopus sativus*).

Сербия Serbia; **сербский** *a.* Serbian.

сервал *m.* (mam.) serval (*Felis serval*).

серв/антный *a.* (math.) serving; **—ер** *m.* (comp.) server; **—из** *m.*, **—изный** *a.* service, set (of tableware); **—ировать** *v.* serve; set (a table); **—ировка** *f.* serving; setting; service, set; **—ис** *m.*, **—исный** *a.* service; **—исная программа** (comp.) utility (program); **—итут** *m.* (law) servitude, right (to).

серво *see* **сервомеханизм; —двигатель** *m.* servomotor; **—канал** *m.* servo channel; **—клапан** *m.* servo valve, pilot valve; **—компенсатор** *m.* (av.) balance tab, (balancing) tab; **—контроллер** *m.* servocontroller; **—контур** *m.* servoloop; **—механизм** *m.* servomechanism, servounit, booster; **—мотор** *m.* servomotor, actuator; **—привод** *m.* servo(-drive); **—регулирование** *n.* servocontrol; **—руль** *m.* (av.) servotab, flying tab; **—система** *f.* servosystem; **—тормоз** *m.* servobrake, power brake; **—управление** *n.* servocontrol; **—управляемый** *a.* servocontrolled; **—усилитель** *m.* servoamplifier.

серго/зин, —син *m.* Sergosin, methiodal sodium.

сердеч/ко *n.* (bot.) corculum, corde (in seeds); **—ник** *m.*, **—никовый** *a.* core, center; mandrel; strand (of cable); heart patient; cardiologist; (bot.) Cardamine; **выдвижной —ник** (foundry) drawback.

сердечн/о-сосудистый *a.* (anat.) cardiovascular; **—ый** *a.* heart, cardiac; cordial, sincere; **—ая мышца** (anat.) myocardium.

сердинка *f.* (ichth.) Black Sea sprat.

сердит/ый *a.* angry; strong; hard (frost); **—ь** *v.* anger; **—ься** *v.* be angry.

сердолик *m.* (min.) carnelian, sard.

сердце *n.* heart; (anat.) cor, cardia; **—биение** *n.* (med.) palpitation; heartbeat; **—видка** (mal.) Cardium; **—видный** *a.* heart-shaped, cordiform, cordate.

сердцевин/а *f.* heart, core, center; (bot.) pith, medulla; pulp (of fruit); **без —ы** pithless; **—ный** *a.* pithy; medullar(y).

сере *dat., prepos. of* **сера.**

серебр/ение *n.* silvering, silver plating; **—еник** *m.* silver smith; **—ён(н)ый** *a.* silver-plated.

серебристо— *prefix* silver, argento—.

серебрист/ый *a.* silvery; silver, argentous; argentiferous (lead); **с. слой, —ая оболочка** (ichth.) argenteal layer.

серебрить *v.* silver (plate); **—ся** *v.* turn silver; shine.

серебр/о *n.* silver, Ag; **азотнокислое с., нитрат —а** silver nitrate; **бромистое с.** silver bromide; **сернистое с., сульфид —а** silver sulfide; **хлористое с.** silver chloride; **цианистое с.** silver cyanide.

серебро/носный *a.* argentiferous, silver-bearing, silver-containing; **—органический** *a.* organosilver; **—плавильный, —плавочный** *a.* silver-refining; **—содержащий** *see* **сереброносный.**

серебрянк/а *f.* silver steel, bright-polished carbon tool steel; (zool.) water spider; silver fox; (ichth.) argentine (*Argentina silus*); chum salmon (*Oncorhynchus keta*); **—овые** *pl.* (ichth.) Argentinidae.

серебряносинеродистый натрий sodium silver cyanide, sodium argentocyanide.

серебрян/ый *a.* silver; **—ых дел мастер** silversmith.

серёг *gen. pl. of* **серьга.**

середин/а *f.* middle, center, midst; mean; **с. полосы** midband; **с. размаха** midrange; **на —е** in the middle, halfway between; **—ка** *f.* middle piece, central portion, the very center; **—ный** *a.* middle, mean, central.

серёдка *see* **середина;** inside.

середняк *m.* average person.

серёж/ка *see* **серьга;** jowl, wattle, dewlap; (bot.) catkin, ament; **—чатый** *a.* amentaceous.

серендибит *m.* (min.) serendibite.

серение *n.* sulfuring, treating with sulfur, sulfur fumigation.

Сёренсена метод (chem.) Sørenson method.

cepe/ть *v.* turn gray; **—ющий** *a.* graying.

сержант-рыбы *pl.* cobias (*Rachycentridae*).

сери— *prefix* seri(ci)— (silk).

сериальн/ый *a.* serial; **—ая структура** (geol.) seriate structure.

сериемы *pl.* (orn.) Cariamidae.

сериес/-двигатель, с.-мотор *m.* (elec.) series motor; **—ный** *a.* series; series-wound; **с.-параллельный** *a.* series-parallel (winding).

серийн/о *adv.* (elec.) in series; **с. выпускающийся** off-the-shelf (equipment); **—ость** *f.* batch production; **—ый** *a.* series, serial; series-produced; assembly-line; lot, batch (production); production (model); standard (equipment); **—ое время** time per batch.

серикоза *f.* sericose, cellulose acetate.

сериметр *m.* silk-testing device; **—ия** *f.* testing silk for tensile strength.

серин *m.* serine, hydroxyalanine.

сериола *f.* (ichth.) yellowtail, amberjack (*Seriola*).

серить *v.* sulfur, treat with sulfur, fumigate with sulfur.

серицин *m.*, **—овый** *a.* sericin, silk glue; **—овая кислота** sericic acid.

серицит *m.* (min.) sericite; **—изация** *f.* sericitization; **—овый** *a.* sericitic.

серия *f.* series, set, bank (of machines); (pulse, etc.) train; order, succession, sequence, range; family; (bot.) sere; **вторичная с.** (bot.) subsere; **—ми** (elec.) in series.

серка *f.* suint, yolk (of wool); (chem.) galipol; white turpentine resin; (zool.) young seal.

сермерсоак *m.* ice-cap; continental ice sheet.

серм/яга *f.*, **—яжина, —яжка** *f.*, **—яжный** *a.* coarse undyed homespun.

серна *f.* (mam.) chamois (*Rupicapra rupicapra*).

серная *f. of* **серный.**

сернисто/аммониевая соль ammonium sulfite; **—водородный** *see* **сероводородный; —калиевая соль** potassium sulfite; **—кальциевая соль** calcium sulfite; **кислая —кальциевая соль** calcium bisulfite.

сернистокисл/ый *a.* sulfurous acid; sulfite (of); **с. натрий** sodium sulfite; **—ая соль** sulfite; **кислая —ая соль** bisulfite.

сернистонатриевая соль sodium sulfite; **кислая с. соль** sodium bisulfite.

сернист/ость *f.* (petrol.) sulfur content; **—о-щелочные стоки** spent sulfidic caustic liquors.

сернист/ый *a.* sulfur(ous); sulfide (of); (petrol.) medium-sulfur, sour; **с. ангидрид** sulfurous anhydride, sulfur dioxide; **с. водород** hydrogen sulfide; **с. газ** sulfur dioxide; **с. голубой** sulfur blue; **с. источник** sulfur spring; **с. натрий** sodium sulfide; **с. углерод** carbon disulfide; **с. цвет** flowers of sulfur, sublimed sulfur; **—ая кислота** sulfurous acid; **—ая медь** copper sulfide; **—ая руда** (min.) sulfide ore; **—ые красители, —ые краски** sulfur dyes; **кислая соль —ой кисло-**

ты bisulfite; **окись —ого алкила** sulfoxide; **соль —ой кислоты** sulfite.

серница *f.* (timber) resinous pocket.

серно/алюминиевая соль aluminum sulfate; **—аммониевая соль** ammonium sulfate.

сернобыки *pl.* (mam.) oryx, gemsboks (*Oryx*).

серноватисто/аммониевая соль ammonium thiosulfate; **—кислый натрий** sodium thiosulfate.

серновинная кислота ethylsulfuric acid, ethyl sulfate.

серножелез/истая соль ferrous sulfate; **—ная соль** ferric sulfate.

серно/жёлтый *a.* sulfur yellow; **—известковый** *a.* sulfur-lime (spray); **—калиевая соль** potassium sulfate; **кислая —калиевая соль** potassium bisulfate; **—кальциевая соль** calcium sulfate; **—кислотное производство** sulfuric acid manufacture; **—кислотчик** *m.* sulfuric acid specialist (or manufacturer).

сернокисл/ый *a.* sulfuric acid; sulfate (of); **с. натрий** sodium sulfate; **кислый с. натрий** sodium bisulfate; **—ая соль** sulfate.

серно/кобальтистая соль cobaltous sulfate; **—кобальтовая соль** cobaltic sulfate.

сернокоза *f.* (mam.) serow (*Capricornis*).

серно/медистая соль cuprous sulfate; **—медная соль** cupric sulfate; **—метиловый эфир** methyl sulfate.

серно/очистительный завод sulfur refinery; **—свинцовистая соль** lead sulfate, plumbous sulfate; **—синеродистый** *see* **серосинеродистый**; **—феноловая кислота** phenolsulfuric acid; **—этиловый эфир** ethyl sulfate.

серн/ый *a.* sulfur(ic); **с. ангидрид** sulfuric anhydride, sulfur trioxide; **с. цвет** flowers of sulfur, sublimed sulfur; **с. чёрный** sulfur black; **с. эфир** ethyl ether; **—ая кислота** sulfuric acid; **—ое железо** ferric sulfide; **—ое молоко** milk of sulfur, precipitated sulfur; **кислая соль —ой кислоты** bisulfate; **соль —ой кислоты** sulfate.

серо— *prefix* sulfur; gray; sero—, serum, serous; *adv.* grayly; **—азот** *m.* nitrogen sulfide; **—бактерии** *pl.* sulfur bacteria; **—белый** *a.* grayish white; young (winter ice); **—бурый** *a.* brownish gray, dun-colored; **—ваккковый конгломерат** (petr.) graywacke; **—вакцина** *f.* (med.) serovaccine; **—ватый** *a.* grayish; (bot.) canescent, hoary.

сероводород *m.* hydrogen sulfide; **—истый, —ный** *a.* hydrosulfide (of); **—ная вода** hydrogen sulfide solution; **—ная кислота** hydrosulfuric acid, hydrogen sulfide; **соль —ной кислоты** sulfide.

серодиагностика *f.* (med.) serodiagnosis.

сероза *f.* (anat.) serosa, serous membrane.

серозём *m.* sierozem, gray desert soil.

серозит *m.* (med.) serositis.

серозн/о— *prefix* sero—, serum; **—ослизистый** *a.* seromucous; **—офибринозный** *a.* (med.) serofibrinous; **—ый** *a.* (med.) serous; **—ая жидкость** serum; **—ая оболочка** serous membrane, serosa.

серокитовые *pl.* (mam.) gray whales (*Eschrichtiidae*).

серология *f.* (med.) serology.

серо/обжигательная печь sulfur kiln, sulfur burner; **—очистка** *f.* sulfur purification; desulfurization; **—профилактика** *f.* serum immunization.

серо/синеродистый *a.* thiocyanate, sulfocyanate (of); **с. барий** barium thiocyanate; **—содержащий** *a.* sulfur-containing.

сероспинка *f.* (ichth.) alewife.

серость *f.* grayness.

серотерапия *f.* (med.) serotherapy.

серотонин *m.* serotonin, 5-hydroxytryptamine.

сероуглерод *m.*, **—ный** *a.* carbon disulfide.

серп *m.* sickle; (anat.) falx.

серпазил *m.* Serpasil, reserpine.

серпантина *see* **серпентина.**

серпен/ие *n.* twisting.

серпентин *m.* (min.) serpentine; **—а** *f.* (roads) hairpin turn; **—изация** *f.* (min.) serpentinization; **—изированный** *a.* serpentinous; **—ит** *m.* serpentinite, serpentine rock; **—овый** *a.* serpentine.

серпетка *f.* pruning knife.

серп/ик *dim. of* **серп;** narrow crescent; **—овидноклеточный** *a.* (med.) sickle-cell; **—овидный** *see* **серпообразный; —овидная пластинка** (anat.) tympanic plate; **—овище** *n.* sickle handle; **—оклюв** *m.* (orn.) Ibis-bill (*Ibidorhyncha*); **—ообразный** *a.* sickle-shaped, crescent-shaped, falciform, falcate.

серпуха *f.* (bot.) saw-wort (*Serratula*).

серпянка *f.* sarp cloth, open canvas.

серраки *pl.* (glacier) ice serrations.

серрановые *pl.* (ichth.) sea basses (*Serranidae*).

сертация *f.* (bot.) certation.

сертификат *m.* certificate; **снабжённый —ом** *a.* certified.

Сертоли клетки (physiol.) Sertoli's cells.

серум *m.* serum.

серусодержащий *see* **серосодержащий.**

серушка *f.* (ichth.) river roach.

серфы *pl.* parasitic wasps (*Serphoidea*).

серы *gen., etc., of* **сера.**

серый *a.* gray; young, winter (ice).

серьг/а *f.* (connecting) link, ring, shackle, stirrup, strap; (horol.) bow; **с. с болтом** clevis; **с —ой** shackle-type.

серьёзн/о *adv.* seriously; **—ость** *f.* seriousness, gravity; **—ый** *a.* serious, grave, of deep concern; sound, solid, basic, important, thorough (research).

серянка *f.* sulfur match; sulfur pot; (timber) resinous cancer.

сесамо/видный, —идный *a.* sesamoid.

сескви— *prefix* sesqui— (one and a half); **—терпен** *m.* sesquiterpene.

сесси/я *f.*, **—онный** *a.* session, sitting; term (of court).

сестон *m.* (biol.) seston, microplankton.

сестр/а *f.* sister; (med.) nurse; **—ин(ский)** *a.* sister's; daughter (chromosome).

сесть *see* **садиться.**

сет *m.* (typ.) set; **—а** *f.* (biol.) seta.

сете/видный *see* **сетеобразный; —вой** *a. of* **сеть;** supply-line; line (frequency); **—вязальный** *a.*, **—вязание** *n.* net weaving; **—й** *gen. pl. of* **сеть; —образный, —подобный** *a.* reticular, retiform, net-like, netted; plexiform (neuroma); **—подъёмный** *a.* (fishing) net-lifting.

сети *gen., pl., etc., of* **сеть.**

Сет-Иль (geog.) Sept Iles.

сетк/а *f.* netting, net(work); sieve, screen; (wire) gauze; strainer, (suction) basket, liner; grid, grate, grating; cage (of elevator); (paper) wire; (comp.) array; (cryst.) lattice; pattern, spacing; (geod.; geog.) graticule, reticule; (incandescent) mantle; (wage) scale; (zool.) reticulum; **с. нитей** cross-hairs; **с.-верхплавка** floating gill-net; **—ообразный** *a.* net-shaped, reticular, reticulated.

сетлер *m.* settler, separator.

сет/ной, —ный *a. of* **сеть; —ок** *gen. pl. of* **сетка; —очка** *dim. of* **сетка; —очник** *m.* (paper) machine operator, screener.

сеточн/ый *a. of* **сетка;** wire gauze (electrode); mesh (electrode); finite-difference (equation); **с. товар** netting; **—ая утечка** (rad.) grid leak; **—ое смещение** grid bias; **с —ым управлением** grid-controlled.

сеттер *m.* setter (dog).

сетчат/ка *f.* meshwork; (anat.) retina; **на —ке** retinal (image); **—о—** *prefix* reticulato—, reticulate(ly); dicty(o)— (net); **—ожилковатый, —онервный** *a.* reticulate-veined, net-veined; **—окрылые** *pl.* (ent.) Neuroptera; **—ость** *f.* reticulation, netting.

сетчат/ый *a.* netted, network, net-shaped, retiform, reticulate(d), reticular, veined; cellular; latticed; wiregauze (electrode); cross-linked (polymer); sieve (plate); perforated (bottom); **с. барабан** revolving screen; **с. узор** reticulation; **с. шоб** mesh weld; **—ая оболочка** (anat.) retina; **—ая структура, —ое строение** reticular structure, reticulation; (met.) network structure.

сет/ь *f.* net(ting), mesh; network, system; circuit; (water) mains; (anat.) rete; reticulum; (telephone) set; **напряжение —и** (elec.) line voltage; **подавать с. на** turn on (power to); **чудесная с.** (zool.) rete mirabile; **электрическая с.** power-supply system.

Сеул (geog.) Seoul.

сефадекс (chem.) Sephadex.

сеча *v.* cutting, etc., *see* **сечь.**

сечен/ие *n.* (cross) section, cut, profile, sectional view; size, gage, diameter; cutting, chopping (off, up); (comp.) cutset (of network section); (anat.) sectio; *suffix* (med.) —(o)tomy (cutting, incision); **с. горизонталей** *see* **сечение рельефа; большого —ия** heavygage (wire); **живое с.** free cross sectional area; **малого —ия** light-gage (wire); **площадь —ия** sectional area; **поперечное с.** cross section; **эффективное с.** radar cross-section.

сеч/енный *a.* cut, chopped (off, up).

сеченовский *a.* (med.) Sechenoff('s).

сеч/ка *f.* cutting, chopping; cutter, chopper, cleaver; chopped straw; crushed grain; **—онка** *f.* (cer.) crackle; **—ь** *v.* cut, chop (off, up); whip, flog; dress, trim; **—ься** *v.* split; (text.) fray, unravel.

сеющий *pr. act. part. of* **сеять; сеющий прибор** *see* **сеялка.**

сеял/ка *f.*, **—очный** *a.* seeder, sower, planter, drill; sifter, screen; (fertilizer) spreader; **рядовая с.** drill; **—ьный** *a.* sowing, seeding; seed (board); sifting; **—ьный рожок** drill.

сея/льщик *m.* sower; sifter, screener; **—нец** *m.* seedling; **—ние** *n.* sowing, etc., *see v.*; **—нный** *a.* sown, seeded, etc., *see v.*; **—ть** *v.* sow, seed, plant; sprinkle; sift; screen; (biol.) make a culture; **—ться** *v.* be sown, etc.; pour; fall (of rain, snow), drizzle.

СЖ *abbr.* **(сахароза, желатин)** saccharose, gelatin; *abbr.* **(спасательный жилет)** inflatable life jacket.

сжарить *v.* roast; fry.

сжат/ие *n.* compression; constriction, contraction, reduction, shrinkage, shrinking; oblateness (of the Earth); condensation; squeezing; packing (of powder); pinch; grip, clutch; **камера —ия** compression chamber; **предел прочности на с.** compression strength; **сопротивление —ию** compressive strength; **степень —ия** compression ratio; **ход —ия** compression stroke (of piston); **эффект —ия** (elec.) pinch effect.

сжат/о *adv.* concisely, in brief form; compactly; **—оспиральный** *a.* close-coiled; **—ость** *f.* conciseness, compactness; compression; **большая степень —ости** high compression ratio; **—ый** *a.* compressed (air, gas); compression; under pressure; condensed, compact, concise, brief; short (time); constricted, pinched; clenched (fist); (geom.) oblate; mowed, reaped, harvested; **—ь** *v.* reap; *see also* **сжимать.**

сжёванный *a.* chewed (up).

сжевать *v.* chew (up or on).

сжечь *see* **сжигать.**

сживаться *v.* get used to.

сжиг/ание *n.* combustion, burning (up), consumption (of fuel); incineration (of rubbish); (acid) digestion; **камера —ания** combustion chamber; **—ательный** *a.* combustion; **—ать** *v.* burn (up), consume; burn out, burn off; set on fire; scorch; digest (in acid).

сжи/дить *see* **сжижать; —жаемость** *f.* liquefiability, etc., *see a.*; **—жаемый** *a.* liquefiable, condensable, compressible; **—жать** *v.* liquefy; condense, compress; **—жение** *n.* liquefaction, etc., *see v.*; **—женный** *a.* liquefied, etc., *see v.*

сжим *m.* clip, grip, clamp, tongs, forceps.

сжим/аемость *f.* compressibility, condensability; contractibility; **коэффициент —аемости** *f.* compressibility factor; **—аемый** *a.* compressible, condensable, coercible; contractible; **—ание** *n.* compression, etc., *see v.*; **—атель** *m.* compressor; (anat.) sphincter, constrictor; **—атель-расширитель** *m.* compressor-expander, compander; **—ать** *v.* compress, condense; shrink, tighten, contract, constrict, squeeze, press, pinch, force together; clench (fist); grip, hug; pack (powder); (med.) strangulate; **—аться** *v.* condense, contract, shrink.

сжимающ/ий *a.* compressing, condensing; sphincter (muscle); **с. ход** compression stroke (of piston); **—ая мышца** (anat.) constrictor; **—ая сила, —ее усилие** compressive force; **—ийся** *a.* constringent, contractile.

сжимки *pl.* clamp, tongs.

сжинать *v.* reap, harvest, mow.

сжиться *see* **сживаться.**

СЖК *abbr.* **(синтетическая жирная кислота)** synthetic fatty acid.

СЖО *abbr.* **(система жизнеобеспечения)** life support system.

СЖС *abbr.* **(синтетический жирный спирт)** synthetic fatty alcohol.

сжуёт *pr. 3 sing. of* **сжевать.**

с.-з., С.-З. *abbr.* [**северо-запад(ный)**].

сзади *adv. and prep. gen.* (from) behind, at the rear (of), in back (of); **вид с.** rear view, end view.

с.з.п. *abbr.* **(сила земного притяжения)** gravitational force.

сзывать *see* **созвать.**

си *n.* (music) B.

Си *abbr.* **(истинный север)** true north.

СИ *abbr.* **(система интернациональная)** International System (of Units).

сиал/о— *prefix* sial(o)— (saliva; salivary glands); **—аденит** *m.* (med.) sial(o)adenitis; **—овая кислота** sialic acid.

сиаль *m.* (geol.) sial (layer of rocks).

сиаманг *m.* (mam.) siamang gibbon.

сиамск/ий *a.* Siam(ese); **с. бензой, —ая камедь** Siam benzoin (resin).

сиарезинол *m.* siaresinol; **—овая кислота** siaresinolic acid.

сиб. *abbr.* **(сибирский).**

сиба *see* **циба—.**

сиббинг *m.* mating of siblings.

сибир/еязвенный *a.*, **—ка** *f.*, **—ская язва** (vet.) anthrax; **—ский** *a.* Siberia(n).

Сибирь Siberia.

сиботаксис *m.* (phys.) cybotaxis.

сибсы *pl.* siblings.

сива/питек *m.* (pal.) Sivapithecus; **—терий** *m.* (pal.) Sivatherium; **—шник** *m.* (ichth.) weed goby.

сивка *f.* gray horse.

сивуха *f.* fusel oil; raw vodka.

сивуч *m.*, **—ий** *a.* (zool.) sea lion.

сивушный *a. of* **сивуха.**

сивый *a.* gray(ish) (horse).

сиг *m.* (ichth.) whitefish (*Coregonus*); **—ан** *m.* (ichth.) spinefoot; **—овые** *pl.* rabbitfishes, spinefeet (*Siganidae*).

сигануть *v.* jump, leap.

сигар/а *f.* cigar; **—ет(к)а** *f.*, **—етный** *a.* cigarette; **—ный** *a.* cigar; **—ообразный** *a.* cigar-shaped.

сигать *see* **сигануть.**

сигбол *m.* Sigbol, antistatic additive used in fuels.

сигла *f.* sigla, logogram, symbol.

сигм/а *f.* sigma, σ; **—овидный,** **—оидальный** *a.* sigmoid(al), C-shaped, S-shaped; **—овидная кишка** (anat.) sigmoid (flexure); **с.-связь** *f.* sigma bond.

сигнал *m.* signal, alarm; signal call, message; signal tower; sign, mark; (mil.) flare; **по —у** on call (detonation); **—изатор** *m.* alarm, signaling device, warning device, annunciator; indicator; (gases) warning component; **—изационный** *a.*, **—изация** *f.*, **—изирование** *n.* signaling, warning, alarm, annunciation; indicating, indication; **—изировать** *v.* (sound a) signal, warn; **—изирующий** *a.* signaling, warning; **—ист** *see* **сигнальщик; —ьно-предупредительный** *a.* alarm (system).

сигнальн/ый *a.* signal(ing), alarm, warning; pilot (light); current awareness (information); **с. ген** genetic marker; **с. звонок** alarm, signal; **с. огонь** beacon; signal light; **с. прибор** alarm; indicator; **с. экземпляр** (typ.) preprint copy; **—ая пластина** (comp.) backplate; **—ые составы** flare components.

сигнальщик *m.* signal man, signaler; (railroad) flagman.

сигнатур/а *f.*, **—ный** *a.* (typ.) signature (mark); (prescription) label; **—ка** *f.* prescription label.

сиго/вые *pl.* (ichth.) Salmonidae; **—вый** *a. of* **сиг; —лов** (ichth.) *see* **сиг.**

сигуатера *f.* (med.) ciguatera, ichthyosarcotoxism.

СИД *abbr.* **(светоизлучающий диод)** light-emitting diode, LED.

сида *f.* (bot.) Sida; **—льцея** *f.* Sidalcea.

сиделка *f.* nurse, attendant.

сиден/ие *n.* sitting, staying; seat(ing); session; **—ье** *n.* seat(ing).

сидеразотит *m.* (min.) siderazotite.

сидер/альный *a.* green (manure); **—ат** *m.* green manure crop; **—ация** *f.* sideration, use of green manure.

сидерит *m.* (min.) siderite, chalybite.

сидерический *a.* (astr.) sidereal.

сидеро— *prefix* sidero— (star; iron); **—з** *m.* (med.) siderosis; **—капсы** *pl.* (bact.) Siderocapsaceae; **—нитовый** *a.* sideronitic (texture); **—пения** *f.* (med.) sideropenia, iron deficiency; **—скоп** *m.* (ophth.) sideroscope; **—сфера** *f.* siderosphere; **—фильный** *a.* siderophile (elements).

сидеть *v.* sit, be seated; occupy, hold; sit up, stay up (with); be; fit.

сидлак *m.* (chem.) seed lac.

Сидн/ей, —и (geog.) Sydney.

сиднон *m.* (chem.) sydnone.

сидр *m.*, **—овый** *a.* cider.

сидячеглазые *pl.* (mal.) pond snails (*Basommatophora*).

сидячие *pl.* (zool.) Sedentaria.

сидя/чий, —щий *a.* sitting, sedentary; sessile, fixed; inserted, set (in).

сие *n. of* **сей.**

сиена *see* **сиенна.**

сиенит *m.* (petr.) syenite; **—овый** *a.* syenitic, syenite.

сиенн/а *f.*, **—ая земля** sienna (pigment); **жённая с.** burnt sienna.

сиенск/ий *a.* sienna; **—ая желть, —ая земля** sienna (pigment).

сиз *sh. m.*, **—а** *sh. f. of* **сизый.**

сизаль *m.*, **—ский** *a.* sisal (hemp); **—нопеньковый** *a.* sisal hemp.

сизарь (orn.) *see* **голубь.**

сизиг/ийный *a.* syzygial; (ocean.) spring, high (tide); **средний уровень малых —ийных вод** mean low water springs; **средний уровень полных —ийных вод** mean high water springs; **—ийский** *a.* (astr.; math.; zool.) syzygial; **—ия** *f.* syzygy.

сизо— *prefix* glauco— (silvery gray); **—ватый** *a.* (bot.) glaucescent; **—воронка** *f.* (orn.) roller (*Coracias*).

сизый *a.* gray-blue, dove-colored.

сии *pl. of* **сей;** these.

СИИ *abbr.* **(система искусственного интеллекта)** artificial intelligence, AI.

сиккатив *m.* siccative, desiccant, drier.

Сикким (geog.) Sikkim.

сиккозак *m.* sikussak, bay ice, old polar fast ice.

сиковка *see* **щиповка.**

сикоз *m.* (med.) sycosis.

сиколка *see* **щиповка.**

сико/мор *m.* (bot.) sycamore; **—н** *m.* (zool.) sycon (in sponges); **—ний** *m.* (bot.) syconium; **—цериловый спирт** sycoceryl alcohol.

сикромо *n.* Sicrome steel.

сил/а *f.* force; power, strength; pull (of gravity); intensity (of light, sound); vigor, energy; **с. действия** efficiency; **с. (химической) связи** binding force; **с. сигнала** (rad.) signal strength; **быть в —ах** *v.* have the power (to), be in a position (to); **вектор —ы** line of force; **в —е valid; в —у** on the strength (of), by virtue (of), because (of); **войти в —у** *v.* come into effect, become effective; **диаграмма сил** stress diagram; **единица —ы** unit of force; **живая с.** kinetic energy; manpower, personnel; **жизненная с.** vitality; **измеритель —ы** dynamometer; **имеющий —у** (law) valid; **лошадиная с.** horsepower; **остаться в —е** *v.* hold good, be valid; **поле сил** force field; **подъёмная с.** (aero.) lift; lifting capacity (of crane, etc.); carrying capacity (of truck, etc.); **подъёмная с. воды** buoyancy of water; **работать через —у** *v.* overwork; **рабочая с.** work force, labor; **реактивная с.** (jet) thrust; **сохранять —у** *v.* be preserved, hold good, be valid (for); **тянущая с.** pull.

силан *m.* silane, silicon hydride; **—ол** *m.* silanol, silicol.

сила-час *m.* horsepower hour.

силевый поток (geol.) sill.

силезский *a.* Silesian.

силекс *m.* Silex (glass).

силен *sh. m. of* **сильный;** (mam.) Масаса.

силён *sh. m. of* **сильный.**

сили *see* **сели.**

силика/алюмогель *m.* aluminosilicate gel; **—гель** *m.* silica gel; **—н** *m.* sil(ic)ane.

силикат *m.* silicate; **—изация** *f.*, **—ирование** *n.* silication; **—ировать** *v.* silicate; **—ный, —овый** *a.* silicate; silica (brick, etc.).

силико— *prefix* silico—, silicon; **—бутан** *m.* silicobutane, tetrasilane; **—вольфрамовая кислота** silicotungstic acid; **—з** *m.* (med.) silicosis; **—метан** *m.* monosilane; **—н** *m.*, **—новый** *a.* silicone; **—пропан**

m. silicopropane, trisilane; —**уксусная кислота** silicoacetic acid; —**этан** *m.* silicoethane, disilane.

силинг *m.* ceiling.

силипур *m.* finely dispersed silica.

силит *m.,* —**овый** *a.* Silit (silicon carbide).

силиться *v.* try.

силиц/ид *m.* silicide; —**ий** *see* **кремний**; —**ил** *m.* silicyl; —**илен** *m.* silicylene.

силковый *a.* of **силок**.

силл *m.* (geol.) sill.

силлеп/сис *m.* (grammar) syllepsis; —**тический** *a.* sylleptic.

силов/ой *a.* power, force; heavy-duty; **с. агрегат** power unit; **с. многоугольник** polygon of forces; **с. привод** actuator; **с. провод** (elec.) power line; **с. следящий привод** servodrive; **с. узел,** —**ая головка** power pack; —**ая линия** line of force; —**ая передача** transmission; —**ая постоянная** force constant; —**ая трубка, трубка** —**ых линий** field tube; force tube; —**ая установка** (mech.) power plant; (rocket) propulsion system; —**ая функция** (av.) mass-flow function; (phys.) force function; —**ая цепь** power circuit; —**ое поле** field of force; —**ые линии (поля)** lines of force; field pattern; **мощный с.** superpower.

силой *adv.* by force.

силок *m.* snare, trap.

силокс/ан *m.,* —**анный** *a.* siloxane; —**ен** *m.* siloxen; —**икон** *m.* siloxicon (a refractory material).

силоме(т)р *m.* dynamometer.

силон *m.,* —**овый** *a.* Kapron, nylon-6.

силоприёмник *m.* (mech.) receiver.

силос *m.* (agr.) silo; silage.

силосель *m.* Sil-O-Cel (heat insulator).

силосн/ый *a.* (agr.) silo, (en)silage; —**ая башня,** —**ая яма** silo; —**ые культуры** (en)silage crops.

силосо/вание *n.* (storing) ensilage; —**ванный корм** ensilage (fodder); —**вать** *v.* ensilage, silo, store in a silo; —**наполнитель** *m.* silo feeder; —**резка** *f.* (en)silage cutter, shredder; —**трамбовщик** *m.* silo packer; —**уборочный** *a.* (en)silage-harvesting; —**хранилище** *n.* silo storage; —**швырялка** *f.* blower.

силосуемость *f.* (en)silage capacity.

силунд *m.* silundum, silicon carbide.

силур *m.,* —**ийский период** (geol.) Silurian period.

силуэт *m.,* —**ный** *a.* silhouette, outline.

силы *gen., pl., etc.,* of **сила;** (mil.) forces; **с. и средства** men and equipment.

силь *see* **сель.**

сильван *m.* sylvan, *alpha*-methylfuran.

сильванит *m.* (min.) sylvanite.

сильве/глицерин *m.* silveglycerin; —**оловая кислота** silveolic acid.

сильвер— *prefix* silver—.

сильвестрен *m.* sylvestrene.

сильвиев водопровод (anat.) aqueduct of Sylvius.

сильвин *m.* (min.) sylvite; —**ит** *m.* (petr.) sylvinite; (med.) inflammation of the aqueduct of Sylvius; —**овая кислота** sylvic acid, abietic acid; —**овокислый** *a.* sylvic acid; sylvate (of).

сильвиновый *a.* (anat.) sylvian.

сильн/ее *comp.* of **сильно;** more; rather, preferably; —**ейший** *superl.* of **сильный;** best.

сильно *adv.* powerfully, strongly, intensely, vigorously, highly, severely, very; densely (wooded); badly; —**действующий** *a.* strong, potent; aggressive, offensive, violent, drastic; —**ионизированный** *a.* highly ionized; —**клееный** *a.* (paper) heavily sized; —**основный** *a.* strongly alkaline; —**связанный** *a.* closely

coupled, tightly coupled; —**точный** *a.* heavy-current, high-current; —**фокусирующий** *a.* strong-focusing; —**щелочной** *see* **сильноосновный**.

сильный *a.* strong, powerful, potent; vigorous; high, intense, sharp, severe (cold, etc.); concentrated; hard, heavy (rain, etc.); violent (storm); significant (effect); high-level (radioactivity); *suffix* -horsepower; (bot.) —**dynamous; исключительно с.** dramatic.

сильфон *m.,* —**ный** *a.* bellows.

сильхром *m.* Silchrome (steel).

сильча (ichth.) *see* **кета.**

силэб *m.* sea lab (underwater laboratory).

сим *abbr.* **(сименс);** *instr.* of **сей.**

сим— *prefix* sym— (with, together).

сима *f.* (geol.) sima; (ichth.) Oncorhynchus masu.

симаруб/а *f.* (bot.) mountain damson (*Simaruba officinalis*); —**идин** *m.* simarubidin; **кора** —**ы,** —**овая кора** simaruba bark, bitter damson.

симба *f.* (ichth.) minnow (*Phoxinus*).

симбатность *f.* (biol.) symbasis; agreement.

симбатный *a.* cymbate, boat-shaped; (math.) symbatic.

симби/оз *m.* (biol.) symbiosis, living together; —**онт** *m.* symbiont; —**отический** *a.* symbiotic; —**отрофный** *a.* (biol.) symbiotrophic.

симблефарон *m.* (med.) symblepharon.

символ *m.* symbol, sign, mark; character, notation; letter (of a code); (binary) digit; **набор** —**ов** (comp.) character set; —**изировать** *v.* symbolize, represent, stand (for); —**изм** *m.* symbolism; —**ика** *f.* (biol.) symbolics (of genes); (math.) symbolism, notation; —**ически** *adv.* (math.) in symbols; —**ический** *a.* symbolic, figurative.

сименс *m.* (elec.) siemen, mho (unit of conductance).

симистор *m.* (elec.) triac.

симмелия *f.* (med.) symmelia.

симметр/изация *f.,* —**ирование** *n.* symmetrization, balancing; —**ирующий** *a.* symmetric(al); balancing; —**ический,** —**ичный** *a.* symmetrical, balanced; double-ended; —**ичность,** —**ия** *f.* symmetry.

симморфоз *m.* (chem.) addition.

симоген *see* **цимоген.**

симпат/изировать *v.* sympathize; —**ин** *m.* (physiol.) sympathin; —**ический** *a.* sympathetic; —**ическая реакция** sympathetic reaction, induced reaction; —**ские чернила** sympathetic ink, invisible ink; —**ичный** *a.* likable; —**ия** *f.* sympathy; liking (for); —**рический** *a.* (biol.) sympatric; —**рия** *f.* sympatry; —**эктомия** *f.* (med.) sympathectomy.

симпетальный *a.* (bot.) sympetalous.

симплекс *m.* (math.) simplex; —**ный** *a.* simplex; one-way (channel).

симплициальный *a.* simplicial.

симпод/иальный *a.* (bot.) sympodial; —**ий** *m.* sympodium.

симпозиум *m.* symposium, workshop.

симпровизировать *v.* improvise.

Симпсона правило (surv., etc.) Simpson's rule.

симптом *m.* symptom, sign; **комплекс** —**ов** syndrome; —**атика** *f.* (med.) symptomatology; —**атический** *a.* symptomatic; —**окомплекс** *m.* syndrome.

симул/ировать *v.* simulate; —**ьтанный** *a.* simultaneous; —**ьтантный** *a.* combined; —**янт** *m.* simulator; (med.) malingerer; —**яция** *f.* simulation.

симфиз *m.* (anat.) symphysis; —**ный** *a.* symphyseal.

син— *prefix* syn— (with, together; at the same time; like).

син/алар *m.* (pharm.) Synalar, fluocinolone acetonide; —**альбин** *m.* sinalbin.

синайский *a.* (geog.) Sinai.

синан/гий *m.* (biol.) synangium; **—дрий** *a.* (bot.) synandrium; **—дрия** *f.* synandry; **—тезис** (bot.) synanthesis, synacme; **—тия** *f.* (bot.) synanthy; **—тропный** *a.* synanthropic.

синап/ин *m.* sinapine; **—иновый** *a.* sinapic (acid); **—иновокислая соль** sinapate.

синапс(ис) *m.* (genetics) synapsis; (physiol.) synapse.

синапта *f.* (zool.) sea cucumber.

синапт/ический *a.* (physiol.) synaptic; **—оспермный** *a.* (bot.) synaptospermous.

сынартроз *m.* (anat.) synarthrosis.

син/афобранховые *pl.* deep-sea eels (*Synaphobranchidae*); **—бранховые** *pl.* swamp eels (*Synbranchidae*).

сингам *m.* (zool.) Syngamus; **трахейный с.** gapeworm; **—ия** *f.* (biol.) syngamy, conjugation; **—оз птиц** *m.* (vet.) gapes.

Сингапур (geog.) Singapore.

синген/ез *m.* syngenesis; **—етический** *a.* syngenetic.

сингиль *m.* mullet (*Mugil*).

синглет *m.*, **—ный** *a.* singlet; single line (spectral line).

сингония *f.* syngony, (crystal) system.

сингулярн/ость *f.* (math.) singularity; **—ый** *a.* singular.

синдактилия *f.* (med.) syndactilia; (zool.) syndactyly.

синдез(ис) *m.* (gen.) syndesis.

синдесм(о)— *prefix* (anat.) syndesm(o)— (connective tissue; ligament); **—оз** *m.* syndesmosis; **—ология** *f.* syndesmology.

синдетикон *m.* syndetic material, liquid glue.

син-диазосоединение *n.* syndiazo compound.

синди/кат *m.* syndicate; **—отактический** *a.* syndiotactic (polymer); **—цированный** *a.* syndicated; **—цировать** *v.* syndicate.

синдром *m.* (med.) syndrome.

сине *sh. n. of* **синий**; *prefix* blue; sine— (without); syne— (together); **—ва** *f.* dark-blue color; (phyt.) blue stain, blue rot; **—ватобледный** *a.* livid; **—ватый** *a.* bluish; **—видение** *n.* (med.) cyanopsia; **—глазка** *f.* day flower (*Commelina communis*); **—гнойная палочка** (bact.) Bacillus pyocyaneus; **—головник** *m.* (bot.) Eryngium; **с.-зелёные водоросли** (bot.) Cyanophyceae; **—калильный** *a.* blue (heat).

синеклиза *f.* (geol.) syneclise.

синекура *f.* sinecure.

синематограф *see* **кинематограф.**

синеморка *f.* (ichth.) Volga shad.

синем/урский, —юрский *a.* (geol.) Sinemurian.

синение *n.* bluing; (met.) blue tempering.

синён(н)ый *a.* blued; blue tempered.

сине/пёрый *a.* blue-finned; **—плодный** *a.* (bot.) cyanocarpous.

синерг/етический *a.* synergetic; **—ида** *f.* (bot.) synergid; **—изм** *m.* synergy, synergism; **—ист** *m.* synergist; **—ический** *a.* synergistic; **—ия** *f.* synergy, correlated action.

синерезис *m.* (gels) syneresis.

синерод *m.* cyanogen; **—истоводородная кислота** hydrocyanic acid.

синеродист/ый *a.* (formerly lower or **—ous**) cyanide (of); **с. водород** hydrogen cyanide; **с. калий** potassium cyanide; **—ая кислота** cyanic acid.

синеродн/ый *a.* (formerly higher or **—ic**) cyanide (of); **—ая медь** cupric cyanide; **—ая ртуть** mercuric cyanide; **—ое железо** ferric cyanide.

синеродо— *prefix* cyan(o)—.

синеродоводород *m.*, **—ная кислота** hydrogen cyanide, hydrocyanic acid, prussic acid; **соль —ной ки-** слоты cyanide; **—ный** *a.* hydrocyanic, hydrocyanide (of).

синеспинка *f.* blueback herring.

синестезия *f.* (physiol.) synesthesia.

синетелка *f.* pearlfish (*Glaucosoma*).

синеть *v.* turn blue.

синефрин *m.* synephrin.

синехвостки *pl.* (orn.) bluetails (*Tarsiger*).

синехия *f.* (med.) synechia, adhesion.

синец *m.* (ichth.) bream (*Abramis*); roach (*Rutilus*).

синеющий *a.* cyanescent, turning dark blue.

синигрин *m.* sinigrin, potassium myronate.

син/ий *a.* (dark) blue; **с. пигмент** cyanin; **—ее пятно** (med.) livor; **—яя болезнь** (med.) morbus caeruleus; **(светописная) —яя копия** blueprint.

синильно— *see* **синеродо—.**

синильн/ый *a.* bluing; dyeing; prussic, hydrocyanic (acid); **соль —ой кислоты** cyanide; **жёлтая —ая соль** potassium ferrocyanide; **красная —ая соль** potassium ferricyanide.

синиперка *see* **ауха.**

синистр/альный *a.* sinistral, left-sided; left-handed; **—ин** *m.* sinistrin.

синить *v.* (dye) blue.

синиц/а *f.* (orn.) tit(mouse) (*Parus*); **—а-чаичка** *f.* blackcapped chickadee; **—евые, —ы** *pl.* tit(mouse) family (*Paridae*).

синкаин *m.* Syncaine, procaine.

синкалин *m.* sincaline, choline.

синкарион *m.* (gen.) synkaryon.

синкарпий *m.* (bot.) syncarp.

синкинезия *f.* (physiol.) synkinesis.

синкл/аза *f.* (geol.) synclase; **—иналь** *f.*, **—инальная складка** syncline; **—инальный** *a.* synclinal; **—инорий** *m.* synclinorium, synclinore.

синкопа *f.* (med.) syncope, faint.

синнематин *m.* synnematin.

синов/иальный *a.* (anat.) synovial; **—иальная жидкость** synovia; **—ит** *m.* (med.) synovitis; **—ия** *f.* synovia.

синодический *a.* synodic, lunar (month).

синойкия *f.* (biol.) synoikia.

синолог *m.* Sinologist.

синоменин *m.* sinomenine.

синоним *m.* synonym; **—ический** *a.* synonymous; **—ический ряд** set of synonyms; **—ия** *f.* synonymy.

синопсис *m.* synopsis.

синопти/к *m.* synoptic meteorologist, weather forecaster; **—ка** *f.* synoptics, synoptic meteorology; **—ческий** *a.* synoptic; weather (map).

синостоз *m.* (med.) synostosis.

синтагма *f.* syntagma, group (of words).

синтакс/ис *m.* syntax; **—ический** *a.* syntactical; **—ический анализ** parsing.

синталин *m.* Synthalin.

синтез *m.* synthesis; (nucl.) fusion; **—атор** *m.* synthesizer; **—ирование** *n.* synthesis; **—ированный** *a.* synthesized; **—ировать** *v.* synthesize.

синтер *m.* sinter (cake); **—ированный** *a.* sintered; **—ировать** *v.* sinter; **—ование** *n.*, **—овочный** *a.* sintering.

синтетаз/а *f.*, **—ный** *a.* (biochem.) synthetase.

синтетический *a.* synthetic.

синт/ин *m.* synthine (synthetic mixture of hydrocarbons); **—ип** *m.* (bot.) syntype; **—ол** *m.* synthol.

синтомицин *m.* synthomycin.

синтон *m.* (chem.; biol.) synthon.

синтониз/ация *f.* syntonization, tuning; **—ированный** *a.* syntonized, tuned; **—ировать** *v.* syntonize, tune.

синтонин *m.* syntonin, muscle fibrin.

синтопия *f.* (anat.) syntopy.

синузия *f.* (biol.) synusia.

синуит *m.* (med.) sinusitis.

синус *m.* (math.) sine; (anat.) sinus; **—ит** *see* **синуит;** **—ный** *a. of* **синус;** sinusoidal (pickup); **—ово-пред-сердный** *a.* (anat.) sinoatrial, sinoauricular; **—овый** *a. of* **синус;** **—овый узел** (cardiac) pacemaker.

синусоид *m.* (hemat.; anat.) sinusoid; **—а** *f.,* **—альная кривая** (math.) sinusoid, sine curve; **—ально** *adv.* sinusoidally; **—альный** *a.* sinusoidal, sine(-shaped).

синус-счётчик *m.* (elec.) sine meter.

синфаз/ирование *n.* synphasing, cophasing, inphasing; **—ность** *f.* inphase state, cophasal state; phase coincidence; coherence; phase balance; **—ный** *a.* inphase, cophasal, cophased; coherent; **—ная антенна** phased array; **—ная составляющая** in-phase component; **—ое возбуждение** excitation in the parallel mode.

синхизит *m.* (min.) synchysite.

синхондроз *m.* (anat.) synchondrosis.

синхонин *m.* cinchonine.

синхорология *f.* (bot.) synchorology.

синхрогенератор *m.* sync generator.

синхродорожка *f.* sprocket holes.

синхрониз/атор *m.* synchronizer, synchromesh unit; **—ационный** *a.,* **—ация** *f.,* **—ирование** *n.* synchronization, synchronizing, timing; **—ированный** *a.* synchronized, simultaneous; **—ировать** *v.* synchronize, bring into step, phase-lock; **—ирующий** *a.* synchronizing; dating, master, clock (pulse).

синхронизм *m.* synchronism, simultaneous occurrence; **выше —а** hypersynchronous; **ниже —а** hyposynchronous; **приводить в с.** *v.* synchronize; **реле выпадения с —а** out-of-step relay.

синхрон/и(сти)ческий *see* **синхронный;** **—ичность** *see* **синхронность;** **—ичный** *see* **синхронный;** **—ия** *see* **синхронность;** **—но** *adv.* in synchronism (with); in step; **—оследящий** *a.* synchronous tracking; **—ность** *f.* synchronism; timing; **выпасть из —ности** get out of step; drop out of phase; **—ный** *a.* synchronous, simultaneous, coincident; parallel; **—ный генератор** (elec.) synchronous generator, alternator; **—оскоп** *m.* synchronoscope.

синхро/сигнал *m.* sync(hronizing) signal; **—скоп** *m.* (elec.) synchroscope; **—смесь** *f.* composite sync pulse; **—трон** *m.,* **—тронный** *a.* (nucl.) synchrotron; **—фазирование** *n.* phase synchronization; **—фазотрон** *m.* (nucl.) synchrophasotron, protonsynchrotron; **—циклотрон** *m.* (nucl.) synchrocyclotron (accelerator), f-m cyclotron.

синцефалон *m.* (zool.) syncephalus.

синцианин *m.* syncyanin (blue pigment).

синцитий *m.* (biol.) syncytium.

синь *f.* blue (pigment); (phyt.) blue stain; *sh. m. of* **синий;** **—га** *f.* (orn.) common scoter (*Melanitta nigra*); *see* **синец;** **—ка** *f.* blue; bluing; blueprint; **жёлтое с.-кали** potassium ferrocyanide; **красное с.-кали** potassium ferricyanide; **жёлтый с.-натр** sodium ferrocyanide; **красный с.-натр** sodium ferricyanide.

син/экология *f.* (bot.) synecology; **—энергетический** *see* **синергетический;** **—эстезия** *f.* (physiol.) synesthesia.

синэстрол *m.* Synestrol, dienestrol.

синю/ха *f.* (med.) cyanosis; (bot.) Polemonium; (ichth.) *see* **синец;** **—шка** *f.* diazo (line color) copy; (ichth.)

(young) salmon, grilse; brook trout; owsianka; **—шность** *f.* cyanosis; **—шный** *a.* cyanotic; **—шная болезнь** *see* **синяя болезнь.**

синя *sh. f. of* **синий.**

синявка *f.* (ichth.) blueback, a local name for many fishes, including salmon, pike, bleak, zope.

синяк *m.* (med.) livor, discoloration; bruise; (bot.) viper's bugloss (*Echium*).

сиомин *m.* siomine, hexamethyleneamine tetraiodide.

сип *m.* (orn.) vulture (*Gyps*); hiss(ing); croak; *past m. sing. of* **сипнуть;** **—ение** *n.* hissing; croaking; **—еть** *v.* speak hoarsely; croak; hiss.

сип/лость *f.* hoarseness; **—лый** *a.* hoarse, husky; **—нуть** *v.* get hoarse.

сиполин *see* **циполин.**

сипота *f.* hoarseness.

сипункулиды *pl.* (zool.) Sipunculoidea.

сипух/и, —овые *pl.* (orn.) barn owls (*Tytonidae*).

Сирак/узы, —ьюс (geog.) Syracuse.

сирена *f.* siren, horn; (med.) sirenomelus; (mam.) sea cow (*Sirenia*); **с. ламантин** (mam.) manatee (*Trichechus*).

сирен/евый *a.* lilac(-colored); syringic (acid); **с. альдегид** syringaldehyde; **—ь** *f.* (bot.) lilac.

сирийский *a.* Syrian.

сиринг/енин *m.* syringenin, oxymethylconiferin; **—ин** *m.* syringin, lilacin; **—ит** *m.* (med.) syringitis, inflammation of auditory tube; **—о—** *prefix* syringo— (tube, fistula); **—овая кислота** syringic acid.

сирихта *f.* (mam.) tarsier.

Сирия Syria.

сирокко *m.* s(c)irocco (wind).

сироп *m.* syrup; **—ный** *a.* syrup(y); **—ообразный** *a.* syrupy, syrup-like, viscous.

сирота *m. and f.* orphan.

сирфы *pl.* flower flies (*Syrphidae*).

сирый *a.* orphaned; abandoned.

сисаль *m.* sisal (hemp).

система *f.* system, method, scheme, arrangement, organization; set; net-work; **с. команд** (comp.) instruction set; **с. координат** (robotics) frame.

систематизация *f.* systematization; classification, filing; arrangement; **—изировать** *v.* systematize; classify, arrange, organize, file; **—ик** *m.* (biol.) taxonomist, classifier; **—ика** *m.* systematism; systemization; taxonomy, classification; **—ически** *adv.* systematically, etc., *see* **систематический;** **—ический** *a.* systematic, methodical; classified (catalog); taxonomic; constant, fixed (error); **—ическая единица** (zool.) taxon; **—ическо-предметный** *a.* classified-subject; **—ично** *adv.* systematically; **—ичность** *f.* systematic nature, order, continuity; **—ичный** *see* **систематический.**

системный *a.* (agr.) paddock (grazing); (med.) systemic.

системотехника *f.* systems engineering.

систерна *see* **цистерна.**

систокс *see* **меркаптофос.**

систол/а *f.* (physiol.) systole; **—ический** *a.* systolic.

сис/ька, —я teat, tit.

ситалл *m.* sital, devitrified glass such as Pyroceram.

ситец *m.* (text.) calico, cotton print.

ситечко *dim. of* **сито.**

ситио— *see* **сито—.**

ситник *m.* coarse white bread; (bot.) rush (*juncus*); **—овый** *a.* rush.

ситный *a.* sifted.

сито *n.* sieve, screen, riddle, bolter, sifter; **шкала сит** mesh gage.

сито— *prefix* screen, sieve; sito— (food); **—видный** *see*

ситообразный; —**видная пластинка** (zool.) cribellum (of spiders, insects); —**видная пористость** pinholes.

ситовина f. (phyt.) rot, putrefaction.

ситовник m. (bot.) Pycreus.

сито/вый a. screen, sieve; particle size (analysis); —**логия** f. sitology, dietetics; —**образный** a. cribriform, cribrose, sieve-like; screen.

сито/стан m. sitostane; —**стерин** m. sitosterol; —**токсин** m. sitotoxin, food poison.

ситочный a. sifter, sieve, screen.

ситро n. fruit drink.

ситуаци/онный a. situation(al); **с. план** site plan, layout plan; —**я** f. situation; (comp.) condition; symbolized map data.

ситус: анализ с. (math.) analysis situs.

ситце/вый a. of **ситец**; —**набивной** a., —**печатание** n., —**печатный** a. cotton printing, calico printing; —**печатник** m. cotton printer.

ситчатый a. screen; sieve (plate); sieve-plate (column); perforated (bottom); **с. барабан** revolving screen.

сиф (comm.) C.I.F. (cost, insurance, freight).

сифили/д m. (med.) syphilid, syphilitic skin lesion; —**с** m. (med.) syphilis; —**тик** m., —**тический** a. syphilitic.

сифон m. siphon; siphon trap; (air) lift; **сливать —ом** siphon (off); —**альный** see **сифонный**; —**ировать** v. siphon (off).

сифонн/ый a. siphon(al); siphonate; **с. запор, с. затвор, с. приёмник** siphon trap; **с. трубопровод, —ая трубка** siphon (tube), siphon tubing.

сифоно— prefix siphono— (siphon, tube); —**вый** a. see **сифонный**; —**гамный** a. (bot.) siphonogamous; —**стела** f. (bot.) siphonostele; —**форы** pl. (zool.) Siphonophora.

сих gen. pl. of **сей**.

сихама f. (ichth.) sihama, northern whiting.

сихнодимит m. (min.) sychnodymite.

сицилийский a. Sicilian.

Сицилия (geog.) Sicily.

сиштоф m. Si-stoff (siliceous by-product of alumina industry).

Сиэтл (geog.) Seattle.

сиюминутный a. immediate, happening right now, current; momentary.

сия f. of **сей**.

сия/ние n. shining, radiation, radiance, brilliance, shine, luminescence, glow, gleam, luster, sheen; aureole, halo; **полярное с., северное с.** aurora borealis; **южное с.** aurora australis; —**ть** shine, (e)radiate, beam; —**ющий** shining, radiant, beaming.

СК abbr. (**салициловая кислота**) salicylic acid; (**синтетический каучук**) synthetic rubber; **ск.** abbr. (**сегнетокерамика; скала; скорость**).

скабиоза f. (bot.) scabious (Scabiosa).

ска/жем (let us) say; —**занное** n. what has been said; —**занный** a. said, spoken; —**зать** v. say, speak, tell; **так —зать** so to speak; —**зуемое** n. (gram.) predicate; —**з(ыв)аться** v. tell, show up; profess to be; —**зываться благоприятно** have a favorable effect (on); —**зываться на** affect, influence.

скак/ание n. skipping, jumping; —**ательный** a. (biol.) saltatory; —**ательный сустав** ankle joint; hock; —**ать** v. skip, jump, leap, bound; gallop, lope.

скак/нуть see **скакать**; —**овой** a. racing, steeplechasing; —**ун** m. jumper; racer; —**уны** pl. tiger beetles.

скала f. rock, crag, cliff; scale (of thermometer, etc.).

скаленоэдр m. (cryst.) scalenohedron; —**ический** a. scalenohedral.

скаленэктомия f. (med.) scalenectomy, resection of scalenus muscle.

скалёпус m. (mam.) mole (Scalopus).

Скалистые горы Rocky Mountains.

скалистый a. rocky, craggy; (med.) petrous.

скалить v. show or bare (one's teeth).

скалк/а f., —**овый** a. ram, plunger; pin, rod, spindle; mangle; rolling pin; cylindrical guideway; **расточная с.** boring bar.

скало— prefix rock, saxi—.

скалозуб/овые pl. (ichth.) puffers (Tetraodontidae); —**ообразные** pl. (ichth.) triggerfishes, etc. (Tetraodontiformes); —**ые** pl. see **скалозубовые**; porcupine fishes (Diodontidae).

скалолазание n. rock climbing.

скал/ообразующий a. (geol.) petrogenic.

скалоп see **скалёпус**.

скалы pl. of **скала**; mountains.

скалыв/ание n. shearing, etc., see v.; shear (fracture), sliding fracture; (nucl.) spallation; **осколок —ания** spallation fragment; **прочность на с.** shearing strength; —**ать** v. shear (off); cleave, split off; spall, chip up; pin together; prick out (outline); —**ающий** a. shearing, etc., see v.; —**ающая сила** shearing force.

скальзывать see **скользить**.

скалькировать v. trace.

скалькулировать v. calculate, estimate.

скальнокрысиные pl. (mam.) dassie rats (Petromyidae).

скальн/ый a. of **скала**; hard, rocky (soil); (bot.) saxatile, rupestrine; —**ые работы** rock excavation.

скальол m. scagliola (imitation stone).

скальп m. scalp; —**ель** m. scalpel; —**ировать** v. scalp.

скальчатый a., **с. поршень** plunger, ram.

скаляр m., —**ный** a. (math.) scalar; —**ное произведение** dot product.

скам/еечка dim. of **скамейка**; —**ейка** f. bench.

скаммон/ий m. scammony (root); **камедь —ии** scammony resin.

скамья f. bench.

сканд. abbr. (**скандинавский**).

скандие/вый a. scandium; —**вая земля** scandia, scandium oxide; —**носный** a. scandium-bearing.

сканд/ий m. scandium, Sc; **окись —ия** scandium oxide; **хлористый с.** scandium chloride; —**ийсодержащий** a. scandium-bearing.

скандинавский a. Scandinavian.

скан(д)иров/ание n. scan(ning); —**анный** a. scanned; (med.) scanning, staccato (speech); —**овать** v. scan; —**овка** f. scan(ning).

сканирующий a. scanning.

сканистор m. (electron.) scanistor.

скань f. filigree (work).

скап m. (ichth.) scup, northern porgy.

скапавший a. trickled off.

скапаноринховые pl. (ichth.) goblin sharks (Scapanorhynchidae).

скапанус m. (mam.) mole.

скапливать v. collect, accumulate, hoard; —**ся** v. collect, accumulate, agglomerate, aggregate; pile up.

скаполит m. (min.) scapolite, wernerite; —**изация** f. scapolitization.

скапотировать v. (av.) nose over.

скапус m. scapus, stem (of feather); (hair) shaft.

скапывать v. dig off, dig away.

скар m. (ichth.) parrotfish.

скарабей *m.* scarab, dung beetle.

скарифи/катор *m.* (agr.) scarifier; **—кационный** *a.*, **—кация** *f.* scarification; **—цировать** *v.* scarify.

скарлатина *f.* (med.) scarlet fever.

скармлива/ние *m.* feeding; **с. на корню** grazing; **—ть** *v.* feed.

скарн *m.*, **—овый** *a.* (petr.) skarn (silicate contact gangue).

скаровые *pl.* (ichth.) parrotfishes (*Scaridae*).

скат *m.* slope, incline, descent, pitch, gradient, declivity; shoulder; edge (of a pulse); ramp; slide, chute, trough; rolling, sliding (down, off); (car) wheel; (ichth.) ray, skate (*Raja*); *see also* **скаты**; (anat.) clivus; **—ать** *v.* roll up; felt, mat.

скатерт/ный *a.*, **—ь** *f.* tablecloth.

скат/ить *v.* roll down; rinse off, sluice; **—иться** *v.* roll down, slide down; be rinsed off; **—ка** *f.* rolling down, sliding down; rolling up; roll; felting, matting; **—ный** *a.* ramp, slide.

скато— *prefix* scato—, skato— (feces); **—вые** *see* **скаты**; **—ксил** *m.* skatoxyl; **—л** *m.* (chem.) skatole, methylindole.

скаты *pl. of* **скат**; (ichth.) Batoidei (skates, rays, torpedoes, guitarfishes, sawfishes, etc.).

скатыв/ание *n.* rolling up, etc., *see v.*; **угол —ания** angle of pitch; (geol.) angle of dip; **—ать(ся)** *v.* roll up; mat, felt; roll down, roll off, slide down; rinse, sluice (off); (ichth.) migrate (downstream).

скафандр *m.* pressure suit, (space) suit; diving suit; clean bench, (laminar-flow) booth.

скафо— *prefix* scapho— (boat-shaped); **—цефалический** *a.* (med.) scaphocephalic.

скача *gerund* skipping, etc., *see* **скакать**.

скач/анный *a.* pumped (off, out); **—ать** *v.* pump (off, out).

скаченный *a.* run-off, tapped, skimmed, slagged (off); sluiced; rolled down.

скачет *pr. 3 sing. of* **скакать**.

скачив/ание *n.* skimming, etc., *see v.*; **—ать** *v.* skim, draw off, tap, drain off, run off, slag off; pump (off, out); rinse, sluice off; flush (slag).

скачк/а *gen. of* **скачок**; *f.* gallop(ing); **—ами** *instr. pl. of* **скачок**; **—и** *pl. of* **скачок**; horse race, racing; **—овый** *a.* saltatory; **—ом** *instr. sing. of* **скачок**; *adv.* abruptly, discontinuously, stepwise.

скачкообразн/о *adv.* by leaps or jumps, jumpwise; spasmodically; **—ость** *f.* spasmodic nature, irregularity, unevenness; **—ый** *a.* spasmodic, jerky, uneven, intermittent; jump, step (function, etc.); (comp.) unit step (input); jump-type, abrupt (process); **—ая перестройка частоты** (commun.) frequency hopping; **—ая работа** skipping.

скач/ок *m.* jump, skip, leap, spring, bound; (math.) saltus; sudden change, drop; step, break, discontinuity (in curve); (potential) difference; shock; (unit) step input; (biol.; med.) saltation; **с. уплотнения** shock (wave); compression wave; **замыкающий с.** terminal shock (wave); **плоский с.** step-shock; **развитие —ками** (biol.) saltatory evolution; **слой —ка** layer of discontinuity; **температурный с.** thermocline; **течение за прямым —ком** flow through a normal shock wave; **—ки** *pl.* skipping; **—ками** in jumps; in stages or steps, by degrees, gradually; **движение —ками** galloping motion; **—ут** *pr. 3 pl. of* **скакать**; **—ущий** *a.* jumping; (med.) saltatory (gait).

скашив/ание *n.* sloping, etc., *see v.*; **с. под углом** beveling; **—ать** *v.* slope, bevel, chamfer, cant, cut aslant, skive, shave off, pare; (agr.) mow down.

СКБ *abbr.* (**синтетический каучук, бутадиеновый**) synthetic butadiene rubber.

скваж/ина *f.* pore, aperture, chink, slit, gap, interstice, rift; (bore; key) hole; well; **боевая с.** emplacement hole (for underground nuclear test); **со —инами** porous; **с.-водоисточник** *f.* water-supply well; **с.-шахта** *f.* shaft well; **—инный** *a. of* **скважина**; well-drilling; **—истость** *f.* porosity; **—истый** *a.* porous; blown; slit(ted); **—ность** *f.* porosity; duty factor; (rad.) on-off (time) ratio; (phys.) relative duration (of pulse); **—ный** *see* **скважистый**.

сквален *m.* squalene, spinacene.

сквамозный *a.* squamous, scaly.

сква/сить *see* **сквашивать**; **—шенный** *a.* fermented, sour(ed); **—шивать** *v.* let sour.

сквер *m.* (city) square, plaza.

скверн/о *adv.* badly, poorly; **ему с.** he is not well; **—ый** *a.* bad, poor.

скверхедный *a.* squarehead (wheat).

сквидж *m.* squeegee, intermediate rubber layer.

сквоз/истый *a.* drafty; not light-tight; **—ить** *v.* blow through; pass, penetrate, show through (of light), shine; not be light-tight; **—ит** there is a draft.

сквозн/ой *a.* through (hole; road; trip); open (weave, etc.); thin (forest); not light-tight; (comp.) ripple-through (carry); **с. ветер** *see* **сквозняк**; **с. камень** (horol.) jewel hole; **—ая коррозия** (met.) perforation; **—ая прокаливаемость** complete penetration hardenability; **—ая работа** (min.) open cut; **—як** *m.* draft, current of air.

сквозь *adv. and prep. acc.* through.

сквор/ец *m.* (orn.) starling (*Sturnus*); myna (*Acridotheres*); **—цовые**, **—цы** *pl.* starling family (*Sturnidae*).

скег *m.* (naut.) skeg (of keel).

скелет *m.* skeleton, frame, shell; **внутренний с.** endoskeleton; **наружный с.** exoskeleton; **—ирование** *n.* skeletonization (of foliage); (med.) extreme emaciation; **—ный** *a.* skeleton, frame; skeletal; **—ная кривая** (comp.) backbone; **—ное вещество** (cyt.; hist.) ground substance.

скеп/сис, **—тицизм** *m.*, **—тичность** *f.* skepticism; **—тик** *m.* skeptic; **—тический**, **—тичный** *a.* skeptical.

скептрон *m.* (electron.) sceptron, spectral comparative pattern recognizer.

скерда *f.* (bot.) Crepis.

скетч *m.* sketch.

СКИ *abbr.* (**синтетический каучук, изопреновый**) synthetic isoprene rubber.

скиа— *prefix* skia— (shadow); **—метр** *m.* skiameter, actinometer.

скиатический *a.* (anat.) sciatic.

скиатрон *m.* (elec.) skiatron, dark trace tube.

скид *m.* pallet, skid.

скидать *see* **скидывать**.

скиддер *m.* skidder.

скид/ка *f.*, **—ывание** *n.* throwing off; allowance, reduction, deduction, discount, rebate; **—ывать** *v.* allow, reduce, deduct; throw off, cast off; take off (clothes).

скимкоультер *m.* (agr.) skim colter.

скин-слой *m.* skin layer.

скинут/ый *a.* deducted; thrown off, cast off; **—ь** *see* **скидывать**.

скин-эффект *m.* (elec.) skin effect.

скио— *prefix* skio— (shade); sci(o)— (shadow); **—фильный** *a.* (zool.) sciophil(ous).

скип/аться, **—еться** *v.* sinter together.

скипджек *m.* (ichth.) skipjack (tuna).

скипидар *m.*, —**ный** *a.* turpentine.

скирд *m.*, —**а** *f.* stack, rick (of hay, etc.); —**овальный** *a.*, —**ование** *n.* stacking, etc., *see v.*; —**ованный** *a.* stacked, etc., *see v.*; —**овать** *v.* stack, rick, pile up; —**овка** *see* **скирдование.**

скирр *m.* (med.) scirrhus.

скис/ание *n.* souring, acidification; —**ать** *v.* (turn) sour, curdle.

С-кислота S acid.

скиснуть *see* **скисать.**

скиф *m.* skiff (boat); Scythian.

скифский ярус (geol.) Scythian stage.

скицировать *v.* sketch, draft.

склад *m.* warehouse, storehouse; (mil.) depot, dump; (lumber) yard; storage, store, stock; habit; physique; mentality; **с. ядерного оружия** nuclear weapons stockpile; **на** —**е** in storage, in stock; —**альный** *a.* storage, storing; —**ень** *m.* hinged, folding object such as a folding knife (**нож-складень**) or chair (**стул-складень**); —**ирование** *n.* storage, warehousing, stockpiling; —**ировать** *v.* store, stockpile.

складк/а *f.* crease, wrinkle, fold, lap, crimp, crinkle, crumple, corrugation, plica(tion); (geol.) fold; ridge; (text.) pleat; **с. местности** (geol.) natural feature; **точка** —**и** plait point (in solubility curve); **с.-взброс, с.-надвиг** *f.* (geol.) overthrust, upthrust fold; **с.-сброс** *f.* fault fold; **с.-сдвиг** *f.* overthrust; —**овыпрямление** *n.* unfolding; —**ообразный** *a.* pliciform; —**ообразование** *n.* folding, fold formation.

складк/ой *a.* folding, collapsible, portable; —**ая линейка** folding rule.

складн/ость *f.* coherence; —**ый** *a.* coherent, well-ordered; well-built.

склад/ок *gen. pl.*; —**очка** *dim.* of **складка.**

складочн/ый *a.* of **склад**; —**ое место** storehouse; (mil.) dump.

складск/ой *a.* warehouse; —**ое хозяйство** stores, supply department.

складчат/о— *prefix* plicato—, ptych(o)— (fold, layer); —**озуб** *m.* free-tailed bat (*Tadarida*); —**ость** *f.* (geol.) folding, puckering; —**ый** *a.* folded, plicate(d), fluted; wrinkled.

складыв/аемое *n.* (math.) addend; —**ание** *n.* adding, addition, etc., *see v.*; —**ать** *v.* add (up), sum up; combine, put together, build up; make up, compose; pack, fold (up), collapse, jackknife; accumulate, pile (up), store; —**аться** *v.* be added, etc.; add up; consist (of); pool (resources); fold, collapse; —**ающий** *a.* adding, etc., *see v.*

скле/енный *a.* glued, etc., *see v.*; agglutinate; compound (lens); —**ивание** *n.* gluing, etc., *see v.*; agglutination; —**ивать** *v.* glue, cement, paste, stick, bond (together); splice; size, dress; agglutinate; conglutinate; (math.) join; —**иваться** *v.* be glued, etc.; adhere; —**ивающий** *a.* gluing, etc., *see v.*; adhesive; —**ивающее вещество** adhesive; agglutinant; —**ить** *see* **склеивать;** —**йка** *see* **склеивание;** splice; adhesive joint; (comp.) patch; (math.) joining, matching.

склёпанный *a.* riveted (together).

склепать *see* **склёпывать.**

склёп/ка *see* **склёпывание;** —**машина** *f.* riveting machine; —**очный** *a.* riveting; —**ывание** *n.* riveting, fastening; —**ывать** *v.* rivet (together), fasten; —**ывающий** *a.* riveting.

склер— *prefix* **склеро**—; —**а** *f.* (anat.) sclera; —**еида** *f.* (bot.) sclereid, grit cell; —**енхима** *f.* (biol.) sclerenchyma; —**ит** *m.* (med.) scleritis; (zool.) sclerite.

склеро— *prefix* sclero— (hard); —**з** *m.* (med.; bot.)

sclerosis, hardening; **рассеянный** —**з** (med.) multiple sclerosis; —**зированный** *a.* sclerosed; —**зный** *a.* sclerous, hard; —**ма** *f.* (med.) scleroma; —**метрический** *a.* sclerometric; —**номный** *a.* scleronomic.

склеропротеин *m.* scleroprotein.

склероскоп *m.* scleroscope.

склероспороз *m.* (phyt.) sclerosporosis.

склероти/ка *f.* (anat.) sclerotic; —**ниоз** *m.* (phyt.) Sclerotinia rot; —**ния** *f.* (phyt.) Sclerotinia; —**новый** *a.* sclerot(in)ic (acid); —**ческий** *a.* (med.; bot.) sclerotic, sclerosed.

склеротомия *f.* (med.) sclerotomy.

склероций *m.* (bot.) sclerotium.

склиз *m.* slide; (text.) (shuttle) race; —**кий** *a.* slippery, slimy; —**ок** *m.* hide of unborn calf.

склон *m.* slope, (hill)side, descent, decline, declivity, embankment (of canal, etc.), flank (of volcano); **вверх по** —**у** uphill; —**ение** *n.* slope, incline, inclination, declivity, dip, pitch, hade (of an ore vein); depression; declination, deflection, variation; (gram.) declension; **магнитное** —**ение** magnetic declination; **стрелка** —**ения** (geol.) dip needle; —**ённый** *a.* inclined, sloped; —**ить** *v. see* **склонять.**

склонн/ость *f.* inclination, tendency, (pre)disposition, propensity, bent, leaning, taste, aptitude, affinity; **иметь с.** *v.* tend, be inclined (to); **с. к заболеваниям** susceptibility to diseases; —**ый** *a.* inclined, (pre)disposed, prone, ready (to).

склоновый *a.* of **склон**; surface (flow).

склоноход *m.* ramp.

склон/ять *v.* incline, bend, bias; —**яться** *v.* dip, incline, bend; yield, comply; be disposed (to), tend (to); —**яющийся** *a.* dipping, etc., *see v.*

склянка *f.* phial, vial, flask, bottle; (naut.) bell, half-hour interval; half-hour interval; (ocean.) brackish ice crust; black ice; **с.-моностат** *f.* pressure gage.

скоб/а *f.* cramp (iron), clamp, cleat, clinch(er); bracket, brace, frame; hook, fastening, strap, catch, claw, detent, detainer; buckle; clip; staple; stirrup, shackle, yoke, link; **измерительная с., калиберная с.** external gage, horseshoe gage, snap gage; **прибить** —**ами** *v.* staple; **скрепить** —**ой** *v.* cramp, clamp; **соединение** —**ой** clasp joint.

скобель *m.* scraper, draw knife.

скобк/а *f.* bracket; *see also* **скоба; брать в** —**и** *v.* bracket; **квадратные** —**и** brackets; **круглые** —**и** parentheses; **фигурные** —**и** braces.

скобл/ение *n.* scraping, etc., *see v.*; abrasion; —**ен(н)ый** *a.* scraped, etc., *see v.*; —**ильный** *a.* scraping, scrape; —**ильный инструмент** scraper; —**ить** *v.* scrape, smooth, plane, shave, pare; file; gouge; (med.) scarify.

скобо/к *gen. pl.* of **скобка**; —**образный** *a.* bracket-shaped; (met.) brace-test (bar); —**чка** *dim.* of **скоб(к)а**; —**чный** *a.* of **скоб(к)а**; —**чная машина** stapler.

скобяной товар hardware.

сков/анность *f.* (med.) constraint, stiffness, paralysis; —**анный** *a.* forged, welded (together); (ice-)bound; —**ать** *see* **сковывать.**

сковка *see* **сковывание.**

сковорода *f.* (frying) pan; (elec.) grill.

сковород/ень, —ник *m.*, **соединение в с.** dovetail (joint); **вязка** —**нем, соединение** —**нем** dovetailing.

сковыв/ание *n.* forging, etc., *see v.*; —**ать** *v.* forge, weld (together); chain, bind; (mil.) hold, paralyze, immobilize; cover with ice, lock (by freezing); —**аться** *v.* be forged, etc.; freeze over.

сковыр/ивать, —нуть, —ять *v.* pick at (scab).

скок *m.* jump(ing), hop(ping), leap(ing).

скол *see* **скалывание;** chip; spalling; cleavage face.

сколачивать *v.* knock together, put together; knock off, strike off.

сколеко— *prefix* scolec(o)— (worm); **—спора** *f.* (bot.) scolecospore.

сколекс *m.* (zool.) scolex (of tapeworm).

скол/ии *pl.* (ent.) Scoliidae; **—и(о)—** *prefix* scoli(o)— (twisted, crooked; curvature); **—иодоновый** *a.* scoliodonic (acid); **—иоз** *m.* (med.) scoliosis; **—иотический** *a.* scoliotic; **—ит** *m.* (ent.) Scolytus.

скол/ка *f.* chipping off, knocking off; pricking out (of pattern); **—ок** *m.* pricked pattern, pricked tracing; copy; chip.

сколопидий *m.* (ent.) scolopidium.

сколотина *f.* buttermilk.

сколотить *see* **сколачивать.**

сколоть *see* **скалывать.**

сколоченный *past pass. part. of* **сколотить;** cohesive.

сколуп/нуть, —(ыв)ать *v.* scrape off.

сколь *see* **сколько; с. бы** *adv.* no matter how (small, etc.); **с. угодно малый** as small as one likes, arbitrarily small.

скольжен/ие *n.* slipping, etc., *see* **скользить;** slip, slide; launching (of ship); stroke (of piston); **боковое с.** side-slip(ping); **зеркало —ия** (geol.) slickenside(s); **кривая —ия** slip curve; **плоскость —ия** sliding surface; **подшипник —ия** sliding bearing; **угол —ия** angle of slide; glancing angle, grazing angle, Bragg angle.

скольз/ить *v.* slip, slide, skid; glide, skim (over); **—кий** *a.* slippery; **—ко** *adv.* (it is) slippery; **—кость** *f.* slipperiness, lubricity, lubricating power; **—ун** *m.* slipper, slide block, guide shoe; **—ящий** *a.* slipping, etc., *see v.*; slipper, slide (block); varying; nonlocalized (vector); glancing (blow); (med.) accordion (graft); **—ящий полёт** gliding; **—ящий сустав** (anat.) saddle joint; **метод —ящих средних** moving-average method.

сколько *adv.* how much, how many? **с. ни** however; **с. раз** how often? **с. столько** as much as, as many as; **с.-нибудь** any (amount); **с.-то** some (amount).

скольтер *m.* (agr.) colter.

скомандовать *v.* order, command.

скомбинировать *v.* combine.

скомбрин *m.* scombrine.

скомк/анный *a.* wrinkled, crumpled; **—ать** *v.* wrinkle, crumple; hurry through, do hastily.

скомпенсировать *v.* compensate.

скомпилировать *v.* compile, collect.

скомплектов/анный *a.* made up (of); staffed; (mach.) gang(ed);**—ать** *v.* make up (a set); staff.

скомпоновать *v.* compose, combine, arrange, put together.

сконденсировать *v.* condense.

сконструиров/анный *a.* constructed, etc., *see v.*; **—ать** *v.* construct, design, engineer, develop; pattern (after).

сконфузить *v.* confuse, disconcert.

С-концевой *m.* (chem.) C-terminal.

сконцентрировать *v.* concentrate.

сконч/авшийся *a.* defunct; deceased; extinct; **—аться** *v.* finish; die.

скоординировать *v.* coordinate.

скопа *f.* (orn.) osprey.

скопарин *m.* scoparin.

скопать *v.* scrape off (by digging).

скопелеевые *pl.* lanternfishes (*Myctophidae*).

скопец *m.* (zool.) eunuch, castrate.

скопившийся *a.* accumulated.

скопиные *pl.* (orn.) osprey family (*Pandionidae*).

скопировать *v.* copy.

скопить *v.* castrate; *see also* **скапливать.**

скопище *n.* crowd (of people).

скопл/ение *n.* accumulation, heap, mass, aggregate; aggregation, stock, conglomeration, agglomerate, congregation, congestion, concentration, crowding, piling, pile(-up), build-up; cluster (of points); (iceberg) herd; swarm, flock; reflux (of steam); (geol.) segregation; (med.) afflux; **—енный** *a.* accumulated, collected; **—яемый** *a.* (ac)cumulative; **—ять** *see* **скапливать.**

скопнить *v.* stack (hay, etc.).

скопол/амин *m.* scopolamine, hyoscine; **—еин** *m.* scopoleine; **—етин** *m.* scopoletin, chrysatropic acid; **—ил** *m.* scopolyl; **—ин** *m.* scopoline; **—иновый** *a.* scopolic (acid); **—ия** *f.* (bot.) Scopolia.

скопом *adv.* together, jointly, en masse.

скопометр *m.* (opt.) scopometer; **—ия** *f.* scopometry.

скопы *pl. of* **скопа,** Pandionidae.

скор *sh. m. of* **скоры.**

скорбный *a.* doleful.

скорбут *m.* (med.) scurvy; **—ный** *a.* scorbutic.

скорбь *f.* sorrow; **мировая с.** Weltschmerz, sentimental pessimism.

скорее *comp. of* **скоро; скорый** sooner, more quickly; rather, preferably; **с. всего** most likely, probably; **как можно с.** as soon as possible.

скорифика/тор *m.* (assaying) scorifier; **—ция** *f.* scorification.

скорлуп/а *f.* (nut)shell, hull, testa; (biol.) putamen; crust; **—ка** *dim. of* **скорлупа; —ный** *a.* shell(y); crustaceous; **—няковый** *a.* (zool.) crustacean; **—оватый** *a.* shell(y); (geol.) conchoidal (structure); **—оватое отслоение** peeling; **—овый** *a.* testaceous, crustacean; **—овая железа** (crust.) maxillary gland; **—ообразный, —чатый** *a.* shell-like, shell-shaped, conchoidal.

скорм *m.* feeding; consumption (of food); **—ить** *v.* feed, give; use up; **—ленный** *a.* fed; used.

скорня/жить *v.* dress furs; trade in furs; **—(жни)чество** *n.* fur dressing; fur trading; **—жный** *a.* fur(rier); **—к** *m.* furrier, fur dresser.

скоро *adv.* soon, promptly, quickly, speedily, rapidly, at a rapid rate; *prefix* quick, rapid, fast.

скоробить *v.* warp, distort.

скороварка *f.* pressure cooker.

скорода *f.* (bot.) chives.

скороморозил/ка *f.* freezer; **—ьный** *a.* freezer; quick-freezing.

скоропашка *f.* (agr.) cultivator.

скоропись *f.* cursive (writing).

скороплодн/ость *f.* early maturity; **—ый** *a.* early-maturing.

скороподъёмность *f.* rate of climb.

скоропортящийся *a.* perishable.

скоропостижный *a.* sudden (death).

скоропреходящий *a.* transitory, short-lived, ephemeral.

скороспел/ка *f.* early-maturing fruit or plant; *f. and m.* prodigy; **—ость** *f.* early ripening, earliness; precociousness; **—ый** *a.* early(-ripening); premature; precocious; praecox.

скорост/емер *m.* speedometer; **—еуменьшитель** *m.* reducing gear; **—ник** *m.* specialist in high-speed methods; fast worker; **—ной** *a.* (high-)velocity, high-speed, rapid, fast; accelerated (training); one-step (process); kinetic; dynamic (friction); impact (tube); rate (equation, etc.); while-you-wait.

скорострельн/ость *f.* (art.) rate of fire; **—ый** *a.* rapid-firing, quick-firing.

скорост/ь *f.* velocity, speed, pace, rapidity, rate; **с. хода** speed; **замедлять с.** *v.* slow down, decelerate; **измеритель —и** speedometer; **коробка —ей** gear box, gear case; **набирать с., развивать с.** *v.* gain speed, speed up, accelerate, gain momentum; **с переменной —ью** variable-speed; **снижать с.** *v.* decelerate; **указатель —и** speedometer.

скоротечн/ость *f.* transience, short duration, rapidity; **—ый** *a.* transient, short-lived, brief, fast; (med.) fulminant; galloping (consumption).

скоросшиватель *m.* binder (for papers).

скорпен/овые *pl.* (ichth.) scorpionfishes (*Scorpaenidae*); **—ообразные** *pl.* (ichth.) Scorpaeniformes; **—ы** *see* **скорпеновые**.

скорпио/идный *a.* scorpioid, coiled like a scorpion's tail; **—н** *m.* (zool.) scorpion; **морской —н** (ichth.) greater weever (*Trachinus draco*); **—ницы** *pl.*, **—овые мухи** scorpion flies (*Mecoptera*).

скорректировать *v.* correct.

скоррелировать *v.* correlate.

скорца *f.* scorza (epidote sand).

скорцонера *f.* (bot.) Scorzonera.

скорчинг *m.* (rubber) scorching.

скорчиться *v.* writhe (in pain).

скор/ый *a.* fast, quick, speedy, rapid, swift; first (aid); approaching, impending; express (transportation); **в —ом времени** soon, in a short time, before long.

скос *m.* bevel, chamfer(ing), slope, slant(ing), incline; taper(ing); feather (wedge); skewback (of propeller blade); (agr.) mowing; **с. потока вверх** (av.) upwash; **с. потока (вниз)** downwash; **коэффициент —а пазов** (elec.) skew factor.

скосарь *m.* (ent.) weevil (*Otiorrhynchus*).

скосить *see* **скашивать**.

скособочиться *v.* list, tilt, cant, be lopsided.

скот *m.* cattle, livestock; **горбатый с.** zebu (*Bos indicus*); **—ина** *f.*, **—иний** *a.* cattle, livestock; **—ник** *m.* cowman, cowhand; **—ный** *a.* cattle, livestock.

ското— *prefix* cattle; **scoto—** (darkness); **—бойня** *f.* slaughter house, abattoir; **—вод** *m.* cattle breeder; **—водство** cattle breeding; **—водческий** *a.* cattle (ranch).

скотография *f.* scotography.

скотозаготовка *f.* state purchase of cattle.

скотома *f.* (med.) scotoma.

ското/могильник *m.* burial ground for animal refuse.

скотопия *f.* (physiol.) night vision.

ското/приёмный *a.* cattle-receiving; **—прогонный** *a.* cattle-driving; **—промышленность** *f.* cattle trade, cattle industry.

скотопсин *m.* (biochem.) scotopsin.

скотосбрасыватель *m.* (rr.) cowcatcher.

скотоскопия *f.* (med.) skiascopy, fluoroscopy.

ското/сырьё *n.* beef cattle; **—торговец** *m.* cattle dealer; **—убойный** *a.* cattle-slaughtering.

скотофобия *f.* scotophobia, fear of the dark.

скотский *a.* cattle, livestock.

Скотта способ (analysis) Scott method.

скофтальмус *m.* (ichth.) turbot (*Scophthalmus*).

скошенн/ый *a.* chamfered, bevel(ed), tapered, canted, biased, skewed, sloped, tilted, oblique, slanted; mitered; mowed (grass); **—ая окклюзия** torsiversion (of tooth).

СКР *abbr.* (**спектр комбинационного рассеяния**) Raman spectrum.

скраб *m.* (bot.) scrub, sclerophyllous bush formation.

скрадывать *v.* conceal, hide; make less noticeable, minimize; muffle (sound); **—ся** *v.* become less noticeable.

скрайбер *m.* (carpentry) scriber.

скрап *m.* scrap (iron); **с.-процесс** (met.) scrap process; **—ный двор** scrap stockyard, scrap pile.

Скраупа синтез (chem.) Skraup synthesis.

скреб *m.* (forestry) scrub, bush.

скрёб *past m. sing. of* **скрести**.

скребень *m.* (zool.) proboscis worm.

скребка *gen. of* **скребок**.

скрёбка *f.* scraper; currycomb.

скреб/ово-ковшовый *a.* scraper (conveyer); **—овый** *a.* scraper, scraping; drag (screen); rake (classifier); **—овый ковш** scraper; **—овый конвейер, —овый транспортер** drag conveyer, rake conveyer, scraper conveyer.

скреб/ли *past pl. of* **скрести**; **—ло** *n.* strickle; doctor, scraping knife; **—машина** *f.* scraper, dehairer (for hides); **—ни** *pl. of* **скребень**; **—ни(-колючего-ловые)** (zool.) Acanthocephala; **—ница** *f.* scrubbing brush; currycomb; **—ной** *a.* scraper; **—нуть** *see* **скрести**; **—ок** *m.* scraper, scrubber; rabble(r); trowel; **скрёбок** *gen. pl. of* **скрёбка**; **—ут** *pr. 3 pl. of* **скрести**; **—ущий** *a.* scraping.

скрежать *v.* grind, gnash (teeth).

скрепа *f.* tie, clamp, clip, clinch, fastener; union, coupling, splice; fastening (together); brace; authentication; **за —ой** countersigned.

скрепер *m.* scraper; **—ист** *m.* scraper operator; **—ный** *a. of* **скрепер**.

скреп/ить *see* **скреплять**; **—ка** *dim. of* **скрепа**; (paper) clip; **—ление** *n.* fastening, etc., *see v.*; reinforcement; scarf, splice, joint, connection; attachment; brace, bond; knitting (of bones); (mil.) hooping; countersignature; **—лённый** *a.* fastened, etc., *see v.*; **—лять** *v.* fasten, make fast, fix, secure; clamp, hold together, tighten; tie, bind, bond, cement, joint, couple, splice; brace, strengthen, reinforce; ratify; countersign; **—лять болтами** bolt together; **—ляющий, —очный** *a.* fastening, etc., *see v.*; **—ляющая машина** stapler.

скрести *v.* scrape, scrub; rake; torment; scratch, claw.

скре/стить *see* **скрещивать**; **—щение** *see* **скрещивание**; **—щённый** *a.* crossed, etc., *see v.*; (biol.) hybrid; cruciate; **—щиваемость** *f.* capacity for hybridization; **—щивание** *n.* crossing, etc., *see v.*; junction; hybridization; (bot.) cross pollination; **родственное —щивание** inbreeding; **—щивать(ся)** *v.* cross (over), twist; intersect; interlace; interbreed, crossbreed, mate; hybridize; **—щивающий(ся)** *a.* crossing, etc., *see v.*

скрив/ить, —лять *v.* bend, twist, warp; **—лённый** *a.* twisted, warped.

скрип *m.* creak, squeaking; **—ение** *n.* creaking; **—еть** *v.* creak, grate, squeak; grind (one's teeth); **пёстрая —ица** parasol mushroom (*Lepiota procera*).

скрипк/а *f.* violin; **—овидный** *a.* fiddle-shaped, pandurate.

скрип/нуть *see* **скрипеть**; **—ун** *m.* long-horned beetle (*Saperda*); (bot.) orpine (*Sedum telephium*); **—учий** *a.* creaking, creaky, crepitant, squeaky, grating, grinding.

скристаллизовать(ся) *v.* crystallize.

скроенный *a.* cut out (by pattern).

скроет *fut. 3 sing. of* **скрыть**.

скроить *v.* cut out (by pattern).

скролл/ер *m.* (comp.) scroll bar; **—инг** *m.* scrolling; **линейка —инга** scroll bar.

скромный *a.* modest, plain.

скротум *m.* (anat.) scrotum.

скрофул/ёз *m.* (med.) scrofula; **—одерма** *f.* scrofuloderma.

скрош/енный *a.* crumbled; **—иться** *v.* crumble.

скроющий *pr. act. part. of* **скрыть.**

скруб *m.* (forestry) scrub, bush.

скруббер *m.* (gas) scrubber, washer; **—ный** *a.* scrubber; scrubbing.

скругл/ение *n.* rounding (off), roundness, curvature, bending radius; **внутренее с.** (met.) fillet; **—ённый** *a.* rounded (off); **—ить, —ять** *v.* round (off).

скрупул *m.* (pharm.) scruple (1.296 gram); **—ёзный** *a.* scrupulous, meticulous.

скрут/ить *see* **скручивать; —ка** *f.* twist(ing); twist joint; joining; splice; **шаг —ки** lay (of cable).

скрученн/о— *prefix* torti— (twisted); strept(o)— (twisted, curved); **—ость** *f.* twistedness; torsion; **—ые** *pl.* (bot.) Contortae.

скруч/енный *a.* twisted, etc., *see v.*; **—иваемость** *f.* (paper) curl; **—ивание** *n.* twisting, etc., *see v.*; torsion; torque failure, twist-off; (phys.; chem.) distortion; contortion; kink; (leaf) curl, roll; **момент —ивания** torque; **прочность на —ивание** torsional strength; **угол —ивания** angle of twist; **—ивать** *v.* twist (together), twine, contort; spin; coil, roll up, curl; buckle, warp; **—ивающий** *a.* twisting, etc., *see v.*; torsion(al); **—ивающий момент** torque, torsional moment; **—ивающая сила, —ивающее усилие** torque, torsional force.

скрыв/ание *n.* concealment, hiding; (mil.) camouflaging; **—ать** *v.* conceal, hide, secrete; camouflage; **—аться** *v.* hide, vanish, disappear; be, occur; **—ающий** *a.* screening, concealing; **—ающийся** *a.* disappearing, vanishing; concealed.

скрын/ица, —я *f.* box, bin, trunk.

скрыт/ие *see* **скрывание; —ники** *pl.* (ent.) Lathridiidae; **—но** *adv.* secretly; *prefix see* **скрыто—; —ноеды** *pl.* (ent.) Cryptophagidae; **—ность** *f.* secrecy, security; concealment; **—ность действия** (mil.) stealth; **—нохоботник** *m.* (ent.) weevil (*Ceutorrhynchus* or *Cryptorhynchus*); **—ный** *a.* concealed, hidden, secret(ive).

скрыто— *prefix* crypto— (hidden); **—генетический** *a.* cryptogenetic; **—жаберные** *pl.* (zool.) Cryptobranchia; **—зернистый** *a.* cryptomerous; (geol.) cryptoplastic, compact; **—корешковый** *a.* (bot.) endorhizal; **—кристаллический** *a.* cryptocrystalline, microcrystalline; **—письменногранитный** *a.* (petr.) cryptographic; **—подзолистый** *a.* cryptopodzolic (soil); **—семянные** *pl.* (bot.) Angiospermae; **—ух** *m.* (mam.) shrew (*Cryptotis*); **—хоботник** *see* **скрытнохоботник.**

скрыт/ый *a.* hidden, concealed, obscured, secret, occult, cryptic; masked (diabetes); saphenous (vein, etc.); latent (heat, image); buried, underground (cable); stored, potential (energy); insidious (disease); **с. период** (med.) incubation; lag-phase; **—ое состояние** latency, latent state; **—ь** *see* **скрывать.**

скрэб *m.* (forestry) scrub, bush(es).

скручи(ва)ть *v.* twist, bend, warp.

скудель *f.* (potter's) clay.

скуд/(н)еть *v.* grow poor, thin (out), decline, diminish; **—но** *adv.* sparsely; **—(н)ость** *f.* sparseness, etc., *see a.*; scarcity; **—ный** *a.* sparse, scarce, scanty; poor, meager, lean (ore); bare, barren (soil); small, short.

скука *f.* boredom, tedium.

скул/а *f.* (anat.) cheekbone, zygoma; (naut.) bilge; **—атник** *m.* (bot.) polypody; **—ить** *v.* whimper; whine; **—овисочный** *a.* zygomaticotemporal; **—овой** *a.* (anat.) zygomatic; (naut.) bilge; **—овая кость** cheekbone, zygoma; **—оглазничный** *a.* zygomaticoorbital; **—олобный** *a.* zygomaticofrontal.

скульпт/ор *m.* sculptor; **—ура** *f.* sculpture, statuary;

(pal.) ornamentation; **—урный** *a.* sculptural, plastic; modeling (clay).

скумбр/ещуковые *pl.* (ichth.) sauries, skippers (*Scomberecidae*); **—иевидные** *pl.* (ichth.) Scombroidei; **—иевые** *pl.* mackerels and tunas (*Scombridae*); **—иевый** *a.*, **—ия** *f.* (ichth.) mackerel.

скумпия *f.* (bot.) smoke tree (*Cotinus*).

скунс *m.*, **—овый** *a.* (zool.) skunk (*Mephitis*).

скуп *sh. m. of* **скупой.**

скупать *v.* buy up, corner.

скупит *m.* (min.) schoepite.

скупить *see* **скупать.**

скупиться *v.* stint, be sparing, grudge.

скуп/ка *f.*, **—ной** *a.* buying up, cornering.

скуп/ой *a.* sparse, poor, meager; sparing, niggardly, stingy; **—ость** *f.* sparseness, etc., *see a.*

скуп/очный *a. of* **скупка; —щик** *m.* buyer.

скутелл/арин *m.* scutellarin; **—ум** *m.* (bot.; zool.) scutellum.

скутер *m.* scooter, outboard-motor boat.

скутум *m.* (bot.; zool.) scutum.

скуч/ать *v.* be bored; feel dull; mope; miss, long (for); **—ен** *sh. m. of* **скучный.**

скученн/ость *f.* congestion, overcrowding; density; **—ый** *a.* congested, crowded, packed, densely clustered, close; conglomerate; dense, compact.

скуч/ивание *n.* crowding, etc., *see v.*; **—и(ва)ть** *v.* crowd, pack, pile together, box up; heap, accumulate; assemble; **—и(ва)ться** *v.* flock together, assemble.

скучн/еть *v.* become melancholy; mope; **—о** *adv. of* **скучный; ему —о** he is bored; **—ый** *a.* tedious, dull; sad.

скушать *v.* eat up.

сл *abbr.* (**сантилитр**) centiliter.

сл *abbr.* (**слабо; следующий; слово**).

СЛ *abbr.* (**соединительная линия**) junction line.

слаб *sh. m. of* **слабый; —еть** *v.* weaken, grow weaker, slacken; diminish, run down; **—еющий** *a.* weakening, wilting; **—ина** *f.* weak spot; slack, sag; **—инка** *dim. of* **слабина.**

слабит/ельное *n.*, **—ельный** *a.* laxative, purgative; cathartic; **—ь** *v.* purge.

слаблинь *m.* (naut.) lacing line.

слабнуть *v.* become weak, weaken.

слабо *adv. and prefix* weakly, feebly, slightly, mildly; loosely; poorly; sub—; astheno— (weak); **очень с.** barely, scarcely; **—активный** *a.* mildly active; (nucl.) warm; **—видение** *n.* poor eyesight; **—возбуждённый** *a.* (elec.) feebly excited, low-excitation; **—волие** *n.* abulia, abnormal lack of initiative; **—высыхающий** *a.* poorly drying; **—запрещённый** *a.* (phys.) nonfavored (transition); **—ионизированный** *a.* slightly ionized; **—кипящий** *a.* light-boiling; **—кисл(отн)ый** *a.* weakly acid(ic), subacid; **—летучий** *a.* not very volatile, heavy; **—наклонный** *a.* slightly inclined; flat (vein); **—натянутый** *a.* slack, loose; **—неоднородный** *a.* slightly nonhomogeneous; **—нервный** *a.* (med.) neurasthenic.

слабо/обогащённый *a.* slightly enriched; **—польный** *a.* (phys.) weak-field; **—проникающий** *a.* soft (X-rays); **—пульсирующий** *a.* ripple (current); **—радиоактивный** *a.* slightly radioactive; **—развитый** *a.* underdeveloped; raw (soil); **—растворимый** *a.* slightly soluble; **—сильный** *a.* weak; **—слышащий** *a.* hard of hearing, hearing impaired.

слабо/сть *f.* weakness, weak point, failing, disadvantage; (med.) asthenia, debility; impotence; **—сучёный** *a.* slack (silk); **—точный** *a.* weak-current; sound (cable; insulator).

слабоум/ие *n.* feeble-mindedness, amentia, dementia; **—ный** *a.* feeble-minded.

слабофокусирующий *a.* weak-focusing.

слабый *a.* weak, feeble, infirm, asthenic, slight, faint, light; soft, mild; low, inefficient, poor; low-power, slight, small; low-level (radioactivity); (math.) removable (discontinuity); dilute (solution); loose, lax, slack; thin (negative).

слав/а *f.* fame, repute; glory; **—ен** *sh. m. of* **славный**; **—иться** *v.* have a reputation (for); **—ка** *f.* (orn.) warbler (*Sylvia*); **—ный** *a.* famous, renowned, distinguished; extraordinary; pleasant.

славян/ин *m.*, **—ка** *f.* Slav; **—ский** *a.* Slav(on)ic.

слаг/аемая *f.*, **—аемое** *n.* component; item, term, sum, summand, addend; **—аемый** *a.* addend; **—ательный** *a.* additive; **—ать** *v.* add, sum up; put together, compose, make (up); join, clasp; fold (up); put off; put down, lay down, resign; **—ать с себя** decline (responsibility); **—аться** *v.* be added, etc.; make up, constitute; **—ающая** *f.* component, constituent; **—ающий** *a.* adding, etc., *see v.*; component, constituent; cumulative.

сладить *see* **слаживать**.

сладк/ий *a.* sweet; **—оватый** *a.* sweetish; **—огорький** *a.* bittersweet; **—огорькость** *f.* bittersweetness; **—огуб** *m.* (ichth.) sweet-lips (*Plectorhynchus*); **—озвучный** *a.* pleasant-sounding, mellifluous; **—окислый** *a.* sweet-sour; **—окорень** *m.* wall fern (*Polypodium vulgare*); **—оплодный** *a.* sweet-fruited; **—ость** *f.* sweetness; **—ости** *pl.* confectionery.

слад/ок *sh. m. of* **сладкий**; **—острастие** *n.* (med.) libido; **—острастный** *a.* voluptuous; **—ость** *f.* sweetness; sweets; **—чайший** *superl. of* **сладкий**.

слаж/енность *f.* coordination, teamwork; **—енный** *a.* coordinated, etc., *see v.*; well ordered; **—ивание** *n.* coordination; arrangement, management; **—ивать** *v.* coordinate; arrange, manage, piece, join; **—иваться** *v.* coordinate, agree.

слазить *v.* climb (up or down).

слайд *m.* (phot.) slide.

слал *past m. sing. of* **слать**.

сламывать *v.* break, demolish.

сланец *m.* (petr.) schist; slate; shale; **глинистый с.** clay shale; **горючий с.** oil shale, bituminous shale.

сланик *see* **стланик**.

сланный *a.* sent.

сланцеват/ость *f.* schistosity, foliated structure, foliation (cleavage), cleavage (structure); jointing; **—ый** *a.* schistose, schistous; foliated; flaky, scaly, slatelike, slaty; shaly; **—ая глина** shale, slate clay.

сланцевидный *a.* slate-like, slaty; schistose, schistous.

сланцев/ый *a.* schist(ose), schistous; slate, slaty, slatelike; foliated, foliaceous, scaly, flaky; shale (oil, tar); **с. пласт** (petr.) schist; **—ая чёрная краска** slate black.

сланц/еперегонный *a.* shale-distilling; **—ы** *pl. of* **сланец**.

слань *f.* flooring (of ship); (flat) dunnage; log paving.

сласти *pl.* sweets, confection(ery); **—ть** *v.* sweeten; taste sweet.

сласть *f.* pleasure.

слать *v.* send.

слащавый *a.* very affectionate; sugary.

слаще *comp. of* **сладкий**.

слева *adv.* from the left, (to the) left, leftwards, left-hand.

слега *f.* pole, lath.

слегание *n.* caking (of soil, etc.).

слегка *adv.* (s)lightly, a little, gently, mildly; **с. толкнуть** *v.* give a slight push.

след *m.* trace, mark, dent; footprint; track, trail, spoor; vestige; pattern (of nuclear fallout); spur (of matrix); (hydr.) wake; **с. инверсии** contrail, vapor trail; **в один с.** single-cut (disc harrowing); **в два —а** double-gang (disc harrowing); **зрительный с.** afterimage; **не с. ему** he should not; **ни —а** not a trace (of), no sign (of); **—ы** *pl.* traces; trace amount; **—ы примеси** (microelectronics) trace impurity; **анализ —ов** trace analysis.

след. *abbr.* **(следовательно; следующий).**

следить *v.* watch, attend, follow, keep track (of), track, observe, monitor, keep an eye on, make sure, be careful; leave tracks; **с. за тем, чтобы** make sure that, take care that, care should be taken to; **с. за тем, чтобы не** care should be taken to avoid.

след. обр. *abbr.* **(следующим образом).**

следован/ие *n.* sequence, succession, following; investigation; movement, running; **в путь —ия** en route; **дальнего —ия** *a.* long-distance; **курс —ия** course; **путь —ия** travel line; **частота —ия импульсов** pulse repetition rate.

следовательно *intr. word and conj.* therefore, consequently, hence; it follows that.

след/овать *v.* follow, go after, come after, succeed, result; recur; (naut.) proceed; head for; conform (to); follow, obey (rules); **—ует** it is necessary, it should, one must; **ему —ует** he should; **из этого —ует** this implies; **как —ует** properly; as follows; **как и —овало ожидать** as was to be expected; **—овой** *a. of* **след**; trace; *prefix* after—; **—овой потенциал** (physiol.) afterpotential; **—ом за** immediately after, (the very) next; **—опыт** *m.* tracker, pathfinder; **—оуказатель** *m.* guide; (agr.) marker.

следственный *a.* inquest, inquiry; **с. материал** evidence.

следствие *n.* consequence, issue, result, effect, conclusion; inquest, investigation; **с. из теоремы, естественное с.** corollary; **причина и с.** cause and effect.

следу/емый *a.* due; **—ет** *pr. 3 sing. of* **следовать**; **—ющее** *n.* the following (procedure).

следующ/ий *a.* following, next, sequent; *suffix* **—bound**; **с. на юг** southbound; **в с. раз** next time; **—им образом** as follows, in the following manner, thus, in this fashion; **в —ей форме** in the following form, as.

следы *pl. of* **след**.

следящ/ий *a.* follow-up, track(ing); servo; **с. за полётом** flight path, tracking (radar); **с. за снарядом** missile-tracking; **с. механизм** servomechanism; follower; **—ая гидропередача** hydraulic servodrive; **—ая система, —ое устройство** servosystem; servomechanism; (comp.) control system.

слежавшийся *a.* caked, compact(ed).

слежаться *see* **слёживаться**.

слеж/ение *n.* following, tracing, tracking; **—ечный** *a.* track.

слёжив/аемость *f.* caking, consolidation; slumping, settling; tendency to cake; **—ание** *n.* caking, agglutination; deterioration in storage; **—аться** *v.* cake, clump, pack, settle, slump; deteriorate.

слежка *f.* surveillance.

слеза *f.* tear, lacrima; drop.

слез/ание *n.* descent; **—ать** *v.* descend, climb down, alight, dismount.

слез/ивый *a.* tearful, lachrymose; **—иться** *v.* water, tear; drip, ooze.

слёз/ка *f.* tear drop; drop; insulating bead; **—ки** *pl.* (bot.) Job's tears (*Coix lachryma*).

слез/ливый *a.* tearful, lachrymose; **—ник** *m.* drip ring; (anat.) lachrimal gland; **—ничок** *m.* lachrimal sac.

слёз/носовой *a.* (anat.) nasolacrimal; **—ный** *a.* tear, lachrymal.

слезо/видный *a.* teardrop; **—гонный** *a.* tear-exciting, lachrimatory; **—образный** *see* **слезовидный**; **—отделение** *n.* tear secretion; **—течение** *n.* (physiol.) lacrimation; (med.) epiphora; **—точивый газ** tear gas.

слезть *see* **слезать**.

слезящийся *a.* watery, running.

слеминг *m.* slamming.

слепень *m.* horsefly, gadfly.

слеп/ец *m.* blind person; **—имость** *f.* glare; **—ить** *v. see* **слепливать**; dazzle, blind.

слеп/ливать, —лять *v.* glue, paste (together); mold, form; **—ливаться, —ляться** *v.* stick together, adhere.

слепни *pl. of* **слепень**.

слеп/нуть *v.* become blind, lose one's sight; **—няки** *pl.* leaf bugs (*Miridae*); **—о** *adv.* blindly; **—оглазковые** *pl.* (ichth.) cavefishes (*Amblyopsidae*); **—ой** *a.* blind, sightless; instrument (flying); (anat.) cecal; blank, control (test); *m.* blind person; **—ой дождь** rain during sunshine; **—ой метод печатания на машинке** touch typing; **—ой мешок** cul-de-sac; **—ая кишка** (anat.) cecum; **—ое пятно** (anat.) papilla nervi optici, blind spot.

слепок *m.* mold, cast; stamp; model, copy, counterpart.

слепокишечный *a.* (anat.) cecal.

слеп/орождённый *a.* congenitally blind; **—ота** *f.* blindness; **куриная —ота, ночная —ота** night blindness, nyctalopia; **—ушонка** *f.* (mam.) mole-vole, mole-lemming (*Ellobius*); **—ыш** *m.* (zool.) mole rat (*Spalax*); **—ящий** *a.* blinding, dazzling; **—ящая яркость** glare.

слесар/ить *see* **слесарничать**; **—ная** *f.* fitter's shop; **—ничать** *v.* be a fitter; do mechanical work, do metal work; assemble (parts); **—новодопроводное дело** plumbing; **—ный** *a.* fitter's; metal working; locksmith's; **—ная обработка** bench work; **—ня** *f.* fitter's shop.

слесарь *m.* fitter, mechanic; assembly worker; locksmith; **с. на сборке** fitter; assembler; **с.-водопроводчик** *m.* plumber; **с.-инструментальщик** *m.* tool maker.

слёт *m.* flying off, etc., *see v.*; flight; swarming out (of bees); assembly; (text.) slub; **—анность** *f.* (av.) formation flying.

слет/ать, —еть *v.* fly off, disappear; fly down, land; fall off; **—аться** *v.* assemble, gather.

слёток *m.* (orn.) fledgling.

слечь *v.* lie down; come down (with an illness).

слешер *m.* slasher; slab saw.

слив *m.* pouring, etc., *see* **сливать**; overflow, decantation, discharge; sink; drain(age); (fuel) dumping, jettisoning.

слива *f.* prune, plum.

слив/ание *n.* pouring, etc., *see v.*; decantation; **—ать** *v.* pour (off, out, over), decant, run off, drain, discharge, discard, jettison, dump; (met.) cast, found; pour together, mix, blend; collate; **—аться** *v.* be poured, etc.; be discharged (to); run together, flow together, unite, fuse, coalesce, combine, blend; **—ающийся** *a.* flowing together, confluent, blending, fusing; **—ка** *see* **сливание**.

сливк/и *pl.* cream; **—ообразный** *a.* creamy; **—ование** *n.* creaming (of latex); **—ователь** *m.* creaming agent; **—оотделитель** *m.* (cream) separator.

сливн/ой *a.* overflow, pouring; mixed; drain (valve, pipe); (med.) confluent; **с. пункт** creamery; **—ая доска** (window) sill; **—ая станция** sewage plant; **—ое отверстие** drain.

слив/ный *see* **сливовый**; **—няк** *m.* plum tree orchard; **—овый** *a.* plum, prune; **—овое масло** plum seed oil.

сливочн/ый *a.* cream(y); **—ое масло** butter; **—ое мороженое** ice cream.

слившийся *a.* coalesced.

сливянка *f.* plum brandy.

слиз *m.* (ichth.) blenny; stoneloach.

слизать *see* **слизывать**.

слизе— *prefix* muci— (mucus); **—вики** *pl.* (bot.) Myxomycetes.

слизев/ой *a.* mucous; slime; mucic (acid); viscous (fermentation); **соль —ой кислоты** mucate; **—ые грибы** (bot.) Myxomycetes.

слизевокисл/ый *a.* mucic acid; mucate (of); **—ая соль** mucate.

слиз/ень *m.* (zool.) slug (*Limax*); **—еподобный** *a.* mucus-like, mucoid; **—етечение** *n.* (phyt.) slime flow; **—и** *pl.*, *etc.*, *of* **слизь**.

слизист/ая *f.* (anat.) mucous membrane; **с. матки** (anat.) endometrium; **—о—** *prefix* muc(o)—, mucous; **—огнойный** *a.* mucopurulent.

слизист/ый *a.* slimy, mucilaginous; mucous; **с. отёк** (med.) myxedema; **—ая железа** (anat.) mucous gland; **—ая оболочка, —ая ткань** (anat.) mucosa, mucous membrane; **—ая сумка** (anat.) bursa mucosa; **—ое вещество** mucin; **—ое истечение** phlegm; **—ые споровики** (zool.) *m.* Myxosporidia.

слиз/кий *a.* slippery, slimy, viscous, mucous; **—ни** *pl. of* **слизень; морские —ни** (ichth.) snailfishes (*Liparidae*); lumpsuckers (*Cyclopteridae*); **—няк** *see* **слизень**; **—ывать** *v.* lick off; **—ь** *f.* mucus, phlegm; slime, mucilage; **первичная —ь** (cyt.) plasson.

слил *past m. sing. of* **слить**.

слин/ялый *a.* faded; **—ять** *v.* fade; (zool.) shed.

слип *m.* (naut.) slip(way); (av.) slipstream.

слип/ание *n.* sticking together, adhesion, agglutination; conglomeration; **—аться** *v.* stick together, adhere, agglutinate; conglomerate; coalesce.

слипер *m.* sleeper (beam foundation).

слипинг-док *m.* railway dock.

слип/нуться *see* **слипаться; —чивый** *a.* adhesive, sticky; **—шийся** *a.* adhering; conglomerate; conglutinate.

слитие *see* **сливание**.

слитко/воз *m.* (met.) ingot buggy, pot car; **—выжиматель** *m.* ingot stripper; **—вый** *a. of* **слиток**.

слитножаберник/и *pl.* (ichth.) swampeels (*Synbranchidae*); **—овые** *pl.* (ichth.) deepsea eels (*Synaphobranchidae*); **—ообразные** *pl.* (ichth.) Synbranchiformes.

слитн/ость *f.* coalescence, fusion, unification; **—очерепные** *pl.* (ichth.) chimaeras (*Holocephali*); **—ый** *a.* coalescent, fused, united, unified; massive (structure); mixed (heredity); concerted (reaction).

слитой *a.* compact (soil).

слит/ок *m.*, **—очный** *a.* (met.) ingot, bar, slab; (gold) bullion.

слит/ый *a.* poured, etc., *see* **сливать; —ь** *see* **сливать**.

слич/ать *v.* compare, collate, check; **—ение** *n.* comparison, collation, checking; **—ённый** *a.* compared, etc., *see v.*; **—ительный** *a.* comparative.

слишком *adv.* too (much), too many; over; **с. много** too many, too much.

слияни/е *n.* fusion, union, blending, merging, consolidation, amalgamation, coalescence; confluence, junction (of rivers); (gametic) syngamy; **порядок —я** (comp.) merge order.

словар/ик *dim. of* **словарь; —ник** *m.* lexicographer; **—ный** *a.* dictionary, lexicographic; **—ный состав** vocabulary; **—ная бумага** (printing) bible paper, India paper; **—ь** *m.* dictionary; glossary; vocabulary.

словацкий *a.* Slovak(ian).

Словения (geog.) Slovenia; **словенский** *a.* Slovenian.

словесн/ый *a.* word, in words, verbal; **с. портрет** word picture, description; **—ая окрошка** (med.) incoherence; **—ая слепота** word blindness, alexia.

слов/ить *v.* catch, grab, capture, trap; **—ленный** *a.* caught, etc., *see v.*

словник *m.* vocabulary, glossary, word list; word book; terminology bank.

словно *conj.* as (if), as though, like.

слов/о *n.* word, term; say, speech, address; **с. в с.** word for word, verbatim; **к —у** by the way; **одним —ом** in short, briefly; **—оизменение** *n.* (gram.) inflection.

словолит/ец *m.* type founder; **—ный** *a.* type-casting; **—ня** *f.* type foundry; **—чик** *m.* type founder.

слово/м *intr.* word in short, briefly; **—образование** *n.* word formation, word building; **—образовательный** *a.* word-forming, word-building; **—производство** *n.* derivation; **—сочетание** *n.* idiom, (idiomatic) phrase, word group; **—творчество** *n.* creation of new words; **—толкование** *n.* interpretation; **—употребление** *n.* word use.

слог *m.* syllable; (comp.) byte; (written) style; **—овой** *a.* syllabic, syllable(-building); **—ообразующий** *a.* syllable-building.

слоеват/ость *f.* schistosity; lamination, sheeting; **—ый** *a.* schistous; slaty; foliated, scaly, flaky.

слоевищ/е *n.* (bot.) thallus; **—евидный**, **—ный** *a.* thalloid; **—ное растение** thallophyte.

слоев/ой *a. of* **слой**; **—ая выемка** (min.) slicing.

слоевцов/ые *pl.* (bot.) Thallophyta; **—ый** *a. see* **слоевищный**; **—ое растение** thallophyte.

сло/ёк *gen. pl. of* **слойка**; **—ение** *n.* foliation; **—ён(н)ый** *a.* foliated; flaky, puff (pastry); **—еобразующий** *a.* (layer-)building.

слож/ен *sh. m. of* **сложный**, **сложенный**; **—ение** *n.* addition, summation; build, configuration, form; (vector) composition; texture, structure; (address) modification; **логическое —ение** (comp.) disjunction; **—енность** *f.* complexity; **—енный** *a.* added, etc., *see v.*; folded; packed; **—ивший** *a.* developed, ready-made; **—ившийся** *a.* stabilized, established; **—имый** *a.* collapsible, folding; (math.) summable; **—ить** *v.* add, sum up; put together, build; make up, compose; fold (up); get rid (of responsibility).

сложно *adv.* complexly, complicatedly; **—слоистый** *a.* (geol.) multiple-bedded; **—сокращённый** *a.* (gram.) abbreviated; **—сочинённый** *a.* compound (sentence).

сложност/ь *f.* complexity, intricacy, complication; multiplicity; **в общей —и** on the whole, after all.

сложноцветные *pl.* (bot.) Compositae.

сложноэфирный *a.* ester.

сложн/ый *a.* complex, complicated, intricate, sophisticated; elaborate, involved, challenging; composite, mixed; multiple(x); multistage, step (rocket); combined; aggregate; (comp.) accumulative (carry); comprehensive; compound; irregular (shape); (surv.) broken (base); *suffix* -syllable; **с. индивид** compound; **с. профиль** configuration; **—ое вещество** compound; **—ое сопротивление** combined strength; **—ое тело** compound; **—ой формы** complex-shaped.

слои *pl. of* **слой**.

слоисто— *prefix* strato—, stratus; **—дождевое облако** nimbostratus (cloud); **—кучевое облако** stratocumulus.

слоистост/ь *f.* lamination, stratification, bedding, layer-

ing, sheeting, foliation; schistosity; (met.) peel(ing); **лишённый —и** *a.* massive.

слоист/ый *a.* laminated, lamellar, lamellate, foliated, flaky, scaly; stratified, layer(ed), bedded; sheeted (zone); schistose (structure); sandwich (panel); layer-built (construction); névé (iceberg); intercalation (compound); *suffix* -ply; **с. напластованный** unconformity (iceberg); **—ое облако** layer cloud, stratus.

слоиться *v.* flake, scale, peel off, exfoliate.

сло/й *m.* layer, stratum, bed, band, seam; lamella, flake, lamina, sheet; ply, thickness; coat(ing), film; (metal) foil; (filter) bed; course; (electron) shell; (hard) pan; (min.) slice; (anat.) tapetum; panniculus; **—ями** in layers; **метод —я** (meteor.) slice method; **отделение —ев** exfoliation; **тонкий с.** film.

слой/ка *f.* (ex)foliation, flaking; **—ноконечная группа** (math.) group with finite layers; **—ность** *f.* number of plies; **—ный** *a. suffix* -layer; **—чатый** *a.* foliate; stratified.

слом *m.* breaking, wrecking, demolition; **металл на с.** scrap metal; **—анный** *a.* broken; truncated (cone); **—ать** *v.* break (up); (med.) fracture; subdue, overcome; **—аться** *v.* break, snap; (med.) fracture; get out of order; **—ить** *see* **сломать**; **—ка** *f.* breaking.

слон *m.* elephant; **морской с.** elephant seal (*Mirounga*); **—ёнок** *m.* elephant calf; **—ик** *m.* (ent.) weevil, snout beetle; (mam.) elephant shrew (*Elephantulus*); **—ик-блошка** leaf miner; **—иха** *f.* elephant cow; **—ка** *f.* (orn.) woodcock; **—овий** *a.* elephant(ine); ivory; **—овость** *f.* (med.) elephantiasis; **—овый** *a.* elephant(ine); ivory; **—овая болезнь** elephantiasis; **—овая кость** ivory; **жжёная —овая кость**, **—овая чернь** ivory black; **—ята** *pl. of* **слонёнок**.

слуга *m.* servant.

служащий *a.* serving; *m.* employee.

служб/а *f.* service, attendance; office, department; duty, job, work, employment; (weather) bureau; **—ы** *pl.* services; outbuildings, annexes; **время —ы**, **срок —ы** service, useful life, life (span), life expectancy; **на —е** at work, on duty.

служебн/ый *a.* employee's, service; official, staff (catalog); content-free, function (word); working (dogs); ancillary; (comp.) housekeeping; utility (program); **с. персонал** staff; **—ое время** working hours; **—ое преступление** violation of duty; **—ое состояние** status; **—ое устройство** (comp.) server; **—ые инстанции** (mil.) chain of command; **—ые часы** office hours.

служ/ение *n.* service; **—итель** *m.* servant, attendant; **—ить** *v.* serve, be employed, work, be (with); work (as).

слуп/ить, **—ливать** *v.* strip, peel.

слух *m.* hearing, ear; rumor, report, news; **есть —и, что; ходят —и** it is rumored that; **—ач** *m.* listener, monitor; (mil.) listening sentry; morse operator.

слухов/ой acoustic, auditory, aural, auricular; dormer (window); *prefix* ot(o)— (ear); **с. анализатор** echolocator (of bats); **с. аппарат** hearing aid; **с. нерв** (anat.) auditory nerve; **с. проход** (anat.) acoustic meatus; **с. пузырёк** (anat.) otocyst; **—ая косточка** (anat.) otolith; **—ая трубка** (tel.) receiver; (anat.) eustachian tube; ear trumpet; **—ое поле** (anat.) area vestibularis.

случ/ай *m.* case, occurrence, incident, instance, occasion, circumstance, situation, event; chance, opportunity; **в —ае** in case (of), in the event (of), it; **в —ае необходимости** as required, if needed; **в других —аях** otherwise; **в идеальном —ае** ideally; **в лучшем —ае** at best; **в общем —ае** in general; **во всяком**

—ae in any case, at any rate; **в таком** —ае in such a situation; in that case, then; **даже в таком** —ае even so; **в тех** —аях when; **в тех** —аях, **если** where; **в тех** —аях, **когда** where, when; **в худшем** —ае at the worst; **в этом** —ае in this instance; **и в том и в другом** —ае in either case, in both cases; **закрыто по** —аю **ремонта** closed for repairs; **к этому** —аю ad hoc; **на всякий с.** in any case; just in case; **на с. аварии** for emergency use; **на с.** in case (of); **ни в каком** —ае on no account, by no means; **ни в коем** —ае **не** under no circumstances; **по** —аю on account (of), owing (to); **при** —ае on occasion; when convenient; **чем в ином** —ае than would otherwise be the case.

случайн/о *adv.* randomly, accidentally, by chance, inadvertently; —**ость** *f.* (math.) contingency; randomness; accident, chance; —**ый** *a.* random, stochastic, chance, accidental, unexpected, incidental, occasional, haphazard, stray, irregular, sporadic; nonrecurrent (waste); —**ая величина** (aut.) stray parameter; (math.) random variable; (stat.) chance value; —**ая переменная величина** random variable; **непрерывная** —**ая величина** continuous random variable; —**ая функция** (math.) function of a random variable; —**ое блуждание** random walk; —**ое воздействие** random input; —**ое совпадение** (nucl.) random coincidence; —**ые данные** (comp.) hash; **система** —**ых причин** (math.) chance-causes system.

случ/ать *v.* couple, pair, mate; —**аться** *v.* couple, pair (with), mate; happen, occur, take place, come about, be the case; *see* **случать;** —**ённый** *a.* coupled, paired, mated; —**ившееся** *n.* occurrence, event, happening; —**ившийся** *a.* having occurred; —**ить** *see* **случать;** —**иться** *v. see* **случаться;** —**ка** *f.,* —**ной** *a.* coupling, pairing, mating, coitus; (gen.) conjugation; —**ная болезнь** (vet.) trypanosomiasis.

слуш/ание *n.* hearing; —**атели** *pl.* audience; —**ать** *v.* listen; hear (a case); —**аться** *v.* listen, pay attention (to); obey; —**имый** *a.* audible.

слущивание *n.* (med.) desquamation, scaling off.

слыть *v.* have a reputation (for), be known (as); be said; pass (for).

слых(ив)ать *v.* hear.

слыш/ать *v.* hear; sense, perceive; —**имость** *f.* audibility; —**имый** *a.* audible; —**но** *adv.* audibly; it is reported, it is said; —**ный** *a.* audible, heard; perceptible (odor).

слэг *m.* slug (unit of mass).

слюд/а *f.* (min.) mica; —**истый** *a.* micaceous, laminated; —**оносный** *a.* mica-bearing; —**ообразный** *a.* micalike, micaceous; —**яной** *a.* mica(ceous).

слюн/а *f.* saliva; —**ить** *v.* wet with saliva, lick; —**ный** *a.* salivary (glands); —**о**— *prefix* sial(o)— (saliva); ptyal(o)— (spittle); —**огон** *m.*, —**огонка** *f.* (bot.) pellitory of Spain (*Anacyclus pyrethrum*); —**огонный** *a.*, —**огонное средство** sialagogue, ptyalogogue; —**оотделение** *n.* salivation; —**особиратель** *m.* saliva trap (in respirator); —**отечение** *n.*, —**оток** *m.* (med.) ptyalism, (hyper)salivation; —**оточивый** *a.* salivating; —**явый** *a.* drooling, slobbery.

сляб *m.* (met.) slab; —**инг** *m.* slab(bing) mill.

сля/гут *fut. 3 pl.*; —**жет** *fut. 3 sing. of* **слечь.**

слякот/ный *a.* slushy; —**ь** *f.* mire, slush.

см *abbr.* (**сантиметр**) centimeter.

см. *abbr.* (**смотри**) see; **с.м., с/м** *abbr.* (**сего месяца**) this month.

смаз/анный *a.* lubricated, etc., *see* **смазывать;** —**ать** *see* **смазывать;** —**ка** *f.* lubricant, grease, oil, tallow; (physiol.) smegma; lubrication, oiling; (mold) coating; **величина** —**ки, значение** —**ки** lubricating value; **первородная** —**ка** (embr.) vernix caseosa; **суставная** —**ка** (physiol.) synovia; —**ной** *a.* lubricated; treated (leather); —**очное** *n.* lubricant.

смазочн/ый *a.* lubricating, lubrication, grease, greasing; **с. жир** (axle) grease; **с. материал** lubricant; —**ая коробка** lubricator, oil can, grease cup; —**ое средство** lubricant.

смазчик *m.* greaser, lubricator, oiler.

смазыв/аемость *f.* lubricating property; —**ание** *n.* lubrication, greasing, oiling; —**ать** *v.* lubricate, grease, oil; smear; blur, obscure; slur; evade (a question); —**ающе-охлаждающий** *a.* cutting (fluid); —**ающий** *a.* lubricating, etc., *see v.*; —**ающее приспособление** lubricator.

смаивать *v.* exhaust.

смак *m.* relish, savor.

смалец *m.* lard.

смалу *adv.* from early childhood.

смалывать *v.* grind (up), mill.

смальт/а *f.* smalt (blue pigment or glass); mosaic enamel; —**ин** *m.* —**ит** *m.* (min.) smaltine, smaltite.

сманеврировать *v.* maneuver.

смани(ва)ть *v.* lure, tempt.

смарагд *m.* (min.) emerald; —**ит** *m.* smaragdite; —**овый** *a.* emerald (green).

смаривать *v.* exhaust; overcome.

смарид/а *f.* (ichth.) picarel; —**ы** *pl.* picarels (*Maenidae*).

смаст *m.* smust, smoke and dust.

смастерить *v.* make, contrive, devise.

сматривать *v.* look (over), examine; watch (over).

сматыв/ание *n.* winding, etc., *see v.*; —**ать** *v.* wind, reel (on); reel off, unreel, unroll, uncoil, run off, pay out.

смах/ивать, —**нуть** *v.* brush off; resemble.

смачив/аемость *f.* wettability; —**аемый** *a.* wettable; —**ание** *n.* wetting, etc., *see v.*; **порог** —**ания** threshold of wettability; —**атель** *m.* wetting agent; —**ать** *v.* wet, moisten, damp(en), humidify, sprinkle; soak, steep, imbue, drench; —**ающий** *a.* wetting, etc., *see v.*; —**ающийся** *a.* wettable (powders).

смачн/о *adv.* with relish; —**ый** *a.* savory, appetizing.

смв, СМВ *abbr.* (**сантиметровые волны**) centimeter waves.

см-г-сек *see* **СГС.**

см/дин *abbr.* (**сантиметр на дину**) centimeter(s) per dyne.

смегма *f.* (physiol.) smegma.

смежать *v.* close (one's eyes).

смежен *sh. m. of* **смежный.**

смежить *see* **смежать.**

смежник *m.* component manufacturer; parts supplier.

смежно *adv.* contiguously; in the vicinity (of); —**сть** *f.* contiguity, adjacency, proximity, juxtaposition.

смежн/ый *a.* adjacent, contiguous, proximate, neighboring, abutting, adjoining; (chem.) vicinal; contact; related, allied; interfacing; **с. класс** (math.) coset, residue class; —**ое нахождение** juxtaposition; —**ые области науки** allied sciences.

смейз *m.* smaze, smoke and haze.

смек/алистый *a.* sharp, keen-witted; —**алка** *f.* sharpness, quick comprehension; —**ать,** —**нуть** *v.* comprehend, catch on.

смел *past m. sing. of* **смелеть; смёл** *past m. sing. of* **смести.**

смелет *fut. 3 sing. of* **смолоть.**

смел/еть *v.* become bold(er); —**о** *adv.* boldly; —**ость** *f.* boldness, daring, audacity; —**ый** *a.* bold, daring, audacious, courageous.

смен/а *f.* change, changing, relay, exchange, interchange, replacing, replacement, renewing, relief; (crop) rotation; alternation; (labor) shift; (educ.) session; **с. зубов** secondary dentition; **с. хозяев** (biol.) heteroecism, change of hosts; **—ить** *see* **сменять.**

сменн/ость *f.* working in shifts; **—осуточный план** planned daily production quota.

смен/ный *a.* (inter)changeable, exchangeable, renewable, replaceable, replacement, detachable, removable; disposable, expendable; plug-in; spare (part); change (gear); (labor) shift, per shift, relief; relay; **—щик** *m.* relief, counterpart on opposite shift.

сменяем/ость *f.* interchangeability; **—ый** *a.* interchangeable, removable, replaceable.

сменять *v.* (inter)change, exchange, replace, remove, renew; relieve; **—ся** *v.* take turns, alternate; work in opposite shifts or watches; supersede; give way (to).

смердеть *v.* stink, reek.

смерз/аемость *f.* freezability; **—ание** *n.* freezing (together); **—ать(ся)** *v.* freeze (together); congeal.

смёрз/лый *a.* frozen, congealed; **—нуть(ся)** *see* **смерзать(ся).**

смери(ва)ть *v.* measure.

смерк/ать, —нуть *v.* darken, grow dark.

смертель/ность *f.* mortality; **—ный** *a.* mortal, fatal, deadly, lethal, killer; **с. исход** fatal outcome, death.

смертн/ик *m.* condemned man; **—ость** *f.* mortality, death rate, die-off; **коэффициент —ости, показатель —ости, процент —ости** death rate; **—ый** *a.* mortal, fatal, deadly; death (penalty); capital (punishment).

смертоносн/ость *f.* deadliness; **—ый** *a.* deadly, lethal, fatal; pestilent.

смерт/ь *f.* death, decease; **объявление о —и** obituary; **удостоверение о —и** death certificate.

смерч *m.* waterspout; tornado, cyclone, dust-devil.

смерять *v.* measure.

смес/еобразование *n.* (engines) carburetion; **внутренее с.** fuel injection; **—и** *gen., pl., etc., of* **смесь;** **—ильный** *see* **смесительный;** **—имость** *f.* miscibility; **—имый** *a.* miscible; **—итель** *m.* mixer, mixing tank, blender; kneader; (rad.) frequency changer; **—ительный** *a.* mixing, blending, agitating, mixer; **—итель-обводитель** *m.* washer-hydrator; **—итель-отстойник** *m.* mixer-settler; **—ить** *see* **смешивать;** **—ок** *gen. pl. of* **смеска.**

смести *v.* sweep away, eliminate; sweep together.

сместит/ель *m.* displacer; **—ельный** *a.* displacing, etc., *see* **смещать; —ь** *see* **смешать.**

смесь *f.* mixture, mix, blend, composite, hybrid, compound, composition; miscellany; (culture) medium; (molding) sand; **составлять с.** *v.* mix, blend, compound.

смет/а *f.*, **составлять —у** *v.* estimate.

сметана *f.* sour cream; paste.

сметание *n.* sweeping away, etc., *see* **сметать.**

сметан/ный *a.* sour cream; pasty; **смётанный** *past pass. part. of* **сметать; —ообразный** *a.* creamy, paste-like, viscous.

смет/ать *v.* sweep away, eliminate; sweep together; stack, pile; (sewing) baste.

смётк/а *f.* sweeping away, etc., *see v.*; comprehension, sharpness; **—и** *pl.* sweepings.

смет/ливость *f.* sharpness, comprehension; **—ливый** *a.* sharp, quick-witted.

сметн/ый *a.* estimate(d), planned; budgetary; **—ая калькуляция** estimation, calculation; **—ая цена** estimate.

смёточный *a.* basting (stitches).

сметчик *m.* estimator.

смётыв/ание *n.* stacking, etc., *see v.*; **—ать** *v.* stack, pile, baste.

сметь *v.* dare, have the courage.

смех *m.* laughter; **мышца —а** (anat.) risorius; **—овой** *a.* risorial.

смеш/анный *a.* mixed, miscellaneous, composite, compound(ed), combined, combination, blended; pooled (serum); (biol.) hybrid, stirred, agitated; joint (committee); **—ать** *see* **смешивать; —ение** *n.* mixture, mixing (together), combination, blend(ing), merging, coalition; confusion; complication; (breeding) cross.

смешив/аемость *f.* miscibility; **—аемый** *a.* miscible; confused; **—ание** *n.* mixing, etc., *see v.*; **—атель** *see* **смеситель; —ать** *v.* mix, blend, combine, merge, compound, compose, stir, agitate; shuffle; mix up, confuse; **—аться** *v.* (inter)mix, (inter)blend, intermingle, merge, coalesce, fuse; be mixed, etc.; **—ающий** *a.* mixing, etc., *see v.*; **—ающий аппарат** mixer; **—ающийся** *a.* (inter)mixing, etc., *see v.*; miscible; **не —ающийся** immiscible.

смеш/ить *v.* amuse; **—ливость** *f.* risibility; **—ливый** *a.* risible, disposed to laugh; **—но** *adv.* ridiculously; comically; it is ridiculous, it is odd; **—ной** *a.* funny, amusing, ludicrous, ridiculous, odd, strange, **—ок** *m.* chuckle.

смещ/ать *v.* displace, shift, dislocate, dislodge; offset, bias; misalign; **—аться** *v.* shift; (geol.) heave; be displaced; **—ающий** *a.* displacing, etc., *see v.*; **—ающее напряжение** bias (voltage); **—ающийся** *a.* slipping.

смещ/ение *n.* displacement, shift(ing), dislodgement, offset; (angular) misalignment; (electron.) bias; movement, migration, (continental) drift; (comp.) dragging (image on screen); disturbance; (geol.) dislocation, slip, heave, upheaval; **с. вперёд** (anat.) anteposition; **с. кпереди** (med.) antedisplacement; **с. матки** (med.) metrectopia; **с. нулевой точки** zero creep; **с. при сдвиге** shear displacement; **с. фаз** phase shift; **напряжение —ения** bias (voltage); **поле —ения** bias field; **постоянное с.** bias; **правило —ения** (nucl.) displacement law; **процесс —ения границ** (phys.) moving boundary; **ток —ения** displacement current, bias current; **—ённый** *a.* displaced, etc., *see* **смещать;** out of line, off-center, offset; biased; misplaced; (med.) ectopic.

сме/ющийся *a.* risorial; **—яться** *v.* laugh (at), ridicule.

СМЖ *abbr.* **(спинномозговая жидкость)** cerebrospinal fluid.

смиг/ивать, —нуть *v.* blink (away).

смила-сапонин *m.* smila-saponin.

смилацин *m.* smilacin, sarsasaponin.

смин/ание *n.* mashing, etc., *see v.*; **—ать** *v.* mash, knead, work; crumple, crush; crease; **—аться** *v.* collapse; **—ающийся** *a.* collapsible; crushing (strip).

смир/ение *n.* suppression (of emotion), submissiveness; **—енность** *f.* humility; **—енный** *a.* submissive, quiet, meek; **—ительная рубашка** (med.) strait jacket; **—ить** *see* **смирять.**

смирна *f.* myrrh (gum).

смирно *adv.* quietly; *imp.* attention!.

смирнский *a.* (geog.) Smyrna; **с. ладан** myrrh (gum).

смир/ный *a.* quiet, gentle; **—ять** *v.* subdue, tame; break, subjugate; suppress, restrain; **—яться** *v.* submit, yield; calm down; resign oneself (to).

Смита процесс (met.) Smith process.

смит/ит *m.* (min.) smithite; **—сонианский** *a.* Smithsonian; **—сонит** *m.* (min.) smithsonite.

СМЛ *abbr.* (**судебно-медицинская лаборатория**) forensic medicine laboratory.

смог *past m. sing. of* **смочь**; smog, smoke and fog.

смоделирова/нный *a.* simulated; **—ть** *v.* (make a) model, simulate.

смоет *fut. 3 sing. of* **смыть**.

сможет *fut. 3 sing. of* **смочь**.

смоква *see* **смоковница**.

смокед-шит *m.* (rubber) smoked sheet.

смоковница *f.* fig (*Ficus carica*); **райская с.** plaintain (*Musa paradisiaca*).

смола *f.* resin, rosin, gum; tar, pitch; **жидкая с.** pitch, tar; **искусственная с.** synthetic resin; **каменноугольная с.** coal tar; **твёрдая с.** rosin.

смолава *f.* (ichth.) striped ruffe.

смолачивать *v.* (agr.) thresh.

смолеватый *a.* resinous; tarry.

смолёвка *f.* (bot.) catchfly (*Silene*); (ent.) pine weevil (*Pissodes*).

смол/евой, —ёвый *a.* resin(ous); tar(ry), tarred; **—ен** *sh. m. of* **смольный**; **—ение** *n.* resinification; tarring; **—енный** *a.* resin(ed); tar(red), pitched.

смоленский *a.* (geog.) Smolensk.

смолёный *see* **смолённый**.

смолистость *f.* resinous nature; resin content; tarriness; (petrol.) tar content.

смолист/ый *a.* resin(ous); gummy; pitchy, tarry; pitch (coal; peat); **—ое масло** oleoresin; **—ые материалы** naval stores.

смолить *v.* resin; (coat with) tar, pitch; **—ся** *v.* become resinous, resinify.

смолка *f.* tarring; resin smudge; resinous sealing compound; (bot.) Viscaria.

смолк/ать, —нуть *v.* grow silent; cease.

смолница *f.* (soils) smolnitz.

смоло/бетон *m.* tar concrete; **—варня** *see* **смолокурня**; **—гон** *m.* tar distiller; **—гонный** *a.* tar-distilling; **—гонщик** *m.* tar distiller; **—доломитовый** *a.* tar-bonded dolomite (refractories).

смолоду *adv.* from one's youth.

смолоистечение *n.* (phyt.) resinosis.

смолокур *m.* tar distiller; **—ение** *n.*, **—(ен)ный** *a.* tar-distilling; **—ня** *f.* tar works, tar distillery.

смолонос *m.* resinous plant; **—ница** *f.* (bot.) Ferula; **—ный** *a.* resiniferous; tar-bearing.

смоло/образование *n.* resin formation; gum formation; gumming; **—образующий** *a.* resin-forming, resin-secreting; gum-forming; **—отделитель** *m.* tar separator; **—отделительный** *a.* (petrol.) tar-stripping; **—перегонный** *a.* tar-distilling; **—подобный** *a.* resinoid; tarry; **—продуктивный** *a.* highly resinous; **—разгонка** *f.* tar distillation; **—садный** *see* **смологонный**; **—семянник** *m.* (bot.) Pittosporum; **—содержащий** *a.* resin-containing; gum-containing, gummy; tar-containing; **—течение** *n.* (phyt.) resinosis.

смолотить *v.* (agr.) thresh.

смолот/ый *a.* ground up, milled; **—ь** *v.* grind up, mill; mince (meat).

смолоченный *a.* (agr.) threshed.

смолт *m.* (ichth.) smolt (a young, silvery salmon as it descends to salt water).

смоль *f.* resin; tar; **—ё** *n.* resinous wood; **—ный** *see* **смоляной**; **—ня** *f.* tar-works, tarring loft; **—няк** *see* **смольё**.

смол/як *see* **смольё**; **—янистый** *a.* tarry.

смолян/ой *a.* resin(ous), resinoid; tar(ry), pitch; coal-tar (dyes); asphalt (lake); (elec.) resinous, negative; **с. желвак** resin deposit (in wood); **с. камень** (petr.) pitch-

stone; **с. клей** resin sizing; **—ая бумага** tar paper; **—ая замазка** bituminous cement; **—ая кислота** resin acid; **соль —ой кислоты** resinate; **—ая масса** resinous compound; **—ая обманка, —ая руда** (min.) pitchblende; **—ое масло** resin oil; tar oil; **—ое число** tar value.

смолянокисл/ый *a.* resin acid; resinate (of); **—ая соль** resinate.

смоляночёрный *a.* pitch-black, piceous.

смоница *f.* (soils) smonitza.

смонтиров/анный *a.* assembled, etc., *see v.*; **с. на салазках** skid-mounted; **—ать** *v.* assemble, erect, build up, set up, fit, mount.

смораживаться *v.* congeal, freeze.

сморить *v.* overcome; exhaust.

сморк/аться, —нуться *v.* blow one's nose.

сморо́д/а, —ин(к)а *f.* currant; **—инник** *m.* currant thicket; **—инный, —иновый** *a.* currant.

сморозь *f.* conglomerated ice.

сморч/ковый *a.*, **—ок** *m.* morel (mushroom).

сморщ/енный *a.* wrinkled, etc., *see v.*; corrugated; **вторично с.** (med.) arteriosclerotic (kidney); **первично с.** contracted (kidney); **—ивание** wrinkling, etc., *see v.*; corrugation; shrinkage; (med.) pyknosis; (med.) kraurosis; **—и(ва)ть** *v.* wrinkle, crinkle, crumple; corrugate; shrivel, shrink; **—и(ва)ться** *v.* wrinkle, crinkle, crumple (up); shrivel, shrink; **—ивающий** *a.* wrinkling, etc., *see v.*; **— иватель** *m.* (anat.) corrugator (muscle).

смот/анный *a.* wound, reeled (on); unreeled, unrolled; **—ать** *see* **сматывать**; **—ка** *see* **сматывание**.

смотр *m.* inspection; review; (mil.) parade; **произвести с.** *v.* inspect, review; **—еть** *v.* inspect; look, view, regard; face; show, appear; **—еть за** superintend, look after, be in charge of, watch (over), keep (order); **если —еть на** when facing; **если —еть со** when viewed from; **—и** *imp. of* **смотреть**; see; **—итель** *m.* keeper, custodian; (game) warden; supervisor, inspector.

смотров/ой *a.* inspection, sight; surveillance, viewing; (auto) service (pit); **с. колодец** man hole; **с. лю(чо)к, —ая дверь, —ое окно, —ое отверстие** sight hole, peep hole, inspection hole; **—ое стекло** sight glass.

смотря *pr. ger. of* **смотреть**; **с. на, с. по** according to, depending on; **не с. на** in spite of, notwithstanding.

смоч/енный *a.* wetted, moistened, humidified; soaked; wet-bulb (thermometer); **—ить** *see* **смачивать**.

смочь *v.* be able, prove able.

смоющий *pr. act. part. of* **смыть**.

СМП *abbr.* (**Северной морской путь**) Northern Sea Route; (**скорая медицинская помощь**) (emergency) first aid.

смрад *m.* stink, stench, offensive odor; **—ный** *a.* stinking, foul-smelling.

см/сек² *abbr.* (**сантиметр на секунду в квадрате**) centimeter per second per second.

смуглый *a.* dark-complexioned, swarthy.

смутить *see* **смущать**.

смутн/о *adv.* indistinctly, not clearly, vaguely; **—ость** *f.* dimness; confusion; **—ый** *a.* dim, vague; hazy, indistinct; confused; troubled; disturbing.

смуш/ек *m.*, **—ка** *f.* astrakhan lambskin; **—ковый** *a.* fur-bearing (sheep).

смущ/ать *v.* disturb, perplex, confuse, embarrass; **—ение** *n.* confusion, embarrassment; **—ённый** *a.* disturbed, confused, embarrassed.

смыв *m.* washing off; (geol.) washout; erosion; sluicing; **—аемый** *a.* wipe-off; **—альный** *a. of* **смыв**; **—ание** *n.* washing (away, off, out); rinsing free (of); **—ать** *v.* wash (away, off, out); rinse free (of); **—ка** *see*

смывание; wash solution; cleaning fluid; (paint) remover; **—ной** *a.* wash(ing); flushing; washed off; **—очный** *a.* wash(ing).

смык *see* **смыкание;** joint; **—ание** *n.* join(t)ing, etc., *see v.*; linkage, connection; closure; (sylv.) canopy; (dental) occlusion; (microelectronics) punch-through; **—ать** *v.* join(t), link, couple; close (up), heal; fit in, clamp; (surv.) adjust (traverse); **—аться** *v.* join, fuse, interlock; close, draw together, come together; wink, blink; disregard; **—ающийся** *a.* (bot.) connivent; converging.

смыли(ва)ть *v.* lather, use up (soap).

смысл *m.* sense, meaning, significance, purport; **в —е** in the sense (of), in a . . . sense, in terms (of), from the standpoint (of); **в некотором —е** in a sense; **в том —е, что** in (the sense) that; **в широком —е** in the broad sense; **в этом —е** in this respect; **здравый с.** common sense; **иметь с.** be worthwhile; **нет —а** there is no point (in); **по —у** according to the terms (of); **—ить** *v.* understand, comprehend; have know-how; **—овой** *a.* of **смысл;** semantic; **—овое соответствие** relevancy.

смыт/ость *f.* erodibility; **—ый** *a.* washed (away, off, out), eroded; **—ь** *see* **смывать.**

смычка *f.* joint(ing), coupling, union, shackle; clamp; chain length.

смыч/ковый *a.*, **—ок** *m.* bow (for a stringed instrument).

смышлёный *a.* bright, intelligent.

смягч/ать *v.* soften, plasticize; mitigate, moderate, modify; cushion, damp; subdue, tone down (color); degrade (spectrum); alleviate (pain); **—аться** *v.* be softened, etc.; soften; ease off, relax, decrease, abate; grow mild; **—ающий** *a.* softening, etc., *see v.*; extenuating (circumstances); **—ающее средство** *see* **смягчитель; —ение** *n.* softening, etc., *see v.*; moderation; extenuation; (linguistics) palatalization; **—ённый** *a.* softened, etc., *see v.*; **—итель** *m.* softener, softening agent; plasticizer; emollient; **—ительный** *see* **смягчающий; —ить** *see* **смягчать.**

смятен/ие *n.* confusion, commotion; **—ный** *a.* (emotionally) disturbed, anxious; confused, perplexed.

смят/ие crumpling, etc., *see v.*; collapse; **напряжение —ия** bearing stress; **прочность на с.** bearing strength; **—ый** *a.* crumpled, etc., *see v.*; **—ь** *v.* crumple, crush; beat down, trample; knead, work; disrupt; **—ься** *v.* crumple, collapse, get out of shape.

сн *abbr.* **(стен)** sthene (unit of force equal to 1000 newtons); **сн.** *abbr.* **(снизу)** from the bottom.

СН *abbr.* **(среднее напряжение)** average voltage; **(строительные нормы)** building code.

сна *gen.* of **сон.**

снаб/дить, —жать *v.* supply, furnish, provide; outfit, equip, fit (with); deliver, feed; **—жающий** *a.* supplying, etc., *see v.*; supply, delivery; **—жён** *sh. m.* of **снабжённый; —женец** *m.* supplier; **—жение** *n.* supplying, etc., *see v.*; provision, procurement, supply, delivery, feed; outfit; **—жение электроэнергией** electricity service; power supply; **материально-техническое —жение** (mil.) logistics; procurements; **—жённый** *a.* supplied, etc., *see v.*; (complete) with, incorporating, featuring; **—жённый наконечником** tipped (with); **—жённый ногтями** (anat.) unguiculate; **—женский** *a.* supply(ing).

снадобье *n.* home remedies, drug.

Снайдера, снайдеровский *a.* Snyder('s).

снайпер *m.* (mil.) sniper, sharpshooter.

снайтов/ать, —ить *v.* lash.

снаружи *adv.* on the outside, on the exterior, externally, outwardly.

снаряд *m.* apparatus, equipment, implement(s), tool(s); machine, vehicle; dredge; (art.) shell, round, shot, projectile, missile; **—ить** *v. see* **снаряжать; с.-ловушка** *m.* decoy missile; **с.-мишень** *m.* target drone; **—ный** *a.* of **снаряд;** adapter (plug); **—остойкий** *a.* shellproof, missile-proof; **с.-перехватчик** *m.* interceptor missile; **с.-приманка** *m.* decoy missile; **с.-ракета** *m.* rocket missile; **с.-спутник** *m.* satellite (vehicle).

снаряж/ать *v.* equip, furnish, fit out, outfit; load, charge (with explosive); actuate (mine); **—аться** *v.* get ready, prepare; **—ение** *n.* equipping, etc., *see v.*; equipment, outfit, gear, tackle; (naut.) harness rigging; support; implements; **—ение взрывателем** fuzing; **личное —ение** accoutrement(s); **—ённый** *a.* equipped, etc., *see v.*

снаст/и *pl.* tackle, equipment; **—ить** *v.* (naut.) equip, rig out; **—ный** *a.* hook-and-line (fishing); **—ь** *f.* tackle, equipment, gear, outfit; implement, tool; rope, cordage, rigging; **—и** *pl.* cordage, rigging.

сначала *adv.* (at) first, to start with, initially; from the beginning; anew, again.

снашив/ание *n.* wear (and tear), abrasion; **—ать** *v.* wear out, abrade; bring together.

СНГ *abbr.* **(Содружество независимых государств)** Commonwealth of Independent States, CIS.

сне *prepos.* of **сон.**

снеббер *m.* (min.) snubber.

снег *m.* snow; (dry) ice; **граница вечного —а** snow line; **мокрый с.** sleet; **талый с.** slush.

снегирь *m.* (orn.) bullfinch (*Pyrrhula pyrrhula*).

снего— *prefix* chion(o)—, snow; **—борьба** *f.* snow control, snow removal; **—вал** *m.* snow plow; (forestry) snow crush; **—вание** *n.* refrigeration with snow; (agr.) snow retention; **—вой** *a.* snow; **—вая граница** snow line; **—задержание** *n.* snow fence; (agr.) snow retention; **—задерживающий** *a.* snow-retaining; **—защита** *f.* snow fence; snow protection; **—лом** *m.* (forestry) snow breakage; snowbreak; **—любивый** *a.* (bot.) snow-loving, chionophilous; **—мер** *m.* snow sampler, snow gage; **—мерный** *a.* snow-measuring; **—мёт** *m.* snow blower; **—накопление** *n.* snowpack; **—отвал** *m.* snowbreak.

снегоочиститель *m.* snow-removing machine, snow plow; **пневматический с.** snow blower; **—ный** *a.* snow-removal.

снего/пад *m.* snowfall; **—пах** *m.* snow plow; **—пахание** *n.* snow plowing; **—погрузчик** *m.* snow loader; **—подобный** *a.* snow-like, snowy; **—ступ** *m.* snowshoe; **—таялка** *f.* snow melter; **—таяние** *n.* snow melt(ing); **—уборка** *f.* snow removal; **—уборочный** *a.* snow-removal; **—уборочная машина, —уборщик** *m.* snow plow; **—уплотнитель** *m.* snow-compacting roller; **—ход** *m.* snow-going vehicle, snowmobile.

снедок *m.* (bot.) chervil (*Anthriscus cerefolium*).

снеж/инка *f.* snow flake; **—ить** *v.* snow; **—ник** *m.* (geol.) firn, névé basin; **—ница** *f.* meltwater puddle; **—нобелый** *a.* snow-white; **—ноягодник** *m.* snowberry; **—ный** *a.* snow(y); (bot.) nival, chionic; snowflurry (charge); pre-névé (iceberg); **—ная буря** snowstorm; **—ная крупа** soft hail; **—ная плесень** (phyt.) snow mold, bacterial brown rot; **—ок** *m.* light snow; **—ура** *f.* snow slush.

Снейк Snake River.

Снелля закон (phys.) Snell's law.

снес/ение *n.* demolishing, etc., *see* **сносить;** demolition;

removal; **—ённый** *a.* demolished, etc., *see* **сносить;**
—ти *see* **сносить.**

снет/ковый *a.,* **—ок** *m.* (ichth.) smelt (*Osmerus*); silver-
sides (*Atherina*).

сниж/ать *v.* reduce, lower, decrease, bring down, depress, drop, lessen; cut (price); impair, be detrimental
(to); **—аться** *v.* decrease, come down, sink, drop, descend, decline, fall (off), diminish, abate, be relieved;
—ение *n.* reduction, lowering, etc., *see v.*; decrease,
loss (of), drop (in), depression; descent, decline; deterioration; degradation; (hearing) impairment; (rad.) down
lead (of antenna); **—енный** *a.* reduced, etc., *see v.*

снизать *see* **снизывать.**

снизить *see* **снижать.**

снизка *f.* stringing together.

снизойти *see* **снисходить.**

снизу *adv.* underneath, (from) below, from the bottom; **с.
вверх** from the bottom up; upward (compatibility,
etc.); **вид с.** bottom view; **подача с.** underfeed.

снизывать *v.* string together.

сним/аемость *f.* removability, detachability; **—аемый**
a. removable, detachable; **—ание** *n.* removing, etc.,
see v.; removal; peeling; picking, harvesting; **—ать** *v.*
remove, take off, take down, take away; strip (off),
skim (off); lift off, detach, slip off; release; take (readings); plot (a curve); relieve (pressure); compensate;
gather (crop), harvest; photograph, copy, rent, lease;
—ать мерку take measurements, measure; **—ать с
работы** dismiss, discharge; **—аться** *v.* be removed,
etc.; come off; (phot.) take; **—аться с места** take off,
start; **—ающий** *a.* removing, etc., *see v.*; **—ающийся**
a. erasable, removable; stripping; **—ающееся покрытие** stripcoat.

снимок *m.* print, photograph; copy, counterpart; *suffix*
—graph.

СНиП *abbr.* (**строительные нормы и правила**) construction standards and specifications, building codes.

снисходит/ельный *a.* condescending; lenient; **—ь** *v.*
condescend; make allowance (for).

снисхождение *n.* condescension.

сниться *v.* dream.

сница *f.* (stub) pole, short tongue.

снова *adv.* again, anew, afresh; re—; **с. пускать** *v.* restore to operation; **с. установить** *v.* reset (for); **начать с.** *v.* make a fresh start.

снов/альный *a.* (text.) warp(ing); **—альщик** *m.* warper;
—ание *n.,* **—ка** *f.* warping; **—ать** *v.* warp; scurry
around; shuttle to and fro.

сновидение *n.* dream.

сногсшибательный *a.* hard (blow); stunning (blow).

сном *instr. of* **сон; лечение с.** sleep therapy.

сноп *m.* sheaf, bundle; cone, shaft, beam (of light), shower
(of sparks), jet (of flame); **—овидный** *a.* sheaf-like;
—овый *a. of* **сноп; —овязалка** *f.,* **—овязальная
машина, —овязка** *f.* (agr.) binder; **—онос** *m.* sheaf
carrier; **—ообразный** *a.* sheaf-like; **—оподаватель**
m. sheaf elevator; **—осушилка** *f.* drying barn; **—о-
уравнитель** *m.* butt adjuster, butter (of binder).

сн彂ров/истый *a.* skillful, dextrous; **—ка** *f.* skill, knack.

снос *m.* pulling down, etc., *see v.*; demolition, removal;
(av.; naut.) drift, deflection; (min.) stripping system;
terrace, bench (of open-cut mine); **измеритель —а**
driftmeter; **продольный с.** (naut.) surge, surging;
—ен *sh. m. of* **сносный; —ить** *v.* pull down, demolish, wreck, tear down, take down; take, bring down,
bring together, pile up; carry away, wash away; blow
off; wear out; suffer, endure; **—иться** *v.* be pulled
down, etc.; wear out; confer, communicate.

сноска *f.* reference, footnote; demolition, tearing down;
bringing down.

сносный *a.* tolerable; passable.

снотворн/ый *a.,* **—ое средство** soporific.

снохождение *n.* somnambulism.

сношен/ие *n.* relation, connection, communication, deal-
ings; (biol.) coitus; **поддерживать —ия** *v.* keep in
touch (with).

сношенный *past pass. part. of* **сносить.**

снуёт *pr. 3 sing. of* **сновать.**

снук/и, —овые *pl.* (ichth.) snooks, rabalos, glassfishes
(*Centropomidae*).

снулый *a.* fixed, restrained; motionless; sluggish.

сныть *f.* (bot.) Aegopodium.

снэк *m.* (ichth.) snoek, barracouta.

снэппер *m.* (ichth.) snapper (*Lutjanus*).

снюх/(ив)аться *v.* sniff each other (of dogs); come to
terms, reach an understanding.

снят *see* **снеток.**

снят/ие *n.* removing, etc., *see* **снимать;** removal; release
(of pressure); *prefix* un—, de—; **с. зажима** unclamp-
ing; **с. окалины** descaling; **с. урожая** harvesting;
—ой *a.* skim (milk).

сняток *see* **снеток.**

снят/ый *a.* removed, etc., *see* **снимать;** derived; stripped
(emulsion); skim(med) milk; **с. затылок** cutting clearance; **со —ым затылком** cleared; **—ь** *see* **снимать.**

со *see* **с; со— ** *see* **с—.**

СО *abbr.* (**социальное обеспечение**) social security.

соавтор *m.* coauthor, joint author, collaborator; **—ство**
n. collaboration.

соапсток *m.* soap stock.

соаренда *f.* joint lease.

собак/а *f.* dog (*Canis familiaris*); dog family (*Canis*);
енотовидная с. raccoon dog (*Nyctereutes procyo-
noides*); **кустарниковая с.** bush dog (*Speothos vena-
ticus*); **летучая с.** flying fox (bat) (*Pteropus*); **морская с.** (ichth.) spiny dogfish (*Squalus acanthias*); **—и**
pl. dogs (*Canidae*); **—и-рыбы** (ichth.) puffers (*Tetraodontidae*); **—оводство** *n.* dog breeding.

собач/ата *pl.* puppies; **—ий** *a.* dog, canine; **—ий зуб**
canine tooth, cuspid; (bot.) Bermuda grass; **—ка** *f.*
dim. of **собака**; (mech.) dog, catch, stop, detent, arresting device; click, trip, pawl, releasing cam; trigger (of
gun); (ichth.) round goby; **клиновые —ки** (ichth.)
Clinidae; **луговая —ка** prairie dog (*Cynomys*); **морские —ки** (ichth.) Blenniidae; **чешуйчатые —ки**
Clinidae; **—ковые** *pl.* (ichth.) Blenniidae; **—ьи** *see*
собаки; —ья *f. of* **собачий; —ья петрушка** dog's
parsley (*Aethusa synapium*); **—ья чума** distemper;
—ья ямка (anat.) fossa canina.

соберёт *fut. 3 sing. of* **собрать.**

собес *m.* social security department.

собесед/ник *m.,* **—ница** *f.* interlocutor; **—ование** *n.* discussion.

собир/ание *n.* gathering, etc., *see* **собирать;** collection,
agglomeration; **—атель** *m.* collector, collecting agent;
gatherer; (elec.) conductor.

собирательн/ый *a.* collecting, collective; **с. приёмник,
с. сосуд** collecting vessel, receiver, reservoir; drip pan,
collecting basin; stock tub; **—ая линза** condensing
lens, condenser, converging lens; **—ая полоса, —ая
шина** (elec.) busbar, collecting bar.

собирательство *n.* collecting.

собир/ать *v.* gather, collect, pick; pick up, catch; accumulate, stock; assemble, set up, erect, rig, mount, fit
(up), join; put together, make up, build up; congregate,
agglomerate; **—аться** *v.* be gathered, etc.; gather, col-

lect, congregate, meet; agglomerate; intend, plan, get ready (to); **—ающий** *a.* gathering, etc., *see v.*; converging (lens); **—ающийся** *a.* congregating; intending, planning.

соблазн/ительный *a.* tempting; **—ить, —ять** *v.* tempt.

соблю/дать, —сти *v.* observe, keep, maintain, adhere (to), fulfill, meet (condition), comply (with); **—дение** *n.* observance, keeping, maintenance, adherence.

собой *instr. of* **себя.**

собол/еводство *n.*, **—еводческий** *a.* sable breeding; **—евый, —ий, —иный** *a.*, **—ь** *m.* (zool.) sable (*Martes zibellina*); **американский —ь** (American) marten.

собою *instr. of* **себя.**

собран/ие *n.* gathering, assembly, meeting, conference, board; collection, accumulation, congregation, complex; collected works; code (of laws); **—ный** *a.* gathered, etc., *see* **собирать;** self-disciplined (person); conglomerate; **в —ном виде** assembled.

собрат *m.* colleague, fellow member; **с. по ремеслу** fellow worker, coworker.

собрать *see* **собирать.**

собрер/ол *m.* sobrerol, pinol hydrate; **—он** *m.* sobrerone, pinol.

собственни/к *m.* owner, proprietor; **—ческий** *a.* proprietary.

собственно *adv.* properly, strictly, correctly; **с. говоря** strictly speaking; **с. кожа** (anat.) true skin, corium; **—ручный** *a.* autographic; holographic.

собственност/ь *f.* property, estate, possessions; ownership; **иметь в —и** *v.* own, possess; **право —и** proprietary rights.

собственно-хрящевое соединение костей (anat.) synchondrosis.

собственн/ый *a.* own, characteristic; natural, inherent, fundamental; self—; eigen—; internal (friction, resistance, etc.); proper (motion; name); intrinsic (conductivity); rest, stationary (mass); in-house; (comp.) home (address); **с. вес** gravity; **—ая масса** rest mass; **—ая нота** (sound) fundamental tone; **—ая функция** eigenfunction, fundamental function; **—ая частота** fundamental frequency; natural frequency; **—ая энергия** self-energy; **—ое значение** (math.) eigenvalue; **—ое колебание** natural oscillation, proper oscillation; **—ое поле** self-field (of a cell); **—ое состояние** eigenstate; **—ое число** eigenvalue; **—ым весом** by gravity.

событ/ие *n.* event, occurrence; **—ия** *pl.* events, developments.

собьёт *fut. 3 sing. of* **сбить.**

сов—, сов. *abbr.* (**советский**) Soviet.

сова *f.* owl; **белая с.** snowy owl (*Nyctea scandiaca*); **болотная с.** short-eared owl (*Asio flammeus*); **ушастая с.** long-eared owl (*Asio otus*); **ястребиная с.** hawk owl (*Surnia ulula*).

совать *v.* thrust, shove, push; **—ся** *v.* intrude, interfere.

совёнок *m.* owlet.

совенталь *m.* sovental (detergent).

соверш/ать *v.* accomplish, effect, perform, achieve, execute, fulfill; commit; **—аться** *v.* be accomplished; come about; **—ение** *n.* accomplishment, completion, performance, achievement, fulfillment.

совершенно *adv.* quite, completely, entirely, fully, thoroughly, wholly, totally, perfectly, precisely; to all intents and purposes; **с. верно** precisely, absolutely, right; **с. секретно** top secret; **—летие** *n.* majority, full age; **достигнуть —летия** *v.* come of age; **—летний** *a.* adult, of age; **—ротые (рыбы)** *pl.* (ichth.) Teleostomi.

совершенный *a.* perfect, ideal, complete, thorough, absolute; black (radiator); (gram.) perfective.

совершенств/о *n.* perfection, ideal; efficiency; **в —е** to perfection; **верх —а** acme of perfection; **—ование** *n.* perfecting, etc., *see v.*; improvement, development; proficiency; **стадия —ования** generation; **—овать** *v.* perfect, improve, develop, refine; **—оваться** *v.* be perfected, improve, progress.

совершит/ель *m.* accomplisher, performer; **—ь** *see* **совершать.**

совест/ливый, —ный *a.* conscientious, scrupulous; **—ь** *f.* conscience.

совет *m.* council, board, committee; Soviet; advice, counsel, opinion, recommendation; **—ник** *m.* adviser, counselor; **—овать** *v.* advise, counsel, recommend, suggest; **—оваться** *v.* consult, take counsel, discuss.

советск/ий *a.*, **—о—** *prefix* Soviet; **С. Союз** Soviet Union; **—ая власть** the Soviet Government; **—ое государство** the Soviet State.

советчик *see* **советник.**

совещ/ание *n.* conference, meeting; consultation, counsel, deliberation; communication; **—ательный** *a.* consultative, deliberative, advisory; **—аться** *v.* take counsel, confer.

совиден *m.* vinyl chloride-vinylidene chloride copolymer (Soviet equivalent of Saran).

сов/иноголовки *see* **совки; —иные** *pl.* owls (*Strigidae*); **—иный** *a. of* **сова; —ка** *f.* (orn.) screech owl (*Otus*); cutworm (*Agrotis*); *gen. of* **совок; стеблёвая —ка** stem borer; **—ки** *pl.* owlet or cutworm moths (*Noctuidae*); *pl. of* **совка.**

совкаин *m.* Sovcaine, percaine.

совков/ый *a.* scoop(-type), trowel(-type); **—ая лопата** shovel.

совлад/ать *v.* control, get the better (of); **—елец** *m.* joint owner; **—ение** *n.* joint ownership, joint property.

совместим/ость *f.* compatibility; (electrical) connectivity; **—ый** *a.* compatible, combinable, consistent.

совместительство *n.* plurality (of professions); **—вать** *v.* hold two or more positions.

совместить *see* **совмещать.**

совместно *adv.* in common, jointly, together, in combination, in conjunction (with); **владеть с., использовать с.** *v.* share; **работающий с.** collaborating, cooperating; jointly operating; **ставить с.** *v.* class (with); **—сть** *f.* compatibility; consistency (of equations).

совместн/ый *a.* joint, common, cooperative; co—, combined; compatible; (math.) simultaneous, (comp.) collateral; **с. объём** co-volume; **—ая полимеризация** copolymerization; **—ая работа** teamwork, collaboration, cooperation; **—ое действие** joint action, cooperation; **—ое обучение** coeducation; **—ое осаждение** coprecipitation.

совмещ/ать *v.* combine, join, integrate; match, make coincident (with); blend, fuse; (geom.) superpose; **—аться** *v.* be combined, etc.; be compatible; coincide; **—ающийся** *a.* coinciding; superposable; **—ение** *n.* combining, combination, etc., *see v.*; coincidence; alignment; overlay; overlap; contact; plurality (of professions); **точное с.** exact registration; **—ённый** *a.* combined, blended, etc., *see v.*

совнутри *adv.* from within.

совок *m.* shovel, scoop, trowel; dust pan; *gen. pl. of* **совка.**

совокуп/ительный *a.* (zool.) copulative; **—ительная сумка** (zool.) bursa copulatrix; **—иться** *see* **совокупляться; —ление** *n.* copulation; **—ляться** *v.* copulate; combine.

совокупн/о *adv.* jointly; **—ость** *f.* series, set, aggregate; collection; totality; combination, conjunction; assembly (of parts); (math.; stat.) population; pattern (of electric charges); **в —ости** in the aggregate, in total, together; **—ый** *a.* joint, combined, collective, cumulative, aggregate; simultaneous (equations).

совол *m.* chlorinated biphenyl.

совообразные *pl.* owls (*Strigiformes*).

совпа/дать *v.* coincide, be coincident (with), be in line (with), match, accord closely; concur, conform, tally, agree; **с. во времени** synchronize; be synchronized, happen at the same time; **с. по фазе** be in phase; **с. частично** overlap; **точно с.** (printing) register; **—да́ющий** *a.* coincident(al), concurrent, congruent, corresponding; **—дающий осями** coaxial; **—дающий по фазе** cophasal, in phase; **—дение** *n.* coincidence, concurrence, conformity, congruence, concordance, correspondence, accord(ance); agreement, match(ing), fit; hit (in computer search); superposition; **—дение при наложении** (math.) congruence; **линия —дения** match line; **отсчёт —дения, счёт —дений** (instr.) coincidence counting; **с —дением по току** (comp.) coincident-current; **схема —дения** coincidence circuit; **—сть** *see* **совпадать**.

совпрен *m.* sovprene, chloroprene rubber.

современн/ик *m.* contemporary; **—ость** *f.* contemporaneousness, the present time, modernity; **—ый** *a.* contemporary, contemporaneous, modern, up-to-date, recent, advanced, state-of-the-art, present(-day), current.

совсем *adv.* altogether, absolutely, entirely; quite; **с. не** not in the least, not at all; **с. не то** nothing of the sort.

совторгфлот *m.* Soviet merchant marine.

совулканизация *f.* covulcanization.

совхоз *m.*, **—ный** *a.* sovkhoz, state farm.

совы *pl.* (orn.) Strigiformes; *see also* **сова**.

совьёт *fut. 3 sing. of* **свить**.

соглас/ен *sh. m. of* **согласный**; **—ие** *n.* consent, compliance, concurrence, assent, accord, agreement, congruence; (geol.) conformity; **в —ии** in accordance (with); **находиться в —ии** *v.* agree; **общее —ие** consensus; **—ительный** *a.* conciliatory; **—иться** *see* **соглашаться**.

согласн/о *adv. and prep. dat.* concordantly, in harmony; in accordance (with), according (to), in conformance (with); to suit; by; to; from; under; as per (order); **с. наблюдениям** as observed; **с. указаниям** as directed; **—ость** *f.* concord(ance); consistency; **—ый** *a.* conforming (to), in agreement (with), consistent (with); cumulative; consonant (letter).

согласов/ание *n.* concordance, agreement, conformity, correspondence, coordination, matching; consent, approval; adjustment; trade-off, fair; (math.) congruence; **—анность** *f.* concordance, agreement, harmony, compatibility, consistency; coordination; match; consensus; consent; **—анность действия** teamwork; **—анный** *a.* adjusted, etc., *see v.*; coordinate(d); simultaneous; consistent; approved; **—(ыв)ать** *v.* adjust; coordinate, correlate, match, fit; conciliate; accommodate, comply; submit for approval; trade off, fair; **—(ыв)аться** *v.* be adjusted, etc.; conform, be in keeping (with), be in line (with), agree, be consistent (with), correlate; match, fit, check (with); comply; cohere; **не —(ыв)аться** disagree (with), be at variance (with), be inconsistent.

согласующ/ий *pr. act. part. of* **согласов(ыв)ать**; **—ие переходы** (wave guides) impedance-matching transformers; **—ийся** *a.* conforming; compatible; adjusted, coordinated; simultaneous; approved.

соглаш/ать *v.* persuade, induce; **—аться** *v.* consent, agree, comply (with); coincide; **не —аться** differ, dis-

agree; **—ение** *n.* agreement, understanding, arrangement, contract.

согнать *see* **сгонять**.

согнут/о *prefix* campylo—, curved; **—осеменной** *a.* (bot.) campylospermous; **—ый** *a.* bent, curved; **—ь** *v.* bend, curve, twist; fold.

согосподствующий *a.* (bot.) codominant.

согрев/ание *n.* warming, heating; **—атель** *m.* heater; **—ательный** *a.* heating; **—ать** *v.* warm, heat; **—аться** *v.* get warm; **—ающее** *n.* hot drink; **—ающий** *a.* warming, heating.

согрет/ый *a.* warmed, heated; **—ь** *see* **согревать**.

согреш/ение *n.* error; **—ить** *v.* err.

сода *f.* soda, sodium carbonate; **с. бикарбонат, с. для теста** sodium bicarbonate, baking soda; **с. для стирки** washing soda, sodium carbonate; **аммиачная с.** ammonia soda, Solvay soda; **двууглекислая с.** sodium bicarbonate; **жжёная с., кальцинированная с.** soda ash (anhydrous sodium carbonate); **каустическая с.** caustic soda, sodium hydroxide; **обезвоженная с.** soda ash; **питьевая с.** sodium bicarbonate; **прокалённая с.** soda ash; **углекислая с.** sodium carbonate.

Содди-Фаянса закон Soddy-Fajans law.

содейств/ие *n.* assistance, cooperation; concurrence; **—овать** *v.* assist, help, aid, cooperate; contribute, further, forward, expedite, promote.

содержание *n.* content(s), percentage, concentration, capacity, volume (of a body), area (of a surface); (bact.) count; maintenance, upkeep, care, keeping; subject matter (of book); scope (of meaning); (min.) assay; housing (system); allowance, salary, pay; **с. жира** fat content; **с. и форма** form and contents; **краткое с.** summary; **кубическое с.** volume; **процентное с.** percentage, per cent content; **руда богатая —м** a rich ore; **с большим —м, с высоким —м** rich (in), high (in); **с низким —м** low (in), low-grade (ore), poor (in); **техническое с.** maintenance work; **уголь с высоким —м золы** high-ash coal.

содерж/ать *v.* contain, hold, include, comprise, incorporate; keep, support, maintain, care (for), take care (of); **с. в себе** contain, include, incorporate; **с. мало** be poor (in), be low (in); **с. много** be rich (in); **—аться** *v.* be contained, etc.; occur, be found, be present; **—ащий** *a.* containing, etc., *see v.*; *suffix* **—(и)ferous, -bearing, -containing; **—ащий много пузырьков** (anat.) vesiculose; **не —ащий** free (of); **не —ащий урана** uranium-free; **—имое** *n.* contents; **—имость** *f.* capacity, volume.

содов/ая *f.* soda water; **—о—** *prefix* soda; **—о-известковое умягчение** (water softening) soda-lime process; **—ый** *a.* soda.

содоклад *m.* coreport, joint report; supplementary paper; **—чик** *m.* reader of a joint or supplementary report.

содок/оз *m.*, **—у** *f.* rat-bite fever.

содомия *f.* (med.) sodomy.

содосодержащий *a.* containing soda.

содр/анный *a.* stripped, skinned, barked; **—ать** *see* **сдирать**.

содрог/ание *n.* shudder(ing), tremor; **—ать** *v.* shake, vibrate; **—аться, —нуться** *v.* shudder.

содружеств/енный *a.* concomitant, accompanying, attending; (med.) consensual (reaction), crossed (reflex); **—енное движение** (med.) synkinesis; **—енное косоглазие** (med.) concomitant strabismus; **—о** *n.* concord; collaboration; commonwealth; *see also* **СНГ**; **—о наций** (British) commonwealth.

соев/ище *n.* soybean field; **—ый** *a. of* **соя**, soybean.

соединен/ие *n.* connection, connecting, etc., *see* **соединять(ся);** (chem.) compound; combination; (con)junction, coalescence, coalition, fusion; (mech.) coupling, union, joint, seam, bond, link; splice; (elec.) contact; line, lead; (tel.) call; (gen.) conjugation; (anat.) junctura; (mil.) formation, (task) force; **с. на клею** glued joint; **с. на резьбе** threaded joint; **с. осей** axis coupling; **с. плодов** (med.) *suffix* —pagus; **с. плодов головами** (med.) craniopagus; **—ия** *pl. of* **соединение;** (math.) (permutations and) combinations; (elec.) routing, wiring; **в —иях** combined; **в —ии с** in connection with; **вес —ия** combining weight; **вступать в с., входить в с.** enter into combination, combine (with), react; **место —ия** joint, junction; **неподвижное с. костей** (anat.) synostosis; **объём —ия** combining volume; **реакция —ия** addition reaction; combination; **с непосредственным —ием** direct-coupled; **схема —ия** (elec.) circuit diagram; **теплота —ия** heat of combination; **с.-зигзаг** *n.* (elec.) zigzag connection.

Соединённые Штаты United States.

соедин/ённый *a.* connected, etc., *see* **соединять;** joint; **—итель** *m.* connector, bond, coupler, coupling, fastener; (elec.) jumper.

соединительнотканн/ый *a.* (anat.) connective tissue; **—ая оболочка (мышцы)** perimysium.

соединительн/ый *a.* connecting, coupling, binding, joint; conjunctive; combining (volume; weight); draw (bar); flange, collar (nut); (elec.) junction (box); splice (plate); (cartography) adjustment (curve); connective (tissue); (anat.) anastomotic; (gram.) connective (particle); copulative (conjunction); **с. зажим** (elec.) connecting terminal, connector; **с. провод** (elec.) jumper; **с. фланец** flange coupling; **—ая деталь** coupling piece, adapter; **—ая коробка** (elec.) junction box; **—ая линия** (tel.) trunk (line); **—ая муфта** connector, sleeve; **—ая оболочка** (anat.) conjunctiva; **—ая трубка** nipple; **—ая тяга** coupling rod, tie (rod); **—ая часть** joint; connecting piece, connection; **—ое звено** link, coupling.

соедин/ить *see* **соединять;** **—яемый** *a.* connectable; combinable; connected; combined; **—ять** *v.* connect, join, unite, consolidate, draw together, coordinate, link, couple, bridge, fasten, attach, splice; bind, combine, fix; bond; blend, fuse, amalgamate; joint, articulate; assemble, build up; engage, mesh, put in gear; **с. в** (elec.) connect up, connect to; **—ять в себе** combine; **—яться** *v.* be connected, etc.; connect (with), combine, unite, join, couple; congregate, aggregate; coalesce, fuse, blend; engage, mesh (of gears); **—яться повторно** recombine; **—яющий** *a.* communicating, (re)uniting.

соек *gen. pl. of* **сойка.**

сожал/ение *n.,* **—еть** *v.* regret.

сож/гут *fut. 3 pl. of* **сжечь;** **—жение** *n.* combustion, burning; cremation; **анализ —жением** combustion analysis; **—жённый** *a.* burned, scorched; **—жечь** *see* **сжечь;** **—игательный** *a.* combustion.

сожитель *m.* (biol.) symbiont, cohabitant; **—ство** *n.* symbiosis, cohabitation; **—ствовать** *v.* live together, cohabit.

сожмёт *fut. 3 sing. of* **сж(им)ать.**

созваниваться *v.* (tel.) get in touch, call.

созвать *see* **созывать.**

созвездие *n.* (astr.) constellation.

созвониться *see* **созваниться.**

созвуч/ие unison, agreement, accord, concord, consonance, harmony; **—ный** *a.* unison; consonant (with); in keeping (with), in harmony (with), in tune (with).

созд/аваемый *a.* produced, etc., *see v.;* due (to); **—авание** *n.* producing, etc., *see v.;* creation, establishment; **—аватель** *see* **создатель;** **—авать** *v.* produce, generate, give rise (to), evolve, develop, devise; create, make, form, build (up), set up, found, establish; **—аваться** be produced, etc., *see* **создавать;** arise, spring up; **—ание** *see* **создавание;** advent; growth; creature; **—атель** *m.* originator, founder, creator, maker; **—ать** *see* **создавать.**

созерцать *v.* contemplate.

созид/ание *n.* erection, construction, building; creation, foundation; **—атель** *m.* builder; creator, founder; **—ательный** *a.* constructive; creative; **—ать** *see* **создавать.**

созин *m.* sozin (a body protein).

созн/авать *v.* acknowledge, recognize, admit; **—аваться** *v.* confess, admit; **—ание** *n.* consciousness, sense; acknowledgement, admission; **потерять —ание** *v.* lose consciousness; **—ательно** *adv.* consciously, knowingly, deliberately; **—ательность** *f.* consciousness, awareness; **—ательный** *a.* conscious, deliberate; **—ать** *see* **сознавать.**

созовёт *fut. 3 sing. of* **созвать,** *see* **созывать.**

созо/иодол *m.* sozoiodol, sozoidolic acid; **—ловая кислота** sozolic acid, *o*-phenolsulfonic acid.

созре/вание *n.* ripening, etc., *see v.;* **половое с.** puberty; **—вательный** *a.* ripening, etc., *see v.;* **—вать** *v.* ripen, mature; cure (of concrete, etc.); age, season; **—вающий** *see* **созревательный;** **—вший** *a.* ripe, mature; aged, seasoned; digested (sludge); **—лый** *a.* ripe, mature; **—ть** *see* **созревать.**

созыв *m.* call, summons, invitation; **—ать** *v.* call (a meeting), summon, invite; convene.

сои *gen., etc., of* **соя.**

СОИ *abbr.* **(служба обработки информации)** data processing service.

соиздатель *m.* copublisher.

соизменим/ость *f.* (math.) covariance; **—ый** *a.* covariant.

соизмерим/ость *f.* commensurability, commensuration; **—ый** *a.* commensurable, commensurate; comparable.

соизмер/ить, —ять *v.* commensurate.

соиск/ание *n.* competition, rivalry; **—атель** *m.* competitor, rival.

сойдя *pr. ger. of* **сойти.**

сойка *f.* (orn.) jay (*Garrulus*).

сойти *see* **сходить.**

сок *m.* juice, sap; liquor; (furnace) slag.

сокалоин *m.* socaloin.

сокатализатор *m.* cocatalyst.

сокирки *pl.* (bot.) larkspur (*Delphinium consolida*).

сокление *n.* (cyt.) syncytium.

соко/вместилище *n.* (biol.) somatocyst; **—выжиматель** *m.* juice extractor, juicer, squeezer; **—вой, —вый** *a. of* **сок;** pulpy; liquor-tanned; **—гонный** *a.* (pharm.) secretagogue; **—движение** *n.* (bot.) sap flow, sap rise.

сокол *m.* (constr.) float, hawk, (plasterer's) trowel; (orn.) falcon (*Falco*); **—ёнок** *m.* young falcon; **—ий** *a. of* **сокол;** **—иные** *pl.* (orn.) Falconidae; **—иный** *a. of* **сокол;** **—иха** *f.* female falcon; **—ок** *m.* float, hawk; brisket (cut of meat); **—ообразные** *pl.* birds of prey (*Falconiformes*); **с.-сапсан** *see* **сапсан; соколы** *see* **соколиные; —ьник** *m.* falconer.

соко/отделение *n.* (physiol.) secretion; **—отжималка** *see* **соковыжиматель; —подъёмник** *m.* montejus; **—содержание** *n.* (bot.) sap content.

сокр. *abbr.* **(сокращение)** abbreviation.

сократим/ость *f.* (math.) contract(ib)ility, reducibility; **мышечная с.** (physiol.) myotility; **—ый** *a.* contracti(b)le, reducible.

сократитель *m.* (min.) riffle; sampler.

сократительн/ый *a.* contracting, contraction; (met.) concentration; contracti(b)le; retractable; **—ая плавка** concentration smelting.

сократить *see* **сокращать.**

сокращ/аемость *f.* contracti(bi)lity; **—аемый** *a.* contracti(b)le; **—ать** *v.* contract, shorten, abbreviate, abridge, condense; reduce, decrease, curtail, cut (down); shrink; foreshorten (perspective); (fractions) cancel (out); **—аться** *v.* be contracted, etc.; contract, shorten, shrink; drop, decrease, fall, decline; cancel (out); **—ающий** *a.* contracting, etc., *see v.*; decreasing (species); **—ающийся** *a.* contractile; **—ение** *n.* contraction, shortening, etc., *see v.*; abridgement; decrease, curtailment, cut; shrinkage; short cut; (math.) cancellation (of like terms), reduction (of fractions); **—ение сердца** systole; **—ённо** *adv.* in brief, briefly; in abbreviated form; **—ённость** *f.* brevity; **—ённый** *a.* contracted, etc., *see v.*; brief, concise; compact; short(-cut); catchword (title).

сокристаллизация *f.* cocrystallization.

сокровенный *a.* secret, concealed.

сокровищ/е *n.* treasure; **—ница** *f.* treasury, depository, storehouse.

сокруш/ать *v.* crush, smash, shatter, break (up), destroy, demolish; wreck; distress, grieve; **—ение** *n.* crushing etc., *see v.*; destruction, demolition; grief; **—ённый** *a.* crushed, etc., *see v.*; **—ительный** *a.* crushing, etc., *see v.*; destructive, damaging; **—ать** *see* **сокрушать.**

сокрытие *see* **скрытие.**

сок-самотёк *m.* (chem.) (distillation) first runnings; (coal tar) first light oil; (sugar) high green syrup; (whiskey) foreshot.

сокслет *m.* (chem.) Soxhlet apparatus.

сол *m.* (ichth.) sole (*Solea*).

солан/густин *m.* solangustin; **—дрин** *m.* solandrine; **—елловая кислота** solanellic acid; **—идин** *m.* solanidine; **—ин** *m.* solanine; **—ион** *m.* solanione, javanicin; **—овая кислота** solanic acid; **—орубин** *m.* solanorubin; **—тины** *pl.* solantine colors; **—трены** *pl.* solanthrene colors.

соларовое масло *see* **соляровое масло.**

соларсон *m.* Solarson, chloroarsenol.

соласодин *m.* solasodine.

сола/т *m.* solate, liquefied gel; **—ция** *f.* solation, liquefaction of a gel.

солдат *m.* soldier; (ichth.) minnow (*Phoxinus*); **—ик** *m.* tool post; **—ы-рыбы** *see* **белки-рыбы.**

соле— *prefix* halo—, salt; **—вар** *m.* salt plant worker; **—варение** *n.*, **—вар(ен)ный** *a.* salt-making; **—варня** *f.* salt works, saltern; **—вой** *a.* salt, saline; **—вой обмен** (physiol.) mineral balance; **—выносливый** *a.* salt-resistant; (bot.) salt-tolerant; **—добывание** *n.*, **—добывающий** *a.* salt-mining; **—дробилка** *f.* salt crusher; **—евые** *pl.* (ichth.) Soleidae; **—й** *gen. pl. of* **соль; —любивый** *a.* (bot.) halophilous, salt-loving; **—мер** *m.* salinometer, salinity bridge, brine gage; **—мии** *pl.* (zool.) veiled clams (*Solemyidae*); **—накопление** *n.* salt accumulation; **—ние** *n.* salting; corning; pickling; pickled foods.

соленоид *m.*, **—ный** *a.* (elec.) solenoid; **—альный** *a.* solenoidal; tube-like.

солёно-копчёный *a.* kippered (fish).

сол/еносный *a.* saliferous, salt-bearing; **—еностела** *f.* (bot.) solenostele; **—ёность** *f.* saltiness, salinity, salt

content, mineral content; **—еноцит** *m.* (zool.) solenocyte.

солён/ый *a.* salt(y), saline, salt-bearing; briny, brackish; pickled; corned (beef); **с. огурец** pickle; **—ая вода** brine; **—ая капуста** sauerkraut.

соленье *see* **соление.**

солеобраз/ование *n.* salt formation, salification; **—ователь** *m.* salt former, halogen; **—ующий** *a.* salt-forming.

соле/подобный *a.* salt-like, saline; **—разбрасыватель** *m.* salt spreader; **—разработки** *pl.* salt works; **—род** *m.* halogen; **—рос** *m.* (bot.) Salicornia; **—содержание** *n.* salt content, salinity; **—содержащий** *a.* salt-containing, salt-bearing, saliferous; **—содержащая моча** (med.) calcariuria; **—сос** *m.* salt pump; **—стойкий** *a.* (bot.) salt-tolerant; **—стойкость** *f.* salt tolerance; **—устойчивость** *f.* salt tolerance; resistance to salt.

солея *f.* (ichth.) sole (*Solea*).

соли *gen., pl., etc., of* **соль.**

солидар/изироваться *v.* hold (with), share; **—но** *adv.* jointly (and severally); **—ность** *f.* solidarity; **—ный** *a.* jointly (and severally); **—ность** *f.* solidarity; **—ный** *a.* solidary, having common interests; authoritative.

солидн/ость *f.* solidity, firmness, reliability, soundness; **—ый** *a.* solid, firm, reliable, sound, sturdy, substantial.

солидол *m.* (lubricant) grease; **—онагнетатель** *m.* grease gun.

солидус *m.* (met., etc.) solidus.

соликамские соли natural deposits of sodium and potassium salts.

солильн/ый *a.* salting; pickling; **—я** *f.* salt works.

солион *m.* solion (electrochemical sensing and control device).

солитер *m.* solitaire (gem).

солить *v.* salt, brine, pickle, cure.

солифлюкция *f.* solifluction, soil creep.

солка *f.* salting, pickling.

солнечник *m.* (ichth.) sunfish, dory (*Zeus*); (prot.) heliozoan, sun animalcule; **—и** *pl. of* **солнечник; —овые** *pl.* (ichth.) dories (*Zeidae*); **—ообразные** *pl.* (ichth.) Zeiformes.

солнечно-звёздный *a.* solar-sidereal.

солнечнотепловая энергия solar thermal energy.

солнечн/ый *a.* solar, sun; sunny (weather); **с. свет** sunlight; **с. удар** sun stroke; **—ая система** solar system; **—ое сияние** sunshine; **—ое сплетение** (anat.) solar plexus; **—ые часы** sun dial; **обучение —ым светом** insolation.

солнц/е *n.* sun; sunshine; **ложное с.** (astr.) parhelion; anthelion; *prefix* heli(o)— (sun); **по—у** by the sun; clockwise; **—езащитный** *a.* sun (glasses); **—елечение** *n.* heliotherapy; **—елюбивый** *a.* (bot.) heliophilous, sun-loving; **с.-рыба** *see* **рыба, солнечная; —естояние** *n.* (astr.) solstice; **—ецвет** *m.* sunrose (*Helianthemum*).

соло *n.* (music) solo.

соловей *m.* (orn.) nightingale (*Luscinia*).

солов/еть *v.* glaze (of eyes); become drowsy; **—ый** *a.* glazed (eyes); sleepy (person); light bay (horse).

соловь/ёнок *m.* young nightingale; **—и** *pl.* nightingales (*Lusciana*); **—иный** *a. of* **соловей; —иха** *f.* female nightingale.

солод *m.* malt; **затёртый с.** mash; **—елый** *a.* sweetish.

солоди *pl., etc., of* **солодь.**

солод/ильный *a.* malt(ing); **—ить** *v.* malt; sweeten.

солодк/а *f.*, **—овый** *a.* licorice.

солодо/вание *see* **соложение; —вня** *f.* malt house;

—вый *a.* malt; **—вый сахар** malt sugar, maltose; **—дробилка** *f.* malt crusher; **—ращение** *n.* malting; **—сушилка, —сушильня** *f.* malt dryer, malt kiln, malt drying floor.

солодь *f.* (soils) solod, degraded solonetz.

соложение *n.* malting, malt production.

солом/а *f.* straw, chaff; **древесная с.** match-stick wood; **—енно-макулатурный** *a.* mixed-straw (board); **—енный** *a.* straw; straw-colored; **—енная масса** (paper) straw pulp; **—ина** *f.* straw, stalk; (bot.) culm; **—инка** *f.* a straw; **—истый** *a.* (bot.) heavy-stalked, culmiferous; **—ит** *m.* pressed straw (insulation) board; **—ка** *f.* straw, haulm, stem; (match) stick; **—оволокуша** *f.* straw sweep; **—овыдуватель** *m.* straw blower; **—овяз** *m.* straw binder; **—оизмельчитель** *m.* straw shredder; **—окопнитель** *m.* straw collector; **—о-крутка** *f.* straw rope twister.

Соломоновы острова Solomon Islands.

соломо/подъёмник *m.* straw conveyer; **—половокопнитель** *m.* straw and capes collector; **—пресс** *m.* straw baler; **—резка** *f.* straw cutter; **—сбрасыватель** *m.* straw dumper; **—силосорезка** *f.* straw and silage chopper; **—таска** *f.* straw carrier; **—транспортёр** *m.* straw conveyer; **—тряс** *m.* straw shaker, straw rack; (combine) separator.

солон *sh. m. of* **солёный**; **—еть** *v.* become salty; **—ец** *m.* solonetz (alkali soil); salt lake; salt spring; **—ина** *f.*, **—инный** *a.* corned beef; **—ица, —ка** *f.* salt shaker; **—о** *sh. n. of* **солёный**; **—оватость** *f.* saltiness, brackishness; **—оватый** *a.* subsaline, brackish, briny; **—оводный** *a.* (zool.) euhaline, saltwater (fauna).

солонцеват/ость *f.* solonetzicity, alkalinity (of soil); **—ый** *a.* solonetzic, alkaline; saliferous.

солонцовый *a. of* **солонец**.

солончак *m.* solonchak, saline soil; salt marsh; (bot.) saltwort (*Salsola*); **—оватость** *f.* salinity; **—овый** *a.* brackish, briny, saliniferous, salty; saline (soil); (bot.) halophytic.

солор/иновая кислота solorinic acid; **—овая кислота** soloric acid.

Солсбери (geog.) Salisbury.

солур/иновый *a.* solurinic (acid); **—ол** *m.* solurol, nucleotinphosphoric acid.

соль *f.* salt; spec. sodium chloride; (music) G; **с. серной кислоты** sulfate; **с. уксусной кислоты** acetate; **кислая с.** acid salt, bisalt; **основная с.** basic salt, subsalt.

сольбар *m.* a barium polysulfide insecticide and fungicide.

сольв/ат *m.* solvate; **—атация** *f.*, **—атационный** *a.* solvation; **—атированный** *a.* solvated; **—атный** *a.* solvate; **—атохромия** solvatochromism.

сольвент(-нафта) *m.* solvent-naphtha.

сольёт *fut. 3 sing. of* **слить.**

Сольвея способ Solvay process.

сольволи/з *m.* solvolysis; **—тический** *a.* solvolytic, solvation.

Сольвэ способ Solvay process.

сольный *a.* (music) solo.

сольпуги *pl.* (zool.) Solpugida.

сольфатара *f.* solfatara (volcanic orifice).

солюбилизация *f.* solubilization.

солюм *m.* solum, lowest part; (med.) bottom, lowest part; (law) parcel of ground.

солю/сульфон *m.* Sulphetrone, solapsone; **—сурьмин** *m.* Solyusurmin, sodium stibogluconate.

солютре *n.*, **—йский** *a.* (archeol.) Solutrean.

солянк/а *f.* salt shaker; (bot.) halophyte, spec. saltwort (*Salsola*); **—овый** *a.* halophytic.

солян/ой *a.* salt(y), saline; *see also* **соляный**; **с. рассол** brine; **—ая шляпа** (geol.) salt cap; **—о-калочный** *a.* salt-bath tempering, salt-bath (furnace).

солянокисл/ый *a.* hydrochloric acid; chloride (of metals, etc.); hydrochloride (of organic compound); **—ая соль** chloride; hydrochloride.

солян/ый *a.* hydrochloric (acid); **соль —ой кислоты** chloride.

соляр *m.* (petrol.) solar oil (petroleum distillate obtained after kerosene and before lubricating oil); Diesel fuel; **—изация** *f.* solarization; **—ий** *m.* solarium; **—иметр** *m.* solarimeter; **—ит** *m.* (med.) solar plexitis; **—ка** *see* **соляр; —ный** *a.* solar; **—овый** *a.* solar (oil).

сом *m.* (ichth.) sheatfish, catfish (*Silurus*).

сома *f.* (biol.) soma, body; *suffix* **—some**.

сомалийский *a.* (geog.) Somali(land).

сом/атический *a.* (biol.) somatic; **—ато—** *prefix* somato— (body); **—атология** *f.* somatology; **—атомегалия** *f.* (med.) somatomegaly, gigantism; **—атоплазма** *f.* (biol.) somatoplasm; **—атотропный** *a.* (biochem.) somatotropic, growth (hormone); **—ик** *dim. of* **сом; —ит** *m.* somite, body segment.

сомкнут/ость *f.* density, closeness, compactness; **с. полога** (silv.) close stand, crown contact; **—ый** *a.* dense, close, compact; closed, joined; **—ь** *see* **смыкать.**

Соммле реакция (chem.) Sommelet reaction.

сомнамбул *m.* somnambulist; **—изм** *m.* somnambulism.

сомне/ваться *v.* doubt, have doubts, question; **—ние** *n.* doubt; **без —ния** without doubt, no doubt, undoubtedly, without question; **подвергать —нию** *v.* doubt, question.

сомнёт *fut. 3 sing. of* **смять.**

сомнирол *m.* somnirol.

сомнительн/о *adv.* doubtfully; it is doubtful, it is questionable; **—ость** *f.* doubtfulness, uncertainty; **—ый** *a.* doubtful, dubious, questionable, open to question, problematical.

сомнитол *m.* Somnitol.

сомнож/ество *n.* (math.) coset, corresponding set; **—итель** *m.* (co)factor.

сомнол *m.* somnol, chloroethanal alcoholate.

сомовидные *pl.* (ichth.) Siluroidea.

сомов/ий *a. of* **сом; —ина** *f.* catfish (as food); **—ые** *pl.* catfishes, silurids (*Siluridae*); **—ый** *a. of* **сом.**

сомон *m.* salmon (color).

сомы *see* **сомовые.**

сон *m.* sleep; hibernation, dormancy; dream; (acous.) sone (unit of loudness).

Сона (geog.) Saône.

сонар *m.* sonar, sound navigation and ranging.

соневые *pl.* (mam.) dormice (*Gliridae*).

сонерил *m.* Soneryl, Neonal, butethal.

сони *gen., pl., etc., of* **соня.**

соним *m.* (met.) sonim.

Сонина полином (math.) Sonine polynomial.

сонлив/ость *f.* somnolence, drowsiness; **неестественная с.** (med.) coma; **—ый** *a.* somnolent, sleepy, drowsy; **болезненно —ый** *a.* comatose.

сонно-барабанный *a.* (med.) caroticotympanic.

сонн/ый *a.* sleepy; (anat.) carotid, carotic; **с. напиток** soporific; **—ая артерия** (anat.) carotid; **—ая болезнь** (med.) sleeping sickness; **—ая железа** (anat.) carotid body; **—ое зелье** (bot.) mandrake (*Mandragora officinarum*).

сонометр *m.* sonometer, phonometer.

сонорный *a.* resonant, sonorous.

сонорский *a.* (geog.) Sonora.

сон-трава *f.* pasqueflower.

соня *m. and f.* drowsy person; *f.* (zool.) dormouse.

сообитание *n.* (biol.) cohabitation, association.

соображ/ать *v.* understand, grasp; consider, take into consideration; contrive; **—ение** *n.* understanding, consideration, deliberation; reason; **по различным —ениям** for diverse reasons; **принимать в —ение** *v.* take into consideration, allow (for).

сообразит/ельность *f.* quickness, alertness, quick thinking; **—ельный** *a.* quick-witted, alert, bright; **—ь** *see* **соображать.**

сообразн/о *adv. and prep. dat.* in conformity (with), according (to); **—ость** *f.* suitability, suitableness, compatibility, conformity, compliance, congruence, coincidence; consent; **—ый** *a.* suitable, compatible, conformable, congruent, consistent.

сообразов(ыв)ать *v.* adapt, adjust, conform; **—ся** *v.* fit, conform, comply.

сообща *adv.* together, jointly; **действие с.** consolidated action; **действовать с.** *v.* collaborate, pool interests.

сообщ/ать *v.* communicate, inform, advise, report, notify, announce; pass on, transmit; give, furnish, add (to); place on record; **как —ают** reportedly; **—аться** *v.* be in communication (with); be announced; **—ающийся** *a.* communicating.

сообщ/ение *n.* communication, information, message, report, notice, word; (press) release; traffic; service; (elec.) connection, contact; **с. о погоде** weather report; **пути —ения** means of communication; **согласно —ениям** reportedly; are said to; **установить с.** *v.* establish communication; (elec.) connect up; **—ённый** *a.* communicated, etc., *see* **сообщать.**

сообщ/ество *n.* community; (biol.) bioc(o)enosium; association; cooperation; **с. организмов** (biol.) bioc(o)enosis, biotic community; **растительное с.** (bot.) phytoc(o)enosis; **—ить** *see* **сообщать; —ник** *m.* accomplice, partner; (law) accessory; **—ничество** *n.* complicity, participation.

соопылитель *m.* (bot.) copollinator.

соору/дить *see* **сооружать; —жаемый** *a.* under construction; **—жать** *v.* construct, build, erect, install; equip, outift, tool up, arm; **—жение** *n.* construction, building, etc., *see v.*; edifice, structure; **—жения** *pl.* (water) works; (mil.) installations; **оборонительные —жения** defenses; **—жённый** *a.* constructed, etc., *see v.*

сооса/дитель *m.* coprecipitator; **—дить, —ждать** *v.* coprecipitate; **—ждение** *n.* coprecipitation.

соосн/ость *f.* coaxial alignment, coaxiality; **—ый** *a.* coaxial, uniaxial.

соответственно *adv. and prep. dat.* accordingly, correspondingly; consequently; respectively; according to, as per (instructions); **—сть** *f.* conformance, conformity, correspondence; suitability, pertinence.

соответственн/ый *a.* expedient, proper, suitable, pertinent; corresponding, conforming, congruent, homologous; **—ая часть** mate, counterpart; **—ые углы** corresponding angles.

соответств/ие *n.* conformity, compliance, agreement, accord(ance); homology; expediency, fit(ness); (math.) correspondence; **в —ии** in conformity (with), in accordance (with), according (to), by, depending (on); in line (with), to match, to fit; **взаимное с.** congruence; **режим полного —ия** (comp.) what you see is what you get, WYSIWYG; **—овать** *v.* conform (to), comply (with), be in accord (with); correspond (to), match (up), be in line (with), follow, fit, tally, correlate; answer, meet, satisfy (requirement); **—ующий** *a.* con-

forming, etc., *see v.*; appropriate, suitable, pertinent, proper, adequate; respective; specific, characteristic; homologous; **—ующая часть** counterpart, mate; **—ующим образом** suitably, properly, as required.

соответчик *m.* (law) codefendant.

соотечественн/ик *m.*, **—ица** *f.* compatriot.

соотнести *see* **соотносить.**

соотносит/ельность *f.* correlation; **—ельный** *a.* correlative; **—ь** *v.* correlate, relate (to); compare.

соотношен/ие *n.* correlation, relation(ship), connection, correspondence; proportion, ratio; **с. веса** weight ratio; **быть в —ии** *v.* correspond, correlate; **генерирующее с.** generating relation; **установить правильное с.** *v.* coordinate.

сопа *f.* (ichth.) bream (*Abramis sapa*).

сопел *gen. pl.*; **—ьный** *a.* of **сопло.**

сопение *n.* wheezing, snorting, puffing.

соперни/к *m.*, **—ца** *f.* rival, competitor; **—чать** *v.* rival, compete; **—чество** *n.* rivalry, competition; antagonism.

сопеть *v.* wheeze, snort, puff.

сопка *f.* mud volcano; cone-shaped hill.

соплеменн/ик *m.*, **—ица** *f.* member of the same tribe.

сопли *gen., pl., etc.*, of **сопля; —вый** *a.* runny-nosed.

сопло *n.*, **—вой, —вый** *a.* nozzle, jet; orifice, venturi; nipple; (wind tunnel) throat.

соплодие *n.* collective fruit, compound fruit, syncarp(y).

сопло-разбрызгиватель *m.* spray nozzle.

сопля *f.* (physiol.) mucor, mucus.

соподчин/ение *n.* (gram.) coordination; **—ённость** *f.* hierarchy; **—ённый** *a.* (gram.) coordinating; **—ить, —ять** *v.* coordinate.

сопок *gen. pl.* of **сопка.**

сополиконденсация *f.* copolycondensation.

сополимер *m.* copolymer; **—изация** *f.* copolymerization.

соположение *n.* coordinate position.

сопор *m.* (med.) sopor, coma; **—озный** *a.* soporose.

сопостав/имость *f.* comparability; **—имый** *a.* comparable; **—ительный** *a.* comparative; **—ить** *see* **сопоставлять; —ление** *n.* comparison, contrast; juxtaposition; matching; correlation (of data); confrontation; **в —лении с** in comparison (with), as compared (to), versus; **правило —ления** (math.) associative law; **—ленный** *a.* compared, etc., *see v.*; **—лять** *v.* compare, contrast; juxtapose; correlate (data); confront (with).

сопочный *a.* of **сопка.**

соправитель *m.* co-driver, co-operator.

сопрано *n.*, **—вый** *a.* soprano.

сопревать *v.* rot, decay, spoil.

сопредельн/ость *f.* contiguity; **—ый** *a.* contiguous, adjacent.

сопр/елый *a.* decayed, spoiled; **—еть** *see* **сопревать.**

соприкас/ание *see* **соприкосновение; —аться** *v.* touch, come in contact (with); make contact; deal (with); adjoin, border, be adjacent (to), abut; (geom.) osculate; **—аться с** have bearing on; engage, mesh; **—ающий(ся)** *a.* touching, etc., *see v.*; in contact, contiguous; osculatory.

соприкосновен/ие *n.* contact, touch; contiguity, juxtaposition; (geom.) osculation; engagement; **поверхность —ия** contact surface; **—ность** *f.* contiguity; **—ный** *a.* contiguous; implicated (in).

соприкоснуться *see* **соприкасаться.**

сопричастн/ость *f.* association; complicity; **—ый** *a.* participant; implicated, involved.

сопрово/дитель *m.* escort, convoy; **—дительный** *see* **сопровождающий; —дительное письмо** cover(ing) letter; **—дить, —ждать** v. accompany, attend, escort, convoy, go with; follow, track; carry along, entrain; **—ждаться** v. be accompanied, etc.; **—ждающий** a. accompanying, etc., see v.; concomitant, associated; power-follow (current); **—ждение** n. accompanying, etc., see v.; accompaniment; convoy, escort, (comp.) maintenance (of software, files, etc.); **—ждение по дальности** range tracking; **—ждённый** a. accompanied, etc., see v.

сопрограмма f. (comp.) coroutine.

сопромат m. strength of materials.

сопротивлен/ие n. resistance, opposition; (av.) drag; (electron.) impedance; strength (of material); resistor; **с. изгибу** transverse strength, bending strength; **с. износу** resistance to wear, wear resistance; **с. разрыву, с. растяжению** tensile strength; **с. сдвигу, с. срезу** shear(ing) strength; **с. толчку, с. удару** impact strength; **датчик —ия** strain gage; **диаграмма —ия разрыву** tensile stress-strain curve; **коэффициент —ия** (av.) drag coefficient; **линия наименьшего —ия** line of least resistance; **магазин —ия** (elec.) resistance box; **магнитное с.** (elec.) reluctance; **мост —ия** (elec.) Wheatstone bridge; **нагревание —ием** resistance heating; **оказать с.** v. resist; **печь —ия** resistance furnace; **полное с.** (elec.) impedance; (av.) total drag; **провод большого —ия** high-resistance line; **реактивное с.** (elec.) reactance; **реле активного —ия** (electron.) resistance relay; **реле полного —ия** impedance relay; **сварка —ием** resistance welding; **сила —ия** resisting force; **точка предельного —ия** yield point; **удельное с.** (elec.) specific resistance, resistivity.

сопротивл/яемость f. resistance, capacity to resist, strength; (elec.) resistivity, specific resistance; **—яться** v. be resistant (to), resist, oppose; **—яющийся** a. resisting, resistant.

сопроцессор m. (comp.) coprocessor.

сопря/гать v. conjugate, join, pair, couple; combine, (inter)link, connect; (elec.) gang (capacitors); (comp.) interface; track (circuits); **—гающий** a. conjugating, etc., see v.; (cartography) adjustment (curve); **—жение** n. conjugation, joining, etc., see v.; (con)junction, union; interface; **—жение связей** conjugation; **—жённость** see **сопряжение**; contingency; **—жённый** a. conjugated, etc., see v.; (chem.; math.) conjugate; interdependent, associated; adjoint (function); induced (reaction); **—жённая двойная связь** conjugate double bond; **—жённая деталь** mate; **—жённая широта** colatitude; **—жённые слои** conjugate layers; **—жено** (it) involves.

сопрячь see **сопрягать**.

сопутств/ование n. accompaniment; **—овать** v. accompany; be associated with; **—ующий** a. accompanying, associated, attendant, concomitant; co-moving (space); satellite (pulse); (biol.) secondary, accessory (species); **—ующий результат** fallout, spin-off, by-product; **—ующие металлы** metal impurities.

сор m. litter, rubbish, waste, dross, impurity; (geol.) sor, solonchak playa.

соразмер/ение n. matching, etc., see v.; **—ить** see **соразмерять**; **—но** adv. and prep. dat. in proportion (to); **—ность** f. proportion(ality); balance, symmetry; adequacy; **—ный** a. proportional, proportionate, commensurate; balanced; fit, adequate; **—ять** v. match, fit together; proportion, apportion, weigh (out); regulate; **—яться** v. be matched, etc.; match, correspond.

сорб/ат m. sorbate; **—ент** m. (chem.) sorbent; **—инововокислая соль** sorbate; **—иновый** a. sorbic (acid).

сорбир/ование n. sorption; **—ованный** a. sorbed (ab-

sorbed or adsorbed); **—ованное вещество** sorbate; **—овать** v. sorb; **—ующий** a. sorbing; **—ующее вещество** sorbent.

сорбит m. (chem.) sorbitol; **—ный, —овый** a. sorbite, sorbitic; **—ообразный** a. sorbitic.

сорбоза f. sorbose.

сорбц/ионный a., **—ия** f. sorption.

сорв/анный a. stripped, etc., see v.; **—ать** v. strip (thread); tear off, peel off, tear away, tear down; break off, disrupt; **—аться** v. be stripped, etc.; strip; break off, break away, come off; fail, stall.

сорганизов(ыв)ать v. organize.

сорго n., **—вый** a. (bot.) sorghum.

Сорε правило see **Сорэ правило**.

соревн/ование n. competition, rivalry; contest; emulation; **—оваться** v. compete, rival; emulate; **—ующийся** a. competing.

соред/иальный a. (bot.) soredial; **—ия** f. soredium, brood bud.

сориентироваться v. get oriented.

сор/инка f. (dirt) particle, dust particle, speck of dust; **—ить** v. litter.

сорн/ость f. contamination, impurity; **—олуговое растение** meadow weed; **—ый** a. littered; rubbish, waste; dirty; (agr.) weedy; nuisance (fish); (bot.) ruderal; **—ая трава, —(ополев)ое растение** weed; **—ые куры** (orn.) Megapodiidae; **—як** m. weed.

сорога f. (ichth.) roach (Rutilus r.).

сородич m. relative; (gen.) ancestor, allied line.

сорок num., **—а—** prefix forty.

сорока f. (orn.) magpie (Pica); **голубая с.** azure-winged magpie (Cyanopica cyana).

сорокавосьмигранн/ик m. (cryst.) hexoctahedron; **—ый** a. hexoctahedral.

сорок/алетие n. forty years; fortieth anniversary or birthday; **—алетний** a. forty-year; **—ачасовой** a. forty-hour; **—и** pl. of **сорока**; **—овой** a. fortieth; **—ножка** f. (zool.) centipede.

сорокопуты pl. (orn.) shrikes (Laniidae); **ласточковые с.** (orn.) wood swallows (Artamidae).

сорочечный a. of **сорочка**.

сорочий a. of **сорока**.

сорочка f. shirt; jacket; sheath; (anat.) caul; **сердечная с.** (anat.) pericardium.

сорт m. sort, kind, variety, brand; strain, breed, species; nature, quality, grade; **—амент** m. assortment, set; grades, grading; gage (of wire); **с.-анализатор** m. (strain) tester; **с.-донор** (bot.) donor variety; **—имент** see **сортамент**.

сортир/овальный a. sorting, etc., see v.; card-receiving (pocket); **—овальная машина** sorter; grading machine; **—ование** n. sorting, etc., see v.; classification; **—ованный** a. sorted, etc., see v.; **—овать** v. sort, grade, classify; pick (out), select, cull, screen; separate, assort, size; distribute; batch; **—овка** see **сортирование**; sorter, grader, classifier; screen; (rr.) marshalling; **—овка слиянием** (comp.) merge-sort; **—овка-горка** (agr.) gravity separator; **—овочная** f. sorting center; (rr.) marshalling yard, shunting yard; **—овочный** a. sorting, etc., see v.; separatory (funnel); (rr.) shunting; **—овочный аппарат** sorter, separator, grader, classifier; **—овщик** m. sorter, grader; **—ующий** a. sorting, etc., see v.

сорт/ность f. rating; (petrol.) performance number (antiknock rating); grade (of quality); **—ный** a. high-quality; varietal; **—о—** prefix sort, variety; **—овальный** see **сортировочный**; **—оведение** n. research on varieties; **—оводство** n. plant breeding.

сортов/ой *a.* sort, variety; brand; (biol.) strain; section (-shaped); sorted, graded; commercial (timber); select(ed), high-quality; **—ая сталь** section(al) steel, structural steel; **—ые ножницы** cutting tool.

сорто/гибочный *a.* (met.) section-bending; **—изучение** *n.* (biol.) strain investigation; **—испытание** *n.*, **—испытательный** *a.* strain testing; grade-testing, quality-testing; **—обновление** *n.* (gen.) strain renovation; **—опылитель** *m.* (agr.) pollinator; **—правильный** *a.* (met.) section-straightening; **—размер** *m.* grade size; **—сеть** *f.* (biol.) strain-testing system; **—смена** *f.* strain changing; **—улучшающий** *a.* strain-improving; **—участок** *m.* (biol.) strain-testing station; strain-testing plot.

сортутить *see* **сортучивать.**

сортуч/ение *n.* amalgamation; **—енный** *a.* amalgamated; **—и(ва)ть** *v.* amalgamate; **—ка** *f.* amalgam.

сорус *m.* (bot.) sorus.

соры *pl. of* **сор.**

Сорэ правило Soret's principle.

соряд *m.* (bot.) coseries.

сос/альце *n.* (zool.) sucker; haustellum (proboscis); **—альщик** *m.* fluke (parasitic worm); **—альщики** *pl.* Trematoda; **—ание** *n.*, **—ательный** *a.* suction, sucking; **—ательная лопасть** (ent.) labellum; **—ать** *v.* suck; torment, gnaw at (of pain).

сосед *m.*, **—ка** *f.* neighbor; **—ний** *a.* neighboring, adjoining, adjacent; (math.) affine; **—ство** *n.* neighborhood, vicinity, adjacency, proximity; **по —ству** in the vicinity, nearby; **—ствовать** *v.* be next to one another.

сосен *gen. pl. of* **сосна; —ка** *f.* young pine; **—ник** *m.* pine forest.

Со-Сент-Мари *see* **Су-Сент-Мари.**

сосец *see* **сосок.**

сосис/ка *f.* sausage; **—ковидный** *a.* allantoid, sausage-shaped; **—очный** *a.* sausage.

соска *gen. of* **сосок;** (anat.) papilla; nipple (of baby's bottle); pacifier.

соскаблив/ание *n.* scraping off, abrasion; **—ать** *v.* scrape off; pare, shave.

соскакив/ание *n.* jumping off, etc., *see v.*; drop-off; **—ать** *v.* jump off, spring off, come off, slip off, drop off, work off.

соскальзыв/ание *n.* sliding, etc., *see v.*; slide, slip; **—ать** *v.* slide (off), slip (off), run off, skid; launch (ship).

соски *pl. of* **сосок, соска;** papillae.

соско— *prefix* mammi— (breast); thel(o)— (nipple).

соскоб *see* **соскабливание; —лить** *see* **соскабливать.**

соско/видный *a.* mammiform, mammillary; papillose; **—вый** *a. of* **сосок;** mammillary.

соскообразный *see* **сосковидный.**

соскочить *see* **соскакивать.**

соскре/бать, —сти *v.* scrape off.

сослагательный *a.* (gram.) subjunctive.

сосл/анный *a.* exiled, deported; *m.* an exile; **—ать** *v. see* **ссылать.**

сослеп/а, —у *adv.* due to poor eyesight.

сослуживец *m.* colleague, fellow worker.

сосн/а *f.*, **—овый** *a.* pine; **—овая камедь** gum rosin; **—овая смола** pine tar; **—овая шерсть** pine (needle) wool; **—овое масло** pine oil (crude turpentine).

соснуть *v.* doze, nap.

сосняк *m.* pine forest; pine lumber.

сосо/к *m.* (anat.) nipple, teat; papilla; optic disk; **—чек** *dim. of* **сосок;** (anat.) papilla; caruncle; **листовидный**

—чек (anat.) Mayer's organ (on tongue); **—чковатый** *f.* mammillate; **—чковидный** *a.* papillar, nipple-shaped; mammillar(y); **—чковый** *a.* papillary.

сосредоточ/ение *n.* concentration, centering, etc., *see v.*; **—енно** *adv.* intently; **—енность** *f.* concentration; **—енный** *a.* concentrated, etc., *see v.*; (elec.) lumped (constant, etc.); **—ивание** *see* **сосредоточение; —и(ва)ть** *v.* concentrate, center, centralize, focus; localize; lump, mass; converge (fire); **—и(ва)ться** *v.* center, focus.

соссюрит *m.* (min.) saussurite; **—изация** *f.* saussuritization; **—ный, —овый** *a.* saussurite.

состав *m.* composition, constitution, make-up, formation, structure; compound, composite; formulation; formula (of fertilizer, etc.); (charge) mixture; (rocket) fuel; (mold) assembly; body; staff, personnel; amount (of property); **с. команд** (comp.) repertoire; **с. оборудования** (comp.) configuration; **с. плана** plan components; **входить в с.** be(come) part (of), be a member (of); enter into the composition; **подвижной с.** (rr.) rolling stock; **химический с.** chemical composition.

состав/итель *m.* author, composer, compiler; **—ить** *see* **составлять; —ление** *n.* composition, composing, etc., *see v.*; synthesis; *suffix* —ing; **—ление графика** scheduling; **—ление проектов** designing, projecting; **—ление смет** estimating; **—ление таблиц** tabulation; **—ленный** *a.* composed, etc., *see v.*; **—лять** *v.* compose, put together, compile, formulate, draw up, work out; prepare, compound, concoct, mix, combine; fit up, set up, build up, construct, design; constitute, form, comprise, make (up); represent, account (for); amount, come (to), total, run, range (from . . . to), measure; **—лять план** plan; **—ляться** *v.* be composed, etc.; consist, be made up (of); form, organize; add (up to), accumulate.

составляющ/ая *f.*, **—ая часть, —ий элемент** component, ingredient, constituent, integral part; **—ий** *a.* composing, etc., *see* **составлять;** component, constituent; composite (force); partial (fraction).

составн/ой *a.* compound, composite, combined, complicated; tandem (transistor); compounding; built up, sectional, separable, join(t)ed; flexible (pipe); component, constituent; link, chain; telescope, telescopic; **с. цех** batch-mixing section; **—ая деталь** unit; **—ая кривая** compound curve; **—ая часть** component, constituent, ingredient, (integral) part; element (of compound); **твёрдая —ая часть** solid constituent; **—ое ядро** compound nucleus.

состар/енный *a.* aged; **—еться** *v.* age; **—ивание** *n.* aging; **—ившийся** *a.* aged, elderly; **—ить(ся)** *v.* age.

сост/егать, —ёгивать *v.* tack or wire together.

состир(ыв)ать *v.* wash out.

состоян/ие *n.* condition, state, status, position, stage; ability; (weather) condition; (chemical) compound or group; assets; **с. готовности** readiness; **с. спелости** ripeness, maturity; **с. тела** state of aggregation, physical form (of matter); **быть в —ии** *v.* be in position (to), be able (to); **в —ии литья** as cast; **в —ии покоя** at rest; **в —ии поставки** as received; **в свободном —ии** free, in the free state; **в сухом —ии** dry(-state); **диаграмма —ия** phase (equilibrium) diagram; **насыщенное с.** saturated state, saturation; **по —ию на** as of (date); **таблица —ий** (relay) combination table.

состоятельн/ость *f.* competence; solvency; justifiability; consistency; validity, strength (of argument); **—ый** *a.* solvent; well-off, well-grounded, justifiable; consistent.

состоя/ть *v.* consist (of), be made up (of), comprise, be composed (of); include, involve; be, lie (in); **—ться** *v.* consist; happen, take place; **не —ться** fail; **—щий** *a.* consisting, etc., *see v.*

сострагивать *v.* plane off.

сострад/ание *n.* compassion, sympathy; **—ательный** *a.* compassionate.

сострачивать *v.* stitch together, bind.

сострел *m.* (art.) calibration (fire).

costp/игать, —ичь *v.* shear off, cut off.

сострогать *see* **сострагивать.**

сострочить *see* **сострачивать.**

состру́г(ив)ать *v.* plane off, smooth.

состряпать *see* **стряпать.**

состыков(ыв)ать *v.* (space) dock; (elec.) mate, engage; (mech.; constr.) join.

состяз/ание *n.* contest, competition; **—атель** *m.,* **—а-тельница** *f.* competitor; **—ательный** *a.* competing; controversial; **—аться** *v.* compete; cope (with).

сосуд *m.* vessel, receiver, container; jar, can; (vacuum) flask; (biol.) vas; (anat.) *prefix* angio—; **пластика —а** (med.) angioplasty; **склероз —ов** (med.) angiosclerosis; **—ик** *m.* (bot.) vasculum; **—исто-волокнистый** *a.* fibrovascular; **—исто-нервный** *a.* neurovascular; **—истый** *a.* vascular; **—истая оболочка** (anat.) vascular coat, tunica vasculosa; **—одвигательный** *a.* (anat., physiol.) vasomotor; **—ообразующий** *a.* (zool.) vasoformative; **—орасширитель** *m.,* **—орасширяющий** *a.* (physiol.) vasodilator; **—осжимающий, —осуживающий** *a.* vasoconstrictor; **—осшивание** *n.* (med.) angiorrhaphy; **—ы** *pl. of* **сосуд;** (anat.) vasa.

сосулька *f.* icicle.

сосун *m.* suckling; suction pipe; **—ок** *dim. of* **сосун.**

сосуществ/ование *n.* coexistence; **—овать** *v.* coexist; **—ующий** *a.* coexisting; concomitant, accompanying; (chem.) conjugate.

сосущ/ий *a.* sucking; (zool.) suctorial, haustellate; **—ая сила** suction; soil-water strength; **—ие инфузории** (zool.) Suctoria.

сосц/евидный *a.* mammiform, mammillary; papillose; mastoid; **с. отросток** (anat.) mastoid process; **—евидная полость** mastoid antrum; **—евидное отверстие** mastoid foramen; **—ы** *pl.* papillae, nipples, teats.

сосчит(ыв)ать *v.* count, calculate, sum up, add up; number.

сот *m.* honeycomb.

СОТ *abbr.* (**скрытая огневая точка**) (mil.) concealed fire position.

сотая *f.* hundredth (part).

сотвор/ение *n.* creation, making; **—ить** *v.* create, make, fabricate; **—чество** *n.* coauthorship, collaboration.

сотен *gen. pl. of* **сотня; —ный** *a.* hundredth; *suffix* -hundred.

сотерн *m.* sauterne (wine).

сотка *f.* one hundredth.

соткать *v.* weave, spin; **—ся** *v.* interweave.

сотня *f.* one hundred.

сотоварищ *m.* associate, fellow member, fellow worker; **—ество** *n.* company, society; partnership; membership.

сото/видный *a.* honeycomb(ed), cellular; **—вый** *a.* honeycomb, cellular; **—вый мёд** honey in combs; **—вая катушка** (rad.) honeycomb coil.

соток *gen. pl. of* **сотка.**

сотообразный *see* **сотовидный.**

сотопласт *m.* honeycomb(ed) plastic (insulation).

сотрёт *fut. 3 sing. of* **стереть.**

сотрудни/к *m.* collaborator, contributor, colleague, co-worker, associate; staff member; **—чать** *v.* collaborate, contribute, cooperate; **—чество** *n.* collaboration, cooperation.

сотряс/аемость *f.* shakability; seismic vulnerability; **—атель** *m.* shaker.

сотрясательн/ый *a.* shaking, rocking; concussive; shocking; **—ое движение** shaking; **—ое сито** shaking screen, shaker.

сотряс/ать *v.* shake, vibrate, jar, concuss; **—ающийся** *a.* shaking, jigging; **—ение** *n.* shake, shaking, jarring, vibration, pulsation (of sound); percussion; shock, concussion (of brain), (med.) commotio; commotion; **—ти** *see* **сотрясать.**

соты *pl.* honeycomb.

сотый *a.* centesimal, hundredth.

соудар/ение *n.* collision, impact, encounter, impingement, shock; **плотность —ения** collision density; **—яться** *v.* collide, encounter.

соус *m.,* **—ный** *a.* sauce, gravy.

соустье *n.* (med.) anastomosis.

соучаст/вовать *v.* participate, take part in, cooperate, collaborate; **—ие** *n.* participation, cooperation, collaboration; complicity; **—ник** *m.,* **—ница** *f.* participant, associate, collaborator; accomplice, (law) accessory; **—ный** *a.* participating.

соученик *m.,* **—ница** *f.* fellow student.

софа *f.* sofa.

софийский *a.* (geog.) Sofia.

софит *m.* (arch.) soffit.

софлоровый *see* **сафлоровый.**

софокусный *a.* (phys.) confocal.

софор/а *f.* (bot.) Sophora; **—ин** *m.* sophorin (glucoside); sophorine (alkaloid).

соффиони *pl.* (geol.) soffioni.

соха *f.* wooden plow.

соха/тина *f.* elk meat; elk hide; **—тый** *a.* elk; *a.* forked; antlered; **—ч** *see* **лось.**

сохнуть *v.* dry (up), desiccate; wither, shrivel.

сохран/ение *n.* preservation, conservation, retention; constancy; care, custody, maintenance, upkeep; disposal (of radioactive waste); **с. энергии** conservation of energy; **закон —ения импульсов** law of conservation of momentum; **закон —ения массы** law of conservation of matter; **—ённый** *a.* conserved, etc., *see* **сохранять; —ивший** *a.* (having) conserved; **—ившийся** *a.* conserved, etc., *see* **сохранять; —итель** *m.* guardian, custodian; **—ительный** *a.* preservative; **—ить** *see* **сохранять.**

сохранн/о *adv.* safely, securely; it is safe; **—ость** *f.* safety; preservation; integrity; **быть в —ости** be in safekeeping; **—ый** *a.* safe, secure.

сохраняемость *f.* keeping qualities, preservability; (comp.) retention; survival (rate or time).

сохранять *v.* conserve, preserve, retain; store; (comp.) save; maintain, keep, observe; **с. за собой** reserve (for oneself); **с. силу** (math.) hold (true), be valid; **—ся** *v.* be well preserved, keep, last; remain; survive, persist, prevail.

сохший *a.* dried (up), etc., *see* **сохнуть.**

соц— *prefix* social; socialistic.

соцветие *n.* (bot.) raceme, inflorescence.

социал/изация *f.* socialization; **—изм** *m.* socialism; **—истический** *a.* socialistic; **—ьно-бытовой** *a.* social, living (conditions); **—ьный** *a.* social; **—ьное обеспечение** welfare.

социация *f.* (bot.) sociation.

социолог *m.* sociologist; **—ический** *a.* sociological; **—ия** *f.* sociology.

соци/ула *f.* (biol.) sociule; **—я** *f.* socies; **—эта** (biol.) society.

соч. *abbr.* (**сочинение**) composition, paper.

сочевичник *m.* (bot.) bitter vetch (*Orobus*); peavine (*Lathyrus*).

сочен *sh. m. of* **сочный; —ие** *n.* trickle, ooze, oozing, dribble; bleeding (of trees).

сочет/ание *n.* combination, union, conjunction, joining; blend; compromise; (math.) combination, set; **в —ании** in conjunction (with), together (with); **—ания** *pl.* (math.) combination, set; **теория —аний** combinatorics; combinatorial analysis; **—ательность** *f.* (math.) associativity; **—ательный** *a.* associative; combinative; **—ать** *v.* combine, associate, connect, join, unite; blend; match (up); **—ать в себе** combine; **—аться** *v.* be combined, etc.; go together.

сочин/ение *n.* composition, paper; (gram.) coordination; **собрание —ений** collected works; **—итель** *m.* author, composer; **—ительный** *a.* (gram.) coordinating; **—ить, —ять** *v.* compose.

сочить *v.* sap, draw off, tap (trees); **—ся** *v.* drip, ooze (out), trickle, dribble; bleed (of trees).

сочла *past f. sing. of* **счесть.**

сочлен *m.* fellow member.

сочлен/ение *n.* articulation, join(t)ing, etc., *see v.*; joint, link, member; junction; (comp.) (con)catenation; coupling; **—ённый** *a.* articulated, etc., *see v.*; chain; **—ить** *v. see* **сочленять; —ов(ан)ный** *a.* (anat.) articular; **—ять** *v.* articulate, join(t), hinge; couple, connect, (inter)link, (con)catenate.

сочло *past n. sing. of* **счесть.**

сочн/о— *prefix* (bot.) chyl(o)— (succulent); **—олистный** *a.* (bot.) chylophyllous; **—ость** *f.* juiciness, succulence; **—ый** *a.* juicy, succulent; rich (color).

сочтённый *past pass. part. of* **счесть.**

сочувств/енный *a.* sympathetic; **—ие** *n.* sympathy; **—овать** *v.* sympathize.

сошедший *past act. part. of* **сойти.**

сошка *f.* prop, support; rack, rest; (art.) mount, bipod, tripod.

сошлёт *fut. 3 sing. of* **сослать.**

сошлифов/ка *f.* grinding off, abrasion; **—ывать** *v.* grind off, grind away.

сошник *m.* (agr.) plowshare; colter; (anat.) vomer; **—ово-влагалищный** *a.* vomerovaginal; **—ово-нёбный** *a.* vomeropalatine; **—ово-носовой орган** (anat.) Jacobson's organ; **—овый** *a. of* **сошник;** vomerine.

сошный *a. of* **соха.**

сошьёт *fut. 3 sing. of* **сшить.**

сощип/нуть, —(ыв)ать *v.* pinch off.

СОЭ *abbr.* (**скорость оседания эритроцитов**) erythrocyte sedimentation rate, E.S.R.

союз *m.* union, association, alliance; agreement; conjunction.

Союз Советских Социалистических Республик Union of Soviet Socialist Republics (USSR).

союзн/ик *m.*, **—ница** *f.* ally, associate, confederate; **—ый** *a.* union; allied.

соя *f.* soy(a), soybean.

сп *abbr.* (**сантипуаз**) centipoise; **сп, сп.** *abbr.* (**спирт**) alcohol, spec. ethyl alcohol; (**собственный потенциал**) self potential.

СП *abbr.* (**Северный полюс**) North Pole.

спагетти *n.* spaghetti.

спад *m.* decrease, drop, fall(-off); recession, slump; (comp.) decay; slope, incline.

спад/ание *n.* falling, etc., *see v.*; fall, drop, diminution, decrease, abatement; recession; taper; **—ать** *v.* fall

(off), drop, diminish, decrease, abate, go down, decay, die out; (elec.) roll off; recede (of water); slope; collapse; **—аться** *see* **спадать;** fall together, come together; **—ающий(ся)** *a.* falling, etc., *see v.*; decaying (wave); **—ение** *n.* (med.) collapse.

спаек *gen. pl. of* **спайка.**

спаечный *a.* adhesive; (anat.) commissural.

спазм *m.*, **—а** *f.* spasm, convulsion; **—атический, —одический** *a.* spasmodic, convulsive; **—олитин** *m.* spasmolytin, adiphenine hydrochloride; **—отин** *m.* spasmotin, sphacelotoxin; **—отоксин** *m.* spasmotoxin.

спаив/ание *n.* soldering, etc., *see v.*; coagmentation; **—ать** *v.* solder (below 427 °C), braze (above 427 °C); coagment, join together; water (stock); **—аться** *v.* be soldered, etc.; fuse.

спай *m.* soldering; soldered joint; seal; joint, seam, juncture; (thermocouple) junction.

спайк *m.* spike.

спайка *see* **спай;** (biol.) commissure; (med.) adhesion.

спайник *m.* (zool.) Diplozoon.

спайно— *see* **сростно—.**

спайнолепест/ковый, —ный *a.* (bot.) gamopetalous, sympetalous; **—ные** *pl.* Sympetalae.

спайн/ость *f.* cleavage; jointing; cleavability; **—ости** *pl.* cleavage cracks; **—ый** *a. of* **спайность;** cleavable; (biol.) commissural.

спайщик *m.* jointer, splicer; solderer.

спал *past m. sing. of* **спасть; спать.**

спалзывать *v.* creep down, slip (off); (instr.) drift.

спалить *v.* singe, burn.

спа/льн(а)я *f.* bedroom; **—льный** *a.*, **—ньё** *n.* sleeping.

спанандрия *f.* (biol.) spanandry, scarcity of males.

спаниель *m.* spaniel (dog).

спано— *prefix* span(o)— (scarce).

спарагмит *m.* (petr.) sparagmite.

спарассол *m.* sparassol, methyl ester of everninic acid.

спарганоз *m.* (med.; vet.) sparganosis.

спардек *m.* spardeck (of boat).

спаренный *a.* coupled, connected; duplex, twin, paired, dual; (mach.) gang(ed).

спарж/а *f.*, **—евый** *a.* asparagus.

спар/ивание *n.* pairing, etc., *see v.*; copulation; (agr.) covering, serving; **—ивать** *v.* pair, couple, match, mate; (mach.) gang; let spoil; **—иваться** *v.* mate, copulate; **—ивающий** *a.* pairing, etc., *see v.*; **—ить** *see* **спаривать.**

спарнакский *a.* (geol.) Sparnacian.

спаровые *pl.* (ichth.) porgies, sea breams (*Sparidae*).

спартанский *a.* Spartan.

спартеин *m.* sparteine, lupinidine.

спарто *see* **эспарто.**

спарывать *v.* rip off.

спас/аемый *a.* recoverable, reusable; **—ание** *n.* rescue, recovery, salvage; **—атель** *m.* rescuer; rescue ship.

спасательн/ый *a.* rescue, saving, safety; life (belt; boat); salvage (vessel); **—ая лестница** fire escape; (min.) emergency ladder; **—ое дело** rescue work; salvage.

спасать *v.* save, rescue, recover, salvage; **—ся** *v.* save oneself, escape.

спасение *see* **спасание.**

спасибо *particle* thanks (to).

спаситель *m.* rescuer.

спасти *see* **спасать.**

спастический *a.* (med.) spastic.

спасть *see* **спадать.**

спата *f.* (bot.) spathe.

спатулатин *m.* spathulatine.

спать *v.* sleep.

спая *gen. of* **спай.**

спа/янность *f.* unity, solidarity, cohesion; **—янный** *a.* soldered, etc., *see v.;* **—ять** *v.* solder (together); join, unite.

спеет *pr. 3 sing. of* **спеть.**

спейс/ер *m.* spacer; **—истор** *m.* (electron.) spacistor.

спек *m.* cake, clinker; **спёк** *past m. sing. of* **спечь.**

спек/аемость *f.* tendency to cake; coking property (of coal); **—ание** *n.* caking, etc., *see v.;* agglomeration; **—ательный** *a.* caking, etc., *see v.;* **—ать(ся)** *v.* cake, clinker, sinter, coke, frit; agglomerate; (hem.) coagulate; burn, stick; bake; **—ающийся** *a.* caking, etc., *see v.*

спектр *m.* spectrum; **с. комбинационного рассеяния** Raman spectrum; **ядерный с. гамма-резонанса** Mössbauer spectrum.

спектральн/о чистый *a.* spectro-pure; **—ость** *f.* spectrality; **—ый** *a.* spectral, spectrum; spectroscopic (observations); **—ый анализ** spectrum analysis; spectrochemical analysis.

спектро— *prefix* spectro—, spectrum; **—анализатор** *m.* spectrum analyzer; **—болограф** *m.* spectrobolograph; **—визор** *m.* spectrovisor.

спектрогелио/грамма *f.* (astr.) spectroheliogram; **—граф** *m.* spectroheliograph; **—скоп** *m.* spectrohelioscope.

спектрограмма *f.* spectrogram.

спектрограф *m.* spectrograph; **—ический** *a.* spectrographic; **—ия** *f.* spectrography.

спектрометр *m.* spectrometer; **—ический** *a.* spectrometric; **—ия** *f.* spectrometry.

спектрополяриметр *m.* spectropolarimeter.

спектроскоп *m.* spectroscope; **—ически чистый** spectroscopically pure, spec-pure; **—ический** *a.* spectroscopic; **—ия** *f.* spectroscopy.

спектрофотометр *m.* spectrophotometer; **—ический** *a.* spectrophotometric; **—ия** *f.* spectrophotometry.

спектрохим/ический *a.* spectrochemical; **—ия** *f.* spectrochemistry.

спекулировать *v.* speculate.

спекулярит *m.* (min.) specularite, specular hematite.

спекуля/тивный *a.* speculative; **—ция** *f.* speculation, venture.

спёкш/ийся *a.* caked, sintered, baked, parched; **—иеся куски** sinter.

спел *sh. m. of* **спелый.**

спелео— *prefix* spel(a)eo— (cave); **—лог** *m.* speleologist.

спел/ость *f.* ripeness, maturity; **половая с.** (physiol.) puberty; **—ый** *a.* ripe, mature; refined, finished; ready; (agr.) arable (soil).

спер/ва *adv.* at first; at the start; in the first place, firstly; **—воначала, —воначалу** *adv.* at first; **—еди** *adv. and prep. gen.* at the front (of), in front, before; **вид —еди** front view, face.

сперма *f.* sperm(atozoa), semen.

сперматида *f.* (gen.) spermatid.

спермато— *prefix* sperm(at)o— (sperm, seed, germ); **—генез** *m.* (biol.) spermatogenesis; **—гоний** *m.* spermatogonium; **—зоид** *m.* (zool.) spermatozoön; (bot.) spermatozoid; **—логия** *f.* (bot.) spermatology; **—рея** *f.* (med.) spermatorrhea; **—фор** *m.* (gen.) spermatophore; **—цит** *m.* (cyt.) spermatocyte.

спермацет *m.,* **—овый** *a.* (chem.) spermaceti.

сперм/идин *m.* (biochem.) spermidine; **—ий** *see* **сперматозоид.**

спермин *m.* (biochem.) spermine (a leucomaine).

спермиогенез *see* **сперматогенез.**

спермо— *see* **спермато—;** **—дерма** *f.* (bot.) seed coat, spermoderm; **—собиратель** *m.* (med.; vet.) semen

collector; **—тип** *m.* spermotype; **—токсин** *m.* (bioch.; immun.) spermotoxin.

спёртый *a.* close, stuffy; compressed.

спесистор *m.* (electron.) spacistor.

спеть *v.* ripen, mature.

спех *m.* haste, hurry; **к —у** urgent.

спец *m.* specialist, professional; *prefix* special.

специал/изация *f.* specialization; **—изированный** *a.* specialized, special-purpose; **—изировать(ся)** *v.* specialize; **—ист** *m.* specialist, expert; **—ьно** *adv.* specially, expressly, purposely, specifically; **—ьность** *f.* specialty, specialized skill, field, line, department; **—ьный** *a.* special(ized), specific, particular; user-oriented (edition); **—ьная обработка** decontamination; **—ьная сталь** (special) alloy steel.

специи *pl. of* **специя.**

специнструмент(ы) special tools.

специф/ика *f.* specific, characteristic; specificity, specific nature; **—икация** *f.* specification; description; parts list; **—икация по крупности** size specification; **давать —икацию** *v.* specify; **—ицировать** *v.* specify; make a specifications list; classify; **—ический** *a.* specific; distinctive; particular; characteristic (of); **—ичность** *f.* specificity; **—ичный** *see* **специфический.**

специя *f.* spice, seasoning.

спец/кор *m.* special correspondent; **—курс** *m.* (educ.) special course; **—материалы** *pl.* special materials; **—наз** [(силы) специального назначения] (mil.) special forces; **—овка, —одежда** *f.* work outfit, (c)overalls; **—подготовка** *f.* special training; **—сигнал** *m.* siren; **—сплав** *m.* special alloy; **—сталь** (special) alloy steel.

спеч/ённый *a.* caked, etc., *see* **спекать(ся);** **—ь(ся)** *see* **спекать(ся).**

спеш/а *adv.* in haste, hurriedly; **не с.** unhurriedly.

спеши/вание *n.* dismounting; clipping (of queen bee's wings); **—(ва)ть(ся)** dismount.

спеш/ить *v.* hasten, hurry, rush; be fast (of clock); **—ка** *f.,* **—ность** *f.* haste, hurry, urgency; **—но** *adv.* hastily, in haste, hurriedly, urgently; it is urgent; **—ный** *a.* hasty, urgent, pressing; express (mail); **—ная почта** special delivery.

спз *abbr.* (сантипуаз) centipoise.

СПЗУ *abbr.* (стираемое постоянное запоминающее устройство) erasable read-only memory, EROM.

спигел/ин *m.* spigeline; **—ия** *f.* (bot.) worm-grass (*Spigelia*).

СПИД *abbr.* (синдром приобретённого иммуного дефицита) acquired immunodeficiency syndrome, AIDS.

спидометр *m.* speedometer.

спикировать *v.* (av.) dive.

спикул/а *f.* (zool.) spicule; **—ярный** *a.* spicular.

спил *m.* sawing off; saw cut, gash; (cross-)section.

спилантол *m.* spilanthol.

спил/енный *a.* sawed off, etc., *see v.;* **—ивание** *n.* sawing off, etc., *see v.;* **—и(ва)ть** *v.* saw off, saw down; file off, file down; **—ка** *see* **спиливание;** *gen. sing. of* **спилок; —ок** *m.* (leather) split (hide).

спин *m.* (nucl.) spin; *gen. pl. of* **спина.**

спин/а *f.* back, dorsum; **—ой к —е** back to back; **область —ы** dorsal region.

спина/льный *a.* spinal; **—стерин** *m.* spinasterol; **—цен** *m.* spinacene, squalene; **—цин** *m.* spinacine.

спинвалентность *f.* spin valency.

спинель *see* **шпинель.**

спинка *f. dim. of* **спина;** back (edge), dorsum; (ent.) notum, tergum.

спинметка *f.* spin-labeling.

спиннинговая катушка (angler's) spinning reel.

спиннобрюшной *a.* (anat.) dorsoventral.

спинн/ой *a.* back; (anat.) dorsal, spinal; **с. мозг, —ая струна** spinal cord; **с. хребет** spinal column; **с. щит** (zool.) carapace; **—ая пластинка** neural (plate) (in turtles); **—омозговой** *a.* cerebrospinal; spinal (fluid); **—опокрышечный** *a.* spinotectal.

спинов/оврожденный *a.* spin-degenerated; **—ый** *a.* spin.

спинок *gen. pl. of* **спинка.**

спинопёр *m.* (ichth.) featherback (*Notopterus*).

спинор *m.* (phys.) spinor.

спин-орбитальный *a.* (phys.) spin-orbit.

спинорог *m.,* **—и, —овые** *pl.* (ichth.) triggerfish(es) (*Balistidae*).

спиношип *m.,* **—ы(е)** *pl.* spiny eels (*Notacanthidae*).

спин-решёточный *a.* (phys.) spin-lattice; **спин-спиновый** *a.* spin-spin.

спинтарископ *m.* (nucl.) spinthariscope, scintillascope.

спин-эхо *n.* spin echo.

спираденома *f.* (med.) spiradenoma.

спирал/евидный, —еобразный *a.* spiral, helical; **—изация** *f.* (left or right) handedness; (gen.) (relational) coiling.

спираль *f.* spiral, spire, helix, snail; coil (spring); (twist) drill; (mil.) (barbed-wire) concertina; **крутая с.** (av.) corkscrew; **—но** *adv.* in a spiral; *prefix* spiro— (spiral, coiled); **—ность** *f.* spirality; **—ношовный** *a.* spiral-seam (tubes); **—ный** *a.* spiral, helical; coil(ed); volute (pump; siphon); twisted (beam); corkscrew (antenna); coil (spring); **—ная линия** spiral line, helix.

спир/ан *m.,* **—ановый** *a.* spiran, spiro compound; **—атрон** *m.* (electron.) spiratron (traveling-wave tube); **—ацин** *m.* spiracin, methylcarboxylsalicylic acid; **—ема** *f.* (gen.) spireme; **—ейный** *a.* spiraeic (acid); (bot.) spirea; **—ея** *f.* spirea, **—илла** *f.* (bact.) spirillum; **—иллы** *pl.* (bact.) Spirillaceae.

спиро— *prefix* spiro— (spiral, coiled; respiration); **—гира** *f.* (bot.) Spirogyra; **—зал** *m.* Spirosal, monoglycol salicylate; **—ил** *m.* spiroyl; **—метр** *m.* (med.) spirometer; **—пентан** *m.* spiropentane; **—соединения** *pl.* spiro compounds, spirans, **—форм** *m.* Spiroform, acetylsalol; **—хета** *f.* (biol.) spirochaeta; **—хетоз** *m.* (med.) spirochetosis; **—хин** *m.* spirochin; **—цид** *m.* Spirocide, acetarsone; **—циклан** *m.* spirocyclan, spiro compound.

спирт *m.* alcohol, spirit; **древесный с.** wood alcohol, methyl alcohol; **стандартный с.** proof spirit; **—аза** *f.* alcoholase.

спиртн/ой, —ый *see* **спиртовой.**

спирто/альдегид *m.* alcohol aldehyde, hydroxyaldehyde; **—амин** *m.* alcohol amine, hydroxyamine; **—вание** *n.* alcoholization, etc., *see v.*; (text.) bleaching; **—вать** *v.* alcoholize, add alcohol; (wines) fortify; bleach; **—вка** *f.* alcohol lamp, alcohol burner; **—водочный завод** distillery.

спиртов/ой *a.* alcohol(ic); spirit (colors; level; mordant); **—ая смесь** alcoholic mixture.

спирто/завод *m.* distillery; **—кетон** *m.* alcohol ketone, hydroxyketone; **—кислота** *f.* alcohol acid, hydroxyacid.

спирто/ме(т)р *m.* alcoholometer; **—метрический** *a.* alcoholometric; **—метрия** *f.* alcoholometry.

спирто/растворимый *a.* alcohol-soluble; spirit (dye); **—сырец** *m.* crude spirit, raw spirit; (distilling) low wine, singlings; **—устойчивый** *a.* alcohol-resistant, alcohol-fast; **—эфир** *m.* alcohol ether, hydroxyether.

спирт-ректификат *m.* distilled alcohol; **с.-сырец** *see* **спиртосырец.**

спис/ание *see* **списывание; —анный** *a.* copied, etc., *see v.;* **—ать** *v. see* **списывать; —ок** *m.* copy, transcript; list, register, directory, inventory; schedule; (service) record; **вносить в —ок** *v.* record, catalog; **—ывание** *n.* copying, etc., *see v.;* **—ывать** *v.* (make a) copy, transcribe; write off; (naut.) transfer; discharge (personnel); **—ывать девиацию компаса** (av.) swing the compass, (naut.) swing the ship; **—ываться** *v.* be copied, etc.; correspond (with).

спит *pr. 3 sing. of* **спать.**

спит/ой *a.* dilute(d), weak (drink); **—ь** *v.* dilute; drink off.

спих/ивать, —нуть *v.* push off, push out, push together.

спиц/а *f.,* **—евой, —евый** *a.* (wheel) spoke; knitting needle; (traction) wire.

спич *m.* speech.

спичак *m.* (ichth.) sturgeon.

спичечн/ица *f.* matchbox; **—ый** *a.* match; **—ая соломка** matchstick.

спичка *f.* match.

сп. л. *abbr.* **(спектральная линия)** spectral line.

спл *abbr.* **(сополимер)** copolymer.

сплав *m.* (met.) alloy; fusion; melt; (timber) float(ing), drifting, rafting; **с. на алюминиевой основе** aluminum-base alloy; **—ать** *v.* float over, swim over; **—ина** *f.* quaking bog, quagmire; (bot.) floating mat; **—ить** *v. see* **сплавлять; —ка** *see* **сплавливание.**

сплавл/ение *see* **сплавливание; —енный** *a.* alloyed, etc., *see v.;* **—ивание** *n.* alloying, etc., *see v.;* fusion; (geol.) syntexis; **сварка —иванием** fusion welding; **—яемый** *a.* alloyable; fusable; **—яемый материал, —яемая загрузка** melting charge, melt; **—ять** *v.* (met.) alloy; melt, fuse (together); (logging) float, drift, raft, drive; **—яться** *v.* be alloyed, etc.; fuse together, coalesce.

сплав/ной *a. of* **сплав;** floatable; drift (wood); log (raft); **с. катализатор** skeleton catalyst, Raney catalyst; **—ное дело** transport by water; **—ообразование** *n.* alloy formation; **—оспособный** *a.* floatable; **—щик** *m.* log driver, raftsman.

спланировать *v.* plan, project; (av.) glide down.

спланхно— *prefix* (anat.) splanchno— (viscera); **—логия** *f.* splanchnology.

сплачив/ание *n.* joining, etc., *see v.;* joint; **с. в четверть** (carp.) rebate; **—ать(ся)** *v.* join, unite, combine, put together; clamp; scarf; make into a raft.

сплёвывать *v.* spit out, expectorate.

сплен/ит *m.* (med.) splenitis; **—(о)—** *prefix* (anat.) splen(o)— (spleen); **—омегалия** *f.* (med.) splenomegaly, enlargement of the spleen.

сплесень *m.* splice (joint), splicing.

сплёскивать *v.* rinse off; splash out.

сплесн/ение, —ивание *n.* splice, splicing, joining; **—и(ва)ть** *v.* splice, join.

сплеснуть *see* **сплёскивать.**

спле/сти, —тать *v.* splice, intertwine, interlace, (inter)weave, (inter)twist; plait, braid; **—таться** *v.* be spliced, etc., *see* **сплетать;** mesh; **—тение** *n.* splicing, etc., *see v.;* splice; entanglement, complication; tangle; (anat.) plexus, network; **солнечное —тение** solar plexus; **—тённый** *a.* spliced, etc., *see v.*

сплот/ить *see* **сплачивать; —ка** *f.* joining; joint(ing); straight joint; bundling; string; **—ок** *m.* raft; **—очный** *a. of* **сплотка;** float (unit).

сплоч/ение *n.* joining, scarfing; uniting, rallying; unity; **—ённость** *f.* unity, solidarity, cohesion, closeness;

—**ённый** *a.* joined, united; close, packed; compacted (ice edge); —**ённый лёд** close pack-ice.

сплошн/ой *a.* continuous, unbroken, one-piece, entire, integral, uniform; solid, massive, compact; blind (wall); sheet (lightning); clear (cutting); full-scope (survey); broadcast (sowing); fast (ice); **с. характер** uniformity; —**ая среда** continuum; —**ого действия** non-selective, general (pesticide); —**ое покрытие** coating; **бурение —ым забоем** solid drilling; **механика —ых сред** continuum mechanics, flow mechanics; —**ость** *f.* continuity; uniformity (of structure); —**як** *m.* solid mass.

сплошь *adv.* continuously, uninterruptedly; without exception; **с. да рядом, с. и рядом** very often, frequently; completely, entirely.

сплы/вание *n.* coalescence; (soil) fusion; —**(ва)ть** *v.* float (with current); run off, overflow; —**(ва)ться** *v.* float together, run together, blend, merge, mix, fuse.

сплюнуть *see* **сплёвывать.**

сплюснут/ость *see* **сплющенность;** —**ый** *see* **сплющенный;** —**ь** *see* **сплющивать.**

сплюшка *f.* scops owl (*Otus scops*).

сплющ/енность *f.* flatness; oblateness; —**енный** *a.* flattened, etc., *see v.*; oblate; —**ивание** flattening, etc., *see v.*; —**и(ва)ть** *v.* flatten (out), compress, draw down; telescope; upset, jump up; clinch (rivet head); —**и(ва)ться** *v.* be flattened (out), etc.; telescope, collapse; —**ивающий** *a.* flattening, etc., *see v.*

СПМ *abbr.* (**сополимеризация**) copolymerization.

сподо— *prefix* spodo— (ashes); —**грамма** *f.* (bot.) spodogram, record of ash content.

сподручный *a.* handy, convenient.

споенный *a.* watered (stock).

спозаран/ку, —**ок** *adv.* (from) early morning.

споить *v.* water.

спойлер *m.* (aero.) spoiler.

спокоенный *a.* killed (steel).

спокойн/ый *a.* calm, quiet, tranquil, quiescent, resting, at rest, restful; mild; smooth (working); latent; stagnant; (elec.) static; dead, steady (load); killed (steel); still (air).

спокойств/ие, —**о** *n.* calm(ness), quietness, placidity, composure; (atmospheric) stability; **общественное с.** law and order.

сполаживание *n.* flattening.

сполласкив/ание *n.* rinsing (off, out); —**ать** *v.* rinse (off, out).

сполз/ание *n.* sliding off, slipping, creep; (land)slide; (instr.) drift; —**ать,** —**ти** *see* **сползывать.**

сполна *adv.* completely, entirely, in full.

споловинить *v.* halve.

сполос/катель *m.* rinser; (min.) clean-up man; —**кать,** —**нуть** *see* **споласкивать.**

сполох *see* **северное сияние;** lightning flashes.

спонгин *m.* (zool.) spongin.

спонгио/бласт *m.* (embr.) spongioblast; —**цит** *m.* (cyt.) spongiocyte.

спондил/ит *m.* (med.) spondylitis; —**(о)**— *prefix* spondyl(o)— (vertebra); —**оз** *m.* spondylosis.

спонтанн/ость *f.* spontaneity; —**ый** *a.* spontaneous.

спор *m.* dispute, argument, controversy, debate; *sh. m. of* **спорый; об этом нет —у** it is self-evident.

спора *f.* (biol.) spore; **зимняя с.** teleutospore.

спорадич/еский, —**ный** *a.* sporadic.

споранг/иальный, —**иевый** *a.* (bot.) sporangial; —**иеносец** *m.* sporangiophore; —**ий** *m.* sporangium, spore case; —**ин** *m.* sporangin.

спорен *sh. m. of* **спорный.**

спориди/й *m.,* —**я** *f.* (bot.) sporidium.

спор/ить *v.* dispute, argue; —**иться** *v.* succeed; —**ный** *a.* disputable, debatable, questionable, controversial, moot.

споро— *prefix* (biol.) sporo—, spore; —**вики, —вые животные** *pl.* (zool.) Sporozoa; —**вместилище** *see* **спорангий;** —**во-пыльцевой** *a.* (bot.) palynological; —**вость** *f. suffix* —spory; —**вый** *a.* spore; (bot.) cryptogamous; —**вое растение** (bot.) sporophyte; —**генез** *m.,* —**гония** *f. see* **спорообразование;** —**карпий** *m.* (bot.) sporocarp; —**киста** *f.* (zool.) sporocyst; —**листик** *see* **спорофилл;** —**нос(ец)** *m.* sporophore; —**носный** *a.* (bot.) sporiferous; sporogenous; —**образование** *n.* (biol.) spore formation, sporogenesis.

спорость *f.* quickness; profitableness.

споротрихоз *m.* (med.) sporotrichosis.

спороть *v.* rip off.

споро/убивающий *a.* sporicidal; —**филл** *m.* (bot.) sporophyll, spore-bearing leaf; —**фит** *m.* (bot.) sporophyte; —**циста** *f.* (prot.) sporocyst.

спорт *m.* sport, mutation; —**ивный** *a.* sport(s), athletic; race (horse).

спорул/ировать *v.* (biol.) sporulate; —**яция** *f.* sporulation.

споры *pl. of* **спор; спора.**

спорый *a.* quick, fast; profitable, advantageous, successful, rapidly progressing.

спорынья *f.* (phyt.) ergot; smut.

спорыш *m.* (bot.) knotweed (*Polygonum aviculare*).

способ *m.* method, process, means, way(s), procedure, technique, manner, mode, system; **с. бурения** drilling; **с. действия** (biol.) action mechanism; modus operandi; **с. получения** process, making (e.g. iron making); **влажным —ом** wet (process); **механическим —ом** mechanically; by machine; **таким —ом** in this way.

способн/ость *f.* capacity, capability, power, ability, aptitude, talent, faculty; —ability, —ibility, —ivity; **с. делиться** fissionability; **с. к окислению** oxidizability; **продуктивная с.** productivity; —**ый** *a.* capable, able, gifted; in a position (to); —**ый к делению** fissionable.

способств/ование *n.* contribution, aid, assistance; —**овать** *v.* contribute, aid, assist, promote, further, enable, favor, encourage, foster, be conducive (to), make (for); —**ующий** *a.* contributing, etc., *see v.*; instrumental.

спот/кнуться *see* **спотыкаться;** —**ыкание** *n.* stumbling; —**ыкаться,** —**ыкнуться** *v.* stumble.

спохват/иться, —**ываться** *v.* recall suddenly.

СППЗУ *abbr.* (**стираемое программируемое постоянное запоминащее устройство**) erasable programmable read-only memory, EPROM.

спр. *abbr.* (**справочник**) handbook.

справа *adv.* to the right, from the right, on the right; (naut.) to starboard; right-hand; **вид с.** right-side elevation.

справедлив/о *adv.* fairly, justly, rightly, equitably; with good reason; (it) holds true, (it) is true, (it) holds (for); —**ость** *f.* justice, right, fairness; truth, validity; accuracy; **отдать ему —ость** *v.* do him justice; **по —ости** in all fairness; justly; —**ый** *a.* just, fair, right; valid, legitimate; true, correct, accurate.

справ/ить(ся) *see* **справлять(ся);** —**ка** *f.* reference; information, report; (comp.) help; inquiry, search; certificate; **наводить —ки** *v.* make inquiries, inquire, investigate; —**лять** *v.* straighten; rectify; correct, repair; buy; obtain; celebrate; —**лять путь** take a short-cut; —**ляться** *v.* refer; collate; consult, make inquiries, inquire, ask (about); manage, master, cope (with), handle,

справный *a.* in good condition.

справок *gen. pl. of* **справка**.

справочн/ая *f.* information (service); —**ик** *m.* reference book, handbook, manual; directory; —**о-библиограф-ический** *a.* reference (and bibliographical), literature-searching; —**о-информационный** *a.* inquiry, reference (information) —**ый** *a.* reference, information, inquiry, (comp.) help; —**ый кран** try cock, gage cock; —**ый стол** information desk; —**ая таблица** (comp.) look-up table; —**ые данные** reference data; data bank.

спрашив/ается the question arises; —**ать** *v.* ask, demand, inquire; —**аться** *v.* ask permission; be asked.

спредер *m.* spreader.

спрессов/анный *a.* pressed; —**ать, —ывать** *v.* (com)press, force together.

сприн(г)бок *m.* (mam.) springbok (*Antidorcas marsupialis*).

спринклер *m.,* —**ная головка** sprinkler; —**ное оборудование** sprinkler system.

спринц/евание *n.* syringing, injection; (med.) lavage; —**евать** *v.* syringe, inject; (med.) irrigate; —**овка** *f.* syringe; syringing.

спровоцировать *v.* provoke, incite.

спроектиров/анный *a.* designed, etc., *see v.;* —**ать** *v.* design, plan; (math.) project.

спрос *m.* (com.) demand, market; permission; **с. на** demand for; **с. и предложение** supply and demand; —**ить** *see* **спрашивать**.

спрофилировать *v.* profile, shape.

спрошенный *a.* asked; demanded, in demand.

спру *n.* (med.) sprue, catarrhal dysentery.

спрут *m.* (zool.) octopus.

спрыг/ивание *n.* jumping off, etc., *see v.;* —**ивать,** —**нуть** *v.* jump off, jump down, spring down.

спрыс/кивание *n.* spraying, etc., *see v.;* —**кивать** *v.* spray, sprinkle, wet, moisten; —**нутый** *a.* sprayed, etc., *see v.;* —**нуть** *see* **спрыскивать**.

спрягать *v.* harness; (gram.) conjugate.

спрядённый *a.* (text.) spun.

спряжение *n.* (gram.) conjugation.

спрям/ить *see* **спрямлять;** —**ление** *n.* rectification, straightening (out), linearization (of curve); alignment; squaring; —**лённый** *a.* rectified, etc., *see v.;* —**ляемость** *f.* rectifiability; —**ляемый** *a.* rectifiable; —**лять** *v.* rectify, straighten (out), linearize; align; square; —**ляющий** *a.* rectifying, etc., *see v.;* (av.) turning (vane).

спрясть *v.* (text.) spin.

спрята/нный *a.* hidden, etc., *see v.;* —**ть** *v.* hide, conceal; store.

спрячь *v.* harness.

спуаз *abbr.* (**сантипуаз**) centipoise.

спуг/ивать, —**нуть** *v.* scare off.

спуррит *m.* (min.) spurrite.

спуск *m.* lowering, etc., *see v.;* descent; slope, incline, downgrade; chute, drop; discharge, drain, run-off, outlet, escape, vent, bleeding; disposal; re-entry (of satellite); (naut.) launch(ing) (of ship); (chronometer) escapement; trigger, release; (pharm.) cerate; (typ.) imposition; **на** —**е** on the downgrade; —**ание** *n.* lowering, etc., *see v.;* —**ать** *v.* lower, let down, run in(to) (a well), drop; discharge, tap (off), draw off, bleed, drain (off), empty, flush, run off; deflate; unwind; let loose, let out, release, trip, trigger; launch (ship); (typ.) impose; —**аться** *v.* be lowered, etc.; descend, come down, go down; hang (from); slope (down); —**аю-щийся** *a.* descending; hanging; sloping; (comp.) pull-down (menu).

спускн/ой *a. of* **спуск;** bleeding (valve); **с. жёлоб** shoot,

chute, slide; **с. канал** sewer; **с. кран** drain cock, petcock; **с. крючок** trigger, releasing cam; **с. механизм** trigger mechanism, release; —**ая втулка,** —**ая проб-ка** drain plug; —**ая собачка** trigger, release; —**ое действие** trigger action; —**ое отверстие** drain, discharge, tap hole; —**ое приспособление** trigger, release; —**ые сани** launching cradle.

спуск/овой *see* **спускной;** **с. крючок** trigger (of rifle); drain cock (of radiator); —**овая кнопка** (phot.) shutter release; —**овая схема** (aut.) flip-flop, trigger circuit; —**оподъёмный** *a.* hoisting (operations); —**оподъём** *m.* round trip (of instrument).

спуст/ившийся *a.* descended; (av.) landed; —**ить** *see* **спускать**.

спустя *prep. acc.* after, later.

спутанно *adv.* in a tangle; —**волокнистая структура** (geol.) felted texture; —**столбчатый** *a.* diverse columnar; —**сть** *f.* entanglement; confusion.

спут/анный *a.* (en)tangled, intertwined, matted; confused, vague; —**ать** *see* **спутывать**.

спутник *m.* satellite; (anat.) comes; companion; (min.) accessory, associated mineral; **с. земли** earth satellite; **с. специального назначения** dedicated satellite; **искусственный с.** satellite.

спутник-бомбардировщик *m.* bomb-carrying satellite; **с.-заправщик** *m.* refueling satellite; **с.-инспектор** *m.* space control satellite; **с.-истребитель** *m.* interceptor satellite; **с.-ловушка** *m.* decoy satellite; **с.-перехват-чик** *m.* interceptor satellite; **с.-постановщик помех** disperser satellite; **с.-приманка** *m.* decoy satellite; **с.-радиомаяк** *m.* beacon satellite; **с.-ретранслятор** *m.* communication(s) satellite; relay satellite; **с.-связи** communication(s) satellite; **с.-снаряд** *m.* satellite (vehicle); **с.-танкер** *m.* refueling satellite; **с.-фотораз-ведчик** *m.* camera-carrying satellite; **с.-цель** *m.* target satellite.

спут/никовый, —**ничный** *a. of* **спутник;** —**ный** *a.* accompanying; lee (wave); cocurrent; —**ная струя** (av.; naut.) wake.

спутыв/ание *n.* (en)tangling, etc., *see v.;* entanglement; —**ать** *v.* (en)tangle, intertwine, snarl, mat; confuse, mix up; upset (calculation); hobble (animals), tie (up).

спущенный *a.* lowered, etc., *see* **спускать;** flat (tire).

спя/чка *f.* sleep; sleepiness; sopor; dormant state; **зим-няя с.** hibernation; —**щий** *a.* sleeping, dormant, resting; *m.* sleeping person.

ср *abbr.* (**стерадиан**) steradian; **ср.** *abbr.* (**сравни**) compare; (**среда**) Wednesday; (**средний**) average, mean; middle; **с.р.** *abbr.* (**сильно растворимый**) readily soluble; (**спирторастворимый**) alcohol-soluble.

срабатыв/аемость *f.* wearability, durability; —**ание** *n.* wearing away, *see v.;* abrasion, wear (and tear); response (of counter, etc.); (comp.) pickup; **скорость** —**ания** (comp.) operating speed; —**ать** *v.* wear away, abrade, (mach.) operate, function, work, come into action; trip, actuate, trigger; change state (of pulse circuits, logic elements); make, fabricate; draw (water) off or down (from reservoir), lower (water level); deplete (fuel); blow off (of valve); —**аться** *v.* be worn away, etc.; wear (away, out), deteriorate, work well together.

сработ/авшийся *a.* worn out, used up; —**анность** *f.* (degree of) wear; good teamwork; —**анный** *past pass. part. of* **сработать;** —**ать** *see* **срабатывать;** —**ка** *see* **срабатывание;** decrease (of storage); available capacity (of reservoir).

сравнен/ие *n.* comparison, correlation, checking, matching; rating; **блок** —**ия** error detector; **вещество для** —**ия** reference material; **выдерживать с.** *v.* compare favorably; **делать с.** *v.* compare, check (against); **орган —ия** (aut.) comparer, discriminator; **по —ию с** in comparison with, (as) compared to (or with), as against, versus; on, over; from; **признак —ия сходимости** (math.) test of convergence; **электрод —ия** reference electrode.

сравни *imp.* compare; **—ваемый** *a.* comparable; **—вание** *n.* comparing, etc., *see v.*; **—вать** *v.* compare, correlate, check (against), match; contrast, confront (with); level, make even, equal(ize), equate; **—ваться** *v.* be compared, etc.; (be) equal, match, come up (to); line up (of water levels); equate; **—вающий** *a.* comparing, etc., *see v.*; **—вающее устройство** comparator.

сравним/ость *f.* comparability; **—ый** *a.* comparable; comparing favorably (with); (math.) congruent.

сравнительн/о *adv.* comparatively, relatively, fairly; in (or by) comparison; **с. с** versus, against; **—ый** *a.* comparative, relative, respective; comparison (study); reference (sample); **—ый период** (nucl.) comparative lifetime.

сравн/ить, —ять *see* **сравнивать; —яться** *v.* be equalized, become equal, match.

сра/жать *v.* overwhelm; **—жаться** *v.* fight; **—жение** *n.* battle; **—зить(ся)** *see* **сражать(ся).**

сразу *adv.* at once, immediately; at one stroke, then and there; **с. после** right after; **с. после того, как** as soon as, the moment.

срамной *a.* shameful, disgraceful.

срамный *a.* (anat.) pudendal; **с. губы** labia.

сраст/ание *n.* growing together, etc., *see v.*; intergrowth, accretion, concrescence; coalescence, coalition; concretion; union; **двойник —ания** (cryst.) interpenetration twin; **—аться, —ись** *v.* grow together, intergrow, concresce, coalesce, fuse (together), interlock; adhere; (med.) heal, form a scar, knit; **—ить** *see* **сращивать.**

сращ/ение *see* **срастание;** (anat.) symphysis; **—ённый** *a.* joined, etc., *see v.*; **—ивание** *n.* joining, etc., *see v.*; fusion; union, joint, splice; **—ивать** *v.* join, combine, unite, consolidate; joint; splice, piece, bind; (welding) fuse; **—иваться** *see* **срастаться.**

ср. вр. *abbr.* **(среднее время)** (astr.) mean time.

сребробрюшковые *pl.* (ichth.) Leiognathidae.

среброносный *see* **сереброносный.**

сред/а *f.* medium, atmosphere, (working or process) fluid, agent, vehicle; region; surroundings, environment; (biol.) habitat; condition(s); population (of quantum generator); Wednesday; **воздушная с.** atmosphere; **окружающая с.** environment; **сплошная с.** (phys.) the continuum; **условия (внешней) —ы** environment; **факторы —ы** ecological factors.

среди *prep. gen.* in the middle (of), among, of; *prefix* inter—.

средизем/номорский *a.* Mediterranean; sickle-cell (anemia); **—номорье** *n.* coastal area of Mediterranean Sea; **—ный** *a.* inland (sea); Mediterranean (Sea); **—ье** *see* **средиземноморье.**

срединный *a.* middle, mean, median.

средне— *prefix* middle, medium, central; medi(o)—, meso—; average; **—азиатский** *a.* Central Asia(n); **—активный** *a.* medium-active; (nucl.) medium-activity, semi-hot; **—арифметический** *a.* arithmetic mean; **—вековый** *a.* medieval; **—вековье** *n.* Middle Ages; **—взвешенная величина, —взвешенное** *n.* (stat.) weighted average, weighted mean; **—влаголюбивый** *a.* (bot.) mesophytic; **—геометрический** *a.* geometric mean; **—годовой** *a.* average annual; **—горье** *n.* medium-high mountain country; **—грудь** *f.* meso-

thorax; **—девонский отдел** (geol.) Meso-devonic period; **—доступный** *a.* moderate (price); **—дунайский** *a.* Central Danube.

средн/ее *n.* average, mean; *see also under* **средний; с. по времени** time average; **в —ем** on the average; **геометрическое с., пропорциональное с.** geometric mean.

средне/европейский *a.* Central European; **—зернистый** *a.* medium-grained; medium (sand); **—калиберный** *a.* medium-caliber.

среднеквадрат/ический *a.,* **—ичное** *n.,* **—ичный** *a.* (math.) root-mean-square, rms.

среднекубический *a.* root-mean-cube, rmc.

средне/легированный *a.* (met.) medium-alloy; **—линейный** *a.* midline; **—месячный** *a.* average monthly; **—навесной** *a.* mid-mounted; **—плодник** *m.* (bot.) mesocarp; **—прогрессивный** *a.* progressive mean; a mean based on expected improvement in the future; **—серийный** *a.* medium-size; **—сибирский** *a.* Central Siberian; **—сменный** *a.* average (per) shift; **—смертельная доза** median lethal dose, LD$_{50}$; **—сортный** *a.* medium-grade; **—суточный** *a.* daily average; **—твёрдый** *a.* medium-hard; **—тяжёлый** *a.* medium-weight; **—часовой** *a.* hourly average; **—численный, —числовой** *a.* number-average (molecular weight); **—чревный** *a.* (anat.; embr.) mesogastric.

средн/ий *a.* middle, mean, average, medium, median, central; midway, mid- (point, position); medium-sized; neutral (reaction; salt); representative (sample); moderate, middling, intermediate; medium-textured (soil); secondary (school); **С. восток** Middle East; **с. квадратический** (math.) root-mean-square; **с. мозг** (anat.) mesencephalon; **—ее арифметическое** arithmetic mean; **—ее время** local mean time; **—ее время жизни** mean life; **—ее значение** mean (value); **—ее ухо** (anat.) middle ear; **—ее число** mean, average; **выводить —ее число** *v.* average; **—ие данные** (math.; stat.) averages; **—ие сутки** mean solar day; **—им числом** on an average, at an average; **—яя величина** mean (value); **—яя линия** median, center line; **—яя ошибка** standard deviation; **—яя продолжительность жизни** life expectancy; **—яя точка** midpoint, center; **в —ем** on an average, on the average, medium; **выше —его** above average.

средн/ик *m.* (typ.) intercolumn space; (window) mullion; **—яя** *see* **среднее.**

средостен/ие *n.* (anat.) mediastinum; **—(оч)ный** *a.* mediastinal.

средоточие *n.* center (point), (point of) concentration, focus.

средств/о *n.* agent, medium, media, tool, device, aid, equipment; vehicle; **—ант, —ент;** means, way, facility, expedient; (pharm.) remedy; **с. доставки (оружия)** (mil.) (weapon) delivery vehicle; **с. против коррозии** rust preventive; **—а** *pl.* means, facilities; resources, assets, funds, capital; (consumers') goods; (mil.) weapons; equipment, gear; **—а массового поражения** weapons of mass destruction; **—а наблюдения** surveillance systems; **—а передвижения** transport facilities; **—а радиопротиводействия** electronic countermeasures, ECM; **абсорбирующее с.** absorbent; **активирующее с.** activator; **антибиотическое с.** antibiotic; **материальные —а** (mil.) stores; **национальные технические —а контроля** national technical means of (treaty) verification; **ракетные —а** missile systems; **служить —ом** *v.* be instrumental; **технические —а** hardware, components; **транспортное с.** (transporter) vehicle; **ускорительные —а** (rockets) boosters; **финансовые —а** funds.

среды *gen., pl. of* **среда.**

средь *see* **среди.**

срез *m.* cut, slice; (microscopic) section; cut-off; shear, shearing (off); (elec.) trailing edge (of pulse); **плоскость —а** shear plane; **прочность на с.** shearing strength; **частота —а** cut-off frequency.

срез/ание *see* **срезывание; —анный** *a.* cut, sheared; truncated; **—ать** *see* **срезывать; —ающий** *see* **срезывающий; —ка** *see* **срезывание;** *gen. of* **срезок; —ной** *a.* cut off; shear (bolt); **—ок** *m.* slice, section.

срезыв/аемый *a.* in shear; **—ание** *n.* cutting, etc., *see v.*; cut-off; truncation; **—ать** *v.* cut (away, off, down), shear (off), trim, pare; bevel; truncate; level off (hills); **—ающий** *a.* cutting, etc., *see v.*; **—ающая сила** shearing force.

срисов/ать *see* **срисовывать; —ка** *f.,* **—ывание** *n.* copying, reproduction; drawing; **—ывать** *v.* copy, reproduce; draw.

сровн/енный *a.* leveled (off); **—ять** *see* **сравнивать.**

сродн/ить *v.* relate, bring together; **—ый** *a.* innate, natural; homogeneous, allied, congenial; related.

сродственный *a.* related.

сродство *n.* relationship, affinity; **избирательное с.** affinity; **химическое с.** chemical affinity.

сроё/к *m.* (apid) afterswarm; **—нный** *a.* swarmed (of bees).

сроет *fut. 3 sing. of* **срыть.**

сроиться *v.* swarm (of bees).

срок *m.* date, time (interval), term, (fixed) period, duration; deadline; **с. гарантии** warranty; **с. годности** useful life; expiration date; **с. поставки** delivery date; **с. работы, с. службы** (service) life (of equipment); **с. хранения** shelf life; **—ом до** within (given time); **—ом на 10 дней** for (a term of) 10 days; **в срок** on time, by the deadline; **до —а** ahead of schedule; **льготный с.** grace period; **переносить с.** postpone; **раньше —а** ahead of schedule; **родившийся в с.** full-term (baby).

срост *m.* attachment, adhesion.

сростно— *prefix* syn(o)—, sym—, syl— (together; associated); gamo— (fusion); **—лепестный** *a.* (bot.) sympetalous; **—листный** *a.* (bot.) gamophyllous; **—палость** *f.* (med.) syndactyly; **—плодный** *a.* syncarpous; **—челюстные** *pl.* (ichth.) puffers (*Tetraodontidae*).

сросток *m.* attachment, adhesion; joint, junction, splice, splicing; (min.) concretion.

сросшийся *a.* grown together, united; (biol.) (co)adnate.

срочн/о *adv.* urgently, quickly, by express; on a crash basis; **—ослужащий** *m.* (mil.) conscript, draftee; **—ость** *f.* urgency; priority; **—ый** *a.* urgent, pressing; emergency; crash (program); rush (order); prompt (action); special-delivery (letter); (com.) due; **—ое наблюдение** (meteor.) standard observation; **—ые роды** (med.) labor at full term.

сроющий *pr. act. part. of* **срыть.**

ср. ск. *abbr.* (**средняя скорость**) mean velocity, average speed.

сруб *m.* frame(work), crib, cage, timber(ing); felling; cut; **—ание** *n.* felling, etc., *see v.*; **—ать, —ить** *v.* fell, hew, chop down, chop off; chop away; cut down, cut off; frame, build (with wood); **—ка** *see* **срубание; —ленный** *a.* felled, etc., *see v.*; **—овый** *a.* timber; **—овая крепь** (min.) crib.

срыв *m.* break(ing), break-away, separation; interruption; disruption, failure, breakdown; (av.) stall(ing); stripping; **с. генерации** (elec.) quenching of oscillation; **с. дуги** (elec.) blow-out; **с. пламени** (av.) flame-out; **с. потока** flow separation; **реакция —а** stripping reac-

tion; **скорость —а** (av.) stalling speed; **—ание** *n.* breaking, tearing off; picking, plucking; leveling, razing; **—ать** *see* **сорвать, срыть; —ка** *adv.* with a jerk; abruptly; **—ник** *m.* (av.) spoiler; **—ной** *a.* leaf (lettuce); **—у** *see* **срывка; —щик** *m.* disrupter.

срыг/ивать, —нуть *v.* regurgitate.

срыт/ие *n.* demolition, razing; **—ь** *v.* demolish, raze, level; break down; tear off, strip (a thread); blow away.

срядить *see* **сряжать.**

сряду *adv.* one after the other, continuously, in succession, running.

сряжать *v.* equip, fit out, prepare; **—ся** *v.* get prepared; contract, undertake.

сс *abbr.* (**существование сомнительное**) existence doubtful.

сс. *abbr.* (**села**) villages.

СС *abbr.* (**сейсмическая станция**) seismic station; (**схема сравнения**) comparison circuit.

сса/дина *f.* excoriation, abrasion, scratch; **—дить(ся)** *see* **ссаживать(ся); —дка** *f.* shrinkage; **—живать** *v.* excoriate, abrade, scratch; help down; drop, let off (passengers); **—живаться** *v.* get scratched; get off.

ссасывать *v.* suck out, draw out.

ссевшийся *a.* coagulated, clotted; crystallized, granulated (honey).

ссед/ание *n.* shrinking, etc., *see v.*; shrinkage; coagulation; deposition, crystallization (of honey); **—аться** *v.* shrink, contract; coagulate, curdle, clot; settle, sink.

ссек *abbr.* (**сантисекунда**) centisecond.

ссек *m.* (meat) top round; *past m. sing. of* **ссечь; —ание** *n.* chopping off, cleaving; **—ать** *v.* chop off, cleave.

ссел/ение *n.* merger (of villages); **—ить(ся), —ять(ся)** *v.* settle together.

ссесться *see* **сседаться.**

ссеч/ка *f.* clearing; **—ь** *see* **ссекать.**

ссор/а *f.* disagreement, quarrel; **—иться** *v.* disagree, quarrel.

ссосать *see* **ссасывать.**

ссохнуться *see* **ссыхаться.**

ССП *abbr.* (**станция скорой помощи**) first aid station.

СССР *abbr.* (**Союз Советских Социалистических Республик**) Union of Soviet Socialist Republics (USSR).

ссу/да *f.* loan, advance; **безвозвратная с.** grant; **—дить** *see* **ссужать; —дный** *a.* loan, lending; **—до-сберегательный** *a.* savings and loan (bank); **—жать** *v.* loan, lend, advance.

ссутулить(ся) *v.* stoop, hunch.

ссучить *see* **сучить.**

ссыл/ать *v.* banish, exile, deport; **—аться** *v.* be exiled; refer, allude (to), cite, quote; plead (illness); **—аясь на** with reference to; **—ка** *f.,* **—очный** *a.* exile, deportation; transportation; reference, citation; (comp.) access address; **—ьный** *a.* exiled; *m.* exile.

ссып/ание *n.* pouring (of solids); **—ать** *v.* pour (in, together); dump; **—ать в мешки** *v.* bag; **—ка** *f.* pouring; collection; **—ной** *a.* pouring; grain-collecting (center).

ссыхаться *v.* shrink, shrivel, dry up, warp.

ссядется *fut. 3 sing. of* **ссесться.**

ст *abbr.* (**стокс**) stoke(s) (unit of kinematic viscosity).

ст. *abbr.* (**стадия**) stage, phase; (**стандарт**) standard; (**станция**) station; (**старший**) senior; (**статья**) article; (**степень**) degree; (**столб**) column; (**ступень**) grade.

ста *gen. of* **сто.**

стабилиз/атор *m.* stabilizer, balancer, equalizer; regulator; inhibitor; (av.) fin; **с. напряжения** voltage regulator; **с. пламени** (av.) flame holder; **с. частоты** frequency control (circuit); **вертикальный с.** (av.) fin; **гиросиловой с.** fly-wheel; **хвостовой с.** tail fin; —**ация** f. stabilization, stabilizing, etc., see v.; level-off; control; (speed) hold; (phase) lock; —**ация по курсу** (av.) yaw stabilization; —**(ир)ованный** a. stabilized, etc., see v.; —**(ир)овать** v. stabilize, balance, level off, regulate, control; —**ируемый вращением** a. spin-stabilized; —**ируемый оперением** a. fin-stabilized; —**ирующий** a. stabilizing, etc., see v.; anti-hunt; —**ирующее вещество** stabilizer.

стабил/итрон m. (electron.) stabilitron, voltage stabilizing tube; avalanche (break-down) diode; **с. коронного разряда** corona stabilitron, corona tube; —**овольт** m. stabilivolt.

стабильн/ость f. stability; **с. нуля** zero stability; —**ый** a. stable, constant, consistent; firm, rigid.

ставен/ный a., —**ь** m. shutter; lid.

став/ить v. place, put, set, stand; pose, state (a problem), present, offer, issue (a challenge); raise (a question); apply, secure, bond (with adhesive); assign (a probability); lay down (conditions); build, erect, put up, set up, pitch (a tent), organize, stage; run, carry out, perform; make (a diagnosis); regard (as), look upon; —**ка** f. placing, etc., see v.; rate (of pay); headquarters; filling (operation on winding machine); **сдельная —ка** piece(work) rate.

ставн/ик m., —**ой** a., —**ая сеть** fixed net, trap net.

ставня see **ставень.**

ставрид/овые, —ы pl. (ichth.) scads, jacks, horsemack-erels (Carangidae).

ставро— prefix staur(o)— (cross).

ставропольский a. (geog.) Stavropol.

ставрос m. (bot.) stauros.

ставший past act. part. of **стать.**

стагнация f. stagnation, dead season.

стадиальный see **стадийный.**

стадийн/о adv. in stages; —**ость** f. vicissitude, change (by stages); —**ый** a. stage, phase(d), by stages.

стадион m. stadium; (bot.) stade.

стад/ия f. stage, phase; time, interval; (chem.) step; (bot.) stade; **в —ии** under (construction); **в начальной —ии** initially; **на этой —ии** at this stage, at this point; **по —иям** in stages.

стад/ность f. herd instinct; —**ный** a. gregarious; —**о** n. herd, drove, flock; stock; school, shoal (of fish).

стает fut. 3 sing. of **стаять.**

стаж m. experience, record; seniority; length of service; **с. практическим —ем** experienced; —**евый** a. experienced, senior; —**ёр** m. trainee; probationer; intern; —**ирование** see **стажировка;** —**ировать** v. work on probation, get on-the-job training; —**ировка** f. probation; practical experience, on-the-job training; internship.

стаз m. (physiol.) stasis.

стаивать v. melt (away), thaw off, defrost, deice.

стайка dim. of **стая.**

стайн/ость f. gregariousness; —**ый** a. of **стая;** gregarious.

стакан m., —**ный** a. glass, tumbler; beaker; hollow metal cylinder or sleeve; bushing, sleeve; housing, casing, case, shell; tube; body; (well pump) bucket; vessel, pot; —**ный бур** core drill; —**чик** dim. of **стакан;** can, pot; (paper) cup; (analysis) boat, capsule.

стак(к)ер m. stacker.

стаксель m. (naut.) staysail.

стал past m. sing. of **стать.**

сталагмит m. (geol.) stalagmite; —**овый** a. stalagmitic.

сталагмометр m. (phys.) stalagmometer.

сталактит m. (geol.) stalactite; —**овый** a. stalactitic.

стале— prefix steel; ferro— (alloy); —**алюминий** m. ferroaluminum; —**бетон** m., —**бетонный** a. steel concrete; —**вар** m. steel worker; —**варение** n. steel making; —**ватый** a. steely, steel-like; —**делательный** a. steel (mill); —**литейный** a. steel casting; foundry; —**литейный завод, —литейная мастерская** steel foundry, steel mill, steel works; —**литейщик** m. steel founder.

сталеплавиль/ный a. steel smelting; steel (furnace; mill); —**щик** m. steel smelter.

сталеразливочный a. steel-pouring.

стали past pl. of **стать;** gen., pl., etc., of **сталь.**

сталийное время (com.) lay days (for loading and unloading a ship).

Сталинград (geog.) Stalingrad (Soviet name for Volgograd).

сталинит m. stalinite (Soviet tool alloy); tempered safety glass.

сталиров/ание n., —**ка** f. steel plating; —**ать** v. steel-plate.

сталистый a. steely, steel-like; **с. чугун** semisteel, toughened cast iron.

сталкиват/ель m. (conveyor) pusher; (typ.) jogger; —**ь** v. push, shove off; push together, make collide; (typ.) jog; —**ься** v. collide, run (against, into), encounter, impinge (upon); clash, conflict, interfere; face (a challenge).

сталкивающий a. pushing, etc., see **сталкивать.**

стало past n. sing. of **стать; во что бы то ни с.** by all means; **с. быть** conj. consequently, therefore.

сталь f. steel; **специальная с.** special (alloy) steel; —**бетон** m. steel concrete.

стальник m. (bot.) restharrow (Ononis).

стальноголовый a. (ichth.) steelhead (trout).

стальн/ой a. steel; —**осерый** a. steel gray.

Стамбул (geog.) Istanbul.

стамес/ка f., —**очный** a. wood chisel.

стаминодий m. (bot.) staminodium.

стампийский a. (geol.) Stampian (stage).

стамуха f. grounded ice hummock.

стан m. mill; machine; stand, support; camp, station; stature.

станд m. stand.

стандарт m. standard(s), standard specifications, norm(al); gage; sort; **установление —ов** regulation; —**изация** f. standardization; —**изировать, —изов(ыв)ать** v. standardize, calibrate, gage; —**изованный** a. standard(ized); —**ный** a. standard(ized), normal, regular, conventional; common; off-the-shelf; (chem.) reference; prefabricated (house); **с.-титр** m. titrant.

стандерс m. (naut.) stand(ard).

стандовый a. stand; bench (test).

станет fut. 3 sing. of **стать.**

станин/а f., —**ный** a. mount, bed(plate), base, pedestal; bench, stand; frame(work), carcass, casing, case, housing; (elec.) (stator) yoke; column, pillar; (art.) trail.

станиол/евый a., —**ь** m. (metal) foil; tinfoil.

станк/и pl. of **станок;** —**ист** m. machine-gunner; —**о—** prefix lathe, machine; —**овый** a. of **станок;** —**о-инструментальный** a. machine-tool.

станкостро/ение n. machine tool manufacture; —**ительный** a. machine tool manufacturing.

станн/ат m. stannate; —**ил** m. stannyl; —**ин, —ит** m. (min.) stannite, tin pyrites; —**ит** m. (chem.) stannite.

становись! imp. (mil.) fall in!

станов/иться v. become, turn (into), get, grow; go (into position), put oneself (in); get upon, stand on; **—ище** *n.* temporary quarters, camp; **—ление** *n.* formation, making; build-up; **зондирование —лением** build-up sounding; **метод —ления поля** (phys.) induced-field method; **—лять** *v.* form, build up.

становой *a.* of **стан**; chine (bone); **с. винт** (leveling) tripod clamp; **с. хребет** backbone; main support.

становье *see* **становище.**

стан/ок *m.* machine (tool); lathe; bench, stand, mount; (gun) mounting; saddle; (drilling) rig; (saw) horse; (text.) loom; (typ.) press; (livestock) stall, box, stanchion; **с. для резки** cutter; **обработанный на —ке** *a.* machined; **с.-тренога** *m.* tripod (mount).

станочн/ик *m.* machine operator; lathe operator; **—ый** *a.* of **станок.**

станут *fut. 3 pl. of* **стать.**

станц/ионный *a.,* **—ия** *f.* station, post; (service) center; office; plant; (tel.) exchange; (geod.) instrumental setup; (lunar) base; series of observations; data.

стань(те) *imp. of* **стать.**

стапель *m.* (naut.) building slip; berth; stocks; fixture; gantry; **с.-блок** *m.* building block; **—ный** *a. of* **стапель; с.-палуба** *f.* dock floor.

стапливать *v.* melt, fuse; use as fuel; burn up.

стаптывать *v.* wear down; trample.

стар *sh. m. of* **старый.**

стар/ание *n.* endeavor, effort, exertion; care, pains; prospecting; **—атель** *m.* prospector.

старательн/ость *f.* assiduity, application, diligence; **—ый** *a.* painstaking, assiduous, conscientious.

старательс/кий *a.* (min.) prospecting, prospector's; **—тво** *n.* prospecting.

стараться *v.* endeavor, strive, try; seek; tend toward.

стар/е(е) *comp. of* **старый**; older; **—ейший** *superl. of* **старый**; oldest; very old; **—ение** *n.* aging, seasoning; deterioration; (nucl.) storage for decay; **подвергать(ся) —ению** *v.* age, season; **—еть** *v.* age, grow old; become obsolete; **—еющий** *a.* aging, etc., *see v.*; senescent; **—ик** *m.* old man; (apid.) parent colony; (orn.) ancient murrelet (*Synthliboramphus antiquus*); **белоплечий —ик** (mam.) wrinkle-faced bat (*Centurio senex*); **—ика** *f.* litter, mulch; **—иковский** *a. of* **старик; —ина** *f.* old times, antiquity; **—инный** *a.* old (-fashioned), long-established, ancient; **—ить** *v.* age, mature; **—иться** *see* **стареть; —ица** *f.* oxbow (lake), meander, cut-off.

старн-кница stern(post) knee.

старнпост *m.* (shipbuilding) sternpost.

старо *adv.* and *sh. n. of* **старый**; *prefix* old; **—ватый** *a.* oldish, rather old; **—давний** *a.* ancient; **—дубка** *f.* (bot.) false hellebore (*Adonis vernalis*); **—заветный** *a.* old(-fashioned); conservative; **—залежный** *a.* long-fallow (field); **—запашный** *see* **старопахотный; —модный** *a.* old-fashioned, antiquated; **—пахота** *f.* old arable land; **—пахотный** *a.* old arable (soil), long-cultivated; **—пашка, —пашня** *f.* old arable land, mellow soil; **—речье** *n.* old (or dry) river bed; **—садка** *f.* starosadka (accumulation of seasonal layers of salt in a lake); **—сть** *f.* (old) age, senility.

старт *m.* start, take-off, blast-off, lift-off, launch(ing); take-off position; **момент —а** initial time; **—ер** *or* **—ёр** *m.* starter; **автоматический —ер** self-starter; **—ерный** *a.* starter; **—ование** *see* **старт; —овать** *v.* start, take off, blast off, launch.

стартов/ый *a.* start(ing), takeoff, blast-off, launching; booster (motor; rocket); boost (mode); precombustion (chamber); **с. вес** all-up weight, launch weight; **с. двигатель** (rocket) booster; **с. стол** launcher, launch(ing)

pad; **с. ускоритель** booster (rocket); **с. участок** vertical flight phase, launch(ing) phase; **—ая установка, —ое сооружение** launcher.

старт/стопный *a.* start-stop; **—ующий** *see* **стартовый.**

стар/уха *f.* old woman; **—ческий** *a.* senile; **—ческая немочь** (med.) marasmus; **—ческое зрение** presbyopia.

старше *comp. of* **старый**; older; **—классник** *m.* (educ.) upperclassman; **—курсник** *m.* senior.

старш/ий *a.* oldest, senior; superior; (math.) highest (derivative); leading (coefficient); more significant (number); (comp.) most significant (digit); high-order (bit, byte, etc.); dominant; top; maximum; (educ.) upper (class); *m.* chief, head; **с. член** source, leading term; **—ина** *m.* foreman; (mil.) warrant officer; master sergeant; petty officer; **—инство** *n.* seniority; precedence; (math.) significance.

стар/ый *a.* old, ancient; senile; former, past; back (number); weathered (hummock); (educ.) senior; **—ьё** *n.* old things, junk.

Стаса пипетка Stas pipet.

стацит (min.) stasite.

стаскивание мин (mil.) mine pulling.

стаск(ив)ать *v.* pull off, drag over.

стассфуртские соли Stassfurt salts (chiefly potassium chlorides and sulfates).

стат *m.* stat (unit of radioactivity); *prefix* stat— (denotes electrostatic unit); *suffix* —stat (an apparatus); **—ампер** *m.* statampere; **—вольт** *m.* statvolt; **—генри** *m.* stathenry.

стат/ей *gen. pl. of* **стать; статья; —ейка** *f.* short article, item; **—ейный** *a. of* **статья; —и** *gen., pl., etc., of* **стать;** (livestock) points, form.

статив *m.* rack, stand; (tel.) bay; surface gage.

статизм *m.* (control systems) constant-error response.

статика *f.* (mech.) statics.

статикон *m.* staticon tube.

статисти/к *m.* statistician; **—ка** *f.* statistics; **биологическая вариационная —ка** biometrics; **—ческий** *a.* statistic(al).

статич/ески *adv.* statically; **—еско-слуховой** *a.* (anat.) vestibulocochlear (nerve), eighth (nerve); **—еский** *a.* static (aut.) quiescent; steady-state (characteristic); position (error); **—еский расчёт** steady-state analysis; **—ность** *f.* static nature; **—ный** *see* **статический.**

статкулон *m.* (elec.) statcoulomb.

статмокинез *m.* (gen.) stathmokinesis, inhibition of cell division.

стато— *prefix* stato— (standing, fixed); **—лит** *m.* (biol.) statolith.

статом *m.* statohm.

статор *m.,* **—ный** *a.* (elec.) stator; (turbine) stay-ring.

статоскоп *m.* statoscope, altimeter.

статоцист *m.* (biol.) statocyst.

статский *a.* civilian.

статус *m.* standing (position); condition, state; (law) status; **с.-кво** *m.* status quo.

статут *m.,* **—ный** *a.* statute.

статуя *f.* statue.

статфарада *f.* (elec.) statfarad.

стат/ь *v.* begin (to); come (to); become, grow, get; be, exist; stand (at, in, up); rise; take a position; stop; *f.* purpose, reason; figure, shape, build; (livestock) point; **с. с** *v.* happen to; **с какой —и** why (should)? **—ься** *v.* become, happen.

стать/я *f.* (journal) article, paper; item; clause, paragraph, article (of treaty), entry (in dictionary); point (of animal); **с. актива** (com.) asset; **с. пассива** liability;

—и ввоза imports; **—и вывоза** exports; **—и дохода** revenues; **распределять по —ям** itemize.

стафил— *prefix* staphyl(o)— (uvula; staphylococcic); **—иниды** *pl.* rove beetles (*Staphylinidae*); **—ококк** *m.* (bact.) staphylococcus; **—ома** *f.* (med.) staphyloma.

стафисагроин *m.* staphisagroine.

стаханов/ец *m.*, **—ский** *a.* stakhanovite.

стахи— *prefix* stachy— (spike; ear of corn); **—дрин** *m.* stachydrine; **—оза** *f.* stachyose; **—с** (bot.) stachys.

стационар *m.* hospital; (mach.) foundation, base; stationary establishment.

стационарн/ость *f.* stability, permanence; immobility; stagnation (of an industry); **—ый** *a.* stationary, fixed, permanent, nonportable; steady-state (condition; flow; plasma; value); static; inpatient (care); resident (school); **—ый больной** inpatient; **—ая платформа** drilling platform.

стация *f.* (biol.) habitat, eco-area.

стачать *v.* stitch together.

стачечн/ик *m.* striker; **—ый** *a.* strike.

стач/ивать *v.* stitch together; grind down; **—иваться** *v.* wear down; **—ка** *f.* stitching together; seam; strike; **—ной** *a.* stitching, sewing.

стащить *see* **стаскивать.**

стая *f.* flock; shoal, school (of fish); pod (of whales); herd, pack.

стаять *see* **стаивать.**

ств *abbr.* **(сверхтонкое взаимодействие)** (phys.) hyperfine coupling; **констант ств** hyperfine splitting constant.

ствол *m.* trunk, stem, stalk; core, body; tube; (min.) shaft; bore, hole; (gun) barrel; (tool) shaft, shank; high-pressure (fire) hose, branch (of fire hose); (commun.) channel; (nerve) cord; rachis, scapus (of feather); neck (of bottle); **—ик** *dim. of* **ствол**; (ent.) stipes; **—истый** *a.* stem-like, trunk-like; stalky; well-branched; **—о—** *prefix* cormo—, trunk; **—овой** *a. of* **ствол**; truncal, trunk; (min.) cage operator; **—олистный** *a.* (bot.) cormophyllous; **—ы** *pl. of* **ствол**; (anat.) trunci; **—ьный** *a.* gun barrel; **—ьная коробка** breech (of rifle); casing (of submachine gun).

створ *m.* alignment, range, transit; (gage) line; (hydr.) section, site; (channel) mark(s); fold, flap, leaf; **в —е** in line.

створажив/ание *n.*, **—ающийся** *a.* curdling, coagulating; **—ать** *v.* curdle, coagulate.

створить *see* **створять.**

створ/ка *f.* fold, flap, leaf; valve; hinge; door, shutter; (zool.) cusp (of valve); (bot.) glume; **—ный** *a.* folding; valved; alignment, ranging; range, leading (lights); axial (observation).

створож/енный *a.* curdled, coagulated; **—ить** *see* **створаживать.**

створочка *f.* (bot.) valvula.

створчатый *a.* folding, hinged; valved, valvate, valvular; flap, clack (valve); casement (window).

створять *v.* range, align.

стеапс/аза *f.*, **—ин** *m.* steapsase, steapsin.

стеарат *m.* stearate.

стеарил *m.*, **—овый** *a.* stearyl.

стеарин *m.* stearin, glyceryl tristearate.

стеариново/кислый *a.* stearic acid; stearate (of); **—кислая соль** stearate; **—этиловый эфир** ethyl stearate.

стеаринов/ый *a.* stearic; stearin (oil, soap, etc.); **—ая кислота** stearic acid; **соль —ой кислоты** stearate.

стеаро—*prefix* stearo— (tallow, suet; stearic, stearin); **—кисловая кислота** stearoxylic acid, 9,10-dioxooc-tadecanoic acid; **—ловая кислота** stearolic acid, 9-octadecynoic acid; **—н** *m.* stearone, 18-pentatriacontanone; **—нитрил** *m.* stearonitrile, octadecanenitrile.

стеат— *see* **стеато—**; **—ит** *m.* (min.) steatite; **—итовый** *a.* steatite, steatitic; **—о—** *prefix* steat(o)— (fat, oil); **—оз** *m.* (med.) steatosis; **—ор(р)ея** *f.* (med.) steatorrhea.

стебел/ёк *dim. of* **стебель**; (biol.) pedicel.

стебель *m.* stem, stalk, culm; peduncle, pedicel; column; bracket, arm; (tool) shank, shaft; barrel (of micrometer); **—ковый** *a.* stalk-like; having a stalk, pedicellate, peduncular; columnar; **—ный** *a. of* **стебель**; **—чатоглазые** *pl.* (mal.) land snails, etc. (*Stylommatophora*); **—чатый** *see* **стебельковый.**

стебл/е— *prefix* caul(o)— (stem); **—евание** *n.* stooling, sprouting shoots; **—евидный** *a.* stem-like; (bot.) cauliform; **—евой, —ёвый** *a. of* **стебель**; cauline; **—евое растение** (bot.) cormophyte; **—едробилка** *f.* stem crusher; hay crusher; **—еед** *m.* (ent.) Lixus; **—ей** *gen. pl. of* **стебель**; **—екорень** *m.* root(-like part); **—еобъемлющий** *a.* (bot.) amplexicaul(ine); **—еплодный** *a.* caulocarpic; **—еплющилка** *f.* stalk crusher; hay crusher; **—еродный** *a.* caulogenous; **—еруб** *m.* stalk chopper; **—естой** *m.* (agr.) density of stand, plant stand.

стебл/истый *a.* stalky; multiple-stemmed; **—я** *gen. of* **стебель.**

стег/альный *a.* quilting; **—ание** *n.* quilting; lashing.

стёга(н)ный *a.* quilted.

стег(а)нуть *v.* lash.

стегать *v.* stitch, quilt; lash.

стегозавр *m.* (pal.) stegosaurus.

стёж/ка *f.* quilting; seam; **—ок** *m.* stitch.

стек *m.* (comp.) stack; **с. магазиного типа** pushdown stack, last in-first out (LIFO) list; **указатель —а** stack pointer.

стёк *past m. sing. of* **стечь.**

стек/ание *n.* draining, etc., *see v.*; runoff; (charge) leakage; **—ать** *v.* drain (down), run down, run off, run out, flow (off); discharge; drip (off), trickle; leak; **—аться** *v.* be drained, etc.; flow together, converge; gather, collect, accumulate; **—ающий** *a.* draining, etc., *see v.*

стекл/а *gen. and pl. of* **стекло**; *past f. sing. of* **стечь**; **—енеть** *v.* vitrify; become brittle.

стеклить *v.* glaze; glass in.

стекло *n.* glass; (window) pane; windshield; (laboratory) glassware; (lamp) chimney; *past n. sing. of* **стечь**; **с. буры** fused borax; **с. жизни** Vitaglass; **жидкое с., растворимое с.** water glass, potassium or sodium silicate solution.

стекло/бетон *m.* glass concrete; **—блок** *m.* glass block, glass brick; **—бой** *m.* cullet, broken glass; **—вание** *n.* vitrification; (polymers) glass transition.

стекловар *m.* glass maker; **—ение** *n.* glass making, glass manufacture; **—(ен)ный, —очный** *a.* glass-making; glass (furnace; pot).

стекловат/ый *a.* vitreous, glassy; **—ь** *v.* vitrify.

стекловидн/ость *f.* glassiness, vitreousness; **—ый** *a.* glassy, glass-like, vitreous, hyaline; **—ое тело** (anat.) vitreous body (of the eye); **разжижение —ого тела** (med.) synchysis.

стекловолокн/истый *a.* fiberglass; **—ит** *m.* fiber-glass (molding) material; **—о** *n.* fiber glass; glass fiber.

стекло/выдувальщик *m.* glass blower; **—выдувной** *a.* glass-blowing; **—граф** *m.* glass-marking pencil, grease pencil; (typ.) glass duplicating device; **—графия** *f.* glass printing.

стеклодел *m.* glass maker; —**ательный** *a.*, —**ие** *n.*, —**ьный** *a.* glass-making.

слекло/дув *m.* glass blower; —**дувный** *a.* glassblowing; blow (pipe); —**жгут** *m.* glass roving; —**калильный** *a.* glass (furnace); —**керамика** *f.*, —**кристаллический** *a.* glass ceramic; —**лакоткань** *f.* varnished glass cloth; —**масса** *f.* glass melt; —**мат** *m.* glass mat; —**наполнитель** *m.* glass filler; —**обогреватель** *m.* de-icer, defroster; —**образный** *see* **стекловидный**; —**омыватель** *m.* windshield washer; —**основа** *f.* glass base; —**очиститель** *m.* windshield wiper.

стекло/пакет *m.* double glass pane; —**плав** *m.* glass maker; —**плавильный** *a.* glass-melting; glass (furnace; pot).

стеклопласт *m.* fiberglass (plastic) material, fiberglass reinforced laminate; —**ик** *m.*, —**иковый** *a.* fiberglass, fiberglass(-reinforced) plastic.

стекло/подобный *see* **стекловидный**; —**подъёмник** *m.* window raiser; —**пряжа** *f.* (fiberglass) strands, yarn.

стеклоре/жущий *a.* glass-cutting; —**з** *m.* glass cutter; —**з(оч)ный** *a.* glass-cutting.

стекло/рогажка *f.* fiberglass mat(ting); —**рубероид** *m.* fiberglass roofing material; —**тара** *f.* glass containers; —**текстолит** *m.* fiberglass laminate; —**ткань** *f.* fiberglass fabric; —**упрочнитель** *m.* fiberglass reinforcement, fiberglass filler; —**фанера** *f.* fiberglass laminate; —**формовка** *f.*, —**формовочный**, —**формующий** *a.* glass-molding, glass-shaping; —**холст** *m.* fiberglass mat(ting); —**шерсть** *f.* glass wool; —**шифер** *m.* fiberglass (roofing) shingle; —**шпон** *m.* laminated fiberglass sheet.

стеклуемость *f.* vitrifiability.

стеклышко *n.* piece of glass; glass bead; **покровное с.** (micros.) cover glass.

стеклян/истый *a.* hyaloid, pellucid, glass-like; —**ницы** *pl.* clear-winged moths (*Aegeriidae*).

стеклянн/ый *a.* glass, vitreous, hyaline; (elec.) positive; fiberglass (fabric); sand (paper); glassy (eyes); —**ая вата** glass wool, spun glass; —**ая палочка** stirring rod, glass rod; —**ая посуда**, —**ые изделия** glassware.

стекля/рус *m.*, —**русный** *a.* glass bead; —**шка** *f.* piece of glass; glass object.

стековой *a.* of **стек**; **с. список** (comp.) pushdown stack, last in-first out (LIFO) list.

стекольн/ый *a.* glass, vitreous; —**ая замазка** putty; —**ые работы** glazing.

стекольщи/к *m.* glazier; glass maker; glass cutter; —**чий** *a.* glazier's, glazing; glass.

стексировать *v.* cut into steaks.

стёкший *a.* discharged, run out, drained.

стела *f.* (bot.) stele; sign post.

стелаж *see* **стеллаж.**

стелазин *m.* (pharm.) Stelazine, trifluoperazine dihydrochloride.

стел/ек *gen. pl.*; —**ечный** *a.* of **стелька.**

стелидий *m.* (bot.) stelidium.

стелить *v.* spread, strew, lay; —**ся** *v.* spread; creep; float, drift.

стеллаж *m.* shelving, (set of) shelves; rack, stand; stillage; (casks) scantling, trestle; —**и** *pl.* scaffolding; —**ный** *a.* of **стеллаж**; stage (kiln).

стеллион *m.* (herp.) Agama.

стель *see* **стела.**

стелька *f.* inner sole, insole.

стельность *f.* (zool.) pregnancy.

стел/ющийся, —**ящийся** *a.* (bot.) trailing, creeping, prostrate.

стелярный *a.* of **стела.**

стем *m.* (shipbuilding) stem.

стемма *f.* (ent.) stemma, ommatidium, facet (of compound eye).

стемнеть *v.* get dark.

стен *m.* sthene (unit of force).

стен/а *f.* wall, partition, (anat.) paries; side; **обнести —ой** *v.* wall in; **с.-ограда** *f.* boundary wall.

стенбок *m.* (mam.) steenbok (*Raphicerus*).

стенд *m.* stand, bench; (cooling) rack; bed; testing unit; (testing) jig; (exhibit) booth, showcase; **продавать со стенда** sell off the floor; —**ер** *m.* stand pipe; —**овый** *a.* of **стенд**; —**овый доклад** poster (report); —**овое испытание** bench test.

стенический *a.* (med.) sthenic, strong.

стенк/а *f.* wall, partition; (baffle) plate; (boiler) shell; web (of beam); quay; (phys.) (domain) boundary; (anat.) paries; **верхняя с.** (anat.) roof (of orbit); **сдавать у (причальной)** —**и** (naut.) berth; **с двойными —ами** double-walled.

стенко/отрывной *a.* (bot.) septifragal; —**раздельный**, —**разрывной** *a.* septicidal.

стенметр *m.* unit of work equal to one kilojoule.

стенник *m.* (bot.) candytuft (*Iberis*).

стенн/ой *a.* wall(-type), mural; plug-in (unit); (biol.) parietal; building (brick).

стено— *prefix* wall; steno— (narrow, little, close); —**батный** *a.* (zool.) stenobathic; —**вой** *a.* wall, building; —**галинный** *a.* stenohaline, adaptable to a narrow range of salinity.

стенограмм/а *f.*, —**ный** *a.* shorthand report, verbatim account.

стенограф *m.* stenographer; a bark beetle (*Ips stenographus*); —**ировать** *v.* write in shorthand; —**ист** *m.*, —**истка** *f.* stenographer; —**ический** *a.* stenographic, shorthand; verbatim, complete, literal; —**ия** *f.* stenography, shorthand.

стеноз *m.* (med.) stenosis, narrowing, constriction; **с. желудка** gastrostenosis; —**ин** *m.* Stenosine, sodium methanearsonate.

стенок *gen. pl.* of **стенка.**

стенокардия *f.* (med.) stenocardia.

стенолазы *pl.* (orn.) wall creepers (*Tichodroma*).

стенонов проток (anat.) duct of Steno.

стенопейческий *a.* (opt.) stenopaic; pinhole.

стенопись *f.* mural.

стено/спермокарпия *f.* (bot.) stenospermocarpy, seedlessness; —**термический**, —**термный** *a.* (biol.) stenothermal, stenothermic.

стеньг/а *f.*, —**овый** *a.* (naut.) top mast.

степей *gen. pl.* of **степь.**

степенн/ой, —**ый** *a.* of **степень**; (math.) power, exponential (function, etc.); staid, sedate.

степен/ь *f.* degree, extent, level, range; (moisture) content; modulus; rate; step, stage; grade, class; ratio; order (of an equation); (math.) power, exponent; index (of a radical); **с. кислотности** acidity; **с. окисления** oxidation state; **в —и** to the power; **в значительной —и** to a large extent, largely, in large part, to a high degree; **в меньшей —и** to a lesser degree, less; **в слабой —и** to a slight degree, slightly; **в такой же —и, как и** as much as; **второй —и** (math.) quadratic; **до некоторой —и** in some measure, to a certain degree; **корень третьей —и** cube root; **ни в какой —и** in no degree, in no wise, not at all; **первой —и** (math.) linear; **показатель —и** (math.) exponent; coefficient (of wear);

index (of root); **третья с.** (math.) third power, cube; **учёная с.** (university) degree.

спеп/ной *a. of* **степь;** **—няк** *m.* one living on the steppe; **—ь** *f.* steppe, plain.

степс *m.* (naut.) mast step.

стер *m.* stere, cubic meter; *abbr.* (**стерадиан**); *past m. sing. of* **стереть;** **—ад(иан)** *m.* steradian (unit of solid angle).

стеран *m.* (pharm.) Sterane, prednisolone.

стерв/а *f.* carrion, carcass; **—оядные** *pl.* (zool.) scavengers; **—оядный** *a.* carrion-eating, scavenging; **—ятники** *pl.* a genus of vultures (*Neophron*).

стереж/ение *n.* guard, watch, charge; guarding, watching; **—ённый** *past pass. part. of* **стеречь.**

стереида *f.* (bot.) stone cell.

стерео— *prefix* stereo— (solid, three-dimensional; spatial); **—автограф** *m.* stereoautograph; **—адаптер** *m.* stereo-control unit; **—акустика** *f.* stereoacoustics; **—беспорядочный** *a.* atactic, random (polymer); **—бинокль** stereoscope; **—блок** *a.* (polymers) stereoblock; **—гноз** *m.* (physiol.) stereognosis.

стереограф/ический *a.* (geom.) stereographic; **—ия** *f.* stereography.

стереоизомер *m.* stereoisomer; **—ия** *f.* stereoisomerism; **—ный** *a.* stereoisomeric.

стерео/кино *n.* stereoscopic movies; **—компаратор** *m.* stereocomparator.

стереом *m.* (bot.) stereom(e), mechanical tissue.

стереометр *m.* stereometer; **—ический** *a.* stereometric; **—ия** *f.* stereometry, solid geometry.

стерео/механика *f.* stereomechanics; **—модель** *f.* (surv.) stereoscopic model; **—направленный** *a.* stereochemically directed; **—пара** *f.* stereogram, stereoscopic image, relief effect; **—планиграф** *m.* stereoplanigraph; **—препятствие** *n.* steric hindrance; **—регулярный** *a.* stereoregular (polymer).

стереоскоп *m.* stereoscope; **—ический, —ичный** *a.* stereoscopic; **—ичность, —ия** *f.* stereoscopy.

стерео/снимок *m.* stereogram, stereoscopic photograph; **—сополимер** *m.* stereocopolymer; **—специфический** *a.* stereospecific; **—телевидение** *n.* stereotelevision.

стереотип *m.* stereotype, duplicate printing plate; **—ировать** *v.* stereotype; **—ия** *f.* stereotypy, stereotyping; **—ный** *a.* stereotype, stereotypic; **—щик** *m.* stereotypist.

стерео/труба *f.* stereoscopic telescope; **—упорядоченный** *a.* stereospecific; **—физика** *f.* stereophysics.

стереофон/ический *a.* stereophonic; **—ичность, —ия** *f.* stereophonics, binaural effect.

стереоформула *f.* (chem.) conformational formula.

стереофотогра/мметрия *f.* stereophotogrammetry; **—фия** *f.* stereophotography; stereoscopic photograph.

стереохим/ический *a.* stereochemical; spatial (formula); **—ия** *f.* stereochemistry.

стерео/экран *m.* stereo screen; **—эффект** *m.* three-dimensional effect.

стереть *v.* rub out, rub off, erase, efface, obliterate, wipe out, raze, (comp.) delete; wipe off, clean; chafe, abrade; grind, pulverize; **—ся** *v.* be rubbed out, etc.; wear (away, off, out); fray; rub off; disappear.

стеречь *v.* guard, watch (over), take care (of), have charge (of).

стерженёк *dim. of* **стержень;** (biol.) rachilla.

стерженщик *m.* (foundry) core maker.

стержень *m.* rod, bar; stem, shank, shaft; pin, bolt, spindle; strut; tie; (geol.) spine, column; plug; body (of screw); (met.) core; (anat.) trunk; modiolus (of cochlea); (biol.) rachis (of feather); scapus (of hair, etc.); **с. управления**

(nucl.) control rod; **аварийный с.** (nucl.) scram rod; **—ковый** *a.* (bot.) baculiform, rod-shaped; **с.-перемычка** *m.* (met.) wafer core.

стержн/евидный *a.* (biol.) rachiform, rod-shaped; **—евой** *a. of* **стержень;** core (box, rod, etc.); core-type (transformer); bar (magnet, winding); interdigital (magnetron); strut; pivotal (problem); (bot.) main, tap (root); **—еобразный** *a.* rod-like, bar; **—я** *gen. of* **стержень.**

стеригматоцистин *m.* sterigmatocystin.

стерид *see* **стероид.**

стерилампа *f.* sterilamp.

стерил/изатор *m.* sterilizer; **—изационный** *a.* sterilizing, sterilization; **—изация** *f.* sterilization; **—из(ир)овать** *v.* sterilize; **—изованный** *a.* sterilized, sterile; **—изующий** *a.* sterilizing; **—ьность** *f.* sterility; **—ьный** *a.* sterile.

стерины *pl.* sterols (solid alcohols).

стерическ/ий *a.* steric, spatial; **—ое затруднение** steric hindrance.

стерко— *prefix* sterco— (feces); **—билин** *m.* stercobilin, urobilin; **—лит** *m.* (med.) stercolith, fecal concretion; **—рол** *m.* stercorol, coprosterol.

стеркулиевая камедь sterculia gum, Indian tragacanth.

стерлинг *m.,* **—овый** *a.* sterling.

стерля/дь *f.,* **—жий** *a.* (ichth.) sterlet (*Acipenser ruthenus*).

стерналь/гия *f.* (med.) sternalgia; angina pectoris; **—ный** *a.* (anat.) sternal.

стернбергит *m.* (min.) sternbergite.

стерн/евой *a. of* **стернь;** **—ит** *m.* (ent.) sternite, sternal sclerite; **—ум** *m.* (anat.) sternum; **—ь, —я** *f.* (agr.) stubble (field).

стероид *m.,* **—ный** *a.* steroid.

стерол *m.* (chem.) sterol.

стерпеть *v.* bear, tolerate, endure.

стертор *m.* stertor, snoring; **—озный** *a.* stertorous.

стёрт/ость *f.* worn condition; **—ый** *past pass. part. of* **стереть.**

стерх *m.* (orn.) crane (*Grus*).

стесать *see* **стёсывать.**

стесн/ение *n.* hindering, etc., *see v.;* constraint; uneasiness; constriction (of throat); **с. кредита** (com.) money squeeze, tight money; **—ённый** *a.* hindered, etc., *see v.;* labored (breathing); **—ительный** *a.* restrictive; inconvenient; shy; **—ить, —ять** *v.* hinder, hamper, obstruct, impede, restrict, handicap; press together, constrict; crowd; embarrass, constrain, lay constraint (on); **—иться, —яться** *v.* be hindered, etc.; restrict oneself; be shy; be ashamed; crowd (together); become labored (of breathing).

стёсывать *v.* cut off, chop off; plane off.

стетоскоп *m.* (mach.; med.) stethoscope; **—ический** *a.* stethoscopic.

Стефана закон (phys.) Stefan's law.

стефан/ит *m.* (min.) stephanite, brittle silver ore; **—о—** *prefix* stephano— (crown); **—обериксовые** *pl.* (ichth.) spiny pricklefishes (*Stephanoberycidae*); **—ский ярус** (geol.) Stephanian stage.

стехио— *prefix* stoichio— (element); **—логия** *f.* (physiol.) stoichiology; **—метрический** *a.* stoichiometric; **—метрия** *f.* stoichiometry.

стеч/ение *n.* confluence, convergence; concurrence, coincidence; **—ь** *see* **стекать.**

стешет *fut. 3 sing. of* **стесать.**

СТЗ *abbr.* (**система технического зрения**) (robotics) vision.

стиб/(ио)— *prefix* stib(io)— (antimony); **—амин** *m.* Stibamine; **—енил** *m.* stibenyl; **—иат** *m.* stibiate, antimonate; —**ид** *m.* stibide, antimonide; —**иконит** *m.* (min.) stibiconite; —**ил** *m.* stibyl, antimonyl; —**ин** *m.* stibine, antimonous hydride; —**лит** *m.*, —**ляная охра** (min.) stiblite; —**нит** *m.* (min.) stibnite, antimony glance; —**оний** *m.* (chem.) stibonium.

Стивенса перегруппировка (chem.) Stevens rearrangement.

стивидор *m.* (naut.) stevedore.

стигма *f.* (biol.) stigma; —**стерин** *m.* stigmasterol; —**т** *see* **стигма;** —**тизм** *m.* stigmatism; —**тоидный** *a.* (bot.) stigmatoid, stigma-bearing.

стилбестрол *see* **стильбэстрол.**

стилет *m.* stiletto; (biol.; med.) stylet.

стилизованный *a.* stylized; conventionalized.

стилидий *m.* (bot.) stylidium.

стилка *f.* spreading, laying.

стиллинг/ин *m.* stillingine; —**оид** *m.* stillingoid.

стило— *prefix* stylo— (pillar, column); —**гонидия** *f.* (bot.) stylogonidium; —**граф** *m.* stylograph (pen); —**дий** *m.* (bot.) stylodium; —**лит** *m.* (geol.) stylolite; —**литовый** *a.* stylolitic; —**метр** *m.* (met.) spectrophotometer; —**нихия** *f.* (prot.) Stylonichia; —**подий** *m.* (zool.) stylopodium; limb; —**скоп** *m.* spectroscope; —**спора** *f.* (bot.) stylospore; —**стегий** *m.* (bot.) stylostegium.

стилочный *a. of* **стилка.**

Стилтьес формула (math.) Stieltjes' formula.

стиль *m.* style, manner, fashion; **с. работы** modus operandi.

стильб *m.* stilb (unit of brightness).

стильбен *m.* stilbene, toluylene.

стильбэстрол *m.* (diethyl)stilbestrol.

стимул *m.* stimulus, stimulant, spur, incentive; —**ирование** *n.* stimulation; —**ированный человеком** (ecol.) man-induced; —**ировать** *v.* stimulate, spur, encourage, foster, promote, offer incentives; —**ирующий** *a.* stimulating, etc., *see* v.; stimulant; —**ятор** *m.* stimulant; pacemaker; —**ятор роста** growth hormone, growth factor; —**яция** *f.* stimulation.

стипелла *f.* (bot.) stipel.

стипенд/иат *m.* scholarship student; grant holder; —**ия** *f.* stipend, scholarship; grant.

стипитатовая кислота stipitatic acid.

стипт/ицин *m.* Stypticin, cotarnine chloride.

стираемый *a.* washable; (comp.) erasable.

стиракол *m.* Styracol, guaiacol cinnamate.

стиракс *m.*, —**овый** *a.* styrax (balsam); —**овое дерево** (bot.) styrax.

стир/альный *a.* washing, laundering; erasing; **с. порошок** detergent; —**альная машина** washing machine, washer; —**ание** *n.* rubbing out, etc., *see* **стереть;** (comp.) erasure, deletion; obliteration; abrasion; laundering; —**ан(н)ый** *a.* laundered; —**ать** *see* **стереть;** wash, launder; —**ать в порошок** *v.* pulverize; —**аться** *see* **стереться;** wash, be washable.

стирацин *m.* styracine, cinnamyl cinnamate.

стирающий *pr. act. part. of* **стирать;** (comp.) erasing, deleting; play-off, scan-off (beam); —**ся** *a.* erasable; washable.

стирен *m.* styr(ol)ene, phenethylene.

стирил *m.*, —**овый** *a.* styryl; —**овая кислота** styrilic acid; —**овый спирт** styryl alcohol, cinnamic alcohol.

стирка *f.* washing, laundering, laundry.

стирол *m.* styrene; styrol, colloidal silver; **с.-дистиллят** *m.* styrene distillate; —**ен** *see* **стирен;** —**еновый спирт** styrolene alcohol, cinnamic alcohol; **с.-изобутиленовый** *a.* styrene-isobutylene; —**овый** *a.* styrene; **с.-ректификат** *m.* rectified styrene.

стиро/н *m.* styrone, cinnamic alcohol; —**пор** *m.* expanded polystyrene; —**флекс** *m.* polystyrene film; —**фом** *m.* styrofoam (insulation).

стирп (biol.) stirps.

стис/кивать, —**нуть** *v.* squeeze, compress, jam; clutch, grip; clench (teeth).

стифнат *m.* styphnate.

стифнинов/ая кислота styphnic acid, trinitroresorcinol; **соль** —**ой кислоты,** —**окислая соль** styphnate.

стихать *v.* calm down, abate, die down, subside.

стихеевые *pl.* (ichth.) pricklebacks (*Stichaeidae*).

стихидий *m.* stichid(ium) (in algae).

стих/ийный *a.* elemental; spontaneous; natural (disaster); —**ийное движение** elemental upheaval; —**ия** *f.* element.

стихнуть *see* **стихать.**

стихо— *prefix* sticho— (row, line); —**хромная клетка** (cyt.) stichochrome.

стицерин *m.* stycerin; —**овая кислота** styceric acid.

стлан/ец *see* **стланик;** (dew-)retted flax; —**ие** *see* **стланьё;** —**ик** *m.* dwarf tree, elfin tree; creeping vegetation; —**иковый** *a.* (bot.) humistrate; —**ный** *a.* laid out, spread; —**цевый** *a. of* **стланец;** —**ь** *f.* layer; —**ьё** *n.* (dew-)retting.

стлать *see* **стелить.**

стлб. *abbr.* (**столбец**) column.

стлище *n.* (flax) dew-retting area.

сто *num. and prefix* hundred (one) hundred; *prefix* centi—.

стов/аин *m.* Stovaine; —**арсол** *m.* Stovarsol, acetarsone.

стог *m.* (hay)stack, (hay)rick; —**овальщик** *m.* stacker; —**ование** *n.* stacking; —**ованный** *a.* stacked; —**овать** *v.* stack; —**овой** *a. of* **стог;** stack(ed); —**ометание** *n.* stacking; —**омёт;** —**ометатель** *m.* stacker.

стоградусный *a.* centigrade.

стое/к *gen. pl. of* **стойка;** *sh. m. of* **стойкий;** —**чка** *dim. of* **стойка;** stand; prop, support; —**чный** *a. of* **стойка.**

стожары *pl.* (astr.) Pleiades.

стож/ить *v.* stack; —**ок** *dim. of* **стог.**

стоимост/ный *a.*, —**ь** *f.* cost, price, charge(s), fee(s); value, worth; —**ь с установкой** installed cost; **номинальная** —**ь** face value; **падение** —**и** depreciation.

стоит *pr. 3 sing. of* **стоить, стоять; с. только** one need only.

стоить *v.* cost, amount (to), be worth; be worthwhile, pay off.

стоици/зм *m.* stoicism; —**ческий** *a.* stoic.

стой *imp. of* **стоять;** Halt!

стойбищ/е *n.*, —**ный** *a.* pasture corral.

стойка *f.* stand, pedestal, leg; upright, stanchion; column, pillar, post, stake; stem, shank; tine; rest, support, prop, brace, strut, stay; (display) counter, (salad) bar, (buffet) table; bench; bay; rack; (plow) standard; (mil.) picket; *sh. f. of* **стойкий; аппаратурная с.** equipment rack; **испытательная с.** test(ing) jig.

стойкий *a.* stable, resisting, resistant, immune; durable, hardy; steady, persistent; sturdy, firm; **с. к огню** fireproof, fire-resistant; **с. против** —proof; **химически с.** chemically stable.

стойком *see* **стоймя.**

стойкость *f.* stability, resistance, strength, durability, endurance; (radiation) tolerance; (phys.) immunity (to electromigration); steadiness, persistence; sturdiness, firmness; life (of cutting tool); **детонационная с.** antiknock rating (of fuel).

стойло *n.* stall, pen, sty; box, compartment; bay; —**вый** *a. of* **стойло;** barnyard (manure).

стоймя *adv.* upright, on end.

сто́йче *comp. of* **сто́йкий.**

сток *m.* flow, discharge, drainage, escape, effluence, confluence, running together; outlet, run-off, gutter, sewer, drain; sewage, waste (water), effluent; discharge (volume); (phys.) sink; (transistor) drain; **с. серде́чных вен** (anat.) sinus coronarius; **твёрдый с.** silt load.

Сто́ка конве́ртер Stock converter.

стокго́льмский *a.* (geog.) Stockholm.

стокези́т *m.* (min.) stokesite.

сто́кер *m.,* **—ный** *a.* stoker; feeder.

сто́ковый *a. of* **сток.**

стокра́тный *a.* centuple, hundredfold.

Сто́кса зако́н Stokes' law.

стол *m.* table, desk; (assembly) bench; anvil (for hardness testing); (typ.) (ink) plate; board; platform, deck; (launch) pad; food, diet; **монта́жный с.** (cinematography) editor; **набо́рный с.** type case.

столб *m.* column, pillar, post, pole, stake, peg; mast; pylon; (bot.) stele; sharply projecting rock (in Urals and Siberia); **жи́дкий с.** liquid column.

столбене́ть *v.* stiffen, go rigid.

столбе́ц *m.* (typ.; math.) column; bar (of histogram); (bot.) carpophore; (ichth.) gudgeon (*Gobio g.*).

сто́лбик *dim. of* **столб;** (drilling) core; peg; (biol.) style; (anat.) columella; **с. рту́ти** mercury column; **венти́льный с.** (semiconductors) rectifier stack; **конта́ктный с.** (microelectronics) contact bump, protruding contact, tab; **—ови́дный, —обра́зный** *a.* styliform; (med.) nummular (eczema).

столб/и́ть *v.* stake out (boundary); **—лённый** *a.* staked out.

столбня́/к *m.* (med.) tetanus; **—чный** *a.* tetanic, tetanus; stunned, astonished; **—чная па́лочка** (bact.) Clostridium tetani.

столбо/ви́дный *a.* columnar, pillar-like; **—во́й** *a. of* **столб; —чек** *m.* (bot.) carpophore.

столбу́р *m.* (phyt.) big bud.

столбча́к *m.* (petr.) basalt.

столбча́т/ый *a.* columnar, basaltiform; acicular (crystal); palisade (cell, tissue); pillar (mining); **—ая диагра́мма** bar chart, histogram; **—ая кость** (herp.) epipterygoid; **—ая отде́льность** (geol.) columnar structure, basaltic structure.

столе́т/ие *n.* century; centennial; **—ний** *a.* centennial; **—ник** *m.* (bot.) century plant (*Agave americana*).

стол/е́шница *f.* table top; **—и́к** *dim. of* **стол;** (micros.) stage.

столи́ст/венный, —ый *a.* (bot.) centifolious; **—ник** *m.* centifolio.

столи́/ца *f.* capital, metropolis; **—чный** *a.* metropolitan.

столка́ть *v.* push (together).

столкн/ове́ние *n.* collision, impact, impingement; encounter; (mil.) engagement; shock, percussion; spallation, fragmentation; interference; **с. в лоб** head-on collision; **частота́ —ове́ний** collision rate; **—у́ть** *see* **ста́лкивать.**

столко́в(ыв)аться *v.* come to an agreement.

столку́т *fut. 3 pl. of* **столо́чь.**

столо́в/ая *f.* dining room; (mil.) mess (hall); **—ый** *a. of* **стол;** tabular (iceberg); salad (oil); edible (fish); **с. гора́** (geol.) mesa; **с. соль** table salt, sodium chloride; **с. страна́** tableland, plateau.

столо́н *m.* (bot.) stolon, runner.

столообра́зный *a.* tabletop; tabular (iceberg).

столо́чь *v.* grind.

столп *see* **столб;** tower.

столпи́ть(ся) *v.* crowd together.

столчён(ный) *past pass. part. of* **столо́чь.**

столь *adv.* so; **—ко** *adv.* so (much), so many; as much, as many (times); **—ко (же) ско́лько** as much as, as many as; **ещё —ко же** as much again; **—ко-то** so much, so many; so many . . . so many.

столя́р *m.* carpenter, joiner, woodworker, cabinet maker; **—ить** *see* **столя́рничать; —ка** *see* **столя́рная; с.-краснодере́вец** *m.* cabinet maker; **—ная** *f.* carpenter shop, woodworking shop; **—ничать** *v.* do carpentry work, work with wood; **—ничество** *n.* carpentry; **—но-пло́тничный** *a.* carpenter's; **—ный** *a.* carpenter, carpentry, joiner's, woodworking; cabinet (work); panelled (door); **—ная плита́** panel; **—ня** *see* **столя́рная.**

сто́ма *f.* stoma, opening, orifice; **—т(о)—** *prefix* stomat(o)— (mouth); **—ти́т** *m.* (med.) stomatitis; **—толо́гия** *f.* stomatology.

стомие́вые *pl.* scaly dragonfishes (*Stomiatidae*).

сто́мий *m.* (bot.) stomium.

стон *m.,* **—а́ть** *v.* moan, groan.

стоно/г *m.* (bot.) hart's tongue (*Scolopendrium*); **—жка** *f.* (zool.) centipede.

стоп *m.* stop.

стопа́ *f.* foot, pes; ream (of paper); pile, stack; series; **о́бласть —ы** pedal region; **по его́ —м** in his footsteps.

сто́п-а́нкер *m.* stern anchor.

стопе́р *m.* (min.) stoper, stoping drill.

стопи́н *m.* quick match.

сто́пинг *m.* (min.) stoping.

стопи́ть *see* **ста́пливать.**

сто́пка *f.* stack, pile; small glass.

сто́п-кадр freeze-frame.

сто́п-кран *m.* shutoff valve; (rr.) emergency brake.

стопо/ви́дно *adv.* pedately; *prefix* (bot.) pedati—, pedate; **—во́й** *a.* series, serial.

сто́пор *m.* plug, stopper; stop, catch, detent, detainer; checking device, arresting device, pawl.

стопоре́зка *f.* guillotine, trimmer.

стопо́рить *v.* plug, stop(per); fix, lock; (mach.) check, slow down.

стопо́рн/ый *a. of* **сто́пор;** stop(ping), lock(ing), closing; lock (nut); cut-off, check (valve); set (screw); binding (bolt); retaining (pin); **с. кран** stopcock; **с. механи́зм** stop(per), arresting device, lock mechanism; **с. штифт** stop (pin); **—ая про́бка** (met.) stopper head; **—ое приспособле́ние, —ое устро́йство** lock, catch.

сто́пор-ныря́ло *m.* (art.) setback pin.

стопоходя́щий *a.* (zool.) plantigrade.

стопо́чн/ый *a. of* **сто́пка;** stack (casting); **—ые тру́бки** stopper rod sleeves.

стопроце́нтный *a.* (one) hundred per cent; total.

сто́п-сигна́л *m.* stop signal, stop light; brake light; **с.-сте́ржень** *m.* (nucl.) scram rod, shut-off rod.

стопта́ть *see* **ста́птывать.**

стора́кс *see* **стира́кс.**

сторго́в/аться *v.* make a deal, agree on terms; **—ыва́ться** *v.* bargain (with).

сторни́ровать *v.* (com.) correct, reverse (an erroneous entry).

сто́рно *n.* (bookkeeping) correction.

сто́рож *m.* guard, watchman, caretaker; **на —е** on the watch, on the alert; **—еви́к** *m.* coast guard; **—ево́й** *a.* watch, guard; **—и́ть** *v.* (keep) watch (over), guard; **—ка** *f.* guard('s) shack; sentry box; **—о́к** *m.* catch; tongue, cock (of scales).

сторон/а́ *f.* side, flank; (surv.) leg; direction; sense; region, place, land; (law) party; **—о́й** sideways; **вою́-**

ющая с. belligerent, combatant; **в —е** aside, apart; clear (of); **в —у** to the side, laterally; **в другую —у** in the other direction, the other way; **остаться в —е** *v.* be out of the picture; **отложить в —у** *v.* put aside, lay aside; **перемещение в —у** lateral movement, lateral displacement; **повернуть в —у** *v.* turn aside; **уход в —у** (drilling) side tracking; **во все —ы** in different directions; on all sides; **задняя с.** back; **передняя с.** front, face; **с —ы** from the side; laterally; **с другой —ы** on the other hand; **с его —ы** for his part, from his point of view; **с одной —ы** on the one hand, on one side; **со —ы** as viewed from; **он со своей —ы** he for one, for his part.

сторониться *v.* stand aside, make way; shun, avoid.

сторонн/ий *a.* outside, irrelevant, extraneous; *suffix* —hedral, —lateral, -sided; **—ик** *m.* adherent, supporter, advocate; *suffix* —hedron; **—ичество** *n.* siding, adherence, support.

сторцевать *v.* butt-joint.

стосил *m.* (bot.) ginseng (*Panax*).

сто/сильный *a.* one-hundred-horsepower; **—тысячный** *a.* one hundred thousand(th).

стохастич/еский *a.* stochastic, conjectural, probabilistic, random, chance.

сточ/енный *a.* ground off; worn down; **—ить** *v.* grind off; wear down; **—ка** *f.* grinding off; wearing down.

сточн/ый *a. of* **сток;** drip (chamber; edge); **с. колодец** cesspool, sewer; **—ая жидкость** sewage; **—ая канава** gutter; **—ая труба** sewer pipe, drain; **—ое отверстие** run-off, outlet, drain; **—ые воды** effluent; waste water, slops; sewage.

стоя *adv.* upright.

стояк *m.* standpipe, riser, uprise, (smoke)stack; upright; (ocean.) temporarily grounded floe; **литниковый с.** (steel flask) riser.

стоялый *a.* stale, stagnant; long unused.

стоян/ие *n.* standing; stand (of plants); position; **—ка** *f.,* **—очный** *a.* stand, station, quarters; halt; layover, stopover; (train) stop; parking (place), (helicopter) pad; anchorage, berth; camp site, encampment; **—очное время** lay days (in commercial shipping).

сто/ять *v.* stand; (mil.) lie; be idle; be, exist; stay; halt, stop; confront, face; **с. за** stand for, defend; **с. перед** confront; **—ячий** *a.* standing, stationary; vertical, erect; stagnant, still; stand (pipe); floor (lamp); **—ячая волна** (elec.) standing wave; (ocean.) stationary wave.

стоящий *a.* costing; worthwhile; **дорого с.** costly, expensive; **ничего не с.** worthless.

СТП *abbr.* **(средняя точка попадания)** center of impact; **(стандарт предприятия)** factory standard.

стр *abbr.* **(стерадиан)** steradian; **стр.** *abbr.* **(страница)** page; **(строка)** line; **(строящийся)** under construction.

СТР *abbr.* **(система терморегулирования)** temperature monitoring system.

страбизм *m.* (med.) strabismus.

страв/ить *see* **стравливать; —ление** *n.* scouring, pickling, etching, corrosion; **—ленный** *a.* scoured, etc., *see v.;* **—ливание** *n.* scouring, etc., *see v.;* reduction (of pressure), deflation; slippage; **—ливать, —лять** *v.* scour, pickle, etch, corrode; strip (with solvent), cleanse; relieve, reduce (pressure), deflate; blow off; pay out (rope); (over)graze, use (pasture); feed.

страгивать *v.* move aside, displace, shift; rouse (an animal); **—ся** *v.* move aside.

страда *f.* intensified seasonal work, labor at harvesting season.

страд/ание *n.* suffering, pain; **—ать** *v.* suffer, undergo;

be impaired (by); **—ательный** *a.* (gram.) passive; **—ающий** *a.* suffering.

страдн/ой, —ый *a. of* **страда.**

страз *m.,* **—овый** *a.* paste (jewel).

страивать *v.* triple, increase threefold.

страна *f.* country, land, region; **с. света** cardinal point; **с.-хозяйка** host country.

странен *sh. m. of* **странный.**

страни/ца *f.,* **—чный** *a.* page, leaf; **домашняя с.** home page.

странн/ик *m.,* **—ица** *f.* wanderer, migrant; **—ичать** *v.* wander, roam; **—ический** *a.* wandering, wanderer's.

странн/о *adv.* strangely, oddly; it is strange; **как это ни с.** strange as it may seem; **—ость** *f.* strangeness, oddity, singularity, peculiarity; **—ый** *a.* strange, odd, singular, peculiar.

страноведение *n.* regional geography.

странств/ование *n.* migration, wandering; **—овать** *v.* wander, travel, migrate; **—ующий** *a.* wandering, etc., *see v.;* migrant; **—ующий голубь** passenger pigeon; **—ующий лоскут** (med.) jump flap.

страст/ный *a.* passionate; **—оцвет** *m.* passion flower (*Passiflora*); **—ь** *f.* passion, mania.

стратег/ия *f.* strategy; **—егический** *a.* strategic(al).

страти— *prefix* strati— (stratum); **—графический** *a.* stratigraphic; columnar (section); **—графия** *f.* stratigraphy; **—фикация** *f.* stratification, bedding; **—фицированный** *a.* stratified; **—фицировать** *v.* stratify.

страто— *prefix* (meteor.) strato— (stratus); **—лайнер** *m.* (aero.) stratoliner; **—пауза** *f.* stratopause; **—план** *m.* (aero.) high-altitude aircraft; **—стат** *m.* high-altitude balloon; **—сфера** *f.* stratosphere; **—сферный** *a.* stratosphere, stratospheric.

страус *m.,* **—овый** *a.* ostrich (*Struthio camelus*).

страх *m.* fear, fright, apprehension; *prefix* insurance; **на свой с.** at one's own risk; **навязчивый с.** phobia; **под —ом** under penalty (of), on pain (of).

страхов/ание *n.* insurance; **с. от огня** fire insurance; **—атель** *m.* insured party, policy holder; **—ать** *v.* insure; **—ка** *see* **страхование; —ой** *a.* insurance; **—щик** *m.* insurance agent; underwriter.

страш/илки *pl.* (ent.) Phasmatidae; **—ить** *v.* frighten; **—иться** *v.* fear, be in fear (of), be apprehensive; **—но** *adv.* frightfully, extremely; it is dreadful; **—ный** *a.* frightful, dreadful, terrible; extreme, intense (cold, pain, etc.).

стр-во *abbr.* **(строительство).**

стребовать *v.* demand, request.

стрежень *m.* (river) channel line, midstream, race.

стрейнер *m.* (rubber) strainer; **с.-гранулятор** *m.* strainer-pelletizer; **с.-слаббер** *m.* strainer-slabber.

стрек/ательный *a.* (biol.) stinging; **—ательная капсула** (zool.) nematocyst; **—ающие** *pl.* (zool.) Cnidaria.

стрекоз/а *f.,* **—ий, —иный** *a.* dragon fly.

стрекот *m.,* **—ание** *n.* rasping sound; chirr(ing) (of insects), stridulation; clattering (of machinery); **—ать** *v.* stridulate, chirp (of cricket); chatter (of magpie); clatter, rattle.

стрел/а *f.* arrow, pointer, indicator; jib, boom (of derrick); cantilever; rise (of arch); dart; outrigger; **с. подъёма** rise; **с. провеса** sag; **с. прогиба** deflection; **—ец** *m.* (astr.) Sagittarius; **—и(ва)ть** *see* **стрелять.**

стрелк/а *f.* arrow, pointer, needle, indicator, index; hand (of clock); (rr.) switch; spit, tongue (of land); frog (of hoof); (bot.) flower stalk, spike, scape; (zool.) sagitta, arrow worm; **идти в —у** (hort.) form flower stalks; **—и** *pl.* (orn.) New Zealand wrens (*Acanthisittidae*); **—ование** *n.* (bot.) bolting; **—овидный** *a.* scapiform;

—овый *a. of* **стрелка**; shooting; rifle; infantry; **—овое оружие** small arms; **—овые** *pl.* (zool.) Sagittidae; **—ообразный** *a.* scapiform.

стрело— *prefix* sagitti— (arrow).

стреловидн/ость *f.* (av.) sweep(back); **обратная с., отрицательная с.** forward sweep; **положительная с., прямая с.** sweepback; **с переменной —остью** variable-sweep; **—ый** *a.* arrow-like, sagittal, sagittary; (av.) swept(back); **—ый шов** (anat.) sagittal suture.

стреловой *a. of* **стрела**; *m.* crane operator.

стрелок *m.* rifleman; gunner; (orn.) Acanthisitta chloris.

стрелолист *m.* (bot.) Sagittaria; **—ный** *a.* sagittifolious.

стрелоух *m.* (mam.) desert long-eared bat (*Otonycteris*).

стрелочн/ик *m.* (rr.) switchman; **—ый** *a. of* **стрела**; sagittary; (rr.) switch; **—ый (измерительный) прибор** indicator.

стрельб/а *f.* shooting, firing, fire; **—ы** *pl.* firing range practice; **—ище** *n.,* **—ищный** *a.* firing range.

стрельнуть *see* **стрелять**.

стрельчат/ка *f.* (ent.) Acronycta; **—ый** *a.* arrow-shaped, sagittary; gabled, pointed; herringbone (design).

стрел/яние *n.* shooting, firing, discharge, shot; **—яный** *a.* shot, fired, spent (ammunition); **—ять** *v.* shoot, fire, discharge; kill; **—яться** *v.* fight a duel; shoot oneself; **—яющий** *a.* shooting, etc., *see v.*; gun (perforator).

стрем/ена *pl. of* **стремя**; **—енной** *a. of* **стремя**; (anat.) stapedius (muscle); **—ечко** *dim. of* **стремя**; (anat.) stirrup bone, stapes; (zool.) columella.

стремительн/о *adv.* swiftly; impetuously, recklessly, headlong; **—ость** *f.* impetus; impetuosity; rapidity; **—ый** *a.* impetuous, precipitate, rapid, forced (march), abrupt; **—ое движение** rush.

стрем/ить *v.* direct; carry off, drag, sweep away; **—иться** *v.* aim (at), strive (for), attempt, try, seek; approach; tend (to); rush, stream, flow rapidly; **—ление** *n.* striving, quest; aspiration; urge; tendency, inclination, leaning.

стремнина *f.* chute, race, rapids.

стремя *n.* stirrup; (anat.; zool.) stapes.

стремянка *f.* stepladder; bridging board, gangway; U-bolt (for spring).

стрем/янный *a. of* **стремя**; (anat.) stapedial; **—ячко** *see* **стремечко**.

стремящийся *pr. act. part. of* **стремиться**.

стренга *f.* strand.

стренда *see* **стренга**.

стренер *m.* strainer, filter.

стреножи(ва)ть *v.* hobble (a horse), fetter.

стрепет *m.,* **—иный** *a.* (orn.) bustard (*Otis tetrax*).

стрептидин *m.* streptidine.

стрепто— *prefix* strepto— (twisted chain; streptococcus); **—биоза** *f.* streptobiose; **—зим** *m.* streptozyme; **—кокк** *m.* (bact.) streptococcus; **—кокковый** *a.* streptococcal; **—лин** *m.* streptolin; **—мицин** *m.* streptomycin; **—трицин** *m.* streptothricin; **—цид** *m.* Streptocid, sulfanilamide; **—цин** *m.* streptocin.

стресс *m.* (med.) stress; **—орный** *a.* stressful.

стреха *f.* eaves.

стриарный *a.* (anat.) striatal.

стриг *past m. sing. of* **стричь**; **—альный** *a.* shearing; **—аль** *see* **стригальщик**; **—альня** *f.* shearing shed; **—альщик** *m.* shearer.

стриг/ун *m.* a beetle (*Myelophilus*); (mam.) yearling; **—ущий** *a.* cutting, shearing.

стридор *m.* (med.) harsh, high-pitched respiration, stridor.

стриж *m.* (orn.) swift (*Apus*).

стриж/ей *m.* shearer; **—ен(н)ый** *a.* sheared, shorn, clipped; **—ёт** *pr. 3 sing. of* **стричь**.

стрижи(ные) *pl.* (orn.) swifts (*Apodidae*).

стрижка *f.* shearing, clip(ping), cropping, haircut.

стрик *m.* (phyt.) streak.

стрик/тура *f.* (med.) stricture, narrowing; **—ционный** *a.* striction.

стрингер *m.* stringer, longitudinal member.

стриппер *m.* stripper.

стриппинг-колонна *f.* stripper; **с.-секция** *f.* stripping section (of fractionating column).

стрихнидин *m.* strychnidine.

стрихнин *m.,* **—овый** *a.* strychnine; **—овая кислота** strychninic acid.

стрихницин *m.* strychnicine.

стричь *v.* cut, clip, shear, fleece.

строб *m.* (electron.) strobe, gate.

стробил *m.* (bot.) strobile; **—а** *f.* (zool.) strobila.

строб/импульс *m.* gate (pulse), strobe (pulse); **—ирование** *n.* gating, strobing; **ширина —ирования** gate width; **—ировать** *v.* gate, strobe; **—ирующий** *a.* gating, strobing, gate; sampling (oscillograph); **—ирующий импульс** gating pulse, gate; **—ирующая схема** gating circuit, gate.

стробилоидный *a.* strobiloid, cone-shaped.

стробо— *prefix* strobo— (whirling); **—резонанс** *m.* stroboresonance; **—скоп** *m.* stroboscope; **—скопический** *a.* stroboscopic; **—трон** *m.* strobotron.

строг *sh. m. of* **строгий**.

строг/ало *n.* plane; **—аль** *see* **строгальщик**; **—альнокалёвочный станок** molder; **—альный** *a.* planing; **—альный станок** planer, shaper; **—альщик** *m.* planer (operator); **—ание** *n.* planing, shaping; **—аный** *a.* planed; **—ать** *v.* plane, shape, shave, dress (boards).

строг/ий *a.* strict, rigid, exacting, severe, stringent; rigorous (treatment); strong (correlation); close (control); **—о** *adv.* strictly, rigidly, exactly, rigorously; **—ость** *f.* strictness, rigidity, severity.

строев *gen. pl. of* **строй**; **—ик** *m.* construction specialist; **—ой** *a.* construction, building; operational; (mil.) drill, parade (ground); (av.) formation; **—ой лес** timber.

строек *gen. pl. of* **стройка**.

строен *sh. m. of* **строенный**; **стройный**; **строён** *sh. m. of* **строённый**.

строен/ие *n.* building, construction; formation; structure; constitution, composition; fabric, texture, grain; **формула —ия** structural formula.

строенный *a.* built, constructed.

строённый *a.* triple(d), triplex.

строж/айший *superl.;* **—е** *comp. of* **строгий**.

строжка *f.* planing, shaving; (welding) gouging.

строитель *m.* builder, constructor, designer, engineer; **—ный** *a.* building, construction, structural, architectural, civil engineering; **—ный раствор** mortar; **—ная техника** civil engineering; **—ное искусство** architecture; **—ные леса** scaffold(ing); **—ство** *n.* building, construction, erection; project, development; construction site; civil engineering; building trade; **зелёное —ство** park development; landscaping.

стро́ить *v.* build, construct, erect; set up; marshall; form, create; pattern (after); base (on); plot (a curve).

строи́ть *v.* triple, increase threefold.

строиться *v.* be under construction; (mil.) form (up), fall in; parade.

стро/й *m.* system, order, regime; formation, line; column (of ships); line of battle, disposition; commission; (phys.) array (of dislocations); (music) pitch; *prefix and suffix* construction; **с. пеленга** (naut.) bearing; **вступить в с.** *v.* go into production, go into operation, come on stream; join the fleet; (naut.) swing into line; **вы-**

водить из —**я** *v.* put out of commission, disable, render inoperative; **выход из** —**я** failure, breakdown; **выходить из** —**я** *v.* malfunction, break down, fail; (mil.) fall out; **полёт** —**ем** formation flight.

стройка *f.* construction, building; development, project; construction site.

стройный *a.* well-proportioned; harmonious, orderly; (math.) elegant; unified (whole).

стройплощадка *f.* building site.

строк/а *f.* line; row (e.g. of matrix); (comp.) string; **висячая с.** (typ.) widow, orphan; **начать с новой** —**и** *v.* indent, begin a new paragraph; —**оотливная наборная машина** linotype.

строма *f.* (biol.) stroma, binding tissue; (protein) network.

стромате/евые, —**идовые** *pl.* butterfishes (*Stromateidae*).

строматин *m.* (hist.) stromatin; —**ический** *a.* stromatic.

строматология *f.* (geol.) stromatology.

стромболианский *a.* (geol.) strombolian (eruption).

стромейерит *m.* (min.) stromeyerite.

стронгил/иды *pl.* (zool.) Strongylidae; —**оид** *m.* (zool.) Strongyloides.

стронуть(ся) *see* **страгивать(ся).**

стронц/иан *a.* strontia, strontium oxide; —**иановый** *a.* strontianiferous; —**иевый** *a.* strontium; —**ий** *m.* strontium, Sr; **карбонат** —**ия** strontium carbonate; **окись** —**ия** strontium oxide, strontia.

строп *m.* sling, strap; —**а** *f.* (parachute) shroud line, suspension line.

стропил/а *pl.* frame(work), truss; —**ина** *f.,* —**о** *n.,* —**ьная нога,** —**ьная связь** truss piece, rafter.

строп/ить *v.* sling; —**ка** *f.* (naut.) lanyard; —**овка** *f.* slinging.

строфант *m.* strophanthus (seeds); —**идин** *m.* strophanthidin; —**ин** *m.* strophanthin, methylouabain; —**обиоза** *f.* strophanthobiose; —**овая кислота** strophanthic acid.

строфоида *m.* (geom.) strophoid.

строфулус *m.* (med.) strophulus, papular urticaria.

строч/ение *n.* stitching; —**ен(н)ый** *a.* stitched; —**ечный** *a.* stitch(ing); needletype; —**ить** *v.* stitch; jot down, write; —**ка** *f.* stitch(ing); short line; (punched tape) channel; —**ной,** —**ный** *a.* stitched; line; horizontal; lower-case (letter).

строя *gen. of* **строй.**

строящийся *a.* under construction.

струбц/ин(к)а *f.,* —**инок** *m.,* —**ынга,** —**ынка** *f.* screw clamp, C-clamp; lock, latch.

струв/ерит *m.* (min.) strüverite; —**ит** *m.* struvite.

струг *m.* plane; draw knife; (road) grader; plow; adz(e); slicer; (leather) shaver; —**ан(н)ый** *a.* planed; —**ать** *see* **строгать;** —**овидный** *a.* (bot.) runcinate.

струе— *prefix* jet; —**к** *gen. pl. of* **струйка;** —**отклоняющий** *a.* jet-deflecting.

струж/ечный *a.,* —**ка** *f.* shaving(s), cutting(s), chip; (sugar) cossette; abatement; —**ки** *pl.* shavings, cuttings, chips, turnings, filings, borings.

стру/и *gen., pl., etc., of* **струя;** —**истый** *see* **струйчатый;** —**иться** *v.* stream, flow, run; trickle, dribble; spurt, gush; (light) shine; —**й** *gen. pl. of* **струя.**

струйк/а *f.* groove, channel; small jet; (geol.) stria, costella; (hydrogeology) water thread; fluid filament; —**овый** *a. of* **струйка;** stream (lubrication).

струйник *m.* control jet.

струйн/ый *a. of* **струя;** jet; current, flow; running, continuous (recording); fluidic (element); streaming (electrode); ink-jet (printer); **с. аппарат** (rr.) jet blower; **с. насос** jet pump; —**ая техника** fluidics, pure fluid

systems; —**ое течение** jet stream; one-dimensional flow.

струйчат/ость *f.* waviness; (geol.) striations; **следы** —**ости** (geol.) ripple marks; —**ый** *a.* fluid, flowing, moving; striated; rill (irrigation); —**ый прибор** radiator.

структор *m.* (soil) stabilizer.

структур/а *f.* structure, texture, composition, constitution, fabric; (math.) lattice; **с. с дополнениями** complemented lattice; **М-структура** exchange lattice; —**альный** *a.* structural; —**ирование** *n.* structuring, structur(al)ization, structure formation; (polymers) cross-linking; —**ированный** *a.* structur(iz)ed, cross-linked; —**ировать** *v.* structure; cross-link; —**ирующий** *a.* cross-linking; —**ность** *f.* degree of structure; cross-linkage; —**ночувствительный** structure-sensitive; —**ный** *a.* structural; core (drilling); plastic (viscosity); —**ный ген** structural gene, cistron; —**ный режим движения** plug flow; —**ная единица кости** osteon; —**ная сеть,** —**ная сетка** (anat.) network; reticulum; —**ная схема** block diagram; —**ное бурение** core drilling.

структурообраз/ование *see* **структурирование;** structural formation, aggregation (of soil); gelation; —**ователь** *m.* cross-linking agent; (soil) stabilizer; —**ующий** cross-linking; gel-forming, gelling; —**ующее удобрение** (soil) conditioner.

струм/а *f.* (med.) struma, goiter; —**ит** *m.* strumitis, thyroiditis.

струн/а *f.* string, cord; catgut; cross brace; (anat.) chorda; **спинная с.** (anat.) notochord; —**ец** *m.* (zool.) nematode worm (*Ascaris*); —**ка** *dim. of* **струна;** —**ный** *a. of* **струна;** string(ed); cable (hoist); —**ная проволока** string (for musical instrument), piano wire; —**о**— *prefix* chord(o)— (chord; string); —**обетон** *m.* reinforced concrete; —**овидный** *a.* chordoid; string-like; —**цы** *pl.* (zool.) Nematoda.

струп *m.* (med.) scab; (bot.) scurf; **молочный с.** (med.) cradle cap; —**оватый** *a.* scurfy, scaly, scabby.

струсить *v.* take fright, fear.

струч/коватый *a.* (bot.) podded; siliquiform; —**ковый** *a.* pod(-like); leguminous; —**ковый горох** peas in the pod; —**ок** *m.* pod, silique, capsule; —**очек** *m.* (bot.) little pod, silicule; —**очковидный,** —**очкообразный** *a.* silicular.

стру/я *f.* jet, spray, spurt, stream, blast; spout, flow, current (of air, etc.); plume; ray (of light); stria(tion); (ship's) wake; **бить** —**ей** *v.* jet, spout, flush; **винтовая с.** propeller race, slipstream; **действия** —**и** jet action; **масса** —**и** flow mass; **попутная с.** back eddy; wake; **тонкой** —**ей** in a thin stream.

стряпать *v.* cook (a meal); concoct, fabricate.

стря/сать, —**сти** *see* **стряхивать;** —**хивание** *n.* shaking off; —**хивать,** —**хнуть** *v.* shake off, shake down, dislodge.

С.Т.С. *abbr.* (**сверхтонкая структура**) (phys.) hyperfine structure, hfs.

студен/еть *v.* jellify, gel; cool down; —**истый** *a.* jelly-like, gelatinous; pulpy (nucleus); —**истая масса** jelly; —**иться** *see* **студенеть;** —**ость** *f.* coldness, chilliness.

студен/т *m.,* —**тка** *f.,* —**ческий** *a.* student, undergraduate; **с. второкурсник** sophomore; **с. первокурсник** freshman; **с.-медик** medical student.

студен/ый *a.* gelled; gelid, frigid, cold; —**ь** *m.* gel(atin), jelly; cold, frost.

студийный *a. of* **студия.**

студить *v.* gel; cool, refrigerate.

студия *f.* studio.

студне/видный, —образный, —подобный *a.* jelly-like, gel-like, gelatinous.

студни *pl. of* **студень.**

студтит *m.* (min.) studtite.

стуж/а *f.* intense cold, frost; **—енный** *past pass. part. of* **студить; —еный** *a.* chilled.

стук *m.* knock(ing), clatter, rattling, ping(ing); (arch.) stucco; **с. в моторе** motor knock; **—анье** *n.* knocking, etc., *see v.*; **—ать** *v.* knock, strike; rap, beat, thump, rattle.

стукко *n.* (arch.) stucco.

стук/нуть *see* **стукать; —отня** *f.* knocking, rattling (noise).

стул *m.* chair; (anvil) block; mounting, base; ball, block (of soil); stool, fecal discharge; **—ик** *dim. of* **стул; —овой** *a.* bench (tool); **—ьный** *a. of* **стул; —ьчак** *m.* toilet seat; **—ьчик** *m.* stool, bench; **—ья** *pl. of* **стул.**

ступа *f.* mortar.

ступать *v.* step, tread, walk.

ступеевая кислота stuppeic acid.

ступенчато *adv.* stepwise, step by step, in steps or stages, gradually; **—сть** *f.* gradation.

ступенчат/ый *a.* step(ped), step-by-step, in steps or stages, gradual, graduated, graded; step-shaped, step-like; ladder-shaped, scalar; tapering; staggered; multistage, multistep; cascade(-type); (math.) stepwise; (phys.) joggy; variable-speed (gear); shingle (splice); ladder (vein); echelon (grating); **с. выключатель** (elec.) step switch; **с. элеватор** escalator; **—ая реакция** (chem.) step(wise) reaction; **—ое воздействие** (unit) step input; **—ое разложение** stepwise decomposition.

ступен/ь *f.* step, tread (of stairs); rung (of ladder); stage (of development); phase; interval; grade, degree, shade (of a color), level; (rad.; rockets) stage; (transmission) gear; **с. сброса** (geol.) fault bench, fault terrace; **—ями** by degrees, gradually, step by step, in steps, stepwise; in stages; **—ька** *f.* step, tread, footboard; (ladder) rung; (phys.) jog; (distillation) theoretical plate.

ступить *see* **ступать.**

ступ/ица *f.,* **—ичный** *a.* boss, hub, nave (of wheel); spider.

ступка *dim. of* **ступа;** stamp, mortar.

ступня *f.* foot, pes; (anat.) tarsus.

ступок *gen. pl. of* **ступка.**

ступор *m.* (med.) stupor.

ступпа *f.* stupp (in mercury distillation).

стурин *m.* sturine.

стучать *v.* knock, tap, rap; make a racket, clatter, rattle; pound, hammer, bang; ping.

стуш/еваться, —ёвываться *v.* keep in the background; become less noticeable; efface oneself.

стушить *v.* braise (food).

стывший *past act. part of* **стыть.**

стыд *m.* shame, disgrace; **—ить** *v.* put to shame; **—иться** *v.* feel ashamed, lose face; **—но** *adv.* shamefully; it is shameful; **—ный** *a.* shameful.

стык *m.* joint(ing), junction, seam, splice; boundary; butt (joint); **в с.** abutting; **прямой с.** butt joint; **соединение в с., шов в с.** butt joint; **—ать** *see* **стыковать; —нуться** *see* **стыковаться; —ование** *n.* butt-jointing, etc., *see v.*; **—ованный** *a.* butt-jointed, etc., *see v.*; **—овать** *v.* butt-joint, butt(-join); join, couple, splice; **—оваться** *v.* (space) link up (with), dock; meet; (elec.) mate; **—овка** *f.* link-up, docking; joining; (assembly) mating; **—овой** *a. of* **стык;** butt (joint; welding); clamp (bolt); contiguous, abutting; **—овая**

накладка cover plate; **—овочный** *a.* butt-joining (machine); docking; **—овочные испытания** interface tests; **—уемый** *a.* mating, mated; abutting.

сты/лый *a.* cold, cooled; **с. ход** cold working; **—нуть** *v.* cool (off); freeze; **—нь** *f.* cold, frost; **—ть** *see* **стынуть.**

стынка *f.* (ichth.) smelt.

стычка *f.* (mil.) skirmish, clash.

стычный *a. of* **стык;** butt-jointed.

Стьюдента распределение (stat.) Student distribution.

стэн *see* **стен.**

стэнд *see* **стенд.**

Стэнли водопады (geog.) Stanley Falls.

стюард *m.* steward.

Стюарт-Кирхгофа закон Stewart-Kirchhoff law.

стэр *see* **стер.**

стягив/аемость *f.* contractibility; **—ание** *n.* tightening, contraction, etc., *see v.*; shrinkage; **—ать** *v.* tighten, contract, constrict; draw together; tie (up), bind, clamp, shackle; couple; bond; brace; agglutinate; pull off, pull away; subtend (an angle); **—аться** *v.* be tightened, etc.; tighten, contract, shrink; sinter, form clinker or slag; **—ающий** *a.* tightening, etc., *see v.*; tie; astringent; **—ающее средство** astringent.

стяж/ание *n.* acquisition; **—ать** *v.* acquire, get, obtain.

стяж/ение *see* **стягивание;** (min.) concretion, nodule; **—ка** *f.* tightening device, turnbuckle, tie rod, draw bar, coupling, coupler; clamp(ing); brace; tightening; (con str.) covering; **проволочная —ка** stay wire; **—ной** *a.* tightening, tension; coupling, tie; clamp; **—ная муфта** turnbuckle; **—ная тяга** tie rod, tension rod.

стянут/ый *a.* tightened, etc., *see* **стягивать; —ь** *see* **стягивать.**

су-ауру *f.* (vet.) trypanosomiasis.

суб— *prefix* sub—, under—; **—альпийский** *a.* (bot.) subalpine; **—арахноидальный** *a.* (anat.) subarachnoid; **—аренда** *f.* sublease; **—арктика** *f.* subarctic zone; **—арктический** *a.* subarctic; **—атомный** *a.* subatomic; **—ацидный** *a.* (med.) subacid; **—аэральный** *a.* subaerial, in the open air; **—аэратор** *m.* sub-aerator; **—аэрация** *f.* (flotation) subaeration.

суббот/а *f.* Saturday; **—е-воскресный** *a.* weekend; **—ник** *m.* day of unpaid, volunteer labor.

суб/гармоника *f.,* **—гармонический** *a.* (acous.) sub-harmonic, suboctave; **—группа** *f.* subgroup.

СУБД *abbr.* (система управления базой данных) (comp.) database management system, DBMS.

субдуральный *a.* (anat.) subdural.

субер/ан *m.* suberane, suberyl heptane; **—ат** *m.* suberate; **—ен** *m.* suberene; **—ил** *m.* suberyl; **—иловый спирт** *see* **суберол; —ин** *m.* suberin; **—иновая кислота** suberic acid, octanedioic acid; **—иновокислая соль** suberate; **—ол** *m.* suberol, cycloheptanol; **—он** *m.* suberone, cycloheptanone; **—оновый** *a.* suberonic (acid).

субзерно *n.* subgrain.

суб-инспектор *m.* junior inspector.

субклеточный *a.* subcellular.

субконтрагент *m.* subcontractor.

субламин *m.* Sublamine, mercuric sulfate ethylenediamine.

сублетальный *a.* (med.) sublethal; (gen.) semilethal (gene).

сублим/ат *m.* sublimate; spec. corrosive sublimate, mercuric chloride; **—ационный** *a.* sublimation; freeze (drying); **—ация** *f.,* **—ирование** *n.* sublimation; **—ированный** *a.* sublimated; **—ировать** *v.* sublimate, sublime; **—ирующийся** *a.* sublimable.

суб/металлический *a.* submetallic; **—микрон** *m.* submicron; **—микроскопический** *a.* submicroscopic; **—миниатюризация** *f.* subminiaturization; **—несущий** *a.* subcarrier; **—нивальный** *a.* subniveal, under the snow; **—нормальный** *a.* subnormal.

суборь *m.* subor (forest on transitional, relatively poor soils).

субподряд *m.* subcontract; **—ный** *a.* subcontract(ed); **—чик** *m.* subcontractor.

суб/продукты *pl.* by-products; **—рефракция** *f.* subrefraction; **—секвентный** *a.* subsequent.

субсид/ировать *v.* subsidize; **—ия** *f.* subsidy, grant, subvention.

субстан/тивный *a.* substantive, direct (dye); **—ци-(он)альный** *a.* substantial, material; **—ци(он)альная производная** (phys.) material derivative; derivative following the fluid; **—ция** *f.* substance.

субститу/т *m.* substitute; **—ция** *f.* substitution.

суб/страт *m.* substratum; substrate; basement (complex of rocks); **почвенный с.** bedrock; **—ный** *a.* of **субстрат**; **—стратостат** *m.* substratosphere balloon; **—стратосфера** *f.* substratosphere; **—структура** *f.* substructure; **—тангенс** *m.* (geom.) subtangent; **—тенолин** *m.* subtenolin; **—тилизин** *m.* subtilysine; **—тилин** *m.* subtilin.

субтильн/ость *f.* slenderness, frailty; **—ый** *a.* slight, delicate, frail.

субтитр *m.* subtitle.

субтроп/ики *pl.*, **—ический пояс** subtropics; **—ический** *a.* subtropic(al).

суб/трузия *f.* subtrusion; **—фоссильный** *a.* subfossil; **—фосфорный** *a.* hypophosphoric (acid); **—фторид** *m.* subfluoride; **—щелочной** *a.* subalkaline.

субъединица (chem.) subunit.

субъект *m.* subject; person; **—ивность** *f.* subjectivity; **—ивный** *a.* subjective; **—ивная ошибка** personal equation.

суб/ъядерный *a.* subnuclear; **—экваториальные пояса** subequatorial region.

суверен/итет *m.* sovereignty; **—ный** *a.* sovereign.

суводь *f.* whirlpool, eddy.

сувой *m.* whirlpool; vortex; swirled snow hummock; **—ки** *pl.* (zool.) Vorticella.

суген *m.* (ichth.) barbel.

суглин/исто-песчаный *a.* sandy loam; **—истый** *a.* loamy, loam-like; **—ок** *m.* loam; (met.) weak clay; **—ок-супесь** *m.* sandy loam.

сугроб *m.* snow drift, snow bank; **—истый** *a.* drifted, drift-covered.

сугубый *a.* especial, particular.

суд *m.* court, tribunal; **верховный с.** supreme court; **подавать в с.** *v.* institute proceedings (against).

суда *pl.* of **судно**; *gen.* of **суд**.

судак *m.*, **—овый** *a.* (ichth.) pike perch (*Lucioperca*).

судан *m.*, **—овый** *a.* sudan (dye); **—ка** *f.* Sudan grass; **—ский** *a.* Sudan(ese).

судач/ий *a.* of **судак**; **—ок** *see* **судак**.

судеб *gen. pl.* of **судьба**.

судебномедицинский *a.* forensic medicine.

судебн/ый *a.* legal, law, judicial; forensic (medicine; chemistry); **с. порядок** court procedure; **—ым порядком** in legal form; **преследовать —ым порядком** *v.* bring action (against); **с. следователь** examining judge; **—ое разбирательство** lawsuit, trial.

судейский *a.* judicial.

суден *gen. pl.* of **судно**.

судза *f.* (bot.) Perilla.

судидовые *pl.* (ichth.) barracudinas (*Paralepididae*).

судимость *f.* previous convictions, criminal record.

судить *v.* judge, pass judgment on, try, referee, umpire; foresee, conjecture, visualize; form an opinion; **—ся** *v.* go to court.

судмедэкспертиза *f.* forensic medicine.

судно *n.* ship, steamer, boat, vessel, craft; bedpan; **грузовое с.** cargo ship, freighter; **с.-кран** *n.* crane ship; **с.-матка** *n.* aircraft carrier.

судо— *prefix see* **судебный; судовой; —верфь** *f.* shipyard; **—владелец** *m.* ship owner; **—владельческий** *a.* ship owner's.

судово/дитель *m.* navigator; **—дительский** *a.* navigator's; **—ждение** *n.* navigation.

судов/ой *a.* ship, naval, maritime; marine (oil); ship's (papers); **—ые припасы** naval stores.

судок *m.* cruet; lunch box.

судомойка *f.* dishwasher; scullery.

судомойн/ый *a.* dish-washing; utensil-washing; **—ая машина** dish washer.

судо/монтажник *m.* shipwright; **—оборот** *m.* maritime traffic; **—подъёмный** *a.* ship-raising.

судопроизводство *n.* legal procedure.

судо/рабочий *m.* stevedore; **—ремонт** *m.*, **—ремонтный** *a.* ship repair(ing).

судоро/га *f.* cramp, spasm, convulsion; **—жный** *a.* spasmodic, convulsive.

судосборщик *m.* shipwright.

судостро/ение *n.* ship building; **—итель** *m.* ship builder; **—ительный** *a.* ship-building.

судоустройство *n.* judicial system.

судоход/ность *f.* navigability; **—ный** *a.* navigable; maritime; shipping; **—ство** *n.* navigation.

судубрава *f.* oak or pine forest.

судьба *f.* fate, destiny, fortune, luck.

суд/ья *m.* judge, justice, referee; **—я по** judging by, to judge from.

суевер/ие *n.* superstition; **—ный** *a.* superstitious.

суёт *pr. 3 sing.* of **совать**.

сует/а *f.* commotion, fuss; **—иться** *v.* bustle, scurry about; **—ня** *f.* fuss, bustle; vanity.

сужа/ть *see* **суживать; —ющий** *a.* narrowing, etc., *see* **суживать**; necked-down.

сужден/ие *n.* judgment; opinion; **основа —ия** criterion.

суж/ение *n.* narrowing, constriction, etc., *see v.*; taper (of wing); (met.) waist; (med.) stenosis; (anat.) isthmus; angustia; (physiol.) miosis; **—ение артерии** arteriostenosis; **—енный** *a.* narrowed, etc., *see v.*; stenosed; miotic (pupil); **—ивание** *see* **сужение; —иватель** *m.* constrictor; (anat.) sphincter; **—ивать** *v.* narrow, constrict, compress, neck, reduce in area; narrow down, taper; **—иваться** *v.* narrow down, shrink, contract; taper; **—ивающий** *a.* sphincter (muscle); **—ивающийся** *a.* narrowing; tapering; conical (nozzle).

сузанит *see* **сусанит**.

сузить *see* **суживать**.

сузотоксин *m.* susotoxin.

сузу *m.* (mam.) Ganges dolphin.

суицидный *a.* suicidal.

суй *imp.* of **совать**.

суйлюк *m.* suilyuk disease (of horses).

суйма *f.* (geol.) solidified freshly deposited salt.

сук *m.* branch, bough, limb; knot (in wood).

сука *f.* (zool.) bitch; (ichth.) spined loach (*Cobitis taenia*); (orn.) godwit (*Limosa*).

суккулент *m.*, **—ный** *a.* (bot.) succulent.

сукно *n.* (woolen) cloth; felt; **класть под с.** *v.* shelve, file away.

сукновал *m.* (text.) fuller; **—ьный** *a.* fulling; **—ьная глина** fuller's earth; **—ьня** fulling mill, fullery.

сукноделие *n.* cloth manufacture.

суковатый *see* **сучковатый.**

сукон *gen. pl. of* **сукно; —ка** *f.* piece of cloth, rag; **—ный** *a. of* **сукно; —щик** *m.* cloth worker.

сукрови/ца *f.* (med.) sanies, (inflammatory) lymph; ichor; (blood) serum; **—чный** *a.* sanious; ichorous.

сукрол *m.* Sucrol, dulcin; **—ит** *m.* sucrolite (synthetic resin).

сукрольность *f.* pregnancy, gestation period (of rabbits).

сукрутина *f.* (text.) snarl; corkscrew.

суктории *pl.* (prot.) Suctoria.

сукцессия *f.* (biol.) succession.

сукцин— *prefix* succin(o)—; **—амид** *m.* succinamide, butanediamide; **—амил** *m.* succinamyl; **—аминовая кислота** succinamic acid; **—ат** *m.* succinate; **—елит** *m.* succinelite.

сукцинил *m.* succinyl, butanedioyl; **—(о)-янтарный** *a.* succinylsuccinic (acid).

сукцин/имид *m.* succinimide, butanimide; **—ол** *m.* succinol; **—онитрил** *m.* succinonitrile, ethylene cyanide; **—орезинол** *m.* succinoresinol; **—уровая кислота** succinuric acid.

сулем/а *f.,* **—овый** *a.* corrosive sublimate, mercuric chloride sublimate.

сулла *f.* (bot.) Hedysarum.

сулой *m.* swift current; whirlpool; riptide.

султан *m.* (bot.) tassel; coma; anthurus; plume (of smoke, etc.).

султанк/а *m.* (ichth.) red mullet (*Mullus barbatus*); (orn.) gallinule (*Porphyrio*); **—и, —овые** *pl.* (ichth.) Mullidae.

султан(овид)ный *a.* plume-like (grains).

сульванит *see* **сулванит.**

сульгин *m.* Sulfaguine, sulfaguanidine.

сульсен *m.* selenium sulfide.

сультон *m.* sultone.

сульф— *prefix* sulf(o)—, thio—; **—адимезин** *m.* sulfadimesine; **—азид** *m.* sulfazide; **—азин** *m.* sulfadiazine; **—азол** *m.* sulfazole, sulfamethylthiazole; **—актин** *m.* sulfactin; **—альдегид** *m.* sulfaldehyde, thioaldehyde; **—амид** *m.,* **—амидный** *a.* sulfamide; **—амин** *m.* sulfamine; **—аминобензойный** *a.* sulfaminobenzoic (acid).

сульфаминов/ая кислота sulfamic acid; **соль —ой кислоты, —окислая соль** sulfamate; **—окислый** *a.* sulfamic acid; sulfamate (of).

сульфамино/кислота *f.* sulfamic acid; **—л** *m.* sulfaminol, thiooxydiphenylamine.

сульфан *m.* hydrogen polysulfide; **—гидрид** *m.* sulfide (of phosphorus, etc.).

сульфанил/амид *m.* sulfanilamide; **—овая кислота** sulfanilic acid; **—овокислая соль** sulfanilate.

сульфа/нтрол *m.* sulfanthrol; **—пиридин** *m.* sulfapyridine.

сульфат *m.* sulfate; **с. калия** potassium sulfate; **—аза** *f.* sulfatase; **—ация** *f.* sulf(atiz)ation; **—ид** *m.* (biochem.) sulfatide; **—изирующий** *a.* sulfat(iz)ing; **—изирующий обжиг** (met.) sulfate roasting; **—ирование** *see* **сульфатация; —ировать** *v.,* **—ный** *a.* sulfate; **—ная масса** (paper) sulfate pulp; **—остойкий** *a.* sulfate-resistant (cement).

сульфацил *m.* sulfacetamide, N¹-acetylsulfanilamide.

сульфгемоглобин *m.* (biochem.) sulf(met)hemoglobin.

сульфгидр/ат *m.* hydrosulfide; **—ил** *m.* sulfhydryl, mercapto—.

сульфид *m.* sulfide; **с. натрия** sodium sulfide; **—изатор** *m.* sulfidizing agent; **—ин** *m.* Sulfidine, sulfapyridine; **—ирование** *n.* sulfid(iz)ing; **—ированный** *a.* sulfid(iz)ed; **—ировать** *v.* sulfid(iz)e; **—ность** *f.* sulfidity; **—ный** *a.* sulfide.

сульф/икислота *f.* sulfinic acid; **—имид** *m.* sulfimide; **—ин** *m.* sulfine, sulfonium; **—иновый** *a.* sulfinic (acid).

сульфир/ование *n.* sulfonation; sulfur(iz)ation; **—ованный** *a.* sulfonated; sulfurized; **—овать** *v.* sulfonate; sulfurize; **—ующий** *a.* sulfonating; sulfurizing.

сульфит *m.* sulfite; **с. натрия** sodium sulfite; **—ация** *f.* sulfitation (of fruit, etc.); **—ирование** *n.* sulfitization; **—ировать** *v.* (food) sulfur(ize), sulfite; **—новарочный процесс** sulfite cooking, sulfite pulping process; **—но-спиртовая барда** sulfite waste liquor.

сульфит/ный *a.* sulfite; **с. щёлок** sulfite liquor; **—овый** *a.* sulfite; **сульфит-целлюлоза** *f.* sulfite pulp.

сульфкарб/амид *m.* thiocarbamide, thiourea; **—аминовая кислота** thiocarbamic acid; **—анилид** *m.* thiocarbanilide, sulfocarbanilide.

сульфо— *prefix* sulfo—, thio—; **—аммофос** *m.* ammonium sulfate-phosphate fertilizer; **—ароматический** *a.* sulfoaromatic; **—бензойная кислота** sulfobenzoic acid; **—бромид** *m.* sulfobromide; **—группа** *f.* sulfo group; **—йодид** *m.* sulfoiodide; **—ихтиоловая кислота** sulfoichthyolic acid.

сульфокарб/амид *see* **сульфкарбамид; —онат** *m.* sulfocarbonate; **—оновая кислота** sulfocarbonic etc.

сульф/окислота *f.* sulfo acid, sulfonic acid; **—оксид** *m.* sulfoxide; **—оксил** *m.* sulfoxyl; **—оксиловый** *a.* sulfoxylic (acid).

сульфомасса *f.* sulfonated material.

сульфон *m.* sulfone; **—ал** *m.* Sulfonal, sulfonmethane; **—амид** *m.* sulfonamide, sulfamine; **—ат** *m.* sulfonate; **—иевый** *a.,* **—ий** *m.* sulfonium; **—ил** *m.* sulfonyl, sulfuryl.

сульфониров/ание *n.* sulfonation; **—анный** *a.* sulfonated; **—ать** *v.* sulfonate.

сульфонитрат *m.* nitrosulfate.

сульфонов/ая кислота sulfonic acid; **амид —ой кислоты** sulfonamide; **соль —ой кислоты; —окислая соль** sulfonate; **хлорангидрид —ой кислоты** sulfonyl chloride.

сульфо/нокарбоновая кислота sulfonocarboxylic acid, sulfonecarboxylic acid; **—нол** *m.* sulfonol, alkylbenzenesulfonate; **—окись** *f.* sulfoxide; **—оксоль** *m.* a drying oil; **—основание** *n.* sulfur base; **—производные** *pl.* sulfo derivatives; **—салициловая кислота** sulfosalicylic acid; **—соединение** *n.* sulfo compound; **—соль** *f.* sulfo salt, thio salt.

сульфо/уголь *m.* sulfonated coal; **—угольная кислота** sulfocarbonic acid, thiocarbonic acid; **—уксусная кислота** sulfoacetic acid; **—феноловая кислота** phenolsulfonic acid; **—фикация** *f.* (agr., chem.) sulfofication; **—фторид** *m.* sulfofluoride; **—хлорирование** *n.* sulfochlorination.

сульф/оциан *see* **тиоциан; —оэтиловая кислота** ethylsulfonic acid; **—уратор** *m.* sulfonator; **—урил** *m.* sulfuryl, sulfonyl.

сульфур/атор *m.* sulfurator (for applying sulfur fumes); **—иметр** *m.* device for determining fineness of sulfur grains.

сульфуриров/ание *n.* sulfonation; sulfurization; **—анный** *a.* sulfonated; sulfurized, sulfureted; **—ать** *v.* sulfonate; sulfurize, fumigate with sulfur

сульцимид *m.* sulcimide, N¹-cyanosulfanilamide.

сума *f.* bag, pouch.

сумак *see* **сумах.**

сумарезинол *m.* sumaresinol.

сумасброд/ить, —ничать *v.* act without stopping to think, go off half cocked.

сумасш/едший *a.* insane, mad; *m.* madman, lunatic; **с. дом** insane asylum; **—ествие** *n.* madness, insanity.

суматоха *f.* confusion, disorder, bustle.

суматр(ан)ский *a.* Sumatra(n) (camphor).

сумах *m.* (bot.) sumac (*Rhus*); **—ировать** *v.* (leather) (re)tan with sumac; **—овый** *a.* of **сумах.**

сумбул *m.,* **—ьный корень** sumbul, musk root; **—ьная кислота** sumbulic acid, angelic acid.

сумбур *m.* confusion.

сумер/ечные *pl.* (ent.) Crepuscularia; **—ечный** *a.* crepuscular; (biol.) disphotic (zone); (physiol.) mesopic (vision); **—ечное зрение** (med.) hemeralopia; **—ки** *pl.* crepuscule, twilight, dusk.

суметь *see* **уметь;** know how, be able.

сумк/а *f.* bag, sack, pack, satchel, case, carrier, (tool) kit; (zool.) pouch; (anat.) bursa, sac, follicle, capsule; (bot.) ascus; marsupium; **—ообразный** *a.* sack-like, bursiform, box; **—оспора** *f.* (bot.) ascospore.

сумма *f.* sum, amount, total; **контрольная с.** (comp.) hash total; checksum; **с.-разность** *f.* add-subtract (radio direction finder); **—рный** *a.* summary, summarized; total, gross, overall, ultimate; cumulative, aggregate (error); composite (force); resultant; accumulation (curve); stacked (records); **—рные белки** (biochem.) total protein content.

сумматор *m.,* **—ный** *a.,* **—ное устройство** (comp.) adder, accumulator, summator; **полный с.** (comp.) full adder, three-input adder.

суммация *f.* (physiol.) summation.

суммир/ование *n.* summation, summing up, addition; **—овать** *v.* sum up, summarize, add up; **—уемость** *f.* summability; **—ующий** *a.* integrating; cumulative; summation, summing, adding; **—ующий узел; —ующее устройство** summator, adder.

сумо/к *gen. pl. of* **сумка; —чка** *dim. of* **сумка;** (biol.) utricle; **—чный** *a.* of **сум(оч)ка;** capsular; utricular.

сумра/к *m.* dusk, twilight, darkness; **—чный** *a.* dark, dusky, gloomy.

сумской *a.* (geog.) Suma.

сумчат/ые *pl.* (zool.) marsupials; **—ый** *a.* utricular, pitcher-shaped; marsupial; (bot.) ascomycetous; **—ая болезнь** (phyt.) plum pocket; **—ая крыса** (mam.) opossum; **—ая спора** (bot.) ascospore; **—ые грибы** (bot.) Ascomycetes.

сун *m.* sunn, Indian hemp.

сундтит *m.* (min.) sundtite, andorite.

сунду/к *m.,* **—чный** *a.* trunk, chest.

сунженский *a.* (geog.) Sunzha.

сунский *a.* (geog.) Suna (river).

сунуть *see* **совать.**

суп *m.* soup.

супер— *prefix* super— (above, over); **—ам** *m.* ammoniated superphosphate fertilizer; **—баллон** *m.* balloon tire; **—гармонический** *a.* superharmonic; **—генный** *a.* (gen.) supergene; **—гетеродин** *m.* (rad.) superheterodyne; **—жирный** *a.* superfatted (soap); **—иконоскоп** *m.* (electron.) image iconoscope; **—кавитирующий** *a.* supercavitating; **—компактный** *a.* supercompact; **—комплекс** *m.* supercomplex; **—кристальный** *a.* (petr.) supercrustal; **—обложка** *f.* jacket, dust cover, wrapper; **—обмазка** *f.* supercoating;

—оксид *m.* peroxide, hyperoxide; **—ортикон** *m.* (telev.) image orthicon; **—палит** *m.* (mil.) superpalite.

суперпозиц/ионный *a.* superimposed; peek-a-boo, optical coincidence (card); **—ия** *f.* superposition.

суперрегенер/ативный *a.* super-regenerative; **—атор** *m.* super-regenerative receiver; **—ация** *f.* super-regeneration.

супер/рефракция *f.* super-refraction; **—структура** *f.* superstructure; **—финиш** *m.* superfinish; **—фосфат** *m.,* **—фосфатный** *a.* superphosphate (fertilizer); **—фузивный** *a.* (geol.) superfusive; **—функция** *f.* (physiol.) superfunction, hyperfunction; **—центрифуга** *f.* supercentrifuge; **—чаржер** *m.* supercharger; **—элита** *f.* super quality stock seed; **—элитный** *a.* superstock, superior quality.

супес/ковый, —ный *a.,* **—ок, —чаник** *m.,* **—чаный** *a.,* **—ь** *f.* sandy loam.

супин/атор *m.* (anat.) supinator (muscle); (med.) arch support; **—ировать** *v.* supinate.

суплировать *v.* (silk) souple.

суповой *a.* soup.

супон/ь, —я *f.* hame strap.

супоросность *f.* (swine) gestation.

супорт *see* **суппорт.**

суппозитории *pl.* (pharm.) suppositories.

суппорт *m.,* **—ный** *a.* support, rest, carriage, slide; saddle; **продольный с.** main tool slide.

суппурация *f.* (med.) suppuration.

супра— *prefix* supra— (above, over; on the dorsal side of); **—капсулин** *see* **супрарен(ал)ин; —литоральный** *a.* supralittoral, above the high-water mark; **—орбитальный** *a.* (anat.) supraorbital; **—рен(ал)ин** *m.* Supracapsuline, Suprarenaline, Suprarenin (epinephrine); **—стерин** *m.* suprasterol; **—умбиликальный** *a.* supraumbilical, epigastric (reflex); **—фосфат** *m.* supraphosphate, basic slag.

супрессор *m.* (gen.) suppressor, inhibitor.

супротивн/о *adv.* oppositely; *prefix* oppositi—; **—олистный** *a.* (bot.) oppositifolious; **—ый** *a.* (bot.) accumbent, opposite, reverse, contrary, decussate.

супру/г *m.* husband; **—га** *f.* wife; **—жеский** *a.* marital; **—жество** *n.* marriage.

супряга *f.* land-working partnership.

сурамень (bot.) suramen, coniferous forest.

сурамин *m.* (pharm.) suramin sodium.

сураханский *a.* Surakhany (crude oil).

сургуч *m.,* **—ный** *a.* sealing wax.

сурд/ина *f.* (music) sourdine, mute; silencer, muffler, damper; **—инирующий** *a.* muting; **—инка** *see* **сурдина; —о—** *prefix* surdo— (deaf); **—окамера** *f.* anechoic chamber; **—опедагогика** *f.* education of deaf-mutes.

суреп/а, —ица *f.* (bot.) rape; **—ица, —ка** *f.* winter cress (*Barbarea vulgaris*); **—ное масло** rapeseed oil.

сурж/а *f.,* **—ик** *m.* maslin, mixture (of wheat and rye grain).

сурик *m.* minium, red lead; **железный с.** iron minium, iron oxide; red ocher; **свинцовый с.** red lead, minium.

сурикат *m.* (mam.) meerkat (*Suricata*).

суриковый *a.* of **сурик;** cinnabar (red), vermillion.

суринам/ин *m.* surinamine, methyltyrosine; **—ский** *a.* (geog.) Surinam.

сурк/и *pl.,* **—овый** *a.* of **сурок.**

суров/еть *v.* grow (more) severe; **—ость** *f.* severity, austerity, rigor; **—ый** *a.* severe, stern, rigorous, bleak, inclement (climate); hard (frost); (text.) coarse, unbleached; raw (silk); **—ьё** *n.* coarse, unbleached cloth.

суро/к *m.*, **—чий** *a.* (zool.) marmot (*Marmota*); **лесной с.** woodchuck (*Marmota monax*).

суррогат *m.* substitute; (med.) succedaneum; **—ировать** *v.* substitute; **—ный** *a.* substitute(d); artificial; random (antenna).

сурхандарьинский *a.* (geog.) Surkhandarya.

сурч/ина *f.* marmot den; woodchuck hole; **—онок** *m.* young marmot.

сурьм/а *f.* antimony, Sb; (**трёх)хлористая с.** antimony (tri)chloride; **—аорганический** *a.* organoantimony; **—инированный** *a.* stibiated.

сурьмянисто/кислый *a.* antimonous acid; antimonite (of); **с. натрий, —натриевая соль** sodium antimonite; **—кислая соль** antimonite.

сурьмянист/ый *a.* antimonous, antimony, antimonial; antimonide, stibide (of); **с. ангидрид** antimonous hydride, stibine; **—ая кислота** antimonous acid; **соль —ой кислоты** antimonite.

сурьмяно/водород *m.* antimonous hydride, stibine; **—й** *see* **сурьмяный; —калиевая соль** potassium antimonate; **—кальциевая соль** calcium antimonate; **—кислый** *a.* antimonic acid; antimonate (of); **—кислый натрий** sodium antimonate; **—кислая соль** antimonate; **—свинцовая соль** lead antimonate.

сурьмян/ый *a.* antimonic, antimony, antimonial; **с. ангидрид** antimony pentoxide; antimony sulfide; **—ая кислота** antimonic acid; **соль —ой кислоты** antimonate; **—ое масло** butter of antimony, antimony trichloride; **—ое стекло** antimony glass, antimonous oxide; **—ые белила** antimony white (antimony trioxide).

сусак *m.* (bot.) Butomus.

сусаль *f.*, **—ный** *a.* tinsel; **—ное золото** tinsel; gold leaf; mosaic gold; **—ное серебро** tinsel.

сусек *m.* (corn) bin, compartment.

Су-Сент-Мари Sault Sainte Marie.

Су-сити (geog.) Sioux City.

Сусквеганна Susquehanna (river).

сусли/к *m.*, **—ковый, —чий** *a.* suslik, ground squirrel (*Citellus*).

сусло *n.* (grape) must; (brewing) wort; wash; **—мер** *m.* mustmeter.

суслон *m.* sheaves, shock.

сусляный *a. of* **сусло.**

суспен/дированный *a.* suspended; **—дировать, —зировать** *v.* suspend; **—зионный** *a.*, **—зия** *f.* suspension; **—зии** *pl.* suspended matter; **—зоид** *m.* suspensoid, suspension, soliquoid; **—зорий** *m.* (zool.) suspensorium; **—зорный** *a.* suspensory.

сустав *m.* joint, articulation; hinge; *prefix* arthr(o)—(joint); **истинный с.** (med.) diarthrosis; **камень —а** arthrolith, arthritic calculus; **неподвижность —ов** (med.) ankylosis; **неподвижный с.** synarthrosis; **третий с.** (ent., etc.) femur, third joint; **—ной** *a. of* **сустав;** articular; condyloid (process); antarthritic (salve); glenoid (cavity); link (belt); **—ноплечевой** *a.* (anat.) glenohumeral; **—олом** *m.* (vet.) pyemia; **—очный** *a.* jointed, articulated, hinged; telescopic, telescope; flexible (pipe); **—чатоногие, —чатые** *pl.* (zool.) Arthropoda; **—чатый** *see* **суставочный.**

сусук *see* **сузу.**

сути *gen., etc., of* **суть.**

сут/ки *pl.* day, 24 hours; **—ок** *gen. pl. of* **сутки; —очный** *a.* daily, diurnal; **—очный ритм** circadian rhythm; **—очные** *pl.* per diem (expense) allowance.

сутул/ина *f.* curve, bend; **—иться** *v.* stoop; **—(оват)ый** *a.* round-shouldered, stooping.

сутун/ка *f.*, **—очный** *a.* (met.) sheet billet, sheet bar.

сутур/а *f.* suture; **—(аль)ный** *a.* sutural.

сут/ь *f.* substance, gist, essence, essentials, kernel, pith (of the matter); *pr. 3 pl. of* **быть; с. дела** point; **по —и дела** in principle, basically.

суфле *n.* souffle.

суфлёр *m.* breather (of engine).

суфляр *m.* (min.) piper, gas feeder; (geol.) fumarole; **—ный газ** blower gas.

суффикс *m.* (gram.) suffix.

суффозия *f.* (geol.) undermining, collapse from solvent action of water.

сух *sh. m. of* **сухой.**

сухар/ик *dim. of* **сухарь;** (arch.) dentil; **—ный** *a. of* **сухарь;** kaolinic (clay); **—ь** *m.* rusk, dry bread; refractory kaolin clay; (mach.) slide block, slider; (universal-joint) trunnion; dowel; **—и** *pl.* (tongue) dies.

сухмен/ный *a.* very dry; **—ь** *f.* drought; dry place; dry soil.

сухо *adv.* dry(ly); it is dry; *prefix* xero—, dry; **—адиабатический** *a.* (meteor.) dry adiabatic; **—боина** *f.* (timber) seasoning check; **—ватый** *a.* dryish; **—вей** *m.*, **—вейный** *a.* hot, dry wind.

суховер/хий *a.* stagheaded, dry-topped (tree); **—шинник** *m.* stagheaded tree; **—шинный** *see* **суховерхий.**

сухоголовчатый *a.* (bot.) xerocephalous.

сухогрузный *a.* dry-cargo (ship).

суходол *m.*, **—ьный** *a.* dry valley.

сухожарный *a.* dry-heat, hot-air (sterilizer).

сухожил/ие *n.* (anat.) sinew, tendon; **подобный —ию** aponeurotic; **—ьный** *a.* sinewy, tendinous; **—ьное растяжение** lacertus.

сух/ой *a.* dry, arid, barren; dry-bulb (thermometer); **с. остаток** dry residue, total solids; **—ая перегонка** dry distillation, destructive distillation; **—им путём** dry (method); by land, over land; **анализ —им путём** dry analysis; **всасывание в —ую** dry suction.

сухоложский *a.* Sukhoi Log.

сухо/лом *m.* brushwood; **—любивый** *a.* (bot.) xerophilous, drought-resistant; **—мятка** *f.* dry food.

сухонос *m.* (orn.) Chinese goose (*Cygnopsis cygnoides*).

сухопарн/ик *m.* steam dome; steam dryer; boiler room; **—ый колпак** steam dome.

сухо/парый *a.* lean, thin, spare; **—перегонный** *a.* dry-distilled; **—плодный** *a.* (bot.) xerocarpous; **—путный** *a.* overland, (by dry) land, ground; **—путье** *n.* land route; **—разрядный** *a.* dry flash-over; **—смешанный** *a.* dry-mixed.

сухостой *m.* deadwood; dry period (of cow); **—ник** *m.* deadwood; **—ный** *a.* dead standing (tree), deadwood; dry (cow).

сухо/сть *f.* dryness; aridity, barrenness; **с. кожи** (med.) xeroderma; **—та** *f.* dryness; drought; (med.) emaciation; **—тка** *f.* (med.) tabes; **—точный** *a.* tabetic; **—фрукты** *pl.* dried fruits; **—цвет** *m.* (bot.) everlasting; **—щавый** *a.* lean, emaciated; **—ядение** *n.* dry food; **лечение —ядением** (med.) dipsotherapy.

суч/ение *n.* spinning, twisting; **—енный** *part.*, **—ёный** *a.* spun, twisted; **—ильный** *a.* spinning, twist(ing); **—ильщик** *m.* spinner; **—ить** *v.* spin, twist; throw (silk).

суч/коватый *a.* knotty, nodose, gnarled, snagged; **—ковый** *a. of* **сучок; —ковая масса** (paper pulp) screenings; **—корез** *m.* (agr.) extension pruner, tree trimmer; **—корезка** *f.* tree pruner; knot saw; **—ок** *dim. of* **сук** knot, knag, knurl; twig; sprout; **—ья** *pl. of* **сук** brushwood, branches.

суш/а *f.* dry land, continent; **воды —и** inland waters; **окружённый —ей** landlocked; **по —е** by land; **экология —и** terrestrial ecology; **—е** *comp. of* **сухо,**

сухой, drier; **—ек** *gen. pl. of* **сушка; —ение** *n.* drying, desiccation; **—еница** *f.* (bot.) everlastings (*Gnaphalium*); **—енный** *part.*, **—ёный** *a.* dried, desiccated, dehydrated (food); **—енье** *see* **сушение.**

сушил/ка *f.*, **—о** *n.* drier, desiccator, drying kiln, drying chamber, drying plant; **с.-вакуум** vacuum drier.

сушильн/ый *a.* drying; **с. аппарат** drier, desiccator; **с. барабан** rotary drier; **с. пол** drier, drying floor; **с. прибор** drier; **с. станок** drying rack; **с. шкаф** desiccator, drier, drying chamber; **—ая печь** drying oven, drying kiln, drier, desiccator; **—ая полка, —ая тележка** drying rack; **—ое средство** drying agent, drier, desiccant, siccative.

суш/ильня *f.* drying chamber, drying plant; **—ильщик** *m.* drier; **—ина** *f.* dried up tree; **—итель** *m.* drier, drying agent; dehumidifier; **—ить** *v.* dry, desiccate, bake; dehydrate, dehumidify; season, cure, weather; **—иться** *v.* be dried, etc.; dry; **—ка** *f.* drying, etc., *see v.*; desiccation, dehydration; drier, siccative; **—няк** *m.* deadwood; adobe; sun-dried clay brick; **—онка** *f.* (drier) cake; **—ь** *f.* dryness, drought, dry weather; dry matter; empty (honey) comb.

существенн/о *adv.* significantly, etc., *see a.*; **—ое** *n.* an essential; **—ость** *f.* significance; **—ый** *a.* significant, important; substantial, material, considerable, tangible, appreciable; essential, intrinsic; entry, catch (word).

существительное *n.* (gram.) noun.

существ/о *n.* being, creature, organism, animal, nature; essence, point; **по —у** essentially, in essence; in fact; **—ование** *n.* existence, being, subsistence; occurrence; **время —ования** (nucl.) lifetime; **условия —ования** (biol.) habitat; **—овать** *v.* exist, be, live, subsist; be extant; be available; **не —овать** be non-existent; **—ующий** *a.* existing, etc., *see v.*; present-day, current; **всё —ующее** *a.* all that exists.

сущий *a.* existing, which is; real, true.

сущност/ь *f.* substance, nature; essentiality, essence, point; **в —и** virtually; **в —и говоря** practically speaking.

СУЭ *abbr.* (**сероуглеродная эмульсия**) carbon disulfide emulsion.

Суэцкий канал Suez Canal.

сующий *pr. act. part. of* **совать.**

суягность *f.* gestation (of ewe).

сфабриковать *v.* make, devise, concoct.

сфагн/овый *a.*, **—ум** *m.* peat moss (*Sphagnum*).

сфазирован/ие *n.* phasing in; **—ный** *a.* phased.

сфалерокарпий *m.* (bot.) sphalerocarp(ium).

сфальц/евать *v.* fold, crease; rabbet, groove; **—ованный** *a.* folded, etc., *see v.*; **—ованный гормошкой** accordion-fold(ed), fan-folded (paper).

сфацелотоксин *m.* (pharm.) sphacelotoxin, spasmotin.

сфексы *pl.* sphecid wasps (*Sphecoidea*).

сфено— *prefix* sphen(o)— [wedge(-shaped)]; **—ид** *m.* (cryst.) sphenoid; **—идальный** *a.* sphenoid(al).

сфера *f.* sphere, realm, range, scope, domain, province, field, area, zone.

сферидии *pl.* (mal.) sphaeridia.

сферит *m.* (min.) spherite.

сферич/еский *a.* spherical, globular, ball-shaped, orbicular; **—еско-мешотчатый** *a.* (med.) saccular (nerve); **—ность** *f.* sphericity; **—ный** *a. see* **сферический.**

сфероблastoma *f.* (med.) medulloblastoma.

сфероид *m.* spheroid; **—альный** *a.* spheroidal, sphere-shaped; (met.) nodular; **—изация** *f.*, **—изирование** *n.* (met.) spheroidizing, spheroidization; **—изированный** *a.* spheroidized; **—ный** *a.* spheroid, globular.

сферокристалл *m.* spherocrystal, spherical crystal.

сферолит *m.* (cryst.) spherulite, spheroidal aggregate; (med.) spherolith; **—овый** *a.* spherulitic.

сферометр *m.* spherometer; **—ический** *a.* spherometric; **—ия** *f.* spherometry.

сферопласт *m.* (cyt.; bot.) spheroplast.

сферо/тека *f.* (phyt.) powdery mildew (*Sphaerotheca morsuvae*); **—текоустойчивый** *a.* resistant to powdery mildew; **—физин** *m.* spherophysine; **—форин** *m.* spherophorin; **—форус** *m.* (bot.; vet.) Sphaerophorus; **—цитоз** *m.* (med.) spherocytosis, globe cell anemia.

сферулит *see* **сферолит.**

сфигмо— *prefix* (med.) sphygmo— (pulse); **—граф** *m.* sphygmograph; **—манометр** *m.* sphygmomanometer.

сфинго/зин *m.* sphingosine; **—миелин** *m.* sphingomyelin.

сфинкс *m.* sphinx (moth).

сфинктер *m.* (anat.) sphincter.

сфирена *f.* (ichth.) barracuda.

сфокусиров/ание *n.* focusing; **—анный** *a.* focused; critical (illumination); **—ать** *v.* focus.

сформ/ированный *a.* formed, etc., *see v.*; **—иров(ыв)ать** *v.* form, mold, shape; organize, create; **—овать** *v.* form, mold, shape; **—улировать** *v.* formulate.

сфотографировать *v.* photograph.

сфрезеров(ыв)ать *v.* mill.

СФРЮ *abbr.* Socialist Federated Republic of Yugoslavia.

с. х. *abbr.* (**сельское хозяйство**) agriculture; **с-х** *abbr.* (**сельскохозяйственный**) agricultural.

схват *m.* grip(per), grab; **ящик —а** grab (bucket).

схва/тившийся *a.* set (concrete); **—тить** *see* **схватывать; —тка** *f.* seizing; (mil.) skirmish, engagement, clash; **—тки** *pl.* tongs; pangs (of pain); **родовые —тки** labor pains, contractions; **—ткообразный** *a.* spasmodic, paroxysmal; **—ты** *see* **схватки; —тывание** *n.* seizing, etc., *see v.*; coalescence (of metals); setting (of concrete, etc.); **—тывать** *v.* seize, grasp, clutch, catch hold (of), grab; bind, tie, join, fasten; bond (metals); catch (disease); **—тываться** *v.* be seized, etc.; seize; (concrete) set, harden; start up; recall suddenly; enter battle; **—тывающий** *a.* seizing, etc., *see v.*; **—тывающийся** *a.* setting (concrete); **—ченный** *a.* seized, etc., *see v.*

с. х-во *see* **с. х.**

схем/а *f.* scheme, plan, project; regimen; flow sheet, chart, schematic drawing, diagram; system, arrangement, layout, configuration, outline (of text); hook-up, connection, circuit, network; device; (flow) pattern; **с. движения материала, с. технологического потока** flow sheet; **с. соединений** (elec.) connection, hook-up; circuit diagram; communication chart; **интегральная с.** integrated circuit, chip; **принципиальная с.** schematic (diagram), circuit diagram; **составлять —у** *v.* connect, hook up.

схематизировать *v.* schematize, plan; give a rough picture (of).

схемат/изм *m.* schematism, sketchiness; **—ический**, **—ичный** *a.* schematic, diagrammatic, outline; sketchy; **—ичность** *see* **схематизм.**

схем/ный *a. of* **схема; с. элемент** circuit element, component; **—отехника** *f.* circuit design; circuitry; **—ы** *pl.* circuitry.

схизо— *prefix* schiz(o)— (division, cleavage); *see also under* **шизо—; —генный** *a.* schizogenous; **—гония** *f.* (prot.) schizogony; **—карп(ий)** *m.* (bot.) schizocarp(ium); **—френия** *f.* (med.) schizophrenia.

схистоцерка *f.* schistocerca (a locust).

схлест/ать, —нуть *see* **схлёстывать.**

схлёстывать *v.* whip, lash; cross (of wires).

схлопыва/ние *n.*, **—ть** *v.* collapse.

схлынуть *v.* abate, flow away, recede.

сход *m.* descent, descending; gathering, meeting; coming off; (rr.) derailment; (missile) take-off, launching; toe-in (of wheels); tail(ing)s; oversize (material); trimmings; (math.) vanishing point; **с. стружки** chip flow (in cutting).

сходен *sh. m. of* **сходный.**

сходимость *f.* (math.) convergence.

сходить *v.* go down, descend, come down, get off; leave; go and return; come off, peel off; **с. за** pass for; go for, fetch; **с. на нет** dwindle to nothing, vanish; taper down to nothing; **—ся** *v.* meet, join, come together, converge; agree, coincide.

сходка *f.* meeting, assembly.

сходни *pl.* gangplank, gangway, ramp.

сходн/ость *f.* similarity; **—ый** *a.* similar, like, analogous; allied, companion; (bot.) affinis, related; suitable, advantageous.

сходня *see* **сходни.**

сходств/енный *a.* similar, like, compatible; **—о** *n.* similarity, likeness, resemblance, analogy, comparison; coincidence, congruity, compatibility; affinity, relatedness.

схо/ды *pl. of* **сход; —дя** *pr. ger. of* **сходить; не —дя с места** without moving; **—дящийся** *a.* descending, etc., *see* **сходить;** convergent; **—ждение** *n.* convergence, meeting; descent; coming off, leaving; **—жде-ние колёс** toe-in.

схож/есть *f.* similarity; **—ий** *a.* similar, (a)like.

схоластический *a.* scholastic.

схоронить *v.* bury; save, keep.

СХОС *abbr.* (**сельскохозяйственная опытная станция**) agricultural experiment station.

сцапать *v.* seize.

сцарап(ыв)ать *v.* scratch off.

сце/дить *see* **сцеживать; —жа** *f.* blow pit, drainage pit; **—женный** *a.* decanted, etc., *see v.*; **—живание** *n.* decanting, decantation, etc., *see v.*; **—живать** *v.* decant, draw off, drain, tap; filter off, strain.

сцементировать *v.* cement together, bind.

сцена *f.* stage, scene; **—рий** *m.* (AI) script, scenario.

сцентр(ир)овать *v.* center; **—ся** *v.* coincide (of centers).

сцеп *see* **сцепка;** hook, link, chain, bond; **—ить** *see* **сцеплять; —ка** *f.* coupling, etc., *see v.*; coupler, clutch; (tractor) hitch; **—ление** *n.* coupling, etc., *see v.*; linkage; cohesion, coherence; adherence, adhesion; engagement (of gears); chain, series; bond, link; clutch; (gen.) conjunction; attachment; (comp.) concatenation; **сила —ления** cohesive force; **—ленный** *a.* coupled, etc., *see v.*; in gear; **—ленный с полом** sex-linked; **—ляемость** *f.* cohesiveness, adhesiveness; **—лянки** *pl.* (bot.) Conjugatae; **—лять** *v.* couple, (inter)link, hook up, connect; lock; clutch, mesh, engage, put in gear, throw in (clutch); **—ляться** *v.* be coupled, etc.; couple, interlock; adhere, cohere, stick together; mesh, engage (with); **—ляющий** *a.* coupling, etc., *see v.*; **—ляющийся** *a.* cohesive.

сцепн/ой *a.* coupling; **с. брус, с. крюк, с. прибор** drawbar; **—ая муфта** clutch; **—ая тяга, —ое приспособление** drawbar.

сцепок *gen. pl. of* **сцепка.**

сцептрон *see* **скептрон.**

сцепщик *m.* coupler.

сциадо— *see* **сцио—.**

сциеновые *pl.* (ichth.) croakers, etc. (*Sciaenidae*).

Сцилард (phys.) Szilard.

сцилл/а *f.* (bot.) squill (*Scilla*); **—аин** *m.* scillain; **—арен** *m.* scillaren; **—ареназа** *f.* scillarenase; **—аридин** *m.* scillaridin; **—ин** *m.* scillin; **—ипикрин** *m.* scillipicrin; **—ит** *m.* scyllitol; **—итин** *m.* scyllitin; **—итоксин** *m.* scillitoxin.

сцимнол *m.* scymnol.

сцинтилл/ирование *n.* (nucl.) scintillation; **—ирующий** *a.* scintillating; **—ирующее вещество** scintillator; (scintillating) phosphor; **—ограф** *m.* scintillograph, automatic scintillation scanner; **—ометр** *m.* scintillation counter; **—ятор** *m.* scintillator; **—яционный** *a.* scintillation; **—яционный индикатор, —яционный счётчик** scintillation counter; **—яция** *f.* scintillation.

сцио— *prefix* scio— (shade, shadow); **—фильный** *a.* (bot.) sciophilous.

сциф(о)— *prefix* scyph(o)—, scyphi— (cup); **—а** *f.* (bot.) scyphus; **—идные** *pl.* (zool.) Scyphozoa; **—о-видный** *a.* (bot.) scyphiform, cup-shaped.

СЦМ *abbr.* (**специализированная цифровая математическая машина**) special purpose digital computer.

сц. сп. *abbr.* (**сцинтилляционный спектрометр**) scintillation spectrometer.

с.ч., с/ч *abbr.* (**сего числа**) today.

счал *m.* moored vessels; **—и(ва)ть** *v.* moor, lash together; **—ка** mooring; moored vessels; cable.

счастливый *a.* fortunate, lucky, happy; **с. крюк** (oil-well drilling) grab.

счаст/ье *n.* happiness, fortune, chance, luck; **к —ью** fortunately, luckily.

счёл *past m. sing. of* **счесть.**

счерп/нуть, —(ыв)ать *v.* scoop off, skim, ladle out.

счер/тить, —чивать *v.* trace, draw.

счёс *m.*, **—ка** *f.* combing out; (fibers) carding (out); scratching off.

счесать *see* **счёсывать.**

счесть *see* **считать.**

счёсывать *v.* comb out; (fibers) card (out); scratch off.

счёт *m.* account; bill, statement; expense; numeration; counting; score; calculation; **баланс —ов** balance sheet; **быть на хорошем —у** *v.* stand well (with); **в конечном —е** in the final analysis; **за счёт** at the expense (of); by (means of), through; due to, because of; **обратный с.** count-down; **относить за с.** *v.* credit (to), attribute (to); account (for); **круглым —ом** in round figures; **на этот с.** on that score, on that account; **скорость —а** counting rate; **схема —а** counting circuit.

счетверить *v.* combine in fours.

счётно-аналитический *a.* punch(ed)-card, tabulating, computing; **с.-конторский** *a.* bookkeeping and clerical (personnel); **с.-перфорационный** *a.* punch(ed)-card.

счётно-решающ/ий *a.* computing; **с. прибор, —ее устройство** computer.

счётность *f.* denumerability, countability.

счётн/ый *a. of* **счёт;** slide (rule); (math.) denumerable, countable (set); account(ing); **с. диск** counter dial; **с. механизм** (cash) register; **—ая книга** account book; **—ая машина** calculating machine, adding machine; **—ая таблица** register; scale; **—ое устройство** counter; computer.

счето/ведение *see* **счетоводство; —вод** *m.* accountant, bookkeeper; **—водный** *a.*, **—водство** *n.* accounting, bookkeeping.

счёт-фактура *f.* invoice.

счётчик *m.* meter, measuring device; register, indicator, recorder; integrating device; calculator, computer;

(comp.; nucl.) counter; accounting clerk; **с.-зонд** *m.* counter probe; **с. делений** fission counter; **с. импульсов** pulse counter; (impulse) scaler; rate meter; **электрический с.** electric meter.

счёты *pl.* abacus, counting board.

счисл/ение *n.* calculation, reckoning, etc., *see v.;* calculus; **с. пути** (av.; naut.) dead reckoning; **система —ения** notation; (comp.) number system, code; **—енный** *a.* calculated, etc., *see v.;* **—ять** *v.* calculate, reckon; (e)numerate, number, count.

счист/ить *see* **счищать;** **—ка** *f.* scraping off, etc., *see* **счищать.**

счит/анный *a.* counted, etc., *see v.;* **—анье** *n.* counting, etc., *see v.;* **—ать** *v.* count; compute, reckon, calculate; number; rate, regard, think, consider, assume, presume, believe; proofread, compare, check (against); **—ать за** consider as, take for; **если не —ать** *see* **не считая;** **—аться** *v.* be counted, etc.; be thought to be, be held to be; take into consideration, take into account; run into, be; **не —аться** disregard, ignore; **—ающий** *a.* counting, etc., *see v.;* **—ая** *pr. ger.* counting, etc., *see v.;* **—ая на** on the basis of; **не —ая** not counting, apart (from), exclusive (of), except (for), but for, less, minus; **не —аясь** disregarding, regardless (of), in spite (of); **—ка** *f.* proofreading, checking; **—чик** *m.,* **—чица** *f.* proofreader.

считыв/аемость *f.* readability; **—ание** *n.* (comp.) reading, read-out, sensing; computation; **—ание данных** read-out; **время —ания** access time; **сигнал —ания** read(ing) signal, sense signal; **—атель** *m.* reader; **—ать** *v.* read (from, off, out), take readings; compute; **—ающий** *a.* reading, read-out; computing; **—ающее устройство** reader.

счищ/алка *f.* scraper, cleaner; **—ать** *v.* scrape off, clean off, clear, take off, remove; **—енный** *a.* scraped off, etc., *see v.*

с. ш. *abbr.* (**северная широта**) north latitude.

США *abbr.* (**Соединённые Штаты Америки**) United States of America.

сшабрить *v.* scrape off.

сшиб/ать, —ить *v.* knock down, knock off; **—иться** *v.* collide, clash.

сшив *see* **сшивание;** **—альный** *a.* joining, etc., *see v.;* **—ание** *n.* joining, etc., *see v.;* **—ать** *v.* join, sew (together), stitch; (polymers) cross-link; lace (belt); (med.) suture; **—ающий** *a.* joining, etc., *see v.;* **—ка** *see* **сшивание;** seam, joint; suture; lace; clamp bar, clip; **—ка тканей** tissue bridging; **—ной** *a.* stitched, pieced; (belts) laced.

сшинковать *v.* shred, cut fine.

сшит/ый *a.* joined, etc., *see* **сшивать;** **—ь** *see* **сшивать.**

съед/ание *n.* eating, consumption; **—ать** *v.* eat (up), consume, eat away, corrode; **—енный** *a.* eaten, etc., *see v.*

съедет *fut. 3 sing. of* **съехать.**

съедобн/ость *f.* edibility; **—ый** *a.* edible.

съежи(ва)ться *v.* shrivel, shrink; curl up, roll up.

съезд *m.* convention, conference, congress, meeting, assembly, reunion; arrival; (min.) cross-over; (гг.) access track; descent; **наклонный с.** access ramp; **—ить** *v.* go.

съезжать *v.* slide off, come off, come down; **—ся** *v.* convene, meet, assemble.

съём *m.* removal, extraction, withdrawal; taking off, skimming; pick-off; stripping; output, yield; (agr.) picking, harvest(ing); **—ка** *see* **съём;** survey(ing); plan(ning), mapping, plotting; photography; exposure; **делать**

—ку *v.* photograph, expose (film); **производить —ку** *v.* survey.

съёмн/ик *m.* stripper; remover, puller, lifter, extractor, withdrawal tool; (agr.) picker; **—ый** *a.* detachable, removable, dismountable, renewable, replaceable, interchangeable; (paper) couch (roll); adjustable; withdrawable, retrievable; drop (bottom); access (panel); (agr.) ripe, ready to pick.

съём/очный *a.* of **съёмка;** surveying; photographic, camera, filming, shooting; **—щик** *m.* surveyor; lessee, tenant.

съест/ное *n.* food; **—ной** *a.* edible; **—ь** *see* **съедать.**

съехать *see* **съезжать.**

сыворотка *f.* whey; (med., zool.) serum.

сывороточн/ый *a.* whey; (med., zool.) serum, serous; **—ая жидкость** serum; **—ая закваска** (cheese) rennet; **—ая оболочка** serous membrane, serosa.

сыгр(ыв)ать *v.* play, perform.

сызнова *adv.* anew, afresh, again.

сын *m.* son; **—овья** *pl.* sons.

сып/ание *n.* strewing, etc., *see v.;* **—ать** *v.* strew, scatter; pour (bulk material); fall (of snow); **—аться** *v.* run out, pour (of dry material); flake off; (text.) fray; **—ец** *m.* pulverized material; **—кий** *see* **сыпучий;** **—ной** *a.* (med.) exanthematic; **—нотифозный** *a.* typhous; **—нуть** *see* **сыпать;** **—няк** *m.* typhus; **—ок** *sh. m. of* **сыпкий;** **—ун** *m.* fine dry sand.

сыпучесть *f.* friability.

сыпуч/ий *a.* friable, loose, granular, free-flowing, running, drift; bulk (material); (geol.) quick; **мера —их тел** dry measure; **с. песок** quicksand; **—ка** *f.* sypuchka (loose, fine-grained sand).

сыпь *f.* fines; (med.) exanthema, rash, eruption; **аллергическая с.** urticaria; **гнойничковая с.** impetigo; **картофельная с.** (vet.) potato eczema.

сыр *m.* cheese; *sh. m. of* **сырой.**

сырдарьинский *a.* (geog.) Syrdarya.

сыр/естойкий *a.* damp-proof; **—еть** *v.* dampen, grow damp.

сырец *m.* raw material; raw silk; adobe, sun-dried clay brick; **пенька-с.** raw hemp.

сырный *a.* cheese, cheesy, caseous.

сыро— *prefix* raw; wet, damp; cheese.

сыровар *m.* cheese maker; **—ение** *n.* cheese making; **—ня** *f.* cheese dairy.

сыроват/ость *f.* slight dampness; **—ый** *a.* dampish, moist; half-cooked; not quite ripe.

сыровидный *a.* cheese-like.

сыродел/ие *n.,* **—ьный** *a.* cheese-making.

сыродутный процесс (met.) blooming.

сыроежка *f.* (bot.) agaric (*Russula*).

сыр/ой *a.* damp, moist, humid, wet; raw, crude, coarse, untreated; uncooked; uncured (rubber); unripe; green (wood); **с. материал, —ые продукты** raw material(s).

сырок *m.* (ichth.) whitefish (*Coregonus*); cheese curd.

сыромолот *m.* (agr.) wet threshing.

сыромят/ина *see* **сыромять;** **—ник** *m.* (leather) tawer; **—ный** *a.* tawed; tawing; raw (hide); **—ное дубление** tawing; **—чик** *m.* tawer; **—ь** *f.* rawhide; tawed leather.

сыроподобный *a.* cheesy, caseous.

сыросека *f.* brushwood burning.

сыростестойкий *a.* damp-proof, moisture-proof, moisture-resistant.

сырость *f.* damp(ness), moisture, wetness, humidity.

сырт *m.* (geol.) syrt, watershed upland.

сырть *f.* (ichth.) vimba.

сырц/а *f.* slight dampness; *gen. of* **сырец;** **—овый** *a.* raw, crude.

сырь *see* **сырость.**

сырьё *n.* raw material(s), resources, stock; source, starting material; **алмазное с.** rough *or* uncut diamonds.

сыр/евой *a.* of **сырьё;** **—ём** *adv.* raw, in the raw state.

сыт *sh. m. of* **сытый;** **—ен** *sh. m. of* **сытный;** **—ность** *f.* substantiality (of food); **—ный** *a.* satisfying, filling; **—ость** *f.* satiation, repletion; **—ый** *a.* satisfied, satiated, replete; **до —а** to repletion.

сыть *f.* (bot.) cyperus; **съедобная с.** chufa (*Cyperus esculentus*).

сыч *m.* (orn.) owl; **—и** *pl. of* **сыч.**

сычуаньский *a.* (geog.) Szechwan.

сычу/г *m.* (zool.) abomasum; **—жина** *f.,* **—жная закваска** rennet; **—жный фермент** rennin; **—жок** *m.* rennet.

сьерра (geog.) Sierra.

Сьюард (geog.) Seward.

Сьюдад-боливар (geog.) Ciudad Bolivar.

сэбин *m.* sabin (unit of sound absorption).

сэдбюрийский *a.* (geol.) Sudburian; Sudbury (ore).

сэкономить *v.* economize.

сэлопский ярус (geol.) Salopian stage.

сэндвич-соединение *n.* sandwich compound.

сюда *adv.* here, hither.

сюжет *m.* subject, topic.

сюрприз *m.* surprise; booby-trap.

сюрфасография *f.* streamlining.

сядут *fut. 3 pl. of* **сесть.**

сяж/ок *m.* (ent.) antenna; (zool.) feeler, palp; **—ки** *pl. of* **сяжок.**

Сясьстрой (geog.) Siasstroy.

Т

т *abbr.* **(тесла)** tesla unit; **(том)** volume; **(тонна)** ton; **(точка)** point; **(тысяча)** thousand; **Т** *abbr.* **(температура)** temperature; **(титр)** titer; **(тонна-сила)** ton-force; **Т-** *abbr.* **(тера—)** tera— (10¹²); **т, Т** *abbr.* **(твёрдый)** hard; **(технический)** technical.

та *f. of* **тот,** that.

табак *m.* tobacco; **—оводство** *n.,* **—оводческий** *a.* tobacco-growing.

табанить *v.* (rowing) back astern; sheave, backwater.

таба/цин *m.* tabacin; **—чный** *a.* tobacco; tobacco-colored.

табардилло *n.* (med.) murine typhus.

табашир *m.* (bot.) tabasheer (a secretion of bamboo).

таббиит *m.* (min.) tabbyite, wurtzilite.

табель *f.* table, list, catalog, schedule; time board, time sheet, time (clock) card; **—ный** *a.* of **табель;** time (board); **—щик** *m.* timekeeper.

табе/с *m.* (med.) tabes (dorsalis), progressive atrophy; **—тический** *a.* tabetic.

табл. *abbr.* **(таблица)** table.

таблет/изация *f.* pastillation; **—ирование** *n.* tableting; (plastics) preforming; **—ировать** *v.* tablet; preform; **—ировочный** *a.* (compressing and) tableting, tablet-making (machine); **—ка** tablet; pellet; cake, slab; preform; **—очный** *a.* tablet; preforming.

таблитчатый *a.* tabular, flat, discoid.

табли/ца *f.* table, list, chart, scale, schedule; plate; (comp.) spreadsheet; **т. логарифмов** (math.) logarithmic table; **вносить в —цу** *v.* tabulate; **подвижная счётная т.** sliding scale; **представлен в —це** tabulated; **составление —ц** tabulation; **т.-приложение** *f.* appendix table; **—чка** *dim. of* **таблица;** table, tabulation; plate; indicator; board; **—чный** *a. of* **таблица;** tabular, in table form; **—чное задание** tabular definitions (of functions).

табло signal panel, mimic panel; display board, indicator, chart; (rr.) illuminated track diagram.

табопаралич *m.* (med.) taboparesis.

Табс, т. абс. *abbr.* **(температура абсолютная)** absolute temperature.

табул/ирование *n.* tabulation; **—ированный** *a.* tabulated; **—ировать** *v.* tabulate; **—яграмма** *f.* tabulated form; **—ятор** *m.* tabulator, tabulating machine.

табуляты *f.* (zool.) stony corals (*Tabulata*).

табуляция *f.* tabulation.

табун *m.* tabun (lethal gas); (zool.) herd; pod (of whales); **—ный** *a. of* **табун;** gregarious.

табурет *m.,* **—ка** *f.* stool.

таволга *f.* (bot.) Spiraea; Filipendula.

тавот *m.* (lubricating) grease; **—ница** *f.* grease cup; grease gun; **—ный** *a.* grease.

Тавр Taurus Mountains.

тавр/ение *n.* branding, stamping; **—ё(н)ный** *a.* branded, stamped.

таврик *m.* (av.) T-section.

тавр/ить *v.,* **—о** *n.* brand, stamp, mark.

тавро— *prefix* T-, tee-; branding iron; **—бимсовое железо,** **—бульб** *m.,* **—бульбовое железо** T-bulb iron, bulb bar.

тавров/ый *a.* T-, tee; *also a. of* **тавро;** **т. угольник** T-square.

тавто— *see* **тауто—.**

таган *m.* andiron, trivet, stand.

таг/атоза *f.* tagatose.

тагма *f.* (biol.) tagma.

тагуан *m.* (mam.) flying squirrel.

таджикский *a.* (geog.) Tadjik.

таёжный *a. of* **тайга.**

ТАЕМ *abbr.* **(тысячная атомная единица массы)** millimass unit.

тает *pr. 3 sing. of* **таять.**

таз *m.* basin, pan; (anat.) pelvis; **—ик** *dim. of* **таз;** tray; (ent.) coxa.

тазиметр *m.* (elec.) tasimeter.

тазобедренный *a.* (anat.) coxofemoral, hip.

тазовский *a.* (geog.) Taz.

тазо/вый *a. of* **таз;** (anat.) pelvic; **т. пояс** pelvic girdle; **—вая кость** (anat.) hip bone, os coxae; **—мер** *m.* (med.) pelvimeter.

таиландский *a.* (geog.) Thai(land).

таинственный *a.* secret, mysterious.

Таит/и (geog.) Tahiti.

таитянский *a.* Tahitian.

таить *v.* conceal, hide, shelter; **—ся** *v.* be hidden; hide, conceal oneself.

тай *m.* (ichth.) sea bream.

тайваньский *a.* (geog.) Taiwan.

тайга *f.* taiga (coniferous forest).

тайком *adv.* secretly, in secret.

Тайлор *see under* **Тэйлора.**

таймень *m.* (ichth.) taimen (*Hucho taimen*).

таймер *m.* timer, timing unit.

тайм/тактор *m.* time-cycling device; **-чартер** *m.* time charter; **-шит** *m.* time sheet.

таймырский *a.* (geog.) Taimyr.

тайн/а *f.* secret, secrecy, privacy; **—ик** *m.* hiding place, cache; marine trap net.

тайно *adv.* secretly, in secret, confidentially; *prefix* crypto— (hidden); **—брачный** *a.* (bot.) cryptogamic; **—пись** *f.* cryptography.

тайный *a.* secret, hidden; cryptic; covert, clandestine; confidential; security.

тайпотрон *m.* (electron.) typotron.

тайристор *m.* (electron.) thyristor.

тайфун *m.* typhoon.

тайфунник *m.* (ichth.) fulmar, petrel (*Pterodroma*).

так *adv., particle and conj.* so, thus, like this; as, since; then, in that case; **т. держать** (naut.) steady (as you go); **т. же** so, as, in the same way; **т. . . . как** as . . . as; **т. же, как и** as well as, as are, as is, as does, in the same way as; **т. и есть** so it is; **т. или иначе** somehow or other, by some means or other; **т. как** as, because, for, since, inasmuch as, seeing that, being that; **т. например** for instance, thus; **т. сказать** so to speak; **т. точно** exactly, just so; (mil.) yes, sir!; **т., что** so that; **т., чтобы** so as to, so that; **если это т.** if that is so, if that is the case; **и т. далее** and so forth.

такаба *f.* (ichth.) takaba (*Labracoglossa*).

така-диастаза *f.* Taka diastase.

такамагак *m.* tacamahac (resin).

такелаж *m.*, **—ный** *a.* cordage, rigging, tackle; **—ить** *v.* rig out.

также *adv.* also, too, likewise; **т. не** neither; **а т.** and at the same time.

таки *particle* after all; **опять-т.** again.

такин *m.* (mam.) takin (goat) (*Budorcas taxicolor*).

так наз. *abbr.* (**так называемый**) so-called; **так. обр.** *abbr.* (**таким образом**) in such a manner, thus.

таков *a.* such, like; **все они —ы** all of them are alike, they are all like that; **—ой** *a.* such; **если —ой имеется** if any; **как —ой** as such.

так/ой *a.* such; **т. же** such a one, similar; **т. же как и** as; **—им же образом, как и** in the same way as for; **—им образом** in this way, thus; **всё т. же** always the same, still the same; **не т. как** unlike; **что —ое** what is it? what is the matter?

такон/(ий)ский *a.* (geol.) Taconian; **—ит** *m.* (petr.) taconite.

такса *f.* fixed price; tariff, fee, rate; **—тор** *m.* assessor, appraiser; tax collector; **—ция** *f.* fixing of prices; assessment, evaluation; taxation; (forest) inventory.

такси *n.* taxi (cab).

таксин *m.* taxine.

таксиров/ание *n.* price fixing, price freezing; **—ать** *v.* fix prices; estimate, evaluate; (av.) taxi; **—ка** *see* **таксирование; —щик** *see* **таксатор.**

таксис *m.* (biol.) taxis, tropism.

таксит *m.* (petr.) taxite; **—овый** *a.* taxitic.

таксический *a.* (biol.) tactic.

таксовый *a. of* **такса.**

таксодий *m.* (bot.) Taxodium.

таксон *m.* (biol.) taxon; **—омический** *a.* taxonomic; **—омия** *f.* taxonomy, classification.

таксофон *m.* pay telephone.

такт *m.* cycle (of engine); stroke; rate, tempo; time step; beat; time, measure; tact; **т. работы** (mach.) operating cycle.

тактик *m.* tactician; **—а** *f.* tactics, plan, approach; **—о-технические данные** tactical characteristics and specifications.

тактильн/ый *a.* tactile, tangible; **—ая слепота** (med.) astereognosis, tactile amnesia.

тактир/ование *n.* clocking; **—уемый** *a.* clocked.

тактиты *pl.* (petr.) tactites.

тактич/еский *a.* tactic; (mil.) tactical; **—ичность** *f.* tact; **—ный** *a.* tactful.

такто— *prefix* tact(o)— (touch).

тактовый *a. of* **такт;** clock; timing; cadence (signal); (optical communications) framing, frame; **т. генератор** clock.

такто/золь *m.* tactosol; **—ид** *m.* tactoid; **—каталитический** *a.* tactocatalytic; **—метр** *m.* (physiol.) tactometer; **—фаза** *f.* tactophase.

такыр *m.*, **—ный** *a.* takyr (clay-surfaced desert); takyr soil; **—изация** *f.* takyrization; **—овидный** *a.* takyr-like.

тал *m.* (bot.) willow (*Salix*).

талам/ический *a.* (anat.) thalamic; **—о** *prefix* thalamo— (thalamus); **—о-кортикальный** *a.* thalamo-cortical; **—отомия** *f.* (med.) thalamotomy; **—ус** *m.* (anat.) thalamus.

талант *m.* talent, gift, ability; **—ливый** *a.* talented.

талассемия *f.* (med.) thalassemia.

таласский *a.* (geog.) Talas.

талассо— *prefix* thalasso— (sea); **—ма** *f.* (ichth.) wrasse (*Thalassoma*); **—фит** *m.* (bot.) thalassophyte, marine plant; **—фрина** *f.* (ichth.) poison toadfish (*Thalassophryne*).

талатизамин *m.* talatisamine.

талевый *a. of* **таль.**

талеихт *m.* (ichth.) eulachon, candlefish (*Thaleichthys*).

таленит *m.* (min.) thalenite.

талер *m.* (typ.) bed plate, foundation.

тали *gen., pl., etc., of* **таль;** block and tackle; **т. с цепью** hoist chain.

талидомид *m.* (pharm.) thalidomide.

тали/евый *see* **таллиевый; —й** *see* **таллий.**

талик *m.*, **—а** *f.* thawed ground.

таликтрин *m.* thalictrine.

талит *m.* talitol (hexahydric alcohol).

талия *f.* waist, middle.

талл *m.* (bot.) thallus.

таллейохин *m.* thalleioquine.

таллен *m.* thallene.

таллидий *m.* (bot.) thallidium.

таллиевый *a.* thallium, thallic.

талл/ий *m.* thallium, Tl; **хлористый т.** thallous chloride; **хлорный т.** thallic chloride.

таллийорганический *a.* organothallium.

таллин *m.* thalline.

таллинский *a.* (geog.) Tallin.

таллирование *n.* thallation.

таллистый *a.* thallium, thallous.

талло— *prefix* thallo— (young shoot).

талл/овое масло, —ол *m.* tall oil, tallol, liquid rosin.

талл/ом *m.* (bot.) thallome, thallus; **—оспора** *f.* thallospore; **—офит** *m.* (bot.) thallophyte; **—охлор** *m.* thallochlore, lichen chlorophyll; **—ус** *m.* thallus.

таловый *a.* willow.

талоза *f.* talose.

талон *m.* check; coupon; stub (of check); boarding pass.

талоновая кислота talonic acid.

талослизевая кислота talomucic acid.

талофидный элемент thalofide (photoelectric) cell.

талреп *m.* turnbuckle.

талый *a.* melted, thawed; snow melt (water); **т. снег** slush.

талыш(ин)ский *a.* (geog.) Talysh.

тал/ь *f.*, **—и** *pl.* block and tackle, compound pulley, pulley block; hoist.

тальбот *m.* (phys.) talbot (10^7 lumergs).

Тальбота способ Talbot process.

тальвег *m.* (geol.) thalweg, valley profile.

тальк *m.* (min.) talc; **—ит** *m.* talcite; **—овый** *a.* talc-(ous), talcose; talcum (powder); **—овый камень** soapstone; **—овый сланец** talc schist; **—оз** *m.* (med.) talcosis; **—оподобный** *a.* talc-like, talcoid.

тальмень *see* **таймень.**

тальми *n.* talmi gold.

тальник *m.* (bot.) willow (*Salix*).

там *adv.* there; **т., где** where, wherever.

тамандуа *f.* (mam.) tamandua, tree anteater.

тамарикс *m.* (bot.) tamarisk (*Tamarix*).

тамарина *f.* (mam.) marmoset, tamarin.

тамаринд *m.* (bot.) tamarind (*Tamarindus indica*).

тамариск *see* **тармарикс.**

тамбовский *a.* (geog.) Tambov.

тамбур *m.* tambour; vestibule, lobby; (air) lock, lock chamber, trap, double door; reel, drum; (rr.) platform (between cars); **—ин** *m.* tambourine; **—ный** *a. of* **тамбур.**

тамга *f.* seal, stamp.

тамнар *m.* (mam.) wallaby.

тамноловая кислота thamnolic acid.

тамож/енный *a.* customhouse, customs, revenue; custom (duties); **—енное управление** customs; **—ня** *f.* customhouse.

тамошний *a.* of (or in) that place, there; local.

тампи/ко *n.* tampico (a dyewood); **—коловая кислота** tampicolic acid; **—цин** *m.* tampicin (resin).

тампон *m.* plug, pad, wad, lump; (med.) tampon; **—аж** *m.* tamponage; (min.) plugging, stopping up; grouting; **—ация** *f.*, **—ирование** *n.* packing; **—ировать** *v.* tampon, plug up; pack.

тамурия *f.* (med.) thamuria, frequency of urination.

тана *f.* (mam.) tree shrew.

танагр/а *f.*, **—овые, —ы** *pl.* (orn.) tanager(s) (*Thraupidae*).

танато— *prefix* thanato— (death); **—з** *m.* thanatosis.

танатол *m.* thanatol, guaethol.

танацетон *m.* tanacetone.

тангаж *m.* (av.; naut.) pitch(ing).

тангалунга *f.* (mam.) civet.

Танганьика (geog.) Tanganyika.

танген/с *m.* (geom.) tangent; **относящийся к —су** tangential; **т.-буссоль** *f.* tangent compass; **т.-гальванометр** *m.* tangent galvanometer; **—соида** *f.* tangent curve.

тангента *f.* speaking key, push-to-talk key.

тангенциальный *a.* tangent(ial); centrifugal (force).

тангинин *m.* tanghinine.

тандем *m.*, **—ный** *a.* tandem.

тандер *m.* turnbuckle, stretcher; clamp.

танец *m.* dance.

Танжер (geog.) Tangiers.

танжерин *m.* tangerine (fruit).

танзанийский *a.* Tanzania.

танин *see* **таннин.**

танк *m.* tank; **—аж** *m.* tank capacity; tankage (slaughterhouse waste); **—ер** *m.* (oil) tanker; **—ер-заправщик** *m.* refueling tanker; **—ерный** *a.* tanker; **—етка** *f.* (mil.) light tank; **—ист** *m.* tank crew member.

танко— *prefix* tank; **—вый** *a.* tank, armored; **—доступный** *a.* tank-traversable (terrain); **—недоступный** *a.* tank-proof, tank-inaccessible.

танк-тральщик *m.* mine-sweeping tank.

танн/аза *f.* tannase; **—альбин** *m.* Tannalbin, albumin tannate; **—ат** *m.* tannate; **—иген** *m.* tannigen, acetannin; **—ид** *see* **таннин; —ил** *m.* tannyl; **—ин** *m.* tannin, tannic acid; **—иноносный** *a.* tanniniferous; **—иноподобный** *a.* tannic.

танно/зал, —креозот *m.* tannosal, tannocreosote, creosote tannate; **—пин** *m.* Tannopin, urotropine tannin; **—форм** *m.* Tannoform, tannin-formaldehyde.

тантайрон *m.* Tantiron (alloy).

тантал *m.* tantalum, Ta; **—ат** *m.* tantalate; **—истый** *a.* tantalous, tantalum; **—овокислый** *a.* tantalic acid; tantalate (of); **—овокислый натрий, —овонатриевая соль** sodium tantalate; **—овый** *a.* tantalic, tantalum; **—овый ангидрид** tantalic anhydride, tantalum pentoxide; **—овая кислота** tantalic acid; **соль —овой кислоты** tantalate; **—офтористый калий** potassium tantalum fluoride.

тантьема *f.* bonus.

танц/евать, —овать *v.* dance; **—мейстер** *m.* inside calipers.

тапет/альный *a.* (biol.) tapetal; **—ум** *m.* tapetum.

тапиока *f.* tapioca, manioca starch.

тапиолит *m.* (min.) tapiolite.

тапир *m.* (mam.) tapir (*Tapirus*).

тапс/иевая кислота thapsic acid; **—ия** *f.* (bot.) deadly carrot (*Thapsia*).

тар *m.* (mam.) tahr (*Hemitragus jemlaicus*).

тар/а *f.* pack(ag)ing; package, container(s), box, can; case, crate; (com.) tare; **вес в —е** packaged weight, crated weight; **охранная т.** shielding container (for transporting radioactive material).

таракан *m.*, **—ий** *a.* cockroach.

таракса/нтин *m.* taraxanthin; **—стерин** *m.* taraxasterol; **—церин** *m.* taraxacerin; **—цин** *m.* taraxacin.

таран *m.* (mech.) ram; (bot.) knotweed (*Polygonum*); **—ить** *v.* ram.

таранно— *prefix* (anat.) talo— (astragalus, ankle); **—большеберцовый** *a.* talotibial; **—ладьевидный** *a.* talonavicular; **—пяточный** *a.* talocalcanean.

тараннонский *a.* Tarannon (shale).

таранн/ый *a. of* **таран;** collision (bulkhead); **—ая кость** ankle bone, talus.

тарант/изм *m.* (med.) tarantism; **—ул** *m.* (zool.) tarantula.

тарань *f.* (ichth.) roach.

тарахтеть *v.* rattle, clatter, rumble.

тарашка *f.* (ichth.) white bream.

тарбаган *m.* (mam.) marmot; **—чик** *m.* (mam.) jerboa.

таргол *m.* targol (antiknock compound).

тардин *m.* tardin.

тарел/ка *f.* plate, tray, disk; **коэффициент полезного действия —ки** plate efficiency; **теоретическая т.** theoretical plate; **—очка** *dim. of* **тарелка;** flare, flange; **—очный** *a. of* **тарелка; —очный процесс** plate process; **—очная колонна** (petrol.) bubble tower.

тарельчат/ый *a.* plate(-like), disk, tray, pan; scallop (squash); **т. клапан** disk valve; **т. питатель** (revolving) feed table; **—ая колонна** plate column; **—ая колпачковая колонна** bubble tower; **—ая печь** revolving hearth.

тарзальный *a.* (anat., zool.) tarsal.

тарзо— *prefix* (anat.) tarso— (edge of eyelid; instep of foot); **—глазничный** *a.* tarso-orbital; **—тибиальный** *a.* tarsotibial.

тариров/ание *n.* taring, etc., see *v.*; calibration (test); substitution; **—ать** *v.* tare; calibrate, gage; rate; **—ка** *f.*, **—очный** *a.* taring, etc., see *v.*

тариф *m.* tariff, rate(s), charge(s); **основного —a** base-rate (district); **—икационный** *a.*, **—икация** *f.* rating, charging; **—ицировать** *v.* levy a tariff; fix a rate; charge; **—но-квалификационный** *a.* job evaluation;

—ный *a. of* тариф; —ная сетка tariff table; wage scale.

тарконовая кислота tarconic acid.

тармакадам *m.* tar-macadam road.

тарн/ый *a. of* тара; —ое хозяйство packaging service.

таро-крахмал *m.* taro starch.

тарпан *m.* tarpan, Mongolian wild horse, Przewalski's horse.

тарпон *m.* (ichth.) tarpon (*Megalops*); —овые *pl.* Megalopidae.

тарпун *see* тарпон.

тарс— *see* тарз—.

тарсус *m.* (anat.) tarsus.

тартальный *a.* bailing.

тартан *m.* (text.) tartan.

тарт/ание *n.* bailing; —ать *v.* bail (out).

тартр/азин *m.* tartrazine (dye); —аминовая кислота tartramic acid; —ат *m.* tartrate; —иметр *m.* tartrimeter; —онил *m.* tartronyl; —онилмочевина *f.* tartronyl urea; —оновая кислота tartronic acid.

тартуский *a.* (geog.) Tartu.

тартыши *pl.* (ice) growler.

тархониловый спирт tarchonyl alcohol.

тархун *m.* (bot.) tarragon.

тары *pl. of* тар; *gen., pl., etc., of* тара.

тарын *m.* (geol.) ice sill, ice step.

таск/ание *n.* dragging, etc., *see v.*; —ать *v.* drag, draw, tug, pull.

таскыл *m.* taskyl (rounded summit covered with placers).

Тасмания (geog.) Tasmania; тасманово море Tasman Sea.

тасов/ать *v.* shuffle (cards); randomize; —ка *f.* shuffling; randomization.

тат. *abbr.* (татарский); тат— *prefix* Ta(r)tar.

татар/ка *f.* Welsh onion (*Allium fistulosum*); —ник *m.* cotton thistle (*Onopordon*); —ский *a.* Tartar.

Татреспублика the Tartar Autonomous Socialist Soviet Republic.

татуировать *v.* tattoo.

тауберовый *a.* (math.) Tauberian.

таувина *f.* (ichth.) grouper (*Epinephelus tauvina*).

тауерная цепь pull chain.

тауи *m.* (orn.) towhee (*Pipilo*).

таунсендовский *a.* Townsend.

таур/ил *m.* tauryl; —иловая кислота taurylic acid; —ин *m.* taurine, aminoethylsulfonic acid; —окарбаминовая кислота taurocarbamic acid.

таурохол/ат *m.* taurocholate; —евая кислота taurocholic acid; —евокислая соль taurocholate.

тау-сагыз *m.* (bot.) tau-saghyz (*Scorzonera tausaghyz*) (rubber-bearing plant).

таутан *m.* (ichth.) perch.

тауто— *prefix* tauto— (the same).

таутомер *m.* tautomer; —изация *f.* tautomerization; —из(ир)овать *v.* tautomerize; —ия *f.* tautomerism, dynamic isomerism; —ный *a.* tautomeric.

таутомочевина *f.* tautourea.

таутохрон/а *f.* (math.) tautochrone; —изм *m.*, —ность *f.* tautochronism; —ный *a.* tautochronous.

ТАФ *abbr.* (триаммонийфосфат) triammonium phosphate.

тафа *f.* (mam.) marsupial mice (*Phascogale*).

тафелевский *a.* (chem.) Tafel.

тафо— *prefix* taphe—, tapho— (grave, burial); —номия *f.* (pal.) taphonomy.

тафро— *prefix* taphri—, taphro— (ditch, trench); —геналь *f.* (geol.) taphrogen; —генический *a.* taphrogenic; —геосинклиналь *f.* taphrogeosyncline.

тафт/а *f.*, —яной *a.* (text.) tafetta.

тахеометр *see* тахиметр; —ическая съёмка, —ия *f.* (surv.) tacheometry.

тахи— *prefix* tachy— (swift, quick); —генез *m.* (zool.) tachygenesis; —кардия *f.* (med.) tachycardia.

тахиметр *m.* (surv.) tachymeter; —ический *a.* tachymetric; —ия *f.* tachymetry.

тахинин *m.* tachinin.

тахины *pl.* tachina flies (*Larvaevoridae*).

тахипноэ *n.* (med.) tachypnea.

тахистерин *m.* tachysterol.

тахистоскоп *m.* tachistoscope.

тахителический *a.* (biol.) tachytelic.

тахо— *prefix* tacho— (quick, swift); —генератор *m.* tachogenerator, tachometer generator; —генератор переменного тока tachometric alternator; —граф *m.* tachograph, recording tachometer; -интегрирующий *a.* rate-integrating; —метр *m.* tachometer; —метрия *f.* tachometry.

тач/алка *f.* (books) stitcher; —альный *a.*, —ание *n.* stitching; —аный *a.* stitched; —ать *v.* stitch.

тачёк *m.* (ichth.) Black Sea shad.

тач/ечный *a.* wheelbarrow; —ка *f.* wheelbarrow; dolly; stitching; —ной *a.* stitching.

ташка *f.* (mil.) shoulder bag.

ташкентский *a.* (geog.) Tashkent.

тащить *v.* carry (along), drag along, lug, haul, pull, tow, pilfer; —ся *v.* drag along, lag (behind), crawl, creep, plod.

та/ющий *a.*, —яние *n.* thawing, melting; температура —яния melting point; —ять *v.* thaw, melt.

тбилисский *a.* (geog.) Tbilisi.

ТБФ *abbr.* (трибутилфосфат) tributyl phosphate.

тв. *abbr.* (твёрдость; твёрдый).

ТВ *abbr.* (тяжеловодный) heavy-water.

тваддевский *a.* Twaddle (hydrometer).

тваймановский *a.* Twyman (interferometer).

твд *abbr.* (телевидение) television.

твёрд *sh. m. of* твёрдый.

тверде/ние *n.* hardening, solidification, etc., *see v.*; —ние при старении age hardening; —ть *v.* harden, solidify, congeal, set; cure, mature (of concrete); toughen; cake.

твердить *v.* reiterate; т. наизусть *v.* memorize.

твердо— *prefix* scler(o)— (hard).

твёрдо *adv.* firmly, steadfastly; consistently; thoroughly, well; т. стоять на своём *v.* be firm in one's decision.

твердо/вины *pl.* metallic inclusions; —кожие *n.* (med.) scleroderma; —копчёный *a.* thoroughly smoked (food).

твердомер *m.* hardness gage, durometer.

твердопенистый *a.* solid-foam(ed).

твердоплавк/ий *a.* fusible with difficulty, infusible; —ость *f.* infusibility.

твердосплавный *a.* hard-alloy.

твердоплодный *a.* (bot.) sclerocarpous.

твердостекловатый *a.* durovitreous.

твёрдост/ь *f.* hardness, toughness; solidity, rigidity, stiffness, steadiness, firmness, constancy, consistency; resolution, fixedness; т. по Бринелю Brinell hardness; показатель —и hardness number; средней —и medium hard; шкала —и hardness scale, Mohs scale.

твердо/тельный *a.* solid-state; —топливный *a.* solid-propellant (missile); —тянутый *a.* (met.) hard-drawn; —фазный *a.* solid-phase.

твёрд/ый *a.* hard, tough, sclerous, firm, solid, rigid; stable, resolute, constant, steady, consistent; sediment (discharge); hard and fast (rule); fixed (price); т. раст-

вор solid solution; —**ая масса** concretion; —**ая оболочка** (anat.) dura mater; —**ая схема** (electron.) (solid-state) integrated circuit; —**ое состояние** solid state, solidity; **на** —**ых схемах** solid-state; **переводить в** —**ое состояние** v. solidify; —**ое тело** solid; **физика** —**ого тела** solid-state physics; —**ые примеси** particulate matter.

твёрже comp. of **твёрдый**.

тверженный a. repeated.

твин m. a serge-like fabric.

твиндек m. (naut.) 'tweendecks.

твиновый a. of **твин**.

твистор m. (comp.) twistor.

ТВО abbr. (**тепловлажностная обработка**) steam curing, hot-water curing (of concrete).

т. возг. abbr. (**температура возгонки**) sublimation temperature.

твор/ение n. creation; slaking (of lime); —**ён(н)ый** a. slaked; —**ец** m. creator, author; —**ило** n. lime pit, lime vat; opening, manhole; —**ильный** a. slaking.

творить v. create, make, do, shape, produce; slake (lime); —**ся** v. be created, be made, be done; happen; be slaked.

творо/г m. curds; cottage cheese, pot cheese; —**жистый** a. curdled, clotted; caseous; —**жить(ся)** v. curdle, clot, coagulate; —**жный** a. curdy, curdled, coagulated; caseous; pot cheese, cottage cheese.

творчес/кий a. creative; —**тво** n. creative power, creative genius.

т. воспл. abbr. (**точка воспламенения**) ignition point.

ТВР abbr. (**тяжеловодный реактор**) heavy-water reactor.

Твт abbr. (**тераватт**) (elec.) terawatt.

ТВЧ, т.в.ч. abbr. (**ток высокой частоты**) high-frequency current.

т.г. abbr. (**текущего года**) of the current year.

т.д. abbr. (**так далее**) so forth.

те pl. of **то(т), та** those.

т.е. abbr. (**то-есть**) that is.

теаза f. thease.

теамин m. Theamin, theophylline ethanolamine.

театр m. theater.

теб/аин m. thebaine.

тебен/евать v. pasture over the winter; —**ёвка** f., —**ёвочный** a. winter grazing.

теб/енол m. (chem.) thebenol; —**енон** thebenone; —**омолочная кислота** thebolactic acid.

Тевенина теорема (elec.) Thévenin's theorem.

теве/резин m. theveresin; —**тин** m. thevetin.

тевяк m. (mam.) gray seal (*Halichoerus grypus*).

тег m., —**овый** a. (comp.) tag; **разряд** —**а**, —**овый разряд** tag bit.

тегмен m. (biol.) tegmen; —**тальный** a. tegmental.

тегогликол m. tegoglycol.

тегула f. (ent.) tegula.

теел/ин m. theelin, estrone.

тезаур(изм)оз m. (med.) thesaur(ism)osis, storage disease.

тезаурус m. thesaurus.

тезин m. thesine.

тезис m. thesis; summary; position.

теин m. theine; —**изм** m. (med.) theaism.

Тейзена аппарат Theisen cleaner.

тейкрин m. teucrin.

тейлери/оз m. (vet.) theileriasis; —**я** f. (prot.) Theileria.

тейлоровый a. Taylor's.

тейхоевая кислота, тейхоиновая кислота (biochem.) teichoic acid.

тёк past m. sing. of **течь**.

тека f. (biol.) theca; suffix —theca, receptacle; library, archives, collection; —**клеточный** a. (med.) theca cell.

текл/а f., —**и** pl., —**о** n. past tense of **течь**.

текодин m. (pharm.) thecodine.

теко/донтный a. (biol.) thecodont; —**идеи** pl. (pal.) Edrioasteroidea; —**ма** f. (med.) thecoma.

текомин m. tecomin, lapachol.

текостегноз m. (physiol.) thecostegnosis.

текс m. tex (unit of fiber weight).

тексроп m., —**ный** a. texrope, V-belt.

текст m. text, reading matter; wording, copy; **обработка** —**ов** word processing.

текстиль m., —**ный** a. textile, fabric; —**ные изделия** textiles; —**щик** m. textile worker.

текстовинит m. a leather substitute.

текстов/ка f. caption; —**ой** a. (in the) text, textual; —**ый процессор** word processor.

текстолит m., —**овый** a. textolite (resin-impregnated fabric laminate).

текстообработка f. word processing.

текстуальный a. textual.

текстур/а texture, grain; (geol.) texture, fabric, structure; —**диаграмма** f. X-ray fiber pattern; —**ный** a. textural; —**ованный** a. textured; grain-oriented; —**овочный** a. texturing.

тектиты pl. (petr.) tektites.

текто— prefix tecto— (roof; builder); —**генез** m. tectogenesis.

тектон/ика f. tectonics; structural geology; —**ический** a. tectonic, structural; (med.) plastic.

тектоспондиловый a. (anat.) tectospondylous.

тектохинон m. tectoquinone.

тектум m. (anat.) tectum.

текут pr. 3 pl. of **течь**.

текучест/ь f. flow, fluidity, liquid state; viscosity, consistency; yield (of metal); turnover (of labor); **предел** —**и** (mech.) yield stress; (met.) yield limit, creep limit; (petrol.) yield point; **степень** —**и** consistency; **температура начала** —**и** pour point.

текуч/ий a. flowing, fluid; running (water); fluctuating, unstable; **легко т.** (very) liquid; **трудно т.** thick, viscous.

текущ/ий a. flowing, streaming, running, leaking, leaky; current, present; (math.) instantaneous (value); routine, day-to-day; (comp.) active (job); default (drive); **т. ремонт** maintenance; —**ее значение** actual value.

тёкший past act. part. of **течь**.

тел gen. pl. of **тело**; —**а** gen., pl. of **тело**; corpora.

телальгия f. (med.) telalgia, referred pain.

телам dat. pl. of **тело**.

теле— prefix tele— (operating at a distance; remote); —**автоматика** f. (elec.) automatic remote control; —**автоматический** a. telecontrol (system); —**амперметр** m. teleammeter; —**башня** f. television (broadcast) tower; —**вещание** n. television broadcasting.

телеви/дение n. television; **т. с высокой резкостью** high-definition television, HDTV; **кабельное т.** cable television; **передавать по** —**дению** n. televise; —**зионно-управляемый** a. television-controlled; —**зионный** a., —**зия** f. television, video; —**зор** m., —**зорный** a. television set.

телега f. cart, wagon.

телегониометр m. telegoniometer, direction finder.

телегония f. (gen.) telegony.

телеграмма f. telegram, wire, cable, dispatch; **шифрованная т.** cryptogram.

телеграф *m.* telegraph; telegraph office; **—ирование** *n.* telegraphing, telegraphy; **—ировать** *v.* telegraph, wire, cable; **—ист** *m.* telegraph operator; **—ить** *see* **телеграфировать; —ия** *f.* telegraphy; **—но-модулированный** *a.* telegraph-modulated; **—ный** *a.* telegraph(ic).

теледатчик *m.* remote pickup.

телединамометрирование *n.* teledynamometry.

теледу *m.* (mam.) hog badger (*Arctonyx collaris*).

тележ/ечный *a. of* **тележка;** (rr.) truck; **—ка** *f.* hand cart, truck, trolley, car; (mach.) carriage; dolly; (rr.) truck, bogie; (robotics) vehicle; **—ка-грузовик** *f.* truck; **—ка-медведка** *f.* trundle; **—ник** *m.* carter; material(s) handler; **—ный** *a. of* **тележка.**

теле/зритель *m.* televiewer; **—измерение** *n.*, **—измерительный** *a.* telemetering, remote measuring; **—индикатор** *m.* teleindicator.

телейто— *prefix* teleuto— (completion, final); **—кучка** *f.*, **—сорус** *m.* (phyt.) teleutosorus; **—спора** *f.* (bot.) teleutospore.

теле/камера *f.* television camera; **—конференция** *f.* teleconference; **—кино** *n.* televised movies.

телекия *f.* (bot.) oxeye (*Buphthalmum*).

теле/ключатель *m.* remote (control) switch; **—командование** *n.* televised instruction(s); **—контроль** *m.* telecontrol, remote control.

телекс *m.*, **—ный** *a.* telex (message).

телеметеор *m.* (astr.) telescopic meteor.

телеметр *m.* telemeter; **—ирование** *n.*, **—ический** *a.* telemetry; **—ия** *f.* telemetry, telemetering, remote measuring.

телемехан/изация *f.* tele-automation; **—ика** *f.* telemechanics, remote control; **—ический** *a.* telemechanical, remote control.

теле/мотор *m.* telemotor, remote-controlled electric motor; **—набор** *m.*, **—наборный** *a.* teletypesetting.

телёнок *m.* (zool.) calf; **т.-молозивник** *m.* colostrum-fed calf; **т.-молочник, т.-сосун** *m.* unweaned calf.

теленом, —ус *m.* (ent.) Telenomus.

телеобработка *f.* remote processing.

телеологический *a.* (biol.) teleological.

теле/объектив *m.* telephoto lens; **—патия** *f.* telepathy; **—передатчик** *m.* television transmitter; **—передача** *f.* television program, telecast; **—пирометр** *m.* telepyrometer; **—приёмник** *m.* television set; **—психрометр** *m.* telepsychrometer.

теле/регулирование *n.* remote control; **—регулируемый** *a.* remote-controlled; **—рецептор** *m.* telereceptor; **—робототехника** *f.* telerobotics; **—связь** *f.* telecommunication; **—сигнализация** *f.* remote signaling.

телескоп *m.*, **—ировать** *v.* telescope; **—ический** *a.* telescopic; **—ия** *f.* telescopy; **—ный** *a.* telescope, telescopic; **т.-рефрактор** *m.* refracting telescope.

телесный *a.* corporal, bodily; flesh (color); solid, material; solid (angle); (zool.) somatic.

теле/тайп *m.* teletype; teleprinter; **—тайпсеттер** *m.* teletypesetter; **—термометр** *m.* telethermometer; **—управление** *n.* remote control; **—управляемый** *a.* remote-controlled, telecontrolled; drone, pilotless (aircraft); guided (missile); **—факс** *m.* (tele)fax.

телефон *m.* telephone; **т.-автомат** *m.* pay (tele)phone; **—изировать** *v.* establish telephone communication; **—ирование** *n.* telephoning; telephony; **—ировать** *v.* telephone, call; **—ист** *m.*, **—истка** *f.* telephone operator; **—ить** *see* **телефонировать; —ия** *f.* telephony; **—ный** *a.*, **—ный аппарат** telephone; **—ограмма** *f.* telephone message.

телефот *m.* telephote (remote image transmitter); **—огра-**

фический *a.* telephoto(graphic); **—ография** *f.* telephotography; telephotograph; **—ометр** *m.* telephotometer; **—ометрия** *f.* telephotometry.

телец *m.* (zool.) calf; *gen. pl. of* **тельце;** (ichth.) Volga zander.

телецентр *m.* television station.

тели— *prefix* thely— (female); **—бласт** *m.* thelyblast, female pronucleus.

тели/й *m.* (phyt.) teleutosorus; **—о—** *see* **телейто—.**

тели/н *see* **теелин; —т** *m.* (med.) thelitis; **—токия** *f.* (gen.) thelyotoky.

телиться *v.* calve.

телифон *m.* whip scorpion (*Thelyphonus*).

телка *gen. of* **телок.**

тёлка *f.* heifer.

теллур *m.* tellurium, Te; **(дву)хлористый т.** tellurium dichloride; tellurous chloride; **сернистый т.** tellurium sulfide; **хлорный т., четырёххлористый т.** telluric chloride, tellurium tetrachloride.

теллур/ат *m.* tellurate; **—ид** *m.* telluride; **—ий** *m.* tellurium; (astr.) tellurian; **—ил** *m.* telluryl; **—иновая кислота** tellurinic acid.

теллуристо/кислый *a.* tellurous acid; tellurite (of).

теллурист/ый *a.* tellurous, tellurium, telluriferous; telluride (of); **т. ангидрид** tellurous anhydride, tellurium dioxide; **т. водород** hydrogen telluride; **—ая кислота** tellurous acid; **соль —ой кислоты** tellurite.

теллурит *m.* (chem.; min.) tellurite.

теллурический *a.* telluric, earth.

теллуро— *prefix* telluro—.

теллуроводород *m.* hydrogen telluride; **—ный** *a.* hydrotelluride (of); telluride (of); **—ная кислота** hydrotelluric acid; **соль —ной кислоты** telluride.

теллурово/кислый *a.* telluric acid; tellurate (of).

теллуров/ый *a.* telluric, tellurium; **т. ангидрид** telluric anhydride, tellurium trioxide; **—ая кислота** telluric acid; **соль —ой кислоты** tellurate.

теллуро/ний *m.* telluronium; **—новая кислота** telluronic acid; **—рганический** *a.* organotellurium; **—синеродистая кислота** tellurocyanic acid; **—углерод** *m.* carbon telluride; **—фенол** *m.* tellurophenol.

тел/о *n.* body, corpus, soma, solid, substance, matter; (working) fluid; (filter) bed; shaft, shank (of tool); belly (of muscle); housing; core, center (of roll, axle); (math.) field (of sets); **гормон жёлтого —а** progesteron; **жёлтое т.** (anat.) corpus luteum; **жидкое т.** liquid; **простое т.** element; **сложное т.** compound; **твёрдое т.** solid.

тело— *prefix* body; telo— (end, terminal; far); **—ген** *m.* telogen.

тело/движение *n.* exercise, motion; **—дендрий** *m.* (anat.) telodendron.

телок *m.* bull calf.

телол *see* **теелол.**

телолецитальный *a.* (zool.) telolecithal (egg).

телом *m.* (bot.) telome.

теломер *m.* (gen.) telomere; **—изация** *f.* telomerization.

телосложение *n.* build, constitution, physique, habitus.

телоспоридии *pl.* (zool.) Telosporidia.

телофаз/а *f.*, **—ный** *a.* (biol.) telophase.

телофоровая кислота thelophoric acid.

телофрагма *f.* (cyt.) telophragma, Z band.

тельный *a.* body; flesh-colored.

тельсон *m.* (zool.) telson.

тельфаировая кислота telfairic acid.

тельфер *m.* (transportation) telpher, hoist; **—аж** *m.* telpherage.

тельце *n.* corpuscle; body; (fat) globule; **кровяное т.**

blood cell, hemocyte; **направительное т., полярное т.** polar body.

телязиоз *m.* (vet.) telasiosis.

теля/та *pl.* calves; **—тина** *f.* veal; **—тник** *m.* calf pen; calf attendant; **—чий** *a.* calf; veal.

тем *instr. of* **то(т)**; *dat. of* **те**; *adv.* so much the; **т. более, что** the more so (especially) as; **т. лучше** so much the better, all the better; **т. не менее** nevertheless, none the less, in spite of that; **т. самым** thereby, thus; **с т., чтобы** (in order) to; on condition that, provided that.

тема *f.* theme, subject, topic; **—тика** *f.* content(s), subject matter, subject (field); **—тический** *a.* thematic, subject, topical, devoted to a specific topic; **—тический план** syllabus.

тембр *m.*, **—овый** *a.* timbre, tone quality.

тёмен *sh. m. of* **тёмный.**

темен/и *gen. of* **темя**; **—но-затылочный** *a.* (anat.) parietooccipital; **—ной** *a.* (anat.) parietal; sincipital; **—ная кость** parietal bone.

темень *see* **темнота.**

Темза the Thames.

теми *instr. of* **те.**

темляк *m.* loop, strap.

темн/а *sh. f. of* **тёмный**; **—ее** *comp. of* **тёмный, темно,** darker; **—еть** *v.* darken, grow dark; **—еющий** *a.* darkening, turning black.

темнит/ель *m.* dimmer; **—ь** *v.* dim, darken.

темно *adv.* darkly, obscurely; it is dark.

темно—, тёмно— *prefix* dark-, scoto—.

тёмно-багровый *a.* dark purple.

темно/ватый *a.* darkish, rather dark, rather obscure; **—вой** *a.* (phys.) dark (current, etc.); **—волосый** *a.* dark-haired.

тёмно-жёлтый *a.* dark yellow.

темно/зобый *a.* (orn.) dark-throated; **—калильный** *a.* black-hot.

тёмно-красный *a.* dark red.

темно/окрашенный *a.* dark-colored; **—польный** *a.* dark-field (microscopy, etc.).

тёмно-русый *a.* chestnut (colored).

темно/споровый *a.* (bot.) phaeosporous; **—та** *f.* darkness), obscurity; **—хвойный** *a.* dark coniferous, boreal (forest); **—цветный** *a.* dark-colored.

тёмн/ый *a.* dark, dingy, dim, indistinct; obscure, vague (meaning); deep (color); non-luminous (flame); silent (discharge); ignorant; shady, disreputable; **—ая вода** (med.) amaurosis; **—ая комната** (phot.) darkroom; **—ая теплота** obscure heat; **—ое пятно** (astr.) nebula.

темп *m.* tempo, time; rate, frequency; (mil.) momentum (of attack); (mil.) (fire) interval.

темп. абс. *abbr.* (**температура абсолютная**) absolute temperature; **темп. возг.** *abbr.* (**температура возгонки**) sublimation temperature; **темп. воспл.** *abbr.* (**температура воспламенения**) ignition point; **темп. всп.** *abbr.* (**температура вспышки**) flash point.

темпера *f.* tempera (color).

темперамент *m.* temperament.

температур/а *f.* temperature; (boiling; flash; melting) point; **падение —ы, перепад —ы** temperature drop; **предел —ы** temperature limit; **пределы —ы** temperature range; **при высокой —е** high-temperature (process).

температурный *a.* temperature, heat, thermal; **т. интервал** temperature range; **т. режим** temperature schedule; **т. шов** heat crack, expansion joint.

температуропроводность *f.* thermal diffusivity.

температуро/стойкий *a.* heat-resistant, heatproof; **—стойкость** *f.* temperature stability; **—устойчивость** *see* **температуростойкость.**

темперирование *n.* tempering.

темп. зам. *abbr.* (**температура замерзания**) freezing point; **темп. заст.** *abbr.* (**температура застывания**) solidification point.

темпирование *n.* timing (of bomb).

темп. исп. *abbr.* (**температура испарения**) evaporation temperature; **темп. кип.** *abbr.* (**температура кипения**) boiling point; **темп. конд.** *abbr.* (**температура конденсации**) dew point; **темп. крит.** *abbr.* (**критическая температура**) critical temperature.

темплет *m.* template, pattern.

темповый *a. of* **темп.**

темпоральный *a.* temporal.

темп. отв. *abbr.* (**температура отвердения**) solidification temperature; **темп. пл.** *abbr.* (**температура плавления**) melting point.

темп-ра *abbr.* (**температура**).

темп. разл. *abbr.* (**температура разложения**) decomposition temperature; **темп. размягч.** *abbr.* (**температура размягчения**) softening point; **темп. стекл.** *abbr.* (**температура стеклования**) glass transition temperature.

темь *f.* darkness.

темя *n.* (anat.) sinciput; crown (of head); vertex.

тенакуль *m.* (med.; biol.) tenaculum.

теналгия *f.* (med.) tenalgia.

тенар *m.* (anat.) thenar.

тенарова синь Thenard's (cobalt) blue.

тендем *see* **тандем.**

тенденц/иозность *see* **тенденция**; tendentiousness; **—иозный** *a.* tending, conducive; intentional, with a purpose; tendentious; **—ия** *f.* tendency, trend; **иметь —ию, выявить —ию, проявлять —ию** *v.* tend (to), be prone (to), be inclined (to).

тендер *m.*, **—ный** *a.* (rr.; naut.) tender; cutter.

тенд/инит *m.* (med.) tendinitis; **—овагинит** *m.* (med.) tendovaginitis, tenosynovitis.

тене— *prefix* sciado— (shade); scoto— (darkness).

тенев/ой *a.* shadow; shaded, shady; schlieren (photograph); **—ая защита** (nucl.) shadow shielding.

теневынослив/ость *f.* (bot.) tolerance of shade; **—ый** *a.* shade-tolerant.

тенезм *m.* (med.) tenesmus, straining.

теней *gen. pl. of* **тень.**

тенелюбивый *a.* (bot.) shade-loving, sciophilous.

тенерес *m.* lead trinitroresorcinate.

тенёта *pl.* net, snare, trap.

тензи/метр *m.* tensimeter (for vapor pressure); **—метрия** *f.* tensimetry; **—ометр** *m.* tensiometer (for surface tension).

тензо/датчик, —метр *m.* strain gage, tensometer; **—метр сопротивления** resistor element; **—метрический** *a.* strain-measuring, strain-gage; **—метрия** *f.* strain measurement; **—р** *m.*, **—рный** *a.* tensor; **—чувствительность** *f.*, **—эффект** *m.* strain sensitivity; **—чувствительный** *a.* strain-sensitive.

тени *gen., pl., etc., of* **тень.**

тени/аринхоз *m.* (med.) Taeniarhynchus infestation; **—аринхус** *m.* beef tapeworm (*Taeniarhynchus*); **—иды** *pl.* tapeworms (*Taeniidae*).

тениловый спирт thenyl alcohol, thiophenecarbinol.

тенистый *a.* shady, shaded, shadowy; (bot.) umbrosous.

теннесьян *m.* (geol.) Tennessean system.

тено— *prefix* teno— (tendon); **—нит** *m.* (med.) tenonitis; **—ново пространство** (anat.) Tenon's space.

тенор *m.*, **—овый** *a.* (music) tenor.

тенотомия *f.* (med.) tenotomy.

тенрек/и, —овые *pl.* (mam.) Tenrecs, Madagascar "hedgehogs" (*Tenrecidae*).

тенсид *m.* surfactant.

тенсиметр *m.* tensimeter, vapor pressure gage.

тент *m.* awning, canopy; canvas, tarpaulin.

тенторий *m.* (anat.) tentorium.

тень *f.* shade, shadow; (astr.) umbra.

теоброми/ин *m.* theobromine; **—овая кислота** theobromic acid.

теодолит *m.* (surv.) theodolite, transit; **—ный** *a.* theodolite, theodolitic.

теор. *abbr.* (**теоретически**).

теорема *f.* theorem; **обратная т.** converse of a theorem.

теорет/изировать *v.* theorize; **—ик** *m.* theorist; **—ически-вероятностный** *a.* (math.) probabilistic; **—ически** *adv.* theoretically; **—ический, —ичный** *a.* theoretical; **на —ических основаниях** on theoretical grounds, theoretically.

теор/ия *f.*, **т. работы** theory; **выход 85% —ии** the yield is 85% of the theoretical.

теофиллин *m.* theophylline, 1,3-dimethylxanthine.

тёпел *sh. m. of* **тёплый.**

теперешн/ий *a.* present, contemporary, actual; **—ие времена** the present.

теперь *adv.* now, at present; **т. же** at once; **т., когда** now that; **т. о** now for.

тёпленький *a.* tepid.

тепл/еть *v.* get warm, grow warm; **—ить** *v.* warm up, make warm; **—иться** *v.* burn low; gleam, shine; **—ица** *f.*, **—ичный** *a.* hothouse, greenhouse.

тепл/о *n.* heat; *adv.* warm(ly); it is warm; *sh. n. of* **тёплый;** **обмен —а** heat exchange; **отвод —а** cooling.

тепло— *prefix* heat, thermal, thermo—; **—аккумулирующий** *a.* heat-retaining, heat-storage; **—бетон** *m.* thermoconcrete; **—вато** *adv.* tepidly; it is rather warm; **—ватость** *f.* tepidity; **—ватый** *a.* tepid, lukewarm; **—видение** *n.* thermal imaging; **—влагообмен** *m.* heat and moisture exchange; **—водный** *a.* warm-water; (bot.) thermal; **—воз** *m.* (гг.) diesel engine; **—возный** *a.* diesel(-engine).

теплов/ой *a.* heat, thermal, thermic, caloric; **т. поглотитель** heat sink; **т. удар** (med.) heat stroke, thermoplegia; (met.) thermal shock; **т. эквивалент** heat equivalent, calorific value; **т. эффект** heat effect, Joule effect; **т. эффект сгорания** heat of combustion, heat value; **—ая единица** heat unit, thermal unit; **—ая оболочка** heating jacket, steam jacket; **—ая обработка** heat treatment; **—ая станция** thermal power plant; **—ое значение** heat value; **—ое напряжение** thermal stress; **удельный т. поток** heat transfer rate.

тепловоспри/нимающий *a.* heat-absorbing; **—ятие** *n.* heat absorption.

тепловыдел/ение *n.* heat release, heat liberation, evolution of heat; **—яющий** *a.* heat-liberating, heat-generating; (nucl.) fuel (element).

теплогашение *n.* thermoquenching.

теплоёмкость *f.* heat capacity, thermal capacity; **удельная т.** specific heat.

тепло/зависимое сопротивление thermally sensitive resistor, thermistor; **—защита** *f.* heat shield(ing); thermal insulation; **—защитный** *a.* heat-shielding, heat-reflecting; heat (shield); **—звукоизоляционный** *a.* heat-insulating and soundproofing.

теплоизлуч/ающий *a.* heat-radiating; **—ение** *n.* heat radiation.

теплоизол/ирующий, —яционный *a.* heat-insulating, heat-insulation; **—ятор** *m.* heat insulator; **—яция** *f.* heat insulation, thermal insulation.

теплоиспользован/ие *n.* heat utilization; heat consumption; **коэффициент полезного —ия** utilization factor.

теплокровный *a.* (zool.) warm-blooded, homoiothermal.

тепло/лечение *n.* heat therapy; **—любивый** *a.* (biol.) heat-loving; thermophilous.

тепломер *m.* thermometer; calorimeter; heat meter; **—ный** *a.* thermometric; calorimetric.

тепло/накопление *n.* heat build-up; **—напряжение** *n.* heat-release rate; thermal stress; **—напряжённость** *f.* thermal stress; calorific intensity; heat flux density; **—непроницаемый** *a.* heatproof, impervious to heat, athermanous; insulating; **—носитель** *m.* heat carrier, heat-transfer agent; cooling agent, coolant; **—носитель-замедлитель** *m.* coolant-moderator.

теплообмен *m.* heat exchange; heat transfer; **—ник** *m.*, **—ный аппарат** heat exchanger; **—ник-подогреватель** *m.* exchanger-preheater.

теплооборот *m.* thermal economy.

теплообраз/ование *n.* heat production, thermogenesis; heat build-up; **—ователь** *m.* heat producer, heat generator; **—ующий** *a.* heat-producing, heat-generating, thermogenetic, heat-forming.

тепло/отбор *m.* heat take-off; **—отвод** *m.* heat removal, heat dissipation; cooling; **—отводящий** *a.* heat removing, heat-transmitting; cooling; **—отдача** *f.* heat emission; heat transfer; heat exchange; **—отдающий** *a.* heat-liberating, exothermic.

теплопеленгатор *m.* infrared radar; **—ный** *a.* infrared direction-finding.

теплоперед/атчик *m.* heat transmitter; heat-transfer agent; **—ача** *f.* heat transfer; **—ающий** *a.* heat-transfer, heat-transmitting.

теплопере/нос *m.* heat transport; **—пад** *m.* temperature drop; thermal head; **—ход** *m.* heat transfer.

теплопогло/титель *m.* heat absorber; **—тительный, —щательный, —щающий** *a.* heat-absorbing; **—щение** *n.* heat absorption.

теплоподвод *m.* heat supply, heat input.

тепло/поступление *n.* heat input; **—потеря** *f.* heat loss; **—потребляющий** *a.* heat-consuming.

теплопри/ток *m.* heat influx; heat gain; **—ход** *m.* heat input, heat supply.

теплопровод *m.* steam or hot water pipe; heat conductor; **—имость, —ность** *f.* heat conduction, heat transfer; thermal conductivity; **коэффициент —ности** (coefficient of) thermal conductivity; **—ник** *m.* heat conductor; **—ный, —ящий** *a.* heat-conducting, heat-conveying, heat-carrying; diathermic, diathermal, diathermanous; **—ная способность** heat conductivity.

теплопрозрачн/ость *f.* diathermancy; **—ый** *a.* diathermanous, diathermic.

теплопроизвод/ительность *f.* heat value, calorific value, heating efficiency, heat output; **—ящий** *a.* heat-producing, heat-generating.

теплопроницаемость *f.* diathermancy.

тепло/прочный *a.* heat-resistant, refractory; **—регулирующий** *a.* heat-regulating.

теплород *m.* caloric; thermogen; **—ный** *a.* caloric, calorific, thermal.

теплосиловой цикл thermodynamic power cycle.

тепло/смена *f.* thermal cycling; (direct) heat exchange; **—снабжение** *n.* heat supply; **—содержание** *n.* heat content, enthalpy; **—старение** *n.* heat aging.

теплостойк/ий *a.* heatproof, heat-resistant, thermostable; **—ость** *f.* resistance to heat, thermostability.

теплосъём *m.* heat removal, heat extraction; output (of nuclear reactor).

теплот/а *f.* heat, warmth; **единица —ы** heat unit, thermal unit, therm; **удельная т.** specific heat.

теплотворн/ость *f.*, **—ая способность** calorific value, heat value, heating capacity, efficiency (of fuel); **—ый** *a.* calorific, heat-producing.

теплотехник *m.* heat engineer; **т.-печник** *m.* furnace engineer; **—а** *f.* heat technology; heat engineering.

теплотехнический *a.* heat-engineering; power-engineering.

теплоусвоение *n.* heat assimilation.

теплоустойчив/ость *f.* thermal stability; heat retention (of building); **—ый** *see* **теплостойкий.**

теплофизический *a.* thermal (properties).

теплофи/кационный *a.*, **—кация** *f.* district heating, central heating; **—цированный** *a.* centrally heated; **—цировать** *v.* (supply with) heat.

тепло/ход *m.*, **—ходный** *a.* motor boat, diesel boat; producer-gas-powered vessel; **—централь** *f.* central heating plant; **отопление от —централи** district heating; **—чувствительный** *a.* heat-sensitive.

теплоэлектро/генераторный *a.* heat and power generating; **—централь** *f.* central heating and power plant.

теплоэнергетик *m.* thermal power engineer; **—а** *f.* thermal power; heat and power engineering.

теплушка *f.* heated building; heated freight car.

тёплый *a.* warm; thermal.

теплынь *f.* warm weather.

тепляк *m.* (construction) enclosure, housing; winter shelter.

тёр *past m. sing. of* **тереть.**

тера— *prefix* tera— (10^{12}).

тер/аконовая кислота teraconic acid; **—акриловая кислота** teracrylic acid.

терапевт *m.* therapist; **—ика** *f.* therapeutics; **—ический** *a.* therapeutic.

терапиновая кислота terapic acid.

терапия *f.* therapy, therapeutics.

терапоновые *pl.* (ichth.) tigerfishes (*Theraponidae*).

терас— *see* **террас—.**

терато— *prefix* terato— (monster); **—логия** *f.* teratology; **—ма** *f.* (med.; bot.) teratoma, abnormal growth.

терб/ий *m.*, **—иевый** *a.* terbium, Tb; **окись —ия, —иевая земля** terbium oxide, terbia; **хлористый т.** terbium chloride.

тергит *m.* (ent.) tergite.

тердесьен *m.* sienna (pigment).

тере/(б)— *prefix* tere(b)— (turpentine); **—бен** *m.* terebene; **—бентен** *m.* terebenthene; **—бентиловый** *a.* terebentylic (acid).

теребил/ка *f.* (flax) puller; **—ьный** *a.* pulling; **—ьщик** *m.* flax puller.

теребинов/ая кислота tereb(in)ic acid; **—окислая соль** terebate.

тереб/ить *v.* pull, pluck, pick; **—ление** *n.* pulling, picking.

тередо *n.* (mal.) shipworm (*Teredo*).

терескен *m.* (bot.) winterfat (*Eurotia*).

тереть *v.* rub, chafe, polish; grate, grind, shred; **—ся** *v.* rub.

терефтал/евая кислота terephthalic acid, *p*-benzenedicarboxylic acid; **—иловый спирт** terephthalyl alcohol.

тереха *f.* (ichth.) white bream.

терзать *v.* tear to pieces.

терилен *m.* Terylene (synthetic fiber).

тёрка *f.* grater; rasp; huller; (plaster) float; (art.) friction bar, scratcher; (zool.) radula.

тёрли *past pl. of* **тереть.**

терм *m.* term; therm (unit of heat).

терм/ализация *f.* thermalization; **—альгия** *f.* (med.) thermalgia; **—альный** *a.* thermal; **—альные воды** hot springs.

термика *f.* thermal conditions.

термин *m.* term; technicality; **определение —а** definition.

терминал *m.* (comp.) terminal; **—изация** *f.* (gen.) terminalization; **—ьный** *a.* terminal.

терминатор *m.* (astr.) terminator.

термин/овать *v.* term, name, designate; **—ологический** *a.* terminological, nomenclature; **—ология** *f.* terminology, nomenclature; special vocabulary; **-эквивалент** *m.* equivalent term.

термион *m.* (electron.) thermion; **—ный** *a.* thermionic.

термист *m.* heat specialist.

термистор *m.* (electron.) thermistor, thermal resistor; **т.-бусинка** *m.* bead thermistor.

термит *m.* (bombs; welding) Thermit, thermite; (ent.) termite; **—ник** *m.* termite nest; **—ный, —овый** *a. of* **термит; —офильный** *a.* (ent.) termitophilous.

термическ/ий *a.* thermic, thermal, heat; temperature-indicating; **т. глаз** (herp.) heat-sensing organ (of pit viper); **—ая единица** heat unit, thermal unit, therm; **—ая обработка** heat treatment; **—ая стойкость** thermal stability; **—ая цепь** thermoelement; **—ое расширение** heat expansion.

терм/ичность процесса characteristics of the thermal process; **—ия** *f.* thermie (unit of work and energy).

термо— *prefix* therm(o)—, heat; **—автоэлектронная эмиссия** (phys.) thermal field emission; **—активный** *a.* thermosetting (plastics); **—акцептор** *m.* thermal acceptor; **—амперметр** *m.* thermoammeter; **—анализ** *m.* thermal analysis.

термоанемометр *m.* hot-wire anemometer, thermal flowmeter; **—ический** *a.* hot-wire (method).

термо/баллон *m.* temperature sensing element; **—барокамера** *f.* altitude chamber, thermal vacuum chamber; **—барометр** *m.* thermobarometer; **—батарея** *f.* (elec.) thermopile; **—биметаллический** *a.* thermobimetallic; **—весовой** *a.* thermogravimetric; **—вулканизация** *f.* heat vulcanization; **—выделение** *n.* heat evolution; **—выключатель** *m.* thermostatic switch; thermoswitch; **—высвечивание** *n.* thermoluminescence.

термо/гальванометр *m.* (elec.) thermogalvanometer; **—генератор** *m.* thermogenerator; **—гравиметрия** *f.* thermogravimetry; **—граф** *m.* thermograph, temperature recorder; **—датчик** *m.* temperature-sensitive element; **—двигатель** *m.* thermomotor, heat engine, thermomagnetic motor; **—деление** *n.* thermofission; **—дин** *m.* thermodin, phenacetin urethane.

термодинами/ка *f.* thermodynamics; **—ческий** *a.* thermodynamic.

термо/диффузионный *a.*, **—диффузия** *f.* thermal diffusion; (moisture) migration; **—единица** *f.* thermal unit, therm; **—естезия** *f.* (physiol.) thermesthesia, temperature sense; **—зит** *m.* foamed slag, slag pumice; **—извещатель** *m.* heat detector; **—изоляционный** *a.* heat-insulating; **—изоляция** *f.* thermal insulation, heat insulation; **—индикаторный** *a.* heat-indicating.

термоион *m.* (electron.) thermion; **—изация** *f.* thermal ionization; **—ный** *a.* thermionic.

термо/каротаж *m.* (geol.) temperature logging; **—карст** *m.* (geol.) thermokarst; **—карстовый** *a.* thermokarst(ic), frost-thaw; **—катод** *m.* hot cathode, thermionic cathode.

термо/каустика *f.* (med.) thermocautery (cauterization); **—каутер** *m.* cautery (instrument); **—клейстогамия** *f.* (bot.) thermocleistogamy; **—компрессия** *f.* thermocompression (bonding); **—компрессор** *m.* thermocompressor; **—контактный крекинг** fluid coking; **—копирование** *n.* thermographic copying process;

—**лабильный** *a.* thermolabile; —**лиз** *m.* thermolysis; —**литический** *a.* thermolytic; —**люминесценция** *f.* thermoluminescence.

термомагн/етизм *m.* thermomagnetism; —**итный** *a.* thermomagnetic.

термометр *m.* thermometer; **мокрого —а, смоченного —а** wet-bulb (temperature); —**ический** *a.* thermometer, thermometric; —**ия** *f.* thermometry; —**ограф** *m.* thermometrograph, recording thermometer; **т.-праща** *m.* sling thermometer.

термо/механический *a.* thermomechanical; —**мотор** *see* **термодвигатель;** —**намагничивание** *n.* (geol.) thermomagnetization; —**натрит** *m.* (min.) thermonatrite; —**нейтральность** *f.* thermoneutrality; —**обработка** *f.* heat treatment, thermal processing; —**окислительный** *a.* (petrol.) thermooxidative (stability); —**отверждаемый** *a.* thermosetting (resin); —**отрицательный** *a.* thermonegative; —**пара** *f.* thermocouple; —**пауза** *f.* thermopause.

термопласт *m.* thermoplast, thermosoftening plastic; —**икат** *m.* thermally plasticized material; —**икация** *f.* thermal plasticization, thermal softening; —**ический** *a.* thermoplastic, thermosoftening; —**ичность** *f.* thermoplasticity.

термо/плён *m.* film material for packaging, shrink-wrap; —**полимеризация** *f.* heat polymerization; —**положительный** *a.* thermopositive; —**прен** *m.* thermoprene (rubber isomer); —**преобразователь** *m.* thermal converter; —**приёмник** *m.* temperature detector; (thermometer) bulb; —**распад** *m.* thermal degradation; —**реактивный** *a.* thermoreactive, thermohardening, thermosetting.

терморегул/ирующий *a.* thermoregulating, temperature-control; —**ятор** *m.* thermoregulator, temperature-control device, thermostat; —**яция** *f.* thermoregulation.

термо/реле *n.* thermorelay, thermal relay, temperature relay; —**рецептор** *m.* (physiol.) thermoreceptor; —**с** *m.* Thermos (bottle).

термосенсибилиз/ация *f.* thermal sensitization, heat sensitization; —**ированный** *a.* heat-sensitized.

термо/сифон *m.* thermosiphon; —**сифонный** *a.* thermosiphon, gravity-system (cooling).

термосопротивлен/ие *n.* thermal resistance; thermistor.

термо/спай, —сросток *m.* thermocouple junction, thermojunction.

термостабил/изация *f.* thermal stabilization; —**ьность** *f.* thermal stability; —**ьный** *a.* thermostable, heat-resistant.

термо/стакан *m.* thermowell; —**старение** *n.* thermal aging.

термостат *m.* thermostat; incubator (for microorganisms); constant temperature bath or oven; **т. колонки** (chromatography) column oven; —**ирование** *n.* thermostatic control; —**ированный** *a.* thermostatically controlled; constant-temperature; —**ировать** *v.* control thermostatically; —**ируемый** *a.* temperature-controlled; —**ический** *a.* thermostatic.

термостойк/ий *a.* thermostable, thermally stable, heat-resistant, heatproof; —**ость** *f.* thermal stability, heat resistance; (met.) thermal shock resistance.

термо/столбик *m.* (elec.) thermopile; —**стрикция** *f.* thermostriction; —**сушка** *f.* thermal drying, heat drying; —**сфера** *f.* thermosphere; —**таксис** *m.* (physiol.) thermotaxis; —**танк** *m.* thermotank; —**терапия** *f.* thermotherapy, heat treatment; —**ток** *m.* thermoelectric current; —**упругий** *a.* thermoelastic.

термоустойчив/ость *see* **термостойкость;** —**ый** *see* **термостойкий.**

термо/фаза *f.* (bot.) thermophase, vernalization phase; —**физика** *f.* thermophysics; —**физический** *a.* thermophysical; —**фиксация** *f.* thermal fixation, thermal stabilization; —**фильный** *a.* (biol.) thermophilic; —**фон** *m.* thermophone; —**фор** *m.* (instr.) thermophore; (oil) thermofor; —**фосфат** *m.* thermophosphate (fertilizer); —**химический** *a.* thermochemical, chemical heat; —**химия** *f.* thermochemistry; —**хромизм** *m.* thermochromism; —**хромирование** *n.* diffusion chromizing; —**чувствительный** *a.* thermosensitive; thermal (element); —**шкаф** *m.* temperature chamber, oven; —**шум** *m.* (elec.) thermal noise; —**эдс** *m.* thermoelectromotive force; —**эластичный** *a.* thermoelastic.

термоэлектрическ/ий *a.* thermoelectric; **т. столб, —ая батарея** thermopile; —**ая пара, —ая цепь** thermoelectric couple, thermocouple, thermoelement.

термоэлектр/ичество *n.* thermoelectricity; —**огенератор** *m.* thermoelectric generator; —**од** *m.* thermocouple wire, thermoelectrode; —**одвижущая сила** thermoelectromotive force, thermoelectric power; —**озамыкатель, —оизвещатель** *m.* heat-sensitive unit, flame switch; —**он** *m.* thermion, thermoelectron; —**онный** *a.* thermoelectronic, thermionic.

термо/элемент *m.* thermoelement, thermocouple; thermopile (of battery); —**эмиссия** *f.* thermal emission; —**эффект** *m.* thermoeffect; —**ядерный** *a.* thermonuclear; —**ядерная техника** thermonucleonics.

термы *pl. of* **терм, терма.**

тёрн *see* **терновник.**

Тернера, тернеровый *a.* Turner('s).

тернеция *f.* (ichth.) black tetra, blackamoor (*Gymnocorymbus ternetzi*).

тернистый *a.* prickly, thorny.

тернов/ник *m.* (bot.) blackthorn, sloe (*Prunus spinosa*); —**ый** *a.* blackthorn; thorn(y).

тернопольский *a.* (geog.) Ternopol.

тернослива *see* **терновник.**

терофит *m.* (bot.) therophyte, annual plant.

тёрочный *a. of* **тёрка;** grating, grinding.

терп/адиен *m.* terpadiene; —**ан** *m.* terpane, menthane; —**анон** *m.* terpanone.

терпелив/ость *f.* patience, perseverance; —**ый** *a.* patient, persevering.

терпен *m.* terpene.

терпение *n.* patience, perseverance.

терпен/иловая кислота terpenylic acid; —**овый** *a.* terpene; —**ол** *m.* terpenol; —**он** *m.* terpenone.

терпентин *m.,* —**ный, —овый** *a.,* —**ное масло** turpentine.

терп/еть *v.* endure, bear, suffer, tolerate, stand, put up (with); undergo; **время —ит** there is plenty of time.

терпилен *m.* terpilene, terpinylene; —**ол** *m.* terpilenol, terpineol.

терпим/ость *f.* tolerance, toleration, sufferance; —**ый** *a.* tolerant, indulgent, permissive; tolerable, bearable, endurable.

терпин *m.* terpine, dihydroxymenthane; —**гидрат** *m.* terpin hydrate; —**ен** *m.* terpinene; —**еол** *m.* terpineol, lilacin; —**ил** *m.* terpinyl; —**илен** *m.* terpinylene, terpilene; —**иловый** *a.* terpinyl; terpinylic (acid); —**ол** *m.* terpinol; —**олен** *m.* terpinolene.

терпк/ий *a.* tart, sharp, acerbic, sour, astringent; —**ость** *f.* tartness, acerbity, astringency.

терпу/г *m.* rasp, rasping file; (ichth.) rock trout; atka fish, greenling (*Hexagrammos*); —**ги** *pl.* Hexagrammidae; —**говидные** *pl.* Hexagrammoidei; —**говые** *pl.* Hexagrammidae; —**жок** *m.* needle file.

терпче *comp. of* **терпкий.**

терразит *m.* colored building plaster.

терракот/а *f.*, **—овый** *a.* terra cotta.

террамицин *m.* Terramycin, oxytetracycline (antibiotic).

террар/ий, —иум *m.* terrarium.

терра-росса *f.* terra rossa (a red earth).

терраса *f.* terrace; balcony, platform; (geol.) bench.

терра-сиенна *f.* terra sienna, ocher.

террас/ирование *n.* terracing, benching; **—ировать** *v.* terrace, bench; **—ировка** *see* **террасирование**; **—ный** *a.* of **терраса**; terraced, benched; **—овидный** *a.* terrace-like, step, bench; **—овый** *see* **террасный.**

терраццо *n.* terrazzo (mosaic).

терреевая кислота terreic acid.

терри/генный *a.* (geol.) terrigenous, terrestrial; **—кон(ик)** *m.* (rock) dump, waste pile.

территор/иальный *a.* territorial; land-use; **—ия** *f.* territory, region, area, premises.

терский *a.* (geog.) Terek.

тертух *m.* (ocean.) fine brash.

тёртый *a.* grated; ground (pigment).

терфенил *m.* terphenyl, diphenylbenzene.

терция *f.* third; (typ.) columbian, two-line brevier; (music) mediant.

терчуг *see* **терпуг.**

тёрший *past act. part. of* **тереть.**

терьер *m.* terrier (dog).

теря/ть *v.* lose, give up, give off; shed; waste; **—ться** *v.* be lost, escape; disappear; get lost; be at a loss; be offset (by); **—ющийся** *a.* vanishing.

тёс *m.* (thin) planks, battens, deals, boards.

тесак *m.* hatchet; **—ание** *m.* hewing, etc., see *v.*

тёсан(н)ый *a.* hewn, cut, dressed, trimmed; **т. камень** (constr.) ashlar, hewn stone.

тесать *v.* hew, cut, dress, trim, square.

тесём/ка *f.*, **—очный** *a.* tape, band; braid; lace; **система —ок** tab assembly; **—чатый** *a.* tape-like, ribbon-like.

тесен *sh. m. of* **тесный.**

тесина *f.* board, plank.

тёска *see* **тесание.**

тесла *f.* Tesla (unit of magnetic induction).

тесло *n.* adz.

тесн/а *sh. f. of* **тесный; —ина** *f.* gorge, canyon, pass, defile; narrows; **—ить** *v.* restrict, confine; press, squeeze, cram, push, thrust, force back; **—иться** *v.* be pressed, etc.; crowd (together), cluster; **—о** *adv.* narrowly, tightly, closely, intimately; it is tight; **—овато** *adv.* rather tightly, rather closely; **—оватый** *a.* rather narrow, rather crowded; **—ота** *f.* crowded state, closeness; **—ый** *a.* narrow, tight, close; intimate (mixture).

тесовый *a.* deal, plank, board.

тессеральный *a.* (cryst.) tesseral.

тест *m.* test, criterion.

теста *f.* (biol.) testa; seed coat; *gen. of* **тест, тесто.**

тестер *m.* tester, analyzer.

тестикул/а *f.* (anat.) testicle; **—ярный** *a.* testicular.

тестиров/ание *n.* test(ing); **—ать** *v.* test; **—ый** *a.* test.

тест-купон *m.* test coupon (e.g., of laminated plate).

тесто *n.* dough, paste, pulp, viscous mass, (cement) slurry; (pharm.) magma; **—ватый** *a.* pasty, pulp-like; **—месилка** *f.* kneader; **—месильный** *a.* kneading; **—образный** *a.* pasty, paste-like, doughy, semi-liquid.

тестостерон *m.* testosterone.

тест-программа *f.* (comp.) test program, check(ing) routine.

тест-таблица *f.* focusing board; test pattern.

тест-фильм *m.* test film.

тесты *pl.* tests.

тесьм/а *see* **тесёмка**; (anat.) vinculum; **—овидный** *a.* (bot.) fasciated; taeniate.

тетаграмма *f.* (meteor.) thetagram.

тетан/ин *m.* tetanine; **—ия** *f.* (med.) tetany; (vet.) staggers; **—отоксин** *m.* tetanotoxin; **—трен** *m.* tetanthrene, tetrahydrophenanthrene; **—ус** *m.* (med.) tetanus.

тета-ритм (med.) theta wave.

тетартоэдр/ический *a.* (cryst.) tetartohedral; **—ия** *f.* tetartohedry.

тетелин *m.* tethelin.

тетерев *m.* (orn.) black grouse (*Lyrurus tetrix*); **—иные** *pl.* (orn.) grouse family (*Tetraonidae*); **—ятник** *m.* goshawk (*Accipiter gentilis*).

тетёрка *f.* black grouse hen.

тетива *f.* (bow)string; (construction) string board, stringer.

тетра— *prefix* tetra—, quadri—, four-; (ichth.) tetra; **—борат** *m.*, **—борнокислая соль** tetraborate; **—борный** *a.* tetraboric (acid); **—бром** *prefix* tetrabrom(o)—; **—бромбензол** *m.* tetrabromobenzene; **—бромид** *m.* tetrabromide; **—галоидбензол** *m.* tetrahalogenated benzene.

тетрагексаэдр *m.* (cryst.) tetrahexahedron; **—ический** *a.* tetrahexahedral.

тетрагидро— *prefix* tetrahydro—; **—бензол** *m.* tetrahydrobenzene; **—каннабинол** *m.* tetrahydrocannabinol, THC; **—кси** *prefix* tetrahydroxy—; **—фуран** *m.* tetrahydrofurane; **—хинолин** *m.* tetrahydroquinoline.

тетра/гира *f.* (cryst.) fourfold axis of symmetry; **—гон** *m.* (geom.) tetragon; **—гональный** *a.* tetragonal; **—да** *f.* tetrad; **—декан** *m.* tetradecane; **—децил** *m.* tetradecyl; **—диплоид** *m.* (gen.) quadruple diploid.

тетрад/ка *see* **тетрадь; —ный** *a.* of **тетрадь**; (gen.) tetrad; **—ь** *f.* notebook, pad; (print.) signature, section.

тетраз/ан *m.* tetrazane; **—ен** *m.* tetrazene; **—ил** *m.* tetrazyl; **—ин** *m.* tetrazine; **—о** *prefix* tetrazo—; **—ол** *m.* tetrazole; **—он** *m.* tetrazone.

тетра/йод *prefix* tetraiod(o)—; **—йодбензол** *m.* tetraiodobenzene; **—йодид** *m.* tetraiodide; **—йодметан** *m.* tetraiodomethane; **—каин** *m.* tetracaine; **—карбоновый** *a.* tetracarboxylic (acid); **—козан** *m.* tetracosane; **—козановый** *a.* tetracosanic (acid).

тетракокки *pl.* (bact.) Gaffkya tetragena.

тетрал/ин *m.* Tetralin, tetrahydronaphthalene; **—ит** *m.* tetralite, Tetryl; **—ол** *m.* tetralol; **—он** *m.* tetralone.

тетрамер *m.* tetramer; **—ный** *a.* tetramerous.

тетраметил/ен *m.* tetramethylene; **—мочевина** *f.* tetramethylurea.

тетрамин *m.* tetramine.

тетранитро/пентаэритрит *m.* (explosives) pentaerythritol tetranitrate, PETN; **—соединение** *n.* tetranitro compound.

тетранихиды *pl.* (ent.) Tetranychidae, mites.

тетраокси— *prefix* tetrahydroxy—; **—антрахинон** *m.* tetrahydroxyanthraquinone; **—бензол** *m.* tetrahydroxybenzene; **—кислота** *f.* tetrahydroxy acid.

тетраплегия *f.* (med.) quadriplegia.

тетраплоид *m.* (gen.) tetraploid.

тетрархный *a.* (bot.) tetrarch.

тетра/силан *m.* tetrasilane; **—спора** *f.* (bot.) tetraspore; **—сульфид** *m.* tetrasulfide; **—тионат** *m.* tetrathionate; **—тионовый** *a.* tetrathionic (acid).

тетрафенилборнатрий *m.* sodium tetraphenyl borate.

тетрафтор/ид *m.* tetrafluoride; **—метан** *m.* tetrafluoromethane, carbon tetrafluoride; **—этилен** *m.* tetrafluoroethylene.

тетрахлор/бензол *m.* tetrachlorobenzene; **—ид** *m.* tetrachloride; —**метан** *m.* tetrachloromethane, carbon tetrachloride; —**этан** *m.* tetrachloroethane.

тетрахорический *a.* (stat.) tetrachoric.

тетрациклин *m.* tetracycline (antibiotic).

тетрацит *m.* (gen.) tetracyte.

тетраэдр *m.* (cryst.) tetrahedron; —**ический** *a.* tetrahedral.

тетраэтил/аммоний *m.* tetraethylammonium; —**пирофосфат** *m.* tetraethyl pyrophosphate; —**свинец** *m.* tetraethyl lead.

тетридин *m.* Tetridin, Pyrithyldione.

тетрил *m.* (expl.) Tetryl, tetranitromethylaniline.

тетриновая кислота tetrinic acid.

тетрод *m.*, —**ный** *a.* (rad.) tetrode.

тетрон/ал *m.* tetronal, diethylsulfone diethylmethane.

тетурам *m.* tetraethylthiuram disulfide, Antabuse.

тефиграмма *f.* (meteor.) tephigram.

тефия *f.* (astr.) Tethys.

тефлон *m.* Teflon (polytetrafluoroethylene).

тефр/ит *m.* (petr.) tephrite; —**озин** *m.* tephrosin, hydroxydeguelin.

тех *gen. and prepos. of* **те.**

тех— *prefix, see* **технический.**

техасск/ий *a.* (geog.) Texas; —**ая лихорадка** (vet.) Texas fever, bovine piroplasmosis.

тех/кадры *pl.* technical cadres; —**минимум** minimum required technical knowledge.

технеций *m.* technetium, Tc.

техник *m.* technician, technologist; engineer, mechanic; —**а** *f.* technology, technological process; technique, method, procedure, practice; engineering; industry; materiel, equipment; (work) habits; —**а безопасности** safety engineering, industrial safety practices; —**а низких температур** cryogenics; —**а организации производства** production engineering; **электронная —а** electronics; —**о-экономический** *a.* technical and economic; feasibility (study); —**ум** *m.* technical school.

технически *adv.* technically; **т. обоснованный** *a.* based on technical data.

техническ/ий *a.* technical; engineering, mechanical; industrial, commercial(-grade), technical-grade, crude; (тг.) running (speed); large (calorie); **т. контроль** quality control; **т. минимум** minimum required technical knowledge; **т. расчёт** engineering; —**ая вода** industrial water; —**ая единица массы** engineering unit of mass, metric slug; —**ая химия** applied chemistry, industrial chemistry, chemical technology; —**ие культуры** industrial crops; —**ие средства** equipment; (comp.) hardware; —**ие условия** technical specifications, (standard) specifications; **программа —их работ** engineering effort; **указывать —ие условия** *v.* specify; —**ое изготовление** manufacture; —**ое обеспечение** (comp.) hardware; —**ое обслуживание** maintenance.

технолог *m.* technologist, production engineer, process engineer; —**ический** *a.* technological; technical(-grade), crude; production, process(ing), operating; engineering (process); industrial (equipment); straight-flow (production); —**ический поток** production line; —**ическая карта** flow sheet; —**ическая подготовка производства** computer-aided manufacturing; —**ичность** *f.* technological effectiveness; —**ичный** *a.* technologically effective, efficient; —**ия** *f.* technology; engineering; know-how; (foods) processing, canning.

технорук *m.* works manager.

техобслуживание *n.* maintenance.

тех/промфинплан *m.* technical, industrial and financial plan; —**ред** *m.* technical editor; —**снаб** *m.* technical

supply; —**упр** *m.*, —**управление** *n.* technical administration; —**уход** *m.* maintenance.

теций *m.* (bot.) thecium.

тече/безопасный *a.* leakproof; —**искание,** —**испытание** *n.* leak detection, leak testing; —**искатель** *m.* leak detector, leak tester.

течен/ие *n.* current, stream, course, flux, flow, run; streaming, flowing; passage; tendency, trend; **в т.** for, throughout, over (a period of), during, in the course (of); **вверх по —ию, против —ия** upstream, against the current; (**вниз**) **по —ию** downstream, with the current; **медленное т.** ooze, oozing; **обратное т.** reflux; **потенциал —ия** streaming potential; **распределение —ий, система —ий** flow pattern.

течка *f.* (gravity) spout; (discharge) hopper; (zool.) (o)estrus, heat.

течь *v.* flow (along, in, through), pass through, run, stream; leak, escape, trickle, drip; fly, pass (of time); *f.* leak(ing), leaks, leakage, flow, run; (med.) flux; **т. обратно** *v.* reflux; **с —ю** leaky.

тешет *pr. 3 sing. of* **тесать.**

т:ж; Т:Ж *abbr.* (**соотношение твёрдого к жидкому**) solid-to-liquid ratio.

т. зам. *abbr.* (**точка замерзания**) freezing point; **т. заст.** *abbr.* (**точка застывания**) solidification point.

тиаз/ил *m.* thiazyl; —**ин** *m.* thiazine; —**иновые краски** thiazine dyes; —**ол** *m.* thiazole; —**олил** *m.* thiazolyl; —**олин** *m.* thiazoline, dihydrothiazole.

ти/альдин *m.* thialdine; —**амид** *m.* thiamide; —**амин** *m.* thiamine, vitamin B_1; —**антрен** *m.* thianthrene, diphenylene disulfide.

тибетолид *m.* (chem.) exaltolide.

тибетский *a.* (geog.) Tibetan.

тибиальный *a.* (anat.) tibial.

тибон *m.* thibone, thiacetazone.

тигель *m.*, —**ный** *a.* crucible; (typ.) platen.

тиглинов/ая кислота tiglic acid, 2-methyl-2-butenoic acid; **соль —ой кислоты** tiglate; —**ый альдегид** tiglaldehyde.

тигмо— *prefix* thigmo— (touch); —**таксис** *m.* (biol.) thigmotaxis.

тигр *m.* tiger; —**ёнок** *m.* tiger cub; —**иный** *a. of* **тигр;** —**ица** *f.* tigress; —**овый** *a. of* **тигр;** tigrine, marked like a tiger; —**овый глаз** (min.) tigereye; —**оид** *m.* tigroid; —**оидное вещество** (cyt.) Nissl substance; —**оидные глыбки** Nissl bodies; —**олиз** *m.* (med.) tigrolysis.

тиен/ил *m.* thienyl; —**он** *m.* thienone, thienyl ketone.

тик *m.* (mech.) tick(ing); (text.) ticking; teak(wood); (med.) tic; —**анье** tick(ing); —**ать** *v.* tick; —**кер** *m.* (rad.) ticker, chopper; —**овый** *a. of* **тик;** —**овое дерево** teakwood.

тиксотроп/ия, —**ность** *f.* thixotropy (of gels); —**ный** *a.* thixotropic.

тила *f.* (cyt.) tylosis.

тилапия *f.* (ichth.) Tilapia.

тилацин *m.* (zool.) Tasmanian wolf (*Thylacinus cynocephalus*).

Тиле трубка Thiele tube.

тили/адин *m.* tiliadin; —**цин** *m.* tilicin.

тилкальзин *m.* Tylcalsin, calcium acetylsalicylate.

тиллитин *m.* Tyllithin, lithium acetylsalicylate.

тилль *f.* (geol.) till, glacial drift.

тило— *prefix* tyl(o)— (knob, callus); —**з** *m.* (med., bot.) tylosis; —**за** *f.* (chem.) Tylose, methylcellulose; —**образование** *n.* (med., bot.) tylosis; —**форин** *m.* (chem.) tylophorine.

тильда *f.* (typ.) tilde, curl.

тимацетин *m.* thymacetin, thymol phenacetin.

тимбер/ованный *a.* timbered, etc., *see* v.; **—овать** *v.* timber; (naut.) repair, refit; **—овка** *f.* timbering, etc., *see* v.; **—с** *m.* timber.

тимели/евые, —и *pl.* (orn.) babbler family (*Timaliidae*).

тим/ен *m.* (biochem.) thymene; **—иан** *see* **тимьян; —идиловая кислота** thyidylic acid; **—идин** *m.* thymidine; **—идол** *m.* thymidol, methylpropylphenyl menthol; **—ил** *m.*, **—иловый** *a.* thymyl; **—ин** *m.* thymine, 5-methyluracil; **—иновый** *a.* thyminic (acid); **—иноз** *m.* (med.) yaws.

тимо/видин *m.* thymovidin; **—гидрохинон** *m.* thymohydroquinone; **—дин** *m.* thymodin, thymol iodide.

тимол *m.*, **—овый** *a.* (chem.) thymol, 3-hydroxy-*p*-cymene; **—блау** *n.* thymol blue; **—фталеин** *m.* thymolphthalein.

тимо/нуклеиновая кислота *see* **тимуснуклеиновая кислота; —тиновый** *a.* thymotic (acid).

тимофеевка *f.* (bot.) timothy (*Phleum*).

тимо/форм *m.* thymoform; **—хинон** *m.* thymoquinone; **—цит** *m.* (cyt.) thymocyte.

тимпан *m.* (anat.) tympanum; tympanic membrane; **—альный** *a.* tympanal, tympanic; **—ит** *m.* (med.) tympanitis; **—ия** *f.* (med., vet.) tympanites; **—ный** *a.* tympanic; **—ное колесо** tympanium, drum wheel.

тимус *m.* (anat.) thymus; **—нуклеиновая кислота** thymus nucleic acid, desoxyribonucleic acid, DNA.

тимьян *m.*, **—овый** *a.* (bot.) thyme.

тина *f.* slime, mud, mire, ooze, silt, slurry; (pond) scum; (bot.) freshwater algae.

тинаму *pl.* (orn.) Tinamiformes.

тинда *f.* (ichth.) grilse (*Salmo salar*).

тиндаллизация *f.* tyndallization, sterilization.

Тиндаля явление (light) Tyndall effect.

тинист/ость *f.* sliminess; **—ый** *a.* slimy, oozy, muddy.

тинкал *m.* (min.) tincal, crude borax.

тинктура *f.* tincture, infusion.

тиннин *m.* thynnin.

тинный *a. of* **тина;** muddy, slimy; (bot.) conferval, confervaceous.

тино— *prefix* thin(o)— (dune); **—фит** *m.* (bot.) thinophyte, dune plant.

тинтометр *m.* tintometer (colorimeter).

Тинувин П (chem.) Tinuvin P (ultraviolet absorber for plastics).

тио— *prefix* thio— (sulfur); **—альдегид** *m.* thioaldehyde; **—арсенит** *m.* thioarsenite; **—ацетамид** *m.* thioacetamide; **—бензойная кислота** thiobenzoic acid; **—геновый** *a.* thiogenic, sulfur (dyes); **—гликолевый** *a.* thioglycolic (acid); **—изоцианат** *m.* isothiocyanate; **—индиго** *n.* thioindigo.

тиокарб/амат *m.* thiocarbamate; **—амид** *m.* thiocarbamide, thiourea; **—аминовая кислота** thiocarbamic acid; **—онил** *m.* thiocarbonyl.

тио/каучук *m.* thio rubber; **—кетон** *m.* thioketone; **—кислота** *f.* thioacid; **—кол** *m.* Thiocol, potassium guaiacol sulfonate; Thiokol (polysulfide rubber).

тиоксан *m.* thioxane; **—тен** *m.* thioxanthene, methylenediphenylene sulfide; **—тон** *m.* thioxanthone.

тиокс/ен *m.* thioxene, dimethylthiophene; **—илол** *m.* thioxylene.

тио/л *m.* thiol; **—ловая кислота** thiolic acid; **—лютин** *m.* thiolutin; **—молочная кислота** thiolactic acid; **—мочевина** *f.* thiourea, thiocarbamide; **—муравьиная кислота** thioformic acid.

тиомышьяков/ая кислота thioarsenic acid, sulfarsenic acid; **—окислая соль** thioarsenate, sulfarsenate; **—истая кислота** thioarsenious acid, sulfarsenious

acid; **—истокислая соль** thioarsenite, sulfarsenite; **—истоаммониевая соль** ammonium thioarsenite; **—оаммониевая соль** ammonium thioarsenate.

тио/налид *m.* Thionalide; **—нафтен** *m.* thionaphthene, benzothiophene.

тион/еин *m.* thioneine, thiazine; **—ил** *m.* thionyl, sulfinyl; **—ин** *m.*, **—иновый** *a.* thionine, Lauth's violet; **—овая кислота** thionic acid; **—уровая кислота** thionuric acid.

тиоокись *f.* (mono)sulfide (of olefins).

тиооловянн/ая кислота thiostannic acid; **соль —ой кислоты, —окислая соль** thiostannate; **—оаммониевая соль** ammonium thiostannate.

тиопентал-натрий *m.* thiopental-sodium, Pentothal sodium.

тиосерн/ая кислота thiosulfuric acid; **—истая кислота** thiosulfurous acid; **—истокислая соль** thio sulfite; **—окислая соль** thiosulfate; **—онатриевая соль** sodium thiosulfate.

тио/синамин *m.* thiosinamine, allyl thiourea; **—соединение** thio compound; **—соль** *f.* thio salt; **—спирт** *m.* thio alcohol; **—станнат** *m.* thiostannate; **—сульфат** *m.* thiosulfate; **—сульфокислота** *f.* thiosulfonic acid; **—сульфонат** *m.* thiosulfonate.

тиосурьмян/ая кислота thioantimonic acid, sulfantimonic acid; **—истая кислота** thioantimonious acid, sulfantimonious acid; **—истокислая соль** thioantimonite; **—окислая соль** thioantimonate.

тио/толен *m.* thiotolene, methylthiophene; **—углекислая соль** thiocarbonate; **—угольная кислота** thiocarbonic acid; **—уксусная кислота** thioacetic acid; **—урацил** *m.* (pharm.) thiouracil; **—уретан** *m.* thiourethane; **—фан** *m.* thiophane.

тиофен *m.* thiophene, thiofuran; **—ил** *m.* thiophenyl; **—ин** *m.* thiophenine, aminothiophene; **—карбоновая кислота** thiophenecarboxylic acid; **—овый** *a.* thiophenic (acid); **—ол** *m.* thiophenol, phenylmercaptan.

тио/флавон *m.* thioflavone; **—форм** *m.* thioform, basic bismuth dithiosalicylate; **—фос** *m.* Thiophos, parathion (insecticide); **—фосген** *m.* thiophosgene, thiocarbonyl chloride; **—фосфат** *m.* thiophosphate; **—фосфорил** *m.* thiophosphoryl; **—фосфорная кислота** thiophosphoric acid; **—фтен** *m.* thiophthene, bithiophene.

тиохром *m.* thiochrome.

тиоциан *m.* thiocyanogen; **—ат, —ид** *m.* thiocyanate; **—овая кислота** thiocyanic acid, sulfocyanic acid; **—уровая кислота** thiocyanuric acid.

тиоэфир *m.* thio ether.

тип *m.* type, kind, model, design, pattern, make, variety; (biol.) phylum; (oscillation) mode; form, style; class (of ship); **т. вида** (biol.) holotype; **происходить по —у** *v.* follow the pattern; **—аж** *m.* standardization; (biol.) phylum.

типиз/ация *f.* typification, etc., *see* v.; **—ированный** *a.* typified, etc., *see* v.; specialized; **—ировать** *v.* typify, classify by type; standardize.

тип/ический *see* **типичный; —ичность** *f.* typicalness; **—ичный** *a.* typical, characteristic, representative; peculiar (to); **—ия** *f. suffix* —typy (state, process); **—овой** *a. of* **тип;** type, model; standard; typical.

типогенез *m.* (biol.) typogenesis.

типограф *m.* typographer, printer; a bark beetle (*Ips typographus*); **—(иче)ский** *a.* typographic; type (metal); printing (press); printer's (ink, varnish, etc.); **—ия** *f.* printing house, printer's, press; **в —ии** at the printer's, in press; **—щик** *m.* printer.

типо/логия *f.* typology; **—метрия** *f.* point system of type measurement; **—ним** *m.* (biol.) typonym.

типун *m.* (vet.) pip.

типчак *m.* (bot.) fescue (*Festuca sulcata*).

тир *m.* (shooting) gallery, range; tar compound.

тираж *m.* circulation (of journal); printing, number of copies printed, impression, run; figures; edition; **—ировать** *v.* determine the circulation; set the size of a printing; **—ность** *see* **тираж; —ный** *a. of* **тираж.**

тирамин *m.* tyramine.

тиран/ны, —овые *pl.* (orn.) tyrant flycatchers (*Tyrannidae*); **—нозавр** *m.* (pal.) tyrannosaur.

тиратрон *m.*, **—ный** *a.* (electron.) thyratron.

тир-бушон *m.* stopper, plug.

тире *n.* dash; hyphen.

тирезол *m.* thyresol, santalolmethylester.

тирео— *prefix* (anat.) thyr(e)o—, thyroid; **—генный** *a.* thyrogenic; **—глобулин** *m.* thyroglobulin; **—идизм** *m.* (med.) thyroidism; **—идин** *m.* thyroidin; **—идный** *a.* thyroid; **—тропный** *a.* thyrotropic.

тиристор *m.* (electron.) thyristor.

тиркушк/и, —овые *pl.* (orn.) pratincoles (*Glareolidae*).

тиро— *prefix* tyr(o)— (cheese); (anat.) *see* **тирео—.** TIROWATX *v.* tar, pitch.

тироз *m.* (med.) tyrosis; **—ил** *m.* tyrosyl; **—ин** *m.* (biochem.) tyrosine, aminohydroxycinnamic acid; **—иназа** *f.* tyrosinase; **—инуровая кислота** tyrosinuric acid; **—ол** *m.* tyrosol, *p*-hydroxyphenethyl alcohol.

тироксин *m.* thyroxine.

тиролейпин *m.* tyroleucin.

тирольский *a.* Tyrolene.

тиро/токси(ко)н *m.* tyrotoxi(co)n, diazobenzene hydroxide; **—трицин** *m.* tyrothricin; **—цидин** *m.* tyrocidine.

Тирша (med.) Thiersch's (graft, knife, etc.)

тис *m.* yew (tree).

Тиса (geog.) Tisza (river).

тиск/ание *n.* squeezing, etc., *see v.*; **—ать** *v.* squeeze, (com)press; cram; print, insert.

тиск/и *pl.* vise, clamp; **—овый** *a.* vise; clamping, tightening.

тисн/ение *n.* embossing, etc., *see v.*; **—ён(н)ый** *a.* embossed, etc., *see v.*; **—ильный** *a.* embossing, etc., *see v.*; **—ить, —уть** *v.* emboss, impress, (im)print, stamp; tool (leather).

тисовый *a. of* **тис.**

тисоч/ки *dim.*, **—ный** *a. of* **тиски.**

т. исп. *abbr.* (**температура испарения**) vaporization temperature.

тисс *m.* (bot.) yew (tree).

тисса (geog.) Tisza (river).

Тиссена гравиметр Thyssen gravimeter.

Тиссо конденсатор Tissot condenser.

тиссовый *a. of* **тисс.**

титан *m.* titanium, Ti; (astr.) Titan; **двуокись —а** titanium dioxide; **сернокислый т., сульфат —а** titanium sulfate; **—ат** *m.* titanate; **—ил** *m.* titanyl; **—истый** *a.* titanous, titanium, titaniferous; **—ический** *see* **титановый;** **—о—** *prefix* titano—, titanium; **—овокислый** *a.* titanic acid; titanate (of); **—овокислая соль** titanate; **—овый** *a.* titanic, titanium, titaniferous; **—овый ангидрид** titanic anhydride, titanium dioxide; **—овая кислота** titanic acid; **соль —овой кислоты** titanate; **—овая сталь** titanium steel; **—овые белила** titanium white; **—ометрия** *f.* titanium titration; **—органический** *a.* organotitanium; **—офтор(ист)оводородный** *a.* fluorotitanic (acid).

тити *m.* titi monkey (*Callicebus*).

титон *m.*, **—ский ярус** (geol.) Tithonian stage.

титр *m.* titer, titration standard; (text.) titer, metric number; caption; **определять т., устанавливать т.** *v.* titrate; **—атор** *m.* titrator; **—иметр** *m.* titrimeter; **—иметрический** *a.* titrimetric; **—ировать** *see* **титровать.**

титров/альный *a.* titrating, titration; **т. анализ** analysis by titration, volumetric analysis; **—ание** *n.* titration, titrimetry; **приём —ания** titration method; **—анный** *a.* titrated; titrating; **—анный раствор** titration standard, standard solution, titrant; **—ать** *v.* titrate.

титр/ометрический *a.* titrimetric; **—ометрия** *f.* titrimetry; **—уемый** *a.* titrated; titratable; **—уемый раствор** titrate; **—ующий** *a.* titrating; **—ующийся** *a.* titratable.

титубация *f.* (med.) titubation, staggering.

титул *m.* title; title page; **—ованный** *a.* (en)titled; **—овать** *v.* (en)title; **—ьный** *a.* title.

тиурам *m.* thiuram.

тиурет *m.* thiuret.

тиуроний *m.* thiouronium.

тиф *m.* (med.) typhus; **брюшной т.** typhoid fever; **сыпной т.** typhus; Rocky Mountain spotted fever.

тифастерин *m.* typhasterol.

тифдрук *m.* intaglio printing.

тифен *m.* (pharm.) thiphen (hydrochloride).

тифин *pl.* black wasps (*Tiphidae*).

тифлит *m.* (med.) typhlitis.

тифло— *prefix* typhlo— (cecum; blindness); **—гепатит** *m.* (vet.) typhlohepatitis, blackhead (in turkeys); **—педагогика** *f.* education of the visually handicapped.

тифо/зный *a.*, **—ид** *m.* (med.) typhoid.

тифон *m.* signal whistle, blast.

тифотоксин *m.* typhotoxin.

тих *sh. m. of* **тихий**; *past m. sing. of* **тихнуть.**

тихий *a.* quiet, still, noiseless, silent; calm; mild, gentle; slow, sluggish; soft, low (sound); **Т. океан** Pacific Ocean; **т. разряд** (dielectrics) silent discharge, corona.

тих/нуть *v.* quiet down, abate; **—о** *adv.* quietly, etc., *see* **тихий.**

тихоновский *a.* (math.) Tikhonov.

тихонько *adv.* quietly, cautiously.

тихоокеанский *a.* (geog.) Pacific.

тихопланктон *m.* (ocean.) tychoplankton, inshore plankton.

тихоход *m.* slow-moving vehicle; (zool.) sloth; bear animalcule; **—ный** *a.* slow(-moving), low-speed, slow-running.

тиш/айший *superl.*; **—е** *comp. of* **тихий, тихо** quieter; more quietly; **—ина, —ь** *f.* stillness, quiet, silence, calm, mildness.

т.к. *abbr.* (**так как**) since, inasmuch as; **ТК** *abbr.* (**тонкий кишечник**) small intestine; (**трансплантат кожи**) skin graft.

тка/льный *a.* weaving; **—невый** *a.* textile, fabric, cloth; (biol.) tissue, histological; **—невый слой** (biol.) tela; **—нетерапия** *f.* tissue therapy; **—неэквивалентный** *a.* (radiobiol.) tissue equivalent; **—ние** *see* **тканье; —(н)ный** *a.* woven, cloth.

ткан/ь *f.* fabric, cloth; web; texture; (biol.) tissue; **доза в —и** tissue dose (of radiation); **металлическая т.** wire gauze; **основная т.** (biol.) parenchyma; **проволочная т.** wire gauze; **сетчатая т.** netting.

тканьё *n.* weaving; (text.) piqué; **—вое** *n.* pique; **—вый** *a.* cloth; woven; (biol.) tissue; webbing (belt); **—вая доза** tissue dose (of radiation).

т. капл. *abbr.* (**температура каплепадения**) drop point.

тка/ть *v.* weave.

ткацк/ая *f.* weaver's workshop, loom department; **—ий** *a.* weaver's, weaving, loom, textile; **т. станок**

703

loom; **—ое производство** weaving; **—о-прядиль-ный** *a.* weaving and spinning.

ткач *m.* weaver; **общественный т.** (orn.) sociable weaver; **—ество** *n.* weaving; **—иковые** *pl.* weaver birds (*Ploceidae*); **т.-усач** *m.* (ent.) longicorn.

ТКЕ *abbr.* (**температурный коэффициент ёмкости**) temperature coefficient of capacitance.

ткёт *pr. 3 sing. of* **ткать.**

т. кип. *abbr.* (**точка кипения**) boiling point.

т-км, ткм *abbr.* (**тонна-километр**) ton-kilometer.

ткнуть *see* **тыкать.**

т. конд. *abbr.* (**температура конденсации**) dew point.

т. крит. *abbr.* (**температура критическая**) critical temperature.

ТКФ *abbr.* (**тетракальцийфосфат**) tetracalcium phosphate; (**трикальцийфосфат**) tricalcium phosphate; (**трикрезилфосфат**) tricresyl phosphate.

тл *abbr.* (**тесла**) tesla (unit of magnetic induction).

тлёвый *a. of* **тля; т. лев** (ent.) aphis lion, chrysop.

тле/н *m.* decay, decomposition; decayed matter; **—ние** *n.* glowing, etc., *see v.*; decay, decomposition; **—нность** *f.* perishability; **—нный** *a.* perishable; decayed; **—творный** *a.* noxious, putrid; **—ть(ся)** *v.* glow, smolder, burn incompletely; molder, rot, decay; **—ющий** *a.* glowing, etc., *see v.*; **—ющий разряд** (elec.) glow discharge.

тля *f.* (ent.) aphid, plant louse.

тм *abbr.* (**тоннометр**) ton-meter; **тМ** *abbr.* (**тёплая масса воздуха**) warm air mass; **т. м.** *abbr.* (**текущего месяца**) of this month.

тмин *m.* caraway (seed); **воложский т., римский т.** cumin; **чёрный т.** nutmeg flower; **—ный** *a.* caraway; cumin.

ТМО *abbr.* (**термомеханическая обработка**) thermomechanical processing.

ТМТД *abbr.* (**тетраметилтиурам дисульфид**) tetramethylthiuram disulfide; **ТМТМ** *abbr.* (**тетраметилтиурам моносульфид**) tetramethylthiuram monosulfide.

ТН *abbr.* (**трансформатор напряжения**) (voltage) transformer.

т. наз. *abbr.* (**так называемый**) so-called.

ТНК *abbr.* (**тимонуклеиновая кислота**) thymus nucleic acid.

ТНТ *abbr.* (**тринитротолуол**) trinitrotoluene, TNT.

т. н. ч. *abbr.* (**ток низкой частоты**) low-frequency current.

то *n. of* **тот;** that; *conj.* then, in that case; **то есть** that is (to say); **то же** ditto, same; **то ли . . . то ли** either . . . or; **то . . . то** sometimes, at times . . . at others . . . , now . . . now; first . . . then; **то туда, то сюда** hither and thither; **то, что** (the fact) that; **а не то** if not, otherwise, or else; **да и то** even then; **если так, то** if (it is) so, then; **не то, что** not that; **об этом-то** precisely about that.

т.о. *abbr.* (**таким образом**) thus.

тоар *m.*, **—ский ярус** (geol.) Toarcian.

Тобина бронза (met.) Tobin bronze.

тобольский *a.* (geog.) Tobol (river).

т-образный *a.* T-, T-shaped, tee-.

товар *m.* merchandise, goods, wares; commodity, article; **—ы** *pl.* goods, stock; **т. широкого потребления** consumer goods; **запас —ов** stock in trade.

товарищ *m.* companion, partner, fellow, colleague, associate; **т. по торговле** partner in trade; **т. по учению** fellow student; **—ество** *n.* company, partnership, society, association.

товарность *f.* marketability.

товарн/ый *a.* goods, commodity; marketable; commercial; technical (grade); ready-mix (concrete); trade (mark); freight (train); truck (farming); **крытый т. вагон** box car; **—ое движение** freight traffic; **—ое хозяйство** goods economy.

товаровед *m.* merchandising specialist; **—ение** *n.*, **—ный, —ческий** *a.* merchandising.

товаро/обмен *m.* barter; **—оборот** *m.* turnover (of merchandise); **—отправитель** *m.* forwarder of merchandise, consignor; **—пассажирский** *a.* (rr.) freight and passenger; **—подъёмник** *m.* freight elevator; **—получатель** *m.* recipient of merchandise, consignee; **—проводящий** *a.* merchandise supply; **—производитель** *m.* manufacturer.

тогда *adv.* then, at that time; **т. же** at the same time; **т. и только т.** (math.) if and only if; **т. как** while, whereas, when; **т.-то** at that (particular time); **—шний** *a.* of that time, existing at that time, contemporary.

того *gen. of* **то(т); из т., что** from the fact that.

тоди *pl.* (orn.) Todidae.

тождеств/енность *f.*, **—о** *n.* identity; **—енный** *a.* identical, same.

тоже *adv.* also, too, likewise; **т. не** not . . . either.

тожеств/енность, —о *see* **тождественность; —енный** *see* **тождественный.**

тозил *m.* tosyl, tolylsulfonyl.

той *gen., dat., etc., of* **та; т. или иной** that or any other, either, some.

ток *m.* current, stream, flow; (elec.) current; (agr.) threshing floor; **т. крови** bloodstream, circulation; **без —а** without current, dead (wire); **допустимая нагрузка —ом** current-carrying capacity; **переменного —а** alternating current, a-c (motor); **плотность —а** current density; **под —ом** current-carrying, live, energized; **подать т.** *v.* make contact; **постоянного —а** direct current, d-c (motor); **растительный т.** malt floor; **указатель —а** (elec.) current indicator, spec. ammeter.

токай *m.*, **—ское** *n.* Tokay wine.

токарн/ая *f.* lathe shop; **—ичать** *v.* turn, work on a lathe, do lathework.

токарно/винторезный станок screw-cutting lathe; **—карусельный станок** turning and boring lathe; **—механическая** *f.* lathe shop; **—револьверный станок** turret lathe; **—шлифовальный станок** grinding lathe.

токарн/ый *a.* lathe, worked on a lathe; turning; turned; **т. автомат** automatic lathe; **т. полуавтомат** semi-automatic lathe; **т. резец** cutting tool; **т. станок** lathe; **—ая работа** turning, lathework; **—ые стружки** turnings; **—я** *f.* lathe shop.

токарь *m.* turner, lathe hand.

токи *pl. of* **ток.**

токийский *a.* (geog.) Tokyo.

токо— *prefix* (elec.) current; toco— (childbirth, offspring).

токо/вание *n.* (orn.) courtship display; **—вать** *v.* (orn.) court, display.

токоведущий *a.* current-carrying, live.

токовище *n.* (orn.) courting display ground.

токо/вращатель *m.* pole changer; **—вый** *a.* current; **—генераторный** *a.* current-generating; **—дробитель** *m.* current divider.

токология *f.* tocology, obstetrics.

токо/непроводящий *a.* non-current carrying, nonconducting; **—несущий** *a.* current-carrying, live.

токоограничитель *m.* (elec.) current limiter; **—ный** *a.* current-limiting.

токо/отвод *m.* (elec.) lead; terminal; **—подвод** *m.* current supply; **верхний —подвод** top feed(ing); **—прерыватель** *m.* circuit breaker.

токоприёмн/ик *m.* (elec.) current collector, trolley; **—ый** *a.* current-collecting; **—ый ролик** trolley; **—ая дуга** bow collector.

токопровод *m.* (elec.) conduction; conductor; lead(-in) wire, connecting lead; **—ящий** *a.* (current-)conducting, current-carrying.

токопрохождение *n.* circuit diagram.

токосниматель *m.* (elec.) collector.

токособиратель *m.* (elec.) current collector; **—ный** *a.* current-collecting, collector; slip (ring).

токо/съёмник *see* **токоприёмник**; **—управляющий** *a.* current-controlling.

токоферол *m.* tocopherol (vitamin E).

токс— *prefix* tox(ico)— (poison); **—альбумин** *m.* tox-albumin; **—афен** Toxaphene, chlorinated camphene (insecticide); **—емия** *f.* (med.) toxemia; **—икарол** *m.* toxicarol, tephrosin; **—икоз** *m.* (med.) toxicosis; (soil) sickness; **—иколог** *m.* toxicologist; **—икологический** *a.* toxicological; **—икология** *f.* toxicology; **—ин** *m.* toxin; **—истерин** *m.* toxisterol; **—ический** *a.* toxic, poisonous; **—ичность** *f.* toxicity; **—ичный** *a.* toxic.

токсокар/а *f.* a nematode worm (*Toxocara*); **—оз** *m.* (med.) toxocariasis.

тол *see* **толит**; **—амин** *m.* Tolamine, chloramine-T; **—ан** *m.*, **—ановый** *a.* tolan, diphenylacetylene.

толацил *m.* tolacyl; **—амин** *m.* tolacylamine.

толбутамид *m.* (pharm.) tolbutamide.

толевая кровля roofing paper.

толерантн/ость *f.* tolerance; **—ый** *a.* tolerance (dose, etc.).

толиантипирин *m.* toly(anti)pyrine.

толидин *m.* tolidine, dimethylbenzidine.

толиз/аль *m.* tolysal, tolypyrine salicylate; **—ин** *m.* Tolysin, neocinchophen.

толил *m.* tolyl; tolil, dimethylbenzil; **—ен** *m.* tolylene; **—овый спирт** tolyl alcohol, tolylcarbinol.

толимидазол *m.* tolimidazole.

толипирин *m.* tolypyrine, *p*-tolyldimethylpyrazole.

толит *m.* (expl.) tolit, trinitrotoluene.

толк *m.* meaning, sense; use; push, nudge; **—и** *pl.* talk, rumors; **взять в т.** *v.* understand; **с —ом** sensibly, intelligently; **сбить с —у** *v.* confuse, baffle.

толк/ание *n.* pushing, etc., *see v.*; push; **—атель** *m.* pusher, push rod; plunger; follower; lifter; (valve) tappet; expediter; **—ательный** *a.* pushing; pusher-type (furnace); **—ать** *v.* push, thrust, shove; nudge; shake, joggle; **—ач** *see* **толкатель**; pestle, pounder; **—ающий** *a.* pushing, etc., *see v.*; pusher (propeller); push (rod); propelling (force); **—ающий механизм** thrust gear.

толкли *past pl. of* **толочь**.

толкнуть *see* **толкать**; give a push.

толков/ание *n.* interpretation, explanation, comment(ary); **—атель** *m.* interpreter; **—ать** *v.* interpret, explain, comment; discuss; **—ый** *a.* explanatory; sensible; **—ый словарь** glossary, defining dictionary.

толком *adv.* clearly, plainly, sensibly.

толкотня *f.* crush, crowd; jostling.

толкун(чик) *m.* (ent.) dance fly; (ichth.) trumpetfish.

толк/ушка *f.* pestle, pounder, stamp; **—ущий** *pr. act. part. of* **толочь**.

Толленса проба Tollens test.

толовый *a. of* **тол**.

толока *f.* fallow-field grazing.

толокно *n.* oat flour, oatmeal.

толокнянка *f.* (bot.) bearberry (*Arctostaphylos*, spec. *A. uva ursi*).

толоконный *a. of* **толокно**.

толокси— *prefix* toloxy—, cresoxy—.

толочь *v.* stamp, pound, beat, crush, grind, mill, (reduce to) powder, comminute; **—ся** *v.* be stamped, etc.; (ent.) swarm.

толп/а *f.* crowd; **—иться** *v.* crowd, cluster, group.

толпыга *see* **толстолоб(ик)**.

толст *sh. m. of* **толстый**; **—еть** *v.* get fat; **—ить** *v.* fatten; **—о** *adv.* thickly; fat.

толсто— *prefix* thick; **—брюшки** *pl.* (ent.) tent caterpillars; **—ватый** *a.* rather thick; rather fat; **—головки** *pl.* (ent.) common skippers (*Hesperiidae*); **—кожее** *n.* (zool.) pachyderm; **—кожий** *a.* thick-skinned, pachydermatous; **—корый** *a.* thick-barked.

толстолист/ный, —овой *a.* thick-leaved; plate (steel).

толстолоб(ик) *m.* (ichth.) silver carp.

толсто/ножки *pl.* chalcid flies (*Eurytomidae*); **—пластинчатый** *a.* thick-plate, in thick plates; **—рог** *m.* bighorn sheep; **—слойный** *a.* thick(-layered); deep-bed (filter); **—стеный** *a.* thick-walled, heavy-walled; **—та** *f.* thickness; **—тел** *m.* Colobus monkey; **—тный** *a.* thickness.

толстый *a.* thick, heavy (paper), heavy-gage (wire); fat, stout, obese.

толтры *pl.* toltry (sharp-peaked hills running in parallel rows).

толу/амид *m.* toluamide, methylbenzamide; **—анилид** *m.* toluanilide, *a*-phenylacetanilide.

толуанск/ий бальзам tolu, balsam of Tolu; **—ое масло** tolu oil.

толуидин *m.*, **—овый** *a.* toluidine.

толуил *m.* toluyl; **—ен** *m.* toluylene; **—ендиамин** *m.* toluylene diamine; **—еновый** *a.* toluylene; **—овый** *a.* toluyl; **—овая кислота** toluic acid, methylbenzoic acid.

толу/нитрил *m.* tolunitrile, cyanotoluene; **—ол** *m.* toluene, methylbenzene; **—олсульфокислота** *f.* toluenesulfonic acid; **—ольный** *a.* toluene; **—тиазол** *m.* toluthiazole; **—феназин** *m.* toluphenazine.

толухин— *prefix* toluquin—; **—олин** *m.* toluquinoline; **—он** *m.* toluquinone.

толчейная *f.* (met.) stamp mill.

толчейн/ый *a.* stamp; **т. пест** stamp; **т. постав, т. стан** *see* **толчейная**; **т. шлам, т. шлих, —ая муть** ore slime; **—ая мука** pulverized ore.

толч/ение *n.* stamping, etc., *see* **толочь**; comminution; **—ён(н)ый** *a.* stamped, etc., *see* **толочь**; **—ея** *f.* stamp mill, crusher; surge (of waves).

толчки *pl. of* **толчок**.

толчко/мер *m.* bumpometer, impact-measuring device; **—образный** *a.* jerky, jerking; (elec.) shock; **—образное развитие** jump.

толч/ок *m.* push, thrust, impulse, impetus; jerk, jolt, jar, shake, tremor, joggle; kick, percussion, concussion; collision, impact; (elec.) shock; (ionization) burst; (med.) insult, stroke; (heart) beat; **—ки** *pl.* jerks, jerking; bumping; **—ками** by jerks, jerkily, by starts or jolts, percussively, intermittently; **движение —ками** jerky motion; **действующий —ками** pulsating, intermittent; **истечение —ками** intermittent delivery; **влияние —ков** pulsating effect; **дать т.** *v.* start; **образование —ков** bumping; **приёмник —ков** shock absorber.

толщ/а *f.* thickness, mass, layer; (protective) cover; (earth's) crust; (geol.) rock mass, series, strata; **—е**

comp. of **толстый; в —е воды** in open water, pelagic(ally); **—ина** *f.* thickness, width, depth; size, caliber, gage; fatness, obesity, corpulence; **—иной** in thickness, thick; **—иномер** *m.* thickness gage, feeler gage.

толь *m.* roofing paper, tar paper; roofing felt.

только *adv., conj., and particle* only, merely, just, but, solely; was not . . . until, did not . . . until, not . . . except; **не т.** not only; **т.-т.** barely, just; **т.-что** just (now).

толя *gen. of* **толь.**

том *m.* (typ.) volume; *prepos. of* **то(т).**

томас/ирование *n.* basic Bessamer process; **—овский** *a.* (met.) Thomas; basic Bessemer; **т. чугун** Thomas pig (iron), basic pig (iron); **—овый** *see* **томасовский; —фосфат, —шлак** *m.* Thomas slag, basic slag (fertilizer).

томат *m.* tomato; tomato sauce; **—ин** *m.* tomatine; **—ный** *a.* tomato.

томболо *n.* (geol.) tombolo.

томбуй *m.* (anchor) buoy, float.

томильный *a.* (met.) malleablizing; soaking (furnace, pit, zone).

томит *m.* (min.) tomite, sapromyxite.

том/ительность *f.* anguish; weariness; **—ительный** *a.* agonizing; tiresome, wearisome; **—ить** *v.* tire, exhaust, weary, fatigue; torture, torment; soak; (met.) malleabl(e)ize; braise (meat); cure, treat (tobacco); stain (wood); **—иться** *v.* get tired, tire; pine (for); **—ление** *n.* fatigue; soaking; steeping; curing (of tobacco); (met.) malleablizing; **—лёный** *a.* wearied, tired; malleablized, soaked; malleable (cast iron); **—ность** *f.* languor, lassitude; **—ный** *a.* languid; *suffix* **—**volume.

томография *f.* (med.) tomography (X-ray diagnosis).

томорин *m.* Tomorin (rodenticide).

Томсена процесс Thomsen process.

томский *a.* (geog.) Tomsk.

Томсона, томсоновский *a.* (phys.) Thomson (scattering, etc.).

тому *dat. of* **то(т); т. назад** ago.

тон *m.* tone, tint, hue; note; sound.

тональн/о-модулированный *a.* tone-modulated; **—ость** *f.* tonality, key(note); (physiol.) tonicity; **—ость до мажор** key of C major; **—ый** *a.* tone; audio—; voice-frequency, low-frequency.

тонг *m.* joint tongue.

тонгр(ий)ский *a.* (geol.) Tongrian.

тон/евой *a.*; **—ей** *gen. pl. of* **тоня.**

тоненький *see* **тонкий.**

тонер *m.* toner, lake (pigment).

тонет *pr. 3 sing. of* **тонуть.**

тонзил/лит *m.* (med.) tonsillitis; **—ярный** *a.* tonsillar.

тонизир/овать *v.* tone up; **—ующее средство** tonic.

тоника *f.* (acous.) keynote.

тонико-клонический *a.* (med.) tonoclonic (spasm).

тонина *f.* fineness, dispersity.

тонирование *n.* (phot.) toning.

тонит *m.* (expl.) tonite.

тоническ/ий *a.*, **—ое средство** tonic.

тонка *f.* tonka bean; *sh. f. of* **тонкий.**

тонкан *m.* Toncan (iron).

тонк/ий *a.* thin, slender, fine, minute, fine-grained; subtle; meager; intimate (mixture); delicate, precision (adjustment); keen (hearing); light-gage (sheet); gracilis (muscle); (chem.) thorough (drying); **—ая пластинка** lamina; **—ая структура** (phys.) fine structure.

тонко *adv. and prefix* thin(ly), fine(ly); **—бороздчатый** *a.* finely striated; **—волокнистый** *a.* fine-fiber(ed), fine-fibrous; fibrillose; **—волочёный** *a.* fine-drawn.

тонковый *a.* tonka (bean).

тонко/жилковатый *a.* fine-grained (wood); **—зём** *m.* fine earth; **—зернистый** *a.* fine(-grained); **—измельчённый** *a.* finely pulverized, finely divided, fine (powder); **—канальчатый** *a.* fine-tubular; **—кожий** *a.* thin-skinned; **—корый** *a.* thin-barked.

тонколист/ный, —овой *a.* thin leaf, thin-leaved; (met.) sheet.

тонко/мерный *a.* small-dimension; **—нитчатый** *a.* (bot.) velvet-like, byssoid; **—ног** *m.* (bot.) Koeleria; **—ногий** *a.* thin-legged, thin-stemmed; **—оттянутый** *a.* fine-drawn, finely drawn (wire); **—песчаный** *a.* fine-sandy; **—плёночный, —плёнчатый** *a.* thin-filmed, thin-pellicular; **—полосный** *a.* stratified; **—пряд** *m.* (ent.) hepialid moth; **—прядильный** *a.* fine-spinning; **—размолотый, —распылённый** *a.* finely divided, finely pulverized; **—расточный** *a.* fine-boring; **—рунный** *a.* fine-wooled (sheep); **—слоистый, —слойный** *a.* thin-layer; (thinly) laminated, lamellar; thin-bedded; close-grained (wood); **—стебельчатый** *a.* thin-stalked.

тонкостенн/ость *f.* thinness of walls; **—ый** *a.* thin-walled, thin-section.

тонкост/ь *f.* thinness, fineness, sharpness, delicacy; subtlety; **—и** *pl.* details, ins and outs.

тонкотел *m.* langur (monkey) (*Presbytis*).

тонко/тянутый *a.* thin-drawn; **—шёрст(н)ый** *a.* fine-wool(ed).

тонмейстер *m.* (sound) mixer, audio controller.

тонна *f.* ton; **—ж** *m.* tonnage; **т.-километр** *m.* ton-kilometer; **т.-метр** *m.* ton-meter; **т.-миля** *f.* ton-mile; **т.-сила** *f.* ton-force.

тоннель *see* **туннель; —ный** *see* **туннельный.**

тонн/о *— see under* **тонна; —ый** *a. of* **тоня;** *suffix* -ton.

тонов/ой, —ый *a. of* **тон.**

тонография *f.* (ophth.) tonography.

тонок *sh. m. of* **тонкий.**

тонометрия *f.* (ophth.) tonometry.

тонопласт *m.* (cyt.) tonoplast.

тонстудия *f.* sound studio.

тонус *m.* (med.) tone, tonicity.

тонуть *v.* drown, sink.

тонфильм *m.* sound film.

тонч/айший *superl. of* **тонкий;** very fine, capillary; **—ать** *v.* become thinner, become finer.

тоншнейдер *m.* pug mill, clay cutter.

тоньше *comp. of* **тонкий,** thinner, finer.

тоня *f.* fishery; haul; (hydr.) crawl.

топ *m.* (naut.; met.) top, head.

топаз *m.*, **—овый** *a.* (min.) topaz.

топальгия *f.* (med.) topalgia, localized pain.

топ/ание *n.* stamping (of feet); **—ать** *v.* stamp.

топенант *m.* (naut.) (topping) lift, jigger; **т.(-шкентель)** topping line (of derrick).

топи *m.* (mam.) topi (antelope).

топильн/ый *a.* heating; **—ое пространство** combustion chamber, fire chamber; combustion space.

топинамбур *m.* Jerusalem artichoke.

топить *v.* heat; fire, stoke; melt (down), render; drown; sink (a ship); **—ся** *v.* burn; melt; be drowned.

топический *a.* (med.) topical, local.

топк/а *f.* furnace, burner; fire box, combustion chamber; heating, firing, stoking; fire; melting; **автоматическая т., механическая т.** automatic stoking; stoker; **с газовой —ой** gas-heated.

топк/ий *a.* swampy, muddy; suitable for fuel, combustible; **—ость** *f.* swampiness, muddiness.

топл/ение *n.* heating; melting; **—енный** *part.*, **—ёный** *a.* heated, etc., *see* **топить.**

топливн/ик *m.*, **—ое пространство** fire box, heating chamber, combustion chamber; **—ый** *a.* fuel, combustible; **—ая батарея** *f.* fuel cell; **—ая нефть, —ое масло** fuel oil.

топлив/о *n.* fuel; (rocket) propellant; **древесное т.** firewood; **жидкое т.** liquid fuel; fuel oil; **твёрдое т.** solid fuel; solid propellant; **на твёрдом —е, твёрдого —а** solid-propellant (rocket).

топливо/добывающий *a.* fuel (industry); **—дозирующий** *a.* fuel-metering; injector fuel (valve); **-заменитель** *m.* fuel substitute; **—заправочный** *a.* fuel-supply; **—использование** *n.* fuel utilization, fuel efficiency; **—мер** *m.* fuel level indicator, oil gage; **—несущий** *a.* fuel-carrying, fuel-bearing; **—перекачивающий** *a.* fuel-transfer; **—подача** *f.*, **—подающий** *a.* fuel-handling, fuel supply; **—подкачивающий** *a.* fuel-feed, fuel-priming (pump); **—приёмный** *a.* fuel-intake; **—провод** *m.* fuel line; **—регулируемый** *a.* fuel-metering; **—снабжение** *n.* fuel supply; **—содержащий** *a.* fuel-containing; **—хранилище** *n.* fuel storehouse.

топлый *a.* soaked, wet.

топляк *m.* submerged log.

топнуть *see* **топать.**

топо— *prefix* top(o)— (place).

топограф *m.* topographer; surveyor; **—ический** *a.* topographic; **—ический каталог** (library) shelf list; **—ия** *f.* topography.

топовый огонь (naut.) masthead light.

топок *gen. pl. of* **топка;** *sh. m. of* **топкий.**

топол/евый, —иный *a. of* **тополь.**

рополог/изация *f.* (math.) topologization; **—ический** *a.* topologic(al); **—ия** *f.* topology.

тополь *m.* (bot.) poplar (*Populus*).

топор *m.* ax; **—ик** *m.* hatchet; (orn.) puffin (*Fratercula*); **—иковые** *pl.* (ichth.) (silver) hatchetfishes (*Sternoptychidae*); **—ище** *n.* (ax) handle, shaft.

топорн/ость *f.* clumsiness, coarseness; **—ый** *a.* clumsy, coarse, rough(-hewn); ax.

топоровидный *a.* hatchet-shaped.

топорщить(ся) *v.* bristle; puff up.

топос *m.* (mam.) yak.

топот *m.* stamping (of feet), trampling; **—ать** *v.* stamp (feet); patter, clatter.

топотип *m.* (genetics) topotype.

топохим/ический *a.* topochemical, localized reaction; **—ия** *f.* topochemistry.

топоцентрический *a.* topocentric.

топочн/ый *a.* furnace; heating; fire (box); **т. газ** flue gas; fuel gas; **т. порог** fire bridge, baffler; **т. ход, —ая труба** flue; **—ое пространство** fire box, combustion chamber; (inside of) furnace.

топрик *m.* (naut.) davit span.

топтать *v.* trample, tread (upon).

топ/че *comp. of* **топкий; —ь** *f.* swamp, marsh, (quag)mire, bog.

тор *m.* (geom.) tore, torus, anchor ring; torr, Torricelli unit (1 mm of mercury).

торазин *m.* (pharm.) Thorazine, chlorpromazine (hydrochloride).

торакальный *a.* (anat.) thoracic.

торак/о *prefix* thoraco— (thorax, thoracic, chest); **—c** *m.* thorax.

торамин *m.* toramin (ammonium trichlorobutyl malonate).

торба *f.* bag.

торг *m.* trade, trading; bargaining; *prefix see* **торговый;** *suffix* trade, commerce; trading organization; **—и** *pl.* auction; tender(s), bid.

торгов/ать *v.* trade, deal, negotiate, sell; **—аться** *v.* bargain; **—ец** *m.* tradesman, dealer, merchant.

торговл/я *f.* commerce, trade, business, traffic (in); **основные предметы —и** staple commodities.

торгово-промышленный *a.* pertaining to commerce and industry.

торгов/ый *a.* trading, trade, commercial, mercantile; **т. автомат** vending machine; **т. знак** trademark; **т. флот** merchant marine, merchant shipping; **—ая марка** trademark; **—ая палата** Chamber of Commerce, Board of Trade; **—ое дело** business; **—ое качество** commercial grade, technical grade; **—ое предприятие** business (enterprise); **—ое судно** freighter, cargo ship, merchant ship.

торгпред *m.* trade representative; **—ство** *n.* Trade Delegation.

тор/ец *m.* end (plane), butt; face, side; wood paving block; **вид с —ца** end view; **задний т.** back; **подрезать т.** *v.* face.

торжеств/енность *f.* solemnity; **—енный** *a.* solemn, triumphal, gala; grand (meeting); **—о** *n.* triumph, celebration; **—овать** *v.* triumph (over), celebrate.

торзио— *see under* **торсио—.**

тор/ид *m.* thoride; **—иевый** *a.* thorium; **—иевая земля** thoria, thorium oxide; **—ий** *m.* thorium, Th; **окись —ия** thorium oxide, thoria; **сернокислый т., сульфат —ия** thorium sulfate; **хлористый т.** thorium chloride; **эманация —ия** thoron, Tn; **—ийсодержащий** *a.* thorium-bearing; **—ированный** *a.* thoriated; **—истый** *a.* containing thorium.

торица *f.* (bot.) spurry (*Spergula*).

ториччелиева *see* **торричеллиева.**

торический *a.* toric (lens).

торичник *m.* (bot.) Spergularia.

торкрет *m.* (concrete) gunite; guniting; **—бетон** *m.* gunite; **—ирование** *n.* guniting; **—ировать** *v.* gunite; **—ный** *a.* gunite; guniting; **т.-пушка** *f.* concrete gun.

тормаз *see* **тормоз.**

тормо/жение *n.* braking, retardation, etc., *see v.*; brake action, frictional action, drag; (aero.) stagnation; arrest; (distillation column) loading; **способность —жения** (nucl.) stopping power; **—жённый** *a.* braked, etc., *see v.*; **—з** *m.* brake, braking; obstruction; **на —зах** slowly; **—зить** *v.* brake, retard, inhibit, decelerate, slow down; throttle, damp; stop, arrest, check; apply brakes; obstruct, impede.

тормозн/ой *a.* brake, braking; drag; retarding, inhibiting; deceleration (parachute); inhibitory (reflex); stopping; *m.* brakeman; **т. путь** braking distance; **т. (ракетный) двигатель** retrorocket engine; **т. эффект** braking efficiency, retardation efficiency; **—ая двигательная установка** retrorocket, retropackage, braking engine; **—ая колодка** brake shoe; **—ая коробка** brake housing; **—ая ракета** retrorocket; **—ая система** brake assembly; **—ая способность** (nucl.) stopping power; **—ая тяга** brake rod; **—ое излучение** bremsstrahlung, braking radiation; **—ое приспособление** brake, stopping device.

тормозящ/ий *a.* braking, etc., *see* **тормозить; т. агент** inhibitor; **т. момент** braking torque, drag torque; **—ая поверхность** braking surface, brake surface; **—ая сетка** (electron.) barrier grid; **—ее действие** brake action.

торнадо *n.* (meteor.) tornado.

торндайковый *a.* Thorndike.

торный *a.* well-used (road), beaten, smooth (path).

торогуммит *m.* (min.) thorogummite.

тороид *m.* (geom.) toroid; toroidal core choke; (welding) toroidal choke transformer; —**альный** *a.* toroidal; doughnut (coil); **витой** —**альный** *a.* wound-tape (core).

торон *m.* thoron, Tn; thorium emanation.

тороп/ить *v.* hasten, hurry, precipitate, rush, urge (on), push (on, forward); —**иться** *v.* make haste, (be in a) hurry, speed; **не** —**ясь** unhurriedly.

тороплив/о *adv.* hurriedly, with speed; —**ость** *f.* haste, hurry, speed; —**ый** *a.* hasty, hurried, speedy, quick, prompt.

торос *m.* hummock (of ice), hummocked ice, ice reef; —**истость** *f.* hummocking; —**истый** *a.* hummocked; —**ить** *v.* hummock, pile up; —**овый** *a.* of **торос**.

торошен/ие *n.* hummocking (of ice); —**ный** *a.* hummocked, piled up.

торп *m.*, —**а** *f.* (ichth.) brown trout.

Торпа синтез Thorpe synthesis.

торпед/а *f.* (mil.; oil-well drilling) torpedo; —**ирование** *n.* torpedoing; (well) shooting; —**ированный** *a.* torpedoed; shot; —**ировать** *v.* torpedo; shoot; —**ист** *m.* torpedoist, torpedo man; —**ный** *a.* torpedo; —**о** *n.* fore body (of vehicle), cowl; *prefix* torpedo; —**ование** *see* **торпедирование;** —**ометание** *n.* torpedo bombing; —**оносец** *m.* torpedo bomber; —**оносный** *a.* torpedo-carrying; —**ообразный** *a.* torpedo-like.

торпидный *a.* (med.) torpid.

торр *m.* torr (1 mm of mercury column).

торричеллиева пустота Torricellian vacuum (of a barometer).

торс *m.* torso, trunk, body; (math.) torse.

торсио/грамма *f.* torsiogram; —**граф** *m.* torsiograph; —**метр** *m.* torsiometer, torquemeter; —**н** *m.* torsion (bar); —**нный** *a.* torsion.

торсоцветия *f.* (bot.) anthodium.

торт *m.*, —**овый** *a.* pastry.

тортонский *a.* (geol.) Tortonian (substage).

торф *m.* peat, turf; **болотный т.** bog peat; **волокнистый т., моховой т.** fibrous peat, peat moss.

торфо— *prefix* peat; —**вание** *n.* enrichment of soil with peat; —**вать** *v.* apply peat (to soil); —**добывание** *n.*, —**добыча** *f.*, —**добывающий** *a.* peat mining, peat cutting; —**крошка** *f.* peat dust; —**образование** *n.* peat formation; —**перегнойный** *a.* peat-humus; peat (pots); —**подобный** *a.* peat-like, peaty; —**разработка** *f.* peat mining; —**резка** *f.* peat cutter, turf cutter; —**сос** *m.* hydraulic peat mining machine; —**тук** *m.* peat-fertilizer mixture; —**фосфат** *m.* peat phosphate.

торфяник *m.* peat bog; peat soil; peat worker.

торфянист/ый *a.* peaty, turfy; —**ая земля** peaty or black earth, mold.

торфян/ой *a.* peat(y), turf(y), moor; **т. мох** peat moss; —**ая залежь** peat deposit, peat bog; —**ая мука** powdered peat.

торц/а *gen.* of **торец;** —**евание** *n.* facing; paving; —**евать** *v.* face; pave; —**евой** *see* **торцовый;** —**овать** *v.* face; pave; —**овка** *f.* facing; facing lathe; deck saw; woodblock pavement; —**овочный** *a.* facing; —**овый** *a.* front, face; end; (phys.) end-window (counter); plane (surface); socket, box (wrench); crosscut (saw); (geol.) mullion, rodding (structure); blockwood (pavement); —**овый щит** fender, guard; —**овое соединение** edge joint.

торч/ание *n.* protrusion, projection; —**ать** *v.* protrude, project, stick out; —**ащий** *a.* projecting, etc., *see* v.; upright; (bot.) strigillose; —**ком, —мя** *adv.* on end, upright, vertically; —**ок** *m.* protruding object; knot, snag, stump; (oak) seedling.

тоска *f.* anxiety, distress; longing, melancholy.

Тоскана (geog.) Tuscany.

тоскливый *a.* sad, melancholy; depressed.

тот *m.* *pron.*, **та** *f.*, **то** *n.* that; **те** *pl.* those; **тот же** the (self)same; **один и тот же** one and the same; **тот и другой** both, the one and the other; **тот или другой** either; **тот или иной** one or another, specific, particular, given; **ни тот ни другой** neither; **тот, кто** the one who, whoever; **до того** to such an extent, to such a degree, so much; **тому назад** ago; **тому подобное** (and) so forth; such as; similar, like; **к тому же** besides, moreover.

тотальный *a.* total.

тотипотентн/ость *f.* (biol.) totipotence; —**ый** *a.* totipotent(ial).

т. отв. *abbr.* (**точка отвердения**) solidification point, setting point.

тотчас *adv.* immediately, directly, without delay, right away, promptly.

тохлорин *m.* Tochlorine, chloramine-T.

точек *gen. pl.* of **точка.**

точен *sh. m.* of **точный.**

точ/ение *n.* sharpening, etc., *see* **точить;** —**енный** *part.*, —**ёный** *a.* sharpened, etc., *see* **точить.**

точеч/ка *dim.* of **точка;** —**но—** *prefix* point(wise); (welding) spot; —**но-контактный** *a.* point-contact, point-to-point; —**но-плоскостный** *a.* point-junction (transistor); —**но-роликовый** *a.* stitch (welder); —**сваренный** —**сварной** *a.* spot-welded.

точечн/ый *a.* point, punctate; dot; dotted (line); localized (impact); point-source (lamp, etc.); *suffix* —punctate; **т. электрод** point electrode; —**ая коррозия** pitting; —**ая масса** (phys.) point mass; —**ая мутация** (gen.) point mutation; **диаграмма** —**ого преобразования** point-to-point mapping graph.

точил/ка *f.*, —**о** *n.* whetstone, grindstone, sharpener; **круглое** —**о** grinding wheel, polishing wheel.

точ/ильный *a.* sharpening, etc., *see* v.; **т. брусок, т. камень** whetstone, grindstone; **т. материал** abrasive; **т. станок** sharpener, (tool-)grinding machine; lathe; —**ильня** *f.* grind mill; —**ильщик** *m.* sharpener, grinder; —**ильщики** *pl.* (ent.) Anobiidae; —**ить** *v.* sharpen, grind, whet, hone; machine, work, turn (on lathe); (zool.) gnaw, eat; corrode; wear out.

точ/ка *f.* point, dot, period, spot; (typ.) point (0.35146 mm); sharpening, grinding; (anat.) punctum; **т. в** —**ку** exactly, to a T, in the same manner; **т. кипения** boiling point; **т. нулевого заряда** (met.) zero charge potential; **т. с запятой** semicolon; **в трёх** —**ках** three-point; **попасть в** —**ку** *v.* hit the mark; **т.-тире** *n.* dot-and-dash (code); —**кообразный** *a.* dot-shaped, punctiform.

точнее *comp.* of **точно.**

точно *adv.*, *conj.*, *particle*, *and sh. n.* of **точный,** exactly, precisely, closely, accurately, faithfully, carefully, well, duly; conclusively; precision (tooled); indeed, really; as if, as (though); like; **т. определять** *v.* pin-point; **т. отрегулированный** *a.* precision-set; **т. так** exactly so, just so; **т. так же** just so, in exactly the same way; **т. такой** exactly the same.

точност/ь *f.* accuracy, exactness, preciseness, precision; punctuality; fit; trueness, closeness, degree, fineness, delicacy (of adjustment); (elec. comm.) fidelity; **в** —**и** exactly, punctually; **с** —**ью до** correct to, correct within, with an accuracy (of), to the nearest; **с** —**ью до порядка величины** order-of-magnitude (calculation); **с высокой** —**ью** to a high precision; (acous.) high-fidelity.

точн/ый *a.* exact, precise, accurate, correct, punctual, sharp, distinct, explicit, definite, strict, close; faithful, true; direct; fine, delicate, sensitive (adjustment); precision (instrument, tool, work); **—ое дополнение** (comp.) true *or* radix complement; **—ые науки** exact sciences.

точь-в-точь *adv.* exactly, in the same way; word for word.

тошн/ить *v.* feel nauseated; **ему —о** he is nauseated; **—ота** *f.* nausea; **—отворный** *a.* nauseating, nauseous.

тощ/ать *v.* grow thin, waste away; **—ий** *a.* lean, poor (ore, gas); empty; skim (milk), skim-milk; emaciated, thin; (anat.) jejunal; **—ая кишка** (anat.) jejunum.

т. п. *abbr.* (**тому подобное**) similar, like; such as; (and) so forth, (and) so on.

т. пл. *abbr.* (**точка плавления**) melting point.

ТПН *abbr.* (**трифосфопиридиннуклеотид**) triphosphopyridine nucleotide, TPN.

т. пр. *abbr.* (**температура превращения**) transformation temperature, critical point.

тр. *abbr.* (**труды**) transactions.

т-ра *abbr.* (**температура**) temperature.

трабекул/а *f.* (biol.) trabecula; **—ярный** *a.* trabecular.

трав/а *f.* grass, herb, weed; **ароматичные —ы, лекарственные —ы** herbs; **морская т.** seaweed.

травел(л)ер *m.* traveler; portal crane; **—ный** *a.* traveling.

травенеть *v.* overgrow with grass.

траверз *see* **траверс;** **—а** *see* **траверса;** **—ный** *see* **траверсный.**

траверс *m.* crosspiece, crossbeam, crossarm; (mil.) traverse; (naut.) beam; (hydr.) small dam; **—а** *f.*, **—ный** *a.* traverse, yoke; crosspiece, crossbar; (tie) beam, tie piece; stay, brace; transverse member.

травертин *m.* (petr.) travertine.

травиль/ный *a.* etching, etc., *see* **травить; —щик** *m.* etcher.

травин(к)а *f.* blade (of grass).

трав/итель *m.* etching reagent; pickling agent; **—ить** *v.* etch, pickle, corrode, attack, scour, cleanse, dip; stain (wood); poison, exterminate (with poison); pay out (rope), unwind, uncoil; let out (steam, air); slacken, loosen; trample down, damage (crops); graze (a field); hunt (down), hound, persecute; **—ка** *see* **травление;** *dim. of* **трава; —ление** *n.* etching, etc., *see v.*; **—лен(н)ый** *a.* etched, etc., *see v.*; **—ля** *f.* hunt(ing), persecution, baiting.

травм/а *f.* trauma, wound, injury; **—атизировать** *v.* traumatize; **—атизм** *m.* traumatism; traumatic injury; accident; **—атический** *a.* traumatic; **—атовый** *a.* traumatic (acid); **—атология** *f.* traumatology; **—ировать** *v.* traumatize, injure, wound.

травник *m.* (orn.) redshank (*Tringa totanus*).

травный *a. of* **трава.**

траво— *prefix* grass; weed; **—вед** *m.* herbalist; **—косилка** *f.* lawn mower; **—косный** *a.* grasscutting; grass (land); **—нагрузчик** *m.* hay loader; **—очиститель** *m.* weeder; weed killer, herbicide; **—полье** *n.* grassland farming; crop-and-grass rotation; **—польный** *a.* grassland; grass-arable (rotation); **—рез** *m.* (orn.) plant-cutter (*Phytotomus*); **—сейный** *a.* grass-seeded; **—сеяние** *n.* grass cultivation; **—сжигатель** *m.* weed burner; **—смесь** *f.* mixed grass crop; **—стой** *m.* herbage; **—ядный** *a.* herbivorous, grazing (animal); phytophagous.

травяник *m.* (ichth.) goby.

травян/истый *a.* grassy, herbaceous.

травянка *f.* (ichth.) pike (*Esox lucius*).

травян/ой *a.* grass(y); herb(al), herbaceous; **—ая вошь** (ent.) aphid; **—ое дерево** grass tree (*Xanthorrhoea australis*).

травящий *see* **травильный.**

траг/акант, —аниит, —ант *m.*, **—антовая камедь** tragacanth (gum).

траг/едия *f.* tragedy; **—ический, —ичный** *a.* tragic.

традесканция *f.* (bot.) Tradescantia.

традици/онный *a.* traditional; **—я** *f.* tradition.

траектор/ия *f.* trajectory, path, track; orbit, locus; **веер —ий** (mil.) sheaf of fire; **вершина —ии** culminating point; **сноп —ий** (mil.) cone of fire.

тразентин *m.* (pharm.) Trasentine.

т. разл. *abbr.* (**температура разложения**) decomposition temperature; **т. размягч.** *abbr.* (**температура размягчения**) softening point.

трайбология *f.* tribology.

трайлер *see* **трейлер.**

трак *m.* track link, track shoe.

Т-ра кип. *see* **т. кип.**

тракт *m.* highway, road; channel, route; loop, circuit; (anat.) tract.

тракт/ат *m.* treatise; treaty; **—ование** *see* **трактовка; —овать** *v.* treat, examine, consider; discuss, interpret; **—овка** *f.* treatise, treatment, interpretation.

трактовый *a. of* **тракт.**

трактор *m.* tractor; **—изация** *f.* tractorization; **—ист** *m.* tractor driver; **—ный** *a.* tractor; tractor-drawn; **—остроение** *n.* tractor manufacture; **т.-снегоход** *m.* snow tractor; **т.-тягач** *m.* (truck) tractor.

трактотомия *f.* (med.) tractotomy.

трактриса *f.* (geom.) tractrix.

тракция *f.* (med.) traction.

трал *m.* trawl (line), trawl net; (mine)sweep(er); **—ение** *n.* trawling; sweeping; **—ер** *see* **тральщик; —ить** *v.* trawl; sweep; **—мейстер** *m.* (fishing) trawler; **—овый** *a.* trawl(er's); **—ьщик** *m.* minesweeper.

трама *f.* (bot.) trama.

трамбалловский *a.* Trumbull.

трамблёр *m.* distributor (of motor).

трамб/ование *n.* ramming, etc., *see v.*; **—ованный** *a.* rammed, etc., *see v.*; **—овать** *v.* ram, tamp, pack, plug; stamp; **—овка** *f.*, **—овочный** *a.* ramming, etc., *see v.*; ram(mer), tamper, compactor; stamper; **—овщик** *m.* rammer; packer; **—ующий** *a.* ramming, etc., *see v.*

трамвай *m.*, **—ный** *a.* trolley, street car.

трамлёр *see* **трамблёр.**

трамп *m.* (naut.) tramp steamer.

трамплин *m.* spring board; (ski) jump, jumping platform.

транец *m.* transom.

транзистор *m.* (electron.) transistor; **на —ах** transistorized; **т.-бусинка** *m.* bead transistor; **—изация** transistorization; **—ный** *a.* transistor(iz)ed, transistor.

транзит *m.* transit; **—ивность** *f.* (math.) transitivity; **—ивный** *a.* transitive; **—ник** *m.* transit passenger; **—ный** *a.* transit; direct; **—ная связь** tandem operation; **—орный** *a.* transitory, fleeting.

транзитрон *m.* (electron.) transitron.

транквилизатор *m.* (pharm.) tranquilizer, sedative.

транс *m.* (med.) trance.

транс— *prefix* trans— (across); **—активность** *f.* transactivity; trans-effect; **—альдолаза** *f.* (enz.) transaldolase; **—аляскинский нефтепровод** trans-Alaska pipeline; **—аминаза** *f.* transaminase; **—аминирование** *n.* (biochem.) transamination; **—аннулярный** *a.* transannular; **—арктический** *a.* transarctic; **—атлантический** *a.* transatlantic; **—ацетилаза** *f.* (enz.) transacetylase; **—ацилаза** *f.* transacylase.

Трансва/аль, —л (geog.) Transvaal.

трансверсаль *m.* transversal; **—но** *adv.* transversal(ly); **—ный** *a.* transversal.

трансверт/ер, —ор *m.* (elec.) transverter.

транс-влияние *n.* trans-effect.

трансгенация *f.* (gen.) transgenation, (point) mutation.

транс/грессия *f.* (geol.) transgression, unconformability of overlap; advance (of sea); **согласная т.** parallel transgression; **—дуктор** *m.* (elec.) transducer; **—дукция** *f.* (gen.) transduction; **—дюсер** *m.* (elec.) transducer, transductor; **—звуковой** *a.* transonic; **—иверный** *a.* transceiver, transmitter-receiver; **-изомер** *m.* trans-isomer; **-изомерный** *a.* trans-isomeric; **—ильванский** *a.* (geog.) Transylvania(n); **—кетолаза** *f.*, **—кетолазный** *a.* (enz.) transketolase; **—континентальный** *SW1a.* transcontinental; **-конфигурация** *f.* transconfiguration.

транскри/бирование *n.* transcribing, transcription; transliteration; **—бированный** *a.* transcribed; transliterated; **—бировать** *v.* transcribe; transliterate; **—пционный** *a.*, **—пция** *f.* transcription.

транскристалл/изация *f.* transcrystallization; **—итный, —ический** *a.* transcrystalline.

транскюр/иевый *a.*, **—ий** *m.* transcurium.

транслир/овать *v.* translate, relay, retransmit; **—ующий** *a.* translating, relaying.

транслитерация *f.* transliteration.

транслокация *f.* (gen.) translocation.

трансля/тор *m.* (elec. comm.) translator, repeater; **—ция** *f.*, **—ционный** *a.* translation, relay(ing), retransmitting; repeater.

трансметил/аза *f.* (enz.) transmethylase, methyltransferase; **—ирование** *n.* transmethylation.

трансми/ссия *f.*, **—ссионный** *a.* transmission, transmitting; **—ттер** *m.* transmitter.

транс/мутация *f.* (biol.) transmutation; **—оидный** *a.* (chem.) staggered; **—океанский** *a.* transoceanic; **—парант** *m.* (phot.) transparency; ruled paper; **—пирация** *f.* transpiration; **—пирование** *n.*, **—плана** *f.* gliding image plane; **—плантат** *m.* (med.) (skin) graft; transplant; **—плантация** *f.*, **—плантирование** *n.* (med.) transplantation; (bot.) grafting; **—плутоние-вый** *a.*, **—плутоний** *m.* transplutonium.

транспозиция *f. see* **транспонирование.**

трансположение *n.* (gen.) transconfiguration.

транспониров/ание *n.*, **—ка** *f.* transposition; (math.) transpose (of matrix); **—ать** *v.* transpose.

транспорт *m.* transport(ation), conveyance, conveying, hauling; traffic; transit, transfer; (accounting) carrying forward; **—абельность** *f.* (trans)portability; **—абель-ный** *a.* (trans)portable; **—ёр** *m.* transporter, transport vehicle, carrier; conveyer; **ленточный —ёр** conveyer belt; **—ёр-вездеход** *m.* all-terrain transporter; **—ёрный** *a. of* **транспортёр; —ёрный червяк** screw conveyer; **—ёрная лента** conveyer belt.

транспортир *m.* protractor.

транспортир/ование *n.* transport(ation), conveying, conveyance, haulage, shipment; handling (operation); **—ованный** *a.* transported, etc., *see v.*; **—овать** *v.* transport, convey, haul, carry; ship; transfer, handle; **—овка** *see* **транспортирование; при —овке** in transit; **—овочный, —ующий** *a.* transporting, etc., *see v.*; **—овочная лента** conveyer belt.

транспортн/ик *m.* transport worker; transport plane; **—ый** *a. of* **транспорт;** transfer (RNA); **—ая лента** conveyer belt; **—ая накладная** bill of lading, consignment note; **—ая труба** conveyer pipe, pipeline; **—ое движение** traffic; **—ое средство** vehicle, means of transportation.

транссибирский *a.* trans-siberian.

транссуд/ат *m.* (physiol.) transudate; **—ация** *f.* transudation; **—ировать** *v.* transude, exude.

трансуран *m.* transuranium; **—ид** *m.* transuranide; **—овый** *a.* transuranium, transuranic.

трансфер/аза *f.* (enz.) transferase; **—рин** *m.* (biochem.) transferrin, siderophilin.

трансфер/кар *m.* transfer car; **—т** *m.*, **—тный** *a.* transfer.

трансфлюксор *m.* (comp.) Transfluxor.

трансформ(ант)а *f.* transform.

трансформатор *m.* (elec.) transformer; converter; **—ный** *a.* transformer; inductive (coupling; pickup); **т.-по-выситель** *m.* step-up transformer; **т.-понизитель, т.-редуктор** *m.* step-down transformer.

трансформ/ационный *a.*, **—ация** *f.* transformation, conversion; (photogrammetry) rectification; **—изм** *m.* (biol.) transformism; **—ирование** *see* **трансфор-мация; —ированный** *a.* transformed, etc., *see v.*; **—ировать** *v.* transform, convert, change; rectify (aerial print); **—ирующий** *a.* transformation (DNA).

трансфосфорилаза *f.* (enz.) transphosphorylase.

трансфузи/онный *a.*, **—я** *f.* transfusion.

трансцендент/(аль)ный *a.* (math.) transcendental; **—ность** *f.* transcendence.

транш/еекопатель *m.* trench digger, trencher; **плуж-ный т.** trench plow; **—ейный** *a.*, **—ея** *f.* trench, ditch; pit, dug-out.

трап *m.* ladder; gangway, ramp; trap, drain; (gems) trap(-cut) brilliant; **—балка** *f.* ladder davit.

трапец/евидный *see* **трапециевидный; —еидальный** *a.* trapezoid(al); buttress (screw thread); **—иевидный** *a.* trapezoid(al), trapeziform; trapezius (muscle); **—ия** *f.* trapeze, trapezium; map frame, map projection limits; **—оид** *m.* trapezoid; **—оидальный** *see* **трапецеи-дальный.**

трапецоэдр *m.* (cryst.) trapezohedron; **—ический** *a.* trapezohedral.

т-ра плавл. *see* **т. пл.**

трапп *m.*, **—овый** *a.* (petr.) trap(rock).

трапспаут *m.* trap spout.

трасс *m.* (petr.) trass.

трасса *f.* route, course, run (of cable), layout, trace; line, direction; alignment; track, path, orbit, trajectory; location; airway; sketch, draft, plan.

трасс/ант *m.* (com.) drawer (of bill of exchange); **—ат** *m.* drawee.

трассёр *m.* tracer, flare; (analytical chem.) spike.

трассир/ование *n.*, **—овка** *f.* tracing, etc., *see v.*; **—овать** *v.* trace, locate; stake out, mark out; (com.) draw (a bill); **—овка** *f.* tracing, location (survey); laying, laying out, layout; **—ующий** *a.* tracing; (mil.) tracer (bullet).

трассовой *a. of* **трасса, трасс;** intermediate (airfield).

трассология *f.* (criminology) detection, study of clues.

трат/а *f.* expense, expenditure; consumption; waste, wasting; **—ить** *v.* expend, disburse, spend; consume; waste.

тратта *f.* (com.) bill of exchange.

Траубе, траубевский *a.* (physiol.; phys.) Traube's.

траулер *m.*, **—ный** *a.* trawler.

траур *m.* mourning (clothes); **—ница** *f.* willow butterfly (*Vanessa antiopa*); **—ный** *a.* funereal; mournful.

трафарет *m.* stencil, pattern, template, mask; cliché; **т. ввода данных** (comp.) data entry screen; **размечать по —у, —ить** *v.* stencil(ing); **—ка** *f.* stencil(ing); stencil brush; title block (of drawing); **—ность** *f.* banality; **—ный** *a.* stencil(ed); masking (technique); trite, conventional, unoriginal; **—ная печать** stenciling.

траф(ф)ик *m.* traffic.

трах *m.* bang, crash.

трах/еальный *a.* (anat.; bot.) tracheal; **—еи** *pl.* (bot.) tracheids; **—еид** *m.* tracheid; **—еит** *m.* (med.) tracheitis; **—ейнодышащие, —ейные** *pl.* (zool.) Tracheata; **—ейный** *a.* (anat.) tracheal; **—еобронхиальный** *a.* (anat.) tracheobronchial; **—еола** *f.* (biol.) tracheole; **—еомикоз** *m.* (phyt.) tracheomycosis, fungal wilt; **—еоскопия** *f.* tracheoscopy; **—еотомия** *f.* (med.) tracheotomy; **—ея** *f.* (anat.) trachea.

трахинот(ус) *m.* (ichth.) pompano (*Trachinotus*).

трахит *m.* (petr.) trachyte; **—ный, —овый** *a.* trachyte, trachytic.

трахихтовые *pl.* (ichth.) roughies, slime heads (*Trachichthyidae*).

трахома *f.* (med.) trachoma.

траченный *past pass. part. of* **тратить.**

ТРВ *abbr.* (**терморегулирующий вентиль**) heat-regulating valve.

тр-д *abbr.* (**трубопровод**) pipeline.

ТРД *abbr.* (**турбореактивный двигатель**) turbojet engine; **ТРДВ, ТРД-В** *abbr.* (**турбореактивный двигатель, винтовой**) turboprop engine.

тре— *see* **трёх—.**

требов/ание *n.* demand, requirement, requisition, request, claim; **технические —ания** specifications; **—ательность** *f.* demands, exactions; **—ательный** *a.* demanding, exacting, particular; **—ательный листок** (library) call slip; **—ать** *v.* demand, claim, require, need, request, want, ask, call (for); necessitate; consume (time); **—аться** *v.* be demanded, etc.; be necessary, be essential, require; it takes . . . to.

требуемый *a.* required, requisite, specified; wanted, desired.

требу/ха, —шина *f.*, **—шинный** *a.* guts, entrails; offal.

требующий *a.* demanding, etc., *see* **требовать.**

тревог/а *f.* alarm, anxiety, fear, concern; **бить —у** *v.* sound an alarm; **воздушная т.** air-raid warning; **сигнал —и** alarm (signal); **учебная т.** drill.

тревож/ить *v.* alarm, disturb, worry; **—иться** *v.* be alarmed, be anxious, worry; **—ный** *a.* alarm(ing), troubling, uneasy; anxious; **—ный сигнал** alarm; **—ная сигнализация** alarm (system).

трегалоза *f.* (chem.) trehalose.

трегер *m.* (chem.) carrier, medium; support(er), substrate; **—ный** *a.* supported.

трегерит *m.* (min.) trögerite.

тред-юнион *m.* trade union.

трезв/енник *m.* teetotaler; **—енный** *see* **трезвый; —еть** *v.* sober up; **—ость** *f.* soberness.

трезвучие *n.* (phys.) triad, common chord.

трезвый *a.* sober, sound, judicious.

трезуб/ец *m.* trident; **—(чат)ый** *a.* trident(ate), three-pronged.

трейбование *n.* (met.) cupellation.

трейлер *m.* trailer.

трек *m.*, **—овый** *a.* track, trace, trail.

трелевать *v.* (logging) skid, haul, drag, snake; log.

трелёв/ка *f.*, **—очный** *a.* skidding, etc., *see v.*; **—очный захват** trail dogs; **—щик** *m.* skidder, hauler.

трель *f.* (music) trill, quaver, warble; (logging) trail.

трельяж *m.* trellis, lattice (work).

трём *dat. of* **три;** *pr. 1 pl. of* **тереть.**

тремадокский *a.* (geol.) Tremadoc(ian).

трематод/оз *m.* (med.) trematodiasis; **—ы** *pl.* (zool.) Trematoda.

трематом *m.* (ichth.) cod (*Trematomus*).

тремблер *m.* (elec.) trembler.

тремоло *n.* (music) tremolo.

тремор *m.* tremor; **—ный** *a.* tremulous.

трёмстам *dat. of* **триста.**

тремя *instr. of* **три.**

тренаж *m.* training, drill; **—ёр** *m.* trainer, coach; simulator, training equipment.

тренд *m.* trend.

тренер *m.* trainer.

трензель *m.*, **—ный** *a.* swing bracket; snaffle (bit); **большой т.** (met.) quadrant plate; **малый т.** tumbler gear.

трен/ие *n.* friction, rubbing; **т. покоя** friction of rest, static friction; **без —ия** frictionless; **сопротивление от —ия** frictional resistance; **тормоз —ия** friction brake; **физика —ия** tribophysics; **электричество —ия** frictional electricity.

тренинг *m.* training.

трениров/анность *f.* degree of training; **—анный** *a.* trained, etc., *see v.*; **—ать** *v.* train; condition, activate (catalyst); age; **—ка** *f.*, **—очный** *a.* training, etc., *see v.*

трено/га *f.* tripod; three-pole derrick; hobble; **т.-лафет** *m.* tripod mount; **—гий, —жный** *a.* tripod, three-legged; **—жник** *m.* tripod; (zool.) tripus.

трентонский *a.* (geol.) Trenton.

тренцов/альная машина worming machine (for rope); **—ать** *v.* worm.

тренчик *m.* narrow strap.

треншальтер *m.* (elec.) cut-out switch.

трео/за *f.* threose; **—зовая кислота** threosic acid; **—нин** *m.* (biochem.) threonine.

трепал/ка *f.*, **—о** *n.* brake, swingle, scutcher, beater (for fibers); **—ьный** *a.* scutching; **—ьня** *f.* scutching room; **—ьщик** *m.* stripper, beater.

трепан *m.* (surgery) trepan, trephine; (mach.) trepan, trepanning tool; **—ация** trepanation.

трепанг *m.* (zool.) sea cucumber (*Stichopus*).

трепание *n.* scutching, etc., *see* **трепать.**

трепанировать *v.* (mach.; med.) trepan.

трёпанный *a.* scutched, etc., *see v.*

трепануть *v. see* **трепать.**

трёпаный *a.* scutched, swingled; tattered, worn; shaggy.

трепать *v.* scutch, swingle, brake, break, beat (fiber); pull about; fray, tear, wear out; disintegrate; twitch; rumple, tumble; **—ся** *v.* be scutched, etc.; fray.

трепел *m.* (petr.) tripoli(te), diatomite; **—ьный** *a.* tripoli(ne).

трепет *m.* tremble, trepidation, palpitation, shiver; **—ание** *n.* trembling, etc., *see v.*; tremors; fibrillation; **—ать** *v.* tremble, palpitate, quiver, shiver, shake; flicker; throb; **—ный** *a.* trembling, palpitating; flickering.

трепешник *m.* (bot.) Sanicula.

трёпка *f.* scutching, etc., *see* **трепать.**

трепло *n.* scutching blade.

трепонемы *pl.* (bact.) Treponema.

трепых/аться, —нуться *v.* flutter, quiver; flicker, twinkle, glimmer.

треск *m.* crack(le), snap, (de)crepitation, crepitus; crash; (rad.) crackling.

треска *f.* cod (fish) (*Gadus morhua*).

треск/ание *n.* cracking, etc., *see v.*; **—ать** *v.* crack, split, cleave; **—аться** *v.* crack(le), split, cleave, burst; chap.

треско/вые *pl.* (ichth.) codfishes (*Gadidae*); **—вый** *a.* cod; **—вый жир** cod liver oil; **—образные** *pl.* Gadiformes; **—подобные** *pl.* Gadinae.

треск/отня *f.* rattle, continuous crackling; **—учий** *a.* crackling, crepitant.

трескучка *f.* (bot.) regma.

трескучник *m.* (bot.) weld, dyer's weed (*Reseda luteola*).

тресн/увший, —утый *a.* cracked, decrepitated; —уть *v.* crack, fracture, split, burst; chap; —уться *v.* knock, strike, hit (against).

тресок *gen. pl. of* треска.

трест *m.* trust, combine.

треста *f.* stock, treated plant fibers.

трест/ировать *v.* organize into a trust; —овский *a.* trust.

трёт *pr. 3 sing. of* тереть.

трет— *prefix* tertiary.

третей *gen. pl. of* треть.

третейский *a.* arbitral; umpire (analysis); т. суд court of arbitration; т. судья arbitrator.

трети *gen., etc., of* треть.

трет/ий *a.* third; —ья копия triplicate; в —ьих in the third place, thirdly.

третичный *a.* tertiary, ternary; (geol.) Tertiary (period).

третник *m.* soft solder, quick solder.

третной *a.* every four months; mottled.

трет/ь *f.* (a) third, one third; метод —ей (math.) method of thirds.

третье *n. of* третий; *prefix* third; —классник *m.*, —классница *f.* third-grader; —очередной, —разрядный, —сортный *a.* third-rate, insignificant, inferior; —степенный *a.* insignificant, mediocre; tertiary.

третьина *f.* (bot.) buckbean (*Menyanthes trifoliata*).

третья *f.* one third; *f. of* третий; —к *m.* third-year foal, third-year calf; third swarm (of bees); third log (from butt).

треугольн/ик *m.* triangle; (color) gamut; (anat.) trigone, trigonum; соединение —иком (elec.) delta connection; —оплодный *a.* (bot.) trigonocarpous; —ый *a.* triangular, trigonal; pyramid (code); delta (wing).

трефин *m.* (med.) trephine.

трефофрезерный *a.* wobbler milling.

трёх *gen. and prepos. of* три; *prefix* tri—, three, triple; задача т. тел (phys.) three-body problem; —адресный *a.* (comp.) three-address; —аллюрный *a.* three-gaited (horse); —атомный *a.* triatomic; trihydric (alcohol); trivalent; (chem.) three-center (bond); —балльный *a.* (meteor.) three-point; —бороздный, —бороздчатый *a.* (bot.) trisulcate; —братственный *a.* (bot.) triadelphous; —бромистый *a.* tribromide (of); —брусный *a.* (agr.) three-cutterbar; —бугорчатые *pl.* (pal.) Pentotheria; —бугорчатый *a.* (zool.) tritubercular (teeth); —валентность *f.* trivalence; —валентный *a.* trivalent; —ваттный *a.* (elec.) three-watt.

трёхверст/ка *f.* map with a scale of 3 versts to the inch; —ный *a.* three-verst (to the inch).

трёх/вершинный *a.* tricuspid (teeth); —вильчатый *a.* trifurcate.

трёх/винтовой *a.* triple-screw; —водный гидрат trihydrate; —галоид— *prefix* trihalogeno—; —галоид-замещённый *a.* trihalogen(ated); —главый *a.* tricephalous; —главая мышца (anat.) triceps; —гнёздный *a.* three-cell(ed); trilocular, trilobate; —годичный, —годовой *a.* three-year; —горлый *a.* three-necked (bottle).

трёхгранн/ик *m.* (geom.) trihedron; —ый *a.* trihedral; three-surfaced; triquetral (bone); (biol.) triquetrous; three-edged (bayonet).

трёх/дименсионный *a.* three-dimensional; —дневный *a.* three-day; (med.) tertian (fever); —дольный, —дольчатый *a.* trilobate, three-lobed; —домный *a.* (bot.) trioecious.

трёхдюймов/ка *f.* three-inch board; —ый *a.* three-inch; 76-mm (caliber).

трёхжилковый *a.* (bot.) trinervate.

трёхжильный *a.* three-strand, triple (cable).

трёхзамещённ/ые *pl.* trisubstitution products, triderivatives; —ый *a.* trisubstituted; —ый фосфат кальция tricalcium phosphate.

трёх/зарядный *a.* triple-charged; —заходный *a.* triple (thread); —звенный полимер trimer; —значный *a.* three-digit; three-aspect; three-unit (code); three-place (decimal).

трёх/зубые *pl.* (ichth.) Triodontidae; —зуб(чат)ый *a.* trident(ate), three-pronged, triconodont; (ichth.) triodontoid; —йодзамещённый *a.* triiodo (compound); —йодистый *a.* triiodide (of); —камерный *a.* three-chambered, trilocular; (distillation) triple-effect; —каскадный *a.* three-stage; triple-cascade; triple-spool (engine); —килевой *a.* (av.) triple-finned.

трёхкилометров/ка *f.* map with scale of 3 kilometers to the centimeter; —ый *a.* three-kilometer (to the centimeter).

трёх/кислотный *a.* triacid; —клиномерный *a.* (cryst.) triclinic; —колёсный *a.* three-wheeled, tricycle; —колонный *a.* three-column, three-legged; —компонентный *a.* ternary, three-component; —контактный *a.* (elec.) three-pronged, three-pin (plug); —контурный *a.* three-circuit; —корневой *a.* three-rooted; —корпусный *a.* three-unit; triple; triple-effect (evaporator); (naut.) triple-hulled; —красочный *a.* three-color; —кратный *a.* threefold, triple, three-stage; three times (a day); —кремнеземик *m.* trisilicate (group of minerals); —крылый *a.* tripterous; —кулачковый *a.* three-jawed; —ламповый *a.* (rad.) three-tube; —лемешный *a.* three-share, three-furrow (plow).

трёхлет/ие *n.* three-year period; third anniversary; triennial; —ка *see* трёхлеток; —ний *a.* triennial, three-year; —ок *m.* three-year old; three-year period.

трёх/линейка *f.* 7.6 mm-caliber rifle; —линейный *a.* 7.6 mm (caliber); trilinear; —линзовый *a.* three-lens; —листный *a.* trifoliate; —листовой *a.* three-sheet; —лонжеронный *a.* three-spar (wing); —лопастный *a.* three-bladed; three-way (bit); trifoliate; trilobate; —лучевой *a.* (pal.) trilete, triple (slit); (telev.) three-gun; (nucl.) three-pronged (star).

трёх/мерный *a.* three-dimensional; trivariate; т. полимер trimer; —местный *a.* three-man (spacecraft), three-seater; —месячный *a.* three-month, quarterly; —минутный *a.* three-minute; —моторный *a.* trimotor (airplane); —надрезный *a.* trifid; —недельный *a.* three-week; —ниточный *a.* triple-filament; triple (thread); —ногий *a.* three-legged, tripod; —обмоточный *a.* triple-wound; —оборотный *a.* triple (thread); —объективный *a.* three-lens; —окись *f.* trioxide; —оска *f.* six-wheel truck; —основный *a.* tribasic; —осный *a.* triaxial, three-axis; triple-axle, six-wheeled.

трёх/палубный *a.* three-deck; —палый *a.* (zool.) tridactylous; —парный *a.* (bot.) trijugate; —перегородчатый *a.* (biol.) triseptate; —перстка *f.* (orn.) buttonquail, hemipode (*Turnix tanki*); —перстки, —перстковые *pl.* (orn.) Turnicidae; —персткообразные *pl.* Turniciformes; —перстный *see* трехпалый; —планный *a.* three-plane, three-sided; —плечий *a.* three-arm, three-armed.

трёхпол/ка *f.*, —ье *n.* three-field system (of crop rotation); —ьный *a.* three-field; three-crop.

трёх/полюсный *a.* tripolar, triple-pole, three-pole; —проводный *a.* three-wire, three line, triple; —процентный *a.* three-percent; —путный *a.* three-way; three-lane (highway); (rr.) three-track; —раздельный *a.* tripartite, trifid; —размерный *a.* three-dimensional; —разо-

вый *a.* triple, three-time; **—разрядный** *a.* three-digit; **—рёберный** *a.* three-ribbed, tricostate; three-way (drag); **—рядный** *a.* three-row, triserial, triple; (bot.) tristichous; three-range, three-tier; **—светный** *a.* with three rows of windows; **—связный** *a.* triply connected; **—сернистый** *a.* trisulfide (of); **—скальчатый** *a.* triple-plunger (pump); **—следный** *a.* triplegang (mower).

трёхслой/ка *f.* three-ply; **—ные** *pl.* (zool.) Triploblastica; **—ный** *a.* three-ply, three-layer; triple-covered (wire); sandwich (plate).

трёхсмен/ка *f.* three-shift work, around-the-clock operation; **—ный** *a.* three-shift.

трёхсот *gen. of* **триста**; **—летие** *n.* tercentenary; **—ый** *a.* tercentennial; three-hundredth.

трёх/срезный *a.* triple-shear; **—стволка** *f.* three-barrel(ed) gun; **—ствольный** *a.* three-barrel(ed); (drilling) three-shaft; **—створчатый** *a.* three-valved, tricuspid; three-leaved; **—стержневой** *a.* three-rod; three-legged.

трёхсторонн/ий *a.* trilateral, trihedral, three-sided; **—ее измерение** (geod.) trilateration.

трёх/струйный *a.* triple-jet; **—ступенчатый** *a.* three-stage, three-step(ped); triple-cascade; three-speed (gear box); **—суточный** *a.* three-day; **—тактный** *a.* (mach.) three-stroke; **—томник** *m.* three-volume edition; **—томный** *a.* three-volume; **—тонка** *f.* three-ton truck; **—тонный** *a.* three-ton; three-tone; **—трубка** *f.* tribble; **—трубный** *a.* triple (torpedo tube); **—тысячный** *a.* three-thousand; **—тычинковый** *a.* (bot.) triandrous; **—угольный** *see* **треугольный**; **—ударный** *a.* (med.) trigeminal (pulse); **—уровневый** *a.* three-level.

трёхфазн/ый *a.* (elec.) triphase, three-phase; **т. генератор, генератор —ого тока** three-phase generator.

трёхформенн/ость *f.* (cryst.) trimorphism; **—ый** *a.* trimorphous.

трёхфтор/замещённый *a.* trifluoro (compound); **—истый** *a.* trifluoro; trifluoride (of).

трёххвостковые *pl.* (ichth.) tripletails (Lobotidae).

трёххлор/замещённый *a.* trichloro (compound); **—истый** *a.* trichloro; trichloride (of).

трёхходов/ой *a.* three-way, three-pass; (elec.) three-throw; triplex (winding); triple (thread); **т. кран** three-way cock, T-valve; **—ая деталь** T-piece.

трёхцвет/ка *f.* pansy (Viola tricolor); **—ность** *f.* trichromatism; (cryst.) trichroism; **—ный** *a.* tricolor(ed), three-color, trichromatic.

трёх/цилиндровый *a.* three-cylinder; **—часовой** *a.* three-hour; three o'clock; **—частичный** *a.* three-piece.

трёхчетверт/ка *f.* three quarters; **—ной** *a.* three-quarter; **—ьволновый** *a.* three-quarter-wave.

трёхчлен *m.*, **—ное количество** (math.) trinomial; **—истый** *a.* (zool.) triarticulate; **—ный** *a.* trinomial, trinominal, ternary, three-membered.

трёх/шарнирный *a.* three-hinged; **—шарочный** *a.* three-cone, tricone (bit); **—щелевой** *a.* triple-slotted; **—щетинковый** *a.* (bot.) trisetose; **—ъядерный** *a.* trinuclear, trinucleate; tricyclic; **—ъязычный** *a.* trilingual; **—ъярусный, —этажный** *a.* three-story, three-storied; three-tier.

трешеровые *pl.* (ichth.) thresher sharks (Alopiidae).

трещ/ание *n.* crack(l)ing, etc., *see v.*; **—ать** *v.* crack(le), rattle; chirp, chirr; burst, split; **—ётка** *see* **трещотка.**

трещин/а *f.* crack, cleft, fissure, rima, fracture, crevice, slit, split, chink, break, flaw; (geol.) joint, fracture; (timber) shake; **—ка** *dim. of* **трещина**; **—ный** *a. of* **трещина**; interstitial (water); **—ное строение** fracture pattern.

трещиноват/о-кавернозный *a.* (geol.) vuggy-fractured; **—ость** *f.* parting, jointing, fracturing; block disintegration; **—ый** *a.* cracked, full of cracks, crazed, fissured, rimose, fractured, jointy; split, cleft; broken up, crumbling (rock).

трещинообразование *n.* cracking, crazing, splitting.

трещиноустойчив/ость *f.* resistance to cracks; **—ый** *a.* crack-resisting.

трещотк/а *f.* ratchet; rattle, click, clack; **с —ой** ratchet (tool); **сверлильная т.** ratchet drill.

три *num.* three; *prefix* tri—, three; *imp. of* **тереть; —ада** *f.* triad; **—адный** *a.* triad, ternary.

триаз/ан *m.* triazane; **—ен** *m.* triazene; diazoamine; **—ин** *m.* triazine; **—инил** *m.* triazinyl; **—о—** *prefix* triazo—; **—о-бензол** *m.* triazobenzene; **—ол** *m.* triazole, pyrrodiazole; **—олил** *m.* triazolyl; **—олон** *m.* triazolone, ketotriazole; **—осоединение** *n.* triazo compound.

триак *m.* (electron.) triac, triode alternating current thyristor.

триакантин *m.* triacanthine.

триакантовые *pl.* hornfishes (Triacanthidae).

триаконтаэдр *m.* (geom.) triacontahedron; **—ический** *a.* triacontahedral.

триалкил/арсин *m.* trialkyl arsine; **—ьный** *a.* trialkyl(ated).

триамил *m.*, **—овый** *a.* triamyl.

триамино— *prefix* triamino .

триаммоний *m.* triammonium.

триаморфный *a.* (cryst.) triamorphous.

триам/синолон, —цинолон *m.* (pharm.) triamcinolone.

триангель *m.* (rr.) brake beam.

триангул/ирование *n.* (surv.) triangulation; **—ированный** *a.* triangulated; **—ировать** *v.* triangulate; **—ируемый** *a.* triangulable; **—ятор** *m.* triangulator; **—яционный** *a.*, **—яция** *f.* triangulation.

триарил/метан *m.* triarylmethane; **—ьный** *a.* triaryl(ated).

триас *m.*, **—овый** *a.* (geol.) Triassic.

триацет/ат *m.* triacetate; **—ил** *m.* triacetyl; **—илглицерин** *m.* triacetin; **—илцеллюлоза** *f.* cellulose triacetate; **—ин** *m.* triacetin, glyceryl triacetate.

триб *m.* pinion, drive gear.

триба *f.* (biol.) tribe.

трибадия *f.* (psych.) tribadism.

трибензил *m.* tribenzyl.

трибка *f.* pinion, drive gear.

трибо— *prefix* tribo— (friction); **—люминесценция** *f.* triboluminescence; **—метр** *m.* tribometer, friction gage; **—метрия** *f.* tribometry.

трибохимия *f.* tribochemistry.

трибочный *a. of* **триб.**

трибоэлектричес/кий *a.* triboelectric; **—тво** *n.* triboelectricity.

трибром— *prefix* tribrom(o)—; **—бензол** *m.* tribromobenzene; **—замещённый** *a.* tribromo (compound); **—производные** *pl.* tribromo derivatives; **—уксусный** *a.* tribromoacetic (acid).

трибсталь *f.* pinion steel.

трибугорчатый *a.* tritubercular, tricuspid (teeth).

трибуна *f.* tribune; forum; platform, rostrum; (grand) stand.

трибунал *m.* tribunal, court.

трибут/ил *m.* tributyl; **—илбор** *m.* tributyl boron; **—илфосфат** *m.* tributyl phosphate; **—ирин** *m.* tributyrin.

тривалентный *a.* trivalent.

тривалерин *m.* trivalerin, phocenin.

тривариантный *a.* trivariant.

тривиальный *a.* trivial; common (name).

тригалоид— *prefix* trihalo(geno)—; **—бензол** *m.* trihalogenobenzene.

тригамный *a.* (bot.) trigamous.

тригатрон *m.* trigatron (electronic switch).

триггер *m.*, **—ный** *a.* trigger; (electron.) flip-flop; **—ная схема** flip-flop (circuit); **—ная ячейка** (comp.) flip-flop.

тригеминальный *a.* trigeminal (pulse).

три/генный *a.* (gen.) trigenic; **—гибрид** *m.*, **—гибридный** *a.* trihybrid.

тригидрат *m.* trihydrate.

тригир/а *f.* (cryst.) threefold axis of symmetry; **—ный** *a.* trigonal (system).

тригл/а *f.* (ichth.) gurnard, searobin (*Trigla*); **—овые, —ы** *pl.* Triglidae.

триглицерид *m.* triglyceride.

тригон *m.* trigon, trigone; **—альный** *a.* trigonal, triangular; **—додекаэдр** *m.* (cryst.) trigondodecahedron.

тригонеллин *m.* trigonelline, nicotinic methylbetaine.

тригонид *m.* trigonid (of a tooth).

тригонометр/ист *m.* (surv.) triangulator; **—ический** *a.* trigonometric, trigonometrical; **—ия** *f.* trigonometry; **плоская —ия, прямолинейная —ия** plane trigonometry.

три/грамма *f.* trigram (three-letter combination); **—дакна** (mal.) giant marine clam (*Tridacna*); **—декан** *m.* tridecane; **—дециловая кислота** tridecylic acid, tridecoic acid; **—димит** *m.* (min.) tridymite.

тридцати— *prefix* triaconta—, thirty; **—гранник** *m.* triacontahedron; **—двухгранник** *m.* thirty-two-sided polygon; **—летие** *n.* thirty-year period; thirtieth anniversary; **—летний** *a.* thirty-year; thirtieth anniversary.

тридцат/ый *a.* thirtieth; **—ь** *num.* thirty; **—ью** *adv.* thirty times.

триер *m.*, **—ный** *a.* grain cleaner, grader, cylinder (grader); screening machine; sifter; **—ование** *n.* screening, etc., *see v.*; **—ованный** *a.* screened, etc., *see v.*; **—овать** *v.* screen, sort, grade; sift.

триестский *a.* Trieste.

трижды *adv.* three times, three-fold.

тризамещ/ение *n.* trisubstitution; **—ённый** *see* **трёхзамещённый.**

тризм *m.* (med.) trismus.

три/йод— *prefix* triiod(o)—; **—калий** *m.* tripotassium; **—кальцийфосфат** *m.* tricalcium phosphate.

трикапр/ин *m.* tricaprin, glyceryl tricaprinate; **—оин** *m.* tricaproin, glyceryl tricapronate.

трикарбоновый *a.* tricarboxylic (acid).

триклин/ический, —ный *a.* (cryst.) triclinic, anorthic, asymmetric.

трико *n.* (text.) tricot.

триконодонтный *a.* triconodont (teeth).

трикотаж *m.* (text.) tricot, jersey; knitted fabric; tricotwear; **—ник** *m.* tricot knitter; **—ный** *a.* of **трикотаж.**

трикрез/ил *m.* tricresyl; **—илфосфат** *m.* tricresyl phosphate; **—ол** *m.* tricresol.

трилепестный *a.* (bot.) tripetalous.

трилистн/ик *m.* (bot.) trefoil, clover; **—иковидный** *a.* cloverleaf; **—ый** *a.* three-leaved, trifoliate.

трилит *m.* (expl.) trilite, trinitrotoluene.

триллион *m.*, **—ный** *a.* trillion (10^{12}).

трилобит *m.* (pal.) trilobite.

трилон *m.* Trilon (chelating agent).

трима *f.* (bot.) tryma.

тримаран *m.* (naut.) trimaran.

тримезиновая кислота trimesic acid.

тримекаин *m.* trimecaine hydrochloride.

тример *m.* trimer (a polymer); **—ный** *a.* (chem.) trimeric; (bot.) trimerous.

триместр *m.* (educ.) trimester.

триметил *m.* trimethyl; **—амин** *m.* trimethylamine; **—арсин** *m.* trimethyl arsine; **—бензол** *m.* trimethylbenzene; **—бор** *m.* trimethyl boron; **—ен** *m.* trimethylene; **—ксантин** *m.* trimethylxanthine, caffeine; **—овый** *a.* trimethyl.

триметин *m.* trimethadione.

триметрический *a.* (cryst.) trimetric, orthorhombic.

тримм/ер *m.* trimmer; (av.) trim(ming) tab, stabilizer; **—инг-машина** *f.* trimming machine, trimmer.

тримолекулярный *a.* trimolecular.

тримонэцичный *a.* (bot.) trimonoecious.

триморф/изм *m.* trimorphism; **—ный** *a.* trimorphous.

тримужний *a.* (bot.) triandrous.

тринадцат/илетний *a.* thirteen-year; **—ый** *a.* thirteenth; **—ь** *num.* thirteen.

тринарный *a.* ternary; (zool.) trinomial (nomenclature).

тринатрийфосфат *m.* trisodium phosphate.

тринидадский *a.* (geog.) Trinidad.

тринитрат *m.* trinitrate; **т. целлюлозы** trinitrocellulose, pyroxylin.

тринитрин *m.* trinitrin, nitroglycerin.

тринитро— *prefix* trinitro—; **—бензол** *m.* trinitrobenzene; **—ксилол** *m.* trinitroxylene; **—соединение** *n.* trinitro compound; **—толуол** *m.* trinitrotoluene, TNT; **—фенол** *m.* trinitrophenol, picric acid; **—целлюлоза** *f.* trinitrocellulose, pyroxylin; **—этанол** *m.* trinitroethanol; **—эфир** *m.* trinitrate.

тринол *m.* (expl.) trinol, trinitrotoluene.

трином *m.* (math.) trinomial.

трио *see* **трио-стан.**

триод *m.* triode, three-electrode tube; **кристаллический т.** transistor; **на кристаллических —ах, на полупроводниковых —ах** transistor(ized).

триоз/а *f.* triose; **—офосфат** *m.* triosephosphate; **—офорный** *a.* triosephosphoric (acid).

три/окись *f.* trioxide; **—оксазол** *m.* trioxazole; **—оксан** *m.* trioxane, paraformaldehyde; **—окси—** *prefix* trioxy—; trihydroxy—; **—оксибензол** *m.* trihydroxybenzene; **—оксид** *m.* ozonide; **—оксим** *m.* trioxime; **—оксимасляный** *a.* trihydroxybutyric (acid); **—оксиметилен** *m.* trioxymethylene, paraformaldehyde; **—олеин** *m.* triolein, olein; **—олефин** *m.* triolefin.

трионал *m.* trional, sulfonethylmethane.

трио-стан *m.* three-high (rolling) mill.

триостр/енник *m.* (bot.) triglochin; **—иевый** *a.* tricuspidate, three-pointed.

трипальмитин *m.* tripalmitin.

трипан/блау *n.* trypan blue, diamine blue; **—овый** *a.* trypan; **—озомоз** *m.* (vet.) trypanosomiasis; **—осома** *f.* trypanosome (parasitic protozoan); **—рот** *m.* trypan red.

трип/арсамид *m.* tryparsamide; **—афлавин** *m.* Trypaflavine, acriflavine.

трипептид *m.* tripeptide.

триперстовый *a.* (zool.) tridactyl.

триплан *m.* (av.) triplane.

триплегия *f.* (med.) triplegia.

трипл/екс *m.* triplex; laminated safety glass; **—ексный** *a.* triplex; **—ет** *m.*, **—етный** *a.* triplet; triplicate; **—оид** *m.* (biol.) triploid; **—окаулический** *a.* (bot.) triplocaulous.

триппер *m.* (med.) gonorrhea.

трипропил *m.*, **—овый** *a.* tripropyl; **—амин** *m.* tripropylamine.

трипротамин *m.* triprotamine, sturine.

трипс *m.* (ent.) thrips.

трипс/ин *m.* trypsin, trypsase; **—иноген** *m.* trypsinogen; **—ический** *a. of* **трипсин.**

триптамин *m.* (biochem.) tryptamine.

триптан *m.* triptane, trimethylbutane.

триптический *a.* (biochem.) tryptic.

трипто/н *m.* tryptone (a peptone); tripton, debris; **—фан** *m.* tryptophan, indolylalanine.

тририцинолеин *m.* triricinolein.

трисазо— *prefix* trisazo—.

три/сахарид *m.* trisaccharide; **—сектриса** *f.* (math.) trisectrix; **—секция** *f.* trisection; **—сель** *m.* (naut.) trysail; **—семянка** *f.* (bot.) triachenium; **—силан** *m.* trisilane; **—силикат** *m.* trisilicate; **—сомик** *m.* (gen.) trisomic; **—сомия** *f.* trisomy.

триссокл *m.* whiskered anchovy (*Thrissocles*).

три/ста *num.* three hundred; **—стеарин** *m.* tristearin; **—сульфид** *m.* trisulfide; **—сульфокислота** *f.* trisulfonic acid; **—танопия** *f.* (ophth.) tritanopia.

трите *imp. of* **тереть.**

тритетраэдр *m.* (cryst.) tritetrahedron.

тритиан *m.* trithiane.

тритий *m.* tritium (hydrogen isotope).

тритикале wheat-rye hybrids, Triticale.

тритил *m.* trityl, triphenylmethyl.

тритио— *prefix* trithio—; **—карбонат** *m.* trithiocarbonate; **—нат** *m.* trithionate; **—новая кислота** trithionic acid; **—новокислая соль** trithionate; **—угольная кислота** trithiocarbonic acid.

тритицин *m.* triticin (carbohydrate from *Triticum*).

трито/н *m.* (zool.) triton, newt, eft; triton, t (nucleus of tritium); Triton (detergent); (acous.) tritone; **—пин** *m.* tritopine.

тритуберкулярный *a.* tritubercular (teeth), tricuspid.

триумф *m.* triumph; **—альный** *a.* triumphal; **—атор** *m.* victor.

трифенил *m.* triphenyl; **—ен** *m.* triphenylene; **—метан** *m.*, **—метановый** *a.* (dyes) triphenylmethane.

три/феррин *m.* triferrin, iron paranucleinate; **—филин** *m.* (min.) triphylite; **—фолиата** *f.* trifoliate orange; **—фоль** *f.* (bot.) buckbean, bogbean (*Menyanthes trifoliata*).

трифонид *m.* ichneumon fly.

трифтазин *m.* (pharm.) trifluoperazine, Triftazin.

трифтор— *prefix* trifluor(o)—; **—бензол** *m.* trifluorobenzene; **—ид** *m.* trifluoride; **—уксусный** *a.* trifluoroacetic (acid).

трихиаз *m.* (med.) trichiasis.

трихин/а, **—елла** *f.* (zool.) trichina (*Trichinella spiralis*); **—еллёз**, **—оз** *m.* (med.) trichinosis; **—еллёзный**, **—озный** *a.* trichinous.

трихиноил *m.* triquinoyl.

трихит *m.* (min.) trichite.

трихлор— *prefix* trichlor(o)—; **—истый** *a.* trichloride (of); **—метан** *m.* trichloromethane, chloroform; **—(о)уксусная кислота** trichloroacetic acid; **—этан** *m.* trichloroethane; **—этилен** *m.* trichloroethylene.

трихо— *prefix* trich(o)— (hair); **—безоар** *m.* trichobezoar, hair ball; **—грамма** *f.* (ent.) Trichogramma; **—дина** *f.* (prot.) Trichodina; **—диниоз** *m.* (ichth.) trichodiniosis; **—з** *m.* (med.) trichosis; **—микоз** *m.* trichomycosis; **—мицин** *m.* Trichomycin (antibiotic); **—монада** *f.* (zool.) Trichomonas; **—монацид** *m.* trichomonacide; **—мониаз**, **—моноз** *m.* (vet.) tricho-

moniasis; **—рексис** *m.* (med.) trichorrhexis; **—тецин** *m.* trichothecin; **—томия** *f.* trichotomy; **—фития** *f.*, **—фитоз** *m.* (med.) trichophytosis; **—фор** *m.* (cyt.) trichophore; **—цидин** *m.* trichocidin; **—циста** *f.* (prot.) trichocyst.

трихро/изм *m.* (cryst.) trichroism; **—ичный** *a.* trichroic; **—мат** *m.* trichromate; **—матичный** *a.* trichromatic.

три/цепс *m.* (anat.) triceps; **—циан** *m.* tricyanogen; **—циклен** *m.* tricyclene; **—циклический** *a.* tricyclic; **—щетинник** *m.* (bot.) Trisetum; **—эдр** *m.* (geom.) trihedron; **—эдрический** *a.* trihedral.

триэн *m.* tryen, Yatren.

триэтаноламин *m.* triethanolamine.

триэтил *m.* triethyl; **—амин** *m.* triethylamine; **—арсин** *m.* triethyl arsine; **—бор** *m.* triethyl boron; **—висмутин** *m.* triethyl bismuthine; **—овый** *a.* triethyl; **—этоксимоносилан** *m.* triethylsilane ethyl oxide.

триэтокси— *prefix* triethoxy—; **—моносилан** *m.* triethyl silicoformate.

триэцичный *a.* (bot.) trioecious.

тр-к *abbr.* **(треугольник)** triangle.

тРНК *abbr.* transfer RNA.

троакар *m.* (surgery) trocar.

трог *m.* (geol.) glacial trough.

трог/ание *n.* touching, stirring; **т. с места** starting; **скорость —ания** threshold velocity (of soil during wind erosion); **—ательный** *a.* touching, moving; pathetic; **—ать** *v.* touch, affect; disturb; start; **—аться** *v.* touch, be in contact (with); stir, move, budge; start off, take off; taint, spoil; **—аться с места** start; **не —ая с места** without disturbing.

троговая долина *see* **трог.**

трогоны *pl.* (orn.) Trogonidae.

трое *num.* three; *prefix* three, triple; **на т.** in three parts; **—губ** *m.* (ichth.) Opsariichthys; **—к** *gen. pl. of* **тройка; —кратно** *adv.* three times, triply; **—кратный** *a.* three(fold), triple; **—н** *gen. pl. of* **тройня; —пёр** *m.* (ichth.) three-fin blennies (*Tripterygion*); **—тёс** *m.* three-inch nail; **—шипые** *pl.* (ichth.) spikefishes (*Triacanthidae*).

троилит *m.* (min.) troilite.

тро/ить *v.* divide into three; combine in threes; do in triplicate; do three times; **—ично-кодированный** *a.* ternary-coded; **—ичный** *a.* ternary.

тройка *f.* triplet, triad, set of three; trefoil; team of three.

тройник *m.* tee, T-piece, T-joint, T-branch; tripartite; tri-unit measure; (cryst.) trilling; triplet; (elec.) T-junction box, branch box; **доска-т.** *f.* three-inch board; **—овый** *a. of* **тройник;** T-(joint), three-way (pipe); **—овое образование** (cryst.) trilling.

тройнич/ость *f.* triplicity; **—ый** *a.* triple; (anat.) trifacial, trigeminal.

тройн/ой *a.* triple, triplicate, three, tri-, ternary; triangular; **—ая ось** (cryst.) triad axis; trilobate (placenta); **—ая связь** triple bond; **—ая соль** trisalt; **—ая точка** triple point; **—ое деление** (nucl.) ternary fission; **—ое правило** (math.) rule of three; **—я** *f.* triplets.

тройский вес Troy weight.

тройственн/ость *f.* triplicity; **—ый** *a.* triple.

тройчат/ка *f.* triad, group of three; tripartite; **—(н)ый** *a.* tripartite; ternate, arranged in threes.

троллей *m.* (elec.) trolley; **—бус** *m.* trolley bus; **—воз** *m.*, **—кара** *f.* trolley (electric) truck; **—ный** *a.* trolley.

тромб *m.* (med.) thrombus, blood clot; (meteor.) tornado; **—а** *f.* tornado.

тромб/аза *f.*, **—ин** *m.* thrombase, thrombin, zymoplasm; **—иноген** *m.* (hemat.) prothrombin, Factor II; **—оген**

m. thrombogen, serozyme; **—оз** *m.* (med.) thrombosis; coagulation, clotting; **—окиназа** *f.* (enz.) thrombokinase.

тромбон *m.,* **—ный** *a.* trombone.

тромбо/тонин *m.* (biochem.) serotonin; **—флебит** *m.* (med.) thrombophlebitis; **—цит** *m.* thrombocyte, blood platelet.

тром(м)ель *m.* (min.) trommel, revolving sieve, washing drum.

трона *f.* (min.) trona.

тронк *m.* trunk (piston); **—овый** *a.* trunk.

трон/утый *a.* touched, affected; spoiled, tainted; **—уть** *see* **трогать; —уться** *v.* be affected, spoil, go bad; start.

троостит *m.* (met.; min.) troostite.

тропа *f.* path(way), walk, track.

тропа/кокаин *m.* tropacocaine, benzoylpseudotropine; **—н** *m.* tropan, N-methylnortropan; **—нол** *m.* tropanol; **—нолкарбоновый** *a.* tropanolcarboxylic (acid); **—нон** *m.* tropanone.

троп/ат *m.* tropate; **—ацин** *m.* tropacine; **—еин** *m.* tropeine; **—ентан** *m.* tropentane; **—еолин** *m.* tropeolin; **—идин** *m.* tropidine; **—изм** *m.* tropism.

тропик *m.* tropic; circle; **т. Рака** tropic of Cancer; **—ализация** *f.* tropicalization; **—и** *pl.* tropics; **между —ами** intertropical.

троп/ил *m.* tropyl; **—илиден** *m.* tropilidene, 1,3,5-cycloheptatriene; **—илий** *m.* tropylium; **—ин** *m.* (chem.) tropine, N-methyltropoline; (biol.) tropin.

тропинка *f.* little path, footpath.

тропин/карбоновая кислота tropinecarboxylic acid, ecgonine; **—овая кислота** tropic acid.

тропическ/ий *a.* tropic; torrid (zone); tropicalized (equipment); **—ие пояса** tropics.

тропо— *prefix* tropo— [turn(ing), change]; **—вая кислота** tropic acid; **—лон** *m.* (chem.) tropolone; **—миозин** *n.* (biochem.) tropomyosin; **—пауза** *f.* (meteor.) tropopause, top of troposphere; **—сфера** *f.* troposphere; **—сферный** *a.* troposphere, tropospheric; **—фильный** *a.* (bot.) trophophilous, adapted to seasonal changes; **—фит** *m.* trophophyte.

трос *m.* cable, rope, (steel) line; (naut.) hawser; **—ик** *dim. of* **трос; спусковой —ик** (phot.) cable release; **—овый** *a. of* **трос.**

тростильный *a.* twisting, etc., *see* **тростить.**

тростин/а, **—ка** *f.* reed, cane.

тростить *v.* twist together, splice; (text.) slub; throw (silk).

трост/ник *m.* reed, rush; (sugar) cane; **—никововкрысиные** *pl.* cane rats (*Thryonomyidae*); **—никовый** *a.* reed; rush (matting); cane (sugar); **—ь** *f.,* **—яной** *a.* cane; (music) reed.

тротил *m.* (expl.) trotyl, trinitrotoluene.

тротуар *m.,* **—ный** *a.* sidewalk, footpath; pavement, platform; **движущийся т.** conveyer.

троф/ический *a.* trophic, nutrition; **—ный** *a. suffix* trophic; **—о—** *prefix* tropho— (food, nourishment); **—биоз** *m.* (zool.) trophobiosis; **—оневроз** *m.* (med.) trophoneurosis; **—плазма** *f.* (cyt.) trophoplasm; **—цит** *m.* trophocyte, nurse cell.

трохантер *m.* (anat.; ent.) trochanter.

трохо— *prefix* troch(o)— (wheel); **—вая кислота** trochoic acid; **—ида** *f.* (geom.) trochoid; **—ид(аль)ный** *a.* trochoid(al); **—стома** *f.* burrowing sea cucumber (*Trochostoma*); **—сфера** *f.* (zool.) trochosphere, trochophore; **—трон** *m.* trochotron (trochoidal mass spectrometer or electronic beam-switching tube); **—фора** *f.* (zool.) trochophore.

трохус *m.* (mal.) marine snail (*Trochus*).

трощ/ение *n.* twisting, torsion; (text.) slubbing; throwing (of silk); **—ёный** *a.* twisted; slubbed; thrown.

троюродный брат, троюродная сестра second cousin.

трояк/ий *a.* triple, threefold; trimorphous; **—о** *adv.* in three different ways; **—оперистый** *a.* tripinnate.

троян/ский *a.* Troy, Trojan; **—цы** *pl.* (astr.) Trojan group.

тр-р *abbr.* **(трансформатор)** transformer.

труб/а *f.* pipe, tube; flue, funnel, shaft, (smoke) stack; duct, conduit; (anat.) tube, tuba; trumpet; telescope; **т.-качалка** rotary distributor (e.g., for trickling filter); **т.-лаз** *f.* access tube; **т.-сушилка** *f.* tube dryer, pneumatic dryer; **—ач** *m.* (zool.) stentor; (orn.) trumpeter; (orn.) Psophia; **—ить** *v.* trumpet.

трубк/а *dim. of* **труба;** (small-diameter) tube, tubule; (ignition) fuse; (percussion) primer; (tel.) receiver; (anat.) canna, reed; **—ование** *n.* (bot.) stalk shooting, stem extension stage, leaf-tube formation; **—оверт** *m.* (ent.) leaf roller; **—овидный** *see* **трубкообразный; —озуб** *m.* (zool.) aardvark (*Orycteropus*); **—онос** *m.* tube-nosed bat (*Murina*); **—оносный** *a.* tubiferous; **—ообразный** *a.* tubiform, tubular; **—ообразующий** *a.* (biol.) tubiparous (glands); **—орыловые** *pl.* (ichth.) ghost pipefishes (*Solenostomidae*); **—оцветный** *a.* (bot.) tubuliflorous.

трубн/ик *m.* pipe worker; **—о—** *prefix* tubo—, salping(o)— (tube); **—оглоточный** *a.* (anat.) salpingopharyngeal; **—онёбный** *a.* salpingopalatine; **—ояичниковый** *a.* tubo-ovarian; **—ый** *a. of* **труба;** casing (tongs, etc.); tubal (pregnancy); **—ая доска** tube sheet (e.g., of a boiler).

трубо— *prefix* pipe, tube; **—воз-раскладчик** *m.* pipe-laying carrier; **—волочение** *n.,* **—волочильный** *a.* tube-drawing; **—гибочный** *a.* pipe-bending; **—дёр** *m.* tube extractor; **—держатель** *m.* pipe support, tube holder; **—загибочный** *a.* pipe-bending; **—испытательный** *a.* pipe-testing; **—к** *gen. pl. of* **трубка; —клад** *m.* pipe layer; **—литейное производство** pipe casting; **—ловка** *f.* pipe grab; casing spear; **—нарезной** *a.* pipe-threading; **—отвод** *m.* branch pipe; **—отрезной** *a.* pipe-cutting; **—очиститель** *m.* pipe cleaner, tube cleaner, reamer.

трубопровод *m.* pipe(line), main, (supply) line; conduit, duct, piping (system), tubing; manifold (of engine); **—ный** *a. of* **трубопровод; —ная сеть** pipe system, piping; **—чик** *m.* pipe fitter, plumber.

трубопрокат/ка *f.,* **—ный** *a.* pipe rolling, tube rolling; **—чик** *m.* pipe roller.

трубо/расширитель *m.* tube beader, tube expander; **—рез** *m.* pipe cutter, tube cutter; casing knife; **—резный** *a.* pipe-cutting; **—рог** *m.* (zool.) whelk; **—сварочный** *a.* pipe-welding; **—став** *m.* pipefitter; **—укладочный** *a.* pipe-laying; **—укладчик** *m.* pipe layer; **—формовочный** *a.* tube-molding, pipe-molding; **—цвет** trumpet flower; **—чист** *m.* pipe cleaner; chimney sweep; (ichth.) black Amur; **—чка** *dim. of* **трубка;** tubule; sleeve; **—чники** *pl.* (zool.) Tubificidae.

трубочный *a.* pipe, tube; **т. камень** (petr.) pipestone, catlinite.

трубчат/ка *f.* (petrol.) pipe still, tube still; **—ки** *pl.* (ichth.) cornetfishes, flutemouths (*Fistulariidae*); **—окольцевой** *a.* cannular (combustion chamber); **—опластинчатый** *a.* secondary-surface (radiator); **—оцветковый** *a.* (bot.) tubuliflorous.

трубчат/ый *a.* tubular, tubulated; hollow; piping, pipe; core (drill); sleeve (antenna); **т. колодец** Abyssinian well, drilled well; **—ая печь** tube furnace; rotary furnace; (petrol.) tube still.

трубштаг *m.* (naut.) funnel shroud.

трубы *gen., pl., etc., of* **труба**; **т.-зонды** *pl.* (agr.) fumigating tubes.

труд *m.* labor, work, toil; difficulty; (scientific) treatise; **—ы** *pl.* transactions, proceedings (of society), works (of author); **без —а** without difficulty, without effort, easily; **с большим —ом** with great difficulty; **биржа —а** labor bureau; **взять на себя т.** *v.* take the trouble; **положить много —а** *v.* take great pains.

труден *sh. m. of* **трудный**.

трудиться *v.* work, labor, toil.

трудно *adv.* with difficulty, hardly; it is difficult; **—вато** *adv.* with some difficulty; it is rather difficult; **—ватый** *a.* rather difficult; **—доступный** *a.* not easily accessible, hard to reach; difficult (terrain); **—дробимый** *a.* strong, tough; **—обнаруживаемый** *a.* hard to detect; **—обрабатываемый** *a.* churlish, difficult to work; **—определимый** *a.* nondescript, difficult to define; **—плавкий** *a.* hardly fusible; infusible, refractory; **—проходимый** *a.* difficult (terrain); **—растворимый** *a.* weakly soluble; **—сть** *f.* difficulty, hardship; road block; **—текущий** *a.* viscous, thick.

трудный *a.* difficult, hard, laborious, heavy (work).

трудо— *prefix,* **—вой** *a.* labor, work(ing), man-power, occupational (therapy), earned (income); **—вой коллектив** employees, staff; **—вая книга** service record, employment records; **—день** work day; **—ёмкий** *a.* labor-consuming, time-consuming, laborious, arduous; (econ.) labor-intensive; **—ёмкость** *f.* man-hours per job; labor intensity, laboriousness, difficulty; **—любивый** *a.* hard-working, industrious; **—способность** *f.* capacity for work; **восстановление —способности** rehabilitation; **потеря —способности** disability; **—способный** *a.* capable, able-bodied; **—устройство** *n.* specialized employment; (job) placement.

труд/ы *pl. of* **труд**; **—ящийся** *a.* working; *m.* worker; **здравоохранение —ящихся** occupational health.

трукс/еллин *m.* truxelline; **—иллин** *m.* truxilline; **—илловый** *a.* truxillic (acid); **—иновый** *a.* truxinic (acid).

труп *m.* corpse, cadaver, carcass.

трупиал *m.* (orn.) oriole; blackbird; meadowlark; **—овые, —ы** *pl.* Icteridae.

трупножировосковой *a.* adipocerous.

трупн/ый *a.* corpse, cadaverous; **т. (жиро)-воск** adipocere; **т. яд** ptomaine; **—ое окоченение** rigor mortis.

трупо/ед *m.* (zool.) necrophage; **—ядный** *a.* necrophagous.

трусики *pl.* shorts, swim trunks.

трус/ить *v.* be afraid; shake, scatter; **—ливый** *a.* cowardly, timid, pusillanimous, apprehensive; **—ость** *f.* cowardice.

трусца *f.* gentle trot, jog.

трусы *see* **трусики**.

трут *m.* tinder, punk; agaric; *pr. 3 pl. of* **тереть**.

трут/ень *m.*, **—невой** *a.* drone (bee).

трутовидный *a.* tinder-like.

трутовик *m.* (bot.) Polyporus.

трутовка *f.* (bees) laying worker.

Трутона правило Trouton's rule.

трух/а *f.* rot, rotten wood; (hay) dust, chaff; trash, rubbish; **—ляветь, —лявиться** *v.* rot, molder, disintegrate; **—лявый** *a.* rotten, moldering.

трущий(ся) *a.* rubbing, friction.

трущоб/а *f.*, **—ный** *a.* thicket; slum, ghetto.

трэгер *m.* support (for catalyst).

трэк *m.* track.

трюм *m.*, **—ный** *a.* (naut.) bilge, hold.

трюмо *n.* (arch.) pier; pier glass.

трюфель *m.*, **—ный** *a.* (bot.) truffle.

тряп/ица *f.* rag; **—ичник** *m.* ragman; **—ичниковые** *pl.* (ichth.) ragfishes (*Icosteidae*); **—ичный** *a.* rag; **—ка** *f.* rag, piece of waste; **—очка** *dim. of* **тряпка**; **—очный** *a.* rag; **—ьё** *n.* rags.

тряс *past m. sing. of* **трясти**.

тряс/ение *n.* shaking, etc., *see* **трясти(сь)**; **—илка** (mech.) shake(r); **—ильный** *a.* shaking, etc., *see* **трясти**.

трясин/а *f.*, **—ный** *a.* marsh, swamp; quagmire, quaking bog.

тряс/ка *f.* shaking, etc., *see v.*; jolt; **—кий** *a.* shaky; jolting; rough, bumpy (road); **—коформовочный** *a.* (molding) jar-ramming, jarring, jolt-ramming; **—огузка** *f.* (orn.) wagtail (*Motacilla*); **—огузковые** *pl.* pipits and wagtails (*Motacillidae*); **—ти** *v.* shake, jolt, joggle, jar; (av.) buffet; **—тись** *v.* be shaken, etc.; shake, shiver, tremble; **—унка** *f.* quaking grass; **—учий** *a.* shaking, etc., *see v.*; **—учка** *f.* shaker; fever; quaking grass; **—ущийся** *a.* shaking, etc., *see v.*; shaky.

тряхнуть *see* **трясти**.

тс *abbr.* (**тонна-сила**) ton-force.

ТС *abbr.* (**технологическая спецификация**) technical specifications.

тсе-тсе *see* **цеце**.

т. сж. *abbr.* (**температура сжижения**) liquefaction temperature.

ТСК *abbr.* (**термостойкий костюм**) heat-resisting suit.

т. стекл. *abbr.* (**температура стеклования**) glass transition temperature.

тсуг/а *f.* (bot.) hemlock (*Tsuga*); **—иновая кислота** tsugic acid.

тсунами *n.* tsunami.

т/счёт *abbr.* (**текущий счёт**) current account.

тт. *abbr.* (**тома**) volumes.

ТТ *abbr.* (**теоретическая тарелка**) (distillation) theoretical plate; (**технические требования**) technical requirements, specifications.

ТТГ *abbr.* (**тиреотропный гормон**) thyrotropic hormone.

ТТФ *abbr.* (**тимидин трифосфат**) thymidine triphosphate.

ТТХ *abbr.* (**хлористый трифенилтетразол**) triphenyltetrazolium chloride.

ту *acc. of* **та**, that; **ТУ** *abbr.* (**телеуправление**) remote control; (**технические условия**) technical specifications; (**трихлорфеноксиуксусная кислота**) trichlorphenoxyacetic acid.

туалет *m.*, **—ный** *a.* toilet; dress, attire; restroom, lavatory; dressing table; (surgery) scrubbing up; trimming, washing (of butchered carcasses); **—ные изделия** toilet preparations.

туба *f.* (paste) tube; (music) tuba.

туба/вая кислота tubaic acid; **—зид** *m.* Tubazid, isonicotinic acid hydrazide; **—ин** *m.* tubain; **—нол** *m.* tubanol.

туберидий *m.* (bot.) tuberidium (pseudobulb of an orchid).

туберкул *m.* (med.) tubercle; **—ёз** *m.* (med.) tuberculosis; (bot.) olive knot; **—ёз кожи** (med.) tuberculoderma; **—ёзный** *a.* tuberculous, tubercular, consumptive; **—ид** *m.* tuberculid; **—ин** *m.* tuberculin.

тубероз/а *f.* (bot.) tuberose (*Polianthes tuberosa*); **—ный** *a.* tuberose; tuberous, nodular; **—ное масло** tuberose oil.

тубиф/екс *m.* (zool.) an oligochaete (*Tubifex*); **—ициды** *pl.* Tubificidae.

тубокурарин *m.* tubocurarine.

тубонаполнительный *a.* tube-filling.

туботоксин *m.* tubotoxin (rotenone).

тубу/латный *a.* tubulate(d); —**лус** *see* **тубус;** —**лярный** *a.* tubular, tube-shaped; —**с** *m.* tubule, tube, barrel, sleeve, (viewing) hood.

тувинский *a.* (geog.) Tuvinski.

туводная рыба indigenous fish.

туг *sh. m. of* **тугой.**

тугай *m.,* —**ный** *a.* tugai (vegetation-covered bottomland).

туг/о *adv.* tightly, fast; hard, firmly; slowly, with difficulty; fully (inflated); *prefix see* **тугой; ему приходиться т.** he finds it difficult; —**ой** *a.* tight, taut, close; pressure (bandage); difficult; stiff, unyielding; dull; —**озудый** *a.* hard-mouthed (horse); —**онатянутый** *a.* tightly drawn, taut, tense.

тугоплавк/ий *a.* difficultly fusible, high-melting; high-heat, heatproof; infusible, refractory; hard (glass); —**ость** *f.* infusibility, refractoriness.

тугость *f.* tightness, stiffness; slowness.

тугоух/ий *a.* hard of hearing; *m.* partially deaf person; —**ость** *f.* impaired hearing.

тугун *m.* (ichth.) Coregonus tugun.

туда *adv.* there, thither; **т. и обратно** back and forth, to and fro; round-trip (ticket).

туе/вик *m.* (bot.) Thujopsis; —**вый** *a.* thuja (oil); thujic (acid); —**н** *m.* thujene, tanacetone.

туер *m.* chain tug; —**ный** *a.* chain (tug, ferry).

туетин *m.* thujetin.

туже *comp. of* **туго, тугой,** tighter.

тужиться *v.* exert oneself.

тужурка *f.* (uniform) jacket; short coat.

туз *m.* dinghy, scull(er); (cards) ace.

тузем/ец native; —**ный** *a.* native, indigenous.

тузик *see* **туз.**

тузлу/к *m.* brine; —**кование** *n.* preservation in brine; —**ковать** *v.* preserve in brine; —**чный** *a.* brine.

туи *gen., pl., etc., of* **туя.**

туй/ан *m.* thujane, sabinane; —**евый** *see* **туевый;** —**ен** *see* **туен;** —**егенин** *m.* thujigenin; —**ил** *m.,* —**иловый** *a.* thujyl; —**иловый спирт** *see* **туйол;** —**ин** *m.* thujin; —**оид** *m.* thujoid; —**ол** *m.* thujol, hydroxythujene, absinthol; —**он** *m.* thujone, tanacetone; —**ородин** *m.* thujorhodin, rhodoxanthin; —**я** *see* **туя.**

тук *m.* fertilizer.

тукан *m.* (orn.) toucan (*Ramphastos*); —**овые,** —**ы** *pl.* Ramphastidae.

тукаши (mam.) Amazon river dolphin (*Sotalia fluviatilis*).

туковый *a. of* **тук.**

туко/мешалка *f.* fertilizer mixer; —**нагрузчик** *m.* fertilizer loader; —**разбрасыватель** *m.,* —**распределитель** *m.* fertilizer spreader, manure spreader; —**смесь** *f.* fertilizer mixture; —**смешение** *n.* fertilizer mixing.

туко-туко *m.* (mam.) tuco-tuco (*Ctenomys*); *pl.* Ctenomyidae.

тулейка *f.* shank.

тулейный *a. of* **тулья.**

тулес *m.* (orn.) plover (*Squatarola*).

Тулета раствор (min.) Thoulet solution.

тул/ий *m.* thulium, Tm (Tu in former USSR); **окись** —**ия** thulium oxide; **хлористый т.** thulium chloride.

туловище *n.* trunk, body, torso, bulk.

тулузский *a.* (geog.) Toulouse.

тулуп *m.,* —**ный** *a.* sheepskin (coat).

тульский *a.* (geog.) Tula.

тулья *f.* crown (of hat).

туляремия *f.* (med.) tularemia.

тулярин *m.,* —**овый** *a.* (immun.) tularine.

тумак *see* **тунец.**

туман *m.* fog, mist, haze, vapor, spray, film; **лёгкий т.** mist; **сухой т.** haze; —**ить** *v.* fog, darken, make obscure; —**иться** *v.* get foggy, grow dark, become obscure, get dim; —**ность** *f.* fogginess, mistiness, mist, haziness; (astr.) nebula; —**ный** *a.* foggy, misty, hazy, cloudy; nebulous, vague, obscure; —**омер** *m.* fog meter.

туманообраз/ный *a.* fog-like, misty; **высококучевые** —**ные облака** altocumulus nebulosus; **высокослоистые** —**ные облака** altostratus nebulosus; —**ователь** *m.* fog generator; atomizer; —**овательный,** —**ующий** *a.* fog-forming; mist (sprayer).

тумба *f.* curbstone; pedestal, post, column; **причальная т.** (naut.) bollard.

тумблер *m.,* —**ный переключатель** *m.* toggle switch.

тумбовый *a. of* **тумба.**

туменол *m.* Tumenol, ichthammol.

тун(а) *see* **тунец.**

тунг *m.,* —**овый** *a.* tung (tree).

тунгстен *see* **вольфрам.**

тунгус(с)кий *a.* (geog.) Tunguska.

тундр/а *f.,* —**еный,** —**овый** *a.,* —**овая полоса** tundra (treeless plain).

тундрянка *f.* tundra ptarmigan (*Lagopus mutus*).

тунец *m.* (ichth.) tuna (*Thunnus*).

туник/а *f.* (bot.) tunica, coating; —**атный** *a.* tunicate; —**аты** *pl.* (zool.) Tunicata.

тунисский *a.* (geog.) Tunisian.

туницин *m.* (zool.) tunicin.

туннел/естроение *n.* tunnel construction; —**ирование** *n.* (phys.) tunneling; —**ь** *m.* tunnel; duct, conduit; —**ьный** *a.* tunnel; tunnel-type (furnace); duct(ed).

тунца *gen. of* **тунец.**

тунц/еловный *a.* tuna (boat); —**еобразные** *pl.* Thunniformes; —**овые** *pl.* Thunnidae; —**овый** *a.* tuna.

ТУП *abbr.* (**технические условия проектирования**) technical design specifications.

туп *sh. m. of* **тупой.**

тупай/и *pl.* (mam.) tree shrews (*Tupaiidae*); —**я** *f.* tree shrew.

тупеть *v.* become blunt, grow dull.

тупец *m.* (leather) scraper.

тупик *m.* blind alley, impasse, cul-de-sac, dead end; blunt knife; (comp.) lock-up; (rr.) siding; (orn.) puffin (*Fratercula*); **попасть в т.** *v.* be at a loss; **стать в т.** *v.* be perplexed; —**овый** *a. of* **тупик;** —**овая ситуация** (comp.) deadlock, lock-up.

тупить *v.* blunt, dull, take off the edge.

тупо *adv.* bluntly, dully; obtusely.

туповат/ость *f.* bluntness; —**ый** *a.* rather blunt, rather dull, dullish.

тупой *a.* blunt, dull; obtuse (angle).

тупо/конечный *a.* blunt; —**листный** *a.* (bot.) obtusifolious; —**носый** *a.* blunt-nosed, blunt; —**рылка** *f.* (ichth.) gizzard shad (*Dorosoma*); —**рылый** *a.* blunt-nosed; —**сть** *f.* bluntness, dullness; —**угольный** *a.* obtuse-angled; obtuse (triangle); —**умие** *n.* (med.) hebetude; —**умный** *a.* stupid, dull; —**хвостый** *a.* stump-tailed, bobtailed.

тур *m.* round; gabion; mountain goat (*Capra*); auroch (*Bos primigenius*); **Тур** (geog.) Tours.

тур. *abbr.* (**турецкий**) Turkish.

турако *n., pl.* (orn.) touraco(s) (*Musophagidae*).

тура/ноза *f.* turanose; —**цин** *m.* turacin.

турач *m.* (orn.) francolin, black partridge (*Francolinus*).

турачка *f.* (naut.) warping drum.

турбак *m.* (ichth.) chub.

турбеллярии *pl.* (zool.) Turbellaria.

турбидиметр *m.* turbidimeter; **—ический** *a.* turbidimetric, nephelometric (analysis); **—ия** *f.* turbidimetry.

турбин/а *f.* turbine; **т.-компаунд** compound turbine **—ный** *a.* turbine(-driven); turbine-type (mixer, etc.); turbo- (dryer); **—о—** *prefix* turb(in)o—, turbine; **—щик** *m.* turbine specialist.

турбо— *prefix* turbo—, turbine; **—агрегат** *m.* turbounit; **—альтернатор** *m.* turbo-alternator; **—бур** *m.* turbodrill; **—вентилятор** *m.*, **—вентиляторный** *a.* turbofan; **—винтовой** *a.* turboprop (engine); **—воз** *m.* turbine locomotive; **—возбудитель** *m.* (elec.) turboexciter; **—воздуходувка** *f.* turboblower; **—генератор** *m.*, **—генераторный** *a.* (elec.) turbogenerator, turboalternator.

турбо/детандер *m.* turboexpander, turbine expansion engine, centrifugal expander; **—динамо** *n.*, **—динамомашина** *f.* (elec.) turbodynamo; **—долото** *n.* turbobit; **—зубчатый** *a.* turbogear.

турбокомпрессор *m.*, **—ный** *a.* turbocompressor, centrifugal compressor; turbo-supercharger (of piston engine); gas generator (of gas-turbine engine); **—ный воздушно-реактивный** *a.* turbojet (engine).

турбо/лёт *m.* turbojet; **—логуошер** *m.* (min.) turbowasher; **—машина** *f.* turbomachine; **—нагнетатель** *m.* turbosupercharger, turbocompressor; **—насос** *m.*, **—насосный** *a.* turbopump, turbine pump; **—преобразователь** *m.* turboconverter; **—привод** *m.* turbodrive; **с —приводом** turbine-driven; **—прямоточный** *a.* turboram(jet) (rocket engine); **—ракетный** *a.* turborocket; **—реактивный** *a.* turbojet (engine); spinstabilized (missile).

турбостро/ение *n.*, **—ительный** *a.* turbine construction, turbine manufacture.

турбо/трансформатор *m.* turbotransformer; **—холодильник** *m.* cooling turbine; **—эксгаустер** *m.* turbinedriven exhauster; **—электроход** *m.* turbo-electric ship.

турбулентн/ость *f.* turbulence; **—ый** *a.* turbulent, eddy; **схема —ого обмена** boundary layer pattern; **—ое движение** eddy.

турбулиз/атор *m.* turbulator, double-action pump; (petrol.) turbulence agent; **—ация** *f.* turbulization, agitation; **—ирующий** *a.* turbulizing, agitating.

тургайский *a.* (geog.) Turgai (river).

тургесцентный *a.* tumid, turgid, swollen, bloated.

тургор *m.* (bot.) turgor; **—ный** *a.* turgid, swollen.

турель *f.*, **—ный** *a.* turret; ring mount(ing); gun ring; **—ная установка** turret.

турецк/ий *a.* Turkish; **т. боб** kidney bean, scarlet runner bean; **—ое седло** (anat.) sella turcica.

турист *m.*, **—(иче)ский** *a.* tourist.

турк— *prefix* **—естанский** *a.* (geog.) Turkestan; **—менский** *a.* Turkmen.

турма *f.* bin; tower.

турмалин *m.* (min.) tourmaline.

турменн/ый *a. of* **турма**.

турмер/ин *m.* turmerin; **—овая кислота** turmeric acid.

турнбул/лева синь, —ьская синь Turnbull's blue, insoluble Prussian blue.

турне *n.* tour, round, circuit.

турнейский *a.* (geol.) Tournaisian.

турнепс *m.* turnip.

турнерова желть Turner's yellow, Cassel yellow.

турникет *m.*, **—ный** *a.* tourniquet; turnstile.

туронский *a.* (geol.) Turonian.

турпан *m.* (orn.) scoter (*Melanitta*).

турпет *m.* turpeth root; **—ин** *m.* turpethin; **—ный** *a.* turpeth.

турта *f.* (ichth.) Aral roach.

турухтан *m.* (orn.) ruff; **—ка** *f.* reeve (*Philomachus pugnax*).

Турция (geog.) Turkey.

туры *pl. of* **тур**; cattle (*Bos*).

тускарора wild rice (*Zizania aquatica*).

тускл/о *adv.* dimly, without luster; **—(оват)ость** *f.* dimness, lack of luster, dullness, tarnish, cloudiness; **—оватый** *a.* rather dim; **—осерый** *a.* dull gray; **—ый** *a.* dim, lusterless, dull, tarnished, dingy, crepuscular.

тускн/ение *n.* fogging, tarnishing; **—еть, —уть** *v.* grow foggy, tarnish, get dim, get dull; **—еющий** *a.* tarnishing.

Тусон (geog.) Tucson.

Туссена формула (meteor.) Toussaint's formula.

туссоковый *a.* tussock (grass).

туссол *m.* tussol, antipyrine mandelate.

тут *adv.* here; then; (bot.) *see* **тута**; **т. же** then and there, immediately.

тута *f.* (bot.) mulberry (*Morus*).

тутин *m.* tutin.

туто/видный *a.* (bot.) moriform; **—вник** *m.* mulberry (tree); **—водство** *n.*, **—водческий** *a.* mulberry culture; **—вый** *a.* mulberry.

тутокаин *m.* tutocaine, butamin.

туттоновые соли (chem.) Tutton salts.

туф *m.* (petr.) tuff; tufa; **вулканический т.** volcanic tuff; **известковый т.** (calcareous) tufa, travertine.

туф/елька *f.* slipper animalcule, paramecium; **—ельный** *a.*, **—ля** *f.* slipper, shoe.

туфо/бетон *m.* tufaceous concrete; **—вый** *a. of* **туф**; **—вый вулканический** *a.* tufaceous; **—вый известковый** *a.* tufaceous; **—образный, —подобный** *a.* tufa-like, tufaceous.

тухл/ость *f.* putrefaction; **—ый** *a.* putrefied, rotten, spoiled, tainted; **—ятина** *f.* tainted food.

тухнуть *v.* putrefy, spoil; go out, become extinguished.

туч/а *f.*, **—евой** *a.* (storm) cloud; (ent.) swarm; **—ка** *dim. of* **туча**.

тучн/еть *v.* fatten, gain weight; (soils) become more fertile; **—ость** *f.* obesity; fertility, richness (of soil); **—ый** *a.* obese, fat, corpulent; fertile, rich; succulent, full (grain); (biol.) mast (cell).

туша *f.* carcass.

тушащий *a.* extinguishing, etc., *see* **тушить.**

туше *n.* touch.

туш/евальный *a.*, **—ание** *n.* (drawing) shading, etc., *see v.*; **—ёванный** *a.* shaded, etc., *see v.*; **—евать** *v.* shade, wash, tint; **—ёвка** *see* **тушевание**; **—евый** *a. of* **тушь.**

туш/ение *n.* extinguishing, etc., *see v.*; **—ёнка** *f.* canned stewed meat; **—енный** *part.*, **—ёный** *a.* extinguished, etc., *see v.*; **—ение** *see* **тушительный**; **—итель** *m.* extinguisher, sprinkler; quencher, quenching agent; **—ительный** *a.* extinguishing, etc., *see v.*; **—ить** *v.* extinguish, put out (fire); slake, quench; damp; (elec.) switch off, turn off; (food) stew, braize; suppress.

тушка *dim. of* **туша.**

тушканчик *m.* jerboa (a rodent).

тушь *f.*, **китайская т.** India ink.

туя *f.* (bot.) Thuja; *prefix* thuja—, thuya—; **—кетон** *m.* thuyaketone.

ТФП *abbr.* (**модель Томаса-Ферми с поправками**) (phys.) Thomas-Fermi model with corrections, TFC model.

ТХК, ТХУ(К) *abbr.* (**трихлоруксусная кислота**) trichloroacetic acid.

ТХФМ *abbr.* (**трихлорфенолят меди**) copper trichlorophenolate.

тч. *abbr.* (**точка**) point; **т. ч.** *abbr.* (**так что**) so that; **т/ч** *abbr.* (**тонн в час**) tons per hour; **т/ч, ТЧ** *abbr.* (**техническая часть**) technical section, technical unit.

тщательн/о *adv.* carefully, with great care, thoroughly, in detail; closely, intimately; **т. следить за тем, чтобы** *v.* take great care that; **—ость** *f.* care(fulness), attention; exactness; **—ый** *a.* careful, thorough; exacting, meticulous; accurate; close, intimate (mixing).

тщедуш/ие *n.* debility, feebleness, weakness; **—ный** *a.* infirm, feeble, weak.

тщетн/о *adv.* vainly, in vain, to no purpose; **—ость** *f.* uselessness, futility; **—ый** *a.* vain, useless, futile.

тыкать *v.* poke, prod, thrust; **—ся** *v.* knock (against).

тыкв/а *f.* (bot.) pumpkin, squash, gourd; **летняя т., обыкновенная т., столовая т.** summer squash; pumpkin; **—енные** *pl.* Cucurbitaceae; **—енный** *a.* of **тыква**; cucurbitaceous; **—ообразный** *a.* gourd-shaped.

тыкнуть *see* **тыкать.**

тыл *m.* (anat.) back, dorsum; rear (area); (mil.) home front; logistic system, supply system; **с —а** at the rear, from the rear; **—ы** *pl.* supply corps, support units; **—овой** *a.* back, dorsal; rear(-end); logistic; administrative; **—ок** *m.* (tools) back edge; **—ьный** *see* **тыловой.**

тын *m.*, **—овый** *a.* paling; stockade.

тырло *n.* cattle pen.

тыс. *abbr.* (**тысяча**) thousand.

тысяча *num.* thousand.

тысяче— *prefix* thousand, milli—; **—голов** *m.* (bot.) cowherb (*Vaccaria*); **—гранник** *m.* (geom.) chiliahedron; **—кратный** *a.* thousandfold; **—летие** *n.* millenium; thousand-year period; **—летний** *a.* millenial; thousand-year; **—листник** *m.* (bot.) yarrow (*Achillea*); **—ног** *m.*, **—ножка** *f.* (zool.) millepede.

тысячн/ая *f.* (mil.) mil; **—ик** *m.* leading worker; **—ый** *a.* thousandth; of many thousands.

тычет *pr. 3 sing.* of **тыкать.**

тычина *f.* stake, post.

тычин/ка *f.* (bot.) stamen; **жаберная т.** (ichth.) gill raker; **—ковый** *a.* staminal, staminate; **—коносный** *a.* staminate, staminiferous, stamen-bearing; **—ник** *m.* (bot.) androecium; **—очный** *see* **тычинковый; —очная трубка** (bot.) androphore.

тычка *f.* center punch, prick punch.

тыч/ковый *a.*, **—ок** *m.* (masonry) header, bondstone, bonder; blow, hit, shove, prod, knock; peg, pin; **—ковая гайка** castle nut.

тычут *pr. 3 pl.* of **тыкать.**

тьма *f.* dark(ness), obscurity.

Тьюринга машина (comp.) Turing's machine.

ТЭА *abbr.* (**тетраэтиламмоний**) tetraethylammonium; (**триэтаноламин**) triethanolamine.

тэдс, ТЭДС, Т.-Э.Д.С. *abbr.* (**термоэлектродвижущая сила**) thermoelectromotive force.

Тэйлора ряд (math.) Taylor's series.

тэк *m.* (mam.) Asiatic ibex (*Capra siberica*).

тэка *see* **тека.**

тэкс *m.* tack.

ТЭН *abbr.* (**тетранитропентаэритрит**) pentaerythrityl tetranitrate, PETN.

ТЭПФ *abbr.* (**тетраэтилпирофосфат**) tetraethyl pyrophosphate.

ТЭС *abbr.* (**тепловая электростанция**) thermal electric power plant.

тэта *f.* theta (θ); **тэта-пинч** *m.* (phys.) theta-pinch.

ТЭФ *abbr.* (**триэтиленфосфорамид**) triethylenephosphoramide.

ТЭЦ *abbr.* (**теплоэлектроцентраль**) heat and electric power plant.

тюб/ик *m.* tube; **—инг** *m.*, **—овый** *a.* tubing, piping; (min.) tubbing.

тювик *m.* (orn.) Accipiter badius.

тюк *m.*, **укладывать в —и, —овать** *v.* bale, bundle, pack(age); **—овка** *f.* baling, packing; **—овщик** *m.* baler, packer; **—овый** *a.* bale(d), pack(ed); **т.-рулон** *m.* round bale.

тюлевый *a.* of **тюль.**

тюлен/ебойный *a.* seal-hunting; **—евые** *pl.* true seals (*Phocidae*); **—евый** *a.* seal(-skin); **—ёнок** *m.* seal pup; **—и** *pl.* Pinnipedia; **—ий** *a.* seal; **—ий жир** seal oil; **—ина** *f.* seal meat; **—ь** *m.* seal.

тюль *m.* (text.) tulle.

тюлька *f.* Caspian sprat (*Clupeonella delicatula*).

тюльпан *m.*, **—ный, —овый** *a.* (bot.) tulip; **—ообразный** *a.* tulip-shaped, funnel-shaped, funneled; tulip (valve).

тюменский *a.* (geog.) Tyumen.

тюрбо *n.* turbot (flatfish).

тюремный *a.* of **тюрьма.**

Тюри регулятор (elec.) Thury regulator.

тюринг(ен)ский *a.* (geog.) Thuringian.

тюркский *a.* (geog.) Turkic.

тюрьма *f.* prison, jail.

тютень *see* **тигель.**

тютюн *m.* low-grade tobacco.

тюф/як *m.*, **—ячный** *a.* mattress, pad; (hydr.) revetment; (mil.) burster layer.

тявк/ать, —нуть *v.* yap, yelp.

тяг/а *f.* pull, draw, draft; traction, pulling, hauling, haulage; propulsion; (rockets) thrust; (push-)pull rod, (connecting) rod, tie rod; linkage; stay, brace; (laboratory) hood; **искусственная т.** forced draft; **регулятор —и** damper; **с нижней —ой** downdraft; **сила —и** tractive force; (rockets) thrust; **служба —и** transport service; (rr.) rolling stock department; **—соединительная т.** draw bar; **тракторной —и** tractor-drawn.

тяг/альный *a.* pulling, traction; **—ать** *v.* pull, tow; **—ач** *m.* (truck) tractor; tow truck; prime mover.

тягло *n.* tax; **живое т.** draft animals; **—вый** *a.* draft (horse); tax(ed).

тягвооружённость *f.* (aero.) thrust-to-weight ratio.

тягов/ый *a.* traction(al), tractive, drawing, pulling, hauling; draw (bar); drawbar (spring; test); pull (chain, rope); **т. брус** drawbar; **т. двигатель** *m.* (elec.) traction motor; (naut.) propulsion engine; **т. крюк** draw (bar) hook; **т. прибор** drawgear, traction equipment, pulling equipment; **т. стержень** drawbar; **—ая мощность** traction (power); (av.) thrust power (output); **—ое оборудование** haulage equipment; **—ое усилие** pulling force; (rr.) tractive effort.

тягодутьевой *a.* forced-draft.

тягомер *m.* draft gage, draft indicator, suction gage; blast meter, blast indicator; traction dynamometer.

тягост/ный *a.* burdensome, wearisome; distressing; **—ь** *f.* burden.

тягот/а *f.* weight, load, burden, heaviness, hardship; **—ение** *n.* gravitation, gravity, attraction, pull; **коэффициент —ения** gravity constant; **поле —ения** gravitational field; **сила —ения** gravitational force, gravity; **—еть** *v.* gravitate, be attracted; weigh; **—еющий** *a.* gravitating; **—ить** *v.* overload, overwhelm, weigh; hang (upon), hang heavy; **—иться** *v.* feel the weight (of), feel the burden (of).

тягун *m.* (glass) lehr, annealing furnace.

тягуч/есть *f.* ductility; malleability; tenacity, toughness; viscosity (of liquid); **—ий** *a.* ductile; malleable; tenacious, tough; tensile, tractile; viscous (liquid), viscid, ropy.

тягчайший *superl. of* **тяжкий**.

тяж *m.* drawing rod, (brake) rod; strand, cord; (biol.) tenia; gubernaculum; peduncle, fascicle; trace, shaft brace; **сцепной т.** tow bar.

тяжек *sh. m. of* **тяжкий**.

тяжёл *sh. m. of* **тяжёлый**; **—тяжелее** *comp. of* **тяжёлый**.

тяжел/еть *v.* get heavy; **—ить** *v.* make heavy; **—о** *adv.* heavily; with difficulty; it is heavy; it is difficult; *prefix* heavy; **—оватый** *a.* rather heavy.

тяжеловес *m.* (sports) heavyweight; (min.) Siberian topaz; **—ность** *f.* heaviness, etc., see *a.*; **—ный** *a.* heavy, ponderous, unwieldy, clumsy; heavily loaded.

тяжело/водный *a.* heavy-water; **—воз** *m.* heavy draft horse; heavy truck; **—грузный** *a.* heavily loaded; heavy-freight; **—раненый** *a.* seriously wounded; **—суглинистый** *a.* clayey loam (soil); **—ходы** *pl.* (pal.) Gravigrada.

тяжёл/ый *a.* heavy, weighty, ponderous; hard, difficult, burdensome; severe, harsh; close (air); rich (food); serious (illness; problem); (mach.) heavy-duty; substantial; **—ая вода** heavy water, deuterium oxide; **—ая жидкость** gravity solution; **—ая затяжная неврастения** (med.) neurasthenia gravis; **—ая индустрия** heavy in-

dustry; **—ого типа, для —ой работы** heavy-duty (machine).

тяжение *n.* stress.

тяжест/ь *f.* weight, gravity, heaviness, load, burden; severity; **поле —и** gravitational field; **сила —и** (force of) gravity, gravitational force, gravitation; **силой —и** by gravity; **центр —и** center of gravity.

тяжка *f.* (leather) staking.

тяжкий *a.* grave, weighty, serious, severe; heavy; dangerous, distressing.

тяжник *m.* draw band.

тяну/льный *a.* pulling, etc., see *v.*; **—льная машина** (leather) staking machine; **—тый** *a.* pulled, etc., see *v.*; **—ть** *v.* pull, haul, drag; stretch (out), draw (out), extend, reach; lay (cable); suck (in), pull in, draw in; heave; weigh; drag out, delay, protract, procrastinate, prolong, put off; last, continue; **—ться** *v.* be pulled, etc.; stretch, extend, run, range; last, continue, drag on, hold out, linger; strive (to equal); **—чки** *pl.* (televi.) streaks; **—щий** *a.* pulling, tractor (propeller); **—щая сила** pull; **—щийся** *a.* extending, running.

тяньцзиньский *a.* (geog.) Tientsin.

тянь-шаньский *a.* (geog.) Tien Shan (mountain range).

тяп/ание *n.* hacking; **—ать, —нуть** *v.* hack, chop, cut; **—ка** *f.* chopper, cleaver; hoe.

ТЯЭС *abbr.* (**термоядерная электростанция**) thermonuclear electric power plant.

У

у *prep. gen.* by, near, at, on, in; to; with, of; **у него (есть)** he has, he possesses, he owns; **у них на заводе** at their plant; **попросить у него** *v.* ask him.

у— *prefix* de—, ab—, away from.

уабаин *m.* (pharm.) ouabain, G-Strophanthin.

уади *n.* (geol.). wadi (a valley).

уайтрот *m.* white rot (of trees).

уайтхедовский *a.* (math.) Whitehead.

уакари *m.* ouakari monkey (*Cacajao*).

уатт *m.* (elec.) watt; *see also* **ватт**.

Уатта регулятор (elec.) Watt governor.

уаттметр *see* **ваттметр**.

убав/ить *see* **убавлять**; **—ка** *f.*, **—ление** *n.* diminishing, etc., see *v.*; curtailment, reduction, decrease; discount; **—ленный** *a.* diminished, etc., see *v.*; **—лять** *v.* diminish, lessen, decrease; curtail, reduce, abridge, shorten; abate, subdue; **—ляться** *v.* be diminished, etc.; diminish, decrease, drop (down), lessen, abate; **—ляющий** *a.* diminishing, etc., see *v.*

убанги (geog.) Ubangi; (ichth.) Gnathonemus petersi.

убег/ание *n.* running away, etc., see *v.*; runaway; **скорость —ания** runaway speed; second cosmic velocity; **—ать** *v.* run away, escape, make off; boil over; run off, stretch, extend; **—ающий** *a.* running away, etc., see *v.*; runaway.

убедительн/ость *f.* persuasiveness, conclusiveness; **—ый** *a.* persuasive, convincing, conclusive, earnest (request).

убедить *see* **убеждать**.

убежать *see* **убегать**.

убежд/ать *v.* convince, persuade, satisfy; prevail (upon); induce, urge; **—аться** *v.* be convinced, etc.; make sure, ascertain, be sure, ensure (that); see, determine (that); **—ение** *n.* conviction, persuasion; **не поддающийся —ению** inconvincible; **—ённость** *f.* conviction, assurance; **—ённый** *a.* convinced, positive (of), certain.

убежище *n.* refuge, shelter, cover, dugout; sanctuary, asylum.

убел/ённый *a.* whitened, bleached, hoary (with age); **—ивание** *n.* whitening, bleaching; **—и(ва)ть, —ять** *v.* whiten, bleach.

уберегать *v.* preserve, protect, guard, keep safe, safeguard.

уберёт *fut. 3 sing. of* **убрать**.

уберечь *see* **уберегать**.

убив/ание *n.* killing, etc., see *v.*; **—ать** *v.* kill, butcher, slaughter; pack, tamp (down); **—ающий** *a. suffix* —cidal, destroying, **—ающее средство** *suffix* —cide.

убийств/енный *a.* deadly, killing, murderous; **—о** *n.* murder, homicide, assassination; slaughter, butchery.

убиквисты *pl.* (biol.) ubiquists.

убир/аемый *a.* (av.) retractable; **—ание** *n.* removing, etc., see *v.*; removal; retraction; **—ать** *v.* remove, take off, clear; take away, withdraw, retract; dispose (of), put away; put in order, arrange; harvest, reap, gather, pick, pluck; pull (flax); trim, decorate; **—ать породу** (min.) muck; **—аться** *v.* be removed, etc.; clear (away, off), get out of the way, disappear; collapse, fold up; retract; **—ающий** *a.* removing, etc., see *v.*; **—ающийся** *a.* folding(-type), collapsible; retractable, retractile.

убит/ый *a.* killed; inactivated (vaccine); packed, beaten down; depressed, crushed; *m.* the dead; **—ь** *see* **убивать**.

убихинон *m.* ubiquinone, coenzyme Q.

УБК *abbr.* (**универсальный башенный кран**) universal tower crane.

ублюд/ковый, —очный *a.* hybrid; mongrel, cross-bred; **—ок** *m.* hybrid, half-breed; mongrel.

убо/гий *a.* poor, lean (ore); worthless, wretched, squalid; handicapped; *m.* cripple; beggar; **—гая руда** chats (small pieces of stone with ore); **—гость** *f.* leanness, wretchedness, squalor; **—жество** *n.* scantiness, poverty; need; insignificance; wretchedness, squalor; deformity.

убоина *f.* meat; fattened cattle.

убой *m.* slaughter(ing); **—ность** *f.* (mil.) destructive power; lethality; **—ный** *a.* (for) slaughter, slaughtering; dressed (weight of meat); (mil.) destructive, lethal; stopping (power); **—ный пункт** slaughterhouse.

убори́ст/ость *f.* closeness, compactness; **—ый** *a.* close, compact.

убо́рка *see* **убира́ние;** retraction; harvest, harvesting season.

убо́рная *f.* lavatory.

убо́рочн/ая *f.* harvest (time); **—ый** *a.* harvesting; **—ая маши́на** harvester, picker; windrower.

убо́рщик *m.* attendant, janitor, (office) cleaner; (agr.) picker, harvester; windrower.

убр/анный *a.* removed, etc., *see* **убира́ть; —анство** *n.* decoration; **—а́ть** *see* **убира́ть.**

УБТ *abbr.* (утяжелённая бурильная труба) drill collar.

убу́дет *fut. 3 sing. of* **убы́ть.**

убыв/а́ние *n.* diminishing, etc., *see v.*; decrease, reduction, diminution; descent; (exponential) decay; **сортиро́вка по —а́нию** (comp.) descending sort; **—а́ть** *v.* diminish, decrease, lessen, decline, drop; (math.) descend; decay (exponentially); subside, sink, ebb, fall (of tide); wane (of moon); **—а́ющий** *a.* diminishing, etc., *see v.*; last (quarter of moon); **зако́н —а́ющего плодоро́дия** law of diminishing returns.

убы́л *past m. sing. of* **убы́ть.**

убы́ль *f.* decrease, diminution; subsidence, decline, ebb; loss, waste, leak; wear and tear, depreciation; (mil.) casualties; **итти́ на у.** *see* **убыва́ть.**

убыстр/и́ть, —я́ть *v.* speed up, accelerate.

убы́т/ие *see* **убыва́ние;** fall; **—ок** *m.* damage, loss; deficit; disadvantage; **—очность** *f.* unprofitableness; **—очный** *a.* unprofitable, losing; wasteful; detrimental; **—ь** *see* **убыва́ть.**

убьёт *fut. 3 sing. of* **уби́ть.**

УВ *abbr.* (у́гол ве́тра) wind angle; (устро́йство вычита́ния) subtractor; **УВ; у.в.** *abbr.* (уде́льный вес) specific gravity.

ува *f.* (bot.) uva.

уваж/а́ть *v.* respect, esteem; **—е́ние** *n.* respect, regard, deference, appreciation; **с —е́нием** respectfully yours; **—а́тельный** *a.* valid, satisfactory, allowable; worthy of consideration; **—и́ть** *v.* comply (with a request).

ува́л *m.* ridge, spur; slope; departure; (road) rut, pothole; drift (of a boat); (anat.) colline; **—и(ва́)ть** *v.* pile (on); let fall, drop; disperse; lean, tilt; go off course, veer, drift; (text.) full; **—и(ва́)ться** *v.* be piled (on), etc.; fall, tumble; tilt, incline, lean; **—и(ва́)ться под ве́тер** (naut.) fall off to leeward; **—ка** (text.) fulling; **—ьность** *f.* ridginess; (naut.) slackness; **—ьный** *a.* ridgy, spurry; ridge(d); **—ьчивость** *f.* (naut.) slackness; **—я́ть** *v.* full.

ува́р *see* **ува́ривание; —енный** *a.* boiled down, etc., *see v.*; **—ивание** *n.* boiling down, etc., *see v.*; concentration; loss on boiling; **—и(ва́)ть** *v.* boil down, evaporate down, concentrate (cook thoroughly); **—ка** *see* **ува́ривание.**

УВВ *abbr.* (устро́йство для вво́да и вы́вода) input-output device.

УВД *abbr.* (управле́ние возду́шным движе́нием) air traffic control.

уве́альный *a.* (anat.) uveal.

уведёт *fut. 3 sing. of* **увести́.**

уведом/и́тельный *a.* informative; **—и́ть** *see* **уведомля́ть; —ле́ние** *n.* information, notification, advice, notice, message; **—ля́ть** *v.* inform, advise, notify, give notice.

увезти́ *see* **увози́ть.**

уве́ит *m.* (med.) uveitis.

увекове́чи(ва)ть *v.* immortalize, perpetuate.

увёл *past m. sing. of* **увести́.**

увелич/е́ние *n.* increasing, augmentation, etc., *see v.*; increase, increment, rise, gain, growth, expansion; enhancement; magnification, magnifying power; (phot.) enlargement; **у. жёсткости** hardening; **у. ногте́й** (med.) onychauxis, overgrowth or thickening of nails; **с больши́м —е́нием** high-power (microscope); **с ма́лым —е́нием** low-power; **—енный** *a.* increased, etc., *see v.*; **—ивание** *see* **увеличе́ние; —ива́ть** *v.* increase, augment, add, raise, (step) up, scale up; magnify, enlarge; build up, boost, amplify, intensify, enhance; prolong, extend, expand; **—ива́ть втро́е** triple; **—ива́ться** *v.* be increased, etc.; (be on the) increase, rise, grow, become larger; soar, climb; **—ива́ющий** *a.* increasing, etc., *see v.*; **—ива́ющийся** *a.* (bot.) accrescent, increscent.

увеличи́тель *m.* enlarger; magnifier; **—ный** *a.* enlarging, magnifying, augmentative; **—ный аппара́т** enlarger; **—ное стекло́** magnifying glass, magnifier.

увели́чить *see* **увели́чивать.**

увенч/а́ние *n.* crowning; **—анный** *a.* crowned, etc., *see v.*; coronate; **—(ив)а́ть** *v.* crown, cap, crest; complete, finish; **—ива́ющий** *a.* (bot.) coronans, crowning.

увеопароти́т *m.* (med.) uveoparotid fever, Heerfordt's disease.

увере́н/ие *n.* assertion, assurance; **—но** *adv.* confidently, positively; **—ность** *f.* assurance, sureness, confidence, certainty; **мо́жно с —ностью сказа́ть** it is safe to say; **—ный** *a.* assured, sure, confident, positive, certain.

уве́рить *see* **уверя́ть.**

уверну́ть *see* **увёртывать.**

уве́ровать *v.* come to believe.

увёрт/ка *f.* subterfuge, evasion, dodge; **—ливость** *f.* evasiveness; **—ливый** *a.* evasive, elusive; **—ывать** *v.* wrap up, pack up, envelop; turn down, lower; **—ываться** *v.* be wrapped up, etc.; evade, elude, escape, avoid, dodge, shirk.

уверя́ть *v.* assure, persuade, convince; **—ся** *v.* become convinced, make sure.

увеси́ст/ость *f.* heaviness, weightiness; **—ый** *a.* heavy, weighty.

уве́сить *see* **увеш(ив)а́ть.**

увести́ *see* **уводи́ть.**

увеч/ить *v.* maim, cripple, mutilate, disable; **—ность** *f.* disability; **—ный** *a.* crippled, disabled, etc., *see v.*; lame; *m.* cripple; **—ье** *n.* mutilation, severe injury.

увеш(ив)а́ть *v.* hang (over), drape.

увещ/а́ние *n.* exhortation, admonition, admonishment; **—а́тельный** *a.* exhortative, admonitory; **—(ев)а́ть** *v.* exhort, admonish, talk (to).

увива́ть *v.* entwine, wrap around.

увид/а́ть, —еть *v.* see, catch sight (of), set eyes (on); perceive, understand; **—еться** *v.* see each other, meet.

увил/ива́ние *n.* elusion, evasion; **—ива́ть, —ьну́ть** *v.* elude, evade, dodge.

уви/новая кислота́ uvic acid; **—олевый** *a.* uviol, ultra-violet-transmitting (glass); **—осто́йкий** *a.* resistant to ultraviolet rays; **—тиновая кислота́** uvitic acid; **—тоновая кислота́** uvitonic acid.

уви́ть *see* **увива́ть.**

увлажн/е́ние *n.* moistening, etc., *see v.*; humidification; **—еность** *f.* moisture, humidity; **сте́пень —ености** moisture content; **—енный** *a.* moistened, etc., *see v.*; humid; (bot.) irrorate, humectate; **—и́тель** *m.* moistener, mister, humidifier; —**ительный** *a. see* **увлажн-я́ющий**; —**ить**, —**ять** *v.* moisten, damp(en), humidify, wet; (text.) condition; —**я́ющий** *a.* moistening, etc., *see v.*

увлек/а́тель *m.* (azeotropic distillation) withdrawing agent; —**а́тельный** *a.* fascinating, absorbing, interesting, exciting; —**а́ть** *v.* entrain, entrap, carry off, carry along, carry away; absorb, interest, fascinate; —**а́ть при осажде́нии** carry down by precipitation, coprecipitate; —**а́ть пыль водо́й** settle dust with water, sprinkle down; —**а́ться** *v.* be absorbed (in), take a fancy (to); be carried away.

увлеч/е́ние *n.* entrainment, carrying away; interest, enthusiasm; —**ённый** *a.* entrained, etc., *see* **увлека́ть**; —**ь** *see* **увлека́ть**.

УВМ *abbr.* (**управля́ющая вычисли́тельная маши́на**) control computer.

у-во *abbr.* (**устро́йство**).

уво́д *m.* leading away, drift, deflection, creeping; (av.) rake, tilt (of wing); **у. вверх** (art.) climb (of barrel); —**и́ть** *v.* lead away, carry off; discharge, drain off.

уво́з *m.* removal, carrying off, etc., *see v.*; —**и́ть** *v.* remove, carry off, carry away, drive away, take away, abduct.

увола́кивать *v.* carry off, drag (away).

уво́лить *see* **увольня́ть**.

уволо́ч/ить, —**ь** *see* **увола́кивать**.

уволь́н/е́ние *n.* dismissal, discharge; (mil.) leave; **у. в отста́вку** retirement; —**и́тельный** *a.* discharge; —**и́тельная запи́ска** (mil.) pass; —**я́ть** *v.* dismiss, discharge, expel; discard; free, exempt (from); (mil.) grant leave.

УВПД *abbr.* (**указа́тель высоты́ и перепа́да давле́ния**) altitude and pressure-drop indicator.

ВЧ *abbr.* (**ультравысокочасто́тный; ультравысо́кая частота́**) ultra-high frequency; (**усили́тель высо́кой частоты́**) high-frequency amplifier.

увьёт *fut. 3 sing. of* **уви́ть**.

увя́д/ание *n.* wilting, etc., *see v.*; (phyt.) wilt; —**а́ть** *v.* wilt, wither, fade; waste away; —**ший** *a.* wilted, withered; (e)marcid.

увя́з/ать *see* **увя́знуть**, **увя́зывать**; —**ить** *see* **увя́знуть**; —**ка** *see* **увя́зывание**; (stratigraphic) correlation; coordination; —**нуть** *v.* get stuck, sink (in), mire; —**очный** *a.*, —**ывание** *n.* tying up, etc., *see* **увя́зывать**; —**ывать** *v.* tie up, pack up, bale; link up, connect (up), coordinate (with); —**ываться** *v.* be tied up, etc.; tag along.

увя́нуть *see* **увяда́ть**.

уга́д/ать, —**ывать** *v.* guess; —**ывание** *n.* guessing.

уга́й *m.* (ichth.) eastern redfin (*Leuciscus brandti*).

уга́ндский *a.* (geog.) Uganda.

уга́р *m.*, —**ный** *a.* waste, loss; (met.) furnace loss, waste by oxidation, loss in burning; consumption (of fuel); carbon monoxide fumes; **е́дкий у.** corrosive fumes; —**ный газ** carbon monoxide; —**ы** *pl.* (text.) waste, refuse.

уга́с/ание *n.* fading, etc., *see v.*; extinction; —**а́ть** *v.* fade, die away, weaken, fail, grow dim; go out, become extinguished, become extinct; damp off (of seedlings); —**и́ть** *see* **угаша́ть**; —**нуть** *see* **угаса́ть**; —**ший** *a.* extinct, extinguished, quenched.

угаш/а́ть *v.* extinguish, quench, put out; suppress, check; —**енный** *a.* extinguished, etc., *see v.*

Уги ре́акция (chem.) Ugi reaction.

угиба́ть *v.* bend down.

угла́ *gen. of* **у́гол**.

угла́стый *a.* angular.

угле́ *prepos. of* **у́гол**.

угле— *prefix* carbon; coal; —**аммиа́чная соль,** —**аммоние́вая соль** ammonium carbonate; —**ба́риевая соль** barium carbonate; —**ви́дный** *a.* coal-like; —**ви́смутовая соль** bismuth carbonate; —**во́д** *m.*, —**во́дный** *a.* carbohydrate; **просто́й —во́д** monosaccharide; **сло́жный —во́д** polysaccharide.

углеводоро́д *m.* hydrocarbon; —**истый** *a.* hydrocarbon(aceous), containing hydrocarbons; —**истое соедине́ние** hydrocarbon; —**ный** *a.* hydrocarbon; —**ная жи́дкость** *f.* liquid hydrocarbon.

угле/во́з *m.* coal freighter; —**возду́шный** *a.* coal-air; —**волокно́** *n.* carbon fiber.

углевыжига́тельн/ый *a.* charring; —**ая печь** charcoal kiln.

углеграфи́т *m.* graphite.

угле/держа́тель *m.* carbon holder; —**добыва́ющий** *a.*, —**добыча** *f.* coal mining; —**дроби́лка** *f.* coal crusher; —**железистая соль** ferrous carbonate; —**железная соль** ferric carbonate; —**жже́ние** *n.* charcoal burning, charring, carbonization; —**жог** *m.* charcoal burner; —**зерни́стый** *a.* granulated carbon; —**кали́евая соль** potassium carbonate; —**ка́льциевая соль** calcium carbonate.

углекислот/а́ *f.* carbonic acid, carbon dioxide; **соль —ы** carbonate; **твёрдая у.** dry ice.

углеки́сл/ый *a.* carbonic acid; carbonate (of): **у. газ** carbon dioxide; **у. на́трий** sodium carbonate; **у. охлади́тель** carbon dioxide refrigerant, liquid carbon dioxide; —**ая соль** carbonate; **ки́слая —ая соль** acid carbonate, bicarbonate; **основна́я —ая соль** basic carbonate, subcarbonate.

угле/ко́п *m.* coal miner, collier; —**копле́ние** *n.* (geol.) coal formation; —**крези́ловый эфи́р** cresyl carbonate; —**ли́тиевая соль** lithium carbonate; —**магние́вая соль** magnesium carbonate.

углемарганцо́в/ая соль manganic carbonate; —**истая соль** manganous carbonate.

углеме́д/истая соль cuprous carbonate; —**ная соль** cupric carbonate.

угле/мо́йка *f.* coal washer; —**на́триевая соль** sodium carbonate; **ки́слая —на́триевая соль** sodium bicarbonate; —**ни́келевая соль** nickel carbonate; —**но́сность** *f.* coal content, tenor of coal; presence of coal; —**но́сный** *a.* coal-bearing, carboniferous.

углеобжига́тельный *a.* carbonizing, charring; **у. заво́д** charcoal works.

угле/обогати́тельный *a.* coal-concentrating; —**образова́тель** *m.* carbon-forming material; coal-forming material; —**отбо́йная маши́на** coal cutter; —**пла́стик** *m.* carbon-fiber-reinforced plastic; —**пло́тность** *f.* coal concentration per km²; —**погру́зочный** *a.* coal-loading; —**пода́тчик** *m.* coal feeder; stoker; —**про́вод** *m.* (coal) slurry pipeline; —**промы́вочный** *a.* coal-washing; —**промы́шленность** *f.*, —**промы́шленный** *a.* coal mining, coal industry; —**разбо́рка** *f.* sorting of coal; —**разре́з** *m.* (coal) strip mine.

углеро́д *m.* carbon, C; **двуо́кись —а** carbon dioxide; **о́кись —а** carbon monoxide; **четырёххлори́стый у.** carbon tetrachloride.

углероди́ст/ый *a.* carbon(ic), carbonaceous, carboniferous; carbide (of); **у. водоро́д** hydrocarbon; —**ая связь** carbon bond; —**ая сталь** carbon steel; —**ое желе́зо** iron carbide.

углеро́дный *a.* carbon(ic), carbonaceous.

углеродопла́сты *pl.* carbon-filled plastics.

угле/свинцо́вистая соль lead carbonate; —**серебряная соль** silver carbonate; —**фика́ция** *f.* (geol.) coalification, carbonification (metamorphism); **—цинковая соль** zinc carbonate; **—цинковый** *a.* carbon-zinc (cell); **—щелочной** *a.* coal-alkali; **—щелочной реагент** alkali extract of brown coal (drilling mud additive).

угли *pl. of* **уголь.**

углистый *a.* carbonaceous, carbon-like; coal(-like); **у. железняк** (min.) black band iron ore; **у. сланец** (petr.) carbonaceous shale, ampelite.

угл. корр. *abbr.* (угловая корреляция) angular correlation.

угло/бимсовое железо, —бульбовое железо bulb angle iron; **—бульб** *m.* bulb angle.

углов *gen. pl. of* **угол.**

углова́то *adv.* angularly; at an angle; *prefix* gonio—, anguli—; **—зернистый** *a.* angular-grained; **—круглый** *a.* subangular; round-cornered.

угловат/ость *f.* angularity; **—ый** *a.* angular.

углов/ой *a.* angle, angular; corner; **у. коэффициент** gradient, slope; **у. лист** corner plate; **у. сустав** (anat.) ginglymus, hinge joint; **у. эффект** corner effect (of wind); **—ая минута** minute of arc; **—ая ориентация** attitude (of a rocket); **—ая связь** angle brace; **—ая скорость** angular velocity; **—ая частота** angular frequency, radian frequency; **—ое железо** angle iron.

угло/измерительный *a.* goniometric; **у. прибор** (art.) aiming circle; **—м** *instr. of* **угол.**

угломер *m.* goniometer, angle gage; (art.) deflection; **у.-квадрант** *m.* goniometric sight, combined clinometer and azimuth scale; **—ный** *a.* goniometric, angle-measuring; **—ный инструмент** goniometer; **—ный прибор** direction finder.

угломестный *a.* elevation (antenna, etc.).

углу *prepos. of* **угол,** corner.

углуб/итель *m.* depressor (of trawl); **—ить** *see* **углублять; —ка** *see* **углубление.**

углубл/ение *n.* hollow, depression, recess, pocket, pouch, concave, cavity, hole; sump, pit; socket; notch, indentation; slot, rabbet; deepening, sinking, immersion; (naut.) draft; (pal.) fossa; (anat.) alveolus, lacuna, excavatio(n), vallecula; **—ённость** *f.* depth; **—ённый** *a.* deepened, etc., *see v.*; depth (study); fundamental (test); intensive (instruction); **—еньице** *f.* (biol.) alveola; **—ять** *v.* deepen, make deeper, excavate; depress, sink, recess, concave; intensify; **—яться** *v.* deepen, become deeper; dip; go far into; examine closely, investigate.

углы *pl. of* **угол.**

угля *gen. of* **уголь; —к** *m.* black diamond.

угнать *see* **угонять.**

угнездиться *v.* nestle; settle in.

угнести *see* **угнетать.**

угнет/ать *v.* oppress, depress, weigh heavy (on); (chem.) inhibit; **—ение** *n.* oppression; (med.) depression; (chem.) inhibition; **—ённый** *a.* oppressed, depressed, etc., *see v.*

угнуть *v.* bend down.

уговарив/ание *n.* persuasion, urging; **—ать** *v.* persuade, urge, exhort; **—аться** *v.* agree, be persuaded; arrange.

уговор *m.* agreement, understanding; persuasion; **с —ом** on condition; **—ить** *v.* persuade, prevail (upon), induce; **—иться** *v.* come to an agreement; **—ный** *a.* agreed (upon), contracted; stipulated.

угод/а *f.* pleasure, gratification, satisfaction; piece of land; **в —у** to please, to oblige; **—ий** *gen. pl. of* **угодье; —ить** *see* **угождать; как ему —но** as he pleases, as he chooses; **сколько —но** as much as is desired; **что —но** anything at all.

угод/ье *n.* land, area; **—ья** *pl.* grounds; (farming) lands; **лесные —ья** forests; **полевые —ья** arable lands.

угожд/ать *v.* gratify, please, humor; **—ение** *n.* gratification, compliance.

уг/ол *m.* angle; corner; (anat.) angulus; **у. при вершине** point angle (of a drill); **за —лом** around the corner; **под —лом** at an angle, obliquely; angular (adjustment, drive, etc.); **под прямым —лом** at right angles (to); perpendicular (to); right-angle (bend); **сечение под —лом** oblique section; **сдвиг —лов** angular displacement.

уголёк *m.* (illum.) carbon filament; small piece of coal.

уголковый *a. of* **уголок;** V-(antenna).

уголов/ный *a.* criminal, penal; **—щина** *f.* criminal act.

угол/ок *dim. of* **угол;** corner; (structural) angle, section; **—очный** *a.* corner; angle.

уголь *m.* coal; carbon; **активированный у.** activated carbon; **бурый у.** lignite, brown coal; **древесный у.** charcoal; **жирный у.** soft coal, bituminous coal; **ископаемый у.** coal; **каменный у.** (hard) coal; **превращать в у.** *v.* carbonize; **растительный у.** charcoal.

угольник *m.* (try-)square; angle (iron); (pipe) elbow; crank; *suffix* **—гон; листовой у., полосовой у.** corner plate; **стыковой у.** angle bracket; **у.-центроискатель** *m.* center square.

угольн/ый *a.* coal; carbon(ic); carbon-pile (regulator); carbon-filament (lamp); *see also* **угловой;** *prefix* **—гональ; у. ангидрид** carbon dioxide; **у. бассейн** coal field; **у. газ** coal gas; **у. пек** coal tar; **у. район** coal field; **у. рудник** coal mine, colliery; **у. стержень** carbon (of electric arc lamp); **—ая ангидраза** carbonic anhydrase; **сварка —ой дугой** carbon arc welding; **—ая кислота** carbonic acid, carbon dioxide; **соль —ой кислоты** carbonate; **—ая копь** coal mine, colliery.

угольщик *m.* coal miner, collier; coal freighter; charcoal burner.

угон *m.* driving away; (cattle) rustling; hijacking; (rail) creep(ing), sliding; **—ка** *f.* driving away; **—ять** *v.* drive away; hijack; rustle (cattle); **—яться** *v.* overtake, catch up (with), equal.

угор *m.* hillock.

угор/ать, —еть *v.* be poisoned by carbon monoxide; (smelting) decrease, diminish.

угорок *m.* mound, hillock.

угорь *m.* (med.) blackhead, acne, comedo; (ichth.) eel.

угорье *n.* foothill.

уго/стить, —щать *v.* treat, entertain.

угребычковые *pl.* (ichth.) eelgobies (Gobioididae).

угреватый *a.* pimply, pimpled.

угревать *v.* warm up, heat.

угревид/ные *pl.* (ichth.) Anguilloidei; **—ный** *a.* eel-like.

угрев/ой *a. of* **угорь,** blackhead; **—ая сыпь** (med.) acne.

угрёв/ые *pl.* freshwater eels (Anguillidae); **—ый** *a. of* **угорь,** eel.

угреобразные *pl.* (ichth.) Anguilliformes.

угреть *see* **угревать.**

угри *pl. of* **угорь;** (med.) acne; (ichth.) **морские у.** Conger eels; **речные у.** freshwater eels; **—цы** (zool.) Anguillulidae.

угрож/аемый *see* **угрожающий; —ать** *v.* threaten, menace, impend; **—ающий** *a.* threatening, etc., *see v.*; imminent; precarious; emergency (situation); troublesome (zone); aposematic (coloration).

угроза *f.* threat, menace, hazard, danger.

угря *gen. of* **угорь.**

уд. *abbr.* (**удельный**) specific; (**удовлетворительный**) satisfactory, adequate.

уда *f.* hook; fishhook.

удабривать *see* **удобрять.**

удав *m.* (zool.) boa constrictor.

удаваться *v.* succeed, be a success, turn out well; **не у.** fail.

удав/ить *see* **удавливать; —ка** *f.* slip knot, noose, timber hitch; (med.) paraphimosis; **—ление** *n.* strangulation; **—ливать** *v.* strangle, choke.

удал/ение *n.* removing, elimination, etc., *see* **удалять;** removal, withdrawal, extraction (of tooth), disposal, clearance; expulsion; departure, escape; range; de—; (med.) resection, —ectomy; **у. кишки** enterectomy; **у. отходов** waste disposal; **у. серы** desulfurization; **коэффициент —ения** (ballistics) reduction coefficient, r factor; **поле —ения ионов** (instrumentation) clearing field; **—ённость** *f.* remoteness; **—ённый** *a.* removed, etc., *see* **удалять;** remote, outlying, distant; apart, far, away (from); ablated, removed; extirpated; **—ившийся** *a.* withdrawn; escaped; **—итель** *m.* eliminator; (paint) remover, stripper; **—ить** *see* **удалять.**

удалой *see* **удалый.**

удалось *past n. sing. of* **удаться.**

удал/ый *a.* bold, daring, enterprising; **—ь** *f.*, **—ьство** *n.* boldness, daring, enterprise.

удалять *v.* remove, eliminate, extirpate; (med.) ablate; (comp.) delete; extract (teeth); withdraw, draw off, draw out, drain off, run off, discharge, empty; expel, evacuate, drive out, drive off, send away; take away, dispose (of), get rid (of), free (of); clear away, clear out; strip; avert; deprive (of); separate, space; **у. белки** deproteinize; **—ся** *v.* be removed, etc.; withdraw, recede, move away, go away.

удаляющийся *a. suffix* **—fugal** (directed away from); **у. от коры** corticofugal.

удар *m.* blow, stroke, strike, hit, knock, tap; impact, impingement, collision, smash, clash; shock, percussion, kick; impulse; detonation; (sonic) boom; pounding (of valves); (elec.) shock; (sun) stroke; clap (of thunder); beat (of pulse); (mil.) attack, thrust; (hydraulic) hammer; **—ами** percussively; by starts or jolts, jerkily; ~~испытание на у.~~ (met.) ~~impact test; dynamic crush~~ test; **одним —ом** with one blow, at one stroke; **поглотитель —а** shock absorber; **прочность на у.** impact strength; **теория —а** (radiobiol.) hit theory; **точка —а** point of impact.

ударение *n.* stress, emphasis; **делать у. на** *v.* emphasize.

удар/енный *a.* struck, hit, knocked; **—ить** *see* **ударять;** **—ник** *m.* firing pin, striker; pellet; tapper, telegraph key; **—ник** *m.*, **—ница** *f.* shock worker; timpanist.

ударно/-вращательный *a.* percussion-rotary (drilling); **у.-канатный** *a.* churn, cable-tool (drill); **—механический** *a.* mechanical (mine); **—прочный** *a.* impact-resistant, shock-resistant, strong; rugged(ized); **—сжатый** *a.* shock-compressed; **—стойкий** *see* **ударно-прочный; у.-штанговый** *a.* rod-tool (drilling).

ударн/ый *a.* shock; impact, collision; percussion, percussive; (electrochem.) strike; urgent; **у. винт** stop screw, adjusting screw; **у. грохот** impact screen; **у. инструмент** churn drill; **у. колпачок** percussion cap; **у. механизм** percussion mechanism, firing mechanism; **у. перфоратор** percussion drill, hammer drill; **у. раствор** (electrochem.) striking solution; **—ая бригада** shock brigade; **—ая волна** shock wave; **—ая вязкость** impact strength, resilience; **—ая подводная лодка** (mil.) attack submarine; **—ая проба** (met.)

impact test; drop test; hammer test; **—ая сварка** percussion welding; **—ая сила** striking power; force of impact; **—ая стена** deflecting wall, baffle; **—ая трубка** percussion fuse; **—ое действие** shock effect; percussion; **—ое нагружение** shock loading; **—ые темпы** high pressure (of work); **в —ом порядке** with dispatch; **на —ую нагрузку** drop (test).

удар/оглушитель *m.* shock absorber; **—опрочность** *f.* impact strength; **—опрочный** *a.* shock-resistant; **—очувствительность** *f.* sensitivity to shock; **—яемый** *a.* struck, hit; knocked-on (atom).

ударять *v.* strike, hit, knock, kick; chop; attack; **—ся** *v.* strike, hit, knock (against), collide (with), impinge; interfere.

удаться *see* **удаваться.**

удач/а *f.* luck, success, good fortune; **—но** *adv.* successfully, well; **—ный** *a.* lucky, successful, fortunate; suitable, appropriate, felicitous.

уд. в. *see* **уд. вес.**

удваив/ание *n.* (re)doubling; duplication; splitting; **—ать** *v.* (re)double; duplicate; repeat; split; **—аться** *v.* be doubled, (re)double.

уд. вес *abbr.* (**удельный вес**); **уд. вл.** *abbr.* (**удельная влажность**) specific humidity.

удво/ение *see* **удваивание; —енно—** *prefix* bi— (two, twice, doubly); **—еннозубчатый** *a.* (bot.) bidentate, doubly toothed; **—енный** *a.* double(d), twofold, twin; duplicate; **—енный ритм** (med.) coupled rhythm, bigeminy; **—итель** *m.* doubler; duplicator; **—ить** *see* **удваивать.**

удевятерять *v.* multiply by nine.

удел *m.* lot, fate, fortune.

уделать *see* **уделывать.**

удел/ение *n.* allocating, etc., *see* **уделять;** allotment; **—ённый** *a.* allocated, etc., *see* **уделять; —ить** *see* **уделять.**

уделывать *v.* make, prepare; decorate.

удельно *adv.* specifically, very.

удельн/ый *a.* specific, (per) unit; **у. вес** specific gravity; specific weight; density; relative significance; **у. объём** specific volume.

уделять *v.* allocate, allot, distribute; spare, find (time); give, pay, focus, center (attention); place (emphasis).

удерж/ание *see* **удерживание; —анный** *see* **удерживаемый; —ать** *see* **удерживать; —иваемость** *f.* retentivity; adherence (of insecticides); **—иваемый** *a.* retained, etc., *see* v.; **—ивание** *n.* retaining, etc., *see* v.; retention; reservation; containment, confinement; occlusion; **агент —ивания** hold-back agent; **—иватель** *m.* (anat.) retinaculum; **—ивать** *v.* retain, hold, keep (back, down, in place); fix, secure (in position); confine, restrain; withhold; (finance) deduct; detain, delay; maintain; **—ивать за собой** retain, reserve (for oneself); **—иваться** *v.* be retained, etc.; refrain, restrain oneself; hold on, cling; hold out, stand one's ground; **—ивающий** *a.* retaining, etc., *see* v.; (nucl.) hold-back (agent); retentive; **—ивающая способность** retentivity; (distillation) holdup; **—ивающие связи** bilateral constraints.

удесятер/ённый *a.* tenfold, decuple; **—ить, —ять** *v.* multiply by ten.

удешев/ить, —лять *v.* lower the price; mark down.

удив/ительно *adv.* surprisingly, etc., *see a.*; very, greatly, extremely; it is remarkable; **не у., что** it is no wonder that; **—ительный** *a.* surprising, astonishing, amazing; wonderful, admirable, remarkable; **ничего —ительного** no wonder; **—ить** *see* **удивлять; —ление**

n. surprise, wonder, astonishment; **—лённый** *a.* surprised, etc., *see v.*; **—лять** *v.* surprise, astonish, amaze; **—ляться** *v.* be surprised, wonder.

удилище *n.* (fishing) rod.

удило *n.* bit (for horse).

удиль/ный *a.* (fishing) angling; **—щик** *m.* angler; **—щики**, **—щиковые** *pl.* (ichth.) goosefishes, anglerfishes (*Lophiidae*).

удирать *v.* run away, escape.

удить *v.* angle, fish.

УДК *abbr.* (**универсальная десятичная классификация**) universal decimal classification, UDC.

удлин/ение *n.* lengthening, elongation, etc., *see v.*; stretch; **относительное —** relative elongation; (av.) aspect ratio (of wing); **—ённый** *a.* lengthened, etc., *see v.*; prolate; oblong; **—ённый череп** hypsicephalic skull; **—итель** *m.* lengthener, extender, extension (arm), extension piece; drill collar; (commun.) attenuation network, attenuator; **—ительный** *a.* lengthening, etc., *see v.*; extension; **—ить** *see* **удлинять**; **—яемость** *f.* extensibility; **—яемый** *a.* lengthened, etc., *see v.*; extensible; **—ять(ся)** *v.* lengthen, elongate, prolong, extend, stretch out; expand, enlarge; **—яющий** *see* **удлинительный**; **—яющийся** *a.* lengthening, etc., *see v.*; extensible.

удмуртский *a.* (geog.) Udmurtia(n).

уд. об. *abbr.* (**удельный объём**).

удобн/о *adv.* conveniently, easily; comfortably; it is convenient; **—ость** *f.* convenience, ease, facility; comfort; **—ый** *a.* convenient, handy, easy, expedient; comfortable; **—ый случай** favorable occasion, opportunity.

удобо— *prefix* conveniently, well, easily, readily; **—варимость** *f.* digestibility; **—варимый** *a.* easily digestible.

удобоисполним/ость *f.* feasibility, practicability; **—ый** *a.* feasible, practicable, easy to carry out.

удобоносим/ость *f.* portability; **—ый** *a.* portable, easily carried.

удобообрабатываем/ость *f.* workability; **—ый** *a.* workable, easy to handle.

удобообтекаем/ый *a.* streamlined; **—ое тело** streamline.

удобоперевозим/ость *f.* transportability (by vehicle); **—ый** *a.* transportable.

удобопереносим/ость *f.* (trans)portability (by hand); **—ый** *a.* (trans)portable, easily transported.

удобопонятн/ость *f.* comprehensibility; **—ый** *a.* comprehensible, intelligible.

удобо/разрезаемость *f.* sectility; **—разрезаемый** *a.* sectile, easily cut; **—регулируемый** *a.* easily regulated, adjustable.

удобосмешиваем/ость *f.* miscibility; **—ый** *a.* miscible, mixable.

удобоукладываемый *a.* easy to lay; placeable.

удобоуправляем/ость *f.* maneuverability; **—ый** *a.* maneuverable.

удобо/усвояемый *a.* readily assimilated; digestible; **—читаемость** *f.* legibility; readability; **—читаемый** *a.* legible; readable.

удобр/ение *n.* fertilizing, etc., *see v.*; fertilizer, manure; **—енный** *a.* fertilized, etc., *see v.*; **—итель** *m.*, **—ительное вещество** fertilizer; **—ительный** *a.* fertilizing, etc., *see v.*; fertilizer; **—ить, —ять** *v.* fertilize, manure, top-dress, apply fertilizer.

удобство *n.* convenience, accommodation, facility; comfort, ease.

удовлетвор/ение *n.*, **—ённость** *f.* satisfaction; **—ённо** *adv.* with satisfaction; **—ённый** *a.* satisfied, content;

—ительно *adv.* satisfactorily, etc., *see a.*; **—ительность** *f.* satisfactoriness; **—ительный** *a.* satisfactory, adequate, fair, reasonable; **—ить, —ять** *v.* satisfy, meet, (ful)fill (requirements); obey, comply (with); fit, suit, answer (need).

удовольств/ие *n.* gratification, pleasure, enjoyment; **—оваться** *v.* be satisfied, content oneself (with).

удод *m.* (orn.) hoopoe (*Upupa epops*).

удой *m.* milk yield; milking; **—ливость** *f.* milk yield, productivity; **—ливый** *a.* milk-producing; productive (milker); **—ник** *m.* milk pail; **—ность** *see* **удойливость**; **—ный** *a.* productive; per milking; **—ная корова** good milker.

удометр *m.* udometer, rain gage.

удорож/ание *n.* rise in price; **—ать, —ить** *v.* raise the price, mark up.

удостаивать *v.* honor (with), award, confer (a degree), pay (attention); deign, vouchsafe.

удостовер/ение *n.* certificate, testimonial; attestation; **у. личности** identification (card), badge, credential; **в у.** in witness (of); **сортовое у.** certificate; **—итель** *m.* witness, attestor; **—ить, —ять** *v.* certify, attest, bear witness, testify; **—иться, —яться** *v.* ascertain, prove, convince oneself, make sure (of).

удостоить *see* **удостаивать**.

удосужи(ва)ться *v.* find time (for), get around (to).

удотка *f.* (ichth.) spined loach (*Cobitis taenia*).

удочка *f.* (fishing) rod.

уд. р. *abbr.* (**удельная реактивность**) specific reactivity.

удрать *see* **удирать**.

удруж/ать, —ить *v.* do a good turn (to).

удруч/ать *v.* depress, make despondent; **—ённый** *a.* depressed, dejected; **—ить** *see* **удручать**.

удуш/ать *v.* suffocate, choke, asphyxiate, smother, gag, stifle; **—ающий** *a.* suffocating, etc., *see v.*; suffocative (goiter); **—ающее вещество** asphyxiant; **—ение** *n.* suffocation, choking, etc., *see v.*; **—енный** *a.* suffocated, etc., *see v.*; **—ить** *see* **удушать**; **—ливый** *see* **удушающий**; noxious, mephitic; **—ье** *n.* (med.) dyspnea, labored breathing; **свистящее —ье** (vet.) roaring (in horses), laryngeal hemiplegia.

УДФ *abbr.* (**уридиндифосфат**) uridine diphosphate, UDP; **УДФГ** *abbr.* (**уридиндифосфатглюкоза**) uridine diphosphate glucose.

уедин/ение *n.* solitude, seclusion; **—ённый** *a.* isolated, solitary, secluded, remote; **—ить, —ять** *v.* isolate, separate, detach, insulate.

уезд *m.* district.

уездить *see* **уезживать**.

уезжать *v.* go away, depart, leave.

уёк *m.* (ichth.) capelin (*Mallotus villosus*).

уехать *see* **уезжать**.

уж *m.* (zool.) grass snake; *adv. see* **уже**.

ужал/ение *n.* sting(ing); **—енный** *a.* stung; **—ить** *v.* sting.

ужари(ва)ть *v.* roast thoroughly; reduce by roasting.

ужас *m.* horror, dismay, fright; **к своему —у** to one's dismay; **притти в у.** *v.* be horrified; **—ать** *v.* horrify, appall; **—но** *adv.* terribly, horribly, awfully, very; **—нуть** *see* **ужасать**; **—ный** *a.* terrible, horrible, awful, dreadful.

ужать *v.* squeeze, pinch; harvest.

ужгородский *a.* (geog.) Uzhgorod.

уже *comp. of* **узкий, узко**, narrower; *adv.* already; even only; as long ago as; by this time, (by) now; **у. в 1942 г.** as long ago as 1942; **у. давно** long ago; **у. малое количество** even a small amount; **у. не** no longer; **его у. нет** he is no longer here.

ужевидный *a.* snake-like.

ужение *n.* angling (for fish).

ужесточ/ать *v.* toughen, ruggedize; **—ение** *n.* toughening, (electron.) ruggedization; hardening, solidification; **—ить** *see* **ужесточать**.

уживаться *v.* get accustomed (to); agree, get along (with).

ужим *m.* pinch(ing); (rolling) pincher(s); **—ать** *v.* pinch, constrict, squeeze, compress, press down; **—ина** *f.* (casting) pin hole; rattail.

ужин *m.* supper; (agr.) harvest, reaping; **—ать** *v.* eat supper; harvest.

ужиный *a.* of **уж**.

ужиться *see* **уживаться**.

уж/мёт *fut. 3 sing. of* **ужать**, pinch; **—нёт** *fut. 3 sing. of* **ужать**, harvest.

ужовка *f.* (mal.) cowrie.

ужов/ник *m.* (bot.) adder's tongue (*Ophioglossum vulgatum*); (pharm.) symphytum; **—ый** *a. of* **уж**.

УЗ *abbr.* (**ультразвук**) ultrasonics; (**ультразвуковой**) ultrasonic; (**участок заражения**) contaminated area.

уза *f.* propolis, bee glue.

узакон/ение *n.* legalization; ordinance, decree; **—и-(ва)ть**, **—ять** *v.* legalize.

узарин *m.* uzarin.

узбек— *prefix*, **—ский** *a.* (geog.) Uzbek.

узбой *m.* uzboi, relict desert valley.

УЗД *abbr.* (**ультразвуковой диагностический аппарат**) ultrasonic diagnostic apparatus; (**уравнение закона Дальтона**) Dalton's law equation.

узд/а *f.* bridle; check, restraint; **—ечка** *f.* (anat., zool.) frenulum; (orn.) lore(s); **—ечный** *a. of* **узда, уздечка**.

УЗДМ *abbr.* (**уравнение закона действующих масс**) equation of the law of mass action.

узел *m.* node; knot, loop; bundle, pack; (mach.) block, unit, (sub)assembly; joint (connection); cross-link, bond; center; (elec., rr.) junction, terminal; knot (in wood); (anat.) ganglion; **у. обслуживания** (comp.) server; **у. решётки** (cryst.) lattice point; **—ки** *pl. of* **узелок**; **—ковый** *a.* nodular; nodulate(d); **—ок** *dim. of* **узел**; nodule, nodulus; **-родитель** *m.* (math.) parent (node).

узиться *v.* get narrower.

узк/ий *a.* narrow, tight; pencil (beam); highly specialized; **—ое место** bottleneck; (med.) stenosis.

узко *adv.* narrowly, tightly; *prefix* angusti—, sten(o)— (narrow); **—ватый** *a.* somewhat narrow; **—высокий** *a.* tall and narrow, taller than broad; **—габаритный** *a.* narrow-track (tractor); **—голов(чат)ый** *a.* (med.) stenocephalous; **—горлый** *a.* narrow-necked; **—грудость** *f.* (med.) stenothorax; **—колейка** *f.* narrow-gage railroad; **—колейный** *a.* narrow-gage; **—листный** *a.* (bot.) narrow-leaved, angustifoliate; **—лучевой** *a.* narrow-beam; **—надкрылые** *pl.* (ent.) Oedemeridae; **—носый** *a.* narrow-nosed; **—перегородчатый** *a.* (bot.) angustiseptate; **—плёночный** *a.* (phot.) narrow-film (8 and 16 mm); **—плодный** *a.* (bot.) stenocarpous; **—полосица** *f.* strip farming; **—полосный** *a.* narrow-band; narrow-line (emission); **—полосый** *a.* (zool.) narrow-striped (e.g., mongoose); **—родственный** *a.* (gen.) close, affinity (breeding); **—рядный** *a.* (agr.) narrow-row(ed), close-drill.

узкоспециал/изированный *a.* highly specialized; **—ьность** *f.* highly specialized skill.

узко/сть *f.* narrowness; (naut.) narrows, narrow waters; **—телки** *pl.* (ent.) Colydiidae; **—тепловой** *a.* (bot.) stenothermal; **—угольный** *a.* narrow-angle(d); (telev.) partial-scan.

узл/а *gen. of* **узел**; **—ов** *gen. pl. of* **узел**.

узловат/ость *f.* knottiness, nodosity; **—ый** *a.* knotty, nodose, nodular, knobby, torose; (anat.) ganglionic.

узлов/ой *a. of* **узел**; nodal; (med.) interrupted (suture); **у. лист** junction plate, gusset (plate); **у. пункт, —ая станция** junction; **у. шарнир** multiple joint; **—ая система** (zool.) sympathetic nervous system; **—ая точка** junction point; (acous.) node; (math.) (cru)node; **—ое соединение** node.

узло/вязатель *m.* knotter; **—вязательный** *a.* knotting; **—ловитель** *m.* (paper) knotter, knot screen.

узлы *pl. of* **узел**.

узна/вание *n.* recognition; learning, knowledge; **—(ва)ть** *v.* recognize, identify, know; learn, find out; **—(ва)ться** *v.* become well known; **—ющий** *a.* recognizing, etc., *see v.*

узок *sh. m. of* **узкий**.

узор *m.* pattern, design, arrangement, markings, figure; **—ный, —чатый** *a.* figured, ornamented, patterned.

узость *f.* narrowness, tightness.

узурпировать *v.* usurp.

узус *m.* usage, customary practice.

узы *pl.* bonds, ties.

Уилкса земля (geog.) Wilkes Land.

уил/ло(у)биевский *a.* Willoughby (exploration); **—соновский** *a.* Wilson; **—ьямсоновский** *a.* Williamson (reaction).

уинлокский *a.* (geol.) Wenlock.

Уинстон-сейлем Winston-Salem.

уипловский *a.* Whipple.

уипсток *m.* (drilling) whip stock.

уистити *m.* (mam.) marmoset (*Callithrix*).

уитстонов мост (elec.) Wheatstone bridge.

Уитфильда газогенератор Whitfield producer.

Уичито (geog.) Wichita.

уйгурский *a.* (geog.) Uigur(ian).

уйдёт *fut. 3 sing. of* **уйти**.

уймёт *fut. 3 sing. of* **унять**.

уйти *see* **уходить**.

укажет *fut. 3 sing. of* **указать**.

указ *m.* decree, edict, enactment.

указ/ание *n.* indication, hint; direction(s), instruction(s), guideline(s), designation; **согласно —анию** as directed; **—анный** *a.* indicated, etc., *see* **указывать**; mentioned (above); **если не —ано иначе** unless otherwise specified; **как —ано** as (directed), as indicated; **—атель** *m.* indication, sign; (chem.) indicator; indicator, (indicator) dial; pointer, needle, arrow; detector; guide; index, directory, catalog, register; (rr.) timetable, schedule; (street) sign; (comp.) pointer, access address; **—атель уровня** level indicator; depth gage, dipstick.

указатель/ный *a.* indicating, indicatory; **у. механизм** indicator; **у. палец** forefinger, index finger; **—ая пластинка** dial; **—ая стрелка** pointer.

указ/ать *see* **указывать**; **следует у.** it should be noted; **—ка** *f.* pointer, fescue, marker; (art.) marking disk; **—ный** *a.* standard; **—ывать** *v.* indicate, be an indication (of), denote, imply, suggest; point out, point to the fact (that), show, direct, explain, demonstrate; specify, give, list, mention; **на что —ывает** as indicated by; **—ывающий** *a.* indicating, etc., *see v.*

укалывать *v.* prick, puncture.

укат/анный *a.* rolled (smooth); **—ать** *see* **укатывать**; **—ить** *v.* roll away; drive off; **—ка** *f.*, **—ывание** *n.* rolling; **—ывать** *v.* roll (smooth).

укашивать *v.* (agr.) mow (completely).

УКВ *abbr.* (**ультракороткие волны**) ultrashort waves; (**ультракоротковолновый**) ultrashort wave.

укидывать *v.* bestrew, scatter.

укип/ание *n.* boiling down, evaporation; **—ать, —еть** *v.* boil down, concentrate; cook thoroughly.

укис/ать, —нуть *v.* become fully sour.

уклад *m.* structure, order of things, way of life, (social) pattern; (met.) natural steel.

уклад/ка *see* **укладывание**; casting, laying (of concrete); **порядок —ки** (phys.) stacking order; **—очный** *a.* stacking, etc., *see v.*; **—чик** *m.* stacker, etc., *see v.*; (parachute) rigger; **—ывание** *n.* stacking, etc., *see v.*; installation; placement; **—ывать** *v.* stack, pile; pack (up), package, bag; stow, put away; place, set, install, lay; cast, pour (concrete); pave, embed; **—ываться** *v.* be stacked, etc.; pack up; fold (up); fit, go (into), be contained (in); **—ывающий** *a.* stacking, etc., *see v.*

укле/и(ва)ть *v.* glue; **—йка** *f.* gluing; **—йка, —я** *f.* (ichth.) bleak (*Alburnus*).

уклон *m.* slope, dip, slant, incline, declivity, pitch, gradient, grade (of road), downgrade, fall; ramp; taper, bias, canting, bevel; bias, trend, inclination; deviation; **под у.** at a slant, downgrade, downhill; **итти под у.** *v.* slope.

уклон/ение *n.* deviation, deviating, etc., *see v.*; digression, error, aberration, declination; evasion; (gen.) deflexion; **—иться** *see* **уклоняться**; **—оме(т)р** *m.* inclinometer; **—оуказатель** *m.* gradient sign; **—чивость** *f.* evasiveness; **—чивый** *a.* evasive; **—яться** *v.* deviate, vary, digress, diverge (from); swerve (away), deflect; evade, avoid, dodge, shun; **—яющийся** *a.* deviating, etc., *see v.*; aberrant.

уключина *f.* ragbolt; oarlock.

уковка *f.* (met.) forging reduction.

укол *m.* prick(ing), puncture; (med.) injection, shot.

укол/ачивать, —отить *v.* pound, beat down; nail down.

уколот/ый *a.* pricked, punctured; (med.) injected; **—ь** *see* **укалывать**.

укомплектов/ание *n.* completion, completing, etc., *see v.*; **—анный** *a.* completed, etc., *see v.*; complete (with); made up (of), comprising; **—(ыв)ать** *v.* complete; equip, fit out; fill (a quota); assemble, make up (a set); recruit, man, staff, make up the staff (of), bring up to strength.

уконопа/тить, —чивать *v.* caulk (up).

укор *m.* reproach, blame.

укорачив/ание *n.* shortening, contraction, etc., *see v.*; **—ать** *v.* shorten, contract, reduce, abridge, curtail, abbreviate; (chem.) degrade (a chain); take up (belt); **—ающий** *a.* shortening, etc., *see v.*

укорен/ение *n.* implanting, inculcating; rooting, taking root; **—ившийся** *a.* (deep-)rooted, inveterate, of long standing; **—ить, —ять** *v.* implant, inculcate; **—иться, —яться** *v.* take root; **—яющийся** *a.* (bot.) rooting, radicant.

укоризн/а *f.* reproach; **—енный** *a.* reproachful; censurable.

укорить *see* **укорять**.

укор/отитель *m.* (pulse) chopper; **—отить** *see* **укорачивать**; **—очение** *see* **укорачивание**; abbreviation; **—оченный** *a.* shortened, etc., *see* **укорачивать**; chopped (pulse); stub; *prefix* brachy— (short); **—оченный череп** (anat.) brachycephaly.

укорять *v.* reproach, blame.

укос *m.* (agr.) mowing, haying; (hay) crop, yield.

укосина *f.* strut, angle brace, cross brace; cantilever; (crane) boom, jib, outrigger.

укосн/ение *n.* delay, slowness; **—ительный** *a.* slow; **—ительное движение** decelerating motion, deceleration.

укосный *a. of* **укос.**

УКП *abbr.* (**учебно-консультационный пункт**) education and consultation center.

укр— *prefix,* **—аинский** *a.* Ukrainian.

украдкой *adv.* stealthily, by stealth.

украсить *see* **украшать.**

украсть *v.* steal, make off (with); tap.

украш/ать *v.* adorn, decorate, ornament, embellish; **—ение** *n.* decoration, ornament; **—енный** *a.* decorated.

укреп/ительный *see* **укрепляющий**; **—ить** *see* **укреплять**; **—ление** *n.* strengthening, fortification, etc., *see v.*; reinforcement; (mil.) fortification, defense, work; (bridge) head; **—лённый** *a.* strengthened, etc., *see v.*; **—лять** *v.* strengthen, fortify; reinforce, stiffen; fix, set, make fast, fasten, embed; stabilize; consolidate; corroborate, confirm; brace, invigorate; **—ляться** *v.* be strengthened, etc.; become stronger; become entrenched; consolidate (one's position); **—ляющее** *n.* **—ляющее средство** tonic, restorative; **—ляющий** *a.* strengthening, etc., *see v.*; restorative; (chem.) rectifying (section of a fractionation column); (anat.) fixator (muscle); **—ляющая часть** (fractionation) rectifying section.

укроет *fut. 3 sing. of* **укрыть.**

укромный *a.* secluded; comfortable.

укроп *m.*, **—ный** *a.* (bot.) dill (*Anethum graveolens*); fennel (*Foeniculum vulgare*); **аптечный у.** fennel; **душистый у., огородный у., пахучий у.** dill; **—олистный** *a.* bot.) anethifolious.

укро/тить, —щать *v.* subdue, curb, check, restrain, repress; appease, pacify; tame, domesticate; **—щение** *n.* subduing, etc., *see v.*

укрупн/ение *n.* enlarging, etc., *see v.*; enlargement; **—ённый** *a.* enlarged, etc., *see v.*; **—итель** *m.* enlarger; coagulant; **—ить, —ять** *v.* enlarge; extend; coarsen; consolidate, combine; amalgamate; coagulate, flocculate; **—иться, —яться** *v.* become larger; (met.) coarsen; agglomerate.

укру/тить, —чивать *v.* wrap around.

укры/вание *n.* concealing, etc., *see v.*; concealment; **—вательство** *n.* concealment; **—вать** *v.* conceal, hide, cover, sheathe; screen, shelter, house; **—ваться** *v.* be concealed, etc.; seek shelter, hide; **—вистость** *f.* (paints) covering power; **—тие** *see* **укрывание**; cover(ing), shelter, housing; screen; **—тый** *a.* concealed, etc., *see v.*; **—ть** *see* **укрывать.**

уксус *m.* vinegar; **—ник** *m.* (anat.) acetabulum.

уксусно/алюминиевая соль aluminum acetate; **—амиловый эфир** amyl acetate; **—аммониевая соль** ammonium acetate; **—бариевая соль** barium acetate; **—бутиловый эфир** butyl acetate; **—железистая соль** ferrous acetate; **—железная соль** ferric acetate; **—известковая соль, —кальциевая соль** calcium acetate; **—калиевая соль** potassium acetate.

уксуснокисл/ый *a.* acetic acid; acetate (of); **у. калий** potassium acetate; **у. этил** ethyl acetate; **—ая соль** acetate.

уксусно/крезиловый эфир cresyl acetate; **—магниевая соль** magnesium acetate; **—медистая соль** cuprous acetate; **—медная соль** cupric acetate; **—метиловый эфир** methyl acetate; **—натриевая соль** sodium acetate; **—пропиловый эфир** propyl acetate; **—ртутистая соль** mercurous acetate; **—ртутная соль** mercuric acetate; **—свинцовая соль** lead acetate; **—этиловый эфир** ethyl acetate.

уксусн/ый *a.* vinegar; acetic; **у. альдегид** acetaldehyde, ethanal; **у. ангидрид** acetic anhydride; **у. сахар** sugar of lead, lead acetate; **у. шёлк** acetate silk; **у. эфир**

acetic ester, ethyl acetate; **у. эфир целлюлозы** cellulose acetate; **—ая кислота** acetic acid; **ледяная —ая кислота** glacial acetic acid; **амид —ой кислоты** acetamide; **ангидрид —ой кислоты** acetic anhydride; **соль —ой кислоты** acetate; **основная соль —ой кислоты** subacetate; **—ая плёнка** flower of vinegar; **—ая эссенция** vinegar essence; **—ое брожение** acetic fermentation; acetification; **—ое дерево** (bot.) staghorn sumac (*Rhus typhina*).

уксусомёд *m.* (pharm.) oxymel.

укупор/ивание *n.* corking, etc., see *v.*; **—иватель** *m.* (bottle) capping machine; **—и(ва)ть** *v.* cork, cap, stop (up), plug, seal; pack, crate; **—ка** see **укупоривание;** (fuse) box; closure; **—очный** *a.* corking, etc., see *v.*; **—щик** *m.* corker, etc., see *v.*

укус *m.*, **—ить** *v.* bite, sting.

укут/анный *a.* wrapped up, etc., see *v.*; **—ать, —ывать** *v.* wrap up, muffle up, cover; **—ывание** *n.* wrapping up, etc., see *v.*

укушенный *a.* bitten, stung.

УКЧ *abbr.* (**чистая уксусная кислота**) pure acetic acid.

улавлив/ание *n.* catching, etc., see *v.*; catchment; capture, interception; (dust) suppression; recovery (of waste); **—атель** see **уловитель;** **—ать** *v.* catch, capture, (en)trap; pick up, collect, recover; intercept; discover, detect, discern; locate; seize (an opportunity); **—аться** *v.* be caught, etc.; **—ающий** *a.* catching, etc., see *v.*; pickup; entrainment (tower).

ула/дить see **улаживать;** **—женный** *a.* settled, etc., see *v.*; **—живание** *n.* settling, etc., see *v.*; reconciliation; **—живать** *v.* settle, arrange, manage; adjust, fix up, make up; reconcile; **—живаться** *v.* be settled, etc.; work out.

уламывать *v.* prevail (upon), talk (into), persuade.

улар *m.* (orn.) snowcock (*Tetraogallus*).

улёгся *past m. sing. of* **улечься.**

улежать *v.* remain lying; **—ся** *v.* settle down, get compacted.

улеек *m.* (apid.) queen cell.

улей *m.*, **—ный** *a.* beehive, hive.

улекс/ин *m.* ulexine, cytisine.

улёт *m.* flying away, flight, migration (of birds).

улет/ание *n.* flying away, escape; **—ать, —еть** *v.* fly away, escape.

улетуч/енный *a.* volatilized, etc., see *v.*; **—иваемость** *f.* volatility; **—иваемый** *a.* volatile; **—ивание** *n.* volatilization, evaporation; escape, disappearance; **—и(ва)ться** *v.* volatilize, evaporate; escape, disappear; **—ивающийся** *a.* volatilizing, etc., see *v.*; volatile.

улечься *v.* settle (down), get compacted; subside; lie down, go to bed; fit, be contained (in).

улика *f.* evidence, proof.

улит *m.* (orn.) sandpiper (*Tringa*).

улит/ка *f.* (zool.) snail; (anat.) cochlea; helix; spiral conveyer; (mach.) scroll; snail-case housing; **нерв —ки** (anat.) cochlear nerve; **отверстие —ки** (anat.) helicotrema; **—ки** *pl.* (mal.) Gastropoda; **—ковидный** *a.* cochleate; **—ковый** *a. of* **улитки;** **—кообразный** *a.* spiral, helical; conchoidal; **—очный** *a.* snail; helical; scroll.

улица *f.* street; (rr.) (switch) track(s); **зелёная у.** green light.

улич/ать, —ить *v.* convict; expose; detect; **—ение** *n.* conviction; detection; **—итель** *m.* detector.

уличный *a.* street; outdoor.

улов *m.* catch, take, yield; **—имый** *a.* perceptible; audible (sound); **—итель** *m.* catcher, separator, intercep-

tor; trap; detector, locator (of sound); **—ить** see **улавливать.**

уловка *f.* trick, ruse, stratagem.

улов/ление see **улавливание;** **—ленный** *a.* caught, captured, etc., see **улавливать;** **—ный** *a.* caught (fish); good (fishing place).

улож/ение see **укладывание;** (law) code; **—енный** *a.* stacked, etc., see **укладывать;** **—ить** see **укладывать.**

уломать see **уламывать.**

улочка *f.* space between frames (in a beehive).

улус *m.* nomad camp.

улуч/ать, —ить *v.* seize, catch; find.

улучш/аемый *a.* improved, etc., see *v.*; improvable; (met.) heat-treatable; **—ать** *v.* improve, (make) better, ameliorate, upgrade, enhance; refine, develop, adapt; amend; (met.) treat with heat; **—аться** *v.* be improved, etc.; improve, get better; progress; **—ающий** *a.* improving, etc., see *v.*; **—ающее вещество** ameliorant, conditioner, stabilizer; surfactant; **—ающийся** *a.* improving, etc., see *v.*; **—ение** *n.* improving, etc., see *v.*; improvement, amelioration, betterment; refinement, development, adaptation; **термическое —ение** toughening, tempering; **—енный** *a.* improved, etc., see *v.*

улыб/аться *v.*, **—ка** *f.* smile; **мышца —ки** risorius muscle; **—нуться** see **улыбаться.**

улька *f.* (ichth.) bigmouth sculpin (*Ulca bolini*).

ульевой *a. of* **улей.**

улькус *m.* (med.) ulcus, ulcer.

Ульмана реакция Ullman reaction.

ульман(н)ит *m.* (min.) ullmannite.

ульмат *m.* ulmate.

ульмин *m.* ulmin; **—овый** *a.* ulmin, ulmic; **—овая кислота** ulmic acid, geic acid; **—овокислая соль** ulmate.

ульмовский *a.* (math.) Ulm.

ульнарный *a.* (anat.) ulnar, cubital.

ульрихит *m.* (min.; petr.) ulrichite.

ульстерский *a.* (geol.) Ulsterian.

ультимат/ивный *a.* ultimate, final; ultimatum; **—ум** *m.* ultimatum.

ультра— *prefix* ultra—, excessively; **—акустика** *f.* (acous.) ultrasonics.

ултраабиссаль (ocean.) hadal zone, ultra-abyssal zone.

ультравирус *m.* (med.) filterable virus.

ультравысок/ий *a.* ultrahigh; **—очастотный** *a.* ultra-high-frequency, UHF (300–3,000 MHz).

ультразвук *m.* ultrasound; ultrasonics (frequencies above 20,000 Hz); **—овой** *a.* ultrasonic.

ультракислый *a.* (geol.) hyperacid.

ультракоротк/ий *a.* ultrashort; **—оволновый** *a.* ultrashort-wave (wavelength < 10 m).

ультра/красный *a.* infrared; **—малый** *a.* minute, trace.

ультрамарин *m.*, **—овый** *a.* ultramarine (pigment); **—овый жёлтый** ultramarine yellow, barium chromate.

ультрамикровесы *pl.* ultramicrobalance.

ультрамикро/метр *m.* ultramicrometer; **—н** *m.* ultramicron; **—скоп** *m.* ultramicroscope; **—скопический** *a.* ultramicroscopic; **—скопия** *f.* ultramicroscopy; **—химический** *a.* ultramicrochemical.

ультра/основный *a.* ultrabasic; **—полярный** *a.* ultrapolar; **—структура** *f.* ultrastructure (of cells); **—телеметеор** *m.* ultratelemeteor; **—тен** *m.* ultrathene (ethylene vinyl acetate copolymer); **—фильтр** *m.* ultrafilter; **—фильтрация** *f.* ultrafiltration; **—фиолетовый** *a.* ultraviolet (rays); **—центрифуга** *f.* ultracentrifuge; **—центрифугирование** *n.* ultracentrifugation; **—щелочной** *a.* ultrabasic.

ульцерация *f.* (med.) ulceration.

улья *gen. of* **улей.**

ульяновский *a.* (geog.) Ulianovsk.

улягутся *fut. 3 pl. of* **улечься.**

ум *m.* mind, intellect, intelligence, brains; **прийти на ум** *v.* occur (to).

ум. *abbr.* (**умер**) deceased.

у.м. *abbr.* (**уровень моря**) sea level.

умаз(ыв)ать *v.* smear (all over), daub.

умаление *n.* belittling, disparagement; depreciation, decrease, lessening.

умаливать *v.* entreat, implore, beg.

умалить *see* **умалять.**

умалишённый *a.* psychotic, insane, deranged; *m.* psychotic.

умалчивать *v.* say nothing (of), leave unsaid, omit; suppress, hold back.

умалять *v.* belittle, disparage; depreciate; **—ся** *v.* diminish, lessen.

уматывать *v.* wind around, wrap.

умащивать *v.* pave, floor.

умбелл/аровая кислота umbellaric acid; **—атин** *m.* umbellatine; **—иферон** *m.* umbelliferone, 4-hydroxycoumarin; **—овая кислота** umbellic acid, *p*-hydroxycoumaric acid; **—оновый** *a.* umbellonic (acid); **—уловый** *a.* umbellulic (acid); **—улон** *m.* umbellulone.

умбиликаровый *a.* umbilicaric (acid).

умбиликус *m.* (anat.) umbilicus, navel.

умбра *f.* (ichth.) mudminnow (*Umbra krameri*); **земля у.** umber (pigment).

умбриевые *pl.* (ichth.) Umbridae.

умбрин/а *f.* (ichth.) croaker; **—овые** *pl.* croakers, drums (*Sciaenidae*).

умбровые *pl.* (ichth.) mudminnows (*Umbridae*).

умедл/ить, —ять *v.* slow down, decelerate.

умел/ец *m.* skillful worker, expert; **—ость** *f.* skillfulness, expertness; **—ый** *a.* skillful, expert.

умельч/ать, —ить *v.* make fine(r), reduce.

умён *sh. m. of* **умный.**

умение *n.* skill, ability; know-how.

уменьш/аемое *n.* (math.) minuend; **—аемый** *a.* reducible; **—ать** *v.* diminish, lessen, lower, decrease, reduce; cut down, curtail; abate, ease (up), alleviate; minimize; narrow (down); **—ать вдвое** *v.* halve; **—аться** *v.* be diminished, etc.; diminish, lessen, decrease, drop (down, off), fall, decline, go down, abate; taper off, dwindle; contract, shrink; deteriorate; **—ение** *n.* diminution, lessening, decrease, reduction, decline, fall, drop; abatement, attenuation; downsizing; contraction, shrinkage; short-cut; deterioration; **—ение подвижности** immobilization; **—ение скорости** deceleration; **пропорциональное —ение** scaling down; **—енный** *a.* diminished, etc., *see v.*; **—ательный** *a.* diminishing, etc., *see v.*; diminutive; **—ить** *see* **уменьшать.**

умеренн/о *adv.* moderately; **—ость** *f.* moderation; **—ый** *a.* moderate, medium, mild, temperate; **—ый пояс** (meteor.) temperate zone.

умереть *see* **умирать.**

умери(ва)ть *see* **умерять.**

умертвить *see* **умерщвлять.**

умерший *a.* dead, deceased; *m.* the dead, the deceased.

умерщвл/ение *n.* killing, destruction; (med.) mortification (of flesh); **—ять** *v.* kill, destroy, put to death.

умерять *v.* moderate, mitigate, modify, abate, restrain, check; appease; **—ся** *v.* become moderate, become temperate.

умесить *see* **умешивать.**

умест/ительный *a.* spacious, roomy; **—ить** *see* **умещать.**

умести/ость *f.* pertinence, appropriateness, aptness, relevancy; timeliness; **—ый** *a.* pertinent, appropriate, relevant, well-timed, timely.

умёт *m.* refuse, dirt; shelter, trench; steppe farm.

уметь *v.* be able, know how.

умешивать *v.* knead, mix in, work up.

умещ/ать *v.* fit in, put in, pack in, find room (for); **—аться** *v.* be fitted in, etc.; fit in, go in; **—ённый** *a.* fitted in, etc., *see v.*

уминать *v.* (com)press, consolidate; squeeze, tread down; knead, work.

умир/ание *n.* dying, expiration; **—ать** *v.* die (off), expire; **—ающий** *a.* dying.

умир/ить, —отворить, —(отвор)ять *v.* pacify, appease, conciliate.

умнёт *fut. 3 sing. of* **умять.**

умн/еть *v.* grow wiser; **—о** *adv.* intelligently, etc., *see* **умный.**

умнож/ать *v.* multiply; increase, augment, enlarge, expand; **у. на** multiply by; **—аться** *v.* be multiplied, etc.; multiply, increase; **—ающий** *a.* multiplying, etc., *see v.*; (comp.) multiplier; **—ение** *n.* multiplication; rise, increase; breeding (of nuclear fuel); **трубка —ения** *f.* (electron.) multiplier tube; **—енный** *a.* multiplied, etc., *see v.*; **—енный на** multiplied by, times; **—итель** *m.* multiplier, factor; **—ить** *see* **умножать.**

умный *a.* intelligent, clever, smart, quick(-witted); sensible, wise.

УМО *abbr.* (**уровень мёртвого объёма**) minimum operating level, dead storage level (of reservoir).

умоет *fut. 3 sing. of* **умыть.**

умозаключ/ать, —ить *v.* conclude, deduce, infer; **—ение** *n.* conclusion, deduction, inference.

умозр/ение *n.* speculation, theory; **—ительность** *f.* theoretical nature; **—ительный** *a.* speculative, theoretical.

умоисступление *n.* delirium.

умол *m.* grinding; loss in grinding.

умолачивать *v.* thresh, beat.

умолить *see* **умолять.**

умолк/ать, —нуть *v.* fall silent, stop.

умол/от *m.* threshing; yield (of grain); **—отить** *see* **умолачивать; —отный** *a.* high-yielding; **—оченный** *a.* threshed.

умолч/ание *n.* suppression, omission; silence; (comp.) default; **—ать** *see* **умалчивать.**

умолять *v.* supplicate, entreat, implore.

умопомешательство *n.* insanity.

уморение *n.* (furs) alkali treatment.

уморить *v.* kill; exhaust, tire out; **—ся** *v.* be dead tired.

умостить *see* **умащивать.**

умотать *see* **уматывать.**

умрёт *fut. 3 sing. of* **умереть.**

умственн/ый *a.* mental, intellectual; **показатель —ых способностей** intelligence quotient, I.Q.

умудр/ённый *a.* taught, made wiser; **—ить, —ять** *v.* teach, make wiser; **—иться, —яться** *v.* become wiser; contrive, manage, find a way.

УМФ *abbr.* (**уридинмонофосфат**) uridine monophosphate, UMP.

умформер *m.* (elec.) converter; dynamotor; motor generator (set); (steam) transformer.

умчаться *v.* rush away; fly past (of time).

умыв/альн(а)я *f.* washroom, lavatory; **—альник** *m.* basin, wash stand; **—альный** *a.* wash(ing); **—ание** *n.* wash(ing); (pharm.) lotion; **—ать(ся)** *v.* wash (up).

умыс/ел *m.* design, intention; **без —ла** unintentionally; **с —лом** on purpose, intentionally, deliberately; **—лить** *see* **умышлять.**

умыт/ый *a.* washed; **—ь** *see* **умывать.**

умышленн/о *adv.* intentionally, on purpose, purposely, deliberately; **—ость** *f.* deliberateness; **—ый** *a.* intentional, deliberate, designed, premeditated.

умышлять *v.* plot, scheme, contrive.

умя/гчать *v.* soften; supple, make flexible; **—гчение** *n.* softening; **—гчённый** *a.* softened; **—гчитель** *m.* softener, softening agent; **—гчить** *see* **умягчать; —кнуть** *v.* soften, become soft.

умять *see* **уминать.**

унаби *f.* (bot.) Zizyphus, spec. jujube (*Z. jujuba*).

унав/аживание *n.* (agr.) manuring; **—аживать, —о-живать** *v.* manure, top-dress.

унаследов/ание *n.* inheriting; heredity; **—анный** *a.* inherited, hereditary; **—ать** *v.* inherit.

унау *m.* (mam.) two-toed sloth.

УНГ *abbr.* (**уранилнитратгексагидрат**) uranyl nitrate hexahydrate.

унгулиновая кислота ungulinic acid.

ундека/диен *m.* undecadiene; **—лактон** *m.* undecalactone; **—н** *m.* undecane, hendecane; **—нафтеновый** *a.* undecanaphthenic (acid).

ундеколевая кислота undecolic acid.

ундецен *m.* undecene, hendecene; **—ил** *m.* undecenyl; **—овая кислота** undecenoic acid, undecyclic acid.

ундецил *m.,* **—овый** *a.* undecyl, hendecyl; **—ен** *m.* undecylene, hendecene; **—еновая кислота** undecylenic acid, 9-hendecenoic acid; **—овая кислота** undecylic acid, hendecanoic acid; **—овый альдегид** undecylic aldehyde, hendecanal; **—овый спирт** undecylic alcohol, hendecyl alcohol.

ундулирующий *a.* undulating; undulant (fever, etc.).

унести *see* **уносить.**

уни— *prefix* uni— (one, single); **—аксиальный** *a.* uniaxial; **—валентный** *a.* (chem.) univalent; **—вариантный** *a.* univariant.

универмаг *m.* department store; warehouse.

универсал *m.* (astr.; surv.) universal theodolite; wide-range specialist, jack of all trades.

универсально *adv.* universally; *prefix* universal; **у.-наладочный** *a.* universal adjusting; **у.-сборный** *a.* universal assembly; **—сть** *f.* universality, versatility; **у.-фрезерный** *a.* universal milling; **у.-шлифовальный** *a.* universal grinding.

универсальный *a.* universal, all-purpose; multipurpose, general(-purpose), versatile; expansion (bit); department (store); liberal (education); main-frame (computer).

университет *m.,* **—ский** *a.* university.

уни/жать, —зить *v.* lower, reduce; degrade, humiliate; **—жение** *n.* lowering, etc., *see v.*

уни/кальный *a.* unique; **—когерентный** *a.* unicoherent; **—кум** *m.* unique; great rarity; **—курзальный, —курсальный** *a.* unicursal.

унимать *v.* appease, pacify; soothe, calm; stop, staunch (bleeding), alleviate (pain).

уни/модальный *a.* unimodal; **—модулярный** *a.* unimodular; **—он** *m.* union; **—ониды** *pl.* (mal.) Unionidae; **—плоид** *m.* (bot.) monoploid, haploid; **—полярность** *f.* unipolarity; **—полярный** *a.* unipolar; (mach.) acyclic; (nucl.) homopolar (generator); **—потентный** *a.* unipotent; **—рациональный** *a.* unirational; **—сольвентный** *a.* unisolvent.

унисон *m.,* **—ный** *a.* unison.

унитаз *m.* toilet bowl.

уни/тарный *a.* unit(ary); **—терм** *m.* key word, catch word; **—фикация** *f.* unification, unitization; standardization; **—филяр** *m.* unifilar; declinometer; **—филярный** *a.* unifilar; **—фицировать** *v.* unify, unitize; standardize.

униформ/изация *f.,* **—изирование** *n.* uniformization, making uniform; **—изированный** *a.* made uniform, evened (out); **—изировать** *v.* make uniform; even (out); **—ный** *a.* uniform.

уничтож/ать *v.* destroy, annihilate, exterminate, eliminate, dispose (of), do away (with); abolish, nullify, cancel (out), neutralize; demolish, obliterate; extinguish; dissipate, deplete; **—ающий** *a.* destroying, etc., *see v.;* destructive; **взаимно —ающиеся погрешности** compensating errors, etc., *see v.;* **—ение** *n.* destruction, annihilation, etc., *see v.;* disposal (of); abolishment; demolition; **—енный** *a.* destroyed, etc., *see v.;* **—итель** *m.* annihilator; **—ительный** *a.* destructive; **—ить** *see* **уничтожать.**

уния *f.* union.

унос *m.* carrying away, etc., *see v.;* carry-over; entrainment; (boiler) priming; team, crew; **у. массы** ablation; **—имый** *a.* ablative (material); **—ить** *v.* carry away, carry off, carry over; bear, take (away), conduct away.

УНРС *abbr.* (**установка непрерывной разливки стали**) continuous steel-pouring unit.

ун-т *abbr.* (**университет**) university.

унтертон *m.* undertone, subharmonic tone.

унтерцуг *m.* (min.) timber support.

унты *pl.* aviator's boots.

унцевый *a.* (one-)ounce.

унцинариевые *pl.* hookworms (*Uncinariidae*).

унцинатовая кислота uncinatic acid.

унция *f.* ounce (29.86 g).

УНЧ *abbr.* (**ультранизкая частота**) very low frequency, VLF (3–30 kHz).

уны/вать *v.* lose heart, be dejected; **—лый** *a.* dejected, depressed; **—ние** *n.* dejection, melancholy.

уньон *m.* union.

унять *see* **унимать.**

уолтеровский *a.* Walter('s).

уотсоновский *a.* Watson('s).

упа/вший *a.* fallen; **—дать** *see* **упасть.**

упад/ок *m.* decline, decay, degeneration; (urban) blight; fall, decrease, ebb; descent, dip; **у. питания** malnutrition; **у. сил** breakdown, collapse; **приходить в у.** *v.* decline; **—очный** *a.* decadent, degenerate.

упаков/анный *a.* packed, etc., *see v.;* **—ать** *see* **упаковывать; —ка** *f.* pack(ag)ing, etc., *see v.;* package, wrapper; container, crate, (empty) box(es); **—ка в мешки** bagging; **—ка в ящики** boxing, crating; **в —ке** packed, wrapped; **вес в —ке** shipping weight; **картонная —ка** carton; **плотной —ки** close-packed; **—очный** *a.* pack(ag)ing, etc., *see v.;* **—очный коэффициент, —очный множитель** (nucl.) packing fraction; **—щик** *m.* packer; **—ывание** *n.* packing, etc., *see v.;* **—ывать** *v.* pack (up), package, put up, wrap up; bag; bale; box, crate.

упар/енный *a.* boiled down, etc., *see v.;* **—ивание** *n.* boiling down, etc., *see v.;* concentration (by evaporation); **—и(ва)ть** *v.* boil down, concentrate (by evaporation), evaporate, thicken (by boiling), inspissate; steam, stew; **—ка** *see* **упаривание; —очный** *a.* boiling down, etc., *see v.*

упасть *v.* fall (down); go down, decline, deteriorate, degenerate.

упах(ив)ать *v.* till, plow thoroughly.

упвардовский *a.* Upward (chlorine cell).

упёк *m.* thorough baking; weight loss in baking.

упекать *v.* bake thoroughly; send away; **—аться** *v.* lose in baking, bake out.

упереть *see* **упирать.**

упечат(ыв)ать *v.* place, fit in (printed matter); fill in, seal up, close.

упечь *see* **упекать.**

упирать *v.* set, place, fix; rest, prop, lean (against); pilfer; **—ся** *v.* be set, etc.; push, thrust, abut, butt up, lean (against), be against; rest (upon); run into (of road); persist (in); resist.

упис(ыв)ать *v.* write in, fill in.

упит/анность *f.* fatness, obesity; (nutritional) condition; **—анный** *a.* well-fed; fat(tened); **(ыв)ать** *v.* feed up, fatten.

упих/(ив)ать, —нуть *v.* push in.

упишет *fut.* 3 *sing.* of **уписать.**

упла/та *f.* payment, disbursement; **в —ту** on account; **—тить** *see* **уплачивать; —ченный** *a.* paid (off), settled; **—чивать** *v.* pay, disburse.

упле/сти, —тать *v.* entwine; plait together; eat greedily.

уплотн/ение *n.* thickening, condensation, etc., *see v.;* hardening; (soil) compaction; consolidation (of concrete, etc.); (commun.) multiplexing; shrinkage; (math.) refinement; seal, gasket, gland, packing; **частотное у.** frequency division multiplexing; **—ённость** *f.* compactness; **коэффициент —ённости** void factor; **—ённый** *a.* thickened, etc., *see v.;* dense; compact; concise; (agr.) companion, nurse (crop); **—ённый посев** interplanting, planting a companion crop; **—итель** *m.* thickener, etc., *see v.;* seal; weather strip; **—итель энергии** energy-concentrating device; **—ительный** *see* **уплотняющий; —ить, —ять** *v.* thicken, condense, concentrate; compress, squeeze, contract; compact, pack, consolidate; tighten, make tight, make impervious, seal (off, in, out), lute; (gas) blanket; share (a channel); multiplex (channels); **—яться** *v.* be thickened, etc.; thicken, condense, pack, compact, settle; contract, shrink; sinter; **—яющий** *a.* thickening, etc., *see v.;* impermeable; blanketing (gas); **—яющая масса** packing (material).

уплощ/ение *n.* flattening, applanation; **у. основания черепа** (med.) basilar impression, platybasia; **у. стопы** (med.) flatfoot; **—ённый** *a.* flat(tened), depressed, applanate; **—ённый череп** (med.) platycrania.

уплы(ва)ть *v.* swim away, go away, float away; pass away, elapse.

уподоб/ить, —лять *v.* liken, compare; **—ление** *n.* likening, comparison.

упо/ение *n.* rapture; **—ённый** *a.* enraptured.

упол— *prefix see* **уполномоченный.**

уполаживание *n.* flattening.

уполз/ать, —ти *v.* creep away.

уполномоч/ение *n.* authorization; **—енный** *a.* authorized; *m.* authorized agent, representative, delegate; **—и(ва)ть** *v.* authorize, empower, commission.

уполовинить *v.* cut in half.

уполовник *m.* skimmer; (casting) ladle.

уположение *n.* (rr.) diminishing of gradient.

упомин/ание *n.* mention(ing); reference; **—ать** *v.* mention, make mention (of), refer, make reference (to).

упомнить *v.* memorize, store.

упомянут/ый *a.* mentioned, referred (to); **—ь** *see* **упомянуть.**

упор *m.*, **—ка** *f.* rest, prop, support, stay, brace; dog, stop; arresting device, checking device, catch, detent, de-

tainer, pawl; thrust, resistance; (grinder) poppet; **в у.** point-blank, directly (at); **делать у.** *v.* emphasize.

упорно *adv.* persistently; **—сть** *f.* obstinacy, persistence, tenacity.

упорн/ый *a.* stubborn, obstinate, unyielding, persistent, tenacious; stop, thrust; fixed (center); (min.) rusty (gold); *suffix* **—proof, —resistant; у. болт** stop; **у. диск** bearing disk, thrust plate; **у. кулачок** stop, detent; **у. подшипник** thrust bearing; **у. рычаг** stop, detent; **у. торец** anvil; **у. угольник** back square; **у. штифт** stop(pin); **—ая бабка** tailstock; **—ая скоба** stop piece, check clamp; **—ое кольцо** thrust collar.

упор-ограничитель *m.* positive stop(per).

упорство *see* **упорность; —вать** *v.* persist (in); be stubborn.

упорхнуть *v.* fly away.

упорядоч/ение *n.* regulation, ordering, etc., *see v.;* sequencing; order; **у.-разупорядочение** order-disorder transformation; **процессы —ения и разупорядочения** order-disorder phenomena; **теория —ения** sequencing theory; **—енность** *f.* order(liness); (cryst.) ordering; **—енный** *a.* regulated, etc., *see v.;* ordered; **—енное движение** drift; **—и(ва)ть** *v.* regulate, (put in) order, rank; orient; **—ивающий** *a.* regulating, etc., *see v.*

употр. *abbr.* (**употребительный**) customary; (**употребляется**) is used.

употреб/ительность *f.* usualness; frequency (of usage); use; **—ительный** *a.* usual, customary, generally used, popular; **—ить** *see* **употреблять; —ление** *n.* use, utilization, employment, application, usage; **вводить в —ление** *v.* introduce; **вышедший из —ления** *a.* obsolete, outdated; **способ —ления** directions, instructions (for use); **—лённый** *a.* used, etc., *see v.;* **—лять** *v.* use, make use (of), utilize, employ, apply; take (medicine); **—ляться** *v.* be used, etc.; be in use; serve (as); **—ляющий** *a.* using, etc., *see v.*

упр. *abbr.* (**управление, управляющий**).

управ/а *f.* justice; board, council; **—дел** *m.* business manager; **—итель** *m.* manager; **—ить** *see* **управлять.**

управлен/ие *n.* management, government, administration; board, bureau, office, directorate, headquarters; handling, operation, control(ling), regulation; steering, guiding, guidance, direction; (av.) controls; **у. на расстоянии** remote control; **выключатель —ия** master switch; **механизм на —ия** operating gear; steering gear; **пост —ия** pulpit, control position; **пульт —ия** control panel, console; **рычаг —ия** control lever; **с ручным —ием** manually operated; **с электронным —ием** electronically controlled; **система —ия** control system; **устройство —ия** (comp.) control unit, monitor; **щит —ия** control panel.

управленческ/ий *a.* managerial, executive (staff); administrative, administration, management; overhead (expenses); **—о-административный** *a.* administrative (personnel).

управл/яемость *f.* control(lability), manageability; handling, behavior; **—яемый** *a.* controllable, etc., *see v.;* operable; controlled, etc., *see v.;* guided (missile); slaved; **—яемый по радио** radio-controlled; **—ять** *v.* control, regulate, manage, handle, manipulate; run, operate; maneuver, drive, steer, guide, pilot, direct; govern, rule, administer; **—яться** *v.* be controlled, etc.; manage, get along; handle, overcome; **—яющий** *a.* controlling, etc., *see v.;* control; master (joint, pulse, etc.); *m.* manager, superintendent, director; **—яющая машина** control computer; **—яющая последовательность** (comp.)

escape sequence; **—яющая сетка** (rad.) modulation grid; **—яющее воздействие** manipulated variable; **—яющее звено, —яющее устройство** control(ler).

упражн/ение *n.* exercise, practice, drill; **—ять(ся)** *v.* exercise, practice.

упраздн/ение *n.* abolition, elimination; **—ить, —ять** *v.* abolish, eliminate.

упрашивать *v.* beg, entreat, urge.

упревать *v.* be stewed; perspire.

упре/дительный *a.* preceding, etc., see *v.*; preventive; (comp.) look-ahead; **у. механизм** predictor; **—дить, —ждать** *v.* precede; lead, advance; anticipate, forestall, prevent; predict; **—ждающе-пересекающийся** *a.* lead collision (course); **—ждающий** *see* **упредительный**; anticipatory; advanced, pre—; **—ждение** *n.* preceding, etc., see *v.*; anticipation, etc., see *v.*; advance, lead; priority; (comp.) look ahead; **угол —ждения** angle of lead; **—ждённый** *a.* preceded, etc., see *v.*; predicted, future (data); lead (trajectory).

упрёк *m.* reproach, reproof.

упрек/ать, —нуть *v.* reproach, reprove.

упрелый *a.* stewed, cooked; perspired.

упрессов(ыв)ать *v.* press, tamp (down).

упрёт *fut. 3 sing. of* **упереть.**

упреть *see* **упревать.**

упросить *see* **упрашивать.**

упростить *see* **упрощать.**

упроч/ение *n.* stengthening, etc., see *v.*; **—и(ва)ть** *v.* strengthen, consolidate; fix, steady, secure; fortify.

упрочн/ение *n.* strengthening, etc., see *v.*; reinforcement; **механическое у.** (met.) strain hardening; **поверхностное у.** case hardening; **—ённый** *a.* strengthened, etc., see *v.*; high-tenacity; **—итель** *m.* reinforcing agent, reinforcement; **—ить, —ять** *v.* strengthen, toughen, harden; reinforce; ruggedize (instruments); **—яющий(ся)** *a.* strengthening, etc., see *v.*; strain-hardening.

упрощ/ать *v.* simplify; **у. до** reduce to; **—ение** *n.* simplification; **—ённость** *f.* simplicity; **—ённый** *a.* simplified; reduced; short(-cut); **—енский** *a.* oversimplified.

упруг/ий *a.* elastic, springy, resilient, flexible; expansible (gas); compressional (wave); **—ая отдача** recoil; **—ая постоянная** elastic constant; **—ое восстановление** elastic recovery; (met.) springback; **—ое основание** cushion; **—ое последействие** elastic lag, elastic after-effect; (creep test) elastic extension (at beginning), elastic contraction (at end); **—о** *adv.* elastically, resiliently; **—овязкий** *a.* viscoelastic; **—одеформируемый** *a.* elastic-deformation; **—ожидкий** *a.* elastic-fluid; **—опластический** *a.* elastoplastic.

упругост/ь *f.* elasticity, resilience, spring(iness), flexibility; extensibility, expansibility, buoyancy (of gas); (gas) tension; pressure (of dissociation); **у. пара** vapor pressure; **у. при сжатии** compression modulus, bulk modulus of elasticity; **модуль —и** modulus of elasticity; Young's modulus; **объёмная у.** bulk modulus of elasticity; **предел —и** elastic limit; **сила —и** elastic force, elasticity.

упрудить *see* **упруживать.**

упруже *comp. of* **упругий.**

упруживать *v.* dam (up).

упружить *v.* make elastic or springy; **—ся** *v.* be elastic, be springy.

упрягать *v.* harness.

упряж/ечный *a.* harness; **—ка** *f.* harness(ing); team; (min.) shift; **—ная** *f.* harness room; **—ной** *a.* harness; draft (horse); draw (bar), coupling (hook); **—ной при-**

бор draw gear; **—ная тяга** drawbar; **—ь** *f.* harness, gear.

упрям/иться *v.* persist, be obstinate; **—ство** *n.* persistence, obstinacy, perversity; **—ствовать** *v.* persist; **—ый** *a.* persistent, obstinate, stubborn.

упрячь *see* **упрягать.**

УПС *abbr.* **(управление пограничным слоем)** boundary-layer control.

УПТ *abbr.* **(усилитель постоянного тока)** d-c amplifier.

упу/скать, —стить *v.* omit, overlook, let slip, neglect, miss (an opportunity); **—щение** *n.* omission, oversight, neglect; **—щенный** *a.* omitted, etc., see *v.*

УПЧ *abbr.* **(усилитель промежуточной частоты)** intermediate-frequency amplifier.

упырь *m.* (mam.) vampire bat.

упятер/ённый *a.* quintuple, fivefold; **—ить, —ять** *v.* quintuple, increase fivefold.

УР, у.р. *abbr.* **(удельная радиоактивность)** specific radioactivity; **ур.** *abbr.* **(уравнение)** equation; **(уровень)** level; **(урочище)** tract, area.

уравн/ение *n.* equation, relation; *see also* **уравнивание; у. первой степени** simple equation, linear equation; **—енность** *f.* evenness; **—енный, —ённый** *a.* leveled, etc., see *v.*; **—ивание** *n.* leveling, etc., see *v.*; adjustment; equalization, compensation; **—ивать** *v.* level, grade, even, smooth; equalize, compensate, balance, equate, make equal; regulate, adjust; steady; **—ивающий** *a.* leveling, etc., see *v.*; **—иловка** *f.* wage leveling; **—итель** *m.* leveler, equalizer, etc., see *v.*; **—итель хода** governor.

уравнительн/ый *a.* leveling, etc., see **уравнивать;** buffer (piston); expansion (pipe); **у. агрегат** balancer, equalizer; **у. винт** set screw, adjusting screw; **у. маятник** compensator, compensation pendulum; **у. метод** compensation method; **у. чан, —ая башня** surge tank; **—ая обмотка** (elec.) compensating winding.

уравнове/сить *see* **уравновешивать; —шение** *see* **уравновешивание; —шенность** *f.* equilibrium, balance; **—шенный** *a.* (counter)balanced, etc., see *v.*; level, steady, in equilibrium; **—шенный мост(ик)** (elec.) Wheatstone bridge; **—шивание** *n.* (counter)balancing, etc., see *v.*; equilibration; counterweight, counterpoise; compensation; adjustment; (geol.) isostasy; **—шивать** *v.* (counter)balance, counterpoise, counterweigh, balance out, equilibrate, put in equilibrium, equalize; counteract, cancel, neutralize; compensate; adjust, offset; relieve (valve); **—шиваться** *v.* be (counter)balanced, etc.; become equal; **—шивающий** *a.* (counter)balancing, etc., see *v.*; trimming (moment).

уравнять *see* **уравнивать.**

ураган *m.*, **—ный** *a.* hurricane.

ураз/ин *m.* urazine, diurea; **—ол** *m.* urazole, hydrazodicarbonimide; urasol, acetylmethylene-disalicylic acid.

уразуме(ва)ть *v.* comprehend.

Урал Ural (mountains, river, or region).

уралин *m.* Uralin, chloral urethane.

уралит *m.* (min.) uralite; Uralite (a fireproof asbestos material); Uralit (wood preservative); **—изация** *f.* uralitization.

уральский *a.* (geog.) Ural.

урамил *m.* uramil, 5-aminobarbituric acid.

урамин *m.* uramine, guanidine.

уран *m.* uranium, U; **двуокись —а, закись —а** uranium dioxide, uranous oxide; **окись —а** uranic oxide, uranium trioxide.

уран/ат *m.* uranate; **—ид** *m.* uranide.

уранграфитовый *a.* uranium-graphite; **у. кипящий ре-**

актор большой мощности uranium-graphite channel type reactor, RBMK reactor.

уранид *m.* uranide.

уранизм *m.* uranism, homosexuality.

уранил *m.* uranyl; **—овый, —ьный** *a.* uranyl.

уранин *m.* uranin, sodium fluorescein; (min.) pitchblende; **—ит** *m.* (min.) uraninite, pitchblende.

уранисто— *prefix* uranoso—, uranous.

уранист/ый *a.* uranium, uranous.

уранит *m.* (min.) uranite; **—овый** *a.* uranitic.

урано—*prefix* uran(o)— [uranium; the sky; (anat.) palate].

ураново/кислый *a.* uranic acid; uranate (of); **у. натрий, —натриевая соль** sodium uranate; **—кислая соль** uranate.

уранов/ый *a.* uranium, uranic; **у. ангидрид** uranic anhydride, uranium trioxide; **у. блок** (nucl.) slug; **у. жёлтый** uranium yellow, sodium uranate; **у. котёл, у. реактор** nuclear reactor; **у. свинец** uranium lead; **—ая кислота** uranic acid; **соль —ой кислоты** uranate; **—ая слюда** (min.) uran mica, uranite; **—ая смолка, —ая смоляная обманка, —ая смоляная руда** (min.) pitchblende; **—ая соль** uranium salt; **—ая чернь** a group of uranium oxide minerals; **—ые цветы** (min.) zippeite.

урано/графия *f.* uranography, descriptive astronomy; **—добывающий** *a.* uranium-mining; **—метрическая съёмка** method of prospecting for uranium ores; **—метрия** *f.* (astr.) uranometry; **—носный** *a.* uranium-containing, uraniferous; **—пластика** *f.* (med.) palatoplasty; **—рафия** *f.* (med.) staphylorrhaphy; **—содержащий** *see* **ураноносный**; **—шиз** *m.* (med.) uranoschisis, cleft palate.

урансодержащий *see* **ураноносный**.

урао *n.* (min.) urao, trona.

урари *n.* urari, curare; **—н** *m.* curarine.

урасол *see* **уразол**.

урат *m.* urate; **—емия** *f.* (med.) uratemia; **—оз** *m.* uratosis.

урахус *m.* (embr.) urachus.

урацил *m.* (biochem.) uracil, 2,4,dioxopyrimidine.

урбанизация *f.* urbanization.

урбанит *m.* (min.) urbanite.

УРВ *abbr.* **(управляемый ртутный выпрямитель)** controlled mercury-arc rectifier.

урвать *see* **урывать**.

УрВБ *abbr.* **(уровень верхнего бьефа)** upper-water level.

Ур. г.в. *abbr.* **(уровень грунтовых вод)** ground-water level.

ургидроз *m.* (med.) urhidrosis.

ургон *m.*, **—ский ярус** (geol.) Urgonian stage.

уреаза *f.* urease, urase.

урегулиров/ание *n.* regulation, regulating, etc., *see v.*; **—ать** *v.* regulate, regularize; settle (a question); compensate, adjust.

уред(ин)ий *m.* (myc.) uredosorus.

уред(ини)оспора *f.* (myc.) uredospore.

урез *see* **урезка;** **—ать** *see* **урезывать; —ка** *f.* curtailing, etc., *see* **урезывать**; curtailment; abridgement; cut-off portion.

урезони(ва)ть *v.* persuade, reason (with).

урезыв/ание *n.* curtailing, etc., *see v.*; curtailment; **—ать** *v.* curtail, cut down, cut off, cut away; shorten, abridge, reduce.

уреид *m.* ureide.

урема *f.* bottom land deciduous forest.

урем/ический *a.* (med.) uremic; **—ия** *f.* uremia.

урёмный *a. of* **урема**.

уреометр *m.* ureometer, ureameter.

урет *m.* urete; **—ан** *m.*, **—ановый** *a.* urethane, ethyl carbamate.

уретер *m.* (anat.) ureter.

уретидин *m.* uretidine, tetrahydrourete.

уретр/а *f.* (anat.) urethra; **—альный** *a.* urethral; **—ит** *m.* (med.) urethritis; **—о—** *prefix* urethr(o)— (urethra); **—оскоп** *m.* (med.) urethroscope.

уриал *m.* (mam.) red sheep (*Ovis orientalis*).

уридиловая кислота (biochem.) uridylic acid.

уридин *m.* (biochem.) uridine; **—дифосфат** *m.* uridine diphosphate, UDP; **—овый** *a.* uridine; **—трифосфат** *m.* uridine triphosphate, UTP; **—фосфорный** *a.* uridine-phosphoric (acid).

уридроз *see* **ургидроз**.

уриказа *f.* uricase.

урик(ацид)емия *f.* (med.) uricacidemia, lithemia.

уриконский *a.* (geol.) Uriconian.

урин/а *f.* urine; **—оид** *m.* urinoid, cyclohexene-3-one; **—ометр** *m.* urinometer.

ур. м. *abbr.* **(уровень моря)** sea level.

урм/ан *m.*, **—она** *f.* urman, coniferous forest.

урна *f.* urn; (ballot) box; trash can; theca (of mosses).

ур-ние *abbr.* **(уравнение)** equation.

урно/видный *a.* urn-shaped; **—вый** *a. of* **урна**.

урночка *dim. of* **урна**.

уро— *prefix* uro— (urea; urine; urinary tract; urination); **—билин** *m.* urobilin, hydrobilirubin; **—билиноген** *m.* urobilinogen; **—бромогематин** *m.* urobromohematin.

уровенный *a. of* **уровень**.

уров/ень *m.* level, plane, surface; standard; point; (spirit) level; concentration; stage; **у. моря** sea level; **у. стояния** (water) table; **банка —ня** leveling bottle; **в у.** flush (with); **жизненный у.** standard of living; **измеритель —ня** level gage; **на —не** (on a) level (with); **на —не земли** at ground level; **на одном —не** (on a) level (with), on one level; **падение —ня** recession; **поверхность —ня** level surface; **устанавливать по —ню** *v.* level.

уровн/емер *m.* level gage; **—ять** *v.* level, grade, smooth out; **—яться** *v.* level off, become level.

уро/гематин *m.* urohematin; **—генитальный** *a.* (anat.) urogenital; **—генный** *a.* urogenous; **—графия** *f.* urography.

урод *m.* monster, freak; crop, harvest; **—ина** *m. and f.* monster, freak; **—ить** *v.* bear (a crop); **—иться** *v.* ripen; be born; **—ливость** *f.* deformity, abnormality, defect; **—ливый** *a.* deformed, misshapen, abnormal, (med.) teratological; **—ование** *n.* disfigurement, mutilation; **—овать** *v.* disfigure, mutilate, deform, cripple; **—ство** *n.* disfigurement, deformity, malformation; (med.) teratism.

урожай *m.* harvest, crop, yield; **снимать у., собирать у.** *v.* harvest, reap; **—ность** *f.* productivity, yield; **—ный** *a.* fruitful, productive; harvest.

урожать *v.* produce, bear, yield.

урожд/ать *v.* bear (fruit); **—аться** *v.* ripen; be borne, be born; **—ённый** *a.* born.

уроженец *m.* native, indigene.

урозин *m.* urosine, lithium quinate.

урок *m.* lesson; task, assignment.

урокан/ин *m.* urocanin; **—иновая кислота** urocaninic acid; **—овая кислота** urocanic acid, imidazoleacrylic acid.

урокиназа *f.* (enz.) urokinase.

уроксантин *m.* uroxanthin.

уролит *m.* (med.) urolith, urinary calculus.

уролог *m.* (med.) urologist; **—ический** *a.* urological; **—ия** *f.* urology.

урометр *m.* urometer, urinometer.

урон *m.* loss, damage, harm.

уронид *m.* uronide.

уронить *v.* drop.

уро/новая кислота uronic acid; **—порфирин** *m.* uroporphyrin; **—поэз** *m.* (physiol.) uropoiesis; **—протовый** *a.* uroprotic (acid); **—птерин** *m.* uropterin; **—рубин** *m.* urorubin.

уростиль *m.* (zool.) urostyle (in amphibia).

уро/сульфан *m.* (pharm.) Urosulfan, sulfanilylurea; **—токсин** *m.* urotoxin; **—тропин** *m.* urotropin, hexamethylenetetramine; **—фан** *m.* urophan; **—ферин** *m.* uropherine, theobromine lithium; **—фос** *m.* urophosphate (fertilizer); **—хлораловый** *a.* urochloralic (acid); **—хром** *m.* urochrome.

уроч/ище *n.* tract, area; natural boundary, natural landmark, survey mark; **у. обитания** biochore; **—ный** *a.* fixed, determined.

уроэритрин *m.* uroerythrin.

урс/ановая кислота ursanic acid; **—ин** *m.* ursin, arbutin; **—ол** *m.* Ursol, *p*-phenylenediamine; **—оловая кислота, —он** *m.* ursolic acid, urson; **—оновый** *a.* ursonic (acid).

уртикарная сыпь (med.) urticaria, hives.

уругвайский *a.* (geog.) Uruguay(an).

уруме *n.* (ichth.) round herring (*Etrumeus teres*).

уруть *f.* (bot.) Myriophyllum.

урч/ание *n.* rumbling (e.g., of bowels); **—ать** *v.* rumble.

уруш/иновая кислота urushic acid, laccol; **—иол** *m.* urushiol.

урыв/ать *v.* snatch; **—ками** in snatches, at odd moments, by fits and starts; **—очный** *a.* disjointed, irregular.

урю/к *m.*, **—ковый, —чный** *a.* dried apricot.

ус *m.* whisker; barb, tab, tongue; (whale) bone; (carpentry) miter; (bot.) tendril, runner, flagellum; awn (of grass); (ent.) antenna, feeler; (ichth.) barbel; **соединение в ус** miter joint.

усадебный *a.* of **усадьба.**

усад/ить *see* **усаживать; —ка** shrinkage, contraction; subsidence; loss, disappearance; setting, planting; **—ка при обжиге** firing shrinkage; **давать —ку** *v.* shrink; **коэффициент —ки** shrinkage factor.

усадочн/ость *f.* shrinkability; **—ый** *a.* shrink(age); shrinkability; **—ый масштаб** shrink(age) rule; **—ая мера** shrinkage allowance; **—ая раковина** (met.) shrink hole, shrinkage cavity, pipe; **вторичная —ая раковина** inverted piping.

усадьба *f.* farm(stead).

усаж/ать *v.* seat, settle (down); plant, set; **—аться** *v.* take a seat, get settled; **—енный** *a.* sown thickly, covered; **—ивать(ся)** *see* **усажать(ся).**

усал/ивать *v.* (rub with) grease; salt, pickle; **—ить** *v.* (rub with) grease.

усат/ка *f.* bearded wheat; **—ый** *a.* bearded; (bot.) awned, aristate.

усач *m.* longhorn beetle; (ichth.) barbel (*Barbus*).

усв/аивание *n.* assimilation, etc., *see v.;* uptake; learning, mastering; ingestion (of food) (biol.) anabolism; **—аивать** *v.* assimilate; digest; appropriate, adopt, acquire; master, learn, familiarize oneself (with); **—оение** *see* **усваивание; —оенный** *a.* assimilated, etc., *see v.;* **—оить** *see* **усваивать; —ояемость** *f.* assimilability, etc., *see a.;* **—оямый** *a.* assimilable, available, accessible; comprehensible; **—оять** *see* **усваивать.**

усе/вать, —ивать *v.* strew, sow; stud.

усекать *v.* cut off, truncate.

усерд/ие *n.* diligence, assiduity, zeal; **—ный** *a.* diligent, industrious, painstaking, zealous.

усесться *see* **усаживаться.**

усеч/ение *n.* cutting off, truncation; (med.) excision; **—ённый** *a.* cut off, truncated, topped; **—ённый конус** truncated cone, frustum of a cone.

усечь *see* **усекать.**

усе/янный *a.* sown, strewn; studded, dotted; (petr.) sempatic; **—ять** *see* **усевать.**

усидчивый *a.* persevering, assiduous, diligent.

усик *m.* (bot.) tendril; (zool.) antenna, feeler, palp, horn; (ichth.) barbel; whisker; **—и** *pl.* antennae, cirri; **—овидный** *a.* cirriform; tendril-shaped; **—оватый** *a.* antennal; **—оносный** *a.* cirriferous.

усил/ение *n.* strengthening, intensification, reinforcement; growth, rise, gain, increase, boost, amplification; enhancement; **у. действия** (pharm.) potenti(aliz)ation; **коэффициент —ения** (electron.) amplification factor; (elec. commun.) gain; **регулировка —ения** gain control, volume control; **регулятор —ения** automatic gain control, AGC; **с большим —ением** high-gain (amplifier); **с переменным —ением; с регулируемым —ением** variable-gain (amplifier); **способ —ения** cumulative method; **—енно** *adv.* strenuously, hard, intensely; **—енный** *a.* strengthened, etc., *see v.;* super(charge); extensive; urgent (request); high-caloric (diet); **—ивать** *v.* strengthen, intensify, heighten, increase, augment, enhance, boost; (phot.) intensify; amplify, magnify; reinforce, stiffen; promote, aggravate, strain; **—иваться** *v.* be strengthened, etc.; grow stronger, become more pronounced; intensify, increase; exert oneself; **—ивающий** *a.* strengthening, etc., *see v.;* **—ивающий родовую деятельность** (med.) parturifacient.

усил/ие *n.* stress, strain, pull, force; effort, exertion, endeavor; **прилагать —ия** *v.* exert oneself, make efforts, take pains.

усилитель *m.* amplifier; intensifier, booster; reinforcing agent; repeater; **у. на сопротивлениях** resistance-coupled amplifier; **у. напряжения** voltage amplifier, booster; **у. с бегущей волной** traveling-wave accelerator.

усилитель/-автодин *m.* amplidyne-amplifier; **у.-выпрямитель** *m.* amplifier-rectifier; **у.-дискриминатор** *m.* amplifier-discriminator; **у.-инвертор** *m.* amplifier-inverter; **—ный** *a.* strengthening, etc., *see* **усиливать;** amplifier; **—ная лампа** amplifying tube; **у.-ограничитель** *m.* limiting amplifier; **у.-прерыватель** *m.* chopper amplifier; **у.-формирователь** *m.* shaping amplifier.

усилить *see* **усиливать.**

уск/альзывать, —ользать, —ользнуть *v.* slip away, slip off; escape, evade.

ускорен/ие *n.* acceleration, speeding up, hastening; **у. хода** acceleration; **измеритель —ия** accelerometer; **отрицательное у.** deceleration; **сила —ия** accelerating force; **—иемер** *m.* accelerometer; **—ный** *a.* accelerated, speeded up; fast, express; quick (freezing).

ускор/итель *m.* accelerator; accelerant; (rocket) booster; **у. взлёта** take-off unit; **у. на бегущей волне, у. с бегущей волной** traveling-wave accelerator; **с —ителем** boosted (vehicle); **—ительный** *a.* accelerating; boost (engine); **—ить, —ять** *v.* accelerate, speed (up), quicken, hasten; expedite, favor, promote; intensify; **—яющий** *a.* accelerating, etc., *see v.;* step-up; multiplying (gear).

услав ливаться *see* **условиться.**

усластить *v.* sweeten.

услать *see* **усылать.**

услащать *v.* sweeten.

усл. ед. *abbr.* **(условная единица)** arbitrary unit, conventional unit.

усле/дить, —живать *v.* follow, observe.

услов/ие *n.* condition, stipulation, specification; understanding, proviso, clause; circumstance, situation; **—ия** *pl.* conditions; terms (of contract); mode; **в —иях** during, in or under conditions; **в —иях эксплуатации** under operating conditions; **по —ию** according to agreement; **под —ием, при —ии, с —ием** on condition (that), provided, providing, if; **при прочих равных —иях** other conditions being equal; **при сходных —иях** under similar conditions; **ни при каких —иях** under no circumstances; **ставить —ием** *v.* stipulate, condition; (geom.) postulate; **технические —ия** specifications.

услов/иться, —ливаться *v.* agree, arrange, make arrangements, settle, fix, stipulate; contract; **—ленный** *a.* agreed (upon), etc., *see v.*

услов/но *adv.* conditionally, etc., *see a.*; **—огодовой** *a.* standard yearly; **—опостоянный** *a.* constant; **—ость** *f.* conditionality; convention; **—ый** *a.* conditional, provisory, provisional; arbitrary, conventional, agreed (upon), assumed; representative (scale); code (language, signal); hypothetical (problem); nominal (pressure, velocity, etc.); ideal, comparison (fuel); relative (viscosity); quasi—, apparent; **—ый знак** conventional sign or symbol; legend; **изображение —ыми знаками** symbolization; **—ый нулевой уровень** zero reference level.

усложн/ение *n.* complication; **—ённый** *a.* complicated; modified (resin); **—ить, —ять** *v.* complicate.

услуг/а *f.* service, good turn, favor; **к его —ам** at his service, at his disposal.

услышать *v.* hear.

усматривать *v.* find, discover, discern, see, perceive; look (after), attend (to).

усмир/ить, —ять *v.* suppress, put down; appease, pacify.

усмотр/ение *n.* discerning; judgment, discretion; **—еть** *see* **усматривать.**

уснаровая кислота usnaric acid.

усна/стить, —щ(ив)ать *v.* equip (with); fill, (over)load, (over)charge; embellish.

усн/етиновый *a.* usnetinic (acid); **—етовый** *a.* usnetic (acid); **—идиновый** *a.* usnidic (acid); **—иновый** *a.* usn(in)ic (acid).

уснуть *v.* fall asleep; die (of fish).

усовершенствов/ание *n.* improvement, refinement, advance(ment), development; perfecting; adaptation; **—анный** *a.* improved, etc., *see v.*; more elaborate, more sophisticated; **—атель** *m.* improver, developer; **—ать** *v.* improve, refine, develop, perfect, advance; adapt; **—аться** *v.* be improved, etc.; improve, develop.

усовик *m.* (rr.) guard rail, counterrail.

усовка *f.* (carpentry) mitering.

усол *m.* salting, pickling; **—ить** *v.* salt, pickle.

усомниться *v.* doubt, have misgivings.

усоногие *pl.* (zool.) Cirripedia.

усох/ить *see* **усыхать; —ший** *a.* dried.

успе/ваемость *f.* advancement, progress; good results; **—вать** *v.* succeed, be successful, obtain good results; advance, improve, make progress; have time, manage (to); be on time; **—вающий** *a.* succeeding, etc., *see v.*; **—ется** there is still time; **—ть** *see* **успевать.**

успех *m.* success; improvement, progress, advance(ment), gain; **с —ом** successfully, to advantage; **с большим**

—ом very successfully, to great advantage; **—и** *pl.* progress; **делать —и** *v.* succeed; improve, advance, make progress; **добиться —а** *v.* achieve success, succeed.

успешн/о *adv.* successfully, etc., *see v.*; to advantage; **—ость** *f.* success(fulness), effectiveness; **—ый** *a.* successful, effective; advantageous, favorable.

успокаив/ание *n.* quieting, etc., *see v.*; deexcitation; moderation, decrement; **гидравлическое у.** liquid damping; **—ать** *v.* quiet, calm, steady, stabilize; (elec.) damp; soothe, reassure, set at ease; kill (steel); (med.) sedate; **—аться** *v.* be quieted, etc.; calm down; slacken, abate; **—ающий** *a.* quieting, etc., *see v.*; (pharm.) sedative; **—ающее средство** sedative, tranquilizer.

успоко/ение *see* **успокаивание;** attenuation; (steel) killing; **время —ения** transient period, damping time; **—енный** *a.* quieted, etc., *see* **успокаивать;** quiet; **—итель** *m.* arrester; stabilizer, deoscillator; (elec.) damper; (steel) killing agent; (rr.) arrestment; **—ительный** *see* **успокаивающий;** stilling (chamber); **—ительные обмотки** (elec.) damper; **—ить** *see* **успокаивать.**

усредитель *m.* (sewage) equalizer, equalization basin.

усредн/ение *n.* neutralizing, neutralization, etc., *see v.*; blending (of ores); averaging; **—енный** *a.* neutralized, etc., *see v.*; average, mean; **—енный по времени** time-mean (value); **—итель** *m.* neutralizer, neutralizing agent; surge tank; **—ительный** *a.* balancing, equalizing (reservoir); **—ять** *v.* neutralize; average (out); smooth (out); homogenize; **—яющий** *a.* neutralizing, etc., *see v.*

уст. *abbr.* **(устарелый)** obsolete.

уста *f.* (anat.) os, mouth.

устав *m.* statute, regulations, rules, code.

уставать *v.* get tired, tire.

устав/ить *see* **уставливать; —ка** setting, etc., *see v.*; **—ливать, —лять** *v.* set arrange, place, put; fill, cover.

уставный *a.* of **устав;** statute (mile); legal, statutory (reserve); authorized (capital).

устаивать *see* **устоять.**

устал/остный *a.* fatigue; fatigue-testing; **—остная прочность** fatigue strength; **—остная тренировка** fatigue cycling loads; **—ость** *f.* fatigue; **испытание на —ость** fatigue test; **предел —ости** fatigue limit, fatigue point, endurance limit; **—ый** *a.* tired, fatigued; **—ь** *f.* fatigue; **без —и** untiringly, unceasingly.

устанавлив/аемый *a.* adjustable; **—ание** *see* **установка, установление.**

устанавливать *v.* install, erect, build, set up; lay (pipe); mount, fit, put together, assemble; rig up; set, put, place, position, arrange, seat; post (guards); align, adjust, regulate; establish, determine; assay, measure; specify, fix, settle, lay down (rules), stipulate; ascertain, find out, locate, distinguish, define; reach, attain, achieve; (elec.) make (contact); detect (flaws); **у. на** set at; adjust for; **у. по** set by, set to; **—ся** *v.* be installed, etc.; settle (down); adjust; determine, decide.

установ/ившийся *a.* set, settled, steady, smooth, stabilized; stationary; steady-state (error, motion, etc.); sustained (flight); conservative (value); **у. процесс, у. режим** steady-state behavior; **—ить** *see* **устанавливать.**

установк/а *f.* installing, installation, etc., *see* **устанавливать;** adjustment; arrangement; establishment; assembly, mount; (drilling) rig; station, works; facility, plant, unit, set-up; outfit, equipment, apparatus; device, contrivance; system; emplacement; aim, purpose, tendency; *suffix* **—er; у. для опрыскивания** sprayer, spraying unit; **у. для переработки** processing plant; **у. на** adjustment for; **у. на нуль** zero adjustment; **у. на фокус** focusing; **у. по центру** center adjustment; **иметь —у на** v. aim at; **дать —у** v. give indications; **допускающий —у по** adjustable for; **силовая у.** power plant; **точная у.** fine adjustment; **угол —и** setting angle.

установл/ение n. establishment, institution; determination, determining, fixing, ascertainment; assay; adjustment; detection (of flaws); evidence; (elec.) rating; **время —ения** setting time, transient period; **время —ения равновесия** equilibration time; **—енный** a. installed, etc., see **устанавливать;** prescribed, specified; in position; **—енный впереди** front-mounted; **—енный на ракете** rocket-borne; **—енный на спутнике** satellite-mounted; **—енный сзади** rear-mounted; **—ять** see **устанавливать.**

установочн/ый a. adjusting, adjustable, regulating, setting; installing, mounting; set (screw); adaptive (nystagmus); righting (reflex); **—ая мера** reference gage; **—ое приспособление** adjusting device, adjuster; control gear.

установщик m. adjuster, fitter, erector, installer, mounter; setter, setting device; (mine)layer.

устар/еваемость see **устарелость; —евший** see **устарелый; —елость** f. obsolescence, obsoleteness; **—елый** a. obsolete, antiquated, out of date, outdated; **—еть** v. become obsolete.

устать see **уставать.**

устели/-поле n. (bot.) Ceratocarpus; **—ть** v. cover.

устере/гать, —чь v. watch (over), guard.

устилаговая кислота ustilagic acid.

уст/(и)лать v. cover, floor, pave; strew, spread; **—илка** f. covering, etc., see v.

уст/ин m. Ustin, nornidulin; **—ицеаин** m. ustizeain.

уст/ичный see **устьичный; —ный** a. oral, verbal.

устой m. abutment, pier, column; basis, foundation, support; cream (on milk).

устойчив/о adv. stably, steadily, firmly; **—ость** f. stability, steadiness, firmness, rigidity; immunity, resistance, tolerance, endurance; persistence; **—ый** a. stable, steady, firm, rigid; hardy, durable, resistant; sustained; persistent (gas); settled (weather); *suffix* —resistant, —proof, —fast; **—ый к щелочам** alkali-resistant; **—ое осединение** stable compound; **делать —ым** m. stabilize, steady.

усторожить see **устерегать.**

устоять v. resist, hold out (against), withstand; **—ся** v. settle, precipitate; become stabilized; be ready; gather, form cream (of milk).

устраив/ать v. arrange, make arrangements (for), accommodate; organize, set up; make, construct; place, settle, establish, install; suit, be convenient (for); **—аться** v. be arranged, etc.; get established.

устран/ение n. removing, elimination, etc., see v.; removal; release (of inhibition); de—; **у. возбуждения** de-energization; **у. напряжения** stress relief; **у. неисправностей** trouble-shooting; **—ённый** a. removed, etc., see **устранить; —имый** a. removable; **—ить, —ять** v. remove, eliminate, dispose (of), do away (with), get rid (of); clear out, clear away, move away; rectify, remedy, correct (faults); cancel; stop (leak); suppress, overcome, circumvent; separate, uncouple; **—ять девиацию** compensate (a compass); **—иться, —яться** v. be removed, etc.; stand aside, withdraw; separate, uncouple; keep (from).

устраш/ать v. frighten, scare; appall; **—аться** v. be frightened, fear; be deterred; **—ающий** a. frightening;

formidable; **—ение** n. frightening; intimidation; deterrence; **средство —ения** deterrent; **—ить(ся)** see **устрашать(ся).**

устрем/ить see **устремлять; —ление** n. directing, turning; tendency, striving, aspiration; rush; **—лённость** f. trend, tendency; **—лять** v. direct, turn, fix; (math.) let. . .tend toward; **—ляться** v. be directed (at, towards).

устри/ца f. oyster; **—цеводство** n. oyster culture; **—цеобразный червец** oyster-shell scale; **—чник** m. oyster bed; **—чный** a. oyster.

устро/ение n. arrangement; organization; construction; **—енный** a. arranged, etc., see **устраивать; —итель** m. organizer; **—ить** see **устраивать; —йство** n. arrangement, layout, system; organization, establishment; installation; means, device, attachment, appliance, apparatus, mechanism, instrument, equipment, gear; facility; unit; (mach.) working principle; —ing device, —er; **—йство для наблюдения** viewing attachment; **диагностические —йства** (instr.) diagnostics; **зарядное —йство** charger; **пусковой —йство** starter; **ядерное —йство** nuclear device.

уступ m. shelf, ledge, bank, terrace, step; (geol.) bench, scarp, escarpment; berm; offset, stagger; shoulder (of hole); (arch.) projection; niche, recess; spur (of hill); (mil.) echelon; **—ы** pl. (min.) benching; **—ами** benched, terraced; step-like, graduated, graded, gradual; **работа —ами** (min.) benching; **расположенный —ами** arranged in steps, stepped, staggered.

уступ/ать, —ить v. yield, succumb, give in; give up, resign; give way, (con)cede; be second (to), be inferior (to); abate, reduce, take off; **—ка** f. yielding, etc., see v.; (con)cession; abatement, discount; **делать —ки, идти на —ки** v. compromise.

уступ/ный a. (min.) bench(ed); **—ная выемка** benching; **—ообразный** a. benched; stepped, in steps; **—чатый** a. stepped, staggered, terraced.

уступчив/ость f. compliance; **—ый** a. compliant, pliable, yielding.

усть/е n. mouth, issue; opening, aperture, orifice; (biol.) stoma; (anat.) ostium; mouthpiece; entrance; (well) head; (stoke) hole; vent, outflow, discharge; estuary (of river); junction; **—евый** a. mouth; estuarine; **—ице** n. dim. of **устье;** (biol.) stoma; pore; **—ичный** a. stomatal; **—я** pl. of **устье;** ostia.

усугуб/ить see **усугублять; —ление** n. intensifying, aggravation, etc., see v.; increase; **—ленный** a. intensified, etc., see v.; **—лять** v. intensify, aggravate, enhance; redouble; increase, augment.

усуш/ать, —ить v. dry (up), parch; **—ка** drying(-up); shrinkage, loss on drying.

усчит(ыв)ать v. check, verify; deduct, discount; count.

усы pl. of **ус.**

усылать v. send away.

усып/ание n. strewing, scattering; **—анный** a. scattered, etc., see v.; consperse; **—ать** v. strew, scatter, cover, litter.

усып/ительный a. soporific, hypnotic, narcotic; **—ительное средство** soporific; **—ить** see **усыплять; —ление** n. narcosis (of animals); lulling; hypnotism; **—лять** v. lull, make drowsy; hypnotize; narcotize, anesthetize; (vet.) put to sleep, put down; **—ляющий** see **усыпительный.**

усы/хание n. drying, desiccation, shrinking, shrinkage; (phyt.) mal secco; **—хать** v. dry, shrivel, shrink; **—шка** f. shrinkage, loss on drying.

ута/ивание n., **—йка** f. concealment, suppression; **—и(ва)ть** v. conceal, hide, keep secret; suppress.

утаптывать *v.* tread, trample down; pack, tamp down.

утаскивать *v.* drag away; carry, bear, take (away, off); entrain; remove.

утач/ать *v.* stitch up; shorten (a garment) by taking up the hem; **—ивание** *n.* stitching up; grinding down; **—ивать** *v.* stitch up; grind down; **—ка** *f.* stitching up.

утащ/енный *a.* dragged away, etc., *see* **утаскивать**; **—ить** *see* **утаскивать**.

утв. *abbr.* **(утверждённый)** approved.

утварь *f.* utensils, implements; (silver) plate, service.

утвердит/ельно *adv.* affirmatively, in the affirmative; **—ельный** *a.* affirmative, positive; confirming; **—ь** *see* **утверждать**.

утвержд/ать *v.* affirm, assert, maintain, claim; confirm, corroborate; authorize, approve, accept; ratify; sanction; prove; strengthen, consolidate; **—ают, —ается** it is claimed; **—аться** *v.* be affirmed, etc.; **—ение** *n.* affirmation, etc., *see v.*; statement, claim; approval; strengthening; **—ённый** *a.* affirmed, etc., *see v.*

утекать *v.* flow away, flow off, run off; leak, escape; disperse.

утёнок *m.* duckling.

утепл/ение *n.* heating, warming; insulation, keeping warm; **—ённый** *a.* heated, warmed; blanketed (radiator); **—итель** *m.* heater, warmer; (battery) thermal container; thermal blanket; **—ительный** *a.* heating, warming; **—ить, —ять** *v.* heat, warm, insulate.

утерамин *m.* Uteramine, tyramine.

утереть *see* **утирать**.

утеро— *prefix* (anat.) utero— (uterus); **—пластика** *f.* (med.) uteroplasty.

утеря *f.* loss; **—нный** *a.* lost; forfeited; **—ть** *v.* lose; forfeit.

утёс *m.* rock, crag, cliff, bluff.

утесать *see* **утёсывать**.

утёсистый *a.* rocky, craggy; steep.

утесник *m.* (bot.) furze, gorse (*Ulex*).

утесн/ить, —ять *v.* wedge in, squeeze in.

утёсывать *v.* cut down, trim, dress (wood).

утеч/ка *f.* leak(age), leaking (out), outflow, escape, drain, loss, wastage, stray; disclosure (of information); dissipation, dispersion; issue, effluent, runoff; (insurance) ullage; **у. мозгов** brain drain; **коэффициент —ки** leakage factor; **с —кой** leaky, leaking; **ток —ки** (elec.) leakage current; **—ь** *see* **утекать**.

утеш/ать *v.* console, comfort, relieve; **—ение** *n.* consolation, comfort, relief; **—ительный** *a.* consoling, comforting, relieving; **—ить** *see* **утешать**.

утилиз/атор *m.,* **—аторский** *a.* (waste) utilizer, recovery unit; salvager; **—аторство** *n.* recovery; **—ационный** *a.* of **утилизация**; heat-recovery, waste-heat (boiler); **—ация** *f.* utilization, salvaging, recovery; **—ировать** *v.* utilize, salvage, recover, reclaim; **—ируемый** *a.* utilizable, etc., *see v.*; available; utilized, etc., *see v.*

утилита *f.* (comp.) utility (program).

утилитарн/ость *f.* utility, usefulness; **—ый** *a.* utilitarian, useful, practical.

утиль *m.* utility waste, utilizable scrap, salvage, scrap material; (metal) junk; (cer.) bisque; **—завод** *m.* scrap reprocessing plant; **—ный** *a.* of **утиль**; utilized; (cer.) bisque, body (firing); **—резина** *f.* scrap rubber; **—сырьё** *n.,* **—сырьевой** *a. see* **утиль**; **—цех** *see* **утильзавод**; **—щик** *m.* scrap collector, junkman, salvager.

утин/ый *a.* (orn.) duck('s), anatine; *see pl.* Anatidae.

утир/альник *m.* towel; **—ание** *n.* wiping, etc., *see v.*; **—ать** *v.* wipe (away, off), dry, **—ка** *see* **утирание**.

утиск(ив)ать *v.* press in, squeeze in.

утих/ание *n.* abatement, subsidence, dying down; **—ать, —нуть** *v.* abate, subside, quiet down; fade, die away (of noise); cease; **—ший** *a.* abated, moderated.

утихомири(ва)ть *v.* soothe, pacify; **—ся** *v.* settle down.

утка *f.* (orn.) duck (*Anas*); long-necked flask; urinal; (naut.) belaying cleat; *gen. of* **уток**.

уткать *v.* weave a pattern into; enmesh, cover with a net.

уткнуть *v.* stick, thrust, shove (in); bury, hide; **—ся** *v.* be stuck, etc.; run (into), come up (against); concentrate (on).

утко/водство *n.* duck breeding; **—нос** *m.* (zool.) duck-bill platypus (*Ornithorhynchus anatinus*).

утлегарь *m.* (naut.) jib boom.

утлый *a.* fragile, rickety; leaky.

уток *m.* (text.) weft, filling; *gen. pl. of* **утка**.

утол/ение *n.* slaking, quenching (of thirst); satisfaction (of hunger); alleviation (of pain); (med.) sedation; **—ить** *see* **утолять**.

утолочить *v.* trample.

утолочь *v.* pulverize thoroughly.

утол/стить, —щать *v.* thicken, make thicker; **—щение** *n.* thickening, thicker part, swell(ing), intumescence, enlargement, expansion, bulging, bulge, bulb, node; (welding) reinforcement; rib, boss, camber; (anat.) splenium; (text.) nub; **центр(ир)ующее —щение** (art.) bourrelet, guide band; **—щённый** *a.* reinforced; thickened; incrassate; **—щённый череп** pachycephalic skull, pachycephaly.

утолять *v.* slake, quench (thirst); satisfy (hunger); alleviate (pain).

утомительн/ость *f.* tiresomeness; **—ый** *a.* tiresome, fatiguing, tedious.

утом/ить, —лять *v.* fatigue, tire; **—ление** *n.* fatigue; exhaustion, depletion (of soil); **—лённый** *a.* fatigued, tired; **—ляемость** *f.* fatigability, susceptibility to fatigue.

утон/ение *n.* thinning, tapering; thin part; **—ённый** *a.* thinned, taper(ed); **—ить** *see* **утонять**.

утонуть *v.* drown, sink, submerge, founder.

утонч/ать *v.* thin (down), make thinner, attenuate, narrow down, taper; refine; **—аться** *v.* be thinned (down), taper; **—ающийся** *a.* tapering; **—ение** *n.* thinning (down), etc., *see v.*; taper; **—енность, —ённость** *f.* refinement, subtlety; **—енный, —ённый** *a.* thinned (down), etc., *see v.*; subtle, fine; **—ить** *see* **утончать**.

утон/ьшать, —ять *v.* thin, make thinner; **—ьшение** *n.* thinning, tapering.

утоп *m.* deadhead; **—ать** *v.* drown, sink, founder; trample down; **—итель** *m.* depresser, dipper; **—ить** *v.* drown, submerge; bury, embed, sink (into); recess, build in; suppress; warm up.

утопич/еский, —ный *a.* Utopian.

утоплен/ие *n.* drowning, etc., *see* **утопить**; submersion; **—ник** *m.* drowned person; **—ный** *a.* drowned, etc., *see* **утопить**; countersunk (head), flush; built-in; **—ная головка** countersink; **—ного типа** flush(-type).

утопнуть *see* **утонуть**.

утоптать *see* **утаптывать**.

утор *m.* notch; chine, fissure, crevice; croze (of barrel).

утораплива ть *v.* speed up, accelerate.

утор/ить *v.* notch, groove; (coopering) croze; beat (a path); **—ник** *m.* notcher; crozer.

утор опить *see* **утораплива ть**.

уточина *f.* (text.) weft thread.

уточ/ить *v.* grind down; **—иться** *v.* wear down; **—ка** *f.* grinding down; *dim. of* **утка**; (zool.) barnacle; (ichth.) clingfish.

уточн/ение *n.* refinement, improvement; revision; more

exact definition; specification; **—ённый** *a.* refined, etc., *see v.*; **—ить** *v.* refine, improve; specify, make more precise, define more accurately, pinpoint, obtain more accurate (information); verify, check (data).

уточн/омотальный *a.* (text.) cop-winding, weft-winding (machine); **—ый** *a.* weft.

уточнять *see* **уточнить.**

утраивать *v.* treble, triple.

утрамбов/анный *a.* rammed, tamped, packed; **—ка** *f.*, **—ывание** *n.*, **—ывающий** *a.* ramming, tamping, packing; **—(ыв)ать** *v.* ram, tamp, pack.

утра/та *f.* loss; exhaustion, depletion (of soil); **—тить**, **—чивать** *v.* lose; forfeit; **—ченный** *a.* lost; **—чивание** *n.* loss, losing.

утренний *a.* morning, early.

утренник *m.* early morning frost.

утрёт *fut. 3 sing. of* **утереть.**

утрикул *m.* (anat.; bot.) utricle; **—ярный** *a.* utricular, bladder-like.

утриров/ание *n.*, **—ка** *f.* overdoing, exaggeration; **—ать** *v.* overdo, exaggerate, carry too far.

утро *n.* morning.

утроб/а *f.* womb; viscera; **—ный** *a.* uterine; **—ный плод** fetus.

утро/ение *n.* trebling, tripling, triplication; **—енный** *a.* trebled, triple, threefold, three times as great; **—итель** *m.* trebler, tripler; **—ить** *see* **утраивать.**

утром *adv.* in the morning. A M

утру/диться *see* **утруждаться;** **—днить**, **—днять** *v.* make more difficult, complicate, inconvenience; **—ждаться** *v.* take trouble, trouble oneself.

утруска *f.* spillage; weight loss.

утряс/ать, **—ти**, **—ывать** *v.* shake down.

утух/ать, **—нуть** *v.* die out, go out.

утучн/ение *n.* enrichment, fertilization; fattening; **—ить**, **—ять** *v.* enrich, fertilize, manure; fatten.

утуш/ать *v.* extinguish; suppress; **—ить** *v.* extinguish; suppress; stew, braize.

утфель *m.* (sugar) massecuite, fillmass.

утык(ив)ать *v.* set (with); caulk.

утю/г *m.* iron (for pressing); (road) drag, roller, grader; **—гообразный** *a.* iron-shaped, bow(-shaped); **—жение** *n.*, **—жильный** *a.* ironing, etc., *see v.*; planing; **—жить** *v.* iron, press; drag, scrape, grade; **—жка** *see* **утюжение;** **—жный** *a. of* **утюг.**

утягивать *v.* bind, tie; pull in, tighten, draw tight; draw, pull, haul; entrain; keep back, retain.

утяжел/ение *n.* charging, loading; weighting; **—ённый** *a.* heavy; weighted; **—итель** *m.* weighting compound; (leather) filler; **—ить**, **—ять** *v.* charge, load; weight.

утяжина *f.* (met.) shrinkage cavity, shrink hole, pipe; crush; spread (of sheet material).

утя/жка *f.* binding, etc., *see* **утягивать;** (rolling) shear drag; (slab rolling) underfills; (cold drawn tubes) draft; **—нутый** *a.* bound, etc., *see* **утягивать;** **—нуть** *see* **утягивать.**

утят/а *pl. of* **утёнок,** ducklings; **—ина** *f.* duck (meat).

УФ *abbr.* **(узкополосный фильтр)** narrowband filter; **(ультрафиолетовый)** ultraviolet; **(умеренный фронт)** moderate front.

уфимский *a.* (geog.) Ufa.

уфл, УФЛ *abbr.* **(ультрафиолетовые лучи)** ultraviolet rays.

УФО *abbr.* **(ультрафиолетовое облучение)** ultraviolet irradiation; **(ультрафиолетовое освещение)** ultraviolet illumination.

уха *f.* (fish) chowder; *gen. of* **ухо.**

ухаб *m.*, **—ина** *f.* hole, hollow, pit, rut (in road); **—ы** *pl.* ups and downs; **—истый** *a.* rough, uneven, rutty.

ухажив/ание *n.* tending, etc., *see v.*; care, treatment; (mach.) maintenance, service; **—ать** *v.* tend, nurse, take care (of), care (for), attend; handle, treat; (mach.) maintain, service; cure (concrete); cultivate (plants).

ухание *n.* slip (of furnace charge).

ухва/т *m.* shank, grip, tongs, grab; wall hook; **—тить** *see* **ухватывать;** **—тка** *f.* grip; way, trick, manner; **—тный** *a. of* **ухват;** **—тывать** *v.* grip, grasp, seize, catch hold (of); **—тываться за** *v.* seize (an opportunity); **—ченный** *a.* gripped, etc., *see v.*

ухвостье *n.* tailings.

ухи/триться, **—щряться** *v.* contrive, manage, find a way; **—щрение** *n.* device, contrivance, shift, dodge; **—щрённый** *a.* clever.

ух/о *n.* (anat.) ear; (mech.) ear, lug, hanger, eye; **морское у.** (zool.) abalone (*Haliotis*); **наружное у.** (anat.) auricle; **склероз —а** (med.) otosclerosis; **среднее у.** middle ear; **тугой на у.** hard of hearing.

уховертка *f.* (ent.) earwig.

уход *m.* maintenance, care, service, upkeep; attendance, attention; handling, treatment; departure, going away, leaving, resignation, withdrawal; (frequency) drift; run-(ning)-off, escape; loss; shift; deflection (of gyroscope); **у. в сторону** sidetrack; **у. за больными** nursing; **у. и эксплуатация** care and maintenance; **монтёр —а** maintenance man, service man; **не требующий —а** maintenance-free.

уход/ить *v.* depart, go away, leave; go out, run off, issue; escape, leak, seep; recede; withdraw, retreat; retire, resign; pass, elapse (of time); spend, consume; kill; **—ящий** *a.* departing, etc., *see v.*; outgoing; discharge, waste (water).

ухообразный *a.* auricular, ear-shaped.

УХР *abbr.* **(уравнение химического равновесия)** chemical equilibrium equation.

ухтинский *a.* (geog.) Ukhta.

ухудш/ать *v.* deteriorate, degrade, make worse, aggravate, impair, spoil; **—аться** *v.* be deteriorated, etc.; deteriorate, get worse; **—ение** *n.* deterioration, etc., *see v.*; change for the worse, decline; degradation, impairment, negative impact; aggravation (of symptoms); **—енный** *a.* deteriorated, etc., *see v.*; inferior; **—ить** *see* **ухудшать.**

уцеле/вший *a.* surviving; *m.* survivor; **—ть** *v.* survive, remain uninjured, escape destruction, be left intact.

уцен/ённый *a.* (com.) marked down; **—и(ва)ть** *v.* mark down; **—ка** *f.* discount, price reduction.

уцеп/ить(ся), **—лять(ся)** *v.* catch hold (of), seize, grip, grasp, clutch.

уч. *abbr.* **(участковый; участок; учебный; учёный).**

учали(ва)ть *v.* moor, tie up.

участв/овать *v.* take part (in), participate, share (in), have a hand (in), partake, be involved (in), collaborate; **—ующий** *a.* participating; *m.* participant.

участ/ие *n.* share, sharing, part, participation, partnership, collaboration; attention, interest, concern; **при —ии** with the assistance (of), with the cooperation (of); **принимать у.** *v.* take part (in), participate, take interest (in).

участит/ель *m.* amplifier; **—ь** *see* **учащать.**

участковый *a. of* **участок;** sectional; district.

участник *m.* participant, participator, partner, privy (to a contract), party (to an agreement); member; competitor, exhibitor; **у. торгов** bidder, tenderer.

участ/ок *m.* section, part, portion, segment; region, district, locality, site, area, field, space; lot, plot, strip, piece, parcel (of land); division, allotment; leg (of flight); (flight) path; (launching) phase, trajectory, leg; run (of pipe); **у. ассоциации** (bot.) community; **у. цепи** (elec.) subcircuit; **—ками** piecemeal.

участь *f.* lot, portion, destiny, fate.

учащ/ать *v.* make more frequent, increase the frequency (of); thicken; repeat; **—аться** *v.* become more frequent, increase in frequency; **—ение** *n.* increase of frequency; repetition; **—ённый** *a.* more frequent; accelerated, quickened; **—ённое сердце** (med.) tachycardia.

учащий *m.* teacher; *a.* teaching; **—ся** *m.* student; *a.* studying.

уч. г. *abbr.* (**учебный год**) school year.

учёба *f.* studying; studies; training, drill.

учебник *m.* textbook, manual.

учебно/-воспитательный *a.* educational and training; **у.-имитационный** *a.* practice; **у.-методический институт** institute of educational methods; **у.-наглядные пособия** visual study aids; **у.-научный** *a.* scientific training; **у.-опытный** *a.* instructional and experimental; **у.-тренировочный** *a.* (av.) training, trainer.

учебн/ый *a.* educational, training; school; study; instructional; academic; text (book); drill, practice; dummy (ammunition); **у. курс, у. план, —ая программа** curriculum; **—ое время** (school) term; **—ое заведение** educational institution, school.

учёл *past m. sing. of* **учесть.**

учен/ие *n.* teaching, instruction; tuition; learning, studying; apprenticeship, training, (mil.) exercise; science; doctrine; *suffix* —ology; **у. о клетке** cytology; **отдать в у. мастеру** *v.* apprentice; **—ик** *m.*, **—ица** *f.* student; apprentice; trainee; **—ик-лётчик** *m.* student pilot; **—ический** *a.* pupil's, student's; raw, immature; **—ичество** *n.* apprenticeship, training.

учёно *adv.* scientifically; **—сть** *f.* learning, erudition.

учён/ый *a.* scientific; learned, academic, scholarly, erudite; university (degrees); *m.* scientist; **у. совет** scientific council; **—ая степень** academic degree; **у.-атомник, у.-ядерник** *m.* nuclear scientist.

ученье *see* **учение.**

учёс *m.* combings, hatchelling (of hemp).

учесть *see* **учитывать.**

учёт *m.* calculation, estimation; accounting; discount(ing) (of bills); registration; record keeping, metering; follow-up; stock-taking; *see also* **учитывание; у. и контроль (ядерных) материалов** (nuclear) material control and accountancy, MC&A; **у. кадров** personnel records; **у. производительности** (petrol.) gaging; **без —а** ignoring; **бухгалтерский у.** bookkeeping; **вести у.** *v.* take stock; **плановый у.** follow-up; **при —е** if . . . is taken into account; **с —ом** with regard (to), with allowance made (for); based (on); **с должным —ом** with due regard (for); **стать на у.** *v.* register; **хозяйственный у.** accounting.

учетвер/ение *n.* quadrupling; **—ённый** *a.* quadruplicate; quadruple; **—ить, —ять** *v.* quadruple, multiply by four.

учётн/о-издательский лист publisher's sheet (unit of measure); **у.-регистрационный** *a.* enumerative, primary (bibliography); **—ый** *a. of* **учёт; —ый процент** rate of discount.

учётчик *m.* accountant; calculator.

училищ/е *n.*, **—ный** *a.* school.

учимый *a.* educable.

учинение *n.* making, committing.

учин/ить, —ять *v.* make, commit.

учитель *m.*, **—ница** *f.* teacher, instructor; **—ский** *a.* teacher's; magistral; **—ство** *n.* teaching; **—ствовать** *v.* teach, be a teacher.

учитыв/ание *n.* considering; etc., *see v.*; inclusion; **—ать** *v.* consider, take into consideration, take into account, take account (of), allow (for), make allowance (for); keep in mind, keep track (of), follow up; include, incorporate; take stock; discount; **не —ать** disregard, ignore, neglect; **необходимо —ать** allowance must be made (for); **—аться** *v.* be considered, etc.; **—ая** *pr. ger.* considering, etc., *see v.*; **не —ая** disregarding.

учить *v.* teach, instruct, train; learn, study; **—ся** *v.* learn, study.

учли *past pl. of* **учесть.**

учре/дитель *m.* founder, institutor, establisher; **—дить, —ждать** *v.* found, establish, set up, institute, start; **—ждение** *n.* founding, etc., *see v.*; establishment, institution; institute.

уч-ся *abbr.* (**учащийся**) student.

учтёт *fut. 3 sing. of* **учесть.**

уч-ще *abbr.* (**училище**) school.

ушан *m.* (zool.) bat (*Plecotus auritus*).

уша(с)тый *a.* (zool.) long-eared.

ушат *m.* bucket, tub, small vat.

ушедший *past act. part. of* **уйти;** gone, lost; off—.

уш/ей *gen. pl. of* **ухо; —ек** *gen. pl. of* **ушко.**

ушёл *past m. sing. of* **уйти.**

ушестер/ённый *a.* sextuple; **—ить, —ять** *v.* sextuple, increase sixfold.

уши *pl. of* **ухо.**

ушиб *m.* bruise; (med.) contusion; **—ание** *n.* bruising; **—ать, —ить** *v.* bruise, hurt, contuse.

ушив/альник, —атель *m.* lace, leather cord; **—ание** *n.* sewing up; lacing up; (med.) suturing; *suffix* —rrhaphy; **—ание селезёнки** splenorrhaphy, surgical repair of spleen; **—ать** *v.* sew up; take in; lace up.

ушир/ение *n.* widening, broadening, breadth, spread, enlargement, amplification; **у. линии** (spectral) line broadening; **—итель** *m.* broadener; extension; **—ительный** *a.* widening, enlarging; **—ить(ся), —ять(ся)** *v.* widen, enlarge, broaden, spread.

ушить *see* **ушивать.**

ушко *dim. of* **ухо;** eye (ring), eyelet, shackle, ear, lug, loop, handle; (anat., zool.) auricle; eye (of needle, etc.); tab, tag, ansa; **морское у.** (mal.) abalone (*Haliotis*); *prefix* ото—, auri— (ear); **с —м** ansa(ted); **—ватый** *a.* auriculate, eared; **—видный** *a.* ansiform; auricular (nerve, etc.); **—вый** *a. of* **ушко;** pin (joint).

ушкуй *m.* flat-bottomed boat.

ушла *past f. sing. of* **уйти.**

ушлёт *fut. 3 sing. of* **услать.**

ушли *past pl. of* **уйти.**

ушн/ик *m.* (med.) ear specialist; **—ой** *a.* ear, aural, auricular, otic; **—ая боль** earache; **—ая раковина** (anat.) concha of auricle; **—ое зеркало** (med.) otoscope.

ушьёт *fut. 3 sing. of* **ушить.**

ущел/истый *a.* full of ravines; **—ье** *n.* ravine, gorge, canyon; gulch, rift, pass; notch, gap.

ущем/ить *see* **ущемлять; —ление** *n.* pinching, strangulation, etc., *see v.*; **—лённый** *a.* pinched, etc., *see v.*; incarcerated (hernia, etc.); **—лять** *v.* pinch, strangulate, constrict, (med.) incarcerate; jam; infringe (upon).

ущерб *m.* damage, injury, harm; detriment, disadvantage; loss, decline; gibbousness (of moon); **в у.** to the detriment (of); **на —е** on the wane; **наносить у.** *see* **ущерблять; —ать** *v.* decrease, wane; **—ить** *see* **ущерблять; —лённый** *a.* harmed, etc., *see v.*; gibbous (moon); **—лять** *v.* harm, damage, injure, impair; **—ляться** *v.* decrease, wane; **—нуть** *see* **ущербать**; **—ный** *a.* waning, declining.

ущип/нуть, —ывать *v.* pinch, nip (off).

ущуп(ыв)ать *v.* probe, feel (for).

уэббовский *a.* Webb('s).

уэд *m.* (geol.) wadi.

Уэделла море (geog.) Weddell Sea.

уэджвуд *m.* (cer.) Wedgwood.

уэллсовский *a.* Wells.

Уэльс (geog.) Wales; **уэльский** *a.* Welsh.

УЭС *abbr.* (**удельное электрическое сопротивление**) electric(al) resistivity.

уютный *a.* comfortable, cozy.

уязв/имость *f.* vulnerability; **—имый** *a.* vulnerable; **—ить, —лять** *v.* hurt, wound; sting, bite; offend.

уясн/ить, —ять *v.* elucidate, explain, clear up, clarify; size up (situation); understand.

Ф

ф *abbr.* (**фарада**) farad; (**фетмо**) fetmo— (10^{-15}); (**фот**) phot; **ф, ф.** *abbr.* (**форма**) form; (**фунт**) pound; **ф.** *abbr.* (**фут**) foot; **°Ф** *abbr.* (**градусов по Фаренгейту**) degrees Fahrenheit.

фа *n.* (music) F.

фаб— *prefix see* **фабричный**.

фабзав/ком factory committee; **—уч** *m.* factory training school.

фабианол *m.* fabianol.

Фабри болезнь Fabry's disease.

фабрик/а *f.* factory, shop, mill, works, plant; **ф.-кухня** *f.* commercial kitchen; **—ант** *m.* manufacturer, maker, producer; **—аты** *pl.* manufactured goods, (finished) products; **—ация** *f.*, **—ование** *n.* manufacture, manufacturing, production, making, fabrication; **—овать** *v.* manufacture, produce, make, fabricate.

Фабри-Перо интерферометр (opt.) Fabry-Perot interferometer.

Фабрициева сумка bursa of Fabricius (in chick embryos).

фабрично-заводск/ий, —ой *a.* industrial, manufacturing, factory; industrial-training (school).

фабричн/ый *a. of* **фабрика**; industrial, manufacturing; **—ая марка** trademark, brand; **—ая цена** cost price, net cost; **—ое законодательство** labor legislation; **—ое клеймо** nameplate, label; **—ое производство** manufacturing, manufacture.

фавеола *f.* (anat.) faveola.

фавия *f.* star coral (*Favia*).

фавн *m.* (mam.) capuchin monkey (*Cebus*).

фавозный *a.* favose, honeycombed, alveolate.

Фаворского перегруппировка, Ф. реакция (chem.) Faworski rearrangement.

фаг *m.* bacteriophage; *suffix* **—фаг(е)** (eater, swallower).

фагарамид *m.* fagaramide.

фагацид *m.* fagacid (acid resin).

фагеденический *a.* (med.) phagedenic.

фагин *m.* fagine.

фаго— *prefix* phago— (eating, swallowing); **—терапия** *f.* bacteriophagic therapy; **—цит** *m.* phagocyte; **—цитарный** *a.* phagocytic; **—цитоз** *m.* phagocytosis.

ФАД *abbr.* (**флавинаденидинуклеотид**) flavine-adenine dinucleotide.

фаз/а *f.* phase, stage, step; (**находящийся**) **в —е** in phase; **жидкой —ы** liquid-phase; **не в —е** out of phase; **правило фаз** phase rule; **сдвинутый по —е** *a.* phase-shifted; out of phase; **смещение —ы** phase shift; **совпадающий по —е** *a.* in phase; **совпадение фаз** phase coincidence; **твёрдая ф.** solid phase; solids; **угол сдвига фаз** phase (displacement) angle.

фазан *m.* (orn.) pheasant; **—ёнок** *m.* pheasant chick; **—ий** *a. of* **фазан**; **—овые** *pl.* Phasianidae.

фазелин *m.* phaselin.

фазео/лин *m.* phaseolin (protein); phaseoline (alkaloid); **—лунатин** *m.* phaseolunatin; **—лунатиновая кислота** phaseolunatinic acid; **—маннит** *m.* phaseomannite, inosite.

фазии *pl.* (ent.) Phasiidae.

фазин *m.* phasin.

фазиров/ание *n.*, **—ка** phasing; **—анный** *a.* phased; **—ать** *v.* phase.

фаз/ис *see* **фаза**; **—итрон** *m.* (electron.) phasitron; **—ный** *a.* phase; (mach.) phase-wound; **с —ным ротором** slip-ring (motor).

фазо—, —во— *prefix* phase; **—воимпульсный** *a.* pulse-position, pulse-phase; **—вомодулированный** *a.* phase-modulated; **—вонеустойчивый** *a.* phase-unstable; **—вращатель** *m.* phase shifter, phase switcher, phase-shifting circuit.

фазов/ый *a.* phase; **ф. переход** phase transition; **—ая синхронизация** phase locking; **—ая скорость** phase velocity; **—ая характеристика** phase response.

фазо/выравниватель *m.* phase equalizer, phase compensator, phase modifier; **—граф** *m.* phasograph; **—двигающий** *a.* phase-displacing; **—импульсный** *see* **фазововоимпульсный**; **—инвертор** *m.* phase inverter; **—индикатор** *m.* phase indicator, phase monitor; **—компенсатор** *m.* phase compensator, phase advancer; **—метр** *m.* phase meter, phase indicator, power-factor meter; **—модулированный** *a.* phase-modulated; **—опережающий** *a.* (phase-)lead (network); **—преобразователь** *m.* phase converter.

фазораздел/итель *m.* phase separator; **—яющий** *a.* phase-separating.

фазорасщеп/итель *m.* phase splitter; **—ительный, —ляющий** *a.* phase-splitting.

фазо/регулятор *m.* phase regulator, phase shifter; **—сдвигающий, —смещающий** *a.* phase-shift(ing); **—трон** *m.* phasotron, synchrocyclotron, frequency-modulated cyclotron; **—тропия** *f.* phasotropy; **—указатель** *see* **фазометр**; **—частотный** *a.* phase-frequency; **—чувствительный** *a.* phase-sensitive, phase detecting.

фазы *gen., pl., etc. of* **фаза**; **ф. распределения** valve timing.

фай *m.* (text.) faille.

файл *m.*, **—овый** *a.* (comp.) file.

файнс *m.* fines.

файрфильдит *m.* (min.) fairfieldite.

файрфрекс *m.* Firefrax cement.

факел *m.* torch, flare; jet, tongue (of flame); (fuel) spray; (astr.) facula; **ф.-лоцман** pilot flame; **—ьный** *a. of* **факел**.

факит *m.* (ophth.) phakitis.

фако— *prefix* phac(o)— (lens); **—идальный** *a.* (petr.) phacoidal; **—лит** *m.* (geol.) phacolith; (min.) phacolite; **—литовый** *a.* phacolithic; phacolitic; **—маляция**

f. (ophth.) phacomalacia, soft cataract; —**метр** *m.* (opt.) phacometer; —**склероз** *m.* phacosclerosis, hard cataract.

факсимил/е *n.,* —**ьный** *a.* facsimile; —**ьный аппарат** fax machine.

факт *m.* fact.

фактис *m.* (rubber) factice.

фактическ/и *adv.* actually, in fact; practically, virtually, essentially; by facts; —**ий** *a.* actual, real, true, factual, based on facts; practical; —**ий материал,** —**ая сторона,** —**ие данные** the facts; —**ие смоли** existent gum (gasoline).

фактор *m.* factor, coefficient, agent; (pacing) item; —**ы** *pl.* factors, elements; —**иал** *m.* (math.) factorial; —**иальный** *a.* factor(ial).

фактория *f.* trading post.

факторный *a. of* **фактор.**

фактор-пространство *n.* (math.) factor space, coset space.

фактур/а *f.,* —**ный** *a.* (com.) invoice, bill; surface finish, texture; composition.

факультативный *a.* facultative, optional, elective (subject).

факультет *m.* faculty; (university) department, school.

факция *f.* faction.

фал *m.* (naut.) halyard, puller.

фал. *abbr.* **(фениланин)** phenylalanine.

фаланг/а *f.* (anat.) phalanx; (zool.) solpugid, sun spider; (anat.) —**еальный** *a.* phalangeal.

фалангер *m.* (mam.) phalanger.

фаланго/вый *a.* phalangeal; —**ходящие** *pl.* unguligrade animals.

фаланук *m.* small-toothed mongoose (*Eupleres*).

фалда *f.* tail, skirt, flap.

фалерц *see* **фальерц.**

фалинь *m.* (naut.) painter (rope).

Фалло *f.* (med.) Fallot.

фалло— (anat.) phallo— (penis).

фаллопиевы трубы (anat.) Fallopian tubes.

фаллопластика *f.* (med.) phalloplasty.

фалреп *m.* (naut.) manrope, side rope.

фалунит *m.* (min.) fahlunite.

фаль/банд *m.* (petr.) fahlband; —**ерц** *m.* (min.) fahlerz, fahlore, tetrahedrite, gray copper ore.

фальсифи/кация *f.,* —**цирование** *n.* adulteration; forgery, counterfeiting; —**цированный** *a.* adulterated; —**цировать** *v.* falsify, adulterate; counterfeit, forge; —**цирующий** *a.* adulterating; —**цирующее вещество** adulterant.

фальц *m.* rabbet, groove, furrow, channel; fold; seam (of can); —**аппарат,** —**бейн** *m.* folder; —**гебель,** —**гобель,** —**губель** *m.* rabbet plane, fillister; —**евальный** *a.,* —**евание** *n.* rabbeting, etc., *see v.;* —**евание гармошкой** fanfolding; —**евать** *v.* rabbet, groove, chamfer, channel; fold, crease; horn; seam; —**машина** *f.* folder; —**ованный** *a.* fanfold(ed); —**овка** *see* **фальцевание;** rabbet plane, fillister; —**овочный** *a.* rabbeting, etc., *see v.;* seam-closing; bumping (hammer).

фальчик *m.* (bookbinding) hinge.

фальшборт *m.* bulwark.

фальшив/ка *f.* forged document; —**омонетчество** *n.* counterfeiting; —**ость** *f.* falseness; —**ый** *a.* spurious, false, counterfeit (money); pseudo—; jury(-rigged), temporary.

фальшкиль *m.* (naut.) false keel.

фальшфейер *m.* false fire, blue light.

фаля *f.* spring lock.

фаматинит *m.* (min.) famatinite.

фаменский *a.* (geol.) Famennian (stage).

фамилия *f.* family name, surname.

фамильярн/ость *f.* familiarity; —**ый** *a.* familiar, unceremonious.

фаналока *f.* (mam.) Malagasy civet (*Fossa fossa*).

фаналь *m.* fanal (color).

фанат/ик *m.,* —**ический** *a.* fanatic.

фанг *m.* double-rib knit fabric.

фангломерат *m.* (petr.) fanglomerate.

фанер *m.* mouse lemur (*Phaner*).

фанер/а *f.* veneer, plywood; —**ит** *m.* veneer; plywood; (min.) phanerite; —**ка** *f.* sheet of plywood; —**ный** *a.* veneer; plywood; —**ный лист** plywood (sheet); —**ное дерево** plywood; —**о—** *prefix* phanero—, visible; veneer, plywood; —**ование** *n.* veneering; —**ованный** *a.* veneer(ed); —**овать** *v.* veneer; —**овка** *f.* veneering; —**овщик** *m.* veneer applier.

фанерофит *m.* (bot.) phanerophyte.

фанза *f.* (text.) foulard.

фановый *a.* drain, sewage, soil (pipe); sewage-disposal (system).

фанодорм *m.* Phanodorm, cyclobarbital.

фанта/зёп *m.,* —**зёрка** *f.* visionary, dreamer; —**зия** *f.* fantasy, fancy, imagination; —**стика** *f.* fantasy; (science) fiction; —**стический,** —**стичный** *a.* fantastic, imaginary.

фантастрон *m.* (electron.) phantastron.

фантом *m.* (radiology) phantom; model (of body); —**ный** *a.* phantom.

фаопланктон *m.* surface plankton, phaoplankton.

ФАПЧ *abbr.* **(фазовая автоматическая подстройка частоты)** (elec.) phase-lock control, phase-lock(ed) loop, PLL.

фара *f.* headlight; (landing) light.

Фарабефа треугольник (anat.) Farabeuf's triangle.

фарад/а *f.* (elec.) farad (unit of capacitance); —**еевский** *a.* Faraday; —**ей** *m.* faraday (electrochemical constant).

Фарадея явление Faraday effect; **Ф. число** *see* **фарадей.**

фарадизация *f.* (med.) faradization.

фарадиол *m.* faradiol.

фарад/ический *a.* faradic; —**метр** *m.* (elec.) faradmeter.

фараонова змея Pharaoh's serpent (stick of mercuric thiocyanate); **ф. мышь** (zool.) ichneumon.

фара-прожектор *f.* searchlight, spotlight.

фаратсигит *m.* (min.) faratsihite.

фарблак *m.* (color) lake.

фарватер *m.,* —**ный** *a.* fairway, waterway, (navigable) channel.

фаренгейт *m.* Fahrenheit thermometer; **градус Фаренгейта** degree Fahrenheit.

Фарерские острова (geog.) Faroe Islands.

фаринг—, —**о—** *prefix* (anat.) pharyng(o)— (pharynx); —**еальный** *a.* (anat.) pharyngeal; —**ит** *m.* (med.) pharyngitis; —**оскоп** *m.* pharyngoscope.

фарино/за *f.* farinose; —**том** *m.* (grain analysis) farinotome.

фармако— *prefix* pharmaco— (drug, medicine; poison); —**гнозия** *f.* pharmacognosy; —**лог** *m.* pharmacologist; —**логический** *a.* pharmacological; —**логия** *f.* pharmacology; —**пея** *f.* pharmacopoeia; —**химия** pharmaceutical chemistry.

фармацевт *m.* pharmacist, druggist; —**ика** *f.* pharmaceutics; —**ический** *a.* pharmaceutical; —**ические товары** pharmaceuticals, drugs.

фармация *f.* pharmaceutics; pharmacy.

фарнез/ал *m.* farnesal; **—ин** *m.* farnesene; **—еновая кислота** farnesenic acid; **—ол** *m.* farnesol.

фарту/к *m.*, **—чный** *a.* apron; hood, cover, housing; deflector, flap.

фарфор *m.* porcelain, china; **—овидный** *a.* porcelain-like, porcelaneous.

фарфоров/ый *a. of* **фарфор**; **—ая глина** china clay; **—ая посуда**, **—ые изделия** china, porcelain ware; **—ая яшма** (min.) porcelain jasper, porcellanite.

фарфорообжигательная печь porcelain kiln.

фарш *m.* stuffing; sausage meat; **—ированный** *a.* stuffed; **—ировать** *v.* stuff.

фары *pl. of* **фара.**

фас *m.* face, front, facade; (geol.) scarp, escarpment (of fault).

фасад *m.*, **—ный** *a.* facade, face, front; elevation, view; **боковой ф.** side view, profile; **передний ф.** front(al) view.

фас/ет *m.*, **—етка** *f.* facet; face; bevel edge; **—етный** *a.* facet; multi-aspect, multidimensional (classification); beveled (mirror); **—еточный** *a.* facet; (ent.) faceted, compound (eye); **—етчатый** *a.* facet(ed); **—ка** *f.* facet; bevel (edge), edge chamfer(ing); **с —кой** beveled (glass); **снимать —ку** *v.* chamfer.

фасок *gen. pl. of* **фаска.**

фасол/евый *a.*, **—ь** *f.* bean; **почкообразная —ь, обыкновенная —ь** kidney bean(s).

фасон *m.* style, fashion; **—ирование** *n.* shaping, etc., *see v.*; **—ировать** *v.* shape, form, fashion; **—но-токарный станок** shaping lathe, forming lathe.

фасонн/ый *a.* fashioned, shaped, molded; shape, form, profile, contour; irregular, irregularly shaped; section(-shaped); grooved (roll); **ф. калибр** (rolling) section groove; **ф. профиль** (met.) channel section, shaped section; **ф. резец** forming tool, form cutter; shaping tool; **ф. фрезер** profile cutter; **ф. шаблон** curve gage; **—ая гладилка** trowel; **—ая наковальня** die block; **—ая обработка** profiling; **—ая плита** die plate; **—ая сварка** shape welding; **—ая фрезеровка** form milling; **—ая штамповка** molding; **—ое железо** profile iron, structural iron, section steel, shaped steel; **—ое литьё** shaped casting(s); **—ые части** fittings (for pipes, etc.).

фасци/альный *a.* (anat.) fascial; **—ация** *f.* (bot.) fasciation; **—и** *pl.* fasciae; **—ит** *m.* (med.) fasciitis; **—кул** *m.* (anat.) fasciculus; **—ола** *f.* (zool.) fasciola, (liver) fluke; (zool.) fasciola, narrow band; **—олёз** *m.* (vet.) fascioliasis; **—олопсис** *m.* (zool.) a trematode worm (*Fasciolopsis*); **—я** *f.* (anat.) fascia.

фатальн/ость *f.* fatality; **—ый** *a.* fatal; unfortunate, unlucky.

Фатеров сосочек (anat.) Vater's papilla, major duodenal papilla.

фау-1 (mil.) V-1 (German robot bomb); **ф.-2** V-2 (German rocket).

Фаулера раствор Fowler solution (of potassium arsenite); **Ф. ряд** Fowler's series (of helium spectrum lines).

фаун/а *f.* (zool.) fauna; **—истика** *f.* zoological geography; **—овый** *a.* faunal.

фаустпатрон *m.* (mil.) panzerfaust.

фаут *m.* (timber) defect, fault, flaw, rot; **—ный** *a.* defective, faulty, rotten, decayed.

фахаки *pl.* (ichth.) porcupinefishes (*Diodontidae*); puffers (*Tetradontidae*).

фахверк *m.*, **—овое сооружение** framework; **—овый** *a.* framework; frame (building).

фацелия *f.* (bot.) Phacelia.

фацет *see* **фасет.**

фаци/альный *a.* phase; (biol.; geol.) facies, environmental; facial (zonality); **—ация** *f.* (bot.) faciation; **—я** *f.* facies, phase, environment.

фашин/а *f.* fascine, fagot; **—изация** *f.*, **—ная работа** reinforcement with fascines; **—ник** *m.* brushwood, fagot wood; **—ный** *a. of* **фашина.**

фаэтон *m.* (orn.) tropicbird (*Phaëthon*).

фая *gen. of* **фай.**

фаянс *m.*, **—овый** *a.*, **—овая посуда** (cer.) faience, glazed pottery.

Фаянс-Содди правило (nucl.) Fajans-Soddi law.

ФВЧ *abbr.* (**фильтр верхних частот**) highpass filter.

ф. гр. *abbr.* (**фёдоровская группа симметрии**) Fedorov symmetry group.

ФДМ *abbr.* (**фенилдиметилмочевина**) phenyldimethylurea.

феба *f.* (astr.) Phoebe.

фебри/литет *m.* (med.) febris, fever; **—льный** *a.* febrile, feverish; **—фугальный** *a.* febrifugal, antipyretic; **—фугин** *m.* febrifugine (alkaloid).

февраль *m.*, **—ский** *a.* February.

фед *m.* Fed (Soviet miniature camera).

федер/альный *a.* federal; **—ация** *f.* federation, league; **—ион** *m.* (bot.) federion.

фединг *m.* fading, fade-out.

федометр *m.* (dyes) Fademeter.

фёдоровский *a.* Fedorov.

Фезера анализ (nucl.) Feather analysis.

Фейльгена реакция *see* **Фёльгена реакция.**

фейервер/к *m.*, **—очный** *a.* fireworks.

фейеровский *a.* (math.) Fejer.

фейнмановский *a.* (phys.) Feynman.

фейринг *m.* (av.) fairing.

фейфка *f.* tube, pipe.

фейхоа *f.* (bot.) feijoa (*Feijoa sellowiana*).

фекал/ии *pl.* feces, excrements; **—ин** *m.* chlorinated fecal dust used as fertilizer; **—ьный** *a.* fecal; **—ьный тук** *see* **фекалин**; **—ьная масса** feces, excrements.

фекулометр *m.* (starch) feculometer.

фелингов раствор, ф. реактив, —а жидкость (sugar) Fehling solution.

фелин/овый *a.* feline, cat('s); **—оз** *m.* (med.) cat-scratch fever.

фелландрен *m.* phellandrene, 1(7),2-*p*-menthadiene.

фелллановая кислота fellanic acid.

феллема *f.* (bot.) phellem, cork.

фелло— *prefix* phello— (cork); **—ген** *m.* (bot.) phellogen, cork cambium; **—геновая кислота** phellogenic acid; **—дерма** *f.* (bot.) phelloderm; **—идный** *a.* phelloid; **—новая кислота** phellonic acid; **—пластика** *f.* phelloplastics.

Фёльгена реакция (biochem.) Feulgen reaction, Feulgen's test.

фельдшер *m.*, **—ский** *a.* doctor's assistant, surgeon's assistant, paramedic.

фельдшпат *m.* (min.) feldspar; **—изироваться** *v.* feldspathize; **—овый** *a.* feldspar, feldspathic.

фельдъегер/ский *a.*, **—ь** *m.* (mil.) courier, dispatch rider; state messenger.

фельзит *m.* (petr.) felsite; **—овый** *a.* felsite, felsitic.

фелю/га *f.*, **—жный** *a.* (naut.) felucca.

феминиз/ация *f.* (med.) feminization; **—ированный** *a.*

feminized; **—ировать** *v.* feminize, make effeminate; give a feminine form (to); **—ироваться** *v.* take on female characteristics.

фемический *a.* (petr.) femic.

феморальный *a.* (anat.) femoral.

фемто— *prefix* femto— (10^{-15}).

фен *m.* phene, benzene ring; fan; hair dryer.

фён *m.* foehn (wind).

фен— *prefix* phen—.

фенадон *m.* Fenadone, methadone hydrochloride.

феназ/арсиновая кислота phenazarsinic acid; **—ин** *m.* phenazine, dibenzoparadiazine; **—инфуран** *m.* phenazinfuran; **—он** *m.* phenazone; **—оний** *m.* phenazonium.

фенакаин *m.* phenacaine, Holocaine.

фенамин *m.* phenamine (amphetamine).

фенантр/ахинон *m.* phenanthraquinone, phenanthrenequinone; **—ен** *m.* phenanthrene; **—енон** *m.* phenanthr(en)one; **—иазин** *m.* phenanthriazine, **—идин** *m.* phenanthridine, **—идон** *m.* phenanthridone; **—ил** *m.* phenanthryl; **—оксазин** *m.* phenanthroxazine; **—ол** *m.* phenanthrol, hydroxyphenanthrene; **—олин** *m.* phenanthroline; **—он** *m.* phenanthrone.

фенарсазин *m.* phenarsazine.

фенат *m.* phenate.

фенацет/ин *m.* phenacetin, acetophenetide; **—ол** *m.* phenacetol, phenoxyacetone; **—уровая кислота** phenaceturic acid.

фенацил *m.* phenacyl; **—иден** *m.* phenacylidene; **—идин** *m.* phenacylidin; **—овый** *a.* phenacyl.

фенгомазин *m.* phenhomazine.

фенек *m.* (mam.) fennec (*Fennecus zerda*).

фенестрация *f.* (med.) fenestration.

фенет/идин *m.* phenetidine, ethoxyaniline; **—ил** *m.* phenetyl, ethoxyphenyl; **—ол** *m.* phenetole, ethoxybenzene.

фенигрековое семя fenugreek seed.

фенил *m.* phenyl; **—аланин** *m.* phenylalanine; **—амин** *m.* phenylamine, aniline; **—арсенокислота** *f.*, **—арсоновая кислота** phenylarsonic acid; **—ат** *m.* phenylate; **—ацетилен** *m.* phenylacetylene; **—гидразин** *m.* phenylhydrazine; **—ен** *m.* phenylene; **—ендиамин** *m.* phenylenediamine; **—еновый** *a.* phenylene; **—иден** *m.* phenylidene; **—изотиоцианат** *m.* phenyl isothiocyanate; **—ин** *m.* phenindione, 2-phenyl-1,3-indandione.

фенилир/ование *n.* phenylation; **—ованный** *a.* phenylated; **—овать** *v.* phenylate; **—ующий** *a.* phenylating.

фенил/карбинол *m.* phenylcarbinol, benzyl alcohol; **—кетонурия** *f.* (med.) phenylketonuria; **—масляный** *a.* phenylbutyric (acid); **—мочевина** *f.* phenylurea.

фениловый *a.* phenyl(ic); **ф. спирт** phenylic alcohol, phenol; **ф. эфир** phenyl ether, phenoxybenzene; **ф. эфир уксусной кислоты** phenyl acetate.

фенил/он *m.* Phenylone, antipyrine; **—тиомочевина** *f.* phenylthiourea, phenylthiocarbamide, PTC; **—трихлорсилан** *m.* phenyltrichlorosilane; **—уксусная кислота** phenylacetic acid; **—фосфиновая кислота** phenylphosphinic acid; **—фосфористая кислота** phenylphosphorous acid, phosphenylic acid; **—хинолин** *m.* phenylquinoline; **—ьный** *see* **фениловый**; **—этан** *m.* phenylethane, phenylic acid; **—этанол** *m.*, **—этиловый спирт** phenylethanol, phenylethyl alcohol.

фенин *m.* phenin, phenacetin.

фенит *m.* (petr.) fenite; **—изация** *f.* fenitization.

фениц/ин *m.* phoenicin; **—ит** *m.* (min.) phoenicinite, phoenicochroite.

фен/метил *m.* phenmethyl; **—о—** *prefix* (chem.) phen(o)— (phenyl, benzene); pheno— (showing).

фёновый *a.* (meteor.) foehn; phenic (acid).

феногенетика *f.* phenogenetics, developmental genetics.

феноза *f.* (chem.) phenose.

фенокарта *f.* (ecol.) phenological map.

фенокол(л) *m.* (chem.) phenocoll.

фенокопия *f.* (gen.) phenocopy.

фенокрист/(алл) *m.* (petr.) phenocryst, porphyritic crystal; **—аллический** *a.* phenocrystalline, phanerocrystalline.

феноксазин *m.* phenoxazine.

фенокси— *prefix* phenoxy—; **—бензол** *m.* phenoxybenzene, phenyl ether; **—уксусный** *a.* phenoxyacetic (acid).

фенол *m.* phenol, carbolic acid; **—аза** *f.* phenolase; **—оальдегид** *m.*, **—оальдегидный** *a.* phenol-aldehyde; **—овый** *a.* phenol(ic); **—овый красный** phenol red, phenolsulfonphthalein.

фенолог/ический *a.* (biol.) phenological; **—ия** *f.* phenology.

феноло/кетон *m.* phenol(ic) ketone; **—кислота** *f.* phenol(ic) acid; **—спирт** *m.* phenolic alcohol; **—сульфокислота** *f.* phenolsulfonic acid; **—формальдегидный** *a.* phenol-formaldehyde (resins).

фенол/рот *m.* phenol red (indicator); **—серный** *a.* phenolsulfuric (acid); **—сульфоновая кислота** phenolsulfonic acid; **соль —сульфоновой кислоты** phenolsulfonate.

фенолсульфоново/алюминиевая соль aluminum phenolsulfonate; **—кальциевая соль**, **—кислый кальций** calcium phenolsulfonate; **—кислый** *a.* phenolsulfonic acid; phenolsulfonate (of); **—кислая соль** phenolsulfonate, sulfophenylate.

фенолсульфонфталеин *m.* phenolsulfonphthalein, phenol red (indicator).

фенолурия *f.* (med.) phenoluria.

фенол/формальдегидный *a.* phenol-formaldehyde (resins); **—фталеин** *m.* phenolphthalein; **—фталид** *m.* phenolphthalide; **—хинин** *m.* phenolquinine; **—ьный** *a.* phenol(ic); **—ят** *m.* phen(ol)ate.

феном *m.* (ecol.) phenom(e).

феномен *m.* phenomenon; **—альный** *a.* phenomenal; **—ологический** *a.* phenomenological; **—ология** *f.* phenomenology.

фено/н *m.* phenone; **—нафтазин** *m.* phenonaphthazine, benzophenazine; **—пирин** *m.* phenopyrine, antipyrine phenate; **—пласт** *m.* phenoplast (phenol-formaldehyde plastic); **—прен** *m.* phenoprene, 2-phenylbutadiene-1,4; **—салил** *m.* phenosalyl; **—сафранин** *m.* phenosafranine; **—стал** *m.* phenostal, diphenyl oxalate; **—стеклослой** *m.* fiber glass impregnated with phenol-formaldehyde resin; **—тиазин** *m.* phenothiazine, thiodiphenylamine; **—тип** *m.* (biol.) phenotype; **—фаза** *f.* (biol.) phenological phase; **—хинон** *m.* phenoquinone.

фентазин *see* **фенотиазин**.

фентоламин *m.* (pharm.) phentolamine.

фенх/ан *m.* fenchane; **—анол** *see* **фенхол**; **—анон** *see* **фенхон**; **—елевый** *a.*, **—ель** *m.* fennel; **—ен** *m.* fenchene; **—еновый** *a.* fenchenic (acid); **—ил** *m.*, **—иловый** *a.* fenchyl; **—оксим** *m.* fenchoxime; **—ол** *m.* fenchol, fenchyl alcohol; **—оловый** *a.* fencholic (acid); **—он** *m.* fenchone.

фенэтил *m.*, **—овый** *a.* phenethyl; **—амин** *m.* phenethylamine; **—ен** *m.* phenethylene, styrene.

фео— *prefix* ph(a)eo— (dun-colored; dark); **—пласт** *m.*

(bot., gen.) phaeoplast; **—фитин** *m.* (chem.) pheophytin; **—форбид** *m.* (chem.) pheophorbid; **—хром** *m.* pheochrome.

фераза *f.* (biochem.) transferase.

Фервея эффект Verwey effect (in semiconductors).

ферганский *a.* (geog.) Fergana.

Фери калориметр Féry calorimeter.

феринка *f.* (ichth.) Atherina.

ферма *f.* (agr.) farm; (constr.) truss, girder; framework; support.

Ферма принцип Fermat's principle.

фермат *m.* fermate (fungicide).

ферменный *a.* of **ферма** (constr.).

фермент *m.* enzyme, ferment; **—ативный** *a.* fermentative, fermentation, zymotic; enzym(at)ic; **—атор** *m.* fermenter; **—ационный** *a.*, **—ация** *f.* fermentation; **—ёр** *m.* fermenter; **—ировать** *v.* ferment; **—ный** *a.* of **фермент**; **—ология** *f.* enzymology; **ф.-переносчик** *m.* transfer(ring) enzyme, transferase.

фермер *m.* farmer; **—ский** *a.* farm, farmer's; **—ское хозяйство** farm; **—ство** *n.* farming.

ферми *m.* fermi (unit of length).

Ферми график (nucl.) Fermi plot; **возраст по Ф.** Fermi age.

ферми/-газ *m.* Fermi gas; **—евский** *a.* Fermi; **—й** *m.* fermium, Fm; **—он** *m.* (nucl.) fermion; **ф.-частица** fermi particle.

фермовый *see* **ферменный.**

фермуар *m.* clasp, catch, snap; chisel.

фернамбук *m.*, **—овый** *a.* brazilwood.

феромон *m.* (zool.) pheromone.

ферон *m.* pheron (colloidal carrier).

феррат *m.* ferrate.

ферредоксин *m.* ferredoxin.

ферри/магнетизм *m.* ferrimagnetism; **—стор** *m.* (electron.) ferristor.

феррит *m.* ferrite; **—диодный** *a.* ferrite diode (cell); **—ин** *m.* (biochem.) ferritin; **—иновый** *a.* ferritin-bound (iron); **—ный** *a.*, **—овый** *a.* ferrite, ferritic.

феррицианид *m.* ferricyanide.

ферро— *prefix* ferro—, iron; **—алюминий** *m.*(met.) ferroaluminum; **—бор** *m.* (met.) ferroboron; **—ванадий** *m.* (met.) ferrovanadium; **—вольфрам** *m.* (met.) ferrotungsten, tungsten steel; **—динамический** *a.* ferrodynamic; **—кальцит** *m.* (min.) ferrocalcite; **—кобальт** *m.* (met.) ferrocobalt; **—кремний** *m.* ferrosilicon.

ферроксильный *a.* (chem.) ferroxyl (indicator).

ферромагн/етизм *m.* ferromagnetism; **—етик** *m.* ferromagnetic (substance); **—итный** *a.* ferromagnetic; **—итография** *f.* ferromagnetic printing.

ферромагнон *m.* (phys.) ferromagnon, ferromagnetic spin wave.

ферроманган *m.* (met.) ferromanganese.

ферро/марганец *m.* (met.) ferromanganese; **—метр** *m.* ferrometer; **—молибден** *m.* (met.) ferromolybdenum; **—никель** *m.* (met.) ferronickel; **—ниобий** *m.* ferroniobium; **—платина** *f.* (met.) ferroplatinum.

феррорезонанс *m.* ferroresonance; **—ный** *a.* ferroresonant.

ферро/сплав *m.*, **—сплавный** *a.* ferroalloy; **—статический** *a.* ferrostatic; **—типия** *f.* (phot.) ferrotype; **—хелатаза** *f.* (enz.) ferrochelatase, heme synthetase; **—хром** *m.* (met.) ferrochromium; **—цен** *m.* ferrocene, dicyclopentadienyliron; **—цианид** *m.* ferrocyanide; **—электрический** *a.* ferroelectric.

фертилизин *m.* (biochem.) fertilizin.

фертиль/ность *f.* fertility; birth rate; **—ный** *a.* fertile.

ферто/ень, **—инг** *m.* (naut.) mooring (swivel).

ферул/а *f.* (bot.) Ferula; **ф.-альдегид** *m.* (chem.) ferulaldehyde; **—ен** *m.* ferulene; **—овая кислота** ferulic acid.

фестон *m.* festoon; (bot.) scallop; **—ный**, **—чатый** *a.* scalloped.

фетальный *a.* fetal.

Фетера формула Feather's formula.

фето— *prefix* (embr.) feto— (fetus); **—метрия** *f.* fetometry.

фетр *m.*, **—овый** *a.* felt.

ф.-з. *abbr.* (**фабрично-заводской**) factory.

фи phi (Greek letter).

фиалида *f.* (bot.) phialide, sterigma.

фиалк/а *f.*, **—овый** *a.* violet; **трёхцветная ф.** pansy; **—овый корень** orris root.

фиаско *n.* fiasco, failure.

Фиата печь Fiat furnace.

Фибоначчи (math.) Fibonacci.

фибра *f.* fiber; **—тор** *m.* fibrator.

фибрилл/а *f.* fibril, small fiber; **—ировать** *v.* fibrillate; **—овый** *a.* fibrillar, fibrillate; **—ярный** *a.* fibrillar; fibrous (protein); **—яция** *f.* (med.) fibrillation.

фибрин *m.* fibrin; **—овый** *a.* fibrinous; **—оген** *m.* fibrinogen; **—озный** *a.* fibrinogenous, fibrinous; **—олиз** *m.* fibrinolysis; **—олизин** *m.* fibrinolysin.

фибрин-фермент *m.* (enz.) thrombin.

фибробласт *m.* (zool.) fibroblast, lamellar cell; **—ический** *a.* fibroblastic.

фибро/вый *a.* fiber, fibrous; **—з** *m.* (med.) fibrosis, fibrous degeneration; **—зный** *a.* fibrous; scirrhous (carcinoma); **—зное растяжение** (anat.) aponeurosis; **—ин** *m.* fibroin; **—лизин** *m.* fibrolysin; **—лит** *m.*, **—литовый** *a.* (min.) fibrolite; (constr.) fiberboard; **—ма** *f.* (med.) fibroma, fibrous tumor; **—нектин** *m.* (biochem.) fibronectin; **—пластин** *m.* fibroplastin, paraglobulin.

фибулярный *a.* (anat.) fibular.

фиг. *abbr.* (**фигура**) figure, illustration.

фиг/а *f.*, **—овый** *a.* fig.

фигляр *m.* (orn.) bateleur (*Terathopius ecaudatus*).

фигур/а *f.* figure, illustration, diagram; shape, form; pattern; (etch) pit; (av.) maneuver; **—ально** *adv.* figuratively; **—альный** *a.*, **—ативный** *a.* figurative, symbolic; **—ировать** *v.* figure, act (as), play the part (of); appear, occur, be mentioned; **—ка** *dim. of* **фигура.**

фигурн/ый *a.* figure(d); fancy (pattern); irregularly shaped, (complex-)shaped; **ф. контур** irregular outline; **ф. резец** form tool, forming cutter; **—ые скобки** braces.

фидер *m.*, **—ный** *a.* feeder.

Фиджи (geog.) Fiji.

фидуциальный *a.* fiducial.

физ. *abbr.*, **физ—** *prefix* (**физический**).

физал/ин *m.* physalin; **—ис** *m.* (bot.) ground cherry (*Physalis*).

физетеровая кислота physeteric acid, 5,6-tetradecenoic acid.

физетин *m.* fisetin, tetrahydroxyflavone.

физетоленновая кислота physetoleic acid, hypogaeic acid.

физиатрия *f.* (med.) physiatrics; physical therapy.

физик *m.* physicist; **—а** *f.* physics; **—а твёрдого тела** solid-state physics; **—а ядра** nuclear physics; **ф.-атомник** *m.* nuclear physicist.

физико— *prefix* physics—, physical; **ф.-математический** *a.* physicomathematical; **ф.-технический** *a.*

physicotechnical; **ф.-технологический** *a.* physico-technological; **ф.-химический** *a.* physicochemical, physical chemistry.

физик-теоретик *m.* theoretical physicist; **ф.-химик** *m.* physical chemist.

физио— *prefix* physi(o)— (physical; physiological; natural); **—гномия** *f.* physiognomy; face; **—графический** *a.* physiographic; **—графия** *f.* physiography, physical geography.

физиолог *m.* physiologist; **—ический** *a.* physiological; **—ия** *f.* physiology.

физио/пластика *f.* plastic surgery; **—терапевт** *m.* physical therapist; **—терапевтический** *a.*, **—терапия** *f.* physical therapy.

физит *m.* physite, erythrol.

физическ/ий *a.* physical; manual (labor); physics; compound (pendulum); **—ая моделирующая величина** analog quantity; **—ая нагрузка** (med.) exercise; **—ие свойства** physical properties; **—ие элементы** (comp.) components.

физкульт— *prefix,* **—ура** *f.* physical culture, athletics, sports.

физмат *m.* (educ.) department of physics and mathematics.

физо/д(ал)овый *a.* physod(al)ic (acid); **—стигмин** *m.* physostigmine, eserine.

Фика диффузия Fickian diffusion; **Ф. закон** (nucl.) Fick's law.

фико— *prefix* (bot.) phyco— (seaweed, algae); fico—; **—ксантин** *m.* phycoxanthin; **—логия** *f.* phycology, study of algae; **—микоз** *m.* (med.) phycomycosis; **—мицеты** *pl.* (bot.) Phycomycetes; **—феин** *m.* phycophaein; **—хром** *m.* phycochrome; **—церитрин** *m.* phycocerythrin; **—циан** *m.* phycocyanin; **—эритрин** *m.* phycoerythrin.

фикс *m.* fixed price; point; **—аж** *m.* fixing, fixation; fixer, fixative, fixing bath; **—ажный** *a. of* **фиксаж**; stopping, transition (point).

фиксанал *m.* (chem.) primary standard.

фикс/атив *m.* fixative, fixing agent; **—атор** *m.* catch, lock, stop, detent, latch, clamp; locator, guide, index (pin); pull-off, push-off; (chem.) fixative (nitrogen) fixer; **—аторный орган** (biol.) appressor(ium), hold-fast; **—атуар** *m.* pomade; **—ация** *see* **фиксирование**; pull-off, push-off; *suffix* (med.) **—рexy**; **—ация печени** hepatopexy.

фиксир/ование *n.* fixation, fixing, etc., *see v.*; (comp.) holding (beam action); **—ованный** *a.* fixed, etc., *see v.*; (comp.) nonremovable (disk); **—овать** *v.* fix; stop, lock, clamp; secure, make fast, freeze in; hold; anchor; stabilize; immobilize (nuclear waste); locate, position; record, register, note (reading); **—ующий** *a.* fixing, etc., *see v.*; (comp.) holding (beam); **—ующий реагент** *see* **фиксатив**; **—ующая деталь** retainer; **—ующие отверстия** indexing holes (in a printed circuit board).

фикс-пункт *m.* fixed point.

фиктивн/ость *f.* fictitiousness; **—ый** *a.* fictitious, false, imitation, dummy; theoretical, hypothetical; (comp.) null; **—ая операция** (robotics) do-nothing operation.

фикус *m.*, **—ный** *a.* (bot.) fig (*Ficus*).

фикция *f.* fiction.

Филадельфия Philadelphia.

филамент *m.* filament, fiber, thread.

филандер *m.* (mam.) four-eyed opossum (*Philander opossum*).

филант *m.* a sphecid wasp (*Philanthus triangulum*).

филар/иоз *m.* (med.) filariasis; **—иомикоз** *m.* (vet.)

filariomycosis (of fishes); **—ия** *f.* filaria (parasitic nematode).

филата *f.* (min.) cross board (of support).

Филатова(-Пфейфера) болезнь (med.) infectious mononucleosis.

филе *n.*, **—йный** *a.* filet.

филён/ка *f.* panel(ing); slat, dividing strip; **обшивать —кой** *v.* panel; **—очный, —чатый** *a.* panel(led), panel-type; strip(e).

филетический *a.* (biol.) phyletic.

фили *pl. of* **филум**, (biol.) phyla.

филиал *m.* branch (office), affiliated branch, affiliated society; **ф. завода** branch works; **—ьный** *a.* branch, affiliated; **—ьное отделение** branch.

филиация *f.* (biol.) filiation, relationship.

филигран *m.*, **—ный, —овый** *a.* filigree (work); **—ь** *f.* filigree; watermark, watermarked paper.

филиколистная ива tealeaf willow (*Salix phylicifolia*).

филиксовая кислота filixic acid.

филин *m.* eagle owl (*Bubo bubo*).

филиппинский *a.* (geog.) Philippine.

филицин *m.* filicin, filicic acid anhydride; **—овая кислота** filicinic acid.

филлантин *m.* phyllanthin.

филлер *m.* filler, filling material.

филлигенин *m.* phillygenin.

филлин *m.* phyllin.

филлирин *m.* phyllyrin.

филло— *prefix* phyllo— (leaf); **—гемин** *m.* phyllohemin; **—генетический** *a.* phyllogenetic, leaf-producing; **—диевый** *a.* phyllodineous; **—дий** *m.* (bot.) phyllode; **—кладий** *m.* (bot.) phylloclade; **—ксера** *f.* (ent.) phylloxera; **—пиррол** *m.* phyllopyrrole; **—порфирин** *m.* phylloporphyrin; **—спондиловый** *a.* (zool.) phyllospondylous (vertebrae); **—стахис** *m.* (bot.) Phyllostachys; **—стиктоз** *m.* (phyt.) Phyllosticta disease; **—хинон** *m.* phylloquinone, vitamin K_1; **—эритрин** *m.* phylloerythrin.

филлярии *pl.* (bot.) phyllaries.

фило— *prefix* phyl(o)— (phylum; tribe; race; having an affinity for); **—генез** *m.*, **—гения** *f.* (biol.) phylogenesis, phylogeny, race history; **—генетический** *a.* phylogenetic.

филодендрон *m.* (bot.) philodendron.

филоподия *f.* filopodium (of protozoa).

философ *m.* philosopher; **—ический** *a.* philosophic; **—ия** *f.* philosophy.

филум *m.* (biol.) phylum.

фильд— *see under* **филд—**.

фильде/кос *m.* (text.) lisle thread; **—косовый** *a.* lisle; **—перс** *m.*, **—персовый** *a.* high-grade lisle.

фильера *f.* draw plate; die; (text.) spinneret.

фильм *m.*, **—а** *f.* film.

фильмарон *m.* Filmaron, aspidinofilicin.

фильм/о— *prefix,* **—овый** *a.* film; **—отека** *f.* film library; **—офон** *m.* sound recorder; **—пак** *m.* (phot.) film pack.

фильтр *m.* filter, strainer; **тело —а** filter bed; **—ат** *m.* filtrate; **—ационный** *a.*, **—ация** *f.* filtration, filtering; percolation; transmission, permeability; filter loss, leak(age), seepage; flow (of a fluid through porous medium); **ф.-воронка** *f.* settling cone; **ф.-ловушка** *f.* absorption trap.

фильтров/альный *a.* filtering, etc., *see v.*; filter (paper, etc.); **ф. слой** filter bed; **—альная набивка** filter pad; **—альная сетка** filter gauze; **—ание** *n.* filtration, filtering, solids removal; **—анный** *a.* filtered, etc., *see v.*; **—ать** *v.* filter, strain; percolate; **—ка**

see **фильтрация;** —**очный** *see* **фильтровальный;** —**ый** *a.* of **фильтр.**

фильтр/одержатель *m.* filter ring, filter support; —**осный** *a.* air-diffusion, aerating, aeration; **-отстойник** *m.* gravitation filter; **-поглотитель** *m.* filter-absorber; —**пресс** *m.* filter press; —**пробка** *f.* suppression filter; —**уемость** *f.* filterability; —**уемый** *a.* filterable; filtered; —**ующий** *see* **фильтровальный;** —**ующийся** *a.* filterable; filtering.

филяр/ии *pl.* nematode worms (*Filarioidea*); —**и(ат)оз** *m.* (vet.) filariasis.

филярный *a.* filar, thread-like.

ФИМ *abbr.* **(фазоимпульсная модуляция)** pulse-phase modulation.

фимбрия *f.* (zool.) fimbria, fringe-like structure.

фимоз *m.* (med.) phimosis.

фин. *abbr.* **(финансовый; финский).**

финал *m.* end, conclusion; —**ьный** *a.* final.

финанс/ирование *n.* financing; —**ировать** *v.* finance; —**овый** *a.* financial; —**ы** *pl.* finances.

финвал *m.* finback whale.

финик *m.*, —**овый** *a.* date (fruit); **морской ф.** (mal.) sea date (*Lithophaga lithophaga*).

Финикс (geog.) Phoenix.

финиметр *m.* gage for gas cylinders.

фининспектор *m.* assessor.

финифт/евый, —яный *a.* enamel(ed); —**ь** *f.* enamel.

финиш *m.* finish; **момент** —**а** terminal time; —**ер** *m.* finisher, finishing machine; —**ировать** *v.*, —**ный** *a.* finish; —**ная обработка поверхности** surface finish(ing).

финка *see* **финна.**

финляндский *a.* (geog.) Finland's, Finnish.

финн/а *f.* (zool.) cysticercus (larval tapeworm); —**оз** *m.* (med.) cysticercosis; (vet.) measles (of cattle, etc.); —**озный** *a.* cysticercus-infested; measly (meat); —**ы** *pl.* (vet.) measles; cysticerci.

финский *a.* Finnish.

финта *f.* (ichth.) twaite shad (*Alosa fallax*).

фиолетовый *a.* violet; magenta; **ф. пигмент** anthocyanin.

фион *m.* phyone, adenohypophyseal growth hormone.

фиорд *m.*, —**овый** *a.* fiord, fjord.

фирм/а *f.* firm, company; —**енный** *a.* firm, company; trade (catalog); —**енный щиток** nameplate.

фирн *m.* firn, névé (field of granular snow); —**изированный, —овый** *a.* firn (snow); névé (iceberg); permanent snow (field).

фисгармония *f.* (acous.) harmonium.

фискальный *a.* fiscal.

фисташк/а *f.* pistachio nut; —**ово-зелёный** *a.* pistachio-green.

фисташков/ый *a.* pistachio; **ф. лак** mastic varnish; —**ая водка** mastic (liquor); —**ая смола** mastic (resin).

фисташник *m.* pistachio.

фистул/а *f.* (med.) fistula; —**озный, —ьный, —ярный** *a.* fistulous, fistular.

фисци/евая кислота, —он *m.* physcic acid, physcion; —**ол** *m.* physciol.

фит— *prefix* phyt(o)— (plant, vegetable); —**аза** *f.* phytase; —**альбумин** *m.* phytalbumin, vegetable albumin; —**ан** *m.* phytane; —**ен** *m.* phytene; —**еновая кислота** phytenic acid; —**ил** *m.* phytyl.

фитил/едержатель *m.* wick holder; —**ёк** *dim. of* **фитиль;** —**ь** *m.*, —**ьный** *a.* wick, fuse; core.

фитин phytin.

фитинг *m.* fitting, adapter.

фитиновая кислота phytic acid, inositolhexaphosphoric acid.

фито— *see* **фит—;** —**вредитель** *m.* phytopest; —**генический** *a.* phytogenic; —**гормон** *m.* phytohormone; —**графия** *f.* phytography, descriptive botany; —**климат** *m.* plant climate; —**л** *m.* phytol; —**лакка** *f.* (bot.) Phytolacca; —**лакцин** *m.* phytolaccin, phytolaccine (alkaloid); —**лякка** *f.* (bot.) Phytolacca; —**метрия** *f.* phytometry; —**монады** *pl.* (prot.) Phytomonadina; —**н** *m.* (bot.) phyton; —**нцид** *m.* bacteride-fungicide-protozoacide (from plants); —**паразит** *m.* phytoparasite; —**патология** *f.* phytopathology, plant pathology; —**планктон** *m.* phytoplankton; —**стерин** *m.* phytosterol; —**стеролин** *m.* phytosterolin; —**тератология** *f.* phytoteratology, study of monstrous growths in plants; —**токсический** *a.* phytotoxic; —**фаг** *m.* phytophage, plant-eating insect; —**фагия** *f.* phytophagy; —**фармакология** *f.* phytopharmacology; —**фтороз** *m.* (phyt.) phytophthora infection; —**химический** *a.* phytochemical; —**химия** *f.* phytochemistry; —**хром** *m.* (bot.) phytochrome; —**ценоз** *m.* phytocenosis, plant community; —**цидное действие** plant damage (by sprays); —**эдафон** *m.* phytoedaphon (microscopic soil flora).

Фиттига реакция Fittig reaction.

фитэритрин *m.* phyterythrin.

фифи (orn.) wood sandpiper (*Tringa glareola*).

фифленый *a.* serrate(d).

~~**Фицджеральда-Лоренца сокращение**~~ Fitzgeraid-Lorentz contraction.

фицин *m.* (biochem.) ficin.

фиш-балка *f.* (naut.) fish davit; **ф.-блок** *m.* fish block.

Фишера распределение Fisher distribution.

Фишер-Тропша процесс Fischer-Tropsch process.

фишка *f.* plug.

фиш-тали *pl.* (naut.) fish tackle.

ф-ия *abbr.* **(функция)** function.

ф-ка *abbr.* **(фабрика)** factory.

ф.кв.д. *abbr.* **(фунтов на квадратный дюйм)** pounds per square inch, psi.

ф-ла *abbr.* **(формула)** formula.

флавазин *m.* flavazine.

флаван *m.* flavan; —**ол** *m.* flavanol, 3-hydroxyflavone; —**он** *m.* flavanone, 2,3-dihydroflavone; —**трен** *m.* flavanthrene.

флав/аспидовая кислота flavaspidic acid; —**едо** *n.* (phyt.) flavedo; —**иановая кислота** flavianic acid; —**ин** *m.*, —**иновый** *a.* flavin; —**инмононуклеотид** *m.* (biochem.) flavin mononucleotide, FMN; —**ицид** *m.* flavicid.

флаво— *prefix* flav(o)— (yellow); —**ксантин** *m.* flavoxanthin; —**л** *m.* flavol, 2,6-anthracenediol; —**мицин** *m.* flavomycin; —**н** *m.*, —**новый** *a.* flavone, 2-phenylchromone; —**протеид** *m.*, —**протеидный** *a.* flavoprotein; —**пурин** *m.* flavopurin, alizarin X; —**пурпурин** *m.* flavopurpurin, 1,2,6-trihydroxyanthraquinone; —**фенин** *m.* flavophenine; —**фосфин** *m.* flavophosphine.

флаг *m.* flag, banner; (bot.) vexillum; —**дук** *m.* bunting.

флагеллаты *pl.* (zool.) flagellates.

флаг/ман *m.* (mil.) flag officer; —**манский** *a.* flag (ship); —**шток** *m.* flag pole, flagstaff.

флаж/ковый *a.* of **флажок;** —**ный** *a.* of **флаг;** —**ок** *dim. of* **флаг;** (hand) flag; (art.) thumb catch, thumb piece.

флакон *m.* small bottle, flask.

фламандский *a.* (geog.) Flemish.

фламбиров/ание *n.* flambing; (med.) flambage, singeing; **—ать** v. flame, pass through or over a flame; sterilize (with flame); singe (cloth).

фламинго m. and pl., **—вые** pl. (orn.) flamingos (*Phoenicopteridae*).

фланг m., **—овый** a. flank, wing, side.

Фландрия (geog.) Flanders.

фланел/евый a. flannel; **—ет** m. flannelette; **—ь** f., **—ьный** a. flannel.

фланец m. flange, collar, ring, bush.

фланжиров/альный see **фланжировочный**; **—ать** v. flange; **—ка** f. flanging.

фланжировочн/ый a. flange, flanging; **ф. пресс, ф. станок, —ая машина** flanger, flanging machine.

фланк m., **—ировать** v. (mil.) flank; **—ирующий** a. flanking.

фланц/евание n. flanging; **—евать** v. flange; **—евый** a. flange(d); **—ованный** a. flanged.

флат m., **—овая бумага** flat (sheet) paper; **—орезка** f. sheet cutter.

флаттер m., **—ный** a. (av.) flutter.

флашинг-процесс m. flashing process.

флеб—, —о— prefix phleb(o)— (vein); **—ит** m. (med.) phlebitis; **—эктазия** f. phlebectasia, varicosity.

флегма f. phlegm; (fractional distillation) reflux, bottoms, residue.

флегмат/изатор m. retarder, deterrent, stabilizer; (fire) suppressant; **—изация** f. retardation, etc., see v.; **кривая —изации** flammability curve; **—изированный** a. retarded, etc., see v.; insensitive (high explosive); **—изировать** v. retard, moderate, suppress (fire), deter; stabilize; **—ический, —ичный** a. phlegmatic, sluggish.

флегмов/ый a. of **флегма**; **—ое число** reflux ratio.

флегмона f. (med.) phlegmon.

флейто/вые, —рыловые, —рылы pl. (ichth.) trumpetfishes (*Aulostomidae*).

флекс/иметр m. fleximeter; **—ор** m. (anat.) flexor; **—ура** f. (geol.) flexure, fold.

флеп m. flap, cover; rim band.

флёр m. gauze; crepe; **—ница** f. goldeneyed fly (*Chrysopa*).

флец m., **—овый** a. (geol.) fletz, bed.

флигель m. wing, annex.

фликер-фотометр m. flicker photometer.

фликтен/а f. (med.) phlyctena; **—оз** m. phlyctenulosis.

флиндерсин m. flindersin.

Флинта шум (med.) Flint's murmur.

флинт(глас) m. flint glass.

флиппер m. (rubber) flipper.

флицид m. a pyrethrum insecticide.

флиш m. (geol.) flysch.

фло/бафен m. phlobaphene; **—гистон** m. phlogiston; **—гоз** m. (med.) phlogosis, inflammation; **—гозин** m. phlogosin; **—гопит** m. (min.) phlogopite.

флокен m. floc(cule); (met.) flake; **—очувствительный** a. susceptible to flocculation.

флокит m. (min.) flokite.

флоккул/а f. floccule; **—и** pl. flocculi (clouds).

флокс m. (bot.) phlox.

флокул/ирование see **флокуляция**; **—ированный** a. flocculated, flocculent; **—ировать** v. flocculate; **—янт** m. flocculant; **—ятор** m. flocculator; **—яция** f. flocculation.

флор m. (naut.) floor.

флора f. (bot.) flora; **—льный** a. floral.

флорамид m. foramid (urea fertilizer).

флорент/ийский a. Florentine; **ф. лак** Florentine lake, cochineal carmine; **ф. сосуд** settling tank; **—ин** m.

florentine; settling tank; **—ина** f. Florentine flask, separatory tank; **—инский** a. Florentine.

Флоренция (geog.) Florence.

флоресценция f. (bot.) florescence.

флоретин m. phloretin; **—овая кислота** phloretic acid.

флориген m. (biochem.) florigen (hormone).

флорид/ин m., **—иновые глины** Floridin, fuller's earth; **—зин** m., **—зиновый** a. (pharm.) phlorhi(d)zin; **—ка** f. (ichth.) (American) flagfish (*Jordanella floridae*); **—озид** m. (biochem.) floridoside; **—ский** a. Florida, Floridian.

флориз/еин m. phlorizein; **—ин** m. phlor(h)izin.

флорист m. florist; **—ика** f. floristics; horticulture; **—ический** a. floristic; flora(l); horticultural.

флоро/глюцин m. phloroglucinol, 1,3,5-benzenetriol; **—за** f. phlorose, alpha-glucose; **—л** m. phlorol, o-ethylphenol; **—н** m. phlorone, p-xyloquinone.

флорризин see **флоризин**.

флорхинил m. phloroquinyl.

флот m. fleet, navy; **воздушный ф.** air force; **торговый ф.** merchant marine.

флот— prefix (min.) flotation; **—атор** m. floated ore; flotation unit; flotation plant worker; **—аторщик** m. flotation plant worker; **—ационный** a., **—ационное обогащение, —ация** f. flotation.

флотилия f. flotilla, small fleet.

флотир/ование see **флотация**; **—ованный** a. floated (off); **—овать(ся)** v. float (off); **—уемость** f. floatability; **—уемый** a. floatable; **—ующийся** a. floating; floatable.

флотконцентрат m. flotation concentrate.

флото— prefix (min.) flotation; **—гравитационный** a., **—гравитация** f. gravity flotation; **—классификация** f. flotation screening; **—машина** f. flotation machine, flotation cell; **—отсадка** f. flotation jigging; **—реагент** m. flotation agent; **—цех** m. flotation plant.

флотский a. fleet, naval.

флотура f. floater (in glass furnace).

флоэм/а f., **—ный** a. (bot.) phloem.

флу— see also under **флю—**.

флуавил m. fluavil.

флуат m. Fluate (preservative); **—ирование** n. fluating, fluosilicate coating.

флудинг m. flooding.

флукту/ационный a., **—ация** f. fluctuation; **—ировать** v. fluctuate; **—ирующий** a. fluctuating.

флундра f. (ichth.) flounder (*Pleuronectes*).

флуо— see also **флюо—**.

флуор— see also **фтор—**.

флуор/ан m. fluoran; **—антен** m. fluoranthene, idryl; **—ен** m. fluorene, diphenylenemethane, **—еновая кислота** fluorenic acid; **—енол** m. fluorenol, fluorene alcohol; **—енон** m. fluorenone, diphenylene ketone.

флуоресцеин m. fluorescein, resorcinolphthalein; **—калий** m. potassium fluorescein; **—овый** a. fluorescein.

флуоресц/ентный a. fluorescent; fluorescence; **—енция** f. fluorescence; (ichth.) fluorescent disease; **—ирование** n. fluorescence; **—ин** m. fluorescin; **—ировать** v. fluoresce; **—ирующий** a. fluorescent.

флуор/ид m. fluoride; **—ил** m. fluoryl; **—илиден** m. fluorylidene; **—иметр** m. fluorimeter; **—инден** m. fluorindene; **—ит** see **флюорит**; **—ометр** m. fluorometer; **—ометрия** f. fluorometry; **—он** m. fluorone, 3-isoxanthone; **—оскоп** m. fluoroscope; **—офор** m. fluorophore; **—охром** m. (chem.) fluorochrome.

флюат see **флуат**.

флювио— prefix fluvio—, river; **—гляциальный** a. (geol.) fluvioglacial; **—граф** m. fluviograph.

флюг/арка *see* **флюгер;** (chimney) cowl, deflector; (naut.) badge, emblem, colors, arms; **—ер** *m.* weather vane, (wind) vane, anemoscope; (av.) wind sock; flag; **—ерный** *a.* anemotropic; **—ирование** *n.* (av.) feathering; **—ировать** *v.* feather.

флюид *m.* fluid; **—альный** *a.* fluid(al); flow (structure); **—изация** *f.* fluidization; **—изированный** *a.* fluidized; **—изировать** *v.* fluidize; **—ный** *a.* fluid.

флюкс *m.* flux; **—ия** *f.* fluxion; **—метр** *m.* (elec.) fluxmeter; **—ующий** *a.* fluxing, flux.

флюктуация *see* **флуктуация.**

флюкция *see* **флюксия.**

флюмазин *m.* (pharm.) flumazine, fluphenazine.

флюор— *see also* **флуор—.**

флюоризация *f.* fluoridation.

флюорит *m.* (min.) fluorite, fluorspar.

флюоро/глюцин *m.* phloroglucinol; **—графия** *f.* (med.) fluorography; **—роз** *m.* (med.) fluorosis; **—скоп** *m.* fluoroscope; **—хром** *see* **флуорохром.**

флюотан *m.* fluroxene, halothane (anesthetic).

флюс *m.* flux, fusing agent; (phys.) flow; (med.) gumboil; **—ный** *a.* of **флюс; —ование** *n.* fluxing, flux(at)ion; **—ованный** *a.* fluxed, fused; **—овать** *v.* flux, fuse; **—овка** *see* **флюсование; —овый** *a.* of **флюс; —ующий** *a.* fluxing.

флюта *f.* (ichth.) rice eel (*Monopterus albus*).

флютбет *m.* apron (of dam), flood bed, foundation slab; spillway, by-channel.

фля/га *f.* flask, canteen, water bottle; phial; (milk) can; **—жка** *dim. of* **фляга; —ковидный, —кообразный** *a.* flask-shaped; **—жный** *a. of* **фляга.**

флянцевый *see* **фланцевый.**

фляшерия *f.* (vet.) flasheria; (ent.) septicemia.

ФМН *abbr.* **(флавинмононуклеотид)** flavine mononucleotide.

ФНЧ *abbr.* **(фильтр нижних частот)** (elec.) low-pass filter.

фоб/ия *f.* (med.) phobia; **—ность** *f. suffix* —phoby, —phobic nature; **—ный** *a. suffix* —phobic, —phobous, -shunning; **—отаксис** *m.* (zool.) phobotaxis.

фовеальный *a.* foveate, pitted.

Фовлеров раствор (chem.) Fowler's solution.

Фоже газогенератор Faugé producer.

фойе *n.* foyer, lobby.

фок *m.* (naut.) foresail.

фокальный *a.* focal, focus(ed).

фок-мачта *f.* (naut.) foremast.

фокомелия *f.* (med.) phocomelia.

фокометр *m.* (opt.) focometer, focimeter; **—ия** *f.* focometry.

фокус *m.* focus, focal point; (X-rays) focal spot; trick; **приводить в ф., собирать в —е** *v.* (bring into) focus; **установка на ф.** focusing; **—ирование** *n.* focusing; **—ированный** *a.* focused; **—ировать** *v.* (bring into) focus; **—ировка** *f.,* **—ировочный, —ирующий** *a.* focusing; **—ный** *a.* focus, focal; **—ное пятно** focus, focal point; **—ное расстояние** focal length.

фолад(ид)ы *pl.* (mal.) piddocks (*Pholadidae*).

фолас *m.* (mal.) angel wing (*Pholas*).

фол/ацин *m.,* **—евая кислота** *see* **фолиевая кислота.**

фолиант *m.,* **—ный, —овый** *a.* folio; volume.

фоли/арный *a.* (bot.) foliar; **—ация** *f.* foliation.

фолидоз *m.* (zool.) pholidosis, scutellation.

фолиевая кислота folic acid, pteroylglutamic acid, vitamin B_c.

фолио *n.* folio.

фоллетаж *m.* (agr.) apoplexy (grape disease).

фолликул *m.,* **—а** *f.* (anat., bot.) follicle; **—ин** *m.* folliculin, estrone; **—ит** *m.* (med.) folliculitis; **—остимулирующий** *a.* follicle-stimulating; **—ярный** *a.* follicular.

фольварк *m.* farm.

фольг/а *f.,* **—овый** *a.* foil.

фомка *f.* forcer.

фомоз *m.* (phyt.) phomosis.

фон *m.* background; (rad.) hum; (tel.) background noise, crackling; (acous.) phon (unit of volume); (polarography) supporting electrolyte, base electrolyte; (torsion balance) springback; (agr.) preceding crop, preceding fertilization; *prefix see* **фоно—;** *suffix* —phone.

фонареглаз(ов)ые *pl.* (ichth.) lanterneye fishes (*Anomalopidae*).

фонар/ик *dim. of* **фонарь; —ный** *a.,* **—ь** *m.* lantern, lamp, light; skylight; bay window; (mach.) connector, distance piece; (petrol.) mast; **волшебный —ь** slide projector; **карманный —ь, электрический —ь** flashlight; **передовой —ь** headlight.

фон/астения *f.* (med.) phonasthenia; **—ация** *f.* phonation.

фонд *m.* fund(s), resources, capital; stock, holdings, collection; (genetic) pool; **единица —а** stock unit; **основные —ы** fixed capital; **—ирование** *n.* state funding; **—ировать** *v.* allocate funds; **—ируемый** *a.* centrally allocated; **—овый** *a. of* **фонд;** share; stock; **—оотдача** *f.* yield of capital investment; return on capital.

фон/ема *f.* phoneme; **—етика** *f.* phonetics; **—етический** *a.* phonetic; audio (information); **—иатрия** *f.* speech therapy; **—ический** *a.* phonic, acoustic; buzzer (call); **—ия** *f. suffix* —phony, —phonia.

фоно— *prefix* phono— (sound); **—вый** *a. of* **фон;** baseline (studies); **—грамма** *f.* phonogram; sound track; sound record(ing); **—граф** *m.* phonograph; **—графический** *a.* phonographic; **—кардиограф** *m.* (med.) phonocardiograph; **—катетер** *m.* (med.) phonocatheter; **—логия** *f.* phonology; **—мания** *f.* phonomania, homicidal mania; **—метр** *m.* phonometer, sound-level meter; **—н** *m.* phonon (lattice-vibration quantum); **—рецептор** *m.* (zool.) phonoreceptor; **—скоп** *m.* phonoscope; **—тека** *f.,* **—течный** *a.* record and tape library; **—фобия** *f.* phonophobia.

фонтан *m.* fountain, spout; flow; (petrol.) gusher; blowout.

фонтанел/ла, —ь *f.* (anat.) fontanel.

фонтан/ирование *n.* flowing, etc., *see v.;* flow; (phys.) fountain effect; **—ировать** *v.* flow, gush, spout, blow (wild), blow out; **—ирующий** *a.* flowing, etc., *see v.;* **—ирующий слой** fluidized bed; **—ный** *a. of* **фонтан; —ная арматура, —ная ёлка** (petrol.) Christmas tree.

фоны *pl. of* **фон.**

фор— *prefix* fore—, pre—, preliminary.

фораж *m.* (med.) forage.

фораминиферы *pl.* (zool.) Foraminifera.

форвакуум *m.* initial vacuum, forevacuum, rough exhaust; **—ный** *a.* fore(vacuum), rough-vacuum, roughing (pump).

форвальцы *pl.* preliminary roller(s).

форгенин *m.* forgenin, tetramethylammonium formate.

форд *m.* Ford (car).

Форда воронка (viscosity) Ford cup.

фордевинд *m.* (naut.) stern wind; **идти ф.** sail before the wind.

форез *m.* phoresis; **—ия** *f.* (zool.) phoresia.

форелевый *a.* (ichth.) trout.

форелеокунь *m.* (ichth.) troutperch (*Percopsis omiscomaycus*); largemouth bass (*Micropterus salmoides*).

форелленштейн *m.* (petr.) forellenstein, troctolite.

форель *f.*, **—ный** *a.* (ichth.) trout.

форетический *a.* phoretic (electron).

форзац *m.* (typ.) fly leaf.

фориды *pl.* humpbacked flies (*Phoridae*).

фор/камера *f.*, **—камерный** *a.* precombustion chamber, premix chamber, mixing chamber; doghouse (of furnace); injection (spray) cup; **—киль** *m.* (av.) dorsal fin; **—конденсат** *m.* prepolymer; **—контакт** *m.* preliminary catalytic purifier; **—контактирование** *n.* preliminary catalytic purification.

Форлендера правило Vorlander's rule.

форлюк *m.* (naut.) forehatch.

форм/а *f.* form, shape, contour, configuration, pattern; stencil; (casting) mold; structure, build, make, model; (math.) mode; mode (of interaction, etc.); (chem.) species; landform; uniform; **в —е** in (the form of), as; **в окисленной —е** oxidized; **иметь —у** *v.* be in the form (of), be shaped (like); **нижняя ф.** drag mold; **отливать —у** *v.* mold, cast; **придавать —у** *v.* mold, shape, form.

формазил *m.* formazyl; **—карбоновая кислота** formazylcarboxylic acid.

формал *see* **формаль.**

формализ/ация *f.* formalization; **—(ир)овать** *v.* formalize; **—м** *m.* (math.) formalism.

форм/алин *m.*, **—алинный,** **—алиновый** *a.* Formalin (formaldehyde solution); **—аль** *m.* formal, dimethoxymethane; **—альдегид** *m.* formaldehyde, methanal; **—альдоксим** *m.* formaldoxime.

формальн/о *adv.* pro forma; **—ость** *f.* formality; **—ый** *a.* formal.

форм/амид *m.* formamide, methanamide; **—амидин** *m.* formamidine; **—амин** *m.* formamine, hexamethylenetetramine; **—анилид** *m.* formanilide, N-phenylformamide; **—анит** *m.* (min.) formanite; **—анта** *f.* (acous.) formant.

форма-род (bot.) form genus.

формат *m.* size, format; layout; folding; (aspect) ratio; **—ирование** *n.* (comp.) formating; **—ный** *a. of* **формат;** strip (film); **—ный станок** circular trimming saw; **—ная расстановка** arrangement by size.

форматор *m.* shaper; **ф.-вулканизатор** shaper-vulcanizer.

формация *f.* formation, structure; (bot.) association.

формвар *m.* Formvar, polyvinyl formal resin.

форменный *a.* formal, regular, prescribed; positive.

формиат *m.* formate.

формиевые *pl.* (ichth.) butterfishes (*Formionidae*).

формий *see* **формиум.**

формик/арий *m.* formicary, ants' nest; **—ация** *f.* (med.) formication (sensation of small insects crawling on skin).

формил *m.* formyl; **—ирование** *n.* formylation; **—ировать** *v.* formylate; **—овый** *a.* formyl; **—фторид** *m.* formyl fluoride.

формин *m.* Formin, hexamethylenetetramine.

формир/ование *n.* forming, etc., *see* v.; **—ователь** *m.* former; **—ователь такта** oscillator; **—овать** *v.* form, shape, throw (pottery); mold, cast; construct, build up, produce, establish, organize, marshal; activate, raise; **—овка** *see* **формирование; —овочный, —ующий** *a.* forming, etc., *see* v.; **—ующее устройство** former; (pulse) shaper.

формиум *m.* (bot.) New Zealand flax (*Phormium tenax*).

форм-мочевина *f.* urea-formaldehyde (a nitrogenous fertilizer).

формов/альный *see* **формовочный; —ание** *n.* molding, etc., *see* v.; **—анный** *a.* molded, etc., *see* v.; **—ать** *v.* mold, cast; form, shape, model, fashion; (hort.) train; **—ка** *see* **формование;** mold frame; **—ой** *a.* mold(ing), molded; **—очная** *f.* molding room; **—очный** *a.* mold(ing), molder's, molded; form(ing); extruding (machine).

формо/вщик *m.* molder.

формоза *f.* formose, *i*-fructose.

формозский *a.* (geog.) Formosa, Taiwan.

формо/изменение *n.* form changing, deformation; mechanical shaping; **—изменяемость** *f.* susceptibility to form changing; **—импульсный** *a.* (electron.) pulse-shape.

формо/ксим *m.* formoxime; **—литный** *a.* formolite (number); **—ль** *m.* formol.

форм/ообразование *n.* forming, shaping; morphogenesis; **—ообразовательный** *a.* forming, shaping; morphogenic, formative; **—уемость** *f.* formability; moldability; susceptibility to shaping; **—оустойчивость** *f.* dimensional stability.

формула *f.* formula; (patent) claims; **ф. образования** equation for the formation (of).

формулиров/ание *n.* formulating, etc., *see* v.; formula(tion); statement; **—анный** *a.* formulated, etc., *see* v.; **—ать** *v.* formulate, word, phrase; state, enunciate; **—ка** *see* **формулирование.**

формульный *a. of* **формула.**

формуляр *m.* (service) log, logbook, record book; data card; (library) card; blank, form; **—ный** *a. of* **формуляр;** official.

формующий *pr. act. part. of* **формовать.**

формфактор *m.* (elec.) form factor.

форникс *m.* (anat.) fornix.

форон *m.* phorone.

форониды *pl.* (zool.) Phoronidea.

форпик *m.* (naut.) forepeak.

форполимер *m.* prepolymer; **—изация** *f.* preliminary polymerization.

форпост *m.*, **—ный** *a.* (bot.) outpost.

фор/прессование *n.*, **—прессовка** *f.* prepressing, preliminary pressing; **—продукт** *m.* preliminary product, spec. prepolymer.

форсаж *m.* afterburning, boost, reheat(ing) (of engine); **—ный** *a. of* **форсаж;** afterburner (fuel); backing (pump); **—ная камера** afterburner.

форсиров/ание *n.* forcing, etc., *see* v.; augmentation; boost(ing); (mil.) assault crossing; **—анный** *a.* forced, etc., *see* v.; high-speed, high-power, heavy-duty; emergency (level); **—ать** *v.* force, push, boost, speed up, augment; reheat (engine); spike (nuclear reactor); cross (water barrier).

форципрессура *f.* (med.) forcipressure.

форсун/ка *f.*, **—очный** *a.* sprayer, atomizer, pulverizer; jet, injector (orifice); (spray) nozzle, rose; (oil) burner; **—очная сажа** lampblack.

форт *m.* fort; **—ификация** *f.* fortification.

фортка *f.* airport, air vent.

фортоин *m.* Fortoin, methylenedicotoin.

форточ/ка *f.*, **—ный** *a.* air vent, small window; (av.) direct-vision window.

Форт-уэйн (geog.) Fort Wayne; **Ф.-уэрт** Fort Worth.

форфришер *m.* preliminary refining mixer.

форцепсы *pl.* forceps.

фор/шальт-турбина *f.* front turbine; **—шахта** *f.* (min.)

front shaft; —**штевень** *m.* (naut.) stem(post); —**штосс** *m.* adapter.

фосвитин *m.* (biochem.) phosvitin, phosphovitellin.

фосген *m.* phosgene; —**ирование** *n.* phosgenation; —**овый** *a.* phosgene.

фосмука *f.* phosphate rock meal.

фосса *f.* (mam.) fossa (*Cryptoprocta ferox*).

фоссил/изация *f.* (geol.) fossilization; —**изированный** *a.* fossilized; —**изировать** *v.* fossilize; —**ии** *pl.* fossils; —**ьный** *a.* fossil.

фостоновая кислота phostonic acid.

фосф/аген *m.* phosphagen; —**азид** *m.* phosphazide; —**азин** *m.* phosphazine; —**азол** *m.* phosphazol; —**азосоединение** *n.* phosphazo compound; —**азот** *m.* urea-superphosphate; —**амид** *m.* phosphamide; —**анилин** *m.* phosphaniline, phenylphosphine.

фосфат *m.* phosphate; **ф. кальция** calcium phosphate; —**аза** *f.* phosphatase; —**ация** *f.* phosphatization; —**диабет** *m.* (med.) phosphite diabetes; —**ид** *m.* phosphatide; phospholipin; —**идил** *m.* (biochem.) phosphatidyl; —**идная кислота** phosphatidic acid; —**ин** *m.* phosphatin; —**ирование** *n.* phosphating; phosphate coating, parkerizing; —**ный**, —**овый** *a.* phosphate; —**ная порода** phosphate rock; —**шлаки** *pl.* phosphate slag (fertilizer).

фосф/ен *m.* (physiol.) phosphene; —**енил** *m.* phosphenyl; —**енилистый** *a.* phosphenylous (acid); —**ениловый** *a.* phosphenylic (acid); —**ид** *m.*, —**идный** *a.* phosphide; —**ил** *m.* phosphyl.

фосфин *m.* phosphine; phosphorous hydride; —**истая кислота** phosphinous acid, R$_2$POH; —**овая кислота** phosphinic acid, R$_2$PO(OH); —**огруппа** *f.* phosphino group; —**оксид** *m.* phosphine oxide.

фосфит *m.* phosphite.

фосфо— *prefix* phospho—, phosphorus; —**бензол** *m.* phosphobenzene; —**гипс** *m.* phosphogypsum (fertilizer); —**киназа** *f.* phosphokinase; —**кислота** *f.* phospho acid, phosphonic acid.

фосфолип/ид, —**ин** *m.* phospholipid.

фосфо/мутаза *f.* phosphomutase; —**некроз** *m.* (med.) phosphonecrosis; —**ниевый** *a.*, —**ний** *m.* phosphonium; —**нистый** *a.* phosphonous; —**нитрилхлорид** *m.* phosphonitryl chloride; —**новый** *a.* phosphonic; —**протеид** *m.* phosphoprotein.

фосфор *m.* phosphorus, P; phosphor, luminescent material; **красный ф.** red phosphorus; **пятиокись —а** phosphorus pentoxide.

фосфорат *m.* phosphorate.

фосфоресц/ентный *a.* phosphorescent; —**енция** *f.* phosphorescence; —**ирование** *n.* phosphorescing; —**ировать** *v.* phosphoresce; —**ирующий** *a.* phosphorescing, phosphorescent, luminescent; luminous (paint).

фосфориз/ация *f.* phosphorization; —**ировать** *v.* phosphorize.

фосфорил *m.* phosphoryl; —**аза** *f.* phosphorylase; —**ирование** *n.* phosphorylation; —**ировать** *v.* phosphorylate; —**холин** *m.* phosphorylcholine.

фосфористо/калиевая соль, —кислый калий potassium phosphite; —**кислый** *a.* phosphorous acid; phosphite (of); —**кислая соль** phosphite; —**этиловый эфир** ethyl phosphite.

фосфорист/ый *a.* phosphorous; phosphide (of); **ф. ангидрид** phosphorous anhydride, phosphorus trioxide; **ф. водород** hydrogen phosphide, phosphine; —**ая кислота** phosphorous acid; **соль —ой кислоты** phosphite.

фосфорит *m.* (min.) phosphorite; phosphate rock; —**ный**

see **фосфоритовый**; —**ная мука** phosphate fertilizer; —**ование** *n.* (agr.) phosphate fertilizing; —**овый** *a.* phosphorite, phosphoritic; —**оподобный** *a.* phosphoritic.

фосфор/иться *v.* phosphoresce; —**ический** *a.* phosphorescent; —**ичность** *f.* phosphorescence.

фосфорно/алюминиевая соль aluminum phosphate; —**аммониевонатриевая соль** sodium ammonium phosphate.

фосфорноват/ая кислота hypophosphoric acid; **соль —ой кислоты** hypophosphate; —**истая кислота** hypophosphorous acid; **соль —истой кислоты** hypophosphite.

фосфорноватистокальциевая соль; —кислый кальций calcium hypophosphite; —**кислый** *a.* hypophosphoric acid; hypophosphite (of); —**кислая соль** hypophosphite.

фосфорно/вольфрамовая кислота phosphotungstic acid; —**железистая соль** ferrous phosphate; —**кальциевая соль** calcium phosphate.

фосфорнокисл/ый *a.* phosphoric acid; phosphate (of); **ф. кальций** calcium phosphate; —**ая соль** phosphate.

фосфорномолибденов/окислый *a.* phosphomolybdic acid; phosphomolybdate (of); —**ый** *a.* phosphomolybdic (acid); phosphomolybdate (blue).

фосфорн/ый *a.* phosphorus, phosphoric, phosphate; —**ая кислота** phosphoric acid; **соль —ой кислоты**, —**ая соль** phosphate.

фосфоро— *prefix* phosphoro—, phosphorus; —**бактерин** *m.* phosphorobacterin (fertilizer); —**бензол** *m.* phosphorobenzene; —**водород** *m.* hydrogen phosphide; phosphine; —**лиз** *m.* (chem.) phosphorolysis, phosphorolytic cleavage; —**лизический** *a.* phosphorolytic; —**метр** *m.* phosphorometer; —**подобный** *a.* phosphorous, like phosphorus.

фосфорорганический *a.* organophosphorus.

фосфоросветящийся *a.* phosphorescent.

фосфорсодержащий *a.* phosphorized, containing phosphorus.

фосфор-(5)-фтористоводородная кислота hexafluorophosphoric acid.

фосфо/серин *m.* (biochem.) phosphoserine; —**трансфераза** *f.* phosphotransferase; —**триоза** *f.* phosphotriose; —**фераза** *f.* phosphopherase, phosphotransferase; —**энолпировиноградная кислота** phosphoenolpyruvic acid.

фот *m.* phot (unit of luminance); —**изм** *m.* (med.) photism.

фотиния *f.* (bot.) Photinia.

фото *n.* photograph; *prefix* photo—, light; photographic; photoelectric; —**активный** *a.* (chem.) photoactive; —**аллергический** *a.* photoallergic; —**анализатор** *m.* photoanalyzer; —**аппарат** *m.* camera; —**батарея** *f.* photoelectric battery; —**биение** *n.* photobeat; —**бомба** (av.) photoflash bomb, flare; —**бумага** *f.* photographic (printing) paper; —**варистор** *m.* (electron.) photovaristor; —**визуальный** *a.* photovisual.

фотовозбужд/ение *n.* photoexcitation; —**ённый** *a.* photoexcited.

фото/восстановление *n.* photoreduction; —**вспышка** *f.* photoflash; (electronic) flash; —**вулканизация** *f.* photovulcanization; —**гальванический** *a.* photovoltaic; etic; —**гель** *m.* photogel; —**гемотахометр** *m.* (med.) photohematachometer.

фотоген *m.* photogen, boghead naphtha; photogen, phosphorescent plant or animal; photogene, after-image;

—**ический** *a.* photogenic; —**ичный** *a.* photogenic, light-producing; —**овый** *a. of* **фотоген.**

фотограв/ировальный *a.* photo-engraving; —**юра** *f.* photogravure; photoengraving.

фотограмм/а *f.* photogram; —**етрический** *a.* photogrammetric, plotting; —**етрия** *f.* photogrammetry, photographic surveying.

фотограф *m.* photographer; —**ирование** *n.* photographing; photography; —**ировать** *v.* photograph.

фотограф/ический, —ичный *a.* photographic; **ф. аппарат** camera; **ф. снимок** photograph, snapshot; —**ическая плёнка** (photographic) film; —**ия** *f.* photograph; photography; graphic presentation; **моментальная —ия** snapshot.

фото/дейтрон *m.* photodeuteron, —**деление** *n.* (nucl.) photofission; —**дерматит, —дерматоз** *m.* (med.) photodermatitis; photodermatosis; —**детектор** *m.* photodetector; —**динамика** *f.* (biol.) photodynamics; —**диод** *m.* (electron.) photodiode; —**диссоциация** *f.* photodissociation, photolysis; —**дозиметр** *m.* photodosimeter, film badge; —**донесение** *n.* photo-intelligence report.

фото/запись *f.* photographic record(ing); —**затвор** *m.* camera shutter; —**звезда** *f.* photostar (in nuclear emulsion); —**импульс** *m.* photoimpact; —**ионизация** *f.* photoionization; —**источник** *m.* photosource; —**калька** *f.* transparent photosensitive paper; —**камера** *f.* camera; —**карта** *f.* photographic map; —**карточка** *f.* photograph.

фотокат/ализ *m.* photocatalysis; —**ализатор** *m.* photocatalyst; —**од** *m.* photocathode.

фотокимограф *m.* recording camera.

фотокино/плёнка *f.* movie film; —**пулемёт** *m.* aerial camera gun, combat camera.

фотоклейстогамия *f.* (bot.) photocleistogamia.

фотоклистрон *m.* (electron.) photoklystron.

фотоколориметр *m.* photocolorimeter; —**ический анализ, —ия** *f.* photocolorimetry.

фотоконтроль *m.* film-badge monitoring (of personnel).

фотокоп/ирование *n.* photocopying; —**ия** *f.* photocopy, photostat.

фотоксилин *m.* photoxylin.

фото/лаборатория *f.* (phot.) dark room; —**лампа** *f.* darkroom light; photoelectric cell; phototube.

фотолиз *m.* photolysis; **продукт из —а** photolyte.

фото/линия *f.* photoline; —**лит** *m.* photolyte; —**литический** *a.* photolytic.

фотолитограф/ический *a.* photolithographic; —**ия** *f.* photolithography; photoengraving.

фото/любитель *m.,* —**любительский** *a.* (phot.) amateur; —**люк** *m.* camera window; —**люминесценция** *f.* photoluminescence.

фотомагнит/ный *a.* photomagnetic; —**оэлектрический** *a.* photoelectromagnetic.

фото/маска *f.* photomask, photographic mask; —**материал** *m.* photographic material, photographic supplies; —**мезон** *m.* (nucl.) photomeson.

фотометр *m.* photometer; **импульсный ф.** photon-counting photometer; —**ирование** *n.* photometry, photometric evaluation; —**ировать** *v.* take a light reading; measure photometrically; —**ический** *a.* photometric; —**ический контроль** film-badge monitoring (of personnel); —**ия** *f.* photometry.

фото/механический *a.* photomechanical; —**микрограф** *m.* photomicrograph; —**множитель** *m.* (electron.) photomultiplier; —**монтаж** *m.* photomontage, composite photograph; —**морфоз** *m.* (biol.) photomorphosis; —**мюон** *m.* photomuon; —**н** *m.* photon;

—**наблюдение** *n.* photographic observation; —**набор** *m.,* —**наборный** *a.* photocomposing, phototypesetting; —**настия** (bot.) photonasty; —**нейтрон** *m.* (nucl.) photoneutron; —**нный** *a.* photon; —**носчётчик** *m.* photon counter.

фото/оборудование *n.* photographic equipment; —**образование** *n.* (nucl.) photo-production; —**образованный** *a.* photoproduced; —**объектив** *m.* photographic lens; —**окисление** *n.* photooxidation; —**отпечаток** *m.* photograph, print, —**отрицательный** *a.* photonegative; —**отщепление** *n.* photodetachment.

фото/передатчик *m.* picture transmitter; —**передающий** *a.* picture-transmitting; —**перенос** *m.* phototransfer; —**период** *m.* (biol.) photoperiod; —**периодизм** *m.* photoperiodism.

фотопечат/ающий аппарат (comp.) flash photographic printer; —**ь** *f.* photocopying, photographic printing.

фото/пион *m.* photopion; —**пирометр** *m.* photoelectric pyrometer; —**пический** *a.* (physiol.) photopic, light-adapted (eye); —**план** *m.* photomap; controlled photo mosaic; —**пластинка** *f.* (phot.) plate; —**плёнка** *f.* film; —**повторитель** *m.* (microelectronics) step-and-repeat camera, photorepeater, pattern repeater; —**полимеризация** *f.* photopolymerization; —**положительный** *a.* photopositive; —**приёмник** *m.* photodetector.

фотопровод/имость *f.* photoconductivity; —**ник** *m.* photoconductor; —**ящий** *a.* photoconductive.

фото/протон (nucl.) photoproton; —**псин** *m.* (biochem.) photopsin; —**псия** *f.* (ophth.) photopsy; —**пулемёт** *m.* camera gun; —**пьезоэлектрический** *a.* photopiezoelectric; —**разведка** *f.* photographic reconnaissance; —**разложение** *n.* photodecomposition; —**распад** *m.* photodecomposition, photodisintegration; —**расцепление** *n.* (nucl.) photodisintegration.

фотореак/тивация *f.* photoreactivation; —**ция** *f.* (biochem.) photoreaction.

фоторегистр/атор *m.* photorecorder; —**ация** *f.* photographic record; —**ограмма** *f.* streak picture.

фоторезист *m.* photoresist (material); —**ивный** *a.* photoresistive; —**ор** *m.* photoresistor, light-dependent resistor.

фото/реле *n.* photorelay, light relay; —**репортаж** *m.* press photography; —**рецептор** *m.* (biol.) photoreceptor; —**рождение** *n.* (nucl.) photoproduction; —**рождённый** *a.* photoproduced; —**седиментометр** *m.* photosedimentometer.

фотосенсибилиз/ация *m.* photosensitization; —**ированный** *a.* photosensitized; light-catalyzed (reaction).

фотосинт/ез *m.* (bot.) photosynthesis; —**етический** *a.* photosynthetic.

фото/скоп *m.* photoscope (a kind of fluoroscope); —**следящий** *a.* photoelectric servo (system); —**слой** *m.* photosensitive layer; —**смеситель** *m.* (electron.) photomixer; —**снимок** *m.* photograph; —**сопротивление** *n.* photoresistance; photoresistor; —**стабилизатор** *m.* (plastics) light stabilizer; —**старение** *n.* photodegradation; light aging; —**стат** *m.* photostat —**сфера** *f.* (astr.) photosphere.

фотосхема *f.* photosketch; mosaic (photo); **маршрутная ф.** strip mosaic (photo).

фотосъёмка *f.* photographing; photographic surveying.

фото/таксис *m.* (biol.) phototaxis; —**тека** *f.* photograph library, photograph collection.

фототелегр/амма *f.* phototelegram, facsimile; —**аф** *m.* phototelegraph; —**афия** *f.* phototelegraphy, telephotography; —**афный** *a.* phototelegraphic, facsimile.

фото/теодолит *m.* phototheodolite, ballistic camera; —**терапия** *f.* (med.) phototherapy; —**техника** *f.* photographic technology; **—технический** *a.* phototechnical, technical photographic; **—типия** *f.* prototype, collotype; **—ток** *m.* photocurrent, photoelectric current; **—тон** *m.* photographic hue; **—травление** *n.* photoetching; **—транзистор** *m.* optical transistor, optoelectronic transistor; **—трансформатор** *m.* phototransformer, rectifier; **—триангуляция** *f.* phototriangulation; **—тропизм** *m.*, **—тропия** phototropism, phototropy; **—тропический** *a.* phototropic; **—троф** *m.* (biol.) phototroph; **—трофный, —трофический** *a.* phototrophic.

фото/увеличитель *m.* (phot.) enlarger; **—удар** *m.* photoimpact; **—умножитель** *m.* (electron.) photomultiplier; **—упругий** *a.* photoelastic; **—упругость** *f.* photoelasticity; **—фильный** *a.* (biol.) photophilous, lightloving; **—фобия** *f.* photophobia; **—фобный** *a.* photophobic, light-intolerant; **—фор** *m.* photophore, lightemitting organ; **—форез** *m.* photophoresis; **—фосфорилирование** *n.* (bot.) photophosphorylation; **—химический** *a.* photochemical, actinic; **—химия** *f.* photochemistry; **—хромия** *f.* photochromy, color photography; **—хроника** *f.* pictorial review; **—цинкография** *f.* (typ.) photozincography.

фоточувствительн/ость *f.* photosensitivity, photoelectric sensitivity; **—ый** *a.* photosensitive.

фото/шаблон *m.* (microelectronics) mask; **—штамп** *m.* photorepeater, step-and-repeat tool.

фото-эдс *m.* photo-emf; **ф.-эффект** *m.* photovoltaic effect.

фотоэклектор *m.* light trap (for insects).

фотоэлектричес/кий *a.* photoelectric; **—тво** *n.* photoelectricity.

фотоэлектро/движущая сила photoelectromotive force; **—н** *m.* photoelectron; **—нный** *a.* photoelectronic; **—нный умножитель** photomultiplier; **—химический** *a.* photoelectrochemical.

фотоэлемент *m.* photocell, photoelectric cell; phototube; photoemissive element; electric eye, photodetector; **эмиссионный ф.** photoemissive cell.

фотоэм/иссионный *a.* photoemissive; **—иссия** *f.* photoemission, extrinsic photoeffect; **—иттер** *m.* photoemitter.

фотоэстетический *a.* photoesthetic, having sensation of light.

фотоэффект *m.* photoeffect, photoelectric effect; **внешний ф.** extrinsic photoeffect, photoemission; **внутренний ф.** intrinsic photoeffect, photoconductive effect; **порог —а** photoelectric threshold.

фотоядерный *a.* photonuclear.

фотран *m.* (electron.) photran, optical trigger.

фотронрефлектометр *m.* photronreflectometer (for measuring turbidity).

фот-секунда *f.* (illum.) phot-second; **ф.-час** *m.* phot-hour.

фоцен/ин *m.* phocenin, trivalerin; **—овая кислота** phocenic acid, valeric acid.

фоциметр *m.* (phot.) focimeter.

ФП *abbr.* **(фильтр-поглотитель)** absorption filter; **(флавопротеид)** (biochem.) flavoprotein, FP.

ф-р *abbr.* **(фельдшер)** paramedic.

фр. *abbr.* **(фракция)** fraction.

фрагарол *m.* fragarol.

фрагма *f.* (biol.) spurious dissepiment, phragma; **средняя ф.** (ent.) mesophragma.

фрагмент *m.* fragment; **—арный** *a.* fragmentary; incomplete; **—ация** *f.* fragmentation.

фрагмо— *prefix* phragm(o)— (barrier; partition; septum); **—пласт** *m.* (gen.) phragmoplast; **—спора** (bot.) phragmospore, septate spore.

фрадицин *m.* fradicin (antibiotic).

фраза *f.* phrase, sentence; word block.

фразерин *m.* fraserin.

фракс/етин *m.* fraxetin; **—идубильный** *a.* fraxitannic (acid); **—ин** *m.* fraxin.

фрактальный *a.* (math.) fractal.

фрактур/а *f.*, **—ный** *a.* fracture; (typ.) Fraktur.

фракциониров/ание *n.* fractionation; **—анный** *a.* fractionated; fractional (condensation, distillation); **—ать** *v.* fractionate; **—ка** *f.*, **—очный** *a.* fractionating.

фракционн/о *adv.* fractionally; by degrees, in steps; **—ый** *a.* fractional; factional; fractionating (column); selective (oxidation); **—ый состав** distillation (result), distillation curve.

фракция *f.* fraction, cut, batch; faction.

фрамбезия *f.* (med.) frambesia, yaws.

фрамицетин *m.* (pharm.) framycetin, neomycin B.

фраму/га *f.*, **—жный** *a.* fixed frame; transom; fan light.

франгулин *m.* frangulin; **—овый** *a.* frangul(in)ic (acid).

франк *m.* franc (money).

Франка-Кондона принцип Franck-Condon principle; **Ф.-Рида механизм** Frank-Read mechanism.

франкиров/ание *n.* prepayment; **—анный** *a.* prepaid; postpaid; **—ать** *v.* prepay, pay the postage; **—ка** *f.* prepayment.

франклин/изация *f.* (med.) franklinization; **—ит** *m.* (min.) franklinite; **—овский ток** Franklin's current.

франко *adv.* (com.) free, prepaid; **ф. до судна** *see* **франко-судно; ф. место работ** delivered at the job; **ф.-борт судна, ф.-вагон, ф.-рельсы, ф.-судно** free on board, f.o.b.

франкфуртский *a.* Frankfort (black).

франсайеллёз *m.* (vet.) Francisella infection.

франский *a.* (geol.) Frasnian.

Франсуа-Рексрота печь (coking) François-Rexroth furnace.

франц. *abbr.* **(французский)** French.

франций *m.* francium, Fr.

Франция France.

французск/ий *a.* French; **ф. ключ** monkey wrench.

фратрия *f.* (bot.) phratry, subtribe, clan.

фраунгоферовы линии (light) Fraunhofer lines.

фрахт *m.* freight, cargo; freightage; **—ование** *n.* freighting; chartering; **—ователь** *m.* charterer; **—овка** *f.* freightage; **—овщик** *m.* freighter; carrier, shipowner; **—овый** *a. of* **фрахт.**

фрачник *m.* (ent.) borer (*Lixus*).

фреат/ический *a.* (geol.) phreatic; **—о—** *prefix* phreato— (well); **—офит** *m.* (bot.) phreatophyte (deep-rooted plant which obtains its water from the water table).

фрегат *m.* frigate (ship); (orn.) frigatebird (*Fregata*).

Фрёде реактив Fröhde's reagent (for alkaloids).

фрез/а *f.* cutter; (agr.) rototiller; (med.) fraise; **ф.-развёртка** *f.* reamer; **—барабан** *m.* (peat) drum shredder; **—ер** *see* **фреза; —ерный** *a.* milling, cutting; shredded; **—ерный резец** cutter, cutting tool; **—ерная машина** (agr.) rototiller, rotary tiller; **—(ер)овальный** *a.*, **—(ер)ование** *n.* milling, etc., *see v.*; **—(ер)ованный** *a.* milled, etc., *see v.*; **—(ер)овать** *v.* mill, cut; (agr.) (roto)till, break up (soil); **—еровочный** *a.* milling, etc., *see v.*; **—еровщик** *m.* milling machine operator.

фрейбургский *a.* (geog.) Freiburg.

фрейд/изм *m.* Freudian theory; **—овский** *a.* Freudian.

фрейм *m.* (artificial intelligence) frame; **ф. знаний** knowledge frame.

Фрейнд/а метод Freund's method; **—лиха уравнение** Freundlich equation.

фрейфал *m.* free fall, free-falling drill.

фреквентин *m.* frequentin; —**овая кислота** frequentic acid, citromycetin.

френ— *prefix* phren— (mind; diaphragm); —**альгия** *f.* (med.) phrenalgia.

френель *m.* (phys.) fresnel (10^{12} hertz).

френит *m.* (med.) phrenitis.

френо/граф *m.* phrenograph (for recording diaphragm movements); —**кардия** (med.) phrenocardia, neurocirculatory asthenia.

френозин *m.* phrenosin; —**овая кислота** phrenosinic acid, cerebronic acid.

френсисовский *a.* Francis'.

Френье насос Frenier pump.

фреон *m.* Freon (refrigerant).

фригана *f.* phrygana (xerophytic growth of shrubbery, briars, etc.).

фриг/атор *m.* an ice-salt refrigeration system; —**идность** *f.* frigidity; —**ориметр** *m.* frigorimeter; —**ория** *f.* frigorie (unit rate of extraction of heat).

Фрид/ель-Крафтса реакция (chem.) Friedel-Crafts reaction; —**лендера палочка** (med.) Friedländer's bacillus; —**лендера синтез** (chem.) Friedlander synthesis; —**рейха** (med.) Friedreich's (foot, phenomenon, etc.).

фриз *m.* frieze, border, rib; —**овый** *a.* frieze, border(ed); —**ы** *pl.* feathers (of horse).

Фрика печь (elec.) Frick furnace.

фрикативный *a.* fricative (sound).

фрикцион *m.* (friction) clutch; —**ировать** *v.* friction, rubberize; —**ный** *a.* friction(al).

фрикция *f.* friction.

фри-мартин *m.* (gen.; agr.) freemartin.

фрин—*prefix* phryn(o)— (toad); —**ин** *m.* phrynin; —**одерма** *f.* (med.) phrynoderma, toadskin.

фрины *pl.* (zool.) tarantulas, etc. (*Amblypygi*).

Фриса перегруппировка Fries rearrangement (of phenol ethers).

фритредерство *n.* free trade.

фритт/а *f.* (glass) frit; —**ер** *m.* coherer; —**овать** *v.*, —**овый** *a.* (glass) frit.

фришев/альный *a.*, —**ание** *n.* (re)fining, etc., *see v.*; —**ать** *v.* (re)fine; freshen, revive.

фробениусовый *a.* (math.) Frobenius.

фронт *m.*, —**овой** *a.* front; (mil.) force, army group; edge, profile, zone; —**альный** *a.* front(al); front(-mounted); front-end (loader); —**ит** *m.* (med.) inflammation of frontal sinus.

фронто/генез *m.* (meteor.) frontogenesis; —**лиз** *m.* frontolysis, breakdown of atmospheric front.

фронтон *m.*, —**ный** *a.* (arch.) fronton, pediment, gable.

фронтообразование *see* **фронтогенез.**

фр. пат. *see* **франц.** *and* **пат.**

Фруда критерий Froude number.

фрукт *m.* fruit.

фрукти/генин *m.* fructigenin; —**фикация** *f.* fructification.

фрукто— *prefix* fructo—, fruit; —**воз** *m.* fruit freighter; —**вый** *a.* fruit; —**вый сахар** *see* **фруктоза;** —**едовые** *pl.* fruit bats (*Stenoderminae*); —**за** *f.* fruit sugar, fructose; —**замин** *m.* fructosamine; —**зан** *m.* fructosan; —**зид** *m.* fructoside; —**зодифосфорная кислота** fructose diphosphate, FDP; —**зурия** *f.* (med.) fructosuria; —**киназа** *f.* fructokinase; —**сниматель** *m.* fruit picker; —**сушилка** *f.* fruit dryer, fruit dehydrator; —**ядный** *a.* fruit-eating.

ф-с *abbr.* **(фот-секунда)** phot-second.

ФСГ *abbr.* **(фолликулостимулирующий гормон)** follicle-stimulating hormone.

ф-сек *see* **ф-с.**

ф. ст. *abbr.* **(фунт стерлингов)** pound sterling.

фт. *abbr.* **(фут)** foot; **ф-т** *abbr.* **(факультет)** faculty, department.

ФТА *abbr.* **(фенилтрифторацетон)** phenyltrifluoroacetone.

фтал— *prefix* phthal—; —**азин** *m.* phthalazine, 2,3-benzodiazine; —**азол** *m.* phthalylsulfathiazole; —**амид** *m.* phthalamide; —**аминовая кислота** phthalamic acid, o-carbamylbenzoic acid; —**анил** *m.* phthalanil, N-phenylphthalimide; —**ат** *m.*, —**ный** *a.* phthalate.

фталево/бутиловый эфир butyl phthalate; —**кислый** *a.* phthalic acid; phthalate (of); —**кислая соль** phthalate.

фталев/ый *a.* phthalic; **ф. альдегид** phthalic aldehyde, phthalaldehyde; **ф. ангидрид** phthalic anhydride, phthalandione; —**ая кислота** phthalic acid, 1,2-benzenedicarboxylic acid; **соль —ой кислоты** phthalate.

фтал/еин *m.* phthalein; —**ид** *m.* phthalide, isobenzofuranone; —**иден** *m.* phthalidene; —**идил** *m.* phthalidyl.

фталил *m.* phthalyl; —**овый спирт** phthalyl alcohol, 1,2-xylenediol; —**хлорид** *m.* phthalyl chloride.

фтал/имид *m.* phthalimide, 1,3-isoindoledione; —**ин** *m.* phthaline; —**ирование** *n.* phthalation.

фтало— *prefix* phthalo—; —**ил** *m.* phthaloyl; —**н** *m.* phthalone; —**нитрил** *m.* phthalonitrile, dicyanobenzene; —**новая кислота** phthalonic acid, carbobenzoylformic acid; —**фенон** *m.* phthalophenone, diphenylphthalein; —**цианин** *m.*, —**цианиновый** *a.* phthalocyanine.

фталуровая кислота phthaluric acid.

фталь— *see* **фтал**—.

фтанит *m.* (petr.) phthanite.

фти/вазид *m.* phthivazide (antituberculotic); —**зиатрия** *f.* (med.) phthisiology; —**зик** *m.* consumptive (patient); —**зио**— *prefix* phthisio— (phthisis, tuberculosis).

фтириаз *m.* (med.) phthiriasis, Phthirus infestation.

фтор *m.* fluorine, F; *prefix* fluo(ro)—; —**алифатический** *a.* fluoroaliphatic; —**ангидрид** *m.* acid fluoride; —**ангидрид хромовой кислоты** chromyl fluoride; —**апатит** *m.* (min.) fluorapatite; —**ацетат** *m.* fluoroacetate; —**бензол** *m.* fluorobenzene.

фторбор/ная кислота fluoboric acid; —**нокислая соль** fluoborate; —**этилен** *m.* fluoroboroethylene.

фтор/гидрокортизон *m.* (pharm.) fluohydrocortisone, Fludrocortisone; —**динитробензол** *m.* (chem.) fluorodinitrobenzene, Sanger reagent.

фторзамещённый *a.* fluoro—, fluorine substituted.

фторид *m.* fluoride; **ф. азота** nitrogen fluoride; —**ирование** *n.* fluoridation.

фториров/ание *n.* fluorination; —**анный** *a.* fluorinated; —**ать** *v.* fluorinate.

фтористоводородная кислота hydrofluoric acid.

фторист/ый *a.* fluorine; (formerly lower or —ous) fluoride (of); (med.) fluoridized (teeth); **ф. водород** hydrogen fluoride; **ф. кремний** silicon fluoride; **основной ф.** oxyfluoride (of); —**ое соединение** fluoride.

фторкаучук *m.* fluorine-containing elastomer.

фторкортизон *m.* (pharm.) fluohydrocortisone, Fludrocortisone.

фторн/ый *a.* fluorine; (formerly higher or —ic) fluoride (of); —**ое олово** stannic fluoride.

фторо— *prefix* fluoro—; —**апатит** *m.* (min.) fluorapatite; —**бензол** *m.* fluorobenzene; —**борат** *m.* fluoborate.

фтороводород *m.* hydrogen fluoride; —**ный** *a.* hydrofluoric, hydrofluoride (of); —**ная кислота** hydrofluoric acid; **соль —ной кислоты** fluoride.

фтор/окись *f.* oxyfluoride; **—олефин** *m.* fluoro-olefin; **—ометрия** *f.* fluorometry; **—ониобат** *m.* fluoniobate, fluocolumbate.

фторопласт *m.* fluoroplastic; **ф.-3** polychlorotrifluoroethylene (same as Kel-F); **ф.-4** polytetrafluoroethylene (same as Teflon).

фтор/органический *a.* organofluoric; **—осиликат** *m.* fluosilicate; **—отан** *m.*, **—отановый** *a.* halothane, Fluothane (anesthetic); **—отанталат** *m.* fluotantalate; **—отитановый** *a.* fluotitanic (acid); **—оуглерод** *m.* carbon tetrafluoride, tetrafluoromethane; **—оформ** *m.* fluoroform, trifluoromethane; **—ополимер** *m.* fluoropolymer; **—ополиэфир** *m.* fluorinated polyester; **—опроизводные** *pl.* fluorine derivatives; **—осиликат** *m.* fluosilicate; **—осодержащий** *a.* fluorine-containing; **—осополимер** *m.* fluorine-containing copolymer; fluoroelastomer; **—угле(водо)род** *m.* fluorocarbon; **—оуксусный** *a.* fluoroacetic (acid); **—оциан** *m.* cyanogen fluoride; **—оцирконат** *m.* fluozirconate; **—оэластомер** *see* **фторсополимер.**

ФТП *abbr.* **(фарадеево тёмное пространство)** Faraday dark space.

ФТЯ, ФТ-ячейка *abbr.* **(феррит-транзисторная ячейка)** ferrite-transistor cell.

фуга *f.* seam, crack.

фуган/ок *m.*, **—очный** *a.* smoothing plane, jointer.

фугас *m.* (mil.) fougasse, (land) mine; **—ка** *f.* fougasse; high-explosive shell; **—ность** *f.* fugacity; **—ный** *a.* of **фугас**: high-explosive (shell, bomb); demolition (rocket, etc.); **—ное действие** demolition effect, explosive effect; brizance; mine action.

фугат *m.* centrifugate, centrifuged effluent.

фугативность *f.* fugacity.

фуггерит *m.* (min.) fuggerite.

фугетивность *f.* fugacity.

фугин *m.* fugin, fugutoxin.

фугировать *v.* centrifuge.

фугитивность *f.* fugacity.

фугов/ально-склеечный станок combined jointing and gluing machine; **—альный** *a.* jointing; **—альный станок** jointing machine, surface planer; **—ание** *n.* jointing, etc., *see v.*; **—ать** *v.* joint, plane; file (saw teeth); centrifuge; **—ка** *see* **фугование**; jointer; centrifuging.

фуговой фонарь arc lamp.

фуговочный *a.* of **фуговка.**

фугоидный *a.* phugoid, long-period.

фугу *m.* pufferfish (*Fugu*).

Фудзи/сан, —яма (geog.) Mt. Fuji.

фужер *m.* (glass) stemware.

фуз *m.* residue, sediment.

фузаин *m.* fusain, mineral charcoal.

фузар/иновый *a.* fusaric (acid); **—иоз** *m.* (phyt.) fusariose, Fusarium wilt; **—иозный** *a.* fusarial; **—иозное увядание** *m.* Fusarium wilt; **—иум** *m.* Fusarium.

фузоспириллёз *m.* (med.) fusospirillosis; **—ный** *a.* fusospirochetal (sepsis).

Фуко ток (elec.) Foucault current, eddy current.

фуко/за *f.* fucose; **—зидоз** *m.* (med.) fucosidosis; **—идный** *a.* fucoid(al), seaweed-like; **—иды** (bot.) seaweed (*Fucaceae*); **—ксантин** *m.* fucoxanthine; **—новая кислота** fuconic acid.

фуксин *m.* fuchsin(e), magenta red; **—осернистая кислота** fuchsin sulfurous acid (Schiff's reagent).

фуксия *f.* (bot.) fuchsia.

фуксово стекло water glass, sodium silicate solution.

фуксон *m.* fuchsone, quinonediphenylmethane.

фуку/зин *m.* fucusine, fucusamine; **—зол** *m.* fucusol; **—с** *m.* (bot.) Fucus.

фулаксит *m.* phulaxite.

фулл/ерова земля, —еровская земля fuller's earth.

фульв/анол *m.* fulvanol; **—ен** *m.* fulvene, 5-methylenecyclopentadiene; **—овая кислота, —окислота** fulvic acid.

фульг/еновая кислота fulgenic acid; **—ид** *m.* fulgide; **—гурация** *f.* (med.) fulguration (destructuration of living tissue by electric sparks); **—ировать** *v.* fulgurate; come and go like a lightning flash; **—урит** *m.* (petr.) fulgurite.

фулькра *f.* (zool.) fulcrum.

фульмин/ат *m.* fulminate; **ф. ртути** (expl.) fulminate of mercury; **—овая кислота** fulminic acid; **—овокислая соль** fulminate; **—овосеребряная соль** silver fulminate; **—уровая кислота** fulminuric acid, isocyanuric acid; **—уровокислая соль** fulminurate.

фуляр *m.*, **—овый** *a.* (text.) foulard.

фумагиллин *m.* fumagillin.

фумар/аза *f.* (biochem.) fumarase; **—амид** *m.* fumaramide; **—ат** *m.* (chem.) fumarate; **—ил** *m.* fumaryl; **—ин** *m.* fumarine, protopine; Fumarin (a rodenticide); **—овая кислота** fumaric acid, *trans*-butenedioic acid; **—овокислая соль** fumarate; **—оидная конфигурация** fumaroid; **—ола** *f.* (geol.) fumarole, smoke hole; fumarole deposit; **—протоцетраровый** *a.* fumaroprotocetraric (acid).

фумиг/ант *m.* fumigant; **—атин** *m.* fumigatin (antibiotic); **—атор** *m.* fumigator; **—ацин** *m.* fumigacin, helvolic acid; **—ационный** *a.*, **—ация** *f.* fumigation.

фунги— *prefix* fungi—; **—сид** *m.* fungicide; **—статический** *a.* fungistatic; **—стерин** *m.* fungisterol; **—цид** *m.* fungicide; **—цидин** *m.* fungicidin, nystatin.

фунгозный *a.* fungous, fungal.

фундальный *a.* (anat.) fundal; **—ная железа** gastric gland, fundic gland.

фундамент *m.* foundation, substructure, groundwork, bed, base, sole; seat(ing); footing; **—ы марок** (surv.) marker footings; **закреплённый на —е** *a.* stationary.

фундаментальн/о *adv.* fundamentally; **—ость** *f.* fundamentality, solidity; **—ый** *a.* fundamental, solid, substantial; foundation; main, basic (research).

фундаментн/ый *a.* of **фундамент**; **—ая плита** bed plate, base.

фундиров/анный *a.* based; (com.) funded; **—ать** *v.* base.

фундук *m.* hazelnut, filbert.

фундулус *m.* (ichth.) killifish, mummichog (*Fundulus*).

фундус *m.* (bot.) fundus.

фуникулёр *m.* funicular (railway), cable railway; (ski) lift.

фуникул/ит *m.* (med.) funiculitis; **—ус** *m.* (anat., bot.) funiculus.

фуникулярный *a.* (anat.) funicular.

функия *f.* plaintain lily (*Funkia*).

функтор *m.* (math.) functor.

функцион/ал *m.* (math.) functional; **—альный** *a.* functional; nutrient-deficiency (disease); **—ирование** *n.* functioning, operation, etc., *see v.*; **—ировать** *v.* function, operate, run; behave, act; serve (as); **—ирующий** *a.* functioning, etc., *see v.*

функц/ия *f.* function; purpose; **в —ии** as a function (of), against, versus; **выполнять —ию** *see* **функционировать; как ф.** *see* **в функции.**

фунт *m.* pound (Russian: 409.5 g); **ф.-вес** pound-force; **ф.-калория** *f.* centigrade heat unit, Chu; **ф.-масса** *f.* pound-mass; **—овик** *m.* one-pound weight; **—овой** *a.*

(one-)pound; **—офут** *m.* pound-foot, foot-pound; **ф.-сила** *f.* pound force.

фура *f.* wagon, van.

фураж *m.* (agr.) forage, fodder; **сухой ф.** hay; **—ир** *m.* forager; storer; distributor; **—ировать** *v.* forage; **—ировка** *f.* forage, foraging; **—ный** *a. of* **фураж.**

фуразан *m.* furazan, oxdiazole.

фуразолидон *m.* (pharm.) furazolidone (antibacterial).

фуран *m.* fur(fur)an; **—карбоновая кислота** furancarboxylic acid, pyromucic acid; **—овый** *a.* furan; **—оза** *f.* furanose.

фурацилин *m.* Furacin, nitrofurazone.

фургон *m.*, **—ный** *a.* van, truck.

фурка *f.* (biol.) furca, forked structure.

Фурдриниера машина (paper) Fourdrinier machine.

фурил *m.* furyl; furil, difurylglyoxal; **—иден** *m.* furylidene; **—овый спирт** furfuryl alcohol, furfuralcohol.

фурма *f.* (blast furnace) tuyere; (open hearth furnace) oxygen lance.

фурманка *f.* small van.

фурменн/ый *a. of* **фурма; —ая амбразура** tuyere arch; **—ая коробка** tuyere box, blast box.

фурмов/ание *n.* punching; **—щик** *m.* puncher.

фурнель *m.* (min.) a chute.

фурнирный *a.* veneer(ing); inlay.

фурнитур/а *f.*, **—ный** *a.* fittings, accessories.

фуро/диазол *m.* furodiazole, oxdiazole; **—ил** *m.* furoyl; **—илирование** *n.* furoylation; **—ин** *m.* furoin; **—л** *m.*, **—ловый** *a.* furol, furfural, 2-furancarbonal; **—новая кислота** furonic acid, furfurylacetic acid; **—хинолиновый** *a.* furoquinoline.

фурункул *m.* (med.) furuncle, boil; **—ёз** *m.* furunculosis.

фурфур/акролеин *m.* furfuracrolein; **—ал** *m.* furfural, 2-furancarbonal; **—алкоголь** *m.* furfuralcohol, furfuryl alcohol; **—аль** *see* **фурфурал; —амид** *m.* furfuramide, furfuryl amide; **—ан** *m.* fur(fur)an.

фурфурил *m.* furfuryl; **—иден** *m.* furfurylidene, fural; **—овый спирт** furfuryl alcohol, furylcarbinol.

фурфурин *m.* furfurine.

фурфуровый *a.* furfuric; **ф. альдегид** furfuraldehyde, furfural; **ф. спирт** furfuralcohol, furfuryl alcohol.

фурфур/оин *m.* furfuroin, furfuryl-fural; **—ол** *m.* furfural; **—ол-флороглюцид** furfuralphloroglucide; **—ольный** *a.* furfural; **—остильбен** *m.* furfurostilbene.

Фурье ряд (math.) Fourier series; **Ф. преобразование** Fourier transform.

фусоотделитель *m.* sediment separator, tar separator in by-product coking process.

фуст *m.* (arch.) fust, shaft, trunk.

фус/тик *m.* fustic (wood); **—тин** *m.* fustin; **—цин** *m.* fuscin.

фусы *pl.* heavy coal-tar products formed in by-product coking process.

фут *m.* foot (0.305 meter).

футаба *f.* futaba (Japanese vessel for collecting oil spills).

футбол *m.*, **—ьный** *a.* football, soccer.

футболен *m.* (chem.) buckminsterfullerene.

футер *see* **футеровка; —ование** *n.* lining, fettling; **—ованный** *a.* lined, fettled; **—овать** *v.* line, fettle; **—овка** *f.*, **—овочный** *a.* (refractory) lining, fettling, fettle, fritting.

фут-ламберт *m.* (illum.) foot-lambert.

футляр *m.* case, casing, cover, sheath, jacket; (bot.) theca, spore case; box, container, housing; **—окрылые** *pl.* (zool.) New Zealand short-tailed bats (*Mystacinidae*); **—охвостые** *pl.* sheath-tailed bats (*Emballonuridae*); **—чик** *dim. of* **футляр.**

футовый *a.* (one-)foot.

футор *m.* lining; bushing; lining leather; **—ка** *f.* threaded bushing, threaded sleeve, fitting.

фут/-свеча *f.* (illum.) foot-candle; **ф.-тонна** *f.* foot-ton (unit of work); **ф.-фунт** *m.* foot-pound; **—шток** *m.* sounding rod, depth gage, tide gage, foot gage.

фуф/аечный *a.*, **—айка** *f.* sweater, vest.

фуцит *m.* fucitol.

фушунский *a.* (geog.) Fushun.

ФФ *abbr.* (**фенолфталеин**) phenolphthalein.

ФФД *abbr.* (**фенолформалиндициандиамид**) phenol formaldehyde dicyandiamide.

ф-ция *abbr.* (**функция**) function.

ф-ч *abbr.* (**фот-час**) phot-hour.

фырк/анье *n.* chuffing, etc., *see v.*; **—ать, —нуть** *v.* chuff; sniff; snort; **—ающий** *a.* snort, blow (valve).

фырчанье *see* **фырканье.**

фьельд *m.* (geol.) fjeld (plateau).

фьёрд, фьорд *see* **фиорд.**

ФЭ *abbr.* (**фотоэлемент**) photocell.

фэр, ф.э.р., ФЭР *abbr.* (**физический эквивалент рентгена**) physical roentgen equivalent, rep.

ФЭУ *abbr.* (**фотоэлектронный умножитель**) photomultiplier.

фюзеляж *m.*, **—ный** *a.* (av.) fuselage.

фюзен *m.* (petr.) fusain, mineral charcoal; **—изация** *f.* fusainization; **—изированный** *a.* fusainized; **—о—** *prefix* fuso—.

фюльгебель *m.* micrometer.

Х

ХА *abbr.* (**хромель-алюмельный**) chromel-alumel (thermocouple).

хабаровский *a.* (geog.) Khabarovsk.

хабертиоз *m.* (vet.) Chabertia infection.

хавег *m.* Haveg (phenol-formaldehyde resin).

хави— *see* **шави—.**

хадакристалл *m.* chadacryst, enclosed crystal.

хадальный *a.* hadal, ultra-abyssal.

хаживать *see* **ходить.**

хаз *m.* rear end of hide.

хазмо— *prefix* chasmo— (yawning, opening); **—гамия** *f.* (bot.) chasmogamy; **—гамный** *a.* chasmogamic; **—фит** *m.* chasmophyte.

хазовый конец fag end, frayed end.

Хайберский проход (geog.) Khyber Pass.

хайк/а *f.*, **—о** *n.* (ichth.) chum salmon (*Oncorhynchus keta*).

хайло *n.* opening, aperture.

хайнык *m.* (agr.) khynik, cross between domestic yak and cow.

хайпер— *see under* **гипер—.**

хака *f.* (ichth.) Chaca.

хакасский *a.* (geog.) Khakass.

хаки *a. and n.* khaki (color).

хаковые *pl.* (ichth.) Indian catfishes (*Chacidae*).

халаз/а *f.* (bot.; embr.) chalaza; **—ион** *m.* (med.) chalazion, meibomian cyst; **—огамия** (bot.) chalazogamy.

халат *m.* robe, coverall.

халатн/ость *f.* negligence; **—ый** *a.* negligent, careless, remiss.

халва *f.* halva (confectionery).

халдейский *a.* (geog.) Chaldean.

халзан *m.* (orn.) golden eagle.

халикоз *m.* (med.) chalicosis.

халикты *pl.* mining bees (*Halictidae*).

халиловский *a.* Khalilovo; **х. чугун** a naturally alloyed iron.

халко— *see* **халько—**.

халтур/ить *v.* take a second job, moonlight; do careless work; **—ный** *a.* hack (work).

халцедон *m.*, **—овый** *a.* (min.) chalcedony.

халько— *prefix* chalco— (copper); **—алюмит** *m.* (min.) chalcoalumite; **—ген** *m.* chalcogen; **—граф** *m.* chalcograph beetle (*Tomicus chalcographus*); **—графия** *f.* chalcography, line engraving; **—з** *m.* (med.) chalicosis; **—н** *m.* chalcone, benzalacetophenone; **—фильный** *a.* chalcophile (elements).

хальтероидные иглы *pl.* (pal.) halteroid spines.

хальфовый *a.* esparto.

хальциды *pl.* (ent.) Chalcididae.

халява *f.* (glass) muff.

хама *f.* (mal.) jewel box (*Chama*).

хамада *f.* hamada, stony desert.

хамазулен *m.* (pharm.) chamazulene.

хаме— *prefix* (bot.; zool.) chamae— (low, on the ground).

хамелеон *m.* (zool.) chameleon; (chem.) potassium permanganate.

хам/емии *pl.* aphid flies (*Chamaemyidae*); **—еропс** *m.* fan palm (*Chamaerops*); **—овая кислота** chamic acid.

хамефит *m.* (bot.) chamaephyte.

хампсодоно/вые, —подобные *pl.* (ichth.) Champsodontidae.

хамс/а *f.* (ichth.) khamsa, anchovy (*Engraulis*); **—овый** *a. of* **хамса**.

хамсодонтовые *pl.* (ichth.) Champsodontidae.

хандр/а *f.* melancholy; **—ить** *v.* be melancholy, be blue.

Ханкеля функция Hunkel function.

ханос *m.* (ichth.) milkfish (*Chanos c.*); **—овидные** *pl.* (ichth.) snakeheads (*Channoidea*); **—овые** *pl.* milkfishes (*Chanidae*).

ханство *n.* khanate.

Ханта синдром (med.) Hunt's syndrome.

Ханфорд (geog.) Hanford.

хао/с *m.* chaos, disorder, confusion; **—тически** *adv.* chaotically, in disorder, at random; **—тический, —тичный** *a.* chaotic, disorganized, without order, random; turbulent.

хаптагай *m.* (mam.) Bactrian camel.

хара *f.* (bot.) Chara.

хараксовидные *pl.* (ichth.) Characoidei.

характер *m.* character, nature, temperament, type; properties, behavior (of lather, etc.); (chem., phys.) condition, state; pattern (of landscape); method (of operation); degree (of curvature); **—изовать** *v.* characterize; interpret; describe; **—изоваться** *v.* be characterized (by), feature; **—изующий** *a.* characterizing, characteristic, specific.

характеристик/а *f.* characteristic(s), character, property, properties; characterization; (characteristic) curve; diagram; measure, degree; index (of logarithm); response, performance, behavior; rating; **—и** *pl.* characteristic(s), performance; **графическая х., кривая х.** characteristic curve; **техническая х.** specifications.

характеристич/еский, —ный *a.* characteristic; performance; **—еская вязкость** intrinsic viscosity; **—еская диаграмма** performance diagram.

характерн/о *adv.* characteristically; significantly; it is characteristic, it is significant; **—ость** *f.* character, distinguishing feature; strength of character; **—ый** *a.* characteristic, representative, typical; specific, special, peculiar (to), inherent; distinctive, distinguishing; characterized (by); **—ая особенность, —ая черта** characteristic, feature.

характерограф *m.* (elec.) automatic recorder for volt-ampere characteristics.

характрон *m.* (electron.) charactron.

харалес *m.* (bot.) jarales.

харацин/иды, —овые, —ы *pl.* (ichth.) tetras, characins (*Characidae*); **летающие —ы** flying hatchetfishes (*Gasteropelecidae*).

Харди-Вайнберга закон (gen.) Hardy-Weinberg law.

харенгула *f.* (ichth.) little herring (*Harengula*).

харза *f.* (mam.) Himalayan marten (*Martes flavigula*).

хариус *m.* (ichth.) grayling (*Thymallus*); **—овые** *pl.* Thymallidae.

харк/анье *n.* expectoration, spitting; **—ать, —нуть** *v.* expectorate, spit.

харлэкский отдел (geol.) Harlech series.

харовые *pl.* (bot.) Characeae.

хартия *f.* charter.

Хартри-Фока метод (phys.) Hartree-Fock(-Dirac) method, self-consistent-field method.

Хартфорд (geog.) Hartford.

харьковский *a.* (geog.) Kharkov.

хастеллой *m.* (met.) Hastelloy (alloy).

хат/а *f.* hut; **х.-лаборатория** *f.* (agr.) kolkhoz laboratory.

хатангский *a.* (geog.) Khatanga.

хатка *dim. of* **хата**; (beaver) lodge.

хаттский *a.* (geol.) Chattian.

хатыс *m.* (ichth.) species of sturgeon (*Acipenser baeri*).

хатьма *f.* (bot.) Lavatera.

хауз-турбина *f.* house turbine.

Хаукинса элемент Hawkins' cell.

хаулиодовые *pl.* (ichth.) viperfishes (*Chauliodontidae*).

хаульмугр/иловый *a.* chaulmoogryl (alcohol); **—овый** *a.* chaulmoogra (oil); chaulmoogric (acid).

хаунак(с)овые *pl.* anglerfishes (*Chaunacidae*).

хаус *m.* (mam.) jungle cat (*Felis chaus*).

хашам *m.* (ichth.) Caspian asp.

х/б, х/бум *abbr.* (**хлопчатобумажный**) cotton.

хвал/а *f.* praise; **—ебный** *a.* eulogistic, laudatory; **—ен(н)ый** *a.* praised; **—ить** *v.* praise, commend, eulogize.

хвастать(ся) *v.* boast, brag.

хват *m.* (ichth.) asp (*Aspius a.*).

хват/ание *n.* snatching, grasp(ing), seizing; prehension; **—ательный** *a.* grasp(ing); prehensile; raptorial (feet); **—ать** *v.* snatch, seize, catch hold (of), catch, grasp, clutch, bite; carry; suffice, be sufficient, last; **у него не —ает** he is short (of); **—аться** *v.* snatch (at), grasp, get hold (of); **—ающий** *a.* prehensile; **—ить** *v.* suffice, be sufficient; hit, strike, come on suddenly; grasp, grab; suffer, undergo; go too far; **—иться** *v.* remember suddenly; **—ка** *f.* seizing, clutching; grasp, clutch, grip.

х-во, х/во *abbr.* (**хозяйство**) economy; farm, establishment.

хвоевертка *f.* (ent.) Evetria.

хвоевидный *a.* aciculiform.

хвои *gen., etc., of* **хвоя.**

хвойн/ик *m.* (bot.) Ephedra; (young) coniferous forest;

—ка *f.* acicula; **—ые** *pl.* conifers; **—ый** *a.* coniferous, cone-bearing; acerose; coniferyl (alcohol); **—ое дерево** conifer.

хворать *v.* be sick, ail.

хворост *m.* brushwood; slash; **—ина** *f.* stick, dry branch; **—ь** *see* **хворь; —яной** *a.* brushwood.

хвор/ый *a.* sickly, puny; **—ь** *f.* sickliness, illness, ailment.

хвост *m.* tail, cauda; line, queue; shank, shaft (of tool); spike; last runnings (in distillation); **конский х.** (anat.) cauda equina; **заносить х.** *v.* skid; **образование —ей** (chromatography) tailing; **плестись в —е** *v.* lag behind; **спуск на х.** (av.) tail spin.

хвостат/ые *pl.* (zool.) Caudata, Urodela; **—ый** *a.* tailed, caudate.

хвост/ец *m.* (anat.) coccyx; urostyle; (orn.) pygostyle; **—ик** *dim. of* **хвост;** scut; (spermatozoal) cilium; (root) base; (bot.) caudicle; **—ный** *a.* tail.

хвосто— *prefix* ur(o)—, caudi—, caud(o)— (tail); **—видный** *a.* caudiform; **—вик** *m.* (tool) stem, shaft; tail end (of broach); butt (of automatic coupler); (petrol.) liner; **—вой** *a.* tail, caudal, uropygial; rear, posterior, hindmost, butt, end; after; residual, waste, discarded; **—вой усик** (ent.) cercus; **—вой щит** (zool.) pygidium, tail shield; **—вая кость** (anat.) coccyx; **—вая лопасть** (crust.; ent.) telson; **—вая нить** (ent.) cercus; **—вая пластинка** (herp.) pygal (plate); **—кол** *m.* (ichth.) stingray (*Dasyatis*); **—коловые; —колы** *pl.* (ichth.) Dasyatidae, Trygonidae; Urolophidae; **—листный** *a.* (bot.) urophyllous; **—ножки** *pl.* (ent.) springtails (*Collembola*); **—образование** *n.* (chromatography) tailing; **—хранилище** *n.* tailing pond.

хвостцов/ый *a.* (anat.) coccygeal; **—ая кость** coccyx.

хвосты *pl. of* **хвост;** (min.) tails, tailings, residue.

хвощ *m.* (bot.) horsetail (*Equisetum*).

хвоя *f.* coniferous needles or branches.

хевея *f.* (bot.) Hevea; **бразильская х.** para rubber tree (*H. brasiliensis*).

Хевисайда слой Heaviside layer, ionosphere.

Хегелера печь Hegeler furnace.

Хеддльсон (vet.) Huddleson (test for brucellosis).

хедер *m.* (agr.) header, cutter.

хейл—, —о— *prefix* cheil(o)— (lip; edge); **—ёз** *m.* (med.) cheilosis; **—линусы** *pl.* (ichth.) wrasses (*Cheilinus*); **—ит** *m.* (med.) cheilitis; **—омастигоз** *m.* (med.) Chilomastix infection; **—омастикс** *m.* (prot.) Chilomastix; **—опластика** *f.* (med.) cheiloplasty; **—осхиз, —ошизис** *m.* (med.) cheiloschisis, harelip.

хейр/амин *m.* cheiramine; **—антин** *m.* cheiranthin; **—антовая кислота** cheiranthic acid; **—ин** *m.* cheirin; **—инин** *m.* cheirinine; **—о—** *prefix* cheir(o)— (hand); **—олин** *m.* cheirolin; **—оспазм** *m.* cheirospasm.

хек *m.* (ichth.) hake (*Merluccius m.*).

хекер *see* **хэкер.**

хековые *pl.* (ichth.) codfishes, hakes, etc. (*Gadidae*).

хел/ант *m.* chelating agent; **—ат** *m.* chelate, chelate compound; **—атный** *a.* chelate(d); **—атометрия** *f.* chelatometry; **—атообразование** *n.* chelation; **—атообразователь** *m.* chelating agent; **—атохромный** *a.* chelatochrome; **—ация** *f.* chelation.

хелидон/аминовая кислота chelidonamic acid; **—ин** *m.* chelidonine; **—овая кислота** chelidonic acid; pyronedicarboxylic acid; **соль —овой кислоты, —овокислая соль** chelidonate.

хелицер/а (zool.) chelicera, pincer-like appendage; **—овые, —оносные** *pl.* (zool.) Chelicerata.

хело— *see* **гело—.**

хелон *m.* (ichth.) mullet (*Mugil*).

хелонин *m.* chelonin.

хелостомовые *pl.* climbing perches (*Anabantidae*).

Хельбергера печь Helberger furnace.

хельмит *m.* (min.) hielmite.

х.е.м. *abbr.* (**химическая единица массы**) chemical mass unit.

хеми— *see* **хемо—, геми—; —люминесценция** *f.* chemiluminescence.

Хемминга код (math.) Hamming code.

хемо— *prefix* chemo—, chemi(co)—, chemical; **—генные отложения** chemical precipitates (in water); **—з** *m.* (med.) chemosis; **—каустика** *f.* (med.) chemocautery; **—кинезис** *m.* chemokinesis; **—лиз** *m.* chemolysis; **—реология** *f.* chemorheology; **—рецептор** *m.* (physiol.) chemoreceptor; **—синтез** *m.* (physiol.) chemosynthesis; **—смоз** *m.* chemosmosis.

хемосорб/ированный *a.* chemisorbed; **—ционный** *a.*, **—ция** *f.* chemisorption, chemical absorption.

хемо/сфера *f.* chemosphere; **—таксис** *m.* (biol.) chemotaxis; **—троника** *f.* chemotronics; **—тропизм** *m.* chemotropism; **—троф** *m.* (biol.) chemotroph.

хемулоны *pl.* (ichth.) grunts (*Pomadasyidae*).

Хендерсона способ Henderson process.

хенна *f.* henna.

хенодезоксихолевая кислота (biochem.) chenodeoxycholic acid, chenic acid.

хенопод/иевый *a.* chenopodium (oil); **—ин** *m.* chenopodin.

херес *m.* sherry.

хермес *m.* (ent.) Chermes.

херсонский *a.* (geog.) Kherson.

Хертера-Дриффильда характеристика Hurter-Driffield characteristic curve.

херувизм *m.* (med.) cherubism.

хескер *m.* (agr.) husker; **—ный** *a.* husking.

хет/а *f.* chaeta, seta, spine, bristle; **—огнаты** *pl.* (zool.) Chaetognatha.

хетомин *m.* chetomin.

хетоптерус *m.* parchment worm (*Chaetopterus*).

хетотаксия *f.* (zool.) chaetotaxy, bristle pattern.

хетчер *m.* hatcher, incubator.

хеш *m.* (comp.) hash; **—ирование** *n.* hashing; **х.-таблица** hash table.

хиазм *m.*, **—а** *f.* (biol.) chiasm(a); **—одовые** *pl.* (ichth.) (black) swallowers (*Chiasmodontidae*).

хиастоневрия *f.* (mal.) chiastoneuria.

хиатус *m.* hiatus.

хибикон *m.* Hibicon, benzchlorpropamide.

Хивисайда *see* **Хевисайда.**

хидантоин *m.* hydantoin.

хидорусы *pl.* (crust.) Chydoridae.

хижин/а *f.* hut; **—ка** *dim. of* **хижина.**

хи-квадрат *m.* (math.) chi-square.

хикори (ichth.) hickory shad (*Alosa mediocris*).

хил *sh. m. of* **хилый,** *see also* **хилус; —ангиома** *f.* (med.) chylangioma.

хилеть *v.* grow feeble, grow sickly.

хило— *prefix* (physiol.) chyl(o)—, chyle; **—донелла** *f.* (prot.) Chilodonella; **—донеллёз** *m.* chilodonellosis; **—дус** *m.* (ichth.) Chilodus punctatus; **—зный** *a.* chylous.

хилость *f.* feebleness, sickliness, debility.

хилоторакс *m.* (med.) chylothorax.

хилус *m.* (physiol.) chyle.

хилый *a.* feeble, weak, sickly, debilitated.

хим— *prefix* chemical.

химаза *f.* chymase.

химаппарат *m.* chemical apparatus, chemical equipment.

химафилин *m.* chimaphilin.

химбаклаб *m.* chemical and bacteriological laboratory.

химбомба *a.* chemical bomb, gas bomb.

химера *f.* (biol.) chimera; (ichth.) Chimaera.

химеричн/ость *f.* impracticability; **—ый** *a.* impracticable, chimerical, absurd.

химзавод *m.* chemical plant.

хим. зн. *abbr.* (**химический знак**) chemical symbol.

химиз/ация *f.* chemization; **—ировать** *v.* introduce chemical methods and products; **—м** *m.* chemism; chemical aspect, chemical nature, chemistry.

химик *m.* chemist.

химик/алии, —аты *pl.* chemicals.

химик-консультант *m.* consulting chemist.

химико— *prefix* chemico—, chemical; **—аналитический** *a.* analytical (balance).

химик-органик *m.* organic chemist.

химико/спектрографический *a.* spectrochemical; **—термический** *a.* thermochemical; **—технологический** *a.* chemical engineering; **—физический** *a.* physicochemical.

химик-пищевик *m.* food chemist; **х.-эксперт** *m.* consulting chemist.

химиловый спирт chimyl alcohol.

химио— *see* **хемо—**; **—профилактика** *f.* (med.) chemoprophylaxis; **—синтез** *m.* chemosynthesis; **—терапия** *f.* chemotherapy; **—цептор** *m.* chemo(re)ceptor.

химически *adv.* chemically.

химическ/ий *a.* chemical; indelible (pencil); manmade (fibers); **—ая служба** chemical warfare service; **—ая технология** chemical technology; chemical engineering; **—ая физика** physical chemistry; **—ая чистка** dry cleaning; **—ое зажигание** (rockets) spontaneous ignition; **—ое стекло** laboratory glassware; **—ие материалы, —ие препараты, —ие продукты** chemicals.

химическо-физический *a.* physicochemical.

химия *f.* chemistry; **х. растений** phytochemistry; **биологическая х.** biochemistry.

химозин *m.* chymosin, rennin.

химопрепарат *m.* chemical compound, drug.

химотрипсин *m.* chymotrypsin; **—оген** *m.* (biochem.) chymotrypsinogen.

хим/отроника *f.* chemotronics; **—поглотитель** *m.* chemical absorber; **—пром** *m.* chemical industry; **—снаряд** *m.* chemical shell; **—сорбция** *f.* chemical absorption; **—состав** *m.* chemical composition; **—стойкий** *a.* resistant to chemicals; **—стойкость** *f.* resistance to chemicals; **—сырё** *n.* chemical feedstock; **—уголок** *m.* chemistry reading room.

химус *m.* (physiol.) chyme.

химфугас *m.* chemical (land) mine.

химчистка *f.* dry cleaning.

хин——*prefix* quin—, quinine; **—а** *f.* quina, cinchona bark; **—азин** *m.* quinazine, quinoxaline; **—азолин** *m.* quinazoline, phenmiazine; **—азолон** *m.* quinazolone, oxyquinazoline; **—акридин** *m.* quinacridine; **—акрин** *m.* quinacrine hydrochloride, chinacrin hydrochloride; **—ализарин** *m.* quinalizarin.

хинальдин *m.,* **—овый** *a.* quinaldine, 2-methylquinoline; **—овая кислота** quinaldic acid, 2-quinolinecarboxylic acid.

хин/амидин *m.* quinamidine; **—амин** *m.* quinamine; **—амицин** *m.* quinamicine; **—анафтол** *m.* quin(an)-aphthol; **—ат** *m.* quinate; **—гамин** *m.* chloroquine.

—гидрон *m.,* **—гидроновый** *a.* quinhydrone; **—долин** *m.* quindoline; **—ен** *m.* quinene.

хинид/амин *m.* quinidamine; **—ин** *m.* quinidine.

хинизарин *m.,* **—овый** *a.* quinizarin, 1,4-dihydroxyanthraquinone.

хинизатин *m.* quinisatin; **—овая кислота** quinisatinic acid.

хинин *m.* quinine; **—дол** *m.* quinindole; **—овый** *a.* quinine; quininic (acid); **—он** *m.* quininone.

хин/ит *m.* quinite, quinitol, cyclohexanediol; **—ицин** *m.* quinicine.

хиннис *m.* (ichth.) Hynnis goreensis.

хиннодубильный *a.* quinotannic (acid).

хинолиновый *a.* quinoline.

хинн/ый *a.* quinine; **х. корень** (bot.) China root (*Smilax china*); **—ая кислота** quinic acid, hexahydrotetrahydroxybenzoic acid; **соль —ой кислоты** quinate; **—ая кора** cinchona bark; **—ое дерево** (bot.) cinchona.

хино— *prefix* quino— (quina; quinine); **—вин** *m.* quinovin, chinovin; **—воза** *f.* quinovose (glucoside); chinovose (carbohydrate); **—дубильная кислота** quinotannic acid, cinchonatannin; **—зол** *m.* Quinosol, 8-hydroxyquinoline sulfate; **—ид** *m.,* **—идный** *a.* quinoid; **—идин** *m.* quinoidine; **—ил** *m.* quinoyl.

хинок/итиол *m.* hinokitiol, thujaplicin; **—овая кислота** hinokic acid.

хиноксал/ил *m.* quinoxalyl; **—ин** *m.* quinoxaline, quinazine; **—он** *m.* quinoxalone.

хинол *m.* quinol, hydroquinone; **—изин** *m.* quinolizine; **—ил** *m.* quinolyl.

хинолин *m.* quinoline, 1-benzazine; **—карбоновый** *a.* quinolinecarboxylic (acid); **—овый** *a.* quinoline; **—овая кислота** quinoline acid; quinolinic acid, 2,3-pyridinedicarboxylic acid; **—ол** *m.* quinolinol, hydroxyquinoline.

хино/лон *m.* quinolone; **—ль** *see* **хинол**; **—н** *m.* quinone; **—нил** *m.* quinonyl; **—ниминовый** *a.* quinone imine (dyes); **—токсин** *m.* quinotoxine; **—тропин** *m.* quinotropine, urotropine quinate; **—фталон** *m.* quinophthalone; **—хинолин** *m.* quinoquinoline; **—цид** *m.* quinocide (antimalarial).

хинуклидин *m.,* **—овый** *a.* quinuclidine.

хио— *prefix* chio— (snow).

хиодоны *pl.* (ichth.) mooneyes (*Hiodontidae*).

хио/коцин *m.* chiococcine; **—нантин** *m.* chionanthin; **—нантоид** *m.* chionanthoid.

хионо— *prefix* chion(o)— (snow); **—фильный** *a.* chionophilous, bearing winter leaves.

хирад *m.* khirad (polyethylene-base plastic).

хиральн/ость *f.* chirality; **—ый** *a.* chiral, turning the plane of polarization of light to either hand.

хират/ин *m.* chiratin; **—огенин** *m.* chiratogenin.

хиреть *see* **хилеть.**

хирман *m.* khirman, cotton ginning yard.

хиро— *prefix* ch(e)ir(o)— (hand).

хирогале (mam.) a genus of lemurs (*Cheirogaleus*).

хирола *f.* (mam.) Hunter's antelope.

хироним *m.* (bot.) chironym.

хирономидовые *pl.* (ent.) Chironomidae.

хиропластика *f.* (med.) ch(e)iroplasty, plastic surgery on hand.

хиропот *m.* (mam.) saki (*Chiropotes*).

хиропрактика *f.* (med.) chiropractic.

хироптеригий *m.* (zool.) cheiropterygium, pentadactyl limb.

хироптеро— *prefix* chiroptero— (bats); **—фильный** *a.* chiropterophilous, pollinated by bats.

хироскоп *m.* (ophth.) ch(e)iroscope.

хиротип *m.* (biol.) chirotype, type specimen.

хироцентровые *pl.* (ichth.) wolf herrings, dorab (*Chirocentridae*).

хирург *m.* surgeon; **—и** *pl.* (ichth.) surgeonfishes (*Acanthuridae*); **—ический** *a.* surgical; surgeon's; suture (needle); **—ия** *f.* surgery; **—овые** *pl.* (ichth.) Acanthuridae.

хитен/идин *m.* chitenidine; **—ин** *m.* chitenine.

хитёр *sh. m. of* **хитрый.**

хитин *m.* chitin; **—изация** *f.* chitinization; **—овый** *a.* chitin(ous).

хитоза *f.* chitose; **—мин** *m.* chitosamine (glucosamine); **—н** *m.* chitosan.

хитон (mal.) chiton; **—овая кислота** chitonic acid.

хитоны *pl.* (zool.) Loricata.

хитридий *m.* (bot.) chytridium.

хитр/о *adv.* cleverly, etc., *see a.*; **—осплетение** *n.* stratagem; **—ость** *f.* cunning, slyness; intricacy; ingenuity; trick, dodge, stratagem; **—оумие** *n.* finesse; **—оумный** *a.* clever; crafty; **—ый** *a.* clever, sly, cunning, ingenious.

хищ/ение *n.* theft, plunder; misappropriation, embezzlement; tampering; **—нецы** *pl.* (ent.) assassin bugs; **—ник** *m.* predator; **—нический** *a.* carnivorous; predatory; **—ность** *f.* predatory nature, rapacity; carnivorousness; **—ные** *pl.* (zool.) Carnivora; **водные —ные** Pinnipedia; **наземные —ные** Fissipedia; **—ный** *a.* predatory; predaceous (insect); raptorial (bird); carnivorous; **—ные зубы** fangs, canine teeth; **дневные —ные птицы** birds of prey (*Accipitres, Falconiformes*).

хиэна *f.* (ichth.) puntazzo.

хл *abbr.* (**хлороформ**) chloroform.

хлад— *see* **хладно—**; **—агент** *m.* refrigerant; cooling agent, coolant.

хладно— *prefix* cold; cool; refrigeration; **—кровие** *n.* composure, equanimity; **—кровный** *a.* cool, composed; indifferent.

хладноломк/ий *a.* (met.) cold short, cold brittle; **—ость** *f.* cold shortness; cold brittleness.

хладностойк/ий *a.* cold-resistant; **х. состав** antifreeze; **—ость** *f.* cold resistance; (met.) cold strength.

хладо— *see* **хладно—**; **—агент** *see* **хладагент**; **—бойня** *f.* slaughterhouse; **—носитель** *m.* cold carrier; **—стойкий** *see* **хладностойкий**; **—текучесть** *f.* cold flow; **—транспорт** *m.* refrigerated transportation.

хлам *m.* junk, trash, rubbish.

хламид/иевые, —ии *pl.* (biol.) Chlamydiaceae; **—ный** *a.* chlamydeous; **—о—** *prefix* chlamyd(o)— (mantle, cloak, covering); **—оспора** *f.* (bot.) chlamydospore.

хламис *m.* (mal.) scallop (*Chlamys*); (lichens) chlamys, cloak.

хл.-бум *abbr.* (**хлопчатобумажный**).

хлеб *m.* bread, loaf; cereals, grain; **—а** *pl.* grain crop.

хлебать *v.* gulp, swallow.

хлеб/ец *m.* small loaf; **—ина** *f.* beebread.

хлеб/ка *gen. of* **хлебок**; **—нуть** *see* **хлебать.**

хлебн/ый *a. of* **хлеб;** lucrative; frumentaceous; grain (alcohol); **х. амбар** granary; **х. комарик** Hessian fly; **х. спирт** grain alcohol, ethyl alcohol; **—ая мушка** (ent.) grass fly; **—ая плесень** bread mold (*Mucor mucedo*); **—ое дерево** (bot.) bread-fruit (*Artocarpus incisa*); **—ые растения** cereals.

хлебо— *prefix* grain; bread; **—булочный** *a.* baked (goods); **—завод** *m.* bakery; **—заготовительный** *a.*, **—заготовка** *f.* grain storage, grain harvesting; **—закупка** *f.*, **—закупочный** *a.* grain purchasing.

хлебок *m.* sip, mouthful, swallow.

хлебокопнитель *m.* grain stacker.

хлебопаш/енный *a.* agricultural; **—ество** *n.* agriculture; grain farming; **—ествовать** *v.* raise grain.

хлебо/пёк *m.* baker; **—пекарный** *a.* baking; **—пекарня** *f.* bakery; **—печение** *n.* bread baking; **—поставка** *f.* grain delivery (to the state); **—продукты** *pl.* grain products; **—производящий** *a.* grain-producing; **—резка** *f.* bread cutter; **—резный** *a.* bread-cutting; **—роб** *m.* grain grower; **—род** *m.* abundant grain crop; **—родный** *a.* grain-producing; productive, abundant; **—сдаточный** *a.*, **сдача** *f.* grain delivering; **—сольство** *n.* hospitality; **—стой** *m.* stand of grain; **—торговля** *f.* grain trade; **—уборка** *f.*, **—уборочный** *a.* grain harvest(ing); **—фураж** *m.*, **—фуражный** *a.* grain and forage.

хлев *m.* cattle shed, barn, pen.

хлёст *see* **хлестание.**

хлест/ание *n.* whipping, etc., *see v.*; **—ать** *v.* whip, lash, beat, flap; gush (out), spout, flow, pour.

хлёсткий *a.* whipping, lashing; bold, swift.

хлеще *comp. of* **хлесткий.**

хлипкий *a.* weak, poor; pasty, gruel-like.

хлоазма *f.* (med.) chloasma.

хлоп *m.* bang(ing), clap(ping); **—анье** *n.* banging, etc., *see v.*; **—ать** *v.* bang, slam; clap, slap; flap, whip; pop.

хлопко— *prefix* cotton; **—видный** *a.* (bot.) gossypine, cottony; **—вод** *m.* cotton grower; **—водство** *n.*, **—водческий** *a.* cotton-growing.

хлопков/ый *a.* cotton(y); **—ая моль** (ent.) pink cotton bollworm (*Pectinophora gossypiella*); **—ое масло** cottonseed oil; **—ое семя** cottonseed.

хлопко/завод *m.* gin (mill); **—заготовка** *f.* state purchase of cotton; **—комбайн** *m.* cotton combine; **—очёски** *pl.* cotton waste.

хлопкоочист/итель *m.*, **—ительная машина** (cotton) gin; **—ительный** *a.* ginning; **—ительный завод** gin (mill); **—ка** *f.* ginning.

хлопко/прядение *n.*, **—прядильный** *a.* cotton-spinning; **—роб** *m.* cotton grower; **—сеющий** *a.*, **—сеяние** *n.* cotton planting, cotton growing; **—собиратель** *m.* cotton picker; **—сушилка** *f.* cotton dryer; **—трепалка** *f.* batting machine; **—уборка** *f.*, **—уборочный** *a.* cotton picking.

хлопнуть *see* **хлопать.**

хлопок *m.* cotton; floc, flake; clap; **х.-сырец** *m.* raw cotton.

хлопот/ать *v.* (take) trouble; try for; intercede, plead (for); solicit, petition; bustle about; **—ливый** *a.* busy (person); troublesome (business); **—ня** *f.* concern, care; fuss; **—ы** *pl.* trouble, cares.

хлопун *m.* (ichth.) pikeperch (*Lucioperca l.*).

хлопушка *f.* firecracker; gate valve; fly swatter; (bot.) catch fly.

хлопчатник *m.* cotton plant; **—овый** *a.* cotton; cottonseed (oil).

хлопчато— *prefix* cotton.

хлопчатобумажн/ый *a.* cotton; **х. порох** guncotton, pyroxylin; **—ая материя, —ая ткань** cotton (fabric).

хлопчат/ый *a.* cotton, **—ая бумага** cotton (fabric).

хлопь/е *n.* floc, flake; **—ями** in flakes, in flocculent form; **в виде —ев** flocculent; **—евидный, —еобразный** *a.* flaky, flocculent; **—еобразование** *n.* flocculation; **—я** *pl.* flakes; flocs.

хлор *m.* chlorine, Cl, chlorine gas; **гидрат —а** chlorine hydrate; **окись —а** chlorine oxide.

хлор— *prefix* chlor(o)—; chloride; **—агент** *m.* chlorinating agent; **—азид** *m.* chlorazide; **—азин** *m.* Chlorazine; **—азол** *m.* chlorazol; **—акон** *m.* Chloracon, benzchlorpropamide.

хлорал *m.* chloral, trichloroethanal; **—гидрат** *m.* chloral hydrate; **—ид** *m.* chloralide; **—оза** *f.* chloralose, anhydroglucochloral.

хлор/алун *m.* chloralum; **—алуровая кислота** chloraluric acid; **—аль** *see* **хлорал**; **—алюминит** *m.* (min.) chloraluminite; **—амид** *m.* chloramide, chloral amide; **—амил** *m.* amyl chloride; **—амилен** *m.* chloroamylene; **—амин** *m.* chloramine; **—амфеникол** *m.* chloramphenicol, Chloromycetin (antibiotic).

хлорангидрид *m.* acid chloride; **х. стеариновой кислоты** stearyl chloride; **х. уксусной кислоты** acetyl chloride.

хлоранил *m.* chloranil, tetrachloroquinone; **—амид** *m.* chloranilamide; **—ин** *m.* chloraniline; **—овая кислота** chloranilic acid; **—овокислая соль** chloranilate.

хлорантия *f.* (bot.) chloranthy.

хлор/ат *m.* chlorate; **—атор** *m.* chlorinator; **—аурат** *m.* chloraurate.

хлорацет/ат *m.* chloroacetate; **—ил** *m.* chloroacetyl; **—он** *m.* chloroacetone; **—оновая кислота** chloroacetonic acid; **—офенон** *m.* chloroacetophenone, phenacyl chloride.

хлорбенз/ил *m.* chlorobenzyl; benzyl chloride; **—ойная кислота** chlorobenzoic acid; **—ол** *m.* chlorobenzene.

хлор/бромбензол *m.* chlorobromobenzene; **—бутадиен** *m.* chlorobutadiene, chloroprene; **—бутанол** *m.* chlorobutanol; **—бутилкаучук** *m.* chlorinated butyl rubber; **—винил** *m.* vinyl chloride; **—винилиден** *m.* vinylidene chloride; **—газ** *m.* chlorine gas; **—гексидин** *m.* chlorhexidine (antibacterial).

хлоргидр/ат *m.* hydrochloride; chlorine hydrate; **—ин** *m.*, **—иновый** *a.* chlorohydrin; **—ирование** *n.* hydrochlorination.

хлор/дан *m.* chlordan (insecticide); **—елла** *f.* (bot.) Chlorella (alga); **—енхима** *f.* (bot.) chlorenchyma (tissue whose cells contain chlorophyll); **—закись кобальта** cobaltous oxychloride; **—замещённый** *a.* chlorine-substitution, chloro—; **—ид** *m.* chloride; **—ид калия** potassium chloride; **—идемия** *f.* (med.) hyperchloremia; **—идин** *m.* Chloridin, pyrimethamine; **—идный** *a.* chloride; **—изация** *f.* chlorination; **—ил** *m.* chloryl; **—илен** *m.* chlorylene, trichloroethylene; **—ин** *m.* khlorin (a polyvinyl chloride fiber); (biochem.) chlorin (porphin derivative); **—атдифенил** *m.* chlorinated diphenyl; **—инация** *f.* chlorination; **—ион** *m.* chlorion, chloride ion; **—ипривный** *see* **хлоропривный**.

хлорир/ование *n.* chlorination; **—ованный** *a.* chlorinated; **—овать** *v.* chlorinate; **—ующий** *a.* chlorinating.

хлористоводородн/ый *a.* hydrochloride (of); **х. газ** hydrogen chloride; **х. хинин** quinine hydrochloride; **—ая кислота** hydrochloric acid; **соль —ой кислоты** chloride.

хлористо/калиевая соль; —кислый калий potassium chlorite; **—кислый** *a.* chlorous acid; chlorite (of); **—кислая соль** chlorite.

хлорист/ый *a.* chlorine, chlorous; (formerly lower or **—ous**) chloride (of); **х. винил** vinyl chloride; **х. водород** hydrogen chloride; **х. карбонил** carbonyl chloride, phosgene; **х. натрий** sodium chloride; **—ая кислота** chlorous acid; **соль —ой кислоты** chlorite; **основной х.** oxychloride (of).

хлорит *m.* (chem.; min.) chlorite; **—изация** *f.* (min.) chloritization; **—овый** *a.* chlorite; (min.) chloritic.

Хлор-ИФК *abbr.* (изопропил-N-3-хлорфенилкарбамат) isopropyl N-(3-chlorophenyl)carbamate.

хлор/ка *f.* bleaching powder; **—кали** *n.* potassium chlo-

ride; **—кальций** *m.*, **—кальциевый** *a.* calcium chloride; **—ксилол** *m.* chloroxylene; **—лейкемия** *f.*, **—лейкоз** *m.* (med.) chloroleukemia, chloroma; **—масляная кислота** chlorobutyric acid; **—метан** *m.* chloromethane; **—метил** *m.* chloromethyl; methyl chloride; **—метилирование** *n.* chloromethylation; **—мицетин** *see* **хлоромицетин**; **—мочевина** *f.* chlorourea; **—нитробензол** *m.* chloronitrobenzene.

хлорно/аммониевая соль ammonium perchlorate; **—бариевая соль** barium perchlorate; **—ватая кислота** chloric acid; **соль —ватой кислоты** chlorate.

хлорноватисто/калиевая соль potassium hypochlorite; **—кальциевая соль** calcium hypochlorite; **—кислый** *a.* hypochlorous acid; hypochlorite (of); **—кислый натрий** sodium hypochlorite; **—кислая соль** hypochlorite.

хлорноватист/ый *a.* hypochlorous; **х. ангидрид** hypochlorous acid anhydride, chlorine monoxide; **—ая кислота** hypochlorous acid; **соль —ой кислоты** hypochlorite; **—ые эфиры** hypochlorite esters.

хлорновато/алюминиевая соль aluminum chlorate; **—бариевая соль** barium chlorate; **—калиевая соль** potassium chlorate; **—кислый** *a.* chloric acid; chlorate (of); **—кислый натрий, —натриевая соль** sodium chlorate; **—кислая соль** chlorate.

хлорно/калиевая соль, —кислый калий potassium perchlorate; **—кислый** *a.* perchloric acid; perchlorate (of); **—кислая соль** perchlorate.

хлорность *f.* chlorine content, salinity.

хлорн/ый *a.* chlorine; (formerly higher or **—ic**) chloride (of); **х. ангидрид** perchloric anhydride, chlorine heptoxide; **—ая вода** chlorine water; **—ая известь** bleaching powder, calcium hypochlorite mixture; **—ая кислота** perchloric acid; **соль —ой кислоты** perchlorate; **—ая медь** cupric chloride; **—ая ртуть** mercuric chloride; **—ое железо** ferric chloride; **—ое олово** stannic chloride; **основной х.** oxychloride (of); **основная —ая медь** copper oxychloride.

хлоро— *prefix* chlor(o)— (green; chlorine).

хлороводород *m.* hydrogen chloride; **—ный** *see* **хлористоводородный**.

хлоро/генин *m.* chlorogenine, alstonine; **—геновая кислота** chlorogenic acid; **—гидрин** *m.* chlorohydrin; **—гонидия** *f.* (lichens) chlorogonidium, green gonidium; **—з** *m.* (med.; phyt.) chlorosis; **—иодистый** *a.* chloroiodide, iodochloride (of); **—какодил** *m.* cacodyl chloride; **—кальцит** *m.* (min.) chlorocalcite, hydrophilite.

хлорокись *f.* oxychloride; **х. серы** thionyl chloride, sulfinyl chloride; **х. углерода** carbonyl chloride, phosgene; **х. фосфора** phosphorus oxychloride, phosphoryl chloride.

хлоро/ксилен *m.* chloroxylene, xylyl chloride; **—лейцит** *m.* (bot.) chloroleucite; **—ма** *f.* (med.) chloroma, green cancer; **—метр** *m.* chlorometer; **—метрия** *f.* chlorometry; **—мицетин** *m.* Chloromycetin, chloramphenicol.

хлоропаллад/ат *m.*, **—иевокислая соль** chloropalladate; **—иевый** *a.* chloropalladic (acid); **—ит** *m.* chloropalladite.

хлоропласт *m.* (bot.) chloroplast.

хлороплатин/ат *m.* chloroplatinate, platinichloride; **—истая кислота** chloroplatinous acid; **—истокислая соль, —ит** *m.* chloroplatinite, platinochloride; **—овая кислота** chloroplatinic acid; **—овокислая соль** chloroplatinate.

хлоро/прен *m.*, **—преновый** *a.* chloroprene, 2-chloro-1,3-butadiene; **—привный** *a.* chloroprivic, deprived of chlorides; —**производное** *n.* chlorine derivative; —**рафин** *m.* chlororaphin; —**саркома** *m.* (med.) chloroma; —**содержащий** *a.* chlorine-containing; —**тический,** —**тичный** *a.* chlorotic; —**углерод** *m.* carbon (tetra)chloride; —**фаит** *m.* (min.) chlorophaite; —**фан** *m.* (min.) chlorophane.

хлорофил/л *m.* (bot.) chlorophyll; —**лаза** *f.* (biochem.) chlorophylase; —**лин** *m.* chlorophyllin; —**ловый,** —**ьный** *a.* chlorophyll(ous); —**ловое зерно** (bot.) chloroplast(id); —**лоносный** *a.* chlorophylligerous.

хлорофит *m.* (bot.) chlorophyte.

хлороформ *m.,* —**енный** *a.* chloroform, trichloromethane; —**ированный** *a.* chloroformed; —**ировать** *v.* chloroform.

хлор/офос *m.* Trichlorfon, Dipterex (insecticide); —**охин** *m.* (pharm.) chloroquine; —**парафин** *m.* chloroparaffin; —**пентан** *m.* chloropentane; —**пикрин** *m.* chloropicrin; —**платинат** *see* **хлороплатинат;** —**производные** *pl.* chlorine derivatives, chlorine compounds; —**промазин** *m.* (pharm.) chlorpromazine, thorasine; —**пропамид** *m.* chlorpropamide; —**пропан** *m.* chloropropane; —**смесь** *f.* a carbon disulfide-carbon tetrachloride pesticide; —**содержащий** *a.* chlorine-containing; —**стирол** *m.* chlorostyrene; —**сульфоновый** *a.* chlorosulfonic (acid); —**тен** *m.* polychloropinene (insecticide); —**тетрациклин** *m.* chlortetracycline, aureomycin; —**тиазид** *m.* chlorothiazide; —**тиофенол** *m.* chlorothiophenol; —**толуол** *m.* chlorotoluene; —**трианизен** *m.* (pharm.) chlorotrianisene, a synthetic estrogen; —**углеводород** *m.* chlorohydrocarbon.

хлоругольн/ый *a.* chlorocarbonic, chloroformic (acid); —**эфир** —**ой кислоты** chlorocarbonate, chloroformate.

хлоруксусн/ая кислота chloroacetic acid; —**окислая соль** chloroacetate; —**оэтиловый эфир** ethyl chloroacetate; —**ые эфиры** chloroacetic esters.

хлор/фен *m.* chlorophene, chlorinated camphene, Toxaphene; —**фенидим** *m.* N-4-chlorophenyl-N', N'-dimethyl urea (herbicide); —**фенол** *m.* chlorophenol; —**циан** *m.* cyanogen chloride; —**цинк** *m.* zinc chloride; —**цинкиод** *m.* chlorozinc iodurate; —**щавелевая кислота** chlorooxalic acid; —**этан,** —**этил** *m.* chloroethane, ethyl chloride; —**этилен** *m.* chloroethylene, vinyl chloride; —**этиловый эфир** chloroethyl ether; —**этон** *m.* chloretone, chlorobutanol; —**юр** *see* **хлорид;** —**янтарная кислота** chlorosuccinic acid.

хлуп *m.,* —**ь** *f.* (orn.) fluff; tectrices.

хлф. *abbr.* (**хлороформ**) chloroform.

хлын/увший *a.* gushing; irruptive; —**уть** *v.* gush (out), spout, well; rush, pour.

хлыст *m.* whip, switch; trimmed log, bole, trunk; —**ать,** —**нуть** *see* **хлестать;** —**овидный** *a.* vimineous; virgate, wand-shaped; —**овик** *m.* whipworm (parasite) (*Trichuris trichiura*); —**овый** *a. of* **хлыст.**

хлюп *m.,* —**анье** *n.* squelch(ing); —**ать** *v.* squelch; —**кий** *a.* viscous, sticky.

хлябь viscous mud.

ХМ *abbr.* (**хлорат магния**) magnesium chlorate; **хМ** *abbr.* (**холодная масса**) cold (air) mass.

хмар/а *f.* cloud; —**ь** *f.* fog.

хмел/евина *f.* lupulin, humulin; —**евод** *m.* hop grower; —**еводство** *n.,* —**еводческий** *a.* hop growing; —**евой** *a.* hop; brewer's (yeast); —**евая мука** *see* **хмелевина;** —**еграб** *m.* (bot.) hop hornbeam (*Ostrya*); —**ёк** *m.* hop clover; —**елистный** *a.* (bot.) humulifolious, hop-leaved; —**еподобный** *a.* hop-like; —**есушилка** *f.* hop dryer; —**еть** *v.* get intoxicated;

—**еуборочный** *a.* hop-picking; —**ина** *f.* hop cone, hop branch; —**ить** *v.* intoxicate; —**ица** *f.* staminate hop(s), male hop(s); —**ь** *m.* hops; intoxication; —**ьник** *m.* hop field.

хмельницкий *a.* (geog.) Khmelnitski.

хмельн/ое *n.* intoxicating liquor; —**ой** *a.* intoxicating; intoxicated; brewing.

хмур/ить *v.* wrinkle, knit (the brows); —**иться** *v.* scowl, frown; be overcast, grow cloudy; —**ый** *a.* surly, sullen; gloomy, overcast.

хмыз *m.* sprig, twig; underbrush, thicket.

ХН *abbr.* (**химическое нападение**) chemical attack.

хна *f.* henna (dye or plant).

хоана *f.* (anat.) choana.

хобот *m.* (mach.) yoke, overarm; snout, nose, end; (lathe) tool holder; (art.) trail; (zool.) proboscis, trunk; —**ик** *m.* (ent.) proboscis; —**ковый** *a.* (physiol.) lip (reflex); sucking (phenomenon); —**ник** *m.* fruit bat (*Macroglossus*); an oligochaete (*Rhynchelmis*); —**ной** *a. of* **хобот;** —**норылые** *pl.* (ichth.) spiny eels (*Mastacembelidae*); —**ные** *pl.* (mam.) elephants (*Proboscidea*); —**овидный** *a.* (biol.) proboscidiform; —**овый** *a. of* **хобот;** —**ок** *m.* (biol.) proboscis, rostel(lum); —**ообразный** *see* **хоботовидный.**

Х-образные ноги knockknees.

ход *m.* motion, move(ment), travel, progress, headway; run (of fish); migration; course, path, way, passage, conduit; channel; (anat.) duct, meatus; passing, going; rate, speed, gait, pace; functioning, operation, run(ning), working (of furnace), process, procedure; (annual) variation; (leveling) line; (surv.) traverse; (photogrammetry) extension; (ray) diagram; degree (of curvature); (caterpillar) tread, track; action, blow (of press); stroke (of piston); gear, thread, pitch (of screw); shape, trend, dependence (of curve); range (of magnet); entrance (to building, etc.); train (of thought); *suffix* pass; boat, ship; **без** —**а** stationary (drive); (naut.) dead in the water; **быть в** —**у** *v.* run, work, be in operation; **быть на** —**у** *v.* be in operation, run; **в** —**е** during (a process); **в** —**е выполнения** as part (of); **величина** —**а, высота** —**а** delivery head; **временной х.** time dependence (of curve); **давать ход** *see* **пускать в ход; на** —**у** on the go, on the move, in transit, (while) running, without stopping, in progress; in running order; **на полном** —**у** at full speed; **на резиновом** —**у** rubber-tired (vehicle); **неровный х.** wobble; **по** —**у** in the course of; **пускать в х.** *v.* put into operation, put into service; start up, set going, set in motion; (naut.) get underway; **свободный х.** free running, free play; **своим** —**ом** under its own power.

ходатай *m.* mediator, agent; —**ство** *n.* intercession; negotiation; application; —**ствовать** *v.* intercede, intervene; petition; apply, send in an application (for).

Ходжкина болезнь (med.) Hodgkin's disease.

ход/ильный *a.* ambulatory, walking, gressorial (foot), gradatory; —**имость** *f.* life (of tire); —**ить** *v.* go, walk, run, operate, work; pass (of current, etc.); attend; nurse, tend; —**кий** *a.* fast(-moving); in (great) demand, salable, marketable; light (ship); —**кость** *f.* marketability; (naut.) propulsive performance; pick-up (of motor); speed (of horse); —**ный** *a. suffix* going, moving.

ходов/ой *a.* going, running, moving, working, operating; traveling, transient, migratory, mobile; propelling; traction (engine); performance (test); routine (analysis); conning, navigating (bridge); track, path; leading; popular, in demand; salable, marketable; **х. валик** feed shaft; **х. винт** lead screw, leader, guide screw; **х. золотник** throttle valve; **х. механизм** running gear; **х. парк** motor pool; **х. ролик** traveler, traveling roller, runner; **—ая гайка** sliding nut; **—ая пружина** mainspring (of clockwork); **—ая рубка** pilot house; **—ая часть** (mach.) underframe, undercarriage; **—ое колесо** running wheel; (horol.) verge wheel; **—ое судно** ship going upriver.

ходок *m.* pedestrian; delegate; light cart; (min.) conduit, passage (for people); (air) course; *sh. m. of* **ходкий.**

ходоуменьшитель *m.* reducing gear; **—ный** *a.* speed-reducing.

ходул/очники *pl.* (orn.) stilts, etc. (*Recurvirostridae*); **—ьный** *a.* stilt(ed), pretentious; gralliform; **—я** *f.* stilt.

ходуном: ходить х. *v.* shake, rock.

ходы *pl. of* **ход;** (anat.) ductuli; labyrinths (of inner ear).

ход/ьба *f.* walking; **—ячий** *a.* walking; current.

хождение *n.* walking; nursing, caring (for); **иметь х.** *v.* be current, pass.

хоз— *prefix;* **хоз.** *abbr.* (**хозяйственный; хозяйство);** **—единица** *f.* business unit; **—инвентарь** *m.* farm implement; **—расчёт** *m.* cost accounting; self support; **на —расчёте** self-supporting; **—расчётный** *a.* self-supporting; profitability (indicator); **—фекальные воды** municipal or domestic sewage; **—часть** *f.* economic department.

хоз/яин *m.* master; boss; landlord, owner, proprietor; (biol., min.) host; (biol.) vector, carrier, transmitter; **сельский х.** farmer; **—яйка** *f.* mistress, landlady; housewife; **—яйничать** *v.* manage, boss; farm.

хозяйственн/ик *m.* economist; manager, executive; **—о** *adv.* economically; **—ость** *f.* economy, thrift; **—ый** *a.* economic(al); executive (personnel); farm; household; fiscal (year); **—ый расчёт** *see* **хозрасчёт; —ый учёт** accounting.

хозяйство *n.* economy; farm; farming, husbandry, cultivation (of crops); industry; facilities (and management), service(s); system, management; (tool) department, stock; installation; establishment, household; (power) plant; **домашнее х.** household; housework; **коллективное х.** cooperative farm; **лесное х.** forestry; **народное х.** national economy; economics; **общественное х.** public sector; **пастбищное х.** range management; **сельское х.** farming, agriculture; **—вание** *n.* management; **—вать** *see* **хозяйничать.**

хол *— see* **холе—; —ан** *m.* cholane; **—ангит** *m.* (med.) cholangitis; **—андрический** *a.* (biol.) holandric; **—ановый** *a.* cholanic (acid); **—ат** *m.* (chem.) cholate.

Холде(й)на (gen.) Haldane's (rule).

холе— *prefix* chol(e)— (bile); **—вая кислота** cholic acid; **—вокислый** *a.* cholic acid; cholate (of); **—вокислая соль** cholate; **—дохолит** *m.* (med.) choledocholith; **—иновый** *a.* choleic (acid); **—кальциферол** *m.* cholecalciferol, vitamin D_3; **—литиаз** *m.* (med.) cholelithiasis.

холеный *a.* well cared for, sleek.

холер/а *f.* (med.) cholera; **—ический** *a.* choleric; **—ный** *a.* cholera(ic); **—овидный** *a.* choleraic, cholera-like.

холест/ан *m.* cholestane; **—еатома** *f.* (med.) cholesteatoma; **—ен** *m.* cholestene; **—енон** *m.* cholestenone; **—ерил** *m.* cholesteryl.

холестерин *m.* cholesterol; **—емия** *f.* (med.) hypercholesterolemia; **—овокислая соль** cholesterate; **—овокислый** *a.* cholesteric acid; cholesterate (of); **—овый** *a.* cholesterol; cholesteric (acid).

холестерол *m.* cholesterol.

холецист/ит *m.* (med.) cholecystitis; **—олитиаз** *see* **холелитиаз.**

холзан *m.* (orn.) golden eagle.

холин *m.,* **—овый** *a.* choline, bilineurine; **—овая кислота** cholinic acid; **—эстераза** *f.* choline esterase.

холить *v.* care (for), groom (a horse).

холка *f.* (zool.) withers, ridge, crest.

холл *m.* (entrance) hall.

Холла эффект, Х. явление (phys.) Hall effect.

холлардиевые *pl.* (ichth.) Triacanthodidae.

Холлерита карта (comp.) Hollerith (punched) card.

холловский *a.* (phys.) Hall (mobility, etc.).

холм *m.* hill, hillock, mound, hummock, hog-back; (sand) dune; (anat.) mons, mound, elevation, eminence; **лонный х.** pubic mound.

холмий *see* **гольмий.**

холм/ик *m.* hillock, mound, hummock; (anat.) colliculus, monticulus; **семенной х.** seminal colliculus; **яйценосный х.** ovarian cumulus; **—истость** *f.* hilliness; **—истый** *a.* hilly, rolling, undulating; **—иться** *v.* rise in hills; **—овой** *a.* (bot.) growing on low hills.

холмогорский *a.* Kholmogor (cattle).

холо— *prefix* cholo— (bile); holo— (whole); **—гамия** *f.* (cyt.) hologamy; **—гастер** *m.* (ichth.) cavefish; **—гинный** *a.* (gen.) hologynous, hologynic; **—гон** *m.* Chologon, dehydrocholic acid.

холод *m.* cold, chill; **—а** *pl.* cold weather; **градусы —а** degrees of frost, degrees below freezing; **лечение —ом** (med.) cryotherapy; **на —е** low-temperature; **на —у** in the cold; **выдавливание на —у** cold pressing; **насыщать на —у** *v.* saturate in the cold (state); **проба на —у** cold test.

холодеть *v.* grow cold, cool, chill.

холодильник *m.* refrigerator, cooler; freezer; condenser; **х. смешения** mixing condenser; **башенный х.** cooling tower; **вторичный х.** aftercooler; **обратный х.** reflux condenser; **х.-шкаф** *m.* refrigerator.

холодильн/ый *a.* cooling, refrigerating, refrigerative, refrigerant; condensing; freezing (mixture, salt, etc.); **х. агент** cooling agent, coolant; **х. вагон** (rr.) refrigerator car; **х. чан** cooler; **х. шкаф** refrigerator; **—ая машина** refrigerating machine, refrigerator; cooler; **—ая промышленность** refrigeration industry; **—ая техника** refrigeration engineering; **—ая установка** refrigerating plant, cooling plant; freezing plant; cold storage plant; **—ое вещество** refrigerant, refrigerating agent; **—ое дело** refrigeration; **—ое пространство** cooling jacket.

холодиновая кислота cholodinic acid.

холодить *v.* cool, chill, refrigerate.

холоднеть *v.* (meteor.) cool off.

холодно *adv.* cold(ly); it is cold; **—ватый** *a.* rather cold, chilly; **—катаный** *a.* cold-rolled; **—кованый** *a.* cold-forged; **—кровный** *a.* cold-blooded, poikilotherm(al); **—прессованный** *a.* cold-pressed; **—стойкий** *a.* cold-resistant; **—сть** *f.* cold(ness).

холодн/ый *a.* cold, frigid, chilly; winter (season); **х. пояс** frigid zone; **—ые красители** ice colors (azo dyes).

холодовынослив/ость *see* **холодостойкость; —ый** *see* **холодостойкий.**

холодо/к *m.* chill, cold(ness); **—любивый** *a.* cold-loving; **—носитель** *m.* cold carrier, cooling medium; **—производительность** *f.* refrigerating capacity.

холодостойк/ий *a.* cold-resistant; (bot.) hardy; **—ость** *f.* resistance to cold; hardiness.

холодоустойчив/ость *see* **холодостойкость; —ый** *see* **холодостойкий.**

холоиданова кислота choloidanic acid.

холопус *m.* (mam.) sloth (*Choloepus*).

холостить *v.* castrate.

холост/ой *a.* idle, loose(-running), free; no-load, empty, blank, dummy; inert (fuel element); (elec.) dead; single, unmarried; (biol.) barren, sterile; (agr.) castrated, gelded, neutered; **х. заряд** blank cartridge; **х. ролик** idler; **х. ход** idling; **работать на —ом ходу, работать в —ую** *v.* (run) idle, run without load; **—ая проба** blank test, control test; **—ое пятно** (chromatography) reference spot.

холостяк *m.* bachelor.

холоталлин *m.* cholothallin.

холо/фермент *m.* (biochem.) holoenzyme; **—целлюлоза** *f.* holocellulose.

холощ/ение *n.* castration; **—ён(н)ый** *a.* castrated, gelded.

холст *m.* canvas; linen, hemp cloth; (filter) cloth; **грубый х.** sacking; **—ина** *f.* canvas; linen; **—инка** *f.*, **—инковый** *a.* gingham; **—инный, —иновый, —яной** *a.* of холст.

холурия *f.* (med.) choluria.

холщовый *see* **холстинный**.

Хольстеда шов (med.) Halsted's suture.

холява *f.* (glass) muff.

хоминг *m.* (zool.) homing.

хомофит *m.* (bot.) chomophyte.

хомут *m.* collar, yoke, ring, lug, hoop, stirrup, strap; clamp, clip; **—ик** *dim. of* **хомут**; **—ина** *f.* collar pad.

хомя/к *m.* (mam.) hamster (*Cricetus*); **полевой х.** American harvest mouse (*Reithrodontomys*); **рисовый х.** rice rat (*Oryzomys*); **—кообразные** *pl.* Cricetidae (mice, rats, lemmings, voles, hamsters); **—чий** *a.* hamster; **—чок** *m.* hamster (*Cricetulus*); **белоногий —чок** deermouse (*Peromyscus*); **—чьи** *pl.* Cricetidae.

хон *m.* hone, honing head.

Хонгха (geog.) Red River (in China).

хондр— *see* **хондро—**; **—а** *f.* (geol.) chondrule; **—илла** *f.* (bot.) chondrilla; **—альгия** *f.* (med.) chondralgia; **—ин** *m.* (biochem.) chondrin; **—ио—** *see* **хондро—**; **—иом** *m.*, **—иома** *f.* (cyt.) chondriome; **—иосома** *f.* chondriosome; **—ит** *m.* (geol.) chondrite; (med.) chondritis.

хондро— *prefix* chondr(i)o— (grain, grit, granular; cartilage); **—арсенит** *m.* (min.) chondrarsenite; **—бласт** *m.* (anat.) chondroblast; **—генез** *m.* chondrogenesis; **—дин** *m.* chondrodine; **—дистрофия** *f.* (med.) chondrodystrophy.

хондроз *m.* (physiol.) chondrosis; **—амин** *m.* chondrosamine; **—аминовая кислота** chondrosamic acid; **—ин** *m.* chondrosin; **—иновая кислота** chondrosinic acid.

хондро/идный *a.* chondroid, resembling cartilage; **—ин** *m.* chondroine; **—итин** *m.* chondroitin; **—итинсерная кислота** chondroitinsulfuric acid; **—итовая кислота** chondroitic acid; **—логия** *f.* chondrology, study of cartilages; **—ма** *f.* (med.) chondroma; **—маляция** *f.* (med.) chondromalaccia; **—новая кислота** chondronic acid; **—протеид, —протеин** *m.* chondroprotein.

хонинг (mach.) honing; **—овальный** *a.* honing; **—ование** *n.* honing; **—овать** *v.* hone.

хонолиты *pl.* (geol.) chonoliths.

Хонсю (geog.) Honshu.

хопкалит *see* **гопкалит**.

хоппер *m.* hopper; hopper car.

хор *m.* choir; chorus; *gen. of* **хоры**; khor; watercourse, ravine.

хорватский *a.* (geog.) Croatian.

Хорвуда процесс Horwood process.

хорд/а *f.* (anat.; math.) chord; span (of arc); **—альный** *a.* chordal; **—овые** *pl.* (zool.) Chordata; **—овый** *a.* chord; chorded; grid (packing); (zool.) chordate; **—угломер** *m.* milrule, goniometric ruler.

хор/ёвый *a. of* **хорёк**; **—ёк** *m.* (mam.) polecat, ferret, weasel, mink (*Mustela*).

хор/ея *f.* (med.) chorea.

хори *pl. of* **хорь**.

хори/за *f.*, **—зис** *m.* (bot.) chorisis.

хор/(и)оидит *m.* (med.) chor(i)oiditis; **—ион** *m.* (embr., zool.) chorion; **—ия** *f. suffix* —chory, dispersal, distribution; **—ный** *a. suffix* —chorous.

хоро— *prefix* choro— (place); **—графия** *f.* chorography; **—логия** *f.* chorology, biogeography.

хоронить *v.* bury, inter; hide, conceal.

хорош/ее *n.* (the) good; **—енько** *adv.* well, properly; **—еть** *v.* improve; **—ий** *a.* good; high (yield, etc.); **—о** *adv.* well, effectively, highly; fully (equipped); freely, heavily; very, readily (soluble); (it is) good.

хоры *pl.* gallery, balcony.

хорь *see* **хорёк**; **—ки** *pl. of* **хорёк**; **—ковый** *a. of* **хорёк**.

хот/ение *n.* desire, volition; **—еть** *v.* wish, want, desire; **—еться** *v.* be desirable; **ему хочется** he wants, he desires, he would like (to).

хот/ь, —я *conj. and particle* (al)though, even though; at least; **х. бы** if only, even if; **—я** *pr. act. part. of* **хотеть**.

хох/латка *f.* crested fowl, crested bird; (ent.) puss moth; (bot.) Corydalis; **—латки** *pl.* (ent.) Notodontidae; **—латый** *a.* tufted, crested, cristate; **—лач** *m.* (mam.) hooded seal (*Cystophora cristata*); (ichth.) tilefish; **—лить(ся)** *v.* bristle up; **—лушка** *see* **хохлатка**; **—ол** *m.* tuft, crest, hood; **—олок** *see* **хохол**; (bot.) pappus; thistledown.

хохотун: черноголовый х. (orn.) great black-headed gull; black-headed merrymaker (*Larus ichthyaetus*).

хохуля *f.* (mam.) Russian desman (*Desmana moschata*).

хочет *pr. 3 sing. of* **хотеть**.

ХП *abbr.* (**хлоропрен**) chloroprene; (**холодный период**) cold period; **ХП, х.п.** *abbr.* (**химическая промышленность**) chemical industry.

ХПК *abbr.* (**химическая потребность в кислороде**) chemical oxygen demand.

хр *abbr.* (**хронометр**) chronometer; **хр, ХР** *abbr.* (**химическая рота**) chemical company; **хр.** *abbr.* (**хребет**) mountain range.

храбрый *a.* brave, courageous, daring.

храмуля *f.* (ichth.) Varicorhinus.

хран/ение *n.* storing, preservation, etc., *see v.*; storage; custody; **х. на холоду** cold storage; **период —ения, срок —ения** shelf life; **—ённый** *a.* stored, etc., *see v.*; **—илище** *n.* storehouse, storage; warehouse, depot, depository; safe; reservoir; (retrieval) file; (nucl.) storage pit; **—ильность** *f.* storability, keeping qualities; **—имость** *f.* shelf life; **—итель** *m.* keeper, custodian, guardian, (game) warden; **—ить** *v.* store, keep, hold, preserve, conserve, save, guard; **—иться** *v.* be stored, etc.; be kept on deposit.

храп *m.* grab, crampon; snore piece (of pump); snore; snort; **—ение** *n.* snoring, stertor; **—еть** *v.* snore; snort.

храпов/ик *m.* ratchet (gear or wheel); **х. и собачка** ratchet and pawl; **—ой** *a.* ratchet; clamshell (excavator); **—ой механизм** *see* **храповик**; **—ая собачка** pawl.

храпок *m.* strainer; suction basket, snore piece (of pump).

хреб/ет *m.*, **—етный** *a.* (anat.) spine, spinal column, backbone; crest, ridge (of mountain); range, chain (of mountains); **—та** *gen. of* **хребет**; **—товый** *a. of* **хребет**; center; **—тообразный** *a.* ridged.

хрен *m.*, **—овый** *a.* horseradish.

хрестоматия *f.* reader, selections.

хриз— *see* **хризо—**; **—алида** *f.* (zool.) chrysalis, pupa; **—амминовая кислота** chrysamminic acid; **—антема** *f.* (bot.) chrysanthemum; **—антемин** *m.* chrysanthemin; chrysanthemine (alkaloid); **—аробин** *m.* chrysarobin; **—атроповая кислота** chrysatropic acid, scopoletin; **—ен** *m.* chrysene, benzophenanthrene; **—иаз** *m.* (med.) chrysiasis, auriosis; **—ин** *m.* chrysin, 5,7-dihydroxyflavone.

хризо— *prefix* chrys(o)— (golden, gold-colored); **—берилл** *m.* (min.) chrysoberyl; **—идин** *m.* chrysoidin; chrysoidine, 2,4-diaminoazobenzene; **—колла** *f.* (min.) chrysocolla; **—лит** *m.* (min.) chrysolite, olivine; **—монады** *pl.* (zool.) chrysomonadina; **—праз** *m.* (min.) chrysoprase; **—терапия** *f.* (med.) chrysotherapy, treatment with gold salts; **—тил** *m.* (min.) chrysotile.

хризофан/ин *m.* chrysophanin; **—овая кислота**, **—ол** *m.* chrysophanic acid, chrysophanol.

хрип *m.*, **—ение** *n.* hoarseness; rattle, crepitation, rhonchus, rale; **—еть** *v.* speak hoarsely; rattle, crepitate, crackle; **—лый** *a.* hoarse; husky; **—нуть** *v.* become hoarse; **—ота** *f.* hoarseness; **—ы** *pl.* rale(s); **—ящий** *a.* stertorous (respiration).

хром *m.* chromium, (constr.); chrome; chrome leather; *sh. m. of* **хромой**; **закись —а** chromous oxide, chromium monoxide; **соль закиси —а** chromous salt; **окись —а** chromium (III) oxide, chromic oxide; **соль окиси —а** chromic salt; **сернокислый х.** chromium sulfate; **хлористый х.** chromous chloride; **хлорный х.** chromic chloride.

хромазия *f.* (cyt.) chromasie.

хромат *m.* chromate; **—ермография** *f.* chromathermography; **—ид** *m.* (biol.) chromatid; **раскалывание —идов, распад —идов** chromatid break; **—изм** *m.* chromatism, chromatic aberration; **—ика** *f.* chromatics; **—ин** *m.*, **—иновый** *a.* (biol.) chromatin; **—ирование** *n.* chrome plating; chroming, chrome tanning; **—ический, —ичный** *a.* chromatic, color; **—ическая чувствительность** *see* **хроматопсия**; **—ичность** *f.* chromaticity; **—ное наполнение** chromating (anticorrosion treatment).

хромато/грамм *m.*, **—грамма** *f.* chromatogram; **—граф** *m.*, **—графировать** *v.* chromatograph; **—графический** *a.* chromatographic (analysis); **—графия** *f.* chromatography; **—з** *m.* (med.) (abnormal) pigmentation; **—лиз** *m.* (med.) chromatolysis; **—метрия** *f.* chromatometry; **—плазма** *f.* (cyt.) chromatoplasm; **—псия** *f.* (ophth.) chromatopsia, anomalous color vision; **—скоп** *m.* chromatoscope; **—фор** *m.* (biol.) chromatophore, pigment cell.

хроматр/он *m.* chromatron (tube), focus-mask tube; **—оп** *m.* chromatrope.

хромать *v.* limp, be lame; lag behind.

хромаффинный *a.* (cyt.) chromaffine(e), having an affinity for chromium salts.

хромгельб *m.* chrome yellow.

хромидия *f.* (cyt.) chromidium.

хромил *m.* chromyl; **хлористый х.** chromyl chloride.

хромир/ование *n.* chrome-plating, etc., *see v.*; **—ованный** *a.* chrome-plated, etc., *see v.*; **—овать** *v.* chrome-plate, chromize; chrome(-tan); **—овка** *see* **хромирование**; **—овочный** *see* **хромирующий**; **—овщик** *m.*

chrome plater; chrome tanner; **—ующий** *a.* chrome-plating, etc., *see v.*

хромисто/железистая соль ferrous chromite; **—кальциевая соль** calcium chromite; **—кислый** *a.* chromous acid; chromite (of); **—кислая соль** chromite; **—магниевая соль** magnesium chromite; **—синеродистый калий** potassium chromicyanide.

хромист/ый *a.* chromium, chromous, chrome; **—ая кислота** chromous acid; **соль —ой кислоты** chromite; **—ая соль** chromous salt.

хромисы *pl.* (ichth.) coralfishes, spotted damselfishes (*Cichlidae*).

хромит *m.*, **—овый** *a.* chromite.

хромо— *prefix* chromo— [color; pigment(ation); chrome, chromium].

хромово/аммониевая соль ammonium chromate; **—бариевая соль** barium chromate; **—калиевая соль** potassium chromate; **—кислый** *a.* chromic acid; chromate (of); **—кислый свинец** lead chromate; **—кислая соль** chromate.

хромовольфрамовая сталь chrome-tungsten steel.

хромово/медная соль cupric chromate; **—ртутистая соль** mercurous chromate; **—ртутная соль** mercuric chromate.

хромовщик *m.* chrome tanner.

хромов/ый *a.* chromium, chromic, chrome; **х. ангидрид** chromic anhydride, chromium trioxide; **х. жёлтый** chrome yellow; **х. сок, х. экстракт** chrome tan liquor; **—ая кислота** chromic acid; **соль —ой кислоты** chromate; **кислая соль —ой кислоты** bichromate; **хлорангидрид —ой кислоты** chromyl chloride; **—ая кожа** chrome leather; **—ая краска** chrome color; **—ая соль** chromic salt; **—ая сталь** chrome steel, chromium steel; **—ая шпинель** (min.) chrome spinel, picotite; **—ое дубление** chrome tanning; **—ое железо** (met.) ferrochrome; **—ые квасцы** chrome alum, ammonium chromic sulfate.

хромоген *m.*, **—ная группа** chromogen; **—ный** *a.* chromogenic.

хромо/дубильный раствор chrome tan liquor; **—золь** *m.* chromosol dye; **—зома** *see* **хромосома**; **—изомер** *m.* chromoisomer; **—изомерия** *f.* chromoisomerism.

хромой *a.* lame, limping; (med.) claudicant.

хромо/кадмиевая желть chrome cadmium yellow (pigment); **—кислый** *see* **хромовокислый.**

хромолиз *m.* (med.) chrom(at)olysis, dissolution of chromatin.

хромолитограф/ия *f.* chromolithography, color lithography; **—ский** *a.* chromolithographic; **—ский оттиск** chromolithograph, color print.

хромо/марганцевый *a.* chrome-manganese (steel); **—мера** *f.* (cyt.) chromomere, chromatin particle; **—метр** *m.* chromometer, colorimeter; **—молибденовый** *a.* chrome-molybdenum; **—натриевая соль** sodium chromate; **—нема** *f.* (gen.) chromonema; **—никелевый** *a.* chrome-nickel.

хромоногий *a.* lame.

хромопласт *m.* (biol.) chromoplast(id), pigmented plastid.

хромопроте/ид, **—ин** *m.* chromoprotein.

хромопсия *see* **хроматопсия**.

хромоскоп *m.* (ophth.) chromoscope.

хромосом/а *f.* (biol.) chromosome; **неполовая х.** autosome; **половая х.** sex chromosome; **х.-игрек** *f.* Y-chromosome; **х.-икс** *f.* X-chromosome; **—ный** *a.* chromosome, chromosomal; **—ный набор** chromosome complement; karyotype.

хромо/сорб *m.* chromosorb (kieselguhr); **—сфера** *f.* (astr.) chromosphere; **—сферный** *a.* chromospheric.

хромота *f.* lameness, limping; (med.) claudication; **пере-межающаяся х.** intermittent claudication, angina cruris.

хромо/терапия *f.* (med.) chromotherapy, beam therapy; **—тип** *m.* chromotype, color print; **—типия** *f.* color printing; **—трихия** *f.* (med.) chromotrichia, coloration of hair; **—троп** *m.* chromotrope; **—тропия** *f.* chromotropy, chromoisomerism; **—троповая кислота** chromotropic acid; **—фильный** *a.* (biol.) chromophilic, readily stained; **—фор** *m.*, **—форная группа** chromophore; **—форм** *m.* chromoform; **—фотография** *f.* color photography; **—фотометр** *m.* chromophotometer (colorimeter); **—центр** *f.* (gen.) chromocenter, karyosome; **—цит** *m.* (cyt.) chromocyte.

хромпик *m.* bichromate, spec. potassium bichromate; **аммониевый х.** ammonium bichromate.

хром/пикотит *m.* (min.) chrompicotite; **—шпинелид** *m.* chromospinelide.

хронаксия *f.* (physiol.) chronaxy.

хронизатор *m.* timer.

хроник *m.* chronic invalid.

хроник/а *f.* chronicle; news item; newsreel; **—ёр** *m.* chronicler, reporter.

хронир/ование *n.* timing; **—овать** *v.* time; **—ующий** *a.* timing; **—ующее устройство** timer.

хроническ/и *adv.* chronically; **—ий** *a.* chronic, lingering.

хроно— *prefix* chrono— (time); **—грамма** *f.* chronogram; **—граф** *m.* chronograph, timer; **—логический** *a.* chronological; **—логия** *f.* chronology.

хронометр *m.* chronometer, timekeeper; **—аж** *m.* timing, time metering; time study; time card system; time keeping; **—ажист** *m.* timekeeper, time clerk; **—аж-ный** *a.* of **хронометраж;** time (card); **—ирование** *see* **хронометраж; —ировать** *v.* time, do a time study; **—ист** *m.* timekeeper; **—ический** *a.* chronometric, timing; **—ия** *f.* chronometry; **—овый** *a.* of **хронометр.**

хроно/скоп *m.* chronoscope; stopwatch; **—счётчик** *m.* time meter; **—трон** *m.* chronotron (a mass spectrometer).

хруп *m.*, **—анье** *n.* crack(ing), crunch(ing); **—ать(ся)** *v.* crack, crunch.

хрупк/ий *a.* friable, brittle, fragile, frangible; **—ость** *f.* friability, brittleness, frangibility; embrittlement; **тем-пература —ости** breaking point.

хруп/нуть(ся) *see* **хрупать(ся); —ок** *sh. m.* of **хрупкий; —че** *comp.* of **хрупкий.**

хруст *m.* crunch, crackle, crepitation; cartilage.

хрусталик *m.* (anat.) crystalline lens; **склероз —а** (med.) phacosclerosis; **—овый** *a.* lenticular.

хрусталь *m.* crystal; crystal glass, cut glass; **английский х.** flint glass; **горный х.** (min.) rock crystal; **—ный** *a.* crystal(line).

хрустан *m.* (orn.) dotterel (*Charadrius morinellus*).

хруст/ать *see* **хрустеть; —ение** *n.* crunching, etc., *see v.*; **—еть** *v.* crunch, crack(le), crepitate; **—кий** *a.* crunchy; **—нуть** *see* **хрустеть; —ящий** *a.* crackling, etc., *see v.*; crepitant.

хрущ *m.* cockchafer, may beetle; (ichth.) Coregonus ussuriensis; **—ак** *m.* tenebrionid beetle; **мучной —ак**

meal worm; **—ик** *m.* beetle of the Scarabaeidae family.

хр/юкальщики *pl.* (ichth.) grunts, etc. (*Pomadasyidae*); **—юканье** *n.* grunt(ing); **—юкать** *v.* grunt; **—як** *m.* boar.

хряс/к *m.* crunch, crackle; **—кий** *a.* crack(l)ing; **—т-нуть** *v.* crunch, crack(le), rustle.

хрящ *m.* cartilage, cartilago, gristle; gravel, grit; **волок-нистый х.** fibrocartilage; **—и** *pl.* (met.) shot; **—евато—** *prefix* chondr(o)— (grain, grit, granular); **—еватость** *f.* gristliness; **—еватый** *a.* gristly, cartilaginous; gravelly; **—евидный** *a.* chondroid, gristly; **—евина** *f.* gristle.

хрящев/ой *a.* cartilaginous, chondral; gravelly (soil); **х. клей** chondrin; **—ое соединение** (anat.) synchondrosis; **—ая опухоль** (med.) chondroma.

хряще/подобный *a.* chondroid; **—костные, —кос-тистые** *pl.* (ichth.) Chondrostei.

ХСК *abbr.* (**хондроитинсерная кислота**) chondroitin-sulfuric acid.

хтон— *prefix* chthon— (earth); **—изотермический** *a.* (geol.) chthonisothermic.

ХТС *abbr.* (**химико-технологическая система**) chemical engineering system; process system.

худ *sh. m.* of **худой; —ее** *comp.* of **худой; —ение** *n.* growing thin, getting thin; **—еть** *v.* grow thin, lose weight.

худжира *f.* khudzhira (dry, steppe lake).

худо *adv.* badly, ill; *n.* harm, evil.

худоба *f.* thinness, leanness, emaciation.

худож/ественный *a.* artistic; **—ник** *m.* artist, painter.

худ/ой *a.* bad, ill; (med.) malignant; thin, lean, meager, poor; **—ородный** *a.* poor (soil); **—осочие** *n.* (med., vet.) cachexia; **—осочный** *a.* cachectic; **—ощавость** *f.* thinness, emaciation, cachexia; **—ощавый** *a.* thin, lean, emaciated, cachectic; **—шее** *n.* the worst; **—ший** *a.* worse, the worst; **в —шем случае** at the worst.

хуже *comp.* of **худо(й),** worse; **х. всего то, что** the worst of it is that; **ещё х., что** to complicate matters, to make matters worse; **тем х.** so much the worse; **—ть** *v.* get worse.

хульман *m.* (mam.) entellus langur (*Presbytis entellus*).

хундовский *a.* (phys.) Hund's.

хуп/еровский *a.* Hooper('s); **—совый** *a.* Hoopes(').

хурма *f.* (bot.) persimmon.

хурхит *see* **черчит.**

хутия *f.* (mam.) hutia (*Capromys*, etc.).

хутор *m.*, **—ный, —ской** *a.* farm(stead); **—янин** *m.* farmer.

х.ч. *abbr.* (**химически чистый**) chemically pure.

Хьюстон (geog.) Houston.

хэдер *see* **хедер.**

хэкер *m.* (comp.) hacker.

хэммок *m.* hammock (subtropical forest islands in the Everglades).

хэмо/дерма *f.* (mal.) Chaetoderma; **—плевра** *f.* Chaetopleura.

Хэуорса синтез Haworth synthesis.

хэширование *n.* (comp.) hashing.

Хюккель (chem.) Hückel.

Ц

ц *abbr.* (**центнер**) centner; **ц.** *abbr.* (**цена**) price, cost; (**центр**) center; (**цех**) shop, plant; (**цифра**) number; (**цифровой**) numerical, digital; **°Ц** *abbr.* (**градус Цельсия**) degree centigrade.

Цаги трубка a water meter.

цанг/а *f.*, **—и** *pl.*, **—овый** *a.* tongs, tweezers, forceps; holder, clamp; collet chuck; **—овый патрон** collet chuck, spring chuck, draw(-in) chuck.

цапатеро *n.* (ichth.) leatherjacket (*Oligoplites*).

цап/ать *v.* hoe, hack; seize; —ка *f.* hoe, chopper; cornerplate.

цапл/евые, —и herons, egrets, bitterns, etc. (*Ardeidae*); молотоглавые —и hammerkops (*Scopidae*); —я *f.* heron; розовая —я roseate spoonbill (*Ajaia a.*).

цапонлак *m.* cellulose nitrate varnish.

цапф/а *f.* pin, pivot, (pivot) journal (of shaft); trunnion; shank; шаровая ц. ball journal; —енный *a.*, —овый *a.* of цапфа; —овый мост trunnion bascule bridge.

царап/ание *n.* scratching, abrasion; scratches; —анный *a.* scratched, abraded; —ать *v.* scratch, abrade; —ина *f.* scratch, abrasion, mark, notch, score; cicatrix, scar; —инка *dim.* of царапина; —ка *f.* scratch; bark stripper; —нуть *see* царапать.

царг/а *f.* course (of tank wall); ring (of pressure-vessel shell); —овый *a.* of царга; —овая колонна column built up in courses.

царёк *m.* (ichth.) pumpkinseed; goldfish.

царск/ий *a.* czar; basilic, royal, kingly; ц. корень, ц. костыль (bot.) masterwort (*Imperatoria ostruthium*); —ая вена (anat.) basilic vein; —ая водка aqua regia; —ая синь smalt (pigment); —ие кудри (bot.) Turk's-cap lily (*Lilium martagon*).

царств/о *n.* kingdom, empire; —ование *n.*, —овать *v.* reign, rule (over); —ующий *a.* reigning, ruling.

цв. *abbr.* [цвет(ной)].

цве/ль *f.* mold, mustiness; efflorescence; flowers (of wine); —сти *v.* become moldy; effloresce; (bot.) bloom, blossom; flourish, thrive.

цвет *m.* color(ation), tint, hue; flower, blossom, bloom; игра —ов iridescence; коэффициент —а color-distribution coefficient; морские —ы true sea anemones (*Actiniaria*); основные —а, первичные —а primary colors; серный ц. flowers of sulfur; тёмного —а dark-colored.

цвет/ение *n.* (bot.) blooming, blossoming, flowering, florescence; (algal) bloom; flower, blossom; flowers (of wine); efflorescence; anthesis; ц. ногтей (med.) leukonychia; —ень *m.* pollen, beebread; —истый *a.* flowery; colorful; —ить *v.* color, dye, paint (brightly); —ка *gen.* of цветок; —ковые *pl.* flowering plants (*Anthophyta*); —ковый *a.* flowering, phanerogamous, floral; *suffix* —florate, —florous, —anthous.

цветн/ик *m.*, —иковый *a.* flower garden, flower bed; —ой *a.* chromatic, colored; color (photography; reaction; spectrum); floral; stained (glass); tinted (glasses); (met.) nonferrous; —ой пластид chromoplast; —ая литография *a.* chromolithography; —ость *f.* chromaticity; color index; —я *gen.* of цветень.

цвето—*prefix* color; flower; —видный *a.* flower-like; —вод *m.* flower grower; —водство *n.*, —водческий *a.* flower growing, floriculture.

цветов/ой *a.* color; chromatic; chromaticity; —ая реакция на color reaction for; —ая температура (phot.) color temperature.

цвето/воспроизводящий *a.* chromatogenic; —деление *n.* (phot.) color separation; —делённый *a.* color-separation, color-separated; —делительный *a.* color-separating; (cryst.; phys.) dichroic.

цветоед *m.* blossom beetle; curculio.

цветозамещаемый *a.* allochromatic.

цветоизмен/яемость *f.* allochroism, change of color; —яющий *a.* versicolor; —яющийся *a.* allochroic.

цветок *m.* flower, blossom, bloom.

цвето/корректор *m.* color corrector, color scanner; —ложе *n.* (bot.) torus, floral receptacle; —мер *m.* colorimeter; (sugar) decolorimeter; —метр *m.* color-

imeter; —метрический *a.* colorimetric; —метрия *f.* colorimetry; —насыщенность *f.* color saturation; chroma, color quality; —ножка *f.* (bot.) peduncle, pedicel; —нос *m.* floriferous shoot; peduncle; —носный *a.* flower-bearing, floriferous; —ощущение *n.* color sensation, color perception; chromatopsia; порог —ощущения (physiol.) achromatic threshold; —передача *f.* color reproduction; —различение *n.* color discrimination; —расположение *n.* inflorescence, anthotaxis; —рассеяние *n.* chromatic aberration, chromatic dispersion; —стойкий *a.* colorfast; —стойкость, —устойчивость *f.* color fastness; —устойчивый *a.* colorfast.

цветоч/ек *dim.* of цветок; —ник *m.* floriculturist; flower pot; (ent.) boll weevil; —ницы, —ницевые *pl.* (orn.) Coerebidae; —ный *a.* flower(ing), floral; —ный покров (bot.) perianth.

цвет/уха *f.* seed stalk; premature blooming; —ушность *f.* bolting, producing seed prematurely; —ущий *a.* blossoming, flowering; flourishing; efflorescent.

цвиттер-ион *m.* (chem.) zwitterion, amphoteric ion.

ЦВМ *abbr.* (цифровая вычислительная машина), ЦВУ *abbr.* (цифровое вычислительное устройство) (digital) computer.

ЦГС *see* СГС.

ЦДА *abbr.* (цифровой дифференциальный анализатор) (electron.) digital differential analyzer, DDA.

цеаксантин *m.* zeaxanthine.

цеб/иды, —усовые *pl.* (mam.) Cebidae.

цевитаминовая кислота cevitamic acid, ascorbic acid, vitamin C.

цев/ка *f.* bobbin, spool, reel; spindle; (driving) pin, chain link pin; (roller) tooth; (zool.) (tarsometa)tarsus; cannon bone; —очный *a.* of цевка; —очный механизм lantern gear or pinion; —очная шестерня pin gear, lantern gear.

цевьё rod; (art.) foregrip, forearm.

цедил/ка *f.*, —о *n.* filter, strainer.

цедильн/ый *a.* filter(ing), straining; ц. колпак, ц. мешок filter bag; —ая подушка filter pad.

цедить *v.* filter, strain; percolate.

цедр/а *f.* lemon or orange peel; (phyt.) flavedo; —ат *see* цитрон; —ин *m.* cedrin; —ол *m.* cedrol, cedar camphor.

цеж/ение *n.* filtering, filtration, straining; percolation; —енный *part.*, —ёный *a.* filtered, strained; percolated.

цезальпиния *f.* (bot.) Caesalpinia.

цез/иевый *a.*, —ий *m.* cesium, Cs; окись —ия cesium oxide; сернокислый —ий, сульфат —ия cesium sulfate; —ированный *a.* cesium-coated.

цезол *m.* cesol.

Цейзеля реакция Zeisel reaction.

цейлонск/ий *a.* (geog.) Ceylon; —ая болезнь (med.) beriberi.

Цейнера диаграмма Zeuner diagram.

Цейсса линза Zeiss lens.

цейтлупа *f.* high-speed movie camera.

цек *m.* crackle; crazing, craze.

цекальный *a.* (anat.) cecal.

цеков/ание *n.* (mach.) spotfacing; —ать *v.* spotface (make a seat for a bolthead or nut); —ка *f.* spotfacer.

цекотомия *f.* (med.) cecotomy.

цел *sh. m.* of целый.

целакант *m.* (ichth.) coelacanth (*Latimeria chalumnae*); —овые *pl.* Latimeriidae.

цела/неза *f.* Celanese dye; —ноль *m.* celanol dye; —тен *m.* celatene dye.

целебесский *a.* Celebes (Sea).

целеб/ость *f.* curative property; —ый *a.* salutary, curative, medicinal, healing; wholesome, healthful; —ое средство remedy.

цел/евой *a. of* цель; system (programming); target (function); end (product); special-purpose; ц. взнос specific appropriation; —евая установка object; —ей *gen. pl. of* цель.

целен *sh. m. of* цельный.

целенаправленный *see* целеустремлённый.

целентерон *m.* (zool.) coelenteron, gastrovascular cavity.

целесообразн/о *adv.* expediently, etc., *see a.*; it is advisable, it is sound practice; —ость *f.* expediency; advisability; merit; —ый *a.* expedient, expeditious, efficient, suitable, advisable, reasonable.

целестин *m.* (min.) celestine, celestite.

целе/указание *n.* target designation, target indication; point; сетка —указания target-area designator; —установка *f.* aim, object.

целеустремлённ/ость *f.* purpose(fulness), endeavor; —ый *a.* purposeful; goal-seeking.

цели *gen., pl., etc., of* цель.

целиакия *f.* (med.) celiac disease.

целик *m.* pillar, block (of untouched ore); natural soil; (art.) rear sight; wind gage; —и нефти retained oil.

целиком *adv.* wholly, totally, entirely, completely; ц. и полностью fully; ц. из стали all-steel.

целин/а *f.* virgin soil; —ый *a.* virgin (land).

целиноградский *a.* (geog.) Tselinograd.

целио— *prefix* cel(i)o—, coelo— (abdomen); —скопия *f.* cel(i)oscopy.

целит *m.* Celite (diatomaceous earth).

целительн/ость *see* целебность; —ый *see* целебный.

цел/ить(ся) *v.* aim (at), point (at), direct (at), allude (to); —кий *a.* aiming well, true.

целлит *m.* cellite (plastic).

целло/биаза *f.* cellobiase, β-glucosidase; —биоза, —за *f.* cellobiose, cellose; —зольв *m.* Cellosolve, 2-ethoxyethanol; —зольвацетат *m.* Cellosolve acetate; —идин *m.* (micros.) celloidin; —н *m.*, —новый *a.* Cellon (a cellulose acetate plastic); —фан *m.*, —фановый *a.* cellophane.

целлул/оза *see* целлюлоза; —оид *m.*, —оидный, —оидовый *a.* celluloid.

целлюларный *see* целлюлярный.

целлюлит *m.* (med.) cellulitis.

целлюлоз/а *f.*, —ный *a.* cellulose; (paper) pulp; —нобумажный *a.* paper and pulp; —ность *f.* cellulosity.

целлюлоид *see* целлулоид.

целлюлярн/ость *f.* cellularity; —ый *a.* cellular.

цело *adv. and sh. n. of* целый.

целов/ание *n.* kissing; —ать(ся) *v.* kiss.

целогаструла *f.* (embr.) coelogastrula.

цел/ое *n.* the whole, the entire; (math.) integer; в —ом upon the whole, in all, altogether; молекула в —ом the whole molecule; одно ц. с integral with; за одно ц. in block, in one piece, unit; отлитый за одно ц. *see* цельнолитой.

целозия *f.* (bot.) Celosia.

целом *m.* (zool.) coelom; *see also under* целое; —ический *a.* coelomic, having a body cavity; —ический рак (med.) mesothelioma; —ные *pl.* (zool.) Coelomata.

целомудр/енность *f.*, —ие *n.* virginity, chastity; —енный *a.* virgin(al), chaste.

целостат *m.* (astr.) coelostat.

целост/ность *f.* completeness, wholeness, entirety, integrity; область —ности (math.) integral domain;

—ный *a.* complete, whole, entire, undivided, integral; нарушение —и данных (comp.) data corruption; —ь *f.* wholeness, entirety, integrity; в —и completely, entirely; intact.

целотекс *m.* (constr.) Celotex.

целотелий *m.* (embr.) mesothelium.

целочисленн/ость *f.* whole number(s), integer(s); —ый *a.* integral, integer.

цел/ый *a.* whole, entire, integral, unbroken, complete, intact, sound; integer (multiple); ц. и невредимый safe and sound; ц. ряд a (wide) variety; —ая величина integral; —ое число whole number, integer; в —ом as a whole, by and large; по —ым неделям for weeks at a time.

цел/ь *f.* target, goal, aim, mark; object(ive), intention; end, purpose; в —ях for the purpose (of), to find out; для этой —и for this purpose, to do this, with this aim in view; задаваться —ью *v.* aim (at); иметь —ью *v.* be aimed (at), be directed (at); не достигающий —и *a.* ineffectual; отвечать —и *v.* answer the purpose; попадать в ц. *v.* hit the mark, hit home; с —ью with a view (to), in order (to), for (the purpose of), to find, with the object (of), in an effort (to); with a purpose, on purpose; с этой —ью *see* для этой цели; указатель движущихся —ей moving target indicator.

цельзиан *m.* (min.) celsian.

цельзия *f.* (bot.) Celsia.

цельно *adv.* wholly, entirely; in a single piece; *prefix* holo— (whole, complete); all-; —головые *pl.* (ichth.) Holocephali; —деревянный *a.* all-wood; —костные *pl.* (ichth.) Holostei; —крайний *a.* entire, integer; smooth-edged (leaf); —литой *a.* one-piece, solid.

цельно/металлический *a.* all-metal; —молочный *a.* whole-milk (product); —резиновый *a.* all-rubber; —решётчатый *a.* expanded (metal); —стальной *a.* all-steel; —сть *f.* wholeness, entirety, integrity; —тянутый *a.* seamless (pipe); —факельный *a.* forced-draft (burner); —численный *a.* integral.

цельный *a.* whole, entire, integral, total; one-piece, solid; unitized (construction); whole, unskimmed (milk).

цельсий *m.* centigrade thermometer; градус Цельсия degree centigrade.

цем— *prefix*, —ент *m.* cement; —ентаж *m.* cementing.

цементац/ионный, —ия *see* цементирование.

цементиклы *pl.* cementicles (in tooth root).

цементир/ный *a.*, —ование *n.* cementing; (met.) cementation; contact precipitation; поверхностное —ование (met.) case-hardening; —ованный *a.* cemented, etc., *see v.*; cement (steel); —овать *v.* carburize, case-harden; —овка, —овочный *see* цементирование; —ующий *a.* cementing, etc., *see v.*; —ующее вещество cement, bond; (met.) carburizer.

цементн/ый *a.* cement; cementation, carburizing (furnace); ц. камень hydrated (hardened) cement; cement block; ц. раствор cement mortar; —ая затирка cement floor; —ая порода cement rock, cement stone (for cement manufacture); —ая сталь cement(ation) steel, blister steel; —ое молоко cement grout.

цемент/овальный *a.* cement(ing); —ование *see* цементирование; —ованный *see* цементированный; —овать *see* цементировать; —овка *see* цементирование; —овоз *m.* cement carrier (ship or truck); —овочный *a. of* цементирование; —омёт *m.*, -пушка *f.* cement gun, concrete gun; —уемый *a.* cemented; carburizing (steel).

цемзавод *m.* cement plant.

цемянки *pl.* broken brick, rubble, grog.

цен/а *f.* price, value, worth, cost, charge; **ц. без скидки** net price; **ц. деления** scale division, graduating mark; **ц. деления шкалы** scale factor; **—ою** at the cost (of).

ценантий *m.* (bot.) coenanthium.

ценен *sh. m. of* **ценный.**

ценз *m.*, **—овый** *a.* qualification, condition for admission to or inclusion in a group, (age, etc.) requirement; (stat.) census.

цензор *m.* censor; **—ство** *n.* censorship.

цензур/а *f.* censorship; **дозволено —ой** licensed; **—ный** *a.* censorial.

ценит/ель *m.* appraiser, valuer, judge; **—ь** *v.* value, appraise, estimate, rate; appreciate; **высоко —ь** prize, rate high; **слишком высоко —ь** overrate; **—ься** *v.* be valued, etc.

ценн/ик *m.* price list; **—остный** *a.* value, valuational; **—ость** *f.* value, worth; importance; **—ый** *a.* valuable; registered (mail).

цено— *prefix* c(o)eno— (shared); **—бий** *m.* (biol.) coenobium, colony of unicellular organisms; **—вид** *m.* coenospecies.

ценовые соединения —cene compounds, cyclopentadiene derivatives.

цено/генез *m.* (biol.) cenogenesis; **—з** *m.* (med.) cenosis, morbid discharge; **—крепис** *m.* (ent.) chalcid (*Caenocrepis bothynoderi*).

ценолестовые *pl.* (mam.) rat-opossums (*Coenolestoidea*).

ценообразование *n.* pricing, price-setting.

ценотип *m.* coenotype.

цент *m.* (acous.; coin) cent.

центаур/еидин *m.* centaureidin; **—ин** *m.* centaurin (glucoside); centaurine (alkaloid).

центез *m.* (med.) perforation, tapping, centesis; *suffix* **—centesis.**

центи— *see* **санти—.**

центнер *m.* centner, hundredweight (50 kg; USSR—100 kg).

центр *m.* center, focal point, focus, centrum; (cryst.) nucleus, seed; site; (surv.) reference mark; **между —ами** center to center; **по —у** (through the) center; **установка по —у** center adjustment.

централиз/ационный *a.* centralization; control; **—ация** *f.* centralization, centralized control; (rr.) interlocking; **диспетчерская —ация** centralized traffic control; **—м** *m.* centralism; **—ованный** *a.* centralized; **—овать** *v.* centralize.

централ/ит *m.* centralite (solid-fuel stabilizer); **—ь** *f.* central main, central line; **—ьно—** *prefix* central; **—ьный** *a.* central, principal, main; center, centrally located; Equatorial (Africa); (phot.) between-the-lens (shutter); master (catalog); **—ьная полость** atrium (of sponges).

центрарховые *pl.* (ichth.) sunfishes, black basses (*Centrarchidae*).

центратор *m.* centering guide, centralizer.

центрина *f.* (ichth.) Oxynotus centrina.

центриол/ь *m.*, **—а** *f.* (cyt.) centriole.

центрипетальный *a.* centripetal.

центрир/ование *n.* centering, etc., *see v.*; **—ованный** *a.* centered, etc., *see v.*; **—овать** *v.* center, align; centralize; drill center holes; **—овка** *see* **центровка;** **—ующий** *a.* centering, etc., *see v.*; **—ующее острие** center point.

центрифуг/а *f.* centrifuge; spinning machine (for casting concrete pipe); **—альный** *a.* centrifugal; **ц.-грохот** *f.* screen-type centrifuge; **—ирование** *n.* centrifugation, centrifugal separation; spinning; **—ированный** *a.* centrifuged; spun; **—ировать** *v.* centrifuge.

центрический *a.* (biol.) centric.

центробарический *a.* centrobaric.

центробеж/ка *f.* (centrifugal) extractor, centrifuge; **—но** *adv.* centrifugally, by centrifugal means.

центробежн/ый *a.* centrifugal; outward-flow (turbine); rotary (pump); swirl (nozzle); efferent (nerve).

центров/альный *a.* centering; **—анный** *a.* centered, etc., *see v.*; **—ать** *v.* center, mark centers, drill center holes; **—ка** *f.* centering, etc., *see v.*; alignment; central adjustment; **линия —ки** center line; **производить —ку** *v.* center, align; **—ой** *a.* center, central, centric; **—очный** *a.* center(ing); **—очный циркуль** divider calipers.

центро/ида *f.* (astr.) centroid; **—идальный** *see* **центроидаль;** **—идальный** *a.* centroidal; **—клиналь** *f.* (geol.) centrocline; **—клинальный** *a.* centroclinal; **—лецитальный** *a.* (zool.) centrolecithal (ovum).

центролофовые *pl.* (ichth.) ruffs (*Centrolophidae*).

центромер *m.*, **—а** *f.* (gen.) centromere; **—ный** *a.* centromeric.

центроплазма *f.* (gen.) centroplasm.

центроплан *m.* (av.) center (wing) section; **—ный** *a.* center-wing (tank).

центропомовые *pl.* (ichth.) snooks, etc. (*Centropomidae*).

центросома *f.* (biol.) centrosome.

центростремительн/ость *f.* centripetence; **—ый** *a.* centripetal; inward-flow, peripheral(-admission) (turbine); afferent (nerve); **—ая сила** centripetal force.

центротехника *f.* centralized control and management system.

центросфера *f.* (cyt.) centrosphere, attraction sphere.

центура *f.* center bit; (bot.) century, set of 100.

ценур *m.*, **—а** *f.* (zool.) larval state of tapeworm of genus Multiceps, found primarily in sheep, etc.; **—оз** *m.* (vet.) coenurosis, gid; **—ус** *m.* Coenurus cerebralis.

цены *gen., pl. of* **цена.**

ценящий *pr. act. part. of* **ценить.**

цеолит *m.* (min.) zeolite; **—изация** *f.* zeolitization; **—овый** *a.* zeolite, zeolitic; **—ообразный** *a.* zeolitic.

цеорин *m.* zeorin.

цеп *m.* (agr.) flail.

цеп/ей *gen. pl. of* **цепь;** **—екокк** *m.* (bact.) streptococcus; **—енатяжной** *a.* chain-tightening.

цепенеть *v.* grow torpid, become numb; stiffen.

цепень *m.* tapeworm (*Taenia*); **ц.-мозговик** *m.* tapeworm (*Multiceps*).

цеп/еобразный *a.* chain-like; (biol.) caten(ul)ate; **—и** *gen., pl., etc., of* **цепь; —ка** *see* **цепочка.**

цеп/кий *a.* cohesive, adhesive, sticky; clinging, tenacious; clutching, gripping; (zool.) prehensile, scansorial; trailing (plant); **—кость** *f.* cohesiveness, adhesiveness, tenacity; prehensility; **—лять** *v.* hook, catch hold (of); **—ляться** *v.* adhere, cling; clutch, grasp; **—ляющийся** *a.* clinging, etc., *see* **цепляться;** (bot.) climber.

цепн/евые *pl.* Taeniidae; **—и** *pl. of* **цепень** (*Cyclophyllidea*).

цеподолбёжный станок chain-type slotter.

цепн/ой *a. of* **цепь; цеп;** chain; (math.) catenary; continued (fraction); sprocket (wheel); ladder (attenuator; network); membrane (stress); suspension (bridge); **ц. блок** sprocket; **ц. ключ** chain tongs (pipe wrench); **ц. тормоз** drag chain; **ц. транспортёр** chain conveyer; **—ая звёздочка** sprocket wheel; **—ая линия** (math.) catenary; **—ая подача** chain feed; **—ая реакция** (nuclear) chain reaction; **—ое колесо** sprocket wheel; **—ое правило** (math.) chain rule; **—ое превращение**

(nuclear) chain reaction; **с —ым строением** chain (molecule, etc.).

цепнореагирующий *a.* chain-reacting.

цепня *gen. of* **цепень.**

цепок *gen. pl. of* **цепка;** *sh. m. of* **цепкий.**

цепола *f.* (ichth.) bandfish (*Cepola*).

цепо/пробный *a.* chain-testing; **—ченный** *a.*, **—чечный** *a.*, **—чка** *f.* (little) chain, series, network, circuit; **—чковидный, —чкообразный** *a.* chain-like, caten(ul)ate; **—чно-планчатый** *a.* chain-and-plank (conveyer); **—чный** *see* **цепной.**

цеппелин *m.* zeppelin, airship.

цеп/ь *f.* chain, catena; network; bond; (elec.) circuit; (mountain) range; **боковой —и** side-chain (isomerism); **вводить в ц.** *v.* connect (up); **замыкать ц.** *v.* close a circuit, make contact; **с нормальной —ью** open-chain (compound); **с прямой —ью** straight-chain (compound); **с разветвлёнными —ями** branch-chain (molecule); **—ью** *adv.* in a row, in line.

цер/азин *m.* cerasin; **—амид** *m.* (biochem.) ceramide; **—ан** *m.* cerane, isohexacosane.

церанограф *m.* (meteor.) ceraunograph.

церат *m.* cerate; **—идовые** *pl.* (ichth.) sea devils, angler fishes (*Ceratiidae*); **—ин** *m.* ceratin, keratin; **—иназа** *f.* ceratinase; **—одовые** *pl.* (ichth.) barramundas, lungfishes (*Ceratodidae*); **—ония** *f.* (bot.) carob (*Ceratonia*).

церациум *m.* (prot.) a dinoflagellate (*Ceratium*).

цербер/етин *m.* cerberetin; **—идин** *m.* cerberidin; **—ин** *m.* cerberin.

церва *f.* (bot.) weld (*Reseda luteola*).

цервантит *m.* (min.) cervantite.

церви/кальный *a.* (anat.) cervical, neck; **—цит** *m.* (med.) cervicitis.

церебр/альный *a.* (anat.) cerebral, brain; **—ин** *m.* cerebrin; cerebrine, cerebrum siccum; **—иновая кислота** cerebric acid; **—оза** *f.* cerebrose, galactose; **—о-макулярная дегенерация** Tay-Sach's disease; **—он** *m.* cerebron; **—оновая кислота** cerebronic acid; **—оспинальный** *a.* (med.) cerebrospinal.

цере/вистерин *m.* cerevisterol (a yeast sterol); **—зин** *m.* ceresine (wax).

церемон/иальный *a.* ceremonial, ceremonious; **—иться** *v.* stand upon ceremony; **—ия** *f.* ceremony.

церера *f.* (astr.) Ceres.

церид *m.* ceride; **—ин** *m.* ceridin, cerolin.

цериев/ый *a.* cerium, ceric; **—ая земля** ceria, cerium dioxide; **—ая соль** ceric salt.

цериз *m.* cerise, cherry red.

цер/ий *m.* cerium, Ce; **азотнокислая закись —ия** cerous nitrate; **соль закиси —ия** cerous salt; **окись —ия** ceric oxide, cerium dioxide; **соль окиси —ия** ceric salt; **фтористый ц.** cerous fluoride.

церил *m.* ceryl; **—ен** *m.* cerylene; **—овый спирт** ceryl alcohol, 1-hexacosanol.

цериметр/ический *a.* cerimetric (analysis); **—ия** *f.* cerimetry.

цериминозный *a.* (physiol.) ceruminous.

церин *m.* cerin (a sterol); **—овая кислота** cerinic acid, cerotic acid.

цер/истый *a.* cerium, cerous; **—истая соль** cerous salt; **—ит** *m.* (min.) cerite.

церк/а *f.* (ent.) cercus; **—ария** *f.* (zool.) cercaria (stage of trematode development); **—о** *prefix* cerc(o)— (tail); **—оспореллёз** *m.* (phyt.) Cercosporella leaf spot; **—оспороз** *m.* Cercospora leaf spot.

ЦЕРН *abbr.* **(Европейская организация ядерных исследований)** European Organization for Nuclear Research, CERN (initialism from original French name: Conseil européen pour la recherche nucléaire).

цернезьен *m.* (geol.) Cernaysian.

церо— *prefix* cero—, wax; cerium, ceric; **—вый** *see* **цериевый; —зин** *m.* ceresin, cerosinyl cerosate; **—ль** *m.* cerol dye.

церот/ин *m.* cerotin, ceryl cerotate; **—иновая кислота** cerotic acid, heptacosanoic acid; **—ол** *m.* ceryl alcohol.

цесарка *f.* guinea hen.

цестод/оз *m.* (med.) cestodiasis, tapeworm; **—ы** *pl.* (zool.) Cestoda.

цет/ан *m.* cetane, hexadecane; **—ановое число** cetane number (of diesel oil); **—ен** *m.* cetene, hexadecylene.

цетил *m.* cetyl, hexadecyl; **—ен** *m.* cetylene, cetene; **—ид** *m.* cetylide; **—овая кислота** cetylic acid, palmitic acid; **—овый спирт** cetyl alcohol, 1-hexadecanol; **—овый эфир** cetyl ether.

цетин *m.* cetin.

цетрария *f.* (bot.) Cetraria.

цефал—, —о— *prefix* cephal(o)— (head); **—ин** *m.* cephalin, kephalin; **—одий** *m.* (bot.) cephalodium; **—опаг** *m.* (med.) craniopagus; **—оподы** *pl.* (zool.) Cephalopoda, **—оспорин** *m.* cephalosporin; **—оспориоз** *m.* (phyt.) cephalosporium infection; **—ьгия** *f.* (med.) headache, cephalalgia.

цефарантин *m.* cepharanthine.

цефаэлин *m.* cephaeline.

цеф/еида *f.* (astr.) Cepheid; **—ей** *m.* Cepheus.

цех *m.* works, plant, mill; shop, department, unit, section; trade union, guild; **—и** *pl.* works; **—ком** *m.* shop committee.

цехов/ой *a.* of **цех;** working (conditions); **—ое выражение** shop term.

цеховщина *f.* overspecialization.

цехштейн *m.* (geol.) Zechstein, upper division of the Permian.

цеце *f.* tsetse (fly).

цецидий *m.* (bot., zool.) cecidium, gall.

циамелид *m.* cyamelide, s-trioxanetriimine.

циан *m.* cyanogen; *prefix* cyan(o)—, cyanic, cyanide; **—азид** *m.* cyanazide; **—амид** *m.*, **—амидный** *a.* cyanamide; **—амид кальция** calcium cyanamide; **—газ** *m.* hydrogen cyanide.

цианея *f.* (zool.) scyphoid medusa (*Cyanea*).

цианид *m.* cyanide; **чёрный ц.** *see* **цианплав; —ный** *a.* cyanide.

циан/изация *see* **цианирование; —изировать** *v.* cyanide; **—ин** *m.* cyanin; cyanine; **—иновый** *a.* cyanine (dyes); **—ирование** *n.* cyanidation, cyaniding, cyanide process; cyanation.

цианистоводородн/ый *a.* hydrocyanic; hydrocyanide (of); **—ая кислота** hydrocyanic acid; **соль —ой кислоты** cyanide.

цианист/ый *a.* cyanogen, cyano—; (formerly lower or —ous) cyanide (of); hydrocyanic (acid); **ц. водород** hydrogen cyanide; **ц. калий** potassium cyanide.

цианкали *n.* potassium cyanide; **жёлтое ц.** potassium ferrocyanide; **красное ц.** potassium ferricyanide.

циано— *see* **циан—.**

циановодород *m.* hydrogen cyanide; **—ный** *see* **цианистоводородный.**

цианово/калиевая соль potassium cyanate; **—кислый** *a.* cyanic acid; cyanate (of); **—кислый цинк** zinc cyanate; **—кислая соль** cyanate.

цианов/ый *a.* cyanic, cyanogen; (formerly higher or —ic) cyanide (of); **—ая кислота** cyanic acid; **соль —ой кислоты** cyanate; **—ые водоросли** (bot.) Cyanophyceae.

циано/генератор *m.* hydrogen cyanide generator; **—з** *m.* (med.) cyanosis; **—кобаламин** *m.* cyanocobalamine, vitamin B_{12}; **—л** *m.*, **—ловый** *a.* cyanol, aniline; **—метр** *m.* cyanometer; **—псин** *m.* cyanopsin (pigment); **—типия** *f.* cyanotype, blueprint; cyanotypy; **—тический** *a.* (med.) cyanotic; **—уксусная кислота** cyanoacetic acid; **—фицин** *m.* (bot.) cyanophycin (blue coloring matter of algae); **—форм** *m.* cyanoform, tricyanomethane.

циан/плав *m.* calcium and sodium cyanide mixture; **—уксусноэтиловый эфир** ethyl cyanoacetate; **—урамид** *m.* cyanuramide; **—урин** *m.* cyanurin; **—уровая кислота** cyanuric acid; **—этилирование** *n.* cyanoethylation.

циатий *m.* (bot.) cyathium.

циатоцефалёз *m.* (vet.) Cyathocephalus truncatus infection.

циба *f.* ciba (dye); **ц.-краситель** *m.* ciba dye; **—нон** *m.* cibanone dye; **—цет** *m.* cibacet dye.

цибет *see* **циветта**; **—он** *m.* civetone, 9-cyclohepta-decen-1-one.

циботактический *a.* cybotactic.

цивет(т)а *f.* (mam.) civet.

цивилиз/ация *f.* civilization; **—ованный** *a.* civilized; **—овать** *v.* civilize.

цигад/един *m.* zygadenine; **—ит** *m.* (min.) zygadite.

цигайский *a.* (agr.) Tsigai (sheep).

цигейк/а *f.*, **—овый** *a.* fur from Tsigai lamb.

цигер *m.* cheese albumin.

цигота *f.* (biol.) zygote.

цидонин *m.* cydonin (gum).

циез *m.* (physiol.) cyesis, pregnancy.

циейзен *see* **циэйзен.**

циемовые *pl.* (ichth.) snipe-eels (*Cyemidae*).

цикад/а *f.* (ent.) cicada; (bot.) cycad; **—ка** *f.* leaf hopper (*Cicadellida*).

цикатр/икс *m.*, **—иса** *f.* cicatrix, scar.

цикл *m.* cycle; round, circuit; (comp.) loop; ring; period; series; change; **ц. развития** life history; **испытавший ц.** cycled; **разрыв —а** (chem.) ring cleavage.

цикламен *m.* (bot.) cyclamen.

цикл/амин *m.* cyclamin, arthranitin.

цикл/евальный *a.*, **—евание** *n.*, **—ёвка** *f.* scraping; **—евать** *v.* scrape.

циклей *gen. pl. of* **цикля.**

цикл/ид *m.* (geom.) cyclide; **—изация** *f.* cyclization, ring formation.

циклина *f.* scraper.

циклит *m.* cyclite; benzyl bromide; (med.) cyclitis, inflammation of ciliary body.

циклич/еский *a.* cycle, cyclic; continuous; batch (processing); (chem.) ring; (comp.) end-around (carry, etc.); circular-orbit; **—еская кривая** cycle curve; **—еского типа** batch (dissolver); **—еское соединение** cyclic compound; **кривая —еской прочности** stress-number curve; **предел —еской прочности** endurance limit; **—ность** *f.* cycle of operations; (cyclic) recurrence; **—ный** *see* **циклический.**

цикло— *prefix* cyclo—(circle; cycle; cyclic compound); **—бутан** *m.* cyclobutene, tetramethylene; **—бутен** *m.* cyclobutene.

циклование *n.* cycling.

циклогекс/ан *m.* cyclohexane, hexamethylene; **—анол** *m.* cyclohexanol; **—ен** *m.* cyclohexene, tetrahydroben-zene; **—ил** *m.* cyclohexyl.

циклоген/ез *m.* (meteor.) cyclogenesis, development of a cyclone; **—етический** *a.* cyclogenetic.

циклогептан *m.* cycloheptane.

циклогра/мма *f.* (phot.) cyclogram; operating schedule; mission profile; **ц. движений** motion-path cyclogram; **—ф** *m.* cyclograph.

циклоз(ис) *m.* (cyt.) cyclosis.

цикло/ида *f.* (geom.) cycloid; **—ид(аль)ный** *a.* cyclo-id(al); **—каучук** *m.* cyclorubber; **—комплексооб-разователь** *m.* chelating agent; **—лиз** *m.* cyclolysis.

циклометр *m.* cyclometer, revolution counter; **—иче-ский** *a.* cyclometric; **—ия** *f.* cyclometry.

цикломицин *m.* (pharm.) tetracycline.

цикломорфоз *m.* (zool.) cyclomorphosis, cycle of seasonal changes in form.

циклон *m.* (meteor.) cyclone; (min.) cyclone, dust extractor; (fumigation) a cyanide-impregnated absorbent; **—ировать** *v.* cyclone, separate; **—ический** *a.* cyclone, cyclonic; **ц.-классификатор** *m.* cyclone classifier; **—ный** *a. of* **циклон;** **—окс** cyclohexanone peroxide; **—ообразование** *n.* (meteor.) cyclogenesis; (chem.) ring formation; **ц.-сгуститель** *m.* cyclone thickener.

цикло/октан *m.* cycloöctane; **—олефин** *m.* cycloölefin; **—парафин** *m.* cycloparaffin, naphthene.

циклоп *m.* (med.) cyclops; (crust.) waterflea (*Cyclops*).

циклопент/адиен *m.* cyclopentadiene; **—ан** *m.* cyclo-pentane, pentamethylene; **—ен** *m.* cyclopentene; **—ил** *m.* cyclopentyl.

циклоп/ит *m.* (min.) cyclopite; **—ический** *a.* cyclopean, gigantic; **—ия** *f.* (med.) cyclopia; **—олимеризация** *f.* cyclopolymerization.

циклопроп/ан *m.* cyclopropane, trimethylene; **—ил** *m.* cyclopropyl.

цикло/птерин *m.* cyclopterin; **—серин** (chem.) cyclo-serine (antibiotic); **—синхротрон** *m.* (electron.) cyclo-synchrotron; **—строфический** *a.* (meteor.) cyclo-strophic; **—тона** *f.* (ichth.) bristlemouth (*Cyclothone*); **—трон** *m.*, **—тронный** *a.* (nucl.) cyclotron (an accelerator); **—фан** *m.* (chem.) cyclophane.

цикля *f.* scraper.

циковка *f.* counterbore, counterboring.

цикор/ий *m.*, **—иевый** *a.* chicory; **салатный ц.** endive.

цикут/а *f.* (bot.) water hemlock (*Cicuta virosa*); **—ен** *m.* cicutene; **—ин** *m.* cicutine; **—оксин** *m.* cicutoxin.

цилиарный *a.* (anat.; biol.) ciliary.

цилиндр *m.* cylinder, roll(er), drum; (Faraday) cup; (med.) (urinary) cast; **—ический** *a.* cylindrical; spur (gear); columnar; **—ический сустав** (anat.) trochoid joint; **—овый** *a.* cylinder; **—оид** (med.) cylindroid, spurious cast; **—оида** *f.* (geom.) cylindroid.

цилиоэктомия *f.* (med.) ciliectomy.

цимантрен *m.* cymanthrene, cyclopentadienyl tricarbonyl.

цимар/игенин *m.* cymarigenin; **—ин** *m.* cymarin; **—оза** *f.* cymarose, 3-methyldigitoxose.

цимат *m.* Zimate, Ziram, zinc dimethyldithiocarbamate.

цимидин *m.* cymidine, carvacrylamine.

цимицин *m.* cimicin.

цимол *m.* cymene, isopropyltoluene.

цинародий *m.* (bot.) cynarrhodion, hip.

цинга *f.* (med.) scurvy.

цингерон *m.* zingerone.

цинготн/ый *a.* (med.) scorbutic; **—ая трава** scurvy grass (*Cochlearia*).

цинеб *m.* (chem.) Zineb, zinc ethylenebisdithiocarbamate (fungicide).

цинен *m.* cinene, limonene.

цинеол, —ь *m.* cineole, eucalyptole.

цинерария *f.* (bot.) cineraria.

цинк *m.* zinc, Zn; **окись —а** zinc oxide; **сернокислый**

ц., сульфат —**а** zinc sulfate; **хлористый ц.** zinc chloride; **хромовокислый ц.** zinc chromate.

цинк/вейс *m.* zinc white, zinc oxide; —**грау** *n.* zinc gray; —**дибраунит** *m.* (min.) zinc-dibraunite; —**диэтил** *m.* diethylzinc; —**енит** *m.* (min.) zinkenite; —**ит** *m.* (min.) zincite; —**метил** *m.* dimethylzinc.

цинков/альный *a.*, —**ание** *n.* zinc plating, galvanizing; —**анный** *a.* zinc-plated, galvanized; —**ать** *v.* zinc-plate, galvanize.

цинковщик *m.* zinc metallurgist.

цинков/ый *a.* zinc; **ц. жёлтый, ц. крон** zinc yellow, zinc chromate; **ц. купорос** zinc vitriol, zinc sulfate; **ц. цвет** zinc flowers, zinc oxide; **ц. шпат** (min.) zinc spar, smithsonite; —**ая зелёная,** —**ая зелень** zinc green; —**ая мазь** zinc oxide (ointment); —**ая обманка** (min.) zinc blende, sphalerite; —**ая окись** zinc oxide; —**ая окшара** blue powder (zinc dust); —**ая пыль** zinc dust; —**ая шпинель** (min.) zinc spinel, gahnite; —**ое масло** zinc butter, zinc chloride; —**ые белила** zinc white, zinc oxide; —**ые огарки** zinc ash, zinc calx; —**ые цветы** (min.) zinc bloom, hydrozincite.

цинкограф *m.* zincographer; —**ический** *a.* zincographic; —**ия** *f.* zincography, etching on zinc; engraving department.

цинк/одестилляционная печь zinc (distillation) furnace; —**озит** *m.* (min.) zinkosite; —**оплавильный завод** zinc smelter, zinc works; —**органический** *a.* organozinc; —**этил** *see* **цинкдиэтил**.

циннам/ал(ь) *m.* cinnamal; —**еин** *m.* cinnamein, benzyl cinnamate; —**ен** *m.* cinnamene, styrene; —**енил** *m.* cinnamenyl, styryl.

циннамил *m.*, —**овый** *a.* cinnamyl; —**овый спирт** cinnamyl alcohol, cinnamic alcohol.

циннамо/ил *m.* cinnamoyl; —**мум** *m.* cinnamon.

циннвальдит *m.* (min.) zinnwaldite.

цинния *f.* (bot.) zinnia.

цинов/ка *f.*, —**очный** *a.* mat(ting).

циноглоссовые *pl.* (ichth.) Cynoglossidae.

циногнатус *m.* (pal.) Cynognathus.

цинубель *m.* roughing plane.

цинхол *m.* cinchol; —**епидин** *m.* cincholepidine.

цинхон/а *f.* cinchona (bark); —**амин** *m.* cinchonamine; —**ан** *m.* cinchonane; —**идин** *m.* cinchonidine; —**ин** *m.* cinchonine; —**ицин** *m.* cinchonicine, cinchotoxine.

цинхо/тин *m.* cinchotine, hydrocinchonine; —**токсин** *m.* cinchotoxine; —**фен** *m.* cinchophen, atophan.

цинциннатьян *m.* (geol.) Cincinnatian.

ципрея *f.* (mal.) a marine gastropod (*Cypraea*).

циприс *m.* (crust.) cypris (larval stage).

цирен *m.* salt pan.

цирк *m.* circus; (geol.) cirque; (volcanic or lunar) crater, lunar (ring) formation.

циркадный *a.* circadian (rhythm).

циркалой *m.* Zircaloy (alloy).

цирковой *a.* of **цирк**.

циркон *m.* (min.) zircon; —**ат** *m.* zirconate.

циркониев/ый *a.* zirconium; —**ая земля** zirconia, zirconium oxide.

циркон/ий *m.* zirconium, Zr; **двуокись** —**ия** zirconium dioxide, zirconia; **сернокислый ц., сульфат** —**ия** zirconium sulfate.

циркон/ил *m.* zirconyl; —**истый** *a.* zirconium.

цирконов/ый *a.* zirconium, zirconic; **ц. ангидрид** zirconic anhydride, zirconium oxide; **соль** —**ой кислоты** zirconate.

циркообразный *a.* (geol.) cirque, crater.

циркулин *m.* Circulin (antibiotic).

циркулир/овать *v.* circulate; —**ующий** *a.* circulating, circulation; distributing.

циркуль *m.* dividers, compass(es); calipers; **делительный ц., измерительный ц.** dividers; **калиберный ц.** calipers; —**ный** *a.* of **циркуль**; circular; curved.

циркулянт *m.* (math.) circulant.

циркуляр *m.* circular; —**ка** *f.* circular saw; —**ный** *a.* circular; circulatory, circulating.

циркулятор *m.* circulator.

циркуляц/ионный *a.* circulation, circulating; circulatory; —**ия** *f.* circulation; circuit; circling, turning circle; **котёл с** —**ей** circulation boiler.

циркум— *prefix* circum— (around, surrounding); —**полярный** *a.* circumpolar; —**ференция** *f.* circumference; —**цизия** *f.* (med.) circumcision.

циров/ание *n.*, —**ка** *f.* engine turning, guilloche, —**ать** *v.* engine-turn.

циррина *f.* (ichth.) Cirrhina.

цирроз *m.* (med.) cirrhosis.

циррус *m.* (biol.) cirrus.

цирцея *f.* (bot.) Circaea.

цирфея *f.* (mal.) piddock (*Zirfaea*).

цис— *prefix* cis- (on the same side); **ц.-изомер** *cis* isomer; **ц.-полимер** *m. cis* polymer; **ц.-соединение** *n. cis* compound.

циссоида *f.* (math.) cissoid.

цист/а *f.* (biol.) cyst; —**амин** *m.* cystamine, hexamethylenetetramine; —**еин** *m.* cysteine, β-mercaptoalanine; —**еиновая кислота** cysteic acid.

цистерна *f.* cistern, reservoir, tank; **(вагон-)ц.** (rr.) tank car.

цис-терпин *m. cis*-terpine.

цистида *f.* (bot.) cystid(ium).

цист/ин *m.* (biochem.) cystine; —**ит** *m.* (med.) cystitis; —**ицерк** *m.* (zool.) Cysticercus; —**ицеркоз** *m.* cysticercosis, cysticercus infestation; —**о**— *prefix* cyst(o)— (bladder); —**оидеи** *pl.* (pal.) Cystoidea; —**окарпий** *m.* cystocarp (in algae); —**олит** *m.* cystolith, vesical calculus; —**ома** *f.* (med.) cystoma; —**опурин** *m.* cystopurin; —**оскопия** *f.* (med.) cystoscopy; —**отомия** *f.* (med.) cystotomy.

цис-транс-/изомер *m. cis-trans* isomer; —**тест** (gen.) *cis-trans* test.

цистрон *m.* (gen.) cistron.

цитаза *f.* cytase.

цитарин *m.* Citarin.

цитар/ихт *m.* (ichth.) Citharichthys; —**овые** *pl.* (ichth.) Citharidae.

цит/ата *f.*, —**атный** *a.* citation, quotation; —**атничество** *n.* quoting out of text; —**ация** *f.* quoting.

цитварн/ая полынь (bot.) santonica (*Artemisia cina*); —**ое семя** santonica (seed), wormseed.

цити/диловая кислота cytidylic acid; —**дин** *m.* cytidine, cytosine riboside; —**динфосфорный** *a.* cytidinephosphoric (acid); —**зин** *m.* cytisine, ulexine.

цитиров/ание *n.* citation, quotation; —**ать** *v.* cite, quote, extract.

цититон *m.* (pharm.) cytisine solution.

цито urgent (on prescriptions).

цито—*prefix* (biol.) cyto— (cell; cytoplasm); —**бласт** *m.* cytoblast, cell nucleus; —**бластема** *f.* cytoblastema; —**гамия** *f.* cytogamy; —**ген** *m.* cytogene; —**генез** *m.* cytogenesis; —**генетика** *f.* cytogenetics; —**да** *f.* cytode (non-nucleated protoplasmic mass); —**дирезис** *m.* cytodieresis; —**диагностика** *f.* (med.) cytodiagnosis; —**зин** *m.*, —**зиновый** *a.* cytosine; —**кинез** *m.* cytokinesis; —**лиз** *m.* cytolysis, dissolution of cells; —**лизин** *m.* cytolysin; —**логия** *f.* cytology; —**плазма**

f. cytoplasm; **—плазматический** *a.* cytoplasmic; **—сома** *f.* cytosome; **—стом** *m.* cytostome (of protozoa); **—токсин** *m.* cytotoxin; **—фаринкс** *m.* cytopharynx; **—химия** *f.* cytological chemistry; **—хром** *m.* cytochrome; **—центр** *m.* centrosome, cell center.

цитр/ал(ь) *m.* citral; **—ил** *m.* cityryl, lemon oil.

цитрин *m.* citrin, vitamin P; citrine ointment, mercuric nitrate ointment; (min.) citrine; **—ин** *m.* citrinin.

цитро/мицетин *m.* citromycetin, frequentic acid; **—н** *m.* (bot.) citron (*Citrus medica*); **—нат** *m.* candied citron or lemon peel.

цитронелл/а *f.* citronella grass; **—ал(ь)** *m.* citronellal- (dehyde); **—ил** *m.* citronellyl; **—ол** *m.* citronellol.

цитрулл/ин *m.* citrulline; citrullin, colocynthin; **—ол** *m.* citrullol.

цитрус *m.* (bot.) citrus; **—овод** *m.* citrus grower; **—овый** *a. of* **цитрус.**

цифелла *f.* cyphella, dimple (in lichens).

циферблат *m.,* **—ный** *a.* dial (plate), face; **—ный индикатор** dial gage.

цифр/а *f.* digit; cipher, figure, number, numeral, character; **обозначать —ами** *v.* number; **—ация** *f.* numbering; **—о-аналоговый** *a.* digital-to-analog (converter); **—ованный** *a.* numbered, etc., see *v.*; **—ователь** *m.* digitizer; **—овать** *v.* number; digitize; (write in) code, cipher; **—овой** *a. of* **цифра;** digital; numerical (analog, coding); numbered, figured; **—овой вычислитель** digital computer; **—овой преобразователь** digitizer; **—овая вычислительная машина** digital computer; **—овые данные** figures, numerical data.

цих/ласома *f.* (ichth.) Cichlasoma; **—лиды, —ловые** *pl.* (ichth.) Cichlidae.

цицания *f.* (bot.) wild rice (*Zizania*).

цицеро *n.* (typ.) pica.

циэйзен *m.* die, draw plate.

ЦЛ *abbr.* **(центральная лаборатория)** central laboratory.

ЦМ *abbr.* **(цветомер)** colorimeter; **(центр массы)** center of mass.

ЦМД *abbr.* **(цилиндрический магнитный домен)** (phys.) cylindrical magnetic domain, bubble domain.

цмин *m.* (bot.) Helichrysum.

цн *abbr.* **(центнер)** centner.

ЦНИ . . . *abbr.* **(Центральный научно-исследовательский . . .)** Central Scientific Research . . .; **ЦНИИ . . .** *abbr.* **(Центральный научно-исследовательский институт . . .)** Central Scientific Research Institute of . . .

ЦНС, ц.н.с. *abbr.* **(центральная нервная система)** central nervous system.

цойсия *f.* lawn grass (*Zoysia*); **ц.-матрелла** *f.* Manila grass (*Z. matrella*).

цок/анье *n.* clatter, etc., see *v.*; **—ать, —нуть** *v.* click, clatter, rattle.

цокол/евка *f.,* **—евочный** *a.* basing, base; **—ь** *m.,* **—ьный** *a.* foundation, base, pedestal; socle, block; socket, base (of electric bulb).

цокор *m.* (mam.) molerats (*Myospalax*); **—овые** *pl.* Myospalacinae.

ЦПУ *abbr.* **(центральное процессорное устройство)** (comp.) central processing unit, CPU.

ЦТ, Ц. Т., ц.т. *abbr.* **(центр тяжести)** center of gravity.

ЦТСЛ *abbr.* **(цирконат-титанат свинца, модифицированный лантаном)** lead lanthanum zirconate-titanate, PLZT (ferroelectric ceramic).

цуг *m.* train (of waves); tandem (arrangement of horses, oxen); **—овой** *a.* train; tandem; **—ом** *adv.* (in) tandem, one behind the other.

цукат *m.,* **—ный** *a.* candied peel.

цунами *f.* tsunami, seismic sea wave.

цуцик *m.* (ichth.) goby.

цуцугамуши *f.* (med.) scrub typhus.

ЦЧП *abbr.* **(Центрально-чернозёмная полоса)** Central Black Earth Belt.

цык/ать, —нуть *v.* hush, silence.

цынга *see* **цинга.**

цыновка *f.* mat.

цыпл/ёнок *m.* chick, baby chicken; **—ята** *pl.* chicks; **—ячий** *a.* chicken.

цюрихский *a.* (geog.) Zurich.

Ч

ч, ч. *abbr.* **(час)** hour; **ч.** *abbr.* **(часть)** part, unit; **(человек)** man, men; **(через)** through; **(чертёж)** drawing; **(число)** number; date; **(чистый)** pure.

чаба/н *m.* shepherd, sheepherder; **—ний** *a.* shepherd's; **—нить** *v.* shepherd, herd sheep; **—нский** *a.* shepherding; **—рня** shepherd's dwelling.

чаб/ёр *m.* (bot.) savory (*Satureia*); **—рец** *m.* thyme (*Thymus*).

чавк/анье *n.* champing; **—ать** *v.* champ, bite repeatedly.

чави— *see* шави—.

чавыча *f.* chinook salmon (*Oncorhynchus tschawytscha*).

чага *f.* birch mushroom (*Boletus scaber*).

чагас *m.* (vet.) Chagas' disease.

чагеран *m.* (bot.) camel's thorn (*Alhagi*).

Чад (geog.) Chad.

чад *m.* smoke, fumes; **—ить** *v.* smoke, fume; **—ный** *a.* smoking, fuming.

ча/е— *prefix* tea; —ёв *gen. pl. of* **чай.**

чае/вод *m.* tea grower; **—водство** *n.,* **—водческий** *a.* tea-growing; **—обработка** *f.* tea processing; **—подобный** *a.* tea-like; **—сушилка** *f.* tea dryer.

чай *m.* tea plant (*Thea*); tea; infusion.

чайка *f.* (orn.) (sea)gull (*Larus*).

Чайлда закон Child's law.

чайн/ик *m.* teapot; **—огибридный** *a.* hybrid tea (rose); **—ые** *pl.* (bot.) Theaceae; **—ый** *a. of* **чай; —ый куст** *m.,* **—ое дерево** *n.* tea plant (*Thea*).

чайот *m.* (bot.) chayote (*Sechium edule*).

чайский *a.* (geog.) Chaya (river).

чакан *m.* (bot.) cattail, etc. (*Typha*).

чаквала *f.* (herp.) chuckwalla.

чакма *f.* chacma baboon (*Papio ursinus*).

чал *m.* mooring rope, tie rope; **—ить** *v.* moor; **—ка** *f.* mooring; mooring rope.

чалбыш *m.* (ichth.) Siberian sturgeon.

чалм/а *f.* turban, tiara; **—овидный** *a.* (bot.) tiariform.

чало-пегий *a.* piebald (horse).

чалт/ык *m.,* **—ычная почва** chaltyk (old rice soil).

чалый *a.* gray, roan (horse).

чампра *f.* squall, small storm.

чан *m.* vat, tub, tank; trough, pit; **—драсекхаровский** *a.* (astr.) Chandrasekhar's; **—овый** *a. of* **чан; ч.-фильтр** *m.* filter tank.

чап/ада *f.* chapada (table land with grasslands and park forests); **—араль** (bot.) chaparral.

Чапек (microbiol.) Czapek (medium).

чап/олоть, —олочь *f.* (bot.) holy grass (*Hierochloe odorata*); **—ыжник** (bot.) pea shrub (*Caragana*).

чап/рак *m.* (agr.) saddle cloth or blanket; **—ыги** *pl.* plow handles.

Чарлстон (geog.) Charleston.

чаровать *v.* fascinate.

чартер *m.* (com.) charter.

чаруса *f.* grassy bog.

чарующий *a.* fascinating, captivating.

час *m.* hour; **в ч.** at one o'clock; **через ч.** in an hour; **—ами** *adv.* for hours, for a long time; **—ики** *dim. of* **часы.**

часов/ня *f.* (arch.) chapel.

часов/ой *a.* one hour's, an hour's; hourly, per hour; *suffix* -hour; clock; watch; *m.* sentinel, sentry, watch, guard; **ч. механизм** clockwork; **ч. пояс** time zone; **—ая стрелка** hour hand (of clock); **по ч. стрелке** clockwise, from left to right; **против ч. стрелки** counterclockwise, from right to left; **—ое дело** horology; **—ое стекло** watch glass, (large size) clock glass; **—щик** *m.* watch maker, clock maker, horologist; (ent.) furniture beetle (*Anobium*).

час/ом *adv.* sometimes, now and then; **—пром** *m.* watchmaking industry.

част *sh. m. of* **частый.**

частей *gen. pl. of* **часть.**

частенько *adv.* rather often.

части *gen., pl., etc., of* **часть.**

част/ик *m.* fine-mesh net; small fish; **—иковый** *a.* fine-mesh; **—ить** *v.* accelerate; make closer; frequent; do often.

части/ца *f.* particle, bit, grain, fraction, speck, corpuscle; molecule; (chem.) species (ion, radical, etc.); **метод —цы** (meteor.) parcel method; **ч.-мишень** *f.* target particle; **ч. огнеупоров** (met.) brick inclusions; **ч.-предшественник** *m.* precursor; **ч.-снаряд** *f.* projectile particle; **—чка** *f.* (very fine) particle, spicule.

частичн/о *adv.* partially, partly, incompletely; in part, part way; **ч.-видящий** *a.* (*med.*) partially sighted; **ч.-водонапорный** *a.* partial water (drive); **—ый** *a.* partial, fractional, incomplete; preliminary (decontamination); selective; particle, particulate; corpuscular, molecular; **—ый итог** subtotal; **—ый платёж** installment; **—ый разрез** cut-away drawing; **—ая формула** molecular formula.

частник *m.* free-lance worker.

частно— *prefix* private(ly); **—владельческий** *a.* privately owned; **—е** *n.* (math.) quotient; **—капиталистический**, **—предпринимательский** *a.* private enterprise; **—собственнический** *a.* private-owner(ship).

частност/ь *f.* particularity, detail; relative frequency; **в —и** in particular, specifically; in part, among other things.

частн/ый *a.* private; partial; special, specific; peculiar, exceptional, individual, particular; descriptive (ichthyology); (bot.) local (succession); **—ая производная** (math.) partial derivative; **—ая собственность** private property; **—ым образом** privately, confidentially, unofficially.

часто *adv.* often, constantly, frequently; close, thickly, densely; *prefix* crebri— (close); densi— (dense); dasy— (shaggy, rough); русn(о)— (close, compact); *sh. n. of* **частый; —кол** *m.* hedge, enclosure, paling, palisade, fencing.

частомер *m.* (elec.) frequency meter.

часто-проблесковый *a.* quick-flashing.

частость *see* **частота.**

частот/а *f.* frequency, rate; thickness, closeness; spacing, interval; **ч. повторяемости** frequency; **ч. следования импульсов** pulse repetition rate; **ч. среза** cut-off frequency; **большой —ы** high-frequency; **верхних частот** high-pass (filter); **высокой —ы** high-frequency; **деление —ы** scaling down; **диапазон частот** frequency band; **малой —ы** low-frequency; **нижних частот** low-pass (filter); **низкой —ы** low-frequency.

частотно/-временной *a.* time-and-frequency; variable duration frequency (modulation); **ч.-зависимый** *a.* frequency-dependent, frequency-sensitive; **ч.-избирательный** *a.* frequency-selective; **ч.-импульсный** *a.* pulse-frequency; **ч.-модулированный** *a.* frequency-modulated; **ч.-преобразовательный** *a.* frequency conversion, converter (tube); **—сть** *f.* frequency (rate).

частотн/ый *a. of* **частота; —ая коррекция** accentuation (of amplifier); **—ая характеристика** frequency response; **с —ой модуляцией** frequency-modulated, f-m.

частотомер *m.* (elec.) frequency meter.

частух/а *f.* (bot.) water plantain (*Alisma*).

частый *a.* frequent, dense, thick, crowded; (text.) close-woven; quick (pulse).

част/ь *f.* part, portion, share, fraction, proportion; fragment, piece, segment; member, unit, component; area, department, section; detail; quota; step, stage; digit (1/12 of moon's diameter); (silv.) end, log; (statistics) rate; moiety; (anat.) pars, division; **ч. целого** integrant, component; **—ей на** parts per; **—ью** *adv.* part(ly), partially, for the most part; **—ями** piecemeal, in portions; **баллистическая головная ч.** ballistic reentry vehicle; **бо́льшей —ью** for the most part; **бо́льшая ч.** the greater part, the majority; **интегрирование по —ям** (math.) integration by parts; **на —я** apart, to pieces; **одна пятая ч.** one fifth; **по —и** in connection (with); **по —ям** in parts, in installments; piecemeal; partially; **разобрать на —и** *v.* take apart, dismantle.

часы *pl. of* **час;** clock; watch; (sun) dial; meter; **ч.-хронометр** time-keeper, timepiece.

чатала *f.* prop (for fruit trees).

Чатам (geog.) Chatham.

чатертоновский *a.* Chatterton.

чаулмугр— *see* **хаульмугр—.**

чах/лость *f.* weakness, unhealthiness; emaciation; **—лый** *a.* sickly; weak; withered; wilting; stunted, dwarfed (vegetation); **—нуть** *v.* fade away, wither away; weaken, flag; **—нущий** *a.* ailing, diseased (tree); *see* **чахлый.**

чахот/ка *f.* (med.) phthisis, consumption, tuberculosis; **—очный** *a.* consumptive, tubercular.

чачалака *f.* (orn.) chachalaca (*Ortalis*).

чаша *f.* bowl, cup; dish, basin, pan, pot; (anat.) cotyledon; cavity; **ч. оттаивания** thaw basin.

чаше/видный *a.* cup(-shaped), dish(-shaped), bowl(-shaped); saucer(-shaped); scyphate; cyathiform; **—вый** *a. of* **чаша; —к** *gen. pl. of* **чашка; —листик** *m.* (bot.) sepal; **—носный** *a.* (bot.) cupuliferous; cyathium-bearing; **—образный** *see* **чашевидный; —подобный** *a.* (anat.) spheroidal, ball-and-socket (joint); **—цветник** *m.* (bot.) Calycanthus; **—цветный** *a.* calyciflorous.

чашеч/ка *dim. of* **чашка;** cup, bowl, dish; crucible; (bot.) calyx, bell; calycule; (knee) cap; (anat.) calix; caliculus; patella; **—ко—** *prefix* (bot.) calyci—, calc(o)— calyx); **—ковидный** *a.* calyciform, calycine; **—коно-**

сный *a.* calyciferous; **—ный** *a.* of **чашка;** bucket-wheel (rotor); *suffix* —calyculate; calycine; **—ный (микро)манометр** cup (micro)manometer.

чашк/а *f.* cup, bowl, vessel; (Petri) dish; crucible; beaker; hollow; (anat.) calix; pan (of balance); (knee)cap; bob (of pendulum); housing; cistern (of barometer); **(над)-коленная ч.** kneecap, patella; **—ообразный** *a.* cup(-shaped).

чаща *f.* thicket, brushwood, brake; heart (of forest).

чаще *comp.* of **часто, частый,** more often, more frequently; **ч. всего** mostly, most often, most commonly; **как можно ч.** as often as possible.

чащоба *f.* thicket.

чая *gen.* of **чай.**

чв-д *abbr.* (**человеко-день**) man-day, worker-day.

чв-ч *abbr.* (**человекочас**) man-hour, worker-hour.

ЧД *abbr.* (**частота дыхания**) respiration rate.

ч.д.а. *abbr.* (**чистый для анализа**) analytical grade (reagent), chemically pure.

чебак *m.* one of several kinds of small fish, e.g. roach, ide, dace, minnow.

чеб/ёр *abbr.* savory (*Satureia*); **—рец** *m.* thyme (*Thymus*).

Чевиот(-Хилс) (geog.) Cheviot Hills.

чеглок *m.* (orn.) hobby (*Falco subbuteo*).

чего *gen.* of **что,** what.

чеграва *f.* (orn.) Caspian tern (*Hydroprogne tschegrava*).

чедвиковский *a.* (phys.) Chadwick.

чезаровский *a.* (math.) Cesaro.

чей *m. pron.* whose; **ч.-либо, ч.-нибудь** anybody's, somebody's, someone's.

Чейна-Стокса, чейн-стоксовый (med.) Cheyne-Stokes.

чей-то somebody's, someone's.

чек *m.* check; (agr.) check plot; (flooding) basin.

чек/а *f.* pin, cotter (pin), linch pin, splint pin, key, wedge, chock; cross piece; splint; **закрепить —ой** *v.* key.

чекалка *f.* jackal (*Canis aureus*).

чекан *m.* stamping, etc., *see v.*; stamp, punch, die; calking iron, (calking) chisel, calker; (orn.) chat (*Saxicola*); **—ение** *n.* stamping, etc., *see v.*; **—ить** *v.* stamp, impress, imprint, mark; engrave, emboss, chase, chisel, fuller; knurl (edge); mint, coin (money); strike (medals); bead (pipes); calk; (hort.) pinch back, prune; pinch out; chop (cotton); **—ка** *f.* stamping, etc., *see v.*; die stamping; relief work; impression; calking iron; calked seam; riveting punch; fullering tool; **ч.-каменка** (orn.) wheatear; **—ный** *a.* stamped, etc., *see v.*; stamping, etc., *see v.*; chiseled, chased (work); legible, expressive; measured, firm; **—очный** *a.* stamping, etc., *see v.*; **—очный пресс** die press, coining press; **—очный штамп** embossing die; **—щик** *m.* stamper, etc., *see v.*

чеки *pl.* inundated rice fields.

чекмарная соль (geol.) partly solidified, recently deposited salt.

чекмарь *m.* rammer, beater; smoother.

чековый *a.* of **чек.**

чел. *abbr.* (**человек**).

челбух *m.* immature sturgeon.

Челлин/а печь *see* **Кьеллина печь; —и гало** (meteor.) Cellini's halo.

чёлка *f.* (horse's) forelock; (human) bangs.

чёлн *m.* dug-out, canoe; bark, boat.

челн/овидки *pl.* shining fungus beetles (*Scaphidiidae*); **—овидный** *a.* scaphoid, boat-shaped; **—ок** *m.* dug-out, canoe; (weaving) shuttle; bobbin; rabbit; (anat.) cymba; **—ок ушной раковины** (anat.) cymba conchae auriculae; **—оклювы** *pl.* boat-billed herons (*Cochleariidae*); **—окодержатель** *m.* shuttle carrier; **—ок-самолёт** *m.* fly(ing) shuttle; **—ообразный** *a.*

scaphoid, boat-shaped; **—очницы** *pl.* (ent.) Cymbidae; **—очный** *a.* of **челнок;** reciprocating trough (conveyer); (min.) wavy (vein); **—очная кость** navicular bone.

чело *n.* (met.) charge hole.

человек *m.* man, person, human being, individual; **на —а** per man; **разумный ч.** Homo sapiens; **сила —а** manpower; **—одень** *m.* man-day; **—оеды** *pl.* (ichth.) piranha (*Serrasalmidae*); **—олюбец** *m.* philanthropist; **—олюбивый** *a.* philanthropic; **—олюбие** *n.* philanthropy; **—оненавистник** *m.* misanthropist; **—оненавистнический** *a.* misanthropic; **—оненавистничество** *n.* misanthropy; **—ообразный, —оподобный** *a.* man-like, anthropoid; **—оподобные** *pl.* anthropoid apes (*Anthropoidea*); **—осмена** *f.* man-shift; **—оубийство** *n.* homicide, manslaughter; **—оуправляемый** *a.* manned; human (torpedo); **—очас** *m.* man-hour.

человеч/ек *m.* manikin, dummy; **—(еск)ий** *a.* human; **—еский род** mankind; **—ество** *n.* mankind, humanity; **—ина** *m. and f.* human flesh; **—ность** *f.* humanity, humaneness; **—ный** *a.* human, man's; humane.

челта-зандури *f.* (agr.) Triticum timopheevi.

чел-ч *abbr.* (**человекочас**) man-hour.

чёлышко *n.* brisket.

челюст/евидный *a.* (anat.) maxilliform, mandibuliform; **—но-** *prefix* (anat.) maxillo—; **—но-зубной** *a.* maxillodental; **—ной** *a.* jaw, maxillary, mandibular; **—ная кость** maxilla, jawbone; **—ная ножка** (zool.) maxilliped; **—но-подъязычный** *a.* mylohyoid; **—но-ротые** *pl.* jawed vertebrates (*Gnathostomata*); **—ные** *pl.* jawed fishes; **—ь** *f.* jaw, maxilla; dental plate, denture; **верхняя —ь** maxilla; **нижняя —ь** mandible.

челябинский *a.* (geog.) Chelyabinsk.

чем *instr.* of **что,** (with) what; *conj.* than, more; **ч. дальше, тем хуже** from bad to worse; **ч. позже, тем лучше** the later the better.

чём *prepos.* **о ч.?** what about, of what? **он не при ч.** he has nothing to do with it; **остаться не при ч.** *v.* lose.

чембур *m.* (horses) lead rein.

чемерица *f.* (bot.) Veratrum.

чемодан *m.*, **—ный** *a.* suitcase, bag; **—чик** *dim.* of **чемодан.**

чемпедак *m.* (bot.) champedak (*Artocarpus champeden*).

чемпион *m.* champion; **—ат** *m.* championship (tournament); **—ский** *a.* champion.

чемплэн *m.* (geol.) Champlainian period.

чемра *see* **чамра.**

чему *dat.* of **что,** to what; **к ч.** to what; what for, why.

чемыш *m.* salt tree (*Halimodendron*).

чепец *m.* cap; (anat.) tegmentum.

чепманайзинг-процесс *m.* (met.) Chapmanizing process.

чепура *f.* (orn.) cattle egret.

чепрак *m.* back of hide, butt; saddle cloth.

чепух/а *f.* nonsense; **—овый** *a.* nonsensical; trifling, insignificant.

чепыги *pl.* plow handles.

черва *f.* grub (of bee), bee brood; (bot.) dyer's rocket (*Reseda luteola*).

червеедка *f.* (ent.) Pollenia.

червей *gen. pl.* of **червь.**

червеобразн/ые *pl.* (zool.) Apoda; **—ый** *a.* vermiform, vermicular, worm-like; **—ый отросток** (anat.) appendix.

червец *m.* (ent.) scale; **мучнистые —ы** mealy bugs.

черви *pl.* of **червь;** (zool.) worms; **дождевые ч.** Lumbricidae; **кольчатые ч.** Annelida; **кручлие ч.** Nematoda; **ленточные ч.** Cestoda; **плоские ч.** Plathelminthes; **—веть** *v.* become wormy; **—вость** *f.* worminess; **—вый** *a.* wormy, worm-eaten; **—ть** *v.* lay eggs (of bees).

червлёный *a.* dark red, scarlet, purple.

черво— *prefix* vermi—, worm.

червобо/ина *f.* worm-eaten fruit; **—й** *m.* spoilage from worms; **—йный** *a.* worm-infested, worm-eaten.

червовод *m.* silkworm breeder; **—ня** *f.* silkworm breeding house; **—ство** *n.*, **—ческий** *a.* silkworm breeding, vermiculture.

червонный *a.* red; high-carat (gold).

черво/точина *f.* worm hole; dry rot; vermiculation; worm dust; **—точный** *a.* worm-eaten; **—ядный** *a.* vermivorous, worm-eating.

черв/ь *m.* worm; (anat.) vermis; **ч. мозжечка** vermis cerebelli; (zool.) **дождевые —и** Lumbricidae; **капустный ч.** (ent.) cabbage white butterfly; **кольчатые —и** Annelida; **круглые —и** roundworms (*Nematoda*); **ленточные —и** tapeworms (*Cestoda*); **плоские —и** flatworms (*Plathelminthes*); **—яги** *pl.* (herp.) Caeciliidae; **—як** *m.* worm, endless screw, auger; hob (cutting tool); **—яковый**, **—ячий** *a.* worm; **—ячки** *pl.* (chem.) spaghetti (catalyst).

червячно-фрезерный станок worm milling machine.

червячн/ый *a.* worm, screw, auger; **ч. бур** worm auger; **ч. привод** worm gear drive; **—ая машина** extruder; **—ая передача**, **—ое колесо** worm gear.

червячок *dim. of* **червяк**; (anat.) vermis (cerebelli).

черд/ак *m.*, **—ачный** *a.* attic, loft.

черевички *pl.* (bot.) forking larkspur (*Delphinium consolida*).

черед *m.* turn, order, succession, taking turns; line; row; **—а** *see* **черед**; (bot.) bur marigold (*Bidens*).

черед/ование *n.* alternating, rotation, etc., *see v.*; interleaving; interchange; **ч. поколений** heterogenesis; **—овать(ся)** *v.* alternate, take turns, rotate, interchange; (elec.) reverse; **—ом** *adv.* properly, as required; **—ующийся** *a.* alternating, alternate, staggered; cycling; sandwich (winding).

через *prep. acc.* across, over; per, via, by (way of), through, from, at; in (terms of); after; within (a given time); trans—; **ч. борт** overboard; **ч. день** every other day, on alternate days; in a day; **ч. каждый час** at hourly intervals; **ч. кожу** (med.) transdermal.

череззерница *f.* (bot.) partially filled ear.

черему/ха *f.*, **—ховый** *a.* (bot.) bird cherry (*Padus*); **—шник** *m.* bird cherry thicket.

черемша *f.* (bot.) ramson (*Allium ursinum*).

черён *sh. m. of* **чёрный**.

черенки *pl. of* **черенок**.

Черенкова *see* **черенковский**.

черенков/ание *n.* (hort.) propagation by cuttings; (bud) grafting; **—ать** *v.* propagate by cuttings.

черенковский *a.* Cerenkov (radiation).

черен/ковый *a. of* **черенок**; stick (sulfur); (bot.) pedunculate; **—ок** *m.* (hort.) cutting, slip; scion, graft; peduncle, stalk; malleolus, layer; (tool) shank, handle, stock, grip; (mal.) razor clam (*Solen*); **—ок-глазок** bud cutting.

череп *m.* (anat.) skull, cranium; **невральный, осевой ч.** (anat.) neurocranium; **шов —а** (anat.) cranial suture.

черепах/а *f.*, **—овый** *a.* (zool.) tortoise, turtle; tortoise shell.

черепаш/ий *a.* slow; tortoise, turtle, testudinate; **ч. панцырь**, **—ья чешуя** tortoise shell; **—ка** *f.* shield bug (*Eurygaster*); **—ки** *pl.* (ent.) Pentatomidae.

черепи/на *f.* broken tile; **—тчатый** *a.* tiled; roof-tile, tegular; imbricate, overlapping; **—ца** *f.* (roof) tile;

drain tile; **крытый —цей** tiled; **—цеобразный** *a.* imbricate(d), teguliform.

черепичн/ый *a.* tile; (zool.) tegular; **—ая кровля** tile roofing, tiling; **—ая печь** tile kiln; **—ое положение** (comp.) tiling (of windows).

череп/ной *a.* cranial, skull; **ч. свод** (anat.) calvaria; **—ная коробка** cranium; **—ная крыта** tegmen cranii, calvaria; **—нолицевой** *a.* craniofacial; **—номозговой** *a.* cranial; **—ные** *pl.* (zool.) Craniata; **—одержатель** *m.* skull clamp.

череп/ок *m.* crock; shard, fragment; **плавка в —ке** (met.) crock melting; **—ушка** small pot, bowl.

черепокожный *a.* (zool.) testaceous.

черепян/ой, —ый *a.* clay, ceramic.

чересло *n.* (agr.) colter, cutter.

черес/полосица *f.* overlapping (of lands); enclavement; **—полосный** *a.* broken up; strip (logging); **—строчный** *a.* interlaced.

чересчур *adv.* too, excessively.

черешковый *a.* (bot.) stalk(ed), petiolate.

черешн/евый *a.*, **—я** *f.* sweet cherry (*Cerasus avium*).

череш/ок *m.* handle, haft; (bot.) petiole, (leaf) stalk, peduncle; **—очек** (bot.) *dim. of* **черешок**; **—чатый** *a.* petiolate.

черкан *m.* trap, automatic snare.

черкануть *see* **черкнуть**.

черкасский *a. of* **Черкассы** (geog.) Cherkassy.

черкать *v.* cross out, delete.

черкез *m.* (bot.) saltwort (*Salsola richteri*).

черкесский *a.* (geog.) Circassian.

черкнуть *v.* scribble, jot down; streak.

чермет *m.* ferrous metallurgy.

черна *sh. f. of* **чёрный**; (ichth.) grouper (*Epinephelus*).

черн/ение *n.* black(en)ing; **—ён(н)ый** *a.* black(en)ed; nielloed; **—ети** *pl.* (orn.) Aythyinae; **—еть** *v.* become black, blacken, darken; **—еющий** *a.* nigrescent, blackening; **—и** *gen., etc. of* **чернь**.

Черни шов (med.) Czerny's suture.

черниговский *a.* (geog.) Chernigov.

черника *f.* (bot.) whortleberry, bilberry (*Vaccinium myrtillus*).

чернил/а *pl.* ink; **—овыводитель** *m.* ink eradicator; **—оустойчивый** *a.* (paper) ink-resistant; **—ьница** *f.* inkwell.

чернильноорешковая кислота gallic acid; **ч. дубильная кислота** tannic acid.

чернильн/ый *a.* ink; **—ая болезнь** (ichth.) blackspot disease; **—ая железа** (zool.) ink sac; **—ое заболевание** (ichth.) blackspot disease; **ч. камень** inkstone, copperas; **ч. мешок** (zool.) ink sac; **ч. орешек** gallnut, (nut) gall; **ванна —ых орешков** gall steep.

чернить *v.* blacken, smoke; black out.

черни/ца, —чина *f.* whortleberry; **—чник** *m.* whortleberry thicket; **—чный** *a.* whortleberry.

черно *adv. and sh. n. of* **чёрный**; *prefix* atri—, nigri—, melan(o)—; black, dark.

черно/бривцы *pl.* marigolds, **—бровка** *f.* (ichth.) Acanthalburnus microlebis; **—бурый** *a.* dark brown; silver (fox); **—бурая сажа** bister, wood-pulp black; **—был(ь), —быльник** *m.* (bot.) mugwort, wormwood (*Artemisia vulgaris*); **Чернобыль** (geog.) Chernobyl; **—ватый** *a.* blackish, dark; **—вик** *m.* rough copy, draft; **—вица** *f.* black dot, black spot; **—вой** *a.* rough, coarse; draft (copy); preliminary (operation); intermediate; impure, crude (metal); black, blister (copper); (met.) breakdown (die); **—вой (прокатный) стан** (met.) roughing mill, breaking down mill; **—вой проход, —вая проходка** roughing cut; breaking down; —**вой резец** roughing tool; —**вая обработка** roughing out, rough finishing; —**вая прокатка** roughing (down); —**вая форма** (glass) parison mold; —**вые валки** roughing-down rolls, breaking-down rolls.

черноголов/ка *f.* (bot.) self-heal (*Prunella*); —**ник** *m.* burnet (*Poterium*); —**ый** *a.* black-headed, melanocephalous.

черно/горка *f.* (bot.) adonis; —**горский** *a.* (geog.) Montenegrin; —**гривый** *a.* black-maned; —**зелье** *n.* (bot.) black peavine (*Lathyrus niger*).

чернозём *m.*, —**ный** *a.* chernozem, black soil; —**овидный** *a.* chernozem-like; —**ообразование** *n.* chernozem formation.

черно/зобик *m.* (orn.) sandpiper (*Calidris alpina*); —**зобый** *a.* black-throated; —**клён** *m.* (bot.) maple (*Acer tataricum*); —**клювый** *a.* black-billed; —**кожий** *a.* black, negro; —**корень** *m.* (bot.) hound's tongue (*Cynoglossum*); —**корый** *a.* black-barked; —**кровие** *n.* (med.) melanemia; —**кудренник** *m.* black horehound (*Ballota nigra*); —**кудрый** *a.* black-haired; —**лесный** *a.* (bot.) deciduous; —**лесье** *n.* deciduous, hardwood forest; —**лоз** *m.* gray willow (*Salix cinerea*); —**ломкий** *a.* (met.) black-hot short, brittle at black heat; —**морский** *a.* (geog.) Black Sea; —**ногий** *a.* black-footed; —**пёрка** *f.* (ichth.) bream; —**пишущий аппарат** ink writer, inker; —**плёнчатость** *f.* (bacterial) black chaff (of wheat); —**плодный** *a.* melanocarpous, black-fruited; —**пуз** *m.* (ichth.) nase (*Chondrostoma*); —**пурпуровый** *a.* atropurpureous, dark purple; —**пятнистый** *a.* blackspot; —**рабочий** *a.* manual (labor); *m.* manual laborer, unskilled workman; —**реченский** *a.* (geog.) Black River.

черно/семянный *a.* melanospermous; —**слив** *m.* bullage plum; **сухой** —**слив** prune; —**слойный** *a.* black-ringed; —**спинка** *f.* black-backed shad (*Caspialosa kessleri*); —**стебельчатый** *a.* black-stalked.

черно/та *f.* blackness; dark pigmentation, melania; —**тал** *m.* (bot.) laurel-leaf willow (*Salix pentandra*); —**телки** *pl.* darkling beetles (*Tenebrionidae*); —**хвостый** *a.* black-tailed; —**цвет** *m.* (bot.) enchanter's nightshade (*Circaea*); —**цветковый** *a.* black-flowered; —**щетинковый** *a.* black-bristled.

чернушка *f.* (bot.) fennel flower (*Nigella*); mushroom (*Lactarius necator*); (phot.) cross hair; (ent.) Erebia.

чёрн/ый *a.* black; unskilled, manual (labor); rough, coarse; everyday; gross, net (weight); blacktop (road); deciduous (forest); (met.) ferrous; back (entrance); dust (storm); **ч. корень** (bot.) Cynoglossum; Scorzonera; —**ая варка** (paper) black cook; —**ая доска** blackboard; —**ая металлургия** iron and steel industry; ferrous metallurgy; —**ая ножка** (phyt.) stem wilt, black stem rot, damping off; —**ая пелена** (med.) blackout; —**ое дерево** (bot.) ebony (*Diospyros ebenum*); **(абсолютно) —ое тело** (phys.) black body; **коэффициент излучения —ого тела** Stefan-Boltzmann constant.

черныш *m.* (orn.) green sandpiper (*Tringa ochropus*); (bot.) Boletus scaber; (ichth.) goby.

чернышевит *m.* (min.) tschernichewite.

чернь *f.* black (pigment); black enamel; niello (on silver); (phyt.) sooty mold; coniferous taiga; (orn.) *see* **чернеть.**

чернядь *f.* dark red ocher.

черп/ак *m.*, —**аковый** *a.* scoop, ladle, bail(er); (grab) bucket, pail; —**алка** *see* **черпак;** —**ало**— *prefix* ary(teno)— (ladle, jug); —**аловидный** *a.* (anat.) arytenoid; —**алонадгортанный** *a.* (anat.) ary(teno)epi-

glottic (fold); —**альный** *a.*, —**ание** *n.* scooping, etc., *see* v.; —**ать** *v.* scoop, ladle, dip (out), draw out; dredge; —**ачковый, —ачный** *a. of* **черпак;** —**ачный элеватор** bucket dredge; —**ачок** *dim. of* **черпак;** —**нуть** *see* **черпать.**

черстветь *v.* get stale; become hardened or callous.

чёрств/ость *f.* staleness; —**ый** *a.* stale, hard, dry; callous, insensitive.

черт. *abbr.* **(чертёж)** diagram, drawing.

чёрт *m.* devil; **морской ч.** anglerfish, monkfish (*Lophius piscatorius*); Atlantic manta (*Manta birostris*).

черт/а *f.* trait, characteristic, feature, quality; line, mark, scratch, dash; boundary; (min.) streak; —**ы** *pl.* pattern; **в —е** in the boundaries (of); **в общих —ах** in general outline, roughly, in a few words.

чертёж *m.* plan, design; (engineering) drawing; sketch, draft, diagram, representation, outline drawing, illustration, chart; **исполнительные —и** working drawings, as-built drawings; **сборный ч.** assembly drawing; —**ная** *f.* drafting room; —**ник** *m.* draftsman; designer; —**ный** *a.* drafting, drawing, graphic; design; lettering (pen); —**ная игла** drawing point; —**ная кнопка** thumb tack; —**ная линейка** rule(r), straightedge.

черт/илка *f.* scriber, marking tool, scratch awl; drop point; —**ильный** *see* **чертёжный;** —**ить** *v.* draw, sketch, trace, mark, scribe; design, plot; —**ок** *m.* thumbtack.

чертополох *m.* (bot.) thistle (*Carduus*); —**овка** *f.* (ent.) painted lady butterfly (*Pyraemis cardui*).

чёрточка *dim. of* **черта;** dash.

черты *pl. of* **черта.**

Черча (math.) Church's (theorem, etc.).

черчен/ие *n.* drawing, etc., *see* **чертить;** —**ный** *a.* drawn, etc., *see* **чертить.**

черч/иллит *m.* (min.) churchillite, mendipite; —**ит** *m.* churchite.

чесал/ка *f.* (hemp, flax) comb, ripple, hackle; (text.) carding machine; rubbing post; —**о** *n. see* **чесалка;** insecticide applicator (for cattle).

чес/альник *see* **чесальщик;** —**альный** *a.* combing, carding, hackling, rippling; —**альный гребень** comb; —**альщик** *m.* comber, carder.

чёсанец *m.* combed flax.

чесание *see* **ческа.**

чёсан(н)ый *a.* combed, etc., *see* **чесать.**

чесапикский *a.* (geog.) Chesapeake.

чес/ать *v.* comb, hackle, dress, ripple, card; scratch; curry (horse); —**аться** *v.* be combed, etc.; comb one's hair; scratch; itch.

чёска *f.* combing, etc., *see* v.

чесно/к *m.* garlic (*Allium sativum*); —**ковый** *a.* garlic; —**чина** *f.* garlic clove; —**чник** *m.*, —**чница** *f.* garlic mustard (*Alliaria*); —**чницы** (amph.) spade-foot toads, etc. (*Pelobatidae*); —**чно** *prefix* scorodo— (garlic); —**чнолистный** *a.* scorodophyllous; —**чный** *a.* garlic, alliaceous.

чесот/ка *f.* itch; (med.) scabies; mange; —**(оч)ный** *a.* scabious, scab(i)etic, mangy; —**очные клещи** mites.

чествовать *v.* honor, celebrate.

честен *sh. m. of* **честный.**

честер *m.* Chester (breed of pig).

честерьян *m.* (geol.) Chesterian series.

чести/ость *f.* honesty, integrity; —**ый** *a.* honest, upright, straightforward.

честолюб/ивый *a.* ambitious; —**ие** *n.* ambition.

честь *f.* honor; *v.* deem; **отдавать ч.** give credit (to); **считать за ч.** *v.* consider it an honor, deem it a favor; **это делает ему ч.** this does him credit.

чесуч/а *f.*, **—овый** *a.* tussah (silk).

чет *m.* pair, even number; **—а** *f.* pair.

четверг *m.* Thursday.

четвер/ик *m.* 26.24-liter measure; **—ичный** *a.* (stat.) quartile.

четвёрка *f.* (group of) four, team of four; number four (transport); (commun.) quad, tetrad.

четверн/и *pl.* quadruplets; **—ой** *a.* fourfold, quadruple, tetra—; quaternary; tetrad (axis); **—я** *f.* team of four.

четверо *num.* four; *prefix* tetr(a)—, quadri—, quadru—; **их ч.** there are four of them; **—классник** *m.* fourth-grade pupil; **—курсник** *m.* fourth-year student, senior; **—ногий** *a.* quadruped, tetrapod, four-footed; **—ногое** *n.* quadruped; **—рукие** *pl.* (mam.) quadrumanes; **—рукий** *a.* quadrumanous; **—холмия** *pl.* (anat.) corpora quadrigemina; **пластинка —холмия** (anat.) lamina tecti, quadrigeminal plate; **—який** *a.* fourfold, quadruple.

четвертин/а *f.* one quarter; quarter beam; **—ка** *dim. of* **четвертина**; quarter-liter bottle.

четверт/ичный *a.* quaternary; (geol.) Quaternary.

четвёртка *see* **четверть**.

четвертная *f.* unit of measure (dry: 210 liters; liquid: 3 liters; one-fourth yard); **—ной** *a.* one-fourth, quarter; quaternary, four-component.

четвёртый *a.* fourth; **—ая часть** one fourth, a quarter.

четверт/ь *f.* one fourth, quarter; (geom.) quadrant; (arch.) rebate, rabbet; *see also* **четвертная; ч. второго** a quarter past one o'clock; **без —и пять** a quarter to five o'clock.

четверть/волновой *a.* quarter-wave; **—оборотный** *a.* quarter-turn.

чётки *pl.* (med.) (rachitic) beads.

чётк/ий *a.* legible, clear(-cut), distinct, high-definition, sharp; accurate, precise; meticulous; concise; efficient; **—о** *adv.* legibly, etc., *see a.*; **—о выраженный** *a.* clearly defined, well-defined, marked, distinct, pronounced.

чётко/видный, —образный *a.* beaded, moniliform; lenticular (vein).

чёткость *f.* legibility, clearness, sharpness, definition; accuracy; contrast; (fractionating) efficiency.

чётн/о-нечётный *a.* even-odd; **—ость** *f.* (phys.) parity; **—о-чётный** *a.* even-even; **—ый** *a.* even (number).

чёток *sh. m. of* **чёткий**.

чёточн/ик *m.* (bot.) rosary pea (*Torularia*); **—ый** *a.* beaded; **ч. водоподъёмник** chain pump; **—ая жила** (min.) wavy vein; **—ая молния** beaded lightning.

четтертоновский *a.* Chatterton (compound).

чётче *comp. of* **чёткий, чётко.**

четыре *num.* four; *prefix see* **четырёх—; —жды** *adv.* four times, multiplied by four, fourfold; **—ста** four hundred; **—угольник** *see* **четырёхугольник.**

четырёх— *prefix* tetra—, quadri—, four; **—адресный** *a.* (comp.) four-address; **—алкильный** *a.* tetraalkyl(ated); **—арильный** *a.* tetraaryl(ated); **—атомный** *a.* tetraatomic; tetravalent; **—ацильный** *a.* tetraacylated; **—базисный** *a.* tetrabasic; **—бороздный, —бороздчатый** *a.* quadrisulcate; **—бромистый** *a.* tetrabromide (of); **—бугорчатый** *a.* quadritubercular (teeth).

четырёхвалентн/ость *f.* tetravalence; **—ый** *a.* tetravalent.

четырёх/валковый *a.* four-roll(er), four-high (rolling mill); **—вёрстный** *a.* four-verst; having a scale of four versts to the inch; **—весельный** *a.* four-oar; **—вильчатый** *a.* quadrifurcate; **—водный гидрат** tetrahydrate; **—галоидный** *a.* tetrahalogen(ated); **—главый** *a.*

quadriceps; **—глазковые** *pl.* four-eyed fishes (*Anablepidae*); **—гнёздный** (bot.) quadrilocular; **—годичный** *a.* four-year; **—годовик** *m.* four-year-old.

четырёхгранн/ик *m.* (geom.) tetrahedron; **—ый** *a.* tetrahedral; quadrangular; (bot.) four-rowed (spike).

четырёх/диффузорный *a.* four-choke (carburetor); **—дневный** *a.* four-day; recurring every fourth day; quartan (fever); **—жаберные** *pl.* (zool.) Tetrabranchia; **—железистый** *a.* quadriglandular; **—жилковый** *a.* quadrinervate; **—замещённый** *a.* tetrasubstituted; **—звенник** *m.* four-link chain; **—зубообразные** *pl.* (ichth.) Tetraodontiformes; **—зубчатый** *a.* (bot.) quadridentate; **—зубы** *pl.* (ichth.) puffers (*Tetraodontidae*); **—иглый** *a.* four-spine(d); **—йодистый** *a.* tetraiodide (of).

четырёх/камерный *a.* four-chamber; quadrilocular, tetrathalamous; **—клеточный** *a.* quadricellular; **—коленчатый** *a.* four-throw (shaft); **—колёсный** *a.* four-wheel(ed); **—конечный** *a.* four-point; **—корпусный** *a.* quadruple-effect (evaporator); **—косточковый** *a.* (bot.) tetrapyrenous; **—красочный** *a.* four-color; **—кратный** *a.* fourfold, quadruple; **—кремнекислый** *a.* tetrasilicate; tetrasilicic acid; **—круговой** *a.* tetracyclic; **—крылый** *a.* tetrapterous, four-winged; **—крыльник** *m.* (bot.) winged pea (*Tetragonolobus*); **—кулачковый** *a.* four-jawed.

четырёх/лепестный *a.* (bot.) tetrapetalous; **—летие** *n.* four-year period; fourth anniversary; **—летка** *f.* one in the fourth year of its life, age 3+; four-year-old horse; **—летний** *a.* four-year; fourth anniversary; **—листник** *m.* quarterfoil; **—листный** *a.* (bot.) quadrifoliate; **—листочковый** *a.* quadrifoliolate; **—лопастный** *a.* four-blade; (bot.) quadrilobate; **—лучевой** *a.* four-beam; four-rayed; (bot.) quadriradiate; **—мерный** *a.* four-dimensional; quaternary; **—местный** *a.* four-seater (vehicle); **—метильный** *a.* tetramethyl(ated); **—молекулярный** *a.* tetramolecular; **—надрезной, —надрезный** *a.* (bot.) quadrifid, divided into four parts; **—ногий** *see* **четвероногий.**

четырёх/объективный *a.* four-lens; **—окись** *f.* tetroxide; **—основный** *a.* tetrabasic; **—осный** *a.* (cryst.) tetraaxial, four-axis; eight-wheeled; **—остный** *a.* quadriaristate; **—палость** *f.* tetradactyly; **—палый** *a.* (zool.) tetradactyl(ous), four-digited; **—парный** *a.* (anat.) quadrigeminal; (bot.) quadrijugate; **—перегородчатый** *a.* (bot.) quadriseptate; **—перистый** *a.* quadripinnate; **—пёрый** *a.* four-blade (bit); **—пестичный** *a.* (bot.) tetragynous, having four pistils; **—плодолистиковый** (bot.) tetracarpellar; **—полосный** *a.* four-lane (highway); **—полье** *n.* four-field crop rotation; **—польный** fourfold (table); (agr.) divided into four plots for different crops.

четырёхполюсн/ик *m.* quadripole, four-pole; (four-terminal) network; **—ый** *a.* quadripole, quadripolar, four-pole, four-polar.

четырёх/процентный *a.* four per cent; **—прядный** *a.* four-strand; **—раздельный** *a.* quadripartite; **—рассечённый** *a.* quadrisected; **—ребристый** *a.* quadricostate, having four ribs or ridges; **—реечный** *a.* quadruplex (classifier); **—рогий** *a.* quadricorn(ous), four-horn, four-spine; **—рожковый** *a.* four-pronged; **—рукавный** *a.* four-armed; **—рукие** *see* **четверорукие; —рядный** *a.* tetraserial, four-row, (bot.) tetrastichous.

четырёх/секционный *a.* four-compartment; **—семянный** *a.* (bot.) tetraspermous; **—сернистый** *a.* tetra-sulfide (of); **—сильный** *a.* (bot.) tetradynamous; **—скатный** *a.* pyramidal (roof); **—скоростной** *a.* four-speed; **—сложный** *a.* quaternate, in fours, consisting of four; **—слойный** *a.* four-layer(ed); **—со-тый** *a.* four-hundredth; **—сплавный** *a.* quaternary, four-component (alloy); **—ствольный** *a.* quadruple; **—створчатый** *a.* (bot.) quadrivalve.

четырёхсторонн/ий *a.* quadrilateral, four-sided; **—ик** *m.* quadrilateral figure.

четырёх/строчный *a.* four-row; **—ступенчатый** *a.* four-stage, four-step(ped); **—тактный** *a.* (mach.) four-cycle, four-stroke; **—тионовая кислота** tetrathionic acid; **—точечный** *a.* four-point; **—трубный** *a.* four-tube; quadrupled; **—тычиночный** *a.* (bot.) tetrandrous; **—углеродное кольцо** four-carbon ring.

четырёхугольн/ик *m.* tetragon, quadrangle; **—ый** *a.* tetragonal, quadrangular, four-angled; quadrate; **—ая мышца** (anat.) musculus quadratus.

четырёх/уровневый *a.* four-level; **—фазный** *a.* four-phase; **—фтористый** *a.* tetrafluoride (of); **—хлористый** *a.* tetrachloride (of); **—ходовой** *a.* four-way; **—цветковый** *a.* (bot.) quadriflorous, tetranthous; **—цветный** *a.* four-color; **—цикловый** *a.* four-cycle; **—частичный** *a.* four-piece; **—чашелистиковый** *a.* (bot.) tetrasepalous; **—член** *m.* (math.) quaternion; **—члениковые** *pl.* (biol.) Tetramera; **—члениковый** *a.* tetramerous, composed of four parts; **—членный** *a.* four-membered, four-period; (biol.) tetramerous; **—шариковая машина трения** four-ball friction tester; **—шкальный** *a.* four-scale; (cryst.) four-axis (system); **—щетинковый** *a.* quadriset(ace)ous; **—ъядерный** *a.* quadrinucleate; **—элементный** *a.* four-element; cloverleaf (antenna); **—этажный** *a.* four-story; **—этильный** *a.* tetraethyl(ated).

четырнадцат/ый *a.* fourteenth; **—ь** *num.* fourteen.

четь *f.* approximately 1.35 acres.

чефер *m.* chafer (strip).

чефрас *m.* sandalwood.

чех/лик *m.* cap, covering; (bot.) calyptra; **корневой ч.** root cap; **—ликовидный** *a.* hood-shaped; **—лить** *v.* cover; **—ловидность** *f.*, **—ловидная болезнь** *f.* (phyt.) cattail disease, epichloe choke; **—лоноски** *pl.* (ent.) casebearer moths (*Coleophoridae*); bagworm moths (*Psychidae*); **—ол** *m.* case, hood, (protective) cover(ing), shroud; jacket, casing, housing, sheath; can, carrier, pouch; (bot.) spathe, spathella; **—ольницы** *pl.* (ent.) bagworm moths (*Psychidae*); **—ольный** *a. of* **чехол**; **—ольчик** *dim. of* **чехол**; (biol.) indusium.

чехонь *f.* (ichth.) Pelecus cultratus.

чечеви/тчатый *a. see* **чечевицеобразный; —ца** *f.* lens; (bot.) lentil(s); (orn.) scarlet rosefinch (*Carpodacus erythrinus*); **—цеобразный** *a.* lentiform, lens-shaped, lenticular; **—цеобразное ядро** (anat.) lentiform nucleus; **высококучевые —цеобразные облака** (meteor.) altocumulus lenticularis; **—чка** *f.* a lentil; (bot.) lenticel; breathing pore; lenticule (in fungi); **—чный** *a.* lenticular; lentil; pea, bean (ore).

чечен/о-ингушский *a.* (geog.) Chechen(o)-Ingush; **—ский** *a.* Chechen (island).

чечётка *f.* (orn.) redpoll (*Acanthis flammea*); **горная ч.** (orn.) twite.

чечуга *f.* (ichth.) sturgeon, sterlet.

чешет *pr. 3 sing. of* **чесать.**

чешир *m.*, **—ский** *a.* Cheshire (swine).

чешский *a.* Czech; Chesha (river); **ч. лес** Bohemian Forest.

чешуе— *prefix* squam(i)—, lepid(o)—, scale, scaly, flake; **—видный** *see* **чешуеобразный; —крылые** *pl.* (ent.) Lepidoptera; **—крылый** *a.* lepidopterous; **—ноги** *pl.* (herp.) flap-footed lizards (*Pygopodidae*); **—носный** *a.* scale-bearing, scaly, squamiferous; **—образный** *a.* scale-shaped, squamiform, scaly, flake-like; **—съём-**

—ный *a.* (fish-)scaling; **—хвостник** *m.* sickle grass (*Pholiurus*); **—цветные** *pl.* (bot.) glumiflorae.

чеш/уина *f.* (anat.) scale, squama; **—уистый** *a.* scaly, squamous.

чешуй/ка *f. dim. of* **чешуя;** (biol.) squam(ul)a; (ent.) tegula; **полая ч.** (bot.) fornix, arched scale; **ароматические —ки** (ent.) androconia, scent scales; **—ковидный** *a.* squamuliform; **—никовый** *a.* lepidote; **—ница** *f.* (ent.) silverfish.

чешуйчат/ка *f.* (bot.) Agaricus; **—ники, —никовые** *pl.* (ichth.) lungfishes, mud sirens (*Lepidosirenidae*); **—о—** *see* **чешуе—; —о-сосцевидный** *a.* (anat.) squamomastoid; **—ость** *f.* scaliness, flakiness; **—ые** *pl.* (herp.) Squamata; **—ый** *a.* scaly, scaled, squamose, squamosal, lamellar, laminated, foliated, flaky, flaked, platy; (bot.) lepidote; (geol.) imbricate (structure); (petr.) lepidoblastic; pod, husk (corn).

чешу/т *pr. 3 pl. of* **чесать; —щий** *a.* combing; scratching.

чешуя *f.* scale, flake, scute; plate, lamella; squama; husk; (bot.) glume; (tectonic) sliver; **ч. злаков** (bot.) grass palea, grass glume; stragulum; **вильчатая ч.** (biol.) fulcrum; **кроющая ч.** (bot.) bract scale, chaff; **рыбья чешуя** (med.) ichthyosis, scaly skin.

чз, ЧЗ *abbr.* (**частотное зондирование**) frequency sounding.

чибис *m.* (orn.) lapwing.

чивик/анье *n.* chirping, etc., *see v.*; **—ать, —нуть** *v.* chirp, twitter, warble.

чига *f.* (ichth.) sterlet.

чигирь *m.* water-lifting wheel.

чиж *m.* (orn.) siskin (*Carduelis spinus*); **—и** *pl.* goldfinches (*Spinus*); **—ик** barnyard grass.

чизел/евание *n.* (agr.) chiseling, subsoiling; **—евать** *v.* break subsurface soil; **—ь** *m.* chisel (subsoil cultivator).

чий *m.* (bot.) cheegrass (*Stipa splendens*); Lasiogrostis.

чик *m.* (ichth.) pond loach.

чикаг/о *n.*, **—ский** *a.* Chicago.

чик/анье *n.* clipping, etc., *see v.*; snipping noise of scissors; **—ать** *v.* clip, snip; snap off; (orn.) chirp.

чикл *m.* chicle (gum).

чикнуть *see* **чикать.**

Чили Chile.

чили/буха *f.* (bot.) nux vomica (*Strychnos nux-vomica*); **—га** *f.* pea tree (*Caragana*).

чилийский *a.* (geog.) Chile(an).

чилик/анье *n.* chirping, etc., *see v.*; **—ать, —нуть** *v.* chirp, twitter.

чилим *m.* (bot.) water caltrop (*Trapa*); spec. water chestnut (*T. natans*).

чилин *see* **чилийский.**

чин *m.* rank, grade.

чина *f.* peavine, vetchling (*Lathyrus*).

чинар *m.*, **—а** *f.* plane (tree) (*Platanus orientalis*); **—овка** *f.* (orn.) green finch; **—овый** *a. of* **чинар.**

чингил *m.* chingil (rock glacier); **—ь** *m.* salt tree (*Halimodendron*).

чин/енный *part.*, **—ёный** *a.* repaired, etc., *see v.*; **—ить** *v.* repair, fix, mend, patch; sharpen, point; make, do, commit; administer, inflict; put in the way.

чинк *m.* (geol.) chink (scarp).

чинка *f.* mending, repair, overhauling.

чиновн/ик *m.* official, public servant; **—ический** *a.* bureaucratic.

чинтермалическая линия (meteor.) isotherm based on simultaneous observations.

чинук *m.* (meteor.) chinook.

чир *m.* whitefish.

чирей *m.* (med.) boil, furuncle, abscess.

чириканье see **чиликанье**.

чирк/ать, —нуть v. strike (a match).

чирок m. (orn.) teal, duck (*Anas*).

чир/ос see **чирус; —у** m. (mam.) chiru, Tibetan antelope; **—ус** m. (ichth.) mackerel.

чирья gen. of **чирей**.

чисел gen. pl. of **число**.

численн/о adv. numerically; in number; **ч. превосходить** v. outnumber; **—ость** f. number, quantity; count; population; (sample) size; (mil.) strength, complement; **ч. населения** population; **—остью** in number; **—ый** a. numer(ic)al, digital (information); **—ый масштаб** fractional scale, representative fraction.

числитель m. (math.) numerator; **—ное** n., **—ный** a. numeral, number.

числить v. count; **—ся** v. be counted, be reckoned; be (on the list); be itemized.

числ/о n. number, quantity, amount; population; (pulse) count; degree (of freedom); (reflux, gear) ratio; date; value, rate; index; **ч. е** Napier number; **ч. M** Mach number; **без —а** countless, innumerable; undated; **в том —е** among them, including; **видовое ч.** (silv.) form factor; **водяное ч.** (phys.) water equivalent; **входить в ч.** v. be among; **закон больших чисел** law of averages; **к —у . . . относится** among . . . is; **первое ч.** the first of the month; **помечать —ом** v. date; **принадлежать к —у** v. be among, rank among; **сего —а** today, this day.

числовой a. numer(ic)al; digital (coding); number (field); number-scale (axis); (comp.) number-transfer (bus).

ЧИСС abbr. (**частотно-избирательная сейсмическая станция**) frequency-selective seismic station.

чист sh. m. of **чистый**.

чистец m. (bot.) hedge nettle (*Stachys*).

чист/ик m. scraper, clean(s)er; **—ики, —иковые** pl. (orn.) auks, murres, puffins (*Alcidae*); **—илка** f. scraper, clean(s)er; (plow) staff.

чистильник m. (bot.) wild cucumber (*Ecballium elaterium*).

чист/ильный see **чистительный; —ильщик** m. clean(s)er; (ichth.) cleaner wrasse; **—итель** m. clean(s)er; **—ительный** a. clean(s)ing, etc., see v.; **—ить** v. clean(se), wash, scrub, scour, scrape; purify; clear (out); purge (gas pipe); dredge (a canal); weed out; **—ка** f. clean(s)ing, etc., see v.; grooming (of horse); clean-up.

чисто adv. cleanly; prefix clean; pure; **ч. парофазный процесс** true vapor-phase process; **—вик** m. clean, fair, or final copy.

чистов/ой a. clean; finish(ing); final (copy); **ч. стан** finishing mill; **—ая обработка, —ая отделка** finishing (off), finishing (work).

чисто-комплексный a. totally complex.

чистокров/ка f. and m. purebred animal; **—ность** f. purity (of breed); **—ный** a. purebred, thoroughbred, pedigreed.

чисто/линейный a. (biol.) pure-strain; **—ль** m. copper and brass cleanser; **—обрезной** a. clean-cut (timber); **—плотный** a. clean, neat; **—полье** n. open field; **—породный** a. purebred; **—пробный** a. highest quality; **—сердечный** a. frank, sincere; **—смешенный** a. purely mixed.

чистосортн/ость f. (varietal) purity; **—ый** a. pure, selected; clean (timber).

чистот/а f. clean(li)ness; purity; clarity, clearness; (acous.) fidelity; **ч. поверхности** smoothness; (met.) surface roughness; **размер в —е** finished size.

чисто/тел m. (bot.) celandine (*Chelidonium*); **—уст** m. (bot.) Osmunda; **—шерстяной** a. pure-wool; **—ягодичный** a. (med.) frank breech (presentation).

чист/ый a. clean, uncontaminated; pure, unmixed; neat; blank (page); clear (timber); proper (fraction); net (weight, energy, profit); mere (chance); finished, smooth; quiescent (boil); absolute (alcohol); homogeneous (planting, stand of trees); bare, weed-free; **ч. для анализа** analytically pure, analytical grade; **—ая отделка** finish(ing).

чистяк m. (bot.) pilewort (*Ficaria*).

чисщалка see **чищалка**.

чит/аемость f. readability; popularity; **—аемый** a. readable; popular; **—алка** f. reading room; **—альный** a. reading; **—альный аппарат** (microfilm) reader, viewer; **—альня** f. reading room; **—ание** n. reading; **—анный** a. read; **—атель** m. reader; **—ательский** a. reader's; public (catalog); **—ать** v. read; deliver (a lecture); **—ающий** a. reading; **—ающее устройство** optical character reader, character recognition device.

читинский a. (geog.) Chita.

чит/ка f. reading; **—ывать** v. read.

читтагонгский a. (geog.) Chittagong.

Чиуауа (geog.) Chihuahua.

чих m. sneeze, sneezing; **—анье** n. sneezing; (mach.) popping; **—ательный** a. sternutative; **—ать** v. sneeze; **—ирь** m. (vet.) bovine piroplasmosis; **—нуть** v. sneeze; **—ота** f. sneezing (spell); **—отная трава** (bot.) sneezewort (*Achillea ptarmica*).

Чичибабина реакция (chem.) Chichibabin synthesis.

чищ/алка f. scraper, boring spoon; **—е** comp. of **чисто, чистый; —ение** see **чистка; —енный** a. clean(s)ed, etc., see **чистить**.

чия gen. of **чий**.

чкаловит m. (min.) chkalovite.

чл. abbr. (**член**); **ч.-л.** abbr. (**что-либо**).

член m. member, fellow; (math.) term; (anat.) limb; joint; **мужской половой ч.** penis; **—ение** n. dismembering, etc., see **членить; —ик** m. articulus; segment; joint; element; **основной —ик** (mal.; ent.) cardo, basal member, subcoxa.

членист/о adv., prefix articulato— (jointed); arthr(o)— (joint); condyl(o)— (knuckle, joint, knob); **—оногие** pl. (zool.) Arthropoda, **—остебельные** pl. (bot.) horsetails; **—ость** f. articulation, segmentation; **—ый** a. articulated, hinged, jointed, segmented; **—ый луч** (ichth.) segmented ray (of a fin); **—ый плод** (bot.) loment(um).

членить v. articulate, segment; dismember, disjoint; **—ся** v. be dismembered; consist of separate segments or members.

член/-корреспондент m. corresponding member, associate member; **—овредительство** n. maiming, crippling; **—о-мошоночный** a. (anat.) penoscrotal; **—о-раздельный** a. articulate, distinct; **—орасположение** n. attitude (of fetus); **—ский** a. member(ship).

член/-соревнователь m. candidate for membership; **—ство** n. membership.

чл.-корр. abbr. **член-корреспондент**.

ЧМ abbr. (**часовой механизм**) clockwork; (**частотно-модулированный**) frequency-modulated, f-m; (**чрезвычайно мягкий**) extremely soft.

ЧМН abbr. (**черепномозговой нерв**) cranial nerve.

чмок/ать, —нуть v. smack one's lips.

ч.н.м. abbr. (**части на миллион**) parts per million, ppm.

Ч.О. abbr. (**число омыления**) saponification number.

чок/анье n. clanking, etc. see v.; **—ать, —нуть** v. clank, clink; tick (clock); clash; pronounce ц as ч.

Чок-Ривер (geog.) Chalk River.

чомг/а f. (orn.) great crested grebe (*Podiceps cristatus*); **—овые** pl. Podicipedidae.

чоп *m.* tap *or* plug for tank; (ichth.) Aspro zingel; **малый ч.** Aspro streber; **—а** *f.* (ichth.) bream (*Lagodon rhomboides*); **—ик** *m.* zander, pikeperch; **—овые** *pl.* rudderfishes (*Kyphosidae*).

чоппер *m.* chopper, shredder.

Чохральского метод Chochralski method (of crystal growth).

ЧПИ *abbr.* (**частота повторения импульсов**) pulse repetition rate.

ч.р. *abbr.* (**частично растворим**) partially soluble.

чреватый *a.* filled, fraught (with).

чрев/ный *a.* abdominal; splanchnic (nerve); celiac (artery); **—о** *n.* abdomen; womb; **—овещание** *n.* ventriloquism; **—осечение** *n.* (med.) laparotomy, celiotomy; **—оугодние, —оугодничество** *n.* gluttony; **—ье** *n.* (anat.) mesogastrium.

чрез *see* **через; —брюшинный** *a.* (med.) transperitoneal; anterior (nephrectomy).

чрезвычайн/о *adv.* extremely, exceedingly, highly, extra; **—ость** *f.* extreme, excessiveness; **—ый** *a.* extreme, excessive, extraordinary, emergency, special, unusual; **—ая рубка** cutting of deforested area.

чрез/кожный *a.* (med.) percutaneous; **—костный** perosseous; **—лоханочный** transpelvic.

чрезмерн/о *adv.* excessively, etc., *see a.;* **ч. упрощённый** *a.* over-simplified; **—ость** *f.* excess(iveness); **—ый** *a.* excessive, extreme, immoderate, inordinate, redundant, undue, too much, abnormal; over—, hyper—; super—; **—ый разряд** overdischarge; **—ая возбудимость** hyperexcitability; **—ая эксплуатация** overdevelopment.

чрезмыщелковый *a.* (anat.) transcondylar (fracture).

чрен *m.* trough, tub, tank, vat; salt pan.

чрес/плевральный *a.* transpleural, transthoracic; **—пузырный** *a.* transvesical; **—суставной** *a.* transarticular; **—суставная ампутация** disarticulation (amputation or separation at a joint).

ЧСА *abbr.* (**сывороточный альбумин человека**) human serum albumin.

ч. сп. *abbr.* (**чистый спирт**) pure alcohol.

ЧССР *abbr.* Czechoslovak Socialist Republic.

ЧТ *abbr.* (**чрезвычайно твёрдый**) extremely hard.

чт(в) *abbr.* (**четверг**) Thursday.

чтение *n.* reading, perusal.

чт/ец *m.,* **—ица** *f.* reader, lecturer.

что *pron.* which, what(ever); *conj.* that; *adv.* why; **ч. обнаружено** as revealed; **ни за ч.** not for anything, not under any circumstances; **—б(ы)** *conj. and particle* (in order) that, in order to, so that; if one is to; **—б(ы) не** lest; **вместо того, —б(ы)** instead of; **ч.-либо, ч.-нибудь** *pron.* something, anything, whatever; **ч.-то** *pron. and adv.* something; rather, somewhat; somehow; it looks as if.

ЧТТ *abbr.* (**число теоретических тарелок**) number of theoretical plates.

чтущий *a.* deeming.

ЧУ *abbr.* (**читающее устройство**) (comp.) reader.

чуб *m.* tuft of hair, forelock.

чубарый *a.* mottled, speckled, skewbald.

чубук *m.* grape stalk; stem (of pipe); bighorn sheep (*Ovis canadensis*).

чубушник *m.* (bot.) mock orange (*Philadelphus*).

Чувашская АССР the Chuvash Autonomous Soviet Socialist Republic.

чувственный *a.* sensual, sexual.

чувствительн/ость *f.* sensitivity, sensitiveness, sensibility, susceptibility, excitability; esthesia, perception, feeling, sensation, sense; delicacy; response; **ч. к нагреву** heat sensitivity; **ч. по току** current sensitivity; **болевая ч.** algesthesia, pain sensibility; algesthesia, painful sensation; **изменённая ч.** parasthesia, abnormal sensation; dysesthesia, impairment of any sense; **порог —ости** tolerance threshold; **предел —ости** detection limit; **—ый** *a.* sensitive, sensible, susceptible, responsive, delicate; appreciable (error); perceptible; (zool.) sensory; transition (color); **—ый к излучению** radiosensitive; **—ый к кислоте** acid-labile; **сделать —ым** *v.* sensitize.

чувство *n.* feeling, sensation, sense; **ч. давления** baresthesia, pressure sense; **лишиться чувств** *v.* lose consciousness, faint; **обман чувств** illusion; delusion; **органы чувств** (anat.) sense organs; **притти в ч.** *v.* regain consciousness; **—вание** *n.* sensation, feeling; **—вать** *v.* feel, sense, perceive, experience; **—вать себя больным** feel ill.

чувствующий *a.* sentient, sensitive.

чугаевский *a.* Tschugaeff (synthesis).

чугачский *a.* (geog.) Chugach.

чуг.-лит. *abbr.* (**чугунолитейный**).

чуг.-плав. *abbr.* (**чугуноплавильный**).

чугун *m.* cast iron; pig (iron); cast iron pot; **ч. в болванках, ч. в свинках, ч. в чушках** pig iron; **белый ч.** white (pig) iron, chilled iron; **доменный ч.** pig iron; **литейный ч.** cast iron; **магниевый ч.** nodular iron; **серый ч.** gray iron; **штыковой ч.** pig iron.

чугунка *f.* cast iron pot; portable iron stove; a dark-colored, crude salt.

чугун/ный *a. of* **чугун; —ная отливка** cast iron; (pig) iron casting; **—овоз** *m.* hot-metal car; **—овозный ковш** ladle car; **—ок** *m.* small cast iron pot; **—олитейная** *f.* iron foundry; **—олитейный** *a.* iron casting, foundry; **—олитейный завод** iron foundry, iron works; **—олитейщик** *m.* iron founder; **—оплавильный** *a.* iron-smelting; **—оплавильный завод** iron foundry, iron works.

чуда/к *m.* eccentric, person who behaves bizarrely; **—чествовать, —чить** *v.* behave eccentrically *or* bizarrely; **—чка** *f. of* чудак.

чуд/ен *sh. m. of* чудный; **—ён** *sh. m. of* чудной; **—еса** *pl. of* чуда; **—есный** *a.* wonderful, marvelous, miraculous, extraordinary; **—есная палочка** (bact.) Bacillus prodigiosus; **—есная сеть** (zool.) rete mirabile; **—ить** *v.* behave bizarrely; **—иться** *v.* seem, appear; occur, happen; wonder (at); be surprised (at).

чудн/о *adv.* wonderfully, marvelously; oddly, strangely; it is strange; **—ой** *a.* strange, odd, queer; **—ый** *a.* wonderful, marvelous, outstanding; **—ая сеть** (zool.) rete mirabile.

чудо *n.* miracle, wonder.

чудовищ/е *n.* monster, freak; **—ность** *f.* monstrosity, enormity; **—ный** *a.* monstrous, gigantic, enormous; unusual, unnatural.

чужа/к *m.,* **—чка** *f.* stranger.

чужд/аться *v.* avoid, shun; **—ый** *a.* foreign, hostile, alien, extraneous; incomprehensible; devoid, free (of); **—ые виды** strange species, strangers.

чуже/земец *see* **чужестранец; —земный** *a.* alien, foreign, strange, extraneous; **—опыление** *n.* cross fertilization; **—родный** *a.* alien, foreign, outside; species-different; heterologous; (geol.) allogenic; **—странец** *m.* alien, foreigner; **—ядный** *a.* parasitic.

чужой *a.* foreign, strange; extraneous; ecdemic; someone else's; *m.* foreigner, stranger, outsider.

чуйский *a.* (geog.) Chu.

чукотский *a.* (geog.) Chukotsk; **Чукотское море** Chuckchee Sea.

чукучан *m.*, —**овые** *pl.* (ichth.) suckers (*Catostomidae*).

чулан *m.*, —**ный** *a.* pantry; storeroom.

чулара *f.* (ichth.) mullet.

чул/ок *m.* stocking; (mach.) housing; jacket; cable grip, sleeve; (incandescent) mantle; —**ки** *pl.* stockings, hosiery; —**очки** *pl.* socks; —**очник** *m.* stocking maker; —**очновязальный** *a.* hosiery-knitting; —**очный** *a.* stocking, hosiery; —**очные изделия** hosiery.

чулымский *a.* (geog.) Chulym.

чума *f.* (vet.) plague, pest(ilence); **ч. свиней** hog cholera; **водяная ч.** water weed (*Elodea canadensis*); **собачья ч.** distemper.

чуметь *see* чумиться.

чумиза *f.* foxtail millet (*Setaria italica*).

чумиться *v.* (vet.) have the plague, hog cholera or distemper.

чумичка *f.* skimmer, ladle.

чум/ка *f.* (vet.) distemper; —**ной** *a.* pestilential, plague-stricken; —**ная палочка** plague bacillus.

чуни *pl.* work boots.

чураться *v.* avoid, shun.

чур/бак, —**бан** *m.* block, log; chunk, lump; —**ка** *f.* chock, block.

чутк/ий *a.* sensitive, delicate, responsive; cautious, careful, wary; keen (hearing); light (sleep); —**ость** *f.* sensitivity, delicacy; tact.

чуточ/ка *f.* a tiny bit; —**ку** *adv.* very slightly; —**ный** *a.* minute.

чутче *comp. of* чуткий.

чуть *adv. and conj.* hardly, barely, scarcely, slightly, somewhat, a little; just (as), as soon as, when; **ч. (ли) не** almost, nearly; **ч. свет** at daybreak; **ч. только** as soon as; **ч. что** at every opportunity; **ч. что не** all but.

чутьё *n.* sense, the senses; keenness (of senses); perception, feeling, instinct; hearing; scent.

чуть-чуть *adv.* very slightly; a little.

чуфа *f.* (bot.) chufa (*Cyperus esculentus*).

чучел/о *n.* dummy, stuffed animal; scarecrow; follicle; empty glume; cyst; shell; hide, skin; —**ьник** *m.* taxidermist.

чушк/а *f.*, —**овый** *a.* (met.) pig, ingot, bar; (zool.) young sow; —**олом(атель)** *m.* pig breaker.

чушь *see* чепуха.

чуяние *n.* scenting, smelling, hearing.

чуять *v.* smell, scent, feel, sense; perceive quickly; feel keenly.

чхать *see* чихать.

чч. *abbr.* (**части**) parts, units.

чьё *n. pron.* whose.

Чьелина печь *see* Кьеллина печь.

чьи *pl. pron.*; **чья** *f. pron.* whose.

Чэдвика способ Chadwick process.

Чэддока штатив Chaddock support.

чэзи *n.* (geol.) Chazy subdivision.

Чэпмана насос Chapman pump.

Ш

ш. *abbr.* (**широта**) latitude.

шабала *f.* scoop.

шабдар *m.* Persian clover (*Trifolium resupinatum*).

шабер *m.* scraper, strickle; (paper) doctor; **ш.-крючок** hook scraper.

шабли *n.* Chablis (wine).

шаблон *m.* template, gage, pattern; model, copy; (master) form, mold; stencil; (foundry) sweep; bobbin, spool; (elec.) former; **по —у** to gage; template (milling); **изготовлять по —у** *v.* copy; **формовка по —ам** template molding; **ш.-высотомер** *m.* center height gage; —**ировать** *v.* (foundry) strickle, sweep up; **ш.-копир** *m.* cardboard template; —**ный** *a. of* шаблон; (elec.) form(er), preformed, spool (winding); unoriginal; routine; —**одержатель** *m.* pattern holder.

шабмашина *f.* slicer.

шабот *m.* anvil block, anvil bed.

шабр/ение *n.* scraping, scouring; —**ить** *v.* scrape, scour; —**ованный** *a.* scraped, scoured; —**овка** *f.*, —**овочный** *a.* scraping, scouring; —**овочный станок** scraper; —**овщик** *m.* scraper.

шави/бетол *m.* chavibetol, 5-allylguaiacol; —**кол** *m.* chavicol, *p*-allylphenol; —**цин** *m.* chavicine; —**циновая кислота** chavicic acid.

шавозот *m.* chavosot (*p*-allylphenol).

шаг *m.* step, pace; (mech.) pitch, spacing, interval, degree, stage; increment; twist (of rifling); size (of mesh); course (of ship); **ш. вперёд** advance; **ш. за —ом** step by step, stepwise, gradually; **ш. цикла** (comp.) iteration; **с малым —ом** closely spaced; —**ание** *n.* pacing, stepping, walking; course (of a ship); —**ать** *v.* pace, step, walk; —**ающий** *a.* pacing; ambulatory; **с —ающими балками** walking-beam; —**нуть** *v.* take a step.

шаго/вый *a. of* шаг; step(-type), step-by-step; stepping (switch); stepper (motor); —**м** *adv.* at a slow pace, slowly; —**мер** *m.* pedometer, odometer, pace counter; pitch gage.

шагрен/евальный *a.* (leather) pebbling; —**евый** *a. of* шагрень; pale tan; —**евая поверхность** (rubber) crow's feet, flawed surface; —**ировать** *v.* shagreen, pebble; —**ь** *f.* shagreen, pebbled leather.

шадрик *m.* leached ashes, crude potash.

шадринский *a.* (geog.) Shadrinsk.

шаж/ком *adv.* with short, frequent steps; —**ок** *dim. of* шаг; —**ок мыши** (comp.) mickey (unit of mouse movement).

шайба *f.* washer, shim, gasket; disk, collar; plate.

шайбелиит *m.* (min.) szaibelyite.

шайка *f.* small tub.

шайр *m.*, —**ский** *a.* Shire (horse).

шакал *m.* jackal (*Canis aureus*).

шакша *f.* (tanning) bark liquor, ooze, puree; bate, drench (for leather).

шала *f.* unhusked rice, seed rice.

шаланда *f.* scow, barge.

шалаш *m.*, —**ный** *a.* hut; tegurium; bower.

шалашник/и, —**овые** *pl.* (orn.) bowerbirds (*Ptilonorhynchidae*).

шалёвка *f.* thin plank(ing), paneling.

шалевый *a. of* шаль.

шалеть *v.* become insane; be confused.

шалить *v.* play tricks; function improperly.

шалнер *see* шарнир.

шалот *m.* (bot.) shallot (*Allium ascalonicum*).

шалфей *m.*, —**ный** *a.* sage (*Salvia*).

шаль *f.* shawl.

шальной *a.* stray, random; crazy, foolish.

шальтер *m.* switch.

шамбала *f.* (bot.) fenugreek (*Foenumgraecum sativum*).

Шамберлана фильтр (bact.) (Pasteur-)Chamberland filter.

шамберленовый *a.* Chamberlain.

шамбо *n.* sewer, septic tank.

шамкать *v.* mumble.

шамот *m.*, **—ный, —овый** *a.* chamotte, fireclay; grog; mullite; **—ный камень, —ный кирпич** firebrick; **—ная футеровка** refractory lining.

шампакол *m.* champacol, guaiol.

шампан/изировать *v.* (wines) champagnize; **—ский** *a.*, **—ское** *n.* champagne.

шампиньон *m.* (bot.) meadow mushroom (*Agaricus campestris*); **—ница** *f.* mushroom cellar; **—овые** *pl.* Agaricaceae.

Шамплейн *m.* Lake Champlain.

шампунь *m.* shampoo.

шамра *f.* (meteor.) squall.

шамуа *f.* (leather) chamois.

шандор/а *f.* dam timber; shutter (of dam); **—ный** *a.* of шандора; stoplog (dam); **—ный щит** dam walling.

шандра *f.* (bot.) horehound (*Marrubium*).

шанк/ерный *a.* (med.) chancrous; **—р** *m.* chancre; **—роид** *m.* chancroid.

Шаннон *m.* (geog.) Shannon; *see also* **шеннон.**

шанс *m.* chance; **—ы** *pl.* odds; **иметь —ы** *v.* stand a good chance.

Шанхай Shanghai.

шанц/евый *a.* digging (tool); **—овать** *v.* entrench; **—ы** *pl.* fieldwork.

шаньдунский *a.* (geog.) Shantung.

шаньсийский *a.* (geog.) Shansi.

шапагат *m.* twine.

шапирограф *m.* a manifolder.

шап/ка *f.* cap; (geol.) caprock; banner (headline); (page) header; (bot.) mitra; **—овал** *m.* fuller, felt maker.

шапоч/ка *dim. of* **шапка; —ки** *pl.* marigold (*Tagetes*); **—кообразный** *a.* (anat.; bot.) mitral (valve), mitriform; **—ник** *m.* hatter; **—ный** *a.* hat, cap.

шар *m.* ball, globe, sphere, orb; **ш. трасировки** (comp.) trackball; **бледный ш.** (anat.) globus pallidus; **воздушный ш.** balloon; **земной ш.** globe, the earth; **золотой ш.** (bot.) cutleaf coneflower (*Rudbeckia laciniata*); **координатный ш.** (comp.) trackball; **поплавковый ш.** ball float; **снежный ш.** (bot.) snowball, guelder rose (*Viburnum opulus*).

шарас *m.* charas (drug from hemp resin).

шаран, —ец *m.* (ichth.) mirror carp (*Cyprinus carpio*); (ichth.) roach (*Rutilus rutilus*).

Шаргута метод (phys.) Szargut's method.

Шардингера фермент, Ш. энзим (bioch.) Schardinger enzyme.

шар-зонд *m.* (meteor.) sounding balloon.

шариаж *see* **шарьяж.**

шарик *dim. of* **шар;** ball; globule, spherule, pellet, bead; bubble; (thermometer) bulb; (blood) corpuscle; **—овидный** *a.* globose, spherical; globulose; **—овый** *a. of* шарик; ball-type (tool); bead (catalyst); ball-point (pen); **—овый упорный** ball thrust (bearing); **—оносный** *a.* (bot.) globuliferous.

шарикоподшипник *m.*, **—овый** *a.* ball bearing; **упорный ш.** ball thrust bearing.

шарить *v.* probe, search, grope, feel (for); ransack.

Шарко лихорадка (med.) Charcot's fever.

шарлах *m.*, **—овый** *a.* scarlet (pigment).

шарлот *m.* (bot.) shallot (*Allium ascalonicum*).

Шарля закон Charles (gas) law.

шармутьен *m.* (geol.) Charmouthian.

шарнир *m.* hinge, joint, knuckle, articulation, link; **на —е, на —ах** hinged; **универсальный ш.** universal joint, ball-and-socket joint; **—но опертый** *a.* hinged;

—но-закреплённый *a.* hinged, articulated; pivoted, tilting; **—но-коленчатый** *a.* knuckle-joint; **—но-укреплённый** *see* **шарнирно-закреплённый.**

шарнирн/ый *a.* hinge(d), joint(ed), articulate(d); swivel(ed), pivot(ed), tilt(ing), swing(ing); link (belt, chain, etc.); knuckle-joint, hinge-joint; toggle(-action) (shears, etc.); flap (valve); (anat.) ginglymoid; **ш. сустав** (anat.) ginglymus; **ш. узел** (hinged) joint; **ш. четырёхугольник** four-bar linkage; **—ая связь** (hinged) joint; **—ое соединение** swivel joint.

шаровать *v.* (agr.) cultivate.

шаровидн/о *prefix, adv.* globi— (ball), sphaer(o)— (ball, sphere; round); globosely; **—оголовчатый** *a.* round-headed; sphaerocephalous; **—околосный** *a.* (bot.) round-spiked, sphaerostachyous; **—оплодный** *a.* sphaerocarpous; **—оскученный** *a.* (bot.) conglobate; **—ость** *f.* sphericity, globularity; **—оцветковый** *a.* (bot.) sphaeranthous; **—ый** *a.* spherical, spheroidal, globular, ball-like, round; globose; bubble (cap); **—ый сустав** spheroidal joint.

шаров/ики *pl.* (ent.) Cystoidea; **—ка** *f.* (agr.) cultivation; **—ки** *pl.* (ent.) Cyrtidae; **—ница** *f.* globe daisy (*Globularia*).

шаров/ой *a.* ball, sphere, spherical, globe, globular; (geol.) spherulitic; **ш. клапан** ball valve; **ш. слой** (geom.) spherical frustum; **—ая мельница** ball mill; **—ое сочленение, —ое шарнирное соединение,** ball-and-socket joint.

шароголовый *a.* sphaerocephalous.

шароле *n.* Charollais (breed of cattle).

шаро/образный *see* **шаровидный; железо с —образным графитом** nodular iron; **—пилотный** *a.* pilot-balloon.

шарош/ечный *a.* cutting, milling; rolling cutter (bit), rock (bit); **ш. станок** (milling) cutter; mill; **—ечная головка** cutter block; **—ить** *v.* mill; **—ка** *f.* cutter, cone; mill.

шар-пилот *m.* (meteor.) pilot balloon.

шарпит *m.* (min.) sharpite.

шар-рыба (ichth.) puffer (*Cyclichthys orbicularis*).

Шартр (geog.) Chartres.

шартрез *m.* chartreuse (liqueur).

шарф *m.* scarf.

шарьяж *m.* (geol.) overthrust (sheet).

шасси *n.* chassis, underframe, carriage; (av.) landing gear.

шаста слои (geol.) Shasta series.

шаст/алка *f.* grain awner, hummeling machine; **—ание** *n.* awning, separating grain from awns.

шат/ание *n.* swaying; hesitation, vacillation; free play; **—ать** *v.* shake, rock, sway; **—аться** *v.* get loose, be loose, shake, be shaky; loaf; **—ающийся** *a.* shaky, wobbly, loose, wavering.

шатен *m.*, **—ка** *f.* person with dark-red or brown hair.

шатёр *m.* tent; marquee; (agr.) (hay) curing rack; (anat.) fastigium; **—ный** *a. of* шатёр.

шатировка *f.* shading.

шатк/ий *a.* unsteady, wavering, rickety, shaky, precarious; **—ость** *f.* unsteadiness, etc., *see a.*; vacillation.

шатнуть *see* **шатать.**

шатров/идный *a.* effuse, loosely spreading; **—ый** *a.* pyramidal (structure), wedge-shaped; hip(ped) (roof).

шатун *m.* connecting rod, pitman, link, rocker; pump; tiller, guide lever; (vet.) meningitis; (mam.) bear disturbed during hibernation; **—ная шейка** crankpin.

шафлор *see* **сафлор.**

шафран *m.* (bot.) saffron; crocus; **—ный, —овый** *a.* saffron; **—но-жёлтый** *a.* saffron-yellow.

шахмат/но-трубчатый *a.* staggered-tube (radiation);

—ный *a.* chess; checkerboard, checkered, tessellate, staggered, alternate; (min.) chessboard (structure); checkrow (planting); **—ный узор** checkerwork; **в —ном порядке, —ообразный** *a.* checkered, staggered, alternate; **—ы** *pl.* chess.

шахт/а *f.* mine, pit, shaft, well; stack; column; compartment; (silo) chute; **ш.-хранилище** *f.* storage well; **—енный** *a.* of **шахта; —ёр** *m.* miner; **—ёрка** *f.* woman miner; miner's cap; worker's outfit; **—ёрский** *a.* miner's; **—ный** *a.* of **шахта; —ный колодец** dug(-out) well, pit; **—ный ствол** (min.) shaft; **—ная пусковая установка** (missile) silo; **—овый** *a.* of **шахта; —оуправление** *n.* mine management.

шаш/ель, —ень *m.* shipworm, borer.

шаш/ечница *f.* (ent.) nymphalid butterfly (*Melitaea*); **—ечный** *a.* of **шашка;** checkerboard; lined, checkered (rod); **—ка** *f.* (constr.) block, slab, tile; checkers; (expl.) charge; (blasting) cartridge; (rockets) grain; (smoke) pot; saber, sword.

шв. *abbr.* **(шведский)** Swedish.

шва *gen.* of **шов.**

шваб/а *f.,* **чистить —ой** *v.* mop, swab.

Швальбе ядро (cyt.) Schwalbe's nucleus.

шванно/вский *a.* (biol.) Schwann's (cell); **—овская оболочка** (anat.) Schwann's sheath, neurilemma; **—(глио)ма** (med.) schwannoma.

шварт *m.* (med.) adhesion.

швартов *m.,* **—ый** *a.* mooring, hawser (of ship); **—ать** *v.* moor.

Швартца-Кристоффеля интеграл (math.) Schwartz-Christoffel transformations.

швартцембергит *m.* (min.) schwartzembergite.

Шварцвальд the Black Forest.

Шварцмана феномен (med.) Schwartzman phenomenon.

шведка *f.* (ent.) frit fly (*Oscinella*).

шведск/ий *a.* Swedish; **ш. ключ** monkey wrench; **—ая зелень** *see* **Шееле зелень; —ая муха** *see* **шведка; —ая спичка** safety match.

швейник *m.* sewer, garment worker.

швейнфуртская зелень Schweinfurt green, Paris green.

швей/ный *a.* sewing, garment (industry); **—пром** *m.* garment industry.

швейц. *abbr.* **(швейцарский)** Swiss.

Швейцария Switzerland.

швейцарский *a.* Swiss.

швейцеров реактив Schweitzer's reagent (for cellulose).

швелева/ние *n.* low-temperature carbonization, semi-coking; **—ть** carbonize (at low temperature); char.

швермер *m.* (blasting) squib.

шверт *m.,* **—овый** *a.* (naut.) centerboard.

шверц *m.* (naut.) leeboard.

швец *m.* (book) stitcher.

Швеция Sweden.

швиц/евание *n.* (leather) sweating; **—камера** *f.* sweating room; **—кий** *a.* Swiss brown (cattle); **—овать** *v.* sweat, steam.

швом *instr.* of **шов.**

шворень *see* **шкворень.**

шворка *f.* seam, join.

швы *pl.* of **шов.**

швыр/ковые дрова firewood; **—нуть** *see* **швырять; —ок** *m.* rush; hurl; moving target; firewood; **—ялка** *f.* spinner; blower; **—яние** *n.* throwing, flinging; **—ять** *v.* throw, fling.

шевелилка *f.* agitator, stirrer.

шевелин *m.* a heat-insulation material from flax wastes.

шевел/ить, —ьнуть *v.* move, stir, budge; turn, ted (hay); **—иться** *v.* move, stir.

шев/ер *m.,* **—инговальный станок** (mach.) shaver; **—ингование** *n.,* **—инг-процесс** *m.* shaving.

шевиот *m.,* **—овый** *a.* (text.) cheviot; Cheviot (sheep).

Шевреля соль Chevreul's salt, cuprous-cupric sulfite.

шевр/ет *m.,* **—етовый** *a.* chrome-tanned sheepskin; **—о** *n.,* **—овый** *a.* kid (leather).

шеврон *m.* (mil.) chevron, stripe; **—ный** *a.* chevron, herringbone.

шевская смола cobbler's wax.

Шегрена синдром (med.) Sjögren's syndrome.

шеддок *m.* (bot.) shaddock (*Citrus maxima*).

шедовый *a.* shed, ridge and valley (roof); **ш. фонарь** sawtooth skylight.

шедший *past act. part.* of **идти.**

шеек *gen. pl.* of **шейка.**

Шееле зелень, шеелева зелень Scheele's green (acid copper arsenite).

шеелиз(ир)овать *v.* scheelize (treat wine with glycerin).

шеечно— *prefix* cervico—, trachelo— (neck); **—влагалищный** *a.* cervicovaginal; **—пузырный** *a.* cervico-vesical; **ш.-щёчный** *a.* cervicobuccal; **—язычный** *a.* cervicolingual.

Шези формула Chezy's formula.

ше/и *pl.* of **шея; —й** *gen.* of **шея;** *imp.* of **шить.**

шейвер *see* **шевер.**

шей/ка *f.* neck, collar; pin, pivot journal, journal (of shaft); spindle; (anat.) cervix, collum; (bot.) stylidium; (zool.) tail (of crayfish); web (of rail); recess; **—ка зуба** (anat.) collum dentis; **—ка матки** (anat.) uterine neck; **корневая —ка** (bot.) root collar; **пластика —ки матки** (med.) tracheloplasty; **раковые —ки** snakeweed (*Polygonum bistortia*); **с широкой —кой** wide-necked; **—ковый** *a.* of **шейка;** cervical; stylidious.

шейн/о— *prefix* cervico—, trachelo— (neck); *see also under* **шеечно—; —огрудной** *a.* thoracocervical; **—озатылочный** *a.* cervico-occipital; **—оплечевой** *a.* cervicobrachial; **—ый** *a.* neck; (anat.) cervical; jugular; **—ый позвонок** cervical vertebra; **—ая пластинка** (herp.) nuchal plate.

шейхцерия *f.* (bot.) Scheuchzeria.

Шеклтона шельфовый ледник Shackleton Ice Shelf.

шёл *past m. sing.* of **идти.**

шелёвка *f.* thin plank(ing).

шелест *m.* rustle, rustling, murmur; **—еть, —ить** *v.* rustle.

шёлк *m.* silk.

шелко— *prefix* silk; **—видный** *a.* silky, silk-like, with a silky luster, sericeous; **—вина** *f.* silk fiber; silk thread; **—висто—** *prefix, adv.* sericeo— (sericaceous); serico— (silken); **—вистолистный** *a.* sericophyllous; **—вистый** *see* **шелковидный.**

шелков/ица *f.* mulberry (tree) (*Morus*); **—ицелистный** *a.* morifolious; **—ичный** *a.* mulberry; silk (worm); bombic (acid).

шелковка *f.* buckwheat flour.

шелковник *m.* (bot.) Batrachium.

шелковод *m.* silkworm breeder, sericulturist; **—ный** *a.,* **—ство** *n.* silkworm breeding, sericulture.

шёлко/вый *a.* silk, bombycine; silky, sericeous; tissue (paper); **—графия** *f.* silk screening, silk screen printing; **—крутильный** *a.* silk-throwing; silk (mill); **—кручение** *n.* silk throwing; **—крылы** *pl.* (ent.) Endromididae; **—мотальня** *f.* silk-winding department; **—мотание** *n.* silk winding; **—носность** *f.* silk content; **—носный** *a.* silk-bearing; **—обрабатывающий** *a.* silk-processing; **—отделительный** *a.* (zool.) silk (gland); **—отделочный** *a.* silk-finishing.

шелкопряд *m.* silkworm; **кольчатый ш.** tent caterpillar (*Malacosoma neustria*); **непарный ш.** gypsy moth (*Lymantria dispar*); **—ение** *n.*, **—ильный** *a.* silk spinning; **—ильня** *f.* silk mill; **—ы** *pl.* (ent.) Bombycidae; Lasiocampidae.

шёлкотка/цкий *a.*, **—чество** *n.* silk weaving.

шёлк-сырец *m.* raw silk.

шеллак *m.*, **—овый** *a.* shellac.

шеллачный *see* **шеллаковый.**

шеллен *m.* shellene.

шелл/ер *m.* (corn) sheller; **—машина** *f.* hulling mill, decorticator.

шеллоловая кислота shellolic acid.

Шеллонг-Стрисоуэра феномен (med.) Schellong-Strisower phenomenon.

шелохнуть(ся) *v.* move, stir, agitate.

шелудив/еть *v.* become mangy; **—ость** *f.* (phyt.) rhizoctonia disease; **—ый** *a.* mangy, scabby.

шелух/а *f.* peel, rind, coat, skin, jacket, husk, arillus, hull, pod; scale (of fish); shell meal (fertilizer); **—ачатый** *a.* furfuraceous, scurfy; **—овый** *a.* scaly; **—оотделитель** *m.* husk separator.

шелуш/ащийся *a.* desquamative; **—ение** *n.* shelling, etc., *see v.*; exfoliation; desquamation; **—енный** *a.* shelled, etc., *see v.*; **—ильный** *a.* shelling, etc., *see v.*; **—инка** *f.* chaffy scale, ramentum; furfur; **—истый** *a.* (bot.) ramentaceous; **—итель** *m.* sheller, etc., *see v.*; **—ить** *v.* shell, hull, husk, peel, skin; shed; **—иться** *v.* be shelled, etc.; peel, flake, scale (off), exfoliate; desquamate.

шелыга *f.* crown, apex (of arch).

шельтердечный *a.* (naut.) shelter-deck.

шельф *m.* shelf, ledge; **—овый** *a.* shelf, ledge; shelf ice; tabular, névé (iceberg); **—овый ледник** (geol.) ice shelf.

шелюг/а *f.* sharpleaf willow (*Salix acutifolia*); **—ование** *n.* willow planting; **—овать** *v.* plant willows.

шемая *f.* (ichth.) Danube bleak, shemaia (*Chalcalburnus chalcoides*).

шёнбейновский *a.* (chem.) Schönbein.

Шёнгерра способ Schoenherr process.

шенкель *m.* (horse's) thigh.

Шёнлейна-Геноха болезнь Schönlein-Henoch disease, purpura.

шеннон *m.* shannon (unit of information); **—овский** *a.* (artificial intelligence) Shannon's (maze).

шёнфлиевский *a.* (cryst.) Schoenflies.

шепеля/вить *v.* lisp; **—вость** *f.* lisping, parasigmatism; **—вое произношение** lisp; **—ть** *v.* lisp.

шепинг *m.* shaper, shaping machine; shaping.

шепнуть *v.*, **шёпот** *m.* whisper; **шепотком, шёпотом** *adv.* very quietly.

шептала *f.* dried apricots or peaches.

шепт/ание *n.* whispering; **беззвучное ш.** mussitation; **—ать** *v.* whisper.

шёпфовский *a.* Schöpf.

шепчет *pr. 3 sing. of* **шептать.**

шерабадский *a.* (geog.) Sherabad.

шерардия *f.* (bot.) field madder (*Sherardia*).

шербер *m.* (met.) cupel, roasting dish, scorifier; **—ная проба** scorification.

шербет *m.* sherbet; fruit drink.

Шербур *m.* Cherbourg.

шергень *f.* (naut.) declivity board.

шеренга *f.*, **—овый** *a.* rank, file.

шереровский *a.* Scherer.

шереспёр *m.* (ichth.) asp (*Aspius aspius*).

шеретовка *f.* hulling mill.

шерохов/альный *a.*, **—ание** *n.* roughing; buffing, polishing; **—атка** *f.* bottlebrush grass (*Asperella*); **—ато—** *adv., prefix* roughly; scabri—, trachy— (rough); **—атоволосистый** *a.* scabrid; **—атолистный** *a.* rough-leaved; **—атосемянный** *a.* trachyspermous; **—атость** *f.* roughness(es), irregularities; asperities; (med.) scabrities; **—атый** *a.* rough, coarse, broken, irregular, scored, scabrous; (bot.) asperate; **—ики** *pl.* (zool.) Echinodermata; **—ка** *see* **шерохование.**

шерошница *f.* woodruff (*Asperula odorata*).

шерст/е— *prefix* wool; **—евидность** *f.* wool-like appearance; **—еобрабатывающий** *a.* wool-processing; **—еподобный** *a.* wooly, wool-like, fleecy; **—естебельник** *m.* pipewort (*Eriocaulon*); **—ин(к)а** *f.* wool fiber, wool thread; **—исто—** *prefix* lani—, lanati—, eri(o)— (wool); mall(o)— (downy); lachn(o)— (soft hair, down); **—истоплодный** *a.* eriocarpous; **—истость** *f.* wooliness, fleeciness; **—истый** *a.* wooly, fleecy; (bot.) lanate; wool-bearing; shaggy; **—ить** *v.* irritate (the skin); **—ицвет** *m.* (bot.) Erianthus.

шёрст/ка *f.* (zool.) wool, fur, hair, coat; **—ность** *f.* wooliness; wool yield; **—ный** *a.* wooly; wool(-yielding).

шерстняк *see* **шерстицвет.**

шерсто— *prefix* wool; **—бит** *m.* wool carder, wool beater; **—битный** *a.* wool-carding; **—бой** *see* **шерстобит;** **—бойный** *see* **шерстобитный;** **—бойня** *f.* wool-carding factory, wool-beating mill; **—вед** *m.* wool grower; **—ведение** *n.* wool research; **—крылы** *pl.* flying lemurs (*Dermoptera*); **—лапка** *f.* (ent.) Dasychira; **—мер** *m.* (opt.) eriometer; **—моечный, —мойный** *a.* wool-washing; **—мойка, —мойня** *f.* wool washer; wool-washing plant; **—носный** *a.* wool-bearing.

шерстопряд/ение *n.*, **—ильный** *a.* wool-spinning; **—ильня** *f.* wool mill.

шерсто/ткацкий *a.*, **—ткачество** *n.* wool weaving; **—трепальный** *a.* wool-beating; **—цвет** *see* **шерстицвет.**

шерсто/чёс *m.*, **—чесалка** *f.* wool carder; **—чесальный** *a.* wool-carding.

шерст/ь *f.* wool, fleece; (zool.) fur, hair; **древесная ш.** wood fiber, batting; **—як** *m.* (bot.) Eriochloa; **—янка** *f.* cotton fleece; **—яной** *a.* wool(en); **—яной жир** wool fat, wool grease; **—яной пот** suint, yolk; **—яное дерево** silk cotton tree (*Ceiba pentandra*).

шерт *m.* (petr.) chert.

шертинг *m.* (text.) shirting.

шерфование *n.* (leather) trimming.

шерхебель *m.* rough plane, jack plane.

шершав/еть, —иться *v.* get rough, roughen; **—ость** *f.* roughness, asperity; shagginess; **—ый** *a.* rough, asperous; shaggy, hirsute; roughing (mill).

шерш/ень *m.*, **—невой** *a.* (ent.) hornet.

шессилит *m.* (min.) chessylite, azurite.

шест *m.* pole, rod, stick, staff, post, perch, boom, stake.

шеств/ие *n.* procession, train; **—овать** *v.* march.

шестерён/ка *dim. of* **шестерня;** **—(оч)ный, —чатый** *a.* pinion, gear(-driven); gear-type (pump); **—чатый (зубчатый) привод** gearing.

шест/ерик *m.*, **—ёрка** *f.* (group of) six; sextuplet; six-horse team; six-oar boat; number six; six-inch thickness; six-strand rope; six-inch nail; **—ерной** *a.* six(fold); (cryst.) hexad (axis).

шестерн/я *f.* pinion, gear (wheel); six-horse team; **ведущая ш.** drive gear; **коническая ш.** bevel gear; **соединённый —ей** *a.* geared (to).

шестеро *num.* six; **их ш.** there are six of them; **—ногная передача** pinion drive.

шести *gen. of* **шесть.**

шести— *prefix* hex(a)—, sex—, six; **—атомный** *a.* hexatomic; hexavalent; hexahydric (alcohol); **—бороздчатый** *a.* sexsulcate, having six furrows; **—бромистый** *a.* hexabromide; **—валентный** *a.* hexavalent; **—валковый** *a.* (met.) six-high cluster (mill); **—вершинник** *m.* six-pointed star; **—водный гидрат** *a.* hexahydrate; **—гнёздный** *a.* sexlocular.

шестигранн/ик *m.* (geom.) hexahedron, cube; **—ый** *a.* hexahedral, cubic; hexagon(al), sexangular; sexpartite; (bot.) six-rowed.

шестидесяти— *prefix* sixty; **—дневный** *a.* sixty-day; **—летие** *n.* 60-year period; 60th anniversary; **—летний** *a. of* **шестидесятилетие;** sexagenarian.

шести/десятый *a.* sixtieth; **—днёвка** *f.* six-day week; **—дневный** *a.* six-day; (med.) sextan (fever); **—дюймовка** *f.* six-inch gun; **—жаберный** *a.* six-gilled; **—замещённые** *pl.* hexasubstitution products, hexaderivatives; **—зарядный** *a.* six-chambered (revolver); **—зубчатый** *a.* sexdentate; **—косточковый** *a.* hexapyrenous, having six kernels; **—кратный** *a.* sixfold, sextuple; **—круговой** *a.* hexacyclic, arranged in six whorls.

шести/лепестный *a.* hexapetalous; **—летие** *n.* six-year period; **—летний** *a.* six-year; **—листный** *a.* (bot.) hexaphyllous; **—листовка** *f.* sexfollicle; **—листочковый** *a.* sexfoliolate; **—лопастный** *a.* sexlobate.

шестилучев/ой *a.* hexactinal, sexradiate, six-rayed; hexagonal; **—ые** *pl.* (zool.) Hexacorallia.

шести/минутный *a.* six-minute; **—мужный** *a.* (bot.) hexandrous; having six stamens; **—ногий** *a.* (zool.) hexapod, six-legged; **—осевой** *a.* hexaxial; **—основный** *a.* hexabasic; hexahydric (acid); **—палый** *a.* hexadactylous, six-fingered; **—парный** *a.* (bot.) sexjugous; **—пестичный** *a.* (bot.) hexagynous, having six pistils; **—польный** *a.* (agr.) six-field (crop rotation).

шести/раздельный *a.* sexpartite, hexapartite; **—сотый** *a.* six-hundredth; **—ствольный** *a.* sextuple.

шестисторонн/ий *a.* (geom.) hexahedral, six-sided; hexagonal; **—ик** *m.* hexahedron; (cryst.) cube.

шести/точечный *a.* six-point; **—тычинковый** *a.* (bot.) hexandrous, hexastaemenous.

шестиугольн/ик *m.* (geom.) hexagon; **—ый** *a.* hexagonal, sexangular.

шести/фазный *a.* six-phase; **—фтористый** *a.* hexafluoride (of); **—фторо—** *prefix* hexafluoro—; **—хлористый** *a.* hexachloride; **—цветковый** *a.* (bot.) hexanthous; **—часовой** *a.* six-hour; **—чашелистиковый** *a.* (bot.) hexasepalous; **—членный** *a.* six-membered, hexamerous; (bot.) hexaphyllous; **—электродная лампа** *f.* (rad.) hexode.

шестнадцатеричный *a.* (math.) hexadecimal.

шестнадцатигранн/ик *m.* (cryst.) dioctahedron; **—ый** *a.* dioctahedral.

шестнадцат/иричный *see* **шестнадцатеричный; —ый** *a.* sixteenth; **—ь** *num.* sixteen.

шестов/атый *a.* columnar, stalked; (met.) spiky; **—атая структура** (min.) columnar structure; **—ина** *f.* pole, staff, post.

шест/ой *a.* sixth; **в —ых** sixthly, in the sixth place; **одна —ая** one sixth.

шесток *m.* hearth; (poultry) roost, perch.

шесть *num.* six; **—десят** *num.* sixty; **—сот** *num.* six hundred; **—ю** *adv.* multiplied by six.

шетл/андский, —ендский *a.* Shetland.

шеф *m.* chief, master; chef; patron; **—ство** *n.* patronage; **—ствовать** *v.* head, supervise; look (after); be a patron (of); **ш.-электрик** chief electrician.

Шеффера (chem.) Schäffer's (acid, etc.); (math.) Sheffer.

Шеффильд Sheffield.

шея *f.* neck, collum, cervix, throat; collar; vent.

ШЖ *abbr.* (шёлкоотделительная железа) silk gland.

ШЗ *abbr.* (шар-зонд) sounding balloon.

ши *m.* (bot.) shea butter tree (*Butyrospermum parkii*).

шибер *m.* gate (valve), slide valve; slide(r), slide bar; weir (of jigger); damper (of chimney); **—ный** *a.* gate, slide (valve); vane (pump).

шибк/ий *a.* fast, quick; **—о** *adv.* quickly; very, much.

шибл(и)як *m.* (bot.) shibliak, deciduous bush formation.

шибняк *m.* (ichth.) pikeperch.

шибок *sh. m. of* **шибкий.**

шибуол *m.* shibuol.

шивера *f.* stony river bed; rapids.

шиверекия *f.* (bot.) Schivereckia.

шиворот-навыворот *adv.* topsy-turvy; incorrectly.

шигелл/а *f.,* **—ы** *pl.* (bact.) Shigella.

шизо— *prefix* schizo—, split; *see also under* **схизо—; —генез** *m.* (biol.) schizogenesis; **—гония** *f.* schizogony; **—ид** *m.,* **—идный** *a.* schizoid; **—мицеты** *prefix* (bot.) Schizomycetes; **—френия** *f.* (med.) schizophrenia; **—цит** *m.* (hem) schistocyte.

Шика реакция (med.) Schick test.

шик/имен *m.* (bioch.) shikimene, sikimin; **—имовый** *a.* shikimic (acid); **—имол** *m.* shikimol, safrole; **—онин** *m.* shikonin.

шикша *f.* (bot.) crowberry (*Empetrum*).

шил *past m. sing. of* **шить.**

шиллер/изация *f.* (min.) schillerization.

шиллинг *m.* shilling (coin).

шило *n.* awl, pricker; (planting) stick; stylus; (ichth.) Nerophis; **—видно(—)** *adv.* awl-shaped; *prefix* subulato—; **—видный** *a.* awl-shaped, subulate; (anat.) styloid; **—видный отросток** styloid process; **—глоточный** *a.* stylopharyngeal; **—клювки** *pl.* (orn.) avocets (*Recurvirostridae*); **—клювый** *a.* sharp-beaked.

шило/образный *a.* styloid; **ш.-подъязычный** *a.* (anat.) stylohyoid; **—хвостый** *a.* sharp-tailed, awl-tailed; **—хвость** *f.* (orn.) pintail (*Anas acuta*); **ш.-язычный** *a.* styloglossal.

шильбовые *pl.* catfishes (*Shilbeidae*).

шильдик *m.* nameplate, instruction plate.

шильн/ик *m.* (bot.) awlwort (*Subularia*); (mam.) second-year male deer; water plantain; **—ый** *a.* awl; **—ая трава, —як** *m.* (bot.) broom, spec. dyer's broom (*Genista tinctoria*).

шильце *n.* small awl; (bot.) plumule, pip.

Шимана реакция Schiemann reaction.

шимм *m.* shim; **—и** *n.* shimmy; **—ирование** *n.* (instrumentation) shimming.

шимпанзе *n.* (zool.) chimpanzee (*Pan troglodytes*); **карликовый ш.** pygmy chimpanzee (*Pan paniscus*).

шина *f.* tire; iron hoop, (wheel) band; (inner) tube; (elec.) busbar, (collecting) bar; (comp.) bus; (med.) cast, splint; **с резиновыми —ми** rubber-tired; **числовая ш.** number transfer bus.

шина-аэроплан *m.* (med.) airplane splint; **ш.-баллон** *f.* balloon tire; **ш.-гусматик** *f.* block tire; **ш.-лира** (med.) banjo traction splint; **ш.-эластик** *f.* cushion tire, air-core tire.

шиндлериевые *pl.* (ichth.) Schindleriidae.

шинировать *see* **хинировать;** (med.) splint.

шинков/альный *a.*, **—ание** *n.* chopping, shredding; **—ать** *v.* chop, shred; **—ка** *f.*, *see* **шинкование;** shredder, slaw cutter.

шинколобвит *m.* (min.) chinkolobwite, sklodowskite.

шин/ный *a. of* **шина;** band, hoop (iron); **—одержатель** *m.* tire holder; **—ообкатный станок** tire-testing bench.

шиншилл/а *f.*, **—овый** *a.* (zool.) chinchilla.

шиншилула *f.* Altiplano chinchilla mouse (*Chinchillula sahamae*).

шип *m.* pin, dowel; tongue, tenon; journal, pivot; horn, lug, projection; (anat.) spina, aculeus; spine, thorn, prickle; (tire) stud; cleat; bar; stub; crampon; calk(ing); (ichth.) sturgeon; hissing (sound); **ш. и гнездо** tenon and mortise; **подковный шип** calk(ing); **соединение —ом** tenon joint; **соединение —ом в гнездо** mortise joint.

шип/ение *n.* hissing, etc., *see v.*; hiss; whistling; trumpeting (of elephant); grunting (of pig); baying (of ass); humming (of bees); **—еть** *v.* hiss, fizz, sparkle, froth, effervesce; sizzle, spit, sputter; simmer, boil; scratch (of phonograph needle); creak, grate.

шипик *m. dim. of* **шип;** (bot.) small prickle, acicula; **—овый** *a.* aculeate, pointed; **—оговые** *pl.* (ichth.) Denticipitidae; **—ообразный** *a.* spiniform.

шипов/ато *adv.* aculeate, *prefix* spinoso—; **—атозубчатый** *a.* spinosodentate; **—атый** *a.* prickly, thorny, spinose, aculeate, echinate; **—идный** *a.* spinous, spiny, spine-like; **—идный слой** prickle-cell layer (of epidermis); **—ник** *m.*, **—никовый** *a.* dog rose (*Rosa canina*); **—ой** *a. of* **шип.**

шипо/голов *m.* (ichth.) Holacanthus imperator; **—ножка** *f.* (ent.) hydrophilid beetle (*Anacaena*).

шипонос *m.* (zool.) Echinorhyncus; (ichth.) thornback ray (*Raja clavata*); **—ки** *pl.* tumbling flower beetles (*Mordellidae*).

шипорезный *a.* tenoning; dovetailing, dovetail (saw).

шипохвост *m.* (herp.) spiny-tailed lizard (*Uromastix*); **—ы(е)** *pl.* (mam.) scaly-tailed squirrels (*Anomaluridae*); **—ый** *a.* spiny-tailed.

шипощек *m.* (ichth.) thornhead (*Sebastolobus*).

шиппингпортский *a.* Shippingport (reactor).

шипун *m.* (orn.) mute swan (*Cygnus olor*).

шипуч/ее *n.* carbonated drink; **—есть** *f.* frothiness, effervescence; **—ий** *a.* frothy; effervescent, carbonated, soft (drink); sparkling (wine); **—ка** *f.* carbonated drink.

шипящий *a.* hissing, fizzing, sibilant; **ш. звук** hiss.

шир. *abbr.* (**ширина**) width.

шир/е *comp. of* **широкий, широко; —ение** *n.* broadening, etc., *see v.*; **—илка** *f.* expander, stretcher; **—ильный** *see* **ширительный; —ина** *f.* width, breadth, latitude; thickness; amplitude; (tolerance) range; (rail) gage; **по —ине** edgewise, on edge; **пять футов —ины** five feet wide; **—ительный** *a.* broadening, etc., *see v.*; **—ительная машина** stretcher; **—ить** *v.* broaden, widen, enlarge, stretch; (text.) tenter, stenter; **—иться** *v.* be broadened, etc.; broaden, widen, spread, expand.

ширма *f.* screen, shield, blind.

ширмерит *m.* (min.) schirmerite.

широк *m.*, **—а** *f.*, **—и** *pl. sh. forms of* **широкий.**

широк/ий *a.* broad, wide(spread), extensive, spacious, extended; general (public); (anat.) latus; **—ая мышца** (anat.) musculus vastus; **—ая публика** the public at large; **—ого назначения** general-purpose; **товары —ого потребления** consumer goods.

широко *adv.* broadly, widely, extensively; *prefix* broad,

wide, lat(i)—, plat(y)—; eury—; *sh. n. of* **широкий; ш. использовать** *v.* use extensively, make good use (of); **ш. использоваться** *v.* be in common use; **—адаптивный** *a.* euryadaptive; **—ватый** *a.* rather broad; **—ветвистый** *a.* platycladous, broad-branched; **—вещание** *n.*, **—вещательный** *a.* (rad.) broadcast(ing); **—габаритный** *a.* wide; **—головчатый** *a.* (anat.) platycephalic; **—головый** *a.* (anat.) brachycephalic; **—горлый** *a.* wide-necked; **—грудый** *a.* broad-chested.

широко/диапазонный *a.* wide-range; **—захватный** *a.* far-reaching, wide-span, long-range, wide-cut (mower); long-base (drag); **—зубчатый** *a.* latidentate; **—излучатель** *m.* wide-angle (lighting) fitting; wide-beam diffusor; **—клювый** *a.* latirostral, broad-beaked; **—колейка** *f.* wide-gage track; **—колейный** *a.* wide-gage; **—колокольчик** *m.* balloon flower; **—колосый** *a.* broad-spiked; **—кост(н)ый** *a.* big-boned.

ширококрыл/ые *pl.* (pal.) Eurypterida; **—ый** *a.* broadwinged, large-winged.

широколист/(вен)ница *f.* (bot.) Polypodium; **—венный, —(н)ый** *a.* broad-leaved.

широколоб/ка *f.* (ichth.) sculpin, miller's thumb (*Cottus gobio*); **—ки** *pl.* sculpins (*Cottidae*); **—ый** *a.* having a broad forehead.

широколопастный *a.* latilobate, having broad lobes.

широконос/ка *f.* (orn.) shoveler, spoonbill (*Anas clypeata*); **—ый** *a.* broad-nosed; **—ые** *pl.* (mam.) Platyrrhina.

широкоосновный *a.* broad-based.

широко/плечий *a.* broad-shouldered; **—полосатый** *a.* banded; (bot.; zool.) vittate, striped or ridged lengthwise; **—полосный** *a.* wide-band, broadband; wide-range; strip (mill); **—полый** *a.* broad-(b)rimmed; **—пористый** *a.* large-pored; **—профильный** *a.* wide-section; **—раскрывный** *a.* wide-angle; **—распространённый** *a.* widely distributed, widespread.

широкорот *m.* (orn.) broad-mouthed dollarbird (*Eurystomus orientalis*); **—ы** *pl.* (orn.) Euryilaimidae; **—ые** *pl.* (ichth.) gulper eels (*Eurypharyngidae*); **—ый** *a.* wide-mouthed.

широко/рядный *a.* wide-row, broad-row; having widely spaced rows; **—семянный** *a.* platyspermous, flatseeded; **—слойный** *a.* broad-zoned; coarse-grained (wood); **—солевой** *a.* euryhaline, adapted to a wide range of salinity; **—стебельчатый** *a.* platycaulous, broad-stalked; **—тарелочный** *a.* large-disk (insulator); **—тепловой** *a.* eurythermic, adaptable to a wide range of temperature; **—травье** *n.* broad-leaved grasses; **—угольный** *a.* wide-angle (lens); wide-aperture (telescope); full-scan (camera); **—ушка** *f.* (mam.) barbastelle bat (*Barbastella*); **—хвостка** *f.* (orn.) Cetti's warbler (*Cettia cetti*); **—ходовой** *a.* loose (fit), loose-running; **—экранный** *a.* wide-screen.

широт/а *f.* width, breadth, range; (geog.) latitude; **—ноимпульсный** *a.* pulse-duration, pulse-width; **—номодулированный** *a.* width-modulated; **—ный** *a.* latitudinal.

шир/очайший *superl. of* **широкий;** (anat.) latissiums (muscle); **—потреб** *m.* consumer goods; mass consumption; **—ь** *see* **ширина.**

ширяш *m.* (bot.) Eremurus spectabilis.

шисто— *prefix* schisto— (cleft; fissure); *see also under* **шизо; —зоматоз** *m.* (vet.) schistosomiasis; **—церка** *f.* locust (*Schistocerca*); **—цит** *m.* (med.) schistocyte.

шит-асфальт *m.* sheet asphalt.

шитиха *f.* (blasting) squib.

шит/ый *a.* sewn; **—ь** *v.* sew, stitch; **—ьё** *n.* sewing.

Шифа реактив Schiff's reagent, thioacetic acid.

шифер *m.* (petr.) slate; schist; shale; slate shingle, roofing shingle; shiver, clay slate; **—вейс** *m.* flake white (white lead); **—ный** *a.* slate, slaty, slate-like; schist(ose); shale; scaly, flaky, foliated, foliaceous; **—ная чернь** mineral black (graphitic slate); **—ное масло** shale oil.

шифон *m.*, **—ный** *a.* (text.) chiffon.

шифр *m.* code, cipher; (library) classification number; **—атор** *m.* (en)coder; **—овальный** *a.* code, cryptographic; **—овальщик** *m.* coder; **—ование** *n.* (en)coding, etc., *see v.*; **—ованный** *a.* (en)coded, etc., *see v.*; **—овать** *v.* (en)code, write in code, codify, cipher; **—овка** *f.* (en)coding, etc., *see v.*; coded text; **—овщик** *m.* coder; **—ограмма** *f.* coded telegram.

шифтингборд *m.* shifting board.

Шиффа реактив *see* **Шифа реактив.**

Шиффово основание (chem.) Schiff base.

шихан *m.* sharp-pointed hill; spec. shikhan (a limestone-reef monadnock).

шихт/а *f.* (met.) charge, burden, batch, mixture, blend, (melting) stock; **обставлять —у** *v.* mix, blend; **—арник** *m.* mixing shed, stockyard, ore yard.

шихт/овальный *a.*, **—ование** *n.* (met.) burdening, etc., *see v.*; **—овать** *v.* burden, blend, mix, make up a mixture, calculate a charge; laminate; **—овка** *see* **шихтование**; burden, charge; **—овочный** *see* **шихтовальный**; **—овочная машина** reclaimer; **—овый** *a.* of **шихта**; stock (bin); flaky (fracture); **—овый двор** stockyard, bedding plant; mixing shed; **—осмеситель** *m.* reclaimer; **—плац** *see* **шихтовый двор.**

шишак *m.* (mal.) helmet shell (*Cassis cornuta*).

шиш/ек *gen. pl.* of **шишка**; **—ечка** *dim.* of **шишка**; bump, lump; knob, button; **—ечник** *m.* (bot.) Bunium; **—ечниковые** *pl.* (ichth.) pinecone fishes (*Monocentridae*); **—ечный** *a.* of **шишка**; **—ечная болезнь** (ichth.) lump disease, myxoboliosis; **—ка** *f.* bump, lump; tuber, knob; (bot.) cone, strobile; (text.) nep; (anat.) pinea; **ворсовальная —ка** (bot.) fuller's teasel (*Dipsacus fullonum*); **—ко—** *prefix* con(o)—, coni(o)— (cone), strobili—; **—коватый** *a.* bumpy, gnarled, knobby, knotted, tuberous, torose, torous; strobilaceous, cone-like; tuberculate, nodular; **—ковидный** *a.* bumpy, knobby; cone-like, strobiliform; pineal; **—ковидная железа** (anat.) conarium, pineal gland or body; epiphysis; **—ковые** *see* **шишечниковые**; **—коносные** *pl.* conifers; **—коносный** *a.* (bot.) cone-bearing, coniferous, strobiliferous; **—кообразный отросток** (anat.) condyle; **—косушилка**, **—косушильня** *f.* cone kiln; **—коягода** *f.* cypress or juniper cone, galbulus.

шкал/а *f.* scale, range, dial; (time) base; **ш. полутонов**, **ш. серых тонов** gray scale; **ш. твёрдости** hardness scale; **круглая ш.** dial; **полное отклонение стрелки —ы** full-scale deflection; **со —ой** graduated; **—ьный** *a.* of **шкала**; indicating (controller).

шканечный *a.* (naut.) quarterdeck; log (book); **ш. журнал** log(book).

шкант *m.* dowel.

шканцы *pl.* (naut.) quarterdeck.

шкап *see* **шкаф.**

шкатулка *f.* box, case.

шкаф *m.* closet, locker; cupboard, cabinet, case, box; safe; (exhaust) hood; (drying) oven; (ice) chest; **ш.-колонка** column case; **сушильный ш.** desiccator; **—ик** *dim.* of **шкаф**; **—ной**, **—ный** *a.* of **шкаф.**

шкафут *m.* (naut.) waist.

шкаф/-холодильник *m.* refrigerator; **—чик** *dim.* of **шкаф**; locker; (balance) case; (air conditioning) outlet.

шквал *m.* squall, gust of wind, tornado, (snow) flurry; flaw; **—истый**, **—овой**, **—ьный** *a.* squally.

шквар *see* **шкварки**; **—(ин)а** *f.* scoria, dross, scum; (fat extraction) residue; **—ки** *pl.* cracklings, greaves; **—(оч)ный** *a.* low-grade (fat).

шкворень *m.* pin, bolt, pivot, pintle, vertical axle; kingpin.

шкериани *pl.* (bot.) rosebay.

шкерт *m.* binding rope.

шкив *m.* pulley, sheave, block; **ш.-маховик** *m.* flywheel pulley; **—ообразный** *a.* pulley(-like); disk-like, discoid(al); **ш.-редуктор** *m.* reducing pulley.

шкод/а *f.* loss, damage; **—ить** *v.* damage; **—ливый** *a.* harmful.

школ/а *f.* school; plant nursery, seedbed; **—ить** *v.* discipline, school; **—ка** *f.* plant nursery, seedbed; **—оведение** *n.* school management; **—ьник** *m.* student, pupil; **—ьный** *a.* school.

шкот *m.*, **—овый** *a.* (naut.) (rigging) sheet, rope or chain used to set sail angle; **—овый узел** sheet bend; weaver's knot.

шкраб *m.* student worker.

шркебетуха *f.* (ichth.) gray mullet.

шкуна *f.* schooner.

шкур/а *f.* hide, skin, pelt, pelage, fell, pelt wool; **—ить** *v.* sand; **—ка** *dim. of* **шкура**; (prot.) pellicle; (larval) skin; abrasive cloth or paper; **стеклянная —ка** sandpaper; **—ки** *pl.* exuviae (cast-off skin, shells, etc.); **—ный** *a. of* **шкура.**

шла *past f. sing.* of **идти.**

шлаг *m.* explosive shell in a rocket.

шлагбаум *m.* (traffic control) barrier, bar, toll gate, lifting gate, swing gate; turnpike, toll road.

шлак *m.* slag, dross, scoria; cinder, sinter; (coal) clinker; tails, poison (in nuclear reactor); residue, remainder, rest; **волокнистый ш.** slag wool, mineral wool; **спуск —а** slagging off; **топочный ш.** cinder.

шлако/бетон *m.*, **—бетонный** *a.* slag concrete; **—блок** *m.*, **—блочный** *a.* cinder block.

шлаков/ание *n.* slagging, scorification; **—ата** *f.* slag wool; **—атый** *see* **шлаковидный**; **—ать** *v.* (form) slag, scorify, clinker.

шлако/видный *a.* slaggy, scoriaceous, drossy; **—вик** *m.* slag chamber, slag pocket; cross gate; dirt trap; **—вина** *f.* slag inclusion; **—вня** *f.* slag pot; skimmer; (electric furnace) slag pocket; **—воз** *m.* slag car; **—вщик** *m.* cinder pit man.

шлаков/ый *a. of* **шлак**; slaggy; cinder, scoriaceous, drossy; clinker; residual; **ш. камень, ш. кирпич** slag brick, slag block; **—ая вата** slag wool, mineral wool.

шлакообраз/ный *a.* slaggy, scoriaceous; **—ование** *n.* slag formation, scorification; **—овательный** *a.* slag-forming; **—ующий** *a.* slag-forming.

шлакоотдел/ение *n.* slagging, slag removal; **—итель** *m.* slag remover, slag separator, skimmer, skim gate; **—ительный** *a.* slag-removing, front-slagging, continuous-tapping (spout).

шлако/отстойник *m.* slag basin; **—подобный** *a.* slaggy, scoriaceous, drossy; **—портландцемент** *m.* portland blast-furnace cement, slag cement; **—приёмник** *m.* slag catcher, cinder pocket; **—сниматель** *see* **шлакоотделитель**; **—содержащий** *a.* slag-containing, slaggy, containing clinker; **—удаление** *n.* slag removal, slag withdrawal, slag disposal; **—уловитель** *m.* slag trap, cross gate; **центробежный —уловитель** whirl gate; **—устойчивость** *f.* resistance to slag; **—цемент** *m.* slag cement.

шлакующийся *a.* slagging, clinkering.

шлам *m.* slime, mud, ooze, sludge; slurry, pulp; sediment, silt, residue, bottoms, tarry residue (in engine); drilling mud; (drill) cuttings; (cer.) slip; —**бассейн** *m.* sludge pool; —**овый** *a. of* **шлам;** solids-handling (pump); —**овый реактор** slurry (nuclear) reactor; —**омешалка** *f.* slurry mixer.

шламо/образный *a.* slime-like, slimy; slurry; —**образная смесь** slurry (nuclear) reactor; —**образование** *n.* sliming; sludging; —**отделитель** *m.* slime separator; sludge remover; —**отстойник** *m.* slime pit, mud-settling pit; slurry tank; —**разделитель** *m.* slime separator; —**уловитель** *m.* slime trap; sludge extractor.

шланг *m.,* —**овый** *a.* hose, flexible tube, pipe or cable; tubing.

шлёвка *f.* belt loop; supporting ring.

шлеечная машина (text.) thread extractor, thread picker.

шлейка *f.* strap.

шлейф *m.* (elec.) loop, circuit; stub; (measuring) loop; tail (of curve); (geol.) train, trail, strip (of loose deposits); bench; breech-band (of sow); (agr.) leveler, drag, float; **ш.-борона** *f.* smoothing harrow; surface cultivation; **ш.-волокуша** *f.* (agr.) band sweep, drag, slicker; —**ование** *n.* smoothing, etc. *see v.;* —**овать** *v.* smooth, plane; slick, sweep; drag; —**овый** *a. of* **шлейф;** rotating-mirror (oscillograph); **ш.-резонатор** *m.* circuit-resonator.

шлем *m.* helmet; galea; (mech.) neck; (still) head; —**ник** *m.* (bot.) Scutellaria; —**овый** *a.* helmet; —**оносец** *m.,* —**оносный** *a.* (ichth.) staghorn sculpin (*Gymnocanthus*); —**ообразный** *a.* helmet-shaped; —**орогатковые** *pl.* (ichth.) Rhamphocottidae; —**офон** *m.* interphone headset, radio-equipped helmet.

шлёп/анье *n.* slapping, etc., *see v.;* —**ать,** —**нуть** *v.* slap, smack, splash, spank.

шлепок *m.* spank, slap.

шлёт *pr. 3 sing. of* **слать.**

шли *past pl. of* **идти.**

шликер *m.* (met.) dross; (cer.) slip.

Шлиппе соль Schlippe's salt, sodium thioantimonate (V).

шлипс *m.* tool grab, slip socket.

шлир *m.,* —**а** *f.,* —**ы** *pl.* schlieren (regions of varying refraction as in liquids); (glass) thread or tear-shaped flaw; —**ен-методом** schlieren (photography); —**овый** *a.* schlieren; streaky (structure).

шлите *imp. of* **слать.**

шлиф *m.* (micro)section, polished section, slide; cross-sectional view; ground-glass joint; ground edge; (chem.) cone; —**ной** *a. of* **шлиф;** —**ной напильник** smooth(-cut) file.

шлифовальн/ик *m.* (glass) grinding pan; —**ый** *a.* polishing, etc., *see* **шлифовать;** abrasive; —**ый круг** polishing wheel; —**ый материал** abrasive; —**ый станок** grinder; —**я** *f.* polishing room.

шлифов/альщик *m.* polisher, grinder; —**ание** *n.* polishing, etc., *see v.;* abrasion; —**анный** *a.* polished, etc., *see v.;* ground; —**ать** *v.* polish, buff, burnish, grind, abrade, file; —**ка** *see* **шлифование;** finish; —**щик** *m.* polisher, grinder.

шлифу/емый *a.* grindable; —**ющий** *a.* polishing, etc., *see* **шлифовать.**

шлих *m.* (ore) slime, schlich, slick; concentrate; alluvial sand; —**еры** *pl.* dross; —**овой** *a. of* **шлих;** placer (gold), bullion (gold).

шлихта *f.* (text.) size.

Шлихтинг *m.* (phys.) Schlichting.

шлихт/овальный *a.* smoothing, etc., *see v.;* warp-sizing (mach.); —**овальная шкурка** fine emery cloth; —**ование** *n.* smoothing, etc., *see v.;* —**ованный** *a.* smoothed, etc., *see v.;* —**овать** *v.* smooth, plane, finish; dress; (text.) size; (met.) planish; (foundry) blackwash (molds); —**овка** *see* **шлихтование.**

шлихштейн *m.* (met.) lead matte.

шлиц *m.,* —**а** *f.,* —**евать** *v.* slit, slot, groove, spline; —**евой** *a. of* **шлиц;** castle-type, castellated, spline(d); —**евой вал** spline shaft; —**евая ножовка** slitting saw; —**евая фреза** slot cutter; —**евое соединение** splined joint; —**ешлифовальный** *a.* spline-grinding; —**ованный** *a.* slit, slotted, grooved, splined.

шло *past n. sing. of* **идти.**

шлюз *m.,* —**ный** *a.* sluice, lock; gate valve; (comp.) gateway; —**ование** *n.* sluicing, etc., *see v.;* canalization (of rivers); —**ованный** *a.* sluiced, etc., *see v.;* lock (canal); —**овать** *v.* sluice, lock, dam; build sluices; flush; —**овой** *a. of* **шлюз;** —**овой сервер** (comp.) gateway server; **ш.-регулятор** *m.* regulator sluice.

шлюп *m.* (naut.) sloop; —**балка** *f.* davit; —**ка** *f.,* —**очный** *a.* boat.

шлющий *pr. act. part. of* **слать.**

шлям *see* **шлам.**

шлямбур *m.* jumper, drift (borer).

шлямов/ка *f.* slime separator; —**очный** *a.* stripping (machine).

шляп/а *f.* hat; (geol.) cap; —**ка** *f.* cap, bonnet; pileus (of mushroom); head (of nail, etc.); (cartridge) base; —**ник** *m.* hatter; —**ный** *a. of* **шляпа.**

шляпо/видный, —**образный** *a.* hat-shaped; (bot.) pileate, pileiform; —**чный** *a. of* **шляпка;** pileate, crested; —**чные грибы** *pl.* pileate fungi (*Hymenomycetes*).

шлях *m.* road.

шляхтхебель *m.* plane.

шмак *m.* sumac (dye); —**овка** *f.* dyeing with sumac.

шмальт/а *f.* smalt, cobalt blue.

шмат(ок) *m.* piece, lump.

шмел/ежук *m.* (ent.) bumble flower beetle (*Euphora*); —**и** *pl.* (ent.) Bombinae; —**иный** *a.,* —**ь** *m.* (ent.) bumblebee (*Bombus*).

шмидтинский *a.* Schmidt('s).

Шмидта реакция Schmidt reaction.

шмуцтитул *m.* (typ.) section(al) title, bastard title, half title.

шмыг/ать, —**нуть** *v.* dart, run about.

шмяк/ать, —**нуть** *v.* throw with a crash, dash (to the floor).

шнек *m.,* —**овый** *a.* auger; worm (feeder), endless screw; worm conveyer, screw conveyer; **ш.-смеситель** pug mill; —**овый транспортёр** worm conveyer, screw conveyer; —**пресс пелотеза** plodder, screwpress; (cer.) auger.

шнит(т)-/лук *m.* chives (*Allium schoenoprasum*); **ш.-салат** *m.* cut-leaf lettuce.

шноркель *m.* snorkel, snort.

Шнорра земля (min.) Schnorr's earth.

шнур *m.* cord, string, twine; lace, lacing, braid; (elec.) flex, flexible cord, flexible cable; (blasting) fuse; (nucl.) pinch; (bot., zool.) funiculus.

шнур/ковый *a. of* **шнурок;** —**ование** *n.,* —**овка** *f.* lacing, tying; —**овать** *v.* lace, tie; —**овидный** *a.* funiform, cord-like; —**овой** *a.* string, cord, lace; corded (book); cord-circuit (repeater); —**овая книга** statistical seed record; —**овая обработка** stringing (of tobacco); —**ок** *m.* (thin) cord, string, lace, twine; funiculus; (blasting) fuse; —**ки** *pl.* laces.

Шоб/а копёр Schob impact tester; **эластичность по —у** Schob elasticity, percentage rebound.

шов *m.*, **—ный** *a.* seam, joint, junction; weld; (anat.) commissure; (anat., bot.) raphe; (med., bot.) suture; **адгезионный ш.** adhesion joint; **без шва** seamless.

шовин/изм *m.* chauvinism; **—ист** *m.*, **—истка** *f.* chauvinist; **—ист(иче)ский** *a.* chauvinistic.

шовкун *m.* white mulberry (*Morus alba*).

шовный *a.* sutural.

шодди *n.* shoddy (wool).

Шодрона элемент (elec.) Chaudron's thermopile.

Шоиниган-фолс (geog.) Shawinigan Falls.

шок *m.*, **—ировать** *v.* shock; **—кер** *m.* shocker; **—овый** *a.* shock.

шоколад *m.* chocolate; **—ка** *f.* chocolate bar; **—ник** *m.* (bot.) cacao tree (*Theobroma cacao*); **—ный** *a.* chocolate, cocoa; **—ное дерево** *see* **шоколадник**.

шокур *m.* (ichth.) whitefish (*Coregonus*).

шола *f.* shola, evergreen mountain forest.

Шомодьи Somogyi (name).

шомпол *m.*, **—ьный** *a.* ramrod, ram, rammer, tamping stick, tamper, cleaning rod.

шоопирование *n.* schooping, metal pulverization, metal spraying.

Шопарта сустав (anat.) Chopart's joint, articulatio tarsi transversa.

шор *m.* (geol.) sor, solonchak playa.

Шор/а метод (met.) Shore hardness test; **твёрдость по —у** Shore hardness.

шора *f.* (min.) a supporting framework.

шорн/ик *m.* harness maker, saddler; **—ичная** *f.* saddler's room, harness maker's shop; **—ичество** *n.* harness making; **—оседельный** *a.* harness and saddle; saddler's (shop); **—ый** *a.* harness (leather); leather (strap); **—я** *f.* saddler's shop.

шорох *m.* noise, rustling.

шортгорнский *a.* shorthorn (cattle).

шоры *pl. of* **шор**; harness; blinders; *see also* **соры**.

шоссе *n.*, **—йный** *a.*, **—йная дорога** highway, paved road.

шоссиров/ание *n.* highway construction; macadamization; **—ать** *v.* build a highway; macadamize.

Шотки эффект Schottky effect (in semiconductors).

шотл. *abbr.* (**шотландский**) Scotch.

Шотландия Scotland.

шотланд/ка *f.*, **—ская материя** (text.) plaid; **—ский** *a.* Scotch.

шотовское *see* **шоттовское**.

шотт *m.* (geol.) shott, salt depression.

Шоттена реакция Schotten's reaction.

Шоттки *see* **Шотки**.

шоттовское стекло Schott glass, Jena glass.

шофёр *m.* chauffeur, driver, operator.

шпага *f.* sword.

шпагат *m.* (binder) twine.

шпадель *see* **шпатель**.

шпажка *f.* finishing tool.

шпажн/ик *m.* (bot.) Gladiolus; **—ый** *a. of* **шпага**.

шпак *m.* (orn.) starling (*Sturnus vulgaris*).

шпаклев/ание *n.* spackling, etc., *see v.*; **—ать** *v.* spackle, fill (up), putty, stop (holes); (paints) prime.

шпаклёв/ка *see* **шпаклевание**; spackling compound, filler, putty, lute; primer; **—очный** *a. of* **шпаклёвка**; **—щик** *m.* spackler.

шпала *f.* cross tie, sleeper.

шпалер/а *f.* (hort.) espalier; trellis, lattice-work; pergola, arbor; lane (of trees, etc.); tapestry; **—ник** *m.* lane; tapestry maker; **—ный** *a.* trellis, espalier(ed); tapestry;

—ование *n.* trellis training (of vines); **—овать** *v.* espalier.

шпало/носка *f.* sleeper tongs; **—подбивочный** *a.* track-packing; **—подбойка** *f.* packer, tamper; packing; **—разрушитель** *m.* tie breaker; **—резный** *a.* tie-sawing.

шпальт *m.* opening, gap, cleft.

шпан *m.* span piece, bar.

шпанголит *m.* (min.) spangolite.

шпангоут *m.*, **—ный** *a.* (av., naut.) rib, frame, (joint) ring, ring frame support.

шпандырь *m.* shoemaker's stirrup, holding strap.

шпанка *f.* (bot.) black cherry; (zool.) merino sheep; (ent.) Spanish fly (*Lytta vesicatoria*); blister beetle (*Epicauta*).

шпанрама *f.* (text.) (s)tenter, stretcher.

шпанск/ий *a.* Spanish; **—ая пила** pit saw, cleaving saw; **—ие мушки** Spanish flies, cantharides.

шпар/ить *v.* scald; **—ка** *f.* scalding, blanching.

шпарутка *f.* (text.) temple.

шпат *m.* (min.) spar; (vet.) spavin; **бурый ш.** brown spar, ankerite; **горький ш.** bitter spar, dolomite; **дощатый ш.** tabular spar. wollastonite; **заячий шпат** (vet.) curb; **кубический ш.** cube spar, anhydrite; **малиновый ш.** rhodochrosite; **пенистый ш.** foam spar, aphrite; **полевой ш.** feldspar; **синий ш.** blue spar, lazulite; **тяжёлый ш.** heavy spar, barite, barytes.

шпател/евидный *a.* spatulate; **—ь** *m.* spatula; putty knife.

шпатлевать *see* **шпаклевать**.

шпато/видный *a.* (min.) spathiform, spar(ry); **—вый** *a.* spar(ry), spathic; **—вый железняк** spathic iron, siderite, chalybite; **—ая руда** siderite.

шпахтель *m.* spatula.

шпация *f.* (typ.) space; (naut.) spacing.

шпей/за *f.* (met.) speiss; **—скобальт** *m.* (min.) smaltite; **—совый** *a.* speiss.

шпек *see* **шпик**.

шпенёк *m.* pin, peg, prong.

шперак *m.* beak iron, bickern, horn (of anvil).

шпергель *m.* (bot.) spurry (*Spergula*).

шпиатр *m.* type metal.

шпинг *m.*, **—а** *f.* lard.

шпигат *m.* (naut.) drain hole, scupper; (submarine) flood(ing) port.

шпигель *m.*, **—ный** *a.* (met.) spiegel(eisen); specular (cast) iron; cordovan leather.

шпигов/альный *a.*, **—ание** *n.* larding; **—анный** *a.* larded; **—ать** *v.* lard.

шпик *m.*, **—овать** *v.* lard.

шпилевой *a. of* **шпиль.**

шпил/ечный *a. of* **шпилька**; **—ить** *v.* (fasten with a) pin, pin together.

шпиль *m.* spire, steeple; needle, pin, pivot; reel, capstan, windlass.

шпилька *f.* pin, bolt, stud (bolt); splint pin, cotter pin; peg, dowel; nail, tack; (text.) spindle; **соединение на —х** dowel joint; **установочная ш.** dowel pin.

шпинат *m.*, **—ный** *a.* spinach (*Spinacia*).

шпингалет *m.* latch, catch, bolt.

шпиндель *m.*, **—ный** *a.* spindle, pivot, axle, arbor, shaft, mandrel; stem (of valve); **рассверливающий ш.** boring bar; **—ная бабка** headstock.

шпинел/евый *a.* (min.) spinel; **—лид** *m.* spinellide; **—ь** *f.* spinel; **железистая —ь, железная —ь** iron spinel, hercynite.

шпинтон *m.* tail spindle.

шпион *m.* spy; (min.) twist drill; **—аж** *m.* espionage.

шпитц/лутен *m.*, **—лютте** *n.* (ore concentration) spitzlutte.

шпиц *m.* spire, steeple; Spitz (dog); **—бергенский** *a.* (geog.) Spitsbergen; **—евание** *n.* pointing; **—кастен** *m.* (ore concentration) spitzkasten, funnel box, V-vat; **—лютте** *see* **шпитцлутен**; **ш.-масштаб, —метр** *m.* water gage.

шплейзофен *m.*, **—ное гнездо** (met.) refining hearth.

шплинт *m.* split pin, cotter pin, (slotted) pin; key; splint; forelock; **—ованный** *a.* splinted, etc., *see v.*; **—овать** *v.* splint; fasten with a cotter pin; **—овка** *f.* splinting, etc., *see v.*; forelocking; **—овыдёргиватель** *m.* cotter pin extractor.

шпод *m.* (min.) grapnel.

шпон *m.* (typ.) lead; veneer sheet.

шпонка *f.* dowel, peg, pin; key, spline; gib; joint tongue; sheave, pulley, disk; (hydr.) waterproof packing; **на —х** doweled (joint); **направляющая ш.** spline key, feather key; **скользящая ш.** sliding key; **скреплять —ми** *v.* pin, peg, dowel.

шпоночн/о-долбёжный *a.* key-seating, key-slotting; **ш.-пазовый** *a.* key-groove; keyway-slotting; **ш.-фрезерный** *a.* keyway-milling; **—ый** *a. of* **шпонка**; **—ый паз, —ая канавка** keyway, key bed, key slot.

шпор *m.* heel (of mast).

шпор/а *f.* spur; (wheel) lug, cleat; (track) grouser; (hydr.) cut-off wall; (anat.) calcar; **ш. трахеи** (anat.) carina trachea; **относящийся к —е** (anat.) calcarine; **птичья ш.** (bot.) calcar avis; **—ец** *m.* (bot.) spur, calcar.

шпорник *m.* (bot.) larkspur, delphinium (*Delphinium*).

шпор/ный *a.* calcarine; **—ообразный** *a.* spur-shaped; calcarine; **—ца** *f.*, **—це** *n.* (bot.) calcar, spur; **—цевидный** *a.* spur-like, calcariform.

шпред/ер *m.*, **—инг-машина** *f.* (rubber) spreader; **—инго-вание** *n.*, **—ировка** *f.* spreading, rubberizing.

Шпре(е) (geog.) Spree.

шпренгель *m.* tie rod; **—ный** *a.* trussed, strutted; **—ная система** truss.

шприц *m.* syringe, injector, squirt, sprayer, irrigator; (med.) hypodermic syringe; (grease) gun; wash bottle; **—евание** *n.* extrusion, forcing (out); injection; **—евать** *v.* extrude, force (out); **ш.-машина** *f.* extruder; **ш.-насос** injection pump; **—ованный** *a.* extruded, forced (out); **—ометр** *m.* extrudometer; **ш.-пистолет** spray gun; **ш.-процесс** *m.* extrusion process; **ш.-тюбик** *m.* syringe tube; **—уемость** *f.* extrudability.

шпрот *m.*, **—овый** *a.* (ichth.) sprat (*Sprattus sprattus*).

шпрынка *f.* peg (of shuttle).

шпрюит *m.* bridle (of trawl).

ШПУ *abbr.* (**шахтная пусковая установка**) missile silo.

шпул/едержатель *m.* bobbin holder; **—ечный** *a.*, **—ька** *f.*, **—ьный** *a.*, **—я** *f.* (elec.; text.) spool, bobbin.

шпунт *m.* groove, slot, channel, rabbet; tongue and groove; pile; (naut.) bearding; chisel; **ш. и гребень** tongue and groove; **соединение в ш.** tongue and groove joint; **—губель** *see* **шпунтубель**; **—ина** *f.* pile plank, grooved pile, sheet pile.

шпунтов/альный *a.*, **—ание** *n.* grooving, etc., *see v.*; tongue and groove; **—анный** *a.* grooved; **—ать** *v.* groove, rabbet; (groove and) tongue; match; **—ик** *m.* grooving plane, tongue plane; hammerhead chisel; **—ка** *see* **шпунтование**; **—ой, —ый** *a.* groove(d), tongued and grooved; gutter (tile); **—ый ряд** piling; **—ая стенка** sheet piling, sheeting; **—ое соединение** tongue-and-groove joint, tonguing and grooving.

шпунтубель *m.* grooving plane, rabbet plane, tongue plane, bevelling plane.

шпур *m.* (math.) spur (of matrix); (geom.) trace; (min.) blast hole, bore hole; (met.) furnace outlet, gutter.

шпур/овой *a. of* **шпур**.

шрадан *m.* octamethyl pyrophosphoramide (insecticide).

Шрайвера фильтрпресс Shriver filter press.

шрам *m.* scar, gash, slash, cicatrix; **—ик** *m.* cicatricula, small scar.

шрапнель *f.*, **—ный** *a.* (mil.) shrapnel.

шраффировать *v.* shade, hatch, line.

шредер *m.* shredder.

Шрёдера уравнение Schroeder's equation.

шредеровать *v.* shred.

Шрёдингера волновая функция Schrödinger wave function; **Ш. уравнение** Schrödinger equation, wave equation.

Шривпорт (geog.) Shreveport.

шрифт *m.* type, print, font; character; written records, documents; **прямой ш.** Roman type; **ш.-курсив** italics; **—овой** *a.* type; **—олитейный** *a.* type-casting; **—она-борный** *a.* typesetting; **—оотливной** *a.* typecasting.

шропширский *a.* (geog.) Shropshire.

шрот *m.* small shot; grist, groats; oil cake; **ш.-эффект** *m.* (electron.) Schrott effect, shot effect.

шт. *abbr.* (**штат**) state; staff; (**штаб**) staff, headquarters; (**штольня**) adit, gallery; (**штука**) piece; **ш.т.** *abbr.* (**шкала твёрдости**) hardness scale.

штаб *m.* (mil.) staff, headquarters.

штабел/евание *n.* piling, stacking; **—евать** *v.* pile, stack, stockpile; **—ёр** *m.* piler, stacker, stock-piling machine; **—еразборочный** *a.* unstacking, depalletizing; **—еукладчик** *see* **штабелёр**; **—изирование** *see* **штабелевание**; **—ировать** *see* **штабелевать**; **—ь** *m.* pile, heap, stack, stockpile, bing.

штабик *m.* small bar; (molding) fillet; glass rod.

штабист *m.* staff officer.

штаб/-квартира *f.* headquarters; **—ник** *m.* staff officer; **—ной** *a. of* **штаб**; military.

штаг *m.* (naut.) stay; **ш.-блок** *m.* stayblock.

штакетн/ик *m.*, **—ый** *a.* picket (fence).

штамб *m.*, **—овый** *a.* stem, trunk, body (of tree); bole; timber, stock; (root) stock.

штамм *m.* (genetics) strain, line; breed, race.

штамп *m.* stamp, punch, die, press tool; title block (of a drawing); **—овальный** *a.*, **—ование** *n.* stamping, etc., *see v.*; **—ованный** *a.* stamped, etc., *see v.*; stock (phrase); **—овать** *v.* stamp, punch, blank, form; press; impress, emboss; coin; (drop-)forge; die forge; **—ов-ка** *see* **штампование**; stampings; **—овочный** *a.* stamping; **—овальный** *a.* drop; swage (hammer); **—овоч-ный станок** stamp; punching press; **—овочные работы** punchpress work; **—овщик** *m.* stamp operator, puncher; **—овый** *a.* stamp(ing), punch(ing); die (steel); **—овые изделия** stampings; **—овые краски** printing inks.

штамп-форма *f.* stamping mold.

штанга *f.* rod, bar; pole, beam, arm, boom; probe; link; (valve) stem; (sports) weight; **буровая ш.** drill rod, bore rod; **насосная ш.** pump rod.

штан/ген высоты height gage; **—генглубомер** *m.* depth gage; **—генмикрометр** *m.* micrometric gage; **—генрейсмас, —генрейсмус** *m.* (Vernier) height gage; **—генциркуль** *m.* slide gage, sliding calipers, Vernier caliper; beam compass.

штанго/вращатель *m.* rod rotor; **—вый** *a. of* **штанга**; sucker rod (pump); boom (microphone); **—вая крепь** (min.) roof bolting; **—держатель** *m.* rod adapter.

штанг/-удлинитель *m.* push rod; **—щик** *m.* (surv.) rodman, staffman.

штандоль *m.* stand oil, lithographic oil (polymerized linseed oil).

штан/ец *m.* knife blade, cutting tool, cutting die; **—цевание** *n.* stamping out, punching out; **—цмессер** *m.* die.

штаны *pl.* trousers, breeches.

штапель *m.*, **—ка** *f.*, **—ный** *a.* staple.

штап(ик) *m.* beveling plane.

штарк/а смещение Stark displacement; **—овский** *a.* Stark.

штат *m.* state; staff, personnel.

штатив *m.*, **—ный** *a.* support, mount(ing), frame, stand, holder; rack; base, foot; tripod; **ш. для пробирок** test-tube rack.

штатный *a.* state, official; regular, standard; personnel, staff.

штатский *a.* civil(ian); *m.* civilian.

Штаудингера реакция Staudinger reaction.

штауфер *m.*, **—ка** *f.* Stauffer lubricator, (screw-feed) grease cup.

штейгер *m.* mine boss, head miner.

штейн *m.* (met.) matte.

Штейна-Левенталя синдром (med.) Stein-Leventhal syndrome.

штейнаш *m.* stone ash (a mixture of potash and potassium hydroxide).

штейнбок *m.* (mam.) steenbok (*Raphicerus*).

штейнгут *m.* (cer.) white ware.

Штейнмеца закон (elec.) Steinmetz law.

штейнов/ый *a.* (met.) matte; **—ая лётка** (met.) charging thimble.

штеккер *m.*, **—ный** *a.* (elec.) plug, pin (board).

штеклинг *m.* (agr.) steckling, slip.

штемпел/евание *n.* stamping; **—евать** *v.* stamp, impress; postmark; **—ь** *m.*, **—ьный** *a.* stamp; seal; plunger (of press); **почтовый —ь** postmark.

штенгель *m.* stem, stalk; exhaust tube.

штендер *m.* (min.) pillar, support.

штепсел/евать *v.* (elec.) plug in; **—ь** *m.*, **—ьный** *a.*, **—ьная вилка** plug, adapter; **—ьная колодка** receptacle; **—ьная коробка** junction box; **—ьная панель** (comp.) plugboard; **—ьная розетка** (wall) socket; **—ьное гнездо** (switchboard) jack; **—ьное соединение** plug and socket connection.

Штерна-Герлаха эффект Stern-Gerlach effect.

штёфлер *m.* Stöfler (lunar mountain-walled depression).

штиблеты *pl.* boots, shoes.

штибр *m.* fines.

штил/евой *a.* still, calm; **—евая полоса, —ь** *m.* calm.

штирборт *m.* (naut.) starboard.

штирийский *a.* (geog.) Styrian.

Штифеля способ Stiefel process.

штифной *a.* smooth(-cut) (file).

штифт *m.* pin, spike; stem, pivot; stud; dowel, rod, peg; (elec.) plug; tack; **на —ах** doweled; **—ик** *m.* brad; **—овой** *a.* of **штифт**.

штих *m.* shoe size unit (2/3 cm).

штихель *m.* engraving tool, burin, chisel.

штихмас(с) *m.* inside caliper gage, pin gage, end-measuring rod.

штихпробер *m.* fuel meter.

штицеровка *f.* stitching.

Штоббе конденсация Stobbe condensation.

шток *m.* rod (of piston, etc.); plunger, pin, stem; (anchor) stock; (geol.) boss, stock, body, block (of ore); **—верк** *m.* (min.) stockwork; **—лак** *m.* stick lac.

штокроза *f.* (bot.) hollyhock (*Althaea rosea*).

штольн/я *f.*, **—евый** *a.* (min.) gallery, drift, tunnel; adit, entrance; passage.

штольцит *m.* (min.) stolzite.

штоп/альный *a.*, **—ка** *f.* darning, mending; **—ать** *v.* darn, mend.

штопор *m.* corkscrew; (av.) spin; **крутой ш.** (av.) normal spin; **спуск —ом** spinning; **—ить** *v.* spin; **—ный** *a.* of **штопор**; (free-)spinning (wind tunnel); **—овидный, —ообразный** *a.* spiral.

штопфер *m.* plugger (dental instrument).

штор/а *f.* blind, curtain, shade; (phot.) shutter; **—ка** *dim.* of **штора**; shutter; (cockpit) hood; (camouflage) blind.

шторм *m.* storm, gale, tempest; **—ить** *v.* be stormy; **—овать** *v.* weather the storm; **—овой** *a.* of **шторм**; **—овой ветер** gale; **—трап** *m.* rope ladder, sea ladder, Jacob's ladder.

шторн/о-щелевой *a.* (phot.) focal-plane (shutter); **—ый** *a.* of **штора**; focal-plane.

штоссель *m.* rammer; tappet, slide.

штоф *m.*, **—ный** *a.* (text.) damask; old unit of liquid measure (1.23 liter).

штранг-пресс *m.* extruder.

штранц *m.* strand, beach.

штраф *m.* fine, penalty; charge; **—ной** *a.* penal; **—овать** *v.* fine.

штрейкбрехер *m.* strike breaker, scab.

штрек *m.* (min.) drift, drive, gallery; (cross) gate, entry; (adit) level; **выемка —ами** drift mining, drifting; **промежуточный ш.** subdrift; **—обурильный** *a.* tunneling; **—овый** *a.* of **штрек**; gateway, gate-end (conveyer); **—опроходческий** *a.* drifting.

Штреккера реакция Strecker reaction.

штригель *m.* (agr.) weeding harrow.

штрипка *f.* strap.

штрипс *m.*, **—овый** *a.* (met.) strip; (rolling) skelp; **—овая заготовка** feed.

штрих *m.* stroke, line, dash; mark, accent, touch; trait, feature; hatchure; stria, streak, groove, channel; (math.) prime; (Sheffer) stroke symbol; **со —ом** primed; **—диаграмма** *f.* X-ray diffraction diagram; **—ный** *a.* (cross-)hatched, etc., *see v.*; **—оватость** *f.* (phyt.) streak (mosaic); streak disease; striation; **—оватый** *a.* hatched, striated; **—овать** *v.* (cross)hatch, shade; (math.) prime; **—овка** *f.* hatch(ing), hatchure, shading, striation; **—овой** *a.* of **штрих**; broken, dashed (line); lined, checkered (rod); line (copy); **—овой код** barcode; **—передача** *f.* facsimile transmission; **ш.-пунктир** *m.*, **—пунктирная линия** dot-and-dash line; **ш.-точечный пунктир** dot-and-dash line.

штроп *m.* link.

штрутидеа *f.* (orn.) apostle-bird (*Struthidea cinerea*).

Штрюмпеля феномен (med.) Strümpell phenomenon.

штудировать *v.* study.

штука *f.* thing; piece, sample, specimen, item.

штукатур *m.* plasterer; **—ить** *v.* plaster, stucco; **—ка** *f.* plaster(ing), stucco; **—ный** *a.* plaster(ing), stucco; lathe (nail); **—ный раствор** plaster mix.

штуков/ать *v.* piece, patch, repair, mend; fine-draw; **—ка** *f.* piecing, etc., *see v.*

штукофен *m.* (met.) high bloomery furnace.

штуп *m.* stupp, mercurial soot.

штурвал *m.* pilot wheel, helm; steering wheel; (av.) control stick; (pipeline) handwheel, handle; star wheel; turnstile; **—ьная** *f.* pilot's cabin; **—ьный** *a.* of **штурвал**; **—ьчик** *m.* star knob.

штурм *m.* assault, attack.

штурман *m.* navigator; **ш.-корректировщик** *m.* navigator observer; **ш.-оператор РЛС** *m.* radar navigator; **ш.-радист** *m.* radio operator; **—ский** *a.* navigator's; nautical (equipment); **—ская рубка** chart house, pilot house; **—ская служба** navigation.

штурмов/ать *v.* attack, assault, storm, rush; conquer; **—ик** *m.* attack plane; **—ка** *f.* (low-flying) attack; **—ой** *a. of* **штурм**; scaling (ladder); **—щина** *f.* rush work.

штуртрос *m.* (naut.) tiller line.

Штутгарт (geog.) Stuttgart.

штуф *m.*, **—ный** *a.* lump (of ore or rock).

штуцер *m.*, **—ный** *a.* connecting pipe, (pipe) connection, pipe adapter with outside thread, coupling, union, sleeve, nipple; fitting, adapter; (condenser) tube; (oil wells) flow nipple, flow regulator.

штуч/ка *dim. of* **штука**; **—ный** *a. of* **штука**; (by the) piece, per unit; single, individual; inlaid; **—ная плата** piece rate; **—ная работа** piecework.

штыб *m.* culm, coal fines, breeze, coal slack, coal dust, powdered coal; **—оотбрасыватель, —оотвал** *m.* culm remover.

штык *m.* bayonet; spit; (met.) bar, ingot, pig; (agr.) spade's depth.

штыков/ание *n.*, **—ка** *f.* spading up; **—ать** *v.* spade up, turn over (soil).

штыков/ой, —ый *a. of* **штык**; **ш. затвор** bayonet lock, bayonet catch; **ш. контакт** (elec.) plug; **—ая медь** copper bar.

штыр/евой *a. of* **штырь**; collapsible-whip (antenna); **—ёк** *m.* (elec.) aligning plug; (base) pin; **—ь** *m.* pin, dowel; prong; (landing) spike; pintle, pivot pin; probe; cramp (iron), clincher; (electrolyzer) clamp; **центральный —ь** central pivot; king pillar; **—ька** *f. dim. of* **штырь**; pin, sprocket.

штэк-фильтр *m.* (min.) filter drain (perforated pipe in wall).

Штюве диаграмма Stüve diagram.

шуб/а *f.* fur (coat); **—ка** *dim. of* **шуба**; **—ный** *a.* fur; **—ная моль** (ent.) casemaking clothes moth (*Tinea pellionella*).

шубригель *m.* slide gage, sliding calipers.

шубункин *m.* (ichth.) shubunkin, goldfish.

шуг/а *f.* slush ice, sludge, frazil ice, floating anchor ice; **—осброс** *m.* ice chute, ice slide; **—оход** *m.* moving sludge.

шуллю (ichth.) European pikeperch (*Lucioperca lucioperca*).

Шульце-Гарди правило Schulze-Hardy rule (of colloid coagulation).

шум *m.* noise, sound; roar(ing), hum; bruit, (heart) murmur; tinnitus; **ш. над аортой** (med.) aortic murmur; **ш. плеска** splashing sound.

шум/ен *sh. m. of* **шумный**; **—еть** *v.* make noise, be noisy; **—иха** *f.* uproar, racket; spangle, tinsel; **—ливость** *f.* noisiness; **—ливый** *a.* noisy; **—но** *adv.* noisily; **—ность** *f.* noisiness; (signal) interference; **—ный** *a.* noisy, loud; **—овик** *m.* (rad.) sound man; **—овка** *f.* crackle; skimmer, ladle.

шумо/вой *a.* noise, noisy, hum; **ш. фон** background noise; **—глушающий** *a.* sound-suppressing; **—глушение** *n.* noise abatement, sound suppression; **—(за)-глушитель** *m.* muffler, silencer, noise suppressor; (rad.) anti-hum; **—излучение** *n.* noise emission;

—имитационный *a.* noise deceptive, sound (device); **—к** *dim. of* **шум**; **—мер** *m.* noise gage, sound(-level) meter; **—непроницаемый** *a.* soundproof; **—пеленгатор** *m.* (naut.) directional hydrophone, passive sonar, sound locator, submarine detector; **—подавление** *n.* noise suppression; **—подавляющий** *a.* noise-suppressing; **—подобный** *a.* noise-type (signal).

шум/фактор *m.* noise factor; **—ы** *pl.* noise.

шумящий *a.* noisy; roaring (flame); (vet.) emphysematous (carbuncle).

шунт *m.* shunt; by-pass; (biochem.) (glucose oxidative) breakdown.

шунтир/ование *n.* (elec.) shunting, etc., *see v.*; **—ованный** *a.* shunted, etc., *see v.*; **—овать** *v.* shunt, by-pass, bridge; **—ующий** *a.* shunting, etc., *see v.*; by-pass; branch (resistance).

шунт-мотор *m.* shunt-wound motor.

шунто/вать *see* **шунтировать**; **—вой** *a.* shunt; (mach.) shunt-wound; by-pass; (med.) derivative (circulation); **—мер** *m.* shunt meter.

шуров/ание *n.* rabbling, etc., *see v.*; **—анный** *a.* rabbled, etc., *see v.*; **—ать** *v.* rabble, stir, poke; stoke; scrub, scour; **—ка** *see* **шурование**; rabble; **подрезные —ки** (boilers) prickets, blades; **—ой, —очный** *a.* rabbling, etc., *see v.*; rabble; **—очный лом, —очный сокол** rabble, poker; **—очное приспособление** stirrer, rabble.

шуруп *m.* wood screw.

шурующий *pr. act. part. of* **шуровать.**

шурф *m.* perforation, hole; (min.) prospecting pit, (bore) pit; **—обур** *m.* portable drill; **—ование** *n.* prospecting, pitting, pit sampling; **—овать** *v.* prospect, make (test) pits, perforate; **—овка** *see* **шурфование**; **—овочный** *a.* pitting, boring, perforating; **—овщик** *m.* digger, excavator.

шурш/ание *n.*, **—ащий** *a.* crackling, rustling, crepitation; **—ать** *v.* crackle, rustle, crepitate, creak.

шуст *m.* auger.

шут/ить *v.*, **—ка** *f.* jest, joke; **—очный** *a.* laughing, trifling (matter); **—я** *pr. ger.* in jest; easily; **не —я** in earnest.

шуттель-аппарат *m.* shaker, shake table.

шутя *pr. ger. of* **шутить.**

шуцлак *m.* protective lacquer.

шучья трава (bot.) Polygonum amphibium.

шх. *abbr.* (**шахта**) mine, shaft.

шхеры *pl.* sea cliffs, rocks, skerries.

шхуна *f.* schooner.

шь/ёт *pr. 3 sing. of* **шить**; **—ют** *pr. 3 pl.*; **—ющий** *a.* sewing.

шэд *m.*, **американский ш.** (American) shad (*Alosa sapidissima*); **индийский ш.** Chinese herring (*Ilisha elongata*).

шэнноновский *see* **шеннон.**

шэпинг *see* **шепинг.**

шютте *n.* (phyt.) needle cast, needle-shedding disease.

шюттелирование *n.* shuttling.

шюттель-аппарат *see* **шуттель-аппарат.**

шяуляйский *a.* (geog.) Shaulyai (in Lithuania).

Щ

щавелевокисл/ый *a.* oxalic acid; oxalate (of); **щ. анилин** aniline oxalate; **щ. ряд** oxalic acid series; **—ая соль** oxalate; **кислая —ая соль** bioxalate.

щавелево/медная соль cupric oxalate; **—уксусный** *a.* oxalacetic (acid); **—этиловый эфир** ethyl oxalate; **—янтарный** *a.* oxalosuccinic (acid).

щавелев/ый *a.* oxalic; (bot.) sorrel; **—ая кислота** oxalic acid, ethanedioic acid; **соль —ой кислоты** oxalate; **кислая соль —ой кислоты** bioxalate.

щавел/ёк *m.* (bot.) sheep sorrel (*Rumex acetosella*); **—ь** *m.*, **—ьник** *m.*, **—ьный** *a.* sorrel, dock (*Rumex*); **—ьник** *m.* sorrel soup.

щад/итель *m.* shock absorber; **—ительный**, **—ящий** *a.* sparing; gentle, conservative, mild; bland (diet); **—ить** *v.* spare.

щеб/енить *v.* fill with rubble, ballast; **—ёнка** *see* **щебень**; **—ёночный** *a.* rubble; **—ёночный слой** ballast (of road bed); **—ёнчатый** *a.* rubbly.

щебень *m.* rubble, crushed or broken stone, crushed or broken rock, rock debris; chip(ping)s; gravel, ballast; (geol.) detritus; **щ. из бетона** broken concrete; **мелкий щ.** rubble, chippings; **шлаковый щ.** broken slag.

щебет *m.*, **—ание** *n.* (orn.) twitter(ing), chirp(ing); **—ать** *v.* twitter, chirp; **—унья** *f.* chirping bird.

щебн/еватый; **—истый** *a.* schistose; (geol.) rubbly, detrital; stony (clay); skeleton (soil); **—евой** *a. of* **щебень.**

щебрушка *f.* (bot.) basil thyme (*Acinos*).

щеврица *f.* (orn.) pipit (*Anthus*).

щег/лёнок *m.* (orn.) goldfinch fledgeling; **—ловка** *f.* female goldfinch; **—лячий** *a.*, **—ол** *m.* goldfinch (*Carduelis c.*).

щёголь *m.* (orn.) spotted redshank (*Tringa erythropus*); dandy, fop.

щедрин(к)а *f.* pockmark.

щедр/ость, **—ота** *f.* liberality, generosity; **—ый** *a.* liberal, generous.

щей *gen. of* **щи.**

щека *f.* cheek; (vise) jaw; side(piece), side wall; (pulley) face; (crank) web; (harness) cheekpiece; (anat.) cheek, bucca, mala.

щёки *pl.* buccae; (ent.) genae.

щек/овой *a. of* **щека**; overhanging, side (wall); (anat.) buccal; **—одробилка** *f.* (mach.) jawbreaker.

щеколда *f.* latch, catch, pawl, finger, trigger, trip gear, tripping latch; lock, (locking) bar; (window) fastener.

щеко/образный *a.* jaw-shaped; **—рог** *m.* (ichth.) spine-cheek (*Bovichthys*); **—роги**, **—роговые** *pl.* Bovichthyidae.

щёкот *m.* (orn.) warbling, trilling.

щекот/ание *n.* tickling; *see* **щёкот;** **—ать** *v.* tickle; (orn.) warble, trill; **—ка** *f.* tickling; *see* **щёкот; —ливый** *a.* ticklish; delicate.

щел. *abbr.* **(щелочной)** alkaline.

щеле/вание *n.* slotting, slitting; **—ватый** *a.* fissury, fractured; **—видный** *a.* slit-like, rimiform; fissured; chink-shaped; **—вой** *a. of* **щель**; slot(ted); slotting (tool); slit; crevice (corrosion); (biol.) rimose, fissure(d); **—вая программа** (spectroscopy) slit function; **кольцевая —вая форсунка** ring-gap nozzle; **—жаберные** *pl.* (ichth.) hornsharks (*Heterodontidae*); **—зуб** *m.* (mam.) Solenodon; **—зубы(е)** *pl.* Solenodontidae; **—й** *gen. pl. of* **щель**; **—нёбный** *a.* (med.) cleft palate; **—нос(ов)ые** *pl.* (mam.) slit-faced bats (*Nycteridae*); **—образный** *a.* fissure-like, fissuriform.

щел.-зем. *abbr.* **(щелочноземельный).**

щел/и *gen., pl., etc., of* **щель; —ина** *see* **щель; —истый** *a.* rimose, full of fissures; chinky.

щёлк *m.* click, snap.

щёлка *dim. of* **щель.**

щёлк/ание, **—анье** *n.* clicking, etc., *see* v.; (orn.) trill, jug; **—ать**, **—нуть** *v.* click, snap, pop; crack (seeds); chatter (of teeth); flick; (vet.) over-reach (hooves); trill, jug.

щелковск/ий *a.* (chem.) Shchelkovo; **—ая зелень** a Paris green (insecticide).

щелк/отня *f.* clicking; **—ун** *m.* (seed) cracker; (ent.) click beetle; **—унчик** *m.* Limonius; Hypnoidus; **—уны** *pl.* Elateridae.

щёлок *m.* lye, caustic, alkali; liquor; *gen. pl. of* **щёлка; калийный щ.** potassium hydroxide; **натронный щ.** soda liquor, caustic soda solution; **чёрный щ.** black (sulfate) liquor; **—оотделитель** *m.* liquor separator.

щёлоче— *prefix* alkali; **—любивый** *a.* (biol.) basiphilous.

щелочение *n.* alkalization; lixiviation.

щёлоче/растворимость *f.* alkali solubility; **—растворимый** *a.* alkali-soluble; **—стойкий**, **—упорный**, **—устойчивый** *a.* alkali-proof, alkali-resistant; **—стойкость** *f.* alkali resistance or stability.

щёлочить *v.* alkalize; lixiviate.

щёлочка *dim. of* **щель.**

щёлочно— *prefix* alkali—; **—земельный** *a.* alkaline-earth; **щ.-известковый** *a.* (geol.) alkali-lime.

щелоч/ной *a.* alkali(ne), alkalescent, basic; caustic; **—ной резерв** standard bicarbonate; **—ная земля** alkali earth.

щёлоч/но-кислотный *a.* acid-base (equilibrium); **—норастворимый** *a.* alkali-soluble; **—нореагирующий** *a.* alkaline reacting; **—ность** *f.* alkalinity; **—ноупорный**, **—ноустойчивый** *a.* alkali-proof, alkali-resistant, alkali-resisting; **—ь** *f.* alkali, base; lye; caustic; **калиевая —ь** potassium hydroxide.

щелчок *m.* snap, click; **двойной щ.** (comp.) double-click (of mouse button).

щель *f.* chink, slit, slot, crack, fissure, cleft, split; aperture, gap, opening; peephole; (mil.) slit trench, foxhole; (anat.) rima, hiatus; crena, notch; **щ. связи** (radar) coupling aperture; **глазная щ.** (anat.) palpebral fissure.

щем/ить *v.* pinch; smart; **—ление** *n.* pinching; smarting; **—ло** *n.* vise, press; brace (of drill); **—ящий** *a.* pinching; smarting; gripping (pain).

щен/ение *n.* (zool.) whelping, etc., *see* v.; **—иться** *v.* whelp, pup, cub, bear a litter; **—ка** *see* **щенение.**

щённа(я) *a.* pregnant, with pup.

щен/ок *m.* puppy, cub, whelp; **—ята** *pl.*; **—ячий** *a. of* **щенок.**

щеп/а *f.* (wood) chip(s), shavings, splinters, slivers; kindling; (roofing) shingle; **—ально-драночный** *a.* peeling (machine); **—альный** *a.* chipping, etc., *see* v.; **—ан(н)ый** *a.* chipped, etc., *see* v.; **—ать** *v.* chip, splinter, split (off), cleave; bite, sting, smart.

щепетильный *a.* scrupulous, punctilious.

щеп/ить *see* **щепать; —ка** *f.* chip, sliver, splinter, shaving; *pl.* kindling; **—коловитель** *m.*, **—ловка** *f.* (paper) sliver screen; **—ной** *a. of* **щепа; —ные изделия** light wood materials; **—одралка** *f.* chip maker, wood-chipping machine.

щепот/ка, **—очка**, **—ь** *f.* pinch.

щепо/уловитель *m.* sliver catcher; **—чка** *dim. of* **щепка.**

щерб/а *see* **щербин(к)а;** chip; **—атый** *a.* chipped; pockmarked; scarred; **—ин(к)а** *f.* pockmark, pit, scar; cut, crack, chipped place, chink, crevice, gap, breach; notch.

щерить *v.* bare (one's teeth).

щетин/а *f.* bristle, stubble; seta; **—ист(о)—** chaet(o)—; **—истоволосистый** *a.* hispid; **—истолистный** *a.* chaetophyllous, hirtifolious; **—истый** *a.* bristly, setaceous; **—иться** *v.* bristle; **—ка** *f.* chaeta, seta, bristle; **плёнчатая —ка** *f.* (bot.) fimbrilla; **—ко—** *see* **щетино—; —ник** *m.* bristle grass (*Setaria*); **—ный** *a. of* **щетина; —ные** *pl.* (mam.) swine family (*Suidae*);

—о— *prefix* seti—, bristle; **—оватый** *a.* bristly; **—овидный** *a.* setiform; setaceous, bristly; **—озуб-(ов)ые** *pl.* (ichth.) butterflyfishes (*Chaetodontidae*); **—оносный** *a.* setigerous; **—ообразный** *a.* setiform; **—оплодник** *m.* (bot.) Chaetosciadium; **—охвостки, —охвостые** *pl.* (ent.) bristletails, silverfish (*Thysanura*); **—очка** *dim.* of **щетинка,** *f.* fine bristle.

щёт/ка *f.* brush; (windshield) wiper; tuft (of hair); (horse) fetlock; **искрение —ок** (elec.) brush sparking; **—ковидный, —кообразный** *a.* (ent.) strigilate; penicillate; brush-like; **—кодержатель** *m.* brush holder; **—кохвост** *m.* (mam.) vulpine phalanger (*Trichosurus vulpecula*); **—ок** *m. gen. pl.* of **щётка; —очка** *dim.* of **щётка;** *f.* penicillus; tuft; **—очник** *m.* brush maker; **—очный** *a.* of **щётка.**

щеть *f.* (bot.) Nardus stricta.

щецинский *a.* (geog.) Szczecin.

щёч/ка *dim.* of **щека;** *f.* stock, side plate; **—но—** *prefix* (anat.) bucco—; **—но-глоточный** *a.* buccopharyngeal; **—ный** *a.* of **щека;** cheek, buccal, malar, zygomatic; **—ная мышца** (anat.) buccinator.

щи *pl.* cabbage soup.

щикол(от)ка *f.* (anat.) malleolus, ankle.

щип/альный *a.,* **—ание** *n.* plucking, etc., *see v.;* **—ан(н)ый** *a.* plucked, etc., *see v.;* **—ать** *v.* pluck; pinch, nip; shred; nibble, crop, browse (on); **—аться** *v.* be plucked, etc.; pinch; **—ец** *m.* gable; muzzle (of dog); **—ка** *see* **щипание; —нуть** *see* **щипать; —овка** *f.* (ichth.) spined loach (*Cobitis*); **—овки** *pl.* Cobitidae; **—ок** *m.* pinch(ing), nip, tweak; **—еобразный** *a.* forcipate, forceps-like; **—цовый** *a.* of **щипцы;** gable (roof); **—цы** *pl.* forceps, tongs, pincers, pliers; extractor; (electrode) holder; **—чики** *pl.* forceps, pincers, tweezers, nippers.

щирица *f.* (bot.) amaranth.

щит *m.* shield, screen, blind; (switch)board, panel; (hydr.) gate; guard; (display) rack; (ice) sheet; (cloud) canopy; (snow) fence; (zool.) scutum; (pal.) carapace; (turtle) shell; (bot.) shieldwort (*Peltaria*); **щ. от грязи** mudguard; **щ. управления** control panel; **брюшной щ.** plastron (of turtle); **головной щ.** (ent.) clypeus.

щитень *m.* (crust.) tadpole shrimp (*Lepidurus*).

щит/ик *m.* (ent.) scutellum; (bot.) stylostegium; **—ки** *pl.* (zool.) scuta, shields; **—коватый, —ковидный** *a.* (bot.) corymbose; corymbiform; **—ковые** *pl.* (pal.) Ostracodermi; **—ковый** *a.* of **щиток; —коносный** *a.* corymbiferous; **—ни** *pl.* (crust.) Triopsidae; **—ники** *pl.* stink bugs (*Pentatomidae*); **—ница** *f.* (bot.) Clypeola;

—о— *pref. see* **щитовидно—; —овидки** *pl.* (ent.) Ostomatidae; **—овидно—** *pref.* (bot.) peltati—; scuti— (shield); (anat.) thyro—; **—видно-подъязычный** *a.* thyrohyoid; **—овидный** *a.* shield-shaped, scutiform, scutellate; (anat.) thyroid (gland); (bot.) peltate; **—овка** *f.* scale insect; **калифорнийская щ.** San Jose scale; **—овки** *pl.* (ent.) Diaspididae; **—овник** *m.* (bot.) wood fern (*Dryopteris*).

щит/овой *a.* of **щит;** panelboard (construction); **—овой затвор** sluice gate; **—ок** *m.* shield, screen, cover; dashboard, panelboard, (instrument) board; (av.) flap; (biol.) scutellum; (zool.) scutum; (bot.) cyme, corymb; (anat.) apophysis; **—ок-жучок** *m.* (zool.) scute; **—олистник** *m.* (bot.) water pennywort (*Hydrocotyle*); **—олистный** *a.* (bot.) scutifolious; **—омордник** *m.* (herp.) Ancistrodon; **—онадгортанный** *a.* (anat.) thyroepiglottic; **—оносец** *m.* (mam.) armadillo (*Dasypus*); **—носка** *f.* leaf beetle (*Cassida*); **—оноски, —оносковые** *pl.* Cassidinae; **—ообразный** *a.* shield-shaped, scutellate; **—оподъязычный** *a.* (anat.) thyrohyoid; **—охвостики, —охвостые** *pl.* (herp.) Uropeltidae.

щокур *m.* (ichth.) whitefish (*Coregonus*).

щук/а *f.* (ichth.) pike (*Esox*); **—и, —овые** *pl.* Esocidae.

щуп *m.* feeler, probe; dip rod, dip stick; tracer, detector; (met.) test rod, trial rod; thickness gage, clearance gage; (grain) sampler; (zool.) palp, tentacle; **—ак** *see* **щука; —алец** *m.* (text.) feeler; **—альный** *a.* feeler, feeling, probing; **—альце** *n.* (zool.) tentacle, feeler; antenna; **—альцевые** (zool.) *pl.* Tentaculata; **—альцежвалы** *pl.* (zool.) Chelicerae; **—альценогие** *pl.* (zool.) Palpigrada; **—ание, —анье** *n.* feeling, etc., *see v.;* **—ать** *v.* feel, touch, palpate, probe; grope (one's way); **—ик** (zool.) *see* **щупальце;** (tech.) *m.* feeler gage.

щупл/ость *f.* undeveloped state (of seeds); **—ый** *a.* undersized, puny, meager, shriveled.

щур *m.* (orn.) pine grosbeak (*Pinicola*).

щур/ата *pl.* (ichth.) young pikes; **—ёнок** *dim.* of **щука;** *m.* (orn.) bee eater's fledgeling.

щурить *v.* screw up (eyes), squint.

щурк/а *f.* (orn.) bee-eater (*Merops*); **—и, —овые** *pl.* Meropidae.

щуч/ий *a.* of **щука; —ина** *f.* pike flesh; **—ка** *dim.* of **щука;** *f.* tussock grass (*Deschampsia caespitosa*); **—ник** *m.* tussock grass meadow; **—ьи** *pl.* (ichth.) pikes (*Esocidae*); **—ья трава** *f.* water knotweed (*Polygonum amphibium*).

Э

э *abbr.* **(электрон)** electron; **(эрг)** erg; **(эрстед)** oersted; **(эфир)** ether; ester.

эбенов/ые *pl.* (bot.) Ebenaceae; **—ый** *a.* ebony.

Эбергарда явление (phot.) Eberhard effect.

эбонит *m.,* **—овый** *a.* ebonite, hard rubber.

эбул(л)ио/метр *m.* ebulliometer; **—скоп** *m.* ebullioscope; **—скопический** *a.* ebullioscopic, boiling (constant); boiling point (method); **—скопия** *f.* ebullioscopy.

эбурнеация *f.* (med.) eburnation (of bones).

эв *abbr.* **(электрон-вольт)** electron volt.

эв— *prefix* eu—, good, well; (bot., zool.) most typical, ortho—; *see also under* **эй—** and **эу—.**

эвак/опункт *m.* evacuation center; **—приёмник** clearing station; **—уационный** *a.* evacuation; wrecker, salvage (equipment); **—уация** *f.* evacuation; wrecking, clearing away (of damaged vehicles); **—уированный** *a.* evacuated, etc., *see v.;* **—уировать** *v.* evacuate, empty, exhaust; wreck, clear away.

эвальвация *f.* evaluation, estimation.

эвант/иевый, —овый *a.* (bot.) euanthic.

эвапор/атор *m.* evaporator; **—ация** *f.* evaporation, vaporization; **—иметр, —ометр** *m.* (meteor.) evaporimeter; **—иты** *pl.* (geol.) evaporites; **—ография** *f.* evaporography.

эв-барн *abbr.* **(электрон-вольт барн)** electron-volt barn.

эвгедральн/ость *f.* (petr.) euhedral character; **—ый** *a.* euhedral, automorphic.

эвген— *see* **эйген—; —ия** *f.* (bot.) Eugenia; **—ол** *m.* (pharm.) eugenol.

эвглен/а *f.* (prot.) Euglena; **—овые** *pl.* Euglenoidea.

эвгранитовый *a.* (geol.) eugranitic.

эвдиометр *m.* eudiometer; **—ический** *a.* eudiometric; **—ия** *f.* eudiometry, gasometry, gasometric analysis.

эвдорина *f.* (prot.) Eudorina.

эвенкийский *a.* Tungus, Evenk (a Mongoloid people of Eastern Siberia).

эвентуальный *a.* eventual.

эверглейдс *m.* (geog.) Everglades.

эверитова соль *f.* Everitt's salt, potassium ferrous ferrocyanide.

эверман(н)елловые *pl.* saber-toothed fishes (*Evermanellidae*).

эвер/ниин *m.* everniine; **—ниновый** *a.* everninic, evernesic (acid); **—ния** *f.* (bot.) Evernia; **—новый** *a.* evernic (acid); **—нуровый** *a.* evernuric.

эверсманния *f.* (bot.) Eversmannia.

эвипал *m.* (pharm.) Evipal, hexobarbital.

эвисцерация *f.* (med.) evisceration, exenteration.

эвкаин *m.* (chem.) eucaine.

эвкалипт *m.*, **—овый** *a.* (bot.) eucalyptus; **—ол** *m.* (pharm.) eucalyptol, cineole.

эвкар/иды *pl.* (crust.) Eucarida.

эвкариотический *a.* (gen.) eukaryotic.

эвкарпический *a.* (bot.) eucarpic.

эвклидовый *a.* Euclidean.

эв/климакс *m.* (bot.) euclimax.

эв/кодал *m.* Eucodal, dihydrohydroxycodeinone hydrochloride; **—кодеин** *m.* eucodeine, methyl codeine bromide; **—коллоид** *m.* eucolloid, true colloid.

эв/коммия *see* **эйком(м)ия; —конический** *a.* (zool.) eucone.

эвлитораль *f.* (ecol.) eulittoral, upper littoral.

ЭВМ *abbr.* (**электронная вычислительная машина**) computer.

эвмезофильный *a.* (bot.) eumesophilous.

эвменэс *m.* (ent.) wasps (*Eumenes*).

эвнатрол *m.* eunatrol, sodium oleate.

эв/нице *f.* (zool.) palolo worm (*Eunice*); **—ницевые, —нициды** *pl.* Eunicidae; **—ное** *n.* (zool.) Eunoë.

эвод/иамин *m.* evodiamine; **—ия** *f.* (bot.) Euodia.

эвока/тор *m.* (bioch.) evocator; morphogenic hormone; **—ция** (bioch.) evocation.

эвольвент/а *f.* involute (of circle); evolute, evolvent; **—ный** *a.* (mech.) involute (gearing), standard (tooth); **—ная форсунка** involute burner, involute injector; **—ометр** *m.* involute measuring machine.

эволют/а *f.*, **—ный** *a.* (geom.) evolute.

эволюц/ионизм *m.* theory of evolution, evolutionism; **—ионировать** *v.* evolve, develop, unfold; evolutionize; **—ионист** *m.* evolutionist; **—ионист(иче)ский** *a.* evolutionist(ic); **—ионный** *a.* evolution(ary); **—ирующий** *a.* evolving; **—ия** *f.* evolution.

эвпа/рин *m.* euparin; **—торин** *m.* eupatorine (alkaloid); eupatorin (glucoside).

эвплоид/ия *f.* (gen.) euploidy; **—ный** *a.* euploid.

эвпроктис *m.* (ent.) moth (*Euproctis*).

эври— *prefix* eury— (wide, broad); **—батный** *a.* (ecol.) eurybathic; **—бионтный** *a.* (biol.) eurybiontic; **—валент** *m.* (bot.) euryvalent, eurytopic plant; **—галинный** *a.* (biol.) euryhalin(e).

эвригастер *m.* (ent.) Eurygaster.

эври/ксенный *a.* (biol.) euryxenous; **—ксерофильный** *a.* (biol.) euryxerophilous; **—мезофильный** *a.* (biol.) eurymesophilous; **—ойкный** *a.* (ecol.) euryoecic, euryoecious.

эвриптериды *pl.* (pal.) Eurypterida.

эврист/ика *f.*, **—ический** *a.* heuristic.

эври/термный *a.* (biol.) eurythermal; **—томуха** *f.* eurytomid, chalcid fly; **—топный** *a.* (biol.) eurytopic; **—трема** *f.* (zool.) trematode (*Eurytrema*); **—трем(ат)оз** *m.* (vet.) Eurytrema pancreaticum infection; **—трофный** *a.* (biol.) eurytrophic; **—фагический, —фагный** *a.* (zool.) euryphagous; **—фотический** *a.* (biol.) euryphotic; **—хорный** *a.* (bot.) eurychorous, eurychoric.

эвспорангиатный *a.* (bot.) eusporangiate.

эвстатический *a.* (geol.) eustatic.

эвстела *a.* (bot.) eustele.

эвтаксит *m.* (petr.) eutaxite; **—овый** *a.* eutaxitic, banded (structure).

эвтект/ика *f.* eutectic(s); **—ический** *a.* eutectic; **—оид** *m.*, **—оидный** *a.* (met.) eutectoid; **—тоидный распад** eutectoid transition; **—офировый** *a.* eutectophyric.

эвтонический *a.* (chem.) eutonic.

эвтроф *m.* (bot.) eutroph, eutrophic plant; **—ный** *a.* (biol.) eutrophic; (med.) healthily nutritious.

эвфаузи/иды, —евые *pl.*(crust.) krills (*Euphausiacea*).

эвфеника *f.* (ecol.) euthenics.

эвфилл *m.* (bot.) euphyll, true leaf.

эвфорб/ий *m.* euphorbium (resin); **—ин** *m.* euphorbin; **—иновый** *a.* euphorbic (acid).

эвфот/ический *a.* (ocean.) euphotic; **—ометрический** *a.* (bot.) euphotometric.

эвциклический *a.* (bot.) eucyclic.

эвшель *m.* (met.) zaffer (a cobalt oxide).

эгагропил/а *f.* (vet.) hair ball, aegagropila; (bot.) algae (*Aegagropila*); **—ьный** *a.* aegagropilous.

эгализ/атор *m.* (dyeing) leveling agent; **—ированный** *a.* blended; (dyes) leveled; **—ировать** *v.* blend; level; **—ирующий** *a.* blending; leveling.

Эгейское море the Aegean Sea.

эгилопс *m.* (bot.) Aegilops.

эго— *prefix* ego—; **—бронхофония** *f.* (med.) egobronchophony; **—истический, —истичный** *a.* egoistic, self-centered, narrow; **—фония** *f.* (med.) egophony; **—центрический** *a.* egocentric, self-centered.

эгретки *pl.* (orn.) nuptial plume.

эд *abbr.* (**электродвигатель**) electric motor.

ЭДА-комплекс (**электронный донорно-акцепторный комплекс**) EDA (electron-donor-acceptor) complex, adduct.

эдаф/ический *a.* (plant ecology) edaphic, soil (factor); **—ология** *f.* edaphology; **—он** *m.* edaphon, soil fauna; **—онический** *a.* edaphic; **—офит** *m.* (bot.) edaphophyte.

эдеагус *m.* (ent.) aedeagus.

эдельвейс *m.* (bot.) edelweiss (*Leontopodium alpinium*).

эдема *f.* (med.) edema.

эдестин *m.* (bot.) edestin.

эджер *m.* edger.

эдикт *m.* edict.

эдильбаевская овца *f.* (mam.) Edilbaev sheep.

эдификатор *m.* (bot.) edificator.

эдс, э.д.с., ЭДС *abbr.* (**электродвижущая сила**) electromotive force, emf; **э.д.с. Пельтье** Peltier emf.

ЭДТ *abbr.* (**этилендиаминтартрат**) ethylenediaminetartrate; **ЭДТА** *abbr.* (**этилендиаминтетраацетат**) ethylenediaminetetraacetate; **ЭДТК, ЭДТУ** *abbr.* (**этилендиаминтетрауксусная кислота**) ethylenediaminetetraacetic acid.

Эдулджи корреляция *f.* (chem.) Eduljee correlation.

э.е. *abbr.* (**электростатическая единица**) electrostatic unit; (**энтропийная единица**) entropy unit.

э. ед. *abbr.* (**электронная единица**) electronic unit.

эжек/тируемый *a.* ejected; driven (flow); **—тирующий**

a. ejecting; driving (flow); —**тор** *m.* ejector; lift-out attachment, grapnel; beam extractor (accelerator); —**торный** *a.*, —**ция** *f.* ejection.

эзенбековая кислота esenbeckic acid.

эзер/идин *m.* eseridine; —**ин** *m.*, —**иновый** *a.* eserine, physostigmine.

эзо/бе *n.* (bot.) esobe, azonal soil; —**терический** *a.* esoteric; —**тропия** *f.* (ophth.) esotropia.

эзофаг/ит *m.* (med.) esophagitis; —**о** *prefix* (med.) esophag(o)— (esophagus, esophageal); —**огастро**— *prefix* (med.) esophagogastro—; —**омикоз** *m.* (med.) esophagomycosis; —**оскопия** *f.* esophagoscopy; —**остома** *f.* (zool.) Oesophagostomum; —**остомоз, остомиаз** *m.* (med.) esophagostomiasis; (vet.) nodule disease; —**отомия** *f.* (med.) oesophagotomy; —**оцеле** *n.* (med.) esophagocele.

эзофория *f.* (ophth.) esophoria, esodeviation.

эй— *see also* **эв**—; —**галлол** *m.* eugallol, pyrogallol monoacetate.

эйген/величина *f.*, —**верт** *m.* (math.) eigenvalue, proper value; —**ин** *m.* eugenin; —**овая кислота** eugenic acid; —**ол** *see* **эйгенол;** —**период** *m.* eigenperiod.

эйглобулин *m.* (bioch.) euglobulin.

эйд— *see* **эйдо**—.

Эйде *see under* **Биркеланд.**

эйдесмол *m.* eudesmol.

эйдетический *a.* (psych.) eidetic.

эйдо— *prefix* eid(o)—, image, figures, form; —**ген** *m.* (embr.) eidogen; —**номия** *f.* (bot.) eidonomy; —**птометрия** *f.* (ophth.) eidoptometry.

эйзения *f.* an earthworm (*Eisenia*).

Эйзенменгера комплекс *m.* (med.) Eisenmenger complex.

эйкаин *m.* eucaine.

эйкалипт *see* **эвкалипт.**

Эйкен *m.* Eucken (thermal conductivity of gases).

эйкоз/ан *m.* eicosane; —**ановая кислота** eicosanic acid; —**анол** *m.*, —**иловый спирт** eicosanol, eicosyl alcohol; —**ил** *m.* eicosyl; —**илен** *m.* eicosylene.

эйкозоль *m.* a casein paint for leather.

эйколит *m.* (min.) eucolite.

эйком(м)ия *f.* (bot.) gutta percha tree (*Eucommia*).

эйкон/ал *m.* (opt.) eikonal; —**оген** *m.* (phot.) Eikonogen; —**ометр** *m.* (ophth.) eikonometer.

эйкриптит *m.* (min.) eucryptite.

эйкрит *m.* (petr.) eucrite.

эйксант/ин *m.* euxanthin; —**иновая кислота** euxanth(in)ic acid, purreic acid; —**оген** *m.* euxantogen, mangiferin; —**он** *m.* euxanthone, purrone; —**оновая кислота** euxanthonic acid.

эйксенит *m.* (min.) euxenite, polycrase.

эйкупин *m.* Eucupin, *i*-amylhydrocupreine.

эйлер/ианский, —**ов(ский)** *a.* (math.) Eulerian, Euler('s); —**ов(ский) интеграл первого рода** beta function; —**ов период свободных колебаний** Eulerian (free) period; —**ова сила** critical force; —**овы круги** *pl.* (logic) Eulerian circles; Euler diagram.

Эйлер-хельпин (chem.) Euler-Chelpin.

эйл/изит *m.* (petr.) eulysite; —**иптол** *m.* eulyptol; —**итин,** —**итит** *m.* (min.) eulytin, eulytite.

эйм/енол *m.* Eumenol.

Эймери шельфовый ледник *m.* (geog.) Amery Ice Shelf.

эймер/иоз *m.* (med.) Eimeria infection (coccidosis); —**ия** (prot.) Eimeria.

эй/мидрин *m.* Eumydrin, atropine methyl nitrate; —**натрол** *see* **эвнатрол.**

Эйнтховена треугольник *m.* (physiol.) Einthoven's triangle.

эйнштейн *m.* einstein (photochemical unit of energy); —**ий** *m.* einsteinium, Es; —**овский** *a.* Einstein('s).

эйоним/ин *m.* euonymin; —**ит** *m.* euonymit, galactitol.

эй/осмит *m.* euosmite (fossil resin); —**осмия** *f.* (physiol.) euosmia; —**панкреатизм** *m.* (physiol.) eupancreatism.

эйпа/рал *m.* euparal (synthetic resin); —**рин** *m.* euparin; —**тирин** *m.* eupatirin, stevioside; —**торин** *m.* eupatorin.

эйпеп/сия *f.* (physiol.) eupepsia; —**тический** *a.* eupeptic.

эйпирхроит *m.* (min.) eupyrchroite.

эйпноэ *n.* (physiol.) eupnea.

Эйр (geog.) Eyre.

эйрезол *m.* Euresol, resorcinol monoacetate.

эйренис *m.* (herp.) Eirenis.

эйри— *see also under* **эври**—.

Эйри спираль *f.* (opt.) Airy's spiral.

эйритмия *f.* (physiol.) eur(h)ythmia.

эйтаксит *see* **эвтаксит.**

эйтиохроновый *a.* euthiochronic (acid).

эйтроф/ический *a.* (biol.) eutrophic; —**ия** *f.* eutrophia.

Эйфель (geog.) Eifel; —**ский ярус** (geol.) Eifelian stage.

эйфилл/ин *m.* Euphylline, aminophylline; —**ит** *m.* (min.) euphyllite (a mica).

эйфор/бий *see* **эвфорбий;** —**ин** *m.* euphorine, phenylurethane; —**ия** *f.* euphoria.

эйфоти/д *m.* (petr.) euphotide, gabbro; —**ческий** *a.* euphotic, gabbro.

эйфтальмин *m.* euphthalmine, eucatropine.

Эйхгорна гидрометр Eichhorn's hydrometer.

эйхинин *m.* Euquinine, quinine ethylcarbonate.

эйякуляция *f.* (physiol.) ejaculation.

ЭК *abbr.* (**коэффициент энергии**) energy coefficient.

эк *abbr.* (**электрокаротаж**) (petrol.) electrical logging.

э.К. *abbr.* (**эффект Керра**) (phys.) Kerr effect.

эка— *prefix* eka— (one, first); —**да** *f.* (ecol.) ecad; —**элемент** *m.* eka-element.

экболин *m.* ecboline.

экв. *abbr.* [**эквивалент(ный)**].

эквадорский *a.* (geog.) Ecuador(ian).

экватор *m.* equator; —**иал** *m.* equatorial (telescope); —**иально** *adv.* equatorially; —**иальный** *a.* equatorial.

эквационный *a.* (math.) equational.

экв. вл. *abbr.* (**эквивалент влажности**) (agr.) moisture equivalent.

экв. ед. *abbr.* (**эквивалентная единица**) equivalent unit.

экви— *prefix* equi—; —**аффинный** *a.* (math.) equiaffine.

эквивалент *m.* equivalent; counterpart; **э. антенны** dummy antenna; —**ность** *f.* equivalence; —**ный** *a.* equivalent; —**ная масса** mass equivalent; —**ная отражающая поверхность** radar cross-section; **закон —ных отношений** law of definite proportions.

эквидистантный *a.* equidistant.

экви/зетовая кислота equisetic acid, aconitic acid; —**коррелированный** *a.* equicorrelated; —**ленин** *m.* equilenin.

эквилибр *m.* equilibrium, balance; —**ировать** *v.* equilibrate, balance; —**истика** *f.* equilibration, equipoise.

экви/лин *m.* equilin; —**молекулярный** *a.* equimolecular; —**молярный** *a.* equimolar; —**партиция** *f.* equipartition; —**потенциал** *m.*, —**потенциальный** *a.*

equipotential; **—скалярный** *a.* equiscalar; **—фазный** *a.* equiphase; **—фациальный** *a.* equifacial.

экворея *f.* (zool.) Aequorea.

ЭКГ *abbr.* (**электрокардиограмма**) electrocardiogram; (**электрокардиография**) electrocardiography.

экгон/идин *m.* ecgonidine, *dl*-anhydroecgonine; **—ин** *m.* ecgonine, tropinecarboxylic acid.

экдизон *m.* (biochem.) ecdysone.

экер *see* **эккер**

экз. *abbr.* (**экземпляр**).

экз— *see also* **экс—**; **—альгин** *m.* Exalgin, methylacetanilide; **—альтация** *f.* exaltation.

экзам/ен *m.*, **—енационный** *a.* examination; **—енатор, —инатор** *m.* examiner; **—еновать** *v.* examine.

экзантема *f.* (med.) exanthema.

экзарация *f.* (geol.) exaration, furrowing.

экзартикуляция *f.* (med.) exarticulation.

экзархный *a.* (bot.) exarch.

экзацербация *f.* (med.) exacerbation.

экзегетический *a.* (math.) exegetic.

экзема *f.* (med.) eczema; **—тозный** *a.* eczematous.

экземпляр *m.* copy; specimen, sample; model; **в трёх —ах** in triplicate.

экз/ентерация *f.* (med.) exenteration, evisceration; **—ина** *f.* (bot.) ex(t)ine; **—итус** *m.* (pal.) exitus.

экзо— *prefix* exo— (outside, outer); ecto—; **—антиген** *m.* ectoantigen; **—базидий, —базидиум** *m.* (bot.) exobasidium.

экзо/гамия *f.* (biol.) exogamy; **—гаструла** (embr.) exogastrula; **—генный** *a.* exogenous; exogenetic; (geol.) accidental (inclusion); **—генная брекчия** fault breccia; **—генное развитие** exogeny; **—гировый** *a.* crustacean; **—дерма** *f.* (biol.) exodermis.

экзо/кардия *f.* (med.) ectocardia; **—кариогамия** *f.* (gen.) exo(caryo)gamy; **—карп(ий)** *m.* (bot.) exocarp; **—катафория** *f.* (ophth.) exocataphoria; **—кринный** *a.* (physiol.) exocrine; **—кутикула** *f.* (zool.) exocuticle.

экзо/миксис *m.* (gen.) exomixis; **—молекулярный** *a.* intermolecular; **—морфизм** *m.* (geol.) exomorphism; **—морфный** *a.* exomorphic; **—настический** *a.* (bot.) exonastic; **—паразит** *m.* (zool.) ectoparasite; **—пептидаза** *f.* (enz.) exopeptidase; **—перидий** *m.* (bot.) exoperidium; **—плазма** *f.* (zool.) ectoplasm; **—подит** *m.* (zool.) exopodite.

экзо/связь *f.* intermolecular bond; **—скелет** *m.* (zool.) exoskeleton; **—скопический, —скопный** *a.* exoscopic, visible from without; **—смос** *m.* exosmosis; **—смотический** *a.* exosmotic; **—спора** *f.* exospore, conidium; **—спорий** *m.* (bot.) exosporium; ex(t)ine; **—стоз** *m.* (med.) exostosis; **—стом** *m.*, **—стома** *f.* (bot.) exostome; **—сфера** *f.* exosphere, upper layer of terrestrial atmosphere.

экзот *m.* (biol.) exotic (plant); **—ека** *f.* (zool.) exotheca.

экзотерический *a.* exoteric; external.

экзотермич/еский, —ный *a.* exothermic, heat-liberating.

экзотеций *m.* (bot.) exothecium.

экзот/ика *f.* (biol.) exotic (plant); **—ический, —ичный** *a.* exotic; ecdemic; high-energy (fuel); **—ическая глыба** (geol.) erratic block; **—ичность** *f.* exotic nature.

экзо/токсин *m.* (bact.) exotoxin; **—тропия** *f.* (ophth.) exotropia, divergent strabismus, walleye; **—ты** *pl.* (biol.) exotics.

экзо/фермент *m.* exoenzyme; **—фитный** *a.* (bot., med.) exophytic; **—фория** *f.* (ophth.) exophoria, exodeviation; **—фтальм** *m.* (med.) exophthalmos; **—хорион** *m.* (biol.) exochorion; **—циклический** *a.* exocyclic.

экзоэлектрон *m.*, **—ный** *a.* exoelectron; **—ная эмиссия, —ое испускание** exoelectron emission.

экзо/эмиссия *see* **экзоэлектронная эмиссия; —энергетический** *a.* (phys.) exoenergic; **—эргический** *a.* (nucl.) exoergic.

экзувии *pl.* (zool.) exuviae (cast-off skin, shell, etc.).

экзэн/терация *f.* (med.) exenteration; **—цефалический** *a.* exencephalous.

ЭКИ *abbr.* (**электрокимограмма**) electrokymogram, EKY.

эки/вок *m.* equivocality, ambiguity; ambiguous term; **—ловый некроз** (med.) peritonsillar abscess, quinsy.

экипаж *m.* vehicle, carriage, car(t); undercarriage, chassis; crew; (deck) hand; (naval) training center; **без —а** unmanned, robot (satellite); **с —ем** manned, with crew; **—ный** *a.* of **экипаж**; vehicular; **—ная часть** undercarriage.

экипиров/анный *a.* equipped, furnished; **—ать** *v.* equip, furnish, fit out; **—ка** *f.* equipment, fitting out, outfit; housing; **—очный** *a.* equipment.

эккер *m.* (surv.) square, cross-staff (head); **зеркальный э.** optical square; **крестообразный э.** cross-staff, diopter square.

эккри/нный *a.* (physiol.) exocrine, eccrine; **—тический** *a.* eccritic, excretion.

эклампси/зм *m.* eclampsism, preeclampsia; **—я** *f.* eclampsia.

эклектор *m.* selector.

эклиметр *m.* (in)clinometer, elevation meter.

эклип/с *m.* (astr.) eclipse; **—тика** *f.*, **—тический** *a.* ecliptic; **—тическое среднее Солнце** first mean Sun.

эклогит *m.* (petr.) eclogite; **—овый** *a.* eclogite, eclogitic.

эк/мнезия *f.* (psych.) ecmnesia; **—молин** *m.* Ekmolin (antimicrobial).

эко— *prefix* eco— (environment); **—вид** *m.* ecospecies.

эко/генез *m.* ecogenesis; **—дем** *m.* (ecol.) ecodeme; **—зит** *m.* eco(para)site; **—ид** *m.* ecoid; **—климат** *m.* ecoclimate; **—клинальный** *a.* ecoclinal.

эко/лид *m.* Ecolid, chlorisondamine chloride; **—лог** *m.* ecologist; **—логический** *a.* (biol.) ecological; **—логия** *f.* ecology, bionomics; **—логия растительных сообществ** synecology.

эконом/айзер, —изатор *m.* economizer, waste gas heater; **—ансия** *f.* economancy (study of methods of utilization of industrial by-products); **—етр** *m.* econometer; **—етрика** *f.* econometrics; **—ика** *f.* economics; economy, economic structure; **—ист** *m.* economist; **—ить** *v.* economize, save, cut down expenses.

экономическ/ий *a.* economical; commercial; pilot (burner); **—ая игла** economizer (in carburetor).

экономичн/ость *f.* economy; efficiency, effectiveness; husbandry; **—ый** *a.* economical; efficient, effective; economy-type.

эконом/ия *f.* economy, saving, **—ничать** *v.* economize, save; **—ность** *f.* economy; **—ный** *a.* economical; frugal, provident.

экосистема *f.* ecosystem.

эко/тип *m.* (biol.) ecotype; **—тон** *m.* ecotone; **—топ** *m.* ecotope; **—токсикология** *f.* ecological toxicology; **—фен** *m.* ecophene, ecad.

экразер *m.* (med.) écraseur.

экран *m.* screen, shield; display; baffle, deflector; blind; visor; lining (of dam); blanket (of reactor).

экраниз/ация *see v.*; **—ировать** *v.* film, do a documentary; make a screen version (of).

экранир/ование *n.* screening, shielding, insulation; (elec.) screening effect; (electrochem.) shadowing; **коэффициент —ования; постоянная —ования**

screening number, screening constant (of element); —**ованный** *a.* screened, shielded; —**ованная камера** (nucl.) hot cell; —**овать** *v.* screen (off), shield; —**овка** *see* **экранирование**; —**ующий** *a.* screening, shielding; screen (grid); —**ующая фольга** neutron curtain.

экранный *a.* of **экран**; cathode-ray tube (display).

экс *abbr.* (**экспериментальный**).

экс— *prefix* ex—; *see also* **экз—**; —**анол** *m.* polyisobutylene used as a lubricating oil additive.

Экс-ан-Прованс Aix-en-Provence.

эксанталовая кислота ecsantalic acid.

эксгаустер *m.* exhauster, exhaust fan, suction fan, aspirator.

эксерг/ия *f.* exergy, energy loss (by one part of system to another); —**онический,** —**оный** *a.* exergonic.

эксикат/ор *m.* exsiccator, desiccator; —**ы** *pl.* exsiccatae (dried herb, etc.).

эксимер *m.* eximer.

эксит/он *m.,* —**онный** *a.* (phys.) exciton; —**он Ванье** Wannier exciton; —**рон** *m.* excitron.

экскаватор *m.* excavator, power shovel, digger, ditcher, dredge; **кабельный э., канатный э., э.-драглайн** *m.* drag-line excavator; **э.-канавокопатель** *m.* ditch digger; —**ный** *a.* excavator, excavation; —**ные работы** excavation (work); **э.-обратная лопата** back hoe; —**остроение** *n.* excavator manufacture; **э.-струг** *m.* excavator-grader; —**щик** *m.* excavator operator.

экскавация *f.* excavation, digging; cutting (of road).

эксклав *m.* (anat.) exclave.

экскре/ментный *a.* excremental; —**менты** *pl.* excrement, feces;—**торный** *a.* excretory, exocrine; —**ты** *pl.* (physiol.) excreta, excretions; —**ция** *f.* excretion, elimination.

экскурс *m.* digression; —**ант** *m.* sightseer; —**ионный** *a.* of **экскурсия**; —**ировать** *v.* move freely, run out, (mil.) attack; —**ия** *f.* excursion (nuclear reactor); trip, tour; —**овод** *m.* tour guide.

экслибрис *m.* ex libris.

эксосмос *see* **экзосмос**.

эксп. *abbr.* (**экспедиционный**) expeditionary.

экспан/дер, —**дор,** —**зер** *m.* expander; —**зионный,** —**сионный** *a.* expansion; —**сивный** *a.* expansive; —**син** *m.* Expansine, patulin (antibiotic); —**сиометр** *m.* expansion gage; —**сия** *f.* expansion, expanse.

экспед/ировать *v.* expedite, facilitate; dispatch, send; —**итор** *m.* file clerk; dispatcher; forwarding agent; —**иционный** *a.* expeditionary; dispatch; —**иционные исследования** field work; —**иция** *f.* expedition; dispatch office.

экспеллер *m.* expeller.

экспенд/ер *m.* (tire manufacture) expander; —**ирование** *n.* expanding.

эксперимент *m.* experiment, test, trial; **в —е** under experimental conditions; —**ально** *adv.* experimentally; —**альный** *a.* experiment(al); exploratory; tentative; pilot (plant); research (nuclear reactor); measured (value); —**атор** *m.* experimenter; —**аторский** *a.* experimenter's; —**аторство** *n.* experimentation; tendency to experiment; —**ирование** *n.* experimentation; —**ировать** *v.* experiment.

эксперт *m.* expert; examiner, inspector, (livestock) judge; investigator; —**иза** *f.* expert's opinion, consultation; examination, appraisal, estimation; study (of documents); commission of experts; **трудовая —иза** expert medical testimony on work capacity or extent of disability; —**ный** *a.* expert('s).

экспира/тор *m.* expirator; —**торный,** —**ционный** *a.* expiratory; —**ция** *f.* expiration.

эксплант/ат *m.* (biol., med.) explant; —**ация** *f.* explantation.

экспликация *f.* explication, explanation; legend, key (of diagram).

эксплоат— *see* **эксплуат—**.

эксплуата/бильность *f.* exploitability; —**тор** *m.* exploiter; —**торский** *a.* exploiting.

эксплуатационн/ик *m.* maintenance worker; operator; —**о-ремонтный** *a.* maintenance and repair; —**ый** *a.* exploitation, operation(al); producing, operating, working; service, performance, field(test); cruising (power of engine); access (door); use(tax); —**ый режим** operating conditions, working conditions; —**ая вышка** drilling rig, derrick; —**ая надёжность** serviceability; —**ые качества** performance; —**ые объекты** (petrol.) production facilities; —**ые расходы** operating costs, cost of operation, maintenance cost.

эксплуатац/ия *f.* exploitation, operation, running; (mach.) service, maintenance; (petrol.) recovery; (agr.; min.) improvement, working, use, utilization; **вводить в —ию** *v.* put into service, put into operation, commission; **вводиться в —ию** *v.* come on stream; **отдел —ии** maintenance division; **пускать в —ию** *v.* put into service, put on stream; **срок —ии** life (of machine, etc.); **условия —ии** operating conditions, working conditions.

эксплуатиров/ание *see* **эксплуатация**; —**анный** *a.* exploited, etc., *see v.*; —**ать** *v.* exploit, use, operate, run; (mach.) service, maintain; improve, work (land, mine).

экспоз/е *n.* exposé, exposure; summary, abstract; —**иметр** *see* **экспонометр**; —**иционный** *a.,* —**иция** *f.* exposition, exhibition, display; exposure (to light, etc.); exposure time; (bot.) aspect; —**иция затвора** shutter speed; **коэффициент —иции** exposure factor.

экспон/ат *m.,* —**атный** *a.* exhibit; —**ент** *m.* exhibitor; (math.) exponent, index; —**ента** *f.* exponential (curve); —**ентный,** —**енциальный** *a.* exponential; —**ирование** *see* **экспозиция**; —**ированный** *a.* exhibited, etc., *see v.*; —**ировать** *v.* exhibit, show; expose (to light, etc.); irradiate; —**ирующее устройство** projector; —**ометр** *m.* exposure meter; spectral intensitometer, X-ray exposure meter.

экспорт *m.* export(ation); —**ёр** *m.* exporter; —**ирование** *n.* exportation; —**ировать** *v.* export; —**ный** *a.* export(able); —**ная торговля** export.

экспресс *m.* express (train); **э.-анализ** *m.* proximate analysis, quick analysis; —**ивность** *f.* (gen.) expressivity; **э.-информация** *f.* express information service; **э.-лаборатория** *f.* field laboratory; **э.-методом** *adv.* quick (test); —**ность** *f.* rapidity; —**ный** *a.* express; **э.-определение** *see* **экспресс-анализ**; **э.-старение** *n.* accelerated aging.

экспромтом *adv.* impromptu, extempore, without preparation.

экспропри/ация *f.* expropriation; —**ировать** *v.* expropriate, dispossess.

экссуд— *see* **эксуд—**.

экстен/дер *m.* extender, diluent, thinner; —**зометр** *see* **экстенсометр**; —**зор** *m.* (anat.) extensor; —**сивность** *f.* extensiveness; incidence (of attack by a parasite or disease); —**сивный** *a.* extensive; —**сометр** *m.* extensometer; —**сэффективность** *f.* (vet.) efficacy (of anthelmintic).

экстерн *m.* extramural student; —**ат** *m.* independent study.

экстеро(ре)цептор *m.* (zool.) exteroreceptor.

экстерриториальн/ость *f.* extraterritoriality.

экстерьер *m.* exterior; (agr.) conformation.

экстина *f.* (bot.) extine.

экстинкц/ионный *a.* extinction; —**ионный коэффициент** (opt.) extinction coefficient, absorptivity; —**ия** *f.* extinction, optical density.

экстирп/атор *m.* extirpator, cultivator, weeder; —**ация** *f.* extirpation, eradication; —**ировать** *v.* extirpate, eradicate.

экстра— *prefix* extra— (outside of, beyond, in addition).

экстравагантн/ость *f.* extravagance; —**ый** *a.* extravagant, liberal.

экстравагинальный *a.* extravaginal.

экстравазат *m.* (med., geol.) extravasate.

экстра/верзия *f.* (psych.) extraversion; (med.) extroversion; —**гент** *m.* extractant, extracting agent.

экстрагир/ование *n.* extraction, separation; —**ованный** *a.* extracted; —**овать** *v.* extract; —**уемый** *a.* extractable; —**ующий** *a.* extracting, extractive.

экстра/дуральный *a.* extradural; —**капсулярный** *a.* (anat.) extracapsular; —**колумелла** *f.* (zool.) extracolumella; —**ксилярный** *a.* (bot.) extraxylary.

экстракт *m.* extract; —**ант** *m.* extractant, extracting agent; —**ивность** *f.* extract content; —**ивный** *a.* extractive, extractable; —**ивное вещество** extractive; —**ный**, —**овый** *a.* extract; —**ор** *m.* extractor.

экстракци/онный *a.* extraction; —**онная перегонка** extractive distillation; —**онная фосфорная кислота** wet-process phosphoric acid; —**я** *f.* extraction; —**я растворителем** solvent extraction.

экстра/лин *m.* an antiknock additive for gasoline; —**матрикальный** *a.* (bot.) extramatrical; —**нуптиальный** *a.* (bot.) extranuptial.

экстраординарный *a.* extraordinary, unusual, uncommon; **э. профессор** adjunct professor; reader.

экстраоссальный *a.* (anat.) extraosseous.

экстра-пар *m.* extra steam.

экстра/перитонеальный *a.* extraperitoneal; —**пирамидный** *a.* (anat.) extrapyramidal.

экстраполиров/ание *n.* extrapolation; —**анный** *a.* extrapolate(d); —**анный пробег** extrapolated range; —**анное расстояние** (nucl.) extrapolation distance; —**ать** *v.* extrapolate.

экстраполя/тор *m.* predictor; —**ция** *f.* extrapolation.

экстра/систола *f.* (med.) extrasystole; —**ток** *m.* (elec.) extra current; —**флоральный** *a.* (bot.) extrafloral; —**целлюлярный** *a.* extracellular; —**циклический** *a.* (chem.) extracyclic (compound).

экстрем/альный *a.* extreme, extremal; (math.) extremum; optimizing (control); —**ист** *m.*, —**истский** *a.* extremist; —**ум** *m.* extremum, extreme.

экстренн/о *adv.* specially; —**ость** *f.* urgency; —**ый** *a.* special, urgent; emergency; unforeseen (expenses).

экстрорзный *a.* (bot.) extrorse, facing outward.

экстр/удат *m.* extrudate; —**удер** *m.* extruder; —**удирование** *n.* extrusion; —**удировать** *v.* extrude; —**удируемость** *f.* extrudability; —**узия** *f.*, —**юдинг(-процесс)** *m.* extrusion.

эксуд/ат *m.* exudate; —**ация** *f.* exudation.

эксфолиация *f.* exfoliation.

эксцельсиор *m.* excelsior.

эксцентр/ик *m.* (mach.) eccentric; cam; —**иковый** *a.* eccentric; cam (roll); —**иситет**, —**ицитет** *m.* eccentricity; —**ический** *see* эксцентричный; —**ично** *adv.* eccentric (to); —**ичность** *f.* eccentricity; —**ичный** *a.* eccentric, off-center.

эксцесс *m.* excess.

эксцизия *f.* excision, cutting out.

эксципул *m.* (bot.) excipulum, exciple.

экта/зия *f.* (med.) ectasia, expansion, dilation, distention; —**тический** *a.* ectatic.

эктим/а *f.* (med.) ecthyma; —**овидный** *a.* ecthymiform.

экто— *prefix* ecto—(outside, external); —**бласт** *m.* (biol.) ectoblast, epiblast; —**генез** *m.* ectogenesis; —**генный** *a.* ectogenic; (bact.) ectogenous; —**дерма** *f.* (zool.) ectoderm; —**дермальный**, —**дермический** *a.* ectodermal; —**кинетический** *a.* (bot.) ectokinetic.

эктопаразит *m.* (zool.) ectoparasite; —**ный**, —**ический**, *a.* ectoparasitic.

экто/пический *a.* ectopic, abnormally situated; —**пия** *f.* (med.) ectopy, ectopia; displacement; —**плазма** *f.* (biol.) ectoplasm; —**плазматический** *a.* ectoplasmatic; —**пласт** *m.* (bot.) ectoplast; —**спора** *f.* (bot.) ectospore, basidiospore; —**споровый** *a.* ectosporous; —**трофный** *a.* (bot.) ectotrophic; —**флеодный** *a.* (bot.) ectophloe(o)dic; —**флойный** *a.* (bot.) ectophloic.

эктро— *prefix* (congenital absence of a part); —**дактилия** *f.* ectrodactyly; —**мелия** *f.* (physiol.) ectromelia.

эктропион *m.* (med.) ectropion, eversion.

экуадорский *a.* (geog.) Ecuador(ian).

эк/фория *f.* (psych.) ecphoria, recollection; —**химоз** *m.* (med.) ecchymosis.

Экштейна-Эйбнера основание (chem.) Eckstein-Eibner base, ethylideneaniline.

ЭЛ *abbr.* (**электролюминесценция**) electroluminescence; (**электронная лампа**) electron tube; (**эхолот**) sounding device.

эл. *abbr.* (**электрический**) electric(al).

элагат *m.* (ichth.) rainbow runner (*Elagatis bipinnulatus*).

элаидин/овая кислота elaidic acid, *trans*-9-octadecenoic acid; —**овокислая соль** elaidate.

элаил *m.* elayl, ethylene.

элайо— *prefix* el(a)eo—, elaio— (oil); *see also* элаио—; —**метр** *m.* elaiometer (oil-expressing device); —**пласт** *m.* (bot.) elaioplast.

эларсоновая кислота elarsonic acid.

эласмы *pl.* chalcid flies (*Elasmidae*).

элассома *f.* (ichth.) dwarf sunfish (*Elassoma evergladei*).

эластанс *m.* (elec.) elastance.

эластик *m.* elastic, stretch material; rubber.

эластин *m.* elastin (a protein).

эластич/еский, —**ный** *a.* elastic, resilient, springy, flexible, supple; stretch; —**еская оболочка** (anat.) elastica (of notochordal sheath); —**ность** *f.* elasticity, resilience, spring, flexibility.

эласто/вискозиметр *m.* elastoviscometer; —**гель** *m.* elastogel; —**графия** *f.* flexography, aniline rubber plate printing; —**з** *m.* (med.) elastosis; —**кинетика** *f.* elastokinetics; —**мер** *m.* elastomer, elastoplastic; —**мерный** *a.* elastomeric; —**механика** *f.* elastomechanics.

элатер/а *f.* (bot.) elater; (ent.) click beetle; —**ит** *m.* elaterite, mineral caoutchouc.

элбон *m.* Elbon, p-hydroxyphenylurea cinnamate.

эл-в, эл.-в. *see* эв.

эл.-графич. *abbr.* (**электронно-графический**) electron-diffraction.

элевайф *m.* (ichth.) alewife.

элеватор *m.*, —**ный** *a.* elevator, hoist, lift; (grain) elevator.

элев/еза *f.* (poultry) brooder; —**зина** *f.* crab grass (*Eleusine*); —**он** *m.* (av.) elevon, ailavator; —**сине** *see* элевзина.

элегаз *m.* sulfur hexafluoride.

элексир *see* эликсир.

элективный *a.* (med.) elective; (biochem.) selective (culture).

электрет *m.* electret (a dielectric).

электриз/атор *m.* electrizer; **—ация** *f.*, **—ование** *n.* electrification; charging; **—ованный** *a.* electrified; **—овать** *v.* electrify, electrize; charge; **—уемый** *a.* electrified; electrifiable; **—ующийся** *a.* electrifiable.

электрик *m.* electrician; electric blue.

электрифи/кация *f.* electrification; **—цированный** *a.* electrified; **—цировать** *v.* electrify.

электрически *adv.* electrically.

электрическ/ий *a.* electric(al); **э. фонарь** flashlight; **—ая восприимчивость** dielectric susceptibility; **—ая ёмкость** (elec.) capacitance; **—ая отдача** electrical efficiency; **—ая проницаемость** dielectric constant, permittivity; **—ая станция** (electric) power plant; **отрицательно э.** electronegative; **положительно э.** electropositive; **с —им приводом** electrically driven.

электричество *n.* electricity; **э. трения** frictional electricity.

электричка *f.* electric railroad.

электро *n.* electro(type).

электро— *prefix* electro—, electric; **—агрегат** *m.* generating set; **—акустика** *f.* electroacoustics; **—акустический** *a.* electroacoustic; **—анализ** *m.* electroanalysis; **—балансёр** *m.* electric balancer; **—бетон** *m.* electroconcrete; **—биология** *f.* electrobiology; **—бритва** *f.* electric shaver; **—бур** *m.* electric drill; **—бурение** *n.* electric drilling; **—бус** *m.* electrobus; **—бытовые приборы** *pl.* electrical household appliances; **—вагонетка** *f.* electric truck.

электровалентн/ость *f.* electrovalence; **—ый** *a.* electrovalent.

электро/ветер *m.* electric breeze, static breeze, aura; **—взрывание** *n.* electric ignition; electric firing; **—взрыватель** *m.* electric exploder, electric fuse; **—влагомер** *m.* electric hygrometer; **—водокачка** *f.* electric pump.

электровоз *m.* electric locomotive; **—будительный** *a.* electromotive; **—гонка** *f.* electrostatic filter, electrostatic precipitator; **—остроение** *n.* manufacture of electric locomotives.

электро/ворсование *n.* (text.) electric teaseling; **—восковка** *f.* wax stencil film; **—воспламенитель** *m.* electric igniter, electric fuse; **—восстановление** *n.* electrolytic reduction; **—выделение** *n.* (met.) electrowinning; **—выщелачивание** *n.* (chem.) electrolytic leaching; **—вязкостный** *a.* electroviscous.

электрогастро— *prefix* electrogastro—.

электрогемо— *prefix* electrohemo—; **—стаз** *m.* electrohemostasis.

электрогенератор *m.* generator; **—ный** *a.* generator; electricity-generating.

электро/гидравлический *a.* electrohydraulic; **—глазурование** *n.* electroglazing; **—гониометр** *m.* electrogoniometer, phase indicator; **—горелка** *f.* electric burner; **—гравировальный** *a.* electroengraving.

электрограф/ический *a.* electrographic; **—ия** *f.* electrography.

электрогрелка *f.* electrotherm (surgical tool).

электрод *m.* electrode.

электродвигатель *m.* electric motor; **—ный** *a.* electric motor; electromotive.

электро/движок *m.* small electric motor; **—движущий** *a.* electromotive; **—декантация** *f.* electrodecantation; **—дермато—** *prefix* electrodermato—; **—дерматом** *m.* (med.) electrodermatome; **—детонатор** *m.* electric detonator.

электрод-зонд *m.* auxiliary electrode.

электродиа/гностика *f.* electrodiagnosis; **—лиз** *m.* electrodialysis; **—лизатор** *m.* electrodialyzer.

электродинам/ика *f.* electrodynamics; **—ический** *a.* electrodynamic; dynamatic (brake); **—ометр** *m.* electrodynamometer.

электрод-инструмент *m.* tool electrode.

электро/диспергирование *n.* electrodispersion; **—диффузия** *f.* electrodiffusion; **—дный** *a.* electrode; **—додержатель** *m.* electrode holder.

электродо/ение *n.*, **—ильный** *a.* electric milking; **—илка** *f.* electric milking machine; **—йка** *f.* electric milking; electric milking machine.

электро/долбёжник *see* **электродрель**; **—доменная печь** electric blast furnace; **—дрель** *f.* electric drill; **—дренаж** *m.* electric drying and compacting (of soil); **—дуга** *f.*, **—дуговой** *a.* electric arc; **—ёмкость** *f.* electric capacity, electric capacitance; **—жгут** *m.* electric harness; **—закалка** *f.* (met.) electric hardening; **—заклёпка** *f.* electric riveting; **сварка —заклёпками** arc spot welding.

электро/запал *m.* electric fuze; **—защита** *f.* cathodic protection (against corrosion); **—звуковой** *a.* electroacoustic; **—золь** *m.* electrosol; **—изгородь** *f.* electric fence.

электроизмерительный *a.* electric measuring; **э. прибор** electric meter.

электроизол/ирующий, **—яционный** *a.* insulating, dielectric; **—яция** *f.* (electric(al) insulation.

электроимпульсный *a.* electropulse.

электроиндук/тивный *a.* (electro)inductive; **—ция** *f.* (electro)induction.

электро/инструмент *m.* power tool; **—интегратор** *m.* computer-integrator, differential analyzer; **—искровой** *a.* electric-spark; **—искровая обработка** electromachining; **—калориметр** *m.* electrocalorimeter; **—калорический** *a.* electrocaloric; **—капил(л)ярность** *f.* electrocapillarity; **—капил(л)ярный** *a.* electrocapillary; **—кар** *m.*, **—кара** *f.* power truck, battery-operated truck; electric dolly.

электрокардио/грамма *f.* (med.) electrocardiogram; **—графия** *f.* electrocardiography.

электро/карот(т)аж *m.* (min.) electric logging; **—каутер** *m.*, **—каустика** *f.* electrocautery; **—кимограмма** *f.* electrokymogram; **—кинетика** *f.* electrokinetics; **—кинетический** *a.* electrokinetic; **—кислородный** *a.* oxy-electric (cutting); **—клёпка** *f.* electric riveting; **—коагуляция** *f.* electrocoagulation; **—кожный** *a.* electrocutaneous.

электроконтактн/ый *a.* electrocontact, electromechanical; **—ая обработка** (met.) electric discharge machining.

электро/копчение *n.* (food) electric curing; **—коррозия** *f.* electrocorrosion; **—кортикограмма** *f.* electrocorticogram; **—корунд** *m.* synthetic corundum; **—котёл** *m.* electric boiler; **—кратовый** *a.* electrocratic; **—крекинг** *m.* (petrol.) electrocracking; **—кристаллизация** *f.* electrocrystallization; **—культура** *f.* plant culture with electric heat.

электро/лампа *f.* electric lamp; **—лафета** *f.* electric car; **—лебёдка** *f.* electric hoist, electric winch; **—лечение** *n.* electrotherapy.

электролиз *m.* electrolysis; **подвергать —у** *v.* electrolyze; **—атор**, **—ер** *m.* electrolyzer; electrolytic furnace; **—ация** *f.* electrolyzing; **—ный** *a.* electrolytic; **—ованный** *a.* electrolyzed; **—овать** *v.* electrolyze, decompose by electrolysis.

электролиния *f.* electric line.

электролит *m.* electrolyte; salt bath; **—ический**, **—ный** *a.* electrolytic.

электролов *m.* electric fish trap(ping); **—ушка** *f.* electric insect trap.

электролюминесцен/тный *a.* electroluminescent; —**ция** *f.* electroluminescence.

электромагн/етизм *m.* electromagnetism; —**ит** *m.* electromagnet; —**итизация** *f.* electromagnetization; —**итный** *a.* electromagnetic.

электромагнитная единица СГС electromagnetic cgs unit (designated by prefix ab—), emu; **э. е. напряжения** abvolt; **э. е. тока** abampere.

электромашин/а *f.* electric machine; —**ный** *a.* electromechanical; —**ный генератор** generator dynamo; —**ный усилитель** dynamoelectric amplifier, amplidyne.

электромер *m.* electromer; —**ия** *f.* electromerism.

электрометр *m.* electrometer; —**ический** *a.* electrometric; electrometer; —**ия** *f.* electrometry, electrical logging.

электромехани/к *m.* electrician; —**ка** *f.* electromechanics; electrical engineering; —**ческий** *a.* electromechanical.

электромиграция *f.* electromigration.

электромигалка *f.* flashing light; flasher, blinker; flashing traffic indicator; electric gun flash simulator.

электромио/грамма *f.* (med.) electromyogram; —**графия** *f.* electromyography.

электро/мобиль *m.* electric car; —**моделирующий** *a.* electrical analog; —**молокоотсос** *m.* electric breast pump.

электромонт/аж *m.* electric wiring; —**ажник** *m.* electrician; —**ажный** *a.* (installation and) wiring (work); —**ёр** *m.* electrician.

электро/мотор *m.* electric motor; —**мотриса** *f.* electric truck; —**мощность** *f.* electric power.

электрон *m.* electron.

электрона *f.* lantern fish (*Electrona*).

электро/нагрев *m.* electric heating; —**наркоз** *m.* (med.) electronarcosis; —**наседка** *f.* electric incubator; —**насос** *m.* electric pump.

электрон/-вольт *m.* electron-volt (unit of energy); —**ика** *f.* electronics.

электронистагмография *f.* (ophth.) electronystagmography.

электронно— *prefix* electron(ic); *see also under* **электронный.**

электронно/возбуждённый *a.* electron-induced; —**волновой** *a.* electron-wave; —**вычислительная машина** computer; —**грамма** *f.* electron diffraction pattern; **-дырочный** *a.* electron-hole; **-дырочный переход** *p-n*-junction; **-ионный** *a.* electrostatic; **-лучевой** *a.* electron-beam; cathode-ray (tube); **-микроскопический** *a.* electron-microscopic; **-наведённый** *a.* electron-induced.

электронно-оптический *a.* optical-electronic; **э.-преобразователь** image converter (tube), image translator.

электронно/-позитронный *a.* electron-positron; —**разрядный** *a.* electron-discharge; —**световой** *a.* electronic ray (indicator); **-спиновый** *a.* electron spin.

электронн/ый *a.* electron(ic); **э. захват** electron capture; **э. парамагнитный резонанс** electron paramagnetic resonance, EPR; electron spin resonance, ESR; **э. прожектор** electron gun; —**ая плотность** (chem.) charge density; —**ая пушка** electron gun.

электроно/акцепторный *a.* electron-acceptor; —**грамма** *f.* electron-diffraction pattern; —**граф** *m.* electron-diffraction camera; —**графический** *a.* electron-diffraction; —**графия** *f.* electron diffraction (study); —**донор** *m.*, —**донорный** *a.*, —**отдаватель** *m.* electron donor; —**отдающий** *a.* electron-releasing; —**отталкивающий** *a.* electron-repelling; —**подобный** *a.* electron-like; —**сродство** *n.* electron affinity; —**фильный** *a.* electrophilic.

электро/обезболивание *n.* electroanesthesia; —**обеспыливатель** *m.* electric dust suppressor; —**обогрев** *m.* electric heating; —**обогреватель** *m.* electric heater; —**оборудование** *n.* electrical equipment; —**обработка** *f.* electrotreatment (of wool); —**оглушение** *n.* (agr.) stunning with electricity (before slaughtering); —**ожог** *m.* electric burn; —**окраска** *f.* electrostatic painting; —**окрашивание** *n.* electrodyeing; —**оптика** *f.* optical electronics; —**оптический** *a.* electrooptic(al); optoelectronic.

электрооса/дитель *m.* electric precipitator; —**ждение** *n.* electrodeposition, electrolytic precipitation; —**ждённый** *a.* electrodeposited.

электро/освещение *n.* electric lighting; —**осмос** *m.* electroosmosis; —**осмотический** *a.* electroosmotic; —**отрицательность** *n.* electronegativity; —**отрицательный** *a.* electronegative; —**очистка** *f.* electrocleaning; electrical precipitation (of gases); —**пайка** *f.* electric soldering; —**пастух** *m.* electric fence; —**пахота** *f.* electric plowing; —**передача** *f.* power transmission; supply line; —**перенос** *m.* electromigration; —**печать** *f.* electric printing.

электропечь *f.* electric furnace.

электро/пила *f.* power saw; —**пиролиз** *m.* electropyrolysis; —**питание** *n.* power supply; —**питающий** *a.* power; —**плит(к)а** *f.* electric hot plate; —**плуг** *m.* electric plow.

электропневм/атический *a.* electropneumatic; —**оклапан** *m.* electropneumatic valve.

электро/погрузчик *m.* electric fork lift; —**подвижность** *f.* electrophoretic mobility; —**подстанция** *f.* power substation; —**подъёмник** *m.* (electric) elevator; —**поезд** *m.* electric train; —**покрытие** *n.* (met.) electrodeposition, electroplating.

электрополиров/ание *n.* electropolishing; —**анный** *a.* electropolished; —**ать** *v.* electropolish; —**ка** *f.* electropolishing.

электро/положительный *a.* electropositive; —**предохранитель** *m.* electric fuse; —**предприятие** *n.* electrical works; —**прибор** *m.* electric appliance; —**привод** *m.* electric drive.

электропровод *m.* power line; —**имость** *f.* electrical conductivity; —**ка** *f.* (electric) wiring; —**ность** *f.* conductance; —**ный**, —**ящий** *a.* conducting.

электро/прогрев *m.* electric heating; —**проигрыватель** *m.* electric record player, turntable; —**производительность** *f.* electrical efficiency; —**промышленность** *f.* electric industry; —**пульт** *m.* electropanel; —**пунктура** *f.* (med.) electropuncture; —**пылеулавление** *n.* electrical dust precipitation.

электро/разведка *f.* electric geophysical exploration; —**раздражение** *n.* (med.) electrostimulation; —**разрядный** *a.* sputter-ion (pump); capacitive (transducer); **автоматический** —**разъём** quick-disconnect connector, snatch plug; —**распределительный** *a.* power-distributing; —**расцепление** *n.* electrodisintegration; —**реактивный** *a.* ion-plasma jet (engine); —**резка** *f.* (electric) arc cutting; —**ретинограмма** *f.* electroretinogram; —**рыбозаградитель** *m.* electric fish screen.

электросвар/ка *f.*, —**очный** *a.* (electric) arc welding; —**очная** *f.* arc weld shop; —**щик** *m.* arc welder, electric welder.

электро/сверло *n.* electric drill; —**светокультура** *f.* (hort.) fluorescent light gardening; —**свечение** *n.* electroluminescence; —**связь** *f.* electric communication; —**сепарация** *f.* electrostatic or electromagnetic separation; —**сеть** *f.* electric network, power supply network; —**сила** *f.*, —**силовой** *a.* (electric) power;

—синтез *m.* electrosynthesis; **—система** *f.* electric(al) system.

электроскоп, э.-детектор *m.* electroscope; **э.-дозиметр** radioscope; **—ический** *a.* electroscopic; **—ия** *f.* electroscopy.

электро/скребок *m.* electric wiper; **—слаботочный** *a.* weak-current; **—снабжение** *n.* power supply; **—сократимость** *f.* (physiol.) electrocontractility; **—сон** *m.*, **—сонный** *a.* electrosleep, cerebral electrotherapy; **—сопротивление** *n.* electric resistance; **удельное —сопротивление** specific resistance, resistivity; **—сортировка** *f.* electric separation (of seed, grain); electric grader; **—спуск** *m.* electric trigger; **—сродство** *n.* electron affinity; **—сталь** *f.* electric steel.

электро/станция *f.* power plant; **ветровая э., ветряная э.** wind turbine; wind-driven power plant; **вьючная э.** portable generator set.

электростартер *m.* electric starter.

электростати/ка *f.* electrostatics; **—ческий** *a.* electrostatic; **—ческая единица СГС** electrostatic cgs unit (designated by prefix *stat-*, e.g. **э. е. ёмкости** statfarad); **—ческая эмиссия** field emission, cold emission.

электро/стенолиз *m.* electrostenolysis; **—сторож** *m.* electric fence; **—стригальный** *a.*, **—стрижка** *f.* electric shearing, electric clipping; **—стрикция** *f.* electrostriction; **—струя** *f.* electrojet; **—судорожный** *a.* (med.) electroconvulsive; electric shock (therapy); **—сушилка** *f.* electric dryer; **—сушка** *f.* electric drying; **—счётчик** *m.* electric meter; **—таль** *f.* electric hoist.

электротензо/месдоза *f.* strain-gage dynamometer; **—метрия** *f.* electrotensometry.

электротепл/ица *f.* electrically heated greenhouse; **—овой** *a.* electrothermal.

электротерапия *f.* (med.) electrotherapy.

электротерм/ический *a.* electrothermal; **—ия** *f.* electrothermics; **тепловая —оцентраль** steam-electric power plant.

электротехни/к *m.* electrician, electrical engineer; **—ка** *f.* electrical technology, electrical engineering; **—ческий** *a.* electrotechnical, electrical engineering; electrical.

электро/тигель *m.* electric crucible; **—типия** *f.* electrotypy; **—тон(ус)** *m.* (physiol.) electrotonus; **—трактор** *m.* electric tractor; **—трал** *m.* electric trawl; **—трепан** *m.* (med.) electrotrephine; **—тропизм** *m.* (biol.) electrotropism; **—тяга** *f.* electric traction.

электро/угревые *pl.* electric eels (*Electrophoridae*); **—ударный** *a.* electrocontact, electromechanical (mine); **—улавливание** *n.* electric (dust) collection; **—управляемый** *a.* electrically controlled; **—установка** *f.* electric(al) installation; **—утюг** *m.* electric iron; **—физика** *f.* electrophysics; **—физический** *a.* electrophysical.

электрофильн/ость *f.* electrophilicity, electrophilic nature; **—ый** *a.* electrophilic.

электро/фильтр *m.* electrofilter, spec. electrostatic precipitator, Cottrell precipitator; **—фон** *m.* electrophone.

электрофор *m.* electrophorus; **—ез(ис)** *m.* electrophoresis; **—етический** *a.* electrophoretic.

электроформовка *f.* electroforming.

электрофото/графия *f.* electrophotography, xerophotography; **—метр** *m.* electrophotometer; **—метрия** *f.* electrophotometry.

электрофреза *f.* electric rotary tiller.

электрохим/ический *a.* electrochemical; **—ическая защита** cathodic protection; **—ия** *f.* electrochemistry.

электрохирургия *f.* electrosurgery.

электро/ход *m.* electrically powered ship; **—хозяйство** *n.* power plant; **—холодильник** *m.* electric refrigerator; **—хроматография** *f.* (chem.) electrochromatography; **—централь** *f.* power plant; **—цепь зажигания** electrical firing circuit; **—часы** *pl.* electric clock; **—чугун** *m.* electric (furnace) pig iron.

электро/шлаковый *a.* electroslag (welding); **—шлифмашина** *f.* electric grinder; **—шлифовалка** *f.* sander; **—шлифование** *n.* electrolytic grinding; **—щиток** *m.* power panel, (electrical) distribution box; **—щуп** *m.* (text.) electric feeler; **—эндосмос** *m.* electroendosmosis; **—энергетика** *f.* (electrical) power engineering; power industry; **—энергия** *f.* electric energy, electric power.

электроэнцефало/грамма *f.* (med.) electroencephalogram; **—графия** *f.* electroencephalography.

электро/эрозионный *a.* (met.) electro-erosion; **—ядерный** *a.* electronuclear.

электуар/ий, —иум *m.* (pharm.) electuary, confection.

элемент *m.* element; unit, component, member, part; (elec.) cell; (Chaudron's) thermopile; thermocouple; (meteor.) factor; **э.-аналог** homologue; **э. жёсткости** reinforcing member; **э. изображения** (comp.) pixel; **э.-индикатор** *m.* indicator element; **гальванический э.** galvanic cell, voltaic cell; **готовые —ы** prefabricated components; **жидкостный э., наливной э.** wet cell; **периодическая система —ов** periodic system (of the elements); **сухой э.** dry cell; **химический э.** chemical element.

элементарн/ость *f.* elementariness; **—ый** *a.* elementary, elemental, simple; fundamental; ultimate (analysis); **—ая ячейка** (cryst.) unit cell; **—ое звено** monomer unit, mer.

элементный *a.* of **элемент.**

элементоорганический *a.* hetero-organic, organoelemental.

элемецин *m.* elemecin.

элем/и *n.*, **смола э., —иевый** *a.* elemi (gum).

элео— *prefix* el(a)eo— (oil).

элео/маргариновая кислота eleomargaric acid, octadecadienoic acid; **—метр** *m.* elaeometer (oil hydrometer); **—норит** *m.* (min.) eleonorite; **—стеариновая кислота** eleostearic acid, octadecatrienoic acid; **—трисы** *pl.* (ichth.) sleepers (*Eleotridae*).

элерон *m.* (av.) aileron, flap; **э.-закрылок** flap aileron.

элефантиаз(ис) *m.* (med.) elephantiasis.

элизия sea slug (*Elysia*).

эликсир *m.* elixir; **грудной э.** antitussive; **зубной э.** dentifrice water.

элимин/ант *m.* (math.) eliminant; **—атор** *m.* eliminator; **—ация** *f.*, **—ирование** *n.* elimination; **—ированный** *a.* eliminated; elimination; **—ировать** *v.* eliminate.

элимус *m.* wild rye, lyme grass (*Elymus*).

элипс *see* **эллипс.**

элит/а *f.*, **—ный** *a.* (gen.) elite, superior stock, selected varieties.

элитораль *f.*, **—ный** *a.* (ocean.) elittoral.

элитр/а *f.* (zool.) elytron; **—о—** *prefix* elytr(o)— (vagina).

элитры *pl.* (zool.) elythrae.

эллаг/ендубильная кислота, —одубильная кислота ellagitannic acid; **—овая кислота** ellagic acid, gallogen.

эллинг *m.* launch, slipway; shipyard, dock, berth; (av.) hangar; **воздушный э., надувной э.** inflatable structure; **—овый** *a.* of **эллинг;** shipbuilding.

эллипс, —ис *m.* (geom.) ellipse; **э. искажёний** indicatrix; **э. рассеивания** (mil.) fire pattern, shot group; **—овидный** *a.* ellipsoid(al); **—ограф** *m.* ellipsograph; **—оид** *m.* ellipsoid; **—оид рассеивания** (mil.) volume of dispersion; **—оидальный** *a.* ellipsoid(al).

эллиптич/еский *a.* elliptic(al); **э. мешочек** (anat.) utriculus, utricle; **—еско-мешотчатый** *a.* utricular (nerve); **—ность** *f.* ellipticity.

эллобииды *pl.* (mal.) Ellobiidae.

эл. магн. ед. *abbr.* (**электромагнитная единица**) electromagnetic unit.

эл.-микроскопич. *abbr.* (**электронно-микроскопический**) electron-microscopic.

эл-од *abbr.* (**электрод**) electrode.

элодея *f.* (bot.) water thyme (*Elodea*).

элонгация *f.* elongation, stretch.

элопс *m.* (ichth.) tenpounder, etc.; **—овые** *pl.* tarpons, ten-pounders, ladyfishes (*Elopidae*).

эл.-оптич. *abbr.* (**электронно-оптический**) electron-optical, electronic (aberration).

элотрон *m.* a gamma spectrometer using recoil electrons.

э. л. с. *abbr.* (**эффективная лошадиная сила**) effective horsepower, brake horsepower.

Элсмир (geog.) Ellesmere.

эл.-ст. *abbr.* (**электростанция**) power plant.

эл.-ст. ед. *abbr.* (**электростатическая единица**) electrostatic unit.

эл-хим *abbr.* (**электрохимия**) electrochemistry.

эль *m.* ale.

Эльб/а the Elbe (river); **—са реакция** Elbs reaction.

эльдрин *m.* (chem.) aldrin.

Эльзас Alsace; **эльзасский** *a.* Alsatian.

Эльм/а огонь, святого —са огонь (meteor.) St. Elmo's fire.

Эль-Ниньо *n.* El Niño (ocean current).

элю/ант *m.* eluant; **—ат** *m.* eluate; **—ация** *see* **элюирование; —виальный** *a.* (geol.) eluvial; **—вий** *m.* eluvium, residual rock.

элю/ент *m.* elutriator, elutriating agent; **—ирование** *n.* elution, washing, extraction; elutriation (separation of radioactive elements by ion exchanger); **—ировать** *v.* elute, extract; **—ирующий** *a.* eluting; elutriating; **—ирующий раствор** (chem.) eluant; **—триация** *f.* elutriation; **—ционно-разделительный** *a.* elution-partition; **—ция** *see* **элюирование.**

э.м. *abbr.* (**электронная микроскопия**) electron microscopy.

эм. *abbr.* (**эмулься**) emulsion.

ЭМ *abbr.* (**электронный микроскоп**) electron microscope.

эмаграмма *f.* (meteor.) emagram.

эмал/евый *a.* enamel; (dentistry) adamantine; **—евая клетка** ameloblast, enamel cell; **—ирование** *n.* enameling, glazing; **—ированный** *a.* enameled, glazed; enamel (ware); **—ировать** *v.* enamel, glaze; **—ировка** *f.,* **—ировочный** *a.* enameling, glazing; **—ь** *f.* enamel.

эман *m.* eman (unit of radioactivity); **—атор** *m.* emanator; **—ационный** *a.,* **—ация** *f.* emanation, Em; **коэффициент —ации** emanating power; **—ий** *m.* emanation, emanon, Em; **—ирование** *n.,* **—ирующий** *a.* emanating; **—ометр** *m.* emanometer.

эмаскуляция *f.* (med.) emasculation; castration.

эмбарго *n.* (law) embargo.

эмбел/иевая кислота, —ин *m.* embelic acid, embelin.

эмбенский *a.* (geog.) Emba.

эмбии *pl.* (ent.) web-spinners (*Embiidae*).

эмбин/а *f.* (ichth.) surfperch; **—ы, —отоковые** *pl.* (ichth.) surfperches (*Embiotocidae*).

эмбл/ема *f.* emblem; insignia; **—ика** *f.* (bot.) emblic.

эмбол *m.* (med.) embolus, clot; **—ия** *f.* (med.) embolism; **—олалия** *f.* embololalia.

эмбрио— *prefix* embryo—, embryonic.

эмбриоген/ез *m.,* **—ия** *f.* embryogeny; **—етический, —ный** *a.* embryogen(et)ic.

эмбриолог *m.* embryologist; **—ический** *a.* embryological; **—ия** *f.* embryology.

эмбрион *m.* embryo; **—альный** *a.* embryonic, embryonal; **—ия** *f.* embryony.

эмбрио/патия *f.* embryopathy; **—токсон** *m.* (ophth.) embryotoxon; **—томия** *f.* embryotomy; **—троф** *m.* embryotroph.

ЭМГ *abbr.* (**электромиограмма**) (physiol.) electromyogram.

э.м.е. *see* **эл. магн. ед.**

эмеральдин *m.* emeraldin (dye).

эмет/амин *m.* emetamine; **—ик** *see* **рвотный камень; —ин** *m.* emetine; **—ический** *a.* emetic.

ЭМИ *abbr.* (**электромагнитный импульс**) electromagnetic pulse, EMP.

эмигр/ант *m.* emigrant; refugee; **—ационный** *a.* emigration, emigrant; **—ация** *f.* emigration; **—ировать** *v.* emigrate.

эминенция *f.* (anat.) eminence.

эмиссар/ий *m.* (anat.) emissarium, emissary vein; **—ный** *a.* emissary, affording an outlet.

эмисс/ионный *a.* emission, emissive, emitting; **—ионная способность** emissivity; **—ия** *f.* emission; **удельная —ия** emissivity.

эмит(т)/ер *m.,* **—ерный** *a.* emitter; **—ированный** *a.* emitted; **—ировать** *v.* emit, give off; **—ируемый** *a.* emitted; **—ирующий** *a.* emitting, emissive.

эмкар *m.* (vet.) gangrene.

эммелихтовые *pl.* (ichth.) rubyfishes, redbaits (*Emmelichthyidae*).

эммер *m.* (bot.) emmer (*Triticum dicoccum*).

эмметроп *m.* (ophth.) emmetrope; **—ический** *a.* emmetropic; **—ия** *f.* emmetropia.

эмодин *m.* emodin; **—овая кислота** emodinic acid; **—ол** *m.* emodinol.

эмотивн/ость emotivity; **—ый** emotive.

эмоц/иональный *a.* emotional; **—ия** *f.* emotion.

эмпием/а *f.* (med.) empyema; **э. плевры** thoracic empyema; **э. сустава** arth(o)empyesis; **—ный** *a.* empyemic.

эмпиревматический *a.* empyreumatic, tarry.

эмпир/изм *m.* empiricism; **—ик** *m.* empiricist; **—ически** *adv.* empirically; **—ический, —ичный** *a.* empiric(al); experimental; **—ия** *f.* empirism, experience, observation.

эмпис *m.* (ent.) Empis.

эмподий *m.* (zool.) empodium.

эму *m. and pl.* (orn.) emu(s) (*Dromiceidae*).

эмульг/атор *m.* emulsifier, emulsifying agent; **—ация** *f.,* **—ирование** *n.* emulsification; **—ированный** *a.* emulsified; **—ировать** *v.* emulsify; **—ируемость** *f.* emulsifiability; **—ируемый** *a.* emulsifiable; emulsified; **—ирующий** *a.* emulsifying; **—ирующийся** *a.* emulsifiable; **—о-паста** *f.* emulsifiable concentrate.

эмульса/тор *m.* emulsifier; **—ция** *see* **эмульсификация.**

эмульсер *m.* emulsifier.

эмульсин *m.* emulsin, synaptase.

эмульс/ионность *f.* emulsibility; **—ионный** *a.* emulsion; emulsifying (agent); **—ирование** *n.* emulsification; **—ированный** *a.* emulsified; **—ировать** *v.* emulsify; **—ификатор** *m.* emulsifier, emulsifying agent; **—ификация** *f.* emulsification; **—ия** *f.* emulsion; **делать —ию** *v.* emulsify; **концентрат —ии** emulsifiable concentrate; **обратная —ия** inverse emulsion, water-in-oil emulsion; **прямая —ия** normal emulsion; **—оид** *m.* emulsoid; **—ол** *m.* self-emulsifying oil; **—ор** *see* **эмульсификатор.**

эмфизема *f.* (med.) emphysema; **—тозный** *a.* emphysematous.

ЭМХ *abbr.* **(этилмеркурхлорид)** ethylmercuric chloride (fungicide for treating seed).

эмшер *m.* (geol.) Emscherian stage.

эмшерский бассейн, э. колодец Imhoff (septic) tank.

эналид *m.* (bot.) enalid.

эналлягма *f.* (ent.) damselfly (*Enallagma*).

энант *m.* enanthic fiber; **—ема** *f.* (med.) enanthema; **—ил** *m.* enanthyl; **—иловая кислота** heptanoic acid.

энантио— *prefix* enantio— (opposite); **—морф** *m.* (cryst.) enantiomorph; **—морфизм** *m.* enantiomorphism; **—морфный** *a.* enantiomorphous, similar but not superposable; **—тропия** *f.* (cryst.) enantiotropy; **—тропный** *a.* enantiotropic.

энантов/ый *a.* heptanoic (acid, etc.); **э. эфир** enanthic ether, ethyl heptanoate.

энанто/л *m.* enanthol, heptyl alcohol; **—токсин** *m.* enanthotoxin.

энартроз *m.* (anat.) enarthrosis.

энац/ионный *a.* enate, growing out; **—ия** *f.* enation, outgrowth.

энвайронменталистика, энвироника *f.* environmental science.

энгармонический *a.* enharmonic.

энгельманова сосна Engelmann spruce.

энглеровский *a.* Engler's (viscosimeter).

эндартери(и)т *m.* (med.) endarteritis.

эндархный *a.* (bot.) endarch.

эндгаз *m.* endothermic gas.

эндекаэдр *m.* (cryst.) hendecahedron; **—ический** *a.* hendecahedral.

эндем, —ик *m.* endemic animal or plant; endemic (disease); **—ический, —ичный** *a.* endemic, local; **—ия** *f.* endemia; endemic (disease).

эндергон/ический, —ный *a.* endergonic.

эндивий, э. цикорий endive.

эндиол *m.*, **—ьный** *a.* (chem.) enediol.

эндит *m.* (zool.) endite.

эндо— *prefix* endo— (within); **—биотический** *a.* endobiotic; **—бласт** *m.* (embr.) entoderm, endoblast, hypoblast; **—вибратор** *m.* endovibrator, cavity resonator; **—гамический** *a.* endogamous; **—гамия** *f.* (biol.) endogamy; **—генный** *a.* endogenous, endogenic; **—генное развитие** endogeny; **—дерма** *f.* (biol.) endoderm; endodermis; **—зоофит** *m.* endozoophyte; **—зоохорный** *a.* endozoochorous; **—кард(ий)** *m.* (anat.) endocardium; **—кардит** *m.* (med.) endocarditis; **—карп(ий)** *m.* (bot.) endocarp.

эндокрин *m.*, **—ный** *a.* (physiol.) endocrine; **—олог** *m.* endocrinologist; **—ология** *f.* endocrinology; **—опатия** *f.* (med.) endocrinopathy.

эндо/кроцин *m.* endocrocin; **—кси—** *prefix* endoxy—; **—ксилофит** *m.* (zool.) endoxylophyte, parasite living in plants; **—лизин** *m.* (bioch.) endolysin, leukin; **—лимфа** *f.* (anat.) endolymph; **—лимфатический** *a.* endolymphatic; **—литический** *a.* endolithic, living in rock; **—метрий** *m.* (anat.) endometrium; **—метриоз** *m.* (med.) endometriosis; **—метрит** *m.* (med.) endometritis.

эндоми/зий *a.* (anat.) endomysium; **—ксис** (prot.; cyt.) endomixis; **—тоз** *m.* (gen.) endomitosis; **—мицин** *m.* endomycin.

эндоморф *m.* (cryst.) endomorph; **—изм** *m.* endomorphism; **—ный** *a.* endomorphic; **—оз** *m.* endomorphism.

эндо/неврий *m.* (anat.) endoneurium; **—паразит** *m.* endoparasite, internal parasite; **—пептидаза** *m.* (enz.) endopeptidase; **—перидий** *m.* (myc.) endoperidium, inner peridium.

эндоплазм/а *f.* (biol.) endoplasm; **—атический, —енный** *a.* endoplasmic.

эндо/пласт *m.* (cyt.) endoplast, cell nucleus; **—плевра** *f.* (bot.) endopleura, inner seed coat; **—полиплоидия** *f.* (gen.) endopolyploidy; **—скелет** *m.* (anat.) endoskeleton; **—скопия** *f.* (med.) endoscopy.

эндосмо/метр *m.* (phys.) endosmometer; **—с** *m.* endosmosis; **—тический** *a.* endosmotic.

эндо/сперма *f.* (bot.) endosperm; **—спора** *f.*, **—спорий** *m.* endospore; **—споровый** *a.* endosporous; **—ст(еум)** *m.* endosteum; **—стом** *m.*, **—стома** *f.* (bot.) endostome; **—субтилизин** *m.* endosubtilysin; **—телиальный** *a.* (hist.) endothelial; **—телий** *m.* (zool.) endothelium; **—телиома** *f.* endothelioma.

эндотерм/ический, —ный *a.* endothermic, heat-absorbing; **—ичность** *f.* endothermicity.

эндотеций *m.* (bot.) endothecium.

эндо/тия *f.* (phyt.) endothia blight; **—токсин** *m.* endotoxin; **—трофный** *a.* (biol.) endotrophic; **—фермент** *m.* endoenzyme, intracellular enzyme; **—фит** *m.* (bot.) endophyte; **—фитный** *a.* endophytic; **—фтальмит** *m.* (med.) endophthalmitis; **—хондральный** *a.* (anat.) endochondral, cartilaginous (ossification); **—хрома** *f.* (bot.) endochrome (pigment within cell); **—энергетический** *a.* endoergic; **—энзим** *m.* endoenzyme; **—эргический** *a.* endoergic; **—эффект** *m.* endothermal effect.

энеева мышь *f.* (zool.) dwarf mouse opossum (*Marmosa murina*).

энезол *m.* Enesol, methanearsonic acid.

энема *f.* (med.) enema.

энервация *f.* (med.) enervation.

энергатор *m.* hydrotransmitter.

энергети/к *m.* power engineer, power worker; **—ка** *f.* energetics; power engineering; **ядерная э.** nuclear power (industry); **—ческий** *a.* energy, power; energy-producing; power-generating; high-energy; fuel (oil); **—ческий реактор** (nucl.) power reactor.

энергида *f.* (cyt.) energid; active protoplasm.

энергич/еский *a.* energetic, active; **—но** *adv.* energetically, vigorously; **—ный** *a.* energetic, vigorous, lively, active; activated (carbon); **—ная реакция** vigorous reaction.

энерг/ия *f.* energy, power; (germinating) force, vigor; **внутренняя э.** (chem.; phys.) energy content; **внутриядерная э.** nuclear forces, nuclear binding energy; **кинетическая э.** kinetic energy; **э. лобового сопротивления** (aerodyn.) frontal drag; **э. отдачи** recoil energy; **э. связи** (nucl.) binding energy; **получать —ию, снабжаться —ией** *v.* be powered (by).

энерго— *prefix* energy, power; **—база** *f.* power source; **—баланс** *m.* power balance; **—блок** *m.* power(-generating) unit, power supply; **—вооружённость** *f.* power available per productive unit or worker; provision of electric power (to a factory, farm or national economy); (av.) power-to-weight ratio; (ship-building) power to displacement ratio; **—выделение** *n.* release of energy, energy liberation.

энергоёмк/ий *a.* power-consuming; power-intensive; **—ость** *f.* energy capacity, power capacity, energy content (of fuel); power requirement(s).

энергоза/висимый *a.* (comp.) volatile (memory); **—трат** *m.* energy consumption, power consumption.

энерго/машиностроение *n.* power machine(ry) construction; power-plant engineering; power plant industry; **—независимый** *a.* (comp.) nonvolatile (memory); **—обмен** *m.* energy exchange; energy balance, energy metabolism; **—оборот** *m.* energy transformation; **—оборудование** *n.* power equipment; **—объединение** *n.* power pool; **—отдача** *see* **энерговыделение;** **—питание** *n.* power supply; **—поезд** *m.* (rr.) power train, mobile power unit; **—поставляющий** *a.* energy-providing, energy-yielding; **—потеря** *f.* energy loss, dissipation; **—потребление** *n.* energy consumption, power consumption; power requirement; **—пром** *m.* power engineering industry; **—ресурсы** *pl.* energy resources, source of energy; utilities; **—силовая установка** power plant; **—система** *f.* power system, energy system; **—снабжение** *n.* power supply; **—содержание** *n.* energy content; **—станция** *f.* power plant; **—технология** *f.* study of engineering processes with a view to utilizing energy resources (e.g. waste heat) to generate power; **—установка** *f.* power plant; **—хозяйство** *n.* power facilities; **—центр** *m.* power center; **—эквивалентный** *a.* power-equivalent.

энзим *m.*, **—ный** *a.* enzyme; **—атический, —ный** *a.* enzym(at)ic; **—ология** *f.* enzymology.

энзоот/ический *a.* enzootic, endemic; **—ия** *f.* enzootic disease.

энимики *pl.* (geol.) Animikian series.

энин *m.* enin.

энкаусти/ка *f.* encaustic (painting); **—ческий** *a.* encaustic (tile, etc.).

энклав *m.* enclave, inclusion.

энкринит *m.* encrinite (fossil crinoid); **—овый** *a.* encrinitic.

эннеа— *prefix* enne(a)— (nine); **—эдр** *m.* (geom.) enneahedron; **—эдрический** *a.* enneahedral.

эннеатин *m.* enniatin.

энный *a.* some, any, unspecified, *n*th.

эно— *prefix* oen(o)— (wine).

энол *m.* enol; **—аза** *f.* enolase; **—ат** *m.* enolate; **—изация** *f.* enolization; **—ьный** *a.* enol.

энотека *f.* collection of wine samples.

энотера *f.* evening primrose (*Oenothera*).

энофтальм *m.* (ophth.) enophthalmos.

энский *a.* some, a certain.

энтада *f.* (bot.) sea bean (*Entada*).

энтальпия *f.* (phys.) enthalpy.

энтелехия *f.* (biol.) entelechy; full development.

энтер/ит *m.* (med.) enteritis; **—о—** *prefix* entero— (intestine); **—огепатит** *m.* enterohepatitis, histomoniasis; blackhead (of turkeys, etc.); **—окиназа** *f.* enterokinase; **—кокк** *m.* enterococcus, streptococcus of human intestine; **—околит** *m.* (med.) enterocolitis; **—околостомия** *f.* enterocolostomy; **—олит** *m.* enterolith, intestinal calculus; **—оморфа** *f.* green algae (*Enteromorpha*); **—опатия** *f.* enteropathy, intestinal disease; **—опнейсты** *pl.* (zool.) acorn worms, tongue worms; **—отоксемия** *f.* (med.) enterotoxemia; **—отомия** *f.* enterotomy; **—оцель** *m.* (zool.) enterocoel(e).

энто— *prefix* ento—(within, inner); *see also under* **эндо—;** **—дерма** *f.* (embr.) entoderm, endoderm; **—зоон** *m.* entozoon, animal parasite.

энтомо— *prefix* entom(o)— (insect); **—лог** *m.* entomologist; **—логический** *a.* entomological; **—логия** *f.* entomology; **—фильный** *a.* (bot.) entomophilous, pollinated by insects; **—хорный** *a.* entomochoric, dispersed by insects.

энтоп/ический *a.* entopic, in normal position; indirect (factors); **—лазма** *see* **эндоплазма;** **—тический** *a.* (anat.) entoptic, intra-ocular.

энтр. ед. *abbr.* (**энтропийная единица**) entropy unit, eu.

энтроп/ийный *a.* (phys.) entropic, entropy; **—ион** *m.* (med.) entropion, inversion; **—ия** *f.* entropy.

энтузиазм *m.* enthusiasm.

энуклеация *f.* enucleation.

энурез *m.* (med.) enuresis; bedwetting.

энхондриальный *a.* (anat.) enchondral.

энцелад *m.* (astr.) Enceladus.

энцефал, —о— *prefix* encephal(o)—(brain); **—ит** *m.* (med.) encephalitis; **—омиелит** *m.* encephalomyelitis; **—омиело—** *prefix* encephalomyelo—; **—опатия** *f.* encephalopathy.

энциклопед/ический *a.* encyclopedic; **—ия** *f.* encyclopedia.

эо— *prefix* eo—(early, dawn); **—ген** *m.* (geol.) Eogene; **—гиппус** *m.* (pal.) eohippus.

эозин *m.* eosin, tetrabromofluorescein; **—опения** *f.* (med.) eosinopenia; **—офил** *m.* (biol.) eosinophile; **—офилия** *f.* eosinophilia; **—офильный** *a.* eosinophilic.

эозо/йский *a.* (geol.) Eozoic, pre-Cambrian.

эоксен *m.* (ent.) Eoxenos.

эолис *m.* (mal.) sea slug (*Aeolis*).

эолит *m.* (archeol.; geol.) eolith.

эолов/а арфа (acous.) aeolian tones; **—о-обломочный** *a.* (geol.) anemoclastic; **—ый** *a.* aeolian, windborne; **—ый многогранник** ventifact; **—ые отложения** aeolian rocks, wind deposits.

эоцен *m.*, **—овый** *a.* (geol.) Eocene.

ЭП *abbr.* (**электропитание**) power supply; (**электроподогреватель**) electric heater.

эп—*see* **эпи—.**

эпархейский *a.* (geol.) Eparchean.

эпейроген/ез *m.* (geol.) epeirogenesis; **—етический, —ический** *a.* epeirogenic; **—ия** *f.* epeirogeny.

эпенд/има, —ыма *f.* (anat.) ependyma; **—имома** *f.* (med.) ependymoma.

эпи— *prefix* epi— (upon, over); **—бласт** *m.* (biol.) epiblast; **—блема** *f.* (bot.) epiblem(a), rhizodermis; **—болия** *f.* (embr.) epiboly; **—борнеол** *m.* epiborneol, 3-camphanol; **—бранхиальный** *a.* (zool.) epibranchial; **—бромгидрин** *m.* epibromohydrin; **—вальва** *f.* (bot.) epivalve (of diatom).

эпигастральный *a.* epigastric.

эпигеальный *a.* (bot.) epigeal, living near the ground.

эпиген/ез *m.* (biol.; geol.) epigenesis; **—етический** *a.* epigenetic; **—ный** *a.* epigene.

эпигидрин *m.* epihydrin, propylene epoxide; **—овый** *a.* epihydrinic (acid); epihydric (alcohol).

эпигин/ичный, —ный *a.* (bot.) epigynous.

эпигуанин *m.* (bioch.) epiguanine, methylguanine.

эпидем/иология *f.* (med.) epidemiology; **—ический** *a.*, **—ия** *f.* epidemic; outbreak.

эпидерм/а *f.*, **—ис** *m.* (biol.) epidermis; **—ический** *a.* epidermic, epidermal; **—одисплазия** *f.* (med.) epidermodysplasia; **—оидный** *a.* epidermoid (carcinoma); **—олиз** *m.* epidermolysis; **—офития** *f.* (med.) epidermophytosis.

эпи/диаскоп *m.* (opt.) epidiascope

эпидидими/с *m.* (anat.) epididymis; **—т** *m.* (med.) epididymitis.

эпидот *m.*, **—овый** *a.* (min.) epidote, pistacite; **—изация** *f.* epidotization.

эпи/дурит *m.* external meningitis.

эпизио— *prefix* episio— (vulva); **—томия** *f.* (med.) episiotomy.

эпизод *m.* episode; **—ический** *a.* incidental, occasional; casual (inspection); spasmodic.

эпизойный *a.* epizoic, growing on animals.

эпизона *f.* (geol.) epizone, shallow zone.

эпизоо/тический *a.* (vet.) epizootic; **—тия** *f.* epizooty, epizootic disease; **—тология** *f.* epidemiology (of animals other than man); **—хория** *f.* epizoochory.

эпи/каин *m.* epicaine; **—камфора** *f.* epicamphor, 3-camphanone; **—кантус** *m.* (anat.) epicanthus; **—кард(ий)** *m.* (anat.) epicardium; **—карп(ий)** *m.* (bot.) epicarp(ium); **—континентальный** *a.* shallow continental (sea, etc.); **—котиль** *m.* (bot.) epicotyl; **—котильный** *a.* epicatyllary; **—криз** *m.* (med.) epicrisis, secondary crisis; **—ксильный** *a.* epixylous, growing on wood.

эпилеп/сия *f.* (med.) epilepsy; **—тик** *m.*, **—тический** *a.* epileptic; **большой —тический припадок** grand mal epilepsy; **малый —тический припадок** petit mal epilepsy.

эпи/лимнион *m.* epilimnion (upper water layer in lakes); **—лировать** *v.* depilate, remove hair; **—лировочный** *a.* depilatory; **—литический, —литный** epilithic, growing on rocks.

эпиляхна *f.* squash lady beetle (*Epilachna*).

эпиляция *f.* (d)epilation, hair removal, plucking.

эпиматий *m.* (bot.) epimatium (of conifers).

эпимер, —ид *m.* epimer, epimeride (isomer); **—аза** *f.* epimerase; **—ный** *a.* epimeric.

эпи/микрокарта *f.* opaque microcard; **—морф** *m.* (cryst.) epimorph; **—морфоз** *m.* (biol.) epimorphosis; **—настия** *f.* epinasty; **—нефрин** *m.* epinephrine (adrenaline); **—нин** *m.* Epinine; **—параклаз** *m.* (geol.) epiparaclase, overthrust; **—планктонный** *a.* (biol.) epiplanktonic; **—подий** *m.* (bot.; mal.) epipodium; **—положение** *n.* epiposition; **—породы** *pl.* (geol.) epirocks; **—рамноза** *f.* (chem.) epirhamnose.

эпирогенезис *see* **эпейрогенез.**

эпи/скоп *m.* episcope (projector); **—спадия** *f.* (med.) epispadia(s); **—сперм(ий)** *m.* (bot.) episperm; **—спорий** *m.* (bot.) episporium, espispore; **—стаз** *m.* (gen.) epistasis; **—стерн(ум)** *m.* (zool.) episternum; **—строфей** *m.* (anat.) epistropheus, axis; **—таксиальный** *a.* (cryst.) epitaxial; **—таксия** *f.* epitaxy; **—тека** *f.* (bot.) epitheca; **—телиальный** *a.* (biol.) epithelial; **—телиальное тельце** (anat.) parathyroid gland; **—телий** *m.* epithelium; **—телио—** *prefix* epithelio— (epithelium); **—телиома** *f.* epithelioma, epithelial cancer; **—тепловой, —термальный** *a.* epithermal; **—тет** *m.* epithet; **—теций** *m.* (bot.) epithecium; **—трохоида** *f.* (geom.) epitrochoid; **—физ** *m.* (anat.) epiphysis; **—физарный** *a.* epiphysial; **—фильный** *a.* epiphyllous, growing on leaves; **—фит** *m.* (bot.) epiphyte; **—фитный** *a.* epiphytic; **—фитотия** *f.* epiphytoty; **—флеодный** *a.* epiphloedic, growing on bark; **—фрагма** *f.* epiphragma, winter covering; **—хилий** *m.* (bot.) epichilium.

эпихлоргидрин *m.* epichlorohydrin, chloropropylene oxide.

эпицентр *m.* epicenter, zero point; **э. взрыва** ground zero.

эпицикл *m.* (astr.) epicycle; **—ический** *a.* epicyclic; **—оида** *f.* (geom.) epicycloid.

эпиэритроза *f.* epierythrose.

Эплтона слой Appleton layer (of ionosphere).

эпокси— *prefix* epoxy—; **—группа** *f.* epoxy group; **—д** *m.* epoxide, epoxy; **—дирование** *n.* epoxidation; **—дный** *a.* epoxy (resin); **—пластификатор** *m.* epoxy plasticizer; **—смола** *f.* epoxy resin; **—соединение** *n.* epoxy compound; **—цикл** *m.* epoxy ring, epoxy group.

эпоха *f.* epoch, period, time, age.

э. п. р., ЭПР *abbr.* **(электронный парамагнитный резонанс)** electron spin resonance; electron paramagnetic resonance.

эпрувет *m.* test tube.

эпсилон-энтропия *f.* ε-entropy.

эпсом/ит *m.* (min.) epsomite, natural Epsom salt; **—ский** *a.* Epsom.

эпул/ис *m.* (med.) epulis; **—о—** *prefix* epulo—.

эпштейновский *a.* Epstein.

эпюр *m.*, **—а** *f.* epure, diagram, drawing; graphic representation; line; curve.

эпюр/ат *m.* (fractionation) intermediate product; **—ационная колонна** a fractionating column.

эр/а *f.* era; **нашей —ы** anno Domini, A.D.; **до нашей —ы** B.C.

эрагростис *m.* (bot.) lovegrass (*Eragrostis*).

эрб/иевый *a.*, **—ий** *m.* erbium, Er; **—иевая земля, окись —ия** erbia, erbium oxide; **сернокислый —ий** erbium sulfate.

эрг *m.*, **—овый** *a.* erg (unit of work); (geol.) erg, sand desert.

ЭРГ *abbr.* **(электроретинограмма)** electroretinogram.

эргамин *m.* ergamine, histamine.

эргаст/ический *a.* (cyt.) ergastic; **—оплазма** *f.* (cyt.) ergastoplasm, endoplasmic reticulum.

эргин *m.* ergine.

эргметр *m.* (elec.) ergmeter.

эрго— *prefix* ergo— (ergot; work); **—базин** *m.* (biochem.) ergonovine, ergobasine, ergometrine; **—граф** *m.* (med.) ergograph; **—дический** *a.*, **—дическая путь** (phys.) ergodic; **—дичность** *f.* ergodicity; channeled energy; **—зин** *m.* ergosine; **—кальциферол** *m.* ergocalciferol, vitamin D$_2$; **—кристин** *m.* (biochem.) ergocristine; **—метр** *m.* (phys.) ergmeter; **—метрин** *see* **эргобазин; —новин** *m.* ergonovine; **—номика** *f.* ergonomics, human engineering; **—стан** *m.* ergostane; **—стерин** *m.* ergosterol; **—тамин** *m.* ergotamine; **—тизм** *m.* (med.) ergotism; **—тинин** *m.* ergotinine; **—тиновая кислота** ergotic acid; **—токсин** *m.* ergotoxine; **—флавин** *m.* ergoflavin; **—хризин** *m.* ergochrysin.

эрг-сек *abbr.* **(эрг-секунда)** erg-second.

эректор *m.* erector.

эрек/ция *f.* (physiol.) erection; **возбуждающие —цию нервы** (anat.) nervi erigentes, pelvic splanchnic nerves.

эрем *m.* (bot.) eremus; desert community; **—офильный** *a.* eremophilous.

эремурус *m.* (bot.) Eremurus.

эреп/син *m.*, **—таза** *f.* erepsin, ereptase; peptidase.

эретизм *m.* (psych.) erethism.

эрзац *m.* substitute.

Эри Lake Erie.

эриантус *m.* plume grass (*Erianthus*).

эригероновое масло erigeron oil.

эридан *m.* (astr.) Eridanus.

эризи/мин *m.* erysimin; **—пелоид** *m.* (med.) erysipeloid.

эрийский ярус (geol.) Erian stage.

эрик/а *f.* (bot.) heath (*Erica*); **—оидный** ericoid, heathlike.

эриколин *m.* ericolin.

эриксеновский *a.* (met.) Erichsen.

эринит *m.* pentaerythritol tetranitrate.

эрио— *prefix* erio— (wool); **—диктиол** *m.* (biochem.) eriodictyol; **—хорный** *a.* (bot.) eriochorous; **—хромовый** *a.* eriochrome (dye).

эритем/а *f.* (med.) erythema; **—альность** *f.* erythemal factor; **—ный** *a.* erythematous; erythema (dose).

эритр—*see* эритро—; —ен *m.*, —еновый *a.* erythrene, 1,3-butadiene.

эритрина *f.* coral tree (*Erythrina*).

эритриновые *pl.* (ichth.) Erythrinidae.

эритрит *m.* erythrite, cobalt bloom; erythritol.

эритро—*prefix* erythro— (red; erythrocyto—); —бласт *m.* (med.) erythroblast; —глюцин *m.* erythroglucin, erythrol; —декстрин *m.* erythrodextrin; —за *f.* erythrose; —зин *m.* erythrosine.

эритрозонус *m.* (ichth.) glowlight tetra.

эритро/ксилин erythroxyline, cocaine; —круорин *m.* (biochem.) erythrocruorin; —л *m.* erythr(it)ol; —мицин *m.* (pharm.) erythromycin (antibiotic); —плазия *f.* (med.) erythroplasia; —поэз *m.* (hemat.) erythropoiesis, formation of red blood cells; —поэтический *a.* (hemat.) erythropoietic; —филл *m.* (bot.) erythrophyll; —флеин *m.* erythrophleine.

эритроцит *m.* erythrocyte, red blood corpuscle; распад —ов erythrocytolysis; реакция оседания —ов erythrocyte sedimentation test; —осодержащая моча, —урия *f.* erythrocyturia, hematuria, blood in the urine.

эритрулоза *f.* erythrulose.

эрицин *m.* ericin, Mesotan.

эрквеин *m.* herquein (antibiotic).

эркер *m.* bay window.

эрленмейеровский *a.* Erlenmeyer (flask).

эрлифт *m.* air lift; —но-центробежный *a.* airlift-centrifugal.

эрлихин *m.* ehrlichin.

эрлиховский *a.* Ehrlich (side chain theory).

эрмитов/а матрица Hermitian matrix; э. форма (math.) Hermitian form; —о сопряжение (math.) Hermitian conjugate; —ский *a.* Hermitian, Hermite.

эродиров/анный *a.* eroded, weathered; denuded; —ать *v.* erode, wear away.

эроз/ивный *a.* erosive, wearing; corrosive; —иеустойчивый, —ионноустойчивый *a.* erosion-resistant; —ионный *a.* erosion(al); —ия *f.* erosion, weathering (of rocks, etc.).

эро/с, —т *m.* (astr.) Eros; —тизм *m.* (psych.) erotism; —тический, —тичный *a.* erotic.

эрратический *a.* erratic.

Эрроу теорема Arrow's theorem.

эрс *abbr.* (эрстед).

эрстед *m.* (elec.) oersted (magnetic unit); —метр *m.* oerstedmeter.

эрудиция *f.* erudition, learning.

эруковая кислота erucic acid, *cis*-13-docosenoic acid.

эруковидная личинка (ent.) eruca, eruciform larva.

эруптивный *a.* (geol.) eruptive.

эруц/идовая кислота erucidic acid, brassic acid; —иловый спирт erucylic alcohol.

эрштедт *see* эрстед.

Э.С. *abbr.* (энергия связи) binding energy.

эсе *see* эл.-ст. ед.

эскадр/а *f.* squadron; —енный *a.* squadron; fleet; —илья *f.* (air) squadron; —он *m.* squadron.

эскалатор *m.*, —ный *a.* escalator.

эскариоль *m.* (bot.) escarole.

эскарп *m.* scarp, escarpment, cliff; (mil.) one-way tank ditch; —ировать *v.* scarp, cut down; —овый *a. of* эскарп.

эскер *m.* (geol.) esker.

эскиз *m.* sketch, draft, rough drawing, freehand drawing, outline; —ность *f.* sketchiness; —ный *a.* sketch(y), preliminary, conceptual; —ный проект, —ный чертёж sketch, draft, outline.

эскимосский *a.* Eskimo.

эскорпион *m.* (herp.) beaded lizard (*Heloderma horridum*).

эскорт *m.*, —ировать *v.*, —ный *a.* (mil.) escort.

эскул/етин *m.* esculetin, 6,7-dihydroxycoumarin; —етиновая кислота esculetinic acid; —ин *m.*, —иновая кислота esculin, esculinic acid.

эсминец *m.* (mil.) destroyer.

эсо *n.* lizardfish (*Saurida undusquamis*).

эсобразная кривая sigmoid curve.

эспар/то *n.*, —товый *a.* (bot.) esparto (grass); —цет *m.* sainfoin (*Onobrychis*).

эспатит *m.* Espatite (Soviet ion-exchange resin).

эссенци/альный *a.* essential, indispensable, necessary; (med.) idiopathic; —я *f.* essence; летучая э. essential oil, volatile oil.

эст. *abbr.* (эстонский).

эстакад/а *f.* scaffold, bridge, gantry, trestle; platform, loading ramp; service ramp; stockade (breakwater); overpass; —ный *a. of* эстакада; (rr.) elevated; —ный мост trestle bridge.

эстамп *m.* print, plate, engraving.

эстафет/а *f.* express delivery; relay race; —ный *a.* rapid (spread of cracks); —ная проводимость hopping conduction (semiconductors).

эстезио—*prefix* (a)esthesio— (feeling, sensation); —генный *a.* esthesiogenic, sensation-producing; —логия *f.* esthesiology; —метр *m.* (med.) esthesiometer, tactometer.

эстер *see* эфир, сложный; —аза *f.* esterase; —ификация *f.* esterification; —ифицированный *a.* esterified; —олиз *m.* hydrolysis of esters.

эстет *m.* aesthete; (mal.) sense organ; —ический, —ичный *a.* aesthetic; —ические блага amenities; —ичность *f.*, —ство *n.* aestheticism.

эстивация *f.* (biol.) estivation.

эстист *m.* (mil.) signals telegraph operator; teleprinter set.

эстонский *a.* (geog.) Estonia(n).

эстрагол *m.* estragole, *p*-allylanisole.

эстрагон *m.*, —овый *a.* (bot.) tarragon.

эстрада *f.* platform, stage.

эстрадиол *m.* estradiol.

эстрадный *a. of* эстрада.

эстральный *a.* (physiol.) (o)estrous (cycle).

эстр/атриен *m.* estratriene; —ин *see* эстрон; —иол *m.* estriol.

эстрих(гипс) *m.* (constr.) gypsum floor; flooring plaster.

эстро/ген *m.*, —генный гормон estrogen; —н *m.* estrone, folliculin.

эструс *m.* (physiol.) (o)estrus, (o)estrous cycle, heat, rut.

эстуар/иевый *a.* (geol.) estuarine; —ий *m.* estuary, frith, firth.

Эстьена аппарат Estienne apparatus.

эсхинит *see* эшинит.

эта *pron. f.* this, that.

этаж *m.* story, floor, level; здание в пять —ей five-story building; нижний э., первый э. ground floor.

этажерка *f.* set of shelves, rack; bookcase; (micromodule) stack.

этажность *f.* number of stories.

этажный *a.* story, floor; storied; stepped, step-like, graduated, graded, gradual; multiple-stage, multistage; multiple-seated (valve); stack (molding); block (caving); tier (antenna); platen, multidaylight (press); э. выключатель (elec.) floor switch.

этазол *m.* (pharm.) sulfaethidole.

этакридин *m.* (pharm.) ethacridine, ethoxydiaminoacridine lactate, Rivanol.

эталий *m.* (myc.) aethalium.

эталон *m.* standard (of weights or measures); reference; gage, calibration instrument.

эталониров/ание *n.* standardization, standardizing, etc., *see v.;* **—анный** *a.* standardized, etc., *see v.;* **—ать** *v.* standardize, adjust; calibrate; gage, test (instrument).

эталонн/ый *a.* standard; calibrating, calibration; reference (source, etc.); comparison (potentiometer); normal (forest); **э. аппарат** calibrating device; **э. источник** radioactive standard; **—ая кислота** reference acid; **—ая мера** unit prototype; **—ая тактовая частота** clock frequency; **—ое сопротивление** standard resistance.

эталь *m.* ethal, cetyl alcohol.

этам/бутол *m.* (pharm.) ethambutol; **—ид** *m.* ethoxyzolamide, Ethamide; **—инал** *m.* pentobarbital; **—инал-натрий** *m.* pentobarbital (sodium), Nembutal.

этан *m.* ethane; **—алевый** *a.,* **—ал(ь)** *m.* ethanal, acetaldehyde; **—амид** *m.* ethanamide, acetamide; **—диаль** *m.* ethanedial, glyoxal; **—дикарбоновая кислота** ethanedicarboxylic acid; **—дикислота** *f.,* **—диновая кислота** ethanedioic acid, oxalic acid; **—диол** *m.* ethanediol, glycol; **—овый** *a.* ethane; **—овая кислота** ethanoic acid, acetic acid; **—оил** *m.* ethanoyl, acetyl; **—ол** *m.* ethanol, ethyl alcohol; **—оламин** *m.* ethanolamine; **—олиз** *m.* ethanolysis.

этансульфо/кислота *f.,* **—новая кислота** ethanesulfonic acid.

этантиол *m.* ethanethiol, ethyl mercaptan; **—овый** *a.* ethanethiolic (acid).

этап *m.* step, stage, stanza (of development); halting place.

этаперазин *m.* perphenazine, Trilafon.

этап/ирование *n.* (mil.) staging; **—ный** *a. of* **этап**; **—ный пункт** depot.

Этвеша правило (phys.) Eötvös rule.

этез/ии *pl.* etesian winds; **—ийный** *a.* etesian, periodical.

этен *m.* ethene, ethylene; **—ил** *m.* ethenyl; **—иламид** *m.* ethenylamide, acetamidine; **—илиден** *m.* ethenylidene; **—ол** *m.* ethenol, vinyl alcohol.

этео/генез *m.* (biol.) etheogenesis; **—стома** *f.* (ichth.) darter (*Etheostoma*).

этериз/ация *f.* (med.) anesthetization; **—ировать** *v.* anesthetize.

этерифи/кация *f.* esterification; etherification; **—ковать, —цировать** *v.* esterify; etherify.

этернит *m.* Eternit (asbestos shingle).

эти *pron. pl.* these, those.

эти/ден *m.* eth(yl)idene; **—денический паротит** mumps; **—зин** *m.* fenethazine.

этика *f.* ethics.

этикет/ирование *n.,* **—ировка** *f.,* **—ировочный** *a.* labeling; **—ка** *f.* label, tag, nameplate.

этил *m.* ethyl; **бромистый э.** ethyl bromide, bromethane; **перекись —а** ethyl peroxide; **хлористый э.** ethyl chloride, chloroethane.

этил/ал(ь) *m.* ethylal; **—амин** *m.* ethylamine; **—анилин** *m.* ethylaniline; **—ат** *m.* ethylate (ethoxide or alcoholate); **—ацетат** *m.* ethyl acetate; **—бензил** *m.* ethylbenzyl; **—бензол** *m.* ethylbenzene; **—бромид** *m.* ethyl bromide.

этилен *m.* ethylene, ethene; **окись —а** ethylene oxide; **хлористый э.** ethylene chloride; **—гликоль** *m.* ethylene glycol; **—диамин** *m.* ethylenediamine; **—диаминтетрауксусная кислота** ethylenediaminetetraacetic acid, EDTA; **—изация** *f.* ethylene treatment; **—имин** *m.* ethylenimine; **—молочная кислота** ethylene lactic acid; **—ная связь** olefinic linkage; **—овый** *a.* ethylene; **—овая связь** ethylene linkage, double bond; **—хлоргидрин** *m.* ethylene chlorohydrin.

этилиден *m.* ethylidene; **—мочевина** *f.* ethylidene urea.

этилиров/ание *n.* ethylation; **—анный** *a.* ethylated; leaded (gasoline); **—ать** ethylate.

этил/карбонат *m.* ethyl carbonate; **—меркаптан** *m.* ethyl mercaptan; **—меркурхлорид** *m.* ethylmercuric chloride; **—морфин** *m.* ethylmorphine; **—овоспиртовый** *a.* ethyl-alcoholic.

этилов/ый *a.* ethyl; **э. спирт** ethyl alcohol, ethanol; **э. эфир** (ethyl) ether; ethyl ester; **э. эфир уксусной кислоты** ethyl acetate; **—ая жидкость** lead tetraethyl solution.

этилол *m.* ethylol, hydroxyethyl.

этилсерн/ая кислота ethylsulfuric acid; **соль —ой кислоты, —окислая соль** ethylsulfate; **—истая кислота** ethylsulfurous acid; **—окислый** *a.* ethylsulfuric acid; ethylsulfate (of); **—онатриевая соль** sodium ethylsulfate.

этил/сульфокислота *f.,* **—сульфоновая кислота** ethylsulfonic acid; ethanesulfonic acid; **—толуол** *m.* ethyltoluene; **—уретан** *m.* ethyl urethan; **—целлюлоза** *f.* ethylcellulose; **—ьный** *a.* ethyl (group); **—эстренол** *m.* (pharm.) ethylestrenol.

этимо/логический *a.* etymologic(al); **—логия** *f.* etymology; **—н** *m.* etymon; root word.

этин *m.* ethyne, acetylene; **—ил** *m.* ethynyl.

этио— *prefix* etio— (cause); **—генный** *a.* etiogenic, causative.

этиолирова/ние *n.* etiolation, blanching; **—нный** *a.* etiolated; **—ть** *v.* etiolate, bleach by exclusion of sunlight.

этиолог/ический *a.* (med.) etiologic; **—ия** *f.* etiology.

этио/нин *m.* ethionine; **—порфирин** *m.* etioporphyrin; **—тропный** *a.* (med.) etiotropic.

этич/еский, —ный *a.* ethic(al).

этмоид/альный *a.* (anat.; zool.) ethmoid, sieve-like; **—ит** *m.* (med.) ethmoiditis.

этмолит *m.* (geol.) ethmolith.

Этна Mt. Etna.

этн/ический *a.* ethnic; **—о—** *prefix* ethn(o)— (race, tribe); **—оботаника** *f.* ethnobotany, folk botany; **—огенез** *m.* ethnogeny; **—ография** *f.* ethnography.

это *pron. n.* this, that, it.

этокс/алил *m.* ethoxalyl; **—и—** *prefix* ethoxy—; **—игруппа** *f.* ethoxy group; **—илирование** *n.* ethoxylation; **—ильный** *a.* ethoxy (group); **—иуксусный** *a.* ethoxyacetic (acid).

этолог/ический *a.* ethologic(al); **—ия** *f.* ethology.

этот *pron. m.* this, that.

этрол *m.* etrol (a plastic).

этропл/ус, —юс *m.* (ichth.) Etroplus.

Этгеля раствор Öttel's rule.

этюд *m.* study; (music) etude, exercise.

эу— *see also under* **эв—, —эй—; —галинный** *a.* euhaline, stenohaline; **—гермафродит** *m.* euhermaphrodite; **—гетерозис** *m.* euheterosis; **—глифа** *f.* (prot.) Euglypha; **—дендриум** *m.* (zool.) Eudendrium; **—комия** *see* **эйком(м)ия.**

эу/митоз *m.* (gen.) eumitosis, typical mitosis.

эури— *see* **эври—.**

эуриптериды *pl.* (pal.) sea scorpions (*Eurypterida*).

эутроф/икация *f.* eutrophication (of water body); **—ный** *a.* eutrophic.

эу/филлин *m.* (pharm.) aminophylline, Euphyllin; **—хроматин** *m.* (gen.) euchromatin; **—хромосома** *f.* euchromosome, autosome.

эф. *abbr.* **(эфир)** ether.

эфа *f.* (herp.) viper.

эфапс *m.* (anat.) ephapse.

эфармо/з *m.* (biol.) epharmosis; **—нический** *a.* epharmonic, adaptive.

эфебический *a.* (biol.) ephebic, adult.

эфедр/а *f.* (bot.) Ephedra; **—овые** *pl.* (bot.) Ephedraceae.

эфедр/ин *m.* ephedrine.

эфелидоз *m.* (med.) lentigo, freckle.

эфемер *m.* (bot.) ephemeral; **—а** *f.* (ent.) mayfly; **—ида** *f.*, **—идный** *a.* (ent.) ephemerid; (astr.) ephemeris; **—иды** *pl.* (ent.) mayflies (*Ephemeridae*); **—ность** *f.* ephemerality, transient nature; **—ный** *a.* ephemeral, short-lived, transitory, transient; **—овый** *a.* ephemeral plant; **—оид** *m.*, **—оидный** *a.* (bot.) ephemeroid.

эфес *m.* handle (of sword, etc.).

эфесциа *f.* (ent.) Ephestia.

эфидрогамные растения (bot.) ephydrogamicae.

Эфиопия Ethiopia; **эфиопский** *a.* Ethiopian.

эфипп/игер *m.* (ent.) Ephippiger; **—овые** *pl.* (ichth.) spadefishes (*Ephippidae*).

эфир *m.* ester; ether, spec. ethyl ether; **э. уксусной кислоты** acetate; **азотистоэтиловый э.** ethyl nitrite; **простой э.** ether; **сложный э.** ester; **этиловый э.** ethyl ether; **этиловый э. уксусной кислоты** ethyl acetate.

эфир/ат *m.* etherate; **—изатор** *m.* esterifier; **—изация** *f.* (chem.) etherification, esterization; (med.) etherization.

эфирн/омасличный *a.* essential-oil; **—ый** *a.* ester; ether(eal); **—ая смола** ester gum; **—ое (летучее) масло** essential oil; **—ые пары** ether fumes.

эфир/окислота *f.* ether acid; **—омасличный** *a.* aromatic, essential-oil; **—ометр** *m.* (med.) etherometer; **—онос** *m.* essential-oil (bearing) plant; **—оносный** *a.* aromatic; **—ообразование** *n.* esterification; etherification; **—оподобный** *a.* ester-like; ether-like; **—орастворимый** *a.* ether-soluble; **—осоль** *f.* ester salt; **—сульфонат** *m.* chlorophenylchlorobenzenesulfonate, Ovotran.

эфициллин *m.* ephicillin, penethamate.

ЭФК *abbr.* (**экстракционная фосфорная кислота**) wet-process phosphoric acid.

эфлоресценция *f.* efflorescence.

эфотический *see* **эвфотический**.

эфф. *abbr.* (**эффективный**).

эффект *m.* effect, result; impact; capacity.

эффект-доз/а (med.) dose effect; **кривая э.-дозы** dose-response curve, DRC.

эффективн/ость *f.* effectiveness, efficiency; performance; (charge) factor, yield; potency (of medicine); **э. действия** (mil.) lethality, effectiveness; **предел —ости** effective range; **—ый** *a.* effective, efficient; active; considerable; powerful; resultant; productive; profitable; apparent (temperature).

эффект/ный *a.* effective; showy; impressive; **—ор** *m.* (bioch.) effector.

эфф/ерентный *a.* (physiol.) efferent; **—игурация** *f.* (bot.) effiguration; **—лоресценция** *f.* efflorescence; **—луент** *m.* (chem.) effluent.

эффуз/ивный *a.* effusive; **—иометр** *m.* (gases) effusiometer; **—ия** *f.* effusion; **—ный** *a.* effuse; **—ор** *m.* effuser.

эхел/иды, **—овые** *pl.* worm eels (*Echelidae*).

эхи/ин *m.* echiine; **—каучин** *m.* echicaoutchin; **—накозид** *m.* echinacoside; **—нацея** *f.* coneflower (*Echinacea*).

эхино— *prefix* echino— (spiny; sea urchin); **—кактус** *m.* Echinocactus; **—кокк** *m.* echinococcus (tapeworm); **—коккоз** *m.* (med.) echinococcosis; **—псилон** *m.* (bot.) Echinopsilon; **—псин** *m.* (chem.) echinopsine; **—ринх** *m.* echinorhynchus (parasitic worm).

эхит/амин *m.* echitamine, ditaine; **—енин** *m.* echitenine, **—ин** *m.* echitin.

эхиуриды *pl.* (zool.) Echiuroidea.

эхо *n.* echo; **э.-индикатор** *m.* echo indicator; **—камера** *f.* echo chamber; **—кардиография** *f.* ultrasonic cardiography; **—лалия** *f.* (psych.) echolalia; **—ледомер** *m.* ice fathometer; **—лот** *m.* sounding device, echo sounder; (naut.) fathometer; (av.) acoustic altimeter; **измерение —лотом, —лотирование** *n.* echo sounding; **—подобная речь** echolalia; **—праксия** *f.* (med.) echopraxia; **э.-сигнал** *m.* echo (signal), return, blip.

эцезис *m.* (bot.) ecesis.

эци/альный *a.* (bot.) aecium, aecial; **—дий** *m.* aecidium; **—диоспора** *f.* aeci(di)ospore; **—й** *m.* aecium.

э.ч. *abbr.* (**эфирное число**) ester value, ester number.

ЭШ *abbr.* (**эффект Штарка**) Stark effect.

эша/лот *m.* (bot.) shallot.

эшара *f.* (med.) eschar.

эшафот *m.* scaffold.

Эшвил (geog.) Asheville.

эшелетт *m.* (phys.) echelette.

эшелон *m.* (mil.; opt.) echelon; (av.) flight level, cardinal altitude; (transition) level; **воздушно-десантный э.** (mil.) airborne wave; **войнский э.** (mil.) troop transport; **диффракционный э.** echelon grating; **—ирование** *n.* echeloning, disposition in depth; (av.) separation, stacking; **—ировать** *v.* echelon; separate; **—ный** *a. of* echelon; **—ное стекло** echelon lens.

эшерихия *f.* (bact.) Escherichia.

эшинит *m.* (min.) (a)eschynite.

ЭЭГ *abbr.* (**электроэнцефалограмма**) electroencephalogram; (**электроэнцефалография**) electroencephalography.

эякуляция *f.* (physiol.) ejaculation.

Ю

ю, Ю, Ю. *abbr.* (**юг; южный**).

ЮАР *abbr.* (**Южно-Африканская Республика**) South Africa.

юбея *f.* (bot.) coquito (palm) (*Jubaea*).

юбилей *m.*, **—ный** *a.* anniversary.

юб/ка *f.*, **—очный** *a.* skirt; petticoat.

ю.-в., ЮВ, Ю-В, Ю.-В. *abbr.* (**юго-восток; юго-восточный**).

ЮВА *abbr.* (**Юго-Восточная Азия**) Southeast Asia.

ювелир *m.* jeweler; **—ный** *a.* jewelry; meticulous.

ювенильный *a.* juvenile, young; (orn.) juvenal (plumage).

юг *m.* south; **на юг** southward.

югальн/ый *a.* (anat.) jugal; **—ая пластинка** (ent.) tegula; squama.

юган *m.* hay plant (*Prangos pabularia*).

юглон *m.* juglone, 5-hydroxy-14-naphthoquinone; **—овый** *a.* juglonic (acid).

юго— *prefix see* **южно—**.

юго-восток *m.* southeast; **ю.-восточный** *a.* southeast(ern); **ю.-запад** *m.* southwest; **ю.-западный** *a.* southwest(ern).

Югослав/ия *f.* Yugoslavia; **югославский** *a.* Yugoslav(ic), Yugoslavian.

югу/лярный *a.* (anat.) jugular.

югум *m.* (biol.) jugum.

югурт *m.* yogurt.

юдан *m.* (bot.) tamarisk.

юж. *abbr.* (**южный**).

южанин *m.* (—е *pl.*) southerner.

южн. *abbr.* (**южный**).

Южная Америка South America.

южнее *adv.* ad meridiem, towards the south.

южно— *prefix* austro— (south).

южно/-американский *a.* South American; **ю.-африкан-ский** *a.* South African—**бережный** *a.* south coast; —**полярный** *a.* antarctic; **ю.-русский** *a.* South Russian.

южн/ый *a.* austral, meridional, south(ern), southerly; antarctic; negative (pole of magnet); **ю. крест** (astr.) Crux; **Ю. Ледовитый океан** Antarctic Ocean; **ю. полюс** south pole; **ю. полярный круг** antarctic circle—**ое сияние** aurora australis; **Южные Карпаты** Transylvanian Alps, South Carpathians.

юз *m.* slippage, skidding; dragging.

ю.з., ю.-з., ЮЗ, Ю.-З. *abbr.* (**юго-запад; юго-запад-ный**).

ЮЗА *abbr.* (**Юго-Западная Африка**) Southwest Africa.

Юза аппарат Hughes' apparatus.

юзом *adv.* skidding; dragging; **идти ю.** *v.* skid.

юиттовский *a.* Hewitt.

юйюба *see* **ююба.**

юкатанский *a.* (geog.) Yucatan.

юкка *f.* (bot.) yucca, Spanish bayonet—**сапонин** *m.* yuccasaponin.

юкола *f.* sun-cured fish.

Юкон Yukon (river).

Юкспор (geog.) Yukspor.

юкстагломерулярный *a.* (anat.) juxtaglomerular.

юла *f.* (orn.) woodlark (*Lullula arborea*).

юлан *see* **юдан.**

Юлийские Альпы Julian Alps.

юлокротин *m.* yulocrotine.

юлол *m.* julol; —**идин** *m.* julolidine, 1,2,5-6-tetrahydro-julol.

юлить *v.* spin; wheedle; curry favor.

юморка *f.* yellow lucerne, sickle medic(k) (*Medicago falcata*).

юн *sh. m. of* **юный.**

Юнг (med.) Jung; —**а модуль** (phys.) Young's modulus, longitudinal elasticity; —**ерман(н)иевые** *pl.* (bot.) Jungermanniaceae.

юнион *m.* union.

юнипер/ен *m.* juniperene; —**ин** *m.* juniperin; —**овая кислота** juniperic acid, 16-hydroxyhexadecanoic acid; —**ол** *m.* juniperol.

юнкер (морской ю.) *m.* (ichth.) rainbow wrasse (*Coris julis*).

юнко *m.* (orn.) slate-colored junco.

юнона *f.* (astr.) Juno.

юн/ость *f.* youth; adolescence; (geol.) immaturity; —**ошеский** *a.* youthful, young, juvenile; —**ошество** *n.* youth, young people; —**ый** *a.* young, youthful; immature.

ЮП *abbr.* (**южный полюс**).

юпитер *m.* (astr.) Jupiter.

ЮПК *abbr.* (**южный полярный круг**).

юр *m.* height, bluff; **на** —**у** in an exposed place.

Юра the Jura mountains.

юра *see* **юрский период;** *f.* shoal (of fish).

Юра способ Ure's process.

юр/идический *a.* juridical—**исдикция** *f.* jurisdiction; —**исконсульт** *m.* legal adviser—**испруденция** *f.* jurisprudence, science of law; —**ист** *m.* jurist; lawyer; law student.

юркий *a.* brisk, lively; nimble.

юродивый *a.* irresponsible, incompetent.

юрок *sh. m. of* **юркий;** (orn.) brambling, mountain finch; —**ский период** (geol.) Jurassic period.

юрта *f.* yurt, nomad's tent, hut.

юстир *m.*, —**ные весы** assay balance; —**ование** *see* **юстировка;** —**овать** *v.* adjust, correct, align, tune; —**овка** *f.*, —**овочный** *a.* adjustment, correction, alignment; tuning.

юстиция *f.* justice; (bot.) justicia.

ют *m.* (naut.) poop (cabin).

Юта (geog.) Utah; **юта** *f.* jute.

Ютланд/ия *f.* (geog.) Jutland—**ский** *a.* Jutland(ic).

ютовый *a.* of **ют.**

юттия *m.* gyttja, mud (of lake bottom).

юфт/евый *a.*, —**ь** *f.*, —**яной** *a.* Russia leather.

юхта *see* **юфть.**

ю. ш. *abbr.* (**южная широта**) south latitude.

ююба *f.* (bot.) jujube (*Zizyphus*).

Я

я *pron.* I; ego.

ябан/и, —ь (ichth.) sevan trout (*Salmo ischchan*).

ябин *m.* yabine.

яблоко *n.* apple; (eye) ball; (mech.) ball; (bot.) pome; **я.-видный** *a.* pomiform, apple-shaped; —**носный** *a.* pomiferous.

яблон/евый *a.* apple tree; —**евые** *pl.* Pomaceae; —**овка** *f.* apple brandy; —**овый хребет** Yablonovy Mountains; —**ый** *a.*, —**я** *f.* apple tree.

яблочк/о *n. dim. of* **яблоко; серый в** —**ах** dapple-gray (horse).

Яблочкова свеча (illum.) Jablochkoff candle.

яблочно/-зелёный *a.* apple green; pomaceous; —**каль-циевая соль** calcium malate; —**кислый** *a.* malic acid; malate (of); —**кислая соль** malate; —**этиловый эфир** ethyl malate.

яблочн/ый *a.* of **яблоко;** pomaceous; malic (acid); cider (press); **я. шарнир** ball-and-socket joint; **соль** —**ой кислоты** malate.

ябор/анди-листья *pl.* jaborandi; —**идин** *m.* jaboridine; —**ин** *m.* jaborine.

ЯВ *abbr.* (**ядерная вакуоль**) nuclear vacuole; (**ядови-тые вищества**) poisons.

Ява (geog.) Java.

яван/ицин *m.* javanicin (antibiotic); —**ский** *a.* Javanese; —**ское море** Java Sea.

явен *sh. m. of* **явный.**

яви *gen., etc., of* **явь.**

яв/ить(ся) *see* **являть(ся);** —**ка** *f.* appearance, presence, attendance; secret meeting (place); —**ление** *n.* phenomenon, effect; appearance, occurrence; fact; (ionizing) event; (med.) symptom; **химическое** —**ление** chemical phenomenon; —**лять** *v.* show, display, exhibit, manifest; —**ляться** *v.* appear, arrive, make one's appearance; be; seem; provide, offer (means); report (for work); **у него** —**илась мысль** it occurred to him.

явно *adv.* evidently, etc., *see* **явный.**

явно— *prefix* phanero—, ph(a)eno— (visible, apparent); —**брачный** *a.* (bot.) phanerogamous; —**выраженный** *a.* (elec.) salient (pole); —**кристаллический** *a.* phanerocrystalline, obviously crystalline; —**лепестный** *a.*

(bot.) phaenopetalous; **—пластинчатые звёзды** (zool.) starfishes (*Phanerozonia*).

явн/ость *f.* evidence, obviousness, clearness; **—оязычные** *pl.* (amph.) phaneroglossates; **—ый** *a.* evident, obvious, clear, plain, apparent, distinct; certain, unquestionable; (math.) explicit; appreciable (error); (elec.) salient (pole); overt.

явок *gen. pl. of* **явка.**

явор *m.*, **—овый** *a.* sycamore (tree).

явочн/ый *a. of* **явка; —ым порядком, —ым путём** without prior permission.

явский *a.* (geog.) Java(nese).

явств/енность *f.* clearness, distinctness; **—енно** *adv.* openly, frankly; **—енный** *a. see* **явный**; open, frank; **—овать** *v.* be clear, be obvious, be apparent; appear; **что —ует из** as evidenced by.

явь *f.* reality, actuality.

ягель *m.* (bot.) lichen, spec. reindeer moss (*Cladonia rangiferina*).

яглыджа *f.* (bot.) caper spurge (*Euphorbia lathyrus*).

ягн/ение *n.* lambing; **—ёнок** *m.*, **—иться** *v.* lamb; **—ятник** *m.* (orn.) bearded vulture (*Gypaëtus barbatus*); **—ячий** *a.* lamb.

ягод/а *f.*, **—ный** *a.* berry, fruit; **ложная я.** false berry, pseudoberry; **—ица** *f.* breech, buttocks; **нервы —иц** clunial nerves; **—ичный** *a.* breech (presentation); gluteal; pygal; **—ичная мышца** (anat.) gluteus; **—ка** *f.* (bot.) drupelet; **—ковые** *pl.* (bot.) Thymelaeaceae; **—ник** *m.* berry bush; berry patch; **—ница** *f.* berry picker; **—ный** *a.* berry; bacciferous; **—овидный** *a.* berry-like, baccate; **—оводство** *n.* berry growing; **—оносный** *a.* berry-bearing, bacciferous; **—ообразный** *see* **ягодовидный.**

ЯГР *abbr.* (**ядерный гамма-резонанс**).

ягуар *m.*, **—овый** *a.* (zool.) jaguar; **—унди** (zool.) jaguarundi.

ягурт *m.* (food) yogurt.

яд *m.* poison, venom; toxin; virus; **удаление —а** detoxification.

ядар *m.* yadar, subpolar meadow.

яд. ед. *abbr.* (**ядерная единица**) nuclear unit.

ядер *gen. pl. of* **ядро; —но-магнитный** *a.* nuclear-magnetic; **—но-плазменный** *a.* (cyt.) nucleoplasmic; **—но-прецессионный** *a.* spin-precession (magnetometer); **—но-резонансный** *a.* nuclear-resonance; **—ночистый** *a.* nuclear-pure; **—но-энергетический** *a.* nuclear power.

ядерн/ый *a.* nuclear; kernel; **я. гамма-резонанс** Mössbauer spectrum; **я. котёл** nuclear reactor; **я. потенциал** nuclear potential; **я. ракетный двигатель** nuclear propulsion; **я. реактор** nuclear reactor; **я. синтез** nuclear fusion; **я. сок** (cyt.) karyolymph; **я. фильтр** Nuclepore (track-etch) membrane filter; nuclear pore filter; **—ая оболочка** karyotheca, nuclear membrane; **—ая плазма** karyoplasm, nucleoplasm; **—ая силовая установка** nuclear power plant; **—ая техника** nuclear engineering, nucleonics; **—ая физика** nuclear physics; **—ая фотоэмульсия** nuclear emulsion; **—ая функция** (math.) kernel function; **—ое горючее** (nucl.) fuel, fissionable material; **—ое деление** nuclear fission; **—ое топливо** (nuclear) fuel; **—ые организмы** eukaryota.

ядерщик *m.* nuclear physicist.

ядовит/ость *f.* toxicity; virulence, malignity; **—ый** *a.* poisonous, toxic; virulent; venenate, venomous; noxious (gas); **—ый зуб** fang (of snake); **—ое начало** (med.) virus.

ядозубы *pl.* (herp.) Gila monsters (*Helodermatidae*).

ядо/носный *a.* poison-bearing, toxiferous; poisonous, venomous; (bact.) toxigenic; **—образующий** *a.* toxigenic; **—отделительный** *a.* venom (gland).

ядохимикат *m.* toxic material; agricultural chemical (pesticide, fungicide, etc.); **—протравитель** *m.* seed disinfectant.

ядра *pl. of* **ядро.**

ядр/ёный *a.* vigorous, healthy; juicy, succulent, fresh; full (of grains); **—истый** *a.* having big kernels; **—ица** *f.* peeled, whole buckwheat; groats.

ядр/о *n.* nucleus, kernel; (cyt.) karyon; (embr.) nucellus; (gen.) pronucleus; center, core; heartwood; substance, gist; (benzene) ring; ball; (sport) shot; **я. древесины** (bot.) heartwood; **я. дробления** (gen.) synkaryon; **я. семяпочки** ovule, nucellus; **атомное я.** (phys.) atomic nucleus; **двойное я.** (cyt.) amphinucleus; **диффузионное я.** (math.) diffusion kernel; **масса —а** (phys.) nuclear mass; **образование —а** nucleation; **разрыв —а, расщепление —а** ring cleavage; **удаление —а** (biol.) enucleation; **физика атомного —а** nuclear physics.

ядро/вый *a. of* **ядро; —мишень** *n.* target nucleus; **—образование** (cryst.) nucleation; **—продукт** *n.* daughter nucleus, resultant nucleus; **—техника** *f.* nuclear engineering, nucleonics.

ядрышко *dim. of* **ядро;** (biol.) nucleolus, plasmosome; **—вый** *a.* (cyt.) nucleolar, nucleus.

яд-фумигант *m.* respiratory poison; fumigant.

яды *pl. of* **яд.**

яе/ин *m.* (biochem.) yajeine; **—нин** *m.* yajenine.

яз. *abbr.* (**язык**) language.

язв/а *f.* ulcer, sore; (met.) pit; **восточная я.** oriental boil, cutaneous leishmaniasis; **красная я.** (phyt.) coral spot; **сибирская я.** (vet.) anthrax; **—енник** *m.* ulcer patient; (bot.) Anthyllis; **—енный** *a.* ulcer(ous); **—енный распад** (med.) ulceration; **—енная болезнь** ulcers, ulcerous condition; **—ина** *f.* ulcer; (corrosion) pit; (rolling) dimple; **с —инами** pitted.

язевый *a. of* **язь.**

язык *m.* tongue; language; speech; clapper (of bell); **морской я.** (ichth.) sole; **песий я.** (bot.) hound's-tongue (*Cynoglossum officinale*); **пластика —а** (med.) glossoplasty; **пятнистый я.** (ichth.) spotted sole; **собачий я.** *see* **песий я.; средиземноморский я.** (ichth.) Spanish ling; **—ан** (ent.) hummingbird hawk moth (*Macroglossum stellatarum*); **—и** *pl. of* **язык; воробьиные —и** (bot.) strapwort (*Corrigiola littoralis*); **морские —и** (ichth.) soles (*Soleidae*); tonguefishes (*Cynoglossidae*).

язык-ИПЛ *m.* information processing language.

языко— *prefix* lingui—, glosso—, glotto— (tongue; language).

язык-объект *m.* (comp.) object language.

языко/ватость *f.* streakiness; **—вед** *m.* linguist; **—ведение** *n.* linguistics; **—ведческий** *a.* linguistic; **—видный** *a.* linguiform, tongue-shaped; **—вой** *a.* lingual; **—вый** *a. of* **язык;** liguli—; **—глоточный** *a.* (anat.) glossopharyngeal; **—держатель** *m.* tongue depressor; **—знание** *n.* linguistics; **—образный** *see* **языковидный; —творчество** *n.* neology; **—труб** *m.* (bot.) Salpiglossis.

язык-посредник *m.* intermediary language.

языч/ковидный *a.* liguliform; strap-shaped; **—ковые** *pl.* (zool.) tongue worms (*Pentastomidae*); **—ковый** *a.* tongue; (music) reed; (anat.) uvular; (bot.) ligulate, ray; **—колистный** *a.* (bot.) liguifolious; **—кообразный**

see **язычковидный**; **—ник** *m.* (bot.) adder's tongue (*Ophioglossum vulgatum*); **—но—** *prefix* glosso—, linguo— (tongue); **—нонадгортанный** *a.* glossoepiglottic; **—нонёбный** *a.* glossopalatine; **—ный** *a.* tongue; lingual (nerve); linguistic; **—ная кость** (ichth.) entoglossum; **—ок** *dim. of* **язык**; catch, lug; tag; (acous.) reed; (anat.) uvula; (bot.) ligule; (ichth.) sole (*Rhinoplagusia*).

язь *m.* (ichth.) ide, orfe (*Leuciscus idus*).

яиц *gen. pl. of* **яйцо**.

яичек *gen. pl. of* **яичко**.

яич/ко *n.* ovule, egg; (anat.) testis; *dim. of* **яйцо**; под-**вешиватель** **—ка** (anat.) cremaster; **—ковидный**, **—ковый** *a.* testicular; **—ник** *m.* (anat.) ovarium, ovary; egg case; **гормон** **—ника** estrogen; **—никовый** *a.* ovarian; **—ница** *f.* scrambled eggs, omelette; **—ный** *a.* of **яйцо**; yolk-yellow; duck-embryo (vaccine).

яйла *f.* yaila, mountain pasture in Crimea.

яйце— *prefix* egg, ovi—; oö— (egg); **—видный** *a.* egg-shaped, oviform, ovoid, oölitic, oval; **—видный сустав** (anat.) condyloid joint; **—вод** *m.* (anat.) oviduct.

яйцев/ой *a. of* **яйцо**; oviferous; ovarian (follicle); **я. ап-парат** (bot.) oviferous apparatus, egg apparatus; **я. зуб** (orn.; herp.) egg tooth; **я. кокон** egg case, ootheca; **—ая капсула** (ent.) ootheca, egg capsule; **—ая клетка** ovum; **—ая оболочка** (biol.) vitelline membrane; **—ое ядро** (gen.) female pronucleus.

яйцееды *pl.* (ent.) egg eaters, a family of wasps (*Scelionidae*).

яйцеживоро/дящий *a.* (zool.) ovoviviparous; **—ждение** *n.* ovoviviparity.

яйцеклад *m.* (zool.) ovipositor; **—ка** *f.* oviposition, egg laying; **—ные** *pl.* (ent.) Terebrantia; **—ущие** *pl.* egg-laying mammals (*Prototheria*); **—ущий** *a.* oviparous, egg-laying.

яйце/клетка *f.* (zool.) ovicell, egg cell; (bot.) ovule, seed bud; **—носец** (arthropods) oviger; **—ноский** *a.* (agr.) productive (layer); **—носкость** *f.* egg yield; **—носный** *a.* oviferous, ovigerous; productive (layer); **—образный** *see* **яйцевидный**; **—почка** (bot.) sporophydium; **—провод** *m.* (anat.) oviduct.

яйцеро/дность *f.* (zool.) oviparity; **—дный**, **—дящий** *a.* oviparous; **—ждение** *n.* oviparity.

яйцо *n.* egg; (biol.) ovum; **—тумак** *m.* bad egg, rotten egg.

як (mam.) yak (*Bos grunniens*).

якамар/а *f.* (orn.) jacamar (*Galbula*); **—ы** *pl.* Galbulidae.

якан/а *f.* (orn.) Jacana; **—ы** *pl.* Jacanidae.

якоб/иан *m.* (math.) Jacobian (functional determinant); **—иевский**, **—иевый** *a.* Jacobian, Jacobi's; **—сонов орган** (anat.) Jacobson's organ.

якобы *conj. and particle* as if, as though, supposedly.

якор/ёк *dim. of* **якорь**; **пружиняший я.** reed; **—ница** *f.* river barge; **—ный** *a. of* **якорь**; anchor-type; moored (mine); **—ное место** moorage; **с —ными волоска-ми** (bot.) glochidiate; **—цевидный** *a.* (bot.) tribuloid; echinate; *see also* **якорный**; **—цы** *pl.* (bot.) caltrop (*Tribulus*); **—ь** *m.* anchor; (elec.) armature; (acous.) reed.

ЯКР *abbr.* (**ядерный квадрупольный резонанс**) nuclear quadrupole resonance.

яктация *f.* (med.) jact(it)ation.

якулятор *m.* thrower; (bot.) jaculator.

якутский *a.* (geog.) Yakut.

ял *m.* (naut.) yawl.

ялап/а *f.* jalap (root); **—ин** *m.* jalapin, orizabin; **—иновая кислота** jalapic acid; **—иноловая кислота** jalapinolic acid, *d*-11-hydroxyhexadecanoic acid; **—ная смола** jalap resin.

ялик *m.* skiff, dinghy, wherry.

ялов/еть *v.* be barren; be dry (of cow); **—ица** *f.* dry cow; **—ичный** *a.* cowhide; **—ка** *f.* cowhide; dry cow; **—ость** *f.* barrenness, sterility; **—ый** *a.* barren, sterile; dry.

яма *f.* pit, well, depression, hole; ditch, trench; cavity, hollow; (air or gas) pocket; (coal) bin, bunker; (anat.) fossa; (garbage) dump; (fish) pond.

Ямайка, ямайский *a.* (geog.) Jamaica.

ямайцин *m.* jamaicin.

яма-ловушка *f.* trap hole.

ямб/овый *a.* jambul (bark); **—озин** *m.* jambosine; **—улол** *m.* jambulol.

ямистый *a.* full of holes, pitted, bumpy.

ям/ка *dim. of* **яма**; pit, hole, depression; (anat.) foss(ul)a; **с —ками** pitted; **—ки** *pl. of* **ямка**; fossae; **—коголовые** *pl.* (herp.) pit vipers (*Crotalidae*); **—ный** *a. of* **яма**; **—окоп(атель)** *m.* post hole digger; **—очка** *dim. of* **ямка**; (anat.) foveola; vallecula.

ЯМР *abbr.* (**ядерный магнитный резонанс**) nuclear magnetic resonance, NMR.

ямс *m.* (bot.) Chinese yam (*Dioscorea*).

ямчат/ость *f.* pitted condition; (phyt.) pit; **—ый** *a.* pitted, foveate; lacunose.

ямщик *m.* driver.

ямы *gen., pl., etc., of* **яма**.

янв. *abbr.* (**январский, январь**) January.

Янга-Гельмгольца теория (ophth.) Young-Helmholtz theory.

янгонин *m.* yangonin.

Янгстаун (geog.) Youngstown.

янки-машина *f.* (paper) Yankee machine, lick-up machine.

янтак *m.* (bot.) camel's thorn (*Alhagi*).

янтарно/аммониевая соль ammonium succinate; **—жёлтый** *a.* pale yellow, amber yellow; **—кислый** *a.* succinyl; succinate (of); **—кислый алюминий** aluminum succinate; **—кислая соль** succinate; **—этиловый эфир** ethyl succinate.

янтарн/ый *a.* amber; amber-colored; succinic; succinyl; **я. альдегид** succinic aldehyde, succinaldehyde; **я. ан-гидрид** succinic anhydride, succinyl oxide; **—ая кислота** succinic acid, butanedioic acid; **соль —ой кислоты** succinyl chloride; хлорангидрид **—ой кислоты** succinyl chloride; **—ая смола** amber resin; **—ое масло** amber oil.

янтарь *m.* (min.) amber.

янтина *f.* (mal.) violet snail (*Janthina*).

янусовый зелёный Janus green (stain).

Янцзы (geog.) Yangtze (river).

яп. *abbr.* (**японский**) Japanese.

япакон/ин japaconine; **—итин** *m.* japaconitine, acetylbenzoyl japaconine.

япи/гиды, —ксы *pl.* (ent.) Japygidae.

Япония Japan.

японск/ий *a.* Japanese; Japan (lacquer; wax); **—ая речная лихорадка** Japanese river fever, scrub typhus; **—ое лаковое дерево** Japanese wax tree (*Rhus succedanea*); **—ое море** Sea of Japan.

яр *m.* steep bank, gill, ravine; *sh. m. of* **ярый**.

яранга *f.* yaranga (portable dwelling).

яра-яра *f.* (chem.) yara yara, 2-methoxynaphthalene.

ЯРД *abbr.* (**ядерный ракетный двигатель**).

ярд *m.* yard (91.44 cm).

яремн/ый *a. of* **ярмо**; (anat.) jugular; **—ая кость** zygomatic bone; **—ая ямка** (anat.) jugular fossa, suprasternal space.

ярица *f.* spring crop (of wheat or rye).

ярка *sh. f. of* **яркий**; ewe lamb.

ярк/ий *a.* bright, luminous, brilliant; dramatic, spectacular; sharp, clear; strong, intense (light); rich (color); **—о** *adv.* brightly, etc., *see a.*; **—о выраженный** *a.* clearly defined, pronounced, marked; **—окрасный** *a.* bright red; **—о(сте)мер** *m.* brightness meter; **—остномодулированный** *a.* intensity-modulated; **—остный** *a.*, **—ость** *f.* brightness, brilliance, brilliancy, luminance, luminosity, intensity.

ярлы(чо)к *m.* label, tag; trademark.

ярмар/ка *f.*, **—очный** *a.* (agr.) fair.

ярмо *n.* (elec.) yoke; framework, carcass; (anat.) jugum.

яров/изация *f.* vernalization, yarovization (of seeds and bulbs); early stage of growth; **—изированный** *a.* vernalized; **—ое** *n.* summer grain crop; **—ой** *a.* spring (rye, wheat), summer-crop; vernal; summer (annual); **—ой хлеб** summer grain crop; **—ая муха** (ent.) Phorbia genitalis; **—ые** *pl.* summer crops, spring-sown crops; **—ость** *f.* spring habit, summer habit.

ярок *sh. m. of* **яркий**.

ярославский *a.* (geog.) Yaroslav.

ярост/ный *a.* furious, violent; **—ь** *f.* fury, anger, rage; **привести в —ь** infuriate, enrage.

ярра *f.* jarra forest.

ярочка *f.* yearling ewe, ewe lamb.

яруга *f.* ravine, gulch, gully.

ярус *m.* story, floor; deck, tray (of dryer); tier, level; (geol.) stage; (cloud) layer, sheet, stratum; (fishing) long-line; **—ность** *f.* (bot.) vertical stratification; forest canopy; (shipbuilding) tier arrangement; **—ный** *a. of* **ярус**; tier (antenna); multistage; stepped, steplike, graded, graduated, gradual, staged; stratose, tiered, layered; **—оразборочный** *a.* unstacking.

ярутка *f.* (bot.) pennycress (*Thlaspi*).

ярч/айший *superl.*; **—е** *comp. of* **яркий.**

ярый *a.* violent, extreme, furious, raging; ardent; unbleached (wax); young (bees).

ярь *f.* spring crop; verdigris, basic cupric acetate; fury; **я.-медянка** *f.* verdigris.

ясельный *a. of* **ясли.**

ясен *sh. m. of* **ясный.**

ясен/евый *a.* (bot.) ash (tree); **—ец** *m.* dittany (*Dictamnus*); **—ный** *a.*, **—ь** *m.* ash (tree) (*Fraxinus*).

ясколка *f.* chickweed (*Cerastium*).

ясли *pl.* manger, (feeding) rack, crib (for cattle feed); daycare center.

ясменник *m.* (bot.) woodruff (*Asperula*).

ясмон *m.* jasmone.

ясн/а *sh. f. of* **ясный**; **—ее** *comp. of* **ясно, ясный**; **—еть** *v.* clear up; **—о** *adv.* clearly, brightly; in plain terms; distinctly, patently, evidently; it is clear; it is obvious; **—овидение** *n.* clairvoyance; **—овидец** *m.*, **—овидящий** *a.* clairvoyant; **—ость** *f.* clearness, brightness; lucidity; plainness; transparency (of a gem); **внести —ость в** *v.* clear up, clarify.

яснотка *f.* (bot.) deadnettle (*Lamium*).

ясный *a.* clear, bright, distinct, definite, precise; lucid;

explicit; transparent; distinctly audible; obvious, apparent, evident, pronounced; fair (weather).

яссиды *pl.* (ent.) Jassidae.

ястреб(а) *m.* (orn.) hawk (*Accipiter*); **—ёнок** *m.* hawk fledgling; **—инка** *f.* (bot.) hawkweed (*Hieracium*); **—иные** *pl.* (orn.) Accipitridae; **—иный** *a.* hawk; accipitral, hawk-like.

ясты/к *m.*, **—чный** *a.* (ichth.) roe.

ятовь *f.*, **—е** *n.* (ichth.) breeding hole.

ятрен *m.* (pharm.) Yatren, chiniofon.

ятро— *prefix* jatro—; iatr(o)— (medical treatment); **—генный** *a.* iatrogenic, physician-induced (problems); **—фа** *f.* physic nut tree (*Jatropha*); **—фин** *m.* jatrophine; **—химический** *a.* (med.) iatrochemical; **—химия** *f.* iatrochemistry.

ятрышник *m.* (bot.) orchis.

ятулийский *a.* (geol.) Jatulian.

яхобаб *m.* astrakhan hide.

яхонт *m.* gem; **красный я.** ruby; **синий я.** sapphire.

яхт/а *f.*, **—(ен)ный** *a.* yacht.

ячее/к *gen. pl. of* **ячейка**; **—чный** *a. of* **ячейка.**

ячеист/ый *a.* cellular, porous, honeycombed, alveolar, vesicular; brochate (grain); foam (rubber); thecodont (teeth); **я. бетон** cellular concrete; **—ое состояние** porosity.

ячейк/а *f.* nucleus; (biol.) cell; cellula; cavity, pit; caverna; cell, unit, compartment, cubicle; honeycomb; mesh (of screen); stage (in scaling circuit); (standard) register; (anat.) alveole, alveolus; **я. памяти** storage register; **крайняя я.** (apid.) attachment cell; **—овый** *a.* nuclear; cellular; **—ообразный** *a.* cellular, cellulated, honeycomb.

ячея *f.* cell; socket; mesh (of a net).

ячий *a. of* **як.**

ячмене/видный *a.* barley-like; **—волоснец** *m.* (bot.) wood barley (*Hordelymus europaeus*).

ячменный *a.* barley; **я. отвар** barley water; **я. сахар** malt sugar, maltose.

ячмень *m.* barley (*Hordeum*); (med.) sty.

ячн(ев)ый *a.* ground barley.

яшм/а *f.*, **—овый** *a.* (petr.) jasper; **—овая каменная посуда** (cer.) jasperware, Wedgwood; **—оподобный** *a.* jasper-like, jasp(er)oid.

ящер *m.* (mam.) pangolin; **—ёнок** *m.* baby lizard; **—ица** *f.* lizard; **—ицевидный** *a.* lacertine, lizardlike; **—ицы** *pl.* lizards (*Lacertidae*); **—ичный** *a.* lizard; saurian; **—огады** *pl.* (herp.) Rhynchocephalia; **—оголовые** *pl.* (ichth.) lizardfishes (*Synodontidae*); **—ообразные** *pl.* (zool.) Sauropsida; **—отазовые** *pl.* (pal.) Saurischia; **—ы** *pl.* pangolins, scaly anteaters (*Pholidota*).

ящик *m.* box, chest, case, container; bin; cage; drawer (of desk); (rad.) cabinet; tray, pan; **соединительный я.** (elec.) junction box; **я.-решето** *n.* drain box; **я.-сосуд** *m.* (paper) suction (pump) box.

ящич/ек *dim. of* **ящик**; **—ный** *a. of* **ящик**; **—ный калибр** (rolling) box pass; **—ный питатель** hopper (feeder).

ящур *m.* (vet.) foot and mouth disease; **—ка** *f.* (herp.) Eremias; **—ный** *a. of* **ящур.**

ЯЭУ *abbr.* (**ядерно-энергетическая установка**) nuclear power plant.

Яя (geog.) Yaya.